POINT

FORM & R 1997

Compiled by

Jonathan Neesom with Steven Payne

Published 1997 by The Sporting Life
One Canada Square, Canary Wharf, London E14 5AP

ISBN 0 901091 95 2

Irish Point-to-Point Results 1997 are reproduced by courtesy of *The Irish Field*

Editorial and Production by Martin Pickering Bloodstock Services
Cover printed by Colour Splash, London E14
Preliminaries by LBJ Enterprises Ltd, Chilcompton and Aldermaston
Text printed by The Bath Press, Bath and London

Cover picture
Grand Marnier Trophy winner Butler John (Neil Harris) at Lifton on Spring Bank Holiday Monday.

(Photograph: John Beasley)

CONTENTS

REVIEW OF 1997

by Jonathan Neesom

(This article first appeared in *The Sporting Life* on June 10, 1997)

You could not, in all honesty, describe 1997 as a vintage season for point-to-pointing.

After several years of gradual increase in the number of races run, this year's total of 1,474 was a fall of nearly 50 on last season's, while some 150 fewer horses made it to the course.

The drought-like conditions which prevailed from early March through to the beginning of May wreaked havoc with the going at many fixtures and resulted in three meetings being lost to hard ground and a handful of others being unable to muster 20 runners.

There is some consolation to be drawn from a comparison with 1990, the last time similar problems afflicted the sport.

A total of 21 walkovers was at least much less than the 33 which occurred in that season, and the arts of course-management and watering have improved considerably in recent years — those meetings which were willing and able to meet the challenge were often rewarded with decent fields and competitive racing.

Sixty meetings were held on Sundays, an increase of five on last season's record number, and crowds at these again tended to be enormous, even if many of those attending showed little inclination towards the racing on offer.

With the Teme Valley opting for a Saturday, the three remaining mid-week stalwarts were joined by the Weston & Banwell, who drew enthusiasts from far and wide to Cothelstone in mid-May — the market is there for those who take the plunge.

Five new courses and a revived one (Hutton Rudby) appeared and all met with general approval.

Blackforest Lodge and Paxford were unfortunate to draw small fields but both promise to be excellent additions to the list, while a new breed of superhorse turned out at the first of two meetings at Bonvilston.

Five and a half minutes for three miles suggests that these Welsh horses can really shift, although to be fair the race distance was extended for the second effort in early May.

Sponsorship took a decided upturn in 1997, with Greig Middleton and Interlink Express establishing series alongside Land Rover, and the ever-faithful Dodson & Horrell continuing their support of PPORA races throughout the country.

The Greig Middleton ladies' final produced a more than worthy winner in Earthmover, although its staging on a Tuesday afternoon at Chepstow was never likely to attract more than a smattering of pointing fans.

Much worse was the clash between the Interlink Final at Stratford with the all hunter-chase card at Folkestone, a particularly crass piece of race-planning right out of the bottom drawer.

The renamed Wessex area suffered more than most from the weather and contributed six of the season's walkovers as well as 18 of the 70 two-horse races which took place.

If it is harsh to make judgments on an area when the elements conspire to make the sport well-nigh impossible, it has to be pointed out that this region is always more at risk than many others.

Larkhill, Badbury Rings and Barbury Castle, which contribute 11 of the area's scheduled fixtures, are unable to water, and the four meetings held at these venues in successive weeks from the end of March scraped up a total of 70 runners.

The South-East area is in an even worse state, with a collective malaise rapidly descending on the sport in this part of the country.

Three meetings were abandoned, one at very late notice, because of hard ground, while the East Kent at Aldington on Easter Monday reflects little credit on anybody concerned.

Four walkovers — it would have been five but for the intervention of the Welsh-based Bridget Barton — were the inevitable result of ground which was hard and uneven, and whoever was responsible for describing the going at the meeting as "good" just two days beforehand should relinquish the role forthwith.

The last seven meetings which took place in the area raked up a total of 183 runners, with just one of the 43 races managing a field of more than seven — at least spectators were spared the local book-makers' customary rip-off when it came to each-way betting.

All such criticism is rendered trivial by events at Charing on March 8, when the South East Hunts Club meeting was abandoned after one race following the death of Giles Hopper.

The first fatality in the sport for seven years, Hopper's death was the starkest possible reminder that race-riding can exact the severest penalty on its participants, who do it for fun to provide the rest of us with ours.

The Grand Marnier race was noticeably slow in taking off this season but eventually resolved itself into a battle between Butler John and Grimley Gale over the closing weeks.

Butler John's six wins in May eventually proved too much for his rival and provided further evidence, if any was needed, of the skills of Victor Dartnall, who sent out 29 winners during the season, with a strike rate of over 60 per cent.

Dick Baimbridge was never likely to repeat his annus mirabilis of the previous year but still topped the 30 mark for the season, including a win for Dante's Pride, who was transformed from useless to maiden winner during the course of the season.

The loss of those wonderful warriors Di Stefano and Stephens Pet would have taken much of the gloss off the stable's success this season, although Alison Dare's feat in reaching 250 point-to-point wins in an illustrious career deserves the highest praise.

Richard Barber sent out 51 winners in point-to-points during the season, in addition to Earthmover's two prestigious hunter-chase successes but the trainer's greatest moment came at Cheltenham in March.

Fantus' second victory in the Cheltenham Foxhunters' came after a season on the sidelines and a less-than-satisfactory build-up — a fall at the last at Didmarton when in the process of being beaten by The Bounder would scarcely have given much cause for optimism.

To overcome these setbacks, as well as unsuitably fast ground at Cheltenham, reflects enormous credit on all concerned — not least Fantus himself — and producing the horse to perform on the day is very much the training performance of the season.

Mike Roberts also enjoyed a highly-successful season, and it is somewhat ironic that the South-East should produce several of the season's leading horses among the shambles that existed in 1997.

Bitofamixup (the tip for the top in last year's Sporting Life Form & Results), surpassed all expectations with a series of thrilling successes before running a fine race in defeat in the Horse & Hound Championship at Stratford, while in Prince Buck and the impressive

Folkestone winner Storming Lady, Roberts has plenty of ammunition for the future and it would be no surprise to see some or all of these three appear in professional racing.

Damien Duggan's 18 winners have elevated him to the ranks of the leading trainers — while the husband-and-wife team of Richard and Carrie Ford not only trained them, they rode them as well — five winners at Whittington on Easter Saturday being the highlight for them.

Further north, Simon Shirley-Beaven enjoyed a successful season with the likes of Muskora and Orange Ragusa, while among the lesser-known names, Kate Buckett showed that she certainly has the necessary flair.

With Dare unable to muster the necessary fire-power in the closing weeks, and Polly Curling out of the running after a three week lay-off occasioned by a fall at Bitterley in April - "They examined my head for signs of brain-damage but I told them they were looking in the wrong place" — the stage was set for a new ladies' champion to be crowned.

Shirley Vickery and Pip Jones fought it out until the penultimate weekend of the season, when Jones suffered a badly broken leg at Dingley — the latest injury in a career that has seen her triumph over adversity on many occasions.

Nothing should detract from Vickery's championship, however, as she proved herself to be a worthy successor to the Dare-Curling domination of recent years — one fine example of her skill was shown at Cothelstone, where she pinched the members' on Belmount Captain after looking booked for second place throughout the final mile, and her riding exhibits all the talents we have come to expect from our leading ladies.

With reigning champion Jamie Jukes unable to rely on the normally potent service from Bert Lavis' yard, the men's battle also resolved itself into a head-to-head between Julian Pritchard and Tim Mitchell.

When Mitchell rode seven consecutive winners at Woodford and Littlewindsor in late April, it looked as if Pritchard's steady accumulation of success was to be thwarted, but trebles at Maisemore Park and Bredwardine on consecutive weekends in May enabled him to establish a decisive advantage.

Unquoted in the pre-season betting, Pritchard had ridden only one winner when he arrived at the North Hereford in late February — the sixth weekend of the season.

A three-timer there signalled his intentions and the season became a series of tours de force from a man riding at the very peak of his powers.

The list of fine efforts is seemingly endless, although wins on How Friendly at Andoversford, Fort Gale at Maisemore Park and Robero at Bredwardine displayed strength, skill and tactical acumen in large amounts — a worthy and highly-popular champion, and most definitely the rider of the season.

Others also made their mark during the season.

Joe Tizzard, the novice champion of 1996, may only be 17 but is already as good as the rest and his association with The Bounder was one of the real high-spots of the season.

A cast-off from Oliver Sherwood's yard, The Bounder can justifiably be called the best pointer of 1997, and Tizzard's effort on him at the season's first meeting at Barbury Castle, when the fog seemed to lift especially for the crowd's benefit, wins this correspondent's acclaim as the riding performance of the season.

Andrew Dalton enjoyed his best season by some way, while from the ranks of the emerging talents, Ranald Morgan, Rilly Goschen and Polly Gundry all deserve mention for their efforts.

There were plenty of horses who impressed during the season, including Bitofanatter (Northern), Rolier (North-West), Secret Bay (Yorkshire), Perambulate (Devon & Cornwall) and Struggles Glory, who gave the veteran David Robinson all the thrills that a man in his 50s could expect by winning five races and finishing a gallant second to Earthmover in the John Corbet.

You can add to that list the name of Double Thriller, who was an impressive winner of the Lady Dudley Cup, and if he is not a ready-made replacement for Double Silk, then he is at least a worthy successor.

The Lord Grimthorpe Cup at the Middleton attracted a field of 21 but the race concerned only one horse, Ask Antony, who bombed home and has since been sold to race under Rules.

Perhaps the best performance in any of the classics came from Kettles, who overcame her dislike of firm ground to win the Lord

Ashton of Hyde trophy at the Heythrop for the second consecutive year, and is the epitome of gameness.

Television came to point-to-pointing in the shape of the Racing Channel with mixed results. Of the three meetings covered, the Heythrop was a disaster while the New Forest was not an unequivocal success.

Better fortune was enjoyed at Hockworthy, where the cameras were able to cover wins by Magnolia Man, Earthmover and Aller Moor, who subsequently landed the three series' finals, as well as one by the Grand Marnier winner, Butler John.

This meeting, the Tiverton, wins my vote as the pick of the year from those I have attended, not least for its atmosphere and mid-week place in the calendar.

Other meetings worthy of a mention are the Cumberland, Cumberland Farmers, Llangeinor and East Cornwall, consolidating the feeling that the further you go from the metropolis, the better it gets, but in general, the vast majority of the fixtures I have been privileged to attend continue to uphold the idea of an amateur sport run in a professional manner, which is what it should be.

TOP HUNTER CHASERS/ POINT-TO-POINTERS 1997

by Jonathan Neesom

The horses selected here for extended commentary represent those who were, for a variety of reasons, outstanding during 1997 in Hunter chases or point-to-points. This list is not intended to be exhaustive, just a personal opinion of the merits of ten horses in each field; the reader is welcome to disagree with the comments made or to argue the case for any horse that has been omitted!

HUNTER CHASERS

CELTIC ABBEY (40)

Celtic Abbey's performances at Cheltenham and Stratford entitle him to be given the accolade of the season's top hunter-chaser, and yet his year started in disastrous circumstances.

Sent off favourite for a run-of-the-mill race at Hereford in February, Celtic Abbey was never in the hunt on rain-softened ground and after two serious blunders, was pulled up a long way from the finish.

As it also transpired that he suffered a broken blood vessel during the race, the omens could scarcely have looked worse for a horse who should have been at the peak of his powers.

Some of the damage was rectified when he finished a creditable fourth in the Cheltenham Foxhunters a month later, but the turning point came when he was sent to Venetia Williams to prepare for a tilt at the Grand National.

The attempt failed—the Chair claimed him when he was bang in contention—but the skills which have quickly brought the trainer to the forefront of the National Hunt scene soon had their effect on Celtic Abbey.

A return to Cheltenham saw him take on the old course maestro Double Silk at the evening meeting at the end of May.

The betting suggested a close duel was in prospect but the race was decided before the pair headed down the hill for the last time; by this stage Celtic Abbey had seized control of the race and swept to a 30 lengths success in scintillating style.

A planned assault on a valuable handicap at Wolverhampton in mid-May was aborted when the ground there turned into its all-too-familiar state of good to soft with bottomless patches, which just left the Horse & Hound Championship at Stratford with which to finish the season. Runner-up to Proud Sun a year earlier, Celtic Abbey made no mistake this time under a very positive ride from Dai Jones.

Leading before halfway, Celtic Abbey quickened away from his field at the start of the final circuit, and impressively quickened again when Bitofamixup came to challenge three from home. He won by eight lengths from Bitofamixup, with the rest strung out across Warwickshire—a champion's performance in a very fast time.

Celtic Abbey may have been aided by the assistance of a professional trainer but he is a true hunter-chaser, whose rise through the ranks had scarcely been meteoric until the last twelve months. It would be no surprise to see Celtic Abbey in action in the professional world in 1997/8—after all, the Hennessy is fair game for hunter-chasers these days—and it could just be that he still has some improvement left in him.

Given the right conditions—a truly-run race on good or fast ground—Celtic Abbey could well make his mark in the coming months.

FANTUS (39)

If Venetia Williams' training of Celtic Abbey is worthy of high praise, then the skill with which Richard Barber produced Fantus to win a second Cheltenham Foxhunters was an outstanding example of the art.

Unraced since his triumph in 1995, Fantus returned to the fray at Larkhill in February in the Coronation Cup, where his main opponent in the betting was the useful stayer Young Brave. With that horse running moderately, it should have been plain sailing for Fantus, until the talented but unpredictable Brackenfield decided he was in no mood to be cast in the mould of the stable second string—neither for that matter was Polly Curling—and the partnership came again to defeat Fantus at the last.

Returning leg-weary but sound, Fantus continued his Cheltenham build-up with the men's open at the Beaufort, only to run into the season's leading pointer, The Bounder.

If not exactly in the process of being thrashed, Fantus was certainly well beaten in second when falling at the last—not the ideal preparation with the big race 12 days away, but at least his legs had survived the strain of the fast ground at Didmarton.

Despite Barber's record of having sent out two previous Cheltenham Foxhunters winners straight from the point-to-point scene, Fantus was allowed to start at 10–1 for the race, with most people reckoning that the combination of an unsatisfactory build-up and the fast ground enough to put a stop to Fantus' hopes.

The race itself is simple to relate; after Final Pride and Double Silk had set the pace, Tim Mitchell kicked on at the top of the hill to utilise Fantus' stamina.

You knew that the favourite, Cab On Target, would be delivered with his challenge as late as possible and sure enough he loomed up in the straight as the only danger.

Approaching the last, it became as much a matter of courage as ability, and Fantus had a decisive edge here; he dug deep on the run-in and gained a famous victory.

Unlike 1995, Fantus returned from the race sound but with no other obvious target for the rest of the season, and with the ground firming up daily, he was wisely retired, put out to a field to rest on his laurels.

Whether he will be able to complete a unique hat-trick in 1998 will depend not just on his own well-being, but on how many of the season's exciting crop of novices, including the stable's Earthmover, turn out in opposition, but even if he never wins another race, Fantus has carved his place in hunter-chasing's list of greats.

Barber himself sent out 51 point-to-point winners during the season, an astonishing number for the sport, and his skill and success as a trainer inevitably lead to cries of "unfair" from some quarters, where the idea of any semblance of professionalism in performance is seen as sacrilege.

Point-to-pointing has long ceased to be concerned with giving farmers the chance to gallop their hunters against one another, and the development of the sport has seen the emergence of several powerful stables across the country who regularly win plenty of races.

This should be seen as a benefit to the sport, not a drawback, and in an age where we are constantly reminded of the need to "raise standards," the exploits of the leading point-to-point trainers do just that, encouraging the sport to new heights while retaining its basic appeal.

EARTHMOVER (36)

At the head of the list of young pretenders comes Earthmover, who ended the season unbeaten after seven races which stretched over nearly four months.

He made his reappearance in the intermediate at the Great Trethew, and those of us who questioned our sanity for driving to Cornwall at the crack of dawn in early February, were left counting our blessings at witnessing one of the best meetings of the season.

Earthmover did not just beat King Torus and Tinotops (both dual hunter-chase winners themselves later in the season), he obliterated them in the day's fastest time, and established his reputation in one hit.

Four ladies' races followed, each won with style and ease, and that might have been an end to matters but for the return of the rains in early May.

The first final of the Greig Middleton ladies series took place on a Tuesday afternoon at Chepstow on an otherwise all-professional card—not quite the ideal set-up to entice the enthusiasts from around the country—and Earthmover took to regulation fences with no problem.

Cantering into the straight alongside dear old Sams Heritage—whose rejuvenation was one of two miracles conjured up for our delight by Dick Baimbridge in 1997—Earthmover had no trouble easing clear to win untroubled.

The John Corbet was little more than two weeks after and Earthmover took his place in a select field which assembled for the season's novice championship.

Once more it was his ability to quicken which proved decisive in the closing stages as he beat the remarkable Struggles Glory by four lengths after a round of jumping which in all fairness could not be described as faultless.

Earthmover's qualities as a race-horse are his stamina and a turn of foot; the going in 1997 was never really soft enough for him to be completely at ease, which will be worrying news for potential opponents next season—it is hard to see him being beaten in a hunter-chase if conditions are right.

Earthmover's season was also a Tale of Two Pollys—the redoubtable Curling was in the saddle for the first three races, and when she suffered concussion in mid-April, the promising Gundry took over, and kept the ride for the rest of the season.

There is now only one Polly, of course, with the well-publicised Curling-Barber split taking place in May.

A rider does not win three championships and ride over one hundred winners for the same trainer without being the best, and a trainer does not provide those hundred-plus winners without the same credentials, so let's just offer thanks for the memories and wish all concerned the best for the future.

BITOFAMIXUP (36)

It was more in hope than expectation that Bitofamixup was included in these notes last year as the young horse with potential, and after he had finished tailed off in a novice hurdle at Stratford in October, the hope was waning fast. Fortunately, that was but a blip and his reappearance in proper racing at Higham in February saw the transformation from potential to reality in a little over six minutes in the men's open.

Bitofamixup strolled home by a distance in a fast time, and for those of us not present at the meeting, the video evidence confirms the deep impression made upon those who witnessed it in the flesh.

In passing, while it is not the policy of these notes to give free plugs to other agencies, the firm who sell videos of East Anglian meetings do so at a fraction of the cost of most other areas in the country—either they see the service as a labour of love, or other people are making the sort of profits which would reduce chairmen of the privatised utilities to gibbering embarrassment—Gordon Brown should look into it, methinks.

Huntingdon followed soon after Higham for Bitofamixup, and a high-class novices hunter-chase gave him the chance to show his prowess to a wider audience, as he beat off the challenge of the very useful Ask Antony after the last.

The mid-season target for the best novices is quickly becoming the valuable Cuvee Napa at Aintree and Bitofamixup put up another outstanding performance there.

The early departure of favourite Orchestral Suite deprived us of a chance to gauge the relative merits of the pair but Bitofamixup sauntered across the line as runner-up Howayman (two hunter-chase wins and a host of decent performances) was taking the last fence.

A small race at Bangor in May ensured that all parts were working effectively before trainer Mike Roberts opted for the Horse & Hound at Stratford, rather than the John Corbet.

Roberts is in the enviable position of training three highly-promising novices, with Prince Buck (who represented the stable in the John Corbet) and the impressive Folkestone winner Storming Lady, in addition to the stable star, and should he decide to campaign any or all of them under Rules next season, their progress is sure to attract plenty of attention.

Bitofamixup enhanced his reputation in defeat at Stratford; left behind when Celtic Abbey kicked clear on the final circuit, he worked his way into a challenging position three from home but had no answer to the winner's second change of gear. In finishing well clear of horses of the calibre of Mr Boston and Cab On Target, Bitofamixup confirmed his status as a top performer and at only six years old, the best is surely yet to come.

STRUGGLES GLORY (34)

Placed in both efforts in Irish points in 1996, Struggles Glory could not be said to have stood out as a major talent waiting to be snapped up for a fancy price by someone with an open cheque-book. It is another indication that trying to equate Irish point-to-point form with the requirements of racing in England is a futile exercise—many of their top horses flop miserably in England, while the gems are found by looking under the rocks. Struggles Glory is indeed a gem and his performances in 1997 mark him out as a remarkable talent.

Three wide-margin wins in points—the last of which saw him post a record time at Detling—ensured that his reputation had gathered momentum by the time he appeared at Ascot for his hunter-chase debut in April.

A three lengths defeat of the generally disappointing Lurriga Glitter may not sound like the stuff of champions, nor for that matter might the wide-margin win over some second-raters at Huntingdon later in the month, but of course it was the style of victory which caught the attention.

Forcing the pace throughout, Struggles Glory maintained a relentless gallop to the line in both races without appearing to have made any serious exertion at all.

Most remarkable of all, his owner-rider David Robinson is a man for whom the mid-life crisis is but a distant memory, and a rider who is happy to sit and steer, allowing the horse to run unhindered by over-enthusiasm from the saddle. You can say what you like about this school of riding—and most of us have—but you cannot knock success, and five straight wins represent more success than most achieve in a lifetime. Struggles Glory's only defeat came at the hands of Earthmover in the John Corbet—where he was unable to quicken with the winner but stayed on strongly again on the run-in; he looked to have taken little out of himself by the end of the race and it remains a matter of conjecture at present whether a "jockey" would have extracted an immediate response from a horse whose prime asset appears to be relentless galloping.

Rumours abounded late in the season that Robinson was being asked to name his own price by some leading lights in the professional world, but wherever Struggles Glory next appears, he is surely a talent we will enjoy for some years to come.

BLUE CHEEK (29)

Blue Cheek could have easily been named Blue Moon for much of his career, so infrequent were his appearances in the early years, and he looked well past his best after failing to win in a particularly busy four-race season in 1996.

Two appearances in points early in 1997 at least informed of his well-being, although a well-beaten third at the North Hereford in February did little to suggest great glories in the offing.

It was his performance at Ludlow in March which really caught the attention, however; a field of 18 included several noted front-runners, but Blue Cheek took command from the start and galloped some fair rivals into submission with a blistering display of pace-setting in a fast time.

A brief glance at his record in hunter-chases soon reveals that Blue Cheek is not averse to the odd blunder at times and it was a brave decision to head for Aintree and the Foxhunters at the start of April.

This year's renewal was an odd affair with an unusually small field at 14 reduced by four at the first fence, which claimed the well-fancied pair of Chilipour and the ill-fated Country Tarrogen. The favourite, Mr Boston, always appeared to have matters under control but having survived the major perils that the course can present, he fell two from home.

It was at this point that Blue Cheek, who had been outpaced after a mistake four from home, was being urged back into contention by the talented Robert Thornton, and the pair quickly assumed command to win by 17 lengths.

Not surprisingly, Blue Cheek did not appear again after Aintree, but if he never wins another race, his triumph at Aintree will be a testament to his connections' patience, not least that of his owner, Jim Mahon, the highly-popular president of the Point-to-Point Owners & Riders Association.

SECRET BAY (31)

Secret Bay spent his early years eventing but made his mark rapidly in his first season's racing in 1997.

After finishing second on his debut in a maiden at Wetherby, he soon rattled up a hat-trick of wins (including a walkover), before his attentions were turned to hunter-chasing in April.

A win at Hexham against distinctly modest rivals was gained in the manner expected of an odds-on shot but it was his display at Huntingdon at the end of the month which brought him to prominence. Rather like Struggles Glory, who won on the same card, it was not a case of what was beaten—in Secret Bay's example, it was not much at all—but the manner of success.

Jumping well, Secret Bay waited until five from home before leading but easily put a distance between himself and the rest by the line, and for those looking for time comparisons, he recorded an almost identical time as Struggles Glory.

The temptation to take on the leading novices at Stratford was resisted but Secret Bay should have no problem winning more hunter-chases in 1998, and as with many of the young pretenders this season, there is every chance that we have yet to see the best of him.

MISS MILLBROOK (31)

Miss Millbrook may not be the best hunter-chaser in the country but she is the epitome of gameness and her efforts in 1997 were rewarded with three hunter-chase successes as well as narrow victory in one of the season's most exciting point-to-point races.

She opened up with a clear-cut victory at Hereford in February, where she found the soft ground ideal, before blundering her way round Newbury and losing to an in-form Holland House.

She had no realistic chance in the Cheltenham Foxhunters on the prevailing fast ground and was pulled up in the closing stages, but she overcame her dislike of firm ground two weeks later at Llanvapley.

She fought out a terrific finish with the useful Mister Horatio in the men's open before gaining the day near the line in what many spectators considered the best race they had seen for some years.

Firm ground at Chepstow also proved to be her undoing when she failed to put in a serious challenge to the impressive Final Pride, but the season ended in style with wins at Cheltenham and Hereford.

At the former, she again had to overcome unsuitable going to beat a modest field—sheer gameness saw her home—but on good ground at Hereford she emphatically beat some of the best of the second eleven.

Miss Millbrook will never win any of the hunter-chasing's major prizes but will surely find opportunities in 1998—on good or soft ground she is a tough mare to beat in all but the top company.

NODFORM WONDER (32)

Since winning three hurdle races in the autumn of 1992, Nodform Wonder's career under Rules was characterised by some game but unavailing efforts, and at the age of ten his future looked all behind him when he joined the amateur sport in 1997.

Two placed efforts in early season confineds were scarcely the stuff of legends, but he stepped up to take two similar events at Eaton Hall and Tabley, making all on both occasions and winning by a wide margin each time.

Sent to Bangor for a modest hunter-chase in mid-April, Nodform Wonder cruised home under regular rider Richard Bevis, but with the opposition modest, this form as well looked nothing out of the ordinary.

The true nature of his revival only became apparent the second day he went to Bangor, for the prestigious area point-to-point championship. A look through the form beforehand suggested he was a false favourite for the race but from halfway, Nodform Wonder turned the event into a procession, giving the useful and consistent Nothing Ventured 4lbs and a 23 lengths beating. It is some measure of his progress throughout the season that he enjoyed a turn around in form of nearly 50 lengths with fourth-placed Ita's Fellow, who had beaten him in a point 11 weeks previously and had followed up with two more wins.

On this form alone, Nodform Wonder is entitled to take his place among the season's leading performers in hunter-chases, and this bold front-runner will find plenty of other chances to win in 1998 if retaining his zest for racing.

BUZZ O'THE CROWD (31)

The winner of a maiden point in 1994, Buzz O'The Crowd became just one of the familiar faces after, showing no form in two hunter-chase efforts the following year and finishing well-beaten in modest novice chases in 1995/6.

Reappearing at Bratton Down in late April, he finished a respectable third in an average confined, suggesting little had changed, and his only other outing, at Newton Abbot in mid-May, looked an over-ambitious exercise.

With the prolific Phar Too Touchy sent off at 1–3 for this race, it was a case of naming your own odds about the rest, and Buzz O'The Crowd's price of 14–1 did not look over-generous in a race which boasted three previous hunter-chase winners during the season, in addition to Phar Too Touchy.

His performance was a revelation—he was always travelling smoothly under Dominic Alers-Hankey and when he was sent to the front five out, the race was over.

It is true that Phar Too Touchy ran well below form (and was reported to have been in season) but to win by a distance, easing down, was some performance from a horse who had never shown form within 20lbs of this effort.

Just Ben, who had won the confined at Bratton Down, was beaten out of sight in sixth place here, and if you can knock holes in the form of any race, it was impossible not to be impressed with Buzz O'The Crowd's effort.

It could be that he is a spring horse, and certainly the easy ground at Newton Abbot seemed to suit him admirably, but on this form Buzz O'The Crowd would be a match for most hunter-chasers and it will be interesting to see whether he can reproduce this form next season.

TOP POINTERS

THE BOUNDER (35)

The Bounder won just one of his 11 starts over hurdles in the 1995/6 season, after which he was sent packing from Oliver Sherwood's yard reportedly with a less-than-ringing endorsement—"Second-class horse" (trainer), "No chance of staying three miles" (Jamie Osborne).

Four races later, The Bounder is unquestionably the top point-to-pointer of the 1997 season, and a tribute to the skills of three generations of the Tizzard family who own, train and ride him. Appearing on the first day of the season at Barbury Castle, The Bounder not surprisingly figured among the outsiders for the men's open, in which Chilipour and Calling Wild were expected to fight out the finish.

The fog which ensnared the course lifted for this race, and spectators were able to witness a magnificent performance by horse and rider in winning.

Harrying Calling Wild for the first two miles, The Bounder dropped off the leader on the final circuit, as you might expect from a horse whose form under Rules was at the minimum trip.

Joe Tizzard was merely giving him a breather, and, gathered for another effort in the home straight, The Bounder quickened past Calling Wild two out before winning by five lengths in the fastest time of the day.

Any thoughts that this was a flash-in-the-pan display, from a dubious character lulled into showing his worth once only, were soon dispelled when he trotted up at Ottery St. Mary, again in the day's fastest time, before cementing his reputation at Didmarton at the beginning of March. Jumping superbly and making all at the Beaufort, The Bounder was always travelling half a pace too quickly for Fantus, and was still going well in front when that horse fell at the last when four lengths in arrears.

Given Fantus' exploits at Cheltenham 12 days later, The Bounder's performance here was beyond doubt the best seen in a point-to-point in 1997. One final outing at Cothelstone two weeks later saw another facile win and that was his season complete.

It may be that The Bounder will prove best at a bare three miles, and there is no guarantee that he will jump as well under Rules as he has done in points, but if he takes to hunter-chasing in 1998, The Bounder will be a sight to behold—roll on more second-class horses, please!

BUTLER JOHN (31)

Victor Dartnall enjoyed outstanding success in 1996, principally with Phar Too Touchy, who won the Grand Marnier award, and by matching his achievements in 1997, with a strike-rate of over 60%, again showed that he is as good a trainer in the amateur arena as you are likely to find.

Butler John won two of his seven starts in points in 1996 but looked error-prone and a bit of a soft touch at times, an impression left unshaken by his first two attempts this season—he fell in the lead at Wadebridge at the beginning of February and a week later was thrashed in the best race seen at Tweseldown for some years, won by Spacial. The Dartnall stable was not firing in its customary style early-season and Butler John was given five weeks off before reappearing at Wadebridge in mid-March to record his first success of the season in a modest men's open.

Nine more victories followed in the next 11 weeks, including a six-timer in May, as Butler John swept all before him with a series of bold front-running displays.

The art of winning the Grand Marnier involves finding some weak races, and Dartnall had no hestitation in taking in two members races en route to retaining the trophy, but Butler John is no moderate horse benefiting from keen placement—he showed at Hockworthy in mid-April that he has progressed to become a top-flight performer, while his annihilation of the useful ladies' horses Khattaf and Howaryadoon at High Bickington in early May was his most impressive display of the season.

Butler John has shown an ability to handle ground ranging from very firm to soft and is sure to prove hard to beat if back in 1998, while his trainer can savour the prospect of success for others in his yard—the highly-promising hunter-chaser King Torus and the much-improved Four Leaf Clover among them.

GRIMLEY GALE (29)

This really is an admirable mare, and nine victories in 1997 saw her press Butler John until the penultimate week of the season in the Grand Marnier race.

Lightly-raced until this season, Grimley Gale opened up in the modestly-titled moderate race at Tweseldown, where she struggled to beat the virtual no-hoper Fowling Piece, but by the end of the campaign she had proved herself to be a top-class performer, taking each step up in class with ease.

Not the fastest of jumpers in points, Grimley Gale was given something of a lesson in the art of fencing by Stephens Pet at Mollington in May, on that gallant horse's last appearance, but she is a real battler and stayer, attributes which will benefit her if she is sent hunter-chasing in 1998. In four of her victories she was partnered by the season's champion ladies' rider, Shirley Vickery, who was securing her first title.

Riding with all the skill, flair and dash which characterises the best point-to-point riders, Vickery fully deserves her success, and her riding of Arctic Chill to win at Charlton Horethorne in April showed considerable intelligence and nerve. Grimley Gale has several options open to her in 1998, and while she has been known to belt the odd fence in point-to-points, such horses are often the ones who make the transition to hunter-chases more successfully—wherever she is campaigned, further victories await.

BENGERS MOOR (29)

Of the consignment of Richard Barber-trained pointers who will next appear under Rules from Paul Nicholl's yard, Strong Chairman, who was unbeaten from five starts in 1997 may appear to be the most likely prospect, but it will be no surprise if Bengers Moor proves to be the horse with the greatest potential.

The winner of two of his three outings as a five years old, Bengers Moor appeared only twice in 1997, winning on his debut at Didmarton before failing to cope with the useful Slaney Food at Cothelstone two weeks later.

If that does little to suggest future greatness, Bengers Moor's performance at Didmarton was one of the highlights of the season.

Waiting in front on the final circuit in a division of the intermediate race, he quickened away in dramatic style in the short home straight, and numbered Double Thriller and Shuil's Star among his 19 victims.

This was a hugely impressive performance in a decent time, and it is likely that his subsequent defeat was caused through lack of stamina rather than ability.

Bengers Moor should therefore be ideal material for National Hunt racing, where he may well prove most effective at around the two and a half mile mark—certainly it will be surprising if he does not win races, and with only five outings to date, the best is yet to come.

THE ARTFUL RASCAL (28)

The accolade of best point-to-pointer in East Anglia may not carry the weight it once did but The Artful Rascal is a worthy recipient of that honour, and his exploits in 1997 are worthy of special mention.

At 13 years old, and with only two outings in the previous two seasons, it would be natural to assume that the old boy would be a bit of a pushover in 1997, and with his preference for give in the ground it was unlikely that he would be placed to much advantage in a dry spring.

Three outings were all that were managed but in each he thrashed the opposition with disdain. The Artful Rascal's forte is stamina and after an initial win at Horseheath, he romped away with a men's open at Marks Tey over three and a half miles from some perfectly respectable rivals. His final run came at Detling, where despite the fast ground, he stormed home in the grandly-titled Kent Grand National after taking it up half a mile from home.

This race was one of only seven in the country to accept the idea of an area "prestige" race with prize money at double the usual maximum—a notably good innovation which could become a sort of area title race, and one which deserved better than the half-hearted response with which it met. The Artful Rascal should not be discounted on ageist principles should he return in 1998—he has raced less than 30 times in his life and may still possess enough fire to put any upstarts in their place.

BAGALINO (27)

A useful performer on the Flat, Bagalino enjoyed success as a juvenile hurdler in the 1993/4 season, but disappeared after being pulled up in that most demanding of races, the Triumph Hurdle. It was therefore some feat to bring him back after such an absence to win two of his three races in 1997, although his inclusion in these notes owes much to the fact that he was ridden by Julian Pritchard on each occasion.

Bagalino defeated a below-par and near-retirement Scally Muire at Wolverhampton, another old timer Lost Fortune at Upton-on-Severn, before suffering his only defeat at the hands of Shoon Wind at Bitterley in April.

With the ground firming all over the country, it was no surprise that he failed to reappear. Usually, a championship winner has one or two horses to ride during the season who are good for at least half a dozen wins and who form the basis of the successful challenge—Pritchard did not enjoy that luxury and his 37 winners came courtesy of 25 different horses.

That he managed to win the title despite the absence of any multiple winners, or the backing of a major stable, is a rare feat and very much a tribute to his riding throughout the season. Bagalino provided Pritchard with his first winner of the season but it was a treble at the North Hereford and a four timer at the North Ledbury which signalled his intent, and his riding throughout the season was characterised by style, strength and acute tactical awareness—he is a more than worthy champion.

JUST CHARLIE (27)

Just Charlie won six of his eight races in 1997, and if the majority came in less than exalted company, he has proved himself to be a very useful pointer in the process.

Perhaps his best performance was the first at Market Rasen in early February, when he beat Zam Bee and Coolvawn Lady in receipt of two and four pounds respectively.

This was the only occasion on which Just Charlie was in the happy position of receiving weight from rivals—placing him became a task of looking for races in which he would carry penalties, which would nullify the prospect of regular rider David Easterby having to put up overweight.

Easterby did well to keep his weight under such a tight rein throughout the season but is likely to give up the unequal battle with the scales now. Among Just Charlie's feats during the season was humping 12st 12lbs to victory at Easingwold at the end of April, a feat he managed with some ease, and his only reverses came when Easterby mistimed his challenge in the men's open at Stainton on Easter Saturday, and a fall in his final start at Easingwold in May.

Just Charlie will be nine years old in 1998 and should continue to prosper; he is particularly effective on good and fast ground and stays well.

HORNBLOWER (26)

The winner of five of his six starts in points in 1997, in addition to a late-season hunter-chase at Cartmel, Hornblower is a useful, game and consistent pointer and a fine tribute to the training and riding skills of Richard and Carrie Ford.

His only defeat came first time out when he succumbed to the superior fitness of the useful Orange Ragusa at the ever-excellent Cumberland Farmers meeting at Dalston, after which his only worrying time came when he just pipped Lupy Minstrel in a tactical battle at Whittington. In truth, he faced only modest opponents mostly but his hunter-chase debut at Cartmel was full of promise.

Meeting a host of more experienced rivals, he won untroubled with Carrie Ford exercising her neck muscles more than those in her arms on the half-mile run-in—the form might be moderate but there is plenty more to come should he run in hunter-chases again in 1998.

The Ford partnership enjoyed great success in 1997, highlighted by their feat of riding five winners between them at the Vale of Lune meeting on Easter Saturday, and the combination of their talents as a training and riding duo looks destined to take them to the top of the point-to-point world.

BITOFANATTER (26)

Bitofanatter ran only three times in 1995–6 and his sole appearance in

1996 saw him fall at the last fence in his members race when tailed off. Third place in a maiden, a close runner-up in a competitive restricted and a virtual solo round in the same members race comprised his first three runs in 1997—improvement certainly, but nothing out of the ordinary.

It was only when front-running tactics were employed on his last three starts that there was a significant upturn in results.

A restricted success at Lockerbie was followed by two end of season intermediaries, at Mosshouses and Aspatria.

In the first he had little to beat but the Aspatria race was a competitive contest run on ever-softening ground, and if the bare details of victory are solid enough, the manner of success was highly impressive.

Bitofanatter set a strong gallop and had his rivals stretched out before halfway; maintaining the pace throughout the final circuit, he was able to coast home to win unchallenged.

Ridden by the promising Ranald Morgan, Bitofanatter will be ten years old in 1998, but with so little mileage on the clock, he may not have reached his peak yet. There must be every possibility that he could win a novices hunter-chase, at least.

PERAMBULATE (24)

Twenty-five years ago, David Barons ruled the roost in westcountry National Hunt training, and his partnership with Bob Davies saw the rider win three jockeys' titles.

These days, his efforts are concentrated around importing New Zealand-bred horses, most of which are sold immediately, while a few are kept for point-to-pointing before inevitably passing through the sales ring.

In the seventies, Baron's best horse was the hurdler Perambulate, and the name has been handed down to one of this season's most promising pointers, who bears an uncanny resemblance to his namesake.

This latest Perambulate won a division of the maiden at Lemalla in February, a race which received an unexpected boost when the runner-up, Herhorse, won a hunter-chase at Newton Abbot next time out.

Perambulate's only subsequent outing came at Great Trethew in early March, when he survived a blunder two from home to beat the very useful Ticket To The Moon, who showed her worth later in the season by finishing a close second in a decent hunter-chase at Newton Abbot.

Not seen after, Perambulate was sold at Doncaster in May, in the customary Barons' fashion, but this might just be the one which got away—if Perambulate makes just some of the progress you would expect of a five years old, he will be a real force to be reckoned with in 1998.

Raced only on soft ground to date, Perambulate has shown that he is both a battler and a stayer.

INTRODUCTION

This introduction is little changed to that which appeared in previous years but is probably worth re-printing for anyone seeing the book for the first time.

The objective of this form book is to give the racegoer immediate access to all the information that is needed to assess the relative merits of each runner in any race.

To achieve this aim, the contents include:

a. results with 'close-ups' of all meetings in 1997;
b. Irish results of hunter' chases and point-to-points in full;
c. 'at a glance' form of all registered runners in point-to-points and hunter 'chases in 1997;
d. winning amateur riders under Rules and in point-to-points;
e. the weights of winning amateur riders licensed to ride under Rules;
f. course characteristics.

In order to see how a horse ran in all its races at different times of the season, at different courses, on different going and at different distances, the usual procedure is to look in the index for the horse, find the last race in which it ran and then thumb back through the results.

It seems, therefore, eminently sensible to present all this information in an 'at a glance' format, particularly for racegoers at point-to-points where there is little time between the runners being known and the betting market being formed.

This has been done in the Form section where a race rating is given each time a horse ran. From these figures an overall rating is given, not as a historical record of the past season, but as an indication as to how the horse might run in the future when it is one year older.

To ease the task of the racegoer further, the Irish runners are integrated into the main Index of runners rather than into a separate section.

In the Irish results section ratings are given for placed horses. The ratings are on the same scale as those in the main Index and are useful as a guide for horses that subsequently run in the U.K. Care should be taken, however, as there is often a marked difference with some of the younger horses improving significantly while others never run to the same mark again after leaving their professional yards.

The owners of some horses will be disappointed to read that their superb hunter and family pet has been dismissed as 'of no account'. The horse may have run his heart out and given the owner tremendous enjoyment. The comment simply implies that he is not a racehorse who should be treated seriously in the betting market.

Purposely excluded are unregistered hunters. These horses invariably have a rating of 0 and are ineligible to run in any race other than one specifically for hunt members of the host meeting. Their inclusion would clutter up the list to no purpose. Each horse is, of course, able to be found in the results section in the members' race in which it ran.

It is often of interest, particularly in low weighted hunter chases, to know whether or not the usual rider can make the weight and take full advantage of any allowance. It is also sometimes significant as to how much dead weight a horse carries in a point-to-point and the effects of a further penalty of 7 or 10lbs of lead. Consequently the weights are given of all riders who are licensed to ride under Rules who have had at least one success this season, either in a hunter 'chase or in a point-to-point. These weights are incorporated in the table of the record of winning riders.

The book is intended to be used as a working document rather than a library publication. From your local knowledge, if you believe that a race has been assessed wrongly and that horses have been rated either too high or too low then alter them and update as the season progresses. At the end of the book there are blank pages so that horses appearing for the first time next season can be added. These, of course, will be given a rating and, together with every other runner, have the rating updated each week in *Point-to-Point Entries Index.* This is published on Wednesdays to complement the detailed results, which appear on Mondays, in *The Sporting Life.*

Comments and criticisms of this publication will be welcomed. The compiler does not guarantee that each letter will be personally answered but does promise that its contents will be taken fully into consideration before the publication of next year's annual. Write to:

Point-to-Point Feedback, The Sporting Life,
One Canada Square, Canary Wharf, London E14 5AP

HOW TO USE THE RATINGS

Guide to Ratings

10–14	Moderate Form
15–17	Average Maiden Winner
18–19	Average Restricted Winner
20–21	Average Intermediate Winner
22–23	Average Confined Winner
24–26	Average Open Winner
27–29	Very good Pointer/Fair Hunter 'chaser
30–34	Very good Hunter 'chaser
35+	Top Class

Adjustment to Ratings for finding Winners

In Point-to-Points	1 point = 3lbs.
In Hunter 'chases	1 point = 2lbs.

Note: The 5lbs mares allowance and the 7lbs allowance for 5-yr-olds are already taken into account and no further adjustment is necessary.

Other Factors to be taken into account

Ratings, are valueless unless used sensibly, and therefore, must be used in conjunction with the summary given for each horse. This guides the reader, on the evidence available, on the suitability of particular going, distance and type of course. Suppose the comments and ratings of the four main contenders in a race are:

Horse A	25	Best in testing conditions over extreme distances; heavy
Horse B	24	Always needs a couple of runs to come to his best; any
Horse C	26	Useful hunter chaser at 2–2½m; best R/H; firm
Horse D	23	Resolute and consistent; runs less well on heavy

In an early season point-to-point on good ground on a left handed course, Horse D is the most sensible bet even though having the lowest rating.

The rating given after the horse comment in the Index section should be used for early races. Subsequently the rating will be amended weekly in *Point-to-Point Entries Index*.

BETTING

Withdrawn Horse

(a) A bet on a horse withdrawn before it comes under Starter's Orders, will be refunded.

(b) If a horse is withdrawn late, Tattersalls Committee has authorised the following deductions under Rule 4(c) from winnings, based on the price on the withdrawn horse to compensate bookmakers who are obliged to return stakes on the withdrawn horse, as they would have laid shorter odds about the other runners when compiling their book.

If the Current Odds are	Reduction by Bookmaker
3/10 or longer odds on	75p in the £
2/5 to 1/3	70p
8/15 to 4/9	65p
8/13 to 4/7	60p
4/5 to 4/6	55p
20/21 to 5/6	50p
Evens to 6/5	45p
5/4 to 6/4	40p
13/8 to 7/4	35p
15/8 to 9/4	30p
5/2 to 3/1	25p
10/3 to 4/1	20p
9/2 to 11/2	15p
6/1 to 9/1	10p
10/1 to 14/1	5p
over 14/1	No Reduction
2 or more horses being withdrawn	Maximum Reduction 75p in the £

Note: Remember that the full amount of your stake should be returned—it is only the winnings that are subject to a deduction:

Examples:

1. You have a winning bet of £5 at 3–1 but the favourite at even money was withdrawn

stake of £5 returned in full
Winnings of £15 subject to 45p in the £1 deduction
ie. winnings reduced to £8.25
Total Return £13.25

2. You have a winning bet of £6 at 4–6 made before a horse was withdrawn whose price was 4–1

   Stake of £6 returned in full
   Winnings of £4 subject to 20p in the £1 deduction
   ie. winnings reduced to £3.20
   Total Return £9.20

Dead Heat

You will be paid the full odds to half your stake. The other half of your stake is lost.

Example: The prices of two horses that dead heat are even money and 4–1. You have backed both with a stake of £10 on each.

On the even money chance

You have £5 on at evens and win £5
Your return will be £10

On the 4–1 chance

You have £5 on at 4–1 and win £20
Your return will be £25

Point-to-Point Races

MEMBERS', SUBSCRIBERS', FARMERS' or HUNT RACE For horses hunted with the promoting hunt or club.

MAIDEN For horses that have not won a race. They can have qualified from any hunt unless conditions specify certain hunts.

CONFINED For horses hunted with the promoting hunt or one of the confined hunts nominated for the particular meeting.

RESTRICTED For horses that have not won under Rules and have not won an open, intermediate or one restricted point-to-point.

INTERMEDIATE For horses that have not won under Rules, an open or two intermediate point-to-points.

OPEN For any qualified horse, to be ridden by men or women as specified unless mixed (open to both).

CLUB For members' horses.

INDEX TO HUNTS
Point-to-Point

INDEX TO MEETINGS
Point-to-Point

INDEX TO MEETINGS
Hunter Chase

Point-to-Point Results 1997

P-TO-P OWNERS & RIDERS CLUB
Barbury Castle
Sunday January 19th
GOOD TO FIRM

1 Mares (12st)

DOUBTING DONNA 5a ....J Jukes 1
chsd ldrs,poor 5th hlfwy,styd on aft,lft in ld 3 out,ran on
Flame O'Frensi 5a ....Miss J Cumings 2
ld to 9th, chsd ldr to 15th, lft 2nd nxt, fin tired
Gypsy Luck 5a ....Miss P Gundry 3
rear, poor 6th hlfwy, kpt on, nrst fin
Miss Magic 5a *chsd ldrs, poor 4th hlfwy, no prog* ....F Brennan 4
Diamond Wind (USA) 5a *mstks, chsd ldrs til wknd 11th, t.o. & p.u. 3 out* ....A Beedles pu
Normead Lass 5a *alwys bhnd, t.o. & p.u. 14th* ....A Martin pu
All The Jolly 5a 4ow *alwys bhnd, t.o. & p.u. 13th* ....R Jones pu
Phar Too Touchy 5a *(fav) prssd ldr, ld 9th, wll clr whn blnd & u.r. 3 out* ....Miss R Francis ur
Gentle Jester 5a *f 4th* ....A Honeyball f
New Flame 5a *alwys bhnd, t.o. & p.u. last* ....J Trice-Rolph pu
Rusty Hall 7a *blnd 2nd, bhnd til f 6th* ..Miss P Cooper f
11 ran. 15l, 20l, 12l. Time 6m 25.00s. SP 14-1.
Mrs D Hughes (Llangeinor).
Poor Visibility apart from races 3 & 4 - restricted close-ups.

2 Novice Riders Div I (12st)

ALL WEATHER ....M Wilesmith 1
chsd ldrs, 5th hlfwy, prog 13th, ld 2 out, hld on well
Dauphin Bleu (Fr) ....Miss V Roberts 2
(fav) t.d.e. ld to 10th, prssd ldr aft, ev ch 2 out, just hld
Shannon Glen (bl) ....R Dalgety 3
alwys prom, 3rd hlfwy, 5th whn blnd 3 out, styd on wll
Richville *prom, ld 10th-2 out, sn wknd*........M Walters 4
Earl Boon 3ex *mid-div, 6th & pshd alng hlfwy, no prog* ....P Griffiths 5
Glitzy Lady (Ire) 5a *mid-div, 7th & effrt hlfwy, nvr on trms* ....G Smith 6
Real Class *sn wll bhnd, 10th hlfwy, nvr a fctr* ....T Osborne 7
Gallant Effort (Ire) *alwys bhnd, 11th & t.o. hlfwy* ....J Snowden 8
Eyre Point (Ire) *alwys wll bhnd, last & t.o. hlfwy* ....A Honeyball 9
Skinnhill (bl) *prom, 4th hlfwy, 5th & btn whn u.r. last* ....C Mason ur
Origami *rear til u.r. 5th* ....D Davies ur
Pyro Pennant *alwys rear, 9th hlfwy, t.o. & p.u. 14th* ....I Johnson pu
Dick's Cabin 3ow *alwys bhnd, 12th & t.o. hlfwy, p.u. 15th*..........W Pugh pu
Bawnerosh *wll in rear, 8th hlfwy, no ch whn p.u. 2 out* ....D Line pu
14 ran. ½l, 7l, 15l, 2l, ½l, 20l, 1l, 2 fences. Time 6m 22.00s. SP 13-2.
M S Wilesmith (Ledbury).

3 Novice Riders Div II (12st)

PACO'S BOY ....P York 1
alwys prom, chsd ldr 12th, ld flat, lkd hdd nr fin
Bet With Baker (Ire) ....B O'Doherty 2
(fav) mstks, ld 4th, clr aft to 2 out, hdd flat, rallied, lkd wnr
I'm Toby ....Miss S Palmer 3
wll in rear, poor 9th hlfwy, prog 13th, clsd 2 out, nrst fin
Friendly Lady 5a 3ex *cls up til outpcd frm 12th, kpt on agn frm 2 out* ....Miss A Bush 4
Sirisat 5ex *ld to 4th, chsd ldr to 12th, grad wknd frm 3 out* ....Miss T Blazey 5
Trusty Friend *mid-div, 8th hlfwy, no imp ldrs final cct* ....A Brown 6
Dukes Son *in tch, 6th hlfwy, wknd frm 3 out* ..D Smith 7
Midfielder *mid-div, prog & 5th hlfwy, no imp 3 out, sn btn* ....Miss V Roberts 8
High Guardian *blnd 6th, alwys bhnd, t.o. 11th* ....I Johnson 9
Metrostyle 3ow *alwys bhnd, 10th & no ch hlfwy, sn t.o.* ....C James 10
The Country Trader *alwys bhnd, t.o. last hlfwy, p.u. & u.r. apr 2 out* ....J Borrodaile pu
Drumceva *alwys bhnd, blnd 7th, t.o. & u.r. 12th* ....M Wilesmith ur
Electrolyte *chsd ldrs, 6th & wkng whn u.r. 13th* ....G Austin ur
Gt Hayes Pommard *rear whn u.r. 2nd* .....D Howells ur
14 ran. Hd, 2l, 15l, 3l, 3l, 2l, 12l, 2l, 1l. Time 6m 28.00s. SP 33-1.
R H York (Staff College & R.M.A.S. Drag).

4 Men's Open Div I (12st)

THE BOUNDER ....J Tizzard 1
prssd ldr, brthr aft 12th, rnwd effrt to ld 2 out, ran on wl
Calling Wild (Ire) 2ow ....T Mitchell 2
ld, blnd 15th, hdd 2 out, ev ch last, eased whn btn flat
Chilipour 7ex ....J Jukes 3
(fav) hld up, prog 9th, chsd ldng pair 11th, no imp 3 out, wknd
Orujo (Ire) *chsd ldrs, outpcd 12th, onepcd aft, fin 4th, disq* ....P Young 4D
Rusty Bridge 7ex *strgglng frm 8th, sn wll bhnd* ....C Richards 5
Castlebay Lad 4ex *jmpd slwly 5th, in tch til rdn & wknd 10th, t.o. & p.u. 14th* ....M Appleby pu
Cawkwell Dean *in tch, strgglng 10th, 6th & wll btn whn p.u. last* ....R Sweeting pu
Hill Fort (Ire) *t.o. 3rd, p.u. 8th* ....E Williams pu
Aj's Boy 4ow *8s-5/2, mstk 6th, in tch til rdn & wknd 10th, p.u. 12th* ....A Hill pu
9 ran. 5l, 20l, 8l, 20l. Time 6m 16.00s. SP 16-1.
L G Tizzard (Blackmore & Sparkford Vale).
Orujo disqualified - rider not W/I. Original distances.

5 Men's Open Div II (12st)

STILL IN BUSINESS 7ex...............T Mitchell 1
(fav) prog & 3rd hlfwy, ld 2 out, drvn out flat
Qualitair Memory (Ire) 7ex ....J Tizzard 2
prom, 2nd hlfwy, lft in ld apr 12th, hdd 2 out, just hld
Ardbrennan 4ex ....C Bennett 3
rear, 8th hlfwy, nrst fin
Bishops Island 7ex *in tch, 6th hlfwy, onepcd frm 3 out* ....P Young 4
Robusti *bhnd, 8th hlfwy, nvr dang*..........D S Jones 5
Prince Nepal *prom, 4th hlfwy, sn wknd, t.o.* ....G Barfoot-Saunt 6
Granville Grill 4ex *prom, 5th hlfwy, btn whn p.u. 12th* ....J Deutsch pu
Barnaby Boy *in tch in rear, 7th hlfwy, prog & chsng ldrs whn f 15th* ....J P Keen f

Desert Run (Ire) *bhnd, last & wkng whn p.u. 11th* ....T Underwood pu
Fresh Prince *ld til ran out & u.r. bend apr 12th* ....R Wakley ro
Tu Piece *bhnd, 10th hlfwy, p.u. 12th* ....P Howse pu
11 ran. 1l, 6l, ¾l, 25l, 12l. Time 6m 26.00s. SP 7-4.
R G Williams (Cattistock).

6 Ladies

BRACKENFIELD (bl) ....**Miss P Curling** 1
lft in ld 2nd, made most aft, drvn clr 3 out, ran on well
Tinotops ....**Miss S Vickery** 2
(fav) bhnd, gd prog to 15l 3rd hlfwy, chsd wnr 2 out, nrst fin
Sams Heritage ....**Miss A Dare** 3
w.w. prog & 6th hlfwy, styd on frm 14th, nrst fin
Fantastic Fleet (Ire) 7a *prssd wnr til grad wknd apr 2 out* ....Miss P Jones 4
Drummer Boy (Ire) *bhnd, 9th & t.o. hlfwy* ....Miss P Gundry 5
Tangle Baron *prom till 4th & strgglng hlfwy, sn no ch* ....Miss J Cumings 6
Hugli *bhnd, 8th & no ch hlfwy, t.o.* ....Miss L Pearce 7
Run To Form *chsd ldrs, 5th & effrt hlfwy, wknd & p.u. 15th* ....Miss E Wilesmith pu
Gold Diver *rear, 7th & no ch hlfwy, p.u. 14th* ....Miss E Jones pu
Star Oats *ld till blnd & u.r. 2nd* ....Miss S Palmer ur
Great Simplicity *t.o. till p.u. 14th* ....Miss P Cooper pu
Hiram B Birdbath *prom whn blnd & u.r. 4th* ....Miss A Plunkett ur
Dayadan (Ire) *rear whn mstk & u.r. 8th* Miss J Sawyer ur
13 ran. 3½l, 4l, 5l, 30l, 6l, ½l. Time 6m 20.00s. SP 3-1.
Mrs Susan Humphreys (Cattistock).

7 Restricted (12st)

KING TORUS (IRE) ....**J Jukes** 1
prssd ldr clr of rest, ld 3 out, sn clr, ran on well
Pines Express (Ire) ....**J Tizzard** 2
mid-div, 6th hlfwy, ran on strngly aft last, tk 2nd nr fin
Tea Cee Kay ....**A Sansome** 3
ld to 3 out, wknd apr last
Members Cruise *prom, 4th hlfwy, onepcd final cct* ....E Walker 4
Good Looking Guy *rear, 9th hlfwy, no prog* ....A Charles-Jones 5
Mac's Boy *prom, 3rd hlfwy, grad wknd, 5th & no ch whn p.u. last* ....D S Jones pu
Pharrago (Ire) *alwys bhnd, 11th hlfwy, t.o. & p.u. 14th* ....Miss P Cooper pu
Clandon Lad 1ow *blnd & rdr lost iron 1st, bhnd til p.u. 6th* ....T Mitchell pu
Danny Rhy 5a *mid-div, losing tch whn f 11th* E James f
Live Wire (Ire) *alwys bhnd, last & t.o. hlfwy, p.u. 2 out* ....T Cox pu
Swing To The Left (Ire) 5a *bhnd, 10th hlfwy, p.u. 14th* ....Miss J Cumings pu
Stalbridge Bill *mid-div, prog frm 11th, clsng on ldrs whn blnd & u.r. 3 out* ....Miss A Goschen ur
Ridemore Balladeer *(fav) hld up, prog & 5th hlfwy, lost plc & p.u. 13th* ....Miss P Curling pu
Mischievous Imp 3ow *alwys bhnd, 12th & t.o. hlfwy, p.u. 2 out* ....D Line pu
14 ran. 20l, 1l, 2l, 15l. Time 6m 28.00s. SP 6-1.
Nick Viney (Tiverton Staghounds).
J.N.

CAMBRIDGESHIRE HARRIERS
Cottenham
Saturday January 25th
GOOD TO FIRM

8 Confined (12st)

REMO GROVE (IRE) ....**T Lane** 1
made all, drew clr apr 14th, unchal, fin lame
Bervie House (Ire) ....**R Barrett** 2
chsd ldr 6th, hit 3 out, sn rdn & no prog
So Isle 5a ....**M Gingell** 3
chsd ldr to 6th, 3rd & outpcd 14th, no dang aft
Stanwick Farlap 5a 6ex *(fav) in tch, pshd alng 11th, no dang frm 13th* ....T Marks 4
Old Dundalk *bhnd frm 3rd, t.o. & p.u. 14th* ....N King pu
5 ran. 12l, 15l, ½l. Time 6m 7.00s. SP 4-1.
Miss D J Ross (Fitzwilliam).

9 Land Rover Open (12st)

SHEER JEST 7ex ....**A Hill** 1
(fav) hld up, went 2nd 15th, ld apr last, rdn & kpt on flat
Peanuts Pet ....**R Walmsley** 2
chsd ldr, mstk 5th, ld 14th til apr last, onepcd
Faithful Star 7ex ....**R Hunnisett** 3
ld, mstk 7th, hdd 14th, no ch whn blnd 3 out, t.o.
3 ran. 3l, 1 fence. Time 6m 6.00s. SP 2-5.
Mrs Judy Wilson (Pytchley).

10 Intermediate (12st)

SIGN 3ow ....**A Hill** 1
(fav) prom, prssd ldr 14th, rdn apr 3 out, ld nxt, styd on
Salmon Mead (Ire) ....**A Harvey** 2
mid-div, prog 10th, rdn & outpcd 14th, styd on flat
Just A Madam (Ire) 5a ....**Miss E Tomlinson** 3
ld to 3rd, outpcd 14th, 4th whn blnd 2 out, kpt on flat
Horace *pckd 1st,ld 3rd,hit 3 out,hdd nxt, wknd last, bttr for race* ....W Wales 4
Mount Patrick *wll bhnd frm 6th, t.o. & p.u. 9th* ....C Lawson pu
Druid's Lodge *rear, rdn apr 11th, lost tch 13th, p.u. nxt* ....T Bulgin pu
Fiddlers Goodwill *bhnd til f 11th* ....C Ward f
7 ran. 2l, 2l, 6l. Time 6m 6.00s. SP 5-4.
Philip Newton (Pytchley).

11 Ladies

MADRAJ (IRE) ....**Miss H Irving** 1
disp til lft solo 8th
Rousillon To Be *(fav) disp til u.r. 8th*. .Mrs F Needham ur
2 ran. Time 6m 52.00s. SP 6-4.
Bruce Sarson (Warwickshire).

12 Restricted

GRAIN MERCHANT ....**R Walmsley** 1
ld to 4th, 8l 3rd apr 2 out, strng run flat to ld nr fin
Ballydesmond (Ire) ....**A Harvey** 2
(fav) chsd ldr 8th, chal & hit 3 out, ld last, hdd nr fin
Alice Sheer Thorn (Ire) 5a ....**M Gingell** 3
keen hold, ld 4th, jnd 3 out, hdd last, wknd flat
3 ran. ¾l, 5l. Time 6m 28.00s. SP 5-2.
J W Walmsley (Bramham Moor).

13 Open Maiden Div I (12st)

MISTER SPECTATOR (IRE) ....**C Gordon** 1
made all, clr 5th, hit last, unchal
Crestafair 5a ....**Miss H Irving** 2
w.w. prog to 2nd 16th, hit nxt, no hdwy aft
Kendor Pass (Ire) ....**M Tate** 3
chsd ldng pair to 10th, no dang frm 13th
Soon Be Back *mstks, wll bhnd, some prog frm 14th, nvr dang* ....R Barrett 4
Bali Tender *chsd ldr to 15th, grad wknd* ....A Balding 5
Barneys Gold (Ire) *prom whn mstk 4th, bhnd & blnd 11th, t.o.* ....A Bealby 6
Native Mony (Ire) *mid-div, 4th whn mstk 13th, wll btn whn p.u. 3 out* ....S Cowell pu
Trina's Cottage (Ire) *alwys bhnd, t.o. & p.u. 3 out* ....B McKim pu
Hey Bingo 5a *wll bhnd 10th, t.o. & p.u. 12th* ...T Lane pu
Springfield Pet 5a 6ow *n.j.w. alwys bhnd, t.o. & p.u. 3 out* ....K Needham pu
10 ran. Dist, 10l, 1l, 30l, 8l. Time 6m 4.00s. SP 9-2.

P Hughes (East Sussex & Romney Marsh).

14 Open Maiden Div II (12st)

MAKIN' DOO (IRE) ....K Green 1
chsd ldng pair, jnd ldr 14th, ld apr last, styd on und pres
Sunkala Shine ....Miss R Clark 2
ld 4-14th & 16th til aft 3 out,lft in ld nxt,hdd last,no ext
Raincheck ....G Hopper 3
hld up, prog to ld 14-16th, ld, blnd & hdd 2 out, one-pcd flt
Bamboo Pie 5a *ld to 4th, mstk 11th, sn outpcd, no dang aft*..............................S Morris 4
1 Normead Lass 5a *mid-div, lost tch 10th, t.o.* . .A Martin 5
Moon Monkey (Ire) *bhnd whn mstks 6th & 7th, t.o. frm 11th*...................................M Cowley 6
Springfield Rex *bhnd, t.o. 10th, p.u. 13th* . .K Needham pu
7 ran. 1l, nk, 20l, 15l, 12l. Time 6m 13.00s. SP 7-4.
R G Makin (York & Ainsty South).

15 Maiden (12st)

CLAYDONS MONTY ....S R Andrews 1
chsd ldr, ld 10th, hrd prssd whn lft wll clr 2 out
Holding The Aces ....T Lane 2
ld to 10th, ev ch 16th, wknd 3 out, lft 2nd nxt
Ticklebay 5a..............................A Coe 3
alwys bhnd, last & jmpd slwly 13th, lft poor 3rd 2 out
Roscolvin (Ire) 7a *(fav) trckd ldng pair, smooth prog to cls 2nd whn f 2 out,rmntd* ....R Wakley 4
Flapping Freda (Ire) 5a *prom til f 3rd* ....R Gill f
View Point (Ire) *cls up whn f 2nd* ....M Gingell f
Scarlett O'Hara 7a *hmpd 2nd, jmpd slwly 4th, 4th & btn whn ref 3 out* ....A Harvey ref
7 ran. Dist, 1 fence, 1 fence. Time 6m 24.00s. SP 3-1.
Michael A Johnson (Puckeridge).
S.P.

HURSLEY HAMBLEDON
Badbury Rings
Saturday January 25th
GOOD TO FIRM

16 Members (12st)

2 **SKINNHILL 7ex** ....C Mason 1
(fav) made most, drew clr frm 10th, mstk 3 out, easily
Shared Fortune (Ire) *wth wnr to 9th, sn wknd, fence bhnd whn s.u. bnd apr last* ....Daniel Dennis su
2 ran. Time 6m 21.00s. SP 1-5.
P Mason (Hursley Hambledon).

17 Confined (12st)

APATURA KING ....T Mitchell 1
(fav) trckd ldrs, rdn to chs ldr 15th, ld aft last, drvn out
Corly Special ....B Pollock 2
trckd ldrs, ld 11th, hdd & no no ext aft last
Rathmichael ....M Miller 3
ld to 3rd, in tch til outpcd aft 13th, tk poor 3rd flat
Prankster *prom, wth ldr 14th, wknd aft nxt, t.o.* ....T Atkinson 4
Wrekin Hill *bhnd frm 4th, t.o. 11th* . . . .Mrs J Wilkinson 5
Roc de Prince (Fr) *bhnd frm 5th, t.o. & p.u. 11th* ....P Scouller pu
Lake Teereen *mstks, in tch in rear til u.r. 10th* ....T Underwood ur
Bold Bostonian (Fr) *pllng, ld 3-6th, ev ch whn mstk 14th, wknd rpdly, p.u. nxt* ....M Appleby pu
Osmosis *s.s. pllng, ld 6th til nrly u.r. 10th, wknd 13th, p.u. 15th* ....K Nelmes pu
9 ran. 2½l, 30l, 2½l, dist. Time 6m 20.00s. SP Evens.
C E Gibbs (Portman).

18 Ladies

ARCTIC CHILL (IRE) ....Miss S Vickery 1
ld to 2nd, lft in ld 5th, made rest, pshd out & ran on well
6³ **Sams Heritage** ....Miss A Dare 2
(fav) w.w. prog 10th, chsd wnr 15th, styd on, no imp aft last
Spacial (USA) 7ex....................Miss M Hill 3
chsd ldr 5th-15th, grad fdd
Roving Report *outpcd in mid-div, effrt 11th, sn btn, t.o. 15th* ....Mrs A Rucker 4
Daybrook's Gift 7ex *outpcd & bhnd, effrt 10th, sn btn, poor 6th whn f 15th* ....Miss N Allan f
Old Mill Stream 7ex *pllng, ld 2nd til blnd & u.r. 5th* ....Miss P Curling ur
Same Difference (Ire) *last whn nrly u.r. 3rd, t.o. aft til u.r. 12th*............................Miss T Honeyball ur
Pejawi 5a *jmpd lft & sn bhnd,efft 10th,sn btn,poor 4th whn u.r.2 out* ....Miss L Whitaker ur
Front Cover 5a *4th whn f 6th* ....Miss A Goschen f
9 ran. 2l, 15l, 1 fence. Time 6m 6.00s. SP 5-2.
M E Thorne & D G Hobbs (Blackmore & Sparkford Vale).

19 Men's Open (12st)

THE JOGGER 7ex......................J Tizzard 1
(fav) ld to 11th, ld 15th, drew clr 2 out, easily
5³ **Ardbrennan 4ex** ....C Bennett 2
prom, ld 11-15th, prssd wnr aft til wknd 2 out
Arise (Ire) ....N Mitchell 3
hld up, prog to trck ldng pair 11th, sn outpcd, kpt on 3 out
Fosbury 7ex *last & outpcd 3rd, nvr plcd to chal aft* ....T Mitchell 4
Ryming Cuplet 7ex *mid-div, pshd alng hlfwy, sn outpcd, no dang aft* ....L Jefford 5
4 Castlebay Lad 4ex *mstk 5th, in tch to 11th, sn wknd, t.o. & p.u. 15th* ....M Appleby pu
Sea Dreams (Ire) *mstks, prom, 3rd whn f 10th* ....J Barnes f
5 Desert Run (Ire) *in tch to 7th, lost plc rpdly, t.o. & p.u. 13th* ....T Underwood pu
8 ran. 15l, 2½l, 25l, 4l. Time 6m 7.50s. SP 7-4.
Mrs P Tizzard (Blackmore & Sparkford Vale).

20 Maiden Div I (12st)

ORPHAN OLLY ....P York 1
made all, styd on well frm 2 out, comf
Ted's Knight (Ire) ....M Portman 2
(fav) alwys prom, mstk 10th, lft 2nd 2 out, no imp wnr flat
In The Choir 5a................Maj H Carruthers 3
jmpd rght 2nd, last pair til ran on frm 2 out, no dang
Badger Beer 7a *mstk 2nd, last pair, wll bhnd 13th, ran on frm 2 out* ....Miss A Goschen 4
Amaranthine 5a *in tch to 12th, t.o. & p.u. 2 out* ....M Batters pu
Lyrical Seal 5a *w.w. 6th & in tch whn hmpd & u.r. 14th* ....J Maxse ur
Joe Penny *prom, cls 4th whn f 14th*..............B Dixon f
Uncle Bruce *alwys prssng wnr, cls 2nd & ev ch whn f 2 out* ....A Charles-Jones f
Sulason *cls up,lost plc 11th,ralld und pres 15th,wknd 3out,p.u.last* ....M Miller pu
9 ran. 6l, 25l, 2l. Time 6m 26.00s. SP 33-1.
R H York (Windsor Forest).

21 Maiden Div II (12st)

SIT TIGHT ....M Portman 1
(Jt fav) hld up, prog to chs clr ldr 13th, clsd & lft in clr ld last
Dormston Lad 3ow ....C Jowett 2
mid-div, rdn 11th, onepcd aft, lft 2nd last
Tullykyne Bells ....Miss D Stafford 3
mid-div, drppd rear 11th, no prog, lft 3rd last
Cherry Street 5a 2ow *n.j.w. chsd ldr til wknd 13th, t.o. & p.u. 3 out* ....M Batters pu

Lixwm 5a 2ow *(Jt fav) sn wll clr,fnc ahd 15th,tired rpdly 2 out,f last, winded* ....T Lacey f
Tractorias (Ire) *rear, wknd 11th, t.o. & p.u. 15th* ....T Woolridge pu
The Poacher *mstks, prom in chsng grp til ran out & u.r. 13th* ....Daniel Dennis ro
7 ran. 12l, 5l. Time 6m 29.00s. SP 7-4.
Miss S Pilkington (Berks & Bucks).

22 Restricted Div I (12st)

CHISM (IRE) ....M Miller 1
(fav) lft disp apr 4th, ld 3 out, clr last, eased flat,just hld on
Most Vital ....Miss A Goschen 2
lft disp apr 4th til 3 out, ran on agn flat, just faild
Dunamase Dandy (Ire) *ld til p.u. apr 4th, saddle slppd* ....T Lacey pu
3 ran. ½l. Time 6m 47.00s. SP 1-3.
J Webber (Portman).

23 Restricted Div II (12st)

STALBRIDGE GOLD 5a....................Miss A Goschen 1
hld up,prog 11th, chsd clr ldr 2 out, styd on wll to ld flat
7[3] **Tea Cee Kay ....A Sansome 2**
cls up,ld 9th,clr 16th,stmbld bnd apr last,hdd & no ext flat
Elle Flavador 5a....................Miss S Vickery 3
(fav) mstk 5th, chsd ldr, mstk 3 out, wknd & lost 2nd nxt
Celtic Token *t.d.e. ld to 4th, grad outpcd frm 13th* ....J Barnes 4
Just Donald *rear, lost tch 12th, t.o.* ....A Honeyball 5
Mr Sunnyside *chsd ldrs to 12th, wknd, t.o.*...M Batters 6
Dont Rise Me (Ire) *cls up, nrly u.r. 9th, 6th & wkng whn u.r. 12th*....................B Parsons ur
3 Gt Hayes Pommard *s.s. t.o. til p.u. 12th*....D Howells pu
8 ran. 2l, 15l, 4l, 25l, 6l. Time 6m 17.00s. SP 11-2.
C J Barnes (Blackmore & Sparkford Vale).
J.N.

ESSEX FARMERS & UNION
Marks Tey
Sunday January 26th
GOOD TO FIRM

24 Members

GOLDEN FELLOW (IRE) ....A Coe 1
pllng, ld 3rd, made rest, blnd 12th, rdn & styd on wll last
Dynamite Dan (Ire) ....S Cowell 2
(fav) ld to 3rd, chsd wnr aft, 3l down 2 out, no ext
Doctor Dick (Ire)....................T Walsh 3
1st ride, 3rd & in tch 8th, t.o. 3 out
Morstons Magic *1st ride, bhnd til u.r. 9th* ....P Piddington ur
Sheer Hope *pllng, n.j.w. prom early, bhnd 9th, t.o. & p.u. 13th* ....D Hayes pu
Miss Simitar 5a *bhnd frm 3rd, t.o. & p.u. 17th* T Moore pu
6 ran. 5l, 1 fence. Time 6m 56.00s. SP 7-4.
Keith Coe (Essex Farmers & Union).
Restricted close-ups races 1-3, poor visibility.

25 Confined (12st)

CARDINAL RICHELIEU ....Miss L Rowe 1
ld to 8th, chsd ldr aft, ld agn 2 out, styd on well
Craftsman 8ex ....Miss G Chown 2
(fav) chsd ldr, ld 8th-2 out, no ext und pres
Saffron Flame (Ire) ....P Taiano 3
w.w. mstk 9th, 3rd & ch 3 out, btn nxt, eased flat
Malachite Green *trckd ldrs, blnd 11th, lost tch 15th, t.o.*....................S Cowell 4
Major Inquiry (USA) 2ow *alwys rear, lost tch 14th, t.o. & p.u. 3 out*....................W Pewter pu
5 ran. 3l, 20l, 30l. Time 6m 44.00s. SP 8-1.
Christopher Sporborg (Puckeridge).

26 Ladies

ONE FOR THE CHIEF ....Miss A Embiricos 1
chsd ldr 9th, ld 14th, rdn apr last, hld on wll flat
Dunboy Castle (Ire) ....Miss G Chown 2
in tch, rdn 2 out, ev ch last, unable qckn flat
St Gregory (bl)....................Mrs L Gibbon 3
(fav) ld to 2nd, prom, rdn & blnd 2 out, onepcd aft
Wistino *pllng, ld 2-6th, chsd ldrs aft, wknd apr 3 out* ....Miss L Rowe 4
Whats Another 5a 5ow *prom, ld 6-14th, grad wknd* ....Miss K Bridge 5
Profligate *hld up, lost tch 14th, t.o.* .....Miss P Ellison 6
Sarazar (USA) *alwys last, t.o. & p.u. 11th* ....Miss H Pewter pu
Upward Surge (Ire) *bhnd frm 9th, t.o. & p.u. 16th* ....Mrs N Ledger pu
8 ran. ¾l, 1½l, 25l, 12l, 10l. Time 6m 42.00s. SP 9-1.
M A Kemp (Suffolk).

27 Men's Open

SUNNY MOUNT ....S Morris 1
(fav) prom, mstks 1st & 11th, ld 3 out, rdn & ran on strngly last
Over The Edge ....C Ward-Thomas 2
prom, 3rd & rdn 17th, styd on wll flat, not rch wnr
Stede Quarter ....P Bull 3
trckd ldrs, ev ch 3 out, ld brfly nxt, onepcd aft
Airtrak (Ire) *ld to 3 out, wknd nxt* ....A Coe 4
Colonel Kenson *alwys same plc, lost tch 14th, t.o.* ....C Ward 5
Buckshot (Ire) *alwys last, t.o. 14th*..........C Barlow 6
6 ran. 1½l, 2l, 12l, dist, 2l. Time 6m 46.00s. SP 11-10.
J E Greenall (Pytchley).

28 Restricted (12st)

SWEET MERENDA (IRE) 5a............S Cowell 1
mid-div,poor 6th 14th,lft 3rd 3 out,strng run last,ld nr fin
Auchendolly (Ire) ....N Bloom 2
ld 2nd-3rd, outpcd 12th, lft 2nd 3 out, ld flat, hdd nr fin
Fresh Ice (Ire) ....T Lane 3
prom, ld 16th, lft clr 3 out, wknd rpdly apr last, hdd flat
Cool Apollo (NZ) *in tch in rear, blnd 10th, outpcd nxt, kpt on 3 out, no dang*....................G Plenderleith 4
Corn Kingdom *bhnd 7th, nvr trbld ldrs aft*......A Coe 5
Give It A Bash (Ire) 5a *alwys mid-div, 5th & no ch apr 15th* ....T Moore 6
Holmby Mill *(fav) ld,jmpd slwly 1st,ld agn 3rd,blnd & hdd 9th, wknd 15th,t.o.*....................B Pollock 7
Northern Code *chsd ldr, lft in ld 9th, mstk 11th, hdd 16th, btn whn f 3out*....................G Smith f
New York Boy *sn wll bhnd, t.o. & p.u. 14th* ...N Strain pu
9 ran. Nk, 5l, 8l, 12l, 1l, 20l. Time 6m 53.00s. SP 9-2.
B Kennedy (Essex Farmers & Union).

29 Maiden Div I (12st)

BALLYALLIA CASTLE (IRE) ....R Wakley 1
trckd ldrs, ld 3 out, hit last, hld on und pres
Ruperts Choice (Ire) 7a ....C Ward-Thomas 2
mstks, rear, prog 12th, ev ch & blnd 2 out, ran on wll flat
Ludoviciana 5a....................Miss G Chown 3
t.d.e. ld to 4th, ld 15th-3 out, onepcd und pres aft
Burrells Wharf (Ire) *(fav) chsd ldrs going wll, ev ch 3 out, onepcd aft*....................S Morris 4
Remilan (Ire) *w.w. prog 11th, btn apr 3 out, eased* ....P Taiano 5
Alycount (USA) *rear, in tch til u.r. 9th* ......V Coogan ur
Country Parson (Ire) *prom, cls 3rd & going wll whn p.u. aft 15th, lame*....................S R Andrews pu
But Not Quite (Ire) *tubed, hld up, lost tch 13th, t.o. & p.u. 15th*....................P Bull pu
Bishops Tale *keen hld, ld 4th-15th, wkng whn f 17th* ....A Coe f

Regal Bay *bhnd frm 10th, t.o. & p.u. 15th* . . . . W Wales pu
10 ran. ¾l, 3l, 7l, 15l. Time 6m 51.00s. SP 3-1.
A F J Moss (Suffolk).
After Stewards' Inquiry, result stands.

30 Maiden Div II (12st)

EDINBURGH REEL ALE 5a . . . . .R Barrett 1
(fav) jmpd rght, prom, ld 11th, in cmmnd whn lft wll clr 3 out
Regency Cottage . . . . .W Wales 2
rear, prog 9th, 4th & outpcd 14th, lft poor 2nd 3 out
Superforce (bl) *mstks, rmndrs 3rd, t.o. & p.u. 6th, b.b.v.* . . . . .C Ward-Thomas pu
Alapa *prom, ld 7th-11th, 3rd & wkng whn hmpd & u.r. 3 out* . . . . .V Coogan ur
Zoes Pet 5a *mstk 2nd, in tch til u.r. 8th* Miss H Pewter ur
The Prior *rear, prog & in tch 10th, outpcd 13th, t.o. & p.u. 3 out* . . . . .P Rowe pu
Mister Rainman *w.w. prog 9th, chsd wnr 17th, 5l down whn f 3 out* . . . . .T Bulgin f
Go Magic *blnd & u.r. 1st* .S Cowell ur
Bart's Castle *ld to 7th, wknd 10th, t.o. & p.u. 13th* . . . . .A Coe pu
9 ran. Dist. Time 6m 55.00s. SP 2-1.
Mrs Richard Pilkington (Enfield Chace).
S.P.

WEST PERCY & MILVAIN
Alnwick
Sunday January 26th
GOOD

31 Members

WASHAKIE 7ex . . . . .J Walton 1
(fav) chsd ldr to 5th & agn 13th, ld nxt, sn clr, eased flat
Whosthat . . . . .Miss S Lamb 2
ld to 14th, mstk & btn nxt, kpt on
McNay *alwys last, lost tch 10th, abt 12l 3rd whn f 15th* . . . . .R Green f
Donside *chsd ldr 5th til mstk 13th, 3rd whn blnd & u.r. nxt* . . . . .A Robson ur
4 ran. 1l. Time 6m 34.00s. SP 1-3.
Mrs F T Walton (West Percy & Milvain).

32 Restricted

TURBULENT GALE (IRE) . . . . .R Bevis 1
(fav) mstk 8th, ld to 3 out, rallied to ld last, just hld on
Cukeira 5a . . . . .C Paisley 2
jnd ldrs 7th, ld 3 out, mstk nxt, hdd last, rallied flat
Admission (Ire) . . . . .Miss C Metcalfe 3
prom, outpcd 12th, ran on 15th, fin wll, nrst fin
Greenmount Lad (Ire) *mid-div, prog 9th, sn wth ldrs, wknd aft 3 out* . . . . .P Cornforth 4
All Or Nothing 5a *prom, lost plc 7th, t.o. 12th, ran on agn frm 2 out* . . . . .J Ewart 5
Attle *hld up, lost tch 11th, effrt 15th, nvr on trms* . . . . .S Brisby 6
Hoistthestandard 5a *mstk 8th, alwys rear, t.o. 15th* . . . . .T Glass 7
Malvern Cantina *hld up, mid-div hlfwy, no prog whn blnd & u.r. 14th* . . . . .S Swiers ur
By Crikey (Ire) *alwys rear, lost tch 14th, t.o. & p.u. 3 out* . . . . .A Robson pu
Durham Glint *mstks, alwys last, t.o. & p.u. 13th* . . . . .S Bowden pu
Snapper *pllng, chsd wnr 3rd-3 out, 3rd & btn whn f 2 out* . . . . .A Parker f
11 ran. ½l, 1l, 15l, 10l, 8l, 30l. Time 6m 28.00s. SP 6-4.
E E Williams (West Shropshire Drag).

33 Ladies

SOUTHERN MINSTREL . . . . .Miss C Metcalfe 1+
in tch,trckd ldr 13th, outpcd 3 out, ran on last, got up fin
ASTRAC TRIO (USA) . . . . .Miss A Bowie 1+
j.w. prom, ld 9-10th & frm 12th, clr 3 out, jnd post
Lupy Minstrel . . . . .Miss P Robson 3
(fav) trckd ldrs going wll, not quckn 13th, ran on onepcd frm 3out
Roly Prior *cls up til lost tch wth ldrs 14th, styd on wll frm 2 out* . . . . .Mrs V Jackson 4
Houselope Beck *ld to 7th, prom til fdd frm 15th* . . . . .Miss S Forster 5
Rustino *cls up, mstk 12th, effrt to 3rd whn pckd 15th, wknd 2 out* . . . . .Miss R Clark 6
Precarium (Ire) *prssd ldr, ld 7-9th, prom til wknd apr 3 out* . . . . .Miss S Leach 7
Ready Steady *alwys bhnd, nvr a fctr* . . . . .Mrs K Hargreave 8
Schweppes Tonic *mstk 2nd, u.r. 4th*. . .Miss D Laidlaw ur
The Laughing Lord *alwys last, t.o. & p.u. 12th* . . . . .Miss R Shiels pu
Parsons Brig *trckd ldrs til blnd & u.r. 8th* Mrs S Grant ur
Lakeland Edition 5a *u.r. 2nd* . . . . .Miss F Barnes ur
12 ran. Dd-ht, 6l, 10l, 2l, 6l, 10l, 12l. Time 6m 18.00s.
Miss A Bowie / N Chamberlain (Buccleuch / Zetland).
Astrac Trio 4-1, Southern Minstrel 3-1.

34 Men's Open (12st)

COUNTRY TARROGEN 7ex . . . . .N Wilson 1
(fav) j.w. made all, clr 3 out, comf
Castle Tyrant 5a . . . . .P Atkinson 2
chsd wnr to 15th & frm 3 out, no imp nxt
Cot Lane 7ex . . . . .J Tate 3
1st ride, in tch in rear, effrt 15th, styd on wll frm 2 out
King Spring *rear, prog 12th, chsd wnr 15th-3 out, one-pcd* . . . . .A Parker 4
Clare Lad *1st ride, in tch in rear, effrt 15th, btn whn nrly u.r. 2out* . . . . .R Walford 5
Moss Bee *prom to 7th, sn wknd, t.o. & p.u. 12th* . . . . .T Scott pu
Buckaneer Bay *unruly pddck, prom til mstk & wknd 15th, t.o. & p.u. last* . . . . .C Wilson pu
Politico Pot *mstks, prom til wknd & mstk 14th, t.o. & p.u. last* . . . . .S Whitaker pu
Fiscal Policy *mstk & u.r. 1st*. . . . . .R Trotter ur
9 ran. 4l, 1l, ½l, 15l. Time 6m 26.00s. SP 4-7.
Mrs M Cooper (Middleton).

35 Confined (12st)

TOASTER CRUMPET . . . . .Miss P Robson 1
alwys prom, ld 15th, clr last, pshd out, comf
Love Actinium (Ire) 5a . . . . .C Amos 2
in tch, prog 11th, wth wnr 15th, not qckn nxt, styd on
Kinlea 1ow . . . . .P Diggle 3
alwys prom, ld 11-15th, chal 2 out, unable qckn flat
Political Issue *cls up til outpcd 13th, ran on agn 3 out, not qckn nxt* . . . . .P Johnson 4
Little General *prom til onepcd apr 3 out* . . . . .Miss K McLintock 5
Lion Of Vienna *(fav) 6s-3s, rear, strggling whn mstk 11th, effrt 15th, nvr on trms* . . . . .T Scott 6
Murder Moss (Ire) 3ow *rear, lost tch 11th, effrt 15th, sn wknd* . . . . .S Colthard 7
Fish Quay *rear, last & wll bhnd 9th, prog 13th, mstk 15th, wknd* . . . . .Miss S Lamb 8
Young Moss *rear whn blnd 8th, t.o. 13th*. . . . .A Parker 9
Itsalltheonetodev (Ire) 5ex *mstks, ld til ran wd bnd aft 9th, wknd rpdly 15th,p.u.2out* . . . . .R Neal pu
10 ran. 4l, hd, 1l, 4l, 15l, 10l, 8l, 1 fence. Time 6m 30.00s. SP 5-1.
Miss P Robson (Tynedale).

36 Open Maiden Div I

BOULEVARD BAY (IRE) . . . . .N Wilson 1
(fav) hld up wll bhnd, prog frm 10th, ld 3 out, clr last, rdn out
Star Lea . . . . .B Stonehouse 2
chsd ldr 7th til mstk 11th, lft 2nd agn 2 out, styd on flat
Trumpet Hill . . . . .T Morrison 3

out of tch in mid-div, no ch frm 15th, styd on 3 out,nvr nrr
Mapalak 5a *chsd ldrs til grad wknd frm 14th* . .T Scott 4
Bavington *mid-div, no prog 13th, no ch frm 3 out* ....R Morgan 5
Indian River (Ire) *last pair & t.o. til p.u. 4th, dsmntd* ....A Robson pu
Restraint 5a *alwys rear, t.o. 15th, f last* Miss F Barnes f
Bantel Bargain 5a *mstk 3rd, alwys wll bhnd, t.o. & p.u. 11th* ....P Johnson pu
Hurricane Ryan (Ire) *7s-7/2, set mad gallop til ran out apr 7th*..........I McMath ro
Wild Adventure *mstks, prom, 5th whn f 13th*. . .T Glass f
Monynut 5a *rear grp, no prog whn hmpd & u.r. 13th* ....Miss J Wight ur
My Meadowsweet *trckd ldrs, ld 13th-3 out, 2nd & hld whn f nxt*..........C Storey f
Just Takethe Micky *jmp rght,chsd ldr,lft in ld apr 7th,hdd & wknd 13th,p.u.2out* ....A Balding pu
Keep A Secret *last trio, t.o. & p.u. 12th* . . . .P Atkinson pu
Hanleys Call (Ire) *chsd ldrs, 4th whn f 7th* ....M Bradburne f
15 ran. 5l, 20l, 2l, 15l. Time 6m 28.00s. SP 6-4.
J R Burns (Middleton).

37 Open Maiden Div II

POSSTICK MILL 7a..........A Parker 1
hld up bhnd,prog & mstk 10th,chsd ldr 14th,lft clr 3 out
Olive Branch 5a..........Miss S Forster 2
chsd ldrs, no prog 14th, lft 2nd 3 out, styd on
Seymour Fiddles 5a..........C Storey 3
mid-div, lost tch 13th, kpt on 3 out, nrst fin
Bluebell Track 5a *mid-div, no ch frm 13th, kpt on* ....R Trotter 4
Fragrant Lord *alwys bhnd, no dang frm 14th* ....Mrs V Jackson 5
Tropnevad 7ow *alwys bhnd, t.o. 10th* ....J Walton 6
Connor The Second *rear whn f 3rd*. . . . .M Bradburne f
Gallants Delight 5a *ld, clr hlfwy, 30l up whn f 3 out* ....A Robson f
Storm Alive (Ire) *alwys wll bhnd, t.o. & p.u. 15th* ....Miss P Robson pu
Mal's Castle (Ire) 5a *n.j.w. prom to 8th, wknd 10th, t.o. & p.u. 15th* ....P Atkinson pu
Alianne 5a *mstk 1st, alwys last trio, t.o. & p.u. 3 out* ....P Johnson pu
Border Glory *alwys rear, t.o. & p.u. 2 out* R Robinson pu
Primitive Star 5a *not fluent, chsd clr ldr, disp 2nd & wkng whn f 14th*..........P Cornforth f
Bowmans Lodge *(fav) prog 7th, disp dist 2nd 14th til p.u. apr 3 out*..........S Swiers pu
Victor Charlie *prom til grad wknd frm 13th, 7th & no ch whn u.r. 15th* ....N Sutton ur
15 ran. 4l, 15l, 5l, 2l, 1 fence. Time 6m 38.00s. SP 7-2.
Mrs N Hope (Braes Of Derwent).

38 Open Maiden Div III

RIVER RAMBLE 5a ....Miss T Jackson 1
prom, ld 4-6th, blnd 8th, ld apr 3 out where blnd, styd on
Cookie Boy ....S Brisby 2
hld up, mstk 8th, prog 11th, chal 3 out, no ext apr last
Don Tocino ....N Smith 3
ld to 4th, prom aft, 3rd & btn whn mstk 3 out
Press To Sting *ld 6th til apr 3 out, wknd rpdly* ....C Storey 4
Tolmin *alwys bhnd, t.o. 10th, p.u. 3 out* ....Mrs M Fotheringay pu
Aston Warrior 5a *wll bhnd, t.o. last hlfwy, p.u. 15th* ....Mrs K Hargreave pu
Thief's Road *in tch in rear to 14th, bhnd whn p.u. 3 out*..........Miss D Calder pu
Cheap Knight (USA) *pllng, trckd ldrs, mstk 2nd, wknd 15th, p.u. nxt*..........M Ruddy pu
I'm Joking *bhnd, prog & just in tch 13th, sn wknd, p.u. 3 out*..........R Neal pu
Price War *(Jt fav) 5th whn blnd & u.r. 6th*. . . . .R Shiels ur
Linford (Ire) *(Jt fav) mstks, alwys prom, btn 3 out, disp 3rd whn f last*..........R Bevis f
Father O'Callaghan (Ire) *rear, prog hlfwy, 6th & in tch whn mstk & u.r. 12th*..........Miss M Bremner ur
No Justice *last & mstk 1st,effrt 10th,7th & btn whn mstk 15th,p.u. nxt*..........Miss K McLintock pu
Wild Rudolph (Ire) *alwys bhnd, t.o. & p.u. 10th* ....D Wood pu
14 ran. 2l, 10l, 10l. Time 6m 33.00s. SP 6-1.
Mrs G Sunter (Cleveland).
J.N.

NEW FOREST
Larkhill
Saturday February 1st
GOOD TO FIRM

39 Confined (12st)

INDIAN KNIGHT ....C Vigors 1
trckd ldrs, ld 15th, mstk & jnd last, hld on well
Aller Moor (Ire) ....M Miller 2
(fav) hld up, jnd wnr & blnd 3 out, rdn to chal last, just hld
Roaming Shadow ....J Hankinson 3
hld up, prog to prss ldr 13th, outpcd frm 2 out
Mighty Falcon *made most to 15th, sn btn* Miss E Tory 4
2[8] Gallant Effort (Ire) *prom, chsd ldr 10-12th, wknd frm 15th*..........J Snowden 5
17[5] Wrekin Hill *mstks, chsd ldr to 10th, wknd 12th, t.o.* ....Mrs J Wilkinson 6
6 ran. Hd, 15l, 10l, 15l, 12l. Time 6m 9.00s. SP 7-2.
C A Green (South & West Wilts).

40 Open Maiden Div I (12st)

MOSTYN ....Miss P Gundry 1
jmpd lft, made all & sn clr, tiring whn lft wll clr 3 out
5 **Tu Piece ....P Howse** 2
chsd wnr 7-11th, sn wknd, lft poor 2nd 3 out
Walton Thorns *chsd wnr to 7th, wknd 9th, t.o. & p.u. 13th*..........M Munrowd pu
20 Joe Penny *f 1st*..........B Dixon f
Millyhenry *(fav) blnd 3rd,bhnd,prog to chs wnr 11th,clsng whn blnd & u.r.3out* ....J Tizzard ur
5 ran. Dist. Time 6m 14.00s. SP 10-1.
R J Weaver (Berkeley).

41 Open Maiden Div II (12st)

CHASING DAISY 7a..........Miss A Goschen 1
mstk 3rd,chsd ldrs,outpcd frm 14th,mod 4th whn lft clr last
Marginal Margie 5a ....M Munrowd 2
bhnd, kpt on frm 13th, no ch whn lft 2nd last, styd on
Rum Customer ....T Greed 3
(fav) mid-div, outpcd frm 14th, no ch whn lft 3rd last
Nikaroo 5a *ld 2nd-10th, outpcd 14th, no ch whn blnd 2 out*..........Miss M Hill 4
Boddington Hill 5a 1ow *mstks, in tch to 10th, t.o. 13th* ....S Shinton 5
1 Diamond Wind (USA) 5a *prom, ld 10th, jnd 15th, 1l up & going better whn f last* ....A Beedles f
Spinayab 5a 5ow *alwys bhnd, t.o. 12th, p.u. 3 out* ....J Mead pu
Royal Turn *hmpd & u.r. 1st* ....A Honeyball ur
Trecometti 5a *pllng,in tch,chsd ldr 12th,chal 15th,1l down whn f last,dead* ....L Baker f
21[2] Dormston Lad 3ow *ld to 2nd, wknd 13th, t.o. & p.u. 2 out*..........C Jowett pu
The Bold Abbot *4th whn mstk & u.r. 5th* . .Miss S West ur
21 The Poacher *blnd 1st, last whn u.r. 6th*. . . . .H Rowsell ur
False Tail (Ire) 7a *hld up,prog 12th,3rd & no prog 15th,lft in ld & u.r. last*..........J Tizzard ur
13 ran. 12l, 6l, 20l, 20l. Time 6m 14.00s. SP 25-1.
Mrs S Hooper (Blackmore & Sparkford Vale).

42 Mixed Open (12st)

5[1] **STILL IN BUSINESS ....T Mitchell** 1

(fav) mstk 1st, hld up, prog 7th, ld 15th, clr 2 out, eased flat

6[1] **Brackenfield (bl) ....Miss P Curling 2**

trckd ldrs, ld 13th til blnd 15th, no imp on wnr 2 out

Teatrader ....Miss T Blazey 3

prom til outpcd 12th, wll bhnd frm 14th

Alex Thuscombe (v) *last, wll bhnd frm 13th, fin well* ....P Shaw 4

Nearly Splendid *blnd 2nd, p.u. nxt* ....T Greed pu

Jack Sound *made most to apr 13th, wknd rpdly, p.u. last* ....E Williams pu

5[2] Qualitair Memory (Ire) *prssd ldr to 12th,outpcd 14th,ran on 2 out,disp 2nd & f last*..........J Tizzard f

7 ran. 2½l, 20l, nk. Time 5m 57.20s. SP 11-10.

R G Williams (Cattistock).

43 Open Maiden Div III (12st)

JUNIPER LODGE ....S Bush 1

mstk 1st,prom,ld 8-13th,chal & lft in ld aft last,all out

Highway Lad ....P King 2

mstk 6th, ld to 8th, prom aft, outpcd 2 out, fin strngly

Abit More Business (Ire) ....T Mitchell 3

(fav) pllng,hld up,prog to ld 14th,v slw last,sn hdd & nt rcvr

Old Harry's Wife 5a *cls up, mstk 11th, outpcd 2 out, ran on agn flat*..........R Nuttall 4

Tommyknocker (Ire) 7a *alwys rear, t.o. 12th, p.u. 15th* ....Miss P Cooper pu

Sultan Of Swing *hdstr, hld up, ld 13th til blnd nxt, nt rcvr, p.u.3 out* ....Miss P Curling pu

Ten Bob Note *jmpd slwly 1st & 2nd, ref & u.r. nxt* ....M Walters ref

Ishma (Ire) *ref & u.r. 5th* ....D Page ref

Imike *trckd ldrs, 4th & still in tch whn f 3 out, dead* ....A Price f

Cucklington *trckd ldrs, blnd 9th, mstk & u.r. nxt* ....Miss A Goschen ur

10 ran. 1l, ½l, 3l. Time 6m 24.40s. SP 10-1.

Mrs W Jarrett (Beaufort).

44 Open Maiden Div IV (12st)

MISTER ONE ....T Mitchell 1

(fav) hld up, prog 13th, ld 3 out, easily

Jack Sun ....J Snowden 2

ld 2nd, clr 9th, hdd 3 out, kpt on, no ch wth wnr

Lazzaretto ....S Blackwell 3

ld to 2nd, bhnd frm 12th, t.o. 15th, tk poor 3rd nr fin

Dirty Dancer *rear, prog to chs ldrs 12th, wknd 15th, lost poor 3rd nr fin*..........M Wells 4

Flowerhill *prom to 10th, wknd 12th, blnd 13th & p.u.* ....G Barfoot-Saunt pu

23 Dont Rise Me (Ire) 2ow *pllng, hld up, lost tch 14th, poor 4th whn u.r. 3 out* ....B Parsons ur

Bride Run (Ire) *cls up til mstk & u.r. 7th* ....A Price ur

Fix The Spec (Ire) *chsd ldr 9th til wknd 13th, wll bhnd whn p.u. 15th* ....D Page pu

John Robin 7a *pllng, in tch til f 5th* .....T Stephenson f

9 ran. 6l, dist, 1l. Time 6m 15.60s. SP 4-6.

Paul K Barber (Blackmore & Sparkford Vale).

45 Restricted (12st)

7[2] **PINES EXPRESS (IRE) ....Miss S Vickery 1**

(fav) ld 3rd, made most aft, jnd 100 yrds out, hld on well

7[5] **Good Looking Guy ....A Charles-Jones 2**

w.w. in rear, prog 14th, strng chal last 100 yrds, just hld

Nobbutjust (Ire) 5a...................A Beedles 3

alwys prom, outpcd 3 out, strng chal last 100 yrds, just hld

Hungry Jack *in tch in rear, effrt 14th, styd on onepcd frm nxt* ....L Baker 4

Count Balios (Ire) *cls up, prssd wnr 13th-nxt, wknd 15th*..........P Howse 5

Madiyan (USA) *in tch in rear til wknd apr 15th* ....M Bryant 6

Toddling Inn 5a *rear whn hmpd 5th, sn t.o.*.....C Farr 7

Amadeo *ld to 3rd, mstk 10th, in tch whn mstk 13th, wknd, p.u. 15th* ....Miss S Bailey pu

J B Lad *in tch whn f 5th*..........Miss P Gundry f

23[6] Mr Sunnyside *cls up, hmpd & f 5th*..........M Batters f

Balance *mstk 2nd, hmpd nxt, cls up whn b.d. 5th* ....M Walters bd

Antica Roma (Ire) 5a *mid-div whn blnd & u.r. 2nd* ....C Wadland ur

Mister McGaskill *prom, disp whn f 5th*.....P Williams f

Plan-A (Ire) *in tch whn hmpd & u.r. 5th* ...T Woolridge ur

14 ran. Hd, nk, 8l, 2l, 30l, 20l. Time 6m 10.80s. SP 2-1.

Mrs Audrey Kley (Portman).

Count Balios officially placed 4th. Fences 16 & 18 omitted, 16 jumps.

46 P P O R A (12st)

DESERT WALTZ (IRE) ....Miss P Curling 1

(fav) trckd ldr, ld 13th, clr 15th, easily

18 **Front Cover 5a...................Miss S Vickery 2**

mstk 2nd, jmpd lft, outpcd 13th, went 2nd 2 out, no ch wnr

Landsker Missile 5a *ld to 13th, btn whn mstk 3 out, wknd, ref last* ....E Williams ref

3 ran. 12l. Time 6m 2.00s. SP 8-15.

H B Geddes (Beaufort).

J.N.

NORTH CORNWALL
Wadebridge
Saturday February 1st
GOOD

47 Members (12st)

GYMCRAK DAWN ....D Stephens 1

bhnd frm 2nd, 25l down whn lft in ld 12th

Myhamet *(fav) ld til u.r. 12th*..........A Farrant ur

Greenwine (USA) *chsng pair, lft 2nd 10th, u.r. 12th* ....Miss G Underhill ur

Corrib Haven (Ire) *trckd ldrs til u.r. aft 10th, girth broke*..........W Askew ur

4 ran. Time 7m 5.00s. SP 5-2.

A W Perkins (North Cornwall).

48 Men's Open (12st)

FEARSOME ....G Penfold 1

trckd ldrs, ld last, styd on well flat

Bianconi ....L Jefford 2

trckd ldr 7th, lft in ld 14th, hdd last, no ext

Glenform ....L Rowe 3

wll bhnd, lft 3rd 14th

Glencoe Boy *bhnd frm 2nd, wknd 12th, p.u. 14th, dead*..........A Holdsworth pu

Butler John (Ire) 7ex *(fav) ld, going well whn u.r. 14th* ....J Jukes ur

5 ran. 1l, 15l. Time 6m 18.00s. SP 4-1.

G W Penfold (Silverton).

49 Ladies

LARKY MCILROY 5a 5ow.......Miss L Blackford 1

ld/disp til ld aft 9th, mstk 3 out, ran on well

3[8] **Midfielder ....Miss V Roberts 2**

chsng grp, prog 11th, no ext frm nxt

Lucky Ole Son ....Miss P Jones 3

(fav) disp 2nd-9th, grad lost tch 12th, ran on agn flat

Catch The Cross *nvr bttr than 3rd, kpt on onepcd* ....Mrs M Hand 4

Duchess Of Tubber (Ire) 5a *wll bhnd frm 10th, p.u. 2 out* ....Miss S Young pu

5 ran. 6l, 4l, 10l. Time 6m 9.00s. SP 4-1.

D Luxton (Tiverton Foxhounds).

50 Restricted (12st)

MOUNTAIN MASTER ....Miss L Blackford 1

alwys cls up, ld brfly 10th, ld 14th, made rest, ran on well

Hopefull Drummer ....N Harris 2

alwys prom, chal 2 out, unable qckn
1[3] **Gypsy Luck 5a.................Miss J Cumings** 3
(fav) alwys cls up, ld 11-14th, just outpcd clsng stgs
Mrs Wumpkins (Ire) 5a *disp to 2nd, ld 9th-10th, no ext clsng stgs* ....Miss P Jones 4
The Butler *disp to 2nd, prom, ev ch 3 out, wknd last* ....S Slade 5
Sunwind *nvr trbld ldrs*....................D Heath 6
Dark Reflection *bhnd, prog 12th, wknd nxt* ....A O'Connor 7
Sherbrooks *nvr bttr than mid-div* ....M Hoskins 8
Dovedon Princess 5a *nvr a fctr*..........D Stephens 9
Liberty James *s.s. alwys bhnd, p.u. aft 13th*. .L Jefford pu
10 ran. 5l, 1l, 1l, 1l, 3l, 7l, 3l, 10l. Time 6m 17.00s. SP 4-1.
Mrs Sue Rowe (Tiverton Staghounds).

51 Confined (12st)

JUST BERT (IRE) ....Miss S Young 1
(fav) trckd ldrs, ld 3 out, grad asserted
Departure 5a ....J Creighton 2
prom, ld 15th to nxt, hrd rdn & no imp aft
Oneovertheight ....S Kidston 3
ld 2nd-14th, grad fdd
Prince Soloman 3ex *alwys last pair, drvn 3 out, kpt on onepcd*..........................Mrs M Hand 4
4 ran. 5l, 1l, 4l. Time 6m 16.00s. SP Evens.
Mrs J Alford (Eggesford).

52 Intermediate (12st)

BALDHU CHANCE ....J Young 1
made virt all, hld on wll whn chal
6[6] **Tangle Baron 5ex ....Miss J Cumings** 2
(fav) prssd wnr til outpcd 4 out, styd on wll agn frm last
Big Seamus (Ire) ....J Creighton 3
trckd ldrs, effrt 2 out, kpt on wll und pres
Cornish Ways 5ex *wll bhnd frm 3rd, still t.o. whn p.u. 14th* ....Miss S Young pu
4 ran. ½l, ½l. Time 6m 14.00s. SP 2-1.
Terry Long (Fourburrow).

53 Open Maiden Div I (12st)

SCALLYKENNING ....J Young 1
made all, ran out 7th & 14th, rjnd in ld both times, easily
Rose's Lady Day 5a ....D Stephens 2
ran around own pace
Cornish Twoways (Ire) 7a ....Miss S Young 3
nvr trbld wnr
3 ran. 10l, 4l. Time 8m 5.00s. SP 5-1.
J F Weldhen (Fourburrow).
Seven declared runners withdrawn after false start.

54 Open Maiden Div II (12st)

GYPSY GERRY ....L Jefford 1
(Co fav) alwys wll plcd, ld 15th, made rest, styd on well
Brook A Light ....S Slade 2
alwys handy, ld 7th-12th, onepcd aft
Keep Flowing (Ire) ....Miss P Jones 3
(Co fav) ld 5th & agn 12th-15th, styd on und pres
Stretchit *rear til gd prog frm 5 out, nvr nrr*. .G Penfold 4
Jolly Sensible 5a (bl) *nvr bttr than mid-div* ....J Creighton 5
Soul Survivor (Ire) *ld to 5th, grad wknd* ....Miss J Cumings 6
Lawd Of Blisland *(Co fav) alwys chsng ldrs, hrd rdn 4 out, no ext*...........................A Farrant 7
Princess Wenllyan 5a *alwys rear*............R Black 8
Big Reward *jmpd big, alwys bhnd* ....K Crook 9
Cheque Book *mid-div, wknd & p.u. 14th*.......T Cole pu
Riggledown Regent *nvr trbld ldrs, mstk 10th, p.u. nxt* ....A Holdsworth pu
Sonnaura 5a *nvr bttr than mid-div, p.u. aft 14th* ....J Jukes pu
Millwood 7a *alwys rear, p.u. 4 out* ....K Heard pu
13 ran. 4l, 1½l, 2l, 4l, 4l, 1l, 10l, 10l. Time 6m 15.00s. SP 3-1.
C de P Berry (Tiverton Foxhounds).
P.Ho.

OXFORD UNIV HUNT CLUB
Kingston Blount
Saturday February 1st
GOOD TO FIRM

55 Confined (12st)

BROAD STEANE 3ex................A Sansome 1
(fav) hld up, smooth prog to ld 2 out, pshd out
5[4] **Bishops Island 7ex ....P Young** 2
ld 5th til 2 out, no ext whn hdd
Grecian Lark ....G Tarry 3
hld up in tch, nvr able to rch ldrs
The Lorryman (Ire) *alwys prom, not qckn clsng stgs* ....N Mitchell 4
4 Cawkwell Dean 3ex *disp 2nd-4th, lost plc, styd on onepcd*..............................R Sweeting 5
3[3] I'm Toby *ld 2nd-5th, outpcd frm 13th*........A Kinane 6
Rubika (Fr) *ld to 2nd, grad wknd* ....Mrs S Shoemark 7
Sprucefield 4ow *cls up early, wknd aft hlfwy* ....A Barlow 8
17 Lake Teereen *prom early, no ch frm 13th* ....T Underwood 9
Button Your Lip *rear whn p.u. 11th* ....Mrs J Enderby pu
Run For Free 4ow *prom to hlfwy, wkng whn p.u. 3 out* ....A Hill pu
6 Great Simplicity (bl) *chsd ldrs til f 8th* . .Maj O Ellwood f
17 Bold Bostonian (Fr) *chsd ldrs til bhnd & p.u. 15th* ....M Appleby pu
Walkers Point 3ex *nvr a fctr, p.u. aft 11th*....S Astaire pu
Aylesford *bhnd whn f 8th* ....A Tutton f
15 ran. 7l, 5l, 5l, 8l, 8l, 10l, 10l, 12l. Time 6m 12.00s. SP 9-4.
Sir Michael Connell (Grafton).

56 Land Rover Open (12st)

WILD ILLUSION 7ex ....R Lawther 1
(fav) hld up in tch, ld aft 13th, jnd & lft clr 15th
Kingofnobles (Ire) ....R Rogers 2
rear, prog hlfwy, lft 3rd 15th, tk 2nd nr fin
Hackett's Farm ....Julian Pritchard 3
alwys prom, lft 2nd 15th, outpcd aft
Lighten The Load 4ex *chsd ldrs, no imp frm 15th* ....A Wintle 4
3[1] Paco's Boy 4ex *in tch early, wll bhnd frm hlfwy* ....P York 5
19 Castlebay Lad 4ex *ld to 4th, chsd ldrs to hlfwy, wknd* ....M Appleby 6
3 The Country Trader 1ow 7ex *alwys rear*. .J Borradaile 7
Shadow Walker 7ex *in tch early, sn fdd*. . . .O McPhail 8
Stanford Boy *alwys last pair, t.o. hlfwy*.......G Andrew 9
Solar Gem *mostly last, t.o. hlfwy* ....J Mason 10
Lucky Christopher 7ex *chsd ldr,ld 4-6th,sn ld agn,hdd 13th,jnd wnr & ran out 15th* ....G Tarry ro
2[1] All Weather 11ow *sn outpcd, bhnd whn p.u. 13th* ....D Duggan pu
Doran's Town Lad 5a *in tch, ld 6th, sn hdd & wknd, p.u. 14th* ....N Benstead pu
13 ran. 20l, 6l, 4l, 25l, 4l, 8l, 25l, 8l, 6l. Time 6m 12.80s. SP 4-5.
Exors Of The Late Mr G Pidgeon (Grafton).

57 Ladies

BLUE CHEEK 1
alwys prom, ld aft 13th, made rest, drvn out
Larry The Lamb ....Miss G Chown 2
wll bhnd, styd on frm 14th, tk 2nd nr fin
Lake Mission ....Miss G Browne 3
alwys prom, chsd wnr last cct, no imp, lost 2nd flat
Green Archer *wll bhnd til mod prog frm 14th, nrst fin* ....Mrs T Hill 4
Pont de Paix *ld to 13th, grad wknd* . .Miss T Habgood 5
Lily The Lark 5a *chsd ldrs, wknd frm 14th* ....Miss H Irving 6
6 Run To Form *rear, no ch frm 11th*. . .Miss E Wilesmith 7
6 Star Oats *cls up til u.r. 10th*...........Miss S Palmer ur

6 Hiram B Birdbath (bl) *cls up early, bhnd whn p.u. 15th* ....Miss A Plunkett pu
Sperrin View 5a *(fav) prom whn u.r. 2nd* ....Mrs K Sunderland ur
Ace Player (NZ) *cls up to hlfwy, btn whn p.u. 2 out* ....Miss C Ford pu
6 Dayadan (Ire) *rear til p.u. 9th* ....Miss J Sawyer pu
Tomcappagh (Ire) 2ow *alwys bhnd, p.u. 13th* ....Miss S French pu
13 ran. 3l, 4l, 8l, 10l, 12l, 4l. Time 6m 10.50s. SP 3-1.
J Mahon (Croome & West Warwickshire).

58 Members

WARRIOR BARD (IRE) ....M Portman 1
rear, trckd ldrs 6th, ld 9th, made rest, drvn out
Espy ....A James 2
alwys prom, chsd ldr 9th, styd on onepcd
Hill Island ....R Sweeting 3
(fav) ld 5-9th, wknd rpdly, dist 3rd frm 12th
Tarry Awhile *prom to 10th, t.o. & p.u. 2 out* ..J Connell 4
Valibus (Fr) *ld to 5th, sn drppd out, t.o. & p.u. aft 13th* ....P Scouller pu
5 ran. 2l, 25l. Time 6m 18.00s. SP 2-1.
R Stuart-Hunt (Beaufort).

59 Restricted (12st)

4 **AJ'S BOY 4ow...........................A Hill** 1
(fav) sn prom, ld 3rd-5th, ld 10th, made rest, pshd out
Ravensdale Lad ....A Wintle 2
mid-div, 4th hlfwy, chsd wnr 11th, ran on onepcd
20[1] **Orphan Olly ....P York** 3
ld to 3rd, chsd wnr to 11th, rallied flat
Some Tourist (Ire) *wll bhnd, steady prog 13th, wll btn whn lft 4th last*........................N Benstead 4
Brown Baby 5a 9ow *alwys prom, chsng ldrs whn blnd 11th, wknd 15th* ....G Kerr 5
7 Live Wire (Ire) *nvr bttr than mid-div, styd on onepcd* ....T Cox 6
Misty (NZ) *nvr nr ldrs* ....P Young 7
1[4] Miss Magic 5a *s.s. alwys rear, wll bhnd & p.u. aft 13th* ....R Sweeting pu
Colonel Fairfax *alwys bhnd, p.u. aft 11th*......J Trice-Rolph pu
First Command (NZ) *mostly mid-div, no ch whn p.u. 15th*...............................Mrs C Ford pu
Linlake Lightning 5a (bl) *cls up early, fdd & p.u. last* ....Miss H Irving pu
Plateman *s.s. prog to 2nd at 6th, cls 4th whn f 13th* ....F Hutsby f
22 Dunamase Dandy (Ire) *prom, ld aft 5th til mstk & hdd 10th, wknd, p.u. last*..................T Lacey pu
Five Circles (Ire) *nvr rchd ldrs, wll bhnd whn p.u. last* ....M Portman pu
Amerous Lad *sn rear, wll bhnd whn p.u. 2 out* ....R Rogers pu
No Hanky Panky *sn wll bhnd, t.o. whn ref & u.r. 10th* ....R Lawther ref
16 ran. 6l, 1l, 4l, 10l, 20l. Time 6m 16.00s. SP 2-1.
M A Walter (Vale Of Aylesbury).

60 Maiden

DUKE OF LANCASTER (IRE) ....N Sutton 1
(fav) sn wll bhnd, prog frm 13th, poor 6th 15th, qcknd to ld flat
Mrs Moppit 5a.............................R Cope 2
bhnd, prog hlfwy, lft in ld aft 3 out, hdd nr fin
Full Score (Ire) ....J Trice-Rolph 3
alwys prom, chsd ldrs frm 13th, styd on wll flat
Bold Man (NZ) *mid-div, 3rd hlfwy, lost plc, styd on frm 2 out* ....A Sansome 4
Newtown Rambler (Ire) *rear, steady prog to 2nd at 14th, wknd*...............................F Hutsby 5
Woodlands Power *prom to hlfwy, fdd* ..John Pritchard 6
Pukka Sahib *sn prom, chsd ldrs til wknd 14th* ....Miss H Irving 7
Roark's Chukka *cls up, ld 4th til f 7th* ....D Smith f
Cool Rascal 5a *ld to 4th, cls up whn u.r. 7th* ....L Lay ur

13 Trina's Cottage (Ire) *alwys bhnd, p.u. last* ...B McKim pu
Over The Lake (Ire) 5a *alwys wll bhnd, t.o. & p.u. 3 out*...............................R Barrett pu
2 Bawnerosh *alwys wll bhnd, t.o. & p.u. 13th* ....T Underwood pu
Royal Dadda *s.s. alwys wll bhnd, p.u. 3 out* .....A Hill pu
Spring Sabre (bl) *mid-div, prog 6th, lft in ld 14th til ran out bnd apr 2 out* ....R Lawther ro
Fuannae (Ire) *alwys prom, ld 8th til f 14th* ..M Appleby f
Bit Of A Do *nvr seen wth ch, p.u. 14th* .....C Morlock pu
Vally's Spirit *s.s. sn t.o., p.u.* ....Mrs S Shoemark pu
17 ran. Nk, 1½l, 4l, 6l, 4l, 8l, 10l. Time 6m 34.00s. SP 4-1.
R C Irving (Vine & Craven).
H.F.

THURLOW
Horseheath
Saturday February 1st
GOOD TO FIRM

61 Open Maiden (5-7yo) (12st)

LORD KNOX (IRE) ....R Gill 1
ld to 6th, ld agn 15th, made rest, styd on strngly
Andy Gawe (Ire) ....S Cowell 2
chsd wnr, ld 6th til blnd & hdd 15th, wknd apr 2 out
15 **View Point (Ire) ....M Gingell** 3
hld up, blnd 4th, prog to 3rd at 14th, no imp frm nxt
Harbour Light (Ire) *mid-div, mstk 7th, 4th & outpcd 14th, not pshd* ....C Ward-Thomas 4
Joyful Hero 5a *(fav) keen hld, hld up, prog 9th, btn 14th, p.u. 3 out* ....P Bull pu
Thurles Pickpocket (Ire) *f 2nd* ....G Cooper f
Harry Tartar *chsd ldrs to 9th, last whn mstk 12th, p.u. 14th*...............................Capt D Parker pu
Chalinare (Ire) *chsd ldrs, mstk 7th, 3rd whn blnd & u.r. 10th* ....S R Andrews ur
Wise Point (Ire) *mstks, sn wll bhnd, t.o. & p.u. 10th* ....G Lush pu
9 ran. 10l, 15l, 20l. Time 6m 40.00s. SP 6-1.
B G Clark (Puckeridge).

62 Confined (12st)

RIVER MELODY 5a 11ex.................T Moore 1
(fav) hld up, lft 2nd apr 14th, ld 2 out, cruised clr
10[4] **Horace ....W Wales** 2
ld to 5th, lft in ld apr 14th, rdn & hdd 2 out, outpcd
Youcat (Ire) ....I Marsh 3
in tch, chsd ldr brfly 11th, sn strggling, btn whn mstk 3 out
Smart Pal *chsd ldr to 5th, last & losing tch whn f 12th* ....K Needham f
Raise A Loan *j.w. ld 6th til p.u. apr 14th, lame* ....N Bloom pu
5 ran. 10l, 12l. Time 6m 26.00s. SP 5-4.
T W Moore (Essex).

63 Men's Open (12st)

THE ARTFUL RASCAL ....N Bloom 1
(fav) ld 5th, made rest, drew wll clr 14th, easily
Armagret 7ex ....S Cowell 2
hld up, prog 7th, chsd wnr 14th, nvr on trms
Jimmy Mac Jimmy ....C Ward-Thomas 3
prom, chsd wnr 6th-14th, no dang aft
Earlydue 7ex *ld to 2nd, in tch, hit 12th, 4th & no ch frm 14th*...................................T Moore 4
Noble Knight (Ire) *ld 2nd-5th, last frm 9th, t.o. & p.u. 13th* ....C Jarvis pu
5 ran. 25l, 8l, 10l. Time 6m 17.00s. SP 11-10.
M A Kemp (Suffolk).

64 G Middleton Ladies

26[1] **ONE FOR THE CHIEF ....Miss A Embiricos** 1
cls up, ld 6th, made rest, clr frm 15th, comf
26[3] **St Gregory (bl)....................Mrs L Gibbon** 2
(fav) mstks, ld 2nd-6th, chsd wnr 13th-3 out, kpt on
Emsee-H ....Mrs F Needham 3

mid-div, prog 11th, cls 3rd 13th, onepcd frm 3 out
Omidjoy (Ire) 5a *mid-div, prog 9th, disp 2nd 10th-12th, sn outpcd* .... Mrs L Wrighton 4
26 Sarazar (USA) 3ow *jmpd rght 1st, rear, prog 10th, sn lost tch, t.o.* .... Miss H Pewter 5
Nibble *hmpd & nrly u.r. 1st, prog 7th, cls up whn f 9th* .... Miss L Rowe f
12[3] Alice Sheer Thorn (Ire) 5a *keen hld, ld to 2nd, last & wkng whn p.u. 13th* .... Miss E Tomlinson pu
7 ran. 6l, 5l, dist, 20l. Time 6m 21.00s. SP 7-4.
M A Kemp (Suffolk).

65 Restricted (12st)

SPARTANS CONQUEST .... C Ward 1
ld to 5th, cls up, ld & blnd 2 out, clr last
27[5] **Colonel Kenson .... M Gingell 2**
prom, ld 5th-12th & 15th-2 out, onepcd und pres
24[1] **Golden Fellow (Ire) .... A Coe 3**
(fav) mstks, prog to ld 11th, blnd nxt, hdd 15th, btn 2 out
28[4] Cool Apollo (NZ) *prom to 12th, 6th & outpcd 14th, kpt on onepcd* .... G Plenderleith 4
Sunset Run *keen hld, chsd ldrs, mstk 9th, 4th & btn whn ran out 3 out* .... Miss C Tuke ro
Swift Reward 5a *mid-div, rdn & lost plc 9th, t.o. & p.u. 3 out* .... W Wales pu
Sparkling Spirit 5a 3ow *chsd ldrs to 13th, sn strgglng, no ch whn u.r. last* .... I Marsh ur
Aughnacloy Rose *sn bhnd, 8th & no ch whn u.r. 15th* .... N Page ur
30 Go Magic *hld up, prog 8th, blnd 11th, bhnd whn p.u. 3 out* .... S Cowell pu
Forever Freddy *in tch to 6th, reluc & losing plc whn ref & u.r. nxt* .... J Valdes Scott ref
10 ran. 5l, 8l, 5l. Time 6m 28.00s. SP 2-1.
O Vaughan-Jones (West Norfolk).

66 Members

GLENBRICKEN .... K Williams 1
1st ride,chsd ldrs,outpcd 12th,styd on 15th,ld last,sn clr
27[6] **Buckshot (Ire) .... C Barlow 2**
chsd ldr, blnd 3rd, ld 12th til last, sn btn
Linger Hill .... C Ward-Thomas 3
in tch, mstk & rmndr 8th, outpcd 12th, kpt on frm 3 out
Waterloo Andy *1st ride, hld up, 5th & outpcd 13th, kpt on frm 3 out,nvr nr* .... Miss J Cook 4
Cardinal Ralph *alwys bhnd, t.o. & p.u. 14th* .... Miss A Embiricos pu
Notary-Nowell *1st ride, chsd ldrs to 11th, sn bhnd, t.o. & p.u. 3 out* .... Miss N Sell pu
Minehill *(fav) ld to 12th, blnd nxt, rdn 3 out, ev ch whn f nxt* .... N King f
7 ran. 4l, 1½l, ¾l. Time 6m 32.00s. SP 6-1.
Kevin Williams (Thurlow).
S.P.

WETHERBY
Saturday February 1st
GOOD

67 3m 1f Harold Charlton Memorial Hunters' Chase Class H

CAB ON TARGET 11.10 .... Mr S Swiers 1
(fav) held up, tk clr order 10th, trckd ldr from 4 out, rdn to ld final 100 yards.
Teaplanter 11.13 5a................ Mr B Pollock 2
ld to 5th, mstk 8th, led 10th, mistake 4 out, hdd final 100 yards, no ext.
Matt Reid 11.11 7a .... Mr W Morgan 3
in tch, trckd ldr from 10th, ev ch 4 out, fd.
Fordstown (Ire) 11.11 7a *soon bhnd, kept on from 13th, n.d..* .... Mr Jamie Alexander 4
33[1] Southern Minstrel 11.7 7a *in tch till gradually wknd from 12th.* .... Miss C Metcalfe 5
Peajade 11.3 7a *soon bhnd.* .... Miss J Wormall 6
Highlandman 11.3 7a *in tch till outpcd hfwy, no ch after.* .... Mr M Bradburne 7
Tom Log 11.3 7a *mstk 6th, soon bhnd, t.o..* .... Mr W Burnell 8
Kushbaloo 11.11 7a *chsd ldrs to hfwy, soon bhnd, t.o..* .... Mr A Parker 9
No Word 11.3 7a *pulld hrd, led 5th to 10th, wknd quickly, t.o. when blnd 4 out, p.u. before next.* .... Mr I Baker pu
10 ran. 2l, 22l, 14l, 2l, sht-hd, 2l, dist, nk. Time 6m 43.70s. SP 8-13.
N Hurst

EASTON HARRIERS
Higham
Sunday February 2nd
GOOD TO FIRM

68 Members

GILSON'S COVE .... Miss L Rowe 1
(fav) made all, drew clr 10th, easily
Arkay .... R Kerry 2
chsd wnr, lost tch 10th, t.o.
Cosmic Ray *chsd ldrs, wkind 6th, t.o. & p.u. 12th* .... D Page pu
Starchy's Quest 7a *pllng, ran out 2nd, cont, mstk & u.r. 4th* .... R Barr ur
4 ran. Dist. Time 6m 49.00s. SP 1-4.
A Merriam (Easton Harriers).

69 Open Maiden (12st)

13[2] **CRESTAFAIR 5a .... Miss H Irving 1**
sttld bhnd ldrs,prog 8th,mstk 10th,chal 2 out,rdn clr flat
Kellys Nap .... C Ward 2
pllng in mid-div,mstk 5th,prog to ld 15th,hdd & no ext flat
15 **Flapping Freda (Ire) 5a 1ow................ R Gill 3**
hld up rear, last at 12th, clsd 14th, wknd nxt, t.o.
Learner Driver *alwys mid-div, wknd rpdly 8th, p.u. 10th* .... M Gingell pu
29[3] Ludoviciana 5a *(fav) ld til blnd 2nd, ld nxt til f 11th* .... Miss G Chown f
Muddle Head (Ire) *hld up, prog to 4th at 11th, wknd 15th, t.o. & p.u. 2 out* .... S Cowell pu
Stoneyisland (Ire) *prom, lft in ld 2nd, hdd nxt, prom whn mstk & u.r. 13th* .... N Bloom ur
Red Channel (Ire) *s.i.s. disp 5th, lft in ld 11th, hdd 15th, btn whn f 3 out* .... A Hickman f
8 ran. 8l, dist. Time 6m 36.00s. SP 5-1.
Miss H M Irving (Grafton).

70 Men's Open

JUST JACK .... P Jonason 1
trckd ldng pair, chal 4 out, ld aft nxt, qcknd clr, eased
Exclusive Edition (Ire) 5a.................. A Coe 2
(fav) hld up bhnd, clsd 11th, 3rd 13th, disp 4 out, outpcd 2 out
8[4] **Stanwick Farlap 5a .... T Marks 3**
ld to 2nd, ld 7th, jnd 4 out, ev ch nxt, onepcd aft
Nicknavar *prom whn stirrup broke aft 1st & p.u.* .... M Gorman pu
Mara Askari (v) *ld 2nd-7th, wknd rpdly 12th, blnd 15th & p.u.* .... G Hopper pu
5 ran. 2l, 2l. Time 6m 31.00s. SP 9-2.
P Jonason (Cambridgeshire).

71 Ladies

25[2] **CRAFTSMAN .... Miss H Irving 1**
(fav) hld up, mstk 2nd, disp 8th & 12th, drew clr 3 out, blnd last
Professor Longhair .... Miss C Papworth 2
chsd ldrs, outpcd 12th, styd on wll 4 out, tk 2nd cls hm
26 **Upward Surge (Ire) .... Mrs N Ledger 3**

alwys prom, ld 11th, qcknd nxt, hdd & outpcd 16th, dmtd flat
Counterbid *hld up, slw jmp 4th, 3rd at 12th, wknd steadily frm 14th* ....Miss L Rowe 4
Dovehill *prom, ld 4th, blnd & lost plc 6th, mstk 11th, u.r. nxt*....................................Miss P Ellison ur
Laburnum *mid-div, prog 11th, wknd rpdly 13th, p.u. nxt*................................Miss A Embiricos pu
6 ran. 8l, ½l. Time 6m 26.00s. SP 4-7.
G W Paul (Essex & Suffolk).

72 Intermediate (12st)

BILLION DOLLARBILL ....M Gorman 1
prom, ld 2nd-3rd, blnd 11th, prog 16th, ld flat, rdn out
10 **Druid's Lodge ....C Ward-Thomas** 2
chsd ldr, mstk 14th, ld nxt, jnd 2 out, hdd & no ext flat
Bitter Aloe ....R Wakley 3
(fav) ld to 2nd, ld 3rd, jnd 15th, ev ch 3 out, wknd nxt
Aughrim Slopes 5a *s.s. rear whn mstk 3rd, prog 12th, mstk nxt, wknd aft 4 out*.....................W Wales 4
4 ran. 1l, 25l, 25l. Time 6m 23.00s. SP 7-4.
Brian Tetley (Surrey Union).

73 Restricted (12st)

10[2] **SALMON MEAD (IRE) ....A Harvey** 1
(fav) trckd ldr, ld 9th-11th, ld 4 out, sn clr, easily
Beat The Rap ....G Morrison 2
ld at slow pace to 8th, outpcd 12th, styd on agn 4 out
28[5] **Corn Kingdom (bl) ....A Coe** 3
hld up, mstk 5th, prog to ld 8th-9th, ld 11th-4 out, sn btn
3 ran. 6l, 2l. Time 6m 32.00s. SP 2-5.
Christopher Sporborg (Puckeridge).
J.W.

LINCOLNSHIRE UNITED CLUB
Market Rasen Point-To-Point
Sunday February 2nd
GOOD TO FIRM

74 Members

CARLY BRRIN ....N Kent 1
made all, styd on well, und pres frm 2 out
Ways And Means 5a ....K Green 2
(fav) held up, chsd wnr 11th, ev ch 3 out, unable to qckn frm nxt
Golden Moss ....Maj S Robinson 3
chsd wnr til 11th, rmnd 13th, sn lost, tld off
Mister Chippendale *last whn hit 7th, t.o. & p.u. 4 out* ....S Walker pu
4 ran. 2l, dist. Time 6m 28.00s. SP 6-4.
Mrs J R Buckley (Brocklesby).

75 Confined (12st)

JUST CHARLIE 6ex ....D Easterby 1
sn wl bhnd, prog 11th, ld 2 out, hld on, und pres flat
Zam Bee 8ex ....N Bell 2
(fav) ld 3rd, clr 6th, hdd 2 out, rld last, kept on flat
Coolvawn Lady (Ire) 5a 10ex............S Walker 3
prom, chsd ldr, 6th to 3 out, one pcd aft
34[5] Clare Lad *blnd & nrly u.r. 1st, wl bhnd til styd on frm 4 out*.......................................R Walford 4
Alpha One *alwys mid-div, 4th whn blndrd 14th, no dang aft*...P Gee 5
Scole *ld to 3rd, grad lost pl, t.o. frm 14th* ....Miss A Hinch 6
Convincing (v) *prom, 4th & pshd alng 11th, sn bhnd, t.o.*..P Cornforth 7
Friar Street (Ire) *hld up bhnd, prog to 3rd 10th, blndrd 13th, sn wknd, t.o.*..........................G Brewer 8
Ginger Pink 3ow *chsd ldr to 6th, bhnd frm 10th, t.o. & p.u. 3 out*...........................Maj S Robinson pu

Broadcaster *wl bhnd frm 7th, t.o. & p.u. 9th* ....R Chandler pu
10 ran. ½l, 5l, 30l, 6l, 8l, 15l, 20l. Time 6m 23.00s. SP 4-1.
Mrs Susan E Mason (Middleton).

76 P P O R A (12st)

LATHERON (IRE) ....N Wilson 1
w.w., rmdr 6th,prog nxt,ld 14th,lft wll clr 2 out,eased flat
Copper Thistle (Ire) 7ex ....R Hunnisett 2
prom, outpcd 13th, lft 2nd 2 out, kpt on one pace
Elder Prince 4ex..........................P Gee 3
(fav) hld up, hit 5th, prog 14th, lft 3rd 2 out, nvr nr
Douce Indienne 5a *chsd ldrs, blnd 7th, outpcd 11th, no dang aft*...............................T Whittaker 4
Wind Force 7ex *wth ldr to 10th, grad lost pl, no ch frm 14th*...................................S Robinson 5
Ocean Rose 5a *prom, cls 3rd 11th, outpcd frm 13th* ....W Burnell 6
McCartney *chsd ldrs to 11th, sn stugg*..........K Green 7
Cadrillon (Fr) *alwys rr div, nvr on trms* ..Miss A Deniel 8
Sporting Spirit *rr & hit 9th, last frm 13th, t.o.* ....M Kneafsey 9
Whistling Gipsy *mid-div, prog 10th, 4th & outpcd app 14th, t.o. & p.u. last*.......................P O'Keeffe pu
Castletown Count 7a *prog 5th, ld 10-14th, hit 3 out, ev ch whn ran out nxt*..........................S Swiers ro
37 Primitive Star 5a *ld to 10th, wkng whn u.r. 12th* ....P Cornforth ur
12 ran. 7l, 5l, 5l, 10l, 5l, ½l, 10l, dist. Time 6m 26.00s. SP 7-2.
J Sisterson (Middleton).

77 Restricted Div I

PERFECT LIGHT ....R Lee 1
(fav) jmpd rght, made all, sn clr, hit last, unchal
32 **Malvern Cantina ....N Wilson** 2
w.w., prog 7th, chsd wnr 3 out, hrd rdn nxt, no imp
Basil Grey ....P Jenkins 3
prom, chsd wnr 6th-3 out, wl btn nxt
Skyval 5a *hld up bhnd, nvr on trms, t.o. frm 13th* ....K Green 4
Here Comes Charter *hld up, nvr on trms, t.o. frm 12th* ....A Pennock 5
Monarrow (Ire) *1st ride, last frm 11th, t.o.* ....Miss S Buckley 6
War Head *f 1st* ....R Leak f
Banchory *f 1st, dead*..........................D Easterby f
Giorgione (Fr) *jmpt lft, prom til jmp slwly 11th, p.u. aft 12th*...J Turcan pu
9 ran. 10l, 15l, 1 fence, ½l, 1 fence. Time 6m 26.00s. SP 5-2.
R Lee (North Hereford).
One fence omitted last two circuits.

78 Restricted Div II

PATS CROSS (IRE) ....J Byrne 1
lft in ld 3rd, made rest, lft clr 3 out, styd on
City Buzz (Ire) (bl) ....K Needham 2
prom, lft 3rd 3 out, chsd wnr app last, no imp
Ryders Wells ....S Walker 3
in tch, rdn 13th, hit nxt, lft 2nd 3 out, no prog
Its Murphy Man *prom to 11th, grad lost pl* ....J Trice-Rolph 4
Barichste *hld up, prog to jn ldrs 12th, 1/2l 2nd whn ran out 3 out*..........................Maj M Watson ro
The Archorian *ld, clr whn f 3rd, dead*..........G Brewer f
Midnight Service (Ire) *in tch, bln 7th, last frm nxt, p.u. 14th*...W Tellwright pu
32[4] Greenmount Lad (Ire) *(fav) bhnd, hit 4th, prog 7th, u.r. 11th* ....P Cornforth ur
8 ran. 10l, 6l, 8l. Time 6m 31.00s. SP 7-1.
James Byrne (Staintondale).

79 2m 5f Open Maiden Div I

RIVER DON 7a ....P O'Keeffe 1
hld up, mstk 7th, smth prog to ld 2 out, readily
Benbeath ....P Gee 2
keen hld, prom, ld 4 out to 2 out, not pace of wnr

Cuba 7a................................R Barrett 3
chsd ldrs, ev ch frm 11th, no ext app last
Winters Melody 5a *chsd ldrs to 8th, sn wknd, t.o. frm 11th*.................A Pennock 4
Detinu *ld, sn clr, hdd 4 out, wl btn whn f last* A Wintle f
Transcendental (Ire) *20s-5s, mid-div, prog to 3rd 10th, lost pl & p.u. nxt, lame*.................Miss A Deniel pu
Just Shirley 5a *alwys rr, t.o. & p.u. 11th*.....A Balding pu
Little Red *stdyd rr til blndrd & u.r. 3rd*......N Wilson ur
Singh Song 5a *in tch til blndrd & u.r. 3rd*..R Chandler ur
9 ran. 12l, 5l, dist. Time 5m 31.00s. SP 7-2.
Mrs A M Easterby (Middleton).

80 2m 5f Open Maiden Div II

OLIVER HIMSELF ....A Hill 1
(fav) ld to 4th, hit 8th, ev ch 11th, rdn 3 out, lft clr nxt
Kind Of Chic 5a.......................W Burnell 2
blnd 3rd, prssd ldr 4th, outpcd 11th, lft poor 2nd 2 out
Zerose 12a..............................N Kent 3
rr, t.o. 9th, p.u. last, cont'd
Tudor Flight 5a *keen hold, ld 4th, 1/2l ld whn f 2 out*.................................G Markham f
Derring Knight *prom, wkng whn jmpd slwly 8th, p.u. nxt*.................................A Sansome pu
Chummy's Last 5a *w.w., jmpd slwly 7th, prog to 4th whn u.r. 10th*.......................Mrs F Needham ur
Our Wyn-Ston 7a *chsd ldrs til ran out 4th*...S Walker ro
Frumerty 7a *hld up in rr til blndrd & u.r. 4th*..K Green ur
Surprise View 12a *bhnd & mstk 7th, ran out nxt*.................................L Donnelly ro
9 ran. 15l, 1 fence. Time 5m 50.00s. SP 5-4.
Mrs Judy Wilson (Pytchley).
S.P.

NORTH WESTERN HUNT CLUB
Wolverhampton P-To-P Course
Sunday February 2nd
GOOD TO SOFT

81 Maiden Div I

SKY RUNNER ....S Prior 1
in tch, mstk 14th, prog to ld apr 2 out, clr last, pshd out
Dalusaway (Ire) 5a...................C Stockton 2
mid-div, prog 10th, ld 16th til apr 2 out where mstk, no ext
Inglebrook ....G Hanmer 3
s.s. hld up & t.o., ran on 13th, nvr nrr, hopeless task
Penbola (Ire) 7a *prom, ld 10th-16th, wknd, no ch whn mstk 2 out*.................................D Sherlock 4
Mophead Kelly *chsd ldrs til wknd 12th, t.o. & p.u. 14th*.................................J Barlow pu
Eyton Rock *rear, t.o. whn f 11th*.....Miss S Beddoes f
Lydebrook *in tch in rear til u.r. 7th*..........M Wilson ur
Tosawi's Girl (Ire) 5a *in tch til wknd 7th, f nxt* R Burton f
Nights Image (Ire) *(fav) 7s-7/4, prom, cls 3rd whn f 11th*.................................P Blane f
Bubble N Squeek *sn wll bhnd, effrt 13th, nvr rchd ldrs, p.u. 16th*.................................C Barlow pu
Aqueous Rocks *ld to 8th, sn wknd, t.o. & p.u. 11th*.................................M Worthington pu
Lady Pokey 5a *mstks, prom til wknd 12th, t.o. & p.u. 15th*.................................N Gittins pu
Gasmark (Ire) *mstk 1st, prom, ld 8-10th, 2nd whn f nxt*.................................A Crow f
13 ran. 6l, 10l, 12l. Time 6m 44.00s. SP 33-1.
R G E Owen (Cheshire).
One fence omitted final circuit, 17 jumps.

82 Maiden Div II

DOMINO NIGHT (IRE) ....Miss J Elson 1
chsd ldr, ld 16th, sn clr, ran on strngly, imprssv
Noble Angel (Ire) ....A Dalton 2
ld to 16th, sn outpcd & no ch wth wnr aft
Bombadier Jack ....C Barlow 3
prom, clsd up 13th, wknd aft 16th, no ch whn mstk 2 out
Solar Castle (Ire) *slw jmp 2nd, nrly u.r. nxt, t.o. 6th*.................................Miss S Hopkins 4
Analystic (Ire) *alwys bhnd, t.o. 10th*......Miss J Penny 5
Niord *alwys bhnd, t.o. & p.u. 11th*.........C Stockton pu
River Sunset (Ire) *alwys bhnd, t.o. 10th, p.u. 15th*.................................J Barlow pu
Beeworthy 5a *chsd ldrs til lost tch 13th, t.o. & p.u. 16th*.................................A Beedles pu
Maes Gwyn Dreamer *chsd ldrs, 4th whn f 8th* R Bevis f
Ring Bank *chsd ldrs til wknd 11th, t.o. & p.u. 15th*.................................N Gittins pu
Cherry Glen (Ire) *(fav) hld up, prog whn mstk 11th, rdn 13th, btn nxt, p.u. 3 out*.................A Crow pu
11 ran. 25l, 2½l, 30l, 1l. Time 6m 37.00s. SP 4-1.
E Haddock (Meynell & South Staffs).

83 Restricted

ORTON HOUSE ....R Burton 1
chsd ldr, ld 14th, hdd & lft clr 2 out, drvn out
Four Hearts (Ire) ....D Barlow 2
prog 8th, cls up til outpcd 3 out, lft 2nd nxt
Whatwillbewillbe (Ire) ....G Hanmer 3
(fav) w.w. prog 14th, jnd ldrs 3 out, wknd apr nxt
Grants Carouse *jmpd slwly 8th, drppd last 10th, wknd 15th*.................................A Baillie 4
Miss Shaw 5a *ld to 14th, chal agn 3 out, ev ch whn b.d. nxt*.................................C Stockton bd
Sargeants Choice *in tch til wknd rpdly 14th, nrly ref nxt & p.u.*.................................J Barlow pu
Lillybrook 5a *cls up, chal 3 out, ld & going best whn f nxt*.................................J Townson f
Yukon Gale (Ire) *hld up, mstk 4th, prog nxt, hrd rdn & wknd 16th, p.u. 3 out*.................A Crow pu
8 ran. 8l, 20l, 12l. Time 6m 41.00s. SP 12-1.
Mrs A P Kelly (Flint & Denbigh).

84 Members (12st)

FREDDIE FOX 7ex.......................T Garton 1
(fav) chsd ldr 9th, pshd alng frm 11th, kpt on to ld flat, gamely
Howarya Harry (Ire) ....G Hanmer 2
jmpd rght, ld 7th, clr 3 out, hng rght & hdd flat, not qckn
Carniquilla ....C Stockton 3
chsd ldrs, outpcd 12th, kpt on wll frm 3 out, nrst fin, dead
Lady Steel (Ire) 5a *ld 3rd-7th, prom to 11th, sn outpcd*.................................Miss S Baxter 4
Bavard Bay *ld to 2nd, bhnd frm 9th, sn t.o.* L Whiston 5
Foolish Fantasy *ran in sntchs, in tch 11th, wknd nxt, virt p.u. flat*.................................S Prior 6
Side Brace (NZ) *alwys bhnd, t.o. & p.u. 12th*.................................N Swindells pu
Go Again (Ire) *ld 2-3rd, t.o. & p.u. 8th*...Miss T Luder-Gibbs pu
Sirrah Aris (Ire) *rear, mstk 11th & rdn, no respnse, t.o. & p.u. nxt*.................................A Crow pu
9 ran. 1l, 1l, 20l, 25l, 15l. Time 6m 44.00s. SP 7-4.
Mrs A B Garton (Cheshire Forest).
Open ditch omitted from this race onwards. 16 jumps per race.

85 Ladies

OUT THE DOOR (IRE) 7ex ....Miss S Baxter 1
prom, chsd ldr 9th, chal & lft clr 3 out, comf
Cabin Hill ....Miss E James 2
chsd ldr 7-9th, prom aft, lft 2nd 3 out, no imp wnr
6[4] **Fantastic Fleet (Ire) 7a.............Miss P Jones** 3
trckd ldrs, blnd 9th, no imp ldrs frm 12th, lft 3rd 3 out
Sound Forecast *bnhd, poor 7th at 11th, kpt on frm nxt, no dang*.........................Miss D Marfell 4
2[2] Dauphin Bleu (Fr) *(fav) ld to 3rd, lft in ld 5th, jnd & f 3 out*.................................Miss V Roberts f
Man Of Mystery *bhnd frm 8th, last & t.o. 11th, p.u. 3 out*.................................Miss F Hatfield pu

3 Drumceva *bhnd, prog 9th, wknd 12th, t.o. & p.u. 3 out* ....Miss E Wilesmith pu
Bank Place *chsd ldr to 7th, wknd 12th, poor 4th whn u.r. 2 out*....Miss C Thomas ur
The Boiler White (Ire) 7ex *bhnd, last whn u.r. 8th* ....Miss J Froggatt ur
Daphni (Fr) *alwys rear, 8th & no ch at 11th, t.o. & p.u. 3 out*....Miss S Swindells pu
Walter's Lad *plld hrd, ld 3rd, mstk nxt, ran out & u.r. 5th*....Mrs M Wall ro
11 ran. 4l, 12l, 8l. Time 6m 38.00s. SP 5-2.
M Mann (Wheatland).

86 Men's Open (12st)

BAGALINO (USA) ....Julian Pritchard 1
ld 5th, made rest, drew clr aft 3 out, ran on well, easily
Scally Muire 5a 7ex....A Crow 2
(fav) pckd 2nd, bhnd, prog 11th, chsd wnr nxt, ch 3 out,sn btn
Merlyns Choice ....A Woodward 3
bhnd, poor 7th at 11th, styd on well frm nxt, nrst fin
4[5] Rusty Bridge 7ex *ld 3rd-5th, sn pshd alng, outpcd 11th, kpt on frm 13th* ....C Richards 4
Auction Law (NZ) *ld to 3rd, wknd 11th, t.o. & p.u. 3 out* ....L Whiston pu
Charterforhardware 7ex *cls up til rdn & wknd aft 11th, t.o. & p.u. 2 out*....R Burton pu
Daphnis (USA) 7ex *wth wnr 6th til blnd & u.r. 8th* ....S Prior ur
Back The Road (Ire) *w.w. prog to jn wnr 11th, wknd rpdly apr nxt, p.u. 3 out*....G Hanmer pu
Tale Of Endurance (Ire) *alwys bhnd, t.o. & p.u. 12th* ....S Morris pu
9 ran. 10l, 2½l, ¾l. Time 6m 39.50s. SP 7-1.
Miss Jane Fellows (Ledbury).

87 Open Maiden Div I

CONKERDOR ....M Rimell 1
made all, drew wll clr frm 13th, easily
Joyney 5a....Miss C Thomas 2
rear, prog 9th, chsd wnr 2 out, no imp, fin tired
Travel Bound ....D Barlow 3
in tch to 11th, sn wll bhnd, ran on apr last, fin well
2 Pyro Pennant *cls up, 2nd brfly aft 11th, sn outpcd, fin tired*....Miss P Cooper 4
Amazing Air (USA) *(fav) in tch, chsd wnr apr 12th til wknd & blnd 2 out* ....S Blackwell 5
Horsetrader 7a *alwys bhnd, mstk 10th, t.o. & p.u. 12th* ....G Hanmer pu
Welsh Lightning *u.r. 1st*....R Inglesant ur
Brown Bala 5a *in tch in rear, mstk 9th, u.r. 11th* ....J Jukes ur
Coolflugh Hero (Ire) *chsd wnr til wknd rpdly aft 11th, p.u. nxt* ....A Crow pu
Royal Icing 12a *schoold & bhnd, effrt 6th, just in tch whn f nxt* ....P Hanly f
Spirit Prince 7a *tried to ref & u.r. 1st* ....R Evans ur
11 ran. Dist, nk, 1l, 1l. Time 6m 42.00s. SP 5-1.
Giles Smyly (North Cotswold).

88 Open Maiden Div II

MARCH GATE ....D Duggan 1
rear, prog 9th, ld aft 13th, clr 2 out, ran on well
Jack The Td (Ire) ....J Cornwall 2
mstk 10th, ld to aft 13th, sn btn, kpt on to tk 2nd post
Oats For Notes 5a....M Rimell 3
(fav) in tch, chsd ldr 10th, ev ch aft 13th, wknd 2 out, dmtd post
Serdarli 5a *ref 1st*....A Jackson ref
Western Pearl (Ire) *prom to 4th, wll bhnd whn p.u. 11th* ....J Jukes pu
Mr Wilbur *chsd ldr 6-10th, wkng whn mstk 12th & p.u.* ....A Dalton pu
Musical Mail *alwys bhnd, t.o. & p.u. 12th* ....R Ford pu
Toms Choice (Ire) *prom to 4th, bhnd frm 11th, t.o. & p.u. nxt* ....G Barfoot-Saunt pu
Bel Lane 5a *prog 10th, cls up 12th, wknd 3 out, wll btn 4th whn ref last* ....D S Jones ref
Bit Of Rough (Ire) *alwys bhnd, mstks 7 & 8th, t.o. & p.u. 12th*....G Hanmer pu
Musical Vocation (Ire) 5a *mstk 6th, rear til effrt 11th, 5th & no ch whn p.u. 3 out*....A Crow pu
Edina (Ire) 5a *chsd ldr to 6th, wkng whn mstk 8th, t.o. & p.u. 12th, lame*....B Pollock pu
Roger (Ire) 7a *alwys bhnd, mstk 11th, t.o. & p.u. nxt* ....Miss P Cooper pu
13 ran. 20l, sht-hd. Time 6m 49.00s. SP 8-1.
Mrs M D W Wilson (Cotswold).
J.N.

WARWICK
Tuesday February 4th
GOOD TO FIRM

89 3¼m Air Wedding Trophy Hunters' Chase Class H

THE MALAKARMA 12.3 5a ....Mr B Pollock 1
(fav) chsd ldr, nigglд along after one cct, joined lder 6 out, outpcd and rdn 4 out, styd on gamely to lead run-in.
Out For Fun 11.9 7a ....Mr N R Mitchell 2
ld, given breather 6 out, qcknd next, blnd last, hdd and one pace run-in.
3[5] **Sirisat 11.10 7a 1ow ....Miss T Blazey** 3
chsd lding pair, feeling pace when hit 8 out, one pace last 4, no impn.
Corn Exchange 11.9 7a *chasing lding trio when blnd and u.r. 3rd*....Mr M FitzGerald ur
4 ran. 2l, 15l. Time 6m 47.20s. SP 4-6.
Charles Dixey

LUDLOW
Wednesday February 5th
GOOD

90 2½m Pontrilas Hunters' Chase Class H

BEAU DANDY 11.7 7a ....Mr T Marks 1
(fav) alwys handy, hmpd by faller 8th, rcvred to ld after next, made rest, kept on grimly from 2 out.
Hennerwood Oak 11.2 7a....Mr M Munrowd 2
patiently rdn, smooth hdwy to chal from 4 out, ev ch till hit 2 out, kept on same pace run-in.
Billy Bathgate 11.7 7a ....Mr D S Jones 3
nvr far away, left in narrow ld after 8th, hdd after next, rdn and mstk 4 out, soon lost tch.
Hickelton Lad 11.11 3a *chsd ldrs, hrd at work to keep up 5 out, soon lost tch, t.o.*....Mr M Rimell 4
Al Hashimi 11.7 7a *well pld when f 8th.* ..Mr N Ridout f
Pastoral Pride (USA) 11.9 5a *ld, clr 4th, p.u. after 8th, broke blood vessel*....Miss P Curling pu
6 ran. ½l, dist, 30l. Time 5m 2.40s. SP 5-6.
C C Shand Kydd

HUNTINGDON
Thursday February 6th
GOOD

91 3m Duck's Cross Novices' Hunters' Chase Class H

ORCHESTRAL SUITE (IRE) 11.7 7a ..Mr F Hutsby 1
(fav) alwys handy, ld 5 out, styd on well from 2 out.
Lurriga Glitter (Ire) 11.7 7a ....Mr R Wakley 2
held up, hdwy 11th, ld 13th to 6 out, rdn and rallied 2 out, not qckn.
Symbol Of Success (Ire) 11.11 3a (v) Mr M Rimell 3
held up, went 3rd after 4 out, rdn after next, styd on between last 2.
27[3] Stede Quarter 11.11 7a *chsd ldrs, ld after 12th to next, wknd quickly after 5 out. t.o.*....Mr P Bull 4

Green's Van Goyen (Ire) 11.9 5a *ld to 3rd, chsd ldrs till wknd after 11th, bhnd when p.u. before 5 out.* ....Mr T McCarthy pu
Mediane (USA) 11.11 3a *prom when mstk 8th, soon wknd, t.o. after 12th, p.u. after 5 out.* ....Mr Simon Andrews pu
No Joker (Ire) 11.7 7a *mstk 1st, ld 3rd to next, weakening when u.r. 11th.* ....Capt R Hall ur
Not My Line (Ire) 11.9 5a *hdwy 7th, ld 9th to 11th, soon wknd, bhnd when p.u. before 13th.* ....Mr A Sansome pu
Amazon Lily 11.2 7a *ld 4th to 9th, weakening when mstk, swrd and u.r. 11th.* ....Mr M Gorman ur
Rising Sap 11.7 7a *held up, hdwy 9th, ld 11th till after 12th, mstk 4 out, weakening when p.u. before next.* ....Mr A Dalton pu

10 ran. 3½l, hd, dist. Time 6m 27.50s. SP 2-1.
Exors Of The Late Mr G Pidgeon

WINCANTON
Thursday February 6th
GOOD TO FIRM

92 3m 1f 110yds Somerset Hunters' Chase Class H

DOUBLE SILK 12.10 3a..........Mr R Treloggen 1
(fav) ld 2nd, made rest, drew readily clr from 4 out.
Visaga 12.6 7a........................Mr S Lloyd 2
ld to 2nd, chal 8th, hit 12th, chald next, chsd wnr till apr 3 out, went second at last, one pace.
Sonofagipsy 12.6 7a..............Mr R Nuttall 3
in 3rd most of way, rdn from 14th, soon no ch.
Furry Knowe 12.6 7a *mstks 3rd and 4th, hit 8th, hdwy and hit next, fourth and in tch when f 11th.* ....Mr D Pritchard f
Upham Close 11.7 7a *well bhnd 12th, hdwy 16th, chsd wnr 3 out to next, 3rd and weakening when f last.* ....Mrs A Hand f
Jupiter Moon 12.3 7a *soon bhnd, t.o. 9th, p.u. before 12th.* ....Mr R Hicks pu

6 ran. 16l, 2l. Time 6m 56.00s. SP 4-9.
R C Wilkins

BANGOR
Friday February 7th
GOOD

93 2½m 110yds Gilbert Cotton Memorial Hunters' Chase Class H

INCH MAID 11.9 7a...........Miss H Brookshaw 1
held up, hdwy after 6th, ld 3 out, styd on well.
Lord Relic (NZ) 12.0 7a................Mr R Ford 2
trckd ldrs, ld 8th till hdd 3 out, chsd wnr after, no impn.
My Nominee 12.0 7a (bl) ....Mr R Burton 3
(Jt fav) prom, ld 7th to 8th, wknd after 12th, t.o..
Driving Force 12.4 3a (bl) *ld 6th to 7th, driven along after 10th, soon wknd, t.o..* ....Mr M Rimell 4
Palm Reader 12.0 7a *soon well bhnd, t.o. when p.u. before 10th.* ....Mr C J B Barlow pu
Kino 12.0 7a *ld to 4th, wknd after 7th, lost tch and p.u. before 9th.* ....Mr Andrew Martin pu
My Young Man 12.0 7a *(Jt fav) ld 4th to 6th, lost tch before 10th, t.o. when p.u. before 3 out.* ...Mr E James pu
Barkisland 12.0 7a *soon well bhnd, t.o. when p.u. before 11th.* ....Mr J M Pritchard pu
King Of Shadows 11.7 7a *bhnd when b.d. 5th.* ....Mr S Prior bd
Spy's Delight 11.7 7a *blnd and u.r. 2nd.* Mr E Woolley ur
Native Rambler (Ire) 11.7 7a *towards rear when f 5th.* ....Miss E James f

11 ran. 3l, dist, 25l. Time 5m 32.20s. SP 10-1.
S A Brookshaw

NEWBURY
Friday February 7th
GOOD

94 2½m Charles Higgins Memorial Foxhunters' Cup Hunters' Chase Class H

SLIEVENAMON MIST 12.2 5a ....Mr J Jukes 1
hdwy and hit 9th, trckd ldr 12th, chal 4 out, slight ld from next, driven out run-in.
Principle Music (USA) 11.5 7a......Mr A Phillips 2
hdwy 8th, ld 10th, clr apr 12th, hdd 3 out, styd on one pace run-in.
Hobnobber 11.5 7a.................Mr J Docker 3
some hdwy from 3 out, not trbl ldrs.
Flowing River (USA) 11.5 7a *in tch, staying on in 4th when hmpd 12th, soon btn..* ....Mr N R Mitchell 4
23^2 Tea Cee Kay 11.7 5a *bhnd 6th.* ....Mr A Sansome 5
1^2 Flame O'Frensi 11.9 7a *ld to 6th, wknd 10th.* ....Miss J Cumings 6
4 Orujo (Ire) 11.5 7a *prom, ld 6th to 10th, weakening when hmpd 12th.* ....Mr P T Young 7
Charlies Delight (Ire) 11.11 7a 1ow *mstks, soon bhnd, t.o..* ....Mr R Hicks 8
Ramstar 12.5 5a *hdwy 10th, wknd after 12th, t.o. when p.u. before last.* ....Miss P Curling pu
Birchall Boy 11.5 7a *hit 4th, soon bhnd, t.o. when p.u. before 2 out.* ....Miss W Southcombe pu
Idiotic 11.12 5a *(fav) f 2nd.* ....Mr C Vigors f
Pro Bono (Ire) 11.10 7a *with ldrs 6th, chal 10th to 11th, 3rd and rdn when f next.* ....Mr A Dalton f

12 ran. 6l, 26l, 3½l, sht-hd, 26l, 4l. Time 5m 19.70s. SP 5-2.
Nick Viney

EAST CORNWALL
Great Trethew
Saturday February 8th
GOOD TO SOFT

95 Members (12st)

THE KIMBLER 3ex.................Miss S Young 1
(fav) ld to 4th, lft in ld 7th, made rest, rdn out
52 **Cornish Ways ....Miss A Barnett** 2
prssd wnr frm 7th, hit 13th, cls engh 3 out, no imp last
Holly Fare *ld 4th til ref & u.r. 7th* ....C Crosthwaite ref
Linton *8s-4s, mstk 4th, bhnd whn hmpd 7th, t.o. & p.u. 14th* ....Miss P Baker pu

4 ran. 4l. Time 6m 36.00s. SP 1-2.
B R J Young (East Cornwall).

96 Confined (12st)

MILES MORE FUN 5a ....L Jefford 1
16s-6s, w.w. prog to ld 15th, clr 3 out, easily
Senegalais (Fr) 3ex...................M Venner 2
mid-div, outpcd 12th, kpt on frm 3 out, tk 2nd last
Pop Song ....A Farrant 3
ld to 12th & 14th-nxt,btn whn blnd 3 out,wknd,lost 2nd last
Karlimay 5a *(fav) hld up, prog to remote 3rd at 15th, nvr nr ldrs, wknd 2 out* ....K Heard 4
50^7 Dark Reflection *chsd ldr to 7th, strgglng frm 11th, sn t.o.* ....A O'Connor 5
51^4 Prince Soloman 3ex *bhnd frm 6th, t.o. 14th, p.u. 2 out* ....Mrs M Hand pu
52^1 Baldhu Chance *prom, ld 12-14th, wknd rpdly & p.u. 16th* ....J Young pu

7 ran. 20l, 6l, 15l, 8l. Time 6m 17.00s. SP 6-1.
Edward Retter (Dart Vale And South Pool Hrrs).

97 Intermediate (12st)

EARTHMOVER (IRE) ....Miss P Curling 1
trckd ldr 7th, ld 14th, clr apr 2 out, imprssv
7^1 **King Torus (Ire) ....J Jukes** 2
wll in tch, chsd wnr 14th, no imp apr 2 out
6^2 **Tinotops ....Miss S Vickery** 3
(fav) prom, ld 7-14th, outpcd & mstk 16th, no prog aft

Fixed Liability *mid-div,blnd 9th,sn outpcd,poor 4th whn hng rght aft 3 out* .... D Alers-Hankey 4
Southern Flight 5ex *chsd ldrs til poor 4th & no imp frm 13th* .... Miss J Cumings 5
Cautious Rebel *alwys wll bhnd, t.o. 11th* .. J Creighton 6
50[5] The Butler *mid-div til rear & no ch 13th, p.u. nxt* .... S Slade pu
The Apprentice *ld to 7th, wknd rpdly, p.u. 11th* .... T Vaughan pu
Cairneymount 5ex *alwys wll bhnd, t.o. 11th, p.u. 3 out* .... J Tudor pu
The Copper Key *alwys bhnd, t.o. & p.u. 14th* T Greed pu
Diana Moss (Ire) 5a *bhnd, 11th whn u.r. 7th* .. C Heard ur
Hanukkah 5a *t.d.e. alwys wll in rear, t.o. whn mstk 13th, p.u. 15th* .... I Hambly pu
Saint Joseph *alwys bhnd, t.o. & p.u. 11th* .... Miss S Young pu

13 ran. 15l, 10l, 1 fence, 2l, 25l. Time 6m 8.00s. SP 2-1.
R M Penny (Cattistock).

98 Land Rover Open (12st)

KALOORE .... A Farrant 1
(fav) rear, prog 11th, hrd rdn to chs ldr 16th, ld last,jst hld on
Magnolia Man .... N Harris 2
prog 9th, ld apr 14th, hdd last, rallied wll, just faild
The General's Drum 7ex .... K Heard 3
bhnd, prog 10th, chsd ldng pair 16th, no imp nxt
42 Nearly Splendid *ld 4th til apr 14th, sn outpcd, kpt on* .... T Greed 4
Afterkelly 7ex *prom til outpcd frm 15th, sn no dang* .... I Dowrick 5
19[4] Fosbury 7ex *prom, 2nd & rdn 13th, wknd frm 16th, walked in* .... T Mitchell 6
Plain Sailing (Fr) *went prom 10th, cls up til wknd 15th, walked in* .... S Slade 7
January Don (bl) *prom to 7th, sn wknd, t.o. & p.u. 3 out* .... G Barfoot-Saunt pu
Southerly Buster *alwys rear, t.o. 14th, p.u. 3 out* .... S White pu
Charmers Wish 5a 3ow *alwys last pair, mstk 2nd, t.o. 7th, p.u. 13th* .... H Thomas pu
19[5] Ryming Cuplet 7ex *rear whn blnd 4th, rdr lost irons & p.u. nxt* .... L Jefford pu
Touch 'N' Pass *ld to 4th, wkng whn f 11th* ..... J Tudor f
3 Electrolyte *last pair, t.o. 7th, p.u. 16th* .... G Austin pu
48[2] Bianconi *mid-div til u.r. bend aft 9th* .... S Kidston ur

14 ran. Sht-hd, 15l, 6l, 10l, 1l, nk. Time 6m 18.00s. SP 7-4.
Mrs J Alford (Eggesford).

99 Ladies

SECRET FOUR .... Miss T Cave 1
prom, ld aft 13th, drew clr last, ran on well
Slaney Food .... Miss P Curling 2
(fav) prom, chsd wnr 14th, ev ch 2 out, sn btn, eased
Playpen .... Miss S Crooks 3
rear, rpd prog to chal 14th, ev ch 2 out, wknd
Carrick Lanes *bhnd whn mstks 11 & 12th, effrt to 4th at 16th, no prog aft* .... Miss P Jones 4
It's Not My Fault (Ire) *rear, lost tch wth ldrs 13th, one-pcd aft* .... Mrs M Hand 5
Searcy *rear, no prog frm 14th, onepcd* Miss P Gundry 6
49[1] Larky McIlroy 5a *mid-div, 5th whn mstk 13th, btn frm nxt* .... Miss L Blackford 7
Great Pokey *ld to 4th & 8-10th, wknd rpdly 13th, p.u. nxt* .... Miss N Courtenay pu
Celtic Sport (bl) *ld 4-8th & 10th-aft 13th, sn wknd, p.u. 2 out* .... Miss A Plunkett pu
49 Duchess Of Tubber (Ire) 5a *rear, wknd & p.u. 11th* .... Miss S Young pu

10 ran. 6l, 5l, ½l, 12l, 2l, 12l. Time 6m 19.00s. SP 10-1.
P Masterson (Dart Vale And South Pool Hrrs).

100 Restricted (12st)

GIGI BEACH (IRE) .... Miss P Curling 1
(fav) trckd ldrs, mstk 9th, ld 16th, drew clr last, comf
Milled Oats .... A Farrant 2
unruly pddck, alwys prom, ev ch 2 out, no ch wnr last
7 **Swing To The Left (Ire) 5a .... Miss S Vickery 3**
mid-div, prog 14th, jnd wnr 3 out til wknd apr last
95 Holly Fare *2nd outing, alwys rear, no ch 14th, lft 4th by dfctns, t.o.* .... C Crosthwaite 4
Darktown Strutter (bl) *alwys bhnd, p.u. 12th* .... A Holdsworth pu
50[9] Dovedon Princess 5a *mstk 7th, rear, lost tch 13th, p.u. nxt* .... D Stephens pu
Belfry Lad *prom to 10th, wll btn 14th, p.u. last* .... J Creighton pu
7 Mac's Boy *5s-2s, ld to 5th, lost plc & blnd 12th, bhnd whn p.u. 16th* .... D S Jones pu
Play Poker (Ire) *rear, mstk 11th, prog to chs ldrs 14th,4th & btn whn f 2out* .... S Slade f
Springcombe 5a *rear,prog 12th,in tch 14th,wknd 16th,6th & no ch, u.r. 2 out* .... Miss S Eames ur
Lady Lir 5a *in tch, prog to trck ldr 10th til wknd 14th,no ch whn f last* .... Miss S Young f
Dragons Lady 5a *prom, ld 5-6th, rear by 12th, bhnd whn p.u. last* .... G Barfoot-Saunt pu
Mine's A Gin (Ire) *prom, ld 6th-16th, wknd nxt, no ch whn p.u. last* .... Miss J Cumings pu
Boire Ensemble 7a *s.s. t.o. & ref 3rd, cont, p.u. 6th* .... Mrs M Hand pu

14 ran. 4l, 4l, 1 fence. Time 6m 22.00s. SP 7-4.
Mrs Susan Humphreys (Blackmore & Sparkford Vale).

101 Open Maiden Div I Pt I (12st)

THREE AND A HALF .... N Harris 1
prom, ld 11th, drew rght away frm 15th, unchal
Italian Man (Ire) .... G Penfold 2
in tch til outpcd by wnr 15th, lft clr 2nd 2 out
Ask Me Kindly (Ire) .... Mrs M Hand 3
(fav) mstks, prom til outpcd by wnr frm 14th, no ch aft
Katree Runner *in tch til wknd frm 14th, t.o.* .. R Widger 4
44 Dont Rise Me (Ire) *prom, wth ldr whn c.o. by loose horse 9th* .... A Holdsworth co
Amazing Hill (Ire) *last & n.j.w. t.o. & p.u. 13th* C Heard pu
Eurolinkhellraiser (Ire) *w.w. jnd ldrs 13th, wknd & mstks frm 15th, poor 2nd & f 2out* .... T Mitchell f
Midnight Bob *4th whn u.r. 7th* .... J Young ur
Carrarea (Ire) *ld til blnd & wknd 11th, p.u. 13th* .... Miss J Cumings pu

9 ran. Dist, 1l, dist. Time 6m 23.00s. SP 5-1.
J Scott (Devon & Somerset Staghounds).

102 Open Maiden Div I Pt II (12st)

GUNNER BOON .... Miss P Jones 1
(fav) made all, drew clr aft 2 out, comf
Arrogant Lord 7a .... L Jefford 2
prom, lft cls 2nd 14th, no imp wnr aft 3 out
Wicked Pixie (Ire) 12a .... D Stephens 3
schoold, alwys bhnd, t.o. 4th, tk poor 3rd last
Rhyme And Chime *mstks,bhnd,effrt 7th,wknd 10th,sn t.o.,blnd last* .... T Dennis 4
1 All The Jolly 5a *in tch, 4th whn u.r. bend apr 10th* .... R Jones ur
Eserie de Cores (USA) *prom, cls 2nd whn f 14th* .... Miss K Baily f
Lochnaver 5a *prom til f 4th* .... Miss P Gundry f
Belitlir 12a *t.o. 4th, p.u. 10th* .... Miss S Young pu

8 ran. 10l, 2 fences, 4l. Time 6m 32.00s. SP 4-7.
David Brace (Llangeinor).

103 Open Maiden Div II Pt I (12st)

MARION'S OWN (IRE) .... Miss P Curling 1
(fav) chsng grp, disp 16th til lft clr 2 out, all out
Westcountry Lad .... R Woolacott 2
chsng grp, effrt 3 out, lft 2nd nxt, kpt on well
The Ugly Duckling .... S Slade 3
prom in chsng grp, ld aft 13th-3 out, no ext
54[4] Stretchit *n.j.w. in chsng grp, no prog frm 16th* .... G Penfold 4
Sabbaq (USA) *prom in chsng grp, disp 16th, ev ch whn f 2 out* .... I Dowrick f

47 Corrib Haven (Ire) *2nd whn u.r. 3rd*..........W Askew ur
Faster Or Else (NZ) 3ow *33s-12s, chsg grp, rdn & wknd 15th, t.o. & p.u. 2 out*..................T Cole pu
Luney River 5a *clr ldr, blnd 11th, wknd & hdd aft 13th, p.u. 15th*..................................J Young pu
Only Harry *schoold, wll bhnd frm 7th, t.o. & p.u. 11th*..................................Miss S Young pu
9 ran. 2l, 5l, 12l. Time 6m 37.00s. SP 11-8.
Mrs M B Keighley (Cattistock).

104 Open Maiden Div II Pt II (12st)

MY MAN ON DUNDRUM (IRE) ....B O'Doherty 1
prom, ld & blnd 11th, clr 2 out, blnd last, styd on well
Valley's Choice 5a ....L Jefford 2
in tch, chsd wnr 15th, chal aft 3 out, sn no imp
41³ **Rum Customer ....T Greed** 3
(fav) in tch wil wknd frm 16th, walked in
Gamblers Refrain *ld to 5th, prom aft, wknd 3 out, wll btn whn p.u. last*..........................A Holdsworth pu
Spectacular Star (Ire) *6s-3s, in tch til wknd 16th, wll btn whn p.u. last*..............................C Heard pu
Chocolate Buttons 5a *mstks, in tch, effrt 13th, 4th whn f nxt*..................................H Thomas f
Crownhill Cross *wll bhnd frm 10th, t.o. whn ref & u.r. 14th*.................................Miss K Baily ref
Western Fort (Ire) *prom, ld 5th-11th, wknd 13th, p.u. 15th*...............................Miss J Cumings pu
Summerthetime *n.j.w. t.o. 7th, p.u. 10th*.....S Durack pu
9 ran. 10l, dist. Time 6m 36.00s. SP 6-1.
Richard Barber (Cattistock).

105 Open Maiden Div III (12st)

TAMAIMO (IRE) ....T Mitchell 1
prom, ld 15th-3 out, lkd btn nxt, rallied to ld nr fin
Passing Fair 5a ....Miss S Vickery 2
(fav) pllng, ld 3rd-15th & 3 out, lkd wnr nxt, kpt on, hdd nr fin
Sagaville (Ire) ....A Holdsworth 3
alwys prom, blnd 11th, outpcd 14th, tk poor 3rd nr fin
Tall Order (Ire) *mstk 2nd, wth ldrs, 3rd at 12th, wknd 15th, lost 3rd nr fin*..........................J Young 4
Fortitude Star 5a *mid-div, 7th at 12th, wll btn whn f 16th*..................................A Farrant f
Romany Anne 5a *ld to 3rd, prom til outpcd 14th, no ch whn p.u. last*...........................Miss S Young pu
Upton Gale (Ire) *mid-div, wll in tch whn f 11th*..................................D Dennis f
Stony Missile 5a *mstks, alwys wll bhnd, t.o. 11th, p.u. 16th*.............................Miss W Hartnoll pu
Spartans Dina 5a *blnd 7th, in tch in rear til blnd 12th & p.u.*...............................Miss L Blackford pu
Flying Maria 5a *hld up last, just in tch 12th, no ch whn p.u. 16th*..................................C Heard pu
Harmony's Choice *rear, prog to 8th at 12th, lost tch ldrs 14th, p.u. last*.............................N Harris pu
Trolly *in tch, 5th at 12th, wknd & p.u. 15th*....L Jefford pu
53² Rose's Lady Day 5a *alwys bhnd, t.o. & p.u. 13th*..................................D Stephens pu
Penguin 5a *in tch, mstk 9th, 6th at 12th, btn 14th, p.u. 3 out*............................Miss J Cumings pu
Nearly Fair 5a *alwys bhnd, t.o. 13th, p.u. nxt*...T Greed pu
15 ran. 1½l, dist, 1l. Time 6m 30.50s. SP 6-1.
Mrs Susan Humphreys (Cattistock).
J.N.

SOUTH DORSET
Milborne St Andrew
Saturday February 8th
GOOD TO FIRM

106 Restricted (12st)

45 **PLAN-A (IRE) ....T Woolridge** 1
(fav) mid-div, prog 10th, 3rd at 15th, ld 2 out, ran on well
Prince's Gift ....A Phillips 2
in tch, 4th at 15th, chal 2 out, hld flat
23⁴ **Celtic Token ....J Barnes** 3
t.d.e. ld to 14th, rnwd effrt 2 out, wknd apr last
23³ Elle Flavador 5a *hld up, prog 11th, ld 15th-3 out, outpcd frm nxt*..............................R Treloggen 4
Sybillabee 5a 2ow *prom early, outpcd 12th, no ext frm 4 out*..................................M Batters 5
23⁵ Just Donald *alwys rear, t.o. 4 out*.........A Honeyball 6
Final Express 5a 5ow *mid-div, lost tch 12th, plodded round*..................................M Hoskins 7
50³ Gypsy Luck 5a *handy early, losng tch whn u.r. 15th*..................................Miss A Bush ur
Nearly A Mermaid 5a *cls up early, lost tch 13th, t.o. & p.u. 2 out*..................................R Nuttall pu
Vital Legacy *alwys rear, t.o. & p.u. 12th*..................................Miss A Goschen pu
Sue's Quest 5a *in tch early, outpcd frm 12th, t.o. & p.u. 4 out*..................................P King pu
Lady Mouse 5a *sn rear, blnd 7th, t.o. & p.u. nxt*..................................L Baker pu
12 ran. 2l, 10l, 10l, 20l, 3l, 12l. Time 6m 17.00s. SP 5-2.
R W Edwards (Portman).

107 Members

39⁴ **MIGHTY FALCON ....Miss E Tory** 1
(fav) hld up, prog 12th, ld nxt, ran on well frm 3 out
Pabrey ....N Mitchell 2
rear early, prog 12th, prssd wnr 4 out, onepcd frm 2 out
Slaney France (Ire) ....Miss K Lovelace 3
in tch to 12th, outpcd 15th, kpt on frm 2 out
Ainlee Road *alwys rear, styd on frm 15th* ..Mrs S Cuff 4
Smokey Thunder (Ire) *prom to 12th, outpcd nxt, blnd 15th, t.o. 2 out*..................................M Miller 5
Shilgrove Place *ld to 11th, wknd & outpcd aft, t.o.*..................................Col S Allen 6
The Humble Tiller *mid-div til blnd & u.r. 8th*..................................Miss L Knights ur
17⁴ Prankster *cls up, handy 4th whn f 13th*.....T Atkinson f
8 ran. 3l, 12l, 12l, 20l, 25l. Time 6m 27.00s. SP 7-4.
Miss Emma Tory (South Dorset).

108 Mixed Open (12st)

SPITFIRE JUBILEE ....R Nuttall 1
ld/disp to 13th, rdn 15th, disp 3 out, ran on wll frm nxt
18 **Daybrook's Gift ....Miss N Allan** 2
rear, prog 13th, styd on frm 3 out, chal aft last, just hld
17² **Corly Special ....B Pollock** 3
(fav) j.w. alwys prom, ld 14th-3 out, wknd & blnd last
Jimmy Cone *rear, outpcd frm 13th*...Miss A Goschen 4
Temple Mary *handy to 13th, lost tch nxt, outpcd*..................................T Woolridge 5
17³ Rathmichael *disp early, wknd 10th, t.o. & p.u. 4 out*..................................M Miller pu
6 ran. Hd, 6l, 8l, 12l. Time 6m 19.00s. SP 6-4.
Mrs Z S Clark (Blackmore & Sparkford Vale).

109 B F S S (Novice Riders) (12st)

SPRING FUN ....Miss Y Young 1+
alwys prom, disp 5th til ld 2 out, ct post
42⁴ **ALEX THUSCOMBE (bl)..................P Shaw** 1+
prom, disp 12th-2 out, rallied last, forced d/h on line
16¹ **Skinnhill (bl) ....C Mason** 3
mid-div, some prog 15th, nvr on trms
Rapid Rascal *prom, disp 5-10th, lost tch & outpcd aft*..................................Miss S West 4
Met Station (bl) *alwys rear, u.r. 9th*..........J Evans ur
Granville Guest *(fav) 1st ride, hld up, prog 10th, disp 11th til blnd & u.r. 14th*..............Miss C Bryan ur
Sharp Performer (Ire) *plld hrd, ld til ran out bend apr 5th*..................................Miss M Taylor ro
Furry Bear *alwys last, t.o. & p.u. 4 out*.......R Hawker pu
8 ran. Dd-ht, 2l, 15l. Time 6m 21.00s.
David Young / Mrs F Shaw (Portman / Cattistock).
Spring Fun, 9-1. Alex Thuscombe, 2-1.

110 Maiden Div I (12st)

FLYING IMP ....R Nuttall 1
hld up, prog 11th, 3rd at 15th, ld apr last, ran on
Muskerry Moya (Ire) 5a..................B Dixon 2
cls up, disp 12th til ld 14th, hdd apr last, rallied flat
Melling ....Miss A Goschen 3
(fav) ld to 4th, handy til outpcd frm 4 out
1 Gentle Jester 5a *sn rear, t.o. 5th, p.u. 3 out* ....A Honeyball pu
Purbeck Polly 5a *in tch til blnd & u.r. 5th* Mrs A Davis ur
Hod Wood 5a *rear, lost tch 11th, t.o. & p.u. 13th* ....M Miller pu
Georgie Porgie 7a *prom, ld 5th til jnd 12th, f nxt* ....Mrs S Godfrey f

7 ran. ½l, 6l. Time 6m 23.00s. SP 5-1.
Mrs Jane Galpin (Blackmore & Sparkford Vale).

111 Maiden Div II (12st)

RAINBOW FANTASIA (IRE) ....J Wingfield-Digby 1
j.w. handy, 2nd frm 11th til ld aft 2 out, styd on well,lame
2[9] **Eyre Point (Ire) ....A Honeyball** 2
rear, prog 15th, styd on wll 2 out, nrst fin
Vernham Wood ....Maj S Robinson 3
ld til 2 out, wknd apr last
Butts Castle *alwys rear, nvr on trms wth ldrs* ..P King 4
Dancing Barefoot 5a *mid-div til blnd & u.r. 7th* ....J Barnes ur
St Amour *n.j.w. last til p.u. 4th* ....N Mitchell pu
22[2] Most Vital *(fav) in tch, cls 3rd whn f 15th* ....Miss A Goschen f
Feltham Mistress 5a *handy til 13th, lost tch nxt, t.o. & p.u. 4 out* ....E Babington pu

8 ran. 2l, 3l, 20l. Time 6m 37.00s. SP 5-1.
J H Wingfield Digby (South Dorset).

112 Intermediate (12st)

22[1] **CHISM (IRE) ....M Miller** 1
(fav) set slow pace, qcknd 3 out, hdd aft nxt, rallied to ld flat
23[1] **Stalbridge Gold 5a.............Miss A Goschen** 2
hld up in 2nd, chal to ld aft 2 out, hdd flat, ran on
Clobracken Lad ....G Baines 3
j.w. hld up, mstk 15th, ev ch 2 out, rdn last, not qckn
Sandford Orcas *hld up in 3rd, outpcd frm 3 out* ....P Bevins 4

4 ran. ½l, ½l, 8l. Time 6m 39.00s. SP 11-10.
J R Webber (Portman).
D.P.

BADSWORTH
Wetherby Point-To-Point Course
Sunday February 9th
GOOD TO FIRM

113 Confined (12st)

34[3] **COT LANE ....J Tate** 1D
ld to 11th, prom, hrd drvn & styd on gamely to ld flat
12[1] **Grain Merchant ....R Walmsley** 1
mid-div, gd prog to trck ldrs 4 out, lft in ld nxt, hdd flat
75[4] **Clare Lad (v) ....R Walford** 2
prom, ld 11th-15th, onepcd aft
67[8] Tom Log (v) *alwys prom, 2nd at 11th, outpcd frm 3 out* ....W Burnell 3
Squires Tale (Ire) *chsd ldrs, mstk 4th, fdd frm 4 out, t.o.* ....Mrs S Grant 4
Oldhill Wood (Ire) 7ex *plld hrd, rear, prog 11th, wknd 14th, t.o.* ....G Tuer 5
Simply A Star (Ire) 3ex *mid-div, outpcd 10th, t.o. 14th, p.u. 2 out* ....Maj M Watson pu
Skipping Gale *prom til wknd rpdly 10th, sn t.o., p.u. 4 out* ....P Atkinson pu
Another Hooligan *hld up, bhnd 4th, mstk 9th, lost tch 14th, p.u. nxt* ....Mrs F Needham pu
76 Castletown Count 7a *(fav) sttld rear, prog 8th, ld 4 out, going wll whn f nxt* ....S Swiers f

10 ran. ½l, 15l, 3l, 15l, 8l. Time 6m 50.00s. SP 5-1.

114 Open Maiden (5-7yo) Div I (12st)

HARRYS SPECIAL (IRE) ....G Tuer 1
plld hrd, alwys prom, 2nd 3 out, hrd rdn to ld nr fin
Arras-Tina 5a........................S Walker 2
(fav) keen hld, hld up, prog 11th, ev ch 2 out, kpt on flat
Pacific Rambler (Ire) ....N Smith 3
prom, ld 14th til hdd & nt qckn nr fin
79[4] Winters Melody 5a *ld to 3rd, prom, ld 11th-14th, wknd rpdly* ....A Pennock 4
Blacon Point *rear & mstk 2nd, sn lost tch, t.o. 10th* ....Miss S Swindells 5
Mallow Innocence 1ow *s.s. dtchd by 3rd, t.o. 10th, p.u. 14th* ....S Whitaker pu
On The Fly *prom, ld apr 4th, ran wd 7th, hdd 11th, wknd, p.u. 13th* ....P Wilkin pu
Pharlindo (Ire) *trckd ldrs, disp 3rd, blnd & u.r. nxt* ....S Brisby ur

8 ran. Nk, 1l, 25l, dist. Time 7m 15.00s. SP 14-1.
E Tuer (Hurworth).

115 Open Maiden (5-7yo) Div II (12st)

GILLIE'S FOUNTAIN ....A Dalton 1
(Jt fav) mid-div, prog 11th, disp nxt, ld 14th, sn drew clr, eased
38[2] **Cookie Boy ....Miss H Delahooke** 2
(Jt fav) disp til lft in ld 2nd, mstk & jnd 12th, outpcd frm 5 out
Muscoates ....L Donnelly 3
trckd ldrs til wknd frm 13th, virt p.u. flat
Whiskey Ditch 5a *mstk 1st, rear, blnd 6th, lost tch 11th, p.u. nxt* ....S Charlton pu
The Camair Flyer (Ire) *disp ld whn u.r. 2nd* ..P Forster ur
Abbey Moss *mid-div, outpcd 12th, t.o. whn p.u. 4 out* ....Miss J Eastwood pu
Yodeller Bill *twrds rear whn ran out 4th* ......P Wilkin ro
Look Sharpe *s.s. hld up, plld hrd, prog 9th, ev ch whn f 4 out* ....A Bonson f

8 ran. Dist, dist. Time 7m 5.00s. SP 2-1.
J D Callow (Albrighton Woodland).

116 Open Maiden (5-7yo) Div III (12st)

79 **TRANSCENDENTAL (IRE) ....Miss A Deniel** 1
mid-div, prog 14th, chal last, ran on to ld nr fin
Olympic Class ....S Robinson 2
disp til ld 10th, hdd & nt qckn nr fin
Flashlight 1ow......................S Whitaker 3
disp to 10th, trckd ldr aft, not qckn frm 3 out
80 Our Wyn-Ston 7a *prom, ev ch 4 out, onepcd* ....L Donnelly 4
80 Frumerty 7a *(fav) chsd ldrs, fdd frm 4 out*....S Swiers 5
Oliver's Mate (Ire) *prom til wknd 4 out* ....N Tutty 6
Senso (Ire) *rear, lost tch 10th, t.o.* ....K Green 7
Lingcool 5a *rear, lost tch 10th, p.u. nxt*......N Wilson pu
Silly Tinker *alwys handy, ev ch whn blnd & u.r. 3 out* ....C Denny ur
Hard To Break *s.s. rpd prog to go prom 3rd, fdd 10th, t.o. & p.u. 15th* ....N Smith pu
Addington Sharragh 5a *keen hld in rear, prog 10th, wknd 13th, t.o. & p.u. 15th* ....Miss J Binks pu
Kowloon Bay (Ire) *rear, strggling 7th, t.o. 9th, p.u. 12th* ....P Wilkin pu
Yogi's Mistress 5a *mid-div, jmpd slwly 4th, wknd 10th, t.o. & p.u. nxt* ....P Frank pu
West Lutton 7a *prom til wknd 11th, t.o. & p.u. 3 out* ....Maj M Watson pu

14 ran. ½l, 5l, ½l, 15l, 8l, 15l. Time 7m 11.00s. SP 7-1.
Chester Bosomworth (Derwent).

117 Ladies

CUMBERLAND BLUES (IRE) ....Miss A Deniel 1
alwys going wll, chsd ldrs, ld 14th, drew clr frm 2 out

Dark Dawn ....Miss L Foxton 2
hld up, prog 11th, went 2nd 4 out, onepcd aft
Final Hope (Ire) ....Mrs F Needham 3
hld up rear, prog und pres 13th, kpt on onepcd frm 3 out
Clyde Ranger *prom, disp 8th, ld 10th-14th, sn wknd* ....Miss J Eastwood 4
Kellys Diamond *mid-div, some prog 14th, wknd 3 out, t.o.*..............................Miss V Russell 5
La Maja (Ire) 5a *sn lost tch, completed own time* ....Mrs N Wilson 6
Carole's Delight 5a *bckwrd, ld to 3rd, prom, mstk 9th, fdd, t.o. & p.u. 2 out*..................Mrs L Ward pu
Saahi (USA) *prom, ld 3rd til disp 8th, hdd 11th, sn wknd, p.u. 13th*...................Miss K Swindells pu
33[7] Precarium (Ire) *prom whn u.r. 2nd*......Miss S Leach ur
Rualmit (Ire) 5a *(fav) 7/2-6/4, prom whn u.r. 2nd* ....Miss J Wormall ur
10 ran. 15l, 4l, 12l, 8l, 12l. Time 6m 44.00s. SP 10-1.
John Holroyd (Sinnington).

118 P P O R A Restricted (12st)

POLITICAL SAM ....N Smith 1+
chsng grp, prog 13th, ld 2 out, styd on wll, jnd line
36[1] **BOULEVARD BAY (IRE) ....N Wilson** 1+
(fav) hld up rear, prog 7th, gd hdwy 14th, hrd rdn to d/h on post
Ruff Account ....Miss J Eastwood 3
chsd clr ldr, mstk 11th, onepcd frm 3 out
Mandys Lad *j.w. ld & sn wll clr, hdd & wknd rpdly 2 out*..............................S Robinson 4
32[6] Attle *mid-div most of way, und pres & wknd 3 out* ....S Brisby 5
Whispers Hill 5a *prom til fdd 14th, t.o.*......C Mulhall 6
Spartan Juliet 5a *prom til wknd 14th, t.o.*....P Jenkins 7
Earl Gray *rear, lost tch 10th, t.o.*...........M Bennison 8
Rabble Rouser *rear, prog 6th, blnd 10th, sn strgglng, t.o.*...................................P Wilkin 9
Drumcairn (Ire) *rear, lost tch 13th, t.o.*........P Forster 10
The Ultimate Buck *mid-div, wknd rpdly & p.u. 11th* ....R Morney pu
Hillview Lad 1ow *rear, sn dtchd, t.o. & p.u. 14th* ....G Thomas pu
Goodwill Hill *prom til wknd 13th, t.o. & p.u. 4 out* ....D Coates pu
77[2] Malvern Cantina *mid-div whn f 14th*.........S Swiers f
14 ran. Dd-ht, 12l, 5l, 7l, 3l, 2l, 6l, 8l, 25l. Time 6m 56.00s.
David Dickson / J Blake (Middleton / Hurworth).
Boulevard Bay, Evens. Political Sam, 8-1.

119 Men's Open

9[2] **PEANUTS PET ....R Walmsley** 1
wth ldng grp, 2nd 11th, ld apr last, ran on strngly
34[1] **Country Tarrogen ....N Wilson** 2
(fav) disp to 3rd,prom,chal 4 out,ld 2 out,hdd & no ext apr last
Tobin Bronze ....R Tate 3
mid-div, prog 11th, kpt on frm 3 out
75[3] Coolvawn Lady (Ire) 5a *rear, prog 10th, onepcd frm 4 out*.................................S Walker 4
La Fontainbleau (Ire) *prom til lost ground 5th, wll bhnd 10th, t.o.*..........................A Rebori 5
Dalmore *rear, lost tch 10th*................D Coates 6
34[2] Castle Tyrant 5a *prom til fdd frm 13th, virt p.u. flat* ....P Atkinson 7
34 Politico Pot *mid-div, wknd 10th, t.o. & p.u. 12th* ....S Whitaker ur
Highland Friend *rear, strgglng 4th, lost tch 10th, t.o. & p.u. 3 out*.................................N Smith pu
General Brandy *handy whn u.r. 7th*............G Tuer ur
Whinstone Mill *rear, prog 10th, wknd 4 out, p.u. nxt* ....N Kent pu
Mighty Merc *wth ldrs til fdd 13th, t.o. & p.u. 3 out* ....S Gibbon pu
Flip The Lid (Ire) 5a *plld hrd, disp til ld 3rd, hdd 4 out, wknd, p.u. flat, lame*......................N Tutty pu
Polynth *mid-div whn u.r. 4th*...............L Donnelly ur
Carol's Concorde (Ire) *sn rear, t.o. & p.u. 7th* J Saville pu
15 ran. 4l, 15l, ½l, dist, 3l, dist. Time 6m 44.00s. SP 6-1.
J W Walmsley (Bramham Moor).

120 Open Maiden (8yo+)

GOLD CHOICE ....A Ogden 1
plld hrd, made all, sn wll clr, unchal
Secret Bay ....S Swiers 2
alwys in chsng grp, went 2nd 8th, kpt on steadily frm 2 out
Andretti's Heir ....A Bonson 3
alwys in chsng grp, onepcd frm 4 out
Canebreak Boy (Ire) *rear, prog 14th, kpt on frm 3 out, improve*..........................Mrs F Needham 4
Henceyem (Ire) *rear, mstk 4th, nvr dang, t.o.* N Smith 5
Pri Neukin *alwys rear, t.o. & p.u. 11th* ......D Coates pu
14[2] Sunkala Shine *(fav) mid-div,prog 10th,remote 3rd 13th,blnd nxt,sn wknd,p.u.4 out*...........Miss R Clark pu
Persian Lion *rear, sn dtchd, wll bhnd whn p.u. 14th* ....Mrs L Ward pu
Ingleby Flyer 5a *mid-div, wknd 13th, t.o. & p.u. 4 out* ....P Frank pu
Rapid Regent *alwys rear, t.o. & p.u. 11th* ...R Morney pu
Ski Lady 5a *mid-div, mstk 8th, t.o. & p.u. nxt* ....Miss L Horner pu
Smith's Melody *mid-div, wknd 10th, t.o. & p.u. nxt* ....M Haigh pu
Guler-A *alwys rear, t.o. & p.u. 14th*.........S Gibbon pu
Just For Me (Ire) *alwys rear, t.o. & p.u. 11th* N Wilson pu
Rambling Oats *chsng grp, wknd 12th, t.o. & p.u. 2 out* ....Miss A Price pu
Just Jessica 5a *mid-div, lost tch 6th, t.o. & p.u. 10th* ....A Balding pu
The Golly Ollybird 6ow *rear, n.j.w. t.o. & p.u. 11th* ....J Swinburn pu
Gold Talisman 5a *mid-div, wknd 12th, t.o. & p.u. 14th* ....D Barlow pu
18 ran. 7l, dist, 15l, 8l. Time 6m 49.00s. SP 10-1.
Victor Ogden (Bedale).

121 Members

BRECKENBROUGH LAD ....I Bennett 1
disp at slow pace, qcknd to ld apr last
My True Clown ....Miss L Hampshire 2
(fav) disp at slow pace, just outpced apr last
2 ran. 2½l. Time 8m 33.00s. SP Evens.
Mrs M R Bennett (Badsworth).
N.E.

CAMBRIDGE UNIV DRAGHOUNDS
Cottenham
Sunday February 9th
GOOD TO FIRM

122 Members

28[2] **AUCHENDOLLY (IRE) ....S Sporborg** 1
(fav) ld to 5th, prssd ldr aft, ld 2 out, rdn out
Solid (Ire) ....M Barnard 2
ld 5th-2 out, kpt on onepcd flat
Valatch ....J Henderson 3
4th & outpcd by 5th, no prog aft, tk poor 3rd last
Times Leader *in tch wth ldng pair to 10th, steadily wknd*...............................Miss K Hills 4
Royal Quarry *1st ride, raced wd, sn wll bhnd, t.o. last hlfwy* ....W Cursham 5
61[3] View Point (Ire) *jmpd slwly & reluc,bhnd,effrt 12th,sn wknd,t.o. & p.u.16th* ....M Gingell pu
6 ran. 3l, dist, 10l, 1 fence. Time 6m 16.00s. SP 2-5.
Christopher Sporborg (Cambridge University Drag).

123 Intermediate (12st)

10[1] **SIGN 5ex..................................A Hill** 1
(fav) trckd ldrs, chal 15th, mstk nxt, ld 3 out, ran on well
Mister Black (Ire) 3ow ....A Crow 2
chsd ldr 5th, ld aft 10th til 3 out, ev ch last, wknd
72[2] **Druid's Lodge ....C Ward-Thomas** 3

chsd ldrs, 4th & outpcd frm 14th, kpt on to tk 3rd nr fin
62² Horace *mid-div, prog 11th, 3rd & outpcd 15th, no imp ldrs aft* ....W Wales 4
Salty Snacks (Ire) *ld 3rd til aft 10th, wknd frm 14th* ....M Gingell 5
63 Noble Knight (Ire) 10ow *last & sn wll bhnd, t.o. 10th* ....C Jarvis 6
Rarely At Odds *in tch to 11th, sn wknd, t.o. & p.u. 16th* ....S R Andrews pu
Current Attraction 5a *alwys bhnd, t.o. 12th, p.u. 15th* ....M Barnard pu
Cleddau King 6ow *ld to 3rd, sn wknd, t.o. & p.u. 3 out* ....J Buckle pu
Major Neave *mstk 3rd, p.u. nxt, dsmntd* ....G Hopper pu
24² Dynamite Dan (Ire) *hld up, prog & in tch 13th, sn btn, p.u. 16th* ....S Cowell pu
73¹ Salmon Mead (Ire) *rear, nvr on trms wth ldrs, wll bhnd whn p.u. 14th* ....S Sporborg pu
Special Company (Ire) 5a *mid-div, 7th & in tch whn blnd & u.r. 10th* ....R Smith ur

13 ran. 5l, 6l, 1½l, 30l, 20l. Time 6m 6.00s. SP 6-4.
Philip Newton (Pytchley).

124 Men's Open

25¹ **CARDINAL RICHELIEU ....S Sporborg** 1
made all, edgd rght aft last, styd on gamely
62¹ **River Melody 5a ....T Moore** 2
(fav) cls up,trckd wnr aft 3 out,chal last,nt mch room,found nil
27⁴ **Airtrak (Ire) ....R Barrett** 3
prom, prssd wnr 10th til aft 3 out, wknd apr last
Ok Corral (USA) *in tch til outpcd 14th, no imp on ldrs frm 3 out* ....A Greig 4
63² Armagret *rear til prog 10th, outpcd 14th, wknd 2 out* ....S Cowell 5
25 Major Inquiry (USA) *sn rear, 7th & no ch whn u.r. 14th* ....W Pewter ur
Celtic King *last & sn bhnd, p.u. aft 7th* ....H Tregoning pu
30 Alapa *mid-div, outpcd 14th, modest 6th whn u.r. 2 out* ....V Coogan ur
Eden's Close *prssd wnr to 10th, sn wknd, t.o. & p.u. 15th* ....P Keane pu

9 ran. 1½l, 15l, 5l, 6l. Time 6m 4.00s. SP 3-1.
Christopher Sporborg (Puckeridge).
After Stewards' inquiry, result remained unaltered.

125 G Middleton Ladies

RICHARD HUNT ....Miss L Rowe 1
(fav) rear, prog 10th, chal 2 out, ld flat, just hld on
Mountshannon ....Mrs T Hill 2
trckd ldrs, disp 13th til ld aft 3 out, hdd flat, rallied
26⁴ **Wistino ....Mrs L Gibbon** 3
chsd ldr 6th, disp 13th til aft 3 out, wknd apr last
26⁶ Profligate *rear, lost tch hlfwy, kpt on onepcd frm 15th* ....Miss P Ellison 4
64⁴ Omidjoy (Ire) 5a *last pair & alwys wll bhnd, t.o. 10th* ....Mrs L Wrighton 5
66 Notary-Nowell *mid-div, lost tch 11th, t.o. 14th* ....Miss C Savill 6
8³ So Isle 5a *ld to 13th, wknd rpdly & p.u. bef nxt* ....Miss E Tomlinson pu
Raba Riba *prom, cls 3rd whn mstk & u.r. 10th* ....Miss T Spearing ur
Powersurge *rear whn u.r. 1st* ....Miss H Courtney Bennett ur
Warner For Sport *last pair & wll bhnd, mstk 5th, t.o. & p.u. 16th* ....Miss F Worley pu
Monksfort *wll in tch, prog to jn ldrs whn u.r. 13th* ....Miss C Holliday ur

11 ran. Nk, 12l, 20l, 25l, 12l. Time 6m 3.00s. SP 10-11.
Mrs P Rowe (Puckeridge).

126 Restricted (12st)

13¹ **MISTER SPECTATOR (IRE) ....C Gordon** 1
(fav) made all, drew clr aft 2 out, ran on well
15¹ **Claydons Monty ....S R Andrews** 2
chsd wnr, cls engh 14th, hit 2 out, btn whn blnd last
65 **Swift Reward 5a (bl) ....W Wales** 3
chsg grp, lost tch 12th, kpt on frm 3 out, tk 3rd flat
Meadow Cottage *chsng grp, mstk 6th, no prog 13th, onepcd* ....T Stephenson 4
Velka 5a *chsng grp, chsd ldng pair 14th, no imp, wknd flat* ....Mrs S Hickman 5
28 New York Boy *sn bhnd, t.o. 12th, ran on frm 3 out, fin wll* ....N Strain 6
Rayman (Ire) *pllng, chsd ldng pair til wknd & blnd 14th, t.o.* ....J Trice-Rolph 7
Fort Diana *chsng grp til wknd 13th, t.o. & p.u. 3 out* ....M Jones pu
29 Alycount (USA) *jmpd lft 3rd, alwys bhnd, t.o. & p.u. 16th* ....R Wakley pu
69 Learner Driver *n.j.w. & reluc, alwys bhnd, t.o. & p.u. 3 out* ....M Gingell pu
24³ Doctor Dick (Ire) *prom whn blnd & u.r. 2nd* ..S Cowell ur
10 Fiddlers Goodwill *alwys bhnd, t.o. & p.u. 2 out* ....C Ward pu
Tasmanite *alwys bhnd, last & t.o. whn p.u. 12th* ....G Hopper pu
Black Ermine (Ire) *mid-div, pshd alng 9th, no prog, wll bhnd whn p.u. 3 out* ....C Ward-Thomas pu

14 ran. 20l, dist, 3l, 2l, 2l, 20l. Time 6m 9.00s. SP Evens.
P Hughes (East Sussex & Romney Marsh).

127 Open Maiden Div I (12st)

29 **REGAL BAY ....W Wales** 1
cls up, trckd ldr 16th, chal 2 out, drvn to ld flat
Reverend Brown (Ire) ....A Sansome 2
(fav) made most, some slw jmps, jnd last, hdd & no ext flat
True Chimes ....J Owen 3
mstk 3rd, in tch, 4th 3 out, kpt on onepcd
44 John Robin 7a *s.s. & green, prog to prss ldr 8th, wknd 16th* ....T Stephenson 4
Village Copper 7a *16s-8s, in tch, 5th & ch 16th, wknd nxt* ....C Ward-Thomas 5
Allegro Prince *rear, mstks 6 & 13th, sn btn, t.o. whn ran out 3 out* ....L Lay ro
Charlie Andrews *1st ride, mstks 4 & 5th, t.o. 10th, p.u. 13th* ....S Dobson pu
44 Fix The Spec (Ire) *alwys bhnd, t.o. & p.u. 13th* D Page pu
Secret Music *prom, blnd 10th, 3rd whn f nxt* ....Capt D Parker f
Commasarris 7a 5ow *alwys bhnd, t.o. & p.u. 14th* ....P Blagg pu
Scare McClare 5a *10s-5s, in tch in rear, wkng whn mstk 15th, t.o. & p.u. 3out* ....S R Andrews pu

11 ran. 1½l, 20l, 15l, 2l. Time 6m 21.00s. SP 3-1.
David Wales (West Norfolk).

128 Open Maiden Div II (12st)

30 **ZOES PET 5a ....Miss H Pewter** 1
rcd wd,pllng,chsd ldr 11th,hld whn lft in ld 2 out,ran on
30² **Regency Cottage ....W Wales** 2
wth ldrs, 3rd frm 13th til lft 2nd 2 out, no imp wnr
Insulate 5a ....S March 3
in tch in rear til outpcd 14th, no imp ldrs aft
61 Chalinare (Ire) *prom til wknd 14th, walked in* ....S R Andrews 4
Malingerer 5a *pllng, prom to 11th, sn wknd, p.u. 14th* ....M Jones pu
15² Holding The Aces *mstk 10th, made most to 11th, wknd rpdly, p.u. 14th* ....T Marks pu
Bergholt 7a *plld hrd, cls up til 4th & outpcd 14th, wknd, p.u. 3 out* ....A Coe pu
43 Ishma (Ire) *bhnd frm 3rd, t.o. whn crawld 16th & p.u.* ....D Page pu
13⁴ Soon Be Back *(fav) prom, ld 11th, 5l clr whn f 2 out* ....R Barrett f
24 Miss Simitar 5a *in tch til wknd 13th, t.o. & p.u. 16th* ....T Moore pu

10 ran. 4l, dist, 15l. Time 6m 25.00s. SP 20-1.
N J Pewter (Suffolk).
J.N.

COLLEGE VALLEY & N N'LAND
Alnwick
Sunday February 9th
GOOD

129 Members (12st)

SISTER SEVEN (IRE) 5a ....Miss D Laidlaw 1
(Jt fav) made all at steady pace, rdn & qcknd clr flat
Seek And Destroy ....C Storey 2
(Jt fav) trckd wnr, ev ch 3 out, unable qckn flat
2 ran. 3l. Time 6m 38.00s. SP 4-5.
M H Walton (College Valley/Northumberland).

130 Intermediate (12st)

35[7] **MURDER MOSS (IRE) 1ow............S Coltherd** 1
chsd ldr 6th, ld 13th, sn clr, blnd 2 out, rdn out
34 **Fiscal Policy ....H Trotter** 2
ld til aft 3rd, chsd ldrs, went 2nd 3 out, styd on
Farriers Favourite 5a...................A Parker 3
hld up, effrt apr 4 out, kpt on onepcd frm nxt
35[1] Toaster Crumpet 5ex *(fav) alwys same plc, brf efft apr 4 out, wll btn nxt*..................Miss P Robson 4
Hydropic *ld aft 3rd to 13th, wknd apr 4 out, p.u. 2 out* ....Miss K Miller pu
35[9] Young Moss *jmpd rght, cls up to 2nd, sn bhnd, t.o. & p.u. 9th*...............................A Robson pu
Trespasser (Ire) *bhnd & jmpd slwly 8th, reluc aft nxt, ran out 10th*..............................R Morgan ro
7 ran. 3l, 10l, 3l. Time 6m 24.00s. SP 6-1.
S Coltherd (Buccleuch).

131 Restricted (12st)

14[1] **MAKIN' DOO (IRE) ....A Parker** 1
(fav) 7/2-2s, w.w. prog to ld 4 out, hdd last, rallied to ld fin
Denim Blue ....Miss P Robson 2
w.w. prog 14th, rdn to ld last, hdd fin
Jads Lad ....D Reid 3
wth ldr, ld 6th-8th, ev ch 4 out, kpt on onepcd
The Buachaill (Ire) *prom, ld 8th-4 out, onepcd und pres aft*..................................P Craggs 4
32[5] All Or Nothing 5a *in tch, prog & blnd 11th, no hdwy frm 3 out*................................J Ewart 5
35[2] Love Actinium (Ire) 5a *chsd ldrs to 4 out, no hdwy aft* ....Mrs C Amos 6
38[1] River Ramble 5a *ld 2nd-6th, prom to 14th, outpcd frm nxt*...........................Miss T Jackson 7
Panto Lady 5a *sn wll bhnd, t.o. frm 7th, p.u. 3 out* ....Miss S Lamb pu
Green Sheen (Ire) *u.r. 2nd*...................C Wilson ur
Sumpt'n Smart *in tch, prog to chs ldrs 13th, btn apr 4 out, p.u. nxt*..................................R Morgan pu
Miss Cullane (Ire) 5a 6ow *ld to 2nd, bhnd frm 9th, t.o. & p.u. 3 out*.................................R Shiels pu
32 Durham Glint *alwys bhnd, t.o. & p.u. 3 out* S Bowden pu
Ebbzeado Willfurr (Ire) *cls up, 3rd whn mssd mrkr aft 9th, cont, fin 8th* ....J Billinge ro
13 ran. Nk, 2l, 1l, 2½l, 1½l, ½l. Time 6m 25.00s. SP 2-1.
R G Makin (York & Ainsty South).

132 Ladies

MISTY NIGHT 5a ....Miss A Bowie 1
chsd ldrs, lft in ld 11th, made rest, lft clr 3 out, styd on
33 **Parsons Brig ....Miss S Forster** 2
(fav) in tch, 3rd & hit 13th, ev ch 4 out, btn whn lft 2nd nxt
33[3] **Lupy Minstrel ....Miss P Robson** 3
mid-div, outpcd & rmndr 12th, kpt on onepcd frm 3 out
Bow Handy Man *bhnd, styd on frm 3 out, nvr nrr* ....Miss L Plater 4
33[8] Ready Steady *chsd ldr to 4 out, wknd apr nxt* ....Mrs K Hargreave 5
33 Schweppes Tonic *chsd ldrs to 9th, sn wknd, t.o. & p.u. 3 out*..............................Miss D Laidlaw pu
33 The Laughing Lord 1ow *ld til f 11th*.....Miss R Shiels f
Across The Card *in tch, prog 10th, 4l 2nd & clsng whn u.r. 3 out*..............................Miss R Ramsay ur
Craigdale *sn wll bhnd, t.o. & p.u. 3 out* ....Miss M Robinson pu
9 ran. 8l, 3l, hd, 20l. Time 6m 19.00s. SP 9-2.
Mrs M A Bowie (Buccleuch).

133 Men's Open

31[1] **WASHAKIE 3ow........................J Walton** 1
conf rdn, prog 14th, ld 2 out, gd jmp last, ran on strngly
Royal Jester ....C Storey 2
(fav) ld to 2 out, unable to qckn und pres
35[6] **Lion Of Vienna ....T Scott** 3
chsd ldrs, disp 10th-12th, strgglng & mstk nxt, no dang aft
Eastern Pleasure *hld up in tch, prog 9th, outpcd apr 4 out, t.o.*..................................A Robson 4
Strong Measure (Ire) *keen hld, wth ldr to 10th, wknd 13th, t.o. & p.u. 3 out* ....R Morgan pu
35 Itsalltheonetodev (Ire) *t.d.e. hld up, chsd ldr 13th-14th, 3rd & btn whn u.r. 3 out*....................H Trotter ur
6 ran. 3l, 20l, 25l. Time 6m 27.00s. SP 6-4.
Mrs F T Walton (Border).

134 Open Maiden Div I (12st)

SKY MISSILE 5a ....T Oates 1
ld to 4th, chsd ldrs, 3rd & btn whn lft wll clr 4 out
Severe Storm ....C Storey 2
hld up, prog 9th, nvr rchd ldrs, lft poor 2nd 4 out, tired
Buckaroo 5a ....A Parker 3
hld up, prog 9th, nvr on trms, lft poor 3rd 4 out
Pablowmore *(fav) pllng, prom & hit 2nd, lost plc 7th, t.o. 10th, ran on flat*..........................R Green 4
33 Lakeland Edition 5a *sn wll bhnd, t.o. frm 3rd* ....R Robinson 5
36 Bantel Bargain 5a *nvr nr ldrs, poor 7th at 10th, t.o. & p.u. 13th* ....P Johnson pu
Prince Rossini (Ire) *nvr bttr than mid-div, t.o. whn f 4 out* ....B Gibson f
36 Monynut 5a *mid-div, blnd 9th, p.u. nxt* .....A Robson pu
Craig Burn 5a *cls up, ld 4th, clr 6th, 4l up whn f 4 out* ....J Ewart f
Arctic Leader 5a *chsd ldrs,2nd 11th,4l down whn lft in ld, blnd & u.r. 4 out* ....M Ruddy ur
Abbey Lad *jmpd slwly, sn t.o., p.u. 3 out* .....N Swan pu
11 ran. Dist, 4l, 5l, 1 fence. Time 6m 33.00s. SP 10-1.
Gavin Douglas (Jedforest).

135 Open Maiden Div II (12st)

NOTHINGTOTELLME (IRE) ....A Parker 1
(fav) conf rdn, prog 14th, ld 2 out, lft in cmmnd last, ran on
37[4] **Bluebell Track 5a ....R Trotter** 2
alwys prom, 5th 4 out, styd on frm 2 out, sntchd 2nd post
Peelinick ....T Oates 3
mstks, ld 11th-2 out, ev ch whn blnd last, no ext
31 Donside *w.w. prog 10th, ev ch 4 out, btn nxt* ....A Robson 4
Ovahandy Man *in tch, prog 12th, ev ch nxt, wknd 3 out*..................................P Craggs 5
37 Storm Alive (Ire) *bhnd, prog 9th, lost tch 11th, no dang aft*..........................Miss P Robson 6
38 Aston Warrior 5a *wll bhnd frm 3rd, t.o. & p.u. 4 out* ....Mrs K Hargreave pu
Gold Or Bust 5a *rear, mstk 4th, prog & ran wd apr 10th, wknd 12th,p.u.3out* ....Miss T Jackson pu
Annulment (Ire) *pllng, wth ldr, ld 9-11th, wknd rpdly 14th, p.u. 3 out*..........................L Morgan pu
Lethem Laird *ld to 9th, wknd 12th, p.u. 14th* ...T Scott pu
Up And Running *bhnd frm 6th, t.o. & p.u. 4 out* ....C Storey pu

38 Father O'Callaghan (Ire) *rear of main grp, ran on 4 out, 4th whn f last* ....Miss M Bremner f
12 ran. 2l, hd, 6l, 7l, 20l. Time 6m 29.00s. SP Evens.
R A Bartlett (Fife).

136 Open Maiden Div III (12st)

36[2] **STAR LEA ....B Stonehouse 1**
(Jt fav) prom, ld 3 out, steadied last, hld on
Captain Guinness (Ire) ....J Alexander 2
chsd ldrs, ld 12th-14th, ev ch 3 out, kpt on und pres flat
Dillons Bridge (Ire) ....D Wood 3
w.w. prog 10th, 3rd & jmpd slwly 2 out, kpt on flat
Red Hot Boogie (Ire) *chsd ldrs, hmpd 9th, rdn 4 out, kpt on onepcd aft*..............................T Scott 4
Breezy Sea *in tch, prog to ld 14th, hdd 3 out, fdd* ....C Storey 5
36[5] Bavington *mid-div, prog 9th, 6th & outpcd 14th, no dang aft* ....R Morgan 6
Marked Card *tubed, bhnd frm 6th, no dang aft* ....Mrs M Kendall 7
38 Tolmin *bhnd, prog & in tch 10th, outpcd apr 13th* ....Miss M Fotheringham 8
Hooky's Treat 5a *alwys rear, nvr dang* . .M Bradburne 9
Sagaro Belle 5a *in tch to 10th, bhnd frm 13th* ....Miss H Dudgeon 10
36 Indian River (Ire) *ld 3rd-12th, sn wknd, t.o. & p.u. 4 out* ....A Robson pu
31[2] Whosthat *ld, blnd 2nd, hdd nxt, prom whn f 9th* ....Miss S Lamb f
Barrow Knocks *sn m bhnd, t.o. 3rd, p.u. 11th* R Green pu
37 Alianne 5a *bhnd, lost tch 12th, t.o. & p.u. last* ....P Johnson pu
Farriers Fantasy 12a *(Jt fav) mid-div whn blnd & u.r. 4th*..............................A Parker ur
Passim 12a *alwys wll bhnd, t.o. 7th, p.u. 3 out* ....T Morrison pu
16 ran. 1l, ½l, 5l, hd, 10l, 6l, 8l, ½l, 15l. Time 6m 34.00s. SP 2-1.
B Stonehouse (Braes Of Derwent).
S.P.

MIDLAND AREA CLUB
Thorpe Lodge
Sunday February 9th
GOOD TO FIRM

137 Members (12st)

75[5] **ALPHA ONE ....P Gee 1**
mid-div, 2nd at 14th, ld 3 out, ran on well
R N Commander ....J Cornwall 2
ld/disp to 5th, cls up, ld 5 out-nxt, no ext frm 2 out
Ridwan ....Miss S Bonser 3
(fav) n.j.w. outpcd to hlfwy, prog und pres nr fin
74[3] Golden Moss 7ex *rear early, nvr able to rch ldrs* ....Maj S Robinson 4
Phrose *prom, ev ch 5 out, not qckn aft*....A Pickering 5
Vimchase *prom, ld 10th-6 out, in tch whn u.r. nxt* ....S J Robinson ur
Unassuming *cls up, ld 6-9th, wknd, p.u. 5 out* . .D Ingle pu
13 Springfield Pet 5a 1ow *alwys rear, t.o. hlfwy, p.u. 11th* ....K Needham pu
Mysterious Run (Ire) *disp whn ran out 3rd* ....Miss S Samworth ro
9 ran. 2½l, 1l, 30l, 2l. Time 6m 40.00s. SP 8-1.
Mrs R Gee (Grove & Rufford).

138 Men's Open

56 **LUCKY CHRISTOPHER ....G Tarry 1**
(fav) hld up, jnd ldr 3 out, clr nxt, ran on well
Raise An Argument ....N Docker 2
1st ride, j.w. ld til jnd 3 out, ran on onepcd aft
3[6] **Trusty Friend ....A Brown 3**
in tch, no ext frm 3 out
The Difference *mostly 5th & strgglng, ran on frm 3 out, nvr dang*..............................M Chatterton 4
9[3] Faithful Star *ldng grp going wll til wknd rpdly 3 out* ....R Hunnisett 5
5 ran. 4l, 10l, 2l, 20l. Time 6m 45.00s. SP 1-2.
G B Tarry (Grafton).

139 Ladies

85 **THE BOILER WHITE (IRE) 4ow . . .Miss J Froggatt 1**
j.w. 2nd/3rd til ld 6 out, ran on strngly whn chal 2 out
Naughty Nellie 5a.................Mrs J Dawson 2
2nd/3rd til disp 4 out, kpt on onepcd frm 3 out
Nowhiski ....Miss C Tarratt 3
(fav) ld to 11th, in tch whn blnd 4 out, not rcvr
Remalone 5a *alwys rear, lsng tch whn p.u. 14th* ....Mrs C McCarthy pu
4 ran. 2l, 2½l. Time 6m 49.00s. SP 10-3.
Miss J Froggatt (Meynell & South Staffs).

140 P P O R A Restricted (12st)

CAIRNDHU MISTY 5a ....P Gee 1
hld up rear, strng run frm 3 out, ld nxt, sn clr
Miss Solitaire 5a ....G Tarry 2
mstks, mid-div, nrst fin
28[7] **Holmby Mill ....B Pollock 3**
(fav) n.j.w. prom, disp 10th-3 out, onepcd
Miss Cresta 5a *ld 2nd, 20l clr 8th, 10l clr whn f 10th* ....S Morris f
78[3] Ryders Wells *ld to 2nd, lft in ld 10th, disp aft, 2nd & hld whn u.r.2 out* ....J Docker ur
Kamadora *rear, lsng tch whn ref 6th*....S J Robinson ref
Swinging Song *mid to rear, t.o. & p.u. 15th* ....Miss K Gilman pu
7 ran. 8l, 3l. Time 6m 47.00s. SP 8-1.
Mrs R Gee (Grove & Rufford).

141 Maiden (12st)

BUBBLY BOY ....G Tarry 1
(fav) chsng grp, ld 2 out, ran on und pres frm last
13[6] **Barneys Gold (Ire) ....A Bealby 2**
alwys prom, ran on frm 2 out, just faild
Greenacres Rose 5a..........Miss S Phizacklea 3
mid to rear, some late prog frm 3 out, nvr nrr
14 Springfield Rex *mid to rear, kpt on frm 4 out, nrst fin* ....K Needham 4
14[4] Bamboo Pie 5a *clr ldr til wknd & hdd 2 out* . .S Morris 5
Andalucian Sun (Ire) *mid-div, no prog frm 5 out* ....G Brewer 6
Top The Bid *nvr bttr than mid-div* .....Miss C Arthers 7
Casherooski (Ire) *rear, no ch whn p.u. 6 out* ....E Andrewes pu
Mamnoon (USA) *f 3rd* ....J Oldring f
Kiri's Rose (Ire) 5a *f 2nd* ....P Gee f
Greenhil Patchwork *mid-div whn f 10th*.....R Armson f
Mr Freebie (Den) *mid to rear, btn whn p.u. 10th* ....D Ingle pu
12 ran. Hd, 20l, nk, 8l. Time 6m 42.00s. SP 2-1.
G B Tarry (Grafton).
V.S.

TWESELDOWN CLUB
Tweseldown
Sunday February 9th
GOOD TO FIRM

142 Members (12st)

DARTON RI ....T McCarthy 1
(fav) j.w. trckd ldrs, ld 4 out, easily
Sky Venture ....P Bull 2
hld up, prog to ld 11th, hdd 4 out, styd on onepcd
Glen Cherry ....P Scouller 3
chsd ldr, lost plc frm 10th, mstk 15th, sn btn
Raglan Road *not fluent, outpcd in rear, some prog 12th,sn wknd,p.u.3 out*............Miss A Embiricos pu
55[9] Lake Teereen *outpcd in rear, some prog 12th, blnd & btn 3 out, p.u. nxt*......................T Underwood pu
Tompet *hld up, in tch whn blnd & u.r. 11th* . .J Connell ur

Tricksome *chsd ldr, lft in ld 8th, hdd 11th, btn whn f 3 out, dead*................................H Dunlop f
Electric Committee (Ire) *ld, sn clr, tk wrong course bend aft 7th*................................A Wood ro
8 ran. 8l, 12l. Time 6m 24.00s. SP 5-2.
Mrs S Maxse (Hampshire).

143 City Of London

18[4] **ROVING REPORT ....Mrs A Rucker** 1
(fav) hld up last, prog to ld on bit 2 out, easily
55 **Button Your Lip ....Mrs J Enderby** 2
trckd ldr, rdn to disp 3 out, hdd & onepcd nxt
10 **Mount Patrick ....C Lawson** 3
j.w. made most til jnd 3 out, hdd & btn nxt
3 ran. 4l, 15l. Time 6m 36.50s. SP 1-3.
Mrs A Rucker (Worcestershire).

144 Men's Open

19[2] **ARDBRENNAN ....C Bennett** 1
(fav) alwys prom, ld 9th til mstk 11th, ld apr last, rdn out
57 **Star Oats ....A Kinane** 2
pllng, trckd ldrs, ld 11th, hdd apr last, no ext
Beach Bum ....A Charles-Jones 3
hld up, blnd badly 2nd, styd on onepcd frm 4 out
Twist 'N' Scu *j.w. prom til wknd frm 4 out*....C Vigors 4
Diviner (Ire) *mid-div, lost ground frm 12th, t.o. 4 out*................................D Albert 5
The Forties *made most to 9th, wknd rpdly, t.o. 4 out*................................N Earnshaw 6
Folk Dance *hld up, prog 9th, 3rd & ev ch 3 out, wknd nxt, p.u. last*................................P O'Keeffe pu
Banton Loch *twrds rear, outpcd frm 12th, sn t.o., p.u. last*................................J Hankinson pu
Nemuro (USA) *plld, rear, t.o. 9th, ref & u.r. 11th*................................P Scouller ref
9 ran. 1½l, 15l, 1½l, 10l, 3l. Time 6m 24.40s. SP 4-7.
C C Bennett (Vine & Craven).

145 G Middleton Ladies

18[3] **SPACIAL (USA) ....Miss M Hill** 1
j.w. prom, ld 2 out, imprssv
18[1] **Arctic Chill (Ire) ....Miss S Vickery** 2
(fav) prom, ld 6-9th & 15th, blnd 3 out, hdd nxt, no ext
Tudor Henry ....Mrs C Mitchell 3
outpcd in rear, prog frm 9th, styd on onepcd frm 4 out
48 Butler John (Ire) *prom, ld aft 9th-14th, wkng whn mstk 4 out*..........Miss J Cumings 4
On His Own *outpcd in rear, t.o. 12th*................................Miss W Southcombe 5
Ski Nut *outpcd in rear, t.o. 15th*...Miss S Barraclough 6
57 Dayadan (Ire) *immed outpcd, t.o. 4th, u.r. 7th*................................Miss J Sawyer 7
49[2] Midfielder *chsd ldrs, lost tch 12th, p.u. 3 out*................................Miss V Roberts pu
Debjanjo *chsd ldrs, wknd frm 12th, sn t.o., p.u. 3 out*................................Miss P Gundry pu
85[3] Fantastic Fleet (Ire) 7a *ld to 5th, wknd frm 14th, p.u. 3 out*................................Miss P Jones pu
10 ran. 12l, 8l, 15l, 12l, 2l. Time 6m 15.00s. SP 4-1.
Richard J Hill (Wilton).

146 Open Maiden Div I

14[5] **NORMEAD LASS 5a ....A Martin** 1
trckd ldrs,prog to 2nd 15th,ld aft 2 out,mstk last,drvn out
Ally Pally ....P York 2
prom, mstk 15th, ev ch 2 out, no ext
20[2] **Ted's Knight (Ire) ....A Phillips** 3
(fav) blnd badly 1st, rear, styd on thro' btn hrss 4 out, nvr nrr
40[2] Tu Piece *rear, styd on onepcd frm 4 out*....P Howse 4
Jobingo *mstks 3rd & 11th, ld nxt til wknd rpdly aft 2 out*................................Daniel Dennis 5
Colonel Crumpet *rear, rpd prog to ld 3-5th, sn bhnd, t.o. 12th*................................G Casenove 6
Iced Ginger *mid-div, lost ground hlfwy, p.u. aft 11th*................................D Evatt pu
Fever Pitch *plld, ld to 3rd & 6-11th, sn btn, p.u. 3 out*................................B Dixon pu
Weekend Worker *mid-div, in tch whn p.u. 13th, lame*................................A Wintle pu
Celtic Friend (Ire) *rear whn tried to ref & u.r. 2nd*................................M Portman ur
10 ran. 5l, 1½l, 1½l, 15l, 20l. Time 6m 39.80s. SP 25-1.
Ms Felicity Ashfield (Windsor Forest Drag).

147 Open Maiden Div II

FIDDLERS KNAP ....J Hobbs 1
ld to 2nd, alwys prom, ran on to ld apr last, all out
And Why Not ....J Van Praagh 2
10s-6s, j.w. hld up rear,prog to ld 12th,hdd apr last,no ext
Looking ....R Lawther 3
sweating, prom, ld 8-11th, ev ch 3 out, sn wknd
41 Royal Turn *rear, mstks 5 & 7th, styd on onepcd frm 14th*................................A Honeyball 4
River Thrust (Ire) *rear, sn outpcd, t.o. 12th*................................Miss G Young 5
28 Northern Code *(fav) ld 3rd til blnd bdly 7th, wknd rpdly, p.u. 12th*................................G Smith pu
Always Dreaming 5a *mid-div, mstk 11th, 4th & ev ch whn f 4 out*..........................Dr P Pritchard f
Tommy-Gun *prom, wknd 9th, p.u. 12th*.......D Evatt pu
Flights Lane 5a *alwys rear, p.u. 12th*..........B Dixon pu
Nova Star 5a *mstk 1st, t.o. 7th, p.u. 3 out*...C Lawson pu
Bombadier Brown *u.r. 2nd*.........A Charles-Jones ur
Valander 5a *f 2nd*................................P York f
12 ran. 1½l, 12l, 15l, dist. Time 6m 35.50s. SP 9-2.
C P Hobbs (North Cotswold).

148 Moderate (12st)

GRIMLEY GALE (IRE) 5a 5ex............A Wintle 1
(Jt fav) mid-div, mstk 9th, prog 4 out, disp last, ld nr fin, all out
Fowling Piece ....Daniel Dennis 2
alwys prom, ld 13th til jnd last, styd on flat, just hld
Local Manor 5ex.......................H Dunlop 3
mid-div, prog 12th, ev ch 2 out, no ext
58[4] Tarry Awhile *prom, lft in ld 7th, hdd 12th, no ext frm 3 out*................................J Connell 4
Lilac Time 5a *trckd ldrs, ch 15th, onepcd*................................Dr P Pritchard 5
Alias Silver 5ex *mid-div, rmndrs 12th, btn frm 4 out*................................Miss H Irving 6
56[3] Hackett's Farm 5ex *(Jt fav) mid-div, onepcd frm 15th*................................Julian Pritchard 7
Bilbo Baggins (Ire) *n.j.w. in rear, t.o. 13th*..M Gorman 8
Major Man (Ire) *ld, hit 2nd, u.r. 7th*.......Miss C Wates 9
Treaty Bridge *prom, hit 3rd, hmpd & p.u. 5th, lame*................................Miss C Townsley pu
21[1] Sit Tight *rear whn u.r. 11th*..................M Portman ur
7 Stalbridge Bill *mid-div, u.r. 3rd*......Miss A Goschen ur
12 ran. 1l, 12l, 10l, 8l, 3l, 4l, 20l. Time 6m 25.50s. SP 2-1.
R M Phillips (Clifton-On-Teme).
M.J.

HEREFORD
Monday February 10th
GOOD TO SOFT

149 3m 1f 110yds Golden Valley Hunters' Chase Class H

MISS MILLBROOK 11.2 7a ....Mr E Williams 1
held up, hdwy 7th, ld 12th, clr 3 out, blnd last.
Cape Cottage 11.7 7a.............Mr A Phillips 2
in tch, rdn 6 out, chsd wnr 4 out, wknd next.
86[4] **Rusty Bridge 12.5 5a ....Mr R Burton** 3
ld, hit 6th and hdd, wknd six out.
91 Not My Line (Ire) 11.2 5a *prom, ld after 6th to 12th, wknd 4 out*..........................Mr A Sansome 4

Catchapenny 12.3 7a (bl) *prom to 12th, soon bhnd.* ....Mr W Tellwright 5
Some-Toy 11.7 7a *nvr trbl ldrs.*....Miss L Blackford 6
Fiddlers Pike 12.3 7a *prom to 9th, t.o. when p.u. before 3 out.*....Mrs R Henderson pu
Ross Venture 12.3 7a *chsd ldrs, rdn and wknd 6 out.* ....Mr C Stockton pu
45 J B Lad 11.0 7a *bhnd 9th, p.u. before 3 out.* ....Miss P Gundry pu
56[4] Lighten The Load 11.0 7a *alwys rear, p.u. before 3 out.*....Mr A Wintle pu
89 Corn Exchange 11.4 3a *alwys rear, p.u. before 3 out.* ....Mr M Rimell pu
41[5] Boddington Hill 10.11 5a *t.o. when p.u. before 11th.* ....Mr C Vigors pu
Kettles 10.9 7a *nvr better than mid div, rear when blnd and u.r. 3 out.*....Mr R Wakley ur
The Rum Mariner 11.2 5a *prom till wknd 6 out, p.u. before 3 out.*....Mr J Jukes pu
Celtic Abbey 12.0 7a *(fav) mid div, hit 9th, mstk 11th, soon bhnd, p.u. before 5 out*....Mr D S Jones pu
Judy Line 10.9 7a *bhnd hfwy, p.u. before 3 out.* ....Miss V Roberts pu
7 Pharrago (Ire) 11.0 7a *bhnd when p.u. before 8th.* ....Miss E J Jones pu
Forest Fountain (Ire) 11.0 7a *held up, effort 9th, soon bhnd, p.u. before 3 out.*....Mr A Dalton pu
18 ran. 25l, 22l, 2½l, 5l, dist. Time 6m 43.90s. SP 4-1.
D T Goldsworthy

PLUMPTON
Monday February 10th
GOOD TO SOFT

150 3m 1f 110yds Flyaway Challenge Cup Hunters' Chase Class H

LOYAL NOTE 12.2 3a ....Mr Simon Andrews 1
disp ld, not fluent 15th, hit next, ld apr last, ran on well.
Trifast Lad 11.11 3a ....Mr P Hacking 2
made most, hit 16th, hdd apr last, one pace.
27[1] **Sunny Mount 11.7 7a ....Mr S Morris** 3
(fav) held up, prog 13th, ev ch 2 out, one pace.
Annio Chilone 11.7 7a *held up, rdn from 4 out, wknd apr 2 out.*....Mr P O'Keeffe 4
65[2] Colonel Kenson 11.7 7a *ld to 3rd, lost pl 6th, bhnd when blnd badly and u.r. 8th.*....Mr M Gingell ur
5 ran. 2½l, ¾l, 22l. Time 7m 30.00s. SP 7-1.
R Andrews

LINGFIELD
Wednesday February 12th
HEAVY

151 3m R. E. Sassoon Memorial Hunters' Chase Class H

VICOMPT DE VALMONT 12.2 5a ...Mr T Mitchell 1
hdwy 8th, ld last, ran on well.
Avostar 12.2 5a....Mr B Pollock 2
ld, jmpd right from 12th, hdd last.
Fifth Amendment 12.0 7a (bl) ....Mr A Hales 3
chsd ldrs, 5th when blnd 12th, no ch after.
Centre Stage 11.7 7a *t.o. from 5th.*....Mr A Warr 4
Gambling Royal 12.0 7a *second when blnd 9th, 4th when blunded 12th, t.o. when p.u. before 3 out.* ....Dr P Pritchard pu
56[6] Castlebay Lad 11.7 7a *eighth when ref 11th.* ....Mr M Appleby ref
Faringo 12.0 7a *t.o. from 5th, p.u. before 4 out.* ....Mr W Gowlett pu
Holland House 12.2 5a *(fav) chsd ldrs, 3rd when stumbld and u.r. apr 3 out.*....Mr C Vigors ur
27[2] Over The Edge 12.0 7a *bhnd from 9th, t.o. when p.u. before 3 out.*....Mr S Sporborg pu
Amadeus (Fr) 11.7 7a *t.o. when p.u. before 12th.* ....Mr C Ward pu
Colonial Kelly 11.11 3a *blnd 10th, bhnd when p.u. before 11th.*....Mr P Hacking pu
Major Mac 11.7 7a *t.o. when p.u. before 4 out.* ....Mr S Durack pu
Ell Gee 11.2 7a *third when f 7th.*....Miss C Townsley f
13 ran. 12l, dist, dist. Time 7m 12.00s. SP 3-1.
Mrs Bridget Nicholls

MUSSELBURGH
Wednesday February 12th
GOOD TO SOFT

152 3m Fife Hunt Club Cup Class H Hunters' Chase

HOWAYMAN 11.7 7a....Mr A Parker 1
trckd ldrs, ld 4 out, styd on und pres.
130[1] **Murder Moss (Ire) 11.7 7a....Mr M J Ruddy** 2
held up, cld hfwy, ld after 14th to 4 out, chsd wnr after, no impn.
Free Transfer (Ire) 11.9 5a....Mr C Storey 3
in tch, blnd 12th, soon outpcd, rallied before 4 out, mstk 2 out, no ch after.
35[8] Fish Quay 11.7 7a *ld 2nd to 4th, mstk 10th, soon lost tch, t.o.*....Miss S Lamb 4
35[4] Political Issue 11.9 5a *ld to 2nd, led 4th to 7th, lost tch 11th, t.o. when p.u. before four out.*....Mr P Johnson pu
Little Wenlock 12.2 5a *bhnd hfwy, t.o. when p.u. before 2 out.*....Mrs V Jackson pu
Kilminfoyle 11.7 7a *bhnd when mstk 4th, mistake and u.r. next.*....Mr T Scott ur
Master Kit (Ire) 12.0 7a *(fav) keen, ld 7th till after 14th, chsd 1st 2 after, mstk 3 out, rdn after next, no impn when f last.*....Mr J Billinge f
8 ran. 7l, 12l, dist. Time 6m 26.30s. SP 7-2.
Dennis Waggott

SANDOWN
Thursday February 13th
GOOD

153 2½m 110yds Wilfred Johnstone Hunters' Chase Class H

MR BOSTON 12.1....Mr S Swiers 1
(Jt fav) held up in cl tch, shaken up apr 2 out, ld soon after last, pushed out, ran on well.
Howaryasun (Ire) 11.11 7a (v) ....Mr D S Jones 2
ld to 4th, cl up, led 3 out till soon after last, no ext.
56[1] **Wild Illusion 11.11 7a ....Mr R Lawther** 3
(Jt fav) cl up, rdn after 3 out, styd on apr last, one pace.
Poors Wood 11.3 7a *ld 4th to 3 out, hrd rdn apr last, wknd.*....Mr P O'Keeffe 4
Amari King 11.8 7a *held up in cl tch, wknd apr 3 out, t.o.*....Mr C Ward Thomas 5
Royal Irish 10.13 7a *mstk 2nd, lost tch 7th, p.u. before 10th.*....Miss C Townsley pu
6 ran. 5l, ½l, 12l, dist. Time 5m 36.60s. SP 13-8.
M K Oldham

FAKENHAM
Friday February 14th
GOOD

154 2m 5f 110yds Walter Wales Memorial Cup Hunters' Chase Class H

67[1] **CAB ON TARGET 11.10 ....Mr S Swiers** 1
(fav) held up, mstk 6th, hdwy 8th, went 3rd 10th, trckd ldr 4 out, rdn to ld near fin.
19[3] **Arise (Ire) 11.3 7a....Mr E James** 2
held up, chsd ldrs 11th, ld 4 out, rdn 2 out, hdd near fin
94 **Pro Bono (Ire) 11.3 7a....Mr A Dalton** 3
left in ld 8th, hdd 4 out, styd on one pace.
70[1] Just Jack 11.3 7a *chsd ldrs from 10th til wknd after 5 out.*....Mr R Wakley 4

94 Idiotic 11.5 5a *lost tch after 11th, soon bhnd.* ....Mr C Vigors 5
64[3] Emsee-H 11.5 5a *held up, t.o. after 12th.* ....Mr A Sansome 6
Icarus (USA) 11.3 7a (bl) *chsd clr ldr, left 2nd 10th, f next, dead*....................Mr A Rebori f
No More Trix 11.3 7a *in tch when blnd and u.r. 4th.* ....Mr W Burnell ur
Prinzal 11.3 7a *mstks, ld, clr after 4th, blnd and u.r. 8th*....................Mr M Emmanuel ur
Spartan Silver 11.5 7a 2ow *prom to 5th, t.o. 8th, p.u. before 10th*....................Mr N Bloom pu
10 ran. 1¼l, 11l, 18l, ½l, dist. Time 5m 30.20s. SP 4-6.
N Hurst

LANARKS & RENFREWSHIRE
Lanark
Saturday February 15th
GOOD

155 Members

DO A RUNNER ....S Love 1
(fav) ld 6th, drew clr frm 14th
Duncans Dream 7ex ....Miss C Wilson 2
lft in ld aft 4th, hdd 6th, outpcd frm 14th
Crooked Streak *ld til rdr lost control aft 4th, u.r. bef nxt*....................W Shorthouse ur
Explore Mondial (Ire) 5ow *u.r. 2nd*....................S Ramsay ur
4 ran. Dist. Time 7m 0.00s. SP 4-5.
J Love (Lanark & Renfrew).

156 Confined (12st)

ORANGE RAGUSA ....Miss P Robson 1
trckd ldng pair, ld apr 3 out, sn clr
67[4] **Fordstown (Ire) 6ex ....J Alexander** 2
(fav) ld, mstk 11th, outpcd frm 3 out
The Shade Matcher *trckd ldr, upsides whn p.u. aft 14th, lame*....................A Parker pu
Recluse 7ex *bhnd by 4th, p.u. aft 10th*...M Bradburne pu
Tony's Feelings 13ow *u.r. 1st*....................D Reid ur
134[5] Lakeland Edition 5a *wll bhnd by 7th, p.u. 12th* ....R Robinson pu
133 Itsalltheonetodev (Ire) 5ex *raced in 4th, lost tch 14th, poor 3rd whn p.u. 3 out*....................H Trotter pu
7 ran. 20l. Time 6m 33.00s. SP 5-2.
S H Shirley-Beavan (Jedforest).

157 Restricted (12st)

EOSTRE ....P Craggs 1
cls up frm hlfwy, qcknd wll to ld flat
Eastlands Hi-Light ....T Morrison 2
mid-div, rpd prog to ld 3 out, 2l clr last, hdd & no ext flt
131 **Green Sheen (Ire) ....C Wilson** 3
alwys handy, no ext apr last
Lindon Run *ld til 4 out, kpt on onepcd*......R Morgan 4
Royal Fife 5a *nvr rchd ldrs*....................A Parker 5
131[5] All Or Nothing 5a *bhnd by 8th, nvr nr ldrs* ....J Ewart 6
Solwaysands *ldng grp, ld brfly 4 out, wknd frm nxt* ....B Gibson 7
Mandys Special 5a *bhnd by 8th, p.u. 13th*..W Morgan pu
Prime Style *(fav) ldng grp, mstk 11th, cls up whn f 4 out*....................C Gibbon f
Bucklands Cottage 5a *bhnd by 8th, p.u. 12th* ....G McLeod pu
32 Snapper *cls up whn f 8th*....................M Bradburne f
11 ran. 1½l, 1½l, 5l, 15l, 2l, 3l. Time 6m 35.00s. SP 6-1.
Mrs J M Lancaster (Dumfriesshire).

158 G Middleton Ladies

117 **PRECARIUM (IRE) ....Miss S Leach** 1
made most frm 5th, hrd prssd frm 2 out, hld on wll
33[4] **Roly Prior ....Mrs V Jackson** 2
bhnd by 4th, gd prog frm 4 out, chal 2 out, just hld
Very Evident (Ire) ....Miss J Bird 3
alwys handy, no ext frm 3 out
132[5] Ready Steady *bhnd by 4th, jnd ldrs 11th, outpcd frm 3 out*....................Mrs K Hargreave 4
Parliament Hall *(fav) mstks & lost plc hlfwy, prog & chnce 3 out, wknd apr nxt*....................Miss P Robson 5
Lothian Pilot *ld til u.r. 5th*....................Miss S Dickinson ur
Rushing Burn 5a *ld brfly 11th, sn lost plc, bhnd whn p.u. 4 out*....................Miss N Snowden pu
Tannock Brook *bhnd by 4th, t.o. & p.u. 4 out* ....Miss M McMillan pu
8 ran. Sht-hd, 15l, 8l, 15l. Time 6m 29.00s. SP 10-1.
Miss S Leach (Bilsdale).

159 Land Rover Open (12st)

130[2] **FISCAL POLICY ....H Trotter** 1
(fav) ld to 10th, cls up, ld agn 3 out, sn clr
34[4] **King Spring ....A Parker** 2
2nd frm 8th, ld 10th-3 out, no ext
119 Highland Friend 4ex (bl) *2nd to 8th, lost tch 4 out, poor 3rd whn f 2 out*....................N Smith f
3 ran. 7l. Time 6m 37.00s. SP 4-5.
H P Trotter (Berwickshire).

160 2m 5f Open Maiden (5-7yo) Div I

134[4] **PABLOWMORE ....R Green** 1
(fav) not alwys fluent, bhnd til prog 4 out, chal & lft clr 2 out
134 **Abbey Lad ....N Swann** 2
bhnd by 8th, styd on to tk 2nd flat
Tropical Reef (Ire) ....T Morrison 3
hld up, lft poor 2nd 2 out, no imp, dmtd flat
Normans Profit *ldng grp til wknd 4 out* ....T Scott 4
38 Cheap Knight (USA) *ldng grp til wknd 14th* ..M Ruddy 5
Danegeld (Ire) *alwys handy, ld 11th til f 2 out* N Smith f
Davy's Lad *ld to 11th, sn wknd, p.u. 3 out*....A Parker pu
Keirose 5a *alwys handy, cls 2nd whn u.r. 3 out* ....C Paisley ur
Dakeem 12a *sn t.o., p.u. 2 out*....................B Gibson pu
Hetty Bell 12a *sn wll bhnd, p.u. 2 out* ....Mrs K Hargreave pu
10 ran. Dist, 3l, 2l, 20l. Time 5m 52.00s. SP 6-4.
R W Green (Milvain).

161 2m 5f Open Maiden (5-7yo) Div II

37 **GALLANTS DELIGHT 5a ....A Robson** 1
(fav) handy, chsd clr ldr 4 out, ld 2 out, sn clr
Bells Will Ring (Ire) ....T Scott 2
clr ldr til hdd & no ext 2 out
38[3] **Don Tocino ....M Smith** 3
chsng grp, chnce 3 out, no ext frm nxt
Disrespect 5a *ld chsng grp mostly til no ext frm 4 out* ....P Craggs 4
Mr Cosmo (Ire) *in chsng grp, no prog frm 4 out* ....J Billinge 5
36 Restraint 5a *alwys bhnd*....................Miss F Barnes 6
The Pharside (Ire) *sn wll bhnd*....................A Parker 7
135 Lethem Laird *sn wll bhnd* ....C Storey 8
K Walk 5a *bhnd whn p.u. 11th*....................R Morgan pu
136[2] Captain Guinness (Ire) *bhnd whn f 7th*....J Alexander f
Jenny Wood 5a *f 1st*....................M Bradburne f
Rakeira 12a *sn bhnd, p.u. 10th* ....C Paisley pu
Steady Man *u.r. 4th*....................Miss S Nichol ur
The Alleycat (Ire) *sn wll bhnd, p.u. 10th* ....Miss P Robson pu
14 ran. 20l, 3l, 4l, 6l, dist, 2l, 12l. Time 5m 42.00s. SP 7-4.
Mrs C Johnston (Cumberland Farmers).

162 Open Maiden (8yo+)

36[3] **TRUMPET HILL ....T Morrison** 1
mid-div, prog 4 out, styd on to ld flat
Man Of Moreef ....D Wood 2
alwys handy, ld 2 out, hdd & no ext flat
Bitofanatter ....R Morgan 3
mid-div, prog 4 out, not quite rch ldrs
Corston Frisby *(fav) disp ld 7th til no ext frm 2 out* ....A Parker 4
135[2] Bluebell Track 5a *nvr bttr than mid-div*......R Trotter 5
136[8] Tolmin *nvr rchd ldrs* ....A Robson 6

37 Connor The Second 4ow *nvr rchd ldrs* ....P Black 7
Sovereigns Match *made most to 7th, wknd 4 out, eased flat* ....D McLeod 8
136 Sagaro Belle 5a *prom til wknd frm 12th* ....Miss H Dudgeon 9
134 Prince Rossini (Ire) *prom to hlfwy* ....B Gibson 10
Flypie *bhnd til p.u. 14th* ....P Strang-Steel pu
Wester Lad *disp 7th, cls 3rd but hld whn f last* ....C Storey f
135 Annulment (Ire) *cls 4th whn f 11th* ....L Morgan f
136 Barrow Knocks *sn wll bhnd, p.u. 14th* ....R Green pu
Skye Wedding (Ire) 5a *sn t.o., p.u. 11th* ...R Westwood pu
38 Price War *ld/disp early, sn lost tch, p.u. 2 out* R Shiels pu
16 ran. 1l, 5l, 1l, 10l, 10l, 1l, 8l, 8l, 10l. Time 6m 42.00s. SP 10-1.
H M Barnfather (Cumberland Farmers).
R.J.

OLD RABY HUNT CLUB
Witton Castle
Saturday February 15th
FIRM

163 Members

ELLERTON HILL ....**S Swiers** **1D**
(fav) ld til apr 4 out, rdn whn lft clr nxt
76[6] **Ocean Rose 5a** ....**W Burnell** **1**
keen hold, chsd ldr til outpcd 14th, lft 2nd 3 out
Jolly Fellow ....**Miss S Ward** **2**
rear, lost tch 7th, kpt on flat
113 Another Hooligan *sttld 3rd, mstks 2 & 6th, prog to ld apr 4 out, u.r. 3 out* ....Mrs F Needham ur
120 The Golly Ollybird 8ow *rear, not fluent, lost tch 7th, t.o. & p.u. 4 out* ....J Swinburn pu
5 ran. 20l, 15l. Time 6m 26.00s. SP 1-2.

164 Intermediate

75[1] **JUST CHARLIE** ....**Maj M Watson** **1**
(fav) trckd ldr, disp 8th, mstk nxt, ld 14th, prssd 2 out, qcknd
113 **Skipping Gale** ....**P Atkinson** **2**
ld til disp 8th, hdd 14th, rallied 2 out, sn outpcd
Flying Lion ....**S Swiers** **3**
trckd ldrs til onepcd frm 15th
Sharpridge 2ow *trckd ldr, outpcd 14th, lost tch nxt* ....M Mawhinney 4
36 Wild Adventure *plld hrd in rear, mstks 2 & 11th, wknd 14th* ....T Glass 5
118[9] Rabble Rouser 3ow *hld up rear, effrt 14th, sn outpcd, blnd 4 out & p.u.* ....P Wilkin pu
6 ran. 2½l, 15l, 12l, 4l. Time 6m 34.00s. SP 1-2.
Mrs Susan E Mason (Middleton).

165 Ladies

117[1] **CUMBERLAND BLUES (IRE)** ....**Miss A Deniel** **1**
(fav) j.w. made all, drew clr 15th, unchal
33[6] **Rustino** ....**Miss R Clark** **2**
mid-div, prog 10th, kpt on to go remote 2nd 2 out
117[4] **Clyde Ranger** ....**Miss J Eastwood** **3**
chsd ldr til hrd rdn & outpcd 14th
Across The Lake *sttld mid-div, outpcd 11th, t.o.* ....Miss S Brotherton 4
Skolern *s.s. rear, blnd 5th, lost tch 8th, t.o.* ....Miss L Pounder 5
Indie Rock *hld up rear, some prog in 4th whn u.r. 14th* ....Mrs F Needham ur
6 ran. Dist, 8l, 6l, 7l. Time 6m 11.00s. SP Evens.
John Holroyd (Middleton).

166 Men's Open

119[3] **TOBIN BRONZE** ....**R Tate** **1**
hld up rear, gd prog 14th, disp 4 out, ld 2 out, ran on wll
76[1] **Latheron (Ire)** ....**N Wilson** **2**
(fav) hld up & bhnd, prog 14th, hrd rdn & styd on wll 2 out,nvr nr
119 **General Brandy** ....**G Tuer** **3**
ld til disp 4 out, hdd 2 out, onepcd
119[6] Dalmore *mid-div, prog 12th, ev ch 4 out, onepcd* ....D Coates 4
Fast Study *not fluent, prom, fdd frm 14th* S Robinson 5
Misti Hunter (Ire) *rear, some prog 15th, no hdwy aft* ....S Swiers 6
75[7] Convincing *chsd ldr til wknd 12th, t.o.* ....P Cornforth 7
133[4] Eastern Pleasure *keen hld, prom, 2nd at 9th, u.r. nxt* ....N Tutty ur
8 ran. 2l, 1½l, 1l, 10l, 4l, 20l. Time 6m 17.00s. SP 7-2.
G Thornton (York & Ainsty North).

167 Restricted (12st)

118[8] **EARL GRAY** ....**Miss A Deniel** **1**
alwys prom, 2nd 7th, disp 10th, ld 4 out, sn drew clr
118[6] **Whispers Hill 5a** ....**C Mulhall** **2**
rear, rdn 9th, prog 11th, outpcd 3 out, lft 2nd flat
Chapel Island ....**G Tuer** **3**
mid-div most of way, lost plc 14th, kpt on onepcd 3 out
32[7] Hoistthestandard 5a *rear, prog to chs ldrs 11th, fdd 15th, t.o.* ....T Glass 4
118 Goodwill Hill *trckd ldr, mstk 11th, wknd 15th, t.o. & p.u. 3 out* ....D Coates pu
Murton Heights *(fav) alwys prom, 2nd 3 out, no imp whn p.u. flat, lame* ....N Tutty pu
Will Travel (Ire) *ld, disp 10th, hdd & fdd 4 out, wll btn whn p.u. last* ....S Brisby pu
7 ran. 12l, ½l, 15l. Time 6m 24.00s. SP 20-1.
Mrs A Lockwood (Sinnington).

168 Open Maiden (5-7yo) Div I

76 **PRIMITIVE STAR 5a** ....**P Cornforth** **1**
ld to 7th, ld 13th, rdn clr frm 2 out, styd on well
Greystyle ....**N Wilson** **2**
(fav) sttld in 3rd, swishd tail 13th, 2nd nxt, hrd rdn & not qckn
Lakeland Venture 5a ....**N Tutty** **3**
keen hld, trckd ldr, ld 7th-13th, sn wknd, t.o.
Stud Stile Girl 5a *jmpd bdly in rear, lost tch 8th, t.o. & p.u. 12th, dsmntd* ....C Mulhall pu
4 ran. 4l, dist. Time 6m 39.00s. SP 11-4.
J Cornforth (York & Ainsty North).

169 Open Maiden (5-7yo) Div II

116[6] **OLIVER'S MATE (IRE)** ....**N Tutty** **1**
disp to 6th, cls up, disp 13th, ld 3 out, styd on strngly
115 **Yodeller Bill** ....**P Wilkin** **2**
hld up in tch, prog to chal 2 out, unable qckn
116[2] **Olympic Class** ....**S Robinson** **3**
(fav) disp to 6th, ld 10th til disp 13th, hdd & wknd 2 out, lame
Not The Nadger *plld hrd, rear, prog to ld 6th, hdd 10th, wknd, p.u. 13th* ....A Ogden pu
116 Yogi's Mistress 5a *chsd ldrs, slw jmp & lost ground 14th, wknd, t.o. & p.u.last* ....P Frank pu
5 ran. 5l, 15l. Time 6m 48.00s. SP 5-1.
P J Dennis (Hurworth).
N.E.

SOUTH POOL HARRIERS
Ottery St Mary
Saturday February 15th
GOOD

170 Members

96[1] **MILES MORE FUN 5a** ....**A Farrant** **1**
(fav) plld hrd, ld 5th, sn clr, easily
Moze Tidy ....**I Dowrick** **2**
hld up, chsd wnr 10th, outpcd 4 out, blnd 2 out, no imp
First Design ....**Mrs M Hand** **3**
in tch, chsd ldrs to 14th, outpcd aft
Shameless Lady 5a *ld to 4th, lost tch 14th, outpcd aft* ....R Darke 4

Dharamshala (Ire) *handy to 15th, lost tch nxt, outpcd* ....A Holdsworth 5
Miramac *cls up to 5th, lost tch 11th, t.o. 13th* ....R Bateman 6
6 ran. 3l, 8l, 20l, 4l, 25l. Time 6m 36.90s. SP 1-2.
Edward Retter (Dart Vale And South Pool Hrrs).

171 Men's Open

4[1] **THE BOUNDER ....J Tizzard 1**
(fav) j.w. made all, not extndd
48[1] **Fearsome ....G Penfold 2**
hld up, went 2nd 15th, rdn aft, no imp wnr
98[1] **Kaloore ....A Farrant 3**
in tch, chsd alng frm 12th, outpcd frm 3 out
Brabazon (USA) *alwys mid-div, nvr on trms wth ldrs* ....J Scott 4
48[3] Glenform *alwys mid-div, outpcd frm 15th* ....L Rowe 5
Pintail Bay (bl) *in tch, 6th at 13th, wknd 15th, outpcd aft.* ....N Legg 6
98 Charmers Wish 5a *sn rear, t.o. 13th* ....H Thomas 7
5[6] Prince Nepal *chsd wnr to 14th, blnd nxt, p.u. 16th* ....T Hopkins pu
Hensue *in tch to 12th, wknd nxt, p.u. 14th* ....N Harris pu
9 ran. 10l, 6l, 30l, 8l, 1l, 20l. Time 6m 19.90s. SP 4-5.
L G Tizzard (Blackmore & Sparkford Vale).

172 Maiden (12st)

SHREWD THOUGHT (USA) ....A Farrant 1
(fav) j.w. made all, ran on well frm 2 out
101[2] **Italian Man (Ire) ....G Penfold 2**
mid-div early, 4th at 13th, effrt 4 out, no ext frm nxt
Legal Affair 5a....N Harris 3
rear early, prog 14th, nrst fin
Our Neno (NZ) 7a *hld up rear, prog 12th, 6th at nxt, outpcd 3 out* ....J Tizzard 4
Herhorse 5a *alwys mid-div, nvr on trms* ....R Darke 5
103 Only Harry *alwys mid-div, nvr on trms wth ldrs* ....S Slade 6
54 Cheque Book *mstks, prom to 14th, grad lost tch* ....T Cole 7
Regent Son *rear whn ref 7th* ....Miss A Barnett ref
Princess Polly 5a *alwys mid-div, nvr on trms, btn 6th whn u.r. last* ....Miss L Blackford ur
Dance Fever (Ire) *cls up til f 8th* ....R Woolacott f
Mrs Somebody 5a *rear whn f 7th* ....A Holdsworth f
Reptile Princess 5a *mid-div, bhnd whn p.u. 3 out* ....Miss W Hartnoll pu
Devonshire Lad *mid-div, prog 13th, went 2nd 4 out, hld whn whn u.r. 2 out* ....S Kidston ur
Country Madam 5a *in tch, wknd 15th, p.u. 3 out* ....R Treloggen pu
14 ran. 10l, 8l, hd, 30l, 4l, 8l. Time 6m 29.50s. SP 5-2.
George Ball (Lamerton).

173 Confined

EXPRESSMENT ....G Penfold 1
hld up, prog 14th, chal apr last, sn ld & ran on well
96[3] **Pop Song ....J Creighton 2**
ld til apr last, outpcd by wnr
Rasta Man ....A Farrant 3
(fav) in tch, chal 4 out, no ext frm 2 out
49[4] Catch The Cross (bl) *sn bhnd, kpt on onepcd frm 4 out* ....Mrs M Hand 4
Rough Tor *chsd ldr, ev ch 4 out, wknd rpdly aft nxt* ....A O'Connor 5
Cardinal Bird (USA) *last whn ref 5th* ....A Holdsworth ref
50[1] Mountain Master *handy, 4th at 13th, wknd 15th, btn 5th whn u.r. last* ....Miss L Blackford ur
7 ran. 8l, 1l, 12l, 20l. Time 6m 25.00s. SP 7-2.
Miss A S Ross (Eggesford).

174 Ladies

KHATTAF ....Miss J Cumings 1
(fav) cls up, disp 12th til lft clr 4 out, blnd last
47 **Myhamet ....Mrs M Hand 2**
chsd ldrs, lft 2nd 4 out, no imp frm nxt
2[4] **Richville ....Miss R Francis 3**
not fluent, chsd ldrs, 5th at 13th, no ext frm 3 out
99[6] Searcy *alwys handy, 3rd at 13th, outpcd frm 4 out* ....Miss P Gundry 4
False Economy *rear, nvr on trms, outpcd frm 4 out* ....Miss K Scorgie 5
51[1] Just Bert (Ire) *alwys rear, no ch frm 4 out, nrst fin* ....Miss S Young 6
3[4] Friendly Lady 5a *sn bhnd, t.o. whn u.r. 4 out* ....Miss A Bush ur
Kentish Piper *alwys last, t.o. whn tried to run out & u.r. 4 out* ....Mrs R Wharton ur
99 Great Pokey *ld/disp til blnd & u.r. 4 out* ....Miss N Courtenay ur
9 ran. 7l, 6l, ½l, 4l, 2l. Time 6m 21.00s. SP 6-4.
Mrs H C Johnson (Devon & Somerset Staghounds).

175 Restricted Div I (12st)

43[2] **HIGHWAY LAD ....P King 1**
in tch, prog 15th, chal apr last, ld flat, ran on well
Venn Boy ....J Tizzard 2
(fav) ld to 4th & 11th til apr last, onepced flat
106 **Gypsy Luck 5a ....Miss P Gundry 3**
handy, mostly 3rd, outpcd frm 3 out
Churchtown Chance (Ire) 5a *handy, chal 3 out, outpcd & no ext frm nxt* ....A Farrant 4
Call Avondale *cls up to 4 out, wknd frm nxt* M Batters 5
Nodforms Inferno *plld hrd, ld 5th til f 11th.* .G Barfoot-Saunt f
One For The Cross (Ire) *sn bhnd, t.o. & p.u. 14th* ....Miss K Baily pu
Nice To No *alwys mid-div, t.o. & p.u. 15th* ....S Slade pu
Risky Bid 5a *n.j.w. rear til p.u. 15th* ....H Thomas pu
Brooklyn Express 5a *bhnd, t.o. & p.u. 8th* ....S Parfimowicz pu
Belmount Beauty (Ire) 5a *in tch, ev ch 4 out, p.u. nxt, lame* ....I Dowrick pu
Miss Ricus 5a *u.r. 2nd* ....R Treloggen ur
104 Western Fort (Ire) *mid-div early, t.o. 14th, p.u. 2 out* ....Miss J Cumings pu
Heddon Valley *rear whn p.u. 11th* ....J Creighton pu
Tarka Trail *rear til hmpd & p.u. 11th* ....J Young pu
15 ran. 2½l, 4l, 1l, 20l. Time 6m 25.80s. SP 9-2.
M White (Cotley).

176 Restricted Div II (12st)

DOUBLE THRILLER ....J Tizzard 1
(fav) j.w. ld/disp til drew clr 3 out, imprssv
54[1] **Gypsy Gerry ....A Farrant 2**
hld up, prog 12th, went 2nd 14th, ev ch 4 out, outpcd aft
Rosa's Revenge 5a ....G Shenkin 3
alwys prom, outpcd 14th, kpt on onepcd frm 4 out
Newstarsky *mid-div, lost tch 14th, t.o. nxt* ....Miss J Cumings 4
149 Boddington Hill 5a *sn bhnd, t.o. frm 14th* ....C Pennygate 5
Tom's Arctic Dream 5a *f 1st* ....P King f
Redclyffe (USA) *mid-div, lost tch 12th, p.u. 14th* ....B Dixon pu
Bryn's Story *rear whn blnd & u.r. 9th* ....Miss K Allan ur
Stainless Steel *rear til p.u. 14th* ....M Sweetland pu
53[1] Scallykenning (bl) *handy early, lost tch 12th, p.u. 14th* ....J Young pu
50[2] Hopefull Drummer *mid-div, wknd 14th, p.u. 4 out* ....N Harris pu
Mendip Son *rear til p.u. 3 out* ....Miss M Coombe pu
41 Dormston Lad *mid-div til p.u. 11th* ....C Jowett pu
Lake Mariner 5a *mid-div til blnd & u.r. 12th* ....Maj O Ellwood ur
Crucis (Ire) *alwys mid-div, no ch whn p.u. 3 out* ....I Dowrick pu
Another Hubblick *mid-div, lost tch 13th, p.u. 15th* ....T Greed pu
The Bodhran (Ire) *cls up, 3rd whn f 12th* ....R Young f
17 ran. 5l, 6l, dist, dist. Time 6m 25.70s. SP 6-4.
R C Wilkins (Mendip Farmers).
D.P.

UNITED SERVICES
Larkhill
Saturday February 15th
GOOD

177 Members (12st)

46[1] **DESERT WALTZ (IRE) 5ex........D Alers-Hankey** 1
(fav) alwys going wll, trckd ldrs, ld apr 13th, sn clr, canter
45[7] **Toddling Inn 5a..........................C Farr** 2
jmpd lft, ld til apr 13th, chsd wnr vainly aft
20[3] **In The Choir 5a................Maj H Carruthers** 3
bhnd, in tch til apr 13th, jmpd slwly 3 out, tk mod 3rd last
41 Spinayab 5a *in tch, hit 7th, chsd ldr 11th-nxt, 3rd & outpcd apr 15th*............................J Mead 4
Thought Reader (Ire) 5ow *prom til ran out 9th*....................................R Sturgis ro
142 Electric Committee (Ire) *ref to race, tk no part*....................................A Wood ref
6 ran. 10l, 20l, 8l. Time 6m 26.00s. SP 1-5.
H B Geddes (Beaufort).

178 Confined Div I (12st)

STRONG CHAIRMAN (IRE) 1ow........T Mitchell 1
(fav) hld up, jnd ldrs 13th, ld 2 out, drvn & qcknd clr flat
42[3] **Teatrader ....Miss T Blazey** 2
made most, jnd 3 out, hdd nxt, ev ch last, onepcd
17[1] **Apatura King 3ex......................M Miller** 3
hld up mid-div, jnd ldrs 13th, ev ch whn blnd last, not rcvr
43[1] Juniper Lodge *prom, mstk 2nd, chsd ldr 9th-13th, wknd apr 3 out*..........................S Bush 4
39[5] Gallant Effort (Ire) (bl) *chsd ldrs to 13th, sn outpcd*....................................J Snowden 5
107 The Humble Tiller *prom til ran out 4th* Miss L Knights ro
107[6] Shilgrove Place *sn wll bhnd, p.u. 5th*.........S Allen pu
107 Prankster *rear, in tch, strgglng whn hit 14th, t.o. & p.u. last*..................................T Atkinson pu
Rose Of Macmillion 5a *wth ldr, blnd 3rd, lost plc 8th, last whn f 10th*............................E Bailey f
9 ran. 5l, 1l, dist, 5l. Time 6m 5.00s. SP 4-6.
J A Keighley (Blackmore & Sparkford Vale).

179 Confined Div II (12st)

QUIET CONFIDENCE (IRE) 5a....Miss D Stafford 1
made all, clr 2nd, drew rght away frm 12th, unchal, imprssv
55[4] **The Lorryman (Ire) ....N Mitchell** 2
alwys chsng wnr, clsd 9th, outpcd apr 13th, no dang aft
Rustic Sunset ....R Sweeting 3
chsd ldrs, 3rd frm 6th, wkng whn jmpd slwly 13th, t.o.
39[3] Roaming Shadow *hld up, lost tch 7th, some prog frm 14th, nvr on trms, t.o.*..............J Hankinson 4
106[7] Final Express 5a *nvr bttr than mid-div, mod 5th 12th, nvr dang, t.o.*......................M Hoskins 5
Bold Imp *outpcd in mid-div, prog to 4th at 13th, wknd 3 out, t.o.*..............................S Joynes 6
107[3] Slaney France (Ire) 3ow *nvr nr ldrs, t.o. frm 12th*....................................Miss K Lovelace 7
Derring Valley (bl) *reluc, sn bhnd, t.o. & nrly ref 8th, p.u. nxt*....................................S Bush pu
39[1] Indian Knight 3ex *(fav) mid-div til ran out & u.r. 7th*....................................C Vigors ro
Howaryadoon *mid-div til u.r. 6th*..........Miss T Cave ur
Badbury Prince *alwys rear, last & t.o. whn p.u. 12th*....................................Miss D Olding pu
Templerainey (Ire) 8ow *s.s. went prom 5th, 4th & wkng 12th, p.u. nxt*..........................G Maundrell pu
12 ran. Dist, 20l, 10l, nk, 1½l, 1 fence. Time 5m 57.00s. SP 7-2.
Mrs S Kerley (New Forest Buckhounds).

180 Mixed Open

42[2] **BRACKENFIELD (bl).............Miss P Curling** 1
ld, hit 5th, hdd 2 out, rallied und pres to ld last, styd on
Fantus ....T Mitchell 2
(fav) chsd ldr to 3rd & frm 11th,ld 2 out,hdd last,no ext,lame
Prince Of Verona ....R Sweeting 3+
prom, chsd wnr 7-11th, 3rd & outpcd 13th, no dang aft
Young Brave ....M Miller 3+
hld up last, losng tch & rmndr 11th, nvr nr ldrs
Clever Shepherd *chsd wnr 3-7th, 4th & outpcd apr 13th, no ch whn p.u. 3 out*..................R Nuttall pu
Johnny The Fox (Ire) *t.d.e. lost tch 10th, t.o. 14th, p.u. 2 out*..................................C Bennett pu
6 ran. 3l, dist, dd-ht. Time 5m 59.00s. SP 8-1.
Mrs Susan Humphreys (Cattistock).

181 Open Maiden (5-7yo) Div I (12st)

43[3] **ABIT MORE BUSINESS (IRE) ....T Mitchell** 1
(fav) hld up in tch, ev ch 3 out, lft in ld last, ran on
41 **The Bold Abbot ....Miss S West** 2
alwys prom, ev ch 3 out, lft 2nd last, unable qckn
Byron Choice (Ire) ....N Mitchell 3
hld up, prog 10th, ev ch 3 out, btn whn lft 3rd last
Dr Douski 7a *rear & mstk 6th, prog 10th, jnd ldrs 14th, fdd 3 out*....................D Alers-Hankey 4
20 Lyrical Seal 5a *in tch to 14th, outpcd frm nxt* J Barnes 5
Absolutely Average (Ire) *jmpd delib, ld/disp to 6th, wknd 15th, t.o.*..........................H Rowsell 6
20 Sulason *prom to 14th, wknd, t.o. & p.u. 2 out* M Miller pu
The Smiling Girl 5a *u.r. 3rd*..............N Fitzearle ur
43[4] Old Harry's Wife 5a *ld/disp til ld 5th, made rest, 2l up whn f last*..................................R Nuttall f
Horton Country 5a *f 1st*......................P Howse f
Jestastar *prom to 13th, wknd nxt, t.o. & p.u. 2 out*....................................S Bush pu
Nearly An Eye *crashd thro wng & u.r. 3rd*....................................Miss P Curling ro
Noble Protector (Ire) *bdly hmpd & u.r. 1st*....................................Maj G Wheeler ur
43 Cucklington *mstks, alwys rear, t.o. 12th, p.u. 15th*....................................Miss A Goschen pu
Lily Lane 7a *rear, jmpd slwly 7th, lost tch 12th, p.u. 15th*..................................Miss S Vickery pu
Woodlands Beau (Ire) 7a *ref 3rd*.........T Woolridge ref
Baywyn 5a *ran out 1st*..........................R Black ro
17 ran. 2l, 4l, 25l, 10l, 20l. Time 6m 21.00s. SP 7-4.
R G Williams (Taunton Vale).

182 Open Maiden (5-7yo) Div II (12st)

WIRED FOR SOUND ....J Barnes 1
j.w. ld 4th til aft 12th, lft 2nd 3 out, sn ld, drew clr
Zambrano (USA) 7a..............Miss S Duckett 2
in tch, chsd ldr 6th, disp 15th, lft in ld 2 out,sn hdd,wknd
110 **Purbeck Polly 5a ....N Mitchell** 3
last pair,wll bhnd,prog 10th,lft 3rd & chnc whn f 3 out,rmnt
Wild Weather *mid-div whn u.r. 5th*.......Miss S Vickery ur
20 Uncle Bruce *prom, 3rd whn f 5th*....A Charles-Jones f
Gypsy Blues 5a *u.r. 1st*...............Mrs J Wilkinson ur
The Cockertoo *jmpd lft, ld to 4th, cls 2nd whn ref & u.r. 7th*..................................E Bailey ref
Heatherton Park 5a *chsd ldrs, went 2nd 9th, ld apr 13th til ran out 3 out*..........................M Miller ro
44[2] Jack Sun *(fav) prom til pckd & u.r. 3rd*....J Snowden ur
Redhaven Light 5a *mid-div til f 10th*............L Baker f
20[4] Badger Beer 7a *alwys mid-div, last & no ch whn f 15th*..................................R Nuttall f
Rustic Lord 7a *schoold, alwys rear, last & p.u. 14th*....................................T Mitchell pu
12 ran. 10l, Bad. Time 6m 17.00s. SP 25-1.
Mrs Hazel Richardson (Beaufort).
S.P.

VALE OF CLETTWR
Erw Lon
Saturday February 15th
GOOD

183 Members

4 **HILL FORT (IRE)** ....**E Williams** 1
last til jnd ldrs 13th, sn hrd rdn, ld last, all out
Carlowitz (USA) ....**J Comins** 2
n.j.w. chsd ldr, ld 13th-last, not qckn und pres
Plucky Punter ....**J P Keen** 3
(fav) ld to 13th, wknd rpdly, t.o.
3 ran. 2l, dist. Time 6m 23.00s. SP 3-1.
F P Luff (Vale Of Clettwr).

184 Maiden Div I (12st)

HAL'S PRINCE ....**Miss P Jones** 1
(fav) made all, lft clr 3 out, ran on well, unchal
Final Option (Ire) ....**I Johnson** 2
sn wll bhnd, poor 8th at 13th, ran on aft, fin strngly
Cefn Woodsman ....**D S Jones** 3
in tch, 4th & rdn 14th, lft 2nd nxt, no imp
Brynner *trckd wnr 6-14th, btn whn hmpd 3 out, wknd* ....A Price 4
I'm A Bute 5a *t.d.e. mstks, chsd ldrs til wknd 13th* ....J Price 5
102 All The Jolly 5a *6s-3s, trckd ldrs, cls up whn f 12th* ....R Jones f
Jolly Swagman *mstks, chsd wnr to 6th, cls up 12th, wknd rpdly 14th,p.u.nxt* ....G Perkins pu
Popon 5a *mid-div, mstk 8th, sn strgglng, wll bhnd & p.u. 14th* ....J Jukes pu
43 Tommyknocker (Ire) 7a *last pair & t.o. til p.u. 14th* ....Miss P Cooper pu
Peat Potheen *u.r. 1st* ....T Weale ur
Preseli View 5a *in tch, prog 12th, chsd wnr 14th, chnce whn f 3 out* ....M Lewis f
Kerstin's Choice 5a *1st ride, in tch to 13th, poor 6th whn f 2 out* ....P Sheldrake f
Bonus Number (Ire) *n.j.w. sn wll bhnd, t.o. & p.u. 13th* ....K Cousins pu
Dontyoudoda (Ire) *in tch in rear til f 5th* ......W Pugh f
14 ran. 15l, 7l, 8l, 8l. Time 6m 22.00s. SP 9-4.
T L Jones (Tredegar Farmers).

185 Maiden Div II (12st)

RADIO DAYS (IRE) ....**J Jukes** 1
(fav) ld to 2nd & frm 5th, clr 2 out, shkn up & ran on wll flat
Kerry Soldier Blue ....**M FitzGerald** 2
schoold & wll bhnd, ran on 13th, lft 2nd 3 out, no ext last
Wayward Edward ....**J Price** 3
prom, rdn 10th, outpcd 13th, no dang aft, lft 3rd 3 out
3[9] High Guardian *alwys rear, no ch 13th, kpt on* ....I Johnson 4
Bold Alfie *ld 2-5th, chsd wnr to 13th, fdd & eased* ....D S Jones 5
Puttingonthestyle *lost plc 3rd, wknd rpdly & p.u. 9th* ....K Cousins pu
Grampas' Girl (Ire) 5a *prom, 5th & in tch whn ref & u.r. 12th* ....D Davies ref
Miss Montgomery (Ire) 5a *mid-div, 6th & out of tch whn u.r. 11th* ....Miss F Wilson ur
Good Boy Charlie *sn prom, chsd wnr 13th, 2nd & btn whn f 3 out* ....E Williams f
Bus Pass 7a *rear, lost tch hlfwy, t.o. & p.u. 13th* ....P Doorhof pu
Journo's Joy 5a *mstk 2nd, sn rear, t.o. & p.u. 13th* ....A Goldsworthy pu
Alias Parker Jones *jmpd bdly, t.o. 5th, p.u. 2 out* ....R Barton pu
Del's Delight (Ire) 5a *alwys rear, t.o. & p.u. 13th* ....A Price pu
Lillieplant (Ire) 12a *prom til u.r. 9th* ....M Lewis ur
14 ran. 4l, 20l, 1l, 25l. Time 6m 21.50s. SP Evens.
T D Sproat (Pembrokeshire).

186 Maiden Div III (12st)

TRACKMAN (IRE) ....**J Jukes** 1
ld to 3rd, ld 7th, rdn clr 3 out, styd on well
44[3] **Lazzaretto** ....**I Johnson** 2
rear, styd on frm 13th, tk poor 2nd last
Irish Thinker ....**J W Tudor** 3
in tch, chsd wnr 12th, no imp 3 out, wknd & lost 2nd last
Bickerton Poacher *16s-7s, prom, 6th & in tch whn f 12th* ....K Cousins f
1 Rusty Hall 12a *ran out 2nd* ....Miss P Cooper ro
Appeal 5a *prom whn u.r. 4th* ....D Evatt ur
Queen's Equa 5a *in tch to 11th, wknd, blnd 14th & p.u.* ....M Lewis pu
Silk Rascal 5a *ref 2nd* ....T Vaughan ref
Nikitasecondchance 5a *schoold, t.o. til p.u. 10th* ....D Llewellyn pu
Ballyhooly Belle (Ire) 5a *8s-4s, prom til 3rd & btn 13th, p.u. 15th* ....E Williams pu
Buckland Ballad 7a *blnd 5th, sn bhnd, t.o. & p.u. 9th* ....J P Keen pu
Culpeppers Dish *ld 3-7th, wknd 12th, p.u. 14th* ....R Barton pu
Welsh Treasure (Ire) 12a *(fav) prom to 10th, no ch whn p.u. 14th* ....D S Jones pu
13 ran. Dist, 5l. Time 6m 27.00s. SP 5-1.
R E Evans (Pembrokeshire).

187 Men's Open (12st)

MISTER HORATIO ....**M Lewis** 1
prssd ldr, ld 11th, drew clr 15th, rdn out flat
Bullens Bay (Ire) ....**J Llewellyn** 2
trckd ldrs, prog 11th, chsd wnr & outpcd 15th, ran on flat
42 **Jack Sound 7ex** ....**E Williams** 3
chsd ldrs, effrt 13th, rdn & btn nxt
Master Eryl 7ex *chsd ldrs, outpcd 13th, went poor 3rd 2 out, wknd* ....D S Jones 4
5 Barnaby Boy *12s-3s, mid-div, prog 11th, wknd 14th, walked in* ....J P Keen 5
Space Man *chsd ldrs, outpcd frm 12th, no dang aft* ....M FitzGerald 6
Fly Fred *alwys rear, t.o. & p.u. 13th* ....S Lloyd pu
2 Origami *alwys rear, no ch whn ran out 14th* ....D Llewellyn ro
Corry's Caper *wll in rear, brf effrt 11th, t.o. & p.u. 15th* ....J Price pu
Bartondale 5a *alwys rear, lost tch 11th, t.o. & p.u. 14th* ....A Price pu
General Troy *mid-div, wknd 12th, t.o. & p.u. 15th* ....K Cousins pu
Cornish Cossack (NZ) *nvr bttr thn mid-div, no ch 11th, t.o. & p.u. 15th* ....C James pu
Pay-U-Cash *alwys bhnd, t.o. whn ran out 11th* ....G Perkins ro
Curie Crusader (Ire) *mid-div til wknd 9th, t.o. & p.u. 11th* ....J W Tudor pu
Cedar Square (Ire) *(fav) ld to 11th, rdn & wknd 13th, 3rd & wll btn whn p.u. 2 out* ....J Jukes pu
Duchess Of Padua (Ire) 7ex *jmpd bdly, last whn p.u. 6th, lame* ....T Vaughan pu
16 ran. 3l, dist, 6l, 12l, sht-hd. Time 6m 15.00s. SP 7-2.
W D Lewis (Tivyside).

188 Ladies

98 **TOUCH 'N' PASS** ....**Miss A Meakins** 1
in tch, trckd ldr 14th, outjmpd last, ran on to ld nr fin
Busman (Ire) ....**Miss L Pearce** 2
in tch, prog to ld 11th, rdn flat, hdd nr fin
Cherry Island (Ire) ....**Miss E Jones** 3
prom, ld 8-11th, ev ch aft til wknd aft 2 out
Sea Patrol *prom til wknd aft 12th, t.o. nxt* ....Miss B Barton 4

Polish Rider (USA) *ld 2-8th, wknd 10th, sn t.o.* ....Miss R Morgan 5
Harwall Queen 5a *1st ride, t.o. frm 8th* .....Miss J Gill 6
Goolds Gold *(fav) hld up, 6th whn p.u. 6th, lame* ....Miss P Jones pu
Bally Riot (Ire) *sn outpcd in rear, wll bhnd whn p.u. 11th* ....Mrs A Rucker pu
8 ran. ½l, 20l, 1 fence, 1 fence, 10l. Time 6m 19.00s. SP 8-1.
R H P Williams (Llangeinor).

189 Restricted Div I (12st)

TRUE FORTUNE ....J Jukes 1
(fav) mstks, w.w. prog 13th, ld 3 out, drew clr nxt, ran on well
Moonlight Cruise 5a ....G Perkins 2
cls up, effrt 14th, sn outpcd, kpt on to tk 2nd flat
Sister Lark 5a ....E Williams 3
prom, ev ch 14th, sn outpcd, styd on agn flat
Rosieplant 5a *prom, ld 10th-3 out, no ch wnr aft, lost 2nd flat* ....M Lewis 4
Celtic Bizarre 5a *in tch til outpcd 14th, onepcd frm 2 out* ....Miss B Barton 5
Cranagh Moss (Ire) *blnd 3rd, prom til outpcd 15th, btn whn mstk 2 out* ....G Lewis 6
Pick'n Hill (Ire) *in tch in rear, mstk 11th, outpcd frm 14th* ....A Price 7
Flaxridge *in tch in rear, mstk 14th, sn btn, walked in* ....Miss E Tamplin 8
2 Dick's Cabin *ld to 10th, sn wknd, t.o. & p.u. 3 out* ....D S Jones pu
Sea Search *wth ldr to 10th, sn lost plc, t.o. & p.u. 2 out* ....Miss A Meakins pu
Greenfield Tiger (Ire) *alwys last, mstk 7th, t.o. & p.u. 13th* ....C Richards pu
Mackabee (Ire) *in tch in rear to 13th, t.o. & p.u. 2 out* ....T Weale pu
Saffron Moss *in tch til wknd & blnd 11th, wll bhnd whn u.r. 3 out* ....Miss F Wilson ur
186 Appeal 5a *2nd outing, rear, whn mstk 5th, p.u. nxt* ....D Evatt pu
14 ran. 12l, 2l, ½l, 1l, 10l, 2l, 20l. Time 6m 27.00s. SP Evens.
D J Miller (Pembrokeshire).

190 Restricted Div II (12st)

NUTCASE 5a ....A Phillips 1
(fav) trckd ldrs,ld 14th,in cmmnd 2 out,prssd flat, rdn & hld on
50⁴ **Mrs Wumpkins (Ire) 5a..............Miss P Jones 2**
wth ldr, ld 9-13th, chsd wnr 3 out, chal flat, just hld
Wolver's Pet (Ire) ....D S Jones 3
prom, chsd wnr 14th-3 out, rdn & effrt agn last, no ext
Vale Of Oak 5a *alwys bhnd, t.o. hlfwy* ...M FitzGerald 4
I Blame Theparents 5a *prom, ev ch whn p.u. 14th, lame* ....Miss E James pu
Bix *hld up, prog to jn ldrs 13th, wknd 15th, p.u. 2 out* ....P Doorhof pu
Buckley's Court *prom, mstk 9th, ld 13th til blnd nxt, nt rcvr, p.u. 2 out* ....E Williams pu
45 Mister McGaskill *made most to 9th, sn wknd, t.o. & p.u. 13th* ....J Tudor pu
Twilight Tom *in tch til lost plc & p.u. 5th*........A Price pu
Hatterill Ridge *in tch, mstk 9th, sn wknd, t.o. & p.u. 13th* ....C Richards pu
87 Spirit Prince 7a *unruly pddck, jmpd bdly, t.o. til p.u. 13th* ....J Price pu
11 ran. Sht-hd, 4l, dist. Time 6m 24.00s. SP 5-2.
J Graves (Ludlow).

191 Confined

DESMOND GOLD (IRE) ....Miss L Pearce 1
prom, trckd ldr 13th, ld 3 out, clr nxt, rdn out
Archer (Ire) ....M Harris 2
chsd ldr 6-13th, 3rd & rdn whn blnd nxt, kpt on agn last
46 **Landsker Missile 5a..................E Williams 3**
ld, mstk 13th, hdd 3 out, sn btn, lost 2nd last
Polly Pringle 5a *(fav) rear, no ch frm 12th, styd on 3 out, nvr plcd to chal* ....A Price 4
Royal Oats 5a *prom til 4th & strgglng frm 12th, no prog aft* ....D S Jones 5
No Panic *alwys bhnd, t.o. 13th*.......Miss A Meakins 6
49³ Lucky Ole Son *jmpd slwly, bhnd frm 6th, t.o. & p.u. aft 12th* ....Miss P Jones pu
Rusty Music *jmpd bdly, alwys bhnd, t.o. 12th, p.u. last* ....C Richards pu
97 Cairneymount *mstks, rear, rdn & no prog 11th, t.o. & p.u. 14th* ....J Tudor pu
Kelling *alwys bhnd, t.o. & p.u. 13th* ....A Phillips pu
Bancyfelin Boy *alwys bhnd, t.o. & p.u. 14th* . .J P Keen pu
Hill Farm Katie 5a *prom to 6th, sn wknd, t.o. & p.u. 10th* ....J Jukes pu
Astounded *alwys bhnd, t.o. & p.u. 14th* ....J W Tudor pu
13 ran. 5l, 5l, 15l, 3l, 20l. Time 6m 23.00s. SP 12-1.
Keith R Pearce (Carmarthenshire).
J.N.

WAVENEY HARRIERS
Higham
Saturday February 15th
GOOD

192 Members

CREEVES NEPHEW 7ex...........Capt D Parker 1
ld to 3rd, ld 10th, drew clr aft 3 out
Gone For Lunch 7ex...................C Hinsley 2
(fav) ld 3rd-10th, cls 2nd til no ext 3 out
Bodmin 8ow *1st ride, last, losing tch whn u.r. 11th* ....P Cranney ur
3 ran. 20l. Time 6m 58.00s. SP 2-1.
Captain D R Parker (Waveney Harriers).

193 Confined (12st)

FLASHY BUCK ....N Bloom 1
cls up, chal & ld 3 out, made rest, ran on well
70² **Exclusive Edition (Ire) 5a..............A Coe 2**
(fav) cls up, effrt 16th, kpt on last, not trbl wnr
Foxbow (Ire) 7ex......................A Sansome 3
chsd ldrs in tch, chal 4 out, kpt on well frm 2 out
123⁵ Salty Snacks (Ire) *ld til 3 out, wknd rpdly*....M Gingell 4
Couture Quality *mid-div, nvr able to rch ldrs, onepcd 3 out* ....R Wakley 5
70³ Stanwick Farlap 5a *mid-div, nvr on trms* .....T Marks 6
68 Cosmic Ray *immed last, hit 1st, t.o. & p.u. 11th* ....D Page pu
Kumada 5ex *handy, pshd alng 11th, wkng whn p.u. 15th* ....T Moore pu
62 Smart Pal *in rear, sn strgglng & nt fluent, p.u. 12th* ....K Needham pu
72⁴ Aughrim Slopes 5a *mid-div, chsd ldrs und pres frm 15th, no ch whn p.u. 2 out* ....W Wales pu
66² Buckshot (Ire) (bl) *mid-div til blnd & u.r. 5th* ....T Macfarlane ur
123 Dynamite Dan (Ire) *mid-div till f 5th* ....S Cowell f
Ronaldsway *trckd ldr til blnd & u.r. 8th* ...D Parravani ur
Out Of Line 5a *twrds rear whn f 5th*....Miss S French f
14 ran. 3l, 1½l, 6l, 3l, 8l. Time 6m 23.00s. SP 5-1.
Mrs S J Stearn (Suffolk).

194 Men's Open

BITOFAMIXUP (IRE) ....P Hacking 1
conf rdn,hld up,prog 11th,ld on bit aft 16th,sn clr,imprssv
Young Nimrod ....G Wragg 2
hld up, plld up to ldrs 10th, ld 16th-nxt, sn btn
63³ **Jimmy Mac Jimmy ....C Ward-Thomas 3**
mid-div, chsd ldrs 11th, no ch 1st pair aft 4 out, kpt on
Lantern Pike *ld 3rd, brfly hdd 11th, hdd & wknd aft 4 out, bttr for race* ....A Michael 4
Take The Town *mid-div, not pace to trbl ldrs, kpt on frm 3 out* ....M Jones 5
Cockstown Lad *immed last, t.o. 3rd* ..D Featherstone 6
71 Laburnum *alwys rear, wll bhnd 13th* ....C Ward 7

Whats Your Game (bl) *alwys rear*........K Sheppard 8
70 Nicknavar *sn rear, nvr going wll, wll bhnd & p.u. 15th* ....M Gorman pu
Mayday Miracle 5a *in rear til p.u. aft 11th*.....G Lush pu
Eagle Bid (Ire) (h) *(fav) mid-div, jnd ldrs 10th, going wll whn p.u. aft 13th, dsmntd*.............T McCarthy pu
Ragtime Song *chsd ldrs to 12th, wknd, wll bhnd & p.u. 16th*........M Gingell pu
12 ran. Dist, 25l, 4l, 6l, 8l, 1l, 6l. Time 6m 15.00s. SP 5-2.
Mike Roberts (East Sussex & Romney Marsh).

195 Ladies

64² **ST GREGORY** ....**Mrs L Gibbon** **1**
mstks, cls up, clr wth ldr 16th, ld nxt, drvn clr, wll rdn
125 **Powersurge** ....**Miss H Courtney-Bennett** **2**
rear, prog to jnd ldrs 11th,chsd ldrs 14th,kpt on to 2nd fin
71¹ **Craftsman** ....**Mrs C McCarthy** **3**
(fav) ld 3-4th & 6th-16th, 2nd aft til dmtd fin
Pardon Me Mum *cls up in ldng 4, prssd ldr 12-14th, ev ch til outpcd 16th*..................Mrs E Coveney 4
68¹ Gilson's Cove *mid-div, not pace to trbl ldrs* ....Miss S Gritton 5
71³ Upward Surge (Ire) *ld to 3rd & 5-6th, cls 2nd til wknd rpdly 16th*..........Mrs N Ledger 6
93⁴ Driving Force (bl) *cls up til u.r. 12th*.....Miss S Wallin ur
11¹ Madraj (Ire) *mid-div til u.r. 6th*........Miss H Irving ur
70 Mara Askari (v) *rear, not pace ldrs, wll bhnd whn p.u. 15th*..........Miss F Worley pu
Crazy Otto *alwys strgglng rear, p.u. 11th* Miss L Allen pu
71⁴ Counterbid *mid-div til blnd & u.r. 14th*.......Mrs T Hill ur
71² Professor Longhair *immed rear, t.o. 11th, u.r. 15th* ....Miss C Papworth ur
The Man From Lyre (Ire) *mid-div till f 13th* ....Mrs K Warburton f
Wardy Hill 5a *sn strgglng rear, p.u. 11th* Miss C Tuke pu
14 ran. 1l, ½l, 8l, 15l, 8l. Time 6m 16.00s. SP 3-1.
A Howland Jackson (Essex & Suffolk).

196 Open Maiden Div I

57 **TOMCAPPAGH (IRE)** ....**Miss S French** **1**
w.w. cls 2nd frm 8th, ld 16th, ran on wll whn chal flat
Steel Ice ....**N King** **2**
cls up, blnd 7th, wth ldrs 15th, ev ch & rdn 2 out, no ext
Joyful Joan (Ire) 5a ....**R Barrett** **3**
mid-div, chsd ldrs 15th, wknd rpdly nxt
126 Alycount (USA) *alwys rear, p.u. 2 out*.......R Wakley pu
69³ Flapping Freda (Ire) 5a *alwys wll in rear, t.o. & p.u. 2 out*........R Gill pu
69² Kellys Nap *(fav) prom, ld aft 15th, wknd rpdly & p.u. nxt*........C Ward pu
Mutual Memories *set slow pace, ld 5-15th, wknd rpdly, p.u. aft nxt*........S R Andrews pu
69 Stoneyisland (Ire) *mid-div, lost plc 11th, rear & p.u. 3 out*........N Bloom pu
24 Sheer Hope *cls up til wknd rpdly 16th, p.u. 2 out* ....A Coe pu
Reign Dance *n.j.w. in last til p.u. 8th* .....T McCarthy pu
Punnett's Town 5a *disp to 3rd, cls 2nd til lost plc 8th, ran out nxt*........T Hills ro
Cambridge Gold 7a *rear whn ran out 6th*...P Chinery ro
12 ran. ¾l, dist. Time 6m 32.00s. SP 16-1.
Miss S French (Kent & Surrey Bloodhounds).

197 Open Maiden Div II

65 **SPARKLING SPIRIT 5a**...................**I Marsh** **1**
(Jt fav) cls up going wll, effrt 2 out, sn ld, ran on well
Leitrim Cottage (Ire) ....**P Bull** **2**
cls up, chal aft 16th, ev ch til no ext last, improve
Fiddlers Blade 5a......................**P Hacking** **3**
(Jt fav) hld up, prog to ld 11th, ev ch 3 out, no ext last
13 Native Mony (Ire) *cls up til disp 4th to 3 out, wknd nxt* ....S Cowell 4
Borrow Mine (Ire) 7a *mid-div in tch, 5th & btn 15th, ran on nxt, improve*........S Sporborg 5
125 Warner For Sport *prom on outside til wknd rpdly 15th, t.o.*........Miss F Worley 6
124 Alapa *u.r. 1st*........V Coogan ur
29 But Not Quite (Ire) *ld to 3rd, sn lost plc, rear & p.u. 14th*........N Bloom pu
68² Arkay *immed rear, blnd 12th & rdr lost irns, t.o. & p.u. 15th*........R Kerry pu
127 Charlie Andrews *prom, disp 4th-16th, wknd rpdly nxt, p.u. 2 out*........S R Andrews pu
127 Secret Music *mid-div, wknd rpdly 15th, t.o. & p.u. 3 out*........Capt D Parker pu
Lantern Spark (Ire) 5a *rear, losng tch whn ref 14th* ....Miss C Tuke ref
12 ran. 2l, 1l, 8l, 2l, 30l, 1l. Time 6m 32.00s. SP 2-1.
I Marsh (Puckeridge).

198 Restricted (12st)

ELMORE ....**P Hacking** **1**
conf rdn, made virt all, pshd clr 4 out, easily
71 **Dovehill** ....**C Gordon** **2**
prom, cls 2nd at 11th, ev ch til not qckn 16th
Shake Five (Ire) ....**S Sporborg** **3**
(fav) chsd ldrs 11th, lft disp 3rd nxt, nvr able to chal
26⁵ Whats Another 5a *mid-div, not pace to rch ldrs, no ch 14th*........Miss K Bridge 4
65 Aughnacloy Rose *immed last, alwys bhnd, rdr fin wth no irns*........N Page 5
28⁶ Give It A Bash (Ire) 5a *mid-div, wknd 14th, t.o.* ....T Moore 6
73² Beat The Rap *mid-div whn hmpd & u.r. 12th* ....G Morrison ur
Bozo Bailey *sn strgglng in rear, t.o. & p.u. aft 11th* ....N Bloom pu
King Louis *mid-div to 11th, wknd nxt, p.u. 14th* ....W Wales pu
126⁶ New York Boy *mid-div til blnd & u.r. 12th* ....N Strain ur
69¹ Crestafair 5a *trckd ldng pair til f hvly 13th* ....Miss H Irving f
Al Jawwal *mid-div til f 11th*..............R Wakley f
Ballygar Boy (Ire) *blnd & u.r. 1st*............J Buckle ur
148 Sit Tight *prom to 11th, lft disp 3rd aft nxt, wknd 16th, p.u. 2 out*........M Portman pu
14 ran. 15l, 20l, 3l, 30l, 1l. Time 6m 15.00s. SP 8-1.
Mike Roberts (East Sussex & Romney Marsh).
S.B.

WEST SHROPSHIRE DRAGHOUNDS
Weston Park
Saturday February 15th
GOOD

199 Members

KILLATTY PLAYER (IRE) 5a ....**A Crow** **1**
handy, ld 13th, in cmmnd 3 out, ran on well
32¹ **Turbulent Gale (Ire)** ....**M Munrowd** **2**
(fav) ld to 12th, cls 2nd to 3 out, no ext frm nxt, lame
Glenrowan (Ire) ....**R Ford** **3**
alwys mid-div, nvr trbld 1st pair
Leeswood (v) *prom to 12th, outpcd & no ext frm 4 out* ....Mrs C Ford 4
Real Gent *mid-div, no ch wth ldng pair frm 4 out* ....J Lee 5
Renard Quay *cls up to 12th, rdn & wknd 4 out* ....Miss C Wilberforce 6
Le Piccolage *alwys rear, btn whn p.u. last, sore* ....G Hanmer pu
7 ran. 6l, 2l. Time 6m 53.00s. SP 5-1.
Ian Anderson (West Shropshire Drag).

200 Confined

SHOON WIND ....**A Dalton** **1**
(fav) hld up, ld 10th, ran on strgnly whn jnd 3 out, ld nr fin
Inch Fountain (Ire) ....**A Crow** **2**
w.w. mid-div, prog 3 out, lvl last, no ext cls home

Pin Up Boy ....**T O'Leary** 3
alwys chsng grp, no ch wth 1st pair frm 3 out
Nodform Wonder *ld to 9th, cls up to 4 out, outpcd 2 out*..........R Bevis 4
83[1] Orton House *mid-div, nvr pace to rch ldrs*...R Burton 5
Formal *chsd ldrs, btn whn pace incrsd 5 out*..R Owen 6
Tara Boy *alwys rear, p.u. 4 out*..........R Cambray pu
No More The Fool *alwys rear, p.u. 14th*.....L Brennan pu
84[5] Bavard Bay *mid to rear, nvr dang, p.u. 4 out* ....L Whiston pu
Duke Of Impney *mid-div, wknd hlfwy, p.u. 3 out* ....P Saville pu
Bay Owl *nvr bttr than mid-div, t.o. & p.u. 14th* ....M Worthington pu
Forget The Rest *prom early, btn aft 9th, p.u. 11th* ....O Macphail pu
Charlie Chalk *mid-div early, fdd, p.u. 13th* C Stockton pu
Frank The Swank *jmpd slwly, sn t.o., p.u. 14th* ....N Gittins pu
82[1] Domino Night (Ire) 2ow *disp 5th, cls up to 12th, outpcd aft, p.u. 4 out*..........E Haddock pu
Miners Fortune (Ire) *cls up & going wll til fdd 12th, p.u. 14th*..........G Hanmer pu

16 ran. 3l, dist. Time 6m 43.00s. SP 7-4.
J N Dalton (Wheatland).

201 Men's Open (12st)

55[3] **GRECIAN LARK** ....**G Tarry** 1
mid-div, prog 10th, strng chal to ld 3 out, ran on wll
Chip'N'run 7ex ....**J Cornes** 2
prom, ld/disp 3rd til hdd 3 out, ev ch last, no ext flat
First Harvest ....**P Hanly** 3
disp 10th-4 out, outpcd frm 2 out, kpt on
Perhaps (USA) 5a 7ex *mid-div, some late prog, nrst fin*..........A Dalton 4
Garrylucas 7ex *ld to 2nd, prom hlfwy, outpcd 4 out* ....G Hanmer 5
86 Auction Law (NZ) *mid-div, nvr rchd ldrs*.....L Whiston 6
Cwm Arctic 5a *cls up 4th, chsng grp to 6 out, sn btn* ....M Jones 7
Social Vision (Ire) *t.o. til kpt on frm 4 out* ....T Stephenson 8
Stylish Gent *mid to rear, u.r. 12th*..........R Evans ur
86[2] Scally Muire 5a 7ex *(fav) mid-div in tch, p.u. 7th, lame, retired*..........A Crow pu
What A Miss 5a *no ch whn p.u. 11th*.......R Thomas pu
Mount Kinabalu *alwys rear, t.o. & p.u. 14th* D Mansell pu
Fire King *prom to 10th, p.u. 13th*..........E Collins pu
Coolgreen (Ire) *chsng grp to 10th, fdd rpdly, p.u. 13th* ....N Bradley pu
Potato Fountain (Ire) 5a 4ow *chsng grp whn u.r. 8th* ....C Barlow ur
Vision Of Light 5a *in rear, no ch whn p.u. 13th* ....M Munrowd pu

16 ran. 3l, 20l. Time 6m 48.00s. SP 5-2.
J White (Grafton).

202 Ladies

18[2] **SAMS HERITAGE** ....**Miss A Dare** 1
(fav) hld up in tch, ld 5 out, sn in cmmnd, comf
57 **Ace Player (NZ)** ....**Mrs C Ford** 2
w.w. ran on well frm 4 out, nvr nrr
57[5] **Pont de Paix** ....**Miss T Habgood** 3
mstks, mid-div, ran on frm 4 out, nrst fin
85 Bank Place *cls up, 2nd til wknd 4 out* Miss C Thomas 4
139[1] The Boiler White (Ire) 7ow *chsng grp, nvr rchd ldrs, kpt on*..........Miss J Froggatt 5
Tap Dancing *mid-div, no ch wth ldng trio frm 3 out* ....Miss S Pickford 6
Luks Akura *alwys mid-div* ....Miss J Priest 7
Nodforms Dilemma (USA) *mid-div, p.u. aft 5th* ....Miss K Hollinshead pu
Belpenel *made most to 14th, 4th & btn whn u.r. 2 out* ....Miss A Sykes ur
Tipp Down *alwys rear, p.u. 3 out*.....Miss S Sharratt pu
Logical Fun *mid-div early, sn btn, no ch whn p.u. 2 out*..........Miss L Wallace pu
Brockish Bay *hld up rear, lost tch 10th, p.u. nxt* ....Miss S Baxter pu
Moya's Tip Top 5a *chsng grp, cls 3rd whn u.r. 12th* ....Miss C Wilberforce ur

13 ran. 5l, 8l, 2l, 6l. Time 6m 45.00s. SP 1-2.
C G Smedley (Berkeley).

203 Restricted Div I (12st)

NOTHING VENTURED ....**A Beedles** 1
(fav) alwys handy, ld/disp frm 12th, 3l clr 2 out, ran on
83 **Yukon Gale (Ire)** ....**A Crow** 2
w.w. prog 11th, disp 12th-3 out, rdn & not qckn nxt
83 **Miss Shaw 5a** ....**C Stockton** 3
ld to 11th, onepcd frm nxt, outpcd by 1st pair
84[6] Foolish Fantasy *mid-div, some prog frm 5 out, nrst fin* ....S Prior 4
83 Sargeants Choice *cls 2nd to 10th, btn frm 4 out* ....J Barlow 5
Rue de Fort *chsng grp 5th, wknd aft 12th, p.u. 14th* ....J Cornes pu
83[4] Grants Carouse *rear early, no prog frm 12th, wll bhnd & p.u. 2 out*..........A Baillie pu
Twelth Man *prom to hlfwy, sn btn, p.u. 3 out* ..R Bevis pu
Tropical Gabriel (Ire) *mid to rear, btn aft hlfwy, no ch whn p.u. flat*..........Miss J Penney pu
81 Aqueous Rocks *rear, t.o. 10th, p.u. 12th* ....M Worthington pu
85 Daphni (Fr) *mid-div, wknd 12th, sn rear, p.u. 5 out* ....Miss K Swindells pu

11 ran. 2l, dist, 8l, dist. Time 6m 52.00s. SP 7-4.
Countess Goess-Saurau (South Shropshire).

204 Restricted Div II (12st)

FLINTERS ....**A Dalton** 1
prom, ld 4-5th, 2nd aft til ld 3 out, ran on well
Blushing Star ....**N Gittins** 2
ld to 3rd, cls up, ran on onepcd frm 4 out, tk 2nd 2 out
81 **Lydebrook** ....**M Wilson** 3
ld 6th-4 out, no ext frm 2 out
Glen Taylor *alwys rear, fin own time*.......L Whiston 4
Potiphar *cls up to 12th, wknd rpdly, p.u. nxt* ....M Worthington pu
Royle Burchlin *rear & strgglng, p.u. 3 out*...D Barlow pu
Young Parson *mid-div whn u.r. 8th*..........T Marlow ur
82 River Sunset (Ire) *mid to rear, no ch whn p.u. 3 out* ....J Barlow pu
Henrymyson *rear whn p.u. 14th*..........J Cornes pu
Made Of Talent 5a *chsng grp, rdn & no prog 5 out, p.u. 3 out*..........A Crow pu
Mr Bobbit (Ire) *(fav) chsng grp in tch, wknd rpdly 4 out, p.u. nxt*..........R Burton pu
Kayak Point *rear, t.o. & p.u. aft 12th* ....Miss E Guest pu
Idiomatic *t.o. & p.u. 13th*..........R Tilley pu

13 ran. 8l, 5l, dist. Time 6m 57.00s. SP 6-1.
John Halewood (Cheshire).

205 Maiden (5-7yo) Div I (12st)

81 **GASMARK (IRE)** ....**A Crow** 1
(fav) cls 2nd going wll whn lft clr 9th, solo aft
Crafty Gunner ....**M Worthington** 2
rear, some late prog, no ch wth wnr
Agile King ....**J Evans** 3
3rd at 13th, onepcd aft
Rejects Reply *in tch whn f hvly 4th*.........G Hanmer f
81 Tosawi's Girl (Ire) 5a *alwys rear, t.o. & p.u. 14th* ....R Burton pu
Builder Boy *rear, prog to chs wnr 12th, sn btn, p.u. 4 out*..........S Prior pu
Greenacre Girl 5a *mid to rear, no ch whn p.u. 13th* ....D Barlow pu
82 Ring Bank *ld, clr going wll whn u.r. 9th* .....N Gittins ur
Barney Bear *mid to rear, p.u. 12th*..........T Garton pu
Nonny's Boy *s.s. nvr in race, p.u. 10th* ....Miss C Wilberforce pu

10 ran. 25l, dist. Time 7m 3.00s. SP 6-4.
D Pugh (North Shropshire).
2 fences omitted, 16 jumps.

206 Maiden (5-7yo) Div II (12st)

ROLIER (IRE) ....A Dalton 1
mid-div, prog 8th, ld 4 out, sn clr, easily
81 **Nights Image (Ire) ....J Barlow 2**
(fav) cls up, ld 7th til 4 out, outpcd frm 2 out
Crimson Bow 5a ....R Owen 3
mid to rear, no dang to ldng pair
82 Beeworthy 5a *nvr bttr than mid-div, p.u. 4 out* ....A Beedles pu
Societys Stream (Ire) *blnd & u.r. 2nd*..........S Prior ur
88 Musical Vocation (Ire) 5a *ld 4-6th, ev ch til wknd 4 out, p.u. in 4th flat*...........................A Crow pu
Pulltheplug *ld to 3rd, cls up til wknd rpdly 5 out, p.u. 3 out*.....................................R Burton pu
82[4] Solar Castle (Ire) *mid to rear, no ch whn u.r. 14th* ....Miss S Hopkins ur
Broadleaf Clover 5a *rear, t.o. & p.u. 12th* ....M Worthington pu
9 ran. 7l, dist. Time 6m 52.00s. SP 2-1.
T A B Scott (Albrighton).
V.S.

CRANWELL BLOODHOUNDS
Southwell P-To-P Course
Sunday February 16th
GOOD TO SOFT

207 Members

SHERIFF'S BAND ....D Esden 1
(fav) trckd ldr til ld 5th, made rest, rdn out
French Myle (Ire) ....G Smith 2
not fluent, ld to 5th, chsd wnr aft, rdn 15th, onepcd
Lighters Confusion 5a *s.s. jmpd lft, sn wll bhnd, t.o. & p.u. 10th*...........................Miss M Millar pu
3 ran. 2½l. Time 7m 0.00s. SP 4-6.
P J King (Cranwell Bloodhounds).

208 Open Maiden (5-7yo) Div I Pt I (12st)

ARRYSU ....Miss S Sharratt 1
ld til aft 1st, chsd ldr, ld 12th, 15l clr 3 out, unchal
Forever Dreaming (Ire) ....N Wilson 2
(fav) w.w. steady prog 11th,went 2nd apr 3 out,ran on,nt rch wnr
Man Of Wisley (Ire) ....D Ingle 3
rcd freely,ld aft 1st, sn clr, mstks 7 & 10th, hdd 12th,wknd
Calder's Grove *bhnd, brf effrt 11th, last frm 13th, t.o.* ....Miss T McCurrick 4
Towngate *jmpd big 1st, last & rdn 10th, t.o. & p.u. 12th*..............................S R Andrews pu
Bucks Law *bhnd, lost tch 7th, t.o. & p.u. 9th* J Docker pu
Cruikit Rainbow (Ire) 5a *in tch til f 4th*.........K Green f
Mister Kingston *chsng grp, prog to 3rd apr 12th, f 14th* ....B Pollock f
Slumberhill (Ire) *chsd ldng pair 7th-apr 12th, wkng whn blnd 13th, p.u. 3 out* ....P Millington pu
9 ran. 6l, 1 fence, 1 fence. Time 6m 54.00s. SP 6-1.
Miss S Sharratt (Meynell & South Staffs).

209 Open Maiden (5-7yo) Div I Pt II (12st)

114[2] **ARRAS-TINA 5a........................S Walker 1**
(fav) w.w. going wll, 2nd at 8th, ld apr 3 out, rdn nxt, all out
The Auctioneer ....Miss L Rowe 2
ld to 4th & 8th til apr 3 out, rallied nxt, no ext nr fin
Fair Grand ....S Brisby 3
hld up, prog & mstk 9th, rdn 14th, wknd
Tinker Hill *prom to 7th, sn lost plc, t.o. & p.u. 11th* ....M Bond pu
Cuban Skies (Ire) *rear & blnd 7th, lsng tch whn u.r. 12th* ....T Cox ur
Half Sharp 5a *in tch, prog going wll 11th, 4th & btn whn f 13th* ....L Lay f
Roberts Royal *prom, ld apr 5-8th, wknd rpdly & p.u. 12th*...C Stockton pu
7 ran. Nk, 1 fence. Time 6m 55.00s. SP 4-5.
G E Mason (Middleton).

210 Open Maiden (5-7yo) Div II (12st)

BROADWAY SWINGER ....S R Andrews 1
ld/disp til ld 12th, jnd apr 3 out, hld on und pres flat
Irbee 7a...............................A Phillips 2
(fav) chsd ldrs, mstk 15th, ev ch nxt, no ext nr fin
Neelisagin (Ire) ....P Millington 3
mid-div, prog 11th, chsd ldrs 14th, outpcd apr 3 out
114 Mallow Innocence *cls up til apr 12th, grad lost plc, kpt on agn 2 out* ....S Whitaker 4
Troutlet 12a *w.w. prog & in tch 11th, 4th & outpcd apr 3 out* ....M Munrowd 5
Smart Song *ld/disp til apr 12th, grad lost plc* ....M FitzGerald 6
Middleham Pearl 5a *mstk 3rd, bhnd 9th, no dang aft* ....M Bennison 7
Must Be Murphy (Ire) *prom to 11th, sn rdn & wknd, p.u. 14th*..A Dalton pu
Silly Pet *nrly ref 1st, last whn succeeded nxt* ...P Gee ref
Not So Prim 12a *bhnd, prog & in tch whn blnd & u.r. 9th*......................................S Swiers ur
High Intake 7a *alwys rear, lost tch 11th, p.u. nxt* ....N Tutty pu
141 Mr Freebie (Den) *rear, prog 9th, outpcd apr 12th t.o. & p.u. 2 out*.................................D Ingle pu
80[3] Zerose 12a *alwys bhnd, last frm 9th til p.u. 12th* ....P Cornforth pu
Red Rebel 7a *pllng, raced wd, hld up, prog to cls 3rd whn f 13th*..................................T Whitaker f
Willow Brook (Ire) *alwys rear, mstk 7th, t.o. & p.u. 12th*...J Docker pu
15 ran. Hd, 20l, 12l, ½l, 6l, 8l. Time 6m 59.00s. SP 5-1.
Mrs Charlotte Cooke (Cottesmore).

211 Open Maiden (8yo+) Div I (12st)

CORMEEN LORD (IRE) ....J Sharp 1
hld up, steady prog 11th, chsd ldr 15th, ld 2 out, easily
88[2] **Jack The Td (Ire) ....J Cornwall 2**
ld aft 1st, sn wll clr, hit 12th, hdd 2 out, btn & blnd last
13[3] **Kendor Pass (Ire) ....Dr M Tate 3**
prom in chsng grp, lost plc 11th, ran on 3 out, fin well
Duncaha Hero *alwys bhnd, some late prog, nvr dang* ....Miss G Barrow 4
Chorus Of Wings (Ire) *chsd ldrs, wkng & rdn 11th, t.o. 13th*...................................D Crossland 5
88 Musical Mail *ld til aft 1st, chsd ldrs, wkng whn blnd 12th, t.o.*..........................M FitzGerald 6
Race To The Rhythm 5a *hld up, lost tch 10th, p.u. 12th* ....S Morris pu
Ilikehim *prom to 6th, sn wknd, t.o. & p.u. 10th* ....S Whitaker pu
82[2] Noble Angel (Ire) *chsd clr ldr to 15th, wknd rpdly, p.u. nxt*......................................A Dalton pu
Arley Gale 5a *hld up, mstk 7th, prog to 4th at 11th, wknd 14th, p.u. 3 out*.................John Pritchard pu
Sandy King (Ire) *rear, t.o. 7th, p.u. 9th* ....A Baillie pu
Titchwell Milly 5a *in tch to 11th, t.o. & p.u. 15th*..L Lay pu
Chester Ben *(fav) mid-div,prog to 3rd at 11th,jmpd slwly 13th, wknd, p.u.2 out* ....S R Andrews pu
Ms Taaffe 5a *nvr bttr than mid-div, 5th & no ch whn u.r. last* ....Mrs M Bellamy ur
Graham's Choice 5a *schoold, sn t.o., p.u. 12th* ....N Wilson pu
15 ran. 20l, nk, 6l, 30l, 30l. Time 6m 58.00s. SP 5-1.
J C Sharp (Woodland Pytchley).

212 Open Maiden (8yo+) Div II (12st)

ROYAL SEGOS ....C Stockton 1
(fav) ld 4th, made rest, drew clr frm 3 out, easily
120[4] **Canebreak Boy (Ire) (bl) ....Mrs F Needham 2**
in tch, prog 11th, 2nd whn blnd 3 out, no imp aft

88 **Mr Wilbur** ....**A Dalton** 3
prom, chsd ldr 5th til 3 out, wknd
Rovac *hld up, prog 10th, 4th & outpcd 13th, kpt on* ....W Wales 4
Pollytickle 5a *ld to 4th, in tch, prog to 4th at 13th, no hdwy aft*....................................G Smith 5
Smart Mover *hld up in tch, strgglng whn f 12th* ....S Brisby f
Goodheavens Mrtony *prom to 8th, bhnd 12th, t.o. & p.u. 3 out*..................................M Bennison pu
Shining Penny *in tch til f 7th*..............M Bond f
60[6] Woodlands Power *cls up, rdn & outpcd 11th, t.o. & p.u. last*..........................John Pritchard pu
Face The Music *bhnd frm 8th, t.o. & p.u. 14th* ....E Andrewes pu
Sparkling Clown 5a *mstk 1st, bhnd til u.r. 9th* ....Miss C Arthers ur
Inhurst 5a *in tch, went prom 8th, wknd apr 12th, p.u. 3 out*.......................................A Phillips pu
Charlottes Quest 5a *jmpd slwly 1st, alwys bhnd, t.o. & p.u. 14th*...........................M Connors pu
Damis 5a *rear, in tch til rdn & wknd apr 12th, p.u. 14th*.......................................W Burnell pu
14 ran. 20l, 8l, 2l, 10l. Time 6m 58.00s. SP 6-4.
A J Baillie (Meynell & South Staffs).

213 Restricted (12st)

78 **GREENMOUNT LAD (IRE)** ....**P Cornforth** 1
hld up, prog 11th, jnd ldr 3 out, ld cls home
Dark Rhytham ....**S Morris** 2
prom, ld 7th-11th & 13th, jnd 3 out, no ext cls home
78 **Barichste** ....**Maj M Watson** 3
(fav) w.w. prog apr 12th, blnd nxt, ran on 3 out, nvr nrr
59 First Command (NZ) *mid-div, in tch, 6th & outpcd whn blnd 14th, kpt on*...........................A Dalton 4
77[6] Monarrow (Ire) *bhnd, prog 9th, chsd ldrs 13th, no hdwy frm nxt*......................Miss S Buckley 5
Henry Darling *mid-div, went prom 9th, outpcd frm 14th*......................................E Andrewes 6
The Man From Clare (Ire) *chsd ldrs to 11th, sn strgglng, no ch nxt* ....L Lay 7
Mr Gee *in tch til apr 12th, no dang aft*....K Needham 8
77 War Head *alwys bhnd, t.o. & p.u. aft 11th*...W Burnell pu
Miley Pike *in tch to 10th, bhnd whn p.u. 14th*...N Tutty pu
Shannon King (Ire) *chsd ldrs, ld 11th-13th, wknd, p.u. 2 out*..P Hanly pu
White Bullet (USA) *ld 2nd-7th, wknd rpdly 10th, p.u. 12th*...B Pollock pu
Culm Baron *ld to 2nd, grad lost plc, wll bhnd 8th, p.u. 12th*...................................S R Andrews pu
137 Mysterious Run (Ire) *prom, nrly u.r. 5th, wknd 11th, t.o. & p.u. 2 out*......................Miss S Samworth pu
Cahermone Lady (Ire) 5a *bhnd & blnd 10th, t.o. & p.u. 12th*......................................S Whitaker pu
84[4] Lady Steel (Ire) 5a *s.s. f 2nd*..............Miss S Baxter f
16 ran. Sht-hd, 7l, 6l, 3l, 6l, 12l, 5l. Time 6m 53.00s. SP 10-1.
J Cornforth (York & Ainsty North).

214 Confined (12st)

117 **RUALMIT (IRE) 5a 7ex**..................**S Swiers** 1
prom, ld 11th-15th, ld agn 2 out, styd on strngly
Mr Branigan (Ire) ....**T Marks** 2
(Jt fav) in tch, hit 5th, ev ch 15th, onepcd und pres frm 2 out
119[4] **Coolvawn Lady (Ire) 5a 10ex**............**S Walker** 3
(Jt fav) prom, ld 15th-2 out, no ext
138[4] The Difference 6ex *prom to 4th, mid-div aft, nvr trbld ldrs* ....M Chatterton 4
Romany Ark *alwys bhnd, t.o. whn blnd 3 out* ...N Bell 5
Antrim County *ld to 4th, bhnd 8th, t.o. & p.u. 12th* ....J Cornwall pu
76[7] McCartney *alwys rear, last frm 10th, p.u. 13th* N Tutty pu
Soda Popinski (USA) *ld 4th, sn clr, hit 8th, hdd 11th, wknd rpdly, p.u. nxt*............................C Vale pu
Bowery Boy 3ex *f 2nd*...................E Andrewes f
2[6] Glitzy Lady (Ire) 5a *b.d. 2nd*....................G Smith bd
10 ran. 3l, 8l, 15l, 1 fence. Time 6m 50.00s. SP 5-1.
Mrs R White (South Notts).

215 Ladies

CORNER BOY 7ex ....**Mrs J Dawson** 1
(fav) chsng grp, prog to 2nd 7th, ld 3 out, sn clr, easily
Vital Witness (Can) ....**Mrs F Needham** 2
mid-div, prog to 3rd 12th, ev ch 15th, outpcd 3 out, kpt on
Minella Express (Ire) 7ex........**Miss C Spearing** 3
jmpd lft, ld, hdd 3 out, sn outpcd
117[5] Kellys Diamond *mid-div, prog 7th, 4th & onepcd frm 12th*.....................................Miss V Russell 4
76[4] Douce Indienne 5a *mid-div, mod 6th at 9th, nvr nr ldrs*..................................Miss J Eastwood 5
76[8] Cadrillon (Fr) *hld up rear, mstk 2nd, nvr nr ldrs* ....Miss A Deniel 6
Douce Eclair 5a *bhnd, nrly u.r. 8th, nvr on trms* ....Miss L Eddery 7
Kites Hardwicke *alwys rear, last frm 11th* ....Mrs C Behrens 8
Killimor Lad *chsd ldrs to 6th, sn wknd, t.o. & p.u. 11th* ....Miss S Samworth pu
Thistle Monarch 7ex *hld up, prog to mod 6th at 12th, no hdwy aft, p.u. 3 out* ....Miss R Clark pu
85 Man Of Mystery *chsd clr ldr to 7th, grad wknd, p.u. 12th*..................................Miss F Hatfield pu
85 Walter's Lad *s.v.s. fence bhnd whn u.r. 5th* ....Mrs M Wall ur
12 ran. 5l, 2l, 12l, 10l, 12l, 6l, 15l. Time 6m 48.00s. SP 2-1.
Mrs E W Wilson (Brocklesby).

216 Men's Open

TEETON MILL ....**B Pollock** 1
w.w. lft 2nd 7th, ld 4 out, styd on well
Ask Antony (Ire) ....**N Wilson** 2
prog 9th,lost plc 12th,rallied & ev ch 3 out,btn last,eased
75[2] **Zam Bee** ....**N Bell** 3
(fav) prom in chsng grp, ev ch 4 out, onepcd
Penlet *prom to 2nd, rdn 11th, prog 13th, chsd ldrs 3 out, no imp* ....John Pritchard 4
86[3] Merlyns Choice *prom in chsng grp, outpcd apr 12th, no dang aft*................................A Woodward 5
The Point Is *ld, sn clr, hdd 4 out, wknd rpdly, p.u. nxt* ....M Hewitt pu
Bartags Brother *alwys rear, last frm 11th, t.o. & p.u. 14th*......................................S R Andrews pu
Rambling Lord (Ire) *rear, prog 10th, lost tch apr 12th, p.u. 15th*.......................................G Smith pu
86 Daphnis (USA) *in tch till f 7th*...............S Prior f
67 No Word *wth ldr to 4th, 2nd whn p.u. 7th*......I Baker pu
Going Around *prom til wknd apr 12th, t.o. & p.u. 3 out* ....L Lay pu
Gaelic Warrior *alwys rear, lost tch 10th, p.u. 12th* ....S Swiers pu
12 ran. 8l, 9l, 12l, 2½l, 10l. Time 6m 48.00s. SP 5-1.
C R Saunders (Pytchley).
S.P.

FARMERS BLOODHOUNDS
Heythrop
Sunday February 16th
GOOD

217 Members

78[4] **ITS MURPHY MAN** ....**J Trice-Rolph** 1
(fav) made all, lft clr 3 out, comf
Back In A Flash ....**Miss H Irving** 2
mstks, chsd wnr 12th, chal & blnd 3 out, not rcvr
Chinaman ....**A Tutton** 3
chsd wnr to 12th, fdd frm 4 out
Icky's Five *alwys last, bhnd frm hlfwy, no ch aft* ....Miss T Habgood 4
4 ran. 12l, 20l, 3l. Time 7m 17.00s. SP 4-5.
David J Murphy (Farmers Bloodhounds).

218 Intermediate (12st)

46[2] **FRONT COVER 5a................Miss S Vickery** 1
(fav) cls up, trckd ldrs 12th, chal & lft in ld 2 out, sn clr,comf
Springfield Lad 5ex...............Miss E Walker 2
ldng grp, outpcd 15th, kpt on to tk 2nd flat
6[5] **Drummer Boy (Ire) ....Miss P Gundry** 3
in tch, outpcd 3 out, styd on onepcd apr last
French Pleasure 5a *trckd ldrs til outpcd 15th, kpt on* ....P Howse 4
Sudanor (Ire) *ld 5th to 2 out, 2nd & btn whn blnd last, wknd*..........................Julian Pritchard 5
Mitchells Best *bhnd, lost tch 12th, styd on frm 3 out, nrst fin*............................T Stephenson 6
Spartan Pete *in tch til grad wknd frm 14th*...R Burton 7
Bear's Flight 5ex *alwys bhnd, t.o. frm 5th* ....J Hadden Wight 8
Corrianne 5a *ld to 2nd, wknd rpdly & p.u. 10th* ....E Williams pu
Sterling Buck (USA) 7ow *in tch to 11th, wll in rear whn p.u. 2 out*.........................D Duggan pu
Severn Invader 5ex *prom, outpcd aft 14th, btn whn hmpd & u.r. 2 out* ....Miss H Gosling ur
55[8] Sprucefield *alwys rear, wll bhnd whn p.u. last* ....T Illsley pu
Carbery Arctic *2nd whn f 6th, dead* . .G Barfoot-Saunt f
8[2] Bervie House (Ire) *blnd & u.r. 1st*...........R Barrett ur
Apple Nicking 2ow *prom, rdn & wknd 12th, p.u. 14th* ....A Hill pu
Unlucky For Some (Ire) *alwys bhnd t.o. & p.u. 10th* ....M Frith pu
Menature (Ire) *in tch to 11th, wll bhnd whn p.u. 3 out* ....A Sansome pu
58[1] Warrior Bard (Ire) *alwys prom, chal aft 14th, just ld & f 2 out*.......................................M Portman f
Warren Boy *ld 2-5th, wknd 11th, p.u. nxt* Miss P Jones pu
Kington Down *blnd & u.r. 1st*..............M Walters ur
Wot No Cash 7a *alwys rear, t.o. & p.u. 10th* ....R Lawther pu

21 ran. 8l, 4l, 10l, sht-hd, 2l, 6l, 25l. Time 6m 52.00s. SP 5-2.
Stewart Pike (East Devon).
1 fence omitted 2nd circuit. 17 jumps.

219 Ladies

DI STEFANO ....Miss A Dare 1
(fav) not fluent, hld up, prog 12th, chal 2 out, rdn to ld nr fin
57[3] **Lake Mission ....Miss G Browne** 2
ld 4th,prssd but going bttr frm 2 out, hdd & not qckn nr fin
89[3] **Sirisat 9ow ....Miss T Blazey** 3
alwys prom, outpcd by ldng pair 3 out, kpt on wll, gd effrt
57[6] Lily The Lark 5a *prom til outpcd frm 4 out, no prog aft* ....Miss H Irving 4
West Orient *ld to 4th, prom til wknd frm 15th* ....Miss S Hiatt 5
18 Pejawi 5a 2ow *alwys rear, wll bhnd & no ch frm 12th* ....Miss L Whitaker 6
Phelioff *cls up to 8th, wll bhnd frm 12th* ....Miss S Dawson 7
57[4] Green Archer *jmpd slwly, rear by 6th, t.o. 12th, no ch aft*..Mrs T Hill 8
Rip The Calico (Ire) 5a *mid-div, effrt to chs ldng 5 at 14th, no imp, wknd 3 out* ....Miss S Duckett 9
Finally Fantazia 5a *in tch in rear to 7th, t.o. 12th* ....Miss K Holmes 10
55[7] Rubika (Fr) *sn rear, t.o. & p.u. 12th* ..Mrs S Shoemark pu
What A To Do 3ow *in tch to 9th, sn wknd, t.o. & p.u. last* ....Miss L Sweeting pu
Bankroll *reluc to race, t.o. til p.u. 11th* ....Mrs C Chadney pu
55 Great Simplicity (bl) *rear, t.o. & p.u. 12th* ....Miss P Cooper pu
Browned Off *in tch til f 10th* ....Miss P Gundry f
What Chance (Ire) 5a *pckd 1st, in tch til b.d. 10th* ....Miss S Wallin bd

16 ran. Nk, 10l, 8l, 15l, 2l, sht-hd, 2l, 15l, 30l. Time 6m 49.00s. SP 1-3.
Mrs R Onions (Cotswold Vale Farmers).

220 Men's Open

5 **FRESH PRINCE ....D Duggan** 1
chsd ldr, ld 11th, clr 14th, prssd 2 out, ran on well last
Gee Double You ....S Blackwell 2
mid-div, prog 11th, chnce 2 out, onepcd aft
Nether Gobions ....E Williams 3
ld to 11th, chsd wnr aft, chnce 2 out, no ext
Causeway Cruiser *hld up, effrt 12th, nvr rch ldrs, kpt on*..R Lawther 4
Bright Burns (bl) *prom til wknd frm 3 out* ..R Sweeting 5
2[3] Shannon Glen (bl) *prom til wknd frm 15th*...R Dalgety 6
5 Granville Grill *chsd ldrs til wknd frm 15th*...J Deutsch 7
42 Qualitair Memory (Ire) *(fav) chsd ldrs, strgglng frm 15th, no ch aft*..........................J Tizzard 8
56[8] Shadow Walker *alwys rear, t.o. 12th* ...T Stephenson 9
98 January Don (bl) *slw jmp 1st, sn rear, t.o. 12th* ....G Barfoot-Saunt 10
55 Aylesford *alwys bhnd, t.o. 12th* ....A Tutton 11
56[7] The Country Trader *last pair & sn t.o.*....J Borradaile 12
151 Castlebay Lad *alwys rear, t.o. & p.u. 15th* M Appleby pu
93 Kino *rear, prog to chs ldrs 13th, no imp 15th, wknd & p.u. 2 out*..A Martin pu
Sharinski *chsd ldrs til wknd 13th, bhnd whn p.u. 2 out* ....Julian Pritchard pu
Nordic Flash *alwys bhnd, t.o. & p.u. 12th* .....R Cope pu
Major Bugler (Ire) 1ow *alwys last pair, t.o. & p.u. 12th* ....H Chisholm pu
55[2] Bishops Island *blnd & u.r. 1st* ....A Wintle ur
My Best Man *hld up, no prog whn p.u. 11th*.....A Hill pu
Blackwater Lady (Ire) 5a *in tch in rear, eased & p.u. 12th*..P Scouller pu

20 ran. 8l, 1l, 10l, 2l, 15l, 4l, 5l, 25l, 3l, 20l. Time 6m 53.00s. SP 12-1.
Mrs Vanessa Ramm (Cotswold).

221 Interlink Restricted Div I (12st)

SAXON LASS 5a.........................A Martin 1
prom, ld 11th, jnd 3 out, ran on gamely und pres flat
45[2] **Good Looking Guy ....A Charles-Jones** 2
(fav) w.w. prog to prss wnr 3 out, ev ch aft, not qckn flat
59[5] **Brown Baby 5a...........................G Kerr** 3
prom to 14th, lost tch, ran on agn 2 out
Matchlessly 3ow *ld to 4th, cls up aft til fdd frm 15th* ....Miss E Walker 4
No Dozing (Ire) *wll bhnd, t.o. 12th, ran on frm 2 out, fin strngly*..J Barnes 5
Castle Shelley (Ire) *wll bhnd, t.o. 12th, styd on frm 2 out, nvr nrr*..R Smith 6
59 Miss Magic 5a *cls up, prssd wnr 12th-15th, wknd rpdly*..F Brennan 7
109 Furry Bear 1ow *alwys bhnd, t.o. hlfwy*......R Hawker 8
King Of The Clouds 4ow *ld 4th til hdd & f 11th* ....J Hammond f
Viking Flame 5a *alwys bhnd, t.o. & p.u. 14th*...S Bush pu
Archies Oats *reluc to race, t.o. til p.u. 11th*....J Trice-Rolph pu
Sparnova 5a *mid-div, effrt to chs ldrs 12th, btn 14th, p.u. nxt*..R Barrett pu
Le Vienna (Ire) 4ow *tongue-strap, alwys bhnd, t.o. & p.u. 15th* ....S Currey pu
Blue Vapour 5a 4ow *sn rear, bhnd whn f 8th* ....S Shinton f
59 No Hanky Panky *prom to 6th, sn lost plc, p.u. 11th* ....F Hutsby pu

15 ran. 2l, 15l, 2l, 3l, 15l, 4l, 1 fence. Time 7m 4.00s. SP 5-2.
M N J Sparkes (V.W.H.).

222 Interlink Restricted Div II (12st)

59 **PLATEMAN ....F Hutsby** 1
prom, ld 7th, jnd 2 out, hld on gamely flat
Sideliner ....T Stephenson 2
prog 8th, prssd wnr 15th, ev ch last, no ext nr fin
94[5] **Tea Cee Kay ....A Sansome** 3
chsd ldrs, outpcd frm 15th, ran on apr last, nrst fin

Robero *wll bhnd, t.o. 12th, nvr nrr, school* ...Julian Pritchard 4
60[1] Duke Of Lancaster (Ire) *chsd ldrs, outpcd 14th, no dang aft* ...N Sutton 5
Kingsthorpe *alwys rear, no ch frm 14th* ...M Rimell 6
60 Trina's Cottage (Ire) *alwys bhnd, t.o. 12th* ...B McKim 7
Box Of Delights *(fav) mid-div, effrt 12th, 3rd at 15th, btn 2 out, p.u. last* ...E Williams pu
Generator Boy *mstk 4th, alwys rear, t.o. & p.u. 15th* ...G Barfoot-Saunt pu
30[1] Edinburgh Reel Ale 5a *prom til wknd 14th, p.u. 2 out* ...R Barrett pu
59 Five Circles (Ire) *nvr nr ldrs, wll bhnd whn p.u. 3 out* ...M Portman pu
Ballybeggan Parson (Ire) *prom, blnd 9th, sn wknd, t.o. & p.u. 15th* ...R Burton pu
23 Gt Hayes Pommard *ld to 7th, 4th whn u.r. 10th* ...D Howells ur
45[3] Nobbutjust (Ire) 5a *prog 9th, cls up 14th, wknd 3 out, p.u. nxt* ...A Beedles pu
Shelley's Dream 5a *mstk 1st, sn prom, 2nd whn f 10th* ...M Walters f
Miss Dior 5a *alwys bhnd, t.o. & p.u. 14th* ...Miss P Gundry pu
60 Vally's Spirit *wll bhnd til p.u. 9th* ...Mrs S Shoemark pu

17 ran. 2l, 1½l, 30l, 3l, 15l, 1 fence. Time 6m 58.00s. SP 12-1.
K Hutsby (Warwickshire).

223 Interlink Restricted Div III (12st)

45 **ANTICA ROMA (IRE) 5a...C Wadland 1**
hld up rear, prog hlfwy, ld aft 2 out, ran on strngly
The Hon Company ...E Walker 2
prom, ld 10th til aft 2 out, no ch wth wnr aft
45[5] **Count Balios (Ire) ...P Howse 3**
(fav) w.w. prog 9th, chsd ldr 13-15th, onepcd aft
147[3] Looking *chsd ldrs, wknd frm 14th* ...A Sansome 4
Autumn Green (Ire) *prom til wknd 14th, sn bhnd* ...R Burton 5
14[6] Moon Monkey (Ire) *wll bhnd, kpt on frm 15th, no dang* ...M Cowley 6
56 Solar Gem *wll bhnd, effrt 12th, nvr on trms, wknd 2 out* ...J Mason 7
Tudor Oaks 5a *ld 4th-10th, wknd 12th, t.o.* ...Julian Pritchard 8
Di Moda *bhnd til p.u. 11th* ...Miss S Firmin pu
Wotamona 5a *in tch to 12th, wknd & p.u. 15th* R Smith pu
Image Boy (Ire) *alwys rear, t.o. & p.u. 14th* ...E James pu
59 Colonel Fairfax (bl) *ld til mstk 4th, prom to 11th, wknd & p.u. 13th* ...J Trice-Rolph pu
60[4] Bold Man (NZ) *bhnd til p.u. 10th* ...Miss T Honeyball pu
Seminole Princess 5a *mid-div, wknd 12th, p.u. 15th* ...A Charles-Jones pu
60 Roark's Chukka *alwys bhnd, t.o. & p.u. 12th* ..D Smith pu
100 Dragons Lady 5a *f 1st*...G Barfoot-Saunt f
87 Welsh Lightning *chsd ldrs, btn frm 14th, disp poor 4th & u.r. last* ...R Inglesant ur
Royal Bula *alwys bhnd, t.o. & p.u. 12th* ...S Shinton pu
Midnight Miracle 5a *mstks 1st & 2nd, p.u. nxt* L Baker pu

19 ran. 15l, 3l, 25l, 4l, ½l, 12l, 12l. Time 7m 2.00s. SP 10-1.
Mrs K Cockburn (Warwickshire).

224 Maiden (5-7yo) (12st)

BAY HOBNOB ...P Howse 1
trckd ldrs, effrt 14th, ld 2 out, jnd last, pshd clr flat
Butlers Match (Ire) ...A Charles-Jones 2
(fav) w.w. prog 11th, ld 13th, mstk & hdd 2 out, lvl last, kpt on
Imustamit ...R Barrett 3
mid-div, outpcd frm 12th, kpt on onepcd frm 3 out, no dang
Village Remedy 5a *ld 5th-11th, wknd frm 14th, t.o.* ...A Tutton 4
Dip The Lights 5a *rear frm 9th, t.o. & p.u. 15th* ...L Baker pu
1 New Flame 5a *alwys rear, t.o. & p.u. 15th* ...J Trice-Rolph pu
60 Royal Dadda *blnd 5th, in tch, rdn to disp & mstk 9th, sn btn, p.u. 2 out* ...A Hill pu
60 Spring Sabre (bl) *pllng, chsd ldrs to 14th, wknd, 4th & no ch whn p.u. 2 out* ...R Lawther pu
Larkross *ld 2-5th, prom to 13th, bhnd whn p.u. 2 out* ...A Sansome pu
Fighting For Good (Ire) *14s-8s, prog 7th, ld 11-13th, wknd 15th, p.u. 2 out* ...T Illsley pu
Baron's Pearl 5a *mstk 7th, alwys rear, t.o. & p.u. 15th* ...F Hutsby pu
Captain Flashard 7a 2ow *ld til hdd & f 2nd* ...J Hobbs f
Jimmy Morrel *schoold in last, wll bhnd til p.u. 13th* ...T Stephenson pu
Royal Orchard *last pair & alwys bhnd, t.o. & p.u. 13th* ...A Martin pu
Sharp Alice 5a *rear, wknd 12th, t.o. & p.u. nxt* ...O Macphail pu
Gibraltar Queen 12a *hld up, prog to jn ldrs 10th, wknd aft 14th, p.u. 2 out* ...C Wadland pu

16 ran. 1½l, 25l, 25l. Time 7m 12.00s. SP 12-1.
A J Mason (V.W.H.).
J.N.

FOLKESTONE
Wednesday February 19th
SOFT

225 2m 5f Flisher Foods Maiden Hunters' Chase Class H

150[2] **TRIFAST LAD 12.5 3a...Mr P Hacking 1**
(fav) trckd ldr, chal 4 out, ld 2 out, styd on.
Sands Of Gold (Ire) 12.1 7a ...Mr L Lay 2
ld till rdn and hdd 2 out, kept on one pace.
King High 12.1 7a ...Mr C Ward 3
chsd ldrs, one pace from 3 out.
Astound (Ire) 12.1 7a *bhnd till hdwy from 3 out, nvr near to chal.*...Lt-Col R Webb-Bowen 4
Gypsy King (Ire) 12.1 7a *chsd ldrs till wknd 3 out.* ...Mr A Coe 5
151 Ell Gee 11.10 7a *chsd ldrs till hit 9th, soon bhnd, t.o..* ...Miss C Townsley 6
151[4] Centre Stage 12.1 7a *t.o. from 8th.*...Mr A Warr 7
Greybury Lane (Ire) 12.1 7a *blnd and u.r. 2nd.* ...Mr P Bull ur
Dashboard Light 12.5 3a *chsd ldrs till wknd 5 out, t.o. when p.u. before 2 out.*...Mr Simon Andrews pu
Joctor Don (Ire) 11.5 7a *f 1st.*...Mr E Babington f

10 ran. 2½l, 8l, 4l, 1l, dist, 16l. Time 5m 48.60s. SP 11-10.
Mike Roberts

HAYDOCK
Friday February 21st
GOOD

226 3m Walrus Hunters' Chase Class H

93[2] **LORD RELIC (NZ) 12.0 7a ...Mr R Ford 1**
(fav) cl up, ld 2 out, pushed clr after last.
119[2] **Country Tarrogen 12.2 5a...Mr N Wilson 2**
held up, imp hfwy, chasing ldrs when pkd 3 out, kept on apr last.
Glen Oak 11.7 7a ...Mr M P FitzGerald 3
n.j.w., hdwy and in tch 4 out, fd 2 out.
93[3] My Nominee 12.0 7a (bl) *ld 4th, pushed along and hdd 2 out, soon wandered, fd apr last.*...Mr R Burton 4
87[3] Travel Bound 11.9 7a 2ow (bl) *chsd ldrs, lost pl hfwy, well bhnd 5 out.*...Mr D Barlow 5
Will It Last 11.2 7a *soon well bhnd, t.o. when p.u. 11th*...Mr L Brown pu
Mhemeanles 11.7 7a *jmpd poorly, alwys well bhnd, t.o. when p.u. 5 out.*...Mr N R Mitchell pu
Mobile Messenger (NZ) 11.7 7a *ld to 4th, 5th and in tch when f 9th*...Miss S Samworth f
94[8] Charlies Delight (Ire) 11.13 5a *midfield, hdwy 10th, 6th and driven along when f 14th*...Mr A Sansome f
The Major General 12.0 7a *held up, hdwy and in tch 9th, blnd 13th and next, well bhnd when p.u. 3 out.* ...Capt A Ogden pu

152 Master Kit (Ire) 11.11 7a *str hold, chsd ldrs from 5th, 6th and struggling when u.r. 4 out*........Mr J Billinge ur
11 ran. 6l, 13l, 5l, dist. Time 6m 32.00s. SP 9-4.
Mrs H J Clarke

KEMPTON
Friday February 21st
GOOD

227 3m Corinthian Hunters' Chase Class H

19[1] **THE JOGGER 12.0 7a ....Mr J Tizzard** 1
with ldr till ld 3rd, came clr from 4 out, readily.
91 **Mediane (USA) 11.11 3a .....Mr Simon Andrews** 2
reluctant to line up, chsd ldrs 6th, chal 10th to 14th, outpcd after 4 out, styd on again to take 2nd run-in.
153[4] **Poors Wood 11.7 7a ....Mr P O'Keeffe** 3
held up, hdwy and hit 12th, chsd wnr from 4 out till wknd run-in.
67[2] Teaplanter 12.2 5a *(fav) ld to 3rd, in trbl and rdn 10th, hit 12th and wknd*..................Mr B Pollock 4
153[5] Amari King 12.0 7a *chsd ldrs 6th, lost pl 8th, wknd 12th, t.o. when p.u. before 2 out*. ..Mr C Ward Thomas pu
151[3] Fifth Amendment 12.0 7a (bl) *pressed ldrs 3rd and raced wd, wknd 10th, jmpd poorly and tried to refuse in rear till blnd and u.r. 12th*..............Mr A Hales ur
6 ran. 13l, 14l, 14l. Time 6m 23.60s. SP 9-2.
Mrs P Tizzard

BERWICKSHIRE
Friars Haugh
Saturday February 22nd
GOOD

228 Members

159[1] **FISCAL POLICY ....H Trotter** 1
(fav) ld frm 4th, 2l up whn lft clr last
Luckieshiel 5a ....Miss N Snowden 2
s.s. alwys t.o.
131 Miss Cullane (Ire) 5a *u.r. 3rd*..................R Neill ur
The Caffler (Ire) *ld to 4th, chsd wnr aft, 2l down whn u.r. last*..................................W Ramsay ur
4 ran. Dist. Time 6m 43.00s. SP 1-3.
H P Trotter (Berwickshire).

229 Confined (12st)

HAGAR ....M Bradburne 1
alwys handy, ld 3 out, sn clr, comf
Ensign Ewart (Ire) ....C Storey 2
hld up, ldng grp frm 13th, chsd wnr 3 out, no imp
152 **Kilminfoyle 5ex ....T Oates** 3
hld up, prog frm 14th, no imp whn mstk last
Bit Of A Blether (Ire) *(fav) ld 9th til mstk 3 out, no ch aft*......................................A Parker 4
Benghazi *ld early, lost tch 4 out* ....P Craggs 5
134 Arctic Leader 5a *nvr nr ldrs*..................M Ruddy 6
133[3] Lion Of Vienna *prom to hlfwy, sn lost tch* .....T Scott 7
Buck's Delight (Ire) *ld 4th-9th, cls up whn f nxt* ....Miss P Robson f
156 Tony's Feelings 7ex *nvr nr ldrs, t.o. & p.u. 2 out* ....D Reid pu
9 ran. 4l, 5l, 12l, dist, ¾l, dist. Time 6m 32.00s. SP 6-1.
J I A Charlton (Border).

230 Restricted

NOVA NITA 5a ....P Craggs 1
alwys handy, ld 4 out, sn clr, easily
131[2] **Denim Blue ....Miss P Robson** 2
(fav) alwys handy, kpt on to tk 2nd nr fin
157[2] **Eastlands Hi-Light ....T Morrison** 3
alwys in tch, no ext frm 3 out
131 Ebbzeado Willfurr (Ire) *alwys ldng grp, 2nd whn slppd apr 2 out, kpt on well*........................J Billinge 4
158 Tannock Brook *made most til 4 out, sn wknd* A Parker 5
Blakes Folly (Ire) *nvr bttr than mid-div* ....D Wood 6
160[1] Pablowmore *nvr rchd ldrs* ....R Green 7
118 Drumcairn (Ire) *alwys bhnd*................R Morgan 8
162 Flypie *alwys bhnd*....................P Strang-Steel 9
Mighty Express *nvr nr ldrs, p.u. 3 out*......A Robson pu
Fathers Footprints *sn bhnd, p.u. 3 out*.......P Diggle pu
131 Sumpt'n Smart *handy til f 10th* ....L Morgan f
Kings Token *steadied start, plld to ld & f 2nd* J Walton f
167 Will Travel (Ire) *nvr bttr tahn mid-div, bhnd whn p.u. 3 out*..C Bennett pu
161 Steady Man *rear til p.u. 11th*..................T Scott pu
15 ran. 10l, 1l, nk, 15l, 10l, 20l, dist, 6l. Time 6m 33.00s. SP 5-1.
Robert Black (Dumfriesshire).

231 Ladies

132[2] **PARSONS BRIG ....Miss S Forster** 1
(Jt fav) ld/disp frm 10th, slght ld 2 out, styd on wll
33[1] **Astrac Trio (USA) ....Miss A Bowie** 2+
(Jt fav) ld/disp frm 11th, no ext apr last
Funny Feelings 3ow ....Miss D Laidlaw 2+
ld 4th-9th, rmnd handy, ev ch 2 out, no ext apr last
132 Across The Card *s.s. prog to jn ldrs 4 out, no ext apr last*................................Miss R Ramsay 4
Minibrig 5a *nvr quite rchd ldrs* ....Miss P Robson 5
158[3] Very Evident (Ire) *nvr rchd ldrs*............Miss J Bird 6
132 Schweppes Tonic *ld brfly 9th, sn wknd, t.o.* ....Mrs C Amos 7
Rare Fire *ld to 4th, sn wknd, p.u. 13th* Mrs R Davidson pu
132 The Laughing Lord *nvr nr ldrs, p.u. 3 out* ....Miss R Shiels pu
158 Rushing Burn 5a *nvr nr ldrs, p.u. 3 out* ....Miss N Snowden pu
Tod Law 5a *f 2nd* ....Miss S Dickinson f
Mighty Haggis *s.v.s. f 6th*..............Miss M Mahur f
Sudden Sally (Ire) 5a *s.v.s. t.o. til p.u. 3 out* ....Miss M Bremner pu
13 ran. 1½l, dd-ht, ½l, 5l, 2l, dist. Time 6m 41.00s. SP 5-2.
J S Haldane (College Valley & N N'land).

232 Land Rover Open (12st)

SAYIN NOWT 5a........................A Parker 1
(fav) hld up, prog 4 out, just ld 2 out, just hld on
Allezmoss 7ex ....C Storey 2
went 2nd 13th, ld aft 4 out, jst hdd 2 out, styd on wll
Staigue Fort (Ire) 7ex...............H Naughton 3
ld to 4 out, wknd frm nxt
Tartan Tornado 7ex *alwys twrds rear*.......P Johnson 4
Givower *last til some prog 9th, lost tch 4 out* P Diggle 5
Loughlinstown Boy 7ex *2nd til 13th, sn lost tch* ....P Craggs 6
6 ran. Sht-hd, 20l, 5l, 8l, sht-hd. Time 6m 41.00s. SP 4-5.
Dennis Waggott (Dumfriesshire).

233 Open Maiden Div I

WANG HOW ....A Robson 1
hld up, drvn to nrrw ld 3 out, kpt on well
135[4] **Donside ....J Walton** 2
ld 5th til 4 out, upsides last, no ext flat
155 **Explore Mondial (Ire) ....A Parker** 3
hld up, prog to ld brfly 4 out, no ext apr last
135[3] Peelinick *(fav) alwys handy, no ext frm 3 out*. .T Oates 4
Claywalls *nvr nr ldrs*..............................T Scott 5
Hula *ldng grp til wknd 4 out*..................C Storey 6
Lauder Square *alwys wll bhnd*..........M Bradburne 7
115 The Camair Flyer (Ire) *ld to 5th, wknd frm 10th* ....R Morgan 8
Luvly Bubbly *prom early, bhnd by 10th, p.u. 3 out* ....Mrs V Jackson pu
Bagots Park *prom early, bhnd by 9th, p.u. 3 out* ....R Shiels pu
136 Passim 12a *nvr nr ldrs, p.u. 3 out*.........T Morrison pu
38 Wild Rudolph (Ire) *alwys bhnd, p.u. 13th* .....D Wood pu
Respectable Laura 5a *sn bhnd, p.u. 3 out* ....Miss S Forster pu
13 ran. 1l, 2l, 5l, 20l, 2l, dist, 3l. Time 6m 44.00s. SP 8-1.
J C Clark (Lauderdale).

234 Open Maiden Div II

38 **THIEF'S ROAD ....R Shiels** 1

ld 5th, clr 3 out, just hld on
36 **My Meadowsweet ....C Storey** 2
(fav) 3rd hlfwy, clsd on wnr frm 3 out, just faild
162[5] **Bluebell Track 5a ....R Trotter** 3
nvr rchd ldng grp
162 Prince Rossini (Ire) *nvr rchd ldrs* ....B Gibson 4
136 Indian River (Ire) *nvr rchd ldrs* ....T Scott 5
162[9] Sagaro Belle 5a *nvr rchd ldrs* ....T Oates 6
Polly Cinders 5a *5th hlfwy, sn lost tch* ....M Ruddy 7
135 Father O'Callaghan (Ire) *6th hlfwy, sn lost tch* ....Miss M Bremner 8
Bantel Baronet *prom early, bhnd whn p.u. 13th* ....Miss J Hedley pu
Zoflo 5a *ld to 5th, cls up whn p.u. 8th* ....A Parker pu
Hintertux *prom early, bhnd whn p.u. 13th* ....R Green pu
Flower Of Dunblane 5a *sn bhnd, p.u. 2 out* ....Mrs J McGregor pu
Fort Alicia 5a *4th hlfwy, cls up whn f 11th* ....M Bradburne f
Dalmigavie Lad 7a *sn bhnd, p.u. 3 out* ......H Trotter pu
Driminamore (Ire) *2nd hlfwy, 3rd & hld whn f last* ....W Ramsay f
15 ran. Nk, dist, 2l, ½l, 8l, 20l, 20l. Time 6m 45.00s. SP 9-2.
Miss D M M Calder (Berwickshire).

235 Open Maiden Div III

FIDDLERS BRAE ....R Shiels 1
ld 4th-7th, 15l down whn lft in ld 2 out
136[4] **Red Hot Boogie (Ire) ....T Scott** 2
5th hlfwy, lft 2nd 2 out, no imp wnr
Megans Mystery (Ire) *ld 7th, sn clr, mstk 4 out, 15l up whn u.r. 2 out* ....Miss S Forster ur
37 Border Glory *2nd hlfwy, sn lost tch, p.u. 4 out* ....R Robinson pu
37[5] Fragrant Lord *u.r. 7th* ....Mrs V Jackson ur
Sharplaw 5a *sn bhnd, some prog frm hlfwy, bhnd agn whn p.u. 2 out* ....C Storey pu
Thinkaboutthat (Ire) 3ow *ld to 4th, poor 5th whn u.r. 13th* ....J Muir ur
136[9] Hooky's Treat 5a *4th hlfwy, sn wknd, p.u. 3 out* ....M Bradburne pu
Allrite Pet 5a *(fav) u.r. 1st* ....A Parker ur
Political Diamond 5a *sn t.o., p.u. 14th* ....R Green pu
10 ran. 4l. Time 6m 52.00s. SP 3-1.
Miss D M M Calder (Berwickshire).
R.J.

BOLVENTOR HARRIERS
Lemalla
Saturday February 22nd
SOFT

236 Intermediate (12st)

3[2] **BET WITH BAKER (IRE) ....Miss P Curling** 1
keen hld, handy, 2nd at 11th, disp nxt, ld 2 out, clr last
97[2] **King Torus (Ire) ....N Harris** 2
(fav) went 2nd 7th, ld/disp 10th, ev ch til wknd und pres last
Ticket To The Moon 5a ....A Farrant 3
hld up in tch, prog to 3rd 3 out, styng on whn hmpd apr last
Just Ben 10ex *handy, 3rd at 11th, wll plcd til wknd 3 out, bttr for race* ....Miss J Cumings 4
Balmoral Boy (NZ) *5th hlfwy, nvr dang, onepcd frm 15th* ....M Miller 5
Artistic Peace 5a *u.r. 4th* ....D Stephens ur
100[4] Holly Fare *mstks, rear frm 7th, t.o. & ref 16th* ....C Crosthwaite ref
Ballysheil *ld to 8th, lost plc 12th, p.u. 15th* ..S Edwards pu
Ive Called Time 5ex *prom whn blnd & u.r. 1st* T Greed ur
Karicleigh Boy *hdwy 12th, 4th at 15th, wknd nxt, bhnd & p.u. last* ....A Holdsworth pu
45[1] Pines Express (Ire) *mid-div, strggling 12th, rear whn p.u. 15th* ....J Tizzard pu
Karlin's Quest *ld & mstk 1st, sn rear, bhnd & p.u. 10th* ....D Doyne-Ditmas pu
12 ran. 4l, 3l, 20l, 3l. Time 6m 39.00s. SP 2-1.
George W Baker (Mendip Farmers).

237 Confined (12st)

149 **FIDDLERS PIKE ....Mrs R Henderson** 1
j.w. in tch, cls 3rd 16th, ld nxt, drew clr 2 out, styd on
Just My Bill ....C Heard 2
s.s. prog 9th, went 3rd aft 16th, tk 2nd apr last, no ch wnr
96 **Baldhu Chance ....J Young** 3
prog 11th, cls 3rd whn blnd & lost plc 3 out, ran on agn flt
170[2] Moze Tidy 3ex *sn prom, cls 3rd hlfwy, ld 14th-17th, wknd 2 out* ....I Dowrick 4
Lonesome Traveller (NZ) *lost ground steadily frm 9th, rmndrs 12th, wll btn aft* ....Mrs M Hand 5
Cornish Harp *mid-div, 9th at 11th, no ch frm 15th* ....G Shenkin 6
173[2] Pop Song *(fav) ld to 5th, disp 9th-13th, cls 2nd 16th, wknd rpdly, p.u.last* ....A Farrant pu
Queen's Chaplain *mstk 5th, prog to 6th at 9th, lost plc 12th, ref 16th* ....G Penfold ref
96[2] Senegalais (Fr) 3ex *rear whn mstk & u.r. 10th* ....M Venner ur
Querrin Lodge *last frm 6th, wll bhnd whn p.u. last* ....T Greed pu
96[5] Dark Reflection *rear & rmndrs 7th, nvr dang, poor 7th whn u.r. 3 out* ....A O'Connor ur
Roving Rebel *prom, ld 5th, disp 9-11th, lost plc nxt, p.u. aft 16th* ....A Holdsworth pu
Bridge House Boy *mstk 1st, last at 11th, t.o. & u.r. 13th* ....A Oliver ur
13 ran. 7l, 4l, 6l, 8l, 30l. Time 6m 47.00s. SP 12-1.
Mrs R G Henderson (Lamerton).

238 Ladies

99[1] **SECRET FOUR ....Miss T Cave** 1
hld up in tch, prog 13th, chal & ld aft 2 out, pshd clr
174[6] **Just Bert (Ire) ....Miss S Young** 2
alwys prom, 2nd frm 9th til ld aft 3 out, ev ch, no ext last
99 **Celtic Sport (bl) ....Miss A Plunkett** 3
ld til aft 3 out, sn onepcd, eased flat
145[5] On His Own *prom, pckd 10th, lost ground 12th, wll btn frm 17th* ....Miss W Southcombe 4
174 Friendly Lady 5a *sn rear, last at 13th, nrst fin* ....Miss A Bush 5
149[6] Some-Toy *(fav) 6th hlfwy, prog 13th, outpcd 15th, blnd nxt, wknd rpdly* ....Miss L Blackford 6
99[5] It's Not My Fault (Ire) *5th at 9th, outpcd 15th, 5th & wkng 2 out, walked in* ....Mrs M Hand 7
Aristocratic Gold *alwys rear* ....Miss A Barnett 8
102 Eserie de Cores (USA) *rear whn f 12th* ....Miss K Baily f
9 ran. 4l, 12l, 10l, 5l, 3l, 12l, 20l. Time 6m 41.00s. SP 5-2.
P Masterson (Dart Vale And South Pool Hrrs).
One fence omitted final circuit.

239 Land Rover Open (12st)

98[2] **MAGNOLIA MAN ....N Harris** 1
hld up in tch, cls 3rd 17th, qcknd to ld apr last, sn clr
98[3] **The General's Drum 7ex ....K Heard** 2
(fav) wll in tch, 2nd 10th, effrt to disp 3 out, no ext und pres
220[8] **Qualitair Memory (Ire) 7ex ....J Tizzard** 3
ld til jnd 17th, disp 2 out, wknd apr last
171[6] Pintail Bay (v) *6th but in tch 9th, outpcd 15th, nrst fin* ....N Legg 4
Hidden Dollar *prom, 2nd hlfwy, outpcd 15th, 4th 3 out, no ext* ....G Penfold 5
98 Southerly Buster *cls 4th 11th, lost tch wth ldrs 16th* ....S White 6
Pen-Shilmon 7a *blnd 1st, jmpd novicey til p.u. 8th* ....J Young pu
7 ran. 6l, 3l, 8l, 3l, 10l. Time 6m 52.00s. SP 5-2.
Mrs D B Lunt (Tiverton Foxhounds).

240 Restricted Div I (12st)

101[1] **THREE AND A HALF ....N Harris** 1
(fav) prom, disp 15th, ld und pres aft 2 out, lft clr last
He Is ....Miss P Gundry 2
alwys prom, disp 11th-14th, outpcd nxt, lft 2nd last
100 **Springcombe 5a ....Miss S Eames** 3
ld, clr early, wknd & hdd 11th, 5th whn mstk 16th, kpt on
Indian Rabi *keen hld, in tch, 5th at 9th, lost plc aft mstk 13th* ....G Penfold 4
Cedars Rosslare *novice rdn, rear, mstk 11th, t.o. & p.u. 15th*.............................Miss O Green pu
176 Scallykenning (bl) *mid-div, 7th whn hit 10th, blnd 13th, p.u. nxt*.....................................J Young pu
Arble March 5a *whppd round strt, t.o. til p.u. 9th* ....Mrs M Hand pu
106 Vital Legacy *t.o. whn ref 10th*........Miss A Goschen ref
149 Pharrago (Ire) *mstk 4th, rear, 8th hlfwy, bhnd & p.u. 15th*................................Miss P Cooper pu
Dromin Chat (Ire) *chsd ldr to 6th, cls 4th whn mstk 11th, wknd, p.u. 13th* ....T Cole pu
104[1] My Man On Dundrum (Ire) *handy, disp 15th, ev ch but hrd rdn whn ran out last*...............Miss P Curling ro
11 ran. 10l, dist, nk. Time 6m 46.00s. SP 5-4.
J Scott (Devon & Somerset Staghounds).

241 Restricted Div II (12st)

I'MINONIT ....M Miller 1
hld up in tch, prog to disp 16th, hdd nxt, ld last, styd on
7 **Clandon Lad ....T Mitchell** 2
prog 11th, cls 4th at 13th, ld 3 out til last, ran on well
100[2] **Milled Oats ....A Farrant** 3
unruly pddck, mid-div, 6th & rmndrs 13th, 3rd & no ch 2 out
Brown Rebel *mid-div, 6th hlfwy, lost ground steadily frm 13th, p.u. 17th*.................................S Slade pu
Ann's Ambition *prom, ld/disp 11-16th, 3rd 3 out, wknd & p.u. nxt, gd effrt* ....C Heard pu
50[8] Sherbrooks *rear whn mstk 10th, bhnd & p.u. 15th* ....M Hoskins pu
Parditino *rear, mstks, bhnd whn crawld 16th, p.u. nxt* ....Miss V Nicholas pu
175[2] Venn Boy *(fav) ld to 9th, fdd rpdly aft 12th, rear & p.u. 15th*...J Tizzard pu
100[3] Swing To The Left (Ire) 5a *prom, disp 9-14th, lost plc 16th, 5th whn p.u. 2 out*..............Miss J Cumings pu
Pixie In Purple (Ire) *in tch, 5th whn f 14th*. .D Stephens f
Fingal *last whn ran out 4th* ....A Moir ro
11 ran. Sht-hd, 3l. Time 6m 46.00s. SP 3-1.
P S Macrae (Portman).

242 Open Maiden Div I (12st)

RAGTIME BOY ....A Farrant 1
(fav) w.w. prog 9th, 2nd 13th, lft clr 16th, mstk last, unchal
Pilgrim's Mission (Ire) ....D Doyne-Ditmas 2
5th hlfwy, lft 15l 2nd 16th, v tired whn blnd last
Moonbay Lady 5a ....A O'Connor 3
rear, lft remote 3rd by dfctrs 15th, completed own time
176 Tom's Arctic Dream 5a *ld 1st, cls up til disp 6-9th, lost ground 11th, p.u. 13th* ....P King pu
172[7] Cheque Book *not fluent, t.o. 11th, p.u. 15th* ....T Cole pu
101 Dont Rise Me (Ire) *in tch to 9th, rear whn p.u. 15th* ....L Jefford pu
103 Corrib Haven (Ire) *mstk 4th, 5th at 11th, 6th & btn 13th, p.u. 15th*...................................S Slade pu
105 Romany Anne 5a *wll bhnd til p.u. 13th*. .Miss S Young pu
Linda's Prince (Ire) *prog to ld 9th, clr whn f 16th* ....B O'Doherty f
105[3] Sagaville (Ire) *ld 2nd-6th, disp to 9th, 3rd whn stmbld aft 14th & p.u.*............................A Holdsworth pu
10 ran. Dist, Bad. Time 6m 58.00s. SP 4-5.
Mrs Jo Clarke (Tiverton).

243 Open Maiden Div II (12st)

PERAMBULATE (NZ) 7a ....L Jefford 1
not alwys fluent, prog 11th, lft 2nd 16th, ld 2 out, sn clr
172[5] **Herhorse 5a ....R Darke** 2
cls 5th at 10th, lft 3rd 16th, styd on, tk 2nd nr fin
101[4] **Katree Runner ....R Widger** 3
nov rddn,chsd ldr 12th til lft in ld 16th, hdd 2 out,eased
Bedtime Pixie 7a *schoold rear, t.o. 14th, remote 4th aft*...D Stephens 4
105 Fortitude Star 5a *prom, 2nd 7th-11th, lost plc & rmndrs 13th, t.o. & p.u. 16th*...................A Farrant pu
My Prides Way 5a *mid-div, prog whn blnd 9th, immed p.u.*...T Greed pu
146 Fever Pitch *5th hlfwy, lost tch 16th, poor 4th whn ref last*..B Dixon ref
Kirsty's Pal *ran out bend aft 2nd* ....J Young ro
105 Stony Missile 5a *sn bhnd, jmpd slwly, t.o. whn p.u. last* ....Miss W Hartnoll pu
Happy Henry (Ire) *(fav) ld, jnd & f 16th* ......I Dowrick f
102[4] Rhyme And Chime *c.o. bend aft 2nd, cont t.o. til p.u. 7th*..T Dennis pu
102 Belitlir 12a *schoold rear til p.u. 13th* ....Miss S Young pu
12 ran. 10l, ½l, 2 fences. Time 7m 7.00s. SP 3-1.
D H Barons (Dart Vale And South Pool Hrrs).

244 Open Maiden Div III (12st)

111[2] **EYRE POINT (IRE) ....A Honeyball** 1
(fav) hld up mid-div, prog to 2nd 3 out, ld apr last, ran on wll
101 **Midnight Bob ....J Young** 2
ld aft 7th, clr 3 out, hdd apr last, kpt on
105 **Trolly ....L Jefford** 3
in tch, cls 4th whn blnd 16th, wknd, no ch whn mstk last
87[4] Pyro Pennant *ld/disp to 7th, cls up til onepcd frm 3 out*...I Johnson 4
Simply Joyful 5a *in tch til lost plc 15th* ....P King 5
Probation *in tch, 7th hlfwy, wknd, p.u. last*....R Darke pu
172 Dance Fever (Ire) *prom til mstk 13th, rmndrs, bhnd & p.u. 15th* ....R Woollacott pu
175 One For The Cross (Ire) *rear, rmndrs 8th, bhnd & p.u. 12th*...G Penfold pu
I'll Be Bound *disp til 7th, cls 2nd till f 15th* M Burrows f
105 Rose's Lady Day 5a *f 1st* ....D Stephens f
Impetuous Dreamer 5a *rear, n.j.w. f 4th* ....Miss A Goschen f
181 Baywyn 5a *8th hlfwy, nvr dang, t.o. & p.u. last* ....S Kidston pu
12 ran. ½l, 6l, ½l, 3l. Time 7m 6.00s. SP 2-1.
John Honeyball (Taunton Vale Foxhounds).

245 Open Maiden Div IV (12st)

97 **SAINT JOSEPH ....Miss S Young** 1
prom, ld 15th, disp 3 out til drew clr apr last
105 **Harmony's Choice ....N Harris** 2
prog 9th, 2nd at 15th, disp 3 out, wknd nxt
Comedy Gayle ....I Widdicombe 3
in tch, went 3rd at 15th, not chal, improve
54[7] Lawd Of Blisland *ld to 6th,blnd 10th, disp 11-12th, wknd, poor 4th whn f last*......................A Farrant f
110[3] Melling *(fav) mid-div, rdn 12th, no prog, bhnd & p.u. 16th*...B Dixon pu
103 Luney River 5a *keen hold, prom, ld 6th, hdd & wknd 12th, blnd nxt, p.u.*.............................J Young pu
Amicombe Brook 5a *sn rear, t.o. & p.u. 14th* ....Mrs M Hand pu
101 Carrarea (Ire) *alwys wll bhnd, p.u. last* ....Miss J Cumings pu
88 Roger (Ire) 7a *in tch, 6th hlfwy, wknd 12th, bhnd & p.u. 16th* ....Miss P Cooper pu
100 Boire Ensemble 7a *4th whn f 5th*............M Venner f
Mazies Choice 5a *unruly start, rear, blnd 10th, t.o. & p.u. 13th* ....S Slade pu
11 ran. 6l, 30l. Time 6m 54.50s. SP 25-1.
B R J Young (East Cornwall).

Two fences omitted this race.

246 Open Maiden Div V (12st)

147[4] **ROYAL TURN .... A Honeyball 1**
w.w. disp 12th, drew clr apr last, pshd out
103[3] **The Ugly Duckling .... S Slade 2**
(fav) ld/disp, ev ch til no ext apr last
Givus A Hand *lost tch 13th, t.o. & p.u. 16th* ... E Bailey pu
Battle Lord Cisto *cls 2nd whn f 5th* .. D Doyne-Ditmas f
4 ran. 1½l. Time 7m 15.00s. SP 6-4.
John Honeyball (Taunton Vale Foxhounds).
G.T.

BROCKLESBY
Brocklesby Park
Saturday February 22nd
GOOD

247 Members

HENRY GALE 1ow .... P Strawson 1
disp, ld 6th/7th & frm 5 out, drew clr frm nxt
Johnny Be Good .... Maj S Robinson 2
cls up, ld 8th-6 out, outpcd nxt
116[7] Senso (Ire) *w.w., last cls up til u.r. 5 out (ditch)* .... K Green ur
Rymerole *(fav) disp, hrd hld til p.u. qckly 7th* .... Mrs J Dawson pu
4 ran. 30l. Time 6m 50.00s. SP 12-1.
P D F Strawson (Brocklesby).

248 Confined (12st)

SPECIALARRANGEMENT (IRE) .... A Hill 1
(fav) mid-div, prog 10th, 2nd 5 out, ld 3 out, comf
Double Collect .... A Rebori 2
tried to make all, hdd bfr 3 out, no ext
Okeetee .... Miss L Allan 3
mstly 2nd to 5 out, chsd 1st pair gmly, just outpcd
74[2] Ways And Means 5a *nvr dang, ran on pssd wknng rivals frm 7th-4 out* .... K Green 4
113[3] Clare Lad (v) *rear div, prog 6 out, 30l 4th 4 out, ran on onepcd* .... R Walford 5
137[1] Alpha One *mid-div 4th/5th, 5th outpcd 5 out* .... P Gee 6
121[2] My True Clown 1ow *last til gained 2 plcs on flat* .... Miss L Hampshire 7
214 Bowery Boy *4th 1st m, fdd 8th, 8th outpcd 5 out* .... Capt E Andrewes 8
75 Ginger Pink *cls up mstly 3rd til wknd 5 out* .... Maj S Robinson 9
Grey Hussar (NZ) *alwys last pair, rmmndrs 8-9th, gave up 4 out* .... S Walker pu
10 ran. 3l, 9l, 20l, ½l, 30l, 8l, 1l, ½l. Time 6m 16.00s. SP 6-4.
Mrs Judy Wilson (Pytchley).

249 Ladies

117[3] **FINAL HOPE (IRE) .... Mrs F Needham 1**
(fav) made all, 3l clr 3 out, ran on gmly
London Hill .... Miss H Irving 2
2nd frm 5th, chsd wnnr last m, just held off
Try God .... Miss L Allan 3
2nd hrd hld to 4th, cls 3rd til wknd qckly bfr 3 out
139[2] Naughty Nellie 5a *alwys last, not fluent, outpcd 6 out, p.u. 3 out* .... Mrs J Dawson pu
4 ran. 2l, dist. Time 6m 18.00s. SP 11-10.
R Tate (Hurworth).

250 Mens Open

76[2] **COPPER THISTLE (IRE) .... R Hunnisett 1**
(fav) cls up, 3rd frm 12th, outpcd frm 4 out, lft in ld last
138[2] **Raise An Argument .... N Docker 2**
ld 4th, 4th outpcd frm 6 out, lft 2nd last
Kambalda Rambler .... R Armson 3
ld 5th, drew clr frm 4 out, wll clr whn f last, remntd
137[4] Golden Moss *disp brfly, fdd, t.o. 10th, p.u. 3 out, re-stt, completed* .... Maj S Robinson 4
Park Drift 1ow *w.w., prog 8th, 2nd frm 12th til p.u. qckly bfr last* .... R Tate pu
119[5] La Fontainbleau (Ire) *alwys last, rmmdrs 8-9th, t.o. 10th, p.u. 4 out* .... A Rebori pu
6 ran. 5l, 12l, dist. Time 6m 23.00s. SP Evens.
R S Hunnisett (Cottesmore).

251 Interlink Restricted

WISE WIZARD .... E Andrewes 1
cls up, 3rd 4 out, chal nxt, ld 2 out, ran on wll
Beckford .... A Pickering 2
alwys 2nd/3rd, chsd wnnr frm 3 out, just held
213 **White Bullet (USA) .... B Pollock 3**
cls up, ld 11th-3 out, hdd & no ext 2 out
78[2] City Buzz (Ire) *prom bhnd ldrs, 5th 5 out, outpcd nxt* .... K Needham 4
Pokey Grange *ld to 10th, 2nd to 5 out, outpcd nxt* .... Maj S Robinson 5
Sharp To Oblige *alwys rear hlf, outpcd 6 out, ran on onepce* .... S Whitaker 6
The Chap 2ow *alwys rear div, outpcd 6 out, completed own time* .... R Lochman 7
Stride To Glory (Ire) *alwys rear div, outpcd 6 out* .... D Topping 8
137 Vimchase *alwys rear hlf, outpcd 6 out, p.u. 3 out* .... S J Robinson pu
Midge 5a *alwys rear hlf, outpcd 6 out, p.u. 3 out* .... Mrs F Needham pu
Music In The Night *(fav) alwys rear hlf, outpcd 10th, p.u. 2 out* .... F Hutsby pu
Ocean Sovereign *u.r. 1st* .... T Denniff ur
Missile Man *rear div, outpcd 6 out, p.u. 2 out* S Pinder pu
Mount Faber *alwys last trio, outpcd 6 out, p.u. 3 out* .... S Charlton pu
118[3] Ruff Account *3rd to 4th, fdd 7th 5 out, outpcd nxt, p.u. 2 out* .... N Kent pu
Spalease 5a *mid-div, 6th 5 out, outpcd nxt, p.u. 2 out* .... A Hill pu
16 ran. 3l, 1l, 20l, ½l, 5l, 1 fence, ½l. Time 6m 20.00s. SP 6-1.
Mrs F E Gilman (Cottesmore).

252 Open Maiden Div I

CUT A NICHE .... F Hutsby 1
cls up 3rd/4th, cont 4 out, ld aft 2 out, prmsng
211[3] **Kendor Pass (Ire) .... Dr M Tate 2**
ld to 4th & 8th-6 out, outpcd nxt, ran on agn 3 out
79[2] **Benbeath .... P Gee 3**
(fav) alwys prom, ld 5 out, cont 4-2 out, just outpcd
Flying Quest *nvr dang, 5th outpcd 5 out, ran on* .... S Walker 4
60[7] Pukka Sahib *plld hrd, ld 5-7th, 4th outpcd 5 out* .... Miss H Irving 5
141 Casherooski (Ire) *mid-div 1st m, t.o. 6th 10th, p.u. last* .... Capt E Andrewes pu
Educate Me (Ire) *alwys last, t.o. 10th, p.u. 5 out* .... J Burley pu
Stays Fresh *alwys last trio, t.o. 6 out, p.u. 4 out* .... N Kent pu
Handfast Point *mid-div, imprvng whn slppd lndg 12th* .... C Vale f
9 ran. 5l, 2l, 6l, 20l. Time 6m 25.00s. SP 5-2.
Miss J Pidgeon/N Holloway, P Riddley (Bicester With Whaddon Chase).

253 Open Maiden Div II

JOINT ACCOUNT .... Mrs F Needham 1
made all, jmpng vntly rght, bttr spd on flat
Minikino .... C Vale 2
(fav) alwys 2nd, chsd wnnr last m, alwys held
Bugsy Moran (Ire) .... C Millington 3
last hrd hld, 3rd frm 7th, outpcd frm 4 out
Art's Echo (Ire) *alwys last pair, outpcd frm 10th* P Gee 4
Cawkwell Win 5a *3rd 1st m, last pair, outpcd frm 10th* .... K Needham 5
Tiderunner (Ire) *mstly 4th, outpcd 5 out, p.u. 2 out* .... S Walker pu
6 ran. 2l, 20l, 8l, 1 fence. Time 6m 29.00s. SP 6-1.
Mrs F E Needham (Hurworth).

K.B.

NORTH HEREFORDSHIRE
Newtown
Saturday February 22nd
GOOD

254 Members (12st)

77[1] **PERFECT LIGHT ....R Lee** 1
(fav) pllng, jmpd rght, made all & sn clr, unchal
56[2] **Kingofnobles (Ire) ....R Rogers** 2
chsd wnr to 4th,lost tch 10th,ran on 14th,2nd 2 out,nvr nrr
Cathgal ....Miss C Thomas 3
hld up, prog to chs wnr 12th, no imp 3 out, wknd nxt
90[2] Hennerwood Oak 5a *chsd wnr 4th-12th, wknd, t.o.* ....M P Jones 4
I've Copped It (Ire) *t.o. 4th, p.u. 2 out* ....J Rees pu
Asante Sana 5a *u.r. 2nd* ....J Jackson ur
6 ran. 4l, 12l, 1 fence. Time 6m 38.00s. SP 8-11.
R Lee (North Herefordshire).

255 Confined (12st)

STAG FIGHT ....Julian Pritchard 1
ld to 5th & frm 12th, clr 3 out, ran on strngly
56 **All Weather ....M Wilesmith** 2
rear of main grp, 8th hlfwy, ran on 14th, tk 2nd nr fin
218 **Sterling Buck (USA) ....M Rimell** 3
(fav) cls up, prssd wnr 12th-14th, onepcd aft
Pendil's Delight 5a *rear, 9th & no ch at 13th, ran on 15th, nrst fin*......................T Stephenson 4
Just Marmalade *chsd ldrs, pshd alng 10th, no imp frm 14th*................................A Dalton 5
56[9] Stanford Boy *wll bhnd 5th, t.o. 13th, kpt on aft, nrst fin* ....G Andrew 6
143[1] Roving Report 3ex *bhnd frm 6th, no dang aft* ....Mrs A Rucker 7
Oragas *chsd ldrs til lost tch 11th, no prog aft* ....R Burton 8
Sisterly 5a 3ex *prom, cls 3rd at 14th, wknd rpdly frm nxt*..A Wintle 9
Bowl Of Oats (bl) *prom, ld 5th-12th, wknd nxt, p.u. 3 out*..................................S Blackwell pu
Master Donnington *prom to 11th, wknd 13th, p.u. 3 out*..........................Miss E Wilesmith pu
Gold'n Shroud (Ire) *mid-div, wknd hlfwy, last & t.o. whn p.u. 14th*..........................N Oliver pu
201 Potato Fountain (Ire) 5a *alwys bhnd, t.o. whn ref 3 out* ....M P Jones ref
Mr Dennehy (Ire) *1st ride, last til some prog 9th, no ch whn u.r. 15th*..........................M Butcher ur
14 ran. 10l, ½l, 3l, 10l, 12l, nk, 10l, 6l. Time 6m 35.00s. SP 12-1.
Mrs J A Scott (Worcestershire).

256 Men's Open (12st)

OAKLANDS WORD 7ex ....E Williams 1
(fav) prom, trckd ldr 11th, ld 15th, sn clr, drvn out flat
58[3] **Hill Island ....R Sweeting** 2
ld to 15th, sn outpcd, rallied 2 out, ran on flat
218[6] **Mitchells Best ....T Stephenson** 3
rear, prog 10th, outpcd 15th, ran on 2 out, fin well
Ask Frank 7ex *hld up, prog 10th, outpcd frm 15th, no prog 3 out*..............................H Wheeler 4
55[5] Cawkwell Dean *chsd ldr to 11th, prom aft til outpcd frm 15th*......................................L Lay 5
149 Lighten The Load 4ex *hld up, prog 9th, in tch 13th, onepcd frm nxt*............................A Wintle 6
Welsh Singer 4ex *cls up to 11th, wknd 13th, no ch aft* ....R Lawther 7
98 Electrolyte *rear main grp, effrt 12th, sn outpcd & no ch*...G Austin 8
201[5] Garrylucas 7ex *mstk 3d, cls up to 13th, wknd* ....M Munrowd 9
1[1] Doubting Donna 5a *prom, rdn apr 14th, sn wknd, virt p.u. flat*....................................J Jukes 10
Push Along *in tch in rear to 10th, sn strggling, t.o.* ....D Stephens 11
187[4] Master Eryl 7ex *rear, mstks 7 & 8th, t.o. & p.u. 11th* ....Julian Pritchard pu
Silver Age (USA) *blnd & u.r. 2nd*..........S Shinton ur
191 Rusty Music *in tch to 9th, t.o. whn p.u. 3 out* ....C Richards pu
The Dancing Parson 5a *in tch, mstk 6th, sn bhnd, t.o. & p.u. last* ....M Brown pu
19 Sea Dreams (Ire) *f 2nd* ....J Barnes f
Thornhill 5a *alwys bhnd, t.o. & p.u. 13th* .....L Brown pu
17 ran. 2l, 1½l, 8l, 12l, 1l, 8l, 6l, 2l, 12l, 10l. Time 6m 36.50s. SP 4-5.
F P Luff (Tivyside).

257 G Middleton Ladies

215[3] **MINELLA EXPRESS (IRE) 7ex ...Miss C Spearing** 1
ld 2-5th & frm 9th, mstk 11th, made rest, pshd out
Split Second 7ex ....Miss A Dare 2
(fav) trckd ldrs, chsd wnr 3 out, no imp apr last
57[1] **Blue Cheek 7ex................Miss T Spearing** 3
prom, chsd wnr 14th, mstks nxt 2, sn btn
85[4] Sound Forecast *last til prog 12th, no ch aft nxt, styd on wll frm 3 out*..................Miss D Marfell 4
57[7] Run To Form 4ex *prom, cls 4th whn mstk 14th, sn outpcd*.............................Miss E Wilesmith 5
149 Judy Line 5a *hld up in tch, lost plc 13th, sn bhnd, ran on agn 2 out*.........................Miss V Roberts 6
Highway Five (Ire) *mid-div, mstk 9th, outpcd frm 13th, no ch aft* ....Miss E James 7
Lady Llanfair 5a 4ow *in tch to 12th, sn wknd, p.u. aft 3 out* ....Miss A Meakins pu
187 Origami *in tch, 6th & outpcd 13th, no ch aft, ref last* ....Miss S Duckett ref
Dane Rose 5a *in tch to 11th, wknd, 10th & wll btn whn u.r. 3 out*......................Miss A Sheppard ur
Quarter Marker (Ire) *alwys rear, t.o. last whn p.u. 14th* ....Mrs C Ford pu
218 Warren Boy *ld to 2nd & 5-9th, prom til wknd 14th, p.u. last* ....Miss P Jones pu
12 ran. 3l, 10l, 10l, 1l, 8l, 15l. Time 6m 32.00s. SP 7-2.
A Brazier (Croome & West Warwickshire).

258 Restricted Div I (12st)

SCARLET BERRY 5a ....S Blackwell 1
nt alwys fluent, prom, ld 13th, hrd rdn 2 out, drew clr last
Onemoreanwego 5a ....Miss E James 2
sn trckd ldrs, mstk 11th, jnd wnr 15th, swtchd 2 out, no ext
Guarena (USA) ....N Richards 3
wll bhnd, t.o. 10th, tk poor 3rd nr fin
204 Henrymyson *wll bhnd, t.o. 13th, lft poor 3rd 3 out, wknd*..J Cornes 4
Well Bank *prom to 11th, wknd rpdly 13th, p.u. 15th* ....E Walker pu
222[6] Kingsthorpe *mid-div, prog 9th, chsd ldrs 13th, 4th & btn whn f 15th*............................A Phillips f
184[1] Hal's Prince *(fav) mstks 2nd & 11th, ld to 13th, 3rd & btn whn blnd & u.r. 3out* ....Miss P Jones ur
201 Fire King *wth ldr til f 6th*..................E Collins f
Naburn Loch 5a 2ow *alwys wl bhnd, t.o. & p.u. 13th* ....J Hankinson pu
Derring Run 5a *alwys wll bhnd, t.o. last whn u.r. 12th* ....C Yates ur
Tanner *f 1st*..........................M Hammond f
Fruit Field 5a *schoold & mstks,bhnd,some prog 13th,poor 4th whn p.u.2 out*................T O'Leary pu
Dark Delight 5a *hmpd 1st, wll bhnd, t.o. hlfwy, p.u. 14th* ....A Price pu
Irish Venture (Ire) 4ow *hmdp & u.r. 1st*........J Tudor ur
14 ran. 6l, dist, ½l. Time 6m 38.00s. SP 3-1.
P J Sanderson (Clifton On Teme).

259 Maiden Div I (12st)

AGAINST THE AGENT ....H Wheeler 1
pllng, ld 5th, made rest, toyed wth rival frm 2 out
Clovers Last ....D S Jones 2
chsd wnr 5th, chal 3 out, no ch wth wnr frm nxt

Merry Noelle 5a........................J Jukes 3
(fav) trckd ldrs, 3rd at 10th, no imp 1st pair frm 3 out
Layston Pinzal 5a *wll bhnd, effrt whn mstk 12th, nvr on trms aft*..........................Miss S Wallin 4
Mr Suspicious (Ire) *rear, hmpd 9th, no dang aft*...................................M P Jones 5
Central Lass 5a *t.d.e. mid-div, wknd 9th, t.o. & p.u. 12th*...................................S Blackwell pu
How Suir (Ire) *chsd ldrs, 5th at 10th, wknd 12th, t.o. & p.u. 2 out*...............................M Rimell 0
Millstock 5a *alwys rear, t.o. 13th, p.u. 2 out*...................................G Barfoot-Saunt pu
Wolfie Smith *ld to 5th, wknd 10th, t.o. & p.u. 14th*...................................Julian Pritchard pu
Oh Lord (Ire) *chsd ldrs, 4th whn blnd 11th, sn btn, p.u. 14th*...................................J Rees pu
Ribington *prom til f 9th*....................M Harris f
Miss Jcb (Ire) *n.j.w. bhnd, rdn frm 9th, wll t.o. whn p.u. 3 out*............................M FitzGerald pu
Manard 5a *nvr nr ldrs, t.o. & p.u. 13th*...M Hammond pu
Mr Hatchet (Ire) *pllng, hld up, ran out & u.r. 7th*...................................T Stephenson ro
59 Amerous Lad *alwys bhnd, t.o. 12th, p.u. 3 out*...................................R Rogers pu
Hickory Hollow *n.j.w. wll bhnd, t.o. & p.u. 9th*...................................A Dalton pu
Tirley Gale 7a *in tch in rear, u.r. aft 9th*.....S Joynes ur
Shesagud Girl 5a *jmpd bdly, t.o. whn ran out 5th*...................................S Shinton ro
18 ran. 3l, 6l, 25l, 8l. Time 6m 42.00s. SP 4-1.
J P Price (Radnor & West Hereford).

260 Restricted Div II (12st)

PERRYLINE 5a..................Julian Pritchard 1
hld up, prog 9th, ld 2 out, all out
Purple Melody (Ire)............Miss C Spearing 2
(fav) prom 5th, ld 15th-2 out, ran on flat, just faild
126[4] **Meadow Cottage.................T Stephenson 3**
prom, ld 9-13th, onepcd frm 3 out
Bowland Girl (Ire) 5a *prog to trck ldrs 10th, cls up 14th, onepcd frm 2 out*..............Miss E James 4
Chacer's Imp *prom, ld 13th-15th, wknd aft 3 out*...................................H Wheeler 5
Embu-Meru *alwys wll bhnd, t.o. 10th*.........R Tilley 6
Gidgegannup *in tch to 12th, 7th & no ch whn hmpd 14th & p.u.*...........................M Munrowd pu
Varykinov (Ire) *prom, disp whn blnd & u.r. 10th*...................................M Rimell ur
183[1] Hill Fort (Ire) *mid-div, outpcd 13th, 6th & no ch whn blnd & u.r. 14th*..........................E Williams ur
222 Generator Boy *ld 3-9th, wknd 13th, t.o. & p.u. 2 out*...................................J Baimbridge pu
Cussane Cross (Ire) *mstk 3rd & rmndr, bhnd, some prog 13th, no dang, p.u. 2 out*................A Crow pu
81 Eyton Rock *rear whn u.r. 8th*..............R Burton ur
44 Bride Run (Ire) *rear, 9th & no ch whn f 12th*....A Price f
Layston D'Or *prom, f 5th*......................A Dalton f
190 Hatterill Ridge (bl) *ld to 3rd, wknd 9th, t.o. & p.u. aft 13th*...................................C Richards pu
186 Nikitasecondchance 5a *u.r. 1st*..........D Llewellyn ur
16 ran. Hd, 6l, hd, 8l, 25l. Time 6m 39.00s. SP 7-1.
R Fellows (Ledbury).

261 Maiden Div II (12st)

BAPTIST JOHN (IRE)..................M Harris 1
prom, ld 13th, just hdd & lft clr 2 out
Emerald Charm (Ire) 5a.................J Jukes 2
w.w. prog 9th, btn frm 15th, lft 2nd 2 out
Rusty Fellow..........................D Mansell 3
rear, lost tch frm 13th, styd on 2 out, nrst fin
Belle Chapelle 5a *prom, ld 9-13th, wnd 15th*...................................D S Jones 4
Volcanic Roc *schoold & bhnd, effrt to 8th at 13th, nvr nr ldrs*...................................S Blackwell 5
Sheer Power (Ire) *alwys bhnd, t.o. 12th, p.u. last*...................................M FitzGerald pu
41[2] Marginal Margie 5a *bmpd & f 2nd*........M Munrowd f
87[2] Joyney 5a *chsd ldrs to 12th, wknd, p.u. 3 out*...................................Miss C Thomas pu
Blue Rosette *(fav) hld up, steady prog 12th, just ld & f 2 out*..............................Julian Pritchard f
The Blind Judge *alwys bhnd, t.o. 12th, p.u. aft nxt*...................................G Barfoot-Saunt pu
88 Bel Lane 5a *ld to 9th, wknd 12th, wll bhnd & p.u. 15th*...................................E Williams pu
Greenhills Ruby 5a *rear, wknd 10th, t.o. & p.u. 12th*...................................A Dalton pu
87 Brown Bala 5a *mstks, in tch to 11th, sn wknd, t.o. & p.u. 3 out*...............................C Richards pu
Philelwyn (Ire) 5a *mid-div til wknd & p.u. 10th*...................................Miss E James pu
224 Jimmy Morrel *bhnd, 13th whn u.r. 8th*..T Stephenson ur
Tomsson *bhnd, last whn u.r. 8th*............M Rimell ur
16 ran. 20l, 12l, 6l, 6l. Time 6m 39.00s. SP 12-1.
P R M Philips (Worcestershire).

262 Restricted Div III (12st)

102[1] **GUNNER BOON..................Miss P Jones 1**
(fav) made virt all, drew clr apr last, comf
Trevveethan (Ire)......................M Rimell 2
chsd wnr 9th, chal 14th, rdn & no ext 2 out
189 **Mackabee (Ire)........................T Weale 3**
mid-div, prog 11th, mstk 13th, cls up nxt, sn onepcd
59[2] Ravensdale Lad *cls up, ch 14th, sn wknd*....A Dalton 4
For Michael *rear, lost tch 11th, kpt on onepcd frm 14th, no dang*....................Miss J Houldey 5
Glitterbird 5a *prom til wknd aft 13th, poor 5th whn p.u. 2 out*..............................Julian Pritchard pu
Orwell Ross (Ire) *rear, wll bhnd frm 10th, t.o. & p.u. 14th*...................................A Beedles pu
Strong Trace (Ire) *unruly pddck, in tch to 11th, t.o. & p.u. 14th*...................................L Brown pu
Major Bert (Ire) *mid-div, lost tch 12th, t.o. & p.u. nxt*...................................H Wheeler pu
190 Buckley's Court (bl) *mid-div til blnd & u.r. 8th*...................................E Williams ur
177 Thought Reader (Ire) *cls up to 8th, wknd 12th, t.o. & p.u. 14th*...................................R Sturgis pu
Heather Wood 5a *last & n.j.w., t.o. & p.u. 14th*...................................G Barfoot-Saunt pu
Derring Ann 5a *chsd ldr to 9th, lost tch 12th, t.o. & p.u. 14th*...................................D S Jones pu
Dream Lord *h.j.w. last pair & wll bhnd, t.o. & p.u. 14th*...................................J Price pu
Barafundle Bay *mstk 3rd, prom til wknd 11th, t.o. & p.u. 14th*...................................D Llewellyn pu
15 ran. 6l, 16l, 15l, 15l. Time 6m 37.00s. SP 15-8.
David Brace (Llangeinor).

263 Maiden Div III (12st)

ROCKET RADAR...............Julian Pritchard 1
(fav) trckd ldrs, ld 13th, clr 3 out, easily
88 **Western Pearl (Ire)..................S Blackwell 2**
ld 4-9th, lost plc, effrt to chs wnr aft 13th, btn 15th
In The Water..........................M P Jones 3
prom, wth ldr 10-12th, wknd 15th
Distant-Port (Ire) *prom, mstk 8th, ld nxt to 13th, sn wknd*...................................T Stephenson 4
Roscoe's Gemma 5a *ld to 4th, p.u. nxt*...................................Miss J Houldey pu
Bidden 7a *schoold, alwys last pair, t.o. & p.u. 12th*...................................G Barfoot-Saunt pu
Mis-E-Fishant 5a *cls up to 12th, wknd, t.o. & p.u. 2 out*...................................D Mansell pu
Alcofrolic 5a *prom, 4th whn mstk 12th, p.u. nxt, lame*...................................D S Jones pu
End Of The Run *pllng, in tch til ran out 6th*...................................M FitzGerald ro
190 Spirit Prince 7a 3ow *pllng, just in tch to 12th, t.o. & p.u. 15th*...................................J Price pu
Slim Chance 5a *mstk 3rd, t.o. last til p.u. 12th* P Davis pu
11 ran. 15l, 12l, 10l. Time 6m 51.00s. SP Evens.
R Bunn (Ledbury).
J.N.

SINNINGTON
Duncombe Park

Saturday February 22nd
GOOD

264 Members

167[1] **EARL GRAY** ....**Miss A Deniel** 1
hld up in tch, prog 9th, wnt 2nd 11th,ld apr last,ran on wll
Katies Argument 5a...............**Miss J Wilson** 2
ld to 3rd, rmnd prom, outpcd 12th, kpt on frm 3 out
215[6] **Cadrillon (Fr)** ....**M Bennison** 3
prom, jmp lft 2nd, outpcd 9th, kpt on wll frm 3 out
Miami Bear *chsd ldr til ld 3rd,sn wll clr,tired 4 out,hd apr last,wknd* ....L Russell 4
Just A Single (Ire) 3ow *plld hrd in rear, outpcd 10th, t.o. 13th* ....P Wilkin 5
120 Smith's Melody *prom, wnt 2nd 9th, rddn & outpcd 11th, sn wll bhnd, t.o.* ....M Haigh 6
Private Jet (Ire) *(fav) prom, in chsng grp whn u.r. 6th* ....G Markham ur
77[4] Skyval 5a *rear, lost tch 9th, wll bhnd 12th, t.o. whn p.u. 3 out* ....P Atkinson pu
Highwayman *jmp slwly 1st, rear & lost tch 5th, t.o. 7th, p.u. 13th* ....D Collop pu
9 ran. 1l, 8l, 7l, 25l, 5l. Time 6m 22.00s. SP 3-1.
Mrs A Lockwood (Sinnington).

265 Confined (12st)

215[4] **KELLYS DIAMOND** ....**Miss V Russell** 1
hld up,prog 9th,wnt 3rd 4 out,rddn & ran on strgly,ld nr fin
113[5] **Squires Tale (Ire)** ....**Mrs S Grant** 2
mid-div,prog 9th,chsd ldrs 4 out,ld last,hdd & no ext nr fin
113[1] **Cot Lane 3ex** ....**J Tate** 3
prom, lost plc 13th, styd on wll frm 3 out
113[2] Grain Merchant *(fav) alwys prom, not qckn frm 3 out* ....R Walmsley 4
166[4] Dalmore *reluctant to raceg,gd prog 9th,ld 4 out,sn clr,hd & wkndlast*.........................D Coates 5
Master Cornet 7ex *ld til disp 10th, hdd 4 out, steadd fdd* ....Miss S Brotherton 6
Bugley *prom til fdd 12th, sn wll bhnd, t.o.*....P Jenkins 7
164[2] Skipping Gale *prom, disp ld 10th, wknd 14th, t.o.* ....P Atkinson 8
Black Spur *mid-div til lost tch 6th, sn t.o., p.u. 10th* ....Miss A Armitage pu
164[4] Sharpridge 2ow *rear & lost tch 8th, t.o. 10th, p.u. 12th* ....M Mawhinney pu
Stelzer *mid-div, wknd 10th, t.o. & p.u. aft 12th* ....P Halder pu
Nishkina 3ex *prom, til wknd 11th, blndrd 14th, t.o. & p.u. 3 out* ....C Cundall pu
Tooting Times *mid-div, lost tch 8th, t.o. whn p.u. 12th* ....C Mulhall pu
Engaging *prom til lost plc qckly & p.u. 7th* ....Miss T Jackson pu
113 Simply A Star (Ire) 3ex *mid-div, mstk 5th, rider lost reins & p.u. nxt* ....Major M Watson pu
15 ran. ¾l, 3l, 2l, 5l, 5l, 20l, 3l. Time 6m 11.00s. SP 10-1.
Mrs P A Russell (Middleton).

266 Restricted

213[3] **BARICHSTE (bl)**................**Major M Watson** 1
ld to 3rd, prom, mstk 14th, rddn to ld flat, qcknd clr
Blackwoodscountry ....**C Mulhall** 2
prom, disp ld 12th, ld 2 out, hdd & onepcd flat
118[5] **Attle** ....**W Burnell** 3
prom, ld 10th, disp nxt, hdd & onepcd 2 out
118[7] Spartan Juliet 5a *rear, mstk 11th, kpt on frm 3 out* ....P Jenkins 4+
Computer Pickings 5a *towrds rear, blndrd 4 out, kpt on frm 3 out*..............................F Crawford 4+
Make A Line *mid-div thruout, onepcd frm 3 out* ....C Denny 6
G Derek *rear & lost tch 9th, t.o. whn p.u. 13th* ....P Halder pu
77[5] Here Comes Charter *plld hrd,prom,ld 4th til hd bfr 10th,sn wknd,t.o.& p.u.14th* ....A Pennock pu
213 Miley Pike *mid-div til outpcd 10th, t.o. whn p.u. 14th* ....N Tutty pu
Jolly Ghost *rear, lost tch 8th, t.o. 11th, p.u. 14th* ....P Atkinson pu
Level Vibes *mid-div whn u.r. 6th* ....R Abrahams ur
Vale Of York *rear, prog 7th,ld brfly 10th,sn fdd, wll bhnd whn p.u. 4 out* ....Miss R Clark pu
Lartington Lad 5ow *rear whn u.r. 4th*..........E Wilkin ur
Vickyberto 5a *sn detachd, jmp slwly 1st, ref nxt* ....N Wilson ref
114[1] Harrys Special (Ire) *(fav) prom, wnt 3rd 14th, ev ch whn u.r. 2 out* ....G Tuer ur
114 On The Fly 2ow *lost many l stt,rear whn crashd thru wing & u.r. 7th* ....P Wilkin ur
131[7] River Ramble 5a *rear, prog 10th, chsd ldrs & ev ch whn u.r. 3 out* ....Miss T Jackson ur
168[1] Primitive Star 5a *prom,disp 11th,outpcd 13th,rlld 3 out,ev ch whn f 2 out*..................P Cornforth f
Sparky Brown (Ire) *rear & lost tch 5th, t.o. whn p.u. 8th*..............................D Collop pu
19 ran. 5l, 5l, 7l, dd-ht, 7l. Time 6m 16.00s. SP 5-1.
T A Hughes (Middleton).

267 Land Rover Mens Open (12st)

119 **FLIP THE LID (IRE) 5a**...............**N Tutty** 1
mid-div,prog 9th,wnt 2nd 4 out,lft in ld nxt,hld on wll flat
119[1] **Peanuts Pet** ....**R Walmsley** 2
(fav) hld up,gd prog 4 out,lft in 2nd 3 out,chal flat,not qckn
119[7] **Castle Tyrant 5a** ....**P Atkinson** 3
prom til wknd 14th, t.o. frm 3 out
119 Polynth *rear, jmp slwly 7th, wll bhnd 10th, p.u. 12th* ....G Markham pu
78[1] Pats Cross (Ire) *chsd clr ldr til ld 14th, 3l ld whn u.r. 3 out*..............................J Byrne ur
213[1] Greenmount Lad (Ire) *rear & detachd 9th, wll bhnd whn p.u. 13th* ....P Cornforth pu
166[6] Misti Hunter (Ire) *reluctant to race & v slwly away,alwys wll bhd,p.u. 13th*..............S Swiers pu
177 Electric Committee (Ire) *plld hrd, ld & sn clr, hdd 14th, wknd qckly, f 4 out*..............................A Wood f
8 ran. 1l, dist. Time 6m 4.00s. SP 2-1.
Peter Sawney (Cleveland).

268 Ladies Open

117[2] **DARK DAWN** ....**Miss L Foxton** 1
(fav) comf rddn, hld up in rear, prog 3 out, ld last, pushd out
Integrity Boy ....**Miss A Armitage** 2
disp ld to 3rd,in tch whn lft 2nd 4 out,chal last onepcd
215 **Man Of Mystery** ....**Miss F Hatfield** 3
disp til ld 3rd,just ahd whn lft clr 4 out,hd last,onepcd
165[2] Rustino *alwys rear, strgglng 11th, t.o. whn p.u. 14th* ....Miss R Clark 4
158[1] Precarium (Ire) 1ow *settld in 3rd, whn 2nd 6th, prssng ldr whn f 4 out*..............................Miss S Leach f
5 ran. 5l, ½l, 25l. Time 6m 9.00s. SP Evens.
Mrs J M Newitt (Sinnington).

269 Open Maiden (5-7yo)

114 **PHARLINDO (IRE)** ....**W Burnell** 1
keen, prom, ld 6th, qcknd clr last, comf
169[2] **Yodeller Bill** ....**C Mulhall** 2
prom, wnt 2nd 10th, ev ch apr last, not qckn
116 **Lingcool 5a**..............................**N Wilson** 3
ld to 3rd, prom til fdd 14th, hmpd 3 out, t.o.
115 Abbey Moss *prom, ld 3rd, hdd 6th, wknd 12th, t.o. 3 out*..............................Miss J Eastwood 4
208 Cruikit Rainbow (Ire) 5a *prom til wknd 11th, t.o. 3 out* ....M Bennison 5
Lord George *alwys strgglng, t.o. whn p.u. 13th* ....P Atkinson pu

Euro Thyne (Ire) *(fav) mid-div whn mstk 13th, sn fdd, p.u. bfr last, dismntd*..................Miss A Deniel pu
Blank Cheque *mid-div, prog 13th, cls 3rd whn f 3 out*..D Coates f
168³ Lakeland Venture 5a *rear, p.u. 7th, lame*......N Tutty pu
Another Daughter 5a *mid-div, mstk 10th, sn wknd, f 13th*..J Sinnott f
115 Look Sharpe *mid-div, prog 12th, 3rd & ev ch whn f 4 out*..A Bonson f
Daredevil (Ire) *rear & sn detachd, wll bhnd 10th, p.u. 12th*..A Ogden pu
116 Kowloon Bay (Ire) *alwys rear, t.o. whn p.u. 10th*..M Haigh pu
116 West Lutton 7a *rear, mstk 3rd, u.r. nxt*..Major M Watson ur
Ellerton Tony 7a *alwys in rear, wll bhnd 14th, p.u. 2 out*..S Swiers pu
Rambling-Girl 5a *prom, jmp slwly 1st, fdd 10th, lost tch 12th, p.u. 4 out*..........C Gibbon pu

16 ran. 4l, dist, 20l, sht-hd. Time 6m 16.00s. SP 7-1.
Mrs J W Furness (Hurworth).

SUFFOLK
Ampton
Saturday February 22nd
GOOD

270 Members

29¹ **BALLYALLIA CASTLE (IRE) ....N Bloom 1**
(fav) ld to 3rd & 5-15th, rdn 2 out, ran on to ld run in.
195 **Counterbid ....A Sansome 2**
trckd ldrs,ld gng wll 15th,rdn 2 out,nt run on, hdded run in
65⁴ **Cool Apollo (NZ) ....G Plenderleith 3**
chsd ldrs, 4th & outpcd 17th, kpt on onepcd frm nxt.
123⁶ Noble Knight (Ire) *ld 3-5th, blnd 15th, ev ch 17th, wknd appr 2 out*..C Jarvis 4
8 Old Dundalk (bl) *rr, lsng tch & blnd 7th,rdn 12th, no resp, t.o. & p.u. 16th*........................N King pu
124 Major Inquiry (USA) *trkd ldrs, 4th & btn whn p.u. 17th*..G Pewter pu
Foxes Dance 5a *sn wll bhnd, t.o. & p.u. 12th*..D Parravani pu
Georges Ginger Wine *1st ride, in tch til wknd qkly 7th, t.o. & p.u. 12th*........................Miss J Dudley pu

8 ran. ½l, 15l, 8l. Time 6m 43.00s. SP 4-5.
A F J Moss (Suffolk).

271 Confined (12st)

MISTER MAIN MAN (IRE) ....S Sporborg 1
(fav) cls up, ld 3rd, made rest, shkn up & drw clr appr 2 out,easy
154⁶ **Emsee-H 5ex........................A Sansome 2**
w.w. prog 7th, chsd wnr 3 out, sn rdn & no ex
124³ **Airtrak (Ire) 10ex ....R Barrett 3**
alwys prom, chsd wnr 8-3 out, onepcd und press
64 Nibble *chsd ldrs, 4th & rdn appr 3 out, onepcd aft*..A Coe 4
123³ Druid's Lodge *chsd ldrs, mstk 7th, 5th & outpcd 14th, no dang aft*..T Bulgin 5
193 Smart Pal *mid-div, prog 7th, j.s. 9th, 6th & outpcd 14th, no dang aft*........................C Barlow 6
King Cash *hld up, prog to mid-div 14th, nvr rchd ldrs*..S R Andrews 7
El Bae *rr div, mstk 6th, nvr nr ldrs*..........P Taiano 8
194³ Jimmy Mac Jimmy *mstks, chsd ldrs to 6th, no ch & j.s 14th, t.o.*........................C Ward-Thomas 9
122³ Valatch *bhnd frm 7th, t.o.*..............J Henderson 10
Woodhay Hill *cls up to 4th, lst pl nxt, t.o. frm 12th*..J Knowles 11
194 Ragtime Song *prom to 7th, grad lst pl, t.o.*...M Gingell 12
122² Solid (Ire) *ld to 3rd, wknd 12th, t.o. & p.u. 3 out*..M Barnard pu
64⁵ Sarazar (USA) *bhnd, last & p.u. 10th*...Miss H Pewter pu
Unique Tribute *alwys rr, t.o. & p.u. 3 out*..Capt D Parker pu

15 ran. 6l, 3l, 4l, 20l, 2l, ½l, 1½l, 10l, 20l, 8l. Time 6m 39.00s. SP 3-1.
Sir Chippendale Keswick (Puckeridge).

272 Ladies

219⁸ **GREEN ARCHER ....Mrs T Hill 1**
bhnd & j.s 5th, prog to ld 9th, made rest, j.s.2 out,styd on
195¹ **St Gregory (bl)......................Mrs L Gibbon 2**
(fav) chsd wnr frm 7th, 4l down 16th, hd rdn nxt, styd on run in
11 **Rousillon To Be ....Miss L Rowe 3**
ld/disp til ld 7-9th, lst tch wth 1st 2 frm nxt, t.o.
66⁴ Waterloo Andy *sn wll bhnd, sme late prog, nrly snatched 3rd*........................Miss J Cook 4
125⁶ Notary-Nowell (bl) *wth ldrs, rn wde aft 1st, bhnd & rdn 14th, no resp, t.o.*................Miss S Gritton 5
High Beacon (bl) *wth ldrs til wknd qkly 7th, p.u. appr nxt, lame*........................Miss H Pewter pu
57² Larry The Lamb *f 2nd*..............Mrs C McCarthy f

7 ran. 2l, dist, ½l, 25l. Time 6m 34.00s. SP 5-1.
Mrs S D Walter (Vale Of Aylesbury).

273 Land Rover Open (12st)

151 **OVER THE EDGE 7ex ....S Sporborg 1**
made all, pushed clr 3 out, nt extnd
Samsword ....John Pritchard 2
blnd badly 2nd, lft 2nd 12th, rdn 3 out, kpt on one-pcd
223⁷ **Solar Gem ....J Mason 3**
j.s. 1st, in tch, lft 4th 12th, rdn 17th, kpt on
192¹ Creeves Nephew *w.w. in tch, lft 3rd 12th, no prog frm 3 out*........................Capt D Parker 4
138¹ Lucky Christopher 7ex *(fav) prom, no room on inner whn trd to ref & u.r. 12th*....................G Tarry ur
124² River Melody 5a *cls up til badly hmpd & u.r. 12th*..T Moore ur
Cardinal Red 7ex *prom til badly hmpd 12th, nt rcvr, p.u. nxt*........................A Sansome pu

7 ran. 4l, 6l, 10l. Time 6m 51.00s. SP 9-2.
Christopher Sporborg (Puckeridge).
ONE FENCE OMITTED. 19 JUMPS

274 Restricted (12st)

12² **BALLYDESMOND (IRE) ....S Sporborg 1**
(fav) made virt all, rdn & styd on strngly frm 2 out
198⁴ **Whats Another 5a ....Miss K Bridge 2**
chsd ldrs, chsd wnr & ev ch 3 out, onepcd frm nxt
Grassington (Ire) ....S Quirk 3
in tch, prog 7th, 3rd & rdn 3 out, onepcd
128¹ Zoes Pet 5a *cls up, disp ld 3-6th, 4th & mstk 17th, wll btn nxt*........................Miss H Pewter 4
Buckwheat Lad (Ire) *alwys bhnd, mstk 12th, nvr nr ldrs*..A Westrope 5
123 Current Attraction 5a *prom til f 7th*.........M Barnard f
140² Miss Solitaire 5a *n.j.w. sn wll bhnd, t.o. & p.u. 9th*..Mrs C McCarthy pu
64 Alice Sheer Thorn (Ire) 5a *in tch til b.d. 7th*..M Gingell bd
61¹ Lord Knox (Ire) *prom, ld 8-12th, 5th & wkng 16th, t.o. & p.u. 2 out*........................R Gill pu
Courier's Way (Ire) *mstks, in tch bad mstk 9th, last frm nxt til p.u. 14th*........................T Moore pu

10 ran. 2l, 4l, 12l, 10l. Time 6m 43.00s. SP 2-1.
Christopher Sporborg (Puckeridge).

275 Open Maiden (12st)

REEL RASCAL 5a.......................P Keane 1
mid-div, stdy prog to ld appr 3 out, clr nxt, rdn out
Carlinare ....S Cowell 2
in tch, j.s. 7th, prog 9th, chsd wnr 3 out, kpt on wll
15³ **Ticklebay 5a.............................A Coe 3**
chsd ldrs, disp ld 13th til appr 3 out, wknd 2 out
Wolfhill Lad (Ire) *(fav) ld 2-4th & 6th mstk & rmdr 15th, hdded & wknd appr 3 out*..............S R Andrews 4
196 Alycount (USA) *bhnd, mstk 11th, kpt on frm 3 out, nvr nrr*..V Coogan 5
197 Arkay *ld to 2nd & 4-6th, wknd 12th, t.o.*........R Kerry 6
Linlithgow Palace *mid-div, outpcd 11th, no ch whn u.r. last*........................Mrs J Morrison ur

60 Over The Lake (Ire) 5a *rr, rmdrs & hdwy 9th, outpcd 14th, no ch & p.u. 3 out, lame* ....R Barrett pu
61 Harry Tartar *u.r. 5th*..................Capt D Parker ur
Just Mai-Bee 7a *n.j.w. bhnd til p.u. 12th*......C Ward-Thomas pu
10 ran. 2l, 8l, 10l, 5l, dist. Time 6m 56.00s. SP 3-1.
Mrs A Villar (Suffolk).

276 Open Maiden (12st)

PRINCE BUCK (IRE) ....P Hacking 1
(fav) mstks, chsd ldrs, wnt 2nd 13th, ld 2 out, styd on und press
Storming Roy ....H Nicholson 2
prom, ld 13th-2 out, kpt on wll
30 **The Prior ....P Rowe 3**
bhnd, prog 11th, ev ch 17th, no ex appr 2 out
61 Thurles Pickpocket (Ire) *chsd ldrs, ev ch 17th, wknd 3 out*..............................A Coe 4
197 Alapa *pllng, ld 2nd til r.o. nxt*..................V Coogan ro
122[5] Royal Quarry *mstks, wll bhnd frm 10th, t.o. & p.u. 16th* ....Miss A Eaton pu
El Guapo *pllng, lft in ld 3rd, hdded 13th, wkng whn blnd nxt & p.u.*..........................P Chinery pu
126 Fiddlers Goodwill *wth ldrs, mstk 7th, lst pl 11th, wll bhnd whn p.u. 17th*........................C Ward pu
122[4] Times Leader *in tch, 5th & btn whn u.r. 3 out* ....Miss K Hills ur
61 Wise Point (Ire) *sn wll bhnd, t.o. whn r.o. 8th*...G Lush ro
My Shout 7a *hld up, in tch, 6th & ch 16th, outpcd 3 out, p.u. last*..............................S Morris pu
Grangewick Kelly 5a *bhnd 4th, prog 7th, lst pl 11th, t.o. & p.u. 14th*.........................S Dobson pu
12 ran. 3l, 12l, 10l. Time 6m 44.00s. SP 4-5.
Mike Roberts (East Sussex & Romney Marsh).
S.P.

MID SURREY FARMERS DRAGHOUNDS
Charing
Sunday February 23rd
GOOD

277 Members

STRUGGLES GLORY (IRE) ....D Robinson 1
(fav) prom, ld 8th til mstk 11th, ld 14th, sn clr, ran on strngly
Daddy Long Leggs ....R Hubbard 2
prom, ld 11-14th, sn outpcd, fin tired
59[4] **Some Tourist (Ire) ....Miss C Benstead 3**
1st ride, wth ldr to 7th, 3rd & outpcd frm 15th
56 Doran's Town Lad 5a *nrly u.r. 2nd, alwys bhnd, t.o. 13th*...................................N Benstead 4
Devil's Valley *made most to 8th, wknd 12th, t.o. whn ref last*.......................................S Fisher ref
Kelburne Lad (Ire) *hld up, effrt 11th, wkind 15th, poor 4th & p.u. 2 out*..............................P Bull pu
6 ran. 20l, 3l, 1 fence. Time 6m 22.00s. SP 4-5.
D C Robinson (Mid Surrey Farmers Drag).

278 Interlink Restricted

MOUNTAINOUS VALLEY (IRE) ......S R Andrews 1
chsd clr ldr, ld 16th, mstk nxt, drvn out
148 **Stalbridge Bill ....Miss A Goschen 2**
hld up, prog 12th, ev ch whn mstk 3 out, ran on
106[2] **Prince's Gift ....A Phillips 3**
(fav) w.w. prog 12th, 5th & in tch 16th, kpt on one-pcd
Salemhady (Ire) *mstks, in tch, prog 13th, cls up 3 out, no ext*..P Bull 4
126[3] Swift Reward 5a (e/s) *mid-div, lost tch 15th, t.o.* ....W Wales 5
59 Linlake Lightning 5a (bl) *alwys rear, t.o.* Miss H Irving 6
Abdul Emir *alwys rear, lost tch 12th, t.o.*..Mrs L Stock 7
143[3] Mount Patrick *alwys bhnd, t.o.*.............C Lawson 8
Mayfair Maiden 5a *s.s. schoold in last & t.o. til p.u. 13th*...A Hickman pu
146[1] Normead Lass 5a *mid-div, lost tch & p.u. 16th* ....A Martin pu
126 Fort Diana 1ow *mid-div, wknd 11th, t.o. & p.u. 14th* ....M Jones pu
Basher Bill *prom whn mstk 2nd, rear frm 8th, t.o. & p.u. 15th* ....K Giles pu
126 Doctor Dick (Ire) *s.s. 16th whn u.r. 2nd*.......T Walsh ur
Cool Bandit (Ire) *jmpd rght, clr ldr til hdd 16th, ev ch whn u.r. 2 out*.................................T Hills ur
Harmony River (Ire) 5a *chsd ldrs, hmpd 8th, lost tch & p.u. 16th*..........................Miss C Holliday pu
Prime Course (Ire) *prom to 11th, wknd & p.u. 14th* ....C Gordon pu
Croft Court *hld up, prog 11th, nvr rchd ldrs, 6th whn eased & p.u. last*..........................P Hacking pu
17 ran. 2l, 2l, 6l, 1 fence, 4l, 1 fence, 1l. Time 6m 26.50s. SP 7-1.
N W Padfield (Enfield Chace).

279 Confined (12st)

AMERICAN EYRE ....Miss S Gladders 1
trckd ldrs, clsd 16th, rdn nxt, ld last, ran on well
125 **Monksfort ....Miss C Holliday 2**
(fav) t.d.e. prssd ldr, chal & lvl last, not qckn flat
Country Vet 5a ....C Gordon 3
not fluent, in tch, hrd rdn frm 16th, styd on onepcd
Kates Castle 5a *made most, blnd 3 out, mstk nxt, hdd & wknd last*..........................J Van Praagh 4
142[2] Sky Venture 5ex *trckd ldrs, rdn 14th, sn wknd, p.u. last*..P Bull pu
124[4] Ok Corral (USA) 1ow *in tch til rdn & wknd 14th, t.o. & p.u. 16th*..A Greig pu
Saluting Walter (USA) *plld hrd, prom til wknd 8th, stppd 11th*.................................T McCarthy pu
58 Valibus (Fr) 8ex *last pair & wll bhnd til p.u. 10th* ....P Scouller pu
Early Man *trckd ldng pair til eased & p.u. 16th* ....P Hacking pu
Rough Aura *last & t.o. til p.u. 10th*..........P Blagg pu
10 ran. 3l, 2l, 2l. Time 6m 28.00s. SP 16-1.
J S S Hollins (Ashford Valley).

280 Ladies

145[3] **TUDOR HENRY ....Mrs C Mitchell 1**
nrly u.r. 2nd, ld 8th-apr 16th, ld apr last, just hld on
Our Survivor ....Miss C Savell 2
trckd ldrs, rdn 16th, styd on wll flat, just faild
57 **Sperrin View 5a ....Miss S Wallin 3**
(fav) not fluent, trckd ldrs, ld apr 16th til apr last, sn btn
Durbo *trckd ldrs going wll til not qckn frm 16th, one-pcd* ....Mrs E Coveney 4
Thamesdown Tootsie 5a *made most to 8th, outpcd frm 16th*..............................Miss V Lyon 5
145[7] Dayadan (Ire) *jmpd v slowly 1st, alwys rear, t.o. 12th* ....Miss J Sawyer 6
125[4] Profligate *alwys last pair, t.o. 12th*......Miss P Ellison 7
Bright Hour *prom, wkng whn nrly u.r. 10th, t.o. & p.u. 14th*...Miss J Grant pu
143[2] Button Your Lip *alwys bhnd, t.o. & p.u. 14th* ....Mrs J Enderby pu
57 Hiram B Birdbath (bl) *mid-div, 6th & wkng whn p.u. 14th*..................................Miss A Plunkett pu
Paperwork Boy *alwys last pair, t.o. & p.u. 16th* ....Miss F Taylor pu
126[5] Velka 5a *mid-div, 7th & losng tch whn f 12th* ....Mrs S Hickman f
12 ran. Nk, 7l, 6l, 6l, 1 fence, 2l. Time 6m 22.00s. SP 16-1.
J W Mitchell (Garth & South Berks).

281 Men's Open

91[4] **STEDE QUARTER ....P Bull 1**
prom, ld 12th, made rest, rdn clr apr last
Burromariner ....S Cowell 2
alwys prom, prssd wnr frm 12th til no ext apr last
150[4] **Annio Chilone ....P O'Keeffe 3**
made most to 7th, trckd ldrs aft, not qckn frm 2 out
194[5] Take The Town *prom, ld 7th-12th, mstk 14th, outpcd frm nxt*...M Jones 4
144 Nemuro (USA) *trckd ldrs, pshd alng frm 12th, nvr able to chal*...............................P Scouller 5

Yeoman Farmer *hld up, nvr rchd ldrs* ...... P Hacking 6
144 Folk Dance 2ow *mid-div to 8th, rear aft, t.o.* ...... F Jackson 7
151 Faringo *alwys rear, lost tch 12th, t.o.* ...... W Gowlett 8
Oxbow (bl) *hld up, rdn & no prog 13th, t.o. & p.u. last* ...... T McCarthy pu
Darkbrook *alwys bhnd, t.o. & p.u. 14th* ...... G Hopper pu
The Portsoy Loon *wth ldrs til rdn & lost plc 12th, wll bhnd whn p.u. last* ...... A Greig pu
144[1] Ardbrennan *(fav) rear, f 2nd* ...... C Bennett f
12 ran. 5l, ½l, 12l, ½l, 12l, 20l, 6l. Time 6m 29.00s. SP 7-1.
Mrs S Dench (Ashford Valley).
One fence omitted final two circuits, 17 jumps.

282 Intermediate (12st)

SOVEREIGN SPRAY (IRE) ...... P Hacking 1
(fav) trckd ldrs, ld 14th, hrd rdn aft 3 out, all out
112[2] **Stalbridge Gold 5a ...... Miss A Goschen 2**
w.w. trckd wnr 14th, chal & mstk 16th, not qckn 2 out
Greenhill Fly Away ...... P Bull 3
ld to 13th, wknd 15th
148[2] Fowling Piece *novice-rdn, immed bhnd, mstk 5th, t.o. nxt* ...... M Legg 4
More Of It *trckd ldr, ld 13-14th, wknd nxt, p.u. 16th* ...... P Hall pu
King's Maverick (Ire) *hld up in tch, wknd rpdly 15th, p.u. nxt* ...... C Gordon pu
28[1] Sweet Merenda (Ire) 5a *prom til f 10th* ...... S Cowell f
7 ran. 2l, 30l, 1 fence. Time 6m 35.00s. SP 5-2.
S P Tindall (Southdown & Eridge).

283 Open Maiden Div I (12st)

41 **DIAMOND WIND (USA) 5a ...... A Beedles 1**
(fav) made all, drew clr 3 out, comf
Crock D'Or ...... C Gordon 2
alwys prom, 4th & rdn 15th, kpt on to chs wnr apr last
Charlie Kelly ...... P Taiano 3
alwys prom, prssd wnr 9th to 15th, no ext, fin tired
147[2] And Why Not *mid-div, prog 9th, mstk 13th, 3rd & rdn 3 out, no ext, tired* ...... J Van Praagh 4
110[2] Muskerry Moya (Ire) 5a *hld up bhnd, lost tch 13th, t.o.* ...... Miss A Goschen 5
146[5] Jobingo *blnd 2nd, prom til wknd 15th, t.o. & p.u. last* ...... Daniel Dennis pu
69 Red Channel (Ire) *s.s. plld hrd, hld up, some prog 11th, no ch whn p.u. 14th* ...... A Hickman pu
Very Rare (Ire) 5a *hmpd & u.r. 2nd* ...... Miss C Holliday ur
Serious Money (USA) *1st ride, s.s. t.o. til p.u. 15th* ...... Miss C Ewart pu
126 Tasmanite *chsd ldrs, rdn & wknd 12th, 7th whn p.u. 14th* ...... G Hopper pu
Tartan Glory 5a *alwys bhnd, t.o. & p.u. 15th* ...... Mrs N Ledger pu
Run For Brownie (Ire) *prom to 5th, wknd rpdly, p.u. 8th* ...... P Hall pu
128 Soon Be Back *f 2nd* ...... R Barrett f
127 Commasarris 7a 1ow *prssd wnr to 11th, wknd rpdly, t.o. & p.u. 14th* ...... P Blagg pu
Straight Touch 12a *alwys rear, t.o. & p.u. 12th* ...... P O'Keeffe pu
Psamead 7a *s.s. schoold & t.o. til p.u. 12th* ...... P York pu
16 ran. 8l, 5l, 6l, 5l. Time 6m 36.00s. SP 5-2.
Count K Goess-Saurau (Tedworth).
One fence omitted final two circuits, 17 jumps.

284 Open Maiden Div II (12st)

GREYBURY STAR (IRE) ...... P Bull 1
10s-6s, prom, lft in ld 14th, reluc frm 4 out, all out
Shanagore Hill (Ire) ...... P Picton-Warlow 2
ld 6-11th, lft 2nd 14th, plodded on
128 **Ishma (Ire) ...... D Page 3**
sn wll bhnd, t.o. 8th, lft 4th aft 14th, kpt on
Silly Sovereign 5a *sn wll bhnd, t.o. 8th, lft poor 3rd aft 14th, no prog* ...... T Hills 4
Coral Eddy *t.o. 8th, fin own time* ...... Mrs L Stock 5
Wednesdays Auction (Ire) *s.s. t.o. til p.u. 13th* ...... S Garrott pu
Harington Hundreds *prom til wknd 11th, wll bhnd & p.u. 14th* ...... C Gordon pu
Huckleberry Friend 5a *mid-div, 8th & out of tch whn u.r. 9th* ...... P Blagg ur
21 Lixwm 5a *(fav) trckd ldrs til f 10th* ...... C Vigors f
Phaedair *prom til f 10th* ...... M Jones f
General Jackie (Ire) *u.r. 1st* ...... A Hickman ur
196 Reign Dance *8s-4s, made most to 6th, wknd & p.u. 14th, lame* ...... T McCarthy pu
Dad's Delight 5a *u.r. 2nd* ...... Miss A Goschen ur
Half Moon Spinney *sn wll bhnd, t.o. 8th, p.u. 13th* ...... S Cowell pu
Bozen Green (Ire) 7a *sn bhnd, mstk 6th, t.o. 8th, p.u. 12th* ...... S R Andrews pu
Spanish Pal (Ire) *s.s. t.o. til p.u. 11th* Miss S Gladders 0
Martha's Boy (Ire) 4ow *prom, ld 11th, drawing clr whn f 14th* ...... D Robinson f
17 ran. 8l, 6l, 15l, 2 fences. Time 6m 55.00s. SP 6-1.
Mrs D B A Silk (Kent & Surrey Bloodhounds).
J.N.

TAUNTON
Wednesday February 26th
GOOD TO SOFT

285 4¼m 110yds Mitford Slade Challenge Trophy Hunters' Chase Class H

149[3] **RUSTY BRIDGE 12.8 7a ...... Mr R Burton 1**
made all, clr from 9th, hit 3 out, styd on well.
151[1] **Vicompt de Valmont 12.8 7a ...... Mr J Tizzard 2**
(fav) soon well bhnd, rdn along from 7th, hit 22nd, styd on to go 2nd after 2 out, not reach wnr.
149 **Kettles 11.0 7a ...... Mr A Phillips 3**
alwys in tch, effort to cl on ldrs 16th, styd on same pace from 3 out.
219[3] Sirisat 11.12 7a *chsd ldrs, blnd 11th, styd on again from 14th, one pace from 3 out.* ...... Miss T Blazey 4
173[1] Expressment 11.12 7a *hit 6th, bhnd from 12th, t.o..* ...... Mr G Penfold 5
179[5] Final Express 11.0 7a *bhnd from 6th, t.o..* ...... Miss S Vickery 6
Golden Mac 11.5 7a *prom, wknd 17th, t.o. and virtually p.u. run-in.* ...... Major O Ellwood 7
98[4] Nearly Splendid 12.8 7a *hit 6th, blnd 8th, hdwy 17th, t.o. when p.u. before 2 out.* ...... Mr T Greed pu
59[7] Misty (NZ) 11.5 7a *chsd ldrs to 11th, t.o. when p.u. before 3 out.* ...... Mr J M Pritchard pu
98[5] Afterkelly 11.12 7a *bhnd from 12th, t.o. when p.u. before 21st..* ...... Mr I Dowrick pu
54[8] Princess Wenllyan 11.0 7a *hdwy 14th, wknd 18th, t.o. when p.u. before 3 out.* ...... Mr A Holdsworth pu
186[2] Lazzaretto 11.5 7a *t.o. from 5th, p.u. before 23rd.* ...... Mr I Johnson pu
Noisy Welcome 11.7 7a 2ow *f 4th.* ...... Mr M P Jones f
151 Major Mac 11.5 7a *chsd ldrs to 11th, lost tch 15th, t.o. when p.u. before 3 out.* ...... Mr S Durack pu
Conna Moss (Ire) 11.7 5a *mid div till blnd and u.r. 10th.* ...... Mr J Jukes ur
91 Rising Sap 11.5 7a *hit 6th, hdwy 13th, wknd 18th, t.o. when p.u. before 3 out.* ...... Mr A Dalton pu
16 ran. 7l, 3l, ½l, dist, dist. Time 9m 55.50s. SP 20-1.
I K Johnson

HUNTINGDON
Thursday February 27th
GOOD TO SOFT

286 3m Colmworth Hunters' Chase Class H

153[1] **MR BOSTON 12.5 ...... Mr S Swiers 1**
(fav) patiently rdn, steady hdwy to chase ldr final cct, ld before 2 out, styd on strly run-in.
109 **Granville Guest 11.7 7a ...... Mr J Tizzard 2**
settld with chasing gp, gd hdwy to join ldng pair after 3 out, effort and wandered run-in, no ext.
151 **Colonial Kelly 12.4 3a ...... Mr P Hacking 3**

settld in tch, went 2nd hfwy, feeling pace final cct, no impn from 3 out.

150[1] Loyal Note 12.4 3a *not fluent, in tch, went handy after one cct, struggling 6 out, no impn after.* ....Mr Simon Andrews 4

Gay Ruffian 11.7 7a *alwys chasing ldrs, went handy after one cct, struggling 6 out, soon lost tch, t.o.* ....Miss C Dyson 5

125[1] Richard Hunt 11.7 7a *struggling to keep up after one cct, t.o. when p.u. apr 3 out.* ....Miss L Rowe pu

Fire And Reign (Ire) 11.7 7a *n.j.w., feeling pace when f 4th.* ....Mr N King f

Itsgoneoff 11.9 5a *ld and soon clr, not fluent final cct, hdd after 3 out, 3rd when p.u. before next, broke down, destroyed.* ....Mr B Pollock pu

8 ran. 5l, 12l, 1½l, 27l. Time 6m 27.20s. SP 8-11.
M K Oldham

287 3m Langford End Novices' Hunters' Chase Class H

194[1] **BITOFAMIXUP (IRE) 12.2 3a ....Mr P Hacking** 1
(Co fav) chsd ldrs, lost pl 11th, rallied next, ld 5 out, driven out.

216[2] **Ask Antony (Ire) 12.0 5a ....Mr N Wilson** 2
(Co fav) patiently rdn, hdwy hfwy, chsd wnr from 2 out, kept on.

55[1] **Broad Steane 12.0 5a ....Mr A Sansome** 3
(Co fav) chsd ldrs, ld 13th, hdd 5 out, wknd apr 2 out.

Ideal Partner (Ire) 11.12 7a *waited with, imp 9th, wknd 3 out, t.o.* ....Mr J Tizzard 4

225[2] Sands Of Gold (Ire) 11.12 7a *ld to 13th, wknd apr 3 out, t.o.* ....Mr L Lay 5

91[2] Lurriga Glitter (Ire) 11.12 7a *waited with, imp 11th, wknd apr 4 out, t.o.* ....Mr S Joynes 6

214[3] Coolvawn Lady (Ire) 11.7 7a *well pld, hit 13th, wknd after 4 out, t.o.* ....Mr S Walker 7

Multi Line 11.7 7a *sluggish start, rcvred to race in tch to 13th, lost pl, t.o.* ....Miss C Townsley 8

True Steel 12.0 5a *alwys bhnd, t.o. when p.u. before 5 out.* ....Mr J Trice-Rolph pu

250 La Fontainbleau (Ire) 11.12 7a *alwys in rear, t.o. when p.u. before 5 out.* ....Mr A Rebori pu

151 Amadeus (Fr) 11.12 7a *settld midfield, feeling pace 8th, t.o. when p.u. before 13th.* ....Mr C Ward pu

Taura's Rascal 11.12 7a *chasing ldrs when f 7th.* ....Mr F Brennan f

Dad's Pipe 11.12 7a *bhnd when f 3rd.* Mr T E G Smith f

13 ran. 1¼l, 15l, dist, 1l, 3l, dist, 1¼l. Time 6m 30.60s. SP 7-2.
Mike Roberts

LUDLOW
Thursday February 27th
GOOD

288 3m Weatherbys Hunter Chase Planner Hunters' Chase Class H

149[2] **CAPE COTTAGE 11.7 7a ....Mr A Phillips** 1
held up, hdwy 12th, ld 3 out, styd on.

Fox Pointer 11.9 5a..................Mr J Jukes 2
soon trckd ldr, ld apr 5 out, hdd 2 out, one pace.

93[1] **Inch Maid 11.9 7a..............Miss H Brookshaw** 3
(fav) prom till lost pl 5 out, styd on from 2 out.

149 J B Lad 11.7 7a *prom to 6th, bhnd when mstk 9th, t.o.* ....Miss P Gundry 4

223 Welsh Lightning 11.7 7a *mstks in rear, t.o. from 12th.* ....Capt R Inglesant 5

Kingfisher Bay 11.7 7a *bhnd when blnd 11th, soon t.o.* ....Mr G Shenkin 6

144[2] Star Oats 11.7 7a *hit 3rd, ld 5th, soon clr, hit 9th, hdd apr 5 out, wknd quickly, p.u. before next, lame.* ....Mr A Kinane pu

93 King Of Shadows 12.0 7a *ld to 5th, mstk 11th, soon bhnd, t.o. when p.u. before 2 out.* ....Mr S Prior pu

8 ran. 3l, ¾l, dist, dist, sht-hd. Time 6m 9.00s. SP 7-2.
D J Caro

KELSO
Friday February 28th
GOOD TO SOFT

289 3m 1f Alba Country Foods Hunters' Chase Class H

JIGTIME 11.7 7a ....Mr M Bradburne 1
(fav) cl up, ld 12th, strly pressed from 2 out, driven clr after last.

133[2] **Royal Jester 12.7 5a.................Mr C Storey** 2
alwys handy, chal 10th, pushed along from 3 out, styd on same pace.

152[1] **Howayman 11.12 7a.................Mr A Parker** 3
held up, hdwy hfwy, 2nd when hit 2 out, hmpd last, no ext.

152 Little Wenlock 12.3 5a *held up in tch, pushed along to chase lding gp 3 out, one pace between last 2.* ....Mrs V Jackson 4

156[2] Fordstown (Ire) 12.1 7a *ld to 6th, jmpd slowly and lost pl 9th, rallied to chal 14th, driven and no ext between last 2.* ....Mr Jamie Alexander 5

35[5] Little General 12.5 7a *in tch, dropped rear 13th, struggling apr 2 out, soon no dngr.* ....Mr T Scott 6

Savoy 11.12 7a *held up, hit 6th, cld hfwy, pressing wnr when f last.* ....Capt A Ogden f

229 Buck's Delight (Ire) 11.9 3a *ld 6th to 12th, wknd quickly 4 out, p.u. before next.* ....Mr C Bonner pu

8 ran. 12l, 6l, ¾l, 14l, 14l. Time 6m 43.70s. SP 5-2.
J W Hughes

NEWBURY
Friday February 28th
GOOD TO SOFT

290 3m Peter Hamer Memorial Hunters' Chase Class H

151 **HOLLAND HOUSE 12.0 5a...........Mr C Vigors** 1
(fav) made all, hit 5 out and next, clr when mstk 3 out, unchal.

149[1] **Miss Millbrook 11.7 7a.............Mr E Williams** 2
held up, mstk 3rd, blnd and lost pl 11th, left third 3 out, styd on to go 2nd run-in.

112[3] **Clobracken Lad 11.2 7a ....Mr G Baines** 3
chsd wnr to 10th and again 5 out till wknd run-in.

227[2] Mediane (USA) 11.7 3a 1ow (v) *unruly start, ref to race.* ....Mr Simon Andrews r

94[2] Principle Music (USA) 11.2 7a *held up, hdwy when hit 9th, chsd wnr next to 5 out, btn 3rd when blnd and u.r. 3 out.* ....Mr A Phillips ur

Otter River 11.2 7a *alwys bhnd, lost tch after hit 7th, blnd 12th, t.o. when p.u. before last.* ....Mr E James pu

6 ran. 12l, 28l. Time 6m 25.70s. SP 4-5.
E Knight

WARWICK
Saturday March 1st
GOOD

291 3¼m Town Of Warwick Foxhunters' Trophy Hunters' Chase Class H

89[1] **THE MALAKARMA 12.5 5a ....Mr B Pollock** 1
patiently rdn, steady hdwy final cct, jmpd ahd 4 out, styd on strly from between last 2.

226[1] **Lord Relic (NZ) 12.2 5a...................Mr R Ford** 2
(fav) chsd clr ldr, imp to ld apr 7 out, jmpd slowly next, hdd 4 out, rallied from last, fin lame.

Ardesee 11.10 7a...................Mr J Goldstein 3
soon well bhnd, prog final cct, effort 6 out, struggling next, soon btn.

93 My Young Man 11.10 7a *ld and soon well clr, slowed and hdd apr 7 out, wknd rpdly 5 out, t.o. when p.u. before 2 out.* ....Mr E James pu

226 Will It Last 11.5 7a (v) *jmpd slowly, soon t.o. and 2 fences bhnd, jumped slowly and u.r. 6 out.* ....Mr L Brown ur
Cappajune (Ire) 11.9 3a *chasing ldrs when blnd and u.r. 3rd.* ....Mr M Rimell ur
6 ran. 1¾l, 28l. Time 6m 50.40s. SP 9-2.
Charles Dixey

BEAUFORT
Didmarton
Saturday March 1st
GOOD

292 Members

218 **WARRIOR BARD (IRE) ....M Portman** 1
lft in ld 6th, clr 12th, easily
220 **Major Bugler (Ire) ....H Chisholm** 2
in tch til outpcd 11th, tk poor 2nd apr 2 out
179 **Templerainey (Ire) ....G Maundrell** 3
in tch, cls 2nd at 11th, sn btn, lost poor 2nd apr 2 out
262 Thought Reader (Ire) *in tch to 10th, sn strggLng* ....R Sturgis 4
220⁷ Granville Grill 7ex *ld 3rd, clr whn blnd & u.r. 6th* ....J Deutsch ur
45 Amadeo *last til p.u. 4th* ....Miss S Bailey pu
182¹ Wired For Sound *ld to 3rd, 2nd whn p.u. 5th, dsmntd* ....J Barnes pu
177¹ Desert Waltz (Ire) *(fav) in tch til blnd & u.r. 8th* ....D Alers-Hankey ur
Ragtimer *3rd whn blnd & u.r. 3rd* ....S Bush ur
9 ran. Dist, 15l, 4l. Time 6m 15.00s. SP 9-4.
Mrs Robert Puddick (Beaufort).
One fence omitted second circuit. 17 jumps.

293 Intermediate Div I (12st)

178¹ **STRONG CHAIRMAN (IRE) 5ex ....T Mitchell** 1
(fav) w.w. prog 12th, rdn 15th, ld apr last where lft clr
203¹ **Nothing Ventured ....A Beedles** 2
trckd ldrs, effrt 3 out, sn outpcd, lft 2nd last
97⁵ **Southern Flight 5ex....Miss J Cumings** 3
ldng grp, effrt 15th, outpcd 3 out, kpt on
255 Master Donnington *made most to 9th, prom til wknd 3 out, fin tired* ....Julian Pritchard 4
220 Nordic Flash (bl) *prom, blnd & wknd 13th, wll bhnd whn ref last* ....Dr P Pritchard ref
221¹ Saxon Lass 5a *f 1st* ....A Martin f
178 Rose Of Macmillion 5a *alwys rear, t.o. last whn p.u. 11th* ....E Bailey pu
Captain Greg *prom to 6th, 7th & wkng whn u.r. 9th* ....G Barfoot-Saunt ur
218 Apple Nicking *u.r. 1st* ....A Hill ur
Beinn Mohr 5a *cls up til wknd 12th, t.o. & p.u. 2 out* ....E Williams pu
Sebastopol *in tch to 11th, sn wknd, t.o. & p.u. 15th* ....D Stevens pu
218³ Drummer Boy (Ire) *alwys prom, still chsng ldrs whn p.u. aft 2 out, lame* ....Miss P Gundry pu
Rio Cisto 5a *alwys rear, t.o. & p.u. 15th* ....J P Keen pu
106¹ Plan-A (Ire) *prog 6th,ld 9th,hdd aft 2 out,rallied & ev ch whn r.o. last* ....T Woolridge ro
100¹ Gigi Beach (Ire) *hld up bhnd, lost tch 10th, t.o. & p.u. 14th* ....Miss P Curling pu
Dorgan *hmpd 1st, blnd 3rd, last & t.o. til p.u. 9th* ....L Baker pu
16 ran. 15l, 2l, 30l. Time 6m 12.00s. SP Evens.
J A Keighley (Blackmore & Sparkford Vale).

294 Intermediate Div II (12st)

BENGERS MOOR ....Miss P Curling 1
pllng, hld up, prog 7th, ld 12th, qcknd clr apr last
176¹ **Double Thriller ....R Treloggen** 2
(fav) trckd ldrs, effrt to chs wnr 14th, ev ch til outpcd aft 2out
52² **Tangle Baron 5ex ....Miss J Cumings** 3
alwys prom, ev ch 15th, kpt on onepcd
Shuil's Star (Ire) *s.s. wll in rear, no ch 13th, rpd prog aft, nvr nrr* ....P Hamer 4
106³ Celtic Token *made most to 10th, ev ch aft til wknd apr 2 out* ....J Barnes 5
Sunley Street 5a (bl) *nvr nr ldr4s, t.o. frm 14th* ....Miss S Vickery 6
97⁴ Fixed Liability *s.s. alwys wll bhnd, no prog frm 11th* ....D Alers-Hankey 7
123 Special Company (Ire) 5a *chsd ldrs, 6th & outpcd whn blnd 11th, nt rcvr* ....R Smith 8
187 Pay-U-Cash 5ex *alwys rear, t.o.* ....G Perkins 9
187 General Troy *in tch in rear whn blnd bdly 7th, sn bhnd, p.u. 15th* ....K Cousins pu
148⁷ Hackett's Farm 5ex *in tch to 10th, wll btn whn p.u. 14th* ....Julian Pritchard pu
Lonesome Step 5a *alwys rear, t.o. 11th, p.u. 13th* ....A Price pu
Scriven Boy *alwys bhnd, t.o. & p.u. 13th* ....A Beedles pu
Rare Flutter 5a *mid-div, outpcd 11th, 7th & keeping on onepcd whn u.r. 3 out* ....D Renney ur
218⁸ Bear's Flight 5ex *rear whn u.r. 11th* ....J Hadden Wight ur
Todds Hall (Ire) *prom til u.r. 8th* ....A Munro ur
Villains Brief (Ire) *alwys bhnd, t.o. & p.u. 13th* ....R Lawther pu
148¹ Grimley Gale (Ire) 5a *cls up whn u.r. 8th* ....J Jukes ur
Billy-Gwyn *prom, ld 10-12th, wknd rpdly 14th, p.u. nxt* ....J Tudor pu
44⁴ Dirty Dancer *s.s. alwys bhnd, t.o. & p.u. 13th, lame* ....M Wells pu
20 ran. 6l, 2l, hd, 12l, 20l, 15l, 8l, dist. Time 6m 11.00s. SP 6-4.
J R Townshend (Cattistock).

295 Men's Open (12st)

171¹ **THE BOUNDER 7ex ....J Tizzard** 1
j.w. made all, qckncd clr aft 2 out, lft wll clr last
220 **Bishops Island 7ex ....Julian Pritchard** 2
trckd ldrs, prssd wnr 11-12th, 3rd & btn 14th, lft 2nd last
220 **The Country Trader 7ex (bl)....J Borradaile** 3
in tch to 8th, t.o. 12th, lft poor 3rd last
179³ Rustic Sunset *chsd wnr to 8th, 5th & wkng whn u.r. 10th* ....R Sweeting ur
187 Cornish Cossack (NZ) *chsd ldrs, mstk 6th, strgglng 9th, t.o. & p.u. last* ....D S Jones pu
180² Fantus 7ex *(fav) prog 8th,prssd wnr & pshd alng 13th,4l down & btn whn f last* ....T Mitchell f
John Roger *last pair & t.o. til u.r. 9th* ....J Merry ur
187¹ Mister Horatio *mstk 5th, chsd ldrs, 4th & btn frm 12th til f 2 out* ....M Lewis f
Cavalero *unruly pddck, t.o. in last pair til p.u. last* ....L Manners pu
9 ran. Dist, dist. Time 6m 7.00s. SP 11-10.
L G Tizzard (Blackmore & Sparkford Vale).

296 Ladies

97¹ **EARTHMOVER (IRE) ....Miss P Curling** 1
(fav) w.w. out of tch, clsd 13th, ld 2 out, shkn up & ran on well
219² **Lake Mission ....Miss G Browne** 2
set fast pace til hdd 2 out, ran on well flat
Final Pride 5a ....Miss P Jones 3
prssd ldr to 13th, 3rd & btn aft nxt, wknd 2 out
Blessed Oliver 4ex *wll bhnd, ran on frm 11th, 4th & no more imp frm 14th* ....Miss A Plunkett 4
6⁷ Hugli *alwys bhnd, t.o. 11th, fin fast* ....Miss V Roberts 5
219⁹ Rip The Calico (Ire) 5a *alwys bhnd, t.o. 12th* ....Miss S Duckett 6
257 Lady Llanfair 5a *rear main grp, no prog 11th, t.o. & p.u. last* ....Miss A Meakins pu
202⁶ Tap Dancing *rear main grp, t.o. 12th, p.u. 14th* ....Miss S Pickford pu
195 Madraj (Ire) 4ex *alwys bhnd, t.o. & p.u. 13th* ....Miss H Irving pu
Royal Swinger 5a *pcdk 7th, rear, wknd & p.u. 12th* ....Miss S Trotman pu
191 Kelling *chsd ldrs, 5th whn f 8th* ....Miss F Millard f
Gus McCrae *alwys bhnd, 11th whn u.r. 10th* ....Miss L Pearce ur

Riva (NZ) *chsd ldng pair, wkng whn f 11th* Miss M Hill f
13 ran. 5l, 25l, 25l, 3l, 12l. Time 5m 59.00s. SP 1-3.
R M Penny (Cattistock).
Last fence omitted. 17 jumps.

297 Maiden (5-7yo) Div I (12st)

190[4] **VALE OF OAK 5a** .... **M FitzGerald** 1
rear, hmpd 9th & lost tch, ran on 12th, btn whn lft clr flat
Mazzard (Ire) .... **R Treloggen** 2
prom, lft 2nd 9th, no imp whn mstk 3 out, lft 2nd agn flat
147[5] **River Thrust (Ire)** .... **Miss G Young** 3
rear, wll bhnd frm 11th, tk poor 3rd flat
181 Lily Lane 7a *6s-4s, n.j.w. in tch to 10th, sn wknd, t.o.* .... Miss S Vickery 4
Favlient 5a *in tch til b.d. 8th* .... J Barnes bd
181 Horton Country 5a *in tch, mstk 5th, hmpd 8th & 9th, sn bhnd, p.u. last* .... P Howse pu
222 Shelley's Dream 5a *in tch whn u.r. aft 6th* .. M Walters ur
41 False Tail (Ire) 7a *(fav) trckd ldr til f 9th* ...... J Tizzard f
Noble Star 7a *blnd 6th, wknd 10th, t.o. & p.u. 13th* .... S Bush pu
Rosevalley (Ire) *ld, in cmmnd & clr whn u.r. 100 yrds frm fin* .... K Whiting ur
Miss Malachite 12a *in tch til blnd & u.r. 8th* R Lawther ur
11 ran. 6l, dist, 3l. Time 6m 33.00s. SP 7-1.
Miss Scarlett J Crew (V.W.H.).

298 Interlink Restricted Div I

39[2] **ALLER MOOR (IRE)** .... **M Miller** 1
cls up, ld apr last, mstk last & hdd, rallied to ld nr fin
44[1] **Mister One** .... **J Tizzard** 2
(fav) trckd ldrs,ld 11th,hdd apr last,lft in ld last,hdd nr fin
Swansea Gold (Ire) 5a .... **D Alers-Hankey** 3
mstk 1st, ld 7-10th, sn outpcd, kpt on frm 3 out
Kinesiology (Ire) *prom, ld 10-11th, wknd frm 15th* .... R Treloggen 4
Mr Mad *rear, lost tch 11th, t.o. & p.u. 2 out* .. P Hamer pu
223 Colonel Fairfax *prom to 6th, t.o. & p.u. 14th* ... J Trice-Rolph pu
189 Dick's Cabin *ld to 2nd, prom til wknd 11th, t.o. & p.u. 3 out* .... D S Jones pu
176[4] Newstarsky *alwys rear, t.o. & p.u. 2 out* .... Miss J Cumings pu
189[2] Moonlight Cruise 5a *in tch whn f 7th* .... G Perkins f
Savage Oak *rear frm 10th, t.o. & p.u. 14th* .. E Williams pu
182 Uncle Bruce *in tch to 9th, t.o. whn p.u. 2 out* .... A Charles-Jones pu
40[1] Mostyn *n.j.w. ld 2-7th, blnd 9th, wknd, t.o. & p.u. 2 out* .... Miss P Gundry pu
181[1] Abit More Business (Ire) *mid-div, hmpd 7th, nt rcvr & p.u. nxt* .... T Mitchell pu
Bit Of A Citizen (Ire) *chsd ldrs, 4th & outpcd 13th, 5th & wll btn whn p.u. last* .... J Jukes pu
186 Silk Rascal 5a *sn t.o. in last, p.u. 13th* ..... T Vaughan pu
15 ran. ¾l, 25l, 10l. Time 6m 12.00s. SP 7-2.
G Keirle (Portman).

299 Maiden (5-7yo) Div II (12st)

182 **THE COCKERTOO** .... **E Bailey** 1
chsd ldr, ld 11-14th, btn whn lft in ld aft last, hld on
181 **Nearly An Eye** .... **J Tizzard** 2
(fav) w.w. prog to ld 14th, clr whn nrly f last, nt rcvr, unlcky
7[4] **Members Cruise** .... **E Walker** 3
prom, disp 10th, 3rd & outpcd aft 14th
Primitive Girl 5a *rear, prog whn blnd 12th, 4th & no imp frm 14th* .... T Cox 4
Is She Quick 5a *alwys bhnd, t.o. 10th, p.u. 14th* .... M Flynn pu
181[2] The Bold Abbot *nvr nr ldrs, wll bhnd whn u.r. 14th* .... Miss S West ur
182 Wild Weather *ld to 11th, wknd rpdly, p.u. 14th* .... Miss S Vickery pu
222 Gt Hayes Pommard *13th whn f 2nd* .... D Howells f
Prior's Corner 5a *mstk 4th, cls up whn blnd & u.r. 6th* .... S Bush ur
224 New Flame 5a *mid-div, no prog 12th, bhnd whn p.u. 14th* .... J Trice-Rolph pu
181 The Smiling Girl 5a *alwys bhnd, t.o. whn ref 13th* .... N Fitzearle ref
Mankind *prom, blnd 11th & wknd, p.u. 14th* .. L Baker pu
147 Bombadier Brown *alwys bhnd, t.o. 10th, p.u. 15th* .... A Charles-Jones pu
Fraction *last whn hmpd & u.r. 2nd* .. G Barfoot-Saunt ur
14 ran. ¾l, 12l, 25l. Time 6m 17.00s. SP 6-1.
Mrs J M Bailey (Blackmore & Sparkford Vale).

300 Interlink Restricted Div II

PRIDEAUX PRINCE .... **Julian Pritchard** 1
prom,outpcd 14th,ran on 3 out,btn whn lft in ld last,ran on
103[1] **Marion's Own (Ire)** .... **Miss P Curling** 2
(fav) prog to jn ldrs 13th,not qckn 15th,lft 2nd & hmpd last,no ex
222 **Five Circles (Ire)** .... **M Portman** 3
sn prom, outpcd 14th, kpt on onepcd frm 3 out
Tommy O'Dwyer (Ire) *prog 10th, jnd ldr 14th, wknd aft nxt* .... A Hill 4
Ardell Boy *prssd ldr to 11th, onepcd frm 13th* .... Miss P Gundry 5
221 King Of The Clouds *ld 2nd-13th, sn outpcd by ldrs* .... J Hammond 6
221 Viking Flame 5a *alwys rear, no dang frm 14th* S Bush 7
Plas-Hendy *alwys rear, t.o. & p.u. 14th* Miss F Wilson pu
223[2] The Hon Company *mstk 6th, in tch to 11th, wll bhnd whn p.u. 15th* .... E Walker pu
189 Sea Search *nvr nr ldrs, wll bhnd whn p.u. last, dsmntd* .... Miss A Meakins pu
222[2] Sideliner *mid-div, effrt & prog whn f 11th* .... T Stephenson f
Welsh Clover 5a *ld to 2nd, wll bhnd whn p.u. 3 out* .... S Blackwell pu
45 Balance *prom, ld 13th, clr 2 out, 5l up whn f last* .... M Walters f
213[7] The Man From Clare (Ire) *mid-div, no ch frm 14th, wll bhnd whn p.u. last* .... L Lay pu
Country Lord *t.o. in last pair, blnd 9th, p.u. nxt* .... Mrs S Walwin pu
189[3] Sister Lark 5a *alwys rear, t.o. & p.u. 14th* .. E Williams pu
Telephone *alwys last grp, t.o. & p.u. 3 out, dsmntd* .... P Hamer pu
Khandys Slave (Ire) 5a *rear, wknd rpdly & p.u. 12th* .... J Jukes pu
126[7] Rayman (Ire) *prom to 12th, bhnd whn p.u. last* .... R Lawther pu
189[6] Cranagh Moss (Ire) *mstk 1st, t.o. in last pair, p.u. 3 out* .... G Lewis pu
217[1] Its Murphy Man *s.s. prom to 13th, bhnd whn p.u. 2 out* .... J Trice-Rolph pu
224[1] Bay Hobnob *alwys wll in rear, lost tch 11th, p.u. 15th* .... P Howse pu
100 Mine's A Gin (Ire) *in tch, cls 5th whn mstk 12th, sn btn, p.u. last* .... Miss J Cumings pu
23 ran. 5l, 2l, 6l, 6l, 5l, 8l. Time 6m 15.50s. SP 10-1.
Mrs C L Goodinson (Ross Harriers).
J.N.

CHIDDINGFOLD, L'FIELD, COWDRAY
Parham
Saturday March 1st
GOOD

301 Members

ACE OF SPIES .... **Miss A Embiricos** 1
w.w. chal & jmpd 14th & nxt, ld 3 out, drew clr
Pat Alaska .... **Miss C Wates** 2
(fav) ld to 3 out, onepcd
Royal Fireworks *trckd ldr til blnd & u.r. 11th* .... Miss C Nicholls ur
3 ran. 15l. Time 7m 7.00s. SP 2-1.
Mrs S N J Embiricos (Chiddingfold).

302 Confined (12st)

148³ **LOCAL MANOR ....H Dunlop** **1**
mid-div, prog to chal apr 3 out, ld nxt, ran on well
279 **Early Man ....P Hacking** **2**
(fav) 6s-2s, handy, ld apr 3 out, hdd nxt, wknd
Charlton Yeoman ....Mrs D Rowell **3**
rear to 12th, some late prog, tk 3rd cls hm
56⁵ Paco's Boy (bl) *prom, ld 11th-4 out, 3rd aft, steadily wknd, lost 3rd fin* ....P York 4
148⁹ Major Man (Ire) *trckd ldrs, mstk 5th, cls 3rd 4 out, wknd aft*..............................P Bull 5
109³ Skinnhill (bl) *alwys rear, lost tch 14th* ....C Mason 6
282⁴ Fowling Piece *in tch to hlfwy, t.o. 3 out*.....M Legge 7
Trojan Call *mid-div, 5th & losing tch 15th, wll bhnd whn p.u. 2 out*....................Mrs C Mitchell pu
No Inhibitions *ld to 5th, wknd 9th, rear & p.u. 13th* ....A Warr pu
Northern Village *mid-div whn f 2nd* ....P O'Keeffe f
Woody Will *rear, in tch to hlfwy, p.u. aft 15th* ....Mrs E Coveney pu
Linred *mid-div to hlfwy, lost tch & p.u. 14th*.....P Hall pu
Alansford 3ex *ld 5th-11th, grad wknd, wll bhnd whn p.u. 2 out* ....C Gordon pu
Zilfi (USA) *alwys wll in rear, t.o. & p.u. 13th* ....Miss F Worley pu

14 ran. 6l, 10l, nk, 12l, 1l, 10l. Time 6m 45.00s. SP 16-1.
J L Dunlop (Crawley & Horsham).

303 Restricted (12st)

276¹ **PRINCE BUCK (IRE) ....P Hacking** **1**
(fav) made all, styd on well 2 out, drew clr
278 **Croft Court ....Miss C Savill** **2**
alwys prom, 4th & outpcd 4 out, styd on wll to tk 2nd flat
284¹ **Greybury Star (Ire) ....P Bull** **3**
cls up, 2nd 3 out, outpcd by wnr
Gamay *rear, jnd ldrs & blnd 8th & 9th, wknd 2 out, blnd last,tired* ....A Lillingston 4
198² Dovehill *prom to 4 out, bhnd whn p.u. nxt*...C Gordon pu
148⁸ Bilbo Baggins (Ire) *alwys bhnd, t.o. 13th, p.u. 3 out* ....M Gorman pu
Quick Quick Sloe 5a *mid-div, 6th & losing tch whn p.u. 14th*.............................Miss T Cave pu
176 Dormston Lad 4ow *sn rear, lost tch 8th, t.o. & p.u. 15th*..................................C Jowett pu
277³ Some Tourist (Ire) *alwys wll bhnd, p.u. 2 out* ....N Benstead pu
Elmers Marsh 5a (bl) *alwys last, t.o. & p.u. 10th* ....P York pu

10 ran. 20l, 5l, dist. Time 6m 45.00s. SP 7-4.
Mike Roberts (East Sussex & Romney Marsh).

304 G Middleton Ladies

THE WHIP ....Miss C Savill **1**
handy, chsd ldr 14th, ld brfly 2 out, rallied flat, ld line
179 **Howaryadoon ....Miss T Cave** **2**
handy, ld 13th-2 out, ld last, ct line
153 **Royal Irish ....Miss C Townsley** **3**
nvr trbld ldrs, 4th final cct, lft 3rd last
Magsood *alwys rear, wll bhnd whn p.u. 3 out* ....Miss P Ellison pu
280⁵ Thamesdown Tootsie 5a *(Jt fav) ld to 13th, 3rd & btn whn stmbld & u.r. last* ....Miss V Lyon ur
195² Powersurge *trckd ldrs, wknd rpdly 12th, t.o. & p.u. 3 out*.........................Miss H Courtney-Bennett pu
Topping-The-Bill *prom early, bhnd whn p.u. 13th* ....Mrs E Coveney pu
Clover Coin 5a *(Jt fav) wth ldr whn f 2nd* Miss J Grant f
Redelva 5a *last & dtchd whn u.r. 8th*....Mrs D Rowell ur
Saun (Cze) *b.d. 2nd*..................Miss F Worley bd

10 ran. Nk, 20l. Time 6m 48.00s. SP 6-1.
The Hon Mrs C Yeates (East Sussex & Romney Marsh).
One fence omitted final circuit. 17 jumps.

305 Men's Open (12st)

279⁴ **KATES CASTLE 5a.................J Van Praagh** **1**
ld to 12th, agn 4 out, ran on well frm 2 out
225⁷ **Centre Stage ....A Warr** **2**
cls up, chsd ldrs final cct, kpt on same pace 2 out
220 **Blackwater Lady (Ire) 5a 7ex..........P Scouller** **3**
(fav) mid-div, prog to ld aft 12th, hdd 4 out, wknd 2 out
281 Darkbrook 7ex *prom, chsd ldr 6th, rdn & wknd 14th* ....G Hopper 4
144⁶ The Forties *prom early, lost tch 12th, blnd & t.o. 3 out* ....N Earnshaw 5
Glenavey *alwys last, t.o. hlfwy, p.u. 3 out* ......C Hall pu
Rocco 7ex *n.j.w. prom to 5th, bhnd whn p.u. 14th* ....N Jones pu
180 Johnny The Fox (Ire) 4ex *rear til u.r. 9th*....C Bennett ur
225 Greybury Lane (Ire) *wll in tch to 10th, wll bhnd whn p.u. 3 out*..............................P Bull pu

9 ran. 8l, 4l, 30l, 30l. Time 6m 56.00s. SP 4-1.
Ben Van Praagh (Crawley & Horsham).

306 Maiden (12st)

OJONNYO (IRE) ....C Gordon **1**
(fav) cls up, ld 8th-3 out, chal last, rdn clr
Sister Gale 12a...................J Van Praagh **2**
prog to prss ldr 13th, ld 3 out-last, no ext
146² **Ally Pally ....P York** **3**
chsd ldrs, 3rd & und pres 4 out, wknd
Moran Brig *mid-div til u.r. 8th*................J Luck ur
Tamborito (Ire) *alwys rear, lost tch whn p.u. aft 14th* ....S Garrott pu
Miss Pandy 5a *ld to 8th, grad wknd, bhnd whn p.u. 4 out*..................................P Hall pu
283 Very Rare (Ire) 5a *in tch whn f 14th*....Miss C Holliday f
279 Rough Aura *alwys rear, t.o. & p.u. 10th*......P Blagg pu
197² Leitrim Cottage (Ire) *in tch, rmndrs 9th, strgglng aft, 4th & wll btn whn p.u.3out* ....P Bull pu
Miners Medic (Ire) *mid-div, p.u. 10th* ......M Gorman pu
Palmerston's Folly 5a *n.j.w. alwys last, t.o. & p.u. 10th* ....Daniel Dennis pu
Primitive King 7a 2ow *mid-div, clsng whn blnd 14th & p.u.*...................................P Hacking pu

12 ran. 4l, 25l. Time 7m 3.00s. SP 9-4.
S P Tindall (Southdown & Eridge).
G.Ta.

EAST DEVON
Clyst St Mary
Saturday March 1st
HEAVY

307 Members

104² **VALLEY'S CHOICE 5a.................L Jefford** **1**
(fav) hld up, prog 15th, ld 3 out, sn clr
176 **Stainless Steel ....M Sweetland** **2**
ld to 3 out, outpcd aft, fin tired
97 The Copper Key *2nd whn f 7th*.............T Greed f

3 ran. 10l. Time 7m 23.00s. SP 4-7.
S R Stevens (East Devon).

308 Men's Open (12st)

LOST FORTUNE 7ex.................H Wheeler **1**
(fav) hld up, prog 15th, 2nd nxt, ld 3 out, kpt on
239⁴ **Pintail Bay (v).........................N Legg** **2**
w.w. 3rd at 13th, slw jmp 16th, kpt on und pres 3 out
241 **Sherbrooks ....M Hoskins** **3**
prom, disp 6th til ld 14th, hdd 3 out, outpcd
17 Osmosis *evented round, t.o. 2nd* ....K Nelmes 4
171 Prince Nepal *ld/disp to 13th, wknd rpdly, nxt, t.o. & ref 2 out*................................T Hopkins ref
Bridge Express *ld, blnd & u.r. 1st* ....J Creighton ur
256 Sea Dreams (Ire) *bhnd, t.o. & p.u. 13th* ...J Hankinson pu

7 ran. 2l, 6l, dist. Time 7m 17.00s. SP 4-9.
H W Wheeler (North Cotswold).

309 Confined (12st)

STUNNING STUFF ....R Nuttall **1**

ld/disp til clr 12th, wll clr 3 out, tired & crwld last
98 **Bianconi ....J Creighton 2**
(fav) handy, effrt 3 out, alwys hld
Seventh Lock ....Miss L Blackford 3
ld/disp to 11th, chsd wnr aft til wknd 3 out
178[5] Gallant Effort (Ire) *in tch to 3 out, outpcd*. . J Snowden 4
178 Shilgrove Place *sn bhnd, t.o. & p.u. 14th*. . Col S Allen pu
174 Kentish Piper *u.r. 2nd*. . . . . E Clarkson ur
237 Querrin Lodge *sn bhnd, t.o. & p.u. 12th* . . . . . . T Greed pu
7 ran. 2½l, 1l, 10l. Time 7m 27.50s. SP 9-4.
C St V Fox (Blackmore & Sparkford Vale).

310 Intermediate (12st)

AVRIL SHOWERS 5a ....R Atkinson 1
j.w. ld til jnd 13th, clr aft nxt, ran on well
175[1] **Highway Lad ....P King 2**
(fav) w.w. prog 11th, chal 13th, rdn 2 out, alwys hld
171 **Hensue ....N Harris 3**
in tch to 13th, outpcd frm 3 out
51[3] Oneovertheight *in tch to 13th, outpcd aft*. . . . S Kidston 4
107[2] Pabrey *sn bhnd, nvr rchd ldrs* . . . . N Mitchell 5
Batsi *rear til blnd & u.r. 8th* . . . . I Widdicombe ur
236 Ive Called Time 5ex *in tch to 12th, lost plc nxt, t.o. & p.u. 2 out* . . . . T Greed pu
The Criosra (Ire) *1st ride, blnd & u.r. 2nd* . . A Bateman ur
104 Crownhill Cross *ref 2nd*. . . . . Miss R Francis ref
9 ran. 10l, 12l, 20l, 3l. Time 7m 16.00s. SP 3-1.
Mrs R Atkinson (Cattistock).

311 Ladies

174[5] **FALSE ECONOMY ....Miss K Scorgie 1**
made most, ran on well frm 3 out
174[4] **Searcy (bl) ....Miss L Blackford 2**
in tch, chal 2 out-last, not run on
108[4] **Jimmy Cone ....Miss A Goschen 3**
rear, prog 12th, ev ch 3 out, outpcd aft
174[2] Myhamet *(fav) in tch, effrt 3 out, no prog nxt* . . . . Mrs M Hand 4
L'uomo Piu *hld up, prog whn mssd mrkr & p.u. 13th* . . . . Miss K Baker pu
51[2] Departure 5a *chsd ldrs, lost tch 12th, p.u. 14th* . . . . Miss S Gaisford pu
Be My Habitat *in tch to 2 out, 5th & btn whn u.r. last* . . . . Miss L Hawkins ur
21[3] Tullykyne Bells *sn bhnd, t.o. & p.u. 14th* . . . . Miss D Stafford pu
110 Hod Wood 5a *sn bhnd, t.o. & p.u. 2 out* Miss R David pu
9 ran. 1l, 3l, 8l. Time 7m 17.00s. SP 10-1.
Miss G Green (Portman).
16 jumps only from this race onwards

312 Restricted Div I (12st)

175 **MISS RICUS 5a.........................N Harris 1**
(Jt fav) handy, prog 11th, lft in ld 13th, styd on well
176 **Mendip Son ....L Jefford 2**
in tch, effrt 3 out, outpcd nxt
182[3] **Purbeck Polly 5a..................Miss A Davis 3**
hld up, prog 11th, 2nd 13th, ev ch 2 out, wknd apr last
100 Belfry Lad *(Jt fav) in tch to 4 out, wknd aft* J Creighton 4
100 Darktown Strutter (bl) *ld/disp to 7th, lost tch 13th, blnd last*. . . . . A Holdsworth 5
Nikolayevich *sn bhnd, t.o. & p.u. 11th* . . . . A Turner pu
175 Nice To No *cls up to 8th, lost tch & p.u. 12th* . . S Slade pu
176 Lake Mariner 5a *prom, ld 8th til s.u. bend aft 12th* . . . . Maj O Ellwood su
8 ran. 10l, 7l, 20l, ½l. Time 7m 15.50s. SP 3-1.
Miss P J Boundy (Dulverton East).

313 Restricted Div II (12st)

241 **PARDITINO ....Miss V Nicholas 1**
j.w. made all, unchal
Mosside ....N Harris 2
(fav) in tch, 2nd 3 out, no imp on wnr
236 **Artistic Peace 5a...................D Stephens 3**
mid-div, wll bhnd frm 12th
262 Major Bert (Ire) *handy, 2nd to 4 out, wknd nxt* . . . . H Wheeler 4
Third Melody 5a *alwys rear, nvr on trms* . . . . Maj S Robinson 5
176 Redclyffe (USA) *sn rear, t.o. & p.u. 12th*. . . . . . B Dixon pu
106[6] Just Donald *rear til f 11th* . . . . A Honeyball f
242 Dont Rise Me (Ire) *in tch to 12th, outpcd nxt, p.u. last* . . . . L Jefford pu
258 Naburn Loch 5a *prom, lost tch 10th, p.u. 12th* . . . . J Hankinson pu
175 Heddon Valley *rear, f 6th* . . . . J Creighton f
10 ran. 20l, dist, 5l, 20l. Time 7m 13.50s. SP 5-1.
Mrs K R J Nicholas (Tiverton Foxhounds).

314 Maiden Div I

244 **BAYWYN 5a...........................S Kidston 1**
mid-div, lft bttr by dfctns, 2nd & hld whn lft clr last
Carnelia 5a ....J Kwiatkowski 2
sn bhnd, t.o. 11th
Really Neat 5a *prom, ld 6th til blnd & u.r. 11th* . . . . G Beilby ur
104 Gamblers Refrain *ld to 5th, lost tch 10th, ref 12th* . . . . A Holdsworth ref
244 I'll Be Bound *(fav) handy, ev ch whn blnd & u.r. 13th* . . . . M Burrows ur
175 Brooklyn Express 5a *prom, lost tch 6th, t.o. & p.u. 8th* . . . . S Parfimowicz pu
Hill Cruise *alwys prom, lft in ld 3 out, clr whn f last* . . . . B Dixon f
Faraday *rear,prog 11th, 3rd 3 out, wknd nxt, p.u. last* . . . . N Mitchell pu
Renshaw Ings *rear, t.o. & p.u. 11th*. . . . . J Creighton pu
181 Cucklington *prom, ld 4 out, f nxt*. . . . . Miss A Goschen f
245 Mazies Choice 5a *mid-div, blnd & u.r. 7th* . . . . S Slade ur
11 ran. Dist. Time 7m 31.00s. SP 16-1.
R L Black (Dulverton East).

315 Maiden Div II

182 **JACK SUN ....J Snowden 1**
(fav) ld to 3rd, handy, ld 13th, sn clr
Rogerson *cls up, lft in ld 8-12th, wknd 2 out, tired & ref last*. . . . . J Creighton ref
110 Gentle Jester 5a *f 1st* . . . . A Honeyball f
105 Spartans Dina 5a *ld 4th til f 8th* . . . . . Miss L Blackford f
Young Herbert (Ire) *fat, sn bhnd, t.o. & p.u. 13th* . . . . A Holdsworth pu
5 ran. Time 7m 45.00s. SP 4-5.
Ian Snowden

316 Maiden Div III

181 **NOBLE PROTECTOR (IRE) ....Maj G Wheeler 1**
ld 3-11th,wknd nxt,lft bttr by dfctns, kpt on to ld flat
Quince Cross 5a ....M Burrows 2
prom, ld 12-13th, outpcd, lft clr last, wknd & hdd flat
Pallingham Lad (Ire) *prom, ld 13th til apr last, blnd & u.r. last*. . . . . S Kidston ur
176 The Bodhran (Ire) *(fav) hld up, prog 11th, ld apr last, f last, unlucky*. . . . . R Young f
244 Impetuous Dreamer 5a *ld to 2nd, lost tch 5th, blnd 12th & p.u.*. . . . . Miss A Goschen pu
Knight Of Passion 7a *f 1st* . . . . A Farrant f
6 ran. 3l. Time 7m 59.50s. SP 9-4.
G F Wheeler (Blackmore & Sparkford Vale).
D.P.

EAST ESSEX
Marks Tey
Saturday March 1st
GOOD

317 Maiden Div I

69 **LUDOVICIANA 5a.......................P Keane 1**
(fav) ld 4th, made rest, drew wll clr frm 15th, easy
275[4] **Wolfhill Lad (Ire) ....S R Andrews 2**
prom,lft 2nd 9th,chsd wnnr aft,btn whn jmp lft last 3,tired

196 **Flapping Freda (Ire) 5a....................R Gill** 3
mid-div, prog 10th, 3rd 15th, wknd nxt, fin tired
128 Bergholt 7a *in tch, chsd ldng pair 16th, sn wknd, fin tired*.......................................A Coe 4
276 Alapa *styd stt, keen hold, chsd ldrs, 2nd whn f 9th* ....V Coogan f
126 Learner Driver *chsd ldrs to 9th, wknng whn blndrd 13th, t.o. & f 17th*.............................C Ward f
30 Mister Rainman *hld up, prog 8th, outpcd apr 15th, t.o. & p.u. 17th*.................................T Bulgin pu
197 But Not Quite (Ire) (bl) *ld to 4th, chsd ldrs, hmp 9th, p.u. nxt, dead* ....N Bloom pu
196 Sheer Hope (bl) *f 1st*.........................J Townson f
Thereyougo *w.w., some prog 11th, just in tch whn f 14th* ....Mrs F Needham f
196 Cambridge Gold 7a *chsd ldr 4th-8th, 3rd whn f 9th* ....P Chinery f
Dandelion Lad (Ire) 7a *alwys last, t.o. 8th, p.u. apr 11th*...S Morris pu
275 Just Mai-Bee 7a *bhnd 8th, t.o. & jmp slwly 11th, p.u. 13th*...............................C Ward-Thomas pu
13 ran. Dist, 12l, dist. Time 7m 2.00s. SP 6-4.
G W Paul (Essex & Suffolk).

318 Maiden Div II

127² **REVEREND BROWN (IRE)............A Sansome** 1
(fav) chsng grp,wnt 2nd 14th,rdn 3 out,jst ld & lft clr nxt,rdnout
276³ **The Prior ....P Rowe** 2
w.w., stdd prog 11th, 4th 16th, lft 2nd 2 out, no imp on wnr
275² **Carlinare ....S R Andrews** 3
mid-div,prog & blndrd 11th,sn rdn,lft 3rd 2 out,nvr rch ldrs
61² Andy Gawe (Ire) *chsd ldr 5th-14th, wknd apr 16th, t.o.* ....S Cowell 4
Country Barle *jmp wll, ld, sn clr, just hdd whn f 2 out* ....N Bloom f
Mistress Linnet 5a *bhnd, lost tch 8th, t.o. & p.u. apr 11th*.......................................C Ward pu
Loch Irish (Ire) 5a *chsd ldrs to 10th, wknd 13th, t.o. & p.u. 17th* ....A Coe pu
29⁵ Remilan (Ire) *alwys mid-div, lost tch 15th, t.o. & p.u. 3 out*...P Taiano pu
275 Harry Tartar *f 3rd*.....................Capt D Parker f
127⁵ Village Copper 7a *chsd ldr to 5th, wknd 14th, t.o. & p.u. 3 out*.......................C Ward-Thomas pu
197 Lantern Spark (Ire) 5a *f 4th*..................Miss C Tuke f
Kingarth 7a *rear & rmmndrs 3rd, alwys bhnd, t.o. & p.u. 11th*.....................................N King pu
Republican Lady 12a *mstks, t.o. frm 7th til p.u. 10th* ....T Bulgin pu
13 ran. 10l, 1l, 30l. Time 6m 58.00s. SP 5-4.
J M Turner (Suffolk).

319 Confined

123 **SALMON MEAD (IRE) ....S Sporborg** 1
cls up, disp ld 11th, ld 15th, clr 2 out, styd on wll
123⁴ **Horace ....W Wales** 2
(fav) in tch,jnd ldrs 10th,chsd wnr frm 16th,onepcd und pres
271⁸ **El Bae ....P Taiano** 3
prom, 4th & ch 16th, outpcd frm nxt
271⁶ Smart Pal *chsd ldrs to 8th, lost plc 10th, rlld 15th, no hdwy frm nxt* ....K Needham 4
193 Dynamite Dan (Ire) *chsd ldrs to 15th, sn wknd, t.o.* ....S Cowell 5
194 Mayday Miracle 5a *pllng, ld 3rd-7th, wknng & blndrd 10th, p.u. 13th*..............................G Lush pu
124 Celtic King 5ex *chsd ldrs to 14th, wknd, last whn p.u. 3 out* ....H Tregoning pu
271⁷ King Cash *hld up, prog 9th, rddn alng 13th, wknd apr 16th, p.u. 2 out*.......................S R Andrews pu
Exarch (USA) *hld up in tch, gng wll whn f 14th*..A Coe f
Divine Chance (Ire) *rear, jmp slwly 6th & 7th, losng tch whn p.u. 12th*...............................Mrs T Hill pu
154 Spartan Silver *ld til apr 11th, wknd qckly, blndrd 12th, p.u. nxt* ....C Ward-Thomas pu
11 ran. 15l, 12l, 15l, 10l. Time 6m 59.00s. SP 9-4.
Sir C Keswick & C Sporborg (Puckeridge).

320 Members

KILLERY HARBOUR ....T Moore 1
(fav) alwys gng wll, wnt 2nd 10th, ld 2 out, rddn clr flat
Half A Sov ....S March 2
chsd ldr, ld 9th-2 out, onepcd und pres
276 **El Guapo ....P Chinery** 3
ld to 9th, lost plc, wnt 3rd 15th, btn 2 out
198⁵ Aughnacloy Rose *not fluent, in tch to 13th, sn bhnd, t.o.*...R Page 4
4 ran. 3l, 20l, 12l. Time 7m 25.00s. SP 5-4.
W T Fagg (East Essex).

321 Intermediate (12st)

214² **MR BRANIGAN (IRE) ....T Marks** 1
(fav) alwys gng wll, lft 2nd 9th, ld 2 out, drew clr flat
216 **Bartags Brother ....S R Andrews** 2
chsd ldrs, lft 3rd 9th, ev ch 16th, rdn & btn apr last
282 **Sweet Merenda (Ire) 5a ....S Cowell** 3
w.w., lft 4th 9th, ev ch 17th, onepcd und pres
General Picton (v) *disp ld til lft clr 9th, jnd 3 out, hdd nxt, wknd apr last*..................................A Coe 4
123 Cleddau King 7ow *alwys rear div, 5th & no ch 16th, t.o.*...J Buckle 5
273⁴ Creeves Nephew *alwys bhnd, t.o. frm 10th* ....Capt D Parker 6
271⁵ Druid's Lodge *disp ld til f 9th*..............T Bulgin f
Adjalari (Ire) *mid-div to 8th, last & wknng 10th, p.u. apr nxt* ....C Ward pu
Parkers Hills (Ire) *(tuped), mid-div, lost tch 14th, t.o. & p.u. 17th*..................................S Sporborg pu
Mirror Image 5a *alwys rear div, t.o. & p.u. 13th* ....N King pu
10 ran. 10l, ½l, 2l, dist, 25l. Time 6m 57.00s. SP 1-2.
G T H Bailey (Pytchley).

322 3½m Mens Open (12st)

63¹ **THE ARTFUL RASCAL ....S Cowell** 1
(fav) cls up, ld frm 11th, drew wll clr frm 17th, easy
271³ **Airtrak (Ire) 7ex.......................R Barrett** 2
chsd ldrs, wnt 2nd 11th, rdn 17th, no ch wth wnr
63⁴ **Earlydue 7ex ....T Moore** 3
mstks, ld 5-10th, blndrd 12th, 3rd & outpcd frm 17th
271⁹ Jimmy Mac Jimmy *mid-div, 4th & ch 17th, wkng whn blndrd nxt*......................................P Taiano 4
270³ Cool Apollo (NZ) *in tch til outpcd 12th, kpt on frm 17th, nvr dang*..........................G Plenderleith 5
193³ Foxbow (Ire) 7ex *in tch, rdn apr 12th, sn bhnd, t.o.* ....S R Andrews 6
270 Old Dundalk (bl) *rear, lost tch 13th, t.o.* ....N King 7
Saint Bene't (Ire) (bl) *wth ldrs, lost plc qckly 5th, t.o. nxt, p.u. apr 12th*..................................A Coe pu
Cracking Idea (Ire) 7ex *trckd ldrs, cls 4th whn f 14th* ....C Ward-Thomas f
9 ran. 30l, ½l, 8l, ½l, 15l, 1l. Time 7m 41.00s. SP 4-9.
M A Kemp (Suffolk).

323 Ladies

195 **PROFESSOR LONGHAIR ....Miss C Papworth** 1
(fav) hld up, chsd ldrs 11th, 4th 2 out, strng run to ld cls home
125⁵ **Omidjoy (Ire) 5a (bl).............Mrs L Wrighton** 2
prom, disp ld 15th, ld 17th, 3l clr last, hdd cls home
Top Miss 5a ....Miss S French 3
pllng, ld 8-17th, no ext und pres apr last
Lyme Gold (Ire) *ld to 5th, cls up, ev ch 17th, onepcd frm nxt*......................................Mrs T Hill 4
198 Bozo Bailey *hld up, in tch to 13th, t.o. & p.u. 17th* ....Mrs L Gibbon pu
195 The Man From Lyre (Ire) *u.r. 1st*.....Mrs K Warburton ur
195 Wardy Hill 5a *prom, ld 5-8th, blndrd 11th, 5th in tch whn f 15th*.........................Miss E Tomlinson f
7 ran. 2l, 5l, 8l. Time 7m 6.00s. SP 11-10.
A J Papworth (North Norfolk Harriers).

324 Restricted

2111[1] **CORMEEN LORD (IRE) ....J Sharp** 1
(fav) chsd ldr 8th, ld 11th, clr whn hit 16th, comf
Polar Ana (Ire) 5a...............Miss S Gladders 2
rear, prog 13th, mod 6th 15th, wnt 2nd last, nvr nrr
1271[1] **Regal Bay ....W Wales** 3
w.w., prog & pckd 9th, chsd wnr 16th, onepcd und pres
1961[1] Tomcappagh (Ire) *cls up, blndrd 10th, 4th & outpcd 15th, no dang aft*..........Miss S French 4
1221[1] Auchendolly (Ire) *trckd ldrs til rdn & outpcd 14th, no ch frm 16th* ....S Sporborg 5
Oh So Vital *mid-div, prog to 3rd 15th, btn 17th, no ch whn blndrd 2 out*..........A Coe 6
274 Courier's Way (Ire) *bhnd frm 7th, t.o. frm 15th* T Moore 7
66[3] Linger Hill *in tch til 11th, lost tch 14th, t.o.*.....C Ward 8
274 Alice Sheer Thorn (Ire) 5a *chsd ldrs, 5th & wknng apr 15th, t.o.*..........M Gingell 9
126[2] Claydons Monty *prog 9th, chsd wnr 11-15th, sn wknd, p.u. 3 out*..........S R Andrews pu
198 Ballygar Boy (Ire) *ld til apr 11th, wknd qckly, t.o. & p.u. 14th*..........J Buckle pu
Top Of The Range (Ire) *prom to 9th, bhnd whn p.u. 12th*..........P Taiano pu
126 Black Ermine (Ire) *nvr bttr thn mid-div, lost tch 14th, t.o. & p.u. 3 out*..........C Ward-Thomas pu
Tenderman (Ire) *t.d.e., in tch to 10th, t.o. & p.u. 15th*..........S Cowell pu
196 Punnett's Town 5a *s.s., bhnd, jmp rght 4th, t.o. & p.u. 12th*..........T Hills pu
Nanda Devi *alwys rear, last whn f 11th* ....J Knowles f
16 ran. 10l, ½l, 15l, 2l, nk, 15l, 6l, 1l. Time 6m 56.00s. SP 9-4.
Mrs C Harris & C Sharp (Woodland Pytchley).
S.P.

FLINT & DENBIGH
Eaton Hall
Saturday March 1st
GOOD TO SOFT

325 Members

200[6] **FORMAL ....R Owen** 1
cls 2nd til wnt on 13th 10l clr whn lft solo last
260[6] Embu-Meru *(fav) ld to 12th, hdd 13th, in tch 3 out, outpcd, ref last*..........I Lowe ref
Fruit Of Oak (Ire) *alwys 3rd in tch, 2l down whn f 12th*..........A Mackay f
3 ran. Time 6m 41.00s. SP 7-4.
R A Owen (Flint & Denbigh).
finished alone

326 Maiden (5-7yo) Div I

87 **COOLFLUGH HERO (IRE) ....A Crow** 1
(fav) cls up, ld 6th, grdly increased ld 30l 3 out, eased flat
Mintulyar ....A Dalton 2
mid-div, some late prog, nrst at fin
New Cruiser 5a.......................C Barlow 3
chsd ldrs frm 5 out, no imp clsng stgs
Po Cap Eel 5a *mid to rear, nvr dang*......R Thomas 4
Greenacres Girl 5a *t.o. aft ctt, p.u. bfr 12th*....A Wood pu
200 Frank The Swank *ld to 5th, in tch 8th, wknd qckly, p.u. 11th*..........N Gittens pu
199[5] Real Gent *mid-div, f 14th*..........J Lee f
206 Societys Stream (Ire) *f 5th*..........S Prior f
Sheppie's Reality *mid to rear, nvr dang, p.u. 12th*..........I Lowe pu
Rugrat 5a *u.r. 5th*..........Miss G Randle ur
Bobbing Along (Ire) *chsng grp, 3rd 12th, wknd qckly, p.u. 14th*..........M Worthington pu
Banteer Bet (Ire) 12a *mid to rear, p.u. 4 out* A Mitchell pu
Mystic Major 7a *prom, 2nd 8-14th, sn btn, p.u. 3 out*..........D Sherlock pu
Althrey Lad *mid to rear, p.u. 13th*..........G Hanmer pu
14 ran. 20l, 8l, dist. Time 6m 35.00s. SP 7-4.
R H W Major (North Shropshire).

327 Maiden (5-7yo) II

SHARSMAN (IRE) ....A Crow 1
made all, ran on strngly frm 3 out
82[3] **Bombadier Jack ....C Barlow** 2
hld up, some late prog,ran on wll flat to snatch 2nd on line
206[2] **Nights Image (Ire) ....J Barlow** 3
(fav) n.j.w., cls 2nd 6th, in tch til wknd cls home
205 Rejects Reply *hld up in rear, jmp delib, ran on one-pce, not keen*..........G Hanmer 4
81 Lady Pokey 5a *chsng grp, 3rd 9th, ev ch 5 out, not qckn*..........N Gittens 5
205[2] Crafty Gunner *mid-div in tch, ran on 14-15th, sn btn, p.u. 3 out*..........M Worthington pu
Fancytalkintinker (Ire) *rear, nvr dang, p.u. 5 out*..........A Dalton pu
Palladante (Ire) 5a *ldng grp, cls 3rd 10th, fdd, p.u. 4 out*..........D Barlow pu
206 Pulltheplug *prom to hlfwy, wknd qckly, p.u. 5 out*..........R Burton pu
Scally Hill 5a *prom early, t.o. 11th, p.u. 14th*..........A Mitchell pu
Yasgourra (Ire) *alwys towrds rear, p.u. 13th*. .A Jordan pu
11 ran. 8l, sht-hd, 10l, 1l. Time 6m 34.00s. SP 5-2.
E H Crow (North Shropshire).

328 Land Rover Mens Open (12st)

RIVERSIDE BOY 7ex (bl) ....A Crow 1
jmp wll, cls 2nd to 8th, ld 9th, ran on wll frm 4 out, comf
226[4] **My Nominee 7ex.......................R Burton** 2
(fav) alwys 2nd/3rd, nvr on trms wth wnr, ran on onepce frm 4 out
Barkin *t.o. aft 6th, fence bhnd whn f 10th*....J Saville f
Syrus P Turntable *nvr bttr thn 4th, losng tch whn p.u. 13th*..........C Mulhall pu
86 Charterforhardware 7ex *ld to 8th, wknd qckly whn hdd, lost tch 13th, p.u. 5 out*..........R Bevis pu
Stormhead *f 1st*..........C Barlow f
6 ran. 4l. Time 6m 22.00s. SP 4-1.
Miss M E Sherrington (North Staffordshire).

329 Ladies

SOONER STILL (bl) ....Miss S Sharratt 1
chsd ldrs, 2nd 13th, ld 4 out, ran on und pres frm 2 out
117 **Saahi (USA) ....Miss S Swindells** 2
mid-div, lft 3rd 12th, 2nd 2 out, not qckn cls home
202 **Logical Fun ....Miss L Wallace** 3
chsng grp, 2nd 11th, ld 12th, hdd 4 out, ran on one-pce
Running Frau 5a *rear, not go early pce*..........Miss M Mahee 4
202[5] The Boiler White (Ire) 2ow *mid to rear, outpcd, styng on frm 3 out*..........Miss J Froggatt 5
Stephens Pet *(fav) 4th gng easily whn rddr k/o in mid air 10th*..........Miss A Dare ur
202 Moya's Tip Top 5a *mid-div, 4th 4 out, wknd qckly, p.u. last*..........Miss A Price pu
The Parish Pump (Ire) *ld/disp to 6th, 2nd whn u.r. 10th*..........Mrs C Ford ur
188 Bally Riot (Ire) *ld/disp to 6th, clr ldr frm 7th til ran out 12th*..........Mrs A Rucker ro
215 Walter's Lad *rear thruout, no ch whn p.u. 12th*..........Mrs M Wall pu
10 ran. 2l, 6l, 12l, 1l. Time 6m 26.00s. SP 20-1.
R F Rimmer (Cheshire Forest).

330 Confined (12st)

ITA'S FELLOW (IRE) ....Mrs C Ford 1
mid-div, prog 5 out, up sides 2 out,slght ld last,ran on wll
200[4] **Nodform Wonder ....R Bevis** 2
made all, chal strngly by wnr 2 out, jmp lft last, not rcvr
Whatafellow (Ire) 3ex....................A Crow 3

w.w. rear, 10l 3rd 4 out, 2l 3rd & chal 2 out, no ext run in
200 Bavard Bay *prom, nvr far away, outpcd frm 3 out* ....S Prior 4
200 Tara Boy *chsng grp, no imp frm 4 out, onepcd* ....R Cambray 5
201[6] Auction Law (NZ) *cls up to 10th, fdd, onepce frm 4 out* ....L Whiston 6
200 No More The Fool *mid to rear, p.u. 5 out*...L Brennan pu
Golden Fare *mid to rear, p.u. 5 out*....Miss L Wallace pu
200 Forget The Rest *prom thruout, 2nd whn f 13th* ....O McPhail f
201 What A Miss 5a *rear, t.o.& p.u. 11th*.......R Thomas pu
Born Deep *nvr bttr thn mid-div, p.u. 5 out*...D Barlow pu
93 Spy's Delight *f 1st*....E Woolley f
Grindley Brook *t.o., p.u. 11th*....A Gribben pu
Allezscally 5a *hld up, clsr order 11th, short livd efft, p.u. 4 out*....R Burton pu
86 Back The Road (Ire) 5ex *mid-div, nvr gng wll, no ch whn p.u. 3 out*....G Hanmer pu
Journeys Friend (Ire) 7ex *(fav) wth ldrs whn f 7th* ....A Dalton f
16 ran. 2l, 3l, dist, 3l, 4l. Time 6m 26.00s. SP 6-1.
R Prince (Meynell & Sth Staffs).

331 Restricted Div I (12st)

212[1] **ROYAL SEGOS ....A Baillie 1**
trckd ldrs, chal & lft clr 2 out, ran on und pres
262[5] **For Michael ....Miss J Houldey 2**
mid-div, some late prog 5 out, nrst fin
81[2] **Dalusaway (Ire) 5a....C Stockton 3**
chsd ldrs, strng run 2 out, no ext flat
203 Twelth Man *mid-div, ran on onepcd 4 out*.....R Bevis 4
231 Mighty Haggis *ld to 2nd, prom to 12th, onepcd frm 5 out*....Miss M Mahee 5
226[5] Travel Bound *mid-div, nvr rchd ldrs*........D Barlow 6
203 Rue de Fort *lft in ld 5th, hdd 9th, sn btn, p.u. 14th* ....J Cornes pu
Tails U Win *mid to rear, p.u. 5 out*....P Morris pu
April Suprise 5a *alwys mid to rear, no ch whn p.u. 3 out*....G Hanmer pu
218[7] Spartan Pete *mid to rear, p.u. 4 out*........R Burton pu
Charlie Trumper (Ire) *mstks, chsng grp to hlfwy, fdd, p.u. 5 out*....J Saville pu
200 Domino Night (Ire) *(fav) cls up, ld 3-4th, u.r. 5th* ....Miss J Esden ur
Reckless Lord (Ire) *hld up bhnd ldrs, ld 10th, prssd whn f 2 out*....A Crow f
Nancy's Last 5a *mid to rear, no ch whn p.u. 4 out* ....A Mitchell pu
81[1] Sky Runner *alwys rear, t.o. & p.u. 13th*.......S Prior pu
Scally Lass 5a *mid to rear, p.u. 4 out*..M Worthington pu
212 Charlottes Quest 5a *mid-div, f 10th*.......M Connors f
17 ran. ½l, 3l, 2l, 2l, dist. Time 6m 32.00s. SP 3-1.
A J Baillie (Meynell & South Staffs).

332 Restricted Div II (12st)

203[3] **MISS SHAW 5a ....C Stockton 1**
20s-8s, chsng grp, 2nd at last, ran on und pres to ld flat
204 **Royle Burchlin ....D Barlow 2**
ld, 3l clr last, veered lft flat, hdd nr fin
Mr Busker (Ire) ....C Barlow 3
prom, ev ch 4 out, no ext 2 out
T'int (Ire) 5a *mid-div, styd on frm 3 out, nrst fin* ....J Burley 4
204[4] Glen Taylor *mid-div, ran on onepcd frm 5 out* ....L Whiston 5
Rufo's Coup *mid to rear, nvr in race, p.u. 13th* ....T Raynor pu
Callerose *(fav) mid-div hlfwy, prog 14th, chal whn f 2 out*....A Mitchell f
Dromin Mist *mid to rear, nvr dang, p.u. 4 out* ....S Walker pu
223[5] Autumn Green (Ire) *wth ldrs to hlfwy, fdd, p.u. 4 out* ....R Burton pu
204 River Sunset (Ire) *prom to hlfwy, fdd, p.u. 4 out* ....O McPhail pu
Plundering Star (Ire) *mid to rear, p.u. 5 out*....S Prior pu
258[4] Henrymyson *rear whn u.r. 11th*....J Cornes ur
204 Made Of Talent 5a *alwys rear, t.o. & p.u. 12th* A Crow pu
260 Eyton Rock *alwys rear, t.o. & p.u. aft 11th* ....M Worthington pu
The Honest Poacher (Ire) *chsd ldrs, going wll whn f 4 out*....A Dalton f
Little By Little *mid to rear, no ch whn p.u. 5 out* ....J Barlow pu
203 Daphni (Fr) *cls up, 3rd at 10th, 4th & in tch whn f 4 out* ....Miss K Swindells f
Bredinthepurple (Ire) *hld up in tch to 12th, sn btn, p.u. 4 out*....G Hanmer pu
18 ran. ½l, 7l, dist, 25l. Time 6m 26.00s. SP 8-1.
Mrs R Crank (Cheshire Forest).

333 Intermediate (12st)

123[2] **MISTER BLACK (IRE) ....A Crow 1**
j.w. w.w. bhnd runaway ldr, lft clr 10th, unchal
Therewego (Ire) ....M Munrowd 2
hld up in tch, chsd wnr 13th, unable to chal
84[2] **Howarya Harry (Ire) ....G Hanmer 3**
w.w. late prog, running on fin, nvr plcd to chal
Gen-Tech *rear, some prog frm hlfwy, onepcd frm 3 out*....A Gribben 4
204[1] Flinters *cls up, 3rd 10th, chsd wnr 11th, onepcd frm 13th*....A Dalton 5
Trojan Pleasure 5a *t.o. & p.u. 9th*....C Barlow pu
254[1] Perfect Light *(fav) ld, fast pace, 8l up whn f 10th* ....R Lee f
Ledwyche Gate *chsng grp, ev ch 10th, fdd, p.u. 4 out* ....R Evans pu
119 Carol's Concorde (Ire) *mid to rear, nvr dang, p.u. 5 out*....J Saville pu
Mr Goldfinger *mid to rear, no ch whn p.u. 5 out* ....C Mulhall pu
10 ran. 5l, 15l, 1l, 6l. Time 6m 26.00s. SP 5-2.
Mrs N J Hollows (North Shropshire).
V.S.

TYNEDALE
Corbridge
Saturday March 1st
GOOD

334 Members

SHARP OPINION ....Miss P Robson 1
sttld 3rd, lft 2nd 10th, ld last, ran on well
135[6] **Storm Alive (Ire) ....T Scott 2**
chsd ldr, disp 9th til lft clr nxt, wknd & hdd last
136[3] **Dillons Bridge (Ire) ....D Wood 3**
(fav) mstk 1st, mid-div, outpcd 3 out
Able Moss *mid-div, lost tch 9th, t.o. 11th*....P Forster 4
133 Strong Measure (Ire) *keen hld, ld to 9th, disp whn f nxt*....Miss L Plater f
134 Bantel Bargain 5a *rear, lost tch 8th, t.o. & p.u. 11th* ....P Johnson pu
136[6] Bavington *mid-div, mstk 2nd, u.r. 8th*.....R Morgan ur
7 ran. 4l, 15l, dist. Time 6m 22.00s. SP 2-1.
Mrs L Walby (Tynedale).

335 Confined (12st)

129[1] **SISTER SEVEN (IRE) 5a ....Miss D Laidlaw 1**
handy, disp 10th til lft in ld 12th, styd on wll
130[3] **Farriers Favourite 5a....A Parker 2**
rear, prog 3 out, ev ch last, onepcd
130[4] **Toaster Crumpet 3ex....Miss P Robson 3**
mid-div, prog 3 out, ev ch nxt, outpcd
158 Lothian Pilot *ld to 5th, wth wnr 13th til wknd rpdly 2 out*....D Wood 4
Sharp Challenge *prom, ld 5th, disp ld whn f 12th* ....T Glass f
In Demand *(fav) hld up mid-div, f 12th*......P Craggs f
135 Up And Running *rear, jmpd slwly 1st, sn bhnd, rdn 10th, t.o. & p.u. 12th*....Mrs C Amos pu
7 ran. 1½l, 4l, 20l. Time 6m 23.00s. SP 14-1.
M H Walton (College Valley/Northumberland).

336 3m 5f Ladies Open

1321 **MISTY NIGHT 5a ....Miss A Bowie** 1
(fav) mid-div, prog 12th, ld 14th-16th, ld last, ran on strngly
Piper O'Drummond ....Miss P Robson 2
hld up rear, mstk 8th, prog 12th, chal last, not qckn
1324 **Bow Handy Man ....Miss D Laidlaw** 3
mid-div, prog 6th, ld 8th-14th, ld 16th-last, onepcd
2652 Squires Tale (Ire) *prom, drppd rear 13th, kpt on onepcd frm 3 out*..........Mrs S Grant 4
1584 Ready Steady *hld up rear, prog 14th, no imp whn u.r. 2 out*..........Mrs K Hargreave ur
2317 Schweppes Tonic *mid-div, ld 4th-8th, prom til fdd 14th, t.o. & p.u. last*..........Mrs C Amos pu
1654 Across The Lake (bl) *ld to 4th, sn fdd, lost tch 13th, p.u. 2 out*..........Miss S Brotherton pu
2315 Minibrig 5a 2ow *mid-div, prog 10th, ev ch 16th, onepcd whn u.r. 2 out*..........Miss S Forster ur
1582 Roly Prior *alwys prom, ev ch whn f 16th*..........Mrs V Jackson f
9 ran. 1l, 2½l, 6l. Time 7m 45.00s. SP 5-2.
Mrs M A Bowie (Buccleuch).

337 Restricted Div I

LEANNES MAN (IRE) ....C Wilson 1
made all, drew clr frm 2 out, easily
1577 **Solwaysands ....B Gibson** 2
prom, chsd ldr 12th, ev ch 2 out, not qckn
General Delight ....D Wood 3
mid-div, prog 9th, not qckn 3 out
2663 Attle *mid-div, prog 9th, ev ch 14th, wknd rpdly 2 out*..........W Burnell 4
2305 Tannock Brook *prom til outpcd 9th, kpt on frm 2 out*..........T Morrison 5
Jayandoubleu (Ire) *mid-div, mod prog 4 out, sn wknd*..........T Scott 6
2341 Thief's Road *prom til fdd 10th, t.o. 12th*......R Shiels 7
157 Mandys Special 5a *bhnd frm 6th, t.o. 12th*..W Morgan 8
266 River Ramble 5a *rear whn f 4th*.....Miss T Jackson f
1351 Nothingtotellme (Ire) *(fav) rear, mod prog 11th, blnd 14th, sn wknd, p.u. 2 out*..........A Parker pu
230 Kings Token 1ow *prom, mstk 2nd, wknd 10th, t.o. & p.u. 2 out*..........J Walton pu
11 ran. 10l, 4l, 10l, 1l, 2l, 15l, 15l. Time 6m 23.00s. SP 6-1.
Mrs G Reed (Haydon).

338 Restricted Div II

2307 **PABLOWMORE ....R Green** 1
prom, 2nd 13th, ld nxt, clr whn mstk last, styd on well
1314 **The Buachaill (Ire) ....P Craggs** 2
(fav) rear, prog 7th, ld 12th-14th, onepcd frm 2 out
1574 **Lindon Run ....R Morgan** 3
ld to 6th, prom til lft in ld 11th, hdd nxt, fdd 3 out
1361 Star Lea *chsd ldrs, outpcd 13th*........B Stonehouse 4
2664 Computer Pickings 5a *rear & sn bhnd, t.o. 9th*..........F Crawford 5
Sarona Smith 5a 4ow *mid-div, lost plc 5th, wll bhnd whn u.r. 10th*..........Miss J Hutchinson ur
36 Hurricane Ryan (Ire) 1ow *keen hld, rear, prog 4th, ld 6th, clr whn p.u. 11th*..........J McMath pu
1615 Mr Cosmo (Ire) *prom, prssng ldr whn ran out 5th*..........J Billinge ro
36 Keep A Secret *rear & bhnd, t.o. & p.u. last* P Atkinson pu
Kinlochaline 5a *swrvd & u.r. start*..........J Ewart ur
10 ran. 5l, 12l, 7l, 15l. Time 6m 24.00s. SP 6-1.
R W Green (Milvain).

339 3m 5f Land Rover Open (12st)

2291 **HAGAR 7ex.........................M Bradburne** 1
mid-div, gd prog 3 out, ld last, ran on strngly
1323 **Lupy Minstrel 7ex......................A Parker** 2
alwys prom, ld 3 out, hdd last, kpt on
1331 **Washakie 1ow 7ex ....J Walton** 3
(fav) hld up mid-div, prog 3 out, ev ch nxt, onepcd
1661 Tobin Bronze 1ow *hld up rear, prog 13th, went 2nd 4 out, wknd 2 out*..........R Tate 4
2324 Tartan Tornado 7ex *mid-div, drppd rear 16th, sn t.o.*..........P Johnson 5
1134 Tom Log (v) *keen hld, ld to 3 out, wknd rpdly*..........W Burnell 6
Beau Rose *rear, lost tch 11th, p.u. aft 15th*...S Swiers pu
2326 Loughlinstown Boy *mid-div, drppd rear 10th, t.o. & p.u. 13th*..........P Craggs pu
Boreen Owen *prom til wknd 14th, t.o. & p.u. last*..........T Morrison pu
34 Buckaneer Bay *prom til wknd 3 out, p.u. last*..........C Wilson pu
2293 Kilminfoyle 7ex *rear, mstk 4th, t.o. 13th, p.u. 15th*..........T Oates pu
11 ran. 3l, 12l, 1l, 12l, 10l. Time 7m 43.00s. SP 9-4.
J I A Charlton (Border).

340 Maiden (5-7yo) Div I (12st)

1612 **BELLS WILL RING (IRE) ....T Scott** 1
(fav) made all, qcknd clr last, comf
136 **Alianne 5a ....P Johnson** 2
alwys prom, went 2nd 3 out, ev ch nxt, outpcd
235 **Border Glory 1ow.......................R Shiels** 3
alwys prom, ev ch 2 out, sn wknd
Saucy Mint 5a *trckd ldrs, fdd 13th*..........C Storey 4
Jones *rear, lost tch 7th, t.o. 10th, p.u. 12th*..........Miss A Adams pu
1618 Lethem Laird *mid-div, outpcd 12th, t.o. & p.u. 2 out*..........A Robson pu
136 Farriers Fantasy 12a *rear & outpcd 12th, t.o. & p.u. 3 out*..........A Parker pu
Pleasedaspunch (Ire) 7a *mid-div, wknd 8th, t.o. & p.u. 11th*..........Miss D Laidlaw pu
160 Hetty Bell 12a *sn wll bhnd, p.u. 12th* Mrs K Hargreave pu
235 Political Diamond 5a *rear & sn outpcd, t.o. & p.u. 12th*..........R Green pu
10 ran. 6l, 10l, 12l. Time 6m 38.00s. SP 7-4.
Ian Hamilton (Tynedale).

341 Maiden (5-7yo) Div II (12st)

2296 **ARCTIC LEADER 5a.....................M Ruddy** 1
(fav) disp til lft in ld 4th, hdd nxt, ld 10th, clr 12th, imprssv
235 **Hooky's Treat 5a...................M Bradburne** 2
rear, prog 10th, not qckn frm 4 out
160 **Keirose 5a ....C Paisley** 3
chsd ldrs, outpcd 4 out
Political Belle 5a *mid-div, prog 10th, wknd 3 out, t.o.*..........C Wilson 4
1614 Disrespect 5a *prom, ld 5th til hdd & wknd 10th, t.o. & p.u. 4 out*..........P Craggs pu
2334 Peelinick *disp til u.r. 4th*..........T Oates ur
Reskue Line 5ow *mid-div, fdd 12th, f nxt*.....A Shaw f
Bold Echo 12a *rear whn u.r. 8th*..........R Morgan ur
Henry Higgins *rear whn u.r. 1st*..........Miss E Wagg ur
161 The Alleycat (Ire) *rear, t.o. 4th, p.u. 12th*..........Miss P Robson pu
10 ran. 15l, 6l, 10l. Time 6m 34.00s. SP 5-2.
A Gilchrist (Lauderdale).

342 Open Maiden (8yo+) Div I

1367 **MARKED CARD ....Mrs M Kendall** 1
rear, plenty to do 4 out, rdp prog 2 out, ld flat, hld on wl
233 **Luvly Bubbly ....M Bradburne** 2
rear, prog 7th, ld 4 out, hdd nxt, ev ch last, kpt on
Mirror Melody 5a ....T Morrison 3
ld to 6th, prom, ev ch 2 out, sn wknd
Worthy Way *rear, prog 9th going wll, ld 3 out, hdd & wknd last*..........C Storey 4
Are-Oh *(fav) rear, prog 6th, chsd ldrs til outpcd 4 out*..........Miss P Robson 5
135 Aston Warrior 5a *bhnd, t.o. 10th, p.u. nxt*..........Mrs K Hargreave pu
Copper Pan 5a *mid-div, drppd rear 9th, wll bhnd whn p.u. 12th*..........T Scott pu

266 Level Vibes *prom, ld 6th-4 out, wknd rpdly, p.u. 2 out* ....R Abrahams pu
234[4] Prince Rossini (Ire) (bl) *prom, rmndrs 10th, sn wknd, t.o. 12th, p.u. 2 out*....B Gibson pu
Newbrano 5a *mid-div, wknd 12th, t.o. & p.u. 2 out* ....J Carmichael pu
Saigon Lady (Ire) 5a *mid-div, outpcd 13th, t.o. & p.u. 2 out*....A Robson pu
233 Bagots Park *prom til outpcd 12th, t.o. & p.u. 2 out* ....R Shiels pu
12 ran. ½l, 6l, ½l, 15l. Time 6m 36.00s. SP 12-1.
Mrs M A Kendall (Cumberland Farmers).

343 Open Maiden (8yo+) Div II

120[2] **SECRET BAY ....S Swiers** 1
(fav) chsd ldrs, lft in ld 10th, drew clr 4 out, v easily
233[7] **Lauder Square ....M Bradburne** 2
mid-div, kpt on frm 2 out, ran on well flat
162[6] **Tolmin ....A Ogden** 3
mid-div, mod 3rd 11th, onepcd 2 out
162[4] Corston Frisby *prom, lft 2nd 10th, wth wnr til outpcd 4 out*....A Parker 4
Notarius (Fr) *sn rear, lost tch 9th, t.o.* ....Mrs K Hargreave 5
234[5] Indian River (Ire) *mid-div, wknd 11th, t.o.* ....C Wilson 6
234 Bantel Baronet *rear, sn wll bhnd, t.o. & p.u. 12th* ....Miss J Hedley pu
Fast Fun *prom til fdd 8th, t.o. & p.u. 2 out*...R Morgan pu
230 Mighty Express *mid-div, f 3rd*....A Robson f
Billy Buoyant *sn wll bhnd, t.o. & p.u. 12th*....J Walton pu
Capital Letter (Ire) *trckd ldr whn f 10th* ....N Smith f
Mister Buzios *ld til u.r. 10th* ....P Craggs ur
120 Guler-A *prom til b.d. 10th* ....S Gibbon bd
Riding Hills Girl 5a *rear whn f 11th* ....T Scott f
14 ran. Dist, 1l, ½l, 7l, 8l. Time 6m 31.00s. SP 5-4.
S P Dent (Zetland).
N.E.

BURTON
Market Rasen Point-To-Point
Sunday March 2nd
GOOD TO FIRM

344 Members

252[4] **FLYING QUEST ....S Walker** 1
ld/disp til ld apr 14th, sn clr, hdd last, rallied,jst faild
248[4] **Ways And Means 5a ....K Green** 2
(fav) hld up last, went 2nd 14th, clsd 3 out, ld last, eased nr fn
251 **Vimchase ....S J Robinson** 3
ld/disp til apr 14th, sn wll bhnd, t.o.
3 ran. Nk, dist. Time 6m 37.00s. SP 5-2.
J W Lockwood (Burton).

345 Open Maiden Div I (12st)

141 **KIRI'S ROSE (IRE) 5a....P Gee** 1
(fav) in tch, went 2nd 11th, ld apr last, qcknd clr, easily
212[3] **Mr Wilbur ....A Dalton** 2
chsd ldrs, lft 2nd 6th, ld 10th-apr last, no ext
212 **Shining Penny (bl) ....K Green** 3
w.w. steady prog 9th, ev ch 13th, btn apr 2 out
Paddy's Pocket *chsd ldrs 7th, 4th & outpcd apr 14th, t.o.*....D Esden 4
Isola Farnese 5a *mid-div, mstk 4th, blnd & u.r. 6th* ....K Needham ur
147 Northern Code *chsd ldrs to 6th, mid-div whn p.u. 9th* ....G Smith pu
211 Ilikehim *t.d.e. ld til apr 4th,lft clr 6th,hdd apr 11th,wknd,p.u.13th*....S Whitaker pu
120 Rapid Regent *mid-div to 8th, sn wll bhnd, t.o. & p.u. 12th*....R Morney pu
Lac de Gras (Ire) *jmpd bdly, sn wll bhnd, t.o. & p.u. 10th*....A Pennock pu
Fiddle The Books *bhnd frm 3rd, t.o. 9th, p.u. 11th* ....T Marks pu
Gonalston Percy *alwys bhnd, t.o. 9th, p.u. 11th* ....N Kent pu
Kabancy *keen hld, chsd ldr, blnd 3rd, ld apr nxt til f 6th*....J Townson f
Half Each 12a *f 1st* ....T Whitaker f
13 ran. 6l, 10l, dist. Time 6m 39.00s. SP 7-2.
Brian Gee (Grove & Rufford).
Two fences omitted. 16 jumps.

346 Open Maiden Div II (12st)

114[4] **WINTERS MELODY 5a 2ow....A Pennock** 1
prom, lft in ld 6th, drew wll clr apr 14th, unchal
204 **Young Parson ....T Marlow** 2
prom, lft 2nd 6th, outpcd by wnr apr 14th
Petit Primitive 5a ....S Charlton 3
rear, lft 5th at 6th, prog to 3rd 14th, nvr dang
120 Just Jessica 5a *mid-div, lft 3rd 6th, lost tch apr 13th, t.o.*....A Balding 4
120[3] Andretti's Heir 3ow *ld til f 6th* ....A Bonson f
211 Sandy King (Ire) (bl) *prom til apr 7th, sn bhnd, last & p.u. 12th*....A Dalton pu
Wolf Tone *(fav) hld up, last whn bdly hmpd & u.r. 6th* ....R Ford ur
209 Tinker Hill *cls up, 2nd whn f 6th* ....M Bond f
208[3] Man Of Wisley (Ire) *blnd 1st, hvly rstrnd in rear, p.u. 4th*....D Ingle pu
141[4] Springfield Rex *mid-div til b.d. 6th*....K Needham bd
10 ran. Dist, 10l, 8l. Time 6m 41.00s. SP 8-1.
E Pennock (Staintondale).

347 Open Maiden Div III (12st)

141 **MAMNOON (USA) ....N Kent** 1
mid-div, prog 12th, rdn to ld 15th, styd on well 2 out
Adventurus 7a ....A Dalton 2
jmpd slwly 1st, prog 10th, 2nd 3 out, unable qckn und pres
212[5] **Pollytickle 5a 1ow ....G Smith** 3
prom to 5th, in tch, lft 3rd 14th, onepcd frm 3 out
211[5] Chorus Of Wings (Ire) (bl) *cls up, ld apr 7th-9th, wknd frm 3 out*....D Crossland 4
212 Face The Music *ld to 5th, ld 10th-15th, wknd* ....E Andrewes 5
Orinoco Venture (Ire) *hld up, prog 10th, lost tch 13th, bhnd & p.u. 3 out*....R Ford pu
Miss Madelon 12a *hld up bhnd, mstks 4 & 12th, t.o. & p.u. nxt*....S Swiers pu
204 Kayak Point (bl) *cls up, disp 6th-nxt, wknd 13th, p.u. nxt, lame*....Miss E Guest pu
210 Red Rebel 7a *(fav) keen hld, prog to ld 9th-10th, cls 3rd whn ran out 14th*....S Charlton ro
9 ran. 5l, 5l, 6l, 20l. Time 6m 49.00s. SP 20-1.
Rob Woods (Cranwell Bloodhounds).

348 Restricted (12st)

140 **RYDERS WELLS ....S Walker** 1
prom, chsd ldr 9th, ld 3 out, rdn clr, easily
213[6] **Henry Darling ....E Andrewes** 2
mid-div, 4th 2 out, styd on, not trbl wnr
118 **Malvern Cantina ....S Swiers** 3
hld up wll bhnd, prog 11th, mstk 4 out, styd on, nvr nrr
83 Lillybrook 5a *(Jt fav) mid-div, prog 10th, rdn 15th, went 2nd 2 out, no imp wnr*....J Townson 4
203[4] Foolish Fantasy *chsd ldrs, outpcd apr 14th, 5th & no ch apr last*....S Prior 5
Ellerton Park *ld, mstk 10th, hdd 3 out, wknd nxt* ....R Ford 6
Dromin Fox *mstks, alwys bhnd, no ch apr 14th* ....J Dillon 7
213 Cahermone Lady (Ire) 5a 6ow *rear, in tch to 11th, no ch frm 13th*....S Whitaker 8
119 Mighty Merc *chsd ldr to 9th, t.o. & p.u. 15th* S Gibbon pu
203[5] Sargeants Choice *chsd ldrs to 14th, no ch whn s.u. apr last*....J Barlow su
251[8] Stride To Glory (Ire) *chsd ldrs, blnd & u.r. 8th* ....D Topping ur
206[1] Rolier (Ire) *(Jt fav) cls up til slppd & u.r. 5th* ..A Dalton ur

Political Field 5a *alwys rear, blnd 6th, rdn & no rspns 13th, p.u. nxt*....S Charlton pu
13 ran. 20l, 3l, 2l, 7l, 1l, 6l, 3l. Time 6m 36.00s. SP 16-1.
E F Astley-Arlington (Blankney).

349 Ladies

268² **INTEGRITY BOY 7ex....Miss A Armitage** 1
(fav) in tch, lft in ld 12th, drew clr apr 2 out, easily
249 **Naughty Nellie 5a....Mrs J Dawson** 2
chsd ldr 3rd-11th, lft 2nd nxt, btn 2 out, blnd last
195 **Crazy Otto ....Miss L Allan** 3
cls up, lft 3rd 12th, outpcd 15th, nrly sntchd 2nd
Adamare 4ex *ld, blnd & lost irons 12th, p.u. nxt* ....Miss C Tarratt pu
251 Midge 5a *rear, losing tch whn u.r. 13th* ....Miss S Brotherton ur
5 ran. Dist, ½l. Time 6m 45.00s. SP 4-6.
Richard P Watts (Staintondale).

350 Confined (12st)

MR DICK ....S Swiers 1
(fav) in tch, disp ld 14th-nxt, chal & ld last, ran on
266¹ **Barichste (bl)....Maj M Watson** 2
mid-div, jnd ldrs 14th, ld nxt, hdd last, not qckn
76³ **Elder Prince 5ex....P Gee** 3
trckd ldrs, ev ch 14th, rdn & wknd apr last
214⁵ Romany Ark *chsd ldrs, outpcd apr 14th, lft 4th nxt, kpt on*....N Bell 4
Dare Say *alwys bhnd, lost tch 13th, t.o.*....G Brewer 5
118 The Ultimate Buck *rear, lost tch 11th, t.o.*...R Morney 6
121¹ Breckenbrough Lad 6ow *alwys rear, lost tch 13th, t.o.* ....I Bennett 7
Silks Domino *rear, t.o. whn blnd 6th, p.u. 13th* ....C Smith pu
207¹ Sheriff's Band *ld to 14th, 4th & btn whn f nxt, dead* ....D Esden f
214 Soda Popinski (USA) *mid-div, mstk 6th, 6th & btn whn f 14th*....C Vale f
76⁹ Sporting Spirit *prom, chsd ldr 4th til f 12th* ....M Kneafsey f
11 ran. 1l, 8l, 3l, dist, 20l, 15l. Time 6m 34.00s. SP 7-4.
Mrs J Cooper (Middleton).

351 Men's Open (12st)

74¹ **CARLY BRRIN ....S Swiers** 1
chsd ldrs, went 2nd 12th, ld apr 14th, sn clr, unchal
200¹ **Shoon Wind ....A Dalton** 2
(fav) chsd ldrs, 3rd & rdn apr 14th, went 2nd nxt, unable chal
216 **Rambling Lord (Ire) ....G Smith** 3
chsd ldr 11th,blnd nxt,outpcd 14th,3rd & no ch whn blnd last
248⁶ Alpha One *in tch, outpcd apr 14th, styd on well 2 out* ....P Gee 4
216 Daphnis (USA) 7ex *hld up, prog 10th, 4th & btn 14th, no dang aft*....S Prior 5
193⁶ Stanwick Farlap 5a 1ow *rear, in tch to 12th, bhnd frm 14th* ....T Marks 6
154 No More Trix 7ex *prom, disp 4th & btn whn f 14th* ....W Burnell f
Old Money *disp to 5th, wknd 10th, t.o. & p.u. 12th* ....A Pickering pu
265 Simply A Star (Ire) *alwys rear, brf effrt 11th, sn strgglng, t.o. & p.u. last*....Maj M Watson pu
Spring Call (Ire) 7ex *disp 5th til apr 14th, wknd, t.o. & p.u. last*....S J Robinson pu
10 ran. 20l, 2l, 3l, 2l, 8l. Time 6m 33.00s. SP 6-1.
Mrs J R Buckley (Brocklesby).
S.P.

SOUTH DURHAM
Great Stainton
Sunday March 2nd
SOFT

352 Members

164³ **FLYING LION ....Mrs S Grant** 1
(fav) prom, outpcd 14th, styd on 2 out, clsng whn lft clr last
Say Daphne 5a....Miss P Robson 2
rear,blnd 3 out,sn t.o.,lft remote 2nd & guided round last
163³ Jolly Fellow *mid-div, 2nd 7th, disp 3 out, ld nxt, 2l up whn f last* ....Miss S Ward f
164⁵ Wild Adventure *rear, lost tch 15th, f 4 out, dead* ....T Glass f
Japodene 5a *ld til jnd 3 out, hdd nxt, 2nd & hld whn f last*....M Haigh f
5 ran. Dist. Time 7m 0.00s. SP Evens.
John Mackley (South Durham).

353 Confined (12st)

166 **EASTERN PLEASURE ....N Wilson** 1
prom, ld 11th, drew clr 2 out, v easily
264¹ **Earl Gray ....Miss A Deniel** 2
mid-div, outpcd 12th, prog 14th, ev ch 2 out, no imp
166⁵ **Fast Study ....S Robinson** 3
prom, lft in ld 4th, hdd 11th, wknd 2 out
164 Rabble Rouser *mid-div, went 2nd 5th, disp nxt-11th, sn wknd* ....R Edwards 4
265 Black Spur *ld to 2nd, trckd ldr whn ran out 4th* ....Miss P Robson ro
Inconclusive *rear, losing tch whn p.u. 11th* ..A Ogden pu
32³ Admission (Ire) *(fav) prom, ld 2nd til ran out 4th* ....Miss L Horner ro
37 Mal's Castle (Ire) 5a *mid-div, mstk 3rd, bhnd 6th, t.o. & p.u. 11th* ....P Atkinson pu
Crown And Anchor 7a *rear, mstk 3rd, u.r. 6th* ....G Markham ur
9 ran. 8l, 8l, 25l. Time 6m 58.00s. SP 8-1.
Ian Emmerson (Braes Of Derwent).

354 Men's Open

113 **CASTLETOWN COUNT 7a....N Wilson** 1
(fav) hld up, prog 13th, ld 15th, drew wll clr, imprssv
216 **Gaelic Warrior ....N Tutty** 2
prom, ld 3-8th, lft in ld 12th, hdd 15th, onepcd aft
Mr Setaside ....D Coates 3
mid-div, went 2nd 12th, outpcd frm 4 out
265⁵ Dalmore *rear, outpcd 10th, t.o.* ....M Haigh 4
Darika Lad *rear, mstk 11th, lost tch 14th, t.o. & p.u. 2 out* ....C Mulhall pu
166³ General Brandy *sttld 3rd, wknd 14th, t.o. & p.u. 2 out* ....G Tuer pu
267 Pats Cross (Ire) *ld to 3rd, ld agn 8th til crshd thro wing & u.r. 12th*....J Byrne ur
7 ran. 10l, 3l, 25l. Time 6m 41.00s. SP Evens.
Mrs A M Easterby (Middleton).

355 Ladies

CHEEKY POT ....Mrs S Grant 1
rear, lost tch 14th, rpd prog apr last, ld flat
215 **Thistle Monarch ....Miss R Clark** 2
chsd ldr, ld 2 out, sn clr, wknd & hdd flat
67⁵ **Southern Minstrel ....Miss C Metcalfe** 3
rear, prog 8th, outpcd 3 out, kpt on apr last
249¹ Final Hope (Ire) *prom, prog 4 out, no imp frm 2 out* ....Mrs F Needham 4
165¹ Cumberland Blues (Ire) *(fav) ld, jmpd rght, hdd & fdd 2 out*....Miss A Deniel 5
Colonel Popski *alwys mid-div, nvr a dang* Mrs J Barr 6
Crocket Lass 5a 4ow *rear, lost tch 6th, t.o. & p.u. 12th* ....Miss F Hunter pu
Fly For Us 5a *mid-div, prog 8th, wknd 4 out, p.u. nxt* ....Mrs C Ford pu
120 Ski Lady 5a *rear & lost tch 10th, t.o. & p.u. 12th* ....Miss L Horner pu
9 ran. 5l, 2l, 3l, 3l, 2l. Time 6m 41.00s. SP 16-1.
Mrs E I L Tate (Hurworth).

356 Intermediate

TATTLEJACK (IRE) ....Mrs C Ford 1

hld up, prog 13th, went 2nd 4 out, ld apr last, ran on well
264[2] **Katies Argument 5a...............Miss J Wilson** 2
rear & plenty to do 13th, prog 2 out, ran on well flat
Tom The Tank ....C Mulhall 3
(fav) mid-div,prog 11th,ld 15th, sn clr, hdd apr last, eased,lame
167[3] Chapel Island *hld up, prog 11th, went 3rd 3 out, no prog aft*..............G Tuer 4
267 Polynth *mid-div, rdn 11th, outpcd nxt*.....G Markham 5
265[8] Skipping Gale *prom to 9th, sn lost tch*.....P Atkinson 6
118[4] Mandys Lad *plld hrd, ld & sn clr, slw jmp 14th, sn hdd & wknd*..............S Robinson 7
266 On The Fly *prom, wknd 8th, blnd & p.u. aft nxt*..............R Edwards pu
230 Will Travel (Ire) *mid-div, went 2nd 10th, rdn nxt, wknd 14th, p.u. 3 out*..............A Robson pu
9 ran. 10l, hd, 6l, 7l, 2l, 3l. Time 6m 53.00s. SP 7-1.
M Silcock (West Shropshire Draghounds).

357 Open Maiden Div I

269[3] **LINGCOOL 5a...............N Wilson** 1
(fav) made all, drew clr apr last, ran on und pres
Timmoss (Ire)...............A Parker 2
prom, ev ch 3 out, onepcd nxt
266 **Jolly Ghost...............N Smith** 3
alwys prom, ev ch 2 out, onepcd
136 Whosthat *prom til fdd 8th, lost tch 12th, sn bhnd*..............Miss S Lamb 4
343 Capital Letter (Ire) *mid-div, prog 13th, wknd apr 3 out, p.u. nxt*..............G Tuer pu
264[6] Smith's Melody *mid-div, f 4th*..............M Haigh f
120 Just For Me (Ire) *prom, fdd 12th, t.o. & p.u. 3 out*..............J Sinnott pu
Patey Court 5a *rear, prog 10th, wknd 4 out, t.o. & p.u. 2 out*..............C Mulhall pu
Magic Song 5a *prom til wknd 14th, t.o. & p.u. 3 out*..............C Denny pu
210 Not So Prim 12a *prom, fdd 7th, t.o. & p.u. nxt*..N Tutty pu
Mature April 5a *alwys rear, t.o. & p.u. 4 out* P Jenkins pu
80 Surprise View 12a *mid-div, lost tch 12th, p.u. 3 out*..............G Markham pu
269 West Lutton 7a *mid-div, f 3rd*..........Miss A Deniel f
Primitive Way 7a *rear, wll bhnd 14th, p.u. 2 out*..............P Atkinson pu
See More Action 7a *mid-div, drppd rear 10th, t.o. & p.u. 12th*..............Mrs C Ford pu
15 ran. 4l, 1l, 25l. Time 6m 47.00s. SP 2-1.
R Morley (Derwent).
One fence omitted last two races. 17 jumps each race.

358 Open Maiden Div II

THE OXFORD DON ....N Wilson 1
(fav) alwys prom, went 2nd 11th, disp 3 out, ld apr last, ran on
269 **Blank Cheque...............D Coates** 2
prom, disp 3 out, not qckn nxt
162 **Annulment (Ire)...............L Morgan** 3
mid-div, prog to ld 7th, hdd 10th, steadily lost tch
212 Goodheavens Mrtony *prom, lft in ld 5th, hdd 7th, sn fdd*..............M Bennison 4
161[3] Don Tocino *prom, ld 10th, hdd 3 out, sn wknd*..............N Smith 5
269 Lord George *mid-div, fdd 7th, p.u. 9th*.....P Atkinson pu
80 Tudor Flight 5a *rear, prog 8th, ev ch whn f 12th*..............G Markham f
Durham Delight 5a *ld, sn clr, u.r. 5th*......S Bowden ur
209[3] Fair Grand (bl) *rear, lost tch 10th, t.o. 3 out, p.u. nxt*..............A Ogden pu
Killeaney Carr (Ire) *mid-div, lost tch 9th, wll bhnd 11th, t.o. & p.u. 13th*..............Miss P Robson pu
Mr Hook 7a *mid-div, lost tch 8th, p.u. nxt*.....I Brown pu
269 Kowloon Bay (Ire) *sn dtchd, t.o. & p.u. 12th*..............R Edwards pu
168 Stud Stile Girl 5a *f 1st*..............A Robson f
266 Sparky Brown (Ire) *prom, ran out 3rd*.......D Collop ro
14 ran. 6l, dist, 12l, 10l. Time 6m 43.00s. SP 11-4.
Miss C Pinkney (Braes Of Derwent).
N.E.

SOUTH HEREFORDSHIRE
Garnons
Sunday March 2nd
GOOD TO SOFT

359 Members (12st)

KINGS RANK ....H Wheeler 1
jmpd delib, chal 12th, ld nxt, drew clr frm 15th
5[5] **Robusti 7ex...............D S Jones** 2
(fav) ld to 12th, outpcd frm 15th, styd on und pres flat
88[3] **Oats For Notes 5a...............M Rimell** 3
trckd ldrs, effrt 15th, wknd aft 2 out
3 ran. 4l, dist. Time 6m 51.00s. SP 7-2.
Mrs L P Vaughan (South Herefordshire).

360 Confined (12st)

FROZEN PIPE 5a...............J Jukes 1
trckd ldrs, prog 15th, ld & lft clr 2 out
255[8] **Oragas...............R Burton** 2
chsd ldrs til outpcd 11th, lft dist 3rd, tk 2nd flat
255 **Bowl Of Oats...............S Blackwell** 3
prom to 11th, no ch whn lft dist 2nd 2 out
Only In Ireland *ld 2nd-nxt, wknd 10th, p.u. 12th*..............R Inglesant pu
Poinciana *ld frm 7th, 3l up 15th, hdd & f 2 out*..............D Stephens f
McMahon's River 5a 5ex *prom til wknd 11th, t.o. 15th, p.u. nxt*..............C Richards pu
Danbury Lad (Ire) *(fav) trckd ldrs, effrt 14th, no prog nxt, p.u. 2 out*..............Miss A Dare pu
190[1] Nutcase 5a *ld 1st & 4-6th, chsd ldr 15th, lft in btn 2nd whn f 2 out*..............T Stephenson f
260[1] Perryline 5a *prom, ev ch til wknd 15th, p.u. 3 out*..............A Wintle pu
Brighton Beach *alwys last, t.o. whn f 8th* M FitzGerald f
10 ran. Dist, 1l. Time 6m 37.00s. SP 8-1.
Alan P Brewer (North Ledbury).

361 Ladies

219[1] **DI STEFANO ....Miss A Dare** 1
(fav) w.w. clsd 12th, cruised into ld 15th, sn clr
Taurean Tycoon ....Miss S Duckett 2
30l 4th at 7th, effrt to 12l 3rd 14th, won race for 2nd
257[5] **Run To Form ....Miss E Wilesmith** 3
prom to 5th, 25l 2nd 9th, kpt on onepcd 15th
85 Dauphin Bleu (Fr) *ld til u.r. 2nd*.......Miss V Roberts ur
Outcrop 5a *prom, 10l 2nd whn f 8th*...Miss C Thomas f
Peter Pointer *ld 2nd, sn clr, just ld 15th, sn hdd & wknd, p.u. flat*..............Miss E Crawford pu
Opals Son *alwys rear, t.o. 9th, p.u. 11th*..............Miss A Murphy pu
7 ran. Dist, sht-hd. Time 6m 42.00s. SP 1-3.
Mrs R Onions (Berkeley).

362 Men's Open (12st)

DALAMETRE ....M Munrowd 1
ld/disp til def adv aft 15th, styd on well 3 out
Dino Malta (Fr) ....H Wheeler 2
mid-div, prog to chal 14th, ev ch til no ext 2 out
Pat Cullen ....S Blackwell 3
in tch til outpcd 11th, styd on to tk 3rd flat
186[1] Trackman (Ire) *cls up, chal 12th, no ext frm 15th, wknd 3 out*..............J Jukes 4
Saddler's Choice *alwys rear, lost tch 11th, styd on onepcd*..............D Painter 5
Fiddlers Three *(fav) prom, cls 3rd whn f 11th* I Wynne f
Local Customer *ld/disp to 11th, wknd 13th, p.u. 15th*..............D S Jones pu
Members Rights 5a *chsd ldrs to 10th, lost tch nxt, t.o. & p.u. 3 out*..............M Keel pu
85 Drumceva *chsd ldrs til lost tch 11th, t.o. & p.u. 3 out*..............M Wilesmith pu
A Farm Bar *prom til wknd 9th, p.u. 12th*....P Williams pu

Malthouse Lad *in tch to 10th, wknd & p.u. aft 13th* ....D Stephens pu
11 ran. 8l, 10l, 1½l, 1½l. Time 6m 49.00s. SP 10-1.
Mrs J Z Munday (Clifton-On-Teme).

363 P P O R A Div I (12st)

97³ **TINOTOPS** ....**Miss S Vickery** 1
(fav) trckd ldr 8th, ld 15th, 5l up nxt, drew clr
262¹ **Gunner Boon** ....**Miss P Jones** 2
ld til jnd 14th, wknd frm 3 out
Landsker Alfred ....**Miss A Dare** 3
w.w. went cls 3rd 9th, ev ch 13th, wknd nxt, walked in
262 Glitterbird 5a *prom, 4th & in tch whn blnd 11th, p.u. nxt*........Julian Pritchard pu
191⁶ No Panic *10l 5th at 8th, lost tch 11th, p.u. 15th* ....Miss A Meakins pu
200 Charlie Chalk *effrt to 15l 4th at 12th, sn lost tch, p.u. 2 out*........C Stockton pu
6 ran. Dist, dist. Time 6m 38.00s. SP 5-4.
R H H Targett (Blackmore & Sparkford Vale).

364 P P O R A Div II (12st)

202¹ **SAMS HERITAGE 4ex** ....**Miss A Dare** 1
(fav) cls up, ld 7th, alwys in cmmnd, pshd out flat
216⁵ **Merlyns Choice** ....**A Woodward** 2
cls up, went 5l 3rd 14th, chsd wnr nxt, kpt on one-pcd
Sandy Beau 4ex........**D Duggan** 3
made most to 6th, chsd wnr til wknd 14th
220⁹ Shadow Walker 4ex *alwys rear, effrt 13th, no prog 15th*........T Stephenson 4
256 Rusty Music *prom, 4l 3rd at 9th, lost tch 13th* ....C Richards 5
285 Conna Moss (Ire) *rear 5th, 12l 5th at 9th, p.u. aft 13th* ....Miss P Jones pu
221 Le Vienna (Ire) *alwys rear, lost tch 11th, t.o. & p.u. 2 out*........S Currey pu
7 ran. 2l, dist, 10l, 6l. Time 6m 47.00s. SP 2-5.
C G Smedley (Berkeley).

365 2½m Open Maiden Div I (12st)

259 **MANARD 5a** ....**M Hammond** 1
made most, drew clr 3 out, styd on well
Good Boy Fred 7a ....**P Williams** 2
nvr nr ldrs, styd on frm 11th, tk 2nd cls hm
Lindalighter 5a ....**T Stephenson** 3
alwys cls up, rdn into 2nd & ev ch 12th, wknd 2 out
Lakeside Lad 7a *mid-div, kpt on steadily frm 11th* ....M FitzGerald 4
Military Man *(fav) cls up, chsd wnr 11th-3 out, wknd nxt*........M Munrowd 5
Nick The Biscuit *chsd ldrs to 9th, wknd 12th, walked in*........Julian Pritchard 6
208⁴ Calder's Grove *cls 3rd whn u.r. 4th* Miss T McCurrick ur
Tiger Lord *rear frm 4th, t.o. & p.u. 3 out*......J Jukes pu
Silk Oats 5a *prom to 4th, lost tch 10th, p.u. nxt* ....Miss E Wilesmith pu
261 Philelwyn (Ire) 5a *alwys rear, lost tch 7th, t.o. & p.u. 3 out*........Miss E James pu
Welsh Fair 5a *rear frm 6th, no ch 11th, t.o. & p.u. 3 out*........D S Jones pu
186 Culpeppers Dish *prom, disp 4th-6th, wknd 8th, t.o. & p.u. 3 out*........R Barton pu
Tedstone Fox 7a *mid-div, blnd & u.r. 4th*...J Jackson ur
Teigr Pren *t.o. 5th, nrly f nxt & p.u.*.......P Sheldrake pu
14 ran. 20l, 1l, 1½l, 12l, dist. Time 5m 50.00s. SP 6-1.
Mrs J Woodward (Worcestershire).

366 2½m Open Maiden Div II (12st)

BASIL STREET (IRE) 7a ....**T Stephenson** 1
7s-3s, ld 11th, drew clr frm 2 out
103 **Sabbaq (USA)** ....**I Dowrick** 2
(fav) w.w. 6th at 11th, gd prog nxt, ev ch til nt qckn aft 3 out
Stormhill Recruit ....**M P Jones** 3
ld to 3rd, cls up & ev ch 12th, kpt on onepcd frm nxt
201 Vision Of Light 5a *ld 4th-nxt, ev ch aft 11th, no ext nxt* ....M Munrowd 4
Warm Relation (Ire) *mid-div, prog 10th, cls up 12th, wknd nxt*........T Cox 5
111 Feltham Mistress 5a *wth ldrs, cls 2nd at 12th, wknd 3 out*........E Babbington 6
259 Millstock 5a *ld 6-8th, cls 2nd 11th, wknd aft nxt, p.u. last*........G Barfoot-Saunt pu
Astromis (Ire) 5a *chsng ldrs whn blnd & u.r. 10th* ....Julian Pritchard ur
184 Peat Potheen *prog 9th, wknd aft 11th, no ch whn s.u. apr 3 out*........T Weale su
Whats Money 5a *prom, ld 9th-nxt, ev ch whn u.r. 11th* ....A Crow ur
Bright Girl (Ire) 5a *alwys rear, just in tch whn u.r. 10th, dead*........J Jukes ur
Bally Boy 7a *nvr rchd ldrs, t.o. & p.u. 3 out* D S Jones pu
87 Royal Icing 12a *prom to 8th, wknd 11th, p.u. 4 out* ....P Hanly pu
13 ran. 20l, 4l, 2½l, 20l, 10l. Time 5m 39.00s. SP 3-1.
Miss J M Green (Ludlow).

367 2½m Open Maiden Div III (12st)

182² **ZAMBRANO (USA) 7a** ....**S Durack** 1
(fav) trckd ldrs, prog 11th, ld apr last, pshd out
259 **Mr Hatchet (Ire)** ....**T Stephenson** 2
alwys prom, cls 2nd 10th, disp 3 out-nxt, no ext
185 **Alias Parker Jones** ....**R Barton** 3
alwys rear, t.o. 11th, fin 2 fences 4th, promoted
261⁵ Volcanic Roc *cls up, 10l 5th at 11th, 4th & no prog whn f 3 out*........S Blackwell f
Mister Jay Day *ld to 3rd, wknd rpdly 11th, p.u. 3 out* ....J Jukes pu
Kanjo Olda 5a *ld 4th til aft 12th, not qckn nxt, fin 3rd, disq*........M FitzGerald 0
Kits Pride 12a *declined 1st*........D S Jones ref
Lisgarvan Lad (Ire) 7a *rear frm 3rd, rdn 8th, lost tch & p.u. 3 out*........M Munrowd pu
Kristal Haze 12a *rear frm 4th, p.u. 9th*.....P Williams pu
9 ran. 10l, 7l, dist. Time 5m 42.00s. SP 7-4.
D L Williams (Berks & Bucks Drag).
Kanjo Olda disqualified, not W/I. Original distances

368 2½m Open Maiden Div IV (12st)

DAWN INVADER (IRE) ....**J Jukes** 1
prog 10th, chsd ldr 12th, disp 2 out, hung lft flat, all out
105² **Passing Fair 5a** ....**Miss S Vickery** 2
(fav) ld til jnd 2 out, switchd rght & no ext flat
54³ **Keep Flowing (Ire)** ....**Miss P Jones** 3
alwys prom, 3rd 12th, not qckn frm nxt
Who's Your Man (Ire) *prog 9th, ev ch 11th, wknd nxt* ....C Richards 4
The Hollow (Ire) 5a *trckd ldrs in tch, blnd 12th, no ch aft*........R Evans 5
256 Thornhill 5a *nvr rchd ldrs, t.o. 11th*........L Brown 6
258 Derring Run 5a *rear 3rd, blnd & u.r 9th*...R Inglesant ur
185 Grampas' Girl (Ire) 5a *mid-div whn u.r. 5th*...D Davis ur
184 Kerstin's Choice 5a *rear whn u.r. 10th*...P Sheldrake ur
Christmas Thyne (Ire) 7a *chsng ldrs whn blnd & u.r. 7th*........M Munrowd ur
Conimore (Ire) 12a *rear 4th, f 6th*.....Julian Pritchard f
185 Del's Delight (Ire) 5a *hit 3rd, wknd 8th, p.u. aft 10th* ....D S Jones pu
Maiden's Quest 12a *prog to 2nd whn bad mstk 6th, p.u. aft 10th*........M Rimell pu
13 ran. 3l, 3l, 25l, 20l, 20l. Time 5m 36.00s. SP 6-1.
D J Caro (North Ledbury).
P.R.

SOUTH MIDLANDS AREA CLUB
Mollington
Sunday March 2nd
GOOD

369 Members

223¹ **ANTICA ROMA (IRE) 5a** ....**C Wadland** 1

(fav) hld up, prog 13th, rdn to chal 2 out, kpt on, ld post
Sabre King (bl) ....L Lay 2
prom, chsd ldr 10th, ld aft last, hdd post
Copper Bank ....F Hutsby 3
prom, ld 7th, clr 13th, hdd & no ext aft last
220 Kino *chsd ldrs, outpcd 13th, ran on wll frm 3 out, nrst fin* ....A Charles-Jones 4
218 Sprucefield *rear, no ch frm 13th, kpt on frm 3 out* ....A Barlow 5
55[6] I'm Toby *alwys rear, no ch frm 13th, kpt on* ...L Baker 6
Berkana Run *sn t.o.* ....R Bailey 7
55 Walkers Point *sn t.o.* ....S Astaire 8
256[5] Cawkwell Dean *ld to 7th, wknd 13th, bhnd whn p.u. 3 out* ....R Sweeting pu
Smart Teacher (USA) *pllng, prom to 8th, wknd rpdly & p.u. 12th* ....J Trice-Rolph pu
220 Aylesford *mid-div, wknd 11th, t.o. & p.u. last* A Tutton pu
218 Wot No Cash 7a *alwys bhnd, t.o. & p.u. 11th* ....R Lawther pu
Fill The Boot (Ire) *alwys bhnd, t.o. & p.u. 3 out* J Owen pu
13 ran. Hd, 1½l, 3l, 8l, 4l, 1 fence, 10l. Time 6m 32.00s. SP 9-4.
Mrs K Cockburn (Warwickshire).

370 Men's Open

256[2] **HILL ISLAND ....R Sweeting 1**
(fav) made virt all, drew clr aft 2 out, rdn out
220 **My Best Man ....A Hill 2**
trckd ldrs, rdn frm 10th, chal und pres 15th, btn 2 out
216 **Going Around ....L Lay 3**
trckd ldrs going wll, chal 15th, rdn & wknd aft nxt
142 Tompet *hld up last, not keen & bhnd frm 12th, no imp aft* ....J Connell 4
Grand Value *wth wnr til wknd rpdly 11th, t.o. & p.u. 14th* ....C Wadland pu
194[8] Whats Your Game (bl) *pshd alng, prom to 10th, nrly u.r. 11th, t.o. & u.r. 15th* ....K Sheppard ur
6 ran. 8l, 8l, 15l. Time 6m 39.00s. SP 2-5.
Colin Gee (Heythrop).

371 G Middleton Ladies

MAKING TIME 5a ....Miss T Habgood 1
cls up, trckd ldr 15th, ld last, rdn out
219 **What Chance (Ire) 5a ....Miss S Wallin 2**
prom, ld 10th-last, unable qckn flat
219[4] **Lily The Lark 5a ....Miss H Irving 3**
(fav) cls up, trckd ldr 10th-15th, onepcd aft
219 Finally Fantazia 5a *mid-div, outpced 11th, effrt whn mstk 15th, no dang aft* ....Miss K Holmes 4
215[8] Kites Hardwicke *mid-div, outpcd 11th, clsd & in tch 13th, wknd rpdly 2 out* ....Mrs C Behrens 5
219[5] West Orient *jmpd lft, ld 2-10th, btn frm nxt* ....Miss S Hiatt 6
217[4] Icky's Five *ld to 2nd, wknd frm 10th, t.o.* ....Mrs C McCarthy 7
Royal Exhibition *last pair & alwys t.o.* Miss C Ramsey 8
Walkonthemoon 5a *1st ride, t.o. in last pair til p.u. 3 out* ....Miss N McKim pu
9 ran. 1½l, 2l, 25l, 1½l, 15l, 20l, 10l. Time 6m 33.00s. SP 6-1.
R Shepherd (Bicester With Whaddon Chase).

372 Restricted

251 **MUSIC IN THE NIGHT ....F Hutsby 1**
alwys prom, ld 3 out, clr last, rdn out nr fin
221 **Archies Oats ....J Trice-Rolph 2**
alwys prom, prssd ldr 10th, ld 15th-nxt, kpt on well
Needwood Neptune ....A Sansome 3
(Jt fav) w.w. prog 10th, effrt 13th, 3rd & no imp 3 out, fin tired
222[5] Duke Of Lancaster (Ire) *rear grp, no ch frm 11th, t.o. 13th, ran on wll frm 2 out* ....N Sutton 4
218 Unlucky For Some (Ire) *rear grp, no ch frm 11th, kpt on frm 15th, nrst fin* ....C Wadland 5
221[3] Brown Baby 5a *prom to 11th, sn wknd* ....G Kerr 6
221[6] Castle Shelley (Ire) *prssd ldr, ld 10th til mstk 15th, wknd rpdly, crwld last* ....R Smith 7
Damers Treasure *alwys rear, no ch frm 11th, t.o.* ....M Cowley 8
Golden Record *ld to 10th, sn wknd, walked in* ....Miss H Walsgrove 9
Sutton Lass 5a *alwys bhnd, t.o. & p.u. 11th* ..N Waine pu
Whitworth Grey *alwys rear, t.o. & u.r. 15th* ..B McKim ur
Spartan's Saint *alwys bhnd, t.o. & p.u. 12th* P Picton-Warlow pu
Lochinvar Lord (bl) *ldng grp til wknd 11th, no ch whn u.r. 15th, stirrup broke* ....D Renney ur
Full Song 5a *prom to 11th, sn wknd, bhnd whn p.u. 3 out* ....S Morris pu
Dancing Supreme *alwys rear, t.o. & p.u. 11th* ...L Lay pu
Tranquil Lord (Ire) *(Jt fav) rear grp, no ch frm 11th, t.o. & p.u. 2 out* ....D Smith pu
208 Mister Kingston *trckd ldrs, outpcd 12th, no prog, poor 5th whn p.u. 2 out* ....B Pollock pu
210 Willow Brook (Ire) *rear grp, no ch frm 11th, t.o. & p.u. 3 out* ....J Docker pu
Dels Lad *unruly pddck & to post, last til p.u. 8th* ....R Armson pu
19 ran. 3½l, 30l, 3l, 5l, 2l, 8l, 5l, 25l. Time 6m 38.00s. SP 5-1.
Mrs Caroline Price (Bicester With Whaddon Chase).

373 Maiden Div I (12st)

224[2] **BUTLERS MATCH (IRE) ....A Charles-Jones 1**
(fav) trckd ldrs, ld 12th, drew clr aft 2 out, rdn out
Country Brew 5a ....C Marriott 2
cls up, outocd & mstk 13th, no ch 15th, kpt on wll flat
223 **Di Moda ....Miss S Firmin 3**
wll in rear, no ch frm 12th, styd on well frm 3 out, nrst fn
Rivers End (Ire) *prom, ld 9-12th, chsd wnr aft, wknd rpdly aft 2 out* ....A Hill 4
Welsh Rupert (Ire) *trckd ldrs going easily, 3rd & chnce whn blnd 3 out, wknd* ....J Trice-Rolph 5
223 Roark's Chukka *in tch, cls up 10th, sn btn, walked in* ....D Smith 6
Old Father Time *wth ldrs to 12th, wknd rpdly, t.o. & p.u. last* ....L Lay pu
Space Molly 5a *wth ldr til wknd rpdly 9th, t.o. & p.u. 15th* ....M Cowley pu
Another Whistle (Ire) *alwys rear, t.o. 12th, p.u. 15th* ....Miss T Habgood pu
224[4] Village Remedy 5a *f 1st* ....A Tutton f
Bobbin Lace 5a *t.o. til p.u. 4th* ....P Picton-Warlow pu
Deejayef 5a *alwys rear, t.o. & p.u. 2 out* ....N Ridout pu
It's A Scoop *race wd, made most til ran out 9th* ....R Mumford ro
Broad-Thorne *in tch til outpcd 13th, no prog aft, p.u. last* ....John Pritchard pu
14 ran. 25l, 1l, 5l, 8l, dist. Time 6m 47.00s. SP Evens.
Mrs Helen Mobley (Bicester With Whaddon Chase).

374 Maiden Div II (12st)

223 **WOTAMONA 5a ....R Smith 1**
prom, ld 12th, rdn & prssd 2 out, hld on gamely flat
Tell The Boys (Ire) ....A Charles-Jones 2
(fav) cls up going wll, chsd wnr 15th, chal last, no ext nr fin
217[2] **Back In A Flash ....Miss H Irving 3**
alwys prom, chsd wnr 12-15th, ev ch 2 out, no ext
224 Royal Dadda 1ow *in tch, rdn aft 10th, effrt 14th, nvr rchd ldrs* ....A Hill 4
60 Fuannae (Ire) *trckd ldrs, pshd alng 11th, sn outpcd, no imp frm 15th* ....F Brennan 5
Connie Foley *alwys rear, t.o. 12th, walked in* ....Miss S Hiatt 6
Upton Lass (Ire) 5a *prom til wknd 15th, walked in* ....L Lay 7
Truly Optimistic 5a *prom, lft in ld 6th, hdd 12th, wknd rpdly, p.u. 3 out* ....C Wadland pu
Strong Account (Ire) *ld til ran out thro wing 6th* ....A Tutton ro
Magical Manor 5a *last pair til u.r. 4th* ....Mrs C McCarthy ur
Lord Lankie (Ire) *in tch to 11th, bhnd whn p.u. 15th* ....F Hutsby pu

Kickles Lass 5a *prom to 11th, wknd rpdly & f 13th* ....John Pritchard f
Aintgottime (Ire) 7a *pllng, lost plc 5th, effrt 13th, btn 15th, p.u. 2 out* ....R Lawther pu
Blame The Groom (Ire) *1st ride, last & t.o. til p.u. 13th* ....D Buckley pu
14 ran. ½l, 8l, 10l, 10l, 25l, 2l. Time 6m 43.00s. SP 20-1.
Mrs Clare Alderton (Bicester With Whaddon Chase).
J.N.

DONCASTER
Monday March 3rd
GOOD TO FIRM

375 2m 3f 110yds Hambleton Hills Hunters' Chase Class H

94[1] **SLIEVENAMON MIST 11.13 5a ....Mr J Jukes 1**
in tch, hdwy to chase ldr 6th, ld 9th, clr 2 out, styd on well.
195 **Driving Force 12.1 7a (bl) ...Mr A Charles-Jones 2**
mid div, hdwy to chase ldrs 10th, rdn 4 out, left 2nd next, no ch with wnr.
248[2] **Double Collect 11.11 7a ....Mr A Rebori 3**
alwys prom, hit 3rd, rdn along 4 out, one pace next.
Tommys Webb (Ire) 11.7 7a *held up, hdwy to chase ldrs 5 out, soon rdn and no impn*....Mr L Lay 4
90 Al Hashimi 11.7 7a *in tch, rdn along 5 out, soon one pace*....Mr N Ridout 5
216 No Word 11.7 7a *cl up, ld 3rd and soon clr, hdd 9th, wknd after next*....Mr I Baker 6
202 Tipp Down 11.7 7a *chsd ldrs till f 8th, dead.* ....Mr R Thomas f
9[1] Sheer Jest 12.5 3a *(fav) held up, smooth hdwy 5 out, cl 3rd when p.u. lame after 3 out.* ....Mr A Hill pu
The Communicator 11.7 7a (bl) *ld to 3rd, lost pl 8th, t.o. when p.u. before 3 out*....Mr M Munrowd pu
152[3] Free Transfer (Ire) 11.11 3a *in tch, rdn along to chase ldrs when blnd and u.r. 11th.* ....Mr C Bonner ur
Dear Emily 11.9 *mstks, alwys bhnd, t.o. when p.u. before 4 out*....Mr S Swiers pu
11 ran. 20l, 11l, 6l, 20l, dist. Time 4m 55.40s. SP 11-8.
Nick Viney

WINDSOR
Monday March 3rd
GOOD TO FIRM

376 3m Thames Valley Hunters' Chase Class H

CAPO CASTANUM 11.7 7a....Mr A Wintle 1
alwys prom, left 2nd 13th, ld after 4 out, ran on well.
92 **Jupiter Moon 11.7 7a ....Mr J M Pritchard 2**
nvr far away, hdwy to chase wnr from 2 out.
151 **Gambling Royal 11.7 7a ....Dr P Pritchard 3**
chsd ldr, left in ld 13th, hdd after 4 out, wknd next.
Bollinger 11.7 7a *in rear, styd on from 4 out, nvr near to chal*....Mr P O'Keeffe 4
92[3] Sonofagipsy 11.7 7a *in tch till wknd apr 4 out.* ....Mr R Nuttall 5
281[3] Annio Chilone 11.9 5a *bhnd from hfwy, t.o..* ....Mr T McCarthy 6
281[8] Faringo 11.11 7a 4ow *alwys bhnd, soon t.o..* ....Mr W Gowlett 7
Emerald Moon 11.7 7a *in tch till wknd 13th, t.o. when blnd and u.r. 3 out*....Mr D Maitland ur
219 Great Simplicity 11.9 5a (bl) *alwys in rear, p.u. before 9th*....Mr A Sansome pu
154 Prinzal 11.7 7a *slowly away, blnd and u.r. 1st.* ....Mr M Emmanuel ur
179[1] Quiet Confidence (Ire) 11.2 7a *(fav) ld, clr 10th, hit 13th, u.r..*....Miss D Stafford ur
11 ran. 8l, 14l, ¾l, 12l, dist, dist. Time 6m 12.70s. SP 9-2.
D C G Gyle-Thompson

LEICESTER
Tuesday March 4th
GOOD

377 2½m 110yds Squire Osbaldeston Maiden Hunters' Chase Class H

216[1] **TEETON MILL 12.2 5a....Mr B Pollock 1**
(fav) held up, hdwy 6th, ld 9th, driven out.
188[3] **Cherry Island (Ire) 12.2 5a ....Mr J Jukes 2**
held up, hdwy 8th, ev ch apr last, styd on same pace.
Up For Ransome (Ire) 12.0 7a....Mr G Shenkin 3
prom, rdn apr 2 out, ran on one pace.
145[2] Arctic Chill (Ire) 12.0 7a *prom till wknd 4 out.* ....Miss S Vickery 4
223[3] Count Balios (Ire) 12.0 7a *prom, mstk 7th, soon bhnd.* ....Mr P Howse 5
213[2] Dark Rhytham 12.0 7a *hdwy 6th, wknd 3 out.* ....Mr S Morris 6
225 Dashboard Light 12.4 3a *chsd ldrs till wknd apr 3 out.* ....Mr Simon Andrews 7
283[1] Diamond Wind (USA) 11.9 7a *in tch, chsd ldrs 5 out, wknd 3 out.*....Mr A Beedles 8
Pamela's Lad 12.0 7a *alwys in rear.*....Mr G Hanmer 9
251[5] Pokey Grange 12.0 7a *bhnd from 9th.* ....Major S J Robinson 10
195[3] Craftsman 12.0 7a *blnd and u.r. 3rd.* ....Miss A Embiricos ur
211 Noble Angel (Ire) 12.0 7a *pulld hrd, led 4th to apr 6th, weakening when f 9th*....Mr A Dalton f
Judgeroger 12.0 7a *bhnd from 5th, p.u. before 3 out.* ....Mr G Lewis pu
201 Coolgreen (Ire) 12.0 7a *ld to 4th, led apr 6th, hdd 9th, soon lost pl, bhnd when p.u. before four out.* ....Mr N Bradley pu
273[2] Samsword 12.0 7a *alwys in rear, p.u. before 2 out.* ....Mr J I Pritchard pu
15 ran. 3l, 3½l, dist, 3½l, 2l, 21l, ¾l, 5l, dist. Time 5m 19.40s. SP 11-10.
C R Saunders

378 2½m 110yds Melton Hunt Club Hunters' Chase Class H

225[1] **TRIFAST LAD 11.12 3a ....Mr P Hacking 1**
chsd ldrs, lost pl 3rd, tk clr order 9th, ld 2 out, mstk last, styd on well.
257[1] **Minella Express (Ire) 11.12 7a ..Miss C Spearing 2**
(fav) ld, jmpd left, hdd 6 out, ev ch 2 out, styd on same pace run-in.
188[2] **Busman (Ire) 11.8 7a ....Mr D S Jones 3**
prom, chsd ldr 6th, ld six out, mstk 3 out, hdd and hit 2 out, styd on same pace.
250[3] Kambalda Rambler 11.3 7a *raced keenly, soon chasing ldrs, ev ch 2 out, wknd last*....Mr R Armson 4
194[2] Young Nimrod 11.3 7a *held up, effort apr 3 out, soon wknd.* ....Mr G Wragg 5
154[3] Pro Bono (Ire) 11.10 5a *chsd ldrs, mstk 8th, wknd 6 out, p.u. before 2 out.* ....Mr A Sansome pu
6 ran. 2l, 3½l, 5l, 21l. Time 5m 24.00s. SP 5-1.
Mike Roberts

379 3m Arthur Clerke-Brown & Graham Pidgeon Memorial Hunters' Chase Class H

67[7] **HIGHLANDMAN 11.0 7a....Mr Chris Wilson 1**
alwys prom, ld 10th to 6 out, left in ld after 3 out, soon hdd, led run-in, driven out.
67[6] **Peajade 11.0 7a....Miss J Wormall 2**
ld to 10th, led apr 2 out, hdd run-in, styd on und pres.
226[3] **Glen Oak 11.0 7a ....Mr M FitzGerald 3**
alwys prom, reminder 10th, cl up when hmpd 3 out, styd on same pace apr last.
215[1] Corner Boy 11.0 7a *(fav) held up, hdwy 6th, ld and jmpd right 3 out, soon hdd, still ev ch when blundd next, soon btn.* ....Mrs J Dawson 4
272[1] Green Archer 11.0 7a *alwys in rear.* ....Mrs T Hill 5
151[2] Avostar 11.2 5a *prom, lost pl 7th, bhnd when p.u. before 3 out*....Mr B Pollock pu

226[2] Country Tarrogen 11.2 5a *held up, hdwy 7th, ld 6 out, hdd when b.d. 3 out.* .... Mr N Wilson bd
7 ran. ½l, 2½l, 10l, 1¼l. Time 6m 16.90s. SP 66-1.
Mrs Hugh Fraser

380 3m Garthorpe Maiden Hunters' Chase Class H

250[1] **COPPER THISTLE (IRE) 11.12 7a Mr R Hunnisett** 1
alwys prom, left in ld 12th, hdd 4 out, ld again next, ran on well.
198[1] **Elmore 12.2 3a.................... Mr P Hacking** 2
(Jt fav) ld to 4th, led four out, hdd next, outpcd from last.
256[3] **Mitchells Best 12.0 5a............... Mr J Jukes** 3
prom, rdn apr 3 out, styd on same pace.
256[9] Garrylucas 11.12 7a *held up, hrd rdn 3 out, nvr able to chal*........................ Mr G Hanmer 4
216[4] Penlet 11.12 7a *(Jt fav) held up, mstk 6th, hdwy 10th, rdn and btn when pkd 3 out*........... Mr J I Pritchard 5
214[4] The Difference 11.12 7a *alwys in rear.* .... Mr M Chatterton 6
223[6] Moon Monkey (Ire) 11.12 7a *chsd ldrs, rdn 9th, wknd 11th, bhnd when mstk and u.r. 2 out.*.... Mr O McPhail ur
Scale Down (Ire) 12.0 5a *ld 4th till f 12th.* .... Mr A Sansome f
Ollardale (Ire) 11.12 7a *prom, hit 2nd, soon lost pl, pushed along 8th, lost tch 10th, t.o. when p.u. before 5 out.* .... Mr A Dalton pu
9 ran. 11l, 11l, 5l, 1¾l, 6l. Time 6m 21.00s. SP 13-2.
R S Hunnisett

381 2m 1f Thrusters Hunters' Chase Class H

A WINDY CITIZEN (IRE) 11.4 5a... Mr A Sansome 1
(Jt fav) held up, mstk 5th, hdwy 5 out, ld 2 out, rdn out.
139[3] **Nowhiski 11.3 7a.................. Miss C Tarratt** 2
chsd ldrs, rdn apr 2 out, no ext run-in.
108[3] **Corly Special 11.3 7a .... Mr E James** 3
in rear, effort 4 out, not reach ldrs.
90[1] Beau Dandy 12.1 7a *(Jt fav) chsd ldrs, rdn 3 out, one pace apr last.*.......................... Mr T Marks 4
Tumlin Oot (Ire) 11.3 7a *held up, hdwy 5 out, weakening when hmpd 2 out.*.................. Mr Chris Wilson 5
257 Quarter Marker (Ire) 11.3 7a *in tch till wknd 3 out.* .... Mr J M Pritchard 6
Happy Paddy 11.3 7a (bl) *bhnd from 5 out.* .... Mr M Cowley 7
Tbilisi 11.3 7a *reluctant to race, alwys well bhnd, p.u. before 4 out.*.......................... Mr R Munrowd pu
Master Crozina 11.3 7a *mstk 3rd, alwys in rear, bhnd when p.u. before 2 out.* .... Mr P Cornforth pu
How Friendly 11.3 7a *chsd ldrs till f 5 out.* .... Mr M FitzGerald f
291 Cappajune (Ire) 11.2 3a *in tch, mstk 4 out, soon bhnd, p.u. before last*.......................... Mr M Rimell pu
211[2] Jack The Td (Ire) 11.3 7a *ld, hdd when unsighted and u.r. 2 out*.......................... Mr J R Cornwall ur
Michelles Crystal 11.0 7a 2ow *blnd and u.r. 2nd.* .... Mr L Brown ur
13 ran. 2l, 4l, nk, 11l, dist, dist. Time 4m 30.70s. SP 5-2.
Mrs J A Thomson

BANGOR
Wednesday March 5th
GOOD TO SOFT

382 3m 110yds Hugh Peel Challenge Trophy Hunters' Chase Class H

257[7] **HIGHWAY FIVE (IRE) 12.0 7a....... Miss E James** 1
bhnd and nigglд along 5th, cl up 9th, led 4 out to next, pressed ldr, styd on to ld close home.
178[2] **Teatrader 11.7 7a.................. Miss T Blazey** 2
ld to 9th, remained prom, led again 3 out, hrd pressed, slightly hmpd run-in by loose horse, hdd cl home.
288[1] **Cape Cottage 12.0 7a .... Mr R Lawther** 3
(fav) held up, niggld along 9th, hmpd 4 out, ev ch from 2 out, no ext run-in.
200[5] Orton House 11.7 7a *prom, ld 9th to 4 out, pushed along and wknd apr 2 out.* .... Mr R Burton 4
149 Corn Exchange 11.11 3a *cl up when blnd and u.r. 4th.* .... Mr M Rimell ur
189[1] True Fortune 11.9 5a *handy till f 9th.*...... Mr J Jukes f
6 ran. Sht-hd, 1l, 12l. Time 7m 0.10s. SP 20-1.
Lady Susan Brooke

CATTERICK
Wednesday March 5th
GOOD

383 3m 1f 110yds Pytchley Echo Novices' Hunters' Chase Class H

232[1] **SAYIN NOWT 11.2 7a .... Mr A Parker** 1
(fav) not fluent, held up and bhnd, steady hdwy 14th, blnd 3 out, chal next, rdn to ld after last, styd on strly.
267 **Greenmount Lad (Ire) 11.7 7a .... Mr P Cornforth** 2
alwys cl up, disp ld 13th, blnd 4 out, ld next, rdn 2 out, hdd and not qckn after last.
353 **Admission (Ire) 11.7 7a .... Miss L Horner** 3
slowly away, hdwy 6th, chsd ldrs when blnd 11th, rdn apr 3 out, kept on same pace.
230[3] Eastlands Hi-Light 11.7 7a *chsd ldrs, rdn along 4 out, soon one pace, blnd 2 out.* .... Mr T Morrison 4
118[1] Political Sam 11.7 7a *cl up, hit 9th, ld 12th till rdn and hdd apr 3 out, gradually wknd.* .... Mr N F Smith 5
226 Mobile Messenger (NZ) 11.7 7a *prom till outpcd and bhnd from hfwy.* .... Miss S Samworth 6
218 Bervie House (Ire) 11.9 5a *prom, rdn along 12th, wknd from 4 out*.......................... Mr R Ford 7
118[1] Boulevard Bay (Ire) 11.9 5a *trckd ldrs, mstk 3rd, cl up when blnd 5 out, ev ch when blunded 2 out, soon wknd and virtually p.u. flat.* .... Mr N Wilson 8
Galzig 11.7 7a *ld to 12th, wknd before 4 out, bhnd when p.u. before 2 out.* .... Mr W Tellwright pu
Sir Harry Rinus 11.9 5a *chsd ldrs, blnd 10th and soon lost pl, bhnd when blunded 12th and p.u. after.* .... Mr R Hale pu
10 ran. 3½l, 2l, 9l, 14l, 3l, 12l, dist. Time 6m 52.50s. SP 5-2.
Dennis Waggott

TOWCESTER
Thursday March 6th
GOOD TO SOFT

384 3m 1f Banque Arjil Italia Hunters' Chase Class H

227[4] **TEAPLANTER 12.1 5a............. Mr B Pollock** 1
(fav) made most, kept on gamely from 2 out.
237[1] **Fiddlers Pike 11.5 7a.......... Mrs R Henderson** 2
pulld hrd, trckd wnr from hfwy, ev ch 2 out, one pace after.
287[6] **Lurriga Glitter (Ire) 11.5 7a .... Mr S Joynes** 3
prom, chsd ldrs, wknd 4 out, t.o..
Direct 11.11 7a 2ow *bhnd from 10th, t.o..* .... Mr T Edwards 4
285 Major Mac 11.5 7a *bhnd, effort 11th, wknd next, t.o..* .... Mr S Durack 5
219 What A To Do 11.13 7a *prom to 10th, btn 4th when blnd and u.r. last.* .... Miss L Sweeting ur
273[3] Solar Gem 11.5 7a *jmpd poorly in rear, blnd 10th, t.o. when hit 3 out, u.r..* .... Mrs C McCarthy ur
7 ran. 3l, dist, 21l, 9l. Time 6m 59.00s. SP 8-13.
R G Russell

WINCANTON
Thursday March 6th
GOOD

385 3m 1f 110yds Dick Woodhouse Hunters' Chase Class H

98 **RYMING CUPLET 12.0 7a...........Mr L Jefford** 1
disp ld, ld and mstk 6th, hdd 9th, led next, hrd pressed and rdn when left clr 3 out, driven and held on well run-in.
153[3] **Wild Illusion 12.0 7a...............Mr R Lawther** 2
(fav) disp ld to 6th, jmpd slowly 8th, ld 9th to next, jumped slowly 12th, rallied and ev ch last, styd on.
180[3] **Young Brave 12.0 7a..............Mr M G Miller** 3
in tch, hdwy 13th, chsd ldrs and mstk 17th, weakening when blnd 2 out.
290 Mediane (USA) 11.11 3a (v) *ref to race.* ....Mr Simon Andrews l
Tom's Gemini Star 11.7 7a *pressing ldrs when f 9th.* ....Mr E James f
Panda Shandy 11.2 7a *hmpd 9th and lost position, hdwy 13th, chsd wnr 15th, chal 4 out till f next.* ....Mr R Nuttall f
6 ran. 1¾l, 3½l. Time 7m 0.30s. SP 6-1.
Gerald Tanner

AYR
Friday March 7th
SOFT

386 2m 5f 110yds Ayrshire Agricultural Association Hunters' Challenge Cup Nov

230[2] **DENIM BLUE 11.5 5a............Miss P Robson** 1
(fav) chsd ldr, ld 12th, clr 2 out, easily.
Woody Dare 11.3 7a...........Mr Chris Wilson 2
ld, blnd and hdd 12th, chasing wnr when blunded badly 4 out, no ch after.
Frozen Stiff (Ire) 11.5 5a............Mr N Wilson 3
chsd ldrs, mstks 5th and 14th, fd from 4 out.
Canny Chronicle 11.3 7a *chsd ldrs till f 12th.* ....Mr A Parker f
Eli Peckanpah (Ire) 11.3 7a *v unruly start and dismntd, deemed to have ref to race.......*Mr A Robson l
Planning Gain 11.3 7a *started slowly, soon in tch, raced wd, n.j.w., lost touch after 14th, 4th and staying on when f 3 out.* ....Mr M Bradburne f
Molly Grey (Ire) 11.0 5a *blnd 3rd, bhnd, mstks, t.o. when p.u. before 4 out.....................*Mr R Hale pu
7 ran. 21l, 8l. Time 6m 17.30s. SP 9-4.
Mrs L Walby

MARKET RASEN
Friday March 7th
GOOD

387 3m 1f Beaumontcote Hunters' Chase Class H

286[1] **MR BOSTON 12.12 ....Mr S Swiers** 1
(fav) nvr far away, imp and ev ch final cct, edged right and ld before 3 out, drew clr.
351[1] **Carly Brrin 11.12 7a ....Mr C Mulhall** 2
ld 3rd, hdd before 3 out, soon outpcd, no impn when hit last.
67[3] **Matt Reid 12.5 7a.................Mr W Morgan** 3
bhnd, effort after 12th, outpcd before 4 out, no dngr after.
137[2] R N Commander 11.12 7a *ld to 3rd, cl up till lost pl 11th, struggling last 5.* ....Mr J R Cornwall 4
152[4] Fish Quay 11.12 7a *imp to chase wnr after 4th, blnd and lost pl 10th, soon t.o., ref 2 out.* .....Miss S Lamb ref
5 ran. 20l, 7l, dist. Time 6m 44.20s. SP 4-11.
M K Oldham

SANDOWN
Friday March 7th
GOOD

388 3m 110yds Duke Of Gloucester Memorial Hunters' Chase Past And Present Class H

180[1] **BRACKENFIELD 11.11 7a (bl)...Captain D Alers-Hankey** 1
(fav) mstk 1st, ld 4th to 12th, mistake next, led 7 out, drew clr four out, unchal.
231[4] **Across The Card 12.4 7a........Capt W Ramsay** 2
soon well bhnd, t.o. 13th, styd on after 3 out, went 2nd run-in, no ch with wnr.
273[1] **Over The Edge 12.4 7a...........Mr S Sporborg** 3
chsd ldrs, lost pl after 12th, styd on one pace after 4 out.
287 True Steel 11.13 5a *held up, hdwy when mstk 9th, ld 12th, mistake next, hdd 16th, wknd after 2 out, lost 2nd pl run-in, fin tired.* ....Mr J Trice-Rolph 4
91 No Joker (Ire) 11.11 7a *ld to 4th, wknd after 12th, soon t.o., no ch when blnd four out........*Capt R Hall 5
279[1] American Eyre 12.3 7a 6ow *bhnd 10th, t.o. when p.u. before 12th.....................*Mr R Gladders pu
285[7] Golden Mac 11.11 7a *chsd ldrs to 12th, soon bhnd, t.o. when blnd and u.r. 6 out.........*Major O Ellwood ur
7 ran. 26l, 13l, 6l, 4l. Time 6m 42.40s. SP 4-5.
Mrs Susan Humphreys

SANDOWN
Saturday March 8th
GOOD

389 2½m 110yds Dick McCreery Hunters' Chase Class H

372[2] **ARCHIES OATS 11.9 5a........Mr J Trice-Rolph** 1
held up, hdwy 12th, ld last, rdn out and styd on well.
271[1] **Mister Main Man (Ire) 11.7 7a.....Mr S Sporborg** 2
(fav) blnd 4th, hdwy 12th, ev ch when hit last, kept on same pace run-in.
Berrings Dasher 11.7 7a........Major M Watson 3
waited with, chsd clr ldr from 6th, clr order 10th, ld apr 2 out, hdd and hit last, fd run-in.
267 Electric Committee (Ire) 11.7 7a *ld, clr from 3rd, hdd apr 2 out, wknd approaching last.........*Capt A Wood 4
90[4] Hickelton Lad 11.13 7a *blnd 1st, hdwy 10th, wknd apr 3 out.*..........................Major S J Robinson 5
361[2] Taurean Tycoon 11.7 7a *not fluent, bhnd from 7th.* ....Major O Ellwood 6
6 ran. 2½l, 6l, 17l, 1¼l, 4l. Time 5m 29.60s. SP 11-2.
Jon Trice-Rolph

AVON VALE
Barbury Castle
Saturday March 8th
GOOD

390 Maiden Div I (12st)

43 **SULTAN OF SWING ....Miss P Curling** 1
(fav) mid-div, prog 8th, 3rd 3 out, strng run apr last, ld nr fin
Cape Henry ....Dr P Pritchard 2
prom, ld & mstk 6th, clr apr 2 out, hrd rdn apr last,hdd fin
284 **Lixwm 5a ....C Vigors** 3
hld up, prog to chs ldrs 8th, 2nd 10th til wknd 2 out
The Elk 6ow *in tch, mstk 7th, cls 4th at 12th, onepcd frm 3 out.*..................G Maundrell 4
Trimbush *ld to 6th, cls up til wknd 12th, last whn p.u. last*..................................T Lacey pu
Wesshaun 5a 4ow *cls up to 9th, sn wknd, t.o. & jmpd slwly 14th, p.u. 2 out*......................G Chanter pu
297 Favlient 5a *mstks, blnd 2nd, alwys rear, last whn p.u. 13th*...............................J Barnes pu
41[4] Nikaroo 5a *chsd ldrs til wknd 11th, t.o. & p.u. 2 out* ....Miss M Hill pu
Dante's Pride (Ire) *hld up, wll bhnd hlfwy, t.o. & p.u. 2 out*................................Miss A Dare pu
297 Shelley's Dream 5a *rear, blnd & u.r. 10th*...M Walters ur
111 Most Vital *n.j.w. blnd 2nd, alwys rear, t.o. & p.u. 2 out* ....Miss A Goschen pu
First Bash (Ire) *f 1st*.......................M Batters f
146 Celtic Friend (Ire) *hmpd & u.r. 1st*.........M Portman ur

Donald Hawkins 7a 3ow *rear, some prog 11th, nvr nr ldrs, p.u. 2 out*. . . . . P Howse pu
Cloudy House 5a *f 2nd*. . . . . L Baker f
15 ran. 1l, 8l, 2l. Time 6m 22.00s. SP 9-4.
H B Geddes (Beaufort).

391 Members

299 **GT HAYES POMMARD** . . . . . **D Howells** 1
raced wd, jmpd rght, ld to apr 12th, ld last, ran on well
179[4] **Roaming Shadow** . . . . . **J Hankinson** 2
(fav) in tch, chsd ldr 6th, ld apr 12th, blnd & hdd last, wknd
284 **Dad's Delight 5a**. . . . . **Miss A Goschen** 3
w.w. prog 13th, ev ch nxt, blnd 3 out, sn outpcd
112[4] Sandford Orcas *chsd ldrs til 4th & outpcd 15th, no dang aft* . . . . . P Bevins 4
221[5] No Dozing (Ire) *alwys rear, jmpd slwly 2nd lost tch 10th, no ch frm 12th* . . . . . J Byrne 5
Wood Heba *in tch to 12th, 5th & no ch 14th, t.o.* . . . . . R Sharp 6
6 ran. 3l, 15l, ½l, 25l, 20l. Time 6m 40.00s. SP 50-1.
D Howells (Avon Vale).

392 Maiden Div II (12st)

245 **MELLING** . . . . . **N Mitchell** 1
w.w. prog to 3rd 11th, mstk 14th, rdn 2 out, ld nr fin
43 **Ten Bob Note (bl)** . . . . . **M Walters** 2
j.w. ld 4th, 10l clr 12th, wknd 2 out, hdd nr fin
146[4] **Tu Piece** . . . . . **P Howse** 3
chsd ldrs,mstk 9th,5th & outpcd 14th,styd on agn 2 out
314 Cucklington *in tch, prog 11th, 3rd & mstk 15th, one-pcd frm 3 out* . . . . . Miss A Goschen 4
Spanish River *rear, in tch to 8th, p.u. 11th* . . M Batters pu
223 Seminole Princess 5a *ld to 4th, last frm 6th, jmpd slwly 8th, t.o. & p.u. 13th* . . . . . J Merry pu
Noble Comic *(fav) pllng, prom 5th, chsd ldr 12th, wknd rpdly 2 out, p.u. last* . . . . . J Tizzard pu
Bucksum (Ire) 5a *prom, chsd ldr 8th til f 10th* J Barnes f
Nicolinsky 5a *last whn blnd & u.r. 2nd* Miss S Duckett ur
9 ran. 1l, 3l, 4l. Time 6m 31.00s. SP 6-1.
Miss R Dobson (Blackmore & Sparkford Vale).

393 Land Rover Open (12st)

RIP VAN WINKLE . . . . . **J Baimbridge** 1
(fav) chsd ldrs, lft disp 5th, ld 10th, made rest, clr 2 out, easy
Royle Speedmaster . . . . . **T Lacey** 2
sn wll bhnd, nvr nr ldrs, lft poor 2nd last
369 **Aylesford** . . . . . **A Tutton** 3
rear, outpcd 10th, no ch 12th, fin 4th, promoted
292 Granville Grill 2ow 4ex *t.d.e. jmpd lft,ld/disp to 10th,wknd & hit 14th,fin 3rd,disq* . . . . . J Deutsch 4D
385 Mediane (USA) *s.s. sn rcvrd, ld 4th, clr whn f nxt* . . . . . J Luck f
Sandaig *ld to 4th, wknd 9th, last whn p.u. 11th* . . . . . R Pyeman pu
144[4] Twist 'N' Scu *in tch,prog 8th,chsd ldr 12th,2l down 3 out,sn btn,ref last* . . . . . C Vigors ref
7 ran. 30l, 12l, 1 fence. Time 6m 23.00s. SP 4-5.
Dr P P Brown & Mrs S Birks (Berkeley).
Granville Grill disqualified, not W/I.

394 Ladies

DOWN THE MINE . . . . . **Miss A Dare** 1
(fav) made all, rdn & drew clr apr last, styd on strngly
Reef Lark . . . . . **Miss A Goschen** 2
chsd ldrs, mstk 9th, ev ch whn blnd 3 out, kpt on nr fin
145[1] **Spacial (USA)** . . . . . **Miss M Hill** 3
prssd wnr, ev ch apr 2 out, rdn & btn apr last
Foolish Soprano 5a *chsd ldng trio 3rd, mstk 6th, jmpd slwly nxt,wknd & p.u.11th* . . . . . Miss S Duckett pu
219[6] Pejawi 5a *last frm 3rd, t.o. 9th, u.r. 13th* . . . . . Miss L Whitaker ur
5 ran. 8l, 1l. Time 6m 13.00s. SP 8-11.
R T Baimbridge (Berkeley).

395 B F S S (Nov Riders) Div I

255[2] **ALL WEATHER** . . . . . **M Wilesmith** 1
(fav) ld to 1st, chsd ldrs, ev ch 3 out, ld flat, pshd out
295 **Cavalero** . . . . . **L Manners** 2
mid-div, prog 13th, ev ch 2 out, kpt on wll flat
294 **Bear's Flight** . . . . . **J Hadden Wight** 3
chsd ldrs 7th, ld 15th-2 out, onepcd und pres
2[5] Earl Boon *w.w. prog 9th, slght ld 2 out, hdd & wknd und pres flat* . . . . . P Griffiths 4
109 Met Station (bl) *prom, ld apr 4th til aft 11th, wkng whn blnd nxt, p.u. 15th*. . . . . M Walters pu
Le Jacobin *ld 2nd-apr 4th, wknd 10th, t.o. & p.u. last* . . . . . C Lambert pu
239[6] Southerly Buster *prom, ld apr 12th, mstk & hdd 14th, 5th & btn whn u.r. 2 out*. . . . . S White ur
Tango Tom *rear, last whn blnd 8th, soon lost tch, p.u. 11th*. . . . . J Barnes pu
294 Rare Flutter 5a *alwys rear, mstk 7th, no ch frm 12th, t.o. & p.u. 2 out* . . . . . D Renney pu
9 ran. Nk, 1½l, ½l. Time 6m 22.00s. SP 5-4.
M S Wilesmith (Ledbury).

396 Confined (12st)

GUITING GRAY 3ex . . . . . **Miss A Dare** 1
made all, hit 2nd & 6th, drew clr apr 3 out, easily
154[2] **Arise (Ire)** . . . . . **N Mitchell** 2
w.w. in tch, prog to 2nd 11th, rdn & btn apr 2 out
236[1] **Bet With Baker (Ire)** . . . . . **Miss P Curling** 3
(fav) mstk 1st, chsd ldrs 8th, mstk 10th, cls 3rd 12th,outpcd 14th
219 Rubika (Fr) *prom to 2nd, sn bhnd, lft poor 4th 15th, t.o.*. . . . . Mrs S Shoemark 4
39[6] Wrekin Hill *sn wll bhnd, t.o. frm 9th*. . .Mrs J Wilkinson 5
293 Saxon Lass 5a *blnd 1st, chsd ldr to 11th, 4th & wkng whn f 13th* . . . . . J Barnes f
Heathview *mid-div, 6th & outpcd 11th, lft poor 4th 14th, p.u. nxt* . . . . . M Portman pu
218[4] French Pleasure 5a *rear, 7th & pshd alng 10th, no prog, blnd 12th, p.u. aft*. . . . . P Howse pu
Gormless (Ire) *chsd ldrs to 10th, 5th & outpcd 12th, hmpd nxt & p.u.* . . . . . Miss M Hill pu
9 ran. 10l, 20l, 1 fence, 1l. Time 6m 16.00s. SP 9-4.
A M Mason (V.W.H.).

397 B F S S (Nov Riders) Div II

174[3] **RICHVILLE** . . . . . **M Walters** 1
(Jt fav) hld up going wll, prog to 2nd 15th, ld apr 2 out, rdn out
58[2] **Espy** . . . . . **A James** 2
mid-div, prog to 2nd 2 out, hrd rdn apr last, no ext
361[3] **Run To Form** . . . . . **Miss E Wilesmith** 3
chsd ldrs 8th, ld 11th-apr 2 out, onepcd
107[1] Mighty Falcon *(Jt fav) bhnd 4th, prog 11th, went poor 4th 14th, styd on, nvr nrr* . . . . . Miss E Tory 4
295[3] The Country Trader *ld 2nd-8th, 6th & outpcd 12th, no dang aft, t.o.* . . . . . J Borradaile 5
295 John Roger *prom, blnd 7th, 5th & outpcd 14th, no dang aft, t.o.* . . . . . J Merry 6
369[8] Walkers Point *ld to 2nd, ld 8-11th, sn outpcd, t.o. 15th* . . . . . Miss K O'Neill 7
178 Prankster *bhnd frm 4th, no ch whn u.r. 15th* . . . . . T Atkinson ur
292 Amadeo *prom til rdn & lost plc 9th, no ch whn f 13th* . . . . . Daniel Dennis f
179[7] Slaney France (Ire) *bhnd frm 6th, t.o. 12th, p.u. last* . . . . . Miss K Lovelace pu
10 ran. 6l, 1½l, 1l, 1 fence, 3l, 6l. Time 6m 26.00s. SP 5-2.
A Lowrie & P Henderson (Dulverton (West)).
S.P.

BRECON & TALYBONT
Llanfrynach

Saturday March 8th
GOOD

398 Members (12st)

185[2] **KERRY SOLDIER BLUE ....Miss P Jones 1**
2nd til ld 10th, jnd last, qcknd flat
262[3] **Mackabee (Ire) ....T Weale 2**
(fav) hld up, prog 10th, jnd wnr last, no ext flat
257 **Dane Rose 5a 3ex ....Miss A Sheppard 3**
ld early, 3rd frm 11th, wknd 3 out
Astley Jack *ref 1st, cont, fin own time*.......R Cotton 4
Call-Me-Dinky *raced 4th, prog to 3rd 3 out, mstk nxt, wknd & p.u. last* ....J Tudor pu
Takahashi (Ire) *p.u. aft 2nd, dsmntd*.......S Blackwell pu
6 ran. ¾l, 15l, 2 fences. Time 6m 26.00s. SP 2-1.
Mrs Margaret Price (Brecon).

399 Confined (12st)

257[6] **JUDY LINE 5a........................S Shinton 1**
mid-div, steady prog 13th, ld 3 out, sn clr
149 **The Rum Mariner 6ex ....J Jukes 2**
(Jt fav) 3rd to 10th, disp nxt, ld 14th, hdd 3 out, no ext
191[4] **Polly Pringle 5a 3ex ....A Price 3**
hld up, prog 13th, 3rd 3 out, not rch 1st pair
257 Warren Boy *(Jt fav) ld til jnd 11th, ran on onepcd* ....Miss P Jones 4
364[5] Rusty Music *alwys rear, some late prog frm 15th* ....Miss N Richards 5
Equatime 5a *mid-div, styd on onepcd* ....K Cousins 6
93 Native Rambler (Ire) *2nd to 12th, grad lost tch* ....M P Jones 7
Quick Silver Boy 3ex *cls up early, grad wknd*..J Look 8
363 No Panic *nvr bynd mid-div, p.u. 2 out* Miss A Meakins pu
The Last Mistress 5a *last pair til p.u. 3 out* ....J Price pu
Project's Mate 7ex *last pair til p.u. 11th* ...C Richards pu
11 ran. 8l, 2l, 1l, 15l, 3l, 5l, 2l. Time 6m 22.00s. SP 7-1.
K C Lewis (Gelligaer).

400 Men's Open (12st)

187[3] **JACK SOUND 7ex ....E Williams 1**
ld/disp til ld 14th, alwys in cmmnd aft
Sun Of Chance ....P Williams 2
mid-div, onepcd 3rd frm 14th, lft 2nd last
Chiaroscuro ....S Lloyd 3
mostly 4th, wknd 3 out, lft 3rd last
256[6] Lighten The Load 4ex *rear, styd on frm 2 out, no dang* ....A Wintle 4
256[8] Electrolyte *alwys mid-div, nvr dang*.........G Austin 5
288[6] Kingfisher Bay *chsd ldrs to 11th, wknd*....C Richards 6
183[2] Carlowitz (USA) *n.j.w. rear til ref 5th*..........J Price ref
Northern Bluff 7ex *(fav) ld/disp til clr 2nd frm 14th, 4l down & hld whn f last* ....J Jukes f
187[2] Bullens Bay (Ire) *s.u. flat aft 2nd* ....J L Llewellyn su
Laudation (Ire) 7a *n.j.w. in last, p.u. 11th*.....P Hamer pu
10 ran. 20l, 5l, 2l, 2l, 10l. Time 6m 21.00s. SP 3-1.
E L Harries (Pembrokeshire).

401 Ladies

329 **BALLY RIOT (IRE) ....Mrs A Rucker 1**
chsd ldr til ld 3 out, hdd nxt, rallied last, ld flat
Celtic Daughter 5a ....Miss H Jones 2
hld up, went 4th at 11th, ld 2 out, hdd & outpcd last
99[4] **Carrick Lanes ....Miss P Jones 3**
mid-div, some prog 4 out, not rch 1st pair
187 Bartondale 5a *rear, ran on frm 3 out, nvr dang* ....Miss B Williams 4
188[1] Touch 'N' Pass *(fav) rear, no prog 13th* ....Miss A Meakins 5
296 Lady Llanfair 5a *cls up, lost plc hlfwy, no ch aft* ....Miss L Pearce 6
Afaristoun (Fr) *ld, wll clr 15th, wknd rpdly & hdd nxt* ....Miss J Morse 7
359[2] Robusti *tubed, alwys rear* ....Miss E James 8
188[4] Sea Patrol *nvr bynd mid-div* ....Miss B Barton 9
Bobbie's Girl (Ire) 5a *alwys wll in rear* ..Miss J Fowler 10
188[6] Harwall Queen 5a *rear whn f 7th*.........Miss J Gill f
6 Gold Diver *cls up, wknd 14th, p.u. 3 out* ....Miss P Gundry pu
Scared Stiff 5a *ref to race* ....Miss F Wilson 0
West King *last til p.u. 11th* ....Miss E Crawford pu
14 ran. Hd, 3l, 6l, 1l, 3l, 2l, 5l, 10l, 10l. Time 6m 22.00s. SP 6-1.
Mrs A Rucker (Worcestershire).

402 Intermediate Div I (12st)

364 **CONNA MOSS (IRE) ....Miss P Jones 1**
trckd ldrs, rpd prog 3 out, ld nxt, easily
256 **Push Along ....D Stephens 2**
2nd til ld 15th, hdd 2 out, alwys hld
361 **Dauphin Bleu (Fr) ....J Jukes 3**
(fav) ld to 14th, onepcd aft
My Pilot *alwys 4th, no ch frm hlfwy*...........J Price 4
191 Cairneymount *n.j.w. in rear, p.u. 12th*........J Tudor pu
293 Sebastopol *u.r. 2nd* ....I Johnson ur
Lingering Hope (Ire) *f 1st*...................J Comins f
7 ran. 6l, 1l, 25l. Time 6m 25.00s. SP 4-1.
David Brace (Llangeinor).

403 Intermediate Div II (12st)

258[1] **SCARLET BERRY 5a ....S Blackwell 1**
made all, in cmmnd frm 3 out
294[4] **Shuil's Star (Ire) ....P Hamer 2**
(fav) hld up rear, prog 15th, too mch to do
191 **Astounded ....J Tudor 3**
3rd/4th til onepcd frm 15th
191[5] Royal Oats 5a *chsd wnr to 14th, wknd rpdly* ....D S Jones 4
Valiant Friend *rear til p.u. 12th* ....Miss B Barton pu
Merger Mania 7a *ran out 3rd*..........Miss E James ro
186 Queen's Equa 5a *rear, p.u. 9th*...........J P Keen pu
Stickwiththehand *rear, p.u. 11th* ....J Price pu
8 ran. 6l, 15l, 4l. Time 6m 26.00s. SP 2-1.
P J Sanderson (Clifton On Teme).

404 Interlink Resricted Div I (12st)

298 **BIT OF A CITIZEN (IRE) ....E Williams 1**
hld up mid-div, prog to 4th 2 out, drvn to ld nr fin
Inch Empress (Ire) ....J Jukes 2
cls up, ld 14th, hrd rdn & hdd nr fin
258[2] **Onemoreanwego 5a ....Miss E James 3**
(fav) alwys 3rd/4th, outpcd frm 3 out
300 Sister Lark 5a *trckd ldr, ld 11-13th, onepcd aft* ....D S Jones 4
298 Mr Mad *hld up rear, prog 14th, went 2nd 2 out, one-pcd aft*..............................P Hamer 5
362 A Farm Bar *ld to 10th, grad wknd* ....P Williams 6
260 Hill Fort (Ire) *alwys mid-div, onepcd* ....A Wintle 7
184 All The Jolly 5a *rear, p.u. 12th* ....R Jones pu
Linantic *rear whn p.u. 11th* ....Miss P Jones pu
Red Rhapsody 5a *rear, f 5th* ....J Comins f
184 Jolly Swagman *mid-div, 7th at 11th, wknd & p.u. 2 out* ....G Perkins pu
Bay Leader 5a *rear, p.u. 16th* ....Miss E Tamplin pu
260 Bride Run (Ire) *alwys rear, p.u. 2 out* ....A Price pu
365[1] Manard 5a *prom, 3rd at 15th, wknd rpdly & p.u. 2 out* ....M Hammond pu
189[4] Rosieplant 5a *prom early, grad wknd, p.u. 2 out* ....M Lewis pu
Channel Island 5a *mid-div, f 3rd* ....K Cousins f
258 Irish Venture (Ire) *alwys rear, p.u. 3 out*......J Tudor pu
17 ran. ½l, 1l, 2l, 10l. Time 6m 28.00s. SP 5-1.
R Mason (Llangeinor).

405 Interlink Restricted Div II (12st)

260[4] **BOWLAND GIRL (IRE) 5a ....Miss E James 1**
hld up, rpd prog 4 out, ld nxt, drew clr
190[2] **Mrs Wumpkins (Ire) 5a............Miss P Jones 2**
(fav) cls up in 3rd, went 2nd 3 out, outpcd
298 **Moonlight Cruise 5a..................P Williams 3**
mostly 4th/5th, styd on onepcd frm 3 out
185 Journo's Joy 5a *mid-div, prog 15th, nrst fin* ....A Goldsworthy 4

189[5] Celtic Bizarre 5a *mid-div, no prog frm 3 out* ....Miss B Barton 5
Watchit Lad *mid-div, no prog hlfwy* ....M P Jones 6
258 Tanner *trckd ldrs, outpcd frm hlfwy* ....M Hammond 7
Algaihabane (USA) (bl) *lft in ld 5th, hdd 15th, wknd rpdly*....Miss P Gundry 8
189[8] Flaxridge *tongue-strap, ld til f 5th* ....Miss E Tamplin f
Cosa Nostra *alwys rear, p.u. 2 out* ....K Cousins pu
298 Dick's Cabin *rear, p.u. 11th* ....J Tudor pu
Lles Le Bucflow *prom til outpcd 3 out, p.u. last* ....C Richards pu
Hil Lady 5a *alwys rear, p.u. 2 out* ....D S Jones pu
Merry Morn 5a *f 2nd* ....J Jukes f
African Warrior 12a *f 2nd* ....T Vaughan f
15 ran. 5l, 3l, 1l, 5l, 10l, 10l, dist. Time 6m 35.00s. SP 5-1.
R J Scandrett (Radnor & West Hereford).

406 Interlink Restricted Div III (12st)

190[3] **WOLVER'S PET (IRE)** ....**D S Jones** **1**
(fav) trckd ldr, qcknd to ld 2 o ut, drew clr
258 **Hal's Prince** ....**Miss P Jones** **2**
ld 8th, hdd 2 out, onepcd
Reapers Reward 5a....**Miss B Barton** **3**
ld to 7th, prom aft til outpcd 15th
189 Saffron Moss *chsd ldrs, lost tch 15th* ...Miss F Wilson 4
362 Malthouse Lad *mid-div, outpcd frm 14th* ..D Stephens 5
364 Le Vienna (Ire) *tongue-strap, alwys rear, fin own time* ....S Currey 6
Toucher (Ire) *alwys rear, p.u. 8th* ....J Cook pu
189 Greenfield Tiger (Ire) *mid-div, p.u. 12th* ....C Richards pu
240 Pharrago (Ire) *mid-div, p.u. 12th* ....Miss P Cooper pu
Penylan Gold 5a *unruly pddck, rear, p.u. 2nd* ....P Williams pu
293 Rio Cisto 5a *rear whn f 4 out* ....J P Keen f
186 Bickerton Poacher *alwys rear, p.u. last* ....G Perkins pu
Moor Hill Lass (Ire) *f 4th* ....J Comins f
13 ran. 18l, 20l, 3l, 10l, dist. Time 6m 29.00s. SP 6-4.
R W J Willcox (Llangeinor).

407 Maiden Div I (12st)

366[3] **STORMHILL RECRUIT** ....**M P Jones** **1**
(fav) trckd ldrs, disp 3 out, lft in ld apr nxt, all out
185[3] **Wayward Edward** ....**J Price** **2**
trckd ldrs, 3rd 3 out, rallied nxt, onepcd flat
Yarron King ....**I Johnson** **3**
last pair early, late prog, nrst fin
261 Brown Bala 5a (bl) *rear, styd on frm 2 out, no imp* ....C Richards 4
184[4] Brynner *ld to 13th, wknd rpdly, p.u. 2 out* ....A Price pu
Lady Romance (Ire) 5a *prom early, wknd & p.u. 3 out* ....J P Keen pu
Greenfield Maid (Ire) 5a *mid-div, f 8th* ....Miss N Richards f
184 Bonus Number (Ire) *rear, p.u. 11th* ....K Cousins pu
Lady Orr (Ire) 5a *hld up mid-div, prog to disp 3 out, ran out bend apr nxt* ....J Tudor pu
245 Roger (Ire) 7a *f 2nd*....Miss P Cooper f
Davalbury (Ire) 7a *mid-div, blnd 14th, p.u. aft* ....Miss P Jones pu
11 ran. 1l, dist, 10l. Time 6m 43.00s. SP 3-1.
Mrs A Price (Teme Valley (United)).

408 Maiden Div II (12st)

MITTENWALD (IRE) ....**D S Jones** **1**
cls up, 4th at 14th, rpd prog 2 out, ld last
300 **Khandys Slave (Ire) 5a** ....**J Jukes** **2**
hld up, gd prog 14th, ld 3 out, hdd & no ext last
368[4] **Who's Your Man (Ire)** ....**C Richards** **3**
(fav) mostly 2nd til outpcd frm 14th
184[5] I'm A Bute 5a *cls up, 5th at 14th, sn btn*....J Price 4
244[4] Pyro Pennant *mid-div, no prog frm 14th* ....S Shinton 5
365 Tiger Lord *alwys mid-div, no ch frm 14th*....A Price 6
184[2] Final Option (Ire) *alwys last, t.o. hlfwy* ....I Johnson 7
Sweet Mariner *ld to 14th, wknd rpdly, p.u. 2 out* ....S Blackwell pu
184 Tommyknocker (Ire) 7a *rear, p.u. 14th* Miss P Cooper pu
Miswiskers 5a *tongue-strap, rear, p.u. 8th*....S Lloyd pu
Tot Of Rum 5a *f 2nd*....D Stephens f
Miss Clare 5a *alwys rear, p.u. 3 out* ....K Cousins pu
12 ran. 2l, 15l, 1l, 10l, 10l, dist. Time 6m 47.00s. SP 5-2.
Mrs J E Tamplin (Tredegar Farmers).

409 Maiden Div III (12st)

263[3] **IN THE WATER** ....**M P Jones** **1**
trckd ldrs, ld 14th, jnd 2 out, all out flat
366 **Peat Potheen** ....**T Weale** **2**
mid-div, prog 15th, disp 2 out, ev ch, just faild
259 **Ribington** ....**J Jukes** **3**
prom, outpcd frm 3 out
185[4] High Guardian *mid-div, gd prog 14th, onepcd frm nxt* ....I Johnson 4
Heather Boy *(fav) ld 5th-13th, 2nd aft til wknd rpdly 3 out*....Miss P Jones 5
176[5] Boddington Hill 5a *alwys rear* ....S Shinton 6
Trydan *rear, p.u. 11th*....Miss S Robinson pu
367 Mister Jay Day *cls up, gd prog 15th, 3rd & ev ch whn f 2 out* ....A Price f
Stiff Drink *clr ldr til ran out 5th*....Miss K Williams ro
186 Rusty Hall 12a *rear, p.u. 10th*....Miss P Cooper pu
Clansies Girl 5a *rear, p.u. 15th* ....S Lloyd pu
186 Buckland Ballad 7a *mid-div, f 12th* ....K Cousins f
12 ran. Hd, 5l, 4l, 10l, 15l. Time 6m 52.00s. SP 5-1.
Mrs B Brown (Teme Valley).
J.C./P.H.

CUMBERLAND FARMERS
Dalston
Saturday March 8th
GOOD TO SOFT

410 Members (12st)

342[1] **MARKED CARD** ....**Mrs M Kendall** **1**
ld 6-9th, chsd ldr, ld aft 3 out, ran on well flat
Pennine View ....**R Ford** **2**
(fav) w.w. prog 15th,jnd wnr 2 out,ev ch & veerd lft flat,nt qckn
157[6] **All Or Nothing 5a**....**J Ewart** **3**
ld to 6th & 9-12th, sn outpcd & bhnd, ran on agn 2 out
130 Hydropic *cls up, ld 12th, sn clr, hdd & wknd aft 3 out* ....Miss K Miller 4
162[1] Trumpet Hill *alwys last, lost tch 15th, t.o. & p.u. nxt, dsmntd* ....T Morrison pu
5 ran. 2l, 6l, 1l. Time 6m 31.00s. SP 3-1.
Mrs M A Kendall (Cumberland Farmers).

411 Confined (12st)

335[2] **FARRIERS FAVOURITE 5a** ....**A Parker** **1**
w.w. prog 12th, lft 2nd aft 3 out, ld last, drvn out flat
Simon Joseph ....**R Morgan** **2**
trckd ldr, ld 11-14th, lft in ld aft 3 out, hdd last,kpt on
338[1] **Pablowmore** ....**R Green** **3**
jmpd slwly & bhnd, prog frm 14th, styd on wll 2 out,nrst fin
Buckle It Up *prom, outpcd 15th, styd on frm nxt, unable to chal*....C Storey 4
339 Boreen Owen 5ex *prom til outpcd 3 out, kpt on frm nxt* ....T Morrison 5
335 In Demand *(fav) jmpd slwly 4th, nvr going wll, lost tch & btn frm 15th*....P Craggs 6
341[2] Hooky's Treat 5a *chsd ldrs to 14th, wknd aft 3 out* ....M Bradburne 7
Ruecastle *prom to 8th, wknd 11th, t.o.* ....Miss J Hutchinson 8
229[7] Lion Of Vienna *20s-12s, alwys rear, t.o. 15th* ..T Scott 9
231 Rare Fire *t.o. 8th, p.u. 10th*....Miss R Davison pu
334[1] Sharp Opinion *rear & nvr going wll, lost tch 11th, p.u. 15th* ....Miss P Robson pu
343 Fast Fun *alwys bhnd, t.o. last whn p.u. 12th* L Morgan pu
May Run *made most to 11th, wknd 14th, t.o. & p.u. aft 3 out*....Mrs V Jackson pu
162[8] Sovereigns Match *prom, ld 14th, 4l clr whn p.u. aft 3 out* ....D McLeod pu
343 Mighty Express *alwys bhnd, t.o. last whn p.u. 3 out* ....A Ogden pu

Patter Merchant *reluc to race, wll bhnd til p.u. 14th* ....P Hall pu
16 ran. 1½l, 3l, 4l, 4l, 25l, 6l, 25l, 5l. Time 6m 29.00s. SP 9-2.
Mrs J Leckenby (Braes Of Derwent).

412 Ladies

156¹ **ORANGE RAGUSA ....Miss P Robson 1**
(fav) j.w. keen hld, ld 4th, made rest, pshd out & ran on well
336 **Roly Prior ....Mrs V Jackson 2**
prom, chsd wnr 11th-3 out, rallied apr last, ran on
Hornblower ....Mrs C Ford 3
alwys prom, prssd wnr 3 out, unable to qckn apr last
231⁶ Very Evident (Ire) *prog & prom 9th, outpcd 3 out, kpt on agn frm nxt* ....Miss J Bird 4
336 Schweppes Tonic *in tch to 14th, sn wknd, t.o.* ....Mrs C Amos 5
336 Ready Steady *ld to 4th, prom til mstk 13th, sn btn, t.o. & p.u. last* ....Mrs K Hargreave pu
South Stack *last pair, lsng tch whn hmpd & u.r. 14th* ....Miss C Billington ur
329⁴ Running Frau 5a *last pair, losng tch whn blnd & u.r. 14th* ....Miss M Maher ur
8 ran. 2l, 2l, 6l, dist. Time 6m 24.00s. SP 4-6.
S H Shirley-Beavan (Jedforest).

413 Men's Open (12st)

329 **THE PARISH PUMP (IRE) ....R Ford 1**
made all, clr 2 out, pshd out flat
161¹ **Gallants Delight 5a........A Robson 2**
(fav) mstks, hld up, prog to chs wnr 3 out, ran on wll, alwys hld
337² **Solwaysands ....D Gibson 3**
prom til outpcd frm 3 out, sn no ch
229⁵ Benghazi *chsd ldrs, strggling whn mstk 14th, no ch aft* ....A Parker 4
335⁴ Lothian Pilot *prom, chsd wnr 11th-3 out, wknd nxt, blnd last* ....D Wood 5
328 Syrus P Turntable *alwys bhnd, t.o. 15th* ....J Saville 6
155¹ Do A Runner *mstks, nvr going wll, bhnd frm 12th, t.o.* ....S Love 7
Miss Jedd 5a 7ex *prssd wnr til blnd & nrly u.r. 9th, nt rcvr, p.u. 3 out* ....P Craggs pu
Fortinas Flyer 5a (bl) *t.o. & last til p.u. 14th* ....M Bradburne pu
9 ran. 2l, 20l, 3l, 2l, 15l, 8l. Time 6m 29.00s. SP 5-2.
Mrs R Silcock (Vale Of Loon).

414 P P O R A (12st)

131¹ **MAKIN' DOO (IRE) ....A Parker 1**
(fav) alwys going wll, trckd ldrs, ld apr 2 out, rdn out flat
Press For Action ....Miss P Robson 2
ld 2nd, set gd pace, hdd apr 2 out, kpt on well
228² **Luckieshiel 5a........Miss D Calder 3**
plfng,ld to 2nd,4th & outpcd frm 13th,lft poor 3rd apr 2 out
234³ Bluebell Track 5a *in tch to 10th, sn strggling, t.o. 15th* ....R Trotter 4
157¹ Eostre *mstk 3rd, nvr going wll, lost tch 12th, t.o.* ....P Craggs 5
336 Across The Lake 7ex (bl) *chsd ldrs, rdn 11th, sn strggling, t.o. & p.u. 2 out* ....Miss S Brotherton pu
199⁴ Leeswood (v) *chsd ldr,mstks 14 & 15,3rd & btn whn hit mrkr & u.r.apr 2out* ....Mrs C Ford ur
333 Carol's Concorde (Ire) *schoold in last, lost tch 12th, p.u. 2 out* ....J Saville pu
333 Mr Goldfinger *rear, effrt 11th, sn btn, t.o. whn crwld 3 out & p.u.* ....D Sherlock pu
9 ran. 6l, dist, 10l, 8l. Time 6m 28.00s. SP 5-4.
R G Makin (York & Ainsty South).

415 Restricted Div I (12st)

338² **THE BUACHAILL (IRE) ....P Craggs 1**
trckd ldrs, mstk 13th, ld aft 3 out, hld on und pres
162³ **Bitofanatter ....R Morgan 2**
mid-div, 9th hlfwy, prog 13th, prssd wnr apr 2 out, just hld
230⁴ **Ebbzeado Willfurr (Ire) ....J Billinge 3**
mstk 4th,wll bhnd,poor 13th hlfwy,ran on 14th,too mch to do
337⁶ Jayandoubleu (Ire) *alwys prom, ld 11-12th, ev ch 3 out, sn onepcd* ....T Scott 4
230⁸ Drumcairn (Ire) 2ow *rear, prog & 8th hlfwy, effrt to chs ldrs 15th, no imp* ....P Forster 5
231² Funny Feelings *(fav) t.d.e. mstk 6th, prom til outpcd aft 3 out, sn btn* ....Miss D Laidlaw 6
235 Thinkaboutthat (Ire) *ld 2-11th, prom til wknd 3 out* ....J Muir 7
230⁶ Blakes Folly (Ire) *mid-div, 10th hlfwy, prog 15th, kpt on, no dang* ....D Wood 8
Boyup Brook *mstk 1st, alwys bhnd, 17th & t.o. hlfwy* ....T Morrison 9
230⁹ Flypie *alwys rear, 14th & t.o. hlfwy* ....P Strang Steel 10
331 Charlie Trumper (Ire) *mstks, ld to 2nd, 12th & wkng hlfwy, t.o.* ....J Saville 11
337⁸ Mandys Special 5a *chsd ldrs, 7th hlfwy, sn wknd, t.o.* ....L Morgan 12
131³ Jads Lad *alwys bhnd, last & t.o. hlfwy, p.u. 14th* ....D Reid pu
343 Bantel Baronet *sn rear, last & t.o. whn p.u. 10th* ....Miss J Hedley pu
157⁵ Royal Fife 5a *last pair & nvr in race, t.o. & p.u. 15th* ....A Parker pu
233⁶ Hula *prom, ld 12th-aft 3 out, wknd rpdly, 9th whn f 2 out* ....M Bradburne f
342 Newbrano 5a (bl) *mid-div, 11th hlfwy, sn btn, t.o. & p.u. 3 out* ....I Carmichael pu
Slim King *chsd ldrs, 6th hlfwy, sn wknd, t.o. & f 2 out* ....D Woodward f
All Screwed Up (Ire) *mstk 7th, alwys rear, t.o. & p.u. 15th* ....D Sherlock pu
19 ran. ½l, 6l, 6l, 6l, ½l, hd, 6l, dist, 3l, 2l. Time 6m 31.00s. SP 7-2.
Mrs Alix Stevenson (Dumfriesshire).

416 Restricted Div II (12st)

157 **BUCKLANDS COTTAGE 5a........D McLeod 1**
prom, ld 14th til hdd & lft clr 2 out, eased flat
343² **Lauder Square ....M Bradburne 2**
rear, lost tch 14th, ran on wll frm 3 out, nrst fin
157 **Snapper ....A Parker 3**
(fav) hld up, prog 8th, chsd ldrs & outpcd 3 out, sn btn
Whosgotsillyssense 5a *alwys rear, no ch 14th, t.o.* ....C Storey 4
342 Copper Pan 5a *alwys rear, no ch 14th, t.o.*....T Scott 5
Warkswoodman *alwys last, t.o. 11th* ....Miss E Wagg 6
339 Buckaneer Bay *ld to 5th, prom til wknd 15th, wll btn 4th & p.u. 2 out* ....C Wilson pu
Mossiman (Ire) *alwys rear, t.o. whn f 3 out*. .A Robson f
356⁷ Mandys Lad *pllng, ld 5th til mstk 14th, blnd nxt, nt rcvr & p.u.* ....S Robinson pu
338⁴ Star Lea *trckd ldrs, prog 14th, ld & f 2 out* ....B Stonehouse f
341 Peelinick *chsd ldrs, 5th whn u.r. 12th* ....T Oates ur
130 Trespasser (Ire) (bl) *alwys rear, 10th & t.o. whn ref 13th* ....R Morgan pu
12 ran. 2½l, 30l, 30l, 12l, 20l. Time 6m 37.00s. SP 3-1.
J C Hogg (Buccleuch).

417 2½m Open Maiden Div I Pt I (12st)

HIGH HOPES 2ow ....R Shiels 1
ld to 4th, ld 8th, mstk nxt, clr 2 out, pshd out
341 **The Alleycat (Ire) ....C Storey 2**
prom, prssd wnr frm 8th, no imp aft 3 out
334 **Bavington ....R Morgan 3**
rear, 9th & rdn hlfwy, no ch 11th, ran on frm 2 out, nvr nrr
161⁶ Restraint 5a *ld 4-8th, outpcd frm 12th, no imp ldrs aft* ....Miss F Barnes 4
340 Jones *unruly pddck, s.s. jmpd bdly, t.o. 11th* ....Miss A Adams 5
Doc Spot *mid-div, 5th hlfwy, sn lost tch, t.o.* ....S Robinson 6

235 Allrite Pet 5a *(fav) s.s. hld up, prog to trck ldrs 9th, wknd 3 out, virt p.u.*..........................A Parker 7
233 Passim 12a *alwys rear, no ch 11th, t.o.*....T Morrison 8
234[7] Polly Cinders 5a *rear, no ch 11th, t.o. & p.u. 3 out*...M Ruddy pu
Rough House *prom, mstk 11th, sn wknd, t.o. & p.u. 2 out*...A Robson pu
230 Steady Man *s.s. rear til crshd thro wing 4th*...D McLeod ro
11 ran. 10l, 5l, 1½l, 25l, 1l, 6l, 10l. Time 5m 38.00s. SP 9-4.
Miss D M M Calder (Berwickshire).

418 2½m Open Maiden Div I Pt II (12st)

334[2] **STORM ALIVE (IRE)** ....**T Scott** 1
(Jt fav) trckd ldrs, hrd rdn & effrt aft 3 out, styd on to ld nr fin
Arm Ah Man (Ire) ....**C Wilson** 2
(Jt fav) hld up,jnd ldrs 9th,chal 3 out & agn flat,just faild
Romiley Mill ....**D Coates** 3
prssd ldr, ld 3 out, rdn & wknd flat, hdd nr fin
352[2] Say Daphne 5a *wll in tch til wknd aft 3 out*...............................Miss P Robson 4
Imulari *made most to 3 out, wknd & p.u. nxt* P Craggs pu
Conors Bluebird (Ire) *prom til wknd rpdly & p.u. 11th*...............................Mrs K Hargreave pu
161 Rakeira 12a *alwys rear, t.o. & p.u. 10th*......C Paisley pu
338 Kinlochaline 5a *t.o. 5th, p.u. 11th*.............J Ewart pu
Galachlaw *bhnd, mstk 6th, t.o. & p.u. 9th*....R Trotter pu
Percy Special (Ire) *last & t.o. til ran out 4th*....J Davis ro
10 ran. Nk, 1l, 30l. Time 5m 36.00s. SP 7-4.
Mrs Richard Arthur (Tynedale).

419 2½m Open Maiden Div II Pt I (12st)

BUSHMILLER (IRE) ....**A Ogden** 1
ld to 12th, lft in ld aft nxt, in cmmnd whn lft wll clr last
37 **Victor Charlie** ....**N Sutton** 2
chsd ldr to 6th, wknd & blnd 10th, t.o. 3 out, lft 2nd last
358 **Killeaney Carr (Ire)** ....**Miss P Robson** 3
rear,t.o. 10th,kpt on 3 out,3rd & btn whn f last,rmntd
338 Mr Cosmo (Ire) *chsd ldr 6-10th, lft 2nd 3 out, hld whn u.r. last*...............................J Billinge ur
341 Henry Higgins *s.v.s. school & bhnd, t.o. 10th, p.u. last*...............................Miss E Wagg pu
Primitive Streak *trckd ldrs going wll, ld 12th, 4l up whn u.r. aft nxt*...............................P Johnson ur
Don Carlos 7a *blnd & u.r. 1st*......................P Craggs ur
161[7] The Pharside (Ire) *(fav) mstks, 4th whn f 6th*..A Parker f
160[2] Abbey Lad *chsd ldrs, 5th & just in tch whn u.r. 9th*...............................N Swann ur
Cinder Mirage *s.s. mstk 4th, t.o. & p.u. 6th*..A Robson pu
10 ran. Dist, dist. Time 5m 40.00s. SP 6-1.
R A Ross (Braes Of Derwent).

420 2½m Open Maiden Div II Pt II (12st)

HARDEN GLEN ....**Miss D Laidlaw** 1
made all, clr 3 out, easily
358[2] **Blank Cheque** ....**D Coates** 2
mid-div, clsd 11th, chsd wnr & hit 2 out, no imp
233[5] **Claywalls** ....**T Scott** 3
chsd ldr to 6th, ev ch 12th, onepcd aft
235 Megans Mystery (Ire) *(fav) chsd wnr 6th, mstk 8th, wknd aft 3 out*..................................C Wilson 4
340 Pleasedaspunch (Ire) 7a *schoold & wll in rear, nvr nrr, improve*..................................C Storey 5
Ronnies Wedding (Ire) 7a *alwys last, t.o. whn tried ref 4th, school aft*..................................J Saville 6
161 Captain Guinness (Ire) *chsd ldrs, mstk 4th, rdn 9th, sn strgglng*..................................J Alexander 7
True Censation 5a *s.s. last whn tried to ref & u.r. 2nd*..................................D Sherlock ur
8 ran. 8l, 8l, 12l, 5l, 8l, 8l. Time 5m 34.00s. SP 4-1.
M H Walton (College Valley/Northumberland).
J.N.

DERWENT
Charm Park
Saturday March 8th
GOOD TO FIRM

421 Members

265 **NISHKINA** ....**C Cundall** 1
disp til hdd 3rd, ld 11th & disp nxt, ld 15th, kpt on flat
116[1] **Transcendental (Ire) 5ex** ....**Miss A Deniel** 2
(fav) hld up in mid-div, disp 12th,outpcd by wnr 15th,styd on flat
357[1] **Lingcool 5a 5ex** ....**M Morley** 3
prom, ld 6th til rddr lost irons & wd 11th, hdd onepcd 4 out
Dunford Bridge (USA) *mid-div til ld 3rd, hdd 6th & fdd 12th*..................................S Charlton 4
Another Chant *disp to 3rd, fdd 6th, lost tch 10th, t.o. & p.u. 12th*..................................S Swiers pu
Hillmilly 12a *rear, detached 2nd, lost tch 10th, t.o. & p.u. 13th*..................................C Mulhall pu
6 ran. 1l, 6l, 5l. Time 6m 53.00s. SP 7-2.
C J Cundall (Derwent).

422 Confined

164[1] **JUST CHARLIE** ....**D Easterby** 1
(Jt fav) ld to 4th, lft in ld 7th, jnd 4 out, lft wll clr nxt, easily
350[1] **Mr Dick** ....**S Swiers** 2
(Jt fav) hld up in rear, prog 14th, outpcd 4 out, lft poor 2nd 3 out
266 **Here Comes Charter** ....**A Pennock** 3
prom til fdd 13th, lft remt 3rd 3 out
251[7] The Chap *prom,jnd slwly 8th & 9th,wknd qckly 14th,t.o. whn ref 4 out*..................R Lochman ref
Pinewood Lad *prom, ld 4th til ran v wd & p.u. 7th*..................................Miss K Ford pu
163 Another Hooligan *hld up,mstk 5th, prog 11th,disp 4 out,bad mstk & u.r. nxt*..............Mrs F Needham ur
348[8] Cahermone Lady (Ire) 5a *prom whn f 1st* ..S Whitaker f
Strong Words *mid-div whn u.r. 3rd* ....S Pinder ur
8 ran. 15l, 15l. Time 6m 34.00s. SP 6-4.
Mrs Susan E Mason (Middleton).

423 Men's Open

267[2] **PEANUTS PET** ....**R Walmsley** 1
prom, wnt 2nd 10th, prssng ldr & rddn whn lft clr last
264[4] **Miami Bear** ....**L Russell** 2
hld up in rear,prog 4 out,ev ch 2 out,wknng whn lft 2nd last
267 **Misti Hunter (Ire)** ....**S Swiers** 3
prom til stdly fdd frm 3 out, lft 3rd last
353 Black Spur *mid-div, rddn 11th, mstks 13th,sn lost tch,t.o. & p.u. 4 out*..................................P Jenkins pu
Frome Boy *rear, mstks 2nd & 3rd, sn bhnd, t.o. 10th, p.u. nxt*..................................P Johnson pu
354 Pats Cross (Ire) *keen hold, ld just ahd & gng best whn u.r. last*..................................J Byrne ur
354[1] Castletown Count 7a *(fav) rear, prog 5th, trckng ldr whn ran out 9th*..................................N Wilson ro
7 ran. 7l, 2l. Time 6m 28.00s. SP 7-4.
J W Walmsley (Bramham Moor).

424 Restricted Div I (12st)

266[2] **BLACKWOODSCOUNTRY** ....**C Mulhall** 1
(fav) alwys prom, prog to ld last, ran on wll
264[3] **Cadrillon (Fr)** ....**Miss A Deniel** 2
mid-div, prog 4 out, outpcd 2 out, styd on strgly flat
356 **On The Fly** ....**R Edwards** 3
prom, ld 4th til hdd 2 out, kpt on wll
348 Stride To Glory (Ire) 1ow *prom, ld 2 out-last, not qckn*..................................D Topping 4
253[1] Joint Account *pulld hrd, alwys prom, ev ch 3 out, onepcd*..................................Mrs F Needham 5

Sergeant Pepper *hld up & bhnd, prog 10th, mstk 14th, outpcd frm 2 out*..........N Wilson 6
357 Smith's Melody *prom til wknd 11th, sn lost tch, t.o.*..........M Haigh 7
266 G Derek *mid-div til lost tch 11th, t.o. & p.u. last*..........P Halder pu
251[6] Sharp To Oblige 1ow *ld to 4th, prom whn f 11th*..........S Whitaker f
348[6] Ellerton Park *prom, outpcd 9th, wknd 13th, p.u. 4 out (lame)*..........N Smith pu
Canny's Fort 5a 2ow *slwly into stride, sn strggling, wll bhnd 11th, p.u. last*..........S Gibbon pu
353 Crown And Anchor 7a *rear, lost tch 11th, p.u. 13th*..........G Markham pu
12 ran. 1l, 1l, 1l, ½l, 10l, dist. Time 6m 32.00s. SP Evens.
Mrs Winifred A Birkinshaw (Sinnington).

425 Restricted Div II (12st)

343[1] **SECRET BAY ....S Swiers 1**
(fav) sttld mid-div,smth prog 15th,ld 2 out,sn qcknd clr,eased flt
Caman 5a ....Mrs S Grant 2
prom, ld 15th-2 out, no ext
346[1] **Winters Melody 5a..........A Pennock 3**
mid-div, prog 9th, ld 11th-15th, wknd, blndrd last
344[1] Flying Quest *hld up, mstk 3rd, prog 10th, styd on stdly frm 3 out, prmsng*..........S Walker 4
Lyningo *sn in rear, strggng & lost tch 12th*...S Brisby 5
266[6] Make A Line *prom til outpcd frm 4 out*......C Denny 6
251 Ruff Account *prom til outpcd frm 4 out*..........Miss J Eastwood 7
266[4] Spartan Juliet 5a *rear most of the way, strggng 4 out,wll btn whn blndrd 2 out*..........P Jenkins 8
251 Mount Faber *mid-div, lost tch 5 out, t.o.*...S Charlton 9
157 Prime Style 1ow *ld, mstk 1st, blndrd & hdd 11th, wknd qckly 13th, t.o.*..........C Gibbon 10
169[1] Oliver's Mate (Ire) *mid-div, rddn 11th, rear whn f 12th*..........N Tutty f
337 River Ramble 5a *mid-div, wknd 11th, t.o. & p.u. 4 out*..........Miss T Jackson pu
12 ran. 8l, 6l, 3l, 7l, 1½l, 3l, ½l, 5l, 8l. Time 6m 27.00s. SP 4-6.
S P Dent (Zetland).

426 Ladies

268[1] **DARK DAWN ....Miss L Foxton 1**
hld up, prog 11th, ld 2 out, ran on wll, comf
117 **Carole's Delight 5a..........Mrs L Ward 2**
alwys prom, rddn 3 out, ev ch last, kpt on gamely
165 **Indie Rock ....Mrs F Needham 3**
hld up in rear, prog 4 out, ev ch 2 out, not qckn
349[1] Integrity Boy *mid-div, prog 5 out, ev ch 3 out, not qckn frm nxt*..........Miss A Armitage 4
355[5] Cumberland Blues (Ire) *(fav) ld til hdd 2 out, wknd qckly*..........Miss A Deniel 5
268[3] Man Of Mystery *prom, ev ch 4 out, sn fdd*..........Miss S Hatfield 6
355[1] Cheeky Pot *rear, mstk 4th, alwys outpcd* Mrs S Grant 7
215[5] Douce Indienne 5a *mid-div til wknd 11th, wll bhnd 13th*..........Miss J Eastwood 8
355 Ski Lady 5a *mid-div, lost tch 10th, t.o. 13th*..........Miss L Horner 9
355 Crocket Lass 5a *prom early, strggling 8th, sn wll bhnd*..........Miss F Hunter 10
165[5] Skolern (bl) *lost many l stt, alwys wll bhnd, p.u. 3 out*..........Miss L Pounder pu
Oxford Place (bl) *rear & lost tch 9th, t.o. 12th, p.u. 3 out*..........Miss T Jackson pu
12 ran. 2l, 2l, 3l, 8l, 1l, 10l, 8l, 20l, dist. Time 6m 22.00s. SP 11-4.
Mrs J M Newitt (Sinnington).

427 Open Maiden (5-6yo) Div I (12st)

346[3] **PETIT PRIMITIVE 5a..........S Charlton 1**
mid-div, prog 9th, ld 4 out, sn wll clr
Zobejo 7a ....N Smith 2
mid-div, prog 4th 4 out, styd on frm 2 out
357 **Patey Court 5a..........C Mulhall 3**
prom, ev ch 4 out, fddng whn mstks last 2
269[4] Abbey Moss *ld til hdd & wknd qckly 4 out*..........Miss J Eastwood 4
Miss Accounts (Ire) 5a *rear, mstk 2nd, prog 8th, wknd 13th, t.o. frm 3 out*..........Miss A Armitage 5
115 Whiskey Ditch 5a *prom til stdly fdd frm 14th, t.o. & p.u. last*..........M Haigh pu
269 Look Sharpe 3ow *(fav) virt ref to race, stt wll bhnd, alwys t.o. & p.u. 13th*..........A Bonson pu
358 Mr Hook 7a *mid-div, mstk 5th, lost tch 8th, p.u. nxt*..........G Markham pu
Klondyke Maid 5a *prom early, outpcd 8th, wll bhnd 12th, p.u. 4 out*..........P Jenkins pu
Nells Delight 5a *rear & sn strggling, wll bhnd 9th, f 11th*..........P Atkinson f
10 ran. 15l, 1l, 15l, 15l. Time 6m 46.00s. SP 4-1.
Mrs K Ratcliffe (Middleton).

428 Open Maiden (5-6yo) Div II (12st)

80[2] **KIND OF CHIC 5a ....S Swiers 1**
(fav) kn hld,stld 3rd til lft 2nd 5th,ld last,lft clr flat,kpt on
264[5] **Just A Single (Ire) ....R Edwards 2**
ld til hdd last, ran v wd final bnd, rlld fin
79 **Little Red ....T Barry 3**
mid-div, prog 10th, wnt remt 3rd 3 out, nvr nrr
357 West Lutton 7a *rear, prog to chsng grp 10th, mstk nxt, fdd 3 out*..........N Wilson 4
169 Yogi's Mistress 5a *rear, prog to chsng grp 9th, wknd 3 out*..........P Frank 5
Is Red There 7a *mid-div, disp remt 3rd 8th, wknd 10th, t.o. & p.u. 12th*..........N Smith pu
357 Surprise View 12a *alwys in rear, lost tch aft 8th, t.o. & p.u. 10th*..........G Markham pu
210 Zerose 12a *prom in chsng grp, disp remt 3rd 8th, fddng whn u.r. 11th*..........P Cornforth ur
358 Sparky Brown (Ire) 2ow *mid-div, fdd 7th, sn lost tch, t.o. & p.u. 9th*..........D Collop pu
Move In Style *trckd ldr whn f 5th*..........C Gibbon f
10 ran. 5l, 10l, 15l, sht-hd. Time 6m 41.00s. SP 6-4.
Mrs Susan E Mason (Middleton).
Last two races, one fence omitted, 16 jumps.

429 Open Maiden (7yo+)

JUST COMING ....C Mulhall 1
mid-div, prog 12th, ld apr last, sn drew clr, comf
357[3] **Jolly Ghost ....S Charlton 2**
prom, lft 2nd 10th, ld brfly 2 out til apr last, outpcd
Just Johnie ....S Walker 3
prom, wnt 3rd 12th, ev ch 3 out, sn outpcd
Prophet's Choice *prom, lft in ld 10th, hdd 2 out, wknd qckly*..........M Haigh 4
Prickly Trout 5a *rear & sn outpcd, wll bhnd 9th, t.o. 12th*..........M Bennison 5
167[4] Hoistthestandard 5a *mid-div, imprvd 9th, outpcd 12th & sn lost tch, t.o.*..........T Glass 6
120 Persian Lion *ld til f 10th*..........Mrs L Ward f
212 Smart Mover *prom til wknd 9th, lost tch 12th, t.o. & p.u. last*..........S Brisby pu
Timber Topper *rear & sn strggling, t.o. 9th, p.u. 2 out*..........R Edwards pu
266 Lartington Lad *mid-div, fdd 8th, t.o. 10th, p.u. 12th*..........E Wilkin pu
Markham Lad *virt ref to race, stt 2 fences bhnd, alwys t.o. & p.u. 8th*..........R Berry pu
Raike It In 5a *(fav) rear & sn bhnd, t.o. 9th, p.u. nxt*..........S Swiers pu
80 Chummy's Last 5a *nvr gng wll, rear, t.o. 7th, p.u. nxt*..........Mrs F Needham pu
353 Mal's Castle (Ire) 5a *plld hrd, not fluent, alwys rear, lost tch 8th, p.u. 12th*..........P Atkinson pu
14 ran. 5l, 5l, 7l, dist, 2l. Time 6m 28.00s. SP 20-1.
R G P Mason (Middleton).
N.E.

NORTH LEDBURY
Upton-On-Severn
Saturday March 8th
GOOD

430 Members (12st)

220 **SHARINSKI 5ex..................Julian Pritchard** 1
(fav) trckd ldrs, chal 14th, ld 3 out, jnd last, drvn out flat
294 **Hackett's Farm 5ex ....D Duggan** 2
made most frm 5th til 3 out, rallied last, no ext flat
Lady Pendragon 5a ....D Mansell 3
hld up in tch, 3rd 3 out, nvr able to chal
Nanda Moon *ld/disp til grad wknd frm 14th* ....Miss S Jackson 4
4 ran. 3l, 6l, 15l. Time 6m 59.00s. SP 2-5.
Mrs Jo Yeomans (North Ledbury).

431 Confined (12st)

201³ **FIRST HARVEST 5ex ....P Hanly** 1
ld frm 3rd, prssd 3 out, clr last, eased flat
290 **Principle Music (USA) ....M Munrowd** 2
(Jt fav) w.w. prog 12th, chal 3 out, rdn & no ext apr nxt
Viridian 2ex..........................D Duggan 3
mid-div, prog to cls 3rd 10th, not qckn frm 14th
Leigh Boy (USA) *mid-div, lost tch 12th, no ch frm nxt* ....M Rimell 4
Great Uncle *drppd last 9th, lost tch 12th, t.o. 15th* ....Miss T McCurrick 5
256 Master Eryl *ld to 2nd, cls 4th at 11th, outpcd 13th, dist 4th & u.r.2out*..................G Barfoot-Saunt ur
218⁵ Sudanor (Ire) *(Jt fav) last til some prog 8th, no ch 13th, p.u. 15th*..................Julian Pritchard pu
255 Gold'n Shroud (Ire) *chsd ldrs, outpcd 13th, remote 5th whn p.u. 3 out*..................N Oliver pu
255 Mr Dennehy (Ire) *prom, chsd ldr 5-11th, wknd 13th, p.u. 3 out*..................M Butcher pu
9 ran. 6l, 15l, 30l, 10l. Time 6m 44.00s. SP 4-1.
C J Bennett (Ledbury).

432 Mixed Open (12st)

86¹ **BAGALINO (USA) ....Julian Pritchard** 1
(fav) made all, drew clr 3 out, eased flat
308¹ **Lost Fortune ....H Wheeler** 2
cls 2nd at 8th, 8l 4th 13th, effrt nxt, no ext aft 3 out
Master Dancer ....Miss C Dyson 3
chsd ldr, cls 2nd 10th, not qckn frm 14th, kpt on
219 Bankroll *lost 30l start, nvr ct up, fin well* ....Mrs C Chadney 4
Forest Ranger *lost tch 6th, t.o. & p.u. 11th* ....M Munrowd pu
Sayyure (USA) *mostly 4th/5th, outpcd 13th, p.u. 3 out* ....S Bush pu
Emerald Ruler *4l 3rd at 12th, 2l 3rd whn u.r. 3 out* ....P Cowley ur
7 ran. 6l, 8l, 30l. Time 6m 42.00s. SP 11-8.
Miss Jane Fellows (Ledbury).

433 Restricted (12st)

263¹ **ROCKET RADAR ....Julian Pritchard** 1
cls up 8th, prog 13th, ld 3 out, drew clr nxt
Ruth's Boy (Ire) ....Miss S Vickery 2
(fav) ld til hdd & not qckn 3 out, btn frm nxt
261¹ **Baptist John (Ire) ....M Harris** 3
alwys chsng ldrs, not fluent, ev ch til not qckn 15th
Parson Flynn *mid-div, effrt 12th, not chal ldrs* S Bush 4
300 The Hon Company *cls 5th at 8th, outpcd 14th, no ch frm 3 out*..................E Walker 5
Duke Of Plumstead *rear frm 3rd, lost tch & p.u. 10th* ....N Oliver pu
260³ Meadow Cottage *cls up 10th, ev ch whn hit 13th, wknd 15th, p.u. last*..................T Stephenson pu
362 Members Rights 5a *cls 3rd at 7th, outpcd 12th, no ch whn p.u. 2 out*..................M Keel pu
372⁸ Damers Treasure *mid-div whn blnd & u.r. 9th* ....M Cowley ur
213 Shannon King (Ire) *prog 6th, cls 3rd 9th, wknd 12th, p.u. 14th*..................P Hanly pu
258 Kingsthorpe *trckd ldrs, effrt to 4th & ev ch 14th, wknd 3 out, p.u. last*..................M Rimell pu
262 Orwell Ross (Ire) *alwys rear, t.o. 8th, p.u. 11th* ....G Barfoot-Saunt pu
361 Outcrop 5a *disp cls 3rd whn f 5th* ....Miss C Thomas f
300 Sideliner *rear of main grp 9th, blkd & p.u. bef nxt* ....D Duggan pu
331⁴ Twelth Man *rear frm 6th, t.o. 11th, p.u. 3 out* ..R Bevis pu
262⁴ Ravensdale Lad *chsd ldrs, effrt 12th, no prog 15th, p.u. 2 out*..................R Wakeham pu
Parapluie 5a *losing tch 7th, t.o. 11th, p.u. 2 out* ....Miss B Lloyd pu
Gunners Dawn 5a *lost tch 7th, t.o. & p.u. 3 out* ....M Munrowd pu
18 ran. 12l, 6l, 12l, 1½l. Time 6m 44.00s. SP 4-1.
R Bunn (Ledbury).

434 Intermediate (12st)

294⁶ **SUNLEY STREET 5a (bl) ....Miss S Vickery** 1
2nd/3rd,outpcd 12th, 15l 3rd 3 out,ran on strngly to ld flat
255⁹ **Sisterly 5a 5ex ....H Wheeler** 2
(fav) ld til jnd 3 out, 2l up last, not qckn & hdd flat
360 **Nutcase 5a ....T Stephenson** 3
hld up, mstk 10th, prog 12th, chal 3 out, no ext nxt
255³ Sterling Buck (USA) *2nd/3rd til rdn 11th, ev ch whn ptchd lndg 14th, wknd rpdly*..................D Duggan 4
4 ran. 4l, 3l, dist. Time 6m 39.00s. SP 5-2.
J Scammell (Blackmore & Sparkford Vale).

435 Open Maiden Div I (12st)

LETS TWIST AGAIN (IRE) ....Julian Pritchard 1
ld 11th, prssd 3 out, in cmmnd whn lft clr last
201⁸ **Social Vision (Ire) ....T Stephenson** 2
in tch in rear, prog 11th, kpt on, lft 2nd last
Sugi ....I Wynne 3
cls up 8th, chsd ldrs til not qckn 13th, lft 3rd
259² Clovers Last *(fav) ld to 10th, not qckn frm 12th, kpt on onepcd frm 3 out*..................M Harris 4
261² Emerald Charm (Ire) 5a *rear frm 10th, some prog 14th, no ch frm 3 out* ....R Bevis 5
Finesse The King (Ire) *hmpd 2nd, rcvrd, prom to 12th, wkng whn u.r. 15th* ....A Milner pu
Majic Belle 5a (bl) *prom til wknd 11th, t.o. & p.u. 3 out* ....E Walker pu
261³ Rusty Fellow *prom, chsd ldr 14th, lkd hld in 3l 2nd whn f last*..................D Mansell f
Wissywis (Ire) 12a *b.d. 2nd* ....A Wallett bd
210⁶ Smart Song *prom til not qckn 12th, lost tch & p.u. 3 out*..................M Rimell pu
262 Barafundle Bay *mid-div whn f 2nd* ....D Llewellyn f
Firestarter *sn rear, lost tch & p.u. 13th*...Mrs K Bevan pu
Galactic Graham *cls up til wknd 7th, t.o. & p.u. 14th* ....M Munrowd pu
Hectors Way *in tch to 8th, lost plc & outpcd 10th, t.o. & p.u. 15th* ....J Bates pu
14 ran. 12l, 2l, 12l, dist. Time 6m 50.00s. SP 7-2.
Mrs S Bird (Ledbury).

436 Open Maiden Div II (12st)

263 **MIS-E-FISHANT 5a..................D Mansell** 1
alwys chsng ldrs, 4th 14th, lft 2nd 2 out, lft in ld last
259³ **Merry Noelle 5a ....R Bevis** 2
(fav) ld/disp to 6th, ev ch 14th, wknd aft 3 out, lft 2nd
Billy Barter (Ire) ....Miss S Vickery 3
ld 7-12th, cls up til wknd frm 3 out
221⁴ Matchlessly *prom, cls 4th at 12th, outpcd frm 14th* ....Miss E Walker 4
Little Ease (Ire) 12a *t.o. 4th, btn 3 fncs*......J Jackson 5
Bellaghy Bridge 5a *14th & wkng whn f 8th* ....C Yates f
Rootsman (Ire) *rear of ldng grp 9th, in tch til no prog 12th, p.u. 3 out*..................T Stephenson pu
Doctor Briggs (Ire) *mid-div whn p.u. sddnly bef 7th* ....H Wheeler pu
260 Varykinov (Ire) *7s-3s, prog to 2nd 10th, ld 13th, clr whn crmpld lndg last*..................M Rimell f
211⁶ Musical Mail *ld/disp to 6th, wknd 12th, p.u. 3 out* ....R Wakeham pu
Inky 5a *w.w. prog 10th, 6th & no ch 15th, p.u. nxt* ....Julian Pritchard pu

365 Calder's Grove *chsd ldrs, outpcd 11th, p.u. 15th* ....Miss T McCurrick pu
189 Appeal 5a *rear frm 8th, no ch whn p.u. 11th*...D Evatt pu
Domani Hill 5a *chsg ldrs whn blnd & u.r. 6th* I Wynne ur
224 Baron's Pearl 5a *patiently rdn, prog 14th, 8l 2nd whn f 2 out*....................F Hutsby f
367 Lisgarvan Lad (Ire) 7a *u.r. start, rear & rdn 8th, t.o. & p.u. 15th*....................M Munrowd pu
Zaudante (Ire) 5a *in tch to 10th, eased & p.u. 12th* ....M Harris pu
17 ran. 8l, 4l, 20l, dist. Time 6m 55.00s. SP 14-1.
H Turberfield (Ledbury).

437 Open Maiden Div III (12st)

210² **IRBEE 7a ....T Stephenson 1**
s.s. cls 7th at 10th, 2nd 13th, ld 2 out, clr last
261 **Joyney 5a ....Miss C Thomas 2**
prog 12th, 10l 4th whn mstk 3 out, kpt on onepcd
Sylvan Sirocco ....M Harris 3
prom to 2nd, rstrnd, ld 13th-3 out, wknd nxt
368 Christmas Thyne (Ire) 7a *prom to 8th, lost plc, ran on 13th, wknd 3 out*....................M Munrowd 4
201 Mount Kinabalu *ld to 5th, wknd 11th, t.o. & p.u. 3 out* ....D Mansell pu
263² Western Pearl (Ire) *prom, ld 6-12th, not qckn 14th, btn 5th whn f last*....................J Jackson f
261 Blue Rosette *(fav) cls up whn f 7th* ...Julian Pritchard f
299 Prior's Corner 5a *mid-div to 10th, not qckn frm 12th, no ch whn f 3 out*....................S Bush f
Fleeced *prom to 4th, wknd rpdly, t.o. & p.u. 10th* ....C Wilson pu
Corview (Ire) *t.o. 4th, p.u. 10th* ....A Milner pu
All Things Nice 5a *mid-div to 8th, t.o. & p.u. 14th* ....S Joynes pu
260 Nikitasecondchance 5a *cls 8th at 10th, outpcd 13th, dist 6th whn p.u. last*....................G Barfoot-Saunt pu
367³ Alias Parker Jones *in tch to 4th, outpcd 8th, t.o. & p.u. 10th*....................N Oliver pu
Kinlet Crest 5a *rear, t.o. 9th, p.u. 12th*....R Wakeham pu
Chequers Boy *prom til wknd 10th, p.u. 13th*..M Rimell pu
15 ran. 10l, 15l, 15l. Time 6m 59.00s. SP 3-1.
Mrs I Breese (Ludlow).
P.R.

NORTH NORFOLK
Higham
Saturday March 8th
GOOD

438 Open Maiden Div I (12st)

270⁴ **NOBLE KNIGHT (IRE) 4ow....................C Jarvis 1**
disp 3rd, ld 4-7th, ld 16th, drew clr 2 out, v easily
323 **Bozo Bailey ....P Taiano 2**
mostly 3rd/4th, prog to 2nd 15th, onepcd nxt, no ch wnr 3out
196³ **Joyful Joan (Ire) 5a ....R Barrett 3**
(fav) handy in 3rd/4th, not qckn 16th, wknd 3 out
122 View Point (Ire) *mid-div, prog to ld 8th til outpcd 16th, wknd rpdly 3 out*....................M Gingell 4
Royal Battle 5a *jmpd rght, rear, nvr going wll* ....N Bloom 5
321 Mirror Image 5a *alwys rear, outpcd 13th, wll bhnd 16th*....................N King 6
197 Charlie Andrews *mstks, nvr going wll, lost tch rpdly 15th, t.o. & p.u. 3 out*....................S R Andrews pu
317 Cambridge Gold 7a *jmpd slwly 1st, ld 2nd, wd bnd apr 4th, ran out 7th*....................P Chinery ro
8 ran. Dist, 4l, 4l, 2l, 1l. Time 6m 24.00s. SP 7-2.
C Jarvis (Suffolk).

439 Open Maiden Div II (12st)

193 **RONALDSWAY ....D Parravani 1**
trckd ldrs, prog 11th, ld 16th, sn clr, comf
276 **Times Leader ....Miss K Hills 2**
ld 1st, hit 8th, hdd apr 16th, onepcd apr last
196 **Mutual Memories ....S R Andrews 3**
mid-div, hit 7th, chsd ldrs 11th, cls up 14th, onepcd 3 out
283 Soon Be Back *t.o. last at 2nd, schoold rear til ran on 2 out, stewards*....................R Barrett 4
320³ El Guapo *sn rear, outpcd 8th, t.o. & p.u. 16th* ....P Chinery pu
197⁶ Warner For Sport *s.s. rear, blnd 12th & p.u.*..P Taiano pu
15⁴ Roscolvin (Ire) 7a *(fav) trckd ldr, wknd aft 11th, lost plc nxt, no ch & p.u. 2 out*....................R Wakley pu
Chalvey Grove *mid-div til f 9th*....................A Sansome f
Just Chica *mid-div, outpcd aft 11th, rear & p.u. 15th* ....N Bloom pu
318 Lantern Spark (Ire) 5a *mid-div, bhnd frm 11th, t.o. & reluc 14th, p.u. nxt*....................Miss C Tuke pu
I'm Free (Ire) *mid-div, outpcd 7th, dtchd whn p.u. nxt* ....M Gingell pu
11 ran. 10l, 10l, 2l. Time 6m 25.00s. SP 12-1.
James Buckle (Essex & Suffolk).

440 Men's Open

322 **CRACKING IDEA (IRE) ....C Ward-Thomas 1**
trckd ldr, effrt 15th, ld nxt, lft clr 2 out, kpt on
273 **River Melody 5a ....T Moore 2**
(fav) pllng,ld 1st,sttld 3rd,clr wth wnr 16th, blnd 2 out,nt rcvr
194⁶ **Cockstown Lad ....D Featherstone 3**
nrrw ld 2nd til mstk 15th, wknd rpdly nxt, no ch aft
194⁷ Laburnum *cls 2nd at 4th, rmndrs 10th, blnd & wknd 14th, t.o.,dsmntd*....................M Gingell 4
273 Cardinal Red *cls up til drppd rear 11th, slw jmp nxt, lost tch, ref 15th*....................A Sansome ref
5 ran. 3l, dist, 12l. Time 6m 19.00s. SP 4-1.
Mrs P K J Brightwell (Essex & Suffolk).

441 Intermediate

319⁵ **DYNAMITE DAN (IRE) ....A Coe 1**
cls up,clsng whn ran wd apr 3 out,rallied to ld nr fin
62³ **Youcat (Ire) ....I Marsh 2**
ld 3rd, made rest til hdd nr fin
140¹ **Cairndhu Misty 5a ....R Barrett 3**
(fav) cls 2nd til wknd aft 2 out
193⁴ Salty Snacks (Ire) *hld up mid-div, nvr on trms ldrs, outpcd 16th*....................M Gingell 4
Miss Construe 5a *alwys rear, outpcd aft 12th* ....N Bloom 5
193⁵ Couture Quality *ld to 2nd, drppd rear aft, blnd 14th, p.u. nxt*....................R Wakley pu
Pudding 12a *immed last, t.o. 4th, p.u. aft 11th* N King pu
7 ran. 1l, 2l, 3l, 8l. Time 6m 18.00s. SP 11-2.
B Kennedy (Essex Farmers & Union).

442 Ladies

MR WOODCOCK ....Miss A Plunkett 1
conf rdn, ld 6th, made rest, qcknd clr flat
272² **St Gregory (bl) ....Mrs L Gibbon 2**
disp to 3rd, 2nd agn 11th, chsd wnr, chal last, not qckn
202³ **Pont de Paix ....Miss T Habgood 3**
trckd ldrs, outpcd 16th
323¹ Professor Longhair *disp to 2nd, 4th aft, in tch whn hit 13th, no ch aft*....................Miss C Papworth 4
271 Ragtime Song *disp/ld to 5th, last by 8th, hit 13th, t.o.* ....Miss E Tomlinson 5
272⁵ Notary-Nowell *mid-div til u.r. 5th*........Miss N Sell ur
Slight Panic 5a *in tch in rear whn u.r. 10th* ....Miss J Wickens ur
323 Wardy Hill 5a *rear & wd aft 1st, f 5th*.....Miss C Tuke f
8 ran. 2l, 4l, 20l, dist. Time 6m 12.00s. SP Evens.
P A Tylor (Cury Harriers).

443 Ppora Restricted

198³ **SHAKE FIVE (IRE) ....S Sporborg 1**
(fav) cls up, disp 3 out, jnd last, ran on wll flat, all out
198 **New York Boy ....P Taiano 2**
mid-div, mstk 16th, ran on 3 out, chal last, ran on,just hld

274[2] **Whats Another 5a ....Miss K Bridge 3**
disp til ld 3-7th, cls up, chal 3 out, no ext last
323 The Man From Lyre (Ire) *hld up rear,rpd prog to ld 16th,hit nxt,ev ch last,fin lame* ....A Coe 4
213 Culm Baron (bl) *disp to 2nd, ld 8-9th, wknd & last 12th, lost tch & p.u.16th* ....S R Andrews pu
317[1] Ludoviciana 5a *f 1st* ....P Keane f
Tough Minded *j.w. trckd ldrs, ld 11-15th, disp 3 out til p.u. nxt, lame* ....R Wakley pu
7 ran. Nk, 1½l, 1l. Time 6m 18.00s. SP Evens.
Mrs C H Sporborg (Puckeridge).

444 Confined (12st)

271[2] **EMSEE-H 3ex ....A Sansome 1**
mstly 3rd/4th,2nd aft 11th,20l down 15th,ld apr last,sn clr
193[2] **Exclusive Edition (Ire) 5a..................A Coe 2**
mid-div,prog to ld 11th,clr 15th,wknd rpdly nxt,hdd apr last
193[1] **Flashy Buck 3ex.........................N Bloom 3**
(fav) sn rear, nvr going wll, virt t.o. 11th, plodded on
193 Kumada 5ex *ld to 11th, hit nxt, qckly bhnd, t.o. 16th* ....T Moore 4
Another Rhythm *tubed, pllng, prssd ldr whn blnd & u.r. 3rd* ....S Wiltshire ur
154[4] Just Jack 5ex *cls up, hit 9th, blnd & u.r. 11th* ....P Jonason ur
Frank Rich *mid-div, dist 3rd aft 11th, not keen 14th, t.o. & p.u. 2 out* ....C Ward-Thomas pu
Salachy Run (Ire) *rear, ran out bnd bfr 9th* ....N Page ro
8 ran. 6l, dist, 3l. Time 6m 16.00s. SP 4-1.
J M Turner (Suffolk).
S.B.

OAKLEY
Newton Bromswold
Saturday March 8th
GOOD

445 Members

Hawaiian Reef *(fav) ld til ref 4th, cont, ref 6th twice & u.r.* ....M Wells ref
Elder Hays *blnd 2nd & rdr lost irons, u.r. bef nxt* ....G Tawell ur
Major *1st ride, last whn ref & u.r. 1st*...Miss J Robins ref
3 ran.
Race void.

446 Confined (12st)

370[1] **HILL ISLAND 6ex ....R Sweeting 1**
(fav) hld up rear, 3rd at 9th, disp 11th, ld aft 16th, styd on
Fair Crossing ....M Emmanuel 2
alwys chsg ldrs, 3rd apr 16th, tk 2nd 2 out, onepcd
369[5] **Sprucefield ....A Barlow 3**
ld 2nd-3rd, chsd ldrs, ld 7th, hdd 16th, lost 2nd 2 out
218 Severn Invader 3ex *sttld rear, last frm 9th, effrt 14th, fin well* ....Miss H Gosling 4
148[6] Alias Silver *mid-div, no dang frm 16th* ...Miss H Irving 5
370[4] Tompet *ld1st, disp 3rd-apr 7th, lost plc 11th, wknd* ....B McKim 6
293 Apple Nicking *hld up last, prog 11th, mod 5th whn f 16th* ....A Hill f
218 Menature (Ire) *chsd ldrs, cls 2nd at 6th, 3rd 11th, wknd rpdly, p.u. 2 out*....................B Pollock pu
8 ran. 3l, 8l, hd, 15l, 1l. Time 6m 47.00s. SP 4-6.
Colin Gee (Heythrop).

447 Men's Open

273 **LUCKY CHRISTOPHER ....P Picton-Warlow 1**
(Jt fav) hld up rear, 3rd at 9th, ld 2 out, qcknd clr, easily
380[5] **Penlet ....John Pritchard 2**
hld up last, prog to cls 4th at 14th, ld nxt-2 out, no ext
256[7] **Welsh Singer ....R Lawther 3**
lft in ld 2nd, hdd 4th, made most 6th 6th-14th, onepcd
Saraville 5a *chsd ldrs, ld 4th-6th, ev ch 14th, wknd nxt* ....W Wales 4
Admiral Rous *in tch, disp 8th & 12th, wknd 15th, 4th & btn whn f last*..........................C Wadland f
287[3] Broad Steane *(Jt fav) ld til f 2nd* ....J Connell f
6 ran. 4l, 8l, 12l. Time 6m 48.00s. SP 2-1.
B Smith (Grafton).

448 Ladies

125[2] **MOUNTSHANNON ....Mrs T Hill 1**
(fav) hld up, cls up til ld 3 o ut, ran on strngly
Loose Wheels ....Miss K Makinson 2
made most til 3 out, no ext
371[5] **Kites Hardwicke ....Mrs C Behrens 3**
chsd ldrs, 3rd at 14th, styd on well
272[3] Rousillon To Be *rear, last at 14th, sn bhnd* ....Miss L Rowe 4
249[2] London Hill *3rd whn mstk & u.r. 2nd* ....Miss H Irving ur
5 ran. 8l, 1½l, 1 fence. Time 6m 45.00s. SP 8-11.
Mrs T J Hill (Vale Of Aylesbury).

449 P P O R A (12st)

140[3] **HOLMBY MILL ....B Pollock 1**
j.w. made all, drew clr 2 out, imprssv
28[3] **Fresh Ice (Ire) ....T Marks 2**
alwys cls up, effrt 2 out, not pace to chal
274[3] **Grassington (Ire) ....S Quirk 3**
prom, lost plc 7th, went 3rd agn 11th, styd on onepcd
80[1] Oliver Himself *(fav) rear, prog hlfwy, 3rd 13th, no ext 2 out* ....A Hill 4
Supreme Dream (Ire) 5a *ran in sntchs, last at 7th, effrt 3 out, fin well* ....Mrs P Adams 5
324[3] Regal Bay *mid-div, effrt to 5th at 13th, no prog aft* ....W Wales 6
278[6] Linlake Lightning 5a (bl) *tongue-strap, sn prom, wknd 10th, sn bhnd* ....R Lawther 7
371[8] Royal Exhibition *alwys bhnd, t.o.*......Miss C Ramsey 8
Sea Sky 5a *chsd ldr til wknd 13th, bhnd whn p.u. 15th* ....S Morris pu
Smart Beat *cls up, wknd hlfwy, rear & p.u. 15th* ....J Docker pu
274 Miss Solitaire 5a *alwys rear, wll bhnd whn p.u. 3 out* ....P Picton-Warlow pu
221 Sparnova 5a *3rd early, sn lost plc, bhnd & p.u. 3 out* ....T Illsley pu
Anita's Son *last hlfwy, wll bhnd & p.u. 3 out* ....E Andrewes pu
13 ran. 8l, 4l, 25l, ½l, dist, 10l, 12l. Time 6m 46.00s. SP 4-1.
C R Saunders (Pytchley).

450 Maiden Div I

209[2] **THE AUCTIONEER ....Miss L Rowe 1**
(fav) made virt all, styd on well frm 2 out
Teeton Heavens 5a.....................B Pollock 2
rear, 15l 4th at 7th, effrt 12th, onepcd frm 16th
374 **Blame The Groom (Ire) ....D Buckley 3**
chsd wnr, no ext frm 2 out
275 Linlithgow Palace *s.s. cls up til wknd aft 10th, rear & p.u. 15th* ....Mrs J Morrison pu
445 Elder Hays *2nd outing, sn bhnd, p.u. 6th* ...R Lawther pu
276 Grangewick Kelly 5a *cls 3rd whn u.r. 6th* ...S Dobson ur
Novatara 7a *rear, prog 12th, wknd 14th, p.u. nxt* ....S Morris pu
7 ran. 2½l, 20l. Time 7m 4.00s. SP 4-5.
C Bazley (Pytchley).
One fence omitted second circuit. 18 jumps.

451 Maiden Div II

211[4] **DUNCAHA HERO ....Miss G Barrow 1**
ld 2nd-10th, ld 12th-nxt, ld 14th, made rest, drvn clr
224 **Larkross ....B Pollock 2**
alwys prom, ld 10th-12th & 13th-nxt, onepcd 3 out
Bilston George ....S Morris 3
ld 1st, lost plc, lft 3rd 15th, styd on, no imp

The Merry Nun (Ire) 5a *lost plc 6th, ran on hlfwy, cls 3rd whn f 15th* ....J Owen f
373 Bobbin Lace 5a *rear whn f 6th* ......Mrs C McCarthy f
224 Fighting For Good (Ire) *(fav) hld up, cls 4th & ev ch whn hmpd & u.r. 15th* ....T Illsley ur
Half A Chance *cls 3rd til wknd aft 13th, hmpd 15th & p.u.* ....T Marks pu
Manor's Maid 12a 2ow *last til b.d. 6th*.......J Mason bd
8 ran. 8l, 15l. Time 7m 4.00s. SP 4-1.
R Barrow (Pytchley).

452 Maiden Div III

276² **STORMING ROY** ....**H Nicholson** 1
(fav) ld 4th-7th, ld aft 15th, drew clr 2 out
Tombola ....**S Morris** 2
rear, prog to 3rd 11th, ran on 2 out, tk 2nd nr fin
318 **Loch Irish (Ire) 5a** ....**W Wales** 3
ld to 4th, ld 7th-aft 15th, btn whn mstk last, demoted
374 Truly Optimistic 5a *last til mod prog 10th, 4th & no imp 16th* ....C Wadland 4
372 Whitworth Grey *in tch to hlfwy, last whn p.u. 15th* ....B McKim pu
373 Another Whistle (Ire) *chsd ldrs til wknd 11th, bhnd & p.u. 15th* ....R Lawther pu
208 Towngate *rear, wknd 12th, p.u. 15th*.........T Marks pu
The Wayward Gunner *chsd ldrs, in tch whn f 15th* ....A Hill f
On The Quiet 7a *mid-div, wknd 11th, p.u. 14th* ....B Pollock pu
9 ran. 15l, nk, 25l. Time 6m 53.00s. SP 7-4.
J G Nicholson (Woodland Pytchley).
H.F.

SOUTH CORNWALL
Great Trethew
Saturday March 8th
SOFT

453 Confined (12st)

243¹ **PERAMBULATE (NZ) 7a** ....**L Jefford** 1
(6s-3s), ld 14th til blndrd bdly 2 out, ld agn last, gamely
236³ **Ticket To The Moon 5a**..................**K Heard** 2
(fav) cls 5th hlfwy, ld aft 2 out til outjmpd last, no ext
238⁷ **It's Not My Fault (Ire)** ....**A Holdsworth** 3
ld/disp 5-14th, ev ch til not qckn aft 3 out
173³ Rasta Man *prom, disp 12-14th, no prog frm 3 out* ....A Farrant 4
173⁴ Catch The Cross (bl) *ld til 5th, disp til lost plc 12th, no ch frm 14th* ....Mrs M Hand 5
242² Pilgrim's Mission (Ire) *alwys mid-div* D Doyne-Ditmas 6
237 Senegalais (Fr) 3ex *in tch to 13th, wknd* ....Miss V Nicholls 7
236 Ballysheil *bhnd frm 12th*.................S Edwards 8
Linton *sb bhnd, t.o. whn p.u. apr 15th*...Miss P Baker pu
Sancreed *rear frm 8th til p.u. & dismntd apr 13th* ....Miss L Long pu
237 Dark Reflection *ref to race*................C Heard 0
Carrot Bay *mid-div, btn 7th whn p.u. apr 15th* R Darke pu
King Of Cairo *1st ride, sn bhnd, t.o. & p.u. 3 out* ....W Smith pu
13 ran. 2l, 1½l, 1½l, 12l, 25l, 6l, 15l. Time 6m 31.00s. SP 3-1.
D H Barons (Dart Vale And South Pool Hrrs).

454 Ladies

MAJESTIC SPIRIT ....**Miss T Cave** 1
made most, blndrd bdly 12th, clr 14th, styd on strgly
238³ **Celtic Sport (bl)**.................**Miss C Stucley** 2
(fav) chsd ldr, outpcd 14th, styd on onepce clsng stgs
170³ **First Design** ....**Mrs M Hand** 3
3rd frm hlfwy, no ch frm 14th
96⁴ Karlimay 5a *lost tch 12th, no ch frm 14th, t.o.* ....Miss V Nicholls 4
Le Garcon D'Or *rear frm 10th, t.o. p.u. apr 16th* ....Miss K Hurst pu
Jokers Patch *last frm 7th, t.o. p.u. apr 14th* ....Mrs D Gillies pu
Station Express (Ire) *towrds rear, btn 5th whn p.u. apr 15th*............................Miss V Stephens pu
7 ran. 6l, 25l, dist. Time 6m 29.50s. SP 9-4.
Alan Raymond (Blackmore & Sparkford Vale).

455 Men's Open (12st)

SPRING MARATHON (USA) 7ex........**L Jefford** 1
j.w.,in tch, cls 3rd 14th, slght ld 2 out, hld on wll
239¹ **Magnolia Man 4ex**....................**N Harris** 2
(fav) hld up, prog 12th, strng run frm 2 out, just faild
112¹ **Chism (Ire)** ....**M Miller** 3
alwys prom, slght ld 16th, ev ch til hdd & wknd apr 2 out
285 Afterkelly 7ex *prom, ld 13-14th, lost grnd stdly frm nxt* ....I Dowrick 4
171⁴ Brabazon (USA) *5th & rddn 14th, no ch clsng stgs* ....J Scott 5
171⁵ Glenform *ld 2nd-13th, wknd, t.o.*..........L Rowe 6
Pharaoh Blue *lost tch 9th, bhnd whn p.u. apr 15th* ....A Farrant pu
239 Pen-Shilmon 7a *lost grnd frm 12th, last whn p.u. apr 15th* ....A Holdsworth pu
8 ran. ½l, 6l, 25l, 10l, dist. Time 6m 29.00s. SP 4-1.
Mrs Nerys Dutfield (Axe Vale).

456 Intermediate (12st)

240¹ **THREE AND A HALF** ....**N Harris** 1
(fav) hld up, prog 10th, ld 14th, sn clr, easily
236⁴ **Just Ben 10ex** ....**Miss J Cumings** 2
lft in ld 11th, hdd 14th, sn outpcd
307 **The Copper Key** ....**T Greed** 3
hndy, hld in 3rd but styd on stdly clsng stgs
237⁵ Lonesome Traveller (NZ) *mid-div, just in tch frm 14th, no ch frm 16th*............................Mrs M Hand 4
Society Member *5th hlfwy, p.u. aft 13th* .....L Jefford pu
Jet Jockey *towrds rear whn f 9th*..........G Penfold f
236 Karicleigh Boy *prom, ld whn blnrd & u.r. 11th* ....A Holdsworth ur
240 Dromin Chat (Ire) *mstk 4th, rear til p.u. apr 15th* ....T Cole pu
Snitton Stream *ld 5th til f 10th* ......Miss L Blackford f
97 Hanukkah 5a *s.s., bhnd til p.u. apr 15th*....I Hambley pu
Erme Rose (Ire) 5a *ld til 5th, lost plc 14th, p.u. apr 2 out*............................R Nuttall pu
11 ran. 30l, 1½l, 10l. Time 6m 33.00s. SP 5-4.
J Scott (Devon & Somerset Staghounds).

457 Restricted (12st)

241³ **MILLED OATS** ....**A Farrant** 1
hdwy 9th, strng run to ld 2 out, styd on wll
241² **Clandon Lad** ....**T Mitchell** 2
(fav) jmp lft, ld 4th til hdd 2 out, virt walked run in
240⁴ **Indian Rabi** ....**G Penfold** 3
6th hlfwy wnt 3rd apr 3 out, not rch ldrs
246¹ Royal Turn *wnt 3rd 10th, rddn & wknd aft 16th* ....A Honeyball 4
Palace King (Ire) *prom til lost plc 12th, btn 6th whn p.u. apr 15th*............................B Dixon pu
240 Arble March 5a *ld til 4th, sn lost plc, t.o. p.u. apr 13th* ....Mrs M Hand pu
100 Lady Lir 5a *hdwy 10th, losng grnd in 5th whn p.u. apr 15th* ....Miss S Young pu
Sharp Thyne (Ire) *in tch til 10th, rear whn p.u. apr 14th*............................Miss V Stephens pu
8 ran. 20l, 2l, 15l. Time 6m 36.00s. SP 5-1.
Mrs A C Martin (Tiverton Fox Hounds).
Rule 4 applies to all bets 30p in the £.

458 Open Maiden Div I (12st)

105 **PENGUIN 5a**...................**Miss J Cumings** 1
hmp 3rd, ld 12th, clr aft 3 out, unchal, imp
Breeze-Bloc 5a......................**A Farrant** 2
5th 14th, best work clsng stgs, drvn into 2nd cls home
244² **Midnight Bob** ....**J Young** 3

hndy, 3rd 3 out, wnt 2nd 2 out, no ext cls home, imprvd
243[4] Bedtime Pixie 7a *hmp aft 6th, mstk 7th, kpt on und pres clsng stgs, do bttr* ....D Stephens 4
103[4] Stretchit *alwys mid-div* ....G Penfold 5
103[2] Westcountry Lad *5th 12th, hit 14th, sn lost plc* ....R Woolacott 6
Happy Valley 5a *prom early, rear frm 7th, t.o.* ....Miss P Baker 7
245[3] Comedy Gayle *towrds rear, nvr dang, blndrd & u.r. 2 out* ....I Widdicombe ur
243 Stony Missile 5a *ld til 10th, lost plc 12th, bhnd, p.u. 2 out* ....Miss W Hartnoll pu
Golden News *f 3rd* ....P King f
101 Eurolinkhellraiser (Ire) *prom til lost plc 10th, t.o. p.u. apr 15th* ....T Mitchell pu
102[2] Arrogant Lord 7a *(fav) ld 10th, mstk nxt, cls up til wknd 3 out, p.u. apr last* ....L Jefford pu
245[2] Harmony's Choice *b.d. 3rd* ....N Harris bd
243 Belitlir 12a *schoold rear til p.u. apr 9th* Miss S Young pu
314 Mazies Choice 5a *not fluent, rear frm 10th, t.o. p.u. apr 15th* ....S Slade pu

15 ran. 20l, 1½l, 8l, ½l, 1l, dist. Time 6m 39.50s. SP 12-1.
H Messer-Bennetts (Devon & Somerset Stag Hounds).

459 Open Maiden Div II (12st)

244 **PROBATION** ....**R Darke** 1
hld up in tch, cls 3rd 16th, ld apr 2 out, ran on wll
246[2] **The Ugly Duckling** ....**S Slade** 2
made most til 15th, ev ch til not qckn apr 2 out
Jerome Jerome 7a ....**I Dowrick** 3
hld up, 6th 14th, lft 3rd 2 out, imprvd
242 Tom's Arctic Dream 5a *jmp rght, ld til 3rd, lost plc, hmp 11th, f 12th* ....P King f
Moorland Magic (Ire) 12a *ld 8-10th, lost grnd 13th, p.u. apr 16th, imprvd* ....Miss S Young pu
176 Another Hubblick *in tch, 5th 14th, no real prog, p.u. apr 3 out* ....T Greed pu
172 Devonshire Lad *(fav) hld up, slght ld 15th, wknd rpdly aft 3 out, p.u. apr 2 out* ....N Harris pu
Brother Nero (NZ) 7a *hdwy 8th, cls 4th whn f 11th* ....L Jefford f
Horwood Drummer 5a *rear, hmpd 11th, t.o. p.u. apr 14th* ....A Holdsworth pu

9 ran. 4l, 20l. Time 6m 57.00s. SP 7-1.
C Blank/S W May (Dart Vale & South Pool Harriers).

460 Open Maiden Div III (12st)

314 **HILL CRUISE** ....**B Dixon** 1
(fav) in tch, ld apr 14th, clr 3 out, easily
175 **Tarka Trail** ....**J Young** 2
mid-div, wnt 2nd 14th, sn rddn & no imp frm 3 out
243 **My Prides Way 5a** ....**T Greed** 3
8th hlfwy, poor 5th 15th, lft 3rd apr last
238 Eserie de Cores (USA) *bhnd, wnt poor 3rd 15th, disp 3rd whn p.u. apr last* ....N Harris pu
242 Corrib Haven (Ire) *keen hold, jmp lft, ld til aft 13th, wknd qckly, p.u. 3 out* ....S Slade pu
Bucks Flea 5a *rear whn p.u. & dismntd apr 6th* ....G Penfold pu
243 Kirsty's Pal *bhnd whn p.u. apr 9th* ....L Jefford pu
245 Luney River 5a *chsd ldr, hit 7th, sn lost plc, t.o. p.u. apr 13th* ....Miss L Long pu
237[6] Cornish Harp *wnt 4th 10th, in tch whn blndrd & u.r. 14th* ....G Shenkin ur
Proper Cornish *dwelt, ran out 3rd* ....D Stephens ro
Glamorous Guy *t.o. p.u. apr 10th* ....S Parfimowicz pu
315 Spartans Dina 5a *not fluent, 9th hlfwy, t.o. p.u. apr 14th* ....A Holdsworth pu
Jim Crow *prom, 3rd hlfwy, losng grnd in 5th whn p.u. apr 15th* ....P King pu

13 ran. Dist, 10l. Time 6m 45.00s. SP 5-2.
Mrs May Collins (Devon & Somerset Staghounds).

461 Open Maiden Div IV (12st)

366[2] **SABBAQ (USA)** ....**I Dowrick** 1
(fav) trckd ldr, efft & ld aft 2 out, styd on strgly
241 **Ann's Ambition** ....**C Heard** 2
ld til hdd aft 2 out, no ext und pres
170[4] **Shameless Lady 5a** ....**R Darke** 3
hndy, 3rd & ev ch 14th, sn outpcd
Contradict *prom til lost plc aft 13th* ....A Moir 4
243 Fortitude Star 5a *mid-div, sm hdwy 4th 12th, p.u. apr 3 out* ....A Farrant pu
111[4] Butts Castle *sn rear, bhnd whn p.u. apr 15th* ..P King pu
103 Faster Or Else (NZ) *7th hlfwy, bhnd p.u. apr 3 out* ....T Cole pu
245 Amicombe Brook 5a *rear whn f 11th* ....Mrs M Hand f
French Invasion 5a *mid-div whn f 9th* ..S Parfimowicz f
Mrs McClusky (Ire) 12a *schoold rear til p.u. aft 13th* ....L Jefford pu
105 Nearly Fair 5a *rear til p.u. apr 3 out* ....T Greed pu
Cuthaysmayflower 5a *rear & schooling til p.u. apr 11th* ....B Dixon pu

12 ran. 8l, dist, 2l. Time 6m 44.00s. SP 15-8.
A J Dowrick (Quantock Stag).
G.T.

SOUTH EAST HUNTS CLUB
Charing
Saturday March 8th
GOOD

462 Restricted (12st)

277[1] **STRUGGLES GLORY (IRE) 2ow** ....**D Robinson** 1
(fav) cls up, ld 8th, clr 12th, unchal
278 **Harmony River (Ire) 5a** ....**S Cowell** 2
nvr dang, styd on to tk dist 2nd apr last
282[3] **Greenhill Fly Away** ....**P Bull** 3
prom, chsd wnr 8th, lost tch 13th, lost 2nd apr last
Killarney Man *alwys bhnd, t.o. 14th* ....T Hills 4
278 Basher Bill *ld to 5th, sn wknd, t.o. 14th* ....K Giles 5
Kitsbel *t.d.e. immed dtchd, alwys last, p.u. 10th* ....C Gordon pu
278 Fort Diana *prom, ld 5-7th, wknd nxt, bhnd whn p.u. 12th* ....P O'Keeffe pu
278[7] Abdul Emir *rear whn hmpd & u.r. 2nd* ....Mrs L Stock ur
Rushhome 5a 2ow *in tch to 9th, p.u. 11th* ....M Jones pu
The Mill Height (Ire) *mid-div whn blnd & u.r. 2nd* ....G Hopper ur

10 ran. Dist, 6l, 1 fence, 3l. Time 6m 23.00s. SP 2-5.
D C Robinson (Mid Surrey Farmers Drag).
Rest of meeting abandoned. G.Ta.

TANATSIDE
Eyton-On-Severn
Saturday March 8th
GOOD

463 Members

LAKENHEATHER (NZ) ....**G Hanmer** 1
walked over
Mrs Pat Mullen (Tanatside).

464 Intermediate (12st)

333 **LEDWYCHE GATE (bl)** ....**R Evans** 1
hld up,20l 3rd 3 out,ran on strgly frm 2 out,lft in ld last
Comedie Fleur 5a ....**R Burton** 2
chsd ldr in tch,ld brfly 3 out,tired apr last,hmp by faller
331[6] **Travel Bound** ....**D Barlow** 3
settld mid-div, nvr plcd to chal
200 Bay Owl *mid to rear, nvr in race, p.u. 6 out* ....M Worthington pu
Fennorhill 1ow *rear & t.o. 10th, p.u. 13th* ....R Ward-Dutton pu
Secret Castle *rear, p.u. 13th* ....L Brown pu
Jo-Su-Ki *u.r. 2nd* ....P Saville ur
Achieved Ambition (Ire) *rear 10th, t.o. 12th, p.u. 14th* ....P Morris pu
Crunch Time (Ire) *rear 8th, 4th in tch 14th, wknd qckly, p.u. 4 out* ....C Stockton pu

333[1] Mister Black (Ire) 5ex *(fav) ld/disp thruout,hdd 3 out,ran on und pres last,f heavily* ....A Crow f
326 Sheppie's Reality *prom to 8th, sn lost tch, p.u. 4 out* ....S Prior pu
149 Forest Fountain (Ire) *cls up, ev ch whn f 12th* A Dalton f
12 ran. 2½l, 30l. Time 6m 39.00s. SP 7-1.
L Evans (Ludlow).

465 Men's Open (12st)

201[2] **CHIP'N'RUN 7ex ....J Cornes 1**
(fav) cls 2nd til ld 11th, sn clr, ran on strgly
330 **Back The Road (Ire) ....G Hamner 2**
w.w. in rear, prog frm 13th, 2nd 2 out, ran on wll
330[5] **Tara Boy 1ow ....R Cambray 3**
mid-div, ran on frm 5 out, nrst at fin
331 Spartan Pete *rear 10th, some late prog, not trbl ldrs* ....R Burton 4
330 Forget The Rest *chsng grp, strggld whn pce increased 4 out* ....O McPhail 5
330[6] Auction Law (NZ) (bl) *mid to rear 9th, cls order 12th, short lived efft,p.u. 4 out* ....L Whiston pu
330[4] Bavard Bay (bl) *cls up, 2nd 5 out, lost tch, p.u. 3 out* ....A Dalton pu
330 What A Miss 5a *mid-div in tch, sn btn, p.u. 4 out* ....S Prior pu
463[1] Lakenheather (NZ) *rear 10th, t.o. 5 out, p.u. 3 out* ....A Jordan pu
Mr Tittle Tattle 7ex (bl) *ld til hdd 11th, ran on onepce, lost tch & p.u. bfr last* ....D Barlow pu
Bentley Manor *chsng grp, 2nd 13th, bad mstk nxt, sn btn, p.u. 4 out* ....C Stockton pu
Merry Scorpion *f 1st* ....T Marlow f
330[3] Whatafellow (Ire) *f 1st* ....A Crow f
13 ran. 6l, 12l, 8l, 2l. Time 6m 30.00s. SP 4-5.
F Corns (South Shropshire).

466 Ladies

288[3] **INCH MAID 5a 7ex..........Miss H Brookshaw 1**
(fav) j.w., made all, ran on wll, not extnd
Couture Tights ....Miss J Priest 2
w.w., cls order 12th, 2nd 2 out, ran on onepce
Simply Perfect ....Miss K Swindells 3
mid-div early, 3rd 7th, 2nd 10th, ev ch, not qckn frm 3 out
Tytherington *cls up gng wll 12th, outpcd frm 4 out* ....Miss S Talbot 4
329 Moya's Tip Top 5a *mid-div in tch 10th, rear & strglng 12th, rlld,ran on 2 out* ....Miss A Price 5
202 Nodforms Dilemma (USA) *hld up, cls order to 2nd 9th, wknd qckly, p.u. 13th* ....Miss K Hollinshead pu
Montykosky *trckd ldrs to 10th, lost tch 12th, p.u. 4 out* ....Miss L Wallace pu
7 ran. 6l, 12l, 8l, 2l. Time 6m 30.00s. SP 1-3.
S A Brookshaw (North Shropshire).

467 Interlink Restricted Div I

204 **MR BOBBIT (IRE) ....R Burton 1**
chsng grp, hld up, 2nd 12th, ld 5 out, ran on wll und pres
332[3] **Mr Busker (Ire) ....C Barlow 2**
prom,2nd to 5th,ran on wll frm 4 out,tk 2nd last,just outpcd
199[1] **Killatty Player (Ire) 5a..........A Crow 3**
hld up mid-div, prog 10th, cls up & ev ch 4 out, one-pcd
258 Fire King *mid-div, cls order 10th, no imp frm 4 out* ....E Collins 4
260 Cussane Cross (Ire) *mid-div hlfwy, ran on frm 5 out, nrst fin* ....P McAllister 5
331 Rue de Fort *cls up, ld 6th-4 out, lost tch & p.u. 2 out* ....J Cornes pu
Rinky Dinky Doo *ld to 5th, btn 12th, p.u. 5 out* ....P Morris pu
This I'll Do Us (Ire) *t.o. 5th, p.u. 9th* ....A Morley pu
326 Real Gent *f 3rd* ....G Hamner f
331 Domino Night (Ire) 3ow *cls up, 5th & ev ch whn u.r. 13th* ....E Haddock ur
Grecianlid *chsng grp to 10th, no ch whn p.u. 5 out* ....C Stockton pu
332 Little By Little *mid-div, p.u. 3rd* ....A Jordan pu
115[1] Gillie's Fountain *(fav) hld up mid-div, cls order 12th, und pres 5 out, p.u. 3 out* ....A Dalton pu
Bornakanga 5a *alwys rear, p.u. 5 out* ....A Mitchell pu
Faha Point (Ire) 12a *t.o. 5th, p.u. 9th* ....M Rodda pu
15 ran. 1½l, 10l, 10l, 2l. Time 6m 31.00s. SP 5-1.
S J P Furniss (West Shropshire).

468 Interlink Restricted Div II

83[2] **FOUR HEARTS (IRE) ....D Barlow 1**
(fav) alwys 1st trio, ld 9-11th,cls up whn lft clr 12th,ran on wll
332 **Daphni (Fr) ....Miss S Swindells 2**
chsng grp thruout, 2nd 4 out, ran on onepce
330 **Allezscally 5a ....C Stockton 3**
disp to 3rd, hld up mid-div, prog 3rd 5 out, onepcd
262 Strong Trace (Ire) *mid-div, some late prog, nrst fin* ....L Brown 4
59[6] Live Wire (Ire) *chsd wnr to 5th, lft 2nd 13th, onepcd frm 4 out* ....T Cox 5
330 Grindley Brook *wth ldrs whn ran out 6th* ....A Gribben ro
81 Mophead Kelly *j.s., rear early, cls order 10th, wknd, p.u. 2 out* ....A Dalton pu
Silver Fig 5a *clr ldr to 8th,hd 9th,just ld & gng wll whn u.r.12th* ....N Bradley ur
222 Ballybeggan Parson (Ire) *disp to 3rd, cls up in tch 12th, grdly wknd, p.u. 2 out* ....G Hamner pu
Another Chancer *mid-rear, no ch whn p.u. 10th* ....R Evans pu
Ard Rua *alwys rear, p.u. 13th* ....R Burton pu
11 ran. 10l, 8l, 8l, 1l. Time 6m 42.00s. SP 5-2.
D Barlow (Cheshire).

469 2½m Maiden (5-7yo) Div I (12st)

206 **SOLAR CASTLE (IRE) ....P McAllister 1**
w.w. smooth prog to ld 2 out, ran on well
205 **Barney Bear ....T Garton 2**
(fav) chsg grp, cls 2nd 9th, ld 5 out-2 out, no ext
206 **Beeworthy 5a ....L Whiston 3**
ld to 10th, ev ch 3 out, ran on onpcd
205 Tosawi's Girl (Ire) 5a *cls up, 2nd at 8th, mstk nxt, no dang aft* ....R Burton 4
82 Niord *cls up til f 9th* ....C Stockton f
331 Nancy's Last 5a *chsng grp, cls up 9th, fdd 4 out, p.u. 2 out* ....O McPhail pu
King Edward (Ire) *alwys rear, p.u. 8th* ....D Barlow pu
327 Scally Hill 5a *unruly start, lft a fence, p.u. 5th* ....A Dalton pu
Seymours Secret 12a *t.o. & no ch whn u.r. 6th* ....N Gittins ur
9 ran. 5l, 3l, dist. Time 5m 22.00s. SP 4-1.
L A E Hopkins (North Shropshire).

470 2½m Maiden (5-7yo) Div II (12st)

327[2] **BOMBADIER JACK ....C Barlow 1**
(fav) hld up in tch, chal to ld 4 out, sn clr, ran on well
205[3] **Agile King ....G Hanmer 2**
ld to 3rd, cls up til outpcd frm 3 out
206 **Musical Vocation (Ire) 5a..........A Jordan 3**
alwys chsng grp, ev ch 4 out, onepcd
205 Builder Boy *ld 4th til 4 out, outpcd aft* ....C Stockton 4
327 Pulltheplug *mstks, mid-div, onepcd frm 4 out* ....R Burton 5
327 Fancytalkintinker (Ire) *s.s. mostly rear, some late prog* ....A Dalton 6
Roscommon Lad (Ire) 7a *alwys rear, p.u. 9th* L Bland pu
327[3] Nights Image (Ire) *chsd ldrs, wll in tch whn u.r. 6 out* ....P Blane ur
Aralier Man (Ire) *mid-div, nvr trbld ldrs, p.u. 2 out* ....P McAllister pu
327 Yasgourra (Ire) *prom early, losng tch whn p.u. 4 out* ....J Barlow pu
Daftasabrush (Ire) 12a *alwys rear, t.o. & p.u. 9th* ....M Worthington pu

Ishereal (Ire) *mid to rear, no ch whn p.u. 4 out* S Prior pu
12 ran. 12l, 2½l, 15l, 10l, 2l. Time 5m 20.00s. SP 5-2.
R Thomas (West Shropshire Drag).
V.S.

BLANKNEY
Southwell P-To-P Course
Sunday March 9th
GOOD

472 Members (12st)

DRUSO (USA) ....N Squires 1
w.w. clsd 11th, ld nxt, drew clr 3 out, easily
74 **Mister Chippendale ....S Walker** 2
(fav) chsd ldr, blnd 5th & rmndr, ld brfly apr 12th, wll btn 2 out
The Real McCoy 3ow ....D Veasey 3
ld, sn clr, hdd apr 12th, sn lost tch, t.o.
3 ran. 20l, dist. Time 6m 46.00s. SP 3-1.
Mrs M Morris (Blankney).

473 Confined (12st)

324¹ **CORMEEN LORD (IRE) ....J Sharp** 1
(fav) hld up, prog 9th, went 2nd aft 15th, ld 2 out, sn clr,easily
377⁷ **Dashboard Light ....S R Andrews** 2
chsd ldr 3rd, ld 11th, clr apr 3 out, hdd 2 out, sn btn
364² **Merlyns Choice ....A Woodward** 3
mid-div, prog to cls 3rd 12th, kpt on onepcd frm 15th
213 Mysterious Run (Ire) *mid-div, cls 4th at 12th, outpcd 14th, kpt on* ....Miss S Samworth 4
203 Grants Carouse *jmpd lft,ld,jmpd slwly 5th,hdd 11th,ev ch & hit 14th,wknd*........................A Bailey 5
271 Valatch *mid-div to 8th, bhnd frm 10th, t.o.* ....J Henderson 6
75⁶ Scole *last frm 5th, t.o. 9th, p.u. 3 out* ....Miss A Hinch pu
Kemys Commander *in tch, losng plc whn blnd 11th, t.o. & p.u. nxt* ....G Smith pu
Tenelord *chsd ldr to 3rd, 6th & wkng 12th, t.o. & p.u. 2 out, dsmntd* ....S Morris pu
Maison Rouge *in tch til f 9th*...............S Walker f
10 ran. 8l, hd, 4l, 5l, dist. Time 6m 30.00s. SP 4-6.
Mrs C Harris & C Sharp (Woodland Pytchley).

474 Ladies

265¹ **KELLYS DIAMOND ....Miss V Russell** 1
mid-div, prog 12th, chal apr 3 out, ld nxt, hld on well
208¹ **Arrysu ....Miss S Sharratt** 2
ld/disp, just hdd 2 out, hit last, kpt on well
125³ **Wistino ....Miss L Rowe** 3
ld/disp til apr 3 out, onepcd
Subsonic (Ire) *chsd ldrs, 4th & outpcd apr 3 out, onepcd aft*................................Miss C Tarratt 4
215 Killimor Lad *in tch to 14th, sn outpcd* ....Miss S Samworth 5
Gowlaun *chsd ldrs, mstk 12th, cls 3rd & blnd 14th, wknd*..................................Miss L Allan 6
Meritmoore *alwys wll bhnd, t.o. & p.u. 12th, dsmntd* ....Miss F Hatfield pu
215² Vital Witness (Can) *(fav) hld up, prog to mid-div whn b.d. 9th* ....Mrs F Needham bd
Regent Cross *ld/disp to 5th, cls up til wknd 13th, t.o. & p.u. 3 out*..............................Miss J Wormall pu
215⁷ Douce Eclair 5a *bhnd, prog & in tch 11th, 5th & btn whn u.r. 2 out* ....Miss L Eddery ur
117⁶ La Maja (Ire) 5a *pckd 3rd, prog to ld & f 9th* ....Mrs N Wilson f
139 Remalone 5a *bhnd & rdn 4th, mstk 6th, t.o. 9th, p.u. 12th* ....Mrs C McCarthy pu
12 ran. Sht-hd, 8l, 8l, 20l, 10l. Time 6m 28.00s. SP 7-2.
Mrs P A Russell (Middleton).
One fence omitted, 17 jumps.

475 Men's Open (12st)

216 **THE POINT IS ....M Hewitt** 1
t.d.e. ld, sn clr, kpt on gamely frm 3 out
55 **Run For Free ....A Hill** 2
chsd wnr apr 5th, 2l down 15th, hng lft frm nxt, kpt on
339⁴ **Tobin Bronze ....R Tate** 3
(fav) hld up, prog 10th, 8l 3rd apr 3 out, wll btn nxt
248⁵ Clare Lad *chsd ldrs, 6th & outpcd apr 12th, no dang aft* ....R Walford 4
86 Tale Of Endurance (Ire) 7ex (bl) *chsd wnr to 5th, 4th & outpcd 13th, no ch frm nxt*...................S Morris 5
271 Solid (Ire) *bhnd frm 5th, t.o. 12th, p.u. 2 out* M Barnard pu
Rascally 5a 7ex *mid-div, 5th & jmpd slwly 12th, sn rdn, no prog, p.u. 14th*.........................J Townson pu
7 ran. 2l, dist, 15l, 12l. Time 6m 30.00s. SP 9-4.
P S Hewitt (Quorn).

476 P P O R A (12st)

372¹ **MUSIC IN THE NIGHT ....F Hutsby** 1
(fav) 2nd frm 4th,chal & stmbld 3 out,rdn & hit nxt,ld last,ran on
348¹ **Ryders Wells ....S Walker** 2
ld til aft 1st,ld apr 12th,und pres 2 out,hdd last,not qckn
356² **Katies Argument 5a..............Miss J Wilson** 3
rear, in tch to 12th, outpcd, went poor 3rd 3 out
251 Ocean Sovereign *ld aft 1st, clr 4th, hdd apr 12th, no ch whn blnd last*...............................T Denniff 4
353² Earl Gray *mid-div, 4th & rdn 14th, no prog* ....Miss A Deniel 5
Top Odder (Ire) 7a *sn wll bhnd, blnd 4th, t.o. & p.u. 11th* ....P Millington pu
6 ran. 1l, dist, 4l, 2½l. Time 6m 37.00s. SP 4-5.
Mrs Caroline Price (Bicester With Whaddon Chase).

477 Restricted

209¹ **ARRAS-TINA 5a........................S Walker** 1
mid-div, mstk 8th, prog to chal 3 out, ld nxt, rdn & styd on
Give It A Whirl ....M Hewitt 2
ld aft 1st, hdd 2 out, onepcd und pres
251² **Beckford ....A Pickering** 3
prom, chsd ldr 5th, disp 13th-15th, onepcd apr 3 out
251⁴ City Buzz (Ire) *mid-div, in tch til outpcd 14th, no dang aft*..K Needham 4
213⁸ Mr Gee *rear of main grp til outpcd frm 14th* ....Mrs F Needham 5
278⁵ Swift Reward 5a (e/s) *chsd ldr to 5th, rdn & wknd apr 12th*..W Wales 6
78 Midnight Service (Ire) *alwys bhnd, lost tch 7th, nvr on trms* ....W Tellwright 7
251³ White Bullet (USA) *(fav) w.w. prog 7th, mstk 11th, cls 4th nxt, sn strgglng, p.u.14th*................B Pollock pu
Forward View *sn wll bhnd, t.o. & p.u. 13th* ....C Millington pu
210¹ Broadway Swinger *ld to 1st, mstk 3rd, cls 3rd whn blnd 15th, sn btn,p.u. last* ....S R Andrews pu
10 ran. 3l, 10l, 12l, 6l, 10l, 10l. Time 6m 34.00s. SP 5-1.
G E Mason (Middleton).

478 Open Maiden Div I (12st)

347 **RED REBEL 7a...........................N Wilson** 1
hld up, stdy prog 9th, ld 3 out, sn clr, canter
252² **Kendor Pass (Ire) ....M Tate** 2
(fav) ld til aft 1st, grad lost plc, styd on 3 out, not trbl wnr
211 **Chester Ben ....S R Andrews** 3
chsd ldrs, lft in ld 6th, 4l clr 15th, hdd nxt, wknd
252 Educate Me (Ire) *mid-div, ch whn hmpd 15th, sn outpcd*..J Burley 4
116⁴ Our Wyn-Ston 7a *mid-div in tch, hmpd 15th, no ch aft* ....L Donnelly 5
210 Mr Freebie (Den) *hld up, blnd 3rd, prog & in tch 12th, no hdwy 15th* ....Mrs F Needham 6
276 Royal Quarry *chsd ldrs to 7th, rdn & wknd 11th, t.o.* ....Miss A Eaton 7
345 Ilikehim *ld aft 1st, jmpd slwly & hdd 6th, bhnd & p.u. 12th* ....N Kent pu
345³ Shining Penny (bl) *hld up rear, rdn & effrt 11th, sn btn, p.u. 15th*....................................K Green pu

347[3] Pollytickle 5a *prom, chsd ldr 8-13th, cls up whn u.r. 15th* ....G Smith ur
Malenski (Ire) *chsd ldrs, hit 10th, went 2nd 13th, wknd 15th, p.u. 2 out* ....P Millington pu
128 Holding The Aces *mid-div to 4th, lost plc rpdly 7th, p.u. nxt* ....T Marks pu
208 Bucks Law *chsd ldrs to 8th, bhnd 11th, p.u. nxt* ....J Docker pu
Fly The Heights *alwys rear, t.o. & p.u. 14th* ..S Walker pu
Flying Linnet 5a *rear, blnd 5th, t.o. & p.u. aft 11th* ....S Morris pu
Catchphrase *jmpd poorly, sn wll bhnd, t.o. & p.u. 6th* ....K Needham pu
Zodiac Prince 7a *mid-div, blnd 2nd & 3rd, in tch whn f 15th* ....M Harris f
17 ran. 15l, 2l, 20l, 8l, 20l, 5l. Time 6m 37.00s. SP 3-1.
Mrs M E Moody (Middleton).

479 Open Maiden Div II (12st)

29[4] **BURRELLS WHARF (IRE)** ....**S Morris** 1
disp 2nd bhnd clr ldr, clsd 11th, ld apr 2 out, rdn clr
253 **Tiderunner (Ire)** ....**S Walker** 2
mid-div, prog to 4th at 11th, went 2nd & rdn 2 out, onepcd
Themoreyouknow ....**M Harris** 3
disp 2nd bhnd clr ldr, ld apr 12th, hdd apr 2 out, wknd
Royal Balinger 5a *nvr bttr than mid-div, 4th & no ch frm 14th* ....R Armson 4
Cruiser Too *s.s. t.o. whn blnd 5th, p.u. 12th* M Barnard pu
276 Fiddlers Goodwill *chsd ldrs, rdn & wknd 10th, t.o. & p.u. 12th* ....C Ward pu
Percy Pit *ld, hit 1st, sn wll clr, wknd & hdd apr 12th, p.u. 3 out* ....S R Andrews pu
Regal Shadow *hld up, prog 10th, wknd rpdly & p.u. 12th* ....W Wales pu
212[2] Canebreak Boy (Ire) (bl) *(fav) prom in main grp, lost plc 10th, p.u. nxt, dsmntd* ....Mrs F Needham pu
345 Kabancy *raced wd, blnd 5th, t.o. 8th, p.u. 12th* ....P Millington pu
Glad She's Gone *raced wd, chsd ldr to 4th, wkng whn f 6th* ....Miss A Deniel f
Royal Darkness (Ire) *nvr bttr than mid-div, 6th & no ch whn blnd 13th, f nxt* ....Maj M Watson f
You Be King *u.r. 1st* ....M Worthington ur
345 Half Each 12a *schoold, sn wll bhnd, t.o. 4th, p.u. 3 out* ....N Wilson pu
372 Dels Lad *mounted on course, t.o. 4th, p.u. 8th* ....R Barrett pu
15 ran. 6l, 5l, 7l, dist. Time 6m 38.00s. SP 3-1.
M Eley (Fitzwilliam).

480 Open Maiden Div III (12st)

141[2] **BARNEYS GOLD (IRE)** ....**A Bealby** 1
(fav) ld to 5th, ld agn 12th, drew clr apr 3 out, comf
252 **Handfast Point** ....**C Vale** 2
mid-div in tch, styd on frm 15th, fin wll, not rch wnr
210[3] **Neelisagin (Ire)** ....**P Millington** 3
alwys prom, chal apr 3 out, wknd nxt
40 Walton Thorns *prog to trck ldrs 11th, 3rd & outpcd apr 3 out* ....M Munrowd 4
King Keith *w.w. in tch, mstk 12th, no hdwy frm 15th* ....S Walker 5
212[4] Rovac *mid-div, prog 10th, 4th & rdn 14th, wll btn apr 3 out* ....W Wales 6
Busking Along (Ire) *nvr bttr than mid-div, no dang frm 15th* ....H Nicholson 7
Francophile (Ire) *schoold rear, nvr nr ldrs, t.o. 15th* ....N Wilson 8
345 Gonalston Percy *hmpd 2nd, sn wll bhnd, t.o. 6th* ....N Kent 9
141[6] Andalucian Sun (Ire) *bhnd, jmpd slwly 6th, t.o. & p.u. 3 out* ....G Brewer pu
169 Not The Nadger *chsd ldr til ld 5th, hdd apr 12th, p.u. qckly nxt, lame* ....A Ogden pu
210[4] Mallow Innocence *in tch, wknd 12th, t.o. & p.u. 3 out* ....S Morris pu
Rhyming Moppet 5a *f 2nd* ....W Tellwright f
Kellytino 5a *hmpd & u.r. 2nd* ....J Sharp ur

209 Roberts Royal *prom til wknd 13th, bhnd & p.u. 3 out* ....B Pollock pu
331 Charlottes Quest 5a *prom til u.r. 11th* ....M Connors ur
Aaron's Venture *wll bhnd til p.u. 7th* ....J Docker pu
17 ran. 10l, 12l, 3l, 2l, 3l, 2l, dist, dist. Time 6m 34.00s. SP 2-1.
Irvin S Naylor (Quorn).
One fence omitted twice, 16 jumps. S.P.

STAFF COLLEGE & RMA DRAGHOUNDS
Tweseldown
Sunday March 9th
GOOD

481 Members

302[4] **PACO'S BOY (bl)** ....**P York** 1
(fav) j.w. chsd ldr, ld apr last, easily
302 **Trojan Call** ....**Mrs C Mitchell** 2
ld, sn clr, hdd apr last, no ext
287 **Dad's Pipe** ....**T Smith** 3
chsd ldr, outpcd & mstks frm 12th, t.o.
Palace Wolf (NZ) 2ow *ran out 2nd* ....G Barozzi ro
Dad's Dilemma *chsd ldr, wkng whn f 11th* ....D Line f
Sea Mist *caried 14st 1lb, immed t.o. ran out 8th, cont, p.u. aft 12th* ....H Cummins pu
6 ran. 8l, dist. Time 6m 33.00s. SP 4-6.
R H York (Staff College & R.M.A.S. Drag).

482 Ladies

QANNAAS (bl) ....**Miss P Jones** 1
(fav) j.w. made all, easily
219[7] **Phelioff** ....**Miss S Dawson** 2
chsd wnr, no ch frm 14th
238[4] **On His Own** ....**Miss W Southcombe** 3
chsd ldrs, no ch frm 13th, mstk 3 out
145 Debjanjo *chsd ldrs, outpcd 12th, t.o. & p.u. 2 out* ....Miss J Cumings pu
255[7] Roving Report *t.n.p.* ....Mrs A Rucker 0
5 ran. 30l, 8l. Time 6m 17.00s. SP 1-4.
Mrs Ann Leat (Hursley Hambledon).

483 Confined (12st)

142[1] **DARTON RI 6ex** ....**T McCarthy** 1
(fav) ld to 9th, trckd ldrs, ld 15th, pshd out
Myverygoodfriend ....**S Cobden** 2
prom, ld 10-15th, prssd wnr aft, onepcd apr last
Cheeky Cheval ....**M Batters** 3
rear, lost tch 10th, effrt to 3rd 16th, wknd apr last
Old Road (USA) 4ow *prssd wnr, ld 9-10th, wknd rpdly 15th* ....C Coyne 4
278 Normead Lass 5a *chsd ldrs, rdn 8th, wknd 14th, t.o.* ....A Tutton 5
Alone Success *last pair til p..u 8th* ....C Vigors pu
187[6] Space Man *nvr going wll, alwys rear, btn 10th, t.o. & p.u. last* ....M Portman pu
Pure Madness (USA) 3ex *hld up last, jmpd left, t.o. 9th, ran out 11th* ....A Greig ro
8 ran. 4l, 20l, 12l, 15l. Time 6m 25.00s. SP 1-2.
Mrs S Maxse (Hampshire).

484 Men's Open (12st)

294 **GRIMLEY GALE (IRE) 5a** ....**A Wintle** 1
(fav) in tch, blnd 11th, ld 14th, sn clr, ran on well
Pete's Sake ....**C Vigors** 2
prom, ld 10-14th, sn outpcd, kpt on
Old Brig ....**M Miller** 3
prom, wth ldr 12th, outpcd by wnr 15th, kpt on
220 January Don (bl) *ld to 3rd, mstk 11th, outpcd 13th, no dang aft, kpt on* ....G Barfoot-Saunt 4
279 Sky Venture *trckd ldrs going wll, 4th & outpcd whn blnd 15th, wknd* ....P Bull 5
281[7] Folk Dance 3ow 4ex *alwys last, wll bhnd frm 13th, t.o.* ....F Jackson 6
280 Button Your Lip *f 2nd* ....P Atkins f
91 Green's Van Goyen (Ire) 7ex *6/4-3s, trckd ldrs, lost plc hlfwy, sn wll bhnd, p.u. last* ....T McCarthy pu
Abitmorfun *ld 3rd-10th, lost tch 13th, p.u. nxt* C Coyne pu

144[3] Beach Bum *f 1st* .... A Charles-Jones f
10 ran. 12l, 1½l, 10l, 20l, 1l. Time 6m 18.00s. SP 10-11.
R M Phillips (Clifton On Teme).

485 Open Maiden Div I (12st)

60 **COOL RASCAL 5a .... L Lay** **1**
prom, ld 11-15th, ld 2 apr 2 out, sn clr, all out
223[4] **Looking .... R Lawther** **2**
prom,mstk 10th & lost plc,outpcd 15th,ran on 2 out,nvr nrr
Bubbles Galore (Ire) .... T McCarthy **3**
(fav) trckd ldrs, outpcd & nt pshd 15th, effrt 2 out, not qckn
244[5] Simply Joyful 5a *last pair, lost tch 14th, 7th & no ch 3 out, fin strngly* .... P King 4
283[5] Muskerry Moya (Ire) 5a *trckd ldrs, 4th & outpcd 15th, no imp ldrs aft* .... Miss A Goschen 5
252[5] Pukka Sahib *last pair, prog whn mstk 13th, sn lost tch, no dang aft* .... R Smith 6
Mariners Maid 5a *prssd ldr 4-10th, wknd rpdly 13th, p.u. 15th* .... T Woolridge pu
283[4] And Why Not *mstk 1st,in tch,ld 15th,hdd & wknd apr 2 out,no ch & f last* .... J Van Praagh f
261 The Blind Judge *prom til mstk 9th, wknd 11th, last whn f 14th* .... G Barfoot-Saunt f
Ruby's Girl 5a *mstk 1st, made most to 11th, wknd rpdly, t.o. & p.u. 2 out* .... Miss P Gundry pu
284[2] Shanagore Hill (Ire) *dtchd last whn u.r. 1st* .... M Wells ur
11 ran. 2l, 2l, 2l, 3l, 15l. Time 6m 30.00s. SP 12-1.
J Owen (Bicester With Whaddon Chase).

486 B F S S (12st)

274[1] **BALLYDESMOND (IRE) .... S Sporborg** **1**
(fav) chsd ldr, ld 15th, mstk 3 out, rdn & hng lft flat, all out
New Ghost .... Maj O Ellwood **2**
mstks, ld to 15th, prssd wnr aft, unable qckn flat
305 Rocco *alwys last, lost tch whn ref 2 out* ...... A Wood ref
3 ran. 1l. Time 6m 29.00s. SP 2-7.
Christopher Sporborg (Puckeridge).

487 Open Maiden Div II (12st)

BIT OF AN IDIOT .... C Morlock **1**
ld 2nd, set fast pace, drew rght away 15th, imprssv
Colors Of Guidal (Fr) .... P York **2**
sn bhnd, lft poor 4th 10th, kpt on to tk dist 2nd flat
211 **Titchwell Milly 5a .... L Lay** **3**
sn wll bhnd,no ch hlfwy, kpt on frm 16th, went dist 3rd flat
Kala Dawn 5a *ld to 2nd, chsd wnr aft, no ch frm 15th, wknd flat* .... Miss M Tory 4
222[7] Trina's Cottage (Ire) *sn bhnd, t.o. 11th, fin own time* .... A Tutton 5
262[2] Trevveethan (Ire) *(fav) chsd ldng pair, disp 3rd whn f 10th* .... M Rimell f
44 Flowerhill *7th & out of tch whn u.r. 7th* ..... G Barfoot-Saunt ur
Stormy Fashion *sn wll bhnd, t.o. whn blnd 11th & p.u.* .... Maj G Wheeler pu
20 Amaranthine 5a *sn wll bhnd, t.o. & p.u. 16th* .... M Batters pu
182 Redhaven Light 5a *sn bhnd, t.o. last whn f 10th* .... Miss C Osmond f
Sunylad *mstk 2nd, chsd ldng pair, wknd 13th, tired & p.u. aft 3 out* .... M Miller pu
What-A-Brave Run *out of tch in mid-div, poor 5th whn f 10th* .... A Clark f
12 ran. Dist, 2l, 8l, dist. Time 6m 18.00s. SP 5-2.
Mrs D E S Surman (Vale Of Aylesbury).
Last fence omitted, 18 jumps.

488 Restricted (12st)

278[2] **STALBRIDGE BILL .... Miss A Goschen** **1**
(fav) wth ldr, ld & qcknd clr 12th, unchal aft
110[1] **Flying Imp .... R Nuttall** **2**
w.w. rear, mstk 10th, wll bhnd 13th, ran on wll frm 2 out
179[6] **Bold Imp .... M Rimell** **3**
trckd ldrs, outpcd frm 12th, kpt on onepcd frm 3 out
106[5] Sybillabee 5a *in tch, chsd wnr 12th, sn no imp, wknd & lost 2nd flat* .... M Batters 4
223 Dragons Lady 5a *mid-div, lost tch 11th, t.o. 13th* .... G Barfoot-Saunt 5
303 Bilbo Baggins (Ire) *prom to 10th, wll bhnd frm 13th, t.o.* .... M Gorman 6
223 Image Boy (Ire) *in tch, rdn 9th, outpcd 12th, wknd, t.o. & p.u. last* .... E James pu
294 Todds Hall (Ire) 4ow *ld to 12th, sn outpcd, wknd 16th, wll btn whn u.r. last* .... A Munro ur
107[5] Smokey Thunder (Ire) *5th whn blnd 7th, lost tch 11th, t.o. & p.u. 16th* .... M Miller pu
Rossodisera *lft start, crwld 1st & 2nd, ref 3rd, cont, stppd 5th* .... G Giganitesco ref
10 ran. 25l, hd, 1l, 25l, 2l. Time 6m 23.00s. SP 7-4.
Mrs J Frankland (Blackmore & Sparkford Vale).
M.J./J.N.

PLUMPTON
Monday March 10th
GOOD TO SOFT

489 3m 1f 110yds 'Clapper' Challenge Cup Hunters' Chase Class H

376[2] **JUPITER MOON 11.7 7a........ Mr J M Pritchard** **1**
chsd ldrs, ld 16th, hung left run-in, held on well.
286[4] **Loyal Note 12.5 3a........... Mr Simon Andrews** **2**
hdwy 8th, str chal from 2 out, kept on well.
285[2] **Vicompt de Valmont 12.0 5a (bl) ... Mr T Mitchell** **3**
(fav) bhnd, rdn 7th, promising hdwy 14th, chsd ldrs next, one pace from 4 out.
302 Northern Village 11.7 7a *chsd ldrs, mstk 14th, wknd next.* .... Capt D Alers-Hankey 4
227 Fifth Amendment 11.11 7a 4ow (bl) *ld 7th to 16th, wknd quickly, 5th and no ch when ref next.* Mr A Hales ref
304[3] Royal Irish 11.7 7a *in tch till rdn and outpcd 13th, soon bhnd, p.u. before 4 out.* .... Miss C Townsley pu
Ballyandrew 11.7 7a *ld to 7th, lost tch and rdn 13th, p.u. after next.* .... Miss S Gritton pu
7 ran. 1½l, 6l, dist. Time 7m 6.50s. SP 8-1.
The Stanton Seven

STRATFORD
Monday March 10th
GOOD

490 3m Credit Call Cup Novices' Hunters' Chase Class H

91[1] **ORCHESTRAL SUITE (IRE) 11.13 7a Mr F Hutsby** **1**
chsd ldrs, ld 3 out, styd on strly.
King's Treasure (USA) 12.3 7a ...... Mr A Balding **2**
(fav) chsd ldrs, ld 5th, hdd 3 out, outpcd apr last.
287[4] **Ideal Partner (Ire) 11.12 5a (bl) ... Mr R Thornton** **3**
prom, driven along 4 out, wknd apr 2 out.
331[1] Royal Segos 11.11 7a 1ow *ld till 5th, rdn and wknd 4 out.* .... Mr C Stockton 4
294[3] Tangle Baron 11.10 7a *prom, mstk 11th, wknd 5 out.* .... Miss J Cumings 5
149[4] Not My Line (Ire) 11.12 5a *mid div, rdn apr 5 out, soon lost tch.* .... Mr A Sansome 6
351[3] Rambling Lord (Ire) 11.10 7a *held up, n.d..* .... Mr G J Smith 7
285 Rising Sap 11.10 7a *held up, hdwy 10th, wknd 4 out.* .... Mr A Dalton 8
Babil 11.12 5a *prom to 10th, bhnd when p.u. before 4 out.* .... Mr J Trice-Rolph pu
84[1] Freddie Fox 11.13 7a *bhnd from 6th, p.u. before 12th.* .... Mr T Garton pu
145 Fantastic Fleet (Ire) 11.0 7a *held up, hdwy when blundd and u.r. 13th.* .... Mr R Wakley ur
Tellaporky 11.10 7a *held up, mstk 3rd, hdwy 7th, blundd and u.r. 11th.* .... Mr A Middleton ur
12 ran. 14l, 3l, 20l, 1l, 20l, 3l, 3l. Time 6m 12.00s. SP 5-2.
Exors Of The Late Mr G Pidgeon

TAUNTON
Monday March 10th
GOOD

491 3m Somerset Hunters' Chase Class H

FULL ALIRT 11.7 7a .... Miss S Young 1
ld 5th, made rest, hrd pressed last, ran on well.
286² **Granville Guest 12.5 7a .... Mr J Tizzard** 2
(fav) alwys handy, chsd wnr from 12th, str chal when hit last, edged left and wknd run-in.
242¹ **Ragtime Boy 12.0 5a .... Mr A Farrant** 3
held up, hdwy 13th, wknd from 4 out.
Artful Arthur 11.12 7a *held up, rdn after 12th, soon t.o.* .... Mr J Grassick 4
308 Prince Nepal 12.5 7a *left in ld 1st, hit next, hdd 3rd, mstks 6th and next, wknd 13th.* .... Mr G Barfoot-Saunt 5
Mo's Chorister 11.12 7a *ld till f 1st.* .... Miss F Wilson f
174 Great Pokey 12.5 7a *ld 3rd to 5th, remained prom till wknd from 12th, t.o. when p.u. before 3 out.* .... Miss N Courtenay pu
256 Doubting Donna 12.2 5a *held up, reminders apr 11th, prog 13th, cl 4th when blnd and u.r. 15th.* .. Mr J Jukes ur
8 ran. 7l, 17l, 21l, 5l. Time 6m 19.40s. SP 11-2.
B R J Young

SEDGEFIELD
Tuesday March 11th
GOOD

492 3m 3f Win With The Tote Hunters' Chase Class H

379³ **GLEN OAK 11.7 7a .... Mr J M Pritchard** 1
nvr far away, hit 5 out, styd on before last to ld near fin.
67⁹ **Kushbaloo 12.3 7a .... Mr A Parker** 2
(fav) slight ld to 8th, ld again 15th, clr 3 out, shaken up and hdd near fin.
289⁵ **Fordstown (Ire) 12.0 7a ..... Mr Jamie Alexander** 3
disp ld, ld 8th to 15th, outpcd 4 out, styd on from last.
339⁵ Tartan Tornado 12.2 5a *prom, outpcd 4 out, no impn final 2.* .... Mr P Johnson 4
353³ Fast Study 12.3 7a *jmpd badly, held up, imp 8th, struggling 13th, t.o.* .... Mr Simon Robinson 5
84 Side Brace (NZ) 11.7 7a *n.j.w., bhnd, t.o. final cct.* .... Miss S Swindells 6
356⁵ Polynth 11.7 7a *jmpd badly in tch, mstk and lost pl 6th, t.o. final cct, p.u. before last.* .... Mr G Markham pu
7 ran. 1l, nk, 4l, dist, 9l. Time 6m 51.30s. SP 2-1.
R J Mansell

NEWTON ABBOT
Wednesday March 12th
HEAVY

493 2m 5f 110yds Little Town Novices' Hunters' Chase Class H

243² **HERHORSE 11.5 7a .... Mr L Jefford** 1
chsd ldrs, hit 6th, soon rcvred ld 2 out, left well clr last.
171³ **Kaloore 11.10 7a .... Mr R Nuttall** 2
(Jt fav) in rear, rdn and hdwy 6 out, weakening when left 2nd last.
Good King Henry 11.10 7a ..... Mr I Widdicombe 3
in tch till wknd 10th, t.o..
Mecado 11.10 7a (v) *held up, hdwy 8th, wknd 6 out, t.o. when ref 2 out.* .... Mr M Munrowd ref
Absent Minds 11.5 7a *mid div till wknd 9th, t.o. when p.u. before last.* .... Miss S Young pu
309³ Seventh Lock 11.10 7a *trckd ldr, blnd 6th, wknd next, t.o. when p.u. before 4 out.* .... Miss L Blackford pu
Tom's Apache 11.10 7a *mstk 1st, t.o. when p.u. before 10th.* .... Mr I Dowrick pu
176 Bryn's Story 11.10 7a *t.o. 3rd, p.u. before 10th.* .... Major G Wheeler pu
385 Tom's Gemini Star 11.10 7a *bhnd when blnd and u.r. 6th.* .... Mr G Penfold ur
237³ Baldhu Chance 11.10 7a *in tch to 9th, t.o. when p.u. before 4 out.* .... Mr James Young pu
187 Cedar Square (Ire) 11.12 5a *(Jt fav) ld till blnd 2 out, btn when f last.* .... Mr J Jukes f
11 ran. 12l, dist. Time 6m 5.70s. SP 16-1.
Miss A Howard-Chappell

CHELTENHAM
Thursday March 13th
GOOD

494 3¼m 110yds Christies Foxhunter Chase Challenge Cup Class B

295 **FANTUS 12.0 .... Mr T Mitchell** 1
in tch, pressing ldrs when hit 16th, ld after next, strly pressed last, kept on gamely.
154¹ **Cab On Target 12.0 .... Mr S Swiers** 2
(fav) held up, steady hdwy final cct, chal last, kept on till no ext cl home.
What A Hand 12.0 .... Mr P Fenton 3
held up, pushed along to improve final cct, hit 4 out, chsd ldrs after next, soon one pace.
149 Celtic Abbey 12.0 *midfield, hdwy 14th, chsd ldrs 3 out, fd next.* .... Mr D S Jones 4
92¹ Double Silk 12.0 *cl up, ld 9th till after 17th, wknd 3 out.* .... Mr R Treloggen 5
296³ Final Pride 11.9 *set str pace, blnd and hdd 9th, lost tch after 4 out, soon btn.* .... Miss P Jones 6
227¹ The Jogger 12.0 *chsd ldrs, chal hfwy, driven along 5 out, soon btn.* .... Mr J Tizzard 7
Clonrosh Slave 12.0 *well bhnd hfwy, t.o..* .... Mr S H Hadden 8
380¹ Copper Thistle (Ire) 12.0 *jmpd right 5th, well bhnd 10th, soon t.o.* .... Mr R Hunnisett 9
290¹ Holland House 12.0 *held up, pushed along 10th, bhnd when p.u. 6 out.* .... Mr C Vigors pu
328² My Nominee 12.0 (bl) *cl up, rdn and outpcd 6 out, bhnd when p.u. 2 out.* .... Mr R Burton pu
291² Lord Relic (NZ) 12.0 *held up, struggling 14th, bhnd when p.u. 6 out.* .... Mr R Ford pu
Mr Golightly 12.0 *jmpd poorly in rear, t.o. when p.u. 10th.* .... Mrs S Godfrey pu
42¹ Still In Business 12.0 *u.r. 1st.* .... Miss P Curling ur
290³ Clobracken Lad 12.0 *hit 4th, alwys rear, t.o. when p.u. 15th.* .... Mr G Baines pu
286³ Colonial Kelly 12.0 *rear when mstk 12th, blnd next, t.o. when p.u. 6 out.* .... Mr P Hacking pu
290² Miss Millbrook 11.9 *in tch, pushed along when hit 15th and next, soon btn, bhnd when p.u. 2 out.* .... Mr E Williams pu
Tearaway King (Ire) 12.0 *bhnd, jmpd right, hdwy and in tch 13th, hit 17th, lost touch next, p.u. 2 out.* .... Mr E Bolger pu
18 ran. 1¾l, 11l, 7l, 9l, 15l, 18l, 2l, dist. Time 6m 44.70s. SP 10-1.
J A Keighley

FAKENHAM
Friday March 14th
GOOD

495 2m 5f 110yds William Bulwer-Long Memorial Novices' Hunters' Chase Class H

371² **WHAT CHANCE (IRE) 10.11 7a .... Mr A Charles-Jones** 1
held up, hdwy to track ldrs after 9th, cld up after 3 out, ld next, styd on well.
383 **Galzig 11.4 7a 2ow .... Mr W Tellwright** 2
pressed ldr, ld 9th to 11th, ev ch 4 out, rdn and kept on one pace after 2 out.
225⁵ **Gypsy King (Ire) 11.2 7a .... Mr A Coe** 3
alwys chasing ldrs, ev ch 4 out, jmpd slowly next, kept on one pace.

490 Tellaporky 11.2 7a *ld to 9th, pressed ldr, led 11th to 2 out, soon wknd*.....................Mr A Middleton 4
396[2] Arise (Ire) 11.2 7a *(fav) hmpd start and slowly away, hdwy to track ldrs after 8th, ev ch 3 out, soon rdn, wknd after next*.....................Mr N R Mitchell 5
249[3] Try God 11.2 7a *trckd ldrs, ev ch 5 out, rdn and wknd after next*.............................Miss L Allan 6
300 Rayman (Ire) 11.2 7a *bhnd 8th, brief effort after 10th, soon behind*..........................Mr R Lawther 7
322[7] Old Dundalk 11.2 7a (bl) *mstk 7th, soon well bhnd, t.o. when p.u. before last*...................Mr N King pu
322[6] Foxbow (Ire) 11.4 5a *f 3rd*............Mr A Sansome f
192[2] Gone For Lunch 11.2 7a *whipped round start, v slowly away, t.o. when jmpd slowly 5th and p.u.*..
....Mr M Gingell pu

10 ran. 3½l, 2l, 8l, 9l, 11l, 8l. Time 5m 38.50s. SP 7-2.
C W Booth

HEREFORD
Saturday March 15th
GOOD TO FIRM

496 3m 1f 110yds Charlie Knipe Hunters' Chase Class H

PENLEA LADY 11.2 7a ....Mr S Lloyd 1
in tch, mstk 10th, bumped and nearly u.r. 12th, styd on to chase ldr 15th, shaken up and qcknd to ld cl home.
399[2] **The Rum Mariner 11.9 5a ....Mr R Thornton** 2
ld, rdn 3 out, hdd and no ext cl home.
465[1] **Chip'N'run 11.7 7a ....Mr J Cornes** 3
chsd ldr to 15th, wknd 3 out.
286[5] Gay Ruffian 11.7 7a *hdwy 8th, wknd 13th*.
....Miss C Dyson 4
431[1] First Harvest 11.7 7a *hdwy 7th, chsd ldrs when blnd 14th, soon wknd*..........................Mr P Hanly 5
400[6] Kingfisher Bay 11.7 7a *bhnd from 11th, t.o. when p.u. before 13th*..........................Mr G Shenkin pu
382[4] Orton House 11.7 7a *bhnd from 9th, t.o. when p.u. before 15th*...........................Mr R Burton pu
382[2] Teatrader 11.7 7a *hit 6th and bhnd, t.o. when p.u. before 4 out*..........................Miss T Blazey pu
180[3] Prince Of Verona 11.7 7a *(fav) soon outpcd and bhnd, effort 10th, soon wknd, t.o. when p.u. before 15th*.
..................................Mr Rupert Sweeting pu
382[1] Highway Five (Ire) 12.0 7a *soon bhnd, t.o. when p.u. before 15th*...........................Miss E James pu

10 ran. 1¼l, 17l, 16l, 23l. Time 6m 39.00s. SP 7-1.
Mrs S G Addinsell

DUNSTON HARRIERS
Ampton
Saturday March 15th
GOOD TO FIRM

497 Confined (12st)

321 **DRUID'S LODGE ....C Ward-Thomas** 1
alwys 1st 2, ld 15th, made rest, styd on strngly frm 2 out
270[2] **Counterbid ....A Sansome** 2
rr, prog 12th, 4th & nt qkn 3 out, ran on agn appr last.
271[4] **Nibble ....A Coe** 3
trkcd ldrs, gng wll, ev ch & blnd 17th, rdn & btn appr 2 out
Cardinal Black *keen hold, ld/disp til ld 10th, hdded 15th, wknd 3 out*..............................N Bloom 4
319[4] Smart Pal *disp ld to 3rd, prom to 12th, wkng & j.s. 14th, no dang aft*........................K Needham 5
319[3] El Bae *alwys rr div, nvr nr ldrs*.............P Taiano 6
270 Major Inquiry (USA) *chsd ldrs to 10th, wll bhnd frm 16th*.......................................G Pewter 7
193 Buckshot (Ire) *rr, blnd 7th, rmdrs 10th, no resp, t.o. & p.u. 2 out*....................................C Barlow pu
319[1] Salmon Mead (Ire) 3ex *(fav) in tch, jnd ldrs 7th, mstk 9th, rdn & btn 16th, p.u. 3 out*..............S Sporborg pu

9 ran. 6l, ½l, 15l, 8l, 4l, 6l. Time 6m 35.00s. SP 7-1.
D J Lay (Essex & Suffolk).

498 Open Maiden Div I

FAHA MOSS (IRE) ....S R Andrews 1
w.w.disp ld 13th,ld & jmpd lft 3 out,gng best whn lft clrnxt
451 **Fighting For Good (Ire) (bl) ....N Bloom** 2
(fav) trkd ldrs, ld 11th til 3 out, sn rdn & btn
438[6] **Mirror Image 5a..............................N King** 3
chsd ldrs, rdn & btn appr 17th, lft poor 3rd 2 out
438 Cambridge Gold 7a *mstks, made most to 11th, bhnd & hit 14th, t.o.*...............................P Chinery 4
Room To Manouver (Ire) *rcd wde, cls up to 8th, bhnd frm 11th, t.o. whn ref 2 out*..................G Lush ref
317 Sheer Hope *keen hold, prom, blnd 6th,wth wnnr but und press whn f 2 out*........................A Coe f
450 Grangewick Kelly 5a *alwys last, wll bhnd & p.u. 10th*
....S Dobson pu
318 Kingarth 7a *mid div, in tch til 6th & outpcd 16th, t.o. & p.u. 3 out*..........................C Ward-Thomas pu

8 ran. 10l, 6l, dist. Time 6m 50.00s. SP 2-1.
N W Padfield (Enfield Chace).

499 Open Maiden Div II

276[4] **THURLES PICKPOCKET (IRE) ....A Coe** 1
in tch, disp ld 13th, slt ld frm 17th, hld on gamely flat
318[2] **The Prior ....P Rowe** 2
(fav) ld/disp to 17th, unable to qkn appr last
438[2] **Bozo Bailey ....P Taiano** 3
trkd ldrs, cls 4th 15th, unable to qkn und press appr last
318 Harry Tartar *rr, mstks 5th & 7th, rpd prog to cls 3rd 3 out,onepcd aft*......................Capt D Parker 4
128[3] Insulate 5a *alwys mid div, 6th & rdn 16th, nt pace to rch ldrs*...................................S March 5
318 Mistress Linnet 5a *trkd ldrs, cls 3rd & gng wll 15th, btn appr 2 out*..............................C Ward 6
373 Village Remedy 5a *prom, disp ld 7-12th, wkng & hit 13th, no ch aft*.................................A Tutton 7
317 Just Mai-Bee 7a *mstks, disp ld to 7th, wknd 13th, t.o.*
..................................C Ward-Thomas 8
Dilly May Dally 5a *schoold in rr, lst tch 10th, t.o. & p.u. 14th*.......................................N King pu

9 ran. Nk, ½l, ½l, 1½l, 1l, 10l, 30l. Time 6m 49.00s. SP 5-2.
Miss J Stevens (East Anglia Bloodhounds).

500 Ladies

377 **CRAFTSMAN 7ex..................Miss G Chown** 1
ld 2nd-13th, lft in ld nxt, drw clr 2 out, easily
474[4] **Subsonic (Ire) ....Miss C Tarratt** 2
hld up, lft 2nd 14th-nxt, outpcd aft 3 out, kpt on flat
274[4] **Zoes Pet 5a.......................Miss H Pewter** 3
prom, chsd wnr 15th, outpcd aft 3 out, lst 2nd flat
442[2] St Gregory 10ex (bl) *(fav) ld to 2nd, chsd wnr, ld 13th til blnd & u.r. nxt*.......................Mrs L Gibbon ur

4 ran. 10l, ½l. Time 6m 41.00s. SP Evens.
G W Paul (Essex & Suffolk).

501 Men's Open (12st)

388[3] **OVER THE EDGE 7ex ....S Sporborg** 1
(fav) made all, drw clr appr 2 out, easily
319 **Exarch (USA) ....A Coe** 2
hld up, wnt 2nd 14th, ev ch 3 out, sn outpcd.
124[5] **Armagret 7ex ....S Cowell** 3
chsd ldrs, rmdr 5th, rdn appr 17th, wll btn 3 out
440 Cardinal Red 7ex *trkd ldrs til j.s. 8th, reluc & sn wll bhnd, t.o. & ref 16th*......................A Sansome ref

4 ran. 8l, 12l. Time 6m 40.00s. SP 4-7.
Christopher Sporborg (Puckeridge).

502 Restricted (12st)

270[1] **BALLYALLIA CASTLE (IRE) ....N Bloom** 1
(fav) trkd ldrs, outpcd 10th, clsd 14th, ld 2 out, styd on strngly
443 **Ludoviciana 5a..........................P Keane** 2

prom, ld 8th til appr 2 out, no ex
322[5] **Cool Apollo (NZ) ....G Plenderleith** 3
in tch to 15th, sn outpcd, lft poor 3rd 2 out
444 Salachy Run (Ire) *alwys last, t.o & p.u. 13th* ...N Page pu
324 Top Of The Range (Ire) *ld to 8th, prom til 3 out, no ch whn blnd badly 2 out & p.u.* ....C Ward-Thomas pu
5 ran. 5l, 20l. Time 6m 39.00s. SP 4-6.
A F J Moss (Suffolk).

503 B.F.S.S. Nov Riders

438[1] **NOBLE KNIGHT (IRE) ....C Jarvis** 1
chsd ldr, ld 10th, made rest, clr 3 out, hld on gamely flat
302 **Linred ....P Hall** 2
in tch,chsd wnr 13-16th,agn 3 out, hd rdn 2 out, kpt on
369[7] **Berkana Run ....R Bailey** 3
in tch to 12th, poor 5th 16th, ran on frm 3 out,nt rch ldrs
444 Just Jack *(fav) in tch, prog to chs wnr 16th, wknd 3 out, fin tired* ....P Jonason 4
324 Ballygar Boy (Ire) *ld to 10th, grad lst pl, no ch frm 16th* ....J Buckle 5
305 Glenavey *bhnd frm 5th, nvr nr ldrs* ....C Hall 6
278 Doctor Dick (Ire) (bl) *sn wll bhnd, t.o. frm 2nd* T Walsh 7
Obie's Train *alwys bhnd, t.o. & p.u. 17th*....Mrs A Lee pu
443[3] Whats Another 5a *mstks, prom til 5th & outpcd 13th, wll bhnd whn p.u. last* ....Miss K Bridge pu
275[6] Arkay *prom, chsd ldr 6-8th, sn wknd, t.o. whn blnd & u.r. 16th* ....R Kerry ur
324[5] Auchendolly (Ire) *alwys rr, 10th whn u.r. 9th* ....T Macfarlane ur
11 ran. 2l, 10l, 10l, dist, 15l, 2 fences. Time 6m 37.00s. SP 7-2.
C Jarvis (Suffolk).

504 Members

322 **SAINT BENE'T (IRE) (bl) ....N King** 1
(fav) chsd ldr, disp ld 12-14th, rmdr 16th, ld appr 3 out, sn clr
196 **Stoneyisland (Ire) ....N Bloom** 2
ld til appr 3 out, sn wknd
2 ran. 25l. Time 6m 47.00s. SP 4-9.
George Prodromou (Dunston Harriers).
S.P.

HOLDERNESS
Dalton Park
Saturday March 15th
GOOD TO FIRM

505 Members

348[7] **DROMIN FOX ....J Dillon** 1
hld up rear, prog 8th, mstk 4 out, ld last, ran on well
265[6] **Master Cornet ....Miss S Brotherton** 2
(fav) trckd ldr, ld 9th, blnd nxt, hdd last, kpt on
248 **Grey Hussar (NZ) 5ex ....S Walker** 3
mid-div, went 2nd 13th, rdn 16th, outpcd 2 out
426 Oxford Place (bl) *prom, mstk 3rd, wknd 13th, sn bhnd, t.o.*.....................................Miss P Richardson 4
426 Crocket Lass 5a *ld to 9th, fdd, btn whn u.r. 15th* ....Miss F Hunter ur
Auntie Fay (Ire) 5a *not fluent, alwys strgglng, t.o. & p.u. 15th* ....I Baker pu
6 ran. 2l, 5l, dist. Time 7m 12.00s. SP 9-1.
Mrs S Merrington (Holderness).

506 Confined

422[1] **JUST CHARLIE 4ow.....................D Easterby** 1
(fav) prom, ld 6th, made rest, comf
165[3] **Clyde Ranger ....G Markham** 2
mid-div, prog 10th, chsd wnr 14th, outpcd frm 2 out
356[6] **Skipping Gale ....P Atkinson** 3
ld/disp to 6th, outpcd 11th, styd on agn 3 out
265[3] Cot Lane *prom, disp 3rd-6th, not qckn frm 4 out* ....J Tate 4
424[2] Cadrillon (Fr) *rear & mstk 9th, alwys bhnd* ....Miss A Deniel 5
337[4] Attle *mid-div, prog 10th, ev ch 16th, wknd rpdly apr 2 out* ....S Brisby 6
248[7] My True Clown *lost tch 7th, t.o.* ....Miss L Hampshire 7
423[2] Miami Bear *rear, prog 9th, trckd ldrs going wll whn f 15th*...L Russell f
475[4] Clare Lad *prom til fdd 13th, hmpd & u.r. 15th* J Burns ur
339 Beau Rose *prom til outpcd 14th, b.d. nxt*........R Tate bd
265 Tooting Times *plld hrd, mid-div, prog 6th, rdn 12th, sn fdd, p.u. 2 out* ....C Mulhall pu
345 Lac de Gras (Ire) *mid-div, f 1st* ....A Pennock f
China Hand (Ire) 7a *bhnd, bdly hmpd & u.r. 6th* ....R Edwards ur
429 Markham Lad *rear whn u.r. 3rd*..........D Pritchard ur
Braemoss 5a *rear, sn wll bhnd, t.o. & p.u. 12th* ....Miss T Jackson pu
Palmed Off 5a *mid-div, lost tch 5th, ran out nxt* ....A Ogden ro
16 ran. 3l, 10l, 2l, 8l, 1l, dist. Time 6m 58.00s. SP 5-4.
Mrs Susan E Mason (Middleton).

507 Men's Open

423[1] **PEANUTS PET ....R Walmsley** 1
(fav) hld up mid-div, prssd ldr 11th, ld 16th, qcknd clr, easily
267[3] **Castle Tyrant 5a ....P Atkinson** 2
ld to 16th, onepcd
250 **Park Drift ....G Markham** 3
hld up rear, effrt 15th, not qckn 3 out
354[4] Dalmore *rear, outpcd 14th, sn wll bhnd*.....D Coates 4
413[6] Syrus P Turntable *rear, prog 12th, fdd 16th, t.o.* ....C Mulhall 5
423 Black Spur *prom, 3rd whn f 11th* ....P Jenkins f
375[6] No Word *prom til lost plc 8th, bdly hmpd & p.u. 11th* ....I Baker pu
207[2] French Myle (Ire) *prom til outpcd 14th, blnd 3 out, 4th & no ch whn u.r. nxt* ....G Smith ur
8 ran. 12l, 8l, 2½l, 12l. Time 6m 52.00s. SP 4-6.
J W Walmsley (Bramham Moor).

508 Ladies

OSGATHORPE ....Mrs F Needham 1
s.s. trckd ldr, ld 12-14th, ld agn 3 out, sn clr, hld on fin
355[2] **Thistle Monarch ....Miss R Clark** 2
(fav) sttld 3rd,mstk 10th,ld 15th-4 out,outpcd nxt,ran on wll flat
349 **Midge 5a ....Miss S Brotherton** 3
rear, lost tch 7th, wll bhnd 11th
426[5] Cumberland Blues (Ire) *j.w. ld to 12th & 14th-nxt,ld 4 out til wknd & hdd nxt,eased* ....Miss A Deniel 4
4 ran. Hd, 20l, 7l. Time 6m 55.00s. SP 6-1.
R Tate (Hurworth).

509 B F S S (12st)

336[4] **SQUIRES TALE (IRE) ....Mrs S Grant** 1
prom, prog to 2nd 16th, qckn to ld apr last, lft wll clr
339[6] **Tom Log ....C Mulhall** 2
mid-div,lost plc 14th, effrt 16th, onepcd 3 out,lft 2nd last
383[3] **Admission (Ire) ....Miss L Horner** 3
mid-div, mstk 11th, no prog 4 out, lft 3rd last
477[3] Beckford *prom til wknd 15th, t.o.*........A Pickering 4
350[2] Barichste 4ex (bl) *(Jt fav) prom til outpcd & hmpd 15th, sn bhnd, p.u. last* ....Maj M Watson pu
383[2] Greenmount Lad (Ire) 4ex *prom whn ran out 3rd* ....P Cornforth ro
348 Political Field 5a *rear, lost tch 14th, t.o. & p.u. 2 out* ....S Walker pu
269[1] Pharlindo (Ire) *plld hrd, ld, ran wd apr 3rd, disp 10th-14th, f nxt*..............................S Brisby f
422 Strong Words *s.s. alwys rear, wll bhnd 13th, p.u. 15th* ....S Pinder pu
War Horse *rear, t.o. & p.u. 15th*..................A Wood pu
269 Daredevil (Ire) *rear, sn t.o., p.u. 15th* ....A Ogden pu

3581 The Oxford Don *(Jt fav) trckd ldr, disp 10th, ld 14th, lft clr nxt,hdd apr last & f*......................N Wilson f
Last Option 7a *rear & sn wll bhnd, t.o. & p.u. 12th*......................Mrs F Needham pu
13 ran. 15l, 2l, dist. Time 6m 52.00s. SP 9-2.
J G Howse (Bilsdale).

510 Open Maiden (7yo+)

4294 **PROPHET'S CHOICE ....M Haigh** 1
prom,mstk 8th, prog to disp 14th, lft in ld nxt, hld on flat
375 **Dear Emily 5a ....N Smith** 2
mid-div, prog 14th, lft 2nd nxt, chal flat, kpt on wll
342 **Level Vibes ....R Abrahams** 3
ld to 14th, wknd
3584 Goodheavens Mrtony *mid-div, outpcd 9th, t.o. 12th*......................M Bennison 4
Restless Star 5a *rear, strgglng whn ran out 15th*......................S Bowden ro
429 Timber Topper *prom, 4th & in tch whn b.d. 15th*......................H Armstrong bd
346 Andretti's Heir *alwys prom, fdng whn hmpd & p.u. aft 15th*......................A Bonson pu
266 Vale Of York *s.s. mid-div, prog to remote 3rd 15th, no hdwy, p.u. last*......................Miss R Clark pu
Roseberry Star 5a *rear, sn wll bhnd, t.o. 6th, p.u. 12th*......................Miss T Jackson pu
358 Fair Grand (bl) *mid-div whn u.r. 6th*......................S Brisby ur
4293 Just Johnie *(fav) prom, ld & going wll whn f 15th*......................S Walker f
357 Magic Song 5a *rear, lost tch 11th, t.o. & p.u. 13th*......................C Denny pu
Another Delight 5a *lft 20l start, unruly & u.r. bef 1st*......................N Wilson ur
Rosie Blue 5a *rear & sn lost tch, t.o. 6th, p.u. 9th*......................G Tuer pu
14 ran. Hd, dist, 20l. Time 7m 5.00s. SP 12-1.
Mrs R Alderton (Sinnington).
N.E.

NEW FOREST BUCKHOUNDS
Larkhill
Saturday March 15th
GOOD TO FIRM

511 Confined (12st)

3974 **MIGHTY FALCON ....Miss E Tory** 1
disp til ld 13th, clr nxt, easily
Touch Of Winter 5ex ....T Lacey 2
(fav) disp til mstk 13th, found nil aft
Wellington Brown ....Mrs C Mitchell 3
cls up to 12th, btn & jmpd slwly frm nxt, lame
3 ran. 20l, 15l. Time 6m 7.00s. SP 6-4.
Miss Emma Tory (South Dorset).

512 Open Maiden (5-8yo) Div I (12st)

WICKED IMP 7a........................J Jukes 1
mstk 3rd, in tch, prssd ldr 13th, ld 2 out, rdn out flat
181 **Old Harry's Wife 5a ....R Nuttall** 2
(fav) set slw pace, hmpd by loose hrs apr 10th, hdd 2 out, no ext
293 Rose Of Macmillion 5a 1ow *in tch, chsd ldr brfly apr 13th, 3rd whn f 14th*......................Miss D Olding f
458 Golden News *hld up last, u.r. 7th*..............P King ur
390 Most Vital *keen hld, trckd ldr til blnd & u.r. 9th*......................Miss A Goschen ur
The Frosty Fox (Ire) *jmpd slwly 1st, in tch to 13th, wknd rpdly, p.u. 3 out*......................M Miller pu
6 ran. 4l. Time 6m 29.00s. SP 5-2.
Peter Scott (Dulverton West).

513 Open Maiden (5-8yo) Div II (12st)

STILLMORE BUSINESS 1ow..........T Mitchell 1
(fav) trckd ldr 7th, ld aft 4 out, jnd apr last, rdn & styd on wll
390 **First Bash (Ire) ....R Nuttall** 2
hld up last, prog 12th, jnd wnr apr last, rdn & not qckn
294 **Villains Brief (Ire) (bl) ....R Lawther** 3
chsd ldrs, 3rd & outpcd apr 14th, no ch aft
181 Woodlands Beau (Ire) 7a *trckd ldrs til lost plc aft 12th, no dang aft, kpt on*......................T Woolridge 4
Gay Muse 5a 1ow *alwys rear, no ch frm 4 out, sn wll bhnd*......................P King 5
390 Wesshaun 5a 4ow *ld 3rd til aft 4 out, wkng whn blnd nxt, t.o.*......................G Chanter 6
297 Horton Country 5a *alwys rear, t.o. last whn p.u. 4 out*......................P Howse pu
392 Nicolinsky 5a *ld to 3rd, wknd 7th, sn bhnd, p.u. 3 out*......................Julian Pritchard pu
3142 Carnelia 5a 1ow *last whn u.r. 1st*......J Kwiatkowski ur
481 Dad's Dilemma *last whn ran out 2nd*.........T Smith ro
10 ran. 2½l, dist, 1l, 1l, 15l. Time 6m 8.00s. SP 4-6.
R G Williams (Taunton Vale).
One fence omitted, 17 jumps.

514 Mixed Open (12st)

1783 **APATURA KING 1ow ....T Mitchell** 1
(fav) w.w. in tch, ld 15th, sn rdn, styd on wll flat
393 **Mediane (USA) ....A Charles-Jones** 2
trckd ldrs, prssd wnr 2 out, ev ch til not qckn flat
179 **Indian Knight ....C Vigors** 3
cls up, ld 13-15th, wknd 3 out
947 Orujo (Ire) *cls up, jnd wnr 15th, wknd 2 out*......................Julian Pritchard 4
1082 Daybrook's Gift *prom to 4th, lost plc rpdly, t.o. & p.u. 12th*......................Miss N Allan pu
109 Sharp Performer (Ire) *ld to 13th, wknd rpdly 15th, p.u. 2 out*......................M Miller pu
6 ran. 2l, 15l, 1l. Time 5m 59.00s. SP 4-7.
C E Gibbs (Portman).

515 Intermediate (12st)

2362 **KING TORUS (IRE) ....J Jukes** 1
made virt all, clr aft 2 out, hrd rdn & hng lft flat,all out
2932 **Nothing Ventured ....A Beedles** 2
cls up, wth wnr 13th til aft 3 out, styd on wll flat
Thegoose ....P King 3
hld up rear, prog to chs ldng pair 14th,no imp aft,wknd last
3001 Prideaux Prince *wth wnr to 12th, wknd nxt, poor 4th & p.u. last*......................Julian Pritchard pu
1091 Alex Thuscombe (v) *rear whn ran out 3rd* ....P Shaw ro
2822 Stalbridge Gold 5a *in tch in rear to 13th, wll bhnd whn p.u. 3 out*......................Miss A Goschen pu
2481 Specialarrangement (Ire) 5ex *(fav) w.w. prog to 3rd whn mstk 13th, sn btn, p.u. 3 out*......................A Hill pu
293 Plan-A (Ire) *trckd ldrs,mstk 8th,strgglng 13th,no ch whn ref & u.r. 3 out*......................T Woolridge ref
8 ran. 2l, 20l. Time 6m 0.00s. SP 3-1.
Nick Viney (Tiverton Staghounds).

516 Restricted Div I (12st)

4884 **SYBILLABEE 5a ....Daniel Dennis** 1
w.w. prog to ld 13th, clr 3 out, easily
300 **Balance ....M Walters** 2
(fav) many mstks,in tch,effrt to chs wnr 2 out,no imp,mstk last
Neville ....Miss R David 3
ld to 8th, wth ldr to 12th, outpcd 14th, kpt on last
1784 Juniper Lodge *wth ldr, ld 8-13th, 2nd aft til mstk 2 out, wknd*......................S Bush 4
Game Fair *cls up to 14th, wknd rpdly, crwld 3 out & p.u.*......................W Cook pu
222 Nobbutjust (Ire) 5a 1ow *cls up til mstk & u.r. 11th*......................A Beedles ur
Lough Morne 2ow *dtchd last whn mstk & u.r. 2nd*......................Miss A Lock ur
7 ran. 10l, 1½l, 12l. Time 6m 7.00s. SP 14-1.
Mrs D Buckett (Hursley Hambledon).

517 Restricted Div II (12st)

300 **THE MAN FROM CLARE (IRE) ....L Lay** 1
chsd ldrs, 3rd & rdn 2 out, ran on to ld last, drvn out
Daring Duck ....Maj S Robinson 2
alwys prom, disp 13th-last, rdn & kpt on flat
Colourful Boy ....A Charles-Jones 3
hld up, clsd 13th, chsd ldng trio 15th, no imp, lft 3rd last
372 Lochinvar Lord *cls up to 14th, sn wknd, t.o. in 4th whn p.u. last, lame* ....D Renney pu
300⁴ Tommy O'Dwyer (Ire) *in tch to 13th, sn wknd, p.u. 15th* ....A Hill pu
106 Nearly A Mermaid 5a *ld to 3rd, rear whn f 10th* ....R Nuttall f
177³ In The Choir 5a *jmpd v slwly, t.o. til p.u. 13th* ....Maj H Carruthers pu
278³ Prince's Gift *(Jt fav) mstk 7th, nvr going wll, lost tch 13th, p.u. 15th* ....A Phillips pu
7 Ridemore Balladeer *(Jt fav) wth ldr 5th til lft in ld 12th, jnd nxt, hdd & f last, lame* ....T Mitchell f
316¹ Noble Protector (Ire) *ld 3rd, jnd whn f 12th* ....Maj G Wheeler f

10 ran. 2l, 15l. Time 6m 11.00s. SP 20-1.
Mrs R C Matheson (Old Berkshire).

518 Members

311 **TULLYKYNE BELLS ....Miss D Stafford** 1
walked over

M A Kerley (New Forest Buckhounds).
J.N.

QUANTOCK STAGHOUNDS
Cothelstone
Saturday March 15th
GOOD TO SOFT

519 Members

312⁴ **BELFRY LAD ....J Creighton** 1
handy, mstk 11th, lft in ld 13th, unchal
310 **The Criosra (Ire) ....A Bateman** 2
nov rdn, rear, lft poor 2nd 13th, no imp
102 **Lochnaver 5a ....Miss P Gundry** 3
bhnd hlfwy, t.o.
The Golfing Curate *(fav) ld til f 13th* ....I Dowrick f
316 Pallingham Lad (Ire) *prom, cls 2nd whn f 13th* ....S Kidston f

5 ran. Dist, dist. Time 6m 54.00s. SP 7-4.
P T Norman (Quantock Staghounds).

520 Ladies

99² **SLANEY FOOD ....Miss S Vickery** 1
trckd ldr 7th til lft in ld 14th, just ld last, ran on wll
294¹ **Bengers Moor ....Miss P Curling** 2
(fav) w.w. went 2nd 15th, disp & ev ch 2 out, no ext und pres flat
Night Wind ....Mrs A Rucker 3
ld 1st, prom, 3rd but no prog frm hlfwy
257² Split Second *hld up, 5th hlfwy, nvr on trms* ....Miss A Dare 4
389⁶ Taurean Tycoon *alwys mid-div* ....Miss S Duckett 5
Legal Picnic *sn rear, t.o. frm 15th* ....Miss C Bryan 6
311 L'uomo Piu *nov rdn, rear grp, t.o. 16th* ..Miss K Baker 7
47 Greenwine (USA) *nov rdn, not fluent, rear til p.u. 15th* ....Miss G Underhill pu
109⁴ Rapid Rascal *ld 2nd-6th, sn wknd, p.u. 14th* ....Miss S West pu
454² Celtic Sport (bl) *ld 6th til u.r. 14th* .....Miss C Stucley ur
311 Be My Habitat (bl) *nvr dang, t.o. & p.u. 3 out* ....Miss L Hawkings pu
Best Left 5a *t.o. & p.u. 8th* ....Miss W Southcombe pu

12 ran. 2l, 12l, 10l, 2l, 15l, 20l. Time 6m 29.00s. SP 13-2.
Capt T A Forster & M Wiggin (Devon & Somerset Staghounds).

521 Land Rover Open (12st)

295¹ **THE BOUNDER 7ex ....J Tizzard** 1
(fav) made all, modest pace, alwys in cmmnd, clvrly
296 **Riva (NZ) ....N Mitchell** 2
w.w. went 2nd 16th, tried to chal, alwys hld
Feile Na Hinse ....S Durack 3
in tch, went 3rd 17th, no ext
Oh So Windy 5a *chsd wnr til mstk & strggling frm 16th* ....B Pollock 4
Take By Storm (Ire) *hdwy 12th, 4th at 16th, no ch whn p.u. aft 2 out* ....R Payne pu
308 Sea Dreams (Ire) *rear til p.u. 11th* ......J Hankinson pu
Maggies Fellow (Ire) *cls up to 13th, bhnd whn p.u. 16th* ....G Barfoot-Saunt pu
Broad Commitment *lost tch hlfwy, p.u. 13th* ....R Treloggen pu

8 ran. 3l, 5l, 25l. Time 6m 40.00s. SP 2-7.
L G Tizzard (Blackmore & Sparkford Vale).

522 Confined

239³ **QUALITAIR MEMORY (IRE) ....J Tizzard** 1
(fav) handy, disp 3 out, ld nxt, pshd out
457¹ **Milled Oats ....R Widger** 2
cls 5th hlfwy, disp 3 out, 2l 2nd nxt, fin well
310 **Ive Called Time ....T Greed** 3
mid-div, 6th at 14th, ran on steadily, nrst fin
309¹ Stunning Stuff *in tch, 5th at 14th, 3rd 3 out, eased nr fin* ....Miss T Cave 4
Life Peerage (USA) *alwys bhnd* ....Mrs S Barrow 5
Farmer Tom *prom, ld brfly aft 5th, p.u. aft nxt, dsmntd* ....Miss P Curling pu
94⁶ Flame O'Frensi 5a *ld apr 11th til f 15th* ....Miss J Cumings f
308 Bridge Express *made most to apr 11th, lost plc 14th, p.u. 2 out* ....J Creighton pu
309² Bianconi *t.o. & p.u. 9th* ....S Kidston pu
M-Reg *nov rdn, bhnd til p.u. 2 out* ....G Cazenove pu
Suba Lin 5a *bhnd til p.u. 12th* ....M Frith pu
460 Glamorous Guy *u.r. 1st* ....S Parfimowicz ur
294⁷ Fixed Liability (bl) *bhnd til p.u. 13th, b.b.v.* .....D Alers-Hankey pu
312¹ Miss Ricus 5a *bhnd til p.u. 12th* ....R Treloggen pu

14 ran. 1½l, dist, 4l, dist. Time 6m 33.00s. SP 6-4.
C L Tizzard (Blackmore & Sparkford Vale).

523 Restricted Div I (12st)

298³ **SWANSEA GOLD (IRE) 5a........D Alers-Hankey** 1
keen hld, ld 15th, hdd 2 out, ran on to ld flat, gamely
303⁴ **Gamay ....N Mitchell** 2
hld up, prog to 2nd 13th, ld 2 out til hdd flat
467 **This I'll Do Us (Ire) ....A Morley** 3
rear, 8th at 15th, ran on steadily, nrst fin
313⁵ Third Melody 5a *alwys bhnd* ....G Weatherley 4
288⁴ J B Lad *prom til wknd 15th* ....Miss P Gundry 5
240 Cedars Rosslare *nov rdn, alwys strgglng in rear* ....Miss O Green 6
Link Copper *prom til lost ground 11th, p.u. 13th* ....R Treloggen pu
294⁵ Celtic Token *mid-div, mstk 13th, bhnd whn p.u. 2 out* ....J Barnes pu
433² Ruth's Boy (Ire) *(fav) ld til mstk 15th, sn wknd, p.u. 2 out* ....Miss P Curling pu
Windwhistle Lad *in tch, 5th at 13th, prog to 3rd whn f 3 out* ....B Dixon f
312 Lake Mariner 5a *prom til lost plc 15th, bhnd whn p.u. 2 out* ....Maj O Ellwood pu
Olive Basket 5a *bhnd til p.u. 14th* ....Miss W Southcombe pu
300 Mine's A Gin (Ire) *8th hlfwy, rear whn blnd 13th, p.u. nxt* ....Miss J Cumings pu
314¹ Baywyn 5a *rear whn f 12th* ....S Kidston f

14 ran. 1½l, 25l, 15l, 15l, dist. Time 6m 31.00s. SP 3-1.
Mrs H E North (West Somerset Foxhounds).

524 Restricted Div II (12st)

240² **HE IS ....Miss P Curling** 1
prog 9th, lft 2nd 12th, ld nxt, sn clr, comf
468⁵ **Live Wire (Ire) ....T Cox** 2
fmndrs 11th, 3rd at 14th, went 2nd 2 out, fin tired
241 **Venn Boy ....J Tizzard** 3
in tch til rdn 14th, wkng whn hit 3 out
Quicker Jack *s.s. alwys t.o.* ....Miss L Delve 4

303 Quick Quick Sloe 5a *not alwys fluent, lost tch 9th, p.u. 12th* ..... Miss T Cave pu
Miss Gruntled 5a *5th whn hit 13th, bhnd & p.u. 3 out* ..... S Parfimowicz pu
Tangle Kelly *alwys prom, cls 2nd whn blnd & u.r. 12th* ..... S Slade ur
Bewdley Boy *prom, slght ld whn f 12th* ..... Miss P Gundry f
367[1] Zambrano (USA) 7a *(fav) crashd thro' wing 1st* ..... S Durack ro
Lynphord Girl 5a *prom, lft in ld 12th, hdd nxt, btn 3rd whn p.u. 2 out* ..... J Barnes pu

10 ran. Dist, 20l, dist. Time 6m 46.00s. SP 7-4.
T Hamlin (Devon & Somerset Staghounds).
Fences 8 & 15 omitted.

525 Maiden Div I (12st)

299[2] **NEARLY AN EYE** ..... **J Tizzard** 1
(fav) ptntly rdn, prog 13th, cls 2nd 3 out, ld apr nxt, sn clr
Celtic Goblin 5a ..... **D Alers-Hankey** 2
mid-div, prog to ld 16th, hdd apr 2 out, edgd rght flat
314 **Faraday** ..... **N Mitchell** 3
prom, ld 12th-16th, cls 3rd apr 2 out, wknd
246 Givus A Hand *cls 4th hlfwy, lost plc 13th, ran on agn clsng stgs* ..... E Bailey 4
245 Carrarea (Ire) *mid-div, blnd 6th, bhnd frm 9th* ..... Miss J Cumings 5
299 Wild Weather *s.s. alwys trailing* ..... Miss S Vickery 6
Fosabud *f 1st* ..... Miss L Hawkings f
285 Princess Wenllyan 5a *ld, mstk 2nd, hdd 10th, wknd 15th, p.u. 3 out* ..... S Kidston pu
Father Malone (Ire) *p.u. apr 4th* ..... J Creighton pu
And What Else (Ire) *7th at 12th, lost ground & p.u. nxt* ..... B Dixon pu
314 I'll Be Bound (bl) *disp 10-11th, mstks nxt 2, lost tch rpdly & p.u. 15th* ..... M Burrows pu
Grey Jerry *f 1st* ..... B O'Doherty f
Acetylene 12a *bdly hmpd 1st, p.u. nxt* ..... Miss T Cave pu
Diamond Duck 12a *pllng, mid-div, mstk 11th, rear whn p.u. 14th* ..... R Treloggen pu
La Lac (Ire) 5a *rear, blnd 6th, t.o. til p.u. 4 out* ..... Mrs S Godfrey pu

15 ran. 5l, 6l, 3l, 25l, 2l. Time 6m 46.00s. SP 4-6.
Paul K Barber (Blackmore & Sparkford Vale).

526 Maiden Div II (12st)

368[2] **PASSING FAIR 5a** ..... **Miss S Vickery** 1
(fav) keen hld, hld up in tch, ld 3 out, drew clr
297[2] **Mazzard (Ire)** ..... **R Treloggen** 2
ld 6th-9th, ld 13th-17th, sn outpcd
Dollybat 5a ..... **M Frith** 3
ld to 6th, lost plc 12th, ran on agn clsng stgs
Tinker Tailor 7a *keen hld, in tch, cls 4th at 15th, no ext, eased, improve* ..... S Durack 4
Master Buckley *mid-div, no ch frm 13th* ..... T Greed 5
314 Really Neat 5a *mid-div, hmpd & u.r. 6th* ..... G Beilby ur
312 Nikolayevich *bhnd til u.r. 16th* ..... A Turner ur
Warwick Road *in tch to 12th, rear whn p.u. 15th* ..... I Dowrick pu
175 Nodforms Inferno *twrds rear til p.u. 14th* ..... G Barfoot-Saunt pu
Charlottes Billo *bhnd til p.u. 2 out* ..... R Emmett pu
Kimbross *plld hrd, ld 9th-13th, sn wknd, p.u. 15th* ..... N Legg pu
392 Noble Comic *f 1st* ..... J Tizzard f
313 Heddon Valley *in tch whn f hvly 6th* ..... R Widger f
Kiramanda 5a *lost tch 9th, t.o. & p.u. 11th* J Creighton pu
316[2] Quince Cross 5a *plld hrd, f 1st* ..... M Burrows f

15 ran. 10l, hd, 12l, dist. Time 6m 49.00s. SP 5-4.
Mrs C Wilson & M Brickell (Blackmore & Sparkford Vale).

527 Maiden Div III (12st)

MAJOR SHARPE (IRE) 7a ..... **J Tizzard** 1
hld up, steady prog 14th, slght ld last, ran on well
436[3] **Billy Barter (Ire)** ..... **Miss S Vickery** 2
(fav) ld 1st, prom til lft in ld 15th, ev ch til outpcd flat
316 **The Bodhran (Ire)** ..... **R Young** 3
w.w. in tch, ev ch 2 out, not qckn
Expresso Drummer *handy, cls 2nd 16th, ev ch 2 out, no ext, promising* ..... Miss P Curling 4
Bryansbi 5a *rear, 10th at 12th, t.o.* ..... Miss S Lock 5
Sandy Etna (Ire) 5a *ld 2nd-5th, lost plc 13th, eased, t.o.* ..... Mrs K Matthews 6
315 Rogerson *rpd prog to ld 6th, slght ld whn ref 15th* ..... J Creighton ref
Big Arthur (Ire) *rear til p.u. 9th* ..... B Foster pu
312 Nice To No *wll in tch to 14th, wknd, p.u. 2 out* S Slade pu
Joli High Note 5a *sn rear, bhnd & p.u. 13th* ..... Miss T Honeyball pu
Dust Of Life 5a *twrds rear til p.u. 15th* ..... S Durack pu
Crosswell Star (Ire) *twrds rear til p.u. 13th* ..... R Treloggen pu
106 Sue's Quest 5a *jmpd rght, rear hlfwy til p.u. 2 out* ..... G Barfoot-Saunt pu
316 Knight Of Passion 7a *sn rear, not fluent, bhnd & p.u. 13th* ..... D Alers-Hankey pu

14 ran. 2l, ½l, 10l, 30l, ¾l. Time 6m 47.00s. SP 7-2.
Mrs Bridget Nicholls (Blackmore & Sparkford Vale).
G.T.

WESTERN
Wadebridge
Saturday March 15th
GOOD TO FIRM

528 Confined (12st)

311[4] **MYHAMET** ..... **A Farrant** 1
(fav) ld 6th, steadily drew clr, easily
310[4] **Oneovertheight** ..... **N Harris** 2
ld 2nd-6th, styd prom, rdn 12th, no imp aft
313[3] **Artistic Peace 5a** ..... **D Stephens** 3
ld to 2nd, sn bhnd, some late prog
237 Queen's Chaplain (bl) *lost tch 5th, p.u. 10th* G Penfold pu
Martin's Friend *prom til mstk 12th (ditch), wknd rpdly, p.u. nxt* ..... L Jefford pu

5 ran. 15l, 2l. Time 6m 10.00s. SP 4-6.
Paul C N Heywood (North Cornwall).

529 Ladies

238[2] **JUST BERT (IRE)** ..... **Miss S Young** 1
(fav) ld/disp til drew clr frm 2 out
238[8] **Aristocratic Gold** ..... **Miss L Blackford** 2
ld/disp til outpcd frm 2 out

2 ran. 12l. Time 6m 24.00s. SP 1-3.
Mrs J Alford (Eggesford).

530 Men's Open (12st)

145[4] **BUTLER JOHN (IRE)** ..... **N Harris** 1
(fav) made all, 12l clr 12th, not extndd
171[2] **Fearsome 4ex** ..... **G Penfold** 2
alwys 2nd, not pace to trbl wnr
455[6] **Glenform (bl)** ..... **T Cole** 3
3rd frm 2nd, cls up til lost tch 12th
Achiltibuie *alwys bhnd, t.o. & p.u. 3 out* ..... J Young pu

4 ran. 7l, dist. Time 6m 28.00s. SP Evens.
Nick Viney (Exmoor).

531 Open Maiden (12st)

104 **CHOCOLATE BUTTONS 5a** ..... **H Thomas** 1
mid-div, steady prog 11th, ld 15th, made rest
54[2] **Brook A Light** ..... **N Harris** 2
alwys cls up, outpcd frm 3 out
460 **Bucks Flea 5a** ..... **G Penfold** 3
nvr far away, styd on flat, promising
460 Luney River 5a *made most to 15th, fdd* ... Miss L Long 4
460 Spartans Dina 5a *rear til prog 13th, kpt on onepcd frm nxt* ..... Miss L Blackford 5
453 Linton *alwys rear, p.u. 4 out* ..... Miss P Baker pu
172 Reptile Princess 5a *bhnd frm 6th, p.u. 12th* ..... Miss W Hartnoll pu
Aritam (Ire) *(fav) cls up to 12th, p.u. 14th* ..... A Farrant pu
Round Of Drinks *ref to race, t.n.p.* ..... J Young 0

105 Flying Maria 5a *prom early, bhnd in 6th whn f last* ....C Heard f
53[3] Cornish Twoways (Ire) 12a *bhnd 6th, t.o. & p.u. 11th* ....Miss S Young pu
455 Pen-Shilmon 7a *prom early, grad lost tch, bhnd & p.u. last* ....A Holdsworth pu
Mr Kevernair *nvr trbld ldrs, bhnd whn p.u. 2 out* ....T Dennis pu
Kanha 12a *bhnd whn u.r. 12th*....A O'Connor ur
14 ran. 3l, 6l, 1l, 12l. Time 6m 17.00s. SP 12-1.
J R Thomas (Exmoor).

532 Restricted (12st)

176[2] **GYPSY GERRY ....L Jefford** 1
(fav) alwys cls up, 3rd at 12th, ld 14th, made rest, comf
50[6] **Sunwind ....D Heath** 2
alwys prom, onepcd frm 3 out
244[1] **Eyre Point (Ire) ....A Honeyball** 3
alwys prom, kpt on onepcd apr last
176 Hopefull Drummer *rear early, gd prog 15th, ev ch 2 out, no ext*....N Harris 4
Ryme And Run 5a *ld 4th-7th, grad lost tch* ....Miss L Blackford 5
97 The Butler *ld to 4th, sn bhnd*....G Penfold 6
Medias Maid 5a *in 4th at 14th, grad fdd* A Holdsworth 7
240 Scallykenning (bl) *prom early, grad wknd, bhnd frm 15th* ....J Young 8
175 Risky Bid 5a *ld 7-14th, wknd rpdly, p.u. nxt* H Thomas pu
9 ran. 8l, ½l, 2l, 10l, 10l, 12l, 5l. Time 6m 18.00s. SP Evens.
C de P Berry (Tiverton Foxhounds).

533 Intermediate

453 **DARK REFLECTION ....C Heard** 1
bhnd til gd prog 14th, ld 16th, ran on wll whn prssd
95[2] **Cornish Ways ....Miss S Young** 2
alwys cls up, slght ld 14th-16th, kpt on wll und pres
173 **Mountain Master ....Miss L Blackford** 3
(fav) ld/disp til ld 11th-14th, onepcd aft
100 Dovedon Princess 5a *ld/disp to 11th, wknd* ....D Stephens 4
Morchard Milly 5a *trckd ldrs til u.r. 12th* ....J Auvray ur
5 ran. 1l, 10l, 15l. Time 6m 18.00s. SP 7-1.
J D Curnow (Western Hunt).
P.Ho.

CARMARTHENSHIRE
Erw Lon
Sunday March 16th
GOOD TO FIRM

534 Members

OZZIE JONES ....Miss L Pearce 1
ld to 6th, ld 9th, unchal frm 12th
300 **Cranagh Moss (Ire) ....G Lewis** 2
ld 6-9th, strgglng frm 13th
404[5] Mr Mad *(fav) cls up whn f 12th*....P Hamer f
3 ran. 8l. Time 6m 17.00s. SP 3-1.
Keith R Pearce (Carmarthenshire).

535 Confined (12st)

402[1] **CONNA MOSS (IRE) ....Miss P Jones** 1
ld 10th, disp 13th, ld agn nxt, easily
400 **Bullens Bay (Ire) ....J Llewellyn** 2
disp 13th, no imp wnr aft nxt
406[1] **Wolver's Pet (Ire) ....D S Jones** 3
sttld rear, prog 11th, chsd ldrs & hrd rdn 14th, no imp
401[2] Celtic Daughter 5a *(fav) trckd ldrs to 15th, wknd rpdly 2 out, fin tired*....J Jukes 4
399 No Panic *ld to 2nd, cls up to 11th, fdd*....J Price 5
Robbie's Boy *alwys mid-div, bttr for race* ...J P Keen 6
294[9] Pay-U-Cash *in rear, mstk 10th, no dang aft* G Perkins 7
Medieval Queen 5a *in tch til blnd 7th, fdd, p.u. 3 out* ....Miss A Meakins pu
257 Origami (bl) *alwys rear, p.u. 15th* ....A Price pu
294 General Troy *mstk 3rd, in rear aft, p.u. 10th*....J Lilley pu
293 Beinn Mohr 5a *ld 3rd-9th, wknd rpdly, p.u. 14th* ....E Williams pu
294 Billy-Gwyn *mid-div, no ch whn p.u. 3 out* ....J Tudor pu
12 ran. 5l, 1l, 12l, 5l, 3l, 15l. Time 6m 4.00s. SP 4-1.
David Brace (Llangeinor).

536 Ladies

191 **LUCKY OLE SON ....Miss P Jones** 1
(Jt fav) sttld mid-div, prog to ld aft last, rdn out
Kinlogh Gale (Ire) (bl)....Miss H Williams 2
ld aft 12th, kckd clr, hdd aft last, onepcd
362 **Local Customer ....Miss G Gibson** 3
mid-div, prog 11th, rdn 3 out, onepcd
491 Mo's Chorister *ld 1st, trckd ldrs aft, onepcd frm 9th* ....Miss A Meakins 4
Doctor-J (Ire) 2ow *ld 2nd-12th, wknd rpdly aft 3 out* ....Miss S Major 5
296 Gus McCrae *(Jt fav) cls up til fdd frm 11th* ....Miss L Pearce 6
401 Harwall Queen 5a *in rear whn f 15th*....Miss J Gill f
191 Hill Farm Katie 5a *ran out 2nd* ....Miss E Jones ro
401 Bobbie's Girl (Ire) 5a *f 3rd*....Miss J Fowler f
9 ran. 2l, 2l, 1l, 20l. Time 6m 9.00s. SP 3-1.
David Brace (Llangeinor).

537 Men's Open (12st)

401[5] **TOUCH 'N' PASS 7ex ....J Tudor** 1
mid-div, prog 10th, ld aft 2 out, blnd last, styd on well
400 **Northern Bluff 7ex ....J Jukes** 2
(fav) alwys prom, chsd wnr last, ev ch flat, onepcd
400 **Carlowitz (USA) ....J Price** 3
reluc at jmps, ld to 2 out, sn btn
295 Cornish Cossack (NZ) *trckd ldrs to 12th, onepcd aft* ....D S Jones 4
400[5] Electrolyte (bl) *alwys mid-div, no dang* ....G Austin 5
401 Gold Diver *mid-div, btn whn p.u. 13th* ....A Price pu
90[3] Billy Bathgate 1ow *tongue-strap, f 2nd* ....G Perkins f
Derrymoss 7ex (bl) *f 4th*....E Williams f
Princess Lu (Ire) 7ex *nvr nr ldrs, p.u. 13th* ...J P Keen pu
9 ran. 6l, 1l, 12l, 1l. Time 6m 11.00s. SP 2-1.
R H P Williams (Llangeinor).

538 Restricted Div I (12st)

185[1] **RADIO DAYS (IRE) ....J Jukes** 1
(fav) made all, easily
404[7] **Hill Fort (Ire) ....E Williams** 2
chsd wnr, no imp frm 3 out
399[6] **Equatime 5a ....K Cousins** 3
chsd wnr, nvr able to chal
404 Red Rhapsody 5a *nvr nr ldrs, p.u. 12th*....J Comins pu
184 Dontyoudoda (Ire) *alwys rear, p.u. 13th* ....D S Jones pu
5 ran. 12l, 5l. Time 6m 7.00s. SP 1-4.
T D Sproat (Pembrokeshire).

539 Restricted Div II (12st)

300 **TELEPHONE ....P Hamer** 1
mid-div, prog frm 11th, gd jmp 14th, ld 2 out, easily
190 **Mister McGaskill ....P Williams** 2
rear, prog frm 14th, nvr able to chal
406[4] **Saffron Moss ....Miss F Wilson** 3
trckd ldr til fdd 13th, rdn into 3rd flat
405 Flaxridge *tongue-strap, ld to aft 13th, onepcd* ....Miss E Tamplin 4
365 Teigr Pren *mstk 1st, ran green & alwys bhnd* ....P Sheldrake 5
404[4] Sister Lark 5a *prom to 12th, wknd, p.u. nxt* D S Jones pu
362[4] Trackman (Ire) *(fav) prom, ld 14th-2 out, p.u. last, lame* ....J Jukes pu
Eastwood Lad *lft, t.n.p.* ....M Lewis 0
8 ran. 6l, 10l, ½l, dist. Time 6m 12.00s. SP 2-1.
R J Hamer (Llangeinor).

540 Maiden Div I

HOLLOW SOUND (IRE) 5a ....J Jukes 1

made all, unchal frm 14th
Luciman (Ire) ....E Williams 2
(fav) mid-div to 6th, prog & cls up 14th, onepcd
186³ **Irish Thinker ....J Tudor** 3
tongue-strap, mid-div, prog aft 9th, ev ch 13th, wknd 15th
408⁴ I'm A Bute 5a *nvr nr ldrs*....................J Price 4
406 Moor Hill Lass (Ire) *prom to 9th, wknd aft* ...J Comins 5
409⁵ Heather Boy *chsd wnr to 9th, wknd, rear & p.u. 2 out* ....G Lewis pu
Quaker Pep *alwys rear, p.u. 13th*..........P Hamer pu
Its A Doddle 5a *tongue-strap, rear, p.u. 10th* P Wilson pu
184 Preseli View 5a *5th whn mstk 6th, lost reins, p.u. nxt* ....M Lewis pu
184³ Cefn Woodsman *mid-div, prog whn f 11th*. .D S Jones f
Euromill Star 5a *blnd 1st, ref 2nd* ....A Price ref
Mountain Slave 5a *mid-div, prog whn f 14th* ....T Vaughan f
Bushton 7a *alwys rear, ran green, p.u. 13th* J P Keen pu
13 ran. 15l, 8l, dist, 20l. Time 6m 7.00s. SP 7-2.
T D Sproat (Pembrokeshire).

541 Maiden Div II

367 **KRISTAL HAZE 12a....................P Williams** 1
ptntly rdn, prog 3 out, ld aft nxt, ran on
Atheston Gamble ....D S Jones 2
trckd ldr, ld 14th, wknd & hdd aft 2 out
Prince Theo ....M Lewis 3
ld 8th, ld 11-13th, fdd aft
404 All The Jolly 5a *trckd ldrs, u.r. 14th in tch* ....R Jones ur
407 Lady Romance (Ire) 5a *nvr nr ldrs, p.u. 3 out* ....J P Keen pu
Rubblee Bubblee *in tch to 10th, fdd, p.u. 12th* ....E Williams pu
Good Omen *rear, ran green, p.u. 11th* ...P Sheldrake pu
405 Hil Lady 5a *prom, ld 8-10th, ld & f 14th*.........A Price ur
Top Tor 5a *mid-div, no ch whn p.u. 15th* ...T Vaughan pu
Castlemorris (Ire) *(fav) keen hld, hld up, f 4th*. .J Jukes f
10 ran. 8l, 1l. Time 6m 20.00s. SP 20-1.
Mrs K M Dando (Pentyrch).

542 Maiden Div III

368³ **KEEP FLOWING (IRE) ....Miss P Jones** 1
(fav) ld 2nd-5th, ld frm 13th, in cmmnd aft
185⁵ **Bold Alfie ....D S Jones** 2
ld 5-12th, no imp wnr frm 14th
435 **Barafundle Bay ....Miss A Meakins** 3
tongue-strap, sttld rear, prog 12th, nvr nrr
408⁶ Tiger Lord *alwys mid-div, onepcd*............A Price 4
403 Queen's Equa 5a *mid-div, nvr a fctr*.....Miss S Major 5
368 Kerstin's Choice 5a *mstks, alwys rear* ...P Sheldrake 6
Alkarine 7a *mstk 1st, trckd ldrs, ld brfly 12th, wkng whn u.r. 14th* ....J Tudor ur
368 Grampas' Girl (Ire) 5a *mid-div, no ch whn p.u. 15th* ....J P Keen pu
367 Kits Pride 12a (bl) *ref 2nd*....................J Price ref
409 Buckland Ballad 7a *mid-div, nvr dang, p.u. 13th* ....K Cousins pu
368 Del's Delight (Ire) 5a *ld 1st, trckd ldrs to 14th, fdd, p.u. 2 out*..................................E Williams pu
405 African Warrior 12a *f 4th*.................T Vaughan f
Forest Flight (Ire) 7a *mid-div, mstk 6th, p.u. nxt* ....J Comins pu
Mistaken Identity *mstk 3rd, rear, p.u. 12th* ...P Hamer pu
Tiger Sally 5a *rear, u.r. 6th*....................M Lewis ur
15 ran. 4l, 7l, 1l, 2l, dist. Time 6m 23.00s. SP 4-5.
David Brace (Llangeinor).

543 Maiden Div IV

SHE GOES 5a ....A Price 1
prom, ld aft 2 out, ran on gamely
536 **Bobbie's Girl (Ire) 5a ....Miss J Fowler** 2
2nd outing, prog frm 10th, hrd rdn 2 out, no imp flat
183³ **Plucky Punter ....P Williams** 3
ld til aft 2 out, onepcd
365 Culpeppers Dish *nvr nrr than mid-div* .....J Price 4
Gold Tip 5a *trckd ldrs to 12th, wknd, p.u. 2 out* ....Miss R Williams pu

400 Laudation (Ire) 7a *trckd ldr to 9th, fdd, p.u. 12th* ....P Hamer pu
Lynnes Daniella (Ire) 5a *alwys rear, p.u. 6th* ..M Lewis pu
Out On The Town 5a *rear, p.u. 12th*..........J Tudor pu
437 Nikitasecondchance 5a *alwys rear, p.u. 12th* ....D S Jones pu
186 Welsh Treasure (Ire) 12a *(fav) cls up, mstk 10th, p.u. 12th* ....E Williams pu
Flockmaster (Ire) *u.r. 6th in mid-div*..........J P Keen ur
11 ran. ½l, 3l, dist. Time 6m 22.00s. SP 8-1.
William John Day (Gelligaer Farmers).
P.D.

COTTESMORE
Garthorpe
Sunday March 16th
GOOD TO FIRM

544 Members (12st)

251¹ **WISE WIZARD 10ex ....Miss K Gilman** 1
(fav) prom, lft in ld 9th, hdd 3 out, ld appr last, ran on wll
480⁷ **Busking Along (Ire) ....H Nicholson** 2
prom,lft 2nd 9th,disp ld 13th til ld 3 out,hdd & one-pcd last
477 **White Bullet (USA) ....Miss C Tarratt** 3
hld up bhnd, lft poor 3rd 9th, nvr plcd to chall
345 Rapid Regent *ld to 3rd, prom til u.r. 9th* ....R Morney ur
473⁴ Mysterious Run (Ire) *ld 3rd til u.r. 9th* ....Miss S Samworth ur
Skylark Song 5a *s.s. last whn u.r. 2nd* Miss J Holmes 0
6 ran. 1½l, dist. Time 6m 21.00s. SP 4-6.
Mrs F E Gilman (Cottesmore).

545 Confined (12st)

350⁴ **ROMANY ARK ....N Bell** 1
hld up,stdy prog 11th, chall last, ran on to ld cls hme
Miller's Chap ....M Hewitt 2
chsd ldrs 7th, wnt 2nd 12th,ld 2 out til hdd & no ex cls hme
248³ **Okeetee ....Miss L Allan** 3
alwys prom, 4th & ch appr 2 out, onepcd aft
377⁶ Dark Rhytham *(fav) ld til 2 out, wkd und press appr last*....................S Morris 4
351⁴ Alpha One *chsd ldrs til outpcd 13th, no ch frm 3 out* ....P Gee 5
214 Antrim County *chsd ldr 3-12th, wkng whn hit 15th, sn no ch*....................J Cornwall 6
473⁶ Valatch (bl) *nt fluent, alwys bhnd, no ch frm 11th* ....J Henderson 7
250⁴ Golden Moss 5ex *alwys bhnd, no ch frm 11th* ....Maj S Robinson 8
Hostetler 4ow *in tch to 6th, sn bhnd, no ch frm 11th* ....J Stephenson 9
383⁷ Bervie House (Ire) (bl) *mid div til blnd & u.r. 6th* ....R Ford ur
475⁵ Tale Of Endurance (Ire) *chsd ldrs, wnt 2nd aft 15th til nxt, 5th & btn whn f last* ....Miss F Hatfield f
446 Menature (Ire) *bhnd, brf eff 11th, t.o. & p.u. 2 out* ....A Sansome pu
12 ran. 1½l, 3l, 1½l, 20l, 2l, 15l, 3l, 10l. Time 6m 14.00s. SP 8-1.
Mrs A Bell (Belvoir).

546 Ladies

449⁵ **SUPREME DREAM (IRE) 5a ....Mrs P Adams** 1
in tch, chsd ldr 12th to 3 out, rallied appr last,ld cls hme
330 **Spy's Delight ....Mrs F Needham** 2
w.w prog 10th, ld 2 out til hdded & no ex cls hme
426⁶ **Man Of Mystery ....Miss C Tarratt** 3
ld to 2 out, onepcd aft
Knight's Spur (USA) *mid div, prog 11th, outpcd 15th, 4th & no ch frm 3 out* ....Mrs J Parris 4
379⁵ Green Archer *(fav) sn bhnd, j.s. 3rd, sn rddn, poor 8th 15th, styd on, nvr nrr* ....Mrs T Hill 5

474[5] Killimor Lad *chsd ldrs til ran wde appr 12th, grad lot tch*............Miss S Samworth 6
Shouldofdone *prog to chs ldr 7th til appr 12th, sn wknd*............Mrs V Lloyd-Davies 7
473 Scole *chsd ldrs to 4th, grad lst pl, no ch frm 12th*............Miss A Hinch 8
329[5] The Boiler White (Ire) *alwys wll bhnd, t.o. frm 10th*............Miss J Froggatt 9
Smart Rhythm 5a *alwys rr div, t.o frm 10th*............Miss C Arthers 10
448[4] Rousillon To Be (bl) *chsd ldrs til wknd qkly appr 3 out, t.o. & p.u. last*............Miss L Rowe pu
11 ran. 2½l, 3l, 10l, 8l, 6l, 20l, 1l, 20l, 1l. Time 6m 14.00s. SP 10-1.
Mrs Pauline Adams (Pytchley).

547 Land Rover Men's Open (12st)

287[7] **COOLVAWN LADY (IRE) 5a 4ex.........S Walker** 1
disp 2nd plc til apr 3 out,rdn to ld appr last, ran on wll
381[4] **Beau Dandy 7ex........................T Marks** 2
(fav) disp 2nd pl til chsd ldr aft 15th,ld nxt,hdd appr last,no ex
370[2] **My Best Man ....A Hill** 3
prom, hit 7th, sn drvn alng, lost tch wth ldrs 12th, t.o.
370[3] Going Around 7ex *in tch til outpcd 12th, no ch frm nxt*............L Lay 4
349 Adamare 7ex *ld til 3 out, rdn & ev ch whn f nxt*............R Armson f
138[5] Faithful Star 7ex *in tch til 6th & outpcd 12th, t.o. whn u.r. 3 out*............R Hunnisett ur
248[9] Ginger Pink *last frm 8th t.o. & p.u 15th*............Maj S Robinson pu
7 ran. 7l, dist, sht-hd. Time 6m 13.00s. SP 5-1.
W R Halliday (Cranwell Bloodhounds).

548 Restricted

452[1] **STORMING ROY ....H Nicholson** 1
(Jt fav) ld 4th, made most aft, blnd & hdded 3 out, ld last, styd on
449[2] **Fresh Ice (Ire) ....T Lane** 2
(Jt fav) cls up, ld gng wll 3 out, hdd last, nt qckn flat
372[6] **Brown Baby 5a...........................G Kerr** 3
chsd ldrs, 3rd & ev ch 2 out, wknd last
477[5] Mr Gee *in tch, 5th, & rddn 12th, outpcd frm 15th*............K Needham 4
348 Sargeants Choice *chsd ldrs, cls 4th 12th, outpcd frm 14th*............J Barlow 5
372[3] Needwood Neptune *mid div, 6th whn mstk 11th, no ch frm nxt*............A Sansome 6
347[1] Mamnoon (USA) *hld up, nvr nr ldrs, no ch frm 13th*............N Kent 7
384 Solar Gem (bl) *ld til ran wde & hdded appr 4th, cls up til f 9th*............J Mason f
Kerry My Home *rr, last & rddn 10th, no resp, t.o. & p.u. aft 15th*............T Marks pu
480 Rhyming Moppet 5a *sn bhnd, t.o. & p.u. 9th*............W Tellwright pu
10 ran. ½l, 5l, 15l, 8l, 5l, 10l. Time 6m 15.00s. SP 9-4.
J G Nicholson (Woodland Pytchley).
After stewards enquiry. Result stands.

549 Open Maiden Div I (12st)

276 **MY SHOUT 7a...........................S Morris** 1
(fav) w.w prog 13th, lft 4th 3 out, ev ch nxt, ld flat, clvly
372 **Full Song 5a..........................R Thornton** 2
prom, lft in ld 3 out, rddn nxt, hdded & unable to qckn flat
374[7] **Upton Lass (Ire) 5a ....L Lay** 3
prom, lft 2nd 8th, ev ch appr 3 out, wknd appr 2 out
224 Gibraltar Queen 12a *in tch til 12th, lft poor 5th 3 out, kpt on*............C Wadland 4
205 Ring Bank *ld to 4th,lft in ld 8th til aft 15th,ld agn brfly nxt,sn wkd*............N Gittins 5
211 Ms Taaffe 5a *nvr nr ldrs, no ch frm 12th*............Mrs M Bellamy 6
479 Cruiser Too *alwys bhnd, t.o. frm 11th*......M Barnard 7
345 Isola Farnese 5a *jmpd poorly, ld 4th, clr whn u.r. 8th*............N Kent ur
478 Shining Penny (bl) *swrd start, prog to mid div whn blnd & u.r. 7th*............M Bond ur
Star Traveller *t.o. frm 5th til p.u. 3 out*......M Skinner pu
479 Kabancy *pulling, rr, prog to mid div whn hmpd & u.r. 8th*............P Millington ur
374[4] Royal Dadda *chsd ldrs, 3rd & rddn 11th, wknd nxt, hit 14th, p.u. 3 out*............A Hill pu
Ri Ra 5a *alwys rr, t.o. & p.u 3 out*.....Miss S Sharratt pu
141 Greenhil Patchwork *mstks, bhnd frm 5th, t.o. & p.u. 3 out*............R Armson pu
324 Nanda Devi *chsd ldrs til wknd 11th, t.o. & p.u. 3 out*............C Ward pu
480 Aaron's Venture *mid div, prog to ld aft 15th, p.u. appr nxt, lame*............T Lane pu
16 ran. ¾l, 15l, sht-hd, 5l, 10l, 8l. Time 6m 25.00s. SP 3-1.
G T H Bailey & Mrs T Hill (Pytchley).

550 Open Maiden Div II (12st)

372 **MISTER KINGSTON ....B Pollock** 1
ld/disp to 11th,ld appr 3 out, rddn & styd on wll frm 2 out
373[4] **Rivers End (Ire) ....A Hill** 2
in tch, prog 9th, ev ch 3 out, no ex und press frm nxt
260 **Gidgegannup ....J Baimbridge** 3
in tch to 12th, poor 4th 3 out, ran on wll, nt rch ldrs
Grange Missile 5a *chsd ldrs 7th, ld 11th, clr 13th, hdded appr 3 out, wknd*............J Dillon 4
373 Old Father Time *disp ld to 4th, 4th & outpcd 15th, kpt on frm 2 out*............L Lay 5
Cantango (Ire) *(fav) mstks, in tch to 12th, sn strugg, no ch frm 14th*............A Sansome 6
332 River Sunset (Ire) *disp ld 4-11th, wknd appr 13th*............S Prior 7
345[4] Paddy's Pocket *mid div, hit 5th, 4th & hit 14th, wknd, p.u. 2 out*............R Armson pu
253[4] Art's Echo (Ire) *last frm 8th til ran out 12th*............S J Robinson ro
452 Towngate *rr, lost tch 12th, t.o. & p.u. 14th*.....T Lane pu
Stanwick Buckfast *rr, lsing tch whn p.u. appr 12th*............T Marks pu
11 ran. 7l, 3l, 8l, 6l, ½l, 3l. Time 6m 22.00s. SP 9-2.
Mrs S Gee (Pytchley).
S.P.

DART VALE & HALDON HARRIERS
Ottery St Mary
Sunday March 16th
GOOD

551 Members

311 **DEPARTURE 5a.........................J Creighton** 1
made all, blnd 3rd, ran on wll whn chal 3 out
Perfect Stranger ....G Penfold 2
chsd wnr, chal 4 out-nxt, no imp aft
237[4] **Moze Tidy ....I Dowrick** 3
(fav) trckd ldr, chal 4 out, wknd nxt, outpcd
99[3] Playpen *in tch til stmbld & u.r. bend aft 14th*............Miss S Crook ur
4 ran. 6l, 8l. Time 6m 24.50s. SP 5-2.
Mrs J M Whitley (Dart Vale & Haldon Harriers).

552 Men's Open

239[2] **THE GENERAL'S DRUM ....K Heard** 1
(fav) hld up, prog 10th, disp 14th-nxt, ld 16th, styd on well
179[2] **The Lorryman (Ire) ....N Mitchell** 2
ld 3rd-13th, disp aft til hdd 4 out, onepcd aft
239[5] **Hidden Dollar ....G Penfold** 3
trckd ldr to 14th, rdn 4 out, no respns
308[2] Pintail Bay (v) *chsd ldrs, outpcd frm 4 out*......N Legg 4
179 Derring Valley *ld to 3rd, in tch aft, wknd 14th, t.o. & p.u. 2 out*............S Bush pu
Bargain And Sale *in tch to 7th, wknd, p.u. 10th*............I Dowrick pu
6 ran. 5l, 12l, 3l. Time 6m 12.00s. SP 4-7.

Mrs R Fell (Dartmoor).

553 Maiden (12st)

172² **ITALIAN MAN (IRE)** ....**G Penfold** 1
made all, kpt on wll frm 4 out
Damiens Pride (Ire) ....**A Farrant** 2
handy, 3rd at 13th, chsd alng 4 out, styd on well
453⁶ **Pilgrim's Mission (Ire)** ....**D Doyne-Ditmas** 3
mid-div, prog 10th, in tch til wknd 3 out
Drumbanes Pet *alwys mid-div, lost tch 13th, outpcd aft*..........T Greed 4
244³ Trolly *alwys rear, wll bhnd frm 14th*.........J Tizzard 5
Indian Language *bhnd, outpcd & no ch frm 13th*..........Miss L Blackford 6
237 Bridge House Boy *sn bhnd, t.o. 14th*..........A Oliver 7
242 Cheque Book *bhnd, t.o. & p.u. 10th*...........T Cole pu
244 Dance Fever (Ire) *mid-div, lost tch 14th, t.o. & p.u. last*..........R Woolacott pu
172 Mrs Somebody 5a *sn last, t.o. & ref 7th* A Holdsworth ref
54⁵ Jolly Sensible 5a *rear til f 7th*............J Creighton f
172³ Legal Affair 5a *handy, 2nd at 13th, chsd alng 4 out, 2l down whn f nxt*..........N Harris f
Creedy Valley *mid-div, lost tch 12th, p.u. 14th* K Heard pu
459 Brother Nero (NZ) 7a *(fav) 4s-2s, in tch, 3rd & going wll whn f 13th*..........L Jefford f
172 Country Madam 5a *mid-div, outpcd & p.u. 12th*..........R Treloggen pu

15 ran. 7l, 10l, 25l, 2l, 8l, 20l. Time 6m 15.00s. SP 4-1.
G W Penfold (Silverton).

554 Confined

530² **FEARSOME** ....**G Penfold** 1
(Jt fav) in tch, ld 4 out, sn clr
313¹ **Parditino** ....**Miss V Nicholas** 2
mstks, prom til lost plc 14th, rallied 3 out, no imp aft
Parson's Way (bl) ....**A Farrant** 3
(Jt fav) ld to 4 out, onepcd frm nxt
455 Pharaoh Blue (bl) *in tch to 7th, t.o. 13th*.....M Shears 4
Battling Psyche 5a *sn rear, t.o. frm 10th*.......T Cole 5
Faux Pavillon *handy to 13th, wknd nxt & p.u.*..........Miss P Curling pu
Master Decoy *mid-div whn f 4th*............L Jefford f

7 ran. 20l, 5l, dist, 25l. Time 6m 16.00s. SP 7-4.
G W Penfold (Silverton).

555 Ladies

377⁴ **ARCTIC CHILL (IRE)** ....**Miss S Vickery** 1
ld to 7th, 2nd aft, ld agn 4 out, ran on well
292 **Desert Waltz (Ire)** ....**Miss P Curling** 2
(fav) prom, ld 7th-4 out, no ext und pres frm 2 out
311² **Searcy** ....**Miss L Blackford** 3
chsd ldrs, no ch frm 4 out
397¹ Richville *1st ride, alwys mid-div, no ch frm 13th*..........Miss I Dartnell 4
394² Reef Lark *alwys rear, nvr any ch*....Miss A Goschen 5
311³ Jimmy Cone *prom early, lost tch 12th, bhnd frm 4 out*..........Miss J Cumings 6
454 Station Express (Ire) *prom to 12th, lsng tch whn f 15th*..........Miss V Stephens f
Double The Stakes (USA) *mid-div whn u.r. 4th*..........Miss S Gaisford ur
454⁴ Karlimay 5a *rear, t.o. & p.u. 14th*......Miss V Nicholls pu
311 Hod Wood 5a *sn last, jmpd lswly, p.u. 5th*..........Miss R David pu

10 ran. 2l, dist, 12l, 5l, 4l. Time 6m 5.00s. SP 2-1.
M F Thorne (Blackmore & Sparkford Vale).

556 Interlink Restricted Div I (12st)

175⁴ **CHURCHTOWN CHANCE (IRE) 5a** ......**L Jefford** 1
(fav) 3s-6/4, pllng, handy, disp 4 out, lft in ld nxt, easily
457³ **Indian Rabi** ....**G Penfold** 2
mid-div, prog 15th, outpcd 3 out, not trbl wnr aft
299 **The Bold Abbot** ....**Miss S West** 3
mid-div, lft 3rd 3 out, nvr bttr
O So Bossy *hld up, prog 12th, chnce 14th, wknd aft 4 out, gd effrt*..........A Holdsworth 4
313 Redclyffe (USA) *cls up to 13th, wknd nxt, p.u. 4 out*..........B Dixon pu
170⁵ Dharamshala (Ire) *rear & no ch til p.u. 13th*...R Darke pu
Nottarex *prom early, lost tch 10th, t.o. & p.u. 3 out*..........B Wright pu
456 Snitton Stream *ld to 14th, wknd rpdly nxt, p.u. 3 out*..........I Dowrick pu
313² Mosside *alwys mid-div, p.u. 13th*...........N Harris pu
241 Swing To The Left (Ire) 5a *in tch, ld 14th, disp 4 out til f 3 out*..........Miss J Cumings f
Race Against Time 5a *n.j.w. mid-div, lost plc 10th, p.u. nxt*..........Miss A Goschen pu
Kenstown (Ire) *ran out 1st*..........C Heard ro

12 ran. 20l, 4l, 20l. Time 6m 15.00s. SP 6-4.
Paul B Jordain (Western & Banwell).

557 Interlink Restricted Div II (12st)

106⁴ **ELLE FLAVADOR 5a** ....**Miss S Vickery** 1
handy, 2nd at 13th, disp 4 out til lft in ld last
312² **Mendip Son** ....**L Jefford** 2
hd up in tch, effrt 3 out, onpcd frm nxt, lft 2nd last
312⁵ **Darktown Strutter (bl)** ....**J Auvray** 3
ld/disp to 7th, wknd nxt, outpcd aft
456 Jet Jockey *n.j.w. plld hrd in rear, mstk 11th, p.u. nxt*..........G Penfold pu
237 Roving Rebel *mid-div til p.u. 12th*......A Holdsworth pu
Blue Night 5a *pllng, ld 8th-15th, cls up aft, ev ch whn u.r. 2 out*..........J Scott ur
240 My Man On Dundrum (Ire) *(fav) alwys prom, disp 4 out til hit last & u.r.*..........Miss P Curling ur
525 Grey Jerry *sn rear, t.o. & p.u. 14th*.......B O'Doherty pu
Master Laughter *schoold mid-div til p.u. 12th* N Harris pu

9 ran. 2l, dist. Time 6m 32.00s. SP 3-1.
Mrs A B Watts (Blackmore & Sparkford Vale).

558 Intermediate (12st)

453² **TICKET TO THE MOON 5a** ....**A Farrant** 1
(fav) hld up, chal & ld 3 out, styd on well
293³ **Southern Flight 5ex**.............**Miss J Cumings** 2
prom, disp 4 out-nxt, ev ch 2 out, outpcd
310¹ **Avril Showers 5a 5ex** ....**R Atkinson** 3
ld til slw jmp 3 out, rallied aft nxt, not qckn
456 Karicleigh Boy *sn bhnd, no ch frm 14th* A Holdsworth 4
236⁵ Balmoral Boy (NZ) *in tch til stmbld & u.r. bend aft 7th*..........M Miller ur
Henrys No Pushover *handy til wknd 9th, p.u. aft nxt*..........L Jefford pu

6 ran. 2l, 1½l, 25l. Time 6m 12.00s. SP 7-4.
Mrs Janita Scott (South Devon).
D.P.

EGLINTON
Lanark
Sunday March 16th
GOOD TO SOFT

559 Members

415² **BITOFANATTER** ....**R Morgan** 1
(fav) ld frm 11th, sn clr, fin alone
New Problem 5a *ld brfly 7th, lost tch 11th, p.u. aft nxt*..........M Smith pu
411 Patter Merchant *not fluent, made most to 11th, lost tch & p.u. aft 14th*..........P Hall pu

3 ran. Time 6m 59.00s. SP 1-5.
David Caldwell (Eglinton).

560 Confined (12st)

411² **SIMON JOSEPH** ....**R Morgan** 1
2nd hlfwy, 3rd & lkd held 3 out, kpt on to ld flat
230¹ **Nova Nita 5a**.............................**P Craggs** 2
(fav) 3rd hlfwy,wnt 2nd 14th,mstk 3 out,kpt on und 10der handling
413⁴ **Benghazi (bl)**..............................**A Parker** 3
not fluent, clr ld til wknd & jmp slwly last, hdd flat
335³ Toaster Crumpet 3ex *4th hlfwy, nvr rchd ldrs*..........Miss P Robson 4

Bruce's Castle *sn t.o.*..................Miss K Durie 5
Yenoora (Ire) (bl) *lost tch by 9th, p.u. aft nxt* ...J Ewart pu
233[1] Wang How *5th hlfwy, bhnd whn p.u. 2 out* ..A Robson pu
229 Tony's Feelings 7ex *sn bhnd, p.u. aft 11th* ......D Reid pu
8 ran. 1l, 1l, 15l, dist. Time 6m 47.00s. SP 4-1.
Mrs Yda Morgan (Dumfriesshire).

561 Ladies

412[2] **ROLY PRIOR ....Mrs V Jackson 1**
(fav) not fluent, wnt 2nd 9th, disp frm 12th, drew clr 3 out
412[4] **Very Evident (Ire) ....Miss J Bird 2**
bhnd til wnt 3rd 11th, mstk 14th, kpt on, no ch wth wnnr
414[2] **Press For Action ....Miss P Robson 3**
made most til wknd qckly apr 3 out
412 Running Frau 5a *sn bhnd, kpt on frm 4 out, not rch ldrs* ....Miss M Maher 4
289[6] Little General *4th 10th, nvr rchd ldrs* ...Mrs M Kendall 5
Winnie Lorraine 5a *bhnd by 11th, t.o.* ....Miss T Hammond 6
Matrace 5a *3rd 10th, sn wknd, p.u. 13th* ....Miss D Laidlaw pu
7 ran. 25l, 10l, 1l, 5l, dist. Time 6m 42.00s. SP 6-4.
Ian Hamilton (Tynedale).

562 Men's Open

289[3] **HOWAYMAN ....A Parker 1**
(fav) in tch, ld aft 4 out, sn clr, pshd out flat
Todcrag ....T Scott 2
ld 9th-12th, cls up whn mstk 4 out, kpt on & no ch aft
411[5] **Boreen Owen ....T Morrison 3**
ld 12th-4 out, outpcd frm nxt
353[1] Eastern Pleasure *alwys hndy, ch apr 3 out, wknd qckly*..............................A Ogden 4
265 Sharpridge *bhnd whn p.u. aft 8th* ......M Mawhinney pu
Cool It A Bit *disp ld frm 6th til u.r. 8th*.......W Clark ur
413 Miss Jedd 5a *bhnd by 11th, t.o. whn p.u. 2 out* ....P Craggs pu
334 Strong Measure (Ire) *made most til 9th, bhnd by 11th, p.u. 2 out*..............................R Morgan pu
8 ran. 5l, 10l, 25l. Time 6m 51.00s. SP 4-6.
Dennis Waggott (Dumfriesshire).

563 Interlink Restricted (12st)

413[2] **GALLANTS DELIGHT 5a ....A Robson 1**
(fav) alwys in tch, ld 3 out, comf
32[2] **Cukeira 5a ....C Paisley 2**
bhnd til gd hdwy frm 4 out, no imp on wnnr
356 **Will Travel (Ire) ....A Ogden 3**
alwys hndy, kpt on wll frm 3 out
410[1] Marked Card *last 11th, nvr near ldrs* ..Mrs M Kendall 4
419[1] Bushmiller (Ire) *made most til wknd qckly 3 out* ....A Parker 5
331[5] Mighty Haggis *losng tch whn f 13th*......Mrs C Ford f
415 Charlie Trumper (Ire) (bl) *ld brfly 9th, lost tch by 4 out, p.u. 3 out*..............................J Saville pu
230 Sumpt'n Smart *ld brfly 5th, t.o. whn p.u. 2 out* ....R Morgan pu
8 ran. 3l, 1l, 20l, dist. Time 6m 53.00s. SP 4-6.
Mrs C Johnston (Cumberland Farmers).

564 2½m Open Maiden (12st)

419 **DON CARLOS 7a.......................P Craggs 1**
2nd mstly til ld 3 out, sn clr, easily
Shine A Light ....A Ogden 2
ld frm 5th, mstk 4 out, hdd nxt, no ext
115[2] **Cookie Boy ....Miss H Delahooke 3**
same plc virtly thruout, no ch frm 4 out
135[5] Ovahandy Man *(fav) not fluent, 4th frm hlfwy, nvr threaten 1st 2*..............................P Johnson 4
418 Rakeira 12a *nvr nr ldrs*..............................C Paisley 5
418 Kinlochaline 5a *prom til wknd frm 10th*...........J Ewart 6
Turn Of Foot (Ire) *alwys t.o.*..............M Bradburne 7
160[4] Normans Profit *nvr nr ldrs, p.u. 3 out*..........T Scott pu
Houselope Brook 5a *not fluent, bhnd whn p.u. 2 out* ....A Robson pu
160 Dakeem 12a *sn bhnd, t.o. whn p.u. 2 out*......B Gibson pu
340 Hetty Bell 12a *strgglng whn f 8th*....Mrs K Hargreave f
417 Steady Man *ld til 5th, sn wknd, p.u. 3 out* ..D McLeod pu
386 Molly Grey (Ire) 5a *sn bhnd, p.u. 2 out*..........R Hale pu
13 ran. 20l, 15l, 3l, 25l, dist, 20l. Time 5m 59.00s. SP 10-1.
J T H Ainslie (Dumfriesshire).

565 Open Maiden Div I

343 **RIDING HILLS GIRL 5a ....D Wood 1**
3rd hlfwy, disp 2 out, slght ld last, just hld on
343[3] **Tolmin ....A Parker 2**
alwys hndy, ld 12th, jnd 2 out, hdd last, rlld nr line
343[6] **Indian River (Ire) ....J Walton 3**
bhnd early, stdy hdwy frm 11th, not rch ldng pair
162[7] Connor The Second *some hdwy frm 12th, not rch ldrs* ....L Morgan 4
Black And Blues *ld til 12th, wknd frm 4 out*....S Scott 5
Farm Track 5a *sn bhnd, p.u. 11th* ......Miss P Robson pu
Good Profit *t.o. by 9th, p.u. bfr nxt* ....T Scott pu
334[3] Dillons Bridge (Ire) *(fav) 2nd whn u.r. 5th* ...R Morgan ur
340 Lethem Laird *nvr rch ldrs, p.u. 3 out*..........R Shiels pu
341[4] Political Belle 5a *prom to 10th, strgglng whn p.u. 12th* ....P Craggs pu
10 ran. Sht-hd, ¾l, 8l, 12l. Time 7m 11.00s. SP 14-1.
Mrs D McCormack (Braes Of Derwent).

566 Open Maiden Div II

415[7] **THINKABOUTTHAT (IRE) ....J Muir 1**
alwys ldng trio, ld apr 2 out, drew clr flat
419 **Primitive Streak ....P Johnson 2**
(fav) alwys hndy, chal 2 out, no ext flat
419 **Mr Cosmo (Ire) ....J Billinge 3**
ld til apr 2 out, no ext
Madame Beck 5a *kpt on stdly frm 14th, nvr rchd ldrs* ....M Smith 4
411 Mighty Express *bhnd by 11th, kpt on without threatng ldrs*..............................A Ogden 5
233[2] Donside *4th 10th, sn wknd, p.u. bfr last*.......A Robson pu
414 Carol's Concorde (Ire) (bl) *sn drvn alng in rear, p.u. 4 out*..............................J Saville pu
234 Flower Of Dunblane 5a *u.r. 2nd*..............R Hale ur
Copper Dial *u.r. 5th*..............................T Morrison ur
235 Fragrant Lord *bhnd by 11th, p.u. bfr last* ....Mrs V Jackson pu
10 ran. 5l, 10l, 10l, 5l. Time 7m 3.00s. SP 7-1.
James Muir (Buccleuch).
R.J.

ROSS HARRIERS
Garnons
Sunday March 16th
GOOD

567 Members

260 **LAYSTON D'OR ....A Dalton 1**
(fav) w.w. tk clsr ordr 12th, ld 15th, clr 2 out, eased flat
285 **Noisy Welcome ....M P Jones 2**
ld til mstk & hdd 15th, kpt on onepcd aft
433 **Orwell Ross (Ire) ....J Cornes 3**
chsd ldr til outpcd 9th, t.o.
3 ran. 4l, dist. Time 6m 40.00s. SP 2-7.
J W Russell (Ross Harriers).

568 Confined (12st)

360[1] **FROZEN PIPE 5a 3ex...................M Harris 1**
trckd ldrs, chal 2 out, ld last, pshd out flat
363[3] **Landsker Alfred 6ex ....Miss A Dare 2**
(fav) cls up, rdn 2 out, ev ch last, no ext und pres
Crown Jewel ....C Wilson 3
cls 2nd til ld 15th, jnd 2 out, no ext flat
362[1] Dalametre 5ex *ld to 14th, ev ch 2 out, onepcd und pres*..............................M Munrowd 4
Erlemo *alwys rear, last at 9th, styd on onepcd frm 14th*..............................Dr P Pritchard 5

407[1] Stormhill Recruit *chsd ldrs, rdn & outpcd frm 14th* ....M P Jones 6
402 Sebastopol *rear til some prog 12th, no ch frm 15th, t.o.* ....D Stephens 7
364[4] Shadow Walker *mid-div til lost tch 13th, no ch whn p.u. last* ....T Stephenson pu
Morgantwo *ld 1st, cls up til outpcd 9th, t.o. & p.u. last* ....Miss E James pu
Sonny's Song *alwys rear, lost tch 12th, p.u. 15th* ....L Brown pu
431 Gold'n Shroud (Ire) *15l 5th at 12th, lost tch 14th, remote 7th whn u.r. 2 out* ....N Oliver ur
366 Millstock 5a *lft 15l, prog to mid-div 8th, lost tch 13th, p.u. 2 out* ....G Barfoot-Saunt pu
12 ran. ¾l, 5l, 6l, 10l, 6l, dist. Time 6m 28.00s. SP 3-1.
Alan P Brewer (North Ledbury).

569 Men's Open (12st)

328[1] **RIVERSIDE BOY ....A Crow 1**
(fav) ld til 15th, styd on, forged clr flat
191[2] **Archer (Ire) 7ex ....M Harris 2**
chsd ldr,rdn to chal 14th,ld til aft last,stppd flat,cont
380[4] **Garrylucas ....G Hanmer 3**
cls up til outpcd by 1st pair frm 13th, nrly sntchd 2nd
Shareef Star *last frm 7th, completed own time* ....C Yates 4
364[3] Sandy Beau *bhnd til prog 8th, 30l 4th at 12th, t.o. & p.u. 3 out* ....D Duggan pu
399 Project's Mate 7ex *cls up to 6th, wknd 9th, t.o. & p.u. 3 out* ....C Richards pu
The Reprobate (Ire) *wth ldrs to 7th, wknd & p.u. aft 11th* ....E Walker pu
7 ran. Dist, 1l, 2 fences. Time 6m 33.00s. SP 1-2.
Miss M E Sherrington (North Staffordshire).

570 2½m Maiden Div I

MY WEE MAN (IRE) ....G Barfoot-Saunt 1
mid-div, prog to 2nd 14th, ld last, sn clr
365[4] **Lakeside Lad 7a ....A Dalton 2**
prog 9th, rdn & chnc 3 out, no ext frm nxt
259 **Wolfie Smith ....Julian Pritchard 3**
(fav) prom in chsng grp, not qckn 3 out, kpt on flat
Playing The Fool 5a *ld 6th, clr frm 10th, wknd & hdd 2 out, fin tired* ....P Hanly 4
222 Miss Dior 5a *ld 4th-5th, chsd clr ldr til wknd grad 14th* ....Miss P Gundry 5
261 Greenhills Ruby 5a *alwys mid-div, kpt on steadily frm 14th* ....R Burton 6
299 Is She Quick 5a *mid-div to 5th, drppd rear, t.o. & p.u. 12th* ....M Flynn pu
Henrietta Boo Boo 5a *nvr nr ldrs, wll btn whn p.u. last* ....A Phillips pu
359[3] Oats For Notes 5a *mid-div, effrt 11th, gd prog nxt, wknd & p.u. 2 out* ....M Rimell pu
408 Tot Of Rum 5a *last frm 5th, p.u. 7th* ....S Lloyd pu
365 Philelwyn (Ire) 5a *nvr rchd ldrs, runnng on in 6th whn u.r. 12th* ....Miss E James ur
263 Slim Chance 5a *t.o. 5th, p.u. 10th* ....M Munrowd pu
368 Maiden's Quest 12a *alwys rear, lost tch & p.u. aft 10th* ....S Joynes pu
Pick-N-Cruise 12a *alwys rear, no ch frm 10th, p.u. 3 out* ....M Hammond pu
14 ran. 15l, ½l, 8l, 12l, 6l. Time 5m 38.00s. SP 20-1.
G Barfoot-Saunt (Ledbury).

571 2½m Maiden Div II

SAMULE ....Miss P Gundry 1
(fav) chsd ldrs, prog 11th, ld 3 out, kpt on und pres
365[3] **Lindalighter 5a ....T Stephenson 2**
chsd ldrs, rdn 3 out, styd on flat, just hld
A Few Dollars More (Ire) ....D Duggan 3
ld to 3 out, kpt on onepcd
Native Isle (Ire) 7a *alwys rear, no ch 11th, kpt on frm 3 out* ....A Phillips 4
366[4] Vision Of Light 5a *trckd ldrs til outpcd frm 12th* ....M Munrowd 5
263 Spirit Prince 7a *cls up frm 8th, ev ch 11th, wknd frm nxt* ....P Hanly 6
436 Calder's Grove *prom til outpcd 9th, no ch whn p.u. 2 out* ....M Harris pu
366[5] Warm Relation (Ire) *prog 11th, ev ch 3 out, wkng whn f nxt* ....T Cox f
Daisy's Pal 5a *rear frm 5th, in tch til wknd & p.u. 2 out* ....Julian Pritchard pu
437 All Things Nice 5a *prog 8th, wll in tch whn u.r. 11th* ....S Joynes ur
King Paddy (Ire) 7a *rear frm 6th, t.o. & p.u. aft 10th* ....C Richards pu
365 Tedstone Fox 7a *rear whn blnd & u.r. 5th* ....N Oliver ur
A Bit Of Fluff 12a *mid-div whn f 8th* ....M P Jones f
13 ran. Nk, 10l, 8l, 10l, 5l. Time 5m 31.00s. SP 3-1.
Mrs M Harding (Berkeley).

572 Intermediate (12st)

292[1] **WARRIOR BARD (IRE) ....M Portman 1**
(fav) prog 8th, cls up til ld 3 out, drew clr flat
464 **Forest Fountain (Ire) ....A Dalton 2**
hld up til prog 8th, rdn to chal 15th, kpt on und pres
399[1] **Judy Line 5a ....S Shinton 3**
alwys chsng ldrs, not qckn 15th, styd on wll 2 out
Gromit (NZ) *mid-div, effrt 14th, kpt on onepcd frm nxt* ....Julian Pritchard 4
434[4] Sterling Buck (USA) *mid-div, effrt apr 14th, no prog frm nxt* ....D Duggan 5
Durzi *s.s. rdn into mid-div 7th, wknd & p.u. 10th* ....E Walker pu
294 Scriven Boy *lost tch 8th, t.o. & p.u. 11th* ....M Flynn pu
464 Achieved Ambition (Ire) *mstk in rear 6th, 11th whn u.r. 8th* ....A Jordan ur
Sister Emu 5a *prom to 8th, wknd frm 12th, p.u. 2 out* ....P McAllister pu
200[3] Pin Up Boy *cls 3rd whn u.r. 2nd* ....A Crow ur
Charliesmedarlin *ld to 8th, ld 14th til hdd & f 2 out* ....R Burton f
Canny Curate (Ire) *prom to 7th, lost plc & p.u. aft 14th, lame* ....C Barlow pu
403 Merger Mania 7a *prom, ld 9th-13th, mstk & wknd nxt, p.u. 3 out* ....R Evans pu
13 ran. 7l, 2l, 25l, 12l. Time 6m 28.00s. SP 5-2.
Mrs Robert Puddick (Beaufort).

573 Ladies

361[1] **DI STEFANO ....Miss A Dare 1**
(fav) w.w. prog 10th, chal 13th, ld nxt, clr 2 out
Derring Bud ....Miss E James 2
went 3rd 8th, ld 10-12th, outpcd til styd on agn 3 out
Andros Gale (Ire) ....Mrs A Rucker 3
lost 30l strt, prog 12th, styd on to win race for 3rd
304 Thamesdown Tootsie 5a *cls up frm 10th, chal 13th, not qckn frm 3 out* ....Miss V Lyon 4
371 Walkonthemoon 5a *prom in chsng grp, wknd 10th, t.o. & p.u. 14th* ....Miss N McKim pu
433 Outcrop 5a *ld 1st, cls 2nd whn f 3rd* ....Miss A Sykes f
361 Peter Pointer *ld 2nd, set fast pace til ct 10th, wknd & p.u. 3 out* ....Miss E Crawford pu
361 Opals Son *cls 3rd at 5th, wknd & p.u. 10th* ....Miss L Wallace pu
8 ran. 12l, 6l, hd. Time 6m 29.00s. SP 2-7.
Mrs R Onions (Cotswold Vale Farmers).
One fence omitted last two circuits, 16 jumps.

574 Restricted Div I (12st)

467[3] **KILLATTY PLAYER (IRE) 5a ....P McAllister 1**
alwys cls up, rdn to chs ldr 15th, styd on to ld flat
Western Harmony ....Julian Pritchard 2
ld, 3l up 14th, hdd & no ext flat
467 **Real Gent ....R Burton 3**
prom, chsd ldr 13th, kpt on onepcd frm 3 out
405[7] Tanner *chsd ldrs, outpcd 14th, plodded on frm 3 out* ....M Hammond 4
258[3] Guarena (USA) *rear frm 5th, lost tch 11th, t.o. & p.u. 2 out* ....C Richards pu
464 Fennorhill *s.u. bend bef 2nd* ....R Ward-Dutton su

Priory Piper *prom to 10th, wknd nxt, p.u. 15th* ....O McPhail pu
382 Corn Exchange *alwys rear, losing tch whn mstk & u.r. 11th* ....D Duggan ur
374[6] Connie Foley *s.u. bend bef 2nd* ....Miss S Hiatt su
260[2] Purple Melody (Ire) *(fav) 7/4-evens, nvr rchd ldrs, effrt 14th, no prog, p.u. 3 out* ....Miss C Spearing pu
300[3] Five Circles (Ire) *cls up in mid-div to 11th, 20l 4th 14th, p.u. 2 out* ....M Portman pu
223 Royal Bula *last frm 9th, t.o. & p.u. 15th* ....S Shinton pu
Arms Dealer 7a *rear of mid-div whn f 9th* S Blackwell f
It's Pogo *rear frm 11th, no ch whn p.u. 15th* ....G Barfoot-Saunt pu

14 ran. 3l, 9l, 30l. Time 6m 30.00s. SP 6-1.
Ian Anderson (West Shropshire Drag).

575 Restricted Div II (12st)

366[1] **BASIL STREET (IRE) 7a ....A Phillips 1**
(fav) trckd ldrs, qcknd to ld aft 15th, sn in cmmnd
Wooden Minstrel 5a ....Dr P Pritchard 2
cls up, ev ch til not qckn apr 3 out
381 **How Friendly ....Julian Pritchard 3**
cls up frm 11th, ev ch 15th, no ext nxt, lost 2nd cls hm
398[2] Mackabee (Ire) *chsd ldrs til outpcd frm 14th* ..T Weale 4
327[4] Rejects Reply *hld up, prog to cls 4th at 15th, wknd frm nxt* ....G Hanmer 5
259 Shesagud Girl 5a *alwys rear, t.o. 12th* ....S Shinton 6
331[2] For Michael *cls up whn blnd & u.r. 6th* ....Miss J Houldey ur
331 Tails U Win *rear til mstk & u.r. 9th* ....A Jordan ur
345[2] Mr Wilbur *ld 7th-15th, wknd rpdly, p.u. 2 out* A Dalton pu
406 Greenfield Tiger (Ire) *prom til outpcd 7th, t.o. in 7th whn p.u. flat* ....C Richards pu
Priesthill (Ire) *rear whn u.r. 5th* ....D Stephens ur
408 Miswiskers 5a *ld to 6th, wknd 8th, p.u. 12th* ...S Lloyd pu

12 ran. 8l, sht-hd, 20l, 15l, dist. Time 6m 37.00s. SP 11-10.
Miss J M Green (Ludlow).
P.R.

WEST STREET-TICKHAM
Detling
Sunday March 16th
FIRM

576 Members

280 **BRIGHT HOUR ....Miss J Grant 1**
alwys prom, prssd ldr 16th, ld aft 2 out, ran on wll
376 **Emerald Moon ....D Maitland 2**
ld 2nd-5th, lft in ld 7th, hdd aft 2 out, no ext
Bright Crusader ....A Warr 3
in tch, pshd alng 4 out, kpt on
462[5] Basher Bill 4ex *ld to 2nd, wll in tch aft, 3rd last, wknd* ....K Giles 4
Dinnys Delight (Ire) *alwys prom, 3rd & ev ch 3 out, wknd* ....Miss S French 5
462 Abdul Emir *alwys rear, blndrd 11th, 6th & wll btn whn blndrd last* ....Mrs L Stock 6
Tau 4ex *blnrd & u.r. 2nd* ....Miss F McLachlan ur
Netherby Cheese *chsd ldrs, wknd 4 out, p.u. 2 out* ....T Hills pu
462[4] Killarney Man *alwys last, t.o. whn ref last* ...R Barton ref
401[9] Sea Patrol (bl) *(fav) cls up, ld 5th til ran out 7th* ....Miss B Barton ro

10 ran. 6l, 4l, nk, 15l, 1l. Time 6m 16.00s. SP 8-1.
Mrs B Ansell (West Street-Tickham).

577 Confined (12st)

462[1] **STRUGGLES GLORY (IRE) 3ow........D Robinson 1**
(fav) cls up, ld frm 13th, stdly drew clr frm 17th, unchal
279 **Ok Corral (USA) ....A Greig 2**
trckd ldrs,chsd clr ld in 3rd 4 out,kpt on to take 2nd 2 out
278[1] **Mountainous Valley (Ire) ....S R Andrews 3**
nvr nr ldrs, efft 16th, 4th frm 4 out, tk 3rd flat
279[2] Monksfort 5ex *ld 6-13th, chsd wnr aft, stdly outpcd, wknd 2 out* ....S Cowell 4
Rustic Ramble *hld up, prog 15th, poor 5th frm 3 out* ....Miss C Savell 5
302 Woody Will *towrds rear, some hdwy 14th, 5th 4 out, wknd nxt* ....Mrs E Coveney 6
304 Redelva 5a *alwys rear, in tch to 15th* ...Mrs D Rowell 7
281[6] Yeoman Farmer *rear thruout, in tch to 14th* P Hacking 8
305[5] The Forties *alwys rear, last & lost tch 11th* ....N Earnshaw 9
123 Rarely At Odds *alwys rear, t.o. by hlfwy, p.u. 4 out* ....Miss A Sansom pu
Supreme Dealer *ld to 6th, cls aft, mstk 13th, 3rd whn f 15th* ....A Warr f
142 Lake Teereen *p.u. 4th* ....T Underwood pu
279 Saluting Walter (USA) *alwys rear, t.o. whn p.u. 3 out* ....T McCarthy pu
Brunswick Blue (Ire) *trckd ldrs, 4th whn b.d. 15th* ....C Gordon bd
195 Mara Askari (v) *alwys rear, losng tch whn p.u. 14th* ....P O'Keefe pu
142[3] Glen Cherry *prom to 10th, wll in rear whn ref 3 out* ....P Scouller ref
Clean Sweep *alwys towrds rear, 10th whn f 11th* ....M Jones f
322[2] Airtrak (Ire) 7ex *hld up mid-div, imprvd to 2nd whn blndrd & u.r. 4 out* ....R Barrett ur

18 ran. Dist, 12l, 2l, 4l, 5l, 10l, 4l, 3l. Time 5m 56.00s. SP Evens.
D C Robinson (Mid Surrey Farmers Drag).

578 Ladies

195[4] **PARDON ME MUM ....Mrs E Coveney 1**
(fav) alwys prom, 3rd 2 out, hrd rddn to ld last
195[6] **Upward Surge (Ire) ....Mrs N Ledger 2**
cls up, ld 15th, wknd & hdd last
277[4] **Doran's Town Lad 5a........Miss C Benstead 3**
ld to 15th, ev ch 2 out, wknd flat
388 American Eyre *rear, prog 14th, 5th 4 out, kpt on one-pce* ....Miss S Gladders 4
304 Clover Coin 5a *wll in rear, nvr put in race, nrst fin* ....Miss J Grant 5
442 Slight Panic 5a *wll in rear til rpdly jnd pack 6th,in tch final ctt,onepcd* ....Miss J Wickens 6
280[6] Dayadan (Ire) *alwys rear, rmmdrs hlfwy, kpt on one-pce* ....Miss J Sawyer 7
304 Powersurge *cls up, blndrd 11th, grdly wknd frm 14th* ....Miss H Courtney-Bennett 8
280[7] Profligate *trckd ldrs, rddn & ev ch whn bad mstk 3 out,btn whn p.u. nxt* ....Miss P Ellison pu
442 Notary-Nowell *alwys towrds rear, u.r. 14th* ....Miss N Sell ur
323[3] Top Miss 5a *mid-div til pshd alng & wknd 15th, p.u. aft 4 out* ....Miss S French pu

11 ran. 3l, 2l, 3l, 8l, 2l, 3l. Time 6m 7.00s. SP 2-1.
Dr D B A Silk (West Kent).

579 4m Men's Open (12st)

322[1] **THE ARTFUL RASCAL 4ex ....N Bloom 1**
(fav) patiently rdn, prog frm rear 18th, ld 25th, clr 2 out
281[1] **Stede Quarter 7ex ....P Bull 2**
prssd ldr,ld 22nd,hdd 25th,2nd aft,tired & whn blndrd last
376[6] **Annio Chilone 7ex ....P O'Keefe 3**
sweating, ld to 21st, wknd und pres 25th, lft 3rd nxt
281[2] Burromariner *hndy, cls 3rd 23rd, 4th & wkng whn ref 25th* ....S Cowell ref
282 More Of It *mstly mid-div til wknd 19th, no ch whn p.u. 22nd* ....P Hall pu
72[1] Billion Dollarbill *trckd ldrs, chalng whn ran out 3 out* ....M Gorman ro
279 Valibus (Fr) *mid-div,jmp slwly 12th,jn ldr 19th,mstk nxt,btn whn p.u.22nd* ....P Scouller pu
St Laycar *alwys rear, rddn & btn 19th, p.u. 22nd & dismntd* ....A Greig pu
305[2] Centre Stage *rear, t.o. whn p.u. 11th* ....A Warr pu

9 ran. 30l, 1l. Time 8m 6.00s. SP 1-2.
M A Kemp (Suffolk).

580 Restricted (12st)

59³ **ORPHAN OLLY** .... **P York** **1**
alwys prom, ld 14th,made rest,ran on wll whn prssd frm 3 out
280 **Velka 5a** .... **A Hickman** **2**
trckd ldrs, imprvd to prssd wnr 3 out, no ext flat
Cherrygayle (Ire) 5a .... **Miss S French** **3**
hndy, chsd wnr 16th, just outpcd 3 out, ran on wll flat
324² Polar Ana (Ire) 5a *mid-div, hdwy 4 out, 3rd & ev ch nxt, onepce* .... Miss S Gladders 4
403 Valiant Friend (bl) *alwys prom, ld 12-14th, 4th whn ref 17th* .... Miss B Barton ref
462 Fort Diana *in tch to 15th, p.u. 3 out* .... T Hills pu
Cuckoo Pen *mid-div, 4th 4 out, wknd nxt, wll bhnd whn p.u. last* .... M Jones pu
304 Saun (Cze) *alwys rear, mstk 15th, p.u. nxt* .... Miss F Worley pu
284 Huckleberry Friend 5a *alwys rear, mstk 15th, p.u. nxt* .... P Blagg pu
306¹ Ojonnyo (Ire) *(fav) ld to 12th, jmp slwly 14th, wkmng whn p.u. 16th* .... P Hacking pu
41 The Poacher *n.j.w., t.o. whn p.u. 15th* ... Daniel Dennis pu

11 ran. 2l, 1l, 4l. Time 6m 8.00s. SP 5-1.
R H York (Windsor Forest Bloodhounds).

581 Open Maiden (12st)

306 **PRIMITIVE KING 7a** .... **P Hacking** **1**
(fav) rear,prog to trck ldrs 15th,rdn to chal apr last,ld flat
284 **Half Moon Spinney** .... **S Cowell** **2**
mid-div, jnd ldrs 10th, ld 3 out-last, onepcd
Target Time 5a .... **K Giles** **3**
hdwy to 4th 14th, outpcd 4 out, ran on strgly flat
Catabolic (Ire) 7a *rear, prog final ctt, 3rd & ev ch 3 out, no ext apr last* .... P Bull 4
16 Shared Fortune (Ire) *ld 6th, blndrd bdly 17th, hdd 3 out, wknd* .... Daniel Dennis 5
Serious Money 5a (bl) *ref 1st* .... T Hills ref
278 Mayfair Maiden 5a *prom, ld 11-15th, wknng whn f nxt* .... A Hickman f
462 Rushhome 5a *mid-div til wknd & p.u. 14th* ... M Jones pu
Scotch Law *prom to 11th, bhnd whn p.u. 14th* .... Mrs N Ledger pu
Celtic Reg *nvr bttr thn mid-div, 7th whn hmp & f 16th* .... R Barrett f
306 Rough Aura *ld to 6th, wll bhnd 15th, p.u. 3 out* .... P Blagg pu
283 Psamead 7a *alwys rear, last & pshd alng final ctt, bhnd whn p.u. 17th* .... P York pu

12 ran. 1l, 6l, 1l, 6l. Time 6m 13.00s. SP 6-4.
Mr & Mrs M Reed (Crawley & Horsham).

582 Maiden (12st)

284 **PHAEDAIR** .... **M Jones** **1**
trckd ldrs, ld & mstk 4 out, drew clr apr last
283² **Crock D'Or** .... **P Hacking** **2**
hdwy 14th, 2nd 3 out, no pce to chal
406³ **Reapers Reward 5a** .... **Miss B Barton** **3**
alwys prom, ld 10th-4 out, wknd
My Moona 5a *ld til ref & u.r. 6th* .... P York ref
306 Miss Pandy 5a *mid-div whn u.r. 11th* .... P Hall ur
Novasun *alwys rear, lost tch 16th, p.u. 3 out* .... T McCarthy pu
284 General Jackie (Ire) *rear whn p.u. 6th* ..... A Hickman pu
284³ Ishma (Ire) *towrds rear whn b.d. 8th* .... D Page bd
306 Leitrim Cottage (Ire) *mid-div, 5th & btn 3 out, p.u. aft nxt* .... P Bull pu
Fair Caprice 5a *trckng ldrs whn f 8th* ... Miss S French f
324 Punnett's Town 5a *ran out 1st* .... T Hills ro
Squerrey *rear whn ref 8th* .... P McNickle ref
283 Commasarris 7a *2nd til lft in ld 6th,hdd 10th,prom til wknd 3 out,p.u. last* .... P Blagg pu
284 Spanish Pal (Ire) *towrds rear whn c.o. by loose horse 8th* .... Miss S Gladders co
284 Martha's Boy (Ire) *(fav) prom whn blndrd & u.r. 7th* .... D Robinson ur
487 What-A-Brave Run *alwys rear, f 14th* .... A Clarke f

16 ran. 6l, 12l. Time 6m 11.00s. SP 7-1.
Mrs O Hubbard (Old Surrey & Burstow).
G.Ta.

NEWCASTLE
Monday March 17th
GOOD TO FIRM

583 3m Northumberland Hussars Hunters' Chase Class H

355⁴ **FINAL HOPE (IRE) 11.3 7a** .... **Mrs F Needham** **1**
chsd ldrs, ld 13th, styd on well und pres from last.
289⁴ **Little Wenlock 11.8 5a** .... **Mrs V Jackson** **2+**
bhnd, hdwy before 3 out, chal last, no ext und pres clsg stgs.
379¹ **Highlandman 11.6 7a** .... **Mr Chris Wilson** **2+**
ld, hdd 13th, disp ld till outpcd apr last, styd on well und pres towards fin.
336² Piper O'Drummond 11.5 5a *in tch, effort before 3 out, kept on same pace from next.* .... Miss P Robson 4
375 Free Transfer (Ire) 11.5 5a *in tch, outpcd when hmpd 14th, some hdwy after 3 out, wknd after next, fin lame.* .... Mr C Storey 5
339³ Washakie 11.5 5a *(fav) lost tch from 8th, t.o.* .... Mr P Johnson 6
Gathering Time 11.3 7a *soon lost tch, t.o.* Mr A Birch 7
375³ Double Collect 11.3 7a *chsd ldr, weakening when f 14th.* .... Mr A Rebori f

8 ran. ½l, dd-ht, 3l, 21l, 21l, 17l. Time 6m 0.20s. SP 10-1.
R Tate

584 2½m Town & Country Novices' Hunters' Chase Class H

386² **WOODY DARE 12.2 5a** .... **Mr R Thornton** **1**
trckd ldrs, ld 4 out, styd on well from 2 out.
337³ **General Delight 12.0 7a** .... **Mr D Wood** **2**
bhnd early, tk clr order hfwy, effort before 3 out, chsd wnr from next, no impn.
410² **Pennine View 12.2 5a** .... **Mr R Ford** **3**
cl up, disp ld 4 out, ch 2 out, kept on same pace.
340¹ Bells Will Ring (Ire) 12.0 7a *keen, mstks, ld till hdd 4 out, soon wknd, t.o.* .... Mr T Scott 4
381 Master Crozina 12.0 7a *in tch till wknd before 4 out, t.o.* .... Mr P Cornforth 5
381⁵ Tumlin Oot (Ire) 12.0 7a *bhnd, hdwy when blnd 10th, wknd before 4 out, t.o.* .... Mr Chris Wilson 6
Eilid Anoir 12.2 5a *in tch till wknd before 4 out, t.o.* .... Mr R Shiels 7
415⁵ Drumcairn (Ire) 12.2 5a *blnd 1st, soon t.o.* .... Mr P Johnson 8
Count Surveyor 12.0 7a *p.u. lame after 1st.* .... Mr A Parker pu
377³ Up For Ransome (Ire) 12.0 7a *(fav) f 1st.* .... Mr G Shenkin f
338³ Lindon Run 12.0 7a *in tch when blnd and u.r. 9th.* .... Mr R Morgan ur

11 ran. 2l, ½l, 29l, 20l, 19l, 7l, 5l. Time 5m 5.40s. SP 7-1.
P Needham

FONTWELL
Tuesday March 18th
GOOD TO FIRM

585 2m 3f Horse And Hound Charlton Hunt Challenge Cup Hunters' Chase Class H

378³ **BUSMAN (IRE) 11.13 7a** .... **Mr D S Jones** **1**
alwys in tch, challenging when hit 12th, ld next, clr 3 out, unchal.
222³ **Tea Cee Kay 11.9 5a** .... **Mr A Sansome** **2**
alwys prom, ld 4th to 13th, kept on one pace from 2 out.
108¹ **Spitfire Jubilee 11.7 7a** .... **Mr R Nuttall** **3**
(fav) ld to 4th, lost pl 9th, styd on from 2 out.
194 Eagle Bid (Ire) 11.9 5a (h) *held up in tch, hdwy 9th, wknd 2 out.* .... Mr T McCarthy 4

381[3] Corly Special 11.7 7a *prom early, bhnd from 7th.* ....Mr E James 5
221[7] Miss Magic 11.2 7a *trckd ldr, hit 6th, mstk 10th, soon btn*....................Mr F Brennan 6
366[6] Feltham Mistress 11.2 7a *bhnd till hdwy 10th, wknd apr 3 out, p.u. before last*..........Mr E Babington pu
7 ran. 10l, 9l, 1l, 1¾l, ¾l. Time 4m 49.70s. SP 11-4.
Keith R Pearce

EXETER
Wednesday March 19th
GOOD TO FIRM

586 3¼m Robert Webb Travel Hunters' Chase Class H

363[1] **TINOTOPS 11.10 7a..............Miss S Vickery** 1
(fav) trckd ldrs, went 2nd 12th, ld 6 out to next, led again 4 out, mstk 2 out, soon clr, driven out.
285[4] **Sirisat 11.10 7a...................Miss T Blazey** 2
held up, hdwy 10th, chsd ldrs from 6 out, kept on one pace.
291[1] **The Malakarma 12.5 5a ....Mr B Pollock** 3
trckd ldr, ld 12th to 6 out, led again 5 out to next, soon rdn and unable to qckn.
285[1] Rusty Bridge 12.3 7a *ld to 12th, lost pl, rdn and rallied after 6 out, kept on one pace*........Mr R Burton 4
455[5] Brabazon (USA) 11.10 7a *t.o. after 5th, styd on one pace after 5 out*..........................Mr J Scott 5
Baron's Heir 11.10 7a *held up, chsd ldrs from 12th til wknd 4 out.*.............................Mr S Lloyd 6
More Manners 11.10 7a *chsd ldrs, mstk 7 out, soon wknd, bhnd when p.u. after 5 out.*......Mr J Creighton pu
384[2] Fiddlers Pike 11.10 7a *b.d. 1st*.....Mrs R Henderson bd
Knifeboard 11.12 5a *trckd ldrs til wknd after 4 out, p.u. before 2 out*........................Mr A Farrant pu
256 Silver Age (USA) 11.10 7a *blnd and u.r. 1st.* ....Miss P Cooper ur
491[1] Full Alirt 11.12 7a *chsd ldrs to 6 out, soon wknd, bhnd when p.u. before 4 out*..............Miss S Young pu
170[1] Miles More Fun 11.5 7a *held up, pushed along after 7 out, soon wknd, bhnd when p.u. before 4 out.* ....Mr L Jefford pu
12 ran. 12l, 1l, 14l, 21l, 5l. Time 6m 52.30s. SP 5-2.
R H H Targett

LUDLOW
Wednesday March 19th
GOOD TO FIRM

587 2½m Magnus-Allcroft Memorial Trophy Hunters' Chase Class H

257[3] **BLUE CHEEK 11.11 7a.............Mr N Bradley** 1
made virtually all, drew clr from 2 out.
191[3] **Landsker Missile 11.9 7a..........Mr E Williams** 2
chsd wnr thrght, held when blnd 2 out, not rcvr.
378[2] **Minella Express (Ire) 12.0 7a....Miss C Spearing** 3
(fav) alwys prom, one pace apr 4 out.
Tuffnut George 12.0 7a *in tch, hdwy 8th, mstk 11th, no ch from 5 out*..........................Mr A Phillips 4
Great Gusto 11.11 7a *held up rear, hdwy 11th, one pace apr 4 out*......................Miss L Blackford 5
466[3] Simply Perfect 11.7 7a *bhnd, nvr on terms.* ....Miss K Swindells 6
94 Ramstar 12.2 5a *chsd ldrs, mstk 5th, wknd 11th.* ....Miss P Curling 7
288 King Of Shadows 11.11 7a *chsd ldrs till wknd 12th.* ....Mr S Prior 8
369[4] Kino 11.7 7a *alwys bhnd*..........Mr Andrew Martin 9
375[5] Al Hashimi 11.7 7a *mid div till wknd 12th.* ....Mr N Ridout 10
Familiar Friend 12.0 7a (bl) *mid div, wknd 5 out, t.o.*. ....Mr L Lay 11
491 Great Pokey 11.7 7a *slowly away, t.o. 3rd.* ....Miss N Courtenay 12
Winter's Lane 11.7 7a *bhnd, hit 10th, t.o. when p.u. before 12th* ....Capt D Alers-Hankey pu
201 Stylish Gent 11.7 7a *blnd and u.r. 4th*. . . .Mr A Dalton ur
375 The Communicator 11.9 5a (bl) *rear when p.u. after 9th*.....................................Mr C Vigors pu
226 Mhemeanles 11.7 7a *chsd ldrs to 9th, weakening when blnd and u.r. 11th*. ....Mr A Gribbin ur
435 Majic Belle 11.2 7a (bl) *f 2nd*.............Mr A Wintle f
254[4] Hennerwood Oak 11.2 7a *mstk 4th, alwys bhnd, t.o. when p.u. before 2 out*. ....Mr M Munrowd pu
18 ran. 16l, 4l, 10l, hd, 8l, ½l, 3l, 2½l, 1¾l, 6l. Time 4m 53.60s. SP 9-2.
Mrs B Graham

TOWCESTER
Wednesday March 19th
GOOD TO FIRM

588 2¾m Empress Elizabeth Of Austria Open Hunters' Chase Class H

288 **STAR OATS 11.7 7a.................Mr A Kinane** 1
held up, hdwy to ld 2 out, rdn out and styd on well.
389[5] **Hickelton Lad 11.11 7a.............Mr S Durack** 2
ld after 1st to 5th, ev ch apr 2 out, kept on same pace run-in.
376[4] **Bollinger 11.7 7a ....Mr P O'Keeffe** 3
(fav) held up, hdwy to chase ldr from 9th till hit next, soon outpcd, rallied 3 out, one pace next.
226 Charlies Delight (Ire) 11.9 5a *ld till after 1st, regained ld 5th, hdd 2 out, soon btn*..............Mr A Sansome 4
4 ran. 4l, 1½l, 4l. Time 5m 48.50s. SP 7-1.
Hayden Phillips

WINCANTON
Thursday March 20th
GOOD TO FIRM

589 2m 5f Somerton Novices' Hunters' Chase Class H

493 **TOM'S GEMINI STAR 11.7 7a........Mr E James** 1
hdwy 12th, in tch when left cl 2nd and hmpd 4 out, ld next, pushed clr from 2 out.
Vital Song 11.7 7a...............Mr G Matthews 2
prom, slightly outpcd 13th, left in ld 4 out, btn when mstk last.
489[4] **Northern Village 11.7 7a ...Capt D Alers-Hankey** 3
rear, hrd rdn 8th, styd on from 4 out, nvr near ldrs.
238[6] Some-Toy 11.13 7a *in tch when mstk 11th, soon rdn and lost pl.* ....Miss L Blackford 4
293[4] Master Donnington 11.7 7a *in tch till wknd 13th.* ....Mr J M Pritchard 5
490[2] King's Treasure (USA) 11.13 7a *(fav) prom, 3rd when f 6th*................................Mr A Balding f
West Quay 11.7 7a *ld to 3rd, led 13th till p.u. lame apr 4 out*..........................Mr J Creighton pu
Finnigan Free 11.7 7a *rear when p.u. before 7th.* ....Mr M Frith pu
Salvo 11.8 7a 1ow *keen hold, ld 3rd to 13th, cl up when left in ld, mstk and u.r. 4 out*. ......Mr I Dowrick ur
9 ran. 5l, 10l, 5l, 3l. Time 5m 19.50s. SP 33-1.
O J Carter

KELSO
Friday March 21st
GOOD

590 3½m J. Rutherford Earlston Hunters' Chase Class H For Stewart Wight Memorial Trophy

289[1] **JIGTIME 11.4 7a ....Mr M Bradburne** 1
(fav) trckd lding pair, hdwy 16th, ld 3 out, rdn last, ran on strly.
289[2] **Royal Jester 11.11 5a...............Mr C Storey** 2
cl up, rdn along and outpcd apr 4 out, styd on from last, not reach wnr.
412[1] **Orange Ragusa 11.5 5a ....Miss P Robson** 3
ld, rdn along 4 out, hdd next, driven and one pace last.

355[3] Southern Minstrel 11.9 7a *in tch, effort and rdn along 5 out, soon outpcd*..................Miss C Metcalfe 4
492[4] Tartan Tornado 11.11 5a *mstks, alwys rear, bhnd 16th*..............................Mr P Johnson 5
5 ran. 7l, 1¼l, 2½l, dist. Time 7m 13.30s. SP 1-2.
J W Hughes

NEWBURY
Friday March 21st
GOOD TO FIRM

591 3m Alison Associates Hunters' Chase Class H

288[2] **FOX POINTER 11.13 5a..........Mr R Thornton** 1
(fav) j.w, made all, shaken up apr last, qcknd clr.
281 **Ardbrennan 11.11 7a ....Mr E James** 2
cl up, pressed wnr straight, outpcd from 2 out.
385[1] **Ryming Cuplet 12.3 7a ....Mr L Jefford** 3
alwys bhnd, unable to chal final cct.
496 Teatrader 11.11 7a *in tch, bhnd final cct.* ....Miss T Blazey 4
285[5] Expressment 12.3 7a *alwys bhnd, t.o.*...Mr G Penfold 5
317 Alapa 11.11 7a *in cl tch, blnd 4 out, 3rd and held when mstk and u.r. 3 out*...............Mr V Coogan ur
527[3] The Bodhran (Ire) 11.11 7a *f 4th*.........Mr S Durack f
7 ran. 18l, 21l, sht-hd, 12l. Time 5m 58.10s. SP 7-4.
Mrs L T J Evans

LINGFIELD
Saturday March 22nd
GOOD TO FIRM

592 3m Eden Hunters' Chase Class H

494 **COLONIAL KELLY 12.7 5a ....Mr C Vigors** 1
in tch, ld 8th, made rest, left well clr 2 out.
475[2] **Run For Free 12.2 3a..................Mr A Hill** 2
held up, jmpd slowly 10th, soon bhnd, t.o. from 13th, left poor 2nd 2 out.
Loyal Gait (NZ) 11.12 7a *prom, ld after 4th to 7th, wknd from 11th, t.o. when p.u. before 3 out.* ....Mr Andrew Martin pu
378 Pro Bono (Ire) 12.5 7a *held up bhnd ldrs, 4th when blnd and u.r. 8th*...........................Mr A Dalton ur
303[1] Prince Buck (Ire) 12.2 3a *(fav) ld till after 4th, led 7th to next, one l 2nd and rdn when f 2 out.* Mr P Hacking f
5 ran. Dist. Time 6m 17.30s. SP 5-2.
Alan Cowing

CAMBRIDGESHIRE
Horseheath
Saturday March 22nd
FIRM

593 Confined (12st)

319[2] **HORACE ....W Wales** 1
made all, hld on gamely flat
443[1] **Shake Five (Ire) ....S Sporborg** 2
(fav) hld up in 3rd, went 2nd 14th, not qckn 2 out, ran on flat
497[5] **Smart Pal ....J Townson** 3
cls 2nd til outpcd 14th, no ch frm nxt
3 ran. ¾l, 12l. Time 6m 18.00s. SP 7-4.
Mrs A Vaughan-Jones (West Norfolk).

594 P P O R A (12st)

441[1] **DYNAMITE DAN (IRE) ....S Cowell** 1
(fav) nrrw ld to 5th, disp aft til qcknd clr last
319 **Divine Chance (Ire) ....A Coe** 2
disp til slw jmp last, no ext
2 ran. 2l. Time 6m 35.00s. SP 1-4.
B Kennedy (Essex Farmers & Union).

595 Men's Open

501[1] **OVER THE EDGE ....S Sporborg** 1
(fav) made all in nrrw ld, qcknd clr last
440[2] **River Melody 5a ....T Moore** 2
rstrnd in 3rd, clr wth wnr frm 14th, onepcd last
440[3] **Cockstown Lad ....D Featherstone** 3
last til ran on past btn horses to tk 3rd 3 out, nrst fin
495 Foxbow (Ire) *alwys 4th, outpcd 14th* ....A Coe 4
497 Buckshot (Ire) (v) *cls 2nd til outpcd 13th, wknd rpdly 15th, fin tired* ....C Barlow 5
5 ran. 2l, 6l, 2l, 30l. Time 6m 20.00s. SP 4-5.
Christopher Sporborg (Puckeridge).

596 Ladies

DROMIN LEADER ....Miss L Rowe 1
made all, ran on gamely whn prssd last
446[4] **Severn Invader ....Miss H Gosling** 2
(fav) cls 2nd, outpcd frm 14th, ran on agn last, just faild
442[4] **Professor Longhair 2ow ....Miss C Papworth** 3
mostly 3rd, blnd 12th, no ch aft
301[1] Ace Of Spies *mostly last, no ch frm 12th* ....Miss A Embiricos 4
4 ran. Hd, 10l. Time 6m 21.00s. SP 5-2.
J M Turner (Suffolk).

597 Restricted

66[1] **GLENBRICKEN ....Miss A Embiricos** 1
(fav) cls up, ld 11th, made rest, kpt on frm 2 out
449[3] **Grassington (Ire) ....S Quirk** 2
prssd ldr, ld brfly 7-8th, outpcd 15th, ran on agn last
477[6] **Swift Reward 5a ....W Wales** 3
hld up, prog to 2nd at 13th, chsd wnr, no ch 2 out, lost 2nd
502[3] Cool Apollo (NZ) *alwys rear, kpt on onepcd frm 15th* ....G Plenderleith 4
320[1] Killery Harbour *narrw ld til 11th, 2nd to 14th, wknd nxt, no ch 3 out* ....T Moore 5
274 Current Attraction 5a 2ow *1st ride, chsd ldrs til outpcd 9th, t.o. 13th* ....Miss K Thory 6
320[4] Aughnacloy Rose *t.o. 3rd, p.u. aft 13th* ....R Page pu
324 Tenderman (Ire) *alwys rear, bhnd whn p.u. aft 15th, dsmntd* ....A Coe pu
8 ran. 2½l, hd, 10l, 15l, 30l. Time 6m 22.00s. SP 3-1.
Kevin Williams (Thurlow).

598 Open Maiden Div I (12st)

197[5] **BORROW MINE (IRE) 7a.............S Sporborg** 1
(fav) trckd ldr, chal 2 out, ld last, ran on
287 **Amadeus (Fr) ....M Gingell** 2
made all at slw pace, outjmpd last, no ext
317[3] **Flapping Freda (Ire) 5a 2ow................R Gill** 3
alwys 3rd, not pace to chal, blnd 15th, sn btn
3 ran. ½l, 10l. Time 6m 57.00s. SP 4-5.
Mrs C H Sporborg & J Pembroke (Puckeridge).

599 Open Maiden Div II (12st)

318[4] **ANDY GAWE (IRE) ....S Cowell** 1
(fav) ld frm 2nd, nrrw advan & lkd wnr whn lft alone 2 out
439 **Lantern Spark (Ire) 5a ....Miss C Tuke** 2
3rd til lft 2nd aft 9th, prssd wnr 11-16th,u.r. 2out, rmntd
197 Secret Music *ld 1st, cls 2nd aft til u.r. aft 9th* ....Capt D Parker ur
Held To Ransom 7a *n.j.w. lost tch 10th, p.u. nxt* ....P Keane pu
4 ran. Dist. Time 6m 48.00s. SP 4-6.
B Kennedy (Essex Farmers & Union).
S.B.

CRAWLEY & HORSHAM
Parham
Saturday March 22nd
FIRM

600 Members

305[1] **KATES CASTLE 5a 5ex.............J Van Praagh 1**
(fav) 6/4-4/6,ld to 7th & 10-13th,styd on strngly to ld 2 out,easy
389[3] **Berrings Dasher 5ow...................J Ayton 2**
handy, ld frm 13th jmpg wll, hdd 2 out, wknd
302[1] **Local Manor 5ex.......................H Dunlop 3**
s.i.s. sn trckd ldrs, 3rd & pshd alng 3 out, wknd nxt,eased
146 Iced Ginger (v) *mstks, wll in rear whn p.u. 12th* ....D Evatt pu
577[7] Redelva 5a *prom, ld aft 7th-10th, wknd 4 out, bhnd & p.u. 2 out* ....Mrs D Rowell pu
147 Tommy-Gun *prom early, rear whn p.u. 9th* P O'Keefe pu
Ford's Folly 3ow *1st ride, rear whn u.r. 4th* ....Miss K Ford ur

7 ran. 18l, dist. Time 6m 35.00s. SP 4-6.
Ben Van Praagh (Crawley & Horsham).

601 Restricted (12st)

488[6] **BILBO BAGGINS (IRE) ....A Hickman 1**
rear, prog 4 out, ld apr last, ran on well
301 **Royal Fireworks ....A Lillingston 2**
ld, blnd 2nd, hdd 6th, ld 14th-apr last, wknd
July Schoon ....T Underwood 3
(fav) hld up, effrt 13th, outpcd 3 out, saddle slppd
481[3] Dad's Pipe *mstks, just ld 6th, blnd 13th, hdd nxt, fdd, p.u. aft 2 out* ....T Smith pu

4 ran. 9l, nk. Time 6m 39.00s. SP 4-1.
Mrs P A Tetley (Surrey Union).

602 Ladies

304[1] **THE WHIP 4ex...................Miss C Grissell 1**
walked over

The Hon Mrs C Yeates (East Sussex & Romney Marsh).

603 Men's Open (12st)

378[5] **YOUNG NIMROD ....P O'Keefe 1**
(fav) ld, clr 5th, unchal
483 **Pure Madness (USA) ....A Greig 2**
wth rvl to 3rd, not keen aft & drvn alng, t.o. 13th

2 ran. Dist. Time 6m 36.00s. SP 1-3.
G J D Wragg (East Sussex & Romney Marsh).

604 Confined (12st)

577[4] **MONKSFORT 5ex ....Miss C Holliday 1**
(fav) made all, styd on wll frm 3 out
484[5] **Sky Venture 5ex ....P Bull 2**
trckd wnr, jmpd slwly 6th, pshd alng 13th, outpcd
281 **The Portsoy Loon ....A Greig 3**
trckd ldr, rdn 12th, btn 3 out

3 ran. 9l, 11l. Time 6m 32.00s. SP Evens.
Miss C Holliday (Old Surrey & Burstow).

605 Open Maiden (12st)

VULGAN PRINCE ....A Greig 1
(fav) ld 3rd, made rest, styd on well whn prssd frm 4 out
Graphic Designer (Ire) 7ow ....J Hazeltine 2
hld up, jnd wnr 12th, chal 4 out, lvl 2 out, kpt on wll
128 **Malingerer 5a 3ow ....M Jones 3**
alwys prom, pshd alng in 3rd frm 14th, btn 2 out
581 Rough Aura *ld to 3rd, last frm 6th, lost tch whn u.r. 4 out* ....P Blagg ur
582 Ishma (Ire) *cls up, prssd wnr 9th til c.o. loose horse 13th* ....D Page co
Provincial Retreat 7a *in tch til wknd & p.u. aft 2 out* ....P Bull pu
582 Spanish Pal (Ire) *3rd whn u.r. 2nd*....Miss S Gladders ur

7 ran. ½l, 12l. Time 6m 56.00s. SP 5-4.
D R Greig (East Sussex & Romney Marsh).
G.Ta.

DUKE OF BUCCLEUCH'S
Friars Haugh
Saturday March 22nd
GOOD TO FIRM

606 Members (12st)

336[1] **MISTY NIGHT 5a 7ex ....Miss A Bowie 1**
(fav) not fluent, 3rd 9th, ld apr 4 out, pshd out flat
566[1] **Thinkaboutthat (Ire) ....J Muir 2**
ld jmpng wll, blndrd 10th, hdd 4 out, kpt on wll
Harry 21ow ....C Gilholm 3
cls 3rd mstly til grdly lost tch frm 14th
Francis Farrelly 21ow *alwys bhnd*.........G Tweedie 4
Tim Bobbin 21ow *alwys bhnd*...............J Scott 5
Flint 21ow *alwys bhnd*..................J Manclark 6
Toozan Tak (bl) *alwys last*............W Thompson 7
415 Hula 21ow *cls up whn u.r. flat apr 8th* ..Miss F Wilson ur
Sooperstitious *u.r. 1st*..................M Renwick ur

9 ran. 2l, dist. Time 6m 44.00s. SP 1-4.
Mrs M A Bowie (Duke Of Buccleuch's).

607 Restricted

563[3] **WILL TRAVEL (IRE) ....A Robson 1**
hld up in tch, ld apr 3 out, styd on wll
Canister Castle 5ow....................R Shiels 2+
ld/disp to 8th, ld agn brfly 4 out, no ext frm 3 out
416[4] **Whosgotsillyssense 5a................C Storey 2+**
hld up, some hdwy frm 4 out, not trbl wnnr
415[3] Ebbzeado Willfurr (Ire) *not fluent, wnt 3rd 9th, strgglng frm 12th*..............................J Billinge 4
411[8] Ruecastle *ld/disp to 8th, wknng whn u.r. 4 out* ....Miss J Hutchinson ur
563[2] Cukeira 5a *(fav) alwys rear, bhnd whn p.u. bfr 2 out* ....C Paisley pu
228 The Caffler (Ire) *ld 8th til apr 3 out, hld & 3rd whn b.d. last* ....W Ramsay bd
Cool Yule (Ire) *hld up, kpt on wll frm 4 out, 2nd & hld whn f last* ....B Gibson f

8 ran. 10l, dd-ht, 10l. Time 6m 37.00s. SP 5-1.
D V Tate (Braes Of Derwent).

608 P P O R A (12st)

560[4] **TOASTER CRUMPET ....Miss P Robson 1**
hld up, wnt 2nd 4 out, slght ld frm nxt drvn out flat
420[1] **Harden Glen ....Miss D Laidlaw 2**
(fav) ld to 3 out, ev ch whn no ext flat
231 **Tod Law 5a ....C Storey 3**
alwys hndy, no ext frm 3 out
414[3] Luckieshiel 5a *alwys wll bhnd, t.o.*.....Miss D Calder 4
411 Rare Fire *2nd til 7th, lost tch by 9th, t.o.* ....Miss R Davison 5
411[6] In Demand *u.r. 1st*.........................P Craggs ur

6 ran. 1l, 12l, dist. Time 6m 34.00s. SP 4-1.
Miss P Robson (Tynedale).

609 G Middleton Ladies

MUSKORA (IRE) (bl).............Miss P Robson 1
(fav) j.w. in ld, styd on wll
388[2] **Across The Card ....Miss R Ramsay 2**
midfld, styd on to go 2nd apr 2 out, not rch wnnr
561[2] **Very Evident (Ire) ....Miss J Bird 3**
alwys hndy, 2nd 4 out, no ext frm 2 out
336 Minibrig 5a *alwys abt same plc, nvr dang* ....Mrs V Jackson 4
415[6] Funny Feelings *mstly 2nd til wknd frm 14th* ....Miss D Laidlaw 5
386 Planning Gain *bhnd by 7th, nvr dang* ..Miss S Forster 6
Emu Park *s.s., nvr dang*..........Miss S Dickinson 7
412[5] Schweppes Tonic *hndy, wnt 2nd 14th, wknd qckly frm nxt*.................................Mrs C Amos 8
474 La Maja (Ire) 5a *s.s., alwys wll bhnd*....Mrs N Wilson 9
231 The Laughing Lord *nvr a threat, p.u. 4 out* ....Miss R Shiels pu
Tuneful Tom *s.s., t.o. whn p.u. 4 out*......Miss V Burn pu

11 ran. 4l, 4l, 12l, 3l, 1l, 1l, dist. Time 6m 26.00s. SP 2-1.

Mrs F Percy-Davis (Jedforest).

610 Men's Open (12st)

339[1] **HAGAR** ....**M Bradburne** **1**
(fav) hld up, wnt 2nd 4 out, ld nxt, styd on strgly
562[2] **Todcrag** ....**T Scott** **2**
ld 8th-3 out, kpt on wll
228[1] **Fiscal Policy** ....**R Trotter** **3**
alwys just bhnd ldrs, kpt on onepce
383[1] Sayin Nowt 5a *hld up, mstk 5th & 3 out, no dang aft* ....P Craggs 4
232[3] Staigue Fort (Ire) *cls up til lost tch 4 out* . .H Naughton 5
339 Loughlinstown Boy *ld to 8th, sn lost tch, p.u. 4 out* ....J Walton pu
6 ran. 2l, 5l, 7l, 25l. Time 6m 24.00s. SP 6-4.
J I A Charlton (Border).

611 Confined (12st)

229[2] **ENSIGN EWART (IRE)** ....**C Storey** **1**
(Jt fav) mstly 2nd til ld 5 out,hdd brfly nxt,styd on wll frm 3 out
229[4] **Bit Of A Blether (Ire)** ....**P Craggs** **2**
(Jt fav) alwys hndy, ld brfly 4 out, no ext frm 2 out
608 **In Demand** ....**M Bradburne** **3**
alwys hndy, ch 3 out, no ext frm nxt
289 Buck's Delight (Ire) *ld til 5 out, grdly wknd* ....T Scott 4
Green Times 3ex *nvr rchd ldrs* ....W Ramsay 5
387 Fish Quay *last by 8th, nvr dang* ....Miss S Lamb 6
562 Strong Measure (Ire) *alwys bhnd* ....R Morgan 7
560 Yenoora (Ire) *alwys bhnd* ....J Ewart 8
410[4] Hydropic *u.r. 3rd* ....Miss K Miller ur
156 Recluse 7ex (bl) *in tch to hlfwy, bhnd whn p.u. 4 out* ....R Shiels pu
492[3] Fordstown (Ire) 6ex *strgglng in 5th whn u.r. 12th* ....J Alexander ur
11 ran. 2l, 4l, 15l, 20l, 5l, dist. Time 6m 31.00s. SP 5-2.
Major M W Sample (College Valley).

612 Maiden Div I (12st)

420[3] **CLAYWALLS** ....**T Scott** **1**
alwys hndy, ld 4 out, forged clr frm nxt
565 **Dillons Bridge (Ire)** ....**R Morgan** **2**
alwys prom, wnt 2nd aft 2 out, no ch wth wnnr
343 **Mister Buzios** ....**P Craggs** **3**
ld til 4 out, no ext frm nxt
565[3] Indian River (Ire) 4ow *bhnd by 8th, nvr nr ldrs* ....J Walton 4
234 Hintertux *mstly 2nd til wknd frm 10th* ....R Green 5
417 Rough House *nvr nr ldrs* ....B Gibson 6
342[4] Worthy Way *(fav) alwys bhnd* ....C Storey 7
Espley Nipper *strgglng whn f 12th*.......I Carmichael f
415[9] Boyup Brook *cls 2nd whn f 12th* ....T Morrison f
342 Saigon Lady (Ire) 5a 4ow *strgglng whn f 10th* ....A Robson f
162 Price War *bhnd by 7th, p.u. 4 out*............R Shiels pu
37[3] Seymour Fiddles 5a *3rd whn u.r. 5th* ....Mrs C Amos ur
411[7] Hooky's Treat 5a *nvr rchd ldrs, p.u. 4 out* ....M Bradburne pu
Terrorisa 5a *sn t.o., p.u. 4 out*...........Miss J Percy pu
14 ran. 15l, 10l, 15l, 3l, 3l, 5l. Time 6m 35.00s. SP 5-1.
Mrs I Hamilton (Tynedale).

613 Maiden Div II (12st)

415 **FLYPIE** ....**P Strang Steel** **1**
ld frm 8th, made rest, styd on strgly
565[5] **Black And Blues** ....**S Scott** **2**
wnt 2nd 4 out, chal 3 out, no ext apr last
235[2] **Red Hot Boogie (Ire)** ....**T Scott** **3**
made most to 8th, remaind cls up, no ext frm 3 out
411 Fast Fun *ld brfly 4th, cls up til no ext frm 4 out* ....R Morgan 4
234 Driminamore (Ire) *cls up til wknd 3 out*.....W Ramsay 5
234[8] Father O'Callaghan (Ire) *nvr rchd ldrs* ....Miss M Bremner 6
31 McNay *cls up til wknd 12th*...................R Green 7
416[2] Lauder Square *(fav) alwys bhnd*........M Bradburne 8
415 Bantel Baronet *sn bhnd, p.u. 14th*......Miss J Hedley pu
Miss Huntcliffe 5a *loose bfr start, strgglng whn f 10th* ....M Ruddy f
565 Political Belle 5a *mstk & p.u. aft 2nd*...Mrs V Jackson pu
Dynastie D'Auge (Fr) 5a *f 3rd*................R Shiels f
12 ran. 3l, 6l, 5l, 10l, 15l, 3l, 6l. Time 6m 41.00s. SP 50-1.
Mrs C Strang Steel (Lauderdale).

614 Maiden Div III (12st)

416 **PEELINICK** ....**C Storey** **1**
hld up,hdwy 9th,ld 5 out,in cmmnd whn lft virt solo last
415 **Newbrano 5a** ....**I Carmichael** **2**
made most frm 3rd til 5 out, wll hld frm nxt, lft 2nd last
414[4] **Bluebell Track 5a** ....**R Trotter** **3**
4th hlfwy, nvr rchd ldrs, lft 3rd last
417[3] Bavington *nvr rchd ldrs* ....R Morgan 4
Czaryne 5a *ld to 3rd, ld agn brfly 8th, lost tch by 10th* ....Miss J Percy 5
418 Imulari *alwys bhnd*...........................P Craggs 6
342[2] Luvly Bubbly *(fav) alwys bhnd* ....M Bradburne 7
134[3] Buckaroo 5a *hld up, hdwy into cls 2nd 5 out, no ext apr 2 out, f last* ....Miss P Robson f
341[3] Keirose 5a *nvr nr ldrs, p.u. 4 out*...........C Paisley pu
335 Up And Running *losng tch whn f 12th*....Mrs C Amos f
341 Bold Echo 12a *ran out 2nd*...................C Wilson ro
38 No Justice *hndy, cls 2nd whn f 12th* ....Miss K McLintock f
340 Political Diamond 5a *nvr nr ldrs, p.u. 4 out*....T Scott pu
13 ran. Dist, ¾l, 3l, dist, 15l, 10l. Time 6m 33.00s. SP 5-1.
Mrs R L Elliot (Jedforest).
R.J.

HURWORTH
Hutton Rudby
Saturday March 22nd
GOOD TO FIRM

615 Members

480 **NOT THE NADGER** ....**A Ogden** **1**
made all, sn clr, steady 7th, qcknd 3 out, drvn clr flat
425[5] **Lyningo 5ex**..............................**A Wood** **2**
mid-div, prog 11th, mstk 14th, outpcd 3 out, kpt on flat
506[6] **Attle 5ex** ....**N Smith** **3**
chsd clr ldr, clsd up 7th, not qckn frm 3 out
426[9] Ski Lady 5a *rear, mstk 5th, outpcd 7th, nvr dang* ....Miss L Horner 4
356[4] Chapel Island 10ex *alwys prom,ev ch whn wnt wrong side of mrkr aft 4 out & u.r.*..................G Tuer ro
425 Oliver's Mate (Ire) 5ex *(fav) nvr gng wll, rear, strgglng 4 out, sn lost tch, p.u. 2 out* ....N Tutty pu
428[5] Yogi's Mistress 5a *rear,efft 11th,losng tch & rdr lost iron,p.u. aft 15th* ....P Frank pu
Antique Dealer 12a *rear, lost tch 7th, t.o. 12th, p.u. 4 out*.......................................Miss T Gray pu
8 ran. 3l, 3l, 10l. Time 6m 27.00s. SP 8-1.
R T Dennis (Hurworth).

616 Restricted

477[4] **CITY BUZZ (IRE) (bl)**.................**K Needham** **1**
alwys prom, ld 16th, clr 2 out, ran on strgly
425[2] **Caman 5a** ....**Mrs S Grant** **2**
(Jt fav) disp til ld 6th, hdd 16th, onepce frm 3 out
425[9] **Mount Faber** ....**S Charlton** **3**
chsd ldrs til outpcd 14th, prog & ev ch 3 out, onepcd
422 Cahermone Lady (Ire) 5a *mid-div, prog 7th, ev ch 4 out, sn wknd* ....N Kent 4
425[6] Make A Line *mid-div, outpcd 14th* ....C Denny 5
266 Miley Pike *prom til wknd qckly 3 out*...........N Tutty 6
424[4] Stride To Glory (Ire) *rear, lost tch 3 out*.....D Topping 7
265[7] Bugley *disp ld til hdd 6th, prom, rddn 13th, wknd 4 out, t.o.* ....P Jenkins 8
424 Sharp To Oblige (bl) *rear, efft 13th, outpcd & lost tch 16th, t.o.* ....S Whitaker 9

429[6] Hoistthestandard 5a *s.i.s., rear, wll bhnd frm 3 out, t.o.* ....T Glass 10
251 Missile Man *rear, lost tch 8th, t.o. whn p.u. 14th* ....S Pinder pu
348[3] Malvern Cantina *rear, strgglng 14th, t.o. whn p.u. last* ....S Swiers pu
421[2] Transcendental (Ire) *(Jt fav) rear & bhnd, out of tch whn p.u. 14th, saddld slpd* ....Miss A Deniel pu
Mac's Blade (USA) 7a *n.j.w., rear & sn t.o., ref 7th* ....R Edwards ref
14 ran. 10l, ½l, 10l, 2l, 7l, 2l, 6l, 7l, 5l. Time 6m 18.00s. SP 12-1.
John E Needham (Bilsdale).

617 Ladies

426[2] **CAROLE'S DELIGHT 5a....Mrs L Ward** 1
(fav) disp ld til apr last, rlld brfly to ld nr line
474[1] **Kellys Diamond ....Miss V Russell** 2
mid-div, prog 4 out, disp nxt, ld apr last, hdd nr line
426[8] **Douce Indienne 5a....Miss J Eastwood** 3
mid-div, prog 11th, ev ch 3 out, not qckn nxt
426[7] Cheeky Pot *rear & bhnd til rddn & styd on wll frm 3 out* ....Mrs S Grant 4
426[3] Indie Rock *hld up in rear, prog 3 out, ev ch nxt, wknd* ....Mrs F Needham 5
474 Douce Eclair 5a *alwys mid-div, not qckn 3 out* ....Miss L Eddery 6
355[6] Colonel Popski *chsd ldrs, ev ch 4 out, steadd fdd* ....Mrs J Barr 7
268[4] Rustino (bl) *rear & bhnd, brf efft 14th, wknd 16th, t.o.* ....Miss R Clark 8
426 Skolern (v) *disp ld til wknd qckly 3 out, t.o.* ....Miss L Pounder 9
9 ran. Hd, 6l, ½l, 1l, 2l, 3l, 20l, ¾l. Time 6m 14.00s. SP 7-4.
C Holden (Cleveland).

618 Land Rover Open (12st)

354 **GENERAL BRANDY ....G Tuer** 1
mid-div, prog 8th, wnt 2nd 11th, ld 16th, pshd out flat
507[2] **Castle Tyrant 5a 5ex ....P Atkinson** 2
disp ld to 6th, rmnd prom til not qckn frm 2 out
354[2] **Gaelic Warrior ....S Swiers** 3
disp ld to 6th, chsng ldrs whn hit 4 out, onepcd frm 2 out
507[3] Park Drift 7ex *(fav) chsd ldrs, wnt 2nd 3 out, wknd nxt* ....R Tate 4
506 Clare Lad *chsd ldrs til outpcd 8th, wknd frm 4 out* ....R Walford 5
423 Frome Boy 8ow *rear & rmmndrs 6th, alwys strgglng, t.o.* ....P Johnson 6
507[5] Syrus P Turntable *rear & sn detached, t.o.* ...J Saville 7
350[7] Breckenbrough Lad 2ow *rear & sn detached, t.o.* ....I Bennett 8
Srivijaya *plld hrd,disp 6th & ld nxt,hdd & wknd 16th,t.o. & p.u. last*....N Smith pu
353 Inconclusive *s.i.s.,hld up in rear,sn wll bhnd,rddn 13th,t.o. & p.u. 15th* ....A Ogden pu
10 ran. 10l, 1l, 8l, 25l, 3l, 7l, 12l. Time 6m 13.00s. SP 20-1.
E Tuer (Hurworth).

619 Intermediate

509 **GREENMOUNT LAD (IRE) ....P Cornforth** 1
chsd ldrs, disp 10th til ld apr last, ran on strgly
422[2] **Mr Dick ....S Swiers** 2
(fav) prom, disp 5th til rddn & hdd apr last, rlld flat
506[3] **Skipping Gale ....P Atkinson** 3
ld, disp 4-10th, rmnd prom til fdd frm 3 out
352[1] Flying Lion *mid-div til styd on wll frm 2 out*...M Haigh 4
509 Barichste (bl) *mid-div, chsd ldrs to 12th, rddn & wknd 2 out*....M Watson 5
476[5] Earl Gray *alwys rear, lost tch 3 out*.....Miss A Deniel 6
562 Sharpridge *rear, f 7th* ....M Mawhinney f
Grey Realm 5a *disp 4th til lost plcd 6th,prog 5 out,gng wll whn f nxt*....N Smith f
8 ran. ¾l, 12l, 4l, ½l, 2l. Time 6m 20.00s. SP 9-2.
J Cornforth (York & Ainsty North).

620 Open Maiden Div I Pt I

478[2] **KENDOR PASS (IRE) ....M Tate** 1
chsd ldrs til ld apr 14th, qcknd clr whn chal last, easily
210 **High Intake 7a....N Tutty** 2
rear, prog 13th, wnt 2nd 16th, ev ch last, outpcd
357 **Mature April 5a ....P Jenkins** 3
rear, rddn 7th, outpcd 11th, t.o.
424[3] On The Fly *(fav) u.r. on way to post,trckd ldrs,disp 5th,hd apr 14th sn wknd* ....R Edwards 4
429 Persian Lion *ld, disp 5th til hdd 13th, 3rd & fddng whn f 15th*....Miss T Jackson f
358 Tudor Flight 5a *prom whn ran out 4th* ....G Markham ro
428[3] Little Red *prog 7th,chsd ldrs 14th,wknd qckly 16th,t.o & p.u. 3 out*....T Barry pu
116 Addington Sharragh 5a *mstk 1st, alwys rear, lost tch whn ran wd & p.u. aft 8th*....Miss J Binks pu
269 Ellerton Tony 7a *alwys strgglng, t.o. 11th, p.u. nxt* ....S Swiers pu
Royal Charger (Ire) 7a *mid-div, in tch whn b.d. 15th* ....Mrs S Grant bd
10 ran. 6l, dist, 5l. Time 6m 24.00s. SP 9-4.
Dr M P Tate (Middleton).

621 Open Maiden Div I Pt II

343[5] **NOTARIUS (FR) ....Mrs K Hargreave** 1
mid div, prog 12th, ld 3 out, sn clr
418[4] **Say Daphne 5a ....S Whitaker** 2
chsd ldr thruout, ev ch 3 out, onepcd nxt
429 **Chummy's Last 5a ....Mrs F Needham** 3
prom, lost plcd 8th, strgglng 15th
358 Lord George *alwys in rear, lost tch 13th, t.o.* ....P Atkinson 4
Redwood Boy *rear, lost tch 13th, t.o.*....D Raw 5
Lawnswood Quay *strng hold, ld til hdd 3 out, 3rd & btn whn f last*....S Charlton f
427[3] Patey Court 5a *(fav) mid-div, lost tch 4 out, p.u. nxt* ....C Mulhall pu
Hot Move *rear, mstk 1st, efft 11th, outpcd 15th, t.o. whn p.u. 3 out*....G Tuer pu
479 Half Each 12a *prom whn ran out 13th*.....R Walford ro
428[4] West Lutton 7a *rear, efft 12th, outpcd 4 out, btn whn f 2 out*....Maj M Watson f
10 ran. 12l, 5l, 15l, dist. Time 6m 28.00s. SP 4-1.
Mrs A E Juliet Barnett (Braes Of Derwent).

622 Open Maiden Div II Pt I

510[2] **DEAR EMILY 5a....S Swiers** 1
(Jt fav) disp til hdd 7th,trckd ldr til disp 13th,ld 3 out,ran on wll
352 **Japodene 5a ....M Haigh** 2
disp til ld 7th, disp 13th til hdd 3 out, unable to qckn
Ship The Builder ....C Mulhall 3
(Jt fav) hld up in mid-div, prog to go 3rd 13th, ev ch 3 out, onepcd
338 Keep A Secret *prom, mstk 12th, fdd nxt* ...P Atkinson 4
510 Roseberry Star 5a *prom til wknd 14th, t.o.* ....Miss T Jackson 5
509 Last Option 7a *rear & bhnd, mstk 8th, wknd 14th, t.o.* ....Mrs F Needham 6
Greatfull Fred *mid-div, wknd 11th, t.o. & p.u. 13th* ....Miss K Pickersgill pu
506 China Hand (Ire) 7a *mid-div, wknd 9th, t.o. & p.u. 11th* ....H Armstrong pu
427 Mr Hook 7a *mid-div til fdd 12th, t.o. & p.u. 14th* ....G Markham pu
420 True Censation 5a *alwys wll bhnd, t.o. & p.u. 13th* ....J Saville pu
10 ran. 6l, 2½l, 15l, 12l, 15l. Time 6m 24.00s. SP 6-4.
J E Swiers (West Of Yore).

623 Open Maiden Div II Pt II

419[3] **KILLEANEY CARR (IRE) ....S Whitaker** 1
prom,lft 2nd 14th,ch whn mstk last,rlld,just faild,plc 1st
429 **Smart Mover ....A Ogden** 2

ld-5th,2nd & lft in ld 14th,made rest,hld on wll fin,plc 2nd
421[4] **Dunford Bridge (USA) ....S Charlton** 3
mid-div, outpcd 12th, prog 14th, wknd 2 out
418 Percy Special (Ire) *alwys prom, wknd 3 out, t.o.* ....T Barry 4
428[2] Just A Single (Ire) *(fav) prom,ld frm 5th,hung bdly rght apr 7th & 13th whn ran out* ....R Edwards ro
421 Hillmilly 12a *mid-div, jmp slwly 4th, sn lost tch, p.u. 11th* ....W Burnell pu
Madame Defarge 5a *rear, lost tch 11th, t.o. nxt, p.u. 14th*..........Mrs K Hargreave pu
Cute Word 5a *rear & sn wll bhnd, t.o. & p.u. 11th* ....H Arnold pu
510 Rosie Blue 5a *rear & sn strggling, t.o. 12th, p.u. 3 out* ....G Tuer pu

9 ran. ½l, 10l, 25l. Time 6m 26.00s. SP 5-2.
C Dawson (South Durham).
N.E.

LAMERTON
Kilworthy
Saturday March 22nd
GOOD

624 Members

ANVIL CORNER 5a................David Dennis 1
lost plc 9th, 4th whn lft clr 14th
453[5] **Catch The Cross (bl)..............Miss S Young** 2
disp 6-9th, chsd ldr til b.d. 14th, remntd
459[2] **The Ugly Duckling ....S Slade** 3
cls up, in tch whn b.d. 14th, remntd
172[1] Shrewd Thought (USA) *(fav) prom, ld 9th, slght ld whn f 14th*..........A Farrant f
458 Stony Missile 5a *blndrd & u.r. 7th* ....Miss W Hartnoll ur
236 Karlin's Quest *mstk 1st, rear whn crashed thru wing 8th*..........D Doyne-Ditmas ro
Lizzy Gecko 5a *mstk 10th, p.u. apr 14th, cont & ran out immed* ....T Dennis pu

7 ran. Dist, 5l. Time 6m 56.50s. SP 25-1.
Miss Jane Wakeham (Lamerton).

625 Maiden Div I (12st)

531 **FLYING MARIA 5a.......................C Heard** 1
hdwy 5th, cls 2nd 10th, ld 2 out, ran on wll
460 **Eserie de Cores (USA) ....N Harris** 2
alwys prom, cls 4th 11th, ev ch last, not qckn
458[6] **Westcountry Lad ....R Woolacott** 3
bad mstk 3rd, hdwy und pres 16th, onepce clsng stgs
Artic Explorer *mid-div, 7th 16th, nrst fin* .....L Jefford 4
460[2] Tarka Trail *prom til 15th, 6th & no ch 16th, fin wll* ....J Young 5
Sixth In Line (Ire) *mstk 2nd, 8th 11th, t.o.*........T Cole 6
461 Fortitude Star 5a *rear & rmmndrs 10th, t.o. p.u. apr 4 out*..........A Farrant pu
460[3] My Prides Way 5a *towrds rear til f 8th*........T Greed f
456 Hanukkah 5a *s.s., towrds rear til b.d. 8th*...I Hambley bd
242 Romany Anne 5a *ld aft 3rd til 17th, disp 3rd & wkng whn f last*..........Miss S Young f
Cuddle Lover 5a *bhnd til p.u. apr 3 out*...A O'Connor pu
54 Millwood 7a *(fav) hld up, prog 16th, disp 3rd whn f last*..........R Nuttall f
Gaysun 7a *sn bhnd, t.o. til p.u. apr 3 out* .....S Slade pu
Duckin-N-Diving 5a *bhnd til p.u. apr 4 out* ....D Stephens pu

14 ran. 3l, 2l, 12l, 2l, dist. Time 6m 23.50s. SP 7-1.
J S Papworth (South Cornwall).

626 Maiden Div II (12st)

458 **COMEDY GAYLE ....I Widdicombe** 1
mid-div, prog 15th, ld apr last, styd on
Music Of Mourne (Ire) 5a ....David Dennis 2
chsd ldr til 14th,lft in slght ld 2 out,no ext apr last,prom
460 **Corrib Haven (Ire) ....S Slade** 3
pllng, ld & sn clr, hdd aft 15th, wknd
531 Reptile Princess 5a *tongue strap, prom early, sn wknd, bhnd frm 12th* ....Miss W Hartnoll 4
453 King Of Cairo *nov rddn, alwys bhnd* ....W Smith 5
531 Pen-Shilmon 7a *lost tch frm 13th, t.o.*...A Holdsworth 6
458[7] Happy Valley 5a *bhnd til p.u. apr 16th*...Miss P Baker pu
458[2] Breeze-Bloc 5a *(Jt fav) rear til p.u. apr 15th* A Farrant pu
460 Cornish Harp *mid-div, p.u. 14th*...........G Shenkin pu
246 Battle Lord Cisto *bhnd til p.u. apr 15th* ....S Edwards pu
310 Crownhill Cross *rear, mstk 11th, t.o. whn p.u. apr 14th* ....S Kidston pu
243 Rhyme And Chime (bl) *in tch, efft to disp 3 out, f nxt* ....T Dennis f
461 Amicombe Brook 5a *6th hlfwy, rear whn p.u. apr 14th* ....N Harris pu
458[3] Midnight Bob *(Jt fav) hdwy whn hit 11th, disp 15th til jmp lft, swrvd & u.r. 2 out*..........J Young ur

14 ran. 5l, 8l, 30l, 15l, 8l. Time 6m 22.50s. SP 6-1.
Ms S Willcock (Spooners & West Dartmoor).

627 Ladies

238[1] **SECRET FOUR ....Miss T Cave** 1
(fav) hndy, ld 14th, ran on wll clsng stgs
174[1] **Khattaf ....Miss J Cumings** 2
ld 2nd, disp 13-14th, cls 2nd & ev ch whn not qckn flat
551[2] **Perfect Stranger ....Miss L Blackford** 3
wll in tch, disp 13-14th, onepcd frm 3 out
555 Double The Stakes (USA) *4th frm 10th, not pce to chal* ....Miss S Gaisford 4
311[1] False Economy *lost ground stdly frm 11th, no ch* ....Miss K Scorgie 5
My Key Silca *nov rddn, s.s., blndrd & u.r. 2nd* ....Miss L Smale ur
455[4] Afterkelly *1st ride, u.r. 2nd*..........Miss D Ward ur

7 ran. 5l, 2l, 6l, 15l. Time 6m 14.00s. SP 11-10.
P Masterson (Dart Vale & South Pool).

628 Confined (12st)

493[2] **KALOORE 5ex (bl).....................R Nuttall** 1
(fav) mstk 13th,wnt 3rd 14th,cls 2nd nxt til hrd rdn to ld run in
586 **Fiddlers Pike 3ex.............Mrs R Henderson** 2
ld 10th, lkd wnnr til hdd aft last, kpt on gamely
520 **Greenwine (USA) ....Miss G Underhill** 3
nov rddn, in tch, outpcd 15th, kpt on clsng stgs
457 Lady Lir 5a *prog to 5th 13th, ev ch 3 out, onepce* ....Miss S Young 4
456[4] Lonesome Traveller (NZ) *mid-div, 6th & rddn 14th, no ch ldrs*..........N Harris 5
453[4] Rasta Man *ld 4-10th, cls up til wknd 15th*....A Farrant 6
309 Querrin Lodge *8th hlfwy, nvr dang* ....T Greed 7
493 Absent Minds 5a *ld brfly 3rd, prom til lost plcd 10th, t.o.*..........Miss A Barnett 8
552[3] Hidden Dollar *f 1st, (destroyed)* ....G Penfold f
453 Carrot Bay *t.o. p.u. apr 9th*..........R Darke pu
97 Diana Moss (Ire) 5a *nvr gng wll, p.u. apr 7th*. .C Heard pu
Country Gem *bhnd thruout, t.o. p.u. apr 14th* S Slade pu

12 ran. Nk, 2l, nk, 10l, 6l, 25l, 20l. Time 6m 14.00s. SP 6-4.
Mrs J Alford (Eggesford).
Fences 9 & 17 omitted.

629 Men's Open

455[1] **SPRING MARATHON (USA) ....L Jefford** 1
(fav) w.w., trckng ldr, efft til disp last, pshd clr
285 **Nearly Splendid ....T Greed** 2
tried to make all, jnd & jmp lft last, no ext flat
552[1] The General's Drum *p.u. & dismntd aft 2nd*...K Heard pu
Friendly Viking *nvr dang, wll btn 3rd whn ref 15th* ....D Stephens ref
Wise Florizel *last til p.u. apr 14th*..........R Darke pu

5 ran. 3l. Time 6m 16.00s. SP 4-6.
Mrs Nerys Dutfield (Axe Vale).

630 Restricted (12st)

523 **MINE'S A GIN (IRE) ....Miss J Cumings** 1
hdwy 12th, ld 14th, disp 15th, qcknd clr run in
461[2] **Ann's Ambition ....C Heard** 2

prom, hdwy to disp 15th, slght ld last, not qckn
457[4] **Royal Turn ....A Honeyball 3**
hld up, gd hdwy 13th, wnt 3rd 15th, styd on wll
453[8] Ballysheil *ld/disp 5th, ld 9-14th, 4th & onepcd frm 15th* ....S Edwards 4
3071[1] Valley's Choice 5a *in tch, rddn 13th, 5th & onepcd frm 15th*.......................................L Jefford 5
2451[1] Saint Joseph *prog to disp 7-11th, lost ground stdly* ....Miss S Young 6
433[4] Parson Flynn *lft in ld 3rd-5th, cls up til wknd und pres frm 16th*......................................S Slade 7
Uncle James (Ire) *rear, ran on stdly frm 15th, fair debut*......................................A Farrant 8
176[3] Rosa's Revenge 5a (bl) *7th hlfwy, no ch last m* ....T Dennis 9
459[1] Probation *pllng & blndrd 2nd, 10th hlfwy, t.o.* R Darke 10
459 Horwood Drummer 5a *11th hlfwy, t.o.* ..A Holdsworth 11
Maggie Tee 5a *ld & ran out 3rd, saddle slpd*...J Scott ro
460[1] Hill Cruise *(fav) mid-div & not fluent, p.u. apr 14th* ....B Dixon pu
Our Teddis *ld til aft 2nd, c.o. apr nxt* Miss L Blackford co
Huffin And Puffin 7a *bhnd & schooling til p.u. apr 15th*......................................R Nuttall pu
Ballyhasty Lady (Ire) 5a *bhnd til p.u. apr 15th* J Young pu
16 ran. 3l, ½l, 5l, 8l, 1l, 2l, 8l, 1l, 25l, dist. Time 6m 22.00s. SP 7-1.
Mrs H C Johnson (Devon & Somerset Staghounds).

631 Intermediate

522[2] **MILLED OATS ....A Farrant 1**
(fav) hld up, efft 3 out, ld last, ran on strgly
456[2] **Just Ben ....Miss J Cumings 2**
ld 10th, blndrd & lost plc 14th, styd on wll clsng stgs
558[4] **Karicleigh Boy ....A Holdsworth 3D**
cls 2nd 10th til ld 14th,hdd last,wknd,disq lost wtcloth
533[1] **Dark Reflection ....C Heard 3**
s.s., bhnd frm 8th, t.o., fin 4th, promoted
456[3] The Copper Key *ld til 3rd, lost plc 11th, bhnd whn hit 2 out*......................................T Greed 5
Always Lynsey (Ire) 5a 5ow *lost tch 8th, t.o. p.u. aft 10th*......................................B Hurst pu
558 Henrys No Pushover *in tch, 3rd whn mstk 10th, blndrd & u.r. nxt*......................................L Jefford ur
456 Erme Rose (Ire) 5a *lost plc & rmmndrs apr 12th, bhnd whn p.u. apr last*......................................R Nuttall pu
8 ran. 1½l, 1l, 30l, ½l. Time 6m 15.00s. SP Evens.
Mrs A C Martin (Tiverton Foxhounds).
G.T.

LLANGIBBY
Howick
Saturday March 22nd
GOOD TO FIRM

632 Members (12st)

569[2] **ARCHER (IRE) 7ex......................M Harris 1**
(fav) trckd ldr, hrd rdn 3 out, disp last, ld final 50 yrds
399[5] **Rusty Music 7ex...............Miss N Richards 2**
ld, jnd last, hdd & no ext nr fin
2 ran. 1½l. Time 6m 39.00s. SP 1-4.
Paul Green (Llangibby).

633 Restricted Div I (12st)

FRENCH STICK ....E Williams 1
(Jt fav) ld to 7th, 2nd til ld agn 12th, in cmmnd frm 2 out
575[4] **Mackabee (Ire) ....T Weale 2**
(Jt fav) hld up mid-div, prog to 2nd 12th, mstk 3 out, hld aft
Spanish Rouge ....S Blackwell 3
2nd til ld 8th-12th, onepcd aft
260 Generator Boy *mid-div, some prog frm 12th, not rch ldrs*......................................J Baimbridge 4
488[5] Dragons Lady 5a *3rd til wknd frm 12th* ....G Barfoot-Saunt 5
Harry From Barry *7s-7/2, rear til p.u. 14th*.....J Tudor pu
406 Pharrago (Ire) *last pair til ran out 7th* ..Miss P Cooper ro
Lennie The Lion *last & n.j.w., p.u. 9th*.........J Price pu
8 ran. 4l, 15l, 4l, 15l. Time 6m 30.00s. SP 5-2.
Mrs J P Spencer (Clifton On Teme).

634 Restricted Div II (12st)

574 **GUARENA (USA) ....Miss N Richards 1**
hld up, prog 11th, drvn alng 13th, disp 3 out, ld last,qcknd
404[6] **A Farm Bar ....P Williams 2**
2nd frm 4th, disp 8th, strng run 2 out, no ext cls home
Colonel Frazer (Ire) ....G Lewis 3
lft in ld 4th, disp 8th-3 out, outpcd aft
409[1] In The Water *(fav) mid-div, drvn 11th, ran on onepcd* ....M P Jones 4
223[8] Tudor Oaks 5a *ld til f 4th*...............S Blackwell f
Wilton Park 5a *last frm 12th til p.u. 14th*.......A Price pu
409 Clansies Girl 5a *33s-16s, last til p.u. 12th* .....S Lloyd pu
7 ran. 1l, 10l, 5l. Time 6m 36.00s. SP 12-1.
M Lewis (Llangibby).

635 Restricted (12st)

524 **ZAMBRANO (USA) 7a ....S Durack 1**
(fav) hld up mid-div, steady prog 13th, ld 2 out, rdn clr
539[3] **Saffron Moss ....Miss F Wilson 2**
cls 2nd, disp 3 out, mstk nxt, no ext
405 **Cosa Nostra ....K Cousins 3**
ld til jnd 3 out, onepcd frm nxt
405[8] Algaihabane (USA) *3rd til 13th, grad wknd* ..S Shinton 4
405 Lles Le Bucflow *whppd round start, tk no part* ....E Williams 0
Wolfies Wonder 5a *last til blnd & u.r. 9th*..S Blackwell ur
435 Wissywis (Ire) 12a *alwys rear, dist 5th at 10th, p.u. 3 out* ....J Price pu
7 ran. 4l, 3l, 20l. Time 6m 30.00s. SP 4-7.
D L Williams (Berks & Bucks Drag).

636 Confined (12st)

491 **DOUBTING DONNA 5a..................M Harris 1**
4th til prog 12th, disp 3 out, ld nxt, qcknd flat
360 **Poinciana ....D Stephens 2**
cls up til ld 13th, jnd 3 out, hdd nxt, just outpcd
404[1] **Bit Of A Citizen (Ire) ....E Williams 3**
(fav) cls up, 3rd 3 out, rdn & no ext frm nxt
296[5] Hugli *rear, steady prog hlfwy, not rch ldrs* ....Miss L Pearce 4
567[2] Noisy Welcome *last early, some late prog, ran on onepcd* ....M P Jones 5
402[3] Dauphin Bleu (Fr) *ld til 13th, wknd rpdly*.....R Burton 6
535[7] Pay-U-Cash *alwys rear, fin own time*......G Perkins 7
398[3] Dane Rose 5a *rear til f 9th* ....T Weale f
401 Scared Stiff 5a *alwys rear, p.u. 13th*........J P Keen pu
402 Cairneymount 3ex *alwys rear, p.u. 3 out*...T Vaughan pu
187 Curie Crusader (Ire) *cls 2nd whn ran out 8th* ..J Tudor ro
Alfion (Ire) *alwys rear, p.u. 13th* ....D S Jones pu
12 ran. 1l, 4l, 5l, 8l, 12l, dist. Time 6m 23.00s. SP 4-1.
Mrs D Hughes (Llangeinor).

637 Men's Open (12st)

400[1] **JACK SOUND 7ex ....E Williams 1**
(fav) cls up, ld 11th, qcknd 3 out, in cmmnd aft
Al Frolic ....D S Jones 2
mostly 4th, prog 11th to chs wnr 3 out, alwys hld
Adanac ....S Blackwell 3
2nd/3rd til lost plc 14th, ran on well frm 3 out
145 Midfielder *ld to 11th, cls up 3 out, onepcd* ...R Burton 4
568[7] Sebastopol *alwys mid-div* ....D Stephens 5
432 Forest Ranger *last til p.u. 13th*...............J Price pu
537[1] Touch 'N' Pass 7ex *rear, hrd rdn hlfwy, not rch ldrs, p.u. last*......................................J Tudor pu
7 ran. 4l, 5l, 3l, 10l. Time 6m 28.00s. SP 4-5.
E L Harries (Pembrokeshire).

638 Ladies

534[1] **OZZIE JONES** ....**Miss L Pearce** 1
cls up, ld 13th, qcknd clr, ran on well
482 **Roving Report** ....**Mrs A Rucker** 2
mid-div, went 3rd 12th, chal 3 out, alwys hld
466[2] **Couture Tights 3ex** ....**Miss J Priest** 3
(fav) hld up rear, prog hlfwy, unable to chal
Wake Up Luv *2nd til ld 9th, hdd 13th, onepcd aft* ....Miss P Cooper 4
401[4] Bartondale 5a *twrds rear, no prog frm 14th* ....Miss B Williams 5
536[1] Lucky Ole Son 3ex *rear, rdn & no prog frm 13th* ....Miss P Jones 6
401[7] Afaristoun (Fr) *ld to 9th, wknd rpdly, p.u. 13th* ....Miss J Morse pu
Coombesbury Lane 5a *mid-div, wknd & p.u. 3 o ut* ....Miss C Spearing pu
401 West King *last til p.u. 11th*..........Miss E Crawford pu
537[4] Cornish Cossack (NZ) *twrds rear, p.u. 3 out* ....Miss A Meakins pu
10 ran. 4l, 12l, 5l, 10l, 10l. Time 6m 17.00s. SP 5-1.
Keith R Pearce (Carmarthenshire).

639 Maiden Div I (12st)

261 **BEL LANE 5a (bl)**.......................**D S Jones** 1
mostly 2nd/3rd, ld 14th, sn clr
406[5] **Malthouse Lad** ....**D Stephens** 2
10s-6s, mid-div, prog 14th, 2nd 3 out, not rch wnr
285 **Lazzaretto** ....**I Johnson** 3
hld up, ran on to 2nd at 15th, onepcd aft
408 Tommyknocker (Ire) 7a *mid-div, ran on frm 14th, nrst fin*..........Miss P Cooper 4
408 Sweet Mariner *4th/5th til outpcd frm 14th* ..M P Jones 5
406[6] Le Vienna (Ire) *alwys rear* ....S Currey 6
398[4] Astley Jack *cls up, wknd 14th, 4th whn f 2 out* ....R Cotton f
Maytown *alwys rear, p.u. 13th*.........Miss E Jones pu
259 Central Lass 5a *rear til f 14th*............S Blackwell f
404 Jolly Swagman *ld, wll clr 8th, wknd rpdly 13th, f nxt* ....G Perkins f
575 Priesthill (Ire) *alwys rear, p.u. 14th* ....Miss S Duckett pu
540 Quaker Pep (v) *mid-div, f 8th, dead* ....P Hamer f
Saronica-R *rear, p.u. 12th*..........S Shinton pu
186 Ballyhooly Belle (Ire) 5a *(fav) mid-div, no prog whn p.u. 13th*..........E Williams pu
Dinedor Charlie *rear til p.u. 9th*..............J Tudor pu
15 ran. 25l, 10l, dist, 5l, dist. Time 6m 33.00s. SP 4-1.
M R Watkins (Ross Harriers).
Last fence omitted.

640 Maiden Div II Pt I (12st)

541 **TOP TOR 5a**..........................**T Vaughan** 1
(fav) hld up, lft in ld 15th, disp & lft clr 2 out
540[4] **I'm A Bute 5a**............................**J Price** 2
cls up til wknd 13th, styd on agn late
300 **Plas-Hendy**.......................**Miss F Wilson** 3
12s-6s, cls up, ld & clr 13th, blnd 15th, hdd & btn aft
Willow Belle (Ire) 5a *ld to 12th, grad wknd* ..S Shinton 4
409 Trydan *rear, p.u. 12th*.............Miss S Robertson pu
259[5] Mr Suspicious (Ire) *mid-div, cls 4th whn f 14th* ....M P Jones f
398 Takahashi (Ire) *hld up, prog 13th, lft 2nd 15th, disp & f 2 out*..........S Blackwell f
185 Bus Pass 7a *cls up, ran out aft 6th* ....P Doorhof ro
538 Dontyoudoda (Ire) *rear, p.u. 12th*..........J P Keen pu
Rebel Yell (Ire) 5a *rear, p.u. 12th* ....K Cousins pu
10 ran. 25l, 5l, 15l. Time 6m 34.00s. SP 9-4.
R H P Williams (Llangeinor).

641 Maiden Div II Pt II (12st)

407[3] **YARRON KING** ....**I Johnson** 1
(fav) hld up mid-div, prog to ld 15th, styd on
366 **Bally Boy 7a**...........................**D S Jones** 2
rear, prog to 2nd at 16th, chal last, hld flat
406 **Bickerton Poacher** ....**G Perkins** 3
mostly 2nd/3rd, onepcd frm 16th
Prince Itsu *rear til ran out 7th* ....D Stephens ro
406 Toucher (Ire) *mid-div, b.d. 6th*..........J Cook bd
Wooly Town 5a *ld to 6th, wknd & p.u. 12th*. .P Williams pu
Calverstown Star (Ire) *mid-div, hmpd & b.d. 6th* ....M Harris bd
407 Roger (Ire) 7a *ld 6th-13th, wknd rpdly, f 3 out* ....C Pennycate ur
Wyndams Lad (Ire) 2ow *mid-div, b.d. 6th* ....R Cotton bd
9 ran. 4l, 20l. Time 6m 50.00s. SP 2-1.
G A Fynn (Tredegar Farmers).
J.C./P.H.

MENDIP FARMERS
Castle Of Comfort
Saturday March 22nd
GOOD

642 Members (12st)

294[2] **DOUBLE THRILLER** ....**R Treloggen** 1
(fav) jmpd lft, made all, drew clr 2 out, easily
572 **Scriven Boy** ....**M Flynn** 2
chsd wnr, rdn 3 out, onepcd
106 Lady Mouse 5a *hld up, mstk 6th, prog 11th, btn whn jmpd slwly 15th,p.u.nxt*..........B O'Doherty pu
L'artiste *cls up, jmpd slwly 2nd, pshd alng 12th, t.o. & p.u. 14th*..........M Burrows pu
4 ran. 15l. Time 6m 55.00s. SP 1-5.
R C Wilkins (Mendip Farmers).

643 Open Maiden (5-8yo) Div I (12st)

556[3] **THE BOLD ABBOT** ....**Miss S West** 1
ld to 3rd, ld 9th, made rest, clr apr last, styd on
365[5] **Military Man 1ow**.......................**A Phillips** 2
mid-div, chsd ldr 13th, rdn & blnd 2 out, kpt on und pres
243 **Fever Pitch** ....**D Alers-Hankey** 3
cls up, 3rd & ev ch 14th, wknd apr 2 out, fin tired
459 Moorland Magic (Ire) 12a *mid-div, cls 5th at 12th, wknd nxt, p.u. 14th* ....I Dowrick pu
527[6] Sandy Etna (Ire) 5a *cls up til b.d. 8th* Mrs K Matthews bd
Harlequin Bay *s.s. rshd to ld 3rd til apr 7th, 2nd whn f 8th, dead*..........Mrs R Baldwin f
314 Renshaw Ings *prom, ld apr 7th-9th, wknd 11th, p.u. 13th*..........J Creighton pu
458 Eurolinkhellraiser (Ire) *w.w. mstk 2nd, prog whn blnd 13th, btn nxt, p.u. 2 out*..........T Mitchell pu
Funny Farm *(Jt fav) in tch, cls 5th whn b.d. 8th* ....Miss S Vickery bd
40 Millyhenry *(Jt fav) hld up rear, prog & hmpd 8th, wknd apr 15th, p.u. 2 out*..........J Tizzard pu
436[5] Little Ease (Ire) 12a *prom to 4th, grad lost plc, mstk 7th, last whn u.r. 11th* ....J Jackson ur
Perripage *rear & jmpd slwly 4th, last whn blnd 7th, p.u. nxt*..........M Miller pu
12 ran. 3½l, dist. Time 6m 39.00s. SP 6-1.
R A Lissack (South & West Wilts).
One fence omitted, 17 jumps.

644 Open Maiden (5-8yo) Div II (12st)

460 **JIM CROW** ....**P King** 1
made most to apr 13th, rdn 2 out, ld last, hld on gamely
182 **Rustic Lord 7a**.....................**B O'Doherty** 2
trckd ldrs going wll, ld 2 out, ran wd & hdd last, kpt on
571[2] **Lindalighter 5a**.......................**A Phillips** 3
(fav) w.w. in tch, cls 3rd & ev ch 2 out, unable qckn flat
297 False Tail (Ire) 7a *cls up, ld apr 13th-15th, ev ch & rdn 2 out, no ext* ....J Tizzard 4
Droum Ross (Ire) *prom, ld 15th-3 out, 5th & wkng whn blnd nxt*..........Miss C Thomas 5
The Fluter *last pair, steady prog frm 3 out, nvr plcd to chal*..........I Dowrick 6
461 French Invasion 5a *rear, mstk 5th, outpcd 14th, no ch frm 3 out* ....M Frith 7
313 Naburn Loch 5a *chsd ldr, ld brfly 6th, wknd 12th, t.o. & p.u. 15th*..........J Hankinson pu

526 Quince Cross 5a *mid-div, prog to jn ldrs & blnd 10th, wknd 15th, p.u. 2 out* .... M Burrows pu
9 ran. ½l, 1l, 3l, 2l, 3l, 8l. Time 6m 48.00s. SP 12-1.
J M Salter (Axe Vale Harriers).

645 Ladies

296[1] **EARTHMOVER (IRE) .... Miss P Curling** 1
(fav) hld up, prog to ld 8th, made rest, qcknd clr 2 out, easily
434[3] **Nutcase 5a .... Miss S Vickery** 2
trckd ldrs, chsd wnr 9th, rdn & ev ch 3 out, wknd nxt
522[5] **Life Peerage (USA) .... Mrs S Barrow** 3
rear, lost tch 12th, kpt on to tk poor 3rd 2 out
520[6] Legal Picnic *in tch, outpcd 12th, lft poor 3rd 14th, demoted 2 out* .... Miss C Bryan 4
145[6] Ski Nut *ld to 8th, 3rd & outpcd whn blnd & u.r. 14th* .... Miss S West ur
431[5] Great Uncle *wth ldr to 7th, 4th & outpcd 13th, last whn p.u. aft 2 out* .... Miss T McCurrick pu
6 ran. 15l, 15l, 7l. Time 6m 31.00s. SP 1-3.
R M Penny (Cattistock).

646 Men's Open (12st)

293[1] **STRONG CHAIRMAN (IRE) .... T Mitchell** 1
(fav) jmpd lft,trckd ldrs, chal 15th,swtch apr last,ld flat,clvrly
522[1] **Qualitair Memory (Ire) 7ex .... J Tizzard** 2
ld to 9th, mstk 11th, ld 14th, rdn 3 out, hdd & no ext flat
395 **Southerly Buster .... S White** 3
last & jmpd slwly 5th,lost tch 14th,kpt on to poor 3rd flat
491[5] Prince Nepal *chsd ldr, ld 9th, clr 13th, hdd nxt, wll btn whn blnd 3 out* .... J Creighton 4
180 Clever Shepherd 7ex *chsd ldrs, 4th & rdn 14th, no ch nxt, t.o.* .... I Dowrick 5
5 ran. 2l, dist, 2l, 15l. Time 6m 36.00s. SP 4-5.
J A Keighley (Blackmore & Sparkford Vale).

647 Intermediate (12st)

218[1] **FRONT COVER 5a 5ex............ Miss S Vickery** 1
(fav) chsd ldr 3-8th & 12th,ev ch & rdn 3 out,btn whn lft clr last
310[2] **Highway Lad .... P King** 2
chsd ldrs,mstk & lost plc 9th,rdn 14th,no ch & lft 2nd last
575[1] **Basil Street (Ire) 7a.................... A Phillips** 3
mstks, prog 10th, btn 15th, lft poor 3rd last
Ideal *jmpd rght, ld to 10th, last & no ch frm 14th* .... J Rees 4
Neat And Tidy *in tch, ran out & u.r. 5th* .... Miss A Boswell ro
Whitmore *blnd & u.r. 2nd* .... J Tizzard ur
293 Gigi Beach (Ire) *rmndr 8th, ld 10th, hrd rdn 3 out, in cmmnd whn u.r. last* .... Miss P Curling ur
7 ran. Dist, 2l, 1l. Time 6m 31.00s. SP Evens.
Stewart Pike (East Devon).

648 Restricted (12st)

300[2] **MARION'S OWN (IRE) .... Miss P Curling** 1
jnd ldrs 9th, ld 15th, hrd rdn apr last, hng lft, all out
298[4] **Kinesiology (Ire) .... R Treloggen** 2
ld 5th til apr 15th, rdn 3 out, swtchd last, rallied flat
105[1] **Tamaimo (Ire) .... T Mitchell** 3
(fav) w.w. in tch, prog to 3rd 15th, unable qckn apr last
461[1] Sabbaq (USA) *trckd ldrs, mstk 9th, prog & ev ch 15th, onepcd frm 2 out* .... I Dowrick 4
523 Lake Mariner 5a *in tch, chsd ldr brfly 13th, wknd 15th* .... Maj O Ellwood 5
459 Tom's Arctic Dream 5a *ld to 5th, prom til wknd 11th, t.o. & p.u. last* .... P King pu
Electrofane (Ire) *in tch, rdn & outpcd 11th, t.o. & p.u. 15th* .... D Alers-Hankey pu
522 Glamorous Guy *chsd ldr to 4th, last whn blnd 12th, p.u. nxt* .... M Frith pu
8 ran. Hd, 1½l, 6l, 30l. Time 6m 38.00s. SP 6-1.
Mrs M B Keighley (Cattistock).
Objection by 2nd to winner, overruled. S.P.

V W H
Siddington
Saturday March 22nd
FIRM

649 Members

377[8] **DIAMOND WIND (USA) 5a .... A Beedles** 1
(fav) j.w. ld to 3rd & agn 9th, jnd last, pshd out flat
395[2] **Cavalero .... L Manners** 2
hld up, prog 10th, chsd wnr 14th, lvl & mstk last, just hld
585[6] **Miss Magic 5a....................... F Brennan** 3
prom, chsd wnr 9-14th, rdn & btn 3 out, wknd
512 Rose Of Macmillion 5a *ld 3-9th, wknd rpdly, t.o. & p.u. 13th* .... E Bailey pu
396 French Pleasure 5a *trckd ldrs, mstk 12th & rdn, btn whn nrly ref 15th & p.u.* .... P Howse pu
300[7] Viking Flame 5a *mstk 2nd, in tch til wknd 10th, mstk 11th & p.u.* .... S Bush pu
6 ran. Hd, 25l. Time 5m 58.00s. SP Evens.
Count Goess-Saurau And Mr C Leigh (V.W.H.).

650 Confined (12st)

360 **DANBURY LAD (IRE) 3ex .... Miss A Dare** 1
(fav) cls up, disp 13th til ld 3 out, slw jmps last 2, pshd out
Knightly Argus .... M Rollett 2
keen hld, jmpd rght, chsd ldr 9th, disp 13th-3 out, kpt on
446[6] **Tompet .... J Connell** 3
not keen, ld to 13th, sn btn, lft 3rd 15th
572 Durzi *ref & u.r. 1st* .... E Walker ref
Grey Tudor *chsd ldr to 9th, outpcd 14th, 6l 3rd whn blnd & u.r. nxt* .... G Field ur
369[6] I'm Toby *alwys last pair, t.o. 10th, ref 2 out* .... Miss S Palmer ref
Miss Millie 5a *schoold, last til p.u. 10th*. . J Trice-Rolph pu
Bridge Man *not fluent, in tch frm 5-9th, lost plc & p.u. nxt* .... S Bush pu
8 ran. 2l, 25l. Time 6m 7.00s. SP 1-3.
Dr P P Brown & Mrs C Birks (Berkeley).

651 Men's Open (12st)

393 **GRANVILLE GRILL 4ex................ J Deutsch** 1
made all, drew clr aft 3 out, mstk last, rdn out
446[2] **Fair Crossing .... M Emmanuel** 2
chsd wnr, not qckn aft 3 out, kpt on
295[2] **Bishops Island 7ex .... Julian Pritchard** 3
(fav) not fluent, hld up, prog 10th, 3rd & no imp frm 15th
484 Beach Bum *chsd ldng pair,mstk 10th & pshd alng,nt qckn 14th,wknd 2 out* .... A Charles-Jones 4
93 Barkisland *f 2nd*.......................... M Rimell f
397[5] The Country Trader 7ex *chsd ldrs to 8th, wknd 10th, t.o. whn u.r. apr 15th* .... J Borradaile ur
333[2] Therewego (Ire) *mstk 3rd, alwys last, t.o. & p.u. 15th* .... M Munrowd pu
7 ran. 3l, 8l, 15l. Time 5m 53.00s. SP 5-1.
E W Smith (Beaufort).

652 Ladies

364[1] **SAMS HERITAGE .... Miss A Dare** 1
(fav) cls up, trckd ldr 10th, ld 3 out, comf
448[1] **Mountshannon .... Mrs T Hill** 2
ld to 5th, ld 9th-3 out, not qckn aft
371[7] **Icky's Five .... Miss T Habgood** 3
in tch to 10th, t.o. 14th, went dist 3rd 2 out
466[4] Tytherington *lft 25l, rcvrd to ld 5th-9th, wknd 11th, t.o.* .... Miss S Talbot 4
300 Country Lord *last frm 4th, wknd 10th, t.o. & p.u. 3 out* .... Mrs S Walwin pu
5 ran. 4l, dist, 1l. Time 6m 3.00s. SP 4-6.
C G Smedley (Berkeley).

653 Restricted Div I (12st)

377[5] **COUNT BALIOS (IRE)** .... **P Howse** 1
(Jt fav) ld 4th, made most aft, mstks 6th & 3 out, kpt on wll 2 out
435 **Rusty Fellow** .... **D Mansell** 2
rear,effrt 12th,prog to chal 2 out,outjmpd & not qckn aft
485[1] **Cool Rascal 5a** .... **L Lay** 3
trckd ldrs, outpcd 14th, tk poor 3rd last
369 Fill The Boot (Ire) *prom, chsd wnr 10th, mstk 12th, rdn & ev ch 15th, wknd nxt*........J Owen 4
261 Marginal Margie 5a *jmpd slwly 1st, schoold in rear, nvr dang*........M Munrowd 5
450[3] Blame The Groom (Ire) *in tch in rear to 12th, sn bhnd, t.o.*........D Buckley 6
373 Space Molly 5a (bl) *made most to 4th, wth wnr to 9th, sn wknd, t.o.*........P Cowley 7
300 Its Murphy Man *trckd ldrs, outpcd 14th, 5th whn p.u. nxt*........J Trice-Rolph pu
516 Nobbutjust (Ire) 5a *(Jt fav) hld up, mstk 3rd, effrt 12th, nvr rchd ldrs, btn & p.u.3 out*........A Beedles pu
Permit 5a *crawld fences, t.o. til p.u. 6th* ....Miss P Gundry pu

10 ran. 2l, 20l, 1l, 15l, 20l, 8l. Time 5m 56.00s. SP 9-4.
M H Wood (V.W.H.).

654 Mqaiden Div I

299[3] **MEMBERS CRUISE** .... **E Walker** 1
(Jt fav) jmpd rght, chsd ldr 6th, ld 15th, blnd nxt, kpt on und pres
88 **Toms Choice (Ire)** .... **G Barfoot-Saunt** 2
(Jt fav) ld to 15th, sn rdn, ev ch 2 out, no ext
298 **Uncle Bruce** .... **A Charles-Jones** 3
mid-div, 3rd & outpcd frm 12th, kpt on steadily frm 15th
499[7] Village Remedy 5a *alwys rear, t.o. 12th*......A Tutton 4
Roman Romany *f 3rd*........M Rimell f
Daring Daisy 5a *rear frm 5th, t.o. 10th, p.u. 12th* ....Mrs C McCarthy pu
392[3] Tu Piece *chsd ldrs, 6th whn f 8th*........P Howse f
Salmon Poutcher 5a *trckd ldrs, outpcd 11th, no ch 14th, poor 4th & p.u. last*........J Trice-Rolph pu
224 Captain Flashard 7a *prom, 3rd whn u.r. 8th* ..J Hobbs ur
390 Celtic Friend (Ire) *n.j.w. t.o. til p.u. 8th*.....M Portman pu

10 ran. 3½l, 15l, dist. Time 6m 2.00s. SP 3-1.
E W Smith (Beaufort).

655 Restricted Div II (12st)

435[1] **LETS TWIST AGAIN (IRE)** .... **Julian Pritchard** 1
(fav) hld up, prog to ld 10th, drew clr apr 2 out, comf
148[4] **Tarry Awhile** .... **J Connell** 2
prom, ld 7-10th, cls up aft, styd on onepcd frm 2 out
298 **Colonel Fairfax (bl)** .... **J Trice-Rolph** 3
hld up in tch, effrt aft 3 out, hit nxt, no imp aft
Four Rivers *cls up, effrt to chs wnr 13th, ev ch 3 out, rdn & no ext aft*........R Lawther 4
452 Another Whistle (Ire) *alwys rear, outpcd frm 10th, t.o.* ....Miss T Habgood 5
Sungia (Ire) *prom til wknd rpdly 14th, t.o.*.....E Walker 6
Mismetallic 5a *schoold in rear, outpcd 10th, t.o.* ....C Wadland 7
Crestwood Lad (USA) *pllng, ld til ran out 5th* ....M Yardley ro
574 Connie Foley *lft in ld 5th, hdd 7th, prom whn u.r. 9th* ....Miss S Hiatt ur
397[6] John Roger *rear, p.u. 5th*........J Merry pu

10 ran. 6l, 3l, 1l, dist, sht-hd, 8l. Time 6m 1.00s. SP 4-7.
Mrs S Bird (Ledbury).

656 Maiden Div II

373[6] **ROARK'S CHUKKA** .... **D Smith** 1
ld to 12th, ld agn aft 3 out, ran on wll nxt
568[3] **Crown Jewel** .... **C Wilson** 2
(fav) prom, rdn 14th, chal 3 out, ev ch til no ext flat
Jilly Wig (Ire) 12a .... **A Beedles** 3
jmpd slwly early, prom, ld 12th-aft 3 out, wknd apr last
258 Well Bank *alwys prom, rdn & ev ch 15th, wknd aft 3 out*........E Walker 4
485 Ruby's Girl 5a *rear, lost tch 11th, bhnd aft, p.u. 2 out* ....Miss P Gundry pu
299 Bombadier Brown *in tch to 12th, sn wknd, t.o. & p.u. 15th*........A Charles-Jones pu
Carrigbyrne Candy 5a *jmpd slwly, t.o. til p.u. 11th* ....G Barfoot-Saunt pu

7 ran. 2l, 6l, 20l. Time 6m 2.00s. SP 20-1.
D P Smith (Heythrop).
J.N.

WILTON
Badbury Rings
Saturday March 22nd
FIRM

657 Members

MAGIC MOLE 12a .... **Miss M Hill** 1
(Jt fav) prom, blnd 3 out, strng run nxt, ld flat
Elegant Sun .... **Miss R David** 2
ld/disp to 14th, clr nxt, hdd & no ext flat
Newman's Conquest 12a .... **Miss A Goschen** 3
alwys last, blnd 14th, tk 3rd nr fin
303 Dormston Lad *(Jt fav) prom to 3 out, outpcd frm nxt* ....C Jowett 4

4 ran. 1l, 5l, ½l. Time 6m 24.00s. SP 9-4.
Richard J Hill (Wilton).

658 Maiden

INNER SNU 5a........................ **N Mitchell** 1
(fav) hld up, prog 14th, chal 2 out, ld last, ran on und pres
30 **Bart's Castle** .... **Daniel Dennis** 2
ld til hdd apr last, outpcd
111 **Dancing Barefoot 5a** .... **J Barnes** 3
chsd ldr, ev ch 3 out, blnd nxt, no ext
Mountain-Linnet *handy to 14th, lost tch nxt, outpcd* ....T Woolridge 4
487[4] Kala Dawn 5a *in tch til blnd & u.r. 6th*....Miss M Tory ur
391[3] Dad's Delight 5a *in tch to 12th, lost plc nxt, t.o. & p.u. 5 out*........Miss A Goschen pu

6 ran. 2l, 15l, 30l. Time 6m 21.40s. SP 6-4.
S L Mitchell (South Dorset).

659 Men's Open

483[2] **MYVERYGOODFRIEND** .... **S Cobden** 1
j.w. ld to 4 out, disp nxt til ld 2 out, ran on well
514[3] **Indian Knight** .... **N Mitchell** 2
(fav) trckd ldr, chal 3 out, blnd nxt, no ext aft

2 ran. 3l. Time 6m 56.50s. SP 2-1.
S Cobden (Hursley Hambledon).

660 Ladies

394[3] **SPACIAL (USA)** .... **Miss M Hill** 1
ld to 3 out, disp nxt, ran on best und pres
385 **Panda Shandy 5a** .... **Miss A Goschen** 2
(fav) trckd ldr, chal 2 out, onepcd apr last

2 ran. 3½l. Time 5m 59.30s. SP 11-8.
Richard J Hill (Wilton).

661 Restricted (12st)

518[1] **TULLYKYNE BELLS** .... **Miss D Stafford** 1
alwys prom, ld 13th-nxt, rnwd effrt to ld 2 out, kpt on wll
315[1] **Jack Sun** .... **J Snowden** 2
(fav) lft 30l start, prog 11th, disp 13th-nxt, effrt 3 out,nt qckn
372[4] **Duke Of Lancaster (Ire) (bl)** .... **N Sutton** 3
ld to 13th, styd on agn frm 2 out
457 Palace King (Ire) *alwys prom, ld 14th, clr whn blnd 3 out, hdd nxt, onepcd*........R Payne 4

285[6] Final Express 5a *in tch to 13th, outpcd nxt, no dang aft*..........M Hoskins 5
306 Palmerston's Folly 5a *handy til f 8th*....Daniel Dennis f
6 ran. Nk, 4l, 2l, 15l. Time 6m 23.20s. SP 12-1.
M A Kerley (New Forest Buckhounds).

662 Confined

515 **ALEX THUSCOMBE (bl)..........P Shaw 1**
prom, 3rd 4 out, strng run 2 out, ld aft last, styd on
455[3] **Chism (Ire)..........M Miller 2**
(fav) cls up, effrt 4 out, ld nxt, hdd aft last, not qckn
302[6] **Skinnhill..........C Mason 3**
ld to 13th, agn 14th-3 out, outpcd aft
397 Prankster *prom, ev ch 15th, onepcd frm 2 out*..........T Atkinson 4
309[4] Gallant Effort (Ire) *prom early, lost plc 12th, t.o. 15th*..........J Snowden 5
309 Shilgrove Place *sn rear, p.u. 6th*..........S Allen pu
310[5] Pabrey *10s-4s, hld up, prog 12th, ld 13th-nxt, cls 3rd whn f 3 out*..........N Mitchell f
396 Gormless (Ire) *in tch to 14th, wknd nxt, t.o. & p.u. 3 out*..........Miss M Hill pu
8 ran. 1l, 4l, 4l, ½l, 20l. Time 6m 11.00s. SP 3-1.
Mrs Fiona Shaw (Cattistock).
D.P.

SIR W W WYNN'S
Eaton Hall
Sunday March 23rd
GOOD TO FIRM

663 Members

467[2] **MR BUSKER (IRE)..........C Barlow 1**
(fav) ld, lft solo 6th
Extraspecial Brew *2nd til f 6th*..........M Worthington f
2 ran. Time 6m 57.00s. SP 1-8.
C J B Barlow (Sir W W Wynn's).

664 Open Maiden Div I

82 **CHERRY GLEN (IRE)..........A Crow 1**
(fav) hld up rear, prog 5 out, ld 2 out, ran on und pres
464 **Crunch Time (Ire)..........C Stockton 2**
w.w. prog 10th, ld 14th-2 out, ran on, lkd 3rd
326[4] **Po Cap Eel 5a..........G Hanmer 3**
mid-div, prog 12th, ran on und pres 2 out, lkd 2nd
468 Mophead Kelly *mid-div, prog to disp 3 out, not qckn aft*..........A Dalton 4
288[5] Welsh Lightning *rear 12th, some late prog, nvr nrr*..........R Inglesant 5
587 Majic Belle 5a (bl) *chsd ldrs to 12th, grad wknd*..........A Wintle 6
Bowlands Galaxy *prom to 8th, rdn & no rspns 12th*..........R Ford 7
Gold Dam (Ire) (bl) *ld to 13th, onepcd aft, sn btn*..........D Barlow 8
Arctic Red *mid-div, p.u. 5th*..........R Hogan pu
465[4] Spartan Pete *mid-div, rmndrs, p.u. 8th*..........R Burton pu
332 Henrymyson *mid to rear, last whn p.u. 3 out*..J Corrie pu
430[3] Lady Pendragon 5a *prom, 2nd at 7th, disp 10th, wknd 13th, p.u. 3 out*..........D Mansell pu
12 ran. ½l, ½l, 8l, 2l, 2l. Time 6m 30.00s. SP 5-2.
K J Mitchell (North Shropshire).

665 Open Maiden Div II

81 **BUBBLE N SQUEEK..........C Barlow 1**
chsd ldrs, ld 3 out, ran on whn chal last
464[3] **Travel Bound..........D Barlow 2**
ld to 2nd, cls up, lft in ld 12th, hdd apr 3 out, kpt on
480[5] **King Keith..........C Stockton 3**
svrl slw jmps, chsng grp, ev ch 3 out, ran on flat, lkd 2nd
377 Noble Angel (Ire) *whppd round strt, lost 50l, grad made ground, tk 4th flat*..........A Dalton 4
470[5] Pullthepplug *prom, in tch to 5 out, wknd & onepcd aft*..........R Burton 5
360 Only In Ireland *ld 3rd til f 12th*..........R Inglesant f
Parson's Corner *mid to rear, p.u. 4 out*..........Miss C Williams pu
346 Sandy King (Ire) *mid-div, lost tch 12th, p.u. 4 out*..........R Bevis pu
470 Nights Image (Ire) *(fav) f 3rd*..........P Blane f
Hatton Cloud 5a *alwys rear, t.o. & p.u. 4 out, school*..........S Prior pu
469 Seymours Secret 12a *mid to rear, no ch whn p.u. 4 out*..........N Gittins pu
11 ran. 1l, 1½l, 20l, 2l. Time 6m 25.00s. SP 9-2.
C J B Barlow (West Shropshire).

666 Open Maiden Div III

199[3] **GLENROWAN (IRE)..........R Ford 1**
chsd ldr, strng run flat, ld fin
331[3] **Dalusaway (Ire) 5a..........C Stockton 2**
(fav) ld til chal flat, hdd post, lame
327 **Crafty Gunner..........M Worthington 3**
w.w. prog 5 out, ev ch whn mstk 3 out, ran on
409[3] Ribington *chsd ldrs, ev ch 4 out, not qckn* R Thornton 4
81[4] Penbola (Ire) 7a *mid to rear, losng tch whn p.u. 3 out*..........D Sherlock pu
I'll Skin Them (Ire) 5a *mstks, mid to rear, t.o. & p.u. 3 out*..........Mrs C Ford pu
Opulent Trappings 5a *chsng grp, 2nd at 9th, mstk nxt, sn btn, p.u. 3 out*..........J Barlow pu
327 Palladante (Ire) 5a *mid to rear, no ch whn p.u. 3 out*..........D Barlow pu
331 Scally Lass 5a *cls up to 8th, lost tch 10th, t.o. & p.u. 14th*..........Miss J Penney pu
204 Idiomatic *disp to 4th, wknd 10th, p.u. 5 out*....R Tilley pu
10 ran. ½l, 2l, 4l. Time 6m 29.00s. SP 9-2.
R Thomas (West Shropshire Drag).

667 Confined (12st)

330[2] **NODFORM WONDER..........R Bevis 1**
(fav) made most, clr 4th, unchal, easily
464 **Bay Owl..........M Worthington 2**
rear, prog 10th, 2nd 2 out, no imp wnr
332[1] **Miss Shaw 5a..........Miss K Crank 3**
1st ride, mid-div til prog 14th, ran on onepcd
199 Le Piccolage *disp to 3rd, lft 2nd at 10th, no ext 3 out*..........C Barlow 4
492[6] Side Brace (NZ) *mid to rear, poor 6th 4 out, p.u. nxt*..........Miss K Swindells pu
468 Grindley Brook *prom to 10th, wknd rpdly, p.u. 12th*..........A Lake pu
464 Jo-Su-Ki *mid-div early, t.o. 11th, p.u. nxt*....P Saville pu
Bucks Surprise *s.s. sn t.o., no ch whn p.u. 5 out*..........D Dickinson pu
468[1] Four Hearts (Ire) *prom, 3rd at 6th, lost tch & p.u. 4 out*..........D Barlow pu
84 Sirrah Aris (Ire) *disp to 3rd, 10l 2nd whn f 10th* A Crow f
10 ran. 15l, 10l, 4l. Time 6m 18.00s. SP 7-4.
D A Malam (West Shropshire Drag).

668 Men's Open (12st)

494 **MY NOMINEE 7ex (bl)..........R Burton 1**
(fav) made all, lft 25l clr 5 out, eased nr fin
465[3] **Tara Boy..........R Cambrey 2**
10l 3rd at 10th, lft 2nd 5 out, no imp wnr
496[2] The Rum Mariner *6l 2nd & lkd hld whn u.r. 5 out*..........R Thornton ur
3 ran. 10l. Time 6m 21.00s. SP 4-6.
D E Nicholls (North Shropshire).

669 Ladies

412[3] **HORNBLOWER..........Mrs C Ford 1**
(fav) chsg grp til ld 2 out, sn in cmmnd, comf
328 **Charterforhardware..........Miss T Clark 2**
1st ride, ld & sn clr, wknd & hdd 2 out, onepcd aft
329[1] **Sooner Still..........Miss S Sharratt 3**
chsng grp, disp 2nd 3 out, outpcd apr last
466[5] Moya's Tip Top 5a *chsng grp til lost tch 4 out*..........Miss A Price 4

330 Golden Fare *rear by 4th, t.o. & p.u. 11th* ....Miss L Wallace pu
5 ran. 5l, 5l, dist. Time 6m 18.00s. SP 1-3.
N J Barrowclough (North Shropshire).

670 Restricted (12st)

346[2] **YOUNG PARSON ....R Owen 1**
mid-div, prog 10th, trckd ldr til ld 3 out, ran on wll flat
467 **Gillie's Fountain ....A Dalton 2**
w.w. prog & ev ch 4 out, ran on, just held
467 **Rue de Fort ....J Cornes 3**
ld 5th-4 out, unable qckn nxt, no ext last
203[2] Yukon Gale (Ire) *(fav) w.w. prog 5 out, not qckn nxt, nvr able to chal* ....A Crow 4
204[2] Blushing Star *cls up at 10th, in tch 14th, fdd*. .N Gittins 5
Kiltrose Lad *alwys mid-div, nvr rchd ldrs* ....Julian Pritchard 6
468 Ballybeggan Parson (Ire) *prom to hlfwy, lost tch ldrs 4 out* ....G Hanmer 7
468 Another Chancer *mid to rear, fin own time*. . .M Harris 8
332[5] Glen Taylor *strgglng in rear aft 8th* ....Mrs M Wall 9
348[5] Foolish Fantasy (v) *rear, nvr in race* ....S Prior 10
333 Trojan Pleasure 5a *mid to rear, no ch whn p.u. 3 out* ....C Barlow pu
468[3] Allezscally 5a *p.u. 5th, lame* ....C Stockton pu
404[3] Onemoreanwego 5a *u.r. 3rd* ....Miss E James ur
464 Sheppie's Reality *ld to 4th, lost tch 14th, p.u. 3 out* ....O McPhail pu
470 Daftasabrush (Ire) 12a *alwys rear, p.u. 3 out* ....M Worthington pu
15 ran. ½l, 3l, 2l, 8l. Time 6m 20.00s. SP 16-1.
T D Marlow (Flint & Denbigh).

671 3¾m Intermediate (12st)

403[1] **SCARLET BERRY 5a 5ex ....Julian Pritchard 1**
(fav) ld 3rd, strngly chal 3 out, ran on wll und pres
332 **Autumn Green (Ire) (v) ....R Burton 2**
mid-div, prog to 2nd 3 out, ran on und pres, just hld
464[1] **Ledwyche Gate (bl) ....R Evans 3**
ld to 3rd, cls up to 4 out, rdn & sn btn nxt
356[1] Tattlejack (Ire) 5ex *mid-div, nvr dang* ....Mrs C Ford 4
333[5] Flinters *cls up to 12th, btn 4 out, p.u. 2 out* . . .A Dalton pu
332 Plundering Star (Ire) *mid-div, rdn & no imp 14th, wknd & p.u. 16th* ....S Prior pu
574[1] Killatty Player (Ire) 5a 5ex *hld up rear, prog 15th, cls up 4 out, no imp aft, p.u. last* ....A Crow pu
436[1] Mis-E-Fishant 5a *rear, t.o. 11th, no ch whn p.u. 5 out* ....D Mansell pu
8 ran. ½l, 20l, dist. Time 7m 26.00s. SP 6-4.
P J Sanderson (Clifton On Teme).
V.S.

SOUTH WOLD
Brocklesby Park
Sunday March 23rd
GOOD TO FIRM

672 Members (12st)

137 **SPRINGFIELD PET 5a ....K Needham 1**
walked over
Mrs C W Pinney (South Wold).

673 Confined (12st)

344[2] **WAYS AND MEANS 5a 3ex ....K Green 1**
ptntly rdn, prog 14th, ld 2 out, clr last, rdn out
475[3] **Tobin Bronze 8ex ....R Tate 2**
w.w. prog 10th, 2nd apr 3 out, rdn nxt, onepced
351 **Spring Call (Ire) 7ex ....S J Robinson 3**
chsd ldr, ld 5th, mstk & rmndr 10th, hdd 2 out, no ext
476[2] Ryders Wells *(fav) chsd ldrs, blnd bdly 6th, went 2nd 8th-15th, rdn & btn nxt* ....S Walker 4
Cromwell Point *in tch til bhnd 13th, no ch frm 15th* ....C Mulhall 5
350[3] Elder Prince 5ex *w.w. mid-div, prog 12th, ev ch apr 3 out, 4th & btn, f last* ....P Gee f
Majestic Ride *hld up, prog 12th, cls up whn blnd & u.r. 15th* ....R Armson ur
473 Kemys Commander *ld to 5th, cls up whn u.r. 12th* ....G Smith ur
8 ran. 4l, ½l, 5l, 20l. Time 6m 14.00s. SP 6-1.
Mrs S Mollett (Burton).

674 Ladies

448 **LONDON HILL ....Miss H Irving 1+**
mstks, chsd ldrs, went 2nd 7th, ld 3 out, kpt on und pres
422 **ANOTHER HOOLIGAN ....Mrs F Needham 1+**
(fav) w.w. mstk 5th, prog to ld aft 15th, hdd nxt, hit last,kpt on
546[6] **Killimor Lad ....Miss S Samworth 3**
ld 2nd, sn clr, hdd apr 3 out, onepcd
508[3] Midge 5a *ld to 2nd, mstk 6th, chsd ldrs til wknd apr 3 out* ....Miss S Brotherton 4
505 Crocket Lass 5a *mstk 4th, last frm 6th, no ch frm 11th* ....Miss F Hunter 5
5 ran. Dd-ht, 8l, 2l, dist. Time 6m 11.00s.
Mrs A Kemp/ R Tate (Bicester / Hurworth).
Another Hooligan Evens. London Hill 7-4.

675 Land Rover Open (12st)

475[1] **THE POINT IS 4ex ....M Hewitt 1**
made all, kpt on gamely frm 2 out
76[5] **Wind Force 7ex ....S J Robinson 2**
chsd ldr to 14th, rallied & 2nd agn 2 out, no imp flat
385[2] **Wild Illusion 7ex ....F Hutsby 3**
(fav) in tch, rdn alng 10th, chsd wnr 3 out-nxt, no imp apr last
Mr Primetime (Ire) 7ex *chsd ldrs, went 2nd 14th-3 out, onepcd aft* ....N Bannister 4
506 Lac de Gras (Ire) *jmpd rght, t.o. frm 2nd* . . .A Pennock 5
547[1] Coolvawn Lady (Ire) 5a 7ex *w.w. in tch,4th & pshd alng 11th,hit nxt,lost tch & p.u.14th* ....S Walker pu
6 ran. 2l, 2l, 2l, 2 fences. Time 6m 5.00s. SP 3-1.
P S Hewitt (Quorn).

676 Restricted (12st)

544[3] **WHITE BULLET (USA) ....B Pollock 1**
prom, lft 3rd 6th, chsd ldr 14th, ld 2 out, hld on und pres
477[2] **Give It A Whirl ....M Hewitt 2**
disp til ld 5th, hdd 2 out, kpt on gamely und pres
425[4] **Flying Quest ....S Walker 3**
net-muzzle, hld up, prog to 3rd aft 15th, rdn 2 out, fin wll
345[1] Kiri's Rose (Ire) 5a *chsd ldrs, prog 12th, went 3rd brfly apr 3 out, sn wknd* ....P Gee 4
377 Pokey Grange *disp to 5th, chsd ldr to 14th, wknd* ....Maj S Robinson 5
Smashing View *chsd ldrs to 10th, 8th & wkng whn hmpd 12th, t.o.* ....R Hartley 6
422 The Chap *sn wll bhnd, t.o. 6th, p.u. 3 out*. .S Lochman pu
372 Sutton Lass 5a *bhnd, t.o. & p.u. 9th* ....N Waine pu
449[7] Linlake Lightning 5a (bl) *sn wll bhnd, t.o. & p.u. 11th* ....Miss H Irving pu
348[2] Henry Darling *mid-div, 7th & just in tch whn f 12th* ....E Andrewes f
424[5] Joint Account *keen hld, chsd ldrs, 3rd whn u.r. 6th* ....Mrs F Needham ur
252[1] Cut A Niche *(fav) chsd ldrs to 9th, 6th & wkng 13th, p.u. nxt* ....F Hutsby pu
The Red Devil (Ire) *mid-div to 7th,bhnd & rdn 11th,no ch nxt, p.u.3 out,dsmntd* ....W Wales pu
Denby Ryme 7a *sn wll bhnd, last & t.o. whn p.u. 11th* ....S Charlton pu
14 ran. ½l, 1l, 20l, 15l, 20l. Time 6m 4.00s. SP 12-1.
Miss Ruth Matthews (Cottesmore).

677 Maiden

479[2] **TIDERUNNER (IRE) ....S Walker 1**

trckd ldrs, lft in ld 14th, sn hdd, ld agn 2 out, ran on wll
478[3] **Chester Ben ....S R Andrews** 2
(fav) disp to 6th, lft 2nd 14th, sn ld, hdd 2 out, one-pcd
346 **Springfield Rex ....K Needham** 3
chsd ldrs, 4th & outpcd 12th, lft poor 3rd 3 out
247 Senso (Ire) *alwys last, lost tch 10th, t.o.*.......K Green 4
Needwood Joker *disp til ld 6th, 2l up whn u.r. 14th* ....N Kent ur
506 Markham Lad *rear of main grp, clsd 8th, wknd & mstk 12th, u.r. nxt*..........................R Berry ur
Milo Boy *w.w. prog 9th, 3rd & chnc 15th, btn whn f nxt* ....M Mackley f
Albert's Adventure (Ire) *disp til jmpd lft 3rd, in tch whn blnd & u.r. 8th*.....................Maj S Robinson ur

8 ran. 7l, dist, dist. Time 6m 27.00s. SP 9-4.
Mrs M Morris (Blankney).
S.P.

SANDOWN
Tuesday March 25th
GOOD TO FIRM

678 2½m 110yds 'Ubique' Hunters' Chase Class H

389[4] **ELECTRIC COMMITTEE (IRE) 11.5 7a Mr A Wood** 1
ld 3rd, slight mstks 6th and 14th, rdn and styd on well run-in.
587 **Great Pokey 11.5 7a ....Miss N Courtenay** 2
ld to 3rd, outpcd 14th, rallied and ran on run-in.
375[2] **Driving Force 11.13 7a (bl) ..Mr A Charles-Jones** 3
cl up, chsd wnr 13th till wknd run-in.
388[4] True Steel 11.3 5a *(fav) hdwy 7th, mstk next, jmpd slowly and lost pl 9th, btn 13th.*......Mr J Trice-Rolph 4
495[2] Galzig 11.1 7a *rear, hdwy and hit 6th, mstk next, blnd and wknd 13th, 5th and no ch when p.u. apr 3 out.* ....Mr W Tellwright pu
462 The Mill Height (Ire) 11.1 7a *in tch to 6th, t.o. 8th, p.u. before 12th.*...................Mr C Ward Thomas pu

6 ran. 3l, 16l, 9l. Time 5m 24.10s. SP 9-1.
James R Kearsley

ASCOT
Wednesday March 26th
GOOD

679 2m 3f 110yds Mahonia Hunters' Chase Class H

227[3] **POORS WOOD 11.9 5a...........Mr T McCarthy** 1
held up bhnd, hdwy 10th, ld 4 out, clr 2 out, ran on.
376 **Quiet Confidence (Ire) 11.2 7a...Miss D Stafford** 2
(fav) ld 3rd till hdd 4 out, one pace.
376[3] **Gambling Royal 11.7 7a ....Dr P Pritchard** 3
trckd ldrs, mstk 11th, one pace apr 4 out.
94[4] Flowing River (USA) 11.7 7a *held up, blnd 8th, bhnd from 10th, t.o.*.......................Mr N R Mitchell 4
Tom Furze 11.11 7a *ld to 3rd, with ldr to 11th, soon wknd, t.o. when blnd last.*..............Mr M Batters 5
495[4] Tellaporky 11.7 7a *held up, mstks 6th and next, hrd rdn after 9th, bhnd next, t.o.*..........Mr A Middleton 6
588[1] Star Oats 12.1 7a *started slowly, held up in last pl, n.j.w., taild of when p.u. before 2 out.*.....Mr A Kinane pu
587 Familiar Friend 12.1 7a (bl) *trckd ldrs, wknd 10th, t.o. when mstk 3 out, p.u. before next.*..........Mr L Lay pu
381[1] A Windy Citizen (Ire) 11.12 5a *tracking ldrs when f 9th, dead.*..............................Mr A Sansome f

9 ran. 2½l, 5l, 26l, 19l, 2l. Time 4m 59.90s. SP 5-1.
F R Jackson

TOWCESTER
Saturday March 29th
GOOD TO FIRM

680 3m 1f Larry Connell Memorial Hunters' Chase Class H

589[3] **NORTHERN VILLAGE 11.7 7a Mr D Alers-Hankey** 1
held up, mstk 2nd, hdwy 11th, chsd ldr 2 out, styd on to ld near fin.
379 **Avostar 11.9 5a...................Mr B Pollock** 2
ld to 7th, led 9th to 11th, mstk 4 out, led approching 2 out, hrd rdn run-in, hdd near fin.
379[2] **Peajade 11.7 7a.................Miss J Wormall** 3
chsd ldrs, ld 7th to 9th, led 11th to apr 2 out, styd on same pace.
447 Broad Steane 11.9 5a *(fav) held up in tch, hit 6th, rdn apr 2 out, no impn.*..................Mr A Sansome 4
492[1] Glen Oak 11.13 5a *chsd ldrs, rdn apr 2 out, styd on same pace.*.........................Mr R Thornton 5
491[4] Artful Arthur 11.7 7a *patiently rdn, hit 7th, lost tch 6 out, t.o.*.............................Mr J Grassick 6
591[4] Teatrader 11.7 7a *prom to 11th, soon lost pl, t.o..* ....Miss T Blazey 7
548 Solar Gem 11.7 7a (bl) *mstk 1st, in rear when hit 8th, t.o. and p.u. before 6 out.*..........Mrs C McCarthy pu

8 ran. ¾l, 5l, 1¼l, 1½l, 17l, ½l. Time 6m 28.50s. SP 10-1.
L P Dace

ASHFORD VALLEY
Charing
Saturday March 29th
FIRM

681 Members (12st)

578 **PROFLIGATE ....Miss P Ellison** 1
(fav) hld up, lft in ld apr 8th, kpt on strgly frm 2 out
605 **Ishma (Ire) ....D Page** 2
prsd wnr frm 8th,rdn & up sides whn jmp slwly 4 out,no dang
Scarning Gizmo 5a *rear f 2nd*............D Maitland f
302 Zilfi (USA) *prom, just ld whn ran out bnd bfr 8th* ....Miss F Worley ro
283 Serious Money (USA) *ld, jmp slwly 1st, hdd aft 7th, hmp & u.r. bnd bfr 8th*................Miss C Ewart co

5 ran. 6l. Time 6m 35.00s. SP 4-7.
R Dench (Ashford Valley).

682 Restricted (12st)

277 **KELBURNE LAD (IRE) ....P Bull** 1
(fav) ld apr 3rd, mstk 10th, clr 15th, kpt on whn chal 3 out
576[4] **Basher Bill ....K Giles** 2
ld til apr 3rd, 2nd aft, rdn to chal 3 out,ev ch nxt, onepcd
580 **Fort Diana (v)............................T Hills** 3
in tch, chsd ldng pair 15th, wknd 3 out
Golden Pele *alwys rear, t.o. 2 out*............P Hall 4
147 Valander 5a *mstks, in tch to 15th, t.o. 3 out*.....P York 5

5 ran. 2l, 1 fence, 3l, 1 fence. Time 6m 26.00s. SP 5-4.
Mrs D B A Silk (Kent & Surrey Bloodhounds).

683 Land Rover Mens Open (12st)

579[2] **STEDE QUARTER 7ex....................P Bull** 1
(fav) alwys cls, lft in ld 11th, ran on wll whn chal 3 out
577[8] **Yeoman Farmer ....P Hacking** 2
just ld 2nd-5th, chal 3 out, wknd last
484[6] **Folk Dance 5ow 4ex ....F Jackson** 3
alwys rear, in tch to 15th, lft poor 3rd 3 out
579 Burromariner *ld to 2nd, cls aft, 3rd & rddn whn ref 3 out*...S Cowell ref
Slaney Project (Ire) 7a *ld 5th til blndrd & u.r. 11th* ....T Hills ur

5 ran. 6l, 1 fence. Time 6m 19.00s. SP 8-11.
Mrs S Dench (Ashford Valley).

684 Ladies

576[1] **BRIGHT HOUR ....Miss J Grant** 1
(fav) ld to 7th,u.r. nxt,evntlly rejnd,made most aft,held on flat
578[6] **Slight Panic 5a ....Miss J Wickins** 2

ld aft 7th,u.r. 8th,evntlly rejnd,ld 4 out to nxt,ev ch
2 ran. 1½l. Time 12m 27.00s. SP 1-3.
Mrs B Ansell (West Street Tickham).

685 Club

577^5 **RUSTIC RAMBLE .... P Hacking** 1
(fav) held up, rddn 4 out, bttr jmp last, ld & drew clr flat
Barn Elms .... A Hickman 2
ld, clr 3rd, 4l up 2 out, slwd last, hdd & wknd flat
577 **Rarely At Odds .... Miss A Sansom** 3
alwys chsng ldr, kpt on same pce frm 3 out
3 ran. 5l, 1l. Time 6m 19.00s. SP 4-9.
Peter Tipples (East Sussex & Romney Marsh).

686 2½m Open Maiden (5-7yo) (12st)

283 **RED CHANNEL (IRE) .... A Hickman** 1
(fav) ld frm 2nd, alwys gng wll, lft clr 4 out, in command aft
61 **Joyful Hero 5a .... P Bull** 2
not fluent, chsd ldrs final ctt, lft 2nd 4 out,rddn & no imp
581 Celtic Reg *ld to 2nd, cls aft, chal 4 out whn stmbld & u.r.* .... M Jones ur
605 Spanish Pal (Ire) *alwys last, lost tch 7th, p.u. 4 out* .... Miss S Gladders pu
581 Psamead 7a *trckd ldrs, 3rd & btn whn ran out 2 out* .... P York ro
5 ran. 8l. Time 5m 13.00s. SP 5-4.
R Crawley (East Sussex & Romney Marsh).
G.T.

CATTISTOCK
Little Windsor
Saturday March 29th
GOOD TO FIRM

687 Members (12st)

558^3 **AVRIL SHOWERS 5a 7ex .... R Atkinson** 1
(fav) chsd ldr 10th, ld 14th-16th, ld 2 out, pshd out
662^1 **Alex Thuscombe 7ex (v) .... P Shaw** 2
ld to 14th, ld 16th-2 out, kpt on und pres
457^2 **Clandon Lad 5ow .... T Mitchell** 3
w.w. mstk 12th, chal & mstk 3 out, wknd, walked in
648 Electrofane (Ire) *s.s. alwys t.o.* .... Mrs N Joynes 4
523 Olive Basket 5a *mstk 5th, chsd ldr to 10th, sn wknd, t.o. 14th, p.u. 2 out* .... Miss W Southcombe pu
5 ran. 1½l, 30l, 2 fences. Time 6m 28.50s. SP Evens.
Mrs R Atkinson (Cattistock).

688 Interlink Restricted (12st)

390^1 **SULTAN OF SWING .... Miss P Curling** 1
(fav) hng & jmpd lft, hld up, prog to ld 15th, clr 2 out
532^3 **Eyre Point (Ire) .... A Honeyball** 2
in tch, effrt to chs wnr 4 out, no imp apr 2 out
661^5 **Final Express 5a 5ow .... M Hoskins** 3
sn pshd alng, bhnd frm 11th, t.o.
493 Bryn's Story *jmpd lft,chsd ldr,ld brfly aft 14th,wknd rpdly 3 out,u.r.nxt.* .... N Mitchell ur
517 Noble Protector (Ire) *25s-5s,keen hld,mstks,ld to aft 14th,sn wknd,t.o. & p.u.last* .... Maj G Wheeler pu
5 ran. 12l, dist. Time 6m 22.00s. SP 1-2.
H B Geddes (Beaufort).

689 Ladies

555^2 **DESERT WALTZ (IRE) .... Miss P Curling** 1
(fav) hld up, mstk 6th, ld 11th, clr aft 3 out, comf
551^1 **Departure 5a .... Miss S Gaisford** 2
cls up, chsd wnr 12th, no imp aft 3 out
645^4 **Legal Picnic .... Miss C Bryan** 3
ld to 9th, 3rd frm 13th, onepcd frm 15th
627^5 False Economy *prssd ldr, ld 9-11th, not qckn frm 15th* .... Miss K Scorgie 4
514 Daybrook's Gift *in tch, mstk 13th, wknd 15th, t.o. & p.u. last* .... Miss N Allan pu
5 ran. 10l, 8l, 2l. Time 6m 12.50s. SP 2-5.
H B Geddes (Beaufort).

690 Men's Open (12st)

494 **STILL IN BUSINESS 7ex............... T Mitchell** 1
(fav) hld up, ld 10th, drew clr apr 3 out, eased flat
522^4 **Stunning Stuff 7ex .... R Nuttall** 2
ld to 7th, prssd wnr 12th til rdn & outpcd apr 3 out
108^5 **Temple Mary .... T Woolridge** 3
ld 7-10th, lost tch aft 14th, wll bhnd whn blnd 2 out
558 Balmoral Boy (NZ) *cls up til outpcd aft 14th, blnd nxt & p.u.* .... M Miller pu
4 ran. 10l, 20l. Time 6m 15.50s. SP 2-9.
R G Williams (Cattistock).

691 Intermediate (12st)

298^1 **ALLER MOOR (IRE) .... M Miller** 1
(fav) alwys cls up, ld 2 out, drvn out flat
522^3 **Ive Called Time 5ex .... R Nuttall** 2
made most to 2 out, unable to qckn und pres last
515 **Stalbridge Gold 5a............. Miss A Goschen** 3
cls up, jmpd slwly 8th & 9th, ev ch 15th, wknd 3 out
661^1 Tullykyne Bells *hld up, prog 8th, wknd 11th, t.o. 14th, p.u. 3 out* .... Miss D Stafford pu
515 Plan-A (Ire) (bl) *cls up,ld & ran off course aft 14th,cont,ran out & u.r.3 out* .... T Woolridge ro
5 ran. 3l, 20l. Time 6m 18.00s. SP 8-11.
G Keirle (Portman).

692 Open Maiden (12st)

312^3 **PURBECK POLLY 5a .... Mrs A Davis** 1
in tch,mstk 7th,outpcd 15th,styd on wll apr last,ld nr fin
Get Stepping .... J Creighton 2
mstk 4th, cls up, ld 10th, lft clr 3 out, wknd & hdd flat
392^4 **Cucklington .... Miss A Goschen** 3
ran in sntchs, 3rd & outpcd 4 out, lft 2nd nxt, not qckn
526^3 Dollybat 5a *ld to 10th, chsd ldrs to 15th, btn nxt* .... R Treloggen 4
658^4 Mountain-Linnet *prom til wknd frm 15th* .. T Woolridge 5
242 Linda's Prince (Ire) *(fav) mstks, hld up, prog to 2nd 16th, clsng whn blnd & u.r. nxt* .... B O'Doherty ur
Quote 5a *lft 2 fences, cont t.o. til f 11th* .... Miss A McKeowen f
643 Perripage *prom, mstk 10th, sn wknd, p.u. aft 14th* .... M Miller pu
8 ran. 1l, 3l, 8l, 8l. Time 6m 28.50s. SP 8-1.
Mrs Angela Davis (South Dorset).
J.N.

CLEVELAND
Stainton
Saturday March 29th
FIRM

693 Members

429^2 **JOLLY GHOST .... S Charlton** 1
(fav) trckd ldr,ld 4th til hdd 8th,ld 16th,drew clr frm 2 out,easy
620 **Persian Lion .... P Jenkins** 2
keen, ld til hdd 4th, ld 8th-16th, sn outpcd
622^5 **Roseberry Star 5a............... Miss T Jackson** 3
settld in last plc, outpcd 8th, sn lost tch, t.o. 15th
3 ran. 20l, dist. Time 6m 23.00s. SP 2-5.
Miss S Haykin (Cleveland).

694 Confined (12st)

619^2 **MR DICK 3ex .... S Swiers** 1
(fav) alwys prom, ld 15th, prssd 2 out, rddn ran on wll flat
619 **Grey Realm 5a 3ex...................... N Smith** 2

held up, prog 12th, wnt 2nd 3 out, chal nxt, not qckn flat
619[4] **Flying Lion ....M Haigh 3**
alwys chsng ldrs, ev ch 16th, onepcd frm 3 out
584[5] Master Crozina *prom til ld 6th, hdd 15th, fdd frm 3 out* ....P Cornforth 4
619[6] Earl Gray *mid-div, prog to chs ldrs 8th, outpcd frm 4 out* ....Miss A Deniel 5
507[4] Dalmore *alwys in rear, styd on onepce frm 4 out, nvr nrr* ....L Donnely 6
619[3] Skipping Gale *ld til hdd 6th, rmnd prom til grdly fdd frm 4 out* ....P Atkinson 7
673[5] Cromwell Point *prom til outpcd 13th, sn lost tch* ....C Mulhall 8
619 Sharpridge 4ow *prom til lost plc 8th, sn strggling, t.o. & p.u. 15th* ....M Mawhinney pu
352 Jolly Fellow *rear & sn strggling, t.o. 12th, u.r. 14th* ....Miss S Ward ur
509[1] Squires Tale (Ire) *mid-div til outpcd 9th, sn strggling, wll bhnd whh p.u. 16th*..................Mrs S Grant pu
11 ran. 3l, 4l, 6l, 2l, 3l, ½l, 4l. Time 6m 9.00s. SP 6-4.
Mrs J Cooper (Middleton).

695 Restricted

509 **PHARLINDO (IRE) ....W Burnell 1**
held up early, prog 4th, ld 7th, clr 16th, pshd out flat
622[1] **Dear Emily 5a.........................S Swiers 2**
(fav) alwys prom, chsd ldr frm 14th, rddn & not qckn apr last
616[2] **Caman 5a ....Mrs S Grant 3**
disp ld til hdd 7th, rmnd prom til onepcd frm 3 out
615 Chapel Island *mid-div, prog 16th, no further hdwy frm 3 out, sn bttn*..............................G Tuer 4
674[4] Midge 5a *rear, prog into mid-div 8th, mstk 13th, outpcd frm 4 out* ....Mrs F Needham 5
425[8] Spartan Juliet 5a *disp ld to 2nd, settld mid-div, mstk 13th, sn strggling*........................P Jenkins 6
266 Primitive Star 5a *prom, disp ld 3rd-7th, grdly fdd* ....P Cornforth 7
506 Tooting Times (bl) *rear, rddn 7th, lost tch 11th, t.o. & p.u. 15th* ....C Mulhall pu
616[5] Make A Line *alwys rear, wll bhnd 16th, t.o. & p.u. 3 out*....................................C Denny pu
616 Malvern Cantina *rear, blndrd 12th, wll bhnd whn p.u. 3 out, dismntd*..............................N Smith pu
424[6] Sergeant Pepper *plld hrd, held up in rear, prog 8th, mid-div whn p.u. 14th* ....N Wilson pu
11 ran. 4l, 5l, 3l, 7l, 3l, 10l. Time 6m 9.00s. SP 2-1.
Mrs J W Furness (Hurworth).

696 Men's Open

423[3] **MISTI HUNTER (IRE) ....S Swiers 1**
mid-div,2nd 4th,outpcd 16th,ran on strgly apr last,ld flat
618[4] **Park Drift ....R Tate 2**
rear, prog 4th, ld 4 out, hdd & onepcd flat
506[1] **Just Charlie ....D Easterby 3**
(fav) trckd ldr,lost plc qckly 4th,t.o. 11th,ran on strgly 2 out
Knowe Head *ld til hdd & wknd 4 out*........N Wilson 4
Ashdren *settld rear, rddn 14th, sn outpcd, t.o. & p.u. 4 out* ....N Tutty pu
5 ran. 2l, ½l, 15l. Time 6m 10.00s. SP 4-1.
Mrs D Ibbotson (Middleton).

697 Ladies

617[1] **CAROLE'S DELIGHT 5a.............Mrs L Ward 1**
(fav) trckd ldr til disp 6th,lft clr 15th,prssd 3 out,hld on flat
617[4] **Cheeky Pot ....Mrs S Grant 2**
chsd ldrs,outpcd 10th,prog 16th,chal 3 out,mstk nxt,ran on
426[4] **Integrity Boy ....Miss A Armitage 3**
chsd ldrs, outpcd 10th, cls up brfly 16th, wknd 3 out
358[5] Don Tocino *rear, jmp slwly 7th sn lost tch, t.o. & ref 15th*....................................Miss T Gray ref
584[4] Bells Will Ring (Ire) *plld hrd, ld til disp 6th, f 15th, (dead)* ....Mrs V Jackson f
5 ran. ¾l, 15l. Time 6m 6.00s. SP 10-11.
C Holden (Cleveland).

698 Open Maiden (8yo+)

510 **VALE OF YORK ....Miss R Clark 1**
mid-div, prog to ld 12th, hdd 15th, ld agn 3 out, sn wll clr
615[4] **Ski Lady 5a.......................Miss L Horner 2**
ld til hdd 12th, ld 15th-3 out, wknd
510[4] **Goodheavens Mrtony ....Miss A Deniel 3**
settld in 3rd, mstk 7th, outpcd 15th
415 Slim King *sweating, chsd ldr til wknd 11th, sn wll bhnd* ....D Woodward 4
566[5] Mighty Express *(fav) (3s-4/5)rear & nvr gng wll, outpcd 13th, t.o. whn p.u. 4 out* ....A Ogden pu
510 Another Delight 5a *rear & bhnd, not keen 8th, t.o. 11th, p.u. nxt* ....N Wilson pu
6 ran. 10l, 4l, dist. Time 6m 19.00s. SP 5-1.
S B Clark (York & Ainsty South).

699 Open Maiden (5-7yo)

347 **MISS MADELON 12a..................N Wilson 1**
made all, qcknd apr last, comf
620 **Tudor Flight 5a.....................G Markham 2**
(Jt fav) prom, mstk 7th, chsd wnnr frm 12th, outpcd apr last
621[3] **Chummy's Last 5a ....Mrs F Needham 3**
(Jt fav) alwys prom, blndrd 16th, ev ch whn ran wd apr 2 out, sn bttn
623 Cute Word 5a *rear, mstk 3rd, hmp apr 5th, sn wll bhnd, t.o.*..........................Mrs H Arnold 4
419 Abbey Lad *mid-div til slppd up apr 5th*......N Swann su
Gardenia's Song *rear, prog 8th, in tch whn saddle slppd 10th & p.u.*..............................G Tuer pu
623 Rosie Blue 5a *prom,chsd ldr 6th,fdd 12th,wknd,t.o. broke leg & p.u. 4 out*.....................P Jenkins pu
7 ran. 5l, 15l, dist. Time 6m 20.00s. SP 4-1.
Mrs J C Cooper (Middleton).

CLIFTON-ON-TEME
Upper Sapey
Saturday March 29th
GOOD TO FIRM

700 Members

484[1] **GRIMLEY GALE (IRE) 5a 7ex...........A Wintle 1**
(fav) ld to 4th, imprvd to ld agn 15th, lft wll clr nxt, easily
571[5] **Vision Of Light 5a..................M Munrowd 2**
20l 3rd 6th, lost tch wth 1st 2 frm 10th, lft 2nd 2 out
255 **Potato Fountain (Ire) 5a ....T Stephenson 3**
dist 4th 10th, stdy prog frm 3 out gained 3rd run in
Wrenbury Farmer *4th/5th til hlfwy, efft frm 12th,lft 3rd 3 out,outpcd run in* ....O McPhail 4D
Brenner Pass (NZ) *rear frm start, 5th hlfwy, fin own time* ....J Hibbert 4
Monorose 5a *last by 2nd, imprvd 6th hlfwy, t.o. & p.u. 15th*..............................Mrs D Powell pu
Haven Light *ld frm 4th, 3l clr 10th, disp ld whn f 3 out* ....M Harris f
Daisy Lane 5a *mstk in rear, last hlfwy, p.u. aft 4 out* ....D Mansell pu
8 ran. Dist, 30l, 2l, dist. Time 6m 1.00s. SP 2-5.
R M Phillips (Clifton-On-Teme).
Wrenbury Farmer failed to weigh-in rider fined £35.

701 Restricted (12st)

574[2] **WESTERN HARMONY ....Julian Pritchard 1**
(fav) ld frm start, ran on strgly whn chal frm 3 out,drew clr flat
433 **Kingsthorpe ....A Phillips 2**
prog 3rd to 3l 2nd 9th, ev ch whn outpcd frm 2 out
575[3] **How Friendly ....N Oliver 3**

15l last by 6th, efft frm 14th, ran on to take 3rd frm 3 out
Bakmalad *disp 3rd 1st ctt, strggld to go pce hlfwy, no ext frm 15th*............H Wheeler 4
573 Outcrop 5a *5l 2nd til hlfwy, wknd, distant last whn f 3 out*............R Inglesant f
433 Sideliner *5th 1st ctt, strggld frm 9th, p.u. 12th*............T Stephenson pu
6 ran. 4l, 20l, 6l. Time 5m 56.00s. SP 4-7.
R T Baimbridge (Berkeley).

702 Ladies

329 **STEPHENS PET ....Miss A Dare 1**
(fav) made all, drew clr frm 3 out, eased flat
They All Forgot Me ....Miss C Dyson 2
chsd ldr in 2nd plc frm start,8l down mstk 3 out,ran on flat
359[1] Kings Rank (bl) *hmp 1st, 10l 3rd whn ref 4th*............Miss S Duckett ref
638[2] Roving Report *f 1st*............Mrs A Rucker f
4 ran. 5l. Time 6m 8.00s. SP 1-4.
Dr P P Brown (Berkeley).

703 Men's Open (12st)

393[1] **RIP VAN WINKLE ....J Baimbridge 1**
(fav) made all, drew clr frm 15th
434[2] **Sisterly 5a ....A Wintle 2**
efft to take 2nd 11th, ev ch whn outpcd frm 3 out
362 **Drumceva ....M Wilesmith 3**
cls 3rd/4th til pce qcknd hlfwy, wnt clr 3rd 14th, outpcd
430[1] Sharinski 4ex *disp 7-11th, wknd & eased frm 15th*............Julian Pritchard 4
573[2] Derring Bud *reluctant to start, 2 fences bhnd til p.u. 15th*............R Rogers pu
5 ran. 6l, 20l, 20l. Time 5m 52.00s. SP 2-5.
Dr P P Brown/ Mrs S Birks (Berkeley).

704 Intermediate (12st)

572[4] **GROMIT (NZ) ....T Stephenson 1**
efft to disp ld frm 13th, wnt 2l clr apr last, ran on strgly
572[5] **Sterling Buck (USA) ....N Oliver 2**
4l last but ch 17th, ran on strgly to take 2nd flat
360 **Perryline 5a ....A Wintle 3**
efft frm 15th, strng run to hold ev ch 2 out, wknd run in
431 Sudanor (Ire) *(fav) ld til mstk 16th, recvrd wll but outpcd apr last*............Julian Pritchard 4
4 ran. 3l, ½l, 3l. Time 5m 57.00s. SP 7-4.
Miss Sarah Eaton (North Cotswold).

705 Confined

360 **MCMAHON'S RIVER 5a ....Julian Pritchard 1**
8l 3rd 14th, efft apr 3 out, lft clr last
484[4] **January Don (bl) ....G Barfoot-Saunt 2**
10l clr 5th, rmmndrs 11th, wknd frm 15th
573[1] Di Stefano *(fav) disp ld 13th, 10l clr whn crashed thru wing last, (dead)*............Miss A Dare f
635 Wissywis (Ire) 12a 1ow *lost 20l start, last til p.u. 11th*............A Wallett pu
4 ran. 10l. Time 6m 0.00s. SP 7-1.
J V C Davenport (Radnor & West Herefordshire).

706 Open Maiden (12st)

436 **DOCTOR BRIGGS (IRE) ....H Wheeler 1**
ld frm start, lk btn 16th, gd jmp to ld nxt, ran on wll
437[2] **Joyney 5a ....Miss C Thomas 2**
(fav) efft frm 12th to go 4l 3rd 17th, unable to trbl wnnr
390 **Dante's Pride (Ire) ....Miss A Dare 3**
2nd/3rd til lost plc 16th, renewd efft apr last, fin wll
Winter Breeze *prog frm 7th to go 2nd 15th, ev ch til onepcd frm 2 out*............A Wintle 4
487 Flowerhill *cls 5th til 11th, unable to qckn wth ldrs frm 14th*............G Barfoot-Saunt 5
365[6] Nick The Biscuit *cls 3rd/4th til mstk 15th, no ext frm 2 out*............O McPhail 6
568 Millstock 5a *s.s., efft to go 6th 11th, grdly lost tch*............Miss N Stallard 7
True Fred *cls 7th whn f 11th*............R Evans f
407 Greenfield Maid (Ire) 5a *alwys rear, 8th 11th, p.u. 15th*............J Baimbridge pu
254 Asante Sana 5a *strglld frm start, t.o. whn p.u. 15th*............N Oliver pu
368 Conimore (Ire) 12a *mid-div whn bad mstk 5th, p.u. nxt*............J Jackson pu
436 Zaudante (Ire) 5a *lost tch wth ldrs by 12th, p.u. 15th*............R Rogers pu
Cowarne Adventure 7a *last by 11th & p.u. 15th,*............T Stephenson pu
Offley Lass 5a *j.w. in mid-div til p.u. 12th*............Julian Pritchard pu
516 Lough Morne *t.o. by 6th, last by 12th, p.u. 15th*............Miss A Lock pu
15 ran. 3l, 3l, 2l, 10l, 2l, 4l. Time 5m 59.00s. SP 8-1.
Mrs L P Vaughan (V.W.H.).
P.Ma.

ESSEX
High Easter
Saturday March 29th
FIRM

707 Members (12st)

322[4] **JIMMY MAC JIMMY 4ex ....Miss H Barnard 1**
nt fluent, slt ld to 14th, ld agn 2 out, kpt on
444[4] **Kumada 4ex............T Moore 2**
(fav) wth wnr til ld 14th, hdd 2 out, nt qkn und press
2 ran. ¾l. Time 7m 1.00s. SP Evens.
D R Barnard (Essex).

708 Confined

577 **AIRTRAK (IRE) ....A Coe 1**
trkd ldr til ld 6th, mstk & hdd 15th, rdn to ld last,styd on
595[2] **River Melody 5a ....T Moore 2**
(fav) jmpd rt, ld to 6th, ld agn 15th rdn & hdd last, sn btn
502[1] **Ballyallia Castle (Ire) ....N Bloom 3**
chsd ldrs, outpcd & pshd alng 11th, no ch frm 15th, t.o.
3 ran. 2l, dist. Time 6m 36.00s. SP 4-1.
Carols Motors Ltd (Enfield Chace).

709 Ladies

500 **ST GREGORY (bl)............Mrs L Gibbon 1**
(fav) made all, blnd & rmdr 13th, j.s. nxt, clr 2 out,eased nr fin
323[2] **Omidjoy (Ire) 5a (bl)............Mrs L Wrighton 2**
chsd wnr, ev ch 15th, onepcd aft
2 ran. 2l. Time 6m 39.00s. SP 2-7.
A Howland Jackson (Essex & Suffolk).

710 Men's Open (12st)

595[1] **OVER THE EDGE 7ex ....S Sporborg 1**
(fav) j.w. made all, drw clr appr last, easily
440[1] **Cracking Idea (Ire) 7ex............C Ward-Thomas 2**
w.w. hit 3rd, wnt 2nd 7th, ev ch 15th, rdn & btn appr last
444[2] **Exclusive Edition (Ire) 5a............A Coe 3**
trkd ldrs, cls 3rd 14th, outpcd frm nxt
497[7] Major Inquiry (USA) *last frm 4th, lsng tch whn p.u. 11th*............G Pewter pu
501 Cardinal Red 7ex (bl) *wth ldr, j.s. 6th, mstk & lst iron 10th,strugg 14th,p.u.16th*............P Keane pu
5 ran. 5l, 20l. Time 6m 17.00s. SP 4-5.
Christopher Sporborg (Puckeridge).

711 Restricted (12st)

503 **WHATS ANOTHER 5a ....Miss K Bridge 1**

chsd ldrs, ld 12th, made rest, drw clr frm 3 out
443[2] **New York Boy ....P Taiano** 2
in tch,lft 3rd 12th,outpcd 3 out,2nd & wll hld whn mstk nxt
439[1] **Ronaldsway ....D Parravani** 3
(fav) ld to 12th, chsd wnr aft til wknd 3 out, lost 2nd 2 out
576[6] Abdul Emir *chsd ldr to 11th, blnd 9th, cls up whn blnd & u.r. 12th* ....Mrs L Stock ur
198[6] Give It A Bash (Ire) 5a *cls up til f 12th*.........T Moore f
503[7] Doctor Dick (Ire) (bl) *alwys last, mstk & rmdrs 10th, t.o.& j.s.14th, p.u. 16th* ....A Coe pu
6 ran. 15l, 2l. Time 6m 32.00s. SP 6-1.
Mrs G M Bridge (Thurlow).

712 Open Maiden (12st)

29 **BISHOPS TALE ....A Harvey** 1
hld up, prog to 2nd 15th, ld 2out, sn clr, comf
452[3] **Loch Irish (Ire) 5a ....S R Andrews** 2
(fav) chsd ldr til ld 10th, hdd 2 out, onepcd und press
504[2] **Stoneyisland (Ire) ....N Bloom** 3
ld to 10th, 3rd & wkng 3 out
211 Race To The Rhythm 5a *trckd ldrs, 4th & strugg whn hit 16th, no ch aft* ....C Ward-Thomas 4
4 ran. 4l, 15l, 15l. Time 6m 34.00s. SP 9-4.
Mrs Richard Pilkington (Enfield Chace).
S.P.

MONMOUTHSHIRE
Llanvapley
Saturday March 29th
GOOD TO FIRM

713 Members (12st)

187 **FLY FRED ....S Lloyd** 1
(fav) made all, clr hlfwy, easily
Paper Fair 5a ....J Price 2
alwys chsng wnnr, no imp frm hlfwy
575 **Greenfield Tiger (Ire) ....P Hamer** 3
n.j.w., alwys 3rd, ran on onepce
569 Project's Mate 7ex (bl) *in 2nd whn blndrd & u.r. 3rd* ....Miss N Richards ur
4 ran. 10l, 10l. Time 6m 33.00s. SP Evens.
Miss H Lewis (Monmouth).

714 Confined (12st)

400[2] **SUN OF CHANCE 5ex.................P Williams** 1
cls up, ld 6-11th, cls 2nd aft, ld 2 out,blndrd whn clr last
636 **Dane Rose 5a.......................S Blackwell** 2
rear early, stdy prog 13th, 4th 2 out, ran on wll
535 **Beinn Mohr 5a ....E Williams** 3
held up in mid-div,rpd prog to ld 14th,hdd 2 out,no ext last
537 Princess Lu (Ire) *cls up, styd on onepce frm 3 out* ....J P Keen 4
401[8] Robusti (v) *(tubed), prom early, 3rd 11th, grdly wknd* ....D S Jones 5
632[2] Rusty Music 3ex *rear, fin in own time* ....Miss N Richards 6
402[2] Push Along *mid-div, no prog frm 13th* ....D Stephens 7
403[3] Astounded *cls up, ld 12th-nxt, wknd qckly* ....J Tudor 8
Young India 5a *last til p.u. 13th* ....T Vaughan pu
535 General Troy *rear, bad mstk 12th, p.u. 3 out*....J Liley pu
636 Scared Stiff 5a *mid-div, p.u. 10th* ....A Price pu
400[3] Chiaroscuro *rear til p.u. 3 out*...............S Lloyd pu
401[3] Carrick Lanes 5ex *(fav) (6/4-5/2), alwys rear, no ch frm 13th, p.u. last*.........................Miss P Jones pu
539[1] Telephone *ld early, grdly wknd, p.u. & dismntd 13th* ....P Hamer pu
Icecapade (Bel) *mid-div, f 3rd* ....J Cook f
15 ran. 8l, 2l, 8l, 10l, 4l, 2l, 6l. Time 6m 11.00s. SP 5-1.
Miss M Ree (Glamorgan).

715 Men's Open (12st)

494 **MISS MILLBROOK 5a 7ex..............E Williams** 1
(fav) trckd ldr, hrd rdn to disp last, got up cls home
295 **Mister Horatio 7ex.......................M Lewis** 2
j.w., ld 6th, jnd last, just outpcd final 50yds
646[4] **Prince Nepal ....S Shinton** 3
rear early, prog to 3rd 11th, no ch wth 1st 2
Olde Crescent *alwys 3rd/4th, ran on onepce* ....J Comins 4
636 Curie Crusader (Ire) *alwys towrds rear* ....J Tudor 5
496 Kingfisher Bay *ld to 5th, grdly lost plc, p.u. 13th* ....S Lloyd pu
399[3] Polly Pringle 5a *alwys last pair, no ch hlfwy, p.u. 2 out* ....A Price pu
537 Derrymoss 7ex (bl) *last, bad mstk 1st, ref nxt* . . J Price ref
8 ran. Nk, dist, dist, 8l. Time 5m 59.00s. SP 4-6.
D T Goldsworthy (Llangeinor).

716 Ladies

494[6] **FINAL PRIDE 5a ....Miss P Jones** 1
(fav) made all, sn wll clr, easily
638[4] **Wake Up Luv ....Miss P Cooper** 2
2nd til wknd 13th, t.o. whn lft 2nd last
536[4] **Mo's Chorister ....Miss A Meakin** 3
alwys last, fin own time
191[1] Desmond Gold (Ire) *mstly 3rd, drvn to 2nd 13th, blndrd & u.r. nxt*........................Miss L Pearce ur
535[2] Bullens Bay (Ire) *s.s., stdy prog hlfwy, lft 2nd 14th, held whn ref last*.........................Miss E Jones ref
5 ran. Dist, 20l. Time 5m 58.00s. SP 4-7.
Grahame Barrett (South Pembs).

717 Restricted Div I (12st)

640[3] **PLAS-HENDY ....G Lewis** 1
(fav) ld til qcknd clr 13th, easily
404 **Linantic ....Miss P Jones** 2
trckd ldr, onepcd frm 13th
541[1] **Kristal Haze 12a ....P Williams** 3
held up in rear, prog 13th, fin wll, to much to do
635[4] Algaihabane (USA) (bl) *prom in mid-div, ran on onepce* ....S Shinton 4
405[5] Celtic Bizarre 5a *prom in mid-div til lost postn frm 3 out*...Miss B Barton 5
638 West King *last pair, p.u. 3 out* ....J P Keen pu
641 Toucher (Ire) *alwys rear, p.u. 3 out* ....J Cook pu
538 Red Rhapsody 5a *mid-div, wknd & p.u. 3 out* ....J Comins pu
639[2] Malthouse Lad *cls up, ran out 5th* ....D Stephens ro
641 Wooly Town 5a *alwys rear, p.u. 3 out* ......G Perkins pu
639 Priesthill (Ire) *prom til lost plc 12th, p.u. 15th* ....Miss E Crawford pu
633 Lennie The Lion *last til p.u. 4th* ....J Price pu
262 Dream Lord *rear til p.u. 3 out* ....S Lloyd pu
13 ran. 20l, nk, 15l, 2l. Time 6m 12.00s. SP 9-4.
P M Rich (Pentyrch).

718 Restricted Div II (12st)

190 **TWILIGHT TOM ....A Price** 1
trckd ldr til lft in ld aft 11th, made rest, held on wll
404 **Rosieplant 5a ....M Lewis** 2
rear,imprvd to trck ldrs frm 12th,2l down 2 out,alwys held
298 **Savage Oak ....E Williams** 3
alwys 3rd/4th, wnt 2nd 12th-3 out, onepcd
408[7] Final Option (Ire) *last pair til ran on wll frm 3 out* ....I Johnson 4
Killyman (Ire) *mid-div, 10l 4th whn mstk 15th, no further prog*..............................Miss J Mathias 5
Viceroy Of India (Can) *rear til p.u. & dismntd 15th* ....K Cousins pu
639 Maytown *mid-div, f 9th*..............Miss N Richards f
Al Billal *prom to hlfwy, grdly wknd, no ch f 2 out* ....Miss P Cooper f
634 Tudor Oaks 5a *ld til slppd up bnd aft 11th* S Blackwell su
408[1] Mittenwald (Ire) *(fav) mid-div, p.u. 10th & dismntd* ....Miss E Tamplin pu
541 Rubblee Bubblee *mid-div p.u. 3 out* . . . Miss A Meakin pu
575[6] Shesagud Girl 5a *lft start, tk no part* ....S Currey 0

Hardy Wolf *last til p.u. 5th*.................D S Jones pu
13 ran. 3l, 10l, dist, 1l. Time 6m 14.00s. SP 4-1.
L J Williams (Curre).

719 Maiden (5-7yo) Div I (12st)

408[3] **WHO'S YOUR MAN (IRE) ....P Hamer 1**
(Jt fav) j.w. in mid-div, prog 15th to ld nxt, just held on flat
367 **Volcanic Roc ....E Williams 2**
cls up, lft in ld 10th, hdd 3 out, hrd rdn last, just held
409 **Mister Jay Day ....A Price 3**
2nd/3rd til clr 2nd frm 11th, onepcd frm 3 out
639[4] Tommyknocker (Ire) 7a *towrds rear, ran on onepce* ....Miss P Cooper 4
639 Saronica-R *1st ride, alwys last, fin own time* ....Miss S Jones 5
540 Its A Doddle 5a *rear, f 11th*.........Miss S Robinson f
542 Alkarine 7a *(14s-5s), nvr beyond mid-div, p.u. 12th* ....J Tudor pu
409 Stiff Drink *plling in rear, rpd prog frm 6th, lft in ld aft 8th,f 10th*..................S Shinton f
365[2] Good Boy Fred 7a *(Jt fav) cls up, blndrd & u.r. 6th* ....P Williams ur
542 Buckland Ballad 7a *mid-div, f 6th*..........G Perkins f
641 Wyndams Lad (Ire) *towrds rear, p.u. 3 out*...R Cotton pu
639 Dinedor Charlie *alwys rear, p.u. 3 out* .....D S Jones pu
Mo's Keliro 12a *rear, p.u. 3 out* ....Miss A Meakin pu
542 Forest Flight (Ire) 7a *ld til ran out aft 8th* ....J Comins ro
14 ran. ½l, 6l, 3l, dist. Time 6m 30.00s. SP 7-2.
Mr P H Morris (Golden Valley).

720 Maiden (5-7yo) Div II (12st)

185 **MISS MONTGOMERY (IRE) 5a...........J Price 1**
trckd ldr, ld 12th, made rest, qcknd whn chal apr last
Itsstormingnorma 5a................D Stephens 2
mstly 3rd/4th, strng chal frm 3 out, just outpcd
542[5] **Queen's Equa 5a...................Miss S Major 3**
mid-div, prog 3 out, no ext aft
185 Good Boy Charlie *(fav) towrds rear, some prog 13th, onepcd aft*..................D S Jones 4
Dragonara Lad (Ire) 7a *ld til hdd 10th, wknd rpdly, p.u. 12th*..................J Tudor pu
540[5] Moor Hill Lass (Ire) *1st ride, 2nd til f 7th* ....Miss E Roberts f
542[4] Tiger Lord *rear till p.u. 3 out* ....A Price pu
Newchurch Lad *last til f 4th*...........Miss C Davies f
8 ran. 2l, 6l, 1l. Time 6m 19.00s. SP 3-1.
Mrs S M Farr (Ystrad).
One fence omitted second circuit.

NORTH STAFFORDSHIRE
Sandon
Saturday March 29th
GOOD TO FIRM

721 Members

574 **PRIORY PIPER ....M Pennell 1**
(Jt fav) t.o. 9th, 5th & clsng 14th, ran on 2 out, ld last, conf rdn
Very Daring ....Miss S Sharratt 2
(Jt fav) ld to 3rd, in tch, ld 11th-last, no ext
436 **Domani Hill 5a..................Miss L Wallace 3**
chsd ldrs in tch, 2nd 3 out, not qckn apr last
Master Bennett 23ow *trckd ldrs, ev ch 4 out, fdd rpdly*..................C Mellard 4
Worried Pride 13ow *prom, ld 4th-10th at steady pace, btn 3 out*..................M Slater 5
357 See More Action 7a *u.r. apr 1st*.............J Burley ur
6 ran. 3l, 6l, dist, dist. Time 7m 9.00s. SP 2-1.
Mrs L A Ward (North Staffordshire).

722 Open Maiden Div I (12st)

548 **RHYMING MOPPET 5a.............W Tellwright 1**
w.w. clsd 4 out, ld nxt, sn clr
664[2] **Crunch Time (Ire) ....C Stockton 2**
(fav) w.w. off pace, prog 13th, ran on wll, not rch wnr
210 **Must Be Murphy (Ire) ....R Burton 3**
in tch, outpcd 4 out, lft 3rd 2 out
469 Scally Hill 5a *restrnd mid-div, lft 4th 2 out, no prog* ....A Mitchell 4
572 Achieved Ambition (Ire) *rear, t.o. 8th, no ch & p.u. 4 out*..................P Morris pu
469[3] Beeworthy 5a *disp 2nd/3rd, und pres whn f 2 out* ....L Whiston f
549[5] Ring Bank *ld to 4 out, disp 2nd & lkd hld whn b.d. 2 out*..................N Gittins bd
326 Banteer Bet (Ire) 12a 4ow *mid to rear, no ch whn f 4 out*..................J Barlow f
470 Ishereal (Ire) *mid-div, prog 9th, disp 2nd & going wll whn b.d. 2 out*..................S Prior bd
480 Charlottes Quest 5a *rear 4th, losing tch whn f 8th* ....M Connors f
10 ran. 5l, dist, 1l. Time 6m 39.00s. SP 7-1.
E R Hanbury (Quorn).

723 Open Maiden Div II (12st)

665[3] **KING KEITH (bl)......................C Stockton 1**
(fav) hld up,lft 2nd 11th,ld 2 out,v slw last,hdd,ld agn post
436 **Musical Mail ....R Burton 2**
in tch,lft in ld 11th,hdd 2 out,lft in ld aft last, hdd post
470 **Yasgourra (Ire) ....J Barlow 3**
mostly last pair, f 4 out, rmntd
Hyperbole *ld, set str pace, f 11th*.............G Lake f
Maesgwyn Bach 5a *rear, t.o. 12th, p.u. 5 out* ....A Mitchell pu
437 Kinlet Crest 5a *mid to rear, f 10th* ....R Wakeham f
6 ran. Sht-hd, dist. Time 6m 46.00s. SP 1-2.
Mrs C E Whiteway (West Shropshire Draghounds).

724 Ladies

572[2] **FOREST FOUNTAIN (IRE) ....Mrs H Needham 1**
(fav) hld up, prog 12th, ld 3 out, sn in cmmnd
329[3] **Logical Fun (bl) ....Miss L Wallace 2**
cls 2nd, ld 11th, hdd 3 out, not qckn
213 **Lady Steel (Ire) 5a.................Miss S Baxter 3**
ld to 6th, 2nd to 12th, 3rd aft, onepcd
Strong Views *alwys 3rd/4th, t.o. 4 out, no ch whn p.u. aft 2 out*..................Miss J Elston pu
4 ran. 3l, 5l, 4l. Time 6m 32.00s. SP 1-2.
J D Callow (Albrighton Woodland).

725 Men's Open

667[4] **LE PICCOLAGE ....R Burton 1**
cls up, ld 6th, kckd clr 11th, unchal
Emerald Knight (Ire) ....C Stockton 2
(fav) ld at slow pace to 5th, outpcd by wnr 11th, nvr nr aft
490 **Freddie Fox ....T Garton 3**
w.w. alwys 3rd, nvr able to chal
465[2] Back The Road (Ire) *hrd hld in rear, some prog 14th, nrst fin, b.b.v.*..................G Hanmer 4
4 ran. 8l, 2½l, 6l. Time 7m 8.00s. SP 9-1.
S Bradburn (West Shropshire Draghounds).

726 Confined (Nov Rider)

330[1] **ITA'S FELLOW (IRE)....................M Prince 1**
(fav) ld 4th, sn in cmmnd, easily
667 **Bucks Surprise ....D Dickinson 2**
hld up, prog 5 out, 6l 3rd last, tk 2nd post
467 **Domino Night (Ire) ....E Haddock 3**
mostly 2nd in tch, outpcd 4 out, eased & lost 2nd post
330 No More The Fool *mid-div, nvr dang* ......L Brennan 4
467 Rinky Dinky Doo *mid to rear, nvr dang* ......P Morris 5
465 Auction Law (NZ) *prog 5 out, short-lived effrt, sn btn* ....L Whiston 6
670 Trojan Pleasure 5a *chsg grp to hlfwy, sn btn* A Jordan 7

574 Fennorhill *ld to 3rd, fdd rpdly 8th, p.u. 4 out* . . R Ward-Dutton pu
8 ran. 6l, sht-hd, 4l, 15l, 2l, 6l. Time 6m 43.00s. SP 4-6.
R Prince (Meynell & South Staffs).

727 Restricted (12st)

575 **TAILS U WIN** .... **A Jordan** 1
w.w. prog frm rear & lft 2nd 2 out, ld apr last, ran on well
548[5] **Sargeants Choice** .... **J Barlow** 2
cls up, lft in ld 2 out, hdd apr last, wknd
670[9] **Glen Taylor** .... **Mrs M Wall** 3
hld up, onepcd frm 14th, no ch 1st pair
467 Grecianlid *prom hlfwy, onepcd aft* . . . . Miss S Hopkins 4
JJ's Hope *ld to 14th, sn btn, p.u. last* . . Miss J Penney pu
213[4] First Command (NZ) *(fav) prom, ld 14th, going wll whn f 2 out* .... R Burton f
6 ran. 8l, 12l, 12l. Time 6m 43.00s. SP 16-1.
Paul Morris (Albrighton).
V.S.

PERCY
Alnwick
Saturday March 29th
FIRM

728 Members

612[4] **INDIAN RIVER (IRE)** .... **J Walton** 1
(fav) j.w. chsd ldr til ld 4th, qcknd clr 11th, canter
340[4] **Saucy Mint 5a** .... **Mrs D Walton** 2
ld to 4th, outpcd & wll bhnd frm 11th
564 **Houselope Brook 5a** .... **Miss S Lamb** 3
green, alwys last pair, t.o. final m
614 Political Diamond 5a *alwys last piar, t.o. & mstk 2 out, p.u. last* .... Mrs K Hargreave pu
4 ran. Dist, 20l. Time 6m 41.00s. SP 4-6.
Robert Miller-Bakewell (Percy).

729 Restricted

606[2] **THINKABOUTTHAT (IRE)** .... **J Muir** 1
(Jt fav) ld/disp to 4 out,prog agn to disp& mstk 2 out,ld last,ran on
614[1] **Peelinick** .... **C Storey** 2
(Jt fav) alwys prom, went 2nd 13th,ld 4 out,jnd 2 out,hdd last,no ext
Master Mathew .... **Miss D Laidlaw** 3
ld/disp til 3rd frm 13th, kpt on wll frm 3 out
416 Star Lea *alwys prom, handy 4th frm 13th, no imp ldrs aft* .... B Stonehouse 4
560 Wang How *mid-div, prog to 5th at 12th, outpcd frm nxt* .... J Walton 5
415 Jads Lad (bl) *mid-div, lost tch 12th, p.u. 3 out* . . D Reid pu
413 Fortinas Flyer 5a (bl) *alwys rear, t.o. 9th, p.u. nxt* .... M Ruddy pu
564[7] Turn Of Foot (Ire) *alwys rear, t.o. last hlfwy, p.u. 2 out* .... M Bradburne pu
565[1] Riding Hills Girl 5a *mid-div, wknd 12th, lost tch & p.u. 2 out* .... D Wood pu
Bow Tie *climbed 1st & 2nd, ref 3rd, cont, ref 4th, gave up* .... J Ewart ref
10 ran. 1l, 2l, 3l, 3l, 30l. Time 6m 13.00s. SP 5-2.
J F W Muir (Buccleuch).

730 2½m Open Maiden (5-7yo)

566[3] **MR COSMO (IRE)** .... **J Billinge** 1
(fav) alwys prom, ld 9th, clr 3 out, styd on strngly
417[4] **Restraint 5a** .... **Miss F Barnes** 2
ld 2nd-9th, outpcd & 4l 2nd 4 out, no ext
418 **Galachlaw** .... **R Trotter** 3
mid-div, wknd 10th, plggd on onepcd
609 Tuneful Tom *last pair til prog 7th, sn btn, t.o.* .... Miss V Burn 4
564[6] Kinlochaline 5a *rear, t.o. final cct, dead* . . . . . J Ewart 5
419 Henry Higgins *handy 4th til lost tch frm 6th, sn t.o.* .... Miss E Wagg 6
417[5] Jones *alwys last pair, t.o. final cct, p.u. 3 out* .... Miss A Adams pu
Noneofyourbusiness (Ire) 5a *prom, 2l 2nd 6th, outpcd & remote 3rd whn p.u. 3 out* .... T Scott pu
623[4] Percy Special (Ire) *nvr nr ldrs, remote 4th frm 10th til p.u. 3 out* .... T Barry pu
9 ran. 8l, dist, 4l, 1l, 1 fence. Time 5m 23.00s. SP 4-5.
J N R Billinge (Fife).

731 4m Mixed Open (12st)

609[2] **ACROSS THE CARD** .... **Miss R Ramsay** 1
hld up in tch, ld 21st, sn clr, styd on strngly
339[2] **Lupy Minstrel** .... **Miss P Robson** 2
alwys ldng trio, outpcd 21st, rallied wll flat, not rch wnr
614[5] **Czaryne 5a** .... **Miss J Percy** 3
ran in sntchs, prog to 2nd 13th,ld/disp 16th-4out, wknd
336[3] Bow Handy Man *ld/disp til wknd 19th, sn lost tch wth ldrs* .... T Scott 4
560[5] Bruce's Castle *mainly last pair, 6th at 15th, no imp ldrs aft* .... Miss K Durie 5
606[1] Misty Night 5a *(fav) nvr going wll, losing tch whn p.u. 17th, lame* .... Miss A Bowie pu
416[6] Warkswoodman *mainly last pair, wknd final cct, p.u. 20th* .... Mrs H Dickson pu
7 ran. 2l, 25l, dist, 15l. Time 8m 51.00s. SP 5-2.
Major General C A Ramsay (Berwickshire).

732 Confined (12st)

561[5] **LITTLE GENERAL (v)** .... **D Wood** 1
alwys prom, 3rd at 12th, ld last, ran on strngly
608[1] **Toaster Crumpet 3ex** .... **Miss P Robson** 2
alwys prom, chsd ldr 12th-3 out, disp nxt, hdd & no ext last
562[4] **Eastern Pleasure 3ex** .... **R Morgan** 3
chsd ldr, lft in ld 3rd, jnd 2 out, hdd last, no ext flat
611[8] Yenoora (Ire) *alwys last, 15l down 9th, t.o. final m* .... J Ewart 4
335 Sharp Challenge *mstk & u.r. 1st* .... T Glass ur
337[1] Leannes Man (Ire) *(fav) ld til c.o. by loose horse 3rd* .... C Wilson co
6 ran. 1l, nk, dist. Time 6m 12.00s. SP 16-1.
Mrs D McCormack (Braes Of Derwent).

733 Maiden Div I

612 **BOYUP BROOK** .... **T Morrison** 1
trckd ldrs, qcknd clr & mstk 14th, styd on well
613[3] **Red Hot Boogie (Ire)** .... **T Scott** 2
(fav) chsd ldr, ld/disp 10-13th, outpcd nxt, not rch wnr aft
612 **Hooky's Treat 5a** .... **M Bradburne** 3
alwys handy, wknd to 8th 3rd at 14th, rallied 4 out, onepcd
343 Billy Buoyant *rear, no imp on ldrs whn blnd & u.r. 12th* .... J Walton ur
Sunday Pointer *ld 2nd-10th, wkng in 4th 13th, p.u. 3 out* .... Miss S Forster pu
5 ran. 4l, 5l. Time 6m 27.00s. SP 2-1.
J John Paterson (Jedforest).

734 Maiden Div II

566 **DONSIDE** .... **M Bradburne** 1
(fav) prom, ld 9th, hld on wll flat
613[4] **Fast Fun** .... **R Morgan** 2
chsd ldng pair, lft 2nd 10th, und pres 2 out, rallied flat
416[5] **Copper Pan 5a** .... **T Scott** 3
nvr on trms wth ldrs, lft poor 3rd 10th, grad t.o.
Caton Boy *last frm 3rd, t.o. & p.u. 9th* .... Miss J Hollands pu
162 Barrow Knocks *ld to 8th, cls 2nd whn ran out apr 10th* .... R Green ro
613 Political Belle 5a *alwys strgglng, t.o. & p.u. 9th* .... C Wilson pu
6 ran. ½l, dist. Time 6m 23.00s. SP 4-6.
G F White (Percy).

P.B.

SPOONERS & WEST DARTMOOR
Higher Kilworthy
Saturday March 29th
GOOD TO FIRM

735 Members

630[4] **BALLYSHEIL** ....**S Edwards** 1
made all, wll clr 16th, unchal
Christmas Hols ....**Miss K Baily** 2
went poor 2nd aft 15th, no ch
Silver Concord *(fav) rear, p.u. aft 6th, lame*...R Darke pu
Minstrals Boyo *prom til wknd rpdly 13th, t.o. & p.u. 3 out*........L Rowe pu
Prince Warrior *n.j.w. went 2nd 13th, wknd 15th, btn whn f 2 out, winded*........T Cole f
5 ran. Dist. Time 6m 3.50s. SP 9-4.
P M Hunt (Spooners & West Dartmoor).

736 Restricted (12st)

526[1] **PASSING FAIR 5a** ....**Miss S Vickery** 1
(fav) 3s-6/4, cls up, ld 15th, drew clr 2 out, ran on strngly
491[3] **Ragtime Boy** ....**A Farrant** 2
handy, chsd wnr 15th, no ext und pres frm 3 out
624[1] **Anvil Corner 5a**....................**David Dennis** 3
lost tch 10th, t.o.
532[6] The Butler *ld 8-14th, hld in 3rd whn blnd & u.r. 3 out* ....S Slade ur
Kalokagathos *bhnd til p.u. 14th* ....E Clarkson pu
625[6] Sixth In Line (Ire) *bhnd til p.u. 12th*..........T Cole pu
526 Charlottes Billo *t.o. til p.u. 13th*..........R Emmett pu
630 Our Teddis *ld to 8th, wknd, rear & p.u. 13th* S Kidston pu
458[1] Penguin 5a *prom, hng rght thrght, hit 11th, ran out 13th* ....Miss J Cumings ro
461 Mrs McClusky (Ire) 12a *in tch to 13th, wknd 15th, p.u. 3 out, improve*........L Jefford pu
10 ran. 5l, dist. Time 5m 56.50s. SP 6-4.
Mrs C Wilson (Blackmore & Sparkford Vale).

737 Ladies

555[1] **ARCTIC CHILL (IRE)** ....**Miss S Vickery** 1
(fav) handy, ld 8th, qcknd readily 2 out, easily
589[4] **Some-Toy** ....**Miss L Blackford** 2
not fluent, prog to chs wnr 9th, ev ch 3 out, sn out-pcd
626 **Midnight Bob** ....**Miss A Barnett** 3
cls up in 3rd, ev ch til onepcd frm 3 out
Grey Guestino *ld/disp til lost plc rpdly 7th, sn strg-glng, t.o.*........Miss L Delve 4
Lady Leigh 5a *ld/disp to 8th, wknd, p.u. 12th, school* ....Miss R Francis pu
5 ran. 5l, 5l, dist. Time 5m 54.00s. SP 2-5.
M F Thorne & D Hobbs (Blackmore & Sparkford Vale).

738 Confined (12st)

528[1] **MYHAMET 3ex** ....**A Farrant** 1
(fav) handy, disp 13th til ld 16th, sn clr, easily
631[5] **The Copper Key** ....**T Greed** 2
rear, 5th 3 out, styd on to tk 2nd apr last
624 **Karlin's Quest** ....**D Doyne-Ditmas** 3
in tch in 3rd til outpcd frm 3 out
493 Seventh Lock *in tch to 12th, sn wknd* ....Miss L Blackford 4
237 Pop Song *lft in ld 2nd, ld til disp 13th, hdd 15th, wknd, p.u. 2 out*........J Young pu
173 Cardinal Bird (USA) (v) *last whn blnd & u.r. 1st* ....S Kidston ur
Far Too Loud *ld whn ref 2nd, cont, t.o. & p.u. 3 out* ....D Stephens pu
556 Kenstown (Ire) *prom, jmpd rght 5th, lost plc 10th, t.o. & p.u. 12th*........N Harris pu
8 ran. 8l, nk, 25l. Time 6m 4.50s. SP 4-5.
Paul C N Heywood (North Cornwall).
One fence omitted.

739 Men's Open

530[1] **BUTLER JOHN (IRE)** ....**N Harris** 1
(fav) made all, clr hlfwy, unchal
554[3] **Parson's Way (bl)** ....**A Farrant** 2
chsd wnr, no ch frm 4 out
629 Wise Florizel *sn lost tch, t.o. & p.u. 13th*......R Darke pu
3 ran. Dist. Time 5m 54.00s. SP 4-7.
Nick Viney (Exmoor).

740 Maiden Div I (12st)

101[3] **ASK ME KINDLY (IRE)** ....**Mrs M Hand** 1
(Jt fav) w.w. in tch, effrt 16th, strng run to ld aft last
625[2] **Eserie de Cores (USA)** ....**N Harris** 2
cls 2nd til ld 9th, 4l clr 3 out, ct flat, no ext
626[3] **Corrib Haven (Ire)** ....**A Farrant** 3
slght ld 4-9th, cls up til lost plc steadily frm 16th
625 Romany Anne 5a *wll out of tch, fin strngly, too mch to do*........Miss S Young 4
624 Stony Missile 5a *ld 1st, lost plc 8th, t.o. frm 10th* ....Miss W Hartnoll 5
314 Gamblers Refrain *prom, rdn 10th, wkng whn tried to ref 12th, p.u. nxt*........A Holdsworth pu
557 Jet Jockey *rear whn blnd & u.r. 3rd* ....A Oliver ur
Dusty Furlong *t.o. & p.u. 12th* ....Miss K Baily pu
104 Spectacular Star (Ire) *(Jt fav) cls 5th whn blnd & u.r. 6th*........C Heard ur
625 My Prides Way 5a *rear & strgglng til p.u. 12th* ....T Greed pu
Hayne Lass 5a *rear, mstk 2nd, t.o. & p.u. 5th* ....L Jefford pu
626[5] King Of Cairo *rear whn u.r. 7th*..........W Smith ur
553[6] Indian Language *4th hlfwy, lost ground 13th, blnd 3 out, p.u. nxt*........Miss L Blackford pu
524[4] Quicker Jack *sn wll bhnd, t.o. & p.u. 15th* ....Miss L Delve pu
Sea Spirit 12a *mid-div, 6th whn blkd & u.r. 12th* ....R Darke ur
15 ran. 2½l, 30l, 2l, dist. Time 5m 58.00s. SP 7-2.
G M Rowe & Mrs J Fisher (Lamerton).

741 Maiden Div II (12st)

553 **LEGAL AFFAIR 5a** ....**N Harris** 1
(fav) hld up, prog 10th, cls 2nd 12th til ld 15th, lft clr last
461[3] **Shameless Lady 5a** ....**R Darke** 2
cls up til ld 12th-15th, onepcd und pres, lft 2nd last
Ashcombe Valley ....**Miss N Courtenay** 3
twrds rear, 7th at 13th, best work clsng stgs
172 Princess Polly 5a *mid-div, 8th hlfwy, nvr nr to chal* ....Miss L Blackford 4
626[4] Reptile Princess 5a (bl) *tongue-strap, prom, ld 7th-12th, wknd 14th, sn lost tch*.......Miss W Hartnoll 5
554[5] Battling Psyche 5a *rear, mstk 2nd, t.o. & p.u. 12th* ....T Cole pu
Call Me Dickins *handy, mstk 4th, 3rd at 10th, prom whn b.d. nxt*........Miss A Barnett bd
531 Aritam (Ire) *hld up, prog 12th, cls 3rd 15th, disp nxt til f last*........A Farrant f
531 Round Of Drinks *ran green, pllng, ld 2nd-7th, cls up whn f 11th*........Miss K Baily f
553 Brother Nero (NZ) 7a *prog 10th, 5th whn blnd & u.r. 13th*........L Jefford ur
625 Duckin-N-Diving 5a *bhnd, hit 12th, t.o. & p.u. last* ....D Stephens pu
Earlswood *prom whn blnd & u.r. 5th*....A Holdsworth ur
12 ran. 8l, 30l, 5l, 12l. Time 6m 2.50s. SP 6-4.
P R Hill (Silverton).
G.T.

TEDWORTH
Barbury Castle
Saturday March 29th
FIRM

742 Members

396 **HEATHVIEW** .... **M Portman** 1
made all, clr 12th, unchal
488 **Todds Hall (Ire)** .... **A Munro** 2
in tch til wknd rpdly 11th, t.o.
516 **Game Fair** .... **W Cook** 3
rear 6th, t.o. 10th, btn 2f
Far Too Risky *bhnd frm 7th, t.o. & p.u. aft 10th* .... A Beedles pu
511² Touch Of Winter *(fav) trckd wnr, saddl slppd & p.u. apr 9th* .... T Lacey pu
5 ran. Dist, dist. Time 6m 35.00s. SP 5-1.
Mrs Peter Corbett (Tedworth).

743 Restricted (12st)

581⁵ **SHARED FORTUNE (IRE)** .... **Daniel Dennis** 1
walked over
R Gould (Hursley Hambledon).

744 Ladies

442³ **PONT DE PAIX** .... **Miss T Habgood** 1
(fav) made all, mstks 5th & 13th, easily
396⁵ **Wrekin Hill** .... **Mrs J Wilkinson** 2
trckd wnr, effrt 14th, wknd nxt
2 ran. 20l. Time 6m 33.00s. SP 1-4.
Mrs A Murray (Grafton).

745 Men's Open

675³ **WILD ILLUSION** .... **F Hutsby** 1
(fav) w.w. ld 12th, skipped clr 15th, cosily
393² **Royle Speedmaster** .... **T Lacey** 2
alwys prom, pshd up 4 out, unable qckn
662³ **Skinnhill** .... **C Mason** 3
ld to 11th, ran on agn 3 out, lkd to fin 2nd
3 ran. 8l, nk. Time 6m 31.00s. SP 4-9.
Mrs G Pidgeon (Grafton).

746 Confined (12st)

292³ **TEMPLERAINEY (IRE) 2ow** .... **G Maundrell** 1
trckd ldr, ld 13th, qcknd clr, easily
483³ **Cheeky Cheval (bl)** .... **M Batters** 2
(fav) ld til blnd 13th, no ch aft
2 ran. Dist. Time 6m 32.00s. SP 2-1.
Richard J Smith (Beaufort).

747 Open Maiden (12st)

60 **BAWNEROSH** .... **T Underwood** 1
set sedate pace, tk cmmnd 14th, ran on well
513 **Dad's Dilemma** .... **T Smith** 2
not keen early, prog 7th, mstk 14th, nvr nrr
297³ River Thrust (Ire) *(fav) prom, wknd 11th, p.u. 13th* .... Miss G Young pu
3 ran. 15l. Time 6m 47.00s. SP 7-4.
T D B Underwood (Garth & South Berks).
T.S.

UNITED
Brampton Bryan
Saturday March 29th
GOOD TO FIRM

748 Members

569³ **GARRYLUCAS 7ex** .... **G Hanmer** 1
1/1-5/2, made all, rdn 3 out, styd on strngly
360² **Oragas** .... **G Orchard** 2
alwys 3rd, 20l down 15th, sntchd 2nd flat
464² **Comedie Fleur 5a** .... **A Dalton** 3
(fav) trckd ldr, rdn to chal 3 out, no ext nxt, virt p.u. flat
Northern Quay *strgglng frm 6th, t.o. 13th* .... Miss L Macfarlane 4
Wild Edric 7a *4th til mstk & drppd last 6th, p.u. 12th* .... L Brown pu
Jester's Moon 12a *jmpd novicey, prog to 20l 4th whn f flat aft 11th, dead* .... R Evans f
6 ran. 15l, 2l, dist. Time 6m 57.00s. SP 5-2.
J D Lomas (United).

749 Men's Open (12st)

496⁵ **FIRST HARVEST** .... **P Hanly** 1
(fav) 1/3-4/7, cls up, ld 8th, drew wll clr frm 15th
670⁶ **Kiltrose Lad** .... **A Dalton** 2
ld to 7th, rdn & not qckn 13th, went 2nd 15th, blnd last
636⁵ **Noisy Welcome** .... **M P Jones** 3
alwys 4th, 10l down & rdn 12th, went remote 3rd 3 out
Junction Twentytwo *cls up, rdn to chs wnr 13th, mstk & wknd nxt, p.u. last* .... M Rimell pu
4 ran. 15l, 6l. Time 6m 45.00s. SP 4-7.
C J Bennett (Ledbury).

750 Ladies

430⁴ **NANDA MOON** .... **Miss S Jackson** 1
mostly 2nd, rdn 16th, prog nxt, qcknd to ld flat
398 **Call-Me-Dinky** .... **Miss C Thomas** 2
(fav) mostly 3rd, prog to chal last, no ext nr fin
Bumptious Boy .... **Miss S Rooker** 3
ld, 30l clr 13th, ct flat
652⁴ Tytherington *s.s. cls up 4th, outpcd frm 12th, t.o. 15th* .... Miss S Talbot 4
573 Opals Son *last frm 4th, t.o. 12th, p.u. nxt* .... Miss A Murphy pu
5 ran. 1l, 2l, dist. Time 6m 42.00s. SP 12-1.
C F C Jackson (North Ledbury).

751 P P O R A (12st)

351² **SHOON WIND 7ex** .... **A Dalton** 1
(fav) made all, qcknd clr 2 out, readily
568⁵ **Erlemo 4ex (bl)** .... **Dr P Pritchard** 2
not fluent, rdn 15th, chal 3 out, sn btn
Four From The Edge .... **C Dorrington** 3
cls 4th whn mstk 8th, not qckn 14th, kpt on onepcd frm 16th
431⁴ Leigh Boy (USA) *cls up, effrt 11th, sn wknd, p.u. 15th* .... M Munrowd pu
570 Oats For Notes 5a *chsd wnr 3rd, chal 15th, wknd aft nxt, p.u. last* .... M Rimell pu
5 ran. 6l, 4l. Time 6m 38.00s. SP 1-3.
J N Dalton (Wheatland).

752 Confined (12st)

405¹ **BOWLAND GIRL (IRE) 5a** .... **Miss E James** 1
walked over
R J Scandrett (Radnor & West Hereford).

753 Restricted (12st)

635 **LLES LE BUCFLOW** .... **M Munrowd** 1
prog to chal 11th, rdn 16th, ld 2 out, all out
574 **Corn Exchange** .... **M Rimell** 2
mstk 2nd, ld 10th, 5l clr 16th, jnd 2 out, no ext flat
575² **Wooden Minstrel 5a** .... **Dr P Pritchard** 3
cls 4th at 11th, ev ch 15th, not qckn, kpt on
467⁴ Fire King *ld to 9th, lost pld 12th, kpt on onepcd frm 16th* .... E Collins 4
633² Mackabee (Ire) *prog to cls 5th at 15th, wknd aft nxt* .... T Weale 5
670 Onemoreanwego 5a *w.w. prog 8th, 4l 3rd 13th, 10l 3rd whn p.u. aft 16th, lame* .... Miss E James pu
348 Rolier (Ire) *(fav) mid-div whn ran thro' wing 5th* .... A Dalton ro
568⁶ Stormhill Recruit *cls 7th at 11th, lost tch 15th, p.u. aft nxt* .... M P Jones pu
Holly Court 5a *taken steadily in rear til f 6th* .... Miss P Gundry f
9 ran. 1l, 5l, 12l, 20l. Time 6m 40.00s. SP 20-1.
Jeffrey A Smith (Golden Valley).

754 Maiden Div I (12st)

436 **INKY 5a**........................**A Phillips** **1**
30l 4th at 8th, 30l 2nd at 13th, ran on to ld 3 out, comf
470[2] **Agile King**........................**A Dalton** **2**
ld to 5th, 2nd/3rd til prog 16th, no ch wth wnr
435[5] **Emerald Charm (Ire) 5a**..........**M Rimell** **3**
(fav) clr ldr frm 6th, 30l up 15th, hdd 3 out, kpt on und pres
408 Miss Clare 5a *rear frm 4th, ran on steadily frm 15th, nrst fin*........F Cunningham 4
Saxon Smile *wth chsg grp, 3rd frm 11-16th, wknd & p.u. flat*........M Munrowd pu
Farriana 5a *mid-div, lost tch 9th, p.u. nxt*.....P Hanly pu
407[4] Brown Bala 5a (bl) *rear frm 6th, t.o. 13th, p.u. 15th*........Miss E James pu
Young Spring 12a *schoold in rear, p.u. 11th*....T Cox pu
360 Brighton Beach *rear frm 4th, p.u. 9th*...M Hammond pu
9 ran. 4l, 1l, 3l. Time 6m 56.00s. SP 5-2.
M J Hart (Ludlow).

755 Maiden Div II (12st)

CWM BYE........................**A Dalton** **1**
w.w. prog to 4l 3rd at 14th, ld 3 out, kpt on well
643[2] **Military Man**....................**M Munrowd** **2**
(fav) ld 5th til hdd aft 16th, kpt on onepcd und pres
261 **Sheer Power (Ire)**..............**F Cunningham** **3**
last til went 8l 4th at 12th, 30l last 16th, walked in
437 Corview (Ire) *prog to chal 11th, 2l 3rd & ev ch whn f 15th*........A Phillips f
209 Cuban Skies (Ire) *ld to 4th, disp cls 2nd whn ran out wing 13th*........T Cox ro
5 ran. 8l, dist. Time 6m 57.00s. SP 7-4.
Ms B Brown (Teme Valley).
P.R.

VALE OF AYLESBURY
Kimble
Saturday March 29th
GOOD TO FIRM

756 Members

549 **ROYAL DADDA**....................**A Hill** **1**
ld/disp, out jmpd, rdn 17th, ld apr last, lft solo
60[2] Mrs Moppit 5a *(fav) ld/disp, qcknd clr 16th, idld, hdd apr last, u.r. last*........R Cope ur
Bet A Lot 5a *hld up, 2nd 17th, clsng whn f nxt*........Miss T Honeyball f
3 ran. Time 7m 9.00s. SP 9-4.
M P Avery & J Dance (Vale Of Aylesbury).

757 Intermediate (12st)

446[3] **SPRUCEFIELD**....................**A Barlow** **1**
ld aft 1st-3rd, outpcd 13th, no ch whn lft clr bend apr last
369[1] Antica Roma (Ire) 5a *(fav) hld up in tch, p.u. aft 10th, lame*........C Wadland pu
377 Samsword *ld frm 3rd,qcknd clr aft 15th,12l ld whn slpd & u.r.apr last*........R Lawther ur
3 ran. Time 6m 47.00s. SP 4-1.
M H D Barlow (Bicester With Whaddon Chase).

758 Men's Open

651[2] **FAIR CROSSING**..................**M Emmanuel** **1**
alwys 1st pair, ld 4th, made rest, qcknd clr 15th
201[1] **Grecian Lark**....................**G Tarry** **2**
(fav) hld up, mstk 6th, 2nd aft 2 out, no ch wnr
447 **Admiral Rous**....................**C Wadland** **3**
chsd ldrs, 2nd frm 10th til aft 2 out, onepcd
447[3] Welsh Singer *hld up rear, f 4th*..........R Lawther f
393[3] Aylesford *ld 2nd-4th, wknd 10th, last whn p.u. aft 12th*........A Tutton pu
Quite A Miss 5a *alwys bhnd, t.o. & p.u. 13th*..A Martin pu
6 ran. 25l, 8l. Time 6m 26.00s. SP 5-2.
Michael Emmanuel (Vale Of Aylesbury).

759 Ladies

442[1] **MR WOODCOCK**..................**Miss A Plunkett** **1**
(fav) ld 4-11th, & nxt-15th, ld 3 out-nxt, disp last, styd on wll
Radical Views....................**Mrs T Hill** **2**
2nd hlfwy, lost plc, qcknd to ld 2 out, jnd last, hdd nr fin
304[2] **Howaryadoon**....................**Miss T Cave** **3**
prog 13th, ld 15th-3 out, no ext aft
484 Button Your Lip *ld to 3rd, cls up to hlfwy, last at 10th, sn t.o.*........Mrs J Enderby 4
4 ran. ¾l, 6l, 25l. Time 6m 29.00s. SP 4-5.
P A Tylor (Cury Harriers).

760 Interlink Restricted

287 **TAURA'S RASCAL**..................**F Brennan** **1**
rear, prog to ld 11th-2 out, drvn to ld flat
517 **Tommy O'Dwyer (Ire)**..............**A Hill** **2**
prssd ldrs, ld 2 out, jnd last, not qckn & hdd flat
374[1] **Wotamona 5a**....................**R Smith** **3**
chsd ldrs, 4th & not rch ldrs fin cct
Dixons Homefinder *cls up, ld 3-7th, wknd 2 out*........A Barnett 4
274[5] Buckwheat Lad (Ire) *rear, last at 6th, t.o.*..A Westrope 5
Horcum *hld up rear, 4th hlfwy, 5th at 15th, btn & p.u. nxt*........M Frith pu
141[1] Bubbly Boy *(fav) ld to 3rd, 6th hlfwy, last at 12th, p.u. last*........G Tarry pu
7 ran. 2l, 4l, 6l, 20l. Time 6m 43.00s. SP 3-1.
F J Brennan (V.W.H.).

761 Open Maiden

374 **AINTGOTTIME (IRE) 7a**............**R Lawther** **1+**
hld up,ld 12th,sn hdd,ld 16th til wd last bend,got up post
653[4] **FILL THE BOOT (IRE)**..............**J Owen** **1+**
(fav) sttld mid-div, prog 15th, ld apr last, hrd rdn, jnd post
452 **The Wayward Gunner**................**A Hill** **3**
hld up, prog to prss ldrs 16th, onepcd aft
655[5] Another Whistle (Ire) *ld to 11th, lost plc, not qckn frm 16th*........Miss T Habgood 4
Mr Pinball (bl) *prom til blnd 12th, lost plc, not rcvr*........M Cowley 5
Abbey Flyer *alwys last pair, wll bhnd whn p.u. 16th*........T Illsley pu
Miss Precocious 5a *cls 3rd frm 6th til wknd 15th, p.u. 2 out*........C Wadland pu
Multipower *chsd ldrs to hlfwy, in tch whn mstk & u.r. 13th*........D Buckley ur
374 Lord Lankie (Ire) *chsd ldrs, 5th at 12th, wknd & p.u. 3 out*........F Hutsby pu
299 Fraction *mid-div, 8th hlfwy, rear whn p.u. 16th*........A Martin pu
369 Wot No Cash 7a *sn rear, 9th hlfwy, bhnd & p.u. 16th*........M Frith pu
297 Miss Malachite 12a *in tch early, last at 8th, t.o. & p.u. aft 11th*........Miss G Browne pu
12 ran. Dd-ht, 15l, 12l, ½l. Time 6m 45.00s.
Mrs Ian McKie / Miss F Kehoe (Bicester With Whaddon Chase).
Fill The Boot, 3-1. Aintgottime, 6-1. H.F.

VALE OF LUNE
Whittington
Saturday March 29th
SOFT

762 Members

666 **I'LL SKIN THEM (IRE) 5a**..........**Mrs C Ford** **1**
j.s., 2nd 6th, ld/disp frm 9th, lft wll clr 15th
Tips Lad........................**D Greenwood** **2**
lft 20l 3rd 6th, alwys bhnd aft, btn 1 fence
Damers Cavalry *(fav) not alwys fluent, lft in ld 6th, disp til f 15th (dead)*........R Ford f

563 Mighty Haggis *s.s., ld aft 1st, clr 5th, missd mrkr bef nxt*.....Miss M Maher pu
Castle Cross *s.v.s., sn t.o., 2 fences down whn p.u. 3 out*.....G Thomas pu
5 ran. Dist. Time 7m 34.00s. SP 9-2.
M F Lee/A P Lee (Vale Of Lune).

763 Confined

584[3] **PENNINE VIEW** .....**R Ford** 1
(fav) chsd ldr, ld 7th, lft wll clr 15th, eased flat
418[3] **Romiley Mill** .....**D Coates** 2
mid-div, lft dist 2nd 15th, styd on wll, not trble wnnr
328 **Barkin** .....**P Saville** 3
bhnd, t.o. 6th, lft remote 3rd 15th
On Your Way *s.s., alwys t.o., 2 fences bhnd 6th*.....A Gilby 4
Nearctic Bay (USA) 9ow *alwys rear, t.o. 6th, p.u. 11th*.....J Simpson pu
422 Pinewood Lad 4ex *mid-div whn u.r. 3rd*..Miss K Ford ur
328 Stormhead *alwys cls up, 1l 2nd whn f 16th*.....C J B Barlow f
572 Pin Up Boy *ld to 7th, 10l 3rd & lkd btn whn f 14th*.....A Crow f
469 King Edward (Ire) *alwys mid-div, 40l 5th whn p.u. 11th*.....D Barlow pu
9 ran. 25l, 2 fences, 2 fences. Time 7m 15.00s. SP 7-4.
J J Dixon (Cumberland Farmers).

764 G Middleton Ladies

158[5] **PARLIAMENT HALL** .....**Mrs C Ford** 1
ld to 9th & frm 14th, styd on wll whn chal apr 2 out
617[2] **Kellys Diamond** .....**Miss V Russell** 2
(fav) held up, 2nd 15th, ev ch 2 out, no ext
561[4] **Running Frau 5a**.....**Miss M Maher** 3
rear til ran on strgly frm 3 out, fin fast
412 South Stack *cls 2nd til ld 9th, hdd 14th, wknd qckly*.....Miss C Billington 4
329[2] Saahi (USA) *alwys 3rd/4th, 9l down whn f 14th*.....Miss S Swindells f
5 ran. 10l, 10l, 20l. Time 7m 7.00s. SP 2-1.
S H Shirley-Beavan (Jedforest).

765 Land Rover Mens Open (12st)

413[1] **THE PARISH PUMP (IRE) 4ex** .....**R Ford** 1
(fav) ld 8th, wnt clr aft 3 out, eased flat
562[3] **Boreen Owen** .....**A Parker** 2
mid-div, rddn alng 11th, 2nd 13th, ev ch 3 out, no ext
618[7] **Syrus P Turntable** .....**J Saville** 3
alwys 3rd/4th, nvr trbld ldrs
465 Mr Tittle Tattle 7ex (bl) *ld mstly to 8th, cls up til wknd aft 3 out*.....D Barlow 4
618[5] Clare Lad *alwys rear, p.u. 2 out*.....T Whittaker pu
Broguestown Pride (Ire) *last pair throut, nvr dang, p.u. 15th*.....R Hale pu
6 ran. 12l, 20l, 1½l. Time 7m 11.00s. SP 11-10.
R Burgess (Vale Of Lune).

766 Intermediate (12st)

332 **CALLEROSE** .....**R Bevis** 1
4th 11th,lft 2nd 15th,ld nxt,hdd 2 out,qcknd to ld apr last
332[2] **Royle Burchlin (bl)** .....**D Barlow** 2
ld to 15th & apr 2 out, hdd last, outpcd flat
325[1] **Formal** .....**R Owen** 3
alwys cls up, ev ch 3 out, styd on onepcd
476[3] Katies Argument 5a *alwys bhnd, tk 4th aft 2 out*.....Miss J Wilson 4
478[1] Red Rebel 7a *held up, 15l 6th apr 14th, strggld aft*.....R Ford 5
563[4] Marked Card *6l 3rd whn u.r. 7th*.....Mrs M Kendall ur
671 Flinters (bl) *chsd ldr, cls 2nd whn f 14th*. C J B Barlow f
414[1] Makin' Doo (Ire) *(fav) held up, 4l 5th & gng wll whn b.d. 14th*.....A Parker bd
Bunny Hare (Ire) *alwys last, t.o. 11th, p.u. 13th*.....G Thomas pu
427[1] Petit Primitive 5a *mstk 1st, mid-div whn f 6th*.....T Whittaker f
10 ran. 5l, 4l, 30l, 2½l. Time 7m 7.00s. SP 3-1.
R J Bevis (West Shropshire Drag).

767 Open Maiden Div I

208[2] **FOREVER DREAMING (IRE)** .....**R Ford** 1
(fav) mstks,lft 3rd 13th,20l down 3 out,ran on strgly to ld last
417[2] **The Alleycat (Ire)** .....**R Bevis** 2
lft in clr ld 13th,15l up whn mstk 3 out,wknd & hdd apr last
120 **Gold Talisman 5a** .....**D Barlow** 3
ldng grp, lft 2nd 13th, onepcd aft
415 All Screwed Up (Ire) *mstks, bhnd, lft 4th 13th, t.o. 2 out*.....D Sherlock 4
Browlea Lyndene 5a *mstks, rear, t.o. 9th, p.u. 11th*.....P Blane pu
38[4] Press To Sting *ld to 9th, cls 2nd whn f 12th*....R Hale f
564[3] Cookie Boy *chsd ldr, ld 10th, u.r. 13th*.....Miss H Delahooke ur
666 Scally Lass 5a *rear, t.o. 11th, last whn u.r. 13th*.....D Norlander ur
Little Idiot 5a *alwys rear, t.o. 9th, p.u. 11th*...A Parker pu
9 ran. 4l, 8l, 1 fence. Time 7m 22.00s. SP 6-4.
Mrs M Cooper (Middleton).

768 Open Maiden Div II

435[3] **SUGI** .....**I Wynne** 1
alwys cls up, 2l 2nd last, qcknd wll flat
420[2] **Blank Cheque** .....**D Coates** 2
(fav) ld to 15th, lost tch, ran on wll agn to ld last,outpcd flat
665 **Nights Image (Ire)** .....**M Worthington** 3
held up, styd prog to ld apr 3 out, hdd nxt, no ext
120 Rambling Oats *alwys prom, ld 2 out, wknd qckly nxt*.....Miss A Price 4
206[3] Crimson Bow 5a *mstks, 3rd til wknd 13th*....R Owen 5
Keep Them Keen (Ire) *bhnd, nvr dang, p.u. 2 out*.....J Maher pu
325 Fruit Of Oak (Ire) *n.j.w., alwys last pair, t.o. 14th, f 3 out*.....A Crow f
478[5] Our Wyn-Ston 7a *nvr bynd mid-div, p.u. 2 out*.....C J B Barlow pu
419 Cinder Mirage *cls up 1st ctt, wknd & u.r. 15th*.....B Gibson ur
Noreasonatall 12a *mstks, rear, p.u. 11th*..T Whittaker pu
10 ran. 4l, 3l, 20l, 5l. Time 7m 25.00s. SP 9-2.
Ian Wynne (Sir W W Wynn's).

WOODLAND PYTCHLEY
Dingley
Saturday March 29th
GOOD

769 Confined (12st)

321[1] **MR BRANIGAN (IRE)** .....**T Marks** 1
(fav) alwys 1st pair, ld 10th, drew away 2 out, comf
473[2] **Dashboard Light** .....**S R Andrews** 2
w.w. prog frm 8th, 2nd 5 out, only threat 2 out, outpcd
441[2] **Youcat (Ire) 5ow**.....**I Marsh** 3
prog 6 out, 5th 4 out, ran on well, nrst fin
548[1] Storming Roy *mid-div, prog 9th, 3rd 5 out-2 out, no ext*.....H Nicholson 4
547[4] Going Around *abt 5th for 2m, wknd 6 out, 8th 5 out, fin own time*.....L Lay 5
593[1] Horace 3ex *prom bhnd ldrs, 4th 6 out-4 out, outpcd nxt*.....W Wales 6
545[6] Antrim County *ldng trio 1st m, sn fdd, p.u. 12th*.....J Cornwall pu
Joestone *rear div, mstk 3rd, t.o. 8th, p.u. 11th*.....Miss E Godfrey pu
503 Obie's Train 12ow *disp brfly on outside, sn outpcd, bhnd whn u.r. 5th*.....Mrs A Lee ur
Kiltroum (Fr) *t.o. 1st, f 8th*.....J Dillon f
Jerrigo *alwys rear div, p.u. 4 out*.....J Knowles pu

545[2] Miller's Chap *prom 1st cct, 3rd at 11th, wknd 6 out, p.u. last* ....M Hewitt pu
473 Tenelord *ld/disp til wknd frm 12th, 5th & outpcd 5 out, p.u. last*................................S Morris pu
Scraptastic *prom 1st m, fdd, p.u. 11th* ....N Bell pu
14 ran. 7l, 2l, nk, 30l, ½l. Time 6m 33.00s. SP 4-5.
G T H Bailey & W Rowe (Pytchley).

770 Restricted (12st)

477 **BROADWAY SWINGER ....S R Andrews 1**
w.w. hrd hld,rpd prog 10th,ld 5 out, hdd last, rallied flat
548[3] **Brown Baby 5a..........................G Kerr 2**
alwys prom, outpcd brfly 6 out, prog to ld last, ct fin
480[1] **Barneys Gold (Ire) ....A Bealby 3**
prog 8th, 3rd frm 10th, chsd 1st pair 3 out, unable to cls
545[4] Dark Rhytham *w.w. prog 9th, 2nd 12th-3 out, wknd nxt* ....S Morris 4
251 Spalease 5a *prom bhnd ldrs til outpcd frm 6 out, fin own time* ....R Barrett 5
548[4] Mr Gee *alwys rear hlf, last pair at 10th, wll bhnd whn p.u. last*................................K Needham pu
344[3] Vimchase *mid-div whn u.r. 6th* ....S J Robinson ur
550 Paddy's Pocket *disp brfly to 3rd, sn fdd, last pair 10th, p.u. nxt* ....R Armson pu
548 Kerry My Home *twrds rear whn f 3rd*........T Marks f
317 Learner Driver *alwys rear hlf, outpcd 6 out, p.u. 3 out* ....M Gingell pu
550[4] Grange Missile 5a *mid-div, fdd 12th, remote 8th whn p.u. last*................................J Dillon pu
677[1] Tiderunner (Ire) *mid-div, 5th/6th to 12th, outpcd nxt, p.u. 3 out* ....S Walker pu
Diamond Valley (Ire) *disp brfly, sn mid-div, ran on 6 out,6th whn blnd & u.r.2out* ....Miss S Wallin ur
Rough Edge *alwys rear hlf, outpcd 6 out, remote 7th whn p.u. last* ....W Wales pu
Weston Moon (Ire) 5a *ld 4th-12th, fdd nxt, 6th whn p.u. last* ....J Docker pu
Rakish Queen 5a *alwys rear hlf, outpcd 6 out, p.u. nxt* ....Miss H Phizacklea pu
450[1] The Auctioneer *(fav) ld to 3rd, 2nd til blnd & u.r. 10th* ....Miss L Rowe ur
544 Skylark Song 5a *plld hrd, cls up til u.r. 8th* ....Mrs J Holmes ur
18 ran. Sht-hd, 3l, 20l, 30l. Time 6m 34.00s. SP 10-1.
Mrs Charlotte Cooke (Cottesmore).

771 Land Rover Open (12st)

675 **COOLVAWN LADY (IRE) 5a 7ex ....S Walker 1**
cls up, ld 11th, drew clr 6 out, 15l up 2 out, tired flat
250[2] **Raise An Argument 7ex................N Docker 2+**
j.w.chsd ldrs, effrt to 2nd 2 out, ran on gamely
473[3] **Merlyns Choice ....A Woodward 2+**
last to 8th, remote 7th at 11th, steady prog to d/h 2nd post
447[2] Penlet *(fav) mostly 6th, rdn frm 10th, ran on 6 out, not rch 1st trio*..........................John Pritchard 4
Pancratic *3rd brfly to 3rd, sn fdd, t.o. 10th, p.u. 2 out* ....C Millington pu
547 Adamare 7ex *ld to 10th, wknd rpdly nxt, p.u. 4 out* ....R Armson pu
547 Faithful Star 7ex *cls up til wknd 10th, bhnd whn p.u. last*..........................R Hunnisett pu
475 Solid (Ire) *alwys last pair, t.o. last at 10th, p.u. last* ....M Barnard pu
Tudor Fable (Ire) 7ex *alwys prom, 3rd til 2nd 6 out-2 out, wknd rpdly, p.u. last* ....R Sweeting pu
549 Kabancy *abt 8th 1st m, t.o. 10th, p.u. 6 out* ....P Millington pu
10 ran. 4l, dd-ht, 8l. Time 6m 36.00s. SP 3-1.
W R Halliday (Cranwell Bloodhounds).

772 Members

544[2] **BUSKING ALONG (IRE) ....H Nicholson 1**
(fav) alwys 1st pair, ld to 5th & frm 6 out, drew away 2 out
Woodlands Lady 5a...........Miss K Makinson 2
t.o. last thrght
549[6] Ms Taaffe 5a *mostly 4l 3rd, rdn 6 out, f nxt* ....Mrs M Bellamy f
Seaton Mill *alwys 1st pair,ld 6th-12th,outpcd 2 out,p.u.last,stewards*......................M Hewitt pu
4 ran. Dist. Time 6m 58.00s. SP 1-3.
J G Nicholson (Woodland Pytchley).

773 G Middleton Ladies

379[4] **CORNER BOY ....Mrs J Dawson 1**
(fav) cls up, ld 12th, drew away frm 2 out, comf
448[3] **Kites Hardwicke ....Mrs C Behrens 2**
w.w. 5th & rdn 10th, 3rd 6 out, chsd wnr nxt, outpcd 2 out
446[5] **Alias Silver ....Miss H Irving 3**
sn rear hlf, prog 8th, 2nd 6 out, 3rd nxt, no imp
546[1] Supreme Dream (Ire) 5a *nvr dang, 5th/6th for 2m, 4th & onepcd frm 4 out* ....Mrs P Adams 4
448[2] Loose Wheels *cls up to 11th, 5th & outpcd 6 out* ....Miss K Makinson 5
Tinryland *last pair til ref 8th* ....Miss C Elderton ref
384 What A To Do *abt 6th til outpcd & t.o. 10th, p.u. 2 out* ....Miss L Sweeting pu
546[3] Man Of Mystery *first pair, mstly ld to 11th, wknd rpdly 5 out, p.u. 2 out* ....Miss F Hatfield pu
546 Smart Rhythm 5a *alwys last, t.o. 10th, p.u. last* ....Miss C Arthers pu
Toiapan (Ire) *plld hrd, ld 5th, ran out nxt* ....Miss R Gander ro
546[7] Shouldofdone *abt 9th til f 6th*.....Mrs V Lloyd-Davies f
11 ran. 10l, 8l, 4l, dist. Time 6m 34.00s. SP 4-7.
Mrs E W Wilson (Brocklesby).

774 2m 5f Open Maiden (5-7yo) Div I Pt I (12st)

SHADRACH ....A Charles-Jones 1
cls up, ld 6 out, clr 2 out, promising
480[3] **Neelisagin (Ire) ....P Millington 2**
(fav) alwys prom, 3rd 3 out, chsd wnr nxt, no imp
Tinsun ....John Pritchard 3
2nd to 9th, 4th & outpcd 4 out, ran on onepcd
438[4] View Point (Ire) *ld to 10th, 2nd to 3 out, 3rd & outpcd nxt* ....M Gingell 4
The Rebel Parish (Ire) *n.j.w. alwys last pair, t.o. & p.u. aft 2 out* ....Mrs J Dawson pu
Gold Sword *7th & in tch to 9th, 5th & outpcd 6 out, bhnd & f 3 out* ....P Cowley f
478 Bucks Law *cls up to 9th, reluc & outpcd nxt, p.u. 4 out* ....J Docker pu
Sun Setting *in tch til outpcd 6 out, f 3 out* ....Miss L Sweeting f
Chapeau Chinois 5a *last frm 3rd, t.o. 5th, p.u. 10th* ....Miss E Godfrey pu
473 Maison Rouge *nvr dang, 6th & rmndrs 8th, no respns, p.u. 4 out* ....S Walker pu
10 ran. 5l, 10l, 8l. Time 5m 37.00s. SP 4-1.
T J Sunderland (Bicester With Whaddon Chase).

775 2m 5f Open Maiden (5-7yo) Div I Pt II (12st)

478[6] **MR FREEBIE (DEN) ....D Ingle 1**
4th of 5 survivors at 7th, 3rd nxt, ld 4 out, ran on well
141[3] **Greenacres Rose 5a..........Miss S Phizacklea 2**
alwys 1st pair, chsd wnr frm 4 out, alwys hld
Doyden Castle ....W Wales 3
alwys rear hlf, 5th & last frm 6 out, fin own time
549 Star Traveller *2nd/disp til f 5 out*...........M Skinner f
Fearless Bertie *prom til u.r. 4th* ....N Ridout ur
Flying Fellow (Ire) *4th whn u.r. 3rd*.......Miss C Tuke ur
450 Novatara 7a *(fav) mid-div, ran out 4th*.......S Morris ro
Erik The Viking *rear hlf til u.r. 4th*..........R Armson ur
Kings Choir 7a *last til ref 5th* ....T Lane ref
451 Half A Chance *cls 3rd frm 6th, p.u. sddnly 11th* ....T Marks pu
10 ran. 8l, dist. Time 5m 47.00s. SP 6-1.
Mrs M C Banks (South Wold).

776 2m 5f Open Maiden (5-7yo) Div II Pt I (12st)

478 **CATCHPHRASE ....K Needham 1**
w.w. prog 6 out, 2nd 3 out, qcknd & ld last, clvrly, prmsng
479[4] **Royal Balinger 5a 1ow ....T Lane 2**
disp, lft in ld 3 out, hdd & outpcd apr last
439 **I'm Free (Ire) ....M Gingell 3**
disp to 10th, 3rd frm 6 out, no ext frm 2 out
372 Dancing Supreme *ref to race* ....M Turner 0
127 Allegro Prince (bl) *prom bhnd ldrs, 6th & outpcd 6 out, 4th 2 out, p.u. last*..........................R Mumford pu
Mistress Dasher 5a *disp, ld 10th-4 out, ev ch whn f nxt* ....R Sweeting f
141[5] Bamboo Pie 5a *prom whn b.d. 3rd* ....C Vale bd
478 Flying Linnet 5a *prom whn f 3rd*............J Docker f
Ourmanjac *(fav) nvr dang, 5th 6 out-3 out, wknd, p.u. last*.......................................S Morris pu
Right Well (Ire) 7a *alwys rear, t.o. 7th at 9th, p.u. 2 out* ....E Andrewes pu

10 ran. 5l, 4l. Time 5m 44.00s. SP 12-1.
A A Day (Atherstone).

777 2m 5f Open Maiden (5-7yo) Div II Pt II (12st)

480 **MALLOW INNOCENCE ....N Kent 1**
2nd to 9th, 4th & outpcd 6 out, ran on strngly 3 out,ld last
79[3] **Cuba 7a...............................R Barrett 2**
(fav) cls up, 2nd 6 out, disp nxt, ld 2 out, hdd last
478 **Malenski (Ire) ....P Millington 3**
cls up, 3rd frm 6 out, just outpcd apr last
128[2] Regency Cottage *ld to 5 out, disp to 2 out, onepcd apr last*..................................W Wales 4
Colonel Wilkie *6th/7th til outpcd 6 out, fin own time* ....J Dillon 5
Princess Letitia 5a 2ow *alwys last, t.o. 8th, p.u. 5 out* ....J Stephenson pu
478 Fly The Heights *mostly 5th til outpcd 6 out, p.u. last* ....S Walker pu
Teduet *alwys rear, outpcd 6 out, p.u. last* ....T Marks pu

8 ran. 1l, 4l, ½l, 20l. Time 5m 51.00s. SP 12-1.
Mrs Lorraine Lamb (Grove & Rufford).
K.B.

CARLISLE
Monday March 31st
GOOD

778 3¼m John Mckie Maiden Hunters' Chase Class H

611[4] **BUCK'S DELIGHT (IRE) 12.0 7a Mr M Bradburne 1**
alwys prom, ld 5 out, hrd pressed from last, ran on well.
287[2] **Ask Antony (Ire) 12.2 5a...............Mr R Ford 2**
(fav) imp to ld after 3rd, joined final cct, hdd 5 out, rallied gamely from last.
509[3] **Admission (Ire) 12.0 7a ....Miss L Horner 3**
started slowly, soon in tch, effort 13th, no impn final 3.
561[1] Roly Prior 11.9 5a *bhnd and rdn along, imp 6 out, no impn final 4*...........................Mrs V Jackson 4
410[3] All Or Nothing 11.2 7a *mstks in rear, nvr on terms.* ....Mr J Ewart 5
584[2] General Delight 12.0 7a *mid div, rdn 11th, outpcd before 5 out*...............................Mr D Wood 6
357 Just For Me (Ire) 12.2 5a *chsd ldrs, hit 8th, outpcd last 5*.............................Mr M H Naughton 7
231 Rushing Burn 11.9 7a *blnd 1st, imp to chase ldrs 8th, fd 5 out, t.o.*.......................Miss N C Snowden 8
383 Sir Harry Rinus 12.0 7a *jmpd badly in rear, t.o. when p.u. before 2 out*.......................Miss F Barnes pu
157[3] Green Sheen (Ire) 12.0 7a *prom till outpcd 12th, p.u. 3 out*..................................Mr Chris Wilson pu
386[3] Frozen Stiff (Ire) 12.2 5a *chsd ldrs, struggling when hit 10th, soon btn, p.u. 5 out*..............Mr R Shiels pu
566[4] Madame Beck 11.10 7a 1ow *held up, imp to chase ldrs 12th, struggling 5 out, p.u. last*......Mr R M Smith pu
414[5] Eostre 12.0 *ld to 3rd, lost pl 11th, p.u. before 4 out.* ....Mr P Craggs pu
413[3] Solwaysands 11.7 7a *chsd ldrs, struggling final cct, p.u. 4 out*.................................Mr B Gibson pu

14 ran. ½l, 14l, 8l, 1½l, 13l, 29l, dist. Time 7m 4.20s. SP 33-1.
Mrs Richard Arthur

FAKENHAM
Monday March 31st
GOOD

779 2m 5f 110yds Robert Hoare Memorial Novices' Hunters' Chase Class H

490[6] **NOT MY LINE (IRE) 11.9 5a..........Mr W Wales 1**
held up, joined ldr 13th, ld after 2 out, all out.
584 **Up For Ransome (Ire) 11.7 7a.......Mr T J Barry 2**
in tch, hit 3rd, ld 12th till after 2 out, rallied run-in.
678 **Galzig 11.7 7a ....Mr W Tellwright 3**
chsd ldrs, rdn and one pace from 3 out.
318[1] Reverend Brown (Ire) 11.9 5a *(fav) not fluent early, kept on one pace from 3 out*...........Mr A Sansome 4
280[3] Sperrin View 11.2 7a *rear most of way.* Mr A Charles-Jones 5
585[2] Tea Cee Kay 11.7 7a *well pld till rear 8th, soon lost tch.* ....Mr Rupert Sweeting 6
497[4] Cardinal Black 11.7 7a *ld to 3rd, led 7th to 12th, rear when p.u. after 2 out*....................Mr R Wakley pu
65 Sunset Run 11.7 7a (bl) *bhnd till p.u. before 7th.* ....Miss C Tuke pu
769 Scraptastic 11.7 7a *ld 3rd to 7th, rear when f 10th.* ....Mr N M Bell f

9 ran. ½l, 5l, 7l, 4l, 20l. Time 5m 37.90s. SP 20-1.
P C Caudwell

780 3m 110yds Queen's Cup, An Eastern Counties Hunters' Chase Class H

596[1] **DROMIN LEADER 11.7 5a..........Mr W Wales 1**
(fav) chsd ldr, left in ld 4 out, driven out, held on well.
Cherry Chap 11.5 7a............Capt D R Parker 2
held up, joined ldrs 14th, ev ch last, rallied near line.
504[1] **Saint Bene't (Ire) 11.5 7a (bl) ....Mr J G Townson 3**
dropped rear 5th, lost tch 14th, styd on well from 2 out.
545[1] Romany Ark 11.1 7a *dropped rear 4th, hdwy when mstk 13th, no ext from 3 out*................Mr N M Bell 4
503[4] Just Jack 11.5 7a *in tch, rdn and one pace from 3 out.*.......................................Mr N Bloom 5
Tammy's Friend 11.5 7a (bl) *ld, mstk 6th, blnd and u.r. 4 out.*.................................Mr J Ferguson ur
323[4] Lyme Gold (Ire) 11.5 7a *not fluent early, mstk 9th, wknd 14th, p.u. before last*................Mr D Keane pu

7 ran. Hd, 10l, 1l, 10l. Time 6m 34.40s. SP 7-4.
J M Turner

HEREFORD
Monday March 31st
GOOD TO FIRM

781 2m 3f James Daly Hunters' Chase Class H

587[2] **LANDSKER MISSILE 11.2 7a.......Mr N Bradley 1**
(fav) prom, ld 7th, hrd pressed from 3 out till driven clr from last.
679 **Familiar Friend 12.3 7a (bl)...........Mr P Scott 2**
in tch, pressed wnr from 3 out, no ext from last.
360[3] **Bowl Of Oats 11.7 7a (bl)...........Mr A R Price 3**
soon bhnd, mod hdwy 3 out, n.d..
414 Leeswood 11.7 7a (v) *alwys bhnd, struggling from hfwy, nvr a factor*.........................Mrs C Ford 4
Enchanted Man 11.7 7a *bhnd 6th, t.o. when p.u. before 3 out*..................................Mr A Wintle pu

Emrys 11.7 7a *chsd ldrs, wknd 8th, t.o. when p.u. before 2 out*..........................Miss E J Jones pu
90 Pastoral Pride (USA) 11.9 5a *ld to 7th, lost pl quickly 9th, bhnd when p.u. before next*........Miss P Curling pu
569⁴ Shareef Star 11.7 7a (bl) *n.j.w., alwys well bhnd, t.o. when p.u. before 4 out*....................Mr S Joynes pu
627⁴ Double The Stakes (USA) 11.7 7a *in tch, blnd 5th, hdwy to go prom 7th, wknd next, bhnd when p.u. before 10th*..........................Mr J Creighton pu

9 ran. 15l, 30l, 15l. Time 4m 39.00s. SP Evens.
W J Evans

TOWCESTER
Monday March 31st
GOOD TO FIRM

782 2¾m 23rd Year Of The Schilizzi 1906 Sixty Years Commemorative Challenge Cup Hunters' Chase Class H

384¹ **TEAPLANTER 12.0 5a..............Mr B Pollock** 1
(fav) ld to 7th, styd tracking ldr, chal 4 out, led, blnd and hdd next, led again apr last, stayed on gamely.
587⁴ **Tuffnut George 11.7 7a.............Mr A Phillips** 2
trckd wnr, chal 6th, ld next, hdd 3 out but soon left in front again, hded 2 out, soon btn.
588² **Hickelton Lad 11.7 7a..............Mr S Durack** 3
alwys 3rd, lost tch 8th, mstk next, t.o..

3 ran. 19l, dist. Time 5m 37.70s. SP 4-9.
R G Russell

EAST KENT
Aldington
Monday March 31st
HARD

783 Restricted (12st)

580² **VELKA 5a............................A Hickman** 1
(fav) hld up, ld 15th, in cmmnd aft
682² **Basher Bill..............................K Giles** 2
wth ldr frm 2nd, ld 6-10th, agn 12-15th, 2nd best aft
580 **Valiant Friend (bl).................Miss B Barton** 3
ld,jmpd slwly 2nd, hdd 6th, ld 10-12th, 3rd frm 15th,onepcd
576 Killarney Man *last frm 6th, lost tch 12th*........T Hills 4

4 ran. 6l, 8l, 1 fence. Time 6m 45.00s. SP 1-4.
R V Mair (East Sussex & Romney Marsh).

784 Confined (12st)

685² **BARN ELMS..........................A Hickman** 1
(fav) ld, lft solo 9th
576 Sea Patrol *chsd rival til ran out & u.r. 9th* ....Miss B Barton ro

2 ran. Time 7m 1.00s. SP 1-3.
Mrs S J Hickman (East Sussex & Romney Marsh).

785 Ladies

681 **SERIOUS MONEY (USA) ....Miss C Ewart** 1
walked over
Mrs Angus Campbell (Ashford Valley).

786 Men's Open (12st)

AUTHORSHIP (USA).......................T Hills 1
walked over
G M Turnwell (Coakham Bloodhounds).

787 Open Maiden (12st)

581³ **TARGET TIME 5a.........................K Giles** 1
walked over
B Neaves (West Street-Tickham).

788 Members

PRINCE ZEUS ....G Knowles 1
walked over
D G Knowles (East Kent).
G.Ta.

EGGESFORD
Bishopsleigh
Monday March 31st
GOOD

789 Members

628⁶ **RASTA MAN.............................K Heard** 1
(fav) ld til nrly ref & u.r. 3rd, rmntd, disp 5 out,ld last,ran on
Maboy Lady.......................David Dennis 2
lft in ld 3rd, disp 5 out til hdd & no ext last
458 **Mazies Choice 5a.......................K Crook** 3
in tch to 14th, outpcd aft, no ch 4 out
315 Young Herbert (Ire) *sttld rear, lost tch 14th, blnd 4 out, no ch aft*..................................J Auvray 4
Play Risky (Ire) *cls up to 12th, lost tch 14th, p.u. aft nxt* ....R Emmett pu

5 ran. 4l, 30l, 30l. Time 7m 13.00s. SP 1-2.
J Heard (Eggesford).

790 Ladies

627² **KHATTAF.......................Miss J Cumings** 1
(fav) j.w. ld 5th, kpt on wll frm 4 out
951 **The Kimbler.......................Miss S Young** 2
handy, 2nd at 15th, chsd wnr vainly aft
520 **Celtic Sport.......................Miss C Stucley** 3
cls up to 15th, outpcd frm 4 out
627 Afterkelly *sn rear, mod late prog, nvr any ch* ....Miss D Ward 4
454 Le Garcon D'Or *sn rear, wll bhnd frm 14th* ....Miss K Hurst 5
482 Debjanjo *sn rear, t.o. & p.u. 11th* ....Miss R David pu
454¹ Majestic Spirit *ld to 5th, 2nd to 14th, wknd, p.u. 17th* ....Miss T Cave pu

7 ran. 1l, 3l, 12l, dist. Time 6m 34.70s. SP 4-6.
Mrs H C Johnson (Devon & Somerset Staghounds).

791 Confined

522 **FLAME O'FRENSI 5a............Miss J Cumings** 1
j.w. made all, kpt on wll frm 3 out
532¹ **Gypsy Gerry..........................L Jefford** 2
(fav) hld up, 3rd at 14th, effrt 3 out, not qckn frm 2 out, eased
Frosty Reception (bl)...........Miss C Stucley 3
chsd ldr to 17th, wknd nxt, fin tired
Tranquil Waters (USA) *alwys rear, t.o. 17th* ....David Dennis 4
530 Achiltibuie *chsd ldrs til wknd 17th, t.o. nxt* ..G Penfold 5
554⁴ Pharaoh Blue *alwys bhnd, t.o. & p.u. 15th*....K Heard pu

6 ran. 4l, dist, 30l, 4l. Time 6m 38.40s. SP 6-4.
P J Clarke (Devon & Somerset Staghounds).

792 Restricted (12st)

523 **LINK COPPER..........................R Payne** 1
hld up, prog 17th, 3rd 2 out, chal & ld aft last
454³ **First Design..........................L Jefford** 2
alwys prom, disp 4 out til outpcd flat
556 **Swing To The Left (Ire) 5a.......Miss J Cumings** 3
(fav) prom, ld 7th til hdd aft last, no ext
556² Indian Rabi *alwys mid-div, effrt 17th, unable rch ldrs* ....G Penfold 4
307² Stainless Steel *prom early, lost tch 17th, outpcd* ....M Sweetland 5
Remember Mac (bl) *prom early, mid-div 10th, outpcd aft*..................................Miss C Hayes 6
631 Always Lynsey (Ire) 5a *rear whn blnd & u.r. 3rd* ....Miss K Hurst ur
556 Nottarex *mid-div, blnd 8th, rdr lost irons, p.u. nxt* ....B Wright pu
736 Our Teddis *ld til ran out 7th*..................K Crook ro
458 Belitlir 12a *schoold in rear til p.u. 13th*..Miss S Young pu
Robehen 5a *mid-div, no show, p.u. 16th* David Dennis pu

Too Phar Gone 7a *schoold in rear, p.u. 17th* ....A O'Connor pu
State Medlar *alwys mid-div, btn 6th whn ran out last* ....R Woolacott ro
13 ran. 1l, 4l, 20l, 2l, 25l. Time 6m 48.00s. SP 6-1.
Mrs E J Taplin (Devon & Somerset Staghounds).

793 Men's Open

554[1] **FEARSOME** ....**G Penfold** 1
(fav) hld up, prog 17th, chal 2 out, hrd rdn last, ld cls hm
Abbotsham ....**David Dennis** 2
prom, ld/disp 10th til hdd aft last, ran on und pres,jst hld
453[3] **It's Not My Fault (Ire)** ....**L Jefford** 3
handy, mostly 3rd, disp 4 out-last, no ext nr fin
647[4] Ideal *ld to 10th, 2nd aft til wknd 17th* ....J Rees 4
627 My Key Silca *u.r. 3rd* ....K Crook ur
629[2] Nearly Splendid *nvr going wll, bhnd whn p.u. 10th* ....T Greed pu
552 Bargain And Sale *alwys rear, t.o. & p.u. 12th* R Payne pu
7 ran. 1l, 1l, 20l. Time 6m 39.00s. SP Evens.
G W Penfold (Silverton).

794 Open Maiden Div I

557[2] **MENDIP SON** ....**L Jefford** 1
(fav) hld up, lft in ld 12th, kpt on und pres whn chal
458[5] **Stretchit** ....**G Penfold** 2
in tch, 4th at 10th, chal 3 out, no ext aft last
625[5] **Tarka Trail** ....**T Dennis** 3
mid-div, slght chnc 4 out, outpcd aft
461 Nearly Fair 5a *mid-div, effrt 17th, 3rd nxt, dmtd apr last* ....N Legg 4
553[5] Trolly *prom to 17th, wknd* ....David Dennis 5
Be Are *prom to 14th, wknd, p.u. 17th* ....A O'Connor pu
740 Dusty Furlong *prom early, lost tch 7th, t.o. & p.u. 16th* ....Miss K Baily pu
54 Riggledown Regent *sn rear, p.u. 10th* ....J Auvray pu
591 The Bodhran (Ire) *mid-div, outpcd 16th, lost tch nxt, p.u. 3 out* ....R Young pu
553 Creedy Valley *mid-div to 14th, lost tch & p.u. 17th* ....K Heard pu
525[5] Carrarea (Ire) *7s-3s, ld til f 12th* ....Miss J Cumings f
630 Ballyhasty Lady (Ire) 5a *rear whn ref 6th* ....K Crook ref
12 ran. ½l, 12l, 4l, 25l. Time 6m 52.70s. SP 5-4.
Mrs H E Rees (Cattistock).

795 Open Maiden Div II

458 **ARROGANT LORD 7a** ....**L Jefford** 1
(fav) w.w. prog 14th, ld 17th, sn clr, easily
531[3] **Bucks Flea 5a** ....**G Penfold** 2
sn bhnd, prog 15th, chsd wnr vainly frm 4 out
624[3] **The Ugly Duckling** ....**K Heard** 3
alwys prom, 3rd at 15th, nvr on trms frm 4 out
522 Suba Lin 5a *mid-div, chsd ldrs 17th, nvr on trms* ....M Frith 4
526 Nikolayevich *alwys rear, t.o. & p.u. 12th* ....A Turner pu
740 Gamblers Refrain *mid-div til ref 13th* ....J Auvray ref
740 Jet Jockey *ld to 17th, wknd rpdly nxt, p.u. last* ....A O'Connor pu
643 Moorland Magic (Ire) 12a *prom, 2nd to 14th, wknd & p.u. 17th* ....Miss S Young pu
526 Kimbross *alwys mid-div, nvr any ch, bhnd & p.u. 4 out* ....N Legg pu
Haven *mid-div til ran out 7th* ....David Dennis ro
Mellicometti *sn bhnd, no ch & p.u. 17th* ..R Woolacott pu
Oh So Quiet 7a *schoold til p.u. 14th* ..Miss J Cumings pu
12 ran. 10l, 6l, 25l. Time 6m 48.80s. SP Evens.
Mrs C Egalton (East Devon).
D.P.

ESSEX FARMERS & UNION
Marks Tey
Monday March 31st
FIRM

796 Open Maiden Div I

598[2] **AMADEUS (FR)** ....**M Gingell** 1
(fav) alwys prom,ld to 5th & agn 10th,drew clr frm 15th,easy
Bachelor-Carrasco (Ire) ....**S R Andrews** 2
bhnd early, prog to 3rd 6th, chsd wnr frm 15th, wknd nxt
317 Mister Rainman *chsd ldrs,wknd last 9th,prog und pres 11th,p.u. dismntd 13th* ....T Bulgin pu
498[4] Cambridge Gold 7a *mstk 3rd, ld 5th, hdd & wknd qckly 11th, t.o. & p.u. 13th* ....P Chinery pu
Morstons Star *s.s., last whn ran thru wing 3rd* ....S Cowell ro
Paddy A Go Go 12a *bhnd,mstk 2nd,prog to 3rd 11th,wknd frm 14th,t.o. & p.u.16th* ....A Coe pu
6 ran. 15l. Time 7m 3.00s. SP 4-5.
Robert Barr (Easton Harriers).

797 Open Maiden Div II

317[4] **BERGHOLT 7a** ....**A Coe** 1
(fav) held up,prog disp ld 15th,ld 3 out,jnd nxt,qcknd clr bfrlast
Kilcounty (Ire) 5a ....**Mrs P Twinn** 2
pllng, last to 12th, prog trckd ldrs 14th, chal 2 out,outpcd
Mr Boco ....**S R Andrews** 3
chsd ldr, brfly disp 14th, ev ch 4 out, wknd nxt
24 Morstons Magic *ld til jnd 14th, hdd 16th, wknd qckly nxt, t.o. & f 2 out* ....P Piddington f
4 ran. 4l, 15l. Time 7m 2.00s. SP 4-6.
Keith Coe (Essex Farmers & Union).

798 Restricted (12st)

324[7] **COURIER'S WAY (IRE)** ....**T Moore** 1
alwys prom,ld 7th,hdd 3 out,rlld ld last,styd on strng last
711 **Give It A Bash (Ire) 5a** ....**M Gingell** 2
mstk 1st,hdwy to go 2nd 11th,ld 3 out,jnd nxt,hd last,ran on
502 **Top Of The Range (Ire)** ....**C Ward-Thomas** 3
cls up,ld 5th,hdd 7th,disp ld 2 out,just outpcd flat
320[2] Half A Sov *mid-div,und pres 12th,outpcd 14th,styd on agn 3 out,nrst fin* ....S March 4
321[5] Cleddau King *trckd ldrs, last 9th, wknd 14th, t.o.* ....J Buckle 5
599[1] Andy Gawe (Ire) *rear early,mstk 2nd,prog 3rd 15th,wknd qckly nxt,p.u. last* ....S Cowell pu
498[1] Faha Moss (Ire) *(fav) mstks in rear,slght prog to 5th 9th,wknd 11th,p.u. aft 12th* ....S R Andrews pu
7 ran. 1½l, 1l, 1l, 15l. Time 6m 45.00s. SP 7-1.
Mrs C Kendrick/ C M Mills (Essex).

799 Men's Open

124[1] **CARDINAL RICHELIEU** ....**S Sporborg** 1
(fav) trckd ldr,ld 8th,brfly chal 3 out,drew clr 2 out,easily
501[2] **Exarch (USA)** ....**A Coe** 2
held up,prog disp ld 14th,hdd nxt,ev ch 3 out,btn mstk 2 out
497[6] **El Bae** ....**P Taiano** 3
midfld, cls up 10th, outpcd frm 14th
442[5] Ragtime Song (bl) *mstk 1st,slw jmp 7th,hdd nxt,wknd qckly 9th,t.o. & p.u. 11th* ....M Gingell pu
503[5] Ballygar Boy (Ire) *chsd ldr til mstk & u.r. 4th*. J Buckle ur
5 ran. 10l, 5l. Time 6m 51.00s. SP 1-3.
Christopher Sporborg (Puckeridge).

800 Ladies

709[1] **ST GREGORY** ....**Mrs L Gibbon** 1
(fav) made all, slght mstk 12th, rddn clr apr last, easily
596[3] **Professor Longhair** ....**Miss C Papworth** 2
last to 7th, prog disp 10th, ev ch 3 out, outpcd nxt
497[3] **Nibble** ....**Mrs L Wrighton** 3

mstks in rear, last 10th, outpcd 16th, styd on frm 3 out
3 ran. 3l, 2l. Time 6m 37.00s. SP 4-9.
A Howland Jackson (Essex & Suffolk).

801 Confined (12st)

DANCE ON SIXPENCE ....S March 1
chsd ldr,ld 7th,gng wll 11th,ld 15th,jnd 3 out,ran on 3 out
495³ **Gypsy King (Ire) ....A Coe** 2
(fav) midfld,wnt 3rd 11th,chsd wnr 15th,ev ch 2 out,styd on wll
25⁴ **Malachite Green ....S Cowell** 3
alwys prom, cls 2nd 4 out, outpcd nxt, styd on apr last
497 Salmon Mead (Ire) 3ex *mid-div, imprvd disp ld 10th, hdd nxt, wknd frm 4 out* ....S Sporborg 4
710 Major Inquiry (USA) *rear main grp, wknd frm 16th, t.o.* ....G Pewter 5
597 Aughnacloy Rose *v.s.a., t.o. 2nd, cont in own time* ....R Page 6
444 Another Rhythm *qckly ld,30l clr 5th,wknd qckly 6th,hdd 7th,t.o. & p.u. 11th*..................M Gingell pu
193 Cosmic Ray *alwys rear, lost tch 7th, t.o. 10th, blndrd & u.r. 3 out*.................................D Page ur
8 ran. 1l, ¾l, 15l, 30l, 2 fences. Time 6m 40.00s. SP 3-1.
R W Gardiner (East Essex).

802 Intermediate (12st)

497¹ **DRUID'S LODGE 5ex............C Ward-Thomas** 1
(fav) chsd ldrs, prog ld 10th, rddn clr apr last, styd on wll flat
486¹ **Ballydesmond (Ire) ....S Sporborg** 2
held up,prog ld 6th,hdd nxt,und pres 11th,ev ch 3 out,outpcd
593³ **Smart Pal 5ex ....C Barlow** 3
ld 1st, hdd 6th, ld agn nxt, hdd 10th, ev ch 2 out, no ext
499 Dilly May Dally 5a *alwys rear, lost tch 9th, t.o. & p.u. aft 11th*...N King pu
4 ran. 4l, 3l. Time 6m 41.00s. SP 4-5.
D J Lay (Essex & Suffolk).
J.W.

FOUR BURROW
Wadebridge
Monday March 31st
FIRM

803 Members

493 **BALDHU CHANCE ....J Young** 1
(fav) ld 5th, gd jmp 7th, alwys in comm aft, comf
532² **Sunwind ....D Heath** 2
ld 3rd-5th, chsd wnr aft, no imp
457 **Arble March 5a.....................Mrs M Hand** 3
qck away, ld to 3rd, sn lost tch, btn 3 fences
3 ran. 4l, dist. Time 6m 14.00s. SP 1-3.
Terry Long (Four Burrow).

804 Intermediate (12st)

631³ **DARK REFLECTION ....C Heard** 1
(Jt fav) bhnd til rddn to jn ldrs 3 out, ld cls home
533 **Morchard Milly 5a.................A Holdsworth** 2
ld 14th til no ext cls home
533³ **Mountain Master ....Miss L Blackford** 3
(Jt fav) alwys cls up til onepcd aft last
528³ Artistic Peace 5a *wnt down early, alwys prom, ev ch 2 out, fdd aft*..........................D Stephens 4
Roses In May 5a *trcks ldrs til grdly wknd frm 3 out* ....Miss A Barnett 5
528² Oneovertheight *ld til mssd marker aft 14th.* .S Kidston ro
6 ran. ½l, ½l, ½l, 10l. Time 6m 9.00s. SP 6-4.
J D Curnow (Western Hunt).

805 Men's Open (12st)

BIG JIM ....A Farrant 1
(fav) ld 7th, made rest, kpt on wll
47¹ **Gymcrak Dawn ....T Cole** 2
alwys prom, prssd wnr frm 15th til no ext run in
625 **Hanukkah 5a ....I Hambly** 3
nvr bttr plc, kpt on onepcd
Bert House *ld to 7th, styd prom til grdly wknd frm 3 out*..S Kidston 4
533⁴ Dovedon Princess 5a *alwys trllng fld, no ch frm 15th* ....D Stephens 5
5 ran. 3l, dist, 20l, 10l. Time 6m 5.00s. SP 11-8.
Edward Retter (Dart Vale And South Pool Hrrs).

806 Restricted (12st)

532⁴ **HOPEFULL DRUMMER ....N Harris** 1
ld 7th, clr 13th, ran on wll
175³ **Gypsy Luck 5a ....A Farrant** 2
(fav) bhnd til prog 15th, not pce to trbl wnnr
532⁵ **Ryme And Run 5a..............Miss L Blackford** 3
ld to 6th, drppd bck, ran on agn clsng stgs
532⁷ Medias Maid 5a *2nd 7-13th, grdly fdd*. . .A Holdsworth 4
532⁸ Scallykenning (bl) *alwys prom, trckd ldrs til fdd frm 4 out* ....J Young 5
523 Baywyn 5a *alwys rear til p.u. aft 13th* ......S Kidston pu
6 ran. 6l, 2l, 10l, 3l. Time 6m 11.00s. SP 7-4.
W Westacott (Dulverton East).

807 Ladies

TRY IT ALONE ....Miss L Blackford 1
ld 4-7th agn 9th, made rest comf
624² **Catch The Cross ....Mrs M Hand** 2
(fav) alwys prom, 2nd frm 9th, onepcd frm 3 out
Northern Bride 5a................Miss R Francis 3
ld 7-8th, efft short livd, grdly lost tch
529² Aristocratic Gold *alwys cls up, 3rd 9th, 6l 3rd whn u.r. 3 out*..............................Miss A Barnett ur
4 ran. 6l, dist. Time 6m 8.00s. SP 5-4.
M Biddick (North Cornwall).

808 Open Maiden (12st)

527⁵ **BRYANSBI 5a.......................Miss S Lock** 1
chsng grp til lft 2nd 12th,chal 2 out,ld last,kpt on run in
531⁵ **Spartans Dina 5a ....Miss L Blackford** 2
chsd ldr til lft in ld 12th-last, no ext whn chal
625 **Gaysun 7a..........................Mrs M Hand** 3
alwys chsng ldrs, kpt on frm 3 out, promsng
242³ Moonbay Lady 5a *alwys towrds rear til p.u. aft 9th* ....C Heard pu
531⁴ Luney River 5a *plld hrd, race into clr ld til u.r. 12th (ditch)*.................................Miss L Long ur
531² Brook A Light *(fav) towrds rear, clip rnng rail aft 6th, p.u. 9th* ....N Harris pu
244 Rose's Lady Day 5a *nvr a factor, p.u. 4 out* ....D Stephens pu
531 Kanha 12a *alwys towrds rear til p.u. bfr 4 out* ....S Kidston pu
8 ran. 3l, 8l. Time 6m 22.00s. SP 8-1.
Miss S Lock (East Devon).
P.H.

MORPETH
Tranwell
Monday March 31st
GOOD

809 Members

411 **MAY RUN ....Mrs V Jackson** 1
(fav) alwys prom,mainly 3l 2nd 9-14th,qcknd to ld 2 out,6l up last
614² **Newbrano 5a ....I Carmichael** 2
ld til hdd 5th, ld agn 12th til hdd 2 out, outpcd last
614⁶ **Imulari ....P Craggs** 3
in tch 1st ctt, cls 2nd & even ch 4 out, wknd into 3rd 2 out
608⁵ Rare Fire *alwys last, t.o. & p.u. 6th*....Miss S Davison pu

Oisin Dubh (Ire) *chsd ldr til ld 5th, mstk & hdd 11th, disp 2nd whn f 13th* ....J Cookson f
5 ran. 8l, 5l. Time 6m 19.00s. SP 4-5.
W R Middleton (Morpeth).

810 Confined (12st)

411³ **PABLOWMORE ....R Green 1**
ld til hdd 3rd, trckd ldrs til disp ld 3 out,qcknd 5l up nxt
335¹ **Sister Seven (Ire) 5a 3ex ....Miss D Laidlaw 2**
(fav) alwys prom,hdwy to disp ld 3 out,outpcd & 5l 2nd nxt,no ext
Hollow Suspicion (Ire) ....Miss J Percy 3
j.w., ld 3rd til hdd & wknd into 3rd 3 out, lost tch frm nxt
611⁷ Strong Measure (Ire) *in tch 1st ctt, wknd to 4th 12th, outpcd & lost tch frm nxt* ....R Morgan 4
334⁴ Able Moss *hndy 3rd 6th, wknd to 5th 9th & p.u.* ....P Forster pu
5 ran. 10l, dist, dist. Time 6m 10.00s. SP 2-1.
R W Green (Percy).

811 Ladies

WIGTOWN BAY ....Miss N Stirling 1
ld til hdd 5th, cls up til 2l 2nd 2 out, ld last, ran on wll
609⁵ **Funny Feelings ....Miss D Laidlaw 2**
(fav) chsd ldr til hd 5th,ld agn 7th til mstk & hd last,not rcvrd
608³ **Tod Law 5a........................Miss A Bowie 3**
mnly 3rd 1st ctt, cls 2nd 11-14th, wknd to 3rd 2 out
3 ran. 2l, ½l. Time 6m 15.00s. SP 7-2.
Mrs P C Stirling (Fife).
Two w/d not under orders rule 4 to all bets deduct 50p in the £.

812 Men's Open

610² **TODCRAG ....T Scott 1**
(fav) j.w.,cls 2nd til ld 7th,mnly 8l up 8th-2 out,styd on strngly
583⁶ **Washakie ....J Walton 2**
outpcd 1st ctt,gd hdwy frm 13th into 8l 2nd last,not rch wnr
610⁵ **Staigue Fort (Ire) ....H Naughton 3**
ld 3rd-7th, mnly 8l 2nd 8th-2 out, wknd into 3rd last
607¹ Will Travel (Ire) *outpcd in 3rd 1st ctt, wknd into 4th 2 out* ....A Parker 4
590⁵ Tartan Tornado *alwys rear, outpcd final ctt, wnt poor 5th 3 out* ....P Johnson 5
492⁵ Fast Study *alwys rear, no imp final ctt, tk poor 6th run in* ....Simon Robinson 6
507 Black Spur *nvr on terms wth ldrs, poor 6th 3 out, wknd run in* ....P Jenkins 7
7 ran. 8l, 8l, 4l, 15l, 12l, 4l. Time 6m 6.00s. SP 4-6.
Mrs D Scott (Border).

813 Restricted

584 **LINDON RUN ....R Morgan 1**
made virt all, 1l up last & ran on strngly
608² **Harden Glen ....Miss D Laidlaw 2**
(fav) cls 2nd til disp ld 2nd-10th,hdd nxt,disp ld 2 out,hdd last
623¹ **Killeaney Carr (Ire) ....S Whitaker 3**
cls up 1st ctt, 1l 2nd 14th & even ch, wknd into 3rd nxt
416 Buckaneer Bay *towrds rear til disp 3rd hlfwy,no imp on ldrs frm 4 out* ....P Johnson 4
415 Mandys Special 5a *in tch 1st ctt, cls 5th 9th til outpcd & lost tch 12th* ....L Morgan 5
Deise Crusader *rear, 20l 7th 9th, lost tch final ctt & p.u. 4 out* ....P Forster pu
416 Trespasser (Ire) (bl) *cls 3rd 4th, wknd into 6th 9th, outpcd & u.r. 12th* ....P Jenkins ur
7 ran. 3l, 5l, 2l, 20l. Time 6m 10.00s. SP 5-2.
T D Donaldson (Tynedale).

814 Open Maiden (12st)

767 **COOKIE BOY ....Miss H Delahooke 1**
j.w., made virt all, kpt on strngly run in
37⁶ **Tropnevad 4ow (bl) ....J Walton 2**
alwys prom,cls 3rd 9th,styd on strngly last in to 2nd run in
607² **Whosgotsillyssense 5a................C Storey 3**
(fav) alwys prom,cls 2nd 12-14th,1l down 2 out-last,no ext run in
612² Dillons Bridge (Ire) *in tch wth ldrs 1st ctt,cls 6th 9th,wnt 4th 4 out,not rch ld* ....R Morgan 4
Sally Smith 5a *cls up 1st ctt, lost wth ldrs tch frm 4 out* ....Miss J Percy 5
Broughpark Azalea *mid-div whn p.u. 6th* ..S Robinson pu
Stanwick Fort 5a *ld 3rd til ran out nxt* Mrs H Dickson ro
612 Saigon Lady (Ire) 5a *prom 1st ctt,2l 2nd 9th,wknd into 6th 14th,t.o. & p.u. last* ....M Ruddy pu
566 Copper Dial *rear div, t.o. last 5th, p.u. 7th* ....Mrs K Hargreave pu
9 ran. 1l, ½l, 2l, 10l. Time 6m 14.00s. SP 4-1.
J S Delahooke (Zetland).

815 2½m Open Maiden (5-7yo) (12st)

420⁵ **PLEASEDASPUNCH (IRE) 7a............C Storey 1**
rear til hdwy into 5th 8th,wnt 2nd 2 out,fin strgly run in
564² **Shine A Light ....A Parker 2**
(fav) made virt all til hdd run in
233⁸ **The Camair Flyer (Ire) ....M Ruddy 3**
alwys prom, 2l 2nd & ev ch 11th, wknd into 3rd 2 out
621² Say Daphne 5a 3ow *held up til hdwy into cls 3rd 8th, no imp on ldrs frm 3 out* ....S Whitaker 4
340² Alianne 5a *mid-div, nvr nr ldrs final ctt* ....P Johnson 5
418 Conors Bluebird (Ire) *alwys mid-div, styd on wll frm 2 out* ....Mrs K Hargreave 6
613 Dynastie D'Auge (Fr) 5a *mid-div, no imp on ldrs final m* ....T Scott 7
Grey Rock (Ire) 5a *n.j.w., rear div, styd on gmly frm 4 out* ....Miss K Miller 8
564 Hetty Bell 12a *alwys rear div* ....L Morgan 9
612 Espley Nipper *cls 4th hlfwy, wknd qckly & lost tch frm 2 out* ....I Carmichael 10
Little Hawk *6th hlfwy, wknd 10th & lost tch wth ldrs* ....P Jenkins 11
161 K Walk 5a *mid-div til p.u. 7th* ....R Morgan pu
Hansel's Streak 7a *u.r. 1st* ....S Galloway ur
419² Victor Charlie *alwys prom, cls 2nd whn u.r. 7th* ....N Sutton ur
14 ran. 3l, 15l, nk, 6l, 2l, 10l, ½l. Time 5m 12.00s. SP 12-1.
C Storey (College Valley/Northumberland).
15 JUMPS P.B.

NORTH COTSWOLD
Paxford
Monday March 31st
FIRM

816 Members

WILDNITE ....Miss E Walker 1
trckd ldr, lft in ld 15th, ran on gamely
260⁵ **Chacer's Imp ....H Wheeler 2**
(fav) hld up last, effrt apr 2 out, outpcd
Straight Bat *carried 14st, ld til f 15th* ....A Puddy ur
3 ran. 1½l. Time 6m 54.00s. SP 5-2.
Miss L Robbins (North Cotswold).

817 Confined (12st)

490 **FANTASTIC FLEET (IRE) 7a......Julian Pritchard 1**
(fav) hld up rear, prog to 2nd at 12th, ld 3 out, qcknd flat
750³ **Bumptious Boy ....S Hanks 2**
ld til 3 out, rallied, ev ch last, styd on onepcd
Briarland Springer ....M Davis 3
chsd ldr til wknd 13th, sn bhnd
3 ran. 1½l, dist. Time 6m 30.00s. SP 4-9.
Mrs R Mackness (Cotswold).

818 Ladies

HEARTS ARE WILD .... Miss P Gundry 1
chsd ldr, ld 8th-14th, ld nxt, drew clr 3 out, easily
371[6] West Orient .... Mrs J Parris 2
ld to 8th, ld agn 14th-nxt, onepcd aft
520[3] Night Wind .... Mrs A Rucker 3
(fav) hld up last, went 2nd 13th, hit 15th, wknd, t.o.
3 ran. 15l, 25l. Time 6m 10.00s. SP 5-4.
Miss Polly Gundry (Berkeley).

819 Men's Open (12st)

220[3] NETHER GOBIONS 4ex .... Julian Pritchard 1
(fav) hld up, ld 6th-12th, ld 3 out, clr nxt, fin tired
431[3] Viridian 7ex .... M Rimell 2
ld 3-5th, ld 12th-3 out, chal 2 out, no ext flat
651[1] Granville Grill 7ex .... J Deutsch 3
t.d.e. ld to 3rd, chsd ldr til wknd 13th, onepcd aft
651 The Country Trader 7ex *nvr nrr, onepcd.* .... E Walker 4
652[3] Icky's Five *1st ride, alwys last, sn t.o.* ..... M Gregory 5
5 ran. ¾l, 15l, 1½l, 1 fence. Time 6m 19.00s. SP 4-5.
P Clutterbuck (Berkeley).

820 Interlink Restricted (12st)

449[8] ROYAL EXHIBITION .... Miss C Ramsey 1
mostly 2nd, effrt 3 out, ld nxt, styd on well
655[3] Colonel Fairfax (v) .... J Trice-Rolph 2
(fav) ld til hdd 2 out, no ext flat
372[5] Unlucky For Some (Ire) .... C Wadland 3
nrly alwys last, no ch frm 15th, walked in
676 Sutton Lass 5a *chsd ldrs, mstks 4 & 7th, blnd 9th, lost irons, ran out 10th* .... N Waine ro
4 ran. 4l, dist. Time 6m 34.00s. SP 3-1.
Mrs Jayne Barton (Bicester With Whaddon Chase).

821 Open Maiden (12st)

297 ROSEVALLEY (IRE) .... K Whiting 1
(fav) ld 2nd, made rest, unchal
655 Connie Foley .... J Trice-Rolph 2
rear, tk mod 2nd at 15th, styd on
436[4] Matchlessly .... Miss E Walker 3
ld to 2nd, chsd ldrs, onepcd frm 15th
Arctic Line *in tch, wknd aft 11th, p.u. 12th* .... S Green pu
Lizapet (Ire) 12a *hld up rear, f 9th* .... G Barfoot-Saunt f
570[5] Miss Dior 5a *chsd wnr til f 9th* .... Miss P Gundry f
6 ran. Dist, 2l. Time 6m 23.00s. SP 6-4.
A J Whiting (Berkeley).
H.F.

OLD BERKSHIRE
Lockinge
Monday March 31st
FIRM

822 Members

396[4] RUBIKA (FR) .... Mrs S Shoemark 1
made all, sn clr, tired 2 out, gd jmp last, hld on
514[4] Orujo (Ire) .... Miss G Browne 2
chsd clr ldr, clsd frm 3 out, chnc whn outjmpd last,nt qckn
517[1] The Man From Clare (Ire) .... L Lay 3
(fav) mstks, chsd clr ldr, rdn frm 14th, 3rd & btn 3 out
The Holy Golfer *alwys last, t.o. 13th, p.u. 2 out* .... C Smyth pu
4 ran. 2l, 8l. Time 6m 22.50s. SP 6-1.
Mrs Sarah Shoemark (Old Berkshire).

823 Open Maiden (5-7yo)

I'M THE GAFFER .... F Brennan 1
cls up, ld 7th-16th, lft in ld final bnd, drvn out
Salcantay 5a .... J Owen 2
jmpd slwly 1st, cls up, ld 16th til ran wd final bnd,nt rcvr
451[2] Larkross .... L Lay 3
(fav) keen hld & rstrnd, cls up, ev ch 14th, not qckn frm 16th
644 Naburn Loch 5a *blnd 1st, made most to 7th, wknd 14th, p.u. 4 out* .... J Hankinson pu
4 ran. 3l, 4l. Time 6m 45.00s. SP 3-1.
F J Brennan (V.W.H.).

824 Confined (12st)

744[1] PONT DE PAIX 5ex .... F Hutsby 1
(fav) mstks, ld to 10th, ld agn 13th, clr 16th, comf
649[3] Miss Magic 5a .... F Brennan 2
chsd wnr 6th, ld 10-13th, wknd & v tired frm 16th
520[5] Taurean Tycoon .... Miss S Duckett 3
chsd wnr 5-6th, 4th & outpcd 11th, no imp ldrs aft
483[4] Old Road (USA) 1ow *chsd ldrs, 3rd & outpcd 11th, no imp aft, wknd 16th* .... C Coyne 4
Champagne Run *in tch whn s.u. bnd apr 5th* .... R Hawker su
395 Le Jacobin *mstk 2nd, chsd wnr to 5th, sn wknd, t.o. & p.u. 13th* .... C Lambert pu
645 Ski Nut 1ow *sn wll bhnd, no ch hlfwy, t.o. & p.u. last* .... J Hankinson pu
217[3] Chinaman *alwys rear, 5th & no ch frm 11th, t.o. & p.u. last* .... A Tutton pu
8 ran. 25l, 8l, 6l. Time 6m 21.00s. SP Evens.
Mrs A Murray (Grafton).

825 Mixed Open

773 WHAT A TO DO .... Miss L Sweeting 1
(fav) not fluent, made most to 13th, ld agn 16th, sn clr
296 Madraj (Ire) .... Miss H Irving 2
prssd wnr, ld 13-16th, sn wknd, lame
484 Abitmorfun .... C Coyne 3
hld up in tch, ld brfly 9th, not qckn 14th, btn nxt
3 ran. 12l, 20l. Time 6m 38.00s. SP 2-5.
C J R Sweeting (Heythrop).

826 Restricted

516[2] BALANCE .... G Maundrell 1
(fav) trckd ldrs, ld 12th, clr 15th, easily
655[2] Tarry Awhile .... J Connell 2
trckd ldr, ld 8-11th, chsd wnr 14th, not qckn & no imp
676 Linlake Lightning 5a (bl) .... Miss H Irving 3
ld to 8th & 11-12th, 3rd & btn aft 14th
449 Sparnova 5a (bl) *alwys last, effrt 10th, outpcd & mstks frm 13th* .... T Illsley 4
4 ran. 20l, 2½l, 4l. Time 6m 23.50s. SP 4-5.
Richard J Smith (Beaufort).

827 Open Maiden 6yo+

513[3] VILLAINS BRIEF (IRE) .... R Lawther 1
(fav) disp at slow pace til drew clr aft 14th
Wodehouse .... C Coyne 2
disp at slow pace til wknd aft 14th
221 No Hanky Panky *jmpd slwly & rght, lost tch 11th, p.u. nxt, dsmntd* .... F Hutsby pu
3 ran. Dist. Time 6m 44.00s. SP Evens.
Nick Quesnel (Berks & Bucks Drag).
J.N.

SOUTHDOWN & ERIDGE
Heathfield
Monday March 31st
FIRM

828 Members

503[6] GLENAVEY .... C Hall 1
cls up, ld 9-14th, ld agn 4 out, hd prssd whn lft clr last
284 Wednesdays Auction (Ire) .... S Garrott 2
hld up, prog apr 3 out, 1l dwn & clsng whn blnd last,nt rcvr

Sure Pride (USA) ....**P Hall** 3
lft in ld aft 4th-9th & 14th-4 out, onepcd und press
Linger Balinda 5a *chsd ldrs, mstks 10th & 14th, rdn apr 3 out, wl btn nxt*.........................P Bull 4
Boll Weevil *(fav) ld til p.u. aft 4th, saddle slpd* ....M Jones pu
5 ran. 2l, nk, 20l. Time 6m 58.00s. SP 5-2.
C S Hall (Southdown & Eridge).

829 B F S S Nov Riders

685[3] **RARELY AT ODDS** ....**Miss A Sansom** 1
prom, 3rd & rdn apr 4 out, ld last, ran on strngly
503[2] **Linred** ....**P Hall** 2
(fav) disp til j.s.4th, ld 9th til hdd last, onepcd und press flat
605[2] **Graphic Designer (Ire)** ....**J Hazeltine** 3
trkd ldrs, ld brfly apr 4 out, wknd qkly apr 3 out
577[9] The Forties *tubed, disp til ld 4th-9th, 4th & wkng whn blnd & u.r. 14th*.........................N Earnshaw ur
580 Huckleberry Friend 5a *alwys last, hit 6th, lsng tch & hit 10th, t.o. & p.u. 2 out* ....P Blagg pu
5 ran. 1l, 15l. Time 6m 35.00s. SP 7-2.
Mrs S A Sansom (Old Surrey & Burstow).

830 Mixed Open (12st)

601[1] **BILBO BAGGINS (IRE)** ....**M Gorman** 1
hld up last, mstk 6th, rpd hdwy 3 out, ld flat, ran on well
578[4] **American Eyre** ....**Miss S Gladders** 2
rr, last 4 out, ran on frm nxt, nt rch wnr
600[1] **Kates Castle 5a** ....**J Van Praagh** 3
(fav) ld/disp til ld 16th, 8l clr & hit 3 out, hit nxt, hdd flat
579 More Of It *chsd ldrs, 3rd & rdn 15th, blnd nxt, kpt on frm 2 out*.........................P Hall 4
684[1] Bright Hour *chsd ldrs, mstk 11th, pshd alng 13th, wknd 3 out* ....Miss J Grant 5
602[1] The Whip *ld/disp til 15th, 2nd & btn whn f 3 out* ....Miss C Grissell f
6 ran. 2½l, 1l, 1l, 15l. Time 6m 24.00s. SP 7-1.
Mrs P A Tetley (Surrey Union).

831 Restricted (12st)

580[4] **POLAR ANA (IRE) 5a**...........**Miss S Gladders** 1
(fav) j.w. made all, rdn apr last, kpt on
303 **Dovehill** ....**P Bull** 2
n.j.w. outpcd 16th, rallied nxt, no imp frm 2 out
2 ran. 4l. Time 6m 40.00s. SP 2-5.
Mrs P A McIntyre (Ashford Valley).

832 Intermediate (12st)

579 **BILLION DOLLARBILL 5ex** ....**M Gorman** 1
made all, drvn alng 15th, styd on strngly frm 3 out
282[1] **Sovereign Spray (Ire) 5ex** ....**P Hacking** 2
(fav) w.w. effort to chall 4 out, rdn nxt, wll btn apr last
2 ran. 6l. Time 6m 40.00s. SP 4-5.
Brian Tetley & R Baldock (Surrey Union).

833 Open Maiden (12st)

485 **AND WHY NOT** ....**J Van Praagh** 1
(Jt fav) hld up, stdy prog to chal 4 out, ld 2 out, lft wll clr last
600 **Iced Ginger (v)**...........................**D Evatt** 2
disp til lft in ld 4th, hdd & blnd 14th, lft poor 2nd last
Indiway ....**P Bull** 3
in tch lft 3rd 12th, wknd 4 out, lft poor 3rd last
582 Miss Pandy 5a *disp ld til f 4th* ....P Hall f
686 Celtic Reg *(Jt fav) chsd ldr 4th til ld 14th, hdd 2 out, 2l dwn & btn whn f last*.....................M Jones f
Get On Lottie 5a *last pr, mstks 2nd & 6th, lsng tch & j.s 8th, t.o & p.u 10th*....................M Gorman pu
582 What-A-Brave Run *mstks, in tch til blnd & u.r. 12th* ....A Clarke ur
7 ran. 25l, 4l. Time 6m 51.00s. SP 7-4.
Mrs C E Van Praagh (Surrey Union).

S.P.

SOUTH NOTTS
Thorpe Lodge
Monday March 31st
FIRM

834 Members

673 **KEMYS COMMANDER** ....**G Smith** 1
(fav) made all, ran on strngly flat
480[9] **Gonalston Percy (bl)** ....**N Kent** 2
mstly 5l 2nd, prssd ldr frm 6 out, outpcd last, eased
Annascanan 12a *cls up til hit 6th, t.o. 10l frm 8th, eased p.u. 5 out*.........................S Morris pu
3 ran. 10l. Time 7m 1.00s. SP 1-2.
G J Smith (South Notts).

835 Intermediate

673[4] **RYDERS WELLS** ....**S Walker** 1
ld 1st-7th & frm 12th, drew clr frm 2 out, comf
351[6] **Stanwick Farlap 5a** ....**T Marks** 2
mstly 3rd, ld 8-9th, outpcd by ldng pair 3 out, tk 2nd flat
441[3] **Cairndhu Misty 5a**....................**R Barrett** 3
alwys abt 5th, rdn 6 out, chsd 2nd frm 3 out
673 Majestic Ride *cls up 3rd/4th, chal 4 out, outpcd 2 out, hit last, wknd* ....N Kent 4
676[4] Kiri's Rose (Ire) 5a *(fav) cls up, ld 7th & 10-11th, 2nd to 6 out, onepcd nxt*.........................P Gee 5
350[6] The Ultimate Buck *alwys last trio, t.o. 6 out, comp own time* ....R Morney 6
506[7] My True Clown *last frm 5th, t.o. 7th, p.u. 12th* ....Miss L Hampshire pu
7 ran. 10l, ½l, 1½l, 3l, 30l. Time 6m 36.00s. SP 9-4.
E F Astley-Arlington (Blankney).

836 Men's Open (12st)

618[8] **BRECKENBROUGH LAD** ....**I Bennett** 1
cls up mstly 3rd til qcknd to ld 4 out, ran on strngly
673 **Elder Prince** ....**P Gee** 2
(fav) 4th/5th for 2 m, 3rd 4 out, ran on frm 2 out,not rch wnr
Easby Roc (Ire) ....**N Kent** 3
alwys prom, ld 5th-7th & 5 out, chsd wnr nxt, outpcd 2 out
351 Old Money 7ex *ld 3rd-4th & 12th til hit 5 out, wknd qckly, walked in*.........................A Pickering 4
76 Whistling Gipsy *midfld whn f 2nd*............T Lane f
The Announcer *alwys last, rdn frm 5th, t.o. 10th, p.u. 13th*.........................E Andrewes pu
350 Soda Popinski (USA) *cls up 2nd/disp til fdd 8th, t.o. 5th 10th, p.u. 6 out* ....J Docker pu
7 ran. 8l, 4l, 1 fence. Time 6m 36.00s. SP 25-1.
Mrs M R Bennett (Badsworth).

837 G Middleton Ladies

773 **MAN OF MYSTERY** ....**Miss F Hatfield** 1
(fav) trckd ldr, qcknd 4 out, clr nxt, v easily
674[3] **Killimor Lad** ....**Miss S Samworth** 2
tried to make all,brushed aside bfr 3 out,eased whn ch gone
Sanamar ....**Mrs C McCarthy** 3
t.o. mstly 3rd frm 3rd, lft remote 3rd 13th
578 Notary-Nowell *in t.o. pair mstly 4th til ran out 13th (ditch)*.........................Miss N Sell ro
Just Jeeves *last til u.r. 6th*...........Miss A Eaton ur
5 ran. 30l, 2 fences. Time 6m 35.00s. SP 8-13.
D Field/ R Crosby (Quorn).

838 Interlink Restricted (12st)

676[3] **FLYING QUEST** ....**S Walker** 1
(fav) 3rd/4th hrd held til 2nd frm 12th,ld 3 out,sprntd flat,clvy
772[1] **Busking Along (Ire)** ....**H Nicholson** 2
cls up mstly 3rd, chsd wnr frm 2 out, outpcd flat

140 **Swinging Song** ....Miss K Gilman 3
tried to make all, hdd & onepcd 3 out
597[6] Current Attraction 5a 11ow *2nd to 6th, 5th rdn alng 12-13th, t.o. 6 out*..........................Miss K Thory 4
Tremeirchion *back of bunch whn u.r. 2nd* ..M Barnard ur
5 ran. 8l, 6l, 1 fence. Time 6m 43.00s. SP 4-7.
J W Lockwood (Burton).

839 Open Maiden (12st)

480 **ANDALUCIAN SUN (IRE)** ....G Maloney 1
prog 10th, 2nd 12th, ld 6 out, ran on gmly, bttr spd flat
Maltby Son 7a ....T Lane 2
cls up 3rd,chsd wnr 6 out,level 3 out-last,just outpcd,prom
478[4] **Educate Me (Ire)** ....J Burley 3
(Jt fav) alwys prom 3rd/4th, outpcd by 1st pair frm 6 out
478 Ilikehim *ld to 13th, 4th outpcd frm nxt* ....N Kent 4
677 Milo Boy *(Jt fav) mid-div, remmndrs 12-13th, outpcd 5th frm 6 out* ....M Mackley 5
549 Isola Farnese 5a *2nd til mstk 10th, wknd qckly, p.u. 13th* ....M Barnard pu
478[7] Royal Quarry *rear hlf, t.o. 6th 12th, p.u. nxt* ....Miss A Eaton pu
544 Rapid Regent *ldng pair whn f 2nd* ....R Morney f
Bex Boy (Ire) *f 3rd*..............................I Bennett f
80 Derring Knight *rear hlf whn ref 8th*.......E Andrewes ref
The Tide Race 5a *alwys rear hlf, wll bhnd whn p.u. aft 12th* ....P Gee pu
550 Stanwick Buckfast *cls up 5th til f 11th* ....T Marks f
Sandi Devil *rear hlf, t.o. 7th 12th, p.u. nxt* ....D Dickenson pu
479 Dels Lad *alwys rear hlf, bhnd whn p.u. aft 12th* ....J Docker pu
Suny Rose 5a *f 2nd*...............................S Walker f
15 ran. ½l, 30l, 10l, 1l. Time 6m 36.00s. SP 16-1.
A Witcomb (Quorn).
K.B.

SOUTH PEMBROKESHIRE
Lydstep
Monday March 31st
FIRM

840 Members (12st)

403[4] **ROYAL OATS 5a** ....D S Jones 1
(fav) chsd ldr, ld 11th, easily
Redoran 5a ....M Lewis 2
chsd ldrs, nvr able to chal
535 **Medieval Queen 5a** ....Miss A Meakins 3
alwys twrds rear, nvr dang
541[3] Prince Theo *ld to 11th, sn wknd, p.u. 14th, lame* ....C James pu
Forever In Debt 5a (v) *in rear whn ref 6th* ....Miss C Williams ref
Just Ruffled *rear whn ref 5th*..............Miss J Gill ref
6 ran. 10l, 20l. Time 6m 7.00s. SP Evens.
E Tudor Harries (South Pembrokeshire).

841 Open Maiden (5-7yo) Div I

639 **JOLLY SWAGMAN** ....G Perkins 1
mid-div, prog 13th, ld 15th, unchal aft
Lighter Lord ....E Williams 2
alwys 2nd/3rd, no imp wnr, improve
407 **Lady Orr (Ire) 5a**.........................J Tudor 3
sttld rear, prog 14th, nvr nr engh to chal
542[6] Kerstin's Choice 5a *trckd ldr early, wknd 13th, onepcd* ....P Sheldrake 4
542[2] Bold Alfie *(fav) ld to 14th, p.u. nxt, lame*...D S Jones pu
542 Grampas' Girl (Ire) 5a *mid-div, no ch whn p.u. 15th* ....J P Keen pu
539 Eastwood Lad *trckd ldrs, tiring whn f 3 out* ..M Lewis f
437 Alias Parker Jones *alwys rear, p.u. 11th* ......J Price pu
8 ran. Dist, 10l, 2l. Time 6m 13.00s. SP 6-1.
B R Hughes (Llangeinor).

842 Open Maiden (5-7yo) Div II

540 **PRESELI VIEW 5a** ....M Lewis 1
(Jt fav) sttld rear, prog 13th, ld 16th, in cmmnd aft, eased flat
542 **Del's Delight (Ire) 5a** ....J Jukes 2
hld up, prog 12th, ld 14th-aft nxt, onepcd aft und pres
541 **Hil Lady 5a** ....J P Keen 3
(Jt fav) twrds rear, prog 14th, sn ev ch, no imp wnr aft
540 Cefn Woodsman *mid-div, no dang frm 15th* ....D S Jones 4
641[3] Bickerton Poacher *alwys rear, p.u. 7th*.....G Perkins pu
542 Kits Pride 12a (bl) *ref 2nd*................T Vaughan ref
641 Roger (Ire) 7a *u.r. 2nd*.....................S Shinton ur
543 Out On The Town 5a *alwys rear, p.u. 2 out* ...J Tudor pu
543[4] Culpeppers Dish *ld to 14th, fdd, p.u. 2 out*.....J Price pu
405 Merry Morn 5a *f 1st*..........................E Williams f
539[5] Teigr Pren *alwys rear, f 15th* ....P Sheldrake f
Fridays Child 12a *trckd ldr til f 10th*...Miss A Meakins f
12 ran. 1½l, 10l, 10l. Time 6m 12.00s. SP 3-1.
W D Lewis (Tivyside).

843 Men's Open (12st)

637[1] **JACK SOUND 7ex** ....E Williams 1
(fav) ld to 15th, ld agn last, hrd rdn flat, just hld on
637[2] **Al Frolic 5a**..............................D S Jones 2
chsd wnr, ld 16th-last, kpt on und pres, just hld
535 **Origami** ....J P Keen 3
trckd ldrs, ev ch 3 out, onepcd aft, lame
535[5] No Panic *cls up to 12th, no ch aft* ....J Price 4
4 ran. ¾l, 20l, dist. Time 6m 9.00s. SP 1-3.
E L Harries (Pembrokeshire).

844 Ladies

638[1] **OZZIE JONES 3ex** ....Miss L Pearce 1
(fav) ld/disp til ld 11th, sn in cmmnd
188[5] **Polish Rider (USA)** ....Miss R Morgan 2
3rd til chsd wnr 15th, no imp
Mount Falcon 4ow...............Miss C Morgan 3
alwys rear, no dang
536 Harwall Queen 5a *twrds rear, p.u. aft 11th, leather broke* ....Miss J Gill pu
638[6] Lucky Ole Son 5ex *alwys strggling, p.u. last, lame* ....Miss P Jones pu
536[5] Doctor-J (Ire) *ld/disp till f 9th*...........Miss S Major f
6 ran. 25l, dist. Time 5m 58.00s. SP 1-2.
Keith R Pearce (Carmarthenshire).

845 Restricted (12st)

405 **DICK'S CABIN** ....D S Jones 1
ld frm 2nd, unchal, eased flat
539[2] **Mister McGaskill** ....P Williams 2
(fav) sttld rear, prog 4 out, nvr thrtnd wnr
Tims Kick (Ire) 5a ....J Tudor 3
ld to 2nd, chsd wnr aft, wknd 2 out
534[2] Cranagh Moss (Ire) *alwys 3rd/4th, onepcd* ...G Lewis 4
540 Euromill Star 5a *mid-div whn f 6th*..........J P Keen f
5 ran. 6l, 2l, 10l. Time 6m 14.00s. SP 2-1.
W H Pugh (Llangeinor).
Highland Minstrel (fav) withdrawn, not under starter's orders.

846 Intermediate (12st)

535[3] **WOLVER'S PET (IRE)** ....D S Jones 1
trckd ldrs, ld 14th, unchal, easily
363[2] **Gunner Boon** ....Miss P Jones 2
(fav) ld to 14th, no ch wnr aft
536[6] **Gus McCrae 5ex**.................Miss L Pearce 3
alwys 3rd, no dang
636[7] Pay-U-Cash 5ex (bl) *prom to 7th, sn strggling* ....G Perkins 4
4 ran. 5l, 20l, dist. Time 5m 58.00s. SP Evens.
R W J Willcox (Llangeinor).

847 Open Maiden (8yo+)

536² **KINLOGH GALE (IRE) (bl) ....E Williams** 1
(fav) sttld mid-div, prog 12th, ld 14th, sn in cmmnd
636 **Alfion (Ire) ....D S Jones** 2
sttld rear, prog 4 out, kpt on, nvr nrr, improve
407² **Wayward Edward ....J Price** 3
ld/disp to 13th, onepcd aft
408⁵ Pyro Pennant *ld/disp to 13th, ev ch 4 out, wknd rpdly* ....S Shinton 4
640 Dontyoudoda (Ire) (bl) *ld/disp to 11th, fdd, p.u. 14th* ....T Vaughan pu
5 ran. 12l, 8l, dist. Time 6m 14.00s. SP 1-2.
W J Evans (Pembrokeshire).
P.D.

SOUTH SHROPSHIRE
Eyton-On-Severn
Monday March 31st
GOOD TO FIRM

848 Members (12st)

668² **TARA BOY (bl) ....R Cambrey** 1
prom early, steadd 4th, prog 4 out, ran on wll to ld last
670³ **Rue de Fort ....J Cornes** 2
(fav) made all til cght apr last, no ext run in
Ultrason IV (Fr) ....A Beedles 3
mid-div, cls order 10th, ev ch 3 out, not qckn
669 Golden Fare *cls up 8th, lost tch 12th, wll bhnd whn p.u. bfr last* ....Miss L Wallace pu
Board Game *sn t.o., fence bhnd whn p.u. 5 out* ....Miss M Collins pu
Hicky Jigger 5a *cls up to 13th, outpcd 4 out, p.u. 3 out* ....R Burton pu
6 ran. 5l, 25l. Time 6m 34.00s. SP 9-2.
Mrs R Cambray (South Shropshire).

849 Men's Open (12st)

FIBREGUIDE TECH ....R Thomas 1
ld 13th, ran on wll und pres frm 2 out
Squirrellsdaughter 5a 7ex........M Worthington 2
(fav) held up, cls order 7th, 2nd 10th, ev ch 5 out, onepcd
726⁶ **Auction Law (NZ) ....L Whiston** 3
alwys in tch, disp 2nd 3 out, not qckn frm 2 out
377⁹ Pamela's Lad *held up in rear, 3rd 3 out, p.u. 2 out* ....G Hanmer pu
291 Will It Last 5a *ld to 4th, sn btn, t.o. 9th, p.u. 5 out* ....L Brown pu
664 Henrymyson *ld 4-12th, fdd 5 out, no ch whn ref last* ....J Cornes ref
Injunction (Ire) 7ex (bl) *w.w.,cls order 10th,chal whn bad mstk 4 out,4th whn u.r.last* ....C Stockton ur
7 ran. 10l, 2l. Time 6m 32.00s. SP 8-1.
Mrs T R Kinsey (Cheshire Forest).

850 Ladies

280 **HIRAM B BIRDBATH (bl).........Miss A Plunkett** 1
ld to 3rd, ld 5th, made rest, ran on gmly und pres
466 **Nodforms Dilemma (USA) ...Miss K Hollinshead** 2
rear to 12th, cls order 4 out, lkd held in 3rd 2 out
722 **Charlottes Quest 5a...........Miss S Sharratt** 3
cls up, lost tch 10th, tk 3rd run in, wll btn
669⁴ Moya's Tip Top 5a *cls up & ev ch 5 out, sn wknd* ....Miss A Price 4
202⁴ Bank Place *(fav) 2nd frm 9th,chal strngly 3 out,1l down 2 out,broke down last* ....Miss C Thomas pu
666 Palladante (Ire) 5a *cls up, ld 4th, 2nd whn f 6th* ....Miss L Wallace f
6 ran. 20l, 20l, dist. Time 6m 39.00s. SP 4-1.
Steven Astaire (Windsor Forest Drag).

851 Intermediate (12st)

433¹ **ROCKET RADAR ....T Stephenson** 1
(fav) rear, in tch 7th, 3rd 3th, ld 5 out, ran on wll und pres
Mr Pipe Man (Ire) ....A Crow 2
hndy, disp 4-2 out, no ext apr last
467¹ **Mr Bobbit (Ire) ....R Burton** 3
chsng grp, rdn 3 out, not qckn und pres frm 2 out
667² Bay Owl 5ex *held up in rear, some late prog, no imp on 1st 3* ....M Worthington 4
671³ Ledwyche Gate 5ex *mstly 2nd/3rd til outpcd 12th* ....N Harris 5
464 Secret Castle *cls up, ld 5-11th, sn btn, p.u. 13th* ....C Stockton pu
667 Jo-Su-Ki *ld, 25l clr whn u.r. 4th* ....P Saville ur
515 Specialarrangement (Ire) 5ex *w.w., cls order to ld 12th, hdd 5 out, p.u. qckly 4 out* ....A Hill pu
8 ran. 4l, 8l, 5l, 20l. Time 6m 28.00s. SP 7-4.
R Bunn (Ledbury).

852 Restricted (12st)

670⁸ **ANOTHER CHANCER ....M Harris** 1
ld to start, mid-div 9th, rdn & ran on wll to ld 2 out
670⁴ **Yukon Gale (Ire) ....A Crow** 2
(fav) ld to 2nd, cls up, ld 3 out, not qckn frm 2 out
468² **Daphni (Fr) ....Miss K Swindells** 3
alwys chsng grp, unable to rch chal postition
467 Little By Little *mid-div, styng on onepce frm 5 out* ....T O'Leary 4
563 Charlie Trumper (Ire) *in tch wth ldrs til wkng 5 out* ....J Saville 5
670 Allezscally 5a *mid-div, broke leg apr 11th (dead)* ....C Stockton f
670⁵ Blushing Star *mid-div early, ld 9-13th, sn btn whn hdd, p.u. 3 out* ....N Gittins pu
468⁴ Strong Trace (Ire) *rear, poor last 11th, t.o. 13th, p.u. 5 out* ....L Brown pu
203 Aqueous Rocks *cls up, ld 3rd-8th, in tch whn f 13th* ....M Worthington f
Offensive Weapon *mid-div to 5th, rear 8th, t.o. 12th, p.u. 4 out*............................T Stephenson pu
469¹ Solar Castle (Ire) *mstk 2nd, f 4th* ....P McAllister f
11 ran. 20l, 10l, 6l, 25l. Time 6m 33.00s. SP 8-1.
K C G Edwards (Ludlow).

853 Open Maiden (5-7yo) (12st)

470³ **MUSICAL VOCATION (IRE) 5a 4ow ....A Crow** 1
(fav) prom, ld 6th, 30l clr 12th, ran on wll, eased run in, imp
478 **Zodiac Prince 7a......................R Phillips** 2
rear early, ran on frm 13th, nrst fin
574 **Arms Dealer 7a 2ow ....P O'Leary** 3
mid-div 9th, ran on onepce frm 4 out
Take A Right 7a *ld to 2nd, chsng grp to 10th, sn wknd, p.u. 4 out* ....J Cornes pu
572 Merger Mania 7a *cls up, ld 3rd-5th, outpcd, p.u. 5 out* ....T Stephenson pu
549 Ri Ra 5a *mid-div, losng tch whn p.u. 5 out* ....Miss S Sharratt pu
571 Warm Relation (Ire) *rear, p.u. 12th*.............T Cox pu
570⁶ Greenhills Ruby 5a *chsd ldrs, 3rd 10-14th, no ch whn p.u. 4 out* ....R Burton pu
Susies Prince *alwys rear, schooling, p.u. 5 out* ....S Prior pu
Bee-A-Scally 5a *cls 2nd to 8th, hdd chsng grp til tir-ing 4 out, p.u. 3 out* ....C Stockton pu
China Lal 12a *ran out 3rd* ....R Thomas ro
Nickamy Fountain (Ire) *ran out 3rd*.........J Mather ro
Master Muffler 7a *mid-div hlfwy, t.o. whn p.u. 4 out* ....A Beedles pu
13 ran. 15l, 20l. Time 6m 33.00s. SP 2-1.
G L Edwards (North Shropshire).

854 Open Maiden (12st)

572 **CHARLIESMEDARLIN ....R Burton** 1
(fav) j.w., made all, nvr seriously chal
665⁴ **Noble Angel (Ire) ....A Dalton** 2
mid-div, disp 3rd-4th-13th, ran on wll frm 3 out
Scorpotina 5a ....R Thomas 3
chsng grp, in tch til pce increased 4 out

665 Parson's Corner *cls up, outpcd frm 4 out* ....Miss C Williams 4
550[7] River Sunset (Ire) *alwys ldng quintet, onepcd frm 3 out* ....S Prior 5
Gordonstoun *cls up 5th, sn mid-div, schooling* ....Miss S Sharratt 6
368[6] Thornhill 5a *rear, t.o. 12th, p.u. 5 out* ....L Brown pu
566 Carol's Concorde (Ire) *p.u. 4th* ....J Saville pu
470 Aralier Man (Ire) *nvr bttr thn mid-div, rdn 6 out, found little, p.u. 3 out*....................A Crow pu
Riot Lady (Ire) 5a *prom to 9th, lost tch, p.u. 3 out* ....D Barlow pu

10 ran. 4l, 20l, 2l, 4l, 20l. Time 6m 33.00s. SP Evens.
W James Morgan (Albrighton Woodland).

STAINTONDALE
Charm Park
Monday March 31st
FIRM

855 Members (12st)

423 **PATS CROSS (IRE) 5ex ....J Byrne** 1
(fav) ld to 15th, disp nxt, hdd, ld 2 out, hld on
422[3] **Here Comes Charter ....A Pennock** 2
trckd ldr, disp 4 out, ld nxt, hdd 2 out, outpcd flat
Red Spruce *in tch to hlfwy, fdd, bhnd 12th, p.u. 14th* ....P Atkinson pu

3 ran. 2l. Time 6m 35.00s. SP 2-5.
James Byrne (Staintondale).

856 Restricted (12st)

509 **THE OXFORD DON ....N Wilson** 1
(fav) rear, prog 10th, ld 14th, made rest, comf
676 **Joint Account ....Mrs F Needham** 2
cls up, 2nd 4 out, chsd wnr, mstk 2 out, alwys hld
617[6] **Douce Eclair 5a ....Miss L Eddery** 3
last at 10th, prog 14th, onepcd 2 out, lkd 4th
616[7] Stride To Glory (Ire) *ld to 4th, ld 10-13th, onepcd, lkd 3rd* ....D Topping 4
615[2] Lyningo *alwys mid-div, nvr a fctr*..........A Wood 5
506[5] Cadrillon (Fr) *in tch to 10th, rear aft, pst btn horses frm 2 out* ....Miss A Deniel 6
676 The Chap *mid-div to hlfwy, rear & onepcd aft* ....R Lochman 7
510[1] Prophet's Choice *ld 5-10th, wknd, hit 12th, sn rear* ....M Haigh 8

8 ran. 4l, 2l, sht-hd, 5l, 15l, 4l, 5l. Time 6m 23.00s. SP 4-6.
Miss C Pinkney (Braes Of Derwent).

857 Mixed Open (12st)

508[1] **OSGATHORPE ....Mrs F Needham** 1
(fav) 20l 2nd at 5th, prog aft, ld 11-15th, ld 2 out, sn clr, easy
421[1] **Nishkina ....C Cundall** 2
20l 3rd at 5th, trckd ldr 11th, ld 4 out-2 out, outpcd
507 **No Word ....I Baker** 3
ld to 10th, fdd, t.o. 13th

3 ran. 8l, dist. Time 6m 32.00s. SP 2-5.
R Tate (Bilsdale).

858 Intermediate

425[1] **SECRET BAY ....S Swiers** 1
walked over

S P Dent (Zetland).

859 Open Maiden (7yo+)

RISE ABOVE IT (IRE) ....K Green 1
(fav) made all, easily
621[5] **Redwood Boy ....D Raw** 2
chsd wnr, 20l down 10th, no imp, mstk 2 out
677 **Markham Lad ....D Pritchard** 3
in tch to 10th, outpcd 12th, t.o. aft
429[5] Prickly Trout 5a *u.r. 2nd* ....C Mulhall ur

4 ran. Dist, dist. Time 6m 49.00s. SP 4-6.
Mrs P M Jibson (Derwent).

860 Open Maiden (5-6yo)

620[4] **ON THE FLY ....R Edwards** 1
cls up, ld 11th, made rest, styd on
623 **Hillmilly 12a ....S Charlton** 2
alwys prom, chsd wnr 13th, alwys hld
427[4] **Abbey Moss ....Miss J Eastwood** 3
mid-div, lft 3rd 15th, t.o.
505 Auntie Fay (Ire) 5a *s.s. mstks 1st & 2nd, ref 3rd* ....I Baker ref
675[5] Lac de Gras (Ire) *in tch, 5th at 8th, wknd, f 13th* ....A Pennock f
622 China Hand (Ire) 7a *cls up, 3rd at 8th, wknd, f 11th* ....H Armstrong f
621 Patey Court 5a (bl) *ld to 10th, 2nd whn f 12th* ....C Mulhall f
427[2] Zobejo 7a *(fav) rear, prog 12th, 3rd nxt, fdng whn ref 15th*....................N Wilson ref
428 Is Red There 7a *bhnd, nvr a fctr, p.u. 12th*....N Smith pu
622 Mr Hook 7a *alwys wll in rear, not fluent, p.u. 10th* ....I Brown pu
428 Surprise View 12a *sn bhnd, p.u. 10th*.....G Markham pu
699 Gardenia's Song *alwys rear, nvr dang, p.u. 13th* ....G Tuer pu

12 ran. 2l, dist. Time 6m 39.00s. SP 2-1.
M J Brown (Sinnington).
A.C.

TAUNTON VALE
Kingston St Mary
Monday March 31st
FIRM

861 Members

630[3] **ROYAL TURN ....A Honeyball** 1
(fav) made virt all at mod pce, pshd out
554 **Master Decoy ....Miss A Bush** 2
trckd wnr, eft 3 out, ev ch last not qckn

2 ran. Nk. Time 7m 39.50s. SP 1-4.
John Honeyball (Taunton Vale Foxhounds).

862 Confined (12st)

554[2] **PARDITINO ....Miss V Nicholas** 1
prom, ld 16th til aft 3 out, lkd btn til rlld to ld nr post
395[4] **Earl Boon 3ex ....P Griffiths** 2
held up, prog 16th, ld aft 3 out, clr til cght nr post
557[1] **Elle Flavador 5a..................Miss S Vickery** 3
(fav) hdwy to disp aft 16th, ev ch til wknd rpdly aft 3 out
519[2] The Criosra (Ire) *rear, lost tch 15th, t.o.*....A Bateman 4
520[7] L'uomo Piu *ld til ran out 7th* ....Miss K Baker ro
526 Really Neat 5a *rear til f 15th* ....G Beilby f
522 Miss Ricus 5a *lft in ld 7th, slght ld til f 16th* ....R Treloggen f

7 ran. ½l, 12l, 25l. Time 6m 30.00s. SP 9-2.
Mrs K R J Nicholas (Tiverton Foxhounds).

863 Men's Open (12st)

522 **BRIDGE EXPRESS ....N Mitchell** 1
(Jt fav) made virt all, jnd aft 4 out, pshd clr 2 out
310[3] **Hensue ....S Slade** 2
(Jt fav) hndy, disp aft 4 out, ev ch til no ext 2 out
662[4] Prankster *hit 7th, lost tch 13th, blndrd & u.r. 15th* ....T Atkinson ur
519 The Golfing Curate *cls 3rd whn f 6th* ....I Dowrick f

4 ran. 5l. Time 6m 26.40s. SP 2-1.
C T Moate (West Somerset Vale).

864 Ladies Open

482[3] **ON HIS OWN ....Miss W Southcombe** 1
prog 16th, lft in ld apr nxt, clr til virt cght nr post
520 **Rapid Rascal ....Miss S West** 2
ld to 6th,lost pl,ran on agn apr last,strng run flat,unlucky
520 **Be My Habitat 5ow (bl) ....Miss L Hawkings** 3

in tch, chsd ldr til outpcd aft 3 out, rlld cls home
555 Station Express (Ire) *alwys rear, rnng on in 4th whn f last* ....Miss V Stephens f
18 Old Mill Stream *(fav) keen hold, ld 6th til p.u. lame aft 16th*....Miss S Vickery pu
525 And What Else (Ire) *1st ride, bhnd til p.u. aft 8th* ....Miss E Pring pu
6 ran. Hd, 1½l. Time 6m 30.00s. SP 2-1.
P L Southcombe (Cattistock).

865 Restricted (12st)

524 **TANGLE KELLY** ....**S Slade** 1
disp 6th, cls up til ld aft 16th,clr whn lft alone apr 3 out
523 Windwhistle Lad *(fav) disp 6th, ld 11-16th, wknng & p.u. lame apr 3 out* ....B Dixon pu
391[1] Gt Hayes Pommard *ld til jmp slwly 6th, 3rd whn blndrd & u.r. 8th*....D Howells ur
3 ran. Time 6m 34.60s. SP 6-4.
The Fennington Five (Devon & Somerset Staghounds).

866 Open Maiden Div I (12st)

525[3] **FARADAY** ....**N Mitchell** 1
(fav) hit 15th, wnt 2nd nxt, ld apr 3 out, drew clr
526 **Nodforms Inferno** ....**D Alers-Hankey** 2
pllng, ld til hdd apr 3 out, wknd, walked in
512 Golden News *rear, blndrd 7th, p.u. bfr nxt*....P King pu
Better By Half (Ire) *rear, mstk 7th, t.o. p.u. apr 13th* ....S Slade pu
War Baron *towrds rear, 30l 4th whn p.u. apr 13th* ....I Dowrick pu
525 Acetylene 12a *chsd ldr frm 7th, wknd 16th, btn 3rd p.u. apr last*....Miss T Cave pu
104 Summerthetime *last whn f 6th* ....A Moir f
7 ran. Dist. Time 6m 39.50s. SP 5-4.
G B Foot (Seavington).

867 Open Maiden Div II (12st)

KING OF THE MICKS ....**R Emmett** 1
plld hrd,trckd ldr,not fluent,efft & ran on to ld cls home
461 **Butts Castle** ....**S Slade** 2
tried to make all, sn clr, cght cls home
527 **Crosswell Star (Ire)** ....**N Mitchell** 3
rear, wnt remote 3rd aft 14th
647 Neat And Tidy *3rd whn ran out 6th*....Miss A Boswell ro
524 Miss Gruntled 5a *bhnd til p.u. apr 2 out* ....Maj O Ellwood pu
299 The Smiling Girl 5a 2ow (bl) *5th whn blndrd & u.r. 11th*....N Fitzearle ur
6 ran. ¾l, dist. Time 6m 33.70s. SP 8-1.
Mrs Peter Wakely (Axe Vale).
Willsan (fav) w/d not under orders deduct 60p in the £. G.T.

VINE & CRAVEN
Hackwood Park
Monday March 31st
FIRM

868 Members

397[2] **ESPY** ....**A James** 1
(fav) mstk 1st, disp til lft alone 3 out
Huntsmans Holloa *1st ride, mstks 1st & 11th, disp til f 3 out* ....J Goddard f
2 ran. Time 6m 55.00s. SP 1-5.
C James (Vine & Craven).

869 B F S S (Nov Riders) (12st)

394 **PEJAWI 5a** ....**Miss L Whitaker** 1
hld up, smooth prog to jn ldrs 2 out, styd on wll frm last
511[1] **Mighty Falcon** ....**Miss E Tory** 2
(fav) mostly 2nd til ld 12th, disp aft til hdd last, ran on
745[3] **Skinnhill (bl)** ....**C Mason** 3
rear & sn rdn, clsd 7th, disp 12th, outpcd 2 out
Prince's Court *cls up to 8th, wknd, rear last cct* ....Mrs J Kimber 4
178 The Humble Tiller *ld til hdd & f 12th*....Mrs A Bevins f
302[7] Fowling Piece *u.r. 1st*....M Legg ur
6 ran. 3l, 10l, 8l. Time 6m 21.00s. SP 9-1.
Miss L Whitaker (Berks & Bucks Draghounds).

870 Mixed Open (12st)

660[2] **PANDA SHANDY 5a 7ex**....**Miss A Goschen** 1
(fav) j.w. rear til ld brfly 14th, ld 3 out, ran on well
281[5] **Nemuro (USA) 7ex**....**P Scouller** 2
disp to 8th,steadied,ld & mstk 15th,hdd nxt,mstk last,ran on
481[1] **Paco's Boy 7ex (bl)** ....**P York** 3
disp to 8th, hmpd 10th-12th, wknd
Vultoro 7ex *s.s. jmpd lft, ld 10th-12th, wknd, p.u. last* ....T Underwood pu
4 ran. 1l, 30l. Time 6m 26.00s. SP 1-2.
Mrs R H Woodhouse (Portman).

871 Open Maiden (12st)

487[2] **COLORS OF GUIDAL (FR)** ....**P York** 1
(Jt fav) alwys cls up, chal frm 2 out, mstk & lft clr last
485[5] **Muskerry Moya (Ire) 5a** ....**Miss A Goschen** 2
alwys 1st trio, wknd apr 2 out, lft poor 2nd last
Springvilla (Ire) *(Jt fav) ld 5th, narrow ld whn pckd & u.r. last, unlucky*....C Vigors f
657[4] Dormston Lad *ld to 4th, wknd, t.o. & p.u. 14th* ....C Jowett pu
283 Jobingo *nvr bttr than mid-div, wknd & p.u. 14th* ....Daniel Dennis pu
390 Nikaroo 5a *alwys rear, poor 4th last, p.u. flat, dead* ....S Bush pu
513[4] Woodlands Beau (Ire) 7a *cls up 1st cct, in tch whn f 14th*....T Woolridge f
7 ran. 12l. Time 6m 27.00s. SP 5-2.
Nolan D Best (Garth & South Berks).

872 Confined (12st)

742[1] **HEATHVIEW** ....**M Portman** 1
ld 4th, jmpd rght, qcknd & 6l up whn lft clr last
580[1] **Orphan Olly** ....**P York** 2
(fav) alwys last, hrd rdn & mstk 13th, t.o. & lft poor 2nd last
742 Touch Of Winter 5ex *3rd to 11th, chsd wnr aft, p.u. flat* ....T Lacey pu
577 Glen Cherry *ld early, 2nd to 11th, wknd, p.u. last* ....P Scouller pu
4 ran. Dist. Time 6m 22.00s. SP 11-4.
Mrs P Corbett (Tedworth).

873 Restricted (12st)

601[3] **JULY SCHOON** ....**C Vigors** 1
(fav) hld up going wll, clsd 2 out, ld apr last, easily
495[7] **Rayman (Ire)** ....**R Cope** 2
rear til prog to ld 13th, hdd 2 out, no ch wth wnr
Palaman ....**C Pearson** 3
ld 7-12th, mstks 3 out & nxt, fdd
601 Dad's Pipe (bl) *jmpd bdly rght, 2nd early, t.o. hlfwy* ....T Smith 4
Vital Shot 5a *ld to 6th, cls up to 10th, p.u. nxt* ....Mrs R Baldwin pu
41[1] Chasing Daisy 12a *p.u. aft 1st*....Miss A Goschen pu
6 ran. 8l, 15l, 1 fence. Time 6m 21.00s. SP 5-2.
T D B Underwood (Worcestershire).
P.M.

UTTOXETER
Tuesday April 1st
GOOD TO FIRM

874 2m 7f Mount Argus Hunters' Chase Class H

154[5] **IDIOTIC 11.12 5a....................Mr C Vigors** 1
hdwy to chase ldrs 10th, chal 3 out, blnd next, rallied last, rdn to ld near fin.
668[1] **My Nominee 11.10 7a (bl)...........Mr R Burton** 2
(fav) in tch, rdn to chal 3 out, ld next, ridden and ct run- in.
592 **Pro Bono (Ire) 11.12 5a...........Mr A Sansome** 3
soon chasing ldrs, chal from 10th, hit 11th, ev ch 3 out, wknd next.
587[8] King Of Shadows 11.10 7a *made most to 5th, wknd 10th, no ch when blnd 12th, t.o..* ....Mr S Prior 4
490 Babil 11.12 5a *prom till wknd 7th, t.o. when p.u. before 9th*.........................Mr J Trice-Rolph pu
Frank Be Lucky 11.12 5a *chal 3rd till ld 5th, hdd apr 2 out, wknd rpdly and p.u. before last*....Mr R Thornton pu
583 Double Collect 11.10 7a *in tch when blnd and u.r. 7th*..............................Mr N F Smith ur
490[8] Rising Sap 11.10 7a *bhnd when blnd badly 8th, hdwy 11th, hit 4 out, wknd quickley, t.o. when p.u. before last*..............................Mr M Munrowd pu
666 Idiomatic 11.10 7a *t.o. from 5th, p.u. before 10th*...............................Mr D Sherlock pu
9 ran. Nk, 17l, dist. Time 5m 40.00s. SP 4-1.
E Knight

WETHERBY
Tuesday April 1st
GOOD TO FIRM

875 3m 1f Howard Brown Memorial Novices' Hunters' Chase Class H

386[1] **DENIM BLUE 11.7 5a............Miss P Robson** 1
(fav) held up, hdwy to track ldr hfwy, rdn to chal 3 out, styd on und pres to ld run-in, all out.
411 **Sovereigns Match 11.7 5a ....Mr N Wilson** 2
ld, jmpd slowly 4 out, joined next and rdn, hdd run-in, rallied towards fin.
765[3] **Syrus P Turntable 11.5 7a...........Mr J Saville** 3
chsd ldrs till wknd after 14th, t.o..
509[2] Tom Log 11.5 7a *mstk 6th, blnd next, soon lost tch, t.o..* ....Mr W Burnell 4
387[4] R N Commander 11.5 7a *lost tch from hfwy, well t.o..* ....Mr J R Cornwall 5
5 ran. ½l, dist, 18l, dist. Time 6m 30.10s. SP 4-11.
Mrs L Walby

CROOME & WEST WARKS
Upton-On-Severn
Tuesday April 1st
GOOD TO FIRM

876 Members

433 **DAMERS TREASURE (bl) ....M Cowley** 1
ld to 2nd, lft in ld 6th, hdd 15th, lft in ld nxt, styd on
435[4] **Clovers Last ....M Harris** 2
(fav) trckd ldrs, rdn 14th, lft 2nd 3 out, no imp wnr
435 **Hectors Way ....J Bates** 3
prom,blnd 9th,ld 15th,blnd & nrly ran off course nxt,nt rcvr
Steel Street (Ire) *t.o. 4th, btn 3 fncs*..........P Britten 4
Bluff Cove *rear whn u.r. 6th*..................A Chipp ur
432[4] Bankroll 5ex *ld 2nd, clr whn ref 6th*...Mrs C Chadney ref
263[4] Distant-Port (Ire) *t.d.e. ref to race*......T Stephenson 0
7 ran. 4l, 20l, Bad. Time 6m 47.00s. SP 7-1.
O P J Meli (Croome & West Warks).

877 Restricted (12st)

CRUISE A HOOP ....Julian Pritchard 1
prom, ld 7th, drew clr apr 3 out, mstk last, unchal
701 **Sideliner ....T Stephenson** 2
mid-div, effrt 9th, went 5th at 11th, no prog, lft 2nd last
363 **Glitterbird 5a ....A Dalton** 3
prom til 4th & outpcd frm 12th, no prog aft
433 Members Rights 5a *chsd ldr to 5th, outpcd frm 10th, no ch aft* ....M Keel 4
Highland Talk *jmpd bdly, bhnd whn ref 6th* G Densley ref
222 Box Of Delights *trckd ldrs,chsd wnr 11th,mstk 13th,btn 3 out,p.u. nxt,dsmntd* ....E Williams pu
Snippetoff *mstks, sn in rear, wll bhnd whn p.u. 15th* ....Miss F Wilson pu
Saffron Spirit 5a *mid-div, lost tch 9th, poor 8th at 11th, p.u. 13th, dsmntd* ....J Baimbridge pu
392[1] Melling *alwys rear, no ch frm 10th, t.o. & p.u. 15th* ....N Mitchell pu
198 Sit Tight *alwys rear, t.o. & p.u. 11th*........M Portman pu
671 Mis-E-Fishant 5a *last & t.o. til p.u. 11th* ....D Mansell pu
Penly *prom, blnd 8th, sn strggling, wll bhnd & p.u. 15th*..............................John Pritchard pu
881 March Gate *(fav) alwys rear, no ch frm 9th, wll bhnd whn p.u. 13th*.............................M Rimell pu
640 Bus Pass 7a (v) *ld to 7th, 3rd frm 11th, poor 2nd agn apr 2 out, u.r. last*....................P Doorhof ur
542[3] Barafundle Bay *alwys bhnd, t.o. & p.u. 11th* ...J Price pu
543 Nikitasecondchance 5a *rear, 9th & wll bhnd at 11th, p.u. 15th, dsmntd* ....G Barfoot-Saunt pu
All Change *mid-div, 7th & out of tch whn f 9th* T Illsley f
17 ran. Dist, 3l, 2l. Time 6m 31.00s. SP 6-1.
W M A Davies (Ledbury).

878 BFSS Novice Riders (12st)

MISTER GEBO ....Miss C Dyson 1
(fav) in tch, trckd ldr 8th, ld 15th, drew clr apr last
300[6] **King Of The Clouds ....J Hammond** 2
ld 4th, sn clr, hdd 15th, cls engh 2 out, sn btn
Meldon ....J Barnes 3
rear, effrt to poor 4th at 12th, kpt on, nvr dang
568 Shadow Walker *1st ride, alwys bhnd, t.o. 11th, kpt on* ....W Lefonder 4
Kerry Hill *alwys wll bhnd, t.o. 11th*....Miss D Jackson 5
362[5] Saddler's Choice *mid-div, no ch frm 9th, wknd 15th, cllpsd aft race* ....D Painter 6
Ballad Song *ld to 4th, wknd frm 8th, wll bhnd whn u.r 14th*..............................Mrs C Chadney ur
639 Astley Jack 3ow *ref to race* ....R Cotton 0
575 For Michael *rear, prog 7th, 3rd & outpcd frm 10th, wknd 15th, p.u. last* ....Miss J Houldey pu
651 Therewego (Ire) *rear, jmpd lft 9th, ran out & u.r. nxt* ....Mrs R Corn ro
Yorkshire Pop 5a *last whn u.r. 1st* ....N Rudge ur
11 ran. 10l, 15l, 20l, 4l, 3l. Time 6m 44.00s. SP 7-4.
Mrs D J Dyson (Worcestershire).

879 Mixed Open (12st)

652[1] **SAMS HERITAGE ....Miss A Dare** 1
(fav) trckd ldr, ld 8th, qcknd frm 13th, easily
380[3] **Mitchells Best ....T Stephenson** 2
cls up til outpcd 12th, kpt on to tk 2nd aft last
521[4] **Oh So Windy 5a ....B Pollock** 3
cls up, wth wnr 10-13th, outpcd whn mstk 15th, lost 2nd flat
431 Master Eryl *ld to 8th, effrt to cs wnr & mstk 3 out, wknd, walked in* ....Julian Pritchard 4
4 ran. 12l, ½l, dist. Time 6m 40.00s. SP 4-11.
C G Smedley (Berkeley).

880 Confined (12st)

655[1] **LETS TWIST AGAIN (IRE) ....Julian Pritchard** 1
(fav) made all, jmpd lft 9th, clr 2 out, pshd out
568[2] **Landsker Alfred 6ex ....Miss A Dare** 2
mstly chsd wnr, jmpd lft 10th, rdn & no imp 3 out
430[2] **Hackett's Farm ....A Dalton** 3
prom, cls up 12th, sn outpcd by 1st pair
650[2] Knightly Argus *chsd ldrs, mstk 7th, sn pshd alng, bhnd frm 13th*..............................M Rollett 4
Master Bracken *hld up, lost tch 11th, wknd, walked in* ....P Newth 5
Carlton Moor 5a *bhnd frm 9th, sn t.o., walked in* ....Miss S Rooker 6
6 ran. 15l, 15l, 15l, 30l, 30l. Time 6m 33.00s. SP 4-5.
Mrs S Bird (Ledbury).

881 Maiden (12st)

653[2] **RUSTY FELLOW ....D Mansell** 1
chsd ldrs, effrt 3 out, disp 2 out til qcknd clr aft last
390[2] **Cape Henry ....Dr P Pritchard** 2
(fav) mstk 3rd,trckd ldrs going wll,disp 2 out-last,not qckn
212 **Woodlands Power ....John Pritchard** 3
ld/disp til ld 13th, hdd 2 out, hrd rdn & onepcd
437[3] Sylvan Sirocco *chsd ldrs to 15th, grad wknd frm 3 out* ....M Harris 4
435[2] Social Vision (Ire) *hld up, lost tch ldrs 11th, nvr on trms aft* ....T Stephenson 5
568 Sonny's Song *keen hld, mstk 7th,prom to 10th, wknd, p.u. 15th* ....L Brown pu
655 Crestwood Lad (USA) *cls up whn b.d. 5th* ..M Yardley bd
876 Distant-Port (Ire) *2nd attempt, lft 30l, rshd up to jn ldrs whn f 5th* ....J Price f
571[3] A Few Dollars More (Ire) *mstk 10th, ld/disp to 13th, 5th & wkng whn f 3 out*......................M Rimell f
261 Jimmy Morrel *schoold rear, bhnd frm 12th, p.u. 3 out* ....Julian Pritchard pu
Uncle Tom *schoold, rear, chsd ldng grp 13th, no prog & p.u. 3 out*..............................A Dalton pu
437 Chequers Boy *bhnd, last whn blnd 9th, t.o. & p.u. 11th*.............................G Barfoot-Saunt pu
Slaught Boy (Ire) *cls up til f 5th* ....Miss P Gundry f
13 ran. 5l, 5l, 15l, 6l. Time 6m 38.00s. SP 11-4.
Mrs G M Shail (Ledbury).
J.N.

HIGH PEAK HARRIERS
Flagg Moor
Tuesday April 1st
GOOD

882 Stone Wall Members

CARLI'S STAR ....Miss S Rodman 1
(fav)
Arm In Arm ....Mrs A Turner 2
465 **What A Miss 5a....................Mrs L Astell** 3
Kingoftheswingers 5ow 4
Gremlin Spring 28ow 5
Thorneycroft Kittiwake 6
Gretel 7
Dragons Lair 6ow .... ref
8 ran. 4l, 8l. SP 1-2.
Mrs S Rodman (High Peak Harriers).

883 Open Maiden

574[3] **REAL GENT ....C Stockton** 1
chsd ldr to 6th & frm 11th, styd on und pres to ld flat
Concerto Collonges (Fr) ....R Ford 2
prom, chsd ldr 6-11th, ld 3 out, ran green apr last,hdd flat
331 **April Suprise 5a ....G Hanmer** 3
w.w. prog to trck ldrs 9th, 3rd & rdn 3 out, onepcd
549[2] Full Song 5a *(fav) bhnd whn mstk 7th, lost tch 13th, t.o. & p.u. 3 out* ....S Morris pu
664[8] Gold Dam (Ire) (bl) *ld to apr 3 out, wknd rpdly, p.u. last, dsmntd* ....D Barlow pu
670 Sheppie's Reality (bl) *hld up rear, in tch whn f 9th* ....O McPhail f
326 Rugrat 5a *chsd ldrs, 6th & wkng 4 out, t.o. & p.u. last* ....P McAllister pu
347[4] Chorus Of Wings (Ire) *chsd ldrs, cls 4th at 15th, s.u. bnd apr nxt* ....D Crossland su
Top Beauty 5a *mid-div, mstk 2nd, blnd & u.r. nxt* ....Mrs J Dawson ur
326 Althrey Lad *keen hld, prom to 10th, 6th & wkng whn f 12th*.......................................A Jordan f
476 Top Odder (Ire) 7a *blnd 1st, last frm nxt, t.o. 11th, p.u. 15th* ....P Millington pu
Who Doctored Who (Ire) *s.s. rear of main grp whn f 5th* ....M Worthington f
12 ran. 1½l, 8l. Time 7m 29.00s. SP 4-1.
Jonathan A Lee (West Shropshire Drag).

884 Confined

666[1] **GLENROWAN (IRE) ....R Ford** 1
w.w. lft 3rd 14th, ld 3 out, rdn & forged clr apr last
665[1] **Bubble N Squeek ....C Barlow** 2
w.w. lft 2nd 14th, ev ch 3 out, no ext und pres
667 **Side Brace (NZ) (v)...................R Thomas** 3D
chsd ldr 3rd, ld 7th-3 out, wknd, fin 3rd, disq
545[5] **Alpha One ....P Gee** 3
ld to 1st,lft 2nd aft 5th-11th,lost tch,t.o.,fin 4th,prmtd
476[4] Ocean Sovereign *ld til ran wd & hdd aft 5th, last aft, t.o. & p.u. 15th*............................T Denniff pu
671 Killatty Player (Ire) 5a *(fav) lft in ld aft 5th, hdd 7th, 4l down whn blnd & u.r. 14th*...................A Crow ur
6 ran. 5l, 20l, 30l. Time 7m 31.00s. SP 7-2.
R Thomas (West Shropshire Drag).
Side Brace disq, not draw correct weight. Original distances.

885 Ladies

669[1] **HORNBLOWER ....Mrs C Ford** 1
(fav) w.w. 2nd at 15th, ld 3 out, rdn apr last, kpt on
414 **Across The Lake ....Miss S Brotherton** 2
ld to 2nd, bhnd frm 6th, clsd 3 out, kpt on
573[4] **Thamesdown Tootsie 5a ....Miss V Lyon** 3
chsd ldr 2-15th, onepcd aft
Ryton Guard *3rd wh blnd 5th, last frm nxt, t.o. whn blnd & u.r. 12th*...................Miss H Brookshaw ur
669[2] Charterforhardware *ld 2nd, 20l clr 9th, hdd 3 out, wknd, no ch whn f last* ....Miss T Clark f
5 ran. 7l, 1l. Time 7m 22.00s. SP 2-5.
R Burgess (West Shropshire Draghounds).

886 Land Rover Open (12st)

569[1] **RIVERSIDE BOY 4ex (bl) ....A Crow** 1
(fav) ld, sn clr, drew rght away 3 out, heavily eased flat
771 **Kabancy ....P Millington** 2
schoold,immed t.o.,went 2nd 3 out,fin full of rnng,stewards
Rustic Craft (Ire) *chsd wnr, wknd rpdly 3 out, exhstd whn stppd nxt* ....A Brown ref
3 ran. 10l. Time 8m 26.00s. SP 1-8.
Miss M E Sherrington (North Staffordshire).

887 PPORA

FORCE EIGHT ....Mrs J Dawson 1
(fav) ld 6th, clr apr 2 out, comf
771[2] **Merlyns Choice ....A Woodward** 2
last & dtchd 5th, styd on 14th, chnc 3 out, no imp aft
490[7] **Rambling Lord (Ire) ....G Smith** 3
chsd ldrs, 2nd 4 out-2 out, wll btn whn blnd last
332[4] T'int (Ire) 5a *chsd ldrs, mstk 12th, 2nd brfly apr 15th, wknd 3 out* ....J Burley 4
769 Obie's Train *chsd ldrs, 3rd whn u.r. 3rd* ....Mrs A Lee ur
472[2] Mister Chippendale *mid-div, 5th & rdn 11th, wknd whn blnd 12th & p.u.*.........................S Walker pu
Rhine River (USA) (bl) *ld to 6th, prssd wnr til wknd 15th, p.u. 3 out* ....C Stockton pu
766 Petit Primitive 5a *hld up, 6th whn f 6th*.....T Whitaker f
8 ran. 12l, 12l, 12l. Time 7m 26.00s. SP 4-5.
Mrs E W Wilson (Brocklesby).
S.P.

AINTREE
Thursday April 3rd
GOOD

888 3m 1f Cuvee Napa Novices' Hunters' Chase Class B

287[1] **BITOFAMIXUP (IRE) 12.0 ....Mr P Hacking** 1
j.w, held up, smooth hdwy to chase ldr 6 out, ld soon after 4 out, soon qcknd clr, impressive.
562[1] **Howayman 12.0 ....Mr A Parker** 2
in tch, not fluent 4th, trckd ldrs hfwy till outpcd four out, no ch with wnr.

591² **Ardbrennan 12.0....................Mr E James** 3
soon ld, hit 10th, rdn and hdd after 4 out, soon outpcd.
287⁵ Sands Of Gold (Ire) 12.0 *held up, nigg1d along hfwy, mstk 12th, bhnd when jmpd slowly next, t.o..* Mr L Lay 4
384³ Lurriga Glitter (Ire) 12.0 *bhnd, mstk 9th, t.o. 11th.* ....Mr R Wakley 5
490⁵ Tangle Baron 12.0 *soon chasing ldr, lost pl 6 out, wknd quickly after next, t.o..*.........Miss J Cumings 6
589¹ Tom's Gemini Star 12.0 *held up, f 3rd.*.....Mr M Harris f
305 Johnny The Fox (Ire) 12.0 *u.r. 1st.*.......Mr R Lawther ur
490¹ Orchestral Suite (Ire) 12.0 *(fav) chsd ldrs, f 3rd.* ....Mr F Hutsby f

9 ran. Dist, 1l, 11l, 3½l, 4l. Time 6m 33.20s. SP 9-4.
Mike Roberts

TAUNTON
Thursday April 3rd
FIRM

889 3m Wsm Mercedes Benz Vito Hunters' Chase Class H

862 **L'UOMO PIU 12.0 7a...............Mr O McPhail** 1
made all, hit 12th, driven out.
586⁴ **Rusty Bridge 12.0 7a ....Mr R Burton** 2
(fav) chsd wnr, mstk 4th, rdn when hit 2 out, edged left and kept on run-in.
523⁵ **J B Lad 11.7 7a ....Miss P Gundry** 3
held up, hdwy 14th, hit next, staying on when carried left run-in.
Arctic Baron 12.0 7a *held up, prog 9th, 4th and weakening when blnd four out.* ....Miss L Blackford 4
689² Departure 11.2 7a *soon t.o., p.u. before 14th.* ....Mr J Creighton pu
Cleasby Hill 11.7 7a *held up, rdn 10th, bhnd from 13th, t.o. when p.u. after 4 out.*.....Mr D Alers-Hankey pu
493³ Good King Henry 11.7 7a *held up, jmpd slowly 5th, well bhnd from 14th, t.o. when p.u. before 2 out.* ....Mr I Widdicombe pu

7 ran. 1¾l, hd, 12l. Time 5m 53.20s. SP 10-1.
A Barrow

AINTREE
Friday April 4th
GOOD

890 2¾m Martell Fox Hunters' Chase Class B

587¹ **BLUE CHEEK 12.0 ....Mr R Thornton** 1
cl up, mstk 3rd (Chair), jmpd slowly and outpcd 4 out, hdwy from 3 out, ld soon after next, clr last, easily.
583² **Highlandman 12.0 ....Mr Chris Wilson** 2
midfield, chsd ldrs 8th, outpcd after 12th (Canal Turn), styd on apr 2 out, unable to chal.
793² **Abbotsham 12.0 ....Mr E James** 3
jmpd poorly in rear, blnd 10th (Becher's), staying on when hmpd 2 out, n.d..
K C's Dancer 12.0 *held up, cld 6th, lost tch 13th (Valentine's), styd on same pace from 3 out.* ....Mr J M Pritchard 4
603¹ Young Nimrod 12.0 *in tch, chsd ldr from hfwy, drew level 3 out, ld briefly next, driven and wknd run-in.* ....Mr G Wragg 5
378¹ Trifast Lad 12.0 *not fluent in rear, pkd 10th (Becher's), soon lost tch.*...............Mr P Hacking 6
678² Great Pokey 12.0 *soon ld, hdd 5th, mstk 10th (Becher's), soon well bhnd, t.o..*.....Miss N Courtenay 7
611 Fordstown (Ire) 12.0 *chsd ldrs, struggling hfwy, soon t.o..*....................Mr Jamie Alexander 8
376⁷ Faringo 12.0 *bhnd, not fluent, t.o. hfwy.* Mr W Gowlett 9
387¹ Mr Boston 12.0 *(fav) jmpd right, ld 5th, slight ld and going well when f 2 out.* ....Mr S Swiers f
387³ Matt Reid 12.0 (bl) *f 1st.* ....Mr W Morgan f
4³ Chilipour 12.0 *f 1st.*...............Mr J Jukes f
379 Country Tarrogen 12.0 *f 1st.* ....Mr N Wilson f
496 Highway Five (Ire) 12.0 *f 1st.* ....Mr M P Jones f

14 ran. 17l, 1l, 1¾l, 3½l, 18l, 28l, 7l, 1¼l. Time 5m 48.70s. SP 9-2.
J Mahon

SEDGEFIELD
Friday April 4th
GOOD TO FIRM

891 3m 3f Stanley Thompson Memorial Hunters' Chase Class H

619¹ **GREENMOUNT LAD (IRE) 11.2 7a Mr P Cornforth** 1
(fav) chsd clr ldr, ld 6 out, hrd pressed final 2, ran on well.
609⁹ **La Maja (Ire) 10.11 7a ....Mr C Mulhall** 2
jmpd right thrght, held up, imp after 13th, chal 2 out, hit last, kept on same pace.
Upwell 11.4 5a....................Mr P Johnson 3
ld till hdd 6 out, outpcd before 2 out.
765² Boreen Owen 11.2 7a *in tch, reminders after 13th, outpcd 15th.*....................Mr A Parker 4
611⁶ Fish Quay 11.2 7a *in tch, lost pl 13th, soon struggling, p.u. after 2 out.*...............Miss S Lamb pu

5 ran. 6l, 9l, 7l. Time 6m 50.70s. SP 10-11.
J Cornforth

HEREFORD
Saturday April 5th
GOOD TO FIRM

892 2m Garway Novices' Hunters' Chase Class H

NECTANEBO (IRE) 11.7 7a...........Mr M Frith 1
held up and alwys going well, hdwy 6th, chal 3 out till ld after next, soon clr.
493 **Tom's Apache 11.7 7a...............Mr E James** 2
ld, soon clr, hdd after 2 out, soon outpcd.
568⁴ **Dalametre 11.7 7a...............Mr M Munrowd** 3
(fav) hdwy and rdn along 6th, effort 3 out, soon wknd.
Chan The Man 11.7 7a *chsd ldr from 3rd, hit 8th, ev ch when mstk 3 out, soon wknd.* ....Mr M Harris 4
630² Ann's Ambition 11.7 7a *mstks, alwys bhnd.* ....Mr C Heard 5
587 The Communicator 11.9 5a *chsd ldrs, hit 4 out, soon wknd.*....................Mr B Pollock 6
751 Oats For Notes 11.2 7a *alwys bhnd, no ch when mstk 3 out.*....................Mr R Burton 7
381⁷ Happy Paddy 11.7 7a *in tch, mstk and wknd 5th, t.o..* ....Mr M Cowley 8
653⁷ Space Molly 11.2 7a *t.o. from 4th, p.u. before 3 out.* ....Mr P Cowley pu
381 Michelles Crystal 11.2 7a *slowly away, f 3rd.* ....Mr J Goldstein f
585 Feltham Mistress 11.2 7a *in tch, 4th when f 7th.* ....Mr E Babington f

11 ran. 6l, 16l, 2½l, 12l, 2½l, 14l, dist. Time 4m 4.20s. SP 25-1.
Mrs R E Parker

BRAMHAM MOOR
Wetherby Point-To-Point Course
Saturday April 5th
FIRM

893 Members (12st)

506⁴ **COT LANE ....J Tate** 1
(fav) ld til disp 11th, lft dist clr nxt, easily
Orbit ....P Rigal 2
1st ride,sttld 3rd, lost tch 6th, sn t.o., lft poor 2nd 12th
616⁴ Cahermone Lady (Ire) 5a *trckd ldr, disp 11th til f nxt* ....S Whittaker f

3 ran. Dist. Time 7m 22.00s. SP 1-3.
T P Tate (Bramham Moor).

894 Restricted

621[1] **NOTARIUS (FR) ....Mrs K Hargreave** **1**
hld up, mstk 2nd, prog 10th, ld 3 out, drvn out flat
695[2] **Dear Emily 5a ....N Smith** **2**
(fav) ld to 3rd, prom til ld 14th, hdd 3 out, kpt on
856[6] **Cadrillon (Fr) ....Miss A Deniel** **3**
prom, trckd ldr 5th, disp 11th til rdn & onepcd 14th
415[8] Blakes Folly (Ire) *rear, effrt 3 out, sn outpcd* ..D Wood 4
835 My True Clown *mid-div, lost plc 8th, rdn 10th, wll bhnd frm 13th* ....Miss L Hampshire 5
425[3] Winters Melody 5a *prom, ld 3rd, disp 11th til hdd & wknd 14th, bhnd & p.u.2out*...............A Pennock pu
6 ran. 1½l, 10l, ¾l, dist. Time 6m 50.00s. SP 5-1.
Mrs A E Juliet Barnett (Braes Of Derwent).

895 Ladies Open

697[2] **CHEEKY POT ....Mrs S Grant** **1**
(fav) chsd ldr, rdn 10th, clsd 14th, ld 3 out, sn clr
617[8] **Rustino ....Miss R Clark** **2**
made most, clr 5th, prssd 4 out, hdd nxt, outpcd
2 ran. 8l. Time 6m 56.00s. SP 1-5.
Mrs E I L Tate (Hurworth).

896 Men's Open

618[6] **FROME BOY ....P Johnson** **1**
walked over
Peter Johnson (Saltersgate).

897 Intermediate (12st)

732 **SHARP CHALLENGE ....T Glass** **1**
jmpd rght, ld to 5th, outpcd 7th, poor 2nd whn lft clr 2 out
616 **Mac's Blade (USA) 7a ....R Edwards** **2**
sttld 3rd,strgglng 13th,lft 2nd 2 out,rallied flat,just hld
694[5] Earl Gray *(fav) trckd ldr, ld 5th, clr 7th, 20l up whn blnd & u.r. 2 out*.......................Miss A Deniel ur
3 ran. ½l. Time 6m 54.00s. SP 2-1.
Miss J M Stephenson (Border).

898 Open Maiden Div I

693[2] **PERSIAN LION ....Miss T Jackson** **1**
(fav) made all, drew clr 3 out, unchal
623 **Madame Defarge 5a ....Mrs K Hargreave** **2**
trckd ldr, lost plc 5th, outpcd 10th, ran on wll frm 2 out
883 **Top Odder (Ire) 7a..................P Millington** **3**
mid-div, mstk 4th, prog 5 out, ev ch nxt, wknd
266 Vickyberto 5a *keen hld, prom, ev ch 4 out, rdn & wknd nxt, t.o.*..............................N Wilson 4
See More Castles 5a *plld hrd, alwys rear, outpcd 10th, blnd 12th, p.u. nxt* ....P Atkinson pu
622 True Censation 5a *2nd frm 5th, blnd bdly 14th, not rcvr, p.u. nxt*............................J Saville pu
839 Suny Rose 5a *rear, rdn & strgglng 10th, wll bhnd & p.u. 13th*..................................S Walker pu
7 ran. 15l, 8l, 15l. Time 7m 8.00s. SP 7-4.
A Jackson (Cleveland).

899 Open Maiden Div II

JUST A KING ....G Tuer **1**
sttld 3rd,trckd ldr 14th,rdn 3 out,2l down whn lft clr 2 out
698 **Another Delight 5a ....L Donnely** **2**
trckd ldr, disp 3rd-8th, mstk 13th, wknd nxt, lft 2nd 2 out
777[3] **Malenski (Ire) ....P Millington** **3**
(fav) ld/disp, ld 8th, 2l up whn ran out & u.r. 2 out, rmntd
3 ran. Dist, dist. Time 7m 9.00s. SP 3-1.
Miss G Poad (Bedale).
N.E.

CURRE
Howick
Saturday April 5th
FIRM

900 Members

637[5] **SEBASTOPOL ....D Stephens** **1**
(fav) prom, ld 15th, hrd rdn 2 out, just hld on
715 **Kingfisher Bay (v).......................J Price** **2**
ld to 4th, effrt to ld 11-15th, rallied und pres flat
640[4] Willow Belle (Ire) 5a *ld 8-11th, cls 3rd whn s.u. bnd aft 15th*.....................................S Shinton su
717 Priesthill (Ire) *ld 4-8th, last whn u.r. aft 11th* ....Miss E Crawford ur
4 ran. ½l. Time 6m 44.00s. SP Evens.
Derrick Page (Curre).

901 Interlink Restricted Div I (12st)

298 **MOSTYN ....Miss P Gundry** **1**
cls up,ld 13th-3 out, qcknd to ld agn flat
635[3] **Cosa Nostra ....K Cousins** **2**
(fav) disp to 13th, effrt to ld 3 out, hdd & not qckn flat
641[1] **Yarron King ....I Johnson** **3**
hld up last, wll bhnd 6th, sn t.o., tk remote 3rd post
634[3] Colonel Frazer (Ire) *chsd ldng pair, wknd 11th, fence bhnd 15th, lost 3rd post* ....G Lewis 4
435 Firestarter *n.j.w. wll bhnd frm 9th, t.o.*......S Shinton 5
705 Wissywis (Ire) 12a 5ow *disp mod 3rd til slppd & u.r. bnd aft 9th*.................................J Price ur
6 ran. 2½l, dist, nk, 6l. Time 6m 28.00s. SP 5-2.
R J Weaver (Berkeley).

902 Interlink Restricted Div II (12st)

718[3] **SAVAGE OAK ....E Williams** **1**
(fav) disp til ld 3-9th, lft solo 13th, ambld home
717 **Red Rhapsody 5a.....................J Comins** **2**
disp to 3rd,ld 9th til blnd 13th,rdr lost irons & p.u.,cont
2 ran. Dist. Time 7m 19.00s. SP 1-5.
D Gwyn Williams (Llangeinor).

903 Confined (12st)

714[6] **RUSTY MUSIC ....Miss N Richards** **1**
in tch,pshd alng 11th,2nd 15th,rdn to ld last,jst hld on
749[3] **Noisy Welcome ....D S Jones** **2**
(fav) made most, rdn 2 out, hdd last, rallied flat, just faild
714 **Icecapade (Bel) ....Miss E Jones** **3**
disp to 8th, lost plc nxt, effrt 12th, btn aft 15th
824 Champagne Run *in tch to 10th, sn bhnd, t.o. & p.u. last, dsmntd*.............................R Hawker pu
714 Young India 5a *mstks, alwys rear, t.o. & p.u. 14th* ....T Vaughan pu
294 Lonesome Step 5a *rear, prog to jn ldr 10th, wknd 15th, poor 4th whn p.u. last*..................A Price pu
6 ran. Nk, 30l. Time 6m 35.00s. SP 7-2.
P Richards (Llangibby).

904 Land Rover Open (12st)

714[3] **BEINN MOHR 5a ....E Williams** **1**
(fav) chsd ldr, lft disp 10th til ld 2 out, drvn out
637[3] **Adanac ....A Price** **2**
chsd ldr, lft disp 10th til hdd 2 out, no ext flat
715[3] Prince Nepal *ld, reluc & ran out apr 10th, cont & ref 10th*......................................S Shinton ref
3 ran. 2½l. Time 6m 32.00s. SP 4-6.
Mrs C Howell (Llangeinor).

905 Ladies

716[2] **WAKE UP LUV ....Miss P Cooper** **1**
(fav) made all, clr 12th, unchal

844 **Lucky Ole Son 5ex.................Miss P Jones** 2
chsd wnr to 12th & frm 15th, rdn & no imp
717[4] **Algaihabane (USA) (bl)...........Miss P Gundry** 3
in tch, chsd wnr 12-15th, no imp & btn aft
876 Bankroll *reluc, nrly ref 1st, ref 2nd, cont, ref 3rd* ....Mrs C Chadney ref
4 ran. 10l, 12l. Time 6m 24.00s. SP 11-8.
R Williams (Gelligaer Farmers).

906 Intermediate (12st)

399 **THE LAST MISTRESS 5a ....J Price** 1
made all, clr 3 out, comf
633[1] **French Stick ....E Williams** 2
(fav) trckd wnr, no imp 3 out, btn whn blnd nxt
2 ran. 12l. Time 6m 29.00s. SP 3-1.
A J Cook (Llangibby).

907 Maiden Div I (12st)

640[2] **I'M A BUTE 5a ....J Price** 1
ld to 13th,3rd & outpcd aft,lft 2nd apr last,ld flat,all out
706[5] **Flowerhill ....G Barfoot-Saunt** 2
(fav) prom,ld 14th-3 out,btn whn lft in ld apr last,wknd & hdd flt
643 **Little Ease (Ire) 12a ....S Shinton** 3
bhnd & mstks frm 8th, btn 2 fncs
718 Maytown *cls up,ld 13th-nxt,ld 3 out,clr whn u.r. apr last,sddl slppd* ....A Wintle ur
4 ran. 1½l, dist. Time 6m 41.00s. SP 6-4.
T R R Farr (Ystrad).

908 Maiden Div II (12st)

720 **MOOR HILL LASS (IRE) ....G Lewis** 1
ld 4th, mstk 10th, wll clr 13th, unchal
821 **Miss Dior 5a ....Miss P Gundry** 2
ld 3-4th, chsd wnr aft, no ch frm 13th, fin tired
717 **Lennie The Lion ....J Price** 3
disp mod 3rd frm 7th, no ch frm 12th
719[4] Tommyknocker (Ire) 7a *disp mod 3rd frm 7th, no ch 12th, nvr plc to chal* ....S Shinton 4
718 Al Billal *(fav) jmpd slwly, ld to 3rd, rear & rdn 8th, t.o. & p.u. 3 out* ....Miss P Cooper pu
Berkeley Vale 7a *s.s. t.o. whn ref 2nd*.........J Lloyd ref
718 Hardy Wolf *jmpd slwly 4th, alwys bhnd, stppd aft 11th* ....D S Jones pu
7 ran. Dist, dist, ½l. Time 6m 35.00s. SP 7-2.
P J Roberts (Pentyrch).
J.N.

FITZWILLIAM
Cottenham
Saturday April 5th
FIRM

909 Members

835[2] **STANWICK FARLAP 5a.................T Marks** 1
(fav) ld 5th, rdn & hld on flat
838[4] **Current Attraction 5a.............Miss K Thory** 2
ld to 5th, mstk 3 out, ev ch last, unable qckn
2 ran. ½l. Time 6m 27.00s. SP 1-4.
T F G Marks (Fitzwilliam).

910 Confined (12st)

769[6] **HORACE 3ex...........................W Wales** 1
(fav) ld til apr 10th, ld 13th, kpt on und pres flat
595[3] **Cockstown Lad 5ex ....D Featherstone** 2
in tch, pshd alng & outpcd 12th, rallied 15th,kpt on flat
801[4] **Salmon Mead (Ire) 3ex ....S Sporborg** 3
chsd ldr, ld apr 10th-13th, rdn nxt, btn apr last
3 ran. ¾l, 15l. Time 6m 7.00s. SP 6-4.
Mrs A Vaughan-Jones (West Norfolk).

911 Men's Open

126[1] **MISTER SPECTATOR (IRE) ....S R Andrews** 1
made all, shkn up & drew clr 3 out, hrd hld
710[1] **Over The Edge ....S Sporborg** 2
(fav) chsd wnr, outpcd 3 out, kpt on flat
577[2] **Ok Corral (USA) ....A Greig** 3
in tch, rdn 13th, no ch frm 3 out
3 ran. 5l, 8l. Time 6m 1.00s. SP 9-4.
P Hughes (East Sussex & Romney Marsh).

912 Ladies

707[2] **KUMADA ....Miss S Gritton** 1
ld to 5th, ld 11th-14th, ev ch 3 out, ran on to ld nr fin
780[2] **Cherry Chap ....Miss H Pewter** 2
(fav) prssd ldr, ld 5-11th, ld 14th, jnd 3 out, hdd nr fin
497[2] **Counterbid ....Miss L Rowe** 3
w.w. reluc & rmndr 12th, outpcd 16th, no ch aft
3 ran. Hd, 15l. Time 6m 11.00s. SP 8-1.
Mrs J K Marriage (Essex).

913 Interlink Restricted (12st)

324 **CLAYDONS MONTY ....S R Andrews** 1
(fav) w.w. prog to chal 15th, ld apr 2 out, sn clr, easily
150 **Colonel Kenson ....M Gingell** 2
prom, ld 13th til apr 2 out, sn btn
711[3] Ronaldsway *chsd ldr, ld 10th-13th, 3rd & btn whn u.r. 3 out*..........................D Parravani ur
597[2] Grassington (Ire) *made most til ran wd 10th, last frm 13th,t.o. & p.u. 2 out* ....S Quirk pu
4 ran. Dist. Time 6m 10.00s. SP Evens.
Michael A Johnson (Puckeridge).

914 Open Maiden Div I

COPTIC DANCER 5a...................W Wales 1
(Jt fav) ld 2nd-5th, in tch, wnet 2nd 13th, ld 2 out, rdn clr flat
599[2] **Lantern Spark (Ire) 5a (bl)..........Miss C Tuke** 2
(Jt fav) ld 5th, clr 8th, blnd 3 out, hdd nxt, ev ch last, no ext
210 **Silly Pet ....S J Robinson** 3
ld til hmpd 2nd, jmpd slwly 4th, lost tch 13th, no ch aft
The Whole Lot *u.r. 1st* ....J Buckle ur
4 ran. 3l, 20l. Time 6m 28.00s. SP 5-4.
J J Greenwood (West Norfolk).

915 Open Maiden Div II

439 **ROSCOLVIN (IRE) 7a....................N Bloom** 1
keen hld, hld up, prog 3 out, ld last, qcknd clr flat
550[2] **Rivers End (Ire) ....A Hill** 2
(fav) hld up, went 2nd 11th, ld 2 out, hdd last, one-pcd
479 **Regal Shadow ....W Wales** 3
jmpd rght, ld, sn clr, hdd 2 out, wknd
599 Secret Music *keen hld, lft 3rd at 5th, wknd 16th, t.o.* ....Capt D Parker 4
Fragment (Ire) *1st ride, chsd clr ldr to 9th, t.o. & p.u. 15th* ....R Tillyer pu
775 Flying Fellow (Ire) *3rd whn ran out 5th* ....Miss C Tuke ro
6 ran. 3l, dist, dist. Time 6m 28.00s. SP 6-4.
Mrs Julie Read (Suffolk).
S.P.

ROYAL ARTILLERY
Larkhill
Saturday April 5th
FIRM

916 Members

513[6] **WESSHAUN 5a ....G Chanter** 1
made all, dist clr 13th, unchal
692 **Quote 5a......................Miss A McKeowen** 2
alwys 3rd, dist bhnd whn lft 2nd last
Gunner Stream ....S Greany 3

(fav) alwys 2nd, dist bhnd whn blnd & u.r. last, rmntd
3 ran. Dist, dist. Time 6m 29.80s. SP 5-4.
Mrs A G Sims (Royal Artillery).

917 2½m Open Maiden (5-7yo) (12st)

513 **NICOLINSKY 5a** ....**Mrs S Walwin** 1
last til clsd 3 out, ran on to ld nr fin
Scarra Darragh (Ire) 5a.........**A Charles-Jones** 2
ld to 3rd, 2nd aft, ld 3 out, crwld 2 out & last, hdd nr fin
582 My Moona 5a *plld hrd, ld 3rd til blnd & u.r. 4 out* ....P York ur
Exhibition Prince (Ire) *chsd ldrs to 7th, lost tch nxt, p.u. 4 out*....................M Gorman pu
224 Spring Sabre *hld up, prog 10th, lft 2nd 4 out, ld apr nxt & ran out*....................R Lawther ro
512 Most Vital *(fav) unruly start, lft 30l, ran out 2nd* ....N Mitchell ro
6 ran. Nk. Time 5m 35.00s. SP 12-1.
Mrs S J Biggin (Beaufort).

918 Confined (12st)

659² **INDIAN KNIGHT** ....**M Miller** 1
walked over
C A Green (South & West Wilts).

919 Intermediate (12st)

691³ **STALBRIDGE GOLD 5a**..........**Miss A Goschen** 1
walked over
C J Barnes (Blackmore & Sparkford Vale).

920 4m Mixed Open (12st)

98⁶ **FOSBURY** ....**T Mitchell** 1
(fav) trckd ldr, disp 5 out, ld nxt, sn clr, eased flat
662⁵ **Gallant Effort (Ire)** ....**Miss A Goschen** 2
ld to 5 out, blnd nxt, no ext frm 3 out
744² Wrekin Hill *alwys 3rd, t.o. whn ref 3 out* ....Mrs J Wilkinson ref
662 Pabrey *5s-2s, last, jmpd slwly 10th, p.u. nxt, b.b.v* ....N Mitchell pu
4 ran. 4l. Time 8m 1.00s. SP 2-5.
Mrs Susan Humphreys (Cattistock).

921 Restricted (12st)

824² **MISS MAGIC 5a** ....**F Brennan** 1
disp to 2nd, ld 4th, sn clr, easily
No Reply ....**P York** 2
ld 2nd-4th, cls up to 10th, outpcd aft
661³ Duke Of Lancaster (Ire) (bl) *(fav) last, slw jmp 3rd, wll bhnd whn blnd & u.r. 6th*....................N Sutton ur
3 ran. Dist. Time 6m 11.70s. SP 5-4.
F J Brennan (V.W.H.).

922 2½m Kings Troop Members

HAVANA ....**Sgt C Lloyd** 1
(fav)
Henley ....**Bdr M Watson** 2
Hercules ....**Lt C Farr** 3
Huckleberry 4
Highgate 5
Hockenheim .... ur
Homfray .... pu
Huxley .... pu
8 ran. 3l, 2l. SP 2-1.
Capt A Wood (Royal Artillery).
D.P.

BELVOIR
Garthorpe
Sunday April 6th
GOOD TO FIRM

923 Members

380⁶ **THE DIFFERENCE** ....**M Chatterton** 1
(fav) hld up, ld 7-12th, lvl 2 out, ran on best flat
774² **Neelisagin (Ire)** ....**P Millington** 2
handy, ld 13th, jnd 2 out, just hdd und pres flat
546⁸ **Scole** ....**Miss A Hinch** 3
2nd til 5th, chsd ldrs, ev ch 5 out, not qckn
545⁷ Valatch (bl) *ld to 7th, mstk 11th, lost tch 13th, sn t.o.* ....J Henderson 4
4 ran. 1l, 12l, dist. Time 6m 27.00s. SP 4-7.
M G Chatterton (Belvoir).

924 Confined (12st)

676¹ **WHITE BULLET (USA)** ....**B Pollock** 1
chsg grp, lft in ld 10th, 8l clr 13th, comf
545⁹ **Hostetler** ....**J Stephenson** 2
mid-div, lft 3rd 10th, went 2nd flat, no ch wnr
769 **Joestone** ....**Miss E Godfrey** 3
mid-div, prog to 2nd 3 out, no ext & dmtd flat
834¹ Kemys Commander *ld til f 10th*....................G Smith f
Rather Sharp *prom, 2nd at 11th, fdd, p.u. 3 out* ....K Green pu
544¹ Wise Wizard *(fav) hld up, wll in tch whn u.r. 10th* ....Miss K Gilman ur
6 ran. 15l, nk, dist. Time 6m 21.00s. SP 6-4.
Miss Ruth Matthews (Cottesmore).

925 Ladies

545³ **OKEETEE** ....**Miss L Allan** 1
chsd ldr, ld 12th, 4l clr 14th, ran on strngly 3 out
837¹ **Man Of Mystery** ....**Miss F Hatfield** 2
ld to 11th, chsd wnr aft, unable to cls frm 15th
773³ **Alias Silver** ....**Miss H Irving** 3
(fav) mid-div, 3rd at 12th, nvr going wll, no imp
Fenton Bridge *cls up 8th, sn wknd, bhnd & p.u. 2 out* ....Miss R Tutton pu
397⁷ Walkers Point *rear 8th, t.o. 11th, p.u. 2 out* ....Miss K O'Neill pu
Drawn'N'quartered *mid-div, in tch to 14th, wll btn whn p.u. last*....................Mrs J Dawson pu
474 Remalone 5a *mid-div to 5th, sn rear, t.o. 11th, p.u. 3 out*....................Mrs C McCarthy pu
7 ran. 5l, 12l. Time 6m 12.00s. SP 5-2.
B T Crawford (South Nottinghamshire).

926 Men's Open (12st)

587⁹ **KINO** ....**A Martin** 1
chsng grp, ld 13th, sn in cmmnd, ran on well
389² **Mister Main Man (Ire)** ....**S Sporborg** 2
prom, 3rd 6th-12th, went 2nd apr 2 out, ran on one-pcd
771¹ **Coolvawn Lady (Ire) 5a 7ex**.............**S Walker** 3
cls up, 2nd at 13th, no ext frm 2 out
769³ Youcat (Ire) *ld at gd pace to 12th, wknd nxt, kpt on frm 2 out* ....I Marsh 4
836⁴ Old Money 7ex *nvr bttr than mid-div, no dang* ....A Pickering 5
494⁹ Copper Thistle (Ire) 7ex *(fav) mid-div, nvr going wll, nrst fin*....................R Hunnisett 6
771 Pancratic *alwys rear, no imp, p..u 8th*....C Millington pu
769 Kiltroum (Fr) *hrd hld in rear, no rspns whn let go 4th, p.u. 10th* ....P Millington pu
Fighting Mariner *prom, cls 2nd at 6th, grad lost tch, p.u. 3 out*....................John Pritchard pu
Delvin Spirit (Ire) 5a *alwys bhnd, p.u. 10th*...M Hewitt pu
10 ran. 3l, 5l, 20l, 12l, 2l. Time 6m 13.00s. SP 20-1.
Andrew J Martin (Heythrop).

927 Restricted

839¹ **ANDALUCIAN SUN (IRE)** ....**G Maloney** 1
hld up, prog to 2nd at 11th, ld 13th, prssd 3 out, hld on wl
372⁷ **Castle Shelley (Ire)** ....**R Smith** 2
prom, 2nd 14th, chal frm 3 out, ev ch last, just faild
374 **Strong Account (Ire)** ....**A Tutton** 3

ld to 2nd, cls up, ev ch 4 out, outpcd apr nxt
Kingeochy *chsd ldrs to hlfwy, lost tch 12th, no dang aft* ......M Hewitt 4
770 Tiderunner (Ire) *(fav) alwys mid-div, nvr dang* ......S Walker 5
Ha-To-Siee (Ire) *cls up 6th, wknd 9th, p.u. 12th* ......S R Andrews pu
Lucky Landing (Ire) *ld 3rd-12th, wknd rpdly, no ch whn p.u. 3 out* ......A Martin pu
Statfold Solva 5a *prom to 6th, sn bhnd, t.o. & p.u. 10th* ......B Pollock pu
451[1] Duncaha Hero *rear 4th, t.o. 8th, p.u. 10th* ......Miss G Barrow pu
9 ran. Hd, 20l, 20l, 8l. Time 6m 22.00s. SP 5-2.
A Witcomb (Quorn).

928 Open Maiden (5-7yo)

GOLDEN STAR (IRE) ......Maj M Watson 1
(fav) ld 4th-6th, steadied, lft clr 5 out, ran on well
774 **Gold Sword ......John Pritchard** 2
mid-div hlfwy, 4tha t 12th, went 2nd 3 out, not rch wnr
549 **Nanda Devi ......J Knowles** 3
mid-div, lost tch 10th, ran on onepcd
654[4] Village Remedy 5a *ld to 3rd, chsd ldrs aft, 5l 3rd whn f 2 out, rmntd* ......A Tutton 4
886[2] Kabancy *prom, ld 6th, going wll whn f 5 out* ......P Millington f
479 Royal Darkness (Ire) *mid-div, u.r. 8th* ..Miss F Hatfield ur
776 Flying Linnet 5a *u.r. 1st* ......J Docker ur
777 Teduet *mid-div, t.o. & p.u. 4 out* ......T Marks pu
8 ran. 6l, dist, dist. Time 6m 26.00s. SP 3-1.
R Beauchamp (Quorn).
V.S.

BLACKMORE & SPARKFORD VALE
Charlton Horethorne
Sunday April 6th
GOOD

929 Members

646[2] **QUALITAIR MEMORY (IRE) ......J Tizzard** 1
(fav) mstk 7th,ld to 12th,ld agn 14th,hrd rdn flat,just hld on
862[2] **Earl Boon ......Miss P Curling** 2
mstk 9th,trckd ldrs,ld 12-14th,ralld und pres last,jst fld
434[1] **Sunley Street 5a (bl)......Miss S Vickery** 3
mstk 10th,prssd ldr to 12th,ev ch 3 out,wknd nxt,eased
555[6] Jimmy Cone *t.o. til p.u. 8th* ......Miss J Russell pu
Spar Copse *lost tch 7th, t.o. 12th, p.u. 3 out* ......Maj G Wheeler pu
5 ran. Nk, 20l. Time 6m 54.00s. SP 4-6.
C L Tizzard (Blackmore & Sparkford Vale).

930 Intermediate (12st)

647 **GIGI BEACH (IRE) ......T Mitchell** 1
(fav) hld up, prog 9th, ld 13th, pshd out flat
648[1] **Marion's Own (Ire) ......Miss P Curling** 2
hld up, prog 10th, rdn 15th, chsd wnr 2 out, not qckn last
515[3] **Thegoose ......P King** 3
hld up, prog 6th, wth wnr 13th-15th, onepcd frm 2 out
635[1] Zambrano (USA) 7a *4s-2s, hld up, mstk 9th, outpcd frm 13th, effrt 3 out,no imp* ......A Charles-Jones 4
524[3] Venn Boy *hld up, outpcd 13th, nvr on trms aft* ......J Tizzard 5
743[1] Shared Fortune (Ire) *ld to 13th, sn rdn & btn, wknd 2 out* ......Daniel Dennis 6
Braemount Deer (Ire) *cls up to 8th, sn wknd, t.o. & p.u. 14th* ......C Wilson pu
American Black *chsd ldr to 10th, outpcd 14th, wknd & p.u. 2 out* ......Miss T Cave pu
8 ran. 4l, 4l, 12l, 4l, 15l. Time 6m 59.00s. SP 6-4.
Mrs Susan Humphreys (Blackmore & Sparkford Vale).

931 Men's Open (12st)

646[1] **STRONG CHAIRMAN (IRE) ......T Mitchell** 1
(fav) sttld 3rd, effrt to chs ldr 3 out, ld last, pshd out
552[2] **The Lorryman (Ire) 7ex......N Mitchell** 2
ld, 5l clr 3 out, hdd last, ran on
552[4] **Pintail Bay (v)......N Legg** 3
w.w. in rear, prog 13th, disp 2nd 3 out, wknd aft nxt
308[4] Osmosis 2ow *s.s. alwys t.o.* ......K Nelmes 4
521 Take By Storm (Ire) *chsd ldr til blnd 3 out, not rcvr & p.u. nxt, lame* ......R Payne pu
384[5] Major Mac *in tch til wknd rpdly 13th, t.o. & p.u. 3 out* ......A Charles-Jones pu
6 ran. 1½l, 15l, 2 fences. Time 6m 56.00s. SP 2-7.
J A Keighley (Blackmore & Sparkford Vale).

932 Ladies

737[1] **ARCTIC CHILL (IRE) ......Miss S Vickery** 1
(fav) outpcd,4th & strgglng hlfwy,ran on 13th,ld 2 out,styd on wll
679[2] **Quiet Confidence (Ire) 5a......Miss D Stafford** 2
chsd ldr, ld 9th, clr 13th, hdd 2 out, unable qckn
432 **Sayyure (USA)......Miss T Cave** 3
chsd ldrs, went 2nd 12th-aft 15th, wknd apr 2 out
555[5] Reef Lark *outpcd, last & pshd alng hlfwy, t.o. 3 out* ......Miss A Goschen 4
Clandon Jack (v) *blnd 5th, ld to 9th, steadily wknd 12th, p.u. 3 out* ......Miss P Curling pu
520 Best Left 5a *last til ran out 5th* ..Miss W Southcombe ro
6 ran. 2l, dist, 15l. Time 6m 45.50s. SP 4-5.
M F Thorne & D Hobbs (Blackmore & Sparkford Vale).

933 Open Maiden (5-7yo) (12st)

644[4] **FALSE TAIL (IRE) 7a......Miss P Curling** 1
w.w prog 13th, mstk nxt, ld 15th, rdn & qcknd flat
795 **Kimbross ......N Legg** 2
bhnd,blnd 11th,effrt 13th,rdn 3 out,ran on strngly apr last,lkd 3rd
524 **Lynphord Girl 5a......J Barnes** 3
20s-4s, wth ldr to 13th, lost plc, ran on agn 2 out, fin wll, lkd 2nd
644[2] Rustic Lord 7a *(fav) w.w. prog 13th, ev ch apr 2 out, not qckn last* ......B O'Doherty 4
Barton Rose *schoold rear,mstk 12th,prog 14th,ev ch apr 2 out,wknd last* ......S Slade 5
643[3] Fever Pitch *mstk 3rd, in tch, wth wnr 15th-2 out, wknd rpdly* ......D Alers-Hankey 6
687 Olive Basket 5a *prom, ld 13th-15th, wknd apr 2 out* ......Miss W Southcombe 7
525[6] Wild Weather *mstk 8th, alwys rear, last & lost tch whn p.u. 15th* ......Miss S Vickery pu
437 Fleeced *last frm 9th, t.o. & p.u. 12th* ......C Wilson pu
526 Noble Comic *w.w. trckd ldrs going wll 14th, wknd rpdly & p.u. 2 out* ......J Tizzard pu
513 Carnelia 5a *made most to 13th, sn wknd, t.o. & p.u. 2 out* ......Miss A Goschen pu
642 Lady Mouse 5a *jmpd slwly 6th, prom to 8th, rear whn blnd 11th & p.u.* ......Miss T Cave pu
12 ran. 2l, 1½l, 2l, 2l, 15l, ½l. Time 7m 5.00s. SP 7-2.
J A Keighley (Blackmore & Sparkford Vale).

934 Open Maiden (8yo+) (12st)

647 **WHITMORE ......J Tizzard** 1
prom,chsd ldr 9th,15l down 3 out,ran on to ld last,drvn out
658[2] **Bart's Castle ......Daniel Dennis** 2
8s-3s, jmpd rght, ld, clr 8th, rdn & hdd last, no ext
487 **Stormy Fashion ......Maj G Wheeler** 3
chsd ldr to 9th, sn outpcd, t.o. 3 out
692[5] Mountain-Linnet *mid-div, effrt to chs ldrs 11th, no imp 13th, t.o.* ......Miss A Goschen 4
433 Parapluie 5a *mstk 3rd, alwys bhnd, t.o. 10th* ......Miss B Lloyd 5
792 Nottarex *alwys bhnd, t.o. 10th* ......B Wright 6
526 Warwick Road *chsd ldrs, mstk 5th, lost tch 13th, 6th whn p.u. nxt* ......I Dowrick pu

513[5] Gay Muse 5a *alwys rear, 7th & no ch whn blnd 11th, p.u. 3 out* ....P King pu
439 Chalvey Grove *alwys bhnd, t.o. last whn p.u. 11th* ....Miss S Duckett pu
656[2] Crown Jewel *(fav) chsd ldrs, disp 2nd 10-14th, 3rd whn p.u. 2 out, dsmntd* ....C Wilson pu
10 ran. 2½l, dist, 15l, 1 fence, 3l. Time 6m 53.00s. SP 3-1.
E B S Farmer (Blackmore & Sparkford Vale).

935 Restricted (12st)

525[1] **NEARLY AN EYE** ....**J Tizzard** 1
(fav) hld up,trckd ldr 7th,ld 14th,mstk nxt,shkn up 2 out,rdn out
516[3] **Neville** ....**Miss R David** 2
in tch,outpcd 14th,ran on to chs wnr 2 out,chnc last,no ext
523 **Ruth's Boy (Ire)** ....**Miss P Curling** 3
chsd ldr to 7th, rdn & effrt 13th, no imp 2 out, eased
877 Melling (bl) *mid-div, prog to ld 12th-14th, wknd rpdly apr 2 out* ....N Mitchell 4
523 Celtic Token *t.d.e. ld to 12th, btn frm 14th*....J Barnes 5
523[4] Third Melody 5a *n.j.w. alwys bhnd, t.o. & p.u. 3 out* ....G Weatherley pu
644[1] Jim Crow *in tch to 10th, wknd & p.u. 13th*....P King pu
7 ran. 6l, 20l, 10l, 4l. Time 6m 55.00s. SP 1-2.
Paul K Barber (Blackmore & Sparkford Vale).
J.N.

CHESHIRE FOREST
Tabley
Sunday April 6th
GOOD

936 Members

667[3] **MISS SHAW 5a** ....**Miss K Crank** 1
chsd ldrs, mstk 12th, ld 15th, clr 3 out, comf
Alicante (bl) ....**C Stockton** 2
mstk 1st, prog 7th, chsd wnr apr 2 out, kpt on und pres
727 **JJ's Hope** ....**Miss J Penney** 3
ld, blndrd 9th, hdd apr 14th, wknd, lft poor 3rd 2 out
Melsonby *1st ride, alwys mid-div, outpcd frm 10th, t.o.* ....H Hankey 4
763 Nearctic Bay (USA) 14ow *tubed, alwys bhnd, t.o. frm 7th* ....J Simpson 5
Hogies Delight 23ow *sn t.o., blndrd & u.r. last, rmt* ....P Hogarth 6
725[3] Freddie Fox 3ex *(fav) chsd ldr, ld apr 14-15th, 3rd & wll btn & p.u. 2 out* ....T Garton pu
667 Grindley Brook 16ow (bl) *wll bhnd, poor 6th whn u.r. 12th* ....R Walker ur
Willow Wake 14ow *sn t.o., p.u. 15th* ....Miss H Davenport pu
9 ran. 8l, dist, 25l, dist. Time 6m 36.00s. SP 7-4.
Mrs E Crank (Cheshire Forest).

937 Confined (12st)

667[1] **NODFORM WONDER 3ex** ....**R Bevis** 1
(fav) disp til ld 4th, made rest, drew clr frm 3 out, easily
675[4] **Mr Primetime (Ire) 7ex** ....**N Bannister** 2
chsd ldng pair thruout, rddn apr 2 out, kpt on, nvr nr wnnr
546[2] **Spy's Delight** ....**N Rayner** 3
bhnd, kpt on frm 3 out, wnt 3rd flat, nvr nrr
849 Pamela's Lad *prog to chs ldr 10th, rddn & btn 3 out, lost 2nd run in* ....G Hanmer 4
490[4] Royal Segos *alwys mid-div, blndrd 8th, nvr rchd ldrs* ....A Baillie 5
667 Sirrah Aris (Ire) *alwys mid-div, brf efft to 4th 13th, nvr dang* ....A Crow 6
851[4] Bay Owl *disp ld to 4th, chsd ldr to 9th,wknd nxt,p.u. & dismntd 14th* ....M Worthington pu
670[1] Young Parson *bhnd, rddn 12th, 5th & no ch whn u.r. 15th* ....R Owen ur
762 Mighty Haggis *whppd round start, rear whn f 4th* ....H Hankey f
851 Jo-Su-Ki *wiped round start, t.o. whn tried to ref & u.r. 7th* ....P Saville ur
10 ran. 25l, 3l, ½l, 6l, 3l. Time 6m 27.00s. SP 4-6.
D A Malam (West Shropshire Drag).

938 Land Rover Open (12st)

FARDROSS ....**C Stockton** 1
prom, ld 7th, rddn & drew clr apr last, comf
I Haven't A Buck (Ire) ....**R Burton** 2
trckd ldrs gng wll, wnt 2nd 3 out, sn rddn, onepcd
793[4] **Ideal** ....**J Rees** 3
prom, 4th & rddn apr 2 out, no ext
851[2] Mr Pipe Man (Ire) *(fav) mstks, cls up, blndrd 8th, hrd rddn & btn 2 out* ....A Crow 4
725[1] Le Piccolage *rear, some prog to 5th 2 out, nvr trbld ldrs* ....C Barlow 5
765[4] Mr Tittle Tattle 7ex (bl) *prom to 12th, 5th & wknng 14th, t.o.* ....D Barlow 6
726[4] No More The Fool *in tch, rmmndr 12th, sn outpcd, t.o.* ....L Brennan 7
587 Mhemeanles 7ex (bl) *s.s., t.o. 2nd til f 6th*...F Nichols f
Worleston Farrier *tubed,t.d.e.,ld to 6th,lost plcd nxt,no ch 3 out, p.u. last* ....G Hanmer pu
9 ran. 7l, ¾l, 4l, ½l, 30l, 20l. Time 6m 31.00s. SP 4-1.
G W Briscoe (Wheatland).

939 Ladies

885[1] **HORNBLOWER** ....**Mrs C Ford** 1
(fav) prom, ld 13-16th, rddn to ld apr last, styd on
573[3] **Andros Gale (Ire)** ....**Mrs A Rucker** 2
mid-div & gng wll, prog to ld 16th, hdd apr last, no ext
725[2] **Emerald Knight (Ire)** ....**Miss J Penney** 3
rear, prog to trckd ldrs 15th, onepcd apr 2 out
Taurian Princess 5a *w.w. in tch, 5th & outpcd 3 out, kpt on* ....Miss J Priest 4
724[3] Lady Steel (Ire) 5a *severall postitions, disp ld 14th-nxt, wknd 3 out* ....Miss S Baxter 5
764 Saahi (USA) *chsd ldrs til wknd frm 15th* ....Miss K Swindells 6
669[3] Sooner Still (bl) *prom, ld 6-10th, lost plcd & rddn 12th, no dang aft* ....Miss S Sharratt 7
724[2] Logical Fun (bl) *ld to 6th & agn 10-13th, wknd, p.u. last* ....Miss L Wallace pu
Irish Gent *alwys last, u.r. 16th*....Miss M Maher ur
9 ran. 3l, 7l, 8l, 2l, 12l, 25l. Time 6m 28.00s. SP 4-6.
N J Barrowclough (West Shropshire Drag).

940 Restricted (12st)

753 **ROLIER (IRE)** ....**A Dalton** 1
mid-div, ld apr 2 out, ran on strngly
663[1] **Mr Busker (Ire)** ....**C Barlow** 2
(fav) prom, wnt 2nd 9th, ld 16th til apr 2 out, onepcd
205[1] **Gasmark (Ire)** ....**A Crow** 3
ld, sn clr, jmp lft 6th, hdd 16th, wknd 2 out
726[7] Trojan Pleasure 5a *b.d. 3rd* ....A Jordan bd
671 Plundering Star (Ire) (bl) *f 3rd* ....R Bevis f
670[7] Ballybeggan Parson (Ire) *chsd ldr,blndrd 4th & 8th,sn rddn & lost plc,t.o. & p.u.13th* ....R Burton pu
852 Solar Castle (Ire) *w.w., prog 11th, 4th & bttn 3 out, blndrd last, p.u. flat* ....P McAllister pu
Harvest Singer 5a *bhnd, last & blndrd 7th, f nxt* ....J Mather f
My First Man *chsd ldrs to 5th, wknd 7th, t.o. & p.u. apr 11th* ....S Prior pu
9 ran. 6l, 25l. Time 6m 21.00s. SP 4-1.
T A B Scott (Albrighton).
One fence omitted.

941 Open Maiden Div I

666[3] **CRAFTY GUNNER** ....**C Stockton** 1
(fav) hld up, prog to 2nd 14th, chal on bit last, ld flat, clvly
283[3] **Charlie Kelly** ....**P Taiano** 2
lft in ld 1st, kckd clr 13th, hit nxt, hdd flat, onepcd
768 **Fruit Of Oak (Ire)** ....**T O'Leary** 3

rear, blndrd 6th, prog 11th, wnt 3rd 16th, outpcd 3 out

768 Keep Them Keen (Ire) *mstks, mid-div, lost tch 12th, lft poor 4th 3 out* ....J Mather 4
665[2] Travel Bound *ld til blndrd & u.r. 1st*....D Barlow ur
Admiral Villeneuve *cls up to 5th, bhnd 10th, p.u. 13th* ....D Norlander pu
767 Scally Lass 5a *mstks, lost tch 11th, p.u. aft 13th* ....D Sherlock pu
722[4] Scally Hill 5a *chsd ldr 7th til wknd 13th, t.o. whn f 3 out*....A Mitchell f
721[3] Domani Hill 5a *chsd ldrs, 3rd & wknng 14th, 4th whn f 16th* ....Miss L Wallace f
Katie Kitoff 12a *prom, chsd ldr 7-13th, wknng whn ref & u.r. nxt* ....J Barlow ref
775 Erik The Viking *rear, mstk 6th, prog & in tch whn f 13th*....R Armson f

11 ran. 1l, 20l, 3l. Time 6m 44.00s. SP 5-4.
Mssrs N Salmon / G Jones (South Shropshire).

942 Open Maiden Div II

768[2] **BLANK CHEQUE ....D Coates 1**
ld to 10th, disp ld 15th, bttr jmp last, styd on
347[2] **Adventurus 7a ....A Dalton 2**
w.w., prog 11th, disp 15th til outjmpd last, no ext
768[3] **Nights Image (Ire) ....C Stockton 3**
w.w., prog 3rd 9th, rddn & btn apr 2 out, blndrd last
664[3] Po Cap Eel 5a *prom, disp ld 7th til ld 10th, hdd 15th, wknd*....R Thomas 4
723 Maesgwyn Bach 5a *chsd ldrs to 9th, last & blndrd 14th, p.u. 16th* ....D Sherlock pu
Waddle's Rock (Ire) *jmp slwly 2nd & 3rd, in tch til p.u. 12th*....R Burton pu
Harweld 7a *in tch, jmp slwly 7th, hit 14th, lost tch, p.u. apr 2 out*....T O'Leary pu
854 Riot Lady (Ire) 5a *prom to 11th, rmmdrs 13th, sn bhnd, no ch, p.u. last*....S Prior pu

8 ran. 2½l, 20l, 15l. Time 6m 41.00s. SP 3-1.
J Coates (Pendle Forest & Craven).
S.P.

JEDFOREST
Friars Haugh
Sunday April 6th
GOOD TO FIRM

943 Members

413[5] **LOTHIAN PILOT ....T Oates 1**
2nd frm 10th, ld 3 out, grdly forged clr
561[3] **Press For Action ....Mrs C Amos 2**
(fav) ld til 3 out, no ext
411[9] **Lion Of Vienna ....B Gibson 3**
sn bhnd, tk remote 3rd btw last 2
611 Recluse 7ex (bl) *2nd frm 3rd til lost tch frm 10th* ....R Shiels 4
609 The Laughing Lord *cls 2nd whn u.r. 3rd* Miss R Shiels ur

5 ran. 10l, 25l, 25l. Time 6m 35.00s. SP 3-1.
Mrs B Warres (Jedforest).

944 Intermediate (12st)

560[2] **NOVA NITA 5a ....P Craggs 1**
(fav) hld up, wnt 2nd 9th, ld aft 3 out, comf
584[7] **Eilid Anoir ....R Shiels 2**
ld til aft 3 out, no ext frm nxt
729[1] **Thinkaboutthat (Ire) ....J Muir 3**
nvr gng wll, poor 4th 9th, lft 3rd 4 out
131 Panto Lady 5a *sn bhnd, t.o. whn p.u. aft 9th* ....Miss S Lamb pu
730[1] Mr Cosmo (Ire) *2nd til 9th, btn 3rd whn ran out 4 out* ....J Billinge ro

5 ran. 12l, 25l. Time 6m 35.00s. SP 8-13.
Robert Black (Dumfrieshire).

945 Ladies

609[1] **MUSKORA (IRE) (bl) ....Miss P Robson 1**
(fav) sn wll clr, 15l up 3 out, only 3l up whn lft clr 2 out
231[1] **Parsons Brig ....Miss S Forster 2**
strgglng 10th, wnt 3rd 3 out, lft 2nd 2 out, no ch wth wnnr
609[8] **Schweppes Tonic ....Mrs C Amos 3**
in chsng trio til wknd qckly 4 out
609[3] Very Evident (Ire) *wnt 2nd 4 out, cls wll frm 3 out, 3l down whn u.r. 2 out*....Miss J Bird ur
415 Royal Fife 5a *bhnd by 7th, p.u. aft 9th*..Mrs V Jackson pu
609[7] Emu Park *2nd mstly til wknd 4 out, poor 4th whn u.r. 2 out*....Miss S Dickinson ur

6 ran. 10l, 25l. Time 6m 28.00s. SP 4-7.
Mrs F Percy-Davis (Jedforest).

946 Men's Open

812[1] **TODCRAG ....T Scott 1**
(fav) 2nd til ld 12th, drew clr frm 3 out
812[3] **Staigue Fort (Ire) ....H Naughton 2**
ld, mstk 6th, hdd 12th, outpcd frm 3 out
611[5] **Green Times ....W Ramsay 3**
hld up, wnt cls 3rd 4 out, wknd qckly frm nxt
732[4] Yenoora (Ire) *alwys last, t.o.*....J Ewart 4
562 Miss Jedd 5a *10l 4th whn f 8th*....P Craggs f

5 ran. 6l, 25l, dist. Time 6m 32.00s. SP 1-5.
Mrs M Scott (Border).

947 Restricted

612[1] **CLAYWALLS ....T Scott 1**
(fav) 2nd mstly til ld 3 out, sn clr
607[4] **Ebbzeado Willfurr (Ire) ....J Billinge 2**
3rd mstly frm 8th, wnt 4l clr apr 4 out, no ext frm nxt
734[1] **Donside ....J Walton 3**
jmp wll in ld til apr 4 out, sn btn
607 Ruecastle *in tch til no ext frm 4 out*....M Ruddy 4
766 Marked Card *strgglng in rear frm 12th* ....Miss P Robson 5
613[1] Flypie *cls 3rd whn u.r. 8th* ....P Strang Steel ur

6 ran. 8l, 10l, 4l, 25l. Time 6m 40.00s. SP 6-4.
Ian Hamilton (Tynedale).

948 Open Maiden

418[2] **ARM AH MAN (IRE) ....C Wilson 1**
(fav) slght ld frm 12th, forged clr frm 2 out
613[7] **McNay ....T Scott 2**
ld, mstk 11th, hdd nxt, rmnd cls up, outpcd frm 2 out
614 **Buckaroo 5a ....A Parker 3**
not fluent, in tch til wknd frm 4 out
General Jack *alwys rear*....Miss J Percy 4
623[2] Smart Mover *2nd mstly til 12th, wknd frm 4 out, poor 4th whn u.r. last*....S Brisby ur
614 Up And Running *lost tch by 9th, u.r. 12th* Mrs C Amos ur
614 No Justice *(33's-8's), 3rd whn f 6th* Miss K McLintock f

7 ran. 6l, 25l, 15l. Time 6m 38.00s. SP 10-11.
Miss Elizabeth Robinson (Zetland).

949 Mares Maiden

235 **SHARPLAW 5a ....C Storey 1**
15l 3rd 3 out, strng run apr nxt, ld last, sn clr
417[7] **Allrite Pet 5a....A Parker 2**
(fav) slght ld frm 4 out, lft clr apr 2 out, hdd last, no ext
559 **New Problem 5a....M Smith 3**
ld til 4 out, sn btn
728[3] Houselope Brook 5a *sn wll bhnd*....J Walton 4
729 Fortinas Flyer 5a *p.u. aft 1st*....M Ruddy pu
162 Skye Wedding (Ire) 5a *sn bhnd, t.o. whn p.u. 10th* ....R Westwood pu
234 Fort Alicia 5a *prssd ldr frm 4 out til p.u. lame apr 2 out*....M Bradburne pu
Singing Profit 12a *losng tch whn u.r. 10th*....T Scott ur
815[8] Grey Rock (Ire) 5a *u.r. 2nd*....Miss K Miller ur
506 Palmed Off 5a *6th but just in tch whn f 9th*...A Ogden f

10 ran. 5l, dist, 12l. Time 6m 38.00s. SP 6-1.
J P Elliot (Jedforest).
R.J.

SILVERTON
Black Forest Lodge
Sunday April 6th
GOOD

950 Members

5875 **GREAT GUSTO ....Miss L Blackford** 1
(fav) handy, ld 9th, went clr 12th, easily
7382 **The Copper Key ....T Greed** 2
alwys prom, lost plc 10th, rnwd effrt 13th, tk 2nd apr last
7384 **Seventh Lock ....S Kidston** 3
handy to 10th, went 2nd 14th, outpcd frm 2 out
7374 Grey Guestino *ld to 9th, 2nd to 13th, wknd nxt* ....Miss L Delve 4
5236 Cedars Rosslare *sn last, t.o. & p.u. 13th* ...A Jackson pu
8054 Bert House *sn bhnd, t.o. whn hit marker bnd aft 13th, p.u. aft* ....R Woolacott pu
737 Lady Leigh 5a *plld hrd, t.o. & p.u. 10th* Miss R Francis pu
7 ran. 20l, hd, 20l. Time 6m 10.00s. SP 1-2.
Eddie Rice (Silverton).

951 Confined

ANJUBI ....J Creighton 1
(fav) ld/disp til went clr 10th, v easily
6287 **Querrin Lodge ....T Greed** 2
in tch, disp 7th, 3rd aft, tk 2nd apr last
791 **Pharaoh Blue ....M Shears** 3
in tch, disp 7th, 2nd aft, dmtd apr last
3 ran. 25l, ½l. Time 6m 12.50s. SP 2-5.
W H Whitley (South Devon).

952 G Middleton Ladies

645 **GREAT UNCLE ....Miss T McCurrick** 1
j.w. disp to 3rd, 2nd aft, chal 2 out, ld apr last,ran on wl
7915 **Achiltibuie 11ow ....Miss L Smale** 2
plld hrd, ld 4th til 2 out, outpcd apr last
6285 **Lonesome Traveller (NZ) ....Mrs M Hand** 3
(fav) disp to 3rd, disp 2nd aft, prog 14th, ran on, lkd 2nd
3 ran. 4l, ½l. Time 6m 14.00s. SP 7-4.
Miss T McCurrick (Worcestershire).

953 Land Rover Open (12st)

4552 **MAGNOLIA MAN 4ex ....N Harris** 1
(fav) made all, v easily
793 My Key Silca *n.j.w. blnd 6th, 6l down whn p.u. 2 out, dead* ....G Penfold pu
2 ran. Time 6m 47.00s. SP 1-3.
Mrs D B Lunt (Tiverton Foxhounds).

954 Restricted (12st)

6251 **FLYING MARIA 5a......................C Heard** 1
hld up in tch, prog 11th, ld 14th, kpt on, comf
8044 **Artistic Peace 5a ....G Penfold** 2
ld to 14th, chsd wnr vainly aft
Fifth Fusilier ....Miss C Courtenay 3
1st ride, prom to 13th, lost tch, t.o. 3 out
Twice Knightly *blnd 1st, rdr lost irons & injured, p.u. nxt* ....J Creighton pu
4 ran. 4l, dist. Time 6m 27.50s. SP 4-6.
J S Papworth (South Cornwall).

955 Open Maiden Div I (12st)

HOLCOMBE IDEAL 5a ....L Jefford 1
(fav) made all, blnd 11th, dist clr nxt, unchal
Alicott Lad ....Miss L Smale 2
chsd wnr, dist bhnd 10th, t.o. aft
2 ran. Dist. Time 6m 50.00s. SP 2-5.
J R Wescott (Devon & Somerset Staghounds).

956 Open Maiden Div II (12st)

HOLCOMBE HANDFUL ....Miss L Blackford 1
hld up, prog to 2nd 11th, chal 2 out, qcknd clr
6922 **Get Stepping ....N Harris** 2
(fav) ld til aft 2 out, outpcd aft
626 **Happy Valley 5a ....Miss P Baker** 3
chsd ldr to 10th, 3rd aft, outpcd & no imp 2 out
738 Kenstown (Ire) *sttld 3rd, outpcd 14th, no ext 3 out, lame* ....G Penfold 4
4 ran. 5l, 5l, 20l. Time 6m 23.00s. SP 3-1.
J R Wescott (Devon & Somerset Staghounds).
D.P.

TIVYSIDE
Pantyderi
Sunday April 6th
FIRM

957 Members (12st)

784 **SEA PATROL (bl).......................M Lewis** 1
sttld rear, impvd 10th, ld 2 out, ran on
7175 **Celtic Bizarre 5a................Miss B Barton** 2
(fav) jmpd carefully, ld 8th-2 out, rallied aft
8443 **Mount Falcon ....Miss A Webb** 3
1st ride, ld to 8th, sn wknd
3 ran. 1l, dist. Time 6m 9.00s. SP 6-4.
Miss B M Barton (Tivyside).

958 Confined (12st)

7811 **LANDSKER MISSILE 5a 7ex ....E Williams** 1
(fav) made all, unchal
8434 **No Panic ....Miss B Barton** 2
2nd thruout, nvr near to chal
536 Hill Farm Katie 5a *p.u. aft 4th* ....J P Keen pu
3 ran. 8l. Time 6m 6.00s. SP 1-5.
W J Evans (Pembrokeshire).

959 Intermediate (12st)

7042 **STERLING BUCK (USA) ....D Duggan** 1
(fav) disp to 3 out, in comm aft, easy
7833 **Valiant Friend (bl)................Miss B Barton** 2
disp to 3 out, onepcd aft
2 ran. 2l. Time 6m 19.00s. SP 1-4.
D J Clapham (Cotswold Vale).

960 Men's Open (12st)

8171 **FANTASTIC FLEET (IRE) 7a ....E Williams** 1
walked over
Mrs R Mackness (Cotswold Vale).

961 Ladies

637 **TOUCH 'N' PASS ....Miss P Jones** 1
trckd dlr til lft alone 14th
8441 Ozzie Jones *(fav) ld til ran out 14th* ....Miss L Pearce ro
2 ran. Time 6m 13.00s. SP Evens.
R H P Williams (Llangeinor).

962 Restricted (12st)

8471 **KINLOGH GALE (IRE) (bl) ....E Williams** 1
(fav) lft in ld 2nd, unchal aft
6401 **Top Tor 5a ....T Vaughan** 2
chsd wnr frm 2nd, clsng whn mstk 2 out, no ch aft
7013 How Friendly *ld til u.r. 2nd* ....D Duggan ur
3 ran. 3l. Time 6m 43.00s. SP 5-4.
W J Evans (Pembrokeshire).

963 Maiden Div I (12st)

842 **CULPEPPERS DISH ....A Price** 1
ld to 3 out, lkd hld whn lft in ld nxt, kpt on
8414 **Kerstin's Choice 5a.................P Sheldrake** 2
mid-div thruout, nvr near to chal, lft 2nd 2 out

Mr Ffitch ....G Barfoot-Saunt 3
trckd ldr to 14th, sn wknd, fin tired
541 Lady Romance (Ire) 5a *4th/5th thruout, p.u. bfr last* ....J P Keen pu
Southerncrosspatch *(fav) trckd ldrs, ld 3 out, f 2 out, unlucky* ....D S Jones f
Storm Dai Fence (Ire) 12a *alwys in rear & t.o. whn p.u. 10th*....................................D Lewis pu
6 ran. 5l, dist. Time 6m 11.00s. SP 14-1.
Mrs L A Parker (Tivyside).

964 Maiden Div II (12st)

542 **AFRICAN WARRIOR 12a.............T Vaughan** 1
2nd til ld 3 out, rddn out
543 **Laudation (Ire) 7a ....P Hamer** 2
(fav) wll in rear, jmp rght, rpd prog aft 15th,ev ch last,onepcd
842 **Fridays Child 12a ....E Williams** 3
ld til aft 15th, fdd rpdly
543 Lynnes Daniella (Ire) 5a *ref 3rd* ....M Lewis ref
4 ran. 5l, dist. Time 6m 28.00s. SP 5-1.
R H P Williams (Llangeinor).
P.D.

WEST KENT
Penshurst
Sunday April 6th
FIRM

965 Members

577 **CLEAN SWEEP ....M Jones** 1
(fav) hvly restrained, ld 12th, in comm aft
829 **Huckleberry Friend 5a ....P Blagg** 2
set v sedated pce, hvly restrained, hdd 12th,chsd wnr aft
580 **Cuckoo Pen ....T McCarthy** 3
hld up, efft 4 out, nvr pce to chal
3 ran. 4l, 1l. Time 7m 51.00s. SP 1-3.
Mrs G Drury (West Kent).

966 Confined (12st)

577[6] **WOODY WILL ....Mrs E Coveney** 1
alwys cls up, chal 3 out, ld last, ran on wll
683[2] **Yeoman Farmer ....P Hacking** 2
(fav) hld up, drvn up to chal apr last, hld flat
604[2] **Sky Venture 5ex ....P Bull** 3
trckd ldrs, efft 4 out, kpt on onepce
783[2] Basher Bill *alwys wll in tch, 3rd 3 out, kpt on same pce*...K Giles 4
786[1] Authorship (USA) 5ex *ld 9th, chal 3 out, blndrd & hdd last, not rcvrd*...........................P O'Keefe 5
870 Vultoro *immtly detached, p.u. 3rd*......T Underwood pu
281 Oxbow *ld to 9th, p.u. aft nxt lame*........T McCarthy pu
7 ran. 2l, 1l, 1l, 1l. Time 6m 43.00s. SP 4-1.
Mrs Emma Coveney (Old Surrey & Burstow).

967 Men's Open (12st)

579[3] **ANNIO CHILONE 7ex..................P O'Keefe** 1
trckd ldr, lft disp 12th, lft clr 14th & solo 3 out
484 Green's Van Goyen (Ire) 7ex *ld til p.u. lame 12th* ....T McCarthy pu
828[2] Wednesdays Auction (Ire) *alwys last, lost tch 10th, lft poor 2nd 14th, u.r. 3 out* ....S Garrott ur
683[1] Stede Quarter 7ex *(fav) trcks ldr, lft disp 12th til blndrd 14th & p.u. (dead)*.......................P Bull pu
4 ran. Time 6m 44.00s. SP 5-1.
Mrs Liz Champion (Old Surrey & Burstow).

968 Ladies

831[1] **POLAR ANA (IRE) 5a............Miss S Gladders** 1
(fav) hndy, chal 14th, ld 3 out, pshd out flat
280[4] **Durbo ....Mrs E Coveney** 2
ld to 3rd, cls aft, ld 13th, hdd 3 out, rlld flat, alwys hld
684[2] **Slight Panic 5a ....Miss J Wickins** 3
last, rpd prog to ld 8-10th, prom aft, wknd 3 out
495 Old Dundalk *1st ride, ld 3rd-8th agn 10-13th, fdd aft* ....Miss A Hayes 4
785[1] Serious Money (USA) *sn rear, many slow jmps, t.o. & p.u. aft 13th* ....Miss C Ewart pu
5 ran. 1½l, 25l, 10l. Time 6m 45.00s. SP 5-4.
Mrs P A McIntyre (Ashford Valley).

969 Intermediate (12st)

576 **TAU ....A Warr** 1
chsd ldr 7th, drvn up to chal last, ld flat
682[1] **Kelburne Lad (Ire) ....P Bull** 2
(fav) ld to 2nd agn 6th, 4l up 2 out, mstks last 2, hdd flat
829[1] Rarely At Odds *ld 2nd-6th, wth ldr whn sltly hmp & u.r. 7th* ....Miss A Sansom ur
3 ran. 1½l. Time 6m 44.00s. SP 5-2.
Miss Felicity McLachlan (West Street Tickham).

970 Restricted (12st)

747[1] **BAWNEROSH ....T Underwood** 1
ld to 7th agn 3 out, ran gmly & held on
833[1] **And Why Not ....J Van Praagh** 2
(fav) hld up, chal 3 out, und pres nxt, just held
711 **Abdul Emir ....Mrs L Stock** 3
cls up, ld 7th, mstk 10th, hdd 4 out, fdd
787[1] Target Time 5a *alwys last, jmp slwly 14th, t.o. aft, ran on frm 2 out* ....K Giles 4
4 ran. 1l, 20l, 10l. Time 6m 49.00s. SP 5-2.
T D B Underwood (Garth & South Berks).

971 Open Maiden (12st)

833 **CELTIC REG ....M Jones** 1
wth ldr, bndrd 6th, ld 9th, prssd aft til kpt bttr frm 2 out
498[3] **Mirror Image 5a..........................N King** 2
(fav) ld to 9th, prssd wnnr aft til no ext 2 out
Three B's 5a ....P Blagg 3
in tch in rear til outpcd 14th, lft poor 3rd aft 3 out
582 Squerrey *in tch in rear,3rd & rddn 14th,no ch whn p.u. lame aft 3 out* ....P Bull pu
686 Spanish Pal (Ire) *trckng ldrs whn hmp & f 5th* ....Miss S Gladders f
5 ran. 5l, 1 fence. Time 7m 14.00s. SP 2-1.
R Thomson (Ashford Valley).
G.Ta.

KELSO
Monday April 7th
GOOD TO FIRM

972 3m 1f Holland & Holland Buccleuch Cup Maiden Hunters' Chase Class H

563[1] **GALLANTS DELIGHT 11.3 7a 1ow . . Mr A Robson** 1
chsd ldrs, hit 12th, hdwy 14th, chased lder and blnd 3 out, ld last, styd on well.
611[1] **Ensign Ewart (Ire) 11.9 5a..........Mr C Storey** 2
(fav) held up, steady hdwy 14th, chsd ldrs 3 out, effort and rdn next, styd on same pace.
763[1] **Pennine View 11.9 5a.................Mr R Ford** 3
chsd ldr, ld 7th, rdn 2 out, hdd and hit last. wknd run-in.
607 Cool Yule (Ire) 11.7 7a *hit 1st, alwys rear, bhnd from 8th*...Mr B Gibson 4
Lothian Commodore 11.7 7a *in tch, rdn along 15th, soon wknd*.......................Captain A Ogden 5
418[1] Storm Alive (Ire) 11.7 7a *chsd ldrs, hit 9th and soon bhnd, blnd 11th, soon t.o.*.......................Mr T Scott 6
606 Hula 11.7 7a *in tch, hdwy 13th, rdn along and blnd 16th, 4th when b.d. 3 out*.............Mr M Bradburne bd
607[2] Canister Castle 11.9 5a *chsd ldrs, rdn along and blnd 15th and next, wknd and p.u. before 3 out.* Mr R Shiels pu
813[1] Lindon Run 11.7 7a *chsd ldrs, hit 12th, rdn along and blnd 15th, soon wknd and hmpd 3 out, bhnd when f last*..................................Mr R Morgan f

584[6] Tumlin Oot (Ire) 11.9 5a *held up, hit 4th, hdwy to chase ldrs and blnd 8th, blunded 13th and soon bhnd, t.o. when p.u. 3 out* .... Mr N Wilson pu
612 Seymour Fiddles 11.2 7a *mstks, in rear till f 11th.* .... Mr M Ruddy f
732 Leannes Man (Ire) 11.7 7a *ld to 7th, chsd ldr, blnd 9th, driven along in 3rd when f 3 out.* ..... Mr Chris Wilson f
12 ran. 8l, 5l, 19l, 3½l, dist. Time 6m 14.40s. SP 9-2.
Mrs C Johnston

973 3m 1f Stefes Champion Hunters' Chase Class H

NOW YOUNG MAN (IRE) 11.7 7a Mr Chris Wilson 1
in tch till outpcd and rdn along 15th, styd on apr last, ridden run-in to ld near fin.
590[2] **Royal Jester 11.9 5a .... Mr C Storey** 2
(fav) chsd ldr, rdn along apr 3 out, styd on approaching last, ridden and ev ch run-in, no ext near fin.
492[2] **Kushbaloo 12.0 7a .... Mr A Parker** 3
ld, rdn along and blnd 2 out, hdd last 50 yards, no ext.
426[1] Dark Dawn 12.0 7a *held up, steady hdwy 12th, chal and ev ch 2 out, wknd last* .... Miss Lorna Foxton 4
583[2] Little Wenlock 11.9 5a *chsd ldrs till p.u. lame after 9th, dead* .... Mrs V Jackson pu
5 ran. ½l, 2½l, 19l. Time 6m 22.60s. SP 13-2.
Grant C Mitchell

HEYTHROP
Heythrop
Tuesday April 8th
FIRM

974 Members

819[4] **THE COUNTRY TRADER .... J Borradaile** 1
mstk 5th, chsd ldr 8th, ld last, ran on wll, dism aft fin
372 **Tranquil Lord (Ire) .... D Smith** 2
(fav) mstks, w.w. prog 14th, ld aft 2 out, hdd last, no ex, lame
820[2] **Colonel Fairfax .... Miss K Matthews** 3
wll bhnd, prog 10th, hit 13th, ev ch 2 out, onepcd appr last
Sad Old Red *ld, 10l clr 14th, blnd badly 3 out, jmpd lft & hdd nxt, fdd* .... M Davis 4
373[2] Country Brew 5a *chsd ldr to 8th, last frm 12th, rallied & ch 2 out, onepcd* .... C Marriott 5
5 ran. 3½l, 1l, 10l, 10l. Time 6m 55.00s. SP 13-2.
J Borradaile (Heythrop).

975 Intermediate (12st)

653[1] **COUNT BALIOS (IRE) .... P Howse** 1
(fav) chsd ldr, ld appr last, rdn clr flat
749[2] **Kiltrose Lad (bl) .... M Harris** 2
ld, mstk 7th & 10th, hdd appr last, onepcd und press
760 **Horcum .... M Frith** 3
alwys last, lst tch 12th, t.o.
3 ran. 2½l, dist. Time 6m 39.00s. SP 4-9.
M H Wood (V.W.H.).

976 4m Sporting Life Open

285[3] **KETTLES 5a .... A Phillips** 1
(fav) hld up wll bhnd,prog 15th,blnd 20th,chal last,sn ld,styd on
819[3] **Granville Grill .... J Deutsch** 2
t.d.e. jmpd lft, ld til hdd sn aft last, no ex
671[1] **Scarlet Berry 5a .... Julian Pritchard** 3
prom, chsd ldr 7th, ev ch frm 3 out, kpt on onepcd und press
705[2] January Don (bl) *chsd ldrs, rmdrs 6th, 4th & drvn 15th, no ch frm 19th* .... G Barfoot-Saunt 4
745[2] Royle Speedmaster *alwys bhnd, poor 6th whn p.u & dismntd 16th* .... T Lacey pu
880[3] Hackett's Farm *last frm 4th, t.o frm 14th, p.u. 2 out* .... A Dalton pu
671[2] Autumn Green (Ire) (v) *chsd ldr 4-7th, sn lst pl, no ch & j.r. 13th, p.u. 20th* .... R Burton pu
7 ran. 2½l, ½l, dist. Time 8m 17.00s. SP 2-1.
Mrs M R Daniell (Ledbury).

977 3m 5f Sporting Life Ladies

371[1] **MAKING TIME 5a .... Miss T Habgood** 1
walked over
R Shepherd (Bicester With Whaddon Chase).

978 Confined (12st)

596[2] **SEVERN INVADER 3ex .... Miss H Gosling** 1
(fav) trkd ldr frm 6th, ld aft 2 out, sn clr, unextnd
370 **Grand Value .... C Wadland** 2
ld til hdd aft 2 out, no ex
Lad Lane .... J Borradaile 3
chsd ldr til j.s. 6th, last aft, t.o. frm 3 out
3 ran. 3½l, dist. Time 6m 42.00s. SP 1-6.
Mrs E Gosling (Bicester With Whaddon Chase).

979 Open Maiden Div I

654 **SALMON POUTCHER 5a .... J Trice-Rolph** 1
(fav) ld to 3rd & 11-14th, ld appr 2 out, clr last, easily
833 **What-A-Brave Run .... A Charles-Jones** 2
keen hold, ld 3-11th & 14-2 out, sn rddn & btn
2 ran. 20l. Time 7m 2.00s. SP 1-2.
Mrs J L Phelps (Berkeley).

980 Open Maiden Div II

761 **FRACTION .... A Martin** 1
(Jt fav) disp ld til ld appr last, rddn & drw clr flat
The Chairman (Ire) .... J Trice-Rolph 2
(Jt fav) disp ld til appr last, hung lft last, nt run on
2 ran. 2½l. Time 7m 20.00s. SP 4-5.
Mrs F J Marriott (Heythrop).
S.P.

CHEPSTOW
Wednesday April 9th
FIRM

981 3m Earthstoppers Hunters' Chase Class H

737[2] **SOME-TOY 11.8 7a .... Miss L Blackford** 1
steady hdwy from 13th, ld after next, shaken up and ran on well run-in.
889[2] **Rusty Bridge 11.11 7a .... Mr O McPhail** 2
(fav) ld to 10th, soon pushed along, outpcd apr 14th, rallied and hit 4 out, chsd wnr 2 out, one pace run-in.
679[3] **Gambling Royal 11.5 7a .... Dr P Pritchard** 3
soon tracking ldr, chal 8th till ld 10th, hdd after 14th, wknd after 3 out.
825[1] What A To Do 11.8 7a *in tch till wknd 7th, lost touch from 10th* .... Miss L Sweeting 4
807[2] Catch The Cross 11.12 7a (bl) *in tch 7th, styd on 14th, soon wknd* .... Mrs A Hand 5
376[5] Sonofagipsy 11.5 7a (bl) *prom till wknd 7th, n.d. after.* .... Mr N R Mitchell 6
6 ran. 4l, 22l, 9l, ½l, 7l. Time 6m 0.00s. SP 5-1.
John Squire

LUDLOW
Wednesday April 9th
FIRM

982 3m Chase Meredith Memorial Trophy Hunters' Chase Class H

874[2] **MY NOMINEE 11.12 7a (bl) .... Mr R Burton** 1
ld to 2nd, regained ld next, made rest, hrd pressed from 4 out, all out.
382[3] **Cape Cottage 11.12 7a .... Mr A Phillips** 2

held up in tch, chsd wnr from 7th, str chal from 4 out, kept on.
591[1] **Fox Pointer 12.0 5a..................Mr J Jukes** 3
(fav) in tch, chsd wnr from 5th till dived 7th, wknd apr 3 out.
Candle Glow 11.7 7a *ld 2nd to next, chsd wnr after till 5th, rdn 13th, wknd 15th*...............Mr S Morris 4
745[1] Wild Illusion 11.12 7a *bhnd, hdwy apr 12th, wknd 14th, t.o. when p.u. before 4 out*..........Mr F Hutsby pu
572[3] Judy Line 11.2 7a *held up, well bhnd from 10th, t.o. when p.u. before 4 out*..................Mr S Shinton pu
6 ran. Hd, 12l, 5l. Time 5m 57.80s. SP 11-4.
D E Nicholls

ASCOT
Saturday April 12th
GOOD TO FIRM

983 3m 110yds 'Merlin' Novices' Hunters' Chase Class H

577[1] **STRUGGLES GLORY (IRE) 12.0 7a 7ow ...Mr D C Robinson** 1
(fav) cl up, ld 10th, made rest, styd on well.
888[5] **Lurriga Glitter (Ire) 11.7 7a (bl)......Mr R Wakley** 2
chsd ldrs, blnd 12th, lost pl next, hdwy 4 out, styd on well from 2 out, mstk last, no impn.
376[1] **Capo Castanum 12.7 7a.............Mr A Wintle** 3
alwys handy, chsd wnr from 11th till lost pl apr last, one pace.
Balasani (Fr) 11.9 5a *mstk 1st, bhnd till styd on from 2 out, nvr nrr*..........................Mr A Sansome 4
600[2] Berrings Dasher 11.7 7a *alwys handy, driven and wknd from 3 out*.......................Mr M Watson 5
680[1] Northern Village 12.0 7a *with ldrs early, soon held up in mid div, mstk 11th, blnd 15th, soon wknd.* ....Mr D Alers-Hankey 6
514[1] Apatura King 12.0 5a 5ow *alwys bhnd*...Mr T Mitchell 7
830[1] Bilbo Baggins (Ire) 11.7 7a *alwys bhnd, t.o.* ....Mr M Gorman 8
888 Tom's Gemini Star 12.0 7a *held up in tch, hdwy to chase ldrs from 10th, rdn along 15th, driven and held in 4th when blnd and u.r. 2 out*...........Mr E James ur
380[2] Elmore 11.11 3a *mid div, dropped rear 10th, mstk 12th, p.u. before 3 out*..................Mr P Hacking pu
679[1] Poors Wood 12.2 5a *pulld hrd, held up, p.u. before 10th, dismntd*............................Mr T McCarthy pu
796[1] Amadeus (Fr) 11.7 7a *ld to 10th, trckd ldrs, rdn 14th, soon wknd, t.o. when p.u. before last*....Mr M Gingell pu
592 Loyal Gait (NZ) 11.9 5a *mid div when blnd badly 4th (water), bhnd from hfwy, t.o. when p.u. before 15th.* ....Mr J Trice-Rolph pu
977[1] Making Time 11.2 7a *held up, hdwy 10th, mstk 12th, soon wknd, p.u. before 3 out*........Mr Andrew Martin pu
14 ran. 5l, 9l, 11l, 1½l, 2l, 3l, dist. Time 6m 17.20s. SP 3-1.
D C Robinson

BICESTER WITH WHADDON CHASE
Kingston Blount
Saturday April 12th
GOOD TO FIRM

984 Pegasus Members

764[3] **RUNNING FRAU 5a ....Miss M Maher** 1
(fav) trckd ldrs, outpcd 14th, ran on 3 out, ld apr last, sn clr
650[3] **Tompet ....J Connell** 2
ld aft 5th til reluc & hdd 14th, sn outpcd, kpt on agn flat
Celtic Caber ....G Opperman 3
ld to aft 5th, ld 14th til apr last, onepcd
766 Bunny Hare (Ire) *last frm 7th til u.r. 13th*....G Thomas ur
4 ran. 5l, ½l. Time 6m 40.00s. SP 11-10.
Sir Sanderson Temple (Ledbury).

985 Members

369 **CAWKWELL DEAN ....R Sweeting** 1
(fav) j.w. made all, clr 14th, eased flat
826[4] **Sparnova 5a (bl).........................T Illsley** 2
mstks, chsd wnr to 5th & frm 10th, sn rdn, no imp
653[3] **Cool Rascal 5a ....L Lay** 3
sn pshd alng, chsd wnr 5-10th, rdn & wknd 11th, t.o.
820[1] Royal Exhibition *last & out of tch til u.r. bnd aft 8th* ....Miss C Ramsey ur
4 ran. 12l, dist. Time 6m 25.00s. SP Evens.
Neale Hutchinson (Bicester With Whaddon Chase).

986 Confined (12st)

579 **VALIBUS (FR) 8ex.....................P Scouller** 1
ld to 6th, prom, jnd ldr 14th, ld 3 out, hld on well
773[2] **Kites Hardwicke ....Mrs C Behrens** 2
w.w. prog 12th, clsd 3 out, chal last, not qckn flat
577[3] **Mountainous Valley (Ire) ....S R Andrews** 3
(fav) prom, ld 13th, jnd nxt, hdd 3 out, no ext nxt
978[2] Grand Value *ld 6-11th, lost tch frm 13th, t.o.* ....C Wadland 4
877 Penly *mstks, trckd ldrs til 4th & outpcd aft 13th, t.o.* ....John Pritchard 5
759[4] Button Your Lip *chsd ldrs, outpcd frm 9th, brf effrt 14th, sn t.o.*..........................Mrs J Enderby 6
824 Chinaman *wth ldr whn mstk 6th, sn lost plc, t.o. 13th* ....A Tutton 7
820 Sutton Lass 5a *jmpd slwly, sn bhnd, t.o. 13th, p.u. 2 out*.......................................R Lawther pu
756[1] Royal Dadda *svrl slw jmps, sn pshd alng, rdn & no prog 10th, p.u. 15th*...............................A Hill pu
Buladante (Ire) *in tch to 10th, rear nxt, eased & p.u. 13th*...P York pu
10 ran. 1l, 3½l, dist, 6l, 1l, 20l. Time 6m 21.00s. SP 6-1.
P A D Scouller (Garth & South Berks).

987 Men's Open

679[5] **TOM FURZE ....M Batters** 1
keen hld, ld 6th, jnd brfly 15th, clr 2 out, comf
771[4] **Penlet ....John Pritchard** 2
(fav) chsd wnr 11th,ev ch 15th,rdn whn slppd bnd aft 3out,sn btn
Lofty Deed (USA) ....A Charles-Jones 3
jmpd v slwly, lost tch 13th, t.o.
487[5] Trina's Cottage (Ire) *ld to 6th, wknd 13th, t.o.* B McKim 4
4 ran. 6l, 25l, 20l. Time 6m 26.00s. SP 5-2.
Mrs K Buckett (Hursley Hambledon).

988 Ladies

546[5] **GREEN ARCHER ....Mrs T Hill** 1
lft 2nd 4th, rdn 11th, jnd & lft wll clr 14th, unchal
371[4] **Finally Fantazia 5a...............Miss K Holmes** 2
lft 3rd at 4th, rdn & no imp ldrs 12th, lft poor 2nd 14th
819[5] **Icky's Five ....Mrs J Parris** 3
alwys outpcd, t.o. 11th, lft remote 3rd 14th
652 Country Lord *jmpd vry slwly, alwys t.o., tk wrng course aft 13th,rtrcd* ....Mrs S Walwin 4
850[1] Hiram B Birdbath (bl) *lft in ld 4th, jnd whn blnd & u.r. 14th*..................................Miss A Plunkett ur
818[2] West Orient *clr ldr til ran out 4th* ....Miss S Hiatt ro
Fundy (Ire) *(fav) in tch til followed ldr out at 4th* ....Miss T Spearing ro
7 ran. 25l, 25l, 2 fences. Time 6m 21.00s. SP 9-2.
Mrs S D Walter (Vale Of Aylesbury).

989 Intermediate (12st)

873[1] **JULY SCHOON ....T Underwood** 1
hld up,prog 9th,not qckn 14th,ran on & ld aft 2 out,sn clr
516[1] **Sybillabee 5a..........................M Batters** 2
(fav) prom, prssd ldr 7-13th, outpcd nxt, ran on one-pcd 2 out
446 **Apple Nicking ....A Hill** 3
hld up,prog 10th,ld 15th-aft 2 out,btn whn jmpd slwly last
Haydon Hill 5a *s.s. sn prom, mstk 3rd, ld 6-15th, wknd 2 out* ....Miss H Gosling 4

760[4] Dixons Homefinder *ld to 4th, lost plc aft nxt, bhnd frm 12th, t.o.* ....A Barnett 5
975[3] Horcum *chsd ldrs, wknd aft 13th, sn bhnd* C Wadland 6
826[3] Linlake Lightning 5a (bl) *ld 4-6th, bhnd frm 10th, t.o.* ....Miss H Irving 7
7 ran. 12l, 1l, 8l, 25l, 1l, 20l. Time 6m 22.00s. SP 3-1.
T D B Underwood (Worcestershire).

990 Maiden

549[3] **UPTON LASS (IRE) 5a........L Lay** 1
prom, ld aft 13th, rdn clr aft 2 out, kpt on
756 **Bet A Lot 5a........Miss T Honeyball** 2
hld up last pair,ran on 14th,went 2nd last,given no ch
821[2] **Connie Foley........S Green** 3
rear, prog 11th, chsd wnr 15th, no imp 2 out, wknd last
712[2] Loch Irish (Ire) 5a *(fav) cls up, chsd wnr aft 13th, rdn & btn aft 15th* ....S R Andrews 4
928[4] Village Remedy 5a *ld to 13th, wknd nxt* ......A Tutton 5
485[6] Pukka Sahib *prssd ldr, ld brfly 13th, wknd nxt* ....Miss H Irving 6
Totally Optimistic *blnd 5th, last whn blnd 6th & p.u.* ....C Wadland pu
451 Bobbin Lace 5a *in tch whn nrly ref 6th, p.u. nxt* ....Mrs C McCarthy pu
60 Bit Of A Do *w.w. prog whn mstk 10th,sn rdn,in tch 14th,wknd & p.u.3 out*........A Hill pu
686 Psamead 7a (bl) *cls up to 9th, wll bhnd whn nrly ref 14th, p.u. nxt* ....P York pu
Crested Eye 5a *schoold in rear, in tch aft 13th, eased & p.u. nxt*........J Docker pu
11 ran. 6l, 15l, 2l, 3l, 3l. Time 6m 34.00s. SP 6-1.
Mrs M Kimber (Grafton).
J.N.

BRAES OF DERWENT
Tranwell
Saturday April 12th
FIRM

991 Members

812[4] **WILL TRAVEL (IRE) 7ex........C Bennett** 1
(fav) ld til 5th,disp ld 8-9th,ld nxt,1/2l up 4out-2 out,kpt on
813[4] **Buckaneer Bay........Miss A Hicks** 2
cls 2nd til ld 5th,jnd 8-9th,hdd nxt,ev ch 4 out,not rch ldr
565[2] Tolmin *n.j.w., 6l last & u.r. 3rd* ..Miss M Fotheringham ur
3 ran. 1l. Time 6m 19.00s. SP 1-2.
D Tate (Braes Of Derwent).

992 Intermediate (12st)

810[2] **SISTER SEVEN (IRE) 5a........Miss D Laidlaw** 1
walked over
M Walton (College Valley & N N'land).

993 Men's Open

812[5] **TARTAN TORNADO ....P Johnson** 1
towrds rear,wnt 3l 4th 9th,ld 11th,jnd last,ld last 100yds
Music Box........C Wilson 2
alwys prom, 2l 2nd 4 out, disp ld last, no ext last 100yds
946[4] **Yenoora (Ire)........J Ewart** 3
rear div 1st ctt, 4th 3 out, styd on poor 3rd run in
561[6] Winnie Lorraine 5a *(fav) disp ld 3rd-10th,hdd nxt,no imprssn frm 3 out,wknd run in* ....T Scott 4
810[4] Strong Measure (Ire) *disp ld 3rd-10th,hdd nxt,mstk & wknd into 4th 14th,last 3out* ....R Morgan 5
5 ran. 2l, 25l, 4l, 5l. Time 6m 4.00s. SP 3-1.
W J Laws (Tynedale).

994 G Middleton Ladies

992[1] **SISTER SEVEN (IRE) 5a........Miss D Laidlaw** 1
(fav) hld up 1st ctt,smth hdwy frm 14th to ld 3 out,ran on wll
Steele Justice........Miss P Robson 2
ld 8th til jnd 10th, hdd 3 out, outpcd & 3l down nxt
945 **Emu Park........Miss S Dickinson** 3
lft in ld 4th til hdd 6th, ev ch til demoted to 3rd 3 out
945[3] Schweppes Tonic *cls up til ld 6th, hdd 8th, ev ch 14th til wknd 4th 3 out*........Mrs V Jackson 4
894[4] Blakes Folly (Ire) *ld 3rd til mstk & u.r. nxt* ....Mrs K Hargreave ur
5 ran. 3l, ½l, ½l. Time 6m 11.00s. SP 4-5.
M Walton (College Valley & N N'land).

995 Restricted (12st)

694[4] **MASTER CROZINA ....P Cornforth** 1
j.w., ld/disp 5-8th, 1l up 9-14th, drew clr frm 2 out
563 **Sumpt'n Smart ....L Morgan** 2
disp ld 5-8th, mnly 1l 2nd 9-14th, outpcd frm 2 out
607 **The Caffler (Ire)........W Ramsay** 3
(fav) trckd ldrs 1st ctt, disp 3l 3rd 14th, mstk & outpcd 2 out
947 Flypie *rear div 1st ctt, wnt 4th 2 out, no impssn on ldrs apr last*........P Strang Steel 4
947[4] Ruecastle *disp ld 2nd-3rd, hdd nxt, 3l 3rd 9-14th, outpcd frm nxt*........M Ruddy 5
944 Panto Lady 5a *n.j.w., 20l last 9th, lost tch 11th, t.o. & p.u. 3 out* ....Miss S Lamb pu
6 ran. 7l, 5l, 3l, 15l. Time 6m 5.00s. SP 3-1.
J Cornforth (York & Ainsty North).

996 Open Maiden

809[2] **NEWBRANO 5a........I Carmichael** 1
ld 3rd-5th, lft 2nd 13th, qcknd to ld 3 out, hld on gamely
734[2] **Fast Fun ....R Morgan** 2
(fav) mid-div 1st ctt,hdwy & lft in ld 13th til hdd 3 out, no ext
565[4] **Connor The Second 5ow ....P Black** 3
rear 1st ctt,lft 3rd 13th,styd on wll frm 3 out,not rch ldrs
814 Stanwick Fort 5a *cls up,ld 6th til ran wd aft 11th & dmtd to last,f 13th* ....Mrs H Dickson f
Need A Ladder *last 3rd, t.o. 9th & p.u. nxt* P Johnson pu
733 Billy Buoyant *alwys rear div, 7th whn p.u. aft 5th* ....J Walton pu
Another Islay *cls up 1st ctt, 1l 2nd 9th, ld 12th & gng wll whn f 13th* ....P Forster f
728[2] Saucy Mint 5a *prom, ld 5th til hdd nxt, cls 3rd 9th, gng wll whn f 13th* ....C Storey f
8 ran. 2l, hd. Time 6m 14.00s. SP 7-1.
Ian Carmichael (Morpeth).

997 2½m Open Maiden (5-7yo)

949[4] **HOUSELOPE BROOK 5a........J Walton** 1
alwys prom, wnt 2nd 3 out, 2l down & lft in ld last, ran on
613[5] **Driminamore (Ire) ....W Ramsay** 2
(Jt fav) disp ld to 8th, hdd nxt, wknd to 3rd 3 out, lft 2nd last
Tartan Buck (Ire) 5a........Miss D Laidlaw 3
prom, hndy 4th 10th-2 out, outpcd & lft poor 3rd last
948 Up And Running *rear div, last 6th, styd on wll frm 4 out, not trbl ldrs*........D McLeod 4
Little Monkside (Ire) 5a *hndy 5th 6th, nvr nrr ldrs final ctt*........Mrs H Dickson 5
815[3] The Camair Flyer (Ire) *(Jt fav) disp ld to 8th,ld nxt,2l up whn ran out thruwing last*........M Ruddy ro
815 Little Hawk *rear div, wnt 5th 10th, no imprssn on ldrs frm nxt,p.u. last*........R Morgan pu
730 Noneofyourbusiness (Ire) 5a *cls 6th 6th, grdly lost tch final ctt, t.o. & p.u. 4 out*........T Scott pu
8 ran. 5l, 20l, 5l, 6l. Time 5m 13.00s. SP 10-1.
F V White (Percy).
P.B.

CHESHIRE
Alpraham

Saturday April 12th
GOOD TO FIRM

998 Members

766[2] **ROYLE BURCHLIN (bl)** ....**D Barlow** 1
(fav) made all, clr 3 out, easily
763[3] **Barkin** ....**P Saville** 2
chsd ldrs, tk 2nd aft 3 out, nvr dang
766 **Flinters (bl)**..........................**C Barlow** 3
cls up, jmpd slwly 5th & rmndrs, wknd rpdly 3 out
Just Ed 10ow *grad lost tch, t.o. 10th, p.u. 3 out* ....P Arnold pu
4 ran. 20l, 12l. Time 7m 28.00s. SP 4-9.
R A Royle (Cheshire).

999 Open Maiden (12st)

O K FLO JO 5a......................**C Stockton** 1
hld up, 3rd 12th, ld aft 3 out, clr nxt
883 **Rugrat 5a** ....**A Crow** 2
bhnd, 2nd at 8th, ld 14th-3 out, no ext
854[5] **River Sunset (Ire)** ....**S Prior** 3
alwys mid-div, styd on onepcd, not rch ldrs
723 Hyperbole *4th whn f 3rd*...............D Norlander f
941 Travel Bound *(fav) ld to 14th, wknd rpdly, p.u. 2 out* ....D Barlow pu
941[4] Keep Them Keen (Ire) 3ow *rear, in tch til wknd 12th, p.u. 2 out* ....J Mather pu
874 Idiomatic *chsd ldrs, wknd 11th, p.u. 2 out* ..R Thomas pu
Fred Lad *whppd round strt & u.r., t.n.p.* ..P McAllister 0
8 ran. 10l, 15l. Time 7m 31.00s. SP 6-1.
Mrs Ruth Crank (Cheshire).

1000 Interlink Restricted (12st)

884[2] **BUBBLE N SQUEEK** ....**C Barlow** 1
cls up, ld 11th, prssd last, all out
721[1] **Priory Piper** ....**C Stockton** 2
hld up rear,4th at 15th,styd on to chal & mstk last,jst fld
327[1] **Sharsman (Ire)** ....**A Crow** 3
(fav) ld to 3rd & 4-11th, rdn 3 out, no ext
723[1] King Keith *chsd ldr 11th-3 out, no ext* ....S Walker 4
852[4] Little By Little *s.s. 30l bhnd by 1st, prog to 10l 5th 14th, no frthr hdwy* ....T O'Leary 5
727[3] Glen Taylor *chsd ldrs to 10th, wknd, t.o. 15th, tk 6th flat*....................................L Whiston 6
727[4] Grecianlid *cls up to 14th, fdd rpdly, walked in* ....Miss S Hopkins 7
936 Grindley Brook (bl) *ld 3rd, 6l clr whn f nxt* D Norlander f
8 ran. Hd, 12l, 8l, 12l, 25l, hd. Time 7m 24.00s. SP 5-2.
C J B Barlow (Cheshire).

1001 Mixed Open (12st)

937[3] **SPY'S DELIGHT 7ex** ....**N Rayner** 1
(fav) hld up rear, clsd 13th, lft wll clr apr 2 out
884 **Side Brace (NZ)** ....**Miss K Swindells** 2
chsd ldr to 13th, strgglng aft
363 Charlie Chalk *ld, mstk 8th, just ld whn s.u. flat apr 2 out* ....C Stockton su
3 ran. 20l. Time 7m 27.00s. SP 4-5.
N Rayner (Sir W. W. Wynn's).

1002 Confined (12st)

726[1] **ITA'S FELLOW (IRE) 6ex**.............**Mrs C Ford** 1
(fav) ld 6th, clr 14th, easily
884 **Killatty Player (Ire) 5a**...................**A Crow** 2
svrl mstks,ld to 6th,lost plc,tk 2nd 3 out,not trbl wnr
848[3] **Ultrason IV (Fr)** ....**A Beedles** 3
hld up, chsd wnr 14th-16th, no ext
937 Jo-Su-Ki *rear, 10l 4th whn f 13th, dead* .....C Barlow f
4 ran. 8l, 6l. Time 7m 26.00s. SP 1-2.
R Prince (Meynell & South Staffs).

1003 2½m Open Maiden (5-7yo)

469 **NIORD** ....**C Stockton** 1
made all, rdn out whn chal flat
470[4] **Builder Boy** ....**S Walker** 2
mostly 2nd frm 8th, styd on wll, nvr rchd wnr
839[3] **Educate Me (Ire)** ....**J Burley** 3
alwys mid-div, styd on onepcd 3 out, nvr dang
754[2] Agile King *(fav) chsd ldrs, 2nd at 11th, hrd rdn & no ext aft*...................................S Prior 4
763 King Edward (Ire) *mstly 2nd to 8th, grad wknd frm 11th* ....D Barlow 5
767 Browlea Lyndene 5a *cls up to 8th, fdd, t.o. 11th* ....P Blane 6
Sonnen Gift 5a *rear whn ref 2nd* ....T O'Leary ref
853 China Lal 12a *hmpd 1st, rear whn u.r. 3rd*. .R Thomas ur
Sentimentalscally 12a *bhnd whn s.u. flat aft 3rd* ....P McAllister su
940 Harvest Singer 5a *rear whn u.r. 6th*.........J Mather ur
10 ran. 1l, 15l, 2l, 15l, 3l. Time 5m 27.00s. SP 12-1.
B Davies (Cheshire Forest).
R.A.

GLAMORGAN
St Hilary
Saturday April 12th
GOOD TO FIRM

1004 Members

901[2] **COSA NOSTRA** ....**K Cousins** 1
(fav) 2nd til ld 7th, qcknd clr 15th, easily
633 Harry From Barry *3rd til went 2nd 16th, hld whn ref last* ....J Tudor ref
718[5] Killyman (Ire) *ld to 6th, 2nd to 15th, wknd rpdly, p.u. 3 out* ....Miss J Mathias pu
406 Penylan Gold 5a (bl) *4th til f 10th*..........P Williams f
4 ran. Time 6m 16.00s. SP 4-5.
K Cousins (Glamorgan).

1005 Confined (12st)

538[1] **RADIO DAYS (IRE)** ....**J Jukes** 1
(fav) hld up in 3rd, prog to ld 3 out, just hld on und pres flat
632[1] **Archer (Ire)** ....**J Llewellyn** 2
2nd til disp frm 12-15th, hdd nxt, hrd rdn flat, just faild
906[1] **The Last Mistress 5a** ....**J Price** 3
ld to 11th, disp to 15th, wknd frm nxt
Sweet Kildare 5a *hld up in mid-div, prog to 4th 3 out, styd on onepcd*..............................J P Keen 4
718[4] Final Option (Ire) *last til ran on frm 3 out past btn hrss* ....I Johnson 5
843[2] Al Frolic *4th/5th til wknd rpdly frm 15th* ....D S Jones 6
846[4] Pay-U-Cash *alwys last pair*...............G Perkins 7
845[1] Dick's Cabin *rear til p.u. 11th*...............W Pugh pu
715 Derrymoss *mid-div, wknd rpdly 7th, p.u. 9th* ....E Williams pu
903[3] Icecapade (Bel) *rear til p.u. 16th* ....Miss E Jones pu
10 ran. Nk, 20l, 25l, 1l, 2l, 4l. Time 6m 7.00s. SP Evens.
T D Sproat (Pembrokeshire).

1006 G Middleton Ladies

961[1] **TOUCH 'N' PASS 7ex** ....**Miss P Jones** 1
(fav) hld up rear, rpd prog 16th, ld 3 out, sn clr
537 **Gold Diver** ....**Miss P Gundry** 2
mostly 2nd, ld 14th, hdd nxt, ran on onepcd
844[2] **Polish Rider (USA)** ....**Miss R Morgan** 3
hld up mid-div, rpd prog to ld 15th, hdd 3 out, wknd rpdly
844 Doctor-J (Ire) *12s-5s, ld to 6th, ld 10-13th, wknd frm nxt* ....Miss S Major 4
638 Afaristoun (Fr) *cls up, ld 7th-10th, 3rd whn f nxt* ....Miss J Morse f
713 Project's Mate 5ex *rear til p.u. 2out*. .Miss N Richards pu
635[2] Saffron Moss *mid-div, prog to 3rd at 14th, f 16th* ....Miss F Wilson f
7 ran. 15l, 4l, 25l. Time 6m 11.00s. SP 4-7.
R H P Williams (Llangeinor).

1007 Men's Open (12st)

900² **KINGFISHER BAY** .... **J Price** 1
ld to 12th, lost plc, ran on 15th, ld flat
843¹ **Jack Sound 7ex** .... **E Williams** 2
(fav) 2nd til ld 13th, wknd rpdly apr last, hdd flat
714¹ **Sun Of Chance** .... **P Williams** 3
hld up mid-div, some prog 3 out, ran on wll, nrst fin
714⁸ Astounded *alwys mid-div, ran on onepcd* .... J Tudor 4
715⁴ Olde Crescent *twrds rear, styd on onepcd* .. J Comins 5
638 Cornish Cossack (NZ) *tongue-strap, prom til wknd 15th* .... W Pugh 6
904² Adanac *alwys mid-div, btn & p.u. 15th* .... A Price pu
904 Prince Nepal *mid-div, f 4th* .... S Shinton f
903 Young India 5a *s.s. last til p.u. 15th* .... T Vaughan pu
636⁴ Hugli *prom, went 2nd 16th, cls up & ev ch whn s.u. bnd apr 3 out* .... D S Jones su
10 ran. Hd, 8l, 20l, 5l, 6l. Time 6m 10.00s. SP 50-1.
D W Chilcott (Curre).
One fence omitted final circuit.

1008 Restricted (12st)

540¹ **HOLLOW SOUND (IRE) 5a** .... **J Jukes** 1
(fav) 2nd til lft in ld 12th, qcknd 3 out, sn clr
Everso Irish .... **E Williams** 2
cls up in 3rd, went 2nd 3 out, styd on onepcd
719¹ **Who's Your Man (Ire)** .... **D S Jones** 3
prom, lft 2nd 12th, onepcd frm 3 out
841¹ Jolly Swagman *hld up rear, went 4th hlfwy, no frthr prog* .... G Perkins 4
957² Celtic Bizarre 5a *twrds rear, onepcd, nvr dang* .... Miss B Barton 5
720¹ Miss Montgomery (Ire) 5a *mid-div, wknd frm 15th* .... J Price 6
959² Valiant Friend 3ow (bl) *alwys rear* .... R Barton 7
534 Mr Mad *rear til p.u. 14th* .... P Hamer pu
538³ Equatime 5a *ld til f 12th* .... K Cousins f
713³ Greenfield Tiger (Ire) *rear, no ch whn p.u. 16th* .... P Sheldrake pu
845³ Tims Kick (Ire) 5a *mid-div, wknd & p.u. 15th* .. J Tudor pu
11 ran. 7l, 15l, 20l, 2l, 5l, 3l. Time 6m 8.00s. SP 6-4.
T D Sproat (Pembrokeshire).

1009 Maiden (5-7yo) Div I

908³ **LENNIE THE LION** .... **J Price** 1
ld to 14th, ld agn 3 out, ran on well
840² **Redoran 5a** .... **M Lewis** 2
prom, went 2nd 16th, ran on onepcd
842⁴ **Cefn Woodsman** .... **D S Jones** 3
2nd til ld 14th, hdd 3 out, no ext
720² Itsstormingnorma 5a *(fav) cls up in 3rd/4th, onepcd frm 3 out* .... D Stephens 4
720⁴ Good Boy Charlie *mid-div, blnd & u.r. 10th* .... J Lilley ur
720³ Queen's Equa 5a *mid-div, wknd 12th, p.u. 15th* .... Miss S Major pu
639 Ballyhooly Belle (Ire) 5a *mstks in rear til p.u. 7th* .... Miss E Jones pu
842 Merry Morn 5a *twrds rear til p.u. 15th* ..... T Vaughan pu
542 Tiger Sally 5a *rear, f 2nd* .... Miss V Roberts f
963 Storm Dai Fence (Ire) 12a *twrs rear til p.u. 3 out* .... P Sheldrake pu
Chantingo Lad *t.o. last til p.u. 13th* .... A Price pu
11 ran. 7l, 3l, 15l. Time 6m 29.00s. SP 33-1.
T R R Farr (Ystrad).

1010 Maiden (5-7yo) Div II

640 **TAKAHASHI (IRE)** .... **E Williams** 1
(Co fav) prom, lft in ld 14th, qcknd clr 3 out
842³ **Hil Lady 5a** .... **J P Keen** 2
(Co fav) cls up, lft 2nd 14th, ran on onepcd
720 Dragonara Lad (Ire) 7a *n.j.w. ld to 11th, grad wknd, p.u. 16th* .... D S Jones pu
641 Calverstown Star (Ire) *(Co fav) mid-div, mstk 14th, p.u. nxt* .... J Jukes pu
719 Alkarine 7a *rear til p.u. 13th* .... Miss L Pearce pu
719 Stiff Drink *2nd til ld 11th, f 14th* .... J Cook f
964 Lynnes Daniella (Ire) 5a *rear til p.u. 13th* ..... R Barton pu
842 Out On The Town 5a *mid-div, dist 3rd whn ref 3 out* .... J Tudor ref
719 Buckland Ballad 7a *last til p.u. 13th* .... G Perkins pu
640 Rebel Yell (Ire) 5a *rear til p.u. 13th* .... A Price pu
10 ran. 6l. Time 6m 23.00s. SP 5-2.
Mrs M G Wallace (Brecon).

1011 Maiden (8yo+)

543³ **PLUCKY PUNTER** .... **P Williams** 1
made all, ran on strngly whn chal 2 out
847² **Alfion (Ire)** .... **D S Jones** 2
prom, strng chal frm 15th, cls 2nd whn mstk last, no ext
409⁶ **Boddington Hill 5a** .... **I Johnson** 3
rear, lft 3rd by dfctns
900 Priesthill (Ire) *mid-div, onepcd frm 15th* ... D Stephens 4
541 All The Jolly 5a *(fav) mid-div, went 3rd 15th, wknd & p.u. last* .... Miss P Jones pu
900 Willow Belle (Ire) 5a *2nd til lost plc 12th, p.u. 3 out* .... J Price pu
640 Trydan *rear til p.u. 13th* .... G Perkins pu
717 Toucher (Ire) *rear til p.u. 13th* .... J Cook pu
Mississippisteamer (Ire) *whppd round strt, tk no part* .... J Tudor 0
847 Dontyoudoda (Ire) *mid-div, f 12th* .... T Vaughan f
10 ran. Nk, dist, 5l. Time 6m 22.00s. SP 3-1.
J R Jones (Vale Of Clettwr).
J.C./ P.H.

LUDLOW
Bitterley
Saturday April 12th
GOOD TO FIRM

1012 Members

BEYOND THE STARS .... **M Rimell** 1
w.w. prog to chal 13th, ld nxt, kpt on frm 2 out
851⁵ **Ledwyche Gate (bl)** .... **R Evans** 2
ld to 13th, ev ch til no ext frm 3 out, eased flat
587 **Stylish Gent** .... **D Mansell** 3
alwys cls up, prog to chal 15th, wknd frm 2 out
701 Outcrop 5a *cls up, mstks 5 & 7th, wknd 12th, t.o. whn nrly u.r. last* .... R Inglesant 4
647³ Basil Street (Ire) 7a *(fav) blnd & u.r. 1st* ..... A Phillips ur
Crescent Moonshine 5a *last frm 3rd, lost tch 6th, t.o. & p.u. aft 11th* .... R Hawker pu
6 ran. 6l, 6l, dist. Time 6m 17.00s. SP 14-1.
J F H Collett (Ludlow).

1013 Confined (12st)

700¹ **GRIMLEY GALE (IRE) 5a** .... **A Phillips** 1
(fav) hld up, prog 8th, rdn to ld last, eased nr fin
255⁵ **Just Marmalade** .... **R Burton** 2
chsd ldr, ld 7th, rdn & no ext whn hdd 2 out
714 **Chiaroscuro** .... **S Lloyd** 3
alwys cls up, not qckn frm 15th, kpt on onepcd
755¹ Cwm Bye *mid-div, effrt 12th, ev ch nxt, wknd frm 3 out* .... A Dalton 4
465 Bentley Manor *nvr rchd ldrs, kpt on onepcd frm 15th* .... G Hanmer 5
515 Prideaux Prince *alwys rear, rmndrs aft 10th, rdn & no prog 13th* .... Julian Pritchard 6
753 Stormhill Recruit *rear frm 11th, no ch frm 14th* .... M P Jones 7
665 Only In Ireland *ld to 6th, wknd 8th, p.u. 12th* .... R Inglesant pu
Band Leader *mid-div whn f 7th* .... T Stephenson f
Katie Parson 5a *rear frm 8th, no ch whn p.u. aft 14th* .... M Hammond pu
818³ Night Wind *prom, cls 3rd whn f 13th* .... Mrs A Rucker f
753¹ Lles Le Bucflow *mid-div whn b.d. 7th* .... M Munrowd bd
752¹ Bowland Girl (Ire) 5a *prog to cls 4th whn hmpd & u.r. flat aft 13th* .... Miss E James ur
852¹ Another Chancer *rear frm 8th, lost tch & p.u. 15th* .... M Harris pu
14 ran. 2l, 3l, 15l, 12l, 10l. Time 6m 6.00s. SP 10-11.
R M Phillips (Clifton-On-Teme).

1014 Land Rover Open (12st)

751[1] **SHOON WIND** ....A Dalton 1
ld to 3rd, prog to chal 2 out, disp last, rdn out flat
432[1] **Bagalino (USA) 4ex** ....Julian Pritchard 2
(fav) cls up whn wd aft 3rd, chsd ldr, ld 15th, hdd & no ext flat
851[3] **Mr Bobbit (Ire)** ....R Burton 3
chsd ldrs, 12l 4th at 13th, kpt on onepcd frm 15th
781[3] Bowl Of Oats (bl) *20l 8th at 11th, dist 5th whn p.u. 2 out*..............................T Stephenson pu
781 Shareef Star *alwys last, t.o. 7th, p.u. 14th*.....C Yates pu
Polydeuces *cls up, 8l 3rd at 10th, wknd rpdly, p.u. aft 12th*..............................R Inglesant pu
748[1] Garrylucas 7ex *rdn alng frm 10th, no prog 13th, p.u. 15th*..............................G Hanmer pu
634[4] In The Water *in chsng grp, wknd frm 13th, p.u. 15th* ....M P Jones pu
700 Haven Light *ld frm 4th, 10l up 12th, ct aft 14th, wknd & p.u. 2 out*..............................M Harris pu
9 ran. 1l, 10l. Time 6m 10.00s. SP 7-2.
J N Dalton (Wheatland).

1015 Open Maiden (5-7yo) Div I (12st)

436 **ROOTSMAN (IRE)** ....T Stephenson 1
hld up rear, prog 3 out, qcknd to ld last, sn clr
774 **Sun Setting** ....Miss L Sweeting 2
alwys prom, ev ch 3 out, kpt on to tk 2nd flat
755 **Corview (Ire)** ....A Phillips 3
cls 5th at 10th, effrt 3 out, ev ch til wknd apr last
436[2] Merry Noelle 5a *cls up til ld 12th, hdd & wknd aft 2 out*..............................M Harris 4
Bessie's Will 5a *cls up whn c.o. apr 5th*....G Barfoot-Saunt co
262 Heather Wood 5a *ld til ran out 5th*.........D Mansell ro
755 Cuban Skies (Ire) *last & rdn 11th, prog nxt, 5th & wkng whn u.r. 3 out*..............................T Cox ur
570[2] Lakeside Lad 7a *cls up to 9th, 10l 6th whn f 3 out* ....R Burton f
641[2] Bally Boy 7a *mid-div, p.u. sddnly aft 3rd* ....Julian Pritchard pu
326[2] Mintulyar *ld 6th til ran out 12th*.............A Dalton ro
527[4] Expresso Drummer *(fav) blnd & u.r. 2nd* ....Miss P Curling ur
Thoughtful Choice 5a *rear til prog 12th, 15l 5th whn f 2 out*..............................Miss E James f
12 ran. 8l, ¾l, 10l. Time 6m 19.00s. SP 20-1.
Mrs J Morgan (North Ledbury).
One fence omitted, 16 jumps.

1016 Open Maiden (5-7yo) Div II (12st)

LANCASTRIAN JET (IRE) ....M Rimell 1
(fav) alwys prom, mstk 13th, ld 3 out, qcknd clr
644[3] **Lindalighter 5a**.........................A Dalton 2
prog to 5th at 12th, ev ch 15th, not qckn frm nxt
570 **Philelwyn (Ire) 5a** ....Julian Pritchard 3
ld 6th til hdd 3 out, kpt on onepcd
Cashew Chaos 7a *hld up rear, ran on steadily frm 14th, improve* ....M Munrowd 4
254 I've Copped It (Ire) *prom to 13th, not qckn nxt, rdn & no ext frm 15th*..............................J Rees 5
706[6] Nick The Biscuit *alwys mid-div, effrt 13th, no prog frm 15th*..............................O McPhail 6
853 Merger Mania 7a *hld up rear, gd prog 14th, wknd frm 3 out*..............................T Cox 7
881 Distant-Port (Ire) *last frm 7th, t.o. 10th* ..T Stephenson 8
755[2] Military Man *prom whn f 10th*..............A Phillips f
470[6] Fancytalkintinker (Ire) *hld up, prog 12th, cls 2nd nxt, ev ch til wknd 3 out,p.u.nxt*..............................R Burton pu
706 Asante Sana 5a *ld til slw jmp 6th, wknd 8th, t.o. & p.u. 13th*..............................N Oliver pu
706 Zaudante (Ire) 5a *alwys rear, lsng tch whn f 12th* ....R Rogers f
467 Faha Point (Ire) 12a *prom til p.u. aft 4th, saddle slppd* ....M Rodda pu
876[3] Hectors Way *cls 6th at 12th, wknd 14th, no ch whn p.u. 3 out, dsmntd*..............................N Bradley pu
14 ran. 10l, 4l, 6l, 5l, 2l, 2l, dist. Time 6m 24.00s. SP 3-1.
Capt T A Forster (Ludlow).

1017 Ladies

520[4] **SPLIT SECOND 7ex**.................Miss A Dare 1
ld 4th, in cmmnd whn lft clr last
645[2] **Nutcase 5a**.........................Mrs D Smith 2
hld up, effrt 12th, ev ch til just outpcd frm 15th
432[3] **Master Dancer** ....Miss C Dyson 3
ld to 3rd, cls up til outpcd 14th, walked in
520[1] Slaney Food 7ex *(fav) trckd wnr 4th,chal 15th,cls 2nd & hld whn f last,dead*..............................Miss C Thomas f
4 ran. 6l, dist. Time 6m 15.00s. SP 5-4.
Mrs P J Willis (Berkeley).

1018 Open Maiden (8yo+) Div I (12st)

575 **MR WILBUR** ....A Dalton 1
w.w. prog to ld 14th, kpt on, rdn out flat
Ora Pronobis ....T Stephenson 2
ld to 8th, styd prom, rdn 2 out, no ext
881 **Crestwood Lad (USA)** ....M Yardley 3
alwys prom, kpt on onepcd frm 15th
Nordross 5a *trckd ldrs, effrt 12th, ld nxt, not qckn frm 14th* ....G Hanmer 4
634 Wilton Park 5a *rear of main grp, nvr able to chal* ....J Rees 5
Cal's Boy *rear frm 8th, kpt on same pace frm 13th* ....M FitzGerald 6
700 Monorose 5a *alwys rear, t.o. 8th* ....Mrs D Powell 7
Pridewood Golding *ld frm 9th, blnd nxt, hit marker & u.r. apr 13th* ....T Cox ur
Ballyhamage (Ire) *(fav) cls 4th at 6th, prog to ld whn f 12th*..............................M Munrowd f
Roo's Leap (Ire) 5a *rear frm 11th, lost tch & p.u. 15th* ....O McPhail pu
706 True Fred *prom til lost plc 7th, blnd nxt, p.u. 10th* ....S Lloyd pu
754 Farriana 5a *mid-div to 10th, lost tch 13th, p.u. 15th* ....P Hanly pu
877 Barafundle Bay *cls up to 10th, wknd 13th, p.u. 2 out* ....G Barfoot-Saunt pu
13 ran. 4l, 5l, 5l, 12l, ½l, dist. Time 6m 19.00s. SP 7-2.
J D Callow (Albrighton Woodland).

1019 Open Maiden (8yo+) Div II (12st)

754[3] **EMERALD CHARM (IRE) 5a**............M Rimell 1
trckd ldrs, 2l 3rd 14th, rdn to chal last, ld flat
706[3] **Dante's Pride (Ire)** ....Miss A Dare 2
(fav) ld 1st, prog to ld 13th, jnd last, no ext flat
706[4] **Winter Breeze** ....A Phillips 3
prog to cls 2nd 12th, chsd ldr til wknd 2 out
876[2] Clovers Last *cls up to 10th, just outpcd frm 13th, no ch frm 3 out* ....M Harris 4
854[4] Parson's Corner *nvr going pace, t.o. & p.u. 5th* ....Miss C Williams pu
656[4] Well Bank *prom, ev ch 14th, wknd nxt, p.u. 2 out* ....E Walker pu
201[7] Cwm Arctic 5a *ld 2nd-11th, rdn 13th, disp btn 3rd whn f 2 out* ....M P Jones f
Kinlet Spark 5a *in tch til eased & p.u. 8th*....R Burton pu
664[5] Welsh Lightning *mid-div whn mstk & u.r. 4th* ....R Inglesant ur
754 Saxon Smile *prom to 8th, lost tch 10th, p.u. aft nxt* ....Julian Pritchard pu
666[4] Ribington *cls up to 10th, wknd & p.u. 12th* ....M Hammond pu
700 Daisy Lane 5a *lost tch 3rd, p.u. 7th* ....D Mansell pu
12 ran. 1½l, 20l, 2l. Time 6m 13.00s. SP 7-2.
M P Wiggin (Ludlow).
P.R.

PORTMAN
Badbury Rings
Saturday April 12th
FIRM

1020 Restricted (12st)

873 **VITAL SHOT 5a** ....**Mrs R Baldwin** 1
walked over
M C Hillier (Beaufort).

1021 Members (12st)

690[3] **TEMPLE MARY 7ex** ....**T Woolridge** 1
(fav) restrained, disp 10th, blndrd 3 out, wnt aft nxt, rddn out
658 **Kala Dawn 5a**..................**Miss M Tory** 2
jmp lft,made most til jnd 10th,mstk 16th,hd aft 2 out,onepcd
2 ran. 3l. Time 6m 23.70s. SP 2-5.
Andrew Eveleigh (Portman).

1022 Ladies

689[3] **LEGAL PICNIC** ....**Miss C Bryan** 1
hdl up last, prog frm 14th, ld apr last, pshd out
Lavalight ....**Miss A Goschen** 2
jmp rght, trckd ldr til ld apr 11th, hdd last, no ext
657[2] **Elegant Sun** ....**Miss R David** 3
(fav) ld, mstk 4th, hdd 11th, sn wknd, t.o. 3 out
3 ran. 3l, dist. Time 6m 8.90s. SP 7-4.
Ms C Bryan (Blackmore & Sparkford Vale).

1023 Land Rover Mens Open (12st)

585[3] **SPITFIRE JUBILEE 7ex**..................**R Nuttall** 1
(fav) j.w., made all, sn clr, v easy
687[1] **Avril Showers 5a**..................**R Atkinson** 2
not fluent, immmed outpcd, styd on onepce frm 15th
2 ran. 12l. Time 6m 4.60s. SP 4-5.
Mrs Z S Clark (Blackmore & Sparkford Vale).

1024 Open Maiden (12st)

929 **SPAR COPSE** ....**Miss A Goschen** 1
(fav) trckd ldr,cls up frm 11th,ld 14th,lft clr 16th,pshd out
916[2] **Quote 5a**..................**Miss A McKeowen** 2
plld, ld til apr 14th, sn wknd, lft remote 2nd 16th
917 Most Vital *not fluent in rear, rddn 13th, hld in 2nd whn ran out 16th*..................T Woolridge ro
3 ran. Dist. Time 6m 21.60s. SP 4-6.
P E Froud (Blackmore & Sparkford Vale).

1025 Intermediate (12st)

919[1] **STALBRIDGE GOLD 5a 5ex** .....**Miss A Goschen** 1
(fav) disp to 12th, qcknd to ld cls home, all out
391[2] **Roaming Shadow** ....**J Hankinson** 2
j.w., disp til narrow adv 12th, outpcd & hdd cls home
2 ran. Hd. Time 6m 23.10s. SP 2-5.
C J Barnes (Blackmore & Sparkford Vale).
M.J.

PUCKERIDGE
Horseheath
Saturday April 12th
HARD

1026 Members

910[3] **SALMON MEAD (IRE)** ....**S Sporborg** 1
walked over
Christopher Sporborg (Puckeridge).

1027 Open Maiden (12st)

LUCKY VIENNA 5a ....**M Barnard** 1
(Jt fav) j.s 1st, ld & j.s 3rd, 30l clr 9th, lft solo 11th
914 The Whole Lot 3ow *(Jt fav) n.j.w. ld ti j.s & hdd 3rd, lst tch 6th, t.o. whn ref 11th*..................J Buckle ref
2 ran. Time 7m 19.00s. SP 4-5.
H Hill (Fitzwilliam).

1028 Confined (12st)

910[2] **COCKSTOWN LAD 5ex** ....**D Featherstone** 1
(fav) disp ld til ld 15th, clr nxt, unextnd
271 **Sarazar (USA)** ....**G Pewter** 2
nt fluent, disp ld til 15th, sn outpcd
193 Out Of Line 5a *alwys last, lsng tch & hit 11th, t.o. & p.u. 3 out*..................N Bloom pu
3 ran. 20l. Time 6m 39.00s. SP 1-4.
Mrs E R Featherstone (Puckeridge).

1029 Ladies

912[3] **COUNTERBID (bl)** ....**Mrs F Needham** 1
keen hold, ld 4th, made rest, clr 3 out, eased flat
912[1] **Kumada** ....**Miss S Gritton** 2
(fav) ld to 4th, chsd wnr, 2l dwn & hit 15th, no ch wth wnr aft
801[5] **Major Inquiry (USA)** ....**Miss H Pewter** 3
last frm 4th, outpcd 13th, r.o. 3 out, retraced
3 ran. 5l, dist. Time 6m 25.00s. SP 6-4.
J M Turner (Suffolk).

1030 Men's Open

911[2] **OVER THE EDGE** ....**S Sporborg** 1
(fav) disp ld til ld 13th, clr frm nxt, rdn flat, just hld on
710 **Cardinal Red (bl)** ....**P Keane** 2
disp ld til j.s13th & 14th,rallied und press flat,jst faild
2 ran. Hd. Time 6m 25.00s. SP 1-5.
Christopher Sporborg (Puckeridge).

1031 Intermediate (12st)

1026[1] **SALMON MEAD (IRE) 5ex** ....**S Sporborg** 1
w.w. lft 2nd 11th, ld 3 out, 8l clr nxt, hit last, all out
798[1] **Courier's Way (Ire)** ....**T Moore** 2
ld til aft 10th, lft in ld nxt, hdd & blnd 3 out, rlld flat
711[1] Whats Another 5a *(fav) chsd ldr 6th, ld aft 10th, f nxt*..................Miss K Bridge ur
3 ran. 1l. Time 6m 28.00s. SP 7-4.
Christopher Sporborg (Puckeridge).

1032 Restricted (12st)

909[2] **CURRENT ATTRACTION 5a 7ow**....**Miss K Thory** 1
(fav) jmpd wll, disp til ld 2 out, drw clr
838 **Tremeirchion** ....**M Barnard** 2
mstks, wth wnr til wknd appr last
2 ran. 8l. Time 6m 52.00s. SP 4-7.
Miss Katie Thory (Fitzwilliam).
S.P.

TETCOTT
Lifton
Saturday April 12th
FIRM

1033 Confined (12st)

738[1] **MYHAMET 6ex** ....**A Farrant** 1
(fav) lft in ld apr 4th, clr nxt, unchal
804 **Oneovertheight** ....**N Harris** 2
lft remote 3rd apr 4th, ran on to take 2nd cls home
237[2] **Just My Bill** ....**C Heard** 3
lft 2nd apr 4th til wknd aft last
738 Far Too Loud *ref 1st*..................T Dennis ref
803[1] Baldhu Chance *ld 3rd til slppd up bnd apr 4th*..................J Young su
888[6] Tangle Baron 3ex *3rd 1st-2nd, cls 2nd whn slppd up bnd apr 4th*..................Miss J Cumings su
6 ran. 10l, 4l. Time 6m 5.00s. SP 5-4.
Paul C N Heywood (North Cornwall).

1034 Maiden Div I (12st)

461 **FASTER OR ELSE (NZ)** ....**T Cole** 1
towrds rear early, gd prog 12th, chal last, ld cls home
741 **Aritam (Ire)** ....**A Farrant** 2

(fav) made virt all til cght cls home, no ext
553 **Jolly Sensible 5a (bl) ....Miss L Blackford** 3
alwys front rank, prssd ldr 14th, no ext frm nxt
Noble Jakey *alwys cls up til rddn frm 3 out, promsng* ....L Jefford 4
808 Luney River 5a *raced wd, alwys towrds rear* ....Miss L Long 5
624 Lizzy Gecko 5a *prom til wknd 12th, p.u. 2 out* ....T Dennis pu
808 Kanha 12a *alwys rear til p.u. 14th* ....S Kidston pu
7 ran. ½l, 1l, 15l, 20l. Time 6m 15.00s. SP 25-1.
Reg Jones (Spooners & West Dartmoor).

1035 Maiden Div II (12st)

794 **CARRAREA (IRE) ....A Farrant** 1
mid-div til moved up 12th, ld 15th, ran on strgly
737[3] **Midnight Bob ....J Young** 2
(fav) bhnd til tk cls order 5 out, efft 2 out, no ext aft
808[2] **Spartans Dina 5a ....Miss L Blackford** 3
ld 4-6th agn 8-11th, poor jmp 14th, wknd qckly
629 Friendly Viking *alwys abt same plc, kpt on onepcd frm 2 out* ....I Hambly 4
792 Robehen 5a *alwys bhnd, t.o. frm 7th* ....T Dennis 5
736 Sixth In Line (Ire) *front rank til wknd 12th, p.u. aft 14th* ....T Cole pu
Bucktail (NZ) 7a *alwys prom, still cls up whn u.r. 14th* ....L Jefford ur
Fair And Square 12a 6ow *t.o. whn p.u. aft 10th* ....K Heard pu
808[3] Gaysun 7a *ld 1st-4th, ld agn 7th, grdly wknd, p.u. 4 out* ....S Slade pu
741 Earlswood *nvr a factor, wll bhnd whn p.u. aft 12th* ....G Penfold pu
Go Willie Go *bhnd til ref 7th* ....R Young ref
11 ran. 4l, 5l, 2l, dist. Time 6m 13.00s. SP 7-2.
J Atkins/M C Kirby/K Cumins (Devon And Somerset Staghounds).

1036 Ladies

740[4] **ROMANY ANNE 5a ....Miss S Young** 1
hld up, gd prog 15th, ld aft last, comf
689[4] **False Economy ....Miss K Scorgie** 2
(fav) ld/disp to 11th, clr 12th, no ext whn chal
792 **Always Lynsey (Ire) 5a ....Miss K Hurst** 3
ld/disp to 11th, fdd, sn bhnd
Roving Vagabond *slght ld 1st, sn lost tch, bhnd whn ref 14th* ....Miss A Barnett ref
4 ran. 4l, dist. Time 6m 11.00s. SP 11-8.
L Bond (Stevenstone).

1037 Men's Open (12st)

739[2] **PARSON'S WAY 7ex (bl)..........A Farrant** 1
trckd ldr til ld 15th, made rest readly
793 **Bargain And Sale ....I Dowrick** 2
trckd ldrs in 3rd, lft 2nd last, onepcd
586 **Miles More Fun 5a..........L Jefford** 3
(fav) slght ld to 15th, hdd & lkd btn whn f last, rmt
Another Barney 7ex *nvr trbld ldrs, p.u. aft 13th* ....A Moire pu
Harvest Home (Ire) 7a *alwys bhnd til f 12th* ...S Slade f
5 ran. Dist, dist. Time 6m 9.00s. SP 11-8.
Mrs K A Heywood (North Cornwall).

1038 Intermediate (12st)

1033 **TANGLE BARON 3ex ....Miss J Cumings** 1
(fav) 2nd run, made all, lft wll clr 13th, canter
865[1] **Tangle Kelly ....S Slade** 2
alwys bhnd, lft 2nd 13th, kpt on onepcd
930 American Black *chsd ldr, rmmndrs 12th, wknd & p.u. 13th* ....Miss T Cave pu
626 Crownhill Cross *not alwys fluent, wll bhnd whn p.u. 14th* ....S Kidston pu
4 ran. Dist. Time 6m 8.00s. SP 4-6.
P J Clarke (Devon & Somerset Staghounds).

1039 Restricted (12st)

803[2] **SUNWIND ....A Farrant** 1
bhnd til prog 15th, smooth run to ld 3 out,ran on strngly
804[2] **Morchard Milly 5a..........A Holdsworth** 2
ld 7th til hdd 3 out, kpt on und press
806[3] **Ryme And Run 5a..........Miss L Blackford** 3
alwys mid-div, kpt on onepce
736[3] Anvil Corner 5a *alwys towrds, lft 4th by defections* ....D Dennis 4
736 The Butler *prom til wknd 14th, p.u. 2 out* .....S Slade pu
Northern Sensation 5a *nvr trbld ldrs, p.u. aft 13th* ....N Harris pu
628[4] Lady Lir 5a *chsd ldrs til grdly wknd 5 out, p.u. 2 out* ....Miss S Young pu
740[1] Ask Me Kindly (Ire) *(fav) ld 1st til p.u. 7th, dismntd lame* ....Mrs M Hand pu
8 ran. 1½l, 10l, 10l. Time 6m 7.00s. SP 3-1.
David Heath (Four Burrow).
P.Ho.

WEST SOMERSET VALE
Cothelstone
Saturday April 12th
GOOD TO FIRM

1040 Members

645[3] **LIFE PEERAGE (USA) ....Mrs S Barrow** 1
ld to 6th,ld 12th,disp 4 out-2 out,hdd, ld apr last, ran on
692[4] **Dollybat 5a..........M Frith** 2
(fav) chsd ldr,ld 7-12th, disp 4 out til ld 2 out, hdd last,no ext
527 **Dust Of Life 5a ....N Mitchell** 3
alwys 3rd, handy to 13th, lost tch nxt, t.o. 3 out
3 ran. ½l, dist. Time 6m 39.00s. SP 7-4.
Michael James Hayes (West Somerset Vale).

1041 Restricted (12st)

866[1] **FARADAY ....N Mitchell** 1
(fav) disp til clr ldr 5th, jnd 2 out, ld last, ran on well
861[1] **Royal Turn ....A Honeyball** 2
w.w. prog 12th, 2nd nxt, chal 2 out, outpcd flat
823[1] **I'm The Gaffer ....F Brennan** 3
mostly 3rd, nvr on trms wth ldrs, outpcd frm 4 out
688 Bryn's Story *disp to 5th, wknd, last frm 12th, t.o. 3 out* ....Maj G Wheeler 4
4 ran. 2l, dist, 20l. Time 6m 19.30s. SP 6-4.
G B Foot (Seavington).

1042 Mixed Open (12st)

929[1] **QUALITAIR MEMORY (IRE) ....J Tizzard** 1
(fav) trckd ldr, ld 14th, easily
791[3] **Frosty Reception (bl)..........Miss C Stucley** 2
ld til blnd 13th, chsd wnr vainly aft, blnd last
2 ran. 5l. Time 6m 22.00s. SP 1-5.
C L Tizzard (Blackmore & Sparkford Vale).

1043 Intermediate (12st)

760[1] **TAURA'S RASCAL ....F Brennan** 1
n.j.w. made all, clr whn blnd 3 out, kpt on wll und pres
792[1] **Link Copper ....Miss S Jackson** 2
hld up, prog 4 out, tk 2nd 2 out, nrst fin
863[2] **Hensue ....Miss S West** 3
alwys mid-div, lft 2nd 14th, outpcd frm 3 out
687[2] Alex Thuscombe 5ex (v) *(fav) w.w. chsd alng 14th, no ch whn blnd last* ....P Shaw 4
950[4] Grey Guestino *prom early, lost plc 12th, onepcd frm 4 out* ....Miss L Delve 5
642[2] Scriven Boy *cls up, 2nd frm 11th til blnd & u.r. 13th* ....M Flynn ur
648[5] Lake Mariner 5a *hld up, prog 12th, 4th & ev ch whn hmpd & u.r. nxt* ....M Wells ur
7 ran. 2l, 3l, 15l, 25l. Time 6m 19.00s. SP 2-1.
F J Brennan (V.W.H.).

1044 PPORA (12st)

736[1] **PASSING FAIR 5a** ....Miss S Vickery 1
(fav) made all, lft solo 14th
Busteele *chsd ldr, 5l 2nd whn f hvly 14th* ....J Tizzard f
2 ran. Time 6m 34.50s. SP 1-5.
Mrs C Wilson (Blackmore & Sparkford Vale).

1045 Open Maiden (12st)

527[2] **BILLY BARTER (IRE)** ....Miss S Vickery 1
(fav) ld to 5th, 2nd aft til ld 10th, not extndd
527 **Sue's Quest 5a**..........................P King 2
last til prog 13th, hrd rdn 2 out, tk 2nd flat
864 **And What Else (Ire)** ....B Dixon 3
2nd to 5th, 3rd to 10th, chsd wnr agn 14th, blnd 3 out, wknd
795[4] Suba Lin 5a *sttld rear, no ch frm 4 out, nrst fin* ....M Frith 4
Dula Model 5a *s.s. plld hrd, ld 5-9th, wknd rpdly, t.o. & p.u. 4 out* ....J Boscherini pu
Retrieving Mission (Ire) *ref & u.r. 1st* ......M Burrows ref
6 ran. 5l, ½l, 1l. Time 6m 28.70s. SP 2-5.
J C Worrow (Blackmore & Sparkford Vale).
D.P.

DUMFRIESSHIRE
Lockerbie
Sunday April 13th
FIRM

1046 Members

778 **SOLWAYSANDS** ....B Gibson 1
(fav) ld 6th, made rest, kpt on well
561 **Matrace 5a** ....A Parker 2
cls 2nd frm 14th, no ext flat
612[6] **Rough House** ....R Morgan 3
ld to 6th, cls 2nd til 14th, lost tch 3 out
Poynder Park (Ire) *alwys last, lost tch by 13th, p.u. 2 out* ....L Morgan pu
4 ran. 3l, dist. Time 7m 31.00s. SP 2-5.
K Little (Dumfriesshire).

1047 Intermediate (12st)

671[4] **TATTLEJACK (IRE) 5ex (bl)** ....Mrs C Ford 1
(fav) disp to 5th, ld 15th, jnd last, found ext cls hm
Little Glen 5ex..............................T Scott 2
ld 5th-15th, jnd wnr last, no ext cls hm
608[4] **Luckieshiel 5a**...................Miss D Calder 3
cls up til wknd frm 14th
Muffled Mist 5a *alwys last, lost tch 13th, p.u. 4 out* ....C Storey pu
4 ran. ½l, 25l. Time 7m 21.00s. SP 11-10.
M Silcock & T Taylor (West Shropshire Drag).

1048 Ladies

778[4] **ROLY PRIOR** ....Mrs V Jackson 1
ld 3rd-11th, ld 14th, sn clr
731[2] **Lupy Minstrel** ....Miss P Robson 2
(fav) cls up til outpcd frm 14th
943[3] Lion Of Vienna (bl) *alwys last, t.o. & p.u. 4 out* ....Mrs C Ford pu
945 Very Evident (Ire) *ld til ran out 3rd* ....Miss J Bird ro
814[1] Cookie Boy *ld 11th-14th, btn 3rd whn p.u. apr 2 out* ....Miss H Delahooke pu
231 Sudden Sally (Ire) 5a *in tch til wknd frm 14th, p.u. apr last* ....Miss M Bremner pu
6 ran. 10l. Time 7m 14.00s. SP 5-2.
Ian Hamilton (Tynedale).

1049 Men's Open

560[1] **SIMON JOSEPH** ....R Morgan 1
(fav) ld & alwys abt 3l up, comf
411[4] **Buckle It Up** ....C Storey 2
chsd wnr 3rd, nvr quite on trms, fin lame
891[4] **Boreen Owen** ....T Morrison 3
last frm 3rd, clsd slghtly frm 4 out, nvr dang
3 ran. 4l, 1l. Time 7m 16.00s. SP 4-9.
Mrs Yda Morgan (Dumfriesshire).

1050 Restricted

559[1] **BITOFANATTER** ....R Morgan 1
made most, went clr frm 14th, mstk 2 out, unchal
883[2] **Concerto Collonges (Fr)** ....R Ford 2
(fav) 2nd frm 13th, no imp on wnr
762[1] **I'll Skin Them (Ire) 5a** ....Mrs C Ford 3
last at 10th, nvr nr wnr
416[3] Snapper *cls up to 13th, sn lost tch, virt p.u. flat* ....A Parker 4
778 Madame Beck 5a *in tch til wknd 13th, p.u. 3 out* ....M Smith pu
5 ran. 15l, 1½l, dist. Time 7m 18.00s. SP 15-8.
David Caldwell (Eglinton).

1051 Maiden Div I (12st)

949 **GREY ROCK (IRE) 5a**...................P Craggs 1
made most to 8th, ld agn 15th, cosily
767[2] **The Alleycat (Ire)** ....Miss P Robson 2
(fav) last at 9th, prog to chal 2 out, alwys just hld
566 **Flower Of Dunblane 5a**.................A Parker 3
bhnd til prog 4 out, not rch ldng pair
898[2] Madame Defarge 5a *bhnd til some late prog, nvr rchd ldrs* ....Mrs K Hargreave 4
729 Turn Of Foot (Ire) *alwys twrds rear* .....M Bradburne 5
948[4] General Jack *ld 8th-13th, sn wknd* ......Miss J Percy 6
Bi Then (Ire) 5a *prog to trck ldrs whn u.r. 11th* ....Miss H Dudgeon ur
565 Lethem Laird *disp ld early, wknd frm 13th, p.u. 2 out* ....C Storey pu
613[6] Father O'Callaghan (Ire) *cls up til 3 out, wknd rpdly, p.u. last*...........................Miss M Bremner pu
948 No Justice *cls up, ld 13th-15th, sn wknd, p.u. last* ....T Scott pu
10 ran. ½l, 6l, 6l, 15l, 10l. Time 7m 24.00s. SP 9-1.
Mrs B E Miller (Cumberland Farmers).

1052 Maiden Div II (12st)

731[3] **CZARYNE 5a**.......................Miss J Percy 1
alwys handy, ld 4 out, styd on well
814[4] **Dillons Bridge (Ire)** ....R Morgan 2
(fav) alwys handy, chal 2 out, no ext apr last
972 **Seymour Fiddles 5a** ....D McLeod 3
bhnd til prog frm 12th, ch 3 out, wknd apr nxt
949[3] New Problem 5a 3ow *sn clr 2nd, wknd frm 14th, p.u. 3 out* ....M Smith pu
767 Little Idiot 5a *alwys wll bhnd, p.u. 3 out* .....A Parker pu
Templand *chsng grp whn p.u. 10th* ....P Craggs pu
768 Cinder Mirage *sn bhnd, t.o. & p.u. aft 11th* ..B Gibson pu
Read The News 12a 8ow *sn last, t.o. & p.u. 3 out* ....T Morrison pu
729 Bow Tie *sn wll clr, wknd rpdly 4 out, p.u. 2 out* ....J Ewart pu
Tantalum 5a 6ow *alwys bhnd, p.u. 3 out* ...W Spence pu
10 ran. 2l, 15l. Time 7m 17.00s. SP 5-2.
Mrs J D Percy (Tynedale).
R.J.

HAMPSHIRE
Hackwood Park
Sunday April 13th
GOOD TO FIRM

1053 Members (12st)

483[1] **DARTON RI** ....Mrs S Bingham 1
(fav) ld to 6th, outpcd 15th, clsd last, ld flat, readily
873[3] **Palaman** ....C Pearson 2
ld 7th, qcknd 6l clr 4 out, rdn apr last, wknd & hdd flat
2 ran. 1½l. Time 6m 32.00s. SP 1-4.
Mrs S Maxse (Hampshire).

1054 Confined (12st)

868[1] **ESPY** ....**A James** 1
2nd frm 3rd, going wll & narrow ld whn lft clr 2 out
870[3] **Paco's Boy** ....**P York** 2
chsd ldrs, wknd rpdly bef 2 out, lft poor 2nd
489 Royal Irish *chsd ldrs, wknd apr 2 out, ran out & u.r. last*.......................................C Pearson ur
872[1] Heathview 3ex *(fav) jmpd rght, mstk 12th, ld til hdd & f 2 out*...................................M Portman f
4 ran. 30l. Time 6m 20.00s. SP 4-1.
C James (Vine & Craven).

1055 Men's Open (12st)

659[1] **MYVERYGOODFRIEND** ....**S Cobden** 1
(fav) ld 6th, jmpd slwly 14th, ld agn 16th, all out
976[4] **January Don (bl)** ....**M FitzGerald** 2
alwys cls up, chal frm 2 out, just hld
869[3] **Skinnhill (bl)** ....**C Mason** 3
rdn alng, ld to 6th, ld brfly 15th, ran on
825[3] Abitmorfun *alwys last, remote frm hlfwy* ....C Coyne 4
4 ran. Nk, 4l, 1 fence. Time 6m 24.00s. SP 1-2.
S Cobden (Hursley Hambledon).

1056 G Middleton Ladies

932[1] **ARCTIC CHILL (IRE)** ....**Miss S Vickery** 1
(fav) j.w. made all, comf
869[1] **Pejawi 5a** ....**Miss L Whitaker** 2
went 2nd at 11th, no ch wth wnr
824[3] **Taurean Tycoon** ....**Miss S Duckett** 3
chsd wnr to 11th, wknd rpdly 3 out
3 ran. 3l, 30l. Time 6m 23.00s. SP 1-6.
M F Thorne & D Hobbs (Blackmore & Sparkford Vale).

1057 B F S S (12st)

305[3] **BLACKWATER LADY (IRE) 5a 7ex** .....**P Scouller** 1
(fav) ld 4-6th, ld & mstk 2 out, qcknd clr last
633[5] **Dragons Lady 5a**...................**M FitzGerald** 2
ld early, drppd rear, rdn 3 out, ran on wll last
966 **Vultoro 7ex**..........................**T Underwood** 3
ld 6th-2 out, outpcd flat
790 Debjanjo *rear & rmndrs, wknd 3 out, p.u. last* M Miller pu
4 ran. 2l, 3l. Time 6m 25.00s. SP 2-5.
P A D Scouller (Garth & South Berks).

1058 Interlink Restricted (12st)

770[3] **BARNEYS GOLD (IRE)** ....**A Bealby** 1
(fav) 6/4-4/5, ld to 3rd, ld 11th, comf
742[3] **Game Fair** ....**W Cook** 2
alwys 2nd/3rd, chal 2 out, no imp
873[2] **Rayman (Ire)** ....**R Cope** 3
rear, clsd 13th, mstk nxt, wknd
921 Duke Of Lancaster (Ire) *rear, mstk 11th, no dang* ....N Sutton 4
742[2] Todds Hall (Ire) 1ow (bl) *ld 3-10th, wknd rpdly, t.o. & p.u. aft 3 out*...............................A Munro pu
935[2] Neville *s.s. f 2nd*.......................Miss R David f
6 ran. 5l, 6l, 7l. Time 6m 23.00s. SP 4-5.
Irvin S Naylor (Quorn).
One fence omitted final two circuits.

1059 Open Maiden (12st)

871[2] **MUSKERRY MOYA (IRE) 5a**......**Miss A Goschen** 1
jmpd rght, made all, qcknd clr aft 3 out
Mr Drake (Ire) ....**J Owen** 2
(fav) 3rd til lft 2nd 11th, vain pursuit aft
921[2] No Reply *sweating, 2nd til p.u. 11th*...........P York pu
485 The Blind Judge *in rear til u.r. 4 out*.....M FitzGerald ur
Bold Bluff *rear til p.u. 5 out* ....Miss T Honeyball pu
747[2] Dad's Dilemma *rear whn u.r. 3rd*...........T Smith ur
6 ran. 25l. Time 6m 23.00s. SP 3-1.
N W Rimington (Blackmore & Sparkford Vale).
P.M.

LEDBURY
Maisemore Park
Sunday April 13th
GOOD TO FIRM

1060 Members (12st)

819[2] **VIRIDIAN** ....**M Rimell** 1
in tch, mstk 9th, disp 12th, hit nxt, ld 15th, sn wll clr
703[3] **Drumceva** ....**M Wilesmith** 2
chsd ldr 3-11th, outpcd 13th, kpt on to tk 2nd apr last
880[1] **Lets Twist Again (Ire) 3ex** ....**Julian Pritchard** 3
(fav) ld, blnd 11th, hdd 15th, sn rdn & swshd tail, sn btn
Not A Problem *s.s. sn rcvrd, blnd 4th, t.o. 6th, p.u. 14th*.......................................T Leeke pu
Wayside Boy *in tch, rmndr 5th, mstk 8th, rdn & lost tch 11th, p.u. 14th*.......................A Phillips pu
5 ran. 16l, 8l. Time 6m 31.60s. SP 5-2.
D Hine (Ledbury).

1061 Restricted (12st)

753[2] **CORN EXCHANGE** ....**M Rimell** 1
chsd ldrs, blnd 9th, ld 2 out, styd on wll und pres
648[2] **Kinesiology (Ire)** ....**E Williams** 2
(fav) chsd ldr 6th, blnd 11th, rdn apr 2 out, unable qckn apr last
821[1] **Rosevalley (Ire)** ....**K Whiting** 3
mstks, disp til blnd 4th, ld 12th-2 out, no ext
701[2] Kingsthorpe *chsd ldrs, 2nd whn blnd 14th, kpt on onepcd frm 3 out* ....A Phillips 4
313[4] Major Bert (Ire) *chsd ldrs 10th, 5th & chnce 3 out, one-pcd*..H Wheeler 5
935 Third Melody 5a *alwys bhnd, no ch frm 14th* ....G Weatherley 6
881[1] Rusty Fellow *nvr going wll, t.o. 4th, stewards* ....D Mansell 7
Your Opinion *mid-div, lost tch 13th, p.u. 15th, dsmntd* ....M Walters pu
406[2] Hal's Prince *disp clr ld til ld 4th-12th, 2nd whn blnd 15th, p.u. aft*.............................Miss P Jones pu
633[4] Generator Boy *mid-div, wknd apr 14th, no ch whn f 2 out*...J Baimbridge f
254[2] Kingofnobles (Ire) *bhnd frm 8th, t.o. & p.u. 12th* ....R Rogers pu
262 Derring Ann 5a *rear til u.r. 7th*............D S Jones ur
12 ran. 3l, 6l, sht-hd, 2l, 30l, sht-hd. Time 6m 31.00s. SP 12-1.
D Wellon (Cotswold Vale).

1062 Mixed Open (12st)

SULTAN'S SON ....**G Lewis** 1
50s-12s, 2nd til jnd ldr 13th, ld apr last, ran on well
394[1] **Down The Mine** ....**Miss A Dare** 2
(fav) ld, hit 10th, jnd 13th, hdd apr last, onepcd
636[2] **Poinciana** ....**E Williams** 3
cls up, 3rd & mstk 12th, sn rdn, outpcd by ldng pair aft
Notanotherone (Ire) *chsd ldrs, hit 10th, went mod 4th 14th, not trbl ldrs*...............................S Lloyd 4
702 Kings Rank (bl) *jmpd slwly, t.o. 9th, some late prog, nvr dang*.......................................H Wheeler 5
689 Daybrook's Gift (bl) *alwys bhnd, t.o. whn blnd & u.r. 11th*...................................Miss N Allan ur
Penllyne's Pride *chsd ldrs to 6th, sn lost plc, p.u. 10th* ....J Chilton pu
825[2] Madraj (Ire) (bl) *cls up to 6th, wknd 13th, t.o. & p.u. 2 out*..N Ridout pu
749 Junction Twentytwo (bl) *chsd ldrs, 4th & rdn 11th, wknd, t.o. & p.u. 2 out*.......................A Wintle pu
704[3] Perryline 5a *hld up, some prog to poor 7th at 9th, nvr on trms, p.u.2 out*......................Julian Pritchard pu
535[1] Conna Moss (Ire) *mid-div, rmndr 4th, jinked & u.r. 7th* ....Miss P Jones ur
Mac's Gamble *jmpd rght, alwys last, t.o. & p.u. 12th* ....M Harris pu
12 ran. 2l, 10l, 10l, 12l. Time 6m 25.70s. SP 12-1.
J J V Phillips (Tivyside).

1063 B F S S (Nov Riders)

703[2] **SISTERLY 5a .... R Rogers** **1**
chsd ldr 7th, ld 14th, kckd clr, hit last, unchal
395[1] **All Weather .... Miss E Wilesmith** **2**
(fav) prom, cls 3rd at 12th, outpcd 14th, chsd wnr 3 out, no imp
Altnabrocky .... T Gretton **3**
mid-div, prog to 5th at 14th, outpcd, kpt on apr last
924 Kemys Commander *ld to 14th, sn outpcd by wnr, onepcd* .... G Smith 4
869[4] Prince's Court *bhnd, some prog 14th, went mod 5th 2 out, nvr nrr* .... Mrs J Kimber 5
Air Commander *prog 7th, 4th & chnc 14th, wknd nxt* .... Miss D Olding 6
634[1] Guarena (USA) *rear, rmndr 5th, mstk 12th, nvr dang* .... Miss N Richards 7
706[7] Millstock 5a *t.d.e. s.s. alwys rear* ..... Miss N Stallard 8
569 Sandy Beau *s.s. alwys rear, nvr dang* .. Miss A Nolan 9
255[6] Stanford Boy *chsd ldrs, 6th & wkng whn f 15th* .... G Andrew f
817[2] Bumptious Boy *p.u. 1st, dsmntd* .... S Hanks pu
Proplus *prom to 5th, bhnd 12th, p.u. 15th* .. Mrs A Lee pu
700[4] Brenner Pass (NZ) *s.s. hit 1st, last whn f 4th* J Hibbert f
13 ran. 8l, ½l, 6l, 12l, 8l, 1l, ½l, 8l. Time 6m 37.00s. SP 3-1.
Peter Nash (North Herefordshire).

1064 Confined (12st)

877[1] **CRUISE A HOOP .... Julian Pritchard** **1**
(fav) unruly strt, ld 2nd, 3l clr apr 2 out, styd on strngly
880[2] **Landsker Alfred 6ex .... Miss A Dare** **2**
chsd ldrs, went 2nd 15th, 3l down apr 2 out, btn nxt
568[1] **Frozen Pipe 5a 6ex .... M Harris** **3**
w.w. prog 12th, went 3rd 3 out, no prog aft
931[2] The Lorryman (Ire) *prssd wnr, blnd 12th, 4th & wkng 3 out* .... N Mitchell 4
589[5] Master Donnington *chsd ldrs, 5th whn hit 14th, no dang aft* .... Miss E Wilesmith 5
704[1] Gromit (NZ) *hld up in rear, poor 7th & no ch 13th* .... T Stephenson 6
876 Bluff Cove *alwys wll bhnd, t.o. whn blnd 10th* A Chipp 7
Just Ralph *t.o. 8th, p.u. 10th* .... G Barfoot-Saunt pu
651 Barkisland *wll bhnd 9th, t.o. & p.u. 15th* ..... S Joynes pu
650 Grey Tudor *last whn u.r. 5th* .... G Field ur
493 Mecado (v) *rear & jmpd slwly 7th, wll bhnd & p.u. 14th* .... M Munrowd pu
959[1] Sterling Buck (USA) *prog 9th, 4th & rdn 11th, sn wknd, p.u. 2 out* .... M Rimell pu
Hook Line'N'sinker *ld to 2nd, chsd ldrs to 10th, bhnd whn p.u. 15th* .... L Brown pu
13 ran. 8l, 1½l, 15l, 10l, 5l, 2 fences. Time 6m 25.60s. SP 7-4.
W M A Davies (North Cotswold).

1065 Open Maiden Div I (12st)

649 **ROSE OF MACMILLION 5a .... J Jukes** **1**
hld up rear, lft 3rd 14th, lft 2nd 3 out, ld last, all out
881[4] **Sylvan Sirocco .... M Harris** **2**
ld, clr 6th, blnd 14th, hdd apr last, no ext
480[4] Walton Thorns *prom, chsd ldr 10th, rdn 15th, p.u. rpdly nxt, lame* .... M Munrowd pu
717 Malthouse Lad *chsd ldrs, 3rd whn blnd 11th, sn rdn & wknd, p.u. last* .... E Williams pu
823 Naburn Loch 5a *nvr bttr than mid-div, p.u. 15th* .... J Barnes pu
Glenville Breeze (Ire) *trckd ldrs, wknd 11th, t.o. & p.u. 3 out* .... G Lewis pu
700 Wrenbury Farmer *mid-div, mstk 6th, t.o. 12th, p.u. nxt* .... O McPhail pu
1015 Heather Wood 5a *mstks, prom, lost plc 8th, t.o. & u.r. 13th* .... D Mansell ur
390 Shelley's Dream 5a *mstks, hld up, prog to 2nd 12th, 3rd & btn whn f 14th* .... M Walters f
365 Silk Oats 5a *(fav) prog 8th, chsd ldrs 10th, wknd 12th, p.u. 15th* .... Julian Pritchard pu
390 Donald Hawkins 7a *mid-div, lost tch 8th, no ch whn f 14th* .... P Howse f
706 Cowarne Adventure 7a *t.o. 9th, p.u. 14th* .... T Stephenson pu
901[5] Firestarter *ran out & u.r. 2nd* .... N Oliver ro
13 ran. 2½l. Time 6m 41.20s. SP 14-1.
K R Howse (V.W.H.).
Two fences omitted.

1066 Open Maiden Div II Pt I (12st)

RAP UP FAST (USA) .... Julian Pritchard **1**
(fav) ld aft 2nd, clr nxt, kpt on und pres frm 2 out
570[4] **Playing The Fool 5a .... P Hanly** **2**
keen hld, chsd wnr 8th, ev ch apr 2 out, unable qckn
877 **Snippetoff .... M Rimell** **3**
mstks, prog 9th, lft 3rd 12th, sn lost tch, t.o.
934[5] Parapluie 5a *alwys mid-div, blnd 9th, lft poor 4th 14th, t.o.* .... Miss B Lloyd 4
Wee Macgregor *bhnd frm 5th, no ch 10th, p.u. 14th* .... H Wheeler pu
Brother Harold *prom, blnd 5th & 7th, 3rd whn f 12th* .... A Phillips f
570[3] Wolfie Smith *ld to 2nd, wll bhnd 7th, t.o. & p.u. 11th* .... T Stephenson pu
571 King Paddy (Ire) 7a *chsd ldrs,4th & rdn 7th,lft poor 4th 12th,nrly ref nxt,p.u.* .... R Burton pu
706 Conimore (Ire) 12a *t.o. 6th, 4th & no ch whn blnd & u.r. last* .... J Jackson ur
9 ran. ½l, dist, dist. Time 6m 36.40s. SP 4-5.
R T Baimbridge (Berkeley).

1067 Open Maiden Div II Pt II (12st)

641 **PRINCE ITSU .... A Price** **1**
t.d.e. keen hld, ld 4th, made rest, styd on strngly flat
Kilgobbin (Ire) .... D Stephens **2**
(fav) keen hld, hld up, went 2nd 12th, ev ch 3 out, not qckn last
366 **Astromis (Ire) 5a.................. O McPhail** **3**
hld up, jmpd slwly 5th, blnd 15th, 3rd & chnc 2 out, no ext
719 Dinedor Charlie *in tch,mstk 8th,rmndrs 10th,btn whn blnd 2 out, lft 4th last* .... D S Jones 4
1015 Bessie's Will 5a *in tch,jmpd rght 6th,outpcd 13th,rlld 3 out,btn whn ref last* .... G Barfoot-Saunt ref
Derring Tirley *u.r. 1st* .... S Joynes ur
907[3] Little Ease (Ire) 12a *s.s. in tch 7th, last & wkng 13th, p.u. nxt* .... M Munrowd pu
653 Permit 5a *jmpd slwly, ld to 4th, lost plc 10th, last whn f nxt* .... Miss P Gundry f
8 ran. 5l, 10l, 20l. Time 6m 55.30s. SP 6-1.
John Jones (Gelligaer).
S.P.

MIDDLETON
Whitwell-On-The-Hill
Sunday April 13th
GOOD

1068 Restricted Div I (12st)

778[3] **ADMISSION (IRE) .... Miss L Horner** **1**
(Jt fav) hld up, prog 8th, ld 14th, drew clr 3 out, easily
695[3] **Caman 5a .... Mrs S Grant** **2**
trckd ldrs, ld 11th, hdd 13th, kpt on onepcd frm 2 out
620[1] **Kendor Pass (Ire) .... M Tate** **3**
(Jt fav) trckd ldr, disp 4-8th, ld 13th-nxt, wknd 3 out
698[3] Goodheavens Mrtony *mid-div, effrt 13th, no prog frm 4 out* .... Miss A Deniel 4
859[1] Rise Above It (Ire) *ld/disp to 11th, sn wknd, fin tired* .... K Green 5
616[9] Sharp To Oblige *rear whn u.r. 2nd* .... S Whitaker ur
856[5] Lyningo *rear, outpcd 10th, sn wll bhnd, p.u. 4 out* .... S Brisby pu
Carinci *chsd ldrs, fdd 11th, t.o. & p.u. 14th* . G Hanmer pu
856[4] Stride To Glory (Ire) (bl) *mid-div, outpcd 11th, sn lost tch, t.o. & f hvly last* .... D Topping f
777[1] Mallow Innocence *mid-div, outpcd 10th, sn wll bhnd, p.u. 14th* .... N Kent pu

860[1] On The Fly *prom, cls 3rd whn f 8th* ....R Edwards f
509 Political Field 5a *rear, strgglng & rmndrs 10th, t.o. 12th, p.u. 14th* ....S Walker pu
12 ran. 12l, 4l, 10l, 25l. Time 6m 18.00s. SP 5-2.
Mrs J Horner (South Durham).

1069 Restricted Div II (12st)

695[4] **CHAPEL ISLAND** ....**G Tuer** **1**
mid-div, prog to ld 4 out, drew clr 2 out, pshd out
676[6] **Smashing View** ....**R Hartley** **2**
rear, prog 8th, ev ch 14th, unable qckn nxt
615[3] **Attle** ....**W Burnell** **3**
alwys prom, chsd ldr 14th, onepcd nxt
425[7] Ruff Account *(fav) ld to 11th, steadily wknd 4 out* ....Miss J Eastwood 4
427 Look Sharpe *reluc to race, t.o. til jnd main grp 10th, kpt on frm 4 out*.........................A Bonson 5
856[8] Prophet's Choice *mid-div most of way, not qckn frm 4 out* ....M Haigh 6
695 Make A Line *alwys prom, ld 11th til hdd & wknd 4 out* ....C Denny 7
346[4] Just Jessica 5a *prom til fdd frm 12th*.......A Balding 8
616[6] Miley Pike *mid-div, rdn 9th, sn strgglng, t.o. 13th* ....N Tutty 9
898[1] Persian Lion *trckd ldr, wknd rpdly 14th, t.o. & p.u. 3 out* ....Mrs L Ward pu
424 Canny's Fort 5a *blnd 1st, rear, lost tch 10th, t.o. 13th, p.u. 3 out*...............................S Gibbon pu
839 The Tide Race 5a *rear, strgglng 9th, t.o. 13th, p.u. nxt* ....P Gee pu
12 ran. 12l, 5l, 4l, 4l, 2l, 5l, 1l, 7l. Time 6m 24.00s. SP 4-1.
E W & M Tuer (Hurworth).

1070 PPORA

694[2] **GREY REALM 5a**.......................**N Smith** **1**
prom, disp 6th til ld 9-11th, ld 13th, ran on strngly 2 out
383[8] **Boulevard Bay (Ire)** ....**N Wilson** **2**
(fav) prom, disp 5th-9th, going wll 3 out, chnc nxt, not qckn
937[2] **Mr Primetime (Ire)** ....**N Bannister** **3**
mid-div, prog 4th, ld 11th-13th, rdn & outpcd 3 out
477[1] Arras-Tina 5a *mid-div, outpcd 9th, effrt 11th, strgglng 14th*...................................S Walker 4
619[5] Barichste (bl) *ld til disp 5th, hdd nxt, prom til outpcd frm 4 out*..........................Maj M Watson 5
694[6] Dalmore (bl) *mid-div, prog 11th, wknd 4 out* D Coates 6
694 Sharpridge *mid-div, lost tch 5th, t.o. 9th, p.u. 11th* ....M Mawhinney pu
Dashing Dula 5a *rear, mstk 2nd, outpcd 5th, t.o. 9th, p.u. 12th*................................J Sinnott pu
264 Skyval 5a *rear, mstk 4th, outpcd 7th, wll bhnd 10th, p.u. 4 out*...................................K Green pu
9 ran. 6l, 2½l, 8l, 3l, 12l. Time 6m 23.00s. SP 4-1.
R E Barr (Cleveland).

1071 Confined

507[1] **PEANUTS PET** ....**R Walmsley** **1**
(fav) prom, disp 13th, ld nxt, prssd last, hld on wll nr fin
696[1] **Misti Hunter (Ire)** ....**S Swiers** **2**
hld up, prog 11th, ev ch last, rallied nr fin
424[1] **Blackwoodscountry** ....**C Mulhall** **3**
prom, ev ch 14th, not qckn frm 3 out
618[1] General Brandy *mid-div, prog 10th, disp 13th-nxt, sn outpcd* ....G Tuer 4
618[2] Castle Tyrant 5a *ld til disp 7th, hdd 10th, wknd 14th* ....P Atkinson 5
763 Pinewood Lad *rear, lost tch 9th, t.o. nxt* ..Miss K Ford 6
505[4] Oxford Place (bl) *prom til lost plc 9th, wll bhnd whn u.r. 11th*..........................Mrs F Needham ur
897 Earl Gray *mid-div, rdn 9th, lost tch 12th, wll bhnd whn p.u. 2 out*.........................Miss A Deniel pu
874 Double Collect *prom,disp 7th til ld 10th-13th, fdd 4 out,wll btn & p.u.2out* ....N Smith pu
859 Prickly Trout 5a *rear, lost tch 4th, t.o. 8th, p.u. 10th* ....J Sinnott pu
10 ran. ½l, 15l, 3l, 10l, dist. Time 6m 20.00s. SP 4-6.
J W Walmsley (Bramham Moor).

1072 4m S Life Mixed Open (12st)

778[2] **ASK ANTONY (IRE)** ....**N Wilson** **1**
(fav) mid-div, prog to 3rd 13th, ld 18th, sn clr, imprssv
923[1] **The Difference** ....**M Chatterton** **2**
mid-div, prog 4 out, styd on wll 2 out
583[1] **Final Hope (Ire)** ....**Mrs F Needham** **3**
mid-div, mstk 6th, prog 16th, chsd wnr 4 out, one-pcd
694[3] Flying Lion *rear, styd on frm 4 out, nvr dang* M Haigh 4
Thank U Jim *ld to 15th, grad fdd* .....Miss T Jackson 5
895[2] Rustino *prom, went 2nd 13th, ld 16th-18th, no ext* ....Miss R Clark 6
893[1] Cot Lane *prom til fdd frm 14th*................J Tate 7
617[7] Colonel Popski *prom til wknd 16th* ....N Tutty 8
695[6] Spartan Juliet 5a *alwys rear, nvr a fctr*.....P Jenkins 9
875[4] Tom Log (bl) *mid-div, mstk 15th, wknd 18th* W Burnell 10
855[1] Pats Cross (Ire) *ldng grp til wknd frm 18th, t.o.* ....J Byrne 11
856[7] The Chap *mid-div, strgglng 13th, t.o. & p.u. 16th* ....R Lochman pu
875[3] Syrus P Turntable *rear, wll bhnd 18th, p.u. 4 out* ....J Saville pu
885[2] Across The Lake *rear, strgglng 8th, t.o. & p.u. 16th* ....Miss S Brotherton pu
505[2] Master Cornet *prom til fdd 14th, t.o. & p.u. 19th* ....W Bethell pu
766[4] Katies Argument 5a *rear, strgglng whn blnd 13th, sn t.o., p.u. 16th*.........................Miss J Wilson pu
896[1] Frome Boy 5ow *rear, lost tch 6th, t.o. & u.r. 17th* ....P Johnson ur
855[2] Here Comes Charter *mid-div, strgglng 14th, t.o. 19th, p.u. 2 out* ....A Pennock pu
Hurricane Linda 5a *alwys rear, t.o. whn p.u. 4 out* ....S Walker pu
616 Missile Man *rear, lost tch 13th, t.o. & p.u. 16th* ....S Pinder pu
618[3] Gaelic Warrior *prom til wknd 16th, t.o. & p.u. 19th* ....S Swiers pu
21 ran. 20l, sht-hd, 8l, 1l, ½l, 6l, 10l, 2l, 3l, 25l. Time 8m 40.00s. SP Evens.
Jim Burns (Middleton).

1073 2½m 88yds Open Maiden (5-7yo) Div I (12st)

860 **PATEY COURT 5a (bl)**..................**C Mulhall** **1**
mid-div, rdn 6th, prog 8th, ld 11th, kpt on wll flat
699[2] **Tudor Flight 5a**.....................**G Markham** **2**
rear til ran on wll 3 out, nrst fin
722 **Ishereal (Ire)** ....**S Prior** **3**
rear, prog 4 out, ev ch 2 out, not qckn
510 Just Johnie *(fav) alwys prom, ev ch 3 out, onepcd* ....S Walker 4
839[5] Milo Boy *mid-div, mstk 7th, outpcd frm 4 out* ....M Mackley 5
510 Timber Topper *prom til wknd 4 out, t.o. & p.u. 2 out* ....H Armstrong pu
Auntie Chris 5a *mid-div, wknd 11th, t.o. & p.u. 2 out* ....P Gee pu
Corsage *mid-div, lost tch 11th, p.u. last*......K Green pu
429 Raike It In 5a *ld to 7th, wknd rpdly, p.u. 11th*...N Tutty pu
620 Little Red *prom, ld 7th-11th, sn wknd, t.o. & p.u. 2 out* ....T Barry pu
269[2] Yodeller Bill *mid-div, prog 7th, wknd 3 out, wll bhnd whn p.u. last* ....R Edwards pu
860 Is Red There 7a *mid-div, rmndrs 5th, sn strgglng, wll bhnd whn p.u. 2 out* ....W Burnell pu
860 Surprise View 12a *mid-div, outpcd 6th, f nxt* P Halder f
768 Noreasonatall 12a *alwys rear, t.o. & p.u. 2 out* ....T Whitaker pu
Bit Of A Grip (Ire) 7a *rear, strgglng 7th, t.o. & p.u. 11th* ....N Kent pu
676 Denby Ryme 7a *prom til wknd 10th, p.u. 3 out* ....S Charlton pu
620 Royal Charger (Ire) 7a *prom til wknd 4 out, t.o. & p.u. 2 out* ....Mrs S Grant pu
17 ran. 1½l, 3l, 3l, 15l. Time 5m 27.00s. SP 10-1.

D Gill (Bramham Moor).

1074 2½m 88yds Open Maiden (5-7yo) Div II (12st)

160 **DANEGELD (IRE) ....N Smith** 1
(fav) hld up, prog 8th, ld 4 out, hrd prssd flat, just hld on
768 **Our Wyn-Ston 7a ....L Donnely** 2
alwys prom, chal last, ran on wll flat, just faild
Bucks View (Ire) ....G Hanmer 3
rear, prog 11th, ev ch 4 out, not qckn
357 Primitive Way 7a *prom til wknd apr 3 out* . .P Atkinson 4
116 Silly Tinker *mid-div, prog 10th, ev ch 3 out, wknd rpdly* ....C Denny 5
510 Fair Grand (bl) *alwys rear, nvr dang* ....S Brisby 6
417[6] Doc Spot *prom, ld 6th, disp 8th, ld agn 10th, hdd 4 out, wknd rpdly* ....S Robinson 7
860 China Hand (Ire) 7a *rear & strgglng 9th, sn t.o.* ....H Armstrong 8
699[4] Cute Word 5a *alwys rear, t.o. 6th*. . . . . . .Mrs H Arnold 9
839 Bex Boy (Ire) *disp to 6th, losing tch whn u.r. 10th* ....I Bennett ur
79 Just Shirley 5a *rear, strgglng 8th, t.o. & p.u. 10th* ....A Balding pu
509 Strong Words *disp to 6th, steadily fdd, t.o. & p.u. 2 out* ....S Pinder pu
357 Not So Prim 12a *prom, disp 8th-10th, wknd rpdly, p.u. 2 out* ....W Burnell pu
427[5] Miss Accounts (Ire) 5a *prom whn u.r. 5th* ....Miss A Armitage ur
777 Fly The Heights *rear, rmndr 7th, sn t.o., p.u. 2 out* ....S Walker pu
621 Half Each 12a *prom, wknd 9th, u.r. nxt* . . . . .R Walford ur

16 ran. Sht-hd, 4l, 8l, 6l, 8l, 12l, dist, 5l. Time 5m 25.00s. SP 2-1.
Col M J F Sheffield (Bilsdale).

1075 Members (12st)

694[1] **MR DICK ....S Swiers** 1
(fav) prom, disp 13th til hdd 2 out, hrd drvn to ld post
764[2] **Kellys Diamond ....Miss V Russell** 2
prom, ld 9th, disp 13th, ld 2 out, rdn & hdd post
351 **Simply A Star (Ire) (bl).............Maj M Watson** 3
prom til outpcd frm 3 out
695[5] Midge 5a *mid-div, prog to ld 7th, hdd 9th, grad fdd, lost tch 4 out* ....Miss S Brotherton 4
765 Clare Lad 8ow (v) *rear, lost tch 9th, t.o. 11th* . .J Burns 5
Playboy *carried 13st 6lbs, rear, bhnd 11th, t.o. & f 4 out* ....M Hogg f
856[3] Douce Eclair 5a *ld to 7th, prom whn wd apr 10th, cls 4th whn u.r. 2 out* ....Miss L Eddery ur
891[2] La Maja (Ire) 5a *rear, dtchd whn u.r. 10th* ....Mrs N Wilson ur
Political Trout 5a *rear, strggnlg 7th, t.o. 11th, p.u. 14th* ....C Mulhall pu

9 ran. Sht-hd, 8l, dist, 30l. Time 6m 27.00s. SP Evens.
Mrs J Cooper (Middleton).
N.E.

PYTCHLEY
Guilsborough
Sunday April 13th
GOOD TO FIRM

1076 Members

773[4] **SUPREME DREAM (IRE) 5a ....Mrs P Adams** 1
(Jt fav) trckd ldrs, lost plc 12th, prog 16th, ld 3 out, ran on well
449 **Miss Solitaire 5a.........................J Docker** 2
cls up, wth ldr 13th, mstk nxt, chal 3 out, alwys hld
927 **Duncaha Hero ....Miss R Barrow** 3
made most to 13th, effrt & ev ch 16th til wknd apr last
769 Jerrigo *wth ldr, lost plc 11th, effrt to ld 15th-3 out, btn nxt* ....J Knowles 4
449[4] Oliver Himself *hld up last, lost tch 11th, ran on frm 3 out, fin well* ....R Barrett 5
924[2] Hostetler *alwys rear, strgglng frm 12th, no prog 16th* ....J Stephenson 6
770[2] Brown Baby 5a *(Jt fav) 2nd whn u.r. 2nd* . . . . . .G Kerr ur
769 Tenelord *not fluent, w.w. prog & cls up 14th, wknd nxt, p.u. 2 out* ....S Morris pu
773 Toiapan (Ire) *wth ldr, ld 13th, mstk nxt, hdd 15th, wknd & p.u. 3 out* ....B Pollock pu

9 ran. 2l, 12l, 4l, ½l, 5l. Time 6m 34.00s. SP 3-1.
Mrs Pauline Adams (Pytchley).

1077 Confined (12st)

592[2] **RUN FOR FREE ....A Hill** 1
alwys prom.jnd ldr 12th,ld 16th,sn clr,hung lft frm 3 out
770[1] **Broadway Swinger ....S R Andrews** 2
trckd ldrs, effrt to chs wnr apr 3 out, no imp apr last
758[3] **Admiral Rous ....C Wadland** 3
last quartet to 12th, ran on wll frm 16th, nrst fin
769[4] Storming Roy *trckd ldrs, outpcd & mstk 13th, no prog til kpt on frm 2 out* ....H Nicholson 4
545 Menature (Ire) *s.v.s. grad prog frm 6th, tk 4th 2 out, no hdwy aft* ....A Sansome 5
770 Mr Gee *alwys rear, no ch 13th, t.o.* . . . . . . .K Needham 6
926 Pancratic *alwys last pair, t.o.* ....C Millington 7
546 Rousillon To Be (bl) *ld 2nd-9th, sn btn, p.u. 15th* ....T Lane pu
San Remo *alwys rear, t.o. & p.u. 15th* ....Miss S Samworth pu
769 Miller's Chap *mstk 6th, mid-div, btn frm 12th, p.u. 15th* ....M Hewitt pu
Harmony Walk (Ire) *mid-div, rdn 9th, sn btn, t.o. & p.u. 2 out* ....R Armson pu
369[2] Sabre King (bl) *trckd ldrs, blnd 11th, outpcd 13th, no ch & p.u. 2 out* ....L Lay pu
757 Samsword *mid-div, wknd 13th, bhnd whn p.u. 2 out* ....John Pritchard pu
449[1] Holmby Mill *(fav) ld to 2nd, ld 9th-16th, wknd, 6th whn p.u. 2 out* ....B Pollock pu
928 Kabancy 1ow *mstk 5th, last pair & t.o. til p.u. 13th* ....P Millington pu
Local Race (Ire) *prom to 9th, sn lost plc, p.u. 13th* ....J Brook pu

16 ran. 8l, 3l, 5l, sht-hd, 25l, 10l. Time 6m 24.00s. SP 5-1.
Alan Hill (Vale Of Aylesbury).

1078 Ladies

887[1] **FORCE EIGHT ....Mrs J Dawson** 1
(fav) trckd ldr, ld 7th, clr whn mstk 2 out, styd on
680[3] **Peajade ....Miss J Wormall** 2
cls up, chsd wnr 10-12th, 2nd agn 3 out, styd on wll,nvr nrr
885[3] **Thamesdown Tootsie 5a ....Miss V Lyon** 3
cls up, chsd wnr 12th-3 out, onepcd aft
678[3] Driving Force (bl) *mstk 2nd, prog 8th, chsd ldrs aft, wknd 2 out* ....Miss J Johnston 4
968[4] Old Dundalk *in tch to 10th, sn strgglng, t.o.* ....Mrs A Hayes 5
709[2] Omidjoy (Ire) 5a (bl) *in tch to 10th, sn wknd, t.o.* ....Mrs L Wrighton 6
759[2] Radical Views *not fluent, nvr going wll, rear til p.u. 13th* ....Mrs T Hill pu
225[3] King High *last pair, t.o. 8th, p.u. 15th*. . .Miss S Gritton pu
925 Fenton Bridge *pllng, ld to 7th, wknd frm 14th, t.o. & p.u. last* ....Miss R Tutton pu
773 Shouldofdone *raced wd, prom to 9th, sn wknd, t.o. & p.u. 16th* ....Mrs V Lloyd-Davies pu
925 Remalone 5a *mstks, sn wll bhnd, t.o. last whn u.r. 13th* ....Mrs C McCarthy ur

11 ran. 1½l, 12l, 8l, 25l, 25l. Time 6m 24.00s. SP Evens.
Mrs E W Wilson (Brocklesby).

1079 Men's Open

447[1] **LUCKY CHRISTOPHER ....J Docker** 1
(fav) w.w. trckd ldr 16th, ld 3 out, shkn up & sn in cmmnd
446[1] **Hill Island ....R Sweeting** 2
ld 3rd-3 out, ran on wll, no imp wnr
926[2] **Mister Main Man (Ire) ....S Sporborg** 3

w.w. cls engh 15th, outpcd 3 out, no dang aft
708[1] Airtrak (Ire) *ld to 2nd, chsd ldr 9th til blnd 16th, wknd 2 out*.......A Coe 4
926 Kiltroum (Fr) *last whn f 2nd*.......P Millington f
926[3] Coolvawn Lady (Ire) 5a *ld 2-3rd, wth ldr til lost plc rpdly 9th, p.u. 11th, b.b.v*.......T Lane pu
6 ran. 2l, 8l, 15l. Time 6m 28.00s. SP 8-13.
G B Tarry (Grafton).

1080 Restricted Div I (12st)

779[6] **TEA CEE KAY ....A Sansome 1**
(fav) ld to 9th, ld 13th, kckd clr 2 out, styd on
653 **Nobbutjust (Ire) 5a.......A Beedles 2**
w.w. prog 14th, styd on to chs wnr apr last, nrst fin
770 **Rough Edge ....W Wales 3**
mstks, in tch, effrt to chs ldrs 15th, sn outpcd, kpt on wll
712[1] Bishops Tale *pllng, cls up, blnd 12th, chal & ev ch 3 out, wknd nxt*.......R Barrett 4
775[1] Mr Freebie (Den) *wll in tch to 15th, grad wknd* D Ingle 5
701[4] Bakmalad *sn rear, rdn 9th, lost tch 13th, p.u. 16th*.......F Hutsby pu
443 Culm Baron (bl) *sn pshd alng, prom to 10th, wknd, t.o. & p.u. 3 out*.......S R Andrews pu
Dilly's Last 5a *wll in tch to 15th, wknd rpdly & p.u. 3 out*.......R Armson pu
927[4] Kingeochy *prom, ld 9-13th, wknd & p.u. 16th, dsmntd*.......M Hewitt pu
883 Top Beauty 5a *virt ref 1st & p.u. aft*....Mrs J Dawson pu
776 Ourmanjac *rear, mstk 6th, lsng tch whn mstk 13th & p.u.*.......S Morris pu
11 ran. 3l, 8l, ½l, 15l. Time 6m 35.00s. SP 5-2.
C O King (Old Berkshire).

1081 Restricted Div II (12st)

769[2] **DASHBOARD LIGHT ....S R Andrews 1**
(Jt fav) s.s. sn trckd ldrs, ld 15th, drvn clr 2 out, rdn out
760[2] **Tommy O'Dwyer (Ire) ....A Hill 2**
hld up,mstk 10th,prog nxt,chsd wnr 15th,btn 2 out,fin tired
760[3] **Wotamona 5a.......R Smith 3**
mid-div, outpcd 16th, styd on wll agn frm 2 out
550[1] Mister Kingston *(Jt fav) trckd ldng pair, outpcd aft 16th, no ch aft, onepcd*.......B Pollock 4
838[2] Busking Along (Ire) *last pair, in tch to 15th, sn outpcd, kpt on*.......H Nicholson 5
770 Weston Moon (Ire) 5a *mstk 9th, clr ldr til hdd 15th, wknd*.......J Docker 6
826[2] Tarry Awhile *mstks, in tch whn blnd 6th, rear aft, t.o. 14th*.......J Connell 7
477 Forward View *mstks 4th & 8th, in tch to 14th, t.o. & p.u. 2 out*.......C Millington pu
770 Rakish Queen 5a *rear frm 10th, t.o. 14th, p.u. 2 out*.......Miss H Phizacklea pu
222 Edinburgh Reel Ale 5a *wll in rear, effrt & rdn whn mstk 12th, btn nxt, p.u. 3 out*.......R Barrett pu
774 The Rebel Parish (Ire) *prom, lost plc 13th, eased & p.u. 3 out, improve*.......Mrs J Dawson pu
775 Fearless Bertie *mid-div, 9th & just in tch whn f 14th*.......A Charles-Jones f
776[1] Catchphrase *keen hld, prom to 15th, wknd, p.u. 2 out*.......K Needham pu
13 ran. 10l, 8l, 8l, 5l, 2l, 3l. Time 6m 33.00s. SP 2-1.
A D Cooke (Cottesmore).

1082 Maiden Div I

451[3] **BILSTON GEORGE ....T Lane 1**
prog 9th, disp 13th til ld 16th, clr 3 out, hld on flat
839 **Stanwick Buckfast ....T Marks 2**
prog 9th, ld/disp 10-16th, sn outpcd, ran on strngly 2 out
774[3] **Tinsun ....John Pritchard 3**
ld 3-10th, disp 13-16th, chsd wnr aft, onepcd 2 out
Shedoes 5a *in tch, wkng whn blnd 12th & p.u.*.......C Wadland pu
821 Lizapet (Ire) 12a *rear, lost tch 11th, t.o. & p.u. 3 out*.......S Green pu
776[2] Royal Balinger 5a *prom, disp 13th-16th, sn btn, 4th & no ch whn p.u. last*.......R Armson pu
374 Magical Manor 5a *in tch to 12th, sn wknd, t.o. & p.u. 3 out*.......J Oldring pu
774 Chapeau Chinois 5a *wll bhnd frm 9th, t.o. & p.u. 11th*.......Miss E Godfrey pu
761 Wot No Cash 7a *ld to 3rd, in tch to 15th, wknd & p.u. 3 out*.......R Lawther pu
775 Kings Choir 7a *t.o. til p.u. 9th*.......J Docker pu
450[2] Teeton Heavens 5a *(fav) mstks, w.w. in tch whn blnd 15th, 5th & no ch whn p.u. last*.......B Pollock pu
Moonlight Story *t.o. til ref 7th*.......K Needham ref
Krisan 5a *in tch to 11th, wll bhnd frm 13th, p.u. 15th*.......Miss L Allen pu
776 Right Well (Ire) 7a *in tch to 11th, wll bhnd whn p.u. 16th*.......E Andrewes pu
14 ran. 1½l, 4l. Time 6m 45.00s. SP 14-1.
Mrs G M Riley (Fitzwilliam).

1083 Maiden Div II

DOLLY BLOOM 5a ....A Sansome 1
hld up, prog to trck ldr 13th, ld apr last, all out
892 **Space Molly 5a (bl) ....P Cowley 2**
sn ld, kpt on wll frm 3 out, hdd apr last, no ext flat
479 **You Be King ....P O'Keefe 3**
rear whn mstk 9th, prog 11th, ev ch 16th, outpcd nxt, kpt on
881[3] Woodlands Power *(fav) chsd ldrs, rdn 11th, kpt on aft, nvr able to chal*.......John Pritchard 4
899[3] Malenski (Ire) *rear, prog 13th, ev ch 15th, wknd aft 3 out*.......P Millington 5
775 Star Traveller *rear, lost tch 13th, sn t.o., styd on frm 2 out*.......M Skinner 6
654 Daring Daisy 5a *mstk 5th, alwys bhnd, t.o. 13th*.......Mrs C McCarthy 7
839 Isola Farnese 5a *sn rear, wll bhnd 9th, t.o. & p.u. 13th*.......M Barnard pu
761 Miss Precocious 5a *alwys rear, t.o. 14th, p.u. 3 out*.......C Wadland pu
550[5] Old Father Time *chsd ldrs, pshd alng in cls 5th whn f 14th*.......L Lay f
770 Grange Missile 5a *in tch, blnd 13th, sn wknd, t.o. & p.u. last*.......J Dillon pu
Beech Brook *trckd ldr to 11th, wknd & p.u. 15th*.......T Lane pu
253[2] Minikino *prom, wkng whn hmpd 14th, p.u. nxt*.......J Docker pu
777 Princess Letitia 5a *t.o. til p.u. 6th*.......J Stephenson pu
Kintino 5a *f 2nd*.......R Lawther f
15 ran. 2l, 3l, 12l, 1l, 2l, 15l. Time 6m 37.00s. SP 9-2.
Mrs D F Sansome (Grafton).

1084 Maiden Div III

BUCKLELONE 5a.......S Morris 1
sn rear, poor 4th frm 14th, ran on 3 out, ld last, rdn out
775[2] **Greenacres Rose 5a.......Miss S Phizacklea 2**
ld 2nd-8th, ld 15th, clr 3 out, wknd & hdd last
927[3] **Strong Account (Ire) ....A Tutton 3**
(Jt fav) ld to 2nd, prom, chsd ldr 15th, wknd 2 out
776 Allegro Prince *rear, mstk 5th, prog nxt, mod 4th whn ref 13th*.......R Mumford ref
253[3] Bugsy Moran (Ire) *2nd til f 5th*.......C Millington f
224[3] Imustamit *(Jt fav) prom, ld 8th, blnd 14th, hdd nxt, wknd, no ch & p.u. last*.......R Barrett pu
209 Half Sharp 5a *mstks, sn rear, t.o. 13th, p.u. 3 out*.......L Lay pu
839 Dels Lad *in tch to 8th, sn bhnd, t.o. & p.u. 14th*.......J Docker pu
898[3] Top Odder (Ire) 7a *rear, last whn f hvly 12th*.......P Millington f
775 Half A Chance *sn rear, t.o. & p.u. 12th*.......T Marks pu
Barnys Rose Farm *sn rear, last at 9th, t.o. & p.u. 11th*.......A Sansome pu
11 ran. 3l, 12l. Time 6m 43.00s. SP 4-1.
Miss J C Gilbert (Heythrop).
J.N.

HEXHAM
Monday April 14th
FIRM

1085 3m 1f Chevy Chase Maiden Hunters' Chase Class H

858[1] **SECRET BAY 12.7 ....Mr S Swiers 1**
(fav) ld to 4 out, led again 2 out, rdn clr apr last.
779[2] **Up For Ransome (Ire) 12.0 7a ....Mr T J Barry 2**
cl up, ld 4 out, rdn next, hdd 2 out and one pace und pres apr last.
972[4] **Cool Yule (Ire) 12.2 5a............Miss P Robson 3**
alwys rear, bhnd from 14th.
696[2] Park Drift 12.0 7a *trckd ldrs, effort 4 out, rdn next and soon wknd*...............................Mr R Tate 4
778[5] All Or Nothing 11.9 7a *cl up till u.r. 3rd*....Mr J Ewart ur
5 ran. 14l, 19l, 3l. Time 6m 27.70s. SP 4-5.
Stuart Dent

SOUTHWELL
Monday April 14th
GOOD

1086 3m 110yds Jack Russell Novices' Hunters' Chase Class H

715[2] **MISTER HORATIO 11.7 7a...........Mr M Lewis 1**
(Jt fav) chsd ldrs, ld apr 3 out, clr next.
891[1] **Greenmount Lad (Ire) 12.0 7a ....Mr P Cornforth 2**
held up, hdwy 9th, styd on from 2 out, not reach wnr.
846[1] **Wolver's Pet (Ire) 11.7 7a ....Mr D S Jones 3**
held up, hit 8th, hdwy next, chsd wnr 3 out, styd on same pace.
779[1] Not My Line (Ire) 12.2 5a *prom, joined ldr 12th, ld 4 out, soon hdd, one pace from next*.....Mr A Sansome 4
725[4] Back The Road (Ire) 11.9 7a 2ow *held up, nvr near ldrs*...................................Mr G Hanmer 5
675[1] The Point Is 11.7 7a *(Jt fav) ld, hdd 4 out, soon wknd, p.u. before 2 out*.........................Mr P Hewitt pu
510 Andretti's Heir 11.13 7a 6ow *started slowly, hdwy 9th, weakening when blnd and u.r. 3 out.*
....Mr A Bonson ur
377 Judgeroger 11.7 7a *bhnd from 10th, p.u. before 5 out.*
....Mr G Lewis pu
835[1] Ryders Wells 11.7 7a *soon in rear, hit 6th, bhnd when p.u. before 12th*...............................Mr S Walker pu
834[2] Gonalston Percy 11.7 7a (bl) *started slowly, alwys in rear, t.o. and p.u. before 10th*.............Mr N Kent pu
846[2] Gunner Boon 11.9 5a *prom till blnd badly and u.r. 6 out*..Miss P Jones ur
11 ran. 10l, 1¼l, 2½l, dist. Time 6m 23.20s. SP 7-2.
W D Lewis

CHELTENHAM
Wednesday April 16th
GOOD TO FIRM

1087 3¼m 110yds Howard E. Perry Hunters' Chase Class H

494[5] **DOUBLE SILK 12.0 7a..............Mr E Williams 1**
(fav) chsd ldr, ld 3rd, made rest, clr 14th, styd on strly final 2.
981[1] **Some-Toy 11.10 7a ....Miss L Blackford 2**
held up, hdwy to chase wnr 10th, rdn when hit 3 out, one pace.
981[2] **Rusty Bridge 11.10 7a ....Mr R Burton 3**
ld to 3rd, rdn and lost pl 11th, kept on one pace from 2 out.
874[1] Idiotic 11.12 5a *hdwy 7th, mstk and lost pl 10th, rallied 12th, rdn when hit 3 out, fd run-in*.....Mr C Vigors 4
385[3] Young Brave 12.0 7a *hd up, prog 17th, weakening when hit 3 out*...........................Mr M G Miller 5
586[3] The Malakarma 11.12 5a *held up, wknd 11th, t.o..*
....Mr B Pollock 6
889[1] L'uomo Piu 11.7 7a *prom, chsd ldr from 6th to 10th, bhnd from 12th, t.o. when p.u. before 4 out.*
....Mr O McPhail pu
489[1] Jupiter Moon 11.7 7a *held up, blnd and u.r. 5th.*
....Mr J M Pritchard ur
8 ran. 11l, 11l, 3l, 1¾l, 22l. Time 6m 45.60s. SP 15-8.
R C Wilkins

TIVERTON
Hockworthy
Wednesday April 16th
GOOD TO FIRM

1088 Members

953[1] **MAGNOLIA MAN ....N Harris 1**
(fav) hld up, prog 8th, ld 14th, clr aft 2 out, easily
862[1] **Parditino ....Miss V Nicholas 2**
ld 5th-14th, rdn & onepcd frm 2 out
736[2] **Ragtime Boy ....A Holdsworth 3**
w.w. cls engh 14th, not qckn apr 2 out, kpt on
Touching Star (bl) *bckwrd, made most to 5th, wknd 9th, t.o. & p.u. 13th*..........................Miss C Stucley pu
525 Father Malone (Ire) *cls up til mstk & wknd 11th, blnd nxt & p.u.*...L Jefford pu
861[2] Master Decoy *cls up til f 7th*.............Miss A Bush f
6 ran. 8l, 1l. Time 6m 22.00s. SP 1-2.
Mrs D B Lunt (Tiverton Foxhounds).

1089 Confined

739[1] **BUTLER JOHN (IRE) ....N Harris 1**
(fav) made all, hit 10th, wll clr 14th, imprssv
863 **The Golfing Curate ....A Michael 2**
w.w. rear, 6th & out of tch hlfwy, kpt on to tk 2nd nr fin
631[1] **Milled Oats ....A Farrant 3**
sn pshd alng,rdn to chs wnr 13th,no imp,lost poor 2nd flat
691[2] Ive Called Time *chsd ldrs, outpcd frm 10th, no dang aft*...R Nuttall 4
1037[2] Bargain And Sale (bl) *chsd wnr til wknd rpdly 13th, last whn p.u. 2 out*...........................I Dowrick pu
631[2] Just Ben *nvr going wll, lost plc 8th, wll bhnd whn p.u. 13th*...Miss J Cumings pu
806[4] Medias Maid 5a *alwys last, t.o. & p.u. 13th*
....A Holdsworth pu
7 ran. Dist, ½l, 5l. Time 6m 14.50s. SP 8-11.
Nick Viney (Exmoor).

1090 G Middleton Ladies

645[1] **EARTHMOVER (IRE) ....Miss P Gundry 1**
(fav) w.w. prog 8th, trckd ldr 3 out, ld aft nxt, pshd clr
627[1] **Secret Four ....Miss T Cave 2**
svrl slw jmps, made most frm 4th til aft 2 out,no ch wnr aft
890[7] **Great Pokey ....Miss N Courtenay 3**
wth ldr frm 4th-15th, outpcd aft nxt
869[2] Mighty Falcon *chsd ldrs, outpcd 14th, kpt on frm 2 out*
....Miss D Tory 4
1042[2] Frosty Reception *ld to 4th, chsd ldrs til outpcd 12th, nvr on trms aft*..........................Miss C Stucley 5
889 Departure 5a *sn bhnd, t.o. 8th, p.u. 10th*
....Miss S Gaisford pu
807[3] Northern Bride 5a *n.j.w. s.s., t.o. til p.u. 15th*
....Miss R Francis pu
864[3] Be My Habitat (bl) *mstk 4th, sn wll bhnd, t.o. 8th, p.u. 15th*...Miss L Hawkings pu
8 ran. 12l, 15l, 1l, 8l. Time 6m 14.00s. SP 2-5.
R M Penny (Cattistock).

1091 Men's Open

890 **CHILIPOUR ....J Jukes 1**
(fav) w.w. slw jmp 4th & rmndr, ld 14th, clr 2 out, eased flat
793[1] **Fearsome ....G Penfold 2**
w.w. ld 11-14th, no ch wth wnr aft 2 out, kpt on

690[2] **Stunning Stuff ....R Nuttall** 3
wth ldr, ld 8-11th, rdn 3 out, kpt on onepcd
951[1] Anjubi *ld to 8th, disp 2nd apr 2 out, sn btn & eased* ....I Dowrick 4
4 ran. 3l, 1l, 15l. Time 6m 23.00s. SP 2-5.
Nick Viney (Dulverton (West)).

1092 PPORA (12st)

691[1] **ALLER MOOR (IRE) ....T Mitchell** 1
(fav) w.w. ld 11th, clr 14th, rdn out
630[1] **Mine's A Gin (Ire) ....Miss J Cumings** 2
jmpd rght, wth ldr, ld 8-11th, disp 2nd aft, sn outpcd
688[1] **Sultan Of Swing ....N Mitchell** 3
w.w. effrt to chs wnr 14th, no imp 2 out, demoted aft
879[3] Oh So Windy 5a 3ow *cls up to 11th, sn wknd, no ch & p.u. aft 3 out, lame* ....A Hill pu
631 Erme Rose (Ire) 5a *ld to 8th, wknd 12th, t.o. & p.u. 2 out*..........R Nuttall pu
5 ran. 8l, 4l. Time 6m 23.00s. SP 8-11.
G Keirle (Portman).

1093 Interlink Restricted (12st)

557 **MY MAN ON DUNDRUM (IRE) ....T Mitchell** 1
(fav) trckd ldrs, prog to ld 4 out, clr 2 out, drvn out flat
Nearly At Sea 5a ....I Widdicombe 2
hld up, gd prog frm 6 out, chsd wnr 2 out, ev ch, just hld
1039[2] **Morchard Milly 5a......................J Auvray** 3
chsd ldrs, lost plc & rdn hlfwy, sn no ch, kpt on 2 out
935[3] Ruth's Boy (Ire) *ld to 10th, prom aft til wknd 3 out* ....Miss S Vickery 4
930[5] Venn Boy *alwys rear, nvr a fctr* ....N Mitchell 5
795 Jet Jockey *chsd ldrs, ld 10th-4 out, wknd nxt* A Oliver 6
570[1] My Wee Man (Ire) *n.j.w. alwys rear, t.o.*.....G Barfoot-Saunt 7
50 Liberty James *nvr dang, wll bhnd whn p.u. 5 out* ....T Greed pu
Hand Out 5a *prom to 10th, wknd rpdly, t.o. & p.u. last* ....B Dixon pu
792[6] Remember Mac (bl) *prom to 7th, sn bhnd, t.o. & p.u. 10th* ....Miss C Hayes pu
519[1] Belfry Lad *unruly pddck, prom to 9th, sn wknd, t.o. & p.u. last* ....D Alers-Hankey pu
736 Charlottes Billo *n.j.w. t.o. 4th, p.u. 8th*......R Emmett pu
955[1] Holcombe Ideal 5a *mstks, alwys rear, no ch frm 9th, p.u. 5 out* ....L Jefford pu
954 Twice Knightly *prom to 8th, sn wknd, bhnd whn p.u. 5 out*..........I Dowrick pu
741[1] Legal Affair 5a *in tch, prog & ev ch 4 out, wkng whn blnd 2 out & p.u.*..........N Harris pu
630[8] Uncle James (Ire) *hld up, last whn blnd & u.r. 3rd* ....A Farrant ur
16 ran. 1l, 25l, 3l, 1l, 2l, 15l. Time 6m 18.00s. SP 6-4.
Richard Barber (Cattistock).
Open ditch omitted this race on. Fence 11 omitted this race, 15 jumps.

1094 Maiden Div I (12st)

553[4] **DRUMBANES PET ....David Dennis** 1
slw jmp 4th, ld to 6 out, ld 3 out, hrd rdn & styd on
Big Bands Are Back (USA) 7a ......Miss S Young 2
14s-6s,wth wnr clr of rest,ld 6 out-3 out,ev ch last,no ext
525 **I'll Be Bound (v).......................M Burrows** 3
bhnd,mstk 3rd,gd prog frm 6 out,3rd & ch whn hit 2 out,wknd
Girls In Business 5a *chsng grp, mstk 8th, clsd 3 out, rdn & wknd nxt*..........B O'Doherty 4
795 Oh So Quiet 7a *chsng grp, effrt hlfwy, sn no prog, no ch 3 out*..........Miss J Cumings 5
795 Mellicometti *pllng, hld up, nvr on trms, t.o. 4 out* ....R Woolacott 6
934 Warwick Road *ld chsng grp, blnd 9th, wknd 5 out, t.o. & p.u. 3 out* ....N Mitchell pu
527 Knight Of Passion 7a *mstks 5th & 9th, rear, t.o. & p.u. 4 out* ....D Alers-Hankey pu
526[4] Tinker Tailor 7a 5ow *(fav) chsng grp, effrt to 4th 4 out, sn btn, t.o. & p.u. last* ....A Hill pu
459[3] Jerome Jerome 7a *ran out & u.r. 3rd* ....I Dowrick ro
Brook Heights *n.j.w. wll bhnd frm 5th til p.u. 9th* ....L Jefford pu
11 ran. 4l, 15l, 12l, 15l, 15l, 4l. Time 6m 28.00s. SP 8-1.
Mrs C Lawrence (Eggesford).
Fence 11 omitted this race. 15 jumps.

1095 Maiden Div II (12st)

FOUR LEAF CLOVER 5a ....J Jukes 1
(fav) made all, drew wll clr apr last, drvn out flat
459 **Devonshire Lad ....N Harris** 2
chsd wnr, only dngr frm hlfwy, no imp 2 out, eased last
794[2] **Stretchit ....G Penfold** 3
hld up, went mod 3rd at 9th, no imp 1st pair aft
526 Heddon Valley *bhnd, poor 7th at 10th, sn t.o., fin well* ....S Durack 4
934[6] Nottarex *mid-div, poor 8th hlfwy, sn t.o.*.....B Wright 5
866 War Baron *alwys bhnd, poor 9th hlfwy, mls bhnd final cct*..........A Michael 6
740 Indian Language *chsd ldng pair to 9th, sn wknd, t.o. & p.u. last*..........S Kidston pu
526[5] Master Buckley *chsd ldrs, 5th at 8th, lost plc & p.u. nxt*..........T Greed pu
526 Kiramanda 5a *sn wll bhnd, t.o. 8th, p.u. 5 out* ....Miss P Gundry pu
521 Broad Commitment *chsd ldng pair, 5th & wkng whn blnd & u.r. 10th*..........R Emmett ur
Typical Woman (Ire) 5a *n.j.w. & wll bhnd, effrt to poor 6th hlfwy, t.o. & p.u.4 out*..........M Frith pu
11 ran. 15l, 25l, 20l, 12l. Time 6m 17.50s. SP Evens.
F Tyrrell (Dulverton West).
J.N.

AYR
Friday April 18th
GOOD

1096 3m 3f 110yds Royal Scots Dragoon Guards Cup Hunters' Chase Class H

590[1] **JIGTIME 11.2 7a ....Mr M Bradburne** 1
(fav) chsd ldr, ld 10th, clr 4 out, kept on.
973[2] **Royal Jester 11.9 5a...............Mr C Storey** 2
trckd ldrs, hdwy to chase wnr 15th, rdn 3 out, kept on.
590[4] **Southern Minstrel 11.7 7a ......Miss C Metcalfe** 3
held up, hdwy 14th, rdn 5 out, one pace.
973[1] Now Young Man (Ire) 11.7 7a *held up, pushed along and hdwy when hit 15th, soon rdn and btn 4 out.* ....Mr Chris Wilson 4
946[3] Green Times 11.7 7a *prom till lost pl 12th and soon bhnd, t.o. 5 out*..........Major G Wheeler 5
291[3] Ardesee 11.7 7a *made most to 10th, soon wknd and p.u. before 15th*..........Mr A Wintle pu
650 I'm Toby 11.7 7a *alwys bhnd, t.o. when f 15th.* ....Mr A Kinane f
7 ran. 2½l, 12l, 6l, dist. Time 7m 2.50s. SP 4-7.
J W Hughes

BANGOR
Saturday April 19th
GOOD

1097 2½m 110yds Robert Jones 21st Open Hunters' Chase Class H

982[1] **MY NOMINEE 12.0 7a (bl)..........Mr R Burton** 1
(fav) made all, well clr 4 out, eased down run-in.
892[3] **Dalametre 11.7 7a..............Mr M Munrowd** 2
handy, chsd wnr from 7th, no impn from 4 out.
939[6] **Saahi (USA) 11.7 7a..........Miss S Swindells** 3
well bhnd, styd on from 3 out, nvr a factor.
779[3] Galzig 11.7 7a *midfield, mstk 6th, effort to chase ldrs 10th, btn from 4 out.*..........Mr W Tellwright 4

Nadiad 11.7 7a *bhnd, hdwy to chase ldrs 6th, reminders apr 10th, wknd next, no ch when blnd last, t.o.*..........Mr A Wintle 5

587[6] Simply Perfect 11.7 7a *blnd and u.r. 1st.* ....Miss K Swindells ur

874[4] King Of Shadows 12.0 7a *chsd ldrs, lost pl 6th, soon bhnd, t.o. when p.u. before 2 out*..........Mr S Prior pu

943[2] Press For Action 11.9 5a *prom, jmpd right 7th, wknd 9th, t.o. when p.u. before 4 out*..........Mr R Ford pu

924 Rather Sharp 12.2 5a *alwys bhnd, lost tch 9th, t.o. when p.u. before next*..........Mr B Pollock pu

588[4] Charlies Delight (Ire) 11.9 5a *in tch till f 5th.* ....Mr C Vigors f

854 Thornhill 11.2 7a *bhnd, reminders 9th and lost tch, t.o. when p.u. before 3 out.* ....Mr A Wood pu

11 ran. 22l, 2l, 8l, 14l. Time 5m 13.80s. SP 8-13.
D E Nicholls

1098 3m 110yds Jane McAlpine Memorial Hunters' Chase Class H

937[1] **NODFORM WONDER 11.7 7a..........Mr R Bevis 1**
(fav) ld to 4th, led 7th to 8th, led again 10th, mstk 3 out, clr when pkd last, comf.

940[2] **Mr Busker (Ire) 11.7 7a..........Mr C J B Barlow 2**
held up, hdwy to chase wnr before 3 out, no impn.

1087 **Jupiter Moon 11.13 5a..........Mr C Vigors 3**
in tch, outpcd from 5 out, soon no dngr.

496 Orton House 11.7 7a *cl up to 4th, outpcd final cct.* ....Mr R Burton 4

590[3] Orange Ragusa 11.9 5a *prom, ld 4th to 7th, led 8th to 10th, wknd from 13th.* ....Mr R Ford 5

849[1] Fibreguide Tech 11.7 7a *alwys in rear, t.o. when p.u. before 2 out*..........Mr R Thomas pu

758[1] Fair Crossing 12.0 7a *in tch, prom 7th, losing ground when pkd 10th, t.o. when p.u. before 3 out.* ....Mr M Emmanuel pu

680[2] Avostar 11.13 5a *nvr going well, alwys bhnd, no ch when f last*..........Mr B Pollock f

890 Highway Five (Ire) 12.0 7a *alwys bhnd, t.o. when p.u. before 13th.* ....Miss E James pu

9 ran. 5l, 16l, hd, 2½l. Time 6m 21.20s. SP 5-2.
D A Malam

STRATFORD
Saturday April 19th
GOOD

1099 2m 5f 110yds Richardsons Star Site Hunters' Chase Class H for the Baulking Green Trophy

299 **MANKIND 11.7 7a..........Mr L Baker 1**
chsd ldrs, ld 4th to 9th, led 2 out, rdn out.

874[3] **Pro Bono (Ire) 11.9 5a..........Mr A Sansome 2**
alwys prom, ld 9th, hdd and mstk 2 out, styd on same pace.

732[3] **Eastern Pleasure 11.7 7a..........Mr T J Barry 3**
prom till wknd 4 out.

982[3] Fox Pointer 12.0 7a *(fav) ld to 4th, wknd 5 out.* ....Mr O McPhail 4

771 Tudor Fable (Ire) 12.3 7a *alwys bhnd.* ....Mr Rupert Sweeting 5

679[6] Tellaporky 11.7 7a *slowly into stride, alwys bhnd.* ....Mr A Middleton 6

751[2] Erlemo 11.7 7a (bl) *started slowly, alwys well bhnd.* ....Dr P Pritchard 7

432 Emerald Ruler 11.10 5a 1ow *alwys in rear, t.o. and p.u. before 6 out.* ....Mr J Trice-Rolph pu

679 Star Oats 11.7 7a *prom, hit 10th, blnd next, soon wknd, p.u. before 4 out.* ....Mr A Kinane pu

782[2] Tuffnut George 12.3 7a *prom till wknd 6 out, p.u. before 3 out*..........Mr A Phillips pu

874 Frank Be Lucky 11.7 7a *prom, mstks, wknd 5 out, p.u. before 2 out*..........Mr R Wakley pu

982[4] Candle Glow 11.2 7a *chsd ldrs till wknd 7th, p.u. before 10th*..........Mr P Hutchinson pu

376 Prinzal 12.0 *held up, hdwy 5 out, wknd next, p.u. before 3 out.* ....Mr M Armytage pu

851 Secret Castle 11.7 7a *started slowly, alwys bhnd, p.u. before 9th*..........Mr L Brown pu

14 ran. 1½l, dist, 2½l, 13l, 11l, 5l. Time 5m 30.80s. SP 66-1.
J A T de Giles

BEDALE & WEST OF YORE
Hornby Castle
Saturday April 19th
GOOD

1100 Confined (12st)

1072 **HURRICANE LINDA 5a..........S Walker 1**
held up, prog 9th, gng wll 4 out, ld apr nxt, ran on strgly

1069[1] **Chapel Island..........G Tuer 2**
(Jt fav) mid-div, prog 9th, disp 12th til apr 3 out, onepcd frm nxt

1072[4] **Flying Lion..........M Haigh 3**
prom, jnd ldr 4 out, outpcd nxt

894[1] Notarius (Fr) *(Jt fav) held up in rear, efft 14th, wknd nxt*..........Mrs K Hargreave 4

1070[5] Barichste (bl) *prom, disp 13th, hdd & wknd 4 out* ....Maj M Watson 5

166[7] Convincing *ld,disp 6-9th & agn 12th til wknd qckly nxt,t.o. & p.u. last*..........P Cornforth pu

1070 Sharpridge *rear, outpcd 8th, sn strgglng, t.o. 12th, p.u. 3 out*..........M Mawhinney pu

616 Hoistthestandard 5a *prom, disp 6th, ld 9-12th, wknd qckly, t.o. whn p.u. 3 out*..........T Glass pu

694[7] Skipping Gale *rear, rmmndrs 11th, sn outpcd, t.o. 3 out, p.u. last*..........P Atkinson pu

9 ran. 3l, 10l, 8l, 3l. Time 6m 29.00s. SP 3-1.
Lady Hewitt (Middleton).

1101 Restricted (12st)

1074[1] **DANEGELD (IRE)..........N Smith 1**
disp til 3rd, trckd ldrs aft, chal 3 out,ld nxt,ran on gamly

856[2] **Joint Account..........Mrs F Needham 2**
prom, trckd ldr 6th, disp 8th, ld 4 out, hdd 2 out,rlld last

894[2] **Dear Emily 5a..........S Swiers 3**
(fav) disp til 3rd, chsd ldrs aft, ev ch apr 3 out, onepcd

1075 Douce Eclair 5a *rear, strgglng 10th, styd on frm 3 out* ....Miss L Eddery 4

616[3] Mount Faber (bl) *prom, ld 3rd, disp 8th til hdd & wknd 4 out*..........S Charlton 5

1069[3] Attle *alwys chsng ldrs, wknd 3 out*..........W Burnell 6

1072 The Chap *alwys rear, t.o. 11th, p.u. last*...R Lochman pu

1069[7] Make A Line *mid-div til slppd up bnd apr 8th* C Denny su

Spanish Money *rear, lost tch 6th, t.o. 10th, p.u. nxt* ....N Kent pu

1070 Skyval 5a *alwys in rear, jnd rght 2nd, wll bhnd 11th,t.o. & p.u. 4 out*..........K Green pu

616 Transcendental (Ire) *prom til lost plcd 11th, towrds rear whn u.r. 14th*..........Miss A Deniel ur

1068 On The Fly *prom whn ran out 5th rejnd, alwys t.o., p.u. 4 out*..........R Edwards pu

1073[1] Patey Court 5a (bl) *mid-div, rddn 6th, lost tch 11th, t.o. whn p.u. 4 out*..........C Mulhall pu

Dublin Hill (Ire) *reluctant to race & v slwly away, alwys t.o., p.u. last*..........A Bonson pu

14 ran. 1½l, 3l, 10l, 3l, 3l. Time 6m 28.00s. SP 4-1.
Col M J F Sheffield (Bilsdale).

1102 Ladies

617[5] **INDIE ROCK..........Mrs F Needham 1**
held up in mid-div,chal2 out,ld last,ran on wll undpres flat

697[1] **Carole's Delight 5a..........Mrs L Ward 2**
(fav) ld til disp 4th, ld 7th-last, ran on wll flat, just faild

895[1] **Cheeky Pot..........Mrs S Grant 3**
nvr gng wll,rear,outpcd & bhnd 7th,styd on frm 4 out,nrstfin

1052[1] Czaryne 5a *mid-div til wknd frm 4 out*...Miss J Percy 4

617[9] Skolern *prom, jmp slwly 7th, lost plcd 12th, wknd 4 out, t.o.* .... Miss L Pounder 5
1072 Across The Lake (v) *prom,disp 4-7th,chsd ldr aft,wknd qckly 3 out,btn whn f last* .... Miss S Brotherton f
994 Blakes Folly (Ire) *s.i.s., rear, blndrd & u.r. 9th* .... Mrs K Hargreave ur
7 ran. Sht-hd, 6l, 4l, 15l. Time 6m 27.00s. SP 5-2.
R Tate (Hurworth).

1103 Land Rover Mens Open (12st)

1070[1] **GREY REALM 5a** .... **N Smith** 1
(fav) j.w., ld til 12th, ld agn 14th, qcknd clr 3 out, easily
857[1] **Osgathorpe** .... **R Tate** 2
hvly rstrnd in 3rd, chsd ldr 14th, outpcd 3 out, fin tired
812[6] **Fast Study** .... **S Robinson** 3
rear, rddn 10th, wknd 14th, sn t.o.
993[3] Yenoora (Ire) *rear, mstk 11th, lost tch nxt, t.o. & p.u. last* .... J Ewart pu
1075[3] Simply A Star (Ire) (bl) *trckd ldr, ld 12-14th, in tch whn f nxt* .... Maj M Watson f
5 ran. 20l, dist. Time 6m 31.00s. SP 11-10.
R E Barr (Cleveland).

1104 Members

1071[5] **CASTLE TYRANT 5a** .... **G Tuer** 1
(fav) held up in mid-div,wnt 2nd 12th,ld 4 out,ran on wll 2 out
617[3] **Douce Indienne 5a** .... **D Raw** 2
disp til 4th,sttld 3rd til chasd ldr 4 out,not qckn frm 2out
510[3] **Level Vibes** .... **R Abrahams** 3
disp til 6th, chsd ldr aft til outpcd frm 12th
1071[6] Pinewood Lad *disp, ld 6th til wknd qckly frm 4 out, t.o.* .... Miss K Ford 4
621[4] Lord George *plld hrd in rear, blndrd 11th, t.o. 13th, p.u. 4 out* .... P Atkinson pu
948 Smart Mover *rear, mstk 3rd, rmmndrs 13th, strgglng nxt,t.o. & p.u. 2 out* .... S Brisby pu
6 ran. 2l, 15l, 8l. Time 6m 35.00s. SP Evens.
S Clark (Bedale (West Of Yore)).

1105 Open Maiden Div I

1068[4] **GOODHEAVENS MRTONY** .... **Miss A Deniel** 1
prom,disp 6th,ld 9th & disp 13th,ld agn 3 out,styd on wllnxt
1074[5] **Silly Tinker** .... **C Denny** 2
prom, chsd ldr 3 out, mstk nxt, onepcd
116 **Hard To Break** .... **N Smith** 3
ld, disp 6th til hdd 9th, not qckn frm 3 out
1073[4] Just Johnie *(fav) mid-div, prog 9th, wknd 3 out* .... S Walker 4
120 Sunkala Shine *mid-div,prog into 2nd 12th,disp nxt,blndrd 4 out,sn wknd* .... Miss R Clark 5
699 Abbey Lad *rear, prog 11th, wknd 14th, t.o. 3 out* .... N Swann 6
1074[8] China Hand (Ire) 7a *rear, blndrd 3rd, sn t.o., jmp v slwly & p.u. aft 8th* .... H Armstrong pu
1074[6] Fair Grand *rear, rddn 10th, wll bhnd 14th, p.u. 4 out* .... S Brisby pu
1073 Little Red *s.s., rear whn u.r. 2nd* .... S Swiers ur
615 Yogi's Mistress 5a *prom til wknd qckly 11th, ref 13th* .... T Frank ref
897[2] Mac's Blade (USA) 7a *mstks,mid-div,prog 5th,lost plcd 8th,blndrd 11th,f 14th* .... R Edwards f
11 ran. 3l, 8l, 8l, ½l, 10l. Time 6m 40.00s. SP 5-1.
Mrs C Sykes (Sinnington).

1106 Open Maiden Div II

622[6] **LAST OPTION 7a** .... **Mrs F Needham** 1
prom, blndrd 13th, chal 3 out, ld nxt, ran green, kpt on wll
622[2] **Japodene 5a** .... **M Haigh** 2
(fav) ld til 5th, ld agn 8th, hdd 2 out, not qckn
1069[5] **Look Sharpe** .... **A Bonson** 3
keen hold, alwys prom, ev ch 3 out, onepcd
860 Gardenia's Song *mid-div, prog 4 out, wknd 2 out, eased flat* .... G Tuer 4
860 Mr Hook 7a *alwys in rear, nvr dang* .... G Markham 5
622 Greatfull Fred *mid-div, drppd to rear 8th, sn strgglng* .... Miss K Pickersgill 6
1074[7] Doc Spot *rear, mstk 3rd & 7th, wll bhnd frm 4 out, t.o.* .... S Robinson 7
1074 Bex Boy (Ire) *prom,ld 5-8th,blndrd bdly nxt,lost plc qckly,wll bhnd f 14th* .... C Mulhall f
698[2] Ski Lady 5a *saddle slppd & u.r. bfr 1st* Miss L Horner ur
898[4] Vickyberto 5a *mid-div, lost plcd 6th, mstk 8th, t.o. 13th, p.u. 2 out* .... N Wilson pu
10 ran. 6l, 3l, 15l, 8l, 2l, 7l. Time 6m 41.00s. SP 7-1.
R Tate (Bilsdale).
N.E.

DARTMOOR
Flete Park
Saturday April 19th
GOOD TO FIRM

1107 Members

629 **THE GENERAL'S DRUM** .... **K Heard** 1
(fav) trckd ldr, ld 15th-17th & aft 2 out, unimprssv
630[9] **Rosa's Revenge 5a (bl)** .... **G Penfold** 2
ld til 15th, ld 17th til mstk 2 out, no ext
2 ran. 2l. Time 6m 46.00s. SP 1-4.
Mrs R Fell (Dartmoor).

1108 Restricted (12st)

630[5] **VALLEY'S CHOICE 5a** .... **L Jefford** 1
alwys prom, cls 4tha t 15th, ld apr 2 out, hdl on well
736 **Penguin 5a** .... **Miss J Cumings** 2
(fav) ld 7th til ran wd & lost plc bnd aft 3 out,rallied flat
630 **Probation** .... **R Darke** 3
gd hdwy 3 out, cls 2nd & ev ch last, not qckn
556 Mosside *8th at 10th, prog 15th, kpt on und pres clsng stgs* .... N Harris 4
789[2] Maboy Lady *ld to 7th, chsd ldr til wknd 3 out* T Dennis 5
661[4] Palace King (Ire) *5th hlfwy, no ch frm 15th* .... B Dixon 6
1034 Kanha 12a *bhnd frm 10th* .... A O'Connor 7
954[2] Artistic Peace 5a 1ow *u.r. 1st* .... G Penfold ur
688[2] Eyre Point (Ire) *mid-div til blnd & u.r. 11th* .... A Honeyball ur
Church Ride (Ire) *rear grp, 7th at 15th, bhnd & p.u. 2 out* .... P King pu
1039[4] Anvil Corner 5a *in tch, 7th whn blnd & u.r. 12th* .... David Dennis ur
Beaford Game 5a *sn bhnd, not fluent, t.o. & u.r. 12th* .... Miss K Baily ur
955[2] Alicott Lad *rear, bhnd whn p.u. aft 14th* .... Miss A Barnett pu
1035 Go Willie Go *s.s. last whn ref 2nd* .... Miss L Smale ref
14 ran. Nk, 1½l, 3l, 15l, 8l, 25l. Time 6m 46.00s. SP 8-1.
S R Stevens (East Devon).

1109 4m Men's Open (12st)

793 **NEARLY SPLENDID** .... **T Greed** 1
(Jt fav) made all, j.w. clsng stgs, styd on strngly
792[2] **First Design** .... **L Jefford** 2
handy, went 2nd 20th, ev ch til no ext aft 3 out
930[3] **Thegoose** .... **P King** 3
(Jt fav) hld up bhnd, prog 17th, went 3rd last, fin well
790[4] Afterkelly 7ex *chsd ldr til 2 out, sn outpcd* .... M Frith 4
889[4] Arctic Baron 7ex *mid-div, lost plc steadily frm 14th* .... I Widdicombe 5
804[1] Dark Reflection *alwys bhnd* .... C Heard 6
1038 Crownhill Cross *prom til wknd 14th, t.o., walked in* .... S Kidston 7
951[3] Pharaoh Blue 6ow *5th whn mstk 13th, t.o. 17th til u.r. 2 out* .... M Shears ur
741[5] Reptile Princess 5a (bl) *tongue-strap, sn bhnd, n.j.w. t.o. & p.u. 3 out* .... D Doyne-Ditmas pu
9 ran. 12l, 3l, 4l, 10l, 12l, 25l. Time 8m 4.00s. SP 5-2.
S R Stevens (East Devon).

1110 G Middleton Ladies

790[1] **KHATTAF .... Miss J Cumings** 1
(fav) j.w. made most, lft clr apr last, comf
807[1] **Try It Alone .... Miss L Blackford** 2
w.w. gd prog 3 out, outpcd aft 2 out
1035[2] **Midnight Bob .... Miss A Barnett** 3
cls 2nd frm 7th-3 out, ev ch til outpcd nxt
1036[2] False Economy *disp to 5th, prom til wklnd 15th* .... Miss K Scorgie 4
1036[3] Always Lynsey (Ire) 5a *in tch to 11th, wll bhnd frm 15th* .... Miss K Hurst 5
952[2] Achiltibuie 8ow *u.r. 1st* .... Miss L Smale ur
92 Upham Close 5a *cls 3rd at 15th, chal & ev ch whn p.u. aft 2 out, lame* .... Mrs M Hand pu
794 Dusty Furlong *sn rear, jmpd lft, t.o. & p.u. 14th* .... Miss K Baily pu
740[5] Stony Missile 5a *n.j.w. in rear, t.o. & p.u. 12th* .... Miss W Hartnoll pu
9 ran. 6l, 3l, 5l, Bad. Time 6m 35.00s. SP 2-5.
Mrs H C Johnson (Devon & Somerset Staghounds).

1111 Confined (12st)

981[5] **CATCH THE CROSS (bl) .... Mrs M Hand** 1
disp 5th-7th,lft in ld bnd aft 3 out,lft clr 2 out, pshd out
793[3] **It's Not My Fault (Ire) .... L Jefford** 2
(fav) hld up in tch, ev ch til wknd apr 2 out, eased flat
735[2] **Christmas Hols .... Miss K Baily** 3
ld/disp to 7th, rmndrs 14th, lost tch 17th, t.o.
950[3] Seventh Lock *ld 7th til wd bnd aft 3 out, 2l 2nd whn f 2 out* .... Miss L Blackford f
950[2] The Copper Key *5th & in tch whn p.u. 11th, lame* .... T Greed pu
5 ran. 10l, dist. Time 6m 41.00s. SP 11-2.
Reg Hand (Lamerton).

1112 Maiden (12st)

740[2] **ESERIE DE CORES (USA) .... N Harris** 1
prog 12th, 5th at 16th, lft in ld 3 out, kpt on
101 **Amazing Hill (Ire) .... C Heard** 2
steady prog 10th, lft 5l 2nd 3 out, no imp, improve
795[3] **The Ugly Duckling .... S Slade** 3
handy, 5th hlfwy, lft 10l 3rd 3 out, onepcd
740[3] Corrib Haven (Ire) *pllng, ld to 7th, in tch til wknd 15th* .... Mrs M Hand 4
625[4] Artic Explorer *(fav) handy, disp 10-14th, mstk nxt, wknd rpdly, t.o.* .... L Jefford 5
956[3] Happy Valley 5a *f 1st* .... Miss P Baker f
956[2] Get Stepping *ld 7th, disp 10-11th, 10l 2nd & wkng whn f 17th* .... I Dowrick f
553 Cheque Book *sn bhnd, t.o. whn blnd 17th, p.u. apr nxt* .... T Cole pu
553[3] Pilgrim's Mission (Ire) *prog to disp 12th, ld apr 15th, clr whn f 3 out* .... D Doyne-Ditmas f
741[3] Ashcombe Valley *sn rear, t.o. 12t, p.u. 3 out, dsmntd* .... Miss N Courtenay pu
626 Breeze-Bloc 5a *rear, t.o. & p.u. 13th* .... T Greed pu
740 Sea Spirit 12a *sn rear, 8th at 12th, bhnd whn p.u. 17th* .... R Darke pu
1035 Earlswood *b.d. 1st* .... G Penfold bd
13 ran. 15l, 5l, 15l, 5l. Time 6m 36.00s. SP 5-2.
F R Bown (Lamerton).
G.T.

ESSEX & SUFFOLK
Higham
Saturday April 19th
GOOD TO FIRM

1113 Members

802[1] **DRUID'S LODGE .... C Ward-Thomas** 1
(fav) trckd ldr, just ld 11th, lft clr nxt, v easily
Rhu Na Haven .... J Buckle 2
3rd & not fluent, lft 2nd aft 11th, nvr pace to chal, t.o.
502 Salachy Run (Ire) *ld to 11th, ran out bend apr nxt* .... N Page ro
3 ran. Dist. Time 6m 25.00s. SP 1-5.
D J Lay (Essex & Suffolk).

1114 Restricted (12st)

686[1] **RED CHANNEL (IRE) .... A Hickman** 1
plld to ld 3rd, made rest, 8l clr 15th, kpt on 3 out, comf
711[2] **New York Boy .... P Taiano** 2
(fav) trckd wnr, no imp frm 16th, wknd last
801[6] **Aughnacloy Rose .... R Page** 3
last early, 4tha t 13th, ran on 3 out, nrst fin
598[1] Borrow Mine (Ire) 7a *mstly 3rd, nvr pace to chal ldr, wknd last* .... S Sporborg 4
500[3] Zoes Pet 5a *4th & in tch til outpcd aft 11th, last 13th, t.o. 3 out* .... Miss H Pewter 5
5 ran. 5l, ½l, ½l, 30l. Time 6m 24.00s. SP 2-1.
R A Crawley (East Sussex & Romney Marsh).

1115 Men's Open (12st)

710[2] **CRACKING IDEA (IRE) 7ex ..... C Ward-Thomas** 1
(fav) alwys going easily, trckd ldr 4th, ld 15th, sn clr, easily
1031[1] **Salmon Mead (Ire) .... S Sporborg** 2
disp to 4th, ld aft til hdd 15th, sn outpcd, no ch 4 out
579 **St Laycar 3ow .... A Greig** 3
4th & off pace, went 3rd at 10th, rdn 12th, no imp ldrs
1028[1] Cockstown Lad 7ex *disp to 4th, mstks, nvr going wll aft, t.o. 15th, p.u. 3 out* .... D Featherstone pu
4 ran. 15l, dist. Time 6m 17.00s. SP 4-5.
Mrs P K J Brightwell (Essex & Suffolk).

1116 Ladies

800[1] **ST GREGORY (bl) .... Mrs L Gibbon** 1
(fav) made all, eased clr frm 12th, eased flat
272[4] **Waterloo Andy .... Miss J Cook** 2
in tch til not qckn 12th, wknd 14th, no ch aft
2 ran. 15l. Time 6m 25.00s. SP 1-5.
A Howland Jackson (Essex & Suffolk).

1117 Confined (12st)

926[4] **YOUCAT (IRE) .... I Marsh** 1
(Jt fav) cls up, disp 8th til ld 11th, qcknd clr 2 out, ran on wll
593[2] **Shake Five (Ire) .... S Sporborg** 2
(Jt fav) cls up, disp 8-11th, chsd wnr aft, onepcd 2 out
837 **Notary-Nowell (bl) .... R Barrett** 3
cls up, ev ch til rdn aft 13th, sn outpcd
1032[1] Current Attraction 5a 7ow *ld to 7th, sn lost plc, t.o. 13th* .... Miss K Thory 4
595[4] Foxbow (Ire) 7ex *nvr going or jmpng wll, lost tch aft 11th, t.o. 13th* .... A Coe 5
5 ran. 5l, 20l, 30l, 10l. Time 6m 17.00s. SP 6-4.
I Marsh (Puckeridge).

1118 Open Maiden (12st)

439[3] **MUTUAL MEMORIES .... S R Andrews** 1
trckd ldrs, 2nd at 15th, ld apr 2 out, sn clr
A Right Set Two 7a .... N King 2
trckd ldrs, ld aft 7th, hdd apr 2 out, sn btn, promising
915 Fragment (Ire) *last aft 1st, t.o. 3rd, 2 fncs bhnd whn p.u. 3 out* .... R Tillyer pu
499[3] Bozo Bailey *(fav) cls up, wknd aft 14th, p.u. aft 16th, broke down* .... P Taiano pu
990[4] Loch Irish (Ire) 5a *ld to 7th, sn lost plc, wknd 12th, p.u. 3 out* .... W Wales pu
1027 The Whole Lot *rear, hmnpd & u.r. 6th* .... R Barrett ur
915[4] Secret Music *rear, jmpd poorly, nvr dang, t.o. 13th, p.u. 16th* .... Capt D Parker pu
Vital To Me 7a *rear whn u.r. 1st* .... A Coe ur

796 Paddy A Go Go 12a *alwys rear, jmpd poorly, t.o. 12th, p.u. 15th* ....C Ward-Thomas pu
9 ran. 5l. Time 6m 22.00s. SP 5-1.
D Nicholls (Cambridgeshire).
S.B.

HOLCOMBE HARRIERS
Whittingtor
Saturday April 19th
FIRM

1119 Members

ADMIRAL BYNG (FR) ....Miss D Hawkes 1
(fav) hld up, chsd ldr 5th, ld 12th-14th, qcknd to ld flat
Pride Of Erin 14ow.....................P Quinn 2
ld to 12th, ld 14th til hdd & outpcd flat
Bob 14ow...............................J Barlow 3
mid-div, ev ch 3 out, no ext
763[4] On Your Way *cls up til wknd 9th, t.o. 11th* .....A Gilby 4
Big Bird *in tch to 15th, wknd rpdly, t.o. & ref 2 out* ....Miss T Scott ref
5 ran. 2l, 12l, 30l. Time 7m 34.00s. SP 2-1.
Miss D E Hawkes (Holcombe Harriers).

1120 Intermdiate (12st)

998[1] **ROYLE BURCHLIN (bl) ....D Barlow** 1
(fav) jmpd rght, made all, alwys in cmmnd
984 **Bunny Hare (Ire).....................G Thomas** 2
blnd 3rd & 11th, chsd wnr, rdn & no ext 3 out
2 ran. 5l. Time 6m 55.00s. SP 2-11.
R A Royle (Cheshire).

1121 Confined

1047[1] **TATTLEJACK (IRE) (v)................Mrs C Ford** 1
(fav) made most frm 3rd, clr 3 out, easily
998[2] **Barkin ....P Saville** 2
ld to 3rd, cls up to 15th, rdn & wknd nxt
Shuil Saor ....J Saville 3
alwys 3rd, ev ch 3 out, no ext
Chillys Star *rear, blnd 3rd, t.o. 11th, p.u. 3 out* ....J Mather pu
4 ran. 10l, 15l. Time 6m 53.00s. SP 2-5.
M Silcock (West Shropshire Draghounds).

1122 Ladies

939[1] **HORNBLOWER ....Mrs C Ford** 1
(fav) ld to 14th & frm 16th, ran on wll whn chal last
1048[2] **Lupy Minstrel ....Miss P Robson** 2
j.w. ld 14th-nxt, ev ch last, not qckn nr fin
984[1] Running Frau 5a *chsd ldrs, 6l 3rd whn blnd & u.r. 13th*..................................Miss M Maher ur
3 ran. Hd. Time 6m 41.00s. SP 1-2.
N J Barrowclough (West Shropshire Draghounds).

1123 Men's Open (12st)

938[6] **MR TITTLE TATTLE 7ex (bl) ....D Barlow** 1
(fav) ld to 7th & frm nxt, clr 3 out, easily
1049[3] **Boreen Owen ....T Morrison** 2
hld up, gd prog 13th, cls 2nd nxt-3 out, outpcd aft
936 **Freddie Fox 7ex.......................T Garton** 3
chsd ldr, ld 7th-nxt, cls up til blnd 12th, wknd nxt
939 Irish Gent *alwys rear, nvr dang*...........G Thomas 4
4 ran. 6l, 15l, 20l. Time 6m 38.00s. SP 13-8.
H A Shone (Cheshire).

1124 Open Maiden

883 **WHO DOCTORED WHO (IRE) .....M Worthington** 1
lft 30l,n.j.w.,prog & cls 15th,outpcd,ran on& lft solo last
1003[2] **Builder Boy ....C Stockton** 2
(fav) clr to 15th,qcknd nxt,6l up & wkng whn ref last,cont
2 ran. Dist. Time 7m 32.00s. SP 7-2.
Mrs J Griffith (Flint & Denbigh).
R.A.

OLD SURREY & BURSTOW
Penshurst
Saturday April 19th
GOOD TO FIRM

1125 Members

277[2] **DADDY LONG LEGGS ....R Hubbard** 1
ld/disp to 3 out, styd on to ld agn apr last
304 **Topping-The-Bill ....Mrs E Coveney** 2
(fav) pllng & mstks, wth ldr, ld 3 out til apr last, wknd
486 Rocco *cls up whn u.r. 6th* ....K Tork ur
3 ran. 6l. Time 7m 4.00s. SP 9-4.
Mrs O Hubbard (Old Surrey & Burstow).

1126 Confined

830[2] **AMERICAN EYRE 5ex...........Miss S Gladders** 1
(Jt fav) clsd up 12th, chal 4 out, ld apr 2 out, drew clr
1057[3] **Vultoro ....T Underwood** 2
immed dtchd, clsd 7th, ld 9th-apr 2 out, wknd und pres
966[2] **Yeoman Farmer ....P Hacking** 3
hld up, prog to 3rd at 13th, rdn & no imp frm 4 out
577 Supreme Dealer *(Jt fav) ld to 2nd, lft in ld 7-9th, no dang 4 out, onepcd* ....A Warr 4
683 Burromariner *trckd clr ldr, cls up whn reluc 8th & ref 12th*....................................S Cowell ref
277 Devil's Valley *plld into ld 2nd, immed clr, 10l up whn u.r. 7th*..S Fisher ur
6 ran. 8l, 8l, nk. Time 6m 44.00s. SP 3-1.
J S S Hollins (Ashford Valley).

1127 Men's Open (12st)

685[1] **RUSTIC RAMBLE ....P Hacking** 1
(fav) trckd ldrs, chal 3 out, ld apr nxt, rdn out
970[1] **Bawnerosh ....T Underwood** 2
s.i.s. sn handy going wll,ld 12th-4 out,ld brfly 3 out,no ex
1054[2] **Paco's Boy 4ex.........................P York** 3
trckd ldrs, 3rd & ev ch 4 out, wknd 2 out
966[3] Sky Venture *ld 7-12th, agn 4 out-nxt, onepcd* . . .P Bull 4
969[1] Tau *ld to 7th, wth ldr to 12th, rdn & outpcd 4 out, p.u. last*...A Warr pu
968 Serious Money (USA) (bl) *prom til jmpd slwly 4th, n.j.w. aft, wll bhnd whn p.u. 8th* ....M Jones pu
Mr Oriental *in tch, wkng whn p.u. aft 9th* ....G Gigantesco pu
7 ran. 4l, 7l, 3l. Time 6m 46.00s. SP 13-8.
Peter Tipples (East Sussex & Romney Marsh).

1128 Ladies

968[1] **POLAR ANA (IRE) 5a...........Miss S Gladders** 1
(Jt fav) conf rdn,rear,smooth prog 13th,ld 3 out, sn clr, eased flat
966[1] **Woody Will ....Mrs E Coveney** 2
(Jt fav) wll in tch, 4th frm 12th, rdn & styd on 2 out, tk 2nd flat
968[3] **Slight Panic 5a.................Miss J Wickens** 3
cls up, mstk 11th, chsd wnr 3 out, wknd last
969 Rarely At Odds *alwys prom, pshd alng in 5th frm 12th, kpt on onepcd* ....Miss A Sansom 4
970[3] Abdul Emir *mid-div, clsd 7th, ld 12th-3 out, wknd* ....Mrs L Stock 5
788[1] Prince Zeus *alwys rear, wll bhnd frm 3 out* ....Mrs N Ledger 6
306 Tamborito (Ire) *prom to 5th, n.j.w., t.o. 13th* ....Mrs M Rigg 7
828 Boll Weevil *ld to 12th, fdd, t.o. & p.u. aft 2 out* ....Miss J Grant pu
8 ran. 3l, 5l, 6l, 12l, 20l, 20l. Time 6m 39.00s. SP 6-4.
Mrs P A McIntyre (Ashford Valley).

1129 Restricted (12st)

462[2] **HARMONY RIVER (IRE) 5a ....Miss C Holliday 1**
trckd ldrs, chal 4 out, ld nxt, styd on strngly
878[2] **King Of The Clouds ....J Hammond 2**
plld to ld 3rd,hdd & mstk 12th,3rd aft,kpt on,tk 2nd last
971[1] **Celtic Reg ....M Jones 3**
chsd ldr, ld 12th-3 out, wknd nxt
576[3] Bright Crusader *ld to aft 2nd, last frm 12th, wll bhnd whn p.u. aft 2 out* ....A Warr pu
970[2] And Why Not *rear, wll in tch whn stirrup iron broke & p.u. aft 11th* ....J Van Praagh pu
302[5] Major Man (Ire) *(fav) rear, mstks, 4th final cct, nvr dang, p.u. last* ....P Bull pu
6 ran. 7l, 4l. Time 6m 40.00s. SP 4-1.
Miss C Holliday (Old Surrey & Burstow).

1130 Open Maiden (12st)

681[2] **ISHMA (IRE) ....D Page 1**
(fav) rear, rmndrs & prog 13th, ld aft 3 out, kpt on
828[4] **Linger Balinda 5a ....P Bull 2**
alwys cls up, many rmndrs, ld 13th-3 out, hld aft
833 **Miss Pandy 5a ....Miss C Savell 3**
nvr dang, tk 3rd last
971 Spanish Pal (Ire) *rear, 3rd 14th, not pace to chal* ....Miss S Gladders 4
965[2] Huckleberry Friend 5a 1ow *ld til p.u. aft 13th, dead* ....P Blagg pu
5 ran. 2l, 4l. Time 7m 19.00s. SP Evens.
Darren Page (Ashford Valley).
G.Ta.

PENTYRCH
Bonvilston
Saturday April 19th
GOOD

1131 Members

877 **BOX OF DELIGHTS ....E Williams 1**
(Jt fav) trckd ldrs, lft in ld 14th, qcknd clr 2 out
717[3] **Kristal Haze 12a ....P Williams 2**
held up in rear, prog & lft 2nd 14th, alwys held
1007 **Adanac ....A Price 3**
cls 2nd til hmp 14th, no ch aft
719 Its A Doddle 5a *alwys rear, no ch frm hlfwy* ....Miss S Robinson 4
Steel Valley (Ire) 5a *t.o. frm 5th til p.u. 12th* ....Miss E Jones pu
908[1] Moor Hill Lass (Ire) *(Jt fav) ld til f 14th*........G Lewis f
6 ran. 10l, 25l, dist. Time 5m 38.00s. SP 5-2.
Mrs Jeanne Thomas (Pentyrch).

1132 Confined (12st)

1062 **CONNA MOSS (IRE) 3ex..........Miss P Jones 1**
(fav) made all, qcknd whn chal last
902[1] **Savage Oak ....E Williams 2**
prom, wnt 2nd 3 out, chal last, no ext flat
1006[2] **Gold Diver 8ex..................Miss V Roberts 3**
cls up, lost post hlfwy, styd on late
714[4] Princess Lu (Ire) *mid-div, prog to cls 2nd 15th, wknd qckly nxt* ....J P Keen 4
714 Scared Stiff 5a *alwys rear* ....A Price 5
1063[7] Guarena (USA) *alwys rear* ....Miss N Richards 6
715[5] Curie Crusader (Ire) 5ow *alwys rear, t.o. & p.u. last* ....J Tudor pu
716 Desmond Gold (Ire) 3ex *trckd ldrs, cls 3rd, slppd up bnd aft 14th* ....Miss L Pearce su
900[1] Sebastopol *rear til p.u. 13th* ....D Stephens pu
9 ran. 1½l, dist, 5l, 6l, 3l. Time 5m 31.00s. SP 5-4.
David Brace (Llangeinor).

1133 Intermediate (12st)

1086 **GUNNER BOON ....Miss P Jones 1**
(fav) cls up, lft 2nd 15th, ld 2 out, qcknd clr
636[3] **Bit Of A Citizen (Ire) ....E Williams 2**
cls up, ld 15th, hdd 2 out, no ext
715 **Polly Pringle 5a 5ex ....A Price 3**
held up towrds rear, ran on wll frm 3 out, nrst fin
1005[4] Sweet Kildare 5a *mid-div, nvr plcd to chal*....J Jukes 4
716[3] Mo's Chorister *rear, no ch frm hlfwy* ....Miss S Robinson 5
1043 Scriven Boy *alwys last* ....M Flynn 6
938[3] Ideal *ld til hdd apr 15th & f* ....J Rees f
1005 Icecapade (Bel) *prom early, wknd frm 13th, p.u. 2 out* ....Miss E Jones pu
8 ran. 8l, 4l, 15l, dist, dist. Time 5m 30.00s. SP 5-4.
David Brace (Llangeinor).

1134 4m Mixed Open (12st)

714 **CARRICK LANES ....Miss P Jones 1**
made all, qcknd clr 3 out, comf
1005[2] **Archer (Ire) ....J Llewellyn 2**
(fav) prom, rmmndrs hlfwy, 2nd & held frm 3 out
903[1] **Rusty Music ....Miss N Richards 3**
mid-div, rddn alng hlfwy, tk 3rd 3 out, no ch wth wnnr
1007 Prince Nepal *mid-div, imprvd to 2nd hlfwy, no further prog* ....S Shinton 4
1005[7] Pay-U-Cash *cls up, wknd 16th, ran on onepce* ....G Perkins 5
1008 Greenfield Tiger (Ire) *alwys towrds rear*..P Sheldrake 6
1008[7] Valiant Friend (bl) *last til f 17th* ....Miss B Barton f
400[4] Lighten The Load *prom to 17th, grdly wknd & p.u. last* ....E Williams pu
1006 Project's Mate *nvr bynd mid-div, p.u. 2 out* D S Jones pu
903[2] Noisy Welcome 2ow *towrds rear til p.u. 3 out* ....M P Jones pu
10 ran. 25l, 1l, 10l, dist, dist. Time 7m 0.00s. SP 7-2.
David Brace (Llangeinor).

1135 Restricted (12st)

254[3] **CATHGAL ....Miss C Thomas 1**
prom til ld 15th, qcknd whn chal apr last
1057[2] **Dragons Lady 5a ....G Barfoot-Saunt 2**
cls up, ld 13-15th, ran on wll
324 **Black Ermine (Ire) ....J Jukes 3**
held up, prog 14th to chal 2 out, onepcd aft
718[2] Rosieplant 5a *rear early, prog 3 out, nvr nrr* M Lewis 4
1008 Mr Mad *rear early, prog 15th, no ext apr last* ....P Hamer 5
1008 Equatime 5a *ld to 12th, prom aft til wknd 3 out* A Price 6
901[3] Yarron King *alwys rear*..........I Johnson 7
1008[6] Miss Montgomery (Ire) 5a *mid-div, wknd hlfwy, t.o.* ....J Price 8
539[4] Flaxridge *towrds rear, p.u. last*.......Miss E Tamplin pu
717 West King *alwys rear, p.u. 13th* ....J P Keen pu
1008[2] Everso Irish *cls up early, wknd 15th, p.u. last* ....E Williams pu
753[4] Fire King *prom til wknd frm 14th, p.u. flat*....E Collins pu
907[1] I'm A Bute 5a *t.o. frm hlfwy, p.u. 3 out*. .Miss F Wilson pu
542[1] Keep Flowing (Ire) *(fav) mid-div, p.u. 13th (stewards)* ....Miss P Jones pu
14 ran. 4l, sht-hd, 3l, 10l, 4l, 8l, dist. Time 5m 34.00s. SP 5-1.
Richard Mathias (North Hereford).

1136 Open Maiden Div I (12st)

719[3] **MISTER JAY DAY ....A Price 1**
3rd/4th til ld 13th, made rest, qcknd whn chal flat
719 **Good Boy Fred 7a ....P Williams 2**
(fav) trckd ldrs, 2nd 13th, strng chal apr last, alwys held
1018[5] **Wilton Park 5a ....E Williams 3**
held up, steadd prog 12th, 3rd 15th, styd on onepce
1010 Rebel Yell (Ire) 5a *rear, sm prog 14th, ran on onepcd* ....G Lewis 4
1011[3] Boddington Hill 5a *cls up, wknd frm 15th* ...I Johnson 5
1009 Good Boy Charlie *rear early, styd on onepcd frm 3 out* ....D S Jones 6
Glynn Brae (Ire) *alwys mid-div* ....J Heywood 7
Colonial Office (USA) *alwys rear, p.u. 3 out* ....Miss P Jones pu
717 Wooly Town 5a (bl) *rear til p.u. 12th*........G Perkins pu

901 Wissywis (Ire) 12a *cls up to 7th, wknd qckly, p.u. 15th* ....J Price pu
1009 Queen's Equa 5a *ld til ran out apr 13th* ..Miss S Major ro
540 Mountain Slave 5a *rear til p.u. 3 out* ......T Vaughan pu
543 Flockmaster (Ire) *last til p.u. 3 out* ......J P Keen pu
719 Mo's Keliro 12a *rear til f 10th* ....Miss S Robinson f
720 Newchurch Lad *rear til p.u. 3 out* ....Miss C Davis pu
15 ran. 2½l, 25l, 1l, 5l, 1l, dist. Time 5m 37.00s. SP 5-1.
William John Day (Gelligaer Farmers).
One fence omitted.

1137 Open Maiden Div II (12st)

408² **KHANDYS SLAVE (IRE) 5a** ....**J Jukes** 1
(Jt fav) alwys cls up, ld 12th, made rest, comf
963³ **Mr Ffitch** ....**G Barfoot-Saunt** 2
prom early, lost plc hlfwy, ran on frm 3 out, onepcd
Underwychwood (Ire) ....**J Heywood** 3
towrds rear, steadd prog 15th, nrst fin
847³ Wayward Edward *ld to 11th, hdd nxt, alwys chsng wnnr, wknd 2 out* ....J Price 4
1009⁴ Itsstormingnorma 5a *mid-div, prog to 4th 15th, one-pce aft* ....D Stephens 5
963 Southerncrosspatch *n.j.w., in mid-div, wknd frm 14th* ....D S Jones 6
963 Lady Romance (Ire) 5a *rear, p.u. 3 out* ......J P Keen pu
719² Volcanic Roc *cls up, wknd 14th, p.u. 2 out* . .E Williams pu
1011 Mississippisteamer (Ire) 3ow *rear til p.u. 12th* J Tudor pu
1004 Penylan Gold 5a *rear, p.u. 14th* ....P Williams pu
964² Laudation (Ire) 7a *rear & n.j.w., p.u. 15th* ....P Hamer pu
720 Tiger Lord *rear, p.u. 3 out* ....A Price pu
407 Davalbury (Ire) 7a *(Jt fav) rear til p.u. 12th* ....Miss P Jones pu
13 ran. 10l, 5l, ½l, 15l, 8l. Time 5m 35.00s. SP 3-1.
K M Stanworth (Tredegar Farmers).

1138 Open Maiden Div III (12st)

540 **BUSHTON 7a** ....**J P Keen** 1
held up mid-div,prog 13th,wnt 2nd 3 out,hrd rdn to ld flat
1065 **Malthouse Lad** ....**D Stephens** 2
cls up, ld 14th til hdd flat
1005⁵ **Final Option (Ire)** ....**I Johnson** 3
ld brfly 7th, cls 2nd aft til onepcd frm 2 out
639⁶ Le Vienna (Ire) 2ow *rear til some late prog* . .S Currey 4
706 Greenfield Maid (Ire) 5a *alwys rear* ....D S Jones 5
902² Red Rhapsody 5a *ld early, wknng whn bad mstk 11th & p.u.* ....J Comins pu
Moorlough Bay (Ire) *(fav) prom early, ld 10th, hdd nxt, wknd qckly & p.u. last* ....J Price pu
1011 Dontyoudoda (Ire) (bl) *rear, f 13th* ....T Vaughan f
1009 Chantingo Lad *t.o. & p.u. 9th* ....A Price pu
9 ran. 2l, 4l, 15l, 2l. Time 5m 44.00s. SP 6-1.
J L Brown (Llandeilo).

SOUTH & WEST WILTS
Larkhill
Saturday April 19th
FIRM

1139 Members

892 **FELTHAM MISTRESS 5a** ....**E Babington** 1
jmpd rght, blnd 5th, jnd ldr 13th, ld 2 out, rdn out
934⁴ **Mountain-Linnet** ....**Miss A Goschen** 2
(fav) ld, jnd 13th, hdd & mstk 2 out, onepcd
2 ran. 2l. Time 6m 24.00s. SP 7-4.
Donald C Tucker (South & West Wilts).

1140 Open Maiden (12st)

933 **CARNELIA 5a**...................**Miss A Goschen** 1
walked over
J W Kwiatkowski (Blackmore & Sparkford Vale).

1141 Ladies

864² **RAPID RASCAL** ....**Miss S West** 1
(fav) disp clr ld til ld 9th, drew clr apr 13th, unchal
750¹ **Nanda Moon** ....**Miss S Jackson** 2
jmpd slwly early,lost tch 6th,clsd 15th,2nd apr last,nvr nrr
1022² **Lavalight** ....**Miss A Goschen** 3
disp to 9th, prssd wnr til apr 13th, grad wknd
1020¹ Vital Shot 5a *jmpd slwly, alwys last, t.o. 7th* ....Mrs R Baldwin 4
4 ran. 15l, 5l, 1 fence. Time 6m 2.00s. SP 6-4.
Miss S West (Weston & Banwell).

1142 Land Rover Open (12st)

918¹ **INDIAN KNIGHT** ....**M Miller** 1
(fav) trckd ldr, ld apr 15th, sn clr, canter
921¹ **Miss Magic 5a**.......................**F Brennan** 2
disp til ld 3rd, hdd aft 14th, blnd nxt, sn btn
916³ Gunner Stream *cls up, mstk & rdr lost irons 2nd, p.u. nxt, rtrcd, p.u. 7th* ....S Greany pu
3 ran. Dist. Time 6m 1.00s. SP 2-5.
C A Green (South & West Wilts).

1143 B F S S (Nov Riders)

CRUISE FREE ....**L Manners** 1
chsd ldr, rdn apr last, 4l down & btn whn lft solo
916¹ Wesshaun 5a *(fav) ld, 4l clr & in cmmnd whn f last* ....G Chanter f
2 ran. Time 6m 13.00s. SP 5-4.
H J Manners (Berks & Bucks Drag).

1144 Restricted (12st)

1024¹ **SPAR COPSE** ....**Miss A Goschen** 1
(fav) made all, 4l clr whn jmpd slwly 2 out, kpt on
655 **John Roger 1ow** ....**L Manners** 2
alwys 2nd, 5l down & rdn 3 out, kpt on flat, nt rch wnr
Bungle *hld up last, in tch whn f 5th, dead* . .A Charles-Jones f
3 ran. 1½l. Time 6m 15.00s. SP 4-5.
P E Froud (Blackmore & Sparkford Vale).
S.P.

WORCESTERSHIRE
Chaddesley Corbett
Saturday April 19th
GOOD TO FIRM

1145 Members

255¹ **STAG FIGHT 4ex**...............**Julian Pritchard** 1
(fav) ld to 2nd, ld aft 13th, sn clr, eased flat
431 **Mr Dennehy (Ire)** ....**M Butcher** 2
wll bhnd, poor 4th hlfwy, ran on 4 out, tk 2nd flat
404 **Manard 5a** ....**M Hammond** 3
chsd ldng pair, went 2nd 14th, no imp, wknd & lost 2nd flat
877⁴ Members Rights 5a *ld 2nd til aft 13th, strgglng whn mstk nxt, wknd* ....M Keel 4
878⁴ Shadow Walker *sn wll bhnd, no ch frm hlfwy* ....Miss S Smith 5
Poetic Mover *sn bhnd, wknd & p.u. aft 12th* D Painter pu
6 ran. 10l, 1½l, 15l, 10l. Time 6m 54.00s. SP 2-5.
Mrs J A Scott (Worcestershire).

1146 Confined (12st)

976 **HACKETT'S FARM** ....**Julian Pritchard** 1
(fav) ld/disp,qcknd 13th,drew clr 4 out,hrd rdn & lft wl clr 2 out
704⁴ **Sudanor (Ire)** ....**O McPhail** 2
ld/disp, qcknd 13th, hdd 16th, wknd rpdly, lft 2nd 2 out
1064 **Hook Line'N'sinker** ....**L Brown** 3
cls up til outpcd 13th, sn t.o.
952¹ Great Uncle *in tch in rear til outpcd 13th, sn t.o.* ....Miss T McCurrich 4
750⁴ Tytherington *ld 3rd-4th, outpcd 13th, sn t.o.* ....Miss S Talbot 5

1012[3] Stylish Gent *cls up,3rd & outpcd 13th,ran on 4 out,6l down & clsng,f 2out* ....D Mansell f
6 ran. 30l, 2l, 3l, 3l. Time 6m 52.50s. SP 11-10.
Miss Barbara Wilce (North Ledbury).

1147 Sporting Life Open

642[1] **DOUBLE THRILLER** ....**J Tizzard** 1
prssd ldr, ld 11-13th & 15th, shkn up 2 out, ran on well
930[4] **Zambrano (USA) 7a (v)** ....**S Durack** 2
mstk 3rd,trckd ldrs, went 2nd 16th,ev ch 2 out,ran on onepcd
1071[1] **Peanuts Pet** ....**R Walmsley** 3
w.w. effrt 14th, chsd ldrs, 4 out, kpt on onepcd
690[1] Still In Business *(fav) hld up,prog 10th,ev ch 4 out,wknd rpdly nxt,crawld last* ....T Mitchell 4
587[3] Minella Express (Ire) *ld to 11th & 13th-15th, ev ch & mstk 4 out, sn wknd* ....Julian Pritchard 5
703[4] Sharinski *cls up til wknd apr 14th, bhnd & p.u. 16th* ....M Rimell pu
218[2] Springfield Lad *rear, lost tch & rdn 12th, t.o. & p.u. 16th* ....E Walker pu
7 ran. 3l, 12l, 12l, 3l. Time 6m 41.00s. SP 5-1.
R C Wilkins (Mendip Farmers).

1148 Ladies

939[2] **ANDROS GALE (IRE)** ....**Mrs A Rucker** 1
ld 3-5th & 15th-nxt, ld & lft clr 2 out, ran on well
878[1] **Mister Gebo** ....**Miss C Dyson** 2
ld to 3rd & 5th-15th, ld nxt, hdd & blnd 2 out, no ch aft
920[1] **Fosbury** ....**Miss P Gundry** 3
(Jt fav) nvr going wll, bhnd & pshd alng 12th, no prog, t.o., b.b.v.
647[1] Front Cover 5a *(Jt fav) prom til blnd & u.r. 8th* ....Miss S Vickery ur
988 Fundy (Ire) *prom, cls 3rd whn f 12th* ..Miss T Spearing f
5 ran. 20l, dist. Time 6m 42.00s. SP 16-1.
Mrs A Rucker (Worcestershire).

1149 Interlink Restricted (12st)

877[3] **GLITTERBIRD 5a** ....**A Dalton** 1
made all, styd on well frm 3 out
934[1] **Whitmore** ....**J Tizzard** 2
(fav) hld up bhnd, prog to chs wnr 14th, chnc 4 out, no imp nxt
876[1] **Damers Treasure (bl)** ....**M Harris** 3
chsd wnr to 14th, sn rdn & btn
548[7] Mamnoon (USA) *chsd ldrs, rdn 13th, strggling frm 15th* ....R Armson 4
1014 Polydeuces *cls up to 11th, sn wknd, t.o. & p.u. 2 out* ....R Inglesant pu
1013 Katie Parson 5a *mstks, bhnd frm 9th, p.u. 12th* ....M Hammond pu
6 ran. 6l, 30l, 1l. Time 6m 45.00s. SP 5-1.
Mrs C J Chadney (Croome & West Warwickshire).

1150 Open Maiden Div I (12st)

487 **TREVVEETHAN (IRE)** ....**M Rimell** 1
(fav) w.w. prog to chs ldr 14th, ld & lft clr 16th, comf
1019 **Ribington** ....**M Hammond** 2
chsd ldrs to 14th, wknd 16th, lft poor 2nd 2 out
1013 Only In Ireland *ld, clr to 14th, tired whn hdd & f 16th* ....R Inglesant f
706[2] Joyney 5a *rear & not fluent,effrt to chs wnr 4 out,12l down & u.r.2out* ....M FitzGerald ur
181[4] Dr Douski 7a *rear, strggling whn mstk 12th, t.o. & p.u. 3 out* ....Miss E Godfrey pu
Ullington Lord *alwys rear, rdn & wknd 11th, p.u. 13th* ....S Joynes pu
Royal Sweep *ref 1st, cont til ref 6th* ...Miss P Gundry ref
7 ran. Dist. Time 6m 55.50s. SP 5-4.
Giles Smyly (North Cotswold).

1151 Open Maiden Div II (12st)

853[2] **ZODIAC PRINCE 7a** ....**M Harris** 1
(fav) trckd ldr, lft in ld 6th, clr 2 out, blnd last
575[5] **Rejects Reply** ....**G Hanmer** 2
hmpd 3rd, lft 2nd 11th, ev ch 4 out, btn nxt
654 Roman Romany *ld til ref & u.r. 6th* ....M Rimell ref
1016 Asante Sana 5a (v) *in tch, lft 2nd 6th, f 11th* ...N Oliver f
643 Millyhenry *hld up, f 3rd* ....J Tizzard f
5 ran. 8l. Time 7m 14.00s. SP Evens.
R H Philips (Worcestershire).
J.N.

AXE VALE HARRIERS
Stafford Cross
Sunday April 20th
GOOD TO FIRM

1152 Members

935 **JIM CROW** ....**M Miller** 1
(fav) disp til lft clr 4th, lft solo last
648 Tom's Arctic Dream 5a *disp til p.u. bef 4th, reins broke* ....P King pu
792[5] Stainless Steel *chsd wnr, effrt 2 out, ev ch whn p.u. last, lame* ....M Sweetland pu
Lightening News 5a *u.r. 1st* ....S Slade ur
4 ran. Time 6m 29.00s. SP 8-11.
J M Salter (Axe Vale Harriers).

1153 Confined (12st)

932 **CLANDON JACK (v)** ....**T Mitchell** 1
made all, clr 3 out, tired nr fin
920[2] **Gallant Effort (Ire)** ....**Miss A Goschen** 2
chsd ldr, disp 2nd whn lft clr 2nd 14th, no imp
238[5] **Friendly Lady 5a 3ex** ....**Miss A Bush** 3
mid-div, nvr on trms wth ldrs
931[3] Pintail Bay 5ex *mid-div, went 3rd 12th, rdn 2 out, lost 3rd flat* ....N Legg 4
862[4] The Criosra (Ire) *alwys bhnd, t.o. 15th* .....A Bateman 5
931[4] Osmosis *mid-div, lost tch 12th, t.o. 4 out* ....K Nelmes 6
869 The Humble Tiller *sn rear, t.o. & u.r. 15th* ....Mrs A Bevins ur
Highway Jim *1st ride, alwys last, t.o. whn ref 12th* ....Miss M Burrough ref
Chip And Run *6s-7/2, rear whn u.r. bend aft 8th* ....B O'Doherty ur
929[3] Sunley Street 5a (bl) *(fav) 7/2-9/4, chsd ldr, disp 2nd til blnd 12th, p.u. aft* ....Miss S Vickery pu
10 ran. 2l, 25l, 5l, 30l, 25l. Time 5m 55.00s. SP 100-30.
J G Crumpler (Cattistock).

1154 Men's Open (12st)

1042[1] **QUALITAIR MEMORY (IRE) 7ex** ....**J Tizzard** 1
(fav) made all, ran on wll whn chal frm last
1091[4] **Anjubi** ....**I Dowrick** 2
trckd ldr, effrt 2 out, outpcd flat
2 ran. 4l. Time 6m 7.00s. SP 2-7.
C L Tizzard (Blackmore & Sparkford Vale).

1155 Ladies

864 **OLD MILL STREAM** ....**Miss P Gundry** 1
plld hrd, ld 4th-3 out, disp nxt, rdn & ran on well
1056[1] **Arctic Chill (Ire)** ....**Miss S Vickery** 2
(fav) ld to 4th, chsd wnr aft, rdn aft 3 out, disp nxt, wknd flat
864[1] **On His Own** ....**Miss W Southcombe** 3
rear til prog 14th, lft 3rd last, nvr dang
932[4] Reef Lark *alwys rear, no ch frm 12th* Miss A Goschen 4
1090 Be My Habitat (bl) *alwys bhnd, lost tch 12th, t.o.* ....Miss L Hawkings 5
555[3] Searcy *chsd ldrs, 3rd frm 9th, wll btn in 3rd whn f last* ....Miss L Blackford f
6 ran. 10l, dist, 3l, 25l. Time 5m 51.50s. SP 5-2.
Richard Barber (Taunton Vale).

1156 Intermediate (12st)

930[2] **MARION'S OWN (IRE) (bl)** ....**T Mitchell** 1

(fav) hld up, prog 10th, went 2nd 4 out, chal last, ran on,ld flat
647[2] **Highway Lad** .... **P King** 2
ld 3rd til hdd last, onepcd aft
862[3] **Elle Flavador 5a**.................. **Miss S Vickery** 3
alwys prom, cls 3rd til outpcd frm 2 out
1038[2] Tangle Kelly *prom to 13th, lost tch 15th, no ch aft* .... S Slade 4
930[6] Shared Fortune (Ire) *ld to 3rd, prom to 9th, lost tch frm 14th*.......... Daniel Dennis 5
1039[1] Sunwind *hld up, cls 4th & going wll whn u.r. 14th* .... M Frith ur
6 ran. 6l, 15l, 20l, ½l. Time 6m 7.00s. SP 4-6.
Mrs M B Keighley (Cattistock).

1157 Restricted (12st)

892[5] **ANN'S AMBITION** .... **M Frith** 1
alwys prom,2nd at 11th, lft in ld 14th, styd on strngly 2out
933[1] **False Tail (Ire) 7a** .... **J Tizzard** 2
(fav) prom, 3rd at 11th, chsd wnr & slppd final bnd, no prog aft
1041[2] **Royal Turn** .... **A Honeyball** 3
rear, prog 12th, outpcd frm 3 out
1039 The Butler *prom early, lost tch 14th, onepcd aft* .... S Slade 4
1045[3] And What Else (Ire) *sn bhnd, t.o. 14th* .... B Dixon 5
735[1] Ballysheil *ld til went wrong side of omitted fence at 14th, p.u.*.......... S Edwards pu
516[4] Juniper Lodge *prom til 9th, p.u. apr 11th*...... S Bush pu
692[1] Purbeck Polly 5a *rear whn f 6th* .... Mrs A Davis f
687[3] Clandon Lad *hld up, prog 10th, cls 3rd whn s.u. bnd apr 2 out*.......... T Mitchell su
644[7] French Invasion 5a *mid-div, u.r. 7th*.... S Parfimowicz ur
873 Chasing Daisy 12a *prom early, lost tch 10th, t.o. & p.u. 12th* .... Miss A Goschen pu
11 ran. 8l, 5l, 25l, 2l. Time 5m 58.00s. SP 8-1.
Mrs C Hussey (Warwickshire).

1158 Open Maiden (5-7yo) (12st)

1045[2] **SUE'S QUEST 5a**.................. **P King** 1
disp to 3 out, hdd, rnwd effrt nxt, ld apr last, ran on wll
933[6] **Fever Pitch** .... **J Tizzard** 2
(fav) disp to 4 out, outpcd frm 2 out, tk 2nd nr fin
866 **Acetylene 12a**.................. **Miss T Cave** 3
hld up, prog 12th, ld aft 3 out-apr last, onepcd
933[7] Olive Basket 5a *prom til outpcd 15th, lost tch nxt, ran on agn clsng stgs*.......... Miss W Southcombe 4
661 Palmerston's Folly 5a *sn rear, lost tch 12th, p.u. aft 15th*.......... Daniel Dennis pu
5 ran. 10l, 1½l, 2l. Time 6m 10.00s. SP 7-2.
Mrs S E Wall (Weston & Banwell Harriers).
D.P.

GRAFTON
Mollington
Sunday April 20th
GOOD TO FIRM

1159 Members

680[4] **BROAD STEANE** .... **J Connell** 1
(fav) ld 6th, lft virt solo 11th, lft alone 15th
887 Obie's Train 2ow *ld brfly 2nd, bhnd frm 4th, lft dist 2nd 11th, ref 3 out* .... Mrs A Lee ref
925[3] Alias Silver *ld to 2nd, 3l 2nd whn u.r. 11th* .... Miss H Irving ur
927[2] Castle Shelley (Ire) *ld aft 2nd-6th, wknd rpdly & p.u. 11th*.......... R Smith pu
4 ran. Time 6m 32.00s. SP 2-5.
Sir Michael Connell (Grafton).

1160 Intermediate (12st)

515[2] **NOTHING VENTURED** .... **A Beedles** 1
(Jt fav) wth ldr, ld 10th, drew clr aft 2 out, comf
989[1] **July Schoon 5ex**.................. **T Underwood** 2
w.w. prog 13th, effrt to chs wnr aft 2 out, no imp last
1077 **Sabre King (bl)** .... **L Lay** 3
ld to 10th, chsd wnr aft, chnc whn mstk 2 out, wknd rpdly
878 Therewego (Ire) *cls up, rdn 11th, mstk 13th, outpcd frm nxt* .... M Munrowd 4
1080 Bakmalad *chsd ldrs, jmpd slwly 6th & wknd rpdly, p.u. 10th* .... H Wheeler pu
476[1] Music In The Night *(Jt fav) trckd ldrs, cls 3rd 13th, wknd & p.u. 15th, lame* .... F Hutsby pu
1077[5] Menature (Ire) 4ow *s.s. alwys last, t.o. 10th, p.u. 13th* .... J Seth-Smith pu
927 Lucky Landing (Ire) *keen hld, prom to 11th, wknd 13th, t.o. & p.u. 15th* .... A Martin pu
758 Quite A Miss 5a *chsd ldrs, wknd 12th, t.o. & p.u. 3 out* .... B McKim pu
9 ran. 5l, 25l, 5l. Time 6m 25.00s. SP 7-4.
Countess Goess-Saurau (South Shropshire).

1161 Sporting Life Ladies

702[1] **STEPHENS PET 5ex** .... **Miss A Dare** 1
(fav) ld 5th, drew clr aft 2 out, easily
983 **Making Time 5a** .... **Miss T Habgood** 2
w.w. chsd wnr 13th, no imp aft 2 out
1078 Fenton Bridge *jmpd lft, ld to 5th, last frm 13th, wknd rpdly, p.u. last* .... Miss R Tutton pu
3 ran. 5l. Time 6m 28.00s. SP 1-4.
Dr P P Brown (Berkeley).

1162 Confined (12st)

978[1] **SEVERN INVADER 6ex** .... **Miss H Gosling** 1
sttld dtchd last til rpd prog 2 out, ran on wll to ld nr fin
984[2] **Tompet** .... **B McKim** 2
chsd ldrs, effrt & hit 2 out, kpt on wll flat
757[1] **Sprucefield** .... **A Barlow** 3
j.w. ld to 13th, styd on to ld apr last, hdd nr fin
769[5] Going Around *mstks, chsd ldrs, effrt apr 2 out, one-pcd* .... L Lay 4
545 Bervie House (Ire) 3ex *chsd ldr,ld 13th,sn clr,hit 2 out,wknd rpdly & hdd apr last* .... R Barrett 5
926 Fighting Mariner (bl) *prom to 3 out, wknd rpdly nxt* .... John Pritchard 6
389[1] Archies Oats 7ex *(fav) nvr going wll, mstk 10th, sn lost tch, p.u. 13th* .... J Trice-Rolph pu
7 ran. 1l, hd, 5l, 10l, 25l. Time 6m 31.00s. SP 11-8.
Mrs E Gosling (Bicester With Whaddon Chase).

1163 Land Rover Open (12st)

1079[1] **LUCKY CHRISTOPHER 7ex**.......... **J Docker** 1
(fav) made most, qcknd clr 15th, canter
925 **Walkers Point** .... **S Astaire** 2
sn hrd hld in last, ran on to 2nd last, no ch, rider retired
Secret Truth 5a .... **A Martin** 3
pllng, chsd wnr, no dang, wknd apr last
370 Whats Your Game (bl) *mstly 3rd & not fluent, wknd 3 out*.......... K Sheppard 4
4 ran. 8l, 6l, 2l. Time 7m 2.00s. SP 1-7.
G B Tarry (Grafton).

1164 Restricted

1076 **BROWN BABY 5a**.................. **G Kerr** 1
ld 5-8th, trckd ldrs, qcknd to ld apr last, just hld on
827[1] **Villains Brief (Ire) (bl)** .... **R Lawther** 2
trckd ldrs, ld 14th, clr 3 out, hdd apr last, rallied flat
1076[2] **Miss Solitaire 5a**.................. **J Docker** 3
ld to 5th, prom, chsd ldr 3 out, no ext nxt
653 Its Murphy Man *blnd 1st, in tch, onepcd frm 3 out* .... J Trice-Rolph 4
980[1] Fraction *sn bhnd, mstk 9th, clsd 13th, sn outpcd, kpt on frm 2 out*.......... A Martin 5
649[1] Diamond Wind (USA) 5a *(fav) prom, ld 8th-14th, wknd aft 3 out* .... A Beedles 6
1081[7] Tarry Awhile (bl) *chsd ldrs til wknd 14th, walked in* .... J Connell 7
680 Solar Gem *alwys last, t.o. 6th, p.u. 3 out*..... J Mason pu

985² Sparnova 5a (bl) *mstks, cls up to 14th, lost tch und pres, p.u. last*........T Illsley pu
986⁵ Penly *bhnd frm 8th, brf efft 13th, sn wknd, p.u. last*........John Pritchard pu
10 ran. Hd, 8l, 2l, 10l, 1l, 20l. Time 6m 30.00s. SP 9-2.
G R Kerr (Pytchley).

1165 Open Maiden Div I (12st)

1151 **ROMAN ROMANY** ....**M Rimell** 1
made virt all, clr 14th, pshd out flat
990³ **Connie Foley** ....**S Green** 2
alwys chsng wnr, no imp frm 3 out
986 **Buladante (Ire)** ....**T Underwood** 3
hld up, effrt 3 out, tk 3rd last
487³ Titchwell Milly 5a *(fav) chsd wnr, no imp 3 out, 3rd & btn whn mstk nxt*........L Lay 4
1082 Magical Manor 5a *in tch in rear, effrt 11th, not rch ldrs, wknd apr 3 out*........J Oldring 5
1082 Shedoes 5a *chsd ldrs til wknd 14th, t.o.*...C Wadland 6
Dromain 5a *jmpd bdly in last til p.u. 7th*...A Sansome pu
The Birdie Song 5a *alwys rear, lost tch 13th, t.o. & p.u. last*........M Harris pu
451 Manor's Maid 12a *alwys bhnd, t.o. 13th, p.u. 15th*........Mrs C McCarthy pu
9 ran. 10l, 4l, 1½l, 20l, 20l. Time 6m 36.00s. SP 11-2.
G Smyly (North Cotswold).

1166 Open Maiden Div II (12st)

550⁶ **CANTANGO (IRE)** ....**A Sansome** 1
prom, lft in ld 8-10th, ld aft nxt, hrd rdn 2 out, kpt on
980² **The Chairman (Ire)** ....**J Trice-Rolph** 2
pllng, trckd ldrs, prssd wnr 13th, ev ch last, not run on
1083 **Miss Precocious 5a** ....**C Wadland** 3
prom, disp whn blnd 11th, effrt agn 14th, sn btn
Sir Krispin *last til prog to jn ldrs 9th, wknd 12th, p.u. 15th*........T Illsley pu
974⁵ Country Brew 5a *in tch, disp 3rd & outpcd frm 14th, wknd & p.u. last*........C Marriott pu
Captain's Port 5a *jmpd lft, cls up to 12th, wknd rpdly, p.u. 3 out*........M Harris pu
990 Bobbin Lace 5a *prom, disp 10th til hmpd nxt, not rcvr, p.u. aft 12th*........J Docker pu
373 It's A Scoop *ld til p.u. 8th, dsmntd*........L Lay pu
923² Neelisagin (Ire) *(fav) mid-div, lost tch 13th, t.o. & p.u. 3 out*........J Turcan pu
9 ran. 3½l, 25l. Time 6m 42.00s. SP 4-1.
W J Turcan (Fernie).
J.N.

HAYDON
Hexham Point-To-Point Course
Sunday April 20th
GOOD TO FIRM

1167 Members (12st)

997 **NONEOFYOURBUSINESS (IRE) 5a** ....**T Scott** 1
(fav) 15l 3rd at 6th, prog 10th, ld 2 out, ran on well
996 **Stanwick Fort 5a** ....**Mrs H Dickson** 2
n.j.w. ld 3rd til ran wd & hdd 2 out, not rcvr
Hawaiian Prince ....**Miss T Hammond** 3
ld to 3rd, 2l 3rd 15th, outpcd apr 3 out, lost tch
730⁴ Tuneful Tom *alwys rear, no imp final cct* Miss V Burn 4
734³ Copper Pan 5a 3ow *u.r. 1st*........Miss M Blakey ur
5 ran. 1½l, 30l, 12l. Time 7m 9.00s. SP 2-1.
R W Jewitt (Haydon).
Two fences omitted.

1168 Confined (12st)

993⁴ **WINNIE LORRAINE 5a** ....**T Scott** 1
cls up bhnd ldr, ld aft 16th, styd on well
991¹ **Will Travel (Ire)** ....**A Robson** 2
cls up, disp 16th, 3l 2nd nxt, no imp wnr 2 out
Worthy Spark 3ex ....**P Craggs** 3
(fav) j.w. ld til jnd 16th, wknd nxt, rallied 2 out, no ext last
3 ran. 3l, 1l. Time 6m 48.00s. SP 7-1.
R W Jewitt & Miss T Hammond (Haydon).

1169 Restricted (12st)

694 **JOLLY FELLOW** ....**Miss S Ward** 1
prog frm rear to 4th at 12th, chal 3 out, ld last, styd on
1046¹ **Solwaysands** ....**B Gibson** 2
(fav) ld/disp til hdd last, no ext flat
337 **Kings Token** ....**J Walton** 3
rear, prog 15th, tk poor 3rd apr last
235¹ Fiddlers Brae *nvr nr ldrs, styd on frm 4 out, tk poor 4th last*........Miss D Calder 4
991² Buckaneer Bay *alwys prom, ev ch 15th, wknd 3 out, demoted apr last*........T Barry 5
995 Panto Lady 5a *mid-div to 12th, wknd 15th, p.u. last*........Miss S Lamb pu
810 Able Moss *alwys rear, t.o. last whn p.u. 14th*........L Morgan pu
733¹ Boyup Brook *mid-div, blnd & u.r. 5th*........T Morrison ur
972⁶ Storm Alive (Ire) *disp 3rd-9th, cls up til wknd apr 3 out, p.u. last*........T Scott pu
9 ran. 4l, 20l, 6l, 8l. Time 6m 54.00s. SP 7-1.
Miss S M Ward (South Durham).

1170 Men's Open

812² **WASHAKIE** ....**J Walton** 1
alwys cls up, qcknd to ld 2 out, 4l up last, styd on strngly
946¹ **Todcrag** ....**T Scott** 2
(fav) ld til hdd & outpcd 2 out, 4l down last, no imp flat
2 ran. 5l. Time 6m 50.00s. SP 7-4.
Mrs F T Walton (Border).

1171 Ladies

994² **STEELE JUSTICE** ....**Miss P Robson** 1
(fav) made all, mostly 2l up frm 16th, kpt on wll flat
994⁴ **Schweppes Tonic** ....**Mrs V Jackson** 2
cls up til went 2nd 16th, not rch wnr flat
733³ **Hooky's Treat 5a** ....**Miss L Bradburne** 3
cls up til mstk 16th, outpcd 3 out
3 ran. 1½l, 25l. Time 6m 57.00s. SP 1-4.
W Manners (Morpeth).

1172 Open Maiden (8yo+)

698 **MIGHTY EXPRESS** ....**A Ogden** 1
cls up, disp 15th til ld aft nxt, qcknd clr 2 out
996² **Fast Fun** ....**R Morgan** 2
(fav) ld til jnd 12th-16th, sn hdd, outpcd frm 2 out
991 **Tolmin (bl)** ....**A Parker** 3
cls 2nd to 11th, disp 12th-14th, 3rd nxt, outpcd 3 out
996 Billy Buoyant *handy in 4th til went 3rd & mstk 3 out, demoted last*........J Walton 4
4 ran. 6l, 2½l, 10l. Time 7m 8.00s. SP 7-1.
Mrs C Park (Braes Of Derwent).

1173 2½m Open Maiden (5-7yo) (12st)

GRAND ENTRY ....**T Barry** 1
ld, svrl mstks, mainly 4l up frm 3 out, hld on gamely flat
997 **The Camair Flyer (Ire)** ....**M Ruddy** 2
(fav) prom, went 2nd 6th, 4l down frm 3 out til rallied flat
1074 **Miss Accounts (Ire) 5a** ....**Miss A Armitage** 3
handy in 4th til no imp final cct, lft poor 3rd 2 out
859² Redwood Boy *alwys rear, styd on to remote 4th 2 out*........D Raw 4
815 K Walk 5a *chsd ldrs, no imp final cct, t.o.*...R Morgan 5
1003⁶ Browlea Lyndene 5a *alwys prom, cls 3rd 6-9th, outpcd 3 out, p.u. nxt*........P Blane pu
997 Little Hawk *disp handy 3rd whn ran out 4th*...T Scott ro
More Rain (Ire) *6th whn p.u. 6th*........P Craggs pu

With Respect *last, clmbd 2nd & p.u.* ....J Walton pu
9 ran. 1l, dist, 20l, 20l. Time 5m 19.00s. SP 12-1.
Mrs Mary A Meek (Dumfriesshire).
P.B.

MEYNELL & SOUTH STAFFS
Sandon
Sunday April 20th
GOOD TO FIRM

1174 Members

726³ **DOMINO NIGHT (IRE)** ....**E Haddock** 1
(fav) cls up, ld 3rd, sn clr, mstks 3 out & nxt, ran on well
726² **Bucks Surprise** ....**D Dickinson** 2
ld to 2nd, sn outpcd, clsd 4 out, not rch wnr
665 **Sandy King (Ire) 14ow** ....**M Collins** 3
rear, disp 3rd/4th, 3rd frm 2 out, no dang
South Valley Jo's 14ow *rear, disp 3rd/4th, no dang* ....P Southwell 4
4 ran. 4l, dist, 3l. Time 6m 43.00s. SP 8-11.
E Haddock (Meynell & South Staffs).

1175 Confined (12st)

1018¹ **MR WILBUR** ....**A Dalton** 1
hld up mid-div, 3rd 5 out, ld 3 out, in cmmnd apr last, comf
938⁷ **No More The Fool** ....**I Brennan** 2
s.s. mid-div 5th, ld 11th-4 out, ran on onepcd
938 **Worleston Farrier 3ex**.................**G Hanmer** 3
ld to 10th, ev ch til outpcd frm 2 out
936³ JJ's Hope *alwys prom, outpcd frm 3 out* ....Miss J Penney 4
848¹ Tara Boy (bl) *mid-div, t.o. 12th, p.u. 4 out* . .R Cambray pu
936² Alicante (bl) *cls up in 3rd whn f 11th* ....C Stockton f
1002² Killatty Player (Ire) 5a *(fav) prom, 2nd whn u.r. 7th* ....A Crow ur
776 Dancing Supreme *rear, t.o. & p.u. 4 out* ......L Brown pu
8 ran. 4l, 5l, 6l. Time 6m 31.00s. SP 5-1.
J D Callow (Albrighton Woodland).

1176 Men's Open

1086⁵ **BACK THE ROAD (IRE)** ....**G Hanmer** 1
(fav) made all, set gd pace, breather 14th, ran on und pres 2out
849 **Injunction (Ire) (bl)** ....**C Stockton** 2
alwys prom, 2nd at 9th, chsd wnr, hrd rdn 2 out, alwys hld
726⁵ **Rinky Dinky Doo** ....**P Morris** 3
cls up to 9th, fdd 14th
940 Trojan Pleasure 5a *chsng grp to 9th, wknd, rear frm 12th* ....C Barlow 4
Glenmere Prince 7ow *rear 2nd, blnd nxt, ref 4th* ....P Ikin ref
5 ran. 4l, dist. Time 6m 35.00s. SP 4-5.
M Mann (Wheatland).

1177 Ladies

721² **VERY DARING** ....**Miss S Sharratt** 1
ld to 6th, 2nd aft, ld & lft clr last
849² **Squirrellsdaughter 5a**...........**Miss S Beddoes** 2
(fav) hld up, ld 7th til hdd & f last, rmntd
670 Foolish Fantasy *cls 3rd at 10th, fdd rpdly 4 out, ref last (twice)*.....................................Mrs M Wall ref
939⁵ Lady Steel (Ire) 5a *cls 2nd whn slppd bnd aft 2nd* ....Miss S Baxter su
4 ran. Dist. Time 6m 54.00s. SP 10-1.
Miss Rosalind Booth (North Staffordshire).

1178 PPORA

940¹ **ROLIER (IRE)** ....**A Dalton** 1
(fav) hld up rear, clsd 3 out, disp nxt, ld last & lft clr
852² **Yukon Gale (Ire)** ....**A Crow** 2
alwys prom, ld 11th til hdd last, no ext
1062 **Penllyne's Pride** ....**T O'Leary** 3
chsd ldr clr of rest to 10th, sn strgglng
999 Hyperbole *ld at strng pace to 10th, wknd rpdly, p.u. 4 out*...M Worthington pu
941¹ Crafty Gunner *mid-div hlfwy, prog to chal 2 out, lkd hld whn f last* ....C Stockton f
940 Solar Castle (Ire) *nvr dang, p.u. 4 out*.....P McAllister pu
6 ran. 15l, dist. Time 6m 28.00s. SP 4-6.
T A B Scott (Albrighton).

1179 Maiden (12st)

854 **ARALIER MAN (IRE)** ....**A Crow** 1
(fav) trckd ldr, chal apr last, lft clr
839 **Sandi Devil** ....**D Dickinson** 2
nvr nr ldrs, kpt on frm 2 out, lft 2nd last
940 **My First Man** ....**M Worthington** 3
alwys 3rd, nvr able to chal
381 Tbilisi *ld, just ld whn f last*................G Hanmer f
Two Gents *rear, last & in tch whn f 3rd* . . .C Stockton f
Tiger Bright *mid-div, t.o. 8th, p.u. 11th* . . . .R Cambray pu
6 ran. Dist, 15l. Time 6m 53.00s. SP Evens.
D Manning (North Shropshire).
V.S.

PEMBROKESHIRE
Lydstep
Sunday April 20th
GOOD TO FIRM

1180 Members (12st)

1005¹ **RADIO DAYS (IRE)** ....**J Jukes** 1
(fav) ld to 10th, sn ld agn, in cmmnd aft, pshd out
963² **Kerstin's Choice 5a**...................**P Sheldrake** 2
jmpd novicey, ld brfly 10th, chsd wnr aft, kpt on wll
2 ran. 1l. Time 6m 51.00s. SP 1-8.
T D Sproat (Pembrokeshire).

1181 Intermediate (12st)

1064 **STERLING BUCK (USA)** ....**Julian Pritchard** 1
ld 5-7th, ld 11th, clr 2 out, easily
1005 **Dick's Cabin** ....**D S Jones** 2
ld to 5th, cls up aft til 3 out, onepcd aft
1008¹ Hollow Sound (Ire) 5a *(fav) ld 8-10th, cls up til aft 3 out, fdd, p.u. nxt, dsmntd*.......................J Jukes pu
3 ran. Dist. Time 6m 8.00s. SP 2-1.
D J Clapham (Cotswold Vale).

1182 Men's Open (12st)

958¹ **LANDSKER MISSILE 5a 7ex** ....**E Williams** 1
(fav) ld 2nd, unchal
1005⁶ **Al Frolic** ....**D S Jones** 2
ld to 2nd, waited bhnd wnr aft, ev ch 15th, alwys hld
958² **No Panic** ....**J Price** 3
popped around in rear
3 ran. 6l, dist. Time 6m 12.00s. SP 1-2.
W J Evans (Pembrokeshire).

1183 Open Maiden (5-7yo) (12st)

881 **A FEW DOLLARS MORE (IRE)** ...**Julian Pritchard** 1
(fav) ld to 6th, ld 12th, clr frm 2 out
1009³ **Cefn Woodsman** ....**D S Jones** 2
cls up, ev ch 4 out, hrd rdn 2 out, no imp
1009² **Redoran 5a** ....**M Lewis** 3
in tch, onepcd frm 4 out
1067 Bessie's Will 5a *rear whn ref 6th* . . . .G Barfoot-Saunt ref
543² Bobbie's Girl (Ire) 5a *trckd ldrs, ld 6-12th, tried to run out & u.r. 14th*..............................Miss J Fowler ur
1010 Lynnes Daniella (Ire) 5a (bl) *nvr nrr than 5th, p.u. 4 out* ....J P Keen pu
841 Eastwood Lad *mid-div, no ch whn p.u. 2 out* . .J Jukes pu
Lizzie Boon 12a *nvr nrr than 7th, p.u. 8th* ....J Price pu
8 ran. 3l, dist. Time 6m 20.00s. SP 6-4.
D G Duggan (Cotswold Vale).

1184 Ladies

905[2] **LUCKY OLE SON 3ex ....Miss P Jones 1**
(fav) dist 2nd til clsd 3 out, ld apr last where left clr
1008[5] **Celtic Bizarre 5a..................Miss B Barton 2**
ld 6th, sn wll clr, hdd apr last, f last, rmntd
Moving Force *ld til s.u. flat apr 6th* ...Miss C Williams su
1135[8] Miss Montgomery (Ire) 5a *s.u. bef 6th in rear* ....Miss F Wilson su
4 ran. Dist. Time 6m 8.00s. SP 4-6.
David Brace (Llangeinor).

1185 Restricted (12st)

1011[1] **PLUCKY PUNTER ....P Williams 1**
(fav) made all, in no dang frm 3 out, easily
538[2] **Hill Fort (Ire) ....E Williams 2**
alwys chsng wnr, hrd rdn 2 out, alwys hld
1006 **Saffron Moss ....Miss F Wilson 3**
alwys 3rd, no imp wnr
845 Euromill Star 5a (bl) *4th whn f 7th*...........J P Keen f
634 Clansies Girl 5a *jmpd novicey, in rear whn p.u. 11th* ....S Lloyd pu
5 ran. 3l, 4l. Time 6m 17.00s. SP Evens.
J R Jones (Vale Of Clettwr).

1186 Open Maiden (8yo+) (12st)

1011[2] **ALFION (IRE) ....D S Jones 1**
(fav) trckd ldrs, ld 11th, ran on frm 2 out, easily
Nadanny (Ire) ....J Jukes 2
sttld mid-div, prog 12th, ev ch 3 out, onepcd aft, fin sore
877 **Nikitasecondchance 5a ....G Barfoot-Saunt 3**
alwys mid-div, ran on aft last to tk 3rd flat
Pridewood Target *sttld rear, prog 12th, nvr nr to chal, lost 3rd flat, dsmntd*...............Julian Pritchard 4
755[3] Sheer Power (Ire) *trckd ldrs to 11th, fdd, fin tired* ....M FitzGerald 5
1011 All The Jolly 5a *rear whn f 12th* ....Miss P Jones f
540 Heather Boy *ld to 10th, wknd rpdly, p.u. 14th* G Lewis pu
7 ran. 8l, 25l, 1l, 3l. Time 6m 20.00s. SP Evens.
D R Thomas (Llangeinor).
P.D.

QUORN
Garthorpe
Sunday April 20th
GOOD TO FIRM

1187 Members (12st)

1077[6] **MR GEE 3ex ....K Needham 1**
in tch, mstk 3rd, prog 11th, went 2nd 3 out,rdn to ld nr fin
770 **Paddy's Pocket ....T Lane 2**
ld, 10l clr 15th, rdn apr last, ct nr fin
887[3] **Rambling Lord (Ire) 7ex ....G Smith 3**
(fav) in tch, chsd ldr 13th-3 out, btn whn blnd nxt
1083[5] Malenski (Ire) *in tch, chsd ldr 12th-nxt, 4th & wkng 15th*....................................P Millington 4
924[3] Joestone *in tch, outpcd 12th, no ch frm 15th* ....Miss E Godfrey 5
Splashman (USA) *last whn ref 1st (twice)* ....B Townsend ref
Highlander (Ire) *sn wll bhnd, t.o. & jmpd slwly 4th, p.u. 13th*......................................G Maloney pu
449 Sea Sky 5a *chsd ldr to 11th, wknd nxt, p.u. 14th* ....S Morris pu
927 Statfold Solva 5a *chsd ldrs til rdn & wknd aft 11th, p.u. nxt*.................................M Hewitt pu
9 ran. 1½l, 10l, 30l, 4l. Time 6m 17.00s. SP 9-1.
M W Conway (Quorn).

1188 Men's Open

799[1] **CARDINAL RICHELIEU ....S Sporborg 1**
(fav) chsd ldr, lft in ld 11th-aft 15th, rdn apr last, ld nr fin
1079 **Coolvawn Lady (Ire) 5a..................S Walker 2**
lft 2nd 11th, ld aft 15th, 4l clr whn blnd last, hdd nr fin
926[6] **Copper Thistle (Ire) ....R Hunnisett 3**
raced wd, chsd ldrs to 6th, poor 4th at 15th, styd on wll
926[5] Old Money *in tch, 4th & blnd 14th, sn lost tch* ....A Pickering 4
Write The Music (bl) *sn bhnd, t.o. 4th, blnd & u.r. 9th* ....R Speck ur
771 Adamare *in tch, chsd ldrs 8th, wknd 14th, 5th & no ch whn f 3 out*...............................R Armson f
836 Whistling Gipsy *ld, sn wll clr, blnd 8th, wkng whn blnd & u.r. 11th*..................................T Lane ur
913[2] Colonel Kenson *chsd ldrs, pshd alng 11th, 6th & no ch whn hmpd & u.r. 3 out*..................M Gingell ur
886 Rustic Craft (Ire) *sn wll bhnd, t.o. 7th, p.u. 15th* ....A Brown pu
9 ran. ½l, 5l, 30l. Time 6m 14.50s. SP 4-6.
Christopher Sporborg (Puckeridge).

1189 Ladies

924 **WISE WIZARD ....Miss K Gilman 1**
chsd ldr 8th, ld 15th, hdd last, rallied to ld nr fin
1077 **San Remo ....Miss S Samworth 2**
prom,went 2nd 3 out,ld last,lkd wnr til hdd flat,rallied fin
925[2] **Man Of Mystery ....Miss F Hatfield 3**
prom, ld 4th-15th, wknd nxt
773[5] Loose Wheels *prom to 3rd, sn bhnd, last & t.o. 8th* ....Miss K Makinson 4
1078[1] Force Eight *(fav) prom, mstk 2nd, 2nd whn f 6th* ....Mrs J Dawson f
1077 Miller's Chap *ld 2nd-4th, 3rd whn f 6th* Miss J Wormall f
6 ran. Nk, 12l, 2 fences. Time 6m 18.00s. SP 3-1.
Mrs F E Gilman (Cottesmore).

1190 Intermediate

927[1] **ANDALUCIAN SUN (IRE) ....G Maloney 1**
w.w. prog 8th, ld aft 15th, clr nxt, rdn & styd on wll flat
909[1] **Stanwick Farlap 5a ....T Marks 2**
ld/disp til ld 12th, hdd apr 3 out, onepcd und pres
910[1] **Horace ....W Wales 3**
chsd ldrs, 3rd & ev ch apr 3 out, onepcd und pres
835[4] Majestic Ride *rear, prog & in tch 11th, 4th & outpcd 15th, kpt on* ....R Armson 4
913[1] Claydons Monty *(fav) cls up, lost plc 12th, rdn 14th, 6th & btn nxt, kpt on*..................S R Andrews 5
779 Scraptastic *in tch, 5th & outpcd apr 3 out, kpt on one-pcd*..N Bell 6
802[3] Smart Pal *bhnd 7th, jmpd slwly 11th, no ch frm 15th* ....K Needham 7
441[4] Salty Snacks (Ire) *ld/disp to 12th, wknd, last frm 15th, p.u. last*....................................M Gingell pu
8 ran. 4l, 1½l, 6l, ½l, 3l, 30l. Time 6m 19.50s. SP 3-1.
A Witcomb (Quorn).

1191 Restricted (12st)

449[6] **REGAL BAY ....W Wales 1**
chsd ldrs 7th, chal 3 out, ld last, hld on gamely flat
770[4] **Dark Rhytham ....R Thornton 2**
(fav) ld, jnd 3 out, sn rdn, hdd last, unable qckn flat
983 **Amadeus (Fr) ....M Gingell 3**
t.d.e. chsd ldr 4th-3 out, mstk 14th, btn apr 2 out
1081 Forward View *rear, prog to mid-div 9th, outpcd 13th, kpt on 3 out* ....C Millington 4
477[7] Midnight Service (Ire) *chsd ldrs to 4th, 4th & outpcd 13th, no ch aft*..........................W Tellwright 5
1000[4] King Keith *mstks, prog & in tch 11th, sn strgglng, no ch frm 15th*..................................S Walker 6
770 Kerry My Home *jmpd lft, alwys rear, rmndrs 12th, sn lost tch, t.o.*.......................................T Marks 7
839 Rapid Regent *prom to 9th, last & wkng 12th, p.u. nxt* ....E Andrewes pu
8 ran. Hd, 8l, 30l, hd, 3l, 10l. Time 6m 23.50s. SP 6-1.
David Wales (West Norfolk).

1192 Open Maiden Div I (12st)

550[3] **GIDGEGANNUP ....M Munrowd 1**

w.w. prog to 2nd 12th, chal 2 out, ran on to ld nr fin
677^{2} **Chester Ben .... S R Andrews** 2
(fav) ld at steady pace, jnd 2 out, hdd & no ext last 100 yrds
772 **Seaton Mill .... M Hewitt** 3
keen hld, in tch, chsd ldr 9-12th, wknd apr 3 out
926 Delvin Spirit (Ire) 5a *cls up to 9th, sn lost tch, t.o.* .... N Kent 4
774^{4} View Point (Ire) *hld up, chsd ldrs 6th, cls 4th whn f 15th* .... M Gingell f
834 Annascanan 12a *cls up til blnd & u.r. 8th* ...... T Lane ur
6 ran. 1l, 30l, dist. Time 6m 37.00s. SP 9-4.
Mrs A Phipps (Ledbury).

1193 Open Maiden Div II (12st)

883 **FULL SONG 5a .... S Morris** 1
chsd ldrs, ld 8-11th, rdn 13th, 4l down whn lft clr 2 out
1082^{2} **Stanwick Buckfast .... T Marks** 2
(fav) w.w. prog 10th, 3rd & rdn 15th, wll btn whn lft 2nd 2 out
347^{5} **Face The Music .... E Andrewes** 3
bhnd, t.o. frm 14th, lft bad 3rd 2 out, ref last, cont
990^{6} Pukka Sahib *keen hld, cls 4th & rdn 13th, wknd, t.o. & p.u. 3 out* .... Miss H Irving pu
915^{3} Regal Shadow *ld to 8th, wknd 10th, t.o. & p.u. 13th* .... W Wales pu
1082 Royal Balinger 5a *chsd ldrs, p.u. 5th, lame* .... T Lane pu
Witch Doctor *raced wd, t.o. 8th, blnd 11th, p.u. nxt* .... Miss S Phizacklea pu
1082 Chapeau Chinois 5a *chsd ldrs to 3rd, last frm 7th, t.o. & p.u. 11th* .... Miss E Godfrey pu
Dual Or Bust (Ire) *in tch, ld 11th, 4l clr & going wll whn u.r. 2 out* .... M Gingell ur
9 ran. 15l, dist. Time 6m 27.00s. SP 4-1.
G Coombe (Quorn).
S.P.

CHEPSTOW
Tuesday April 22nd
GOOD TO FIRM

1194 3m Dunraven Windows South And West Wales Point-to-Point Championship Hunter Chase Class H

716^{1} **FINAL PRIDE 11.10 5a .... Miss P Jones** 1
(fav) j.w, made all, soon clr, easily.
715^{1} **Miss Millbrook 11.12 7a .... Mr E Williams** 2
hdwy 10th, went 2nd and hit 2 out, nvr near wnr.
585^{1} **Busman (Ire) 12.3 7a .... Mr D S Jones** 3
chsd wnr 12th to 2 out, one pace.
905^{1} Wake Up Luv 11.13 7a *alwys prom, one pace from 4 out* .... Miss P Cooper 4
1005^{3} The Last Mistress 11.5 7a *nvr better than middle division.* .... Mr S Shinton 5
904^{1} Beinn Mohr 11.8 7a *hit 2nd, soon bhnd, t.o..* .... Mr N R Mitchell 6
1007^{1} Kingfisher Bay 12.1 7a *alwys bhnd, t.o. from 11th.* .... Mr J J Price 7
717^{1} Plas-Hendy 11.10 7a *chsd wnr till wknd 12th.* .... Mr G Lewis 8
840^{1} Royal Oats 11.9 3a *f 6th.* .... Mr M Rimell f
636^{1} Doubting Donna 11.7 5a *nvr near ldrs, 6th and no ch when p.u. before last.* .... Mr J Jukes pu
963^{1} Culpeppers Dish 11.5 7a *prom to 6th, bhnd when tried to refuse 9th, p.u. before next.* .... Mr A Price pu
11 ran. 15l, 6l, 1l, ¾l, dist, dist. Time 5m 56.70s. SP 2-1.
Grahame Barrett

COTSWOLD
Andoversford
Wednesday April 23rd
FIRM

1195 Members

1063 **BUMPTIOUS BOY .... S Hanks** 1
(fav) jmpd lft, made all, drew clr frm 3 out, easily
1019 **Well Bank .... E Walker** 2
keen hld, chsd wnr, mstk 14th, rdn & btn apr 2 out
706 **Lough Morne .... Miss A Lock** 3
jmpd lft, lost tch 4th, t.o. 8th
Student Benefit *in tch whn nrly ref 3rd, jmpd slwly nxt, last whn ref 5th* .... David Dennis ref
4 ran. 15l, 2 fences. Time 6m 26.00s. SP 1-3.
R F Hanks (Cotswold).

1196 Confined (12st)

962 **HOW FRIENDLY .... Julian Pritchard** 1
prom, ld 3-8th, chsd ldr 13th, styd on gamely to ld flat
650^{1} **Danbury Lad (Ire) 6ex .... Miss A Dare** 2
(fav) chsd ldrs, ld 8th, rdn last, no ext & hdd nr fin
1160^{2} **July Schoon .... T Underwood** 3
w.w. prog 11th, hit 16th, 3rd & rdn 2 out, kpt on
1055^{2} January Don (bl) *ld, rmndrs 1st, hdd 3rd, rdn 10th, wknd 3 out* .... G Barfoot-Saunt 4
974^{1} The Country Trader 14ex *in tch to 12th, sn strgglng, no ch frm 14th* .... J Borradaile 5
1062^{5} Kings Rank (bl) *rear & jmpd slwly 4th, last whn ref nxt* .... H Wheeler ref
6 ran. Nk, ¾l, 30l, 5l. Time 6m 14.00s. SP 8-1.
D J Clapham (Cotswold Vale).

1197 Ladies

703^{1} **RIP VAN WINKLE .... Miss A Dare** 1
(fav) alwys going wll, ld 13th, drew clr frm 3 out, v easily
296^{6} **Rip The Calico (Ire) 5a .... Miss S Duckett** 2
w.w. prog to 2nd at 16th, sn outpcd, dsmntd aft fin
1062 **Madraj (Ire) (bl) .... Miss H Irving** 3
in tch, ld 12th-13th, 3rd & wkng apr 2 out, fin tired
482^{2} Phelioff *chsd ldr, ld 5th-12th, sn lost plc, t.o. 16th* .... Miss S Dawson 4
638 Coombesbury Lane 5a *ld til jmpd slwly & hdd 5th, 4th whn hit 15th, p.u. aft nxt* .... Miss C Spearing pu
5 ran. 25l, 15l, 30l. Time 6m 10.00s. SP 1-6.
Dr P P Brown & Mrs S Birks (Berkeley).

1198 Land Rover Open (12st)

976^{2} **GRANVILLE GRILL 7ex .... J Deutsch** 1
t.d.e. jmpd lft, ld 3rd, made rest, clr 2 out, styd on wll
819^{1} **Nether Gobions 7ex .... Julian Pritchard** 2
ld & hit 2nd, hdd nxt, prssd wnr, blnd 12th,rdn & btn 2 out
1023^{1} **Spitfire Jubilee 7ex .... R Nuttall** 3
chsd ldng pair, rdn 13th, nvr able to chal
986^{4} Grand Value *ld 1st, sn hdd, 4th & outpcd aft, kpt on frm 2 out.* .... C Wadland 4
388^{1} Brackenfield 8ex (bl) *(fav) not fluent, sn bhnd, t.o. 8th, some prog whn p.u. 13th, lame* .... T Mitchell pu
5 ran. 8l, 15l, 5l. Time 6m 1.00s. SP 8-1.
E W Smith (Beaufort).

1199 Intermediate (12st)

1127^{2} **BAWNEROSH .... T Underwood** 1
(fav) w.w. going wll, went 2nd 11th, hit nxt, ld apr last, styd on
1025^{2} **Roaming Shadow .... J Hankinson** 2
w.w. in tch, prog 3 out, went 2nd last, no imp flat
718 **Tudor Oaks 5a .... Julian Pritchard** 3
ld, sn clr, jmpd slwly 5th, mstk 15th, hdd apr last, no ext
824 Le Jacobin *chsd ldr 3-11th, 4th & wkng apr 2 out* .... C Lambert 4
989^{6} Horcum *chsd ldrs 5th-8th, last frm 10th, no ch 15th* .... M Frith 5
5 ran. 2½l, ¾l, 15l, 15l. Time 6m 15.00s. SP 5-4.
T D B Underwood (Garth & South Berks).

1200 Open Maiden (12st)

BOYS ROCKS .... Julian Pritchard 1

(fav) ld,slw jmps 4 & 5th,hdd 9th,ld apr last,hng lft,all out,lame

1083 **Old Father Time ....L Lay** 2
prom, ld 9th, hdd apr last, onepcd und pres

654 **Tu Piece ....P Howse** 3
in tch, rmndr 12th, outpcd 16th, rallied 2 out, no imp last

571 Calder's Grove *prom, chsd ldr 11th-3 out, onepcd aft* ....Miss T McCurrick 4

907^{2} Flowerhill *prom, ev ch 3 out, sn rdn, btn nxt, dsmntd aft fin*..............................G Barfoot-Saunt 5

917^{2} Scarra Darragh (Ire) 5a *keen hld, chsd ldrs, blnd 6th, wknd apr 2 out* ....A Charles-Jones 6

1059 The Blind Judge 2ow *alwys bhnd, jmpd slwly 4th, p.u. 12th*..................................T Lacey pu

1136 Wissywis (Ire) 12a *alwys last, t.o. 7th, u.r. 13th* ....C Yates ur

8 ran. 2l, 3l, nk, ½l, 10l. Time 6m 30.00s. SP 9-4.
D J Clapham (Cotswold Vale).
S.P.

PERTH
Thursday April 24th
GOOD

1201 3m Perth Hunt Balnakeilly Challenge Cup Hunters' Chase Class H

972^{2} **ENSIGN EWART (IRE) 11.9 5a ....Mr C Storey** 1
towards rear, steady hdwy from 12th, styd on well to ld final 100 yards, all out.

888^{2} **Howayman 11.12 7a.....................Mr A Parker** 2
(fav) prom, ld 13th till hdd final 100 yards, kept on.

1068^{1} **Admission (Ire) 11.7 7a ....Miss L Horner** 3
prom, ev ch 3 out, wknd before last.

890^{8} Fordstown (Ire) 11.8 7a 1ow *ld till hdd 6th, chsd ldrs after, one paced from 15th.* ....Mr Jamie Alexander 4

973^{4} Dark Dawn 11.12 7a *nvr on terms.* ....Miss Lorna Foxton 5

731^{4} Bow Handy Man 11.7 7a *n.d.*.........Miss S Laidlaw 6

731^{1} Across The Card 11.12 7a *soon bhnd.* ....Mr M Bradburne 7

226 Master Kit (Ire) 11.12 7a *held up early, gd hdwy to ld 6th, mstk 11th (water), hdd 13th, wknd quickly, t.o., virtually p.u. run-in.*.......................Mr J Billinge 8

384^{4} Direct 11.12 7a *soon bhnd, t.o. when p.u. before 15th.* ....Mr T Edwards pu

489 Fifth Amendment 11.7 7a (bl) *hmpd 1st, mstk 5th, lost tch and p.u. before 13th.*.................Mr A Hales pu

875^{1} Denim Blue 12.3 5a *f 2nd.*............Miss P Robson f

1072^{5} Thank U Jim 11.7 7a *blnd and u.r. 1st.* ....Miss T Jackson ur

Rusty Blade 11.9 5a *soon bhnd, t.o. when p.u. before 3 out.*..................................Mr R Hale pu

340^{3} Border Glory 11.7 7a *chsd ldrs to hfwy, weakening when blnd and u.r. 15th.*...............Mr M J Ruddy ur

14 ran. Nk, 18l, 3l, 2½l, 12l, 25l, dist. Time 6m 21.50s. SP 11-2.
Major M W Sample

LUDLOW
Friday April 25th
GOOD TO FIRM

1202 2½m Lane Fox And Balfour & Cooke Hunters' Chase Class H for Ludlow Gold Cup

950^{1} **GREAT GUSTO 12.0 7a.........Miss L Blackford** 1
(fav) chsd ldrs, ld apr 10th, clr 5 out, styd on well.

982^{2} **Cape Cottage 12.0 7a..............Mr A Phillips** 2
held up, hdwy 10th, left 2nd 5 out, effort 2 out, no ext run-in.

1146 **Stylish Gent 11.7 7a ....Mr A Dalton** 3
held up, raced keenly, outpcd 10th, soon well bhnd.

878 Ballad Song 11.7 7a *ld to apr 10th, 2nd when blnd badly 5 out, weakening when hit next, mstk 3 out, soon p.u.*..............................Mr M Munrowd pu

1019^{1} Emerald Charm (Ire) 11.6 3a *chsd ldrs till wknd 10th, t.o. when p.u. before 4 out*...............Mr M Rimell pu

5 ran. 3l, dist. Time 5m 15.00s. SP 4-6.
Eddie Rice

WORCESTER
Saturday April 26th
SOFT

1203 2m 7f 110yds Upton Upon Severn Novices' Hunters' Chase Class H

1 **PHAR TOO TOUCHY 11.2 7a.........Mr N Harris** 1
(fav) chsd ldr, ld 6th, made rest, clr from 10th, hit 12th and 2 out, unchal.

1080^{1} **Tea Cee Kay 11.7 7a........Mr Rupert Sweeting** 2
ld to 6th, chsd wnr after till outpcd 8th, went poor 2nd 3 out, t.o..

1157^{1} **Ann's Ambition 11.7 7a...............Mr M Frith** 3
in tch, chsd wnr from 8th, blnd and lost touch 10th, wknd 3 out, left poor 3rd last, t.o..

484^{2} Pete's Sake 11.9 5a *hit 6th, alwys bhnd, t.o. when p.u. before 13th.*.........................Mr C Vigors pu

1062^{1} Sultan's Son 11.7 7a *held up, lost tch from 8th, went poor 3rd 3 out, blnd and u.r. last.*..........Mr G Lewis ur

750^{2} Call-Me-Dinky 11.2 7a *bhnd till p.u. lame and dismntd before 4th.*....................Miss C Thomas pu

888 Johnny The Fox (Ire) 11.7 7a *mstk 1st, bhnd from 6th, t.o. when p.u. before 10th.* ....Mr R Lawther pu

388^{5} No Joker (Ire) 11.7 7a *trckd ldrs, hit 10th, soon bhnd, t.o. when p.u. before 3 out.*...............Mr P Scott pu

1018 Ballyhamage (Ire) 11.7 7a *f 1st.*.......Mr M Munrowd f

1008^{3} Who's Your Man (Ire) 11.7 7a *bhnd when blnd 7th, t.o. when p.u. before 9th.*.......................Mr R Burton pu

10 ran. Dist, dist. Time 6m 27.10s. SP 5-4.
Miss R A Francis

ATHERSTONE
Clifton On Dunsmore
Saturday April 26th
GOOD TO SOFT

1204 Members

1081 **CATCHPHRASE ....K Needham** 1
w.w. chsd ldr frm 11th, ld aft 2 out, clrvly

771^{2} **Raise An Argument 7ex...............N Docker** 2
(fav) j.w. tried to make all, hdd aft 2 out, onepcd

548^{6} **Needwood Neptune ....P Bennett** 3
last pair for 2m,chsd ldng pair frm 11th, unable to cls

773 Smart Rhythm 5a *prom, 2nd 1st m, fdd, last frm 9th, t.o. 11th* ....Miss C Arthers 4

1193 Witch Doctor *cls up 2nd, rdn & wknd 9th, t.o. 12th* ....Miss S Phizacklea 5

1080 Dilly's Last 5a *last, rmndrs 5th, p.u. nxt* ....R Armson pu

6 ran. 4l, 2l, 1 fence, 20l. Time 6m 20.00s. SP 5-2.
A A Day (Atherstone).
One fence omitted all races, 17 jumps.

1205 Confined (12st)

1083^{6} **STAR TRAVELLER ....M Skinner** 1
w.w. 8th at 9th, ran on 6 out, 5th 3 out, ld last, hld on

985^{1} **Cawkwell Dean 3ex ....R Sweeting** 2
(fav) alwys prom, ld 5 out, 10l clr nxt, no ext whn hdd apr last

1162^{5} **Bervie House (Ire) 3ex ....R Barrett** 3
alwys prom, mostly 4th, ran on frm 4 out, not rch 1st pair

1077 Local Race (Ire) *disp/ld to 6 out, onepcd frm 4 out* ....J Brook 4

1063^{4} Kemys Commander *prom, 2nd/disp til 3rd frm 9th, 2nd agn 4 out, wknd nxt*........................G Smith 5

1187^{5} Joestone *alwys 6th/7th, outpcd 5 out*..Miss E Godfrey 6

1063^{5} Prince's Court *alwys rear, t.o. frm 9th*..Mrs J Kimber 7

1076^{6} Hostetler *alwys abt 8th, rdn frm 9th, outpcd 5 out* ....J Stephenson 8

1063 Proplus *rear div frm 4th, t.o. frm 9th*.......Mrs A Lee 9

1188 Rustic Craft (Ire) *alwys last, t.o. frm 7th*......A Brown 10
Autonomous *cls up in 3rd/4th for 2m, fdd, p.u. 4 out*
....A Charles-Jones pu
137 Unassuming *last til p.u. 4th, lame*............D Ingle pu
1189 Miller's Chap *abt 6th whn f 5th*..............M Hewitt f
13 ran. 1½l, 5l, 5l, 8l, ½l, 6l, 6l, 1 fence, 20l. Time 6m 17.00s. SP 14-1.
Miss E Powell (Fernie).

1206 Men's Open

1079² **HILL ISLAND ....R Sweeting** 1
(fav) cls 2nd, jmpd rght, ld 2 out, drew clr
1077¹ **Run For Free ....A Hill** 2
slght ld on innr hanging lft, hdd & outpcd frm 2 out
1190⁴ **Majestic Ride ....R Armson** 3
outpcd frm 4th
3 ran. 10l, 20l. Time 6m 17.00s. SP 4-6.
Colin Gee (Heythrop).

1207 Ladies

1189 **FORCE EIGHT ....Mrs J Dawson** 1
(fav) made most, drew clr frm 2 out, easily
1076¹ **Supreme Dream (Ire) 5a ....Mrs P Adams** 2
cls up,ld brfly 7-8th, outpcd 5 out, ran on 3 out,nt rch wnr
137³ **Ridwan ....Miss S Bonser** 3
mid-div, disp 2nd 4 out, outpcd 2 out
989⁷ Linlake Lightning 5a *mostly 3rd, disp 2nd 4 out, outpcd nxt*..............................Miss H Irving 4
986² Kites Hardwicke *alwys last pair, outpcd 4 out*
....Mrs C Behrens 5
1161 Fenton Bridge *cls 2nd to 8th, wknd rpdly, t.o. last whn p.u. 5 out*............................Miss R Tutton pu
6 ran. 6l, 2l, 7l, 10l. Time 6m 14.00s. SP 1-2.
Mrs E W Wilson (Brocklesby).

1208 Restricted (12st)

1187¹ **MR GEE ....K Needham** 1
cls up til disp 7 out, ld 4 out, ran on gamely
990¹ **Upton Lass (Ire) 5a ....L Lay** 2
cls up 2nd to 9th, chsd wnr frm 4 out, alwys hld
1081⁶ **Weston Moon (Ire) 5a ....J Docker** 3
ld for 2m, hdd & wknd rpdly frm 4 out
727 First Command (NZ) *(fav) alwys last, rmndrs 9th-10th, t.o. 6 out*...............................Mrs C Ford 4
4 ran. 5l, 30l, 2l. Time 6m 22.00s. SP 11-4.
Mrs M W Conway (Quorn).

1209 Open Maiden (12st)

839² **MALTBY SON 7a ....T Lane** 1
(fav) 3rd frm 6th, mstk 4 out, ran on to chal 2 out, all out
1084³ **Strong Account (Ire) ....A Tutton** 2
made most, jnd 2 out, just outpcd flat
1175 **Dancing Supreme ....L Brown** 3
mid-div, prog 10th, 2nd 5 out, just outpcd frm 2 out
1083⁷ Daring Daisy 5a *rear hlf to 10th, ran on past btn hrss last m*..............................Mrs C McCarthy 4
1018³ Crestwood Lad (USA) *disp to 10th, not qckn, 4th & outpcd 5 out*..............................M Yardley 5
723² Musical Mail *prom in abt 4th til no ext frm 10th, outpcd 6 out*..............................Mrs C Ford 6
Dilkush *lost plc 5th, outpcd frm 6 out*........M Wells 7
1084 Half Sharp 5a *prom to 10th, fdd, outpcd 6 out*...L Lay 8
941 Erik The Viking *alwys last trio, outpcd 6 out* R Armson 9
1082 Krisan 5a *prom to 10th, fdd, outpcd 6 out* Miss L Allan 10
1082 Lizapet (Ire) 12a *last frm 10th, p.u. 5 out*
....Miss S Duckett pu
Killiney's Image (Ire) *abt 9th til f 6th*..........R Barrett f
Marmalade *alwys last trio, p.u. 5 out*.........T Illsley pu
374 Kickles Lass 5a *rear hlf whn f 6th*.....John Pritchard f
1150 Ullington Lord *mid-div, 7th at 10th, fdd, p.u. 5 out*
....S Joynes pu
Highfurlong (Ire) *mid-div, 9th at 10th, wknd & p.u. 5 out*..............................Miss H Irving pu
16 ran. ½l, 4l, 3l, 2l, 30l, sht-hd, 6l, hd, 20l. Time 6m 27.00s. SP 6-4.
Mrs R Smith (Bicester With Whaddon Chase).
K.B.

BERKELEY
Woodford
Saturday April 26th
GOOD

1210 Restricted (12st)

299¹ **THE COCKERTOO ....T Mitchell** 1
keen hld, made most frm 4th, drew clr 3 out, not extndd
1080² **Nobbutjust (Ire) 5a...................A Beedles** 2
mid-div, 7th hlfwy, styd on frm 4 out, not trbl wnr
1061 **Generator Boy ....J Baimbridge** 3
bhnd, 10th hlfwy, kpt on frm 4 out, nvr nrr
1135 Everso Irish *prom, blnd 5th, wth wnr 4 out, sn rdn, wknd 2 out*.........................Julian Pritchard 4
871 Springvilla (Ire) *hld up, last hlfwy, prog 15th, kpt on, nvr nrr*...............................C Vigors 5
1061 Your Opinion *prom, 3rd & rdn apr 3 out, wknd*
....M Keen 6
979¹ Salmon Poutcher 5a *ld to 1st, prom, chsd ldr 14th-apr 4 out, grad wknd*.......................J Trice-Rolph 7
877 Sit Tight *prom til wknd apr 4 out*........M Portman 8
1058² Game Fair *chsd ldrs to 7th, last frm 12th, t.o.* W Cook 9
433⁵ The Hon Company *chsd ldrs, wknd 15th, t.o. & p.u. 3 out*...............................E Walker pu
1135² Dragons Lady 5a *ld 2nd-4th, ld 11th-13th, wknd 15th, p.u. 3 out*.........................G Barfoot-Saunt pu
571¹ Samule *u.r. 3rd*......................Miss P Gundry ur
990 Bit Of A Do *f 3rd*.............................R Cope f
527¹ Major Sharpe (Ire) 7a *(fav) hld up rear, in tch whn f 8th*...............................J Tizzard f
14 ran. 4l, 2l, 2l, 5l, 4l, 1l, 20l, 12l. Time 6m 50.00s. SP 5-1.
Mrs J M Bailey (Blackmore & Sparkford Vale).

1211 Members

1064² **LANDSKER ALFRED ....Miss A Dare** 1
(fav) chsd ldrs, ld 11th, made rest, drew clr frm 3 out, easily
524 **Bewdley Boy ....Miss P Gundry** 2
hld up, prog 10th, wth wnr 4 out, wknd apr 2 out
889³ **J B Lad ....J Tuck** 3
raced wd, ld 9th, wide & hdd 11th, outpcd frm 15th
Airborne Taipan *sn wll bhnd, t.o. frm 7th*
....Miss A Clifford 4
1134⁴ Prince Nepal *ld to 3rd, lft in ld 5th-9th, sn wknd, t.o. & p.u. 3 out*...............................T Hopkins pu
Euro Forum 7a *mid-div, prog to 3rd at 10th, blnd 12th, wknd 15th, p.u.2out*...............G Barfoot-Saunt pu
1150 Royal Sweep *raced freely, ld & blnd 3rd, ran out & u.r. 5th*...............................C Dorrington ro
1061³ Rosevalley (Ire) *w.w. in tch whn blnd 10th, 5th & wkng 13th, p.u. 15th*...........................K Whiting pu
8 ran. 12l, 12l, 2 fences. Time 6m 43.00s. SP 4-7.
Dr P P Brown & Mrs S Birks (Berkeley).

1212 Intermediate (12st)

935¹ **NEARLY AN EYE ....T Mitchell** 1
(fav) w.w. went 2nd 12th, rdn to ld & jmpd lft last, styd on
1060³ **Lets Twist Again (Ire) 5ex ....Julian Pritchard** 2
hld up, prog 10th, ld apr 4 out-last, no ext
1064³ **Frozen Pipe 5a 5ex....................M Harris** 3
in tch, blnd 12th, ev ch 2 out, unable qckn und pres
395³ Bear's Flight 5ex *chsd ldrs til 5th & outpcd 14th, no ch frm 4 out*.........................J Hadden Wight 4
Perseverance *chsd ldr 4th, ld apr 7th-apr 4 out, sn wknd*...............................Miss P Gundry 5
1064 Just Ralph *ld til apr 7th, wkng & rdn 10th, t.o. 12th, p.u. 3 out*.........................G Barfoot-Saunt pu
1133⁶ Scriven Boy *chsd ldrs to 11th, 6th & wkng 14th, t.o. & p.u. last*...............................A Beedles pu
224 Sharp Alice 5a *sn bhnd, t.o. & p.u. 12th*.....J Tizzard pu
8 ran. 1½l, 1½l, 30l, 12l. Time 6m 46.00s. SP 4-5.
Paul K Barber (Blackmore & Sparkford Vale).

1213 G Middleton Ladies

1090[1] **EARTHMOVER (IRE) ....Miss P Gundry** 1
(fav) chsd ldr, disp 13th, rdn 3 out, sn ld, styd on strngly
879[1] **Sams Heritage ....Miss A Dare** 2
trckd ldrs,disp 14th-3 out,blnd nxt,tired whn jmpd lft last
496[4] **Gay Ruffian ....Miss C Dyson** 3
in tch to 14th, sn strggling, lft poor 3rd 4 out
759[1] Mr Woodcock *ld to 13th, sn wknd, disp poor 3rd whn u.r. 4 out*..........................Miss A Plunkett ur
280[1] Tudor Henry *w.w. in tch whn u.r. 9th*...Mrs C Mitchell ur
Loch Garanne 5a *s.v.s. trotted to 1st, 2f bhnd whn ref 2nd*...............................Miss P Cooper ref
6 ran. 15l, 20l. Time 6m 42.00s. SP 1-2.
R M Penny (Cattistock).

1214 Men's Open (12st)

931[1] **STRONG CHAIRMAN (IRE) 4ex ....T Mitchell** 1
(fav) alwys going wll, ld 4 out, rdn clr 2 out, easily
1054[1] **Espy 7ex..............................E James** 2
cls up, ld aft 15th, hdd nxt, outpcd 2 out
879[2] **Mitchells Best ....Julian Pritchard** 3
ld to 12th, last & rdn apr 4 out, kpt on onepcd
758 Welsh Singer 4ex *keen hld, chsd ldrs, ld 12th-15th, cls 3rd & blnd nxt, wknd*...............R Lawther 4
1142[1] Indian Knight *rear, in tch to 15th, no dang aft* ....C Vigors 5
5 ran. 8l, 4l, 6l, 15l. Time 6m 50.00s. SP 1-3.
J A Keighley (Blackmore & Sparkford Vale).

1215 Confined (12st)

689[1] **DESERT WALTZ (IRE) 5ex ....T Mitchell** 1
(fav) made all, drew wll clr apr 4 out, heavily eased flat
1093[7] **My Wee Man (Ire) ....G Barfoot-Saunt** 2
jmpd rght, w.w. went 2nd 14th, sn outpcd by wnr
1063[3] Altnabrocky 5ow *chsd ldr to 14th, 3rd & no ch wth wnr whn blnd & u.r. 2 out*...................T Gretton ur
3 ran. 8l. Time 6m 58.00s. SP 1-7.
H B Geddes (Beaufort).

1216 Maiden (12st)

1138 **MOORLOUGH BAY (IRE) ....T Mitchell** 1
bhnd, poor 7th hlfwy, grad clsd, ld 2 out, sn clr
908[2] **Miss Dior 5a ....Miss P Gundry** 2
chsd ldr 9th, ld 13th, wll clr apr 4 out, hdd 2 out,fin tird
1065[2] **Sylvan Sirocco ....M Harris** 3
(fav) ld to 1st, chsd ldr 14th-3 out, no imp aft
988[4] Country Lord *n.j.w. sn wll bhnd, t.o. 7th* Mrs S Walwin 4
1138[4] Le Vienna (Ire) *alwys bhnd, 8th & no ch hlfwy, t.o.* ....S Currey 5
1045 Dula Model 5a *ld 3rd, clr nxt, hdd 13th, wknd, t.o.* ....J Boscherini 6
296 Royal Swinger 5a *u.r. 2nd*..........Miss S Trotman ur
1138[2] Malthouse Lad *chsd ldrs, wknd 15th, t.o. & p.u. 3 out* ....Julian Pritchard pu
1065 Naburn Loch 5a *ld 2nd-3rd, chsd ldr to 9th, sn wknd, t.o. & p.u. 3 out*..........................J Barnes pu
The Coventry Flyer 5a *jmpd bdly, t.o. last whn ref & u.r. 5th*....................................G Field ref
1211 Royal Sweep *2nd outing, chsd ldrs til u.r. 6th* ....C Dorrington ur
1065 Donald Hawkins 7a *mstks, hmpd 2nd, chsd ldrs, lost tch 15th, p.u. 3 out*........................P Howse pu
1067 Permit 5a *prom to 3rd, sn lost plc, t.o. last at 11th, p.u. nxt*..........................G Barfoot-Saunt pu
13 ran. 20l, 10l, 1 fence, 2l, 15l. Time 7m 6.00s. SP 4-1.
A Leigh (Llangibby).
S.P.

FIFE
Balcormo Mains
Saturday April 26th
FIRM

1217 Members

731[5] **BRUCE'S CASTLE ....Miss K Durie** 1
ld brfly apr 9th, trckd ldr til ld agn apr last
Absailor ....Mrs C Lattilla-Campbell 2
made most til hdd apr last, no ext flat
159[2] **King Spring ....P Black** 3
(fav) jmp slwly, wll bhnd thruout
1051[5] Turn Of Foot (Ire) *f 2nd*...............M Bradburne f
4 ran. 2l, dist. Time 7m 17.00s. SP 10-1.
M Walsh (Fife).

1218 Restricted (12st)

995[3] **THE CAFFLER (IRE) ....C Storey** 1
cls 2nd frm 11th, ld apr 2 out, comf
995[2] **Sumpt'n Smart ....R Morgan** 2
ld frm 2nd til apr 2 out, no ext
811[2] **Funny Feelings ....Miss J Laidlaw** 3
(fav) in tch in 3rd plc til wknd qckly apr 2 out
949 Fortinas Flyer 5a *ld to 2nd, lost tch by 10th, p.u. aft 11th*.......................................D McLeod pu
945 Royal Fife 5a *in tch til 13th, strggling whn p.u. apr 15th*...A Parker pu
5 ran. 6l, 25l. Time 6m 57.00s. SP 5-2.
Major General C A Ramsay (Berwickshire).

1219 G Middleton Ladies

1048[1] **ROLY PRIOR ....Mrs V Jackson** 1
(fav) 10l 2nd whn lft in ld 9th, made rest, pshd out flat
609[4] **Minibrig 5a.....................Miss S Forster** 2
trckd wnnr frm 9th, chal 2 out, no ext flat
560 Tony's Feelings *sn clr, 10l ahd whn ran out 9th* ....Miss L Bradburne ro
3 ran. 1½l. Time 7m 2.00s. SP 2-5.
Ian Hamilton (Tynedale).

1220 Land Rover Mens Open (12st)

994[3] **EMU PARK ....J Thompson** 1
trckd ldr til ld 2 out, held on wll
993[1] **Tartan Tornado 7ex.................P Johnson** 2
(fav) set mod pce, hdd 2 out, kpt on onepce
2 ran. ½l. Time 8m 7.00s. SP 7-4.
J D Thompson (Border).

1221 Intermediate

1169[1] **JOLLY FELLOW ....Miss S Ward** 1
walked over
Miss S M Ward (South Durham).

1222 Open Maiden

1051[3] **FLOWER OF DUNBLANE 5a ....A Parker** 1
(fav) ld frm 11th, made rest comf
1052 **Bow Tie ....J Ewart** 2
made most to 11th, 2nd mstly aft, no ext flat
Rallying Cry (Ire) (bl) ....D McLeod 3
held up, wnt 2nd brfly 3 out, wknd apr nxt
996[3] Connor The Second 5ow *last & strggling whn p.u. aft 11th*..P Black pu
949 Singing Profit 12a *in tch til 4 out, bhnd whn p.u. bfr 2 out*.................................Mrs V Jackson pu
1052 Tantalum 5a *disp ld frm 6-9th, cls 2nd whn f nxt* ....W Spence f
6 ran. 4l, 6l. Time 7m 18.00s. SP 7-4.
Mrs Jean McGregor (Fife).
R.J.

LLANGEINOR
Pyle
Saturday April 26th
GOOD TO SOFT

1223 Members

1134[1] **CARRICK LANES 5ex ....Miss P Jones** 1
(fav) ld 5-9th,lost plc & bhnd 13th,rpd prog 2 out,drvn to ld flat
1194[6] **Beinn Mohr 5a 5ex ....E Williams** 2
ld to 5th,ld 9-12th & 14th,clr 3 out,rdn nxt,hdd flat
1007 **Hugli ....Miss S Major** 3
in tch,slw jmp 8th,outpcd 13th,ran on agn 2 out,one-pcd
1007[6] Cornish Cossack (NZ) *in tch to 13th, sn wknd, t.o.* ....W Pugh 4
535 Billy-Gwyn *cls up, ld 12th-14th, rdn & btn 3 out, wknd & p.u. last* ....J Tudor pu
962[2] Top Tor 5a *blnd 1st, nvr going aft, bhnd frm 5th, p.u. 11th* ....T Vaughan pu
6 ran. 4l, 6l, 30l. Time 6m 37.00s. SP 4-7.
David Brace (Llangeinor).

1224 Confined (12st)

1133[2] **BIT OF A CITIZEN (IRE) ....E Williams** 1
w.w. prog 7th, ld 14th, drvn out frm 2 out
1133[3] **Polly Pringle 5a 3ex ....A Price** 2
7s-4s, mstks, ld to 4th, chsd wnr 14th,hrd rdn & no imp last
1007[3] **Sun Of Chance ....P Williams** 3
mstk 6th, ld 5th-14th, 3rd & btn aft, wknd
1182[3] No Panic *prom, mstk 5th, chsd ldr 9-12th, sn wknd, t.o.* ....J Price 4
1132[5] Scared Stiff 5a *rear, mstk 7th, t.o. & p.u. 13th* ....J P Keen pu
1132[1] Conna Moss (Ire) 6ex *(fav) rmndr 3rd, nvr going wll, lost tch 13th, p.u. nxt* ....Miss P Jones pu
1135[4] Rosieplant 5a *w.w. prog to jn ldrs 13th, wknd rpdly nxt, p.u. 3 out* ....J Jukes pu
7 ran. 6l, 25l, 1 fence. Time 6m 32.00s. SP 5-1.
R Mason (Glamorgan).

1225 Ladies

1006[1] **TOUCH 'N' PASS 7ex ....Miss P Jones** 1
(fav) hld up, prog 14th, ld 2 out, jmpd lft last, pshd out
1184 **Miss Montgomery (Ire) 5a ....Miss F Wilson** 2
prssd ldr,ld apr 3 out-2 out,rdn whn hmpd last,no ext flat
638[5] **Bartondale 5a ....Miss B Williams** 3
chsd ldng pair, not qckn 3 out, kpt on agn frm last
1133[5] Mo's Chorister *mstk 7th, sn last, no ch frm 14th* ....Miss A Meakins 4
1006 Afaristoun (Fr) *jmpd slwly 5th, ld to apr 3 out, wknd rpdly* ....Miss J Morse 5
536[3] Local Customer *hld up, outpcd apr 14th, mstk 15th, t.o. & p.u. 2 out* ....Miss G Gibson pu
6 ran. 6l, 4l, 25l, 15l. Time 6m 37.00s. SP 2-5.
R H P Williams (Llangeinor).
After stewards' inquiry, placings unaltered.

1226 Men's Open (12st)

1194 **DOUBTING DONNA 5a ....J Jukes** 1
ld 6-7th, prssd ldr, ld 14th, rdn clr frm nxt, ran on wll
1182[1] **Landsker Missile 5a 7ex..............E Williams** 2
(fav) ld 7-14th, sn btn, mstk 3 out, wknd & eased
1007[4] **Astounded ....J Tudor** 3
cls up til wknd frm 11th, t.o.
1057[1] Blackwater Lady (Ire) 5a 7ex *last whn mstks 2nd & 3rd, sn t.o.* ....P Scouller 4
1132[3] Gold Diver *ld to 6th, rdn & wknd nxt, p.u. 11th* ....P Williams pu
1007[5] Olde Crescent *bhnd frm 7th, t.o. 12th, p.u. 3 out* ....J Comins pu
6 ran. Dist, dist, 20l. Time 6m 30.00s. SP 2-1.
Mrs D Hughes (Llangeinor).

1227 Restricted (12st)

1135 **KEEP FLOWING (IRE) ....Miss P Jones** 1
(fav) mstk 9th,ld nxt-12th,mstk 15th,ran on to ld apr last,all out
842[1] **Preseli View 5a.........................M Lewis** 2
mid-div,prog 13th,rdn 3 out,drvn to chal & mstk last,no ext
1184[2] **Celtic Bizarre 5a..................Miss B Barton** 3
mostly last trio til ran on frm 13th, nvr nrr
1135[3] Black Ermine (Ire) *cls up,rmndr 9th,chsd ldr 14th,ld 2 out-apr last,wknd* ....J Jukes 4
1185[2] Hill Fort (Ire) *chsd ldrs, no prog frm 14th, sn btn* ....J P Keen 5
1010[1] Takahashi (Ire) *prom, ld 12th-2 out, wknd rpdly, walked in* ....E Williams 6
1135 Flaxridge *pllng, made most 2nd-10th, wknd rpdly 12th, p.u. 15th* ....Miss E Tamplin pu
1135[6] Equatime 5a *wth ldrs to 10th, sn wknd, p.u. 15th* ....A Price pu
405[3] Moonlight Cruise 5a *lost plc 4th, sn wll in rear, t.o. last whn p.u. 12th* ....P Williams pu
1008[4] Jolly Swagman *rear,gd prog to chs ldrs 13th, wknd rpdly & p.u. nxt* ....G Perkins pu
1004 Harry From Barry *last trio til p.u. 6th* ....J Tudor pu
1004 Killyman (Ire) *alwys twrds rear, wll bhnd aft 13th, p.u. 3 out* ....Miss J Mathias pu
1131 Moor Hill Lass (Ire) *wth ldrs, disp whn ran out & u.r. 6th* ....G Lewis ro
1008 Tims Kick (Ire) 5a *mid-div, wknd 13th, t.o. & p.u. 15th* ....Miss S Major pu
964[1] African Warrior 12a *ld to 2nd, wknd frm 9th, t.o. & p.u. 15th* ....T Vaughan pu
15 ran. 2l, 6l, ½l, 20l, 8l. Time 6m 44.00s. SP 2-1.
David Brace (Llangeinor).

1228 Intermediate (12st)

382 **TRUE FORTUNE ....J Jukes** 1
(fav) w.w. trckd ldr 15th, hrd rdn to chal last,ld und pres post
1133[1] **Gunner Boon 5ex..................Miss P Jones** 2
ld 7-8th, ld aft 14th, rdn & jnd last, hdd post
1133 **Ideal ....J Rees** 3
ld to 7th, cls up aft, rdn 3 out, wknd nxt
903 Lonesome Step 5a *bhnd frm 4th, t.o. & p.u. 14th* ....A Price pu
1132[2] Savage Oak *ld 8th-aft 14th, rdn & mstk nxt, wknd, p.u. last, lame* ....E Williams pu
5 ran. Hd, 25l. Time 6m 32.00s. SP Evens.
D J Miller (Pembrokeshire).

1229 Open Maiden Div I (12st)

1137[3] **UNDERWYCHWOOD (IRE) ....J Jukes** 1
(fav) made virt all, rdn clr 2 out, eased flat
540[3] **Irish Thinker ....J Tudor** 2
prssd wnr, ev ch whn mstk 15th, sn rdn, btn 2 out, eased
1009 **Storm Dai Fence (Ire) 12a...........P Sheldrake** 3
rear, pshd alng 10th, went poor 3rd 13th, no dang
1011[4] Priesthill (Ire) *chsd ldrs, mstk 8th, wknd rpdly aft 12th, p.u. aft nxt* ....D Stephens pu
842 Bickerton Poacher *bltd bef start, in tch, wknd & mstk 10th, t.o. & p.u. 3 out* ....G Perkins pu
1010 Stiff Drink *disp whn blnd & u.r. 1st* ....A Price ur
1136 Mountain Slave 5a *chsd ldrs, no ch frm 12th, poor 4th whn u.r. 2 out* ....T Vaughan ur
842 Roger (Ire) 7a *chsd ldrs til wknd 8th, t.o. & p.u. 14th* ....I Johnson pu
543 Welsh Treasure (Ire) 12a *blnd 2nd, effrt to go 3rd whn mstk 11th, wknd & p.u. 13th* ....Miss G Gibson pu
1136 Mo's Keliro 12a *mstks, last & wkng whn ran out & u.r. 12th* ....Miss A Meakins ro
719 Forest Flight (Ire) 7a *f 1st* ....J Comins f
11 ran. 15l, 25l. Time 6m 46.00s. SP Evens.
D Davies (Banwen Miners).

1230 Open Maiden Div II (12st)

1009 **MERRY MORN 5a ....J Jukes** 1
in tch, prssd ldr 14th, rdn apr last, styd on to ld flat
1136[5] **Boddington Hill 5a....................I Johnson** 2
prom, ld 10th, rdn 15th, lkd wnr til hdd & no ext flat

1016[5] **I've Copped It (Ire)** ....**J Rees** 3
chsd ldrs, lost tch hlfwy, t.o. 13th, tk poor 3rd nr fin
1067[2] Kilgobbin (Ire) *(fav) trckd ldrs,3rd & in tch 13th, no imp nxt, wknd, sddl slppd* ....D Stephens 4
Jaki's Roulette 5a *blnd 1st, t.o. whn ref 4th* ..J P Keen ref
1010 Dragonara Lad (Ire) 7a *mstks, ld to 10th, wknd rpdly & p.u. 12th* ....J Tudor pu
Ceffyl Gwyn *t.o. 4th, p.u. 10th*..................J Price pu
1180[2] Kerstin's Choice 5a *chsd ldr til wknd aft 12th, t.o. & p.u. 14th* ....P Sheldrake pu
841 Alias Parker Jones *t.o. 4th, p.u. 6th*...........A Price pu
964[3] Fridays Child 12a *prom til wknd rpdly 6th, p.u. 8th* ....E Williams pu
10 ran. 2l, dist, 2l. Time 6m 44.00s. SP 4-1.
E L Harries (Pembrokeshire).

1231 Open Maiden Div III (12st)

1136[2] **GOOD BOY FRED 7a**..................**P Williams** 1
(fav) trckd ldrs, ld 3 out, clr nxt, pshd out
1010 **Alkarine 7a** ....**J Tudor** 2
mstk 7th, prog to ld aft 13th-3 out, sn btn, eased
847[4] **Pyro Pennant**..........................**I Johnson** 3
2nd whn mstk 8th, sn bhnd, kpt on onepcd frm 15th
1136[7] Glynn Brae (Ire) *ld til mstk 5th, ld 7th-aft 13th, rdn & reluc aft, sn btn*.............................J Hayward 4
1131 Steel Valley (Ire) 5a *ld 5-7th, wknd 13th, t.o.*....J Cook 5
1186 All The Jolly 5a *trckd ldrs, ev ch 13th, wknd rpdly nxt, p.u. 3 out*................................Miss P Jones pu
1183 Lizzie Boon 12a *schoold, cls up frm 6th, ev ch whn f 13th* ....J Price f
7 ran. 10l, 6l, 1l, 25l. Time 6m 57.00s. SP 4-5.
Mrs J Williams (Pentyrch).
J.N.

TEME VALLEY
Brampton Bryan
Saturday April 26th
GOOD

1232 Members

1018 **TRUE FRED** ....**M P Jones** 1
cls up, ld 13th, drew clr frm 16th
574[4] **Tanner** ....**M Hammond** 2
(fav) ld to 2nd, ld 5th-13th, rdn & no ext 15th
1014 **In The Water** ....**M Worrall** 3
slw jmp & last frm 3rd, lost tch frm 12th
Seven Cruise *ld 3rd-nxt, cls 3rd whn blnd & u.r. 11th* ....R Jones ur
4 ran. 12l, dist. Time 7m 13.00s. SP 5-2.
Mrs A Price (Teme Valley).

1233 Confined (12st)

1013 **BOWLAND GIRL (IRE) 5a 3ex** ......**Miss E James** 1
alwys cls up, ld 2 out, blnd last, all out, lkd 2nd
1013[3] **Chiaroscuro** ....**S Lloyd** 2
6th & rdn 10th, styd on frm 15th, lkd to ld post
1063[1] **Sisterly 5a 3ex**....................**Miss S Vickery** 3
(fav) cls up, ld 13th til hdd aft 3 out, rallied und pres flat
568 Gold'n Shroud (Ire) *rear til ran on 16th, nrst fin* ....N Oliver 4
668 The Rum Mariner *ld to 12th, rdn 15th, not qckn nxt, kpt on frm 2 out* ....D S Jones 5
1178[3] Penllyne's Pride *in tch til wknd 11th, crwld nxt & p.u.* ....T O'Leary pu
1002[3] Ultrason IV (Fr) *prog 8th, 15l 6th at 13th, no ch frm 16th, p.u. 2 out*.............................A Dalton pu
938[2] I Haven't A Buck (Ire) *trckd ldrs, cls 5th at 9th, wknd 15th, p.u. 3 out* ....R Burton pu
8 ran. Sht-hd, hd, 1l, 1½l. Time 6m 57.00s. SP 12-1.
R J Scandrett (Radnor & West Hereford).

1234 Men's Open (12st)

1060[1] **VIRIDIAN** ....**M Rimell** 1
trckd ldr, ld 13th, 2l up 16th, rdn & maintained adv
1014[1] **Shoon Wind** ....**A Dalton** 2
(fav) ld to 12th, chsd wnr aft, rallied 2 out, eased flat
1147 Sharinski 4ex *cls up in 3rd, 4l down 9th, lost tch 12th, t.o. & p.u. 3 out*..........................O McPhail pu
939 Logical Fun (bl) *alwys last, clsd to 6l 4th at 10th, outpcd 12th, p.u. 2 out* ....L Brennan pu
4 ran. 5l. Time 6m 51.00s. SP 5-2.
D Hine (Ledbury).

1235 Intermediate (12st)

1044[1] **PASSING FAIR 5a** ....**Miss S Vickery** 1
(fav) prog to cls 3rd 13th,chsd ldr 15th, ld 3 out,kpt on und pres
1061[1] **Corn Exchange** ....**M Rimell** 2
trckd ldr til ld 15th, hdd 3 out, kpt on & rallied flat
1014 **Haven Light** ....**A Dalton** 3
hld up, prog 9th, effrt 14th, no ch wth 1st pair frm 16th
1146[2] Sudanor (Ire) *ld til hdd & rdn 15th, wknd frm nxt* ....O McPhail 4
937 Young Parson *12l 6th at 8th, wkng whn blkd & f 14th* ....R Owen f
1013 Lles Le Bucflow *s.s. nvr rchd ldrs, no ch whn p.u. 15th*.......................................M Munrowd pu
1014[3] Mr Bobbit (Ire) *mid-div, cls 5th whn ran out 14th* ....R Burton ro
1012 Basil Street (Ire) 7a *chsd ldrs, no prog frm 14th, t.o. & p.u. 3 out*..............................A Phillips pu
1061 Derring Ann 5a *mid-div, not qckn 13th, t.o. & p.u. 2 out*..D S Jones pu
1013 Another Chancer *s.s. effrt & prog 12th, in tch whn ran out 14th* ....R Bevis ro
10 ran. 2½l, dist, hd. Time 6m 52.00s. SP Evens.
Mrs C Wilson (Blackmore & Sparkford Vale).

1236 Ladies

1013[1] **GRIMLEY GALE (IRE) 5a**..........**Miss S Vickery** 1
(fav) trckd ldr 4th, ld brfly 11th, ld 13th, rdn clr frm 3 out
976[3] **Scarlet Berry 5a** ....**Miss E James** 2
disp til ld 3rd, hdd 11th, ld nxt-13th, not qckn frm 15th
1060[2] **Drumceva** ....**Miss E Wilesmith** 3
alwys 3rd, outpcd frm 7th, no ch frm 12th
750 Opals Son *disp to 2nd, ran wd aft 4th, t.o. & p.u. 12th* ....Miss D Skyrme pu
4 ran. 15l, dist. Time 6m 58.00s. SP 8-11.
R M Phillips (Worcestershire).

1237 Interlink Restricted (12st)

1015[1] **ROOTSMAN (IRE)** ....**T Stephenson** 1
(fav) hld up, prog 15th, qcknd to ld last, sn clr
1045[1] **Billy Barter (Ire)** ....**Miss S Vickery** 2
trckd ldrs, cls 3rd 15th, rdn to ld 2 out, hdd & no ext last
1000[2] **Priory Piper** ....**C Stockton** 3
hld up, prog 12th, ld 3 out, hit nxt & hdd, kpt on flat
1135 Fire King *ld/disp 7th-15th, not qckn nxt, kpt on onepcd* ....Miss C Thomas 4
1019 Cwm Arctic 5a *cls up til 15th, grad wknd frm nxt* ....J Jackson 5
1061[4] Kingsthorpe *mid-div, effrt to chs ldrs whn hit 13th, wknd 15th, p.u.3out*.........................A Phillips pu
878[5] Kerry Hill *alwys rear, wknd 11th, t.o. & p.u. 3 out* ....Miss D Jackson pu
976 Autumn Green (Ire) (v) *n.j.w. alwys rear, p.u. last* ....G Hanmer pu
380 Ollardale (Ire) *rear frm 8th, lost tch 13th, p.u. 3 out* ....A Dalton pu
639[1] Bel Lane 5a (v) *ld 4th-nxt, cls up til wknd 15th, p.u. aft nxt*...D S Jones pu
1013[7] Stormhill Recruit *in tch til outpcd 13th, t.o. & p.u. last* ....M P Jones pu
1145[3] Manard 5a *slppd bdly 1st, nvr rchd ldrs, p.u. 3 out* ....M Hammond pu
940[3] Gasmark (Ire) *made most frm 6th til hdd 3 out, p.u. last*...A Crow pu
13 ran. 5l, nk, 10l, 12l. Time 7m 3.00s. SP 2-1.
Mrs J Morgan (Ledbury).

1238 Open Maiden Div I Pt I (12st)

1015[4] **MERRY NOELLE 5a....................R Bevis 1**
cls up 11th, chal 3 out, ran on und pres to ld last
1151[2] **Rejects Reply ....G Hanmer 2**
rear til gd prog 14th, ev ch frm 3 out, no ext cls hm
1067[3] **Astromis (Ire) 5a....................O McPhail 3**
hld up, prog frm 16th, ld 2 out-last, wknd flat
1018 Farriana 5a *cls 4th at 8th, ld 15th til hdd 2 out, wknd flat*....................P Hanly 4
754[4] Miss Clare 5a *alwys mid-div, effrt 16th, no ext frm nxt*....................N Oliver 5
1015 Bally Boy 7a *chsd ldrs, ev ch 15th, wknd aft nxt*....................D S Jones 6
1065 Heather Wood 5a *ld frm 5th til hdd aft 12th, wknd & p.u. 15th*....................T O'Leary pu
1019 Saxon Smile *cls up to 8th, lost plc & p.u. 11th*....................Miss S Jackson pu
1150[2] Ribington *ld to 4th, prom til wknd 15th, p.u. aft nxt*....................M Hammond pu
1015[3] Corview (Ire) *(fav) mid-div & rdn 8th, no prog 11th, p.u. aft nxt*....................A Phillips pu
10 ran. ½l, 2½l, 3l, 15l, 12l. Time 7m 22.00s. SP 7-2.
M P Wiggin (Ludlow).

1239 Open Maiden Div I Pt II (12st)

1016[8] **DISTANT-PORT (IRE) ....T Stephenson 1**
hld up just in tch, prog 16th, ld 2 out, clr last
1019[3] **Winter Breeze ....Miss S Vickery 2**
alwys cls up, not qckn apr 3 out, lft 2nd nxt
1016[7] **Merger Mania 7a ....D Mansell 3**
pllng, cls up til lost tch 15th, no ch nxt, fin fast
1018 Pridewood Golding *w.w. prog 8th, ld 14th, ev ch til wknd 2 out*....................T Cox 4
1150 Only In Ireland *ld til 14th, ld nxt, wknd rpdly & p.u. aft 16th*....................C Stockton pu
1066 Brother Harold *prom til wknd 11th, p.u. aft nxt*....................A Dalton pu
1016 Military Man *cls up til wknd 15th, p.u. 3 out*....................Miss E James pu
Fort Gale (Ire) *(fav) sttld mid-div, prog 14th, ld 3 out, hdd & f nxt*....................M Rimell f
Money Don't Matter 12a *nrly f 2nd, in tch til wknd & ran off course aft 11th*....................J Jackson ro
9 ran. 8l, 10l, 15l. Time 7m 18.00s. SP 8-1.
Miss P Morris (Croome & West Warwickshire).

1240 Open Maiden Div II (12st)

1066[2] **PLAYING THE FOOL 5a....................P Hanly 1**
hld up, prog 9th, ld 15th, qcknd clr apr last
1016[2] **Lindalighter 5a....................A Dalton 2**
(fav) hld up frm 4th, effrt wth wnr 13th, no ext frm 2 out
1067[4] **Dinedor Charlie ....D S Jones 3**
prom, cls 2nd whn mstk 15th, wknd aft
570 Henrietta Boo Boo 5a *cls up to 13th, wknd 15th, p.u. 2 out*....................A Phillips pu
1019 Welsh Lightning *cls up frm 7th, wknd 15th, no ch whn p.u. last*....................M Rimell pu
754 Brown Bala 5a (bl) *ld til aft 14th, wknd & p.u. 3 out*....................M Hammond pu
1151 Asante Sana 5a (bl) *mid-div whn blnd & u.r. 6th*....................N Oliver ur
Manley Girl (Ire) *rear frm 3rd, wknd 13th, p.u. 15th*....................G Hanmer pu
1066 Conimore (Ire) 12a *cls up whn ran out 3rd*..J Jackson ro
1065 Firestarter *cls up, chsd ldrs 12th til mstk & u.r. 15th*....................S Shinton ur
1016 Faha Point (Ire) 12a 2ow *prom whn mstk 8th, f 10th*....................D Mansell f
Miss Panoo 5a *rear frm 4th, in tch til mstk 13th, eased & p.u. nxt*....................O McPhail pu
12 ran. 12l, dist. Time 7m 21.00s. SP 3-1.
C J Bennett (Ledbury).
One fence omitted last two circuits, 17 jumps. P.R.

TIVERTON STAGHOUNDS

Bratton Down
Saturday April 26th
GOOD TO SOFT

1241 Members

515[1] **KING TORUS (IRE) ....Miss L Dartnall 1**
(fav) made virt all, eased near fin
804[3] **Mountain Master ....Miss L Blackford 2**
prssd wnnr frm 12th, styd on onepce frm nxt
1093[3] **Morchard Milly 5a....................J Auvray 3**
cls up til lost ground 4 out
1093 Remember Mac (bl) *20l bhnd frm 6th, nvr nrr*....................Miss C Hayes 4
4 ran. 2½l, dist, dist. Time 6m 35.00s. SP 2-5.
Nick Viney (Tiverton Staghounds).

1242 Ladies

1090[2] **SECRET FOUR ....Miss T Cave 1**
(fav) alwys cls up, ld 12th, made rest, kpt on wll run in
1154[2] **Anjubi ....Miss L Blackford 2**
rear til gd prog 12th, chal 2 out, ran on onepce
586 **Full Alirt 5a ....Miss S Young 3**
alwys prom, efft to chal 15th, no ext frm nxt
1062 Daybrook's Gift (v) *alwys towrds rear*....Miss N Allan 4
662 Gormless (Ire) *ld 6-12th, wknd qckly, p.u. 3 out*....................Miss J Cumings pu
1034[5] Luney River 5a *ld to 6th, ran wd, grdly lost tch, p.u. 12th*....................Miss L Long pu
6 ran. Dist, 4l, dist. Time 6m 26.00s. SP 4-6.
P Masterson (Dart Vale And South Pool Hrrs).

1243 Men's Open

1089[1] **BUTLER JOHN (IRE) ....N Harris 1**
made all, nvr serously chal
1033[2] **Oneovertheight ....S Kidston 2**
alwys chsng grp, tk 2nd 3 out, not trbl wnnr
591[5] **Expressment ....G Penfold 3**
chsng grp til no ext frm 2 out
1033 Baldhu Chance *chsd wnnr 4-14th, fdd frm nxt*....................J Young 4
629[1] Spring Marathon (USA) *(fav) bhnd, mstk (ditch), p.u. & dismntd 12th*....................L Jefford pu
531[1] Chocolate Buttons 5a *bhnd, mvd up whn mstk 9th, lost irons, p.u. bfr 2 out*....................H Thomas pu
6 ran. Dist, 2l, dist. Time 6m 30.00s. SP 5-4.
Nick Viney (Exmoor).

1244 Confined (12st)

1089 **JUST BEN 3ex ....Miss J Cumings 1**
(fav) ld 5th, made rest, pshd out cls home
646[3] **Southerly Buster ....S White 2**
alwys prom, chal 2 out, kpt on wd cls home
Buzz O'The Crowd ....A Moir 3
alwys cls up, styd on onepcd aft last
1043[3] Hensue *alwys prom, ev ch 3 out, no ext cls home*....................R Treloggen 4
1153[3] Friendly Lady 5a 3ow *bhnd til some late prog, not near to chal*....................Miss A Bush 5
630[7] Parson Flynn *ldng grp til grdly wknd 12th,stop to walk run in, (dead)*....................S Slade 6
1040[1] Life Peerage (USA) *midfld whn u.r. 5th.* .Mrs S Barrow ur
Rosea Plena 5a *midfld whn u.r. 5th*........S Kidston ur
889 Cleasby Hill *nvr trbld ldrs, p.u. aft 12th*......D Alers-Hankey pu
Deviosity (USA) 3ex *sn bhnd, t.o. whn p.u. 12th*....Lt-Col R Webb-Bowen pu
525 Fosabud *sn bhnd til p.u. aft 12th*....Miss L Hawkings pu
1089 Bargain And Sale 5ex (bl) *raced up wth pce early, sn lost tch, p.u. 15th*....................I Dowrick pu
Baman Powerhouse *trckd ldrs til wknd frm 15th, p.u. aft 2 out*....................J Young pu
Carumu 5a *ld til slppd up bnd aft 4th* ...David Dennis su
14 ran. 3l, 1½l, 8l, 10l, dist. Time 6m 36.00s. SP 6-4.
Roger Persey (Devon & Somerset Staghounds).

1245 Intermediate (12st)

630[6] **SAINT JOSEPH** ....**Miss S Young** 1
alwys gng wll, ld 14th, drew clr, imprssv
1088[2] **Parditino 5ex** ....**Miss V Nicholas** 2
alwys prom, efft 2 out, no imprssn
1038[1] **Tangle Baron 10ex**..............**Miss J Cumings** 3
(fav) ld/disp to 14th, outpcd frm nxt
862 Miss Ricus 5a *mid-div til moved up 3 out, efft short lived*......................................N Harris 4
1093 Liberty James *nvr bttr then mid-div* ....T Greed 5
171[7] Charmers Wish 5a *nvr trbld ldrs, bhnd whn p.u. 12th* ....H Thomas pu
1089 Medias Maid 5a *ld/disp til wknd 12th, p.u. bfr 3 out* ....A Holdsworth pu
1108 Alicott Lad *alwys off the pce til p.u. 10th* ....Miss L Smale pu
241 Fingal *bhnd til p.u. 10th* ....S Kidston pu
9 ran. Dist, 1½l, 10l, 10l. Time 6m 52.00s. SP 9-1.
B Young/Miss S & K Young (East Cornwall).

1246 Open Maiden (5-7yo) (12st)

1095[3] **STRETCHIT** ....**G Penfold** 1
alwys cls up, disp ld 12th til lft in ld 2 out, ran on wll
I Like The Deal 5a...............**Miss J Cumings** 2
alwys prom, wnt 2nd 2 out, styd on, promsng
Sam's Successor ....**S Kidston** 3
mid-div til gd hdwy 15th, styd on up hill fin
557 Grey Jerry *ld/disp til 12th, kpt on onepcd run in* ....B O'Doherty 4
866 Golden News *prom early, grdly wknd & p.u. 11th* ....S Slade pu
1045 Retrieving Mission (Ire) *in chsng grp whn f 14th* ....N Mitchell f
792 Belitlir 12a *wth ldrs til wknd 13th, p.u. 3 out* ....Miss S Young pu
1015 Expresso Drummer *(fav) mstks, nvr trbld ldrs, p.u. apr 2 out*..............................I Widdicombe pu
1088 Master Decoy *ld/disp til 12th, ev ch whn f 2 out* ....L Jefford f
1094 Jerome Jerome 7a *among chsng grp whn b.d. 14th* ....I Dowrick bd
Joy Street 5a *bhnd whn p.u. 13th* ....T Greed pu
Spanish Jest *bhnd whn p.u. 10th* ......S Parfimowicz pu
794 Ballyhasty Lady (Ire) 5a *nvr trbld ldrs, p.u. aft 12th* ....J Young pu
Mrs Green 5a *f 3rd*...................A Holdsworth f
1108 Go Willie Go *u.r. 1st* ....R Young ur
I'm Foxy 5a *prom early, mid-div whn ran out thru wing 14th*..................................A Farrant ro
16 ran. 4l, 10l, hd. Time 6m 53.00s. SP 2-1.
G W Penfold (Silverton).
P.H.

YORK & AINSTY
Easingwold
Saturday April 26th
GOOD TO SOFT

1247 Confined (12st)

696[3] **JUST CHARLIE 12ex**.................**D Easterby** 1
in tch, disp 11-14th, ld nxt, made all aft, comf
1071[3] **Blackwoodscountry** ....**C Mulhall** 2
cls up, tk 2nd 2 out, outpcd by wnnr
995[1] **Master Crozina** ....**P Cornforth** 3
disp, ld 9th-nxt, disp 11-14th, hdd no ext
1075[1] Mr Dick 6ex *(fav) mid-div, tk 4th 14th, styd on same pce* ....S Swiers 4
1071 Earl Gray *mid-div, hit 13th, onepcd, nvr dang* ....Miss A Deniel 5
265 Stelzer *mid-div, wknd 12th, p.u. 3 out*......L Donnelly pu
1100 Skipping Gale *disp to 8th, fdd, p.u. 2 out* ......G Tuer pu
1075 La Maja (Ire) 5a *rear, mstk 8th, wll bhnd whn ref last* ....N Wilson ref
1105 Mac's Blade (USA) 7a *alwys wll in rear, errors, t.o., p.u. 10th*..................................R Edwards pu
9 ran. 8l, 1½l, 2l, 4l. Time 6m 3.00s. SP 5-2.
Mrs Susan E Mason (Middleton).

1248 Men's Open

1147[3] **PEANUTS PET** ....**R Walmsley** 1
(fav) trcks ldr, error 13th, drvn out flat, styd on wll
696[4] **Knowe Head** ....**N Wilson** 2
ld & made all to last, hdd outpcd run in
1085[4] **Park Drift** ....**R Tate** 3
cls up, tk 3rd 2 out, no ch ldng pair
1103[3] Fast Study *mid-div, onepcd, tk 4th run in* S Robinson 4
696 Ashdren *in tch, 2nd 14th, fdd 4 out* ....N Tutty 5
1072 Frome Boy *alwys rear, t.o. 13th, late efft*...P Johnson 6
1100 Sharpridge *alwys wll bhnd, p.u. 8th* ....M Mawhinney pu
351 No More Trix *mstk 3rd, rear aft, p.u. 4 out* ..W Burnell pu
8 ran. 6l, 25l, 12l, 2l, 2l. Time 6m 8.00s. SP 4-7.
J W Walmsley (Bramham Moor).

1249 G Middleton Ladies

1103[2] **OSGATHORPE** ....**Mrs F Needham** 1
in tch, ld 3 out, styd on wll
508[4] **Cumberland Blues (Ire)** ....**Miss A Deniel** 2
ld to 14th, 3rd aft, tk 2nd flat, held by wnnr
1078[2] **Peajade** ....**Miss J Wormall** 3
(Jt fav) cls up, ld 4 out, hdd, no ext run in
1075[2] Kellys Diamond *(Jt fav) mid-div, prog, tk 2nd 4 out, fdd aft*...............................Miss V Russell 4
1102[3] Cheeky Pot (bl) *alwys same plc, onepcd thruout* ....Mrs S Grant 5
674[5] Crocket Lass 5a *rewar, t.o., p.u. 13th* ..Miss S Hunter pu
6 ran. 4l, 3l, 10l, 15l. Time 6m 4.00s. SP 4-1.
R Tate (Bilsdale).

1250 Restricted (12st)

1068[2] **CAMAN 5a**...........................**Mrs S Grant** 1
trckd ldr, ld last, styd on wll
1101[3] **Dear Emily 5a**..........................**S Swiers** 2
mid-div, prog 10th, tk 2nd 3 out, outpcd by wnnr
691[1] **Miss Madelon 12a** ....**N Wilson** 3
(fav) ld & made all to 2 out, hdd & no ext
1101[5] Mount Faber (bl) *mid-div, 4th 3 out, nvr dang* ....S Charlton 4
695 Sergeant Pepper *mid-div, hit 11th, nvr a factor, 5th 13th*..N Smith 5
1069 Persian Lion *prom early, fdd 12th, onepcd aft* ....Mrs L Ward 6
1101 Skyval 5a *mid-div, 10th 10th, same plc thruout* ....K Green 7
1069[6] Prophet's Choice *prom early, mstks, fdd frm hlfwy* ....M Haigh 8
1048 Cookie Boy *cls up, 4th 14th, wknd rpdly 4 out* ....Miss H Delahooke 9
1072 Here Comes Charter *alwys rear, no ext, p.u. 14th* ....A Pennock pu
1075[4] Midge 5a *rear early, mstks, p.u. 11th* ....Miss S Brotherton pu
1068 Lyningo *mid-div, fdd 10th, p.u. 14th* ....S Brisby pu
615[1] Not The Nadger *cls up, outpcd hlfwy, p.u. 4 out* ....A Ogden pu
1120[2] Bunny Hare (Ire) *s.s., wll in rear, f 3 out*....G Thomas f
1101 Dublin Hill (Ire) *bhnd early, prog 10th, fdd whn u.r. 4 out*..A Bonson ur
15 ran. 2l, 15l, 20l, 20l, 8l, 10l, 2l, 4l. Time 6m 4.00s. SP 3-1.
J A V Duell (South Durham).

1251 Open Maiden Div I

1074[2] **OUR WYN-STON 7a**...................**L Donnely** 1
(fav) cls up, hit 13th, disp 2 out, ld last, drew clr, comf
1104 **Smart Mover** ....**S Brisby** 2
ld to 3 out, disp nxt, hdd, outpcd flat
1106[5] **Mr Hook 7a** ....**P Holder** 3
mid-div, prog 14th, lft dist 3rd 3 out
860 Lac de Gras (Ire) *in tch, error 4th, wknd, p.u. 14th* ....A Pennock pu
1105 China Hand (Ire) 7a *cls up, 2nd 12th, fdd 4 out, p.u. 2 out*..R Edwards pu
1105[2] Silly Tinker *prom, 3rd whn f 3 out, lkd btn* ...C Denny f

Always Fresh 12a *alwys wll bhnd, nvr a factor, p.u. 14th* ....C Mulhall pu
899[2] Another Delight 5a *rear, rmmndrs 10th, t.o. p.u. 14th* ....N Wilson pu
Newton Wold 12a *slow jmp 1st, rear, ref 6th* S Swiers ref
9 ran. 5l, dist. Time 6m 25.00s. SP 11-10.
Mrs P A Russell (Middleton).

1252 Open Maiden Div II

1086 **ANDRETTI'S HEIR ....A Bonson** 1
ld to 9th agn frm 4 out, drew clr flat, easily
697 **Don Tocino ....N Smith** 2
in tch, 2nd frm 4 out, outpcd by wnnr
699[3] **Chummy's Last 5a ....Mrs F Needham** 3
mid-div, hit 13th, tk 3rd run in
1074 Not So Prim 12a *prom, ld 10-14th, hdd, no ext aft* ....W Burnell 4
1105 Fair Grand *mid-div, 5th 4 out, nvr dang* .....A Ogden 5
1106 Ski Lady 5a *rear, mstks, completed own time* ....Miss L Horner 6
1073[2] Tudor Flight 5a *(fav) in tch, 4th 6th, u.r. nxt* ....G Markham ur
859[3] Markham Lad *ref 2nd* ....D Pritchard ref
860[3] Abbey Moss *in tch whn f 5th* ....S Charlton f
9 ran. 15l, 2½l, 3l, 20l, 10l. Time 6m 23.00s. SP 7-2.
T S Sharpe (York & Ainsty).

1253 Members (12st)

673[2] **TOBIN BRONZE ....R Tate** 1
(fav) trckd ldr, ld 4-2 out, disp last, styd on wll
1072 **Gaelic Warrior 5ex ....S Swiers** 2
ld 5-14th, hdd, disp last, just btn flat
1072 **Tom Log (bl) ....W Burnell** 3
mid-div, outpcd by ldrs, dist 3rd 3 out
1101 The Chap *bhnd early, 4th frm 14th, nvr a factor* ....R Lochman 4
1101 Make A Line *alwys rear, 5th frm 14th, onepcd* ....C Denny 5
1100 Convincing (v) *cls up, error 12th, wknd, p.u. 14th* ....P Cornforth pu
1074 Strong Words *ld to 4th, fdd, hit 11th, p.u. 13th* ....Miss S Musgrave pu
7 ran. Nk, dist, 10l, 8l. Time 6m 14.00s. SP 4-6.
G Thornton (York & Ainsty North).
A.C.

MID DEVON
Black Forest Lodge
Sunday April 27th
FIRM

1254 Members

1109 **PHARAOH BLUE (bl)..................M Shears** 1
(fav) made all, alwys in cmmnd
An Buchaill Liath (Ire) ....Miss A Barnett 2
alwys abt 6l bhnd wnr, nvr able to chal
2 ran. 6l. Time 6m 54.00s. SP 1-2.
M Shears (Mid Devon).

1255 Confined (12st)

950 **BERT HOUSE ....S Kidston** 1
ld 11th, made rest, ran on wll whn chal
556 **Dharamshala (Ire) ....Mrs M Hand** 2
(fav) prog 14th, no imp on wnr frm 2 out
1111[3] **Christmas Hols ....Miss K Baily** 3
ld to 11th, kpt on onepcd aft
1244 Deviosity (USA) 3ex (bl) *wll bhnd frm 14th, sn t.o.* ..Lt-Col R Webb-Bowen 4
4 ran. 10l, 8l, dist. Time 6m 14.00s. SP 9-4.
A J Cottle (Silverton).

1256 Men's Open

1088[1] **MAGNOLIA MAN ....N Harris** 1
(fav) hld up, rpd prog 5 out, ld aft last, rdn out
1037[1] **Parson's Way ....A Farrant** 2
ld 2nd, hdd 14th, slght ld agn nxt-last, no ext flat
1033[3] **Just My Bill ....C Heard** 3
mostly 2nd, slght ld 14th-nxt, outpcd aft
1091[2] Fearsome *trckd ldrs, no ext frm 3 out* ......G Penfold 4
4 ran. 2l, 3l, ½l. Time 5m 59.00s. SP 4-5.
Mrs D B Lunt (Tiverton Foxhounds).

1257 Ladies

1141[1] **RAPID RASCAL ....Miss S West** 1
(fav) trckd ldrs, ld 7th-9th, drppd bck, rallied to ld agn flat
George Lane ....Miss A Barnett 2
ld/disp to 6th, ld 9th, hdd & no ext aft last
1110[3] **Midnight Bob ....Miss K Baily** 3
hld up, steady prog 13th, ev ch last, just outpcd
1242[4] Daybrook's Gift (bl) *wll bhnd, rpd prog frm 3 out, too much to do* ....Miss N Allan 4
1110 Achiltibuie *cls up til f 3 out* ....Mrs M Hand f
5 ran. 1½l, 1½l, 2l. Time 6m 9.00s. SP 5-4.
Miss S West (Weston & Banwell).

1258 Intermediate (12st)

1043[2] **LINK COPPER ....Miss L Blackford** 1
ld 6th til blnd 11th,ld 15th,jnd 2 out,styd on wll flat
456[1] **Three And A Half 5ex ....N Harris** 2
(fav) bhnd til prog 7th, ld 11th-15th,jnd wnr 2 out,wknd flat,lame
951[2] **Querrin Lodge ....T Greed** 3
cls up to 11th, sn bhnd
1153[5] The Criosra (Ire) 5ex *nvr trbld ldrs, t.o. 9th* A Bateman 4
631 Karicleigh Boy *ld til ran out 3rd*........A Holdsworth ro
5 ran. 1½l, dist, dist. Time 6m 14.00s. SP 5-2.
Mrs E J Taplin (Devon & Somerset Staghounds).

1259 Restricted (12st)

1093[2] **NEARLY AT SEA 5a..................I Widdicombe** 1
hld up, prog 5 out, ld last, ran on wll und pres
236 **Holly Fare ....C Crosthwaite** 2
mid-div til prog 3 out, fin fast
1039 **Northern Sensation 5a..................N Harris** 3
ld/disp, clr 7th, hdd last, no ext
1039[3] Ryme And Run 5a *nvr nrr*..........Miss L Blackford 4
950 Cedars Rosslare *alwys rear, nvr dang*. .Miss O Green 5
1108 Artistic Peace 5a *nvr seen wth ch, p.u. 3 out* ....G Penfold pu
1108[5] Maboy Lady *ld/disp to 6th, grad wknd, p.u. 2 out* ....David Dennis pu
7 ran. 3l, nk, 10l, 10l. Time 6m 13.00s. SP 1-3.
C J Down (East Devon).

1260 Open Maiden Div I (12st)

1094 Warwick Road (bl) *alwys bhnd, t.o. & p.u. last* ....I Dowrick 0
1093[6] Jet Jockey *made all, sn clr, unchal*..........A Oliver 0
1035 Sixth In Line (Ire) *f 9th*..................T Cole 0
1110 Dusty Furlong *nvr nr ldrs, fin 4th* ....Miss K Baily 0
1034[2] Aritam (Ire) *(fav) chsng grp, 4th whn f 12th*...A Farrant 0
1095 Indian Language *alwys bhnd, fin 8th* ....S Kidston 0
1040[2] Dollybat 5a *chsd wnr 7th, no imp, demoted apr last, fin 3rd* ....M Frith 0
1095 Master Buckley *nvr dang, fin 5th*............T Greed 0
867[3] Crosswell Star (Ire) *alwys rear, fin 6th*.......J Barnes 0
808 Brook A Light *chsd ldrs, went 2nd apr last, no imp wnr, fin 2nd*..................N Harris 0
789[4] Young Herbert (Ire) *alwys bhnd, fin 7th* ......J Auvray 0
Merlin The Monkey *alwys bhnd, f 12th* ......S Durack 0
12 ran. 10l, 15l, 15l, 12l, 15l. Time 6m 9.00s.
Race void, runners went wrong side of missed fence.

1261 Open Maiden Div II (12st)

298 **NEWSTARSKY ....Miss J Cumings** 1
10s-4s, alwys prom, ld 14th, made rest, hld on gamely
1112 **Get Stepping ....R Widger** 2
(Jt fav) prom, outpcd 3 out, rallied last, just faild
1112[3] **The Ugly Duckling ....S Slade** 3

ld/disp frm 7th, clr 10th, hdd 14th, fdd frm 2 out
1095[5] Nottarex *alwys mid-div, no dang* .... B Wright 4
1094[6] Mellicometti *twrds rear of ldrs, onepcd frm 3 out* .... R Woolacott 5
Red Is The Rose 5a *prom to 7th, lost plc, nvr nr ldrs aft* .... D Alers-Hankey 6
789[3] Mazies Choice 5a *alwys rear, nvr dang* ..... K Crook 7
741 Call Me Dickins *alwys bhnd, p.u. aft 10th* .... Miss A Barnett pu
1035[3] Spartans Dina 5a *(Jt fav) t.d.e. pllng, ran out 3rd* .... Miss L Blackford ro
1095 Kiramanda 5a *alwys rear, p.u. 3 out* G Barfoot-Saunt pu
557 Master Laughter *bhnd frm 3rd, p.u. aft 10th* .... Miss R Francis pu
1094 Brook Heights *mostly mid-div, wknd 10th, p.u. aft 12th* .... L Jefford pu
12 ran. Hd, 5l, 2l, 6l, 3l, 12l. Time 6m 16.00s. SP 4-1.
R G Westacott (Devon & Somerset Staghounds).
P.Ho.

GROVE & RUFFORD
Southwell P-To-P Course
Sunday April 27th
GOOD

1262 Open Maiden Div I (12st)

942[2] **ADVENTURUS 7a .... A Dalton** 1
mid-div, prog 10th, lft disp 2 out, ld apr last, styd on
1083[3] **You Be King .... R Thornton** 2
(fav) ld til disp 4th,hdd 3 out,lft disp nxt,hdd & no ex apr last
1073 **Auntie Chris 5a .... P Gee** 3
prom, ev ch 3 out, onepcd
549 Shining Penny *alwys mid-div, onepcd frm 3 out* .... K Green 4
1073 Bit Of A Grip (Ire) 7a 2ow *mid-div, drppd rear 11th, sn wll bhnd* .... G Hanmer 5
1073 Noreasonatall 12a *prom til lost plc 11th, sn strgglng* .... T Whittaker 6
941 Katie Kitoff 12a 7ow *prom, disp 9th, mstk 13th & sn lost plc, t.o.* .... J Barlow 7
Raticosa 12a *rear, mstk 10th, t.o. 14th, p.u. 4 out* .... Miss J Eastwood pu
1192[4] Delvin Spirit (Ire) 5a *prom til wknd 10th, t.o. & p.u. 12th* .... N Kent pu
914[3] Silly Pet *mid-div, prog to disp 4th, hdd 9th, fdd, t.o. & p.u. 3 out* .... S Robinson pu
Carlingford Lad (Ire) *mid-div whn u.r. 5th* E Andrewes ur
677[3] Springfield Rex *prom, disp 9th til ld 3 out, going wll whn f 2 out* .... K Needham f
898 Suny Rose 5a *alwys rear, mstk 8th, t.o. 3 out, p.u. last* .... S Walker pu
1192 Annascanan 12a *prom, jmpd slwly 12th, losng plc whn f 14th* .... S Morris f
Shakinallover (Ire) 7a *alwys rear, t.o. & p.u. 2 out* .... A Phillips pu
15 ran. 2l, 4l, 10l, 10l, 1l, 15l. Time 6m 40.00s. SP 2-1.
A N Dalton (Albrighton).

1263 Restricted (12st)

1191[5] **MIDNIGHT SERVICE (IRE) (bl) .... W Tellwright** 1
prom, trckd ldr 10th, ld apr 12th-2 out, rallied to ld last
670[2] **Gillie's Fountain .... A Dalton** 2
(fav) hld up rear,prog 11th,went 2nd 3 out,ld nxt,hdd last,nt qckn
1068[3] **Kendor Pass (Ire) .... M Tate** 3
trckd ldr til lost plc 10th, onepcd frm 3 out
1068 Mallow Innocence *mid-div, mstk 14th, strgglng 3 out* .... N Kent 4
1105[1] Goodheavens Mrtony *prom, rdn 11th, strgglng frm 3 out, t.o.* .... Miss A Deniel 5
1101[4] Douce Eclair 5a *mid-div, mstks 10th & nxt, strgglng whn p.u. 13th, lame* .... Miss L Eddery pu
1068 Carinci *ld til apr 12th, chsd ldr aft, wknd rpdly & p.u. 3 out* .... G Hanmer pu
927[5] Tiderunner (Ire) *rear, strgglng 13th, sn lost tch, p.u. 4 out* .... S Walker pu
1027[1] Lucky Vienna 5a *rear, jmpd slwly 5th, sn wll bhnd, p.u. 12th* .... J Henderson pu
9 ran. 2½l, 15l, 1l, 10l. Time 6m 23.00s. SP 16-1.
Mrs D E H Turner (Belvoir).

1264 Intermediate (12st)

1100[1] **HURRICANE LINDA 5a 7ex .... S Walker** 1
hld up rear, prog 11th, ld 2 out, drvn & hld on wll nr fin
1178[1] **Rolier (Ire) .... A Dalton** 2
(fav) hld up rear, prog 8th, ld 3 out-nxt, rallied wll flat
1070[4] **Arras-Tina 5a .... W Burnell** 3
mid-div, prog 8th, ev ch 3 out, not qckn
1013[2] Just Marmalade *alwys prom, ld 10th til hdd & wknd 3 out* .... R Burton 4
937[5] Royal Segos *prom, disp 6th-10th, chsd ldr aft, fdd 14th, t.o.* .... A Baillie 5
766[3] Formal 4ow *rear, dtchd 7th, hmpd 9th, sn wll bhnd, p.u. 3 out* .... R Owen pu
395 Rare Flutter 5a *mid-div, rdn 10th, wll bhnd 12th, p.u. 2 out* .... D Renney pu
Kingquillo (Ire) *disp to 4th, prom til wknd rpdly 7th, wll bhnd & p.u. 9th* .... G Hanmer pu
763 Pin Up Boy *disp til ld 4th, disp 6-10th, fdd rpdly, p.u. 2 out* .... A Crow pu
9 ran. Sht-hd, 4l, 8l, 15l. Time 6m 17.00s. SP 7-2.
Lady Hewitt (Middleton).

1265 Men's Open

201[4] **PERHAPS (USA) 5a .... A Dalton** 1
mid-div, prog to 2nd at 9th, lft in ld 2 out, styd on
1013[5] **Bentley Manor .... G Hanmer** 2
mid-div, prog to ld 13th, hdd 3 out, lft 2nd nxt
1103 **Simply A Star (Ire) (bl) .... Maj M Watson** 3
prom til wklnd 13th, wll bhnd 4 out, t.o.
1072[2] The Difference *alwys rear, t.o. 4 out* .... M Chatterton 4
1075[5] Clare Lad (v) *mid-div, outpcd 6th, lost tch 12th, t.o. 14th, p.u 3 out* .... R Walford pu
1188[4] Old Money *prom, disp 5-8th, rdn 11th, wknd rpdly 14th, p.u. 3 out* .... A Pickering pu
1071 Double Collect *ld til disp 5th, ld 8-13th, wknd rpdly, p.u. 3 out* .... A Rebori pu
Syd Green (Ire) *(fav) hld up, prog 11th, ld going easily 3 out, f nxt* .... S Walker f
8 ran. 6l, dist, 3l. Time 6m 19.00s. SP 6-1.
Mrs P Tollit (Worcestershire).

1266 Ladies

773[1] **CORNER BOY .... Mrs J Dawson** 1
(fav) trckd ldr, ld apr 5th, made rest, clr 3 out, not extndd
1013 **Night Wind .... Mrs A Rucker** 2
rear, effrt to go 2nd 4 out, onepcd nxt
1189[2] **San Remo .... Miss S Samworth** 3
ld til apr 5th,chsd wnr,lost plc 10th, rallied 4 out,sn wknd
1064 Mecado (v) *rear, mstk 3rd, rdn 10th, wknd 14th, t.o.* .... Miss J Priest 4
1189[3] Man Of Mystery *sttld in 3rd, chsd wnr 10th, wknd 4 out, p.u. nxt* .... Miss F Hatfield pu
5 ran. 5l, 15l, 7l. Time 6m 21.00s. SP 1-3.
Mrs E W Wilson (Brocklesby).

1267 Members

835[5] **KIRI'S ROSE (IRE) 5a .... P Gee** 1
(fav) trckd ldrs, ld 10th, drew clr 13th, unchal
550 **Art's Echo (Ire) .... Miss E Suttcliffe** 2
last, stgglng 13th, styd on to tk 2nd nr fin
884 **Ocean Sovereign .... T Denniff** 3
sttld 3rd, ld apr 5th-10th, onepcd frm 13th
836[3] Easby Roc (Ire) *ld til apr 5th, chsd wnr aft, wknd rpdly 3 out, p.u.last* .... N Kent pu
4 ran. 15l, ½l. Time 6m 40.00s. SP 4-5.
Brian Gee (Grove & Rufford).

1268 Open Maiden Div II (12st)

1074[3] **BUCKS VIEW (IRE)** ....**G Hanmer** 1
(Jt fav) mid-div, prog 6th, ld 12th, drew clr 3 out, easily
622[3] **Ship The Builder** ....**S Brisby** 2
(Jt fav) hld up, prog 11th, chsd wnr 3 out, not qckn
1003[3] **Educate Me (Ire)** ....**J Burley** 3
mid-div, prog 6th, ev ch 4 out, outpcd
1074 Half Each 12a *prom til grad fdd frm 14th* ...R Walford 4
1073[5] Milo Boy *trckd ldr, ld 6th til disp 9th, ld 10-12th, wknd 4 out* ....M Mackley 5
839[4] Ilikehim *ld to 6th, disp 9th-nxt, wknd rpdly 12th, p.u. 3 out* ....N Kent pu
1174[3] Sandy King (Ire) *prom til wknd 9th, t.o. nxt, p.u. 12th* ....D Dickinson pu
381 Jack The Td (Ire) *f 1st* ....J Cornwall f
1069 The Tide Race 5a *mid-div, wknd 8th, t.o. 10th, p.u. 12th* ....P Gee pu
Reaper *twrds rear whn b.d. 1st*.............M Haigh bd
677 Albert's Adventure (Ire) *rear, mstk 2nd, lost tch 6th, t.o. & p.u. 9th*..........................P McAllister pu
253[5] Cawkwell Win 5a *rear, bhnd 5th, t.o. 7th, p.u. nxt* ....K Needham pu
1251 Newton Wold 12a *rear, wll bhnd 12th, p.u. 14th* ....W Burnell pu

13 ran. 12l, 12l, 3l, 15l. Time 6m 31.00s. SP 9-4.
Mr Hocknell (West Shropshire Draghounds).
N.E.

SEAVINGTON
Little Windsor
Sunday April 27th
GOOD TO FIRM

1269 Members

1041[1] **FARADAY** ....**N Mitchell** 1
(fav) made all, mstk 5th, clr whn lft solo aft 14th
314 Brooklyn Express 5a *chsd wnr to 8th & frm nxt, wkng whn p.u. 14th*...........................M Sweetland pu
1157 French Invasion 5a *chsd wnr 8th til blnd nxt, wknd 12th, crwld 14th & p.u.*..................S Parfimowicz pu

3 ran. Time 6m 50.50s. SP 1-6.
G B Foot (Seavington).

1270 2½m Open Maiden (5-7yo) (12st)

525[4] **GIVUS A HAND** ....**T Mitchell** 1
ld to 3rd, prom, mstk 13th, rdn to ld apr 2 out, drvn out
871 **Woodlands Beau (Ire) 7a** ....**T Woolridge** 2
prom, ld 11th til apr 2 out, ev ch last, no ext flat
Barrow Street ....**J Tizzard** 3
jmpd lft,chsd ldr 5th,lft in ld 8-11th, wknd 3 out,fin tired
867 Miss Gruntled 5a *jmpd v slwly, sn bhnd, t.o. & p.u. 9th*...................................S Parfimowicz pu
With Intent 7a *(fav) pllng, ld 3rd til blnd & u.r. 8th* ....L Jefford ur
181 Sulason *prom to 11th, wknd rpdly 13th, last whn ref 3 out* ....M Miller ref
1094[4] Girls In Business 5a *sn bhnd, t.o. & p.u. aft 11th, dsmntd*.......................................B O'Doherty pu
933 Noble Comic *trckd ldrs, ev ch 13th, 4th & btn whn blnd & u.r. nxt*.................................N Mitchell ur
658 Dad's Delight 5a *chsd ldng grp til lost tch 12th, 5th & no ch whn u.r. 3 out* ....Miss A Goschen ur
Zoom 5a *schoold in last, t.o. 5th, p.u. 9th*......A Moir pu

10 ran. 2l, 20l. Time 5m 23.00s. SP 11-4.
Mrs J M Bailey (Blackmore & Sparkford Vale).

1271 Men's Open (12st)

929[2] **EARL BOON** ....**T Mitchell** 1
(fav) trckd ldr, ld 14th, qcknd clr 16th, easily
1091[3] **Stunning Stuff 7ex**.....................**R Nuttall** 2
ld to 14th, rdn & not qckn 16th, no ch wnr aft
872 **Touch Of Winter 7ex**...................**C Vigors** 3
cls up in last til not qckn 15th, wknd nxt

3 ran. 12l, 12l. Time 6m 31.00s. SP 4-7.
J A Keighley (Blackmore & Sparkford Vale).

1272 Ladies

1148 **FRONT COVER 5a**...............**Miss S Vickery** 1
(fav) trckd ldr, ld 3 out, blnd nxt, rdn out
1022[1] **Legal Picnic** ....**Miss C Bryan** 2
ld to 3 out, ev ch aft nxt, btn whn mstk last

2 ran. 8l. Time 6m 31.50s. SP 1-8.
Stewart Pike (East Devon).

1273 Intermediate (12st)

1023[2] **AVRIL SHOWERS 5a 5ex** ....**R Atkinson** 1
(fav) made all, shkn up 2 out, rdn & kpt on apr last
1092[3] **Sultan Of Swing** ....**T Mitchell** 2
jmpd lft, trckd wnr, pshd alng 16th, rdn & no imp apr 2 out

2 ran. 5l. Time 6m 34.00s. SP 4-7.
Mrs R Atkinson (Cattistock).

1274 PPORA (Nov Riders) (12st)

1090[4] **MIGHTY FALCON** ....**Miss E Tory** 1
cls up, ld aft 14th, clr nxt, styd on strngly
1056[2] **Pejawi 5a** ....**Miss L Whitaker** 2
plld into ld 8-9th, steadied, effrt to chs wnr 3 out, no imp
1055[3] **Skinnhill 1ow (bl)** ....**C Mason** 3
ld 6-8th, ld 10th til aft 14th, rdn & onepcd aft
1153[6] Osmosis *mstk 9th,w.w.,steady prog to chs ldrs 15th,wknd nxt,walkd in*.........................K Nelmes 4
903 Champagne Run *sn bhnd, t.o. 8th, p.u. 15th* ....R Hawker pu
Rallye Stripe *ld to 6th, sn wknd, t.o. 10th, p.u. 3 out* ....Col S Allen pu
1153 Highway Jim *chsd ldrs til wknd 14th, t.o. & p.u. 2 out* ....Miss M Burrough pu
1153 Chip And Run *(fav) ld & pckd 9th, hdd nxt, lost plc aft 14th, 4th & btn, f 2out*.....................B O'Doherty f

8 ran. 15l, ½l, 1 fence. Time 6m 31.00s. SP 5-2.
Miss Emma Tory (South Dorset).

1275 Restricted (12st)

1095[1] **FOUR LEAF CLOVER 5a**.................**J Jukes** 1
(fav) ld to 3rd, lft in ld aft 7th, clr 15th, easily
1157 **Clandon Lad** ....**T Mitchell** 2
hld up last, prog hlfwy, chsd wnr 3 out, no imp, fin tired
1058[4] **Duke Of Lancaster (Ire)** ....**N Sutton** 3
jmpd slwly in rear, kpt on frm 14th, nrst fin
688[3] Final Express 5a (bl) *lft 2nd aft 7th, pshd alng frm 12th, no imp, dmtd 3 out*..............Miss S Vickery 4
1157 Ballysheil *ld 3rd til ran off course aft 7th*...S Edwards ro
630 Hill Cruise *chsd ldrs, 4th whn f 11th*..........B Dixon f
688 Noble Protector (Ire) *jmpd bdly, in tch to 12th, last whn f 3 out, dead*.........................Maj G Wheeler f
1139[1] Feltham Mistress 5a *3rd whn u.r. 5th* ....E Babington ur
1140[1] Carnelia 5a *blnd & u.r. 2nd* ....Miss A Goschen ur

9 ran. 30l, ½l, 4l. Time 6m 33.00s. SP 4-5.
A Lowrie & P Henderson (Dulverton West).
J.N.

WEST NORFOLK
Fakenham P-To-P Course
Sunday April 27th
GOOD

1276 Members

1080[3] **ROUGH EDGE** ....**W Wales** 1
(fav) made all, rdn apr last, styd on well
800[2] **Professor Longhair 14ex**.......**Miss C Papworth** 2
blnd 1st, chsd wnr 11th, ev ch 3 out, no ext apr last
196 **Kellys Nap** ....**C Ward** 3
blnd 8th, chsd wnr to 11th, wknd apr 3 out, dsmntd aft fin

Kelly's Manor *bhnd & blnd 1st, t.o. 5th* .... S Hulse 4
Silverspina 5a *chsd ldrs, jmpd slwly 3rd, wkng whn slw jmp 10th, p.u. 15th* .... N Bloom pu
Carat *sn wll bhnd, t.o. 5th, p.u. 13th* ..... A Humphrey pu
Sporting Louella *alwys abt same plc, 5th & t.o. at 10th, u.r. 15th* .... Miss A Ringwood ur
7 ran. 4l, dist, 1 fence. Time 6m 40.00s. SP 4-5.
David Wales (West Norfolk).

1277 Confined

594[2] **DIVINE CHANCE (IRE) .... A Sansome** 1
ld 3rd, clr nxt, drew right away 2 out, easily
801[1] **Dance On Sixpence .... S March** 2
chsd ldrs, blnd 5th, 4th & rdn 15th, went mod 2nd flat
802[2] **Ballydesmond (Ire) .... S Sporborg** 3
ld to 3rd, chsd wnr til rdn & btn apr 2 out
1081[1] Dashboard Light *(fav) prog 5th, went 3rd 11th, blnd nxt & 15th, no hdwy 3 out* .... S R Andrews 4
780 Tammy's Friend (bl) *rear, jmpd slwly 4th, blnd nxt, prog 10th, nvr nr ldrs* .... J Ferguson 5
1031[2] Courier's Way (Ire) *mstks, in tch, blnd & rmndrs 6th, sn lost plc, no dang aft* .... T Moore 6
1113[2] Rhu Na Haven *rear, t.o. frm 8th* .... J Buckle 7
1028[2] Sarazar (USA) (v) *blnd 1st, chsd ldrs, lost plc 9th, p.u. apr 15th* .... G Pewter pu
271 Unique Tribute *mid-div, lost tch 11th, p.u. 13th* .... Capt D Parker pu
1028 Out Of Line 5a *rear, jmpd slwly 3rd, t.o. 8th, p.u. 13th* .... N Bloom pu
10 ran. 20l, nk, 3l, 15l, 5l, 1 fence. Time 6m 18.00s. SP 33-1.
J M Turner (Suffolk).

1278 Restricted (12st)

779[4] **REVEREND BROWN (IRE) .... A Sansome** 1
(fav) prom, ld apr 13th, rdn apr last, styd on
1080[4] **Bishops Tale .... R Barrett** 2
hld up, prog & mstk 10th, went 2nd apr 2 out, one-pcd
198 **Al Jawwal .... R Wakley** 3
mid-div, blnd 10th, 4th & ch 3 out, onepcd und pres
1118[1] Mutual Memories *hld up, prog to 2nd & going wll 13th, wknd apr 2 out* .... S R Andrews 4
503 Auchendolly (Ire) *alwys bhnd, last & mstk 8th, nvr on trms* .... T Macfarlane 5
798[4] Half A Sov (bl) *ld 2nd-12th, wknd, p.u. 15th* ... S March pu
1191[7] Kerry My Home *rear 5th, rmndrs 8th, no rspns, t.o. & p.u. 13th* .... T Marks pu
1114[2] New York Boy *mstk 5th, bhnd frm 10th, t.o. & p.u. 2 out* .... P Taiano pu
927 Ha-To-Siee (Ire) *ld to 2nd, wknd 9th, t.o. & p.u. 15th* .... Miss L Allen pu
1118 Secret Music *chsd ldrs to 9th, bhnd frm 13th, nrly ref 15th & p.u.* .... Capt D Parker pu
1082[1] Bilston George *chsd ldrs, blnd 11th, 5th & wkng 15th, no ch whn u.r. last* .... T Lane ur
11 ran. 2l, 3l, 30l, 8l. Time 6m 25.00s. SP 7-4.
J M Turner (Suffolk).

1279 Men's Open (12st)

1113[1] **DRUID'S LODGE .... C Ward-Thomas** 1
chsd ldr, ld 4th, made rest, rdn apr last, styd on well
780[5] **Just Jack .... P Jonason** 2
in tch, prog 9th, went 2nd 13th, chal 2 out, no ext last
1030[1] **Over The Edge 7ex .... S Sporborg** 3
(fav) ld to 4th, 3rd whn mstk & rmndr 13th, no imp 3 out
1190[2] Stanwick Farlap 5a 2ow *chsd ldrs, 4th & pshd alng 12th, no dang frm 15th* .... T Marks 4
503[3] Berkana Run *bhnd, prog & in tch 12th, no ch frm 15th* .... R Bailey 5
1163[4] Whats Your Game (bl) *jmpd slwly, sn bhnd, t.o. & p.u. 6th* .... K Sheppard pu
780 Lyme Gold (Ire) 7ex *chsd ldrs, lost plc & rdn 7th, mstk 10th, last & p.u. 14th* .... A Sansome pu
7 ran. 2l, 15l, 1l, 1l. Time 6m 21.00s. SP 3-1.
D J Lay (Essex & Suffolk).

1280 Ladies

1116[1] **ST GREGORY (bl) .... Mrs L Gibbon** 1
(fav) prom, mstk 6th, ld 12-15th, ld 3 out, drew clr frm nxt
1029[2] **Kumada .... Miss S Gritton** 2
ld til jmpd slwly 3rd,ld 8-12th & 15th,blnd & hdd nxt,onepcd
1029[3] **Major Inquiry (USA) (bl) .... Miss H Pewter** 3
prom, ld 3-8th, wknd apr 15th
1078[4] Driving Force (bl) *f 1st* .... Miss J Johnson f
1188 Whistling Gipsy *plld hrd, hld up, blnd 13th, ev ch 2 out, btn whn u.r. last* .... Miss L Allen ur
1078[6] Omidjoy (Ire) 5a (bl) *bdly hmpd & u.r. 1st* .... Mrs L Wrighton ur
6 ran. 5l, 15l. Time 6m 35.00s. SP 4-7.
A Howland Jackson (Essex & Suffolk).

1281 Open Maiden (5-7yo) Div I (12st)

478 **HOLDING THE ACES .... T Lane** 1
ld to 13th, ld apr 3 out, sn clr, rdn out
499[4] **Harry Tartar .... Capt D Parker** 2
(fav) rear,jnd ldrs 8th,mstk 13th & outpcd,kpt on to poor 2nd flat
928 **Teduet .... T Marks** 3
chsd ldr 8th, ld 13th til apr 3 out, no ext
1084 Top Odder (Ire) 7a *jmpd slwly 3rd, chsd ldrs 8th, blnd 9th & 14th, btn 3 out* .... P Millington 4
Live Connection (Ire) *jmpd bdly, sn bhnd, t.o. whn blnd 9th, p.u. aft* .... P Taiano pu
498 Kingarth 7a *mstks, chsd ldr to 8th, sn bhnd, t.o. & p.u. 12th* .... C Ward pu
Ballad (Ire) 7a *in tch til blnd & u.r. 10th* .... T Bulgin ur
Sapling 5a *rear, prog 11th, hit nxt, last & strgglng whn f 15th* .... N King f
8 ran. 15l, hd, nk. Time 6m 40.00s. SP 7-2.
G Vergette (Cottesmore).

1282 Open Maiden (5-7yo) Div II (12st)

777[4] **REGENCY COTTAGE .... W Wales** 1
ld 3rd, made rest, jnd 3 out, ld & gd jmp last, styd on
318 **Village Copper 7a .... C Ward-Thomas** 2
in tch, trckd ldrs 12th, outpcd 3 out, kpt on agn frm nxt
439 **Just Chica .... N Bloom** 3
ld; jmpd rght 2nd, hdd nxt, disp 3 out-apr last, one-pcd
599 Held To Ransom 7a *alwys bhnd, rdn 14th, sn no ch* .... R Wakley 4
1118 The Whole Lot *cls up, jmpd slwly 3rd, 5th whn blnd 13th, wknd, p.u. 15th* .... P Keane pu
Bantry Bay 7a *rear, mstk 4th, 6th & in tch whn blnd & u.r. 9th* .... A Coe ur
914[2] Lantern Spark (Ire) 5a (bl) *chsd ldrs, mstk 1st, jmpd slwly 4th, 4th & btn whn u.r. 2out* .... Miss C Tuke ur
Storming Lady 5a *(fav) cls up whn bmpd & u.r. 2nd* .... P Hacking ur
8 ran. 1½l, hd, 1 fence. Time 6m 38.00s. SP 5-2.
David Wales (West Norfolk).

1283 Open Maiden (8yo+)

1083 **BEECH BROOK .... T Lane** 1
chsd ldrs, ld 14th, drew clr apr last
275[5] **Alycount (USA) .... R Wakley** 2
alwys bhnd, no ch frm 11th, went poor 3rd 2 out,lft 2nd last
941[2] **Charlie Kelly .... P Taiano** 3
(fav) chsd ldrs, 4th & rdn 12th, sn lost tch, t.o.
591 Alapa *s.s. hld up, prog to 2nd 14th, btn 2 out, u.r. last* .... V Coogan ur
770 Learner Driver *mid-div, mstks 6th & 11th, lost tch, p.u. 3 out* .... C Ward pu
598[3] Flapping Freda (Ire) 5a *jmpd slwly, alwys bhnd, t.o. 12th, p.u. 3 out* .... R Gill pu

712[3] Stoneyisland (Ire) *ld to 14th, sn wknd, p.u. 3 out* ....N Bloom pu
439[2] Times Leader *mid-div, 7th whn blnd 13th, sn lost tch, p.u. 3 out*................................M Gingell pu
833[3] Indiway *mid-div in tch, mstk 9th, wknd 12th, p.u. 15th, lame*..P Bull pu
9 ran. Dist, 15l. Time 6m 31.00s. SP 12-1.
Mrs Emma Holman-West (Fitzwilliam).
S.P.

HUNTINGDON
Tuesday April 29th
GOOD

1284 3m Robert Lenton Memorial Hunters' Chase Class H

973[3] **KUSHBALOO 11.7 7a ....Mr A Parker 1**
(Jt fav) trckd ldr 5th, ld after 8th, rdn apr last, styd on well run-in.
1087[4] **Idiotic 12.2 5a ....Mr C Vigors 2**
(Jt fav) not fluent, held up, prog 12th, rdn to chase wnr after 3 out, ev ch last, veered left und pres run-in, not qckn.
780[1] **Dromin Leader 12.2 5a ....Mr A Sansome 3**
keen hold, cl up, chsd wnr 11th, rdn apr 2 out, 3rd and held when mstk two out, wknd.
926[1] Kino 11.7 7a *waited with, hmpd 12th and lost tch, rpd prog and mstk next, gradually wknd from 15th.* ....Mr Andrew Martin 4
1128[2] Woody Will 11.7 7a *in tch to 12th, soon wknd, t.o. 3 out*......................................Mrs E Coveney 5
1277[5] Tammy's Friend 11.7 7a (bl) *not fluent, ld till after 8th, mstk next, cl up when u.r. 12th*.........Mr J Ferguson ur
6 ran. 2l, 25l, 16l, dist. Time 6m 6.50s. SP 13-8.
Mr & Mrs Raymond Anderson Green

1285 3m Geoffrey Bevan Memorial Novices' Hunters' Chase Class H

1085[1] **SECRET BAY 12.7 ....Mr S Swiers 1**
(fav) ld to 4th, steadied, trckd ldr 8th, led 15th, soon clr, v easily.
278 **Cool Bandit (Ire) 11.7 7a...............Mr T Hills 2**
jmpd right, ld 6th to 15th, no ch with wnr after.
1127 **Tau 11.7 7a...........................Mr A Warr 3**
rear, lost tch 11th, kept on und pres from 3 out.
1117[3] Notary-Nowell 11.7 7a (bl) *mid div, effort to chase ldng pair 13th, no impn*...............Mr R J Barrett 4
1190[7] Smart Pal 11.7 7a *chsd ldrs till wknd 12th, soon t.o.*. ....Mrs F Needham 5
832[1] Billion Dollarbill 11.7 7a *soon pushed along in rear, rdn and struggling 10th, t.o. and p.u. before 3 out.* ....Mr M Gorman pu
1030[2] Cardinal Red 12.2 5a (bl) *prom till reluctant to race and lost pl rpdly from 10th, t.o. and p.u. before 15th.* ....Mr A Sansome pu
761[5] Mr Pinball 11.7 7a (bl) *n.j.w., soon t.o., p.u. before 16th*.......................................Mr M Cowley pu
983 Loyal Gait (NZ) 11.7 7a *mstk 8th, alwys rear, t.o. and p.u. before 16th*..................Mr Andrew Martin pu
1083[2] Space Molly 11.2 7a (bl) *ld 4th to 6th, wknd 8th, well bhnd when f 12th*.........................Mr P Cowley f
10 ran. Dist, 3l, dist, dist. Time 6m 5.00s. SP 2-5.
Stuart Dent

1286 3m Huntingdon Restricted Series Novices' Hunters' Chase Final Class H

983[1] **STRUGGLES GLORY (IRE) 12.0 7a Mr D C Robinson 1**
(fav) ld to 2nd, led 8th, drew clr 2 out, ran on strly.
911[1] **Mister Spectator (Ire) 12.1 3a ....Mr Simon Andrews 2**
ld 2nd to 8th, pressed wnr after, mstk 12th, ev ch 3 out, wknd next, well btn when blnd last.
1043[1] **Taura's Rascal 11.7 7a ....Mr F Brennan 3**
trckd ldrs, blnd 12th, rdn and in tch 15th, wknd 2 out, fin tired.
708[3] Ballyallia Castle (Ire) 11.7 7a *chsd ldrs till blnd badly 12th, soon well bhnd, styd on from 3 out, nvr nrr.* ....Mr N Bloom 4
303[3] Greybury Star (Ire) 11.7 7a *chsd ldrs, struggling when mstk 12th, soon lost tch*....................Mr P Bull 5
913 Grassington (Ire) 11.7 7a *alwys rear, no ch from 11th.* ....Mr Scott Quirk 6
1164[7] Tarry Awhile 11.10 7a 3ow *soon pushed along in mid div, lost tch from 11th, no ch after*........Mr J Connell 7
1117[4] Current Attraction 11.2 7a *alwys rear, t.o. 14th, p.u. after 3 out*..............................Miss C Tuke pu
798[2] Give It A Bash (Ire) 11.2 7a *chsd ldrs, jmpd slowly 11th, soon wknd, t.o. and p.u. before 2 out.* ....Mr T Moore pu
303 Some Tourist (Ire) 11.7 7a *slowly into stride, alwys bhnd, t.o. and p.u. before 3 out*........Mr N Benstead pu
10 ran. 20l, 3l, 5l, 9l, 4l, 29l. Time 6m 5.80s. SP 8-13.
D C Robinson

1287 2½m 110yds Dr. Wakes-Miller 60th Birthday Hunters' Chase Class H

375[1] **SLIEVENAMON MIST 12.2 5a ....Mr J Jukes 1**
(fav) held up, prog to chase ldng pair 11th, ld apr 2 out where mstk, driven clr.
1029[1] **Counterbid 11.9 5a (bl)...........Mr A Sansome 2**
chsd ldr 5th, rdn and ev ch apr 2 out, unable to qckn.
291 **My Young Man 11.7 7a.............Mr E James 3**
ld and set gd pace, mstk 9th, hdd and wknd apr 2 out.
378[4] Kambalda Rambler 11.7 7a *mid div, lost tch with ldrs 10th, kept on one pace from 3 out, no dngr.* ....Mr R Armson 4
1086[4] Not My Line (Ire) 12.0 5a *chsd ldrs, no prog from 12th*......................................Mr W Wales 5
1099 Candle Glow 11.7 7a *mstks, chsd ldr to 5th, prom till wknd 12th*.........................Mr P Hutchinson 6
1099[5] Tudor Fable (Ire) 11.12 7a *mid div, lost tch when mstk 9th, no dngr after*................Mr Rupert Sweeting 7
1064[4] The Lorryman (Ire) 11.7 7a *mstks, mid div, lost tch 9th, t.o.*...................................Mr N R Mitchell 8
837[2] Killimor Lad 11.7 7a *alwys bhnd, t.o. from 9th.* ....Miss S Samworth 9
891 Fish Quay 11.7 7a *alwys bhnd, t.o. from 9th.* ....Miss S Lamb 10
966[4] Basher Bill 11.7 7a *alwys bhnd, last & t.o. when p.u. after 11th*..............................Mrs E Coveney pu
578[2] Upward Surge (Ire) 11.7 7a *chsd ldrs to 10th, soon wknd, t.o. and p.u. before 2 out*.........Mrs N Ledger pu
1161[2] Making Time 11.2 7a *mstks, alwys bhnd, t.o. and p.u. before 13th*.........................Miss T Habgood pu
1160 Lucky Landing (Ire) 11.7 7a *mid div, lost tch 9th, t.o. and p.u. before 12th*...............Mr Andrew Martin pu
14 ran. 9l, 13l, 8l, 12l, 4l, 2l, 17l, ¾l, 5l. Time 5m 1.90s. SP 4-11.
Nick Viney

CHELTENHAM
Wednesday April 30th
GOOD TO FIRM

1288 2m 5f Evesham Maiden Hunters' Chase Class H

589[2] **VITAL SONG 11.7 7a............Mr G Matthews 1**
made all, left clr 13th, mstk next, ran on well from 2 out.
888[3] **Ardbrennan 11.7 7a.................Mr E James 2**
held up, prog when mstk 11th, left 2nd 13th, rdn apr 3 out, unable to qckn from next.
494 **Clobracken Lad 11.7 7a ....Mr G Baines 3**
n.j.w., in tch, rdn 11th, soon outpcd, styd on well after 3 out.
1147[1] Double Thriller 11.11 3a *(fav) soon cl up, chsd wnr 9th, mstk next, shaken up and one pace after 4 out.* ....Mr R Treloggen 4
1098[4] Orton House 11.7 7a *prom to 8th, weakening when mstk 11th, t.o. when hmpd 14th*..........Mr R Burton 5

1177[1] Very Daring 11.7 7a *bhnd from 8th, t.o. when hmpd 14th.* ....Miss S Sharratt 6
1150[1] Trevveethan (Ire) 11.11 3a *mstk 1st, held up, prog 8th, 5th and in tch when hmpd and u.r. 13th.* ..Mr M Rimell bd
1195[2] Well Bank 11.7 7a *mstks, in tch till rdn and wknd 11th, no ch when f 14th.* ....Mr E Walker f
983[5] Berrings Dasher 11.7 7a *rear, prog 10th, no impn on ldrs after 4 out, fith and well btn when p.u. near fin, dismntd.* ....Mr M Watson pu
1159[1] Broad Steane 11.9 5a *trckd wnr 5th to 9th and from 11th, cl 2nd when f 13th.* ....Mr A Sansome f
10 ran. 4l, 6l, 2l, dist, dist. Time 5m 18.70s. SP 11-2.
G Matthews

1289 3m 1f 110yds Colin Nash Memorial United Hunts' Challenge Cup Hunters' Chase Class H

1194[2] **MISS MILLBROOK 11.5 7a ....Mr E Williams 1**
(fav) trckd ldr 7th, ld 12th till mstk 15th, rdn and mistake 4 out, rallied to ld 2 out, driven out.
680[5] **Glen Oak 11.10 7a ....Mr J M Pritchard 2**
waited with, pushed along after 11th, prog to chase ldrs 13th, not qckn after 3 out, styd on to chase wnr run-in.
1206[1] **Hill Island 11.10 7a ....Mr Rupert Sweeting 3**
ld 6th to 12th, led again 15th, rdn and hdd 2 out, no ext last .
649[2] Cavalero 11.10 7a *blnd 2nd, in tch, chsd ldrs 12th, cl 4th when mstk 3 out, soon btn, eased run-in.* ....Mr A Charles-Jones 4
1211[3] J B Lad 11.10 7a *mstks, ld 4th till 6th, weakening when blnd 14th, t.o. and p.u. before 17th.* ....Miss P Gundry pu
680[7] Teatrader 11.10 7a *ld to 4th, wknd 12th, t.o. and p.u. before 3 out* ....Miss T Blazey pu
6 ran. 3l, 2½l, 30l. Time 6m 40.60s. SP 11-10.
D T Goldsworthy

1290 4m 1f Wragge & Co Hunters' Chase Class H

1087[3] **RUSTY BRIDGE 11.11 7a ....Mr R Burton 1**
(Jt fav) ld to 20th, pressed ldr after, rdn 4 out, led again last, driven and held on gamely.
1087[6] **The Malakarma 11.13 5a ....Mr B Pollock 2**
chsd wnr to 12th, rdn to go 2nd again 18th, ld 20th, soon hrd ridden, hdd last, styd on gamely.
1087[5] **Young Brave 12.0 7a ....Mr M G Miller 3**
waited with, prog going easily 18th, trckd lding pair 22nd, ch 4 out, rdn and one pace after.
489[2] Loyal Note 12.1 3a *chsd ldrs, pushed along 18th, blnd 22nd, rdn and no impn next.* ..Mr Simon Andrews 4
680[6] Artful Arthur 11.7 7a *bhnd, lost tch 14th, rdn and t.o. 17th, styd on from 23rd, no dngr.* ....Mr J Grassick 5
983[2] Lurriga Glitter (Ire) 11.7 7a (bl) *prog to chase ldrs 8th, no impn from 17th, one pace from 22nd.* ..Mr R Wakley 6
976[1] Kettles 11.2 7a *(Jt fav) not alwys fluent, waited with, effort after 15th, nvr reach ldrs, no ch from 22nd.* ....Mr A Phillips 7
890[4] K C's Dancer 11.7 7a *chsd wnr 12th till 20th, wknd 4 out, bhnd when p.u. before 2 out.* ....Mr J M Pritchard pu
780[3] Saint Bene't (Ire) 11.7 7a (v) *rdn 8th, alwys bhnd, t.o. 17th, p.u. before 3 out.* ....Mr A Coe pu
383[6] Mobile Messenger (NZ) 11.7 7a *alwys bhnd, t.o. from 17th, p.u. run-in, lame.* ....Miss S Samworth pu
10 ran. 1¼l, 13l, 12l, 5l, 2½l, 8l. Time 8m 37.40s. SP 4-1.
I K Johnson

1291 3¼m 110yds Cheltenham Champion Hunters' Chase Class H

494[4] **CELTIC ABBEY 11.7 7a ....Mr D S Jones 1**
trckd ldr, ld 15th, drew right away after 3 out, impressive.
1087[1] **Double Silk 12.3 3a ....Mr R Treloggen 2**
(fav) ld to 15th, soon rdn, one pace after 3 out, eased when no ch run-in.
591[3] **Ryming Cuplet 11.10 7a ....Mr L Jefford 3**
chsd ldrs, blnd 5th, lost tch lding pair from 14th, soon bhnd.
1087[2] Some-Toy 11.10 7a *chsd ldrs, mstk 9th, struggling from 12th, soon t.o.* ....Miss L Blackford 4
4 ran. 30l, 14l, 2½l. Time 6m 44.90s. SP 11-8.
G J Powell

1292 2m 5f Golden Harvest Hunters' Chase Class H

586[1] **TINOTOPS 11.7 7a ....Miss S Vickery 1**
cl up, trckd ldr 11th, ld after 3 out, driven out run-in.
586 **Knifeboard 11.7 7a ....Mr J M Pritchard 2**
waited with in rear, gd prog from 10th, mstk 4 out, chsd wnr and mistake last, ran on.
1097[1] **My Nominee 12.0 7a (bl) ....Mr R Burton 3**
(fav) jmpd right, made most till after 3 out, rdn and unable to qckn.
628[3] Greenwine (USA) 11.7 7a *cl up, chsd ldr 9th til jmpd slowly next, rdn and not qckn after 4 out.* ....Miss L Blackford 4
Fight To Win (USA) 11.7 7a *prom, ev ch and going easily 13th, fd after 4 out.* ....Mr J Grassick 5
1099 Frank Be Lucky 11.11 3a *pressed ldr to 9th, cl up after til rdn and wknd after 4 out.* ....Mr R Thornton 6
1175 Tara Boy 11.7 7a *rear, jmpd slowly 5th, rdn 8th, soon well bhnd, kept on und pres from 3 out.* ....Mr R Cambray 7
1097 Simply Perfect 11.7 7a *mstk 6th, lost pl 8th, nvr on terms after.* ....Miss K Swindells 8
679[4] Flowing River (USA) 11.7 7a *mid div, lost tch with ldrs 12th, no prog after.* ....Mr N R Mitchell 9
1090[3] Great Pokey 11.7 7a *alwys rear, t.o. from 13th.* ....Miss N Courtenay 10
751 Leigh Boy (USA) 11.7 7a *reminder 6th, bhnd from 10th, t.o. and p.u. before 2 out.* ....Mr N H Oliver pu
822[2] Orujo (Ire) 11.11 3a *mstks, bhnd, effort 10th, soon btn, t.o. and p.u. before 2 out.* ....Mr A Hill pu
12 ran. 2l, 1¼l, 9l, 4l, 9l, 2½l, 2½l, sht-hd, 30l. Time 5m 20.20s. SP 7-4.
R H H Targett

1293 2m 110yds Overbury Hunters' Chase Class H

1099[2] **PRO BONO (IRE) 11.13 5a ....Mr A Sansome 1**
(fav) held up in cl tch, mstk 5th, ld 3 out, pushed clr last, hrd rdn and kept on near fin.
Master Crusader 11.7 7a ....Mr S Durack 2
held up last, gd prog to press wnr 3 out, ev ch next, rallied and edged left run-in, styd on.
960[1] **Fantastic Fleet (Ire) 11.5 3a ....Mr R Thornton 3**
mstks, ld 3rd till 7th, mistake 4 out and lost pl, rallied und pres apr 2 out, soon not qckn.
781[2] Familiar Friend 12.0 7a (bl) *ld to 3rd, led 7th till 3 out, wknd apr last.* ....Mr L Lay 4
892[1] Nectanebo (Ire) 11.11 7a *keen hold, held up, in tch when u.r. 7th.* ....Mr M Frith ur
5 ran. 1½l, 6l, 2½l. Time 4m 21.90s. SP 6-4.
P C Caudwell

KELSO
Wednesday April 30th
GOOD TO FIRM

1294 3m 1f Charlie Brown United Border Hunters' Chase Class H

1170[1] **WASHAKIE 11.12 ....Mr J Walton 1**
(fav) soon bhnd, some hdwy to chase ldrs after 13th, styd on well from 2 out, ld last, all out.
1201[7] **Across The Card 11.11 7a ....Mr M Bradburne 2**
bhnd, styd on from 3 out, chsd wnr final 200 yards, no impn.
1201 **Rusty Blade 11.7 5a ....Mr R Hale 3**
chsd ldr, blnd 9th, rdn after 13th, ch last, kept on same pace.
1096[5] Green Times 11.7 5a *soon bhnd, n.d.* ....Mr C Storey 4
875[2] Sovereigns Match 11.7 5a *ld, clr 2 out, wknd quickly and hdd last, soon btn.* ....Mr N Wilson 5

815[2] Shine A Light 11.5 7a *trckd ldrs, blnd 8th, wknd quickly after 13th, t.o. when p.u. before last.* ....Captain A Ogden pu
6 ran. 1¼l, 3½l, 18l, 3½l. Time 6m 16.80s. SP 2-1.
Mrs F T Walton

BANGOR
Friday May 2nd
GOOD

1295 3m 110yds Eastern Destiny Novices' Hunters' Chase Class H for the James Griffith Memorial Trophy

888[1] **BITOFAMIXUP (IRE) 12.4 3a ....Mr P Hacking** 1
(fav) nvr far away, ld 14th, clr apr 2 out, easily.
1086[1] **Mister Horatio 11.11 7a ....Mr M Lewis** 2
prom, jmpd slowly 3rd, outpcd when hit 14th, rdn to chase clr wnr apr 3 out, no ch when mstk last.
1097[5] **Nadiad 11.7 7a......................Mr A Wintle** 3
cl up, outpcd and bhnd 14th, no ch when pkd 2 out.
1132 Desmond Gold (Ire) 11.7 7a *set slow pace, jmpd slowly 3rd, qcknd apr 12th, hit and hdd 14th, soon wknd, t.o.*. ....Mr D S Jones 4
4 ran. 25l, 4l, dist. Time 6m 26.10s. SP 1-4.
Mike Roberts

HEREFORD
Saturday May 3rd
GOOD

1296 2m 3f Jail-Break Hunters' Chase Class H

YQUEM (IRE) 11.7 7a ....Mr R Wakley 1
held up, hdwy 6th, ld 3 out, rdn when left clr last.
1293[4] **Familiar Friend 12.0 7a (bl) ....Mr L Lay** 2
held up, hdwy 9th, wknd apr 3 out, left poor 2nd last.
1226[2] **Landsker Missile 11.9 7a ....Mr N Bradley** 3
(fav) alwys prom, rdn 4 out, wknd next, left 3rd last.
1099[6] Tellaporky 11.7 7a (bl) *slowly away, n.j.w., t.o. from 6th.* ....Mr A Middleton 4
1287[3] My Young Man 12.0 7a *ld 2nd rdn and hdd 3 out, ev ch till hit and u.r. last.* ....Mr E James ur
1099 Tuffnut George 12.0 7a *ld to 2nd, prom till wknd 9th, t.o. when p.u. before 2 out.* ....Mr A Phillips pu
1235[4] Sudanor (Ire) 11.7 7a *in tch when blnd 8th, soon bhnd, t.o. when p.u. before 4 out.* ......Mr M Munrowd pu
393 Twist 'N' Scu 11.7 7a *jmpd slowly 5th, t.o. when p.u. before 10th*.. ....Mr R Lawther pu
1097 Thornhill 11.2 7a *slowly away, in rear when f 5th.* ....Mr A Wood f
1018 Roo's Leap (Ire) 11.2 7a *bhnd from 7th, t.o. when p.u. before 9th*.. ....Mr O McPhail pu
1099[1] Mankind 11.11 7a *in tch to 8th, soon bhnd, t.o. when p.u. before 3 out.* ....Mr L Baker pu
11 ran. 15l, ¾l, dist. Time 4m 52.70s. SP 7-1.
J J Boulter

HEXHAM
Saturday May 3rd
FIRM

1297 3m 1f Gilesgate Subaru And Ssangyong 10th Anniversary Heart Of All England Maiden Hunters' Chase Class H

1249[2] **CUMBERLAND BLUES (IRE) 11.7 7a ......Miss A Deniel** 1
made all, rdn 2 out, styd on well from last.
1188[2] **Coolvawn Lady (Ire) 11.2 7a.........Mr S Walker** 2
in tch, hdwy to chase ldrs 7th, effort and disp ld 2 out, soon rdn and one pace last.
1168[2] **Will Travel (Ire) 11.7 7a.............Mr A Robson** 3
(fav) chsd wnr, rdn 4 out, wknd after next.
1085[3] Cool Yule (Ire) 11.9 5a *bhnd till some hdwy from 2 out, nvr a factor.* ....Miss P Robson 4
1220[1] Emu Park 11.7 7a *in tch till wknd from 10th, t.o..* ....Mr J Thompson 5
811[3] Tod Law 11.4 5a *alwys bhnd, t.o. from hfwy.* ....Mr C Storey 6
1172[2] Fast Fun 11.7 7a *chsd ldrs to 7th, soon lost pl and bhnd, t.o. when p.u. before 3 out.* ....Mr R Morgan pu
947[3] Donside 12.0 *chsd ldrs till s.u. after 4th..* .Mr J Walton su
8 ran. 4l, 7l, 22l, dist, 20l. SP 4-1.
John L Holdroyd

WARWICK
Saturday May 3rd
GOOD TO FIRM

1298 2½m 110yds Willoughby de Broke Challenge Trophy Novices' Hunters' Chase

LORD KILTON 11.7 7a ....Mr M Cowley 1
keen hold early, chsd ldr, not fluent 3rd, lost tch 10th, rallied between final 2, ld run-in, ran on.
987[1] **Tom Furze 11.12 7a................Mr M Batters** 2
ld clr from 10th, in command when eased from 2 out, hdd run-in, rdn and ran on well, just failed.
2 ran. Nk. Time 5m 37.00s.
Mrs D Cowley

ALBRIGHTON
Weston Park
Saturday May 3rd
GOOD

1299 Members

1264[2] **ROLIER (IRE) ....A Dalton** 1
(fav) alwys handy, 2nd 10th, ld 5 out, sn in cmmnd, easily
850[2] **Nodforms Dilemma (USA) ...Miss K Hollinshead** 2
ld 4th-13th, chsd wnr at onepcd aft, lame
1000[6] **Glen Taylor ....Mrs M Wall** 3
ld to 3rd, 3rd & outpcd frm 5th, no dang aft
999[3] River Sunset (Ire) *alwys rear, no ch whn p.u. 4 out* ....S Prior pu
4 ran. 15l, 8l. Time 7m 14.00s. SP 1-5.
T A B Scott (Albrighton).

1300 Confined (12st)

1196[3] **JULY SCHOON ....T Underwood** 1
(fav) w.w. rear 4th, steady prog, 2nd 13th, ld aft 2 out,ran on
884[1] **Glenrowan (Ire) 3ex ....R Ford** 2
hld up, 20l bhnd 4 out, ran on wll und pres, just faild
936[1] **Miss Shaw 5a ....C Stockton** 3
mid-div 12th, prog nxt, ev ch & rdn 2 out, ran on
1175[3] Worleston Farrier 3ex *chsd ldr, ld 11th til aft 2 out, wknd apr last* ....G Hanmer 4
1174[2] Bucks Surprise *ld into start, mostly rear, nvr in race* ....D Dickinson 5
1175[2] No More The Fool *mid-div, prog 11th, mstk & wknd 5 out, p.u. 2 out* ....L Brennan pu
1178 Hyperbole *ld at strng pace to 10th, btn frm 12th, t.o. nxt, p.u. 14th* ....M Worthington pu
1175 Killatty Player (Ire) 5a 6ow *n.j.w. in tch 4 out, rdn & no rspns, 5th & p.u. last* ....A Crow pu
8 ran. ½l, ½l, dist, 4l. Time 6m 57.00s. SP 2-1.
T D B Underwood (Worcestershire).

1301 Men's Open

1176[2] **INJUNCTION (IRE) (bl)................C Stockton** 1
(fav) cls 2nd til ld 13th-2 out, reluc whn lft clr last
1123[3] **Freddie Fox ....T Garton** 2
alwys 3rd & onepcd, lft 2nd at last
937[4] **Pamela's Lad ....G Hanmer** 3
hld up rear, prog to 2nd at 14th, ld 2 out, f last,rmntd

1215 Altnabrocky *ld to 12th,3rd nxt,lost tch 4 out, no ch whn p.u. 2 out,lame* ....T Gretton pu
4 ran. 20l, dist. Time 7m 6.00s. SP Evens.
R Cowie (Cheshire Forest).

1302 Ladies

1122[1] **HORNBLOWER** ....**Mrs C Ford** **1**
(fav) chsng grp, ld 4th, unchal
1266[2] **Night Wind** ....**Mrs A Rucker** **2**
3rd, prog 4 out, ran on, not rch wnr
Fell Mist ....**Miss A Sykes** **3**
ld to 4th, chsd wnr to 4 out, wknd & onepcd nxt
Commodity Broker *alwys rear, nvr in tch wth ldng pair, ran on nr fin* ....Miss J Priest 4
202[2] Ace Player (NZ) *in tch whn f 4th* ......Miss S Beddoes f
5 ran. 6l, dist, nk. Time 6m 53.00s. SP 2-5.
N J Barrowclough (West Shropshire Draghounds).

1303 Restricted (12st)

854[1] **CHARLIESMEDARLIN** ....**R Burton** **1**
(fav) j.w. made all, sn clr, eased flat
1000[5] **Little By Little** ....**T O'Leary** **2**
prog 12th, chsd wnr 4 out, ran on onepcd
1176[3] Rinky Dinky Doo 1ow *3rd to 13th, rear whn p.u. 5 out* ....P Morris pu
1003[1] Niord *chsd wnr, mstks & tiring 4 out, p.u. 2 out* ....C Stockton pu
1178[2] Yukon Gale (Ire) *f heavily 1st*..................A Crow f
Bocock's Pride (Ire) *hrd hld in rear, lost tch 7th, blnd 12th, p.u. nxt* ....P McAllister pu
6 ran. 7l. Time 7m 5.00s. SP 1-3.
W James Morgan (Albrighton Woodland).
One fence omitted, 17 jumps.

1304 Open Maiden (12st)

1165[3] **BULADANTE (IRE)** ....**A Crow** **1**
handy, trckd ldr 12th, hrd rdn to ld last, ran on well
1050[2] **Concerto Collonges (Fr)** ....**R Ford** **2**
(fav) cls up, ld 12th, sn clr, hdd & not qckn nr fin
1179 Tbilisi *hrd hld, ld 4th til ref to race apr 8th* ..G Hanmer ref
664[4] Mophead Kelly *ld 10-12th, wknd, p.u. 15th* C Stockton pu
942 Maesgwyn Bach 5a *mid-div to hlfwy, 3rd 5 out, lost tch nxt, p.u. 3 out* ....D Sherlock pu
722[3] Must Be Murphy (Ire) *alwys rear, t.o. 5th, p.u. 10th* ....R Burton pu
1240 Faha Point (Ire) 12a *alwys rear, t.o. 11th, p.u. 15th, school*........................D Mansell pu
1179[3] My First Man *ld to 3rd, wknd rpdly 8th, p.u. 10th* ....M Worthington pu
8 ran. 1½l. Time 7m 4.00s. SP 6-1.
T D B Underwood (Garth & South Berks).
V.S.

CAMBRIDGE UNIV UNITED HUNTS
Cottenham
Saturday May 3rd
FIRM

1305 Members

1117[2] **SHAKE FIVE (IRE)** ....**S Sporborg** **1**
(fav) w.w. trckd ldr 12th,chal last,rdn & found little flat,ld fin
1279[4] **Stanwick Farlap 5a**..................**T Marks** **2**
trckd ldr, ld 7th, rdn 2 out, kpt on onepcd, hdd nr fin
1263 **Lucky Vienna 5a** ....**J Henderson** **3**
last & jmpd slwly, t.o. 11th, tk dist 3rd 3 out
1113 Salachy Run (Ire) *ran wd on bnds, ld to 7th, wknd 13th, t.o. & p.u. aft 3 out*........................N Page pu
4 ran. Nk, dist. Time 6m 15.00s. SP 4-9.
Mrs C H Sporborg (Puckeridge).

1306 Intermediate (12st)

1206[3] **MAJESTIC RIDE** ....**R Armson** **1**
mod 3rd til chsd ldr 14th,blnd 3 out,ld last,all out
1205[3] **Bervie House (Ire) 5ex** ....**R Barrett** **2**
trckd ldr, ld 9th, clr but reluc frm 12th, hdd last, rallied
1286 **Current Attraction 5a 10ow**........**Miss K Thory** **3**
made most to 9th, wknd 13th, t.o.
1117[1] Youcat (Ire) 5ex *(fav) jmpd slwly & nvr going, last frm 4th, t.o. & p.u. 13th* ....I Marsh pu
4 ran. Hd, dist. Time 6m 4.00s. SP 9-1.
Rob Woods (Cranwell Bloodhounds).

1307 Men's Open

708[2] **RIVER MELODY 5a** ....**T Moore** **1**
(fav) prssd ldr, ld 7th, clr frm 12th, easily
1115 **Cockstown Lad** ....**D Featherstone** **2**
not fluent, ld to 7th, lost tch wth wnr 12th, t.o.
2 ran. Dist. Time 6m 13.00s. SP 1-3.
T W Moore (Essex).

1308 G Middleton Ladies

1280[1] **ST GREGORY (bl)**..................**Mrs L Gibbon** **1**
(fav) made all, clr apr last, pshd out flat
1197 **Coombesbury Lane 5a**...........**Miss S Duckett** **2**
chsd wnr 10th-3 out, not qckn, ran on agn flat
1128[3] **Slight Panic 5a**..................**Miss J Wickens** **3**
chsd wnr 5th til blnd 10th,2nd agn 3 out,no imp,dmtd nr fin
1197[4] Phelioff *chsd wnr to 3rd, mstk 11th, sn lost tch* ....Miss S Dawson 4
Lewesdon Princess 5a *chsd wnr 3-5th, last frm 7th, no ch 14th* ....Miss S Gladders 5
5 ran. 2l, 1l, 15l, ¾l. Time 6m 3.00s. SP 1-4.
A Howland Jackson (Essex & Suffolk).

1309 Restricted

915[1] **ROSCOLVIN (IRE) 7a**..................**N Bloom** **1**
(fav) hld up in tch, trckd ldr 14th, ld 3 out, hrd hld
1278 **Kerry My Home** ....**T Marks** **2**
jmpd lft 1st cct, ld 10th-3 out, kpt on, no ch wth wnr
1114[3] **Aughnacloy Rose** ....**R Page** **3**
last frm 7th, t.o. 13th, tk poor 3rd apr last
1032[2] Tremeirchion *ld to 10th, 3rd & in tch whn blnd 16th, wknd rpdly* ....M Barnard 4
4 ran. Nk, 25l, 15l. Time 6m 21.00s. SP 2-7.
Mrs Julie Read (Suffolk).

1310 Open Maiden (12st)

1077 **KABANCY** ....**P Millington** **1**
(fav) plld hrd, ld 4-6th, rstrnd til ld 3 out, sn wll clr
1118 **Fragment (Ire)** ....**T Moore** **2**
set funereal pace to 4th, ld 6th-3 out, immed btn
2 ran. Dist. Time 6m 38.00s. SP 4-11.
Miss P Zygmant (Cottesmore).
J.N.

DEVEN & SOMERSET STAGHOUNDS
Holnicote
Saturday May 3rd
GOOD

1311 Members

FELLOW SIOUX ....**I Dowrick** **1**
bhnd, gd prog frm 13th, ld 3 out, shkn up flat
1245[3] **Tangle Baron** ....**Miss J Cumings** **2**
(fav) made most to 3 out, outpcd aft, kpt on und pres
Tuffnut Tom ....**J Scott** **3**
prssd ldr to 9th, bhnd frm 15th, effrt 3 out, sn wknd
1090[5] Frosty Reception *mid-div, grad fdd frm 15th* ....Miss C Stucley 4
Dollys Best 5a *bhnd frm 2nd, t.o. 10th, ran round own pace*........................Miss C Hayes 5
1261[5] Mellicometti *prom early, 3rd & losing tch whn u.r. 15th*........................Miss K Minns ur
Pipers Zeta *rear 8th, p.u. aft 14th* ....R Widger pu
7 ran. 1l, 15l, 15l, dist. Time 6m 32.00s. SP 2-1.
T B Stevens (Devon & Somerset Staghounds).

1312 Intermediate (12st)

1109[3] **THEGOOSE** .... **P King** 1
(fav) j.w. hld up in 3rd, jmpd into ld 2 out, sn clr
1156[4] **Tangle Kelly** .... **S Slade** 2
made most til outjmpd 2 out, no ch wnr aft
1245 **Charmers Wish 5a** .... **H Thomas** 3
prssd ldr til wknd frm 2 out
3 ran. 3l, 15l. Time 6m 39.00s. SP 1-3.
A Palmer (Cotley).

1313 Confined (12st)

1274 **CHIP AND RUN** .... **T Mitchell** 1
tongue-strap, trckd ldrs, clsd 12th, ld flat, ran on
1245[2] **Parditino 3ex** .... **Miss V Nicholas** 2
ld 5th-9th, ld nxt, clr whn blnd last, not rcvr, hdd flat
1258[2] **Three And A Half** .... **S Slade** 3
(fav) ld to 5th, cls up aft, no ext frm 3 out
1244 Bargain And Sale 5ex *prom, ld brfly 9-10th, lost tch 13th* .... I Dowrick 4
1157[4] The Butler *nvr nr ldrs, t.o. 10th* .... K Crook 5
1244 Life Peerage (USA) *mid div whn u.r. 3rd* .... Mrs S Barrow ur
1244 Cleasby Hill 5ex *not fluent, rmndrs 4th, bhnd frm 6th, p.u. aft 14th* .... A Honeyball pu
7 ran. 2l, 12l, dist, dist. Time 6m 22.00s. SP 9-4.
Richard Barber (Tiverton Foxhounds).
Two fences omitted, 17 jumps.

1314 Open Maiden Div I (12st)

526[2] **MAZZARD (IRE)** .... **R Treloggen** 1
(fav) rear, prog 12th, rdn last, ld nr fin
1139[2] **Mountain-Linnet** .... **T Woolridge** 2
mid-div, prog 12th, ev ch last, just outpcd nr fin
553 **Dance Fever (Ire)** .... **R Woolacott** 3
alwys prom, ld 16th til hdd & no ext aft last
485[4] Simply Joyful 5a *mid-div, prog 10th, no ext apr last* .... P King 4
1244 Fosabud *prom, ld 12th-16th, grad wknd* .... Miss L Hawkings 5
1216[6] Dula Model 5a *ld to 12th, wknd rpdly* .... J Boscherini 6
525 Princess Wenllyan 5a 8ow *sn bhnd, p.u. 10th* R Black pu
Berkley Street 5a *sn bhnd, not alwys fluent, p.u. aft 12th* .... J Tizzard pu
8 ran. Hd, 3l, 6l, 10l, dist. Time 6m 34.00s. SP 4-5.
Mrs L Treloggen (Weston & Banwell).

1315 Open Maiden Div II (12st)

1157[5] **AND WHAT ELSE (IRE)** .... **S Slade** 1
alwys prom, ld 4 out, jnd nxt, lft in ld 2 out, ran on
1245[5] **Liberty James** .... **T Greed** 2
(Jt fav) bhnd & mstks, stdy prog 3 out, no ch wnr, lft 2nd nxt
Fledermaus .... **R Widger** 3
bhnd & rdn 12th, styd on onepcd frm 3 out
1151 Millyhenry *alwys rear, some prog 13th, onepcd frm nxt* .... J Tizzard 4
1021[2] Kala Dawn 5a *ld, clr 12th, hdd 4 out, grad wknd* .... Miss M Tory 5
527 Big Arthur (Ire) *(Jt fav) ld chsng grp, chal 3 out, ran out nxt whn ev ch* .... I Dowrick ro
Sansnip *alwys rear, u.r. 16th* .... N Mitchell ur
7 ran. 20l, 4l, 2l, 6l. Time 6m 29.00s. SP 9-2.
Mrs D A Wetherall (Tiverton Foxhounds).

1316 Mixed Open (12st)

1148[3] **FOSBURY 7ex** .... **T Mitchell** 1
raced off pace, prog to ld 13th, disp aft til ld agn nr fin
1154[1] **Qualitair Memory (Ire) 7ex** .... **J Tizzard** 2
(fav) ld/disp til hdd & just outpcd flat
1025[1] **Stalbridge Gold 5a** .... **Miss A Goschen** 3
rear, prog 14th, not qckn frm 3 out
Unscrupulous Gent *ld/disp to 13th, sn lost tch, t.o.* .... Mrs E Huttinger 4
4 ran. ½l, 4l, dist. Time 6m 32.00s. SP 6-4.
Mrs Susan Humphreys (Cattistock).

1317 Restricted (12st)

1059[1] **MUSKERRY MOYA (IRE) 5a** ...... **Miss A Goschen** 1
ld, clr 13th, unchal aft
1241[4] **Remember Mac (bl)** .... **Miss C Hayes** 2
bhnd, rpd prog 12th, styd prom til no ext frm 16th
1035[1] **Carrarea (Ire)** .... **Miss J Cumings** 3
(fav) ld/disp frm 2nd til ld 9th, hdd 12th, lost tch rpdly
1043 Lake Mariner 5a *sn bhnd, t.o. 2nd, some prog whn u.r. 2 out* .... M Wells ur
806 Baywyn 5a *bhnd frm 4th, p.u. aft 14th* .... S Slade pu
5 ran. 15l, dist. Time 6m 40.00s. SP 6-4.
N W Rimington (Blackmore & Sparkford Vale).
P.Ho.

GELLIGAER FARMERS
Bonvilston
Saturday May 3rd
GOOD

1318 Members (12st)

1134 **LIGHTEN THE LOAD** .... **J Jukes** 1
(fav) rear & rmndrs hlfwy, 30l last 4 out, hrd rdn nxt, ld flat
404 **Bay Leader 5a** .... **Miss E Tamplin** 2
mid-div, rpd prog to ld 2 out, hdd & no ext flat
543[1] **She Goes 5a** .... **A Price** 3
hld up mid-div, prog 14th, ev ch 2 out, onepcd
1067[1] Prince Itsu *trckd ldrs, ld 3 out, blnd nxt, not rcvr* .... D Stephens 4
1007 Young India 5a *rear til p.u. 13th* .... T Vaughan pu
Martiya 5a *rear til p.u. 12th* .... Miss P Cooper pu
1133 Icecapade (Bel) *prom early, lost plc hlfwy, p.u. 2 out* .... Miss E Jones pu
1132[4] Princess Lu (Ire) *lft in ld 7th, hdd 3 out, wknd rpdly, p.u. last* .... S Shinton pu
1229 Stiff Drink *ld til ran out apr 7th* .... J Cook ro
9 ran. 1½l, dist, 10l. Time 6m 22.00s. SP 4-5.
J S Payne (Gelligaer).

1319 Intermediate (12st)

403[2] **SHUIL'S STAR (IRE)** .... **P Hamer** 1
mostly 3rd/4th, prog 3 out, ld last, qcknd flat
1228[2] **Gunner Boon 5ex** .... **Miss P Jones** 2
(fav) chsd ldr, ld 2 out, hdd last, outpcd flat
1228[3] **Ideal** .... **Miss C Thomas** 3
ld to 2 out, styd on onepcd
1224[2] Polly Pringle 5a 5ex *nvr bynd mid-div, no dang* .... A Price 4
1185[3] Saffron Moss *twrds rear, rmndrs 12th, no prog aft* .... J Price 5
1132[6] Guarena (USA) *rear & rmndrs hlfwy, t.o. & p.u. 2 out* .... Miss N Richards pu
1135 West King *mid-div, f 5th* .... J P Keen f
1196[1] How Friendly 5ex *mid-div, prog to 4th at 12th, wknd & p.u. last* .... M Rimell pu
8 ran. 2½l, 4l, 10l, 20l. Time 6m 9.00s. SP 5-2.
R Mason (Carmarthen).
Open ditch omitted from this race on. 16 jumps per race.

1320 Confined (12st)

1223[3] **HUGLI** .... **D S Jones** 1
(Jt fav) cls up, ld 9th-11th, ld 3 out, qcknd clr
1223[2] **Beinn Mohr 5a 3ex** .... **E Williams** 2
hld up mid-div, prog 12th, ev ch 3 out, hrd rdn flat, onepcd
1225[3] **Bartondale 5a** .... **Miss B Williams** 3
rear, prog hlfwy, ld 12th-nxt, styd on onepcd
1194[4] Wake Up Luv 5ex *ld 6th-8th, chsd ldrs aft, no prog 3 out* .... Miss P Cooper 4
Harken Premier *rear til p.u. 2 out* .... A Price pu
Ruffinswick *last til p.u. 10th* .... J Price pu
1063[9] Sandy Beau *rear til p.u. 11th* .... M Rimell pu

399[4] Warren Boy *(Jt fav) ld to 5th, grad lost tch, p.u. 2 out* ....Miss P Jones pu
8 ran. 12l, ½l, dist. Time 6m 7.00s. SP 3-1.
G Hearse (Llangeinor).

1321 Mixed Open (12st)

1223[1] **CARRICK LANES ....Miss P Jones 1**
(fav) mid-div, rmndrs 12th, prog 3 out, ld nxt, ran on well
713[1] **Fly Fred ....S Lloyd 2**
2nd til lft in ld 7th-12th, styd on onepcd
1211 **Prince Nepal ....S Shinton 3**
cls up, ld 13th til hdd 2 out, wknd rpdly
1196[4] January Don (bl) *rear & rdn alng, not trbl ldrs* ....G Barfoot-Saunt 4
1134 Project's Mate (bl) *nvr bynd mid-div, no dang* ....Miss N Richards 5
1226 Gold Diver *ld to 5th, wknd & p.u. 3 out* Miss P Gundry pu
1063[6] Air Commander *rear whn s.u. flat aft 6th* ....Miss D Olding su
1224 Scared Stiff 5a *rear whn s.u. flat aft 6th* ....E Roberts su
1226 Olde Crescent *ld 6th til ran out nxt, rjnd, p.u. 9th* ....J Comins pu
Pretoria Dancer 7a *mid-div, rmndrs hlfwy, wknd & p.u. 2 out* ....M Rimell pu
10 ran. 5l, 25l, 5l, dist. Time 6m 15.00s. SP 4-9.
David Brace (Llangeinor).

1322 Restricted (12st)

1131[1] **BOX OF DELIGHTS ....E Williams 1**
rear, prog to 4th hlfwy, chsd ldr 13th, ld 3 out, sn clr
1183[1] **A Few Dollars More (Ire) ....M Rimell 2D**
prom, ld 9th-apr 13th, onepcd aft, fin 2nd, disq
1137[1] **Khandys Slave (Ire) 5a ....Miss P Jones 2**
ld to 8th, grad wknd, no ch frm 13th, fin 3rd, plcd 2nd
1135[7] **Yarron King ....I Johnson 3**
rear, some late prog, no dang, fin 4th, plcd 3rd
1009[1] Lennie The Lion *rear, no prog frm hlfwy* ....J Price 5
1065[1] Rose Of Macmillion 5a *last early, some prog 7th, p.u. 12th* ....A Price pu
404[2] Inch Empress (Ire) *(fav) 2s-1/1, mid-div, blnd 8th, p.u. 11th* ....J Jukes pu
1227 Jolly Swagman *prom,3rd at 9th, ld apr 13th, hdd nxt,poor 4th & p.u.flat* ....D S Jones pu
1131[2] Kristal Haze 12a *rear, p.u. 11th* ....P Williams pu
9 ran. Dist, 5l, 10l, 5l. Time 6m 7.00s. SP 3-1.
Mrs Jeanne Thomas (Pentyrch).
A Few Dollars More disq, not W/I. Original distances.

1323 Open Maiden Div I

KINGUSSIE FLOWER 12a....M Rimell 1
prom, ld 4 out, qcknd clr 2 out
1230[2] **Boddington Hill 5a ....I Johnson 2**
cls up, ld 11th-4 out, styd on onepcd
1137 **Lady Romance (Ire) 5a ....S Shinton 3**
cls up, lost plc hlfwy, lft 3rd by dfctns
1136 Queen's Equa 5a *10s-6s, rear, prog hlfwy, nrst fin* ....Miss S Major 4
1229 Mo's Keliro 12a *rear, styd on onepcd frm 3 out* ....Miss A Meakins 5
1138 Red Rhapsody 5a *nvr bynd mid-div, no dang* ....J Comins 6
1137 Mississippisteamer (Ire) *mid-div early, lost tch whn p.u. 2 out* ....D S Jones pu
1137 Penylan Gold 5a (bl) *prom to 7th, wknd rpdly, p.u. 11th* ....P Williams pu
1216[5] Le Vienna (Ire) *last til p.u. 2 out* ....S Currey pu
841[3] Lady Orr (Ire) 5a *rear til p.u. 2 out* ....J Tudor pu
1183 Lynnes Daniella (Ire) 5a (bl) *mid-div, p.u. 7th* J P Keen pu
1010 Out On The Town 5a *mid-div, wknd & p.u. 2 out* ....E Williams pu
541 Castlemorris (Ire) *(fav) ld to 11th, 3rd aft til blnd 3 out, p.u. nxt* ....J Jukes pu
1136[4] Rebel Yell (Ire) 5a *rear til p.u. 3 out* ....K Cousins pu
14 ran. 10l, 30l, 15l, 10l, dist. Time 6m 22.00s. SP 4-1.
Mrs Vanessa Ramm (Cotswold).

1324 Open Maiden Div II

1137[2] **MR FFITCH ....G Barfoot-Saunt 1**
5s-3s, chsd ldrs, ran on frm 2 out, ld flat
1138[3] **Final Option (Ire) ....I Johnson 2**
prom, ld 13th til hdd & no ext flat
1138[5] **Greenfield Maid (Ire) 5a ....D S Jones 3**
prom, lost tch hlfwy, lft 3rd by dfctns
1229 Priesthill (Ire) *hld up mid-div, prog to 2nd at 11th, sn lost tch* ....D Stephens 4
908 Al Billal *rear, p.u. 2 out* ....Miss P Cooper pu
Red Neck *rear til p.u. 2 out* ....A Price pu
1011 Toucher (Ire) *rear, p.u. 10th* ....J Cook pu
1230 Dragonara Lad (Ire) 7a *ld to 11th, wknd rpdly, p.u. nxt* ....J Tudor pu
1200 The Blind Judge *alwys rear, p.u. 12th* ....G Lewis pu
1131[4] Its A Doddle 5a *rear, p.u. 2 out* ....Miss A Meakins pu
1229 Bickerton Poacher *mid-div, prog 4 out, cls 3rd whn f last* ....G Perkins f
407 Bonus Number (Ire) *rear, p.u. 10th* ....K Cousins pu
1186[2] Nadanny (Ire) *(fav) cls up, ld 12th, hdd nxt, lsng tch & p.u. 2 out* ....J Jukes pu
1136 Flockmaster (Ire) *rear til p.u. 13th* ....S Shinton pu
1231 Lizzie Boon 12a *rear, f 6th* ....J Price f
1240 Miss Panoo 5a *rear, p.u. 9th* ....M Rimell pu
16 ran. 1½l, dist, dist. Time 6m 29.00s. SP 3-1.
M Howells (Tredegar Farmers).
J.C./P.H.

HARKAWAY CLUB
Chaddesley Corbett
Saturday May 3rd
GOOD TO FIRM

1325 Members

1233 **PENLLYNE'S PRIDE ....J Chilton 1**
walked over
J S Chilton (North Shropshire).

1326 Restricted

1165[1] **ROMAN ROMANY ....Julian Pritchard 1**
(fav) made all,hit 1st,slw jmp 4th,in cmmnd whn blnd last,drvn out
1129[2] **King Of The Clouds ....J Hammond 2**
chsd wnr 3-5th & agn 7th, lft ev ch last, onepcd
1145[4] Members Rights 5a *chsd wnr til blnd 3rd & agn 5-7th,mstk 10th,sn bhnd,u.r.14th* ....M Keel ur
3 ran. 1l. Time 6m 14.00s. SP 4-7.
D R E Bevan (North Cotswold).

1327 G Middleton Ladies

1062[2] **DOWN THE MINE ....Miss A Dare 1**
(fav) ld 3rd, made rest, 4l clr 4 out, comf
1148[2] **Mister Gebo ....Miss C Dyson 2**
ld to 3rd, prssd wnr til 15th, onepcd aft
1147[5] **Minella Express (Ire) ....Miss C Spearing 3**
alwys 3rd, hit 4th & 15th, effrt apr 3 out, no prog nxt
3 ran. 4l, 10l. Time 6m 9.00s. SP 4-6.
R T Baimbridge (Berkeley).

1328 Men's Open

1145[1] **STAG FIGHT ....Julian Pritchard 1**
(fav) disp til ld 3rd, 4l clr 4 out, rdn nxt,drvn out,dsmntd aft
1014 **Garrylucas ....A Dalton 2**
disp til blnd 3rd, hit 12th, rdn apr 3 out, no real imp
2 ran. 3l. Time 6m 21.00s. SP 1-3.
Mrs J A Scott (Worcestershire).

1329 Confined (12st)

1146[5] **TYTHERINGTON ....Miss S Talbot 1**
prssd ldr to 10th,last 12th,lft poor 2nd 3 out,lft solo nxt
1212[2] **Lets Twist Again (Ire) 3ex ....Julian Pritchard 2**

(fav) w.w. went 2nd 12th, pshd alng nxt,jnd ldr 4 out,f nxt,rmntd
1195[1] Bumptious Boy *disp til ld 4th,clr 11th,jnd & lft clr 3 out,blnd & u.r. nxt* ....S Hanks ur
1146[3] Hook Line'N'sinker *4th whn blnd & u.r. 3rd*...L Brown ur
1175[1] Mr Wilbur 3ex *hld up, prog whn f 11th*......A Dalton f
5 ran. Dist. Time 6m 24.00s. SP 66-1.
Miss S H Talbot (Albrighton Woodland).

1330 Maiden (12st)

1019[2] **DANTE'S PRIDE (IRE)**...............**Miss A Dare** 1
(fav) chsd ldr, ld 11th, made rest, lft wll clr last
1216 **Royal Swinger 5a**................**Miss S Trotman** 2
raced freely,prom,blnd 6th,sn bhnd, went poor 3rd 12th,t.o.
1209[5] Crestwood Lad (USA) 4ow *ld to 11th, chal wnr apr 3 out, 1l down whn blnd & u.r. last*...........M Yardley ur
1240 Asante Sana 5a (bl) *hld up, lft 3rd 6th, lost tch 11th, reluc aft, p.u. 3 out*.....N Oliver pu
1216 Royal Sweep *hld up, 5th whn blnd & u.r. 3rd* ....C Dorrington ur
1145[2] Mr Dennehy (Ire) *in tch whn s.u. aft 6th* ....M Butcher su
6 ran. Bad. Time 6m 23.00s. SP 1-2.
G J Fisher (Berkeley).
S.P.

LAUDERDALE
Mosshouses
Saturday May 3rd
FIRM

1331 Members

THE ODIN LINE (IRE)....................**W Kerr** 1
made all, drew clr frm 11th, v easily
995[4] **Flypie**..........................**P Strang Steel** 2
(fav) went 2nd at 10th, grad lost tch frm nxt
814 Saigon Lady (Ire) 5a *cls 3rd whn f 11th*.....M Ruddy f
More Banter *2nd til 10th, sn strgglng, t.o. & p.u. aft 12th*....G Barr pu
Armet Prince *last whn ref 2nd*..............J Dunn ref
5 ran. Dist. Time 6m 47.00s. SP 9-4.
W Kerr (Lauderdale).

1332 Intermediate (12st)

1050[1] **BITOFANATTER**......................**R Morgan** 1
(fav) made all, drew wll clr frm 2 out
1221[1] **Jolly Fellow**.......................**Miss S Ward** 2
hld up, went 2nd 13th, outpcd frm 2 out
944[3] **Thinkaboutthat (Ire) 2ow**................**J Muir** 3
2nd til 13th, sn btn
1169 Panto Lady 5a *3rd to 6th, t.o. 12th, p.u. 2 out* ....Miss S Lamb pu
4 ran. Dist, 6l. Time 6m 37.00s. SP 4-7.
David Caldwell (Eglinton).

1333 Ladies

811[1] **WIGTOWN BAY**.................**Miss N Stirling** 1
(fav) slght ld virt thro'out, styd on gamely
1171[2] **Schweppes Tonic**................**Mrs V Jackson** 2
trckd wnr, ld brfly aft 3 out, mstk last, no ext
2 ran. 2l. Time 6m 48.00s. SP 4-5.
Mrs P C Stirling (Fife).

1334 Restricted (12st)

1218[3] **FUNNY FEELINGS**....................**C Storey** 1
(fav) alwys cls up, mstk 7th, ld 3 out, just hld on
997[1] **Houselope Brook 5a 5ow**...............**J Walton** 2
mostly 2nd frm 11th, kpt on wll flat, just faild
Mini Cruise.............................**T Scott** 3
ld til wknd 3 out
338 Sarona Smith 5a 7ow *sn rear, t.o. 9th, p.u. aft 12th* ....J Hutchinson pu
729[5] Wang How *hld up in tch, chal 2 out, disp 2nd & hld whn f last*....A Robson f
5 ran. ½l, dist. Time 6m 39.00s. SP 5-4.
Mrs J R Scott (College Valley & N N'land).

1335 Men's Open (12st)

946[2] **STAIGUE FORT (IRE) 7ex**..............**H Norton** 1
ld to 4th, made most frm 7th, kpt on wll flat
1220[2] **Tartan Tornado 7ex**..................**P Johnson** 2
sn bhnd, went 2nd 14th, chal 3 out, outpcd apr last
1168[1] **Winnie Lorraine 5a 7ex**................**T Scott** 3
(fav) went 2nd 9th, ld brfly 11th, wknd 3 out
1052 New Problem 5a *ld 4th-7th, wknd rpdly 11th, p.u. aft nxt*....M Smith pu
4 ran. 3l, dist. Time 6m 30.00s. SP 7-4.
T R P S Norton (College Valley & N N'land).

1336 Open Maiden Div I (12st)

996 **ANOTHER ISLAY**......................**R Morgan** 1
alwys 1st trio, went 2nd 3 out, ld apr last, comf
1222 **Tantalum 5a**.............................**T Scott** 2
alwys 1st trio, ld 13th til apr last, no ext
1222[3] **Rallying Cry (Ire)**....................**D McLeod** 3
(fav) not alwys fluent, some prog frm 3 out, not rch ldng pair
996 Saucy Mint 5a *made most til 13th, no ext frm 3 out* ....C Storey 4
814 Copper Dial *t.o. frm 7th*..................J Ewart 5
1172[4] Billy Buoyant *sn bhnd, p.u. aft 11th*........J Walton pu
1222 Singing Profit 12a *sn bhnd, 15l 4th at 9th, nvr rchd ldrs, p.u. 2 out*.....Mrs V Jackson pu
7 ran. 4l, 6l, 1l, dist. Time 6m 47.00s. SP 3-1.
P Forster & D Scott (Haydon).

1337 Open Maiden Div II (12st)

1052[2] **DILLONS BRIDGE (IRE)**...............**R Morgan** 1
(fav) hdl up in tch, hrd rdn 3 out, ld apr last, all out
1050 **Madame Beck 5a**......................**M Smith** 2
alwys handy, made most frm 13th til hdd apr last
1172[3] **Tolmin (bl)**............................**A Parker** 3
made most to 9th, hrd rdn to sty in tch, no ext frm 2 out
234[6] Sagaro Belle 5a *ld 9th-13th, wknd apr 2 out*...T Scott 4
Polly's Lady 5a *bhnd frm 4th, t.o.*..........T Morrison 5
Halls Burn *jmpd violently rght 1st, out of control, p.u. 5th*....M Ruddy pu
Alsina *forced wd & p.u. aft 1st*........Miss S Forster pu
7 ran. 3l, 10l, 4l, dist. Time 6m 43.00s. SP 4-5.
Mrs M Armstrong (Tynedale).
R.J.

MODBURY HARRIERS
Flete Park
Saturday May 3rd
GOOD

1338 Members

1111[2] **IT'S NOT MY FAULT (IRE)**.........**Miss S Vickery** 1
walked over
P D Jones (Modbury Harriers).

1339 Restricted (12st)

1112[1] **ESERIE DE CORES (USA)**............**S Kidston** 1
(fav) handy, ld 13th, styd on strngly
1107[2] **Rosa's Revenge 5a (bl)**...............**G Shenkin** 2
raced wd, cls 2nd mstly, fdd frm 2 out
1108[3] **Probation**..............................**R Darke** 3
slght ld to 13th, lost tch steadily frm 15th
Newski Express 5a *blnd 2nd, prog 13th, cls up til wknd 3 out, p.u. nxt*.....L Jefford pu
1245 Medias Maid 5a (bl) *not fluent, lost tch 12th, p.u. apr 3 out*....A Holdsworth pu
1108[4] Mosside *mstk & lost plc 12th, t.o. & p.u. 15th* N Harris pu
6 ran. 10l, 15l. Time 6m 43.50s. SP 2-1.
F R Bown (Lamerton).

1340 4m Ladies

790[3] **CELTIC SPORT (bl)** .... **Miss T Cave** 1
made all in 4/5l ld, styd on gamely
1109[1] **Nearly Splendid** .... **Miss L Blackford** 2
(fav) chsd wnr, ev ch til no ext 2 out, fin tired
1109[2] **First Design** .... **Miss S Vickery** 3
trckd ldrs in 3rd, lost tch frm 19th
1155[4] Reef Lark 2ow *mostly 4th, lost tch 19th* Miss O Green 4
529[1] Just Bert (Ire) *bhnd frm 12th, f 17th* ..... Miss S Young f
5 ran. 12l, 25l, 8l. Time 7m 56.00s. SP 5-1.
Mrs A C Martin (Tiverton Foxhounds).

1341 Men's Open (12st)

1089[2] **THE GOLFING CURATE** .... **A Michael** 1
steady prog 14th, chsd ldr 16th, lft in ld last
628[1] **Kaloore (bl)** .... **R Nuttall** 2
sn rear, alwys bhnd, lft 2nd last
1243[4] **Baldhu Chance** .... **J Young** 3
ld/disp to 10th, sn wknd, t.o. 3 out
738 Cardinal Bird (USA) (v) *ref 2nd* .... T Cole ref
1243[1] Butler John (Ire) *(fav) prom, ld 10th, 5l clr but und pres whn f last* .... N Harris f
5 ran. 12l, 20l. Time 6m 39.00s. SP 14-1.
T Wheeler & J Turner (Quantock Staghounds).

1342 Confined (12st)

1256[3] **JUST MY BILL** .... **C Heard** 1
ld/disp 10th til slght ld 3 out, drew clr und pres nxt
1033[1] **Myhamet 9ex** .... **N Harris** 2
(fav) hld up in tch, prog 16th, ev ch til no ext 2 out
1111[1] **Catch The Cross 3ex (bl)** .... **Miss S Vickery** 3
ld/disp to 3 out, cls up til onepcd aft nxt
1255[3] Christmas Hols *wll in tch til wknd 14th, t.o. 16th* .... Miss K Baily 4
1112[4] Corrib Haven (Ire) *f 1st* .... Miss L Blackford f
1258 Karicleigh Boy *ld/disp til aft 3 out, wknd nxt, lost tack & p.u. last* .... A Holdsworth pu
6 ran. 4l, 6l, 30l. Time 6m 47.00s. SP 7-2.
Mrs K Heard (North Cornwall).
Two fences omitted this race, 18 jumps.

1343 Open Maiden (12st)

741[2] **SHAMELESS LADY 5a** .... **R Darke** 1
(fav) hld up in tch, ld 11th, styd on wll clsng stgs
1093 **Uncle James (Ire)** .... **M Frith** 2
gd prog 15th, went 2nd 3 out, ev ch nxt, not qckn, prmsng
1112 **Happy Valley 5a** .... **Miss P Baker** 3
in tch, mstk 12th, 4th whn hit 3 out, onepcd
1261 Call Me Dickins (bl) *not alwys fluent, lft in ld aft 6th, hdd 11th, lost tch 4out* .... Miss A Barnett 4
1108[7] Kanha 12a *6th hlfwy, not rch ldrs* .... A O'Connor 5
1109[7] Crownhill Cross *prog to 2nd at 10th, cls up & ev ch til wknd apr 2 out* .... S Kidston 6
1110 Stony Missile 5a *5th hlfwy, wknd 15th, t.o.* .... Miss W Hartnoll 7
741[4] Princess Polly 5a *mid-div, bhnd whn p.u. apr 2 out* .... I Widdicombe pu
1269 Brooklyn Express 5a *rear, t.o. & p.u. 12th* .... S Parfimowicz pu
1242 Luney River 5a *keen hld, ld til p.u. aft 6th* .... Miss L Long pu
461[4] Contradict *mid-div whn u.r. 10th* .... A Moir ur
Roving Gypsy 12a *sn rear, bhnd whn p.u. 12th* .... A Holdsworth pu
1035 Gaysun 7a *sn twrds rear, t.o. & p.u. 16th* ..... N Harris pu
13 ran. 2½l, 15l, 8l, 2½l, 3l, 15l. Time 6m 57.00s. SP 5-2.
R Darke (Dart Vale & South Pool).
G.T.

PENDLE FOREST & CRAVEN
Gisburn
Saturday May 3rd
GOOD TO FIRM

1344 Members

1072 **SYRUS P TURNTABLE** .... **J Saville** 1
ld to 7th, cls up til wknd 14th, lft clr 16th, fin tired
Alex-Path .... **T Whittaker** 2
rear, t.o. 13th, lft 2nd 16th, plodded on
1070[3] Mr Primetime (Ire) *(fav) ld 7th, clr 14th, dist up whn ref & u.r. 16th* .... N Bannister ref
3 ran. 12l. Time 7m 48.00s. SP 4-1.
Miss P Fitton (Pendle Forest & Craven).

1345 P P O R A Maiden

1173[3] **MISS ACCOUNTS (IRE) 5a** ...... **Miss A Armitage** 1
hld up, prog 10th, ld aft 2 out, styd on well
1268[3] **Educate Me (Ire)** .... **J Burley** 2
cls up, ld 3 out til apr last, outpcd
1104[3] **Level Vibes** .... **R Abrahams** 3
ld 5th-15th, no ext
1252[6] Ski Lady 5a *mid-div, nvr trbld ldrs* ..... Miss L Horner 4
1252[5] Fair Grand (bl) *rear, nvr bynd mid-div* .... S Brisby 5
1173 Browlea Lyndene 5a *cls up to 12th, wknd rpdly, p.u. 15th* .... J Barlow pu
1179 Two Gents *alwys last trio, p.u. 15th* .... C Barlow pu
1250 Bunny Hare (Ire) *alwys bhnd, rear whn c.o. 12th* .... G Thomas co
1069[2] Smashing View *nvr bynd mid-div, wll btn 4th whn ran out wing last* .... R Hartley ro
1003[5] King Edward (Ire) *ldng grp, wknd 14th, p.u. 16th* .... D Barlow pu
509 War Horse *alwys rear, p.u. 13th* .... A Ogden pu
763[2] Romiley Mill *(fav) ld to 5th, cls 2nd whn u.r. nxt* .... D Coates ur
898 True Censation 5a *rear whn f 6th* .... J Saville f
13 ran. 4l, 30l, 6l, 25l. Time 7m 18.00s. SP 12-1.
Richard P Watts (Staintondale).

1346 G Middleton Ladies

1201 **THANK U JIM** .... **Miss T Jackson** 1
made all, clr aft 2 out, easily
1102 **Across The Lake (v)** .... **Miss S Brotherton** 2
chsd wnr to 7th, 3rd aft til lft 2nd 2 out
1249 Crocket Lass 5a *alwys rear, mstk & u.r.aft 6th* .... Miss F Hunter ur
1072[3] Final Hope (Ire) *(fav) not fluent,cls 2nd 7th-2 out,wknd rpdly,p.u. last,lame* .... Mrs F Needham pu
114[5] Blacon Point *rear, t.o. 12th, p.u. 14th* .... Miss S Swindells pu
5 ran. 15l. Time 7m 18.00s. SP 7-4.
Mrs G Sunter (Cleveland).

1347 Men's Open (12st)

1123[1] **MR TITTLE TATTLE 7ex (bl)** .... **D Barlow** 1
made all, hld on wll whn chal flat
1248[1] **Peanuts Pet 7ex** .... **R Walmsley** 2
(fav) alwys cls up, 2nd 12th, ev ch & rdn apr last, not qckn
1000[1] **Bubble N Squeek** .... **C Barlow** 3
chsd wnr til wknd 15th, slw jmp 2 out
1264 Formal *mid-div, nvr trbld ldrs* .... R Owen 4
1001[1] Spy's Delight 7ex *alwys mid-div, nvr dang* .. N Rayner 5
1070[6] Dalmore *in tch, 4l 3rd at 14th, wknd rpdly* ... D Coates 6
1122 Running Frau 5a *bhnd, some prog 12th, wknd 15th* .... G Thomas 7
1253[4] The Chap *alwys rear, wknd 12th, p.u. 15th* .... R Lochman pu
8 ran. Hd, 20l, nk, 8l, 2l, 3l. Time 7m 12.00s. SP 3-1.
H A Shone (Cheshire).

1348 Interlink Restricted

1250 **DUBLIN HILL (IRE)** .... **A Bonson** 1
hld up, ld 14th, styd on wll whn chal apr last
1250[9] **Cookie Boy** .... **Miss H Delahooke** 2
cls up, ld 12th-nxt, ev ch last, no ext
1250 **Lyningo** .... **S Brisby** 3
chsng ldrs, ev ch 12th, no dang to 1st pair aft
1250 Midge 5a *cls up to 13th, wknd aft* .. Miss S Brotherton 4
1074[4] Primitive Way 7a *alwys bhnd, nvr trbld ldrs* .... P Atkinson 5
1237 Autumn Green (Ire) *(fav) chsng grp, n.j.w. blnd 8th & 12th, sn rear* .... D Coates 6

1250 Not The Nadger *ld to 6th, wknd 12th, p.u. 15th, lame* ....A Ogden pu
1252 Markham Lad *alwys rear, t.o. 5th, p.u. 9th* D Pritchard pu
1101[6] Attle *wth ldrs whn u.r. 5th* ....W Burnell ur
1106[1] Last Option 7a *cls up, ld 6th-8th, cls 2nd & ev ch whn f 3 out*....Mrs F Needham f
10 ran. 2½l, 8l, 5l, 25l, 5l. Time 7m 19.00s. SP 7-1.
R H Knowles (Middleton).

1349 Confined (12st)

1072[7] **COT LANE 3ex (bl) ....J Tate 1**
(fav) ld 5-12th, ld 14th-nxt, ld agn 2 out, styd on well last
1248 **No More Trix ....W Burnell 2**
mid-div, prog 14th, strng chal aft 2 out, outpcd aft
1120[1] **Royle Burchlin 3ex (bl)....D Barlow 3**
ld to 5th & 12th-14th, ld 16th, hdd & wknd nxt
1001 Charlie Chalk 3ex *mid-div, lost plc 14th, 7th 3 out, styd on onepcd nxt* ....I Wynne 4
852[3] Daphni (Fr) *chsng ldrs, 5l 4th at 13th, fdd* ....Miss K Swindells 5
618 Inconclusive *mid-div, rdn 12th, nvr dang* ....A Ogden 6
1104[2] Douce Indienne 5a (bl) *mid-div, 4l 3rd at 14th, wknd rpdly aft*....Miss J Eastwood 7
1121[2] Barkin 3ex *rear, t.o. 5th, slw jmp 13th, blkd & u.r. nxt* ....P Saville ur
1175[4] JJ's Hope *chsd ldrs, 7l 5th at 12th, rmndrs 14th, btn 6th & p.u. 16th*....Miss J Penney pu
1121[3] Shuil Saor *alwys rear, nvr trbld ldrs, p.u. 3 out* ....J Saville pu
998[3] Flinters (bl) *alwys last trio, t.o. 8th, p.u. 14th* C Barlow pu
11 ran. 6l, 4l, 15l, 4l, 5l, ¾l. Time 7m 8.00s. SP 5-2.
T P Tate (Bramham Moor).
R.A.

FERNIE
Dingley
Sunday May 4th
GOOD

1350 Members

1205[1] **STAR TRAVELLER ....M Skinner 1**
(fav) rcd wd, disp to 4th, lft 2nd 12th, lft wll clr 15th
Harlequin Jack ....P Hutchinson 2
jnd ldrs 10th,wknd 12th,lft poor 2nd 15th,ref last,cont
1077[7] Pancratic *disp til ld 4th, 4l clr whn f 12th*. .C Millington f
1083 Grange Missile 5a *hit 3rd,wnt 2nd 9th,lft in ld 12th,clr whn blnd & u.r. 15th* ....J Dillon ur
1160 Menature (Ire) *cls up til blnd & u.r. 6th*. . .J Seth-Smith ur
5 ran. Dist. Time 7m 14.00s. SP 2-5.
Miss E M Powell (Fernie).

1351 Confined (12st)

887[2] **MERLYNS CHOICE ....A Woodward 1**
bhnd, wnt mod 3rd 12th, styd on to ld apr last, sn drew clr
1164[1] **Brown Baby 5a....G Kerr 2**
ld 4th, hdd aft 11th, lft clr nxt, hdd apr last, no ext
1205[5] Kemys Commander *ld 1st, last frm 5th til p.u. 8th* ....G Smith pu
1205 Miller's Chap *ld 2nd-4th, disp 2nd whn f 8th*. .M Hewitt f
1077 Harmony Walk (Ire) *rear, mod 3rd & rddn 10th, t.o. & p.u. 15th*....R Armson pu
851 Specialarrangement (Ire) 3ex *(fav) chsd ldrs,ld aft 11th,slppd & hdd nxt,wknd 3 out,p.u.last* ....A Hill pu
1190[6] Scraptastic *rcd wd, chsd ldrs til f 4th*....N Bell f
7 ran. 5l. Time 6m 46.00s. SP 3-1.
A Woodward (South Nottinghamshire).

1352 2½m Open Maiden (5-7yo) Div I

DAYTIME DAWN (IRE) ....S Morris 1+
ld to 11th agn 13th, lft clr 3 out, rddn last, cght nr fin
1081 **FEARLESS BERTIE ....A Charles-Jones 1+**
rear, pshd alng 9th, outpcd 11th, wnt 2nd 2 out, ld nr fin
990[5] **Village Remedy 5a ....A Tutton 3**
prom, disp ld 8-10th, wknd 12th, lft poor 3rd last
853 Ri Ra 5a *chsd ldrs, blnd 4th, strggIng whn blnd & u.r. 12th*....Miss S Sharratt ur
1262 Springfield Rex *(fav) chsd ldrs, blnd 11th,lft 2nd & blnd 3 out,btn nxt,p.u. last*....K Needham pu
1084 Half A Chance *wth ldrs to 7th, wknng whn hit 9th, p.u. aft*....T Marks pu
Fawsley Manor 5a *prog 9th, ld 11th, pkd nxt, hdd 13th, ev ch whn f 3 out*....J Docker f
1082 Right Well (Ire) 7a *alwys rear, t.o. & p.u. apr 11th* ....E Andrewes pu
Tonto Mactavish 7a *j.v.s., sn t.o., ref 4th thrice* ....G Maloney ref
9 ran. Dd-ht, 12l. Time 5m 46.00s. SP 4-1.
R Wale/ Miss J Johnston (Pytchley/N. Cotswold).
S.P. of Fearless Bertie 8/1.

1353 2½m Open Maiden (5-7yo) Div II

1081 **THE REBEL PARISH (IRE) ....Mrs J Dawson 1**
(fav) ld til blnd & hdd 12th, ld agn 3 out, styd on strngly
1262[3] **Auntie Chris 5a....P Gee 2**
chsd ldr 3rd, ld 12th-3 out, rddn & onepcd aft
1209 **Highfurlong (Ire) ....Miss H Irving 3**
chsd ldrs til 3rd & outpcd frm 12th
498[2] Fighting For Good (Ire) *chsd ldrs til 4th & wknng 12th, t.o. 2 out*....L Lay 4
1278 Secret Music (bl) *mstk 2nd, prom til f 11th* ....Capt D Parker f
928 Flying Linnet 5a *mstk 4th, jnd ldrs 7th, p.u. qckly 12th, (lame)*....T Lane pu
373 Broad-Thorne *alwys bhnd, p.u. 9th, (lame)* ....John Pritchard pu
1281[4] Top Odder (Ire) 7a *hld up, mstk 8th, outpcd 11th, last whn f 3 out* ....P Millington f
1209 Krisan 5a *in tch, blnd 10th, last aft, t.o. & p.u. 2 out* ....R Armson pu
9 ran. 5l, 25l, 20l. Time 5m 52.00s. SP 5-2.
Mrs E W Wilson (Brocklesby).

1354 Mixed Open (12st)

1079[3] **MISTER MAIN MAN (IRE) ....S Sporborg 1**
made all, 5l clr 2 out, rddn out
758[2] **Grecian Lark ....G Tarry 2**
(fav) w.w., chsd ldr 14th, sn rddn alng, not pce to chal
302 **Alansford ....P Bull 3**
mstk 6th, chsd ldr til blnd 14th, sn outpcd
3 ran. 4l, dist. Time 6m 47.00s. SP 6-4.
Sir Chippendale Keswick (Puckeridge).

1355 Interlink Restricted

928[1] **GOLDEN STAR (IRE) ....Maj M Watson 1**
chsd ldrs, ld 12th, rddn & styd on wll frm 2 out
1276[1] **Rough Edge ....W Wales 2**
w.w., mstk 6th, prog 8th, ev ch 2 out, unable to qckn last
1081 **Rakish Queen 5a ....Miss H Phizacklea 3**
rcd wd, prog 10th, chsd ldng pr 3 out, no prog aft
1083[1] Dolly Bloom 5a *(fav) chsd ldrs, blnd 15th, 4th & rddn 3 out, sn btn* ....A Sansome 4
1191[4] Forward View *prom til p.u. 8th (lame)*....P Hutchinson pu
1193[1] Full Song 5a (bl) *ld, clr 2nd, rddn & reluc 10th, hdd 12th, wknd, p.u. 14th*....S Morris pu
1204[4] Smart Rhythm 5a *chsd ldrs to 7th, last frm 11th, t.o. & ref last*....Miss C Arthers ref
1204 Dilly's Last 5a *rear whn p.u. 6th* ....R Armson pu
1210[8] Sit Tight *w.w.,prog to 4th 10th,wknng whn blnd 3 out,t.o. & p.u. last*....M Portman pu
278 Prime Course (Ire) *mid-div, 6th & wknng 12th, p.u. apr 2 out*....P Bull pu
1287 Lucky Landing (Ire) *chsd ldrs to 11th, t.o. & p.u. 2 out* ....A Martin pu
798 Faha Moss (Ire) *last whn mstk 6th, t.o. & p.u. 14th* ....S R Andrews pu
12 ran. 2l, 8l, 3l. Time 6m 45.00s. SP 6-1.
R Beauchamp (Quorn).

1356 Open Maiden Div I

1082 **TEETON HEAVENS 5a ....B Pollock** 1
(Jt fav) mstks,2nd whn blnd 12th,lft in ld 14th-2 out,ld last,ran on
1084 **Bugsy Moran (Ire) ....P Millington** 2
rear, prog & blnd 11th, lft 2nd 14th, ld 2 out-last, wknd
1268[5] **Milo Boy ....M Mackley** 3
chsd ldrs, lft poor 4th 14th, kpt on frm 2 out, not rch ldrs
479[3] Themoreyouknow *(Jt fav) ld, hit 12th, 10l clr & gng wll whn f 14th*.................................M Harris f
1281[2] Harry Tartar *in tch til outpcd 9th, rddn 11th, no resp, p.u. 15th* ....Capt D Parker pu
1262 Carlingford Lad (Ire) *alwys bhnd, t.o. & jmpd slwly 7th, p.u. apr 9th*.........................E Andrewes pu
1192[3] Seaton Mill *chsd ldrs, 3rd whn f 6th* ....M Hewitt f
1166 Bobbin Lace 5a *chsd ldrs, lft 3rd 14th, sn wknd, p.u. apr 2 out* ....J Docker pu
1084 Barnys Rose Farm *last whn p.u. aft 5th (b.b.v.)* ....A Sansome pu
9 ran. 8l, ½l. Time 6m 56.00s. SP 2-1.
Mrs Joan Tice (Pytchley).

1357 Open Maiden Div II

1204[5] **WITCH DOCTOR ....Miss S Phizacklea** 1
disp ld to 3rd, chsd ldr til ld apr 2 out, ran on gamely
1163[3] **Secret Truth 5a ....A Martin** 2
pllng, ld 3rd til apr 2 out, no ext und pres
1165 **The Birdie Song 5a.....................M Harris** 3
n.j.w., disp ld to 2nd, outpcd 14th, no dang aft
1209 Kickles Lass 5a *mstks, in tch, wknng & blnd 14th, rn wd 2 out, walked in* ....John Pritchard 4
1187[4] Malenski (Ire) *(fav) hld up, in tch, cls 3rd & gng wll whn f 3 out*...............................P Millington f
5 ran. 3l, 15l, 30l. Time 7m 21.50s. SP 10-1.
R W Phizacklea (Atherstone).
S.P.

EXETER
Monday May 5th
GOOD

1358 2m 7f 110yds West Of England Open Hunters' Chase Class H

1091[1] **CHILIPOUR 10.13 7a.................Mr L Baker** 1
(fav) held up, hit 5th, hdwy 7th, ld 11th, all out.
1274[1] **Mighty Falcon 10.13 7a.............Miss E Tory** 2
soon in tch, ld 9th to 11th, rallied to go 2nd 3 out, chal next, kept on und pres.
890[3] **Abbotsham 10.13 7a...................Mr E James** 3
held up in rear, hit 6th, hdwy apr 9th, went 2nd before 4 out, wknd next.
1242[2] Anjubi 10.13 7a *trckd ldrs, outpcd 10th, styd on one pace from 3 out*............................Mr R Widger 4
1198[3] Spitfire Jubilee 10.13 7a *ld to 9th, rdn and wknd 3 out*. ....Mr R Nuttall 5
1214[5] Indian Knight 10.13 7a *trckd ldr to 9th, weakening when hit 5 out, t.o.*...................Mr M G Miller 6
Killelan Lad 10.13 7a *alwys in rear, hit 10th, t.o. when p.u. before 4 out*...................Miss K Di Marte pu
1110[2] Try It Alone 10.13 7a *alwys bhnd, rdn apr 9th, t.o. when p.u. before 4 out*..................Mr G Shenkin pu
8 ran. Nk, 8l, 2½l, 12l, dist. Time 6m 0.10s. SP 4-6.
Nick Viney

SOUTHWELL
Monday May 5th
GOOD TO SOFT

1359 3m 110yds Double Decker Fun Bus Hunters' Chase Class H

890[6] **TRIFAST LAD 12.0 3a..............Mr P Hacking** 1
(fav) chsd clr ldr, hdwy 5 out, rdn to ld after 3 out, held on well from last.
1287[4] **Kambalda Rambler 11.7 7a ....Mr R Armson** 2
held up and bhnd, gd hdwy before 4 out, chal 2 out, ev ch last, kept on.
1201 **Fifth Amendment 11.11 3a (bl)....Mr R Thornton** 3
ld and soon well clr, rdn along 5 out, hdd after 3 out, soon wknd.
1096[3] Southern Minstrel 11.7 7a *in tch, rdn along 13th, bhnd from 4 out*.....................Miss C Metcalfe 4
1262[4] Shining Penny 11.0 7a *bhnd and mstk 5th, blnd 12th and p.u. after*.............................Mr K Green pu
1268[2] Ship The Builder 11.0 7a *prom, chsd ldr 4th till f 11th*. ....Mr T Whitaker f
1130[1] Ishma (Ire) 11.0 7a *in rear, blnd 2nd, bhnd when ref 9th*.......................................Mr D Page ref
7 ran. ½l, 25l, 8l. Time 6m 56.50s. SP 11-10.
Mike Roberts

TOWCESTER
Monday May 5th
GOOD TO FIRM

1360 2¾m Ironsides Solicitors Novices' Hunters' Chase Class H

1162[1] **SEVERN INVADER 11.7 7a ....Miss H Gosling** 1
(fav) plenty to do 4 out, steady hdwy from next, styd on to ld after 2 out, readily.
1203[2] **Tea Cee Kay 11.9 5a ....Mr A Sansome** 2
ld till after 4th, styd with ldr till led again after 7th, rdn and hdd after 2 out, stayed on same pace.
1188[3] **Copper Thistle (Ire) 12.0 7a ......Mr R Hunnisett** 3
chsd ldrs till dropped rear 7th, styd on from 3 out, not reach lders.
1286[3] Taura's Rascal 11.7 7a *chsd ldrs, hit 7th and 11th, hit 3 out and soon wknd, no ch when jmpd badly right last*...................................Mr F Brennan 4
1100[5] Barichste 11.7 7a (bl) *t.o. from 5th, p.u. before last*. ....Mr M Watson pu
1014 Shareef Star 11.7 7a (v) *jmpd badly till tried to refuse and f 4th*...............................Mr A Wood f
1199[2] Roaming Shadow 11.7 7a *ld after 4th till after 7th and wknd rpdly, t.o. when p.u. before 2 out*....Mr J Barnes pu
7 ran. 10l, 3l, 30l. Time 5m 52.20s. SP 9-4.
Mrs Miles Gosling

BANWEN MINERS
Pantyderi
Monday May 5th
GOOD

1361 Members

BELL GLASS (FR) ....D S Jones 1
3rd at 4th, ld 11th, clr last, easily
1229[1] **Underwychwood (Ire) ....J Jukes** 2
(fav) rear til prog 11th, chsng wnr last, no imp
Dandelion ....J Hayward 3
ld to 11th, wknd
1231[4] Glynn Brae (Ire) *chsd wnr to 10th, wknd, p.u. 14th* ....Miss M Headon pu
4 ran. 3l, 8l. Time 6m 32.00s. SP 2-1.
G Walters (Banwen Miners).
Visibility limited to one fence for 1st five races.

1362 Confined (12st)

1226[1] **DOUBTING DONNA 5a 5ex ....J Jukes** 1
(fav) 2nd at 3rd, in ld at 11th, easily
1224 **Conna Moss (Ire) ....Miss P Jones** 2
in ld at 3rd, 2nd at 11th, fin tired
1224[4] **No Panic ....J Price** 3
in rear, mstk 3rd, dist 3rd at fin
1182[2] Al Frolic *3rd til 11th, fin v tired*...........D S Jones 4
4 ran. 10l, dist, dist. Time 6m 10.00s. SP 6-4.
Mrs D Hughes (Llangeinor).

1363 Men's Open (12st)

1321[1] **CARRICK LANES 7ex** ....**J Jukes** 1
3rd til 11th, in ld & rdn out last
1007[2] **Jack Sound 7ex** ....**E Williams** 2
(fav) in ld 3rd, disp 11th, 2nd & hrd rdn last, no ext
1181[1] **Sterling Buck (USA)** ....**M Rimell** 3
chsd ldr, disp 11th, 3rd & btn last
1225 Local Customer *alwys rear* ....J P Keen 4
4 ran. 1l, dist, 5l. Time 6m 4.00s. SP 7-4.
David Brace (Llangeinor).

1364 Ladies

1225[2] **MISS MONTGOMERY (IRE) 5a** .....**Miss F Wilson** 1
2nd at 3rd, 6l 2nd at 11th, ld & clr last
1006[3] **Polish Rider (USA)** ....**Miss R Morgan** 2
rear at 3rd & 11th, no dang to wnr last
1225[1] **Touch 'N' Pass 7ex** ....**Miss P Jones** 3
(fav) in ld 3rd & 11th, f 3 out, rmntd
1184 Moving Force *3rd at 3rd, p.u. aft mssd 8th* ....Miss C Williams pu
1184[1] Lucky Ole Son 7ex *4th at 3rd, 3rd at 11th, p.u. 2 out* ....Miss V Roberts pu
5 ran. 4l, dist. Time 6m 12.00s. SP 8-1.
Mrs S M Farr (Ystrad).

1365 Restricted (12st)

1061 **HAL'S PRINCE** ....**Miss P Jones** 1
(Jt fav) 2nd at 3rd & 11th, hrd rdn & ld last
1227 **Moonlight Cruise 5a**..................**P Williams** 2
rear at 3rd, 9th at 11th, ran on aft last, not rch wnr
1135[5] **Mr Mad** ....**P Hamer** 3
(Jt fav) 6th at 3rd, 3rd at 11th, onepcd aft last
1227[5] Hill Fort (Ire) *5th at 3rd, 7th at 11th, no dang aft* ....J Cook 4
1227[3] Celtic Bizarre 5a *7th at 3rd, 6th at 11th, nvr nr ldrs* ....Miss B Barton 5
1186[1] Alfion (Ire) *3rd at 3rd, cls 4th at 11th, fin v tired* ....D S Jones 6
1227[6] Takahashi (Ire) *8th at 3rd, 5th at 11th, fin 2nd, disq* ....E Williams 0
1230 Kerstin's Choice 5a *4th at 3rd, rear at 11th, p.u. 3 out* ....P Sheldrake pu
1194 Culpeppers Dish *ld 3rd, 2nd at 11th, s.u. 14th* A Price su
1230[1] Merry Morn 5a *rear, f 7th*..............J Jukes f
10 ran. 3l, 4l, 6l, 1l, 1l. Time 6m 7.00s. SP 3-1.
T L Jones (Tredegar Farmers).
Takahashi disqualified for missing fence 14!

1366 Intermediate (12st)

1235[2] **CORN EXCHANGE** ....**M Rimell** 1
(fav) ld 8th, dist clr aft 15th, unchal
1133[4] **Sweet Kildare 5a** ....**J Jukes** 2
ld 5th-7th, chsd wnr aft, no ch frm 15th
1134[5] **Pay-U-Cash** ....**G Perkins** 3
ld til aft 2nd, sn lost plc, no dang
962[1] Kinlogh Gale (Ire) (bl) *chsd ldrs, effrt aft 15th, sn onepcd*..............E Williams 4
1181[2] Dick's Cabin *ld 3rd-5th, wknd frm 11th, p.u. 3 out* ....D S Jones pu
1223 Billy-Gwyn *alwys rear, p.u. 2 out* ....J Tudor pu
6 ran. Dist, dist, 1l. Time 6m 30.00s. SP 4-7.
D Wellon (Cotswold Vale).

1367 Open Maiden Div I (12st)

1137[6] **SOUTHERNCROSSPATCH** ....**D S Jones** 1
ld/disp, ran on best aft last
1239 **Fort Gale (Ire)** ....**M Rimell** 2
(fav) mid-div, prog 12th, disp ld 2 out, hrd rdn & no ext last
1136[3] **Wilton Park 5a** ....**E Williams** 3
3rd til mstk 11th, lost plc, styd on onepcd 3 out
Itspantotime 5a *nvr nrr than 5th, p.u. 16th* ....D Stephens pu
1323 Lady Orr (Ire) 5a *ld/disp to 13th, wknd, p.u. 2 out* ....J Tudor pu
1323 Lynnes Daniella (Ire) 5a *trckd ldrs, f 8th* .....J P Keen f
842 Teigr Pren *mstks, alwys mid-div, wll btn & p.u. 3 out* ....P Sheldrake pu
7 ran. 2l, dist. Time 6m 45.00s. SP 7-4.
Keith R Pearce (Carmarthenshire).

1368 Open Maiden Div II (12st)

1137 **VOLCANIC ROC** ....**E Williams** 1
steady prog to ld 11th, clr 15th, unchal
1229[2] **Irish Thinker** ....**J Tudor** 2
(Jt fav) rear, prog 10th, chsd wnr 12th, hrd rdn 2 out, no imp
1229[3] **Storm Dai Fence (Ire) 12a**..........**P Sheldrake** 3
mid-div, rpd prog frm 15th, styd on wll flat
1183[2] Cefn Woodsman *(Jt fav) ld/disp to 10th, wknd, fin tired* ....D S Jones 4
1137[5] Itsstormingnorma 5a *mid-div, effrt 13th, fdd rpdly 15th* ....D Stephens 5
1231 All The Jolly 5a *ld/disp to 10th, p.u. nxt*....M Rimell pu
1229 Mountain Slave 5a *alwys rear, p.u. 14th* ...T Vaughan pu
1229 Welsh Treasure (Ire) 12a *n.j.w. rear til p.u. 7th* ....Miss G Gibson pu
8 ran. 2l, 2l, 10l, 10l. Time 6m 41.00s. SP 3-1.
Mrs N A Warner (Ross Harriers).
P.D.

COTLEY
Cotley Farm
Monday May 5th
GOOD TO FIRM

1369 Members

1108[6] **PALACE KING (IRE)** ....**B Dixon** 1
held up, prog 4 out, disp nxt, ld last, all out
1274 **Highway Jim** ....**Miss M Burrough** 2
in tch, chal 4 out, disp nxt, rddn & just held
1156[2] **Highway Lad** ....**P King** 3
(fav) ld til 4 out, hdd & wknd frm 3 out
866 Summerthetime *last til lost cth 10th, wknd & p.u. apr 12th*..............A Moir pu
4 ran. Nk, 25l. Time 6m 52.00s. SP 5-2.
Mrs P Strawbridge (Cotley).

1370 BFSS (Novice Riders)

1109[4] **AFTERKELLY** ....**Miss C Stucley** 1
chsd ldr, ld 12th, ran on wll frm 2 out
397 **Slaney France (Ire)** ....**Miss K Lovelace** 2
cls 4th til 12th, wnt 2nd 14th, no further prog frm 2 out
1143 **Wesshaun 5a**.........................**G Chanter** 3
ld til 11th, hdd nxt, lost tch frm 4 out
1043[4] Alex Thuscombe (v) *(fav) held up, prog 12th, cls 2nd whn u.r. nxt* ....P Shaw ur
4 ran. 6l, 20l. Time 6m 47.40s. SP 2-1.
Mrs E M W Lloyd (Dulverton East).

1371 Mixed Open (12st)

1273[1] **AVRIL SHOWERS 5a** ....**R Atkinson** 1
(fav) disp to 9th, trckd ldr til ld 3 out, ran on wll, easily
1142 **Gunner Stream** ....**G Chanter** 2
ld/disp to 3 out, outpcd aft
2 ran. 15l. Time 6m 53.40s. SP 1-10.
Mrs R Atkinson (Cattistock).

1372 Intermediate

989[2] **SYBILLABEE 5a**......................**M Batters** 1
(Jt fav) ld/disp til wnt clr 12th, ran on wll frm 3 out, easily
1269[1] **Faraday** ....**N Mitchell** 2
(Jt fav) ld/disp to 12th, chsd wnnr aft, lost tch frm 3 out
920 Pabrey *alwys 3rd, wll bhnd whn ref 2 out*...T Mitchell ref
3 ran. Dist. Time 6m 41.00s. SP 6-4.
Mrs K Buckett (Hursley Hambledon).

1373 Open Maiden (12st)

934³ **STORMY FASHION** .... **Maj G Wheeler** 1
7s-4s, ld/disp til wnt clr 14th, ran on wll frm 3 out
Willsan 1ow .... **T Mitchell** 2
(fav) hld up,prog 11th,wnt 2nd4 out,ev ch 2out,wknd aft,eased flat
1261⁶ **Red Is The Rose 5a** .... **D Alers-Hankey** 3
in tch, 3rd 10th, ev ch 3 out, wknd & outpcd frm nxt
1270 Miss Gruntled 5a *ld/disp to 13th, lost tch nxt, outpcd frm 3 out* .... S Parfimowicz 4
1158 Palmerston's Folly 5a *sn rear, t.o. whn p.u. 4 out* .... D Denny pu
461 Cuthaysmayflower 5a *prom early, lost tch 10th, p.u. apr 12th* .... B Dixon pu
6 ran. 8l, 6l, dist. Time 6m 43.90s. SP 4-1.
R Read (Seavington).

1374 Restricted (12st)

648⁴ **SABBAQ (USA)** .... **I Dowrick** 1
(fav) w.w., prog 12th, wnt 2nd nxt, ld 4 out, ran on wll, easily
1157³ **Royal Turn** .... **A Honeyball** 2
w.w., prog 14th, disp 4 out, ev ch 2 out, rddn & held aft
1093⁵ **Venn Boy** .... **J Tizzard** 3
in tch, chal 4 out, ev ch nxt, outpcd frm 2 out
1275² Clandon Lad *held up, prog 10th, ev ch 3 out, wknd & onepcd frm nxt* .... T Mitchell 4
1093⁴ Ruth's Boy (Ire) *ld to 14th, hdd & outpcd aft* .... Miss P Curling 5
808¹ Bryansbi 5a *cls up, 2nd 12th, wknd 14th, lost tch & p.u. 2 out* .... Miss S Lock pu
1275 Carnelia 5a *prom early, lost tch 12th, t.o. & p.u. 2 out* .... Miss A Goschen pu
7 ran. 1½l, 3l, 6l, 4l. Time 6m 33.00s. SP 6-4.
A J Dowrick (Quanstock Stag Hounds).
D.P.

ENFIELD CHACE
Northaw
Monday May 5th
FIRM

1375 Members (12st)

1190 **SALTY SNACKS (IRE)** .... **M Gingell** 1
disp ld til lft solo 9th
1285⁴ Notary-Nowell (bl) *trckd ldrs til blnd & u.r. 5th* .... R Barrett ur
Blues Breaker 5a *1st ride, pllng, last til u.r. 3rd* .... P Haslam ur
Target Moon 7ow *1st ride, u.r. 1st* ..... Miss C Phillips ur
986³ Mountainous Valley (Ire) 7ex *(fav) disp ld til f 9th* .... S R Andrews f
5 ran. Time 7m 5.00s. SP 5-2.
J S Ruddy (Enfield Chace).

1376 Confined (12st)

1115² **SALMON MEAD (IRE) 3ex** .... **S Sporborg** 1
ld 5-7th, ld agn 14th, clr 3 out, blnd last,hld on und press
1277² **Dance On Sixpence 3ex** .... **S March** 2
(fav) ld to 5th, & agn 8th, pckd 13th, hdd nxt, rddn 2 out, kpt on
1277 Sarazar (USA) (v) *alwys last, lsng tch whn blnd & lst irons 12th, p.u. aft* .... G Pewter pu
3 ran. ½l. Time 6m 5.00s. SP 6-4.
Sir Chippendale Keswick (Puckeridge).

1377 Men's Open (12st)

1351 **KEMYS COMMANDER 7ex** .... **G Smith** 1
ld, clr 9th, fence ahd whn lft solo 14th
1125 Rocco 7ex *reluc to race, lft 200 yds, ref 2nd* M Jones ref
1285 Cardinal Red 7ex (bl) *(fav) chsd wnr, j.s. 9th, reluc aft, t.o. 12th, ref 14th* .... P Keane ref
3 ran. Time 6m 20.00s. SP 5-4.
G J Smith (South Notts).

1378 Ladies

1276² **PROFESSOR LONGHAIR 3ex** ... **Miss C Papworth** 1
ld to 2nd, last & outpcd 10th,hdwy 13th, chall last, ld flat
1308¹ **St Gregory 7ex (bl)** .... **Mrs L Gibbon** 2
(fav) w.r.s. lst 30l, ld 8-10th, agn 15th, rdn 3 out, hdd flat
1280³ **Major Inquiry (USA) (bl)** .... **Miss H Pewter** 3
in tch, last & outpcd 12th,clsd apr 3 out, wnt 3rd nr fin
1280² Kumada 3ex *ld 4-8th,ld 10th til mstk & hdd 15th,sn rdn, no ex apr last* .... Miss S Gritton 4
1280 Omidjoy (Ire) 5a (bl) *chsd ldrs, rmdrs 9th, 3rd & outpcd 12th, last & btn 3 out* .... Mrs L Wrighton 5
5 ran. Nk, 4l, nk, 12l. Time 6m 6.00s. SP 7-2.
A J Papworth (North Norfolk).

1379 Restricted (12st)

1278⁵ **AUCHENDOLLY (IRE)** .... **T Macfarlane** 1
chsd ldrs, lft 2nd appr 8th, ld appr 3 out, sn clr,
1278 **Half A Sov** .... **S March** 2
chsd ldr, ld appr 8th,hdd appr 3 out, no ch whn f last, rmtd
462³ Greenhill Fly Away *(fav) ld til appr 8th, sn p.u. (lame)* .... P Bull pu
1283 Flapping Freda (Ire) 5a 2ow *jmpd slwly, t.o 4th til p.u. appr 11th* .... R Gill pu
1127 Mr Oriental *nt fluent, lft poor 3rd appr 8th, p.u. 10th* .... G Gigantesco pu
Tidal Reef (Ire) 7a *last whn nrly ref 2nd, succeeded nxt* .... P York ref
6 ran. Dist. Time 6m 13.00s. SP 5-2.
S Macfarlane (Puckeridge).

1380 Open Maiden (12st)

1193 **DUAL OR BUST (IRE)** .... **M Gingell** 1
(fav) made all, rdn clr aft last, comf
1353⁴ **Fighting For Good (Ire) (bl)** .... **N Bloom** 2
chsd ldr to 8th & agn 14th, rdn 2 out, onepcd
1282 **Lantern Spark (Ire) 5a (bl)** .... **P Taiano** 3
keen hold, mstks, chsd ldr 8-14th, rdn 15th, onepcd
686² Joyful Hero 5a *alwys last, in tch til rdn & btn 3 out, p.u. last* .... P Bull pu
4 ran. 2l, 2l. Time 6m 15.00s. SP 8-11.
J S Ruddy (Enfield Chace).
S.P.

NORTH SHROPSHIRE
Eyton-On-Severn
Monday May 5th
GOOD TO FIRM

1381 Members (12st)

854² **NOBLE ANGEL (IRE)** .... **L Whiston** 1
cls up,ld 3rd,made rest,ran on und pres frm 3 out.
1178 **Solar Castle (Ire)** .... **P McAllister** 2
prom, outpcd hlfwy, ran on frm 5 out
1325¹ **Penllyne's Pride (bl)** .... **R Burton** 3
ld to 2nd, cls up in tch 10th,sn outpcd,t.o. 12th,btn fence
332 Eyton Rock *hndy to 4th, qckly lost tch 6th, p.u. nxt* .... T O'Leary pu
938⁴ Mr Pipe Man (Ire) *(fav) w.w.,2nd 10th,chal & ev ch 4 out,3rd & btn whn ref last* .... A Crow ref
5 ran. 1½l, dist. Time 6m 27.00s. SP 5-2.
P Whiston (North Shropshire).

1382 Intermediate (12st)

1235 **MR BOBBIT (IRE)** .... **R Burton** 1
cls up, lft in ld 6th, jnd 3 out, ran on wll frm 2 out

1235 **Another Chancer** ....**M Harris** **2**
prom,2nd 7-13th,drpd back 5th,ran on frm 2 out,tk 2nd flat
748[3] **Comedie Fleur 5a**......................**G Hanmer** **3**
hld up in rear, clsr order 5 out, jnd 3 out, hdd bfr last
1233 Ultrason IV (Fr) 5ex *mstly 3rd, outpcd frm 3 out* ....A Beedles 4
1237[3] Priory Piper *(fav) n.j.w., w.w. in rear, found nil frm 4 out* ....C Stockton 5
1304 Tbilisi *ref to race*...................................A Jordan ref
572 Sister Emu 5a *made running til f 6th* ....P Saville f
7 ran. 2½l, 2l, 5l, 5l. Time 6m 38.00s. SP 2-1.
S T P Furness (West Shropshire Drag).

1383 Men's Open (12st)

1160[1] **NOTHING VENTURED** ....**A Beedles** **1**
prom, cls 2nd whn lft in ld 4 out, ran on wll, comf
1098 **Fibreguide Tech** ....**G Hanmer** **2**
held up bhnd 1st 2, lft 2nd 4 out, cls up 3 out,not qckn
886[1] Riverside Boy 7ex *(fav) alwys ld & 2l clr whn hit 4 out & f* ....A Crow f
3 ran. 10l. Time 6m 26.00s. SP 11-10.
Countess Goess-Saurau (South Shropshire).

1384 G Middleton Ladies

1148 **FUNDY (IRE)** ....**Miss C Spearing** **1**
(fav) ld to 6th, 2nd to 12th, ld 13th, sn in commd, easily
1097[3] **Saahi (USA)** ....**Miss S Swindells** **2**
hld up in rear,prog 13th,2nd 4 out,ran on one-pcd,alwys held
1146[4] **Great Uncle** ....**Miss T McCurrich** **3**
chsd ldrs, nvr bttr thn 3rd, strgglng frm 3 out
988 Hiram B Birdbath (bl) *prom 5th, ld 7-12th, hdd & wknd 13th, not run on frm 3 out* ....Miss A Plunkett 4
848 Golden Fare *cls up in tch to 13th, fdd & p.u. 3 out* ....Miss L Wallace pu
329 Walter's Lad *rear 6th, t.o. whn p.u. 13th* ..Miss M Wall pu
6 ran. 7l, 20l, 8l. Time 6m 32.00s. SP Evens.
A J Brazier (Croome & West Warwickshire).

1385 Restricted (12st)

1303[2] **LITTLE BY LITTLE** ....**T O'Leary** **1**
alwys cls 3rd, ld 4 out, hrd rddn frm 2 out, just held on
326[1] **Coolflugh Hero (Ire)** ....**A Crow** **2**
(fav) ld to 7th,cls 2nd to 3 out,chal strngly nxt,ran on und prss
1263 Carinci *prom, 2nd to 8th, ld 9-14th, wknd qckly, p.u. 4 out* ....G Hanmer pu
1124[1] Who Doctored Who (Ire) *alwys rear, detached & p.u. 12th* ....M Worthington pu
4 ran. ½l. Time 6m 32.00s. SP 7-1.
D Pugh (North Shropshire).

1386 2½m Open Maiden (5-7yo) (12st)

942 **HARWELD 7a 8ow**.......................**A Crow** **1**
(fav) held up,prog frm 8th,strng late run frm 2 out,ld flat,allout
1240 **Henrietta Boo Boo 5a**................**D Sherlock** **2**
alwys cls up, ld 4 out til hdd run in, ran on wll.
1160 **Quite A Miss 5a**.......................**A Martin** **3**
mid-div early,rear 8th,some late prog,rnng on
942 Riot Lady (Ire) 5a *wll in tch wth ldr to 10th, no ext clsng stgs* ....D Barlow 4
1015 Cuban Skies (Ire) *prom, 3rd 4 out, fdd, onepcd* ....G Hanmer 5
852 Aqueous Rocks *ld to 10th, wknd 2 out, p.u. nxt* ....M Worthington pu
941[3] Fruit Of Oak (Ire) *hit 2nd hrd & u.r.*..........T O'Leary ur
Splint *chsng grp, wll in tch 10th, sn btn, p.u. 2 out* ....A Beedles pu
8 ran. Hd, 3l, 6l, 4l. SP 5-2.
E H Crow (North Shropshire).
Due to heavy rain visability was poor. V.S.

RADNOR & WEST HEREFORD
Cursneh Hill
Monday May 5th
GOOD TO FIRM

1387 Members (12st)

1238 **RIBINGTON** ....**M Hammond** **1**
made most at v slow pcd frm 6th, qcknd apr last, just hld on
1233[1] **Bowland Girl (Ire) 5a 13ex**.........**Miss E James** **2**
(fav) trckd reluc ldr frm 6th, qcknd apr last, rddn & just held
Highland Chase ....**K Goodman** **3**
ld 2n-5th, 10l 3rd 13th, ld brfly apr 3 out, sn outpcd
3 ran. Sht-hd, 4l. Time 8m 21.00s. SP 4-1.
W S Layton (Radnor & West Hereford).

1388 Confined (12st)

1233[3] **SISTERLY 5a 3ex**.......................**A Wintle** **1**
(fav) trckd ldr cls up til ld 15th, pshd clr 2 out, comf
1146[1] **Hackett's Farm 3ex**.............**Julian Pritchard** **2**
ld 1st & agn 7th, hdd aft 14th, no ext und pres
1232[1] **True Fred** ....**M P Jones** **3**
wnt 2l 2nd 11th, ev ch til outpcd frm 14th
1232 Seven Cruise *ld 2nd-6th, wknd 11th, mstk nxt, t.o. & p.u. 15th* ....R Jones pu
4 ran. 5l, 5l. Time 6m 19.00s. SP 4-5.
Peter Nash (North Hereford).

1389 Men's Open (12st)

1198[2] **NETHER GOBIONS 7ex** ....**Julian Pritchard** **1**
(fav) made all, 4l up 10th, fence ahd frm 2 out
1232[3] **In The Water** ....**M P Jones** **2**
chsd wnnr, rddn 12th, lost tch frm nxt
2 ran. Dist. Time 6m 27.00s. SP 1-8.
P Clutterbuck (Berkeley).

1390 Intermediate (12st)

1235 **LLES LE BUCFLOW** ....**S Lloyd** **1**
chsd ldrs, rddn 12th, styd on to ld last
901[1] **Mostyn** ....**Miss P Gundry** **2**
(Jt fav) made most til hdd 15th, ld agn 2 out, no ext apr last
1062 **Perryline 5a** ....**Julian Pritchard** **3**
prog frm rear 11th, ld 15th, slw jmp nxt, sn bttn
1235[3] Haven Light *(Jt fav) cls 2nd/disp til efft to ld 14th, wknd qckly & p.u. aft nxt* ....A Dalton pu
4 ran. 1½l, 2l. Time 6m 24.00s. SP 4-1.
J Smith (Golden Valley).

1391 Ladies

1236[1] **GRIMLEY GALE (IRE) 5a 7ex**......**Miss S Vickery** **1**
(fav) ld 1st & frm 9th, drew clr aft 14th, not extnd
1141[2] **Nanda Moon** ....**Miss S Jackson** **2**
cls up, chsd ldr 13th, lost tch nxt, held on for 2nd
1272[2] **Legal Picnic** ....**Miss C Bryan** **3**
mostly last, chal for 2nd frm 15th, onepcd
Fergal's Delight (bl) *ld til hdd 9th, wknd & p.u. 14th* ....Miss E James pu
4 ran. 8l, hd. Time 6m 24.00s. SP 2-7.
R M Phillips (Clifton On Teme).

1392 Interlink Restricted (12st)

1208[4] **FIRST COMMAND (NZ)** ....**A Dalton** **1**
trckd ldrs til prog 12th, ld frm nxt, pshd out flat
1202 **Emerald Charm (Ire) 5a**..................**R Bevis** **2**
(fav) held up, efft to chs wnnr 13th, mstk & no ext frm 2 out
1235 **Derring Ann 5a**.....................**M Hammond** **3**
s.s., cght up 7th, ev ch 14th, kpt on onepcd frm nxt
1237 Kingsthorpe *cls up til lost plc 7th, efft & ev ch 13th, wknd frm nxt*..............................A Phillips 4

1199[3] Tudor Oaks 5a *ld to 12th, wknd 14th, t.o. & p.u. 2 out* ....Julian Pritchard pu
1237 Stormhill Recruit *drppd last 8th, strgglng 11th, p.u. 13th* ....M P Jones pu
6 ran. 2l, 3l, 15l. Time 6m 33.00s. SP 6-1.
R Newey (Ludlow).

1393 Open Maiden (12st)

1239[2] **WINTER BREEZE ....Miss S Vickery** 1
(Jt fav) cls up, efft & rddn 14th, chal last, ld flat, all out
1016[3] **Philelwyn (Ire) 5a ....Julian Pritchard** 2
(Jt fav) ld frm 4th til wknd & jmp lft last, sn bttn
1209[6] **Musical Mail ....A Dalton** 3
cls up til just outpcd 13th, styd on to 3rd aft 2 out
1239[4] Pridewood Golding *alwys cls up, cls 3rd & ev ch 15th, wknd frm nxt* ....T Cox 4
1239[3] Merger Mania 7a 2ow *held up, cls 5th 11th, 8l 5th 13th, no ch frm 15th* ....D Mansell 5
1240 Welsh Lightning *last frm 8th, lost tch & p.u. 11th* ....R Bevis pu
1238 Saxon Smile *ld 2nd til p.u. & dismntd bfr 4th* ....Miss S Jackson pu
1240 Brown Bala 5a (bl) *cls up til wknd 13th, t.o. & p.u. aft 15th* ....M Hammond pu
1238[5] Miss Clare 5a *chsd ldrs, cls 6th whn mstk & u.r. 11th* ....N Oliver ur
9 ran. 2l, 2l, 6l, 15l. Time 6m 35.00s. SP 2-1.
R M Phillips (Worcestershire).
P.R.

STEVENSTONE
High Bickington
Monday May 5th
GOOD

1394 Members (12st)

1257 **ACHILTIBUIE ....G Penfold** 1
(fav) keen hld, chsd ldr, hit 13th, cruised home 2nd, awarded race
1245 **Alicott Lad ....Miss L Smale** 2
ld to 5th, sn wknd, not fluent, t.o.
1036[1] Romany Anne 5a *ld 5th, mssd mrkr aft 7th, cont in ld, eased, disq* ....Miss S Young 0
1035 Fair And Square 12a 8ow *jmpd novicey, disp 2nd whn f 8th* ....K Heard f
4 ran. 2½l, dist. Time 7m 1.00s. SP 10-11.
G Heal (Stevenstone).
Original distances.

1395 Restricted (12st)

792[4] **INDIAN RABI ....A Holdsworth** 1
made virt all, ran on wll clsng stgs
1246[1] **Stretchit ....G Penfold** 2
handy, rmndr 15th, hdwy nxt, chal und pres 3 out, styd on
803[3] **Arble March 5a ....N Harris** 3
twrds rear, 8th at 15th, nrst fin
1259[5] Cedars Rosslare *in tch, 5th at 15th, onepcd* ....Miss O Green 4
1243 Chocolate Buttons 5a *prog to cls 2nd at 15th, ev ch til wknd 2 out* ....H Thomas 5
1275 Ballysheil *cls 4th 14th-17th, onepcd aft* ....S Edwards 6
1043[5] Grey Guestino *trckd ldr, wknd 14th, sn outpcd* ....Miss L Delve 7
556 Race Against Time 5a *prom til wknd rpdly 7th, last whn jmpd slwly 14th, p.u. nxt* ....J Scott pu
1108[2] Penguin 5a *(fav) hld up, prog 11th, mstks 13th & nxt, 5th whn u.r. 2 out* ....Miss J Cumings ur
9 ran. 1½l, 8l, 6l, 1½l, 1l, 2l. Time 6m 43.50s. SP 8-1.
Mrs E M Roberts (Silverton).

1396 Mixed Open (12st)

1341 **BUTLER JOHN (IRE) 7ex ....N Harris** 1
(fav) cls up, ld 9th, hit 15th, sn drew wll clr, unchal
1110[1] **Khattaf ....Miss J Cumings** 2
jmpd rght, prog 10th, cls 2nd 12th-15th, 3rd aft, ran on fin
759[3] **Howaryadoon ....Miss T Cave** 3
mstk 7th, prog to chs wnr 16th, wknd nr fin
1256[4] Fearsome 7ex *rmndrs 8th, 5th hlfwy, nvr dang, styd on clsng stgs* ....G Penfold 4
1256[2] Parson's Way 7ex (bl) *ld to 9th, prom til wknd 14th, no ch 16th* ....K Heard 5
587 Winter's Lane *prom til slppd bnd apr 7th,mstks 12 & nxt, lost tch,p.u.15th* ....S Slade pu
1111 Seventh Lock *rmndrs hlfwy, rear, p.u. apr 16th* ....S Kidston pu
7 ran. Dist, 1½l, 12l, 15l. Time 6m 32.00s. SP 5-4.
Nick Viney (Exmoor).

1397 Confined (12st)

1245[1] **SAINT JOSEPH ....Miss S Young** 1
(fav) went 2nd 10th, cls up whn lft clr 3 out, comf
1255[1] **Bert House 3ex ....S Kidston** 2
ld til blnd & rdr lost irons 3 out, not rcvr
791[4] **Tranquil Waters (USA) ....David Dennis** 3
2nd to 10th, in tch til rdn 15th, fdd
3 ran. 20l, 30l. Time 6m 41.00s. SP 2-5.
B R J Young (East Cornwall).

1398 Intermediate (12st)

789[1] **RASTA MAN ....K Heard** 1
handy, 2nd at 14th, mstk nxt, ld 16th, sn clr, pshd out
952[3] **Lonesome Traveller (NZ) ....L Jefford** 2
chsd ldr, slppd bend apr 14th, ev ch 3 out, styd on onepcd
1156 **Sunwind ....M Frith** 3
hld up, went 4th at 16th, lft 3rd 3 out, tired & mstk nxt
1092[2] Mine's A Gin (Ire) *prog to 3rd at 12th, wknd 15th, no ch clsng stgs* ....Miss J Cumings 4
1275[1] Four Leaf Clover 5a *(fav) hld up, f 4th* ....N Harris f
1038 American Black (bl) *ld to 16th, wkng whn f nxt* ....Miss T Cave f
1312[2] Tangle Kelly *prom, cls 3rd at 11th, hit 13th, lost tch 14th, p.u.aft 16th* ....S Slade pu
7 ran. 11l, 12l, 5l. Time 6m 38.00s. SP 4-1.
J Heard (Eggesford).

1399 Open Maiden Div I (12st)

1095[2] **DEVONSHIRE LAD ....N Harris** 1
(fav) trckd ldr, ld 16th, slght ld whn lft clr last, drvn out
625[3] **Westcountry Lad ....R Woolacott** 2
handy, cls 4th at 14th, went 2nd und pres last, ran on
1094[2] **Big Bands Are Back (USA) 7a ......Miss S Young** 3
ld to 16th, cls up & ev ch til wknd last
1260 Dusty Furlong *raced wd, 6th hlfwy, mstk 12th, wll bhnd frm nxt* ....Miss K Baily 4
Supreme Warrior *mid-div, mstk 9th, p.u. 12th* ....S Kidston pu
553[2] Damiens Pride (Ire) *hld up in tch,3rd frm 13th,effrt to disp ld whn ran out last* ....K Heard ro
933[5] Barton Rose *prog to 6th at 8th, mstk 12th, btn 5th whn p.u. 16th* ....S Slade pu
1260 Merlin The Monkey *bhnd til p.u. 8th, school* ...J Scott pu
1246 Joy Street 5a *rear til p.u. 12th* ....T Greed pu
1246 Ballyhasty Lady (Ire) 5a *prog 7th, 3rd whn blnd 11th, p.u. nxt* ....J Young pu
1246 Mrs Green 5a *schoold rear til p.u. 9th* ..A Holdsworth pu
1246 I'm Foxy 5a *mid-div, 8th at 10th, p.u. 12th* .....M Frith pu
12 ran. 3l, 8l, dist. Time 6m 46.00s. SP 9-4.
Mrs D B Lunt (Tiverton Foxhounds).
Stewards Inquiry into possible interference, placings unaltered.

1400 Open Maiden Div II (12st)

795[2] **BUCKS FLEA 5a ....G Penfold** 1
(Jt fav) in tch, prog to ld apr 14th, steadily drew clr 3 out
1244 **Carumu 5a ....David Dennis** 2

handy, cls 2nd & ev ch 13th, rdn & outpcd frm 3 out
1045[4] **Suba Lin 5a ....M Frith** 3
mid-div, 5th hlfwy, poor 3rd frm 16th
795 Gamblers Refrain *ld til s.u. bend apr 2nd* ....A Holdsworth su
1244 Baman Powerhouse *ld 7th, slwd by flagwavers 9th, ld 11-13th,wknd,p.u. 17th*.......................J Young pu
1260 Sixth In Line (Ire) *c.o. bend apr 2nd*...........T Cole co
1342 Corrib Haven (Ire) *jmpd lft,lft in ld apr 2nd-7th,ld 10-11th,wknd,p.u.16th,lame* ....S Slade pu
625 Fortitude Star 5a *sn bhnd & rmndrs, not fluent, t.o. & p.u. 12th* ....K Heard pu
1261[4] Nottarex *b.d. bend apr 2nd*..................B Wright bd
664[6] Majic Belle 5a *b.d. bend apr 2nd*.........R Woolacott bd
1260 Aritam (Ire) *(Jt fav) c.o. bend apr 2nd*.........N Harris co
1246 Belitlir 12a *immed t.o. & schoold, wll bhnd & p.u. 14th* ....Miss S Young pu
950 Lady Leigh 5a *rmndrs 5th, t.o. 9th, p.u. 12th* S Kidston pu
1246 Go Willie Go *bhnd whn u.r. 3rd*.........Miss L Smale ur
14 ran. 8l, 15l. Time 6m 47.00s. SP 2-1.
G W Penfold (Stevenstone).
G.T.

WARWICKSHIRE
Ashorne
Monday May 5th
GOOD

1401 Open Maiden Div I

1166[2] **THE CHAIRMAN (IRE) ....J Trice-Rolph** 1
cls up, trckd ldr 15th, chal last, pshd out to ld nr fin
1209[2] **Strong Account (Ire) ....A Tutton** 2
(fav) ld 6-9th & frm 14th, hrd rdn last, hdd nr fin
1083[4] **Woodlands Power (bl)............John Pritchard** 3
keen hld,prom,ld 12-14th,wkng whn blnd nxt,lft poor 3rd last
1209 Lizapet (Ire) 12a *mid-div, effrt 12th, wknd nxt, t.o.* ....S Green 4
1166[3] Miss Precocious 5a *cls up, ev ch 15th, wknd nxt, poor 3rd whn u.r. last*..............C Wadland ur
1166 Sir Krispin *12s-4s, rear, prog to chs ldrs 12th, wknd nxt, p.u. 2 out*..............T Illsley pu
1239 Brother Harold *mstk 2nd, ld to 6th & frm 9-12th, wknd rpdly nxt, p.u. 15th* ....L Brown pu
1239 Military Man *hmpd & u.r. 1st*..............M Munrowd ur
917 Spring Sabre (bl) *lft strt, cont t.o. til p.u. 5th* R Lawther pu
1166 Captain's Port 5a *alwys rear, rdn & t.o. 11th, p.u. 15th* ....H Wheeler pu
1165[5] Magical Manor 5a *chsd ldrs, outpcd 13th, 5th & btn whn f 15th*..............J Oldring f
1209 Ullington Lord *alwys rear, t.o. 11th, p.u. 13th* ....S Joynes pu
373 Deejayef 5a *alwys bhnd, t.o. 11th, p.u. 13th* ..N Ridout pu
1212 Sharp Alice 5a *alwys rear, t.o. 11th, p.u. 14th* ....T Stephenson pu
Lady Kilton 5a *s.s. jmpd bdly, t.o. til p.u. 9th* ....P Cowley pu
15 ran. Hd, 25l, 30l. Time 6m 37.00s. SP 8-1.
V C Webster (Warwickshire).

1402 Open Maiden Div II

1209[4] **DARING DAISY 5a ....Mrs C McCarthy** 1
in tch, prog to ld 14th, hdd 2 out, kpt on to ld nr fin
1150 **Joyney 5a.......................Miss C Thomas** 2
(fav) prog 10th,lft 2nd 15th,ld 2 out,hrd rdn & hdd nr fin
Lottie The Lotus 5a ....M Gregory 3
schoold,prog 10th,chsd ldrs aft,nvr askd to chal,fin strngly
485[2] Looking *mstks, ld/disp to 14th, onepcd frm 3 out* ....R Lawther 4
1209[7] Dilkush *mstk 6th, prom, cls 4th whn hmpd 15th, wknd 2 out*..............M Wells 5
881 Sonny's Song (v) *wll bhnd frm 8th, cont t.o.* ..L Brown 6
1288 Well Bank *ld/disp to 14th, cls 2nd & ev ch whn f nxt* ....E Walker f
1165[6] Shedoes 5a *chsd ldrs to 12th, wknd & p.u. 14th* ....C Wadland pu
1082[3] Tinsun *chsd ldrs, rdn 11th, wknd & p.u. 13th, dead* ....John Pritchard pu
1165 Dromain 5a *jmpd bdly, t.o. whn blnd & u.r. 6th* ....J Docker ur
1330 Mr Dennehy (Ire) *8th whn f 7th*..............M Butcher f
11 ran. Hd, 3l, 4l, 20l, 1 fence. Time 6m 40.50s. SP 5-1.
T B Brown (Grafton).

1403 Confined (12st)

1208[1] **MR GEE ....K Needham** 1
w.w. prog 13th, gd run to ld aft last, ran on well
1162[4] **Going Around ....L Lay** 2
trckd ldrs, effrt 15th, rdn to chal 2 out,mstk last,styd on
Sandybraes ....F Hutsby 3
prom,trckd ldr 10th,ld 15th til wknd & hdd aft last
1017[3] Master Dancer *chsd ldrs, 5th & in tch 15th, onepcd aft* ....Miss C Dyson 4
1162[2] Tompet *chsd ldr 7-10th, not qckn aft frm 15th, kpt on* ....J Connell 5
1329 Hook Line'N'sinker *in tch, rmndr aft 11th, wknd 14th* ....S Joynes 6
1198[4] Grand Value *lft in ld apr 3rd til 4th, wknd 8th, t.o. & p.u. 3 out*..............C Wadland pu
650 Durzi *ref 1st*..............E Walker ref
978[3] Lad Lane *t.o. 4th, p.u. 11th*..............J Borradaile pu
Caroles Express 5a *schoold, prog & in tch 10th, sn wknd, p.u. 14th* ....Miss S Duckett pu
987[3] Lofty Deed (USA) 7ex *crwld 3rd, mstk nxt, alwys bhnd, t.o. & p.u. 2 out*..............A Charles-Jones pu
878 Yorkshire Pop 5a *ld til s.u. bnd apr 3rd*......L Brown su
591 Aj's Boy *(fav) ld 4th til mstk & hdd 15th, wknd & p.u. last, dsmntd*..............A Hill pu
1077 Samsword *ref to race* ....John Pritchard 0
14 ran. 2l, 2½l, 2l, 4l, 20l. Time 6m 36.00s. SP 6-1.
M W Conway (Quorn).

1404 Members

1165[2] **CONNIE FOLEY ....J Trice-Rolph** 1
poor last, lft 3rd 13th, ld 15th, all out
1164 **Penly ....A Westrope** 2
chsd ldrs, lft 2nd 13th,ev ch 15th,wknd,rdr lost irons
587 Al Hashimi *s.u. bnd apr 3rd*..............N Ridout su
1162[6] Fighting Mariner (bl) *prom,lft in ld apr 13th,lost plc rpdly nxt,s.u.bnd apr 2 out*..............John Pritchard su
1077[3] Admiral Rous 5ex *cls up, ld 12th til ran out apr nxt* ....C Wadland ro
369[3] Copper Bank *(fav) prom, ev ch whn ran out apr 13th* ....F Hutsby ro
1205[4] Local Race (Ire) *t.d.e. ld to 12th, s.u. bend apr nxt* ....J Brook su
7 ran. 12l. Time 7m 0.00s. SP 5-1.
D Hiatt (Warwickshire).
Remainder of meeting abandoned - course unsafe. J.N.

ZETLAND
Witton Castle
Monday May 5th
GOOD TO SOFT

1405 Confined (12st)

1264[1] **HURRICANE LINDA 5a 3ex ....S Walker** 1
(fav) held up in rear, prog 3 out, chal last, ld flat, drvn out
1101[1] **Danegeld (Ire) ....N Smith** 2
mid-div, prog to disp ld 4 out, hdd & not qckn flat
1168[3] **Worthy Spark 3ex.......................P Craggs** 3
prom, ld 5th til disp 4 out, hdd & not qckn apr last
1100[2] Chapel Island *mid-div, prog 11th, ev ch 3 out, wknd nxt, eased flat*..............G Tuer 4
1247[4] Mr Dick 6ex *towrds rear, ran wd apr 13th, wknd 3 out* ....S Swiers 5
1099[3] Eastern Pleasure 3ex *prom, chsd ldr 14th, wknd apr 4 out*..............T Barry 6
1100[3] Flying Lion *mid-div,chsd ldrs 6th,mstk 11th,lost plc & strgglng 13th,t.o* ....M Haigh 7

972 Lindon Run *ld til 5th, chsd ldr aft, wknd 14th, t.o.* ....R Morgan 8
1247[5] Earl Gray *prom til lost plcd 5th, rear 8th, lost tch 15th, t.o.* ....Miss A Deniel 9
1104[4] Pinewood Lad *rear, detached whn u.r. 7th* ....Miss K Ford ur
10 ran. 1l, 1l, 15l, 4l, 2l, 12l, 2l, 5l. Time 6m 12.00s. SP 6-4.
Lady Hewitt (Middleton).

1406 Restricted

1348 **LAST OPTION 7a....Mrs F Needham 1**
mid-div,prog 12th,disp 15th,ld 3 out,prssd flat,ran on wll
1250[2] **Dear Emily 5a....S Swiers 2**
(fav) chsd ldrs,ld 14th til disp nxt,hdd 3 out,rlld flat
1263[5] **Goodheavens Mrtony ....Miss A Deniel 3**
alwys hndy, chal 14th, outpcd frm 4 out, fin tired
348 Mighty Merc *prom, disp 4th, ld nxt, disp 10th, hdd & fdd 14th* ....S Gibbon 4
584[8] Drumcairn (Ire) *rear, strgglng 12th, t.o. 14th* ....Miss P Robson 5
1250[6] Persian Lion *ld, disp 4th to nxt, chsd ldr til fdd 11th,t.o. & p.u. 4 out* ....Mrs L Ward pu
1247 La Maja (Ire) 5a *rear, prog 7th, disp 10th til hdd & wknd 14th, p.u. 3 out* ....N Wilson pu
1250[7] Skyval 5a *alwys in rear, strgglng 12th, t.o. & p.u. 4 out* ....P Atkinson pu
266 Harrys Special (Ire) *towrds rear, lost tch 13th, p.u. 15th* ....G Tuer pu
1101 Patey Court 5a *j.s.1st,mid-div,rear 6th,sn strgglng,wll bhnd whn p.u. 13th* ....C Mulhall pu
10 ran. 1l, 15l, nk, 20l. Time 6m 17.00s. SP 9-2.
R Tate (Hurworth).

1407 Men's Open

1247[1] **JUST CHARLIE 4ow....D Easterby 1**
(fav) ld, disp 7th, ld 4 out, drew clr 2 out, eased flat
1248[4] **Fast Study ....S Robinson 2**
settld in 3rd til chsd wnr 3rd,disp 7th,hdd & outpcd 4 out
1248[5] **Ashdren ....N Tutty 3**
keen hold, last til mod prog into 3rd 12th, no ch frm 2 out
765 Broguestown Pride (Ire) *chsd wnnr til settld in 3rd 3rd, wknd 12th, t.o.* ....P Craggs 4
4 ran. 7l, 10l, 30l. Time 6m 27.00s. SP 1-8.
Mrs Susan E Mason (Middleton).

1408 Ladies

945[1] **MUSKORA (IRE) (h)....Miss P Robson 1**
(fav) made all, drew clr 14th, hrd drvn & styd on wll flat
1102 **Blakes Folly (Ire) ....Mrs K Hargreave 2**
rear, outpcd 15th, styd on wll frm 2 out, tk 2nd cls home
1249[4] **Kellys Diamond ....Miss V Russell 3**
chsd wnr to 10th,outpcd 13th,prog into 2nd 4 out,onepcd last
1249[1] Osgathorpe *settld 3rd, chsd wnr 10th til wknd qckly 4 out* ....Mrs F Needham 4
1249[5] Cheeky Pot *rear,outpcd 9th,prog 13th,ev ch 15th til wknd nxt,p.u. 2 out* ....Mrs S Grant pu
5 ran. 2½l, sht-hd, 25l. Time 6m 11.00s. SP Evens.
Mrs F Percy-Davis (Jedforest).

1409 Open Maiden (12st)

1073 **TIMBER TOPPER ....C Mulhall 1**
prom, disp 4 out til ld & lft clr last, styd on wll
1173[2] **The Camair Flyer (Ire) ....M Ruddy 2**
prom, ld 11th-4 out, lft 2nd last, kpt on
1251[2] **Smart Mover ....S Brisby 3**
(fav) prom til fdd frm 4 out
1073 Corsage *towrds rear whn p.u. 7th* ....N Tutty pu
1251 China Hand (Ire) 7a *mid-div til wknd 15th, jmp v slwly nxt & p.u.* ....H Armstrong pu
1262 Raticosa 12a *rear, wll bhnd whn jmp v slwly 14th & p.u.* ....Miss J Eastwood pu
1106 Vickyberto 5a *mid-div til lost plcd 7th, rddn nxt, t.o. whn p.u. 13th* ....N Wilson pu
1173[5] K Walk 5a *chsd ldr til wknd qckly 4 out, t.o. whn p.u. last* ....R Morgan pu
1252[3] Chummy's Last 5a *rear div whn u.r. 10th* ....Mrs F Needham ur
131 Durham Glint *rear & sn detached, t.o. 7th, p.u. 3 out* ....S Bowden pu
1268 Reaper *f 1st (dead)* ....M Haigh f
1173 Little Hawk *ld til hdd 11th, wknd qckly, t.o. whn p.u. 4 out* ....T Scott pu
Sand Direct (Ire) *in rear whn f 4th* ....A Ogden f
1106[4] Gardenia's Song *mid-div til wknd 13th, t.o. whn p.u. 15th* ....G Tuer pu
1247 Mac's Blade (USA) 7a *prom, disp 4 out til hdd & 2l down whn f last* ....R Edwards f
15 ran. 5l, 25l. Time 6m 23.00s. SP 7-1.
P Wilkin (Bilsdale).

1410 Members

STILLTODO 5a ....C Wilson 1
(fav) made all, qcknd clr 2 out, pshd out
1069 **Canny's Fort 5a....S Gibbon 2**
trckd wnr til drppd back 3rd 13th,outpcd 15th,tk 2nd flat
1106[7] **Doc Spot ....S Robinson 3**
settld in 3rd, chsd wnr 13th til outpcd 2 out,wknd last
3 ran. 10l, 2l. Time 6m 38.00s. SP 1-3.
W R Wilson (Zetland).
N.E.

WINCANTON
Tuesday May 6th
FIRM

1411a 2m 5f R. K. Harrison Insurance Brokers Novices' Hunters' Chase Class H

1288[3] **CLOBRACKEN LAD 11.7 7a....Mr G Baines 1**
(Jt fav) made all, staying on well when hit 3 out, ran on run-in.
1258[1] **Link Copper 11.7 7a ....Miss L Blackford 2**
alwys chasing wnr, chal 9th and 4 out, rallied again last, one pace.
662[2] **Chism (Ire) 11.7 7a ....Mr M G Miller 3**
(Jt fav) went 3rd after 8th, hdwy to chase ldrs 11th, one pace from 3 out.
1270[3] Barrow Street 11.7 7a *raced in 3rd till dropped back to 4th at 8th, rdn 11th, wknd 13th.* ....Mr J Tizzard 4
4 ran. 2l, 3l, 27l. Time 5m 15.20s. SP 15-8.
T J Swaffield

CHEPSTOW
Wednesday May 7th
GOOD

1411b 3m Jorrocks Novices' Hunters' Chase Class H

1203[1] **PHAR TOO TOUCHY 11.7 7a....Mr N Harris 1**
(fav) made all, shaken up run-in, ran on well.
289 **Savoy 11.7 7a ....Captain A Ogden 2**
held up, hdwy to chase wnr from 9th, reminders apr 2 out, no impn.
1134[2] **Archer (Ire) 11.7 7a ....Mr M Harris 3**
chsd wnr to 9th, wknd 11th, t.o..
1203 Sultan's Son 11.7 7a *in cl tch till outpcd after 8th, t.o..* ....Mr G Lewis 4
4 ran. 4l, 19l, 17l. Time 6m 8.70s. SP 8-11.
Miss R A Francis

UTTOXETER
Wednesday May 7th
GOOD TO SOFT

1412 3¼m Mobilefone Group Novices' Hunters' Chase Class H

1272[1] **FRONT COVER 11.2 7a .... Miss S Vickery 1**
(Jt fav) trckd ldrs, shaken up after 16th, ld next, soon clr, easily.
1264[5] **Royal Segos 11.7 7a .... Mr C Stockton 2**
ld to 4 out, rdn and one pace from next.
1263[2] **Gillie's Fountain 11.7 7a .... Mr A Dalton 3**
settld rear, in tch till rdn and wknd 4 out, left poor 3rd 2 out.
983[4] Balasani (Fr) 11.9 5a *mstk 6th, last when b.d. 8th.* .... Mr A Sansome bd
1086 Ryders Wells 11.7 7a *jinked and u.r. 2nd.* .... Mr S Walker ur
610[3] Fiscal Policy 11.7 7a *blnd and u.r. 1st.* ... Mr R Trotter ur
1264[4] Just Marmalade 11.7 7a *chsd lding pair till cannoned into by loose horse and b.d. 8th.* .... Mr R Burton bd
1288[6] Very Daring 11.7 7a *in tch till b.d. 8th.* Miss S Sharratt bd
1174[1] Domino Night (Ire) 11.7 7a *keen hold, chsd ldr to apr 4 out, 3rd and weakening when f 2 out. Dead.* .... Mr G Hanmer f
1002[1] Ita's Fellow (Ire) 11.7 7a *(Jt fav) keen hold, cl up, mstk 7th, b.d. 8th.* .... Mrs C Ford bd
10 ran. 13l, dist. Time 7m 1.50s. SP 5-2.
Stewart Pike

1413 4¼m Bradshaw Bros. Open Hunters' Chase Class H for the Uttoxeter Premier Trophy

1290[2] **THE MALAKARMA 12.0 5a (bl)...... Mr B Pollock 1**
alwys prom and going well, ld 19th, clr 3 out, rdn out run- in.
1291[3] **Ryming Cuplet 11.12 7a .... Mr L Jefford 2**
reminder 4th, prog 10th, chsd ldr 12th to 19th, chased wnr after next, styd on und pres.
1290[1] **Rusty Bridge 12.2 3a .... Mr R Thornton 3**
ld to 7th, lost pl 11th, rdn and lost tch 18th, kept on und pres from 4 out.
1096[2] Royal Jester 12.2 5a *rear, struggling from 16th, t.o. from 5 out.* .... Mr C Storey 4
1249[3] Peajade 11.7 7a *mstks 7th and 8th, struggling after, t.o. and p.u. before 19th.* .... Miss J Wormall pu
494 Holland House 12.4 3a *(fav) mstks, ld 7th to 19th, weakening when blnd 3 out, 4th and well btn when f last.* .... Mr C Bonner f
491[2] Granville Guest 11.7 7a *trckd ldrs going well till rdn and no response 18th, t.o. and p.u. before 4 out.* .... Mr J Tizzard pu
7 ran. 7l, 17l, dist. Time 9m 1.50s. SP 11-2.
Charles Dixey

SEDGEFIELD
Friday May 9th
GOOD TO FIRM

1414 2m 5f Guy Cunard Hunters' Chase Class H

1086[2] **GREENMOUNT LAD (IRE) 12.3 7a Mr P Cornforth 1**
nvr far away, rdn after 13th, slight ld between last 2, hdd and hit last, soon ld again, styd on well.
495[1] **What Chance (Ire) 11.12 7a Mr A Charles-Jones 2**
nvr far away, ld last, soon hdd, no ext.
1248[2] **Knowe Head 12.9 5a .... Mr N Wilson 3**
(fav) ld till hdd between last 2, no ext.
1169[5] Buckaneer Bay 12.2 5a *lost tch from 7th, no dngr after.* .... Mr R Hale 4
1097 Press For Action 12.5 5a *chsd ldr to 11th, wknd quickly after next.* .... Miss P Robson 5
1297 Donside 12.7 *soon well bhnd, t.o.* .... Mr J Walton 6
6 ran. ¾l, 19l, 12l, 11l, dist. Time 5m 18.00s. SP 5-2.
J Cornforth

STRATFORD
Friday May 9th
GOOD

1415 3m John And Nigel Thorne Memorial Cup Class H Hunters' Chase

1284[4] **KINO 11.7 7a .... Mr Andrew Martin 1**
outpcd 6th, hdwy to chase ldr 11th, wknd 3 out, left poor 2nd after 2 out, left in ld last, lucky.
1292[7] **Tara Boy 11.7 7a .... Mr R Cambray 2**
rear and mstk 5th, nvr reached ldrs, left poor 2nd when hmpd 2 out, soon one pace.
890[9] **Faringo 11.7 7a .... Miss C Grissell 3**
jmpd slowly 2nd, alwys bhnd, left poor 3rd at last.
226 The Major General 12.3 7a *held up in tch, lost position 11th, hdwy to chase ldr 4 out, going well upsides when left clr 2 out, u.r. last, rmt.* ..... Captain A Ogden 4
1410[1] Stilltodo 11.2 7a *ld to 14th, soon wknd, tailed of.* .... Mr Chris Wilson 5
1289[3] Hill Island 11.7 7a *(fav) chsd ldr most of way till ld 14th, rdn, still slight ld but held when f 2 out.* .... Mr Rupert Sweeting f
6 ran. 8l, 5l, 5l, dist. Time 6m 26.30s. SP 10-1.
Andrew J Martin

NEWTON ABBOT
Saturday May 10th
GOOD

1416 2m 5f 110yds Totnes And Bridgetown Novices' Hunters' Chase Class H

1241[1] **KING TORUS (IRE) 11.9 5a .... Mr J Jukes 1**
(fav) alwys prom, ld 10th, rdn 2 out, all out.
558[1] **Ticket To The Moon 11.2 7a.... Mr J M Pritchard 2**
held up in tch, hdwy to press wnr from 4 out, no ext apr last.
1242[3] **Full Alirt 11.9 7a .... Miss S Young 3**
held up in rear, hdwy 9th, one pace from 3 out.
1295[2] Mister Horatio 12.0 7a *held up, hdwy 9th, wknd apr 2 out.* .... Mr M Lewis 4
493[1] Herhorse 11.9 7a *held up, hdwy when hit 5 out, weakening when mstk 3 out.* .... Mr L Jefford 5
1342[2] Myhamet 11.7 7a *held up, hdwy 5 out, nvr near to chal.* .... Mr N Harris 6
1292[9] Flowing River (USA) 11.7 7a (bl) *prom, ld 4th to 10th, weakend quickly, t.o. when p.u. before 2 out.* .... Mr N R Mitchell pu
1339 Newski Express 11.2 7a *f 2nd.* .... Mr G Shenkin f
1203[3] Ann's Ambition 11.7 7a *alwys bhnd, t.o. when p.u. before 2 out.* .... Mr M Frith pu
983 Tom's Gemini Star 12.0 7a *held up, hdwy when blnd 4 out, p.u. before next.* .... Mr T Dennis pu
626[1] Comedy Gayle 11.7 7a *alwys bhnd, t.o. when p.u. after 9th.* .... Mr I Widdicombe pu
1311[1] Fellow Sioux 11.7 7a *pulld hrd, prom till wknd 10th, t.o. when p.u. before 2 out.* .... Mr I Dowrick pu
1035[4] Friendly Viking 11.7 7a *alwys bhnd, t.o. when p.u. after 9th.* .... Mr R Darke pu
1485[4] Barrow Street 11.7 7a (v) *ld to 4th, weakend 9th, t.o. when p.u. before 2 out.* .... Mr J Tizzard pu
14 ran. 1¾l, 9l, nk, 4l, nk. Time 5m 28.60s. SP 11-8.
Nick Viney

WARWICK
Saturday May 10th
GOOD

1417 3¼m Normandy Novices' Hunters' Chase Class H

592 **PRINCE BUCK (IRE) 12.4 3a .... Mr P Hacking 1**
(fav) made all, mstk 2nd, styd on strly.
1228[1] **True Fortune 11.7 7a .... Mr D S Jones 2**
alwys prom, chsd wnr 13th, rdn 3 out, soon btn.
1053[1] **Darton Ri 11.7 7a .... Mr J Maxse 3**
prom, lost pl 6th, soon well bhnd, no ch when hmpd run-in, fin 4th, placed 3rd.
1412 Very Daring 11.7 7a *chsd ldrs, rdn after 13th, soon wknd, fin 3rd, pld 4th.* .... Miss S Sharratt 4

1149[3] Damers Treasure 11.7 7a (bl) *chsd ldrs, mstk 2nd, hit 11th, soon bhnd,* .... Mr M Harris 5
1149 Polydeuces 11.7 7a *held up in tch, jmpd right 4th and 5th, chsd wnr next, wknd 12th, p.u. before 14th.* .... Capt R Inglesant pu
1265[2] Bentley Manor 11.7 7a *held up, rdn and lost tch 10th, p.u. before 4 out* .... Mr G Hanmer pu
480 Kellytino 11.2 7a *held up, hdwy and in tch when blnd and u.r. 12th* .... Mr P Scott ur
8 ran. 19l, dist, 3l, 20l. Time 6m 47.90s. SP 4-6.
Mike Roberts
After a stewards inquiry, the 3rd and 4th places were reversed.

BILSDALE
Easingwold
Saturday May 10th
GOOD TO FIRM

1418 Members

1405[2] **DANEGELD (IRE)** .... **N Smith** 1
(fav) rear,prog 12th, ld 4 out, sn clr, ran wd apr 2 out,rdn out
1409[1] **Timber Topper** .... **C Mulhall** 2
chsd ldrs, disp 11th, ld nxt-4out,prssd wnr 2 out,kpt on wll
Singing Sam .... **M Haigh** 3
sttld 3rd, lft 2nd 7th, disp 11th-nxt, sn wknd
1248 Sharpridge *rear, lost tch 7th, t.o. 9th* ... M Mawhinney 4
812[7] Black Spur *ld til ran out 7th* .... Miss A Armitage ro
1106[6] Greatfull Fred *chsd ldr, lft in ld 7th, hdd & lost plc 11th, u.r. 14th* .... Miss K Pickersgill ur
6 ran. ½l, 20l, dist. Time 6m 12.00s. SP 1-3.
Col M J F Sheffield (Bilsdale).

1419 Confined (12st)

1247[2] **BLACKWOODSCOUNTRY** .... **C Mulhall** 1
(fav) mid-div, prog 6th, ld 4 out, jnd last, styd on und pres flat
1405[5] **Mr Dick 6ex** .... **S Swiers** 2
alwys prom, ev ch 2 out, styd on wll flat
1250[1] **Caman 5a** .... **Mrs S Grant** 3
prom, ld 14th-nxt, chal agn last, outpcd flat
1406[4] Mighty Merc *rear, prog to 2nd at 4th, steadily wknd frm 14th* .... S Gibbon 4
1405[9] Earl Gray (bl) *ld to 14th, sn rdn, wknd nxt, t.o. & p.u. 2 out* .... Miss A Deniel pu
1405[4] Chapel Island 3ow *mid-div, hit 3rd, f 7th* ...... G Tuer f
1348[4] Midge 5a *prom early, rear & strgglng 8th, t.o. 10th, p.u. 14th* .... Miss S Brotherton pu
1250[8] Prophet's Choice *not fluent, rear, wll bhnd 8th, t.o. 10th, p.u. nxt* .... M Haigh pu
8 ran. 1l, 2l, 15l. Time 6m 6.00s. SP 7-4.
Mrs Winifred A Birkinshaw (Sinnington).

1420 Men's Open

1253[2] **GAELIC WARRIOR** .... **S Swiers** 1
prom, ld 3rd, drew clr 2 out, comf
1407[3] **Ashdren** .... **N Tutty** 2
rear, clsd up 7th, lft 2nd 14th, ev ch apr 2 out, sn btn
1349[2] **No More Trix** .... **W Burnell** 3
ld to 3rd, chsd wnr aft, lost plc 12th, sn strgglng
1248[6] Frome Boy 2ow *mid-div, rdn 4th, sn strgglng, t.o. 8th* .... P Johnson 4
1407[1] Just Charlie *(fav) sttld in 3rd, blnd 6th & lost plc, prog to 2nd 12th, f 14th* .... D Easterby f
5 ran. 10l, 25l, dist. Time 6m 10.00s. SP 7-2.
Mrs D Ibbotson (York & Ainsty South).

1421 Restricted

1267[1] **KIRI'S ROSE (IRE) 5a** .... **P Gee** 1+
prom, lft in ld 7th, jnd 2 out, styd on wll flat
1101[2] **JOINT ACCOUNT** .... **Mrs F Needham** 1+
(fav) mid-div, prog 12th, chal going wll 2 out, rdn & ran on flat
1250[4] **Mount Faber (bl)** .... **N Smith** 3
rear, prog 8th, chsd ldr 11th, outpcd frm 2 out
1406 Persian Lion *disp to 3rd, chsd ldr aft, wknd 13th, t.o. 3 out* .... Mrs L Ward 4
1406[3] Goodheavens Mrtony *prom til outpcd & rmndrs 11th, mstk 13th, t.o. & p.u. last* .... Miss A Deniel pu
1252[1] Andretti's Heir *disp til ld 3rd, u.r. 7th* ...... A Bonson ur
1251[1] Our Wyn-Ston 7a *twrds rear, prog 10th,blnd 13th,wknd apr 3 out,p.u. nxt,lame* .... L Donnely pu
1250[5] Sergeant Pepper *s.s. rear til p.u. 5th, lame* .. S Swiers pu
8 ran. Dd-ht, 10l, 20l. Time 6m 14.00s.
Brian Gee/ Mrs F Needham (Grove & Rufford/ Bilsdale).
Kiri's Rose, 7-2. Joint Account, 6-4.

1422 Ladies

1408[4] **OSGATHORPE** .... **Mrs F Needham** 1
chsd ldrs, disp 11th-14th, ld agn last, styd on wll
1102[2] **Carole's Delight 5a** .... **Mrs L Ward** 2
prom,chsd ldr 7th,lft in ld 9th,jnd 11-14th,hdd last,kpt on
1408[3] **Kellys Diamond** .... **Miss V Russell** 3
mid-div, prog 14th, ev ch 3 out, outpcd nxt
1405[7] Flying Lion *1st ride, mid-div, drppd rear 7th, t.o. 13th* .... Miss H Kinsella 4
1408 Cheeky Pot *rear, u.r. 6th* .... Mrs S Grant ur
1346[1] Thank U Jim *(fav) ld to 6th, trckng ldr whn s.u. bef nxt* .... Miss T Jackson su
349[2] Naughty Nellie 5a *rear,prog to ld 6th, sn wll clr, ran out apr 9th,rjnd,f 13th* .... Mrs J Dawson f
7 ran. 1l, 6l, dist. Time 6m 28.00s. SP 4-1.
R Tate (Bilsdale).
Last race abandoned - course unsafe. N.E.

CUMBERLAND
Aspatria
Saturday May 10th
GOOD

1423 Members

730[2] **RESTRAINT 5a** .... **Miss F Barnes** 1
ld, mstk 14th, hdd nxt, ld 16th, pshd out
1123[2] **Boreen Owen** .... **T Morrison** 2
(fav) carried 13st, trckd wnr to 14th, 2nd agn 3 out, not qckn nxt
Heavenly Hoofer .... **R Hale** 3
last til prog to ld 15th-16th, rdn & wknd 2 out
3 ran. 2l, 4l. Time 6m 44.00s. SP 3-1.
J Barnes (Cumberland).

1424 Restricted

415[4] **JAYANDOUBLEU (IRE)** .... **T Scott** 1
made virt all, rdn & jnd 2 out, hld on gamely nr fin
1051[1] **Grey Rock (Ire) 5a** .... **P Craggs** 2
(fav) alwys prom, trckd wnr 4 out, rdn & ev ch 2 out, just faild
1169[4] **Fiddlers Brae** .... **Miss D Calder** 3
sn wll bhnd,gd prog frm 12th,chsd ldng pair 3 out,ran on
947[5] Marked Card *chsd ldrs, outpcd frm 13th, no imp frm 16th* .... Mrs M Kendall 4
1218[2] Sumpt'n Smart *mid-div, no prog 13th, kpt on onepcd* .... L Morgan 5
768[1] Sugi *rear, outpcd frm 12th, no ch aft, kpt on frm 3 out* .... I Wynne 6
1085 All Or Nothing 5a *sn wll bhnd, last & no ch 11th, fin strngly* .... J Ewart 7
1337[1] Dillons Bridge (Ire) *mstks, rear, effrt to chs ldng grp 12th, sn lost tch* .... R Morgan 8
729[3] Master Mathew *mstk 7th, prssd wnr to 12th, wknd 14th* .... Miss D Laidlaw 9
1169 Boyup Brook *sn prom, jnd wnr 13th-nxt, 3rd & btn whn blnd 3 out, wknd* .... T Morrison 10
1169[2] Solwaysands *prom to 13th, wknd rpdly, walked in* .... B Gibson 11
1334 Sarona Smith 5a *prom to 5th, sn wknd, t.o. & p.u. 12th* .... Miss J Hutchinson pu
1172[1] Mighty Express *alwys rear, t.o. & p.u. 15th* .. A Ogden pu
1050[3] I'll Skin Them (Ire) 5a *alwys wll in rear, no ch frm 13th, p.u. 15th* .... Mrs C Ford pu

1222[1] Flower Of Dunblane 5a *alwys rear, t.o & p.u. 3 out* ... A Parker pu
1169[3] Kings Token *hld up, prog to trck ldrs 11th, lost plc & p.u. 15th* ... J Walton pu
Queen Ofthe Knowes 12a *schoold in last til u.r. 5th* ... C Storey ur
17 ran. Sht-hd, 4l, 20l, 1l, ½l, 3l, 4l, 4l, 3l, 20l. Time 6m 21.00s. SP 7-1.
W A Crozier (Haydon).

1425 Ladies

415[1] **THE BUACHAILL (IRE) ... Mrs V Jackson 1**
t.d.e. chsd ldr, mstk 11th, clsd 16th, ld aft 3 out, sn clr
1294[2] **Across The Card ... Miss R Ramsay 2**
last til prog to mod 4th at 12th, kpt on to tk 2nd flat
Just For Kicks ... Mrs N Craggs 3
in tch, chsd ldng pair 14th, no imp, kpt on flat
764[1] Parliament Hall *(fav) not fluent, ld, wll clr frm 5th til wknd & hdd aft 3 out* ... Miss P Robson 4
778[8] Rushing Burn 5a *chsng grp til wknd 11th, t.o. 15th* ... Miss N Snowden 5
1297[6] Tod Law 5a *chsng grp til mstk & wknd 11th, t.o. 15th* ... Miss A Bowie 6
6 ran. 12l, ½l, 5l, 25l, ½l. Time 6m 32.00s. SP 9-4.
Mrs Alix Stevenson (Dumfriesshire).

1426 Men's Open

1412 **FISCAL POLICY ... R Trotter 1**
alwys prom, ld 14th, clr 2 out, kpt on wll
766 **Makin' Doo (Ire) ... A Parker 2**
(fav) in tch, prog 12th, ev ch 14th-3 out, no ext und pres
611[2] **Bit Of A Blether (Ire) ... P Craggs 3**
trckd ldr to 12th, mstk 14th, grad wknd
1123[4] Irish Gent *not fluent in last, no ch frm 11th, kpt on* ... G Thomas 4
1347[4] Formal *chsd ldrs, 6th & strggling 11th, no ch aft* ... R Owen 5
1294[4] Green Times *rear, 7th & strggling 11th, no ch aft* ... C Storey 6
1349[6] Inconclusive *10s-5s, chsd ldrs til 5th & wkng 11th, t.o. & p.u. 16th* ... A Ogden pu
1335[3] Winnie Lorraine 5a *ld to 14th, sn wknd, no ch whn s.u. bnd apr 3 out* ... T Scott su
1407[4] Broguestown Pride (Ire) *mstk 6th, 8th & wkng 11th, last whn p.u. 15th* ... R Ford pu
9 ran. 2½l, 25l, 8l, sht-hd, 20l. Time 6m 42.00s. SP 6-1.
H P Trotter (Duke Of Buccleuch's).

1427 Intermediate (12st)

1332[1] **BITOFANATTER 5ex ... R Morgan 1**
made all, wll clr frm 10th, eased flat, imprssv
732[2] **Toaster Crumpet 5ex ... Miss P Robson 2**
chsd wnr 10-13th, no imp, kpt on to go 2nd agn 2 out
944[1] **Nova Nita 5a 5ex ... P Craggs 3**
(fav) w.w. prog to chs wnr 13th, no imp, dmtd 2 out
1332[3] Thinkaboutthat (Ire) *bhnd frm 7th, t.o. 11th, kpt on frm 3 out* ... J Muir 4
1332[2] Jolly Fellow *last & wll bhnd 7th, t.o. 11th, cont mls bhnd.* ... Miss S Ward 5
1051[6] General Jack *bhnd frm 7th, t.o. 11th, p.u. 13th* ... Miss J Percy pu
1405[8] Lindon Run *chsd wnr to 10th, sn rdn, 4th & wkng whn p.u. 14th* ... P Jenkins pu
7 ran. 20l, 10l, 12l, 2 fences. Time 6m 43.00s. SP 2-1.
David Caldwell (Eglinton).

1428 Open Maiden Div I

KEEPER'S CALL (IRE) 7a ... A Parker 1
schoold & mstks,prog 12th,2nd 14th,ld 2 out,ran on well
949[2] **Allrite Pet 5a ... R Morgan 2**
(fav) prom, ld 8th-2 out, ev ch last, ran on flat
1173 **More Rain (Ire) ... P Craggs 3**
chsd ldrs, 4th & outpcd 13th, no prog aft, t.o.
815 Victor Charlie *plling, mid-div, 5th & btn 13th, sn t.o.* ... C Storey 4
734 Barrow Knocks *jmpd slwly, made most 3rd-8th, sn btn, t.o.* ... R Green 5
613 Bantel Baronet *ld til mstk 3rd, sn bhnd, t.o. & p.u. 11th* ... Miss J Hedley pu
Moyne Cross *alwys rear, last & t.o. whn p.u. 15th* ... Miss D Calder pu
999 Keep Them Keen (Ire) *rear, lost tch 11th, t.o. last whn f 16th* ... J Barlow f
1337 Alsina *9s-5s, mstks, alwys rear, no ch 13th, t.o. & p.u. 2 out* ... T Morrison pu
1336 Singing Profit 12a *n.j.w. alwys bhnd, last whn p.u. 12th* ... T Scott pu
1409 Sand Direct (Ire) *chsd ldr 8th-15th, wknd rpdly & mstks aft, p.u. 2 out* ... A Ogden pu
11 ran. 2½l, dist, 20l, 10l. Time 6m 54.50s. SP 4-1.
R G Makin (York & Ainsty South).

1429 Open Maiden Div II

1304[2] **CONCERTO COLLONGES (FR) ... R Ford 1**
(fav) 3s-6/4,prom,disp 10th til ld 13th,wll clr 3 out,ran on wll
767 **Press To Sting ... C Storey 2**
9s-5s,prom,3rd frm 10th til chsd wnr & 6l 2nd 16th,btn nxt
1294 **Shine A Light ... A Ogden 3**
prom, ld/disp 8th-13th, blnd nxt, wknd 4 out
1297 Fast Fun *alwys bhnd, t.o. & p.u. 12th* ... R Morgan pu
1218 Fortinas Flyer 5a *n.j.w. last & t.o. til p.u. 11th* ... D McLeod pu
1337[3] Tolmin *mid-div & out of tch, wknd & p.u. 12th* ... A Robson pu
Lanton Moor 5a *blnd 6th, t.o. nxt, p.u. 12th* .. P Craggs pu
343[4] Corston Frisby *hld up, prog 8th, 4th & no imp ldrs 13th, t.o. & p.u. last* ... A Parker pu
341 Disrespect 5a *made most to 8th, sn wknd, t.o. & p.u. 12th* ... Miss M Macmillan pu
420[4] Megans Mystery (Ire) *prom til wknd rpdly 10th, t.o. & p.u. 13th* ... J Walton pu
1409 Durham Glint *rear, effrt 11th, 5th & no ch whn f 13th* ... S Bowden f
1171[3] Hooky's Treat 5a *u.r. 2nd* ... Miss L Bradburne ur
853 Nickamy Fountain (Ire) (bl) *t.o. 7th, p.u. 12th* . J Barlow pu
1052 Read The News 12a *alwys bhnd, t.o. & p.u. 14th* ... T Morrison pu
815[7] Dynastie D'Auge (Fr) 5a *mstk 5th, alwys bhnd, t.o. 12th, p.u. last* ... T Scott pu
15 ran. 25l, 25l. Time 6m 48.50s. SP 6-4.
Les Streeton (Pytchley).
J.N.

EAST ANGLIAN BLOODHOUNDS
Marks Tey
Saturday May 10th
GOOD

1430 Confined (12st)

1286 **GIVE IT A BASH (IRE) 5a ... T Moore 1**
hld up, prog 7th, disp 3 out, ld nxt, ran on wll last
1376[2] **Dance On Sixpence ... S March 2**
trckd ldrs, lft in ld aft 10th, jnd 4 out, hdd nxt, ran on
1306[3] **Current Attraction 5a 9ow ... Miss K Thory 3**
alwys rear, last at 9th, t.o. 12th, ran on 3 out, tk 3rd fin
1279[1] Druid's Lodge *(fav) chsd ldrs, 4th at 9th, 2nd 14th, disp 4 out, sn outpcd,eased* ... N Bloom 4
1305 Salachy Run (Ire) *ld 1st, 6l clr 6th, tried to run out & hdd aft 10th, sn btn* ... N Page 5
801 Cosmic Ray *alwys rear, mstks 3rd & 7th, wknd 10th, p.u. last* ... D Page pu
1309[3] Aughnacloy Rose *rear whn p.u. 3rd, stirrup broke* ... R Page pu
7 ran. 2½l, 20l, hd, 20l. Time 6m 53.00s. SP 12-1.
Miss S Wilson (Essex & Suffolk).

1431 Open Maiden (12st)

1379 **FLAPPING FREDA (IRE) 5a (bl) .... M Gingell** 1
(Jt fav) made virt all, jmpd rght, prssd 2 out, drew clr last, easily

1310^{2} **Fragment (Ire) (bl) .... T Moore** 2
trckd wnr, chal & ev ch whn mstk 2 out, hld aft

1281 **Ballad (Ire) 7a .... T Bulgin** 3
rear, prog to chs ldrs 14th, outpcd 16th, styd on 2 out

1282 Bantry Bay 7a *sttld rear, going wll 11th, lost tch 14th, p.u. 3 out* .... A Coe pu

1276 Silverspina 5a *(Jt fav) last whn ref 1st* .... N Bloom ref

1281 Sapling 5a *alwys rear, some prog to 3rd at 11th, outpcd 14th, p.u. 3out* .... N King pu

6 ran. 2l, hd. Time 6m 59.00s. SP 5-2.
B G Clark & Mrs V Storey (Puckeridge).

1432 Members

801^{2} **GYPSY KING (IRE) .... A Coe** 1
(fav) made all at sedate pace, drew clr 12th, canter

1118 **Paddy A Go Go 12a .... S R Andrews** 2
chsd wnr, jmpd delib, lost tch 12th

2 ran. Dist. Time 7m 23.00s. SP 1-6.
Mrs Lulu Wrighton (East Anglian Bloodhounds).

1433 Men's Open

1117^{5} **FOXBOW (IRE) (bl) .... A Sansome** 1
chsd ldrs,disp 7th,clr nxt,drvn 3 out,wknd last, jst hld on

1279^{3} **Over The Edge .... S Sporborg** 2
(fav) ld to 4th,went 2nd 12th,outpcd 3 out,styd on nxt,just faild

1279 **Lyme Gold (Ire) (bl) .... P Keane** 3
prom, ld & mstk 4th, jnd 7th, hdd nxt, blnd 10th, wknd 15th

1310^{1} Kabancy *s.s. alwys last, mstk 3rd, wknd 10th, p.u. 12th* .... S R Andrews pu

4 ran. Nk, 20l. Time 6m 47.00s. SP 4-1.
J M Turner (Suffolk).

1434 Ladies

1378^{1} **PROFESSOR LONGHAIR .... Miss C Papworth** 1
(fav) ld to 4th,mstk 9th,ld 11th-14th,outpcd,ran on to ld last

1378^{3} **Major Inquiry (USA) (bl) .... Miss H Pewter** 2
chsd wnr,ld 4th-11th,ld 14th,clr 4 out,hdd last,ran on flat

596^{4} **Ace Of Spies .... Miss A Embiricos** 3
hld up, prog 9th, last frm 14th, outpcd nxt, styd on 2 out

3 ran. 1l, 2l. Time 6m 57.00s. SP 4-9.
A J Papworth (North Norfolk).

1435 Intermediate (12st)

1355^{2} **ROUGH EDGE .... W Wales** 1
hld up rear,prog 10th,chsd ldr 4 out,chal 2 out,ld last,r.o.

1286^{4} **Ballyallia Castle (Ire) .... N Bloom** 2
(fav) chsd ldr,prog to ld 4 out,prssd 2 out,outjmpd last,ran on

1305^{1} **Shake Five (Ire) .... S Sporborg** 3
hld up, prog 11th, 3rd & ev ch 3 out, sn outpcd

1277^{6} Courier's Way (Ire) *ld, clr & mstk 6th, hdd 16th, wknd frm 3 out* .... T Moore 4

1285^{5} Smart Pal 5ex *alwys prom, ld brfly 16th, sn outpcd, onepcd 2 out* .... K Needham 5

1309^{4} Tremeirchion *alwys rear, lost tch 10th, t.o. 13th, mstk & p.u. aft nxt* .... M Barnard pu

1431 Silverspina 5a *2nd outing,mid-div,slw jmps 1st & 2nd,wknd 10th,p.u.13th* .... N King pu

Tell Tale (Ire) 7a *rear whn hmpd 2nd, mstk nxt, last 10th, p.u. nxt* .... T Bulgin pu

8 ran. Nk, 15l, ½l, 2l. Time 6m 53.00s. SP 3-1.
David Wales (West Norfolk).
J.W.

MINEHEAD & WEST SOMERSET

Holnicote
Saturday May 10th
GOOD

1436 Members (12st)

1311^{3} **TUFFNUT TOM .... R Payne** 1
(fav) ld/disp til ld 2 out, blnd & hdd last, rallied to ld nr fin

795 **Nikolayevich .... A Turner** 2
ld/disp til outpcd aft 3 out, ran on & lft in ld last,hdd fn

1244^{2} **Southerly Buster .... S White** 3
in tch til outpcd 17th, ran on clsng stgs

557 Blue Night 5a *w.w. effrt & ld 3 out, hdd & mstk nxt, sn btn* .... J Scott 4

1144^{1} Spar Copse 13ow *1st ride, lost tch 6th, t.o.* ... P Froud 5

5 ran. Nk, 2l, 6l, dist. Time 6m 52.50s. SP 7-4.
Mrs R Lamacraft (Minehead Harriers).

1437 Open Maiden (12st)

1315^{4} **MILLYHENRY .... J Tizzard** 1
ld/disp frm 4th, ld 16th-3 out, ld agn nxt, sn clr

1260 **Dollybat 5a .... M Frith** 2
hld up, went 2nd 17th, ld nxt til mstk & hdd 2 out, no ext

1314^{4} **Simply Joyful 5a .... P King** 3
ld/disp to 13th, lost plc 16th, onepcd clsng stgs

1246^{3} Sam's Successor *mid-div, 7th at 12th, nvr dang* .... N Harris 4

1088 Father Malone (Ire) *in tch to 14th, wkng whn hit 17th, no ch aft* .... L Jefford 5

1311^{5} Dollys Best 5a 3ow *t.o. 8th, p.u. 13th* ... Miss C Hayes pu

Another Kav (Ire) 5a *20s-4s, twrds rear whn f 4th* .... J Price f

1246 Retrieving Mission (Ire) *(fav) cls 3rd at 10th, cls 2nd whn hit 16th, p.u. nxt, dead* .... N Mitchell pu

Leejay Luki *twrds rear, bhnd whn b.d. 16th* .... A Honeyball bd

1261 Kiramanda 5a *keen hld, prom til lost ground 14th, wkng whn f 16th* .... G Barfoot-Saunt f

1216 Permit 5a *6th hlfwy, bhnd 13th til p.u. 16th* .... Miss A Goschen pu

Weycroft Valley 5a *sn bhnd, t.o. & p.u. 12th* ... B Dixon pu

692 Perripage *prom til lost plc 11th, bhnd whn p.u. 16th* .... M Miller pu

1400 Go Willie Go *s.s. t.o. & ref 3rd* .... R Young ref

14 ran. 5l, 20l, 15l, 3l. Time 6m 42.00s. SP 9-2.
L G Tizzard (Quantock Staghounds).

1438 Ladies

1155^{1} **OLD MILL STREAM .... Miss P Gundry** 1
(fav) j.w. ld frm 5th, drew clr apr 2 out, comf

1316^{3} **Stalbridge Gold 5a .... Miss A Goschen** 2
6th hlfwy, prog 11th, went 2nd 15th, rdn & no ext 2 out

1257^{1} **Rapid Rascal .... Miss S West** 3
slght ld 2-6th, wll in tch til outpcd 15th, kpt on

1394 Romany Anne 5a *5th hlfwy, lost ground 11th, ran on cls home* .... Miss S Young 4

1156^{3} Elle Flavador 5a *keen hld, prom, 2nd whn mstk 14th, wknd 3 out, mstk last* .... Miss S Vickery 5

1340^{1} Celtic Sport (bl) *rear, t.o. 9th til p.u. 15th, dsmntd, lame* .... Miss C Stucley pu

1212^{5} Perseverance *4th whn stirrup iron broke & u.r. 12th* .... Miss J Cumings ur

7 ran. 6l, 5l, hd, 1½l. Time 6m 29.00s. SP 4-5.
Richard Barber (Taunton Vale).
Three fences omitted from this race onwards, 17 jumps per race.

1439 Restricted (12st)

1374^{2} **ROYAL TURN .... A Honeyball** 1
hld up in tch, effrt 15th, ld apr last, styd on strngly

1061^{2} **Kinesiology (Ire) .... R Treloggen** 2
(fav) ld to 14th, ld agn aft nxt, ev ch til not qckn apr last

1210 **Samule .... G Barfoot-Saunt** 3

tongue-strap, 4th whn hit 10th, 5th at 13th, kpt on
1211[2] Bewdley Boy *prog 10th, ld 14th-nxt, sn wknd* ....Miss P Gundry 4
1317[2] Remember Mac (bl) *sn twrds rear, bhnd frm 12th* ....Miss C Hayes 5
567[3] Orwell Ross (Ire) *bhnd frm 5th, p.u. 14th* ....H Wells pu
1216[1] Moorlough Bay (Ire) *chsd ldr to 13th, lost ground aft 15th, p.u. last* ....T Mitchell pu
1315[1] And What Else (Ire) *prom til lost plc 8th, t.o. & p.u. 15th* ....S Slade pu
1094[3] I'll Be Bound (v) *rear, 8th hlfwy, bhnd whn p.u. 14th* ....M Burrows pu
9 ran. 5l, 5l, 5l, dist. Time 6m 36.50s. SP 15-2.
John Honeyball (Taunton Vale Foxhounds).

1440 Men's Open (12st)

1271[1] **EARL BOON ....T Mitchell 1**
(fav) ld 2nd-aft nxt, ld aft 10th, forged clr frm 3 out
1244[4] **Hensue ....N Harris 2**
hld up, went 2nd apr 11th, ev ch til no ext frm 3 out
521[2] Riva (NZ) *raced keenly, ld & clr by 6th, wknd rpdly, blnd 10th,p.u.nxt* ....N Mitchell pu
3 ran. 8l. Time 6m 42.00s. SP 10-11.
J A Keighley (Blackmore & Sparkford Vale).

1441 Confined (12st)

1398 **FOUR LEAF CLOVER 5a ....J Jukes 1**
(fav) sn prom, disp 9th til ld 12th, mstk 15th, drew clr 2 out
1244[1] **Just Ben 6ex ....Miss J Cumings 2**
disp 9th-12th, cls up & ev ch til outpcd 2 out
1398 **Tangle Kelly ....S Slade 3**
ld 1st, prom til ld 8-9th, grad fdd frm 12th
1155 Searcy 5ex *6s-7/2, twrds rear, 5th hlfwy, poor 4th frm 11th, some prog* ....Miss L Blackford 4
1311[4] Frosty Reception 3ex (bl) *in tch til lost plc 8th, no ch frm 11th* ....Miss C Stucley 5
1087 L'uomo Piu 7ex *ld 2-8th, sn wknd, bhnd frm 11th, p.u. 2 out* ....T Mitchell pu
1258[4] The Criosra (Ire) *sn trailing, t.o. 3rd, p.u. 2 out* ....A Bateman pu
7 ran. 8l, 25l, 8l, 8l. Time 6m 34.50s. SP 4-5.
Mrs K A Hanbury (Dulverton West).
G.T.

SURREY UNION
Peper Harow
Saturday May 10th
GOOD TO FIRM

1442 Members

1129 **AND WHY NOT 3ex ....J Van Praagh 1**
(fav) mstk 1st, hld up, ld 12th, clr last, rdn out
1054 **Royal Irish ....P Townsley 2**
jmpd slwly 3rd,ld to 12th,ev ch & rdn 3 out,blnd nxt,onepcd
829 **The Forties 3ow ....N Earnshaw 3**
tubed, prssd ldr to 9th, wknd 11th, lft poor 3rd last
1115[3] St Laycar 3ex *trckd ldrs, 3rd & rdn 13th, btn 3 out, p.u. last, lame* ....A Greig pu
4 ran. 2l, dist. Time 7m 0.00s. SP Evens.
Mrs C E Van Praagh (Surrey Union).

1443 Restricted (12st)

1303 **BOCOCK'S PRIDE (IRE) ....T Underwood 1**
(Jt fav) conf rdn, lft 2nd 14th, chal & ld last, ran on
1355 **Prime Course (Ire) ....P Bull 2**
chsd ldr, lft in ld 14th, slppd apr 2 out, hdd last, no ext
582[1] Phaedair *(Jt fav) u.r. going to strt, ld til stmbld & u.r. 14th* ....R Hubbard ur
3 ran. 2l. Time 7m 23.00s. SP Evens.
T Underwood & C Shankland (Teme Valley).

1444 Men's Open (12st)

986[1] **VALIBUS (FR) 2ow ....P Scouller 1**
chsd ldr, ld 12th, made rest, styd on wll frm 2 out
1285 **Billion Dollarbill ....M Gorman 2**
in tch, outpcd 10th, rallied 13th, 2nd 3 out, kpt on flat
983[6] **Northern Village 7ex ....D Alers-Hankey 3**
(fav) chsd ldrs, jmpd slwly 3rd & 4th, blnd 14th, unable qckn 2out
1300[1] July Schoon *hld up bhnd, prog 12th, chnc 3 out, 4th & hld whn blnd nxt* ....T Underwood 4
830[3] Kates Castle 5a *ld, hit 10th, hdd 12th, sn rdn, wknd 3 out, p.u. last* ....J Van Praagh pu
5 ran. ½l, 3l, 3l. Time 6m 49.00s. SP 5-1.
P A D Scouller (Garth & South Berks).

1445 Ladies

1396[3] **HOWARYADOON ....Miss T Cave 1**
(fav) in tch, disp 11th, ld 3 out, hit last, rdn out
1284[5] **Woody Will ....Mrs E Coveney 2**
prssd ldr, ld 6th-3 out, kpt on wll, cllpsd & died aft race
1128[5] **Abdul Emir ....Mrs L Stock 3**
in tch, chsd ldrs frm 6th, mstk 10th, outpcd frm 13th
1308[5] Lewesdon Princess 5a *keen hld, chsd ldrs to 6th, last frm 9th, no ch frm 12th* ....Miss S Gladders 4
1278 New York Boy *bhnd frm 4th, pshd alng 10th, nvr nr ldrs* ....Miss C Savell 5
830[5] Bright Hour *made most to 6th, 4th & wkng 12th, no ch whn u.r. 14th* ....Miss J Grant ur
6 ran. ½l, 20l, 10l, 7l. Time 6m 53.00s. SP 1-2.
Dr S G F Cave (Blackmore & Sparkford Vale).

1446 Open Maiden (12st)

605 **PROVINCIAL RETREAT 7a ....P Bull 1**
(fav) 5/2-5/4,chsd ldrs,went 2nd & hit 13th, ld 15th, rdn clr flat
1130[2] **Linger Balinda 5a ....J Van Praagh 2**
chsd ldr 4th, ld & blnd 12th, hdd 15th, sn hrd rdn, outpcd
Armed Force ....T Hills 3
hung & jmpd rght, ld, clr to 8th, hdd 12th, wknd nxt, t.o.
917 Exhibition Prince (Ire) *chsd ldr to 3rd,jmpd slwly nxt,4th & rdn 13th,t.o.& p.u.3out* ....M Gorman pu
833 Get On Lottie 5a 3ow *mid-div to 8th, wll bhnd frm 10th, p.u. 13th* ....M Jones pu
1130[4] Spanish Pal (Ire) *hld up, prog to 4th & in tch whn blnd & u.r. 10th* ....Miss S Gladders ur
1379 Tidal Reef (Ire) 7a *alwys bhnd, jmpd slwly 3rd, t.o. & p.u. 13th* ....P York pu
7 ran. 5l, 2 fences. Time 7m 15.00s. SP 5-4.
C G Squance (Surrey Union).

1447 Confined (12st)

1126[4] **SUPREME DEALER ....A Warr 1**
ld to 2nd, ld apr 13th, kpt on gamely frm 2 out
783[1] **Velka 5a ....A Hickman 2**
chsd ldrs,mstk 10th,went 2nd 13th,ev ch & blnd 2 out,no ext
1126[2] **Vultoro ....T Underwood 3**
(fav) tubed, hld up, wll bhnd, prog 12th, rdn 3 out, wll btn nxt
1128[4] Rarely At Odds *tongue-strap, chsd ldrs, 4th & in tch whn u.r. 12th* ....Miss A Sansom ur
576[2] Emerald Moon *ld 2nd, sn clr, blnd 7th, hdd apr 13th, wknd, p.u. 15th* ....T Hills pu
1126[3] Yeoman Farmer *alwys rear, jmpd slwly 3rd, t.o. last at 9th, p.u. 12th* ....Miss S Gladders pu
6 ran. 4l, 15l. Time 6m 57.00s. SP 3-1.
L J Bowman (Kent & Surrey Bloodhounds).
S.P.

VALE OF AYLESBURY
Kingston Blount
Saturday May 10th
GOOD

1448 Confined (12st)

1206[2] **RUN FOR FREE 3ex.........................A Hill** 1
(fav) hld up, prog 6th, ld 11th-aft 2 out, drvn to ld last,lft clr
1289 **Teatrader ....Miss T Blazey** 2
cls up, ld 6th, sn hdd, chsd ldrs, 4th 2 out, ran on
1205[2] **Cawkwell Dean 3ex ....R Sweeting** 3
ld 3rd-aft nxt, ld 7-10th, 5th at 13th, ran on flat
1404 Copper Bank *rear to hlfwy, prog to 4th at 11th, 3rd at 14th, wknd 3 out* ....F Hutsby 4
1403 Grand Value *ld to 2nd, wknd 6th, rear whn p.u. 12th* ....C Wadland pu
Bright As A Button *alwys prom, went 2nd at 14th, ld aft 2 out, hdd & ref last*......................G Tarry ref
1159 Obie's Train 7ow *alwys wll bhnd, t.o. 8th, p.u. aft 11th* ....Mrs A Lee pu
1162[3] Sprucefield *chsd ldrs to 11th, wknd rpdly, p.u. 15th* ....A Barlow pu
Indian Crow *in tch to hlfwy, grad wknd, bhnd whn p.u. last* ....J Trice-Rolph pu
9 ran. 20l, 3l, ¾l. Time 6m 32.00s. SP 2-1.
Alan Hill (Vale Of Aylesbury).

1449 Restricted

1164[2] **VILLAINS BRIEF (IRE) ....R Lawther** 1
hld up, prog aft 5th, ld 7-10th, qcknd to ld flat
1288 **Trevveethan (Ire) ....M Rimell** 2
(fav) mid-div, prog 10th, ld 12th-aft last, not qckn
1210 **The Hon Company ....E Walker** 3
bhnd, last at 7th, prog 11th, 5th at 15th, nrst fin
1210[7] Salmon Poutcher 5a *ld 4th, sn hdd, lost plc, 6th 2 out, ran on wll flat* ....J Trice-Rolph 4
1275[3] Duke Of Lancaster (Ire) *ld to 4th, ld 6th, 2nd nxt, ld 10th-nxt, wknd 12th* ....N Sutton 5
1208[2] Upton Lass (Ire) 5a *mostly mid-div, prog to 2nd at 11th, 3rd at 15th, wknd*..........................L Lay 6
1144[2] John Roger *in tch, 2nd at 5th, wll bhnd frm 7th, styd on*..L Manners 7
Muskerry Miss (Ire) 5a *alwys bhnd, t.o. & p.u. aft 13th* ....A Charles-Jones pu
8 ran. 1l, 12l, hd, 4l, 6l, 4l. Time 6m 42.00s. SP 5-2.
Nick Quesnel (Berks & Bucks Drag).

1450 Ladies

1384[1] **FUNDY (IRE) ....Miss T Spearing** 1
(fav) ld til aft 5th, ld 9th, made rest, drew clr frm 2 out,easily
1058[3] **Rayman (Ire) ....Miss S Duckett** 2
rear, prog to ld aft 5th-9th, cls 2nd til outpcd 2 out
1207[4] **Linlake Lightning 5a ....Miss H Irving** 3
tongue-strap, 2nd til aft 7th, chsd ldrs, not qckn frm 15th
1384[4] Hiram B Birdbath (bl) *mid-div, clsd 7th, no ch frm 12th, rear whn p.u. last* ....Mrs C McCarthy pu
547[3] My Best Man *cls up, 3rd at 5th, wknd nxt, t.o. & p.u. aft 15th* ....Mrs T Hill pu
989[4] Haydon Hill 5a *s.v.s. last til aft 5th, some prog, wknd 8th, p.u. aft 15th*......................Miss H Gosling pu
1164 Sparnova 5a *sn bhnd, last frm 5th, t.o. & p.u. aft 15th* ....Miss T Habgood pu
7 ran. 20l, 10l. Time 6m 30.00s. SP 4-7.
A J Brazier (Croome & West Warwickshire).

1451 Men's Open (12st)

1354[2] **GRECIAN LARK ....G Tarry** 1
(fav) hld up in mid-div, qcknd to ld 15th-nxt, ld 2 out, drvn out
1214[4] **Welsh Singer 4ex.....................R Lawther** 2
in tch, cls 2nd at 14th, ld 3 out-nxt, just outpcd
1403 **Lofty Deed (USA) 7ex..........A Charles-Jones** 3
2nd til aft 9th, cls up, ld aft 13th,sn hdd, kpt on flat
1078 Radical Views *blnd 2nd, hld up, qcknd to ld 14th, hdd nxt, wknd rpdly* ....A Hill 4
1055[4] Abitmorfun 3ow *ld to aft 13th, last nxt, sn t.o.* ....C Coyne 5
5 ran. 1½l, 10l, 15l, 1 fence. Time 6m 42.00s. SP 4-7.
J White (Grafton).

1452 Open Maiden

1285 **MR PINBALL (bl)........................P Cowley** 1
ld 2nd-5th, ld 9th-13th, ld aft 14th, styd on
1209 **Marmalade ....R Sweeting** 2
alwys prom, 5l 2nd at 9th, lost plc nxt, onepcd frm 15th
1402[4] Looking *ld 1st, ld 5-8th, ran out bend apr nxt* ....R Lawther ro
1210 Bit Of A Do *hld up,lft 3rd 9th,2nd nxt,ld 13th-aft nxt,wknd,p.u.2 out*..........................A Hill pu
1209[8] Half Sharp 5a *t.d.e. mid-div, f 5th*..............L Lay f
1402 Mr Dennehy (Ire) *(fav) sn prom, chsd ldr til blnd & u.r. 7th* ....M Harris ur
1352 Fawsley Manor 5a *rear whn ran throgh wing 4th* ....J Docker ro
Tuts Lad *alwys bhnd, last at 5th, t.o. & p.u. aft 10th* ....C Coyne pu
Boozing Gunner *hmpd & p.u. 4th*....A Charles-Jones pu
9 ran. 7l. Time 6m 51.00s. SP 25-1.
Mrs D Cowley (Pytchley).

1453 Members

990[2] **BET A LOT 5a ....Miss T Honeyball** 1
(fav) ld 3rd & agn 7th, ld/disp til qcknd clr aft 3 out
986 **Royal Dadda ....A Hill** 2
ld to 3rd, ld nxt, ld/disp til outpcd aft 3 out
1401 Spring Sabre *reluc to start, cls 3rd til ref 9th* ....R Lawther ref
3 ran. 5l. Time 7m 15.00s. SP 4-7.
Mrs A M Murray (Vale Of Aylesbury).
H.F.

COTSWOLD VALE FARMERS
Maisemore Park
Sunday May 11th
GOOD

1454 Members

1289[2] **GLEN OAK 7ex........................D Duggan** 1
(fav) chsd ldr to 6th & frm 13th, ld 15th, blnd nxt, sn clr
1062 **Junction Twentytwo (bl) ....O McPhail** 2
ld to 15th, hrd rdn & wknd, fin exhausted
1067 **Derring Tirley ....S Joynes** 3
mstks, chsd ldr 9-13th, wknd rpdly, t.o.
1063[8] Millstock 5a *chsd ldr 6-9th,outpcd12th,ran on 2 out,disp 2nd & f last* ....Miss N Stallard f
1324 The Blind Judge *jmpd slwly 3rd & sn t.o., 2 fncs bhnd whn f last*..........................G Barfoot-Saunt f
5 ran. 25l, dist. Time 6m 46.00s. SP 1-6.
R J Mansell (Cotswold Vale Farmers).

1455 Confined (12st)

1064[1] **CRUISE A HOOP 3ex............Julian Pritchard** 1
(fav) ld & mstk 2nd, mstks 10 & 14th, shkn up 2 out, ran on well
1321 **Pretoria Dancer 7a.....................M Rimell** 2
chsd wnr 10-12th & agn 3 out, chnc nxt, btn & slw jmp last
1211[1] **Landsker Alfred 6ex ....Miss A Dare** 3
blnd 4th, effrt to chs wnr 12th-3 out, 3rd & btn aft
1326 Members Rights 5a *bhnd frm 8th, t.o. aft 13th, kpt on frm 3 out* ....M Keel 4
1329 Bumptious Boy *chsd wnr 8-10th, wknd aft 13th, t.o. 3 out*..S Hanks 5
1274 Champagne Run *sn bhnd, t.o. & jmpd slwly 4th, ref 6th*..R Hawker ref
1194[7] Kingfisher Bay *ld to 2nd, rdn & wknd aft 11th, t.o. & p.u. 15th*..J Price pu
1330 Royal Sweep *jmpd slwly, t.o. til ref 4th* . .C Dorrington ref
8 ran. 4l, 10l, 30l, 2l. Time 6m 34.00s. SP 1-2.
W M A Davies (Ledbury).

1456 Ladies

1017[1] **SPLIT SECOND** ....**Miss A Dare** 1
(fav) trckd ldrs, ld 13th, rdn aft 2 out, ran on well
1293[3] **Fantastic Fleet (Ire) 7a**..........**Miss C Thomas** 2
hld up, trckd wnr 14th, ev ch apr last, not qckn
1319 **West King** ....**Miss P Gundry** 3
cls up til wknd 14th, t.o.
219 Browned Off *jmpd rght & slwly, ld to 13th, t.o. aft nxt* ....Miss H Bevan 4
1321 Scared Stiff 5a *jmpd slwly, rear til ran out & u.r. 7th* ....Miss E Roberts ro
5 ran. 2½l, dist, dist. Time 6m 43.00s. SP 1-4.
Mrs P J Willis (Berkeley).

1457 Men's Open (12st)

1234[1] **VIRIDIAN 7ex**...................**Julian Pritchard** 1
(fav) ld to 8th, ld 13th, canter
1455 **Champagne Run (bl)** ....**R Hawker** 2
2nd outing, nrly ref 7th, ld 8th til nrly ref 13th, no ch
2 ran. 9l. Time 7m 17.00s. SP 1-12.
Denis Hine (Ledbury).

1458 P P O R A (12st)

1327[1] **DOWN THE MINE 7ex**...............**Miss A Dare** 1
(fav) made all, clr 15th, ran on well
1210[4] **Everso Irish** ....**Julian Pritchard** 2
cls up, outpcd 13th, effrt to chs wnr 15th, no imp 2 out
1320 Sandy Beau 4ex *bhnd frm 8th, t.o. & p.u. 15th* ....Miss A Nolan pu
1366[1] Corn Exchange *chsd wnr, cls 3rd whn blnd & u.r. 14th*..........M Rimell ur
1212[3] Frozen Pipe 5a *chsd wnr to 15th, p.u. nxt, lame* ....M Harris pu
1370[2] Slaney France (Ire) 1ow *pckd 2nd, t.o. 7th, p.u. 11th* ....Miss K Lovelace pu
6 ran. 8l. Time 6m 33.50s. SP 8-13.
R T Baimbridge (Berkeley).

1459 Open Maiden Div I (12st)

1356 **THEMOREYOUKNOW** ....**M Harris** 1
(fav) ld to 2nd, trckd ldrs, ld 13th, ran on well frm 2 out
1238[2] **Rejects Reply** ....**G Hanmer** 2
hld up,prog frm 10th, chsd wnr 15th, rdn & chnc 2 out,no ext
1330 **Crestwood Lad (USA)** ....**M Yardley** 3
mstk 8th, chsd ldr 3rd-10th, wknd 14th
1324 Bickerton Poacher *mstk 7th, prog & in tch 12th, wknd 14th, t.o.*..........G Perkins 4
1216[4] Country Lord *alwys last, t.o. 7th* ....Mrs S Walwin 5
1320 Ruffinswick *alwys rear, lost tch 9th, t.o. & p.u. 15th* ....J Price pu
1018[6] Cal's Boy *25s-5s, ld 2nd-13th, wknd 15th, wll btn & p.u. 2 out* ....A Dalton pu
1330[2] Royal Swinger 5a *mstk 5th, lost tch 9th, 10th whn u.r. 11th*..........Miss S Trotman ur
King Fowler (Ire) *w.w. prog 8th, jnd ldrs 13th, ev ch whn f nxt*..........A Wintle f
1304 Must Be Murphy (Ire) *in tch whn mstk 11th, wknd & p.u. 13th*..........R Burton pu
1401 Ullington Lord (bl) *prom to 10th, wknd 12th, t.o. & p.u. 15th* ....S Joynes pu
1240 Firestarter *rear, prog 10th, lost tch 14th, poor 4th whn f last* ....S Shinton f
12 ran. 3½l, 20l, 15l, 2 fences. Time 6m 45.50s. SP 11-4.
M H Weston (Worcestershire).

1460 Open Maiden Div II (12st)

1367[2] **FORT GALE (IRE)** ....**Julian Pritchard** 1
(fav) alwys cls up, prog to chal ldr aft 3 out, hrd rdn to ld post
1016[6] **Nick The Biscuit** ....**O McPhail** 2
in tch,prog 11th,ld 15th,jnd apr 2 out,kpt on wll, hdd post
1393[3] **Musical Mail** ....**R Burton** 3
alwys prom, ld 9th-14th, wknd aft 3 out
1323[2] Boddington Hill 5a *chsd ldrs til outpcd frm 13th, 5th & no ch apr 3 out* ....I Johnson 4
573 Peter Pointer *ld to 9th, ld 14th-nxt, wknd 3 out* ....A Wintle 5
1183 Bessie's Will 5a *alwys rear, t.o. & p.u. 15th* G Barfoot-Saunt pu
1401 Brother Harold *chsd ldrs to 12th, sn wknd, t.o. & p.u. 3 out*..........L Brown pu
1324[4] Priesthill (Ire) *in tch to 10th, sn wknd, t.o. & p.u. 14th* ....D Stephens pu
1437 Another Kav (Ire) 5a *16s-7s, hld up, rear whn f 4th* ....J Price f
368[5] The Hollow (Ire) 5a *wll in tch to 12th, sn wknd, wll bhnd & p.u. 3 out* ....R Bevis pu
1330 Asante Sana 5a (v) *n.j.w. alwys rear, t.o. 9th, p.u. 12th* ....N Oliver pu
1216[2] Miss Dior 5a *prom til mstk & u.r. 11th.* .Miss P Gundry ur
570 Maiden's Quest 12a *alwys rear, p.u. 11th* ...A Phillips pu
1239 Money Don't Matter 12a *rear, in tch whn mstk 12th, 5th & wll btn whn u.r. 15th*..........T Stephenson ur
1066[4] Parapluie 5a *f 1st*..........Miss B Lloyd f
1200[6] Scarra Darragh (Ire) 5a *w.w. rear, mstk 12th, sn btn, wll bhnd & p.u. 14th*..........A Charles-Jones pu
16 ran. Sht-hd, 20l, 15l, 1l. Time 6m 40.50s. SP 9-4.
D J Clapham (Cotswold Vale Farmers).
J.N.

ISLE OF WIGHT & THAMES VALLEY
Tweseldown
Sunday May 11th
GOOD TO FIRM

1461 Members (12st)

934[2] **BART'S CASTLE** ....**Daniel Dennis** 1
(fav) made all, rdn whn lft virt solo 3 out
869 **Fowling Piece** ....**M Legge** 2
jmpd delib in rear, t.o. 6th, lft remote 2nd 3 out
The Hon Rose 5a *chsd wnr, ev ch whn f 3 out* ....T Woolridge f
3 ran. Dist. Time 6m 11.50s. SP 4-7.
Miss A M Reed (Isle Of Wight).

1462 Confined (12st)

1214[2] **ESPY 3ex** ....**E James** 1
(fav) j.w. w.w. ld 13th, drvn out flat
585[5] **Corly Special** ....**B Pollock** 2
trckd ldrs, 2nd & ev ch frm 15th, no ext flat
1199[1] **Bawnerosh** ....**T Underwood** 3
hld up, effrt 15th, onepcd frm 3 out
1127[3] Paco's Boy *sn outpcd in rear, rdn 10th, no ch frm 14th*..........P York 4
486[2] New Ghost (v) *made most to mstk 13th, wknd rpdly, p.u. 4 out, lame*..........Miss A Goschen pu
1296 Twist 'N' Scu *mostly cls 2nd, wknd 8th, p.u. 12th, lame*..........R Lawther pu
6 ran. 5l, 15l, 8l. Time 6m 10.00s. SP 13-8.
C James (Vine And Craven).

1463 Mixed Open

1391[1] **GRIMLEY GALE (IRE) 5a**...............**A Wintle** 1
(fav) hld up, prog 10th, ld 14th, mstk last, easily
1288[2] **Ardbrennan** ....**E James** 2
made most til hrd rdn & hdd 14th, mstk nxt, onepcd 2 out
488[1] **Stalbridge Bill** ....**Miss A Goschen** 3
chsd ldrs, outpcd frm 12th, no ch frm 15th
1055[1] Myverygoodfriend *chsd ldrs, outpcd frm 12th, sn btn* ....S Cobden 4
1308[4] Phelioff *mostly cls 2nd to 11th, outpcd & sn btn, t.o. 4 out*..........Miss S Dawson 5
5 ran. 8l, 15l, 1½l, 25l. Time 6m 7.00s. SP 8-13.
R M Phillips (Clifton-On-Teme).

1464 Novice Riders

1274[2] **PEJAWI 5a** .... **Miss L Whitaker** 1
j.w. ld 9th, mstk 12th, rdn out flat
1274[3] **Skinnhill (bl)** .... **C Mason** 2
chsd ldrs, pshd alng 13th, styd on onepcd frm 3 out, retired
824[4] **Old Road (USA)** .... **M Keen** 3
cls up, onepcd 15th, sn btn
1205[9] Proplus *prom, lft in ld 7-9th, wknd 13th*..... Mrs A Lee 4
1279 Whats Your Game (bl) *n.j.w. t.o. whn ref 9th* ..... M Stevens ref
1163[2] Walkers Point *bhnd whn u.r. 7th*....... Miss K O'Neill ur
1288 Broad Steane *(fav) ld til blnd & u.r. 7th* ..... J Connell ur
7 ran. 8l, 20l, 15l. Time 6m 15.00s. SP 4-1.
Miss L Whitaker (Berks & Bucks Draghounds).

1465 Open Maiden

1314[2] **MOUNTAIN-LINNET** .... **Miss A Goschen** 1
(fav) trckd ldr, mstk 13th, ld 15th, easily
871 **Jobingo** .... **Daniel Dennis** 2
ld, ran wd bend aft 14th & hdd, btn 2 out
2 ran. 15l. Time 6m 27.00s. SP 4-9.
Major R P Thorman (South & West Wilts).

1466 Restricted (12st)

1286[7] **TARRY AWHILE** .... **J Connell** 1
mostly cls 2nd, ld 4 out, all out flat
1210[2] **Nobbutjust (Ire) 5a**.................... **A Beedles** 2
(fav) trckd ldrs, rmndrs hlfwy, 2nd 4 out, ev ch last, no ext
1374 **Carnelia 5a**..................... **Miss A Goschen** 3
mostly narrow ld to 15th, rdn & sn btn
985[3] Cool Rascal 5a *trckd ldrs, in tch whn p.u. 12th, lame* ..... L Lay pu
1304[1] Buladante (Ire) *hld up, prog 14th, 4th & ev ch whn blnd & u.r. nxt*........ T Underwood ur
5 ran. 1½l, 12l. Time 6m 14.00s. SP 8-1.
Sir Michael Connell (Grafton).
M.J.

LLANDEILO FARMERS
Erw Lon
Sunday May 11th
GOOD TO SOFT

1467 Members

1362[3] **NO PANIC** .... **G Lewis** 1
chsd ldr, mstk 14th, ld nxt, easily
1227 **Equatime 5a** .... **P Williams** 2
ld to 15th, jmpd rght, btn whn mstk 2 out
1138[1] Bushton 7a *(fav) hld up, chal 13th, f 15th whn going wll*..... J P Keen f
3 ran. 9l. Time 6m 37.00s. SP 2-1.
C R Johnson (Llandilo Farmers).

1468 Intermediate (12st)

1319[2] **GUNNER BOON 5ex** .... **Miss P Jones** 1
ld to 14th, lft in ld 16th, drew clr 2 out
1322[1] **Box Of Delights** .... **E Williams** 2
(fav) sttld rear, prog 11th, ev ch 4 out, onepcd frm 2 out
1322 **Jolly Swagman** .... **D S Jones** 3
nvr nrr than 3rd, onepcd
1134 Valiant Friend (bl) *cls up early, t.o. & p.u. 8th* ..... Miss B Barton pu
Deal Me One *trckd ldrs to 9th, sn wknd, p.u. 13th* ..... J Jukes pu
1366 Billy-Gwyn *prom, ld 14th, p.u. 16th, dsmntd, lame* ..... J Tudor pu
1235 Basil Street (Ire) 7a (bl) *mid-div, rear whn p.u. 15th* ..... A Phillips pu
7 ran. 2l, dist. Time 6m 11.00s. SP 7-4.
David Brace (Llangeinor).

1469 Men's Open (12st)

1319[1] **SHUIL'S STAR (IRE)** .... **P Hamer** 1
made all, clr 3 out, ran on well
1363[1] **Carrick Lanes 7ex** .... **T Mitchell** 2
cls up, hrd rdn 3 out, nvr able to chal
1411[4] **Sultan's Son** .... **G Lewis** 3
cls up, ev ch 4 out, hrd rdn, onepcd 2 out
1320[1] Hugli *chsd wnr, disp brfly 15th, ev ch 3 out, drvn & wknd nxt* ..... D S Jones 4
1320[2] Beinn Mohr 5a *cls up, ev ch 14th, mstk nxt, wknd 3 out* ..... E Williams 5
1362[1] Doubting Donna 5a 4ex *(fav) chsd wnr early, lost plc, p.u. aft 10th* ..... J Jukes pu
6 ran. 5l, 1½l, 3l, 5l. Time 6m 10.00s. SP 2-1.
R Mason (Carmarthen).

1470 Ladies

1364[3] **TOUCH 'N' PASS 7ex** .... **Miss P Jones** 1
(fav) sttld mid-div, prog 13th, ld 2 out, easily
535[4] **Celtic Daughter 5a** .... **Miss E Jones** 2
ld 11th-16th, hrd rdn aft, no ch wth wnr
Aegean Fanfare (Ire) .... **Miss E James** 3
chsd ldr to 14th, onepcd frm nxt
1362[4] Al Frolic *nvr nrr than 4th, no imp ldrs 2 out* ..... Miss L Pearce 4
1363[4] Local Customer *ld 5-11th, ev ch to 15th, onepcd aft* ..... Miss G Gibson 5
1006[4] Doctor-J (Ire) *ld to 5th, blnd 12th, sn wknd* ..... Miss S Major 6
1225[5] Afaristoun (Fr) *alwys mid-div, wknd & p.u. 13th* ..... Miss J Morse pu
1364[2] Polish Rider (USA) *rear, f 10th*........ Miss R Morgan f
1365[5] Celtic Bizarre 5a *rear, p.u. 14th* .... Miss B Barton pu
9 ran. 8l, 2l, 20l, 5l, 5l. Time 6m 9.00s. SP 4-6.
R H P Williams (Llangeinor).

1471 Restricted (12st)

1365[6] **ALFION (IRE)** .... **D S Jones** 1
ld 4th, clr frm 3 out, easily
1318[3] **She Goes 5a** .... **A Price** 2
trckd ldr, ev ch 16th, easily hld aft
1227[4] **Black Ermine (Ire)** .... **J Jukes** 3
(fav) sttld rear, prog 11th, nvr able to chal
1227 Tims Kick (Ire) 5a *trckd ldr til mstk 14th, no ext aft* ..... T Vaughan 4
1365 Kerstin's Choice 5a *alwys twrds rear, t.o.* ..... P Sheldrake 5
1365[3] Mr Mad *ld to 4th, wn lost plc, p.u. 15th* ...... P Hamer pu
1365[2] Moonlight Cruise 5a *mid-div whn f 12th*.... P Williams f
1179[1] Aralier Man (Ire) *chsd ldrs, 7th whn f 12th* ..... A Crow f
1367 Lynnes Daniella (Ire) 5a *rear, p.u. 9th* .... J P Keen pu
9 ran. 8l, 2l, 1l, dist. Time 6m 21.00s. SP 10-1.
D R Thomas (Llangeinor).

1472 PPORA (Novice Riders (12st)

1017[2] **NUTCASE 5a** .... **D Sherlock** 1
ld 9th, in cmmnd whn lft clr last, fin tired
1364 **Lucky Ole Son** .... **Miss V Roberts** 2
twrds rear, rpd prog 2 out, fin fast, lft 2nd last
1227 **Killyman (Ire)** .... **Miss J Mathias** 3
trckd ldrs, ev ch 15th, wknd rpdly 2 out
1135 I'm A Bute 5a *alwys twrds rear, onepcd* ..... Miss F Wilson 4
1364 Moving Force *ld, ran wd bend & mssd 5th* ..... Miss C Williams ro
1388[1] Sisterly 5a *(fav) ld 5-9th, chsd wnr aft, hld whn f last* ..... R Rogers f
1134[3] Rusty Music *f 4th*................. Miss N Richards f
1365[4] Hill Fort (Ire) *3rd whn c.o. 5th*............... J Cook co
1223 Top Tor 5a *chsd ldrs to 11th, fdd, p.u. 15th* T Vaughan pu
9 ran. Dist, 4l, dist. Time 6m 19.00s. SP 3-1.
N Shutts (Ludlow).

1473 Open Maiden

1323 **OUT ON THE TOWN 5a** .... **E Williams** 1
prom til ld 13th, clr 2 out, styd on wll
1065 **Glenville Breeze (Ire)** .... **Miss P Jones** 2
(Co fav) mid-div, prog 14th, chsd wnr 2 out, no imp
1368[4] **Cefn Woodsman** .... **D S Jones** 3

(Co fav) trckd ldrs til hmpd 11th, no dang aft
407 Brynner *mid-div to 11th, 20l 6th at 16th, p.u. 2 out* ....A Price pu
1323 Mississippisteamer (Ire) *f 4th* ....J P Keen f
1386 Fruit Of Oak (Ire) *alwys prom, 2nd & btn whn f last* ....A Crow f
1137 Laudation (Ire) 7a *ld to 12th, wknd rpdly, p.u. nxt* ....M Lewis pu
1231² Alkarine 7a *(Co fav) mid-div, 15l 4th at 16th, p.u. 2 out* ....J Tudor pu
1137 Tiger Lord *alwys rear, p.u. 12th*............T Vaughan pu
1367 Teigr Pren *n.j.w. alwys rear, p.u. 12th* ....P Sheldrake pu
542 Mistaken Identity *alwys twrds rear, p.u. 12th* P Hamer pu
1368³ Storm Dai Fence (Ire) 12a *(Co fav) rear, jmpd novicey, p.u. 12th* ....J Jukes pu
Fast Flow (Ire) 12a *f 4th* ....Miss A Meakins f
13 ran. 16l, 5l. Time 6m 25.00s. SP 16-1.
Keith James (Glamorgan).
P.D.

MELTON HUNT CLUB
Garthorpe
Sunday May 11th
GOOD TO SOFT

1474 Members (12st)

1198¹ **GRANVILLE GRILL 7ex................J Deutsch** 1
(fav) t.d.e. jmpd lft, made all, hld on gamely flat
1263¹ **Midnight Service (Ire) (bl)..........W Tellwright** 2
chsd ldrs, went 2nd 9th, pckd 3 out, ev ch last, no ext
1309² **Kerry My Home ....T Marks** 3
chsd wnr to 5th & 8-9th, 3rd & outpcd frm 13th, lame
1306¹ Majestic Ride *hld up, jmpd slwly 7th, blnd 12th, mod 4th nxt, nvr on trms* ....G Maloney 4
1350 Menature (Ire) *in tch til 5th & outpcd apr 13th, t.o.* ....J Seth-Smith 5
1355 Forward View *cls up, chsd wnr 5-7th, rdn 10th, wknd 13th, p.u. 2 out* ....P Hutchinson pu
6 ran. ¾l, dist, 12l, 12l. Time 6m 35.00s. SP 1-2.
E W Smith (Beaufort).

1475 Club

1351 **HARMONY WALK (IRE) ....R Armson** 1
prom, chsd ldr 7th, ld 13th, clr 2 out, styd on wll
Blue Is The Colour (Ire) ....S Walker 2
(fav) w.w. prog 6th, chsd wnr 2 out, no imp flat
1192¹ **Gidgegannup ....M Munrowd** 3
mid-div, prog 9th, disp apr 3 out, wknd nxt
1305² Stanwick Farlap 5a *chsd ldrs, 4th & rdn apr 3 out, onepcd*............T Marks 4
1196⁵ The Country Trader *nvr bttr than mid-div, mod 6th at 13th, kpt on, nt rch ldrs* ....J Borradaile 5
1348 Attle *hld up, 8th hlfwy, nvr trbld ldrs* ....W Burnell 6
1205⁸ Hostetler *prom to 4th, sn bhnd, last hlfwy, t.o.* ....J Stephenson 7
1204² Raise An Argument *rear frm 4th, 9th hlfwy, t.o.* ....N Docker 8
760⁵ Buckwheat Lad (Ire) *alwys rear, 10th hlfwy, t.o. & p.u. 3 out*............A Westrope pu
1355 Full Song 5a *disp to 8th, 5th hlfwy, wknd 12th, t.o. & p.u. 2 out*............S Morris pu
1355 Dilly's Last 5a *t.n.p.* ....T Lane 0
1403 Samsword *disp til ld 8-13th, wknd, t.o. & p.u. last* ....John Pritchard pu
1355³ Rakish Queen 5a *raced wd, in tch to 8th, t.o. & p.u. last*............Miss H Phizacklea pu
13 ran. 5l, 8l, 12l, 2l, 20l, 20l, 1l. Time 6m 37.00s. SP 33-1.
H Morton (Quorn).

1476 Ladies

1102¹ **INDIE ROCK ....Mrs F Needham** 1
patiently rdn, prog to 2nd 3 out, ld last, ran on well
1207¹ **Force Eight ....Mrs J Dawson** 2
(fav) chsd ldng pair, went 2nd 13th, ld apr 3 out, hdd last,onepcd
1207² **Supreme Dream (Ire) 5a ....Mrs P Adams** 3
last frm 3rd, pckd 8th, went mod 3rd apr 2 out, nvr dang
1266 Man Of Mystery *chsd ldr til ld 3-13th, wknd rpdly, p.u. 3 out*............Miss F Hatfield pu
1266³ San Remo *ld to 3rd, hit 11th, ld 13th-apr 3 out, wknd, p.u. nxt* ....Miss S Samworth pu
5 ran. 1l, 20l. Time 6m 37.00s. SP 2-1.
R Tate (Hurworth).

1477 Novice Championship

1204¹ **CATCHPHRASE ....K Needham** 1
in tch,ld 13th,wd & hdd aft 3 out,lft clr & blnd nxt
1166¹ **Cantango (Ire) ....A Sansome** 2
chsd ldrs, blnd 8th, rmndr 10th, lost tch 13th,lft 2nd 2 out
1149⁴ **Mamnoon (USA) ....R Armson** 3
in tch, ld 11-13th, wknd apr 15th, lft poor 3rd 2 out, tired
1191¹ Regal Bay *w.w. in tch, rdn & wknd apr 13th, p.u. 3 out* ....W Wales pu
1351 Scraptastic *hit 1st, ld to 11th, wknd 13th, p.u. 3 out* ....N Bell pu
1406¹ Last Option 7a *(fav) trckd ldrs, mstks 6th & 14th, lft in ld apr 2 out, u.r. 2out* ....Mrs F Needham ur
6 ran. Dist, 15l. Time 6m 50.00s. SP 3-1.
A A Day (Atherstone).

1478 Men's Open (12st)

1297² **COOLVAWN LADY (IRE) 5a.............S Walker** 1
(fav) trckd rival, ld 11th, drvn & ran on wll flat
987² **Penlet ....John Pritchard** 2
ld to 11th, ev ch 3 out, unable qckn aft
2 ran. ½l. Time 6m 52.50s. SP 2-5.
W R Halliday (Cranwell Bloodhounds).

1479 Open Maiden (12st)

1282 **STORMING LADY 5a..................P Hacking** 1
(fav) trckd ldrs 8th, ld 11th, clr 3 out, styd on, comf
653⁵ **Marginal Margie 5a ....M Munrowd** 2
rear, prog to chs ldr 12th,ev ch & outjmpd 3 out, onepcd aft
1357 **Malenski (Ire) ....T Lane** 3
w.w. prog to 3rd at 15th, no imp aft
1402⁵ Dilkush *chsd ldrs, 4th & outpcd 15th, no ch aft* ....M Wells 4
1356³ Milo Boy *rear, prog to mid-div whn blnd 11th, no ch aft* ....M Mackley 5
1019 Parson's Corner *ld to 5th, chsd ldrs to 11th, wkng & blnd 13th, t.o.* ....Miss C Williams 6
Underway (Fr) *mstks, alwys last, blnd 10th, p.u. aft* ....S Morris pu
1350 Grange Missile 5a *chsd ldrs to 11th, sn wknd, p.u. 15th* ....T Marks pu
677 Needwood Joker *hld up in tch, lost tch 12th, t.o. & p.u. 2 out*............K Green pu
1267² Art's Echo (Ire) *alwys rear, lost tch 12th, t.o. & p.u. 2 out*............S J Robinson pu
1356 Seaton Mill *prom, ld 5-11th, sn wknd, p.u. 15th* ....M Hewitt pu
1262⁵ Bit Of A Grip (Ire) 7a *chsd ldrs, lost plc & blnd 10th, t.o. & p.u. 3 out* ....S Walker pu
12 ran. 6l, 30l, 2l, 10l, 1 fence. Time 6m 45.00s. SP 6-4.
Mike Roberts (East Sussex & Romney Marsh).
S.P.

SOUTH DEVON
Ottery St Mary
Sunday May 11th
GOOD

1480 Members

1358⁴ **ANJUBI ....Miss L Blackford** 1
(fav) disp early, clr ld 7th, unchal aft
310 **Batsi ....I Widdicombe** 2
hld up, prog 13th, went 2nd nxt, no imp wnr
Druid Blue ....Miss S Gaisford 3

disp to 6th, prom to 13th, wknd 3 out
1037 Another Barney *cls up til p.u. aft 9th, dead* ....A Moir pu
1258³ Querrin Lodge *in tch to 10th, losng ground whn p.u. 13th* ....T Greed pu
Bonny Barosy 5a *jmpd slwly, alwys rear, t.o. & p.u. 12th* ....R Darke pu
6 ran. Dist, 25l. Time 6m 34.00s. SP 1-3.
W H Whitley (South Devon).

1481 Confined (12st)

1398² **LONESOME TRAVELLER (NZ)** ....**N Harris** 1
ld/disp to 3 out, rallied apr last, ran on to ld nr fin
1398¹ **Rasta Man** ....**K Heard** 2
hld up, prog 13th, ld 3 out, wknd flat, hdd nr fin
1338¹ **It's Not My Fault (Ire)** ....**L Jefford** 3
alwys prom, disp 4th-4 out, ev ch nxt, onepcd 2 out
1398⁴ Mine's A Gin (Ire) *mid-div, prog 12th, ev ch 3 out, not qckn nxt* ....Miss J Cumings 4
1395² Stretchit *mid-div, prog 14th, ev ch 3 out, outpcd frm nxt* ....G Penfold 5
1416 Comedy Gayle *handy, 5th at 13th, lost plc 15th, rallied 3 out, sn btn* ....I Widdicombe 6
1033 Far Too Loud *ref 1st* ....A O'Connor ref
1396 Seventh Lock *alwys mid-div, nvr on trms, p.u. 2 out* ....S Kidston pu
1241² Mountain Master *prom early, lost tch 10th, t.o. & p.u. 2 out* ....Miss L Blackford pu
1313² Parditino *(fav) alwys rear & outpcd, no ch whn p.u. 2 out* ....Miss V Nicholas pu
1343 Roving Gypsy 12a *rear whn u.r. 3rd* ....A Holdsworth ur
Morchard Gem 12a *rear whn ran out 6th* ....J Auvray ro
12 ran. 1l, 2l, 2l, 2l, 1½l. Time 6m 23.00s. SP 10-1.
Reg Hand (Lamerton).

1482 Ladies

1358³ **ABBOTSHAM** ....**Miss S Vickery** 1
(fav) ld to 9th, disp nxt til ld 15th, sn clr
589 **Salvo** ....**Miss J Cumings** 2
chsd ldr, disp 10th-14th, onepcd aft
1396⁴ **Fearsome** ....**Miss T Cave** 3
chsd ldng pair, rdn 3 out, not qckn nxt
627³ Perfect Stranger *hld up, prog 12th, nvr on trms frm 4 out* ....Miss L Blackford 4
Skerry Meadow *alwys last, t.o. 15th* ....Miss O Green 5
5 ran. 10l, 1l, 15l, dist. Time 6m 17.00s. SP 10-11.
O J Carter (Axe Vale).

1483 Restricted (12st)

624 **SHREWD THOUGHT (USA)** ....**Miss P Curling** 1
(fav) ld til blnd & jnd 3 out, ran on agn frm nxt
753³ **Wooden Minstrel 5a** ....**Dr P Pritchard** 2
handy, prog 13th, 2nd nxt, jnd wnr 3 out, outpcd aft
1400¹ **Bucks Flea 5a** ....**G Penfold** 3
rear, prog 12th, rdn 4 out, onepcd 2 out
1259² Holly Fare *mid-div, prog 14th, ev ch 4 out, outpcd aft* ....C Crosthwaite 4
1313⁵ The Butler *chsd ldr to 13th, wknd 4 out, p.u. 2 out* ....S Slade pu
1259⁴ Ryme And Run 5a *sn bhnd, t.o. & p.u. 14th* ....Miss L Blackford pu
1241³ Morchard Milly 5a *mid-div early, 4th at 13th, lost tch 15th, blnd 2 out & p.u.* ....A Holdsworth pu
1261¹ Newstarsky *t.d.e. s.s. alwys mid-div, nvr on trms, p.u. 15th* ....Miss J Cumings pu
1255² Dharamshala (Ire) *alwys mid-div, nvr on trms, p.u. 3 out* ....L Jefford pu
630 Maggie Tee 5a *mid-div til p.u. 14th* ....I Dowrick pu
Carnival Kid *mid-div whn s.u. bend aft 2nd* ...T Greed su
1275⁴ Final Express 5a (bl) *alwys mid-div, no ch whn p.u. 14th* ....Miss S Vickery pu
1093 Twice Knightly *alwys rear, t.o. & p.u. 2 out* ..R Widger pu
241 Pixie In Purple (Ire) *hld up, cls 3rd at 10th, p.u. 12th, dsmntd* ....K Heard pu
1245 Fingal *alwys rear, t.o. & p.u. 14th* ....S Kidston pu
15 ran. 3l, nk, 8l. Time 6m 25.70s. SP 5-4.
Mssrs Ball, Fisher & Evanses, Mrs Coleman (Lamerton).

1484 Men's Open (12st)

1396¹ **BUTLER JOHN (IRE) 7ex** ....**N Harris** 1
(fav) made all, clr 4 out, v easily
1243³ **Expressment 7ex** ....**G Penfold** 2
hld up, prog 14th, rdn 3 out, tk 2nd cls hm
1342¹ **Just My Bill** ....**C Heard** 3
w.w. prog 13th, ran on und pres frm 3 out
631 Henrys No Pushover *n.j.w. chsd ldrs, 2nd at 12th, tired 2 out, dmtd flat* ....L Jefford 4
1321³ Prince Nepal *cls up to 13th, lost tch 15th, t.o. & p.u. 2 out* ....S Slade pu
1313⁴ Bargain And Sale *chsd ldr to 12th, outpcd aft, p.u. 4 out* ....I Dowrick pu
1243² Oneovertheight *alwys last, t.o. & p.u. 14th* ..S Kidston pu
7 ran. 10l, 1l, 1l. Time 6m 24.50s. SP 1-4.
Nick Viney (Exmoor).

1485 Open Maiden Div I (12st)

1270 **NOBLE COMIC** ....**J Tizzard** 1
hld up, prog 14th, 2nd 3 out, chal last, ran on to ld nr fin
458 **Harmony's Choice** ....**N Harris** 2
(Jt fav) handy, ld 14th, wknd & hdd nr fin
1261³ **The Ugly Duckling** ....**S Slade** 3D
ld to 14th, cls up aft, not qckn 2 out, fin 3rd, disq
1112² **Amazing Hill (Ire)** ....**C Heard** 3
hld up in tch, 4th at 14th, onepcd 3 out, fin 4th, promoted
1399⁴ Dusty Furlong *alwys mid-div, nvr on trms, outpcd* ....Miss K Baily 5
1394² Alicott Lad *sn last, t.o. 7th* ....R Young 6
1315² Liberty James *rear, nvr on trms, bhnd & p.u. 3 out* ....T Greed pu
1254² An Buchaill Liath (Ire) *2nd to 12th, wknd, bhnd & p.u. 3 out* ....Miss A Barnett pu
1400 Aritam (Ire) *(Jt fav) alwys mid-div, nvr on trms, p.u. 2 out* ....K Heard pu
795 Haven *ran out 1st* ....A O'Connor ro
Morchard Mill 7a *bhnd whn f 7th* ....J Auvray f
Raki Crazy *10s-4s, mid-div, nvr on trms, p.u. 2 out* ....Miss S Vickery pu
Horton *sn rear, bhnd whn p.u. 8th* ....I Dowrick pu
13 ran. ½l, 2l, 8l, 10l, dist. Time 6m 32.00s. SP 12-1.
R E Dimond (Blackmore & Sparkford Vale).
The Ugly Duckling disq, not W/I. Two fences omitted, 17 jumps.

1486 Open Maiden Div II (12st)

1399 **DAMIENS PRIDE (IRE)** ....**K Heard** 1
(Co fav) hld up, prog 13th, 3rd nxt, ld 3 out, ran on
1210⁵ **Springvilla (Ire)** ....**M Miller** 2
(Co fav) hld up, prog 4 out, chal 2 out, no ext aft
1112 **Pilgrim's Mission (Ire)** ....**Miss W Hartnoll** 3
mid-div, styd on frm 15th, not rch ldrs
1315⁵ Kala Dawn 5a *alwys mid-div, nvr on trms* ....Miss M Tory 4
1343³ Happy Valley 5a *sn rear, t.o. & p.u. 14th* Miss P Baker pu
1261² Get Stepping *handy to 14th, lost tch nxt, p.u. 3 out* ....R Widger pu
1152 Tom's Arctic Dream 5a *plld hrd, ld to 13th, disp nxt, ld 15th, going wll, f 4 out* ....P King f
1400 Baman Powerhouse *mid-div whn s.u. bend apr 11th* ....J Young su
1400² Carumu 5a *alwys mid-div, outpcd & p.u. 15th* ....David Dennis pu
1260 Master Buckley (bl) *f 1st* ....T Greed f
1246² I Like The Deal 5a *hld up,prog 9th,lft in ld 4 out,jnd nxt,p.u. 2 out, dsmntd* ....Miss J Cumings pu
1343⁶ Crownhill Cross *mid-div, no ch whn p.u. 15th* ....S Kidston pu
1246 Master Decoy *(Co fav) alwys mid-div, nvr on trms, p.u. 3 out* ....L Jefford pu
531 Mr Kevernair *mid-div, nvr on trms, p.u. 15th* T Dennis pu
1261 Master Laughter *alwys mid-div, bhnd whn p.u. 3 out* ....N Harris pu
1246 Spanish Jest *sn rear, t.o. & p.u. 11th* ...S Parfimowicz pu
Derring Katie 12a *rear whn f 7th* ....A Cooksley f
17 ran. 1½l, 4l, 25l. Time 6m 34.60s. SP 3-1.

Paul C N Heywood (Lamerton).
D.P.

TOWCESTER
Monday May 12th
GOOD TO SOFT

1488 2m 110yds Hartwell Land Rover Hunters' Chase Class H

1287^{5} **NOT MY LINE (IRE) 11.11 5a......Mr A Sansome** **1**
ld to 5th, led 7th, styd on well.
1296 **My Young Man 11.6 7a..............Mr E James** **2**
hdwy 3rd, ld 5th to 7th, hit 3 out, no hdway after.
1293 **Nectanebo (Ire) 11.9 7a..............Mr M Frith** **3**
mstks, held up in rear, hdwy from 4 out, one pace from 2 out.
1275 Feltham Mistress 11.1 7a *held up, hdwy 4 out, rdn apr 2 out, one pace*..................Mr E Babington 4
1296^{1} Yquem (Ire) 11.9 7a *(fav) in tch till wknd quickly apr 2 out*..............................Mr N R Mitchell 5
1404 Al Hashimi 11.6 7a *nvr on terms*.........Mr N Ridout 6
1099 Emerald Ruler 11.6 7a *in tch, rdn 4 out, soon wknd.* ....Mr P Cowley 7
1287^{9} Killimor Lad 11.6 7a *alwys bhnd. y* Miss S Samworth 8
1349 Shuil Saor 11.6 7a *alwys bhnd, t.o.*.......Mr J Saville 9
857^{3} No Word 11.6 7a *alwys bhnd, t.o.*.........Mr I Baker 10
1280 Driving Force 11.6 7a (bl) *prom to 7th, t.o. when p.u. before last*.....................Mr A Charles-Jones pu
782^{3} Hickelton Lad 11.6 7a *alwys bhnd, t.o. when p.u. before 2 out*..............................Mr S Durack pu
1097 King Of Shadows 11.6 7a *prom to 5th, t.o. when p.u. before 3 out*................................Mr S Prior pu
1296^{2} Familiar Friend 11.6 7a (bl) *prom till wknd quickly 3 out, p.u. before last*........................Mr L Lay pu
1097^{2} Dalametre 11.6 7a *bhnd from 6th, t.o. when p.u. before last*...........................Mr M Munrowd pu
1355 Lucky Landing (Ire) 11.6 7a *alwys towards rear, t.o. when p.u. before last*..............Mr Andrew Martin pu

16 ran. 8l, 10l, ¾l, 2l, 4l, 1l, 7l, 12l, 15l. Time 4m 19.00s. SP 14-1.
P C Caudwell

1489 3m 1f Land Rover Gentlemans Championship Hunters' Chase Class H

1256^{1} **MAGNOLIA MAN 11.2 7a ....Mr N Harris** **1**
held up, steady hdwy from 11th, ld apr 2 out, styd on strly.
1163^{1} **Lucky Christopher 11.9 5a ....Mr G Tarry** **2**
(fav) alwys in tch, trckd ldr, short of room and switched left on bend apr 2 out, rdn and kept on one pace.
1122^{2} **Lupy Minstrel 11.11 7a ....Mr A Parker** **3**
ld to 4th, led 8th till hdd apr 2 out, rdn and kept on one pace.
1107^{1} The General's Drum 11.7 7a *held up in rear, mstk 6th, wknd 4 out, t.o.*.........................Mr K Heard 4
1344^{1} Syrus P Turntable 11.2 7a *prom, reminders after 9th, soon wknd, t.o. when p.u. before last*......Mr J Saville pu
1357^{2} Secret Truth 10.11 7a *mstk 1st, ld 4th to 8th, wakened quickly, t.o. when p.u. before 11th*...Mr Andrew Martin pu

6 ran. 5l, 6l, 30l. Time 6m 47.70s. SP 9-4.
Mrs D B Lunt

CHEPSTOW
Tuesday May 13th
GOOD

1490 3m Greig Middleton Ladies Championship Hunters' Chase Class H

1213^{1} **EARTHMOVER (IRE) 11.2 7a ......Miss P Gundry** **1**
(fav) held up, hdwy to track ldr apr 7th, ld after 13th, mstk 2 out, shaken up and qcknd clr run-in.
1213^{2} **Sams Heritage 11.9 5a..............Miss A Dare** **2**
held up, hdwy 9th, went 2nd after 13th, ev ch last, outpcd run-in.
1266^{1} **Corner Boy 11.11 7a..............Mrs J Dawson** **3**
pulld hrd, mstks,, trckd ldr till apr 8th, weakening when hit 5 out, btn when blnd 3 out, t.o..
1481^{1} Lonesome Traveller (NZ) 11.2 7a *in tch till wknd 13th, t.o.*....................................Mrs A Hand 4
1110^{4} False Economy 11.11 7a *prom to 7th, t.o. when ref 4 out.*...............................Miss K Scorgie ref
1327^{2} Mister Gebo 11.7 7a *alwys bhnd, t.o. when p.u. before 2 out.*.............................Miss C Dyson pu
1297^{1} Cumberland Blues (Ire) 11.11 7a *ld, jmpd right, hdd after 13th, soon btn, t.o. when p.u. before 3 out.* ....Miss A Deniel pu

7 ran. 9l, dist, 26l. Time 6m 22.70s. SP 1-2.
R M Penny

HEREFORD
Wednesday May 14th
GOOD

1491 3m 1f 110yds Brockhampton Hunters' Chase Class H

1289^{1} **MISS MILLBROOK 11.9 7a ....Mr E Williams** **1**
(fav) hdwy 10th, ld 14th, driven out run-in.
1359^{1} **Trifast Lad 12.4 3a ....Mr P Hacking** **2**
hdwy 10th, chsd wnr from 3 out, styd on apr last but no impn on winner.
1413^{3} **Rusty Bridge 12.0 7a..............Mr O McPhail** **3**
ld till after 1st, rdn from 10th, styd on again from 2 out, tk 3rd run-in.
1363^{2} Jack Sound 11.7 7a *chsd ldr to 3 out, soon wknd.* ....Mr D S Jones 4
1288^{1} Vital Song 12.0 7a *ld after 1st till mstk and hdd 14th, wknd 4 out.*............................Mr G Matthews 5
1289 J B Lad 11.7 7a *hdwy 12th, wknd 4 out.* ....Miss P Gundry 6
567^{1} Layston D'Or 11.7 7a *alwys bhnd.*......Mr A Charles-Jones 7
1292^{3} My Nominee 12.0 7a (bl) *hdwy 11th, wknd 14th.* ....Mr R Burton 8
1358 Killelan Lad 11.7 7a *slowly away and jmpd poorly in rear, soon t.o., p.u. before 8th.*........Miss K Di Marte pu
1467^{1} No Panic 11.7 7a *hdwy 11th, soon wknd, t.o. when blnd and u.r. 4 out.*......................Mr G Lewis ur
1324 Al Billal 11.7 7a *soon t.o., p.u. before 12th.* ....Miss P Cooper pu

11 ran. 3½l, 21l, 1¾l, 2l, ¾l, 18l, 22l. Time 6m 26.50s. SP 2-1.
D T Goldsworthy

WESTON & BANWELL
Cothelstone
Wednesday May 14th
GOOD TO FIRM

1492 Members

BELMOUNT CAPTAIN ....Miss S Vickery **1**
w.w. chsd ldr 12th, rdn 16th, ld last, all out
1438^{3} **Rapid Rascal ....Miss S West** **2**
(fav) ld to 6th, ld 12th, rdn & hdd last, not qckn
1314^{6} Dula Model 5a *ld 6th til hdd & blnd 12th, sn wknd, p.u. 2 out*..........................J Boscherini pu
1486 Derring Katie 12a *s.s. nrly ref 1st, succeeded 2nd* ....A Cooksley ref

4 ran. ½l. Time 6m 21.00s. SP 9-4.
Mr & Mrs R Tucker (Weston & Banwell).

1493 Men's Open (12st)

521^{3} **FEILE NA HINSE ....M Frith** **1**
wth ldr, ld 15th, jnd 2 out, lft clr aft last
1362^{2} **Conna Moss (Ire) ....J Jukes** **2**
(fav) made most to 15th, rdn & ev ch 2 out til eased flat, lame

2 ran. 7l. Time 6m 37.50s. SP 9-4.
Mrs L Roffe-Silvester (Quantock Staghounds).

1494 Restricted (12st)

1215^{2} **MY WEE MAN (IRE) ....G Barfoot-Saunt** **1**

prog 9th, chsd ldr 15th, lft clr apr nxt, comf
1210[3] **Generator Boy** ....**Julian Pritchard** **2**
hld up bhnd, steady prog 13th, went 2nd 2 out, no ch wth wnr
1373[1] **Stormy Fashion** ....**Maj G Wheeler** **3**
jmpd rght, ld to 14th, onepcd aft
1483 The Butler *chsd ldrs, 6th & rdn 12th, poor 4th & no ch frm 16th* ....S Slade 4
1395[7] Grey Guestino *chsd ldr to 11th, wknd 13th, sn wll bhnd* ....Miss L Delve 5
1158[1] Sue's Quest 5a *(fav) chsd ldrs, 5th & rdn 12th, sn btn & bhnd* ....P King 6
1395[6] Ballysheil *mstk 1st, in tch til p.u. 6th, saddle broke* ....S Edwards pu
1483 Newstarsky *rear whn blnd & u.r. 3rd* Miss J Cumings ur
1210[9] Game Fair *prom to 6th, sn wknd, t.o. & p.u. 13th* ....W Cook pu
1369[1] Palace King (Ire) *alwys bhnd, t.o. & p.u. 13th* R Payne pu
1374[3] Venn Boy *prom, trckd ldr 11th, ld 14th, 1l up whn s.u. bnd apr 16th* ....J Tizzard su

11 ran. 20l, ½l, 12l, 8l, 3l. Time 6m 16.50s. SP 8-1.
G Barfoot-Saunt (Ledbury).
One fence omitted final two circuits, 17 jumps.

1495 Ladies

1194[1] **FINAL PRIDE 5a** ....**Miss P Jones** **1**
(fav) made all, drew clr & blnd 13th, dist up 3 out, imprssv
1441[4] **Searcy (bl)** ....**Miss S Vickery** **2**
prssd wnr to 12th, no ch frm 14th, wknd 3 out, fin tired
1358[2] **Mighty Falcon** ....**Miss E Tory** **3**
outpcd, t.o. 6th, kpt on frm 16th, nvr nrr
1374 Bryansbi 5a *last & t.o. frm 3rd, lft v dist 4th last* ....Miss S Lock 4
1369[2] Highway Jim *outpcd, t.o. 6th, bad 4th whn u.r. last* ....Miss M Burrough ur
1141[3] Lavalight *chsd ldng pair, dist bhnd whn ran out 6th* ....Miss A Goschen ro

6 ran. Dist, 5l, 1 fence. Time 6m 1.50s. SP 1-3.
Grahame Barrett (South Pembrokeshire).

1496 Confined (12st)

1481 **PARDITINO 3ex** ....**Miss V Nicholas** **1**
cls up, ld 8th, jnd 13th-aft 3 out, clr nxt, comf
1109[5] **Arctic Baron** ....**Miss S Vickery** **2**
ld to 2nd,ld 6-8th, rdn & outpcd 12th, kpt on to tk 2nd flat
1439[1] **Royal Turn** ....**A Honeyball** **3**
trckd ldrs, jnd wnr 13th til aft 3 out, wknd apr last
1371[1] Avril Showers 5a 5ex *(fav) prom til lost plc 10th, nvr on trms wth ldrs aft* ....R Atkinson 4
1317 Lake Mariner 5a *prog & prom 8th, outpcd frm 13th, no imp frm 16th* ....L Jefford 5
1311[2] Tangle Baron 3ex *rear & nvr going wll, wll bhnd frm 13th, t.o.* ....J Tizzard 6
1441[5] Frosty Reception 3ex *in tch to 10th, wll bhnd 13th, f 3 out* ....Miss C Stucley f
1313 Cleasby Hill *ld 2-6th, wknd 8th, p.u. 11th* ....I Dowrick pu
1095 Typical Woman (Ire) 5a *pckd 6th, last whn mstk & u.r. 9th* ....M Frith ur

9 ran. 6l, 2l, 10l, 10l, 12l. Time 6m 13.00s. SP 5-1.
Mrs K R J Nicholas (Tiverton Foxhounds).

1497 Open Maiden Div I (12st)

1260 **CROSSWELL STAR (IRE)** ....**J Barnes** **1**
mid-div,outpcd 10th,gd prog 3 out,swtchd apr last,ld nr fin
1343[2] **Uncle James (Ire)** ....**R Widger** **2**
prom, lft in ld 13th, jnd 3 out, hrd rdn & hdd nr fin
1270[2] **Woodlands Beau (Ire) 7a** ....**T Woolridge** **3**
mstks,rear,prog 14th,clsd 3 out,chal nxt,ran on,just hld fin
1400[3] Suba Lin 5a *hld up last,wll bhnd 12th,rpd prog 3 out,chnc apr last,no ex* ....M Frith 4
1314[5] Fosabud *prom, lft 2nd 13th, jnd ldr 3 out til wknd apr last* ....Miss L Hawkings 5
877 Highland Talk 8ow *jmpd slwly 6th, sn bhnd, t.o. 13th* ....G Densley 6
1400 Gamblers Refrain *ld to 6th, wknd 12th, nrly ref nxt, p.u. 14th* ....A Holdsworth pu
1373[3] Red Is The Rose 5a *mid-div til u.r. 7th* ....D Alers-Hankey ur
1460 Another Kav (Ire) 5a *pllng,not fluent,2nd til ld 6th,4l up whn blnd & u.r. 13th* ....J Price ur
512[2] Old Harry's Wife 5a *hld up, lost tch 10th, no prog 15th, p.u. 2 out* ....R Nuttall pu

10 ran. ½l, ½l, 4l, ½l, 1 fence. Time 6m 26.00s. SP 25-1.
A J Sendell (Taunton Vale Foxhounds).

1498 Open Maiden Div II (12st)

MIGHTY GALE (IRE) ....**Miss S Vickery** **1**
(fav) n.j.w. in tch, chsd ldr 13th, ld 2 out, pshd out
1270 **Dad's Delight 5a** ....**Miss A Goschen** **2**
ld to 2 out, rdn & kpt on onepcd
1315 **Sansnip** ....**N Mitchell** **3**
rear, mstk 13th, nvr rchd ldrs, styd on to tk 3rd last
1274 Rallye Stripe *prom, mstk 12th, 3rd & chnc 16th, wknd 2 out* ....Col S Allen 4
1269 French Invasion 5a *mstks, chsd ldr to 13th, sn btn* ....S Parfimowicz 5
1314 Berkley Street 5a *chsd ldng grp, jmpd slwly 9th, sn bhnd, t.o.* ....J Tizzard 6
1369 Summerthetime *alwys rear, t.o. & u.r. 10th* ....A Moir ur
1437 Go Willie Go *t.o. & ref 2nd* ....Miss L Smale ref
Watercombe Cracker 5a *alwys rear, t.o. & p.u. 11th* ....R Emmett pu

9 ran. 4l, 12l, 6l, 7l, 1 fence. Time 6m 36.00s. SP 6-4.
E Dauncey (Blackmore & Sparkford Vale).
J.N.

PERTH
Thursday May 15th
GOOD TO SOFT

1499 2½m 110yds Linlithgow & Stirlingshire Hunt Novices' Hunters' Chase Class H

1411[2] **SAVOY 11.7 7a** ....**Captain A Ogden** **1**
(fav) nvr far away, effort before 2 out, styd on well to ld near fin.
1201[2] **Howayman 11.12 7a** ....**Mr A Parker** **2**
cl up, disp ld from 8th, ld before 3 out, hdd towards fin.
1201[8] **Master Kit (Ire) 11.12 7a** ....**Mr J Billinge** **3**
cl up on outside till wknd before 2 out.
1297[3] Will Travel (Ire) 11.7 7a *ld to 8th, struggling 5 out, t.o..* ....Mr A Robson 4
Reed 11.7 7a *cl up, ld 8th till hdd before 3 out, btn when blnd badly 2 out* ....Mr O McPhail 5
813[2] Harden Glen 11.7 7a *mstks, chsd lding bunch till blnd and lost tch 5 out* ....Miss S Laidlaw 6
1217[3] King Spring 11.9 5a *alwys bhnd and detatched, t.o. when p.u. before 4 out* ....Mrs V Jackson pu
1201 Denim Blue 12.3 5a *hmpd start, saddle slpd and soon p.u.* ....Miss P Robson pu

8 ran. Nk, 18l, 21l, 3l, dist. Time 5m 15.10s. SP 11-8.
Robert Ogden

AINTREE
Friday May 16th
GOOD

1500 3m 1f Aintree Novices' Hunters' Chase Class H

1412[1] **FRONT COVER 11.7 7a** ....**Miss S Vickery** **1**
(fav) nvr far away, reminder apr 5 out, soon ld, clr 3 out, unchal.
1233[5] **The Rum Mariner 11.7 7a** ....**Mr D S Jones** **2**
ld, jmpd right thrght, mstk 13th, hdd 5 out, wknd apr 3 out, soon no dngr.
1417[4] **Very Daring 11.7 7a** ....**Miss S Sharratt** **3**
held up, struggling from hfwy, soon t.o..

1476 San Remo 11.7 7a (bl) *cl up till outpcd 11th, soon well bhnd, t.o.* . . . . . . Miss S Samworth 4
778 Frozen Stiff (Ire) 11.7 7a (bl) *almost u.r. 1st, held up, blnd and u.r. rider 4th.* . . . . . . Mr T J Barry ur
1359 Ship The Builder 11.7 7a *bhnd, some hdwy and mod 3rd when blnd and u.r. 13th.* . . . . . . Mr T Whitaker ur
6 ran. Dist, dist, 3l. Time 6m 33.30s. SP 4-9.
Stewart Pike

FOLKESTONE
Friday May 16th
GOOD

1501 3¼m Nigel Collison Fuels Novices' Hunters' Chase Class H for the Guy Peate Memorial Challenge Trophy

1354[1] **MISTER MAIN MAN (IRE) 12.0 7a Mr S Sporborg 1**
(fav) ld to 3 out, led again next, rdn last, held on und pres run- in.
1203 **No Joker (Ire) 12.0 7a . . . . . . Mr P Scott 2**
trckd wnr till after 12th, effort to ld 3 out, hdd next, mstk last, rallied well und pres.
1128[1] **Polar Ana (Ire) 11.9 7a . . . . . . Miss S Gladders 3**
jmpd left, in tch, prog to chase wnr after 12th till 15th, ev ch after 3 out, soon wknd.
1444 Kates Castle 11.9 7a *prom till 4th and weakening when blnd 3 out, no ch after.* . . . . . . Mr J Van Praagh 4
579 Centre Stage 12.0 7a *jmpd slowly 4th and 5th, alwys bhnd, t.o. from 10th.* . . . . . . Mr A Warr 5
1445 Bright Hour 12.0 7a *nvr near ldrs, bhnd from 13th, t.o. and p.u. before 3 out.* . . . . . . Miss J Grant pu
1127[1] Rustic Ramble 12.4 3a *started slowly, nvr going well, t.o. and p.u. before 13th.* . . . . . . Mr P Hacking pu
1446[2] Linger Balinda 11.9 7a (bl) *prom to 10th, weakening in 5th when blnd 13th, t.o. and p.u. before 3 out.* . . . . . . Mr P Bull pu
1435[2] Ballyallia Castle (Ire) 12.0 7a *trckd ldrs, 5th when f 7th.* . . . . . . Mr N Bloom f
1127 Serious Money (USA) 12.0 7a *jmpd v slowly, alwys t.o., ref 13th.* . . . . . . Miss C Savell ref
10 ran. ½l, 13l, 14l, dist. Time 6m 38.50s. SP 13-8.
Sir Chippendale Keswick

1502 2m 5f Kent And Surrey Bloodhounds Challenge Cup Maiden Hunters' Chase Class H

1479[1] **STORMING LADY 11.13 3a . . . . . . Mr P Hacking 1**
alwys going well, trckd ldr 10th, ld after next, drew well clr after 3 out, impressive.
967 **Wednesdays Auction (Ire) 12.2 5a . . Mr T McCarthy 2**
last when pkd 1st, soon well bhnd, t.o. 7th, kept on from 11th, tk poor 2nd after last.
784[1] **Barn Elms 12.0 7a . . . . . . Mr A Hickman 3**
chsd ldr after 6th till 10th, wknd 3 out, fin tired.
1447[1] Supreme Dealer 12.0 7a *chsd ldr till after 6th, weakening when mstk 9th, soon well bhnd.* . . . . . . Mr A Warr 4
1378[4] Kumada 12.0 7a *nvr going well, alwys bhnd, t.o. 8th, p.u. before 3 out.* . . . . . . Miss S Gritton pu
1210[6] Your Opinion 12.0 7a *prom, cl 4th when blnd and u.r. 10th.* . . . . . . Mr M Walters ur
1286[2] Mister Spectator (Ire) 12.4 3a *(fav) n.j.w. and nvr going well, lost pl 5th, well bhnd when p.u. before 7th, lame.* . . . . . . Mr Simon Andrews pu
1309[1] Roscolvin (Ire) 11.7 7a *mstks, held up, bhnd from 7th, t.o. and p.u. before 2 out.* . . . . . . Mr P Bull pu
1285[2] Cool Bandit (Ire) 12.0 7a *ld and soon clr, hdd after 11th, 2nd and well btn when blnd and u.r. 2 out.* . . . . . . Mr T Hills ur
1379 Mr Oriental 12.0 7a *mstks, rear from 6th, t.o. when f 9th.* . . . . . . Mr G Gigantesco f
10 ran. Dist, 7l, 14l. Time 5m 12.20s. SP 2-1.
Mike Roberts

1503 3¼m IBS Appeal Open Hunters' Chase Class H for the Royal Judgement Challenge Trophy

1457[1] **VIRIDIAN 12.4 3a . . . . . . Mr M Rimell 1**
(fav) chsd ldr 11th, chal from 5 out, level and going better when left well clr 2 out, eased run-in.
1415[3] **Faringo 12.0 7a (bl) . . . . . . Miss C Grissell 2**
ld to 5th, soon pushed along, chsd ldr to 11th, wknd after next, left poor 2nd 2 out.
1448[2] **Teatrader 11.8 7a 1ow . . . . . . Miss T Blazey 3**
bhnd, hmpd 7th, no prog from 13th, soon t.o., left poor 3rd 2 out.
1202[2] Cape Cottage 12.7 7a *waited with, 5th and in tch when b.d. 7th.* . . . . . . Mr A Phillips bd
1188[1] Cardinal Richelieu 11.7 7a *started slowly, well bhnd, some prog when p.u. before 12th, lame.* . . . . . . Mr S Sporborg pu
1286[6] Grassington (Ire) 11.7 7a (v) *trckd ldrs, 4th when f 7th.* . . . . . . Mr Scott Quirk f
1433[1] Foxbow (Ire) 11.9 5a (bl) *chsd ldr, ld 5th, rdn and joined when f 2 out.* . . . . . . Mr A Sansome f
7 ran. 19l, 7l. Time 6m 38.00s. SP 6-4.
Denis Hine
Fence 14 was omitted.

1504 3m 7f Shepherd Neame United Hunts Open Champion Hunters' Chase Class H

1454[1] **GLEN OAK 11.10 7a . . . . . . Mr J M Pritchard 1**
(fav) waited with, prog to chase ldr after 14th, pushed along 3 out, ld after next, styd on well.
586[2] **Sirisat 11.7 7a . . . . . . Miss T Blazey 2**
ld till after 2 out, not qckn, wknd run-in.
1285[3] **Tau 11.7 7a . . . . . . Mr A Warr 3**
chsd ldr to 13th, soon wknd, no ch from 15th, tk poor 3rd near fin.
1126[1] American Eyre 11.7 7a *settld in 4th, outpcd after 14th, no impn ldrs next.* . . . . . . Miss S Gladders 4
302[2] Early Man 11.11 3a *settld in 3rd, chsd ldr 13th till mstk next, mistake and wknd 15th, p.u. before 3 out.* . . . . . . Mr P Hacking pu
5 ran. 12l, 24l, 1½l. Time 7m 58.10s. SP 4-6.
R J Mansell
Fences three, ten and 17 omitted this race.

1505 2m 5f Grant's Cherry Brandy South East Champion Novices' Hunters' Chase Final Class H

1317[1] **MUSKERRY MOYA (IRE) 11.9 7a Miss A Goschen 1**
made all, joined 2 out, shaken up and ran on well apr last.
1278[1] **Reverend Brown (Ire) 12.2 5a . . . . . Mr A Sansome 2**
(fav) chsd wnr, mstk 9th, rdn 3 out, joined winner next, wknd rpdly and jmpd last slowly, lame.
1278[4] **Mutual Memories 12.4 3a . . . . Mr Simon Andrews 3**
keen hold, chsd ldrs, mstk 9th, soon struggling, tk poor 3rd und pres near fin.
1114[1] Red Channel (Ire) 12.0 7a *started slowly, pulld hrd and held up, prog to chase ldrs 7th, mstk 11th, wknd 3 out.* . . . . . . Mr A Hickman 4
1278[2] Bishops Tale 12.0 7a *started v slowly, bhnd, rdn after 7th, no prog 9th, soon t.o.* . . . . . . Mr R J Barrett 5
1460 Scarra Darragh (Ire) 11.9 7a *several slow jumps, alwys bhnd, t.o. from 11th.* . . . . . . Mr A Charles-Jones 6
1442[1] And Why Not 12.0 7a *f 1st.* . . . . . . Mr J Van Praagh f
1359 Ishma (Ire) 12.0 7a *prom to 3rd, soon wknd, t.o. and p.u. before 9th.* . . . . . . Mr D Page pu
8 ran. 29l, 18l, 1¼l, 23l, 11l. Time 5m 23.20s. SP 8-1.
N W Rimington

1506 2m 5f Pett Farm Equestrian Services United Hunts Open Challenge Cup Hunters' Chase Class H

1287[1] **SLIEVENAMON MIST 12.9 5a . . . . . . Mr J Jukes 1**
(fav) held up bhnd, prog to chase ldr after 10th, ld apr 2 out, soon clr, eased run-in.
1287[2] **Counterbid 12.2 5a (bl) . . . . . . Mr A Sansome 2**
ld, jmpd slowly 1st and soon hdd, led again 4th, rdn and hded apr 2 out, no ch with wnr.
302 **No Inhibitions 12.0 7a . . . . . . Mr A Warr 3**

prom, chsd ldr briefly 10th, outpcd when mstk next, no dngr after.
1279[2] Just Jack 12.4 3a *mstk 2nd, prom, chsd ldr after 8th till 10th, outpcd from next.* ......Mr Simon Andrews 4
1447 Emerald Moon 12.0 7a *in tch to 10th, soon outpcd and bhnd.* ......Mr T Hills 5+
828[3] Sure Pride (USA) 12.0 7a *alwys bhnd, t.o. from 9th.* ......Mr P G Hall 5+
1128 Boll Weevil 12.0 7a *ld after 1st till 4th, chsd ldr till after 8th, wknd, t.o. and p.u. before 2 out.* ......Miss J Grant pu
890[5] Young Nimrod 12.0 7a *waited with, 6th when u.r. 5th.* ......Mr G Wragg ur
8 ran. 6l, 22l, 13l, nk, dd-ht. Time 5m 17.40s. SP 4-11.
Nick Viney

STRATFORD
Friday May 16th
GOOD

1507 3m Interlink Express Restricted Point-to-Point Final Novices' Hunters' Chase Class H For the Gay and Eve Sheppard Memorial Challenge Trophy

1092[1] **ALLER MOOR (IRE) 11.7 7a ......Mr J Tizzard 1**
held up, steady hdwy to go 2nd 3 out, ld next, tied up run-in, all out.
523[1] **Swansea Gold (Ire) 11.2 7a...Mr D Alers-Hankey 2**
ld to 4th, led 8th, clr four out, wknd and hdd 2 out, rallied gamely run-in.
1058[1] **Barneys Gold (Ire) 11.7 7a ......Mr A Bealby 3**
trckd ldrs till lost pl 8th, styd on from 4 out, left poor 3rd last.
1351[2] Brown Baby 11.3 7a 1ow *pulle hrd, ld 4th to 8th, wknd apr four out.* ......Mr G Kerr 4
1392[1] First Command (NZ) 11.7 7a *chsd ldrs till wknd 12th, t.o. when p.u. before 3 out.* ......Mr A Dalton pu
1259[1] Nearly At Sea 11.2 7a *mstks in rear, t.o. when p.u. after 11th.* ......Mr L Jefford pu
1477[3] Mamnoon (USA) 11.7 7a *bhnd, rdn after 10th, p.u. after next.* ......Mr R Armson pu
1382[1] Mr Bobbit (Ire) 11.7 7a *prom early, hit 6th, t.o.when p.u. after 3 out.* ......Mr R Burton pu
972[1] Gallants Delight 11.7 7a *(fav) held up, hdwy when mstk 10th, hit 12th, rallied 5 out, btn 3rd when blnd and u.r. last.* ......Mr A Robson ur
1224[1] Bit Of A Citizen (Ire) 11.2 7a *held up, hdwy 11th, btn 3rd when blnd and u.r. 3 out.* ......Mr E Williams ur
10 ran. ½l, 18l, 21l. Time 6m 8.00s. SP 9-4.
G Keirle

BANGOR
Saturday May 17th
GOOD

1508 3m 110yds North Western Area Point-to-Point Championship Final Hunters' Chase Class H for the Wynnstay Hunt Challenge Cup

1098[1] **NODFORM WONDER 12.0 7a ......Mr R Bevis 1**
(fav) ld till apr 3rd, regained ld 5th, pkd badly 10th, clr from 12th, unchal.
1383[1] **Nothing Ventured 11.10 7a ......Mr A Beedles 2**
in tch, hdwy to chase wnr 9th, no ch with clr winner from 12th.
1301[3] **Pamela's Lad 11.10 7a ......Mr G Hanmer 3**
bhnd, hdwy to chase ldrs 13th, no impn und pres.
1412 Ita's Fellow (Ire) 11.10 7a *midfield, effort to chase ldrs 13th, soon no impn.* ......Mrs C Ford 4
1292[8] Simply Perfect 11.10 7a *midfield, effort 13th, nvr reached challenging position.* ......Miss S Swindells 5
1415[2] Tara Boy 11.10 7a *alwys in rear, struggling 5 out, nvr a factor.* ......Mr R Cambray 6
1300[2] Glenrowan (Ire) 11.12 5a *alwys well bhnd, nvr a factor.* ......Mr R Ford 7
1347[5] Spy's Delight 11.10 7a *in tch, mstk 5th, hmpd by faller 10th, lost touch from 5 out, t.o.* ......Mr H Rayner 8
1383[2] Fibreguide Tech 11.10 7a *midfield till f 10th.* ......Mr R Thomas f
1300 No More The Fool 11.10 7a *slowly into stride, alwys bhnd, t.o. 12th, p.u. before 5 out.* ......Mr L Brennan pu
1382[4] Ultrason IV (Fr) 11.10 7a *handy till 9th, lost tch from 12th, t.o. when p.u. before last.* ......Mr R Burton pu
1381[1] Noble Angel (Ire) 11.10 7a *prom, ld apr 3rd till hdd 5th, mstk and lost pl 9th, soon lost tch, t.o. when p.u. before 12th.* ......Mr S Prior pu
12 ran. 23l, 12l, 9l, 6l, 10l, 3l, 30l. Time 6m 26.10s. SP 5-4.
D A Malam

BORDER
Corbridge
Saturday May 17th
GOOD TO SOFT

1509 Intermediate (12st)

1427[3] **NOVA NITA 5a 5ex ......P Craggs 1**
mid-div, prog 10th, chsd ldr 13th, hld whn lft clr last
416[1] **Bucklands Cottage 5a ......D McLeod 2**
rear, prog 12th, outpcd 3 out, lft 2nd last
1427[4] **Thinkaboutthat (Ire) ......J Muir 3**
prom, chsd ldr 4th til fdd 10th, wll btn
1424[1] Jayandoubleu (Ire) *(fav) prom, ld 4th, 3l clr & going wll whn f last, rmntd* ......T Scott 4
1414[6] Donside *ld to 4th, sttld in 3rd aft, fdd 11th, t.o. 3 out* ......J Walton 5
1427[5] Jolly Fellow 5ex (bl) *rear, prog 10th, chsd ldr 11th til f nxt, dead* ......Miss S Ward f
1406[5] Drumcairn (Ire) *rear, dtchd frm 7th, t.o. & p.u. 10th* ......M Ruddy pu
1427[2] Toaster Crumpet 5ex *rear whn f 3rd* ..Miss P Robson f
1334[1] Funny Feelings *prom til outpcd 11th, f nxt* ...C Storey f
1348[1] Dublin Hill (Ire) 7ow *mid-div, prog 12th, ev ch 2 out, sn wknd, 3rd & u.r. last* ......A Bonson ur
10 ran. 15l, 3l, 10l, 15l. Time 6m 8.00s. SP 5-2.
Robert Black (Dumfriesshire).

1510 Restricted

1418[2] **TIMBER TOPPER ......C Mulhall 1**
hld up,prog 9th,ld 2 out, clr & jmpd slwly last,ran on wll
1331[1] **The Odin Line (Ire) ......W Kerr 2**
disp til ld 4th, disp 10th til ld 10th, hdd & onepcd 2 out
1424[2] **Grey Rock (Ire) 5a ......P Craggs 3**
(fav) disp to 4th, chsd ldr til disp 10th-12th, onepcd
1424[5] Sumpt'n Smart *prom til outpcd frm 4 out* ...L Morgan 4
1348[3] Lyningo (bl) *mid-div, mstk 2nd, rmndrs 11th, sn wknd, t.o.* ......S Brisby 5
1421[4] Persian Lion *prom til fdd 14th, t.o.* ......Mrs L Ward 6
1336[1] Another Islay *mid-div til wknd 14th, t.o.* ......R Morgan 7
Overstep *jmpd lft, rear, t.o. 7th, p.u. 13th*...D McLeod pu
1421 Andretti's Heir *mid-div, prog 6th, outpcd frm 4 out, 4th & wll btn, f last* ......A Bonson f
1424 Mighty Express *rear, lost tch 14th, t.o. & p.u. nxt* ......A Ogden pu
972 Canister Castle *twrds rear whn u.r. 3rd.* ......T Scott ur
1217 Turn Of Foot (Ire) *rear, dtchd 9th, t.o. & p.u. 13th* ......M Bradburne pu
1334[2] Houselope Brook 5a *twrds rear, blnd 13th, f nxt* ......J Walton f
13 ran. 4l, 4l, 5l, 20l, 10l, 12l. Time 6m 10.00s. SP 9-2.
P Wilkin (Bilsdale).

1511 Ladies

1422 **THANK U JIM ......Miss T Jackson 1**
disp to 5th,chsd ldr aft, ld 9th-4 out, rallied last, ld fin
1425[3] **Just For Kicks ......Mrs N Craggs 2**
rear, dtchd 4th, rpd prog 4 out, ld last, hdd nr fin
1422[2] **Carole's Delight 5a ......Mrs L Ward 3**
ran in sntchs, disp to 5th,prog 13th,chal last,wknd flat

1425[2] Across The Card *mid-div, prog 4 out, ev ch whn mstk 2 out, sn btn*........................Miss R Ramsay 4
1425[1] The Buachaill (Ire) *(fav) prom til outpcd 9th,prog 12th,ld 4 out til wknd & hdd last*.......Mrs V Jackson 5
1408[2] Blakes Folly (Ire) *rear, prog 6th, ev ch 3 out, sn wknd*..................................Mrs K Hargreave 6
1347[7] Running Frau 5a *rear, dtchd 4th, t.o. 11th*..................................Miss M Maher 7
810[3] Hollow Suspicion (Ire) *mid-div, prog to ld 5th-9th, ev ch til wknd 3 out*..........................Miss J Percy 8
1201[6] Bow Handy Man *mid-div, wknd 11th, t.o. & p.u. 13th, retired*..............................Miss D Laidlaw pu
1499 Denim Blue *prom til lost plc 6th, rear whn p.u. 11th, dsmntd*..............................Miss P Robson pu
10 ran. ¾l, 7l, ½l, 5l, 8l, 20l, ½l. Time 6m 8.00s. SP 4-1.
Mrs G Sunter (Cleveland).

1512 Men's Open

1426[1] **FISCAL POLICY** ....**R Trotter** **1**
mid-div, prog 5th, disp 7th-10th, ld 4 out, lft clr last
1349[1] **Cot Lane (bl)**..............................**J Tate** **2**
ld til disp 7th, ld 10th-4 out, onepcd nxt, lft 2nd last
1426[3] **Bit Of A Blether (Ire)** ....**P Craggs** **3**
prom til wknd 3 out
1426[4] Irish Gent *rear, strgglng 9th, t.o. 12th*......G Thomas 4
1426 Inconclusive *mid-div til outpcd 9th, wll bhnd frm 4 out*..A Ogden 5
1407[2] Fast Study *prom til u.r. 10th*.............S Robinson ur
1426[6] Green Times *prom til rdn & wknd 10th, sn wll bhnd, p.u. last*.................................C Storey pu
1294[1] Washakie *(fav) mid-div, prog 10th, chsd wnr 2 out, ev ch whn ran out last*.........................J Walton ro
1488[9] Shuil Saor *rear, t.o. 11th, p.u. 13th*..........J Saville pu
1335[2] Tartan Tornado *rear, wll bhnd 6th, t.o. & p.u. 4 out*..P Johnson pu
10 ran. 12l, 3l, 20l, ½l. Time 6m 13.00s. SP 11-4.
H P Trotter (Berwickshire).

1513 Open Maiden Div I

1428[2] **ALLRITE PET 5a** ....**R Morgan** **1**
(fav) prom, jnd ldr 4 out, ld nxt, hrd drvn & ran on wll flat
1337[2] **Madame Beck 5a**.......................**M Smith** **2**
prom, rmndrs 10th, ev ch apr last, not qckn
1429 **Durham Glint** ....**A Ogden** **3**
mid-div,prog 6th,chsng ldr whn blnd 12th, mstk 2 out,sn btn
612 Terrorisa 5a *rear, prog into mid-div 10th, outpcd frm 4 out*.................................Miss J Percy 4
1106[3] Look Sharpe *alwys twrds rear, onepcd frm 3 out, nvr dang*..................................A Bonson 5
1173[4] Redwood Boy *mid-div, drppd rear 8th, wll bhnd frm 4 out*...D Raw 6
1336[3] Rallying Cry (Ire) (bl) *mid-div, jmpd slwly 6th, wknd 11th, p.u. 14th*.........................D McLeod pu
1334[3] Mini Cruise *ld til jnd 4 out, hdd nxt, wknd rpdly, p.u. last*...T Scott pu
Rum Rebel *alwys rear, t.o. 3 out, p.u. last*....J Walton pu
Phoza Moya (Ire) *prom til wknd rpdly 12th, ref 14th*..................................M Bradburne ref
1345 True Censation 5a *prom til lost plc 4th, wll bhnd 6th, p.u. 8th*.................................J Saville pu
1428[3] More Rain (Ire) *prom til wknd 3 out, f nxt*....P Craggs f
1424 Queen Ofthe Knowes 12a *rear, t.o. 9th, p.u. nxt*..C Storey pu
13 ran. 7l, 1½l, 7l, 1½l, 10l. Time 6m 26.00s. SP 6-4.
Dennis Waggott (Dumfriesshire).

1514 Open Maiden Div II

1429[2] **PRESS TO STING** ....**C Storey** **1**
(fav) prom, disp 11th-14th, ld nxt, qcknd clr last, easily
1251[3] **Mr Hook 7a** ....**G Markham** **2**
rear, prog 3 out, ev ch nxt, outpcd by wnr
1348[5] **Primitive Way 7a**....................**P Atkinson** **3**
alwys prom, ev ch 3 out, sn wknd
1429 Disrespect 5a *rear, prog 13th, in tch whn blnd 4 out, sn btn*.......................Miss M Macmillan 4
1429 Hooky's Treat 5a *alwys in mid-div, strgglng 4 out*..M Bradburne 5
1337[4] Sagaro Belle 5a *prom, lost plc 12th, sn strgglng*..T Scott 6
1429 Fast Fun *mid-div, wknd 4 out, t.o.*..........R Morgan 7
1427 General Jack *prom, ld 9th, disp 11th til ld 14th, hdd nxt, wknd rpdly*.........................Miss J Percy 8
1429 Fortinas Flyer 5a (bl) *rear, wll bhnd whn p.u. 7th*..M Ruddy pu
1429 Tolmin *rear whn p.u. 8th*....................A Parker pu
1167[2] Stanwick Fort 5a *prom whn u.r. 2nd*...Mrs H Dickson ur
479 Percy Pit *plld hrd, ld & sn clr, wknd rpdly & hdd 9th, p.u. nxt*...P Craggs pu
1428[5] Barrow Knocks *s.s. alwys rear, t.o. 14th, p.u. 3 out*..R Green pu
1429 Megans Mystery (Ire) *mid-div, prog 12th, f nxt*..J Walton f
1428 Alsina *rear, wll bhnd 13th, p.u. 3 out*...Miss S Forster pu
Ellfiedick 5a *alwys rear, t.o. 7th, p.u. 10th* Miss T Gray pu
1173 With Respect *rear, t.o. 7th, p.u. 12th*......P Johnson pu
17 ran. 12l, 4l, nk, 3l, 12l, 1l, 8l. Time 6m 28.00s. SP 7-4.
A H Mactaggart (Jedforest).
One fence omitted, 17 jumps.

1515 Members (12st)

1424 **SARONA SMITH 5a 9ow** ......**Miss J Hutchinson** **1**
ld & sn clr,steadied 5th,hdd 4 out,rallied to ld last,hld on
1425[6] **Tod Law 5a 7ex**..........................**T Scott** **2**
(fav) sttld 3rd, prog to ld 4 out, faltered & hdd last, rallied
1336 **Billy Buoyant** ....**J Walton** **3**
chsd ldr, mstk 14th, ev ch 2 out, onepcd
1428 Bantel Baronet *rear, prog 8th, wknd rpdly 2 out, walked in*..............................Miss J Hedley 4
Raffles *1st ride, alwys last, lost tch 10th, t.o. 12th*..Miss D Edminson 5
5 ran. ½l, 7l, 20l, 5l. Time 6m 45.00s. SP 7-1.
Mrs F T Walton (Border).
N.E.

DULVERTON WEST
Bratton Down
Saturday May 17th
GOOD TO SOFT

1516 Confined

1484[1] **BUTLER JOHN (IRE)** ....**N Harris** **1**
(fav) prog to ld apr 8th, sn clr, pshd out flat
1089[3] **Milled Oats** ....**R Widger** **2D**
handy, went 2nd apr 12th, chsd wnr, fin 2nd, disq
1436[3] **Southerly Buster** ....**S White** **2**
raced wd, in tch til outpcd 15th, lft 3rd 3 out, kpt on
1395[1] **Indian Rabi** ....**G Penfold** **3**
ld to 7th, wkng whn mstks 12th & 13th, t.o. 15th
1312[3] Charmers Wish 5a *last, lost tch 12th, t.o. & p.u. last*..H Thomas pu
1374[1] Sabbaq (USA) *hld up, prog 14th, disp 3rd whn blnd & u.r. 3 out*.................................I Dowrick ur
6 ran. 6l, 20l, 25l. Time 6m 26.50s. SP 1-3.
Nick Viney (Dulverton (West)).
Milled Oats disq, rider not W/I. Original distances.

1517 Mixed Open (12st)

1316[1] **FOSBURY** ....**T Mitchell** **1**
j.w. ld 2nd, slght ld til hdd 100yrds out, ld agn nr fin
1292[1] **Tinotops** ....**Miss S Vickery** **2**
(fav) trckd ldr, rdn 2 out, ran on to ld 100 yrds out, hdd post
1397[1] **Saint Joseph** ....**Miss S Young** **3**
in tch, 5th & outpcd aft 16th, styd on wll clsng stgs
1489[4] The General's Drum *prog to 3rd at 15th, outpcd 3 out, sn wknd & eased*..............................K Heard 4
1341[1] The Golfing Curate *prog 14th, in tch 16th, onepcd frm nxt*...A Michael 5
1370 Alex Thuscombe (v) *in tch til wknd 14th, sn btn*..P Shaw 6

1482[3] Fearsome *handy, 2nd brfly aft 13th, sn wknd, t.o.* ....G Penfold 7
1244 Rosea Plena 5a *lost tch 11th, jmpd rght 13th, t.o. & p.u. 16th* ....S Kidston pu
8 ran. Hd, 15l, 6l, 4l, 8l, 25l. Time 6m 31.00s. SP 5-2.
Mrs Susan Humphreys (Cattistock).

1518 PPORA (12st)

1416[1] **KING TORUS (IRE) 4ex ....J Jukes 1**
(fav) ld to 9th, cls 2nd til ld agn 2 out, kpt on gamely und pres
1313[3] **Three And A Half ....N Harris 2**
prom til ld 9th, hdd 2 out, styd on wll und pres flat
1312[1] **Thegoose ....P King 3**
cls 3rd frm 8th til outpcd 3 out, eased flat
1458 Slaney France (Ire) *svrl pstns, in tch to 13th, wll btn frm 16th* ....Miss K Lovelace 4
1397[3] Tranquil Waters (USA) *in tch til rdn & wknd 14th* ....David Dennis 5
1153 The Humble Tiller *not fluent, sn strggling, t.o.* ....P Bevins 6
1156[1] Marion's Own (Ire) (v) *hld up, prog to 4th at 14th, p.u. nxt, lame* ....T Mitchell pu
7 ran. 2l, dist, 25l, 2l, 20l. Time 6m 32.00s. SP 4-6.
Nick Viney (Tiverton Staghounds).

1519 Restricted (12st)

1437[1] **MILLYHENRY ....J Tizzard 1**
prog 9th, ld 13th-16th, disp nxt til pshd clr apr last
1340[3] **First Design ....A Holdsworth 2**
6th hlfwy, prog 15th, went 3rd 3 out, fin strngly
1439[4] **Bewdley Boy ....Miss P Gundry 3**
ld/disp 3rd-9th, lost plc, prog to disp 3 out, no ext last
1395[4] Cedars Rosslare *rear, rmndrs 11th, 7th 2 out, nrst fin* ....Miss O Green 4
1395[3] Arble March 5a *s.s. rear, 12th at 15th, nrst fin* ....Mrs M Hand 5
1339 Medias Maid 5a *prog to 3rd at 12th, 2nd whn mstk 14th, wknd rpdly* ....Miss L Pope 6
1483[3] Bucks Flea 5a *sn rear, 11th at 15th, no ch aft* ....G Penfold 7
1483[2] Wooden Minstrel 5a *ld 2nd, disp 3rd-9th, mstk 11th, wknd, t.o. & p.u. 2 out* ....Dr P Pritchard pu
1088[3] Ragtime Boy (bl) *mid-div, mstk 8th, rmndrs 11th, bhnd & p.u. 14th* ....Miss P Curling pu
1395[5] Chocolate Buttons 5a *9th at 12th, nvr dang, t.o. & p.u. last* ....H Thomas pu
1259[3] Northern Sensation 5a *mid-div, 8th at 10th, bhnd & p.u. 2 out* ....S Kidston pu
1093 Holcombe Ideal 5a *3rd hlfwy, wknd 13th, t.o. & p.u. 16th* ....L Jefford pu
1237[2] Billy Barter (Ire) *(fav) prom, disp 8th-12th, 4th & outpcd 15th, no ch & p.u. last* ....Miss S Vickery pu
1374[4] Clandon Lad (v) *hld up, prog 12th, went 3rd & mstk 16th, wknd, 4th last,p.u.* ....J Jukes pu
792[3] Swing To The Left (Ire) 5a *tubed, rear, blnd 11th, t.o. & p.u. 14th* ....R Nuttall pu
15 ran. 5l, 5l, 4l, 5l, 8l, 1½l. Time 6m 35.00s. SP 4-1.
L G Tizzard (Quantock Staghounds).

1520 Open Maiden Div I (12st)

1486[3] **PILGRIM'S MISSION (IRE) ....R Darke 1**
(fav) handy, ld 14th, clr 3 out, hld on wll, all out
Lord Spider 7a ....Miss P Gundry 2
bhnd, last at 10th, gd prog 13th, chsd wnr 3 out, promising
1400 **Belitlir 12a ....Miss S Young 3**
rear, poor 8th at 14th, fin wll, sntchd 3rd post
1108 Church Ride (Ire) *mid-div, some prog to 3rd & jmpd slwly 3 out, onepcd* ....P King 4
1437[2] Dollybat 5a *9th hlfwy, prog 14th, went 3rd apr 2 out, fdd* ....M Frith 5
Location *prom til 7th, rear whn p.u. 13th* ....N Harris pu
1497 Red Is The Rose 5a *slght ld to 9th, wknd, bhnd & p.u. 14th* ....J Tizzard pu
Dixton Hill *rmndrs & jmpd slwly 4th, bhnd & p.u. 7th* ....G Penfold pu
1485 Haven *s.s. bhnd & jmpd poorly til ref 3rd* ....K Crook ref
1486 Carumu 5a *mid-div, 8th hlfwy, nvr dang, btn 6th whn p.u. 2 out* ....David Dennis pu
1481 Roving Gypsy 12a *rear til p.u. 14th, schooling* ....A Holdsworth pu
1399 Barton Rose *prom, cls 3rd whn hit 12th, cls 2nd & ev ch whn f 16th* ....S Slade f
1498 Summerthetime *prog 5th, ld 9-10th, wd bnd apr nxt, mstk 12th, p.u. 14th* ....N Legg pu
1311 Mellicometti *prom, ld 11th-13th, wknd rpdly 16th, p.u. nxt* ....L Jefford pu
1399 Ballyhasty Lady (Ire) 5a *rear, pckd 2nd, t.o. whn tried to ref & u.r. 12th* ....J Young ur
1481 Morchard Gem 12a *twrds rear whn f 10th* ..S Kidston f
1399 I'm Foxy 5a *mid-div, 10th hlfwy, bhnd & p.u. 3 out, schooling* ....R Widger pu
17 ran. 3l, 10l, nk, 1l. Time 6m 42.50s. SP 7-4.
A G Masters (East Cornwall).

1521 Open Maiden Div II (12st)

1399[3] **BIG BANDS ARE BACK (USA) 7a ...Miss S Young 1**
made all, clr 2 out, easily
1486 **Get Stepping ....Miss S Vickery 2**
prom, cls 3rd at 12th, chsd ldr 16th, no imp
1315[3] **Fledermaus ....R Widger 3**
6th hlfwy, no ch ldrs, just hld 3rd
1400 Sixth In Line (Ire) *rear, 10th at 12th, nrst fin* ....T Cole 4
1095 Broad Commitment *sn prom, 2nd whn blnd 12th, lost ground steadily* ....R Treloggen 5
1400 Nottarex *rear, poor 8th at 14th, t.o.* ....B Wright 6
1485 Liberty James *f 8th, dead* ....T Greed f
1343[4] Call Me Dickins (bl) *prom whn u.r. 2nd* Miss A Barnett ur
1416 Friendly Viking *rear, 10th at 12th, p.u. apr nxt* ....I Hambly pu
1485[2] Harmony's Choice *(fav) in tch til f 9th* ....N Harris f
County Bash 5a *schoold rear, p.u. 8th* ....C Heard pu
1246 Expresso Drummer *prog to 5th at 11th, 4th at 14th, fdd, p.u. flat* ....Miss P Curling pu
1483 Fingal *in tch, 4th at 12th, wknd nxt, bhnd & p.u. 3 out, lame* ....S Kidston pu
1437 Leejay Luki *mid-div, 7th at 12th, bhnd & p.u. flat* ....A Honeyball pu
1437 Weycroft Valley 5a *t.o. & p.u. 11th* ....S Slade pu
1485 Morchard Mill 7a *u.r. 2nd* ....A Holdsworth ur
16 ran. 20l, dist, hd, 3l, 30l. Time 6m 39.50s. SP 3-1.
A G Fear (Tiverton Foxhounds).
Poor visibility this race. G.T.

GOLDEN VALLEY
Bredwardine
Saturday May 17th
GOOD

1522 Members

1390[1] **LLES LE BUCFLOW ....S Lloyd 1**
(fav) not fluent, cls 2nd, jnd ldr & lft alone 14th, reluc nxt
1203 **Who's Your Man (Ire) ....M FitzGerald 2**
made most til jnd & f 14th, rmntd
2 ran. 15l. Time 7m 24.00s. SP 4-6.
Jeffrey A Smith (Golden Valley).

1523 Confined (12st)

1329[2] **LETS TWIST AGAIN (IRE) 3ex....Julian Pritchard 1**
(fav) ld 4-6th, ld 12th, prssd frm 2 out, pshd out flat
1390 **Haven Light ....A Dalton 2**
hld up bhnd, prog 7th, chsd wnr apr 2 out, no ext flat
1233[4] **Gold'n Shroud (Ire) ....A Wintle 3**
cls up, chsd wnr 14th-apr 2 out, kpt on und pres
1403[4] Master Dancer *ld to 4th & 6th-12th, wknd 15th* ....Miss C Dyson 4
1063 Stanford Boy *rear, last but in tch whn u.r. 11th* ....G Andrew ur
1202[3] Stylish Gent *jmps slwly 7th, in tch to 12th, wknd, t.o. & p.u.3 out, lame* ....D Mansell pu

1321[5] Project's Mate 7ex (bl) *mstk 6th, sn drppd out, t.o. & p.u. 11th*............D S Jones pu
7 ran. 1l, 2½l, 20l. Time 6m 39.00s. SP 4-7.
Mrs S Bird (Ledbury).

1524 Men's Open (12st)

1389[1] **NETHER GOBIONS 7ex ....Julian Pritchard 1**
(fav) chsd ldr, ld apr 10th, made rest, styd on wll frm 2 out
1411[3] **Archer (Ire) ....M Harris 2**
in tch, rdn to chs wnr frm 10th, no imp aft 3 out, not qckn
1469 **Doubting Donna 5a...................E Williams 3**
nvr going wll, rmndrs 7th, went poor 3rd 3 out, no dang
1328[2] Garrylucas 4ex *in tch, rdn 12th, sn btn, jmpd slwly 14th, t.o. 3 out*............A Dalton 4
1321[2] Fly Fred *chsd ldrs, 3rd & wkng 13th, t.o. & p.u. last*............S Lloyd pu
816[1] Wildnite *in tch in rear, rdn & wknd 12th, p.u. 15th*............E Walker pu
1472 Moving Force *pllng, ld to apr 10th, wknd rpdly, p.u. 12th*............D S Jones pu
1455[2] Pretoria Dancer 7a *hld up last, sn wll bhnd, t.o. 8th, p.u. 12th*............M Rimell pu
8 ran. 12l, 20l, 15l. Time 6m 33.00s. SP 6-4.
P Clutterbuck (Berkeley).

1525 Ladies

1197[1] **RIP VAN WINKLE ....Miss A Dare 1**
(fav) ld aft 5th, made rest, shkn up last, ran on well
1387[2] **Bowland Girl (Ire) 5a ....Miss E James 2**
mstks 5th & 12th, chsd wnr 10th, ev ch last, ran on
1445[1] **Howaryadoon ....Miss T Cave 3**
prom til 3rd & outpcd frm 14th, no imp ldrs aft
1456[2] Fantastic Fleet (Ire) 7a *hld up, not fluent, in tch 13th, outpcd frm 14th*............Miss C Thomas 4
1213[3] Gay Ruffian *prom to 13th, sn outpcd & btn*............Miss C Dyson 5
1470[5] Local Customer *mstk 9th, in tch to 12th, sn wknd, t.o. 15th*............Miss G Gibson 6
1302[3] Fell Mist *cls up, wkng whn blnd 13th, p.u. nxt*............Miss A Sykes pu
Most Interesting 5a *in tch to 12th, t.o. 15th, p.u. last*............Miss P Jones pu
1237 Bel Lane 5a (v) *ld til ran wd bnd aft 5th, sn bhnd, t.o. 13th, p.u. last*............Miss J Houldey pu
9 ran. 2l, 15l, 4l, 4l, 30l. Time 6m 31.00s. SP 1-3.
Dr P P Brown & Mrs S Birks (Berkeley).

1526 Restricted (12st)

1237 **OLLARDALE (IRE) (bl)...................J Tudor 1**
mstks, prom, ld 9th, kicked clr 14th, unchal, eased flat
1392[3] **Derring Ann 5a ....D S Jones 2**
prog to chs wnr 11th, ev ch 13th, outpcd & mstks frm nxt
1322 **A Few Dollars More (Ire) ....M Rimell 3**
ld to aft 2nd, prom, mstk 10th, rdn & outpcd frm 13th
1458[2] Everso Irish *hld up, prog & in tch 12th, 4th & outpcd 14th, no prog aft*............Julian Pritchard 4
1237[4] Fire King *mid-div, lost tch 13th, no dang aft*............Miss C Thomas 5
1084[1] Bucklelone 5a *w.w. prog & mstk 8th, lost tch 13th, sn wll bhnd*............S Morris 6
1417[5] Damers Treasure *bhnd frm 5th, t.o. 12th*.....M Harris 7
1324[1] Mr Ffitch *in tch, wknd 8th, t.o. & p.u. 11th*..G Barfoot-Saunt pu
433 Meadow Cottage *mid-div, u.r. 4th*...Miss C Spearing ur
1403 Yorkshire Pop 5a *pllng, ld aft 2nd-9th, wknd rpdly, p.u. 12th*............L Brown pu
1178 Crafty Gunner *(fav) mstks, rear, prog to chs ldrs 11th, wknd 13th, p.u. 3 out*............C Stockton pu
852 Offensive Weapon *rear & rdn 11th, sn t.o., p.u. 3 out*............O McPhail pu
1412[3] Gillie's Fountain *prom til rdn & btn 13th, wll bhnd whn p.u. 2 out*............A Dalton pu
13 ran. 12l, 4l, 6l, 10l, 6l, 30l. Time 6m 37.00s. SP 14-1.
Wilfred S Littleworth (Golden Valley).

1527 Open Maiden Div I (12st)

222[4] **ROBERO ....Julian Pritchard 1**
(fav) w.w. prog 13th, ld 3 out, rdn out flat
1460[2] **Nick The Biscuit ....O McPhail 2**
w.w. prog to ld 15th-nxt, chsd wnr aft, not qckn last
1230[4] **Kilgobbin (Ire) ....D Stephens 3**
hld up rear, prog to chs ldng pair aft 15th, no imp 2 out
Itsthejonesboy *made most to 15th, sn wknd, fair debut*............Miss P Jones 4
1323[3] Lady Romance (Ire) 5a *prom to 10th, rear frm 13th, sn t.o.*............S Shinton 5
1459[2] Rejects Reply *hld up last, nvr put in race, ref 8th*............A Dalton ref
1367[3] Wilton Park 5a *nrly ran out 2nd, in tch in rear whn ran out 8th*............A Price ro
1324[3] Greenfield Maid (Ire) 5a *prom til wknd rpdly 13th, p.u. 15th*............J Tudor pu
1238[6] Bally Boy 7a *prom, mstk 12th, lost plc & p.u. 15th*............D S Jones pu
754 Young Spring 12a *ran wd bend apr 3rd & p.u., dsmntd*............A Jordan pu
719 Wyndams Lad (Ire) 4ow *in tch whn ran out 8th*............R Cotton ro
1262 Shakinallover (Ire) 7a *hld up rear,lost tch 13th, 6th & no ch whn p.u. 3 out,school*............A Phillips pu
1324 Miss Panoo 5a *mstks, cls up to 12th, wknd, t.o. & p.u. 2 out*............N Oliver pu
13 ran. 3l, 10l, 20l, 20l. Time 6m 57.00s. SP 7-4.
Tom Hayes (Clifton On Teme).

1528 Open Maiden Div II (12st)

1393[5] **MERGER MANIA 7a..................D Mansell 1**
rear of main grp, ran on 15th, ld apr 2 out, sn clr, eased
1401 **Military Man ....A Phillips 2**
prom, ld 15th til apr 2 out, no ext aft
1402[2] **Joyney 5a.......................Miss C Thomas 3**
alwys handy, ld 13th-15th, styd on onepcd frm 2 out
405[6] Watchit Lad *prssd ldr to 12th, lost plc 15th, kpt on agn 2 out*............M P Jones 4
1238[3] Astromis (Ire) 5a *trckd ldrs, prog to chal 3 out, ev ch apr nxt, wknd*............O McPhail 5
1393 Miss Clare 5a *chsd ldng pair to 12th, outpcd 15th, no imp ldrs aft*............N Oliver 6
1393[4] Pridewood Golding *ld to 13th, steadily wknd*...T Cox 7
1460 Money Don't Matter 12a *mstk 8th, alwys bhnd, t.o. 12th*............T Stephenson 8
1402[6] Sonny's Song (bl) *alwys rear, t.o. 12th, p.u. 14th*............L Brown pu
1460 The Hollow (Ire) 5a *mstk 6th, chsd ldrs to 12th, wknd & p.u. 15th*............R Bevis pu
1388 Seven Cruise *sn wll in rear, bhnd whn u.r. bend apr 10th*............R Jones ur
Clobeever Boy *hld up, wll in rear whn f 10th*............G Barfoot-Saunt f
1460 Asante Sana 5a *alwys rear, rdn & lost tch 12th, t.o. & p.u. 3 out*............M Munrowd pu
1393[2] Philelwyn (Ire) 5a *(fav) w.w. prog to trck ldrs 13th, no imp 3 out, wknd & p.u. last*............Julian Pritchard pu
1324 Flockmaster (Ire) *alwys bhnd, t.o. & p.u. 10th*............S Shinton pu
Humphrey *t.o. 10th, p.u. 12th*............D S Jones pu
Lastofthe Littles 7a *u.r. 1st*............M Rimell ur
17 ran. 8l, sht-hd, 5l, 7l, 2l, 6l, 15l. Time 6m 48.00s. SP 14-1.
W I Owens (Middleton).
J.N.

FAKENHAM
Sunday May 18th
GOOD

1529 3m 110yds Hood, Vores And Allwood Hunters' Chase Class H For Essandem Trophy

1284[3] **DROMIN LEADER 11.13 5a ....Mr A Sansome 1**
made all, clr after 3 out, all out.
1403[3] **Sandybraes 11.5 7a ....Mr F Hutsby 2**
chsd wnr thrght, hit 13th, blnd 3 out, rdn apr last, no impn.
1115[1] **Cracking Idea (Ire) 11.11 7a. .Mr C Ward Thomas 3**
held up, hdwy 9th, outpcd 3 out, styd on und pres run-in.
1284 Tammy's Friend 11.5 7a (bl) *prom, outpcd 3 out, styd on apr last.* ....Mr R Wakley 4
1482[1] Abbotsham 11.5 7a *chsd ldrs, rdn 5 out, wknd 3 out.* ....Miss P Gundry 5
1358[1] Chilipour 12.3 5a *(fav) prom, blnd 13th, rdn 3 out, no impn apr last, eased run-in*..............Mr J Jukes 6
1433[3] Lyme Gold (Ire) 11.11 7a (bl) *alwys in rear.* ....Mr D Keane 7
1377 Cardinal Red 11.11 7a *soon bhnd, tried to refuse 10th, p.u. before next*..............Mr N King 8
1482[5] Skerry Meadow 11.5 7a *hit 1st, soon well bhnd, blnd 6th, p.u. after 10th*..............Miss V Roberts 9
9 ran. 5l, ½l, 1¼l, 12l, 2l, dist. Time 6m 13.80s. SP 6-1.
J M Turner

1530 2m 5f 110yds West Norfolk Maiden Hunters' Chase Class H

1435[1] **ROUGH EDGE 12.2 5a..............Mr W Wales 1**
(fav) held up, hdwy 10th, hit next, chsd ldr 3 out, ld last, styd on well.
1478[1] **Coolvawn Lady (Ire) 11.9 7a.........Mr S Walker 2**
alwys prom, ld 9th, hdd and no ext last.
1296[4] **Tellaporky 12.0 7a..............Mr A Middleton 3**
held up, hdwy 4 out, not reach ldrs.
1283[1] Beech Brook 12.0 7a *chsd ldrs, pkd 10th, mstk 6 out, wknd 4 out*..............Mr T Lane 4
1474[5] Menature (Ire) 12.2 5a *held up, hdwy 12th wknd next.* ....Mr A Sansome 5
1485 Raki Crazy 12.0 7a *bhnd when blnd 3rd, hdwy 10th, wknd 4 out*..............Miss P Gundry 6
214 McCartney 12.0 7a *mid-divison, hdwy and hit 11th, wknd apr 4 out.*..............Mr K Green 7
1192[2] Chester Ben 12.4 3a *made most to 9th, wknd 4 out.* ....Mr Simon Andrews 8
1283 Alapa 12.0 7a *blnd and u.r. 2nd.*..............Mr V Coogan ur
1278[3] Al Jawwal 12.0 7a *in rear when hit 4th, p.u. before next*..............Mr R Wakley pu
1191[2] Dark Rhytham 12.0 7a *prom to 10th, p.u. before 4 out.*..............Mr S Morris pu
11 ran. 6l, 7l, 12l, 22l, sht-hd, 28l, 2½l. Time 5m 28.40s. SP 5-2.
David Wales

BICESTER WITH WHADDON CHASE
Mollington
Sunday May 18th
GOOD TO SOFT

1531 Members

1448 **SPRUCEFIELD ....A Barlow 1**
ld to aft 2nd, wth ldr, ld 10th-2 out, styd on to ld flat
761[1] **Fill The Boot (Ire) ....J Owen 2**
(fav) mstk 6th,hldup,prog to ld 2 out,hng lft,wknd & hdd flat
988[3] **Icky's Five ....Miss T Habgood 3**
cls up til outpcd frm 15th, kpt on 2 out
1199[5] Horcum *in tch til last & jmpd slwly 13th, kpt on frm 2 out*..............Miss C Ramsey 4
877 All Change *in tch, chsd ldr 12th-3 out, ev ch nxt, wknd* ....T Illsley 5
1464 Walkers Point *made most aft 2nd-10th, wknd 15th, t.o.* ....Miss K O'Neill 6
6 ran. 3l, 2l, sht-hd, 3l, 25l. Time 6m 46.00s. SP 2-1.
M H D Barlow (Bicester With Whaddon Chase).

1532 Confined (12st)

1404 **ADMIRAL ROUS ....C Wadland 1**
in tch, prog 13th, chsd ldr aft 2 out, ld flat, ran on wll
1448[1] **Run For Free 6ex ....A Hill 2**
(fav) cls up,pshd alng 14th,ld apr 2 out,hng lft aft, hdd flat
1279[5] **Berkana Run ....R Bailey 3**
prom til outpcd frm 15th, no imp ldrs aft
1403[2] Going Around *trckd ldrs, not qckn 15th, no prog aft* ....L Lay 4
1147 Springfield Lad *in tch in rear to 15th, kpt on agn frm 2 out*..............Miss E Walker 5
1403[5] Tompet *jmpd lft, prssd ldr to 10th, wknd 15th* ....J Connell 6
Sunshine Manor *pllng, ld to apr 2 out, wknd rpdly, walked in*..............G Tarry 7
986 Sutton Lass 5a 3ow *sn last, t.o. 9th, mls bhnd whn ref last*..............N Wain ref
1444[4] July Schoon 3ex *hld up,prog 5th,lost plc 11th,no imp 13th, bhnd & p.u.last*..............T Underwood pu
1403 Lad Lane 2ow *alwys last pair, t.o. 12th, p.u. 3 out* ....J Borradaile pu
1404[1] Connie Foley *rear, lost tch 12th, t.o. & p.u. 3 out* ....J Trice-Rolph pu
11 ran. ¾l, 15l, 4l, 1l, 15l, 2l. Time 6m 35.00s. SP 6-1.
Mrs R Hurley (Warwickshire).

1533 P P O R A (12st)

1449[2] **TREVVEETHAN (IRE) ....M Rimell 1**
(fav) hld up, prog to jn ldrs 13th, ld apr 2 out, clr last, comf
1450[2] **Rayman (Ire) ....Mrs T Hill 2**
prog 5th, ld aft 8th-15th, ld nxt-apr 2 out, no ext
1393[1] **Winter Breeze ....Miss S Vickery 3**
alwys prom, ld 15th-nxt, onepcd apr 2 out
1466 Buladante (Ire) *hld up, prog 11th, ev ch 14th, not qckn nxt, onepcd*..............T Underwood 4
760 Bubbly Boy *last & mstk 6th, nvr on trms aft, no ch frm 13th*..............J Oldring 5
1477[2] Cantango (Ire) *cls up to 11th, rmndr & sn wknd, t.o.* ....E Andrewes 6
1451[5] Abitmorfun 7ex *ld to 5th, prssd ldr to 11th, wknd rpdly, t.o.*..............C Coyne 7
1404[2] Penly 1ow *prom to 11th, sn wknd, 6th & t.o. whn u.r. 2 out*..............A Westrope ur
8 ran. 6l, 2½l, 4l, 20l, 20l, 1 fence. Time 6m 41.00s. SP Evens.
Giles Smyly (North Cotswold).

1534 Men's Open

1448 **BRIGHT AS A BUTTON ....G Tarry 1**
in tch, outpcd 15th, ran on nxt, ld 2 out, drvn out
1415 **Hill Island ....R Sweeting 2**
(fav) trckd ldrs, ld 13th-2 out, ev ch flat, no ext und pres
1451[4] **Radical Views ....A Hill 3**
w.w. cls up 14th, pshd alng nxt, ev ch apr 2 out,wknd last
1488[6] Al Hashimi *trckd ldr 8th til aft 3 out, wknd nxt* ....N Ridout 4
1360[3] Copper Thistle (Ire) *not fluent, ld to 2nd, lost plc 15th, no dang aft*..............R Hunnisett 5
1475[5] The Country Trader (bl) *ld 2nd, sn clr, hdd 13th, sn wknd*..............J Borradaile 6
1478[2] Penlet *last, lost tch 10th, t.o. 13th, p.u. 2 out* ....John Pritchard pu
7 ran. 1½l, 8l, 3l, 12l, 15l. Time 6m 32.00s. SP 10-1.
Sir Michael Connell (Grafton).

1535 Ladies

1463[1] **GRIMLEY GALE (IRE) 5a..........Miss S Vickery 1**
(fav) ld to 4th, prssd ldr, rdn to ld 3 out, clr nxt, ran on wll
1161[1] **Stephens Pet ....Miss A Dare 2**
ld 5th-3 out, eased whn btn apr last, collapsed & died aft
1287 **Making Time 5a ....Miss T Habgood 3**
trckd ldng pair, mstk 6th, outpcd & mstk 12th, sn t.o.
1450[3] Linlake Lightning 5a *in tch, pshd alng 10th, lft bhnd frm 12th, t.o.*..............Miss H Irving 4
Tekla (Fr) *immed dtchd, t.o. 7th, p.u. 11th* ....Miss D Olding pu

573 Walkonthemoon 5a *in tch, pshd alng 10th, sn wknd, t.o. & p.u. 13th*........................Miss N McKim pu
6 ran. 30l, 15l, 20l. Time 6m 23.00s. SP 10-11.
R M Phillips (Worcestershire).

1536 Intermediate (12st)

1449¹ **VILLAINS BRIEF (IRE) (bl) ....R Lawther** 1
(fav) chsng grp, prog & chsd ldr 13th, ld 2 out, ran on wll flat
1403¹ **Mr Gee ....K Needham** 2
w.w. rear, grad prog frm 13th, chal & ev ch last,onepcd flat
1064⁶ **Gromit (NZ) ....T Stephenson** 3
sttld rear,rdn & prog 10th,effrt to chal & ev ch last,no ext
1443¹ Bocock's Pride (Ire) *hld up,prog to chs ldr 11-13th,cls up apr 2 out,wknd,wlkd in* ....T Underwood 4
1319³ Ideal *mstk 6th, chsd clr ldr to 11th, sn wknd, t.o. & p.u. 2 out*...........................Miss C Thomas pu
1326¹ Roman Romany *ld, clr to 11th, hdd & wknd 2 out, p.u. last*.............................M Rimell pu
1401¹ The Chairman (Ire) *hld up, last & lost tch 8th, p.u. aft 10th*..................................J Trice-Rolph pu
1356 Carlingford Lad (Ire) *chsng grp to 9th, wknd rpdly, t.o. & p.u. 13th*.............................E Andrewes pu
8 ran. 3l, 1½l, 30l. Time 6m 39.00s. SP 2-1.
Nick Quesnel (Berks & Bucks Drag).

1537 Open Maiden

1386³ **QUITE A MISS 5a........................A Martin** 1
prom,ld 8th-aft 3 out,lft 2nd nxt,styd on to ld flat
1479⁴ **Dilkush ....M Wells** 2
in tch,prog 12th,chal 3 out,lft in ld nxt,nt run on,hdd flat
1356 **Bobbin Lace 5a........................J Docker** 3
chsd ldrs, wknd 13th, t.o. 3 out, lft poor 3rd nxt
1402 Dromain 5a *prom, mstk 10th, wkng whn mstk 13th, t.o.*...............................Mrs C McCarthy 4
1357³ The Birdie Song 5a *mstks in rear, lost tch 13th, t.o.* ....M Harris 5
451 The Merry Nun (Ire) 5a *rear til hmpd & u.r. 5th* ....J Owen ur
1192 View Point (Ire) *in tch, jnd ldrs & jmpd slwly 13th, sn wknd, t.o. & p.u.2out*......................A Dalton pu
1401 Captain's Port 5a *alwys bhnd, rdn & no prog 11th, t.o. & p.u. 3 out* ....Julian Pritchard pu
1352³ Village Remedy 5a *ld to 8th, wknd 10th, t.o. & p.u. last* ....A Tutton pu
Just Like Madge 5a *t.d.e.,in tch,prssd ldr 13th,ld aft 3 out,lkd wnr & u.r. nxt* ....G Tarry ur
1479 Seaton Mill *in tch til wknd & p.u. 11th*.......M Hewitt pu
1015² Sun Setting *(fav) trckd ldrs til f 5th* ....R Sweeting f
1401 Deejayef 5a *in tch til b.d. 5th*..............N Ridout bd
1401 Lady Kilton 5a *alwys rear, t.o. 12th, p.u. 2 out* ....P Cowley pu
14 ran. 1½l, dist, 5l, 10l. Time 6m 46.00s. SP 6-1.
C W Loggin (Bicester With Whaddon Chase).
J.N.

WHEATLAND
Wolverhampton P-To-P Course
Sunday May 18th
GOOD TO SOFT

1538 Confined

1349³ **ROYLE BURCHLIN ....D Barlow** 1
made all, prssd 4 out, ran on wll frm nxt
1381 **Mr Pipe Man (Ire) ....T O'Leary** 2
mid-div, prog 13th, ran on frm 3 out, not rch wnr
1472¹ **Nutcase 5a...........................A Phillips** 3
(fav) chsd wnr, lvl 4 out, outpcd & btn nxt
1381³ Penllyne's Pride *ref to race*................J Chilton 0
466 Montykosky *mid-div, t.o. 9th, p.u. nxt*. .Miss L Wallace pu
1349 Flinters (bl) *prom early, mid-div 9th, wknd rpdly, p.u. 13th*..................................D Sherlock pu
1382 Sister Emu 5a *rear, t.o. whn f 4 out* ....P Saville f
1382² Another Chancer *cls 2nd/3rd til blnd 5 out, sn btn, p.u. 3 out*....................................M Harris pu
8 ran. 12l, 8l. Time 6m 44.00s. SP 4-1.
R A Royle (Cheshire).

1539 Men's Open (12st)

1288⁵ **ORTON HOUSE ....R Burton** 1
handy, prog to ld 4 out, ran on strngly nxt, comf
887 **Rhine River (USA) (bl) ....S Prior** 2
ld to 5 out, not qckn, btn frm nxt
1351¹ **Merlyns Choice ....A Woodward** 3
(fav) sn rear, nvr going wll, wll t.o. 6 out, ran on to 3rd flat
1301² Freddie Fox 7ex *in tch, onepcd frm 3 out*....T Garton 4
1349 Barkin *2nd at 5th, lost tch 14th, u.r. nxt*.......P Saville ur
5 ran. 10l, 10l, ½l. Time 6m 53.00s. SP 2-1.
Mrs A P Kelly (Flint & Denbigh).

1540 Ladies

1470¹ **TOUCH 'N' PASS 7ex ....Miss P Jones** 1
(fav) cls up, ld 10-11th, ld agn 5 out, ran on wll und pres
1470³ **Aegean Fanfare (Ire) ....Mrs C Ford** 2
rear, in tch, clsd 13th, disp 4 out, lvl last, just faild
1302⁴ **Commodity Broker ....Miss J Priest** 3
alwys handy, ev ch 3 out, outpcd frm nxt
1384 Golden Fare *made most to 10th & 11-14th, fdd 4 out* ....Miss L Wallace 4
1384³ Great Uncle *chsng grp, cls up 5 out, lost tch nxt* ....Miss T McCurrick 5
5 ran. Hd, 10l, 15l, 1l. Time 6m 43.00s. SP 1-2.
R H P Williams (Llangeinor).

1541 Open Maiden (12st)

999² **RUGRAT 5a ....T O'Leary** 1
alwys prom, smooth prog to ld apr 3 out, ran on wll
1479³ **Malenski (Ire) ....B Pollock** 2
hld up, prog 5 out, ran on, nrst fin
1209³ **Dancing Supreme ....L Brown** 3
alwys prom, ev ch 4 out, not qckn apr last
1386⁴ Riot Lady (Ire) 5a *alwys ldng quartet, no ext frm 4 out* ....D Barlow 4
1239 Only In Ireland *handy, ld 6th-4 out, sn wknd* ....R Inglesant 5
1382 Tbilisi *ref to race*...........................A Jordan 0
1386² Henrietta Boo Boo 5a *(fav) chsng grp, 3rd at 14th, sn btn, p.u. 3 out*.............................A Phillips pu
666 Opulent Trappings 5a *ref 1st*..............J Barlow ref
469² Barney Bear *mid to rear, no ch whn p.u. 3 out* ....T Garton pu
1386⁵ Cuban Skies (Ire) *mid-div to 13th, wknd, no ch & p.u. 2 out*....................................G Hanmer pu
1003 Sentimentalscally 12a *cls up to 6th, lost tch 13th, btn whn u.r. 5 out*.........................P McAllister ur
1429 Nickamy Fountain (Ire) (bl) *mid to rear, p.u. 4 out* ....K O'Meara pu
1459 Firestarter *mid to rear, no ch whn p.u. 5 out* S Shinton pu
721 See More Action 7a *ld til ran out 5th*..........R Ford ro
1304 My First Man *rear, t.o. 12th, p.u. nxt*. . .M Worthington pu
15 ran. 10l, 10l, 8l. Time 6m 42.00s. SP 4-1.
G L Edwards (North Shropshire).

1542 Restricted (12st)

1368¹ **VOLCANIC ROC ....E Williams** 1
(fav) chsd ldr til ld 9th, made rest, comf
1475 **Rakish Queen 5a ....Miss H Phizacklea** 2
rear, prog 14th, chsd wnr nxt, no imp frm 2 out
1381² **Solar Castle (Ire) ....P McAllister** 3
hld up in tch, clsd on ldrs 4 out, onepcd frm nxt
1357¹ Witch Doctor *cls up early, 3rd at 10th, 2nd at 13th, mstk nxt, sn t.o.*..................Miss S Phizacklea 4
331 Sky Runner *ld til blnd 9th, sn wknd, p.u. 4 out*. .S Prior pu
1385 Who Doctored Who (Ire) *prom, 2nd at 10th, btn frm 14th, p.u. nxt*.........................M Worthington pu
6 ran. 8l, ½l, dist. Time 6m 46.00s. SP 7-4.
Mrs N A Warner (Ross Harriers).

1543 Members

OVER THE DOOR 12a..................G Hanmer 1
(fav) hld up, ld apr 3 out, 3l up whn lft alone 3 out
1296 Thornhill 5a *ld til apr 3 out, btn whn u.r. 3 out* ....L Brown ur
2 ran. Time 8m 10.00s. SP 1-2.
M Mann (Wheatland).
V.S.

NEWTON ABBOT
Wednesday May 21st
GOOD

1544 3¼m 110yds Mike Howard & Dick Spencer Memorial Hunters' Chase Class H

1244³ **BUZZ O'THE CROWD 11.0 7a........Mr D Alers-Hankey** 1
alwys handy, ld 16th, soon clr, unchal.
1292⁵ **Fight To Win (USA) 11.0 7a........Mr J Grassick** 2
waited with, imp 13th, lost pl 15th, styd on to take poor 2nd 2 out, t.o..
1416 **Tom's Gemini Star 11.7 7a.......Miss V Roberts** 3
held up, hit 13th, soon lost tch, mod prog from 3 out, t.o..
1292² Knifeboard 11.0 7a *held up, hdwy 8th, outpcd apr 15th, t.o..* ....Mr E Williams 4
1411¹ Phar Too Touchy 11.5 7a *(fav) hdwy to go prom 5th, ld 7th, hit next, mstk and hdd 16th, soon wknd, t.o., fin distressed.* ....Mr N Harris 5
1441² Just Ben 11.0 7a *chsd ldrs to 12th, soon wknd, t.o..* ....Miss J Cumings 6
1484² Expressment 11.7 7a *alwys bhnd, t.o..* ..Mr G Penfold 7
1415¹ Kino 11.10 7a *made most to 7th, weakening when hit 15th, t.o. when blnd badly and almost u.r. 3 out, p.u. before next.* ....Mr Andrew Martin pu
884³ Alpha One 11.0 7a *alwys bhnd, t.o. from 8th, p.u. before 14th..* ....Miss K Di Marte pu
1491⁶ J B Lad 11.0 7a *prom, jmpd slowly 4th, bhnd from 11th, t.o. when hit 16th, blnd and u.r. next.* ....Mr S Shinton ur
1291⁴ Some-Toy 11.10 7a *alwys bhnd, t.o. 8th, p.u. before 4 out.* ....Miss L Blackford pu
11 ran. Dist, 11l, 4l, 4l, 13l, 23l. Time 6m 39.00s. SP 14-1.
B J Williams

CARTMEL
Saturday May 24th
GOOD

1545 3¼m Dodson & Horrell Maiden Hunters' Chase Class H for the Fraser Cup

888⁴ **SANDS OF GOLD (IRE) 11.7 7a.........Mr L Lay** 1
alwys prom, hit 3 out, hrd driven to ld entering straight, kept on.
1509⁴ **Jayandoubleu (Ire) 11.7 7a ....Mr T Scott** 2
ld to 12th, cl up, outpcd last, kept on one pace straight, no impn on wnr.
1300⁴ **Worleston Farrier 11.7 7a ....Mr G Hanmer** 3
went to post early, cl up, hit 8th, ld 12th, clr after last till tired and hdd entering straight, no ext.
1297⁴ Cool Yule (Ire) 11.9 5a *in rear, hmpd by faller 11th, pushed along apr 4 out (water), soon styd on, nearest fin.* ....Miss P Robson 4
778⁷ Just For Me (Ire) 11.9 5a *midfield, hit 7th, rdn apr 4 out, kept on one pace, no impn on ldrs.* ....Mr M H Naughton 5
1334 Wang How 11.7 7a *in tch early, bhnd and no ch when mstk 3 out.* ....Mr A Robson 6
1297⁵ Emu Park 11.7 7a *bhnd, hdwy 9th (water), in tch when hit 12th, wknd 4 out (water).* ....Mr J Thompson 7
1539¹ Orton House 11.7 7a *alwys bhnd, struggling from 13th, nvr a factor.* ....Mr R Burton 8
1425⁵ Rushing Burn 11.2 7a *soon bhnd, t.o..* ....Miss N C Snowden 9
1510 Canister Castle 11.7 7a *alwys bhnd, lost tch final cct, t.o.* ....Mr D R McLeod 10
1499 King Spring 11.9 5a *alwys bhnd, t.o. when p.u. before 4 out (water).* ....Mrs V Jackson pu
1424⁷ All Or Nothing 11.2 7a *bhnd, jmpd slowly 2nd, hdwy from 12th to chase ldrs, rdn along when blnd and u.r. 3 out.* ....Mr J Ewart ur
1417² True Fortune 11.9 5a *(fav) in tch, hdwy to go cl up 7th, f 11th.* ....Mr J Jukes f
1345 Bunny Hare (Ire) 11.7 7a *midfield when blnd and u.r. 2nd.* ....Mr R Forristal ur
14 ran. 2½l, hd, 2½l, 1¾l, 19l, 9l, 4l, 20l, dist. Time 6m 30.40s. SP 5-1.
Brett Badham

HEXHAM
Saturday May 24th
GOOD TO FIRM

1546 2½m 110yds Flying Ace Hunters' Chase Class H

1499² **HOWAYMAN 12.2 5a ....Mr R Ford** 1
(fav) held up, left 3rd 3 out, ld before last, soon clr.
1490 **Cumberland Blues (Ire) 12.0 7a....Miss A Deniel** 2
nvr far away, left in ld and hmpd 3 out, hdd next, one pace from last.
1499³ **Master Kit (Ire) 12.0 7a.........Mr M Bradburne** 3
nvr far away, left 2nd 3 out, ld next, hdd before last, soon outpcd.
1499⁵ Reed 11.7 7a *bhnd, rdn hfwy, nvr on terms.* ....Mr O McPhail 4
1414³ Knowe Head 12.0 7a *cl up, mstk 7th, struggling final cct, t.o. when p.u. before last.* ....Mr S Brisby pu
1414⁴ Buckaneer Bay 11.9 5a *bhnd, blnd 8th, p.u. before next.* ....Mr R Hale pu
1511¹ Thank U Jim 11.7 7a *with ldr, ld 8th, f 3 out.* ....Miss T Jackson f
1500 Frozen Stiff (Ire) 11.9 5a *soon t.o., p.u. before 9th.* ....Mr N Wilson pu
1514 Percy Pit 11.9 5a *ld to 8th, p.u. before 10th.* ....Mr P Johnson pu
1424 Kings Token 12.0 *soon t.o., p.u. before 9th.* ....Mr J Walton pu
10 ran. 12l, 10l, 22l. Time 5m 7.10s. SP 10-11.
Dennis Waggott

DULVERTON EAST
Mounsey Hill Gate
Saturday May 24th
GOOD

1547 Members (12st)

1440² **HENSUE ....R Treloggen** 1
(fav) chsd ldrs, ld 9th, made rest, blnd last, hld on und pres
1370¹ **Afterkelly 7ex...................Miss C Stucley** 2
alwys prom, ld 7-9th, blnd 17th, rallied 2 out, styd on flat
1483 **Morchard Milly 5a.................A Holdsworth** 3
ld to 7th, chsd wnr aft 9th, ev ch 3 out, btn last
1439 I'll Be Bound *keen hld, in tch, prog 11th, 4th & btn frm 17th* ....L Jefford 4
1439⁵ Remember Mac (bl) *blnd 2nd & 5th, bhnd aft, 5th & no ch frm 15th* ....Miss C Hayes 5
557³ Darktown Strutter (bl) *chsd ldrs to 11th, rmndrs & lost plc nxt, p.u. 16th* ....Miss L Pope pu
River Stream 5a *t.d.e. prom til wknd 12th, p.u. 16th* ....M Burrows pu
1437⁴ Sam's Successor *bhnd frm 10th, lost tch 12th, t.o. & p.u. 16th* ....N Harris pu
1317 Baywyn 5a *alwys last, jmpd slwly 3rd, lost tch 11th, p.u. 15th* ....S Kidston pu
9 ran. 1l, 3l, 20l, 30l. Time 6m 43.80s. SP 11-10.
Miss P J Boundy (Dulverton East).

1548 Ladies

1525[1] **RIP VAN WINKLE ....Miss A Dare 1**
(fav) chsd ldng pair, prog to ld 14th, sn clr, unextndd
1495[2] **Searcy (bl) ....Miss L Blackford 2**
ld, clr 5th, hdd 14th, no ch wth wnr aft, blnd last, tired
1496[2] **Arctic Baron ....Miss S Vickery 3**
mid-div, 6th & drvn alng 12th, plodded on, tk 3rd nr fin
1495 Lavalight *chsd ldrs, jmpd slwly 5th, 3rd & wkng 16th, dmtd fin* ....Miss A Goschen 4
1438[4] Romany Anne 5a *alwys mid-div, some prog to 4th at 14th, nvr nr ldrs* ....Miss S Young 5
1492[2] Rapid Rascal *chsd ldr to 13th, sn drpppd out, t.o.* ....Miss S West 6
1257[4] Daybrook's Gift *hmpd & u.r. 2nd* ....Miss N Allan ur
Senor Tomas *alwys bhnd, t.o. & p.u. 13th* ....Miss C Stucley pu
1155[5] Be My Habitat 4ow (bl) *sn wll bhnd, t.o. 6th, p.u. 9th* ....Miss L Hawkings pu
1496[1] Parditino *blnd & u.r. 2nd*............Miss V Nicholas ur
10 ran. 20l, 4l, 3l, 8l, 4l. Time 6m 33.10s. SP 1-4.
Dr P P Brown & Mrs S Birks (Berkeley).

1549 Men's Open (12st)

1516[1] **BUTLER JOHN (IRE) 7ex ....N Harris 1**
(fav) made virt all, blnd 4th, clr whn nrly u.r. 9th, solo 15th
1457[2] Champagne Run (bl) *svrl slw jmps, disp til jmpd slwly 5th, t.o. & ref 15th* ....R Hawker ref
2 ran. Time 7m 1.70s. SP 1-8.
Nick Viney (Exmoor).

1550 Intermediate (12st)

1416 **FELLOW SIOUX ....Miss S Vickery 1**
(fav) w.w. going wll, prog to ld 17th, hrd rdn & hld on wll flat
1339[1] **Eserie de Cores (USA) ....S Kidston 2**
in tch, chsd ldr 14th, ev ch 3 out, rdn nxt,unable qckn flat
1516[3] **Indian Rabi ....A Holdsworth 3**
cls up, hit 6th, 5th & outpcd 13th, no dang aft, tk 3rd 2out
1484 Oneovertheight *ld to 17th, 3rd & btn nxt, blnd & dmtd 2 out* ....Miss L Blackford 4
1495 Highway Jim *bhnd, last frm 11th, p.u. 16th* ....Miss M Burrough pu
1480[2] Batsi *alwys bhnd, lost tch 10th, t.o. & p.u. 2 out* ....I Widdicombe pu
1360 Roaming Shadow 5ow *rear, in tch to 15th, wll bhnd whn p.u. 2 out*..........................J Hankinson pu
1441[3] Tangle Kelly *prom, chsd ldr 9-14th, sn strgglng, p.u. 2 out*....................................S Slade pu
1436[1] Tuffnut Tom *mid-div, 6th & in tch whn f 12th* . . .J Scott f
9 ran. ¾l, 20l, 1l. Time 6m 37.00s. SP 10-11.
S T R Stevens (Devon & Somerset Staghounds).

1551 Restricted Div I (12st)

1439[3] **SAMULE ....G Barfoot-Saunt 1**
5s-11/4, in tch, chsd ldr 15th, ld 2 out, hdd last, ld post
1481[5] **Stretchit ....G Penfold 2**
mid-div, prog to ld apr 15th, hdd 2 out, ld last, hdd post
1519[5] **Arble March 5a.....................Mrs M Hand 3**
chsd ldrs to 10th, sn strgglng, went mod 3rd flat
1496[5] Lake Mariner 5a *hld up mid-div, prog to 3rd at 17th, btn 2 out, dmtd flat*..............................L Jefford 4
1494 Palace King (Ire) *trckd ldrs, outpcd 15th, btn whn blnd 17th, t.o.*.....................................D Alers-Hankey 5
1519[4] Cedars Rosslare *bhnd frm 6th, last whn p.u. 13th* ....Miss O Green pu
1494 Ballysheil *cls up, 3rd whn p.u. 11th, lame* . .S Edwards pu
1494 Venn Boy *(fav) mstks, chsd ldrs, 3rd & blnd 10th, 5th & no ch whn p.u.last* ....J Tizzard pu
1519 Northern Sensation 5a *bhnd frm 11th, t.o. & p.u. 15th* ....N Harris pu
1519 Billy Barter (Ire) (bl) *ld to apr 15th, sn fdd, p.u. 3 out* ....Miss S Vickery pu
1465[1] Mountain-Linnet *chsd ldrs til f 14th* . .Miss A Goschen f
1485[6] Alicott Lad *alwys bhnd, p.u. 11th, dsmntd* ....Miss L Smale pu
1497[1] Crosswell Star (Ire) *mstks, alwys bhnd, bdly hmpd 14th, t.o. & p.u. 16th* ....J Barnes pu
13 ran. Sht-hd, 25l, nk, 25l. Time 6m 36.90s. SP 11-4.
Mrs M Harding (Berkeley).

1552 Restricted Div II (12st)

1483 **RYME AND RUN 5a............Miss L Blackford 1**
chsd ldrs, went 2nd 15th, ld nxt, clr 2 out, styd on
1481[6] **Comedy Gayle ....I Widdicombe 2**
in tch, 5th at 13th, went 2nd apr 2 out, onepcd
1485[1] **Noble Comic ....J Tizzard 3**
hld up bhnd, prog 12th, chsd ldng pair 17th, btn nxt, tired
1519[7] Bucks Flea 5a *rmndrs 3rd, last & rdn 12th, kpt on, nvr dang*.................................G Penfold 4
1466[2] Nobbutjust (Ire) 5a *nvr bttr than mid-div, 8th at 13th, no prog* ....A Beedles 5
1519 Holcombe Ideal 5a *alwys mid-div, no ch frm 15th* ....L Jefford 6
1494 Newstarsky *bhnd frm 11th, blnd 13th, p.u. 15th* ....Miss J Cumings pu
1494[3] Stormy Fashion *tubed, ld to 5th, ld 11-16th, wknd rpdly, p.u. 3 out* ....Maj G Wheeler pu
1483 Carnival Kid *ran out 3rd* ....J Boscherini ro
648 Glamorous Guy *alwys bhnd, last whn blnd & u.r. 9th* ....S Parfimowicz ur
1399[1] Devonshire Lad *(fav) chsd ldr, ld 6-11th, 2nd whn p.u. 14th, lame*..............................N Harris pu
1498[1] Mighty Gale (Ire) *chsd ldrs, wknd apr 14th, last whn p.u. 3 out* ....Miss S Vickery pu
12 ran. 6l, 10l, 10l, 4l, 10l. Time 6m 37.90s. SP 25-1.
A Cottel (Spooners & West Dartmoor).

1553 Open Maiden Div I (12st)

1486 **MASTER DECOY ....L Jefford 1**
trckd ldrs,disp 13th,ld 15th,fence clr whn f last,rmtd in ld
1315 **Big Arthur (Ire) (bl)...................N Mitchell 2**
(fav) prog 10th,lft 2nd & reluc 17th,lft solo 2out-last, stll btn
1486 **Tom's Arctic Dream 5a ....P King 3**
rcd freely,ld to 8th,chsd ldrs,3rd & btn whn u.r.3out,rmntd
1497[5] Fosabud *chsd ldrs, 5th & wkng whn p.u. 15th* ....Miss L Hawkings pu
1520 Location *bhnd frm 5th, lost tch 10th, p.u. 15th* ....S Kidston pu
1400 Majic Belle 5a *prom, ld 12th-15th, 2nd & btn whn swrvd & u.r. 17th* ....Miss L Blackford ur
1373[4] Miss Gruntled 5a *blnd 4th, bhnd aft, 10th whn ref 11th* ....S Parfimowicz ref
556 Snitton Stream *raced freely, clr wth ldr, ld 8-12th, wknd, p.u. 14th*..........................R Widger pu
1520[3] Belitlir 12a *bhnd, 8th & losing tch 10th, p.u. 12th* ....Miss S Young pu
1486 Master Laughter *bhnd frm 6th, lost tch 11th, p.u. 14th* ....N Harris pu
1498[6] Berkley Street 5a *alwys last, t.o. 10th, p.u. 14th* ....J Tizzard pu
11 ran. 6l, dist. Time 7m 1.10s. SP 4-1.
M K J Reed (Tiverton Foxhounds).

1554 Open Maiden Div II (12st)

1416 **BARROW STREET ....J Tizzard 1**
w.w. prog 12th,ld aft 3 out,sn clr,tired & jnd last,all out
1486 **Master Buckley ....Miss S Vickery 2**
chsd clr ldrs, 2nd & hrd rdn 2 out, ev ch last, no ext flat
1486 **Baman Powerhouse ....J Young 3**

hld up bhnd, prog 12th, chsd ldrs 17th, btn last, fin tired

1460 Miss Dior 5a *(fav) t.d.e. rear of main grp, 6th whn blnd 17th, kpt on, nvr nrr* .... Miss P Gundry 4

1521[6] Nottarex *chsd ldrs to 6th, grad lost plc, kpt on frm 3 out* .... B Wright 5

1314 Princess Wenllyan 5a *ld to 3rd, clr 2nd aft, blnd 15th, wknd 17th, p.u. 2 out* .... S Kidston pu

1497 Another Kav (Ire) 5a *in tch, 4th at 10th, lost plc rpdly nxt, p.u. 12th* .... G Penfold pu

1497[4] Suba Lin 5a *chsd ldng pair til p.u. 14th, lame* .. M Frith pu

1373 Cuthaysmayflower 5a *alwys rear, lost tch 11th, p.u. 14th* .... D Alers-Hankey pu

1399 Joy Street 5a *bhnd frm 8th, t.o. & p.u. aft 11th* .... T Greed pu

Fossy Bear 12a *schoold, alwys bhnd, p.u. 11th* .... Miss S Young pu

1492 Derring Katie 12a *sn wll bhnd, almost ref 5th, succeeded nxt* .... A Cooksley ref

1498 Go Willie Go *sn wll bhnd, t.o. & p.u. 7th* Miss L Smale pu

1520 I'm Foxy 5a (bl) *t.d.e. ld 3rd, clr whn blnd 16th, hdd aft 3 out, wknd, p.u. nxt* .... R Widger pu

14 ran. 1½l, 7l, 4l, ½l. Time 6m 51.60s. SP 13-2.
C L Tizzard (Blackmore & Sparkford Vale).
S.P.

TREDEGAR FARMERS
Bassaleg
Saturday May 24th
GOOD

1555 Members

1365[1] **HAL'S PRINCE** .... **Miss P Jones** 1
(fav) ld to 9th, ld 11th, mstk 14th, clr 2 out, rdn out

1227 **Flaxridge** .... **Miss E Tamplin** 2
chsd wnr 4th, ld 9-11th, no imp aft 3 out

1324[2] **Final Option (Ire)** .... **I Johnson** 3
lost tch frm 8th, tk bad 3rd 13th, no dang

1458 Sandy Beau *lost tch 8th, mstks & t.o. final cct* .... M FitzGerald 4

1473 Brynner *5th whn mstk 3rd & p.u.* .... A Price pu

1138 Chantingo Lad *n.j.w., t.o. til ref 7th* .... J Cook ref

6 ran. 8l, dist, 6l. Time 6m 32.00s. SP 4-11.
T L Jones (Tredegar Farmers).

1556 Restricted (12st)

1471[3] **BLACK ERMINE (IRE)** .... **E Williams** 1
(fav) lft in ld 7th, ld/disp aft, ld 2 out, hrd rdn & wknd flat, hldon

1227 **African Warrior 12a** .... **Miss P Jones** 2
rear, lost tch ldrs 12th, ran on 15th, fin strngly, just faild

1160 **Bakmalad** .... **H Wheeler** 3
rear, lost tch ldrs 12th, ran on 15th, ev ch flat, nt qckn fin

1525 Bel Lane 5a (bl) *ld to 3rd, ld/disp 8th-aft 2 out, wknd* .... D S Jones 4

1322[3] Yarron King *p.u. aft 3rd, dsmntd* .... I Johnson pu

1472 Hill Fort (Ire) *rear, f 3rd* .... J Cook f

1318[2] Bay Leader 5a *in tch til wknd 12th, t.o. & p.u. 14th* .... Miss E Tamplin pu

1227 Harry From Barry *ld 3rd til jinked & u.r. apr 7th* .... J Tudor ur

1387[1] Ribington *chsd ldng pair 8th, rdn & btn 12th, t.o. & p.u. 2 out* .... M Hammond pu

1322[5] Lennie The Lion *rear whn u.r. 6th* .... J Price ur

1471[4] Tims Kick (Ire) 5a *lost tch 6th, ran wd bend aft 8th, p.u. nxt* .... T Vaughan pu

1467 Bushton 7a *in tch whn f 4th* .... J P Keen f

1473 Teigr Pren *n.j.w. sn wll bhnd, t.o. & p.u. 11th* .... P Sheldrake pu

13 ran. Hd, nk, 6l. Time 6m 35.00s. SP 11-4.
B Mason (Essex & Suffolk).

1557 Confined (12st)

1471[1] **ALFION (IRE)** .... **D S Jones** 1
prom, jnd ldr 12th, rdn 14th, ld 3 out, all out flat, jst hld on

1318 **Icecapade (Bel)** .... **A Wintle** 2
trckd ldng grp, 3rd frm 11th, ran on 2 out, fin wll, just faild

1469[5] **Beinn Mohr 5a 8ex** .... **E Williams** 3
prom, ld 7th, jnd 12th, rdn 14th, hdd 3 out, no ext flat

1223[4] Cornish Cossack (NZ) *sn dtchd, t.o. frm 11th* W Pugh 4

1366[2] Sweet Kildare 5a *ld to 7th, wknd 11th, sn t.o.* .... Miss P Jones 5

1456 Scared Stiff 5a *sn dtchd, t.o. 11th, p.u. 15th* .. A Price pu

1233[2] Chiaroscuro *(fav) prom til slppd & u.r. aft 9th* S Lloyd ur

1456[3] West King *sn dtchd, t.o. 11th, stppd aft nxt* .... J Price pu

1472 Rusty Music 3ex *sn dtchd, wll bhnd in 7th whn u.r. 10th* .... Miss N Richards ur

9 ran. Hd, 1l, dist, 15l. Time 6m 23.00s. SP 5-1.
D R Thomas (Llangeinor).

1558 Ladies

1470[2] **CELTIC DAUGHTER 5a** .... **Miss E Jones** 1
chsd ldr, ld apr 14th, jnd apr 2 out, ran on strngly last

1540[1] **Touch 'N' Pass 7ex** .... **Miss P Jones** 2
(fav) w.w. chsd ldr 14th, chal apr 2 out, ran wd bef last, no ext

1391[2] **Nanda Moon 3ex** .... **Miss S Jackson** 3
held up last, effrt 11th, outpcd nxt, t.o.

1525[6] Local Customer *clr ldr til wknd & hdd apr 14th, t.o.* .... Miss G Gibson 4

1364[1] Miss Montgomery (Ire) 5a 3ex *n.j.w. cls up to 11th, wknd rpdly, p.u. 15th* .... Miss F Wilson pu

5 ran. 7l, dist, 3l. Time 6m 17.00s. SP 4-1.
Mrs E A Webber (Pembrokeshire).

1559 P P O R A Nov Riders (12st)

1319 **HOW FRIENDLY 5ex** .... **M FitzGerald** 1
(fav) ld to 3rd, trckd ldr 5th, ld 15th, hld on flat

1472[2] **Lucky Ole Son 7ex** .... **Miss N Richards** 2
ld 3-4th, lft in ld nxt-15th, ev ch & blnd 2 out, ran on flat

1556 **Hill Fort (Ire)** .... **I Johnson** 3
2nd outing, n.j.w. bhnd frm 9th, t.o. 12th, r.o. aft last, cont

1472[4] I'm A Bute 5a *ld 4th til ran out nxt* ..... Miss F Wilson ro

4 ran. 1l, dist. Time 6m 40.00s. SP 8-11.
R J Mansell (Ledbury).

1560 Men's Open (12st)

1524[3] **DOUBTING DONNA 5a 7ex** .... **D S Jones** 1
prom, ld 12th, clr 14th, pshd out, unchal

1363[3] **Sterling Buck (USA)** .... **Julian Pritchard** 2
(fav) prom, wth wnr 12th-nxt, sn outpcd, no imp frm 15th

1318[1] **Lighten The Load 4ex** .... **A Wintle** 3
w.w. clsd 12th, rdn nxt, onepcd frm 15th

1536 Ideal *ld to 12th, strggling frm 14th* .... E Williams 4

1470[6] Doctor-J (Ire) 7ex *pllng, trckd ldrs, rdn 13th, sn strggling* .... J Tudor 5

1365 Culpeppers Dish *in tch to 9th, sn wknd, t.o. 12th* .... D Stephens 6

1131[3] Adanac *bhnd frm 4th, t.o. & p.u. 11th* .... A Price pu

7 ran. 12l, 6l, 4l, 10l, 1 fence. Time 6m 24.00s. SP 5-2.
Mrs D Hughes (Llangeinor).

1561 Open Maiden Div I (12st)

1368[2] **IRISH THINKER** .... **J Tudor** 1
(fav) cls up, ld 12th, clr 2 out, pshd out

842 **Kits Pride 12a** .... **Miss L Pearce** 2
jmpd slwly 8th, prog 11th, chsd wnr nxt, unable qckn aft 3 out

1460[4] **Boddington Hill 5a** .... **I Johnson** 3
prom, lost plc 10th, outpcd 12th, kpt on onepcd frm 15th

1459 Ruffinswick *in tch to 11th, wknd rpdly nxt, t.o. aft til p.u. 2 out* .... J Price pu

1324 Red Neck *t.d.e. last & schoold, t.o. & p.u. 12th* A Price pu

1323[6] Red Rhapsody 5a *in tch to 11th, 5th & wkng whn f 13th* ....J Comins f
1136 Wooly Town 5a *t.o. 6th, p.u. nxt* ....Miss A Meakins pu
Fortunes Leap 7a *mstks, ld to 12th, wknd rpdly, p.u. 14th* ....G Lewis pu
1230 Alias Parker Jones *in tch to 11th, wknd rpdly nxt, p.u. 14th* ....D S Jones pu
9 ran. 4l, 6l. Time 6m 33.00s. SP Evens.
W Tudor (Llangeinor).

1562 Open Maiden Div II (12st)

1473 **ALKARINE 7a**....**Julian Pritchard** 1
(fav) trckd ldrs, 2nd 3 out, qcknd to ld apr nxt, drvn out
1009 **Ballyhooly Belle (Ire) 5a (bl)**....**E Williams** 2
mstks & svrl rmndrs, ld to apr 2 out, no ext aft
1361 **Glynn Brae (Ire)** ....**Miss M Headon** 3
mostly 2nd frm 5th, rdn & not qckn 3 out, not run on nxt
1323[4] Queen's Equa 5a *chsd ldrs til lost tch 12th, jmpd slwly aft, t.o.* ....Miss S Major 4
1323 Le Vienna (Ire) *alwys bhnd, svrl slw jmps, t.o. 12th* ....S Currey 5
Leinthall Thistle (Ire) 5a *alwys bhnd, t.o. 12th* N Oliver 6
1471[5] Kerstin's Choice 5a *wth ldr whn blnd 4th, p.u. nxt, dead* ....P Sheldrake pu
1471 Lynnes Daniella (Ire) 5a *mstks, chsd ldrs, wknd 13th, t.o. & p.u. 2 out* ....T Vaughan pu
8 ran. 3l, 15l, 20l, 1l, 2½l. Time 6m 40.00s. SP 7-4.
Gareth Richards (Llangeinor).
J.N.

BERKS & BUCKS DRAGHOUNDS
Kingston Blount
Sunday May 25th
GOOD TO FIRM

1563 Members

1464[1] **PEJAWI 5a** ....**Miss L Whitaker** 1
j.w. made all, ran on wll frm 2 out
1536[1] **Villains Brief (Ire)** ....**Miss L Marsh** 2
(fav) 1st ride, trckd wnr 6th, mstk 15th, not qckn frm 2 out
Polar Region ....**C Vigors** 3
7s-5/2, jmpd slwly, chsd wnr to 6th, outpcd frm 14th
1449[7] John Roger *trckd ldng trio, jmpd slwly 11th, wknd aft 13th* ....L Manners 4
1316[4] Unscrupulous Gent *t.o. frm 6th, btn 3 fences* ....N Lampard 5
5 ran. 5l, 20l, 25l, Bad. Time 6m 20.00s. SP 7-4.
Miss L Whitaker (Berks & Bucks Draghounds).

1564 Confined (12st)

1532[7] **SUNSHINE MANOR** ....**G Tarry** 1
mstk 2nd,ld to 3rd,lft in ld nxt,qcknd aft 2 out,pshd out
1203 **Pete's Sake 3ex** ....**C Vigors** 2
hld up, prog to chs wnr 10th, ev ch 3 out, rdn & no ext nxt
1462[1] **Espy 6ex** ....**E James** 3
(fav) w.w. prog to 3rd frm 10th, rdn & not qckn aft 3 out
1462[3] Bawnerosh *hld up, clsd up 12th, outpcd 14th, mstks & wknd aft* ....T Underwood 4D
1533[7] Abitmorfun (bl) *mstk 2nd, chsd wnr to 10th, wknd rpdly, t.o.* ....C Coyne 5
1448 Obie's Train 11ow (bl) *ld 3rd til ran off course apr nxt* ....Mrs A Lee ro
1156[5] Shared Fortune (Ire) *pllng, in tch to 13th, sn wknd, poor 5th whn p.u. last* ....Daniel Dennis pu
7 ran. 5l, 2½l, 30l, 1 fence. Time 6m 17.00s. SP 7-4.
G B Tarry (Grafton).
Bawnerosh disq, rider not W/I.

1565 Men's Open

1463[2] **ARDBRENNAN** ....**E James** 1
(fav) cls up, ld 10th, abt 4l clr frm 14th, rdn out
1451[3] **Lofty Deed (USA)** ....**A Charles-Jones** 2
w.w. chsd wnr 13th, rdn aft 3 out, unable to chal
1464[3] **Old Road (USA)** ....**M Keen** 3
ld to 10th, last aft nxt, lft bhnd frm 13th
1461[2] Fowling Piece *cls up til lft bhnd aft 13th, no ch aft* ....M Legge 4
4 ran. 6l, 20l, 3l. Time 6m 16.00s. SP 2-9.
C C Bennett (Vine & Craven).

1566 Ladies

1533[2] **RAYMAN (IRE)** ....**Mrs T Hill** 1
(fav) hld up in tch, qcknd on innr to ld 3 out, sn clr, comf
1308[2] **Coombesbury Lane 5a**....**Miss C Spearing** 2
svrl slw jmps, prom, chal 14th, ev ch & mstk 3 out, sn btn
1450 **Hiram B Birdbath (bl)** ....**Mrs C McCarthy** 3
made most to 3 out, sn outpcd
1535 Walkonthemoon 5a *in tch to 13th, no imp nxt, wknd rpdly apr last* ....Miss N McKim 4
1531[3] Icky's Five *1st ride, mstk 8th, sn bhnd, t.o. 13th* ....Miss J Bachelor 5
5 ran. 15l, 1½l, 30l, 12l. Time 6m 17.00s. SP 1-2.
M P Avery (Bicester With Whaddon Chase).

1567 Restricted (12st)

1461[1] **BART'S CASTLE** ....**Daniel Dennis** 1
jmpd rght,made all,sn clr,dist up hlfwy,tired 2 out,unchal
1453[1] **Bet A Lot 5a**....**Miss T Honeyball** 2
(fav) chsng grp, went 2nd apr 2 out, ran on, no ch wnr
1449 **Muskerry Miss (Ire) 5a**....**A Charles-Jones** 3+
prom in chsng grp, 2nd brfly 14th, sn no prog & dmtd
1533[4] **Buladante (Ire)** ....**T Underwood** 3+
hld up, in chsng grp whn mstk 15th, no dang, kpt on flat
1449[5] Duke Of Lancaster (Ire) *chsng grp, no prog 15th, wknd 3 out* ....R Wakley 5
1445[4] Lewesdon Princess 5a *chsng grp, wknd 3 out* ....Miss S Gladders 6
1285 Loyal Gait (NZ) *mostly chsd wnr til aft 3 out, 3rd & wll btn whn f nxt* ....P Atkins f
1430 Aughnacloy Rose *blnd 7th & drppd last, t.o. 13th, p.u. 2 out* ....R Page pu
8 ran. 25l, 15l, dd-ht, 3l, 5l. Time 6m 12.00s. SP 5-1.
Miss A M Reed (Isle Of Wight).

1568 Open Maiden (12st)

1465[2] **JOBINGO** ....**Daniel Dennis** 1
jmpd rght,hld up,prog to ld 10th,lft clr 13th,unchal aft
1435 **Tell Tale (Ire) 7a** ....**T Bulgin** 2
mid-div, prog 13th, chsd wnr 15th, no imp til ran on flat
1452[2] **Marmalade** ....**J Owen** 3
in tch, lft 2nd 13th, no imp on wnr, dmtd & onepcd frm 15th
1353 Top Odder (Ire) 7a *mstk 2nd,rear,some prog to poor 4th & slw jmp 15th,fin tired* ....B Pollock 4
374[5] Fuannae (Ire) *prom til blnd 7th & 8th, sn rear, no ch 13th, t.o.* ....F Brennan 5
987[4] Trina's Cottage (Ire) *made msot frm aft 2nd-10th, sn wknd, t.o.* ....B McKim 6
1459[5] Country Lord *ld to aft 2nd, wknd 9th, t.o. 13th* ....Mrs S Walwin 7
1446 Spanish Pal (Ire) *alwys last trio, t.o. 13th* ....Miss S Gladders 8
1486[2] Springvilla (Ire) *(fav) not fluent, prom, 3l 2nd whn blnd & u.r. 13th* ....C Vigors ur
1446 Tidal Reef (Ire) 7a *prog & prom 9th, wknd 13th, t.o. & p.u. 15th* ....P York pu
1452 Boozing Gunner *schoold in last trio, p.u. 11th* ....A Charles-Jones pu
11 ran. 15l, 8l, 25l, 15l, 3l, 10l, 6l. Time 6m 27.00s. SP 20-1.
Mrs C Poland (Isle Of Wight).

J.N.

FONTWELL
Monday May 26th
GOOD TO FIRM

1569 3¼m 110yds Fontwell Park Hunters' Chase Class H

1495[3] **MIGHTY FALCON 11.0 7a............Miss E Tory** 1
ld 3rd till mstk and hdd 10th, lost pl 13th, rear 15th, plenty to do 4 out, gd hdwy to ld last, soon clr.
1054 **Heathview 11.7 7a ....Mr M Portman** 2
hdwy 9th, ld 12th to 15th, mstk next, led apr 3 out to last, soon outpcd.
1201[4] **Fordstown (Ire) 11.7 7a .....Mr Jamie Alexander** 3
ld to 3rd, mstk and outpcd 16th, styd on from 2 out.
1491[2] Trifast Lad 12.4 3a *(fav) settld towards rear, shaken up and hdwy 14th, effort and chal apr last, wknd run-in*...Mr P Hacking 4
1529[4] Tammy's Friend 11.0 7a (bl) *keen hold, prom, ld 10th to 12th, wknd apr last*. ....Mr A Wintle 5
1504[4] American Eyre 11.0 7a *alwys rear, lost tch 15th, p.u. before 4 out*. ....Miss S Gladders pu
1506[3] No Inhibitions 11.7 7a *chsd ldrs till wknd quickly 4 out, bhnd when p.u. before last*. ....Mr A Warr pu
1525[3] Howaryadoon 11.0 7a *blnd 3rd, rear after, bhnd when p.u. before 3 out*..................Miss T Cave pu
592[1] Colonial Kelly 12.2 5a *hdwy to ld 15th, hdd apr 3 out, wknd 2 out, bhnd when p.u. lame run-in*. ..Mr C Vigors pu
1502 Mr Oriental 11.0 7a *mid div, jmpd slowly 2nd, rear when bridle slpd and u.r. after next.* Mr G Gigantesco ur

10 ran. 13l, 3l, nk, 2½l. Time 6m 44.30s. SP 9-2.
Miss Emma Tory

HEREFORD
Monday May 26th
GOOD

1570 3m 1f 110yds Clive Maiden Hunters' Chase Class H

1501[2] **NO JOKER (IRE) 11.10 7a............Mr P Scott** 1
(fav) bhnd, hdwy 4 out, ld last, styd on well.
1480[1] **Anjubi 11.10 7a...................Mr S Mulcaire** 2
chsd ldrs, ld 9th to 11th, led 6 out to 4 out, led apr last, soon hdd and no ext.
1416 **Ann's Ambition 11.10 7a ....Mr M Frith** 3
alwys prom, ld 4 out, hdd and no ext apr last.
1500[2] The Rum Mariner 11.10 7a *ld 3rd to 9th, led 11th to 6 out, wknd 4 out*. ....Mr D S Jones 4
1503[3] Teatrader 11.10 7a *ld to 3rd, wknd 4 out.* Mr S Durack 5
1474[4] Majestic Ride 11.10 7a *prom to 9th, bhnd when p.u. before 3 out*. ....Mr R Armson pu
1358[6] Indian Knight 11.10 7a *in rear when blnd and u.r. 6 out*. ....Mr E James ur
1485[2] Link Copper 12.0 3a *hit 1st, bhnd from 5th, p.u. before 6 out*. ....Mr R Treloggen pu
1458 Corn Exchange 12.0 3a *prom till wknd 5 out, blnd badly 3 out, p.u. before next*. ....Mr M Rimell pu
1190[1] Andalucian Sun (Ire) 11.10 7a *soon well bhnd, saddle slpd, tried to refuse and u.r. 5th*. .....Mr P G Moloney ur
1443[2] Prime Course (Ire) 11.10 7a *mstk 3rd, bhnd from 9th, p.u. before 6 out*..........................Mr P Bull pu
1449[4] Salmon Poutcher 11.7 5a *bhnd from 7th, p.u. after 10th*.................................Mr J Trice-Rolph pu
1528[4] Watchit Lad 11.12 7a 2ow *in rear when hit 8th, t.o. and p.u. before 2 out*..................Mr M P Jones pu
1290[6] Lurriga Glitter (Ire) 11.12 5a (bl) *soon well bhnd, p.u. before 4 out*...................................Mr R Ford pu

14 ran. 3l, 4l, 22l, 26l. Time 6m 27.30s. SP 7-2.
Brigadier R W S Hall

WETHERBY
Monday May 26th
GOOD TO FIRM

1571 2½m 110yds Guy Cunard Hunters' Chase Class H

1491[8] **MY NOMINEE 12.0 7a (bl)...........Mr R Burton** 1
prom, ld after 7th, hit 3 out, rdn next and styd on gamely.
1512 **Shuil Saor 11.2 7a ....Mr C Mulhall** 2
held up, steady hdwy 11th, prom next, rdn 2 out, kept on.
1508[5] **Simply Perfect 11.7 7a.........Miss K Swindells** 3
alwys chasing ldrs, effort and ev ch 4 out, rdn next, one pace and hit last.
1488[1] Not My Line (Ire) 12.2 5a *ld to 3rd, cl up, effort and ev ch 4 out, driven next, held when blnd last.* ....Mr W Wales 4
1419[3] Caman 11.2 7a *in tch till outpcd 5 out, styd on from 2 out, nearest fin*. ....Mrs S Grant 5
1476[1] Indie Rock 11.2 7a *mid div, hdwy 4 out, soon rdn and no impn from next*. ....Mrs F Needham 6
1202[1] Great Gusto 11.11 7a *(fav) trckd ldrs, hdwy 8th, cl up when blnd 10th, rdn along apr 4 out, wknd before next*. ....Miss L Blackford 7
1544 Alpha One 11.7 7a *alwys bhnd*.......Miss K Di Marte 8
1421 Goodheavens Mrtony 11.2 7a *reminders in rear hfwy, soon well bhnd*. ....Miss A Deniel 9
1489 Syrus P Turntable 11.2 7a *bhnd from hfwy.* ....Mr J Saville 10
1405[6] Eastern Pleasure 11.2 7a *prom, rdn along 4 out, weakening when f 2 out*. ....Mr T J Barry f
1529[2] Sandybraes 11.7 7a *bhnd and rdn along 6th, p.u. before next*. ....Mr F Hutsby pu
1488 No Word 11.7 7a *cl up, ld 3rd to after 7th, wknd 10th, bhnd when p.u. lame before 2 out*. ....Mr I Baker pu
1106[2] Japodene 10.11 7a *alwys rear, well bhnd when p.u. before 4 out*. ....Mr M Haigh pu
1420[1] Gaelic Warrior 11.9 *mid-divisoon, hdwy to chase ldrs 10th, rdn after next and weakening when p.u. after 4 out*. ....Mr S Swiers pu

15 ran. 1¼l, 2l, 1l, 1l, 11l, 1¼l, 7l, 13l, 10l. Time 5m 4.30s. SP 4-1.
D E Nicholls

ALBRIGHTON WOODLAND
Chaddesley Corbett
Monday May 26th
FIRM

1572 Members

1460[3] **MUSICAL MAIL ....M FitzGerald** 1
(fav) trckd ldr, ld 13th, clr 15th, pshd out
1329[1] **Tytherington 4ex ....Miss S Talbot** 2
ld to 13th, not qckn aft nxt, kpt on
1200 **Wissywis (Ire) 12a.......................C Yates** 3
alwys last, lost tch 12th, t.o.

3 ran. 8l, dist. Time 6m 30.00s. SP 2-5.
J R Sutcliffe (Albrighton Woodland).

1573 Ladies

1535[1] **GRIMLEY GALE (IRE) 5a.........Miss S Vickery** 1
(fav) prom, ld 6th, made rest, ran on well frm 3 out
355 **Fly For Us 5a ....Mrs C Ford** 2
w.w. prog 10th, prssd wnr aft nxt, rdn & no ext 2 out
1525[2] **Bowland Girl (Ire) 5a ....Miss E James** 3
svrl mstks, in tch til 3rd & outpcd frm 12th, no imp aft
1476[3] Supreme Dream (Ire) 5a *in tch til 4th & outpcd 12th, no imp ldrs aft* ....Mrs P Adams 4
1321 Gold Diver *prom, ld whn blnd & u.r. 4th* ....Miss P Gundry ur
1456[4] Browned Off *n.j.w. made most to 6th, wknd 11th, t.o. & p.u. aft 3 out* ....Miss H Bevan pu

6 ran. 3l, 15l, 3l. Time 5m 59.00s. SP 1-4.
R M Phillips (Worcestershire).

1574 Confined (12st)

1237 **GASMARK (IRE) ....A Phillips** 1

12s-13/2,trckd ldr 3rd,ld & qcknd 14th,rdn 3 out,ran on wll

1536[3] **Gromit (NZ) ....Julian Pritchard 2**
(Jt fav) trckd ldrs,effrt 12th,chsd wnr 15th,rdn 3 out,ran on onepcd
906[2] **French Stick ....E Williams 3**
ld to 14th, outpcd frm nxt
1532 July Schoon 3ex *hld up, outpcd aft 11th, no ch aft* ....T Underwood 4
1511[7] Running Frau 5a *raced wd, in tch to 10th, wknd aft nxt, t.o. 15th* ....G Thomas 5
1524 Wildnite *prom til wknd 12th, 4th & wll btn whn p.u. last, dsmntd* ....Miss E Walker pu
1403[6] Hook Line'N'sinker *rear, mstk 10th & rdn, sn wnd, p.u. 13th* ....S Joynes pu
1329 Mr Wilbur 3ex *(Jt fav) not fluent,hld up,outpcd aft 11th,no ch aft,mstk 2 out &p.u.* ....A Dalton pu
8 ran. 2l, 25l, 15l, 10l. Time 6m 3.00s. SP 13-2.
D Pugh (North Shropshire).

1575 Men's Open (12st)

1149[1] **GLITTERBIRD 5a..........................A Dalton 1**
not fluent,prom,lft 2nd aft 6th,ld 11th,pshd clr apr last
1455[5] **Bumptious Boy ....S Hanks 2**
chsd ldrs, went 2nd aft 15th, cls engh 2 out, sn btn
1524[4] **Garrylucas 4ex ....G Hanmer 3**
chsd ldrs,mstk 9th,effrt 12th,2nd 14th-nxt,wknd,crwld last
Cosmic Force (NZ) *chsd ldrs, effrt 12th, wknd frm 15th* ....M Harris 4
1512[4] Irish Gent 7ex *alwys bhnd, t.o. 12th, nvr nrr* H Hankey 5
1523 Stanford Boy 1ow *alwys bhnd, t.o. 12th, p.u. 14th* ....N Andrew pu
1234 Sharinski 4ex *mstk 3rd, alwys bhnd, rdn & no rspns 10th, t.o. & p.u. 12th* ....M Munrowd pu
1524[1] Nether Gobions 7ex *(fav) prom,ld & slppd up bend aft 6th,rmntd,cont til p.u. 15th* ....Julian Pritchard pu
1541[5] Only In Ireland *made most to 11th, wknd 14th, poor 4th whn f 2 out* ....R Inglesant f
1433 Kabancy *alwys bhnd, t.o. & p.u. 12th, dsmntd* ....G Barfoot-Saunt pu
10 ran. 6l, 20l, 1½l, 12l. Time 6m 1.00s. SP 3-1.
Mrs Caroline Chadney (Croome & West Warwickshire).

1576 PPORA

1523[2] **HAVEN LIGHT ....A Dalton 1**
hld up,prog 7th,ld 12-14th & 15th-nxt,ld apr last,drvn out
1455[3] **Landsker Alfred ....Miss A Dare 2**
(fav) prom,slw jmp 4th,ld 9-12th,ld 3 out-last,rallied flat
1404 **Fighting Mariner (bl) ....John Pritchard 3**
made most to 9th, wknd 12th, lft poor 3rd apr last
1464[4] Proplus *prom til wknd 8th, t.o. frm 12th* ....Mrs A Lee 4
1538 Penllyne's Pride (v) *s.s. sn prom, wknd 10th, t.o. 12th* ....T O'Leary 5
Crawn Hawk *alwys rear, wll bhnd frm 7th, t.o. & p.u. 13th* ....K Needham pu
1472 Sisterly 5a *prom, ld 14th-nxt, wknd 3 out, 3rd & no ch whn p.u. last* ....Miss S Vickery pu
1388[2] Hackett's Farm *trckd ldrs til 5th & lost tch 11th, p.u. nxt* ....Julian Pritchard pu
1366 Dick's Cabin *s.s. alwys bhnd, t.o. last whn p.u. 11th* ....E Williams pu
1532[5] Springfield Lad *alwys bhnd, t.o. & p.u. 12th* ....Miss E Walker pu
1474[2] Midnight Service (Ire) (bl) *mstk 5th, alwys rear, t.o. & p.u. 12th* ....W Tellwright pu
1536[4] Bocock's Pride (Ire) *pllng, ran out aft 3rd, dsmntd* ....M Harris ro
12 ran. 1½l, dist, 25l, hd. Time 5m 59.00s. SP 8-1.
Mrs J P Spencer (Clifton On Teme).

1577 Open Maiden Div I (12st)

1528[7] **PRIDEWOOD GOLDING ....T Cox 1**
hld up, rpd prog to ld 12th, clr aft 15th, mstk 2 out, tired
1187[2] **Paddy's Pocket ....T Lane 2**
ld to 12th, chsd wnr aft, wknd 3 out, fin tired
1486[4] **Kala Dawn 5a..........................Miss M Tory 3**
in tch til lost plc 9th, went poor 3rd aft 13th, plodded on
1460 Parapluie 5a *last & sn dtchd, t.o. 12th* ...Miss B Lloyd 4
1528 Sonny's Song *alwys rear, t.o. frm 12th*......M Rodda 5
Inteabadun 7a *jmpd slwly, in tch til wknd 11th, t.o. & p.u. 13th* ....S Price pu
934 Chalvey Grove *rear, 9th whn u.r. 10th* Miss S Duckett ur
1528 Seven Cruise *chsd ldrs til wknd aft 11th, t.o. & p.u. 3 out* ....R Jones pu
1528[5] Astromis (Ire) 5a *(fav) w.w. prog to 3rd at 9th, strgglng 11th, wknd & p.u. 13th* ....Julian Pritchard pu
1216 The Coventry Flyer 5a *jmpd badly, alwys rear, t.o. whn f 13th* ....M Keel f
1380[2] Fighting For Good (Ire) (bl) *chsd ldr to aft 11th, cls 3rd whn f 12th* ....A Charles-Jones f
11 ran. 15l, nk, 1 fence, 4l. Time 6m 16.00s. SP 8-1.
E A Thomas (North Hereford).

1578 Open Maiden Div II (12st)

1527[2] **NICK THE BISCUIT ....Julian Pritchard 1**
(fav) ld to 2nd, chsd ldr, ld 13th, wll clr 3 out, comf
1527 **Rejects Reply ....G Hanmer 2**
pllng,in tch,3rd & mstk 14th,sn outpcd,went 2nd 2 out,no imp
1459 **Cal's Boy ....M FitzGerald 3**
ld 2nd-13th, chsd wnr aft, btn aft 15th, wknd 2 out
Take Achance On Me 7a *slw jmps 1st & 2nd, in tch til wnd 12th, t.o.* ....M Munrowd 4
1460 Bessie's Will 5a *pllng,slw jmp 4th,in tch,wknd & nrly ref 12th,p.u. & dsmntd* ....G Barfoot-Saunt pu
1454[3] Derring Tirley *in tch wil wknd & mstk 11th, slw jmp nxt & p.u.* ....S Joynes pu
1527 Young Spring 12a *jmpd slwy 2nd, nrly ref 3rd & u.r. aft* ....A Jordan ur
7 ran. 12l, 7l, 1 fence. Time 6m 23.00s. SP 4-7.
S W Rudge (Clifton-On-Teme).
J.N.

SOUTH TETCOTT
Lifton
Monday May 26th
GOOD

1579 Confined (12st)

790[2] **THE KIMBLER 3ex..................Miss S Young 1**
alwys prom, ld 2 out, ran on well
1484[3] **Just My Bill 3ex ....C Heard 2**
(Jt fav) s.s. mid-div hlfwy, prog 15th, chal 2 out, kpt on wll flat
1416[6] **Myhamet 9ex..........................K Heard 3**
(Jt fav) ld 13th-2 out, outpcd aft
1483[4] Holly Fare *nvr bttr than mid-div, styd on onepcd flat* ....C Crosthwaite 4
1480[3] Druid Blue *ld 6th-13th, no ext frm nxt* Miss S Gaisford 5
1518[5] Tranquil Waters (USA) *bhnd frm 7th, nvr dang* ....David Dennis 6
1394[1] Achiltibuie *alwys rear, p.u. 15th* ....G Penfold pu
530[3] Glenform (bl) *nvr trbld ldrs, p.u. 13th*..........T Cole pu
1397[2] Bert House 3ex *ld to 5th, lost tch rpdly, p.u. nxt* ....S Kidston pu
9 ran. 3l, 4l, 2l, 20l, 3l. Time 6m 9.00s. SP 7-2.
B R J Young (East Cornwall).

1580 Men's Open

1549[1] **BUTLER JOHN (IRE) ....N Harris 1**
(fav) ld 2nd, ld agn 4th, drew rght away, unextndd
1481[3] **It's Not My Fault (Ire) ....L Jefford 2**
chsng grp frm hlfwy, nvr able to chal wnr
1550[4] **Oneovertheight ....S Kidston 3**
rear, some late prog, nrst fin
1517[4] The General's Drum *alwys bhnd, past btn horses nr fin* ....K Heard 4
1516[2] Southerly Buster *nvr nr ldrs, rdn 13th, no prog* ....S White 5

1358 Try It Alone *nvr on terms, p.u. aft 15th, lame* . .S Slade pu
1484 Bargain And Sale *prom, grad wknd hlfwy, p.u. 4 out* ....T Greed pu
1341[3] Baldhu Chance *ld 1st, sn hdd, chsng grp aft, fdd & p.u. 4 out* ....J Young pu
8 ran. Dist, 3l, 8l, 3l. Time 5m 54.00s. SP 1-3.
Nick Viney (Exmoor).

1581 Ladies

1548 **PARDITINO ....Miss V Nicholas** 1
mid-div, prog 3 out, chal nxt, ld last, ran on und pres
1396[5] **Parson's Way ....Miss P Curling** 2
made most til hdd last, no ext flat
1342[3] **Catch The Cross ....Mrs M Hand** 3
nvr nrr than 3rd, unable to chal
1494[5] Grey Guestino *nvr trbld ldrs, onepcd* . . . .Miss L Delve 4
1396[2] Khattaf *(fav) rear, prog 10th, wknd 13th, p.u. nxt, lame*....................Miss J Cumings pu
1438[2] Stalbridge Gold 5a *rear, rdn 11th, no prog, p.u. last* ....Miss A Goschen pu
1519[6] Medias Maid 5a *prssd ldr til wknd 12th, p.u. 2 out* ....Miss L Pope pu
7 ran. 1l, 10l, 3l. Time 5m 55.00s. SP 7-2.
Mrs K R J Nicholas (Tiverton Foxhounds).

1582 Intermediate (12st)

1342 **KARICLEIGH BOY ....A Holdsworth** 1
ld 2nd-4th, ld 7th, made rest, just hld on
533[2] **Cornish Ways ....Miss S Young** 2
mid-div, prog 10th, effrt & ev ch flat, just faild
1481[4] **Mine's A Gin (Ire) ....Miss J Cumings** 3
prom til lost ground 9th, rallied 4 out, unable to chal
1496[3] Royal Turn *(fav) rear, prog 4 out, chal 2 out, sn btn* ....A Honeyball 4
1520[1] Pilgrim's Mission (Ire) *mstks 1st 4 fncs, mid-div aft,effrt 4 out,no ext frm 2 out*....................R Darke 5
1547[3] Morchard Milly 5a *cls up til wknd 4 out, kpt on one-pcd frm 2 out*....................S Kidston 6
1366[3] Pay-U-Cash *lost tch 6 out, t.o. & p.u. 2 out* . .G Perkins pu
1153 Sunley Street 5a *blnd 1st, alwys bhnd aft, p.u. 2 out* ....N Mitchell pu
1552 Carnival Kid *ld 5th, ran out bend & u.r. apr nxt* ....J Boscherini ur
1466[3] Carnelia 5a *ld 1st, ld 6th, wknd frm 10th, p.u. 2 out* ....Miss A Goschen pu
10 ran. Sht-hd, 2l, 1l, 3l, 10l. Time 6m 4.00s. SP 10-1.
Philip Rogers (Silverton).

1583 Open Maiden Div I (12st)

1108 **BEAFORD GAME 5a ....Miss K Baily** 1
20s-4s, ld 1st, ld agn 4 out, ran on well
1485 **Aritam (Ire) ....K Heard** 2
(fav) rear, prog 6th, chal 2 out, just outpcd flat
1498[2] **Dad's Delight 5a....................Miss A Goschen** 3
alwys prom, wknd 4 out
1521 Friendly Viking *nvr nrr, fin own time* . . . . .I Hambly 4
St Julien (Ire) *nvr trbld ldrs, t.o. 6th, p.u. 12th* ....N Mitchell pu
Myitsu *ld 2nd to 4 out, 2nd & lkd btn whn u.r. nxt* ....Miss P Jones ur
531 Cornish Twoways (Ire) 12a *alwys wll bhnd, p.u. 12th* ....Miss S Young pu
1480 Bonny Barosy 5a *alwys bhnd, p.u. 10th* . . . . . .R Darke pu
1394 Fair And Square 12a *mostly rear, p.u. aft 12th* ....L Jefford pu
1520 Morchard Gem 12a *nvr going wll, bhnd whn p.u. 12th* ....A Holdsworth pu
1554 Go Willie Go *mid-div, f 9th* ....J Young f
11 ran. 1l, 25l, 12l. Time 6m 5.00s. SP 4-1.
L W Wickett (Torrington Farmers).

1584 Open Maiden Div II (12st)

1521 **FINGAL ....S Kidston** 1
ld/disp 5th-2 out, lkd btn aft, rallied to ld und pres flat
1521 **County Bash 5a ....C Heard** 2
mid-div, rpd prog frm 4 out, just faild
1485[5] **Dusty Furlong ....Miss K Baily** 3
ld/disp 5th til drew clr 2 out, hdd last, sn wknd
1485 The Ugly Duckling *alwys prom, found nil frm 2 out* ....S Slade 4
1521[4] Sixth In Line (Ire) *rear, steady prog frm 13th, onepcd frm 3 out*....................T Cole 5
1486 Happy Valley 5a *nvr nr ldrs to chal* . . . . .Miss P Baker 6
1521 Leejay Luki *nvr bttr than mid-div, no dang 3 out* ....A Honeyball 7
1485 An Buchaill Liath (Ire) *nvr trbld ldrs, t.o. & p.u. 2 out* ....K Heard pu
1527[4] Itsthejonesboy *(Jt fav) ld 1st til almost ran out aft 5th, no dang aft, p.u. 4 out* ....Miss P Jones pu
1260 Brook A Light *(Jt fav) mid-div, p.u. rpdly 4 out* ....N Harris pu
808 Rose's Lady Day 5a *nvr nr ldrs, p.u. 10th*. . .G Penfold pu
Gambling Man *alwys bhnd, p.u. aft 13th* . . . . .W Smith pu
1554 Fossy Bear 12a *alwys bhnd, p.u. aft 9th* Miss S Young pu
13 ran. 1l, 1l, 3l, 10l, 20l, 3l. Time 6m 13.00s. SP 25-1.
Mrs L J Skitt (South Devon).

1585 Members

1486 **CROWNHILL CROSS ....S Kidston** 1
(fav) lft solo 3rd
741 Round Of Drinks *20l bhnd whn u.r. 3rd*. . .Miss K Baily ur
2 ran. Time 6m 47.00s. SP 2-5.
F R Bown (South Tetcott).
P.Ho.

CARTMEL
Wednesday May 28th
GOOD TO FIRM

1586 3¼m Jennings Cumberland Ale Hunters' Chase Class H for the Horace D. Pain Memorial Trophy

1302[1] **HORNBLOWER 11.7 7a (v) ....Mrs C Ford** 1
(fav) ld till after 6th, remained cl up, regained ld 4 out (water), drew clr from last, pushed out.
1569[3] **Fordstown (Ire) 11.11 7a . . . .Mr Jamie Alexander** 2
prom, ld after 6th, hdd 4 out (water), one pace.
1511[4] **Across The Card 11.11 7a . . . . . .Mr M Bradburne** 3
held up and bhnd, late hdwy, nvr nrr.
1359[4] Southern Minstrel 12.0 7a *bhnd, some hdwy final cct, n.d.*....................Miss C Metcalfe 4
1489[3] Lupy Minstrel 12.2 5a *held up, mstk 10th, effort 13th, nvr troubld ldrs.* ....Miss P Robson 5
1382[5] Priory Piper 11.7 7a *steadied start, bhnd, mstk 3rd, nvr on terms.* ....Mr G Hanmer 6
1499[4] Will Travel (Ire) 11.7 7a *cl up till gradually wknd from 14th.*....................Mr A Robson 7
1571[8] Alpha One 12.0 7a *in tch, mstk 2nd, lost pl 7th, struggling and bhnd when blnd badly 13th, not rcvr, p.u. after next, dismntd.*....................Miss K Di Marte pu
1513 Rallying Cry (Ire) 11.7 7a (bl) *bhnd, mstk 2nd and 4th, lost tch 6th, p.u. after 8th, dismntd.* . . .Mr D R McLeod pu
1509 Drumcairn (Ire) 11.7 7a (bl) *n.j.w., in tch, prom 7th, driven along and wknd 12th, blnd next, p.u. before 14th.* ....Mr M J Ruddy pu
10 ran. 6l, 3½l, 12l, 7l, 3½l, hd. Time 6m 35.80s. SP 11-8.
N J Barrowclough

UTTOXETER
Thursday May 29th
GOOD TO FIRM

1587 2m 5f Britannia Brighter Savers Novices' Hunters' Chase Class H for the Feilden Challenge Cup

1518[1] **KING TORUS (IRE) 12.1 5a ....Mr J Jukes** 1
(fav) chsd ldrs, ld apr 4 out, comf.
1545 **True Fortune 11.7 7a ....Mr D S Jones** 2
alwys prom, chsd wnr 4 out, styd on.
1505[1] **Muskerry Moya (Ire) 11.8 7a . . . .Miss A Goschen** 3
ld to apr 4 out, wknd next, fin lame.

1530[3] Tellaporky 11.8 7a 1ow *well bhnd til styd on from 2 out, nvr nrr.* ....Mr A Middleton 4
1526[4] Everso Irish 11.7 7a *alwys bhnd.* ....Mr J Barnes 5
1500[3] Very Daring 11.7 7a *alwys bhnd.* ....Miss S Sharratt 6
1012[1] Beyond The Stars 11.11 3a *prom till f 7th.* ....Mr M Rimell f
1543 Thornhill 11.2 7a *t.o. from 5th, p.u. before 6 out.* ....Mr R Widger pu
1530 Dark Rhytham 11.7 7a *ld to 2nd, remained handy til mstk and wknd 6 out, p.u. before 2 out.* ....Mr T Lane pu
437[4] Christmas Thyne (Ire) 11.0 7a *mid div, rdn 8th, soon bhnd, t.o. and p.u. before 4 out.* ....Mr A Phillips pu
Dragons Bay (Ire) 12.0 *started slowly, held up and bhnd, steady hdwy 5 out, 5th when p.u. before 3 out.* ....Mr S Swiers pu
11 ran. 1½l, 28l, 11l, 14l, 25l. Time 5m 14.40s. SP 10-11.
Nick Viney

STRATFORD
Friday May 30th
GOOD

1588 3½m Horse And Hound Champion Novices' Hunters' Chase Class H for the John Corbet Cup

1490[1] **EARTHMOVER (IRE) 11.7 7a ......Miss P Gundry** 1
(fav) held up in mid-field, hit 13th, steady prog from 16th, ld after 3 out, soon clr, ran on well.
1286[1] **Struggles Glory (Ire) 11.13 7a 6ow ..Mr D C Robinson** 2
ld till after 3 out, styd on run-in.
1469[1] **Shuil's Star (Ire) 11.7 7a.............Mr P Hamer** 3
held up and bhnd, hit 6th, gd hdwy 16th, cl 3rd when hmpd 4 out, one pace from next.
1417[1] Prince Buck (Ire) 11.11 3a *in tch, chsd ldr from 8th to 16th, wknd from 3 out, tiring when mstk next.* ....Mr P Hacking 4
1414[1] Greenmount Lad (Ire) 11.7 7a *held up, mstks 7th and next, soon bhnd, t.o.* ....Mr P Cornforth 5
1544[3] Tom's Gemini Star 11.7 7a *blnd 2nd, alwys bhnd, t.o. when f 4 out.* ....Miss V Roberts f
1544[5] Phar Too Touchy 11.2 7a *prom, mstk 2nd, hit 13th, soon bhnd, p.u. before 16th.* ....Mr N Harris pu
1416[4] Mister Horatio 11.7 7a *prom, chsd ldr from 16th, challenging when blnd and u.r. 4 out.* ....Mr M Lewis ur
1360[4] Taura's Rascal 11.7 7a *mid div, hit 10th, blnd badly 15th, bhnd when p.u. before 17th.* ....Mr F Brennan pu
9 ran. 4l, 9l, 12l, dist. Time 7m 1.60s. SP 7-4.
R M Penny

MARKET RASEN
Saturday May 31st
GOOD TO FIRM

1589 2¾m 110yds Geostar Hunters' Chase Class H

1546[2] **CUMBERLAND BLUES (IRE) 11.11 7a.....Miss A Deniel** 1
(fav) ld till hdd 4 out, rallied to ld run in, gamely.
1571[6] **Indie Rock 11.3 7a.............Mrs F Needham** 2
chsd ldrs, ld 4 out, hit last, soon hdd, kept on well.
1359[2] **Kambalda Rambler 12.3 7a ....Mr R Armson** 3
nvr far away, ev ch 4 out, outpcd after next.
1571[2] Shuil Saor 11.3 7a *held up, steady hdwy 9th, rdn 4 out, blnd next, soon btn.* ....Mr C Mulhall 4
1419 Earl Gray 11.3 7a (bl) *soon bhnd, nvr on terms.* ....Miss J Eastwood 5
1586 Alpha One 12.0 7a *in tch, dropped rear and struggling 8th, n.d. after* ....Miss K Di Marte 6
1479 Needwood Joker 11.3 7a *alwys well bhnd.* ....Mr K Green 7
1353[2] Auntie Chris 10.12 7a *whipped round and u.r. start.* ....Mr P Gee ur
1500 Ship The Builder 11.3 7a *jmpd badly in rear, soon struggling, t.o. when p.u. before 2 out.* ....Mr S Brisby pu
1489 Secret Truth 10.12 7a *chsd wnr, weakening when hit 10th, t.o. when p.u. before 3 out.* ....Mr Andrew Martin pu
10 ran. ½l, 10l, 5l, 16l, dist, 1¼l. Time 5m 39.50s. SP 11-8.
John L Holdroyd

STRATFORD
Saturday May 31st
GOOD

1590 3m Spillers Horse Feeds Ladies' Hunters' Chase Class H

1546 **THANK U JIM 10.7 7a ....Miss T Jackson** 1
ld to 3rd, styd upsides till regained ld after 6 out, set str pace after, stayed on well from 2 out.
1495[1] **Final Pride 10.9 3a ....Miss P Jones** 2
(fav) with ldr, ld 3rd till hdd after 6 out, pressed wnr after, kept on same pace from 2 out.
1320[4] **Wake Up Luv 10.7 7a.............Miss P Cooper** 3
struggling to go pace and well bhnd hfwy, str run from 3 out, fin well.
1490 Mister Gebo 10.7 7a *struggling and driven along after one cct, relentless prog to chase lding pair final circuit, kept on one pace from 3 out.* ....Miss C Dyson 4
1438[1] Old Mill Stream 10.7 7a *driven along with chasing gp, effort hfwy, struggling final cct, nvr a threat.* ....Miss P Gundry 5
1414[2] What Chance (Ire) 10.5 7a *struggling and driven along before hfwy, t.o. final cct.* ....Mrs K Sunderland 6
1491 No Panic 10.7 7a *t.o. before hfwy, virtually p.u. after last.* ....Miss A Meakins 7
1490[2] Sams Heritage 10.9 5a *chsd clr lding pair till p.u. lame before 12th.* ....Miss A Dare pu
1488 Hickelton Lad 10.10 7a *struggling and well bhnd before hfwy, t.o. when p.u. before 2 out.* ....Miss S Duckett pu
9 ran. 3½l, 4l, ½l, 20l, 24l, dist. Time 5m 52.20s. SP 16-1.
Mrs G Sunter

1591 3½m 38th Year Of The Horse And Hound Cup Final Champion Hunters' Chase Class B

1291[1] **CELTIC ABBEY 12.0 ....Mr D S Jones** 1
(fav) with ldr, ld 10th, qcknd to go clr final cct, styd on strly from 3 out, eased towards fin.
1295[1] **Bitofamixup (Ire) 12.0 ....Mr P Hacking** 2
patiently rdn, relentess prog final cct, ch and driven along apr 3 out, no ext from next.
890 **Mr Boston 12.0.....................Mr N Wilson** 3
waited with, tk clr order hfwy, driven along when pace qcknd final cct, no impn from 4 out.
1504[1] Glen Oak 12.0 *chsd ldrs, feeling pace and driven along final cct, no impn on lders from 4 out.* ....Mr J M Pritchard 4
494[2] Cab On Target 12.0 *patiently rdn, tk clr order hfwy, feeling pace when not fluent 6 out, no ch after.* ....Mr S Swiers 5
1503 Cape Cottage 12.0 *alwys chasing ldrs, struggling to hold pl final cct, soon lost tch.* ....Mr A Phillips 6
1491[3] Rusty Bridge 12.0 *ld till hdd 10th, lost pl quickly final cct, t.o.* ....Mr R Burton 7
1504[2] Sirisat 12.0 *well pld for a cct, lost tch quickly apr 6 out, t.o.* ....Miss T Blazey 8
1529[5] Abbotsham 12.0 *reminders to keep up from 5th, t.o. when p.u. before 5 out.* ....Mr R Thornton pu
1489[2] Lucky Christopher 12.0 *struggling to go pace when nearly u.r. 7th, hit next, t.o. till p.u. between last 2.* ....Mr G Tarry pu
1489[1] Magnolia Man 12.0 *soon struggling, t.o. when p.u. before 4 out.* ....Mr N Harris pu
11 ran. 8l, 17l, 10l, 8l, 1¼l, 22l, 6l. Time 6m 49.20s. SP 13-8.
G J Powell

EXMOOR
Bratton Down
Saturday May 31st
FIRM

1592 Members

1580[1] **BUTLER JOHN (IRE) ....Miss J Cumings** 1
(fav) made, all, sn clr, jmpd rght 11th, easily
1580 **Bargain And Sale ....R Treloggen** 2
3rd til chsd wnr 14th, no imp, fin tired
1516 **Charmers Wish 5a....................H Thomas** 3
last til went 3rd 15th, no more prog, collpsd & died aft
1520 Red Is The Rose 5a *chsd wnr to 14th, sn wknd, t.o. & ref last* ....D Alers-Hankey ref
4 ran. 25l, 3l. Time 6m 7.00s. SP 1-6.
Nick Viney (Exmoor).

1593 B F S S (12st)

1440[1] **EARL BOON 4ex.......................T Mitchell** 1
(fav) ld to 8th, trckd ldr, ld aft 16th, clr last, comf
1516 **Milled Oats ....R Widger** 2
not fluent, ld 8th-aft 16th, outpcd aft 2 out, lft 2nd last
1518[4] **Slaney France (Ire) ....Miss K Lovelace** 3
cls up to 9th, wknd 12th, t.o. 15th, tk poor 3rd agn fin
1321 Air Commander *last & sn bhnd, t.o. 14th, went poor 3rd 2 out,eased nr fin*.................Miss D Olding 4
1550 Tuffnut Tom *trckd ldrs,effrt & pckd 2 out,went 5l 2nd & f last,rmntd* ....J Scott 5
5 ran. 7l, dist, ½l, 12l. Time 6m 5.50s. SP 4-9.
J A Keighley (Blackmore & Sparkford Vale).

1594 Intermediate (12st)

1496[6] **TANGLE BARON 10ex...........Miss J Cumings** 1
prom, ld 9th, styd on wll frm 2 out, just hld on
1570 **Link Copper 5ex ....Miss L Blackford** 2
ld 5th til mstk nxt,3rd & outpcd 15th,styd on flat,jst faild
1518[2] **Three And A Half 5ex..................S Kidston** 3
(fav) trckd ldrs,rdn to prss wnr 14th,ev ch til no ext last,dsmntd
100 Play Poker (Ire) *trckd ldrs, not qckn 14th, mod 6th 2 out, fin well* ....S Slade 4
1517[6] Alex Thuscombe 5ex (v) *ld to 5th, prom til outpcd 15th, no imp aft, kpt on, dsmntd*..............P Shaw 5
1547[1] Hensue *ld 6th-9th, lost plc 12th, strggling frm 15th* ....R Treloggen 6
1550 Roaming Shadow *wll in tch til outpcd aft 14th, wknd 2 out, dsmntd*..............................J Hankinson 7
1322 Rose Of Macmillion 5a *n.j.w. in tch in rear to 11th, wkng whn p.u. 13th* ....L Jefford pu
522 M-Reg 5ex *sn last, t.o. 9th, f 14th*........G Cazenove f
1439 And What Else (Ire) *bhnd frm 9th, t.o. & p.u. 14th* ....C Heard pu
10 ran. 1l, 1½l, 12l, ½l, 4l, 12l. Time 6m 4.50s. SP 5-1.
P J Clarke (Devon & Somerset Staghounds).

1595 Ladies

1552[1] **RYME AND RUN 5a 3ow........Miss L Blackford** 1
(fav) trckd ldr 11th, ld 14th, clr 3 out, easily
1090 **Departure 5a ....Miss S Gaisford** 2
last & dtchd til ran on to chs wnr aft 3 out, no imp
1340[4] **Reef Lark ....Miss A Goschen** 3
s.s. not fluent, outpcd 10th, effrt 14th, onepcd frm 3 out
1548[6] Rapid Rascal *mstk 9th, prssd ldr to 11th, outpcd frm 15th*..Miss S West 4
1548 Daybrook's Gift (v) *ld, rdn 12th, hdd 14th, wknd rpdly 16th, p.u. 2 out* ....Miss S Vickery pu
5 ran. 7l, 1l, 10l. Time 6m 3.00s. SP 11-10.
A Cottle (Spooners & West Dartmoor).

1596 4m Men's Open

1517[1] **FOSBURY ....T Mitchell** 1
(fav) j.w. ld 7th, abt 6l clr final cct, easily
1551[3] **Arble March 5a........................L Jefford** 2
chsd wnr 10th-4 out, 2nd agn 2 out, kpt on und pres
1548[5] **Romany Anne 5a..................I Widdicombe** 3
last til prog 13th, chsd wnr 4 out-2 out, wknd, dsmntd
1496[4] Avril Showers 5a *ld to 7th, cls up til lost tch 20th, no ch aft*..R Atkinson 4
1547[2] Afterkelly *pshd alng 7th, last & lost tch 13th, t.o. & p.u. 17th*.....................................T Dennis pu
5 ran. 8l, 8l, 10l. Time 8m 6.00s. SP 1-6.
Mrs Susan Humphreys (Cattistock).

1597 Open Maiden (12st)

1553 **SNITTON STREAM ....Miss S Vickery** 1
j.w. made all, 30l clr hlfwy, unchal
1554[3] **Baman Powerhouse ....J Young** 2
rear, prog 10th, chsd wnr aft 15th, no imp frm 2 out
794 **Creedy Valley ....L Jefford** 3
10s-7/2, chsng grp, effrt & blnd 15th, 3rd frm nxt, kpt on
1520[5] Dollybat 5a *prom/ld chsng grp, no prog 14th, 4th & no ch aft nxt* ....M Frith 4
1554 I'm Foxy 5a (bl) *hld up in chsng grp, prom 12th, wknd aft 14th, no ch aft*...............................R Widger 5
1554[5] Nottarex *mstk 7th, chsng grp til wknd 12th, t.o. 14th* ....B Wright 6
1498[4] Rallye Stripe *s.s. sn prom in chsng grp, wknd 11th, t.o. 14th*.................................Col S Allen 7
1483 Maggie Tee 5a *sn rear of chsng grp, lost tch 12th, t.o. & p.u. aft 14th* ....Miss S Young pu
1486 I Like The Deal 5a *(fav) jmpd slwly 2nd, immed lost tch, t.o. last & p.u. aft 5th* ....Miss J Cumings pu
1547 Sam's Successor *prom in chsng grp, 2nd brfly 10th, lost plc 13th, p.u. 15th* ....S Kidston pu
1520 Mellicometti *rear of chsng grp, lost tch 12th, t.o. & p.u. 15th*...S Slade pu
1583 Morchard Gem 12a *last when f heavily 8th* ....A Holdsworth f
12 ran. 25l, 2l, 20l, 25l, 10l, 25l. Time 6m 5.00s. SP 12-1.
W H Whitley (Dartmoor).
J.N.

YSTRAD TAF FECHAN
Bassaleg
Saturday May 31st
FIRM

1598 Members (12st)

1557[5] **SWEET KILDARE 5a ....J P Keen** 1
(fav) jmpd lft, ld 2nd, clr 4th, pshd out whn chal last, comf
1556 **Lennie The Lion ....J Price** 2
mstks, ld to 2nd, blnd 15th, rdn & ev ch last, onepcd
2 ran. 1l. Time 6m 34.00s. SP 2-5.
V J Thomas (Ystrad).

1599 Restricted (12st)

1470 **CELTIC BIZARRE 5a ....Miss B Barton** 1
(fav) jmpd lft, made all, clr 4th, blnd 8th, unchal
1472 **Top Tor 5a ....T Vaughan** 2
alwys 2nd, mstk 2nd, rdn apr 11th, sn t.o.
2 ran. Dist. Time 6m 28.00s. SP 5-6.
R R Smedley (Tivyside).

1600 Confined (12st)

1557[3] **BEINN MOHR 5a 8ex ....E Williams** 1
(fav) w.w. went 2nd 9th, ld 12th, drew clr 4 out, easily
1557 **Rusty Music 3ex................Miss N Richards** 2
ld to 8th, last nxt, regained 2nd 13th, no ch wth wnr
1557[4] **Cornish Cossack (NZ) ....W Pugh** 3
tongue-strap, disp 5th, ld 8-12th, last & wkng nxt
3 ran. 15l, 20l. Time 6m 20.00s. SP 2-7.
Mrs C Howell (Llangeinor).

1601 Mixed Open (12st)

1560[2] **STERLING BUCK (USA) ....M FitzGerald** 1
(fav) chsd rival, rmndr 11th, ld nxt, sn drew clr

1321 **Olde Crescent** ....**J Comins** 2
ld, clr 4th, hdd 12th, sn btn, blnd 14th, t.o.
2 ran. Dist. Time 6m 23.00s. SP 1-8.
D J Clapham (Ledbury).

1602 Intermediate (12st)

1557^{2} **ICECAPADE (BEL)** ....**E Williams** 1
chsd ldr 4th,ld 12th,rdn 3 out,clr whn blnd last,rdn out
1559^{1} **How Friendly 5ex** ....**M FitzGerald** 2
(fav) w.w. chsd wnr 13th, rdn whn squeezed 3 out, alwys hld,dsmntd
1576 **Dick's Cabin (bl)** ....**J Price** 3
tubed, mounted on course, ld 2nd, clr 4th, hdd 12th, wknd
1555^{3} Final Option (Ire) *alwys last, lost tch 11th, no ch 14th, p.u. 2 out, dsmntd*.........................I Johnson pu
1560^{4} Ideal *2nd whn ran out 3rd* ....Miss C Thomas ro
5 ran. 3l, dist. Time 6m 12.00s. SP 7-4.
P Riddick (Gelligaer).

1603 Open Maiden (12st)

1561^{3} **BODDINGTON HILL 5a** ....**I Johnson** 1
(fav) ld 2nd,slw jmp 5th,hdd nxt,ld 10th,lft clr 13th,unchal,dsmnt
1561 **Ruffinswick** ....**J Price** 2
prom, ld 6th-10th, wknd apr 12th, lft poor 2nd aft nxt
1562^{6} Leinthall Thistle (Ire) 5a *7s-3s, alwys wll bhnd, blnd 9th, lost tch 11th, p.u. 14th* ....N Oliver pu
1460 Priesthill (Ire) *in tch, 4th whn u.r. 4th* Miss E Crawford ur
1367 Lady Orr (Ire) 5a *hld up,prog 10th,2nd & going wll whn crawld 13th,p.u. lame* ....J Tudor pu
1555 Chantingo Lad *ld til hit 2nd, chsd ldrs, blnd 11th, 3rd & no ch, p.u. 15th* ....A Price pu
6 ran. Dist. Time 6m 32.00s. SP 11-10.
B A Hall (Gelligaer Farmers).
S.P.

HARBOROUGH HUNTS CLUB
Dingley
Sunday June 1st
GOOD TO FIRM

1604 Members

1475^{7} **HOSTETLER** ....**J Stephenson** 1
disp frm 9th til plodded clr aft 2 out
1474 **Forward View** ....**P Hutchinson** 2
mstks 6th & 14th, lft in ld 8th, disp aft til no ext 2 out
1350 Pancratic *made most til 8l clr & s.u. bend apr 9th* ....G Morrison su
1573^{4} Supreme Dream (Ire) 5a *(fav) cls up til u.r. 5th* ....Mrs P Adams ur
4 ran. 4l. Time 6m 50.00s. SP 7-1.
Mrs Sally Norris (Pytchley).

1605 Restricted (12st)

1460^{1} **FORT GALE (IRE)** ....**Julian Pritchard** 1
(fav) conf rdn in rear, smooth prog to ld apr 2 out, pshd out flat
1355^{4} **Dolly Bloom 5a** ....**A Sansome** 2
in tch,outpcd aft 15th,effrt to chs wnr aft 2 out,alwys hld
1526 **Meadow Cottage** ....**T Stephenson** 3
w.w. prog to ld & pckd 14th, hdd apr 2 out, onepcd
1578^{1} Nick The Biscuit *w.w. prog to ld 13th-14th, outpcd aft nxt, kpt on* ....A Dalton 4
1542^{2} Rakish Queen 5a *pllng, raced wd, cls up til not qckn aft 15th*............................Miss H Phizacklea 5
1507 Mamnoon (USA) *cls up til wknd 14th, sn bhnd* ....R Armson 6
1576 Crawn Hawk *made most til f 11th*.........K Needham f
1556^{3} Bakmalad *f 1st* ....H Wheeler f
1475 Full Song 5a *prom til wknd 14th, bhnd whn p.u. 2 out* ....S Morris pu
1505^{5} Bishops Tale *prom,mstk 10th, lft in ld nxt-13th, wknd sddnly & p.u. 15th* ....A Coe pu
1572^{3} Wissywis (Ire) 12a *bhnd, dtchd last whn f 8th*. .C Yates f
1567 Aughnacloy Rose *mstk 3rd & immed bhnd, t.o. & p.u. 6th* ....R Page pu
1533^{3} Winter Breeze *wll in tch til p.u. 11th, dsmntd* ....Miss S Vickery pu
13 ran. 2l, 10l, 1l, 3l, 15l. Time 6m 38.50s. SP 2-1.
D J & C B Clapham (Cotswold Vale Farmers).
One fence omitted final circuit, 17 jumps.

1606 Ladies

779^{5} **SPERRIN VIEW 5a** ....**Mrs K Sunderland** 1
raced wd,alwys prom,ld going well 2 out,sn clr, easily
1530^{2} **Coolvawn Lady (Ire) 5a**...........**Miss F Hatfield** 2
trckd ldrs going wll, cls 4th whn pckd 3 out, onepcd aft
1511^{2} **Just For Kicks** ....**Mrs N Craggs** 3
rear, hmpd 6th, 9th & no ch hlfwy, ran on 3 out, nrst fin
1476^{2} Force Eight *(fav) ld to 5th, ld aft 13th-2 out, wknd, lame* ....Miss A Dare 4
1535^{4} Linlake Lightning 5a *ldng grp til grad fdd frm 15th* ....Miss H Irving 5
1488^{8} Killimor Lad *ld 5th-aft 13th, wknd aft 3 out* ....Miss S Samworth 6
1434^{1} Professor Longhair 2ow *bhnd whn hmpd 6th, t.o. aft, no prog* ....Miss C Papworth 7
1532^{2} Run For Free *hmpd 6th, nvr going wll aft, poor 8th hlfwy, p.u. 13th*.............................Mrs T Hill pu
1463^{5} Phelioff *rear whn hmpd & u.r. 6th* ....Miss S Dawson ur
1573^{2} Fly For Us 5a *cls up, chal 3 out, wknd aft nxt, 5th & btn whn p.u. last*.............................Mrs C Ford pu
1540^{4} Golden Fare *prom til b.d. 6th*..........Miss L Wallace bd
1403 Caroles Express 5a *hld up rear, 7th & out of tch whn blnd & u.r. 11th*......................Miss S Duckett ur
1559^{2} Lucky Ole Son *prom, 4th whn f 6th* ......Miss P Jones f
13 ran. 15l, 5l, 8l, 3l, 7l, ½l. Time 6m 27.50s. SP 10-1.
Mrs Helen Mobley (Bicester With Whaddon Chase).
One fence omitted final circuit, 17 jumps.

1607 Men's Open

1234^{2} **SHOON WIND** ....**A Dalton** 1
(fav) j.w. ld to 2nd & frm 5th, clr 3 out, pshd out
1532^{6} **Tompet** ....**B McKim** 2
chsd ldrs,styd on frm 10th,3rd at 14th,chsd wnr last,nvr nrr
1539^{3} **Merlyns Choice** ....**A Woodward** 3
sn pshd alng, outpcd frm 5th, wll bhnd 8th, kpt on frm 3 out
1524 Pretoria Dancer 7a *ld 3-5th, chsd wnr to 12th,, wknd & mstk nxt, fin tired* ....M Rimell 4
1576^{5} Penllyne's Pride (v) *ld 2nd-3rd, wknd 9th, cont mls t.o.* ....G Barfoot-Saunt 5
1539 Barkin *sn last & dtchd, t.o. 8th, u.r. 14th* ......P Saville ur
1575 Sharinski (bl) *prom til rdn & reluc frm 9th, t.o. & p.u. 12th* ....T Stephenson pu
1534^{1} Bright As A Button *pshd alng,chsd wnr 12th,no imp 3 out,lost 2nd & ref last*..........................G Tarry ref
1565^{2} Lofty Deed (USA) *ref & u.r. 1st*........Julian Pritchard ref
9 ran. 7l, 25l, 20l, 1 fence. Time 6m 29.00s. SP 4-6.
J N Dalton (Wheatland).

1608 Intermediate

1448^{3} **CAWKWELL DEAN** ....**L Lay** 1
prom, ld aft 10th, clr 3 out, hrd prssd last, all out nr fin
1536^{2} **Mr Gee** ....**K Needham** 2
bhnd,poor 7th at 10th,ran on 13th,styd on wl flat,nt rch wnr
1564^{1} **Sunshine Manor** ....**G Tarry** 3
(fav) ld to aft 10th, mstks final cct, rallied 2 out, no ext last
1438^{5} Elle Flavador 5a *raced in 5th, mstk 8th, ran on 14th, chal 2 out, no ext last* ....Miss S Vickery 4
1430^{3} Current Attraction 5a *chsd ldng trio to 8th, sn wknd, t.o. 10th*...................................Miss K Thory 5
1570 Majestic Ride *bhnd, 7th whn hit 8th, t.o. & mstk 11th, p.u. nxt* ....R Armson pu

1466[1] Tarry Awhile *ldng trio til wknd apr 2 out, p.u. last* ....J Connell pu
1570 Andalucian Sun (Ire) *sn bhnd & jmpd slwly, 7th & t.o. whn ref 13th*........G Maloney ref
1421[1] Kiri's Rose (Ire) 5a *mstks,chsd ldng trio frm 8th,no imp 15th,wknd 2 out,p.u.last*........P Gee pu
1379[1] Auchendolly (Ire) *last & wll bhnd, t.o. hlfwy, p.u. 3 out* ....T Macfarlane pu
856[1] The Oxford Don *2nd whn f 2nd*........R Hunnisett f
11 ran. ¾l, 3l, ½l, 1 fence. Time 6m 38.00s. SP 14-1.
Neale Hutchinson (Bicester With Whaddon Chase).

1609 Open Maiden

1452 **FAWSLEY MANOR 5a ....R Armson 1**
mid-div,prog & mstk 11th,ran on & ld aft 2out,sn clr,rdn out
1541[2] **Malenski (Ire) ....B Pollock 2**
prom, chsd ldr 15th, ev ch aft 2 out, sn no ext, fin tired
1577[2] **Paddy's Pocket ....T Lane 3**
ld 2nd til aft 2 out, wknd & slw jmp last, fin tired
1589 Auntie Chris 5a *ran in sntchs, 3rd at 10th, sn lost plc, no dang frm 15th*........P Gee 4
1536 Carlingford Lad (Ire) *tongue-strap, prom, chsd ldr 10-15th, wknd aft 3 out, tired*........E Andrewes 5
1401[4] Lizapet (Ire) 12a *ld to 2nd, wknd aft 11th, sn t.o.* ....S Green 6
1076 Toiapan (Ire) *rear whn hmpd & u.r. 2nd*........P Ikin ur
Bowlands Country *(fav) sn wll bhnd, some prog 12th, 7th & clsng grad whn f 14th*........R Ford f
1352 Ri Ra 5a *prom, 4th whn u.r. 6th*......Miss S Sharratt ur
1537 Seaton Mill *rear, lost tch 10th, p.u. nxt*......M Hewitt pu
1537[3] Bobbin Lace 5a *f 2nd*........J Docker f
1537[4] Dromain 5a *in tch til blnd & u.r. 4th*..Mrs C McCarthy ur
1528[8] Money Don't Matter 12a *jmpd badly, t.o. til p.u. 10th* ....Julian Pritchard pu
1195[3] Lough Morne *cls up, mstk 15th, wknd aft, p.u. 2 out* ....Miss A Lock pu
14 ran. 15l, hd, 8l, 5l, 1 fence. Time 6m 46.50s. SP 8-1.
G B Tarry (Pytchley).
One fence omitted final circuit, 17 jumps. J.N.

TORRINGTON FARMERS
Umberleigh
Saturday June 7th
FIRM

1610 Members (12st)

1584[3] **DUSTY FURLONG ....Miss K Baily 1**
(fav) trckd ldr, ld apr 13th, sn clr, drvn & all out, lame
1483 **Dharamshala (Ire) ....A Jones 2**
1st ride,cls up,nrly u.r. 10th,wknd & mstks frm 13th,lame
Fitzroy *ld to apr 13th, wknd, blnd 3 out & p.u.* ..T Cole pu
3 ran. Dist. Time 6m 52.00s. SP 4-5.
Mrs Katie Squire (Torrington Farmers).

1611 Men's Open

1593[1] **EARL BOON ....T Mitchell 1**
(fav) j.w. trckd ldr, ld 8th-aft 12th, ld 3 out, sn clr, easily
1598[1] **Sweet Kildare 5a ....J P Keen 2**
wll in rear til prog 13th, styd on to go 2nd aft 2 out,no ch
1601[1] **Sterling Buck (USA) ....Julian Pritchard 3**
ld to 8th & aft 12th-3 out, sn btn
1557[1] Alfion (Ire) *mstk 2nd, trckd ldrs, drvn to chal aft 12th, wknd 14th*........D S Jones 4
1600[1] Beinn Mohr 5a *prom til 4th & rdn aft 12th, strgglng frm nxt*........E Williams 5
1608 Majestic Ride *alwys rear, lost tch 12th, t.o. & ref 2 out, cont*........G Maloney 6
1607 Lofty Deed (USA) *ref 1st (twice)*.....A Charles-Jones ref
1594[6] Hensue *in tch in rear til s.u. btwn 4th & 5th*...N Harris su
8 ran. 15l, 4l, ½l, 4l, Bad. Time 6m 15.00s. SP 1-3.
J A Keighley (Blackmore & Sparkford Vale).

1612 Ladies

1571[7] **GREAT GUSTO ....Miss L Blackford 1**
(fav) prom, ld 10th, sn clr, unchal
1581 **Medias Maid 5a ....Miss L Pope 2**
hld up, chsd wnr 11th, no imp, mstk 2 out, fin tired
1548[4] **Lavalight (bl) ....Miss A Goschen 3**
prom til lost tch frm 9th, 3rd & no prog final cct
1552 Newstarsky *20s-6s, rear whn mstk 7th, sn wll bhnd, t.o.*........Miss J Cumings 4
1590[3] Wake Up Luv *ld to 10th, sn strgglng, disp mod 3rd whn s.u. bnd apr 13th*........Miss P Cooper su
5 ran. Dist, 2l, dist. Time 6m 14.00s. SP 4-9.
R C H Racing (Silverton).

1613 Restricted (12st)

1374[5] **RUTH'S BOY (IRE) (bl) ....Miss P Curling 1**
(fav) 3s-2s, ld aft 4th, sn clr, 25l up 13th, blnd 3 out, imprssv
1605[3] **Meadow Cottage ....T Stephenson 2**
ld to 2nd, prom in chsng grp, chsd wnr 13th, nvr any imp
1488[4] **Feltham Mistress 5a ....A Charles-Jones 3**
chsng grp, 5th & no ch 14th, styd on to tk 3rd 2 out
1519 Ragtime Boy *out of tch til jnd chsng grp 7th, 6th & no ch 14th, styd on*........Miss L Pope 4
1605[6] Mamnoon (USA) *last & sn mls bhnd, jmpd slwly 5th, t.o. aft*........G Maloney 5
1526 Mr Ffitch *rear & sn pshd alng, t.o. 12th, p.u. 3 out* ....G Barfoot-Saunt pu
1582[6] Morchard Milly 5a *alwys wll bhnd, 11th & t.o. whn u.r. 12th*........J Auvray ur
Prince Rua *alwys last pair, t.o. & p.u. aft 12th* ....Miss P Cooper pu
1552 Stormy Fashion *hld up, sn wll bhnd, no prog hlfwy, poor 5th & p.u. last*........Maj G Wheeler pu
1551 Mountain-Linnet *prom in chsng grp, chsd wnr 7th-13th, wknd, p.u. 2 out*........T Woolridge pu
1584[1] Fingal *alwys rear, 9th at 7th, wknd & p.u. 11th* ....S Kidston pu
1560[6] Culpeppers Dish *ld to aft 4th, chsng grp til wknd 12th, t.o. & p.u. 2 out*........D S Jones pu
1605 Winter Breeze *6s-3s, chsng grp, effrt to 3rd at 14th, sn wknd, p.u. 2 out*........E Williams pu
13 ran. 25l, 2l, 10l, dist. Time 6m 9.00s. SP 2-1.
Capt T A Forster (Devon & Somerset Staghounds).

1614 Confined

1550[1] **FELLOW SIOUX ....Miss S Vickery 1**
(fav) hld up, ld 8th, clr aft 13th, easily
1580[3] **Oneovertheight ....S Kidston 2**
lft in ld aft 6th-8th,blnd 13th,no ch aft, rdn & reluc 2 out
1594[1] Tangle Baron *ld til ran out aft 6th* ....Miss J Cumings ro
3 ran. 15l. Time 6m 33.00s. SP 10-11.
T B Stevens (Devon & Somerset Staghounds).

1615 Open Maiden (12st)

1583[2] **ARITAM (IRE) ....K Heard 1**
(fav) t.d.e. trckd ldrs,ld 14th,clr & rdn apr 2 out,drvn out flat
1554[4] **Miss Dior 5a ....Miss P Gundry 2**
ld aft 5th-14th,lost plc,ran on to chs wnr 2 out,clsng flat
1578 **Bessie's Will 5a ....G Barfoot-Saunt 3**
trckd ldrs, effrt aft 12th, 4th & btn whn mstk 14th, wknd
1547 River Stream 5a *alwys bhnd, t.o. final cct, tk poor 4th 2 out*........M Burrows 4
1473 Mississippisteamer (Ire) *chsd ldrs, nvr able to chal, wknd & blnd 3 out, t.o.*........D S Jones 5
1584[6] Happy Valley 5a *bhnd, 10th whn hmpd & f 7th* ....Miss P Baker f
1402 Well Bank *ld 2nd-aft 5th, wknd 12th, 5th & btn whn blnd & u.r. nxt*........E Walker ur
1230 Ceffyl Gwyn *20s-10s, sn bhnd, t.o. & p.u. 9th*...J Price pu

1577 Fighting For Good (Ire) (bl) *prom, wth wnr 14th-nxt, wknd rpdly aft 3 out, p.u. last* .... L Lay pu
1553 Berkley Street 5a (bl) *ld 1st, blnd nxt & drppd rear, t.o. & p.u. 11th* .... R Nuttall pu
1583 Go Willie Go *rear, 7th whn f 7th, dead* .... J Young f
11 ran. 2l, 25l, dist, hd. Time 6m 24.00s. SP 7-4.
T Hughes, W Coleman & N Beer (Lamerton).
J.N.

Irish Point-to-Point Results 1997

(Reproduced by Courtesy of *The Irish Field*)

SOUTH UNION FOXHOUNDS
Rochestown
Thursday January 9th
SOFT

1 - Adjacent Maiden

No Problem [16]........................D Keane 1
made all, rdn out
Jimmy The Tailor [14]*chsd wnr, rdn & not qckn apr last* 2
Father O'Reilly*nvr dang* 3
Also: Madam Aside (4)
4 ran. 4l, 15l, 2l. SP Evens.

2 - Open Lightweight

Deep Heritage [25]......................E Bolger 1
trckd ldr, ld 2 out, sn clr
Clonrosh Slave [19]*ld to 2 out, sn btn* 2
Awbeg Rover [16]*alwys last, nvr dang* 3
3 ran. 15l, 6l. SP 1-3.

3 - Maiden 5 & 6yo

Hyelord [16] ....C Murphy 1
in tch, ld 2 out, rdn clr
Hugo Henry [10]*prom, lft in ld 3 out, hdd nxt, sn btn* 2
Shenanigans*in tch, 3rd & ev ch 2 out, sn btn, fin 4th, promoted* 3
Also: Jack Dory (4), Old Decency (f), Superior Call (pu), Ship Of Shame (f), Ceasars Reign (pu), St Larry (pu), Inch Cross (pu), Mount Nugent Jack (bd), Oscars Link (0)
12 ran. 20l, 2l, 4l. SP 5-1.

4 - Maiden 7yo+

Royal Barge [15]........................J Barcoe 1
prom, ld 2 out, drvn out
Buck Run [15]*prom, chal 2 out, just held* 2
Prophets Thumb*alwys bhnd, t.o.* 3
Also: An Fear Dubh (4), Beau Cinq (ur), Nelpha (pu), Pure Energy (pu), The Cass Man (pu), Radical-Times (pu)
9 ran. ½l, dist, 8l. SP 5-4.

5 - Winners Of Two

Tearaway King [30].....................E Bolger 1
made all, easily
Lady Elise [20]*hrd rdn to chs wnr 2 out, no imp* 2
Sharoujack*t.o.* 3
Also: Fair Revival (4)
4 ran. 12l, dist, 20l. SP 1-4.

6 - Mares Maiden 7yo+

Tanhoney [16]..........................D O'Brien 1
hld up, prog to chal 2 out, ld aft last, sn clr
Ballinvuskig Lady [14]*prom, ld 2 out-flat, no ext* 2
Beetalot [12]*chsd ldrs, onepcd frm 2 out* 3
Also: Push Gently [10] (4), Rock On Rosies (5), Glistening Waters (ur), Holiday Time (pu), Trimmer Lady (pu), Marys Friend (f)
9 ran. 6l, 5l, 5l. SP 3-1.

UNITED FOXHOUNDS
Lisgoold
Saturday January 11th
HEAVY

7 - Confined Maiden

Nan's Pet [15]........................W O'Sullivan 1
ld 3 out, styd on well flat
Glenselier [12]*chsd ldrs, no imp wnr aft 3 out* 2
Supreme Forward [11]*chsd ldrs, no imp on wnr frm 3 out* 3
Also: Bright Prospect (4), Geragh Road (pu), Supreme Odds (pu), Frightening Child (pu), Garryross (pu), Strong Ambition (pu), Queenofclubs (f), Big Spender (pu), Minstrels Quay (pu), Princess Diga (pu), Woodfield Boss (pu)
14 ran. 6l, 3l, dist. SP 6-4.

8 - Adjacent Maiden 5yo

Clash Of The Gales [17]...............B Hallahan 1
ld aft 2 out, jmpd lft last, styd on well
Brush The Flag [13]*styd on to chs wnr last, no imp* 2
Wayward King [12]*in ld 2 out, sn hdd & wknd* 3
Also: Irish Frolic [11] (4), Inch Champion (pu), Into The Clan (pu), Barnane Walk (pu), Coole Abbey (pu), Kilcully Jake (pu), Hazy Mist (pu), Donna (pu), Wishing William (pu), Arthur (f), Harbour Leader (pu)
14 ran. 8l, 4l, 3l. SP 8-1.

9 - Open Lightweight

What A Hand [30] ....J McNamara 1
w.w. prog to chal 2 out, ld apr last, rdn out
Caddy Man [29]*ld to apr last, styd on well* 2
Castlewhite [22]*no imp 1st pair aft 2 out* 3
Also: Warning Call [21] (4), Upshepops (pu), Derry's Diamond (pu)
6 ran. 1½l, 15l, 3l. SP 11-10.

10 - Mares Maiden 6yo+

Farran Garrett [16]..................J McNamara 1
made all, well clr 3 out, wknd last, just hld on
Cush Princess [16]*chsd wnr 2 out, fin wll, just faild* 2
Greenflag Princess [10]*chsd ldrs, no imp frm 2 out* 3
Also: Idiot's Surprise (4), Shuil Na Mhuire (5), Lady Of Means (6), Macklette (7), Jenaway (f), Strange Secret (pu), Mandoora (pu), Annerene (pu), Donnrua (pu), Sea Breta (pu), Bawnavinogue Lady (pu), Blame Barney (su)
15 ran. Nk, 20l, 10l. SP 6-1.

11 - Maiden 6yo+ I

Mountain Hall [19]......................P Fenton 1
ld 5 out, shkn up apr last, sn qcknd clr
Danger Flynn [14]*chsd ldrs, ev ch 2 out, sn outpcd* 2
The Right Attitude [13]*chsd ldrs, ev ch 2 out, sn outpcd* 3
Also: Hanigans Bridge [11] (4), Diamond Melody (5), Valley Tingo (pu), Master Jake (pu), Vice Captain (pu), Icantsay (pu), Noddis Dilemma (pu)
10 ran. 6l, 2l, 6l. SP 5-4.

12 - Maiden 6yo+ II

Bob Treacy [18] ....A Costello 1
ld 3 out-2 out, rallied to ld flat
The Village Way [18]*ld 2 out til hdd & no ext flat* 2
Scrouthea*t.o.* 3
Also: The Big Fella (pu), Black Fountain (pu), Leamlara Jet (pu), Sparky Joe (pu), La Charente (pu), Ardavillan Prince (pu), Clongeel Lord (pu)
10 ran. ½l, dist. SP 5-1.

13 - Winners Of One

Summerhill Express [21] ....**T Lombard** 1
in tch, ld apr 2 out, hrd rdn, all out ....
Inniscein [21]*prog 2 out, chal last, just hld*........... 2
Fine Affair [19]*wth wnr apr 2 out til no ext last* 3
Also: Slavica [18] (4), Shesadinger [15] (5), Gaye Bard [12] (6), The Pulpit (pu), Fethard Orchid (pu), Wejem (pu), Round Tower Lady (pu), Maypole Fountain (pu), Coolbawn Rose (pu), Hill View Cottage (pu), Drimeen (pu), Tack Room Lady (pu), Rt (pu)
17 ran. Hd, 4l, 3l, 8l. SP 3-1.

MUSKERRY FOXHOUNDS
Aghabullogue
Sunday January 12th
HEAVY

14 - Maiden 5yo

Brush Me Up [21] ....**P Coleman** 1
trckd ldrs, ld aft 2 out, sn clr, easily ....
Regal Absence [10]*chsd wnr apr last, no imp* 2
Not For Parrot [10]*chsd ldrs, rdn & no imp 2 out* 3
Also: Roughshod (4), Avondale Illusion (5), In The Stocking (6), Prestige Lord (7), Lars On Tour (pu), Billymac (pu), Kilcaw (f), Pluvius (f), Rock On Lord (f)
12 ran. Dist, 2l, 5l. SP 5-1.

15 - Winners Of One

Lough Lein Spirit [21]....................**N Fehily** 1
ld 4 out, sn clr, easily................................
No Swap [12]*no imp on wnr frm 3 out*............... 2
Molls Choice [11]*no imp on wnr frm 3 out*........... 3
3 ran. 10l, 2l. SP 4-6.

16 - Open Lightweight

2² **Clonrosh Slave [19]** ....**S Hadden** 1
chsd ldr, ld apr last, kpt on..........................
Tommy The Duke [18]*chsd ldrs, kpt on onepcd frm 2 out*.. 2
Elwill Glory [13]*ld to apr last, wknd*................. 3
Also: Cooladerra Lady (4)
4 ran. 4l, 12l, dist. SP 3-1.

17 - Maiden 6yo+ I

Torduff Express [16] ....**J Cullen** 1
prom, chsd ldr 2 out, styd on to ld nr fin...............
Short Circuit [16]*prom, ld 3 out, hrd rdn & hdd nr fin* 2
Finnow Thyne [15]*prom, ev ch 3 out, not qckn, styd on agn flat*... 3
Also: Clashview (4), Knockadooma (5), First Mohikin (6), Clon Caw (pu), Bartlemy King (pu), Itsajungleoutthere (f)
9 ran. ½l, 1l, dist. SP 7-2.

18 - Maiden 6yo+ II

Pancho's Tango [18]......................**D Daly** 1
prom, ld hlfwy, easily ....
Croi [12]*chsd wnr 5 out, no imp*..................... 2
Tullys Ball*nvr dang* 3
Also: 4³ Prophets Thumb (4), Slaney Stream (pu), The Snuffman (pu), Prince Owen (pu), High Charges (pu), Round Pound (pu), Empowerment (pu)
10 ran. 15l, 20l, 5l. SP 6-4.

19 - Mares Maiden

Claudia Electric [16]....................**N Fehily** 1
w.w. prog to ld apr 2 out, pshd out ....
Leaping Three [14]*in tch, chsd wnr apr last, onepcd* 2
Dont Tell Nell [12]*in tch, went 3rd apr last, onepcd* ... 3
Also: Miss Josephine (4), Tonmarie Chance (5), 10 Jenaway (6), Highland Call (7), Glitter Girl (pu), 6 Holiday Time (pu), Electric Can (pu), Peggys Leg (pu), Dereenavurrig (pu), Fireblends (f)
13 ran. 3l, 5l, 15l. SP 3-1.

20 - Adjacent Maiden

Buckshee [15] ....**M Scanlon** 1
prom, ld 2 out, jnd last, drvn out flat.................
Chevin Lad [14]*rear, ran on apr last, nrst fin* 2
Dohney Boy [14]*prom, wth wnr last, no ext flat*....... 3
Also: Classis King [13] (4), 1³ Father O'Reilly [11] (5), Lisselan Lass (6), Heronimus Bosch (f), Ashburton Lord (bd), Tekroc (pu), Running Wolf (pu), Poachers Lamp (su), Dromod Magic (pu), Allwan (pu)
13 ran. 1l, 1l, 2l, 6l. SP 6-1.

COUNTY LIMERICK
Patrickswell
Sunday January 12th
SOFT

21 - Winners Of One

An Oon Iss An Owl [19]...................**R Flavin** 1
prom, ld 2 out, drvn out...............................
Givemeyourhand [18]*prom, chal apr last, no ext flat* 2
Only One [15]*prom, ev ch 2 out, onepcd*............. 3
Also: Aylesbury Beau [14] (4), Run For Fun [12] (5), Not A Razu (6), Tantum Bonum (7), Carolines Minstrel (pu), Badalka (pu), Starlight Fountain (f), Camogue Bridge (pu)
11 ran. 3l, 5l, 1½l, 5l. SP 11-2.

22 - Maiden 5yo

Vital Issue [17].........................**P Fenton** 1
trckd ldrs, ld 3 out, styd on well......................
Florida Light [14]*chsd ldrs, went 2nd 2 out, no imp wnr*.. 2
Dashing Buck [11]*chsd ldrs, onepcd frm 3 out*....... 3
Also: Livin Joy (pu), Lord Esker (pu), Rockholm Lad (pu), My Uncle Batt (pu), All But (f), King Of The Suir (pu), Sam Quale (pu), Over Eager (pu), Take My Side (pu), Bucks Son (pu)
13 ran. 10l, 10l. SP 3-1.

23 - Maiden 6yo

Brostaig Ort [16].........................**R Flavin** 1
chsd ldr 3 out, lft in ld nxt, hld on well ....
Belhabour [16]*chsd ldrs, lft 2nd 2 out, just held flat* ... 2
3 **Mount Nugent Jack [13]***prom, onepcd frm 2 out*..... 3
Also: The Scrub [10] (4), Knockannig Bay (pu), Matchmaker Seamus (pu), Court Amber (pu), Master Finbar (pu), Stelinjo (pu), West Of The Moon (f), Awalkintheclouds (pu), Spikes The Man (f), Keepthemguessing (pu)
13 ran. ½l, 10l, 8l. SP 10-1.

24 - Open Lightweight

Flashing Steel [29].......................**P Fenton** 1
prom, ld 4 out, clr 2 out, pshd out ....
Aiguille [21]*prom, chsd wnr 3 out, no imp* 2
Lottoleigh [19]*prom, onepcd frm 3 out* 3
Also: Fort View (4), River Wild (pu), Wharfingar (pu), 4 Beau Cinq (pu), Way Home (pu), Whats The Mark (pu), Emarrceeveess (pu), Gabrielle's Boy (pu), Cahercon (pu)
12 ran. 10l, 5l, dist. SP 1-3.

25 - Mares Maiden 5 & 6yo

Golly Miss Molly [15] ....**B Clohessy** 1
chsd ldrs, styd on to ld last, drvn out ....
The Buck Pony [13]*ld to last, no ext flat*............. 2
Scklepp [13]*chsd ldrs, styd on onepcd frm 2 out*...... 3
Also: Kildea Duchess [12] (4), American Conker (ro), Shuil Flossy (ur), Killone River (pu), Snugville Sally (pu), Hill Of Grace (pu), Springtime Mist (f), Fardrum (pu), Palmrock Queen (f), Micro Villa (pu)
13 ran. 4l, ½l, 1l. SP 7-1.

26 - Mares Lightweight

Just A Breeze [22] ....**T Cloke** 1
hld up, ld 3 out, comf..................................
Silent Sneeze [17]*ld to 3 out, no ch wth wnr aft* 2

Ahead Of My Time [15]*chsd ldrs, onepcd frm 3 out* .. 3
Also: 5³ Sharoujack [15] (4), Ballinaclash Pride [13] (5), What A Choice (6), Argideen Bonnie (pu), Borreeva (pu), Sentimental Crush (pu), Don't Waste It (pu), Buxom Orlov (pu)
11 ran. 6l, 5l, ½l. SP Evens.

WESTMEATH HARRIERS
Slanemore
Sunday January 19th
HOLDING

27 - Winners Of Three

Dixon Varner [24]........................**E Bolger** 1
hld up, prog 5 out, ld apr last, shkn up flat ....
Miller King [22]*prom, ld 6 out-apr last, styd on flat*.... 2
Ozier Hill [20]*mid-div, styd on frm 2 out, nrst fin* 3
Also: Find Out More [14] (4), Slaney Goodness [12] (5), Annie's Arthur [10] (6), The Real Bavard (ro), Dennistownthriller (pu), Ossie Murphy (pu), Dead Reckoning (pu), Sanford Heights (pu), Manhattan Prince (pu), Musical Waves (f), Downs Delight (pu), Trimmer Princess (pu), Tuskar Flop (f), Carrigans Lad (pu)
17 ran. ¾l, 6l, 20l, 5l, 6l. SP 1-2.

28 - Maiden 5 & 6yo I

Arrienzio [17]..........................**G Harford** 1
hld up, prog to ld apr last, ran on well ....
Rock On Bud [13]*rear, styd on 2 out, tk 2nd nr fin* 2
Malt Man [13]*prom, ld 4 out, wknd & hdd apr last* 3
Also: Drumlongfield [11] (4), Ollies Boy (5), Crunchy Nut (6), 23 Master Finbar (7), Waitnow (ur), Bracker (pu), Ballysadare Bay (f), Montys Delight (f), Zaffield (pu), Punters Fortune (pu), Millsofballysodare (pu)
14 ran. 8l, 1½l, 1½l, 5l, 4l, 6l. SP 10-1.

29 - Maiden 5 & 6yo II

On Deadly Ground [16]..................**S Mahon** 1
prom, lft in ld aft 2 out, lft clr last......................
Cotton Eyed Jimmy [13]*3rd 5 out, onepcd 2 out, lft 2nd last*.. 2
Mr Chataway [12]*ld 5 out, blnd 2 out, sn hdd & not rcvr*.. 3
Also: The Toor Trail (pu), Colemans River (ur), Shuil Mor (f), 23 Spikes The Man (pu), Tap Practice (pu), 23 Stelinjo (pu), Just Supreme (f), Willie B Brave [15] (f), Court Thyne (pu), Smiling Minstrel (pu), 3 Inch Cross (pu)
14 ran. 6l, 2l. SP 8-1.

30 - Open Lightweight

5¹ **Tearaway King [30]**.....................**E Bolger** 1
hld up, prog to ld apr 2 out, easily ....
Life Of A King [22]*rear, styd on 2 out, tk 2nd last*..... 2
21³ **Only One [19]***ld to 6th, ld 4 out-apr 2 out, wknd*....... 3
Also: Ounavarra Creek [17] (4), Voldi [13] (5), Mischievous Andy [11] (6), Lislary Lad [11] (7), The Committee (8), Maid For Dancing (f), 24 Gabrielle's Boy (pu), Shandonagh Bridge (pu), Borrismore Flash (f), Station Man (pu)
13 ran. 7l, 6l, 5l, 10l, 6l, ¾l, 4l. SP 4-5.

31 - Mares Maiden I

Tempestuous Lady [15] ....**A Fleming** 1
prom, lft in ld 3 out, lft clr nxt.........................
Kilone Abbess [13]*chsd ldrs, no imp 3 out, lft 2nd nxt* 2
Castlevigganlady*t.o*.. 3
Also: Golden Mist (ur), Miss Annagaul (f), Lady Sylvie (f), Hollymead (pu), Make A Move (f), 25³ Scklepp (pu), Buckskins Babe (pu), Snobs Casino (pu), 25 Hill Of Grace (ur), Miners Sunset (pu), Farlough Lady (pu)
14 ran. 6l, dist. SP 10-1.

32 - Mares Maiden II

Sister Nora [16]..........................**L Gracey** 1
prom, ld aft 2 out, in cmmnd whn lft clr last............
Sally Willows*nvr dang, lft 2nd last* 2
Pharavo [14]*ld to aft 2 out, btn whn f last, rmntd* 3
Also: Vermont River (4), Glenpine (pu), Pingo Sloo (ur), 25 Palmrock Queen (pu), Macken Money (f), Dowhatyouhavetodo (pu), Josalady (ur), Haveafewmanners (f), 6 Push Gently (pu), Gerrys Delight (f), Ballyroe Hill (pu)
14 ran. 25l, 5l, 3l. SP 5-2.

33 - Mares Maiden III

Vintage Classic [16].....................**A Martin** 1
trckd ldrs, ld 2 out, comf ....
Rosetown Girl [14]*chsd wnr 2 out, no imp*........... 2
Maries Call [12]*chsd ldrs, onepcd 3 out*............ 3
Also: Harvest Time [11] (4), Proud Princess (pu), 25 Springtime Mist (pu), Billie's Mate (pu), Snowtown Actress (pu), Clonfert Sue (pu), Can She Do It (ur), Mullaghea Lass (f), Buzz About (ur), Woodbinesandroses (pu), 6³ Beetalot (pu)
14 ran. 2½l, 6l, 3l. SP 2-1.

34 - Maiden 7yo+ I

Up And Under [17]...................**N Geraghty** 1
made all, unchal...
Deerpark King*chsd ldrs, no imp wnr 3 out*........... 2
Charlie Hawes*chsd ldrs, no imp wnr 3 out*............ 3
Also: Herb Superb (f), 4 Nelpha (pu), Is This The One (f), Wilbar (pu), Tom Haggard (pu), Bathurst (pu), Forabby (f), Carnmore House (pu), Greedy Johno (pu), Twin Track (pu)
13 ran. 25l, nk. SP 3-1.

35 - Maiden 7yo+ II

Oul Larry Andy [16] ....**A Ross** 1
in tch, ld apr last, styd on ....
Rushing Waters [15]*in tch, chsd wnr last, kpt on*..... 2
Inactualfact [13]*ld to apr last, wknd*................ 3
Also: Ordain [11] (4), Christimatt (5), 18 Slaney Stream (6), Crossword (pu), Bold Boreen (pu), Moynalvy Future VI (pu), Derryowen (pu), Grafy Hill (f), Trimfold (pu), Knockanoran (ur)
13 ran. 2l, 6l, 4l, 10l, 2l. SP 3-1.

36 - Maiden 7yo+ III

Dromod Point [15]......................**H Cleary** 1
prom, ld 2 out, styd on well ....
Normous [11]*chsd wnr aft 2 out, outpcd* 2
Donals Choice [10]*chsd ldrs, onepcd apr 2 out* 3
Also: 4 The Cass Man (4), Cool It (pu), La Mancha Boy (pu), Lisduff Pride (pu), Martin de Porres (pu), Paddy Red (f), Hasty Hours (f), Laurelvale (f), Poulgillie (f), Pats Farewell (f)
13 ran. 10l, 3l, 3l. SP 5-1.

37 - Mares Lightweight

26¹ **Just A Breeze [23]** ....**T Cloke** 1
hld up, ld 2 out, clr last, comf..........................
Credit Transfer [20]*ld to 2 out, no ch wth wnr aft*..... 2
Missing Lady [16]*chsd ldr to 3 out, sn btn*........... 3
Also: Arctic Treasure [15] (4), Chene Rose (pu), Melodic Lady (pu), Slemish Mist (f), 21 Run For Fun (f), Yes Boss (pu), Trimmer Wonder (f), Royal Star (pu), Porter Tastes Nice (pu)
12 ran. 5l, 10l, 3l. SP 3-1.

KILLEAGH HARRIERS
Killeagh
Sunday January 19th
GOOD

38 - Confined Maiden

Lord Of All [15] ....**P Crowley** 1
prom, disp last, just hld on.............................
12 **Black Fountain [15]***prom, disp last, just hld nr fin*.... 2
Via Del Quatro [14]*prom, disp last, no ext nr fin*...... 3
Also: 10 Shuil Na Mhuire [11] (4), 19 Miss Josephine (5), 4 Pure Energy (6), Mr Who (7), Gluais Linn (8), 12 Ardavillan Prince (9), 8 Donna (pu)
10 ran. Hd, 2l, 10l. SP 6-1.

39 - Maiden 5yo I

Good Lord Frank [16] ....R Flavin 1
hld up, prog 3 out, ld nxt, styd on well ....
Deejaydee [15]*prom, ld 3 out-nxt, no ext flat ....* 2
14[2] **Regal Absence [12]***nvr nrr ....* 3
Also: Jolly Decent (4), 8 Arthur (5), Little Buckie (6), Cirvin (7), As Sharp Again (8), Neily Joe (f), 3 Ceasars Reign (pu), Bricanmore (f), Westcourt (pu), 14 Pluvius (pu), Le Hearty Step (pu)
14 ran. 2l, 10l, 10l. SP 6-1.

40 - Maiden 5yo II

Dynamic Design [15].....................T Hyde 1
prom, ld 2 out, styd on well ....
Monteba [14]*prom, chsd wnr 2 out, no ext flat ......* 2
8 **Irish Frolic [14]***chsd ldrs, styd on wll apr last ....* 3
Also: 14 In The Stocking (4), Kelly's Perk (5), Springford (6), Foolsandtheirmoney (pu), Clonageera (pu), Identify In Crisis (f), Just A Playboy (pu), Westons Way (pu), Bridge Party (pu), Fountain Bid (pu)
13 ran. 2l, ½l, 15l. SP 7-4.

41 - Winners Of One

13 **Slavica [20] ....J Shaw** 1
prom, ld 4 out, comf.......................................
13 **Gaye Bard [17]***chsd wnr 3 out, no imp ....* 2
13 **Shaws Cross [14]***chsd ldrs, onepcd frm 3 out.........* 3
Also: 7[1] Nan's Pet [13] (4), 13 Drimeen [11] (5), McFepend (6), John's Right (7), 13 Shesadinger (8), 13 Hill View Cottage (9), 5 Fair Revival (pu), 9 Derry's Diamond (pu), 13 Round Tower Lady (pu), Sandy Pearl Two (pu), Keelson (pu), Black Abbey (f), Mandy's Treasure (pu), Bold Brew (pu), 13 Wejem (pu), Parish Ranger (pu)
19 ran. 3l, 10l, 3l. SP 6-1.

42 - Maiden 6yo I

Old Trafford [20]......................J Moloney 1
cls up, ld 4 out, easily ....
20 **Ashburton Lord [14]***chsd wnr 3 out, no imp ....* 2
11 **Valley Tingo***nvr dang...................................* 3
Also: 20 Poachers Lamp (4), Prospect Star (5), 3[3] Shenanigans (ur), Remmy Cruz (pu), 12 Sparky Joe (pu), Major Bill (pu), Mineral Al (pu), Coopers Clan (pu), Moonvoor (f), 18 The Snuffman (pu), Ten Bob Down (f)
14 ran. 12l, 25l, 5l. SP 8-11.

43 - Maiden 6yo II

Jeepers [17]...........................J Moloney 1
prom, ld 3 out, styd on well ....
Santa Jet [15]*chsd wnr 2 out, kpt on ....* 2
Skimabit [14]*chsd ldrs, styd on frm 2 out ....* 3
Also: Phar Desert (4), Never Heard (ur), Call Me Paris (pu), Colmans Hatch (f), Aireys Man (f), Cullaun (pu), Max Lad (f), Tidaro Fairy (pu), Major Above All (pu), Tom Deely (pu), 7 Minstrels Quay (f)
14 ran. 4l, 2l, dist. SP 6-4.

44 - Open Lightweight

Chalwood [23] ....T Lombard 1
ld 5 out, clr 2 out, comf ....
Mr K's Winterblues [17]*rear, kpt on to chs wnr apr last, no imp ....* 2
V'soske Gale [11]*in tch, ev ch 3 out, sn wknd ....* 3
Also: Father Pat (4), Master Kemal (5), Castle White (pu)
6 ran. 15l, 15l, 7l. SP 2-1.

45 - Mares Maiden 6yo I

7 **Queenofclubs [15] ....J Collins** 1
prom, ld 2 out, styd on und pres ....
Oriental Beauty [15]*in tch, chal last, no ext flat ......* 2
Right Then Rosie [12]*chsd ldrs, onepcd frm 2 out.....* 3
Also: 10 Macklette [11] (4), 19 Glitter Girl (pu), Dusky Run (f), 25 Shuil Flossy (f), Lipstick Lady (pu), Flowery Fern (pu), 10 Strange Secret (pu), Ballyhest Fountain (pu), Merry Castle (pu)
12 ran. 1l, 8l, 2l. SP 3-1.

46 - Mares Maiden 6yo II

One Woman [15] ....M Phillips 1
prom, ld & lft clr 4 out, easily ....
Kilcannon Sophie [10]*lft 2nd 4 out, no imp on wnr aft* **Lady Of Iron***t.o. ....* 3
Also: Brinny Princess (pu), Fountain Moss (pu), Loveable Lady (f), 25 American Conker (pu), 19 Fireblends (f), 19 Electric Can (pu), Vulthyne (pu), 10[3] Greenflag Princess (f)
11 ran. 15l, dist. SP 3-1.

DUNGARVAN HARRIERS
Kilossera
Sunday January 26th
SOFT

47 - Maiden 5yo

Viking Buoy [17]....................J McNamara 1
prom, ld 2 out, styd on well flat ....
8[3] **Wayward King [13]***chsd ldrs, chal apr last, sn btn ....* 2
22 **Over Eager [13]***chsd ldrs, chal apr last, sn btn ....* 3
Also: 3 Ship Of Shame (4), Pejays Duca (pu), 14 Lars On Tour (pu), 8 Kilcully Jake (pu), 39 Neily Joe (pu), Green Hills Glory (pu), Baltic Lake (pu), 14[3] Not For Parrot (f), Blacknock (pu), Charleys Run (pu), Bavard Jet (f), Welsh March (pu), Irish Spirit (pu), Desert Melody (pu), Strong Red Pine (pu)
18 ran. 8l, 1½l, dist. SP 3-1.

48 - Mares Maiden 5 & 6yo

Mardon [15]...........................J Sheehan 1
prom, disp frm last til line...............................
7 **Bright Prospect [15] ....D Leahy** 1
prom, disp from last til line...............................
45 **Strange Secret [13]***chsd ldrs, onepcd frm last.......* 3
Also: Bella Brownie (4), Fair Fontaine (5), Making The Cut (pu), Just Be Lucky (pu), 20 Lisselan Lass (pu), 7 Strong Ambition (pu), Frosty Morn (f), 14 Rock On Lord (pu), 38 Gluais Linn (pu), Goolds Opal (pu), 46 Brinny Princess (pu), Paros Leader (pu), Leamlara Rose (pu), 45 Ballyhest Fountain (pu), 46 Fountain Moss (pu), Ronkino (pu)
19 ran. Dd-ht, 5l, dist. SP 6-1.

49 - Winner Of Two

12[1] **Bob Treacy [19] ....A Costello** 1
chsd ldrs, chal 4 out, ld last, all out.....................
Lucky Town [19]*chsd ldrs, ld 4 out-last, just hld flat...* 2
8[1] **Clash Of The Gales [19]***chsd ldrs, chal 4 out, ev ch last, kpt on well...* 3
Also: 13 Maypole Fountain [18] (4), 13[2] Inniscein [14] (5), 41 Shesadinger [12] (6), Prayon Parson [10] (7), Digacre (8), 26 Sharoujack (9), 21 Tantum Bonum (pu), 18[1] Pancho's Tango (pu), 41 Hill View Cottage (bd), 41 Bold Brew (pu), Garramoss (f), Ashley Heights (pu)
15 ran. ¾l, 1l, 3l. SP 12-1.

50 - Confined Maiden

Magical Approach [18] ....D Costello 1
ld 4 out, clr last, easily ....
42 **Shenanigans [12]***chsd wnr 3 out, no imp...........* 2
The Territorian*nvr dang, t.o. ....* 3
Also: Welsh Lane (4), Grey Horizon (f), Key Idea (pu), 11 Hanigans Bridge (pu), Papuite (ur), 42 Moonvoor (f), Mr Goodbye (pu), 10 Bawnavinogue Lady (pu)
11 ran. 10l, dist, dist. SP 6-4.

51 - Open Lightweight

2[1] **Deep Heritage [24] ....E Bolger** 1
cls up, ld 3 out, easily ....
16[2] **Tommy The Duke [19]***prom, ld 5 out-3 out, no ch wnr aft ....* 2
Lacken Cross [10]*t.o. ....* 3
Also: Kilara (4), Table Rock (5), Dromgurrihy Lad (pu), Run For Niall (pu), Waterloo King [27] (pu)
8 ran. 6l, dist, dist. SP 2-5.

52 - Maiden 7yo+ I

4 **Radical-Times [15]**....................T Lombard 1
prom, ld 3 out, kpt on well
Royal Arctic [13]*chsd wnr 2 out, no imp flat* 2
Sarcoid [10]*chsd ldrs, onepcd frm 2 out* 3
Also: 17 Clashview (4), 4² Buck Run (5), 7 Woodfield Boss (6), Shimano (7), Mitidebe (f), Send It In (f), 11³ The Right Attitude (pu), Brian Og (pu), Tyo Mo Chara (pu), 20 Father O'Reilly (f), 17 Bartlemy King (pu)
14 ran. 6l, 10l, 10l. SP 20-1.

53 - Maiden 7yo+ II

35² **Rushing Waters [16]**....................E Bolger 1
raced wd, trckd ldrs, ld apr last, styd on well
11² **Danger Flynn [13]***prom, ld 2 out-last, no ext* 2
Big Bo [10]*prom, onepcd frm 2 out* 3
Also: 20³ Dohney Boy (4), 18 Prophets Thumb (5), Saol Sona (6), 7 Garryross (pu), Garacillin (pu), Rook's Rock (pu), Barnadown (pu), Sir Frederick (pu), 24 River Wild (pu), Earl Of Mirth (pu)
13 ran. 8l, 8l, 4l. SP 6-1.

54 - Maiden 7yo+ III

34² **Deerpark King [17]** ....P Crowley 1
prom, ld 2 out, drvn out
17 **Itsajungleoutthere [17]***prog to chal 2 out, just hld flat*
4 **An Fear Dubh [14]***ran on frm 2 out, nvr nrr* 3
Also: 11 Noddis Dilemma (4), 24 Fort View (5), Bold Chevalier (pu), 12³ Scrouthea (pu), Maltese Cross (pu), Lostyndyke (pu), 18 Prince Owen (pu), Baybuck (pu), 7² Glenselier (pu), 18³ Tullys Ball (pu)
13 ran. ½l, 8l, 20l. SP 5-1.

CARLOW FARMERS
Ballon
Sunday January 26th
GOOD TO SOFT

55 - Winners Of One I

Haven't An Ocean [18]....................J Berry 1
prog to chal 2 out, ld flat, rdn out
Bobbit Back On [16]*ld to aft last, no ext flat* 2
Priceless Buck [15]*chsd ldrs, onepcd frm 2 out* 3
Also: Speckled Glen [14] (4), Roseland [10] (5), Satalda (6), The Bug Hill (7), Shillelagh Oak (8), Miss Lurgan (9), Silver Buckle (10), Louis de Palmer (11), Kilmisten Breeze (pu), Back Withavengance (pu), Clare To Here (ur), Airecco (pu), 27 Downs Delight (pu), Threeandabit (ur), Hellofahooly (pu), M T Pockets (pu)
19 ran. 4l, 3l, 4l, 15l, 3l, dist, 8l, 4l, 6l, 10l. SP 2-1.

56 - Winners Of One II

Andy's Birthday [20] ....M Phillips 1
prom, ld 3 out, comf
41 **Keelson [18]***chsd wnr 2 out, no imp* 2
Master Julian [15]*chsd ldrs, onepcd 2 out* 3
Also: 36³ Donals Choice [13] (4), 37 Run For Fun (5), 36 The Cass Man (pu), Mr Balda (pu), Lucky Statement (pu), Lanngara (su), Big Murt (pu), Mariners Quest (ur), 36 Poulgillie (pu), Black Fashion (f), 46 Vulthyne (pu), Spring Beau (pu), Stoney Piper (pu), Percusionist (pu), 17¹ Torduff Express (pu), 34 Forabby (pu)
19 ran. 2l, 10l, 5l, 20l. SP 5-1.

57 - Maiden 5yo I

28 **Montys Delight [18]** ....A Martin 1
raced wd, prom, chal 2 out, ld flat, drvn out
McIlhatton [17]*ld 6th til aft last, no ext flat* 2
22 **All But [14]***chsd ldr 5th-2 out, onepcd* 3
Also: 39 Ceasars Reign (4), 8 Into The Clan (5), Nicholls Cross (6), 29 Tap Practice (7), Cottage Counsel (8), Bart Eile (pu), Freestyler (ro), Cappaduff (f), Kabwee Star (pu), Hilltop Duke (pu), What A Storm (pu)
14 ran. 3l, 10l, 20l, ½l, 3l, 10l, 20l. SP 6-4.

58 - Maiden 5yo II

28 **Waitnow [16]** ....G Elliott 1
cls 4th 5 out, ld & lft clr last
Bramble Wood*cls 3rd 5 out, wknd & lft 2nd last* 2
Bothar Fada*nvr dang, t.o.* 3
Also: Templemartin (ur), Just Hold On (f), Apollodorus (ur), Ard Na Gaoithe (pu), Manver (ur), 39 Westcourt (pu), 14 Kilcaw (f), Swan Point (pu), Blasket Sound (pu), Glacial King (pu), 28 Bracker [14] (f)
14 ran. 25l, dist. SP 5-1.

59 - Open Lightweight

24¹ **Flashing Steel [30]**....................P Fenton 1
disp til ld 6 out, drew clr frm 2 out, comf
30² **Life Of A King [22]***prog to chs wnr 3 out, btn frm nxt* 2
Oh So Grumpy [14]*chsd wnr 5 out-3 out, wknd* 3
Also: 16¹ Clonrosh Slave [12] (4), 30 Lislary Lad [11] (5), Barna Lad (6), Cahills Hill (pu), Killiney Graduate (pu), 24 Emarrceevess (pu), Strata Ridge (pu), The H'penny Marvel (pu), 30 Mischievous Andy (pu), 30 Borrismore Flash (pu), Famous Stout (pu), Irish Stout (pu), Harveysland (pu), Crowded House (f), Where's Sam (pu), 36 Martin de Porres (pu), 36 Pats Farewell (pu)
20 ran. 20l, dist, 5l, 4l, dist. SP 2-5.

60 - Mares Maiden 7yo+ I

Strong Dream [17] ....A Coyle 1
ld 5th, made rest, styd on well flat
33 **Proud Princess [13]***chsd wnr 3 out, no imp nxt* 2
Ballynagussaun [13]*chsd ldrs, onepcd frm 3 out* 3
Also: Ferriters Pub [12] (4), 6 Trimmer Lady [11] (5), Fortunes Cast (6), 10 Lady Of Means (7), 33 Clonfert Sue (8), Hows She Going (f), Cappagh Glen (ro), 33 Mullaghea Lass (pu), Dysart Abbey (f), 6 Rock On Rosies (pu), Penny Bug (pu), 26 Buxom Orlov (pu), 33 Buzz About (pu), Trembles Choice (pu), Areyouthereyet (pu)
18 ran. 10l, 1l, 2l, 3l, 12l, 20l, 12l. SP 5-2.

61 - Mares Maiden 7yo+ II

37 **Yes Boss [18]**....................S McGonagle 1
w.w. prog to ld aft 3 out, styd on well
32 **Push Gently [14]***chsd ldrs, styd on onepcd frm 2 out* 2
26 **Borreeva [13]***chsd ldrs, styd on onepcd frm 2 out* 3
Also: Dusty Rose [11] (4), Codology [10] (5), Kings Alibi (6), 36 Hasty Hours (7), Eadie (f), Cynical Wit (ur), 33 Beetalot (pu), Flashy Leader (pu), Young Bebe (pu), 6 Glistening Waters (f), 32 Josalady (pu), Brennan For Audits (pu), Why Emerald (pu), Full Holiday (ur), Hayestown Hope (ur)
18 ran. 6l, 4l, 6l, 4l, 6l, 30l. SP 7-4.

62 - Mares Lightweight I

41¹ **Slavica [20]** ....J Shaw 1
prom, ld 3 out, rdn & styd on wll
9 **Upshepops [19]***prom, ev ch 2 out, no ext flat* 2
13 **Tack Room Lady [18]***prom, ev ch 2 out, no ext flat* 3
Also: 26 Ballinaclash Pride (4), No One Knows (5), Whocantellya (pu), Rejmas (pu), Key Of The Nile (pu), 37 Royal Star (pu), 45 Lipstick Lady (pu), 37 Arctic Treasure (pu), 32 Haveafewmanners (pu), Top Flight Travel (pu)
13 ran. 2l, 1½l, 20l, dist. SP 7-4.

63 - Mares Lightweight II

30 **Maid For Dancing [20]** ....R Fowler 1
prog to ld 4 out, easily
15³ **Molls Choice [17]***chsd wnr 2 out, no imp aft* 2
21 **Aylesbury Beau [17]***chsd ldrs, kpt on onepcd frm 2 out* 3
Also: 32 Gerrys Delight (4), The Executrix (pu), Rachels Plan (su), Bold Irene (pu), Ring Mam (pu), Athas Liath (pu), I Love To Fly (pu), 15² No Swap (pu), Crows Cross (f), Raheen Cross (pu)
13 ran. 2l, 1l, dist. SP 6-4.
Winner subsequently disaqulified - inelgible to run in the race.

64 - Maiden 6yo I

3 **Old Decency [19]........................A Martin** 1
prom, ld apr 2 out, comf
42³ **Valley Tingo [16]***prom, ev ch 2 out, sn no ext* 2
28 **Ollies Boy [11]***nvr dang, tk 3rd flat* 3
Also: Johnstheman (4), Tullibardniceneasy (5), Ballyday Step (6), 28 Master Finbar (7), Jorodec (ur), Clearly Visible (f), Sweetmount Lad (pu), Cash Flow (f), Broad Valley (pu), 17 Knockadooma (pu), 29 Spikes The Man (pu), 29 Colemans River (f), Gee Thanks (ur)
16 ran. 2l, 15l, 5l, 15l, 2l, 4l. SP 4-6.

65 - Maiden 6yo II

Royal Oasis [17]........................G Elliott 1
cls up, ld apr 2 out, styd on well
43 **Colmans Hatch [15]***prom, ev ch 2 out, no ext* 2
Hum 'N' Haw [14]*chsd ldrs, onepcd frm 2 out* 3
Also: Wild Buck [13] (4), 23 Awalkintheclouds [11] (5), 29 Stelinjo (6), Brother Day (7), Forgoodnessjake VI (pu), Berts Cabin (ur), Castle Glow (pu), Sweet Perk (f), Kinnefad King (pu), Carnmore Supreme (ur), Buck River (f), Skidrow River (ur), The Crazy Chick (pu)
16 ran. 5l, 2l, 1½l, 6l, 20l, dist. SP 4-1.

66 - Maiden 6yo III

Little Minute [17]........................A Martin 1
made all, comf
28 **Crunchy Nut [15]***chsd wnr 4 out, no imp frm 2 out* 2
11 **Vice Captain [13]***chsd ldrs, onepcd frm 2 out* 3
Also: 28 Drumlongfield [10] (4), Sweet Castlehyde (5), Some Man (6), 32 Pingo Sloo (pu), Laras Boy (pu), Sir Larry (pu), Shes Bizarre (f), Jolly Jape (pu), 42 Coopers Clan (pu), Na Moilltear (pu), Altobrook (pu), Irregular Planting (pu), Buck And A Half (f)
16 ran. 3l, 6l, 10l, 15l, 8l. SP 5-1.

EAST DOWN
Tyrella
Saturday February 1st
GOOD TO SOFT

67 - Winners Of Two

Some View [18]........................A Martin 1
hld up, prog 4 out, chal & ld last, hld on
It Ain't Easy [18]*lft in ld hlfwy, hdd last, rallied und pres flat* 2
28¹ **Arrienzio [15]***prog to disp 4 out, rdn & btn aft 2 out* 3
Also: Hiltonstown Lass (4D), Chariot Del (4), McClatchey (5), Captains View (6), Knocans Pride (7), Thefirstone (pu), Copper End (pu), 27² Miller King (f)
11 ran. ½l, 5l, dist, nk, 15l, 10l, 2l. SP 7-1.

68 - Maiden 5 & 6yo

Demoniac (Fr) [15]........................A Martin 1
made all, styd on wll frm 2 out
28² **Rock On Bud [13]***lft 2nd hlfwy, chal 2 out, sn no ext* 2
G I Joe*nvr dang* 3
Also: Ireby VI (ur), Opening Quote (ur)
5 ran. 2l, dist. SP 2-1.

69 - Open Lightweight

Gale Griffin [19]........................L Lennon 1
prom, ld 6 out, in cmmnd whn lft clr last
62 **Arctic Treasure [16]***rear, styd on & lft 2nd last, no dang* 2
Bonquist*nvr dang, t.o.* 3
Glenshane Pass*ld to 6 out, wknd, t.o.* 3
Also: 30³ Only One (ro), 34 Bathurst [17] (f)
6 ran. 6l, dist, dd-ht. SP 5-2.

70 - Maiden 5yo

It'snotsimple [12]........................R Marrion 1
chsd ldr, ld 5 out, drvn out
Ballindante [11]*n.j.w. chsd wnr 3 out, no ext flat* 2
Also: Hi Jamie (f), McAuley Jo (pu), Buckie Thistle (f)
5 ran. 2l. SP 8-1.

71 - Maiden 6yo

Willy Wee [15]........................W Ewing 1
chsd ldng pair, disp 4 out, ld & lft clr 2 out
Cardinals Folly*no dang, 5th & no ch whn lft 2nd 2 out* 2
Ngala*no dang, 6th & no ch whn lft 3rd 2 out* 3
Also: Tullyallenstar (pu), Windmill Star (bd), Cool Swallow (f), The Bleary Flyer (ur), Bannagh Mor (f), Risk-A-Dinge (pu), Crottys Bridge (f)
10 ran. Dist, 3l. SP 2-1.

72 - Maiden 7yo+

Hi Dixie [16]........................A Fleming 1
chsd ldng pair, ld aft 2 out, sn clr
Listrakelt [12]*rear, styd on frm 2 out, nvr nrr* 2
Half Scotch [12]*rear, styd on frm 2 out, nvr nrr* 3
Also: Tyrella Clear View [11] (4), 36 La Mancha Boy [10] (5), Bright Lad (6), 31³ Castleviganlady (7), Welshmans Canyon (8), Rovet (pu), Scotts Cross (pu), Iveagh Lady (pu), Damolly Rose (ur), 36 Laurelvale (f), Foyle Boreen (f), Loch Saland (ur), Longmore Boy (ur), 35 Trimfold (pu)
17 ran. 10l, 1l, 2l, 4l, 30l, 5l, dist. SP 2-1.

UNITED FOXHOUNDS
Carrigtwohill
Sunday February 2nd
GOOD TO SOFT

73 - Confined Maiden I

7 **Supreme Odds [15]........................J McNamara** 1
prom, ld 4 out, styd on well
Looks Like Trouble [14]*chsd wnr 3 out, no imp flat* 2
Rio Star [13]*chsd ldrs, onepcd frm 2 out* 3
Also: Irish Rover [10] (4), Bayloughbess (5), 43 Call Me Paris (6), 6 Marys Friend (7), 43 Phar Desert (8), 7 Big Spender (9), 7 Princess Diga (pu), Gale Tan (f), Persian (pu), Dexter Lass (pu), Carhoo Surprise (pu), 12 Leamlara Jet (pu)
15 ran. 3l, 2l, 8l. SP 5-1.

74 - Confined Maiden II

53³ **Big Bo [15]........................M Budds** 1
prom, ld 2 out, drvn out
Gaelic Glen [14]*chsd ldrs, ev ch last, no ext flat* 2
54 **Glenselier [13]***chsd ldrs, onepcd apr last* 3
Also: Bitofabreeze (4), 11 Master Jake (5), 43 Minstrels Quay (ur), 12 Clongeel Lord (pu), 11 Icantsay (pu), 46³ Lady Of Iron (pu), 7 Frightening Child (pu), Moss Pac (f), Shady Prince (pu), Curley Gale (ur), 7 Geragh Road (ro), 52 Woodfield Boss (f)
15 ran. 2l, 3l, 20l. SP 5-2.

75 - Winners Of One

11¹ **Mountain Hall [21]........................T Lombard** 1
ld 5 out, clr last, ran on well
41 **Wejem [19]***chsd ldrs, hrd rdn 2 out, styd on* 2
49² **Lucky Town [19]***prog to join wnr 4 out, btn apr last* 3
Also: 41² Gaye Bard [13] (4), Pearl Dante [11] (5), 41 John's Right (6), 49 Garramoss (7), Magnum Express (pu), 45¹ Queenofclubs (pu), 41 Round Tower Lady (pu), Takeithandy (pu), 21 Carolines Minstrel (pu), Prudence Sarn (f), 13 The Pulpit (pu), 27 Trimmer Princess (pu), 13 Fethard Orchid (pu), Roman Gale (pu), 41 Parish Ranger (pu)
18 ran. 4l, ½l, 20l. SP 3-1.

76 - Maiden 5yo I

Perky Lad [18]........................T Nagle 1
prom, ld 2 out, hld on well flat
22³ **Dashing Buck [18]***cls up, chal 2 out, just hld* 2
8 **Harbour Leader [17]***chsd ldrs, ran on wll apr last, nrst fin* 3
Also: 57 Ceasars Reign [14] (4), Gortroe Guy [12] (5), Newmarket Cheddar (pu), Parsons Green Boy (pu), Zarante (pu), Johnny Claw (pu), 40 Clonageera (pu), 40 Identify In Crisis (pu), 3 Jack Dory (f), Pure Air (ref), 47 Green Hills Glory (pu), 47 Desert Melody (f)
15 ran. Hd, 2l, 8l. SP 3-1.

77 - Maiden 5yo II

8 **Wishing William [17]** .... **P Crowley** 1
cls up, ld 3 out, sn clr, rdn out flat ....
40³ **Irish Frolic [16]***chsd wnr 3 out, kpt on onepcd frm nxt* 2
Supreme Citizen [13]*chsd ldrs, onepcd aft 3 out* 3
Also: Dinan (4), Coalquay Coup (5), Supreme Shamrock (pu), Dingdust (pu), Leap Year Man (pu), 39 Arthur (f), 40 Just A Playboy (pu), 22 My Uncle Batt (f), For Paul (pu), Bumper To Bumper (pu), Briary Boy (pu), 14 Prestige Lord (f)
15 ran. 4l, 8l, 20l. SP 5-1.

78 - Open Lightweight

27³ **Ozier Hill [23]** .... **J Berry** 1
disp 4 out, hrd drvn to ld flat ....
51¹ **Deep Heritage [23]***disp 4 out til no ext und pres flat* .. 2
41 **Derry's Diamond [21]***chsd ldrs, styd on wll frm 2 out* 3
Also: 13 Ashton Court [17] (4), Mack A Day [15] (5), 26² Silent Sneeze [12] (6), Shirgale (7), 37 Trimmer Wonder (8), Okdo (9), Sumakano (10), Looking Ahead (11), Quayside Buoy (pu), Contera (pu), 27 Slaney Goodness (pu), Albert's Fancy (pu), Slaney Encore (pu)
16 ran. 1l, 4l, 10l. SP 3-1.

79 - Mares Maiden 5yo I

38³ **Via Del Quatro [15]** .... **T Lombard** 1
prom, ld 2 out, hld on well ....
48 **Rock On Lord [15]***chal 2 out, just hld flat* 2
48 **Goolds Opal [14]***prom, onepcd frm 2 out* 3
Also: 38 Donna (pu), 19 Tonmarie Chance (pu), Sup A Brandy (pu), Cnoc-Breac (f), 8 Hazy Mist (pu), Mary Marry Me (pu), Little Roo (pu), Nissan Star (pu)
2 ran. Nk, 3l. SP 2-1.

80 - Mares Maiden 5yo II

48 **Fair Fontaine [16]** .... **J Moloney** 1
w.w. prog to ld aft 2 out, sn clr ....
Beehive Queen [12]*ld 3 out til aft nxt, no ext* 2
Ardfert Minstrel [11]*chsd ldrs, onepcd frm 2 out* 3
Also: Bawn Beag (4), Craggy Island (f), Little Santa (bd), Fair Ophelia (pu), Catrionas Lady (pu), 48 Just Be Lucky (f), Steady Woman (pu)
10 ran. 8l, 3l, 8l. SP 5-4.

81 - Maiden 6yo I

23² **Belhabour [18]** .... **E Bolger** 1
ld 5 out, v easily ....
O'Donnell Abu [12]*chsd wnr 3 out, no ch aft* 2
17² **Short Circuit [10]***chsd ldrs, onepcd & no ch frm 3 out* 3
Also: Island Echo [10] (4), 43 Max Lad (5), 42 Poachers Lamp (6), Goolds Diamond (f), 38² Black Fountain (pu), Bosco's Touch (pu), Mickeys Dream (pu)
10 ran. 8l, 6l, nk. SP 7-4.

82 - Maiden 6yo II

3² **Hugo Henry [15]** .... **D Murphy** 1
made all, hrd prssd flat, styd on well ....
Mr Freeman [14]*prog to chal aft last, no ext nr fin* 2
Johnny's Echo [14]*prog to chal aft last, no ext nr fin.* .. 3
Also: Shining Leader (4), 42 Remmy Cruz (5), Metro Fashion (ur), 12 The Big Fella (pu), 65 Skidrow River (f), Timmy Tuff (pu), 17 First Mohikin (pu)
10 ran. 2l, nk, dist. SP 6-4.

WEST WATERFORD
Tallow
Sunday February 9th
SOFT

83 - Confined Maiden

Knock Leader [16] .... **E Gallagher** 1
prom, ld 3 out, comf ....
Teads Boreen [13]*chsd wnr 2 out, no imp apr last* 2
Robin Of Loxley*nvr dang* 3
Also: Hillview Lass (4), 10 Sea Breta (5), 10 Mandoora (6), Miss Metal (7), Gleeming Lace (8), 42 Major Bill (9), Gale Dante (pu), Running Solo (pu), Regal Gossip (pu), Con's Nurse (pu), Classie Claire (pu), 19 Dereenavurrig (pu), 46² Kilcannon Sophie (pu), Erinsborough (pu), Noras Gale (pu)
18 ran. 3l, 15l, dist. SP 5-4.

84 - Maiden 5yo I

57³ **All But [18]** .... **B Hamilton** 1
made all, clr 3 out, unchal ....
77 **Bumper To Bumper [14]***chsd wnr 4 out, no imp aft* ... 2
57 **Freestyler [10]***nvr dang* 3
Also: 8 Inch Champion (4), 58 Manver (5), 40 In The Stocking (6), 8 Coole Abbey (7), 76 Desert Melody (8), 76 Zarante (9), Ahead Of The Posse (10), 58 Glacial King (pu), 47 Lars On Tour (pu), 39 As Sharp Again (f), All A Joke (pu), 47 Charleys Run (ro), Dawdante (pu)
16 ran. 10l, 15l, 10l. SP 2-1.

85 - Maiden 5yo II

76³ **Harbour Leader [19]** .... **E Gallagher** 1
hld up, prog to ld apr 2 out, sn clr, comf ....
40² **Monteba [12]***prom, ld 4 out til apr 2 out, no ch wth wnr aft* 2
Cabille*t.o.* 3
Also: 47 Kilcully Jake (4), 57 Hilltop Duke (f), 50 Mr Goodbye (pu), Clashbridane (pu), 20 Running Wolf (pu), 77 My Uncle Batt (f), Jolly Paddy (pu), 40 Springford (pu), Jolly Man (pu), 14 Roughshod (ur), 58³ Bothar Fada (pu), 76 Pure Air (pu), Ballygowan Beauty (pu)
16 ran. 20l, dist, 2l. SP 2-1.

86 - Maiden 6yo I

I'll Say Nothing [19] .... **R Flavin** 1
trckd ldrs, ld apr last, sn clr, tired nr fin ....
Corkers Flame [16]*chsd ldrs, styd on well apr last, nrst fin* 2
50² **Shenanigans [14]***chsd ldrs, onepcd frm 2 out* 3
Also: 65² Colmans Hatch [12] (4), 82 The Big Fella (5), 50 Hanigans Bridge (6), Playmore (pu), West Trix VI (ro), Jolly Lad (pu), 82 Remmy Cruz (pu), Doolans Stand (pu), 74 Minstrels Quay (ur), 7³ Supreme Forward (pu)
13 ran. 1l, 4l, 6l. SP 5-4.

87 - Maiden 6yo II

Cromogue Minstrel [17] .... **R Lee** 1
prom, ld 5 out, clr 3 out, easily ....
23 **Matchmaker Seamus [11]***chsd ldrs, onepcd frm 3 out* 2
81 **Island Echo***nvr dang* 3
Also: 3 Oscars Link (4), 74 Master Jake (5), 42 Mineral Al (f), 50 Grey Horizon (f), Foreshore Man (f), Flashing Rock (pu), 43 Major Above All (pu), 82 First Mohikin (pu), 64² Valley Tingo (f), 81² O'Donnell Abu (pu)
13 ran. 15l, 20l, 1l. SP 4-1.

88 - Open Lightweight

21¹ **An Oon Iss An Owl [21]** .... **R Flavin** 1
prog to ld aft 3 out, sn in cmmnd ....
62² **Upshepops [18]***prom, disp 3 out, sn hdd & onepcd* ... 2
75 **Parish Ranger [16]***prom, disp 3 out, sn hdd & btn* 3
Also: 9 Warning Call [14] (4), 49 Shesadinger [12] (5), 44 Master Kemal (6), 49 Sharoujack (pu), 51 Waterloo King [27] (pu), Princess Bavard (pu)
9 ran. 3l, 6l, 4l. SP 6-4.

89 - Winners Of One

60¹ **Strong Dream [18]** .... **A Coyle** 1
prom, disp whn lft alone 2 out ....
Also: 3¹ Hyelord (pu), Lordinthesky (pu), 75 The Pulpit (pu), 23¹ Brostaig Ort (ur), 49 Prayon Parson (pu), 62³ Tack Room Lady (f), 55 Silver Buckle (pu), Pintex (pu), 4¹ Royal Barge (f)
10 ran. SP 2-1.

90 - Mares Maiden 5 & 6yo I

64 **Tullibardniceneasy [16]** .... **A Coyle** 1
alwys prom, ld 2 out, styd on und pres...............
Bay Lough [16]*prom, chal last, just hld*............. 2
45 **Macklette [13]***chsd ldrs, onepcd frm 2 out*........... 3
Also: 46 Greenflag Princess [13] (4), 74 Lady Of Iron [10] (5), 50 Papuite (pu), Orafeno (pu), Marys Delight (pu), Over The Glen (pu), Happy Hula Girl (pu), Kamatra Eyre (pu), Prettymaid (pu), Princess Thyne (pu), 46 Electric Can (pu), 48 Brinny Princess (pu), Northcha Lady (f), Onmeown (pu), 45³ Right Then Rosie (pu), 33 Billie's Mate (pu)
19 ran. 1l, 10l, hd. SP 3-1.

91 - Mares Maiden 5 & 6yo II

19² **Leaping Three [16]** .... **P Crowley** 1
w.w. prog to ld 2 out, sn clr ....
Zaffaran Run [13]*rear, styd on to chs wnr last, no imp flat*.. 2
48 **Ballyhest Fountain***t.o.*................................ 3
Also: 48 Ronkino (4), Mocklershill Lady (pu), 56 Black Fashion (pu), Lifes Treasure (f), Comely Maiden (pu), Barenises Rose (pu), 32 Ballyroe Hill (pu), Fools Courage (pu), Woodville Princess (pu), Munta (pu), Cottage Breeze (pu), Kinnahalla (pu), 1 Madam Aside (pu), 80 Craggy Island (pu), Wild Noble (pu)
18 ran. 8l, dist, dist. SP 7-4.

BRAY HARRIERS
Ashford
Sunday February 9th
GOOD TO SOFT

92 - Open Farmers

27 **Dennistownthriller [18]**................. **D Whelan** 1
made all, rdn out flat............................
59 **Harveysland [16]***lft 2nd 4 out, kpt on onepcd aft*...... 2
59 **Killiney Graduate [12]***nvr dang, lft 3rd 2 out*......... 3
Also: Stylish Stepper (4), 63 I Love To Fly (5), 55 Kilmisten Breeze (pu), Cloughan Boy (f), 59 Famous Stout (pu), Cute Agreement (pu), Ardent Spirit (ref), Killenagh Moss (pu), Glenroe Gal (f)
12 ran. 4l, 10l, dist, 1l. SP 5-4.

93 - Winners Of Two

55¹ **Haven't An Ocean [21]**.................... **J Berry** 1
hld up, prog to ld 3 out, in cmmnd whn lft clr last.......
36¹ **Dromod Point [19]***rear, styd on 2 out, lft 2nd last, clsng flat*.. 2
Lovable Outlaw [16]*nvr nrr* 3
Also: Impeccable Buck (f), 62 Royal Star (f), 58¹ Waitnow (f), 67 Miller King (f), 53¹ Rushing Waters (f), Native Blood VI (pu)
9 ran. 2l, 10l. SP 1-2.

94 - Maiden 5 & 6yo I

Hidden Hollow [16] .... **J P Berry** 1
cls up, ld 3 out, styd on well....................
Eddie [15]*cls up, chal whn mstks 2 out & last, no ext*.. 2
81 **Max Lad [14]***prom, onepcd frm 2 out*................ 3
Also: 29 Smiling Minstrel [11] (4), 66 Drumlongfield (5), Ballylennon Bounty (pu), 66 Sir Larry (pu), 55 Airecco (f), Dianas Son (pu), Rare House (pu), Annie Leap (pu), 65 Awalkintheclouds (pu), Magillen (pu)
13 ran. 4l, 1l, 10l. SP 6-1.

95 - Maiden 5 & 6yo II

64 **Spikes The Man [15]**.................. **J Dempsey** 1
hld up, prog 4 out, styd on frm last, ld nr fin ....
Frostbitten [15]*prom, ld 6 out, clr apr last, hdd nr fin* 2
Ringaheen [13]*chsd ldrs, onepcd frm 3 out*.......... 3
Also: 66 Coopers Clan [11] (4), Out Of Actons (f), 55 Back Withavengance (f), 65 Castle Glow (pu), 65 Kinnefad King (pu), Chas Randall (pu), Speedy O'Dee (pu), Whitestown Boy (pu), No Other Hill (f)
12 ran. Hd, 6l, 6l. SP 8-1.

96 - Mares Maiden I

61 **Beetalot [15]**......................... **D Valentine** 1
chsd ldr 5 out, styd on und pres to ld nr fin...........
61 **Codology [15]***ld 6 out, clr 4 out, wknd & hdd nr fin*.... 2
31 **Lady Sylvie [14]***prog 3 out, clsng whn blnd last, not rcvr*.. 3
Also: 60² Proud Princess [13] (4), 37 Melodic Lady [10] (5), 63 The Executrix (bd), 37 Porter Tastes Nice (pu), 60 Areyouthereyet (pu), Wunwabbitwun (pu), Royal Dilemma (f), Gales Fountain (pu), 61³ Borreeva (f), 63 Rachels Plan (pu), Pepsa Morfee (pu), 65 Sweet Perk (pu), Legganhall (f), Bellas Fashion VI (f), Miner's Son (f)
18 ran. 1l, 2l, 2l, 10l. SP 2-1.

97 - Mares Maiden II

55 **Miss Lurgan [16]**.................... **J McNamara** 1
prom, ld 4 out, styd on well, comf....................
61² **Push Gently [13]***prog to chs wnr 3 out, no imp nxt*.... 2
33 **Woodbinesandroses [11]***ld to 4 out, sn outpcd*...... 3
Also: Kilmurray Buck (4), 60³ Ballynagussaun (5), Spritly Lady (f), 61 Young Bebe (ur), Pede Gale (pu), Mauras Girl (f), Over The Tavern (pu), Killaligan Kim (f), 33 Can She Do It (pu), Miss Barnamire (pu), 64 Broad Valley (f), 62 Lipstick Lady (pu), 63 Gerrys Delight (pu), 63 Raheen Cross (f), Pierpoints Choice (pu)
18 ran. 6l, 4l, 10l, 20l. SP 4-1.

98 - Mares Maiden III

45² **Oriental Beauty**......................... **J P Berry** 1
bhnd, lft 2nd 4 out, no ch whn lft alone last...........
31 **Make A Move [15]***ld 6 out, lft clr 4 out, wll clr whn f last, rmntd*.. 2
Also: 46 Fireblends (f), 62 Key Of The Nile (pu), Shanes Bay (ref), Catch The Mouse (pu), Be My Mot (f), 56 Mariners Quest (pu), Sky Rainbow (f), 61 Kings Alibi (f), 32 Macken Money (f), Davids Pride (pu), Supreme Gold (pu), Imlistening (pu), Lost Coin (pu), 55 Roseland (f), Corshanna River (pu), Nervous Kate (f)
18 ran. Dist. SP 6-1.

99 - Maiden 7yo+ I

55² **Bobbit Back On [16]** .... **J Nash** 1
prom, ld 5 out, lft clr 2 out, styd on ....
Bourbon County [13]*chsd ldrs, btn whn lft 2nd 2 out*.. 2
35 **Knockanoran [11]***chsd ldrs, no prog frm 3 out*....... 3
Also: 59 Cahills Hill [11] (4), The Moderator (pu), 18² Croi (pu), 56 Lucky Statement (pu), Docummins (ur), 56 Percusionist (f), Almauritia (f), Regular Beat (pu), 56 Forabby (pu), Stoneyacre (pu), 56 Mr Balda (pu), Snowberry River (pu), Change The Script (f), 34 Herb Superb (f), 56 Donals Choice (ur), Mancha Boy (f)
19 ran. 6l, 6l, ½l. SP 4-6.

100 - Maiden 7yo+ II

52² **Royal Arctic [15]**.......................... **P Kelly** 1
hld up, prog to ld 3 out, all out.....................
35 **Grafy Hill [14]***prom, ld 5 out til mstk 3 out, kpt on* 2
55 **Shillelagh Oak [14]***chsd ldrs, styd on wll flat* 3
Also: 55 Louis de Palmer (pu), 55 Clare To Here (pu), 50³ The Territorian (f), 55 The Bug Hill (pu), 27 Tuskar Flop (pu), 52 Shimano (pu), 34 Nelpha (pu), 35 Ordain (pu), Sail On Sam (f), Benalf (pu), Gradle (pu), Bit Of A Character (f), 35 Moynalvy Future VI (pu), Galloping Giggs (pu)
17 ran. 2l, 1l. SP 5-4.

101 - Nomination

Alimar [14] .... **A Evans** 1
ld 5 out, sn clr, easily.............................
Siamsa Brae*no ch wth wnr frm 3 out*............... 2
Paps Last Hope*no ch wth wnr frm 3 out*.............. 3
Also: 59 Martin de Porres (4), 66 Laras Boy (ur), Slow Beet (pu), Ashplant (pu), 59 Strata Ridge (pu), Arctic Party (pu)
9 ran. Dist, 4l, 10l. SP 4-6.

STONEHALL HARRIERS
Askeaton

Sunday February 9th
GOOD

102 - Confined Maiden

Oneofourown [15]......................B Hassett 1
prog 2 out, ld aft last, drvn out.........................
23 **Court Amber [14]***prom, ld 3 out till aft last, no ext.....* 2
Ballybeggan Lady [11]*chsd ldrs, onepcd frm 2 out....* 3
Also: 43 Tom Deely (4), 52 Mitidebe (5), Donna King (pu), 22 Livin Joy (ro), Villa Alba (pu), Scallybuck (pu)
9 ran. 2l, 10l, 8l. SP 4-1.

103 - Maiden 5yo I

Doctor Darling [17]......................D Quinn 1
cls up, chal last, styd on wll to ld flat.................
47 **Bavard Jet [15]***disp 4 out til hdd & no ext flat.........* 2
22² **Florida Light [14]***disp 4 out til hdd & wknd flat.........* 3
Also: 76 Ceasars Reign [11] (4), Loslomos (5), Titatium (6), 47 Blacknock (7), Glin Castle (pu), 47³ Over Eager (f), Kissanes Pride (pu), Nineteenofive (pu), King Of Clare (pu), Duke Of Tulla (f)
13 ran. 4l, 2l, 7l. SP 8-1.

104 - Maiden 5yo II

39 **Bricanmore [17]......................J McNamara** 1
trckd ldrs, lft in ld 5 out, clr 2 out, styd on well.........
39² **Deejaydee [14]***chsd wnr apr 3 out, no imp frm nxt.....* 2
Lakefield Rambler [10]*chsd ldrs apr 3 out, sn no imp* 3
Also: Cast No Shadow (pu), 76 Parsons Green Boy (pu), Anodfromalord (co), Caher Society (ro), 76 Johnny Claw (pu), Court Ramble (pu), 40 Foolsandtheirmoney (pu), Telecom Affair (pu), Suave (pu)
12 ran. 6l, 12l. SP Evens.

105 - Open Lightweight

Risk Of Thunder [26]......................E Bolger 1
hld up, prog to ld 2 out, easily.........................
I Haven't A Buck [20]*ld to 2 out, no ch wth wnr aft....* 2
Light Argument [17]*chsd ldr, onepcd aft 3 out........* 3
Also: Fools With Horses [14] (4), Granny Bid (5), Brunswick Maid (pu), 60 Dysart Abbey (pu)
7 ran. 4l, 8l, 6l. SP 1-5.

106 - Maiden 6yo+ I

Cathair Neidin [17]......................J McNamara 1
prom, ld 3 out, sn clr.................................
64 **Johnstheman [13]***chsd wnr aft 3 out, no imp nxt.....* 2
Dare To Deel [10]*chsd ldrs, onepcd frm 3 out.........* 3
Also: 65 Buck River (4), Call Me Ogan (f), 43 Never Heard (pu), Twilight Hour (pu), Willbrook (pu), Mr Campus (f), 29 Court Thyne (pu), Mirromark (pu), 17 Clon Caw (f), The Slippery Bear (pu), Tomasins Choice (pu), Charming Moss (pu), General Ari (pu), 81 Bosco's Touch (pu), Sweeney Lee (pu)
18 ran. 12l, 10l, 6l. SP 2-1.

107 - Maiden 6yo+ II

27 **Dead Reckoning [17]......................E Bolger** 1
chsd ldrs, chal apr last, styd on to ld nr fin............
Ecologic [17]*prom, ld 3 out, hrd rdn & hdd nr fin.....* 2
52³ **Sarcoid [14]***chsd ldrs, onepcd frm 2 out...........* 3
Also: 34³ Charlie Hawes [14] (4), 34 Carnmore House [11] (5), 82² Mr Freeman (6), Independence Day (7), 54 Baybuck (8), Some Swop (pu), The Works (pu), Churchtown Drum (pu), Belville Pond (f), 53 River Wild (ur), 59 Barna Lad (pu), Terry McCann (pu), 66 Jolly Jape (pu), Brickhill Lad (pu)
17 ran. ½l, 8l, ½l. SP 5-1.

108 - Winners Of One

50¹ **Magical Approach [19]......................D Costello** 1
cls up, ld 3 out, sn clr, comf.........................
21² **Givemeyourhand [14]***rear, styd on 2 out, tk 2nd flat..* 2
Shareza River [13]*rear, kpt on onepcd frm 2 out.....* 3
Also: 42¹ Old Trafford [13] (4), Runabout [12] (5), 56 Big Murt (pu), 21 Starlight Fountain (f), 49 Digacre (pu), 63² Molls Choice (pu), 26 Don't Waste It (pu)
10 ran. 10l, 4l, 1l. SP 3-1.

109 - Mares Maiden 5 & 6yo I

Thadys Remedy [16]......................R Hurley 1
chal & lft in ld 3 out, styd on well aft..................
33 **Harvest Time [15]***ld 5 out til mstk 3 out, no ext apr last.......................................* 2
33² **Rosetown Girl [12]***chsd ldrs, onepcd frm 3 out.......* 3
Also: My New Merc [12] (4), Derrygallon Fancy (5), 62 Top Flight Travel (6), 45 Glitter Girl (7), Lucky Fifteen (f), 33 Springtime Mist (pu), 65 Carnmore Supreme (pu), 65 Forgoodnessjake VI (pu), Serenas Serenade (pu)
12 ran. 3l, 8l, ½l. SP 5-1.

110 - Mares Maiden 5 & 6yo II

25 **Snugville Sally [18]......................D Costello** 1
prom, ld 4 out, styd on well aft.........................
Iona Flyer [14]*chsd wnr 2 out, no imp...............* 2
Ardnataggle [13]*chsd ldrs, onepcd frm 2 out.........* 3
Also: 31 Scklepp [11] (4), Strong Wishes (5), Pharmacy Trio (6), Manley Girl (7), 45 Shuil Flossy (pu), Gayley Gale (su), Boarding Society (pu), 66 Sweet Castlehyde (f), The Hairy Lord (pu)
12 ran. 7l, 2l, 6l. SP 6-4.

COUNTY DOWN
Loughbrickland
Saturday February 15th
SOFT

111 - Mares Maiden 5yo

92 **Cute Agreement [15]......................A Martin** 1
chsd ldrs, chal & lft clr last...........................
70² **Ballindante [13]***chsd ldrs, 4th & btn whn lft 2nd last..* 2
98 **Macken Money [15]***prom, chal & f last, rmntd........* 3
Also: Lan-Paula (pu), Lady Zaffaran (pu), 32 Dowhatyouhavetodo (f), Principal Peace (f), 27 Musical Waves (f), Blue Alliance (pu), Forever Grey (ur), 70 Buckie Thistle (pu)
11 ran. 6l, dist. SP 2-1.

112 - Winners Of Two I

Sharimage [18]......................P Graffin 1
chsd ldrs, jnd ldr 4 out, ld apr last, ran on wll..........
Uncle Art [16]*ld 5 out, jnd nxt, hdd & no ext apr last..* 2
Raleagh Muggins [15]*chsd ldrs, onepcd frm 3 out.....* 3
Also: Stanley Steamer [14] (4), 69 Only One [10] (5), 71 Windmill Star (6), 71³ Ngala (7), 67 Thefirstone (8), Flodart (pu), Sametoyou (pu), 32¹ Sister Nora (f), Mandingo (pu), Mystic Rose (f), Roselynhill (pu), 71 The Bleary Flyer (ur), Mysterious Beau (pu), 59 Irish Stout (f), Secret Door (f), Drumrock Lady (f)
19 ran. 4l, 3l, 3l, 10l, 6l, 6l, 8l. SP 6-1.

113 - Winners Of Two II

27 **Manhattan Prince [18]......................L Gracey** 1
chsd ldrs, chal 2 out, drvn to ld flat...................
Hilton Mill [18]*chsd ldrs, ld 2 out, hrd rdn & hdd flat..* 2
71¹ **Willy Wee [13]***prom, ld 3 out-nxt, sn btn............* 3
Also: Floruceva (ur), Bridge End (f), 37 Chene Rose (pu), Golden Start (pu), 71 Cool Swallow (pu), Bobby Blazer (pu), Three Town Rock (pu), The Convincer (pu), River Magnet (f), Morans Forge (pu), Glenalla Bella (pu), Serious Note (pu), 32 Glenpine (pu), Drumiller Hill Lad (pu), Emmas Gamble (pu)
18 ran. ½l, 12l. SP 5-1.

114 - Maiden 5yo

Major Sponsor [15]......................B Hamilton 1
made all, clr 3 out, styd on.............................
28 **Zaffield [12]***chsd wnr 3 out, no imp.................* 2
Flanaghans Way*nvr dang, t.o.........................* 3
Also: Tullamore (pu), Righteye (pu), Lord Basil (f), Picton (f), 58 Swan Point (f), Ballydavid (pu), Ballymenagh (pu), Track O'Profit (pu)
11 ran. 6l, dist. SP 5-2.

115 - Open Lightweight I

Funny Ye Know [19]....................**P Graffin** 1
trckd ldr, ld & lft clr last....................
The Boolya [18]*chsd ldrs, btn whn lft 2nd last, styd on*
34 **Wilbar [17]***chsd ldrs, lft 3rd last, styd on*.............. 3
Also: 69[3] Glenshane Pass (4), Ballywoodock VI (pu), 30 The Committee [18] (f), 37[3] Missing Lady (pu), Captains Bar (pu), Karen's Leader (pu), 92 Famous Stout (pu), Neely (pu)
11 ran. 2l, 2l, dist. SP 5-1.

116 - Open Lightweight II

61[1] **Yes Boss [20]** ....**C McGivern** 1
trckd ldrs, ld 3 out, rdn clr apr last....................
Mr Five Wood [17]*prog to chal 2 out, sn rdn & onepcd*
Captain Brandy [17]*prog to chal 2 out, sn onepcd*... 3
Also: Colin's Hatch [15] (4), 69[2] Arctic Treasure (5), Lacken Beau (pu), 69[1] Gale Griffin (pu), 27 Find Out More (ur), Rias Rascal (pu), 67 Hiltonstown Lass (pu)
10 ran. 4l, 1l, 6l, dist. SP 6-1.

117 - Maiden 6yo I

Anns Display [15].....................**I Buchanan** 1
made most, hdd 2 out, ld last, ran on well.............
68[2] **Rock On Bud [14]***lft 2nd 5 out, ld 2 out-last, no ext flat*
Newtown Road*b.d. 4th, rmntd, t.o*.................. 3
Also: King Sol (pu), Carnmoon (pu), Not Found Yet (pu), Capail Mor (pu), 29 Willie B Brave (f), Bluagale (pu), Pharbrook Lad (pu), 64 Colemans River (pu), Moses Man (pu), Barnagan (pu), Strong Time (f)
14 ran. 4l, dist. SP 5-1.

118 - Maiden 6yo II

68[3] **G I Joe [14]**...........................**P Buchanan** 1
bhnd, lft 2nd 3 out, ld aft nxt, clr & u.r. last, rmntd......
66 **Some Man***bhnd, kpt on to 2nd aft 2 out, lft ev ch last, wknd*.. 2
Oneedin Glory*ld to 4 out, lft in ld nxt, wknd rpdly & hdd aft 2 out*.. 3
Also: Dancing Mike (pu), 94 Drumlongfield (f), Castlewood Lodge (pu), 68 Ireby VI (pu), North City (pu), Panda Nova (pu), Pats Boreen (f), 29 Shuil Mor (pu)
11 ran. 6l, 10l. SP 16-1.

119 - Maiden 7yo+ I

Cebu Gale [14] ....**G Clugston** 1
prom, ld 2 out, kpt on..............................
Pauls Point [13]*chsd ldrs, styd on onepcd frm 2 out*.. 2
100 **Ordain [11]***chsd ldrs, styd on onepcd frm 2 out*...... 3
Also: 72 Longmore Boy (4), 72 Damolly Rose (pu), 59 Where's Sam (f), 36 Paddy Red (f), Wind Of Glory (pu), 27 Ossie Murphy (pu), 72 Iveagh Lady (pu), Danny Mann (pu), 72 Castlevigganlady (pu), 72 Rovet (pu), Florida Or Bust (pu), 32 Vermont River (f), Collooney Squire (pu), 67 Copper End (f), 34 Is This The One (su), Dernamay (pu)
19 ran. 2l, 4l, 4l. SP 3-1.

120 - Maiden 7yo+ II

35 **Christimatt [14]** ....**P Buchanan** 1
prog 3 out, ld aft last, styd on well....................
Desmond River [12]*ld 3 out til aft last, wknd*.......... 2
Ardbei*chsd ldrs, no imp frm 2 out*.................. 3
Also: 72[2] Listrakelt (4), Dawn Dieu (pu), Barchester (pu), Island Harriet (f), Tassagh Boy (bd), Greet The Greek [10] (pu), Emerald Breffni (f), You Said It (pu), Skinny Minnie (pu), Gold Leader (pu), 33[3] Maries Call (f), 34 Tom Haggard (pu), Cinq Frank (f), 72 Scotts Cross (pu), Dunturk View (pu)
18 ran. 4l, 10l, dist. SP 3-1.

IVEAGH HARRIERS
Maralin
Saturday February 22nd
SOFT

121 - Open Lightweight

78[2] **Deep Heritage [23]**.......................**E Bolger** 1
prog to ld 5 out, pshd out..........................
59 **Crowded House [21]***prog to chs wnr 3 out, rdn & kpt on well*.. 2
115[2] **The Boolya [20]***chsd ldrs, outpcd 4 out, styd on agn last*.. 3
Also: 30 Voldi [13] (4), 27 Annie's Arthur [12] (5), 116 Arctic Treasure [11] (6), 115 Glenshane Pass (7), 115 Ballywoodock VI (8), Runaco (pu)
9 ran. 2½l, 3l, 20l, 2l, 2l, 6l, dist. SP 2-5.

122 - Maiden 7yo+ I

72[3] **Half Scotch [15]** ....**A Sronge** 1
lft in ld 5 out, unchal..............................
Ash Brae*nvr dang, lft 2nd by dfctns* 2
69[3] **Bonquist***nvr dang, lft 3rd by dfctns*.................. 3
Also: Tip The Skip (4), The Golam (pu), 101 Martin de Porres (pu), Mannix (f), Highland Buck (pu), 59 Pats Farewell (f), 120 Barchester (pu), 120 Dunturk View (pu), 35[3] Inactualfact (co), Mourne Miner (pu), The Majors Hollow (f), 119 Copper End (bd), 27 The Real Bavard (pu), 72 Bright Lad (pu)
17 ran. Dist, 4l, hd. SP 5-1.

123 - Maiden 7yo+ II

Norton's Bridge [16].....................**J Quinn** 1
prom, ld 5 out, drew clr frm 2 out....................
Ballycastle Bay [14]*prog to jn wnr aft 3 out, outpcd frm nxt*... 2
120[2] **Desmond River [10]***chsd ldrs, onepcd final cct*...... 3
Also: 100[2] Grafy Hill (4), 99 Snowberry River (5), 119[3] Ordain (6), Creme Supreme (pu), 36[2] Normous (pu), Tiger Dolly (pu), Twilight Invader (pu), 119 Iveagh Lady (pu), A Bit Of A Rascal (pu), Hot Summers (f), Dhu Bond (pu), 93 Native Blood VI (pu), Greenan Hill (pu), Deerfield (pu)
17 ran. 6l, 12l, 6l, 3l, ½l. SP 7-1.

124 - Winners Of One

120[1] **Christimatt [19]** ....**I Buchanan** 1
rear, prog 5 out, sn ld, in cmmnd whn lft clr last.......
Hall's Mill*disp til chsd ldr 5 out-nxt, wknd, lft 2nd last*.. 2
Also: 112 Mysterious Beau (pu), 112 Sister Nora (pu), 113 The Convincer (pu), Castledell (pu), Wayside Spin (pu), 96 Legganhall (pu), 101 Arctic Party (pu), 81[1] Belhabour (f), 67 McClatchey (pu), 20[1] Buckshee (pu), 113 Drumiller Hill Lad (pu)
13 ran. Dist. SP 5-1.

125 - Mares Maiden 6 & 7yo I

62 **Haveafewmanners [17]**...............**C McGivern** 1
made all, clr 2 out, ran on well......................
113 **Glenalla Bella [10]***rear, kpt on to chs wnr 2 out, no imp*.. 2
Mutual Decision*prom til wknd aft 3 out*............ 3
Also: 63 Bold Irene (4), 113 Bobby Blazer (5), Mystic Moment (pu), 113 Floruceva (f), Conors Lass (pu), 71 Tullyallenstar (pu), Taconas Gift (f), Nancy Hill (pu), Spring Trix (pu), Maccarrons Run (pu), Flame Of Gold (pu), Marino Rose (ur), 72 Loch Saland (pu)
16 ran. 25l, 15l, 15l, 6l. SP 3-1.

126 - Mares Maiden 6 & 7yo II

113 **Golden Start [15]** ....**C Andrews** 1
ld 3 out, hld on wll nr fin..........................
112 **Ngala [15]***chsd wnr 2 out, chal last, just hld*......... 2
Maid O'Tully [13]*chsd ldrs, styd on onepcd apr last*.. 3
Also: 112 Roselynhill (pu), 112 The Bleary Flyer (pu), 112 Secret Door (pu), Ellies Pride (pu), 71 Risk-A-Dinge (f), 112 Windmill Star (f), 97 Gerrys Delight (f), 98 Shanes Bay (pu), 119 Dernamay (pu), Kilbricken Sunset (pu), 71 Crottys Bridge (pu), Go Jenny (pu), Bann View (pu)
16 ran. Nk, 6l. SP 3-1.

127 - Maiden 5 & 6yo I

65³ Hum 'N' Haw [16]......................M Scanlon 1
w.w. ld 3 out, drew clr nxt
113 Bridge End [10]*nvr dnag, kpt on to tk 2nd apr last* 2
Native Cove*nvr dang, kpt on to tk 3rd last*............ 3
Also: 117 Moses Man (4), Cascum Lad (pu), 118 Ireby VI (pu), Fairtree (pu), Miners Bay (pu), Russell Lodge (pu), 114 Righteye (pu), 117 Strong Time (pu), 117 Barnagan (pu)
12 ran. 15l, 15l, 8l. SP 6-4.

128 - Maiden 5 & 6yo II

117 Willie B Brave [15] ....J Quinn 1
hld up, ld 5 out-2 out, ld last, sn clr
114 Ballydavid [10]*prog 4 out, ld 2 out til wknd rpdly last* .. 2
Also: 94 Rare House (pu), 117 King Sol (pu), 118 Castlewood Lodge (pu), 68 Opening Quote (pu), Golfing Man (pu), 117 Capail Mor (f), Legal Whisper (pu), Chase The Sun (pu), Corn Beat (pu)
11 ran. 14l. SP 6-4.

129 - Adjacent Lightweight

Denfield [19] ....I Buchanan 1
ld hlfwy, jnd last, just hld on
113¹ Manhattan Prince [19]*3rd 5 out, prog to chal last, just hld* 2
113 Serious Note*nvr dang, lft poor 3rd aft 2 out* 3
Also: Millerman (pu), Myrtlefield Ann (pu), 113 Emmas Gamble (pu), 119 Wind Of Glory (pu), Jingle Jack (pu), 112² Uncle Art (pu), 119 Castlevigganlady (su)
10 ran. Hd, dist. SP 5-4.

AVONDHU FOXHOUNDS
Knockenard
Saturday February 22nd
HOLDING

130 - Mares Winners Of Two I

88 Shesadinger [18] ....K O'Sullivan 1
prog 3 out, ld apr last, styd on well
89 The Pulpit [16]*in tch, ld 2 out til apr last, no ext* 2
13¹ Summerhill Express [15]*cls up, chal & blnd 2 out, not rcvr* 3
Also: 73¹ Supreme Odds [15] (4), 75 Fethard Orchid [15] (5), 78 Shirgale [13] (6), 41 Sandy Pearl Two [11] (7), 63 No Swap (ur), Glenbower Queen (pu), 56 Run For Fun (f), 21 Badalka (pu), All Style (pu), 109¹ Thadys Remedy (pu)
13 ran. 5l, 3l, 1l, 1l, 6l, 5l. SP 6-1.

131 - Mares Winners Of Two II

108 Don't Waste It [18] ....J McNamara 1
cls up, chal 3 out, ld nxt, sn clr
Glenview Rose [15]*in tch, chal 3 out, outpcd frm nxt*.. 2
78³ Derry's Diamond [12]*nvr dang* 3
Also: 108 Molls Choice [11] (4), Penny Bride (f), 79¹ Via Del Quatro (pu), 78 Looking Ahead (pu), 89 Tack Room Lady (pu), 89 Pintex (pu), 46¹ One Woman (f), 89¹ Strong Dream (pu)
11 ran. 10l, 10l, 3l. SP 6-1.

132 - Maiden 5 & 6yo I

47 Welsh March [18].....................A Costello 1
ld, hdd & lft in ld 4 out, jnd & lft clr last
82 Metro Fashion*nvr dang, lft poor 2nd last* 2
83 Gleeming Lace*nvr dang, lft poor 3rd last* 3
Also: Jack Hackett (4), Imperial Dawn (5), Tourig Bit (pu), 76 Newmarket Cheddar (f), Some Other Knight (pu), Bill Joyce (pu), 81 Goolds Diamond [18] (ur), Sliabh Luchra Boy (pu), 84 All A Joke (pu), 20 Tekroc (f)
13 ran. Dist, 5l, 20l, 25l. SP 7-4.

133 - Maiden 5 & 6yo II

103 Over Eager [20] ....D Costello 1
w.w. prog to ld 2 out, sn clr
86² Corkers Flame [10]*cls up, disp 3 out-nxt, sn btn* 2
85 Mr Goodbye*nvr dang* 3
Also: 74 Geragh Road (4), 40 Bridge Party (5), 43³ Skimabit (f), Vancouver Island (f), 106 Tomasins Choice (pu), West Coast Cooler (pu), 104 Suave (pu), Tom's Tune (bd), The Bell Tree (f), 86³ Shenanigans (f)
13 ran. Dist, 2l, 5l, 20l. SP 2-1.

134 - Open Lightweight

Slaney Wind [22].........................M Hogan 1
made all, styd on well frm last
49 Ashley Heights [21]*chsd wnr 3 out, ev ch last, no ext flat* 2
89 Lordinthesky [18]*chsd ldrs, onepcd frm 3 out*......... 3
Also: Pharditu [11] (4), 78 Okdo (5), 75 Garramoss [11] (6), Dante Lad (pu), 88 Princess Bavard (pu), 51 Run For Niall (pu), 49 Maypole Fountain (pu), Miners Melody (pu)
11 ran. 3l, 8l, 20l, hd, 4l. SP 4-1.

135 - Maiden 7yo+ I

54 Noddis Dilemma [17] ....D Costello 1
4th 5 out, chal 3 out, rallied flat, ld nr fin
53² Danger Flynn [17]*3rd 5 out, disp 3 out til hdd nr fin*... 2
74² Gaelic Glen [16]*2nd 5 out, disp 3 out-last, styd on* 3
Also: Tooth Pick [15] (4), Girlough Castle [10] (5), 74 Icantsay (6), 52 Father O'Reilly (7), 52 Brian Og (8), 74³ Glenselier (9), 107 Baybuck (pu), 54 Maltese Cross (pu), 99³ Knockanoran (pu), Storm Reef (pu)
13 ran. ½l, 1½l, 4l, 15l, 1l, 1l, 5l, 8l. SP 3-1.

136 - Maiden 7yo+ II

83² Teads Boreen [16] ....M Budds 1
disp til ld 4 out, drew clr 2 out
Weak Moment [10]*chsd wnr 4 out, ev ch 2 out, sn btn*
Loach Croga*nvr nrr* 3
Also: 53 Prophets Thumb (4), 53 Barnadown (5), 54 Prince Owen (6), Cloneen Adventure (f), 52 Clashview (pu), Toytown King (pu), 12 La Charente (f), No Such Parson (pu), Irish Display (f)
12 ran. 20l, 6l, dist, 1l, 25l. SP 4-1.

137 - Adjacent Maiden

47² Wayward King [18] ....P Cashman 1
made all, clr 3 out, easily
90³ Macklette [13]*chsd wnr 4 out, no imp nxt* 2
84 Coole Abbey [10]*chsd ldrs, no imp aft 4 out* 3
Also: 60 Lady Of Means (4), Speightstown Boy (pu), Royal Dale (pu), Colmans Hope (pu), Grange Pine (f), 60 Cappagh Glen (pu)
9 ran. 10l, 10l, 15l. SP 4-7.

138 - Mares Maiden 6yo+ I

48 Bella Brownie [15] ....E Gallagher 1
prog hlfwy, ld 2 out, styd on well
61 Dusty Rose [11]*bhnd, kpt on frm 2 out, no dang*...... 2
10 Blame Barney*ld hlfwy til 2 out, wknd*.............. 3
Also: 60 Ferriters Pub (4), Brogeen Dubh (pu), Coolbawn Bramble (pu), 74 Curley Gale (pu), Miss Betsy (pu), Dons Pride (pu), 102³ Ballybeggan Lady (f), Derrygra Fountain (pu), Faithful Pal (pu), 105 Dysart Abbey (pu), 109 Glitter Girl (f), 96² Codology (pu), 102 Villa Alba (f), 26 Sentimental Crush (pu)
17 ran. 12l, 10l, dist. SP 5-1.

139 - Mares Maiden 6yo+ II

97² Push Gently [15].........................J Cullen 1
chsd ldrs, styd on frm 2 out, ld flat
10² Cush Princess [14]*cls up, ld aft 2 out, hdd & no ext flat*.............. 2
61 Why Emerald [13]*ld 5 out til aft 2 out, no ext*......... 3
Also: 6² Ballinvuskig Lady (4), Victim Of Slander (5), 56 Vulthyne (6), 10 Idiot's Surprise (7), 60 Trimmer Lady (8), 83 Mandoora (f), 19 Jenaway (pu), 48 Paros Leader (pu), 46 American Conker (f), Red Mollie (pu), Clochban Clonroche (pu), Saratoga Sal (f), 61 Glistening Waters (pu), Aine Hencey (pu)
17 ran. 4l, 4l, dist, 2l, 1l, 5l, 20l. SP 6-1.

DUHALLOW FOXHOUNDS
Kildorrery

Sunday February 23rd
HEAVY

140 - Adjacent Maiden

107[3] **Sarcoid [15]** .... **E Fehily** 1
trckd ldrs, ld 3 out, clr nxt, comf
107 **Mr Freeman***chsd ldrs, no imp on wnr aft 2 out* 2
Function Dream*nvr dang* 3
Also: 79 Cnoc-Breac (f), Davids Sister (pu), Little Simba (pu), 90 Onmeown (pu), 80 Just Be Lucky (pu), Castlemore Leader (pu), 106 Never Heard (pu), 19 Holiday Time (pu), 47 Irish Spirit (pu), 138[3] Blame Barney (ur), Jake The Peg (pu)
14 ran. 20l, 4l. SP 2-1.

141 - Maiden 5yo I

14 **Avondale Illusion [16]** .... **T Lombard** 1
chsd ldrs, prog 2 out, ld alst, styd on well ....
84[2] **Bumper To Bumper [15]***prom, ld 3 out-last, no ext flat* 2
Maxine's Fountain [13]*chsd ldrs, onepcd frm 2 out* .. 3
Also: 80 Fair Ophelia (pu), 79 Sup A Brandy (pu), 80 Catrionas Lady (pu), Electric Avenue (pu), 76 Clonageera (pu), 22 Sam Quale (pu), Viking Rod (pu), Cottage Girl (pu), Mohera King (pu)
12 ran. 1½l, 4l. SP 7-2.

142 - Maiden 5yo II

85 **Jolly Man [16]** .... **E Gallagher** 1
prom, ld 3 out, styd on well ....
85 **Pure Air [12]***prom, chsd wnr 2 out, no imp* 2
103 **Loslomos [11]***chsd ldrs, onepcd frm 3 out* 3
Also: Rios King (4), 47 Neily Joe (5), 84 Dawdante (6), Jimmy Dan (7), 84 Lars On Tour (pu), 77 Leap Year Man (pu), Close To Tears (f), Knocklawn (pu), Dukestown (pu)
12 ran. 10l, 4l, 20l. SP 5-2.

143 - Mares Maiden 6yo

90 **Greenflag Princess [16]** .... **J Sheehan** 1
ld hlfwy, sn clr, easily ....
Royal Chapeau [10]*prog to chs wnr 3 out, sn no imp* 2
83 **Regal Gossip***prog to 3rd 3 out, sn no imp* 3
Also: Bright Choice (f), Eurogal (pu), 91 Ronkino (pu), 48 Lisselan Lass (pu), 48 Leamlara Rose (pu), No Refund (pu), 91[3] Ballyhest Fountain (pu)
10 ran. 10l, 15l. SP 5-4.

144 - Open Lightweight

51[2] **Tommy The Duke [20]** .... **P Costello** 1
ld 6 out, styd on wll frm 3 out ....
Henleydown [17]*chsd wnr 4 out, ev ch 2 out, no ext* .. 2
59 **Clonrosh Slave [17]***prog & in tch 5 out, onepcd frm 3 out* 3
Also: 75[2] Wejem [13] (4), Crazy Dreams (5), 78 Quayside Buoy (pu), 88 Waterloo King [27] (pu), Scarteen Lower (pu)
8 ran. 5l, ¾l, 10l. SP 9-4.

145 - Winners Of Two

75 **Gaye Bard [18]** .... **J Sheehan** 1
made all, easily ....
88 **Warning Call [12]***chsd wnr, nvr able to chal* 2
52[1] **Radical-Times***chsnd ldng pair, nvr able to chal* 3
Also: Get Cracking (pu), 75 Carolines Minstrel (pu)
5 ran. 15l, 20l. SP 2-1.

146 - Maiden 6yo

12[2] **The Village Way [19]** .... **N Fehily** 1
trckd ldrs, ld 6 out, clr 4 out, easily ....
20[2] **Chevin Lad***nvr dang, lft poor 2nd last* 2
Also: Stags Rock (pu), 106 Twilight Hour (pu), 86 Remmy Cruz (pu), 86 Jolly Lad (f), 86 The Big Fella (pu), 82[3] Johnny's Echo (pu), The Stag (f), 102[2] Court Amber (pu), 43 Cullaun (f)
11 ran. Dist. SP 5-4.

WEXFORD FOXHOUNDS
Wexford Point-To-Point Course
Sunday February 23rd
SOFT

147 - Winners Of Two

100[1] **Royal Arctic [18]** .... **P Kelly** 1
prog 4 out, lft 2nd nxt, hrd rdn to ld flat ....
93 **Miller King [18]***ld, jnd & lft clr 3 out, wknd & hdd flat* .. 2
92 **I Love To Fly***nvr dang, t.o.* 3
Also: Tomeko (4), Serla Sister (5), 92 Ardent Spirit (6), Mitchelstown River (pu), 56[1] Andy's Birthday (f), 66[1] Little Minute (f), 56 Torduff Express (pu), Harry's Secret (pu), Sandfair (pu), 89 Royal Barge (f), 75 Trimmer Princess (f), 89 Silver Buckle (pu), 93[3] Lovable Outlaw (pu)
16 ran. 1l, dist, 4l, 10l, 12l. SP 5-1.

148 - Maiden 5yo

94[2] **Eddie [17]** .... **D O'Brien** 1
prom, ld 6 out, lft clr 3 out, unchal aft ....
57 **Kabwee Star***nvr dang, lft poor 2nd 2 out, ref & u.r. last, rmntd* 2
58 **Apollodorus***prom to 4 out, 2nd & btn whn f 2 out, rmntd* 3
Also: 58[2] Bramble Wood (f), Friars Island (f), Brave Noddy (ur), Carrys Clover (pu), Satquaid (pu), 57 Bart Eile (f), Magikoopa (pu), 94 Annie Leap (pu), 95 Speedy O'Dee (pu), Electric Fencer (pu)
13 ran. Dist, hd. SP 4-5.

149 - Open Lightweight

78[1] **Ozier Hill [21]** .... **J Berry** 1
prog 5 out, ld nxt, comf ....
78 **Mack A Day [18]***mid-div, lft 2nd 2 out, kpt on* 2
92[2] **Harveysland***ld to 3 out, wknd* 3
Also: 78 Trimmer Wonder (4), Watercourse [22] (pu), 92 Killenagh Moss (f), 92[3] Killiney Graduate (f), 92[1] Dennistownthriller (pu), 78 Albert's Fancy (pu)
9 ran. 6l, dist, dist. SP 4-7.

150 - Mares Maiden 5yo I

Definitely Maybe [17] .... **P Crowley** 1
cls up, ld apr last, comf ....
98 **Nervous Kate [13]***ld 5 out til apr last, sn no ext* 2
Winning Rhythm [13]*cls up, onepcd apr last* 3
Also: 91 Kinnahalla [11] (4), 91 Black Fashion (f), Running On Thyne (f), 25[2] The Buck Pony (f), Torduff Star (f), Torduff Bay (f), 96 Wunwabbitwun (pu), 90 Over The Glen (f), Strathfield Lass (pu)
12 ran. 2l, ½l, 6l. SP 4-1.

151 - Mares Maiden 5yo II

97[3] **Woodbinesandroses [15]** .... **P Kelly** 1
prom, ld 3 out, lft clr apr last ....
96[3] **Lady Sylvie [12]***bhnd, ran on wll apr last, nvr nrr* 2
Traceytown*t.o.* 3
Also: Cost-A-Lot (4), No Speed Limit (pu), 90 Prettymaid (pu), 91 Barenises Rose (f), Americo Lady (pu), 98 Imlistening (pu), 98 Supreme Gold (su), 91 Ballyroe Hill (ref), Oh Donna (f)
12 ran. 10l, dist, dist, dist. SP 5-1.

152 - Maiden 6yo I

Beatin Side [16] .... **C Murphy** 1
prom, ld 3 out, jnd & lft clr last ....
87 **Foreshore Man [15]***in tch, chal & blnd last, not rcvr* .. 2
Esquimau*nvr dang, t.o.* 3
Also: Newbog Lad (4), 95 Coopers Clan (f), 95[2] Frostbitten (f), 101 Laras Boy (f), 66 Buck And A Half (pu), 94 Airecco (f), Just Joe (f), 29 Inch Cross (f), 56 Lanngara (pu), The Podger (f), Catstown River (pu)
14 ran. 6l, dist, 4l. SP 3-1.

153 - Maiden 6yo II

Brambledale [16] .... **K O'Donnell** 1
hld up, prog 4 out, lft in ld nxt, styd on well...........
94[3] **Max Lad [14]***prog 3 out, chal & mstk last, no ext flat* .. 2
95[3] **Ringaheen [10]***ld hlfwy til apr 3 out, sn btn* 3
Also: North Kilkenny (f), General Perk (pu), 95 Castle Glow (pu), Invader General (pu), 94 Awalkintheclouds (pu), 86 West Trix VI (pu), Orphan Spa (pu), 66[3] Vice Captain (pu), 95 Chas Randall (pu), 82 Skidrow River (pu), Mile Mill (pu)
14 ran. 6l, 12l. SP 4-1.

154 - Maiden 7yo+ I

100[3] **Shillelagh Oak [16]** .... **J Dempsey** 1
cls up, chal 2 out, disp aft last, ld nr fin ....
99[2] **Bourbon County [16]***cls up, disp 2 out til hdd nr fin* .. 2
99 **Donals Choice [14]***ld to aft 2 out, no ext* 3
Also: Lord Amethyst [12] (4), 100 Shimano [10] (5), Noble Leader (pu), 99 Percusionist (pu), Dos Deegan (f), Cuckroo (pu), 101 Ashplant (pu), 100 The Bug Hill (pu), Regal Fellow (pu), 34 Twin Track (f)
13 ran. Hd, 4l, 4l, 6l. SP 3-1.

155 - Maiden 7yo+ II

100 **Bit Of A Character [12]**.................. **W Codd** 1
chsd ldrs, 3rd & btn whn lft clr last ....
100 **Benalf***chsd ldrs, 4th & no ch whn lft 2nd last*.......... 2
99 **Forabby***t.o., lft 3rd last*.............................. 3
Also: Hey Chief [14] (4), 99 The Moderator (pu), 56 The Cass Man (pu), 101 Slow Beet (pu), 34 Greedy Johno (pu), Captain Deen (pu), Little Len (ur), Boker Hill (pu), 99 Lucky Statement (pu), Bree Hill [14] (f), To The Hilt (pu)
14 ran. 8l, dist, dist. SP 8-1.

156 - Maiden 7yo+ III

55 **Hellofahooly [16]** .... **J P Berry** 1
prom, ld 3 out, lft clr nxt ....
Over The Barrow*chsd ldrs, lft poor 2nd 2 out* 2
101[2] **Siamsa Brae***ld to 3 out, wknd rpdly* 3
Also: 100 Louis de Palmer (4), Course Sprite (pu), 30 Station Man (pu), Four Zeros (f), Set A Way (f), Bronc (pu), Ross Quay (f), Deep Appeal (f), Cottiers Den (pu), 99 Change The Script (f)
13 ran. Dist, 10l, 2l. SP 4-1.

EAST CLARE
Killaloe
Sunday February 23rd
HEAVY

157 - Winners Of One

93 **Rushing Waters [18]**.................... **R Hurley** 1
ld hlfwy, blnd last, styd on wll ....
108[3] **Shareza River [17]***chsd wnr 2 out, ev ch aft last, no ext*... 2
River Of Dreams [15]*chsd ldrs, onepcd frm 2 out* 3
Also: 105 Fools With Horses [10] (4), 110[1] Snugville Sally (5), 92 Cloughan Boy (pu), 84[1] All But (f), Ballybriken Castle (pu), 47[1] Viking Buoy (ro)
9 ran. 1½l, 5l, 15l. SP 7-1.

158 - Maiden 5yo

104 **Telecom Affair [14]**.................... **B Hassett** 1
chsd ldrs, rdn & strgglng 2 out, kpt on to ld last........
22 **Rockholm Lad [13]***chsd ldrs, lft in ld 2 out, wknd & hdd last* 2
Also: 58 Ard Na Gaoithe (pu), 104 Anodfromalord (f), 77 Dingdust (pu), 47 Pejays Duca (f), Deel Sound (pu), 104 Cast No Shadow (pu), Wortagamble (f), 103 Duke Of Tulla (f)
10 ran. 2l. SP Evens.

159 - Mares Maiden 5yo

110[2] **Iona Flyer [15]**........................ **P Cashman** 1
prom, chal last, ld flat, all out.........................
91[2] **Zaffaran Run [15]***in tch, chal last, just hld flat*......... 2
98 **Be My Mot [14]***ld 6 out, clr 2 out, wknd & hdd last* 3
Also: 109 Springtime Mist [10] (4), 110 Scklepp (5), Loch Lomond (6), 91 Mocklershill Lady (pu), Una Juna (pu), Rossy Orchestra (pu), Deerpark Lass (pu)
10 ran. ¾l, 2l, 12l. SP 7-4.

160 - Maiden 6yo+ I

106[2] **Johnstheman [18]**....................... **E Bolger** 1
hld up, ld 6 out, drew clr aft 2 out ....
Kincora [10]*chsd wnr 6 out, ev ch 3 out, btn nxt* 2
Also: 24 Cahercon (bd), 107 Carnmore House (pu), Claddagh Crystal (pu), Meldante VI (pu), Premium Brand (pu), 106 The Slippery Bear (f), Ballyluckamore (pu), Just Harvey (bd)
10 ran. 25l. SP 5-4.

161 - Maiden 6yo+ II

107[2] **Ecologic [16]**............................ **R Hurley** 1
made all, styd on und pres apr last ....
107 **Charlie Hawes [14]***chsd wnr 4 out, chal 2 out, no ext flat*... 2
87 **O'Donnell Abu [12]***chsd ldrs, onepcd frm 2 out* 3
Also: 107 Barna Lad (4), 23 Knockannig Bay (pu), Sammy Sunshine (pu), Park West (pu), 102 Tom Deely (pu), 42 Prospect Star (pu), 107 Terry McCann (pu)
10 ran. 7l, 5l, dist. SP 1-2.

162 - Mares Maiden 6yo+ I

109[3] **Rosetown Girl [16]** .... **E Bolger** 1
ld 5 out, sn clr, comf...................................
Aerlite Classic*chsd wnr 3 out, no imp*............... 2
36 **Lisduff Pride***chsd ldrs, no ch frm 3 out* 3
Also: Handy Sally (pu), 96 Borreeva (pu), Phartoomanny (pu), 60 Clonfert Sue (pu), 65 The Crazy Chick (pu), Rainproof (pu), 109 Lucky Fifteen (pu), 10 Annerene (f), Autumn Fern (pu)
12 ran. Dist, 6l. SP 2-1.

163 - Mares Maiden 6yo+ II

Easter Bard [15] .... **R Flavin** 1
ld 4 out, styd on well ....
98 **Kings Alibi [10]***chsd wnr 3 out, no imp*............. 2
Lothian Magic*nvr dang* 3
Also: 110 Shuil Flossy (f), Miss Lynch (pu), Miss Outlaw (pu), 109 Carnmore Supreme (pu), 139 Aine Hencey (pu), 32[3] Pharavo (pu), 63 Ring Mam (f), Executive Opal (f)
11 ran. 15l, 25l. SP 2-1.

164 - Open Lightweight

30[1] **Tearaway King [30]**...................... **E Bolger** 1
made all, easily ....
Man With A Plan VI*t.o. hlfwy, lft 2nd apr last*......... 2
Also: 108 Runabout (pu)
3 ran. Dist. SP 1-12.

KILWORTH & ARAGLEN
Kilworth
Saturday March 1st
HEAVY

165 - Maiden 4yo

Excuse Me Sir [16] .... **W O'Sullivan** 1
made all, in cmmnd whn lft wll clr last...............
Ramona Style*nvr dang, lft poor 2nd last*............ 2
Curragh Lord*nvr dang, lft poor 3rd last*.............. 3
Also: Another Test (4), Swept Aside (f), Stay West [14] (f), Chelsea Tric (pu)
7 ran. Dist, 4l, 20l. SP 6-4.

166 - Mares Maiden 6yo+ I

Penstal Lady [17] .... **J McNamara** 1
prog to ld 2 out, styd on well flat.....................
83 **Kilcannon Sophie [15]***ld 3 out-nxt, onepcd aft* 2
Beat That [14]*chsd ldrs, onepcd frm 2 out*........... 3
Also: Menalma [13] (4), 19 Highland Call [11] (5), Aroundthevalley (6),

137 Lady Of Means (7), Change The Pace (8), 143 Bright Choice (9), Msadi Mhulu (10), 143 No Refund (11), La Kestrel (12), Kerries Jake (pu), Blazey Lady (pu), 48 Fountain Moss (pu), 83 Miss Metal (f), 138 Miss Betsy (pu), Merry River (bd), 143 Leamlara Rose (pu)
19 ran. 5l, 2l, 3l. SP 7-2.

167 - Mares Maiden 6yo+ II

162 **Phartoomanny [16]**......................**J Collins** 1
prom, ld 3 out, styd on well frm nxt
Pima [13]*chsd wnr 3 out, no imp nxt* 2
74 **Frightening Child***nvr dang* 3
Also: 26 Argideen Bonnie (4), Creative Thought (f), Shamron (f), Dante Alainn (pu), Glen Of Bargy (pu), Celtic Course (pu), Fahoora (f), 140 Castlemore Leader (pu), Miss Thimble (pu), 140 Little Simba (pu), 73 Princess Diga (pu), Skipping Chick (pu), 73 Marys Friend (pu), 139 Glistening Waters (pu), Lorglane Lady (f)
18 ran. 7l, dist, 10l. SP 8-1.

168 - Open Lightweight

85¹ **Harbour Leader [24]**..................**E Gallagher** 1
w.w. prog to ld apr 2 out, sn qcknd clr
144¹ **Tommy The Duke [18]***prom till onepcd aft 3 out* 2
134² **Ashley Heights [12]***ld 5 out til apr 2 out, sn btn* 3
Also: 134 Okdo (4), 134 Dante Lad (pu), 51 Kilara (pu), Too Covers (pu), 157 Viking Buoy (f), 75 Pearl Dante (pu)
9 ran. 8l, 20l, 15l. SP 5-4.

169 - Adjacent Maiden 5yo+

85² **Monteba [15]**..........................**P Cashman** 1
cls up, lft in ld 3 out, drvn out
133 **Skimabit [15]***prog to chal last, just hld flat* 2
136³ **Loach Croga [13]***prog to chal last, sn not qckn* 3
Also: 137 Speightstown Boy (4), 137 Royal Dale (5), 143 Ronkino (f), 137 Grange Pine (ur), Deciding Dance (pu), 86 Playmore (pu), Jennys Pearl (pu), Julias Boy (pu), Familyvalue (pu), Glenfinsh (pu), 54 Tullys Ball (f)
14 ran. 1l, 5l, dist. SP 2-1.

170 - Winners Of Two

133¹ **Over Eager [21]** ....**D Costello** 1
trckd ldrs, ld aft 3 out, ran on strngly
131 **One Woman [14]***ld to aft 3 out, sn onepcd* 2
134³ **Lordinthesky [12]***chsd ldrs, onepcd frm 3 out* 3
Also: 131 Pintex (4), 75 Queenofclubs (f)
5 ran. 10l, 5l, dist. SP 2-5.

171 - Maiden 5yo+ I

136 **La Charente [15]**..........................**B Walsh** 1
prom, ld 4 out, sn clr, easily
146 **Cullaun [10]***chsd ldrs, styd on onepcd frm 2 out* 2
132 **Tekroc***effort to chs wnr 3 out, wknd nxt* 3
Also: 74 Clongeel Lord (4), 73 Irish Rover (5), Man Of Hope (6), 132 Imperial Dawn (pu), Carry On Brendan (pu), 136 Cloneen Adventure (f), 73 Big Spender (pu), 158 Wortagamble (pu), Money Matters (pu)
12 ran. 10l, 4l, 10l. SP 10-1.

172 - Maiden 5yo+ II

Chapel Road [16]........................**J Moloney** 1
disp til ld 3 out, easily
Chelsea King [12]*disp to 3 out, onepcd aft* 2
133 **Shenanigans***disp to 3 out, wknd* 3
Also: Laurintinium (pu), Chamsy (pu), 52 Tyo Mo Chara (f), Lord Egross (pu), Lingering On (pu), Sheer Mischief (pu), 50 Moonvoor (pu), 160 Cahercon (pu)
11 ran. 8l, dist. SP 8-1.

FERMANAGH HARRIERS
Enniskillen
Saturday March 1st
SOFT

173 - Adjacent Lightweight

115 **Missing Lady [19]**....................**C McCarren** 1
made all, styd on wll flat
120 **Listrakelt [17]***chsd wnr frm 2 out, onepcd last* 2
115 **Famous Stout [16]***chsd ldrs, onepcd frm 2 out* 3
Also: 121 Voldi [10] (4), 116 Find Out More (5), 122 Highland Buck (6), 126 Dernamay (pu), The Conawarey (pu), 97 Can She Do It (pu)
9 ran. 4l, 3l, 20l, 12l, dist. SP 8-1.

174 - Winners Of Two

112¹ **Sharimage [17]** ....**P Graffin** 1
ld 7th, mstk nxt, hdd flat, rallied to ld nr fin
112 **Stanley Steamer [17]***ld til blnd 7th, chal & blnd last, ld flat, hdd nr fin* 2
121 **Annie's Arthur***nvr dang* 3
Also: Indexia (pu), My Man (pu), 124 Castledell (pu), 126¹ Golden Start (pu), 128¹ Willie B Brave (pu), 124 Wayside Spin (pu), 117¹ Anns Display (pu), 118¹ G I Joe (f)
11 ran. ¾l, dist. SP 2-1.

175 - Maiden 5 & 6yo I

114 **Lord Basil [15]**.............................**K Ross** 1
prog to chal apr 2 out, ev ch whn lft clr last
Pull The Lever [12]*cls up, outpcd 2 out, kpt on agn flat* 2
Private Power [12]*prom, lft in ld 3 out, jnd & hmpd last, not rcvr* 3
Also: 117 Not Found Yet (4), 118 Dancing Mike (pu), Allistragh Lad (pu), 117 Carnmoon (pu), 127 Russell Lodge (pu), Parman (pu), 114 Swan Point (f), 128 Golfing Man (ur), Ballymichael (pu), 127 Miners Bay (f), 114 Tullamore (pu)
14 ran. 7l, 5l, dist. SP 12-1.

176 - Maiden 5 & 6yo II

117 **Bluagale [13]**............................**R Patton** 1
ld to 4 out, wll btn whn lft in ld last, all out
118 **Panda Nova [12]***prom, ld 4 out-2 out, btn whn lft ev ch last, no ext* 2
117² **Rock On Bud***trckd ldrs 4 out, blnd nxt, wknd* 3
Also: 114 Track O'Profit (pu), Easy Feelin [16] (f), Ollar House (pu), Sand de Vince (pu), Cabra Boy (pu), 129 Millerman (f), 114³ Flanaghans Way (ur), 114 Picton (pu), Reds Paradise (pu), Galannick (pu)
13 ran. 2l, dist. SP 20-1.

177 - Open Lightweight

High Star [21] ....**I Buchanan** 1
made all, jnd last, hrd rdn & hld on well
24² **Aiguille [21]***prssd wnr 3 out, lvl last, just hld flat* 2
121² **Crowded House [11]***prssd wnr till wknd 3 out* 3
Also: 116³ Captain Brandy (4), 116 Colin's Hatch (pu), Shanecracken (pu), Cabra Towers (pu), Ballybollen (pu), 115 Captains Bar (ur), 124¹ Christimatt (pu)
10 ran. Nk, dist, 8l. SP 3-1.

178 - Mares Maiden 5yo+ I

96 **Pepsa Morfee [15]** ....**R McNally** 1
in tch, drvn to ld apr last, styd on
125² **Glenalla Bella [13]***prog 3 out, styd on to go 2nd flat* .. 2
126 **Bann View [13]***rear, ran on 2 out, nvr nrr* 3
Also: 120 Gold Leader (4), 126 The Bleary Flyer (ro), 121 Runaco (pu), Executive Babe (ref), Star Flyer (f), Drumree (f), 111 Lan-Paula (pu), Tierfergus (pu), Princess Cataldi (pu), Ballywee Penny (f), Dawns Choice (ur), 122 Mourne Miner (pu), Carlies Wood (ur)
16 ran. 4l, 1½l, 15l. SP 10-1.

179 - Mares Maiden 5yo+ II

Welsh Sitara [16] ....**I Buchanan** 1
ld 3rd, clr 2 out, styd on well
111 **Forever Grey***chsd wnr, blnd 3 out, wknd nxt* 2
126³ **Maid O'Tully***nvr dang* 3
Also: 123 Tiger Dolly (pu), 125 Spring Trix (pu), 125 Flame Of Gold

(pu), Sounds Confident (f), 125 Bobby Blazer (pu), Ollar Lady (pu), 126 Windmill Star (pu), 125 Maccarrons Run (pu), Kan-Ann (f), 31 Snobs Casino (pu), 125 Nancy Hill (pu), 111 Blue Alliance (pu)

15 ran. Dist, 10l. SP 7-4.

180 - Maiden 7yo+

Baby Jamie [18]........................C McGivern 1
hld up, prog 4 out, chal apr last, hrd rdn to ld nr fin ....
115³ **Wilbar [18]***prom, ld 4 out, hdd und pres flat ....* 2
120³ **Ardbei***chsd ldrs, wknd 2 out ....* 3

Also: 123 Ordain (4), 119 Longmore Boy (5), 119 Florida Or Bust (6), 112 Mandingo (7), 120 Emerald Breffni (pu), 119 Where's Sam (pu), 119 Paddy Red (pu), Stackie Boy (pu), 120 You Said It (pu), Athabasca (pu), Atticall Lady (f), 119 Is This The One (f)

15 ran. ½l, dist, 1l, 3l, 25l, 1½l. SP 2-1.

KILKENNY FOXHOUNDS
Gowran Point-To-Point Course
Sunday March 2nd
HEAVY

181 - Adjacent Maiden 6yo+ I

64 **Cash Flow [18]..........................P Fenton** 1
trckd ldrs, ld 3 out, clr whn blnd last, comf ....
Tea Box [14]*ld to hlfwy, kpt on to chs wnr last ....* 2
153 **Chas Randall***ld hlfwy to 3 out, wknd rpdly ....* 3

Also: 154 Noble Leader (f), Great Reminder (f), Mineral River (pu), Zanagale (ro), 132² Metro Fashion (ur), 153 Orphan Spa (ur), 65 Stelinjo (pu), 153 Castle Glow (pu)

11 ran. 8l, dist. SP 6-4.

182 - Adjacent Maiden 6yo+ II

Cheval de Guerre [17]...................P Fenton 1
prom, chal 2 out, ld apr last, comf.....................
Gladstone [13]*prom, ld 5 out-apr last, onepcd ....* 2
152 **Airecco [11]***prom, chal 3 out, btn apr last...........* 3

Also: 99 Croi (bd), Forold (pu), 87 Mineral Al (f), 152 Catstown River (f), 136 Barnadown (f), 64 Master Finbar (pu), Gallant Gale (pu)

10 ran. 8l, 6l. SP 6-4.

183 - Winners Of Two

147 **Andy's Birthday [20] ....M Phillips** 1
ld hlfwy, drew clr apr 2 out.............................
93² **Dromod Point [17]***prssd wnr frm hlfwy til no ext 2 out*
Oatflake [12]*chsd ldng pair hlfwy, wknd 4 out.........* 3

Also: 112 Only One (4), 153¹ Brambledale (5)

5 ran. 10l, 15l, dist, dist. SP 2-1.

184 - Maiden 5yo

84 **Manver [18]...........................M Scanlon** 1
hld up, prog 4 out, ld apr last, sn clr...................
148 **Brave Noddy [13]***prom, ld 3 out til apr last, no ch wth wnr aft ....* 2
85 **Bothar Fada [13]***rear, styd on wll frm 2 out, nvr nrr...* 3

Also: 133 The Bell Tree [10] (4), Dvvit (5), Paddy Casey (pu), 84 Ahead Of The Posse (pu), 148 Bart Eile (f), 84³ Freestyler (pu), 148 Friars Island (pu), Make Up Your Mind (pu), 84 Glacial King (pu), 148 Magikoopa (pu), Cool River (pu), Robinstown (f), Current Scandal (pu), 148 Bramble Wood (ur)

17 ran. 15l, ½l, 10l, dist. SP 6-1.

185 - Open Lightweight

78 **Slaney Goodness [22] ....J Quigley** 1
made all, clr 2 out, styd on well.........................
Furry Star [16]*prog 3 out, chsd wnr apr last, no imp ..* 2
149 **Watercourse [12]***chsd ldrs, no imp frm 3 out ....* 3

Also: Selkoline [11] (4), Noble Melody (5), Siraidan (pu), 92 Glenroe Gal (pu), Castle Dawn (pu), 155 To The Hilt (pu), 96¹ Beetalot (pu), Celtic Air (pu), 156 Four Zeros (pu), 98 Davids Pride (pu), 66 Na Moilltear (pu), 120 Cinq Frank (f), Lark River (pu), 149 Killenagh Moss (pu)

17 ran. 15l, 10l, 4l, 25l. SP 6-1.

186 - Mares Maiden 5yo I

150 **Kinnahalla [16]........................D O'Brien** 1
hld up, ld aft 3 out, comf ....
150 **Torduff Star [13]***prog to chal 2 out, sn no imp on wnr* 2
101³ **Paps Last Hope***nvr dang ....* 3

Also: 97 Pierpoints Choice (4), Bramhall Princess (ro), Rainbow Trix (f), 151 No Speed Limit (pu), 90 Northcha Lady (f), 150 Strathfield Lass (pu), 159 Scklepp (ur), 159 Mocklershill Lady (ur), 150 Black Fashion (ref)

12 ran. 4l, 15l, 10l. SP 6-1.

187 - Mares Maiden 5yo II

Linda Babe [13] ....J Keville 1
chsd ldrs, wll btn whn lft in ld last.......................
151³ **Traceytown [11]***chsd ldrs, 3rd & no ch whn lft 2nd last ....* 2
159 **Springtime Mist***nvr dang.................................* 3

Also: 96 The Executrix (f), Murphys Cross (ur), 150 The Buck Pony (pu), 150 Running On Thyne (ur), Inch Hill (f), Up The Slaney (pu), Olympic Lady [15] (ref), 96 Rachels Plan (pu), 98 Mariners Quest (pu)

12 ran. 6l, 10l. SP 8-1.

188 - Unplaced Maiden 6yo+

119 **Vermont River [17] ....D O'Brien** 1
prom, ld 4 out, drew clr frm 2 out ....
98² **Make A Move [14]***chsd wnr 3 out, no imp frm nxt......* 2
97 **Young Bebe***nvr dang.....................................* 3

Also: 97 Spritly Lady (4), 32² Sally Willows (bd), Time To Smile (pu), 64 Ballyday Step (pu), Ballylime Again (pu), Hardtobegood (pu), 90 Marys Delight (pu), 139 Red Mollie (pu), 60 Buzz About (ur), 138² Dusty Rose (f)

13 ran. 10l, 15l, 20l. SP 6-1.

WEST WATERFORD
Lismore
Sunday March 2nd
HEAVY

189 - Confined Maiden 5yo+

48³ **Strange Secret [15] ....T Byrne** 1
prom, ld apr last, sn clr...................................
132³ **Gleeming Lace [12]***prom, ld 3 out, mstk nxt, sn hdd & outpcd..* 2
83 **Sea Breta [12]***chsd ldrs, onepcd frm 3 out ....* 3

Also: 90 Right Then Rosie (4), Cottage Lass (pu), 83 Major Bill (f), 83 Running Solo (pu), Brill Star (pu), 139 Mandoora (f), 90 Princess Thyne (f), 83 Hillview Lass (f), 83 Erinsborough (pu), 11 Diamond Melody (pu)

13 ran. 8l, 1l, 10l. SP 8-1.

190 - Maiden 4yo

John Ireland [16] ....J Moloney 1
ld 5th, drew clr flat, easily...............................
Marble City [13]*chsd wnr, chal last, sn outpcd ....* 2
Ludden Chief [11]*chsd ldrs, onepcd frm 2 out ....* 3

Also: Bad Influence (ref)

4 ran. 6l, 4l. SP Evens.

191 - Maiden 5yo I

8² **Brush The Flag [19].......................N Fehily** 1
prom, ld 5 out, lft clr last, styd on strngly..............
39 **Cirvin [14]***rear, ran on apr last, tk 2nd flat ....* 2
Knock It Back [14]*chsd ldr, lft 2nd last, no ch wth wnr* 3

Also: Coming Through [12] (4), 133 West Coast Cooler (5), Royal Tommy (pu), 132 Tourig Bit (pu), Rith Dubh [17] (ur), 141 Viking Rod (co), Mickthecutaway (ur), Dangan Lad (USA) (pu)

11 ran. 15l, hd, 4l. SP 2-1.

192 - Maiden 5yo II

Bramblehill Duke [16].................T Lombard 1
made all, hld on wll nr fin ....

76 Jack Dory [16]*prog to chal & mstk 2 out, rallied flat, just faild* 2
Wild Bavard [11]*chsd ldrs, onepcd frm 2 out* 3
Also: 133³ Mr Goodbye (4), 85 Jolly Paddy (5), Tommys Pride (pu), Bushy Ranger (ur), 84 Zarante (f), Uncle Archie (f), Dalus Executive (f)
10 ran. Nk, 15l, 2l. SP 9-4.

193 - Open Lightweight

49 Pancho's Tango [22]........................**D Daly** 1
made all, lft clr 3 out, comf
130 Shirgale [18]*lft 2nd 3 out, kpt on wll, no imp wnr* 2
134 Miners Melody [14]*nvr dang* 3
Also: 149² Mack A Day [14] (4), 144 Crazy Dreams [10] (5), 168 Viking Buoy (pu), 16 Cooladerra Lady (pu), 88³ Parish Ranger (pu)
8 ran. 3l, 12l, 1l. SP 5-4.

194 - Winners Of One

86¹ I'll Say Nothing [21]........................**R Flavin** 1
hld up, prog 2 out, ld flat, sn clr
132¹ Welsh March [19]*in tch, ld 2 out, hdd & outpcd flat* 2
147 Royal Barge [14]*chsd ldrs, no imp frm 2 out* 3
Also: 75 Round Tower Lady (pu), Up The Banner VI (pu), 134 Garramoss (pu), 74¹ Big Bo (pu), Cozy Cottage (pu), 130 Supreme Odds (pu)
9 ran. 6l, 15l. SP 2-1.

195 - Mares Maiden 5yo

80² Beehive Queen [16]....................**T Lombard** 1
prom, ld 5 out, styd on well
141 Electric Avenue [15]*chsd wnr 3 out, kpt on wll flat* 2
Skipthecuddles [10]*chsd ldrs, lost tch aft 3 out* 3
Also: Cash Ville (4), Ballyknock Lass (pu), Blackwater Heights (pu), 142 Knocklawn (pu), Kacey's Annie (f), Sally Meadows (f), 80 Steady Woman (pu), Woodville Native (ur)
11 ran. 3l, 20l, 15l. SP Evens.

COUNTY CLARE
Quin
Sunday March 2nd
HOLDING

196 - Maiden 5yo

103² Bavard Jet [16]...........................**E Bolger** 1
made all, clr 2 out, easily
22 King Of The Suir [10]*rear, ran on 3 out, tk 2nd nr fin* 2
142³ Loslomos [10]*chsd wnr 4 out, no imp, dmtd nr fin* 3
Also: Garryspillane (4), Welsh Lad (5), 103 Blacknock (pu), 104 Court Ramble (pu), 158 Duke Of Tulla (pu)
8 ran. 15l, nk, 5l. SP 4-5.

197 - Confined Maiden 5yo+

163 Pharavo [14]...........................**B Hassett** 1
made all, unchal
106 General Ari*ran out 5th, cont t.o., lft 2nd 3 out* 2
Also: Storm Man (pu), Fontana Lad (pu)
4 ran. Dist. SP 2-1.

198 - Maiden 6yo

146 Court Amber [14] ....**D O'Meara** 1
ld 4th, kpt on wll frm 2 out
133 Tom's Tune [12]*chsd wnr 5 out, no imp frm 2 out* 2
Bite Back*chsd ldrs, no ch frm 3 out* 3
Also: 128 Legal Whisper (4), Tulira Hill (pu), 152 Laras Boy (pu)
6 ran. 4l, dist, dist. SP 6-4.

199 - Open Lightweight

105¹ Risk Of Thunder [24].....................**E Bolger** 1
made all, unchal
49 Tantum Bonum [16]*chsd ldrs, styd on rm 2 out, nvr able to chal* 2
Ballinaveen Bridge*nvr dang* 3
Also: Mounthenry Star (4)
4 ran. 10l, 20l, dist. SP 1-7.

200 - Mares Maiden 5yo+ I

109 My New Merc [15]....................**S Hennessy** 1
prom, ld 5 out til apr last, rdn to ld flat, styd on wll
162² Aerlite Classic [14]*in tch, chsd wnr 5 out, ld apr last, hdd & no ext flat* 2
163 Carnmore Supreme [11]*chsd ldrs, onepcd frm 2 out* 3
Also: Reinskea (4), 105 Granny Bid (5), 138 Villa Alba (co), Violets Lord (f), 138 Sentimental Crush (f), 163 Miss Lynch (pu), 162 Lucky Fifteen (pu)
10 ran. 4l, 8l, 20l. SP 3-1.

201 - Mares Maiden 5yo+ II

Lottover [15]...........................**B Hassett** 1
prom, ld 4 out, pshd out
163² Kings Alibi [13]*ld to 4 out, no ext flat* 2
162 Rainproof [13]*chsd ldrs, kpt on onepcd frm 2 out* 3
Also: 162³ Lisduff Pride [11] (4), 110³ Ardnataggle (5), Miss Jake (6), Killbally Castle (pu), Norman Road (pu), Ballycar Princess (pu), 110 Boarding Society (pu)
10 ran. 4l, ¾l, 5l. SP 11-10.

202 - Maiden 7yo+

Deep Refrain [15] ....**B Hassett** 1
prog 3 out, lft in ld nxt, just hld on
160 Premium Brand [15]*prog 3 out, lft 2nd nxt, styd on flat, just faild* 2
160 Carnmore House [14]*prog 3 out, lft 3rd nxt, styd on, nrst fin* 3
Also: Mask River [10] (4), 106 Sweeney Lee (5), 61 Full Holiday (ur), 161 Barna Lad (f), 99 Regular Beat (f), 163 Miss Outlaw (ur), 122 Tip The Skip (f), 107 River Wild (f), 161 Park West (pu), 160 The Slippery Bear (f), Here Now (pu), Slaney Fayre (pu), Carrig Heather (f)
16 ran. Nk, 2l, 10l. SP 2-1.

DERRYGALLON HARRIERS
Listowel Point-To-Point Course
Sunday March 2nd
SOFT

203 - Maiden 5yo

77 Prestige Lord [16] ....**P Crowley** 1
trckd ldrs, ld 2 out, styd on well
104² Deejaydee [15]*cls up, ld 5 out, rdn & hdd 2 out, no ext flat* 2
141³ Maxine's Fountain [10]*disp to 3 out, sn btn* 3
Also: 85 Kilcully Jake (4), 158 Ard Na Gaoithe (pu), 104 Johnny Claw (pu), 77 Arthur (f)
7 ran. 2l, 15l, dist. SP 5-1.

204 - Mares Maiden 5yo

159² Zaffaran Run [18] ....**D Costello** 1
trckd ldr hlfwy, ld 4 out, sn clr, easily
79 Little Roo [10]*ld hlfwy to 4 out, no ch wth wnr aft* 2
140 Cnoc-Breac [10]*wll bhnd til ran on frm 2 out, nvr nrr* 3
Also: Furry Island [10] (4), 109 Derrygallon Fancy (5), 80 Bawn Beag (ur), 90 Happy Hula Girl (pu), Tom Said (pu), 141 Cottage Girl [12] (f), Miss Fashion (pu)
10 ran. 20l, 2l, 1l, dist. SP 5-4.

205 - Open Lightweight

Two In Tune [22]...........................**D Keane** 1
trckd ldr, ld 3 out, sn clr, easily
48¹ Bright Prospect [16]*clr ldr til hdd 3 out, no ch wth wnr aft* 2
2³ Awbeg Rover [13]*nvr nr ldng pair, kpt on* 3
Also: 108 Starlight Fountain (pu), Kilcullys-Pride (ur)
5 ran. 10l, 10l. SP 1-3.

206 - Maiden 6yo+

140 Never Heard [14] ....E O'Grady 1
trckd ldrs, 4th 3 out, lft 2nd last, kpt on to ld flat........
135³ Gaelic Glen [14]*prom, ld 5 out-3 out, lft in ld last, sn hdd & no ext* 2
87³ Island Echo [12]*prog 5 out, ev ch 3 out, sn onepcd ...* 3
Also: Galways Granite [12] (4), 133 Tomasins Choice (pu), Ballybeggan Boy (pu), 135 Brian Og (f), 106 Bosco's Touch (pu), 106 Clon Caw (pu), 140² Mr Freeman (f), 160 Just Harvey (pu), 133 Vancouver Island (pu)
12 ran. 1l, 6l, ¾l. SP 5-1.

207 - Mares Maiden 6yo+

138 Brogeen Dubh [15]..................C O'Donovan 1
2nd 5 out, ld 3 out, clr apr last, drvn out...............
Geneva Steele [14]*ld 5 out-3 out, rallied last, no ext flat...* 2
139 Victim Of Slander [13]*3rd 5 out, kpt on onepcd frm 2 out...* 3
Also: 38 Shuil Na Mhuire (4), 138 Ballybeggan Lady (pu), 109 Serenas Serenade (pu), Dante's Whistle (pu), Sandys Girl (pu), 140 Holiday Time (pu), Miss Catherine (pu), Crashland (pu), 163 Executive Opal (pu), 143 Lisselan Lass (pu), 140 Blame Barney (pu)
14 ran. 2l, 3l, 20l. SP 7-1.

208 - Winners Of One

108 Digacre [16] ....J McNamara 1
prog 4 out, chal nxt, styd on to ld flat ....
144² Henleydown [16]*prom, ld 5 out, hdd flat, no ext ......* 2
91¹ Leaping Three [15]*chsd ldrs, not qckn 3 out, kpt on flat...* 3
Also: Carbery Minstrel [14] (4), 162¹ Rosetown Girl [14] (5), 25¹ Golly Miss Molly [11] (6), 130 Fethard Orchid (7)
7 ran. ½l, 1l, 2l, 1l, 8l, 6l. SP 9-1.

EAST DOWN
Tyrella
Saturday March 8th
GOOD TO FIRM

209 - Confined Lightweight

126 Ellies Pride [17].........................W Ewing 1
in tch, ld 2 out, styd on wll ....
122³ Bonquist [14]*chsd ldrs, kpt on to tk 2nd nr fin ....* 2
Sideways Sally [14]*ld to 2 out, sn btn.....................* 3
Also: 113 Morans Forge (ur), Cluan Goill (pu), 122 Bright Lad (ref)
6 ran. 8l, ½l. SP 5-1.

210 - Maiden 5 & 6yo

117 Pharbrook Lad [14] ....B Hamilton 1
chsd ldr to 2 out, lft 2nd agn last, hrd rdn to ld flat......
71 Bannagh Mor [14]*lft in ld 2nd, mstk 2 out, hdd & no ext flat...* 2
71² Cardinals Folly [12]*mid-div, nvr nrr ....* 3
Also: Sherwin (4), Ballinavary VI (5), 118² Some Man (6), 128 Chase The Sun (7), Four North (pu), One Eleven (pu), 175 Tullamore (pu), Jimyril (f), 128² Ballydavid (ro), 176 Ollar House (pu), 175² Pull The Lever (pu)
14 ran. Hd, 6l, dist, 2l, 3l, 4l. SP 10-1.

211 - Open Lightweight

177 Captain Brandy [19] ....D Christie 1
chsd ldrs, ld 4 out, clr 2 out, just hld on ....
116² Mr Five Wood [19]*sn rdn to chs ldrs, chsd wnr 2 out, chal last, just hld ....* 2
116 Lacken Beau [19]*prog to 3rd 2 out, chal last, just hld* 3
Also: 121³ The Boolya [19] (4), 116 Gale Griffin [16] (5), 121 Glenshane Pass (pu), 121 Arctic Treasure (pu), Itsuptome VI (pu), Fay Lin (pu), 123 Deerfield (pu)
10 ran. Nk, nk, ½l, 10l. SP 3-1.

212 - Mares Maiden 5yo+

Killmurray Buck [15] ....R Barnwell 1
prog hlfwy, ld 4 out, clr apr last, rdn out ....
178 Carlies Wood [13]*mid-div, styd on 2 out, tk 2nd nr fin* 2
173 Dernamay [13]*prog to 3rd 3 out, chal nxt, sn no ext...* 3
Also: 129 Castlevigganlady [11] (4), 126 Crottys Bridge (5), 178 Runaco (6), Kitzberg (7), 126 Roselynhill (8), 126 Shanes Bay (pu), 125 Bold Irene (pu), 111² Ballindante (pu), 173 Can She Do It (pu), 113 Cool Swallow (pu), 126 Risk-A-Dinge (f), Shantallow (pu), 179 Nancy Hill (pu), Microtelle Rose (f), 179 Kan-Ann (pu)
18 ran. 4l, ½l, 6l, 3l, 5l, 15l, 10l. SP 5-2.

213 - Winners Of Two

129¹ Denfield [19] ....I Buchanan 1
cls up, ld 3 out, in cmmnd whn lft clr last..............
68¹ Demoniac (Fr) [15]*cls up, mstks 3 out & nxt, btn whn hmpd last, kpt on ....* 2
113³ Willy Wee [15]*cls up, onepcd aft 2 out...............* 3
Also: 124² Hall's Mill [12] (4), 112 Thefirstone (pu), 124 The Convincer (f), 121 Ballywoodock VI (pu), 116 Hiltonstown Lass (f)
8 ran. 6l, 1l, 8l. SP 1-2.

214 - Maiden 7yo+

122 The Golam [15] ....L McBratney 1
cls up, chal apr last, hrd rdn to ld flat.................
72 La Mancha Boy [14] 2D
180 Florida Or Bust [12]*trckd ldr to 4 out, onepcd aft, fin 3rd, promoted.......* 2
122² Ash Brae*nvr nrr, fin 4th, promoted ....* 3
Also: A Monkey For Dick (4), 123 Creme Supreme (5), 120 Scotts Cross (6), Blue Bay (pu), Freemanstown (f), Best Interest (ur), 122 Copper End (bd), 174 Indexia (ro), 180 Ordain (pu), Boreen Boy (ur)
14 ran. 4l, 4l, 15l, 2l, 5l, dist. SP 10-1.

KILLINICK HARRIERS
Lingstown
Sunday March 9th
GOOD

215 - Winners Of One

155 Bree Hill [19] ....P Crowley 1
rear, prog & pshd alng 5 out, lft 2nd 2 out, lft clr last....
94¹ Hidden Hollow [15]*nvr dang, styd on frm 3 out, lft 2nd last* 2
147 Sandfair [12]*nvr dang, lft bttr by dfctns..............* 3
Also: 139¹ Push Gently [12] (4), 193 Viking Buoy [10] (5), 162 Borreeva (6), 151¹ Woodbinesandroses (7), 183³ Oatflake (8), 166¹ Penstal Lady (9), Maks Dream (10), 130 Sandy Pearl Two (11), Rufo's Rapper (pu), 147 Little Minute (f), 132 Bill Joyce (pu), 156¹ Hellofahooly (pu), Sapphire 'N' Silver (pu), 182 Mineral Al (pu), 89 Hyelord (ur)
18 ran. 6l, 10l, 1l, 6l, 5l, 2l, 2l, 10l, 4l, 3l. SP 5-1.

216 - Open Lightweight

149¹ Ozier Hill [21]..............................J Berry 1
prog 4 out, ld 2 out, drvn out ....
134¹ Slaney Wind [20]*prom, ld 4 out-2 out, kpt on well.....* 2
Visible Difference [17]*mid-div, lft 3rd 2 out, no imp ldrs ....* 3
Also: 37² Credit Transfer [16] (4), O Ghluin Go Ghluin [15] (5), 149 Trimmer Wonder [12] (6), 149³ Harveysland [11] (7), 149 Albert's Fancy [10] (8), 185 Selkoline (9), 92 Kilmisten Breeze (pu), 147¹ Royal Arctic (f)
11 ran. 1l, 10l, 3l, 1½l, 10l, 2l, 2l, 2l. SP 1-2.

217 - Mares Maiden 5 & 6yo I

151 Supreme Gold [16]......................P Crowley 1
trckd ldrs, chal apr last, hrd rdn to ld flat.............
188 Spritly Lady [16]*prom, ld 3 out, hdd & no ext flat .....* 2
139 Vulthyne [14]*chsd ldrs, styd on onepcd frm 2 out .....* 3
Also: 90 Billie's Mate [14] (4), 98 Corshanna River (5), 185 Davids Pride (6), Thieving Sands (f), 187 Running On Thyne (pu), Jembato

(pu), 151 Oh Donna (pu), 97 Over The Tavern (pu), Sharlene (f), 97 Lipstick Lady (pu), 90² Bay Lough (ur), 187 Murphys Cross (pu), 150² Nervous Kate (pu), 188 Hardtobegood (pu), Coolroedolly (pu)
18 ran. ½l, 6l, 1l, dist, 5l. SP Evens.

218 - Mares Maiden 5 & 6yo II

151 **Imlistening [15]**........................**J Berry** 1
prom, ld apr last, rdn out
98 **Roseland [14]***disp til ld 4 out, hdd apr last, kpt on* 2
96 **Porter Tastes Nice [14]***prom, chal apr last, kpt on* 3
Also: 10 Donnrua (4), 150 Over The Glen (5), 187 Rachels Plan (6), 139 Clochban Clonroche (7), 151 Americo Lady (8), 151 Prettymaid (9), 150 Wunwabbitwun (10), Perkys Plonker (11), Kyle Lamp (pu), 150 Torduff Bay (pu), 186 Black Fashion (f), Keeragh (pu), 96 Sweet Perk (f), 151 Cost-A-Lot (f), Josie's Turn (pu)
18 ran. 2l, ½l, dist, 12l, 2l, 10l, 1l, dist, 2l, 10l. SP Evens.

219 - Maiden 5 & 6yo I

Solvang [15]........................**E Gallagher** 1
trckd ldrs, chal 2 out, ld last, hld on
152 **Frostbitten [15]***prom, ld 5 out-last, rallied flat*........ 2
Dunaree [12]*prog 5 out, styd on onepcd frm 2 out* 3
Also: 153³ Ringaheen (4), 152 Buck And A Half (5), 64 Gee Thanks (6), 148 Speedy O'Dee (pu), 148 Annie Leap (pu), 153 Skidrow River (pu), 152 Newbog Lad (pu), 148³ Apollodorus (pu), Just Hang On (pu), 148 Satquaid (pu), Go Like The Devil (pu), 153 Invader General (pu), 94 Smiling Minstrel (pu), 181 Great Reminder (pu)
17 ran. ½l, 10l, 8l, 2l, dist. SP 5-2.

220 - Maiden 5 & 6yo II

57 **Nicholls Cross [16]**..................**K O'Donnell** 1
in tch, prog to ld apr last, pshd out
152 **Inch Cross [14]***ld to apr last, onepcd* 2
181 **Orphan Spa [14]***chsd ldrs, styd on onepcd apr last* 3
Also: Bergkamp [11] (4), 65 Berts Cabin [10] (5), Victory Song (6), 152 Coopers Clan (7), 50 Welsh Lane (pu), Society Lad (pu), 184 Free-styler (pu), Pondernot (f), 86 Colmans Hatch (pu), 181 Metro Fashion (pu), 184 Bart Eile (pu), Shanacoole Pride (f), Law Pursuit (pu), Lonely Castle (pu), 152 Just Joe (pu)
18 ran. 2l, 1l, 10l, 3l, 8l, 25l. SP 6-1.

221 - Maiden 7yo+ I

156 **Ross Quay [15]**......................**E Gallagher** 1
prog 5 out, chal 2 out, ld last, kpt on
135 **Knockanoran [14]***prog 5 out, ld 2 out-last, no ext flat* 2
52 **Buck Run [13]***prog 5 out, styd on onepcd frm 2 out* 3
Also: 167 Glen Of Bargy [11] (4), 53 Garacillin (5), 98 Lost Coin (6), 156² Over The Barrow (pu), Dunamanagh Express (pu), 154 Lord Amethyst (pu), 156 Cottiers Den (f), 155 Little Len (pu), 154 Cuckroo (pu), Weavers Window VI (pu), The Grey Major [15] (ur), 188 Buzz About (pu), Baytownghost (pu)
16 ran. 2l, 4l, 5l, 12l, 10l. SP Evens.

222 - Maiden 7yo+ II

154² **Bourbon County [16]**..................**D Whelan** 1
prog 3 out, ld nxt, rdn clr last
155 **Boker Hill [13]***prom, ld 3 out-nxt, sn onepcd* 2
182 **Barnadown [11]***nvr dang, kpt on frm 2 out* 3
Also: 154 Shimano [10] (4), 61 Hasty Hours (5), River Bargy (6), 139 Trimmer Lady (7), Gypsy Rover (pu), 166 Blazey Lady (pu), 98 Sky Rainbow (pu), Sharons Choice (f), 61 Cynical Wit (pu), Marked Well (pu), 138 Codology (pu), 155 Greedy Johno (pu), Oneoftheclan (pu)
16 ran. 10l, 5l, 5l, 4l, 1½l, 15l. SP 5-4.

223 - Maiden 7yo+ III

155 **Captain Deen [16]**.....................**J P Berry** 1
hld up, prog 4 out, lft 2nd 2 out, ld last, styd on
Corrigeen Rambler [13]*chsd ldng pair, 2nd 4 out, ld 2 out-last, wknd*.... 2
154 **Twin Track***prog 4 out, hmpd 2 out, wknd* 3
Also: 155 Slow Beet (4), 156 Set A Way (pu), 155² Benalf (f), Prima-Cosa (pu), 100 Clare To Here (pu), Sparkes Cross (pu), Miss Day (pu), Barrystown Lady (pu), Young Blossom (pu), 156 Louis de Palmer (f), 56 Stoney Piper (pu), 56 Poulgillie (pu)
15 ran. 8l, dist, dist. SP Evens.

224 - Nomination

149 **Dennistownthriller**......................**J Roche** 1
made most, lft clr last
164² **Man With A Plan VI***chsd wnr 3 out, chnc whn u.r. last, rmntd* 2
185¹ **Slaney Goodness***t.o.* 3
Also: 90¹ Tullibardniceneasy (f), Gandon Lady (f), 61 Hayestown Hope (pu)
6 ran. Dist, 10l. SP Evens.

SOUTH WESTMEATH
The Pigeons
Sunday March 9th
GOOD TO SOFT

225 - Confined

157 **Cloughan Boy [14]**.....................**A Fleming** 1
chsd ldrs, lft in ld 3 out, kpt on
Black Boreen [13]*chsd ldrs, hmpd 3 out, not rcvr* 2
Castlepook*nvr dang* 3
Also: Niamhs Glory (f), 201² Kings Alibi (f), 202 Regular Beat (pu)
6 ran. 5l, 25l. SP 3-1.

226 - Maiden 5 & 6yo

94 **Magillen [14]**........................**G Harford** 1
prom, chsd ldr 2 out, lft in ld flat
95 **No Other Hill [13]***prom, ld 3 out, clr nxt, wknd rpdly & hdd flat* 2
High Thyne*nvr dang* 3
Also: 201 Miss Jake (4), Summerhill Flier (f), Camla Lad (f), 64³ Ollies Boy (pu), Cois Inbhir (pu), 111 Musical Waves (f), 128 Corn Beat (bd), Over The Plough (f)
11 ran. 3l, dist, dist. SP 3-1.

227 - Mares Maiden 5yo+ I

125 **Mystic Moment [16]**.................**B Hamilton** 1
prog 6 out, ld 2 out, rdn out
120 **Maries Call [14]***prog 5 out, chsd wnr 2 out, kpt on* 2
Ardeedale [10]*ld 5th to 2 out, sn outpcd* 3
Also: 124 Legganhall (4), 138 Dysart Abbey (5), 96 Areyouthereyet (6), 31 Golden Mist (f), Heather Queen (ur), Simpsons Kid (f), 111 Lady Zaffaran (f), 97 Ballynagussaun (f), Gliding Away (pu)
12 ran. 4l, 12l, 15l, 15l, 4l. SP 5-1.

228 - Mares Maiden 5yo+ II

119 **Damolly Rose [14]**....................**L Lennon** 1
w.w. 2nd 4 out, ld last, hld on flat
162 **Handy Sally [14]***4th 4 out, chal last, just hld*.... 2
113 **Glenpine [14]***prog to chs ldrs 2 out, chal last, kpt on* .. 3
Also: 96 Proud Princess [12] (4), Lady Fleck [11] (5), 60 Fortunes Cast (6), 186 Bramhall Princess (7), Foyle Valley Lady (8), 31 Buckskins Babe (pu), 66 Shes Bizarre (ro), 124 Arctic Party (pu), Mystical Lord (pu)
12 ran. ½l, 1l, 2l, 4l, dist, 5l, 10l. SP 6-1.

229 - Winners Of One

160¹ **Johnstheman [18]**....................**P Graffin** 1
trckd ldr, ld 4 out, lft clr nxt, unchal aft
157 **Ballybriken Castle***ld to 4 out, sn btn, lft 2nd nxt* 2
199³ **Ballinaveen Bridge***nvr dang*.... 3
Also: 35¹ Oul Larry Andy (f), 108 Big Murt (ro)
5 ran. 25l, 2l. SP 4-5.

230 - Open Lightweight

173¹ **Missing Lady [19]**..................**C McCarren** 1
prom, ld 2 out, styd on well
174³ **Annie's Arthur [18]***prom, chal 2 out, no ext flat* 2
173 **Voldi [17]***ld hlfwy to 2 out, no ext aft*.... 3
Also: 147 Mitchelstown River (4), 27 Carrigans Lad (5), Palmura (ro)

6 ran. 1½l, 2l, dist, dist. SP 6-4.

231 - Maiden 7yo+ I

161² **Charlie Hawes [15]**..............**A Younghusband** 1
trckd ldr, ld 5 out, styd on well
99 **Almauritia [12]***rear, kpt on to chs wnr apr last, no imp* 2
202 **Mask River***nvr dang* 3
Also: 180 Paddy Red (4), 100 Tuskar Flop (5), 162 Clonfert Sue (6), Biddys Boy (pu), Cassfinn (pu), 202 Miss Outlaw (f), 154 Percusionist (pu), Baileys Gate (pu), 202 Park West (pu)
12 ran. 10l, 8l, 8l, 3l, dist. SP 2-1.

232 - Maiden 7yo+ II

202² **Premium Brand [15]**....................**P Graffin** 1
trckd ldr, ld 2 out, hrd rdn last, hld on
123 **Normous [14]***prog to chal aft 2 out, ev ch, no ext nr fin* 2
Call Me Joe [14]*mid-div, styd on frm 2 out, nvr nrr* 3
Also: 72 Laurelvale (4), 119 Rovet (5), 202³ Carnmore House (6), 99 Docummins (ur), Test The Jockey (f), Tullyhoniver (pu), 156³ Siamsa Brae (pu), 122 Inactualfact (pu), 107 Belville Pond (f)
12 ran. 2l, 1l, dist, 3l, dist. SP 2-1.

WEST CARBERY
Skibbereen
Sunday March 9th
GOOD TO SOFT

233 - Maiden 4yo

Forest Tribe [13]...........................**D Murphy** 1
ld hlfwy, in cmmnd whn lft wll clr last
Ivy Mist*nvr dang, t.o. & lft 2nd last* 2
Also: The Bandon Car (f)
3 ran. Dist. SP 2-1.

234 - Mares Maiden 5yo+ I

139² **Cush Princess [16]**....................**T Lombard** 1
made all, drvn clr aft 2 out
73³ **Rio Star***chsd wnr hlfwy, chal & blnd 2 out, wknd* 2
207 **Holiday Time***nvr dang* 3
Also: 80³ Ardfert Minstrel (4), 167 Marys Friend (5), 79 Nissan Star (6), 48 Frosty Morn (pu), 79 Hazy Mist (pu), 189³ Sea Breta (f), Lamanaugh Lady VI (f)
10 ran. Dist, 3l, 3l. SP 6-4.

235 - Mares Maiden 5yo+ II

138 **Curley Gale [15]**.........................**M Cronin** 1
prom, ld 2 out, kpt on well
166 **Highland Call [13]***chsd wnr 2 out, no ext last* 2
138 **Faithful Pal [12]***effort to chal 2 out, no ext apr last* 3
Also: 166 Merry River [10] (4), 139 Paros Leader (pu), 143³ Regal Gossip (pu), 167 Little Simba (f), 139 Idiot's Surprise (pu), 166 La Kestrel (f), 138 Derrygra Fountain (pu)
10 ran. 6l, 3l, 7l. SP 4-1.

236 - Winners Of Two

143¹ **Greenflag Princess [20]**...............**J Sheehan** 1
ld 4th, clr 4 out, comf
49 **Inniscein [16]***effort 4 out, kpt on onepcd frm nxt, no imp wnr* 2
1¹ **No Problem [15]***chsd wnr 4 out, sn no imp* 3
Also: 145³ Radical-Times [12] (4), 205 Kilcullys-Pride (5), 15¹ Lough Lein Spirit (f)
6 ran. 5l, 2l, 10l. SP 2-1.

237 - Mares Lightweight

131 **Tack Room Lady [19]**..................**T Lombard** 1
made all, styd on wll frm 3 out
134 **Pharditu [16]***prog to chal & ev ch 3 out, btn frm nxt* 2
130² **The Pulpit [13]***nvr nrr* 3
Also: 131³ Derry's Diamond (4), 167¹ Phartoomanny (f), 130 No Swap (pu), 144 Scarteen Lower (pu)
7 ran. 8l, 8l, 20l. SP 9-4.

238 - Adjacent Maiden

139 **Ballinvuskig Lady [15]**.................**K Beecher** 1
ld to 3 out, kpt on agn to ld flat
146 **The Stag [14]***trckd ldr, ld 3 out, clr whn jmpd slwly last, sn hdd* 2
136 **Clashview [11]***nvr nrr* 3
Also: 146 Stags Rock (4), 203 Arthur (5), 81³ Short Circuit (6), Lovely Hurling (7), 135 Girlough Castle (pu), Carlingford Pit (f), 135 Father O'Reilly (pu), 136 Prophets Thumb (f), 207 Lisselan Lass (pu), 82 Timmy Tuff (pu), Tom The Boy VI (pu)
14 ran. 2l, 10l, 5l. SP 3-1.

239 - Maiden 5yo+

85 **Clashbridane [15]**.......................**E Fehily** 1
prog to ld 4 out, hrd rdn last, just hld on
137³ **Coole Abbey [15]***prog to chs wnr 3 out, ev ch & hrd rdn flat, just hld* 2
76 **Gortroe Guy [11]***ld to 4 out, outpcd aft 2 out* 3
Also: The Rising Buck VI (pu), 141 Clonageera (pu), 133² Corkers Flame (pu), 140 Jake The Peg (pu), Straight Angle (pu)
8 ran. Nk, 10l. SP 6-1.

LIMERICK FOXHOUNDS
Greenmount
Sunday March 9th
SOFT

240 - Winners Of Three

131¹ **Don't Waste It [20]**..................**J McNamara** 1
prom, ld aft 2 out, ran on well
197¹ **Pharavo [17]***clr ldr til hdd aft 2 out, no ext* 2
163¹ **Easter Bard [15]***chsd ldrs, onepcd frm 2 out* 3
Also: 130 Thadys Remedy (4), 208 Golly Miss Molly [12] (5), Meneduke (6), 194 Cozy Cottage (7), 170 Queenofclubs (pu), 200¹ My New Merc (pu), 159¹ Iona Flyer (f)
10 ran. 5l, 5l, 6l. SP 3-1.

241 - Maiden 5yo

141² **Bumper To Bumper [16]**..............**D O'Meara** 1
prom, ld 4 out, lft clr 2 out, styd on wll
47 **Ship Of Shame***chsd ldrs, lft 2nd 2 out, no imp* 2
85 **My Uncle Batt***t.o* 3
Also: 191 Viking Rod (f), Pacificblue (pu), Dothali (pu), 158 Anodfromalord (pu), 84 Charleys Run (pu), 196 Welsh Lad (f), Sporadic Verse (f), 104 Caher Society (pu), 133 Bridge Party (pu), 133 Suave (pu)
13 ran. 15l, dist. SP 6-4.

242 - Maiden 7yo+

100 **The Territorian [15]**...................**J Moloney** 1
chsd ldrs, ld apr 2 out, styd on wll
136 **No Such Parson [12]***chsd ldrs, kpt on onepcd frm 2 out* 2
161 **Sammy Sunshine***nvr dang, onepcd frm 2 out* 3
Also: 169 Speightstown Boy (4), 202 River Wild (5), 136 Irish Display (pu), Have Another (pu), Boulea Boy (ro), 24 Beau Cinq (pu), Stand Alone (ref), 171 Man Of Hope (pu), Scheamin N Dreamin (pu)
12 ran. 8l, 10l, 1l. SP 3-1.

243 - Maiden 6yo

Mac's Legend [16].....................**D Costello** 1
made all, clr 2 out, styd on wll
160² **Kincora [14]***rear, styd on 2 out, tk 2nd flat* 2
Royal Leader [10]*chsd wnr halfwy, rdn & btn aft 3 out* 3
Also: 161 Tom Deely [10] (4), 137 Colmans Hope (5), Executive Fontaine (pu), 106³ Dare To Deel (pu), 198 Tulira Hill (pu), Well Doctor (pu), 189 Major Bill (pu), 160 Meldante VI (pu), 160 Ballyluckamore (pu), 198³ Bite Back (pu), Dark Opal (pu)

14 ran. 5l, 15l, nk. SP Evens.

244 - Open Lightweight

205³ Awbeg Rover [19] ....B Moran 1
hld up, prog to ld 2 out, sn clr ....
168² Tommy The Duke [17]*made most to 2 out, not qckn* .. 2
157² Shareza River [16]*chsd ldrs, onepcd frm 3 out* 3
Also: 37¹ Just A Breeze [15] (4), Hopefully True (ro), 199 Mounthenry Star (pu), 105³ Light Argument (pu)
7 ran. 5l, 3l, 3l. SP 10-1.

245 - Mares Maiden

204 Furry Island [15] ....G Mulcaire 1
chsd ldrs, ld aft 3 out, styd on flat ....
163³ Lothian Magic [14]*prog 3 out, chal nxt, no ext flat* 2
159 Loch Lomond*nvr dang, t.o.* 3
Also: 163 Ring Mam (4), 143² Royal Chapeau (pu), 201 Norman Road (pu), Tiernys Island (f), 110 The Hairy Lord (pu), 163 Shuil Flossy (pu), Hang In There (pu), Aglish Pride (f)
11 ran. 3l, dist, 3l. SP 8-1.

TYNAN & ARMAGH
Farmacaffley
Saturday March 15th
SOFT

246 - Confined Lightweight

173² Listrakelt [16] ....J McGurgan 1
hld up, prog 3 out, ld last, styd on wll ....
176 Track O'Profit [15]*prog 3 out, styd on to chs wnr flat, no imp* 2
173 Highland Buck [15]*chsd ldrs, onepcd apr last* 3
Also: 212³ Dernamay [15] (4), 120 Tassagh Boy [10] (5), Blueilier (6), Lady Of Gortmerron (pu)
7 ran. 3l, ½l, ½l, 15l, 4l. SP 2-1.

247 - Maiden 5 & 6yo I

175 Swan Point [16] ....A Martin 1
5th 6 out, trckd ldr 2 out, ld last, easily ....
Vintage Choice [13]*4th 6 out, lft in ld nxt, hdd last, no ch wth wnr* 2
174 My Man [12]*nvr dang, styd on frm 2 out* 3
Also: 127² Bridge End [11] (4), 127 Barnagan [11] (5), 127 Fairtree (6), 127 Moses Man (7), 128 Capail Mor (8), 175 Dancing Mike (9), Pharniskey (pu), Regar (pu), Whatcanido (pu), Nijapajo (pu), 210 Ollar House (f), 175 Russell Lodge (pu), 175 Ballymichael (pu), 118 Shuil Mor (pu)
17 ran. 4l, 4l, 4l, 1l, 12l, 10l, dist, 2l. SP Evens.

248 - Maiden 5 & 6yo II

Rambling Sam [15] ....J Gault 1
w.w. prog 3 out, chal flat, sn ld, ran on ....
127³ Native Cove [14]*ld 5 out til hdd & no ext flat* 2
127 Righteye [14]*prog 2 out, chal last, no ext flat* 3
Also: 175³ Private Power [12] (4), Roscrily William [11] (5), 176² Panda Nova [10] (6), 175 Parman (7), 175 Allistragh Lad (8), 210 Ballydavid (9), 175 Golfing Man (10), Dexter Gordon (pu), Gold Signal (pu), All The Better (pu), 127 Cascum Lad (pu), 176 Reds Paradise (pu), Dennett Lough (pu)
16 ran. 2l, ½l, 4l, 3l, 3l, 1½l, 12l, 2l, ½l. SP 16-1.

249 - Open Lightweight

211¹ Captain Brandy [23] ....D Christie 1
trckd ldr, ld 2 out, styd on wll ....
211 The Boolya [18]*chsd ldrs, onepcd frm 2 out* 2
115¹ Funny Ye Know [18]*ld to 2 out, sn btn* 3
Also: 177 Captains Bar [18] (4), 177 Shanecracken (5), 211³ Lacken Beau (6), 185 Glenroe Gal (7), 211 Itsuptome VI (8), Limeridge (9), Prince Yaza (pu), Elegant Isle (pu), 211 Fay Lin (pu), Manhattan Jewel (pu)
13 ran. 10l, 2l, 1l, 30l, 4l, 30l, 15l, dist. SP 3-1.

250 - Mares Maiden 5yo+ I

178³ Bann View [15] ....I Buchanan 1
in tch, went 3rd 2 out, chal last, jnd ldr post ....
178 Gold Leader [15]..........................P Graffin 1
prom, disp 5 out, ld 3 out, jnd post ....
178² Glenalla Bella [12]*4th 5 out, chsd ldr 2 out, outpcd apr last* 3
Also: 178 Star Flyer [12] (4), 178 Mourne Miner [12] (5), 179 Maccarrons Run (pu), 212 Shantallow (pu), Blue Gas (pu), 125 Tullyallenstar (pu), 214 Blue Bay (pu), Caladonian Light (pu), 178 Tierfergus (pu), Hillview Susie (pu), 179 Bobby Blazer (f), 126² Ngala (pu), 120 Island Harriet (pu), 112 Drumrock Lady (pu), Rosemary Ann (pu)
18 ran. Dd-ht, 6l, ½l, nk. SP Evens.

251 - Mares Maiden 5yo+ II

Leane [15] ....P Graffin 1
prog to ld 3 out, drw clr apr last, styd on wll ....
125 Floruceva [13]*prom, ld 4 out-nxt, ev ch 2 out, onepcd apr last* 2
Scoil Hill [11]*chsd ldrs, cls up 2 out, onepcd* 3
Also: 120 Skinny Minnie (pu), 115 Karen's Leader (pu), Jinxey Glen (pu), Lizzies Corner (f), 178 Drumree (pu), Hillview Lizzie (pu), 179 Ollar Lady (pu), 126 Secret Door (pu), Land Forlorn (pu), Touch Of Autumn (pu), 179² Forever Grey (pu), 178 Princess Cataldi (pu), 179 Blue Alliance (pu), 113 Three Town Rock (co)
17 ran. 6l, 6l. SP 4-1.

252 - Winners Of Two

180¹ Baby Jamie [20]..........................A Martin 1
raced wd, trckd ldrs, chal 2 out, ld flat, comf. ....
119¹ Cebu Gale [17]*ld hlfwy till hdd & no ext flat* 2
174 Golden Start [10]*prom, chsd ldr hlfwy til mstk 3 out, wknd* 3
Also: 129² Manhattan Prince [10] (4), 112³ Raleagh Muggins [10] (5), 178¹ Pepsa Morfee (6), 113 Chene Rose (pu), 124 Mysterious Beau (pu), 124 Drumiller Hill Lad (f), 112 Sametoyou (pu), 213 Ballywoodock VI (pu), 122¹ Half Scotch (pu), 129 Uncle Art (pu), 176¹ Bluagale (pu), 174 G I Joe (pu)
15 ran. 2l, 20l, ½l, 1l, dist. SP 6-4.

253 - Maiden 7yo+ I

122 Pats Farewell [15] ....P Graffin 1
ld to 6 out, ld 3 out, mstk nxt, sn clr, fin tired ....
180 Where's Sam [12]*chsd ldrs, kpt on to chs wnr apr last, no imp* 2
214 La Mancha Boy*chsd ldrs, ld 6 out, sn clr, hdd 3 out, wknd rpdly nxt.* 3
Also: 123 Dhu Bond (pu), 119² Pauls Point (pu), Cougar D'Avelot (pu), 120 Dawn Dieu (pu), 214 Scotts Cross (pu), Onemans Choice (pu), 122 Mannix (pu), Captains Friend (pu), 214 Indexia (ro), 123 A Bit Of A Rascal (pu), 129 Wind Of Glory (f)
14 ran. 10l, dist. SP 3-1.

254 - Maiden 7yo+ II

180² Wilbar [17]............................J O'Connell 1
hld up, ld 3 out, drew clr last ....
232 Inactualfact [12]*ld/disp to 3 out, onepcd aft* 2
123² Ballycastle Bay [12]*effort to chs ldrs 3 out, onepcd aft nxt* 3
Also: 180 Mandingo [10] (4), 180 You Said It (5), 180 Emerald Breffni (6), 120 Greet The Greek (7), 179 Tiger Dolly (pu), Nature Perfected (pu), 120 Tom Haggard (ro), Leslieshill (pu), 180 Stackie Boy (pu), 173 The Conawarey (pu), Partyonjason (pu)
14 ran. 12l, 1l, 6l, 3l, 25l, 10l. SP Evens.

CLOYNE HARRIERS
Cloyne
Sunday March 16th
GOOD

255 - Maiden 4yo

Lanmire [16] ....E Bolger 1
made all, sn clr, easily ....
Lisdoyleladya*nvr dang, chsd wnr 3 out, no ch ....* 2
Billy The Snake*nvr dnag, no ch frm 4 out............* 3
Also: Glacial Dancer (4), 165² Ramona Style (pu), The Coppeen Lord (pu), 165³ Curragh Lord (pu), Moscow Squeaker (pu)
8 ran. Dist, 3l, 4l. SP Evens.

256 - Winners Of One I

137¹ **Wayward King [18] ....P Cashman** 1
prom, ld hlfwy, styd on wll und pres flat...............
75³ **Lucky Town [17]***prssd wnr 6 out, ev ch last, no ext flat...* 2
82¹ **Hugo Henry [10]***chsd ldng pair 6 out, no imp ....* 3
Also: 102¹ Oneofourown (4), 75 John's Right (5), 237 Scarteen Lower (6), 147 Trimmer Princess (7), 75 Prudence Sarn (f), 87¹ Cromogue Minstrel (pu), Sleepy Rock (ro), Burkean Melody (pu)
11 ran. 1½l, 20l, 2l. SP 7-2.

257 - Winners Of One II

221¹ **Ross Quay [18].......................E Gallagher** 1
chsd ldrs, lft in ld 4 out, sn clr ....
136¹ **Teads Boreen [14]***chsd ldrs, lft wth ev ch 4 out, sn outpcd...* 2
138¹ **Bella Brownie***nvr dang...............................* 3
Also: Proscenium (pu), 168 Pearl Dante (bd), 41 Fair Revival (pu), 237 Phartoomanny (f), 78 Sumakano (pu), 130 Glenbower Queen (pu)
9 ran. 10l, 10l. SP 5-1.

258 - Adjacent Maiden 5yo+

207 **Shuil Na Mhuire [15] ....B Walsh** 1
w.w. ld 3 out, sn clr ....
166 **Menalma***nvr dang, no ch wnr frm 2 out ....* 2
195 **Blackwater Heights***nvr dang ....* 3
Also: 38 Mr Who (pu), 192 Uncle Archie (pu), 38 Pure Energy (pu), 132 All A Joke (pu), Missing Mama (pu), 48 Gluais Linn (pu)
9 ran. Dist, 5l. SP 3-1.

259 - Open Lightweight

27¹ **Dixon Varner [26]........................E Bolger** 1
made all, clr 2 out, comf ....
168¹ **Harbour Leader [22]***w.w. chsd wnr 3 out, no imp frm nxt...* 2
Carry On Shoon [19]*chsd ldrs, onepcd frm 3 out .....* 3
Also: 145² Warning Call (4), 194 Big Bo (5), Radical River (6), 145 Get Cracking (7), Father-Pat (8), All Sytle (ur), 131 Looking Ahead (ur), 193 Cooladerra Lady (pu)
11 ran. 10l, 8l, dist. SP 5-4.

260 - Maiden 5yo+ I

169 **Tullys Ball [16] ....J Sheehan** 1
ld 5th, styd on wll frm 2 out..............................
Persian Packer [14]*chsd wnr 3 out, no imp frm nxt...* 2
85 **Springford***nvr dnag, t.o. ....* 3
Also: Hazy Sea (pu), 172 Sheer Mischief (pu), Another Berry (pu), 172 Lord Egross (pu), 189 Running Solo (pu), Dante's Reward (pu), 171 Carry On Brendan (pu), 135 Icantsay (pu), 152 The Podger (pu), 132 Sliabh Luchra Boy (pu), 20 Dromod Magic (pu)
14 ran. 5l, dist. SP 6-4.

261 - Maiden 5yo+ II

84 **As Sharp Again [16] ....P Cashman** 1
made all, lft clr 4 out, unchal ....
192 **Tommys Pride***nvr dang, lft poor 2nd 3 out ....* 2
Glentoralda*nvr dang, t.o. ....* 3
Also: 142 Jimmy Dan (4), 171 Clongeel Lord (pu), 64 Jorodec (ur), 192 Jolly Paddy (pu), Wintry Willow (pu), Fernboy (pu), Forrest Fuse (ur), 77 Just A Playboy (pu), 103 Nineteenofive (pu), Proud Carlingford (pu), Festive Teak (f)
14 ran. Dist, 8l, dist. SP 3-1.

262 - Maiden 5yo+ III

191² **Cirvin [18] ....J Sheehan** 1
hld up, prog to ld 2 out, sn clr, easily ....
169² **Skimabit [11]***chsd wnr aft 2 out, no ch ....* 2
135 **Glenselier***nvr dang, t.o. ....* 3
Also: 53 Garryross (4), 73 Phar Desert (5), 133 Geragh Road (6), Bearys Cross (7), 86 Minstrels Quay (8), 192 Bushy Ranger (f), Nattico (ur), 192 Zarante (pu), 172 Lingering On (pu), 191 Coming Through (pu), 172 Laurintinium (bd)
14 ran. 20l, dist, ½l. SP 7-4.

263 - Mares Maiden 5 & 6yo I

90 **Lady Of Iron [16] ....N O'Neill** 1
prom, ld hlfwy, in cmmnd whn lft clr last ....
166 **Leamlara Rose***nvr dang, wll btn whn lft 2nd last.......* 2
Marians Own*nvr dang ....* 3
Also: Julies Joy (f), 90 Electric Can (f), 19 Peggys Leg (f), 204 Happy Hula Girl (f), Nellie Gale (pu), 235 Paros Leader (pu), 187 The Buck Pony (pu), Some Shock (pu), 195 Woodville Native [14] (f), 169 Grange Pine (pu)
13 ran. 20l, 20l. SP 5-1.

264 - Mares Maiden 5 & 6yo II

140 **Just Be Lucky [16] ....D Murphy** 1
ld 5 out-3 out, rallied to ld apr last, sn clr ....
195 **Ballyknock Lass [11]***prog to ld 3 out, hdd & wknd apr last ....* 2
141 **Catrionas Lady***t.o.* 3
Also: 109 Forgoodnessjake VI (4), Divine Rapture (f), 189 Princess Thyne (pu), 91 Comely Maiden (f), 83 Gale Dante (pu), Black Spring (ur), Everlaughing (pu), 167 Lorglane Lady (pu), 90 Papuite (pu)
12 ran. 15l, dist, 4l. SP 4-1.

NORTH KILKENNY
Ballyragget
Sunday March 16th
GOOD TO SOFT

265 - Adjacent Maiden 5yo+

182 **Croi [15] ....M Scanlon** 1
prog to ld 4 out, drvn out....................................
153 **North Kilkenny [14]***ld 6 out-4 out, rallied & ev ch whn mstk last, no ext ....* 2
Grey Venture*nvr dang.......................................* 3
Also: 155 The Cass Man (4), 181 Zanagale (5), 182 Master Finbar (6), 167 Creative Thought (f), 217 Murphys Cross (pu), Royal Stock (ur), 182 Forold (pu), Helluvagale (f), Determined Okie (pu), 148 Carrys Clover (pu), Barraby (f), 63 Crows Cross (pu)
15 ran. 3l, 20l, 2l. SP 6-1.

266 - Open Lightweight

183¹ **Andy's Birthday [23] ....M Phillips** 1
prog to ld 5 out, clr last, comf...........................
216 **Royal Arctic [18]***chsd wnr 4 out, btn apr last.........* 2
134 **Run For Niall***nvr dang, lft poor 3rd last ....* 3
Also: Ballyquin Belle (pu), 216 Selkoline (pu), 230 Palmura (pu), 30 Ounavarra Creek [17] (ur)
7 ran. 8l, dist. SP Evens.

267 - Winners Of One

174² **Stanley Steamer [18] ....C McCarren** 1
prom, ld 5 out, styd on wll apr last ....
186¹ **Kinnahalla [15]***prog to prss wnr 2 out, no ext apr last* 2
168 **Dante Lad***nvr dang, t.o.*..................................... 3
Also: 194 Up The Banner VI (pu), 55³ Priceless Buck (pu), 215 Oatflake (pu)
6 ran. 8l, dist. SP 6-4.

268 - Maiden 5 & 6yo I

Tommy Wynn [17] ....C McGivern 1
made all, clr 2 out, comf ....
219 **Ringaheen [12]***chsd wnr 3 out, no imp ....* 2
181² **Tea Box [12]***chsd ldrs, onepcd frm 3 out ....* 3
Also: 181 Stelinjo (4), Joe Rattle (pu), Rising Paddy (pu), 65 Brother

Day (pu), Mr Buster (pu), 184 Make Up Your Mind (pu), 184 Robinstown (pu)

10 ran. 10l, 1l, 10l. SP 6-1.

269 - Maiden 5 & 6yo II

184 Bramble Wood [16] ....K O'Donnell 1
prom, ld 3 out, styd on well
146 The Big Fella [13]*prom, chsd wnr 3 out, no imp nxt...* 2
Also: Henley Knapp (pu), Say Nowt (pu), 182 Catstown River (f), 220 Society Lad (pu), Loudy Rowdy (pu), Burton Hall (pu), Beet Man (pu), Androscoggin (f)

10 ran. 8l. SP Evens.

270 - Mares Maiden 5 & 6yo I

217 Billie's Mate [16] ....P Colville 1
prog to ld aft 3 out, styd on wll
217[3] Vulthyne [13]*chsd wnr 2 out, no imp* 2
218 Donnrua [10]*chsd ldrs, onepcd 3 out* 3
Also: 218 Black Fashion (4), Segundo (5), 217 Corshanna River (6), Amber Dolly (pu), Dunhill Lady (pu), Heres Holly (pu), 218 Rachels Plan (f), 218 Keeragh (pu)

11 ran. 10l, 10l, 15l. SP 4-1.

271 - Mares Maiden 5 & 6yo II

217 Bay Lough [16]........................C Murphy 1
prom, ld 4 out, clr 2 out, styd on
Halsway Lane [10]*chsd ldrs, kpt on onepcd frm 2 out* 2
25 Micro Villa [10]*chsd wnr aft 4 out, no imp* 3
Also: Stalmonta (4), 245 Ring Mam (5), 186 Rainbow Trix (f), 186 Mocklershill Lady (pu), 166[3] Beat That (pu), 187[3] Springtime Mist (pu), Betseale (pu), Scottish Match (pu)

11 ran. 15l, nk, dist. SP 9-2.

272 - Maiden 7yo+ I

232[3] Call Me Joe [16]..........................D Cullen 1
prom, ld 4 out, drew clr last
227 Gliding Away [14]*prog to jn ldrs 3 out, ev ch apr last, no ext* 2
156 Deep Appeal [12]*rear, kpt on frm 2 out, nrst fin* 3
Also: 61 Brennan For Audits (4), Cool Top (5), Rosmere (6), 166 Aroundthevalley (7), 167 Dante Alainn (pu), 139 Saratoga Sal (pu), 156 Station Man (pu)

10 ran. 6l, 6l, 10l. SP Evens.

273 - Maiden 7yo+ II

154 Dos Deegan [14]...........................P Kelly 1
ld/disp til drew clr frm 3 out
223 Louis de Palmer [10]*chsd ldrs, went 2nd apr last, no imp wnr* 2
221 Garacillin*nvr dang* 3
Also: 223 Barrystown Lady (4), 188 Dusty Rose (pu), 227 Dysart Abbey (pu), 221 Cuckroo (pu), 182[2] Gladstone (ur), 242 Boulea Boy (pu), 221 Cottiers Den (pu)

10 ran. 15l, 4l, 10l. SP 5-2.

COUNTY GALWAY
Athenry
Sunday March 16th
GOOD

274 - Maiden 4yo

Portland Row [17]........................J Quinn 1
made all, ran on well frm 3 out
190[2] Marble City [14]*prom, chsd wnr 5 out, no imp aft 3 out* 2
Manacured*t.o.* 3
Also: Clounties Lady (4), Gingers Girl (f), Gordons Bay (pu), Another Mistake (pu), Five Mile Dancer (pu), Queen Of Silver (pu), 190[3] Ludden Chief (f), Nice Approach (pu)

11 ran. 5l, dist, dist. SP 4-1.

275 - Maiden 5yo+

99 Herb Superb [18] ....E Ewing 1
prom, ld 4 out, sn drew clr
202 Barna Lad*3rd 4 out, no imp on wnr aft* 2
171 Imperial Dawn*chsd wnr 4 out, sn no imp* 3
Also: 100 Gradle (4), Larrigan (5), 196[2] King Of The Suir (6), 176 Galannick (pu), 198[2] Tom's Tune (pu), 103 Ceasars Reign (f), O Curry King (pu), Ongoing Dilemma (f), 106 Court Thyne (ro), Sock Hop (pu), 158 Cast No Shadow (pu), 196 Duke Of Tulla (ur), 231[2] Almauritia (pu), 59 The H'penny Marvel (f)

17 ran. Dist, ½l, 15l, 6l, dist. SP 6-1.

276 - Open Lightweight

193[3] Miners Melody [23]...................A Costello 1
made all, drew clr aft 2 out, comf
244 Light Argument [19]*rear, styd on frm 2 out, no ch wth wnr* 2
199[2] Tantum Bonum [17]*prog to chs wnr 3 out, btn next* 3
Also: 229[3] Ballinaveen Bridge [13] (4), 230 Carrigans Lad [11] (5)

5 ran. 10l, 5l, 8l, 5l. SP 4-5.

277 - Mares Maiden 5yo+ I

201 Lisduff Pride [16]......................D Costello 1
prom, rdn to ld 2 out, styd on well
163 Aine Hencey [12]*chsd ldrs, styd on onepcd frm 2 out* 2
207 Executive Opal*nvr dang, onepcd frm 3 out* 3
Also: 25 Killone River (4), Sound Vision (pu), 179 Sounds Confident (ur), Glencaoin (pu), 200[3] Carnmore Supreme (pu), 228 Lady Fleck (f), 201 Ballycar Princess (pu), Howesshecutting (f), Lissnashe (pu)

12 ran. 12l, 10l, 20l. SP 3-1.

278 - Mares Maiden 5yo+ II

228[2] Handy Sally [16].......................J Meagher 1
hld up, prog 2 out, ld apr last, sn clr
San-France [12]*prom, ld 2 out, hdd & wknd apr last* 2
200 Reinskea*nvr dang, t.o.* 3
Also: Bunny Lightening (pu), 159 Deerpark Lass (pu), 226 Miss Jake (pu), Mistic Highway (pu), Swiss Thyne (f), 200 Miss Lynch (pu), 200[2] Aerlite Classic (pu), 200 Lucky Fifteen (f)

11 ran. 12l, dist. SP 3-1.

279 - Winners Of Two

208[1] Digacre [20] ....A McNamara 1
chsd ldrs, ld aft 2 out, pshd out
229[1] Johnstheman [17]*ld to aft 2 out, onepcd* 2
194[2] Welsh March [13]*not fluent, chsd ldrs, no imp frm 3 out* 3
Also: 198[1] Court Amber (4)

4 ran. 10l, 12l, dist. SP 5-1.

280 - Confined Maiden 5yo+

106 Charming Moss [15]...................B Murphy 1
in tch, ld 3 out, drew clr aft nxt
231[3] Mask River [12]*ld to 3 out, sn outpcd, kpt on* 2
191 Dangan Lad (USA) [12]*hld up, prog to chal 3 out, no ext nxt* 3
Also: 232 Carnmore House (4), 226 Camla Lad (5), 231 Cassfinn (pu), 231 Miss Outlaw (pu), 232 Test The Jockey (bd), Sheshia (f), 231 Park West (pu), Trembling Lady (f), Pigeonstown (f)

12 ran. 7l, 1l, 10l, 12l. SP 8-1.

KILDARE FOXHOUNDS
Punchestown P-To-P Course
Monday March 17th
GOOD TO SOFT

281 - Confined Lightweight

56[3] Master Julian [18] ....J Robinson 1
made all, hld on wll flat
Lineker [22]*w.w. clsd 4 out, chal last, no ext nr fin* 2

62 **No One Knows***prog 4 out, sn btn* 3
Also: 31 Miss Annagaul (4), 147 Ardent Spirit (5), 223 Poulgillie (6), 64 Clearly Visible (pu), 55 Downs Delight (pu), 231 Percusionist (ro), Polls Gale (pu), Susies Delight (pu), Tamer's Run (pu), The Dance (pu)
13 ran. ½l, 25l, 10l, 2l, 20l. SP 4-1.

282 - Winners Of One I

231 **Tuskar Flop [15]**.........................**J Quinn** 1
prom, ld 5 out, clr 3 out, easily......................
95[1] **Spikes The Man [11]***effort to chs ldrs 5 out, kpt on onepcd*.. 2
65 **Wild Buck***bhnd til ran on frm 2 out, no dang*.......... 3
Also: 36 Cool It (4), 55 M T Pockets (5), 59 Mischievous Andy (6), 67 Captains View (7), Radical Dual (8), 185 Four Zeros (9), 188 Time To Smile (10), Clover Nook (11), 232 Docummins (f), 123 Native Blood Vl (f)
13 ran. 10l, 12l, 3l, 6l, 15l, 1l, nk, dist, 8l, 5l. SP 3-1.

283 - Winners Of One II

107[1] **Dead Reckoning [20]**....................**E Bolger** 1
hld up, prog 5 out, ld nxt, ran on wll last..............
29[3] **Mr Chataway [17]***chsd ldrs, went 2nd apr 2 out, no imp apr last*... 2
154 **Regal Fellow [15]***chsd ldrs, onepcd frm 3 out*......... 3
Also: 154[3] Donals Choice [10] (4), Wayforward (5), 232 Siamsa Brae (6), 214 Boreen Boy (f), 232 Tullyhoniver (pu), 96 Bellas Fashion Vl (pu), 147[3] I Love To Fly (pu), 97 Miss Barnamire (pu), Tommy Pink (pu), 188[3] Young Bebe (pu)
13 ran. 6l, 5l, 20l, 5l, 25l. SP 4-5.

284 - Open Lightweight

59[3] **Oh So Grumpy [21]**......................**P Barrett** 1
ld hlfwy, easily...
149 **Killiney Graduate [10]***chsd wnr hlfwy, no ch*........ 2
Slaney Supreme*t.o.*....................................... 3
Also: 177 Cabra Towers (su), 185[2] Furry Star (bd), Slaney Bacon (ur), 92 Stylish Stepper (pu)
7 ran. Dist, dist. SP 4-5.

285 - Maiden 5yo

70 **Hi Jamie [17]**............................**A Martin** 1
trckd ldr, ld & mstk last, drvn out.....................
Thats Dedication [17]*made most til hdd last, kpt on wll*.. 2
184 **Glacial King [14]***rear, styd on wll frm 2 out, nvr nrr*... 3
Also: Kings Stride (4), Bonnie Buckskin (pu), 226 Corn Beat (pu), 184 Dvvit (pu), 220 Freestyler (pu), 184 Friars Island (pu), Halco (pu), 184 Magikoopa (pu), 191 Mickthecutaway [16] (f), 226[2] No Other Hill (pu), 185 Siraidan (pu)
14 ran. ½l, 8l, dist. SP 5-1.

286 - Mares Maiden 5 & 6yo

187 **Up The Slaney [15]**......................**P Cloke** 1
hld up, prog 4 out, chal 2 out, ld last, drvn out.........
151[2] **Lady Sylvie [14]***prom, ld apr 2 out-last, no ext flat*.... 2
186[3] **Paps Last Hope [13]***rear, styd on wll frm 2out, nrst fin*.. 3
Also: 111[3] Macken Money [12] (4), 186[2] Torduff Star (5), 55 Threeandabit (6), 227 Legganhall (7), Mandy Still (8), 186 Pierpoints Choice (9), Anotherfling (pu), 228 Bramhall Princess (pu), 218 Cost-A-Lot (pu), 228[3] Glenpine (ur), 166[2] Kilcannon Sophie (ur), 226 Musical Waves (pu), 217 Over The Tavern (pu), Princess Amanda (pu), 228 Shes Bizarre (ur)
18 ran. 1l, 2l, 2l, 10l, 8l, nk, 12l, 3l. SP 6-1.

287 - Maiden 6yo+

152[2] **Foreshore Man [17]**....................**P Crowley** 1
prog 4 out, ld 2 out, lft clr last.......................
Boutrus [13]*chsd ldrs, 4th 2 out, btn whn lft 2nd last*.. 2
232 **Laurelvale [12]***chsd ldrs, 5th & btn 2 out, lft 3rd last*... 3
Also: Time To Be [11] (4), 231 Clonfert Sue (5), 228 Fortunes Cast (6), 223 Miss Day (7), An Tain Shioc (ur), 227 Areyouthereyet (pu), 215 Borreeva (ur), 117 Colemans River (pu), 66[2] Crunchy Nut (co), Danodile Vl (pu), Electric Johnjo (pu), Mysterys Pride (pu), Slaney Delight (pu), 221 The Grey Major [15] (f), 223 Young Blossom (pu)
18 ran. 12l, 2l, 4l, 10l, 1l, 30l, 20l, 6l, 2l. SP 5-4.

NORTH DOWN
Comber
Saturday March 22nd
GOOD TO SOFT

288 - Confined Lightweight

252 **Half Scotch [16]**........................**A Stronge** 1
trckd ldng pair, chal 3 out, ld nxt, styd on..............
129[3] **Serious Note [14]***prog to chs ldng pair 3 out, chal apr last, onepcd*.. 2
174 **Anns Display [12]***prom, ld aft 4 out-2 out, sn btn*..... 3
Also: 249 Elegant Isle (4), 129 Myrtlefield Ann (pu), Brookview Vl (pu), 250 Blue Bay (pu)
7 ran. 4l, 8l, dist. SP 4-1.

289 - Maiden 5yo+

Inver Red [14]..........................**P Graffin** 1
prom, ld 6 out, mstk last, just hld on....................
214 **Copper End [14]***prom, chsd wnr 3 out, chal & blnd last, rallied*... 2
247 **Bridge End [13]***prom, chsd wnr 5 out-3 out, onepcd aft*.. 3
Also: 248 Panda Nova [11] (4), 115 Neely (5), 210 Ballinavary Vl (6), 180 Longmore Boy (7), 254 Greet The Greek (pu), 253 Mannix (pu), Lee Highway (pu), 248 Cascum Lad (pu), 253 Onemans Choice (pu), Glenhugh (pu)
13 ran. ½l, 2l, 6l, 20l, 15l, 6l. SP 6-4.

290 - Winners Of Two

252 **Bluagale [18]**............................**R Patton** 1
made all, lft clr last, all out...........................
67[1] **Some View [17]***raced wd, hld up, chsd wnr 2 out, chal & mstk last,nr rcvr*....................................... 2
227[1] **Mystic Moment [16]***chsd wnr 5 out-2 out, onepcd*.... 3
Also: 177 Christimatt [12] (4), 252 Chene Rose (5), 250[1] Gold Leader (6), Royal Aristocrat (7), 252 Drumiller Hill Lad (pu), 174 Wayside Spin (pu)
9 ran. 2l, 4l, 12l, 12l, 25l, 8l. SP 16-1.

291 - Open Lightweight

276 **Carrigans Lad [14]**....................**B Hamilton** 1
disp at slw pace, mstk 2 out, styd on.................
249[1] **Captain Brandy [13]***disp at slw pace, rdn 4 out, no ext last*.. 2
Also: 211 Glenshane Pass (f)
3 ran. 2½l. SP 10-1.

292 - Mares Maiden 5yo+

251 **Secret Door [14]**.......................**A Stronge** 1
chsd ldrs, prog 4 out, ld 2 out, clr last, kpt on..........
179 **Windmill Star [12]***prom, 2nd 4 out, no imp on wnr flat*
178 **Lan-Paula [10]***nvr dang, kpt on frm 3 out*............ 3
Also: 250 Star Flyer [10] (4), 212 Ballindante (5), 251 Drumree (6), 250 Shantallow (7), 212 Crottys Bridge (8), 251 Touch Of Autumn (9), 227 Lady Zaffaran (10), 212 Microtelle Rose (pu), 125 Taconas Gift (pu), 178 Ballywee Penny (pu), 251 Lizzies Corner (f), 251 Hillview Lizzie (pu), 251 Skinny Minnie (pu), 251 Jinxey Glen (f)
17 ran. 4l, 6l, ½l, 10l, 10l, nk, 3l, 12l, 3l. SP 8-1.

293 - Unplaced Maiden 5yo+

247 **Whatcanido [13]**..........................**N Toal** 1
trckd ldrs, ld flat, styd on...............................
210 **Sherwin [12]***prog to chal & mstk 2 out, kpt on onepcd flat*.. 2
248 **Parman [11]***ld 6 out-flat, no ext*......................... 3
Also: 248 Golfing Man (4), 247 Moses Man (5), Mr Duncan (pu), Gawngadinn (pu), Native Prince (f), 214 A Monkey For Dick (f), 254 Leslieshill (pu)
10 ran. 3l, 4l, 15l, 15l. SP 12-1.

SCARTEEN FOXHOUNDS
Tipperary P-To-P Course
Sunday March 23rd
GOOD

294 - Confined Maiden 5yo+

196[3] **Loslomos [14]** ....**D Duggan** 1
mid-div, styd on frm 2 out, chal last, sn ld, rdn out .....
241[2] **Ship Of Shame [13]***prom, ld 5 out til hdd & no ext flat* 2
275 **Ceasars Reign [13]***prom, chal 2 out, not qckn apr last* 3
Also: Midnight Society [11] (4), Woodview Lady (5), 172 Tyo Mo Chara (6), 203 Ard Na Gaoithe (7), 141 Sam Quale (8), 207 Serenas Serenade (9), 242 Stand Alone (10), 243 Tulira Hill (pu), At The Crossroads (pu), 196 Garryspillane (ur), 106 Mr Campus (pu)
14 ran. 2l, 1l, 7l, 9l, 6l, 7l, hd, 12l, 15l. SP 7-2.

295 - Mares Maiden 5yo+ I

204 **Cottage Girl [17]** ....**B Hassett** 1
prom, ld 2 out, comf ....
26 **What A Choice [14]***prom, chsd wnr apr last, no imp* .. 2
245[2] **Lothian Magic [13]***chsd ldrs, styd on onepcd frm 2 out* 3
Also: Storm Of Protest [13] (4), 201[3] Rainproof [10] (5), 245 Shuil Flossy (6), 277[3] Executive Opal (7), 280 Test The Jockey (8), Persian Moss (9), 235 Idiot's Surprise (10), 265 Determined Okie (pu), Whatalook (pu), Killinane Beauty (pu), 218 Sweet Perk (pu), 245 Norman Road (pu)
15 ran. 2l, 3l, 1l, 8l, 6l, 5l, 2l, ½l, ½l. SP 9-4.

296 - Mares Maiden 5yo+ II

271[3] **Micro Villa [15]**.......................**S Hennessy** 1
prom, ld 2 out, all out nr fin ....
277 **Sounds Confident [15]***hld up, prog 5 out, mstk 3 out, ran on, just faild* 2
218[2] **Roseland [13]***chsd ldrs, onepcd frm 2 out* 3
Also: 60 Buxom Orlov [11] (4), 280[2] Mask River [11] (5), 271 Ring Mam (6), 273 Dusty Rose (pu), 271 Mocklershill Lady (pu), 245 The Hairy Lord (pu), 277 Glencaoin (pu), Creative Flight (pu), Rowdledy (pu), 278[3] Reinskea (pu), 280 Trembling Lady (pu)
14 ran. Nk, 5l, 4l, ½l, 15l. SP 7-4.

297 - Maiden 5yo

Inis Cara [17] ....**P Fenton** 1
trckd ldrs, ld 3 out, ran on well ....
Gowan Gowan [15]*in tch, chsd wnr apr last, styd on*.. 2
241 **Caher Society [15]***chsd ldrs, styd on onepcd frm 2 out*.. 3
Also: 148[2] Kabwee Star [13] (4), 241[3] My Uncle Batt (5), 241 Sporadic Verse (6), 103 King Of Clare (7), 158 Deel Sound (8), 104 Parsons Green Boy (pu), 241 Anodfromalord (pu), 158 Dingdust (pu), Real To Real (pu), Cauteen River (f), 158 Pejays Duca (pu), 241 Pacificblue (pu), 275 Ongoing Dilemma (pu), 196 Court Ramble (pu), 47 Not For Parrot (pu)
18 ran. 3l, 1l, 5l, 15l, 3½l, 9l, 10l. SP 6-4.

298 - Winners Of One

157[3] **River Of Dreams [18]** ....**D Quinn** 1
cls up, ld 2 out, styd on well...........................
232[1] **Premium Brand [15]***mid-div, onepcd 2 out, lft 2nd last* 2
276 **Ballinaveen Bridge [14]***rear, kpt on onepcd frm 2 out, 5th & no ch whn lft 3rd last* 3
Also: 75 Takeithandy [12] (4), 142[2] Pure Air (5), 240 Cozy Cottage (pu), 267 Up The Banner VI (ur), 277 Lady Fleck (pu), 231[1] Charlie Hawes [16] (ur), 158[1] Telecom Affair [14] (f)
10 ran. 5l, 3l, 7l, 15l. SP 6-4.

299 - Mares

208 **Rosetown Girl [20]** ....**D Costello** 1
trckd ldrs, ld 2 out, drvn out ....
240[2] **Pharavo [18]***ld to 2 out, no ext flat* 2
237[2] **Pharditu [16]***chsd ldrs, onepcd frm 2 out* 3
Also: 240 Thadys Remedy [15] (4), 240 Golly Miss Molly (pu), 215 Penstal Lady (pu), Knocktoran Lady (pu), 245[1] Furry Island (f)
8 ran. 5l, 5l, 3l. SP 5-1.

300 - Maiden 6yo+ I

273 **Gladstone [14]**.........................**M Phillips** 1
ld 6 out, drvn out frm last ....
Not Convinced [13]*chsd wnr 2 out, not qckn flat* 2
66 **Irregular Planting [12]***chsd ldrs, not qckn apr last* .. 3
Also: 219 Buck And A Half [10] (4), 243 Tom Deely [10] (5), Tullaghfin (6), Glencush Peak (pu), 243 Well Doctor (pu), 161[3] O'Donnell Abu (ro), 243[3] Royal Leader (pu), 206 Tomasins Choice (pu), 243 Dark Opal (pu), 275 Larrigan (pu)
13 ran. 4l, 4l, 2l, 1l, 25l. SP 7-2.

301 - Maiden 6yo+ II

197 **Fontana Lad [15]**.........................**W Ewing** 1
mstks, in tch, ld 2 out, hrd rdn & kpt on ....
242[2] **No Such Parson [14]***rear, effrt to chs wnr apr last, no ext*.. 2
197[2] **General Ari [14]***prom, ev ch 2 out, no ext*........... 3
Also: 206 Ballybeggan Boy [12] (4), 107 Some Swop [10] (5), 242[3] Sammy Sunshine (6), 265 Forold (pu), 146 Johnny's Echo (f), Triple Action (su), 166 Msadi Mhulu (pu), Full Moon Fever (pu), Mr Connie Vee (pu), 161 Terry McCann (pu)
13 ran. 4l, ½l, 6l, 5l, 25l. SP 4-1.

DUHALLOW FOXHOUNDS
Dromahane
Sunday March 23rd
GOOD

302 - Confined Maiden 5yo+

206 **Mr Freeman [13]** ....**D Costello** 1
chsd ldrs, rdn 5 out, ld 2 out, kpt on ....
203[3] **Maxine's Fountain [12]***in tch, chsd wnr aft 2 out, onepcd* 2
167 **Castlemore Leader [11]***in tch, styd on onepcd frm 2 out*.. 3
Also: Dromod Hero (4), Karens King (5), 262 Laurintinium (6), 234[3] Holiday Time (7), 207 Dante's Whistle (8), 239 Jake The Peg (9), 261 Proud Carlingford (10), 58 Westcourt (11), Theairyman (pu), 234 Lamanaugh Lady VI (pu), 142 Leap Year Man (ur), Coolyline Star (ur)
15 ran. 3l, 2l, 8l. SP 2-1.

303 - Maiden 4yo

King On The Run [15] ....**T Lombard** 1
prom, ld 4 out, sn clr, kpt on...........................
Churchtown Glen [13]*prog to chs wnr 2 out, nrst fin* 2
Bright Buck [13]*prom, kpt on onepcd frm 2 out* 3
Also: Hickeys Tavern [10] (4), Deny's Run (5), Laganside (6), Jolly Short Neck (7), 190 Bad Influence (8), Macfarly (pu), Homo Dorney (ur), Mucky Man (pu)
11 ran. 4l, ½l, 10l. SP 6-4.

304 - Mares Maiden 5yo+ I

137[2] **Macklette [16]**.......................**K O'Sullivan** 1
cls up, ld 5 out, sn clr, easily ....
91 **Craggy Island [12]***chsd wnr 4 out, no imp* 2
Supreme Fountain [12]*chsd ldrs, onepcd frm 3 out* .. 3
Also: 207 Blame Barney (4), 235 Regal Gossip (5), 195[3] Skipthecuddles (6), Dante's Toi (7), Black Swanee (pu), 204 Bawn Beag (f), 20 Allwan (pu), 166 Bright Choice (pu), Ore Galore (pu), 245 Tiernys Island (pu), Ann Black (f), 234 Marys Friend (f), Kings Run (pu), 264 Black Spring (pu), Muriels Pride (pu)
18 ran. 8l, 1l, 20l. SP 3-1.

305 - Mares Maiden 5yo+ II

137 **Cappagh Glen [15]** ....**T Lombard** 1
cls up, chal last, ld flat, hld on ....
207 **Ballybeggan Lady [15]***cls up, chal last, kpt on flat, just hld* 2

245 Aglish Pride [15]*prom, ld 2 out-flat, no ext nr fin* 3
Also: 263 Nellie Gale [10] (4), 189 Right Then Rosie (pu), 166 No Refund (pu), 166 Kerries Jake (pu), 235 La Kestrel (f), 235 Little Simba (ur), 195² Electric Avenue (pu), 245 Royal Chapeau (pu), Sometimes Quickly (pu), Supreme Caution (ur), 264 Comely Maiden (pu), 138 Glitter Girl (pu), 79³ Goolds Opal (pu), 143 Ballyhest Fountain (pu)
17 ran. Nk, ½l, 15l. SP 3-1.

306 - Open Lightweight

121¹ Deep Heritage [26] .... **E Bolger** 1
prom, ld 5 out, comf
244 Mounthenry Star [19]*chsd wnr 4 out, nvr able to chal*
237 Derry's Diamond [15]*nvr dang, kpt on onepcd* 3
Also: 168 Okdo [14] (4), 259³ Carry On Shoon (5), 89 Prayon Parson (6), 88 Sharoujack (7), 144 Quayside Buoy (8), 216 Trimmer Wonder (9), 193² Shirgale (10), 130¹ Shesadinger (pu), 185 Killenagh Moss (f)
12 ran. 2½l, 10l, 2l. SP 2-5.

307 - Maiden 5yo+ I

136² Weak Moment [14] .... **K O'Sullivan** 1
cls up, ld 2 out, sn clr, hld on
220 Metro Fashion [14]*prog 3 out, chal last, no ext flat* ... 2
191 West Coast Cooler [14]*prog 2 out, chal last, no ext flat* 3
Also: 171³ Tekroc [13] (4), By Him Self (5), 171 Cloneen Adventure (6), 262 Nattico (pu), 87 First Mohikin (pu), Paddys Ring (pu)
9 ran. 1l, nk, 3l. SP 5-2.

308 - Maiden 5yo+ II

191³ Knock It Back [17] .... **T Lombard** 1
prom, ld 3 out, easily
Arleneseoin [13]*chsd wnr 2 out, no imp aft* 2
242 Speightstown Boy [10]*chsd ldrs, onepcd frm 2 out* ... 3
Also: 136 Toytown King (4), 203 Kilcully Jake (5), Thornpark Leader (6), 238 Lovely Hurling (7), 132 Newmarket Cheddar (pu), 239² Coole Abbey (f), 135 Baybuck (pu)
10 ran. 8l, 8l, 10l. SP 4-5.

309 - Winners Of One

235¹ Curley Gale [17] .... **M Cronin** 1
rear, rpd prog 2 out, styd on to ld flat
141 Brush Me Up [17]*prom, ld 3 out, clr nxt, hdd & no ext flat* 2
256 Scarteen Lower [16]*prom, chsd ldr 2 out, styd on onepcd* 3
Also: 170 Pintex [13] (4), 206¹ Never Heard (pu), 170³ Lordinthesky (pu), 256 Burkean Melody (pu), 263¹ Lady Of Iron (pu), 208 Carbery Minstrel (pu), 208 Fethard Orchid (pu)
10 ran. ½l, 2l, 10l. SP 8-1.

ORIEL HARRIERS
Dundalk Point-To-Point Course
Sunday March 23rd
SOFT

310 - Mares Maiden 7yo+

228 Proud Princess [14] .... **A Fleming** 1
5th & rdn 4 out, chsd ldr 2 out, ld flat, styd on
33 Snowtown Actress [10]*ld 6 out, clr 4 out, wknd & hdd flat* 2
212 Shanes Bay [10]*nvr nr ldrs, kpt on frm 2 out* 3
Also: 227² Maries Call [10] (4), 227 Ballynagussaun (5), Denel de (pu), 227³ Ardeedale (f), 251 Land Forlorn (f), 253 Scotts Cross (f), 212 Castlevigganlady (ur), 251 Princess Cataldi (pu), You'llbesuprised (pu), The Break (pu), 179 Spring Trix (f), 283 Miss Barnamire (f), 272 Brennan For Audits (f)
16 ran. 12l, ½l, 1½l, 6l. SP 12-1.

311 - Maiden 5 & 6yo

220² Inch Cross [16] .... **J Cullen** 1
prom, ld 7th, mstk 3 out, rdn out
287 Crunchy Nut [14]*prog to chs wnr 4 out, no ext aft 2 out* 2
247² Vintage Choice*ld to 7th, btn 4 out, fin 4th, promoted* .. 3
Also: 285 Kings Stride (4), Currow Hill (5), 118 North City (6), 43 Tidaro Fairy (pu), Newtown Henry (pu), Walterstown Boy (ur), Needsmoretime (pu), 128 Opening Quote (pu), 210 One Eleven (ur), Diddle Di (pu), Well Ted (f), Country Practice (pu), 198 Legal Whisper (ur), 248² Native Cove (0)
17 ran. 5l, 10l, 11l, 30l, dist, 20l. SP 5-2.

312 - Mares Maiden 5 & 6yo

111 Dowhatyouhavetodo [15] .... **S Mahon** 1
ld 6 out, styd on wll apr last
212 Bold Irene [14]*cls up, chal 2 out, no ext flat* 2
250 Ngala*prssd wnr 6 out-2 out, wknd, lft 3rd last* 3
Also: Smart As (pu), 228 Mystical Lord (pu), High Church Annie (f), 227 Simpsons Kid (f), 246 Lady Of Gortmerron (pu), 250 Rosemary Ann (pu), 212 Runaco (pu), 286 Macken Money (f), Berkeley Supreme (pu), 126 Gerrys Delight (bd), 286 Pierpoints Choice (f), 125 Marino Rose (f)
15 ran. 3l, 15l. SP 4-1.

313 - Open Lightweight

31¹ Tempestuous Lady [21] .... **A Fleming** 1
hld up, prog 4 out, ld aft 2 out, styd on well
177³ Crowded House [18]*chsd ldr, ld apr 2 out til aft 2 out, onepcd* 2
230¹ Missing Lady [16]*prog whn blnd 3 out, onepcd aft* 3
Also: 177 Colin's Hatch [15] (4), 249 Shanecracken [13] (5), 230³ Voldi [10] (6), Tully Boy (7), Beau Beauchamp (8), 211 Arctic Treasure (pu), 249 Itsuptome VI (pu), 225³ Castlepook (f)
11 ran. 6l, 5l, 1½l, 6l, 10l, dist, 20l. SP 6-1.

314 - Winners Of Two

215 Push Gently [18] .... **J Cullen** 1
chsd ldr 4 out, lft in ld nxt, drew clr apr last
67³ Arrienzio [12]*rdn 4 out, lft 2nd nxt, ev ch & mstk 2 out, sn btn* 2
230² Annie's Arthur*prom til fdd frm 4 out* 3
Also: 147² Miller King (4), 214¹ The Golam (5), 252³ Golden Start (f), 252² Cebu Gale (f), 282 Captains View (ur), 282¹ Tuskar Flop (pu)
9 ran. 20l, 10l, 2l, dist. SP 7-1.

315 - Maiden 7yo+ I

123³ Desmond River [15] .... **L Lennon** 1
chsd ldrs, chal 2 out, ld last, drvn out
180³ Ardbei [15]*chsd ldr, ld 3 out-last, no ext und pres* 2
223 Benalf*ld til mstk & hdd 3 out, btn frm nxt* 3
Also: 202 Tip The Skip (4), 214 Ordain (5), Zinzan Bank (pu), 231 Biddys Boy (pu), 232 Rovet (ur), 214² Florida Or Bust (ur), 283 Boreen Boy (pu), 185 Celtic Air (pu)
11 ran. ½l, 20l, 25l, dist. SP 5-2.

316 - Maiden 7yo+ II

214 Best Interest [15] .... **J Quinn** 1
made all, clr 3 out, unchal
119 Collooney Squire*chsd ldrs, no imp frm 3 out* 2
254² Inactualfact*chsd ldrs, no prog frm 4 out* 3
Also: 231 Baileys Gate (f), 254 Stackie Boy (ur), 119 Danny Mann (pu), 254 Emerald Breffni (ur), Derrysand (bd), 254 Partyonjason (bd), 254 Nature Perfected (f)
10 ran. Dist, 6l. SP 6-4.

KILLEAGH HARRIERS
Inch
Wednesday March 26th
GOOD

317 - Confined Maiden 5yo+

135² Danger Flynn [15] .... **K O'Sullivan** 1
mid-div, prog 4 out, ld nxt, styd on well
74 Woodfield Boss [12]*cls up, chsd wnr 3 out, no imp nxt* 2

262 Garryross*chsd ldrs, btn frm 3 out* 3
Also: 258[2] Menalma (4), 262 Geragh Road (5), Immediate Action (6), Kilcounty Colleen (pu), Kambalda Bay (f), 258 Pure Energy (pu), 258 Missing Mama (pu), 261 Fernboy (pu), Lucky Jeff (pu), 83 Con's Nurse (pu), Marys Twin (pu), Pharn N Wide (pu), 261 Jolly Paddy (pu), 189 Brill Star (pu), Electric Spark (pu)
18 ran. 8l, 15l, 10l. SP Evens.

318 - Mares Maiden 6yo+ I

Annie Buckers [16]......................E Bolger 1
ld 5 out, clr 2 out, unchal............................
234[2] Rio Star [10]*chsd wnr 3 out, no imp*................ 2
166 Change The Pace*nvr dang* 3
Also: 189 Hillview Lass (4), Pharding (pu), 286 Kilcannon Sophie (pu), 218 Clochban Clonroche (pu), 139 Jenaway (pu), Cuddies Porter (pu), Suite Cottage Lady (pu), 91 Woodville Princess (pu)
11 ran. 15l, 20l, 15l. SP 7-4.

319 - Mares Maiden 6yo+ II

167 Shamron [14] ....B Hallahan 1
made most, clr 3 out, hld on...........................
235 Merry River [13]*chsd wnr 2 out, kpt on, nrst fin* 2
264 Everlaughing [10]*chsd ldrs, onepcd frm 3 out* 3
Also: 235[3] Faithful Pal (4), Born Natural (pu), 207[3] Victim Of Slander (pu), 302 Holiday Time (pu), 83 Dereenavurrig (pu), 235 Derrygra Fountain (pu), Black Serene (pu)
10 ran. 2l, 10l, 15l. SP 6-1.

320 - Open Lightweight

41 McFepend [20]........................T Lombard 1
prom, ld 4 out, drew clr 2 out, unchal aft.............
256 John's Right [14]*prom, ev ch 4 out, sn outpcd* 2
193 Mack A Day [12]*chsd ldrs, btn frm 4 out*............ 3
Also: 259 Looking Ahead (4), 193 Parish Ranger (5), 237[3] The Pulpit (6), 257 Glenbower Queen (7), 259 Cooladerra Lady (8), 306 Okdo (pu), 236 Kilcullys-Pride (pu)
10 ran. 20l, 6l, 8l. SP 3-1.

321 - Maiden 5yo I

192 Mr Goodbye [14] ....J McNamara 1
chsd ldr, ld 2 out, blnd & hdd last, rallied to ld flat......
142 Dawdante [14]*prog 3 out, chsd wnr aft nxt, lft in ld last, hdd flat*.................................... 2
261 Just A Playboy [12]*chsd ldrs, kpt on oepcd frm 2 out* 3
Also: Step In Line (4), 192 Dalus Executive (pu), Ford Classic (pu), 91 Madam Aside (pu), 258 Uncle Archie (f), 195 Kacey's Annie (f), 263 Grange Pine (pu), 262 Bushy Ranger (pu)
11 ran. ½l, 5l, 25l. SP 7-2.

322 - Maiden 5yo II

39 Jolly Decent [16].....................E Gallagher 1
prom, ld 4 out, comf.................................
Asthefellasays [12]*chsd wnr 3 out, no imp frm nxt* ... 2
84 Inch Champion [10]*chsd ldrs, onepcd frm 3 out*...... 3
Also: 262 Bearys Cross [10] (4), Pio'r (pu), Hold The Queen (pu), Dewdrop Lady (pu), 184 The Bell Tree (pu), 79 Mary Marry Me (pu), Ri Na Gaoithe (f), 239[3] Gortroe Guy (su)
11 ran. 10l, 5l, ½l. SP 11-10.

323 - Winners Of Two

257 Pearl Dante [17]...........................D Daly 1
hld up, prog 5 out, ld 2 out, mstk last, hld on...........
258[1] Shuil Na Mhuire [16]*prog 3 out, ran on wll flat, just faild*.. 2
242[1] The Territorian [16]*chsd ldrs, styd on onepcd frm 2 out*... 3
Also: 257[2] Teads Boreen [15] (4), Pharways (pu), Peafield (pu), Roses Luck (f)
7 ran. 1l, 1l, 2l. SP 4-5.

324 - Maiden 6yo+

260 Carry On Brendan [15] ....J Baragry 1
prom, ld 2 out, kpt on well ....
222[3] Barnadown [15]*chsd ldrs, chal 2 out, just hld flat*..... 2
107 Jolly Jape [12]*chsd ldrs, onepcd frm 2 out*........... 3
Also: 262 Minstrels Quay (4), 220 Welsh Lane (pu), Minileader (pu), Colligan Falls (pu), 169 Playmore (pu), 243 Major Bill (pu), 307 Cloneen Adventure (pu), 171 Irish Rover (pu), 146 Jolly Lad (pu), 262 Phar Desert (pu), 172 Moonvoor (pu)
14 ran. ¾l, 10l, 10l. SP 2-1.

COUNTY DOWN
Loughbrickland
Saturday March 29th
SOFT

325 - Winners Of Two

113[2] Hilton Mill [20] ....R Patton 1
chsd ldr, ld 5 out, drew clr last......................
290 Chene Rose [15]*chsd ldrs, ev ch 3 out, btn apr last*... 2
125[1] Haveafewmanners [11]*ld, rdr mstk fin cct early, hdd 5 out, sn btn*.. 3
Also: Forever Gold (pu), 176 Sand de Vince (f)
5 ran. 10l, 12l. SP 5-4.

326 - Winners Of One

254[1] Wilbar [18]............................J O'Connell 1
prog 5 out, sn ldd, blnd 2 out, kpt on...............
252 Raleagh Muggins [16]*ld hlfwy til aft 5 out, rnwd effrt aft 2 out, no ext*.................................... 2
209[1] Ellies Pride*nvr dang* 3
Also: 252 Uncle Art (pu), Che Amigo (pu)
5 ran. 4l, 25l. SP 4-6.

327 - Open Lightweight

313 Colin's Hatch [17] ....L Lennon 1
hld up, prog 2 out, rdn to ld nr fin ....
249 Captains Bar [17]*ld hlfwy til hdd & no ext nr fin*...... 2
313 Itsuptome VI*prom, ev ch 2 out, sn wknd* 3
Also: 288 Elegant Isle (pu), 249[2] The Boolya (ur), 313[2] Crowded House (f)
6 ran. Nk, 30l. SP 8-1.

328 - Maiden 5 & 6yo

210[2] Bannagh Mor [15].........................R Patton 1
ld to last, rallied to ld nr fin ....
176 Flanaghans Way [15]*prog to chs wnr aft 4 out, ld last, hdd nr fin*... 2
176[3] Rock On Bud [14]*prog to 4th 4 out, styd on onepcd frm 2 out*... 3
Also: 293[3] Parman (4), 248 Allistragh Lad (5), 248 Roscrily William (6), 175 Miners Bay (7), 247 Russell Lodge (8), 248 Dexter Gordon (pu), 247 Barnagan (pu), Up The Road (pu), 210 Tullamore (ur), 247 Nijapajo (pu), 311 One Eleven (f), 289 Cascum Lad (ur), 114 Ballymenagh (f)
16 ran. Sht-hd, 3l, 25l, 3l, 5l, 6l, 30l. SP 3-1.

329 - Mares Maiden 5yo+

251 Three Town Rock [16] ....I Buchanan 1
disp 3rd til drew clr frm hlfwy, unchal ....
250 Drumrock Lady [11]*prom til lost plc 4 out, ran on to chs wnr apr last, no imp* 2
250 Bobby Blazer*nvr nrr* 3
Also: 292 Touch Of Autumn (4), 250[3] Glenalla Bella (5), 250 Island Harriet (6), 292[2] Windmill Star (7), Drumfair VI (pu), Roseoree (pu), 292 Microtelle Rose (pu), Knock Road (pu), 251 Forever Grey (pu), Denarii (pu), 250 Hillview Susie (pu), Supreme Flight (ur), 312 Runaco (pu), 310 Castlevigganlady (pu), 312 High Church Annie (f)
18 ran. 12l, 6l, 3l, 2l, 3l, 4l. SP 2-1.

330 - Maiden 7yo+ I

316[3] Inactualfact [13]..........................L Lennon 1
made all, just hld on ....

253 **Pauls Point [13]***prog 3 out, chsd wnr last, clsd flat, just faild* 2
316² **Collooney Squire [11]***chsd wnr til wknd last* 3
Also: 293 A Monkey For Dick (4), 253 A Bit Of A Rascal (ur), 293 Leslieshill (pu), 254 Tom Haggard (pu), 209 Morans Forge (pu), 129 Emmas Gamble (pu), 180 Athabasca (ur), 253 Wind Of Glory (pu)
11 ran. ½l, 6l, dist. SP 3-1.

331 - Maiden 7yo+ II

254 **You Said It [15]** .... I Buchanan 1
ld 3rd, clr 3 out, hld on wll flat
254 **Mandingo [15]***prog hlfwy, chsd wnr 2 out, ev ch flat, just hld* 2
246³ **Highland Buck***chsd wnr til wknd 2 out* 3
Also: 289 Neely (4), Moyavo Lad (pu), 253² Where's Sam (pu), 289 Glenhugh (pu), 214 Creme Supreme (pu), 289 Onemans Choice (pu), 214³ Ash Brae (pu), 315 Ordain (pu)
11 ran. 1l, 20l, 8l. SP 6-4.

DERRYGALLON HARRIERS
Liscarroll
Saturday March 29th
GOOD

332 - Maiden 4yo I

Man Of Steele [16] .... A Costello 1
prom, ld 2 out, styd on well
Stormey Tune [15]*prog to chs wnr apr last, styd on* 2
274 **Ludden Chief [14]***prom, kpt on onepcd frm 2 out* 3
Also: Madam Sioux [14] (4), Good Time Abbey (5), 303 Laganside (6), Waydante (7), Honor Mission (ur), Baile Staibhne (pu), Duskanto (pu), Garrison Friendly (pu), Carlos The Jackal (f)
12 ran. 2l, ½l, 1l. SP 4-1.

333 - Maiden 4yo I

His Song [17] .... P Fenton 1
prom, ld 3 out, ran on well
274 **Nice Approach [14]***prog 3 out, styd on wll frm nxt* 2
255² **Lisdoylelady [11]***in tch, onepcd frm 3 out* 3
Also: Lord-A-Dee (4), 255 Curragh Lord (5), Adramore Belle (6), Cap It If You Can (f), 303 Homo Dorney (pu), Rare Harvest (pu), Judys Thigh (pu), Cartons River (pu)
11 ran. 8l, 10l, 10l. SP Evens.

334 - Open Lightweight

259¹ **Dixon Varner [29]** .... E Bolger 1
made most, clr 2 out, easily
Irene's Call [21]*chsd wnr, ld brfly apr 3 out, no ch wth wnr frm nxt* 2
299³ **Pharditu [17]***chsd ldrs, onepcd frm 3 out* 3
Also: 266 Ounavarra Creek (pu), Myalup (pu)
5 ran. 5l, 10l. SP 1-4.

335 - Maiden 5yo

76² **Dashing Buck [17]** .... A Costello 1
alwys prom, rdn to ld apr last, styd on
Little Duke [16]*prom, ld 4 out til apr last, no ext* 2
57 **Into The Clan [11]***chsd ldrs, no imp frm 3 out* 3
Also: 184³ Bothar Fada (4), 77² Irish Frolic (5), 261 Forrest Fuse (f), Executive Flame (pu), French Gale (pu), Star Of Annagh (pu), Hodders Folly (f), 238 Arthur (f), Tudor Royal (pu), Vain Minstrel (f)
13 ran. 2l, 15l, 2l. SP 4-6.

336 - Winners Of One

277¹ **Lisduff Pride [18]** .... D Costello 1
prom, 2nd & btn whn lft clr last
239¹ **Clashbridane [15]***prom, onepcd 2 out, lft 2nd last* 2
140¹ **Sarcoid [14]***chsd ldrs, onepcd frm 3 out, lft 3rd last* 3
Also: 309³ Scarteen Lower [14] (4), 207¹ Brogeen Dubh [12] (5), 309 Never Heard (6), 309² Brush Me Up (7), 259 Get Cracking (8), 267³ Dante Lad (9), I'm Happy Now (pu), 256 Oneofourown [19] (f), 257 Sumakano (pu)
12 ran. 10l, 2l, 1l. SP 3-1.

337 - Maiden 6yo+

202 **Slaney Fayre [17]** .... B Hassett 1
trckd ldrs, ld apr last, rdn out
206³ **Island Echo [16]***prog 2 out, chsd wnr aft last, styd on* 2
301 **Ballybeggan Boy [13]***prom, ld 3 out-apr last, sn btn* 3
Also: 169³ Loach Croga [11] (4), I'vegotyounow (5), 238 Stags Rock (6), 206² Gaelic Glen (7), 171² Cullaun (8), 206 Galways Granite (9), 262 Lingering On (10), 308 Baybuck (11), 302 Dromod Hero (f), Midnight Magic (f), 302 Karens King (ro), 302 Theairyman (pu), 301 Mr Connie Vee (pu), Natlash (pu), 238² The Stag (pu)
18 ran. 2l, 8l, 4l. SP Evens.

338 - Mares Maiden 6yo+

302 **Dante's Whistle [16]** .... D Murphy 1
disp 5 out, hrd rdn to ld flat
294 **Midnight Society [15]***disp 5 out till no ext flat* 2
305 **Glitter Girl [10]***chsd ldrs, no imp frm 4 out* 3
Also: Coming Soon (4), Salty Bay (5), 263² Leamlara Rose (6), 278 Lucky Fifteen (7), 238 Lisselan Lass (8), 263 Peggys Leg (9), 295 Shuil Flossy (10), 305 No Refund (f), 264 Divine Rapture (pu), Dawn Pageant (pu), 263 Paros Leader (pu), Ballynagleragh (pu), 263 Electric Can (ur), 263 Julies Joy (pu)
17 ran. 2l, 15l, 2l. SP 5-2.

SHILLELAGH & DISTRICT
Tinahely
Sunday March 30th
GOOD TO SOFT

339 - Mares Maiden 5yo+

98 **Catch The Mouse [14]** .... J Winterbotham 1
prog 5 out, ld 3 out, styd on flat
221 **Lost Coin [13]***chsd ldrs, chal last, no ext flat* 2
221 **Buzz About [13]***rear, styd on frm 2 out, nvr nrr* 3
Also: 138 Ferriters Pub [11] (4), 222 Trimmer Lady [10] (5), 270 Rachels Plan (6), 60 Penny Bug (7), 46 Loveable Lady (8), 187 Mariners Quest (9), 310 Miss Barnamire (10), 98 Key Of The Nile (pu), 62 Whocantellya (f), Riverrunsthroughit (f), 218 Wunwabbitwun (pu), 222 Sky Rainbow (pu), 217 Running On Thyne (f), Faircrest (pu), 185 Noble Melody (pu)
18 ran. 1l, 1l, 6l, 4l, 6l, 5l, 2l, 3l, 10l. SP 12-1.

340 - Winners Of Two

215 **Sandy Pearl Two [15]** .... P Cloke 1
made all, lft clr 2 out, kpt on
270¹ **Billie's Mate [14]***chsd ldrs, lft 2nd 2 out, styd on* 2
Also: 131 Strong Dream (ur), 215 Rufo's Rapper (pu), Slaney Saucy (f), 284³ Slaney Supreme (pu), 147 Torduff Express (f)
7 ran. 3l. SP 14-1.

341 - Maiden 7yo+

315³ **Benalf [15]** .... D Valentine 1
made all, prssd frm 3 out, drvn out
221² **Knockanoran [14]***prom, chal 3 out, mstk last, no ext flat* 2
273² **Louis de Palmer [11]***prom, ev ch 3 out, sn outpcd* 3
Also: 283 Siamsa Brae [10] (4), 272³ Deep Appeal (5), Up The Rock (6), 265 The Cass Man (7), 223 Clare To Here (pu), 221 Lord Amethyst (pu), 154 The Bug Hill (pu), 54 Lostyndyke (f), 221 Over The Barrow (pu), Clohamon Bridge (pu), 122 Barchester (pu), 222 Shimano (pu), 185 To The Hilt (pu)
16 ran. 2l, 8l, 3l, 6l, 5l, 3l. SP 4-1.

342 - Open Lightweight

216 **Albert's Fancy [14]** .... J Quigley 1
ld at slw pace, qcknd clr 2 out
216 **Kilmisten Breeze [10]***wth wnr til onepcd frm 2 out* 2
2 ran. 5l. SP 1-2.

343 - Maiden 5 & 6yo

219[2] **Frostbitten [16]** .... **W Codd** 1
ld 3rd, made rest, clr 4 out, unchal ....
268 **Stelinjo [10]** *chsd ldrs, styd on to go 2nd apr last, no ch wth wnr* 2
220 **Coopers Clan** *chsd wnr 5 out til wknd apr last* 3
Also: 220 Bart Eile (4), 219 Newbog Lad (5), 182[3] Airecco (6), 184[2] Brave Noddy (pu), 215 Mineral Al (pu), 268 Joe Rattle (pu), 219 Annie Leap (pu), 181 Castle Glow (f), 265 Master Finbar (f), 261 Nineteenofive (pu)
13 ran. 20l, 10l, 1l, 2l, 20l. SP 5-4.

344 - Mares Maiden 5yo+

150[3] **Winning Rhythm [14]** .... **P Kelly** 1
chsd ldrs, hrd rdn 2 out, styd on und pres to ld flat .....
222 **Hasty Hours [14]** *prom, ld 2 out til hdd flat* 2
286[3] **Paps Last Hope [13]** *chsd ldrs, styd on 2 out, ev ch last, no ext* 3
Also: 221 Weavers Window VI [12] (4), 281 Polls Gale (5), 61 Josalady (6), 217 Lipstick Lady (7), 97 Broad Valley (ur), 286 Mandy Still (bd), 270 Amber Dolly (bd), Edermine Sunset (bd), Regular Rose (pu), 295 Sweet Perk (pu), 286 Cost-A-Lot (pu), 224 Gandon Lady (pu), 217[2] Spritly Lady (ur), 223 Sparkes Cross (pu), 265 Murphys Cross (f), 264 Forgoodnessjake VI (pu)
19 ran. ½l, 1l, 5l, 12l, 25l, 2l. SP 3-1.

SOUTH COUNTY DUBLIN
Naas Point-To-Point Course
Sunday March 30th
GOOD

345 - Winners Of Two

213[2] **Demoniac (Fr) [20]** .... **A Martin** 1
trckd ldrs, ld 2 out, qcknd clr last ....
174 **Willie B Brave [17]** *prom, outpcd 3 out, ran on to chal apr last, alwys hld* 2
314 **Miller King [16]** *ld to 2 out, styd on* 3
Also: 215 Maks Dream [14] (4), Rat Race [13] (5), 240[3] Easter Bard [11] (6), 314 Captains View (pu), 267 Oatflake (pu)
8 ran. 2l, 1½l, 5l, 2l, 5l. SP 11-8.

346 - Open Lightweight

313[1] **Tempestuous Lady [22]** .... **A Fleming** 1
trckd ldng pair, lft 2nd & hmpd apr 3 out, hrd rdn to ld last
313[3] **Missing Lady [19]** *ld, lft clr apr 3 out, hdd & no ext last*
284 **Furry Star [16]** *nvr dang, kpt on onepcd frm 2 out* 3
Also: 249 Glenroe Gal [11] (4), 281 Ardent Spirit (5), 284[2] Killiney Graduate (6), Camden Court (su), Fair Notice (pu)
8 ran. 4l, 10l, 15l, 8l, 20l. SP 9-10.

347 - Maiden 5 & 6yo

Rashkin [15] .... **P Crowley** 1
prog 2 out, chal last, ld flat, styd on ....
311 **Well Ted [15]** *mstks, trckd ldrs, chal & mstk last, styd on* 2
219 **Go Like The Devil [15]** *lft in ld 5-10th, ld apr last, hdd & no ext flat* 3
Also: 285 Bonnie Buckskin [14] (4), 226[3] High Thyne [10] (5), 220 Berts Cabin (6), 219 Gee Thanks (7), 311 Diddle Di (pu), Eagle Vail (pu), King Of Glen (f), Millas Delight (pu), 311 Walterstown Boy (ur)
12 ran. Hd, ½l, 2l, 12l, 5l, 20l. SP Evens.

348 - Maiden 7yo+

287 **The Grey Major [16]** .... **M Hickey** 1
rear, prog 2 out, ld flat, clvrly ....
Venerdi Santo [14] *ld 4th-2 out, ld apr last, hdd & no ext flat* 2
283 **Wayforward [14]** *chsd ldrs, ev ch apr last, onepcd* 3
Also: 283[3] Regal Fellow [14] (4), 315 Tip The Skip [13] (5), 273[3] Garacillin [11] (6), 275 The H'penny Marvel (7), 282 M T Pockets (8), 275 Almauritia (9), 221[3] Buck Run (10), 265 Zanagale (11), 232[2] Normous (12), Derryvella Lad (13), 185 Castle Dawn (14), 287[2] Boutrus [13] (f), 282 Cool It (su), Doctor On Call (bd), 283 Tullyhoniver (f)
18 ran. ½l, nk, ½l, 3l, 5l, 5l, 10l, 15l, 5l. SP Evens.

349 - Mares Maiden 5yo+ I

286[2] **Lady Sylvie [16]** .... **A Martin** 1
cls up, ld 2 out, comf ....
55 **Satalda [12]** *chsd wnr 2 out, no imp* 2
Nucklewood [11] *rear, styd on 2 out, nvr nrr* 3
Also: 187 The Executrix (4), 301 Msadi Mhulu (5), Sparkling Rosie (6), 286 Anotherfling (pu), Cherishthelady (ur), 286 Glenpine (f), 270 Heres Holly (f), Meigs Battle (pu), 286 Shes Bizarre (pu)
12 ran. 8l, 2l, 7l, 12l, dist. SP 4-9.

350 - Mares Maiden 5yo+ II

225 **Kings Alibi [14]** .... **F Kiernan** 1
chsd ldr, ld 6th, clr 5 out, fin tired ....
286 **Princess Amanda [13]** *wll bhnd, styd on frm 2 out, lft 2nd last, nvr nrr* 2
286 **Bramhall Princess [10]** *nvr dang* 3
Also: 228 Foyle Valley Lady (4), 286 Legganhall (5), 227 Heather Queen (f), 281 Miss Annagaul (f), 286 Musical Waves (f), 217 Sharlene (f), Shove Over (f), 281 Susies Delight (pu), Vanity Quest (f)
12 ran. 3l, 8l, 30l, 10l. SP 7-1.

351 - Maiden 5yo+

285 **Mickthecutaway [15]** .... **A Fleming** 1
trckd ldrs, ld 2 out, sn clr ....
282 **Radical Dual [11]** *ld to 2 out, no ch wth wnr aft* 2
281 **Percusionist** *nvr dang* 3
Also: 315 Boreen Boy (4), 311 Legal Whisper (5), 275 Gradle (6), 283[2] Mr Chataway (ur), Sally's Image (pu), 287 Time To Be (pu), 283 Young Bebe (f)
10 ran. 6l, 5l, 30l, dist. SP 4-5.

COUNTY CLARE
Dromoland
Sunday March 30th
GOOD TO FIRM

352 - Maiden 5yo

102 **Scallybuck [16]** .... **D Costello** 1
ld 4 out til mstk 2 out, ld apr last, ran on wll ....
294 **Garryspillane [14]** *chsd wnr 4 out, lft in ld 2 out-apr last, no ext* 2
280 **Pigeonstown [11]** *chsd ldrs, onepcd frm 3 out* 3
Also: Crack Regiment [11] (4), 261[2] Tommys Pride (5), 241 Suave (pu), 297 Deel Sound (bd), Dangan Hill (f), Ruck 'n Maul (pu), Hemero (pu), 260 Sliabh Luchra Boy (pu)
11 ran. 3l, 10l, 1l. SP 10-3.

353 - Maiden 6yo+ I

280 **Carnmore House [15]** .... **F Hanley** 1
prom, ld 3 out, styd on wll ....
300 **Tom Deely [14]** *chsd wnr 2 out, no ext frm last* 2
239 **Corkers Flame [13]** *chsd ldrs, onepcd frm 2 out* 3
Also: 301[3] General Ari [11] (4), 202 Sweeney Lee (5), 242 River Wild (pu), 301 Sammy Sunshine (pu), 225 Regular Beat (pu), Electric Eddie (pu), 300 O'Donnell Abu (f), 280 Cassfinn (pu), 294 Mr Campus (pu), 301[2] No Such Parson (pu), 301 Terry McCann (f), Healing Thought (pu), Swanees Tune (pu), Tinosmill (pu)
17 ran. 3l, 4l, 5l. SP 10-1.

354 - Maiden 6yo+ II

Hunters Chorus [17] .... **R Lee** 1
jnd ldr 5 out, ld apr last, sn clr ....
52 **Send It In [13]** *rear, styd on frm 2 out, tk 2nd flat* 2
206 **Bosco's Touch** *ld to apr last, wknd* 3
Also: 275 Tom's Tune (4), 280 Camla Lad (5), Diamond In The Ruff (6), Just My Harry (7), 232 Belville Pond (pu), Ethelwood VI (pu), 242 Scheamin N Dreamin (pu), Danikar (pu), 106 Call Me Ogan (pu), 275 Sock Hop (pu), Wonder Dawn (pu), Lone Survivor (f), 242 Beau Cinq (pu), Florida Mist (pu)
17 ran. 8l, 20l, dist. SP 3-1.

355 - Mares Maiden 5yo+ I

295[2] What A Choice [16]....................J Moloney 1
ld hlfwy, styd on wll frm 2 out..........................
201 Ardnataggle [15]*chsd wnr 4 out, no imp apr last .....* 2
Steffi Liz [10]*chsd ldrs, no prog frm 3 out ....* 3
Also: 79 Tonmarie Chance (4), 294 Woodview Lady (5), Derry Lark (pu), 271 Springtime Mist (pu), 305 Little Simba (pu), 204 Derrygallon Fancy (pu), 280 Sheshia (f), 202 Full Holiday (0), 277 Sound Vision (pu), Bornacurra Katie (pu), Delmiano (pu)
14 ran. 2½l, 15l, 20l. SP 6-4.

356 - Mares Maiden 5yo+ II

278 Swiss Thyne [15]..........................R Lee 1
made all, styd on wll flat..............................
277[2] Aine Hencey [14]*lft 2nd 5 out, ev ch last, no ext.......* 2
Sunczech [13]*chsd ldrs, kpt on frm 2 out, unable to chal...* 3
Also: 278 Bunny Lightening (pu), 302 Lamanaugh Lady VI (f), Gusty Venture (f), Renty (f), 186 Scklepp (pu), 305[2] Ballybeggan Lady (f), 278 Deerpark Lass (f), 277 Howesshecutting (pu), 277 Killone River (f), 278 Aerlite Classic (pu)
13 ran. 1l, 3l. SP 4-1.

357 - Winners Of One

256[2] Lucky Town [21]..........................E Bolger 1
ld to 5 out, ld 2 out, sn clr ....
164 Runabout [15]*rear, kpt on frm 2 out, tk 2nd flat........* 2
244[3] Shareza River [14]*chsd ldr, ld 5 out til mstk 2 out, lame ....* 3
Also: 240 Iona Flyer [13] (4), 278[1] Handy Sally [11] (5), 299 Furry Island (6), 299 Knocktoran Lady (pu), 224[2] Man With A Plan VI (pu), The Defender (pu), 21 Camogue Bridge (pu), 202[1] Deep Refrain (f)
11 ran. 10l, 3l, 2l. SP 7-4.

358 - Open Lightweight

199[1] Risk Of Thunder [28] ....E Bolger 1
ld/disp til drew clr 2 out, easily ....
205 Starlight Fountain [22]*with wnr to 2 out, sn btn.......* 2
279[2] Johnstheman [20]*nvr dang ....* 3
Also: 276[3] Tantum Bonum [16] (4)
4 ran. 8l, 5l, 10l. SP 1-6.

359 - Nomination

Grey Tide ....D Hassett 1
ld 4 out, styd on ....
Mr Barney*chsd wnr 4 out, no imp last ....* 2
298 Up The Banner VI*nvr dang ....* 3
Also: 300 Glencush Peak (pu)
4 ran. 3½l, 20l. SP 4-1.

ROUTE HARRIERS
Limavady
Tuesday April 1st
GOOD

360 - Mares Maiden 6yo+

292 Crottys Bridge [15]..................L McBratney 1
prog 5 out, ld flat, styd on ....
179[3] Maid O'Tully [13]*prog 5 out, ld 2 out-flat, no ext ....* 2
250 Blue Gas [12]*prog 5 out, ld 3 out-nxt, onepcd apr last* 3
Also: 312[3] Ngala [10] (4), 254 Tiger Dolly (5), 125 Loch Saland (6), 250 Tierfergus (7), 250 Maccarrons Run (pu), 212[2] Carlies Wood (ur), 292 Taconas Gift (pu), 251 Ollar Lady (pu), 292 Ballywee Penny (f), 251 Karen's Leader (f), 212 Cool Swallow (f), 179 Flame Of Gold (ur), Bolesa's Joy (pu)
16 ran. 2l, 2l, 4l, 3l, 1l, dist. SP 6-1.

361 - Winners Of Two

289[1] Inver Red [18] ....G Clugston 1
made all, kpt on wll frm 2 out..........................
213[3] Willy Wee [17]*chsd ldrs, chal 2 out, no ext flat.........* 2
290 Christimatt [16]*chsd ldrs, chal 2 out, onepcd ....* 3
Also: 210[1] Pharbrook Lad (4), Ballypollard (pu), 310 Denel de (f)
6 ran. 3l, 3l, dist. SP 5-2.

362 - Open Lightweight

249 Lacken Beau [20] ....R Arthur 1
trckd ldr, ld 6 out, in cmmnd aft 3 out ....
249 Prince Yaza [16]*effort to chs wnr 3 out, sn no imp ....* 2
291[2] Captain Brandy [10]*ld to 6 out, btn frm 3 out ....* 3
Also: 249 Limeridge (4), 331 Ordain (5), 253 Dhu Bond (pu)
6 ran. 10l, 15l, 20l, 25l. SP 7-4.

363 - Maiden 4 & 5yo

296[2] Sounds Confident [18] ....W Ewing 1
cls up, ld 4 out, clr & mstk 2 out, easily ....
246[2] Track O'Profit [10]*nvr dang, tk 2nd apr last ....* 2
Dreamingagain*nvr dang ....* 3
Also: Mr Peoples (pu), Raymar Dancer (pu), Templepatrick (pu), 177 Ballybollen (pu), 292 Lizzies Corner (f), Whinveagh (f), 289 Lee Highway (pu)
10 ran. 20l, 10l. SP Evens.

364 - Confined Lightweight

249 Fay Lin [12]...........................D Christie 1
trckd ldr, ld 3 out, kpt on ....
210 Pull The Lever [11]*ld to 3 out, unable to qckn aft.....* 2
310 Land Forlorn*nvr dang....................................* 3
Also: Winter Ramble [13] (f)
4 ran. 2l, 20l. SP 6-4.

365 - Winners Of One

316[1] Best Interest [20] ....J Quinn 1
made all, easily ....
209[3] Sideways Sally [11]*chsd wnr, nvr on trms..........* 2
Also: Moybeg (pu), Spartan Park (pu), 213 Hiltonstown Lass (su), 316 Stackie Boy (pu), 247 Shuil Mor (pu), 288[3] Anns Display (pu), 252 Mysterious Beau (pu), 247 Dancing Mike (pu), 331 Where's Sam (f), A Bit Of A Monkey (pu)
12 ran. 25l. SP 4-5.

EAST ANTRIM
Loughanmore
Friday April 4th
GOOD

366 - Maiden 7yo+

Man Of Iron [15]...........................A Martin 1
prog 4 out, chal 2 out, ld & lft clr last ....
289 Longmore Boy [13]*alwys prom, 3rd & btn whn lft 2nd last, kpt on...* 2
316 Emerald Breffni*nvr dang, lft poor 3rd last ....* 3
Also: 331 Neely (4D), 253[3] La Mancha Boy (4), 293 Mr Duncan (f), 31 Farlough Lady (f), Autumn Day (f), 253 Captains Friend (pu), 155 Hey Chief [15] (ur), 365 A Bit Of A Monkey (pu), 292 Star Flyer (pu), 310 Scotts Cross (pu), 289 Mannix (pu), 365 Where's Sam (pu), 292 Drumree (f), 330 A Bit Of A Rascal (pu)
17 ran. 2l, dist, 3l. SP 5-2.

367 - Winners Of Two

215[2] Hidden Hollow [19]......................A Martin 1
w.w. went 2nd 2 out, ld last, sn clr.....................
315[1] Desmond River [14]*prom, ld 4 out-last, no ch wth wnr*
290 Drumiller Hill Lad [13]*chsd ldrs, onepcd frm 3 out ...* 3
Also: 147 Harry's Secret [11] (4), 290 Wayside Spin (5)
5 ran. 5l, 2½l, 6l, 5l. SP Evens.

368 - Mares Lightweight

290[3] Mystic Moment [20] ....B Hamilton 1
prog to 2nd 4 out, lft clr nxt..........................
314 Golden Start*mstks, nvr dang, lft poor 2nd 3 out.......* 2

292[1] **Secret Door***nvr dang, t.o.* 3
Also: 313 Arctic Treasure (4), Tashalin (pu), 211 Gale Griffin (f)
6 ran. Dist, 25l, 4l. SP 2-1.

369 - Maiden 4 & 5yo

293[2] **Sherwin [15]** .... **R Patton** 1
prog to 2nd 4 out, lft clr 2 out, unchal aft ....
Victoria's Boy [12]*rear, kpt on & lft 2nd 2 out, no imp wnr* 2
363 **Ballybollen [11]***lft 3rd 2 out, no prog* 3
Also: Rocket Man [10] (4), 248 Reds Paradise (5), Tee Aitch Kay (pu), Raleagh Native (pu), 328 Up The Road (ro), Culnaveigh (pu), Proan Hill (pu), Micklimar (f)
11 ran. 6l, 3l, 3l, 20l. SP 5-2.

370 - Mares Maiden 5 & 6yo

329 **Touch Of Autumn [15]** .... **R Patton** 1
made all, in cmmnd whn lft wll clr last ....
Riverdance Rosie*nvr dang, lft poor 2nd last* 2
Gerry Delight*nvr dang, lft poor 3rd last* 3
Also: 329 Denarii (pu), 97 Raheen Cross (f), 360[2] Maid O'Tully [12] (f), 363 Whinveagh (pu), 250 Caladonian Light (pu), 292 Jinxey Glen (pu), 329[3] Bobby Blazer (pu), 329 High Church Annie (pu), 329 Roseoree (pu), 360 Flame Of Gold (pu), 288 Myrtlefield Ann (pu)
14 ran. Dist, 25l. SP 5-1.

371 - Unplaced Maiden

The Rural Dean [12] .... **B Potts** 1
chsd ldr 3 out, jmpd slwly nxt, kpt on to ld flat ....
Golden Bar [11]*ld hlfwy, wknd & mstk last, sn hdd & btn* 2
247 **Fairtree***nvr dang, t.o.* 3
Also: 328 Miners Bay (pu), 289 Ballinavary VI (pu), Castle Stephen (pu), Sebrimar (pu), 104 Foolsandtheirmoney (pu), 247 Ollar House (f), 111 Buckie Thistle (f), 175 Carnmoon (f), 328 One Eleven (pu), 328 Barnagan (pu)
13 ran. 2l, dist. SP 8-1.

EAST ANTRIM
Loughanmore
Saturday April 5th
GOOD

372 - Winners Of Two

331 **Creme Supreme [15]** .... **G McKeeven** 1
in tch, prog 5 out, ld 2 out, kpt on ....
250 **Mourne Miner [13]***ld/disp to 5 out, kpt on* 2
289 **Greet The Greek [12]***nvr nrr* 3
Also: Troubled Man [12] (4), 252 Ballywoodock VI [11] (5), 330 Athabasca (f), 360 Ballywee Penny (pu), Fernisky (pu), 292[3] Lan-Paula (su), 248 Gold Signal (pu), Zieg (pu)
11 ran. 4l, 2l, ½l, 2l. SP 5-2.

373 - 5 & 6yo Final

290[1] **Bluagale [16]** .... **R Patton** 1
made all, clr 2 out, comf ....
364[2] **Pull The Lever [12]***in tch, ev ch 3 out, btn nxt* 2
311 **Native Cove [10]***in tch, ev ch 3 out, sn btn* 3
3 ran. 10l, 6l. SP 4-6.

374 - Open Lightweight

311[1] **Inch Cross [22]** .... **J Cullen** 1
trckd ldrs, ld last, styd on wll ....
326[1] **Wilbar [21]***prom, ld 3 out-last, unable qckn flat* 2
327 **Crowded House [18]***bhnd, ran on 2 out, nrst fin.* 3
Also: 249[3] Funny Ye Know [15] (4), 313 Shanecracken [15] (4), 362[1] Lacken Beau [12] (6), 364[1] Fay Lin (7), 334 Ounavarra Creek (8), 291 Glenshane Pass (pu), 327 The Boolya (ur)
10 ran. 2l, 6l, 6l, dd-ht, 8l, 25l. SP 7-2.

375 - Maiden 5yo+

112 **Flodart [15]** .... **K Ross** 1
wll bhnd, prog 5 out, ld 3 out, styd on wll ....
246 **Dernamay [10]***disp to 3 out, sn outpcd, kpt on* 2
289[3] **Bridge End***rear, effrt 5 out, 3rd 3 out, no imp aft* 3
Also: 325 Forever Gold (4), 289 Panda Nova (5), 369 Up The Road (pu), 328[3] Rock On Bud (bd), 331 Moyavo Lad (pu), 364 Winter Ramble [13] (pu), 178 The Bleary Flyer (f)
10 ran. 15l, 4l, 2l, 2l. SP 12-1.

376 - Mares Winners Of Two

288[2] **Serious Note [16]** .... **A Martin** 1
hld up, prog 3 out, ld last, comf ....
124 **Sister Nora [13]***chsd ldrs, ld brfly apr last, no ext* 2
368[2] **Golden Start [11]***mstks, chsd ldrs, ld 3 out-apr last, sn btn* 3
Also: 365 Hiltonstown Lass [11] (4), 290 Gold Leader (5), 288[1] Half Scotch (6), 360[1] Crottys Bridge (pu), 360 Carlies Wood (pu), 274[1] Portland Row (pu)
9 ran. 6l, 6l, ½l, 6l, 1l. SP 3-1.

377 - Unplaced Maiden

72 **Trimfold [11]** .... **G Martin** 1
chsd ldr, wll btn whn lft in ld last, hld on ....
326 **Che Amigo [11]***chsd ldrs, wll btn whn lft 2nd last, just hld flat* 2
328 **Cascum Lad***nvr dang, lft 3rd last* 3
Also: 35 Bold Boreen (4), 209 Bright Lad (pu), 329 Hillview Susie [14] (f), 218 Torduff Bay (f), 329 Knock Road (pu), 366 A Bit Of A Monkey (pu), 330 A Monkey For Dick (pu), 328 Russell Lodge (pu), 330 Morans Forge (pu), 330 Leslieshill (pu), 312 Lady Of Gortmerron (pu), 330 Tom Haggard (pu), 365 Shuil Mor (pu), Supreme Lancer (pu)
17 ran. ½l, 10l, dist. SP 12-1.

UNITED FOXHOUNDS
Ballynoe
Sunday April 6th
GOOD

378 - Confined Maiden

260[2] **Persian Packer [15]** .... **D Murphy** 1
hld up, prog 3 out, ld apr last, styd on wll ....
324 **Minstrels Quay [13]***prom, ld 3 out-apr last, no ext.* 2
260 **Icantsay [13]***prom, onepcd frm 2 out* 3
Also: 319[3] Everlaughing [10] (4), 317[3] Garryross (5), 317[2] Woodfield Boss (6), 317 Fernboy (7), 324 Cloneen Adventure (8), 337 Lingering On (9), 317 Jolly Paddy (10), 45 Flowery Fern (pu), 322[3] Inch Champion (pu), 48 Strong Ambition (pu), 167 Skipping Chick (f)
14 ran. 3l, 1l, 8l. SP 5-2.

379 - Maiden 4 & 5yo

302[2] **Maxine's Fountain [14]** .... **W O'Sullivan** 1
prom, ld 2 out, hld on well ....
322[2] **Asthefellasays [13]***prom, chal 2 out, no ext flat* 2
294 **Sam Quale [10]***nvr nrr* 3
Also: 322 Bearys Cross (4), 169 Royal Dale (5), 343 Joe Rattle (pu), 303 Mucky Man (pu), 261 Jimmy Dan (ur)
8 ran. 2l, 10l, 10l. SP 2-1.

380 - Mares Final

236[1] **Greenflag Princess [21]** .... **E Gallagher** 1
trckd ldr hlfwy, ld 3 out, easily ....
234[1] **Cush Princess [15]***ld to 3 out, no ch wth wnr nxt* 2
309[1] **Curley Gale [13]***nvr dang* 3
Also: 240 Queenofclubs (4), 304[1] Macklette (5), 257 Phartoomanny (6), 319[1] Shamron (7), 309 Lady Of Iron (su), 319 Victim Of Slander (pu), 204[2] Little Roo (pu)
10 ran. 20l, 6l, 20l. SP 7-4.

381 - Maiden 6yo+

Pops Academy [15] .... **E Gallagher** 1
prog 4 out, ld 2 out, styd on wll ....
260 **Sheer Mischief [14]***ld 3 out-nxt, onepcd* 2

260 Dante's Reward [11]*chsd ldrs, onepcd frm 2 out* 3
Also: 308 Toytown King [10] (4), 324 Playmore (5), 307 Nattico (pu), 260 Another Berry (pu), Lord Vince (pu), 337 Midnight Magic (f), 172 Chamsy (f), 317 Lucky Jeff (pu), Cool-Lan-Sir (pu)
12 ran. 3l, 10l, 2l. SP 4-1.

382 - Open Lightweight

194 Garramoss [18]......................**K O'Sullivan** 1
prom, ld & mstk 2 out, styd on wll
320² John's Right [15]*prom, no ext frm 2 out* 2
323 Pharways [12]*chsd ldrs, onepcd frm 3 out* 3
Also: 334 Myalup [12] (4), 309 Carbery Minstrel (5), 323 Peafield (6), 306 Sharoujack (pu), 320 Cooladerra Lady (pu), 336 Dante Lad (pu), 259 Radical River (pu)
10 ran. 10l, 10l, 1l. SP 7-1.

383 - Mares Maiden 5yo+ I

83 Classie Claire [15] ....**E Gallagher** 1
prom, ld 2 out, styd on wll flat
305 Royal Chapeau [12]*in tch, chsd wnr 2 out, no ext apr last* 2
318² Rio Star*chsd ldrs, onepcd 3 out* 3
Also: 138 Dons Pride (4), 189 Mandoora (pu), 263³ Marians Own (bd), Valparaiso (pu), 318 Hillview Lass (pu), 80 Little Santa (pu), Out The Nav (f), 245³ Loch Lomond (pu), Klagunfurt (f), 264 Lorglane Lady (f), 305 Ballyhest Fountain (f)
14 ran. 10l, 8l, 2l. SP 7-1.

384 - Mares Maiden 5yo+ II

304² Craggy Island [15]....................**K Beecher** 1
prom, ld 4 out-apr last, rallied to ld flat
304 Blame Barney [14]*chsd ldrs, ld apr last, hdd & no ext flat*........ 2
Rossi Beg [13]*chsd ldrs, styd on onepcd aft 2 out* 3
Also: 317 Con's Nurse (4), 166 Lady Of Means (5), 304 Marys Friend (6), 263 Some Shock (pu), 322 Hold The Queen (pu), 264 Gale Dante (pu), 235² Highland Call (pu), An Caipin (pu), 169 Jennys Pearl (pu), 263 Woodville Native (pu), Miss Sarajevo (pu)
14 ran. 2l, 3l, dist. SP 5-1.

ISLAND FOXHOUNDS
Camolin
Sunday April 6th
GOOD

385 - Confined Maiden

Loch Garman Arms [14] ....**J Brennan** 1
hld up, prog 5 out, chal & mstk 2 out, sn ld, styd on wll
344 Spritly Lady [13]*ld to aft 2 out, hng lft & no ext flat*.... 2
99 Mr Balda [10]*prssd ldr to 3 out, no ext* 3
Also: 223 Stoney Piper (4), Mary Hand (5), 377 Torduff Bay (pu), Star Hand (pu), Final Statement (pu)
8 ran. 4l, 10l, 10l, dist. SP 8-1.

386 - Open Lightweight

216¹ Ozier Hill [22]..........................**J Berry** 1
hld up, prog to jn ldr 3 out, drew clr aft nxt
224¹ Dennistownthriller [18]*ld 5 out-nxt, kpt on onepcd*... 2
216 Harveysland [18]*ld 4 out, jnd nxt, outpcd aft 2 out* 3
Also: 342¹ Albert's Fancy [16] (4), 306 Trimmer Wonder (5), 284 Slaney Bacon (pu), 216² Slaney Wind (pu)
7 ran. 3l, ½l, 6l, dist. SP 1-2.

387 - Winners Of Two

147 Lovable Outlaw [20] ....**J Berry** 1
hld up, prog 4 out, ld nxt, comf
75 Magnum Express [16]*prog 4 out, styd on onepcd frm 2 out* 2
340 Torduff Express [14]*prog 3 out, nvr nrr* 3
Also: 306 Killenagh Moss [12] (4), 340 Strong Dream [11] (5), 341¹ Benalf (6), 340² Billie's Mate (7), 215 Woodbinesandroses (ro), 256 Trimmer Princess (pu), 342² Kilmisten Breeze (pu), All-Together (pu)
11 ran. 5l, 4l, 6l, 2½l, 12l, 5l. SP 5-4.

388 - Mares Maiden 5yo+ I

339² Lost Coin [14] ....**J Brennan** 1
bhnd, prog to ld 4 out, hld on nr fin
218 Over The Glen [14]*chsd ldrs, outpcd 3 out, ran on flat, just hld* 2
218³ Porter Tastes Nice [14]*chsd ldrs, chal 3 out, no ext flat* 3
Also: 339 Ferriters Pub [12] (4), 151 Barenises Rose (5), 339 Riverrunsthroughit (6), 344 Forgoodnessjake VI (7), Priory Street (8), 344 Weavers Window VI (f), 339 Rachels Plan (pu), 339 Loveable Lady (pu), 186 No Speed Limit (ur), Becca's Rose (f), 217 Hardtobegood (bd), Joyces Hope (pu), 344 Lipstick Lady (pu)
16 ran. Nk, 1l, 6l, 12l, 1l, 30l, 12l. SP 7-2.

389 - Mares Maiden 5yo+ II

217 Oh Donna [15] ....**H Cleary** 1
chsd ldrs, ld aft 5 out, clr 2 out, comf
272 Aroundthevalley [12]*chsd ldrs, styd on onepcd frm 2 out*........ 2
Shelmalier [12]*bhnd til ran on 2 out, nvr nrr* 3
Also: 339 Miss Barnamire [10] (4), 296³ Roseland [10] (5), 344 Josalady (6), 272 Rosmere (7), Riverfort (pu), 339 Whocantellya (pu), 217 Thieving Sands (ur), 344 Sparkes Cross (f), 319 Born Natural (ur), 344 Regular Rose (pu), Right And Reason (pu), Sweet Sandra (pu)
15 ran. 5l, ½l, 6l, ½l, 10l, 8l. SP 5-2.

390 - Maiden 4 & 5yo

285³ Glacial King [15] ....**H Cleary** 1
chsd ldrs 4 out, rdn to ld nr fin
274³ Manacured [15]*ld 4 out til hdd nr fin*........ 2
343 Bart Eile [15]*chsd ldrs 4 out, chal last, ev ch til no ext nr fin*........ 3
Also: Inch Way [14] (4), 219 Apollodorus [12] (5), 219 Satquaid [10] (6), Mrs Daniels (7), Mysterious Woman (pu), She's A Flyer (pu), Morrajay (pu), 343 Nineteenofive (pu), The Crucible (pu)
12 ran. Nk, nk, 4l, 5l, 6l, 10l. SP 4-5.

391 - Maiden 6yo+

156 Change The Script [13]..................**P Cloke** 1
cls up, chal last, ld nr fin
324² Barnadown [13]*prom, ld apr last, hdd nr fin* 2
343 Newbog Lad [13]*ld, mstk 3 out, hdd apr nxt, kpt on wll*........ 3
Also: 343 Castle Glow [13] (4), 300 Buck And A Half [10] (5), 223³ Twin Track (6), 260 The Podger (7), 221 Little Len (8), 324 Welsh Lane (9), 287 Electric Johnjo (f), 341³ Louis de Palmer (f), 341 The Bug Hill (pu), 269 Loudy Rowdy (pu)
13 ran. Nk, nk, ½l, 10l, 8l, 1½l, 20l, 4l. SP 4-1.

WESTMEATH FOXHOUNDS
Castletown-Geoghegan
Sunday April 6th
GOOD TO SOFT

392 - Adjacent Lightweight

313 Tully Boy [12].......................**D McCartan** 1
chsd ldrs, styd on frm 2 out, ld nr fin
349 Glenpine [12]*ld 4 out til hdd & no ext nr fin* 2
348 Almauritia [10]*prom, onepcd frm 2 out*.............. 3
Also: 350 Musical Waves (4), 313 Castlepook (5)
5 ran. 1l, 4l, 8l, ½l. SP 4-1.

393 - Maiden 4 & 5yo

22 Take My Side [17] ....**E Bolger** 1
made all, sn clr, unchal
285 Friars Island*rear, styd on frm 2 out, tk remote 2nd flat* 2
Rise To It*nvr dang* 3
Also: 285 No Other Hill (4), 274 Another Mistake (pu), The Bishops Sister (pu), Yohanna (pu)
7 ran. Dist, hd, 4l. SP Evens.

394 - Mares Maiden 5yo+

278[2] **San-France [13]........................A Martin** 1
prog 5 out, ld last, hld on
356[2] **Aine Hencey [13]***lft 2nd 5 out, rdn to ld 2 out-last, no ext* 2
Native Oasis*lft in ld 5 out, hdd 2 out, sn wknd* 3
Also: 310 Ballynagussaun (4), 349 Sparkling Rosie (5), 227 Golden Mist (6), 351 Sally's Image (pu), Niamhs Dream (pu), 278 Miss Jake (pu), 312 Smart As (pu), 349 Cherishthelady (f), 349 Anotherfling (pu), 312 Mystical Lord (pu), 356 Howesshecutting (pu)
14 ran. 1l, 20l, 3l, 5l, 6l. SP Evens.

395 - Open Lightweight

358[1] **Risk Of Thunder [28]...................E Bolger** 1
made all, v easily
275[1] **Herb Superb [20]***chsd wnr 5 out, mstk 3 out, hrd rdn & no imp* 2
279[1] **Digacre [11]***nvr dang* 3
Also: 313 Voldi [11] (4), 291[1] Carrigans Lad [11] (5), 298[2] Premium Brand (6), 266 Palmura (pu)
7 ran. 3l, dist, nk, ½l, 6l. SP 1-2.

396 - Winners Of Two

314[2] **Arrienzio [16]........................G Harford** 1
not fluent, chsd ldr 4 out, mstk 2 out, drvn to ld fin
272[1] **Call Me Joe [16]***ld 4 out til hdd fin* 2
Kate Gale*nvr dang, t.o.* 3
Also: Dearmistershatter (pu)
4 ran. Nk, dist. SP Evens.

397 - Maiden 6yo+ I

348[3] **Wayforward [16]........................T Angel** 1
made virt all, lft clr 3 out, lft clr last
Eoins Lad [10]*nvr dang, kpt on 2 out, lft 2nd last* 2
296 **Mask River***wth wnr whn mstk 3 out, sn wknd* 3
Also: Parsons Fort (4), Free And Equal (5), Loch Bran Lad (pu), 287[3] Laurelvale (pu), Sir Gandouge [15] (co), Babs Who (ur), Master Dempsey (pu), Dock Strike (pu)
11 ran. 15l, 8l, 1l, 5l. SP 3-1.

398 - Maiden 6yo+ II

351 **Gradle [13]........................W McLernon** 1
trckd ldrs, chal & lft in ld 3 out, just hld on
347 **High Thyne [13]***prog to chs wnr aft 3 out, chal last, just hld* 2
348 **Cool It***ld til mstk 3 out, wknd* 3
Also: 311 Tidaro Fairy (f), Unevano (f), 295 Test The Jockey (pu), Weekend Warrior (pu), Regal Optimist (f), Woodlawn Express (pu), Colins Glen (pu), 315 Biddys Boy (f)
11 ran. Nk, dist. SP 4-1.

TIPPERARY FOXHOUNDS
Clonmel Point-To-Point Course
Sunday April 6th
FIRM

399 - Maiden 4yo

Castle Arrow [11]......................M Phillips 1
chsd ldrs, lft 2nd 2 out, lft in ld last
303 **Jolly Short Neck [11]***chsd clr ldr, lft in ld 2 out, blnd & hdd last* 2
Also: 332 Honor Mission [12] (ur), All Girls (f), Deebert House (f)
5 ran. 3l. SP 2-1.

400 - Maiden 5yo

297 **Parsons Green Boy [11]............J McNamara** 1
disp, lft clr aft 3 out, lft clr agn nxt
Josh The Boss*last, lft 2nd aft 3 out, chal & blnd nxt, mstk last* 2
Also: 322 The Bell Tree (pu)
3 ran. 7l. SP 4-1.

401 - Mares Maiden 5yo+

344[2] **Hasty Hours [15]......................P Crowley** 1
chsd ldrs, prog to ld 2 out, sn clr
304 **Skipthecuddles [11]***nvr dang, kpt on to tk 2nd last* 2
318 **Jenaway [11]***nvr dang, kpt on to tk 3rd last* 3
Also: Orlas Fancy (4), 265 Creative Thought (5), 271 Scottish Match (6), 344 Amber Dolly (f), 270 Dunhill Lady (pu), 299 Golly Miss Molly (f), Solo Minstrel (pu), 355 Full Holiday (f), 356 Aerlite Classic (pu)
12 ran. 8l, nk, 10l. SP Evens.

402 - Winners Of One

298[3] **Ballinaveen Bridge [15]................F Hanley** 1
cls up, ld 2 out, styd on wll
296[1] **Micro Villa [14]***cls up, chsd wnr 3 out, no ext last* 2
306 **Prayon Parson***t.o.* 3
Also: 130 Badalka (4)
4 ran. 4½l, dist, 12l. SP 2-1.

403 - Maiden 6yo+

220 **Victory Song [14]...................J McNamara** 1
chsd ldrs, chal 2 out, ld apr last, styd on
Deep Bit [13]*rear, styd on aft 3 out, tk 2nd flat* 2
337[3] **Ballybeggan Boy [13]***chsd ldrs, ld 4 out-apr last, no ext* 3
Also: Natures Gentleman [10] (4), 301 Some Swop (5), 354 Beau Cinq (6), 269 Society Lad (7), 219 Invader General (pu), 294 Tulira Hill (f)
9 ran. 2l, 1l, 8l. SP 4-1.

404 - Open Lightweight

266[3] **Run For Niall [17]..................S Hennessy** 1
chsd ldr, ld 2 out, kpt on
224[3] **Slaney Goodness [16]***ld to 2 out, not qckn* 2
2 ran. 2l. SP 2-1.

WICKLOW FOXHOUNDS
Camolin
Sunday April 13th
GOOD TO SOFT

405 - Maiden 7yo+

341[2] **Knockanoran [15]........................P Cloke** 1
in tch, ld 2 out, styd on wll
391 **The Bug Hill [13]***mid-div, styd on apr last, nrst fin* 2
391[2] **Barnadown [12]***chsd ldrs, onepcd frm 2 out* 3
Also: 341 To The Hilt [12] (4), Kazmar [11] (5), 385 Final Statement [11] (6), 222 River Bargy (7), 100 Nelpha (8), 385[3] Mr Balda (pu), 391 Little Len (f), Tramps Heartbreak (pu), Daddy Warbucks (bd), 294 Tyo Mo Chara (pu), Spinans Hill (pu), 385 Stoney Piper (pu)
15 ran. 4l, 4l, nk, 1½l, ½l, 5l, 15l. SP 3-1.

406 - Mares Maiden 5yo+ I

Kilfane [18]............................P Crowley 1
hld up, prog to ld 2 out, sn clr
388[2] **Over The Glen [13]***cls up, ev ch 2 out, sn not qckn* 2
388 **Barenises Rose***bhnd, styd on onepcd frm 2 out* 3
Also: 389 Miss Barnamire (4), 263 The Buck Pony (5), 388 Riverrunsthroughit (6), 388[3] Porter Tastes Nice (7), 388 Weavers Window VI (8), 401 Amber Dolly (9), 217 Jembato (pu), 339 Wunwabbitwun (pu), Catherine's Pet (pu), 344 Cost-A-Lot (f), Braca Brook (pu), Neeto (pu), 389 Sparkes Cross (pu)
16 ran. 10l, 20l, 4l, 20l, nk, 3l, 5l, 4l. SP 4-1.

407 - Mares Maiden 5yo+ II

221 **Glen Of Bargy [15]....................D O'Brien** 1
hld up bhnd, prog 5 out, ld last, styd on wll
388 **Hardtobegood [13]***prog 4 out, ev ch aft 2 out, no ext* 2
389[3] **Shelmalier [11]***prom, onepcd frm 2 out* 3
Also: 389 Riverfort (4), 344 Polls Gale (5), Windgates Zone (6), Ten Past Eleven (f), 339 Running On Thyne (pu), 389 Thieving Sands (pu), 388 Joyces Hope (pu), 344 Edermine Sunset (pu), Hi Hi Young Fella (pu), 339 Trimmer Lady (ur), 338 Dawn Pageant (pu), 385[2] Spritly

Lady (pu)
15 ran. 4l, 6l, 6l, 12l, 5l. SP 3-1.

408 - Winners Of One

170² One Woman [19] ....M Phillips 1
hld up, prog 4 out, ld 2 out, styd on wll.............
183² Dromod Point [15]*cls up, lft 2nd 2 out, no imp wnr aft* 2
215¹ Bree Hill [13]*mid-div, rdn hlfwy, onepcd frm 4 out* ... 3
Also: Slaney Sauce [12] (4), 157 All But (5), 387 Woodbinesandroses (6), 387 Trimmer Princess (7), 387 All-Together (pu), 49 Bold Brew (bd), 385¹ Loch Garman Arms (pu), Even Call (f)
11 ran. 10l, 6l, 3l, 8l, 5l, 6l. SP 7-2.

409 - Maiden 5 & 6yo

Crabapple Hill [16] ....D O'Brien 1
prom, ld 3 out, lft clr last.............................
390³ Bart Eile [14]*chsd ldrs, btn whn lft 2nd last* 2
391 Castle Glow [13]*chsd ldrs, btn whn lft 3rd last* 3
Also: 403 Society Lad [11] (4), Glitter Paddy (5), 95 Back Withavengance (6), Our Brew (pu), 285 Freestyler (ro), 390 Satquaid (pu), 215 Bill Joyce [15] (ro), Touching Down (pu), 106 Buck River (pu), Royal Victor (f), 285 Siraidan (ro)
14 ran. 4l, 2l, 6l, 5l, 3l. SP 10-1.

410 - Open Lightweight

386³ Harveysland [17]........................C Donnelly 1
prom, ld 2 out, hld on wll ....
387 Killenagh Moss [17]*prssd wnr 2 out, just hld* 2
340¹ Sandy Pearl Two [14]*chsd ldrs, onepcd frm 2 out* 3
Also: 386 Albert's Fancy [11] (4), 185³ Watercourse [22] (pu), 346 Killiney Graduate (pu)
6 ran. 1l, 10l, 10l. SP 7-2.

411 - Nomination

388¹ Lost Coin [16] ....J Brennan 1
in tch, ld 3 out, styd on wll ....
314¹ Push Gently [13]*chsd wnr aft 3 out, hrd rdn & no imp* 2
387 Kilmisten Breeze*nvr dang* 3
Also: 186 Strathfield Lass (pu), Strawberry Lamp (pu), Ballycarsha (pu)
6 ran. SP 6-20.

LOUTH FOXHOUNDS
Tallanstown
Sunday April 13th
FIRM

412 - Adjacent Lightweight

314 Tuskar Flop [15] ....D Boylan 1
ld 3 out-apr last, ld flat, all out........................
395 Voldi [15]*ld to 3 out, ld apr last where blnd, hdd & no ext flat*.......... 2
Pigeon Hill Buck [14]*chsd ldrs, ev ch 2 out, no ext last* 3
Also: 345 Captains View (ur), 351 Boreen Boy (pu), Moygrehan Girl (f), 345 Rat Race (pu), 398³ Cool It (pu), 396 Dearmistershatter (ur)
9 ran. 1l, 2l. SP 3-1.

413 - Maiden 5 & 6yo

311² Crunchy Nut [15] ....G Elliott 1
lft 2nd 5 out, mstk 3 out, ld apr nxt & lft clr, styd on .....
328 Allistragh Lad [10]*ld to apr 2 out, sn btn* 2
Nobodywantsme*nvr dang* 3
Also: 371 Ballinavary VI (4), 311 North City (5), 363³ Dreamingagain (su), 311 Newtown Henry (f), 292 Lady Zaffaran (pu), Crow Road (f), Cardinal Belle (pu), 377 Supreme Lancer (f), 347 Walterstown Boy (f), Amistar (pu), 391 Electric Johnjo (pu)
14 ran. 15l, 12l, 10l, 30l. SP 6-4.

414 - Open Lightweight

362³ Captain Brandy [19] ....D Christie 1
chsd ldrs, ld 3 out, comf ....
314³ Annie's Arthur [13]*effrt to chs wnr apr 2 out, sn btn* .. 2
395 Palmura [11]*ld to 3 out, wknd* 3
Also: 327³ Itsuptome VI (4), 395 Carrigans Lad (ur)
5 ran. 15l, 5l, 6l. SP 2-1.

415 - Mares

349¹ Lady Sylvie [18] ....A Martin 1
hld up last, ld apr last, sn clr, easily..................
312¹ Dowhatyouhavetodo [14]*trckd ldr, ld 3 out-apr last, no ch wth wnr* 2
229² Ballybriken Castle*ld to 3 out, wknd*.................... 3
3 ran. 7l, 15l. SP 4-7.

416 - Mares Maiden 5yo+

394 Ballynagussaun [14] ....M O'Connor 1
prom, ld 4 out, lft clr 2 out, kpt on ....
312² Bold Irene [12]*prom, btn whn lft 2nd 2 out* 2
360 Ngala*alwys bhnd*.. 3
Also: 394 Sparkling Rosie (f), 350 Susies Delight (pu), High River Den (pu), 370 Flame Of Gold (pu), 377 Lady Of Gortmerron (pu), Cloghran Native (ref), 361 Denel de (pu), 394 Cherishthelady (f), Mainshear (pu)
12 ran. 6l, 25l. SP 7-1.

417 - Maiden 7yo+

391 Twin Track [14].............................A Martin 1
chsd ldr 5 out, ld apr 2 out, styd on.....................
331³ Highland Buck [13]*rear, prog to chs wnr apr 2 out, no imp last*.. 2
348 Tip The Skip [10]*rear, prog to 3rd apr 2 out, no imp aft* 3
Also: 377 Bright Lad (pu), Mersey Racing (f), Persian Life (f), 366 Neely (bd), 366 Mr Duncan (pu), 315 Zinzan Bank (pu), 315 Rovet (pu)
10 ran. 3l, 8l. SP 11-4.

CARBERY FOXHOUNDS
Innishannon
Sunday April 13th
GOOD TO FIRM

418 - Maiden 5yo+

238³ Clashview [15] ....M Fehily 1
ld/disp til drew clr last...................................
337 Stags Rock [13]*ld/disp to last, no ext* 2
238 Short Circuit [12]*cls up, ev ch apr last, no ext* 3
Also: 81 Poachers Lamp [11] (4), 305 Comely Maiden (5), 321 Ford Classic (pu), Hilltown House (f)
7 ran. 5l, 2l, 3l. SP 7-2.

419 - Mares Maiden 5yo+

Tearfull [15] ....N Fehily 1
prom, ld 2 out, styd on wll...............................
338 Salty Bay [14]*chsd wnr 2 out, no ext last* 2
318 Pharding [11]*chsd ldrs, onepcd frm 2 out*............ 3
Also: 383 Little Santa (4), 338 Coming Soon (pu), 338 Lisselan Lass (pu), 195 Cash Ville (ur), 319 Faithful Pal (pu), 238 Carlingford Pit (pu), 384 Gale Dante (pu), 380 Victim Of Slander (pu), Balaltrama (pu), 304 Regal Gossip (pu)
13 ran. 3l, 10l, 6l. SP 8-1.

420 - Open Lightweight

334² Irene's Call [17].......................K O'Sullivan 1
hld up, prog 2 out, ld last, just hld on ....
320¹ McFepend [17]*prom, ld 3 out-last, rallied* 2
382² John's Right [15]*chsd ldrs, onepcd frm 2 out* 3
Also: 306³ Derry's Diamond [12] (4), 306 Quayside Buoy (pu), 320 Glenbower Queen (pu), 382 Cooladerra Lady (pu)
7 ran. Hd, 5l, 10l. SP 5-4.

421 - Winners Of One

75 **Roman Gale [16]........................N Fehily** 1
chsd ldr 4 out, ld last, rdn out........................
309 **Burkean Melody [15]***ld to last, no ext.................* 2
Lord Harry [13]*in tch, styd on wll frm 2 out ....* 3
Also: 336 Scarteen Lower [10] (4), 194 Round Tower Lady (5), 306 Carry On Shoon (pu), Chestnut Shoon (pu), 257 Proscenium (f)
8 ran. 1l, 6l, 10l. SP 4-1.

422 - Maiden 6yo+

324 **Jolly Lad [15].......................K O'Sullivan** 1
in tch, chal 2 out, ld last, hld on........................
403² **Deep Bit [15]***in tch, ld 2 out-last, no ext ....* 2
341 **Deep Appeal [13]***prom, onepcd frm 2 out ....* 3
Also: 353³ Corkers Flame [10] (4), Lazy Acres (5), 324 Minileader (pu), 171 Big Spender (pu), 261 Clongeel Lord (pu), 317 Brill Star (f), Apple Saft (pu)
10 ran. ½l, 5l, 10l. SP 3-1.

423 - Maiden 4 & 5yo

321 **Step In Line [14]........................N Fehily** 1
not fluent, in tch, chal 2 out, ld nr fin....................
39 **Pluvius [14]***ld 3 out, hdd & no ext nr fin...............* 2
239 **Clonageera [10]***chsd ldrs, onepcd apr 2 out ....* 3
Also: 85 Running Wolf (4), Nomerose (pu), Public Interest (pu), 260 Lord Egross (pu), 263 Happy Hula Girl (ur), Northern Talent (pu), Ardfert Fountain (pu), 378 Inch Champion (pu)
11 ran. 1l, 10l, dist. SP 6-4.

LIMERICK FOXHOUNDS
Kilmallock
Sunday April 13th
GOOD

424 - Maiden 4yo

274 **Clounties Lady [15]..................G Mulcaire** 1
cls up, ld 3 out, sn clr...................................
255 **Glacial Dancer [10]***chsd ldrs, went 2nd apr last, no ch wth wnr...* 2
303 **Hickeys Tavern***ld to 3 out, wknd.......................* 3
Also: 333 Cap It If You Can (4), Glenstal Forest (5), 333³ Lisdoylelady (f), 333 Cartons River (pu), 379 Mucky Man (pu), Lime Tree Road (f), All Right Clark (pu)
10 ran. 15l, 15l, ¾l. SP 6-1.

425 - Maiden 5yo

335 **Irish Frolic [15]........................D Turner** 1
prom, ld 3 out, styd on wll...................................
297 **Sporadic Verse [13]***chsd wnr aft 3 out, no imp apr last ....* 2
379³ **Sam Quale [12]***chsd ldrs, kpt on onepcd frm 3 out ....* 3
Also: 297² Gowan Gowan (4), 352 Hemero (5), 352 Deel Sound (6), 304 Black Swanee (pu), 297 My Uncle Batt (su), 322 Gortroe Guy (f), 297 Ongoing Dilemma (pu), 275 O Curry King (pu), 297 Real To Real (pu)
12 ran. 4l, 1½l, 10l. SP 9-2.

426 - Winners Of One

196¹ **Bavard Jet [16]..........................E Bolger** 1
prom, ld apr last, styd on wll ....
353¹ **Carnmore House [14]***ld hlfwy til apr last, no ext .....* 2
336 **Oneofourown [11]***chsd ldrs, onepcd frm 2 out ....* 3
Also: 357² Runabout (4), Hi-Way's Gale (5), 336 Brogeen Dubh (pu), Grannys Cottage (pu), 357 The Defender (pu), 357 Camogue Bridge (pu)
9 ran. 3l, 8l, 5l. SP 11-10.

427 - Open Lightweight

256¹ **Wayward King [23] ....P Cashman** 1
lft in ld 6 out, kpt on wll, jnd post.......................
357¹ **Lucky Town [23].........................E Bolger** 1
prog 5 out, chal last, jnd ldr post.........................
244 **Hopefully True [11]***nvr dang, t.o.....................* 3
Also: 309 Fethard Orchid [10] (4), 358² Starlight Fountain (pu), 336¹ Lisduff Pride (pu), 88² Upshepops (pu), 320 Looking Ahead (f), 357 Furry Island (f), 403 Beau Cinq (pu)
10 ran. Dd-ht, dist, 3l. SP 6-4.

428 - Mares Maiden

305³ **Aglish Pride [20] ....E Bolger** 1
ld/disp, mstk 3 out, sn drew clr, easily................
295 **Persian Moss [14]***prog to chs wnr aft 3 out, sn no imp* 2
296 **Rowdledy***nvr dang ....* 3
Also: 271 Stalmonta (4), 355 Derry Lark (5), Mistress Gale (6), 79 Donna (7), 384 Jennys Pearl (ur), 304 Tiernys Island (pu), 356 Bunny Lightening (pu), At The Corssroads (pu), 338² Midnight Society (pu), 353 Swanees Tune (pu), 356 Renty (pu)
14 ran. 20l, 20l, 5l. SP 4-6.

429 - Maiden 6yo+ I

354³ **Bosco's Touch [15].....................J Collins** 1
made all, lft clr 3 out, kpt on..............................
135 **Tooth Pick [13]***prom, ev ch whn blnd 3 out, no ext aft* 2
Mandril [11]*prom, kpt on onepcd frm 2 out.............* 3
Also: Sound Barrier [10] (4), High Pilgrim (5), 337 Theairyman (pu), 300 Well Doctor (pu), 242 Irish Display (pu), An Cearc Dearg (pu), 353 Sweeney Lee (pu), 287 Slaney Delight (pu)
11 ran. 6l, 6l, 2l. SP 6-1.

430 - Maiden 6yo+ II

348 **Derryvella Lad [15].....................J Boland** 1
chsd ldr, lft in ld 5 out, styd on wll.......................
300² **Not Convinced***chsd ldrs, lft 2nd 5 out, sn no imp ....* 2
275² **Barna Lad***nvr dang ....* 3
Also: 354 Just My Harry (4), 347 Millas Delight (5), 265³ Grey Venture (6), Emyvale Boy (pu), 243 Dare To Deel (pu), Silent Pond (pu), 337 Karens King (pu)
10 ran. 20l, 15l, 5l. SP 10-1.

MID-ANTRIM HARRIERS
Ballymena
Saturday April 19th
GOOD TO SOFT

431 - Winners Of Two

67 **Chariot Del [17].........................A Martin** 1
trckd ldr, mstk 3 out, ld apr last, sn clr..................
375 **Forever Gold [14]***rear, styd on frm 2 out, tk 2nd flat...* 2
328 **Roscrily William [11]***ld to apr last, wknd ....* 3
Also: 292 Ballindante [11] (4), 360 Cool Swallow (5), 247 Ballymichael (6), 365 Spartan Park (pu), World O Good (f)
8 ran. 10l, 10l, nk, dist, 3l. SP 5-2.

432 - Mares Maiden 5yo+

375² **Dernamay [14].........................B Dougan** 1
prom, chsd ldr 4 out, ld aft 2 out, just hld on...........
372² **Mourne Miner [14]***ld, clr 7th, hdd aft 2 out, rallied, just hld ....* 2
360 **Karen's Leader [12]***prom, onepcd frm 3 out ....* 3
407² **Hardtobegood [12]***prom, 3rd whn mstk 3 out, sn out-pcd ....* 3
Also: 366 Star Flyer (5), 329 Runaco (6), 123 Iveagh Lady (7), Barbaras Mews (pu), 368 Tashalin (pu), 416³ Ngala (pu), 369 Culnaveigh (pu), 360 Loch Saland (f), 372 Fernisky (pu), 370 Maid O'Tully (pu), 292 Shantallow (pu)
15 ran. Nk, 6l, dd-ht, dist, 1l, dist. SP 8-1.

433 - Open Lightweight

374 **Shanecracken [19]................P McCrickard** 1
hld up, prog to 2nd aft 4 out, ld flat, styd on.............
361¹ **Inver Red [18]***ld 4 out, mstk last, sn hdd & no ext.....* 2
374 **The Boolya [16]***rear & sn rdn, kpt on frm 2 out ....* 3
Also: 374 Lacken Beau [16] (4), 372 Ballywoodock VI [12] (5), 374 Fay Lin [10] (6), Kalavo (pu), 374 Glenshane Pass (pu)
8 ran. 1l, 6l, ½l, 12l, 4l. SP 6-1.

434 - Winners Of One

290 **Royal Aristocrat [15]..................B Hamilton** 1
made all, clr apr last, kpt on
326 **Uncle Art [14]***chsd wnr, chal 3 out-nxt, kpt on agn flat* 2
Also: 325[3] Haveafewmanners (f), 365 Anns Display (f)
4 ran. 2l. SP 6-1.

435 - Maiden 4 & 5yo

369[3] **Ballybollen [14]........................P Graffin** 1
chsd ldr, ld aft 3 out, mstk nxt, kpt on
363 **Mr Peoples [13]***clr ldr til hdd 3 out, kpt on onepcd* 2
Crookedstone [11]*prog to 3rd 4 out, ld & blnd 3 out, sn hdd, mstk last, wknd* 3
Also: 377 Russell Lodge (4), 328 Tullamore (5), 363 Templepatrick (6), Satco Prince (f), 369 Reds Paradise (ur), 413 Dreamingagain (pu), Musical Breeze (pu)
10 ran. 4l, 6l, 6l, 5l, 10l. SP 6-4.

436 - Maiden 6yo+

366[2] **Longmore Boy [15]....................R Patton** 1
made all, clr apr last, styd on wll
331 **Ash Brae [10]***chsd wnr 3 out, sn no imp* 2
360 **Tiger Dolly***nvr dang* 3
Also: 325 Sand de Vince (4), 289[2] Copper End (5), 377 Tom Haggard (6), 366 Scotts Cross (7), 226 Ollies Boy (f), 331 Onemans Choice (pu), 417 Mr Duncan (pu), 377 A Bit Of A Monkey (pu), 372 Athabasca (pu), Magoney (pu), Lord Sammy (pu), 316 Partyonjason (ro), 371 Carnmoon (pu), 371 Castle Stephen (ur), 371 Sebrimar (ro), 123 Twilight Invader (pu)
19 ran. 15l, 6l, 3l, 8l, 8l, 12l. SP 4-1.

MEATH & TARA
Summerhill
Sunday April 20th
GOOD

437 - Confined

395[2] **Herb Superb [21]........................W Ewing** 1
in tch, ld 4 out, clr 2 out, styd on
374[2] **Wilbar [20]***in tch, chal 4 out, kpt on frm 2 out, no imp flat* 2
351[2] **Radical Dual [13]***nvr dang* 3
Also: 412 Captains View (4), 417 Rovet (5), 412 Cool It (6), 330[3] Collooney Squire (ur), 412 Moygrehan Girl (pu), 394 Niamhs Dream (pu), 93 Royal Star (pu)
10 ran. 4l, 20l, dist, 3l, dist. SP 4-5.

438 - Maiden 4 & 5yo

347[2] **Well Ted [16]............................P Graffin** 1
3rd 6 out, chal & lft clr 2 out, rdn clr
350[2] **Princess Amanda [14]***mid-div, styd on frm 3 out, nrst fin* 2
393[2] **Friars Island [12]***chsd ldr 6 out, onepcd frm 3 out* 3
Also: 350 Shove Over (4), 311 Currow Hill (5), Beet Five (pu), Coca Berry Moon (pu), 347 Eagle Vail (f), 311 Needsmoretime (pu), 225 Niamhs Glory (pu), Onthelist (ur), 344[3] Paps Last Hope (ur), 393 The Bishops Sister (ur), Tracys Trot (ur), Boyne Valley Hero (pu), Dainty Daisy (f), 274 Five Mile Dancer (pu)
17 ran. 5l, 5l, dist, 25l. SP 3-1.

439 - Open Lightweight

346[3] **Furry Star [16]...........................A Cash** 1
ld 4 out, lft clr apr last, styd on
366[1] **Man Of Iron [14]***chsd ldrs, lft 2nd apr last, no imp wnr*
Local Whisper [13]*ld to 4 out, onepcd frm 2 out* 3
Also: 230 Mitchelstown River (pu), 414[3] Palmura (pu)
5 ran. 5l, 2l. SP 4-1.

440 - Maiden 6yo

287 **An Tain Shioc [13] ....A Ross** 1
prog 4 out, chal 2 out, ld last, styd on
343[3] **Coopers Clan** 2D
Glastryturn [11]*lft 2nd 5 out, onepcd frm 2 out, fin 3rd, promoted* 2
The Sutty Fox*chsd ldr 4 out, wknd 2 out, fin 4th, promoted* 3
Also: 397 Dock Strike (ur), 397[2] Eoins Lad (ro), Maeve's Magic (pu), 412[3] Pigeon Hill Buck (f)
8 ran. 1l, 3l, 10l. SP 10-1.

441 - Winners Of Two

396[2] **Call Me Joe [16].........................D Cullen** 1
trckd ldr 6 out, chal 3 out, ld flat, just hld on
Only Four [16]*hld up, prog 6 out, chal apr last, just hld* 2
314 **The Golam [15]***3rd 6 out, ld aft nxt, hdd & no ext flat* 3
Also: 412[1] Tuskar Flop [12] (4), 414[2] Annie's Arthur (5), 290[2] Some View (pu), Red Hugh (pu), Divilabetter (pu), Purcell (pu)
9 ran. Nk, 3l, 10l, 15l. SP 3-1.

442 - Mares Lightweight

365[2] **Sideways Sally [17] ....E Magee** 1
made all, rdd out
376[1] **Serious Note [15]***chsd wnr to 4 out, went 2nd agn apr last, no imp* 2
344[1] **Winning Rhythm [14]***chsd wnr 4 out-apr last, no ext* 3
3 ran. 3l, 2l. SP 4-1.

DONERAILE HARRIERS
Dromahane
Sunday April 20th
GOOD

443 - Confined Maiden 5yo+

172[2] **Chelsea King [16] ....T Nagle** 1
trckd ldr 4 out, ld 2 out, easily
338[3] **Glitter Girl [12]***ld 4 out-2 out, sn outpcd* 2
337[2] **Island Echo [10]***chsd ldrs, rdn 3 out, onepcd* 3
Also: 356 Ballybeggan Lady (4), 142 Neily Joe (5), 419 Coming Soon (pu), 430 Silent Pond (pu), 304 Ann Black (pu), 429 Theairyman (f), 302 Proud Carlingford (pu), 384[2] Blame Barney (pu)
11 ran. 4l, 5l, 8l. SP 5-2.

444 - Maiden 5yo

379[2] **Asthefellasays [16]...................P Cashman** 1
prom, ld 2 out, sn drew clr
321[2] **Dawdante [12]***in tch, chsd wnr aft 2 out, no imp* 2
352 **Tommys Pride***chsd ldrs, onepcd frm 3 out* 3
Also: 84 In The Stocking (4), 379 Bearys Cross (5), 307[3] West Coast Cooler (pu), 308 Newmarket Cheddar (ur), Brittas Boy (pu), 40 Fountain Bid (pu)
9 ran. 10l, 10l, nk. SP 4-1.

445 - Mares Maiden 5 & 6yo

Phildante [18]..........................M Budds 1
made all, clr 5 out, unchal
378 **Strong Ambition***chsd wnr, no ch frm 5 out* 2
384 **Con's Nurse***nvr dang* 3
Also: 378 Skipping Chick (4), 425 Black Swanee (pu), Stuarts Point (pu), 428 Jennys Pearl (pu), 338 Ballynagleragh (pu), 321 Grange Pine (pu), 383 Ballyhest Fountain (pu)
10 ran. Dist, 3l, 3l. SP 5-1.

446 - Open Lightweight

Celtic Buck [19]........................P O'Keeffe 1
prom, ld 4 out, comf
382 **Myalup [14]***chsd wnr 3 out, no imp* 2
382 **Sharoujack [13]***chsd ldrs, onepcd frm 3 out* 3
Also: 420 Glenbower Queen [12] (4), 382[1] Garramoss (ur)
5 ran. 4l, 3l, 2l. SP 4-6.

447 - Maiden 6yo+

422 Corkers Flame [15] ....N Fehily 1
prom, ld 3 out, styd on und pres ....
403 Natures Gentleman [14]*chsd wnr 3 out, chal nxt, no ext flat.* 2
422³ Deep Appeal [13]*cls up, chal 2 out, onepcd last......* 3
Also: 54 Bold Chevalier [12] (4), 429² Tooth Pick [11] (5), 381 Charnsy (6), 381 Playmore (7), Estevez (f), 223 Prima-Cosa (pu), 206 Clon Caw (f), 381 Another Berry (pu), 381 Toytown King (pu), 337 Loach Croga (pu), 135 Maltese Cross (pu), 378 Lingering On (pu), 378 Fernboy (pu), 422 Lazy Acres (pu)
17 ran. 2l, 2l, 1l. SP 5-1.

448 - Winners Of One

421³ Lord Harry [18] ....E Fehily 1
ld 5 out, styd on wll frm 2 out ....
420³ John's Right [16]*effrt to chal 2 out, sn onepcd ....* 2
208² Henleydown [13]*nvr dang.............................* 3
Also: 323 Roses Luck (pu), 336 I'm Happy Now (pu), 400¹ Parsons Green Boy (pu)
6 ran. 4l, 10l. SP 6-4.

LIMERICK HARRIERS
Friarstown
Sunday April 20th
GOOD

449 - Confined Maiden 5yo+

403 Some Swop [13]......................J McNamara 1
ld 5th, made rest, styd on wll ....
425 Hemero [11]*chsd wnr 3 out, no imp.................* 2
341 Lostyndyke*nvr dang..............................* 3
Also: 428 Renty (4), 243 Ballyluckamore (5), 24 Wharfingar (pu), Water Dancer (ro)
7 ran. 6l, 15l, 20l. SP 4-1.

450 - Maiden 4 & 5yo

308² Arleneseoin [14] ....E Bolger 1
made all, hld on wll flat.............................
203² Deejaydee [14]*chsd wnr 3 out, chal last, just hld ......* 2
425 My Uncle Batt [11]*chsd ldrs, onepcd frm 2 out.......* 3
Also: Millbrook Warrior (ro), Belcher Island (ro), 352 Ruck 'n Maul (ro), 77 For Paul (pu)
7 ran. Nk, 8l. SP Evens.

451 - Winners Of Three

426¹ Bavard Jet [19]..........................E Bolger 1
prom, ld 3 out, jnd last, hrd rdn & just hld on ....
Baby Jake [19]*in tch, hrd rdn to chal last, just faild ...* 2
402³ Prayon Parson [17]*chsd ldr to 3 out, styd on onepcd frm nxt* 3
Also: 358 Tantum Bonum [14] (4), 427³ Hopefully True (pu), 402¹ Ballinaveen Bridge (f)
6 ran. Hd, 1½l, 10l. SP 4-6.

452 - Maiden 6yo+

Loughlander [16] ....P Fenton 1
prom, disp 5 out, mstk 3 out, ld last, sn clr ....
324³ Jolly Jape [12]*chsd ldrs, styd on frm 2 out, tk 2nd flat* 2
403³ Ballybeggan Boy [10]*prom, disp 5 out-last, wknd .....* 3
Also: 353 O'Donnell Abu (4), 430³ Barna Lad (5), 353 Mr Campus (6), 301 Full Moon Fever (7), 430 Dare To Deel (8), 405 Stoney Piper (pu), 397 Parsons Fort (pu), Doc Hollywood (f), Colonel Smithers (bd), Grove Cross (pu), 354 Scheamin N Dreamin (pu), 429 An Cearc Dearg (pu)
15 ran. 7l, 5l, 4l. SP 7-4.

453 - Mares Maiden

Flying In The Gale [14] ....P Fenton 1
made all, jnd last, styd on wll.........................
355² Ardnataggle [13]*prog 3 out, jnd wnr last, no ext flat ..* 2
388 Forgoodnessjake VI [10]*nvr nrr ....* 3
Also: 428 Mistress Gale (4), 428 Tiernys Island (5), 201 Boarding Society (6), Dromin Hill (7), 394² Aine Hencey (pu), Menestream (pu), 355 Sheshia (f), Pharcebos (pu), 294 At The Crossroads (f), 356³ Sunczech (pu), 277 Ballycar Princess (pu), 159 Rossy Orchestra (f)
15 ran. 1½l, 8l, 8l. SP 3-1.

454 - Mares Lightweight

427 Upshepops [16] ....B Moran 1
prom, ld 2 out, styd on wll.............................
420 Derry's Diamond [13]*chsd wnr 2 out, no imp last ....* 2
427 Looking Ahead*chsd ldrs til wknd 2 out ....* 3
Also: 240 My New Merc (4), 355¹ What A Choice (5), 427 Fethard Orchid (6), 426 Hi-Way's Gale (7), 105 Brunswick Maid (pu), 357 Knocktoran Lady (pu)
9 ran. 8l, 15l, hd. SP 5-1.

LAOIS FOXHOUNDS
Ballacolla
Sunday April 20th
GOOD

455 - Open Lightweight

Knocknacarra Lad [15]..................N O'Neill 1
chsd ldr hlfwy, styd on und pres apr last, ld flat........
244 Just A Breeze [14]*ld hlfwy til hdd & not qckn flat.....* 2
272 Station Man [11]*ld to hlfwy, sn btn ....* 3
3 ran. 2l, 10l. SP 2-1.

456 - Maiden 4 & 5yo

335³ Into The Clan [15]......................M Phillips 1
chsd ldr & mstk 4 out, chal & lft clr 2 out ....
Good Counsel [10]*nvr dang, lft 2nd 2 out, no ch wth wnr* 2
Butterfield Boy*nvr dang.............................* 3
Also: Joes Favourite (4), 265 Barraby (5), 269 Burton Hall (pu), 424 Cartons River (ur), 303 Bad Influence (f), Chesnut Charley (su), Mr Whalebone (f), Dollys First (pu), 424 Lime Tree Road (f)
12 ran. 15l, 20l, dist, hd. SP 2-1.

457 - Winners Of Two

387³ Torduff Express [15] ....J Cullen 1
disp til ld 4 out, jnd & lft clr 2 out ....
339¹ Catch The Mouse*disp to 4 out, sn btn, lft poor 2nd 2 out* 2
Also: 408 Slaney Sauce [15] (ur)
3 ran. 25l. SP 9-10.

458 - Mares Maiden 6yo+

310 Maries Call [14] ....D O'Brien 1
hld up, prog 3 out, chal nxt, ld flat, kpt on ....
188 Red Mollie [14]*hld up, prog 3 out, ld last, hdd & no ext flat.* 2
407 Trimmer Lady [13]*prom, ld 3 out-last, kpt on.........* 3
Also: 185 Lark River [12] (4), 310 Brennan For Audits [11] (5), 389 Rosmere [10] (6), 287 Miss Day (pu), Ardtrix (ref), Orlas Choice (f), 394³ Native Oasis (pu), 388 Priory Street (pu), 419 Victim Of Slander (pu), 407 Dawn Pageant (f), 349 Heres Holly (pu), 296 Creative Flight (f), 407³ Shelmalier (f), 273 Barrystown Lady (f)
17 ran. ½l, 1l, 2½l, 3l. SP 4-1.

459 - Maiden 6yo+

391 Loudy Rowdy [14] ....J Berry 1
chsd ldrs, rdn 4 out, ld 2 out, all out ....
300³ Irregular Planting [13]*3rd 5 out, chal last, not qckn nr fin* 2
343² Stelinjo [12]*ld 5 out-2 out, styd on flat ....* 3
Also: 405² The Bug Hill [10] (4), 405 Daddy Warbucks (5), 343 Master Finbar (pu), 341 The Cass Man (pu), Wonderful News (pu), 385 Star Hand (pu), 243 Executive Fontaine (pu), C'murra (f), 95 Kinnefad King (pu), High Island (pu), 243 Bite Back (pu), Mullinello (pu)
15 ran. 2l, 4l, 5l, 20l. SP Evens.

460 - Mares Maiden 4 & 5yo

390² **Manacured [17]........................C Murphy** 1
made all, clr 4 out, easily
424 **Cap It If You Can [12]***chsd wnr 4 out, no imp* 2
Laurelhill Lady [11]*rear, styd on frm 3 out, nvr nrr* 3
Also: Member That (4D), Siobhans Princess (pu), 399 Honor Mission (f), Glacial Lady (pu), 312 Simpsons Kid (pu), Quah (f), 399 All Girls (pu), 406 Catherine's Pet (pu), Natures Storm (f), 406 Amber Dolly (f), Ballyday Dazy (pu), Valover (pu), 356 Scklepp (pu), Pride Of Poznan (pu)
17 ran. 10l, 4l. SP 2-1.

NEWRY HARRIERS
Taylorstown
Saturday April 26th
GOOD

461 - Maiden 4 & 5yo I

369 **Micklimar [16] ....A Martin** 1
chsd ldr, ld 4 out, clr last, comf
460³ **Laurelhill Lady [14]***prog 3 out, chsd wnr apr last, no imp flat* 2
416 **Lady Of Gortmerron [12]***prog 3 out, chas wnr nxt til apr last, no ext* 3
Also: 435 Russell Lodge (4), 438 Boyne Valley Hero (5), 413 Lady Zaffaran (6), 363 Lizzies Corner (f), 363 Lee Highway (f), Windsor Fountain (f), 431 Ballymichael (pu), Triail Do Laimh (pu)
11 ran. 4l, 6l, 20l, 20l, 10l. SP 6-4.

462 - Maiden 4 & 5yo II

369 **Raleagh Native [15]..................I Buchanan** 1
chsd ldr, ld apr last, styd on wll
329 **Forever Grey [12]***ld til apr last, no ext flat* 2
312 **Macken Money***prom til wknd 3 out* 3
Also: 369 Proan Hill (f), 413 Cardinal Belle (pu), 432 Culnaveigh (pu), 435 Reds Paradise (pu), Ceary Weary (ro), Millbrook Road (pu), Porcha (ref)
10 ran. 8l, dist. SP 2-1.

463 - Maiden 6yo

366 **Drumree [14]........................I Buchanan** 1
prog 5 out, ld apr last, styd on wll
436 **Ollies Boy [12]***prom, ld 6 out-apr last, no ext* 2
293 **Moses Man***nvr nrr* 3
Also: 329 Windmill Star (4), 370 Bobby Blazer (pu), 377³ Cascum Lad (pu), 436 Sebrimar (pu), 373² Pull The Lever (pu)
8 ran. 4l, 8l, 4l. SP 16-1.

464 - Maiden 7yo+

330² **Pauls Point [14] ....I Buchanan** 1
trckd ldng pair, ld 6 out, styd on wll
366³ **Emerald Breffni [12]***prog 3 out, chsd wnr apr last, no imp flat* 2
417 **Neely***nvr nrr* 3
Also: 209 Cluan Goill (4), 329 Microtelle Rose (5), 316 Nature Perfected (pu), 366 Where's Sam (pu), 436 A Bit Of A Monkey (pu), 366 Captains Friend (pu), 432 Iveagh Lady (pu), 436 Twilight Invader (pu), 437 Collooney Squire (pu), 364³ Land Forlorn (pu), 436 Mr Duncan (f), 376 Carlies Wood (pu)
15 ran. 4l, 8l, 2l, 10l. SP 6-4.

465 - Open Lightweight

177¹ **High Star [18] ....I Buchanan** 1
ld 6 out, clr 3 out, styd on wll
433 **Fay Lin [15]***chsd ldrs, kpt on frm 2 out* 2
373¹ **Bluagale [14]***chsd wnr 5 out, no ext aft 3 out* 3
Also: 433³ The Boolya [13] (4), 412² Voldi [13] (5), 361³ Christimatt [12] (6), 325² Chene Rose [10] (7), 376 Half Scotch [10] (8), 415¹ Lady Sylvie (pu), 433 Ballywoodock VI (pu)
10 ran. 4l, 2l, 4l, nk, 2l, 6l, nk. SP 1-3.

466 - Winners Of One

376² **Sister Nora [17]..........................L Gracey** 1
hld up, prog 5 out, chsd ldr 3 out, hrd rdn to ld nr fin
375¹ **Flodart [17]***ld, hrd rdn flat, hdd nr fin* 2
434 **Anns Display***chsd ldr to 3 out, wknd* 3
Also: 368³ Secret Door (pu), 367 Wayside Spin (pu), 326³ Ellies Pride (pu), 434² Uncle Art (pu), 213 The Convincer (pu), 331¹ You Said It (pu)
9 ran. ½l, dist. SP 5-1.

467 - Unplaced Maiden 6yo+

436 **Castle Stephen [12] ....R Arthur** 1
ld to 2 out, lft in ld apr last, all out
330 **Wind Of Glory [11]***chsd ldrs, lft 2nd apr last, kpt on* 2
329 **Island Harriet***bhnd, kpt on frm 2 out, nvr nrr* 3
Also: 360 Tierfergus (4), 253 Dawn Dieu (f), 416 Denel de (pu), 372 Ballywee Penny (pu), 416 Flame Of Gold (pu), 416 High River Den (pu), 377 Hillview Susie (pu), 432 Loch Saland [13] (su), 366 Mannix (f), Emma's Gamble (pu), 371 One Eleven (pu), 341 Barchester (bd), 436 Tom Haggard (f), 375 The Bleary Flyer (pu), 329 Supreme Flight (pu), Nicole's Hope (pu)
19 ran. 2l, 8l, 6l. SP 12-1.

WARD UNION
Tattersalls
Sunday April 27th
SOFT

468 - Maiden 6yo+

417 **Persian Life [15]....................N Geraghty** 1
ld 8th, lft clr 3 out, unchal aft
440 **Eoins Lad [10]***chsd ldrs, lft 2nd 3 out, no imp wnr* 2
377² **Che Amigo***nvr dang* 3
Also: 398 Tidaro Fairy (4), Ballinmusic (pu), 371² Golden Bar (f), 348 M T Pockets (f), 331² Mandingo (pu), 436 Partyonjason (pu), Schnapps (f), 397 Sir Gandouge (pu), 417³ Tip The Skip (f), Toarlite (pu), 398 Unevano (pu)
14 ran. 15l, 25l, 10l. SP 3-1.

469 - Open Lightweight

441 **Tuskar Flop [19] ....P Burke** 1
chsd ldr 5 out, ld last, drvn out
374¹ **Inch Cross [18]***ld 5 out-last, no ext flat* 2
442¹ **Sideways Sally [14]***ld to 5 out, sn btn* 3
Also: 327² Captains Bar [12] (4)
4 ran. 3l, 12l, 5l. SP 5-1.

470 - Maiden 4 & 5yo

438 **Onthelist [15]......................M O'Connor** 1
made most to 6 out, ld apr last where lft clr
456 **Joes Favourite***5th 5 out, nvr dang, wll btn 4th whn lft 2nd last* 2
251³ **Scoil Hill [14]***prom, ld 6 out-apr last, btn whn f last, rmntd* 3
Also: 413 Amistar (pu), Blue Castle (f), Dean Deifir (pu), 390 Inch Way (f), 438 Needsmoretime (pu), Oriel Dancer [14] (f), 438 The Bishops Sister (pu), Try A Bluff (pu), 413 Walterstown Boy (pu), 390 Mysterious Woman (pu)
13 ran. 20l, 12l. SP 3-1.

471 - Adjacent

437² **Wilbar [21].........................J O'Connell** 1
ld 5 out, sn clr, easily
183 **Only One [15]***ld to 5 out, sn btn* 2
413³ **Nobodywantsme [13]***nvr dang* 3
Also: 437 Rovet (4), 441 Purcell (pu)
5 ran. 20l, 4l, 10l. SP 4-6.

472 - Mares Maiden 5yo+

438 **Paps Last Hope [14]...................D Valentine** 1
chsd ldrs, prog to ld 5 out, mstk last, styd on
329² **Drumrock Lady [12]***alwys prom, chsd wnr 5 out, no imp frm 2 out* 2
392² **Glenpine [10]***3rd 5 out, no imp frm 2 out* 3
Also: 438 Beet Five (4), 458 Ardtrix (pu), Gandouges Lass (pu), 126 Kilbricken Sunset (pu), 438² Princess Amanda (pu), Rare Sally (pu),

370[2] Riverdance Rosie (pu), 370 Roseoree (pu), 394 Sally's Image (pu), Slade Valley High (pu), 310[2] Snowtown Actress (pu), 416 Sparkling Rosie (f)

15 ran. 5l, 7l, dist. SP 4-1.

473 - Winners Of One

345[2] Willie B Brave [17] .... A Martin 1
ld 6 out, styd on wll flat
441 Divilabetter [15]*chsd wnr 4 out, kpt on wll flat* 2
416[1] Ballynagussaun*nvr dang, t.o.* 3
Also: Captain's View (f)

4 ran. 3l, dist. SP 8-11.

KILLEADY HARRIERS
Corrin
Sunday April 27th
GOOD

474 - Maiden 5 & 6yo

379 Jimmy Dan [15] .... E Fehily 1
chsd ldr, ld last, sn clr
Rio's King [13]*ld to last, outpcd* 2
238 Timmy Tuff [11]*chsd ldrs, onepcd 2 out* 3
Also: 459 Star Hand (4), 91 Cottage Breeze (pu)

5 ran. 5l, 6l, dist. SP 3-1.

475 - Winners Of One

421[2] Burkean Melody [18] .... G Crowley 1
made all, clr 3 out, styd on wll
382 Radical River [14]*bhnd, styd on to chs wnr flat, no imp* 2
382[3] Pharways [14]*chsd wnr 3 out, no imp* 3
Also: 382 Peafield [12] (4), 418[1] Clashview (5), 380 Macklette (6), 421 Proscenium (pu), 338[1] Dante's Whistle (pu), 419[1] Tearfull (pu)

9 ran. 10l, 1l, 4l. SP 6-1.

476 - Confined Maiden 5yo+

337 The Stag [15] .... N Fehily 1
not fluent, chsd ldr, ld 3 out, sn clr
353 No Such Parson*ld to 3 out, wknd* 2
64 Knockadooma*nvr dang, t.o.* 3
Also: 418 Comely Maiden (4), 423[3] Clonageera (5), 419 Carlingford Pit (pu), 20 Classis King (pu), Some Day (pu), Athnowen (pu)

9 ran. Dist, 20l, dist. SP 4-6.

477 - Open Lightweight

420[2] McFepend [20] .... N Fehily 1
hld up, ld 2 out, sn drew clr
454[3] Looking Ahead [14]*made most to 2 out, no ch wnr aft*
446 Glenbower Queen*nvr dang.* 3
Also: 446[3] Sharoujack (4), 420 Quayside Buoy (pu)

5 ran. 12l, 20l, 5l. SP 1-3.

478 - Unplaced Maiden 5yo+

452 Stoney Piper [13] .... H Cleary 1
prog 3 out, ld apr last, styd on
443 Neily Joe [10]*ld 5 out-apr last, sn btn* 2
422 Minileader*nvr nrr* 3
Also: 77 Coalquay Coup (4), 418 Ford Classic (5), 305 La Kestrel (f), Supremcan (pu), 384 An Caipin (pu), 381 Cool-Lan-Sir (pu)

9 ran. 8l, 8l, 10l. SP 8-1.

479 - Mares Maiden 5yo+

383 Dons Pride [14] .... J Collins 1
prom, ld 3 out, styd on wll.
445 Ballyhest Fountain [11]*mstks, chsd wnr 2 out, no imp* 2
319[2] Merry River*prom, ev ch 3 out, wknd.* 3
Also: 384 Lady Of Means (4), 378 Everlaughing (5), 419 Little Santa (pu), 207 Miss Catherine (pu), Daring Day (f), 423 Happy Hula Girl (pu), Lomond Hill (pu), 419[2] Salty Bay (f), 384 Woodville Native (f)

12 ran. 8l, 6l, 6l. SP 10-1.

WATERFORD FOXHOUNDS
Kill
Sunday April 27th
HEAVY

480 - Open Lightweight

457[1] Torduff Express [19] .... D O'Brien 1
chsd ldrs, chal last, hrd rdn to ld flat
446[2] Myalup [19]*ld 5 out til hdd flat, kpt on wll* 2
374 Ounavarra Creek [17]*chsd ldrs, styd on onepcd frm 2 out* 3
Also: 411[1] Lost Coin [15] (4), 420 Cooladerra Lady [12] (5), 323[1] Pearl Dante (6), 446 Garramoss (pu)

7 ran. 1l, 2l, 8l. SP 6-4.

481 - Confined Maiden 5yo+

Minella Lass [15] .... D O'Brien 1
prom, ld 4 out, lft clr last
409 Society Lad*nvr dang, lft poor 2nd last* 2
Another Frosty [15]*chsd wnr 3 out, chal & f last, rmntd* 3
Also: Black Is Beautiful (pu), Carbery Boy (pu), 456 Dollys First (pu), Eupaba (pu), Hill Diamond (pu), Mrs Maginn (pu), 447 Estevez (pu)

10 ran. Dist, dist. SP 5-2.

482 - Maiden 5yo+ I

191 Royal Tommy [16] .... P Maloney 1
trckd ldrs, ld 2 out, comf
335 Bothar Fada [13]*chsd wnr 2 out, no imp.* 2
405 River Bargy [10]*chsd ldrs, onepcd 2 out* 3
Also: 447 Maltese Cross (4), 456 Burton Hall (5), 378[2] Minstrels Quay (pu), Real Value (pu), 459 High Island (pu), 456 Chesnut Charley (ro), 241 Bridge Party (pu), 275[3] Imperial Dawn (pu), Tara's Unyoke (pu), 43[2] Santa Jet (f), Ballamon Boy (pu)

14 ran. 4l, 10l, 3l. SP 4-1.

483 - Maiden 5yo+ II

261 Wintry Willow [15] .... A Costello 1
prom, ld 2 out, styd on wll.
54 Scrouthea [12]*chsd wnr 2 out, no imp last.* 2
409[3] Castle Glow [11]*in tch, onepcd 2 out* 3
Also: Templevalley [10] (4), 142 Dukestown (5), Buckle Up (6), Not For Profit (pu), Ruben James (pu), Buckhill (pu), Tully View (pu), Rushmore (pu), 390 Morrajay (pu)

12 ran. 6l, 3l, 2l. SP 8-1.

484 - Maiden 5yo+ III

324 Moonvoor [14] .... P Maloney 1
made all, clr 3 out, unchal
172[3] Shenanigans [12]*chsd wnr 3 out, nvr able to chal* 2
Knockanard*chsd ldrs, onepcd frm 3 out* 3
Also: 447 Another Berry (4), 405 Final Statement (pu), Clara Wood (pu), 381 Lord Vince (pu), 381 Lucky Jeff (pu), 381 Nattico (pu), 456 Mr Whalebone (pu), 280[3] Dangan Lad (USA) (pu), 181 Mineral River (pu), More People (pu)

13 ran. 3l, 10l, dist. SP 6-1.

485 - Maiden 4yo

Only For If [14] .... S Wrynn 1
prom, disp 2 out, hrd rdn to ld flat
332 Waydante [13]*prom, disp 2 out til no ext und pres flat* 2
390 Mrs Daniels*nvr nrr* 3
Also: Lacken Star (4), 332 Laganside (5), 333 Adramore Belle (6), Charlie Fudd (7), Musical Sling (pu), Ballinafauna (f), Stormin To Glory (pu), Cool Cleric (f), Forest Ore (f), 333 Curragh Lord (pu), Ashfield Run (pu), Sean Connors (pu)

15 ran. 2l, 15l, ½l. SP 4-1.

486 - Winners Of One

323[3] **The Territorian [19]**....................**J Moloney** 1
hld up, prog to ld 2 out, sn clr
443[1] **Chelsea King [15]***prom, ev ch 2 out, sn btn*.......... 2
317[1] **Danger Flynn [10]***chsd ldrs til wknd 2 out*........... 3
Also: 378[1] Persian Packer (4), Slaney Cuisine (pu), 384[1] Craggy Island (pu), Brownrose Lad (pu), 448 Roses Luck (pu), 323 Teads Boreen (pu), 408 Loch Garman Arms (pu)
10 ran. 8l, 15l, 25l. SP 5-1.

487 - Mares Maiden 5yo+ I

458 **Lark River [15]**..........................**D Whelan** 1
prom, ld 4 out, clr 2 out, unchal
317 **Menalma***chsd ldrs, no imp frm 2 out*.............. 2
272 **Cool Top***chsd ldrs, no prog frm 3 out*............... 3
Also: 166 Miss Metal (4), Buck's Serenade (pu), 271 Beat That (pu), 38 Miss Josephine (pu), Lady Sparky (pu), 304 Ore Galore (f), 234 Sea Breta (pu), Bucktime (pu), 305 Nellie Gale (pu), Glenmore Star (pu), 356 Killone River (pu)
14 ran. 20l, nk, dist. SP 7-2.

488 - Mares Maiden 5yo+ II

339[3] **Buzz About [14]**..........................**J Murphy** 1
chsd ldr 4 out, ld last, styd on
296 **Dusty Rose [12]***ld 6 out-last, no ext flat*............. 2
389[2] **Aroundthevalley***t.o.*................................ 3
Also: 401 Creative Thought (f), 407 Hi Hi Young Fella (pu), 264[2] Ballyknock Lass (pu), Mellefont (pu), Skipcarl (pu), 91 Munta (pu), 169 Familyvalue (pu), 295 Determined Okie (pu), 383 Valparaiso (pu), Seaside Lady (pu), Ratoath Gale (pu)
14 ran. 6l, dist. SP 6-1.

GOLDEN VALE
Thurles Point-To-Point Course
Sunday April 27th
SOFT

489 - Maiden 4yo

332 **Garrison Friendly [17]**...................**E Bolger** 1
hld up, prog 6 out, ld 2 out, sn clr
Gran Turismo [12]*chsd ldrs, styd on frm 3 out, no imp wnr*.......... 2
424 **Glenstal Forest***nvr dang, t.o.*...................... 3
Also: 450 Millbrook Warrior (4D), 399[2] Jolly Short Neck (pu), 460 All Girls (f), 424 All Right Clark (pu), Native Cannon (f)
8 ran. 10l, dist, 6l. SP 6-4.

490 - Maiden 5 & 6yo

430 **Grey Venture [15]**........................**B Moran** 1
prog 4 out, ld 2 out, sn clr
452[2] **Jolly Jape [10]***prom, ld 4 out-2 out, sn btn*........... 2
Over The Country*nvr dang*........................... 3
Also: 352[3] Pigeonstown (pu), Castleve (f), Laemni (pu), 352 Suave (pu), 459 Executive Fontaine (pu), 430 Just My Harry (pu)
9 ran. 15l, 10l. SP 6-1.

491 - Winners Of One

357 **Deep Refrain [18]**.......................**B Hassett** 1
made all, comf
395 **Premium Brand [14]***chsd wnr 4 out, nvr able to chal* 2
457 **Slaney Sauce [14]***chsd ldrs, styd on frm 2 out, no imp wnr*.......... 3
Also: 459 Mullinello (4), Hurricane Murphy (f)
5 ran. 1½l, hd, dist. SP 6-4.

492 - Open Lightweight

427[1] **Lucky Town [23]**...........................**E Bolger** 1
disp, ld 5 out, drew clr 3 out
455[2] **Just A Breeze [14]***prog to chs wnr 3 out, sn btn*...... 2
Also: 404[1] Run For Niall (pu), Tinerana Boy (pu)
4 ran. 15l. SP 4-6.

493 - Mares Maiden 5yo+

Rural Run [17]..........................**C Murphy** 1
ld 2nd, clr 5 out, unchal
Curraheigh*chsd wnr 4 out, nvr dang*.............. 2
428 **Derry Lark***chsd wnr 4 out, nvr dang*................ 3
Also: 401[3] Jenaway (4), 460 Amber Dolly (5), 355 Delmiano (6), 355[3] Steffi Liz (pu), Ashshanora (bd), Kate's Machine (pu), 445 Ballynagleragh (pu), 271 Betseale (pu), Hardy Cracker (f), 385 Mary Hand (f), 460 Valover (pu), 453 At The Crossroads (f), 453 Menestream (pu), 458 Creative Flight (pu), 460 Scklepp (pu)
18 ran. Dist, 2l, dist. SP 7-2.

494 - Mares Winners Of One

454[2] **Derry's Diamond [15]**...................**J Baragry** 1
lft in ld 5 out, sn clr
131[2] **Glenview Rose [11]***lft 2nd 5 out, sn outpcd*.......... 2
387 **Billie's Mate [10]***cls up til outpcd frm 5 out*.......... 3
Also: 267[2] Kinnahalla (4), 150[1] Definitely Maybe (pu), 415[3] Ballybriken Castle (pu), 401 Golly Miss Molly (f), 454 Knocktoran Lady (f), 402[2] Micro Villa (pu), 454 Brunswick Maid (pu), 345 Easter Bard (pu), 408 Trimmer Princess (pu)
12 ran. 12l, 3l, 2l. SP 8-1.

BREE FOXHOUNDS
Wexford Point-To-Point Course
Friday May 2nd
GOOD

495 - Winners Of Two

215 **Hyelord [18]**............................**C Murphy** 1
made virt all, clr 2 out, mstk last
299 **Penstal Lady [12]***chsd wnr 3 out, no imp*............. 2
441[1] **Call Me Joe***nvr dang*................................ 3
Also: 407[1] Glen Of Bargy (4), 411[2] Push Gently (5), 486 Loch Garman Arms (pu), 478[1] Stoney Piper (pu)
7 ran. 20l, 20l, 2½l, ¾l. SP 5-4.

496 - Maiden 4 & 5yo

409 **Touching Down [15]**...................**D Whelan** 1
in tch, ld last, comf
347 **King Of Glen [14]***ld 3 out-last, sn outpcd*............ 2
343 **Annie Leap***nvr nrr*................................... 3
Also: 470 Inch Way (4), 265 Helluvagale (5), 409[2] Bart Eile (6), 390 Apollodorus (7), 409 Siraidan (8), Brewery Lane (f), 409 Satquaid (pu), 482 Chesnut Charley (f), 409 Freestyler (ro), 50 Key Idea (pu), My Belief (pu), 485 Charlie Fudd (pu), Niralda (ro)
16 ran. 1½l, 20l, hd, 5l, 2l, 15l, 15l. SP 6-4.

497 - Maiden 6yo

391 **Buck And A Half [15]**....................**K Roche** 1
prom, ld 2 out, styd on wll
483[3] **Castle Glow [14]***in tch, chal 2 out, no ext flat*........ 2
391 **The Podger***nvr dang*................................. 3
Also: 220 Pondernot (4), 409 Back Withavengance (5), 389 Roseland (6), 440 Coopers Clan (7), 45 Dusky Run (pu), 482 Tara's Unyoke (pu), 407 Windgates Zone (f), Moss Tree (f), 411 Strawberry Lamp (f), 488 Determined Okie (ref), Ali's Dipper (bd), 481[2] Society Lad (pu), 391 Welsh Lane (f), 409 Our Brew (f), Smitten Not Bitten (pu), 218 Josie's Turn (pu)
19 ran. ¾l, 12l, ¾l, 6l, 10l, 8l. SP 6-1.

498 - Open Lightweight

469[2] **Inch Cross [20]**...........................**J Cullen** 1
cls up, ld 2 out, styd on wll flat
410 **Albert's Fancy [17]***ld to 2 out, onepcd*.............. 2
410[1] **Harveysland [17]***chsd ldrs, kpt on onepcd frm 2 out*.. 3
Also: 480 Lost Coin (4), 97[1] Miss Lurgan (pu), Owen Gowla (pu), 410[2] Killenagh Moss (pu), 391[1] Change The Script (f), Mighty Statement (ref)
9 ran. 1½l, nk, dist. SP 7-2.

499 - Maiden 7 & 8yo I

I Have You Now [15] ....J McNamara 1
ld 5 out, jnd 3 out, lft clr last
341 Siamsa Brae*nvr dang, lft poor 2nd last* 2
405 To The Hilt*nvr dang, lft poor 3rd last* 3
Also: 488² Dusty Rose (4), Blazing Crack (f), 222 Blazey Lady (ro), 488 Hi Hi Young Fella (ur), 339 Penny Bug (pu), 459 Daddy Warbucks [14] (f), 339 Noble Melody (ur), 422 Brill Star (pu), Doogles Son (pu)
12 ran. Dist, 4l, 10l. SP 4-1.

500 - Maiden 7 & 8yo II

405 Tramps Heartbreak [15] ....P Cloke 1
made most, clr apr last, all out flat
459 The Bug Hill [15]*prog 2 out, chal flat, just hld* 2
487³ Cool Top [12]*rear, styd on frm 2 out, nrst fin* 3
Also: 391 Louis de Palmer (4), 458 Miss Day (5), 458³ Trimmer Lady (6), 405 Little Len (ro), 223 Set A Way (f), 383 Out The Nav (f), 273 Cuckroo (pu), 406 Sparkes Cross (pu)
11 ran. ½l, 8l, 8l, 20l, 5l. SP 2-1.

501 - Mares Maiden 5yo

406 Braca Brook [16] ....E Gallagher 1
prom, ld 6 out, comf
493 Mary Hand [13]*chsd wnr 4 out, no imp* 2
385 Torduff Bay [10]*chsd ldrs, onepcd 4 out* 3
Also: 346 Fair Notice (4), 460 Quah (5), 389 Regular Rose (6), 406 Neeto (7), 493 Valover (8), 407 Running On Thyne (f), 407 Joyces Hope (pu), 390 She's A Flyer (pu), Orogale (pu), 488 Seaside Lady (pu), 349 Meigs Battle (pu)
14 ran. 10l, 10l, 4l, 20l, hd, 2½l, 15l. SP 6-1.

KILLULTAGH, OLD ROCK & C'TER
Lennymore
Saturday May 3rd
GOOD TO FIRM

502 - Winners Of Three

464² Emerald Breffni [12] ....A Harris 1
ld hlfwy, made rest, rdn out
462 Ceary Weary*rdn to chs wnr 5 out no imp* 2
Also: 464 Nature Perfected (pu)
3 ran. 5l. SP 4-5.

503 - Winners Of Two

433² Inver Red [18] ....P Graffin 1
lft in ld hlfwy, clr 2 out, hld on
465 Christimatt [17]*chsd ldrs, 2nd 3 out, hrd rdn & clsd flat, nrst fin* 2
465 Chene Rose [15]*wth wnr hlfwy-3 out, styd on agn flat* 3
Also: 326² Raleagh Muggins [12] (4), 466 Uncle Art (5), 466² Flodart (su), 465 Ballywoodock VI (pu)
7 ran. 1l, 6l, 8l, 10l. SP Evens.

504 - Mares Final

370¹ Touch Of Autumn [18] ....R Patton 1
trckd ldr, ld 3 out, sn clr
467 Hillview Susie [10]*ld to 3 out, sn btn* 2
Also: 432 Shantallow (pu), 432 Star Flyer (ur), 376 Gold Leader (f)
5 ran. 20l. SP 4-5.

505 - Open Lightweight

431¹ Chariot Del [19] ....W Ewing 1
chsd ldr, ld 4 out, styd on wll
414¹ Captain Brandy [17]*chsd ldng pair, 2nd 4 out, no imp wnr frm 2 out* 2
374 Funny Ye Know [16]*ld to 4 out, sn outpcd, kpt on* 3
Also: 327¹ Colin's Hatch (4), 433 Glenshane Pass (5), 362² Prince Yaza (6)
6 ran. 3l, 4l, dist, 3l, 15l. SP 7-1.

506 - Maiden 4 & 5yo

462² Forever Grey [15] ....W Ewing 1
pllng, made all, clr 2 out, hld on
311³ Vintage Choice [14]*chsd wnr 5 out, clsd flat, unable to chal* 2
431 Ballindante [11]*chsd ldrs, styd on onepcd frm 2 out* 3
Also: 461 Lady Zaffaran (4D), 432 Runaco (4), 370 Caladonian Light (f), Kingarriff Girl (pu), 462 Culnaveigh (bd), Mole Star (f), Rose Grey (f), 370 Whinveagh (pu), 461³ Lady Of Gortmerron (pu)
12 ran. 4l, 8l, 20l, 10l. SP 2-1.

507 - Maiden 6yo+ I

432² Mourne Miner [14] ....R Patton 1
ld to hlfwy, rallied 2 out, ld flat
413 Supreme Lancer [14]*chsd ldr 4 out, ld nxt, not run on & hdd flat* 2
440² Glastryturn [11]*nvr nrr* 3
Also: 468 Tidaro Fairy [11] (4), Sligo Champion [11] (5), 436 Lord Sammy (6), 436 Scotts Cross (7), 463 Sebrimar (pu), 467 Nicole's Hope (pu), 463² Ollies Boy (pu), Torr Head (ro), 436 Athabasca (pu), Nepe's Melody (ur), 464³ Neely (ur), 467 Barchester (pu), 180 Is This The One (f), 440³ The Sutty Fox (pu), 467 Flame Of Gold (pu)
18 ran. ½l, 8l, 1l, ½l, dist, 2l. SP 5-1.

508 - Maiden 6yo+ II

468 Golden Bar [14] ....L Gracey 1
ld 6 out, lft clr last
464 Microtelle Rose*chsd wnr 6 out-4 out, mstk 2 out, wknd, lft 2nd last* 2
431³ Roscrily William [13]*chsd wnr 4 out, chnc whn u.r. last, rmntd* 3
Also: 463 Cascum Lad (4), 467³ Island Harriet (5), 372³ Greet The Greek (6), 464 A Bit Of A Monkey (7), 436² Ash Brae (f), 328 Parman (f), 464 Twilight Invader (ur), 467 High River Den (pu), 464 Cluan Goill (f), 467 Dawn Dieu (f), 436 Carnmoon (f), 436 Sand de Vince (f), 360³ Blue Gas (pu), 463³ Moses Man (pu), 468 Ballinmusic (pu)
18 ran. 20l, dist, 2l, 6l, 6l, dist. SP 5-2.

STONEHALL HARRIERS
Ballysteen
Saturday May 3rd
GOOD

509 - Confined Maiden 5yo+

243 Meldante VI [14] ....L Temple 1
ld/disp, ld 5 out, styd on wll
300 Royal Leader [12]*prom, chsd wnr 4 out, no imp 2 out* 2
353 Sammy Sunshine*nvr dang* 3
Also: 452 Doc Hollywood (4), 425 Deel Sound (5), 295³ Lothian Magic (pu), 275 Court Thyne (su)
7 ran. 6l, 15l, 6l, ¾l. SP 4-1.

510 - Maiden 4 & 5yo

Tipping Away [14] ....R Flavin 1
prssd ldr, ld 4 out, hld on
335 Executive Flame [14]*ld, tried run out 5 out, hdd nxt, rallied last, just hld* 2
490 Castleve*t.o.* 3
Also: 449² Hemero (4), Coole Lower (pu), Scalp Hunter (f), Kings Response (pu), 453 Rossy Orchestra (pu)
8 ran. ½l, dist, dist. SP 2-1.

511 - Open Lightweight

451¹ Bavard Jet [19] ....E Bolger 1
prom, chal 3 out, hrd rdn to ld nr fin
299¹ Rosetown Girl [19]*prom, ld 3 out, hrd rdn, hdd nr fin* 2
454¹ Upshepops [17]*prom, ld 4 out-nxt, onepcd* 3
Also: 492 Tinerana Boy [14] (4), 451 Ballinaveen Bridge [12] (5), 454 Hi-Way's Gale (6), 494 Brunswick Maid (ur), 427 Starlight Fountain (pu)
8 ran. Hd, 6l, 10l, 6l, 8l. SP Evens.

512 - Maiden 6yo+

202 **Here Now [14]**......................**P Cashman** 1
prog 4 out, ld 2 out, styd on
452 **Parsons Fort [11]***ld 6th-2 out, sn btn*.......... 2
Bashindora*nvr nrr*.......... 3
Also: 429 High Pilgrim (4), 452 Colonel Smithers (5), 452³ Ballybeggan Boy (pu), 242 Man Of Hope (pu), 430² Not Convinced (pu), 449 Ballyluckamore (f)
9 ran. 8l, 6l, hd, 3l. SP 4-1.

513 - Winners Of One

21 **Not A Razu [18]**......................**E Bolger** 1
ld 4 out, comf
424¹ **Clounties Lady [15]***chsd wnr 4 out, nvr able to chal*.. 2
449¹ **Some Swop***nvr dang, t.o.*.......... 3
Also: 429¹ Bosco's Touch (su)
4 ran. 3½l, dist. SP 5-4.

514 - Mares Maiden 5yo+

453 **Aine Hencey [13]**......................**R Hurley** 1
mid-div, prog 5 out, chal last, ld nr fin
428² **Persian Moss [13]***ld 5 out, wknd & hdd nr fin*.... 2
487 **Miss Metal [11]***chsd ldrs, styd on onepcd frm 2 out*... 3
Also: 453³ Forgoodnessjake VI (4), 453 Mistress Gale (5), 493 Delmiano (6), 25 Kildea Duchess (7), 453 Boarding Society (pu), 449 Renty (pu), 162 The Crazy Chick (pu), Miss Florida (f), Pay The Piper (pu), 295 Killinane Beauty (pu), 453 Dromin Hill (pu), 493 Ashshanora (0), 317 Pharn N Wide (f)
16 ran. 1l, 5l, 6l, 25l, 25l, 2l. SP 4-1.

MUSKERRY FOXHOUNDS
Dromahane
Sunday May 4th
GOOD

515 - Maiden 5 & 6yo

484² **Shenanigans [14]**..................**J McNamara** 1
prom, disp 3 out til ld flat, styd on
171 **Money Matters [13]***prom, disp 3 out til no ext flat*.... 2
243 **Colmans Hope [10]***chsd ldrs, onepcd frm 3 out*...... 3
Also: 85³ Cabille (4), 484 Another Berry (5), 444 Brittas Boy (pu), 430 Karens King (pu), 444 In The Stocking (f), 482 Real Value (pu), 220 Shanacoole Pride (pu), 444 Newmarket Cheddar (f), 474 Star Hand (pu), 447 Chamsy (pu), Aughnabroga (pu), Timmyjohn (pu), 77³ Supreme Citizen (f), 444 Fountain Bid (pu), 474² Rio's King (ro), 378 Jolly Paddy (pu)
19 ran. 2l, 10l, 10l. SP 8-1.

516 - Winners Of Two

448¹ **Lord Harry [19]**......................**E Fehily** 1
in tch, ld apr last, sn clr, rdn out
145¹ **Gaye Bard [15]***rear, styd on apr last, tk 2nd flat*...... 2
421 **Carry On Shoon [15]***ld til apr last, onepcd*.......... 3
Also: 426 Brogeen Dubh [12] (4), 486² Chelsea King (ur), 320 The Pulpit (pu), 475² Radical River (pu)
7 ran. 5l, nk, 10l. SP 3-1.

517 - 4yo Championship

489¹ **Garrison Friendly [18]**..................**E Bolger** 1
hld up, prog to ld 2 out, sn clr
Royal Curragh [13]*ld to 2 out, kpt on*.......... 2
332² **Stormey Tune [12]***chsd ldrs, onepcd frm 2 out*...... 3
Also: 332 Good Time Abbey (4), 255 The Coppeen Lord (5), Coppeen Jewel (f), 423 Ardfert Fountain (pu), 423 Northern Talent (pu), One Clean Sweep (pu), 456 Cartons River (pu), Finnisk Dream (pu), Denis Agustine (pu), Meandyou (pu)
13 ran. 6l, 3l, 10l. SP 4-5.

518 - Open Lightweight

427¹ **Wayward King [23]**..................**P Cashman** 1
prom, ld 6 out, styd on wll
320³ **Mack A Day [19]***chsd ldrs, lft 2nd 4 out, no imp on wnr*.......... 2
16³ **Elwill Glory***ld to hlfwy, wknd*.......... 3
Also: 446¹ Celtic Buck (pu), 477³ Glenbower Queen (pu), 421¹ Roman Gale (f)
6 ran. 5l, dist. SP 6-4.

519 - Mares Maiden 5yo+

140³ **Function Dream [14]**....................**B Walsh** 1
prom, ld apr last, hld on flat
487 **Ore Galore [14]***prom, ld 3 out-apr last, kpt on wll*..... 2
487² **Menalma [12]***chsd ldrs, onepcd frm 2 out*.......... 3
Also: 443² Glitter Girl (4), 487 Nellie Gale (5), 384 Marys Friend (6), 476 Some Day (pu), 478 La Kestrel (pu), 445 Black Swanee (pu), Innishfea (f), Langretta (pu), 488 Valparaiso (pu), 79² Rock On Lord (pu), 487 Lady Sparky (pu), 419 Balaltrama (pu), 143 Eurogal (pu), 476 Carlingford Pit (pu)
17 ran. ½l, 5l, 10l. SP 3-1.

520 - Maiden 7yo+

459 **C'murra [15]**......................**M Phillips** 1
ld 3 out, comf
206 **Brian Og [12]***chsd wnr 2 out, no imp*.......... 2
447 **Tooth Pick [12]***prom, onepcd frm 3 out*.......... 3
Also: 308³ Speightstown Boy (4), 422 Clongeel Lord (5), Trakswayboy (pu), 447 Loach Croga (pu), Stratton Park (pu), 337 Baybuck (pu), 482 Maltese Cross (pu), 483 Buckhill (pu), 447³ Deep Appeal (ur)
12 ran. 4l, ½l, 15l. SP 5-4.

BALLYMACAD
Oldcastle
Sunday May 4th
GOOD TO SOFT

521 - Adjacent

468¹ **Persian Life [23]**....................**N Geraghty** 1
made all, clr 2 out, styd on strngly
471¹ **Wilbar [21]***chsd wnr 5 out, no imp frm 2 out*.......... 2
441 **Annie's Arthur [11]***t.o.*.......... 3
Also: 397¹ Wayforward (pu), 471 Purcell (pu), 468 Schnapps (pu), Very Best (pu)
7 ran. 6l, dist. SP 5-4.

522 - Maiden 4 & 5yo

470 **Try A Bluff [14]**......................**A Fleming** 1
prog 4 out, ld 2 out, mstk last, kpt on
461 **Boyne Valley Hero [13]***prssd ldr to 3 out, effrt agn last, no ext flat*.......... 2
438³ **Friars Island [12]***ld to 2 out, sn onepcd*.......... 3
Also: 393 No Other Hill (4), 57 What A Storm (5), 470 Walterstown Boy (6), 311 Country Practice (su), Over The Hill (pu)
8 ran. 1l, 3l, 10l, 4l, 5l. SP 12-1.

523 - Winners Of Two

494 **Easter Bard**..........................**D Cullen** 1
walked over

524 - Open Lightweight

469¹ **Tuskar Flop [21]**................**Claire O'Donnell** 1
ld 5th, made rest, styd on wll
Swordbender [18]*chsd wnr 4 out, btn aft 2 out, kpt on*
465 **Voldi***t.o.*.......... 3
Also: 439 Palmura (pu)
4 ran. 4l, dist. SP 6-4.

525 - Mares Maiden 5yo+

472 **Sparkling Rosie [13]**................**M O'Connor** 1
hld up, ld 6 out-3 out, rallied to ld flat
472³ **Glenpine [13]***in tch, ld 3 out, clr whn mstk last, hdd flat*.......... 2

432 Tashalin*nvr dang* 3
Also: 472 Rare Sally (4), 188 Ballylime Again (5), 460 Siobhans Princess (6), 472 Ardtrix (pu), 440 Dock Strike (pu), 437 Moygrehan Girl (f), 507 Nepe's Melody (pu), Slade Valley Lady (pu), 407 Thieving Sands (pu)
12 ran. 1l, 20l, 2l, 3l, 2l. SP 2-1.

526 - Maiden 7yo+

397 Laurelvale [14] ....**K Donohue** 1
lft in ld 4th, hrd prssd whn lft clr apr 2 out, kpt on
471 Rovet [13]*chsd ldrs, lft 2nd apr 2 out, kpt on, chnc last, no ext* 2
417² Highland Buck*nvr dang* 3
Also: 348 Boutrus (pu), 473² Divilabetter (f), 221 Dunamanagh Express (f), 397 Loch Bran Lad (ro), 437³ Radical Dual (ro), 468 Unevano (f), 398 Weekend Warrior (pu)
10 ran. 2l, 20l. SP 8-1.

EAST GALWAY
Eyrecourt
Sunday May 4th
GOOD TO SOFT

527 - Maiden 4 & 5yo

482 Imperial Dawn [14] ....**D Costello** 1
made all, styd on frm 2 out
490 Pigeonstown [13]*chsd wnr 5 out, kpt on onepcd* 2
Native Chief [12]*chsd ldrs, onepcd frm 3 out* 3
Also: Roll With It (4), Killimor Castle (pu), 425 Gowan Gowan (ur)
6 ran. 2½l, 2l, 25l. SP 5-2.

528 - Open Lightweight

451² Baby Jake [21]..........................**B Hassett** 1
in tch, ld 3 out, comf
455¹ Knocknacarra Lad [15]*prom, ev ch 3 out, not trbl wnr frm nxt* 2
427 Lisduff Pride [14]*in tch, ev ch 3 out, onepcd aft* 3
Also: 397 Babs Who (4), 465 Lady Sylvie (ur)
5 ran. 1½l, 3l, dist. SP 1-2.

529 - Maiden 6yo+

354² Send It In [16] ....**D Costello** 1
prom, ld 3 out, in cmmnd whn lft clr last
459³ Stelinjo*chsd ldrs, btn 3 out, lft 2nd last* 2
443 Silent Pond*nvr dang* 3
Also: 405 Spinans Hill (4), 452 O'Donnell Abu (5), Donna Fountain (pu), Serenade Star (pu), 452 Barna Lad (f), Gaelic Chance (pu), 459 Kinnefad King (f), 459² Irregular Planting [13] (f), Buckcharles VI (pu), 354 Belville Pond (pu), Pimpernels Spread (pu)
14 ran. 20l, 15l, 4l. SP 6-1.

530 - Winners Of One

425¹ Irish Frolic [15]...........................**D Turner** 1
w.w. ld 2 out, in cmmnd aft
Dysart O'Dea [13]*ld 3 out-nxt, no ext* 2
494 Ballybriken Castle*ld to 3 out, wknd* 3
3 ran. 2l, 15l. SP 4-7.

531 - Mares Maiden 5yo+

487 Killone River [12].......................**D Costello** 1
hmpd & lost plc 6th, prog 4 out, lft in ld 2 out, all out
356 Deerpark Lass [12]*chsd ldrs, lft 2nd 2 out, ev ch flat, just hld* 2
458 Heres Holly*nvr nrr* 3
Also: Cloone Star VI (4), Mighty Marble (ur), 493 Kate's Machine (pu), 460 Member That (ur), 453 Sheshia (f), 277 Carnmore Supreme (pu), 493³ Derry Lark (pu), 401 Scottish Match (f)
11 ran. Nk, 10l, dist. SP 7-2.

532 - Unplaced Maiden 5yo+

348 The H'penny Marvel [15]................**D Costello** 1
prom, ld 3 out, in cmmnd whn lft clr last
What Sand [11]*chsd ldrs, btn frm 3 out, lft 2nd last* 2
490 Just My Harry [11]*ld to 3 out, sn btn, lft 3rd last* 3
Also: 490 Laemni (4), 482 Bridge Party (5), 482 Burton Hall [13] (f), 300 Larrigan (f), Kerdiff Park (pu), 297 King Of Clare (pu)
9 ran. 8l, 2l, nk. SP 5-4.

MUSKERRY FOXHOUNDS
Dawstown
Monday May 5th
GOOD

533 - Adjacent Maiden 5yo+

443 Theairyman [13] ....**K Taylor** 1
hld up, rpd prog 2 out, ld nr fin
476² No Such Parson [13]*ld til hdd nr fin* 2
444³ Tommys Pride [12]*prom, ev ch last, no ext flat* 3
Also: Ten Castles [10] (4), 474³ Timmy Tuff (5), Silver Gale (6), 335 Star Of Annagh (pu), 515 Supreme Citizen (pu), Knocknagore (f), Good View (ur)
10 ran. ½l, 1l, 6l. SP 14-1.

534 - Maiden 4 & 5yo

483 Dukestown [15] ....**J McNamara** 1
w.w. ld 3 out, sn clr
Arguably*nvr dang, lft poor 2nd flat* 2
321³ Just A Playboy*t.o.* 3
Also: Saminski (pu), 239 The Rising Buck VI (pu), 476 Athnowen (pu), Churchtown Valley (pu), 423 Nomerose (pu), Cardinal Way (pu), Electric Bridge (pu), Sip Of Brandy (pu), 335 Vain Minstrel (pu), 192³ Wild Bavard [12] (ur), Leon Garcia (f)
14 ran. Dist, dist. SP 3-1.

535 - Open Lightweight

477² Looking Ahead [22] ....**P Crowley** 1
ld 6 out, clr nxt, unchal
480³ Ounavarra Creek [11]*nvr dang, lft poor 2nd apr 2 out*
480² Myalup [11]*nvr dang, poor 3rd frm 2 out* 3
Also: 480 Pearl Dante (4), 477 Quayside Buoy (pu), 477¹ McFepend (pu), Calmos (pu)
7 ran. Dist, ½l, 4l. SP 10-1.

536 - Maiden 6yo+

337 Gaelic Glen [13]......................**E Gallagher** 1
chsd ldr 2 out, hrd rdn to ld flat
418² Stags Rock [12]*ld 3 out, wknd & hdd flat* 2
Also: 366 Hey Chief (pu), 484 Lucky Jeff (pu), Tafadali (pu), Dangerous Dan (pu), 307 Tekroc (pu), Buck McGrath (pu)
8 ran. 1l. SP 4-1.

537 - Winners Of Two

336 Sumakano [17]..........................**T Lombard** 1
rear, ran on frm 2 out, ld nr fin
379¹ Maxine's Fountain [17]*ld 5 out, clr 2 out, hdd nr fin* 2
475¹ Burkean Melody*t.o.* 3
Also: Cailin Chuinne (f)
4 ran. ½l, dist. SP 3-1.

538 - Mares Maiden 5yo+

445 Skipping Chick [16]....................**P Crowley** 1
w.w. prog to ld 2 out, sn clr
479² Ballyhest Fountain*ld 4 out-2 out, sn btn* 2
319 Holiday Time*chsd ldrs, onepcd frm 3 out* 3
Also: 445³ Con's Nurse (4), 317 Marys Twin (5), 167 Princess Diga (pu), 383 Mandoora (pu), The Big Bay Mare (pu), 384 Some Shock (pu), 264 Princess Thyne (pu), 338 No Refund (pu), 167 Celtic Course (pu), 383 Loch Lomond (pu), 519 Carlingford Pit (f), Amandawill (pu), 479 Salty Bay (f), 487 Miss Josephine (pu)
17 ran. 20l, nk. SP 3-1.

KILMOGANNY FOXHOUNDS

Clonmel Point-To-Point Course
Saturday May 10th
GOOD TO SOFT

539 - Mares Maiden 4 & 5yo

Nancy Hanks [16] ....J McNamara 1
trckd ldrs, chal & lft clr 2 out, comf ....
493 **Betseale [12]***chsd ldrs, lft 3rd 2 out, kpt on* 2
479 **Woodville Native [12]***chsd ldrs, lft 2nd 2 out, wknd flat* 3
Also: 487 Bucktime (4), 479 Happy Hula Girl (5), 501 Meigs Battle (ur), Moyle Rover (bd), 460 Honor Mission (f), Unyoke Lady (f), 501 Quah (pu), 478 Ford Classic (pu), 493 Hardy Cracker (f), Queen Biddy (ur), 501 Seaside Lady (pu), 501³ Torduff Bay (pu), 485³ Mrs Daniels (f)
16 ran. 10l, ½l, 25l, 20l. SP 5-2.

540 - Maiden 4 & 5yo

496² **King Of Glen [15]........................C Murphy** 1
prom, ld 3 out, clr aft nxt, styd on ....
482² **Bothar Fada [12]***prom, ld 4 out-nxt, mstk 2 out, eased whn btn* 2
461 **Triail Do Laimh***prom til outpcd aft 4 out* 3
Also: 482 Ballamon Boy (4), 496 Satquaid (pu), 424 Mucky Man (pu), Baile An Daingan (pu), 481 Dollys First (f)
8 ran. 8l, 10l, 12l. SP 5-4.

541 - Winners Of One

494 **Micro Villa [19]..........................M Phillips** 1
prog 3 out, ld nxt, drew clr flat ....
501¹ **Braca Brook [16]***prog to chal 3 out, sn ld, hdd nxt, no ext flat* 2
479¹ **Dons Pride [13]***prom, ld 3 out, sn hdd & onepcd* 3
Also: 484¹ Moonvoor [12] (4), 454 Fethard Orchid (5), 497 Dusky Run (pu), 426 Grannys Cottage (pu), 345 Maks Dream (pu), 486 Brown-rose Lad (0)
9 ran. 5l, 8l, 4l, 2l, 25l. SP 7-2.

542 - Winners Of Two

491¹ **Deep Refrain [19] ....B Hassett** 1
trckd ldrs, ld aft 3 out, pshd out ....
494 **Kinnahalla [16]***rear, prog to chal 2 out, no imp wnr flat* 2
410³ **Sandy Pearl Two [13]***ld to aft 3 out, sn btn* 3
Also: 528 Lady Sylvie (4), 491³ Slaney Sauce (5), 417¹ Twin Track (f)
6 ran. 1½l, 10l, 15l, 1l. SP Evens.

543 - Open Lightweight

480¹ **Torduff Express [20]....................D O'Brien** 1
prom, ld 4 out, mstk 2 out, hdd last, sn ld agn, ran on wll
518 **Celtic Buck [18]***alwys prom, ld last, sn hdd & no ext..* 2
498² **Albert's Fancy [17]***prom, ev ch 2 out, onepcd last....* 3
Also: 484 Mineral River [11] (4), 498³ Harveysland (ur), 495 Push Gently (ro)
6 ran. 4l, 1l, 15l. SP 5-4.

544 - Maiden 6yo+ I

405³ **Barnadown [14]...........................B Doyle** 1
hld up, prog 4 out, lft in ld 2 out, styd on ....
407 **Polls Gale***ld til hmpd 5 out, wknd & lft 2nd 2 out.......* 2
499 **Blazing Crack***nvr dang*.......... 3
Also: 500 Cuckroo (4), Clonmel High (f), 493 Jenaway (f), 301 Johnny's Echo (pu), 458 Barrystown Lady (pu), 488³ Aroundthevalley (pu), 354 Lone Survivor (f), 512³ Bashindora (pu), Comic Act (pu), Drusilla (f)
13 ran. 15l, 7l, 8l. SP 4-1.

545 - Maiden 6yo+ II

Lucky Hero [17] ....M Kavanagh 1
prom, ld 3 out, drew clr last, pshd out ....
497 **Pondernot [13]***in tch, ev ch 2 out, sn outpcd, kpt on...* 2
497² **Castle Glow [12]***not fluent, hld up, prog to chal 2 out, wknd last* 3
Also: 500 Louis de Palmer [10] (4), 407 Spritly Lady (5), 497³ The Podger (6), 482 High Island (7), 482³ River Bargy (8), 459 Wonderful News (bd), Nash Na Habhainn (f), 481 Estevez (ro), 497 Our Brew (pu)
12 ran. 7l, 4l, 6l, 6l, 1l, 3l, 10l. SP 3-1.

NORTH TIPPERARY
Stereame
Sunday May 11th
SOFT

546 - Winners Of One

Hope's Delight [17] ....R Flavin 1
cls up, ld apr last, rdn out ....
426² **Carnmore House [16]***ld til apr last, no ext* 2
494 **Golly Miss Molly [11]***lost tch 4 out, kpt on onepcd frm 2 out* 3
Also: 499¹ I Have You Now (4), 509¹ Meldante VI (5), 494 Trimmer Princess (6), Handball (f), 512¹ Here Now (pu), 520¹ C'murra (f), 357 Handy Sally (bd), 472¹ Paps Last Hope (pu)
11 ran. 3l, 15l, 5l, 2l, 2l. SP 10-1.

547 - Mares Maiden 5 & 6yo

270³ **Donnrua [16]...........................P Colville** 1
trckd ldrs, ld 3 out, styd on flat ....
110 **Pharmacy Trio [15]***alwys prom, ev ch 3 out, no ext last* 2
349³ **Nucklewood [10]***prom, ld 5 out-3 out, sn btn* 3
Also: 538² Ballyhest Fountain (4), 493 Creative Flight (5), 510 Rossy Orchestra (6), 453 Ballycar Princess (7), 514 Ashshanora (pu), Jenobi (f), 453² Ardnataggle (ro), 453 Pharcebos (pu), Gra-Bri (pu), Poor Skin (pu), 531³ Heres Holly (pu), 514 Kildea Duchess (pu), 497 Ali's Dipper (pu)
16 ran. 4l, 15l, 2l, dist, 15l, 8l. SP 5-1.

548 - Maiden 7yo+

512² **Parsons Fort [15]........................R Hurley** 1
made virt all, styd on wll flat ....
520³ **Tooth Pick [14]***prog 3 out, chal und pres last, no ext flat* 2
500² **The Bug Hill [11]***prog 6 out, rdn & no ext 2 out* 3
Also: 491 Hurricane Murphy [10] (4), Ten Pence Princess (5), 458 Rosmere (6), 392³ Almauritia (7), 509³ Sammy Sunshine (8), 544 Jenaway (9), 452 Scheamin N Dreamin (pu), 430 Emyvale Boy (pu), 544 Aroundthevalley (pu), 449³ Lostyndyke (pu), 351³ Percusionist (pu), 481³ Another Frosty (f), 520 Deep Appeal (pu), 427 Beau Cinq (pu), Without A Penny (pu), 536 Dangerous Dan (pu)
19 ran. 3l, 8l, 2l, 10l, 4l, 20l, 20l. SP 6-1.

549 - Open Lightweight

334¹ **Dixon Varner [30]........................E Bolger** 1
ld 5 out, sn clr, easily ....
404² **Slaney Goodness [18]***chsd wnr 5 out, nvr any imp ...* 2
Two Covers*nvr dang* 3
Also: 455³ Station Man (4), Exile On Main St (pu), 511 Brunswick Maid (pu)
6 ran. 15l, 15l, 20l. SP 1-5.

550 - Unplaced Maiden 5yo+

532 **King Of Clare [13].......................B Hassett** 1
disp til ld aft 3 out, kpt on ....
536 **Hey Chief [11]***disp til aft 3 out, sn btn* 2
514 **Renty***nvr dang* 3
Also: 532 Bridge Party (4), 493 At The Crossroads (ur), 223 Slow Beet (pu), 509 Deel Sound (pu), 354 Camla Lad (pu)
8 ran. 4l, 20l, 5l. SP 5-1.

551 - Maiden 5 & 6yo

294² **Ship Of Shame [16] ....J McNamara** 1
prog to 2nd 4 out, disp apr 2 out til ld nr fin ....

85 Ballygowan Beauty [16]*prog to disp apr 2 out, just hld nr fin*.......... 2
184 Cool River [15]*ld, rdn & hdd apr 2 out, styd on agn flat*.......... 3
Also: 510² Executive Flame (4), 483 Tully View (f), 496 My Belief (pu), Linger Jet (pu), 490 Executive Fontaine (pu), 354 Danikar (pu), 468 Toarlite (pu), 425 Real To Real (pu), 171 Wortagamble (pu), 352 Crack Regiment (pu), 443³ Island Echo (pu)
14 ran. ¾l, 2l, 20l. SP 4-1.

COUNTY SLIGO
Sligo Point-To-Point Course
Sunday May 11th
SOFT

552 - Maiden 4 & 5yo

522³ Friars Island [15]..........G Harford 1
hld up, prog to ld aft 2 out, styd on wll..........
522 No Other Hill [12]*in tch, ev ch 2 out, sn btn*.......... 2
522² Boyne Valley Hero*prom til wknd 2 out*.......... 3
Also: Queens Sermon (4), 470 Dean Deifir (5), 470 The Bishops Sister (ur), 460 Glacial Lady (f), 363² Track O'Profit (f), 483 Not For Profit (pu), Out Of The Clouds (pu), 506 Mole Star (pu)
11 ran. 8l, 15l, 10l, 10l. SP 3-1.

553 - Open Lightweight

521² Wilbar [22]..........J O'Connell 1
hld up, prog 5 out, ld 2 out, pshd out..........
505 Colin's Hatch [17]*in tch, chsd wnr 2 out, nvr able to chal*.......... 2
505² Captain Brandy [15]*prom, onepcd frm 2 out*.......... 3
Also: 524³ Voldi [13] (4), 414 Carrigans Lad (pu)
5 ran. 4l, 10l, 6l. SP 4-6.

554 - Maiden 6yo+

482 Santa Jet [15]..........A Costello 1
ld, lft clr 3 out, jnd last, styd on wll flat..........
508 Parman [14]*wll bhnd, rpd prog 2 out, jnd wnr last, wknd flat*.......... 2
532³ Just My Harry*t.o.*.......... 3
Also: 508 Moses Man (f), 468 Sir Gandouge (f), 508 Island Harriet (f), We All Need Dreams (f), 526² Rovet (pu), 231 Paddy Red (pu), Pabelo (pu), Tour Ballyee (pu)
11 ran. 3l, dist. SP 5-4.

555 - Winners Of Two

513¹ Not A Razu [18]..........P Graffin 1
made all, shkn up & drew clr flat..........
521³ Annie's Arthur [15]*chsd ldrs, rdn to chal last, sn no ext*.......... 2
503 Raleagh Muggins [14]*chsd ldrs, rdn to chal last, sn btn*.......... 3
Also: 252 Manhattan Prince (pu), 426 The Defender (pu), 351¹ Mickthecutaway (pu)
6 ran. 3l, 4l. SP Evens.

556 - Mares Maiden 5yo+

472 Kilbricken Sunset [14]..........I Cochrane 1
4th whn lft 2nd 3 out, sn ld, rdn clr flat..........
531 Carnmore Supreme [12]*5th whn lft 3rd 3 out, sn prssd wnr, no ext last*.......... 2
525 Siobhans Princess*t.o.*.......... 3
Also: 472² Drumrock Lady (f), 472 Roseoree (f), 464 Land Forlorn (pu), 458² Red Mollie (pu), 525 Ardtrix (pu), 531 Scottish Match (pu), 312 Rosemary Ann (pu)
10 ran. 7l, dist. SP 8-1.

557 - Unplaced Maiden 7yo+

315 Celtic Air [13]..........P Kelly 1
raced wd, in tch, ld 2 out, styd on wll..........
491 Mullinello [12]*in tch, chsd wnr 2 out, no imp last*.......... 2
298 Lady Fleck*n.j.w. t.o.*.......... 3
Also: 353 Regular Beat (f), 365 Moybeg (pu), Evaris VI (pu), 467 Denelde (pu), 508 Cluan Goill (pu), 507 Is This The One (pu), 508 Ballinmusic (pu), 531 Sheshia (pu), 526 Loch Bran Lad (pu)
12 ran. 3l, dist. SP 5-1.

UNITED FOXHOUNDS
Ballindenisk
Sunday May 11th
GOOD

558 - Confined Maiden 5yo+

483 Buckle Up [14]..........M Budds 1
prom, ld apr 2 out, hld on well..........
447 Toytown King [14]*in tch, chal last, alwys hld nr fin*.......... 2
445² Strong Ambition [13]*in tch, chal last, no ext flat*.......... 3
Also: 378³ Icantsay [10] (4), 444² Dawdante (5), 383³ Rio Star (6), 261³ Glentoralda (7), 422 Big Spender (pu), 73 Bayloughbess (pu), 383 Marians Own (ur), 318 Cuddies Porter (pu), 317 Geragh Road (pu), 520 Trakswayboy (pu), 304³ Supreme Fountain (pu), 482 Minstrels Quay (pu), 538 Princess Diga (pu)
16 ran. Nk, 2l, 8l. SP 5-1.

559 - Maiden 4 & 5yo

490³ Over The Country [15]..........C Murphy 1
prom, ld 3 out, styd on wll..........
241 Charleys Run [14]*in tch, chal 2 out, mstk last, no ext* 2
533³ Tommys Pride [13]*prom, kpt on onepcd frm 2 out*.......... 3
Also: 489 Millbrook Warrior (4), 515 Cabille (5), Sovereign Cottage (6), 534 Athnowen (7), 423 Lord Egross (8), 519 Innishfea (pu), Aislings Pride (pu), 534 The Rising Buck VI (pu), 534 Saminski (pu), 534 Electric Bridge (pu), 517 Finnisk Dream (pu), 517 Meandyou (pu)
15 ran. 2l, 2l, 15l. SP Evens.

560 - Open Lightweight

528² Knocknacarra Lad [18]..........E Gallagher 1
trckd ldr, ld last, styd on wll..........
518³ Elwill Glory [14]*ld to last, no ext*.......... 2
535³ Myalup [12]*chsd ldrs, onepcd frm 2 out*.......... 3
Also: 535 Calmos (4)
4 ran. 3l, 6l, 10l. SP 4-6.

561 - Mares Maiden 5yo+

519³ Menalma [15]..........M Budds 1
prom, ld 3 out, clr nxt, unchal..........
419 Regal Gossip*chsd ldrs, kpt on onepcd frm 2 out, no ch wnr*.......... 2
538 No Refund*chsd ldrs til btn frm 2 out*.......... 3
Also: 488 Skipcarl (4), 519 La Kestrel (5), 500³ Cool Top (pu), 73 Carhoo Surprise (f), Irish Pride (pu), 479 Daring Day (pu), 487 Buck's Serenade (pu), 519 Marys Friend (pu), 519 Balaltrama (pu), 338 Paros Leader (pu), 514 Pharn N Wide (ro), 538 Carlingford Pit (pu), Foherish Mist (pu), 499 Penny Bug (pu), 514³ Miss Metal (pu), 383 Lorglane Lady (pu)
19 ran. 20l, 10l, ½l. SP 6-1.

562 - Winners Of One

513 Bosco's Touch [16]..........J Collins 1
made all, hld on wll nr fin..........
516 The Pulpit [16]*chsd wnr, clsd last, just hld*.......... 2
475 Macklette [13]*chsd ldrs, no prog frm 2 out*.......... 3
Also: 475 Clashview [13] (4), 475 Peafield [11] (5), 516 Brogeen Dubh (pu), 494 Knocktoran Lady (pu), 448 I'm Happy Now (pu), 475 Tearfull (pu)
9 ran. ½l, 6l, ½l. SP 2-1.

563 - Maiden 6yo+

189 Diamond Melody [18]..........E Gallagher 1
trckd ldrs, ld 2 out, sn clr..........
499 Daddy Warbucks [14]*prom, kpt on onepcd frm 2 out* 2
520 Clongeel Lord [10]*nvr able to chal*.......... 3
Also: 422² Deep Bit [10] (4), 83³ Robin Of Loxley (pu), 484 Clara Wood (pu), 520 Speightstown Boy (pu), 512 Man Of Hope (pu), 520 Stratton Park (pu), 536 Buck McGrath (pu), 515 Another Berry (pu), 476³ Knockadooma (pu), 533 Knocknagore (pu), 422 Apple Saft (pu)

14 ran. 10l, 10l, ½l. SP Evens.

UNITED FOXHOUNDS
Bartlemy
Sunday May 18th
GOOD

564 - Confined Maiden 5yo+

558 **Minstrels Quay [13]**..................K O'Sullivan 1
prom, ld apr 2 out, hld on wll
260 **Hazy Sea [13]***in tch, chal apr last, just hld* 2
558 **Glentoralda [12]***in tch, chal apr last, no ext flat* 3
Also: 515 Aughnabroga [11] (4), 479 Everlaughing (5), 558 Icantsay (6), 558³ Strong Ambition (7), 558 Cuddies Porter (8), 558² Toytown King (f), 558 Big Spender (pu)
10 ran. ½l, 3l, 1½l. SP 6-1.

565 - Mares Maiden 4 & 5yo I

485² **Waydante [15]**......................J McNamara 1
prog 3 out, hrd rdn to ld nr fin
538 **Con's Nurse [15]***prom, ld apr 2 out, hdd nr fin* 2
547 **Ardnataggle [14]***prog 3 out, styd on wll flat* 3
Also: 488 Ratoath Gale [14] (4), 559 Innishfea [12] (5), 519 Rock On Lord (6), 510 Coole Lower (7), 519 Black Swanee (pu), 488 Munta (pu), 561 Skipcarl (f), Rose Malt (pu)
11 ran. 1l, nk, ¾l. SP 5-4.

566 - Mares Maiden 4 & 5yo II

514 **Miss Florida [13]**....................J McNamara 1
prom, 2nd & btn whn lft clr last
538 **Some Shock***chsd ldrs, 3rd & no ch whn lft 2nd last* 2
539 **Queen Biddy***nvr dang* 3
Also: 538 Princess Thyne (4), 445 Grange Pine (5), 559 Aislings Pride (pu), 488 Ballyknock Lass [15] (f), 539 Ford Classic (ur), 460 Catherine's Pet (f), Inch Hostess (f), 531² Deerpark Lass (0)
11 ran. 12l, 12l, 3l. SP 7-2.

567 - Open Lightweight

537¹ **Sumakano [23]**........................T Lombard 1
4th til prog 3 out, ld nxt, ran on well
535 **Pearl Dante [19]***set fast pace to 2 out, sn btn* 2
535¹ **Looking Ahead [17]***chsd ldr to 2 out, sn btn* 3
Also: 518² Mack A Day [15] (4), 560¹ Knocknacarra Lad [13] (5), 494¹ Derry's Diamond (6), 518 Glenbower Queen (pu), 486¹ The Territorian (pu), 480 Cooladerra Lady (f), 451 Hopefully True (f)
10 ran. 12l, 5l, 6l. SP 3-1.

568 - Maiden 4 & 5yo

58 **Blasket Sound [16]**.....................C Murphy 1
in tch, ld apr 2 out, styd on wll
425³ **Sam Quale [14]***in tch, chal 2 out, no ext last* 2
484 **More People [13]***chsd ldrs, onepcd frm 2 out* 3
Also: Another One Jasper (4), 77 Briary Boy (5), Scrahan Cross (6), 483 Templevalley (7), Bally Banter (pu), 241 Viking Rod (pu), 534³ Just A Playboy (pu), 197 Storm Man (pu), Bodalmore Spring (pu), 332 Carlos The Jackal (pu), 40 Kelly's Perk (pu), 551 Real To Real (su), Spin City (f), Arbour Hill (pu), Bold Taedy (pu)
18 ran. 3l, 3l, 12l. SP 3-1.

569 - Winner Of One

Know Something VI [17]................D Murphy 1
prom, ld 4 out, kpt on well
236 **Radical-Times [12]***chsd wnr 2 out, no imp* 2
544¹ **Barnadown [10]***chsd ldrs till btn frm 2 out* 3
Also: 486 Craggy Island (4), 511 Hi-Way's Gale (5), 445¹ Phildante (co), 533¹ Theairyman (pu), 421 Chestnut Shoon (pu), 194 Supreme Odds (pu), 172¹ Chapel Road (f), 546³ Golly Miss Molly (pu)
11 ran. 15l, 6l, 2l. SP 5-1.

570 - Maiden 6yo+ I

563 **Robin Of Loxley [14]**...................T Lombard 1
prom, ld 2 out, hld on wll flat
499³ **To The Hilt [14]***chal 2 out, just hld flat* 2
547 **Ballyhest Fountain [13]***chsd ldrs, styd on onepcd apr last* 3
Also: Out The Way [12] (4), Another Planet [11] (5), 484 Nattico (6), 319 Black Serene (7), 563 Stratton Park (f), 561 Foherish Mist (pu), Pinball Rock (pu), Pamellas Star (pu), Bit Of A Lady (pu), 428 Midnight Society (pu), 146 Twilight Hour (pu)
14 ran. ½l, 3l, 4l. SP 6-1.

571 - Maiden 6yo+ II

515³ **Colmans Hope [15]**.................J Motherway 1
prom, ld 2 out, styd on wll
Boreen Lass [14]*prog 3 out, chal last, no ext flat* 2
478³ **Minileader***nvr dang* 3
Also: 548 Dangerous Dan (4), Amber's Delight (5), Fornido (6), Candy Is Dandy (7), Michael's Society (8), 563 Man Of Hope (ro), 561 Paros Leader (pu), 458 Dawn Pageant (pu), 497 Determined Okie (pu)
12 ran. 4l, dist, 2l. SP 6-4.

572 - Maiden 6yo+ III

520² **Brian Og [15]**..........................M Walsh 1
prom, disp 2 out til ld nr fin
381² **Sheer Mischief [15]***prom, disp 2 out til hdd nr fin* 2
536² **Stags Rock [10]***prom til wknd 2 out* 3
Also: Careformenow (USA) (4), 514 Mistress Gale (5), 561 Carhoo Surprise (6), 488 Mellefont (7), Little Paddle (pu), 519 Some Day (pu), 548 Beau Cinq (f), 499 Noble Melody (pu), 561 Irish Pride (pu), 487 Glenmore Star (pu)
13 ran. Nk, 15l, 1l. SP 9-2.

WESTMEATH & LONGFORD
Castletown-Geoghegan
Sunday May 18th
HOLDING

573 - Mares Open

498 **Miss Lurgan [18]**........................K Roche 1
in tch, ld 2 out, clr last, eased nr fin
525¹ **Sparkling Rosie [16]***rear, styd on wll frm 2 out, not rch wnr* 2
492² **Just A Breeze [16]***bhnd, styd on frm 2 out, nrst fin* 3
Also: 542³ Sandy Pearl Two [16] (4), 543 Push Gently [15] (5), 528³ Lisduff Pride [12] (6), 530³ Ballybriken Castle (pu)
7 ran. ½l, nk, 1l, 2l, 8l. SP 6-1.

574 - Maiden 4 & 5yo

496 **Bart Eile [16]**..........................J Brennan 1
in tch, ld 3 out, drew clr flat
496 **Inch Way [13]***bhnd, kpt on frm 3 out, no dang* 2
515 **In The Stocking [10]***prom til fdd frm 3 out* 3
Also: 552³ Boyne Valley Hero (pu), Eyre Eile (pu), 552 Glacial Lady (pu), 496 Helluvagale (pu), 470² Joes Favourite (pu), Mr Flowers (pu), 522 Over The Hill (pu), 552 Queens Sermon (pu), Sally's Call (pu), Take A Little (pu), 522 Walterstown Boy (pu)
14 ran. 10l, 10l. SP 4-1.

575 - Mares Maiden I

493 **Steffi Liz [14]**..........................B Hassett 1
prom, 2nd whn lft clr 2 out, unchal aft.
514 **Forgoodnessjake VI [11]***ld to 5 out, 4th & btn whn lft 2nd 2 out* 2
547 **Poor Skin***alwys bhnd, t.o.* 3
Also: 388 Becca's Rose (4), Chillbabychill (pu), Coolure Queen (pu), 525 Dock Strike (pu), 500 Miss Day (pu), 525 Moygrehan Girl (pu), 545 Nash Na Habhainn (ro), 472 Princess Amanda (pu), 525 Rare Sally (pu), 472 Riverdance Rosie (f), 525 Slade Valley Lady (pu), 525³ Tashalin (pu)
15 ran. 6l, 20l, dist. SP 5-1.

576 - Mares Maiden II

497 Windgates Zone [14]..................**B Hamilton** 1
cls up, ld apr 2 out, hld on flat
531 Mighty Marble [13]*prom, lost plc 4 out, ran on agn apr last* 2
556 Red Mollie [13]*bhnd, ran on frm 2 out, nrst fin* 3
Also: 509 Lothian Magic [13] (4), 501² Mary Hand [11] (5), 547 Rossy Orchestra [10] (6), 525² Glenpine (7), 432³ Hardtobegood (8), 525 Ballylime Again (pu), 472 Beet Five (pu), 458 Brennan For Audits (pu), 556² Carnmore Supreme (pu), 557³ Lady Fleck (pu), Noble Proposal (pu), 539³ Woodville Native (pu)
15 ran. 2l, ½l, 1l, 5l, 3l, 6l, 25l. SP 12-1.

577 - Open Lightweight

553 Voldi [19]..........................**Susan Vance** 1
chsd ldr, ld 2 out, hld on
521¹ Persian Life [19]*ld, blnd 5th, hdd 2 out, no ext flat* 2
549² Slaney Goodness [14]*chsd ldrs, no prog frm 3 out* 3
Also: 549³ Two Covers [14] (4), 439¹ Furry Star (pu), 529 Kinnefad King (pu)
6 ran. 1½l, 12l, nk. SP 10-1.

578 - Winners Of Two

555² Annie's Arthur [18]......................**J Vance** 1D
chal & slppd aft 2 out, rallied to ld last, fin 1st, disq.
546² Carnmore House [16] ....**F Hanley** 1
made most to last, no ext, fin 2nd, promoted
491² Premium Brand [15]*chsd ldrs, unable to chal frm 2 out, fin 3rd, promoted* 2
Also: 387 Benalf (pu), 552¹ Friars Island (pu), 555 Mickthecutaway (pu), 524 Palmura (pu), 521 Wayforward (f)
8 ran. 4l, 1l. SP 3-1.

579 - Maiden 6yo+ I

529 Barna Lad [15].....................**Lulu Olivefalk** 1
prom, ld 3 out, mstk last, styd on
554 Paddy Red [14]*chsd wnr 3 out, no ext flat* 2
529 Spinans Hill*chsd ldrs, no prog 3 out* 3
Also: Brosna Queen (pu), 512 Colonel Smithers (pu), 544 Cuckroo (pu), 548 Emyvale Boy (pu), George Finglas (pu), 557 Loch Bran Lad (pu), 397 Master Dempsey (pu), 468 Partyonjason (pu), 440 Pigeon Hill Buck (pu), 509² Royal Leader (pu)
13 ran. 1½l, 20l. SP 3-1.

580 - Maiden 6yo+ II

468 Tip The Skip [15] ....**P Casey** 1
prom, ld 2 out, styd on
529 Gaelic Chance [14]*rear, ran on frm 2 out, nrst fin* 2
526 Radical Dual [10]*chsd ldrs, onepcd frm 2 out* 3
Also: 545 Louis de Palmer (4D), 507 Tidaro Fairy (4), 532 Laemni (5), 557 Regular Beat (pu), 398 Regal Optimist (pu), 521 Schnapps (pu), 549 Station Man (pu), 551 Toarlite (pu), 526 Unevano (pu)
12 ran. 3l, 12l, 8l, 3l, 6l. SP 5-2.

NORTH DOWN
Comber
Saturday May 24th
GOOD

581 - Confined Lightweight

503 Uncle Art [12] ....**B Hamilton** 1
made all, unchal
508 Sand de Vince*chsd wnr, nvr able to chal* 2
Also: 464¹ Pauls Point (su)
3 ran. 10l. SP 5-4.

582 - Open Lightweight

553³ Captain Brandy [20] ....**D Christie** 1
ld hlfwy, styd on wll
577¹ Voldi [16]*chsd wnr hlfwy, no imp frm 2 out* 2
Also: 505 Glenshane Pass (f), Florida Way (pu)
4 ran. 3l. SP Evens.

583 - Maiden 5yo+

507² Supreme Lancer [16] ....**J Smyth** 1
ld 6 out, lft clr 2 out, unchal
464 Where's Sam*nvr dang, lft poor 2nd 2 out* 2
554² Parman*nvr dang, lft poor 3rd 2 out* 3
Also: 507 Lord Sammy (4), 375 Winter Ramble [13] (5), 554 Sir Gandouge (6), 554 Moses Man (ur), 507 Neely (ur), 436 Copper End (ur), 508 Twilight Invader (pu), 467² Wind Of Glory (ur), 508³ Roscrily William (pu), 579² Paddy Red (co)
13 ran. Dist, 10l, 5l, 3l, dist. SP 5-2.

584 - Winners Of Two

503³ Chene Rose [20]......................**I Buchanan** 1
ld hlfwy, lft clr apr 2 out, styd on well
578 Annie's Arthur [17]*chsd ldrs, lft 2nd apr 2 out, no imp wnr* 2
434¹ Royal Aristocrat [15]*disp to hlfwy, onepcd frm 5 out* 3
Also: 461¹ Micklimar [13] (4), 507¹ Mourne Miner (5), 502¹ Emerald Breffni (f), 473³ Ballynagussaun (ref)
7 ran. 6l, 5l, 5l, dist. SP 2-1.

585 - Unplaced Maiden 5yo+

507 Barchester [12] ....**L Lennon** 1
prom, ld 3 out, styd on
461 Lee Highway [11]*chsd wnr 2 out, no ext flat* 2
508 Carnmoon [11]*chsd ldrs, styd on onepcd apr last* 3
Also: 557 Cluan Goill [10] (4), 467 Loch Saland (5), 506 Runaco (6), 507 Sebrimar (7), Mister Malone (8), 467 One Eleven (pu), 432 Fernisky (pu), 377 Bold Boreen (pu), 552 Out Of The Clouds (pu), 429 Sound Barrier (f), 467 Tom Haggard (pu), 175 Not Found Yet (ro)
15 ran. 2l, ½l, 2l, 8l, dist, 2l, ½l. SP 5-1.

586 - Mares Maiden 5yo+

575 Riverdance Rosie [15]...................**J Quinn** 1
prom, ld apr 2 out, styd on wll
556 Land Forlorn [12]*chsd wnr 2 out, no imp last* 2
575 Tashalin 3D
507 Scotts Cross [11]*chsd ldrs, onepcd frm 2 out, fin 4th, promoted* 3
Also: 554 Island Harriet (4), 506 Lady Zaffaran (5), 461 Windsor Fountain (6), 508 Blue Gas (pu), 526 Dunamanagh Express (pu), 557 Evaris VI (ur), 366 Farlough Lady (ref), 556 Rosemary Ann (pu), 463 Bobby Blazer (pu)
13 ran. 5l, hd, 2l, 10l, dist, 1l. SP 4-5.

ORMOND FOXHOUNDS
Ballingarry
Sunday May 25th
GOOD

587 - Winners Of Two

542² Kinnahalla [19].........................**D O'Brien** 1
in tch, chal last, sn ld, styd on wll
554¹ Santa Jet [18]*in tch, ld 3 out til aft last, no ext* 2
546 Meldante VI [16]*ld to 3 out, sn onepcd* 3
Also: Builders Line [11] (4), 578¹ Carnmore House [11] (5), 548¹ Parsons Fort [10] (6), 546 Handy Sally (pu), 573 Lisduff Pride (pu), 546 Handball (pu), 495 Glen Of Bargy (pu), 517¹ Garrison Friendly (f), 546 Trimmer Princess (pu), 530² Dysart O'Dea (f), 574 Sally's Call (pu)
14 ran. 3l, 6l, 15l, 1l, 1l. SP 6-1.

588 - Maiden 4 & 5yo I

57 Cottage Counsel [15] ....**A Fleming** 1
made all, rdn out flat
539 Honor Mission [13]*chsd ldrs, lft 2nd 2 out, unable chal* 2
510³ Castleve [13]*nvr nrr* 3
Also: 574 Glacial Lady [10] (4), 568 Another One Jasper (5), Boherbee (pu), 551 Executive Flame (f), 540² Bothar Fada (pu), 568 Spin City (f), Shargan (pu)
10 ran. 4l, 15l, ½l, 10l. SP 6-1.

589 - Maiden 4 & 5yo II

484 **Dangan Lad (USA) [15]**.................**D Costello** 1
chsd ldr 2 out, hrd rdn, kpt on to ld nr fin..............
551² **Ballygowan Beauty [15]***prom, ld apr 2 out, clr apr last, hdd nr fin*.. 2
Grand Canyon [13]*nvr nrr*.......................... 3
Also: 58 Just Hold On [11] (4), Carro Valley (f), 551 My Belief (pu), 527 Roll With It (ur), Laura's Melody (pu), 527³ Native Chief (pu), 527² Pigeonstown (pu)
10 ran. ½l, 5l, 6l. SP 4-1.

590 - Mares Maiden 5yo+ I

539² **Betseale [16]**...........................**M Phillips** 1
in tch, ld apr 2 out, drew clr flat.......................
453 **Sunczech [12]***chsd wnr 2 out, no imp flat*............ 2
565³ **Ardnataggle [11]***chsd ldrs, onepcd frm 2 out*......... 3
Also: 576² Mighty Marble [11] (4), 547 Heres Holly (5), 576³ Red Mollie (6), Killena Star (f), 141 Fair Ophelia (ro), 547 Gra-Bri (f), 539 Moyle Rover (pu), 493 Ballynagleragh (f), Arctic Pond (f), 501 She's A Flyer (pu), 497 Strawberry Lamp (pu), 570 Pamellas Star (pu), 547² Pharmacy Trio (bd)
16 ran. 9l, 3l, 1l, 12l, dist. SP 3-1.

591 - Mares Maiden 5yo+ II

497 **Roseland [15]**...........................**D Whelan** 1
chsd ldr apr 2 out, btn whn lft in ld last, kpt on.........
531 **Member That [14]***chsd ldrs, btn whn lft 2nd last, no ext*.. 2
272² **Gliding Away***nvr dang, lft 3rd last*.................... 3
Also: 545 Spritly Lady (4), 575 Nash Na Habhainn (5), 556³ Siobhans Princess (6), 539 Quah (pu), 548 Aroundthevalley (pu), 541 Dusky Run (f), 575 Slade Valley Lady (pu), 544 Drusilla (pu), 493² Curraheigh [16] (ur), 501 Joyces Hope (ur), 576 Glenpine (f), 531 Cloone Star VI (pu)
15 ran. 3l, 20l, 2l, 1l, dist. SP 6-1.

592 - Open Lightweight

492¹ **Lucky Town [26]**..........................**E Bolger** 1
w.w. ld last, easily......................................
579¹ **Barna Lad [17]***lft in ld 3 out, hdd last, no ch wth wnr*.. 2
535² **Ounavarra Creek [16]***chsd ldrs, onepcd frm 3 out*.... 3
Also: 526¹ Laurelvale (4), 580 Station Man (5), 543 Mineral River (f), 528¹ Baby Jake (f)
7 ran. 3l, 3l, dist, dist. SP 2-5.

593 - Maiden 6yo+ I

572 **Careformenow (USA) [15]**..............**C Murphy** 1
made all, kpt on wll flat..................................
Abbey Actor [15]*prog 2 out, hmpd apr last, no ext flat*
545³ **Castle Glow [13]***jnd wnr 2 out, ev ch til wknd flat*..... 3
Also: 161 Prospect Star (4), 529 Buckcharles VI (5), 548 Scheamin N Dreamin (pu), Treasure Gale (pu), 405 Mr Balda (pu), 554³ Just My Harry (pu), 554 Pabelo (pu), Lord Coolroe (pu), 512 Ballybeggan Boy (pu), 548³ The Bug Hill (ur), 548 Almauritia (f), 526 Boutrus (pu), 579 George Finglas (pu), 579 Pigeon Hill Buck (pu)
17 ran. 1l, 6l, 10l, 25l. SP 6-4.

594 - Maiden 6yo+ II

499 **Doogles Son [16]**..........................**P Kelly** 1
made all, clr 2 out, comf..................................
550² **Hey Chief [13]***chsd wnr 2 out, no imp aft*............ 2
545² **Pondernot [12]***chsd ldrs, onepcd frm 3 out*........... 3
Also: 545 River Bargy [10] (4), Hill Of Tulla (f), Flowing Gold (f), 579 Loch Bran Lad (ro), 481 Eupaba (pu), 529 Belville Pond (pu), 529 Serenade Star (pu), 580³ Radical Dual (pu), 498 Mighty Statement (pu), 579 Emyvale Boy (pu), 580² Gaelic Chance (bd), 529 Pimpernels Spread (pu), 353 Tinosmill (pu)
16 ran. 7l, 3l, 4l. SP 6-1.

595 - Unplaced Maiden 5yo+

551 **Crack Regiment [14]**....................**B Hassett** 1
made all, hld on wll flat..................................
500 **Set A Way [14]***chsd ldrs, chal last, no ext nr fin*...... 2
544 **Clonmel High [13]***chsd ldrs, kpt on onepcd frm 2 out* 3
Also: 548 Hurricane Murphy [11] (4), 483 Morrajay (5), 580 Toarlite (6), 577 Kinnefad King (7), 574 Over The Hill (pu), 406 Weavers Window VI (pu), 571 Fornido (pu), 337 Mr Connie Vee (f), 570 Another Planet (pu), 493 Amber Dolly (pu), 568 Real To Real (pu), 484 Final Statement (pu), 580 Tidaro Fairy (pu), 450 For Paul (f)
17 ran. ½l, 3l, 5l, 20l, 5l, dist. SP 6-1.

DUHALLOW FOXHOUNDS
Dromahane
Sunday May 25th
GOOD TO FIRM

596 - Confined Maiden

551 **Island Echo [14]**........................**P Crowley** 1
in tch, chsd ldr 3 out, ld last, rdn out...................
204³ **Cnoc-Breac [12]***in tch, ld 3 out-last, no ext*.......... 2
533 **Ten Castles***in tch til onepcd frm 4 out*.............. 3
Also: 529³ Silent Pond (4), 478² Neily Joe (5), 565 Black Swanee (6), Ellen's Pride (f), 515 Brittas Boy (pu)
8 ran. 5l, 10l, ½l. SP 4-1.

597 - Maiden 4yo

517 **Coppeen Jewel [12]**.....................**E Fehily** 1
cls up, ld 3 out-last, no ext, fin 2nd, promoted.........
489 **Native Cannon [13]***hld up, prog 3 out, ld last, sn clr, fin 1st disq*.. 2
424³ **Hickeys Tavern [10]***chsd ldrs, onepcd aft 3 out*...... 3
Also: 559 Millbrook Warrior (4), Sycamore Cove (ro), 534 Cardinal Way (pu), 534 Sip Of Brandy (f)
7 ran. 4l, 3l, 2l. SP 4-1.

598 - Open Lightweight

205¹ **Two In Tune [18]**.....................**K O'Sullivan** 1
chsd ldrs, hrd rdn to chal last, ld nr fin...............
530¹ **Irish Frolic [18]***prom, ld 2 out, hdd nr fin*............ 2
516¹ **Lord Harry [17]***chsd ldrs, styd on wll frm 2 out, nrst fin*.. 3
Also: 546¹ Hope's Delight [16] (4), 560² Elwill Glory [13] (5), 567 Cooladerra Lady [11] (6), 573³ Just A Breeze (7), 543² Celtic Buck (8), 486 Teads Boreen (f), 543³ Albert's Fancy (pu)
10 ran. Hd, 2l, 3l. SP 3-1.

599 - Mares Maiden 6yo+

443 **Ballybeggan Lady [14]**.................**P Crowley** 1
hld up, prog to ld aft 3 out, sn clr.......................
561 **Cool Top***chsd ldrs, onepcd frm 3 out*................. 2
561 **Daring Day***clr ldr til hdd aft 3 out, wknd*.............. 3
Also: 570 Black Serene (4), 519 Langretta (5), 572 Irish Pride (6), 572 Mistress Gale (7), 538 Miss Josephine (8), 570³ Ballyhest Fountain (9), 570 Foherish Mist (10), 572 Mellefont (11), Minor Setback (pu), 538 The Big Bay Mare (su), 445 Stuarts Point (pu), 558 Princess Diga (pu), 169 Ronkino (f), 547 Ali's Dipper (f)
17 ran. 20l, 10l, 2l. SP 6-1.

600 - Winners Of One

546 **C'murra [16]**..........................**P Maloney** 1
made all, clr 4 out, mstks last 3, styd on...............
572¹ **Brian Og [14]***chsd wnr 4 out, kpt on, nvr able to chal*.. 2
569 **Chestnut Shoon [13]***chsd ldrs, onepcd frm 4 out*..... 3
Also: 494² Glenview Rose [12] (4), 570¹ Robin Of Loxley (5), 510¹ Tipping Away (pu)
6 ran. 4l, 3l, 2l. SP 5-4.

601 - Maiden 5yo+

563² **Daddy Warbucks [15]**.................**T Lombard** 1
prom, disp 3 out til ld flat, drvn out....................
534 **Wild Bavard [14]***prom, disp 3 out til hdd & no ext flat* 2
544³ **Blazing Crack***nvr nrr*................................ 3
Also: Monday's News (4), 544 Bashindora (pu), 87 Master Jake (f), 570 Stratton Park (pu), 571 Man Of Hope (ro), Henry The Lad (pu), 532² What Sand (bd), 558 Geragh Road (pu), 563³ Clongeel Lord (f),

570 Pinball Rock (pu), The Gothic (pu)
14 ran. 2l, 20l, 2l. SP 7-4.

SOUTH UNION
Kinsale
Saturday May 31st
FIRM

602 - Maiden 4 & 5yo

574³ In The Stocking [13] ....**K Ross** 1
prom, ld 4 out, styd on wll
540 Dollys First [11]*chsd wnr 3 out, no imp last* 2
568 Arbour Hill [11]*chsd ldrs, styd on onepcd frm 3 out* 3
Also: 559³ Tommys Pride [11] (4), 321 Uncle Archie (pu), 476 Clonageera (pu), 568 Briary Boy (pu), 444 West Coast Cooler (pu), 601 Monday's News (pu), To Darn Hot (pu), Flighty Leader (pu)
11 ran. 4l, ½l, ½l. SP 6-1.

603 - Winners Of One

562 Tearfull [15]............................**C Murphy** 1
prom, ld 3 out, clr last, styd on wll
569² Radical-Times [11]*prom, wth wnr 3 out-nxt, no ext* 2
599 Foherish Mist*prom til fdd 3 out* 3
Also: 572³ Stags Rock (pu), 562 Clashview (pu)
5 ran. 10l, 4l. SP 4-1.

604 - Ladies Winner Of Two

541 Moonvoor [18]......................**Lillian Doyle** 1
w.w. ld 3 out, clr last, comf
573 Push Gently [15]*chsd wnr 2 out, no imp.* 2
573² Sparkling Rosie [14]*prom, onepcd frm 3 out* 3
Also: 564¹ Minstrels Quay [13] (4), 569 Craggy Island (f), Walyunga (pu), 600³ Chestnut Shoon (bd)
7 ran. 6l, 4l, 2l. SP 6-4.

605 - Open Lightweight

567 Knocknacarra Lad [19] ....**P Crowley** 1
in tch, prog to ld 2 out, rdn out
598 Albert's Fancy [17]*prom, ld 4 out-2 out, no ext* 2
577³ Slaney Goodness [16]*prom, wth ldr 3 out-nxt, no ext* 3
Also: 598 Cooladerra Lady [10] (4), 546 Paps Last Hope (5), 555 Manhattan Prince (pu), Sir L Munny (pu), 542 Lady Sylvie (pu)
8 ran. 4l, 3l, 20l. SP 7-4.

606 - Mares Maiden 4 & 5yo

565 Ratoath Gale [15] ....**E Bolger** 1
made all, clr 2 out, comf
355 Tonmarie Chance [12]*prog to trck wnr 3 out, sn no imp* 2
575 Becca's Rose [10]*nvr nrr* 3
Also: 591² Member That (4), Target Practice (5), 566 Princess Thyne (6), 566 Catherine's Pet (7), 589 Carro Valley (pu), 590 Arctic Pond (f), 596² Cnoc-Breac (pu), 566 Ford Classic (f), 576 Mary Hand (pu), 596 Black Swanee (f), 566 Deerpark Lass (pu), 204 Miss Fashion (co)
15 ran. 4l, 6l, 3l. SP 5-4.

607 - Unplaced Maiden 6yo+ I

558 Bayloughbess [13] ....**T Lombard** 1
in tch, ld 3 out, styd on
571 Candy Is Dandy [10]*chsd wnr 2 out, no imp* 2
571 Amber's Delight [10]*prom, onepcd frm 2 out* 3
Also: 599 Irish Pride (4), 595 Another Planet (5), 378 Cloneen Adventure (6), 563 Clara Wood (pu), 571 Determined Okie (pu), 570 Bit Of A Lady (pu), 476 Comely Maiden (pu), 572 Carhoo Surprise (f), 579 Colonel Smithers (pu), 500 Out The Nav (su), Regal Mist (bd)
14 ran. 6l, 1l, 8l. SP 8-1.

608 - Unplaced Maiden 6yo+ II

595 Mr Connie Vee [13].....................**P O'Keeffe** 1
hld up, prog to ld 2 out, sn clr
557 Ballinmusic*prom, ev ch 2 out, sn outpcd.* 2
570 Nattico*chsd ldrs, no prog frm 2 out* 3
Also: 561 La Kestrel (4), 599 Mistress Gale (5), 348 Zanagale (6), 572 Glenmore Star (pu), 590 Killena Star (pu), 484 Lord Vince (pu), 591 Nash Na Habhainn (pu), 338 Lucky Fifteen (pu), 324 Colligan Falls (pu), 563 Knocknagore (pu)
13 ran. 10l, 6l, 2l. SP 5-2.

SOUTH UNION
Kinsale
Sunday June 1st
FIRM

609 - Maiden 4yo

Sheeghee [14] ....**B Doyle** 1
chsd ldr 2 out, styd on to ld flat
Cebosupremo [14]*prog to ld 3 out, hdd & no ext flat* 2
303 Macfarly [12]*chsd ldrs, onepcd frm 3 out* 3
Also: 597 Millbrook Warrior (4), 489 Jolly Short Neck (5), 588 Boherbee (6), 517 Northern Talent (pu), 489 All Right Clark (0)
8 ran. ½l, 5l, 8l. SP 3-1.

610 - Maiden 6yo+ I

353 Healing Thought [16]..................**B Hassett** 1
prog 3 out, ld apr last, sn clr
593 Ballybeggan Boy [12]*prog 3 out, ev ch nxt, sn outpcd*
583² Where's Sam [10]*prog 3 out, ev ch nxt, sn outpcd* 3
Also: 378 Woodfield Boss [10] (4), 593 Prospect Star (5), 607 Bit Of A Lady (pu), 548 Deep Appeal (pu), 595² Set A Way (ur), Des The Architect (pu), 603³ Foherish Mist (pu), 551 Linger Jet (pu), 607² Candy Is Dandy (pu)
12 ran. 10l, 4l, ½l. SP 5-1.

611 - Maiden 6yo+ II

599 Ballyhest Fountain [13] ....**B O'Sullivan** 1
chsd ldrs, ld last, styd on well
575² Forgoodnessjake VI [10]*ld 3 out-last, wknd* 2
601³ Blazing Crack*chsd ldrs, no prog 2 out.* 3
Also: 599³ Daring Day (4), 608² Ballinmusic (5), 593 George Finglas (6), 579 Cuckroo (pu), 563 Speightstown Boy (pu), 487 Sea Breta (pu), 576 Hardtobegood (pu)
10 ran. 8l, 5l, 1l. SP 8-1.

612 - 4m Open Lightweight

511 Ballinaveen Bridge [18] ....**F Hanley** 1
ld to hlfwy, ld 2 out, drew clr last
562² The Pulpit [12]*ld hlfwy-2 out, sn btn* 2
560³ Myalup [11]*alwys 3rd, no prog 4 out* 3
Also: 604² Push Gently (pu)
4 ran. 15l, 4l. SP 3-1.

613 - Open Lightweight

605² Albert's Fancy [18] ....**J Quigley** 1
ld 4 out, drvn out flat
386 Slaney Wind [17]*chsd wnr 3 out, chal nxt, no ext flat* 2
605 Manhattan Prince [13]*chsd ldrs, onepcd frm 3 out* 3
Also: 605³ Slaney Goodness [11] (4), 567 Hopefully True (5)
5 ran. 1½l, 10l, 5l. SP 3-1.

614 - Winners Of One

538¹ Skipping Chick [17]...................**P Crowley** 1
hld up, prog to chal 2 out, ld last, drvn out
562 Peafield [17]*ld to last, just hld flat* 2
542 Slaney Sauce [15]*chsd ldrs, onepcd frm 2 out* 3
Also: 574¹ Bart Eile [14] (4), 605 Paps Last Hope [13] (5), 587 Trimmer Princess [10] (6), 457² Catch The Mouse (7), Shegoes (8), 604³ Sparkling Rosie (9), 556¹ Kilbricken Sunset (10), 447¹ Corkers Flame (ur), 587³ Meldante VI (ro)
12 ran. 1l, 5l, 2l. SP 6-4.

615 - Maiden 5yo+

601 Clongeel Lord [14]..................S O'Callaghan **1**
chsd ldr 2 out, chal last, ld flat, rdn out ....
564 Toytown King [13]*ld 3 out, wknd & hdd flat ....* **2**
533 Timmy Tuff [11]*chsd ldrs, onepcd frm 2 out..........* **3**
Also: 563 Knockadooma (4D), More Booze (pu), 576 Lothian Magic (pu), 571[3] Minileader (pu)
7 ran. 2l, 5l, 1l. SP 6-1.

Index to Point-to-Point Runners 1997

KEY TO INDEX

HORSE'S NAME	Colour	Sex	Age	Breeding	Owner

Last year's record and Merit Rating for each race
Position (Rating) — **Bold** indicates Hunter Chase — **NH** other NH races
Race Number — Date — Course — Left or Right Handed
(cross refers to Results Section)
Type of Race (refer to Results Section)
Distance to nearest furlong
No. of Runners — Going — Close-up — Finishing Position — Merit Rating for the race
Horse Comment .... **Merit Rating**
(This rating should be used until updated in Point-to-Point Entries Index)

AARON'S VENTURE b.g. 6 Ra Nova - Aberaeron Girl by Neltino — J R Holt

480	9/3	Southwell P'	(L)	MDO 3m	17	G	*wll bhnd til p.u. 7th*	P	0
549	16/3	Garthorpe	(R)	MDO 3m	16	GF	*mid div, prog to ld aft 15th, p.u. appr nxt, lame*	P	0

Dead **14**

ABBEY ACTOR (Irish) — I 593[2]

ABBEY FLYER b.g. 5 Minster Son - Miss Felham by Malinowski (USA) — Mrs J Woollatt

761	29/3	Kimble	(L)	MDO 3m	12	GF	*alwys last pair, wll bhnd whn p.u. 16th*	P	0

Not yet of any account **0**

ABBEY LAD b.g. 7 State Diplomacy (USA) - Another Pin by Pinza — Ernie Fenwick

134	9/2	Alnwick	(L)	MDO 3m	11	G	*jmpd slwly, sn t.o., p.u. 3 out*	P	0
160	15/2	Lanark	(R)	MDO 2m 5f	10	G	*bhnd by 8th, styd on to tk 2nd flat*	2	0
419	8/3	Dalston	(R)	MDO 2 1/2m	10	GS	*chsd ldrs, 5th & just in tch whn u.r. 9th*	U	-
699	29/3	Stainton	(R)	MDO 3m	7	F	*mid-div til slppd up apr 5th*	S	-
1105	19/4	Hornby Cast'	(L)	MDO 3m	11	G	*rear, prog 11th, wknd 14th, t.o. 3 out*	6	0

Distant 2nd on only show of ability & struggles to stay; novice ridden **10**

ABBEY MOSS ch.g. 6 Executive Man - Mickley Vulstar by Sea Moss — Charlie Peckitt

1996 P(0),P(0)

115	9/2	Wetherby Po'	(L)	MDO 3m	8	GF	*mid-div, outpcd 12th, t.o. whn p.u. 4 out*	P	0
269	22/2	Duncombe Pa'	(R)	MDO 3m	16	G	*prom, ld 3rd, hdd 6th, wknd 12th, t.o. 3 out*	4	0
427	8/3	Charm Park	(L)	MDO 3m	10	GF	*ld til hdd & wknd qckly 4 out*	4	0
860	31/3	Charm Park	(L)	MDO 3m	12	F	*mid-div, lft 3rd 15th, t.o.*	3	0
1252	26/4	Easingwold	(L)	MDO 3m	9	GS	*in tch whn f 5th*	F	-

Beat just two others in 3 completions and shows no stamina yet. **0**

ABBOTSHAM b.g. 12 Ardross - Lucy Platter (FR) by Record Token — O J Carter

1996 **F(NH),P(NH),P(NH),2(NH),4(NH),4(NH),F(NH)**

793	31/3	Bishopsleigh	(R)	OPE 3m	7	G	*prom, ld/disp 10th til hdd aft last, ran on und pres,jst hld*	2	21
890	4/4	Aintree	(L)	HC 2 3/4m	14	G	*jmpd poorly in rear, blnd 10th (Becher's), staying on when hmpd 2 out, n.d..*	3	22
1358	5/5	Exeter	(R)	HC 2m 7f 110yds	8	G	*held up in rear, hit 6th, hdwy apr 9th, went 2nd before 4 out, wknd next.*	3	21
1482	11/5	Ottery St M'	(L)	LAD 3m	5	G	*(fav) ld to 9th, disp nxt til ld 15th, sn clr*	1	24
1529	18/5	Fakenham	(L)	HC 3m 110yds	9	G	*chsd ldrs, rdn 5 out, wknd 3 out.*	5	13
1591	31/5	Stratford	(L)	HC 3 1/2m	11	G	*reminders to keep up from 5th, t.o. when p.u. before 5 out.*	P	0

Retains ability & quite useful at best; can win points at 13; Any. **23**

ABDUL EMIR b.g. 10 Ovac (ITY) - Azul by Majority Blue — Mrs Lisa Stock

1996 **U(NH),P(NH),8(NH),8(NH),P(NH)**

278	23/2	Charing	(L)	RES 3m	17	G	*alwys rear, lost tch 12th, t.o.*	7	0
462	8/3	Charing	(L)	RES 3m	10	G	*rear whn hmpd & u.r. 2nd*	U	-
576	16/3	Detling	(L)	MEM 3m	10	F	*alwys rear, blndrd 11th, 6th & wll btn whn blndrd last*	6	0
711	29/3	High Easter	(L)	RES 3m	6	F	*chsd ldr to 11th, blnd 9th, cls up whn blnd & u.r. 12th*	U	-
970	6/4	Penshurst	(L)	RES 3m	4	F	*cls up, ld 7th, mstk 10th, hdd 4 out, fdd*	3	0

1128 19/4 Penshurst (L) LAD 3m 8 GF *mid-div, clsd 7th, ld 12th-3 out, wknd* 5 0
1445 10/5 Peper Harow (L) LAD 3m 6 GF *in tch, chsd ldrs frm 6th, mstk 10th, outpcd frm 13th* 3 11

Maiden winner 94; no form under Rules after; well beaten all starts 97; non-stayer 10

ABIT MORE BUSINESS(IRE) b.g. 6 Henbit (USA) - Driven Snow by Deep Run R G Williams
1996 4(0),2(14)
43 1/2 Larkhill (R) MDO 3m 10 GF *(fav) pllng,hld up,prog to ld 14th,v slw last,sn hdd & nt rcvr* 3 14
181 15/2 Larkhill (R) MDO 3m 17 G *(fav) hld up in tch, ev ch 3 out, lft in ld last, ran on* 1 15
298 1/3 Didmarton (L) RES 3m 15 G *mid-div, hmpd 7th, nt rcvr & p.u. nxt* P 0

Fortunate winner & problems next start; top stable; more needed for Restricted hopes; Good. 16

ABITMORFUN ch.g. 11 Baron Blakeney - Mary Mile by Athenius Christopher Shankland
1996 6(13),**6(0)**,3(14),**8(0),4(NH),5(NH)**
484 9/3 Tweseldown (R) OPE 3m 10 G *ld 3rd-10th, lost tch 13th, p.u. nxt* P 0
825 31/3 Lockinge (L) MXO 3m 3 F *hld up in tch, ld brfly 9th, not qckn 14th, btn nxt* 3 0
1055 13/4 Hackwood Pa' (L) OPE 3m 4 GF *alwys last, remote frm hlfwy* 4 0
1451 10/5 Kingston Bl' (L) OPE 3m 5 G *ld to aft 13th, last nxt, sn t.o.* 5 0
1533 18/5 Mollington (R) XX 3m 8 GS *ld to 5th, prssd ldr to 11th, wknd rpdly, t.o.* 7 0
1564 25/5 Kingston Bl' (L) CON 3m 7 GF *(bl) mstk 2nd, chsd wnr to 10th, wknd rpdly, t.o.* 5 0

Beaten last 31 races & completely lost interest now 0

A BIT OF A MONKEY (Irish) — **I** 365^{P}, **I** 366^{P}, **I** 377^{P}, **I** 436^{P}, **I** 464^{P}, **I** 508,
A BIT OF A RASCAL (Irish) — **I** 123^{P}, **I** 253^{P}, **I** 330^{U}, **I** 366^{P}

A BIT OF FLUFF b.m. 5 Green Adventure (USA) - Cantabile by Bustino Lady Susan Brooke
571 16/3 Garnons (L) MDN 2 1/2m 13 G *mid-div whn f 8th* F -

A brief debut season 0

ABLE MOSS ch.g. 13 Le Moss - Banish Misfortune by Master Owen Miss B Morant
334 1/3 Corbridge (R) MEM 3m 7 G *mid-div, lost tch 9th, t.o. 11th* 4 0
810 31/3 Tranwell (L) CON 3m 5 G *hndy 3rd 6th, wknd to 5th 9th & p.u.* P 0
1169 20/4 Hexham Poin' (L) RES 3m 9 GF *alwys rear, t.o. last whn p.u. 14th* P 0

No longer of any account 0

ABSAILOR b.g. 13 Kambalda - Tarsilogue by Tarqogan C Latilla-Campbell
1996 **10(NH),8(NH)**
1217 26/4 Balcormo Ma' (R) MEM 3m 4 F *made most til hdd apr last, no ext flat* 2 10

Revived for quick thrash in members but no prospects in proper races now 10

ABSENT MINDS br.m. 11 Lir - Forgotten by Forlorn River B R J Young
1996 3(10)
493 12/3 Newton Abbot (L) HC 2m 5f 110yds 11 HY *mid div till wknd 9th, t.o. when p.u. before last.* P 0
628 22/3 Kilworthy (L) CON 3m 12 G *ld brfly 3rd, prom til lost plcd 10th, t.o.* 8 0

Rarely appears & needs to concentrate on maidens - no real prospects of a win, though. 10

ABSOLUTELY AVERAGE(IRE) b.g. 7 Montelimar (USA) - Dr Shadad by Reform Mrs S Maxse
1996 **10(NH)**
181 15/2 Larkhill (R) MDO 3m 17 G *jmpd delib, ld/disp to 6th, wknd 15th, t.o.* 6 0

Fair form under Rules & good enough for maiden win but ran badly only start; best watched 12

ACE OF SPIES b.g. 16 He Loves Me - Belle Bergere by Faberge II Mrs S N J Embiricos
301 1/3 Parham (R) MEM 3m 3 G *w.w. chal & jmpd 14th & nxt, ld 3 out, drew clr* 1 11
596 22/3 Horseheath (R) LAD 3m 4 F *mostly last, no ch frm 12th* 4 12
1434 10/5 Marks Tey (L) LAD 3m 3 G *hld up, prog 9th, last frm 14th, outpcd nxt, styd on 2 out* 3 13

Game old stick; still tries & members again at 17 not beyond him 12

ACE PLAYER(NZ) b.g. 9 Full On Aces (AUS) - C'est La Vie (NZ) by Dubassoff (USA) Brian Bebb
1996 **6(NH),11(NH),2(NH)**
57 1/2 Kingston Bl' (L) LAD 3m 13 GF *cls up to hlfwy, btn whn p.u. 2 out* P 0
202 15/2 Weston Park (L) LAD 3m 13 G *w.w. ran on well frm 4 out, nvr nrr* 2 20
1302 3/5 Weston Park (L) LAD 3m 5 G *in tch whn f 4th* F -

Hurdles winner 95; ran well 2nd start but interrupted season; could win modest ladies at best 20

ACETYLENE b.m. 5 Miner's Lamp - Cherry Morello by Bargello Dr S G F Cave
525 15/3 Cothelstone (L) MDN 3m 15 GS *bdly hmpd 1st, p.u. nxt* P 0
866 31/3 Kingston St' (R) MDO 3m 7 F *chsd ldr frm 7th, wknd 16th, btn 3rd p.u. apr last* P 0
1158 20/4 Stafford Cr' (R) MDO 3m 5 GF *hld up, prog 12th, ld aft 3 out-apr last, onepcd* 3 11

Placed in weak races but shows some promise; could win in 98 if not running out of gas 13

ACHIEVED AMBITION(IRE) gr.g. 9 Derring Rose - In Paris by Last Fandango — Mrs S Davies

1996 F(-),**P(0)**

464	8/3	Eyton-On-Se'	(L)	INT	3m	12	G	*rear 10th, t.o. 12th, p.u. 14th*	P	0
572	16/3	Garnons	(L)	INT	3m	13	G	*mstk in rear 6th, 11th whn u.r. 8th*	U	-
722	29/3	Sandon	(L)	MDO	3m	10	GF	*rear, t.o. 8th, no ch & p.u. 4 out*	P	0

No completions in 5 attempts 96/7 & looks safely ignored 0

ACHILTIBUIE b.g. 13 Roscoe Blake - Gorgeous Gertie by Harwell — G Heal

1996 **5(NH),5(NH),9(NH)**

530	15/3	Wadebridge	(L)	OPE	3m	4	GF	*alwys bhnd, t.o. & p.u. 3 out*	P	0
791	31/3	Bishopsleigh	(R)	CON	3m	6	G	*chsd ldrs til wknd 17th, t.o. nxt*	5	0
952	6/4	Black Fores'	(R)	LAD	3m	3	G	*plld hrd, ld 4th til 2 out, outpcd apr last*	2	10
1110	19/4	Flete Park	(R)	LAD	3m	9	GF	*u.r. 1st*	U	-
1257	27/4	Black Fores'	(R)	LAD	3m	5	F	*cls up til f 3 out*	F	-
1394	5/5	High Bickin'	(R)	MEM	3m	4	G	*(fav) keen hld, chsd ldr, hit 13th, cruised home 2nd, awarded race*	1	11
1579	26/5	Lifton	(R)	CON	3m	9	G	*alwys rear, p.u. 15th*	P	0

Winning chaser; old character who does not stay & handed race on plate; no follow up at 14 11

ACROSS THE CARD b.g. 9 Lir - Cornish Susie by Fair Season — Major General C A Ramsay

1996 2(17),1(15),3(12),1(21),**1(21)**,3(17),U(-),**3(16)**

132	9/2	Alnwick	(L)	LAD	3m	9	G	*in tch, prog 10th, 4l 2nd & clsng whn u.r. 3 out*	U	-
231	22/2	Friars Haugh	(L)	LAD	3m	13	G	*s.s. prog to jn ldrs 4 out, no ext apr last*	4	20
388	7/3	Sandown	(R)	HC	3m 110yds	7	G	*soon well bhnd, t.o. 13th, styd on after 3 out, went 2nd run-in, no ch with wnr.*	2	23
609	22/3	Friars Haugh	(L)	LAD	3m	11	GF	*midfld, styd on to go 2nd apr 2 out, not rch wnnr*	2	21
731	29/3	Alnwick	(L)	MXO	4m	7	F	*hld up in tch, ld 21st, sn clr, styd on strngly*	1	24
1201	24/4	Perth	(R)	HC	3m	14	G	*soon bhnd.*	7	0
1294	30/4	Kelso	(L)	HC	3m 1f	6	GF	*bhnd, styd on from 3 out, chsd wnr final 200 yards, no impn.*	2	22
1425	10/5	Aspatria	(L)	LAD	3m	6	G	*last til prog to mod 4th at 12th, kpt on to tk 2nd flat*	2	17
1511	17/5	Corbridge	(R)	LAD	3m	10	GS	*mid-div, prog 4 out, ev ch whn mstk 2 out, sn btn*	4	20
1586	28/5	Cartmel	(L)	HC	3 1/4m	10	GF	*held up and bhnd, late hdwy, nvr nrr.*	3	20

Tough, consistent, stays all day; gets left behind now; 4m open again in 98/confineds available; Any ... 22

ACROSS THE LAKE b.g. 13 Over The River (FR) - Golden Highway by Royal Highway — Mrs D R Brotherton

1996 3(20),5(18),1(19),2(19),3(19),1(23),P(0),2(22),3(17)

165	15/2	Witton Cast'	(R)	LAD	3m	6	F	*sttld mid-div, outpcd 11th, t.o.*	4	0
336	1/3	Corbridge	(R)	LAD	3m 5f	9	G	*(bl) ld to 4th, sn fdd, lost tch 13th, p.u. 2 out*	P	0
414	8/3	Dalston	(R)	XX	3m	9	GS	*(bl) chsd ldrs, rdn 11th, sn strgglng, t.o. & p.u. 2 out*	P	0
885	1/4	Flagg Moor	(L)	LAD	3m	5	G	*ld to 2nd, bhnd frm 6th, clsd 3 out, kpt on*	2	18
1072	13/4	Whitwell-On'	(R)	MXO	4m	21	G	*rear, strgglng 8th, t.o. & p.u. 16th*	P	0
1102	19/4	Hornby Cast'	(L)	LAD	3m	7	G	*(vis) prom,disp 4-7th,chsd ldr aft,wknd qckly 3 out,btn whn f last*	F	-
1346	3/5	Gisburn	(R)	LAD	3m	5	GF	*(vis) chsd wnr to 7th, 3rd aft til lft 2nd 2 out*	2	13

Staying ladies pointer but deteriorated badly in 97; win at 14 looks beyond him 13

ADAMARE br.g. 13 Chukaroo - Coxmoore Sweaters by Wynkell — H Morton

1996 P(0),1(23),2(16),P(0),1(19),2(19),F(-)

349	2/3	Market Rase'	(L)	LAD	3m	5	GF	*ld, blnd & lost irons 12th, p.u. nxt*	P	0
547	16/3	Garthorpe	(R)	XX	3m	7	GF	*ld til 3 out, rdn & ev ch whn f nxt*	F	-
771	29/3	Dingley	(R)	OPE	3m	10	G	*ld to 10th, wknd rpdly nxt, p.u. 4 out*	P	0
1188	20/4	Garthorpe	(R)	OPE	3m	9	GF	*in tch, chsd ldrs 8th, wknd 14th, 5th & no ch whn f 3 out*	F	-

Dual winner 96 but fell to pieces 97 & unlikely to revive at 14 13

ADANAC b.g. 14 Buckskin (FR) - Rosslea by Klairon — Barton L Williams

1996 U(-),P(0),1(14),3(13),4(14),S(-),P(0)

637	22/3	Howick	(L)	OPE	3m	7	GF	*2nd/3rd til lost plc 14th, ran on well frm 3 out*	3	16
904	5/4	Howick	(L)	OPE	3m	3	F	*chsd ldr, lft disp 10th til hdd 2 out, no ext flat*	2	14
1007	12/4	St Hilary	(R)	OPE	3m	10	GF	*alwys mid-div, btn & p.u. 15th*	P	0
1131	19/4	Bonvilston	(R)	MEM	3m	6	G	*cls 2nd til hmp 14th, no ch aft*	3	0
1560	24/5	Bassaleg	(R)	OPE	3m	7	G	*bhnd frm 4th, t.o. & p.u. 11th*	P	0

Dual Members winner 95/96; outclassed in half-decent races 97 & forlorn hope for a win at 15 11

ADDINGTON SHARRAGH ch.m. 6 Gildoran - Hands Off by Nearly A Hand — Miss Joanne Binks

1996 **10(NH),P(NH)**

116	9/2	Wetherby Po'	(L)	MDO	3m	14	GF	*keen hld in rear, prog 10th, wknd 13th, t.o. & p.u. 15th*	P	0
620	22/3	Hutton Rudby	(L)	MDO	3m	10	GF	*mstk 1st, alwys rear, lost tch whn ran wd & p.u. aft 8th*	P	0

Novice ridden and looks to need firm guidance 0

ADJALARI(IRE) b.g. 6 Al Nasr (FR) - Adjanada by Nishipour (FR) — Mrs Nigel Wrighton

321 1/3 Marks Tey (L) INT 3m 10 G *mid-div to 8th, last & wknng 10th, p.u. apr nxt* P 0

Ex-Irish; no signs of ability in England yet 0

ADMIRAL BYNG(FR) ch.g. 10 Caerleon (USA) - Pig Tail by Habitat — Miss D E Hawkes

1119 19/4 Whittington (L) MEM 3m 5 F *(fav) hld up, chsd ldr 5th, ld 12th-14th, qcknd to ld flat* 1 11

Flat winner; novice ridden to win dreadful race & yet to prove any real ability is retained 11

ADMIRAL ROUS b.g. 6 Rousillon (USA) - Bireme by Grundy — Mrs R Hurley

1996 3(0)

447 8/3 Newton Brom' (R) OPE 3m 6 G *in tch, disp 8th & 12th, wknd 15th, 4th & btn whn f last* F -
758 29/3 Kimble (L) OPE 3m 6 GF *chsd ldrs, 2nd frm 10th til aft 2 out, onepcd* 3 13
1077 13/4 Guilsborough (L) CON 3m 16 GF *last quartet to 12th, ran on wll frm 16th, nrst fin* 3 20
1404 5/5 Ashorne (R) MEM 3m 7 G *cls up, ld 12th til ran out apr nxt* r -
1532 18/5 Mollington (R) CON 3m 11 GS *in tch, prog 13th, chsd ldr aft 2 out, ld flat, ran on wll* 1 22

Flat winner 94; improved late season; stays well; could upgrade to Opens; G/F-G/S 23

ADMIRAL VILLENEUVE b.g. 9 Top Ville - Great Tom by Great Nephew — M J Brown

1996 **4(NH),6(NH),F(NH),3(NH),3(NH)**

941 6/4 Tabley (R) MDO 3m 11 G *cls up to 5th, bhnd 10th, p.u. 13th* P 0

Placed in novice chases 96; good enough for Maiden win but best watched at present. 10

ADMISSION(IRE) br.g. 7 Glow (USA) - Admit by Welsh Pageant — Mrs J Horner

1996 1(14),2(16),**3(22),U(-),3(20)**

32 26/1 Alnwick (L) RES 3m 11 G *prom, outpcd 12th, ran on 15th, fin wll, nrst fin* 3 19
353 2/3 Great Stain' (L) CON 3m 9 S *(fav) prom, ld 2nd til ran out 4th* r -
383 5/3 Catterick (L) HC 3m 1f 110yds 10 G *slowly away, hdwy 6th, chsd ldrs when blnd 11th, rdn apr 3 out, kept on same pace.* 3 22
509 15/3 Dalton Park (R) XX 3m 13 GF *mid-div, mstk 11th, no prog 4 out, lft 3rd last* 3 14
778 31/3 Carlisle (R) HC 3 1/4m 14 G *started slowly, soon in tch, effort 13th, no impn final 3.* 3 21
1068 13/4 Whitwell-On' (R) RES 3m 12 G *(Jt fav) hld up, prog 8th, ld 14th, drew clr 3 out, easily* 1 21
1201 24/4 Perth (R) HC 3m 14 G *prom, ev ch 3 out, wknd before last.* 3 19

Consistent; stays; 2 wins, 8 places - all completions 96/7; should win Confined; Good 21

ADRAMORE BELLE (Irish) — **I** 333[6], **I** 485[6]

ADVENTURUS b.g. 5 Green Adventure (USA) - Florella by Royal Fountain — A N Dalton

347 2/3 Market Rase' (L) MDO 3m 9 GF *jmpd slwly 1st, prog 10th, 2nd 3 out, unable qckn und pres* 2 12
942 6/4 Tabley (R) MDO 3m 8 G *w.w., prog 11th, disp 15th til outjmpd last, no ext* 2 14
1262 27/4 Southwell P' (L) MDO 3m 15 G *mid-div, prog 10th, lft disp 2 out, ld apr last, styd on* 1 13

Steadily improving; beat modest field but strong Restricted chance in 98; Good; sold May 97 18

AEGEAN FANFARE(IRE) br.g. 8 Trojan Fen - Sweet Melody by Alcide — Nick Shutts

1996 **1(NH),3(NH),5(NH),14(NH)**

1470 11/5 Erw Lon (L) LAD 3m 9 GS *chsd ldr to 14th, onepcd frm nxt* 3 17
1540 18/5 Wolverhampt' (L) LAD 3m 5 GS *rear, in tch, clsd 13th, disp 4 out, lvl last, just faild* 2 19

Winning Irish hurdler; late to appear but ran well both starts; Ladies likely if ready in 98 21

AERLITE CLASSIC (Irish) — **I** 162[2], **I** 200[2], **I** 278[P], **I** 356[P], **I** 401[P]

AFARISTOUN(FR) b.g. 13 Top Ville - Afrique (FR) by Exbury — Miss Joanne Morse

1996 P(0),4(17),2(17),7(0),3(14),F(-),4(0)

401 8/3 Llanfrynach (R) LAD 3m 14 G *ld, wll clr 15th, wknd rpdly & hdd nxt* 7 15
638 22/3 Howick (L) LAD 3m 10 GF *ld to 9th, wknd rpdly, p.u. 13th* P 0
1006 12/4 St Hilary (R) LAD 3m 7 GF *cls up, ld 7th-10th, 3rd whn f nxt* F -
1225 26/4 Pyle (R) LAD 3m 6 GS *jmpd slwly 5th, ld to apr 3 out, wknd rpdly* 5 0
1470 11/5 Erw Lon (L) LAD 3m 9 GS *alwys mid-div, wknd & p.u. 13th* P 0

Does not stay & readily grinds to a halt now - no winning prospects 10

A FARM BAR b.g. 10 Arkan - Evening Bar by Pardigras — P Dando

1996 P(0)

362 2/3 Garnons (L) OPE 3m 11 GS *prom til wknd 9th, p.u. 12th* P 0
404 8/3 Llanfrynach (R) INT 3m 17 G *ld to 10th, grad wknd* 6 0
634 22/3 Howick (L) RES 3m 7 GF *2nd frm 4th, disp 8th, strng run 2 out, no ext cls home* 2 13

Maiden winner 95; lightly-raced; beaten in bad race & disappeared; best watched 12

A FEW DOLLARS MORE(IRE) ch.g. 7 Tremblant - Spanish Natalie by Imperial Fling (USA) — D G Duggan

571 16/3 Garnons (L) MDN 2 1/2m 13 G *ld to 3 out, kpt on onepcd* 3 12
881 1/4 Upton-On-Se' (R) MDN 3m 13 GF *mstk 10th, ld/disp to 13th, 5th & wkng whn f 3 out* F -
1183 20/4 Lydstep (L) MDO 3m 8 GF *(fav) ld to 6th, ld 12th, clr frm 2 out* 1 14
1322 3/5 Bonvilston (R) RES 3m 9 G *prom, ld 9th-apr 13th, onepcd aft, fin 2nd, disq* 2D 13
1526 17/5 Bredwardine (R) RES 3m 13 G *ld to aft 2nd, prom, mstk 10th, rdn & outpcd frm 13th* 3 14

Won poor race & well beaten in both Restricteds; more needed in 98; good stable 15

AFRICAN WARRIOR b.m. 5 Exodal (USA) - Sandy Looks by Music Boy R H P Williams

405	8/3	Llanfrynach	(R)	RES	3m	15	G	*f 2nd*	F	-
542	16/3	Erw Lon	(L)	MDN	3m	15	GF	*f 4th*	F	-
964	6/4	Pantyderi	(L)	MDN	3m	4	F	*2nd til ld 3 out, rddn out*	1	0
1227	26/4	Pyle	(R)	RES	3m	15	GS	*ld to 2nd, wknd frm 9th, t.o. & p.u. 15th*	P	0
1556	24/5	Bassaleg	(R)	RES	3m	13	G	*rear,lost tch ldrs 12th,ran on 15th,fin strngly,just faild*	2	14

Won a ghastly contest; much improved last start but more needed in competitive company 14

AFTERKELLY b.g. 12 Le Moss - Vamble by Vulgan Mrs T White

1996 **3(21)**,2(22),4(15),2(20),2(24)

98	8/2	Great Treth'	(R)	OPE	3m	14	GS	*prom til outpcd frm 15th, sn no dang*	5	17
285	26/2	Taunton	(R)	HC	4 1/4m 110yds	16	GS	*bhnd from 12th, t.o. when p.u. before 21st.*	P	0
455	8/3	Great Treth'	(R)	OPE	3m	8	S	*prom, ld 13-14th, lost grnd stdly frm nxt*	4	13
627	22/3	Kilworthy	(L)	LAD	3m	7	G	*1st ride, u.r. 2nd*	U	-
790	31/3	Bishopsleigh	(R)	LAD	3m	7	G	*sn rear, mod late prog, nvr any ch*	4	16
1109	19/4	Flete Park	(R)	OPE	4m	9	GF	*chsd ldr til 2 out, sn outpcd*	4	17
1370	5/5	Cotley Farm	(L)	XX	3m	4	GF	*chsd ldr, ld 12th, ran on wll frm 2 out*	1	16
1547	24/5	Mounsey Hil'	(R)	MEM	3m	9	G	*alwys prom, ld 7-9th, blnd 17th, rallied 2 out, styd on flat*	2	17
1596	31/5	Bratton Down	(L)	OPE	4m	5	F	*pshd alng 7th, last & lost tch 13th, t.o. & p.u. 17th*	P	0

Useful in his prime but mostly schoolmaster 97 & may struggle to win again; stays extra well; Any 15

AGAINST THE AGENT ch.g. 7 Buckley - Calametta by Oats J P Price

259	22/2	Newtown	(L)	MDN	3m	18	G	*pllng, ld 5th, made rest, toyed wth rival frm 2 out*	1	16

Very lightly raced; hacked up only start 97 & could prove useful if standing regular racing 18

AGILE KING b.g. 6 Rakaposhi King - My Aisling by John de Coombe J W Evans

1996 5(0),F(-),U(-),7(0)

205	15/2	Weston Park	(L)	MDN	3m	10	G	*3rd at 13th, onepcd aft*	3	0
470	8/3	Eyton-On-Se'	(L)	MDN	2 1/2m	12	G	*ld to 3rd, cls up til outpcd frm 3 out*	2	11
754	29/3	Brampton Br'	(R)	MDN	3m	9	GF	*ld to 5th, 2nd/3rd til prog 16th, no ch wth wnr*	2	12
1003	12/4	Alpraham	(R)	MDO	2 1/2m	10	GF	*(fav) chsd ldrs, 2nd at 11th, hrd rdn & no ext aft*	4	0

Good at completing but doubtful stayer & form weak; may find short Maiden in 98 13

AGLISH PRIDE (Irish) — **I** 245[F], **I** 305[3], **I** 428[1]

AHEAD OF MY TIME (Irish) — **I** 26[3]

AHEAD OF THE POSSE (Irish) — **I** 84, , **I** 184[P]

AIGUILLE (Irish) — **I** 24[2], **I** 177[2]

AINE HENCEY (Irish) — **I** 139[P], **I** 163[P], **I** 277[2], **I** 356[2], **I** 394[2], **I** 453[P], **I** 514[1]

AINLEE ROAD b.g. 11 Indian King (USA) - Corcomroe by Busted M T Lockyer

107	8/2	Milborne St'	(L)	MEM	3m	8	GF	*alwys rear, styd on frm 15th*	4	0

Of no account 0

AINTGOTTIME(IRE) ch.g. 5 Decent Fellow - Spoonbender by Mr Bigmore Mrs F Kehoe

374	2/3	Mollington	(R)	MDN	3m	14	G	*pllng, lost plc 5th, effrt 13th, btn 15th, p.u. 2 out*	P	0
761	29/3	Kimble	(L)	MDO	3m	12	GF	*hld up,ld 12th,sn hdd,ld 16th til wd last bend,got up post*	1	15

Shows promise; unlucky not to win modest race outright; should progress if ready in 98 16

AIR COMMANDER br.g. 12 Strong Gale - Southern Slave by Arctic Slave G J Chamberlain

1996 3(17),U(-)

1063	13/4	Maisemore P'	(L)	XX	3m	13	GF	*prog 7th, 4th & chnc 14th, wknd nxt*	6	0
1321	3/5	Bonvilston	(R)	MXO	3m	10	G	*rear whn s.u. flat aft 6th*	S	-
1593	31/5	Bratton Down	(L)	XX	3m	5	F	*last & sn bhnd, t.o. 14th, went poor 3rd 2 out,eased nr fin*	4	0

Deteriorated further in 97 & looks a spent force now 0

AIRECCO (Irish) — **I** 55[P], **I** 94[F], **I** 152[F], **I** 182[3], **I** 343[6]

AIREYS MAN (Irish) — **I** 43[F]

AIRTRAK(IRE) b.g. 8 Strong Gale - Deep Khaletta by Deep Run T J Clemence

1996 **F(NH),4(NH),B(NH),6(NH),4(NH)**

27	26/1	Marks Tey	(L)	OPE	3m	6	GF	*ld to 3 out, wknd nxt*	4	19
124	9/2	Cottenham	(R)	OPE	3m	9	GF	*prom, prssd wnr 10th til aft 3 out, wknd apr last*	3	19
271	22/2	Ampton	(R)	CON	3m	15	G	*alwys prom, chsd wnr 8-3 out, onepcd und press*	3	21
322	1/3	Marks Tey	(L)	OPE	3 1/2m	9	G	*chsd ldrs, wnt 2nd 11th, rdn 17th, no ch wth wnr*	2	20
577	16/3	Detling	(L)	CON	3m	18	F	*hld up mid-div, imprvd to 2nd whn blndrd & u.r. 4 out*	U	-
708	29/3	High Easter	(L)	CON	3m	3	F	*trkd ldr til ld 6th, mstk & hdd 15th, rdn to ld last,styd on*	1	19
1079	13/4	Guilsborough	(L)	OPE	3m	6	GF	*ld to 2nd, chsd ldr 9th til blnd 16th, wknd 2 out*	4	15

Winning chaser; fair & consistent pointer; one paced; better chances in Confineds in 98; G-F 21

AISLINGS PRIDE (Irish) — I 559^{P}, I 566^{P}

AJ'S BOY b.g. 9 Broadsword (USA) - Elmolyn by St Elmo — M A Walter

4 19/1 Barbury Cas' (L) OPE 3m 9 GF *8s-5/2, mstk 6th, in tch til rdn & wknd 10th, p.u. 12th* P 0
59 1/2 Kingston Bl' (L) RES 3m 16 GF *(fav) sn prom, ld 3rd-5th, ld 10th, made rest, pshd out* 1 21
1403 5/5 Ashorne (R) CON 3m 14 G *(fav) ld 4th til mstk & hdd 15th, wknd & p.u. last, dsmntd* P 0

Lightly raced; quite useful but injured last start & will miss 98 22

ALANSFORD ch.g. 10 Carlingford Castle - Inneen Alainn by Prince Hansel — Miss Maud Ryder
1996 3(15),2(17),2(16),1(20),1(21)

302 1/3 Parham (R) CON 3m 14 G *ld 5th-11th, grad wknd, wll bhnd whn p.u. 2 out* P 0
1354 4/5 Dingley (R) MXO 3m 3 G *mstk 6th, chsd ldr til blnd 14th, sn outpcd* 3 0

Dual winner 96 but interrupted season 97 & no form; best watched 18

ALAPA b.h. 10 Alzao (USA) - Gay Folly by Wolver Hollow — A B Coogan
1996 r(-),r(-),P(0),r(-),2(13),r(-)

30 26/1 Marks Tey (L) MDN 3m 9 GF *prom, ld 7th-11th, 3rd & wkng whn hmpd & u.r. 3 out* U -
124 9/2 Cottenham (R) OPE 3m 9 GF *mid-div, outpcd 14th, modest 6th whn u.r. 2 out* U -
197 15/2 Higham (L) MDO 3m 12 G *u.r. 1st* U -
276 22/2 Ampton (R) MDO 3m 12 G *pllng, ld 2nd til r.o. nxt* r -
317 1/3 Marks Tey (L) MDN 3m 13 G *styd stt, keen hold, chsd ldrs, 2nd whn f 9th* F -
591 21/3 Newbury (L) HC 3m 7 GF *in cl tch, blnd 4 out, 3rd and held when mstk and u.r. 3 out.* U -
1283 27/4 Fakenham P-' (L) MDO 3m 9 G *s.s. hld up, prog to 2nd 14th, btn 2 out, u.r. last* U 12
1530 18/5 Fakenham (L) HC 2m 5f 110yds 11 G *blnd and u.r. 2nd.* U -

Disastrous figures shield some ability; good enough to win Maiden but urgently needs help from above 13

ALBERT'S ADVENTURE(IRE) ch.g. 7 Le Moss - Berry Street by Class Distinction — C Cottingham
1996 r(-),F(-),P(0),r(-)

677 23/3 Brocklesby ' (L) MDN 3m 8 GF *disp til jmpd lft 3rd, in tch whn blnd & u.r. 8th* U -
1268 27/4 Southwell P' (L) MDO 3m 13 G *rear, mstk 2nd, lost tch 6th, t.o. & p.u. 9th* P 0

Yet to complete the course 0

ALBERT'S FANCY (Irish) — I 78^{P}, I 149^{P}, I 216, , I 342^{1}, I 386^{4}, I 410^{4}, I 498^{2}, I 543^{3}, I 598^{P}, I 605^{2}, I 613^{1}

AL BILLAL b.h. 9 Enchantment - Liana Louise by Silly Season — R Williams

718 29/3 Llanvapley (L) RES 3m 13 GF *prom to hlfwy, grdly wknd, no ch f 2 out* F -
908 5/4 Howick (L) MDN 3m 7 F *(fav) jmpd slwly, ld to 3rd, rear & rdn 8th, t.o. & p.u. 3 out* P 0
1324 3/5 Bonvilston (R) MDO 3m 16 G *rear, p.u. 2 out* P 0
1491 14/5 Hereford (R) HC 3m 1f 110yds 11 G *soon t.o., p.u. before 12th.* P 0

No real hopes & favourite in a dire contest 0

ALCOFROLIC b.m. 8 Brando - Champagne Peri by The Malster — P J Houldey
1996 R(-),4(13)

263 22/2 Newtown (L) MDN 3m 11 G *prom, 4th whn mstk 12th, p.u. nxt, lame* P 0

Placed in 96 but problems only start 97 & best watched if reappearing 12

ALEX-PATH b.g. 14 Warpath - Alexandra by Song — Mrs S G Currie
1996 P(0),P(0),3(12),4(0),P(0)

1344 3/5 Gisburn (R) MEM 3m 3 GF *rear, t.o. 13th, lft 2nd 16th, plodded on* 2 0

No longer of any account 0

ALEX THUSCOMBE ch.g. 9 Takachiho - Portate by Articulate — Mrs Peter Shaw
1996 5(10),2(13),1(15),5(14),1(19)

42 1/2 Larkhill (R) MXO 3m 7 GF *(vis) last, wll bhnd frm 13th, fin well* 4 20
109 8/2 Milborne St' (L) XX 3m 8 GF *(bl) prom, disp 12th-2 out, rallied last, forced d/h on line* 1 18
515 15/3 Larkhill (R) INT 3m 8 GF *(vis) rear whn ran out 3rd* r -
662 22/3 Badbury Rin' (L) CON 3m 8 F *(bl) prom, 3rd 4 out, strng run 2 out, ld aft last, styd on* 1 20
687 29/3 Little Wind' (R) MEM 3m 5 GF *(vis) ld to 14th, ld 16th-2 out, kpt on und pres* 2 18
1043 12/4 Cothelstone (L) INT 3m 7 GF *(fav) (vis) w.w. chsd alng 14th, no ch whn blnd last* 4 13
1370 5/5 Cotley Farm (L) XX 3m 4 GF *(fav) (vis) held up, prog 12th, cls 2nd whn u.r. nxt* U -
1517 17/5 Bratton Down (L) MXO 3m 8 GS *(vis) in tch til wknd 14th, sn btn* 6 15
1594 31/5 Bratton Down (L) INT 3m 10 F *(vis) ld to 5th, prom til outpcd 15th, no imp aft, kpt on, dsmntd* 5 17

Moderate, tough & consistent; novice ridden; problem last start; can win again if fit 98; G-F 20

ALFION(IRE) b.g. 8 Saxon Farm - Knockeevan Girl by Tarqogan — D R Thomas
1996 **R(NH),6(NH),P(NH),P(NH),4(NH),F(NH),P(NH)**

636 22/3 Howick (L) CON 3m 12 GF *alwys rear, p.u. 13th* P 0

847	31/3 Lydstep	(L) MDO 3m	5 F	*sttld rear, prog 4 out, kpt on, nvr nrr, improve*	2	0
1011	12/4 St Hilary	(R) MDN 3m	10 GF	*prom, strng chal frm 15th, cls 2nd whn mstk last, no ext*	2	15
1186	20/4 Lydstep	(L) MDO 3m	7 GF	*(fav) trckd ldrs, ld 11th, ran on frm 2 out, easily*	1	13
1365	5/5 Pantyderi	(L) RES 3m	10 G	*3rd at 3rd, cls 4th at 11th, fin v tired*	6	13
1471	11/5 Erw Lon	(L) RES 3m	9 GS	*ld 4th, clr frm 3 out, easily*	1	16
1557	24/5 Bassaleg	(R) CON 3m	9 G	*prom,jnd ldr 12th,rdn 14th,ld 3 out,all out flat,jst hld on*	1	19
1611	7/6 Umberleigh	(L) OPE 3m	8 F	*mstk 2nd, trckd ldrs, drvn to chal aft 12th, wknd 14th*	4	0

Poor under Rules; much improved & ran well 97; won modest races; could upgrade; just stays 3m; G/F-S 21

AL FROLIC b.g. 10 Alzao (USA) - Fun Frolic by Sexton Blake — D S Jones

637	22/3 Howick	(L) OPE 3m	7 GF	*mostly 4th, prog 11th to chs wnr 3 out, alwys hld*	2	18
843	31/3 Lydstep	(L) OPE 3m	4 F	*chsd wnr, ld 16th-last, kpt on und pres, just hld*	2	18
1005	12/4 St Hilary	(R) CON 3m	10 GF	*4th/5th til wknd rpdly frm 15th*	6	0
1182	20/4 Lydstep	(L) OPE 3m	3 GF	*ld to 2nd, waited bhnd wnr aft, ev ch 15th, alwys hld*	2	18
1362	5/5 Pantyderi	(L) CON 3m	4 G	*3rd til 11th, fin v tired*	4	0
1470	11/5 Erw Lon	(L) LAD 3m	9 GS	*nvr nrr than 4th, no imp ldrs 2 out*	4	10

Poor hurdler; ran well in small fields in 97 but doubtful stayer; may find small race 17

ALGAIHABANE(USA) b.g. 11 Roberto (USA) - Sassabunda by Sassafras (FR) — R Hares

1996 3(0)

405	8/3 Llanfrynach	(R) RES 3m	15 G	*(bl) lft in ld 5th, hdd 15th, wknd rpdly*	8	0
635	22/3 Howick	(L) RES 3m	7 GF	*3rd til 13th, grad wknd*	4	0
717	29/3 Llanvapley	(L) RES 3m	13 GF	*(bl) prom in mid-div, ran on onepce*	4	0
905	5/4 Howick	(L) LAD 3m	4 F	*(bl) in tch, chsd wnr 12-15th, no imp & btn aft*	3	11

Maiden winner 93; lightly raced since & well beaten in poor race last start 10

AL HASHIMI b.g. 13 Ile de Bourbon (USA) - Parmesh by Home Guard (USA) — Bruce Sarson

1996 **6(12),3(12),4(21),5(0),5(17),5(19)**

90	5/2 Ludlow	(R) HC 2 1/2m	6 G	*well pld when f 8th.*	F	-
375	3/3 Doncaster	(L) HC 2m 3f 110yds	11 GF	*in tch, rdn along 5 out, soon one pace.*	5	10
587	19/3 Ludlow	(R) HC 2 1/2m	18 GF	*mid div till wknd 12th.*	10	14
1404	5/5 Ashorne	(R) MEM 3m	7 G	*s.u. bnd apr 3rd*	S	-
1488	12/5 Towcester	(R) HC 2m 110yds	16 GS	*nvr on terms.*	6	14
1534	18/5 Mollington	(R) OPE 3m	7 GS	*trckd ldr 8th til aft 3 out, wknd nxt*	4	17

Ran surprisingly well final start but well past his prime now & another win most unlikely; G-F 13

ALIANNE ch.m. 7 Alias Smith (USA) - Anne de Bretagne by Ardross — Miss C M Martin

1996 P(0),P(0),6(0),P(0)

37	26/1 Alnwick	(L) MDO 3m	15 G	*mstk 1st, alwys last trio, t.o. & p.u. 3 out*	P	0
136	9/2 Alnwick	(L) MDO 3m	16 G	*bhnd, lost tch 12th, t.o. & p.u. last*	P	0
340	1/3 Corbridge	(R) MDN 3m	10 G	*alwys prom, went 2nd 3 out, ev ch nxt, outpcd*	2	12
815	31/3 Tranwell	(L) MDO 2 1/2m	14 G	*mid-div, nvr nr ldrs final ctt*	5	0

Ran much her best race 3rd start but lacks stamina; will find a win hard to come by 11

ALIAS PARKER JONES gr.g. 6 Alias Smith (USA) - Fidessa by Fine Blade (USA) — Mrs L A Parker

185	15/2 Erw Lon	(L) MDN 3m	14 G	*jmpd bdly, t.o. 5th, p.u. 2 out*	P	0
367	2/3 Garnons	(L) MDO 2 1/2m	9 GS	*alwys rear, t.o. 11th, fin 2 fences 4th, promoted*	3	0
437	8/3 Upton-On-Se'	(R) MDO 3m	15 G	*in tch to 4th, outpcd 8th, t.o. & p.u. 10th*	P	0
841	31/3 Lydstep	(L) MDO 3m	8 F	*alwys rear, p.u. 11th*	P	0
1230	26/4 Pyle	(R) MDO 3m	10 GS	*t.o. 4th, p.u. 6th*	P	0
1561	24/5 Bassaleg	(R) MDO 3m	9 G	*in tch to 11th, wknd rpdly nxt, p.u. 14th*	P	0

Totally devoid of ability 0

ALIAS SILVER gr.g. 10 Alias Smith (USA) - Duresme by Starry Halo — Mrs S K Edmunds

1996 P(0),3(0),1(14),5(12),4(11),1(17),4(11),3(13)

148	9/2 Tweseldown	(R) XX 3m	12 GF	*mid-div, rmndrs 12th, btn frm 4 out*	6	0
446	8/3 Newton Brom'	(R) CON 3m	8 G	*mid-div, no dang frm 16th*	5	12
773	29/3 Dingley	(R) LAD 3m	11 G	*sn rear hlf, prog 8th, 2nd 6 out, 3rd nxt, no imp*	3	15
925	6/4 Garthorpe	(R) LAD 3m	7 GF	*(fav) mid-div, 3rd at 12th, nvr going wll, no imp*	3	13
1159	20/4 Mollington	(R) MEM 3m	4 GF	*ld to 2nd, 3l 2nd whn u.r. 11th*	U	-

Dual winner 96; outclassed in better company 97; Members only real hope at 11; G-F 15

ALICANTE b.g. 10 Alzao (USA) - Safe And Happy by Tudor Melody — Dick Chapman

1996 **8(NH),12(NH),10(NH),6(NH)**

936	6/4 Tabley	(R) MEM 3m	9 G	*(bl) mstk 1st, prog 7th, chsd wnr apr 2 out, kpt on und pres*	2	12
1175	20/4 Sandon	(L) CON 3m	8 GF	*(bl) cls up in 3rd whn f 11th*	F	-

Poor hurdler under Rules & little to enthuse about in brief pointing season 13

ALICE SHEER THORN(IRE) ch.m. 7 Sheer Grit - Rugged Thorn by Rugged Man — M J Gingell

1996 **10(NH)**

12	25/1	Cottenham	(R)	RES	3m	3	GF	*keen hold, ld 4th, jnd 3 out, hdd last, wknd flat*	3	12
64	1/2	Horseheath	(R)	LAD	3m	7	GF	*keen hld, ld to 2nd, last & wkng whn p.u. 13th*	P	0
274	22/2	Ampton	(R)	RES	3m	10	G	*in tch til b.d. 7th*	B	-
324	1/3	Marks Tey	(L)	RES	3m	16	G	*chsd ldrs, 5th & wknng apr 15th, t.o.*	9	0

Ex-Irish; last on only placing & no other form; finished early 10

ALICOTT LAD ch.g. 7 All Fair - Lydacott Star by Lyrello — Miss L J Smale

955	6/4	Black Fores'	(R)	MDO	3m	2	G	*chsd wnr, dist bhnd 10th, t.o. aft*	2	0
1108	19/4	Flete Park	(R)	RES	3m	14	GF	*rear, bhnd whn p.u. aft 14th*	P	0
1245	26/4	Bratton Down	(L)	INT	3m	9	GS	*alwys off the pce til p.u. 10th*	P	0
1394	5/5	High Bickin'	(R)	MEM	3m	4	G	*ld to 5th, sn wknd, not fluent, t.o.*	2	0
1485	11/5	Ottery St M'	(L)	MDO	3m	13	G	*sn last, t.o. 7th*	6	0
1551	24/5	Mounsey Hil'	(R)	RES	3m	13	G	*alwys bhnd, p.u. 11th, dsmntd*	P	0

Placings meaningless & looks a hopeless cause - problems last start as well 0

ALIMAR (Irish) — **I** 101[1]

ALI'S DIPPER (Irish) — **I** 497[B], **I** 547[P], **I** 599[F]

AL JAWWAL ch.g. 7 Lead On Time (USA) - Littlefield by Bay Express — Mrs P King

1996 1(15),F(-),P(0)

198	15/2	Higham	(L)	RES	3m	14	G	*mid-div til f 11th*	F	-
1278	27/4	Fakenham P-'	(L)	RES	3m	11	G	*mid-div, blnd 10th, 4th & ch 3 out, onepcd und pres*	3	16
1530	18/5	Fakenham	(L)	HC	2m 5f 110yds	11	G	*in rear when hit 4th, p.u. before next.*	P	0

Maiden winner 96; interrupted season 97; could win Restricted if all went well 98; Good 16

ALKARINE gr.g. 5 Alias Smith (USA) - Colly Cone by Celtic Cone — Gareth Richards

1996 **P(NH),P(NH)**

542	16/3	Erw Lon	(L)	MDN	3m	15	GF	*mstk 1st, trckd ldrs, ld brfly 12th, wkng whn u.r. 14th*	U	-
719	29/3	Llanvapley	(L)	MDN	3m	14	GF	*(14s-5s), nvr beyond mid-div, p.u. 12th*	P	0
1010	12/4	St Hilary	(R)	MDN	3m	10	GF	*rear til p.u. 13th*	P	0
1231	26/4	Pyle	(R)	MDO	3m	7	GS	*mstk 7th, prog to ld aft 13th-3 out, sn btn, eased*	2	0
1473	11/5	Erw Lon	(L)	MDO	3m	13	GS	*(Co fav) mid-div, 15l 4th at 16th, p.u. 2 out*	P	0
1562	24/5	Bassaleg	(R)	MDO	3m	8	G	*(fav) trckd ldrs, 2nd 3 out, qcknd to ld apr nxt, drvn out*	1	13

Found a bad race last start; improvement needed to figure in Restricteds in 98; Good 14

ALL A JOKE (Irish) — **I** 84[P], **I** 132[P], **I** 258[P]

ALL BUT (Irish) — **I** 22[F], **I** 57[3], **I** 84[1], **I** 157[F], **I** 408[5]

ALL CHANGE b.g. 6 Cavalier Servente - Bubbly Isle by Military — T C Illsley

877	1/4	Upton-On-Se'	(R)	RES	3m	17	GF	*mid-div, 7th & out of tch whn f 9th*	F	-
1531	18/5	Mollington	(R)	MEM	3m	6	GS	*in tch, chsd ldr 12th-3 out, ev ch nxt, wknd*	5	10

Not disgraced 2nd start & may do better with experience 12

ALLEGRO PRINCE ch.g. 7 Regal Steel - Fritillaria by Bargello — Mrs J Marles

1996 **7(NH),8(NH),P(NH),P(NH)**

127	9/2	Cottenham	(R)	MDO	3m	11	GF	*rear, mstks 6 & 13th, sn btn, t.o. whn ran out 3 out*	r	-
776	29/3	Dingley	(R)	MDO	2m 5f	10	G	*(bl) prom bhnd ldrs, 6th & outpcd 6 out, 4th 2 out, p.u. last*	P	0
1084	13/4	Guilsborough	(L)	MDN	3m	11	GF	*rear, mstk 5th, prog nxt, mod 4th whn ref 13th*	R	-

Error-prone & unenthusiastic to date 0

ALLER MOOR(IRE) b.g. 6 Dry Dock - Boggy Peak by Shirley Heights — G Keirle

1996 P(0),2(15),1(18),8(0)

39	1/2	Larkhill	(R)	CON	3m	6	GF	*(fav) hld up, jnd wnr & blnd 3 out, rdn to chal last, just hld*	2	20
298	1/3	Didmarton	(L)	RES	3m	15	G	*cls up, ld apr last, mstk last & hdd, rallied to ld nr fin*	1	21
691	29/3	Little Wind'	(R)	INT	3m	5	GF	*(fav) alwys cls up, ld 2 out, drvn out flat*	1	19
1092	16/4	Hockworthy	(L)	XX	3m	5	GF	*(fav) w.w. ld 11th, clr 14th, rdn out*	1	20
1507	16/5	Stratford	(L)	HC	3m	10	G	*held up, steady hdwy to go 2nd 3 out, ld next, tied up run-in, all out.*	1	25

Useful; tough & improving still; responds to pressure; could win more H/Chases 98; G/F-S 27

ALLEZMOSS b.g. 11 Le Moss - Allitess by Mugatpura — Joint Ownership Terminated

1996 **12(NH)**

232	22/2	Friars Haugh	(L)	OPE	3m	6	G	*went 2nd 13th, ld aft 4 out, jst hdd 2 out, styd on wll*	2	25

Formerly high-class Irish performer; retains ability but disappeared after good effort 23

ALLEZSCALLY b.m. 10 Scallywag - Catherine Tudor by Tudor Wood — K Wynne

330	1/3	Eaton Hall	(R)	CON	3m	16	GS	*hld up, clsr order 11th, short livd efft, p.u. 4 out*	P	0
468	8/3	Eyton-On-Se'	(L)	RES	3m	11	G	*disp to 3rd, hld up mid-div, prog 3rd 5 out, onepcd*	3	12
670	23/3	Eaton Hall	(R)	RES	3m	15	GF	*p.u. 5th, lame*	P	0

852	31/3	Eyton-On-Se'	(L)	RES	3m	11	GF	*mid-div, broke leg apr 11th (dead)*	F	-

Dead **13**

ALL GIRLS (Irish) — I 399^{F}, I 460^{P}, I 489^{F}

ALLISTRAGH LAD (Irish) — I 175^{P}, I 248, , I 328^{5}, I 413^{2}

ALL OR NOTHING ch.m. 9 Scorpio (FR) - Kelton Lass by Lord Nelson (FR) — N M L Ewart

1996 7(0),3(13),6(0),U(-),2+(14),1(14)

32	26/1	Alnwick	(L)	RES	3m	11	G	*prom, lost plc 7th, t.o. 12th, ran on agn frm 2 out*	5	11
131	9/2	Alnwick	(L)	RES	3m	13	G	*in tch, prog & blnd 11th, no hdwy frm 3 out*	5	0
157	15/2	Lanark	(R)	RES	3m	11	G	*bhnd by 8th, nvr nr ldrs*	6	0
410	8/3	Dalston	(R)	MEM	3m	5	GS	*ld to 6th & 9-12th, sn outpcd & bhnd, ran on agn 2 out*	3	14
778	31/3	Carlisle	(R)	HC	3 1/4m	14	G	*mstks in rear, nvr on terms.*	5	17
1085	14/4	Hexham	(L)	HC	3m 1f	5	F	*cl up till u.r. 3rd.*	U	-
1424	10/5	Aspatria	(L)	RES	3m	17	G	*sn wll bhnd, last & no ch 11th, fin strngly*	7	11
1545	24/5	Cartmel	(L)	HC	3 1/4m	14	G	*bhnd, jmpd slowly 2nd, hdwy from 12th to chase ldrs, rdn along when blnd and u.r. 3 out.*	U	-

Maiden winner 96 - only success from 24 attempts; novice ridden & needs stronger handling **14**

ALL RIGHT CLARK (Irish) — I 424^{P}, I 489^{P}, I 609,

ALLRITE PET b.m. 6 Alias Smith (USA) - Munster Glen by Furry Glen — Dennis Waggott

235	22/2	Friars Haugh	(L)	MDO	3m	10	G	*(fav) u.r. 1st*	U	-
417	8/3	Dalston	(R)	MDO	2 1/2m	11	GS	*(fav) s.s. hld up, prog to trck ldrs 9th, wknd 3 out, virt p.u.*	7	0
949	6/4	Friars Haugh	(L)	MDN	3m	10	GF	*(fav) slght ld frm 4 out, lft clr apr 2 out, hdd last, no ext*	2	14
1428	10/5	Aspatria	(L)	MDO	3m	11	G	*(fav) prom, ld 8th-2 out, ev ch last, ran on flat*	2	13
1513	17/5	Corbridge	(R)	MDO	3m	13	GS	*(fav) prom, jnd ldr 4 out, ld nxt, hrd drvn & ran on wll flat*	1	15

Expensive to follow but gradually improving; could upgrade in 98; just stays 3m to date **16**

ALL SCREWED UP(IRE) b.g. 7 Henbit (USA) - Princess Umm by Duky — Stuart Currie

415	8/3	Dalston	(R)	RES	3m	19	GS	*mstk 7th, alwys rear, t.o. & p.u. 15th*	P	0
767	29/3	Whittington	(L)	MDO	3m	9	S	*mstks, bhnd, lft 4th 13th, t.o. 2 out*	4	0

Tailed off last when completing & shows no promise yet **0**

ALL STYLE (Irish) — I 130^{P}

ALL SYTLE (Irish) — I 259^{U}

ALL THE BETTER (Irish) — I 248^{P}

ALL THE JOLLY b.m. 9 Bay Express - Whisper Gently by Pitskelly — Robert Jones

1	19/1	Barbury Cas'	(L)	XX	3m	11	GF	*alwys bhnd, t.o. & p.u. 13th*	P	0
102	8/2	Great Treth'	(R)	MDO	3m	8	GS	*in tch, 4th whn u.r. bend apr 10th*	U	-
184	15/2	Erw Lon	(L)	MDN	3m	14	G	*6s-3s, trckd ldrs, cls up whn f 12th*	F	-
404	8/3	Llanfrynach	(R)	INT	3m	17	G	*rear, p.u. 12th*	P	0
541	16/3	Erw Lon	(L)	MDN	3m	10	GF	*trckd ldrs, u.r. 14th in tch*	U	-
1011	12/4	St Hilary	(R)	MDN	3m	10	GF	*(fav) mid-div, went 3rd 15th, wknd & p.u. last*	P	0
1186	20/4	Lydstep	(L)	MDO	3m	7	GF	*rear whn f 12th*	F	-
1231	26/4	Pyle	(R)	MDO	3m	7	GS	*trckd ldrs, ev ch 13th, wknd rpdly nxt, p.u. 3 out*	P	0
1368	5/5	Pantyderi	(L)	MDO	3m	8	G	*ld/disp to 10th, p.u. nxt*	P	0

Figures speak for themselves **0**

ALL THINGS NICE ch.m. 6 Sweet Monday - Penny's Affair by Chingnu — Mrs M R Daniell

437	8/3	Upton-On-Se'	(R)	MDO	3m	15	G	*mid-div to 8th, t.o. & p.u. 14th*	P	0
571	16/3	Garnons	(L)	MDN	2 1/2m	13	G	*prog 8th, wll in tch whn u.r. 11th*	U	-

Some signs 2nd start but season lasted 8 days **10**

ALL-TOGETHER (Irish) — I 387^{P}, I 408^{P}

ALLWAN (Irish) — I 20^{P}, I 304^{P}

ALL WEATHER b.g. 11 Air Trooper - Modom by Compensation — M S Wilesmith

1996 P(0),6(12),1(19),**2(23)**,1(19)

2	19/1	Barbury Cas'	(L)	XX	3m	14	GF	*chsd ldrs, 5th hlfwy, prog 13th, ld 2 out, hld on well*	1	24
56	1/2	Kingston Bl'	(L)	OPE	3m	13	GF	*sn outpcd, bhnd whn p.u. 13th*	P	0
255	22/2	Newtown	(L)	CON	3m	14	G	*rear of main grp, 8th hlfwy, ran on 14th, tk 2nd nr fin*	2	19
395	8/3	Barbury Cas'	(L)	XX	3m	9	G	*(fav) ld to 1st, chsd ldrs, ev ch 3 out, ld flat, pshd out*	1	19
1063	13/4	Maisemore P'	(L)	XX	3m	13	GF	*(fav) prom, cls 3rd at 12th, outpcd 14th, chsd wnr 3 out, no imp*	2	16

Quite able at best & fulfilled 96 comments; goes well fresh; likes Barbury; can win again; G-S **23**

ALLY PALLY ch.g. 6 Town And Country - Drivers Bureau by Proverb — R H York

146	9/2	Tweseldown	(R)	MDO	3m	10	GF	*prom, mstk 15th, ev ch 2 out, no ext*	2	11
306	1/3	Parham	(R)	MDN	3m	12	G	*chsd ldrs, 3rd & und pres 4 out, wknd*	3	0

Fair debut in weak race but disappointed other start & vanished; may do better if fit 98 .... **12**

ALMAURITIA (Irish) — **I** 99F, **I** 2312, **I** 275P, **I** 348, , **I** 3923, **I** 548, , **I** 593F

ALONE SUCCESS br.g. 14 Strong Gale - Tabankulu by Selko — Mrs Michael Ennever

483 9/3 Tweseldown (R) CON 3m 8 G *last pair til p..u 8th* P 0

No longer of any account 0

ALPHA ONE ch.g. 12 Belfalas - Clonaslee Foam by Quayside — D F Bassett

1996 P(0),R(-),R(-)

75 2/2 Market Rase' (L) CON 3m 10 GF *alwys mid-div, 4th whn blndrd 14th, no dang aft* 5 0
137 9/2 Thorpe Lodge (L) MEM 3m 9 GF *mid-div, 2nd at 14th, ld 3 out, ran on well* 1 16
248 22/2 Brocklesby ' (L) CON 3m 10 G *mid-div 4th/5th, 5th outpcd 5 out* 6 0
351 2/3 Market Rase' (L) OPE 3m 10 GF *in tch, outpcd apr 14th, styd on well 2 out* 4 15
545 16/3 Garthorpe (R) CON 3m 12 GF *chsd ldrs til outpcd 13th, no ch frm 3 out* 5 12
884 1/4 Flagg Moor (L) CON 3m 6 G *ld to 1st,lft 2nd aft 5th-11th,lost tch,t.o.,fin 4th,prmtd* 3 0
1544 21/5 Newton Abbot (L) HC 3 1/4m 110yds 11 G *alwys bhnd, t.o. from 8th, p.u. before 14th.* P 0
1571 26/5 Wetherby (L) HC 2 1/2m 110yds 15 GF *alwys bhnd.* 8 10
1586 28/5 Cartmel (L) HC 3 1/4m 10 GF *in tch, mstk 2nd, lost pl 7th, struggling and bhnd when blnd badly 13th, not rcvr, p.u. after next, dismntd.* P 0
1589 31/5 Market Rasen (R) HC 2 3/4m 110yds 10 GF *in tch, dropped rear and struggling 8th, n.d. after.* 6 0

Changed hands & briefly revived 97; changed hands again after 6th start & best ignored now 0

ALSINA b.g. 6 Alias Smith (USA) - Tersina by Lighter — Peter Innes

1337 3/5 Mosshouses (L) MDO 3m 7 F *forced wd & p.u. aft 1st* P 0
1428 10/5 Aspatria (L) MDO 3m 11 G *9s-5s, mstks, alwys rear, no ch 13th, t.o. & p.u. 2 out* P 0
1514 17/5 Corbridge (R) MDO 3m 17 GS *rear, wll bhnd 13th, p.u. 3 out* P 0

Late to appear & no signs of ability yet 0

ALTHREY LAD b.g. 6 Celestial Storm (USA) - Fleetwood Lass by Lochnager — F Lloyd

326 1/3 Eaton Hall (R) MDN 3m 14 GS *mid to rear, p.u. 13th* P 0
883 1/4 Flagg Moor (L) MDO 3m 12 G *keen hld, prom to 10th, 6th & wkng whn f 12th* F -

No cause for encouragement yet 0

ALTNABROCKY b or br.g. 13 Ovac (ITY) - Lady Talisman by Continuation — Mrs N Gretton

1063 13/4 Maisemore P' (L) XX 3m 13 GF *mid-div, prog to 5th at 14th, outpcd, kpt on apr last* 3 16
1215 26/4 Woodford (L) CON 3m 3 G *chsd ldr to 14th, 3rd & no ch wth wnr whn blnd & u.r. 2 out* U -
1301 3/5 Weston Park (L) OPE 3m 4 G *ld to 12th,3rd nxt,lost tch 4 out, no ch whn p.u. 2 out,lame* P 0

Members winner 95; missed 96; problems last start could spell the end 12

ALTOBROOK (Irish) — **I** 66P

ALWAYS DREAMING ch.m. 7 Farajullah - Lady Almscliffe by Plenty Spirit — Miss Sarah George

1996 B(-),P(0),P(0)

147 9/2 Tweseldown (R) MDO 3m 12 GF *mid-div, mstk 11th, 4th & ev ch whn f 4 out* F -

Some promise only start 97 but yet to complete & finished very early 10

ALWAYS FRESH b.m. 5 Exorbitant - Cassandra Moor Vii by Damsire Unregistered — D Westwood

1251 26/4 Easingwold (L) MDO 3m 9 GS *alwys wll bhnd, nvr a factor, p.u. 14th* P 0

Schooled on debut & may do better 10

ALWAYS LYNSEY(IRE) b.m. 8 Mansooj - Kilcurley Lass by Huntercombe — Brian Hurst

631 22/3 Kilworthy (L) INT 3m 8 G *lost tch 8th, t.o. p.u. aft 10th* P 0
792 31/3 Bishopsleigh (R) RES 3m 13 G *rear whn blnd & u.r. 3rd* U -
1036 12/4 Lifton (R) LAD 3m 4 F *ld/disp to 11th, fdd, sn bhnd* 3 0
1110 19/4 Flete Park (R) LAD 3m 9 GF *in tch to 11th, wll bhnd frm 15th* 5 0

Last on both completions & no prospects 0

ALYCOUNT(USA) ch.g. 9 Alydar (USA) - Dancers Countess (USA) by Northern Dancer — A B Coogan

29 26/1 Marks Tey (L) MDN 3m 10 GF *rear, in tch til u.r. 9th* U -
126 9/2 Cottenham (R) RES 3m 14 GF *jmpd lft 3rd, alwys bhnd, t.o. & p.u. 16th* P 0
196 15/2 Higham (L) MDO 3m 12 G *alwys rear, p.u. 2 out* P 0
275 22/2 Ampton (R) MDO 3m 10 G *bhnd, mstk 11th, kpt on frm 3 out, nvr nrr* 5 0
1283 27/4 Fakenham P-' (L) MDO 3m 9 G *alwys bhnd, no ch frm 11th, went poor 3rd 2 out,lft 2nd last* 2 0

Did better for substitute rider last start but "form" amounts to virtually nil 0

AMADEO ch.g. 11 Le Moss - Pops Girl by Deep Run — Mrs Carrie Janaway

1996 P(0),2(10),4(16),U(-),P(0),5(0)

45 1/2 Larkhill (R) RES 3m 14 GF *ld to 3rd, mstk 10th, in tch whn mstk 13th, wknd, p.u. 15th* P 0

292 1/3 Didmarton (L) MEM 3m 9 G *last til p.u. 4th* P 0
397 8/3 Barbury Cas' (L) XX 3m 10 G *prom til rdn & lost plc 9th, no ch whn f 13th* F -

Deteriorated 97 & looks virtually finished now 0

AMADEUS(FR) b.g. 9 Pamponi (FR) - Katy Collonge (FR) by Trenel — Robert Barr
1996 **2(18)**

151 12/2 Lingfield (L) HC 3m 13 HY *t.o. when p.u. before 12th.* P 0
287 27/2 Huntingdon (R) HC 3m 13 GS *settld midfield, feeling pace 8th, t.o. when p.u. before 13th.* P 0
598 22/3 Horseheath (R) MDO 3m 3 F *made all at slw pace, outjmpd last, no ext* 2 12
796 31/3 Marks Tey (L) MDO 3m 6 F *(fav) alwys prom,ld to 5th & agn 10th,drew clr frm 15th,easy* 1 11
983 12/4 Ascot (R) HC 3m 110yds 14 GF *ld to 10th, trckd ldrs, rdn 14th, soon wknd, t.o. when p.u. before last.* P 0
1191 20/4 Garthorpe (R) RES 3m 8 GF *t.d.e. chsd ldr 4th-3 out, mstk 14th, btn apr 2 out* 3 13

Placed in H/Chase 96; changed hands 97; found right opening to score but will struggle to upgrade 14

AMANDAWILL (Irish) — **I** 538[P]

AMARANTHINE b.m. 10 Sunley Builds - Warm Up by Hot Brandy — M D P Butler

20 25/1 Badbury Rin' (L) MDN 3m 9 GF *in tch to 12th, t.o. & p.u. 2 out* P 0
487 9/3 Tweseldown (R) MDO 3m 12 G *sn wll bhnd, t.o. & p.u. 16th* P 0

Of no account 0

AMARI KING b.g. 13 Sit In The Corner (USA) - Maywell by Harwell — M Ward-Thomas
1996 **3(24)**,**4(23)**,**1(25)**,**2(25)**,**F(-)**

153 13/2 Sandown (R) HC 2 1/2m 110yds 6 G *held up in cl tch, wknd apr 3 out, t.o..* 5 0
227 21/2 Kempton (R) HC 3m 6 G *chsd ldrs 6th, lost pl 8th, wknd 12th, t.o. when p.u. before 2 out.* P 0

H/Chase winner 96; season lasted 8 days 97 & could be finished now 18

AMAZING AIR(USA) ch.g. 7 Air Forbes Won (USA) - Amoriah (USA) by Norcliffe (CAN) — Paul C Blackwell
1996 4(0)

87 2/2 Wolverhampt' (L) MDO 3m 11 GS *(fav) in tch, chsd wnr apr 12th til wknd & blnd 2 out* 5 0

Fair debut in 96 but only one run again in 97 & time passing 13

AMAZING HILL(IRE) b.g. 7 Amazing Bust - Cox Hill — Mrs W S Cook

101 8/2 Great Treth' (R) MDO 3m 9 GS *last & n.j.w. t.o. & p.u. 13th* P 0
1112 19/4 Flete Park (R) MDN 3m 13 GF *steady prog 10th, lft 5l 2nd 3 out, no imp, improve* 2 10
1485 11/5 Ottery St M' (L) MDO 3m 13 G *hld up in tch, 4th at 14th, onepcd 3 out, fin 4th, promoted* 3 10

.... 13

AMAZON LILY ch.m. 10 Man Of France - Lady Amazon by Spartan General — Mrs J E Eales
1996 **2(19)**

91 6/2 Huntingdon (R) HC 3m 10 G *ld 4th to 9th, weakening when mstk, swrd and u.r. 11th.* U -

2nd in H/Chase only run 96; 5 runs in 4 seasons & soon disappeared 97; R/H; Soft 19

AMBER DOLLY (Irish) — **I** 270[P], **I** 344[B], **I** 401[F], **I** 406, , **I** 460[F], **I** 493[5], **I** 595[P]

AMBER'S DELIGHT (Irish) — **I** 571[5], **I** 607[3]

AMERICAN BLACK b.g. 9 Lepanto (GER) - Cherry Morello by Bargello — Mrs D Fox-Ledger
1996 6(16),P(0)

930 6/4 Charlton Ho' (L) INT 3m 8 G *chsd ldr to 10th, outpcd 14th, wknd & p.u. 2 out* P 0
1038 12/4 Lifton (R) INT 3m 4 F *chsd ldr, rmmndrs 12th, wknd & p.u. 13th* P 0
1398 5/5 High Bickin' (R) INT 3m 7 G *(bl) ld to 16th, wkng whn f nxt* F -

Dual winner 95 but nothing 96/7 & blinkers no help; can only be watched now 11

AMERICAN CONKER (Irish) — **I** 25, , **I** 46[P], **I** 139[F]

AMERICAN EYRE gr.g. 12 Step Together (USA) - Jane Eyre by Master Buck — J S S Hollins
1996 3(16),2(17),3(18),2(16),4(14),**4(12)**

279 23/2 Charing (L) CON 3m 10 G *trckd ldrs, clsd 16th, rdn nxt, ld last, ran on well* 1 19
388 7/3 Sandown (R) HC 3m 110yds 7 G *bhnd 10th, t.o. when p.u. before 12th.* P 0
578 16/3 Detling (L) LAD 3m 11 F *rear, prog 14th, 5th 4 out, kpt on onepce* 4 16
830 31/3 Heathfield (R) MXO 3m 6 F *rr, last 4 out, ran on frm nxt, nt rch wnr* 2 18
1126 19/4 Penshurst (L) CON 3m 6 GF *(Jt fav) clsd up 12th, chal 4 out, ld apr 2 out, drew clr* 1 19
1504 16/5 Folkestone (R) HC 3m 7f 5 G *settld in 4th, outpcd after 14th, no impn ldrs next.* 4 0
1569 26/5 Fontwell (R) HC 3 1/4m 110yds 10 GF *alwys rear, lost tch 15th, p.u. before 4 out.* P 0

Consistent, safe & reliable in points; one paced; no show in H/Chases; can win another point; G-F 19

AMERICO LADY (Irish) — **I** 151[P], **I** 218,

AMEROUS LAD b.g. 12 Amboise - Falla Dalla by Blandford Lad — B R W Phillips

1996 7(0),4(12),P(0)

59	1/2	Kingston Bl'	(L)	RES	3m	16 GF	*sn rear, wll bhnd whn p.u. 2 out*	P	0
259	22/2	Newtown	(L)	MDN	3m	18 G	*alwys bhnd, t.o. 12th, p.u. 3 out*	P	0

No show in 97 & too old now **0**

AMICOMBE BROOK ch.m. 8 Oats - Pic-A-Path by Warpath — Miss Tracy Turner

245	22/2	Lemalla	(R)	MDO	3m	11 S	*sn rear, t.o. & p.u. 14th*	P	0
461	8/3	Great Treth'	(R)	MDO	3m	12 S	*rear whn f 11th*	F	-
626	22/3	Kilworthy	(L)	MDN	3m	14 G	*6th hlfwy, rear whn p.u. apr 14th*	P	0

No signs of ability yet **0**

AMISTAR (Irish) — **I** 413P, **I** 470P

A MONKEY FOR DICK (Irish) — **I** 214⁴, **I** 293F, **I** 330⁴, **I** 377P

ANALYSTIC(IRE) br.g. 7 Kambalda - Burlington Miss by Burlington II — Ken Liscombe

1996 U(-),F(-),P(0),F(-),F(-)

82	2/2	Wolverhampt'	(L)	MDN	3m	11 GS	*alwys bhnd, t.o. 10th*	5	0

Tailed off last only start 97 & disappeared **0**

AN BUCHAILL LIATH(IRE) gr.g. 8 Roselier (FR) - Buckette Lady by Buckskin (FR) — F J Cox

1996 **14(NH),B(NH),7(NH),P(NH),F(NH)**

1254	27/4	Black Fores'	(R)	MEM	3m	2 F	*alwys abt 6l bhnd wnr, nvr able to chal*	2	0
1485	11/5	Ottery St M'	(L)	MDO	3m	13 G	*2nd to 12th, wknd, bhnd & p.u. 3 out*	P	0
1584	26/5	Lifton	(R)	MDO	3m	13 G	*nvr trbld ldrs, t.o. & p.u. 2 out*	P	0

Poor under Rules & no better in points either **0**

AN CAIPIN (Irish) — **I** 384P, **I** 478P

AN CEARC DEARG (Irish) — **I** 429P, **I** 452P

ANDALUCIAN SUN(IRE) ch.g. 9 Le Bavard (FR) - Sun Spray by Nice Guy — A Witcomb

1996 P(0),F(-),2(10),U(-),P(0),6(0)

141	9/2	Thorpe Lodge	(L)	MDN	3m	12 GF	*mid-div, no prog frm 5 out*	6	0
480	9/3	Southwell P'	(L)	MDO	3m	17 G	*bhnd, jmpd slwly 6th, t.o. & p.u. 3 out*	P	0
839	31/3	Thorpe Lodge	(L)	MDO	3m	15 F	*prog 10th, 2nd 12th, ld 6 out, ran on gmly, bttr spd flat*	1	16
927	6/4	Garthorpe	(R)	RES	3m	9 GF	*hld up, prog to 2nd at 11th, ld 13th, prssd 3 out, hld on wl*	1	16
1190	20/4	Garthorpe	(R)	INT	3m	8 GF	*w.w. prog 8th, ld aft 15th, clr nxt, rdn & styd on wll flat*	1	18
1570	26/5	Hereford	(R)	HC	3m 1f 110yds	14 G	*soon well bhnd, saddle slpd, tried to refuse and u.r. 5th.*	U	-
1608	1/6	Dingley	(R)	INT	3m	11 GF	*sn bhnd & jmpd slwly, 7th & t.o. whn ref 13th*	R	-

Reformed with novice rider to score hat-trick; reverted to old ways last start; hard to place 98 .... **18**

ANDRETTI'S HEIR ch.g. 11 Andretti - Mounemara by Ballymore — T S Sharpe

1996 U(-),P(0),F(-),**5(12)**

120	9/2	Wetherby Po'	(L)	MDO	3m	18 GF	*alwys in chsng grp, onepcd frm 4 out*	3	0
346	2/3	Market Rase'	(L)	MDO	3m	10 GF	*ld til f 6th*	F	-
510	15/3	Dalton Park	(R)	MDO	3m	14 GF	*alwys prom, fdng whn hmpd & p.u. aft 15th*	P	0
1086	14/4	Southwell	(L)	HC	3m 110yds	11 G	*started slowly, hdwy 9th, weakening when blnd and u.r. 3 out.*	U	-
1252	26/4	Easingwold	(L)	MDO	3m	9 GS	*ld to 9th agn frm 4 out, drew clr flat, easily*	1	14
1421	10/5	Easingwold	(L)	RES	3m	8 GF	*disp til ld 3rd, u.r. 7th*	U	-
1510	17/5	Corbridge	(R)	RES	3m	13 GS	*mid-div, prog 6th, outpcd frm 4 out, 4th & wll btn, f last*	F	-

Clumsy but gained deserved win in weak race; likes Easingwold; Restricted looks beyond him **14**

ANDROSCOGGIN (Irish) — **I** 269F

ANDROS GALE(IRE) b.g. 8 Strong Gale - Sirrahdis by Bally Joy — Mrs A Rucker

1996 **4(NH),4(NH),5(NH),P(NH),2(NH),3(NH)**

573	16/3	Garnons	(L)	LAD	3m	8 G	*lost 30l strt, prog 12th, styd on to win race for 3rd*	3	18
939	6/4	Tabley	(R)	LAD	3m	9 G	*mid-div & gng wll, prog to ld 16th, hdd apr last, no ext*	2	22
1148	19/4	Chaddesley '	(L)	LAD	3m	5 GF	*ld 3-5th & 15th-nxt, ld & lft clr 2 out, ran on well*	1	22

Winning chaser; consistent in points but hampered by rider; more placings than wins in 98; G-F **22**

AND WHAT ELSE(IRE) ch.g. 8 Parliament - San Patrice by Random Shot — Mrs D A Wetherall

1996 2(15),**9(0)**,6(0),P(0),P(0)

525	15/3	Cothelstone	(L)	MDN	3m	15 GS	*7th at 12th, lost ground & p.u. nxt*	P	0
864	31/3	Kingston St'	(R)	LAD	3m	6 F	*1st ride, bhnd til p.u. aft 8th*	P	0
1045	12/4	Cothelstone	(L)	MDO	3m	6 GF	*2nd to 5th, 3rd to 10th, chsd wnr agn 14th, blnd 3 out, wknd*	3	10
1157	20/4	Stafford Cr'	(R)	RES	3m	11 GF	*sn bhnd, t.o. 14th*	5	0
1315	3/5	Holnicote	(L)	MDO	3m	7 G	*alwys prom, ld 4 out, jnd nxt, lft in ld 2 out, ran on*	1	16
1439	10/5	Holnicote	(L)	RES	3m	9 G	*prom til lost plc 8th, t.o. & p.u. 15th*	P	0
1594	31/5	Bratton Down	(L)	INT	3m	10 F	*bhnd frm 9th, t.o. & p.u. 14th*	P	0

Found right race to score (probably lucky) but non-stayer & Restricted most unlikely 14

AND WHY NOT ro.g. 9 Baron Blakeney - Tamana Dancer by Gay Fandango (USA) — Mrs C E Van Praagh

1996 **12(NH)**,**U(NH)**,**P(NH)**,**5(NH)**,**6(NH)**,**6(NH)**

147	9/2	Tweseldown	(R)	MDO	3m	12	GF	*10s-6s, j.w. hld up rear,prog to ld 12th,hdd apr last,no ext*	2	14
283	23/2	Charing	(L)	MDO	3m	16	G	*mid-div, prog 9th, mstk 13th, 3rd & rdn 3 out, no ext, tired*	4	10
485	9/3	Tweseldown	(R)	MDO	3m	11	G	*mstk 1st,in tch,ld 15th,hdd & wknd apr 2 out,no ch & f last*	F	-
833	31/3	Heathfield	(R)	MDO	3m	7	F	*(Jt fav) hld up, stdy prog to chal 4 out, ld 2 out, lft wll clr last*	1	13
970	6/4	Penshurst	(L)	RES	3m	4	F	*(fav) hld up, chal 3 out, und pres nxt, just held*	2	13
1129	19/4	Penshurst	(L)	RES	3m	6	GF	*rear, wll in tch whn stirrup iron broke & p.u. aft 11th*	P	0
1442	10/5	Peper Harow	(L)	MEM	3m	4	GF	*(fav) mstk 1st, hld up, ld 12th, clr last, rdn out*	1	12
1505	16/5	Folkestone	(R)	HC	2m 5f	8	G	*f 1st.*	F	-

Doubtful stayer but found 2 soft races on Firm; same again best hope in 98 15

ANDY GAWE(IRE) b.g. 7 Good Thyne (USA) - Miss Fion by He Loves Me — B Kennedy

61	1/2	Horseheath	(R)	MDO	3m	9	GF	*chsd wnr, ld 6th til blnd & hdd 15th, wknd apr 2 out*	2	10
318	1/3	Marks Tey	(L)	MDN	3m	13	G	*chsd ldr 5th-14th, wknd apr 16th, t.o.*	4	0
599	22/3	Horseheath	(R)	MDO	3m	4	F	*(fav) ld frm 2nd, nrrw advan & lkd wnr whn lft alone 2 out*	1	12
798	31/3	Marks Tey	(L)	RES	3m	7	F	*rear early,mstk 2nd,prog 3rd 15th,wknd qckly nxt,p.u. last*	P	0

Ex-Irish; no signs of stamina & won desperate race; 98 chances slim 12

ANDY'S BIRTHDAY (Irish) — **I** 56[1], **I** 147[F], **I** 183[1], **I** 266[1]

AN FEAR DUBH (Irish) — **I** 4[4], **I** 54[3]

ANITA'S SON b.g. 10 Anita's Prince - Jubilaire by Gala Performance (USA) — Mrs B F Abraham

1996 5(0),U(-)

449	8/3	Newton Brom'	(R)	XX	3m	13	G	*last hlfwy, wll bhnd & p.u. 3 out*	P	0

Very lightly raced & shows no ability 0

ANJUBI b.g. 12 Sunyboy - Dyna Bell by Double Jump — W H Whitley

1996 4(16),4(20),**4(22)**

951	6/4	Black Fores'	(R)	CON	3m	3	G	*(fav) ld/disp til went clr 10th, v easily*	1	19
1091	16/4	Hockworthy	(L)	OPE	3m	4	GF	*ld to 8th, disp 2nd apr 2 out, sn btn & eased*	4	14
1154	20/4	Stafford Cr'	(R)	OPE	3m	2	GF	*trckd ldr, effrt 2 out, outpcd flat*	2	17
1242	26/4	Bratton Down	(L)	LAD	3m	6	GS	*rear til gd prog 12th, chal 2 out, ran on onepce*	2	16
1358	5/5	Exeter	(R)	HC	2m 7f 110yds	8	G	*trckd ldrs, outpcd 10th, styd on one pace from 3 out.*	4	20
1480	11/5	Ottery St M'	(L)	MEM	3m	6	G	*(fav) disp early, clr ld 7th, unchal aft*	1	19
1570	26/5	Hereford	(R)	HC	3m 1f 110yds	14	G	*chsd ldrs, ld 9th to 11th, led 6 out to 4 out, led apr last, soon hdd and no ext.*	2	21

Consistent, safe & found 2 easy chances 97; outclassed in good company; easy 3m best; should win 98 20

ANNASCANAN b.m. 5 Ra Nova - Aberaeron Girl by Neltino — G A Coombe

834	31/3	Thorpe Lodge	(L)	MEM	3m	3	F	*cls up til hit 6th, t.o. 10l frm 8th, eased p.u. 5 out*	P	0
1192	20/4	Garthorpe	(R)	MDO	3m	6	GF	*cls up til blnd & u.r. 8th*	U	-
1262	27/4	Southwell P'	(L)	MDO	3m	15	G	*prom, jmpd slwly 12th, losng plc whn f 14th*	F	-

Learning so far & needs to brush up on the jumping; some hope last start 0

ANN BLACK (Irish) — **I** 304[F], **I** 443[P]

ANNERENE (Irish) — **I** 10[P], **I** 162[F]

ANNIE BUCKERS (Irish) — **I** 318[1]

ANNIE LEAP (Irish) — **I** 94[P], **I** 148[P], **I** 219[P], **I** 343[P], **I** 496[3]

ANNIE'S ARTHUR (Irish) — **I** 27[6], **I** 121[5], **I** 174[3], **I** 230[2], **I** 314[3], **I** 414[2], **I** 441[5], **I** 521[3], **I** 555[2], **I** 578, , **I** 584[2]

ANNIO CHILONE b.g. 11 Touching Wood (USA) - Alpine Alice by Abwah — Mrs Liz Champion

1996 **2(NH)**,**6(NH)**

150	10/2	Plumpton	(L)	HC	3m 1f 110yds	5	GS	*held up, rdn from 4 out, wknd apr 2 out.*	4	15
281	23/2	Charing	(L)	OPE	3m	12	G	*made most to 7th, trckd ldrs aft, not qckn frm 2 out*	3	20
376	3/3	Windsor	(R)	HC	3m	11	GF	*bhnd from hfwy, t.o..*	6	0
579	16/3	Detling	(L)	OPE	4m	9	F	*sweating, ld to 21st, wknd und pres 25th, lft 3rd nxt*	3	20
967	6/4	Penshurst	(L)	OPE	3m	4	F	*trckd ldr, lft disp 12th, lft clr 14th & solo 3 out*	1	18

Ex-plodding chaser; too slow even for SE points & bloddless win; Confined possible at 12; G-F 18

ANN'S AMBITION b.g. 10 Ovac (ITY) - Faultless Girl by Crash Course — N A Whittle

1996 **8(NH)**,**3(NH)**,**P(NH)**

241	22/2	Lemalla	(R)	RES	3m	11	S	*prom, ld/disp 11-16th, 3rd 3 out, wknd & p.u. nxt, gd effrt*	P	0
461	8/3	Great Treth'	(R)	MDO	3m	12	S	*ld til hdd aft 2 out, no ext und pres*	2	13
630	22/3	Kilworthy	(L)	RES	3m	16	G	*prom, hdwy to disp 15th, slght ld last, not qckn*	2	16
892	5/4	Hereford	(R)	HC	2m	11	GF	*mstks, alwys bhnd.*	5	0
1157	20/4	Stafford Cr'	(R)	RES	3m	11	GF	*alwys prom,2nd at 11th, lft in ld 14th, styd on strngly 2out*	1	18

1203 26/4 Worcester (L) HC 2m 7f 110yds 10 S *in tch, chsd wnr from 8th, blnd and lost touch 10th, wknd 3 out, left poor 3rd last, t.o..* 3 0
1416 10/5 Newton Abbot (L) HC 2m 5f 110yds 14 G *alwys bhnd, t.o. when p.u. before 2 out.* P 0
1570 26/5 Hereford (R) HC 3m 1f 110yds 14 G *alwys prom, ld 4 out, hdd and no ext apr last.* 3 19

Oddly campaigned but decent performance when winning; should stick to points early 98; G-F 19

ANNS DISPLAY (Irish) — I 117[1], I 174[P], I 288[3], I 365[P], I 434[F], I 466[3]

ANNULMENT(IRE) br.g. 8 Miner's Lamp - Inneen Alainn by Prince Hansel Mrs Yda Morgan

1996 **P(NH)**

135 9/2 Alnwick (L) MDO 3m 12 G *pllng, wth ldr, ld 9-11th, wknd rpdly 14th, p.u. 3 out* P 0
162 15/2 Lanark (R) MDO 3m 16 G *cls 4th whn f 11th* F -
358 2/3 Great Stain' (L) MDO 3m 14 S *mid-div, prog to ld 7th, hdd 10th, steadily lost tch* 3 0

Well-beaten last start but showed glimmer of hope; finished early 10

ANODFROMALORD (Irish) — I 104, , I 158[F], I 241[P], I 297[P]

AN OON ISS AN OWL (Irish) — I 21[1], I 88[1]

ANOTHER BARNEY ch.g. 13 Stetchworth (USA) - Another Reef by Take A Reef D A Roxburgh

1037 12/4 Lifton (R) OPE 3m 5 F *nvr trbld ldrs, p.u. aft 13th* P 0
1480 11/5 Ottery St M' (L) MEM 3m 6 G *cls up til p.u. aft 9th, dead* P 0

Dead 0

ANOTHER BERRY (Irish) — I 260[P], I 381[P], I 447[P], I 484[4], I 515[5], I 563[P]

ANOTHER CHANCER ch.g. 6 Scallywag - Acuity by Sharp Edge K C G Edwards

1996 P(0),1(15),P(0)

468 8/3 Eyton-On-Se' (L) RES 3m 11 G *mid-rear, no ch whn p.u. 10th* P 0
670 23/3 Eaton Hall (R) RES 3m 15 GF *mid to rear, fin own time* 8 0
852 31/3 Eyton-On-Se' (L) RES 3m 11 GF *ld to start, mid-div 9th, rdn & ran on wll to ld 2 out* 1 18
1013 12/4 Bitterley (L) CON 3m 14 GF *rear frm 8th, lost tch & p.u. 15th* P 0
1235 26/4 Brampton Br' (R) INT 3m 10 G *s.s. effrt & prog 12th, in tch whn ran out 14th* r -
1382 5/5 Eyton-On-Se' (L) INT 3m 7 GF *prom,2nd 7-13th,drpd back 5th,ran on frm 2 out,tk 2nd flat* 2 19
1538 18/5 Wolverhampt' (L) CON 3m 8 GS *cls 2nd/3rd til blnd 5 out, sn btn, p.u. 3 out* P 0

Maiden winner 96; wildly inconsistent & suspect temperament; both good runs at Eyton; hard to predict 18

ANOTHER CHANT b.g. 7 Chas Sawyer - Golden Chorus by Golden Mallard D A D Brydon

1996 P(0),3(0)

421 8/3 Charm Park (L) MEM 3m 6 GF *disp to 3rd, fdd 6th, lost tch 10th, t.o. & p.u. 12th* P 0

Placed in 96 but rarely seen & no great ability 0

ANOTHER DAUGHTER b.m. 6 Royal Vulcan - Dereks Daughter by Derek H Mrs J N Askew

1996 **9(NH)**

269 22/2 Duncombe Pa' (R) MDO 3m 16 G *mid-div, mstk 10th, sn wknd, f 13th* F -

Very lightly raced & debut pointing season soon ended 0

ANOTHER DELIGHT ch.m. 10 Politico (USA) - Another Tudor by Tudor Cliff Miss M Wilkin

510 15/3 Dalton Park (R) MDO 3m 14 GF *lft 20l start, unruly & u.r. bef 1st* U -
698 29/3 Stainton (R) MDO 3m 6 F *rear & bhnd, not keen 8th, t.o. 11th, p.u. nxt* P 0
899 5/4 Wetherby Po' (L) MDO 3m 3 F *trckd ldr, disp 3rd-8th, mstk 13th, wknd nxt, lft 2nd 2 out* 2 0
1251 26/4 Easingwold (L) MDO 3m 9 GS *rear, rmmndrs 10th, t.o. p.u. 14th* P 0

Not enthusiastic & placing meaningless; safely ignored 0

ANOTHERFLING (Irish) — I 286[P], I 349[P], I 394[P]

ANOTHER FROSTY (Irish) — I 481[3], I 548[F]

ANOTHER HOOLIGAN gr.g. 8 Scallywag - Chumolaori by Indian Ruler R Tate

1996 U(-),4(0),1(16),2(18),P(0),2(16),1(20)

113 9/2 Wetherby Po' (L) CON 3m 10 GF *hld up, bhnd 4th, mstk 9th, lost tch 14th, p.u. nxt* P 0
163 15/2 Witton Cast' (R) MEM 3m 5 F *sttld 3rd, mstks 2 & 6th, prog to ld apr 4 out, u.r. 3 out* U -
422 8/3 Charm Park (L) CON 3m 8 GF *hld up,mstk 5th, prog 11th,disp 4 out,bad mstk & u.r. nxt* U 22
674 23/3 Brocklesby ' (L) LAD 3m 5 GF *(fav) w.w. mstk 5th, prog to ld aft 15th, hdd nxt, hit last,kpt on* 1 19

Dual winner 96; able but error-prone; sore last start & vanished; win more 98 if fit; G/F-S 21

ANOTHER HUBBLICK ch.g. 6 Nearly A Hand - Sue Lark by Sir Lark T Hubbard

1996 **P(NH),F(NH),10(NH)**

176 15/2 Ottery St M' (L) RES 3m 17 G *mid-div, lost tch 13th, p.u. 15th* P 0
459 8/3 Great Treth' (R) MDO 3m 9 S *in tch, 5th 14th, no real prog, p.u. apr 3 out* P 0

No signs of real ability & finished early 0

ANOTHER ISLAY b.g. 6 Tobin Lad (USA) - Coincidence Girl by Manacle — Miss S Craven

1996 **13(NH)**

996	12/4	Tranwell	(L) MDO 3m	8	F	*cls up 1st ctt, 1l 2nd 9th, ld 12th & gng wll whn f 13th*	F	-
1336	3/5	Mosshouses	(L) MDO 3m	7	F	*alwys 1st trio, went 2nd 3 out, ld apr last, comf*	1	15
1510	17/5	Corbridge	(R) RES 3m	13	GS	*mid-div til wknd 14th, t.o.*	7	0

Landed poor race in good style; disappointed other start but may upgrade on Firm in 98 16

ANOTHER KAV(IRE) b.m. 7 Andretti - Kavrag by Roga Navarro (ITY) — E A McGuinness

1996 **10(NH),9(NH),13(NH),5(NH),8(NH)**

1437	10/5	Holnicote	(L) MDO 3m	14	G	*20s-4s, twrds rear whn f 4th*	F	-
1460	11/5	Maisemore P'	(L) MDO 3m	16	G	*16s-7s, hld up, rear whn f 4th*	F	-
1497	14/5	Cothelstone	(L) MDO 3m	10	GF	*pllng,not fluent,2nd til ld 6th,4l up whn blnd & u.r. 13th*	U	-
1554	24/5	Mounsey Hil'	(R) MDO 3m	14	G	*in tch, 4th at 10th, lost plc rpdly nxt, p.u. 12th*	P	0

Has some ability but blundered away supporters' cash each time; best watched 12

ANOTHER MISTAKE (Irish) — **I** 274^{P}, **I** 393^{P}

ANOTHER ONE JASPER (Irish) — **I** 568^{4}, **I** 588^{5}

ANOTHER PLANET (Irish) — **I** 570^{5}, **I** 595^{P}, **I** 607^{5}

ANOTHER RHYTHM b.g. 13 Music Boy - Just You Wait by Nonoalco (USA) — D J E Scott

444	8/3	Higham	(L) CON 3m	8	G	*tubed, pllng, prssd ldr whn blnd & u.r. 3rd*	U	-
801	31/3	Marks Tey	(L) CON 3m	8	F	*qckly ld,30l clr 5th,wknd qckly 6th,hdd 7th,t.o. & p.u. 11th*	P	0

No longer of any account 0

ANOTHER TEST (Irish) — **I** 165^{4}

ANOTHER WHISTLE(IRE) b.f. 8 Whistling Deer - Alfarouse by Home Guard (USA) — Miss T Habgood

373	2/3	Mollington	(R) MDN 3m	14	G	*alwys rear, t.o. 12th, p.u. 15th*	P	0
452	8/3	Newton Brom'	(R) MDN 3m	9	G	*chsd ldrs til wknd 11th, bhnd & p.u. 15th*	P	0
655	22/3	Siddington	(L) RES 3m	10	F	*alwys rear, outpcd frm 10th, t.o.*	5	0
761	29/3	Kimble	(L) MDO 3m	12	GF	*ld to 11th, lost plc, not qckn frm 16th*	4	0

Well-beaten both completions & much more needed for any chance 10

AN TAIN SHIOC (Irish) — **I** 287^{U}, **I** 440^{1}

ANTICA ROMA(IRE) ch.m. 8 Denel (FR) - Struell Course by Green Shoon — Mrs K Cockburn

1996 1(15),4(10)

45	1/2	Larkhill	(R) RES 3m	14	GF	*mid-div whn blnd & u.r. 2nd*	U	-
223	16/2	Heythrop	(R) RES 3m	19	G	*hld up rear, prog hlfwy, ld aft 2 out, ran on strngly*	1	19
369	2/3	Mollington	(R) MEM 3m	13	G	*(fav) hld up, prog 13th, rdn to chal 2 out, kpt on, ld post*	1	20
757	29/3	Kimble	(L) INT 3m	3	GF	*(fav) hld up in tch, p.u. aft 10th, lame*	P	0

Maiden winner 96; improved; won competitive races; problem last start; Confined if fit 98; Good 20

ANTIQUE DEALER br.m. 5 Silly Prices - Frayland by Sallust — Mrs F M Gray

615	22/3	Hutton Rudby	(L) MEM 3m	8	GF	*rear, lost tch 7th, t.o. 12th, p.u. 4 out*	P	0

Not yet of any account 0

ANTRIM COUNTY ch.g. 12 Deep Run - Gothic Arch by Gail Star — J R Cornwall

1996 6(13),P(0),**4(0)**,**4(0)**,2(17),**P(0)**,**P(0)**,**5(0)**

214	16/2	Southwell P'	(L) CON 3m	10	GS	*ld to 4th, bhnd 8th, t.o. & p.u. 12th*	P	0
545	16/3	Garthorpe	(R) CON 3m	12	GF	*chsd ldr 3-12th, wkng whn hit 15th, sn no ch*	6	11
769	29/3	Dingley	(R) CON 3m	14	G	*ldng trio 1st m, sn fdd, p.u. 12th*	P	0

Looks finished now 10

ANVIL CORNER ch.m. 8 Smackover - Douraine by Doubtless II — Miss Jane Wakeham

1996 P(0),2(11),5(0),U(-)

624	22/3	Kilworthy	(L) MEM 3m	7	G	*lost plc 9th, 4th whn lft clr 14th*	1	10
736	29/3	Higher Kilw'	(L) RES 3m	10	GF	*lost tch 10th, t.o.*	3	0
1039	12/4	Lifton	(R) RES 3m	8	F	*alwys towrds, lft 4th by defections*	4	0
1108	19/4	Flete Park	(R) RES 3m	14	GF	*in tch, 7th whn blnd & u.r. 12th*	U	-

Handed Members when rest fell & struggling since; Restricted looks beyond her 12

APATURA KING ch.g. 7 Button Bright (USA) - Apatura Iris by Space King — C E Gibbs

1996 1(17),1(19),3(11)

17	25/1	Badbury Rin'	(L) CON 3m	9	GF	*(fav) trckd ldrs, rdn to chs ldr 15th, ld aft last, drvn out*	1	20
178	15/2	Larkhill	(R) CON 3m	9	G	*hld up mid-div, jnd ldrs 13th, ev ch whn blnd last, not rcvr*	3	21
514	15/3	Larkhill	(R) MXO 3m	6	GF	*(fav) w.w. in tch, ld 15th, sn rdn, styd on wll flat*	1	22
983	12/4	Ascot	(R) HC 3m 110yds	14	GF	*alwys bhnd.*	7	14

Fair performer now; tough & responds to pressure; should win more points if fit 98; G-F 23

APOLLODORUS (Irish) — **I** 58^{U}, **I** 148^{3}, **I** 219^{P}, **I** 390^{5}, **I** 496,

APPEAL ch.m. 7 Sunley Builds - Pastures Green by Monksfield — Chris Wall
1996 P(0),P(0),4(10),F(-)
186 15/2 Erw Lon (L) MDN 3m 13 G *prom whn u.r. 4th* U -
189 15/2 Erw Lon (L) RES 3m 14 G *2nd outing, rear, whn mstk 5th, p.u. nxt* P 0
436 8/3 Upton-On-Se' (R) MDO 3m 17 G *rear frm 8th, no ch whn p.u. 11th* P 0
Makes no appeal on 97's performances 0

APPLE NICKING b.g. 10 Nickel King - Apple Crumble by Pony Express — Mrs M Upstone
1996 F(-),3(0),P(0),P(0),2(15),1(16),1(20)
218 16/2 Heythrop (R) INT 3m 21 G *prom, rdn & wknd 12th, p.u. 14th* P 0
293 1/3 Didmarton (L) INT 3m 16 G *u.r. 1st* U -
446 8/3 Newton Brom' (R) CON 3m 8 G *hld up last, prog 11th, mod 5th whn f 16th* F -
989 12/4 Kingston Bl' (L) INT 3m 7 GF *hld up,prog 10th,ld 15th-aft 2 out,btn whn jmpd slwly last* 3 17
Dual winner late 96; ran passably last start but little otherwise; best watched at 11 17

APPLE SAFT (Irish) — **I** 422^{P}, **I** 563^{P}

APRIL SUPRISE b.m. 11 Saunter - Kefhalik by Precipice Wood — Dr A J Cooper
1996 2(11),3(0)
331 1/3 Eaton Hall (R) RES 3m 17 GS *alwys mid to rear, no ch whn p.u. 3 out* P 0
883 1/4 Flagg Moor (L) MDO 3m 12 G *w.w. prog to trck ldrs 9th, 3rd & rdn 3 out, onepcd* 3 11
Placed in 3 of 4 races 96/7 but unlikely to win at 12 12

AQUEOUS ROCKS b.g. 6 Precious Metal - Bala Lake by Dumbarnie — Cecil W Wardle
81 2/2 Wolverhampt' (L) MDN 3m 13 GS *ld to 8th, sn wknd, t.o. & p.u. 11th* P 0
203 15/2 Weston Park (L) RES 3m 11 G *rear, t.o. 10th, p.u. 12th* P 0
852 31/3 Eyton-On-Se' (L) RES 3m 11 GF *cls up, ld 3rd-8th, in tch whn f 13th* F -
1386 5/5 Eyton-On-Se' (L) MDO 2 1/2m 8 GF *ld to 10th, wknd 2 out, p.u. nxt* P 0
Yet to complete & shows no stamina 0

ARALIER MAN(IRE) ch.g. 6 Roselier (FR) - Ara Go On by Sandalay — E H Crow
1996 U(-)
470 8/3 Eyton-On-Se' (L) MDN 2 1/2m 12 G *mid-div, nvr trbld ldrs, p.u. 2 out* P 0
854 31/3 Eyton-On-Se' (L) MDO 3m 10 GF *nvr bttr thn mid-div, rdn 6 out, found little, p.u. 3 out* P 0
1179 20/4 Sandon (L) MDN 3m 6 GF *(fav) trckd ldr, chal apr last, lft clr* 1 11
1471 11/5 Erw Lon (L) RES 3m 9 GS *chsd ldrs, 7th whn f 12th* F -
Won a ghastly race (possibly fortunate) & looks a lesser light from a powerful yard 11

ARBLE MARCH gr.m. 8 Baron Blakeney - Eventime by Hot Brandy — D G Congdon
1996 P(0),3(16),4(10),P(0)
240 22/2 Lemalla (R) RES 3m 11 S *whppd round strt, t.o. til p.u. 9th* P 0
457 8/3 Great Treth' (R) RES 3m 8 S *ld til 4th, sn lost plc, t.o. p.u. apr 13th* P 0
803 31/3 Wadebridge (L) MEM 3m 3 F *qck away, ld to 3rd, sn lost tch, btn 3 fences* 3 0
1395 5/5 High Bickin' (R) RES 3m 9 G *twrds rear, 8th at 15th, nrst fin* 3 13
1519 17/5 Bratton Down (L) RES 3m 15 GS *s.s. rear, 12th at 15th, nrst fin* 5 14
1551 24/5 Mounsey Hil' (R) RES 3m 13 G *chsd ldrs to 10th, sn strgglng, went mod 3rd flat* 3 11
1596 31/5 Bratton Down (L) OPE 4m 5 F *chsd wnr 10th-4 out, 2nd agn 2 out, kpt on und pres* 2 18
Maiden winner 95; changed hands 97; consistent; ran well last start; too slow for Restricted win 15

ARBOUR HILL (Irish) — **I** 568^{P}, **I** 602^{3}

ARCHER(IRE) b.g. 9 Roselier (FR) - Suir Valley by Orchardist — P Green
1996 **5(NH),6(NH),8(NH),U(NH),5(NH)**
191 15/2 Erw Lon (L) CON 3m 13 G *chsd ldr 6-13th, 3rd & rdn whn blnd nxt, kpt on agn last* 2 19
569 16/3 Garnons (L) OPE 3m 7 G *chsd ldr,rdn to chal 14th,ld til aft last,stppd flat,cont* 2 19
632 22/3 Howick (L) MEM 3m 2 GF *(fav) trckd ldr, hrd rdn 3 out, disp last, ld final 50 yrds* 1 13
1005 12/4 St Hilary (R) CON 3m 10 GF *2nd til disp frm 12-15th, hdd nxt, hrd rdn flat, just faild* 2 20
1134 19/4 Bonvilston (R) MXO 4m 10 G *(fav) prom, rmmndrs hlfwy, 2nd & held frm 3 out* 2 14
1411 7/5 Chepstow (L) HC 3m 4 G *chsd wnr to 9th, wknd 11th, t.o..* 3 18
1524 17/5 Bredwardine (R) OPE 3m 8 G *in tch, rdn to chs wnr frm 10th, no imp aft 3 out, not qckn* 2 18
Winning chaser; able but ungenuine; all out to win bad race; should continue to frustrate 19

ARCHIES OATS ch.g. 8 Oats - Archetype by Over The River (FR) — Jon Trice-Rolph
1996 1+(14),4(0),P(0),P(0)
221 16/2 Heythrop (R) RES 3m 15 G *reluc to race, t.o. til p.u. 11th* P 0
372 2/3 Mollington (R) RES 3m 19 G *alwys prom, prssd ldr 10th, ld 15th-nxt, kpt on well* 2 18
389 8/3 Sandown (R) HC 2 1/2m 110yds 6 G *held up, hdwy 12th, ld last, rdn out and styd on well.* 1 23
1162 20/4 Mollington (R) CON 3m 7 GF *(fav) nvr going wll, mstk 10th, sn lost tch, p.u. 13th* P 0
Maiden winner 96; well-placed to win H/Chase but vanished after poor effort; options limited 98; Gd ... 21

ARCTIC BARON b.g. 12 Baron Blakeney - Learctic by Lepanto (GER) A C Raymond

1996 2(18),2(20),2(20),2(18),**5(0)**

889	3/4	Taunton	(R)	HC	3m	7	F	*held up, prog 9th, 4th and weakening when blnd four out.*	4	14
1109	19/4	Flete Park	(R)	OPE	4m	9	GF	*mid-div, lost plc steadily frm 14th*	5	14
1496	14/5	Cothelstone	(L)	CON	3m	9	GF	*ld to 2nd,ld 6-8th, rdn & outpcd 12th, kpt on to tk 2nd flat*	2	18
1548	24/5	Mounsey Hil'	(R)	LAD	3m	10	G	*mid-div, 6th & drvn alng 12th, plodded on, tk 3rd nr fin*	3	17

Finished 18 of 19 starts 94-7 but hard ride & very one paced; hard to see a win at 13; F-S 17

ARCTIC CHILL(IRE) b.g. 7 Tremblant - Lady Zalona by Arctic Slave M F Thorne

1996 1(20),2(21),1(24),F(-)

18	25/1	Badbury Rin'	(L)	LAD	3m	9	GF	*ld to 2nd, lft in ld 5th, made rest, pshd out & ran on well*	1	25
145	9/2	Tweseldown	(R)	LAD	3m	10	GF	*(fav) prom, ld 6-9th & 15th, blnd 3 out, hdd nxt, no ext*	2	23
377	4/3	Leicester	(R)	HC	2 1/2m 110yds	15	G	*prom till wknd 4 out.*	4	13
555	16/3	Ottery St M'	(L)	LAD	3m	10	G	*ld to 7th, 2nd aft, ld agn 4 out, ran on well*	1	26
737	29/3	Higher Kilw'	(L)	LAD	3m	5	GF	*(fav) handy, ld 8th, qcknd readily 2 out, easily*	1	25
932	6/4	Charlton Ho'	(L)	LAD	3m	6	G	*(fav) outpcd,4th & strgglng hlfwy,ran on 13th,ld 2 out,styd on wll*	1	27
1056	13/4	Hackwood Pa'	(L)	LAD	3m	3	GF	*(fav) j.w. made all, comf*	1	25
1155	20/4	Stafford Cr'	(R)	LAD	3m	6	GF	*(fav) ld to 4th, chsd wnr aft, rdn aft 3 out, disp nxt, wknd flat*	2	23

High-class Ladies horse now; stays; well-ridden; win plenty more if fit 98; G/F-S 27

ARCTIC LEADER b.m. 7 Supreme Leader - Le Roilelet by Le Bavard (FR) A Gilchrist

134	9/2	Alnwick	(L)	MDO	3m	11	G	*chsd ldrs,2nd 11th,4l down whn lft in ld, blnd & u.r. 4 out*	U	-
229	22/2	Friars Haugh	(L)	CON	3m	9	G	*nvr nr ldrs*	6	0
341	1/3	Corbridge	(R)	MDN	3m	10	G	*(fav) disp til lft in ld 4th, hdd nxt, ld 10th, clr 12th, imprssv*	1	16

Decent start & beat bad field decisively; finished early; should upgrade if fit 98 17

ARCTIC LINE b.g. 9 Green Ruby (USA) - Sally Ann III by Port Corsair S R Green

1996 P(0),6(0),4(0),P(0),P(0)

821	31/3	Paxford	(L)	MDO	3m	6	F	*in tch, wknd aft 11th, p.u. 12th*	P	0

Lost all 28 points & soon vanished in 97 (thankfully) 0

ARCTIC PARTY (Irish) — **I** 101^{P}, **I** 124^{P}, **I** 228^{P}

ARCTIC POND (Irish) — **I** 590^{F}, **I** 606^{F}

ARCTIC RED ch.g. 10 Deep Run - Snow Sweet by Arctic Slave Mrs M J Hogan

664	23/3	Eaton Hall	(R)	MDO	3m	12	GF	*mid-div, p.u. 5th*	P	0

A brief appearance of no promise 0

ARCTIC TREASURE (Irish) — **I** 37^{4}, **I** 62^{P}, **I** 69^{2}, **I** 116^{5}, **I** 121^{6}, **I** 211^{P}, **I** 313^{P}, **I** 368^{4}

ARDAVILLAN PRINCE (Irish) — **I** 12^{P}, **I** 38,

ARDBEI (Irish) — **I** 120^{3}, **I** 180^{3}, **I** 315^{2}

ARDBRENNAN b.g. 10 Deep Run - Callan River by Harwell C C Bennett

1996 1(27),F(-),3(14),1(22),**F(-),U(-)**

5	19/1	Barbury Cas'	(L)	OPE	3m	11	GF	*rear, 8th hlfwy, nrst fin*	3	22
19	25/1	Badbury Rin'	(L)	OPE	3m	8	GF	*prom, ld 11-15th, prssd wnr aft til wknd 2 out*	2	21
144	9/2	Tweseldown	(R)	OPE	3m	9	GF	*(fav) alwys prom, ld 9th til mstk 11th, ld apr last, rdn out*	1	22
281	23/2	Charing	(L)	OPE	3m	12	G	*(fav) rear, f 2nd*	F	-
591	21/3	Newbury	(L)	HC	3m	7	GF	*cl up, pressed wnr straight, outpcd from 2 out.*	2	20
888	3/4	Aintree	(L)	HC	3m 1f	9	G	*soon ld, hit 10th, rdn and hdd after 4 out, soon outpcd.*	3	22
1288	30/4	Cheltenham	(L)	HC	2m 5f	10	GF	*held up, prog when mstk 11th, left 2nd 13th, rdn apr 3 out, unable to qckn from next.*	2	25
1463	11/5	Tweseldown	(R)	MXO	3m	5	GF	*made most til hrd rdn & hdd 14th, mstk nxt, onepcd 2 out*	2	21
1565	25/5	Kingston Bl'	(L)	OPE	3m	4	GF	*(fav) cls up, ld 10th, abt 4l clr frm 14th, rdn out*	1	21

Useful 2nd-class pointer; well-ridden 97; one paced; best easy 3m; should win again; G/F-S 23

ARDEEDALE (Irish) — **I** 227^{3}, **I** 310^{F}

ARDELL BOY b.g. 9 Cisto (FR) - Muses Doom by Fate J E Grey

1996 2(15),1(16)

300	1/3	Didmarton	(L)	RES	3m	23	G	*prssd ldr to 11th, onepcd frm 13th*	5	12

Maiden winner 96; lightly-raced & disappeared after fair run 97; best watched 16

ARDENT SPIRIT (Irish) — **I** 92^{R}, **I** 147^{6}, **I** 281^{5}, **I** 346^{5}

ARDESEE ch.g. 17 Le Coq D'Or - Katie Little by Nulli Secundus R J Peake

291	1/3	Warwick	(L)	HC	3 1/4m	6	G	*soon well bhnd, prog final cct, effort 6 out, struiggling next, soon btn.*	3	17
1096	18/4	Ayr	(L)	HC	3m 3f 110yds	7	G	*made most to 10th, soon wknd and p.u. before 15th.*	P	0

Gallant old stager but looks to have reached the end now 13

ARDFERT FOUNTAIN (Irish) — I 423^{P}, I 517^{P}

ARDFERT MINSTREL (Irish) — I 80^{3}, I 234^{4}

ARD NA GAOITHE (Irish) — I 58^{P}, I 158^{P}, I 203^{P}, I 294,

ARDNATAGGLE (Irish) — I 110^{3}, I 201^{5}, I 355^{2}, I 453^{2}, I 547, , I 565^{3}, I 590^{3}

ARD RUA ch.g. 6 Ardent Lodger - Tom's Niece by Right Honourable Gentl — Mrs A P Kelly

468	8/3	Eyton-On-Se'	(L)	RES	3m	11	G	*alwys rear, p.u. 13th*	P	0

No sign of ability yet 0

ARDTRIX (Irish) — I 458^{R}, I 472^{P}, I 525^{P}, I 556^{P}

ARE-OH ch.g. 8 Noalto - Miss Racine by Dom Racine (FR) — W Manners

1996 5(0),2(10),4(13)

342	1/3	Corbridge	(R)	MDO	3m	12	G	*(fav) rear, prog 6th, chsd ldrs til outpcd 4 out*	5	0

Always finishes but painfully slow & brief appearance 97 spells problems 12

AREYOUTHEREYET (Irish) — I 60^{P}, I 96^{P}, I 227^{6}, I 287^{P}

ARGIDEEN BONNIE (Irish) — I 26^{P}, I 167^{4}

ARGUABLY (Irish) — I 534^{2}

A RIGHT SET TWO ch.g. 5 Island Set (USA) - Super Sol by Rolfe (USA) — Jim Short

1118	19/4	Higham	(L)	MDO	3m	9	GF	*trckd ldrs, ld aft 7th, hdd apr 2 out, sn btn, promising*	2	13

Last of 2 finishers but looks the part & should have winning chances in 98 14

ARISE(IRE) b.g. 8 Rising - What's The Point by Major Point — J J Boulter

19	25/1	Badbury Rin'	(L)	OPE	3m	8	GF	*hld up, prog to trck ldng pair 11th, sn outpcd, kpt on 3 out*	3	20
154	14/2	Fakenham	(L)	HC	2m 5f 110yds	10	G	*held up, chsd ldrs 11th, ld 4 out, rdn 2 out, hdd near fin*	2	25
396	8/3	Barbury Cas'	(L)	CON	3m	9	G	*w.w. in tch, prog to 2nd 11th, rdn & btn apr 2 out*	2	23
495	14/3	Fakenham	(L)	HC	2m 5f 110yds	10	G	*(fav) hmpd start and slowly away, hdwy to track ldrs after 8th, ev ch 3 out, soon rdn, wknd after next.*	5	14

Quite able but non-stayer & hard to place; finished early; better chances under Rules; G-F 22

ARISTOCRATIC GOLD gr.g. 11 Nishapour (FR) - Lady Broke by Busted — J F Weldhen

1996 P(0),2(19),5(0),4(16),3(0),4(0),P(0),4(15)

238	22/2	Lemalla	(R)	LAD	3m	9	S	*alwys rear*	8	0
529	15/3	Wadebridge	(L)	LAD	3m	2	GF	*ld/disp til outpcd frm 2 out*	2	14
807	31/3	Wadebridge	(L)	LAD	3m	4	F	*alwys cls up, 3rd 9th, 6l 3rd whn u.r. 3 out*	U	-

1 win & 15 places in points; ungenuine & most unlikely to find another chance 12

ARITAM(IRE) b.g. 8 Aristocracy - Tamu by Malinowski (USA) — T D H Hughes

1996 **11(NH),P(NH)**

531	15/3	Wadebridge	(L)	MDO	3m	14	GF	*(fav) cls up to 12th, p.u. 14th*	P	0
741	29/3	Higher Kilw'	(L)	MDN	3m	12	GF	*hld up, prog 12th, cls 3rd 15th, disp nxt til f last*	F	-
1034	12/4	Lifton	(R)	MDN	3m	7	F	*(fav) made virt all til cght cls home, no ext*	2	14
1260	27/4	Black Fores'	(R)	MDO	3m	12	F	*(fav) chsng grp, 4th whn f 12th*	0	0
1400	5/5	High Bickin'	(R)	MDO	3m	14	G	*(Jt fav) c.o. bend apr 2nd*	C	-
1485	11/5	Ottery St M'	(L)	MDO	3m	13	G	*(Jt fav) alwys mid-div, nvr on trms, p.u. 2 out*	P	0
1583	26/5	Lifton	(R)	MDO	3m	11	G	*(fav) rear, prog 6th, chal 2 out, just outpcd flat*	2	13
1615	7/6	Umberleigh	(L)	MDO	3m	11	F	*(fav) t.d.e. trckd ldrs,ld 14th,clr & rdn apr 2 out,drvn out flat*	1	0

Very expensive to follow till winning season's final race; not 100% genuine; restrictecd chances slim .. 14

ARKAY ch.g. 7 Good Times (ITY) - Evening Crystal by Evening All — Russell C Kerry

1996 U(-),U(-),4(0),3(0)

68	2/2	Higham	(L)	MEM	3m	4	GF	*chsd wnr, lost tch 10th, t.o.*	2	0
197	15/2	Higham	(L)	MDO	3m	12	G	*immed rear, blnd 12th & rdr lost irns, t.o. & p.u. 15th*	P	0
275	22/2	Ampton	(R)	MDO	3m	10	G	*ld to 2nd & 4-6th, wknd 12th, t.o.*	6	0
503	15/3	Ampton	(R)	XX	3m	11	GF	*prom, chsd ldr 6-8th, sn wknd, t.o. whn blnd & u.r. 16th*	U	-

Yet to beat another horse in 4 completions; useless 0

ARLENESEOIN (Irish) — I 308^{2}, I 450^{1}

ARLEY GALE ch.m. 9 Scallywag - Lady Letitia by Le Bavard (FR) — Mrs A D Pritchard

1996 F(-),4(10),P(0)

211	16/2	Southwell P'	(L)	MDO	3m	15	GS	*hld up, mstk 7th, prog to 4th at 11th, wknd 14th, p.u. 3 out*	P	0

Placed in 96 but brief season 97; doubtful stayer 11

ARMAGRET b.g. 12 Mandrake Major - Friendly Glen by Furry Glen — B Kennedy

1996 6(0),1(24),5(13),1(22),3(16)

63	1/2	Horseheath	(R)	OPE	3m	5	GF	*hld up, prog 7th, chsd wnr 14th, nvr on trms*	2	21

124 9/2 Cottenham (R) OPE 3m 9 GF *rear til prog 10th, outpcd 14th, wknd 2 out* 5 15
501 15/3 Ampton (R) OPE 3m 4 GF *chsd ldrs, rmdr 5th, rdn appr 17th, wll btn 3 out* 3 16

Dual winner 96; consistent & safe but needs easy 3m; finished early; best watched at 13; G-S 19

ARM AH MAN(IRE) b.r.g. 7 Mandalus - Peacocks Call by Peacock (FR) Miss Elizabeth Robinson
1996 2(15)

418 8/3 Dalston (R) MDO 2 1/2m 10 GS *(Jt fav) hld up,jnd ldrs 9th,chal 3 out & agn flat,just faild* 2 15
948 6/4 Friars Haugh (L) MDO 3m 7 GF *(fav) slght ld frm 12th, forged clr frm 2 out* 1 15

Very lightly-raced but confirmed promise when winning; Restricted on cards if racing regularly 98 17

ARMED FORCE b.g. 10 Shernazar - Skittish (USA) by Far North (CAN) R S Eagleton

1446 10/5 Peper Harow (L) MDO 3m 7 GF *hung & jmpd rght, ld, clr to 8th, hdd 12th, wknd nxt, t.o.* 3 0

Disarmed 0

ARMET PRINCE b.g. 6 Ovac (ITY) - Verona Queen by Majestic Streak Mrs G R Dun

1331 3/5 Mosshouses (L) MEM 3m 5 F *last whn ref 2nd* R -

A very brief debut 0

ARM IN ARM b.g. 12 Pas de Seul - Social Partner by Sparkler Miss Rosalind Booth

882 1/4 Flagg Moor (L) MEM 3m 8 G 2 0

Just a potter over the stone walls in 97 0

ARMS DEALER ch.g. 5 Broadsword (USA) - Hot Hostess by Silly Season Mrs Eugenie Collie

574 16/3 Garnons (L) RES 3m 14 G *rear of mid-div whn f 9th* F -
853 31/3 Eyton-On-Se' (L) MDO 3m 13 GF *mid-div 9th, ran on onepce frm 4 out* 3 0

Well-beaten last of 3 when completing but should do better if ready in 98 10

AROUNDTHEVALLEY (Irish) — I 166[6], I 272, , I 389[2], I 488[3], I 544[P], I 548[P], I 591[P]

ARRAS-TINA b.m. 7 State Diplomacy (USA) - Arras Style by Nicholas Bill G E Mason
1996 F(-),F(-)

114 9/2 Wetherby Po' (L) MDO 3m 8 GF *(fav) keen hld, hld up, prog 11th, ev ch 2 out, kpt on flat* 2 15
209 16/2 Southwell P' (L) MDO 3m 7 GS *(fav) w.w. going wll, 2nd at 8th, ld apr 3 out, rdn nxt, all out* 1 17
477 9/3 Southwell P' (L) RES 3m 10 G *mid-div, mstk 8th, prog to chal 3 out, ld nxt, rdn & styd on* 1 18
1070 13/4 Whitwell-On' (R) XX 3m 9 G *mid-div, outpcd 9th, effrt 11th, strggling 14th* 4 14
1264 27/4 Southwell P' (L) INT 3m 9 G *mid-div, prog 8th, ev ch 3 out, not qckn* 3 18

Improved & enjoyed good season; best runs at Southwell; should upgrade; G/S-G/F 21

ARRIENZIO (Irish) — I 28[1], I 67[3], I 314[2], I 396[1]

ARROGANT LORD b.g. 5 Arctic Lord - Warham Fantasy by Barolo Mrs C Egalton
1996 **14(NH)**

102 8/2 Great Treth' (R) MDO 3m 8 GS *prom, lft cls 2nd 14th, no imp wnr aft 3 out* 2 13
458 8/3 Great Treth' (R) MDO 3m 15 S. *(fav) ld 10th, mstk nxt, cls up til wknd 3 out, p.u. apr last* P 0
795 31/3 Bishopsleigh (R) MDO 3m 12 G *(fav) w.w. prog 14th, ld 17th, sn clr, easily* 1 16

Bolted up in easy race & disappeared; Restricted likely if fit in 98; G-S 17

ARRYSU b.g. 6 Derring Rose - New Dawning by Deep Run Miss Sandra E Bowerman
1996 **5(NH),9(NH)**

208 16/2 Southwell P' (L) MDO 3m 9 GS *ld til aft 1st, chsd ldr, ld 12th, 15l clr 3 out, unchal* 1 17
474 9/3 Southwell P' (L) LAD 3m 12 G *ld/disp, just hdd 2 out, hit last, kpt on well* 2 20

Promising; just beaten last start; finished early; Ladies likely if fit 98; G-G/S, so far 22

ARTFUL ARTHUR b.g. 11 Rolfe (USA) - Light Of Zion by Pieces Of Eight Mrs Pat Beck
1996 **9(NH),P(NH),9(NH),6(NH),F(NH),5(NH),F(NH),5(NH),11(NH),6(NH),3(NH),P(NH)**

491 10/3 Taunton (R) HC 3m 8 G *held up, rdn after 12th, soon t.o..* 4 10
680 29/3 Towcester (R) HC 3m 1f 8 GF *patiently rdn, hit 7th, lost tch 6 out, t.o..* 6 11
1290 30/4 Cheltenham (L) HC 4m 1f 10 GF *bhnd, lost tch 14th, rdn and t.o. 17th, styd on from 23rd, no dngr.* 5 15

Aptly named; avoids exertion & lands rider in hot water for whip abuse; safely ignored 13

ARTHUR (Irish) — I 8[F], I 39[5], I 77[F], I 203[F], I 238[5], I 335[F]

ARTIC EXPLORER b.g. 6 Arctic Lord - Happy Wonder by Levanter Mrs B C Willcocks
1996 **P(NH)**

625 22/3 Kilworthy (L) MDN 3m 14 G *mid-div, 7th 16th, nrst fin* 4 10
1112 19/4 Flete Park (R) MDN 3m 13 GF *(fav) handy, disp 10-14th, mstk nxt, wknd rpdly, t.o.* 5 0

Fair debut but disappointed other start; worth another chance in 98 13

ARTISTIC PEACE b.m. 10 Prince Of Peace - Rising Artist by Mandamus Mrs Diane Jackson
1996 P(0),P(0),F(-),5(0),1(0),3(10)

236	22/2	Lemalla	(R)	INT	3m	12	S	*u.r. 4th*	U	-
313	1/3	Clyst St Ma'	(L)	RES	3m	10	HY	*mid-div, wll bhnd frm 12th*	3	0
528	15/3	Wadebridge	(L)	CON	3m	5	GF	*ld to 2nd, sn bhnd, some late prog*	3	14
804	31/3	Wadebridge	(L)	INT	3m	6	F	*wnt down early, alwys prom, ev ch 2 out, fdd aft*	4	15
954	6/4	Black Fores'	(R)	RES	3m	4	G	*ld to 14th, chsd wnr vainly aft*	2	11
1108	19/4	Flete Park	(R)	RES	3m	14	GF	*u.r. 1st*	U	-
1259	27/4	Black Fores'	(R)	RES	3m	7	F	*nvr seen wth ch, p.u. 3 out*	P	0

Won a joke contest in 96; ran better 97; likes Wadebridge; not threatening to win Restricted 13

ART'S ECHO(IRE) b.g. 8 Orchestra - Wesleyan by Great Nephew — C T Pogson

253	22/2	Brocklesby '	(L)	MDO	3m	6	G	*alwys last pair, outpcd frm 10th*	4	0
550	16/3	Garthorpe	(R)	MDO	3m	11	GF	*last frm 8th til ran out 12th*	r	-
1267	27/4	Southwell P'	(L)	MEM	3m	4	G	*last, stgglng 13th, styd on to tk 2nd nr fin*	2	0
1479	11/5	Garthorpe	(R)	MDO	3m	12	GS	*alwys rear, lost tch 12th, t.o. & p.u. 2 out*	P	0

Some promise 95; missed 96; no danger in 97 & will struggle to find a chance 10

ASANTE SANA gr.m. 6 Scallywag - Paddy Will by Dublin Taxi — Mrs E Weaver

1996 P(0),U(-),P(0),P(0)

254	22/2	Newtown	(L)	MEM	3m	6	G	*u.r. 2nd*	U	-
706	29/3	Upper Sapey	(R)	MDO	3m	15	GF	*strglld frm start, t.o. whn p.u. 15th*	P	0
1016	12/4	Bitterley	(L)	MDO	3m	14	GF	*ld til slw jmp 6th, wknd 8th, t.o. & p.u. 13th*	P	0
1151	19/4	Chaddesley '	(L)	MDO	3m	5	GF	*(vis) in tch, lft 2nd 6th, f 11th*	F	-
1240	26/4	Brampton Br'	(R)	MDO	3m	12	G	*(bl) mid-div whn blnd & u.r. 6th*	U	-
1330	3/5	Chaddesley '	(L)	MDN	3m	6	GF	*(bl) hld up, lft 3rd 6th, lost tch 11th, reluc aft, p.u. 3 out*	P	0
1460	11/5	Maisemore P'	(L)	MDO	3m	16	G	*(vis) n.j.w. alwys rear, t.o. 9th, p.u. 12th*	P	0
1528	17/5	Bredwardine	(R)	MDO	3m	17	G	*alwys rear, rdn & lost tch 12th, t.o. & p.u. 3 out*	P	0

Never completes & a leading contender for "worst pointer of the year" award 0

ASH BRAE (Irish) — I 122^{2}, I 214^{3}, I 331^{P}, I 436^{2}, I 508^{F}

ASHBURTON LORD (Irish) — I 20^{B}, I 42^{2}

ASHCOMBE VALLEY gr.g. 9 Almutanabbi - Lady Of Egremont by Hill Farmer — Major Ranulf Rayner

1996 P(0),P(0),F(-),2(14),F(-),4(0),6(0)

741	29/3	Higher Kilw'	(L)	MDN	3m	12	GF	*twrds rear, 7th at 13th, best work clsng stgs*	3	0
1112	19/4	Flete Park	(R)	MDN	3m	13	GF	*sn rear, t.o. 12t, p.u. 3 out, dsmntd*	P	0

Well-beaten when 3rd & problems after; prospects not good 11

ASHDREN b.g. 10 Lochnager - Stellaris by Star Appeal — J D Jemmeson

1996 **11(NH),13(NH)**

696	29/3	Stainton	(R)	OPE	3m	5	F	*settld rear, rddn 14th, sn outpcd, t.o. & p.u. 4 out*	P	0
1248	26/4	Easingwold	(L)	OPE	3m	8	GS	*in tch, 2nd 14th, fdd 4 out*	5	0
1407	5/5	Witton Cast'	(R)	OPE	3m	4	GS	*keen hold, last til mod prog into 3rd 12th, no ch frm 2 out*	3	12
1420	10/5	Easingwold	(L)	OPE	3m	5	GF	*rear, clsd up 7th, lft 2nd 14th, ev ch apr 2 out, sn btn*	2	17

Lightly-raced under Rules; ran passably last start but weak race needed; barely stays 15

ASHFIELD RUN (Irish) — I 485^{P}

ASHLEY HEIGHTS (Irish) — I 49^{P}, I 134^{2}, I 168^{3}

ASHPLANT (Irish) — I 101^{P}, I 154^{P}

ASHSHANORA (Irish) — I 493^{B}, I 514, , I 547^{P}

ASHTON COURT (Irish) — I 13^{P}, I 78^{4}

ASK ANTONY(IRE) gr.g. 7 Roselier (FR) - Lady Casita by Paddy's Stream — Jim Burns

216	16/2	Southwell P'	(L)	OPE	3m	12	GS	*prog 9th,lost plc 12th,rallied & ev ch 3 out,btn last,eased*	2	26
287	27/2	Huntingdon	(R)	HC	3m	13	GS	*(Co fav) patiently rdn, hdwy hfwy, chsd wnr from 2 out, kept on.*	2	29
778	31/3	Carlisle	(R)	HC	3 1/4m	14	G	*(fav) imp to ld after 3rd, joined final cct, hdd 5 out, rallied gamely from last.*	2	26
1072	13/4	Whitwell-On'	(R)	MXO	4m	21	G	*(fav) mid-div, prog to 3rd 13th, ld 18th, sn clr, imprssv*	1	28

Very useful; stays extra well; idles in front; sold to race under Rules & should win; Good 29

ASK FRANK b.g. 11 Seymour Hicks (FR) - West Bank by Martinmas — Mrs R A Price

1996 1(26),2(25),U(-),2(22),2(15)
256 22/2 Newtown (L) OPE 3m 17 G *hld up, prog 10th, outpcd frm 15th, no prog 3 out* 4 21

Good & consistent pointer at best but soon vanished 97; 1st time out best chance if appearing 98 21

ASK ME KINDLY(IRE) b.g. 9 Furry Glen - Kindly by Tarqogan G M Rowe
1996 **P(NH),2(NH),P(NH)**
101 8/2 Great Treth' (R) MDO 3m 9 GS *(fav) mstks, prom til outpcd by wnr frm 14th, no ch aft* 3 10
740 29/3 Higher Kilw' (L) MDN 3m 15 GF *(Jt fav) w.w. in tch, effrt 16th, strng run to ld aft last* 1 16
1039 12/4 Lifton (R) RES 3m 8 F *(fav) ld 1st til p.u. 7th, dismntd lame* P 0

Confirmed ability when winning but problem other start; best watched 15

AS SHARP AGAIN (Irish) — **I** 39, , **I** 84^{F}, **I** 261^{1}
ASTHEFELLASAYS (Irish) — **I** 322^{2}, **I** 379^{2}, **I** 444^{1}
ASTLEY JACK gr.g. 11 Belfort (FR) - Brigado by Brigadier Gerard R J Cotton
1996 P(0),U(-),P(0),F(-),0(0),P(0),P(0),U(-),P(0)
398 8/3 Llanfrynach (R) MEM 3m 6 G *ref 1st, cont, fin own time* 4 0
639 22/3 Howick (L) MDN 3m 15 GF *cls up, wknd 14th, 4th whn f 2 out* F -
878 1/4 Upton-On-Se' (R) XX 3m 11 GF *ref to race* 0 0

Maintains his own unique standards 0

ASTON WARRIOR ch.m. 10 Roman Warrior - Steeple Delight Vii Mrs Susan Corbett
38 26/1 Alnwick (L) MDO 3m 14 G *wll bhnd, t.o. last hlfwy, p.u. 15th* P 0
135 9/2 Alnwick (L) MDO 3m 12 G *wll bhnd frm 3rd, t.o. & p.u. 4 out* P 0
342 1/3 Corbridge (R) MDO 3m 12 G *bhnd, t.o. 10th, p.u. nxt* P 0

No sign of any ability yet 0

ASTOUND(IRE) ch.g. 6 Avocat - Clement Queen by Lucifer (USA) Miss Suzannah Cotterill
1996 3(15),P(0),2(17),3(0)
225 19/2 Folkestone (R) HC 2m 5f 10 S *bhnd till hdwy from 3 out, nvr near to chal.* 4 15

Dead 15

ASTOUNDED ch.g. 10 Radical - Swining Ears Vii L Thomas
1996 **4(NH),13(NH),5(NH),5(NH),F(NH)**
191 15/2 Erw Lon (L) CON 3m 13 G *alwys bhnd, t.o. & p.u. 14th* P 0
403 8/3 Llanfrynach (R) INT 3m 8 G *3rd/4th til onepcd frm 15th* 3 12
714 29/3 Llanvapley (L) CON 3m 15 GF *cls up, ld 12th-nxt, wknd qckly* 8 0
1007 12/4 St Hilary (R) OPE 3m 10 GF *alwys mid-div, ran on onepcd* 4 10
1226 26/4 Pyle (R) OPE 3m 6 GS *cls up til wknd frm 11th, t.o.* 3 0

Ex-Irish; lacks stamina & well-beaten all starts 97; unlikely to win at 11 12

ASTRAC TRIO(USA) ro.g. 7 Timeless Moment (USA) - Fairway Flag (USA) by Fairway Phantom (USA) Mrs M A Bowie
1996 3(17),U(-),3(17),3(16),2(15),4(10),1(20)
33 26/1 Alnwick (L) LAD 3m 12 G *j.w. prom, ld 9-10th & frm 12th, clr 3 out, jnd post* 1 23
231 22/2 Friars Haugh (L) LAD 3m 13 G *(Jt fav) ld/disp frm 11th, no ext apr last* 2 20

Ladies winner 96; ran very well both starts 97; can win again if fit 98; Good 22

ASTROMIS(IRE) b.m. 6 Torus - Fast Money by Captain James Tom Hayes
366 2/3 Garnons (L) MDO 2 1/2m 13 GS *chsng ldrs whn blnd & u.r. 10th* U -
1067 13/4 Maisemore P' (L) MDO 3m 8 GF *hld up, jmpd slwly 5th, blnd 15th, 3rd & chnc 2 out, no ext* 3 0
1238 26/4 Brampton Br' (R) MDO 3m 10 G *hld up, prog frm 16th, ld 2 out-last, wknd flat* 3 11
1528 17/5 Bredwardine (R) MDO 3m 17 G *trckd ldrs, prog to chal 3 out, ev ch apr nxt, wknd* 5 0
1577 26/5 Chaddesley ' (L) MDO 3m 11 F *(fav) w.w. prog to 3rd at 9th, strgglng 11th, wknd & p.u. 13th* P 0

Some ability but non-stayer at present & does not like Firm; hard to place 13

ATHABASCA (Irish) — **I** 180^{P}, **I** 330^{U}, **I** 372^{F}, **I** 436^{P}, **I** 507^{P}
ATHAS LIATH (Irish) — **I** 63^{P}
ATHESTON GAMBLE gr.g. 7 Olympic Casino - Dessert by Rice Pudding Mrs Cherry J Stratford
541 16/3 Erw Lon (L) MDN 3m 10 GF *trckd ldr, ld 14th, wknd & hdd aft 2 out* 2 10

Missed 96; ran passably only start 97 but time passing now 10

ATHNOWEN (Irish) — **I** 476^{P}, **I** 534^{P}, **I** 559,
AT THE CORSSROADS (Irish) — **I** 428^{P}
AT THE CROSSROADS (Irish) — **I** 294^{P}, **I** 453^{F}, **I** 493^{F}, **I** 550^{U}
ATTICALL LADY (Irish) — **I** 180^{F}
ATTLE b.g. 8 Oats - Knockananna by Torus J W Furness

1996 2(14),2(0),U(-),1(14),4(15),2(15)

32	26/1	Alnwick	(L)	RES	3m	11	G	*hld up, lost tch 11th, effrt 15th, nvr on trms*	6	0
118	9/2	Wetherby Po'	(L)	RES	3m	14	GF	*mid-div most of way, und pres & wknd 3 out*	5	11
266	22/2	Duncombe Pa'	(R)	RES	3m	19	G	*prom, ld 10th, disp nxt, hdd & onepcd 2 out*	3	15
337	1/3	Corbridge	(R)	RES	3m	11	G	*mid-div, prog 9th, ev ch 14th, wknd rpdly 2 out*	4	11
506	15/3	Dalton Park	(R)	CON	3m	16	GF	*mid-div, prog 10th, ev ch 16th, wknd rpdly apr 2 out*	6	11
615	22/3	Hutton Rudby	(L)	MEM	3m	8	GF	*chsd clr ldr, clsd up 7th, not qckn frm 3 out*	3	13
1069	13/4	Whitwell-On'	(R)	RES	3m	12	G	*alwys prom, chsd ldr 14th, onepcd nxt*	3	12
1101	19/4	Hornby Cast'	(L)	RES	3m	14	G	*alwys chsng ldrs, wknd 3 out*	6	12
1348	3/5	Gisburn	(R)	RES	3m	10	GF	*wth ldrs whn u.r. 5th*	U	-
1475	11/5	Garthorpe	(R)	XX	3m	13	GS	*hld up, 8th hlfwy, nvr trbld ldrs*	6	0

Maiden winner 96; safe but slow & runs out of gas; Restricted continue to prove elusive 13

AUCHENDOLLY(IRE) b.g. 7 Mandalus - Advance Notice by Le Bavard (FR) Christopher Sporborg

1996 2(10),3(0),3(10),3(0),1(14),3(0),4(0)

28	26/1	Marks Tey	(L)	RES	3m	9	GF	*ld 2nd-3rd, outpcd 12th, lft 2nd 3 out, ld flat, hdd nr fin*	2	15
122	9/2	Cottenham	(R)	MEM	3m	6	GF	*(fav) ld to 5th, prssd ldr aft, ld 2 out, rdn out*	1	13
324	1/3	Marks Tey	(L)	RES	3m	16	G	*trckd ldrs til rdn & outpcd 14th, no ch frm 16th*	5	10
503	15/3	Ampton	(R)	XX	3m	11	GF	*alwys rr, 10th whn u.r. 9th*	U	-
1278	27/4	Fakenham P-'	(L)	RES	3m	11	G	*alwys bhnd, last & mstk 8th, nvr on trms*	5	0
1379	5/5	Northaw	(L)	RES	3m	6	F	*chsd ldrs, lft 2nd appr 8th, ld appr 3 out, sn clr,*	1	15
1608	1/6	Dingley	(R)	INT	3m	11	GF	*last & wll bhnd, t.o. hlfwy, p.u. 3 out*	P	0

Maiden winner 96; modest & found 2 poor races; changed hands after 3rd race; hard to win again 13

AUCTION LAW(NZ) ch.g. 13 Pevero - High Plateau (NZ) by Oncidium Ron Whiston

1996 4(17),P(0),4(0),3(13),2(21),3(15),3(17)

86	2/2	Wolverhampt'	(L)	OPE	3m	9	GS	*ld to 3rd, wknd 11th, t.o. & p.u. 3 out*	P	0
201	15/2	Weston Park	(L)	OPE	3m	16	G	*mid-div, nvr rchd ldrs*	6	0
330	1/3	Eaton Hall	(R)	CON	3m	16	GS	*cls up to 10th, fdd, onepce frm 4 out*	6	0
465	8/3	Eyton-On-Se'	(L)	OPE	3m	13	G	*(bl) mid to rear 9th, cls order 12th, short lived efft,p.u. 4 out*	P	0
726	29/3	Sandon	(L)	CON	3m	8	GF	*prog 5 out, short-lived effrt, sn btn*	6	0
849	31/3	Eyton-On-Se'	(L)	OPE	3m	7	GF	*alwys in tch, disp 2nd 3 out, not qckn frm 2 out*	3	15

Old plodder who is well past his sell-by date now 12

AUGHNABROGA (Irish) — **I** 515[P], **I** 564[4]

AUGHNACLOY ROSE gr.g. 9 Derring Rose - Tower Road by Polaroid D Etheridge

1996 8(0),P(0),6(0),4(0),5(0),2(10),3(0),1(13)

65	1/2	Horseheath	(R)	RES	3m	10	GF	*sn bhnd, 8th & no ch whn u.r. 15th*	U	-
198	15/2	Higham	(L)	RES	3m	14	G	*immed last, alwys bhnd, rdr fin wth no irns*	5	0
320	1/3	Marks Tey	(L)	MEM	3m	4	G	*not fluent, in tch to 13th, sn bhnd, t.o.*	4	0
597	22/3	Horseheath	(R)	RES	3m	8	F	*t.o. 3rd, p.u. aft 13th*	P	0
801	31/3	Marks Tey	(L)	CON	3m	8	F	*v.s.a., t.o. 2nd, cont in own time*	6	0
1114	19/4	Higham	(L)	RES	3m	5	GF	*last early, 4tha t 13th, ran on 3 out, nrst fin*	3	12
1309	3/5	Cottenham	(R)	RES	3m	4	F	*last frm 7th, t.o. 13th, tk poor 3rd apr last*	3	0
1430	10/5	Marks Tey	(L)	CON	3m	7	G	*rear whn p.u. 3rd, stirrup broke*	P	0
1567	25/5	Kingston Bl'	(L)	RES	3m	8	GF	*blnd 7th & drppd last, t.o. 13th, p.u. 2 out*	P	0
1605	1/6	Dingley	(R)	RES	3m	13	GF	*mstk 3rd & immed bhnd, t.o. & p.u. 6th*	P	0

Maiden winner 96; no hopes of a follow-up now 0

AUGHRIM SLOPES ch.m. 10 Le Bavard (FR) - Fine Artist Paul Rackham

72	2/2	Higham	(L)	INT	3m	4	GF	*s.s. rear whn mstk 3rd, prog 12th, mstk nxt, wknd aft 4 out*	4	0
193	15/2	Higham	(L)	CON	3m	14	G	*mid-div, chsd ldrs und pres frm 15th, no ch whn p.u. 2 out*	P	0

Dead 17

AUNTIE CHRIS ch.m. 7 Bold Owl - Basin Street by Tudor Melody Patrick Gee

1073	13/4	Whitwell-On'	(R)	MDO	2 1/2m 88yds	17	G	*mid-div, wknd 11th, t.o. & p.u. 2 out*	P	0
1262	27/4	Southwell P'	(L)	MDO	3m	15	G	*prom, ev ch 3 out, onepcd*	3	11
1353	4/5	Dingley	(R)	MDO	2 1/2m	9	G	*chsd ldr 3rd, ld 12th-3 out, rddn & onepcd aft*	2	12
1589	31/5	Market Rasen	(R)	HC	2 3/4m 110yds	10	GF	*whipped round and u.r. start.*	U	-
1609	1/6	Dingley	(R)	MDO	3m	14	GF	*ran in sntchs, 3rd at 10th, sn lost plc, no dang frm 15th*	4	0

Has some ability but ungenuine & a win should continue to prove elusive 12

AUNTIE FAY(IRE) ch.m. 6 Fayruz - Auntie Ponny by Last Fandango S P Hudson

1996 F(-),**R(-)**,P(0),P(0),P(0),P(0)

505	15/3	Dalton Park	(R)	MEM	3m	6	GF	*not fluent, alwys strgglng, t.o. & p.u. 15th*	P	0
860	31/3	Charm Park	(L)	MDO	3m	12	F	*s.s. mstks 1st & 2nd, ref 3rd*	R	-

No completions in 8 starts 96/7 & no intention of breaking the sequence 0

AUTHORSHIP(USA) b or br.g. 11 Balzac (USA) - Piap (USA) by L'aiglon (USA) G M Turnwell

1996 **F(NH)**

786 31/3 Aldington (L) OPE 3m 1 HD *walked over* 1 0

966 6/4 Penshurst (L) CON 3m 7 F *ld 9th, chal 3 out, blndrd & hdd last, not rcvrd* 5 13

Very lightly-raced these days; unlucky 2nd start but form weak; best watched if appearing at 12 15

AUTONOMOUS b.g. 12 Milford - Mandrian by Mandamus — Mrs Kate Whitehead

1996 1(10),2(16),**R(-)**,4(19)

1205 26/4 Clifton On ' (L) CON 3m 13 GS *cls up in 3rd/4th for 2m, fdd, p.u. 4 out* P 0

Members winner 96; brief appearance 97 could spell the end 11

AUTUMN DAY (Irish) — **I** 366^{F}

AUTUMN FERN (Irish) — **I** 162^{P}

AUTUMN GREEN(IRE) ch.g. 9 Le Moss - Judy Green by Green God — S J P Furniss

1996 P(0),4(0),4(11),4(0),3(14),1(15),3(12)

223 16/2 Heythrop (R) RES 3m 19 G *prom til wknd 14th, sn bhnd* 5 0

332 1/3 Eaton Hall (R) RES 3m 18 GS *wth ldrs to hlfwy, fdd, p.u. 4 out* P 0

671 23/3 Eaton Hall (R) INT 3 3/4m 8 GF *(vis) mid-div, prog to 2nd 3 out, ran on und pres, just hld* 2 17

976 8/4 Heythrop (R) OPE 4m 7 F *(vis) chsd ldr 4-7th, sn lst pl, no ch & j.r. 13th, p.u. 20th* P 0

1237 26/4 Brampton Br' (R) RES 3m 13 G *(vis) n.j.w. alwys rear, p.u. last* P 0

1348 3/5 Gisburn (R) RES 3m 10 GF *(fav) chsng grp, n.j.w. blnd 8th & 12th, sn rear* 6 0

Maiden winner 96; visor worked 1st time but not after; stays but unlikely to win again 14

AVONDALE ILLUSION (Irish) — **I** 14^{5}, **I** 141^{1}

AVOSTAR ch.g. 10 Buckskin (FR) - Starcat by Avocat — R G Russell

151 12/2 Lingfield (L) HC 3m 13 HY *ld, jmpd right from 12th, hdd last.* 2 26

379 4/3 Leicester (R) HC 3m 7 G *prom, lost pl 7th, bhnd when p.u. before 3 out.* P 0

680 29/3 Towcester (R) HC 3m 1f 8 GF *ld to 7th, led 9th to 11th, mstk 4 out, led approching 2 out, hrd rdn run-in, hdd near fin.* 2 22

1098 19/4 Bangor (L) HC 3m 110yds 9 G *nvr going well, alwys bhnd, no ch when f last.* F -

Useful winning H/Chaser 95; missed 96; not as good now & ran poorly twice; best watched 21

AVRIL SHOWERS b.m. 8 Vital Season - April's Crook by Crozier — Mrs R Atkinson

1996 2(18),3(17),1(20),2(18),3(13),1(21),4(12),2(18)

310 1/3 Clyst St Ma' (L) INT 3m 9 HY *j.w. ld til jnd 13th, clr aft nxt, ran on well* 1 20

558 16/3 Ottery St M' (L) INT 3m 6 G *ld til slw jmp 3 out, rallied aft nxt, not qckn* 3 22

687 29/3 Little Wind' (R) MEM 3m 5 GF *(fav) chsd ldr 10th, ld 14th-16th, ld 2 out, pshd out* 1 19

1023 12/4 Badbury Rin' (L) OPE 3m 2 F *not fluent, immmed outpcd, styd on onepce frm 15th* 2 15

1273 27/4 Little Wind' (R) INT 3m 2 GF *(fav) made all, shkn up 2 out, rdn & kpt on apr last* 1 19

1371 5/5 Cotley Farm (L) MXO 3m 2 GF *(fav) disp to 9th, trckd ldr til ld 3 out, ran on wll, easily* 1 18

1496 14/5 Cothelstone (L) CON 3m 9 GF *(fav) prom til lost plc 10th, nvr on trms wth ldrs aft* 4 15

1596 31/5 Bratton Down (L) OPE 4m 5 F *ld to 7th, cls up til lost tch 20th, no ch aft* 4 10

Solid, consistent & safe; veteran-ridden; 6 wins, 10 places - all starts 96/7; H/Chase possible; Any 23

AWALKINTHECLOUDS (Irish) — **I** 23^{P}, **I** 65^{5}, **I** 94^{P}, **I** 153^{P}

AWBEG ROVER (Irish) — **I** 2^{3}, **I** 205^{3}, **I** 244^{1}

A WINDY CITIZEN(IRE) ch.m. 8 Phardante (FR) - Candolcis by Candy Cane — Mrs J A Thomson

1996 P(0),**1(22),2(22),F(-),2(27),3(21),2(23),3(24),U(-),7(0),5(12)**

381 4/3 Leicester (R) HC 2m 1f 13 G *(Jt fav) held up, mstk 5th, hdwy 5 out, ld 2 out, rdn out.* 1 22

679 26/3 Ascot (R) HC 2m 3f 110yds 9 G *tracking ldrs when f 9th, dead.* F -

Dead 23

AYLESBURY BEAU (Irish) — **I** 21^{4}, **I** 63^{3}

AYLESFORD b.g. 6 Efisio - My Myra by Auction Ring (USA) — Miss S Willis

1996 P(0),5(0)

55 1/2 Kingston Bl' (L) CON 3m 15 GF *bhnd whn f 8th* F -

220 16/2 Heythrop (R) OPE 3m 20 G *alwys bhnd, t.o. 12th* 11 0

369 2/3 Mollington (R) MEM 3m 13 G *mid-div, wknd 11th, t.o. & p.u. last* P 0

393 8/3 Barbury Cas' (L) OPE 3m 7 G *rear, outpcd 10th, no ch 12th, fin 4th, promoted* 3 0

758 29/3 Kimble (L) OPE 3m 6 GF *ld 2nd-4th, wknd 10th, last whn p.u. aft 12th* P 0

Shows no real ability 0

BABIL b.g. 12 Welsh Pageant - Princess Eboli by Brigadier Gerard — Mrs C Hicks

1996 **P(0),6(18)**

490 10/3 Stratford (L) HC 3m 12 G *prom to 10th, bhnd when p.u. before 4 out.* P 0

874 1/4 Uttoxeter (L) HC 2m 7f 9 GF *prom till wknd 7th, t.o. when p.u. before 9th.* P 0

Ran one fair race 96 but nothing in 97 & may be finished now 13

BABS WHO (Irish) — I 397^{U}, I 528^{4}

BABY JAKE (Irish) — I 451^{2}, I 528^{1}, I 592^{F}

BABY JAMIE (Irish) — I 180^{1}, I 252^{1}

BACHELOR-CARRASCO(IRE) b or br.g. 6 Le Bavard (FR) - Harvull by Harwell — O Brolly

796 31/3 Marks Tey (L) MDO 3m 6 F *bhnd early, prog to 3rd 6th, chsd wnr frm 15th, wknd nxt* 2 0

Last of 2 finishers in weak race - may do better 10

BACK IN A FLASH ch.g. 8 St Columbus - Julie de Fortisson by Entanglement — Peter Nichols

217 16/2 Heythrop (R) MEM 3m 4 G *mstks, chsd wnr 12th, chal & blnd 3 out, not rcvr* 2 0
374 2/3 Mollington (R) MDN 3m 14 G *alwys prom, chsd wnr 12-15th, ev ch 2 out, no ext* 3 13

Lightly-raced; ran well both starts but finished early; should go close if fit 98 14

BACK THE ROAD(IRE) ch.g. 9 Mister Lord (USA) - Salvation Sue by Mon Capitaine — M Mann

1996 P(0),P(0),P(0),P(0),2(16),**4(16)**,1(20),1(0),**U(-)**

86 2/2 Wolverhampt' (L) OPE 3m 9 GS *w.w. prog to jn wnr 11th, wknd rpdly apr nxt, p.u. 3 out* P 0
330 1/3 Eaton Hall (R) CON 3m 16 GS *mid-div, nvr gng wll, no ch whn p.u. 3 out* P 0
465 8/3 Eyton-On-Se' (L) OPE 3m 13 G *w.w. in rear, prog frm 13th, 2nd 2 out, ran on wll* 2 20
725 29/3 Sandon (L) OPE 3m 4 GF *hrd hld in rear, some prog 14th, nrst fin, b.b.v.* 4 12
1086 14/4 Southwell (L) HC 3m 110yds 11 G *held up, nvr near ldrs.* 5 0
1176 20/4 Sandon (L) OPE 3m 5 GF *(fav) made all, set gd pace, breather 14th, ran on und pres 2out* 1 20

Open winner 96; well-ridden to win weak race but usually outclassed; tubed & b.b.v. once 19

BACK WITHAVENGANCE (Irish) — I 55^{P}, I 95^{F}, I 409^{6}, I 497^{5}

BADALKA (Irish) — I 21^{P}, I 130^{P}, I 402^{4}

BADBURY PRINCE b.g. 11 Le Bavard (FR) - Ellen Mavourneen by Tiepolo II — A J Chamberlain

1996 **P(NH)**

179 15/2 Larkhill (R) CON 3m 12 G *alwys rear, last & t.o. whn p.u. 12th* P 0

Of no account 0

BADGER BEER b.g. 5 Town And Country - Panda Pops by Cornuto — Mrs R H Woodhouse

20 25/1 Badbury Rin' (L) MDN 3m 9 GF *mstk 2nd, last pair, wll bhnd 13th, ran on frm 2 out* 4 0
182 15/2 Larkhill (R) MDO 3m 12 G *alwys mid-div, last & no ch whn f 15th* F -

Some promise on debut but vanished after fall; should do better if fit 98 12

BAD INFLUENCE (Irish) — I 190^{R}, I 303, , I 456^{F}

BAGALINO(USA) ch.g. 7 Lyphard (USA) - Bag Of Tunes (USA) by Herbager — Miss Jane Fellows

86 2/2 Wolverhampt' (L) OPE 3m 9 GS *ld 5th, made rest, drew clr aft 3 out, ran on well, easily* 1 24
432 8/3 Upton-On-Se' (R) MXO 3m 7 G *(fav) made all, drew clr 3 out, eased flat* 1 25
1014 12/4 Bitterley (L) OPE 3m 9 GF *(fav) cls up whn wd aft 3rd, chsd ldr, ld 15th, hdd & no ext flat* 2 22

Flat/hurdles winner; very lightly raced; able but needs give; can win more if fit 98 26

BAGOTS PARK ro.g. 8 Alias Smith (USA) - Newfield Green by Deep Run — S J Leadbetter

1996 3(0),3(13),P(0),6(0)

233 22/2 Friars Haugh (L) MDO 3m 13 G *prom early, bhnd by 9th, p.u. 3 out* P 0
342 1/3 Corbridge (R) MDO 3m 12 G *prom til outpcd 12th, t.o. & p.u. 2 out* P 0

Placed twice in 96 but brief season of no promise in 97 0

BAILE AN DAINGAN (Irish) — I 540^{P}

BAILE STAIBHNE (Irish) — I 332^{P}

BAILEYS GATE (Irish) — I 231^{P}, I 316^{F}

BAKMALAD ch.g. 11 Kambalda - Joyspir by Master Buck — N L Stevens

1996 2(17),4(14),3(18),3(16),3(12)

701 29/3 Upper Sapey (R) RES 3m 6 GF *disp 3rd 1st ctt, strggld to go pce hlfwy, no ext frm 15th* 4 0
1080 13/4 Guilsborough (L) RES 3m 11 GF *sn rear, rdn 9th, lost tch 13th, p.u. 16th* P 0
1160 20/4 Mollington (R) INT 3m 9 GF *chsd ldrs, jmpd slwly 6th & wknd rpdly, p.u. 10th* P 0
1556 24/5 Bassaleg (R) RES 3m 13 G *rear,lost tch ldrs 12th,ran on 15th,ev ch flat,nt qckn fin* 3 14
1605 1/6 Dingley (R) RES 3m 13 GF *f 1st* F -

Placed in 9 of 13 races 95-7 but not interested now & Restricted most unlikely 12

BALALTRAMA (Irish) — I 419^{P}, I 519^{P}, I 561^{P}

BALANCE b.g. 9 Balinger - Dance Partner by Manicou — Richard J Smith

1996 F(-),P(0),1(14),U(-),2(16),3(17)

45 1/2 Larkhill (R) RES 3m 14 GF *mstk 2nd, hmpd nxt, cls up whn b.d. 5th* B -
300 1/3 Didmarton (L) RES 3m 23 G *prom, ld 13th, clr 2 out, 5l up whn f last* F 21
516 15/3 Larkhill (R) RES 3m 7 GF *(fav) many mstks,in tch,effrt to chs wnr 2 out,no imp,mstk last* 2 15

826 31/3 Lockinge (L) RES 3m 4 F *(fav) trckd ldrs, ld 12th, clr 15th, easily* 1 19

Maiden winner 96; quite able; sometimes jumps badly; Intermediate if fit 98; G-F 20

BALASANI(FR) b.g. 11 Labus (FR) - Baykara by Direct Flight J G O'Neill

1996 **7(NH),9(NH),12(NH),1(NH)**

983 12/4 Ascot (R) HC 3m 110yds 14 GF *mstk 1st, bhnd till styd on from 2 out, nvr nrr.* 4 17
1412 7/5 Uttoxeter (L) HC 3 1/4m 10 GS *mstk 6th, last when b.d. 8th.* B -

Former top staying hurdler; failed to take to H/Chasing 19

BALDHU CHANCE ch.g. 9 Chaparly (FR) - Galla Currency by Galeopsis Terry Long

1996 3(13),4(0),S(-),1(15),P(0),1(19),1(17),4(10),F(-),3(12),5(15)

52 1/2 Wadebridge (L) INT 3m 4 G *made virt all, hld on wll whn chal* 1 18
96 8/2 Great Treth' (R) CON 3m 7 GS *prom, ld 12-14th, wknd rpdly & p.u. 16th* P 0
237 22/2 Lemalla (R) CON 3m 13 S *prog 11th, cls 3rd whn blnd & lost plc 3 out, ran on agn flt* 3 17
493 12/3 Newton Abbot (L) HC 2m 5f 110yds 11 HY *in tch to 9th, t.o. when p.u. before 4 out.* P 0
803 31/3 Wadebridge (L) MEM 3m 3 F *(fav) ld 5th, gd jmp 7th, alwys in comm aft, comf* 1 16
1033 12/4 Lifton (R) CON 3m 6 F *ld 3rd til slppd up bnd apr 4th* S -
1243 26/4 Bratton Down (L) OPE 3m 6 GS *chsd wnnr 4-14th, fdd frm nxt* 4 0
1341 3/5 Flete Park (R) OPE 3m 5 G *ld/disp to 10th, sn wknd, t.o. 3 out* 3 12
1580 26/5 Lifton (R) OPE 3m 8 G *ld 1st, sn hdd, chsng grp aft, fdd & p.u. 4 out* P 0

Modest but won 5 of 20 races 96/7 (4 at Wadebridge); should find another small chance; Any 18

BALI TENDER ch.g. 6 Balidar - Highest Tender by Prince Tenderfoot (USA) Terry Wharton

1996 **7(NH),U(NH)**

13 25/1 Cottenham (R) MDO 3m 10 GF *chsd ldr to 15th, grad wknd* 5 0

Well-beaten but not disgraced only start; vanished after 10

BALLAD(IRE) b.g. 5 Salluceva - Song Of Love by Raise You Ten G H Barber

1281 27/4 Fakenham P-' (L) MDO 3m 8 G *in tch til blnd & u.r. 10th* U -
1431 10/5 Marks Tey (L) MDO 3m 6 G *rear, prog to chs ldrs 14th, outpcd 16th, styd on 2 out* 3 0

Close 3rd in very bad race 2nd start; should do better but needs to 11

BALLAD SONG br.g. 14 Ballad Rock - Apt by Ragusa Mrs Caroline Chadney

878 1/4 Upton-On-Se' (R) XX 3m 11 GF *ld to 4th, wknd frm 8th, wll bhnd whn u.r 14th* U -
1202 25/4 Ludlow (R) HC 2 1/2m 5 GF *ld to apr 10th, 2nd when blnd badly 5 out, weakening when hit next, mstk 3 out, soon p.u..* P 0

No longer of any account 0

BALLAMON BOY (Irish) — I 482^{P}, I 540^{4}

BALLINACLASH PRIDE (Irish) — I 26^{5}, I 62^{4}

BALLINAFAUNA (Irish) — I 485^{F}

BALLINAVARY VI (Irish) — I 210^{5}, I 289^{6}, I 371^{P}, I 413^{4}

BALLINAVEEN BRIDGE (Irish) — I 199^{3}, I 229^{3}, I 276^{4}, I 298^{3}, I 402^{1}, I 451^{F}, I 511^{5}, I 612^{1}

BALLINDANTE (Irish) — I 70^{2}, I 111^{2}, I 212^{P}, I 292^{5}, I 431^{4}, I 506^{3}

BALLINMUSIC (Irish) — I 468^{P}, I 508^{P}, I 557^{P}, I 608^{2}, I 611^{5}

BALLINVUSKIG LADY (Irish) — I 6^{2}, I 139^{4}, I 238^{1}

BALLYALLIA CASTLE(IRE) ch.g. 8 Carlingford Castle - Clonsilla by Clever Fella A F J J Moss

1996 **6(NH),12(NH),4(NH),10(NH),4(NH),3(NH)**

29 26/1 Marks Tey (L) MDN 3m 10 GF *trckd ldrs, ld 3 out, hit last, hld on und pres* 1 16
270 22/2 Ampton (R) MEM 3m 8 G *(fav) ld to 3rd & 5-15th, rdn 2 out, ran on to ld run in.* 1 17
502 15/3 Ampton (R) RES 3m 5 GF *(fav) trkd ldrs, outpcd 10th, clsd 14th, ld 2 out, styd on strngly* 1 19
708 29/3 High Easter (L) CON 3m 3 F *chsd ldrs, outpcd & pshd alng 11th, no ch frm 15th, t.o.* 3 0
1286 29/4 Huntingdon (R) HC 3m 10 G *chsd ldrs till blnd badly 12th, soon well bhnd, styd on from 3 out, nvr nrr.* 4 17
1435 10/5 Marks Tey (L) INT 3m 8 G *(fav) chsd ldr,prog to ld 4 out,prssd 2 out,outjmpd last,ran on* 2
1501 16/5 Folkestone (R) HC 3 1/4m 10 G *trckd ldrs, 5th when f 7th.* F -

Poor hurdler; improved in points & found fair races; stays; one paced; should win Confined; G-F 20

BALLYANDREW b.g. 12 Leading Man - Dunoon Court by Dunoon Star A H B Hodge

1996 **U(-),5(10)**,5(10)

489 10/3 Plumpton (L) HC 3m 1f 110yds 7 GS *ld to 7th, lost tch and rdn 13th, p.u. after next.* P 0

Retired 16

BALLY BANTER (Irish) — I 568^{P}

BALLYBEGGAN BOY (Irish) — I 206^{P}, I 301^{4}, I 337^{3}, I 403^{3}, I 452^{3}, I 512^{P}, I 593^{P}, I 610^{2}

BALLYBEGGAN LADY (Irish) — I 102^{3}, I 138^{F}, I 207^{P}, I 305^{2}, I 356^{F}, I 443^{4}, I 599^{1}

BALLYBEGGAN PARSON(IRE) b.g. 8 The Parson - Papadrim — P E Mills

1996 F(-),P(0),1(15),P(0),P(0)

222	16/2	Heythrop	(R)	RES	3m	17	G	*prom, blnd 9th, sn wknd, t.o. & p.u. 15th*	P	0
468	8/3	Eyton-On-Se'	(L)	RES	3m	11	G	*disp to 3rd, cls up in tch 12th, grdly wknd, p.u. 2 out*	P	0
670	23/3	Eaton Hall	(R)	RES	3m	15	GF	*prom to hlfwy, lost tch ldrs 4 out*	7	0
940	6/4	Tabley	(R)	RES	3m	9	G	*chsd ldr,blndrd 4th & 8th,sn rddn & lost plc,t.o. & p.u.13th*	P	0

Maiden winner 96; made mistakes & no show in 97; ground against; best watched 12

BALLYBOLLEN (Irish) — I 177^{P}, I 363^{P}, I 369^{3}, I 435^{1}

BALLY BOY b.g. 5 Green Adventure (USA) - Gold Willow by Goldfella — M R Watkins

366	2/3	Garnons	(L)	MDO	2 1/2m	13	GS	*nvr rchd ldrs, t.o. & p.u. 3 out*	P	0
641	22/3	Howick	(L)	MDN	3m	9	GF	*rear, prog to 2nd at 16th, chal last, hld flat*	2	10
1015	12/4	Bitterley	(L)	MDO	3m	12	GF	*mid-div, p.u. sddnly aft 3rd*	P	0
1238	26/4	Brampton Br'	(R)	MDO	3m	10	G	*chsd ldrs, ev ch 15th, wknd aft nxt*	6	0
1527	17/5	Bredwardine	(R)	MDO	3m	13	G	*prom, mstk 12th, lost plc & p.u. 15th*	P	0

2nd in a terrible race & insufficient stamina yet - may do better 11

BALLYBRIKEN CASTLE (Irish) — I 157^{P}, I 229^{2}, I 415^{3}, I 494^{P}, I 530^{3}, I 573^{P}

BALLYCAR PRINCESS (Irish) — I 201^{P}, I 277^{P}, I 453^{P}, I 547,

BALLYCARSHA (Irish) — I 411^{P}

BALLYCASTLE BAY (Irish) — I 123^{2}, I 254^{3}

BALLYDAVID (Irish) — I 114^{P}, I 128^{2}, I 210, , I 248,

BALLYDAY DAZY (Irish) — I 460^{P}

BALLYDAY STEP (Irish) — I 64^{6}, I 188^{P}

BALLYDESMOND(IRE) br.g. 6 Forties Field (FR) - Tony's Mount by Choral Society — Christopher Sporborg

12	25/1	Cottenham	(R)	RES	3m	3	GF	*(fav) chsd ldr 8th, chal & hit 3 out, ld last, hdd nr fin*	2	14
274	22/2	Ampton	(R)	RES	3m	10	G	*(fav) made virt all, rdn & styd on strngly frm 2 out*	1	17
486	9/3	Tweseldown	(R)	XX	3m	3	G	*(fav) chsd ldr, ld 15th, mstk 3 out, rdn & hng lft flat, all out*	1	14
802	31/3	Marks Tey	(L)	INT	3m	4	F	*held up,prog ld 6th,hdd nxt,und pres 11th,ev ch 3 out,outpcd*	2	16
1277	27/4	Fakenham P-'	(L)	CON	3m	10	G	*ld to 3rd, chsd wnr til rdn & btn apr 2 out*	3	17

Irish Maiden winner 96; modest, one paced & consistent 97; may find Intermediate on long track; G-S 18

BALLYGAR BOY(IRE) b.g. 7 Roselier (FR) - Knock Off — James Buckle

1996 **9(NH),P(NH)**

198	15/2	Higham	(L)	RES	3m	14	G	*blnd & u.r. 1st*	U	-
324	1/3	Marks Tey	(L)	RES	3m	16	G	*ld til apr 11th, wknd qckly, t.o. & p.u. 14th*	P	0
503	15/3	Ampton	(R)	XX	3m	11	GF	*ld to 10th, grad lst pl, no ch frm 16th*	5	0
799	31/3	Marks Tey	(L)	OPE	3m	5	F	*chsd ldr til mstk & u.r. 4th*	U	-

Ex-Irish; well-beaten only completion & no prospects 0

BALLYGOWAN BEAUTY (Irish) — I 85^{P}, I 551^{2}, I 589^{2}

BALLYHAMAGE(IRE) br.g. 9 Mandalus - Deep Slaney by Deep Run — J T Evans

1018	12/4	Bitterley	(L)	MDO	3m	13	GF	*(fav) cls 4th at 6th, prog to ld whn f 12th*	F	-
1203	26/4	Worcester	(L)	HC	2m 7f 110yds	10	S	*f 1st.*	F	-

Going well when falling first start & may atone if fit 98 13

BALLYHASTY LADY(IRE) ch.m. 7 Castle Keep - Ariawell by Harwell — Trevor Woodman

630	22/3	Kilworthy	(L)	RES	3m	16	G	*bhnd til p.u. apr 15th*	P	0
794	31/3	Bishopsleigh	(R)	MDO	3m	12	G	*rear whn ref 6th*	R	-
1246	26/4	Bratton Down	(L)	MDO	3m	16	GS	*nvr trbld ldrs, p.u. aft 12th*	P	0
1399	5/5	High Bickin'	(R)	MDO	3m	12	G	*prog 7th, 3rd whn blnd 11th, p.u. nxt*	P	0
1520	17/5	Bratton Down	(L)	MDO	3m	17	GS	*rear, pckd 2nd, t.o. whn tried to ref & u.r. 12th*	U	-

Yet to complete & looks highly suspect 0

BALLYHEST FOUNTAIN (Irish) — I 45^{P}, I 48^{P}, I 91^{3}, I 143^{P}, I 305^{P}, I 383^{F}, I 445^{P}, I 479^{2}, I 538^{2}, I 547^{4}, I 570^{3}, I 599, , I 611^{1}

BALLYHOOLY BELLE(IRE) b.m. 7 Flower Robe - Maybe Yes by Crozier — R Mason

186	15/2	Erw Lon	(L)	MDN	3m	13	G	*8s-4s, prom til 3rd & btn 13th, p.u. 15th*	P	0
639	22/3	Howick	(L)	MDN	3m	15	GF	*(fav) mid-div, no prog whn p.u. 13th*	P	0
1009	12/4	St Hilary	(R)	MDN	3m	11	GF	*mstks in rear til p.u. 7th*	P	0
1562	24/5	Bassaleg	(R)	MDO	3m	8	G	*(bl) mstks & svrl rmndrs, ld to apr 2 out, no ext aft*	2	12

Well-backed twice but hard ride & makes mistakes; winning prospects slim 11

BALLYKNOCK LASS (Irish) — I 195^{P}, I 264^{2}, I 488^{P}, I 566^{F}

BALLYLENNON BOUNTY (Irish) — I 94^{P}

BALLYLIME AGAIN (Irish) — I 188^{P}, I 525^{5}, I 576^{P}

BALLYLUCKAMORE (Irish) — I 160^{P}, I 243^{P}, I 449^{5}, I 512^{F}

BALLYMENAGH (Irish) — I 114^{P}, I 328^{F}

BALLYMICHAEL (Irish) — I 175^{P}, I 247^{P}, I 431^{6}, I 461^{P}

BALLYNAGLERAGH (Irish) — I 338^{P}, I 445^{P}, I 493^{P}, I 590^{F}

BALLYNAGUSSAUN (Irish) — I 60^{3}, I 97^{5}, I 227^{F}, I 310^{5}, I 394^{4}, I 416^{1}, I 473^{3}, I 584^{R}

BALLYPOLLARD (Irish) — I 361^{P}

BALLYQUIN BELLE (Irish) — I 266^{P}

BALLY RIOT(IRE) br.g. 9 Riot Helmet - Ballybrack by Golden Love — Mrs A Rucker

1996 **F(NH),2(NH),1(NH),3(26)**

188	15/2	Erw Lon	(L)	LAD	3m	8 G	*sn outpcd in rear, wll bhnd whn p.u. 11th*	P	0
329	1/3	Eaton Hall	(R)	LAD	3m	10 GS	*ld/disp to 6th, clr ldr frm 7th til ran out 12th*	r	-
401	8/3	Llanfrynach	(R)	LAD	3m	14 G	*chsd ldr til ld 3 out, hdd nxt, rallied last, ld flat*	1	21

Ex-Irish, where useful; disappointed after decent win; poorly ridden; best watched 21

BALLYROE HILL (Irish) — I 32^{P}, I 91^{P}, I 151^{R}

BALLYSADARE BAY (Irish) — I 28^{F}

BALLYSHEIL b.g. 11 Roi Guillaume (FR) - Paldamask by Native Prince — P M Hunt

1996 5(0),3(11),4(12),2(18),3(0)

236	22/2	Lemalla	(R)	INT	3m	12 S	*ld to 8th, lost plc 12th, p.u. 15th*	P	0
453	8/3	Great Treth'	(R)	CON	3m	13 S	*bhnd frm 12th*	8	0
630	22/3	Kilworthy	(L)	RES	3m	16 G	*ld/disp 5th, ld 9-14th, 4th & onepcd frm 15th*	4	14
735	29/3	Higher Kilw'	(L)	MEM	3m	5 GF	*made all, wll clr 16th, unchal*	1	15
1157	20/4	Stafford Cr'	(R)	RES	3m	11 GF	*ld til went wrong side of omitted fence at 14th, p.u.*	P	0
1275	27/4	Little Wind'	(R)	RES	3m	9 GF	*ld 3rd til ran off course aft 7th*	r	-
1395	5/5	High Bickin'	(R)	RES	3m	9 G	*cls 4th 14th-17th, onepcd aft*	6	10
1494	14/5	Cothelstone	(L)	RES	3m	11 GF	*mstk 1st, in tch til p.u. 6th, saddle broke*	P	0
1551	24/5	Mounsey Hil'	(R)	RES	3m	13 G	*cls up, 3rd whn p.u. 11th, lame*	P	0

Has ability but inconsistent & unlucky 97; problem last start; Restricted hard to find; L/H 14

BALLYWEE PENNY (Irish) — I 178^{F}, I 292^{P}, I 360^{F}, I 372^{P}, I 467^{P}

BALLYWOODOCK VI (Irish) — I 115^{P}, I 121, , I 213^{P}, I 252^{P}, I 372^{5}, I 433^{5}, I 465^{P}, I 503^{P}

BALMORAL BOY(NZ) b.g. 9 Prince Simbir (NZ) - Barbee's Dream (NZ) by Silver Dream — M G Miller

1996 2(18),5(15),5(0),5(15),6(11),1(19),4(0)

236	22/2	Lemalla	(R)	INT	3m	12 S	*5th hlfwy, nvr dang, onepcd frm 15th*	5	15
558	16/3	Ottery St M'	(L)	INT	3m	6 G	*in tch til stmbld & u.r. bend aft 7th*	U	-
690	29/3	Little Wind'	(R)	OPE	3m	4 GF	*cls up til outpcd aft 14th, blnd nxt & p.u.*	P	0

Restricted winner 96; usually consistent but problem last start 97; best watched; G-Hy 17

BALTIC LAKE (Irish) — I 47^{P}

BAMAN POWERHOUSE b.g. 9 Bold Owl - Bella Abzug by Karabas — Graham Kivell

1996 P(0),P(0),3(0),6(0),P(0),P(0)

1244	26/4	Bratton Down	(L)	CON	3m	14 GS	*trckd ldrs til wknd frm 15th, p.u. aft 2 out*	P	0
1400	5/5	High Bickin'	(R)	MDO	3m	14 G	*ld 7th, slwd by flagwavers 9th, ld 11-13th,wknd,p.u. 17th*	P	0
1486	11/5	Ottery St M'	(L)	MDO	3m	17 G	*mid-div whn s.u. bend apr 11th*	S	-
1554	24/5	Mounsey Hil'	(R)	MDO	3m	14 G	*hld up bhnd, prog 12th, chsd ldrs 17th, btn last, fin tired*	3	11
1597	31/5	Bratton Down	(L)	MDO	3m	12 F	*rear, prog 10th, chsd wnr aft 15th, no imp frm 2 out*	2	11

Improved 97 & first real form last two starts; non-stayer & will find it hard to win 12

BAMBOO PIE b.m. 7 Bamboo Saucer - Vulrory's Pie by Saucy Kit — Mrs H Connors

14	25/1	Cottenham	(R)	MDO	3m	7 GF	*ld to 4th, mstk 11th, sn outpcd, no dang aft*	4	0
141	9/2	Thorpe Lodge	(L)	MDN	3m	12 GF	*clr ldr til wknd & hdd 2 out*	5	0
776	29/3	Dingley	(R)	MDO	2m 5f	10 G	*prom whn b.d. 3rd*	B	-

Speedy but no stamina yet & finished early 11

BANCHORY ch.g. 8 Dunbeath (USA) - Filwah by High Top — Mrs A M Easterby

77	2/2	Market Rase'	(L)	RES	3m	9 GF	*f 1st, dead*	F	-

Dead 0

BANCYFELIN BOY ch.g. 10 Old Lucky - Eve Darlin by Arcticeelagh — Miss A L Williams

1996 2(11),1(18),3(13),**P(0)**,**P(0)**

191	15/2	Erw Lon	(L)	CON	3m	13 G	*alwys bhnd, t.o. & p.u. 14th*	P	0

Confined winner 96; soon finished in 97 & best watched at 11 15

BAND LEADER b or br.g. 10 Orchestra - Quick Frozen by Arctic Slave — Mrs S M Lloyd

1013 12/4 Bitterley (L) CON 3m 14 GF *mid-div whn f 7th* F -

Dead **0**

BANK PLACE ch.g. 10 Sheer Grit - Shatana by Tarboosh (USA) — E F Birchall

1996 **P(NH),P(NH)**

85 2/2 Wolverhampt' (L) LAD 3m 11 GS *chsd ldr to 7th, wknd 12th, poor 4th whn u.r. 2 out* U -
202 15/2 Weston Park (L) LAD 3m 13 G *cls up, 2nd til wknd 4 out* 4 12
850 31/3 Eyton-On-Se' (L) LAD 3m 6 GF *(fav) 2nd frm 9th,chal strngly 3 out,1l down 2 out,broke down last* P 0

Poor under Rules; unlucky last start but problems as well **15**

BANKROLL b.g. 10 Chief Singer - Very Nice (FR) by Green Dancer (USA) — R Sumner

1996 **0(NH),6(NH),R(NH)**

219 16/2 Heythrop (R) LAD 3m 16 G *reluc to race, t.o. til p.u. 11th* P 0
432 8/3 Upton-On-Se' (R) MXO 3m 7 G *lost 30l start, nvr ct up, fin well* 4 0
876 1/4 Upton-On-Se' (R) MEM 3m 7 GF *ld 2nd, clr whn ref 6th* R -
905 5/4 Howick (L) LAD 3m 4 F *reluc, nrly ref 1st, ref 2nd, cont, ref 3rd* R -

Winning chaser; always quirky & took complete control in points **0**

BANNAGH MOR (Irish) — **I** 71[F], **I** 210[2], **I** 328[1]

BANN VIEW (Irish) — **I** 126[P], **I** 178[3], **I** 250[1]

BANTEER BET(IRE) ch.m. 5 Black Minstrel - Deirdre Elizabeth by Salluceva — C H Gittins

326 1/3 Eaton Hall (R) MDN 3m 14 GS *mid to rear, p.u. 4 out* P 0
722 29/3 Sandon (L) MDO 3m 10 GF *mid to rear, no ch whn f 4 out* F -

Tailed off both starts & no promise yet **0**

BANTEL BARGAIN b.m. 8 Silly Prices - Yellow Peril by Mljet — A S Nelson

36 26/1 Alnwick (L) MDO 3m 15 G *mstk 3rd, alwys wll bhnd, t.o. & p.u. 11th* P 0
134 9/2 Alnwick (L) MDO 3m 11 G *nvr nr ldrs, poor 7th at 10th, t.o. & p.u. 13th* P 0
334 1/3 Corbridge (R) MEM 3m 7 G *rear, lost tch 8th, t.o. & p.u. 11th* P 0

Lightly raced & shows no ability **0**

BANTEL BARONET b.g. 9 Tickled Pink - Bantel Bouquet by Red Regent — Mrs K Hedley

234 22/2 Friars Haugh (L) MDO 3m 15 G *prom early, bhnd whn p.u. 13th* P 0
343 1/3 Corbridge (R) MDO 3m 14 G *rear, sn wll bhnd, t.o. & p.u. 12th* P 0
415 8/3 Dalston (R) RES 3m 19 GS *sn rear, last & t.o. whn p.u. 10th* P 0
613 22/3 Friars Haugh (L) MDN 3m 12 GF *sn bhnd, p.u. 14th* P 0
1428 10/5 Aspatria (L) MDO 3m 11 G *ld til mstk 3rd, sn bhnd, t.o. & p.u. 11th* P 0
1515 17/5 Corbridge (R) MEM 3m 5 GS *rear, prog 8th, wknd rpdly 2 out, walked in* 4 0

Well-beaten in bad race on only completion **0**

BANTON LOCH br.g. 10 Lochnager - Balgownie by Prince Tenderfoot (USA) — J D Hankinson

1996 P(0),4(13),1(17),**P(0)**

144 9/2 Tweseldown (R) OPE 3m 9 GF *twrds rear, outpcd frm 12th, sn t.o., p.u. last* P 0

Restricted winner 96; soon vanished 97; best watched **14**

BANTRY BAY b.g. 5 Infantry - Breac Ban by Laurence O — E G M Cannon

1282 27/4 Fakenham P-' (L) MDO 3m 8 G *rear, mstk 4th, 6th & in tch whn blnd & u.r. 9th* U -
1431 10/5 Marks Tey (L) MDO 3m 6 G *sttld rear, going wll 11th, lost tch 14th, p.u. 3 out* P 0

Not completely disgraced but no tangible signs of ability yet **0**

BAPTIST JOHN(IRE) b.g. 9 The Parson - Corrielek by Menelek — P R M Philips

1996 P(0),P(0),F(-),3(12),4(11)

261 22/2 Newtown (L) MDN 3m 16 G *prom, ld 13th, just hdd & lft clr 2 out* 1 15
433 8/3 Upton-On-Se' (R) RES 3m 18 G *alwys chsng ldrs, not fluent, ev ch til not qckn 15th* 3 12

Confirmed 96 promise when scoring; ran well in fair Restricted but vanished; chances if fit 98 .... **17**

BARAFUNDLE BAY ch.g. 8 Afzal - Vinca by French Vine — Lt-Col John Bulkeley

262 22/2 Newtown (L) RES 3m 15 G *mstk 3rd, prom til wknd 11th, t.o. & p.u. 14th* P 0
435 8/3 Upton-On-Se' (R) MDO 3m 14 G *mid-div whn f 2nd* F -
542 16/3 Erw Lon (L) MDN 3m 15 GF *tongue-strap, sttld rear, prog 12th, nvr nrr* 3 10
877 1/4 Upton-On-Se' (R) RES 3m 17 GF *alwys bhnd, t.o. & p.u. 11th* P 0
1018 12/4 Bitterley (L) MDO 3m 13 GF *cls up to 10th, wknd 13th, p.u. 2 out* P 0

3rd in weak race on only completion & not threatening to win yet **10**

BARBARAS MEWS (Irish) — **I** 432[P]

BARCHESTER (Irish) — **I** 120[P], **I** 122[P], **I** 341[P], **I** 467[B], **I** 507[P], **I** 585[1]

BARENISES ROSE (Irish) — **I** 91P, **I** 151F, **I** 388⁵, **I** 406³

BARGAIN AND SALE br.g. 12 Torenaga - Miss Woodville by Master Buck — D J Minty

1996 6(16),P(0),2(17),7(0),4(0),P(0),1(19),3(18),5(16),P(0)

552	16/3	Ottery St M'	(L)	OPE	3m	6	G	*in tch to 7th, wknd, p.u. 10th*	P	0
793	31/3	Bishopsleigh	(R)	OPE	3m	7	G	*alwys rear, t.o. & p.u. 12th*	P	0
1037	12/4	Lifton	(R)	OPE	3m	5	F	*trckd ldrs in 3rd, lft 2nd last, onepcd*	2	0
1089	16/4	Hockworthy	(L)	CON	3m	7	GF	*(bl) chsd wnr til wknd rpdly 13th, last whn p.u. 2 out*	P	0
1244	26/4	Bratton Down	(L)	CON	3m	14	GS	*(bl) raced up wth pce early, sn lost tch, p.u. 15th*	P	0
1313	3/5	Holnicote	(L)	CON	3m	7	G	*prom, ld brfly 9-10th, lost tch 13th*	4	0
1484	11/5	Ottery St M'	(L)	OPE	3m	7	G	*chsd ldr to 12th, outpcd aft, p.u. 4 out*	P	0
1580	26/5	Lifton	(R)	OPE	3m	8	G	*prom, grad wknd hlfwy, p.u. 4 out*	P	0
1592	31/5	Bratton Down	(L)	MEM	3m	4	F	*3rd til chsd wnr 14th, no imp, fin tired*	2	0

Open winner 96; fell to pieces in 97 & looks finished 0

BARICHSTE ch.g. 9 Electric - Be Sharp by Sharpen Up — T A Hughes

1996 r(-),P(0),1(14),P(0),7(0),P(0)

78	2/2	Market Rase'	(L)	RES	3m	8	GF	*hld up, prog to jn lrds 12th, 1/2l 2nd whn ran out 3 out*	r	-
213	16/2	Southwell P'	(L)	RES	3m	16	GS	*(fav) w.w. prog apr 12th, blnd nxt, ran on 3 out, nvr nrr*	3	17
266	22/2	Duncombe Pa'	(R)	RES	3m	19	G	*(bl) ld to 3rd, prom, mstk 14th, rddn to ld flat, qcknd clr*	1	19
350	2/3	Market Rase'	(L)	CON	3m	11	GF	*(bl) mid-div, jnd ldrs 14th, ld nxt, hdd last, not qckn*	2	21
509	15/3	Dalton Park	(R)	XX	3m	13	GF	*(Jt fav) (bl) prom til outpcd & hmpd 15th, sn bhnd, p.u. last*	P	0
619	22/3	Hutton Rudby	(L)	INT	3m	8	GF	*(bl) mid-div, chsd ldrs to 12th, rddn & wknd 2 out*	5	14
1070	13/4	Whitwell-On'	(R)	XX	3m	9	G	*(bl) ld til disp 5th, hdd nxt, prom til outpcd frm 4 out*	5	13
1100	19/4	Hornby Cast'	(L)	CON	3m	9	G	*(bl) prom, disp 13th, hdd & wknd 4 out*	5	11
1360	5/5	Towcester	(R)	HC	2 3/4m	7	GF	*(bl) t.o. from 5th, p.u. before last.*	P	0

Maiden winner 96; blinkers worked when winning but effect soon wore off; best watched; G-G/F 16

BARKIN b.g. 14 Crash Course - Annie Augusta by Master Owen — Peter Saville

1996 F(-),5(13),4(10),1(16),3(11),1(18)

328	1/3	Eaton Hall	(R)	OPE	3m	6	GS	*t.o. aft 6th, fence bhnd whn f 10th*	F	-
763	29/3	Whittington	(L)	CON	3m	9	S	*bhnd, t.o. 6th, lft remote 3rd 15th*	3	0
998	12/4	Alpraham	(R)	MEM	3m	4	GF	*chsd ldrs, tk 2nd aft 3 out, nvr dang*	2	10
1121	19/4	Whittington	(L)	CON	3m	4	F	*ld to 3rd, cls up to 15th, rdn & wknd nxt*	2	14
1349	3/5	Gisburn	(R)	CON	3m	11	GF	*rear, t.o. 5th, slw jmp 13th, blkd & u.r. nxt*	U	-
1539	18/5	Wolverhampt'	(L)	OPE	3m	5	GS	*2nd at 5th, lost tch 14th, u.r. nxt*	U	-
1607	1/6	Dingley	(R)	OPE	3m	9	GF	*sn last & dtchd, t.o. 8th, u.r. 14th*	U	-

Dual winner 95/6; deteriorated now & win at 15 most unlikely; G-S 11

BARKISLAND b.g. 13 Prince Regent (FR) - Satlan by Milan — Graham Treglown

93	7/2	Bangor	(L)	HC	2 1/2m 110yds	11	G	*soon well bhnd, t.o. when p.u. before 11th.*	P	0
651	22/3	Siddington	(L)	OPE	3m	7	F	*f 2nd*	F	-
1064	13/4	Maisemore P'	(L)	CON	3m	13	GF	*wll bhnd 9th, t.o. & p.u. 15th*	P	0

No longer of any account 0

BARNABY BOY b.g. 9 Ayyabaan - Owen's Hobby by Owen Anthony — J L Brown

1996 P(0),3(14),1(15),1(17),1(17)

5	19/1	Barbury Cas'	(L)	OPE	3m	11	GF	*in tch in rear, 7th hlfwy, prog & chsng ldrs whn f 15th*	F	-
187	15/2	Erw Lon	(L)	OPE	3m	16	G	*12s-3s, mid-div, prog 11th, wknd 14th, walked in*	5	0

Won 3 in 96; brief season 97 & finished early; Confined possible if fit 98; G-F 19

BARNADOWN (Irish) — **I** 53P, **I** 136⁵, **I** 182F, **I** 222³, **I** 324², **I** 391², **I** 405³, **I** 544¹, **I** 569³

BARNAGAN (Irish) — **I** 117P, **I** 127P, **I** 247⁵, **I** 328P, **I** 371P

BARNA LAD (Irish) — **I** 59⁶, **I** 107P, **I** 161⁴, **I** 202F, **I** 275², **I** 430³, **I** 452⁵, **I** 529F, **I** 579¹, **I** 592²

BARNANE WALK (Irish) — **I** 8P

BARN ELMS ch.g. 10 Deep Run - Leara by Leander — Mrs S J Hickman

1996 3(15),F(-),3(0),6(11),4(13)

685	29/3	Charing	(L)	XX	3m	3	F	*ld, clr 3rd, 4l up 2 out, slwd last, hdd & wknd flat*	2	15
784	31/3	Aldington	(L)	CON	3m	2	HD	*(fav) ld, lft solo 9th*	1	0
1502	16/5	Folkestone	(R)	HC	2m 5f	10	G	*chsd ldr after 6th till 10th, wknd 3 out, fin tired.*	3	15

Non-stayer & handed joke race on plate; fortunate to find another 13

BARNEY BEAR b.g. 6 Scorpio (FR) - Nutt's Corner by Cantab — Mrs A B Garton

205	15/2	Weston Park	(L)	MDN	3m	10	G	*mid to rear, p.u. 12th*	P	0
469	8/3	Eyton-On-Se'	(L)	MDN	2 1/2m	9	G	*(fav) chsg grp, cls 2nd 9th, ld 5 out-2 out, no ext*	2	13
1541	18/5	Wolverhampt'	(L)	MDO	3m	15	GS	*mid to rear, no ch whn p.u. 3 out*	P	0

Fair effort 2nd start (weak race) but yet to show suficient stamina 11

BARNEYS GOLD(IRE) ch.g. 8 Orchestra - Fair Corina by Menelek — Irvin S Naylor

1996 r(-),3(10),F(-),3(0),P(0),P(0)

13	25/1 Cottenham	(R) MDO 3m	10 GF	*prom whn mstk 4th, bhnd & blnd 11th, t.o.*	6	0
141	9/2 Thorpe Lodge	(L) MDN 3m	12 GF	*alwys prom, ran on frm 2 out, just faild*	2	15
480	9/3 Southwell P'	(L) MDO 3m	17 G	*(fav) ld to 5th, ld agn 12th, drew clr apr 3 out, comf*	1	17
770	29/3 Dingley	(R) RES 3m	18 G	*prog 8th, 3rd frm 10th, chsd 1st pair 3 out, unable to cls*	3	18
1058	13/4 Hackwood Pa'	(L) RES 3m	6 GF	*(fav) 6/4-4/5, ld to 3rd, ld 11th, comf*	1	17
1507	16/5 Stratford	(L) HC 3m	10 G	*trckd ldrs till lost pl 8th, styd on from 4 out, left poor 3rd last.*	3	19

Vastly improved in ability & attitude; solid performances; should upgrade if retaining desire; G-F 20

BARNYS ROSE FARM ch.g. 8 Saxon Farm - Red Rose III by St Elmo — Mrs Joan Tice

1084	13/4 Guilsborough	(L) MDN 3m	11 GF	*sn rear, last at 9th, t.o. & p.u. 11th*	P	0
1356	4/5 Dingley	(R) MDO 3m	9 G	*last whn p.u. aft 5th (b.b.v.)*	P	0

No sign of ability & problems already 0

BARON'S HEIR b.g. 10 Town And Country - Lady London by London Gazette — Mrs J L Livermore

1996 3(16),3(15),4(13),2(16),1(17),**2(19)**

586	19/3 Exeter	(R) HC 3 1/4m	12 GF	*held up, chsd ldrs from 12th til wknd 4 out.*	6	0

Consistent in 96 (Open winner) but brief appearance 97; best watched 17

BARON'S PEARL gr.m. 7 Baron Blakeney - Pearly's Orphan by Precipice Wood — Mrs K M Price

224	16/2 Heythrop	(R) MDN 3m	16 G	*mstk 7th, alwys rear, t.o. & p.u. 15th*	P	0
436	8/3 Upton-On-Se'	(R) MDO 3m	17 G	*patiently rdn, prog 14th, 8l 2nd whn f 2 out*	F	13

Promise 2nd start (large but weak field); promptly vanished; chances if fit 98 14

BARRABY (Irish) — I 265[F], I 456[5]

BARROW KNOCKS b or br.g. 9 - Birsley Wood by Flatbush — W J Drummond

136	9/2 Alnwick	(L) MDO 3m	16 G	*sn m bhnd, t.o. 3rd, p.u. 11th*	P	0
162	15/2 Lanark	(R) MDO 3m	16 G	*sn wll bhnd, p.u. 14th*	P	0
734	29/3 Alnwick	(L) MDN 3m	6 F	*ld to 8th, cls 2nd whn ran out apr 10th*	r	-
1428	10/5 Aspatria	(L) MDO 3m	11 G	*jmpd slwly, made most 3rd-8th, sn btn, t.o.*	5	0
1514	17/5 Corbridge	(R) MDO 3m	17 GS	*s.s. alwys rear, t.o. 14th, p.u. 3 out*	P	0

Last on only completion & ability level on zero 0

BARROW STREET b.g. 7 Sula Bula - Kerry Street by Dairialatan — C L Tizzard

1996 P(0),4(0),P(0),r(-),7(0)

1270	27/4 Little Wind'	(R) MDO 2 1/2m	10 GF	*jmpd lft,chsd ldr 5th,lft in ld 8-11th, wknd 3 out,fin tired*	3	0
1485	6/5 Wincanton	(R) HC 2m 5f	4 F	*raced in 3rd till dropped back to 4th at 8th, rdn 11th, wknd 13th.*	4	0
1416	10/5 Newton Abbot	(L) HC 2m 5f 110yds	14 G	*(vis) ld to 4th, weakend 9th, t.o. when p.u. before 2 out.*	P	0
1554	24/5 Mounsey Hil'	(R) MDO 3m	14 G	*w.w. prog 12th,ld aft 3 out,sn clr,tired & jnd last,all out*	1	14

Carried home by Joe Tizzard when winning; non-stayer & future prospects poor 13

BARRYSTOWN LADY (Irish) — I 223[P], I 273[4], I 458[F], I 544[P]

BARTAGS BROTHER br.g. 10 Homeboy - Barline by Lauso — M W Gore

216	16/2 Southwell P'	(L) OPE 3m	12 GS	*alwys rear, last frm 11th, t.o. & p.u. 14th*	P	0
321	1/3 Marks Tey	(L) INT 3m	10 G	*chsd ldrs, lft 3rd 9th, ev ch 16th, rdn & btn apr last*	2	18

Dual winner 95; missed 96; retains ability but season lasted 2 weeks; G-S 17

BART EILE (Irish) — I 57[P], I 148[F], I 184[F], I 220[P], I 343[4], I 390[3], I 409[2], I 496[6], I 574[1], I 614[4]

BARTLEMY KING (Irish) — I 17[P], I 52[P]

BARTONDALE br.m. 12 Oats - Miss Boon by Road House II — L J Williams

187	15/2 Erw Lon	(L) OPE 3m	16 G	*alwys rear, lost tch 11th, t.o. & p.u. 14th*	P	0
401	8/3 Llanfrynach	(R) LAD 3m	14 G	*rear, ran on frm 3 out, nvr dang*	4	18
638	22/3 Howick	(L) LAD 3m	10 GF	*twrds rear, no prog frm 14th*	5	0
1225	26/4 Pyle	(R) LAD 3m	6 GS	*chsd ldng pair, not qckn 3 out, kpt on agn frm last*	3	14
1320	3/5 Bonvilston	(R) CON 3m	8 G	*rear, prog hlfwy, ld 12th-nxt, styd on onepcd*	3	17

Veteran stage now & no longer threatening to win in competitive races 16

BARTON ROSE b.g. 6 Derring Rose - Barton Sauce by Saucy Kit — Mrs S J Evans

933	6/4 Charlton Ho'	(L) MDO 3m	12 G	*schoold rear,mstk 12th,prog 14th,ev ch apr 2 out,wknd last*	5	12
1399	5/5 High Bickin'	(R) MDO 3m	12 G	*prog to 6th at 8th, mstk 12th, btn 5th whn p.u. 16th*	P	0
1520	17/5 Bratton Down	(L) MDO 3m	17 GS	*prom, cls 3rd whn hit 12th, cls 2nd & ev ch whn f 16th*	F	-

Showed promise all 3 starts & should hit the target if all goes well in 98 15

BART'S CASTLE ch.g. 11 Carlingford Castle - Tavojina by Octavo (USA) — Miss A M Reed

30	26/1 Marks Tey	(L) MDN 3m	9 GF	*ld to 7th, wknd 10th, t.o. & p.u. 13th*	P	0
658	22/3 Badbury Rin'	(L) MDN 3m	6 F	*ld til hdd apr last, outpcd*	2	13

934 6/4 Charlton Ho' (L) MDO 3m 10 G *8s-3s, jmpd rght, ld, clr 8th, rdn & hdd last, no ext* 2 15
1461 11/5 Tweseldown (R) MEM 3m 3 GF *(fav) made all, rdn whn lft virt solo 3 out* 1 15
1567 25/5 Kingston Bl' (L) RES 3m 8 GF *jmpd rght,made all,sn clr,dist up hlfwy,tired 2 out,unchal* 1 22

Ex-Irish; much improved; romped home last start; best R/H; can win Confined at 12; G-F 20

BASHER BILL b.g. 14 Maystreak - Rugby Princess by El Gallo K D Giles

1996 P(0),5(0),2(10),F(-),5(0),2(13),**7(0)**,1(12),**5(0)**

278 23/2 Charing (L) RES 3m 17 G *prom whn mstk 2nd, rear frm 8th, t.o. & p.u. 15th* P 0
462 8/3 Charing (L) RES 3m 10 G *ld to 5th, sn wknd, t.o. 14th* 5 0
576 16/3 Detling (L) MEM 3m 10 F *ld to 2nd, wll in tch aft, 3rd last, wknd* 4 10
682 29/3 Charing (L) RES 3m 5 F *ld til apr 3rd, 2nd aft, rdn to chal 3 out,ev ch nxt, onepcd* 2 12
783 31/3 Aldington (L) RES 3m 4 HD *wth ldr frm 2nd, ld 6-10th, agn 12-15th, 2nd best aft* 2 12
966 6/4 Penshurst (L) CON 3m 7 F *alwys wll in tch, 3rd 3 out, kpt on same pce* 4 13
1287 29/4 Huntingdon (R) HC 2 1/2m 110yds 14 G *alwys bhnd, last & t.o. when p.u. after 11th.* P 0

Members winner 96; placed in poor races on Firm & Members win at 15 unlikely 11

BASHINDORA (Irish) — **I** 512^{3}, **I** 544^{P}, **I** 601^{P}

BASIL GREY gr.g. 8 Grey Ghost - Lady Buttons by New Brig S G Jones

1996 F(-),2(10),3(10),3(0),1(15),4(12)

77 2/2 Market Rase' (L) RES 3m 9 GF *prom, chsd wnr 6th-3 out, wl btn nxt* 3 10

Members winner 96; brief appearance 97; best watched 14

BASIL STREET(IRE) b.g. 5 Glenstal (USA) - Pockatello by Commanche Run Miss J M Green

1996 **13(NH)**,**2(NH)**,**4(NH)**

366 2/3 Garnons (L) MDO 2 1/2m 13 GS *7s-3s, ld 11th, drew clr frm 2 out* 1 17
575 16/3 Garnons (L) RES 3m 12 G *(fav) trckd ldrs, qcknd to ld aft 15th, sn in cmmnd* 1 19
647 22/3 Castle Of C' (R) INT 3m 7 G *mstks, prog 10th, btn 15th, lft poor 3rd last* 3 12
1012 12/4 Bitterley (L) MEM 3m 6 GF *(fav) blnd & u.r. 1st* U -
1235 26/4 Brampton Br' (R) INT 3m 10 G *chsd ldrs, no prog frm 14th, t.o. & p.u. 3 out* P 0
1468 11/5 Erw Lon (L) INT 3m 7 GS *(bl) mid-div, rear whn p.u. 15th* P 0

Started very well but 3 races in 20 days bottomed him out; may revive when fresh 98; G-S 19

BATHURST (Irish) — **I** 34^{P}, **I** 69^{F}

BATSI b.g. 13 Battlement - Bright Upham by Paridel Mrs E A Hext

1996 P(0),P(0),**P(0)**

310 1/3 Clyst St Ma' (L) INT 3m 9 HY *rear til blnd & u.r. 8th* U -
1480 11/5 Ottery St M' (L) MEM 3m 6 G *hld up, prog 13th, went 2nd nxt, no imp wnr* 2 0
1550 24/5 Mounsey Hil' (R) INT 3m 9 G *alwys bhnd, lost tch 10th, t.o. & p.u. 2 out* P 0

No longer of any account 0

BATTLE LORD CISTO ch.g. 9 Cisto (FR) - Battle Lady Ivor by Bigivor Miss E A Cork

1996 **17(NH)**,**P(NH)**,**P(NH)**

246 22/2 Lemalla (R) MDO 3m 4 S *cls 2nd whn f 5th* F -
626 22/3 Kilworthy (L) MDN 3m 14 G *bhnd til p.u. apr 15th* P 0

No ability under Rules or in points yet 0

BATTLING PSYCHE ch.m. 13 Tom Noddy - Keep Fighting by Baltus John Nicholls

554 16/3 Ottery St M' (L) CON 3m 7 G *sn rear, t.o. frm 10th* 5 0
741 29/3 Higher Kilw' (L) MDN 3m 12 GF *rear, mstk 2nd, t.o. & p.u. 12th* P 0

An elderly maiden destined to stay that way 0

BAVARD BAY b or br.g. 13 Le Bavard (FR) - Winterwood by Bargello P R Whiston

1996 **6(NH)**,**4(NH)**,**6(NH)**,**2(NH)**,**4(NH)**,**7(NH)**,**7(NH)**

84 2/2 Wolverhampt' (L) MEM 3m 9 GS *ld to 2nd, bhnd frm 9th, sn t.o.* 5 0
200 15/2 Weston Park (L) CON 3m 16 G *mid to rear, nvr dang, p.u. 4 out* P 0
330 1/3 Eaton Hall (R) CON 3m 16 GS *prom, nvr far away, outpcd frm 3 out* 4 0
465 8/3 Eyton-On-Se' (L) OPE 3m 13 G *(bl) cls up, 2nd 5 out, lost tch, p.u. 3 out* P 0

Blinkers no help last start & vanished early - looks finished now 0

BAVARD JET (Irish) — **I** 47^{F}, **I** 103^{2}, **I** 196^{1}, **I** 426^{1}, **I** 451^{1}, **I** 511^{1}

BAVINGTON b.g. 6 Meadowbrook - Bargello's Lady by Bargello Ian Hamilton

1996 P(0)

36 26/1 Alnwick (L) MDO 3m 15 G *mid-div, no prog 13th, no ch frm 3 out* 5 0
136 9/2 Alnwick (L) MDO 3m 16 G *mid-div, prog 9th, 6th & outpcd 14th, no dang aft* 6 0
334 1/3 Corbridge (R) MEM 3m 7 G *mid-div, mstk 2nd, u.r. 8th* U -
417 8/3 Dalston (R) MDO 2 1/2m 11 GS *rear, 9th & rdn hlfwy, no ch 11th, ran on frm 2 out, nvr nrr* 3 10
614 22/3 Friars Haugh (L) MDN 3m 13 GF *nvr rchd ldrs* 4 0

Not totally disgraced but looks slow & yet to threaten a win 11

BAWNAVINOGUE LADY (Irish) — I 10^{P}, I 50^{P}

BAWN BEAG (Irish) — I 80^{4}, I 204^{U}, I 304^{F}

BAWNEROSH b.g. 11 Callernish - Hightown Jackie — T D B Underwood

2 19/1 Barbury Cas' (L) XX 3m 14 GF *wll in rear, 8th hlfwy, no ch whn p.u. 2 out* P 0
60 1/2 Kingston Bl' (L) MDN 3m 17 GF *alwys wll bhnd, t.o. & p.u. 13th* P 0
747 29/3 Barbury Cas' (L) MDO 3m 3 F *set sedate pace, tk cmmnd 14th, ran on well* 1 10
970 6/4 Penshurst (L) RES 3m 4 F *ld to 7th agn 3 out, ran gmly & held on* 1 13
1127 19/4 Penshurst (L) OPE 3m 7 GF *s.i.s. sn handy going wll,ld 12th-4 out,ld brfly 3 out,no ex* 2 16
1199 23/4 Andoversford (R) INT 3m 5 F *(fav) w.w. going wll, went 2nd 11th, hit nxt, ld apr last, styd on* 1 15
1462 11/5 Tweseldown (R) CON 3m 6 GF *hld up, effrt 15th, onepcd frm 3 out* 3 12
1564 25/5 Kingston Bl' (L) CON 3m 7 GF *hld up, clsd up 12th, outpcd 14th, mstks & wknd aft* 4D 10

Late developer; found weak contests for successful season; harder to place at 12; Firm 16

BAYBUCK (Irish) — I 54^{P}, I 107, , I 135^{P}, I 308^{P}, I 337, , I 520^{P}

BAY HOBNOB b.g. 6 Buzzards Bay - Woody Isle by Precipice Wood — A J Mason

1996 P(0),P(0),P(0)

224 16/2 Heythrop (R) MDN 3m 16 G *trckd ldrs, effrt 14th, ld 2 out, jnd last, pshd clr flat* 1 17
300 1/3 Didmarton (L) RES 3m 23 G *alwys wll in rear, lost tch 11th, p.u. 15th* P 0

Beat subsequent winner when scoring; no show other start & vanished; may upgrade if fit 98 16

BAY LEADER b.m. 9 Leander - Cascade Bay Vii — G I Isaac

1996 5(0),6(0),1(0),3(0),P(0),5(0),4(0)

404 8/3 Llanfrynach (R) INT 3m 17 G *rear, p.u. 16th* P 0
1318 3/5 Bonvilston (R) MEM 3m 9 G *mid-div, rpd prog to ld 2 out, hdd & no ext flat* 2 13
1556 24/5 Bassaleg (R) RES 3m 13 G *in tch til wknd 12th, t.o. & p.u. 14th* P 0

Members winner 96; ran best race same contest 97 but shows very little apart 10

BAY LOUGH (Irish) — I 90^{2}, I 217^{U}, I 271^{1}

BAYLOUGHBESS (Irish) — I 73^{5}, I 558^{P}, I 607^{1}

BAY OWL b.g. 13 Paico - Dietrich by Sardis — Mrs A P Glassford

1996 F(-),4(0),P(0),3(14),P(0),7(0)

200 15/2 Weston Park (L) CON 3m 16 G *nvr bttr than mid-div, t.o. & p.u. 14th* P 0
464 8/3 Eyton-On-Se' (L) INT 3m 12 G *mid to rear, nvr in race, p.u. 6 out* P 0
667 23/3 Eaton Hall (R) CON 3m 10 GF *rear, prog 10th, 2nd 2 out, no imp wnr* 2 16
851 31/3 Eyton-On-Se' (L) INT 3m 8 GF *held up in rear, some late prog, no imp on 1st 3* 4 15
937 6/4 Tabley (R) CON 3m 10 G *disp ld to 4th, chsd ldr to 9th,wknd nxt,p.u. & dismntd 14th* P 0

Dual winner 95; well-beaten since & problems last start could spell the end 14

BAYTOWNGHOST (Irish) — I 221^{P}

BAYWYN b.m. 6 Pragmatic - Samantha Whiskers by Old Lucky — R L Black

181 15/2 Larkhill (R) MDO 3m 17 G *ran out 1st* r -
244 22/2 Lemalla (R) MDO 3m 12 S *8th hlfwy, nvr dang, t.o. & p.u. last* P 0
314 1/3 Clyst St Ma' (L) MDN 3m 11 HY *mid-div, lft bttr by dfctns, 2nd & hld whn lft clr last* 1 10
523 15/3 Cothelstone (L) RES 3m 14 GS *rear whn f 12th* F -
806 31/3 Wadebridge (L) RES 3m 6 F *alwys rear til p.u. aft 13th* P 0
1317 3/5 Holnicote (L) RES 3m 5 G *bhnd frm 4th, p.u. aft 14th* P 0
1547 24/5 Mounsey Hil' (R) MEM 3m 9 G *alwys last, jmpd slwly 3rd, lost tch 11th, p.u. 15th* P 0

Won a joke race & shows no real ability 0

BEACH BUM gr.g. 11 Scallywag - St Lucian Breeze by Vivify — Mrs Judy Young

144 9/2 Tweseldown (R) OPE 3m 9 GF *hld up, blnd badly 2nd, styd on onepcd frm 4 out* 3 16
484 9/3 Tweseldown (R) OPE 3m 10 G *f 1st* F -
651 22/3 Siddington (L) OPE 3m 7 F *chsd ldng pair,mstk 10th & pshd alng,nt qckn 14th,wknd 2 out* 4 15

Ran two passable races but win at 12 most unlikely now 15

BEAFORD GAME ch.m. 7 Northern Game - Langton Cadera by Langton Gold Abbot — L W Wickett

1108 19/4 Flete Park (R) RES 3m 14 GF *sn bhnd, not fluent, t.o. & u.r. 12th* U -
1583 26/5 Lifton (R) MDO 3m 11 G *20s-4s, ld 1st, ld agn 4 out, ran on well* 1 14

Beat subsequent winner when landing the punt on 1st ever completion; more needed for Restricteds .. 15

BE ARE ch.g. 11 North Street - Tandys Tonic by Full Of Beans — B F W Rendell

794 31/3 Bishopsleigh (R) MDO 3m 12 G *prom to 14th, wknd, p.u. 17th* P 0

Rarely runs & has never finished 0

BEAR'S FLIGHT ch.g. 10 Royal Vulcan - Semi-Colon by Colonist II — Mrs J Hadden-Wight

1996 U(-),r(-),3(17),P(0),7(0)

218 16/2 Heythrop (R) INT 3m 21 G *alwys bhnd, t.o. frm 5th* 8 0
294 1/3 Didmarton (L) INT 3m 20 G *rear whn u.r. 11th* U -

395 8/3 Barbury Cas' (L) XX 3m 9 G *chsd ldrs 7th, ld 15th-2 out, onepcd und pres* 3 17

1212 26/4 Woodford (L) INT 3m 8 G *chsd ldrs til 5th & outpcd 14th, no ch frm 4 out* 4 10

Still retains some ability but novice-ridden 96/7 & no wins - unlikely to break sequence 15

BEARYS CROSS (Irish) — **I** 262, , **I** 322^{4}, **I** 379^{4}, **I** 444^{5}

BEATIN SIDE (Irish) — **I** 152^{1}

BEAT THAT (Irish) — **I** 166^{3}, **I** 271^{P}, **I** 487^{P}

BEAT THE RAP b.g. 11 Wolverlife - Juries Slip by Super Slip Mrs R J Morrison

1996 P(0),1(12),6(0),4(10),**8(0),6(0)**,5(0),**4(NH),5(NH),4(NH)**

73 2/2 Higham (L) RES 3m 3 GF *ld at slow pace to 8th, outpcd 12th, styd on agn 4 out* 2 14

198 15/2 Higham (L) RES 3m 14 G *mid-div whn hmpd & u.r. 12th* U -

Maiden winner 96; non-stayer & finished early 97; best watched 12

BEAU BEAUCHAMP (Irish) — **I** 313,

BEAU CINQ (Irish) — **I** 4^{U}, **I** 24^{P}, **I** 242^{P}, **I** 354^{P}, **I** 403^{6}, **I** 427^{P}, **I** 548^{P}, **I** 572^{F}

BEAU DANDY ch.g. 10 Le Bavard (FR) - Best Dressed by Pumps (USA) C C Shand Kydd

1996 3(14),4(10),1(22),1(23),**4(17),1(22),1(25),P(0)**

90 5/2 Ludlow (R) HC 2 1/2m 6 G *(fav) alwys handy, hmpd by faller 8th, rcvred to ld after next, made rest, kept on grimly from 2 out.* 1 23

381 4/3 Leicester (R) HC 2m 1f 13 G *(Jt fav) chsd ldrs, rdn 3 out, one pace apr last.* 4 21

547 16/3 Garthorpe (R) XX 3m 7 GF *(fav) disp 2nd pl til chsd ldr aft 15th,ld nxt,hdd appr last,no ex* 2 23

Dual H/Chase winner 96; won 9 of last 17; best R/H, sub 3m; should revive 98; Any, best Good 26

BEAU ROSE b.g. 14 Beau Charmeur (FR) - Rosantus by Anthony Miss C A Blakeborough

1996 5(0),3(0),2(16),5(0),2(14),P(0)

339 1/3 Corbridge (R) OPE 3m 5f 11 G *rear, lost tch 11th, p.u. aft 15th* P 0

506 15/3 Dalton Park (R) CON 3m 16 GF *prom til outpcd 14th, b.d. nxt* B -

Brief season 97 & could be finished now 10

BECCA'S ROSE (Irish) — **I** 388^{F}, **I** 575^{4}, **I** 606^{3}

BECKFORD b.g. 8 Stanford - Combe Hill by Crozier P D F Strawson

1996 U(-),1(13),S(-),7(12),P(0)

251 22/2 Brocklesby ' (L) RES 3m 16 G *alwys 2nd/3rd, chsd wnnr frm 3 out, just held* 2 18

477 9/3 Southwell P' (L) RES 3m 10 G *prom, chsd ldr 5th, disp 13th-15th, onepcd apr 3 out* 3 14

509 15/3 Dalton Park (R) XX 3m 13 GF *prom til wknd 15th, t.o.* 4 0

Maiden winner 96; improved 97; ran well 1st start & could win Restricted on that form if fit 98 16

BEDTIME PIXIE ch.g. 5 Lir - Celerity Lady by Lighter D Stephens

243 22/2 Lemalla (R) MDO 3m 12 S *schoold rear, t.o. 14th, remote 4th aft* 4 0

458 8/3 Great Treth' (R) MDO 3m 15 S *hmp aft 6th, mstk 7th, kpt on und pres clsng stgs, do bttr* 4 0

Finished early but showed distinct promise & should go close if fit in 98 13

BEE-A-SCALLY ch.m. 6 Scallywag - Beringa Bee by Sunley Builds Mrs C E Whiteway

1996 P(0)

853 31/3 Eyton-On-Se' (L) MDO 3m 13 GF *cls 2nd to 8th, hdd chsng grp til tiring 4 out, p.u. 3 out* P 0

Ran prominently only start 97 but 2 outings in 2 seasons so far 10

BEECH BROOK b.g. 8 Relkino - Brinkwood by Precipice Wood Mrs Emma Holman-West

1083 13/4 Guilsborough (L) MDN 3m 15 GF *trckd ldr to 11th, wknd & p.u. 15th* P 0

1283 27/4 Fakenham P-' (L) MDO 3m 9 G *chsd ldrs, ld 14th, drew clr apr last* 1 16

1530 18/5 Fakenham (L) HC 2m 5f 110yds 11 G *chsd ldrs, pkd 10th, mstk 6 out, wknd 4 out.* 4 13

Bolted up from bad field when winning; not disgraced in H/Chase; Restricted possible in 98 17

BEEHIVE QUEEN (Irish) — **I** 80^{2}, **I** 195^{1}

BEETALOT (Irish) — **I** 6^{3}, **I** 33^{P}, **I** 61^{P}, **I** 96^{1}, **I** 185^{P}

BEET FIVE (Irish) — **I** 438^{P}, **I** 472^{4}, **I** 576^{P}

BEET MAN (Irish) — **I** 269^{P}

BEEWORTHY b.m. 7 Gunner B - Miss Starworthy by Twilight Alley J Swinnerton

1996 U(-),P(0),P(0),3(13)

82 2/2 Wolverhampt' (L) MDN 3m 11 GS *chsd ldrs til lost tch 13th, t.o. & p.u. 16th* P 0

206 15/2 Weston Park (L) MDN 3m 9 G *nvr bttr than mid-div, p.u. 4 out* P 0

469 8/3 Eyton-On-Se' (L) MDN 2 1/2m 9 G *ld to 10th, ev ch 3 out, ran on onpcd* 3 12

722 29/3 Sandon (L) MDO 3m 10 GF *disp 2nd/3rd, und pres whn f 2 out* F -

Placed in 2 of 8 starts 96/7 (only completions) & more needed for a win 12

BEINN MOHR b.m. 10 Rymer - Misty Sky by Hot Brandy Mrs C Howell
1996 5(0),P(0),3(0),6(0),4(10),1(20),1(20),5(11)

293	1/3	Didmarton	(L)	INT	3m	16	G	*cls up til wknd 12th, t.o. & p.u. 2 out*	P	0
535	16/3	Erw Lon	(L)	CON	3m	12	GF	*ld 3rd-9th, wknd rpdly, p.u. 14th*	P	0
714	29/3	Llanvapley	(L)	CON	3m	15	GF	*held up in mid-div,rpd prog to ld 14th,hdd 2 out,no ext last*	3	15
904	5/4	Howick	(L)	OPE	3m	3	F	*(fav) chsd ldr, lft disp 10th til ld 2 out, drvn out*	1	15
1194	22/4	Chepstow	(L)	HC	3m	11	GF	*hit 2nd, soon bhnd, t.o..*	6	0
1223	26/4	Pyle	(R)	MEM	3m	6	GS	*ld to 5th,ld 9-12th & 14th,clr 3 out,rdn nxt,hdd flat*	2	18
1320	3/5	Bonvilston	(R)	CON	3m	8	G	*hld up mid-div, prog 12th, ev ch 3 out, hrd rdn flat, onepcd*	2	18
1469	11/5	Erw Lon	(L)	OPE	3m	6	GS	*cls up, ev ch 14th, mstk nxt, wknd 3 out*	5	18
1557	24/5	Bassaleg	(R)	CON	3m	9	G	*prom, ld 7th, jnd 12th, rdn 14th, hdd 3 out, no ext flat*	3	19
1600	31/5	Bassaleg	(R)	CON	3m	3	F	*(fav) w.w. went 2nd 9th, ld 12th, drew clr 4 out, easily*	1	18
1611	7/6	Umberleigh	(L)	OPE	3m	8	F	*prom til 4th & rdn aft 12th, strggling frm nxt*	5	0

Dual winner 96; changed hands; hard ride; found 2 soft races; tough & should win again 19

BELCHER ISLAND (Irish) — **I** 450,

BELFRY LAD b.g. 9 Ayyabaan - Sarah's Joy by Full Of Hope P T Norman

100	8/2	Great Treth'	(R)	RES	3m	14	GS	*prom to 10th, wll btn 14th, p.u. last*	P	0
312	1/3	Clyst St Ma'	(L)	RES	3m	8	HY	*(Jt fav) in tch to 4 out, wknd aft*	4	0
519	15/3	Cothelstone	(L)	MEM	3m	5	GS	*handy, mstk 11th, lft in ld 13th, unchal*	1	13
1093	16/4	Hockworthy	(L)	RES	3m	16	GF	*unruly pddck, prom to 9th, sn wknd, t.o. & p.u. last*	P	0

Maiden winner 95; missed 96; won poor race 97 & Restricted unlikely in 98 13

BELHABOUR (Irish) — **I** 23[2], **I** 81[1], **I** 124[F]

BELITLIR b.m. 5 Lir - Kimberley Ann by St Columbus B R J Young

102	8/2	Great Treth'	(R)	MDO	3m	8	GS	*t.o. 4th, p.u. 10th*	P	0
243	22/2	Lemalla	(R)	MDO	3m	12	S	*schoold rear til p.u. 13th*	P	0
458	8/3	Great Treth'	(R)	MDO	3m	15	S	*schoold rear til p.u. apr 9th*	P	0
792	31/3	Bishopsleigh	(R)	RES	3m	13	G	*schoold in rear til p.u. 13th*	P	0
1246	26/4	Bratton Down	(L)	MDO	3m	16	GS	*wth ldrs til wknd 13th, p.u. 3 out*	P	0
1400	5/5	High Bickin'	(R)	MDO	3m	14	G	*immed t.o. & schoold, wll bhnd & p.u. 14th*	P	0
1520	17/5	Bratton Down	(L)	MDO	3m	17	GS	*rear, poor 8th at 14th, fin wll, sntchd 3rd post*	3	11
1553	24/5	Mounsey Hil'	(R)	MDO	3m	11	G	*bhnd, 8th & losing tch 10th, p.u. 12th*	P	0

An extensive education so far & looks sure to improve in 98 14

BELLA BROWNIE (Irish) — **I** 48[4], **I** 138[1], **I** 257[3]

BELLAGHY BRIDGE b.m. 10 Dublin Taxi - Red Solitaire by Red God Mrs C Yates

436	8/3	Upton-On-Se'	(R)	MDO	3m	17	G	*14th & wkng whn f 8th*	F	-

Of no account 0

BEL LANE b.m. 8 Brotherly (USA) - Bow Lane by Idiot's Delight M R Watkins
1996 P(0),4(14),2(14),2(0)

88	2/2	Wolverhampt'	(L)	MDO	3m	13	GS	*prog 10th, cls up 12th, wknd 3 out, wll btn 4th whn ref last*	R	-
261	22/2	Newtown	(L)	MDN	3m	16	G	*ld to 9th, wknd 12th, wll bhnd & p.u. 15th*	P	0
639	22/3	Howick	(L)	MDN	3m	15	GF	*(bl) mostly 2nd/3rd, ld 14th, sn clr*	1	15
1237	26/4	Brampton Br'	(R)	RES	3m	13	G	*(vis) ld 4th-nxt, cls up til wknd 15th, p.u. aft nxt*	P	0
1525	17/5	Bredwardine	(R)	LAD	3m	9	G	*(vis) ld til ran wd bnd aft 5th, sn bhnd, t.o. 13th, p.u. last*	P	0
1556	24/5	Bassaleg	(R)	RES	3m	13	G	*(bl) ld to 3rd, ld/disp 8th-aft 2 out, wknd*	4	12

Headgear worked when winning (large but desperate bunch); little other form & Restricted unlikely 13

BELLAS FASHION VI (Irish) — **I** 96[F], **I** 283[P]

BELLE CHAPELLE ch.m. 9 Lighter - Bredon Belle by Conwyn Mrs S M Newell

261	22/2	Newtown	(L)	MDN	3m	16	G	*prom, ld 9-13th, wnd 15th*	4	0

Not disgraced only start 97 but very lightly-raced & time passing 10

BELL GLASS(FR) gr.g. 11 Bellypha - Greener Pastures (FR) by Rheingold G Walters
1996 P(0),P(0)

1361	5/5	Pantyderi	(L)	MEM	3m	4	G	*3rd at 4th, ld 11th, clr last, easily*	1	13

Useful to 95 but rarely seen since; popped up to doddle Members - same again only chance 98 14

BELLS WILL RING(IRE) b.g. 7 Roselier (FR) - Chapel Bells by River Beauty Ian Hamilton

161	15/2	Lanark	(R)	MDO	2m 5f	14	G	*clr ldr til hdd & no ext 2 out*	2	13
340	1/3	Corbridge	(R)	MDN	3m	10	G	*(fav) made all, qcknd clr last, comf*	1	15
584	17/3	Newcastle	(L)	HC	2 1/2m	11	GF	*keen, mstks, ld till hdd 4 out, soon wknd, t.o..*	4	10
697	29/3	Stainton	(R)	LAD	3m	5	F	*plld hrd, ld til disp 6th, f 15th, (dead)*	F	-

Dead 15

BELMOUNT BEAUTY(IRE) b or br.m. 8 Sheer Grit - Kakala by Bargello G B Foot
1996 1(13),P(0)

175 15/2 Ottery St M' (L) RES 3m 15 G *in tch, ev ch 4 out, p.u. nxt, lame* P 0

Maiden winner 96; problems only start 97; best watched **15**

BELMOUNT CAPTAIN ch.g. 12 Le Bavard (FR) - The Brown Link by Rugged Man Joint Ownership Terminated

1492 14/5 Cothelstone (L) MEM 3m 4 GF *w.w. chsd ldr 12th, rdn 16th, ld last, all out* 1 15

Winning chaser; well-ridden to scrape home but unlikely to figure at 13 .... **16**

BELPENEL ch.g. 11 Pharly (FR) - Seldovia by Charlottown Miss S Evans

202 15/2 Weston Park (L) LAD 3m 13 G *made most to 14th, 4th & btn whn u.r. 2 out* U -

Ladies winner 95; missed 96; can only be watched if reappearing **17**

BELVILLE POND (Irish) — **I** 107^F, **I** 232^F, **I** 354^P, **I** 529^P, **I** 594^P

BE MY HABITAT ch.g. 8 Be My Guest (USA) - Fur Hat by Habitat A L Hawkings

1996 P(0),F(-),P(0),4(0),U(-),P(0),5(0)

311 1/3 Clyst St Ma' (L) LAD 3m 9 HY *in tch to 2 out, 5th & btn whn u.r. last* U -
520 15/3 Cothelstone (L) LAD 3m 12 GS *(bl) nvr dang, t.o. & p.u. 3 out* P 0
864 31/3 Kingston St' (R) LAD 3m 6 F *(bl) in tch, chsd ldr til outpcd aft 3 out, rlld cls home* 3 16
1090 16/4 Hockworthy (L) LAD 3m 8 GF *(bl) mstk 4th, sn wll bhnd, t.o. 8th, p.u. 15th* P 0
1155 20/4 Stafford Cr' (R) LAD 3m 6 GF *(bl) alwys bhnd, lost tch 12th, t.o.* 5 0
1548 24/5 Mounsey Hil' (R) LAD 3m 10 G *(bl) sn wll bhnd, t.o. 6th, p.u. 9th* P 0

Ran surprisingly well 3rd start but only 4 completions from 13 outings 96/7 & will not win **10**

BE MY MOT (Irish) — **I** 98^F, **I** 159^3

BENALF (Irish) — **I** 100^P, **I** 155^2, **I** 223^F, **I** 315^3, **I** 341^1, **I** 387^6, **I** 578^P

BENBEATH b.g. 7 Dunbeath (USA) - Steelock by Lochnager Brian Gee

1996 2(14),F(-),5(0)

79 2/2 Market Rase' (L) MDO 2m 5f 9 GF *keen hld, prom, ld 4 out to 2 out, not pace of wnr* 2 12
252 22/2 Brocklesby ' (L) MDO 3m 9 G *(fav) alwys prom, ld 5 out, cont 4-2 out, just outpcd* 3 13

Ran well both starts but vanished early; good enough to win if fit 98 .... **14**

BENGERS MOOR b.g. 6 Town And Country - Quilpee Mai by Pee Mai J R Townshend

1996 1(16),2(20),1(20)

294 1/3 Didmarton (L) INT 3m 20 G *pllng, hld up, prog 7th, ld 12th, qcknd clr apr last* 1 24
520 15/3 Cothelstone (L) LAD 3m 12 GS *(fav) w.w. went 2nd 15th, disp & ev ch 2 out, no ext und pres flat* 2 25

Highly talented; may prove best under 3m & sure to make his mark under Rules; G-S **30**

BENGHAZI b or br.g. 13 Politico (USA) - Numerous by New Brig A M Thomson

1996 **5(NH),P(NH),F(NH),5(NH),P(NH)**

229 22/2 Friars Haugh (L) CON 3m 9 G *ld early, lost tch 4 out* 5 0
413 8/3 Dalston (R) OPE 3m 9 GS *chsd ldrs, strggling whn mstk 14th, no ch aft* 4 13
560 16/3 Lanark (R) CON 3m 8 GS *(bl) not fluent, clr ld til wknd & jmp slwly last, hdd flat* 3 20

Old stager; ran remarkably well at Lanark but unlikely to rpeat the feat at 14 .... **17**

BENTLEY MANOR ch.g. 8 M Double M (USA) - Sally Chase by Sallust M A Lloyd

1996 **P(NH),2(NH),R(NH)**

465 8/3 Eyton-On-Se' (L) OPE 3m 13 G *chsng grp, 2nd 13th, bad mstk nxt, sn btn, p.u. 4 out* P 0
1013 12/4 Bitterley (L) CON 3m 14 GF *nvr rchd ldrs, kpt on onepcd frm 15th* 5 0
1265 27/4 Southwell P' (L) OPE 3m 8 G *mid-div, prog to ld 13th, hdd 3 out, lft 2nd nxt* 2 19
1417 10/5 Warwick (L) HC 3 1/4m 8 G *held up, rdn and lost tch 10th, p.u. before 4 out.* P 0

Ran well 3rd start but little other encouragement & may disappoint in 98 .... **16**

BERGHOLT b.g. 5 Reprimand - Kina (USA) by Bering Keith Coe

128 9/2 Cottenham (R) MDO 3m 10 GF *plld hrd, cls up til 4th & outpcd 14th, wknd, p.u. 3 out* P 0
317 1/3 Marks Tey (L) MDN 3m 13 G *in tch, chsd ldng pair 16th, sn wknd, fin tired* 4 0
797 31/3 Marks Tey (L) MDO 3m 4 F *(fav) held up,prog disp ld 15th,ld 3 out,jnd nxt,qcknd clr bfrlast* 1 11

Won a terrible race; much more needed & yet to prove he stays; time on his side, at least **13**

BERGKAMP (Irish) — **I** 220^4

BERKANA RUN ch.g. 12 Deep Run - Geraldine's Pet by Laurence O R J Bailey

1996 9(0),U(-),P(0),U(-)

369 2/3 Mollington (R) MEM 3m 13 G *sn t.o.* 7 0
503 15/3 Ampton (R) XX 3m 11 GF *in tch to 12th, poor 5th 16th, ran on frm 3 out,nt rch ldrs* 3 11
1279 27/4 Fakenham P-' (L) OPE 3m 7 G *bhnd, prog & in tch 12th, no ch frm 15th* 5 13
1532 18/5 Mollington (R) CON 3m 11 GS *prom til outpcd frm 15th, no imp ldrs aft* 3 16

Dual winner 93; lost last 19 races; ran better in 97 but should extend losing sequence **13**

BERKELEY SUPREME (Irish) — **I** 312^P

BERKELEY VALE ch.g. 5 Brotherly (USA) - Minadonna by Don Enrico (USA) G C Lloyd

908 5/4 Howick (L) MDN 3m 7 F *s.s. t.o. whn ref 2nd* R -

Good stable but has shown no aptitude yet **0**

BERKLEY STREET b.m. 6 Lepanto (GER) - Kerry Street by Dairialatan E Vickery

1314 3/5 Holnicote (L) MDO 3m 8 G *sn bhnd, not alwys fluent, p.u. aft 12th* P 0
1498 14/5 Cothelstone (L) MDO 3m 9 GF *chsd ldng grp, jmpd slwly 9th, sn bhnd, t.o.* 6 0
1553 24/5 Mounsey Hil' (R) MDO 3m 11 G *alwys last, t.o. 10th, p.u. 14th* P 0
1615 7/6 Umberleigh (L) MDO 3m 11 F *(bl) ld 1st, blnd nxt & drppd rear, t.o. & p.u. 11th* P 0

.... **0**

BERRINGS DASHER ch.g. 10 Slippered - Lady Actress by Arctic Slave J A C Ayton
1996 P(0),P(0),2(16),3(18),2(18),**2(17)**

389 8/3 Sandown (R) HC 2 1/2m 110yds 6 G *waited with, chsd clr ldr from 6th, clr order 10th, ld apr 2 out, hdd and hit last, fd run-in.* 3 20
600 22/3 Parham (R) MEM 3m 7 F *handy, ld frm 13th jmpg wll, hdd 2 out, wknd* 2 13
983 12/4 Ascot (R) HC 3m 110yds 14 GF *alwys handy, driven and wknd from 3 out.* 5 16
1288 30/4 Cheltenham (L) HC 2m 5f 10 GF *rear, prog 10th, no impn on ldrs after 4 out, fith and well btn when p.u. near fin, dismntd.* P 0

Has ability but not good enough for H/Chases & does not stay 3m; problems last start **17**

BERT HOUSE b.g. 11 Brianston Zipper - Salmon Spirit by Big Deal A J Cottle
1996 P(0),F(-),P(0),U(-),P(0)

805 31/3 Wadebridge (L) OPE 3m 5 F *ld to 7th, styd prom til grdly wknd frm 3 out* 4 0
950 6/4 Black Fores' (R) MEM 3m 7 G *sn bhnd, t.o. whn hit marker bnd aft 13th, p.u. aft* P 0
1255 27/4 Black Fores' (R) CON 3m 4 F *ld 11th, made rest, ran on wll whn chal* 1 15
1397 5/5 High Bickin' (R) CON 3m 3 G *ld til blnd & rdr lost irons 3 out, not rcvr* 2 16
1579 26/5 Lifton (R) CON 3m 9 G *ld to 5th, lost tch rpdly, p.u. nxt* P 0

Non-stayer but found bad race - similar needed for any future chance **15**

BERTS CABIN (Irish) — **I** 65U, **I** 2205, **I** 3476

BERVIE HOUSE(IRE) br.g. 9 Strong Gale - Bramble Hill by Goldhill Mrs Judy Wilson
1996 P(0),P(0),6(12),2(18),**F(-)**,**P(0)**

8 25/1 Cottenham (R) CON 3m 5 GF *chsd ldr 6th, hit 3 out, sn rdn & no prog, subs promoted* 1 16
218 16/2 Heythrop (R) INT 3m 21 G *blnd & u.r. 1st* U -
383 5/3 Catterick (L) HC 3m 1f 110yds 10 G *prom, rdn along 12th, wknd from 4 out.* 7 0
545 16/3 Garthorpe (R) CON 3m 12 GF *(bl) mid div til blnd & u.r. 6th* U -
1162 20/4 Mollington (R) CON 3m 7 GF *chsd ldr,ld 13th,sn clr,hit 2 out,wknd rpdly & hdd apr last* 5 12
1205 26/4 Clifton On ' (L) CON 3m 13 GS *alwys prom, mostly 4th, ran on frm 4 out, not rch 1st pair* 3 17
1306 3/5 Cottenham (R) INT 3m 4 F *trckd ldr, ld 9th, clr but reluc frm 12th, hdd last, rallied* 2 19

Frustrating; sole win from last 13 outings courtesy of Jockey Club; ungenuine; hard to win on merit **17**

BESSIE'S WILL ch.m. 6 Chilibang - Empress Corina by Free State Mrs M Scale

1015 12/4 Bitterley (L) MDO 3m 12 GF *cls up whn c.o. apr 5th* C -
1067 13/4 Maisemore P' (L) MDO 3m 8 GF *in tch,jmpd rght 6th,outpcd 13th,rlld 3 out,btn whn ref last* R -
1183 20/4 Lydstep (L) MDO 3m 8 GF *rear whn ref 6th* R -
1460 11/5 Maisemore P' (L) MDO 3m 16 G *alwys rear, t.o. & p.u. 15th* P 0
1578 26/5 Chaddesley ' (L) MDO 3m 7 F *pllng,slw jmp 4th,in tch,wknd & nrly ref 12th,p.u. & dsmntd* P 0
1615 7/6 Umberleigh (L) MDO 3m 11 F *trckd ldrs, effrt aft 12th, 4th & btn whn mstk 14th, wknd* 3 0

Unpleasant & last start offers no real encouragement **10**

BEST INTEREST (Irish) — **I** 214U, **I** 3161, **I** 3651

BEST LEFT br.m. 7 Gennaro (FR) - Right Lady by Right Flare P L Southcombe
1996 R(-),**P(NH)**

520 15/3 Cothelstone (L) LAD 3m 12 GS *t.o. & p.u. 8th* P 0
932 6/4 Charlton Ho' (L) LAD 3m 6 G *last til ran out 5th* r -

Shows neither ability nor aptitude **0**

BET A LOT ch.m. 8 Balinger - Crimson Flag by Kinglet Mrs A M Murray
1996 P(0),4(0)

756 29/3 Kimble (L) MEM 3m 3 GF *hld up, 2nd 17th, clsng whn f nxt* F -
990 12/4 Kingston Bl' (L) MDN 3m 11 GF *hld up last pair,ran on 14th,went 2nd last,given no ch* 2 11
1453 10/5 Kingston Bl' (L) MEM 3m 3 G *(fav) ld 3rd & agn 7th, ld/disp til qcknd clr aft 3 out* 1 10
1567 25/5 Kingston Bl' (L) RES 3m 8 GF *(fav) chsng grp, went 2nd apr 2 out, ran on, no ch wnr* 2 14

First substantial form in 97; novice-ridden; do better with stronger handling; Restricted possible **16**

BETSEALE (Irish) — **I** 271P, **I** 493P, **I** 5392, **I** 5901

BETTER BY HALF(IRE) br.g. 9 Strong Gale - Belle Bavard by Le Bavard (FR) J F Symes

1996 P(0),P(0),F(-),P(0)

866 31/3 Kingston St' (R) MDO 3m 7 F *rear, mstk 7th, t.o. p.u. apr 13th* P 0

Yet to complete the course 0

BET WITH BAKER(IRE) br.g. 7 Ovac (ITY) - Moate Gypsy by Fine Blade (USA) George W Baker

1996 P(0),2(11),1(15),1(20),3(21)

3 19/1 Barbury Cas' (L) XX 3m 14 GF *(fav) mstks, ld 4th, clr aft to 2 out, hdd flat, rallied, lkd wnr* 2 19
236 22/2 Lemalla (R) INT 3m 12 S *keen hld, handy, 2nd at 11th, disp nxt, ld 2 out, clr last* 1 25
396 8/3 Barbury Cas' (L) CON 3m 9 G *(fav) mstk 1st, chsd ldrs 8th, mstk 10th, cls 3rd 12th,outpcd 14th* 3 17

Dual winner 96; beat hot field 2nd start 97; finished early; Opens if fit 98; G-S 25

BEWDLEY BOY ch.g. 8 Brando - Quiet Queen by Richboy J E Grey

1996 1(15),2(17),P(0)

524 15/3 Cothelstone (L) RES 3m 10 GS *prom, slght ld whn f 12th* F -
1211 26/4 Woodford (L) MEM 3m 8 G *hld up, prog 10th, wth wnr 4 out, wknd apr 2 out* 2 17
1439 10/5 Holnicote (L) RES 3m 9 G *prog 10th, ld 14th-nxt, sn wknd* 4 13
1519 17/5 Bratton Down (L) RES 3m 15 GS *ld/disp 3rd-9th, lost plc, prog to disp 3 out, no ext last* 3 17

Maiden winner 96; fair form 97 & consistent; should find Restricted 98; G-S 17

BEX BOY(IRE) ch.g. 6 Mon Tresor - Calcine by Roan Rocket C Warde-Aldam

839 31/3 Thorpe Lodge (L) MDO 3m 15 F *f 3rd* F -
1074 13/4 Whitwell-On' (R) MDO 2 1/2m 88yds 16 G *disp to 6th, losing tch whn u.r. 10th* U -
1106 19/4 Hornby Cast' (L) MDO 3m 10 G *prom,ld 5-8th,blndrd bdly nxt,lost plc qckly,wll bhnd f 14th* F -

Yet to complete the course 0

BEYOND THE STARS b.g. 6 Jupiter Island - MCA Lucky Star by Lucky Wednesday J C Collett

1996 **P(NH),8(NH),11(NH),10(NH),9(NH)**

1012 12/4 Bitterley (L) MEM 3m 6 GF *w.w. prog to chal 13th, ld nxt, kpt on frm 2 out* 1 17
1587 29/5 Uttoxeter (L) HC 2m 5f 11 GF *prom till f 7th.* F -

Strange season; decent effort in Members but off 7 weeks; could certainly win Confineds 19

BIANCONI b.g. 11 I'm A Star - Coach Road by Brave Invader (USA) D Luxton

1996 P(0),4(13)

48 1/2 Wadebridge (L) OPE 3m 5 G *trckd ldr 7th, lft in ld 14th, hdd last, no ext* 2 18
98 8/2 Great Treth' (R) OPE 3m 14 GS *mid-div til u.r. bend aft 9th* U -
309 1/3 Clyst St Ma' (L) CON 3m 7 HY *(fav) handy, effrt 3 out, alwys hld* 2 15
522 15/3 Cothelstone (L) CON 3m 14 GS *t.o. & p.u. 9th* P 0

Lightly raced these days; stays; finished early; hard to win again 15

BICKERTON POACHER ch.g. 7 Gabitat - On Tour by Queen's Hussar S A James

186 15/2 Erw Lon (L) MDN 3m 13 G *16s-7s, prom, 6th & in tch whn f 12th* F -
406 8/3 Llanfrynach (R) RES 3m 13 G *alwys rear, p.u. last* P 0
641 22/3 Howick (L) MDN 3m 9 GF *mostly 2nd/3rd, onepcd frm 16th* 3 0
842 31/3 Lydstep (L) MDO 3m 12 F *alwys rear, p.u. 7th* P 0
1229 26/4 Pyle (R) MDO 3m 11 GS *bltd bef start, in tch, wknd & mstk 10th, t.o. & p.u. 3 out* P 0
1324 3/5 Bonvilston (R) MDO 3m 16 G *mid-div, prog 4 out, cls 3rd whn f last* F -
1459 11/5 Maisemore P' (L) MDO 3m 12 G *mstk 7th, prog & in tch 12th, wknd 14th, t.o.* 4 0

Would have gone close 6th start but little other form & will find it hard to win 11

BIDDEN ch.g. 5 Most Welcome - True Nora by Ahonoora J S Warner

263 22/2 Newtown (L) MDN 3m 11 G *schoold, alwys last pair, t.o. & p.u. 12th* P 0

A brief educational season 0

BIDDYS BOY (Irish) — **I** 231P, **I** 315P, **I** 398F

BIG ARTHUR(IRE) b.g. 8 Royal Fountain - Rockholm Rosie by Tudor Rocket Brian D Foster

1996 **7(NH)**

527 15/3 Cothelstone (L) MDN 3m 14 GS *rear til p.u. 9th* P 0
1315 3/5 Holnicote (L) MDO 3m 7 G *(Jt fav) ld chsng grp, chal 3 out, ran out nxt whn ev ch* r -
1553 24/5 Mounsey Hil' (R) MDO 3m 11 G *(fav) (bl) prog 10th,lft 2nd & reluc 17th,lft solo 2out-last, stll btn* 2 0

Some ability but irresolute & beaten by remounter last start; may continue to frustrate 13

BIG BANDS ARE BACK(USA) b.g. 5 Alleged (USA) - Jetta J (USA) by Super Concorde (USA) A G Fear

1996 **7(NH),P(NH),P(NH)**

1094 16/4 Hockworthy (L) MDN 3m 11 GF *14s-6s,wth wnr clr of rest,ld 6 out-3 out,ev ch last,no ext* 2 12
1399 5/5 High Bickin' (R) MDO 3m 12 G *ld to 16th, cls up & ev ch til wknd last* 3 13
1521 17/5 Bratton Down (L) MDO 3m 16 GS *made all, clr 2 out, easily* 1 16

Speedy & romped home last start; may improve; needs easy 3m; Restricted possible 18

BIG BO (Irish) — I 53^{3}, I 74^{1}, I 194^{P}, I 259^{5}

BIG JIM b.g. 9 Strong Gale - Archetype by Over The River (FR) — Edward Retter

805 31/3 Wadebridge (L) OPE 3m 5 F *(fav) ld 7th, made rest, kpt on wll* 1 20

Broke duck in weak race; much more to prove & options severely limited now 17

BIG MURT (Irish) — I 56^{P}, I 108^{P}, I 229,

BIG REWARD b.g. 8 Big Connaught - Wardbrook by Damsire Unknown — K F Crook

1996 P(0),5(0),2(12),5(0),P(0),3(12),2(13),4(0)

54 1/2 Wadebridge (L) MDO 3m 13 G *jmpd big, alwys bhnd* 9 0

Placed 4 times in 96 but no show only start 97; best watched 10

BIG SEAMUS(IRE) ch.g. 7 Carlingford Castle - Galla's Pride by Quayside — Mrs J M Whitley

1996 2(14),1(12),2(12),6(0),1(18)

52 1/2 Wadebridge (L) INT 3m 4 G *trckd ldrs, effrt 2 out, kpt on wll und pres* 3 17

Dual winner 96; hard ride & vanished 3rd week 97; best in blinkers; G-F 18

BIG SPENDER (Irish) — I 7^{P}, I 73, , I 171^{P}, I 422^{P}, I 558^{P}, I 564^{P}

BILBO BAGGINS(IRE) ch.g. 9 Beau Charmeur (FR) - Hiking by Royal Highway — Mrs P A Tetley

1996 6(0),**6(0)**,4(11),5(0),P(0)

148 9/2 Tweseldown (R) XX 3m 12 GF *n.j.w. in rear, t.o. 13th* 8 0
303 1/3 Parham (R) RES 3m 10 G *alwys bhnd, t.o. 13th, p.u. 3 out* P 0
488 9/3 Tweseldown (R) RES 3m 10 G *prom to 10th, wll bhnd frm 13th, t.o.* 6 0
601 22/3 Parham (R) RES 3m 4 F *rear, prog 4 out, ld apr last, ran on well* 1 13
830 31/3 Heathfield (R) MXO 3m 6 F *hld up last, mstk 6th, rpd hdwy 3 out, ld flat, ran on well* 1 19
983 12/4 Ascot (R) HC 3m 110yds 14 GF *alwys bhnd, t.o..* 8 0

Changed hands & remarkably revived 97; good performance 5th start; may struggle to follow up; Firm 17

BILLIE'S MATE (Irish) — I 33^{P}, I 90^{P}, I 217^{4}, I 270^{1}, I 340^{2}, I 387, , I 494^{3}

BILLION DOLLARBILL ch.g. 9 Nicholas Bill - Rest Hill Dolly by Balinger — Brian Tetley

1996 2(16),1(16),2(20),2(21),2(13),5(0)

72 2/2 Higham (L) INT 3m 4 GF *prom, ld 2nd-3rd, blnd 11th, prog 16th, ld flat, rdn out* 1 19
579 16/3 Detling (L) OPE 4m 9 F *trckd ldrs, chalng whn ran out 3 out* r -
832 31/3 Heathfield (R) INT 3m 2 F *made all, drvn alng 15th, styd on strngly frm 3 out* 1 17
1285 29/4 Huntingdon (R) HC 3m 10 G *soon pushed along in rear, rdn and struggling 10th, t.o. and p.u. before 3 out.* P 0
1444 10/5 Peper Harow (L) OPE 3m 5 GF *in tch, outpcd 10th, rallied 13th, 2nd 3 out, kpt on flat* 2 20

Dependable, solid & improved in 97; stays; no show in H/Chase; win Confineds 98; G/S-F 21

BILL JOYCE (Irish) — I 132^{P}, I 215^{P}, I 409,

BILLY BARTER(IRE) g. 7 Tanfirion - Dia Glas — J C Worrow

1996 **15(NH),13(NH),U(NH),9(NH),P(NH),F(NH)**

436 8/3 Upton-On-Se' (R) MDO 3m 17 G *ld 7-12th, cls up til wknd frm 3 out* 3 0
527 15/3 Cothelstone (L) MDN 3m 14 GS *(fav) ld 1st, prom til lft in ld 15th, ev ch til outpcd flat* 2 14
1045 12/4 Cothelstone (L) MDO 3m 6 GF *(fav) ld to 5th, 2nd aft til ld 10th, not extndd* 1 14
1237 26/4 Brampton Br' (R) RES 3m 13 G *trckd ldrs, cls 3rd 15th, rdn to ld 2 out, hdd & no ext last* 2 15
1519 17/5 Bratton Down (L) RES 3m 15 GS *(fav) prom, disp 8th-12th, 4th & outpcd 15th, no ch & p.u. last* P 0
1551 24/5 Mounsey Hil' (R) RES 3m 13 G *(bl) ld to apr 15th, sn fdd, p.u. 3 out* P 0

Scrambled home from subsequent winners but found out in tougher races; blinkers no help 16

BILLY BATHGATE ch.g. 11 Gala Performance (USA) - Royal River by Fury Royal — B R Hughes

1996 **P(NH)**

90 5/2 Ludlow (R) HC 2 1/2m 6 G *nvr far away, left in narrow ld after 8th, hdd after next, rdn and mstk 4 out, soon lost tch.* 3 0
537 16/3 Erw Lon (L) OPE 3m 9 GF *tongue-strap, f 2nd* F -

A light of former days 0

BILLY BUOYANT b.g. 8 Silly Prices - Rebrona by Rebel Prince — Mrs F T Walton

343 1/3 Corbridge (R) MDO 3m 14 G *sn wll bhnd, t.o. & p.u. 12th* P 0
733 29/3 Alnwick (L) MDN 3m 5 F *rear, no imp on ldrs whn blnd & u.r. 12th* U -
996 12/4 Tranwell (L) MDO 3m 8 F *alwys rear div, 7th whn p.u. aft 5th* P 0
1172 20/4 Hexham Poin' (L) MDO 3m 4 GF *handy in 4th til went 3rd & mstk 3 out, demoted last* 4 0
1336 3/5 Mosshouses (L) MDO 3m 7 F *sn bhnd, p.u. aft 11th* P 0
1515 17/5 Corbridge (R) MEM 3m 5 GS *chsd ldr, mstk 14th, ev ch 2 out, onepcd* 3 0

Beaten in bad race last start & yet to show any real ability 0

BILLY-GWYN ch.g. 8 Netherkelly - Irish Holiday by Simbir — W Tudor

294 1/3 Didmarton (L) INT 3m 20 G *prom, ld 10-12th, wknd rpdly 14th, p.u. nxt* P 0

535 16/3 Erw Lon (L) CON 3m 12 GF *mid-div, no ch whn p.u. 3 out* P 0
1223 26/4 Pyle (R) MEM 3m 6 GS *cls up, ld 12th-14th, rdn & btn 3 out, wknd & p.u. last* P 0
1366 5/5 Pantyderi (L) INT 3m 6 G *alwys rear, p.u. 2 out* P 0
1468 11/5 Erw Lon (L) INT 3m 7 GS *prom, ld 14th, p.u. 16th, dsmntd, lame* P 0

Dual winner 95; missed 96; unable to recapture form & may be finished now 13

BILLYMAC (Irish) — I 14P
BILLY THE SNAKE (Irish) — I 2553
BILSTON GEORGE b.g. 8 Tudorville - Summer Jasmine Vii by Damsire Unregistered Mrs G M Riley

451 8/3 Newton Brom' (R) MDN 3m 8 G *ld 1st, lost plc, lft 3rd 15th, styd on, no imp* 3 0
1082 13/4 Guilsborough (L) MDN 3m 14 GF *prog 9th, disp 13th til ld 16th, clr 3 out, hld on flat* 1 13
1278 27/4 Fakenham P-' (L) RES 3m 11 G *chsd ldrs, blnd 11th, 5th & wkng 15th, no ch whn u.r. last* U -

Beat a large but undistinguished field (slow time) & much more needed for Restricted hopes 98 14

BIRCHALL BOY br.g. 9 Julio Mariner - Polarita by Arctic Kanda P L Southcombe
1996 1(15),5(0),**3(12)**

94 7/2 Newbury (L) HC 2 1/2m 12 G *hit 4th, soon bhnd, t.o. when p.u. before 2 out.* P 0

Maiden winner 96; always lightly raced & soon vanished 97; best watched 16

BISHOPS ISLAND b.g. 11 The Parson - Gilded Empress by Menelek Lord Vestey
1996 **F(NH),5(NH),6(NH),2(NH),4(NH),3(NH)**

5 19/1 Barbury Cas' (L) OPE 3m 11 GF *in tch, 6th hlfwy, onepcd frm 3 out* 4 23
55 1/2 Kingston Bl' (L) CON 3m 15 GF *ld 5th til 2 out, no ext whn hdd* 2 23
220 16/2 Heythrop (R) OPE 3m 20 G *blnd & u.r. 1st* U -
295 1/3 Didmarton (L) OPE 3m 9 G *trckd ldrs, prssd wnr 11-12th, 3rd & btn 14th, lft 2nd last* 2 22
651 22/3 Siddington (L) OPE 3m 7 F *(fav) not fluent, hld up, prog 10th, 3rd & no imp frm 15th* 3 21

Winning chaser; useful pointer; novice-ridden mostly; ill at ease last start; win if fit 98; Good 23

BISHOPS TALE b.g. 7 Derring Rose - Lilac Silk by Tycoon II Mrs Richard Pilkington
1996 **13(NH)**

29 26/1 Marks Tey (L) MDN 3m 10 GF *keen hld, ld 4th-15th, wkng whn f 17th* F -
712 29/3 High Easter (L) MDO 3m 4 F *hld up, prog to 2nd 15th, ld 2out, sn clr, comf* 1 14
1080 13/4 Guilsborough (L) RES 3m 11 GF *pllng, cls up, blnd 12th, chal & ev ch 3 out, wknd nxt* 4 13
1278 27/4 Fakenham P-' (L) RES 3m 11 G *hld up, prog & mstk 10th, went 2nd apr 2 out, onepcd* 2 17
1505 16/5 Folkestone (R) HC 2m 5f 8 G *started v slowly, bhnd, rdn after 7th, no prog 9th, soon t.o..* 5 0
1605 1/6 Dingley (R) RES 3m 13 GF *prom,mstk 10th, lft in ld nxt-13th, wknd sddnly & p.u. 15th* P 0

Won a poor Maiden & showed nasty symptoms after; non-stayer; pulls very hard; L/H; Firm 15

BITE BACK (Irish) — I 1983, I 243P, I 459P
BI THEN(IRE) b.m. 8 Henbit (USA) - Twitchit by Crash Course Mrs J G Dudgeon

1051 13/4 Lockerbie (R) MDN 3m 10 F *prog to trck ldrs whn u.r. 11th* U -

In touch when departing & may do better if ready 98 10

BIT OF A BLETHER(IRE) b.g. 8 Strong Gale - Chatty Actress by Le Bavard (FR) Mrs Alix Stevenson
1996 F(-)

229 22/2 Friars Haugh (L) CON 3m 9 G *(fav) ld 9th til mstk 3 out, no ch aft* 4 14
611 22/3 Friars Haugh (L) CON 3m 11 GF *(Jt fav) alwys hndy, ld brfly 4 out, no ext frm 2 out* 2 20
1426 10/5 Aspatria (L) OPE 3m 9 G *trckd ldr to 12th, mstk 14th, grad wknd* 3 13
1512 17/5 Corbridge (R) OPE 3m 10 GS *prom til wknd 3 out* 3 19

Dual winner 95; one run only 96 & interrupted season 97; has ability & may do better 98 20

BITOFABREEZE (Irish) — I 744
BIT OF A CHARACTER (Irish) — I 100F, I 1551
BIT OF A CITIZEN(IRE) b.f. 6 Henbit (USA) - Boreen Citizen R Mason
1996 **10(NH)**

298 1/3 Didmarton (L) RES 3m 15 G *chsd ldrs, 4th & outpcd 13th, 5th & wll btn whn p.u. last* P 0
404 8/3 Llanfrynach (R) INT 3m 17 G *hld up mid-div, prog to 4th 2 out, drvn to ld nr fin* 1 17
636 22/3 Howick (L) CON 3m 12 GF *(fav) cls up, 3rd 3 out, rdn & no ext frm nxt* 3 18
1133 19/4 Bonvilston (R) INT 3m 8 G *cls up, ld 15th, hdd 2 out, no ext* 2 18
1224 26/4 Pyle (R) CON 3m 7 GS *w.w. prog 7th, ld 14th, drvn out frm 2 out* 1 20
1507 16/5 Stratford (L) HC 3m 10 G *held up, hdwy 11th, btn 3rd when blnd and u.r. 3 out.* U -

Irish Maiden winner 96; consistent in 97; responds to pressure; should win more 98; G-S 22

BIT OF A DO b.g. 7 Idiot's Delight - Deep Dora by Deep Run Mrs D E S Surman

60 1/2 Kingston Bl' (L) MDN 3m 17 GF *nvr seen wth ch, p.u. 14th* P 0
990 12/4 Kingston Bl' (L) MDN 3m 11 GF *w.w. prog whn mstk 10th,sn rdn,in tch 14th,wknd & p.u.3 out* P 0
1210 26/4 Woodford (L) RES 3m 14 G *f 3rd* F -
1452 10/5 Kingston Bl' (L) MDO 3m 9 G *hld up,lft 3rd 9th,2nd nxt,ld 13th-aft nxt,wknd,p.u.2 out* P 0

No signs of stamina & yet to complete 0

BIT OF A GRIP(IRE) b.g. 5 Lancastrian - For Love Nor Money by Golden Love — J E Cottingham

1073 13/4 Whitwell-On' (R) MDO 2 1/2m 88yds 17 G *rear, strgglng 7th, t.o. & p.u. 11th* P 0
1262 27/4 Southwell P' (L) MDO 3m 15 G *mid-div, drppd rear 11th, sn wll bhnd* 5 0
1479 11/5 Garthorpe (R) MDO 3m 12 GS *chsd ldrs, lost plc & blnd 10th, t.o. & p.u. 3 out* P 0

Well-beaten only completion but could do better with experience 0

BIT OF A LADY (Irish) — I 570^{P}, I 607^{P}, I 610^{P}

BITOFAMIXUP(IRE) br.g. 6 Strong Gale - Geeaway by Gala Performance (USA) — Mike Roberts

1996 P(0),2(11),1(16),1(17),**14(NH)**

194 15/2 Higham (L) OPE 3m 12 G *conf rdn,hld up,prog 11th,ld on bit aft 16th,sn clr,imprssv* 1 32
287 27/2 Huntingdon (R) HC 3m 13 GS *(Co fav) chsd ldrs, lost pl 11th, rallied next, ld 5 out, driven out.* 1 30
888 3/4 Aintree (L) HC 3m 1f 9 G *j.w, held up, smooth hdwy to chase ldr 6 out, ld soon after 4 out, soon qcknd clr, impressive.* 1 34
1295 2/5 Bangor (L) HC 3m 110yds 4 G *(fav) nvr far away, ld 14th, clr apr 2 out, easily.* 1 32
1591 31/5 Stratford (L) HC 3 1/2m 11 G *patiently rdn, relentess prog final cct, ch and driven along apr 3 out, no ext from next.* 2 36

Top-class performer; stays & quickens; could make his mark under Rules; G/S-F 36

BITOFANATTER ch.g. 9 Palm Track - Little Ginger by Cawston's Clown — David Caldwell

1996 U(-)

162 15/2 Lanark (R) MDO 3m 16 G *mid-div, prog 4 out, not quite rch ldrs* 3 13
415 8/3 Dalston (R) RES 3m 19 GS *mid-div, 9th hlfwy, prog 13th, prssd wnr apr 2 out, just hld* 2 17
559 16/3 Lanark (R) MEM 3m 3 GS *(fav) ld frm 11th, sn clr, fin alone* 1 15
1050 13/4 Lockerbie (R) RES 3m 5 F *made most, went clr frm 14th, mstk 2 out, unchal* 1 18
1332 3/5 Mosshouses (L) INT 3m 4 F *(fav) made all, drew wll clr frm 2 out* 1 21
1427 10/5 Aspatria (L) INT 3m 7 G *made all, wll clr frm 10th, eased flat, imprssv* 1 24

Finally came good with a vengeance in 97; gallops & stays; could win H/Chase; G/S-F 26

BIT OF AN IDIOT b.g. 9 Idiot's Delight - Deep Dora by Deep Run — Mrs D E S Surman

1996 P(0),3(16),2(16)

487 9/3 Tweseldown (R) MDO 3m 12 G *ld 2nd, set fast pace, drew rght away 15th, imprssv* 1 20

Flew home & disappeared; Restricted formality if back in 98 22

BIT OF ROUGH(IRE) b.g. 7 Roselier (FR) - Win Em All by General Ironside — Miss Denise Foode

1996 **10(NH),P(NH),9(NH)**

88 2/2 Wolverhampt' (L) MDO 3m 13 GS *alwys bhnd, mstks 7 & 8th, t.o. & p.u. 12th* P 0

Seems aptly named 0

BITTER ALOE b.g. 8 Green Desert (USA) - Sometime Lucky by Levmoss — Mrs Julie Read

1996 2(17),1(18)

72 2/2 Higham (L) INT 3m 4 GF *(fav) ld to 2nd, ld 3rd, jnd 15th, ev ch 3 out, wknd nxt* 3 11

Restricted winner 96; very lightly raced & finished 3rd weekend 97; Good; best watched 16

BIX b or br.g. 6 Adbass (USA) - Valiant Dancer by Northfields (USA) — J Parfitt

1996 r(-),F(-),1(16)

190 15/2 Erw Lon (L) RES 3m 11 G *hld up, prog to jn ldrs 13th, wknd 15th, p.u. 2 out* P 0

Maiden winner 96; headstrong & vanished after one run 97; best watched 16

BLACK ABBEY (Irish) — I 41^{F}

BLACK AND BLUES b.h. 11 Music Boy - Blackeye by Busted — Stuart Scott

565 16/3 Lanark (R) MDO 3m 10 GS *ld til 12th, wknd frm 4 out* 5 0
613 22/3 Friars Haugh (L) MDN 3m 12 GF *wnt 2nd 4 out, chal 3 out, no ext apr last* 2 12

Alternates between occasional pointing efforts & Flat racing with little success in either 12

BLACK BOREEN (Irish) — I 225^{2}

BLACK ERMINE(IRE) br.g. 6 Wylfa - Corston Velvet by Bruni — Mrs P K J Brightwell

1996 1(15),5(0)

126 9/2 Cottenham (R) RES 3m 14 GF *mid-div, pshd alng 9th, no prog, wll bhnd whn p.u. 3 out* P 0
324 1/3 Marks Tey (L) RES 3m 16 G *nvr bttr thn mid-div, lost tch 14th, t.o. & p.u. 3 out* P 0
1135 19/4 Bonvilston (R) RES 3m 14 G *held up, prog 14th to chal 2 out, onepcd aft* 3 15
1227 26/4 Pyle (R) RES 3m 15 GS *cls up,rmndr 9th,chsd ldr 14th,ld 2 out-apr last,wknd* 4 14
1471 11/5 Erw Lon (L) RES 3m 9 GS *(fav) sttld rear, prog 11th, nvr able to chal* 3 12
1556 24/5 Bassaleg (R) RES 3m 13 G *(fav) lft in ld 7th,ld/disp aft,ld 2 out,hrd rdn & wknd flat,hldon* 1 14

Maiden winner 96; changed hands twice since; lucky last start & barely stays; hard to win again 16

BLACK FASHION (Irish) — I 56^{F}, I 91^{P}, I 150^{F}, I 186^{R}, I 218^{F}, I 270^{4}
BLACK FOUNTAIN (Irish) — I 12^{P}, I 38^{2}, I 81^{P}
BLACK IS BEAUTIFUL (Irish) — I 481^{P}
BLACKNOCK (Irish) — I 47^{P}, I 103, , I 196^{P}
BLACK SERENE (Irish) — I 319^{P}, I 570, , I 599^{4}
BLACK SPRING (Irish) — I 264^{U}, I 304^{P}

BLACK SPUR b.r.g. 15 Spur On - Ravenside by Marcus Superbus — T R Beadle

265	22/2	Duncombe Pa'	(R)	CON	3m	15	G	*mid-div til lost tch 6th, sn t.o., p.u. 10th*	P	0
353	2/3	Great Stain'	(L)	CON	3m	9	S	*ld to 2nd, trckd ldr whn ran out 4th*	r	-
423	8/3	Charm Park	(L)	OPE	3m	7	GF	*mid-div, rddn 11th, mstks 13th,sn lost tch,t.o. & p.u. 4 out*	P	0
507	15/3	Dalton Park	(R)	OPE	3m	8	GF	*prom, 3rd whn f 11th*	F	-
812	31/3	Tranwell	(L)	OPE	3m	7	G	*nvr on terms wth ldrs, poor 6th 3 out, wknd run in*	7	0
1418	10/5	Easingwold	(L)	MEM	3m	6	GF	*ld til ran out 7th*	r	-

No longer of any account 0

BLACK SWANEE (Irish) — I 304^{P}, I 425^{P}, I 445^{P}, I 519^{P}, I 565^{P}, I 596^{6}, I 606^{F}
BLACKWATER HEIGHTS (Irish) — I 195^{P}, I 258^{3}

BLACKWATER LADY(IRE) b.m. 8 Torus - Adventure Run by Deep Run — P A D Scouller

220	16/2	Heythrop	(R)	OPE	3m	20	G	*in tch in rear, eased & p.u. 12th*	P	0
305	1/3	Parham	(R)	OPE	3m	9	G	*(fav) mid-div, prog to ld aft 12th, hdd 4 out, wknd 2 out*	3	17
1057	13/4	Hackwood Pa'	(L)	XX	3m	4	GF	*(fav) ld 4-6th, ld & mstk 2 out, qckn d clr last*	1	20
1226	26/4	Pyle	(R)	OPE	3m	6	GS	*last whn mstks 2nd & 3rd, sn t.o.*	4	0

Unbeaten in 4 Irish points 96 (all modest races); disappointing in England; much to prove 98; G/F 19

BLACKWOODSCOUNTRY b.g. 7 Town And Country - Sweet Spice by Native Bazaar — Mrs Winifred A Birkinshaw

1996 3(12),3(13),1(16),P(0),F(-)

266	22/2	Duncombe Pa'	(R)	RES	3m	19	G	*prom, disp ld 12th, ld 2 out, hdd & onepcd flat*	2	17
424	8/3	Charm Park	(L)	RES	3m	12	GF	*(fav) alwys prom, prog to ld last, ran on wll*	1	17
1071	13/4	Whitwell-On'	(R)	CON	3m	10	G	*prom, ev ch 14th, not qckn frm 3 out*	3	17
1247	26/4	Easingwold	(L)	CON	3m	9	GS	*cls up, tk 2nd 2 out, outpcd by wnnr*	2	18
1419	10/5	Easingwold	(L)	CON	3m	8	GF	*(fav) mid-div, prog 6th, ld 4 out, jnd last, styd on und pres flat*	1	20

Maiden winner 96; consistent, stays & one paced; Confineds again likely 98; G/F-G/S 22

BLACON POINT b.g. 6 Rakaposhi King - Doris Blake by Roscoe Blake — J S Swindells

114	9/2	Wetherby Po'	(L)	MDO	3m	8	GF	*rear & mstk 2nd, sn lost tch, t.o. 10th*	5	0
1346	3/5	Gisburn	(R)	LAD	3m	5	GF	*rear, t.o. 12th, p.u. 14th*	P	0

An interrupted season of no promise 0

BLAKES FOLLY(IRE) gr.g. 9 Sexton Blake - Welsh Folly by Welsh Saint — R H M Hargreave

1996 F(-),3(14),4(10),4(10),3(14),3(13)

230	22/2	Friars Haugh	(L)	RES	3m	15	G	*nvr bttr than mid-div*	6	0
415	8/3	Dalston	(R)	RES	3m	19	GS	*mid-div, 10th hlfwy, prog 15th, kpt on, no dang*	8	0
894	5/4	Wetherby Po'	(L)	RES	3m	6	F	*rear, effrt 3 out, sn outpcd*	4	13
994	12/4	Tranwell	(L)	LAD	3m	5	F	*ld 3rd til mstk & u.r. nxt*	U	-
1102	19/4	Hornby Cast'	(L)	LAD	3m	7	G	*s.i.s., rear, blndrd & u.r. 9th*	U	-
1408	5/5	Witton Cast'	(R)	LAD	3m	5	GS	*rear, outpcd 15th, styd on wll frm 2 out, tk 2nd cls home*	2	21
1511	17/5	Corbridge	(R)	LAD	3m	10	GS	*rear, prog 6th, ev ch 3 out, sn wknd*	6	15

Maiden winner 95; well beaten in Restricteds but astounding 6th start in 97; win Ladies if repeating ... 19

BLAME BARNEY (Irish) — I 10^{S}, I 138^{3}, I 140^{U}, I 207^{P}, I 304^{4}, I 384^{2}, I 443^{P}

BLAME THE GROOM(IRE) b.g. 7 Shy Groom (USA) - Peak by High Top — Mrs Ian McKie

374	2/3	Mollington	(R)	MDN	3m	14	G	*1st ride, last & t.o. til p.u. 13th*	P	0
450	8/3	Newton Brom'	(R)	MDN	3m	7	G	*chsd wnr, no ext frm 2 out*	3	0
653	22/3	Siddington	(L)	RES	3m	10	F	*in tch in rear to 12th, sn bhnd, t.o.*	6	0

Novice-ridden & shows no great promise yet 0

BLANK CHEQUE b.g. 7 Idiot's Delight - Quickapenny by Espresso — D J Coates

1996 r(-),P(0),R(-),8(0)

269	22/2	Duncombe Pa'	(R)	MDO	3m	16	G	*mid-div, prog 13th, cls 3rd whn f 3 out*	F	-
358	2/3	Great Stain'	(L)	MDO	3m	14	S	*prom, disp 3 out, not qckn nxt*	2	14
420	8/3	Dalston	(R)	MDO	2 1/2m	8	GS	*mid-div, clsd 11th, chsd wnr & hit 2 out, no imp*	2	13
768	29/3	Whittington	(L)	MDO	3m	10	S	*(fav) ld to 15th, lost tch, ran on wll agn to ld last,outpcd flat*	2	13
942	6/4	Tabley	(R)	MDO	3m	8	G	*ld to 10th, disp ld 15th, bttr jmp last, styd on*	1	15

Gradually got act together; beat subsequent winner last start; Restricted chance if staying sweet 17

BLASKET SOUND (Irish) — I 58^{P}, I 568^{1}

BLAZEY LADY (Irish) — I 166^{P}, I 222^{P}, I 499,

BLAZING CRACK (Irish) — I 499^{F}, I 544^{3}, I 601^{3}, I 611^{3}

BLESSED OLIVER ch.g. 7 Relkino - Oca by O'Grady — Mrs David Plunkett

1996 **3(NH),5(NH),3(NH),F(NH)**

296	1/3	Didmarton	(L)	LAD	3m	13	G	*wll bhnd, ran on frm 11th, 4th & no more imp frm 14th*	4	11

NH Flat winner; no chance in hot Ladies & promptly vanished; has some ability 17

BLUAGALE (Irish) — I 117^{P}, I 176^{1}, I 252^{P}, I 290^{1}, I 373^{1}, I 465^{3}

BLUE ALLIANCE (Irish) — I 111^{P}, I 179^{P}, I 251^{P}

BLUE BAY (Irish) — I 214^{P}, I 250^{P}, I 288^{P}

BLUEBELL TRACK b or br.m. 11 Saher - Douriya — A R Trotter

37	26/1	Alnwick	(L)	MDO	3m	15	G	*mid-div, no ch frm 13th, kpt on*	4	0
135	9/2	Alnwick	(L)	MDO	3m	12	G	*alwys prom, 5th 4 out, styd on frm 2 out, sntchd 2nd post*	2	0
162	15/2	Lanark	(R)	MDO	3m	16	G	*nvr bttr than mid-div*	5	10
234	22/2	Friars Haugh	(L)	MDO	3m	15	G	*nvr rchd ldng grp*	3	0
414	8/3	Dalston	(R)	XX	3m	9	GS	*in tch to 10th, sn strgglng, t.o. 15th*	4	0
614	22/3	Friars Haugh	(L)	MDN	3m	13	GF	*4th hlfwy, nvr rchd ldrs, lft 3rd last*	3	0

Dead 10

BLUE CASTLE (Irish) — I 470^{F}

BLUE CHEEK b or br.g. 11 Strong Gale - Star Streaker by Star Moss — J Mahon

1996 U(-),**5(19)**,**2(24)**,U(-)

57	1/2	Kingston Bl'	(L)	LAD	3m	13	GF	*alwys prom, ld aft 13th, made rest, drvn out*	1	24
257	22/2	Newtown	(L)	LAD	3m	12	G	*prom, chsd wnr 14th, mstks nxt 2, sn btn*	3	23
587	19/3	Ludlow	(R)	HC	2 1/2m	18	GF	*made virtually all, drew clr from 2 out.*	1	32
890	4/4	Aintree	(L)	HC	2 3/4m	14	G	*cl up, mstk 3rd (Chair), jmpd slowly and outpcd 4 out, hdwy from 3 out, ld soon after next, clr last, easily.*	1	29

Very speedy & useful & claimed major prize; best under 3m; should win more H/Chases at 12 if fit;G-F 29

BLUE GAS (Irish) — I 250^{P}, I 360^{3}, I 508^{P}, I 586^{P}

BLUEILIER (Irish) — I 246^{6}

BLUE IS THE COLOUR(IRE) ch.g. 8 The Parson - Avocan by Avocat — Miss E M Hewitt

1996 1(14),1(20)

1475	11/5	Garthorpe	(R)	XX	3m	13	GS	*(fav) w.w. prog 6th, chsd wnr 2 out, no imp flat*	2	17

Unbeaten in 2 starts 96; late to appear 97; still prove useful if right 98; Soft 21

BLUE NIGHT b.m. 8 Latest Model - Midinette by Midsummer Night II — Mrs E Scott

1996 U(-),1(15)

557	16/3	Ottery St M'	(L)	RES	3m	9	G	*pllng, ld 8th-15th, cls up aft, ev ch whn u.r. 2 out*	U	-
1436	10/5	Holnicote	(L)	MEM	3m	5	G	*w.w. effrt & ld 3 out, hdd & mstk nxt, sn btn*	4	10

Maiden winner 96; lightly-raced & interrupted season 97; best watched 14

BLUE ROSETTE b.g. 8 Lucky Wednesday - Cadenette by Brigadier Gerard — K R Dance

1996 P(0),2(0),2(13)

261	22/2	Newtown	(L)	MDN	3m	16	G	*(fav) hld up, steady prog 12th, just ld & f 2 out*	F	16
437	8/3	Upton-On-Se'	(R)	MDO	3m	15	G	*(fav) cls up whn f 7th*	F	-

Changed hands 97; unlucky 1st start but a jinx horse & may continue to frustrate 15

BLUE VAPOUR ch.m. 8 Royal Match - Clan Royal by Royal Smoke — G I Isaac

221	16/2	Heythrop	(R)	RES	3m	15	G	*sn rear, bhnd whn f 8th*	F	-

No show on debut 0

BLUFF COVE ch.g. 15 Town Crier - Dolly Dickins by Double-U-Jay — Sam Hatfield

876	1/4	Upton-On-Se'	(R)	MEM	3m	7	GF	*rear whn u.r. 6th*	U	-
1064	13/4	Maisemore P'	(L)	CON	3m	13	GF	*alwys wll bhnd, t.o. whn blnd 10th*	7	0

Useful in his day but a spent force now 0

BLUSHING STAR b.g. 10 Le Bavard (FR) - Vulstar by Vulgan — S M Graves

204	15/2	Weston Park	(L)	RES	3m	13	G	*ld to 3rd, cls up, ran on onepcd frm 4 out, tk 2nd 2 out*	2	15
670	23/3	Eaton Hall	(R)	RES	3m	15	GF	*cls up at 10th, in tch 14th, fdd*	5	12
852	31/3	Eyton-On-Se'	(L)	RES	3m	11	GF	*mid-div early, ld 9-13th, sn btn whn hdd, p.u. 3 out*	P	0

Ran well enough 1st 2 starts but problem last outing; best watched 14

BOARD GAME b.g. 12 Angel Aboard - Rusty Lowe by Rustam — A Beedles

1996 6(0),1(16)

848 31/3 Eyton-On-Se' (L) MEM 3m 6 GF *sn t.o., fence bhnd whn p.u. 5 out* P 0

Restricted winner 96; always lightly-raced & looks finished now 0

BOARDING SOCIETY (Irish) — I 110[P], I 201[P], I 453[6], I 514[P]

BOBBIE'S GIRL(IRE) ch.m. 7 Roselier (FR) - Ballinattin Girl by Laurence O — Miss J C Fowler

401 8/3 Llanfrynach (R) LAD 3m 14 G *alwys wll in rear* 10 0
536 16/3 Erw Lon (L) LAD 3m 9 GF *f 3rd* F -
543 16/3 Erw Lon (L) MDN 3m 11 GF *2nd outing, prog frm 10th, hrd rdn 2 out, no imp flat* 2 13
1183 20/4 Lydstep (L) MDO 3m 8 GF *trckd ldrs, ld 6-12th, tried to run out & u.r. 14th* U -

Pipped in weak race 3rd start; novice-ridden & may need stronger handling 12

BOBBING ALONG(IRE) ch.g. 6 Over The River (FR) - Ballymore Status by Status Seeker — Mrs A P Glassford

326 1/3 Eaton Hall (R) MDN 3m 14 GS *chsng grp, 3rd 12th, wknd qckly, p.u. 14th* P 0

Bobbed along well enough for 2m & should do better if ready in 98 10

BOBBIN LACE b.m. 8 St Columbus - Grecian Lace by Spartan General — G B Tarry

373 2/3 Mollington (R) MDN 3m 14 G *t.o. til p.u. 4th* P 0
451 8/3 Newton Brom' (R) MDN 3m 8 G *rear whn f 6th* F -
990 12/4 Kingston Bl' (L) MDN 3m 11 GF *in tch whn nrly ref 6th, p.u. nxt* P 0
1166 20/4 Mollington (R) MDO 3m 9 GF *prom, disp 10th til hmpd nxt, not rcvr, p.u. aft 12th* P 0
1356 4/5 Dingley (R) MDO 3m 9 G *chsd ldrs, lft 3rd 14th, sn wknd, p.u. apr 2 out* P 0
1537 18/5 Mollington (R) MDO 3m 14 GS *chsd ldrs, wknd 13th, t.o. 3 out, lft poor 3rd nxt* 3 0
1609 1/6 Dingley (R) MDO 3m 14 GF *f 2nd* F -

All over the place so far but may follow stable's usual pattern & improve with experience 10

BOBBIT BACK ON (Irish) — I 55[2], I 99[1]

BOBBY BLAZER (Irish) — I 113[P], I 125[5], I 179[P], I 250[F], I 329[3], I 370[P], I 463[P], I 586[P]

BOB TREACY (Irish) — I 12[1], I 49[1]

BOCOCK'S PRIDE(IRE) ch.g. 8 Amoristic (USA) - Pride Of Ednego by Gail Star — Miss Julia Oakey

1303 3/5 Weston Park (L) RES 3m 6 G *hrd hld in rear, lost tch 7th, blnd 12th, p.u. nxt* P 0
1443 10/5 Peper Harow (L) RES 3m 3 GF *(Jt fav) conf rdn, lft 2nd 14th, chal & ld last, ran on* 1 12
1536 18/5 Mollington (R) INT 3m 8 GS *hld up,prog to chs ldr 11-13th,cls up apr 2 out,wknd,wlkd in* 4 0
1576 26/5 Chaddesley ' (L) XX 3m 12 F *pllng, ran out aft 3rd, dsmntd* r -

Ex-Irish; found terrible Restricted; looks non-stayer; problems last start; best watched 14

BODALMORE SPRING (Irish) — I 568[P]

BODDINGTON HILL b.m. 9 St Columbus - Dane Hole by Past Petition — B A Hall

1996 5(0),2(0),F(-),2(15),4(0),4(0),4(0),6(0),2(13)

41 1/2 Larkhill (R) MDO 3m 13 GF *mstks, in tch to 10th, t.o. 13th* 5 0
149 10/2 Hereford (R) HC 3m 1f 110yds 18 GS *t.o. when p.u. before 11th.* P 0
176 15/2 Ottery St M' (L) RES 3m 17 G *sn bhnd, t.o. frm 14th* 5 0
409 8/3 Llanfrynach (R) MDN 3m 12 G *alwys rear* 6 0
1011 12/4 St Hilary (R) MDN 3m 10 GF *rear, lft 3rd by dfctns* 3 0
1136 19/4 Bonvilston (R) MDO 3m 15 G *cls up, wknd frm 15th* 5 0
1230 26/4 Pyle (R) MDO 3m 10 GS *prom, ld 10th, rdn 15th, lkd wnr til hdd & no ext flat* 2 13
1323 3/5 Bonvilston (R) MDO 3m 14 G *cls up, ld 11th-4 out, styd on onepcd* 2 12
1460 11/5 Maisemore P' (L) MDO 3m 16 G *chsd ldrs til outpcd frm 13th, 5th & no ch apr 3 out* 4 0
1561 24/5 Bassaleg (R) MDO 3m 9 G *prom,lost plc 10th,outpcd 12th,kpt on onepcd frm 15th* 3 10
1603 31/5 Bassaleg (R) MDO 3m 6 F *(fav) ld 2nd,slw jmp 5th,hdd nxt,ld 10th,lft clr 13th,unchal,dsmnt* 1 10

Finally broke her duck in desperate race; painfully slow; Restricted looks impossible 12

BOHERBEE (Irish) — I 588[P], I 609[6]

BOIRE ENSEMBLE b.g. 5 Tout Ensemble - Howard's Secret Vii by Damsire Unregistered — M S Venner

100 8/2 Great Treth' (R) RES 3m 14 GS *s.s. t.o. & ref 3rd, cont, p.u. 6th* P 0
245 22/2 Lemalla (R) MDO 3m 11 S *4th whn f 5th* F -

Yet to assemble the ensemble 0

BOKER HILL (Irish) — I 155[P], I 222[2]

BOLD ALFIE br.g. 7 Sulaafah (USA) - Miss Boldly by Flandre II — D R Thomas

1996 F(-)

185 15/2 Erw Lon (L) MDN 3m 14 G *ld 2-5th, chsd wnr to 13th, fdd & eased* 5 0
542 16/3 Erw Lon (L) MDN 3m 15 GF *ld 5-12th, no imp wnr frm 14th* 2 12
841 31/3 Lydstep (L) MDO 3m 8 F *(fav) ld to 14th, p.u. nxt, lame* P 0

Ran reasonably 1st 2 starts but always lightly-raced & problems again 12

BOLD BLUFF b.g. 8 Welsh Beacon - Good Alibi by Fleece — Miss T Honeyball

1059 13/4 Hackwood Pa' (L) MDO 3m 6 GF *rear til p.u. 5 out* P 0

Rarely seen & shows nothing **0**

BOLD BOREEN (Irish) — **I** 35^{P}, **I** 377^{4}, **I** 585^{P}

BOLD BOSTONIAN(FR) b.g. 9 Never So Bold - Miss Boston (FR) by River River (FR) — Miss L K Hilder

17	25/1 Badbury Rin'	(L) CON 3m	9 GF	*pllng, ld 3-6th, ev ch whn mstk 14th, wknd rpdly, p.u. nxt*	P	0
55	1/2 Kingston Bl'	(L) CON 3m	15 GF	*chsd ldrs til bhnd & p.u. 15th*	P	0

Season lasted a week & comprised very little **0**

BOLD BREW (Irish) — **I** 41^{P}, **I** 49^{P}, **I** 408^{B}

BOLD CHEVALIER (Irish) — **I** 54^{P}, **I** 447^{4}

BOLD ECHO b.m. 5 Silly Prices - Fair Echo by Quality Fair — D Sundin

341	1/3 Corbridge	(R) MDN 3m	10 G	*rear whn u.r. 8th*	U	-
614	22/3 Friars Haugh	(L) MDN 3m	13 GF	*ran out 2nd*	r	-

Needs more education **0**

BOLD IMP bl.g. 12 Dubassoff (USA) - Woodlands Girl by Weepers Boy — J T Heritage

1996 U(-),**4(21)**,**6(13)**,1(11)

179	15/2 Larkhill	(R) CON 3m	12 G	*outpcd in mid-div, prog to 4th at 13th, wknd 3 out, t.o.*	6	0
488	9/3 Tweseldown	(R) RES 3m	10 G	*trckd ldrs, outpcd frm 12th, kpt on onepcd frm 3 out*	3	12

Members winner 96; lightly raced & finished early 97; Restricted too tough at 13 .... **15**

BOLD IRENE (Irish) — **I** 63^{P}, **I** 125^{4}, **I** 212^{P}, **I** 312^{2}, **I** 416^{2}

BOLD MAN(NZ) b.g. 10 So Bold (NZ) - If It Wishes (NZ) by Zamazaan — R E Baskerville

1996 P(0),F(-),4(0),2(0)

60	1/2 Kingston Bl'	(L) MDN 3m	17 GF	*mid-div, 3rd hlfwy, lost plc, styd on frm 2 out*	4	11
223	16/2 Heythrop	(R) RES 3m	19 G	*bhnd til p.u. 10th*	P	0

Lightly raced & finished early after no show; poor at best **10**

BOLD TAEDY (Irish) — **I** 568^{P}

BOLESA'S JOY (Irish) — **I** 360^{P}

BOLLINGER ch.g. 11 Balinger - Jolly Regal by Jolly Good — Mrs J T Gifford

1996 **15(NH)**,**4(NH)**

376	3/3 Windsor	(R) HC 3m	11 GF	*in rear, styd on from 4 out, nvr near to chal.*	4	16
588	19/3 Towcester	(R) HC 2 3/4m	4 GF	*(fav) held up, hdwy to chase ldr from 9th till hit next, soon outpcd, rallied 3 out, one pace next.*	3	15

Winning chaser; beaten in bad H/Chase last start & vanished; champagne unlikely in future **16**

BOLL WEEVIL b.g. 11 Boreen (FR) - Lavenham Lady by Precipice Wood — L J Bowman

1996 **P(NH)**

828	31/3 Heathfield	(R) MEM 3m	5 F	*(fav) ld til p.u. aft 4th, saddle slpd*	P	0
1128	19/4 Penshurst	(L) LAD 3m	8 GF	*ld to 12th, fdd, t.o. & p.u. aft 2 out*	P	0
1506	16/5 Folkestone	(R) HC 2m 5f	8 G	*ld after 1st till 4th, chsd ldr till after 8th, wknd, t.o. and p.u. before 2 out.*	P	0

Looks past it now **0**

BOMBADIER BROWN b.g. 6 K-Battery - Peace Keeper by Wolver Hollow — Major Paul Greenwood

147	9/2 Tweseldown	(R) MDO 3m	12 GF	*u.r. 2nd*	U	-
299	1/3 Didmarton	(L) MDN 3m	14 G	*alwys bhnd, t.o. 10th, p.u. 15th*	P	0
656	22/3 Siddington	(L) MDN 3m	7 F	*in tch to 12th, sn wknd, t.o. & p.u. 15th*	P	0

Learning so far & nothing to show for it yet **0**

BOMBADIER JACK b.g. 7 Primitive Rising (USA) - Palmister by Palm Track — R Thomas

1996 U(-),3(10)

82	2/2 Wolverhampt'	(L) MDN 3m	11 GS	*prom, clsd up 13th, wknd aft 16th, no ch whn mstk 2 out*	3	10
327	1/3 Eaton Hall	(R) MDN 3m	11 GS	*hld up, some late prog,ran on wll flat to snatch 2nd on line*	2	13
470	8/3 Eyton-On-Se'	(L) MDN 2 1/2m	12 G	*(fav) hld up in tch, chal to ld 4 out, sn clr, ran on well*	1	15

Gradually improved & won weak race comfortably; vanished after; Restricted chances if fit 98; G-S **16**

BONNIE BUCKSKIN (Irish) — **I** 285^{P}, **I** 347^{4}

BONNY BAROSY b or br.m. 6 Derring Rose - Baresca by Bargello — Mrs Janita Scott

1480	11/5 Ottery St M'	(L) MEM 3m	6 G	*jmpd slwly, alwys rear, t.o. & p.u. 12th*	P	0
1583	26/5 Lifton	(R) MDO 3m	11 G	*alwys bhnd, p.u. 10th*	P	0

Late to appear & shows nothing yet **0**

BONQUIST (Irish) — **I** 69^{3}, **I** 122^{3}, **I** 209^{2}

BONUS NUMBER(IRE) br.g. 8 Roselier (FR) - Nelly Gleason by Gleason (USA) — Mrs Caroline Dix

1996 4(0),U(-),P(0),P(0)

184	15/2	Erw Lon	(L)	MDN	3m	14	G	*n.j.w. sn wll bhnd, t.o. & p.u. 13th*	P	0
407	8/3	Llanfrynach	(R)	MDN	3m	11	G	*rear, p.u. 11th*	P	0
1324	3/5	Bonvilston	(R)	MDO	3m	16	G	*rear, p.u. 10th*	P	0

Looks useless **0**

BOOZING GUNNER b.g. 6 Artillery Flight - Verona Brandy by Hot Brandy — H J Manners

1452	10/5	Kingston Bl'	(L)	MDO	3m	9	G	*hmpd & p.u. 4th*	P	0
1568	25/5	Kingston Bl'	(L)	MDO	3m	11	GF	*schoold in last trio, p.u. 11th*	P	0

Yet to open fire **0**

BORDER GLORY ch.g. 6 Derrylin - Boreen's Glory by Boreen (FR) — Mrs Murray Scott

1996 9(0),U(-),P(0)

37	26/1	Alnwick	(L)	MDO	3m	15	G	*alwys rear, t.o. & p.u. 2 out*	P	0
235	22/2	Friars Haugh	(L)	MDO	3m	10	G	*2nd hlfwy, sn lost tch, p.u. 4 out*	P	0
340	1/3	Corbridge	(R)	MDN	3m	10	G	*alwys prom, ev ch 2 out, sn wknd*	3	0
1201	24/4	Perth	(R)	HC	3m	14	G	*chsd ldrs to hfwy, weakening when blnd and u.r. 15th.*	U	-

3rd in weak race & no other form - much more needed **10**

BOREEN BOY (Irish) — I 214^{U}, I 283^{F}, I 315^{P}, I 351^{4}, I 412^{P}

BOREEN LASS (Irish) — I 571^{2}

BOREEN OWEN b.g. 13 Boreen (FR) - Marble Owen by Master Owen — David Alan Harrison

1996 6(0),3(13),3(14),**3(16)**,1(13),5(12),**P(0)**,**P(0)**,2(10),8(10)

339	1/3	Corbridge	(R)	OPE	3m 5f	11	G	*prom til wknd 14th, t.o. & p.u. last*	P	0
411	8/3	Dalston	(R)	CON	3m	16	GS	*prom til outpcd 3 out, kpt on frm nxt*	5	15
562	16/3	Lanark	(R)	OPE	3m	8	GS	*ld 12th-4 out, outpcd frm nxt*	3	18
765	29/3	Whittington	(L)	OPE	3m	6	S	*mid-div, rddn alng 11th, 2nd 13th, ev ch 3 out, no ext*	2	17
891	4/4	Sedgefield	(L)	HC	3m 3f	5	GF	*in tch, reminders after 13th, outpcd 15th.*	4	11
1049	13/4	Lockerbie	(R)	OPE	3m	3	F	*last frm 3rd, clsd slghtly frm 4 out, nvr dang*	3	16
1123	19/4	Whittington	(L)	OPE	3m	4	F	*hld up, gd prog 13th, cls 2nd nxt-3 out, outpcd aft*	2	17
1423	10/5	Aspatria	(L)	MEM	3m	3	G	*(fav) carried 13st, trckd wnr to 14th, 2nd agn 3 out, not qckn nxt*	2	11

Open winner 96; very safe but slow now & turned over at 1/3 final start **14**

BORNACURRA KATIE (Irish) — I 355^{P}

BORNAKANGA ch.m. 7 Remezzo - Big Bunty by Marine Corps — Mrs G McLachlan

467	8/3	Eyton-On-Se'	(L)	RES	3m	15	G	*alwys rear, p.u. 5 out*	P	0

No show on debut **0**

BORN DEEP ch.g. 11 Deep Run - Love-In-A-Mist by Paddy's Stream — H A Shone

1996 **3(NH)**,**2(NH)**,**P(NH)**,**4(NH)**

330	1/3	Eaton Hall	(R)	CON	3m	16	GS	*nvr bttr thn mid-div, p.u. 5 out*	P	0

Winning chaser; should be good enough for points but vanished quickly; best watched **15**

BORN NATURAL (Irish) — I 319^{P}, I 389^{U}

BORREEVA (Irish) — I 26^{P}, I 61^{3}, I 96^{F}, I 162^{P}, I 215^{6}, I 287^{U}

BORRISMORE FLASH (Irish) — I 30^{F}, I 59^{P}

BORROW MINE(IRE) b.g. 5 Borovoe - Jasmine Girl by Jasmine Star — Mrs C H Sporborg

197	15/2	Higham	(L)	MDO	3m	12	G	*mid-div in tch, 5th & btn 15th, ran on nxt, improve*	5	11
598	22/3	Horseheath	(R)	MDO	3m	3	F	*(fav) trckd ldr, chal 2 out, ld last, ran on*	1	12
1114	19/4	Higham	(L)	RES	3m	5	GF	*mstly 3rd, nvr pace to chal ldr, wknd last*	4	12

Fulfilled promise by beating subsequent winners; form weak but should have Restricted chances **16**

BOSCO'S TOUCH (Irish) — I 81^{P}, I 106^{P}, I 206^{P}, I 354^{3}, I 429^{1}, I 513^{S}, I 562^{1}

BOTHAR FADA (Irish) — I 58^{3}, I 85^{P}, I 184^{3}, I 335^{4}, I 482^{2}, I 540^{2}, I 588^{P}

BOULEA BOY (Irish) — I 242, I 273^{P}

BOULEVARD BAY(IRE) b.g. 6 Royal Fountain - Cairita by Pitcairn — Lady Helen Smith

1996 B(-),P(0),2(13),2(12),P(0),P(0),P(0)

36	26/1	Alnwick	(L)	MDO	3m	15	G	*(fav) hld up wll bhnd, prog frm 10th, ld 3 out, clr last, rdn out*	1	17
118	9/2	Wetherby Po'	(L)	RES	3m	14	GF	*(fav) hld up rear, prog 7th, gd hdwy 14th, hrd rdn to d/h on post*	1	19
383	5/3	Catterick	(L)	HC	3m 1f 110yds	10	G	*trckd ldrs, mstk 3rd, cl up when blnd 5 out, ev ch when blunded 2 out, soon wknd and virtually p.u. flat.*	8	0
1070	13/4	Whitwell-On'	(R)	XX	3m	9	G	*(fav) prom, disp 5th-9th, going wll 3 out, chnc nxt, not qckn*	2	18

Fulfilled promise early season; just stays 3m; should upgrade if fit early 98; Good **21**

BOURBON COUNTY (Irish) — I 99^{2}, I 154^{2}, I 222^{1}

BOUTRUS (Irish) — I 287^{2}, I 348^{F}, I 526^{P}, I 593^{P}

BOWERY BOY b.g. 10 Broadsword (USA) - Bowery Babe by Tantivy J R Knight
1996 P(0),2(15),P(0),2(13)

214	16/2	Southwell P'	(L)	CON	3m	10	GS	*f 2nd*	F -
248	22/2	Brocklesby '	(L)	CON	3m	10	G	*4th 1st m, fdd 8th, 8th outpcd 5 out*	8 0

Season lasted 6 days in 97 - can only be watched if returning in 98 13

BOW HANDY MAN ch.g. 15 Nearly A Hand - Bellemarie by Beau Chapeau D Sundin
1996 6(13),1(22),**U(-)**,1(23),**P(0)**

132	9/2	Alnwick	(L)	LAD	3m	9	G	*bhnd, styd on frm 3 out, nvr nrr*	4 0
336	1/3	Corbridge	(R)	LAD	3m 5f	9	G	*mid-div, prog 6th, ld 8th-14th, ld 16th-last, onepcd*	3 20
731	29/3	Alnwick	(L)	MXO	4m	7	F	*ld/disp til wknd 19th, sn lost tch wth ldrs*	4 0
1201	24/4	Perth	(R)	HC	3m	14	G	*n.d..*	6 13
1511	17/5	Corbridge	(R)	LAD	3m	10	GS	*mid-div, wknd 11th, t.o. & p.u. 13th, retired*	P 0

Retired 15

BOWLAND GIRL(IRE) b.m. 8 Supreme Leader - El Marica by Buckskin (FR) R J Scandrett
1996 F(-),3(13),P(0),2(15),2(13),U(-),3(13),1(13)

260	22/2	Newtown	(L)	RES	3m	16	G	*prog to trck ldrs 10th, cls up 14th, onepcd frm 2 out*	4 17
405	8/3	Llanfrynach	(R)	RES	3m	15	G	*hld up, rpd prog 4 out, ld nxt, drew clr*	1 16
752	29/3	Brampton Br'	(R)	CON	3m	1	GF	*walked over*	1 0
1013	12/4	Bitterley	(L)	CON	3m	14	GF	*prog to cls 4th whn hmpd & u.r. flat aft 13th*	U -
1233	26/4	Brampton Br'	(R)	CON	3m	8	G	*alwys cls up, ld 2 out, blnd last, all out, lkd 2nd*	1 19
1387	5/5	Cursneh Hill	(L)	MEM	3m	3	GF	*(fav) trckd reluc ldr frm 6th, qcknd apr last, rddn & just held*	2 0
1525	17/5	Bredwardine	(R)	LAD	3m	9	G	*mstks 5th & 12th, chsd wnr 10th, ev ch last, ran on*	2 23
1573	26/5	Chaddesley '	(L)	LAD	3m	6	F	*svrl mstks, in tch til 3rd & outpcd frm 12th, no imp aft*	3 17

Maiden winner 96; much improved; tricky ride; good chances in Ladies 98; Good 23

BOWLANDS COUNTRY b.g. 6 Town And Country - Kilbride Madam by Mandalus J W Campion
1996 **17(NH),2(NH),2(NH),7(NH)**

1609	1/6	Dingley	(R)	MDO	3m	14	GF	*(fav) sn wll bhnd, some prog 12th, 7th & clsng grad whn f 14th*	F -

Placed in hurdles & should be up to a win if fit in 98; sure to stay; good stable 14

BOWLANDS GALAXY b.g. 7 Scorpio (FR) - Kilbride Madam by Mandalus J W Campion

664	23/3	Eaton Hall	(R)	MDO	3m	12	GF	*prom to 8th, rdn & no rspns 12th*	7 0

Good stable but well-beaten only start & not rateable yet 0

BOWL OF OATS ch.g. 11 Oats - Bishop's Bow by Crozier A P Gent
1996 **P(NH),3(NH),P(NH)**

255	22/2	Newtown	(L)	CON	3m	14	G	*(bl) prom, ld 5th-12th, wknd nxt, p.u. 3 out*	P 0
360	2/3	Garnons	(L)	CON	3m	10	GS	*prom to 11th, no ch whn lft dist 2nd 2 out*	3 12
781	31/3	Hereford	(R)	HC	2m 3f	9	GF	*(bl) soon bhnd, mod hdwy 3 out, n.d..*	3 0
1014	12/4	Bitterley	(L)	OPE	3m	9	GF	*(bl) 20l 8th at 11th, dist 5th whn p.u. 2 out*	P 0

Winning chaser but looks well past it now 12

BOWMANS LODGE b.g. 6 Primitive Rising (USA) - Keldholme by Derek H Miss C J Raines

37	26/1	Alnwick	(L)	MDO	3m	15	G	*(fav) prog 7th, disp dist 2nd 14th til p.u. apr 3 out*	P 0

Going sweetly on debut till stopped & vanished; chances if fit 98 13

BOW TIE b.g. 6 Meadowbrook - Teviot Lady by New Brig J G B Murray

729	29/3	Alnwick	(L)	RES	3m	10	F	*climbed 1st & 2nd, ref 3rd, cont, ref 4th, gave up*	R -
1052	13/4	Lockerbie	(R)	MDN	3m	10	F	*sn wll clr, wknd rpdly 4 out, p.u. 2 out*	P 0
1222	26/4	Balcormo Ma'	(R)	MDO	3m	6	F	*made most to 11th, 2nd mstly aft, no ext flat*	2 10

2nd in weak race but at least going the right way & should have chances in 98 12

BOX OF DELIGHTS br.g. 9 Idiot's Delight - Pretty Useful by Firestreak Mrs Jeanne Thomas
1996 P(0)

222	16/2	Heythrop	(R)	RES	3m	17	G	*(fav) mid-div, effrt 12th, 3rd at 15th, btn 2 out, p.u. last*	P 0
877	1/4	Upton-On-Se'	(R)	RES	3m	17	GF	*trckd ldrs,chsd wnr 11th,mstk 13th,btn 3 out,p.u. nxt,dsmntd*	P 0
1131	19/4	Bonvilston	(R)	MEM	3m	6	G	*(Jt fav) trckd ldrs, lft in ld 14th, qcknd clr 2 out*	1 16
1322	3/5	Bonvilston	(R)	RES	3m	9	G	*rear, prog to 4th hlfwy, chsd ldr 13th, ld 3 out, sn clr*	1 23
1468	11/5	Erw Lon	(L)	INT	3m	7	GS	*(fav) sttld rear, prog 11th, ev ch 4 out, onepcd frm 2 out*	2 18

Fragile but quite able; top stable; romped home twice & should upgrade; Good 23

BOYNE VALLEY HERO (Irish) — **I** 438P, **I** 4615, **I** 5222, **I** 5523, **I** 574P

BOYS ROCKS ch.g. 9 Lighter - Nelodor by Nelcius D J Clapham
1996 5(0)

1200	23/4	Andoversford	(R)	MDO	3m	8	F	*(fav) ld,slw jmps 4 & 5th,hdd 9th,ld apr last,hng lft,all out,lame*	1 12

Found a dire race & owed success to rider; problems & much more needed if fit 98 13

BOYUP BROOK ch.g. 8 Meadowbrook - Terrona Lady — J John Paterson

415	8/3	Dalston	(R)	RES	3m	19 GS	*mstk 1st, alwys bhnd, 17th & t.o. hlfwy*	9	0
612	22/3	Friars Haugh	(L)	MDN	3m	14 GF	*cls 2nd whn f 12th*	F	-
733	29/3	Alnwick	(L)	MDN	3m	5 F	*trckd ldrs, qcknd clr & mstk 14th, styd on well*	1	12
1169	20/4	Hexham Poin'	(L)	RES	3m	9 GF	*mid-div, blnd & u.r. 5th*	U	-
1424	10/5	Aspatria	(L)	RES	3m	17 G	*sn prom, jnd wnr 13th-nxt, 3rd & btn whn blnd 3 out, wknd*	10	0

Found a poor race to open his score; struggles to stay & will need weak Restricted 14

BOZEN GREEN(IRE) ch.g. 5 Mister Lord (USA) - Little Grannie Vii by Damsire Unregistered — H B Hodge

284	23/2	Charing	(L)	MDO	3m	17 G	*sn bhnd, mstk 6th, t.o. 8th, p.u. 12th*	P	0

Showed nothing on debut but by top sire & may do better in 98 0

BOZO BAILEY gr.g. 7 Hadeer - Perceive (USA) by Nureyev (USA) — Mrs Lucy Gibbon

1996 P(0),7(0),P(0)

198	15/2	Higham	(L)	RES	3m	14 G	*sn strgglng in rear, t.o. & p.u. aft 11th*	P	0
323	1/3	Marks Tey	(L)	LAD	3m	7 G	*hld up, in tch to 13th, t.o. & p.u. 17th*	P	0
438	8/3	Higham	(L)	MDO	3m	8 G	*mostly 3rd/4th, prog to 2nd 15th, onepcd nxt, no ch wnr 3out*	2	0
499	15/3	Ampton	(R)	MDO	3m	9 GF	*trkd ldrs, cls 4th 15th, unable to qkn und press appr last*	3	12
1118	19/4	Higham	(L)	MDO	3m	9 GF	*(fav) cls up, wknd aft 14th, p.u. aft 16th, broke down*	P	0

Touched off when 3rd but ran into real trouble last start 12

BRABAZON(USA) b.g. 12 Cresta Rider (USA) - Brilliant Touch (USA) by Gleaming (USA) — Mrs E Scott

1996 4(19),5(15),5(12)

171	15/2	Ottery St M'	(L)	OPE	3m	9 G	*alwys mid-div, nvr on trms wth ldrs*	4	10
455	8/3	Great Treth'	(R)	OPE	3m	8 S	*5th & rddn 14th, no ch clsng stgs*	5	10
586	19/3	Exeter	(R)	HC	3 1/4m	12 GF	*t.o. after 5th, styd on one pace after 5 out.*	5	10

Ran well 1st start 96 but poorly since & finished early 97; best watched at 13 13

BRACA BROOK (Irish) — I 406[P], I 501[1], I 541[2]

BRACKENFIELD ch.g. 11 Le Moss - Stable Lass by Golden Love — Mrs Susan Humphreys

1996 **P(NH),3(NH),4(NH),5(NH),U(NH)**

6	19/1	Barbury Cas'	(L)	LAD	3m	13 GF	*(bl) lft in ld 2nd, made most aft, drvn clr 3 out, ran on well*	1	27
42	1/2	Larkhill	(R)	MXO	3m	7 GF	*(bl) trckd ldrs, ld 13th til blnd 15th, no imp on wnr 2 out*	2	27
180	15/2	Larkhill	(R)	MXO	3m	6 G	*(bl) ld, hit 5th, hdd 2 out, rallied und pres to ld last, styd on*	1	31
388	7/3	Sandown	(R)	HC	3m 110yds	7 G	*(fav) (bl) mstk 1st, ld 4th to 12th, mistake next, led 7 out, drew clr four out, unchal.*	1	31
1198	23/4	Andoversford	(R)	OPE	3m	5 F	*(fav) (bl) not fluent, sn bhnd, t.o. 8th, some prog whn p.u. 13th, lame*	P	0

Useful winning chaser; very able but unpredictable; should return 98; blinkers essential; G-F 28

BRACKER (Irish) — I 28[P], I 58[F]

BRAEMOSS br.m. 6 Ovac (ITY) - Brave'n Easy by Brave Invader (USA) — G Rooks

506	15/3	Dalton Park	(R)	CON	3m	16 GF	*rear, sn wll bhnd, t.o. & p.u. 12th*	P	0

No encouragement 0

BRAEMOUNT DEER(IRE) ch.g. 9 Whistling Deer - Vanda — E J P Kane

930	6/4	Charlton Ho'	(L)	INT	3m	8 G	*cls up to 8th, sn wknd, t.o. & p.u. 14th*	P	0

Ran in a hot race but time already left him behind 0

BRAMBLEDALE (Irish) — I 153[1], I 183[5]

BRAMBLEHILL DUKE (Irish) — I 192[1]

BRAMBLE WOOD (Irish) — I 58[2], I 148[F], I 184[U], I 269[1]

BRAMHALL PRINCESS (Irish) — I 186, , I 228, , I 286[P], I 350[3]

BRAVE NODDY (Irish) — I 148[U], I 184[2], I 343[P]

BRECKENBROUGH LAD b.g. 10 Uncle Pokey - Fabulous Beauty by Royal Avenue — Mrs M R Bennett

1996 2(0),7(0),U(-),P(0),P(0)

121	9/2	Wetherby Po'	(L)	MEM	3m	2 GF	*disp at slow pace, qcknd to ld apr last*	1	0
350	2/3	Market Rase'	(L)	CON	3m	11 GF	*alwys rear, lost tch 13th, t.o.*	7	0
618	22/3	Hutton Rudby	(L)	OPE	3m	10 GF	*rear & sn detached, t.o.*	8	0
836	31/3	Thorpe Lodge	(L)	OPE	3m	7 F	*cls up mstly 3rd til qcknd to ld 4 out, ran on strngly*	1	19

Uusually looks hopeless but 25/1 shock last start; don't rely on a repeat 17

BREDINTHEPURPLE(IRE) b.g. 8 Lancastrian - Pedigree Corner by Pollerton — Miss C A Smithson

332	1/3	Eaton Hall	(R)	RES	3m	18 GS	*hld up in tch to 12th, sn btn, p.u. 4 out*	P	0

Irish Maiden winner 96; looked to meet a problem only start 97 10

BREE HILL (Irish) — I 155[F], I 215[1], I 408[3]

BREEZE-BLOC ch.m. 7 Sunley Builds - Sunny Breeze by Roi Soleil — M Shears
1996 P(0),F(-),P(0)
458 8/3 Great Treth' (R) MDO 3m 15 S *5th 14th, best work clsng stgs, drvn into 2nd cls home* 2 11
626 22/3 Kilworthy (L) MDN 3m 14 G *(Jt fav) rear til p.u. apr 15th* P 0
1112 19/4 Flete Park (R) MDN 3m 13 GF *rear, t.o. & p.u. 13th* P 0
Ran well 1st start 97 but badly after; may do better on Soft in 98 13

BREEZY SEA ch.g. 7 Mljet - Polly Peril by Politico (USA) — D J Fairbairn
136 9/2 Alnwick (L) MDO 3m 16 G *in tch, prog to ld 14th, hdd 3 out, fdd* 5 0
Showed plenty of promise but promptly vanished 13

BRENNAN FOR AUDITS (Irish) — I 61P, I 272⁴, I 310F, I 458⁵, I 576P
BRENNER PASS(NZ) ch.g. 13 Kaioi Lad (AUS) - Irish Star (NZ) by Rangong — J Hibbert
700 29/3 Upper Sapey (R) MEM 3m 8 GF *rear frm start, 5th hlfwy, fin own time* 4 0
1063 13/4 Maisemore P' (L) XX 3m 13 GF *s.s. hit 1st, last whn f 4th* F -
No longer of any account 0

BREWERY LANE (Irish) — I 496F
BRIAN OG (Irish) — I 52P, I 135, , I 206F, I 520², I 572¹, I 600²
BRIARLAND SPRINGER b.g. 14 Maori King - Briarland Bramble by Abyss — G N Avis
817 31/3 Paxford (L) CON 3m 3 F *chsd ldr til wknd 13th, sn bhnd* 3 0
No longer of any account 0

BRIARY BOY (Irish) — I 77P, I 568⁵, I 602P
BRICANMORE (Irish) — I 39F, I 104¹
BRICKHILL LAD (Irish) — I 107P
BRIDE RUN(IRE) ch.g. 8 Le Moss - Mariner's Run by Deep Run — Mrs C M Marles
1996 P(0),2(10),3(11)
44 1/2 Larkhill (R) MDO 3m 9 GF *cls up til mstk & u.r. 7th* U -
260 22/2 Newtown (L) RES 3m 16 G *rear, 9th & no ch whn f 12th* F -
404 8/3 Llanfrynach (R) INT 3m 17 G *alwys rear, p.u. 2 out* P 0
Placed twice in 96 but nothing 97 & finished early; should stick to Maidens 10

BRIDGE END (Irish) — I 113F, I 127², I 247⁴, I 289³, I 375³
BRIDGE EXPRESS b.g. 10 Pony Express - Elysium Dream Vii — C T Moate
1996 6(0),P(0),2(19),1(15),**F(-)**,6(12)
308 1/3 Clyst St Ma' (L) OPE 3m 7 HY *ld, blnd & u.r. 1st* U -
522 15/3 Cothelstone (L) CON 3m 14 GS *made most to apr 11th, lost plc 14th, p.u. 2 out* P 0
863 31/3 Kingston St' (R) OPE 3m 4 F *(Jt fav) made virt all, jnd aft 4 out, pshd clr 2 out* 1 18
Intermediate winner 96; effective only in weak races & found similar in 97 15

BRIDGE HOUSE BOY ch.g. 6 Sunyboy - Danny D'Albi by Wrens Hill — Andrew Oliver
237 22/2 Lemalla (R) CON 3m 13 S *mstk 1st, last at 11th, t.o. & u.r. 13th* U -
553 16/3 Ottery St M' (L) MDN 3m 15 G *sn bhnd, t.o. 14th* 7 0
No signs of ability yet & last when finishing 0

BRIDGE MAN gr.g. 7 Scallywag - Starbridge by Space King — W Bush
650 22/3 Siddington (L) CON 3m 8 F *not fluent, in tch frm 5-9th, lost plc & p.u. nxt* P 0
No promise on one brief appearance 0

BRIDGE PARTY (Irish) — I 40P, I 133⁵, I 241P, I 482P, I 532⁵, I 550⁴
BRIGHT AS A BUTTON ch.g. 13 True Song - Bright Exploit by Exploitation — Sir Michael Connell
1996 P(0),P(0),2(21),3(20),4(19),2(18),R(-),R(-),P(0)
1448 10/5 Kingston Bl' (L) CON 3m 9 G *alwys prom, went 2nd at 14th, ld aft 2 out, hdd & ref last* R 20
1534 18/5 Mollington (R) OPE 3m 7 GS *in tch, outpcd 15th, ran on nxt, ld 2 out, drvn out* 1 22
1607 1/6 Dingley (R) OPE 3m 9 GF *pshd alng,chsd wnr 12th,no imp 3 out,lost 2nd & ref last* R -
Still has ability & won well but very quirky & refused 4 of last 6; win at 14 possible; G-S 21

BRIGHT BUCK (Irish) — I 303³
BRIGHT BURNS b.g. 12 Celtic Cone - Chanter Mark by River Chanter — Colin Gee
1996 3(24),1(23),3(14),**3(22)**,1(18),**8(12)**,**4(17)**,1(19)
220 16/2 Heythrop (R) OPE 3m 20 G *(bl) prom til wknd frm 3 out* 5 18
Fair pointer to 96 but soon vanished 97 & best watched if returning at 13 19

BRIGHT CHOICE (Irish) — I 143F, I 166, , I 304P

BRIGHT CRUSADER b.g. 11 Lepanto (GER) - Snowdra's Daughter by Down Cloud — Mrs N Simm

1996 5(0),4(10),P(0)

576 16/3 Detling (L) MEM 3m 10 F *in tch, pshd alng 4 out, kpt on* 3 10
1129 19/4 Penshurst (L) RES 3m 6 GF *ld to aft 2nd, last frm 12th, wll bhnd whn p.u. aft 2 out* P 0

Very modest performer at best & even poor Members beyond him now 10

BRIGHT GIRL(IRE) ch.m. 6 Going Broke - Bright Proverb by Proverb — C H Warner

366 2/3 Garnons (L) MDO 2 1/2m 13 GS *alwys rear, just in tch whn u.r. 10th, dead* U -

Dead 0

BRIGHT HOUR ro.g. 12 Kabour - Amber Vale by Warpath — Mrs B Ansell

1996 4(0),5(10),3(10),5(14),3(15),4(0),**5(0)**

280 23/2 Charing (L) LAD 3m 12 G *prom, wkng whn nrly u.r. 10th, t.o. & p.u. 14th* P 0
576 16/3 Detling (L) MEM 3m 10 F *alwys prom, prssd ldr 16th, ld aft 2 out, ran on wll* 1 13
684 29/3 Charing (L) LAD 3m 2 F *(fav) ld to 7th,u.r. nxt,evntlly rejnd,made most aft,held on flat* 1 0
830 31/3 Heathfield (R) MXO 3m 6 F *chsd ldrs, mstk 11th, pshd alng 13th, wknd 3 out* 5 12
1445 10/5 Peper Harow (L) LAD 3m 6 GF *made most to 6th, 4th & wkng 12th, no ch whn u.r. 14th* U -
1501 16/5 Folkestone (R) HC 3 1/4m 10 G *nvr near ldrs, bhnd from 13th, t.o. and p.u. before 3 out.* P 0

Broke 5 year barren spell & followed up in farcical Ladies; Members only chance in 98 12

BRIGHT LAD (Irish) — I 72⁶, I 122P, I 209R, I 377P, I 417P

BRIGHTON BEACH b.g. 9 Push On - Phyllis Jane by Lepanto (GER) — Vizard Racing

360 2/3 Garnons (L) CON 3m 10 GS *alwys last, t.o. whn f 8th* F -
754 29/3 Brampton Br' (R) MDN 3m 9 GF *rear frm 4th, p.u. 9th* P 0

No signs of ability & no spring chicken 0

BRIGHT PROSPECT (Irish) — I 7⁴, I 48¹, I 205²

BRILL STAR (Irish) — I 189P, I 317P, I 422F, I 499P

BRINNY PRINCESS (Irish) — I 46P, I 48P, I 90P

BRITTAS BOY (Irish) — I 444P, I 515P, I 596P

BROADCASTER b.g. 9 Broadsword (USA) - Rosepic by Seaepic (USA) — Richard Chandler

1996 P(0),8(10),3(0)

75 2/2 Market Rase' (L) CON 3m 10 GF *wl bhnd frm 7th, t.o. & p.u. 9th* P 0

Finished early 96 & brief appearance 97 could spell the end 0

BROAD COMMITMENT b.g. 6 Broadsword (USA) - Delegation by Articulate — Mrs H J Greenslade

521 15/3 Cothelstone (L) OPE 3m 8 GS *lost tch hlfwy, p.u. 13th* P 0
1095 16/4 Hockworthy (L) MDN 3m 11 GF *chsd ldng pair, 5th & wkng whn blnd & u.r. 10th* U -
1521 17/5 Bratton Down (L) MDO 3m 16 GS *sn prom, 2nd whn blnd 12th, lost ground steadily* 5 0

Shows some speed but well-beaten last start - much more needed 0

BROADLEAF CLOVER b.m. 6 Broadleaf - Clover Honey Bee by Winden — Mrs J M Worthington

206 15/2 Weston Park (L) MDN 3m 9 G *rear, t.o. & p.u. 12th* P 0

Very green on debut 0

BROAD STEANE b.g. 8 Broadsword (USA) - Banbury Cake by Seaepic (USA) — Sir Michael Connell

1996 1(19),3(21),1(20),1(24),2(21),**2(25)**

55 1/2 Kingston Bl' (L) CON 3m 15 GF *(fav) hld up, smooth prog to ld 2 out, pshd out* 1 25
287 27/2 Huntingdon (R) HC 3m 13 GS *(Co fav) chsd ldrs, ld 13th, hdd 5 out, wknd apr 2 out.* 3 24
447 8/3 Newton Brom' (R) OPE 3m 6 G *(Jt fav) ld til f 2nd* F -
680 29/3 Towcester (R) HC 3m 1f 8 GF *(fav) held up in tch, hit 6th, rdn apr 2 out, no impn.* 4 19
1159 20/4 Mollington (R) MEM 3m 4 GF *(fav) ld 6th, lft virt solo 11th, lft alone 15th* 1 20
1288 30/4 Cheltenham (L) HC 2m 5f 10 GF *trckd wnr 5th to 9th and from 11th, cl 2nd when f 13th.* F -
1464 11/5 Tweseldown (R) XX 3m 7 GF *(fav) ld til blnd & u.r. 7th* U -

Useful but ineptly campaigned; often novice-ridden; should stick to sub 3m H/Chases; G/S-G/F 24

BROAD-THORNE ch.g. 6 Broadsword (USA) - Alithorne by Kinglet — Brian Gurney

373 2/3 Mollington (R) MDN 3m 14 G *in tch til outpcd 13th, no prog aft, p.u. last* P 0
1353 4/5 Dingley (R) MDO 2 1/2m 9 G *alwys bhnd, p.u. 9th, (lame)* P 0

Not disgraced 1st start but problems only other run; could do better if fit 98 10

BROAD VALLEY (Irish) — I 64P, I 97F, I 344U

BROADWAY SWINGER b.g. 6 Sulaafah (USA) - River Culm by Royal Salmon — Mrs Charlotte Cooke

1996 U(-),P(0),U(-)

210 16/2 Southwell P' (L) MDO 3m 15 GS *ld/disp til ld 12th, jnd apr 3 out, hld on und pres flat* 1 16

477 9/3 Southwell P' (L) RES 3m 10 G *ld to 1st, mstk 3rd, cls 3rd whn blnd 15th, sn btn,p.u. last* P 0
770 29/3 Dingley (R) RES 3m 18 G *w.w. hrd hld,rpd prog 10th,ld 5 out, hdd last, rallied flat* 1 19
1077 13/4 Guilsborough (L) CON 3m 16 GF *trckd ldrs, effrt to chs wnr apr 3 out, no imp apr last* 2 21

Fulfilled 96 comments; shows right attitude; improved; should win Intermediate; G-S 22

BROCKISH BAY ch.g. 10 Le Bavard (FR) - Almanac by London Gazette Miss S E Baxter
1996 4(11),6(12),1(17),F(-),4(15),P(0)
202 15/2 Weston Park (L) LAD 3m 13 G *hld up rear, lost tch 10th, p.u. nxt* P 0

Restricted winner 96; brief appearance 97 bodes ill; L/H; best watched 14

BROGEEN DUBH (Irish) — I 138P, I 207¹, I 336⁵, I 426P, I 516⁴, I 562P

BROGUESTOWN PRIDE(IRE) b.g. 9 Kemal (FR) - Una's Pride by Raise You Ten S H Shirley-Beavan
765 29/3 Whittington (L) OPE 3m 6 S *last pair throut, nvr dang, p.u. 15th* P 0
1407 5/5 Witton Cast' (R) OPE 3m 4 GS *chsd wnnr til settld in 3rd 3rd, wknd 12th, t.o.* 4 0
1426 10/5 Aspatria (L) OPE 3m 9 G *mstk 6th, 8th & wkng 11th, last whn p.u. 15th* P 0

Good stable but showed nothing at all 0

BRONC (Irish) — I 156P

BROOK A LIGHT ch.g. 6 Lighter - Elmley Brook by Paddy's Stream W Westacott
1996 P(0),4(0),7(0),B(-)
54 1/2 Wadebridge (L) MDO 3m 13 G *alwys handy, ld 7th-12th, onepcd aft* 2 13
531 15/3 Wadebridge (L) MDO 3m 14 GF *alwys cls up, outpcd frm 3 out* 2 14
808 31/3 Wadebridge (L) MDO 3m 8 F *(fav) towrds rear, clip rnng rail aft 6th, p.u. 9th* P 0
1260 27/4 Black Fores' (R) MDO 3m 12 F *chsd ldrs, went 2nd apr last, no imp wnr, fin 2nd* 0 12
1584 26/5 Lifton (R) MDO 3m 13 G *(Jt fav) mid-div, p.u. rpdly 4 out* P 0

Ran well 3 times (inc void race) but disappointed last start; may atone 98 14

BROOK HEIGHTS b.g. 6 Golden Heights - Heluva Season by High Season Paul O J Hosgood
1094 16/4 Hockworthy (L) MDN 3m 11 GF *n.j.w. wll bhnd frm 5th til p.u. 9th* P 0
1261 27/4 Black Fores' (R) MDO 3m 12 F *mostly mid-div, wknd 10th, p.u. aft 12th* P 0

Shows nothing to enthuse about to date 0

BROOKLYN EXPRESS b.m. 8 Sula Bula - Lady Brooklyn by Streak E J Legg
1996 F(-),P(0)
175 15/2 Ottery St M' (L) RES 3m 15 G *bhnd, t.o. & p.u. 8th* P 0
314 1/3 Clyst St Ma' (L) MDN 3m 11 HY *prom, lost tch 6th, t.o. & p.u. 8th* P 0
1269 27/4 Little Wind' (R) MEM 3m 3 GF *chsd wnr to 8th & frm nxt, wkng whn p.u. 14th* P 0
1343 3/5 Flete Park (R) MDO 3m 13 G *rear, t.o. & p.u. 12th* P 0

Shows no ability at all 0

BROOKVIEW VI (Irish) — I 288P

BROSNA QUEEN (Irish) — I 579P

BROSTAIG ORT (Irish) — I 23¹, I 89U

BROTHER DAY (Irish) — I 65, , I 268P

BROTHER HAROLD ch.g. 8 Brotherly (USA) - Miss Kewmill by Billion (USA) John Eaton
1066 13/4 Maisemore P' (L) MDO 3m 9 GF *prom, blnd 5th & 7th, 3rd whn f 12th* F -
1239 26/4 Brampton Br' (R) MDO 3m 9 G *prom til wknd 11th, p.u. aft nxt* P 0
1401 5/5 Ashorne (R) MDO 3m 15 G *mstk 2nd, ld to 6th & frm 9-12th, wknd rpdly nxt, p.u. 15th* P 0
1460 11/5 Maisemore P' (L) MDO 3m 16 G *chsd ldrs to 12th, sn wknd, t.o. & p.u. 3 out* P 0

Makes mistakes & shows no stamina 0

BROTHER NERO(NZ) br.g. 5 Roman Empire - End Of The Road (NZ) by Double Nearco (CAN) D H Barons
459 8/3 Great Treth' (R) MDO 3m 9 S *hdwy 8th, cls 4th whn f 11th* F -
553 16/3 Ottery St M' (L) MDN 3m 15 G *(fav) 4s-2s, in tch, 3rd & going wll whn f 13th* F -
741 29/3 Higher Kilw' (L) MDN 3m 12 GF *prog 10th, 5th whn blnd & u.r. 13th* U -

Clear signs of ability but error-prone at present; should make amends if ready in 98 14

BROUGHPARK AZALEA b.g. 8 Song - Slip The Ferret by Klairon S J Robinson
1996 **F(NH),4(NH),6(NH)**
814 31/3 Tranwell (L) MDO 3m 9 G *mid-div whn p.u. 6th* P 0

Dead 0

BROWLEA LYNDENE gr.m. 6 Arkan - Mountainette by Peter Wrekin S J Manning
767 29/3 Whittington (L) MDO 3m 9 S *mstks, rear, t.o. 9th, p.u. 11th* P 0
1003 12/4 Alpraham (R) MDO 2 1/2m 10 GF *cls up to 8th, fdd, t.o. 11th* 6 0
1173 20/4 Hexham Poin' (L) MDO 2 1/2m 9 GF *alwys prom, cls 3rd 6-9th, outpcd 3 out, p.u. nxt* P 0

1345 3/5 Gisburn (R) MDN 3m 13 GF *cls up to 12th, wknd rpdly, p.u. 15th* P 0

Last on only completion & no stamina 0

BROWN BABY br.m. 11 Full Of Hope - Funny Baby by Fable Amusant G R Kerr
1996 4(10),4(0),**P(0)**,5(10),**F(-)**,**10(0)**
59 1/2 Kingston Bl' (L) RES 3m 16 GF *alwys prom, chsng ldrs whn blnd 11th, wknd 15th* 5 13
221 16/2 Heythrop (R) RES 3m 15 G *prom to 14th, lost tch, ran on agn 2 out* 3 13
372 2/3 Mollington (R) RES 3m 19 G *prom to 11th, sn wknd* 6 0
548 16/3 Garthorpe (R) RES 3m 10 GF *chsd ldrs, 3rd & ev ch 2 out, wknd last* 3 16
770 29/3 Dingley (R) RES 3m 18 G *alwys prom, outpcd brfly 6 out, prog to ld last, ct fin* 2 19
1076 13/4 Guilsborough (L) MEM 3m 9 GF *(Jt fav) 2nd whn u.r. 2nd* U -
1164 20/4 Mollington (R) RES 3m 10 GF *ld 5-8th, trckd ldrs, qcknd to ld apr last, just hld on* 1 17
1351 4/5 Dingley (R) CON 3m 7 G *ld 4th, hdd aft 11th, lft clr nxt, hdd apr last, no ext* 2 17
1507 16/5 Stratford (L) HC 3m 10 G *pulle hrd, ld 4th to 8th, wknd apr four out.* 4 12

Novice-ridden 97 & improved; ended losing sequence of 36; staying better; hard to find chance at 12 .. 18

BROWN BALA b or br.m. 8 Balinger - Brown Veil by Don't Look Mrs J A Skelton
1996 F(-),P(0),P(0),3(0),P(0)
87 2/2 Wolverhampt' (L) MDO 3m 11 GS *in tch in rear, mstk 9th, u.r. 11th* U -
261 22/2 Newtown (L) MDN 3m 16 G *mstks, in tch to 11th, sn wknd, t.o. & p.u. 3 out* P 0
407 8/3 Llanfrynach (R) MDN 3m 11 G *(bl) rear, styd on frm 2 out, no imp* 4 0
754 29/3 Brampton Br' (R) MDN 3m 9 GF *(bl) rear frm 6th, t.o. 13th, p.u. 15th* P 0
1240 26/4 Brampton Br' (R) MDO 3m 12 G *(bl) ld til aft 14th, wknd & p.u. 3 out* P 0
1393 5/5 Cursneh Hill (L) MDO 3m 9 GF *(bl) cls up til wknd 13th, t.o. & p.u. aft 15th* P 0

Last on only completion in 97 & a no-hoper 0

BROWNED OFF br.g. 8 Move Off - Jenifer Browning by Daring March Mrs C Bevan
1996 **P(NH)**
219 16/2 Heythrop (R) LAD 3m 16 G *in tch til f 10th* F -
1456 11/5 Maisemore P' (L) LAD 3m 5 G *jmpd rght & slwly, ld to 13th, t.o. aft nxt* 4 0
1573 26/5 Chaddesley ' (L) LAD 3m 6 F *n.j.w. made most to 6th, wknd 11th, t.o. & p.u. aft 3 out* P 0

Should be pensioned-off 0

BROWN REBEL b.g. 11 Royal Boxer - Brown Rose by Rose Knight Mrs A G Lawe
1996 5(10),P(0)
241 22/2 Lemalla (R) RES 3m 11 S *mid-div, 6th hlfwy, lost ground steadily frm 13th, p.u. 17th* P 0

Maiden winner 95; only 3 runs 96/7 & can only be watched 11

BROWNROSE LAD (Irish) — **I** 486[P], **I** 541,

BRUCE'S CASTLE b.g. 11 Beau Charmeur (FR) - Maid In The Mist by Pry M Walsh
1996 2(0)
560 16/3 Lanark (R) CON 3m 8 GS *sn t.o.* 5 0
731 29/3 Alnwick (L) MXO 4m 7 F *mainly last pair, 6th at 15th, no imp ldrs aft* 5 0
1217 26/4 Balcormo Ma' (R) MEM 3m 4 F *ld brfly apr 9th, trckd ldr til ld agn apr last* 1 11

Plods round now & won bad race for Members; same again only chance 98 10

BRUNSWICK BLUE(IRE) b.g. 9 Sarab - Lanata by Charlottown Mrs D M Stevenson
577 16/3 Detling (L) CON 3m 18 F *trckd ldrs, 4th whn b.d. 15th* B -

In touch in a decent race & would have prospects in weak area if fit 98 16

BRUNSWICK MAID (Irish) — **I** 105[P], **I** 454[P], **I** 494[P], **I** 511[U], **I** 549[P]

BRUSH ME UP (Irish) — **I** 14[1], **I** 309[2], **I** 336,

BRUSH THE FLAG (Irish) — **I** 8[2], **I** 191[1]

BRYANSBI b.m. 13 Golden Passenger - Psidium's Gal by Psidium Miss S Lock
527 15/3 Cothelstone (L) MDN 3m 14 GS *rear, 10th at 12th, t.o.* 5 0
808 31/3 Wadebridge (L) MDO 3m 8 F *chsng grp til lft 2nd 12th,chal 2 out,ld last,kpt on run in* 1 11
1374 5/5 Cotley Farm (L) RES 3m 7 GF *cls up, 2nd 12th, wknd 14th, lost tch & p.u. 2 out* P 0
1495 14/5 Cothelstone (L) LAD 3m 6 GF *last & t.o. frm 3rd, lft v dist 4th last* 4 0

Broke her duck in very poor race; outclassed after & no prospects in Restricteds 11

BRYNNER ch.g. 11 Deep Run - Laharden Lady by Laurence O Mrs A D Heal
184 15/2 Erw Lon (L) MDN 3m 14 G *trckd wnr 6-14th, btn whn hmpd 3 out, wknd* 4 0
407 8/3 Llanfrynach (R) MDN 3m 11 G *ld to 13th, wknd rpdly, p.u. 2 out* P 0
1473 11/5 Erw Lon (L) MDO 3m 13 GS *mid-div to 11th, 20l 6th at 16th, p.u. 2 out* P 0
1555 24/5 Bassaleg (R) MEM 3m 6 G *5th whn mstk 3rd & p.u.* P 0

Little ability & no stamina 0

BRYN'S STORY b.g. 10 Push On - Lido Legend by Good Light G D Blagbrough

1996 P(0),1(13),P(0),P(0)

176	15/2 Ottery St M'	(L) RES	3m	17 G	*rear whn blnd & u.r. 9th*	U	-
493	12/3 Newton Abbot	(L) HC	2m 5f 110yds	11 HY	*t.o. 3rd, p.u. before 10th.*	P	0
688	29/3 Little Wind'	(R) RES	3m	5 GF	*jmpd lft,chsd ldr,ld brfly aft 14th,wknd rpdly 3 out,u.r.nxt*	U	-
1041	12/4 Cothelstone	(L) RES	3m	4 GF	*disp to 5th, wknd, last frm 12th, t.o. 3 out*	4	0

Maidenw inner 96; predictably struggling since & no real prospects now; Soft 11

BUBBLE N SQUEEK ch.g. 8 Celtic Cone - Booterstown by Master Owen — C J B Barlow

1996 3(0),5(0)

81	2/2 Wolverhampt'	(L) MDN	3m	13 GS	*sn wll bhnd, effrt 13th, nvr rchd ldrs, p.u. 16th*	P	0
665	23/3 Eaton Hall	(R) MDO	3m	11 GF	*chsd ldrs, ld 3 out, ran on whn chal last*	1	15
884	1/4 Flagg Moor	(L) CON	3m	6 G	*w.w. lft 2nd 14th, ev ch 3 out, no ext und pres*	2	17
1000	12/4 Alpraham	(R) RES	3m	8 GF	*cls up, ld 11th, prssd last, all out*	1	18
1347	3/5 Gisburn	(R) OPE	3m	8 GF	*chsd wnr til wknd 15th, slw jmp 2 out*	3	15

Quite progressive & twice won tight finishes; stays; Intermediate/Confined likely; G-G/F 20

BUBBLES GALORE(IRE) ch.g. 6 Hubbly Bubbly (USA) - New Top by New Brig — Mrs D H McCarthy

1996 P(0),P(0),**3(15)**

485	9/3 Tweseldown	(R) MDO	3m	11 G	*(fav) trckd ldrs, outpcd & nt pshd 15th, effrt 2 out, not qckn*	3	12

Showed considerable promise last start 96 but stable out of form 97; should atone in 98 if all well 15

BUBBLY BOY ch.g. 10 St Columbus - Spartan Lace by Spartan General — G B Tarry

1996 2(10)

141	9/2 Thorpe Lodge	(L) MDN	3m	12 GF	*(fav) chsng grp, ld 2 out, ran on und pres frm last*	1	15
760	29/3 Kimble	(L) RES	3m	7 GF	*(fav) ld to 3rd, 6th hlfwy, last at 12th, p.u. last*	P	0
1533	18/5 Mollington	(R) XX	3m	8 GS	*last & mstk 6th, nvr on trms aft, no ch frm 13th*	5	0

Fulfilled promise when winning but ran badly other starts; best watched at present 14

BUCK AND A HALF (Irish) — **I** 66[F], **I** 152[P], **I** 219[5], **I** 300[4], **I** 391[5], **I** 497[1]

BUCKANEER BAY b.g. 10 Buckskin (FR) - Down All The Coves by Athenius — S I Pittendrigh

1996 **11(NH),13(NH),15(NH),F(NH),14(NH),7(NH),9(NH),13(NH),8(NH),6(NH),P(NH),7(NH),3(NH),P(NH)**

34	26/1 Alnwick	(L) OPE	3m	9 G	*unruly pddck, prom til mstk & wknd 15th, t.o. & p.u. last*	P	0
339	1/3 Corbridge	(R) OPE	3m 5f	11 G	*prom til wknd 3 out, p.u. last*	P	0
416	8/3 Dalston	(R) RES	3m	12 GS	*ld to 5th, prom til wknd 15th, wll btn 4th & p.u. 2 out*	P	0
813	31/3 Tranwell	(L) RES	3m	7 G	*towrds rear til disp 3rd hlfwy,no imp on ldrs frm 4 out*	4	14
991	12/4 Tranwell	(L) MEM	3m	3 F	*cls 2nd til ld 5th,jnd 8-9th,hdd nxt,ev ch 4 out,not rch ldr*	2	12
1169	20/4 Hexham Poin'	(L) RES	3m	9 GF	*alwys prom, ev ch 15th, wknd 3 out, demoted apr last*	5	0
1414	9/5 Sedgefield	(L) HC	2m 5f	6 GF	*lost tch from 7th, no dngr after.*	4	11
1546	24/5 Hexham	(L) HC	2 1/2m 110yds	10 GF	*bhnd, blnd 8th, p.u. before next.*	P	0

Normally out of his depth & last when 2nd in Members; same race only chance 98 12

BUCKAROO b.m. 6 Escapism (USA) - Come On Clover by Oats — K Anderson

1996 P(0),F(-)

134	9/2 Alnwick	(L) MDO	3m	11 G	*hld up, prog 9th, nvr on trms, lft poor 3rd 4 out*	3	0
614	22/3 Friars Haugh	(L) MDN	3m	13 GF	*hld up, hdwy into cls 2nd 5 out, no ext apr 2 out, f last*	F	13
948	6/4 Friars Haugh	(L) MDO	3m	7 GF	*not fluent, in tch til wknd frm 4 out*	3	0

Shows some ability but yet to put it all together; may do better in 98 13

BUCKCHARLES VI (Irish) — **I** 529[P], **I** 593[5]

BUCKHILL (Irish) — **I** 483[P], **I** 520[P]

BUCKIE THISTLE (Irish) — **I** 70[F], **I** 111[P], **I** 371[F]

BUCKLAND BALLAD b.g. 5 Regal Sting (USA) - Country Ballad by Country Retreat — N B Jones

186	15/2 Erw Lon	(L) MDN	3m	13 G	*blnd 5th, sn bhnd, t.o. & p.u. 9th*	P	0
409	8/3 Llanfrynach	(R) MDN	3m	12 G	*mid-div, f 12th*	F	-
542	16/3 Erw Lon	(L) MDN	3m	15 GF	*mid-div, nvr dang, p.u. 13th*	P	0
719	29/3 Llanvapley	(L) MDN	3m	14 GF	*mid-div, f 6th*	F	-
1010	12/4 St Hilary	(R) MDN	3m	10 GF	*last til p.u. 13th*	P	0

Uniformly without hope at present 0

BUCKLANDS COTTAGE gr.m. 8 Roaring Riva - Nothing Happened by General Ironside — J C Hogg

1996 P(0),1(13)

157	15/2 Lanark	(R) RES	3m	11 G	*bhnd by 8th, p.u. 12th*	P	0
416	8/3 Dalston	(R) RES	3m	12 GS	*prom, ld 14th til hdd & lft clr 2 out, eased flat*	1	16
1509	17/5 Corbridge	(R) INT	3m	10 GS	*rear, prog 12th, outpcd 3 out, lft 2nd last*	2	14

Maiden winner 96; maintained progress with fortunate win; both wins Dalston; can upgrade; G/S 18

BUCKLE IT UP b.g. 12 Buckskin (FR) - The Hofsa by Varano — A H Mactaggart

1996 5(14),6(0),2(16),P(0),2(20)

411 8/3 Dalston (R) CON 3m 16 GS *prom, outpcd 15th, styd on frm nxt, unable to chal* 4 16
1049 13/4 Lockerbie (R) OPE 3m 3 F *chsd wnr 3rd, nvr quite on trms, fin lame* 2 17

Safe but slow now & needs modest Confined in deep mud for any winning chance at 14 17

BUCKLELONE b.m. 8 Buckley - Speakalone by Articulate Miss J C Gilbert
1996 P(0),3(0),3(12),P(0),2(0),P(0)

1084 13/4 Guilsborough (L) MDN 3m 11 GF *sn rear, poor 4th frm 14th, ran on 3 out, ld last, rdn out* 1 13
1526 17/5 Bredwardine (R) RES 3m 13 G *w.w. prog & mstk 8th, lost tch 13th, sn wll bhnd* 6 0

Found ideal race on seasonal debut; disappointing & Restricted most unlikely 13

BUCKLE UP (Irish) — I 483^6, I 558^1

BUCKLEY'S COURT b.g. 8 Buckley - Wing On by Quayside R Weston
1996 3(0),1(12),3(17),r(-),2(10),F(-)

190 15/2 Erw Lon (L) RES 3m 11 G *prom, mstk 9th, ld 13th til blnd nxt, nt rcvr, p.u. 2 out* P 0
262 22/2 Newtown (L) RES 3m 15 G *(bl) mid-div til blnd & u.r. 8th* U -

Maiden winner 96; season lasted week 97 & signs unpromising; L/H 14

BUCK MCGRATH (Irish) — I 536^P, I 563^P

BUCK RIVER (Irish) — I 65^F, I 106^4, I 409^P

BUCK RUN (Irish) — I 4^2, I 52^5, I 221^3, I 348,

BUCK'S DELIGHT(IRE) br.g. 9 Buckskin (FR) - Ethel's Delight by Tiepolo II Mrs Richard Arthur

229 22/2 Friars Haugh (L) CON 3m 9 G *ld 4th-9th, cls up whn f nxt* F -
289 28/2 Kelso (L) HC 3m 1f 8 GS *ld 6th to 12th, wknd quickly 4 out, p.u. before next.* P 0
611 22/3 Friars Haugh (L) CON 3m 11 GF *ld til 5 out, grdly wknd* 4 13
778 31/3 Carlisle (R) HC 3 1/4m 14 G *alwys prom, ld 5 out, hrd pressed from last, ran on well.* 1 26

Dual winner 95; missed 96; shock H/Chase success (beat good horse); hard to predict; G-Hy 24

BUCKS FLEA b.m. 8 Buckley - Flea Pit by Sir Lark G W Penfold
1996 3(12),3(14)

460 8/3 Great Treth' (R) MDO 3m 13 S *rear whn p.u. & dismntd apr 6th* P 0
531 15/3 Wadebridge (L) MDO 3m 14 GF *nvr far away, styd on flat, promising* 3 12
795 31/3 Bishopsleigh (R) MDO 3m 12 G *sn bhnd, prog 15th, chsd wnr vainly frm 4 out* 2 12
1400 5/5 High Bickin' (R) MDO 3m 14 G *(Jt fav) in tch, prog to ld apr 14th, steadily drew clr 3 out* 1 16
1483 11/5 Ottery St M' (L) RES 3m 15 G *rear, prog 12th, rdn 4 out, onepcd 2 out* 3 17
1519 17/5 Bratton Down (L) RES 3m 15 GS *sn rear, 11th at 15th, no ch aft* 7 10
1552 24/5 Mounsey Hil' (R) RES 3m 12 G *rmndrs 3rd, last & rdn 12th, kpt on, nvr dang* 4 10

Finished 10 of last 11 starts & deserved win in modest race; one paced; Restricted chances 98; G-F ... 17

BUCKSHEE (Irish) — I 20^1, I 124^P

BUCKSHOT(IRE) b.g. 9 Le Moss - Buckfast Lass by Buckskin (FR) P Gunn
1996 **P(NH),P(NH)**

27 26/1 Marks Tey (L) OPE 3m 6 GF *alwys last, t.o. 14th* 6 0
66 1/2 Horseheath (R) MEM 3m 7 GF *chsd ldr, blnd 3rd, ld 12th til last, sn btn* 2 13
193 15/2 Higham (L) CON 3m 14 G *(bl) mid-div til blnd & u.r. 5th* U -
497 15/3 Ampton (R) CON 3m 9 GF *rr, blnd 7th, rmdrs 10th, no resp, t.o. & p.u. 2 out* P 0
595 22/3 Horseheath (R) OPE 3m 5 F *(vis) cls 2nd til outpcd 13th, wknd rpdly 15th, fin tired* 5 0

Winning chaser; novice-ridden & well in decline already; hard to see another win 11

BUCKSKINS BABE (Irish) — I 31^P, I 228^P

BUCKS LAW br.g. 7 Buckley - Speakalone by Articulate J H Docker

208 16/2 Southwell P' (L) MDO 3m 9 GS *bhnd, lost tch 7th, t.o. & p.u. 9th* P 0
478 9/3 Southwell P' (L) MDO 3m 17 G *chsd ldrs to 8th, bhnd 11th, p.u. nxt* P 0
774 29/3 Dingley (R) MDO 2m 5f 10 G *cls up to 9th, reluc & outpcd nxt, p.u. 4 out* P 0

No signs of ability & omens unpromising 0

BUCK'S SERENADE (Irish) — I 487^P, I 561^P

BUCKS SON (Irish) — I 22^P

BUCKS SURPRISE ch.g. 9 Hard Fought - Lady Buck by Pollerton Mrs L E Morton
1996 **P(NH),5(NH),6(NH),P(NH)**

667 23/3 Eaton Hall (R) CON 3m 10 GF *s.s. sn t.o., no ch whn p.u. 5 out* P 0
726 29/3 Sandon (L) CON 3m 8 GF *hld up, prog 5 out, 6l 3rd last, tk 2nd post* 2 15
1174 20/4 Sandon (L) MEM 3m 4 GF *ld to 2nd, sn outpcd, clsd 4 out, not rch wnr* 2 12
1300 3/5 Weston Park (L) CON 3m 8 G *ld into start, mostly rear, nvr in race* 5 0

Winning chaser; on the slide in 96 & looks to have own ideas firmly in place now; Soft 14

BUCKSUM(IRE) b.m. 6 Buckskin (FR) - Cothill Lady (IRE) by Orchestra O Titcomb

1996 F(-),P(0),P(0)
392 8/3 Barbury Cas' (L) MDN 3m 9 G *prom, chsd ldr 8th til f 10th* F -
Yet to copmplete from 4 starts 96/7 0

BUCKS VIEW(IRE) b.g. 7 Buckskin (FR) - Our View by Our Mirage
1074 13/4 Whitwell-On' (R) MDO 2 1/2m 88yds 16 G *rear, prog 11th, ev ch 4 out, not qckn* 3 14
1268 27/4 Southwell P' (L) MDO 3m 13 G *(Jt fav) mid-div, prog 6th, ld 12th, drew clr 3 out, easily* 1 15
Promising; trotted up in fair time & should find Restricted in his grasp in 98; Good, so far 18

BUCKTAIL(NZ) b.g. 5 Conquistarose (USA) - Sans Tache (NZ) by First Consul (USA) D H Barons
1035 12/4 Lifton (R) MDN 3m 11 F *alwys prom, still cls up whn u.r. 14th* U -
Right connections & showed ability; should make his mark if ready in 98 15

BUCKTIME (Irish) — I 487[P], I 539[4]

BUCKWHEAT LAD(IRE) br.g. 9 Over The River (FR) - Buckwheat Lass by Master Buck Mrs J H Westrope
1996 4(0),1(15),2D(14),2(14),F(-),8(0)
274 22/2 Ampton (R) RES 3m 10 G *alwys bhnd, mstk 12th, nvr nr ldrs.* 5 0
760 29/3 Kimble (L) RES 3m 7 GF *rear, last at 6th, t.o.* 5 0
1475 11/5 Garthorpe (R) XX 3m 13 GS *alwys rear, 10th hlfwy, t.o. & p.u. 3 out* P 0
Maiden winner 96; changed hands & safely ignored now 0

BUGLEY b.g. 12 Grey Ghost - Girl Sunday by Derek H H S Fletcher
265 22/2 Duncombe Pa' (R) CON 3m 15 G *prom til fdd 12th, sn wll bhnd, t.o.* 7 0
616 22/3 Hutton Rudby (L) RES 3m 14 GF *disp ld til hdd 6th, prom, rddn 13th, wknd 4 out, t.o.* 8 0
Rarely seen now & soundly thrashed both starts 97 0

BUGSY MORAN(IRE) b.g. 7 Buckskin (FR) - Rusheen's Girl by Dusky Boy J R Millington
253 22/2 Brocklesby ' (L) MDO 3m 6 G *last hrd hld, 3rd frm 7th, outpcd frm 4 out* 3 0
1084 13/4 Guilsborough (L) MDN 3m 11 GF *2nd til f 5th* F -
1356 4/5 Dingley (R) MDO 3m 9 G *rear, prog & blnd 11th, lft 2nd 14th, ld 2 out-last, wknd* 2 0
Failed to stay in weak contest last start - may conceivably do better in 98 12

BUILDER BOY ch.g. 7 Sunley Builds - Geordie Lass by Bleep-Bleep Mrs C E Whiteway
1996 P(0),F(-),F(-),P(0)
205 15/2 Weston Park (L) MDN 3m 10 G *rear, prog to chs wnr 12th, sn btn, p.u. 4 out* P 0
470 8/3 Eyton-On-Se' (L) MDN 2 1/2m 12 G *ld 4th til 4 out, outpcd aft* 4 0
1003 12/4 Alpraham (R) MDO 2 1/2m 10 GF *mostly 2nd frm 8th, styd on wll, nvr rchd wnr* 2 13
1124 19/4 Whittington (L) MDO 3m 2 F *(fav) clr to 15th,qcknd nxt,6l up & wkng whn ref last,cont* 2 0
Threw away golden chance last start & win will prove elusive - not eligible for short Maidens 98 11

BUILDERS LINE (Irish) — I 587[4]

BULADANTE(IRE) b.g. 8 Phardante (FR) - Bulabos by Proverb T D B Underwood
986 12/4 Kingston Bl' (L) CON 3m 10 GF *in tch to 10th, rear nxt, eased & p.u. 13th* P 0
1165 20/4 Mollington (R) MDO 3m 9 GF *hld up, effrt 3 out, tk 3rd last* 3 10
1304 3/5 Weston Park (L) MDO 3m 8 G *handy, trckd ldr 12th, hrd rdn to ld last, ran on well* 1 17
1466 11/5 Tweseldown (R) RES 3m 5 GF *hld up, prog 14th, 4th & ev ch whn blnd & u.r. nxt* U -
1533 18/5 Mollington (R) XX 3m 8 GS *hld up, prog 11th, ev ch 14th, not qckn nxt, onepcd* 4 14
1567 25/5 Kingston Bl' (L) RES 3m 8 GF *hld up, in chsng grp whn mstk 15th, no dang, kpt on flat* 3 0
Beat decent prospect when scoring (not owner-ridden); should find Restricted in Sandhurst 98; Good .. 16

BULLENS BAY(IRE) b.g. 8 Hallodri (ATA) - Coolgreen Lolly by Blue Chariot J Milton
1996 **3(NH),3(NH),2(NH),3(NH),P(NH)**
187 15/2 Erw Lon (L) OPE 3m 16 G *trckd ldrs, prog 11th, chsd wnr & outpcd 15th, ran on flat* 2 25
400 8/3 Llanfrynach (R) OPE 3m 10 G *s.u. flat aft 2nd* S -
535 16/3 Erw Lon (L) CON 3m 12 GF *disp 13th, no imp wnr aft nxt* 2 17
716 29/3 Llanvapley (L) LAD 3m 5 GF *s.s., stdy prog hlfwy, lft 2nd 14th, held whn ref last* R -
Winning hurdler; ran well 1st start but disappointing after & has reverted to Rules 20

BUMPER TO BUMPER (Irish) — I 77[P], I 84[2], I 141[2], I 241[1]

BUMPTIOUS BOY b.g. 13 Neltino - Bellardita by Derring-Do R F Hanks
1996 P(0),2(16),U(-),P(0),2(10),3(0)
750 29/3 Brampton Br' (R) LAD 3m 5 GF *ld, 30l clr 13th, ct flat* 3 16
817 31/3 Paxford (L) CON 3m 3 F *ld til 3 out, rallied, ev ch last, styd on onepcd* 2 13
1063 13/4 Maisemore P' (L) XX 3m 13 GF *p.u. 1st, dsmntd* P 0
1195 23/4 Andoversford (R) MEM 3m 4 F *(fav) jmpd lft, made all, drew clr frm 3 out, easily* 1 12
1329 3/5 Chaddesley ' (L) CON 3m 5 GF *disp til ld 4th,clr 11th,jnd & lft clr 3 out,blnd & u.r. nxt* U -
1455 11/5 Maisemore P' (L) CON 3m 8 G *chsd wnr 8-10th, wknd aft 13th, t.o. 3 out* 5 0

1575 26/5 Chaddesley ' (L) OPE 3m 10 F *chsd ldrs, went 2nd aft 15th, cls engh 2 out, sn btn* 2 17

Usually brushed aside now but doddled home in Members & same again best hope at 14 14

BUNGLE b.g. 7 Afzal - Jolly Girl by Jolly Me H J Manners

1144 19/4 Larkhill (R) RES 3m 3 F *hld up last, in tch whn f 5th, dead* F -

Dead 0

BUNNY HARE(IRE) ch.g. 9 Callernish - Maggie Pickens by Beau Chapeau Keith Thomas

766 29/3 Whittington (L) INT 3m 10 S *alwys last, t.o. 11th, p.u. 13th* P 0
984 12/4 Kingston Bl' (L) MEM 3m 4 GF *last frm 7th til u.r. 13th* U -
1120 19/4 Whittington (L) INT 3m 2 F *blnd 3rd & 11th, chsd wnr, rdn & no ext 3 out* 2 12
1250 26/4 Easingwold (L) RES 3m 15 GS *s.s., wll in rear, f 3 out* F -
1345 3/5 Gisburn (R) MDN 3m 13 GF *alwys bhnd, rear whn c.o. 12th* C -
1545 24/5 Cartmel (L) HC 3 1/4m 14 G *midfield when blnd and u.r. 2nd.* U -

Beaten in a match only completion; no prospects & making a fool of himself in summer jumping after ... 0

BUNNY LIGHTENING (Irish) — **I** 278P, **I** 356P, **I** 428P

BURKEAN MELODY (Irish) — **I** 256P, **I** 309P, **I** 421², **I** 475¹, **I** 537³

BURRELLS WHARF(IRE) ch.g. 6 Jamesmead - Granny Grumble by Politico (USA) G Vergette

29 26/1 Marks Tey (L) MDN 3m 10 GF *(fav) chsd ldrs going wll, ev ch 3 out, onepcd aft* 4 13
479 9/3 Southwell P' (L) MDO 3m 15 G *disp 2nd bhnd clr ldr, clsd 11th, ld apr 2 out, rdn clr* 1 16

Decisive win 2nd start & should certainly upgrade if ready in 98 19

BURROMARINER b.g. 13 Julio Mariner - Ever Joyful by Aureole Mrs A Blaker

1996 2(17),1(15),1(19),1(21),1(22),R(-),1(20)

281 23/2 Charing (L) OPE 3m 12 G *alwys prom, prssd wnr frm 12th til no ext apr last* 2 20
579 16/3 Detling (L) OPE 4m 9 F *hndy, cls 3rd 23rd, 4th & wkng whn ref 25th* R -
683 29/3 Charing (L) OPE 3m 5 F *ld to 2nd, cls aft, 3rd & rddn whn ref 3 out* R -
1126 19/4 Penshurst (L) CON 3m 6 GF *trckd clr ldr, cls up whn reluc 8th & ref 12th* R -

Won 5 in 96 but reverted to old habits in 96 - looks finished now 12

BURTON HALL (Irish) — **I** 269P, **I** 456P, **I** 482⁵, **I** 532F

BUSHMILLER(IRE) b.g. 7 Down The Hatch - Blue Cloak by Majority Blue R A Ross

419 8/3 Dalston (R) MDO 2 1/2m 10 GS *ld to 12th, lft in ld aft nxt, in cmmnd whn lft wll clr last* 1 14
563 16/3 Lanark (R) RES 3m 8 GS *made most til wknd qckly 3 out* 5 0

Ex-Irish; fortunate win on debut & yet to prove he stays 3m 14

BUSHTON b.g. 5 High Season - Rusty Fern by Rustingo J L Brown

540 16/3 Erw Lon (L) MDN 3m 13 GF *alwys rear, ran green, p.u. 13th* P 0
1138 19/4 Bonvilston (R) MDO 3m 9 G *held up mid-div,prog 13th,wnt 2nd 3 out,hrd rdn to ld flat* 1 13
1467 11/5 Erw Lon (L) MEM 3m 3 GS *(fav) hld up, chal 13th, f 15th whn going wll* F -
1556 24/5 Bassaleg (R) RES 3m 13 G *in tch whn f 4th* F -

Won a bad race in slow time & nothing very concrete in his form yet - time on his side 14

BUSHY RANGER (Irish) — **I** 192U, **I** 262F, **I** 321P

BUSKING ALONG(IRE) br.g. 8 Phardante (FR) - Buskins Reward by Little Buskins J G Nicholson

1996 **P(NH),6(NH),F(NH),4(NH)**

480 9/3 Southwell P' (L) MDO 3m 17 G *nvr bttr than mid-div, no dang frm 15th* 7 0
544 16/3 Garthorpe (R) MEM 3m 6 GF *prom,lft 2nd 9th,disp ld 13th til ld 3 out,hdd & onepcd last* 2 14
772 29/3 Dingley (R) MEM 3m 4 G *(fav) alwys 1st pair, ld to 5th & frm 6 out, drew away 2 out* 1 13
838 31/3 Thorpe Lodge (L) RES 3m 5 F *cls up mstly 3rd, chsd wnr frm 2 out, outpcd flat* 2 13
1081 13/4 Guilsborough (L) RES 3m 13 GF *last pair, in tch to 15th, sn outpcd, kpt on* 5 0

Safe & steady; novice-ridden & could be up to Restricted win with stronger handling; G-F 15

BUSMAN(IRE) ch.g. 8 Be My Guest (USA) - Cistus by Sun Prince Keith R Pearce

1996 3(20),**2(21)**,3(20),2(22),1(24),1(23),**1(24)**

188 15/2 Erw Lon (L) LAD 3m 8 G *in tch, prog to ld 11th, rdn flat, hdd nr fin* 2 24
378 4/3 Leicester (R) HC 2 1/2m 110yds 6 G *prom, chsd ldr 6th, ld six out, mstk 3 out, hdd and hit 2 out, styd on same pace.* 3 24
585 18/3 Fontwell (R) HC 2m 3f 7 GF *alwys in tch, challenging when hit 12th, ld next, clr 3 out, unchal.* 1 25
1194 22/4 Chepstow (L) HC 3m 11 GF *chsd wnr 12th to 2 out, one pace.* 3 23

Useful & versatile; won 4, placed 7 - last 11 starts; win more 98; Any, best G-S 26

BUS PASS ch.g. 5 Itsu (USA) - Ridgeway Girl by Mr Bigmore J Parfitt

185 15/2 Erw Lon (L) MDN 3m 14 G *rear, lost tch hlfwy, t.o. & p.u. 13th* P 0
640 22/3 Howick (L) MDN 3m 10 GF *cls up, ran out aft 6th* r -
877 1/4 Upton-On-Se' (R) RES 3m 17 GF *(vis) ld to 7th, 3rd frm 11th, poor 2nd agn apr 2 out, u.r. last* U -

Ran fair race last start & has Maiden possibilities if fit 98 14

BUSTEELE b.g. 13 Bustino - Narration (USA) by Sham (USA) — R Hardy
1996 P(0),3(15),P(0)

1044	12/4 Cothelstone	(L)	XX	3m	2	GF	*chsd ldr, 5l 2nd whn f hvly 14th*	F	-

Looks finished now 0

BUTLER JOHN(IRE) b.g. 8 The Parson - Corrielek by Menelek — Nick Viney
1996 1(24),P(0),U(-),2(22),2(21),2(21),1(25)

48	1/2 Wadebridge	(L)	OPE	3m	5	G	*(fav) ld, going well whn u.r. 14th*	U	-
145	9/2 Tweseldown	(R)	LAD	3m	10	GF	*prom, ld aft 9th-14th, wkng whn mstk 4 out*	4	15
530	15/3 Wadebridge	(L)	OPE	3m	4	GF	*(fav) made all, 12l clr 12th, not extndd*	1	23
739	29/3 Higher Kilw'	(L)	OPE	3m	3	GF	*(fav) made all, clr hlfwy, unchal*	1	24
1089	16/4 Hockworthy	(L)	CON	3m	7	GF	*(fav) made all, hit 10th, wll clr 14th, imprssv*	1	25
1243	26/4 Bratton Down	(L)	OPE	3m	6	GS	*made all, nvr serously chal*	1	24
1341	3/5 Flete Park	(R)	OPE	3m	5	G	*(fav) prom, ld 10th, 5l clr but und pres whn f last*	F	25
1396	5/5 High Bickin'	(R)	MXO	3m	7	G	*(fav) cls up, ld 9th, hit 15th, sn drew wll clr, unchal*	1	30
1484	11/5 Ottery St M'	(L)	OPE	3m	7	G	*(fav) made all, clr 4 out, v easily*	1	26
1516	17/5 Bratton Down	(L)	CON	3m	6	GS	*(fav) prog to ld apr 8th, sn clr, pshd out flat*	1	28
1549	24/5 Mounsey Hil'	(R)	OPE	3m	2	G	*(fav) made virt all, blnd 4th, clr whn nrly u.r. 9th, solo 15th*	1	25
1580	26/5 Lifton	(R)	OPE	3m	8	G	*(fav) ld 2nd, ld agn 4th, drew rght away, unextndd*	1	29
1592	31/5 Bratton Down	(L)	MEM	3m	4	F	*(fav) made, all, sn clr, jmpd rght 11th, easily*	1	25

Grand Marnier winner; speedy, front-runs & very useful; good stable; win plenty more; G/S-F 30

BUTLERS MATCH(IRE) ch.g. 7 Matching Pair - Millys Last by Cheval — Mrs Helen Mobley
1996 3(0),P(0)

224	16/2 Heythrop	(R)	MDN	3m	16	G	*(fav) w.w. prog 11th, ld 13th, mstk & hdd 2 out, lvl last, kpt on*	2	16
373	2/3 Mollington	(R)	MDN	3m	14	G	*(fav) trckd ldrs, ld 12th, drew clr aft 2 out, rdn out*	1	15

Wide-margin winner from poor lot; lightly-raced & can upgrade if fit 98; Good 18

BUT NOT QUITE(IRE) b.g. 9 Nearly A Nose (USA) - Rosa Perfecta — Derek J Harding-Jones
1996 U(-),P(0),P(0),P(0)

29	26/1 Marks Tey	(L)	MDN	3m	10	GF	*tubed, hld up, lost tch 13th, t.o. & p.u. 15th*	P	0
197	15/2 Higham	(L)	MDO	3m	12	G	*ld to 3rd, sn lost plc, rear & p.u. 14th*	P	0
317	1/3 Marks Tey	(L)	MDN	3m	13	G	*(bl) ld to 4th, chsd ldrs, hmp 9th, p.u. nxt, dead*	P	0

Dead 0

BUTTERFIELD BOY (Irish) — **I** 456^3

BUTTON YOUR LIP b.g. 15 Le Bavard (FR) - High Energy by Dalesa — Mrs J Enderby
1996 F(-),3(16),1+(13),4(0),4(10),P(0),U(-)

55	1/2 Kingston Bl'	(L)	CON	3m	15	GF	*rear whn p.u. 11th*	P	0
143	9/2 Tweseldown	(R)	XX	3m	3	GF	*trckd ldr, rdn to disp 3 out, hdd & onepcd nxt*	2	13
280	23/2 Charing	(L)	LAD	3m	12	G	*alwys bhnd, t.o. & p.u. 14th*	P	0
484	9/3 Tweseldown	(R)	OPE	3m	10	G	*f 2nd*	F	-
759	29/3 Kimble	(L)	LAD	3m	4	GF	*ld to 3rd, cls up to hlfwy, last at 10th, sn t.o.*	4	10
986	12/4 Kingston Bl'	(L)	CON	3m	10	GF	*chsd ldrs, outpcd frm 9th, brf effrt 14th, sn t.o.*	6	0

Dead-heated in poor race 96 but just goes through the motions now 10

BUTTS CASTLE b.g. 8 Reving - Celtic Express by Pony Express — J F Symes

111	8/2 Milborne St'	(L)	MDN	3m	8	GF	*alwys rear, nvr on trms wth ldrs*	4	0
461	8/3 Great Treth'	(R)	MDO	3m	12	S	*sn rear, bhnd whn p.u. apr 15th*	P	0
867	31/3 Kingston St'	(R)	MDO	3m	6	F	*tried to make all, sn clr, cght cls home*	2	16

Missed 96; set up for last start & just caught in poor race; could win in 98 14

BUXOM ORLOV (Irish) — **I** 26^P, **I** 60^P, **I** 296^4

BUZZ ABOUT (Irish) — **I** 33^U, **I** 60^P, **I** 188^U, **I** 221^P, **I** 339^3, **I** 488^1

BUZZ O'THE CROWD br.g. 10 Sousa - Dotted Swiss by Super Slip — B J Williams
1996 **6(NH),3(NH),5(NH),3(NH),4(NH)**

1244	26/4 Bratton Down	(L)	CON	3m	14	GS	*alwys cls up, styd on onepcd aft last*	3	16
1544	21/5 Newton Abbot	(L)	HC	3 1/4m 110yds	11	G	*alwys handy, ld 16th, soon clr, unchal.*	1	31

Looked nothing special in points & under Rules but blazed home in fantastic style; hard to predict 29

BY CRIKEY(IRE) b.g. 7 Treasure Hunter - Jamie's Lady by Ashmore (FR) — A J Wight
1996 R(-),**5(NH),8(NH)**

32	26/1 Alnwick	(L)	RES	3m	11	G	*alwys rear, lost tch 14th, t.o. & p.u. 3 out*	P	0

Not disgraced in hurdle in 96 but shows nothing in points 0

BY HIM SELF (Irish) — **I** 307^5

BYRON CHOICE(IRE) ch.g. 7 Le Bavard (FR) - Miss Cynthia by Dawn Review — E B Swaffield
1996 U(-)

181	15/2 Larkhill	(R)	MDO	3m	17	G	*hld up, prog 10th, ev ch 3 out, btn whn lft 3rd last*	3	13

Decent effort only start 97 but only 2 runs to date; top stable 13

CABILLE (Irish) — I 85[3], I 515[4], I 559[5]

CABIN HILL ch.g. 11 Roselier (FR) - Bluejama by Windjammer (USA) Mrs A Price

1996 **4(NH)**

85	2/2 Wolverhampt'	(L)	LAD	3m	11	GS	*chsd ldr 7-9th, prom aft, lft 2nd 3 out, no imp wnr*	2	21

Winning hurdler; ran well only start but disappeared; best watched 20

CAB ON TARGET br.g. 11 Strong Gale - Smart Fashion by Carlburg N Hurst

1996 **2(NH)**

67	1/2 Wetherby	(L)	HC	3m 1f	10	G	*(fav) held up, tk clr order 10th, trckd ldr from 4 out, rdn to ld final 100 yards.*	1	32
154	14/2 Fakenham	(L)	HC	2m 5f 110yds	10	G	*(fav) held up, mstk 6th, hdwy 8th, went 3rd 10th, trckd ldr 4 out, rdn to ld near fin.*	1	26
494	13/3 Cheltenham	(L)	HC	3 1/4m 110yds	18	G	*(fav) held up, steady hdwy final cct, chal last, kept on till no ext cl home.*	2	37
1591	31/5 Stratford	(L)	HC	3 1/2m	11	G	*patiently rdn, tk clr order hfwy, feeling pace when not fluent 6 out, no ch after.*	5	23

Top-class H/Chaser 97; needs kid-glove handling; should win more at 12 but not in highest class; Gd .. 33

CABRA BOY (Irish) — I 176[P]

CABRA TOWERS (Irish) — I 177[P], I 284[S]

CADDY MAN (Irish) — I 9[2]

CADRILLON(FR) br.g. 7 Le Pontet (FR) - Jenvraie (FR) by Night And Day Mrs A Lockwood

1996 2(15),1(13),9(0),5(12),11(0),P(0),P(0)

76	2/2 Market Rase'	(L)	XX	3m	12	GF	*alwys rr div, nvr on trms*	8	0
215	16/2 Southwell P'	(L)	LAD	3m	12	GS	*hld up rear, mstk 2nd, nvr nr ldrs*	6	0
264	22/2 Duncombe Pa'	(R)	MEM	3m	9	G	*prom, jmp lft 2nd, outpcd 9th, kpt on wll frm 3 out*	3	13
424	8/3 Charm Park	(L)	RES	3m	12	GF	*mid-div, prog 4 out, outpcd 2 out, styd on strgly flat*	2	16
506	15/3 Dalton Park	(R)	CON	3m	16	GF	*rear & mstk 9th, alwys bhnd*	5	11
856	31/3 Charm Park	(L)	RES	3m	8	F	*in tch to 10th, rear aft, pst btn horses frm 2 out*	6	10
894	5/4 Wetherby Po'	(L)	RES	3m	6	F	*prom, trckd ldr 5th, disp 11th til rdn & onepcd 14th*	3	13

Members winner 96; very safe but a plodder; may find Restricted eventually; G-F 15

CAHERCON (Irish) — I 24[P], I 160[B], I 172[P]

CAHERMONE LADY(IRE) ch.m. 6 Cardinal Flower - Altaghaderry Rose S H Robertshaw

213	16/2 Southwell P'	(L)	RES	3m	16	GS	*bhnd & blnd 10th, t.o. & p.u. 12th*	P	0
348	2/3 Market Rase'	(L)	RES	3m	13	GF	*rear, in tch to 11th, no ch frm 13th*	8	0
422	8/3 Charm Park	(L)	CON	3m	8	GF	*prom whn f 1st*	F	-
616	22/3 Hutton Rudby	(L)	RES	3m	14	GF	*mid-div, prog 7th, ev ch 4 out, sn wknd*	4	14
893	5/4 Wetherby Po'	(L)	MEM	3m	3	F	*trckd ldr, disp 11th til f nxt*	F	-

Irish Maiden winner 96; ran well when 4th (beat 6 others) but clumsy & stamina doubtful 13

CAHER SOCIETY (Irish) — I 104, , I 241[P], I 297[3]

CAHILLS HILL (Irish) — I 59[P], I 99[4]

CAILIN CHUINNE (Irish) — I 537[F]

CAIRNDHU MISTY ch.m. 10 Abednego - Ah Well by Silver Cloud Mrs R Gee

1996 P(0),3(13)

140	9/2 Thorpe Lodge	(L)	RES	3m	7	GF	*hld up rear, strng run frm 3 out, ld nxt, sn clr*	1	16
441	8/3 Higham	(L)	INT	3m	7	G	*(fav) cls 2nd til wknd aft 2 out*	3	18
835	31/3 Thorpe Lodge	(L)	INT	3m	7	F	*alwys abt 5th, rdn 6 out, chsd 2nd frm 3 out*	3	15

Lightly raced; ran well all starts 97; Intermediate chances in fit at 11 18

CAIRNEYMOUNT b.g. 11 Croghan Hill - Glentoran Valley by Little Buskins Robert Williams

1996 F(-),r(-),4(12),3(0),U(-),2(11),r(-),1(16),1(19),1(18),4(17)

97	8/2 Great Treth'	(R)	INT	3m	13	GS	*alwys wll bhnd, t.o. 11th, p.u. 3 out*	P	0
191	15/2 Erw Lon	(L)	CON	3m	13	G	*mstks, rear, rdn & no prog 11th, t.o. & p.u. 14th*	P	0
402	8/3 Llanfrynach	(R)	INT	3m	7	G	*n.j.w. in rear, p.u. 12th*	P	0
636	22/3 Howick	(L)	CON	3m	12	GF	*alwys rear, p.u. 3 out*	P	0

Won 3 in 96 but completely fell to pieces in 97 0

CALADONIAN LIGHT (Irish) — I 250[P], I 370[P], I 506[F]

CALDER'S GROVE b.g. 7 Jupiter Island - Thatched Grove by Thatching Miss L A Perratt

1996 **P(NH),P(NH),8(NH),2(NH),5(NH)**

208	16/2 Southwell P'	(L)	MDO	3m	9	GS	*bhnd, brf effrt 11th, last frm 13th, t.o.*	4	0
365	2/3 Garnons	(L)	MDO	2 1/2m	14	GS	*cls 3rd whn u.r. 4th*	U	-
436	8/3 Upton-On-Se'	(R)	MDO	3m	17	G	*chsd ldrs, outpcd 11th, p.u. 15th*	P	0

571 16/3 Garnons (L) MDN 2 1/2m 13 G *prom til outpcd 9th, no ch whn p.u. 2 out* P 0
1200 23/4 Andoversford (R) MDO 3m 8 F *prom, chsd ldr 11th-3 out, onepcd aft* 4 10

Highly modest & just scrapes a rating - winning prospects very slim 10

CALL AVONDALE br.g. 9 Homeboy - Collectors Girl by Mr Bigmore — Mrs W J Coombes
1996 6(10),P(0)
175 15/2 Ottery St M' (L) RES 3m 15 G *cls up to 4 out, wknd frm nxt* 5 0

Ran well seasonal debuts 96/7 but time passing him by now 12

CALLEROSE b.g. 10 Callernish - Tarqogan's Rose by Tarqogan — R J Bevis
1996 P(0),U(-),1(16),**2(21)**
332 1/3 Eaton Hall (R) RES 3m 18 GS *(fav) mid-div hlfwy, prog 14th, chal whn f 2 out* F -
766 29/3 Whittington (L) INT 3m 10 S *4th 11th,lft 2nd 15th,ld nxt,hdd 2 out,qcknd to ld apr last* 1 22

Maiden winner 96; able & won fair Intermediate; worth trying in H/Chase again; stays 22

CALLING WILD(IRE) b.g. 7 Callernish - Chestnut Vale by Pollerton — J A Keighley
1996 3(18),1(21),2(24),1(24)
4 19/1 Barbury Cas' (L) OPE 3m 9 GF *ld, blnd 15th, hdd 2 out, ev ch last, eased whn btn flat* 2 29

Beaten by season's top pointer only start; will race under Rules 97/8 - should win 30

CALL ME DICKINS gr.g. 8 Rusticaro (FR) - Bad Start (USA) by Bold Bidder — Ms E J Kessler
741 29/3 Higher Kilw' (L) MDN 3m 12 GF *handy, mstk 4th, 3rd at 10th, prom whn b.d. nxt* B -
1261 27/4 Black Fores' (R) MDO 3m 12 F *alwys bhnd, p.u. aft 10th* P 0
1343 3/5 Flete Park (R) MDO 3m 13 G *(bl) not alwys fluent, lft in ld aft 6th, hdd 11th, lost tch 4out* 4 0
1521 17/5 Bratton Down (L) MDO 3m 16 GS *(bl) prom whn u.r. 2nd* U -

Well beaten on 2 completions from 11 starts 94-7 - they'll be calling him something else 0

CALL-ME-DINKY b.m. 14 Mart Lane - Call-Me-Sally — C A Fuller
398 8/3 Llanfrynach (R) MEM 3m 6 G *raced 4th, prog to 3rd 3 out, mstk nxt, wknd & p.u. last* P 0
750 29/3 Brampton Br' (R) LAD 3m 5 GF *(fav) mostly 3rd, prog to chal last, no ext nr fin* 2 16
1203 26/4 Worcester (L) HC 2m 7f 110yds 10 S *bhnd till p.u. lame and dismntd before 4th.* P 0

Unraced 95/6; good effort 2nd start but last outing should signal the end 12

CALL ME JOE (Irish) — **I** 232[3], **I** 272[1], **I** 396[2], **I** 441[1], **I** 495[3]
CALL ME OGAN (Irish) — **I** 106[F], **I** 354[P]
CALL ME PARIS (Irish) — **I** 43[P], **I** 73[6]
CALMOS (Irish) — **I** 535[P], **I** 560[4]

CAL'S BOY b.g. 8 Green Ruby (USA) - Green Gypsy by Creetown — Miss E Murray
1018 12/4 Bitterley (L) MDO 3m 13 GF *rear frm 8th, kpt on same pace frm 13th* 6 0
1459 11/5 Maisemore P' (L) MDO 3m 12 G *25s-5s, ld 2nd-13th, wknd 15th, wll btn & p.u. 2 out* P 0
1578 26/5 Chaddesley ' (L) MDO 3m 7 F *ld 2nd-13th, chsd wnr aft, btn aft 15th, wknd 2 out* 3 0

Not enough stamina - even on short courses - & winning prospects slight at present 11

CALVERSTOWN STAR(IRE) b.g. 7 Torus - Mistress Victoria — V Hughes
641 22/3 Howick (L) MDN 3m 9 GF *mid-div, hmpd & b.d. 6th* B -
1010 12/4 St Hilary (R) MDN 3m 10 GF *(Co fav) mid-div, mstk 14th, p.u. nxt* P 0

No sign of stamina or ability yet 0

CAMAN br.m. 10 Callernish - Chilly For June by Menelek — J A V Duell
1996 P(0),6(0),4(0),P(0),5(0),P(0),9(0),U(-),5(0),7(0),8(0)
425 8/3 Charm Park (L) RES 3m 12 GF *prom, ld 15th-2 out, no ext* 2 13
616 22/3 Hutton Rudby (L) RES 3m 14 GF *(Jt fav) disp til ld 6th, hdd 16th, onepce frm 3 out* 2 17
695 29/3 Stainton (R) RES 3m 11 F *disp ld til hdd 7th, rmnd prom til onepcd frm 3 out* 3 16
1068 13/4 Whitwell-On' (R) RES 3m 12 G *trckd ldrs, ld 11th, hdd 13th, kpt on onepcd frm 2 out* 2 17
1250 26/4 Easingwold (L) RES 3m 15 GS *trckd ldr, ld last, styd on wll* 1 20
1419 10/5 Easingwold (L) CON 3m 8 GF *prom, ld 14th-nxt, chal agn last, outpcd flat* 3 19
1571 26/5 Wetherby (L) HC 2 1/2m 110yds 15 GF *in tch till outpcd 5 out, styd on from 2 out, nearest fin.* 5 16

Vastly improved 97; consistent, safe & stays; should win Confined at 11 if maintaining form; G/S-F 20

CAMBRIDGE GOLD ch.g. 5 Charmer - Celtic Sonata by Music Boy — A Chinnery
196 15/2 Higham (L) MDO 3m 12 G *rear whn ran out 6th* r -
317 1/3 Marks Tey (L) MDN 3m 13 G *chsd ldr 4th-8th, 3rd whn f 9th* F -
438 8/3 Higham (L) MDO 3m 8 G *jmpd slwly 1st, ld 2nd, wd bnd apr 4th, ran out 7th* r -
498 15/3 Ampton (R) MDO 3m 8 GF *mstks, made most to 11th, bhnd & hit 14th, t.o.* 4 0
796 31/3 Marks Tey (L) MDO 3m 6 F *mstk 3rd, ld 5th, hdd & wknd qckly 11th, t.o. & p.u. 13th* P 0

Beaten miles on only completion & shows no aptitude 0

CAMDEN COURT (Irish) — **I** 346S
CAMLA LAD (Irish) — **I** 226F, **I** 2805, **I** 3545, **I** 550P
CAMOGUE BRIDGE (Irish) — **I** 21P, **I** 357P, **I** 426P
CANDLE GLOW ch.m. 9 Capitano - Fused Light by Fury Royal Mrs P J Hutchinson
1996 **P(0),9(0)**,3(16),1(24),**1(22),4(16)**

982	9/4 Ludlow	(R) HC	3m	6	F	*ld 2nd to next, chsd wnr after till 5th, rdn 13th, wknd 15th.*	4	20
1099	19/4 Stratford	(L) HC	2m 5f 110yds	14	G	*chsd ldrs till wknd 7th, p.u. before 10th.*	P	0
1287	29/4 Huntingdon	(R) HC	2 1/2m 110yds	14	G	*mstks, chsd ldr to 5th, prom till wknd 12th.*	6	11

H/Chase winner 96; late to appear & well below form 97; Confineds best hope if fit 98; G-F 18

CANDY IS DANDY (Irish) — **I** 571, , **I** 6072, **I** 610P
CANEBREAK BOY(IRE) ch.g. 8 Le Moss - Scatty Kate R Tate

120	9/2 Wetherby Po'	(L) MDO	3m	18	GF	*rear, prog 14th, kpt on frm 3 out, improve*	4	0
212	16/2 Southwell P'	(L) MDO	3m	14	GS	*(bl) in tch, prog 11th, 2nd whn blnd 3 out, no imp aft*	2	11
479	9/3 Southwell P'	(L) MDO	3m	15	G	*(fav) (bl) prom in main grp, lost plc 10th, p.u. nxt, dsmntd*	P	0

Promising 1st 2 starts but problems last outing; should win if fit 98 14

CANISTER CASTLE b.g. 9 Gypsy Castle - Vultop by Vulgan Slave Miss Z A Green
1996 4(13),3(0),3(11),2(12),**P(0)**,1(15)

607	22/3 Friars Haugh	(L) RES	3m	8	GF	*ld/disp to 8th, ld agn brfly 4 out, no ext frm 3 out*	2	14
972	7/4 Kelso	(L) HC	3m 1f	12	GF	*chsd ldrs, rdn along and blnd 15th and next, wknd and p.u. before 3 out.*	P	0
1510	17/5 Corbridge	(R) RES	3m	13	GS	*twrds rear whn u.r. 3rd*	U	-
1545	24/5 Cartmel	(L) HC	3 1/4m	14	G	*alwys bhnd, lost tch final cct, t.o..*	10	0

Maiden winner 96; over-ambitious campaign 97 & will struggle to win Restricted 14

CANNY CHRONICLE b or br.g. 9 Daring March - Laisser Aller by Sagaro Miss C E J Dawson
1996 P(0),**F(-)**,P(0)

386	7/3 Ayr	(L) HC	2m 5f 110yds	7	S	*chsd ldrs till f 12th.*	F	-

Very useful novice hurdler in 92 but has shown nothing since 0

CANNY CURATE(IRE) b.g. 8 The Parson - Lisa Martin by Black Minstrel B Wilberforce
1996 B(-),4(0),5(0)

572	16/3 Garnons	(L) INT	3m	13	G	*prom to 7th, lost plc & p.u. aft 14th, lame*	P	0

Some promise in 96 but disappeared with problems in 97 0

CANNY'S FORT ch.m. 8 Fort Nayef - Canny's Tudor by Tudor Cliff P F Gibbon
1996 P(0),F(-),5(0),F(-)

424	8/3 Charm Park	(L) RES	3m	12	GF	*slwly into stride, sn strggling, wll bhnd 11th, p.u. last*	P	0
1069	13/4 Whitwell-On'	(R) RES	3m	12	G	*blnd 1st, rear, lost tch 10th, t.o. 13th, p.u. 3 out*	P	0
1410	5/5 Witton Cast'	(R) MEM	3m	3	GS	*trckd wnr til drppd back 3rd 13th,outpcd 15th,tk 2nd flat*	2	10

Finished 2 of 7 races 96/7 & last start proves nothing 0

CAN SHE DO IT (Irish) — **I** 33U, **I** 97P, **I** 173P, **I** 212P
CANTANGO(IRE) b.g. 7 Carlingford Castle - Judy Can Dance by Northern Guest (USA) W J Turcan
1996 2(14),F(-),3(0),F(-)

550	16/3 Garthorpe	(R) MDO	3m	11	GF	*(fav) mstks, in tch to 12th, sn strugg, no ch frm 14th*	6	0
1166	20/4 Mollington	(R) MDO	3m	9	GF	*prom, lft in ld 8-10th, ld aft nxt, hrd rdn 2 out, kpt on*	1	13
1477	11/5 Garthorpe	(R) XX	3m	6	GS	*chsd ldrs, blnd 8th, rmndr 10th, lost tch 13th,lft 2nd 2 out*	2	0
1533	18/5 Mollington	(R) XX	3m	8	GS	*cls up to 11th, rmndr & sn wknd, t.o.*	6	0

Struggled home in weak Maiden & well-beaten after; Restricted prospects slim 14

CAPAIL MOR (Irish) — **I** 117P, **I** 128F, **I** 247,
CAPE COTTAGE ch.g. 13 Dubassoff (USA) - Cape Thriller by Thriller D J Caro
1996 **R(-),2(24),P(0)**

149	10/2 Hereford	(R) HC	3m 1f 110yds	18	GS	*in tch, rdn 6 out, chsd wnr 4 out, wknd next.*	2	23
288	27/2 Ludlow	(R) HC	3m	8	G	*held up, hdwy 12th, ld 3 out, styd on.*	1	25
382	5/3 Bangor	(L) HC	3m 110yds	6	GS	*(fav) held up, niggld along 9th, hmpd 4 out, ev ch from 2 out, no ext run-in.*	3	19
982	9/4 Ludlow	(R) HC	3m	6	F	*held up in tch, chsd wnr from 7th, str chal from 4 out, kept on.*	2	27
1202	25/4 Ludlow	(R) HC	2 1/2m	5	GF	*held up, hdwy 10th, left 2nd 5 out, effort 2 out, no ext run-in.*	2	23
1503	16/5 Folkestone	(R) HC	3 1/4m	7	G	*waited with, 5th and in tch when b.d. 7th.*	B	-
1591	31/5 Stratford	(L) HC	3 1/2m	11	G	*alwys chasing ldrs, struggling to hold pl final cct, soon lost tch.*	6	22

Revived early 97 but threw in towel twice at Ludlow after; still able but early 98 only chance; Good 23

CAPE HENRY b.g. 10 Dubassoff (USA) - Cape Mandalin by Mandamus — T F Sage

1996 3(18)

390	8/3	Barbury Cas'	(L)	MDN 3m	15	G	*prom, ld & mstk 6th, clr apr 2 out, hrd rdn apr last,hdd fin*	2	17
881	1/4	Upton-On-Se'	(R)	MDN 3m	13	GF	*(fav) mstk 3rd,trckd ldrs going wll,disp 2 out-last,not qckn*	2	14

Easily good enough for a win but only 4 runs in career & time running out; one paced 16

CAPITAL LETTER(IRE) b.g. 8 Tumble Gold - Willetta by Will Somers — Henry Bell

1996 **F(NH),F(NH),12(NH),P(NH),P(NH)**

343	1/3	Corbridge	(R)	MDO 3m	14	G	*trckd ldr whn f 10th*	F	-
357	2/3	Great Stain'	(L)	MDO 3m	15	S	*mid-div, prog 13th, wknd apr 3 out, p.u. nxt*	P	0

Switches between pointing & Rules with singular lack of success 0

CAP IT IF YOU CAN (Irish) — I 333^{F}, I 424^{4}, I 460^{2}

CAPO CASTANUM ch.g. 8 Sula Bula - Joscilla by Joshua — D C G Gyle-Thompson

1996 **8(NH),13(NH),4(NH),U(NH),1(NH),2(NH)**

376	3/3	Windsor	(R)	HC 3m	11	GF	*alwys prom, left 2nd 13th, ld after 4 out, ran on well.*	1	24
983	12/4	Ascot	(R)	HC 3m 110yds	14	GF	*alwys handy, chsd wnr from 11th till lost pl apr last, one pace.*	3	23

Winning chaser; found soft race at Windsor; struggles in better company; better off in handicaps 24

CAPPADUFF (Irish) — I 57^{F}

CAPPAGH GLEN (Irish) — I 60, , I 137^{P}, I 305^{1}

CAPPAJUNE(IRE) b.f. 9 Codebreaker - Hainault — M D Killick

291	1/3	Warwick	(L)	HC 3 1/4m	6	G	*chasing ldrs when blnd and u.r. 3rd.*	U	-
381	4/3	Leicester	(R)	HC 2m 1f	13	G	*in tch, mstk 4 out, soon bhnd, p.u. before last.*	P	0

Ex-Irish; season lasted 3 days - should be capable of better if fit 98 16

CAPTAIN BRANDY (Irish) — I 116^{3}, I 177^{4}, I 211^{1}, I 249^{1}, I 291^{2}, I 362^{3}, I 414^{1}, I 505^{2}, I 553^{3}, I 582^{1}

CAPTAIN DEEN (Irish) — I 155^{P}, I 223^{1}

CAPTAIN FLASHARD ch.g. 5 Kinglet - Bowtina by Rugantino — C P Hobbs

224	16/2	Heythrop	(R)	MDN 3m	16	G	*ld til hdd & f 2nd*	F	-
654	22/3	Siddington	(L)	MDN 3m	10	F	*prom, 3rd whn u.r. 8th*	U	-

A clear round is the first priority 0

CAPTAIN GREG ch.g. 10 Cardinal Flower - Pottlerath by Paddy's Stream — Miss E Schaad

293	1/3	Didmarton	(L)	INT 3m	16	G	*prom to 6th, 7th & wkng whn u.r. 9th*	U	-

Misdsed 95/6 & seems virtually untrainable 0

CAPTAIN GUINNESS(IRE) ch.g. 7 Bulldozer - Fine Bess by Fine Blade (USA) — Jamie Alexander

136	9/2	Alnwick	(L)	MDO 3m	16	G	*chsd ldrs, ld 12th-14th, ev ch 3 out, kpt on und pres flat*	2	0
161	15/2	Lanark	(R)	MDO 2m 5f	14	G	*bhnd whn f 7th*	F	-
420	8/3	Dalston	(R)	MDO 2 1/2m	8	GS	*chsd ldrs, mstk 4th, rdn 9th, sn strggIng*	7	0

Fair 1st run but disappointed after & vanished; best watched 12

CAPTAINS BAR (Irish) — I 115^{P}, I 177^{U}, I 249^{4}, I 327^{2}, I 469^{4}

CAPTAINS FRIEND (Irish) — I 253^{P}, I 366^{P}, I 464^{P}

CAPTAIN'S PORT b.m. 7 Welsh Captain - Port'n Lemon by Hot Brandy — R Rainbow

1166	20/4	Mollington	(R)	MDO 3m	9	GF	*jmpd lft, cls up to 12th, wknd rpdly, p.u. 3 out*	P	0
1401	5/5	Ashorne	(R)	MDO 3m	15	G	*alwys rear, rdn & t.o. 11th, p.u. 15th*	P	0
1537	18/5	Mollington	(R)	MDO 3m	14	GS	*alwys bhnd, rdn & no prog 11th, t.o. & p.u. 3 out*	P	0

Shows no ability 0

CAPTAIN'S VIEW (Irish) — I 473^{F}

CAPTAINS VIEW (Irish) — I 67^{6}, I 282, , I 314^{U}, I 345^{P}, I 412^{U}, I 437^{4}

CARBERY ARCTIC b.g. 12 Le Bavard (FR) - Arctic Straight by Straight Lad — John Eaton

1996 3(17),3(19),3(18),2(20),2(23)

218	16/2	Heythrop	(R)	INT 3m	21	G	*2nd whn f 6th, dead*	F	-

Dead 20

CARBERY BOY (Irish) — I 481^{P}

CARBERY MINSTREL (Irish) — I 208^{4}, I 309^{P}, I 382^{5}

CARDINAL BELLE (Irish) — I 413^{P}, I 462^{P}

CARDINAL BIRD(USA) b.g. 10 Storm Bird (CAN) - Shawnee Creek (USA) by Mr Prospector (USA) — F R Bown

1996 P(0),5(0),P(0),R(-),R(-),3(16),P(0),P(0),R(-),P(0),R(-)

173	15/2	Ottery St M'	(L)	CON	3m	7	G	*last whn ref 5th*	R	-
738	29/3	Higher Kilw'	(L)	CON	3m	8	GF	*(vis) last whn blnd & u.r. 1st*	U	-
1341	3/5	Flete Park	(R)	OPE	3m	5	G	*(vis) ref 2nd*	R	-

Completely took control in 97 & should be pensioned off now 0

CARDINAL BLACK br.g. 11 Cardinal Flower - Clockonocra by Shall We Dance — R Fox

497	15/3	Ampton	(R)	CON	3m	9	GF	*keen hold, ld/disp til ld 10th, hdded 15th, wknd 3 out*	4	12
779	31/3	Fakenham	(L)	HC	2m 5f 110yds	9	G	*ld to 3rd, led 7th to 12th, rear when p.u. after 2 out.*	P	0

Useful in 93; missed 95/6 & unable to recover form; can only be watched if returning 15

CARDINAL RALPH b.g. 13 Ovac (ITY) - Alice Minkthorn by Party Mink — Kevin Williams

66	1/2	Horseheath	(R)	MEM	3m	7	GF	*alwys bhnd, t.o. & p.u. 14th*	P	0

No longer of any account 0

CARDINAL RED b.g. 10 The Parson - Rose Ravine by Deep Run — J M Turner

1996 3(21),P(0),1(20),6(0),4(16),U(-),1(21),**1(20)**

273	22/2	Ampton	(R)	OPE	3m	7	G	*prom til badly hmpd 12th, nt rcvr, p.u. nxt*	P	0
440	8/3	Higham	(L)	OPE	3m	5	G	*cls up til drppd rear 11th, slw jmp nxt, lost tch, ref 15th*	R	-
501	15/3	Ampton	(R)	OPE	3m	4	GF	*trkd ldrs til j.s. 8th, reluc & sn wll bhnd, t.o. & ref 16th*	R	-
710	29/3	High Easter	(L)	OPE	3m	5	F	*(bl) wth ldr, j.s. 6th, mstk & lst iron 10th,strugg 14th,p.u.16th*	P	0
1030	12/4	Horseheath	(R)	OPE	3m	2	HD	*(bl) disp ld til j.s13th & 14th,rallied und press flat,jst faild*	2	20
1285	29/4	Huntingdon	(R)	HC	3m	10	G	*(bl) prom till reluctant to race and lost pl rpdly from 10th, t.o. and p.u. before 15th.*	P	0
1377	5/5	Northaw	(L)	OPE	3m	3	F	*(fav) (bl) chsd wnr, j.s. 9th, reluc aft, t.o. 12th, ref 14th*	R	-
1529	18/5	Fakenham	(L)	HC	3m 110yds	9	G	*soon bhnd, tried to refuse 10th, p.u. before next.*	8	0

H/Chase winner; would not do a tap most starts 97 & safely ignored now 12

CARDINAL RICHELIEU ch.g. 10 Cardinal Flower - Knockane Rose by Giolla Mear — Christopher Sporborg

25	26/1	Marks Tey	(L)	CON	3m	5	GF	*ld to 8th, chsd ldr aft, ld agn 2 out, styd on well*	1	24
124	9/2	Cottenham	(R)	OPE	3m	9	GF	*made all, edgd rght aft last, styd on gamely*	1	25
799	31/3	Marks Tey	(L)	OPE	3m	5	F	*(fav) trckd ldr,ld 8th,brfly chal 3 out,drew clr 2 out,easily*	1	20
1188	20/4	Garthorpe	(R)	OPE	3m	9	GF	*(fav) chsd ldr, lft in ld 11th-aft 15th, rdn apr last, ld nr fin*	1	21
1503	16/5	Folkestone	(R)	HC	3 1/4m	7	G	*started slowly, well bhnd, some prog when p.u. before 12th, lame.*	P	0

Missed 95/6; useful & returned in fine form; lame last start but will hopefully return 24

CARDINALS FOLLY (Irish) — I 71[2], I 210[3]

CARDINAL WAY (Irish) — I 534[P], I 597[P]

CAREFORMENOW(USA) (Irish) — I 572[4], I 593[1]

CARHOO SURPRISE (Irish) — I 73[P], I 561[F], I 572[6], I 607[F]

CARINCI b.g. 10 Bishop Of Orange - Prairie Stream by Paddy's Stream — Mrs B Shaw

1068	13/4	Whitwell-On'	(R)	RES	3m	12	G	*chsd ldrs, fdd 11th, t.o. & p.u. 14th*	P	0
1263	27/4	Southwell P'	(L)	RES	3m	9	G	*ld til apr 12th, chsd ldr aft, wknd rpdly & p.u. 3 out*	P	0
1385	5/5	Eyton-On-Se'	(L)	RES	3m	4	GF	*prom, 2nd to 8th, ld 9-14th, wknd qckly, p.u. 4 out*	P	0

Some speed but no stamina 0

CARLIES WOOD (Irish) — I 178[U], I 212[2], I 360[U], I 376[P], I 464[P]

CARLINARE b.g. 7 Sousa - Demetria (GER) by Basalt (GER) — Harry Hobson

275	22/2	Ampton	(R)	MDO	3m	10	G	*in tch, j.s. 7th, prog 9th, chsd wnr 3 out, kpt on wll*	2	12
318	1/3	Marks Tey	(L)	MDN	3m	13	G	*mid-div,prog & blndrd 11th,sn rdn,lft 3rd 2 out,nvr rch ldrs*	3	13

Ran well enough both starts but season lasted a week; could win if fit 98 13

CARLINGFORD LAD(IRE) b.g. 7 Carlingford Castle - Raby by Pongee — A Godrich

1996 r(-)

1262	27/4	Southwell P'	(L)	MDO	3m	15	G	*mid-div whn u.r. 5th*	U	-
1356	4/5	Dingley	(R)	MDO	3m	9	G	*alwys bhnd, t.o. & jmpd slwly 7th, p.u. apr 9th*	P	0
1536	18/5	Mollington	(R)	INT	3m	8	GS	*chsng grp to 9th, wknd rpdly, t.o. & p.u. 13th*	P	0
1609	1/6	Dingley	(R)	MDO	3m	14	GF	*tongue-strap, prom, chsd ldr 10-15th, wknd aft 3 out, tired*	5	0

Ran better last start (1st completion) but still no signs of stamina 0

CARLINGFORD PIT (Irish) — I 238[F], I 419[P], I 476[P], I 519[P], I 538[F], I 561[P]

CARLOS THE JACKAL (Irish) — I 332[F], I 568[P]

CARLOWITZ(USA) b.g. 9 Danzig (USA) - Aunt Carol (USA) by Big Spruce (USA) — Mrs J Sidebottom

1996 P(0),P(0),F(-),R(-),1(19),R(-)

183 15/2 Erw Lon (L) MEM 3m 3 G *n.j.w. chsd ldr, ld 13th-last, not qckn und pres* 2 11
400 8/3 Llanfrynach (R) OPE 3m 10 G *n.j.w. rear til ref 5th* R -
537 16/3 Erw Lon (L) OPE 3m 9 GF *reluc at jmps, ld to 2 out, sn btn* 3 19

Open winner 96; highly temperamental & wouldn't go a yard in 97; unlikely to consent again 13

CARLTON MOOR gr.m. 10 Mandrake Major - Greyburn by Saintly Song Miss S J Rooker

880 1/4 Upton-On-Se' (R) CON 3m 6 GF *bhnd frm 9th, sn t.o., walked in* 6 0

Of no account 0

CARLY BRRIN br.g. 12 Carlin - Bios Brrin by Pitpan Mrs J R Buckley

1996 2(15),2+(20),P(0),1(21),F(-),**P(0),6(14)**

74 2/2 Market Rase' (L) MEM 3m 4 GF *made all, styd on well, und pres frm 2 out* 1 19
351 2/3 Market Rase' (L) OPE 3m 10 GF *chsd ldrs, went 2nd 12th, ld apr 14th, sn clr, unchal* 1 23
387 7/3 Market Rasen (R) HC 3m 1f 5 G *ld 3rd, hdd before 3 out, soon outpcd, no impn when hit last.* 2 21

Market Rasen specialist & ran well all starts 97; finished early; can win at 13 if fit; G-F 22

CARNELIA ch.m. 7 Scorpio (FR) - Broon's Lady by Rapid River J W Kwiatkowski

314 1/3 Clyst St Ma' (L) MDN 3m 11 HY *sn bhnd, t.o. 11th* 2 0
513 15/3 Larkhill (R) MDO 3m 10 GF *last whn u.r. 1st* U -
933 6/4 Charlton Ho' (L) MDO 3m 12 G *made most to 13th, sn wknd, t.o. & p.u. 2 out* P 0
1140 19/4 Larkhill (R) MDO 3m 1 F *walked over* 1 0
1275 27/4 Little Wind' (R) RES 3m 9 GF *blnd & u.r. 2nd* U -
1374 5/5 Cotley Farm (L) RES 3m 7 GF *prom early, lost tch 12th, t.o. & p.u. 2 out* P 0
1466 11/5 Tweseldown (R) RES 3m 5 GF *mostly narrow ld to 15th, rdn & sn btn* 3 12
1582 26/5 Lifton (R) INT 3m 10 G *ld 1st, ld 6th, wknd frm 10th, p.u. 2 out* P 0

No real ability, no stamina & won in the only manner possible 0

CARNIQUILLA gr.g. 12 Carnival Night - Tranquilla by Hul A Hul C J Stockton

84 2/2 Wolverhampt' (L) MEM 3m 9 GS *chsd ldrs, outpcd 12th, kpt on wll frm 3 out, nrst fin, dead* 3 16

Dead 17

CARNIVAL KID b.g. 7 Latest Model - Easter Carnival by Pardigras Mrs M D Best

1996 **13(NH)**

1483 11/5 Ottery St M' (L) RES 3m 15 G *mid-div whn s.u. bend aft 2nd* S -
1552 24/5 Mounsey Hil' (R) RES 3m 12 G *ran out 3rd* r -
1582 26/5 Lifton (R) INT 3m 10 G *ld 5th, ran out bend & u.r. apr nxt* U -

Late to appear & found variety of ways of exiting rapidly 0

CARNMOON (Irish) — **I** 117P, **I** 175P, **I** 371F, **I** 436P, **I** 508F, **I** 5853

CARNMORE HOUSE (Irish) — **I** 34P, **I** 1075, **I** 160P, **I** 2023, **I** 2326, **I** 2804, **I** 3531, **I** 4262, **I** 5462, **I** 5781, **I** 5875

CARNMORE SUPREME (Irish) — **I** 65U, **I** 109P, **I** 163P, **I** 2003, **I** 277P, **I** 531P, **I** 5562, **I** 576P

CAROLE'S DELIGHT b.m. 10 Idiot's Delight - Fishermans Lass by Articulate C Holden

1996 5(14),2(18),1(20),4(17),1(20),P(0),3(20),3(18)

117 9/2 Wetherby Po' (L) LAD 3m 10 GF *bckwrd, ld to 3rd, prom, mstk 9th, fdd, t.o. & p.u. 2 out* P 0
426 8/3 Charm Park (L) LAD 3m 12 GF *alwys prom, rddn 3 out, ev ch last, kpt on gamely* 2 22
617 22/3 Hutton Rudby (L) LAD 3m 9 GF *(fav) disp ld til apr last, rlld brfly to ld nr line* 1 21
697 29/3 Stainton (R) LAD 3m 5 F *(fav) trckd ldr til disp 6th,lft clr 15th,prssd 3 out,hld on flat* 1 21
1102 19/4 Hornby Cast' (L) LAD 3m 7 G *(fav) ld til disp 4th, ld 7th-last, ran on wll flat, just faild* 2 21
1422 10/5 Easingwold (L) LAD 3m 7 GF *prom,chsd ldr 7th,lft in ld 9th,jnd 11-14th,hdd last,kpt on* 2 20
1511 17/5 Corbridge (R) LAD 3m 10 GS *ran in sntchs, disp to 5th,prog 13th,chal last,wknd flat* 3 20

Consistent & game; 9 wins, 17 places, last 32 starts; best on easy courses; can win again. Any 22

CAROLES EXPRESS ch.m. 9 Scottish Reel - Peregrine Falcon by Saulingo G Ivall

1403 5/5 Ashorne (R) CON 3m 14 G *schoold, prog & in tch 10th, sn wknd, p.u. 14th* P 0
1606 1/6 Dingley (R) LAD 3m 13 GF *hld up rear, 7th & out of tch whn blnd & u.r. 11th* U -

Flat winner; no signs in points & withdrawn at start once 0

CAROLINES MINSTREL (Irish) — **I** 21P, **I** 75P, **I** 145P

CAROL'S CONCORDE(IRE) b.g. 9 Sexton Blake - Princess Concorde by Great Heron (USA) Mrs Carol A Cowell

119 9/2 Wetherby Po' (L) OPE 3m 15 GF *sn rear, t.o. & p.u. 7th* P 0
333 1/3 Eaton Hall (R) INT 3m 10 GS *mid to rear, nvr dang, p.u. 5 out* P 0
414 8/3 Dalston (R) XX 3m 9 GS *schoold in last, lost tch 12th, p.u. 2 out* P 0
566 16/3 Lanark (R) MDO 3m 10 GS *(bl) sn drvn alng in rear, p.u. 4 out* P 0
854 31/3 Eyton-On-Se' (L) MDO 3m 10 GF *p.u. 4th* P 0

No lift-off here 0

CARRAREA(IRE) ch.g. 7 Clearly Bust - Margaret's Joy by Paddy's Birthday — J Atkins

101 8/2 Great Treth' (R) MDO 3m 9 GS *ld til blnd & wknd 11th, p.u. 13th* P 0
245 22/2 Lemalla (R) MDO 3m 11 S *alwys wll bhnd, p.u. last* P 0
525 15/3 Cothelstone (L) MDN 3m 15 GS *mid-div, blnd 6th, bhnd frm 9th* 5 0
794 31/3 Bishopsleigh (R) MDO 3m 12 G *7s-3s, ld til f 12th* F -
1035 12/4 Lifton (R) MDN 3m 11 F *mid-div til moved up 12th, ld 15th, ran on strgly* 1 16
1317 3/5 Holnicote (L) RES 3m 5 G *(fav) ld/disp frm 2nd til ld 9th, hdd 12th, lost tch rpdly* 3 0

Clumsy but put it together when winning (A Farrant); more needed for Restricteds 15

CARRICK LANES b.g. 10 Oats - Once Bitten by Brave Invader (USA) — David Brace

1996 2(22),2(22),1(22)

99 8/2 Great Treth' (R) LAD 3m 10 GS *bhnd whn mstks 11 & 12th, effrt to 4th at 16th, no prog aft* 4 19
401 8/3 Llanfrynach (R) LAD 3m 14 G *mid-div, some prog 4 out, not rch 1st pair* 3 20
714 29/3 Llanvapley (L) CON 3m 15 GF *(fav) (6/4-5/2), alwys rear, no ch frm 13th, p.u. last* P 0
1134 19/4 Bonvilston (R) MXO 4m 10 G *made all, qcknd clr 3 out, comf* 1 22
1223 26/4 Pyle (R) MEM 3m 6 GS *(fav) ld 5-9th,lost plc & bhnd 13th,rpd prog 2 out,drvn to ld flat* 1 19
1321 3/5 Bonvilston (R) MXO 3m 10 G *(fav) mid-div, rmndrs 12th, prog 3 out, ld nxt, ran on well* 1 20
1363 5/5 Pantyderi (L) OPE 3m 4 G *3rd til 11th, in ld & rdn out last* 1 24
1469 11/5 Erw Lon (L) OPE 3m 6 GS *cls up, hrd rdn 3 out, nvr able to chal* 2 23

Useful, consistent & stays very well; well-ridden; good season & win more 98; G/S-G/F 24

CARRIGANS LAD (Irish) — I 27P, I 230[5], I 276[5], I 291[1], I 395[5], I 414U, I 553P

CARRIGBYRNE CANDY ch.m. 9 Cruise Missile - Running Light by Deep Run — J de Lisle Wells

656 22/3 Siddington (L) MDN 3m 7 F *jmpd slwly, t.o. til p.u. 11th* P 0

Showed nothing & already in middle-age 0

CARRIG HEATHER (Irish) — I 202F

CARROT BAY b.g. 11 Spitsbergen - Gold Harp by Tormento — M B Ogle

1996 **6(NH),4(NH),P(NH),P(NH),P(NH)**

453 8/3 Great Treth' (R) CON 3m 13 S *mid-div, btn 7th whn p.u. apr 15th* P 0
628 22/3 Kilworthy (L) CON 3m 12 G *t.o. p.u. apr 9th* P 0

No longer of any account 0

CARRO VALLEY (Irish) — I 589F, I 606P

CARRY ON BRENDAN (Irish) — I 171P, I 260P, I 324[1]

CARRY ON SHOON (Irish) — I 259[3], I 306[5], I 421P, I 516[3]

CARRYS CLOVER (Irish) — I 148P, I 265P

CARTONS RIVER (Irish) — I 333P, I 424P, I 456U, I 517P

CARUMU b.m. 8 Henricus (ATA) - Flame Song by True Song — Mrs S A Murch

1996 P(0),P(0),P(0),S(-),5(0),7(0),3(0)

1244 26/4 Bratton Down (L) CON 3m 14 GS *ld til slppd up bnd aft 4th* S -
1400 5/5 High Bickin' (R) MDO 3m 14 G *handy, cls 2nd & ev ch 13th, rdn & outpcd frm 3 out* 2 13
1486 11/5 Ottery St M' (L) MDO 3m 17 G *alwys mid-div, outpcd & p.u. 15th* P 0
1520 17/5 Bratton Down (L) MDO 3m 17 GS *mid-div, 8th hlfwy, nvr dang, btn 6th whn p.u. 2 out* P 0

2nd of 3 finishers in chaotic contest & no other form; unlikely to win 12

CASCUM LAD (Irish) — I 127P, I 248P, I 289P, I 328U, I 377[3], I 463P, I 508[4]

CASHEROOSKI(IRE) b.g. 9 Ballad Rock - Kachela by Kalamoun — Mrs B F Abraham

141 9/2 Thorpe Lodge (L) MDN 3m 12 GF *rear, no ch whn p.u. 6 out* P 0
252 22/2 Brocklesby ' (L) MDO 3m 9 G *mid-div 1st m, t.o. 6th 10th, p.u. last* P 0

Placed in Maiden in 95; missed 96 & nothing in 97 0

CASHEW CHAOS b.g. 5 Neltino - Blakeney Sound by Blakeney — Nick Shutts

1016 12/4 Bitterley (L) MDO 3m 14 GF *hld up rear, ran on steadily frm 14th, improve* 4 0

Beat subsequent winners & gives every sign of scoring himself in 98 14

CASH FLOW (Irish) — I 64F, I 181[1]

CASH VILLE (Irish) — I 195[4], I 419U

CASSFINN (Irish) — I 231P, I 280P, I 353P

CASTLE ARROW (Irish) — I 399[1]

CASTLEBAY LAD br.g. 14 Crozier - Carbery Star by Kelmal (FR) — Michael Appleby

1996 R(-),4(15),2(22),3(15),3(14),4(14)

4 19/1 Barbury Cas' (L) OPE 3m 9 GF *jmpd slwly 5th, in tch til rdn & wknd 10th, t.o. & p.u. 14th* P 0
19 25/1 Badbury Rin' (L) OPE 3m 8 GF *mstk 5th, in tch to 11th, sn wknd, t.o. & p.u. 15th* P 0
56 1/2 Kingston Bl' (L) OPE 3m 13 GF *ld to 4th, chsd ldrs to hlfwy, wknd* 6 0
151 12/2 Lingfield (L) HC 3m 13 HY *eighth when ref 11th.* R -

220 16/2 Heythrop (R) OPE 3m 20 G *alwys rear, t.o. & p.u. 15th* P 0

Useful in his day but looks finished now 0

CASTLE CROSS ch.g. 10 Carlingford Castle - Siba Vione by Dusky Boy Keith Thomas
1996 P(0),F(-),P(0),P(0),4(0)

762 29/3 Whittington (L) MEM 3m 5 S *s.v.s., sn t.o., 2 fences down whn p.u. 3 out* P 0

No longer of any account 0

CASTLE DAWN (Irish) — **I** 185^{P}, **I** 348,

CASTLEDELL (Irish) — **I** 124^{P}, **I** 174^{P}

CASTLE GLOW (Irish) — **I** 65^{P}, **I** 95^{P}, **I** 153^{P}, **I** 181^{P}, **I** 343^{F}, **I** 391^{4}, **I** 409^{3}, **I** 483^{3}, **I** 497^{2}, **I** 545^{3}, **I** 593^{3}

CASTLEMORE LEADER (Irish) — **I** 140^{P}, **I** 167^{P}, **I** 302^{3}

CASTLEMORRIS(IRE) b.g. 6 Clearly Bust - Ballycastle by Ballyciptic D Evans

541 16/3 Erw Lon (L) MDN 3m 10 GF *(fav) keen hld, hld up, f 4th* F -
1323 3/5 Bonvilston (R) MDO 3m 14 G *(fav) ld to 11th, 3rd aft til blnd 3 out, p.u. nxt* P 0

Expensive to follow so far but should do better in 98 10

CASTLEPOOK (Irish) — **I** 225^{3}, **I** 313^{F}, **I** 392^{5}

CASTLE SHELLEY(IRE) b.g. 8 Carlingford Castle - Briarsfield Lady by Cheval C W Booth

221 16/2 Heythrop (R) RES 3m 15 G *wll bhnd, t.o. 12th, styd on frm 2 out, nvr nrr* 6 0
372 2/3 Mollington (R) RES 3m 19 G *prssd ldr, ld 10th til mstk 15th, wknd rpdly, crwld last* 7 0
927 6/4 Garthorpe (R) RES 3m 9 GF *prom, 2nd 14th, chal frm 3 out, ev ch last, just faild* 2 16
1159 20/4 Mollington (R) MEM 3m 4 GF *ld aft 2nd-6th, wknd rpdly & p.u. 11th* P 0

Irish Maiden winner 96; touched off 3rd start but problems last outing; barely stays 16

CASTLE STEPHEN (Irish) — **I** 371^{P}, **I** 436^{U}, **I** 467^{1}

CASTLETOWN COUNT b.g. 5 Then Again - Pepeke by Mummy's Pet Mrs A M Easterby

76 2/2 Market Rase' (L) XX 3m 12 GF *prog 5th, ld 10-14th, hit 3 out, ev ch whn ran out nxt* r 23
113 9/2 Wetherby Po' (L) CON 3m 10 GF *(fav) sttld rear, prog 8th, ld 4 out, going wll whn f nxt* F -
354 2/3 Great Stain' (L) OPE 3m 7 S *(fav) hld up, prog 13th, ld 15th, drew wll clr, imprssv* 1 23
423 8/3 Charm Park (L) OPE 3m 7 GF *(fav) rear, prog 5th, trckng ldr whn ran out 9th* r -

Flat winner; able but wayward; finished early; hard to beat consenting in 98 25

CASTLE TYRANT b.m. 8 Idiot's Delight - Coolek by Menelek S Clark
1996 2(14),1(15),1(20),4(17),4(15),2(21),1(21),**P(0)**

34 26/1 Alnwick (L) OPE 3m 9 G *chsd wnr to 15th & frm 3 out, no imp nxt* 2 21
119 9/2 Wetherby Po' (L) OPE 3m 15 GF *prom til fdd frm 13th, virt p.u. flat* 7 0
267 22/2 Duncombe Pa' (R) OPE 3m 8 G *prom til wknd 14th, t.o. frm 3 out* 3 15
507 15/3 Dalton Park (R) OPE 3m 8 GF *ld to 16th, onepcd* 2 20
618 22/3 Hutton Rudby (L) OPE 3m 10 GF *disp ld to 6th, rmnd prom til not qckn frm 2 out* 2 19
1071 13/4 Whitwell-On' (R) CON 3m 10 G *ld til disp 7th, hdd 10th, wknd 14th* 5 13
1104 19/4 Hornby Cast' (L) MEM 3m 6 G *(fav) held up in mid-div,wnt 2nd 12th,ld 4 out,ran on wll 2 out* 1 17

Won 3 in 96; consistent & safe but struggling in Opens 97; ground against; may perk up 98 20

CASTLEVE (Irish) — **I** 490^{F}, **I** 510^{3}, **I** 588^{3}

CASTLEVIGGANLADY (Irish) — **I** 31^{3}, **I** 72, , **I** 119^{P}, **I** 129^{S}, **I** 212^{4}, **I** 310^{U}, **I** 329^{P}

CASTLE WHITE (Irish) — **I** 44^{P}

CASTLEWHITE (Irish) — **I** 9^{3}

CASTLEWOOD LODGE (Irish) — **I** 118^{P}, **I** 128^{P}

CAST NO SHADOW (Irish) — **I** 104^{P}, **I** 158^{P}, **I** 275^{P}

CATABOLIC(IRE) b.g. 5 Lancastrian - Cousin Flo by True Song Dr D B A Silk

581 16/3 Detling (L) MDO 3m 12 F *rear, prog final ctt, 3rd & ev ch 3 out, no ext apr last* 4 12

Promising debut but vanished; should win if fit in 98 15

CATCHAPENNY br.g. 12 True Song - Quickapenny by Espresso W Tellwright
1996 U(-),3(16),**3(20)**,3(10),**3(28)**

149 10/2 Hereford (R) HC 3m 1f 110yds 18 GS *(bl) prom to 12th, soon bhnd.* 5 14

Thorough stayer but soon vanished 97 & can only be watched at 13 15

CATCHPHRASE ch.h. 7 Baron Blakeney - Aldington Miss by Legal Eagle A A Day

478 9/3 Southwell P' (L) MDO 3m 17 G *jmpd poorly, sn wll bhnd, t.o. & p.u. 6th* P 0
776 29/3 Dingley (R) MDO 2m 5f 10 G *w.w. prog 6 out, 2nd 3 out, qcknd & ld last, clvrly, prmsng* 1 14
1081 13/4 Guilsborough (L) RES 3m 13 GF *keen hld, prom to 15th, wknd, p.u. 2 out* P 0
1204 26/4 Clifton On ' (L) MEM 3m 6 GS *w.w. chsd ldr frm 11th, ld aft 2 out, clrvly* 1 17

1477 11/5 Garthorpe (R) XX 3m 6 GS *in tch,ld 13th,wd & hdd aft 3 out,lft clr & blnd nxt* 1 17

Good start & found right races; possibly fortunate last start but should upgrade in 98; G-G/S,so far 20

CATCH THE CROSS gr.g. 11 Alias Smith (USA) - Juliette Mariner by Welsh Pageant Reg Hand

1996 3(14),3(14),7(12),2(16),4(18),1(17),3(15),5(14),2(21),10(0),3(20)

49 1/2 Wadebridge (L) LAD 3m 5 G *nvr bttr than 3rd, kpt on onepcd* 4 11
173 15/2 Ottery St M' (L) CON 3m 7 G *(bl) sn bhnd, kpt on onepcd frm 4 out* 4 13
453 8/3 Great Treth' (R) CON 3m 13 S *(bl) ld til 5th, disp til lost plc 12th, no ch frm 14th* 5 13
624 22/3 Kilworthy (L) MEM 3m 7 G *(bl) disp 6-9th, chsd ldr til b.d. 14th, remntd* 2 0
807 31/3 Wadebridge (L) LAD 3m 4 F *(fav) alwys prom, 2nd frm 9th, onepcd frm 3 out* 2 16
981 9/4 Chepstow (L) HC 3m 6 F *(bl) in tch 7th, styd on 14th, soon wknd.* 5 10
1111 19/4 Flete Park (R) CON 3m 5 GF *(bl) disp 5th-7th,lft in ld bnd aft 3 out,lft clr 2 out, pshd out* 1 17
1342 3/5 Flete Park (R) CON 3m 6 G *(bl) ld/disp to 3 out, cls up til onepcd aft nxt* 3 17
1581 26/5 Lifton (R) LAD 3m 7 G *nvr nrr than 3rd, unable to chal* 3 18

Always finishes but avoids success expertly; both wins 96/7 at Flete; sold June 97 17

CATCH THE MOUSE (Irish) — **I** 98P, **I** 339[1], **I** 457[2], **I** 614,

CATHAIR NEIDIN (Irish) — **I** 106[1]

CATHERINE'S PET (Irish) — **I** 406P, **I** 460P, **I** 566F, **I** 606,

CATHGAL b.g. 12 Crozier - Mawnie by Mon Capitaine Richard Mathias

1996 P(0),2(14),3(0),**4(0)**,**3(17)**,**U(-)**,2(15),U(-),1(15),**6(16)**

254 22/2 Newtown (L) MEM 3m 6 G *hld up, prog to chs wnr 12th, no imp 3 out, wknd nxt* 3 13
1135 19/4 Bonvilston (R) RES 3m 14 G *prom til ld 15th, qcknd whn chal apr last* 1 17

Maidenw inner 96; did well to find Restricted at 12; Members best hope at 13; needs easy 3m 17

CATON BOY b.g. 16 Astor Boy - Stonebow Lady by Windjammer (USA) A J Hogarth

734 29/3 Alnwick (L) MDN 3m 6 F *last frm 3rd, t.o. & p.u. 9th* P 0

Poor old thing 0

CATRIONAS LADY (Irish) — **I** 80P, **I** 141P, **I** 264[3]

CATSTOWN RIVER (Irish) — **I** 152P, **I** 182F, **I** 269F

CAUSEWAY CRUISER ch.g. 11 Crested Lark - Andromeda II by Romany Air J Tredwell

1996 4(19),1(22),1(27),2(22),1(28),U(-),**P(0)**

220 16/2 Heythrop (R) OPE 3m 20 G *hld up, effrt 12th, nvr rch ldrs, kpt on* 4 19

Useful at best but off course early in 97 (ground against); can win at 12; quickens; G-S 23

CAUTEEN RIVER (Irish) — **I** 297F

CAUTIOUS REBEL ch.g. 10 Shy Groom (USA) - Riot Girl by Right Boy Mrs L Roberts

1996 1(17),4(0),2(15),P(0),F(-),1(16)

97 8/2 Great Treth' (R) INT 3m 13 GS *alwys wll bhnd, t.o. 11th* 6 0

Dual winner 9 but quickly vanished 97; goes well fresh but best watched 15

CAVALERO b.g. 8 Afzal - Jolly Lass by Jolly Me H J Manners

1996 **P(NH)**,**U(NH)**,**F(NH)**,**F(NH)**,**P(NH)**

295 1/3 Didmarton (L) OPE 3m 9 G *unruly pddck, t.o. in last pair til p.u. last* P 0
395 8/3 Barbury Cas' (L) XX 3m 9 G *mid-div, prog 13th, ev ch 2 out, kpt on wll flat* 2 18
649 22/3 Siddington (L) MEM 3m 6 F *hld up, prog 10th, chsd wnr 14th, lvl & mstk last, just hld* 2 18
1289 30/4 Cheltenham (L) HC 3m 1f 110yds 6 GF *blnd 2nd, in tch, chsd ldrs 12th, cl 4th when mstk 3 out, soon btn, eased run-in.* 4 13

Ran well last 3 starts & should find chances in 98; easy 3m best; G-F 20

CAWKWELL DEAN b.g. 11 Boco (USA) - Cawkwell Duchess by Duc D'Orleans Neale Hutchinson

1996 2(21),3(14),2(10),2(20),1(19),3(12),3+(19),1(20)

4 19/1 Barbury Cas' (L) OPE 3m 9 GF *in tch, strgglng 10th, 6th & wll btn whn p.u. last* P 0
55 1/2 Kingston Bl' (L) CON 3m 15 GF *disp 2nd-4th, lost plc, styd on onepcd* 5 15
256 22/2 Newtown (L) OPE 3m 17 G *chsd ldr to 11th, prom aft til outpcd frm 15th* 5 15
369 2/3 Mollington (R) MEM 3m 13 G *ld to 7th, wknd 13th, bhnd whn p.u. 3 out* P 0
985 12/4 Kingston Bl' (L) MEM 3m 4 GF *(fav) j.w. made all, clr 14th, eased flat* 1 20
1205 26/4 Clifton On ' (L) CON 3m 13 GS *(fav) alwys prom, ld 5 out, 10l clr nxt, no ext whn hdd apr last* 2 19
1448 10/5 Kingston Bl' (L) CON 3m 9 G *ld 3rd-aft nxt, ld 7-10th, 5th at 13th, ran on flat* 3 16
1608 1/6 Dingley (R) INT 3m 11 GF *prom, ld aft 10th, clr 3 out, hrd prssd last, all out nr fin* 1 20

Dual winner 96; slow to find form 97; solid & game at best; can win at 12; G/F-S 20

CAWKWELL WIN b.m. 6 Boco (USA) - Cawkwell Duchess by Duc D'Orleans T W Garfield

1996 P(0),F(-),F(-)

253 22/2 Brocklesby ' (L) MDO 3m 6 G *3rd 1st m, last pair, outpcd frm 10th* 5 0
1268 27/4 Southwell P' (L) MDO 3m 13 G *rear, bhnd 5th, t.o. 7th, p.u. nxt* P 0

Interrupted season & beaten miles only completion 0

CEARY WEARY (Irish) — **I** 462, , **I** 502^{2}

CEASARS REIGN (Irish) — **I** 3^{P}, **I** 39^{P}, **I** 57^{4}, **I** 76^{4}, **I** 103^{4}, **I** 275^{F}, **I** 294^{3}

CEBOSUPREMO (Irish) — **I** 609^{2}

CEBU GALE (Irish) — **I** 119^{1}, **I** 252^{2}, **I** 314^{F}

CEDAR SQUARE(IRE) b.h. 6 Dancing Dissident (USA) - Freidnly Ann by Artaius (USA) Miss J L Nicholls
1996 3(0),1(16),1(23),1(25)

187 15/2 Erw Lon (L) OPE 3m 16 G *(fav) ld to 11th, rdn & wknd 13th, 3rd & wll btn whn p.u. 2 out* P 0
493 12/3 Newton Abbot (L) HC 2m 5f 110yds 11 HY *(Jt fav) ld till blnd 2 out, btn when f last.* F 22

Highly promising in 96 but stable out of form 97 & finished early; can revive 98 & win Opens; G-S 24

CEDARS ROSSLARE b.g. 12 Black Minstrel - Sea Guest by Arctic Que P H Green

240 22/2 Lemalla (R) RES 3m 11 S *novice rdn, rear, mstk 11th, t.o. & p.u. 15th* P 0
523 15/3 Cothelstone (L) RES 3m 14 GS *nov rdn, alwys strgglng in rear* 6 0
950 6/4 Black Fores' (R) MEM 3m 7 G *sn last, t.o. & p.u. 13th* P 0
1259 27/4 Black Fores' (R) RES 3m 7 F *alwys rear, nvr dang* 5 0
1395 5/5 High Bickin' (R) RES 3m 9 G *in tch, 5th at 15th, onepcd* 4 11
1519 17/5 Bratton Down (L) RES 3m 15 GS *rear, rmndrs 11th, 7th 2 out, nrst fin* 4 16
1551 24/5 Mounsey Hil' (R) RES 3m 13 G *bhnd frm 6th, last whn p.u. 13th* P 0

Made a fair schoolmaster but no winning chances at 13 12

CEFFYL GWYN gr.g. 10 Scallywag - Must Improve by Lucky Brief F H Williams
1996 U(-)

1230 26/4 Pyle (R) MDO 3m 10 GS *t.o. 4th, p.u. 10th* P 0
1615 7/6 Umberleigh (L) MDO 3m 11 F *20s-10s, sn bhnd, t.o. & p.u. 9th* P 0

Twice backed in 3 outings 96/7 but shows nil ability 0

CEFN WOODSMAN b or br.g. 6 Tigerwood - Orange Pop by Gimlet D R Thomas
1996 P(0),P(0),P(0),4(0),7(0)

184 15/2 Erw Lon (L) MDN 3m 14 G *in tch, 4th & rdn 14th, lft 2nd nxt, no imp* 3 0
540 16/3 Erw Lon (L) MDN 3m 13 GF *mid-div, prog whn f 11th* F -
842 31/3 Lydstep (L) MDO 3m 12 F *mid-div, no dang frm 15th* 4 0
1009 12/4 St Hilary (R) MDN 3m 11 GF *2nd til ld 14th, hdd 3 out, no ext* 3 0
1183 20/4 Lydstep (L) MDO 3m 8 GF *cls up, ev ch 4 out, hrd rdn 2 out, no imp* 2 13
1368 5/5 Pantyderi (L) MDO 3m 8 G *(Jt fav) ld/disp to 10th, wknd, fin tired* 4 0
1473 11/5 Erw Lon (L) MDO 3m 13 GS *(Co fav) trckd ldrs til hmpd 11th, no dang aft* 3 0

Placed 7 times to date but very modest & lacks stamina; may strike lucky eventually 12

CELTIC ABBEY b.g. 9 Celtic Cone - Cagaleena by Cagirama G J Powell
1996 1(24),**2(34)**

149 10/2 Hereford (R) HC 3m 1f 110yds 18 GS *(fav) mid div, hit 9th, mstk 11th, soon bhnd, p.u. before 5 out.* P 0
494 13/3 Cheltenham (L) HC 3 1/4m 110yds 18 G *midfield, hdwy 14th, chsd ldrs 3 out, fd next.* 4 30
1291 30/4 Cheltenham (L) HC 3 1/4m 110yds 4 GF *trckd ldr, ld 15th, drew right away after 3 out, impressive.* 1 38
1591 31/5 Stratford (L) HC 3 1/2m 11 G *(fav) with ldr, ld 10th, qcknd to go clr final cct, styd on strly from 3 out, eased towards fin.* 1 39

Season's top H/Chaser; outstanding wins last 2 starts; stays well; G-F, does not like Soft 40

CELTIC AIR (Irish) — **I** 185^{P}, **I** 315^{P}, **I** 557^{1}

CELTIC BIZARRE b.m. 9 Celtic Cone - Charity Bazzar by Native Bazaar R R Smedley
1996 2(10),4(11),3(12),1(11),P(0),3(0)

189 15/2 Erw Lon (L) RES 3m 14 G *in tch til outpcd 14th, onepcd frm 2 out* 5 13
405 8/3 Llanfrynach (R) RES 3m 15 G *mid-div, no prog frm 3 out* 5 11
717 29/3 Llanvapley (L) RES 3m 13 GF *prom in mid-div til lost postn frm 3 out* 5 0
957 6/4 Pantyderi (L) MEM 3m 3 F *(fav) jmpd carefully, ld 8th-2 out, rallied aft* 2 11
1008 12/4 St Hilary (R) RES 3m 11 GF *twrds rear, onepcd, nvr dang* 5 0
1184 20/4 Lydstep (L) LAD 3m 4 GF *ld 6th, sn wll clr, hdd apr last, f last, rmntd* 2 16
1227 26/4 Pyle (R) RES 3m 15 GS *mostly last trio til ran on frm 13th, nvr nrr* 3 14
1365 5/5 Pantyderi (L) RES 3m 10 G *7th at 3rd, 6th at 11th, nvr nr ldrs* 5 14
1470 11/5 Erw Lon (L) LAD 3m 9 GS *rear, p.u. 14th* P 0
1599 31/5 Bassaleg (R) RES 3m 2 F *(fav) jmpd lft, made all, clr 4th, blnd 8th, unchal* 1 13

Runs regularly, very safe & found a 3rd desperate race to add to her tally; Members only hope 98 14

CELTIC BUCK (Irish) — **I** 446^{1}, **I** 518^{P}, **I** 543^{2}, **I** 598,

CELTIC CABER b.g. 11 Pragmatic - Cruises Royal by Pitpan Miss T Habgood
1996 2(10)

984 12/4 Kingston Bl' (L) MEM 3m 4 GF *ld to aft 5th, ld 14th til apr last, onepcd* 3 10

2nd in Pegasus Members 96; only 3rd in 97! 10

CELTIC COURSE (Irish) — **I** 167^P, **I** 538^P

CELTIC DAUGHTER b.m. 8 Celtic Cone - Onaea by Prince de Galles — Mrs E A Webber

1996 1(13),1(16),P(0),3(18),3(0),**P(0)**,1(19),**U(-)**

401 8/3 Llanfrynach (R) LAD 3m 14 G *hld up, went 4th at 11th, ld 2 out, hdd & outpcd last* 2 21
535 16/3 Erw Lon (L) CON 3m 12 GF *(fav) trckd ldrs to 15th, wknd rpdly 2 out, fin tired* 4 13
1470 11/5 Erw Lon (L) LAD 3m 9 GS *ld 11th-16th, hrd rdn aft, no ch wth wnr* 2 18
1558 24/5 Bassaleg (R) LAD 3m 5 G *chsd ldr, ld apr 14th, jnd apr 2 out, ran on strngly last* 1 23

Won 3 in 96; interrupted season 97 but showed true worth final start; win more Ladies 98; G/F-G/S 23

CELTIC FRIEND(IRE) ch.g. 6 Celtic Cone - Pal Alley by Pals Passage — Robert Puddick

146 9/2 Tweseldown (R) MDO 3m 10 GF *rear whn tried to ref & u.r. 2nd* U -
390 8/3 Barbury Cas' (L) MDN 3m 15 G *hmpd & u.r. 1st* U -
654 22/3 Siddington (L) MDN 3m 10 F *n.j.w. t.o. til p.u. 8th* P 0

Not very friendly so far 0

CELTIC GOBLIN b.m. 9 Swinging Rebel - Goblins Thimbles by Roi Soleil — M H Dare

1996 U(-),P(0)

525 15/3 Cothelstone (L) MDN 3m 15 GS *mid-div, prog to ld 16th, hdd apr 2 out, edgd rght flat* 2 13

Beat plenty of subsequent winners only start 97 but rarely appears; good enough for a win 15

CELTIC KING ch.g. 13 Kingshaven - Celtic Siren by Welsh Pageant — C W C Tregoning

1996 P(0),3(16),2(18),1(22),4(14),**P(0)**,2(19)

124 9/2 Cottenham (R) OPE 3m 9 GF *last & sn bhnd, p.u. aft 7th* P 0
319 1/3 Marks Tey (L) CON 3m 11 G *chsd ldrs to 14th, wknd, last whn p.u. 3 out* P 0

Open winner 96; changed hands & looks finished now 0

CELTIC REG ch.g. 7 Celtic Cone - Another Molly by Choral Society — R Thomson

1996 **9(NH)**,**F(NH)**

581 16/3 Detling (L) MDO 3m 12 F *nvr bttr thn mid-div, 7th whn hmp & f 16th* F -
686 29/3 Charing (L) MDO 2 1/2m 5 F *ld to 2nd, cls aft, chal 4 out whn stmbld & u.r.* U -
833 31/3 Heathfield (R) MDO 3m 7 F *(Jt fav) chsd ldr 4th til ld 14th, hdd 2 out, 2l dwn & btn whn f last* F 12
971 6/4 Penshurst (L) MDO 3m 5 F *wth ldr, bndrd 6th, ld 9th, prssd aft til kpt bttr frm 2 out* 1 10
1129 19/4 Penshurst (L) RES 3m 6 GF *chsd ldr, ld 12th-3 out, wknd nxt* 3 12

Clumsy & found desperate race when winning; even SE Restricteds will need more improvement 13

CELTIC SPORT br.g. 12 Celtic Cone - Bell-Amys by Blandford Lad — Mrs A C Martin

1996 3(24),1(24),1(25)

99 8/2 Great Treth' (R) LAD 3m 10 GS *(bl) ld 4-8th & 10th-aft 13th, sn wknd, p.u. 2 out* P 0
238 22/2 Lemalla (R) LAD 3m 9 S *(bl) ld til aft 3 out, sn onepcd, eased flat* 3 19
454 8/3 Great Treth' (R) LAD 3m 7 S *(fav) (bl) chsd ldr, outpcd 14th, styd on onepce clsng stgs* 2 20
520 15/3 Cothelstone (L) LAD 3m 12 GS *(bl) ld 6th til u.r. 14th* U -
790 31/3 Bishopsleigh (R) LAD 3m 7 G *cls up to 15th, outpcd frm 4 out* 3 21
1340 3/5 Flete Park (R) LAD 4m 5 G *(bl) made all in 4/5l ld, styd on gamely* 1 24
1438 10/5 Holnicote (L) LAD 3m 7 G *(bl) rear, t.o. 9th til p.u. 15th, dsmntd, lame* P 0

Decent staying pointer at best; declined a little 97 & last start could spell problems; G-S 19

CELTIC TOKEN ch.g. 8 Celtic Cone - Ready Token (SWE) by Record Token — Mrs Kin Lundberg-Young

1996 P(0),U(-),U(-),7(0),1(16)

23 25/1 Badbury Rin' (L) RES 3m 8 GF *t.d.e. ld to 4th, grad outpcd frm 13th* 4 12
106 8/2 Milborne St' (L) RES 3m 12 GF *t.d.e. ld to 14th, rnwd effrt 2 out, wknd apr last* 3 15
294 1/3 Didmarton (L) INT 3m 20 G *made most to 10th, ev ch aft til wknd apr 2 out* 5 16
523 15/3 Cothelstone (L) RES 3m 14 GS *mid-div, mstk 13th, bhnd whn p.u. 2 out* P 0
935 6/4 Charlton Ho' (L) RES 3m 7 G *t.d.e. ld to 12th, btn frm 14th* 5 0

Maiden winner 96; blazes away but easily caught; ran in fair races & may find easy chance 98 15

CENTRAL LASS gr.m. 9 Glasgow Central - Fast Gold by Goldfella — K Bayliss

1996 P(0),P(0)

259 22/2 Newtown (L) MDN 3m 18 G *t.d.e. mid-div, wknd 9th, t.o. & p.u. 12th* P 0
639 22/3 Howick (L) MDN 3m 15 GF *rear til f 14th* F -

Yet to complete the course 0

CENTRE STAGE b.g. 11 Pas de Seul - All Beige by Ballycipitic — L J Bowman

1996 P(0),**4(0)**,P(0),1(20),2(20)

151 12/2 Lingfield (L) HC 3m 13 HY *t.o. from 5th.* 4 0
225 19/2 Folkestone (R) HC 2m 5f 10 S *t.o. from 8th.* 7 0
305 1/3 Parham (R) OPE 3m 9 G *cls up, chsd ldrs final cct, kpt on same pace 2 out* 2 17
579 16/3 Detling (L) OPE 4m 9 F *rear, t.o. whn p.u. 11th* P 0
1501 16/5 Folkestone (R) HC 3 1/4m 10 G *jmpd slowly 4th and 5th, alwys bhnd, t.o. from 10th.* 5 0

2nd class pointer at best; ground against 97; could win Confined in Soft early 98 19

CHACER'S IMP b.g. 8 Noble Imp - Chacer by Quartette — Mrs E Adams

1996 2(13),**F(-)**,4(10),1(16),**P(0)**

260 22/2 Newtown (L) RES 3m 16 G *prom, ld 13th-15th, wknd aft 3 out* 5 14
816 31/3 Paxford (L) MEM 3m 3 F *(fav) hld up last, effrt apr 2 out, outpcd* 2 0

Maiden winner 96; changed hands; disappointing 2nd run & vanished; L/H; best watched; G-S 14

CHALINARE(IRE) ch.g. 7 Hatim (USA) - Lady Harford by Great Heron (USA) — Harry Hobson

61 1/2 Horseheath (R) MDO 3m 9 GF *chsd ldrs, mstk 7th, 3rd whn blnd & u.r. 10th* U -
128 9/2 Cottenham (R) MDO 3m 10 GF *prom til wknd 14th, walked in* 4 0

Season lasted 8 days & no signs of stamina yet 0

CHALVEY GROVE b.g. 9 New Member - My Molly by Averof — G Ivall

1996 U(-),P(0),P(0)

439 8/3 Higham (L) MDO 3m 11 G *mid-div til f 9th* F -
934 6/4 Charlton Ho' (L) MDO 3m 10 G *alwys bhnd, t.o. last whn p.u. 11th* P 0
1577 26/5 Chaddesley ' (L) MDO 3m 11 F *rear, 9th whn u.r. 10th* U -

Yet to complete & looks to have no prospects 0

CHALWOOD (Irish) — I 44[1]

CHAMPAGNE RUN b.g. 12 Runnett - Tolaytala by Be My Guest (USA) — Richard Hawker

1996 P(0),5(0),P(0),3(0),P(0),P(0)

824 31/3 Lockinge (L) CON 3m 8 F *in tch whn s.u. bnd apr 5th* S -
903 5/4 Howick (L) CON 3m 6 F *in tch to 10th, sn bhnd, t.o. & p.u. last, dsmntd* P 0
1274 27/4 Little Wind' (R) XX 3m 8 GF *sn bhnd, t.o. 8th, p.u. 15th* P 0
1455 11/5 Maisemore P' (L) CON 3m 8 G *sn bhnd, t.o. & jmpd slwly 4th, ref 6th* R -
1457 11/5 Maisemore P' (L) OPE 3m 2 G *(bl) 2nd outing, nrly ref 7th, ld 8th til nrly ref 13th, no ch* 2 0
1549 24/5 Mounsey Hil' (R) OPE 3m 2 G *(bl) svrl slw jmps, disp til jmpd slwly 5th, t.o. & ref 15th* R -

Specialises in turning out to prevent walkovers but completely in control of the rider 0

CHAMSY (Irish) — I 172^{P}, I 381^{F}, I 447^{6}, I 515^{P}

CHANGE THE PACE (Irish) — I 166, , I 318^{3}

CHANGE THE SCRIPT (Irish) — I 99^{F}, I 156^{F}, I 391^{1}, I 498^{F}

CHANNEL ISLAND b.m. 8 Cisto (FR) - Channel Ten by Babu — Mrs P M Williams

1996 P(0)

404 8/3 Llanfrynach (R) INT 3m 17 G *mid-div, f 3rd* F -

2 runs in 2 seasons & the briefest of sightings 97 0

CHAN THE MAN b.g. 6 Krisinsky (USA) - Channel Ten by Babu — Mrs Sandra Worthington

1996 **P(NH)**,**5(NH)**

892 5/4 Hereford (R) HC 2m 11 GF *chsd ldr from 3rd, hit 8th, ev ch when mstk 3 out, soon wknd.* 4 12

Well-beaten 4th in weak H/chase; won desperate novice chase later in season 14

CHANTINGO LAD b.g. 6 Rustingo - Chantry Rose by Ben Novus — Mrs S E Warman

1009 12/4 St Hilary (R) MDN 3m 11 GF *t.o. last til p.u. 13th* P 0
1138 19/4 Bonvilston (R) MDO 3m 9 G *t.o. & p.u. 9th* P 0
1555 24/5 Bassaleg (R) MEM 3m 6 G *n.j.w., t.o. til ref 7th* R -
1603 31/5 Bassaleg (R) MDO 3m 6 F *ld til hit 2nd, chsd ldrs, blnd 11th, 3rd & no ch, p.u. 15th* P 0

Lacks running or jumping ability 0

CHAPEAU CHINOIS ch.m. 6 Catch The Thatch - Sin Nian by Tudorville — Miss E B Godfrey

774 29/3 Dingley (R) MDO 2m 5f 10 G *last frm 3rd, t.o. 5th, p.u. 10th* P 0
1082 13/4 Guilsborough (L) MDN 3m 14 GF *wll bhnd frm 9th, t.o. & p.u. 11th* P 0
1193 20/4 Garthorpe (R) MDO 3m 9 GF *chsd ldrs to 3rd, last frm 7th, t.o. & p.u. 11th* P 0

Unpromising - seems to stay about a mile 0

CHAPEL ISLAND b.g. 10 Glen Quaich - Cashelgarran by Never Say Die — E W & M Tuer

1996 4(15),5(15),1(18),3(14),2(18),4(15),4(13),2(17),**3(12)**

167 15/2 Witton Cast' (R) RES 3m 7 F *mid-div most of way, lost plc 14th, kpt on onepcd 3 out* 3 12
356 2/3 Great Stain' (L) INT 3m 9 S *hld up, prog 11th, went 3rd 3 out, no prog aft* 4 12
615 22/3 Hutton Rudby (L) MEM 3m 8 GF *alwys prom,ev ch whn wnt wrong side of mrkr aft 4 out & u.r.* r -
695 29/3 Stainton (R) RES 3m 11 F *mid-div, prog 16th, no further hdwy frm 3 out, sn bttn* 4 14
1069 13/4 Whitwell-On' (R) RES 3m 12 G *mid-div, prog to ld 4 out, drew clr 2 out, pshd out* 1 18
1100 19/4 Hornby Cast' (L) CON 3m 9 G *(Jt fav) mid-div, prog 9th, disp 12th til apr 3 out, onepcd frm nxt* 2 18
1405 5/5 Witton Cast' (R) CON 3m 10 GS *mid-div, prog 11th, ev ch 3 out, wknd nxt, eased flat* 4 16
1419 10/5 Easingwold (L) CON 3m 8 GF *mid-div, hit 3rd, f 7th* F -

Consistent, safe & found modest Restricted; just stayd 3m; may win Confined at 11; G/S-F 18

CHAPEL ROAD (Irish) — **I** 172^{1}, **I** 569^{F}

CHARIOT DEL (Irish) — **I** 67^{4}, **I** 431^{1}, **I** 505^{1}

CHARLEYS RUN (Irish) — **I** 47^{P}, **I** 84, , **I** 241^{P}, **I** 559^{2}

CHARLIE ANDREWS ch.g. 7 Teofane - Royal Feature by King's Equity — R Andrews

1996 F(-),P(0),P(0)

127	9/2 Cottenham	(R) MDO	3m	11	GF	*1st ride, mstks 4 & 5th, t.o. 10th, p.u. 13th*	P	0
197	15/2 Higham	(L) MDO	3m	12	G	*prom, disp 4th-16th, wknd rpdly nxt, p.u. 2 out*	P	0
438	8/3 Higham	(L) MDO	3m	8	G	*mstks, nvr going wll, lost tch rpdly 15th, t.o. & p.u. 3 out*	P	0

Yet to complete & shows no ability 0

CHARLIE CHALK b.g. 10 Le Bavard (FR) - Blissful Hour by Hardicanute — Mrs R A Schofield

1996 P(0),7(0),3(11),1(19),P(0),2(17)

200	15/2 Weston Park	(L) CON	3m	16	G	*mid-div early, fdd, p.u. 13th*	P	0
363	2/3 Garnons	(L) XX	3m	6	GS	*effrt to 15l 4th at 12th, sn lost tch, p.u. 2 out*	P	0
1001	12/4 Alpraham	(R) MXO	3m	3	GF	*ld, mstk 8th, just ld whn s.u. flat apr 2 out*	S	-
1349	3/5 Gisburn	(R) CON	3m	11	GF	*mid-div, lost plc 14th, 7th 3 out, styd on onepcd nxt*	4	12

Confined winner 96; declined in 97 & ran badly; stays; mistakes; best watched 14

CHARLIE FUDD (Irish) — **I** 485, , **I** 496^{P}

CHARLIE HAWES (Irish) — **I** 34^{3}, **I** 107^{4}, **I** 161^{2}, **I** 231^{1}, **I** 298^{U}

CHARLIE KELLY b.g. 8 Netherkelly - Changan by Touch Paper — T P Whales

1996 4D(0),2(10)

283	23/2 Charing	(L) MDO	3m	16	G	*alwys prom, prssd wnr 9th to 15th, no ext, fin tired*	3	12
941	6/4 Tabley	(R) MDO	3m	11	G	*lft in ld 1st, kckd clr 13th, hit nxt, hdd flat, onepcd*	2	13
1283	27/4 Fakenham P-'	(L) MDO	3m	9	G	*(fav) chsd ldrs, 4th & rdn 12th, sn lost tch, t.o.*	3	0

Safe & always completes but struggles to stay; may eventually find a race 13

CHARLIES DELIGHT(IRE) b.g. 9 Welsh Term - Pilgrim Soul by Tudor Melody — Mrs C Hicks

1996 **9(NH),P(NH),U(NH),5(NH),F(NH),8(NH),9(NH)**

94	7/2 Newbury	(L) HC	2 1/2m	12	G	*mstks, soon bhnd, t.o..*	8	0
226	21/2 Haydock	(L) HC	3m	11	G	*midfield, hdwy 10th, 6th and driven along when f 14th.*	F	-
588	19/3 Towcester	(R) HC	2 3/4m	4	GF	*ld till after 1st, regained ld 5th, hdd 2 out, soon btn.*	4	14
1097	19/4 Bangor	(L) HC	2 1/2m 110yds	11	G	*in tch till f 5th.*	F	-

No stamina & last on both completions (inc bad H/Chase); prospects grim 11

CHARLIESMEDARLIN b.g. 6 Macmillion - Top Cover by High Top — W James Morgan

572	16/3 Garnons	(L) INT	3m	13	G	*ld to 8th, ld 14th til hdd & f 2 out*	F	-
854	31/3 Eyton-On-Se'	(L) MDO	3m	10	GF	*(fav) j.w., made all, nvr seriously chal*	1	15
1303	3/5 Weston Park	(L) RES	3m	6	G	*(fav) j.w. made all, sn clr, eased flat*	1	18

Promising; beat little but did it in style; one to note; G-G/F, so far 22

CHARLIE TRUMPER(IRE) ch.g. 9 Denel (FR) - Karazend by Karabas — Mrs E J Harrison

1996 **P(NH)**

331	1/3 Eaton Hall	(R) RES	3m	17	GS	*mstks, chsng grp to hlfwy, fdd, p.u. 5 out*	P	0
415	8/3 Dalston	(R) RES	3m	19	GS	*mstks, ld to 2nd, 12th & wkng hlfwy, t.o.*	11	0
563	16/3 Lanark	(R) RES	3m	8	GS	*(bl) ld brfly 9th, lost tch by 4 out, p.u. 3 out*	P	0
852	31/3 Eyton-On-Se'	(L) RES	3m	11	GF	*in tch wth ldrs til wkng 5 out*	5	0

Does not stay & shows no real ability 0

CHARLOTTES BILLO b.g. 7 Aragon - Daring Display by Daring March — R J Emmett

526	15/3 Cothelstone	(L) MDN	3m	15	GS	*bhnd til p.u. 2 out*	P	0
736	29/3 Higher Kilw'	(L) RES	3m	10	GF	*t.o. til p.u. 13th*	P	0
1093	16/4 Hockworthy	(L) RES	3m	16	GF	*n.j.w. t.o. 4th, p.u. 8th*	P	0

Started badly & went downhill from there 0

CHARLOTTES QUEST ch.m. 11 Scallywag - Finwood by Ashmore (FR) — M A Connors

212	16/2 Southwell P'	(L) MDO	3m	14	GS	*jmpd slwly 1st, alwys bhnd, t.o. & p.u. 14th*	P	0
331	1/3 Eaton Hall	(R) RES	3m	17	GS	*mid-div, f 10th*	F	-
480	9/3 Southwell P'	(L) MDO	3m	17	G	*prom til u.r. 11th*	U	-
722	29/3 Sandon	(L) MDO	3m	10	GF	*rear 4th, losing tch whn f 8th*	F	-
850	31/3 Eyton-On-Se'	(L) LAD	3m	6	GF	*cls up, lost tch 10th, tk 3rd run in, wll btn*	3	0

Tailed off in weak Ladies on only completion & shows no promise 0

CHARLTON YEOMAN b.g. 12 Sheer Grit - Bell Walks Breeze by Flaming Breeze (CAN) — Mrs D Rowell

1996 P(0),4(10),2(14),5(0)

302	1/3 Parham	(R) CON	3m	14	G	*rear to 12th, some late prog, tk 3rd cls hm*	3	15

Chase winner 93; well beaten in points in 96 & soon vanished in 97 12

CHARMERS WISH b.m. 13 Beau Charmeur (FR) - Velvet's Wish by Three Wishes — J R Thomas

1996 6(0),P(0),3(12),3(13),P(0),3(0)

98	8/2 Great Treth'	(R) OPE 3m	14 GS	*alwys last pair, mstk 2nd, t.o. 7th, p.u. 13th*	P	0
171	15/2 Ottery St M'	(L) OPE 3m	9 G	*sn rear, t.o. 13th*	7	0
1245	26/4 Bratton Down	(L) INT 3m	9 GS	*nvr trbld ldrs, bhnd whn p.u. 12th*	P	0
1312	3/5 Holnicote	(L) INT 3m	3 G	*prssd ldr til wknd frm 2 out*	3	10
1516	17/5 Bratton Down	(L) CON 3m	6 GS	*last, lost tch 12th, t.o. & p.u. last*	P	0
1592	31/5 Bratton Down	(L) MEM 3m	4 F	*last til went 3rd 15th, no more prog, collpsd & died aft*	3	0

Dead **12**

CHARMING MOSS (Irish) — **I** 106[P], **I** 280[1]

CHARTERFORHARDWARE b.g. 11 Furry Glen - Vulgan Thistle by Vulgan — M F Williams

1996 **12(NH),3(NH),4(NH),3(NH),3(NH),F(NH),P(NH),6(NH)**

86	2/2 Wolverhampt'	(L) OPE 3m	9 GS	*cls up til rdn & wknd aft 11th, t.o. & p.u. 2 out*	P	0
328	1/3 Eaton Hall	(R) OPE 3m	6 GS	*ld to 8th, wknd qckly whn hdd, lost tch 13th, p.u. 5 out*	P	0
669	23/3 Eaton Hall	(R) LAD 3m	5 GF	*1st ride, ld & sn clr, wknd & hdd 2 out, onepcd aft*	2	18
885	1/4 Flagg Moor	(L) LAD 3m	5 G	*ld 2nd, 20l clr 9th, hdd 3 out, wknd, no ch whn f last*	F	-

Winning chaser; gave good debut ride 3rd start but too wily to win again now **16**

CHASE THE SUN (Irish) — **I** 128[P], **I** 210,

CHASING DAISY b.m. 5 Lyphento (USA) - Blue Breeze (USA) by Blue Times (USA) — Mrs S Hooper

41	1/2 Larkhill	(R) MDO 3m	13 GF	*mstk 3rd,chsd ldrs,outpcd frm 14th,mod 4th whn lft clr last*	1	15
873	31/3 Hackwood Pa'	(L) RES 3m	6 F	*p.u. aft 1st*	P	0
1157	20/4 Stafford Cr'	(R) RES 3m	11 GF	*prom early, lost tch 10th, t.o. & p.u. 12th*	P	0

Very fortunate winner on debut; absent 8 weeks after & showed nothing; best watched **13**

CHAS RANDALL (Irish) — **I** 95[P], **I** 153[P], **I** 181[3]

CHE AMIGO (Irish) — **I** 326[P], **I** 377[2], **I** 468[3]

CHEAP KNIGHT(USA) ch.g. 6 Spend A Buck (USA) - Courtly Courier (USA) by Raise A Native — S Coltherd

1996 **P(NH),8(NH)**

38	26/1 Alnwick	(L) MDO 3m	14 G	*pllng, trckd ldrs, mstk 2nd, wknd 15th, p.u. nxt*	P	0
160	15/2 Lanark	(R) MDO 2m 5f	10 G	*ldng grp til wknd 14th*	5	0

Ran out of steam twice & disappeared **0**

CHEEKY CHEVAL ch.g. 12 Cheval - Miss Charlottgoir by Charlottesvilles Flyer — Mrs D Buckett

1996 7(0),P(0),3(0),2(14),3(11),P(0)

483	9/3 Tweseldown	(R) CON 3m	8 G	*rear, lost tch 10th, effrt to 3rd 16th, wknd apr last*	3	11
746	29/3 Barbury Cas'	(L) CON 3m	2 F	*(fav) (bl) ld til blnd 13th, no ch aft*	2	0

Well-beaten all starts 96/7 (inc. tailed off in a match); no prospects now **10**

CHEEKY POT b.g. 9 Petoski - Pato by High Top — Mrs E I L Tate

1996 4(18),3(17),P(0),6(12),5(13),1(20)

355	2/3 Great Stain'	(L) LAD 3m	9 S	*rear, lost tch 14th, rpd prog apr last, ld flat*	1	22
426	8/3 Charm Park	(L) LAD 3m	12 GF	*rear, mstk 4th, alwys outpcd*	7	14
617	22/3 Hutton Rudby	(L) LAD 3m	9 GF	*rear & bhnd til rddn & styd on wll frm 3 out*	4	19
697	29/3 Stainton	(R) LAD 3m	5 F	*chsd ldrs,outpcd 10th,prog 16th,chal 3 out,mstk nxt,ran on*	2	21
895	5/4 Wetherby Po'	(L) LAD 3m	2 F	*(fav) chsd ldr, rdn 10th, clsd 14th, ld 3 out, sn clr*	1	19
1102	19/4 Hornby Cast'	(L) LAD 3m	7 G	*nvr gng wll,rear,outpcd & bhnd 7th,styd on frm 4 out,nrstfin*	3	19
1249	26/4 Easingwold	(L) LAD 3m	6 GS	*(bl) alwys same plc, onepcd thruout*	5	11
1408	5/5 Witton Cast'	(R) LAD 3m	5 GS	*rear,outpcd 9th,prog 13th,ev ch 15th til wknd nxt,p.u. 2 out*	P	0
1422	10/5 Easingwold	(L) LAD 3m	7 GF	*rear, u.r. 6th*	U	-

Ladies winner 96 (blinkered); started 97 well but form fell away; best watched; F-S **18**

CHELSEA KING (Irish) — **I** 172[2], **I** 443[1], **I** 486[2], **I** 516[U]

CHELSEA TRIC (Irish) — **I** 165[P]

CHENE ROSE (Irish) — **I** 37[P], **I** 113[P], **I** 252[P], **I** 290[5], **I** 325[2], **I** 465, , **I** 503[3], **I** 584[1]

CHEQUE BOOK ch.g. 9 Nestor - Vulgan's Joy by Vulgan Slave — A Cole

54	1/2 Wadebridge	(L) MDO 3m	13 G	*mid-div, wknd & p.u. 14th*	P	0
172	15/2 Ottery St M'	(L) MDN 3m	14 G	*mstks, prom to 14th, grad lost tch*	7	0
242	22/2 Lemalla	(R) MDO 3m	10 S	*not fluent, t.o. 11th, p.u. 15th*	P	0
553	16/3 Ottery St M'	(L) MDN 3m	15 G	*bhnd, t.o. & p.u. 10th*	P	0
1112	19/4 Flete Park	(R) MDN 3m	13 GF	*sn bhnd, t.o. whn blnd 17th, p.u. apr nxt*	P	0

Last on only completion- cheque's bounced **0**

CHEQUERS BOY b.g. 6 Sweet Monday - Some Kathy by Some Hand — Alun Corfield

437	8/3 Upton-On-Se'	(R) MDO 3m	15 G	*prom til wknd 10th, p.u. 13th*	P	0
881	1/4 Upton-On-Se'	(R) MDN 3m	13 GF	*bhnd, last whn blnd 9th, t.o. & p.u. 11th*	P	0

No promise yet **0**

CHERISHTHELADY (Irish) — **I** 349^{U}, **I** 394^{F}, **I** 416^{F}

CHERRY CHAP b.g. 12 Kabour - Mild Wind by Porto Bello — J M Bowles
1996 5(12),3(18),2(22),1(21),**P(0)**

780	31/3	Fakenham	(L)	HC	3m 110yds	7	G	*held up, joined ldrs 14th, ev ch last, rallied near line.*	2	20
912	5/4	Cottenham	(R)	LAD	3m	3	F	*(fav) prssd ldr, ld 5-11th, ld 14th, jnd 3 out, hdd nr fin*	2	17

Consistent & moderate pointer; season lasted 5 days 97; best watched if back at 13; G-F 17

CHERRYGAYLE(IRE) b or br.m. 7 Strong Gale - Julia's Pauper by Pauper — P Mercer
1996 1(10)

580	16/3	Detling	(L)	RES	3m	11	F	*hndy, chsd wnr 16th, just outpcd 3 out, ran on wll flat*	3	17

Maiden winner only start 96; ran well only start 97 & would win Restricted if racing regularly 16

CHERRY GLEN(IRE) ch.f. 6 Executive Perk - Cherry Run — K J Mitchell

82	2/2	Wolverhampt'	(L)	MDN	3m	11	GS	*(fav) hld up, prog whn mstk 11th, rdn 13th, btn nxt, p.u. 3 out*	P	0
664	23/3	Eaton Hall	(R)	MDO	3m	12	GF	*(fav) hld up rear, prog 5 out, ld 2 out, ran on und pres*	1	14

Placed Irish Maidens 96; struggled home from poor rivals when winning; much more to prove 15

CHERRY ISLAND(IRE) ch.g. 9 King Persian - Tamar Di Bulgaria (ITY) by Duke Of Marmalade (USA) — Mrs Heather Gibbon
1996 1(15),3(16),2(13),1(18),1(22)

188	15/2	Erw Lon	(L)	LAD	3m	8	G	*prom, ld 8-11th, ev ch aft til wknd aft 2 out*	3	18
377	4/3	Leicester	(R)	HC	2 1/2m 110yds	15	G	*held up, hdwy 8th, ev ch apr last, styd on same pace.*	2	25

Won 3 in 96; ran well at Leicester but stable out of form after; could win H/Chase 98; G-S 26

CHERRY STREET b.m. 8 Cruise Missile - New Cherry by New Brig — Mrs J E Purdie
1996 F(-),P(0)

21	25/1	Badbury Rin'	(L)	MDN	3m	7	GF	*n.j.w. chsd ldr til wknd 13th, t.o. & p.u. 3 out*	P	0

Yet to complete & very lightly raced 0

CHESNUT CHARLEY (Irish) — **I** 456^{S}, **I** 482, , **I** 496^{F}

CHESTER BEN ro.g. 8 Alias Smith (USA) - Saleander by Leander — M Barthorpe

211	16/2	Southwell P'	(L)	MDO	3m	15	GS	*(fav) mid-div,prog to 3rd at 11th,jmpd slwly 13th, wknd, p.u.2 out*	P	0
478	9/3	Southwell P'	(L)	MDO	3m	17	G	*chsd ldrs, lft in ld 6th, 4l clr 15th, hdd nxt, wknd*	3	10
677	23/3	Brocklesby '	(L)	MDN	3m	8	GF	*(fav) disp to 6th, lft 2nd 14th, sn ld, hdd 2 out, onepcd*	2	12
1192	20/4	Garthorpe	(R)	MDO	3m	6	GF	*(fav) ld at steady pace, jnd 2 out, hdd & no ext last 100 yrds*	2	13
1530	18/5	Fakenham	(L)	HC	2m 5f 110yds	11	G	*made most to 9th, wknd 4 out.*	8	0

Promise in 95; missed 96; expensive in 97 & touch of the slows; should strike lucky 14

CHESTNUT SHOON (Irish) — **I** 421^{P}, **I** 569^{P}, **I** 600^{3}, **I** 604^{B}

CHEVAL DE GUERRE (Irish) — **I** 182^{1}

CHEVIN LAD (Irish) — **I** 20^{2}, **I** 146^{2}

CHIAROSCURO b.g. 11 Idiot's Delight - Lampshade by Hot Brandy — Edward D Perry
1996 **13(NH)**

400	8/3	Llanfrynach	(R)	OPE	3m	10	G	*mostly 4th, wknd 3 out, lft 3rd last*	3	15
714	29/3	Llanvapley	(L)	CON	3m	15	GF	*rear til p.u. 3 out*	P	0
1013	12/4	Bitterley	(L)	CON	3m	14	GF	*alwys cls up, not qckn frm 15th, kpt on onepcd*	3	18
1233	26/4	Brampton Br'	(R)	CON	3m	8	G	*6th & rdn 10th, styd on frm 15th, lkd to ld post*	2	18
1557	24/5	Bassaleg	(R)	CON	3m	9	G	*(fav) prom til slppd & u.r. aft 9th*	U	-

Modest hurdler/chaser; unlucky 4th start & may make amends at 12 in small race; Good 18

CHILIPOUR gr.g. 10 Nishapour (FR) - Con Carni by Blakeney — Nick Viney
1996 2(25),1(25),1(24),1(25),P(0),1(0),1(27),1(25),**1(26)**,**1(29)**,**1(30)**

4	19/1	Barbury Cas'	(L)	OPE	3m	9	GF	*(fav) hld up, prog 9th, chsd ldng pair 11th, no imp 3 out, wknd*	3	25
890	4/4	Aintree	(L)	HC	2 3/4m	14	G	*f 1st.*	F	-
1091	16/4	Hockworthy	(L)	OPE	3m	4	GF	*(fav) w.w. slw jmp 4th & rmndr, ld 14th, clr 2 out, eased flat*	1	22
1358	5/5	Exeter	(R)	HC	2m 7f 110yds	8	G	*(fav) held up, hit 5th, hdwy 7th, ld 11th, all out.*	1	24
1529	18/5	Fakenham	(L)	HC	3m 110yds	9	G	*(fav) prom, blnd 13th, rdn 3 out, no impn apr last, eased run-in.*	6	13

Very useful in 96 but troubled 97; best easy 3m; may return to best; G/F-S 27

CHILLBABYCHILL (Irish) — **I** 575^{P}

CHILLYS STAR b.g. 7 Chilibang - Aquarian Star by Cavo Doro — Mrs J Rimmer

1121	19/4	Whittington	(L)	CON	3m	4	F	*rear, blnd 3rd, t.o. 11th, p.u. 3 out*	P	0

Of no account 0

CHINA HAND(IRE) ch.g. 5 Salt Dome (USA) - China Blue by Ahonoora — M J Brown

506	15/3	Dalton Park	(R)	CON	3m	16	GF	*bhnd, bdly hmpd & u.r. 6th*	U	-
622	22/3	Hutton Rudby	(L)	MDO	3m	10	GF	*mid-div, wknd 9th, t.o. & p.u. 11th*	P	0
860	31/3	Charm Park	(L)	MDO	3m	12	F	*cls up, 3rd at 8th, wknd, f 11th*	F	-
1074	13/4	Whitwell-On'	(R)	MDO	2 1/2m 88yds	16	G	*rear & strgglng 9th, sn t.o.*	8	0
1105	19/4	Hornby Cast'	(L)	MDO	3m	11	G	*rear, blndrd 3rd, sn t.o., jmp v slwly & p.u. aft 8th*	P	0
1251	26/4	Easingwold	(L)	MDO	3m	9	GS	*cls up, 2nd 12th, fdd 4 out, p.u. 2 out*	P	0
1409	5/5	Witton Cast'	(R)	MDO	3m	15	GS	*mid-div til wknd 15th, jmp v slwly nxt & p.u.*	P	0

Beaten miles on only completion & looks useless 0

CHINA LAL b.m. 5 Rakaposhi King - Doris Blake by Roscoe Blake — J S Swindells

853	31/3	Eyton-On-Se'	(L)	MDO	3m	13	GF	*ran out 3rd*	r	-
1003	12/4	Alpraham	(R)	MDO	2 1/2m	10	GF	*hmpd 1st, rear whn u.r. 3rd*	U	-

Safely negotiated 4 fences in 2 outings 0

CHINAMAN b.g. 8 Noalto - Diorina by Manacle — Mrs J Shirley

1996 **5(NH),4(NH),8(NH),9(NH),4(NH),P(NH)**

217	16/2	Heythrop	(R)	MEM	3m	4	G	*chsd wnr to 12th, fdd frm 4 out*	3	0
824	31/3	Lockinge	(L)	CON	3m	8	F	*alwys rear, 5th & no ch frm 11th, t.o. & p.u. last*	P	0
986	12/4	Kingston Bl'	(L)	CON	3m	10	GF	*wth ldr whn mstk 6th, sn lost plc, t.o. 13th*	7	0

No stamina & no prospects in points 0

CHIP AND RUN b.g. 11 Strong Gale - Pampered Run by Deep Run — Richard Barber

1996 **P(NH)**

1153	20/4	Stafford Cr'	(R)	CON	3m	10	GF	*6s-7/2, rear whn u.r. bend aft 8th*	U	-
1274	27/4	Little Wind'	(R)	XX	3m	8	GF	*(fav) ld & pckd 9th, hdd nxt, lost plc aft 14th, 4th & btn, f 2out*	F	-
1313	3/5	Holnicote	(L)	CON	3m	7	G	*tongue-strap, trckd ldrs, clsd 12th, ld flat, ran on*	1	21

Novice-ridden twice & Tim Mitchell aboard last start; top yard but no more than moderate at best; Gd .. 20

CHIP'N'RUN gr.g. 11 Cruise Missile - Fairytale-Ending by Sweet Story — F D Cornes

1996 P(0),P(0),P(0),1(22),U(-),1(24),U(-),P(0),1(24),1(23),**P(0)**

201	15/2	Weston Park	(L)	OPE	3m	16	G	*prom, ld/disp 3rd til hdd 3 out, ev ch last, no ext flat*	2	23
465	8/3	Eyton-On-Se'	(L)	OPE	3m	13	G	*(fav) cls 2nd til ld 11th, sn clr, ran on strgly*	1	25
496	15/3	Hereford	(R)	HC	3m 1f 110yds	10	GF	*chsd ldr to 15th, wknd 3 out.*	3	15

Won 4 in 96; Eyton specialist; useful at best but finished early 96 & may be best watched at 12; F-S 23

CHISM(IRE) br.g. 6 Euphemism - Melody Gayle Vii by Damsire Unregistered — H Wellstead

1996 P(0),1(16)

22	25/1	Badbury Rin'	(L)	RES	3m	3	GF	*(fav) lft disp apr 4th, ld 3 out, clr last, eased flat,just hld on*	1	16
112	8/2	Milborne St'	(L)	INT	3m	4	GF	*(fav) set slow pace, qcknd 3 out, hdd aft nxt, rallied to ld flat*	1	18
455	8/3	Great Treth'	(R)	OPE	3m	8	S	*alwys prom, slght ld 16th, ev ch til hdd & wknd apr 2 out*	3	20
662	22/3	Badbury Rin'	(L)	CON	3m	8	F	*(fav) cls up, effrt 4 out, ld nxt, hdd aft last, not qckn*	2	20
1485	6/5	Wincanton	(R)	HC	2m 5f	4	F	*(Jt fav) went 3rd after 8th, hdwy to chase ldrs 11th, one pace from 3 out.*	3	0

Quite able but ungenuine; finds little in front; should win Confined; not one to trust; F-S 22

CHOCOLATE BUTTONS b.m. 8 Button Bright (USA) - Man Maid by Mandamus — J R Thomas

1996 S(-),P(0),2(12),U(-),F(-),7(0)

104	8/2	Great Treth'	(R)	MDO	3m	9	GS	*mstks, in tch, effrt 13th, 4th whn f nxt*	F	-
531	15/3	Wadebridge	(L)	MDO	3m	14	GF	*mid-div, steady prog 11th, ld 15th, made rest*	1	15
1243	26/4	Bratton Down	(L)	OPE	3m	6	GS	*bhnd, mvd up whn mstk 9th, lost irons, p.u. bfr 2 out*	P	0
1395	5/5	High Bickin'	(R)	RES	3m	9	G	*prog to cls 2nd at 15th, ev ch til wknd 2 out*	5	10
1519	17/5	Bratton Down	(L)	RES	3m	15	GS	*9th at 12th, nvr dang, t.o. & p.u. last*	P	0

Finally found right race to score; little after & will struggle in Restricteds 14

CHORUS OF WINGS(IRE) ch.g. 9 Kemal (FR) - Super Sayanarra by Laurence O — D Crossland

211	16/2	Southwell P'	(L)	MDO	3m	15	GS	*chsd ldrs, wkng & rdn 11th, t.o. 13th*	5	0
347	2/3	Market Rase'	(L)	MDO	3m	9	GF	*(bl) cls up, ld apr 7th-9th, wknd frm 3 out*	4	0
883	1/4	Flagg Moor	(L)	MDO	3m	12	G	*chsd ldrs, cls 4th at 15th, s.u. bnd apr nxt*	S	-

Not disgraced 2nd start but more needed & time passing 11

CHRISTIMATT (Irish) — **I** 35^{5}, **I** 120^{1}, **I** 124^{1}, **I** 177^{P}, **I** 290^{4}, **I** 361^{3}, **I** 465^{6}, **I** 503^{2}

CHRISTMAS HOLS b.g. 11 Young Generation - Foston Bridge by Relkino — Mrs V Greatrex

1996 4(0),P(0),P(0),6(12)

735	29/3	Higher Kilw'	(L)	MEM	3m	5	GF	*went poor 2nd aft 15th, no ch*	2	0
1111	19/4	Flete Park	(R)	CON	3m	5	GF	*ld/disp to 7th, rmndrs 14th, lost tch 17th, t.o.*	3	0

1255 27/4 Black Fores' (R) CON 3m 4 F *ld to 11th, kpt on onepcd aft* 3 10
1342 3/5 Flete Park (R) CON 3m 6 G *wll in tch til wknd 14th, t.o. 16th* 4 0

Meaningless placings in weak races & does not stay 10

CHRISTMAS THYNE(IRE) b.g. 5 Good Thyne (USA) - Shady Lady by Proverb Dave Dixon

368 2/3 Garnons (L) MDO 2 1/2m 13 GS *chsng ldrs whn blnd & u.r. 7th* U -
437 8/3 Upton-On-Se' (R) MDO 3m 15 G *prom to 8th, lost plc, ran on 13th, wknd 3 out* 4 0
1587 29/5 Uttoxeter (L) HC 2m 5f 11 GF *mid div, rdn 8th, soon bhnd, t.o. and p.u. before 4 out.* P 0

Well-beaten last on only completion & more stamina needed to figure in 98 10

CHUMMY'S LAST b.m. 7 Palm Track - Chumolaori by Indian Ruler R Tate

1996 P(0),U(-),F(-),r(-),P(0),U(-),P(0),F(-),4(10)

80 2/2 Market Rase' (L) MDO 2m 5f 9 GF *w.w., jmpd slwly 7th, prog to 4th whn u.r. 10th* U -
429 8/3 Charm Park (L) MDO 3m 14 GF *nvr gng wll, rear, t.o. 7th, p.u. nxt* P 0
621 22/3 Hutton Rudby (L) MDO 3m 10 GF *prom, lost plcd 8th, strgglng 15th* 3 0
699 29/3 Stainton (R) MDO 3m 7 F *(Jt fav) alwys prom, blndrd 16th, ev ch whn ran wd apr 2 out, sn bttn* 3 0
1252 26/4 Easingwold (L) MDO 3m 9 GS *mid-div, hit 13th, tk 3rd run in* 3 0
1409 5/5 Witton Cast' (R) MDO 3m 15 GS *rear div whn u.r. 10th* U -

Well-beaten in modest races & not threatening to win; has finished 4 of 15 starts 10

CHURCH RIDE(IRE) b.g. 8 King's Ride - Church Brae by The Parson Mrs G Greenwood

1108 19/4 Flete Park (R) RES 3m 14 GF *rear grp, 7th at 15th, bhnd & p.u. 2 out* P 0
1520 17/5 Bratton Down (L) MDO 3m 17 GS *mid-div, some prog to 3rd & jmpd slwly 3 out, onepcd* 4 11

Missed 96 & modest form in short 97 campaign; stamina doubts 12

CHURCHTOWN CHANCE(IRE) b.m. 7 Fine Blade (USA) - Churchtown Breeze by Tarqogan Paul B Jordain

1996 P(0),4(0),1(12),2(18),5(15)

175 15/2 Ottery St M' (L) RES 3m 15 G *handy, chal 3 out, outpcd & no ext frm nxt* 4 14
556 16/3 Ottery St M' (L) RES 3m 12 G *(fav) 3s-6/4, pllng, handy, disp 4 out, lft in ld nxt, easily* 1 20

Maiden winner 96; maintained progress with clear-cut win; finished early but Intermediate on cards ... 20

CHURCHTOWN DRUM (Irish) — I 107P
CHURCHTOWN GLEN (Irish) — I 303²
CHURCHTOWN VALLEY (Irish) — I 534P
CINDER MIRAGE ch.g. 6 Mirror Boy - Meall Mhor by Fez M Lee

419 8/3 Dalston (R) MDO 2 1/2m 10 GS *s.s. mstk 4th, t.o. & p.u. 6th* P 0
768 29/3 Whittington (L) MDO 3m 10 S *cls up 1st ctt, wknd & u.r. 15th* U -
1052 13/4 Lockerbie (R) MDN 3m 10 F *sn bhnd, t.o. & p.u. aft 11th* P 0

Shows no promise yet 0

CINQ FRANK (Irish) — I 120F, I 185F
CIRVIN (Irish) — I 39, , I 191², I 262¹
CITY BUZZ(IRE) br.g. 7 Phardante (FR) - Tourin Neofa by Teofane John E Needham

1996 F(-),5(10),1(12),B(-),9(0),P(0)

78 2/2 Market Rase' (L) RES 3m 8 GF *(bl) prom, lft 3rd 3 out, chsd wnr app last, no imp* 2 14
251 22/2 Brocklesby ' (L) RES 3m 16 G *prom bhnd ldrs, 5th 5 out, outpcd nxt* 4 13
477 9/3 Southwell P' (L) RES 3m 10 G *mid-div, in tch til outpcd 14th, no dang aft* 4 10
616 22/3 Hutton Rudby (L) RES 3m 14 GF *(bl) alwys prom, ld 16th, clr 2 out, ran on strgly* 1 20

Maiden winner 96; much improved last start 97 & won fair Restricted; can win Confined; blinkers 20

CLADDAGH CRYSTAL (Irish) — I 160P
CLANDON JACK ro.g. 12 Arkan - Brackens Marella by Rugantino J G Crumpler

932 6/4 Charlton Ho' (L) LAD 3m 6 G *(vis) blnd 5th, ld to 9th, steadily wknd 12th, p.u. 3 out* P 0
1153 20/4 Stafford Cr' (R) CON 3m 10 GF *(vis) made all, clr 3 out, tired nr fin* 1 21

Very useful to 95; missed 96; game performance when winning; just stays 3m; top stable; G/F-S 22

CLANDON LAD b.g. 7 Impecunious - Madam's Choice by New Member J G Crumpler

1996 2(18),U(-),F(-),2(15),F(-),B(-),2(18)

7 19/1 Barbury Cas' (L) RES 3m 14 GF *blnd & rdr lost iron 1st, bhnd til p.u. 6th* P 0
241 22/2 Lemalla (R) RES 3m 11 S *prog 11th, cls 4th at 13th, ld 3 out til last, ran on well* 2 20
457 8/3 Great Treth' (R) RES 3m 8 S *(fav) jmp lft, ld 4th til hdd 2 out, virt walked run in* 2 14
687 29/3 Little Wind' (R) MEM 3m 5 GF *w.w. mstk 12th, chal & mstk 3 out, wknd, walked in* 3 10
1157 20/4 Stafford Cr' (R) RES 3m 11 GF *hld up, prog 10th, cls 3rd whn s.u. bnd apr 2 out* S -
1275 27/4 Little Wind' (R) RES 3m 9 GF *hld up last, prog hlfwy, chsd wnr 3 out, no imp, fin tired* 2 12
1374 5/5 Cotley Farm (L) RES 3m 7 GF *held up, prog 10th, ev ch 3 out, wknd & onepcd frm nxt* 4 16
1519 17/5 Bratton Down (L) RES 3m 15 GS *(vis) hld up, prog 12th, went 3rd & mstk 16th, wknd, 4th last,p.u.* P 0

Maiden winner 95; placed 8 times 96/7 but does not stay & getting worse now; G/F-S 14

CLANSIES GIRL b.m. 6 Comme L'etoile - Compelling by Mandamus — K R Staley

409	8/3	Llanfrynach	(R)	MDN	3m	12	G	*rear, p.u. 15th*	P	0
634	22/3	Howick	(L)	RES	3m	7	GF	*33s-16s, last til p.u. 12th*	P	0
1185	20/4	Lydstep	(L)	RES	3m	5	GF	*jmpd novicey, in rear whn p.u. 11th*	P	0

No signs of ability & should stick to Maidens **0**

CLARA WOOD (Irish) — **I** 484^{P}, **I** 563^{P}, **I** 607^{P}

CLARE LAD ch.g. 14 Garda's Revenge (USA) - Sea Dike by Dike (USA) — Mrs G B Walford

1996 7(0),F(-),4(0),7(0),U(-),4(0),4(0)

34	26/1	Alnwick	(L)	OPE	3m	9	G	*1st ride, in tch in rear, effrt 15th, btn whn nrly u.r. 2out*	5	13
75	2/2	Market Rase'	(L)	CON	3m	10	GF	*blnd & nrly u.r. 1st, wl bhnd til styd on frm 4 out*	4	11
113	9/2	Wetherby Po'	(L)	CON	3m	10	GF	*(vis) prom, ld 11th-15th, onepcd aft*	2	15
248	22/2	Brocklesby '	(L)	CON	3m	10	G	*(vis) rear div, prog 6 out, 30l 4th 4 out, ran on onepcd*	5	13
475	9/3	Southwell P'	(L)	OPE	3m	7	G	*chsd ldrs, 6th & outpcd apr 12th, no dang aft*	4	0
506	15/3	Dalton Park	(R)	CON	3m	16	GF	*prom til fdd 13th, hmpd & u.r. 15th*	U	-
618	22/3	Hutton Rudby	(L)	OPE	3m	10	GF	*chsd ldrs til outpcd 8th, wknd frm 4 out*	5	0
765	29/3	Whittington	(L)	OPE	3m	6	S	*alwys rear, p.u. 2 out*	P	0
1075	13/4	Whitwell-On'	(R)	MEM	3m	9	G	*(vis) rear, lost tch 9th, t.o. 11th*	5	0
1265	27/4	Southwell P'	(L)	OPE	3m	8	G	*(vis) mid-div, outpcd 6th, lost tch 12th, t.o. 14th, p.u 3 out*	P	0

Schoolmaster 96/7 & does not threaten to win now **12**

CLARE TO HERE (Irish) — **I** 55^{U}, **I** 100^{P}, **I** 223^{P}, **I** 341^{P}

CLASHBRIDANE (Irish) — **I** 85^{P}, **I** 239^{1}, **I** 336^{2}

CLASH OF THE GALES (Irish) — **I** 8^{1}, **I** 49^{3}

CLASHVIEW (Irish) — **I** 17^{4}, **I** 52^{4}, **I** 136^{P}, **I** 238^{3}, **I** 418^{1}, **I** 475^{5}, **I** 562^{4}, **I** 603^{P}

CLASSIE CLAIRE (Irish) — **I** 83^{P}, **I** 383^{1}

CLASSIS KING (Irish) — **I** 20^{4}, **I** 476^{P}

CLAUDIA ELECTRIC (Irish) — **I** 19^{1}

CLAYDONS MONTY b.g. 8 Majestic Maharaj - Butterfly Lilly by Sidon — Michael A Johnson

15	25/1	Cottenham	(R)	MDN	3m	7	GF	*chsd ldr, ld 10th, hrd prssd whn lft wll clr 2 out*	1	13
126	9/2	Cottenham	(R)	RES	3m	14	GF	*chsd wnr, cls engh 14th, hit 2 out, btn whn blnd last*	2	16
324	1/3	Marks Tey	(L)	RES	3m	16	G	*prog 9th, chsd wnr 11-15th, sn wknd, p.u. 3 out*	P	0
913	5/4	Cottenham	(R)	RES	3m	4	F	*(fav) w.w. prog to chal 15th, ld apr 2 out, sn clr, easily*	1	16
1190	20/4	Garthorpe	(R)	INT	3m	8	GF	*(fav) cls up, lost plc 12th, rdn 14th, 6th & btn nxt, kpt on*	5	13

Modest but solid; best easy 3m; both wins Cottenham; may find another chance 98; G-F **18**

CLAYWALLS b.g. 6 Meadowbrook - Lady Manello by Mandrake Major — Ian Hamilton

1996 5(0),4(0)

233	22/2	Friars Haugh	(L)	MDO	3m	13	G	*nvr nr ldrs*	5	0
420	8/3	Dalston	(R)	MDO	2 1/2m	8	GS	*chsd ldr to 6th, ev ch 12th, onepcd aft*	3	10
612	22/3	Friars Haugh	(L)	MDN	3m	14	GF	*alwys hndy, ld 4 out, forged clr frm nxt*	1	15
947	6/4	Friars Haugh	(L)	RES	3m	6	GF	*(fav) 2nd mstly til ld 3 out, sn clr*	1	16

Steadily improving; clear-cut winner twice; should upgrade 98 if ready; G/S-G/F **19**

CLEAN SWEEP br.g. 10 Deep Run - The Charwoman by Menelek — Mrs G Drury

1996 F(-),4(10),1(11)

577	16/3	Detling	(L)	CON	3m	18	F	*alwys towrds rear, 10th whn f 11th*	F	-
965	6/4	Penshurst	(L)	MEM	3m	3	F	*(fav) hvly restrained, ld 12th, in comm aft*	1	10

Won a bad Maiden in 96 & followed up in similar Members in 97; lucky to find another **11**

CLEARLY VISIBLE (Irish) — **I** 64^{F}, **I** 281^{P}

CLEASBY HILL ch.g. 12 Avocat - Strandhill by Bargello — Mrs F J Walker

1996 U(-),4(11),P(0),P(0)

889	3/4	Taunton	(R)	HC	3m	7	F	*held up, rdn 10th, bhnd from 13th, t.o. when p.u. after 4 out.*	P	0
1244	26/4	Bratton Down	(L)	CON	3m	14	GS	*nvr trbld ldrs, p.u. aft 12th*	P	0
1313	3/5	Holnicote	(L)	CON	3m	7	G	*not fluent, rmndrs 4th, bhnd frm 6th, p.u. aft 14th*	P	0
1496	14/5	Cothelstone	(L)	CON	3m	9	GF	*ld 2-6th, wknd 8th, p.u. 11th*	P	0

No longer of any account **0**

CLEDDAU KING b.g. 11 Push On - Karatina (FR) by Dilettante II — James Buckle

1996 4(0),U(-)

123	9/2	Cottenham	(R)	INT	3m	13	GF	*ld to 3rd, sn wknd, t.o. & p.u. 3 out*	P	0
321	1/3	Marks Tey	(L)	INT	3m	10	G	*alwys rear div, 5th & no ch 16th, t.o.*	5	0
798	31/3	Marks Tey	(L)	RES	3m	7	F	*trckd ldrs, last 9th, wknd 14th, t.o.*	5	0

Beaten miles both completions & a total no-hoper now **0**

CLEVER SHEPHERD b.g. 12 Broadsword (USA) - Reluctant Maid by Relko — P C Browne

1996 **U(NH),U(NH)**

180 15/2 Larkhill (R) MXO 3m 6 G *chsd wnr 3-7th, 4th & outpcd apr 13th, no ch whn p.u. 3 out* P 0
646 22/3 Castle Of C' (R) OPE 3m 5 G *chsd ldrs, 4th & rdn 14th, no ch nxt, t.o.* 5 0

Winning chaser; disappointing in points & can only be watched if returning at 13 12

CLOBEEVER BOY b.g. 7 Shaab - Clover Bee Mrs J Spear
1996 4(13),B(-)

1528 17/5 Bredwardine (R) MDO 3m 17 G *hld up, wll in rear whn f 10th* F -

Promise in 96; appeared as se˜ ˏon ending in 97; should not be written off just yet 12

CLOBRACKEN LAD ch.g. 9 Shaab - Clover Bee by The Bo'sun T J Swaffield
1996 P(0),5(17),1(18),**2(20)**,**2(19)**,**P(0)**

112 8/2 Milborne St' (L) INT 3m 4 GF *j.w. hld up, mstk 15th, ev ch 2 out, rdn last, not qckn* 3 18
290 28/2 Newbury (L) HC 3m 6 GS *chsd wnr to 10th and again 5 out till wknd run-in.* 3 19
494 13/3 Cheltenham (L) HC 3 1/4m 110yds 18 G *hit 4th, alwys rear, t.o. when p.u. 15th.* P 0
1288 30/4 Cheltenham (L) HC 2m 5f 10 GF *n.j.w., in tch, rdn 11th, soon outpcd, styd on well after 3 out.* 3 23
1485 6/5 Wincanton (R) HC 2m 5f 4 F *(Jt fav) made all, staying on well when hit 3 out, ran on run-in.* 1 0

Placed in 4 H/Chases before finding soft race; moderate at best & hard to place now; G/S-F 21

CLOCHBAN CLONROCHE (Irish) — I 139P, I 218, , I 318P
CLOGHRAN NATIVE (Irish) — I 416R
CLOHAMON BRIDGE (Irish) — I 341P
CLONAGEERA (Irish) — I 40P, I 76P, I 141P, I 239P, I 4233, I 4765, I 602P
CLON CAW (Irish) — I 17P, I 106F, I 206P, I 447F
CLONEEN ADVENTURE (Irish) — I 136F, I 171F, I 3076, I 324P, I 378, , I 6076
CLONFERT SUE (Irish) — I 33P, I 60, , I 162P, I 2316, I 2875
CLONGEEL LORD (Irish) — I 12P, I 74P, I 1714, I 261P, I 422P, I 5205, I 5633, I 601F, I 6151
CLONMEL HIGH (Irish) — I 544F, I 5953
CLONROSH SLAVE (Irish) — 494, , I 22, I 161, I 594, I 1443
CLOONE STAR VI (Irish) — I 5314, I 591P
CLOSE TO TEARS (Irish) — I 142F
CLOUDY HOUSE gr.m. 8 Grey Desire - Scenic Villa by Top Ville J A T de Giles

390 8/3 Barbury Cas' (L) MDN 3m 15 G *f 2nd* F -

A brief appearance 0

CLOUGHAN BOY (Irish) — I 92F, I 157P, I 2251
CLOUNTIES LADY (Irish) — I 2744, I 4241, I 5132
CLOVER COIN ch.m. 10 St Columbus - Clover Doubloon by Tudor Treasure M E T Davies
1996 1(22),2(18),2(20)

304 1/3 Parham (R) LAD 3m 10 G *(Jt fav) wth ldr whn f 2nd* F -
578 16/3 Detling (L) LAD 3m 11 F *wll in rear, nvr put in race, nrst fin* 5 13

Lightly-raced; consistent pointer to 96 but out of sorts 97; best fresh; may win 98; G/F-S 18

CLOVER NOOK (Irish) — I 282,
CLOVERS LAST b.g. 11 Push On - Clover Bees Baby by Rugantino Mrs S M Newell

259 22/2 Newtown (L) MDN 3m 18 G *chsd wnr 5th, chal 3 out, no ch wth wnr frm nxt* 2 13
435 8/3 Upton-On-Se' (R) MDO 3m 14 G *(fav) ld to 10th, not qckn frm 12th, kpt on onepcd frm 3 out* 4 0
876 1/4 Upton-On-Se' (R) MEM 3m 7 GF *(fav) trckd ldrs, rdn 14th, lft 2nd 3 out, no imp wnr* 2 10
1019 12/4 Bitterley (L) MDO 3m 12 GF *cls up to 10th, just outpcd frm 13th, no ch frm 3 out* 4 0

Busiest ever season but very slow & lost golden chance in Members; hard to win at 12 11

CLUAN GOILL (Irish) — I 209P, I 4644, I 508F, I 557P, I 5854
CLYDE RANGER b.g. 10 Kemal (FR) - Clyde Avenue by Peacock (FR) I Bray

117 9/2 Wetherby Po' (L) LAD 3m 10 GF *prom, disp 8th, ld 10th-14th, sn wknd* 4 16
165 15/2 Witton Cast' (R) LAD 3m 6 F *chsd ldr til hrd rdn & outpcd 14th* 3 11
506 15/3 Dalton Park (R) CON 3m 16 GF *mid-div, prog 10th, chsd wnr 14th, outpcd frm 2 out* 2 18

Useful winning chaser to 95 but disappointing in points & finished early; good enough to win 18

C'MURRA (Irish) — I 459F, I 5201, I 546F, I 6001
CNOC-BREAC (Irish) — I 79F, I 140F, I 2043, I 5962, I 606P
COALQUAY COUP (Irish) — I 775, I 4784
COCA BERRY MOON (Irish) — I 438P

COCKSTOWN LAD b.g. 11 Main Reef - Pasadena Girl by Busted — Mrs E R Featherstone

1996 3(21),5(13),5(12),1(23),3(19),U(-),P(0)

194	15/2	Higham	(L) OPE	3m	12	G	*immed last, t.o. 3rd*	6	0
440	8/3	Higham	(L) OPE	3m	5	G	*nrrw ld 2nd til mstk 15th, wknd rpdly nxt, no ch aft*	3	12
595	22/3	Horseheath	(R) OPE	3m	5	F	*last til ran on past btn horses to tk 3rd 3 out, nrst fin*	3	18
910	5/4	Cottenham	(R) CON	3m	3	F	*in tch, pshd alng & outpcd 12th, rallied 15th,kpt on flat*	2	17
1028	12/4	Horseheath	(R) CON	3m	3	HD	*(fav) disp ld til ld 15th, clr nxt, unextnd*	1	15
1115	19/4	Higham	(L) OPE	3m	4	GF	*disp to 4th, mstks, nvr going wll aft, t.o. 15th, p.u. 3 out*	P	0
1307	3/5	Cottenham	(R) OPE	3m	2	F	*not fluent, ld to 7th, lost tch wth wnr 12th, t.o.*	2	0

Specialises in weak races on Firm ground; declined in 97 & may struggle to win again 14

CODOLOGY (Irish) — **I** 61[5], **I** 96[2], **I** 138[P], **I** 222[P]

COIS INBHIR (Irish) — **I** 226[P]

COLEMANS RIVER (Irish) — **I** 29[U], **I** 64[F], **I** 117[P], **I** 287[P]

COLINS GLEN (Irish) — **I** 398[P]

COLIN'S HATCH (Irish) — **I** 116[4], **I** 177[P], **I** 313[4], **I** 327[1], **I** 505[4], **I** 553[2]

COLLIGAN FALLS (Irish) — **I** 324[P], **I** 608[P]

COLLOONEY SQUIRE (Irish) — **I** 119[P], **I** 316[2], **I** 330[3], **I** 437[U], **I** 464[P]

COLMANS HATCH (Irish) — **I** 43[F], **I** 65[2], **I** 86[4], **I** 220[P]

COLMANS HOPE (Irish) — **I** 137[P], **I** 243[5], **I** 515[3], **I** 571[1]

COLONEL CRUMPET br.g. 8 Scorpio (FR) - Adeney Lass by Space King — Oliver Helmsley

146	9/2	Tweseldown	(R) MDO	3m	10	GF	*rear, rpd prog to ld 3-5th, sn bhnd, t.o. 12th*	6	0

Distant last only start & vanished 0

COLONEL FAIRFAX gr.g. 9 Alias Smith (USA) - Mistress Meryll by Tower Walk — Mrs N R Matthews

1996 5(0),3(0),P(0),**P(0)**,4(10),1(14)

59	1/2	Kingston Bl'	(L) RES	3m	16	GF	*alwys bhnd, p.u. aft 11th*	P	0
223	16/2	Heythrop	(R) RES	3m	19	G	*(bl) ld til mstk 4th, prom to 11th, wknd & p.u. 13th*	P	0
298	1/3	Didmarton	(L) RES	3m	15	G	*prom to 6th, t.o. & p.u. 14th*	P	0
655	22/3	Siddington	(L) RES	3m	10	F	*(bl) hld up in tch, effrt aft 3 out, hit nxt, no imp aft*	3	14
820	31/3	Paxford	(L) RES	3m	4	F	*(fav) (vis) ld til hdd 2 out, no ext flat*	2	11
974	8/4	Heythrop	(R) MEM	3m	5	F	*wll bhnd, prog 10th, hit 13th, ev ch 2 out, onepcd appr last*	3	13

Maiden winner 96; only success from 26 starts; no stamina or spine; unlikely to win Restricted 14

COLONEL FRAZER(IRE) b.g. 9 Buckskin (FR) - Tabitha Bay by Laurence O — Ray Perkins

1996 P(0),P(0),F(-),2(13),1(12),F(-),P(0)

634	22/3	Howick	(L) RES	3m	7	GF	*lft in ld 4th, disp 8th-3 out, outpcd aft*	3	10
901	5/4	Howick	(L) RES	3m	6	F	*chsd ldng pair, wknd 11th, fence bhnd 15th, lost 3rd post*	4	0

Won terrible Maiden 96 & continues to struggle badly in Restricteds 11

COLONEL KENSON ch.g. 11 Avocat - Bryophila (FR) by Breakspear II — Robert Barr

1996 4(0),3(0),2(14),**5(0)**,**7(0)**

27	26/1	Marks Tey	(L) OPE	3m	6	GF	*alwys same plc, lost tch 14th, t.o.*	5	0
65	1/2	Horseheath	(R) RES	3m	10	GF	*prom, ld 5th-12th & 15th-2 out, onepcd und pres*	2	17
150	10/2	Plumpton	(L) HC	3m 1f 110yds	5	GS	*ld to 3rd, lost pl 6th, bhnd when blnd badly and u.r. 8th.*	U	-
913	5/4	Cottenham	(R) RES	3m	4	F	*prom, ld 13th til apr 2 out, sn btn*	2	0
1188	20/4	Garthorpe	(R) OPE	3m	9	GF	*chsd ldrs, pshd alng 11th, 6th & no ch whn hmpd & u.r. 3 out*	U	-

Generally safe but well-beaten all starts 96/7 & unlikely to reverse the trend at 12 14

COLONEL POPSKI ch.g. 15 Niniski (USA) - Miss Jessica by Milesian — J O Barr

1996 P(0),3(19),6(11),7(0),**P(0)**

355	2/3	Great Stain'	(L) LAD	3m	9	S	*alwys mid-div, nvr a dang*	6	16
617	22/3	Hutton Rudby	(L) LAD	3m	9	GF	*chsd ldrs, ev ch 4 out, steadd fdd*	7	16
1072	13/4	Whitwell-On'	(R) MXO	4m	21	G	*prom til wknd 16th*	8	12

Still gives it a go but non-winner since 94 & a win at 16 impossible 13

COLONEL SMITHERS (Irish) — **I** 452[B], **I** 512[5], **I** 579[P], **I** 607[P]

COLONEL WILKIE b.g. 6 Broadsword (USA) - Peticienne by Mummy's Pet — Ian Gilbert

777	29/3	Dingley	(R) MDO	2m 5f	8	G	*6th/7th til outpcd 6 out, fin own time*	5	0

Last to finish but may do better 0

COLONIAL KELLY ch.g. 9 Netherkelly - Nepal by Indian Ruler — Cockerell Cowing Racing

1996 1(30),**1(25)**,**F(-)**,**2(27)**,**1(23)**

151	12/2	Lingfield	(L) HC	3m	13	HY	*blnd 10th, bhnd when p.u. before 11th.*	P	0
286	27/2	Huntingdon	(R) HC	3m	8	GS	*settld in tch, went 2nd hfwy, feeling pace final cct, no impn from 3 out.*	3	23

494	13/3	Cheltenham	(L)	HC	3 1/4m 110yds	18	G	*rear when mstk 12th, blnd next, t.o. when p.u. 6 out.*	P	0
592	22/3	Lingfield	(L)	HC	3m	5	GF	*in tch, ld 8th, made rest, left well clr 2 out.*	1	27
1569	26/5	Fontwell	(R)	HC	3 1/4m 110yds	10	GF	*hdwy to ld 15th, hdd apr 3 out, wknd 2 out, bhnd when p.u. lame run-in.*	P	0

Dual H/Chase winner 96; below best 97 & problems last start; best watched; G-S 26

COLONIAL OFFICE(USA) ch.g. 11 Assert - Belles Oreilles (CAN) by Nentego — Graham Richards

1136	19/4	Bonvilston	(R)	MDO	3m	15	G	*alwys rear, p.u. 3 out*	P	0

No show & too old 0

COLORS OF GUIDAL(FR) b.g. 7 Nathor (FR) - My Fair Lizia (FR) by Free Round (USA) — Nolan D Best

487	9/3	Tweseldown	(R)	MDO	3m	12	G	*sn bhnd, lft poor 4th 10th, kpt on to tk dist 2nd flat*	2	0
871	31/3	Hackwood Pa'	(L)	MDO	3m	7	F	*(Jt fav) alwys cls up, chal frm 2 out, mstk & lft clr last*	1	13

Fortunate scorer but beat subsequent winner & may have Restricted chances if fit 98 15

COLOURFUL BOY b.g. 8 Afzal - Jolly Girl by Jolly Me — H J Manners

1996 P(0),P(0),F(-),1(14),4(11),4(12)

517	15/3	Larkhill	(R)	RES	3m	10	GF	*hld up, clsd 13th, chsd ldng trio 15th, no imp, lft 3rd last*	3	10

Maiden winner 96; brief appearance in points 97; best watched 14

COMEDIE FLEUR b.m. 9 Martinmas - Welsh Flower by Welsh Saint — Miss Caroline Nicholas

1996 1(0),P(0)

464	8/3	Eyton-On-Se'	(L)	INT	3m	12	G	*chsd ldr in tch,ld brfly 3 out,tired apr last,hmp by faller*	2	19
748	29/3	Brampton Br'	(R)	MEM	3m	6	GF	*(fav) trckd ldr, rdn to chal 3 out, no ext nxt, virt p.u. flat*	3	10
1382	5/5	Eyton-On-Se'	(L)	INT	3m	7	GF	*hld up in rear, clsr order 5 out, jnd 3 out, hdd bfr last*	3	18

Lightly raced; maintains ability but beaten at odds-on in Members; may perk up 98; Any 18

COMEDY GAYLE b.g. 10 Lir - Follifoot's Folly by Comedy Star (USA) — Ms Sue Willcock

245	22/2	Lemalla	(R)	MDO	3m	11	S	*in tch, went 3rd at 15th, not chal, improve*	3	0
458	8/3	Great Treth'	(R)	MDO	3m	15	S	*towrds rear, nvr dang, blndrd & u.r. 2 out*	U	-
626	22/3	Kilworthy	(L)	MDN	3m	14	G	*mid-div, prog 15th, ld apr last, styd on*	1	15
1416	10/5	Newton Abbot	(L)	HC	2m 5f 110yds	14	G	*alwys bhnd, t.o. when p.u. after 9th.*	P	0
1481	11/5	Ottery St M'	(L)	CON	3m	12	G	*handy, 5th at 13th, lost plc 15th, rallied 3 out, sn btn*	6	16
1552	24/5	Mounsey Hil'	(R)	RES	3m	12	G	*in tch, 5th at 13th, went 2nd apr 2 out, onepcd*	2	16

Late starter but creditable season; should have Restricted chance 98; Good 18

COMELY MAIDEN (Irish) — **I** 91[P], **I** 264[F], **I** 305[P], **I** 418[5], **I** 476[4], **I** 607[P]

COMIC ACT (Irish) — **I** 544[P]

COMING SOON (Irish) — **I** 338[4], **I** 419[P], **I** 443[P]

COMING THROUGH (Irish) — **I** 191[4], **I** 262[P]

COMMASARRIS gr.g. 5 Joli Wasfi (USA) - Lucy Aura by Free State — Miss M D M Howie

127	9/2	Cottenham	(R)	MDO	3m	11	GF	*alwys bhnd, t.o. & p.u. 14th*	P	0
283	23/2	Charing	(L)	MDO	3m	16	G	*prssd wnr to 11th, wknd rpdly, t.o. & p.u. 14th*	P	0
582	16/3	Detling	(L)	MDN	3m	16	F	*2nd til lft in ld 6th,hdd 10th,prom til wknd 3 out,p.u. last*	P	0

No signs of stamina yet 0

COMMODITY BROKER b.g. 12 Tycoon II - Lost Bid by Fine Bid — Miss C A Smithson

1302	3/5	Weston Park	(L)	LAD	3m	5	G	*alwys rear, nvr in tch wth ldng pair, ran on nr fin*	4	10
1540	18/5	Wolverhampt'	(L)	LAD	3m	5	GS	*alwys handy, ev ch 3 out, outpcd frm nxt*	3	16

Has ability but very lightly raced (missed 96) & best watched at 13 16

COMPUTER PICKINGS b.m. 10 Taufan (USA) - Ricciola (USA) by Stage Door Johnny — John E Wright

1996 2(18),5(13),P(0),10(0),1(17)

266	22/2	Duncombe Pa'	(R)	RES	3m	19	G	*towrds rear, blndrd 4 out, kpt on frm 3 out*	4	12
338	1/3	Corbridge	(R)	RES	3m	10	G	*rear & sn bhnd, t.o. 9th*	5	0

Members winner 96; consistently disappoints in Restricteds & finished early 13

CONCERTO COLLONGES(FR) br.g. 7 El Badr - Mariane Collonge (FR) by Cap Martin (FR) — Les Streeton

883	1/4	Flagg Moor	(L)	MDO	3m	12	G	*prom, chsd ldr 6-11th, ld 3 out, ran green apr last,hdd flat*	2	14
1050	13/4	Lockerbie	(R)	RES	3m	5	F	*(fav) 2nd frm 13th, no imp on wnr*	2	13
1304	3/5	Weston Park	(L)	MDO	3m	8	G	*(fav) cls up, ld 12th, sn clr, hdd & not qckn nr fin*	2	16
1429	10/5	Aspatria	(L)	MDO	3m	15	G	*(fav) 3s-6/4,prom,disp 10th til ld 13th,wll clr 3 out,ran on wll*	1	16

Made up for narrow defeats with clear-cut win; thorough stayer; good yard; should prosper 98 20

CONIMORE(IRE) b.m. 5 Convinced - Island More by Mugatpura — Tom Hayes

368	2/3	Garnons	(L)	MDO	2 1/2m	13 GS	*rear 4th, f 6th*	F	-
706	29/3	Upper Sapey	(R)	MDO	3m	15 GF	*mid-div whn bad mstk 5th, p.u. nxt*	P	0
1066	13/4	Maisemore P'	(L)	MDO	3m	9 GF	*t.o. 6th, 4th & no ch whn blnd & u.r. last*	U	-
1240	26/4	Brampton Br'	(R)	MDO	3m	12 G	*cls up whn ran out 3rd*	r	-

Yet to complete the course 0

CONKERDOR b.g. 6 El Conquistador - Lolly Spider by Rugantino — Giles Smyly

1996 **13(NH),10(NH),19(NH)**

87	2/2	Wolverhampt'	(L)	MDO	3m	11 GS	*made all, drew wll clr frm 13th, easily*	1	16

A little promise in Bumbers & sluiced home in modest Maiden; Restricted on cards if fit 98 18

CONNA MOSS(IRE) b.g. 8 Le Moss - Glitter On by Even Money — David Brace

285	26/2	Taunton	(R)	HC	4 1/4m 110yds	16 GS	*mid div till blnd and u.r. 10th.*	U	-
364	2/3	Garnons	(L)	XX	3m	7 GS	*rear 5th, 12l 5th at 9th, p.u. aft 13th*	P	0
402	8/3	Llanfrynach	(R)	INT	3m	7 G	*trckd ldrs, rpd prog 3 out, ld nxt, easily*	1	20
535	16/3	Erw Lon	(L)	CON	3m	12 GF	*ld 10th, disp 13th, ld agn nxt, easily*	1	20
1062	13/4	Maisemore P'	(L)	MXO	3m	12 GF	*mid-div, rmndr 4th, jinked & u.r. 7th*	U	-
1132	19/4	Bonvilston	(R)	CON	3m	9 G	*(fav) made all, qcknd whn chal last*	1	20
1224	26/4	Pyle	(R)	CON	3m	7 GS	*(fav) rmndr 3rd, nvr going wll, lost tch 13th, p.u. nxt*	P	0
1362	5/5	Pantyderi	(L)	CON	3m	4 G	*in ld at 3rd, 2nd at 11th, fin tired*	2	17
1493	14/5	Cothelstone	(L)	OPE	3m	2 GF	*(fav) made most to 15th, rdn & ev ch 2 out til eased flat, lame*	2	15

Dual winner 95; missed 96; inconsistent but quite useful at best; badly lame last start; G/F-S 21

CONNIE FOLEY b.g. 11 Floriferous - Get A Bike by Orchardist — D Hiatt

374	2/3	Mollington	(R)	MDN	3m	14 G	*alwys rear, t.o. 12th, walked in*	6	0
574	16/3	Garnons	(L)	RES	3m	14 G	*s.u. bend bef 2nd*	S	-
655	22/3	Siddington	(L)	RES	3m	10 F	*lft in ld 5th, hdd 7th, prom whn u.r. 9th*	U	-
821	31/3	Paxford	(L)	MDO	3m	6 F	*rear, tk mod 2nd at 15th, styd on*	2	0
990	12/4	Kingston Bl'	(L)	MDN	3m	11 GF	*rear, prog 11th, chsd wnr 15th, no imp 2 out, wknd last*	3	0
1165	20/4	Mollington	(R)	MDO	3m	9 GF	*alwys chsng wnr, no imp frm 3 out*	2	11
1404	5/5	Ashorne	(R)	MEM	3m	7 G	*poor last, lft 3rd 13th, ld 15th, all out*	1	10
1532	18/5	Mollington	(R)	CON	3m	11 GS	*rear, lost tch 12th, t.o. & p.u. 3 out*	P	0

Non-stayer & handed Members on plate when rest defected; no further prospects 10

CONNOR THE SECOND b.g. 9 Pollerton - Pinkworthy Pond by Le Bavard (FR) — R H Black

1996 P(0),P(0)

37	26/1	Alnwick	(L)	MDO	3m	15 G	*rear whn f 3rd*	F	-
162	15/2	Lanark	(R)	MDO	3m	16 G	*nvr rchd ldrs*	7	0
565	16/3	Lanark	(R)	MDO	3m	10 GS	*some hdwy frm 12th, not rch ldrs*	4	10
996	12/4	Tranwell	(L)	MDO	3m	8 F	*rear 1st ctt,lft 3rd 13th,styd on wll frm 3 out,not rch ldrs*	3	13
1222	26/4	Balcormo Ma'	(R)	MDO	3m	6 F	*last & strgglng whn p.u. aft 11th*	P	0

Gradually getting to grips until last start; novice-ridden; more needed to win 12

CONORS BLUEBIRD(IRE) b.g. 6 Bluebird (USA) - My Natalie by Rheingold — Mrs Susan Corbett

418	8/3	Dalston	(R)	MDO	2 1/2m	10 GS	*prom til wknd rpdly & p.u. 11th*	P	0
815	31/3	Tranwell	(L)	MDO	2 1/2m	14 G	*alwys mid-div, styd on wll frm 2 out*	6	0

Signs of promise 2nd start & should go closer in 98 13

CONORS LASS (Irish) — **I** 125P

CON'S NURSE (Irish) — **I** 83P, **I** 317P, **I** 384[4], **I** 445[3], **I** 538[4], **I** 565[2]

CONTERA (Irish) — **I** 78P

CONTRADICT b.g. 7 Derring Rose - Contrary Lady by Conwyn — S Hornby

1996 4(0)

461	8/3	Great Treth'	(R)	MDO	3m	12 S	*prom til lost plc aft 13th*	4	0
1343	3/5	Flete Park	(R)	MDO	3m	13 G	*mid-div whn u.r. 10th*	U	-

Only 3 runs in 2 seasons & yet to show any sparkle 0

CONVINCING ch.g. 13 Formidable (USA) - Star Of Bagdad (USA) by Bagdad — J Cornforth

1996 5(15),P(0),2(20),4(13),4(12),**4(13)**

75	2/2	Market Rase'	(L)	CON	3m	10 GF	*(vis) prom, 4th & pshd alng 11th, sn bhnd, t.o.*	7	0
166	15/2	Witton Cast'	(R)	OPE	3m	8 F	*chsd ldr til wknd 12th, t.o.*	7	0
1100	19/4	Hornby Cast'	(L)	CON	3m	9 G	*ld,disp 6-9th & agn 12th til wknd qckly nxt,t.o. & p.u. last*	P	0
1253	26/4	Easingwold	(L)	MEM	3m	7 GS	*(vis) cls up, error 12th, wknd, p.u. 14th*	P	0

1 win from last 41 starts & deteriorated badly in 97 0

COOKIE BOY b.g. 6 Ra Nova - Gypsy Heather by Bivouac — J S Delahooke

1996 P(0),F(-),P(0),P(0)

38	26/1	Alnwick	(L)	MDO	3m	14 G	*hld up, mstk 8th, prog 11th, chal 3 out, no ext apr last*	2	14
115	9/2	Wetherby Po'	(L)	MDO	3m	8 GF	*(Jt fav) disp til lft in ld 2nd, mstk & jnd 12th, outpcd frm 5 out*	2	0

564	16/3	Lanark	(R)	MDO	2 1/2m	13	GS	*same plc virtly thruout, no ch frm 4 out*	3	0
767	29/3	Whittington	(L)	MDO	3m	9	S	*chsd ldr, ld 10th, u.r. 13th*	U	-
814	31/3	Tranwell	(L)	MDO	3m	9	G	*j.w., made virt all, kpt on strngly run in*	1	15
1048	13/4	Lockerbie	(R)	LAD	3m	6	F	*ld 11th-14th, btn 3rd whn p.u. apr 2 out*	P	0
1250	26/4	Easingwold	(L)	RES	3m	15	GS	*cls up, 4th 14th, wknd rpdly 4 out*	9	0
1348	3/5	Gisburn	(R)	RES	3m	10	GF	*cls up, ld 12th-nxt, ev ch last, no ext*	2	15

Tries hard & deserved win; novice-ridden & may find Restricted chance eventually 16

COOLADERRA LADY (Irish) — **I** 16^{4}, **I** 193^{P}, **I** 259^{P}, **I** 320, , **I** 382^{P}, **I** 420^{P}, **I** 480^{5}, **I** 567^{F}, **I** 598^{6}, **I** 605^{4}

COOL APOLLO(NZ) b.g. 10 Gay Apollo - Maple Leaf (NZ) by King's Troop — G W Plenderleith

1996 7(0),5(0),3(0),P(0),**6(14)**,5(0),**P(0)**,6(0)

28	26/1	Marks Tey	(L)	RES	3m	9	GF	*in tch in rear, blnd 10th, outpcd nxt, kpt on 3 out, no dang*	4	11
65	1/2	Horseheath	(R)	RES	3m	10	GF	*prom to 12th, 6th & outpcd 14th, kpt on onepcd*	4	12
270	22/2	Ampton	(R)	MEM	3m	8	G	*chsd ldrs, 4th & outpcd 17th, kpt on onepcd frm nxt.*	3	12
322	1/3	Marks Tey	(L)	OPE	3 1/2m	9	G	*in tch til outpcd 12th, kpt on frm 17th, nvr dang*	5	15
502	15/3	Ampton	(R)	RES	3m	5	GF	*in tch to 15th, sn outpcd, lft poor 3rd 2 out*	3	11
597	22/3	Horseheath	(R)	RES	3m	8	F	*alwys rear, kpt on onepcd frm 15th*	4	12

Maiden winner 95; finished 15 of 17 races since but does not threaten now; finished early 12

COOL BANDIT(IRE) b.g. 7 Lancastrian - Madam Owen — D Curtis

278	23/2	Charing	(L)	RES	3m	17	G	*jmpd rght, clr ldr til hdd 16th, ev ch whn u.r. 2 out*	U	16
1285	29/4	Huntingdon	(R)	HC	3m	10	G	*jmpd right, ld 6th to 15th, no ch with wnr after.*	2	18
1502	16/5	Folkestone	(R)	HC	2m 5f	10	G	*ld and soon clr, hdd after 11th, 2nd and well btn when blnd and u.r. 2 out.*	U	-

Irish Maiden winner 95; quite able but hard ride & non-stayer; best watched 16

COOLBAWN BRAMBLE (Irish) — **I** 138^{P}

COOLBAWN ROSE (Irish) — **I** 13^{P}

COOL CLERIC (Irish) — **I** 485^{F}

COOLE ABBEY (Irish) — **I** 8^{P}, **I** 84, , **I** 137^{3}, **I** 239^{2}, **I** 308^{F}

COOLE LOWER (Irish) — **I** 510^{P}, **I** 565,

COOLFLUGH HERO(IRE) b.g. 6 Torus - Mossy's Niece by Le Bavard (FR) — R H W Major

87	2/2	Wolverhampt'	(L)	MDO	3m	11	GS	*chsd wnr til wknd rpdly aft 11th, p.u. nxt*	P	0
326	1/3	Eaton Hall	(R)	MDN	3m	14	GS	*(fav) cls up, ld 6th, grdly increased ld 30l 3 out, eased flat*	1	16
1385	5/5	Eyton-On-Se'	(L)	RES	3m	4	GF	*(fav) ld to 7th,cls 2nd to 3 out,chal strngly nxt,ran on und prss*	2	16

Ex-Irish; romped home in modest race; off 2 months after & should win Restricted in 98 18

COOLGREEN(IRE) ch.g. 9 Andretti - Emanuela by Lorenzaccio — Neil Allen

1996 **3(NH),5(NH)**

201	15/2	Weston Park	(L)	OPE	3m	16	G	*chsng grp to 10th, fdd rpdly, p.u. 13th*	P	0
377	4/3	Leicester	(R)	HC	2 1/2m 110yds	15	G	*ld to 4th, led apr 6th, hdd 9th, soon lost pl, bhnd when p.u. before four out.*	P	0

Ex-Irish winning pointer; disappointing & brief season; best watched 15

COOL IT (Irish) — **I** 36^{P}, **I** 282^{4}, **I** 348^{S}, **I** 398^{3}, **I** 412^{P}, **I** 437^{6}

COOL IT A BIT b.g. 12 Mandalus - Burlington Miss by Burlington II — W Kerr

1996 P(0),P(0),1(18),B(-),P(0),3(14),P(0)

562	16/3	Lanark	(R)	OPE	3m	8	GS	*disp ld frm 6th til u.r. 8th*	U	-

Changed hands 97 & soon vanished; may be finished now 10

COOL-LAN-SIR (Irish) — **I** 381^{P}, **I** 478^{P}

COOL RASCAL gr.m. 11 Scallywag - Cool Gipsy by Romany Air — A J Owen

1996 P(0),3(0),2(14),3(10),2(13),4(0),3(0)

60	1/2	Kingston Bl'	(L)	MDN	3m	17	GF	*ld to 4th, cls up whn u.r. 7th*	U	-
485	9/3	Tweseldown	(R)	MDO	3m	11	G	*prom, ld 11-15th, ld 2 apr 2 out, sn clr, all out*	1	14
653	22/3	Siddington	(L)	RES	3m	10	F	*trckd ldrs, outpcd 14th, tk poor 3rd last*	3	13
985	12/4	Kingston Bl'	(L)	MEM	3m	4	GF	*sn pshd alng, chsd wnr 5-10th, rdn & wknd 11th, t.o.*	3	0
1466	11/5	Tweseldown	(R)	RES	3m	5	GF	*trckd ldrs, in tch whn p.u. 12th, lame*	P	0

Placed 12 times before hitting the jackpot; non-stayer & problems last start 13

COOL RIVER (Irish) — **I** 184^{P}, **I** 551^{3}

COOLROEDOLLY (Irish) — **I** 217^{P}

COOL SWALLOW (Irish) — **I** 71^{F}, **I** 113^{P}, **I** 212^{P}, **I** 360^{F}, **I** 431^{5}

COOL TOP (Irish) — **I** 272^{5}, **I** 487^{3}, **I** 500^{3}, **I** 561^{P}, **I** 599^{2}

COOLURE QUEEN (Irish) — **I** 575^{P}

COOLVAWN LADY(IRE) b.m. 8 Lancastrian - African Nelly by Pitpan — W R Halliday

1996 P(0),F(-),2(10),1(22),1(23),**6(0)**,F(-),1(23),3(24),2(26)

75	2/2	Market Rase'	(L)	CON	3m	10	GF	*prom, chsd ldr, 6th to 3 out, one pcd aft*	3	23
119	9/2	Wetherby Po'	(L)	OPE	3m	15	GF	*rear, prog 10th, onepcd frm 4 out*	4	21
214	16/2	Southwell P'	(L)	CON	3m	10	GS	*(Jt fav) prom, ld 15th-2 out, no ext*	3	22
287	27/2	Huntingdon	(R)	HC	3m	13	GS	*well pld, hit 13th, wknd after 4 out, t.o..*	7	0
547	16/3	Garthorpe	(R)	XX	3m	7	GF	*disp 2nd plc til apr 3 out,rdn to ld appr last, ran on wll*	1	24
675	23/3	Brocklesby '	(L)	OPE	3m	6	GF	*w.w. in tch,4th & pshd alng 11th,hit nxt,lost tch & p.u.14th*	P	0
771	29/3	Dingley	(R)	OPE	3m	10	G	*cls up, ld 11th, drew clr 6 out, 15l up 2 out, tired flat*	1	23
926	6/4	Garthorpe	(R)	OPE	3m	10	GF	*cls up, 2nd at 13th, no ext frm 2 out*	3	21
1079	13/4	Guilsborough	(L)	OPE	3m	6	GF	*ld 2-3rd, wth ldr til lost plc rpdly 9th, p.u. 11th, b.b.v*	P	0
1188	20/4	Garthorpe	(R)	OPE	3m	9	GF	*lft 2nd 11th, ld aft 15th, 4l clr whn blnd last, hdd nr fin*	2	21
1297	3/5	Hexham	(L)	HC	3m 1f	8	F	*in tch, hdwy to chase ldrs 7th, effort and disp ld 2 out, soon rdn and one pace last.*	2	22
1478	11/5	Garthorpe	(R)	OPE	3m	2	GS	*(fav) trckd rival, ld 11th, drvn & ran on wll flat*	1	19
1530	18/5	Fakenham	(L)	HC	2m 5f 110yds	11	G	*alwys prom, ld 9th, hdd and no ext last.*	2	20
1606	1/6	Dingley	(R)	LAD	3m	13	GF	*trckd ldrs going wll, cls 4th whn pckd 3 out, onepcd aft*	2	22

Incredibly tough now; won 6 of 24 races 96/7; needs easy 3m; inconsistent; win more 98 G/S-F 23

COOLYLINE STAR (Irish) — **I** 302^{U}

COOL YULE(IRE) ch.g. 9 Good Thyne (USA) - Sleigh Lady by Lord Gayle (USA) R W Thomson

607	22/3	Friars Haugh	(L)	RES	3m	8	GF	*hld up, kpt on wll frm 4 out, 2nd & hld whn f last*	F	15
972	7/4	Kelso	(L)	HC	3m 1f	12	GF	*hit 1st, alwys rear, bhnd from 8th.*	4	13
1085	14/4	Hexham	(L)	HC	3m 1f	5	F	*alwys rear, bhnd from 14th.*	3	14
1297	3/5	Hexham	(L)	HC	3m 1f	8	F	*bhnd till some hdwy from 2 out, nvr a factor.*	4	11
1545	24/5	Cartmel	(L)	HC	3 1/4m	14	G	*in rear, hmpd by faller 11th, pushed along apr 4 out (water), soon styd on, nearest fin.*	4	18

Ex-Irish pointer; looks very slow & should stick to Restricteds in 98 - chances at best 16

COOMBESBURY LANE b.m. 11 Torus - Nimble Rose by Furry Glen N F Williams

1996 F(-),3(10),1(17),P(0),F(-),S(-)

638	22/3	Howick	(L)	LAD	3m	10	GF	*mid-div, wknd & p.u. 3 o ut*	P	0
1197	23/4	Andoversford	(R)	LAD	3m	5	F	*ld til jmpd slwly & hdd 5th, 4th whn hit 15th, p.u. aft nxt*	P	0
1308	3/5	Cottenham	(R)	LAD	3m	5	F	*chsd wnr 10th-3 out, not qckn, ran on agn flat*	2	18
1566	25/5	Kingston Bl'	(L)	LAD	3m	5	GF	*svrl slw jmps, prom, chal 14th, ev ch & mstk 3 out, sn btn*	2	12

Open winner 96; problems now & jumps slowly; unlikely to win at 12; best watched 14

COOPERS CLAN (Irish) — **I** 42^{P}, **I** 66^{P}, **I** 95^{4}, **I** 152^{F}, **I** 220, , **I** 343^{3}, **I** 440, , **I** 497,

COPPEEN JEWEL (Irish) — **I** 517^{F}, **I** 597^{1}

COPPER BANK b.g. 9 True Song - Copperclown by Spartan General Mrs H Hutsby

1996 U(-),1(20),P(0)

369	2/3	Mollington	(R)	MEM	3m	13	G	*prom, ld 7th, clr 13th, hdd & no ext aft last*	3	20
1404	5/5	Ashorne	(R)	MEM	3m	7	G	*(fav) prom, ev ch whn ran out apr 13th*	r	-
1448	10/5	Kingston Bl'	(L)	CON	3m	9	G	*rear to hlfwy, prog to 4th at 11th, 3rd at 14th, wknd 3 out*	4	15

Bombed home in Restricted in 96 but lightly raced & yet to repeat; win Confined at best; Soft 20

COPPER DIAL ch.g. 11 My Chopin - Copper Tinsell by Crooner G H D Hopes

1996 P(0)

566	16/3	Lanark	(R)	MDO	3m	10	GS	*u.r. 5th*	U	-
814	31/3	Tranwell	(L)	MDO	3m	9	G	*rear div, t.o. last 5th, p.u. 7th*	P	0
1336	3/5	Mosshouses	(L)	MDO	3m	7	F	*t.o. frm 7th*	5	0

No sign of talent 0

COPPER END (Irish) — **I** 67^{P}, **I** 119^{F}, **I** 122^{B}, **I** 214^{B}, **I** 289^{2}, **I** 436^{5}, **I** 583^{U}

COPPER PAN ch.m. 10 True Song - Copperclown by Spartan General R W Jewitt

1996 F(-),U(-),3(10),4(0)

342	1/3	Corbridge	(R)	MDO	3m	12	G	*mid-div, drppd rear 9th, wll bhnd whn p.u. 12th*	P	0
416	8/3	Dalston	(R)	RES	3m	12	GS	*alwys rear, no ch 14th, t.o.*	5	0
734	29/3	Alnwick	(L)	MDN	3m	6	F	*nvr on trms wth ldrs, lft poor 3rd 10th, grad t.o.*	3	0
1167	20/4	Hexham Poin'	(L)	MEM	3m	5	GF	*u.r. 1st*	U	-

Changed hnads 97 but made no difference - does not stay 0

COPPER THISTLE(IRE) b.g. 9 Ovac (ITY) - Phantom Thistle by Deep Run R S Hunnisett

1996 2(24),1(27),2(29),1(28),1(24),**2(16)**,1(28),**P(0)**

76	2/2	Market Rase'	(L)	XX	3m	12	GF	*prom, outpcd 13th, lft 2nd 2 out, kpt on one pace*	2	22
250	22/2	Brocklesby '	(L)	OPE	3m	6	G	*(fav) cls up, 3rd frm 12th, outpcd frm 4 out, lft in ld last*	1	20
380	4/3	Leicester	(R)	HC	3m	9	G	*alwys prom, left in ld 12th, hdd 4 out, ld again next, ran on well.*	1	21
494	13/3	Cheltenham	(L)	HC	3 1/4m 110yds	18	G	*jmpd right 5th, well bhnd 10th, soon t.o..*	9	0
926	6/4	Garthorpe	(R)	OPE	3m	10	GF	*(fav) mid-div, nvr going wll, nrst fin*	6	11
1188	20/4	Garthorpe	(R)	OPE	3m	9	GF	*raced wd, chsd ldrs to 6th, poor 4th at 15th, styd on wll*	3	19

1360 5/5 Towcester (R) HC 2 3/4m 7 GF *chsd ldrs till dropped rear 7th, styd on from 3 out, not reach ldrs.* 3 19
1534 18/5 Mollington (R) OPE 3m 7 GS *not fluent, ld to 2nd, lost plc 15th, no dang aft* 5 13

Top-class pointer 96; changed hands; novice-ridden; remarkable H/Chase win but mostly feeble now .. 19

COPTIC DANCER b.m. 8 Sayf El Arab (USA) - Copt Hall Royale J J Greenwood
1996 P(0)
914 5/4 Cottenham (R) MDO 3m 4 F *(Jt fav) ld 2nd-5th, in tch, wnet 2nd 13th, ld 2 out, rdn clr flat* 1 10

Won a terrible race only start; only 2 runs to date & much more needed for proper races 12

CORAL EDDY b.g. 10 Current Magic - Blue Coral by Long Till D Marsh
1996 U(-),5(0),U(-),8(0),U(-)
284 23/2 Charing (L) MDO 3m 17 G *t.o. 8th, fin own time* 5 0

Of no account 0

CORKERS FLAME (Irish) — **I** 86^{2}, **I** 133^{2}, **I** 239^{P}, **I** 353^{3}, **I** 422^{4}, **I** 447^{1}, **I** 614^{U}

CORLY SPECIAL b.g. 10 Lyphard's Special (USA) - Courreges by Manado A R Hunt
1996 **4(NH),11(NH)**
17 25/1 Badbury Rin' (L) CON 3m 9 GF *trckd ldrs, ld 11th, hdd & no no ext aft last* 2 19
108 8/2 Milborne St' (L) MXO 3m 6 GF *(fav) j.w. alwys prom, ld 14th-3 out, wknd & blnd last* 3 19
381 4/3 Leicester (R) HC 2m 1f 13 G *in rear, effort 4 out, not reach ldrs.* 3 18
585 18/3 Fontwell (R) HC 2m 3f 7 GF *prom early, bhnd from 7th.* 5 15
1462 11/5 Tweseldown (R) CON 3m 6 GF *trckd ldrs, 2nd & ev ch frm 15th, no ext flat* 2 17

Winning hurdler; does not stay 3m & looked unenthusiastic at times; hard to see a win 18

CORMEEN LORD(IRE) ch.g. 8 Mister Lord (USA) - Sand-Pit Cross by Pitpan J C Sharp
1996 P(0),3(0),4(0),3(0),2(16),5(10)
211 16/2 Southwell P' (L) MDO 3m 15 GS *hld up, steady prog 11th, chsd ldr 15th, ld 2 out, easily* 1 18
324 1/3 Marks Tey (L) RES 3m 16 G *(fav) chsd ldr 8th, ld 11th, clr whn hit 16th, comf* 1 18
473 9/3 Southwell P' (L) CON 3m 10 G *(fav) hld up, prog 9th, went 2nd aft 15th, ld 2 out, sn clr,easily* 1 20

Romped to rapid hat-trick & much improved; could upgrade again if ready 98; G-S 23

CORN BEAT (Irish) — **I** 128^{P}, **I** 226^{B}, **I** 285^{P}

CORNER BOY br.g. 10 Callernish - Rescued by Sir Herbert Mrs E W Wilson
1996 **F(NH)**
215 16/2 Southwell P' (L) LAD 3m 12 GS *(fav) chsng grp, prog to 2nd 7th, ld 3 out, sn clr, easily* 1 26
379 4/3 Leicester (R) HC 3m 7 G *(fav) held up, hdwy 6th, ld and jmpd right 3 out, soon hdd, still ev ch when blundd next, soon btn.* 4 17
773 29/3 Dingley (R) LAD 3m 11 G *(fav) cls up, ld 12th, drew away frm 2 out, comf* 1 24
1266 27/4 Southwell P' (L) LAD 3m 5 G *(fav) trckd ldr, ld apr 5th, made rest, clr 3 out, not extndd* 1 24
1490 13/5 Chepstow (L) HC 3m 7 G *pulld hrd, mstks,, trckd ldr till apr 8th, weakening when hit 5 out, btn when blnd 3 out, t.o..* 3 16

Useful winning chaser; easy winner of 3 points but out of control in H/Chases; hard to beat Ladies 98 .. 26

CORN EXCHANGE b.g. 9 Oats - Travellers Cheque by Kibenka D Wellon
89 4/2 Warwick (L) HC 3 1/4m 4 GF *chasing lding trio when blnd and u.r. 3rd.* U -
149 10/2 Hereford (R) HC 3m 1f 110yds 18 GS *alwys rear, p.u. before 3 out.* P 0
382 5/3 Bangor (L) HC 3m 110yds 6 GS *cl up when blnd and u.r. 4th.* U -
574 16/3 Garnons (L) RES 3m 14 G *alwys rear, losing tch whn mstk & u.r. 11th* U -
753 29/3 Brampton Br' (R) RES 3m 9 GF *mstk 2nd, ld 10th, 5l clr 16th, jnd 2 out, no ext flat* 2 16
1061 13/4 Maisemore P' (L) RES 3m 12 GF *chsd ldrs, blnd 9th, ld 2 out, styd on wll und pres* 1 19
1235 26/4 Brampton Br' (R) INT 3m 10 G *trckd ldr til ld 15th, hdd 3 out, kpt on & rallied flat* 2 18
1366 5/5 Pantyderi (L) INT 3m 6 G *(fav) ld 8th, dist clr aft 15th, unchal* 1 21
1458 11/5 Maisemore P' (L) XX 3m 6 G *chsd wnr, cls 3rd whn blnd & u.r. 14th* U -
1570 26/5 Hereford (R) HC 3m 1f 110yds 14 G *prom till wknd 5 out, blnd badly 3 out, p.u. before next.* P 0

Found form with a venageance 97 & won well twice; needs easy 3m; Confined on cards if same mood 98; 21

CORNISH COSSACK(NZ) br.g. 10 Wolverton - Cotton Bud (NZ) by Balkan Knight J M B Pugh
1996 8(0),2(15),7(11),3(18),5(0),2(0),3(0)
187 15/2 Erw Lon (L) OPE 3m 16 G *nvr bttr thn mid-div, no ch 11th, t.o. & p.u. 15th* P 0
295 1/3 Didmarton (L) OPE 3m 9 G *chsd ldrs, mstk 6th, strgglng 9th, t.o. & p.u. last* P 0
537 16/3 Erw Lon (L) OPE 3m 9 GF *trckd ldrs to 12th, onepcd aft* 4 14
638 22/3 Howick (L) LAD 3m 10 GF *twrds rear, p.u. 3 out* P 0
1007 12/4 St Hilary (R) OPE 3m 10 GF *tongue-strap, prom til wknd 15th* 6 0
1223 26/4 Pyle (R) MEM 3m 6 GS *in tch to 13th, sn wknd, t.o.* 4 0
1557 24/5 Bassaleg (R) CON 3m 9 G *sn dtchd, t.o. frm 11th* 4 0
1600 31/5 Bassaleg (R) CON 3m 3 F *tongue-strap, disp 5th, ld 8-12th, last & wkng nxt* 3 0

Just goes through the motions now 10

CORNISH HARP br.g. 8 Prince Of Peace - Gold Harp by Tormento — M B Ogle

1996 P(0),P(0)

237	22/2	Lemalla	(R) CON 3m	13	S	*mid-div, 9th at 11th, no ch frm 15th*	6	0
460	8/3	Great Treth'	(R) MDO 3m	13	S	*wnt 4th 10th, in tch whn blndrd & u.r. 14th*	U	-
626	22/3	Kilworthy	(L) MDN 3m	14	G	*mid-div, p.u. 14th*	P	0

Tailed off last on only completions 96/7 0

CORNISH TWOWAYS(IRE) b.m. 5 Mandalus - Greek Tan by Pitpan — R J S Linne

53	1/2	Wadebridge	(L) MDO 3m	3	G	*nvr trbld wnr*	3	0
531	15/3	Wadebridge	(L) MDO 3m	14	GF	*bhnd 6th, t.o. & p.u. 11th*	P	0
1583	26/5	Lifton	(R) MDO 3m	11	G	*alwys wll bhnd, p.u. 12th*	P	0

Last when completing & shows no ability yet 0

CORNISH WAYS b.g. 9 Foolish Ways - Decoyanne by Decoy Boy — R J S Linne

1996 4(0),1(13),F(-),P(0)

52	1/2	Wadebridge	(L) INT 3m	4	G	*wll bhnd frm 3rd, still t.o. whn p.u. 14th*	P	0
95	8/2	Great Treth'	(R) MEM 3m	4	GS	*prssd wnr frm 7th, hit 13th, cls engh 3 out, no imp last*	2	11
533	15/3	Wadebridge	(L) INT 3m	5	GF	*alwys cls up, slght ld 14th-16th, kpt on wll und pres*	2	15
1582	26/5	Lifton	(R) INT 3m	10	G	*mid-div, prog 10th, effrt & ev ch flat, just faild*	2	16

Intermediate winner 96; gradually improving & touched off last start; should find a race 98; Good 17

CORN KINGDOM b.g. 11 Oats - Rosa Ruler by Gambling Debt — D W Clark

1996 6(10),F(-),5(0),P(0),2(16)

28	26/1	Marks Tey	(L) RES 3m	9	GF	*bhnd 7th, nvr trbld ldrs aft*	5	11
73	2/2	Higham	(L) RES 3m	3	GF	*(bl) hld up, mstk 5th, prog to ld 8th-9th, ld 11th-4 out, sn btn*	3	13

Maiden winner 94; season lasted week in 97 & best watched at 12 14

CORRIANNE ch.m. 10 Balidar - Serdarli by Miami Springs — Mrs P A Wallis

1996 P(0),P(0),3(15),P(0),5(0),P(0),P(0),**P(0)**

218	16/2	Heythrop	(R) INT 3m	21	G	*ld to 2nd, wknd rpdly & p.u. 10th*	P	0

No longer of any account 0

CORRIB HAVEN(IRE) b.g. 9 Farhaan - Group Problem by Divine Gift — M Weir

47	1/2	Wadebridge	(L) MEM 3m	4	G	*trckd ldrs til u.r. aft 10th, girth broke*	U	-
103	8/2	Great Treth'	(R) MDO 3m	9	GS	*2nd whn u.r. 3rd*	U	-
242	22/2	Lemalla	(R) MDO 3m	10	S	*mstk 4th, 5th at 11th, 6th & btn 13th, p.u. 15th*	P	0
460	8/3	Great Treth'	(R) MDO 3m	13	S	*keen hold, jmp lft, ld til aft 13th, wknd qckly, p.u. 3 out*	P	0
626	22/3	Kilworthy	(L) MDN 3m	14	G	*pllng, ld & sn clr, hdd aft 15th, wknd*	3	10
740	29/3	Higher Kilw'	(L) MDN 3m	15	GF	*slght ld 4-9th, cls up til lost plc steadily frm 16th*	3	0
1112	19/4	Flete Park	(R) MDN 3m	13	GF	*pllng, ld to 7th, in tch til wknd 15th*	4	0
1342	3/5	Flete Park	(R) CON 3m	6	G	*f 1st*	F	-
1400	5/5	High Bickin'	(R) MDO 3m	14	G	*jmpd lft,lft in ld apr 2nd-7th,ld 10-11th,wknd,p.u.16th,lame*	P	0

Headstrong & burns himself out; problem last start; unlikely to win 10

CORRIGEEN RAMBLER (Irish) — **I** 223²

CORRY'S CAPER b.g. 12 Mandalus - Glad Rain by Bahrain — J Turnbull

187	15/2	Erw Lon	(L) OPE 3m	16	G	*wll in rear, brf effrt 11th, t.o. & p.u. 15th*	P	0

Quite useful in 95 but missed 96 & brief appearance 97 suggests ore problems 16

CORSAGE ch.g. 6 Good Times (ITY) - Carnation by Runnymede — L A Mullaney

1996 P(0),3(0)

1073	13/4	Whitwell-On'	(R) MDO 2 1/2m 88yds	17	G	*mid-div, lost tch 11th, p.u. last*	P	0
1409	5/5	Witton Cast'	(R) MDO 3m	15	GS	*towrds rear whn p.u. 7th*	P	0

Two brief campagins so far & no tangible signs of ability 0

CORSHANNA RIVER (Irish) — **I** 98ᴾ, **I** 217⁵, **I** 270⁶

CORSTON FRISBY b.g. 8 Idiot's Delight - Corston Lass — R A Bartlett

162	15/2	Lanark	(R) MDO 3m	16	G	*(fav) disp ld 7th til no ext frm 2 out*	4	13
343	1/3	Corbridge	(R) MDO 3m	14	G	*prom, lft 2nd 10th, wth wnr til outpcd 4 out*	4	0
1429	10/5	Aspatria	(L) MDO 3m	15	G	*hld up, prog 8th, 4th & no imp ldrs 13th, t.o. & p.u. last*	P	0

Not disgraced in all 3 starts; should go much closer in 98 if staying the trip 13

CORVIEW(IRE) b.g. 6 Corvaro (USA) - Rich View by Candy Cane — P T Cartridge

1996 P(0)

437	8/3	Upton-On-Se'	(R) MDO 3m	15	G	*t.o. 4th, p.u. 10th*	P	0
755	29/3	Brampton Br'	(R) MDN 3m	5	GF	*prog to chal 11th, 2l 3rd & ev ch whn f 15th*	F	-
1015	12/4	Bitterley	(L) MDO 3m	12	GF	*cls 5th at 10th, effrt 3 out, ev ch til wknd apr last*	3	11

1238 26/4 Brampton Br' (R) MDO 3m 10 G *(fav) mid-div & rdn 8th, no prog 11th, p.u. aft nxt* P 0

Two promising runs but lame last start; may have chances if fit 98 13

COSA NOSTRA b.g. 11 Furry Glen - The Very Thing — K Cousins

1996 5(0),2(0),P(0)

405 8/3 Llanfrynach (R) RES 3m 15 G *alwys rear, p.u. 2 out* P 0
635 22/3 Howick (L) RES 3m 7 GF *ld til jnd 3 out, onepcd frm nxt* 3 13
901 5/4 Howick (L) RES 3m 6 F *(fav) disp to 13th, effrt to ld 3 out, hdd & not qckn flat* 2 14
1004 12/4 St Hilary (R) MEM 3m 4 GF *(fav) 2nd til ld 7th, qcknd clr 15th, easily* 1 13

Very modest at best but landed Members for 3rd time & best chance again in 98 14

COSMIC FORCE(NZ) b.g. 13 Diagramatic (USA) - Cosmic Lass (NZ) by Roselander — M H Weston

1996 **P(NH)**,**3(NH)**

1575 26/5 Chaddesley ' (L) OPE 3m 10 F *chsd ldrs, effrt 12th, wknd frm 15th* 4 10

Too old now 11

COSMIC RAY b.g. 12 Comedy Star (USA) - Hey Skip (USA) by Bold Skipper (USA) — Darren Page

68 2/2 Higham (L) MEM 3m 4 GF *chsd ldrs, wkind 6th, t.o. & p.u. 12th* P 0
193 15/2 Higham (L) CON 3m 14 G *immed last, hit 1st, t.o. & p.u. 11th* P 0
801 31/3 Marks Tey (L) CON 3m 8 F *alwys rear, lost tch 7th, t.o. 10th, blndrd & u.r. 3 out* U -
1430 10/5 Marks Tey (L) CON 3m 7 G *alwys rear, mstks 3rd & 7th, wknd 10th, p.u. last* P 0

Of no account 0

COST-A-LOT (Irish) — **I** 151⁴, **I** 218ᶠ, **I** 286ᴾ, **I** 344ᴾ, **I** 406ᶠ

COT LANE ch.g. 12 Remainder Man - Smokey Princess by My Smokey — T P Tate

1996 1(20),6(0),**4(10)**,2(22),7(12)

34 26/1 Alnwick (L) OPE 3m 9 G *1st ride, in tch in rear, effrt 15th, styd on wll frm 2 out* 3 21
113 9/2 Wetherby Po' (L) CON 3m 10 GF *ld to 11th, prom, hrd drvn & styd on gamely to ld flat* 1D 20
265 22/2 Duncombe Pa' (R) CON 3m 15 G *prom, lost plc 13th, styd on wll frm 3 out* 3 20
506 15/3 Dalton Park (R) CON 3m 16 GF *prom, disp 3rd-6th, not qckn frm 4 out* 4 14
893 5/4 Wetherby Po' (L) MEM 3m 3 F *(fav) ld til disp 11th, lft dist clr nxt, easily* 1 15
1072 13/4 Whitwell-On' (R) MXO 4m 21 G *prom til fdd frm 14th* 7 15
1349 3/5 Gisburn (R) CON 3m 11 GF *(fav) (bl) ld 5-12th, ld 14th-nxt, ld agn 2 out, styd on well last* 1 21
1512 17/5 Corbridge (R) OPE 3m 10 GS *(bl) ld til disp 7th, ld 10th-4 out, onepcd nxt, lft 2nd last* 2 20

Good schoolmaster in 97 & retains form well; stays very well; can win at 13; F-S 21

COTTAGE BREEZE (Irish) — **I** 91ᴾ, **I** 474ᴾ

COTTAGE COUNSEL (Irish) — **I** 57, , **I** 588¹

COTTAGE GIRL (Irish) — **I** 141ᴾ, **I** 204ᶠ, **I** 295¹

COTTAGE LASS (Irish) — **I** 189ᴾ

COTTIERS DEN (Irish) — **I** 156ᴾ, **I** 221ᶠ, **I** 273ᴾ

COTTON EYED JIMMY (Irish) — **I** 29²

COUGAR D'AVELOT (Irish) — **I** 253ᴾ

COUNT BALIOS(IRE) b.g. 8 Trojan Fen - Soyez Sage (FR) by Grundy — M H Wood

1996 P(0),1(16),6(11)

45 1/2 Larkhill (R) RES 3m 14 GF *cls up, prssd wnr 13th-nxt, wknd 15th* 5 15
223 16/2 Heythrop (R) RES 3m 19 G *(fav) w.w. prog 9th, chsd ldr 13-15th, onepcd aft* 3 13
377 4/3 Leicester (R) HC 2 1/2m 110yds 15 G *prom, mstk 7th, soon bhnd.* 5 12
653 22/3 Siddington (L) RES 3m 10 F *(Jt fav) ld 4th, made most aft, mstks 6th & 3 out, kpt on wll 2 out* 1 20
975 8/4 Heythrop (R) INT 3m 3 F *(fav) chsd ldr, ld appr last, rdn clr flat* 1 18

Maiden winner 96; found ideal races on Firm when winning; needs easy 3m; can win Confined; G-F 20

COUNTERBID gr.g. 10 Celio Rufo - Biddy The Crow by Bargello — J M Turner

1996 2(22),2(20),P(18),4(14),**4(0)**,**4(17)**,**3(17)**

71 2/2 Higham (L) LAD 3m 6 GF *hld up, slw jmp 4th, 3rd at 12th, wknd steadily frm 14th* 4 14
195 15/2 Higham (L) LAD 3m 14 G *mid-div til blnd & u.r. 14th* U -
270 22/2 Ampton (R) MEM 3m 8 G *trckd ldrs,ld gng wll 15th,rdn 2 out,nt run on, hdded run in* 2 17
497 15/3 Ampton (R) CON 3m 9 GF *rr, prog 12th, 4th & nt qkn 3 out, ran on agn appr last.* 2 17
912 5/4 Cottenham (R) LAD 3m 3 F *w.w. reluc & rmndr 12th, outpcd 16th, no ch aft* 3 12
1029 12/4 Horseheath (R) LAD 3m 3 HD *(bl) keen hold, ld 4th, made rest, clr 3 out, eased flat* 1 19
1287 29/4 Huntingdon (R) HC 2 1/2m 110yds 14 G *(bl) chsd ldr 5th, rdn and ev ch apr 2 out, unable to qckn.* 2 23
1506 16/5 Folkestone (R) HC 2m 5f 8 G *(bl) ld, jmpd slowly 1st and soon hdd, led again 4th, rdn and hded apr 2 out, no ch with wnr.* 2 25

Dead 23

COUNTRY BARLE b.g. 9 Town And Country - Pelant Barle by Prince Barle — Mrs Irene Hodge

318 1/3 Marks Tey (L) MDN 3m 13 G *jmp wll, ld, sn clr, just hdd whn f 2 out* F 15

Decent debut & may have won; injured but should win if fit 98 15

COUNTRY BREW ch.m. 9 Country Retreat - Totally Tiddly by French Vine Major C Marriott
1996 P(0),P(0),4(10),P(0)

373 2/3 Mollington (R) MDN 3m 14 G *cls up, outocd & mstk 13th, no ch 15th, kpt on wll flat* 2 0
974 8/4 Heythrop (R) MEM 3m 5 F *chsd ldr to 8th, last frm 12th, rallied & ch 2 out, onepcd* 5 0
1166 20/4 Mollington (R) MDO 3m 9 GF *in tch, disp 3rd & outpcd frm 14th, wknd & p.u. last* P 0

Slow & struggles to stay; unlikely to win 10

COUNTRY GEM b.g. 6 Town And Country - Auto Elegance by Brave Shot W R Britton

628 22/3 Kilworthy (L) CON 3m 12 G *bhnd thruout, t.o. p.u. apr 14th* P 0

No promise 0

COUNTRY LORD ch.g. 8 Town And Country - Nearly A Lady by Nearly A Hand Ms Sarah Walwin
1996 **P(NH)**

300 1/3 Didmarton (L) RES 3m 23 G *t.o. in last pair, blnd 9th, p.u. nxt* P 0
652 22/3 Siddington (L) LAD 3m 5 F *last frm 4th, wknd 10th, t.o. & p.u. 3 out* P 0
988 12/4 Kingston Bl' (L) LAD 3m 7 GF *jmpd vry slwly, alwys t.o., tk wrng course aft 13th,rtrcd* 4 0
1216 26/4 Woodford (L) MDN 3m 13 G *n.j.w. sn wll bhnd, t.o. 7th* 4 0
1459 11/5 Maisemore P' (L) MDO 3m 12 G *alwys last, t.o. 7th* 5 0
1568 25/5 Kingston Bl' (L) MDO 3m 11 GF *ld to aft 2nd, wknd 9th, t.o. 13th* 7 0

Bumbles around with veteran rider 0

COUNTRY MADAM b.m. 6 Town And Country - Happy Manda by Mandamus K R J Nicholas

172 15/2 Ottery St M' (L) MDN 3m 14 G *in tch, wknd 15th, p.u. 3 out* P 0
553 16/3 Ottery St M' (L) MDN 3m 15 G *mid-div, outpcd & p.u. 12th* P 0

Some promise on debut but yet to develop - may do better in 98 12

COUNTRY PARSON(IRE) ch.g. 8 The Parson - Fisalmar Isle Vii D Morgan
1996 **7(NH),10(NH)**

29 26/1 Marks Tey (L) MDN 3m 10 GF *prom, cls 3rd & going wll whn p.u. aft 15th, lame* P 0

Unfortunate 1st appearance & will hopefully have chances to do better 13

COUNTRY PRACTICE (Irish) — I 311P, I 522S

COUNTRY TARROGEN b.g. 8 Town And Country - Sweet Spice by Native Bazaar Mrs M Cooper
1996 **U(-),11(0),5(19)**

34 26/1 Alnwick (L) OPE 3m 9 G *(fav) j.w. made all, clr 3 out, comf* 1 25
119 9/2 Wetherby Po' (L) OPE 3m 15 GF *(fav) disp to 3rd,prom,chal 4 out,ld 2 out,hdd & no ext apr last* 2 26
226 21/2 Haydock (L) HC 3m 11 G *held up, imp hfwy, chasing ldrs when pkd 3 out, kept on apr last.* 2 29
379 4/3 Leicester (R) HC 3m 7 G *held up, hdwy 7th, ld 6 out, hdd when b.d. 3 out.* B -
890 4/4 Aintree (L) HC 2 3/4m 14 G *f 1st.* F -

Dead 29

COUNTRY VET b.m. 11 Town And Country - Ginnett by Owen Anthony John Pyecroft
1996 2(19),P(0),2(18),P(0)

279 23/2 Charing (L) CON 3m 10 G *not fluent, in tch, hrd rdn frm 16th, styd on onepcd* 3 17

Quite useful at best but finished early 96 & brief show 97; stays; needs give 18

COUNT SURVEYOR ch.g. 10 Corawice - Miss Magello by Bargello T R Beadle

584 17/3 Newcastle (L) HC 2 1/2m 11 GF *p.u. lame after 1st.* P 0

The briefest of appearances 0

COUNTY BASH b.m. 6 Shaab - Treloweth Julie by Flandre II Mrs W S Cook

1521 17/5 Bratton Down (L) MDO 3m 16 GS *schoold rear, p.u. 8th* P 0
1584 26/5 Lifton (R) MDO 3m 13 G *mid-div, rpd prog frm 4 out, just faild* 2 12

Possibly unlucky 2nd start (weak race) & should go one better in 98 14

COURIER'S WAY(IRE) b.g. 6 Riberetto - Coursing Bird by Crash Course Mrs C Kendrick

274 22/2 Ampton (R) RES 3m 10 G *mstks, in tch bad mstk 9th, last frm nxt til p.u. 14th* P 0
324 1/3 Marks Tey (L) RES 3m 16 G *bhnd frm 7th, t.o. frm 15th* 7 0
798 31/3 Marks Tey (L) RES 3m 7 F *alwys prom,ld 7th,hdd 3 out,rlld ld last,styd on strng last* 1 15
1031 12/4 Horseheath (R) INT 3m 3 HD *ld til aft 10th, lft in ld nxt, hdd & blnd 3 out, rlld flat* 2 16
1277 27/4 Fakenham P-' (L) CON 3m 10 G *mstks, in tch, blnd & rmndrs 6th, sn lost plc, no dang aft* 6 0
1435 10/5 Marks Tey (L) INT 3m 8 G *ld, clr & mstk 6th, hdd 16th, wknd frm 3 out* 4 13

Irish Maiden winner 96; found modest Restricted; handles Firm & could win again 98 17

COURSE SPRITE (Irish) — I 156P

COURT AMBER (Irish) — **I** 23^{P}, **I** 102^{2}, **I** 146^{P}, **I** 198^{1}, **I** 279^{4}

COURT RAMBLE (Irish) — **I** 104^{P}, **I** 196^{P}, **I** 297^{P}

COURT THYNE (Irish) — **I** 29^{P}, **I** 106^{P}, **I** 275, , **I** 509^{S}

COUTURE QUALITY ro.g. 11 Absalom - Miss Couture by Tamerlane — Mrs T W Bridges

1996 5(0),U(-),**5(10)**,**7(12)**,P(0),**P(0)**,U(-)

193 15/2 Higham (L) CON 3m 14 G *mid-div, nvr able to rch ldrs, onepcd 3 out* 5 14
441 8/3 Higham (L) INT 3m 7 G *ld to 2nd, drppd rear aft, blnd 14th, p.u. nxt* P 0

Lost last 19 starts & finished early 97 10

COUTURE TIGHTS b.g. 12 Mummy's Game - Miss Couture by Tamerlane — M A Lloyd

1996 6(0),4(13),1(18),3(16),2(21)

466 8/3 Eyton-On-Se' (L) LAD 3m 7 G *w.w., cls order 12th, 2nd 2 out, ran on onepce* 2 20
638 22/3 Howick (L) LAD 3m 10 GF *(fav) hld up rear, prog hlfwy, unable to chal* 3 14

Solid pointer at best but interrupted season 96 & short campaign 97; best fresh; do well to win at 13 ... 18

COWARNE ADVENTURE ch.g. 5 Green Adventure (USA) - Ticover by Politico (USA) — Mrs S A Godsall

706 29/3 Upper Sapey (R) MDO 3m 15 GF *last by 11th & p.u. 15th,* P 0
1065 13/4 Maisemore P' (L) MDO 3m 13 GF *t.o. 9th, p.u. 14th* P 0

No signs of ability 0

COZY COTTAGE (Irish) — **I** 194^{P}, **I** 240, , **I** 298^{P}

CRABAPPLE HILL (Irish) — **I** 409^{1}

CRACKING IDEA(IRE) b.g. 9 The Parson - Game Sunset by Menelek — Mrs P K J Brightwell

1996 **4(NH)**,**1(NH)**,**U(NH)**,**5(NH)**,**7(NH)**

322 1/3 Marks Tey (L) OPE 3 1/2m 9 G *trckd ldrs, cls 4th whn f 14th* F -
440 8/3 Higham (L) OPE 3m 5 G *trckd ldr, effrt 15th, ld nxt, lft clr 2 out, kpt on* 1 23
710 29/3 High Easter (L) OPE 3m 5 F *w.w. hit 3rd, wnt 2nd 7th, ev ch 15th, rdn & btn appr last* 2 21
1115 19/4 Higham (L) OPE 3m 4 GF *(fav) alwys going easily, trckd ldr 4th, ld 15th, sn clr, easily* 1 22
1529 18/5 Fakenham (L) HC 3m 110yds 9 G *held up, hdwy 9th, outpcd 3 out, styd on und pres run-in.* 3 20

Winning chaser 96; solid enough in points & won 2 soft races; should win again 98; G-F 23

CRACK REGIMENT (Irish) — **I** 352^{4}, **I** 551^{P}, **I** 595^{1}

CRAFTSMAN b.g. 11 Balinger - Crafty Look by Don't Look — G W Paul

1996 1(25),1(23),3(20),1(18),2(21)

25 26/1 Marks Tey (L) CON 3m 5 GF *(fav) chsd ldr, ld 8th-2 out, no ext und pres* 2 25
71 2/2 Higham (L) LAD 3m 6 GF *(fav) hld up, mstk 2nd, disp 8th & 12th, drew clr 3 out, blnd last* 1 22
195 15/2 Higham (L) LAD 3m 14 G *(fav) ld 3-4th & 6th-16th, 2nd aft til dmtd fin* 3 22
377 4/3 Leicester (R) HC 2 1/2m 110yds 15 G *blnd and u.r. 3rd.* U -
500 15/3 Ampton (R) LAD 3m 4 GF *ld 2nd-13th, lft in ld nxt, drw clr 2 out, easily* 1 22

Useful pointer at best; likes to dictate; goes well fresh; made mistakes 97; G/F-S 23

CRAFTY GUNNER ch.g. 7 Gunner B - Craftsmans Made by Jimsun — Ms M Teague

205 15/2 Weston Park (L) MDN 3m 10 G *rear, some late prog, no ch wth wnr* 2 0
327 1/3 Eaton Hall (R) MDN 3m 11 GS *mid-div in tch, ran on 14-15th, sn btn, p.u. 3 out* P 0
666 23/3 Eaton Hall (R) MDO 3m 10 GF *w.w. prog 5 out, ev ch whn mstk 3 out, ran on* 3 13
941 6/4 Tabley (R) MDO 3m 11 G *(fav) hld up, prog to 2nd 14th, chal on bit last, ld flat, clvly* 1 14
1178 20/4 Sandon (L) XX 3m 6 GF *mid-div hlfwy, prog to chal 2 out, lkd hld whn f last* F 18
1526 17/5 Bredwardine (R) RES 3m 13 G *(fav) mstks, rear, prog to chs ldrs 11th, wknd 13th, p.u. 3 out* P 0

Steadily progressed but ran badly last start (sweating); should make amends in Restricted 98; Good ... 18

CRAGGY ISLAND (Irish) — **I** 80^{F}, **I** 91^{P}, **I** 304^{2}, **I** 384^{1}, **I** 486^{P}, **I** 569^{4}, **I** 604^{F}

CRAIG BURN b.m. 8 Arkan - Burning Mirage by Pamroy — N M L Ewart

1996 U(-),2(0),4(0),6(0)

134 9/2 Alnwick (L) MDO 3m 11 G *cls up, ld 4th, clr 6th, 4l up whn f 4 out* F -

Unfortunate only start 97 but vanished & still hase plenty to prove 13

CRAIGDALE b.g. 6 Mirror Boy - Craigie Way by Palm Track — Robert Robinson

132 9/2 Alnwick (L) LAD 3m 9 G *sn wll bhnd, t.o. & p.u. 3 out* P 0

Of no account 0

CRANAGH MOSS(IRE) ch.g. 8 Le Moss - Cranagh Lady by Le Bavard (FR) — Iwan Thomas

1996 1(14),3(15),U(-),4(0),3(0)

189 15/2 Erw Lon (L) RES 3m 14 G *blnd 3rd, prom til outpcd 15th, btn whn mstk 2 out* 6 10
300 1/3 Didmarton (L) RES 3m 23 G *mstk 1st, t.o. in last pair, p.u. 3 out* P 0
534 16/3 Erw Lon (L) MEM 3m 3 GF *ld 6-9th, strgglng frm 13th* 2 10

845 31/3 Lydstep (L) RES 3m 5 F *alwys 3rd/4th, onepcd* 4 0

Maiden winner 96; downhill since & runs as if something amiss 10

CRASHLAND (Irish) — I 207P

CRAWN HAWK b.r.g. 12 Croghan Hill - Gin An Tonk by Osprey Hawk P C Shires

1996 F(-),U(-),4(15)

1576 26/5 Chaddesley ' (L) XX 3m 12 F *alwys rear, wll bhnd frm 7th, t.o. & p.u. 13th* P 0
1605 1/6 Dingley (R) RES 3m 13 GF *made most til f 11th* F -

Maiden winner 95; very late to appear 97 & time may well have passed him by now 13

CRAZY DREAMS (Irish) — I 144⁵, I 193⁵

CRAZY OTTO ch.g. 11 Nearly A Hand - Papa's Paradise by Florus F Allan

1996 4(18),3(18),P(0),6(0)

195 15/2 Higham (L) LAD 3m 14 G *alwys strgglng rear, p.u. 11th* P 0
349 2/3 Market Rase' (L) LAD 3m 5 GF *cls up, lft 3rd 12th, outpcd 15th, nrly sntchd 2nd* 3 12

Ladies winner 95; deteriorated further 97 & another win beyond him now 12

CREATIVE FLIGHT (Irish) — I 296P, I 458F, I 493P, I 547⁵

CREATIVE THOUGHT (Irish) — I 167F, I 265F, I 401⁵, I 488F

CREDIT TRANSFER (Irish) — I 37², I 216⁴

CREEDY VALLEY b.g. 6 Old Jocus - Jubilee Leigh by Hubble Bubble Mrs S Prouse

553 16/3 Ottery St M' (L) MDN 3m 15 G *mid-div, lost tch 12th, p.u. 14th* P 0
794 31/3 Bishopsleigh (R) MDO 3m 12 G *mid-div to 14th, lost tch & p.u. 17th* P 0
1597 31/5 Bratton Down (L) MDO 3m 12 F *10s-7/2, chsng grp, effrt & blnd 15th, 3rd frm nxt, kpt on* 3 11

Well-backed in weak race last start & showed enough to suggest win on the cards in 98 14

CREEVES NEPHEW b or br.g. 13 Trimmingham - Charlotts Fancy by Charlottesvilles Flyer Captain D R Parker

1996 P(0),8(0),P(0)

192 15/2 Higham (L) MEM 3m 3 G *ld to 3rd, ld 10th, drew clr aft 3 out* 1 0
273 22/2 Ampton (R) OPE 3m 7 G *w.w. in tch, lft 3rd 12th, no prog frm 3 out* 4 13
321 1/3 Marks Tey (L) INT 3m 10 G *alwys bhnd, t.o. frm 10th* 6 0

Won a joke contest & last in other 2 starts 0

CREME SUPREME (Irish) — I 123P, I 214⁵, I 331P, I 372¹

CRESCENT MOONSHINE b.m. 10 Bohemond - Magenta Girl by Southcoates Boy Mrs J Wilcox

1012 12/4 Bitterley (L) MEM 3m 6 GF *last frm 3rd, lost tch 6th, t.o. & p.u. aft 11th* P 0

Of no account 0

CRESTAFAIR ch.m. 9 Crested Lark - Karafair by Karabas Miss H M Irving

1996 4(0),F(-),4(10),P(0),3(15),U(-),3(15)

13 25/1 Cottenham (R) MDO 3m 10 GF *w.w. prog to 2nd 16th, hit nxt, no hdwy aft* 2 13
69 2/2 Higham (L) MDO 3m 8 GF *sttld bhnd ldrs,prog 8th,mstk 10th,chal 2 out,rdn clr flat* 1 15
198 15/2 Higham (L) RES 3m 14 G *trckd ldng pair til f hvly 13th* F -

Dead 14

CRESTED EYE b.m. 6 Crested Lark - Miss Shut Eye by Homeboy Mrs D E King

990 12/4 Kingston Bl' (L) MDN 3m 11 GF *schoold in rear, in tch aft 13th, eased & p.u. nxt* P 0

Eye-catching debut & sure to do better in 98 13

CRESTWOOD LAD(USA) ch.g. 8 Palace Music (USA) - Sweet Ellen (USA) by Vitriolic (USA) W O Yardley

655 22/3 Siddington (L) RES 3m 10 F *pllng, ld til ran out 5th* r -
881 1/4 Upton-On-Se' (R) MDN 3m 13 GF *cls up whn b.d. 5th* B -
1018 12/4 Bitterley (L) MDO 3m 13 GF *alwys prom, kpt on onepcd frm 15th* 3 12
1209 26/4 Clifton On ' (L) MDO 3m 16 GS *disp to 10th, not qckn, 4th & outpcd 5 out* 5 12
1330 3/5 Chaddesley ' (L) MDN 3m 6 GF *ld to 11th,chal wnr apr 3 out,1l down whn blnd & u.r. last,rmntd* 3 13
1459 11/5 Maisemore P' (L) MDO 3m 12 G *mstk 8th, chsd ldr 3rd-10th, wknd 14th* 3 0

Runs passably but does not stay & a win most unlikely 11

CRIMSON BOW b.m. 7 Balinger - Crimson Flag by Kinglet R A Owen

1996 U(-),P(0)

206 15/2 Weston Park (L) MDN 3m 9 G *mid to rear, no dang to ldng pair* 3 0
768 29/3 Whittington (L) MDO 3m 10 S *mstks, 3rd til wknd 13th* 5 0

Last both times & shows no real promise 0

CROCK D'OR b.g. 7 Heights Of Gold - Pegleg by New Member H Macdonald

1996 r(-),2(10)

283 23/2 Charing (L) MDO 3m 16 G *alwys prom, 4th & rdn 15th, kpt on to chs wnr apr last* 2 14
582 16/3 Detling (L) MDN 3m 16 F *hdwy 14th, 2nd 3 out, no pce to chal* 2 12

Ran well both starts (fair races) & will certainly win if ready in 98 15

CROCKET LASS b.m. 14 Cagirama - Lady Crocket by Arrigle Valley — Miss Fiona M Hunter
1996 U(-),2(0),8(0),3(0),2(0),8(0)

355 2/3 Great Stain' (L) LAD 3m 9 S *rear, lost tch 6th, t.o. & p.u. 12th* P 0
426 8/3 Charm Park (L) LAD 3m 12 GF *prom early, strgglng 8th, sn wll bhnd* 10 0
505 15/3 Dalton Park (R) MEM 3m 6 GF *ld to 9th, fdd, btn whn u.r. 15th* U -
674 23/3 Brocklesby ' (L) LAD 3m 5 GF *mstk 4th, last frm 6th, no ch frm 11th* 5 0
1249 26/4 Easingwold (L) LAD 3m 6 GS *rewar, t.o., p.u. 13th* P 0
1346 3/5 Gisburn (R) LAD 3m 5 GF *alwys rear, mstk & u.r.aft 6th* U -

No longer of any account 0

CROFT COURT b.g. 6 Crofthall - Queen Of Dara by Dara Monarch — Alan Cowing
1996 P(0),1(13),2(14)

278 23/2 Charing (L) RES 3m 17 G *hld up, prog 11th, nvr rchd ldrs, 6th whn eased & p.u. last* P 0
303 1/3 Parham (R) RES 3m 10 G *alwys prom, 4th & outpcd 4 out, styd on wll to tk 2nd flat* 2 14

Maiden winner 96; impossible task 2nd start 97 & Restricted certain if fit 98 17

CROI (Irish) — I 18², I 99ᴾ, I 182ᴮ, I 265¹

CROMOGUE MINSTREL (Irish) — I 87¹, I 256ᴾ

CROMWELL POINT gr.h. 11 Another Realm - Miss Eliza by Mountain Call — P Sadler
1996 7(0),**P(0)**,7(14),6(0),2+(19),3(18),6(10),**P(0)**,**5(14)**,**6(0)**,3(15)

673 23/3 Brocklesby ' (L) CON 3m 8 GF *in tch til bhnd 13th, no ch frm 15th* 5 0
694 29/3 Stainton (R) CON 3m 11 F *prom til outpcd 13th, sn lost tch* 8 0

Confined winner 95; disappointing since & beaten last 27 races; best avoided now 0

CROOKEDSTONE (Irish) — I 435³

CROOKED STREAK bl.g. 12 Majestic Streak - Hartfell by Lord Nelson (FR) — John Shearer
1996 2(12),P(0)

155 15/2 Lanark (R) MEM 3m 4 G *ld til rdr lost control aft 4th, u.r. bef nxt* U -

Gives the crowd some fun in his annual Members jaunt 0

CROSSWELL STAR(IRE) ch.g. 6 Salluceva - Margaret Hulse by Arctic Chevalier — A J Sendell
1996 F(-)

527 15/3 Cothelstone (L) MDN 3m 14 GS *twrds rear til p.u. 13th* P 0
867 31/3 Kingston St' (R) MDO 3m 6 F *rear, wnt remote 3rd aft 14th* 3 0
1260 27/4 Black Fores' (R) MDO 3m 12 F *alwys rear, fin 6th* 0 0
1497 14/5 Cothelstone (L) MDO 3m 10 GF *mid-div,outpcd 10th,gd prog 3 out,swtchd apr last,ld nr fin* 1 13
1551 24/5 Mounsey Hil' (R) RES 3m 13 G *mstks, alwys bhnd, bdly hmpd 14th, t.o. & p.u. 16th* P 0

Forced home in blanket finish to modest race & more needed for Restricted chances in 98 15

CROSSWORD (Irish) — I 35ᴾ

CROTTYS BRIDGE (Irish) — I 71ᶠ, I 126ᴾ, I 212⁵, I 292, , I 360¹, I 376ᴾ

CROWDED HOUSE (Irish) — I 59ᶠ, I 121², I 177³, I 313², I 327ᶠ, I 374³

CROWN AND ANCHOR b.g. 5 Lord David S (USA) - Mescalin by Politico (USA) — W Brown

353 2/3 Great Stain' (L) CON 3m 9 S *rear, mstk 3rd, u.r. 6th* U -
424 8/3 Charm Park (L) RES 3m 12 GF *rear, lost tch 11th, p.u. 13th* P 0

Not yet of any account 0

CROWNHILL CROSS ch.g. 6 Dutch Treat - Royal Cross by Royal Smoke — F R Bown
1996 P(0),**6(NH)**,**10(NH)**,**8(NH)**

104 8/2 Great Treth' (R) MDO 3m 9 GS *wll bhnd frm 10th, t.o. whn ref & u.r. 14th* R -
310 1/3 Clyst St Ma' (L) INT 3m 9 HY *ref 2nd* R -
626 22/3 Kilworthy (L) MDN 3m 14 G *rear, mstk 11th, t.o. whn p.u. apr 14th* P 0
1038 12/4 Lifton (R) INT 3m 4 F *not alwys fluent, wll bhnd whn p.u. 14th* P 0
1109 19/4 Flete Park (R) OPE 4m 9 GF *prom til wknd 14th, t.o., walked in* 7 0
1343 3/5 Flete Park (R) MDO 3m 13 G *prog to 2nd at 10th, cls up & ev ch til wknd apr 2 out* 6 0
1486 11/5 Ottery St M' (L) MDO 3m 17 G *mid-div, no ch whn p.u. 15th* P 0
1585 26/5 Lifton (R) MEM 3m 2 G *(fav) lft solo 3rd* 1 0

Of no account & won a nothing contest 0

CROWN JEWEL b.g. 10 Standard Bearer (USA) - Perfect Blue by Blue Lightning — W D'Arcy

568 16/3 Garnons (L) CON 3m 12 G *cls 2nd til ld 15th, jnd 2 out, no ext flat* 3 19
656 22/3 Siddington (L) MDN 3m 7 F *(fav) prom, rdn 14th, chal 3 out, ev ch til no ext flat* 2 14
934 6/4 Charlton Ho' (L) MDO 3m 10 G *(fav) chsd ldrs, disp 2nd 10-14th, 3rd whn p.u. 2 out, dsmntd* P 0

Sensational debut but downhill after & lame last start; novice-ridden; best watched if returning 13

CROW ROAD (Irish) — I 413^{F}

CROWS CROSS (Irish) — I 63^{F}, I 265^{P}

CRUCIS(IRE) gr.g. 6 Kalaglow - Brave Advance (USA) by Bold Laddie (USA) — J W Haydon
1996 P(0),4(10),F(-),F(-)

176 15/2 Ottery St M' (L) RES 3m 17 G *alwys mid-div, no ch whn p.u. 3 out* P 0

Fragile & may be finished now 0

CRUIKIT RAINBOW(IRE) gr.m. 6 Celio Rufo - Little Gort by Roselier (FR) — Mrs Sheila Walker

208 16/2 Southwell P' (L) MDO 3m 9 GS *in tch til f 4th* F -
269 22/2 Duncombe Pa' (R) MDO 3m 16 G *prom til wknd 11th, t.o. 3 out* 5 0

Last when finishing & no signs of ability yet 0

CRUISE A HOOP b.g. 8 Cruise Missile - Hoopoe by Tower Walk — W M A Davies
1996 P(0),3(12),F(-),F(-),6(0),5(0),2(14),1(16)

877 1/4 Upton-On-Se' (R) RES 3m 17 GF *prom, ld 7th, drew clr apr 3 out, mstk last, unchal* 1 23
1064 13/4 Maisemore P' (L) CON 3m 13 GF *(fav) unruly strt, ld 2nd, 3l clr apr 2 out, styd on strngly* 1 23
1455 11/5 Maisemore P' (L) CON 3m 8 G *(fav) ld & mstk 2nd, mstks 10 & 14th, shkn up 2 out, ran on well* 1 21

Maiden winner 96; vastly improved; well-ridden; needs easy 3m; could win Open on 97 form; G-F 24

CRUISE FREE b.g. 8 Cruise Missile - Lyons Charity by Impecunious — H J Manners
1996 5(0),3(0),3(10),7(0),**4(NH)**

1143 19/4 Larkhill (R) XX 3m 2 F *chsd ldr, rdn apr last, 4l down & btn whn lft solo* 1 10

Fortunate winner of joke race & has no further prospects 10

CRUISER TOO b.g. 10 Cruise Missile - Delegation by Articulate — D Stephens

479 9/3 Southwell P' (L) MDO 3m 15 G *s.s. t.o. whn blnd 5th, p.u. 12th* P 0
549 16/3 Garthorpe (R) MDO 3m 16 GF *alwys bhnd, t.o. frm 11th* 7 0

Last when finishing & looks talentless 0

CRUNCH TIME(IRE) ch.g. 8 Erin's Hope - Grishkin's Bliss by Charlottesville — K Wynne

464 8/3 Eyton-On-Se' (L) INT 3m 12 G *rear 8th, 4th in tch 14th, wknd qckly, p.u. 4 out* P 0
664 23/3 Eaton Hall (R) MDO 3m 12 GF *w.w. prog 10th, ld 14th-2 out, ran on, lkd 3rd* 2 13
722 29/3 Sandon (L) MDO 3m 10 GF *(fav) w.w. off pace, prog 13th, ran on wll, not rch wnr* 2 13

Ran passably in modest Maidens (odds-on last start); may go one better if fit 98 14

CRUNCHY NUT (Irish) — I 28^{6}, I 66^{2}, I 287, , I 311^{2}, I 413^{1}

CUBA b.g. 5 Soviet Star (USA) - Rosetta Stone by Guillaume Tell (USA) — Philip Newton

79 2/2 Market Rase' (L) MDO 2m 5f 9 GF *chsd ldrs, ev ch frm 11th, no ext app last* 3 10
777 29/3 Dingley (R) MDO 2m 5f 8 G *(fav) cls up, 2nd 6 out, disp nxt, ld 2 out, hdd last* 2 12

Fair efforts to date; good stable; should win if ready 98 15

CUBAN SKIES(IRE) b.g. 7 Strong Gale - Express Film — N G King
1996 **13(NH),10(NH),9(NH)**

209 16/2 Southwell P' (L) MDO 3m 7 GS *rear & blnd 7th, lsng tch whn u.r. 12th* U -
755 29/3 Brampton Br' (R) MDN 3m 5 GF *ld to 4th, disp cls 2nd whn ran out wing 13th* r -
1015 12/4 Bitterley (L) MDO 3m 12 GF *last & rdn 11th, prog nxt, 5th & wkng whn u.r. 3 out* U -
1386 5/5 Eyton-On-Se' (L) MDO 2 1/2m 8 GF *prom, 3rd 4 out, fdd, onepcd* 5 0
1541 18/5 Wolverhampt' (L) MDO 3m 15 GS *mid-div to 13th, wknd, no ch & p.u. 2 out* P 0

No form under Rules & last on only completion in points 0

CUCKLINGTON b.g. 6 El Conquistador - Belmore by Homeboy — B Pike

43 1/2 Larkhill (R) MDO 3m 10 GF *trckd ldrs, blnd 9th, mstk & u.r. nxt* U -
181 15/2 Larkhill (R) MDO 3m 17 G *mstks, alwys rear, t.o. 12th, p.u. 15th* P 0
314 1/3 Clyst St Ma' (L) MDN 3m 11 HY *prom, ld 4 out, f nxt* F -
392 8/3 Barbury Cas' (L) MDN 3m 9 G *in tch, prog 11th, 3rd & mstk 15th, onepcd frm 3 out* 4 12
692 29/3 Little Wind' (R) MDO 3m 8 GF *ran in sntchs, 3rd & outpcd 4 out, lft 2nd nxt, not qckn* 3 11

Possibly unlucky 3rd start but looks less than enthusiastic & placed in weak races 11

CUCKOO PEN br.g. 12 Swing Easy (USA) - Peachy by Reliance II — Miss Janet Menzies
1996 P(0)

580 16/3 Detling (L) RES 3m 11 F *mid-div, 4th 4 out, wknd nxt, wll bhnd whn p.u. last* P 0
965 6/4 Penshurst (L) MEM 3m 3 F *hld up, efft 4 out, nvr pce to chal* 3 0

No longer of any account 0

CUCKROO (Irish) — I 154^{P}, I 221^{P}, I 273^{P}, I 500^{P}, I 544^{4}, I 579^{P}, I 611^{P}

CUDDIES PORTER (Irish) — I 318^{P}, I 558^{P}, I 564,

CUDDLE LOVER b.m. 7 Morgans Choice - Mandover by Mandamus — Mrs Jane M Wickett

625	22/3 Kilworthy	(L) MDN 3m	14	G	*bhnd til p.u. apr 3 out*	P	0

No encouragement on debut 0

CUKEIRA ch.m. 8 Cruise Missile - Keira by Keren — R Paisley

1996 F(-),2(11),F(-),1(15),2(16),2(13)

32	26/1 Alnwick	(L) RES 3m	11	G	*jnd ldrs 7th, ld 3 out, mstk nxt, hdd last, rallied flat*	2	19
563	16/3 Lanark	(R) RES 3m	8	GS	*bhnd til gd hdwy frm 4 out, no imp on wnnr*	2	17
607	22/3 Friars Haugh	(L) RES 3m	8	GF	*(fav) alwys rear, bhnd whn p.u. bfr 2 out*	P	0

Maiden winner 96; 2 good runs 97 but unhappy on ground last start; should win Restricted if fit 98 19

CULLAUN (Irish) — I 43P, I 146F, I 1712, I 337,

CULM BARON b.g. 9 Baron Blakeney - Culm Port by Port Corsair — D Morgan

213	16/2 Southwell P'	(L) RES 3m	16	GS	*ld to 2nd, grad lost plc, wll bhnd 8th, p.u. 12th*	P	0
443	8/3 Higham	(L) RES 3m	7	G	*(bl) disp to 2nd, ld 8-9th, wknd & last 12th, lost tch & p.u.16th*	P	0
1080	13/4 Guilsborough	(L) RES 3m	11	GF	*(bl) sn pshd alng, prom to 10th, wknd, t.o. & p.u. 3 out*	P	0

Maiden winner 95; missed 96 & looks finished now 0

CULNAVEIGH (Irish) — I 369P, I 432P, I 462P, I 506B

CULPEPPERS DISH b.g. 6 Lochnager - Faint Praise by Lepanto (GER) — Mrs L A Parker

186	15/2 Erw Lon	(L) MDN 3m	13	G	*ld 3-7th, wknd 12th, p.u. 14th*	P	0
365	2/3 Garnons	(L) MDO 2 1/2m	14	GS	*prom, disp 4th-6th, wknd 8th, t.o. & p.u. 3 out*	P	0
543	16/3 Erw Lon	(L) MDN 3m	11	GF	*nvr nrr than mid-div*	4	0
842	31/3 Lydstep	(L) MDO 3m	12	F	*ld to 14th, fdd, p.u. 2 out*	P	0
963	6/4 Pantyderi	(L) MDN 3m	6	F	*ld to 3 out, lkd hld whn lft in ld nxt, kpt on*	1	10
1194	22/4 Chepstow	(L) HC 3m	11	GF	*prom to 6th, bhnd when tried to refuse 9th, p.u. before next.*	P	0
1365	5/5 Pantyderi	(L) RES 3m	10	G	*ld 3rd, 2nd at 11th, s.u. 14th*	S	-
1560	24/5 Bassaleg	(R) OPE 3m	7	G	*in tch to 9th, sn wknd, t.o. 12th*	6	0
1613	7/6 Umberleigh	(L) RES 3m	13	F	*ld to aft 4th, chsng grp til wknd 12th, t.o. & p.u. 2 out*	P	0

Fortunate winner of bad race & no other form; will struggle in 98 10

CUMBERLAND BLUES(IRE) b.g. 8 Lancastrian - Tengello by Bargello — John L Holdroyd

1996 P(0),F(-),5(10),0(0),P(0),1(0),**8(0)**,**2(16)**

117	9/2 Wetherby Po'	(L) LAD 3m	10	GF	*alwys going wll, chsd ldrs, ld 14th, drew clr frm 2 out*	1	25
165	15/2 Witton Cast'	(R) LAD 3m	6	F	*(fav) j.w. made all, drew clr 15th, unchal*	1	25
355	2/3 Great Stain'	(L) LAD 3m	9	S	*(fav) ld, jmpd rght, hdd & fdd 2 out*	5	17
426	8/3 Charm Park	(L) LAD 3m	12	GF	*(fav) ld til hdd 2 out, wknd qckly*	5	17
508	15/3 Dalton Park	(R) LAD 3m	4	GF	*j.w. ld to 12th & 14th-nxt,ld 4 out til wknd & hdd nxt,eased*	4	12
1249	26/4 Easingwold	(L) LAD 3m	6	GS	*ld to 14th, 3rd aft, tk 2nd flat, held by wnnr*	2	20
1297	3/5 Hexham	(L) HC 3m 1f	8	F	*made all, rdn 2 out, styd on well from last.*	1	24
1490	13/5 Chepstow	(L) HC 3m	7	G	*ld, jmpd right, hdd after 13th, soon btn, t.o. when p.u. before 3 out.*	P	0
1546	24/5 Hexham	(L) HC 2 1/2m 110yds	10	GF	*nvr far away, left in ld and hmpd 3 out, hdd next, one pace from last.*	2	23
1589	31/5 Market Rasen	(R) HC 2 3/4m 110yds	10	GF	*(fav) ld till hdd 4 out, rallied to ld run in, gamely.*	1	25

Much improved; front-runner; probably best R/H; more Ladies; possibly H/Chases in 98; G-F 25

CURIE CRUSADER(IRE) gr.g. 6 Belfort (FR) - Katysue by King's Leap — J Tudor

187	15/2 Erw Lon	(L) OPE 3m	16	G	*mid-div til wknd 9th, t.o. & p.u. 11th*	P	0
636	22/3 Howick	(L) CON 3m	12	GF	*cls 2nd whn ran out 8th*	r	-
715	29/3 Llanvapley	(L) OPE 3m	8	GF	*alwys towrds rear*	5	0
1132	19/4 Bonvilston	(R) CON 3m	9	G	*alwys rear, t.o. & p.u. last*	P	0

Last when finishing & of no account in points 0

CURLEY GALE (Irish) — I 74U, I 138P, I 2351, I 3091, I 3803

CURRAGH LORD (Irish) — I 1653, I 255P, I 3335, I 485P

CURRAHEIGH (Irish) — I 4932, I 591U

CURRENT ATTRACTION b.m. 11 Paddy's Stream - Chorabelle by Choral Society — Miss Katie Thory

1996 7(16),F(-),9(0),5(18),1(15)

123	9/2 Cottenham	(R) INT 3m	13	GF	*alwys bhnd, t.o. 12th, p.u. 15th*	P	0
274	22/2 Ampton	(R) RES 3m	10	G	*prom til f 7th*	F	-
597	22/3 Horseheath	(R) RES 3m	8	F	*1st ride, chsd ldrs til outpcd 9th, t.o. 13th*	6	0
838	31/3 Thorpe Lodge	(L) RES 3m	5	F	*2nd to 6th, 5th rdn alng 12-13th, t.o. 6 out*	4	0
909	5/4 Cottenham	(R) MEM 3m	2	F	*ld to 5th, mstk 3 out, ev ch last, unable qckn*	2	11
1032	12/4 Horseheath	(R) RES 3m	2	HD	*(fav) jmpd wll, disp til ld 2 out, drw clr*	1	10
1117	19/4 Higham	(L) CON 3m	5	GF	*ld to 7th, sn lost plc, t.o. 13th*	4	0
1286	29/4 Huntingdon	(R) HC 3m	10	G	*alwys rear, t.o. 14th, p.u. after 3 out.*	P	0
1306	3/5 Cottenham	(R) INT 3m	4	F	*made most to 9th, wknd 13th, t.o.*	3	0
1430	10/5 Marks Tey	(L) CON 3m	7	G	*alwys rear, last at 9th, t.o. 12th, ran on 3 out, tk 3rd fin*	3	11

1608 1/6 Dingley (R) INT 3m 11 GF *chsd ldng trio to 8th, sn wknd, t.o. 10th* 5 0

Schoolmaster in 97; won a nothing race & only Members on Firm offers any hope in 98 11

CURRENT SCANDAL (Irish) — **I** 184^P

CURROW HILL (Irish) — **I** 311^5, **I** 438^5

CUSH PRINCESS (Irish) — **I** 10^2, **I** 139^2, **I** 234^1, **I** 380^2

CUSSANE CROSS(IRE) gr.g. 9 Roselier (FR) - Regency Cherry by Master Buck G J Jones

260 22/2 Newtown (L) RES 3m 16 G *mstk 3rd & rmndr, bhnd, some prog 13th, no dang, p.u. 2 out* P 0
467 8/3 Eyton-On-Se' (L) RES 3m 15 G *mid-div hlfwy, ran on frm 5 out, nrst fin* 5 12

Missed 95/6 & unable to recapture form; can only be watched 13

CUT A NICHE ch.g. 7 Callernish - Cut And Thrust by Pardal Miss Jennifer Pidgeon
1996 P(0),2(10)

252 22/2 Brocklesby ' (L) MDO 3m 9 G *cls up 3rd/4th, cont 4 out, ld aft 2 out, prmsng* 1 16
676 23/3 Brocklesby ' (L) RES 3m 14 GF *(fav) chsd ldrs to 9th, 6th & wkng 13th, p.u. nxt* P 0

Very lightly-raced; scored well but disappointed after; may upgrade if ready 98 16

CUTE AGREEMENT (Irish) — **I** 92^P, **I** 111^1

CUTE WORD ch.m. 6 Hasty Word - Cute Miss by Space King Mrs H M Arnold

623 22/3 Hutton Rudby (L) MDO 3m 9 GF *rear & sn wll bhnd, t.o. & p.u. 11th* P 0
699 29/3 Stainton (R) MDO 3m 7 F *rear, mstk 3rd, hmp apr 5th, sn wll bhnd, t.o.* 4 0
1074 13/4 Whitwell-On' (R) MDO 2 1/2m 88yds 16 G *alwys rear, t.o. 6th* 9 0

Last on both completions & shows nothing 0

CUTHAYSMAYFLOWER ch.m. 9 North Street - May's Baby by Full Of Beans Miss D J Curtis

461 8/3 Great Treth' (R) MDO 3m 12 S *rear & schooling til p.u. apr 11th* P 0
1373 5/5 Cotley Farm (L) MDO 3m 6 GF *prom early, lost tch 10th, p.u. apr 12th* P 0
1554 24/5 Mounsey Hil' (R) MDO 3m 14 G *alwys rear, lost tch 11th, p.u. 14th* P 0

Yet to get involved & already quite old 0

CWM ARCTIC b.m. 10 Cisto (FR) - Menel Arctic by Menelek Mrs B Brown
1996 **P(NH),U(NH),7(NH),F(NH),P(NH)**

201 15/2 Weston Park (L) OPE 3m 16 G *cls up 4th, chsng grp to 6 out, sn btn* 7 0
1019 12/4 Bitterley (L) MDO 3m 12 GF *ld 2nd-11th, rdn 13th, disp btn 3rd whn f 2 out* F -
1237 26/4 Brampton Br' (R) RES 3m 13 G *cls up til 15th, grad wknd frm nxt* 5 0

No form under Rules; not disgraced 2nd start but should concentrate on Maidens 11

CWM BYE ch.g. 6 Hubbly Bubbly (USA) - To Oneiro by Absalom Ms B Brown
1996 U(-),2(14)

755 29/3 Brampton Br' (R) MDN 3m 5 GF *w.w. prog to 4l 3rd at 14th, ld 3 out, kpt on well* 1 12
1013 12/4 Bitterley (L) CON 3m 14 GF *mid-div, effrt 12th, ev ch nxt, wknd frm 3 out* 4 13

Confirmed promise; beaten in decent Confined & Restricted likely in 98; only 4 runs to date 17

CYNICAL WIT (Irish) — **I** 61^U, **I** 222^P

CZARYNE ch.m. 9 Czarist - Tyne Bridge by Red Bridge Mrs J D Percy
1996 5(0),2(11)

614 22/3 Friars Haugh (L) MDN 3m 13 GF *ld to 3rd, ld agn brfly 8th, lost tch by 10th* 5 0
731 29/3 Alnwick (L) MXO 4m 7 F *ran in sntchs, prog to 2nd 13th,ld/disp 16th-4out, wknd* 3 13
1052 13/4 Lockerbie (R) MDN 3m 10 F *alwys handy, ld 4 out, styd on well* 1 16
1102 19/4 Hornby Cast' (L) LAD 3m 7 G *mid-div til wknd frm 4 out* 4 17

Safe & won 7m+ Maiden; could find stamina test Restricted in 98 16

DADDY LONG LEGGS ch.g. 10 Over The River (FR) - Mary Deen by Avocat Mrs O Hubbard
1996 **8(NH),2(NH),6(NH),P(NH),P(NH)**

277 23/2 Charing (L) MEM 3m 6 G *prom, ld 11-14th, sn outpcd, fin tired* 2 12
1125 19/4 Penshurst (L) MEM 3m 3 GF *ld/disp to 3 out, styd on to ld agn apr last* 1 12

Won a virtual match 2nd start; yet to prove much but Restricted possible in weak area 14

DADDY WARBUCKS (Irish) — **I** 405^B, **I** 459^5, **I** 499^F, **I** 563^2, **I** 601^1

DAD'S DELIGHT b or br.m. 6 Lyphento (USA) - Fashion Lady by Heres Mrs P J Awdry

284 23/2 Charing (L) MDO 3m 17 G *u.r. 2nd* U -
391 8/3 Barbury Cas' (L) MEM 3m 6 G *w.w. prog 13th, ev ch nxt, blnd 3 out, sn outpcd* 3 0
658 22/3 Badbury Rin' (L) MDN 3m 6 F *in tch to 12th, lost plc nxt, t.o. & p.u. 5 out* P 0
1270 27/4 Little Wind' (R) MDO 2 1/2m 10 GF *chsd ldng grp til lost tch 12th, 5th & no ch whn u.r. 3 out* U -
1498 14/5 Cothelstone (L) MDO 3m 9 GF *ld to 2 out, rdn & kpt on onepcd* 2 10
1583 26/5 Lifton (R) MDO 3m 11 G *alwys prom, wknd 4 out* 3 0

Does not stay & 2nd in a bad Maiden; will need fortune to score 11

DAD'S DILEMMA b.g. 6 Impecunious - Paddy's Pipe by Paddy's Stream Terry E G Smith

481	9/3 Tweseldown	(R) MEM 3m	6	G	*chsd ldr, wkng whn f 11th*	F	-
513	15/3 Larkhill	(R) MDO 3m	10	GF	*last whn ran out 2nd*	r	-
747	29/3 Barbury Cas'	(L) MDO 3m	3	F	*not keen early, prog 7th, mstk 14th, nvr nrr*	2	0
1059	13/4 Hackwood Pa'	(L) MDO 3m	6	GF	*rear whn u.r. 3rd*	U	-

Well beaten in virtual match & unpromising so far 0

DAD'S PIPE b.g. 7 Nearly A Hand - Paddy's Pipe by Paddy's Stream Terry Ernest Smith

1996 3(13),1(12),2(15)

287	27/2 Huntingdon	(R) HC 3m	13	GS	*bhnd when f 3rd.*	F	-
481	9/3 Tweseldown	(R) MEM 3m	6	G	*chsd ldr, outpcd & mstks frm 12th, t.o.*	3	0
601	22/3 Parham	(R) RES 3m	4	F	*mstks, just ld 6th, blnd 13th, hdd nxt, fdd, p.u. aft 2 out*	P	0
873	31/3 Hackwood Pa'	(L) RES 3m	6	F	*(bl) jmpd bdly rght, 2nd early, t.o. hlfwy*	4	0

Members winner 96; disappointing in 97 & can only be watched now 10

DAFTASABRUSH(IRE) b.m. 5 Brush Aside (USA) - Grey Squirrell by Golden Gorden J W Beddoes

470	8/3 Eyton-On-Se'	(L) MDN 2 1/2m	12	G	*alwys rear, t.o. & p.u. 9th*	P	0
670	23/3 Eaton Hall	(R) RES 3m	15	GF	*alwys rear, p.u. 3 out*	P	0

Just a couple of educational efforts to date 0

DAINTY DAISY (Irish) — I 438F

DAISY LANE b.m. 8 Mart Lane - Alto Sax by Prince de Galles Miss P Kerby

1996 F(-)

700	29/3 Upper Sapey	(R) MEM 3m	8	GF	*mstk in rear, last hlfwy, p.u. aft 4 out*	P	0
1019	12/4 Bitterley	(L) MDO 3m	12	GF	*lost tch 3rd, p.u. 7th*	P	0

Yet to complete from 3 outings 96/7 0

DAISY'S PAL b.m. 6 Governor General - Pallomere by Blue Cashmere A Bunn

1996 P(0),P(0)

571	16/3 Garnons	(L) MDN 2 1/2m	13	G	*rear frm 5th, in tch til wknd & p.u. 2 out*	P	0

Yet to complete from 3 outings 96/7 0

DAKEEM b.m. 5 Silly Prices - Rilin by Ribston K Little

160	15/2 Lanark	(R) MDO 2m 5f	10	G	*sn t.o., p.u. 2 out*	P	0
564	16/3 Lanark	(R) MDO 2 1/2m	13	GS	*sn bhnd, t.o. whn p.u. 2 out*	P	0

Schooling & shows nothing yet 0

DALAMETRE b.g. 10 Dutch Treat - Composite by Compensation Mrs J Z Munday

1996 **2(NH)**

362	2/3 Garnons	(L) OPE 3m	11	GS	*ld/disp til def adv aft 15th, styd on well 3 out*	1	20
568	16/3 Garnons	(L) CON 3m	12	G	*ld to 14th, ev ch 2 out, onepcd und pres*	4	19
892	5/4 Hereford	(R) HC 2m	11	GF	*(fav) hdwy and rdn along 6th, effort 3 out, soon wknd.*	3	13
1097	19/4 Bangor	(L) HC 2 1/2m 110yds	11	G	*handy, chsd wnr from 7th, no impn from 4 out.*	2	18
1488	12/5 Towcester	(R) HC 2m 110yds	16	GS	*bhnd from 6th, t.o. when p.u. before last.*	P	0

Changed hands 97; never reached expected level but found modest Open & may win again; tricky ride 20

DALMIGAVIE LAD b.g. 5 Dancing High - Moschata by Star Moss A R Trotter

234	22/2 Friars Haugh	(L) MDO 3m	15	G	*sn bhnd, p.u. 3 out*	P	0

Just an educational run to date 0

DALMORE b.g. 11 Runnett - Fade To Grey by Gay Fandango (USA) Mrs S J Gospel

119	9/2 Wetherby Po'	(L) OPE 3m	15	GF	*rear, lost tch 10th*	6	10
166	15/2 Witton Cast'	(R) OPE 3m	8	F	*mid-div, prog 12th, ev ch 4 out, onepcd*	4	19
265	22/2 Duncombe Pa'	(R) CON 3m	15	G	*reluctant to raceg,gd prog 9th,ld 4 out,sn clr,hd & wkndlast*	5	16
354	2/3 Great Stain'	(L) OPE 3m	7	S	*rear, outpcd 10th, t.o.*	4	10
507	15/3 Dalton Park	(R) OPE 3m	8	GF	*rear, outpcd 14th, sn wll bhnd*	4	16
694	29/3 Stainton	(R) CON 3m	11	F	*alwys in rear, styd on onepce frm 4 out, nvr nrr*	6	17
1070	13/4 Whitwell-On'	(R) XX 3m	9	G	*(bl) mid-div, prog 11th, wknd 4 out*	6	0
1347	3/5 Gisburn	(R) OPE 3m	8	GF	*in tch, 4l 3rd at 14th, wknd rpdly*	6	11

Consistent but missed 96 & beaten all 26 starts 92-7; likely to extend sequence 13

DALUSAWAY(IRE) b.m. 8 Mandalus - Head Away by Regular Guy L Oakes

1996 3(0)

81	2/2 Wolverhampt'	(L) MDN 3m	13	GS	*mid-div, prog 10th, ld 16th til apr 2 out where mstk, no ext*	2	13

331 1/3 Eaton Hall (R) RES 3m 17 GS *chsd ldrs, strng run 2 out, no ext flat* 3 16
666 23/3 Eaton Hall (R) MDO 3m 10 GF *(fav) ld til chal flat, hdd post, lame* 2 14

Unfortunate last start in many senses; good enough to win if fit in 98 15

DALUS EXECUTIVE (Irish) — **I** 192[F], **I** 321[P]

DAMERS CAVALRY b.g. 14 Stanford - Margery (FR) by Cadmus II R Burgess

762 29/3 Whittington (L) MEM 3m 5 S *(fav) not alwys fluent, lft in ld 6th, disp til f 15th (dead)* F -

Dead 0

DAMERS TREASURE ch.g. 11 General Ironside - Dalmond by Diamonds Are Trump (USA) O P J Meli

1996 9(0),3(0),6(11),**3(10),7(0)**

372 2/3 Mollington (R) RES 3m 19 G *alwys rear, no ch frm 11th, t.o.* 8 0
433 8/3 Upton-On-Se' (R) RES 3m 18 G *mid-div whn blnd & u.r. 9th* U -
876 1/4 Upton-On-Se' (R) MEM 3m 7 GF *(bl) ld to 2nd, lft in ld 6th, hdd 15th, lft in ld nxt, styd on* 1 11
1149 19/4 Chaddesley ' (L) RES 3m 6 GF *(bl) chsd wnr to 14th, sn rdn & btn* 3 0
1417 10/5 Warwick (L) HC 3 1/4m 8 G *(bl) chsd ldrs, mstk 2nd, hit 11th, soon bhnd,* 5 0
1526 17/5 Bredwardine (R) RES 3m 13 G *bhnd frm 5th, t.o. 12th* 7 0

Very poor now but clear round enough to complete Members double; safely ignored now 10

DAMIENS PRIDE(IRE) b.g. 7 Bulldozer - Riopoless by Royal And Regal (USA) Paul C N Heywood

553 16/3 Ottery St M' (L) MDN 3m 15 G *handy, 3rd at 13th, chsd alng 4 out, styd on well* 2 14
1399 5/5 High Bickin' (R) MDO 3m 12 G *hld up in tch,3rd frm 13th,effrt to disp ld whn ran out last* r 16
1486 11/5 Ottery St M' (L) MDO 3m 17 G *(Co fav) hld up, prog 13th, 3rd nxt, ld 3 out, ran on* 1 16

Ran well in all three races (decent events) & deserved win; should upgrade in 98; Good 18

DAMIS b.m. 8 Damister (USA) - Tuft Hill by Grundy Mrs V Payne

212 16/2 Southwell P' (L) MDO 3m 14 GS *rear, in tch til rdn & wknd apr 12th, p.u. 14th* P 0

No promise yet 0

DAMOLLY ROSE (Irish) — **I** 72[U], **I** 119[P], **I** 228[1]

DANBURY LAD(IRE) b.g. 9 Bustinetto - Clyzari by Pinzari Dr P P Brown

1996 3(16),1(21),1(21),1(20),2(18)

360 2/3 Garnons (L) CON 3m 10 GS *(fav) trckd ldrs, effrt 14th, no prog nxt, p.u. 2 out* P 0
650 22/3 Siddington (L) CON 3m 8 F *(fav) cls up, disp 13th til ld 3 out, slw jmps last 2, pshd out* 1 18
1196 23/4 Andoversford (R) CON 3m 6 F *(fav) chsd ldrs, ld 8th, rdn last, no ext & hdd nr fin* 2 19

Won 5 of last 10 but owes much to placing; unimpressive in 97 & may struggle to maintain record; F-S 20

DANCE FEVER(IRE) ch.g. 7 Orchestra - Dance Away by Red God D Woollacott

172 15/2 Ottery St M' (L) MDN 3m 14 G *cls up til f 8th* F -
244 22/2 Lemalla (R) MDO 3m 12 S *prom til mstk 13th, rmndrs, bhnd & p.u. 15th* P 0
553 16/3 Ottery St M' (L) MDN 3m 15 G *mid-div, lost tch 14th, t.o. & p.u. last* P 0
1314 3/5 Holnicote (L) MDO 3m 8 G *alwys prom, ld 16th til hdd & no ext aft last* 3 13

1st form last start in weak race & should go close to a win in 98 14

DANCE ON SIXPENCE b.g. 9 Lidhame - Burning Ambition by Troy R W Gardiner

801 31/3 Marks Tey (L) CON 3m 8 F *chsd ldr,ld 7th,gng wll 11th,ld 15th,jnd 3 out,ran on 3 out* 1 19
1277 27/4 Fakenham P-' (L) CON 3m 10 G *chsd ldrs, blnd 5th, 4th & rdn 15th, went mod 2nd flat* 2 17
1376 5/5 Northaw (L) CON 3m 3 F *(fav) ld to 5th, & agn 8th, pckd 13th, hdd nxt, rddn 2 out, kpt on* 2 18
1430 10/5 Marks Tey (L) CON 3m 7 G *trckd ldrs, lft in ld aft 10th, jnd 4 out, hdd nxt, ran on* 2 16

Winning selling hurdler; consistent in 2nd class races but easily brushed aside; may win again 19

DANCING BAREFOOT ch.m. 8 Scallywag - High Venture by High Award J T Heritage

1996 **7(NH),P(NH),8(NH),12(NH)**

111 8/2 Milborne St' (L) MDN 3m 8 GF *mid-div til blnd & u.r. 7th* U -
658 22/3 Badbury Rin' (L) MDN 3m 6 F *chsd ldr, ev ch 3 out, blnd nxt, no ext* 3 0

Not disgraced 2nd start but vanished; may go close in 98 12

DANCING MIKE (Irish) — **I** 118[P], **I** 175[P], **I** 247, , **I** 365[P]

DANCING SUPREME ch.g. 7 Nestor - Vulgan's Joy by Vulgan Slave Mrs B Stokes

1996 F(-)

372 2/3 Mollington (R) RES 3m 19 G *alwys rear, t.o. & p.u. 11th* P 0
776 29/3 Dingley (R) MDO 2m 5f 10 G *ref to race* 0 0
1175 20/4 Sandon (L) CON 3m 8 GF *rear, t.o. & p.u. 4 out* P 0
1209 26/4 Clifton On ' (L) MDO 3m 16 GS *mid-div, prog 10th, 2nd 5 out, just outpcd frm 2 out* 3 14
1541 18/5 Wolverhampt' (L) MDO 3m 15 GS *alwys prom, ev ch 4 out, not qckn apr last* 3 0

Ran well enough when 3rd in big field but not certain to take the vital leap to victory in 98 13

DANDELION LAD(IRE) ch.g. 5 Phardante (FR) - Jocks Fancy by Patch Mrs P Rowe

317 1/3 Marks Tey (L) MDN 3m 13 G *alwys last, t.o. 8th, p.u. apr 11th* P 0

Shows nothing yet 0

DANEGELD(IRE) b.g. 6 Danehill (USA) - Julip by Track Spare Col M J F Sheffield

160 15/2 Lanark (R) MDO 2m 5f 10 G *alwys handy, ld 11th til f 2 out* F -
1074 13/4 Whitwell-On' (R) MDO 2 1/2m 88yds 16 G *(fav) hld up, prog 8th, ld 4 out, hrd prssd flat, just hld on* 1 16
1101 19/4 Hornby Cast' (L) RES 3m 14 G *disp til 3rd, trckd ldrs aft, chal 3 out,ld nxt,ran on gamly* 1 19
1405 5/5 Witton Cast' (R) CON 3m 10 GS *mid-div, prog to disp ld 4 out, hdd & not qckn flat* 2 20
1418 10/5 Easingwold (L) MEM 3m 6 GF *(fav) rear,prog 12th, ld 4 out, sn clr, ran wd apr 2 out,rdn out* 1 18

Consistent & improving; ran in competitive races; unsuited going last run; upgrade in 98; G-S 23

DANE ROSE b.m. 11 Full Of Hope - Roella by Gold Rod Mrs Roger Guilding
1996 P(0),4(0),3(15),1(17),4(15),**7(NH),6(NH),4(NH)**

257 22/2 Newtown (L) LAD 3m 12 G *in tch to 11th, wknd, 10th & wll btn whn u.r. 3 out* U -
398 8/3 Llanfrynach (R) MEM 3m 6 G *ld early, 3rd frm 11th, wknd 3 out* 3 10
636 22/3 Howick (L) CON 3m 12 GF *rear til f 9th* F -
714 29/3 Llanvapley (L) CON 3m 15 GF *rear early, stdy prog 13th, 4th 2 out, ran on wll* 2 16

Restricted winner 96; only one good run 97 & then vanished; may struggle if back at 12 15

DANGAN HILL (Irish) — **I** 352^{F}
DANGAN LAD(USA) (Irish) — **I** 191^{P}, **I** 280^{3}, **I** 484^{P}, **I** 589^{1}
DANGER FLYNN (Irish) — **I** 11^{2}, **I** 53^{2}, **I** 135^{2}, **I** 317^{1}, **I** 486^{3}
DANGEROUS DAN (Irish) — **I** 536^{P}, **I** 548^{P}, **I** 571^{4}
DANIKAR (Irish) — **I** 354^{P}, **I** 551^{P}
DANNY MANN (Irish) — **I** 119^{P}, **I** 316^{P}
DANNY RHY ch.m. 8 Rymer - Danny D'Albi by Wrens Hill C James

7 19/1 Barbury Cas' (L) RES 3m 14 GF *mid-div, losing tch whn f 11th* F -

Disappeared on 1st day of season 0

DANODILE VI (Irish) — **I** 287^{P}
DANTE ALAINN (Irish) — **I** 167^{P}, **I** 272^{P}
DANTE LAD (Irish) — **I** 134^{P}, **I** 168^{P}, **I** 267^{3}, **I** 336, , **I** 382^{P}
DANTE'S PRIDE(IRE) ch.g. 8 Phardante (FR) - Una's Pride by Raise You Ten G J Fisher
1996 P(0),P(0),P(0),P(0),P(0),P(0),6(0)

390 8/3 Barbury Cas' (L) MDN 3m 15 G *hld up, wll bhnd hlfwy, t.o. & p.u. 2 out* P 0
706 29/3 Upper Sapey (R) MDO 3m 15 GF *2nd/3rd til lost plc 16th, renewd efft apr last, fin wll* 3 13
1019 12/4 Bitterley (L) MDO 3m 12 GF *(fav) ld 1st, prog to ld 13th, jnd last, no ext flat* 2 15
1330 3/5 Chaddesley ' (L) MDN 3m 6 GF *(fav) chsd ldr, ld 11th, made rest, lft wll clr last* 1 14

Scrambled home in poor race - Baimbridge's latest miracle; another needed for Restricted success 14

DANTE'S REWARD (Irish) — **I** 260^{P}, **I** 381^{3}
DANTE'S TOI (Irish) — **I** 304,
DANTE'S WHISTLE (Irish) — **I** 207^{P}, **I** 302, , **I** 338^{1}, **I** 475^{P}
DAPHNI(FR) ch.g. 6 Bad Conduct (USA) - Ragniole (FR) by Mondain (FR) Mrs Jan Wood
1996 B(-),F(-),P(0),1(15)

85 2/2 Wolverhampt' (L) LAD 3m 11 GS *alwys rear, 8th & no ch at 11th, t.o. & p.u. 3 out* P 0
203 15/2 Weston Park (L) RES 3m 11 G *mid-div, wknd 12th, sn rear, p.u. 5 out* P 0
332 1/3 Eaton Hall (R) RES 3m 18 GS *cls up, 3rd at 10th, 4th & in tch whn f 4 out* F -
468 8/3 Eyton-On-Se' (L) RES 3m 11 G *chsng grp thruout, 2nd 4 out, ran on onepce* 2 15
852 31/3 Eyton-On-Se' (L) RES 3m 11 GF *alwys chsng grp, unable to rch chal postition* 3 0
1349 3/5 Gisburn (R) CON 3m 11 GF *chsng ldrs, 5l 4th at 13th, fdd* 5 10

Maiden winner 96; changed hands & only one fair run 97; best watched 14

DAPHNIS(USA) b.g. 8 Lead On Time (USA) - Dancing Vaguely (USA) by Vaguely Noble Miss M C Holt
1996 **8(NH),7(NH)**

86 2/2 Wolverhampt' (L) OPE 3m 9 GS *wth wnr 6th til blnd & u.r. 8th* U -

216 16/2 Southwell P' (L) OPE 3m 12 GS *in tch till f 7th* F -
351 2/3 Market Rase' (L) OPE 3m 10 GF *hld up, prog 10th, 4th & btn 14th, no dang aft* 5 16

Winning hurdler 95; unlikely to stay & finished early; best watched 14

DAREDEVIL(IRE) b.g. 6 Balinger - Kilgabriel Rose by Flower Robe Victor Ogden

269 22/2 Duncombe Pa' (R) MDO 3m 16 G *rear & sn detachd, wll bhnd 10th, p.u. 12th* P 0
509 15/3 Dalton Park (R) XX 3m 13 GF *rear, sn t.o., p.u. 15th* P 0

Schooling to date 0

DARE SAY b.g. 14 Kris - Pampered Dancer by Pampered King P Hudson
1996 6(0),6(12),3(12),U(-),3(18)

350 2/3 Market Rase' (L) CON 3m 11 GF *alwys bhnd, lost tch 13th, t.o.* 5 0

No longer of any account 0

DARE TO DEEL (Irish) — I 106³, I 243ᴾ, I 430ᴾ, I 452,

DARIKA LAD gr.g. 9 Belfort (FR) - Lindrake's Pride by Mandrake Major S V McLaughlin
1996 **P(NH)**

354 2/3 Great Stain' (L) OPE 3m 7 S *rear, mstk 11th, lost tch 14th, t.o. & p.u. 2 out* P 0

No longer of any account 0

DARING DAISY b.m. 9 Balinger - Avado by Cleon T B Brown
1996 P(0)

654 22/3 Siddington (L) MDN 3m 10 F *rear frm 5th, t.o. 10th, p.u. 12th* P 0
1083 13/4 Guilsborough (L) MDN 3m 15 GF *mstk 5th, alwys bhnd, t.o. 13th* 7 0
1209 26/4 Clifton On ' (L) MDO 3m 16 GS *rear hlf to 10th, ran on past btn hrss last m* 4 13
1402 5/5 Ashorne (R) MDO 3m 11 G *in tch, prog to ld 14th, hdd 2 out, kpt on to ld nr fin* 1 14

Steadily improved & scraped home in weak Maiden; more needed for Restricted hopes at 10 15

DARING DAY (Irish) — I 479ᶠ, I 561ᴾ, I 599³, I 611⁴

DARING DUCK br.g. 9 Daring March - Bois Le Duc by Kalydon Mrs P H K McNaught

517 15/3 Larkhill (R) RES 3m 10 GF *alwys prom, disp 13th-last, rdn & kpt on flat* 2 15

Ran well only start & good enough for Maiden win but rarely seen 15

DARKBROOK b.g. 10 Green Shoon - Pitpan Lass by Pitpan M J Footer
1996 7(0),F(-),P(0)

281 23/2 Charing (L) OPE 3m 12 G *alwys bhnd, t.o. & p.u. 14th* P 0
305 1/3 Parham (R) OPE 3m 9 G *prom, chsd ldr 6th, rdn & wknd 14th* 4 0

No longer of any account 0

DARK DAWN b.g. 13 Pollerton - Cacodor's Pet by Chinatown Mrs J M Newitt
1996 **P(0),P(NH),1(28),U(-),5(NH)**

117 9/2 Wetherby Po' (L) LAD 3m 10 GF *hld up, prog 11th, went 2nd 4 out, onepcd aft* 2 21
268 22/2 Duncombe Pa' (R) LAD 3m 5 G *(fav) comf rddn, hld up in rear, prog 3 out, ld last, pushd out* 1 23
426 8/3 Charm Park (L) LAD 3m 12 GF *hld up, prog 11th, ld 2 out, ran on wll, comf* 1 24
973 7/4 Kelso (L) HC 3m 1f 5 GF *held up, steady hdwy 12th, chal and ev ch 2 out, wknd last.* 4 17
1201 24/4 Perth (R) HC 3m 14 G *nvr on terms.* 5 17

Game veteran; good partnership with novice rider & could win more Ladies at 14; G/S-F 23

DARK DELIGHT br.m. 6 Idiot's Delight - Starlight Beauty by Scallywag L J Williams

258 22/2 Newtown (L) RES 3m 14 G *hmpd 1st, wll bhnd, t.o. hlfwy, p.u. 14th* P 0

No delight yet 0

DARK OPAL (Irish) — I 243ᴾ, I 300ᴾ

DARK REFLECTION b.g. 11 Looking Glass - Ellers Gorse by Jock Scot J D Curnow
1996 P(0),1(12),2(13)

50 1/2 Wadebridge (L) RES 3m 10 G *bhnd, prog 12th, wknd nxt* 7 0
96 8/2 Great Treth' (R) CON 3m 7 GS *chsd ldr to 7th, strgglng frm 11th, sn t.o.* 5 0
237 22/2 Lemalla (R) CON 3m 13 S *rear & rmndrs 7th, nvr dang, poor 7th whn u.r. 3 out* U -
453 8/3 Great Treth' (R) CON 3m 13 S *ref to race* 0 0
533 15/3 Wadebridge (L) INT 3m 5 GF *bhnd til gd prog 14th, ld 16th, ran on wll whn prssd* 1 15
631 22/3 Kilworthy (L) INT 3m 8 G *s.s., bhnd frm 8th, t.o., fin 4th, promoted* 3 10
804 31/3 Wadebridge (L) INT 3m 6 F *(Jt fav) bhnd til rddn to jn ldrs 3 out, ld cls home* 1 16
1109 19/4 Flete Park (R) OPE 4m 9 GF *alwys bhnd* 6 10

Completed nap-hand of Wadebridge wins in best ever season 97; modest; may find another chance; G-F 15

DARK RHYTHAM br.g. 8 True Song - Crozanna by Crozier G A Coombe
1996 P(0),F(-),3(10),1(15),1(15)

213 16/2 Southwell P' (L) RES 3m 16 GS *prom, ld 7th-11th & 13th, jnd 3 out, no ext cls home* 2 19
377 4/3 Leicester (R) HC 2 1/2m 110yds 15 G *hdwy 6th, wknd 3 out.* 6 11
545 16/3 Garthorpe (R) CON 3m 12 GF *(fav) ld til 2 out, wkd und press appr last* 4 18
770 29/3 Dingley (R) RES 3m 18 G *w.w. prog 9th, 2nd 12th-3 out, wknd nxt* 4 11
1191 20/4 Garthorpe (R) RES 3m 8 GF *(fav) ld, jnd 3 out, sn rdn, hdd last, unable qckn flat* 2 16
1530 18/5 Fakenham (L) HC 2m 5f 110yds 11 G *prom to 10th, p.u. before 4 out.* P 0
1587 29/5 Uttoxeter (L) HC 2m 5f 11 GF *ld to 2nd, remained handy til mstk and wknd 6 out, p.u. before 2 out.* P 0

Dual winner 96; barely stays but could find Restricted on easy course - concentrate on them 98 17

DARKTOWN STRUTTER ch.g. 11 Pas de Seul - Princess Henham by Record Token R W Pincombe
1996 F(-),P(0),1(13),2(12),P(0),3(0),P(0)

100 8/2 Great Treth' (R) RES 3m 14 GS *(bl) alwys bhnd, p.u. 12th* P 0
312 1/3 Clyst St Ma' (L) RES 3m 8 HY *(bl) ld/disp to 7th, lost tch 13th, blnd last* 5 0
557 16/3 Ottery St M' (L) RES 3m 9 G *(bl) ld/disp to 7th, wknd nxt, outpcd aft* 3 0
1547 24/5 Mounsey Hil' (R) MEM 3m 9 G *(bl) chsd ldrs to 11th, rmndrs & lost plc nxt, p.u. 16th* P 0

Shock Maiden winner 96 - predictably out of his depth since 10

DARTON RI b.g. 14 Abednego - Boogie Woogie by No Argument Mrs S Maxse
1996 1(21),2(19),1(21),U(-),3(14)

142 9/2 Tweseldown (R) MEM 3m 8 GF *(fav) j.w. trckd ldrs, ld 4 out, easily* 1 21
483 9/3 Tweseldown (R) CON 3m 8 G *(fav) ld to 9th, trckd ldrs, ld 15th, pshd out* 1 20
1053 13/4 Hackwood Pa' (L) MEM 3m 2 GF *(fav) ld to 6th, outpcd 15th, clsd last, ld flat, readily* 1 16
1417 10/5 Warwick (L) HC 3 1/4m 8 G *prom, lost pl 6th, soon well bhnd, no ch when hmpd run-in, fin 4th, placed 3rd.* 3 12

Tweseldown specialist & retains form well; won 5 of last 8 points & more possible at 15; G/F-G/S 20

DASHBOARD LIGHT b.g. 7 Idiot's Delight - Good Lady by Deep Run A D Cooke
1996 P(0),2(14),1(14),3(17),F(-),P(0)

225 19/2 Folkestone (R) HC 2m 5f 10 S *chsd ldrs till wknd 5 out, t.o. when p.u. before 2 out.* P 0
377 4/3 Leicester (R) HC 2 1/2m 110yds 15 G *chsd ldrs till wknd apr 3 out.* 7 0
473 9/3 Southwell P' (L) CON 3m 10 G *chsd ldr 3rd, ld 11th, clr apr 3 out, hdd 2 out, sn btn* 2 16
769 29/3 Dingley (R) CON 3m 14 G *w.w. prog frm 8th, 2nd 5 out, only threat 2 out, outpcd* 2 18
1081 13/4 Guilsborough (L) RES 3m 13 GF *(Jt fav) s.s. sn trckd ldrs, ld 15th, drvn clr 2 out, rdn out* 1 19
1277 27/4 Fakenham P-' (L) CON 3m 10 G *(fav) prog 5th, went 3rd 11th, blnd nxt & 15th, no hdwy 3 out* 4 16

Maiden winner 96; short on stamina but improved again 97; well-ridden; easy Confined possible 20

DASHING BUCK (Irish) — I 22^{3}, I 76^{2}, I 335^{1}
DASHING DULA b.m. 11 Oats - Swift Wood by Precipice Wood Mrs J N Askew

1070 13/4 Whitwell-On' (R) XX 3m 9 G *rear, mstk 2nd, outpcd 5th, t.o. 9th, p.u. 12th* P 0

Rarely seen & looks finished now 0

DAUPHIN BLEU(FR) b.g. 11 Direct Flight - Shabby (FR) by Carmarthan (FR) Miss Victoria Roberts
1996 1(15),1(22),2(22),2(26)

2 19/1 Barbury Cas' (L) XX 3m 14 GF *(fav) t.d.e. ld to 10th, prssd ldr aft, ev ch 2 out, just hld* 2 24
85 2/2 Wolverhampt' (L) LAD 3m 11 GS *(fav) ld to 3rd, lft in ld 5th, jnd & f 3 out* F -
361 2/3 Garnons (L) LAD 3m 7 GS *ld til u.r. 2nd* U -
402 8/3 Llanfrynach (R) INT 3m 7 G *(fav) ld to 14th, onepcd aft* 3 17
636 22/3 Howick (L) CON 3m 12 GF *ld til 13th, wknd rpdly* 6 0

Promising dual winner 96 but lost confidence 97; may revive at 12 but best watched 19

DAVALBURY(IRE) ch.g. 5 Ore - Better Again by Deep Run T L Jones

407 8/3 Llanfrynach (R) MDN 3m 11 G *mid-div, blnd 14th, p.u. aft* P 0
1137 19/4 Bonvilston (R) MDO 3m 13 G *(Jt fav) rear til p.u. 12th* P 0

Fair debut but problems last start; may do better at 6 12

DAVIDS PRIDE (Irish) — I 98^{P}, I 185^{P}, I 217^{6}
DAVIDS SISTER (Irish) — I 140^{P}
DAVY'S LAD b.g. 6 Respect - Colisfare by Coliseum Mrs E Borthwick
1996 P(0),P(0),P(0)

160 15/2 Lanark (R) MDO 2m 5f 10 G *ld to 11th, sn wknd, p.u. 3 out* P 0

Yet to complete & no stamina 0

DAWDANTE (Irish) — I 84^{P}, I 142^{6}, I 321^{2}, I 444^{2}, I 558^{5}
DAWN DIEU (Irish) — I 120^{P}, I 253^{P}, I 467^{F}, I 508^{F}
DAWN INVADER(IRE) b.g. 6 Fine Blade (USA) - Kova's Daughter by Brave Invader (USA) D J Caro

1996 **14(NH),10(NH),P(NH)**

368	2/3	Garnons	(L)	MDO	2 1/2m	13	GS	*prog 10th, chsd ldr 12th, disp 2 out, hung lft flat, all out*	1	16

No form under Rules but ideal pointing debut; should upgrade if fit & stays 3m in 98 17

DAWN PAGEANT (Irish) — I 338P, I 407P, I 458F, I 571P

DAWNS CHOICE (Irish) — I 178U

DAYADAN(IRE) b.g. 7 Shernazar - Dayanata by Shirley Heights — R H York

6	19/1	Barbury Cas'	(L)	LAD	3m	13	GF	*rear whn mstk & u.r. 8th*	U	-
57	1/2	Kingston Bl'	(L)	LAD	3m	13	GF	*rear til p.u. 9th*	P	0
145	9/2	Tweseldown	(R)	LAD	3m	10	GF	*immed outpcd, t.o. 4th, u.r. 7th*	U	-
280	23/2	Charing	(L)	LAD	3m	12	G	*jmpd v slowly 1st, alwys rear, t.o. 12th*	6	0
578	16/3	Detling	(L)	LAD	3m	11	F	*alwys rear, rmmdrs hlfwy, kpt on onepce*	7	11

Beat only two others when completing & looks worthless 0

DAYBROOK'S GIFT b.g. 14 Daybrook Lad - Current Gift by Current Coin — Miss N K Allan

1996 P(0),2(19),9(0),1(21),4(16),1(16),1(21),4(17),2(20),7(0)

18	25/1	Badbury Rin'	(L)	LAD	3m	9	GF	*outpcd & bhnd, effrt 10th, sn btn, poor 6th whn f 15th*	F	-
108	8/2	Milborne St'	(L)	MXO	3m	6	GF	*rear, prog 13th, styd on frm 3 out, chal aft last, just hld*	2	21
514	15/3	Larkhill	(R)	MXO	3m	6	GF	*prom to 4th, lost plc rpdly, t.o. & p.u. 12th*	P	0
689	29/3	Little Wind'	(R)	LAD	3m	5	GF	*in tch, mstk 13th, wknd 15th, t.o. & p.u. last*	P	0
1062	13/4	Maisemore P'	(L)	MXO	3m	12	GF	*(bl) alwys bhnd, t.o. whn blnd & u.r. 11th*	U	-
1242	26/4	Bratton Down	(L)	LAD	3m	6	GS	*(vis) alwys towrds rear*	4	0
1257	27/4	Black Fores'	(R)	LAD	3m	5	F	*(bl) wll bhnd, rpd prog frm 3 out, too much to do*	4	13
1548	24/5	Mounsey Hil'	(R)	LAD	3m	10	G	*hmpd & u.r. 2nd*	U	-
1595	31/5	Bratton Down	(L)	LAD	3m	5	F	*(vis) ld, rdn 12th, hdd 14th, wknd rpdly 16th, p.u. 2 out*	P	0

Fair performer to 96 but declined rapidly 2nd half of 97 & looks finished now 11

DAYTIME DAWN(IRE) b.g. 6 Rashar (USA) - Ard Clos by Ardoon — R Wale

1996 **5(NH),7(NH),4(NH),13(NH),9(NH)**

1352	4/5	Dingley	(R)	MDO	2 1/2m	9	G	*ld to 11th agn 13th, lft clr 3 out, rddn last, cght nr fin*	1	13

Modest under Rules; lucky to be given D/H on debut in weak race; more needed for Restricted 14

DEAD RECKONING (Irish) — I 27P, I 1071, I 2831

DEAL ME ONE ch.g. 8 Push On - Martian Wisdom by Aggressor — Mrs M A Jukes

1996 U(-),P(0),P(0)

1468	11/5	Erw Lon	(L)	INT	3m	7	GS	*trckd ldrs to 9th, sn wknd, p.u. 13th*	P	0

Maiden winner 94; no form since 0

DEAN DEIFIR (Irish) — I 470P, I 5525

DEAR EMILY b.m. 9 Uncle Pokey - Malmar by Palm Track — J E Swiers

1996 **4(NH),4(NH),7(NH),4(NH),5(NH),3(NH),4(NH),3(NH),3(NH),4(NH),5(NH),5(NH)**

375	3/3	Doncaster	(L)	HC	2m 3f 110yds	11	GF	*mstks, alwys bhnd, t.o. when p.u. before 4 out.*	P	0
510	15/3	Dalton Park	(R)	MDO	3m	14	GF	*mid-div, prog 14th, lft 2nd nxt, chal flat, kpt on wll*	2	14
622	22/3	Hutton Rudby	(L)	MDO	3m	10	GF	*(Jt fav) disp til hdd 7th,trckd ldr til disp 13th,ld 3 out,ran on wll*	1	15
695	29/3	Stainton	(R)	RES	3m	11	F	*(fav) alwys prom, chsd ldr frm 14th, rddn & not qckn apr last*	2	17
894	5/4	Wetherby Po'	(L)	RES	3m	6	F	*(fav) ld to 3rd, prom til ld 14th, hdd 3 out, kpt on*	2	16
1101	19/4	Hornby Cast'	(L)	RES	3m	14	G	*(fav) disp til 3rd, chsd ldrs aft, ev ch apr 3 out, onepcd*	3	17
1250	26/4	Easingwold	(L)	RES	3m	15	GS	*mid-div, prog 10th, tk 2nd 3 out, outpcd by wnnr*	2	19
1406	5/5	Witton Cast'	(R)	RES	3m	10	GS	*(fav) chsd ldrs,ld 14th til disp nxt,hdd 3 out,rlld flat*	2	18

Highly consistent but beaten 5l or less in Restricteds; frustrating; may follow up eventually; G/S-F 18

DEARMISTERSHATTER (Irish) — I 396P, I 412U

DEBJANJO b.g. 9 Critique (USA) - Miss White (FR) by Carwhite — K A Hicks

145	9/2	Tweseldown	(R)	LAD	3m	10	GF	*chsd ldrs, wknd frm 12th, sn t.o., p.u. 3 out*	P	0
482	9/3	Tweseldown	(R)	LAD	3m	5	G	*chsd ldrs, outpcd 12th, t.o. & p.u. 2 out*	P	0
790	31/3	Bishopsleigh	(R)	LAD	3m	7	G	*sn rear, t.o. & p.u. 11th*	P	0
1057	13/4	Hackwood Pa'	(L)	XX	3m	4	GF	*rear & rmndrs, wknd 3 out, p.u. last*	P	0

Of no account 0

DECIDING DANCE (Irish) — I 169P

DEEBERT HOUSE (Irish) — I 399F

DEEJAYDEE (Irish) — I 392, I 1042, I 2032, I 4502

DEEJAYEF ro.m. 6 True Song - Rochester Way by Waterfall — David J Forsyth

373	2/3	Mollington	(R)	MDN	3m	14	G	*alwys rear, t.o. & p.u. 2 out*	P	0
1401	5/5	Ashorne	(R)	MDO	3m	15	G	*alwys bhnd, t.o. 11th, p.u. 13th*	P	0
1537	18/5	Mollington	(R)	MDO	3m	14	GS	*in tch til b.d. 5th*	B	-

Looks unpromising **0**

DEEL SOUND (Irish) — I 158^{P}, I 297, , I 352^{B}, I 425^{6}, I 509^{5}, I 550^{P}

DEEP APPEAL (Irish) — I 156^{F}, I 272^{3}, I 341^{5}, I 422^{3}, I 447^{3}, I 520^{U}, I 548^{P}, I 610^{P}

DEEP BIT (Irish) — I 403^{2}, I 422^{2}, I 563^{4}

DEEP HERITAGE (Irish) — I 2^{1}, I 51^{1}, I 78^{2}, I 121^{1}, I 306^{1}

DEEP REFRAIN (Irish) — I 202^{1}, I 357^{F}, I 491^{1}, I 542^{1}

DEERFIELD (Irish) — I 123^{P}, I 211^{P}

DEERPARK KING (Irish) — I 34^{2}, I 54^{1}

DEERPARK LASS (Irish) — I 159^{P}, I 278^{P}, I 356^{F}, I 531^{2}, I 566, , I 606^{P}

DEFINITELY MAYBE (Irish) — I 150^{1}, I 494^{P}

DEISE CRUSADER b.g. 10 Farhaan - Rugged Maid by Rugged Man — J P Henderson

1996 6(0)

813	31/3	Tranwell	(L)	RES	3m	7	G	*rear, 20l 7th 9th, lost tch final ctt & p.u. 4 out*	P	0

Maiden winner 95; rarely seen since & shows nothing now **0**

DELMIANO (Irish) — I 355^{P}, I 493^{6}, I 514^{6}

DEL'S DELIGHT(IRE) b.m. 6 Mister Majestic - Adell by Fordham (USA) — A Simpson

185	15/2	Erw Lon	(L)	MDN	3m	14	G	*alwys rear, t.o. & p.u. 13th*	P	0
368	2/3	Garnons	(L)	MDO	2 1/2m	13	GS	*hit 3rd, wknd 8th, p.u. aft 10th*	P	0
542	16/3	Erw Lon	(L)	MDN	3m	15	GF	*ld 1st, trckd ldrs to 14th, fdd, p.u. 2 out*	P	0
842	31/3	Lydstep	(L)	MDO	3m	12	F	*hld up, prog 12th, ld 14th-aft nxt, onepcd aft und pres*	2	13

Gradually improved & fair effort last start; should go one better in 98 .... **14**

DELS LAD b.g. 6 Ilium - Krystle Saint by St Columbus — D J Wheatley

372	2/3	Mollington	(R)	RES	3m	19	G	*unruly pddck & to post, last til p.u. 8th*	P	0
479	9/3	Southwell P'	(L)	MDO	3m	15	G	*mounted on course, t.o. 4th, p.u. 8th*	P	0
839	31/3	Thorpe Lodge	(L)	MDO	3m	15	F	*alwys rear hlf, bhnd whn p.u. aft 12th*	P	0
1084	13/4	Guilsborough	(L)	MDN	3m	11	GF	*in tch to 8th, sn bhnd, t.o. & p.u. 14th*	P	0

Mum was able but a headbanger; son is just the latter at present **0**

DELVIN SPIRIT(IRE) ch.m. 8 Rhoman Rule (USA) - Solarina by Solinus — S Kitching

926	6/4	Garthorpe	(R)	OPE	3m	10	GF	*alwys bhnd, p.u. 10th*	P	0
1192	20/4	Garthorpe	(R)	MDO	3m	6	GF	*cls up to 9th, sn lost tch, t.o.*	4	0
1262	27/4	Southwell P'	(L)	MDO	3m	15	G	*prom til wknd 10th, t.o. & p.u. 12th*	P	0

Beaten miles on only completion & looks useless **0**

DEMONIAC(FR) (Irish) — I 68^{1}, I 213^{2}, I 345^{1}

DENARII (Irish) — I 329^{P}, I 370^{P}

DENBY RYME ch.g. 5 Rymer - True Bond by True Song — J R Hinchliffe

676	23/3	Brocklesby '	(L)	RES	3m	14	GF	*sn wll bhnd, last & t.o. whn p.u. 11th*	P	0
1073	13/4	Whitwell-On'	(R)	MDO	2 1/2m 88yds	17	G	*prom til wknd 10th, p.u. 3 out*	P	0

No real signs of ability yet but time on his side & looks the part **0**

DENEL DE (Irish) — I 310^{P}, I 361^{F}, I 416^{P}, I 467^{P}, I 557^{P}

DENFIELD (Irish) — I 129^{1}, I 213^{1}

DENIM BLUE ch.g. 8 Mandrake Major - Delphinium by Tin King — Mrs L Walby

1996 2(14),2(12),1(16),3(14),U(-)

131	9/2	Alnwick	(L)	RES	3m	13	G	*w.w. prog 14th, rdn to ld last, hdd fin*	2	0
230	22/2	Friars Haugh	(L)	RES	3m	15	G	*(fav) alwys handy, kpt on to tk 2nd nr fin*	2	17
386	7/3	Ayr	(L)	HC	2m 5f 110yds	7	S	*(fav) chsd ldr, ld 12th, clr 2 out, easily.*	1	21
875	1/4	Wetherby	(L)	HC	3m 1f	5	GF	*(fav) held up, hdwy to track ldr hfwy, rdn to chal 3 out, styd on und pres to ld run-in, all out.*	1	19
1201	24/4	Perth	(R)	HC	3m	14	G	*f 2nd.*	F	-
1499	15/5	Perth	(R)	HC	2 1/2m 110yds	8	GS	*hmpd start, saddle slpd and soon p.u..*	P	0
1511	17/5	Corbridge	(R)	LAD	3m	10	GS	*prom til lost plc 6th, rear whn p.u. 11th, dsmntd*	P	0

Maiden winner 96; improved & won 2 poor H/Chases; problem last start; hard to place if fit 98; G/F-S .. **20**

DENIS AGUSTINE (Irish) — I 517^{P}

DENNETT LOUGH (Irish) — I 248^{P}

DENNISTOWNTHRILLER (Irish) — I 27^{P}, I 92^{1}, I 149^{P}, I 224^{1}, I 386^{2}

DENY'S RUN (Irish) — I 303^{5}

DEPARTURE ch.m. 10 Gorytus (USA) - La Gravotte (FR) by Habitat — Mrs J M Whitley

1996 P(0),5(14),4(15),1(15),1(20),3(13),4(12),2(18),F(-)

51 1/2 Wadebridge (L) CON 3m 4 G *prom, ld 15th to nxt, hrd rdn & no imp aft* 2 18

311 1/3 Clyst St Ma' (L) LAD 3m 9 HY *chsd ldrs, lost tch 12th, p.u. 14th* P 0

551 16/3 Ottery St M' (L) MEM 3m 4 G *made all, blnd 3rd, ran on wll whn chal 3 out* 1 17

689 29/3 Little Wind' (R) LAD 3m 5 GF *cls up, chsd wnr 12th, no imp aft 3 out* 2 18

889 3/4 Taunton (R) HC 3m 7 F *soon t.o., p.u. before 14th.* P 0

1090 16/4 Hockworthy (L) LAD 3m 8 GF *sn bhnd, t.o. 8th, p.u. 10th* P 0

1595 31/5 Bratton Down (L) LAD 3m 5 F *last & dtchd til ran on to chs wnr aft 3 out, no imp* 2 13

Dual winner 96; inconsistent & needs to dictate; novice-ridden mostly 97; Members again best chance 15

DEREENAVURRIG (Irish) — I 19^{P}, I 83^{P}, I 319^{P}

DERNAMAY (Irish) — I 119^{P}, I 126^{P}, I 173^{P}, I 212^{3}, I 246^{4}, I 375^{2}, I 432^{1}

DERRING ANN b.m. 7 Derring Rose - Andantino by Another River — R B Davies

1996 5(10),F(-),P(0),1(15),0(0)

262 22/2 Newtown (L) RES 3m 15 G *chsd ldr to 9th, lost tch 12th, t.o. & p.u. 14th* P 0

1061 13/4 Maisemore P' (L) RES 3m 12 GF *rear til u.r. 7th* U -

1235 26/4 Brampton Br' (R) INT 3m 10 G *mid-div, not qckn 13th, t.o.& p.u. 2 out* P 0

1392 5/5 Cursneh Hill (L) RES 3m 6 GF *s.s., cght up 7th, ev ch 14th, kpt on onepcd frm nxt* 3 15

1526 17/5 Bredwardine (R) RES 3m 13 G *prog to chs wnr 11th, ev ch 13th, outpcd & mstks frm nxt* 2 15

Maiden winner 96; not threatening in Restricteds & temperament suspect 15

DERRING BUD br.g. 13 Derring Rose - Tarune by Tarqogan — Lady Susan Brooke

1996 3(17),3(18),**2(NH),P(NH),3(NH),3(NH)**

573 16/3 Garnons (L) LAD 3m 8 G *went 3rd 8th, ld 10-12th, outpcd til styd on agn 3 out* 2 20

703 29/3 Upper Sapey (R) OPE 3m 5 GF *reluctant to start, 2 fences bhnd til p.u. 15th* P 0

Old character; still has ability but keeps it mostly well hidden now 15

DERRING KATIE b.m. 5 Derring Rose - Katiesylver by Cruise Missile — A Cooksley

1486 11/5 Ottery St M' (L) MDO 3m 17 G *rear whn f 7th* F -

1492 14/5 Cothelstone (L) MEM 3m 4 GF *s.s. nrly ref 1st, succeeded 2nd* R -

1554 24/5 Mounsey Hil' (R) MDO 3m 14 G *sn wll bhnd, almost ref 5th, succeeded nxt* R -

Started late & showed all the wrong signs 0

DERRING KNIGHT b.g. 7 Derring Rose - Arctic Servant by Goldhill — Nick Pomfret

1996 2(0),3(10),P(0),R(-),P(0),R(-),**11(NH),5(NH)**

80 2/2 Market Rase' (L) MDO 2m 5f 9 GF *prom, wkng whn jmpd slwly 8th, p.u. nxt* P 0

839 31/3 Thorpe Lodge (L) MDO 3m 15 F *rear hlf whn ref 8th* R -

Ungenuine & not worth persevering with now 0

DERRING RUN b.m. 7 Derring Rose - Corbitt Coins by Deep Run — F L Matthews

1996 **P(0)**

258 22/2 Newtown (L) RES 3m 14 G *alwys wll bhnd, t.o. last whn u.r. 12th* U -

368 2/3 Garnons (L) MDO 2 1/2m 13 GS *rear 3rd, blnd & u.r 9th* U -

Useless 0

DERRING TIRLEY b.g. 7 Derring Rose - Tic-On-Rose by Celtic Cone — Donald Smith

1067 13/4 Maisemore P' (L) MDO 3m 8 GF *u.r. 1st* U -

1454 11/5 Maisemore P' (L) MEM 3m 5 G *mstks, chsd ldr 9-13th, wknd rpdly, t.o.* 3 0

1578 26/5 Chaddesley ' (L) MDO 3m 7 F *in tch wil wknd & mstk 11th, slw jmp nxt & p.u.* P 0

Beaten miles on only completion & signs unpromising 0

DERRING VALLEY b.g. 12 Derrylin - Chalke Valley by Ragstone — A A King

1996 **5(NH),6(NH),3(NH),P(NH),7(NH),6(NH),P(NH)**

179 15/2 Larkhill (R) CON 3m 12 G *(bl) reluc, sn bhnd, t.o. & nrly ref 8th, p.u. nxt* P 0

552 16/3 Ottery St M' (L) OPE 3m 6 G *ld to 3rd, in tch aft, wknd 14th, t.o. & p.u. 2 out* P 0

No longer of any account 0

DERRYGALLON FANCY (Irish) — I 109^{5}, I 204^{5}, I 355^{P}

DERRYGRA FOUNTAIN (Irish) — I 138^{P}, I 235^{P}, I 319^{P}

DERRY LARK (Irish) — I 355^{P}, I 428^{5}, I 493^{3}, I 531^{P}

DERRYMOSS b.g. 11 Le Moss - Derrynaflan by Karabas — W J Evans

1996 **P(NH),P(NH),F(NH)**

537 16/3 Erw Lon (L) OPE 3m 9 GF *(bl) f 4th* F -

715 29/3 Llanvapley (L) OPE 3m 8 GF *(bl) last, bad mstk 1st, ref nxt* R -

1005 12/4 St Hilary (R) CON 3m 10 GF *mid-div, wknd rpdly 7th, p.u. 9th* P 0

No longer of any account 0

DERRYOWEN (Irish) — I 35P
DERRYSAND (Irish) — I 316B
DERRY'S DIAMOND (Irish) — I 9P, I 41P, I 78³, I 131³, I 237⁴, I 306³, I 420⁴, I 454², I 494¹, I 567⁶
DERRYVELLA LAD (Irish) — I 348, , I 430¹
DESERT MELODY (Irish) — I 47P, I 76F, I 84,

DESERT RUN(IRE) ch.g. 9 Deep Run - Another Dutchess by Master Buck — S N Burfield
1996 **8(NH),P(NH)**

5	19/1	Barbury Cas'	(L)	OPE	3m	11	GF	*bhnd, last & wkng whn p.u. 11th*	P 0
19	25/1	Badbury Rin'	(L)	OPE	3m	8	GF	*in tch to 7th, lost plc rpdly, t.o. & p.u. 13th*	P 0

Finished by 2nd Saturday & looks a forlorn hope now 0

DESERT WALTZ(IRE) ch.h. 8 Gorytus (USA) - Desert Pet by Petingo — H B Geddes
1996 1(24),1(22),1(23),1(26),2(22),2(22),2(25),2(25),2(25)

46	1/2	Larkhill	(R)	XX	3m	3	GF	*(fav) trckd ldr, ld 13th, clr 15th, easily*	1 24
177	15/2	Larkhill	(R)	MEM	3m	6	G	*(fav) alwys going wll, trckd ldrs, ld apr 13th, sn clr, canter*	1 23
292	1/3	Didmarton	(L)	MEM	3m	9	G	*(fav) in tch til blnd & u.r. 8th*	U -
555	16/3	Ottery St M'	(L)	LAD	3m	10	G	*(fav) prom, ld 7th-4 out, no ext und pres frm 2 out*	2 25
689	29/3	Little Wind'	(R)	LAD	3m	5	GF	*(fav) hld up, mstk 6th, ld 11th, clr aft 3 out, comf*	1 23
1215	26/4	Woodford	(L)	CON	3m	3	G	*(fav) made all, drew wll clr apr 4 out, heavily eased flat*	1 24

Useful & highly consistent; won 11, 2nd in 8 of 20 races; sure to win more; G/S-F 27

DESMOND GOLD(IRE) b.g. 9 Tumble Gold - Stylish Princess by Prince Tenderfoot (USA) — Keith R Pearce
1996 **18(NH),8(NH)**

191	15/2	Erw Lon	(L)	CON	3m	13	G	*prom, trckd ldr 13th, ld 3 out, clr nxt, rdn out*	1 21
716	29/3	Llanvapley	(L)	LAD	3m	5	GF	*mstly 3rd, drvn to 2nd 13th, blndrd & u.r. nxt*	U -
1132	19/4	Bonvilston	(R)	CON	3m	9	G	*trckd ldrs, cls 3rd, slppd up bnd aft 14th*	S -
1295	2/5	Bangor	(L)	HC	3m 110yds	4	G	*set slow pace, jmpd slowly 3rd, qcknd apr 12th, hit and hdd 14th, soon wknd, t.o..*	4 0

Winning hurdler; well-revived to win Confined; unfortunate after; could perk up again early 98 20

DESMOND RIVER (Irish) — I 120², I 123³, I 315¹, I 367²
DES THE ARCHITECT (Irish) — I 610P
DETERMINED OKIE (Irish) — I 265P, I 295P, I 488P, I 497R, I 571P, I 607P

DETINU ch.g. 6 Hasty Word - Knocksharry by Palm Track — A J Chambers
1996 F(-),P(0),5(0)

79	2/2	Market Rase'	(L)	MDO	2m 5f	9	GF	*ld, sn clr, hdd 4 out, wl btn whn f last*	F -

Lightly raced & yet to achieve anything substantial 10

DEVIL'S VALLEY ch.g. 14 Lucifer (USA) - Barrowvale by Valerullah — S Fisher

277	23/2	Charing	(L)	MEM	3m	6	G	*made most to 8th, wknd 12th, t.o. whn ref last*	R -
1126	19/4	Penshurst	(L)	CON	3m	6	GF	*plld into ld 2nd, immed clr, 10l up whn u.r. 7th*	U -

No longer of any account 0

DEVIOSITY(USA) b.g. 10 Spectacular Bid (USA) - Reinvestment (USA) by Key To The Mint (USA) — Lt-Col R I Webb-Bowen
1996 5(0),4(11),1(17)

1244	26/4	Bratton Down	(L)	CON	3m	14	GS	*sn bhnd, t.o. whn p.u. 12th*	P 0
1255	27/4	Black Fores'	(R)	CON	3m	4	F	*(bl) wll bhnd frm 14th, sn t.o.*	4 0

Confined winner 96; season lasted a weekend in 97 & could be finished now 0

DEVONSHIRE LAD b.g. 6 Sergeant Drummer (USA) - Alice Rairthorn by Romany Air — Mrs D B Lunt
1996 F(-),P(0),C(-),P(0)

172	15/2	Ottery St M'	(L)	MDN	3m	14	G	*mid-div, prog 13th, went 2nd 4 out, hld whn whn u.r. 2 out*	U -
459	8/3	Great Treth'	(R)	MDO	3m	9	S	*(fav) hld up, slght ld 15th, wknd rpdly aft 3 out, p.u. apr 2 out*	P 0
1095	16/4	Hockworthy	(L)	MDN	3m	11	GF	*chsd wnr, only dngr frm hlfwy, no imp 2 out, eased last*	2 14
1399	5/5	High Bickin'	(R)	MDO	3m	12	G	*(fav) trckd ldr, ld 16th, slght ld whn lft clr last, drvn out*	1 17
1552	24/5	Mounsey Hil'	(R)	RES	3m	12	G	*(fav) chsd ldr, ld 6-11th, 2nd whn p.u. 14th, lame*	P 0

Improved & won decent Maiden; problem last start; hopefully fit in 98 - Restricted very likely; Good 18

DEWDROP LADY (Irish) — I 322P
DEXTER GORDON (Irish) — I 248P, I 328P
DEXTER LASS (Irish) — I 73P

DHARAMSHALA(IRE) b.g. 9 Torenaga - Ambitious Lady by Status Seeker — P D Jones
1996 5(10),P(0),P(0),2(11),2(14),1(14)

170	15/2	Ottery St M'	(L)	MEM	3m	6	G	*handy to 15th, lost tch nxt, outpcd*	5 0
556	16/3	Ottery St M'	(L)	RES	3m	12	G	*rear & no ch til p.u. 13th*	P 0

1255	27/4 Black Fores'	(R) CON	3m	4	F	*(fav) prog 14th, no imp on wnr frm 2 out*	2	12
1483	11/5 Ottery St M'	(L) RES	3m	15	G	*alwys mid-div, nvr on trms, p.u. 3 out*	P	0
1610	7/6 Umberleigh	(L) MEM	3m	3	F	*1st ride,cls up,nrly u.r. 10th,wknd & mstks frm 13th,lame*	2	0

Maiden winner 96; struggled badly in 97 & finished lame 10

DHU BOND (Irish) — I 123^P, I 253^P, I 362^P

DIAMOND DUCK ch.m. 5 Vital Season - Some Moor by Some Hand — Kevin J Legg

525	15/3 Cothelstone	(L) MDN	3m	15	GS	*pllng, mid-div, mstk 11th, rear whn p.u. 14th*	P	0

May sparkle more in 98 0

DIAMOND IN THE RUFF (Irish) — I 354^6

DIAMOND MELODY (Irish) — I 11^5, I 189^P, I 563^1

DIAMOND VALLEY(IRE) b.g. 9 Bustinetto - Dalmond by Diamonds Are Trump (USA) — Robert Thame

1996 2(17),2(18),U(-)

770	29/3 Dingley	(R) RES	3m	18	G	*disp brfly, sn mid-div, ran on 6 out,6th whn blnd & u.r.2out*	U	-

Lightly raced now; quite able but can only be watched if returning in 98 15

DIAMOND WIND(USA) b.m. 9 Wind And Wuthering (USA) - Diamond Oyster by Formidable (USA) — Count Goess-Saurau And Mr C Leigh

1	19/1 Barbury Cas'	(L) XX	3m	11	GF	*mstks, chsd ldrs til wknd 11th, t.o. & p.u. 3 out*	P	0
41	1/2 Larkhill	(R) MDO	3m	13	GF	*prom, ld 10th, jnd 15th, 1l up & going better whn f last*	F	17
283	23/2 Charing	(L) MDO	3m	16	G	*(fav) made all, drew clr 3 out, comf*	1	17
377	4/3 Leicester	(R) HC	2 1/2m 110yds	15	G	*in tch, chsd ldrs 5 out, wknd 3 out.*	8	0
649	22/3 Siddington	(L) MEM	3m	6	F	*(fav) j.w. ld to 3rd & agn 9th, jnd last, pshd out flat*	1	19
1164	20/4 Mollington	(R) RES	3m	10	GF	*(fav) prom, ld 8th-14th, wknd aft 3 out*	6	10

Decent performances for late starter; just stays 3m; lame last start & possibly retired 19

DIANA MOSS(IRE) b.m. 8 Le Moss - El Diana by Tarboosh (USA) — J S Papworth

1996 P(0),5(0),U(-),2(12),B(-),2(15),4(14),1(14),1(17)

97	8/2 Great Treth'	(R) INT	3m	13	GS	*bhnd, 11th whn u.r. 7th*	U	-
628	22/3 Kilworthy	(L) CON	3m	12	G	*nvr gng wll, p.u. apr 7th*	P	0

Dual winner late 96 but no show 97 & can only be watched now 14

DIANAS SON (Irish) — I 94^P

DICK'S CABIN br.g. 10 Strong Gale - Lady Park by No Argument — W H Pugh

2	19/1 Barbury Cas'	(L) XX	3m	14	GF	*alwys bhnd, 12th & t.o. hlfwy, p.u. 15th*	P	0
189	15/2 Erw Lon	(L) RES	3m	14	G	*ld to 10th, sn wknd, t.o. & p.u. 3 out*	P	0
298	1/3 Didmarton	(L) RES	3m	15	G	*ld to 2nd, prom til wknd 11th, t.o. & p.u. 3 out*	P	0
405	8/3 Llanfrynach	(R) RES	3m	15	G	*rear, p.u. 11th*	P	0
845	31/3 Lydstep	(L) RES	3m	5	F	*ld frm 2nd, unchal, eased flat*	1	13
1005	12/4 St Hilary	(R) CON	3m	10	GF	*rear til p.u. 11th*	P	0
1181	20/4 Lydstep	(L) INT	3m	3	GF	*ld to 5th, cls up aft til 3 out, onepcd aft*	2	12
1366	5/5 Pantyderi	(L) INT	3m	6	G	*ld 3rd-5th, wknd frm 11th, p.u. 3 out*	P	0
1576	26/5 Chaddesley '	(L) XX	3m	12	F	*s.s. alwys bhnd, t.o. last whn p.u. 11th*	P	0
1602	31/5 Bassaleg	(R) INT	3m	5	F	*(bl) tubed, mounted on course, ld 2nd, clr 4th, hdd 12th, wknd*	3	10

Irish Maiden winner 96; won ghastly race; form only at Lydstep; last run suggests hatful of problems ... 12

DIDDLE DI (Irish) — I 311^P, I 347^P

DIGACRE (Irish) — I 49, , I 108^P, I 208^1, I 279^1, I 395^3

DILKUSH b.g. 8 Dunbeath (USA) - Good Try by Good Bond — S C Wells

1996 P(0)

1209	26/4 Clifton On '	(L) MDO	3m	16	GS	*lost plc 5th, outpcd frm 6 out*	7	0
1402	5/5 Ashorne	(R) MDO	3m	11	G	*mstk 6th, prom, cls 4th whn hmpd 15th, wknd 2 out*	5	0
1479	11/5 Garthorpe	(R) MDO	3m	12	GS	*chsd ldrs, 4th & outpcd 15th, no ch aft*	4	0
1537	18/5 Mollington	(R) MDO	3m	14	GS	*in tch,prog 12th,chal 3 out,lft in ld nxt,nt run on,hdd flat*	2	12

Improved by his standards 97 but threw away golden chance last start - lucky to find another 12

DILLONS BRIDGE(IRE) b.g. 8 Le Bavard (FR) - Colour Clown by Random Shot — Mrs M Armstrong

136	9/2 Alnwick	(L) MDO	3m	16	G	*w.w. prog 10th, 3rd & jmpd slwly 2 out, kpt on flat*	3	0
334	1/3 Corbridge	(R) MEM	3m	7	G	*(fav) mstk 1st, mid-div, outpcd 3 out*	3	11
565	16/3 Lanark	(R) MDO	3m	10	GS	*(fav) 2nd whn u.r. 5th*	U	-
612	22/3 Friars Haugh	(L) MDN	3m	14	GF	*alwys prom, wnt 2nd aft 2 out, no ch wth wnnr*	2	10
814	31/3 Tranwell	(L) MDO	3m	9	G	*in tch wth ldrs 1st ctt,cls 6th 9th,wnt 4th 4 out,not rch ld*	4	13
1052	13/4 Lockerbie	(R) MDN	3m	10	F	*(fav) alwys handy, chal 2 out, no ext apr last*	2	15
1337	3/5 Mosshouses	(L) MDO	3m	7	F	*(fav) hdl up in tch, hrd rdn 3 out, ld apr last, all out*	1	15
1424	10/5 Aspatria	(L) RES	3m	17	G	*mstks, rear, effrt to chs ldng grp 12th, sn lost tch*	8	10

Expensive to follow but eventually struggled home in weak race; reliability may see another chance ... 15

DILLY MAY DALLY ch.m. 6 Don't Dilly Dally - Vulravina by Vulgan — D H Holland

499 15/3 Ampton (R) MDO 3m 9 GF *schoold in rr, lst tch 10th, t.o. & p.u. 14th* P 0
802 31/3 Marks Tey (L) INT 3m 4 F *alwys rear, lost tch 9th, t.o. & p.u. aft 11th* P 0

Plenty of dallying so far 0

DILLY'S LAST br.m. 9 Saunter - Delilah Dell by The Dell — Mrs S Buckler

1996 U(-),P(0),5(12),P(0)

1080 13/4 Guilsborough (L) RES 3m 11 GF *wll in tch to 15th, wknd rpdly & p.u. 3 out* P 0
1204 26/4 Clifton On ' (L) MEM 3m 6 GS *last, rmndrs 5th, p.u. nxt* P 0
1355 4/5 Dingley (R) RES 3m 12 G *rear whn p.u. 6th* P 0
1475 11/5 Garthorpe (R) XX 3m 13 GS *t.n.p.* 0 0

No longer of any account 0

DI MODA ch.g. 10 Buzzards Bay - Diamond Talk by Counsel — Miss Sharon Firmin

1996 F(-),12(0),5(0),11(0)

223 16/2 Heythrop (R) RES 3m 19 G *bhnd til p.u. 11th* P 0
373 2/3 Mollington (R) MDN 3m 14 G *wll in rear, no ch frm 12th, styd on well frm 3 out, nrst fn* 3 0

Plodded on when distant 3rd last start but much more needed to figure 10

DINAN (Irish) — I 77[4]

DINEDOR CHARLIE ch.g. 7 Rustingo - Dinedor Lady by Cavo Doro — Richard J Williams

639 22/3 Howick (L) MDN 3m 15 GF *rear til p.u. 9th* P 0
719 29/3 Llanvapley (L) MDN 3m 14 GF *alwys rear, p.u. 3 out* P 0
1067 13/4 Maisemore P' (L) MDO 3m 8 GF *in tch,mstk 8th,rmndrs 10th,btn whn blnd 2 out, lft 4th last* 4 0
1240 26/4 Brampton Br' (R) MDO 3m 12 G *prom, cls 2nd whn mstk 15th, wknd aft* 3 0

Last on both completions but may just be getting to grips with what is required 10

DINGDUST (Irish) — I 77[P], I 158[P], I 297[P]

DINNYS DELIGHT(IRE) b.g. 8 Sandhurst Prince - Buonas by Orchestra — Miss K M Pickering

576 16/3 Detling (L) MEM 3m 10 F *alwys prom, 3rd & ev ch 3 out, wknd* 5 0

Well beaten in a bad race 0

DINO MALTA(FR) ch.g. 6 Bad Conduct (USA) - Sri Lanka III (FR) by Yelpana (FR) — Mrs K M Price

1996 **10(NH),6(NH),2(NH),2(NH),5(NH)**

362 2/3 Garnons (L) OPE 3m 11 GS *mid-div, prog to chal 14th, ev ch til no ext 2 out* 2 17

Placed in fair novice chases 96; ran passably only start but signs look unpromising 17

DIP THE LIGHTS b.m. 7 Lighter - Honey Dipper by Golden Dipper — J A T de Giles

1996 F(-),3(0),3(0),r(-),5(0)

224 16/2 Heythrop (R) MDN 3m 16 G *rear frm 9th, t.o. & p.u. 15th* P 0

No real ability & soon vanished in 97 0

DIRECT b.g. 14 The Parson - Let The Hare Sit by Politico (USA) — J A C Edwards

1996 3(10),**1(22),F(-),P(0)**

384 6/3 Towcester (R) HC 3m 1f 7 GS *bhnd from 10th, t.o..* 4 0
1201 24/4 Perth (R) HC 3m 14 G *soon bhnd, t.o. when p.u. before 15th.* P 0

H/Chase winner 97; looks finished now 11

DIRTY DANCER b.g. 8 Sizzling Melody - Stratch (FR) by Thatch (USA) — J H Forbes

1996 P(0),2(0)

44 1/2 Larkhill (R) MDO 3m 9 GF *rear, prog to chs ldrs 12th, wknd 15th, lost poor 3rd nr fin* 4 0
294 1/3 Didmarton (L) INT 3m 20 G *s.s. alwys bhnd, t.o. & p.u. 13th, lame* P 0

Does not stay & problems to boot 0

DISRESPECT b.m. 7 Respect - Miss Sunny by Sunnyboy — W G Macmillan

1996 5(0),P(0),U(-)

161 15/2 Lanark (R) MDO 2m 5f 14 G *ld chsng grp mostly til no ext frm 4 out* 4 11
341 1/3 Corbridge (R) MDN 3m 10 G *prom, ld 5th til hdd & wknd 10th, t.o. & p.u. 4 out* P 0
1429 10/5 Aspatria (L) MDO 3m 15 G *made most to 8th, sn wknd, t.o. & p.u. 12th* P 0
1514 17/5 Corbridge (R) MDO 3m 17 GS *rear, prog 13th, in tch whn blnd 4 out, sn btn* 4 10

Not disgraced when 4th twice but will need to step up to figure in 98 12

DISTANT-PORT(IRE) b.g. 7 Phardante (FR) - Quayville by Quayside — Miss P Morris

1996 **12(NH),13(NH)**

263 22/2 Newtown (L) MDN 3m 11 G *prom, mstk 8th, ld nxt to 13th, sn wknd* 4 0
876 1/4 Upton-On-Se' (R) MEM 3m 7 GF *t.d.e. ref to race* 0 0
881 1/4 Upton-On-Se' (R) MDN 3m 13 GF *2nd attempt, lft 30l, rshd up to jn ldrs whn f 5th* F -

1016	12/4	Bitterley	(L)	MDO	3m	14	GF	*last frm 7th, t.o. 10th*	8	0
1239	26/4	Brampton Br'	(R)	MDO	3m	9	G	*hld up just in tch, prog 16th, ld 2 out, clr last*	1	13

Looked mad as a hatter until beating 3 subsequent winners last start; impossible to predict 15

DI STEFANO b.g. 9 Chief Singer - Doree Moisson (FR) by Connaught — Mrs R Onions

1996 1(23),1(23),1(25),1(25),1(26),1(25),1(27)

219	16/2	Heythrop	(R)	LAD	3m	16	G	*(fav) not fluent, hld up, prog 12th, chal 2 out, rdn to ld nr fin*	1	26
361	2/3	Garnons	(L)	LAD	3m	7	GS	*(fav) w.w. clsd 12th, cruised into ld 15th, sn clr*	1	26
573	16/3	Garnons	(L)	LAD	3m	8	G	*(fav) w.w. prog 10th, chal 13th, ld nxt, clr 2 out*	1	25
705	29/3	Upper Sapey	(R)	CON	3m	4	GF	*(fav) disp ld 13th, 10l clr whn crashed thru wing last, (dead)*	F	-

Was a top-class pointer 29

DIVILABETTER (Irish) — I 441^{P}, I 473^{2}, I 526^{F}

DIVINE CHANCE(IRE) b.g. 9 The Parson - Random What by Random Shot — M R Churches

1996 U(-),2(16),6(11),**8(0)**

319	1/3	Marks Tey	(L)	CON	3m	11	G	*rear, jmp slwly 6th & 7th, losng tch whn p.u. 12th*	P	0
594	22/3	Horseheath	(R)	XX	3m	2	F	*disp til slw jmp last, no ext*	2	14
1277	27/4	Fakenham P-'	(L)	CON	3m	10	G	*ld 3rd, clr nxt, drew right away 2 out, easily*	1	23

Sulked in 96/7 till bolting home last start (fast time); may repeat trick late 98 21

DIVINER(IRE) b.g. 8 Lancastrian - Paupers Spring by Pauper — Peter Oldfield

144	9/2	Tweseldown	(R)	OPE	3m	9	GF	*mid-div, lost ground frm 12th, t.o. 4 out*	5	12

Novice-ridden & well beaten only start; best watched if reappearing 10

DIVINE RAPTURE (Irish) — I 264^{F}, I 338^{P}

DIXONS HOMEFINDER b.g. 13 Strong Gale - Julia Too by Golden Horus — J L Barnett

1996 P(0),F(-),F(-),P(0),4(16)

760	29/3	Kimble	(L)	RES	3m	7	GF	*cls up, ld 3-7th, wknd 2 out*	4	12
989	12/4	Kingston Bl'	(L)	INT	3m	7	GF	*ld to 4th, lost plc aft nxt, bhnd frm 12th, t.o.*	5	0

Maiden winner 94; too old now 11

DIXON VARNER (Irish) — I 271^{1}, I 259^{1}, I 334^{1}, I 549^{1}

DIXTON HILL b.g. 9 Pitpan - Miss Silly by Silly Season — M Weir

1996 **P(NH),12(NH),P(NH),P(NH)**

1520	17/5	Bratton Down	(L)	MDO	3m	17	GS	*rmndrs & jmpd slwly 4th, bhnd & p.u. 7th*	P	0

No ability under Rules & unpromising in points 0

DO A RUNNER ch.g. 10 Le Moss - Polarville by Charlottesvilles Flyer — J Love

155	15/2	Lanark	(R)	MEM	3m	4	G	*(fav) ld 6th, drew clr frm 14th*	1	12
413	8/3	Dalston	(R)	OPE	3m	9	GS	*mstks, nvr going wll, bhnd frm 12th, t.o.*	7	0

Restricted winner 95; missed 96; doddled home in Members but looks to have problems again 14

DOC HOLLYWOOD (Irish) — I 452^{F}, I 509^{4}

DOCK STRIKE (Irish) — I 397^{P}, I 440^{U}, I 525^{P}, I 575^{P}

DOC SPOT b.g. 7 Doc Marten - Detonate by Derring-Do — S J Robinson

1996 P(0),5(0),F(-),P(0),3(0)

417	8/3	Dalston	(R)	MDO	2 1/2m	11	GS	*mid-div, 5th hlfwy, sn lost tch, t.o.*	6	0
1074	13/4	Whitwell-On'	(R)	MDO	2 1/2m 88yds	16	G	*prom, ld 6th, disp 8th, ld agn 10th, hdd 4 out, wknd rpdly*	7	0
1106	19/4	Hornby Cast'	(L)	MDO	3m	10	G	*rear, mstk 3rd & 7th, wll bhnd frm 4 out, t.o.*	7	0
1410	5/5	Witton Cast'	(R)	MEM	3m	3	GS	*settld in 3rd, chsd wnr 13th til outpcd 2 out,wknd last*	3	0

Placed 4 times 95-7 but does not stay & a win looks impossible 0

DOCTOR BRIGGS(IRE) ch.g. 8 King Of Clubs - Great Meadow by Northfields (USA) — Mrs L P Vaughan

436	8/3	Upton-On-Se'	(R)	MDO	3m	17	G	*mid-div whn p.u. sddnly bef 7th*	P	0
706	29/3	Upper Sapey	(R)	MDO	3m	15	GF	*ld frm start, lk btn 16th, gd jmp to ld nxt, ran on wll*	1	15

Beat subsequent winners when scoring & could upgrade if fit in 98; tubed 16

DOCTOR DARLING (Irish) — I 103^{1}

DOCTOR DICK(IRE) b.g. 8 Orchestra - Miss Allright by Candy Cane — B Kennedy

1996 F(-),U(-),3(10),4(11),P(0)

24	26/1	Marks Tey	(L)	MEM	3m	6	GF	*1st ride, 3rd & in tch 8th, t.o. 3 out*	3	0
126	9/2	Cottenham	(R)	RES	3m	14	GF	*prom whn blnd & u.r. 2nd*	U	-
278	23/2	Charing	(L)	RES	3m	17	G	*s.s. 16th whn u.r. 2nd*	U	-
503	15/3	Ampton	(R)	XX	3m	11	GF	*(bl) sn wll bhnd, t.o. frm 2nd*	7	0
711	29/3	High Easter	(L)	RES	3m	6	F	*(bl) alwys last, mstk & rmdrs 10th, t.o.& j.s.14th, p.u. 16th*	P	0

Maiden winner 95; mistakes, headstrong & outclassed in Restricteds 0

DOCTOR-J(IRE) ch.g. 7 Jareer (USA) - Velvet Breeze by Windjammer (USA) — Gareth Richards

1996 **9(NH),14(NH),5(NH),5(NH),5(NH),5(NH)**

536	16/3	Erw Lon	(L)	LAD	3m	9	GF	*ld 2nd-12th, wknd rpdly aft 3 out*	5	0
844	31/3	Lydstep	(L)	LAD	3m	6	F	*ld/disp till f 9th*	F	-
1006	12/4	St Hilary	(R)	LAD	3m	7	GF	*12s-5s, ld to 6th, ld 10-13th, wknd frm nxt*	4	0
1470	11/5	Erw Lon	(L)	LAD	3m	9	GS	*ld to 5th, blnd 12th, sn wknd*	6	0
1560	24/5	Bassaleg	(R)	OPE	3m	7	G	*pllng, trckd ldrs, rdn 13th, sn strggilng*	5	0

Hurdles winner 95; gone to pieces now & safely ignored **10**

DOCTOR ON CALL (Irish) — **I** 348^{B}

DOCUMMINS (Irish) — **I** 99^{U}, **I** 232^{U}, **I** 282^{F}

DOHNEY BOY (Irish) — **I** 20^{3}, **I** 53^{4}

DOLLYBAT b.m. 8 Battle Hymn - Come On Doll by True Song — Mrs Carolyn Atyeo

1996 P(0),6(0),4(0),3(0),P(0),P(0),S(-),P(0)

526	15/3	Cothelstone	(L)	MDN	3m	15	GS	*ld to 6th, lost plc 12th, ran on agn clsng stgs*	3	13
692	29/3	Little Wind'	(R)	MDO	3m	8	GF	*ld to 10th, chsd ldrs to 15th, btn nxt*	4	0
1040	12/4	Cothelstone	(L)	MEM	3m	3	GF	*(fav) chsd ldr,ld 7-12th, disp 4 out til ld 2 out, hdd last,no ext*	2	10
1260	27/4	Black Fores'	(R)	MDO	3m	12	F	*chsd wnr 7th, no imp, demoted apr last, fin 3rd*	0	0
1437	10/5	Holnicote	(L)	MDO	3m	14	G	*hld up, went 2nd 17th, ld nxt til mstk & hdd 2 out, no ext*	2	12
1520	17/5	Bratton Down	(L)	MDO	3m	17	GS	*9th hlfwy, prog 14th, went 3rd apr 2 out, fdd*	5	11
1597	31/5	Bratton Down	(L)	MDO	3m	12	F	*prom/ld chsng grp, no prog 14th, 4th & no ch aft nxt*	4	0

Good at completing now but very modest & will need fortune to win **12**

DOLLY BLOOM b.m. 9 Crested Lark - Lucky Sandy by St Columbus — Mrs D F Sansome

1996 F(-),P(0),P(0),2(13),3(11),2(10),2(15)

1083	13/4	Guilsborough	(L)	MDN	3m	15	GF	*hld up, prog to trck ldr 13th, ld apr last, all out*	1	16
1355	4/5	Dingley	(R)	RES	3m	12	G	*(fav) chsd ldrs, blnd 15th, 4th & rddn 3 out, sn btn*	4	15
1605	1/6	Dingley	(R)	RES	3m	13	GF	*in tch,outpcd aft 15th,effrt to chs wnr aft 2 out,alwys hld*	2	15

Found ideal race seasonal debut & ran well after; not 100% genuine but may find Restricted in 98; GF **18**

DOLLYS BEST ch.m. 10 Crawter - Dollys Speedy Vii — W J Hayes

1311	3/5	Holnicote	(L)	MEM	3m	7	G	*bhnd frm 2nd, t.o. 10th, ran round own pace*	5	0
1437	10/5	Holnicote	(L)	MDO	3m	14	G	*t.o. 8th, p.u. 13th*	P	0

No sign of ability **0**

DOLLYS FIRST (Irish) — **I** 456^{P}, **I** 481^{P}, **I** 540^{F}, **I** 602^{2}

DOMANI HILL b.m. 6 Rakaposhi King - Whinberry Hill by Hill Farmer — Mrs Susie Guild

1996 **U(NH),15(NH)**

436	8/3	Upton-On-Se'	(R)	MDO	3m	17	G	*chsg ldrs whn blnd & u.r. 6th*	U	-
721	29/3	Sandon	(L)	MEM	3m	6	GF	*chsd ldrs in tch, 2nd 3 out, not qckn apr last*	3	0
941	6/4	Tabley	(R)	MDO	3m	11	G	*chsd ldrs, 3rd & wknng 14th, 4th whn f 16th*	F	-

2nd start counts for nothing & no real signs yet **0**

DOMINO NIGHT(IRE) b.g. 7 Buckskin (FR) - Frying Pan by Pitpan — E Haddock

1996 **6(NH),F(NH)**

82	2/2	Wolverhampt'	(L)	MDN	3m	11	GS	*chsd ldr, ld 16th, sn clr, ran on strngly, imprssv*	1	17
200	15/2	Weston Park	(L)	CON	3m	16	G	*disp 5th, cls up to 12th, outpcd aft, p.u. 4 out*	P	0
331	1/3	Eaton Hall	(R)	RES	3m	17	GS	*(fav) cls up, ld 3-4th, u.r. 5th*	U	-
467	8/3	Eyton-On-Se'	(L)	RES	3m	15	G	*cls up, 5th & ev ch whn u.r. 13th*	U	-
726	29/3	Sandon	(L)	CON	3m	8	GF	*mostly 2nd in tch, outpcd 4 out, eased & lost 2nd post*	3	15
1174	20/4	Sandon	(L)	MEM	3m	4	GF	*(fav) cls up, ld 3rd, sn clr, mstks 3 out & nxt, ran on well*	1	14
1412	7/5	Uttoxeter	(L)	HC	3 1/4m	10	GS	*keen hold, chsd ldr to apr 4 out, 3rd and weakening when f 2 out. Dead.*	F	-

Dead **16**

DONALD HAWKINS ch.g. 5 Vital Season - Hungerdown Lady by New Member — R J Francome

390	8/3	Barbury Cas'	(L)	MDN	3m	15	G	*rear, some prog 11th, nvr nr ldrs, p.u. 2 out*	P	0
1065	13/4	Maisemore P'	(L)	MDO	3m	13	GF	*mid-div, lost tch 8th, no ch whn f 14th*	F	-
1216	26/4	Woodford	(L)	MDN	3m	13	G	*mstks, hmpd 2nd, chsd ldrs, lost tch 15th, p.u. 3 out*	P	0

Showed just enough to suggest some hope for the future **10**

DONALS CHOICE (Irish) — **I** 36^{3}, **I** 56^{4}, **I** 99^{U}, **I** 154^{3}, **I** 283^{4}

DON CARLOS b.g. 5 El Conquistador - Enborne Blues by Oats — J T H Ainslie

419	8/3	Dalston	(R)	MDO	2 1/2m	10	GS	*blnd & u.r. 1st*	U	-
564	16/3	Lanark	(R)	MDO	2 1/2m	13	GS	*2nd mstly til ld 3 out, sn clr, easily*	1	15

Bolted home 2nd start & must have bright prospects if back in 98 .... **18**

DONNA (Irish) — **I** 8^{P}, **I** 38^{P}, **I** 79^{P}, **I** 428,

DONNA FOUNTAIN (Irish) — I 529[P]

DONNA KING (Irish) — I 102[P]

DONNRUA (Irish) — I 10[P], I 218[4], I 270[3], I 547[1]

DONSIDE gr.g. 9 Alias Smith (USA) - Delnadamph by Royal Palace — G F White

31	26/1	Alnwick	(L)	MEM	3m	4	G	*chsd ldr 5th til mstk 13th, 3rd whn blnd & u.r. nxt*	U	-
135	9/2	Alnwick	(L)	MDO	3m	12	G	*w.w. prog 10th, ev ch 4 out, btn nxt*	4	0
233	22/2	Friars Haugh	(L)	MDO	3m	13	G	*ld 5th til 4 out, upsides last, no ext flat*	2	14
566	16/3	Lanark	(R)	MDO	3m	10	GS	*4th 10th, sn wknd, p.u. bfr last*	P	0
734	29/3	Alnwick	(L)	MDN	3m	6	F	*(fav) prom, ld 9th, hld on wll flat*	1	13
947	6/4	Friars Haugh	(L)	RES	3m	6	GF	*jmp wll in ld til apr 4 out, sn btn*	3	10
1297	3/5	Hexham	(L)	HC	3m 1f	8	F	*chsd ldrs till s.u. after 4th.*	S	-
1414	9/5	Sedgefield	(L)	HC	2m 5f	6	GF	*soon well bhnd, t.o..*	6	0
1509	17/5	Corbridge	(R)	INT	3m	10	GS	*ld to 4th, sttld in 3rd aft, fdd 11th, t.o. 3 out*	5	0

Scraped home in poor race & usually easily beaten; unlikely to win Restricted 13

DONS PRIDE (Irish) — I 138[P], I 383[4], I 479[1], I 541[3]

DON TOCINO b.g. 7 Dominion - Mrs Bacon by Balliol — Henry Bell

1996 **9(NH),6(NH),F(NH)**

38	26/1	Alnwick	(L)	MDO	3m	14	G	*ld to 4th, prom aft, 3rd & btn whn mstk 3 out*	3	11
161	15/2	Lanark	(R)	MDO	2m 5f	14	G	*chsng grp, chnce 3 out, no ext frm nxt*	3	12
358	2/3	Great Stain'	(L)	MDO	3m	14	S	*prom, ld 10th, hdd 3 out, sn wknd*	5	0
697	29/3	Stainton	(R)	LAD	3m	5	F	*rear, jmp slwly 7th sn lost tch, t.o. & ref 15th*	R	-
1252	26/4	Easingwold	(L)	MDO	3m	9	GS	*in tch, 2nd frm 4 out, outpcd by wnnr*	2	10

Good at completing but no stamina & well beaten; unlikely to win 12

DONT RISE ME(IRE) b.g. 8 Don't Forget Me - Raise A Plum (USA) by Raise A Cup (USA) — M R Churches

23	25/1	Badbury Rin'	(L)	RES	3m	8	GF	*cls up, nrly u.r. 9th, 6th & wkng whn u.r. 12th*	U	-
44	1/2	Larkhill	(R)	MDO	3m	9	GF	*pllng, hld up, lost tch 14th, poor 4th whn u.r. 3 out*	U	-
101	8/2	Great Treth'	(R)	MDO	3m	9	GS	*prom, wth ldr whn c.o. by loose horse 9th*	C	-
242	22/2	Lemalla	(R)	MDO	3m	10	S	*in tch to 9th, rear whn p.u. 15th*	P	0
313	1/3	Clyst St Ma'	(L)	RES	3m	10	HY	*in tch to 12th, outpcd nxt, p.u. last*	P	0

A chapter of accidents 0

DONT TELL NELL (Irish) — I 19[3]

DON'T WASTE IT (Irish) — I 26[P], I 108[P], I 131[1], I 240[1]

DONTYOUDODA(IRE) ch.g. 8 Orchestra - Palaska by Mountain Call — J M B Pugh

184	15/2	Erw Lon	(L)	MDN	3m	14	G	*in tch in rear til f 5th*	F	-
538	16/3	Erw Lon	(L)	RES	3m	5	GF	*alwys rear, p.u. 13th*	P	0
640	22/3	Howick	(L)	MDN	3m	10	GF	*rear, p.u. 12th*	P	0
847	31/3	Lydstep	(L)	MDO	3m	5	F	*(bl) ld/disp to 11th, fdd, p.u. 14th*	P	0
1011	12/4	St Hilary	(R)	MDN	3m	10	GF	*mid-div, f 12th*	F	-
1138	19/4	Bonvilston	(R)	MDO	3m	9	G	*(bl) rear, f 13th*	F	-

Definitely more don't than do 0

DOOGLES SON (Irish) — I 499[P], I 594[1]

DOOLANS STAND (Irish) — I 86[P]

DORAN'S TOWN LAD b.m. 10 Tumble Gold - Thomastown Girl by Tekoah — Nigel Benstead

56	1/2	Kingston Bl'	(L)	OPE	3m	13	GF	*in tch, ld 6th, sn hdd & wknd, p.u. 14th*	P	0
277	23/2	Charing	(L)	MEM	3m	6	G	*nrly u.r. 2nd, alwys bhnd, t.o. 13th*	4	0
578	16/3	Detling	(L)	LAD	3m	11	F	*ld to 15th, ev ch 2 out, wknd flat*	3	17

Novice-ridden; ran remarkably well last start but vanished; best watched 15

DORGAN b.g. 6 Lighter - Lovelyroseofclare — J A T de Giles

1996 **13(NH),20(NH)**

293	1/3	Didmarton	(L)	INT	3m	16	G	*hmpd 1st, blnd 3rd, last & t.o. til p.u. 9th*	P	0

No signs of ability under Rules or in debut point 0

DORMSTON LAD b.g. 9 Pragmatic - March At Dawn by Nishapour (FR) — Mrs R Jowett

1996 P(0),6(0),P(0),3(10),3(11),P(0)

21	25/1	Badbury Rin'	(L)	MDN	3m	7	GF	*mid-div, rdn 11th, onepcd aft, lft 2nd last*	2	10
41	1/2	Larkhill	(R)	MDO	3m	13	GF	*ld to 2nd, wknd 13th, t.o. & p.u. 2 out*	P	0
176	15/2	Ottery St M'	(L)	RES	3m	17	G	*mid-div til p.u. 11th*	P	0
303	1/3	Parham	(R)	RES	3m	10	G	*sn rear, lost tch 8th, t.o. & p.u. 15th*	P	0
657	22/3	Badbury Rin'	(L)	MEM	3m	4	F	*(Jt fav) prom to 3 out, outpcd frm nxt*	4	0
871	31/3	Hackwood Pa'	(L)	MDO	3m	7	F	*ld to 4th, wknd, t.o. & p.u. 14th*	P	0

Placed in weak races 96/7 & no real winning chances 10

DOS DEEGAN (Irish) — I 154[F], I 273[1]

DOTHALI (Irish) — **I** 241[P]

DOUBLE COLLECT b or br.g. 11 Kambalda - Halcyon Years by Royal Highway Mrs M D Rebori

248	22/2 Brocklesby '	(L) CON	3m	10	G	*tried to make all, hdd bfr 3 out, no ext*	2	22
375	3/3 Doncaster	(L) HC	2m 3f 110yds	11	GF	*alwys prom, hit 3rd, rdn along 4 out, one pace next.*	3	18
583	17/3 Newcastle	(L) HC	3m	8	GF	*chsd ldr, weakening when f 14th.*	F	-
874	1/4 Uttoxeter	(L) HC	2m 7f	9	GF	*in tch when blnd and u.r. 7th.*	U	-
1071	13/4 Whitwell-On'	(R) CON	3m	10	G	*prom,disp 7th til ld 10th-13th, fdd 4 out,wll btn & p.u.2out*	P	0
1265	27/4 Southwell P'	(L) OPE	3m	8	G	*ld til disp 5th, ld 8-13th, wknd rpdly, p.u. 3 out*	P	0

H/Chase winner 95; missed 96; started well but lost form after & ground against; best watched 17

DOUBLE SILK b.g. 13 Dubassoff (USA) - Yellow Silk by Counsel R C Wilkins

1996 **1(33),2(33),1(36)**

92	6/2 Wincanton	(R) HC	3m 1f 110yds	6	GF	*(fav) ld 2nd, made rest, drew readily clr from 4 out.*	1	30
494	13/3 Cheltenham	(L) HC	3 1/4m 110yds	18	G	*cl up, ld 9th till after 17th, wknd 3 out.*	5	27
1087	16/4 Cheltenham	(L) HC	3 1/4m 110yds	8	GF	*(fav) chsd ldr, ld 3rd, made rest, clr 14th, styd on strly final 2.*	1	31
1291	30/4 Cheltenham	(L) HC	3 1/4m 110yds	4	GF	*(fav) ld to 15th, soon rdn, one pace after 3 out, eased when no ch run-in.*	2	27

One of the greats & still has some fire; 7 wins at Cheltenham but looks ready for retirement now 31

DOUBLE THE STAKES(USA) b.g. 8 Raise A Man (USA) - Je'da Qua (USA) by Fleet Nasrullah Mrs J M Whitley

1996 4(0),P(0)

555	16/3 Ottery St M'	(L) LAD	3m	10	G	*mid-div whn u.r. 4th*	U	-
627	22/3 Kilworthy	(L) LAD	3m	7	G	*4th frm 10th, not pce to chal*	4	19
781	31/3 Hereford	(R) HC	2m 3f	9	GF	*in tch, blnd 5th, hdwy to go prom 7th, wknd next, bhnd when p.u. before 10th.*	P	0

Showed up well 2nd start but does not stay & ran badly in H/Chase; best watched 15

DOUBLE THRILLER b.g. 7 Dubassoff (USA) - Cape Thriller by Thriller R C Wilkins

176	15/2 Ottery St M'	(L) RES	3m	17	G	*(fav) j.w. ld/disp til drew clr 3 out, imprssv*	1	22
294	1/3 Didmarton	(L) INT	3m	20	G	*(fav) trckd ldrs, effrt to chs wnr 14th, ev ch til outpcd aft 2out*	2	22
642	22/3 Castle Of C'	(R) MEM	3m	4	G	*(fav) jmpd lft, made all, drew clr 2 out, easily*	1	20
1147	19/4 Chaddesley '	(L) OPE	3m	7	GF	*prssd ldr, ld 11-13th & 15th, shkn up 2 out, ran on well*	1	26
1288	30/4 Cheltenham	(L) HC	2m 5f	10	GF	*(fav) soon cl up, chsd wnr 9th, mstk next, shaken up and one pace after 4 out.*	4	22

Good prospect; stays & potentially very useful; longer H/Chase on cards in 98; Good 27

DOUBTING DONNA gr.m. 11 Tom Noddy - Dewy's Quince by Quorum Mrs D Hughes

1996 7(0),3(18),10(0),6(11),P(0),B(-),2(13),2(19)

1	19/1 Barbury Cas'	(L) XX	3m	11	GF	*chsd ldrs,poor 5th hlfwy,styd on aft,lft in ld 3 out,ran on*	1	21
256	22/2 Newtown	(L) OPE	3m	17	G	*prom, rdn apr 14th, sn wknd, virt p.u. flat*	10	0
491	10/3 Taunton	(R) HC	3m	8	G	*held up, reminders apr 11th, prog 13th, cl 4th when blnd and u.r. 15th.*	U	-
636	22/3 Howick	(L) CON	3m	12	GF	*4th til prog 12th, disp 3 out, ld nxt, qcknd flat*	1	20
1194	22/4 Chepstow	(L) HC	3m	11	GF	*nvr near ldrs, 6th and no ch when p.u. before last.*	P	0
1226	26/4 Pyle	(R) OPE	3m	6	GS	*ld 6-7th, prssd ldr, ld 14th, rdn clr frm nxt, ran on wll*	1	24
1362	5/5 Pantyderi	(L) CON	3m	4	G	*(fav) 2nd at 3rd, in ld at 11th, easily*	1	22
1469	11/5 Erw Lon	(L) OPE	3m	6	GS	*(fav) chsd wnr early, lost plc, p.u. aft 10th*	P	0
1524	17/5 Bredwardine	(R) OPE	3m	8	G	*nvr going wll, rmndrs 7th, went poor 3rd 3 out, no dang*	3	13
1560	24/5 Bassaleg	(R) OPE	3m	7	G	*prom, ld 12th, clr 14th, pshd out, unchal*	1	22

Inconsistent but enjoyed good season; useful at best; can win more at 12; unpredictable; G/F-S 23

DOUCE ECLAIR b.m. 11 Warpath - Sweet Clare by Suki Desu Mrs J E Eddery

1996 2(16),4(11),3(13),6(11),3(10),8(0),8(0)

215	16/2 Southwell P'	(L) LAD	3m	12	GS	*bhnd, nrly u.r. 8th, nvr on trms*	7	0
474	9/3 Southwell P'	(L) LAD	3m	12	G	*bhnd, prog & in tch 11th, 5th & btn whn u.r. 2 out*	U	-
617	22/3 Hutton Rudby	(L) LAD	3m	9	GF	*alwys mid-div, not qckn 3 out*	6	17
856	31/3 Charm Park	(L) RES	3m	8	F	*last at 10th, prog 14th, onepcd 2 out, lkd 4th*	3	17
1075	13/4 Whitwell-On'	(R) MEM	3m	9	G	*ld to 7th, prom whn wd apr 10th, cls 4th whn u.r. 2 out*	U	-
1101	19/4 Hornby Cast'	(L) RES	3m	14	G	*rear, strgglng 10th, styd on frm 3 out*	4	14
1263	27/4 Southwell P'	(L) RES	3m	9	G	*mid-div, mstks 10th & nxt, strgglng whn p.u. 13th, lame*	P	0

Schoolmaster in 97 & performed well; badly lame last start & may be finished now 13

DOUCE INDIENNE gr.m. 12 Warpath - Sweet Clare by Suki Desu J F Thompson

76	2/2 Market Rase'	(L) XX	3m	12	GF	*chsd ldrs, blnd 7th, outpcd 11th, no dang aft*	4	16
215	16/2 Southwell P'	(L) LAD	3m	12	GS	*mid-div, mod 6th at 9th, nvr nr ldrs*	5	13
426	8/3 Charm Park	(L) LAD	3m	12	GF	*mid-div til wknd 11th, wll bhnd 13th*	8	11
617	22/3 Hutton Rudby	(L) LAD	3m	9	GF	*mid-div, prog 11th, ev ch 3 out, not qckn nxt*	3	19
1104	19/4 Hornby Cast'	(L) MEM	3m	6	G	*disp til 4th,sttld 3rd til chasd ldr 4 out,not qckn frm 2out*	2	16

1349	3/5	Gisburn	(R)	CON	3m	11	GF	*(bl) mid-div, 4l 3rd at 14th, wknd rpdly aft*	7	0

Restricted winner 95; missed 96; mostly outlcassed 97 & blinkers no help; hard to win at 13 16

DOVEDON PRINCESS gr.m. 10 Baron Blakeney - Grace Of Langley by Foggy Bell — D Stephens

1996 P(0),3(13),P(0),2(15),1(13),P(0),4(12),3(15),7(0),9(0),P(0)

50	1/2	Wadebridge	(L)	RES	3m	10	G	*nvr a fctr*	9	0
100	8/2	Great Treth'	(R)	RES	3m	14	GS	*mstk 7th, rear, lost tch 13th, p.u. nxt*	P	0
533	15/3	Wadebridge	(L)	INT	3m	5	GF	*ld/disp to 11th, wknd*	4	0
805	31/3	Wadebridge	(L)	OPE	3m	5	F	*alwys trling fld, no ch frm 15th*	5	0

Maiden winner 96 but well-beaten in 97 & finished early 11

DOVEHILL gr.g. 11 Pragmatic - Arconist by Welsh Pageant — Mrs A Hickman

1996 3(0)

71	2/2	Higham	(L)	LAD	3m	6	GF	*prom, ld 4th, blnd & lost plc 6th, mstk 11th, u.r. nxt*	U	-
198	15/2	Higham	(L)	RES	3m	14	G	*prom, cls 2nd at 11th, ev ch til not qckn 16th*	2	16
303	1/3	Parham	(R)	RES	3m	10	G	*prom to 4 out, bhnd whn p.u. nxt*	P	0
831	31/3	Heathfield	(R)	RES	3m	2	F	*n.j.w. outpcd 16th, rallied nxt, no imp frm 2 out*	2	11

Maiden winner 95; ran well 2nd start but unlikely to win at 12 12

DOWHATYOUHAVETODO (Irish) — **I** 32^{P}, **I** 111^{F}, **I** 312^{1}, **I** 415^{2}

DOWNS DELIGHT (Irish) — **I** 27^{P}, **I** 55^{P}, **I** 281^{P}

DOWN THE MINE b.g. 11 Le Moss - Zauditu by Menelek — R T Baimbridge

1996 1(26),1(27),2(22),2(25)

394	8/3	Barbury Cas'	(L)	LAD	3m	5	G	*(fav) made all, rdn & drew clr apr last, styd on strngly*	1	26
1062	13/4	Maisemore P'	(L)	MXO	3m	12	GF	*(fav) ld, hit 10th, jnd 13th, hdd apr last, onepcd*	2	23
1327	3/5	Chaddesley '	(L)	LAD	3m	3	GF	*(fav) ld 3rd, made rest, 4l clr 4 out, comf*	1	23
1458	11/5	Maisemore P'	(L)	XX	3m	6	G	*(fav) made all, clr 15th, ran on well*	1	23

Very useful pointer; ground against in 97 & should win more in wetter year; G/F-S, prefers Soft 26

DOYDEN CASTLE b.g. 6 Revlow - Cool Brae by Rymer — A W K Merriam

775	29/3	Dingley	(R)	MDO	2m 5f	10	G	*alwys rear hlf, 5th & last frm 6 out, fin own time*	3	0

Tailed off when last to finish but may do better 0

DRAGONARA LAD(IRE) b.g. 5 Mazaad - Marsh Benham by Dragonara Palace (USA) — D Gibbs

720	29/3	Llanvapley	(L)	MDN	3m	8	GF	*ld til hdd 10th, wknd rpdly, p.u. 12th*	P	0
1010	12/4	St Hilary	(R)	MDN	3m	10	GF	*n.j.w. ld to 11th, grad wknd, p.u. 16th*	P	0
1230	26/4	Pyle	(R)	MDO	3m	10	GS	*mstks, ld to 10th, wknd rpdly & p.u. 12th*	P	0
1324	3/5	Bonvilston	(R)	MDO	3m	16	G	*ld to 11th, wknd rpdly, p.u. nxt*	P	0

Runs out of puff at halfway & cannot jump 0

DRAGONS BAY(IRE) b.g. 8 Radical - Logical View by Mandalus — P C W Owen

1587	29/5	Uttoxeter	(L)	HC	2m 5f	11	GF	*started slowly, held up and bhnd, steady hdwy 5 out, 5th when p.u. before 3 out.*	P	0

Given public schoolings, including one H/Chase & should benefit in due course 22

DRAGONS LADY b.m. 8 Dragon Palace (USA) - Lady Hamshire by Proverb — J S Warner

1996 U(-),4(0),4(13),2(11),1(15)

100	8/2	Great Treth'	(R)	RES	3m	14	GS	*prom, ld 5-6th, rear by 12th, bhnd whn p.u. last*	P	0
223	16/2	Heythrop	(R)	RES	3m	19	G	*f 1st*	F	-
488	9/3	Tweseldown	(R)	RES	3m	10	G	*mid-div, lost tch 11th, t.o. 13th*	5	0
633	22/3	Howick	(L)	RES	3m	8	GF	*3rd til wknd frm 12th*	5	0
1057	13/4	Hackwood Pa'	(L)	XX	3m	4	GF	*ld early, drppd rear, rdn 3 out, ran on wll last*	2	15
1135	19/4	Bonvilston	(R)	RES	3m	14	G	*cls up, ld 13-15th, ran on wll*	2	15
1210	26/4	Woodford	(L)	RES	3m	14	G	*ld 2nd-4th, ld 11th-13th, wknd 15th, p.u. 3 out*	P	0

Maiden winner 96; slow to find any form 97 & disappointing; looks hard ride now 14

DRAWN'N'QUARTERED b.g. 10 Decent Fellow - Pencil Lady by Bargello — Mrs E W Wilson

1996 3(20),F(-),4(15)

925	6/4	Garthorpe	(R)	LAD	3m	7	GF	*mid-div, in tch to 14th, wll btn whn p.u. last*	P	0

Dual winner 94; disappointing since & may be finished now 12

DR DOUSKI b.g. 5 Newski (USA) - Doucement by Cheval — Mrs S Cobden

181	15/2	Larkhill	(R)	MDO	3m	17	G	*rear & mstk 6th, prog 10th, jnd ldrs 14th, fdd 3 out*	4	0
1150	19/4	Chaddesley '	(L)	MDO	3m	7	GF	*rear, strgglng whn mstk 12th, t.o. & p.u. 3 out*	P	0

Not disgraced 1st start but absent 9 weeks after; may do better 10

DREAMINGAGAIN (Irish) — **I** 363^{3}, **I** 413^{S}, **I** 435^{P}

DREAM LORD br.g. 6 Arctic Lord - Warham Fantasy by Barolo — Mrs Anne Curtis

1996 **18(NH)**

262 22/2 Newtown (L) RES 3m 15 G *h.j.w. last pair & wll bhnd, t.o. & p.u. 14th* P 0
717 29/3 Llanvapley (L) RES 3m 13 GF *rear til p.u. 3 out* P 0

No signs of ability yet 0

DRIMEEN (Irish) — **I** 13P, **I** 415

DRIMINAMORE(IRE) b.g. 7 Buckskin (FR) - Miss Blue Jay by Blue Refrain — Major General C A Ramsay

234 22/2 Friars Haugh (L) MDO 3m 15 G *2nd hlfwy, 3rd & hld whn f last* F -
613 22/3 Friars Haugh (L) MDN 3m 12 GF *cls up til wknd 3 out* 5 0
997 12/4 Tranwell (L) MDO 2 1/2m 8 F *(Jt fav) disp ld to 8th, hdd nxt, wknd to 3rd 3 out, lft 2nd last* 2 12

Ran well on debut but struggling to stay at present; may do better 12

DRIVING FORCE ch.g. 11 Be My Native (USA) - Frederika (USA) by The Minstrel (CAN) — Mrs Helen Mobley

93 7/2 Bangor (L) HC 2 1/2m 110yds 11 G *(bl) ld 6th to 7th, driven along after 10th, soon wknd, t.o..* 4 0
195 15/2 Higham (L) LAD 3m 14 G *(bl) cls up til u.r. 12th* U -
375 3/3 Doncaster (L) HC 2m 3f 110yds 11 GF *(bl) mid div, hdwy to chase ldrs 10th, rdn 4 out, left 2nd next, no ch with wnr.* 2 22
678 25/3 Sandown (R) HC 2 1/2m 110yds 6 GF *(bl) cl up, chsd wnr 13th till wknd run-in.* 3 15
1078 13/4 Guilsborough (L) LAD 3m 11 GF *(bl) mstk 2nd, prog 8th, chsd ldrs aft, wknd 2 out* 4 15
1280 27/4 Fakenham P-' (L) LAD 3m 6 G *(bl) f 1st* F -
1488 12/5 Towcester (R) HC 2m 110yds 16 GS *(bl) prom to 7th, t.o. when p.u. before last.* P 0

Winning 2m chaser; always moody & no great interest in H/Chases; unlikely to do much at 12 15

DROMAIN ch.m. 8 St Columbus - Lucky Diamond by Eborneezer — Mrs D F Sansome

1165 20/4 Mollington (R) MDO 3m 9 GF *jmpd bdly in last til p.u. 7th* P 0
1402 5/5 Ashorne (R) MDO 3m 11 G *jmpd bdly, t.o. whn blnd & u.r. 6th* U -
1537 18/5 Mollington (R) MDO 3m 14 GS *prom, mstk 10th, wkng whn mstk 13th, t.o.* 4 0
1609 1/6 Dingley (R) MDO 3m 14 GF *in tch til blnd & u.r. 4th* U -

Needs to learn to jump first 0

DROMGURRIHY LAD (Irish) — **I** 51P

DROMIN CHAT(IRE) b.g. 9 Miner's Lamp - Coolishall Again by Push On — A Cole

1996 **P(NH)**,P(0),P(0)

240 22/2 Lemalla (R) RES 3m 11 S *chsd ldr to 6th, cls 4th whn mstk 11th, wknd, p.u. 13th* P 0
456 8/3 Great Treth' (R) INT 3m 11 S *mstk 4th, rear til p.u. apr 15th* P 0

4 runs in 2 seasons & no signs of real ability 0

DROMIN FOX b.g. 11 The Parson - Kilcor Rose by Pitpan — Mrs S Merrington

348 2/3 Market Rase' (L) RES 3m 13 GF *mstks, alwys bhnd, no ch apr 14th* 7 10
505 15/3 Dalton Park (R) MEM 3m 6 GF *hld up rear, prog 8th, mstk 4 out, ld last, ran on well* 1 12

Revived to cause surprise in Members but easily beaten otherwise 13

DROMIN HILL (Irish) — **I** 453, , **I** 514P

DROMIN LEADER b.g. 12 Crash Course - Astral Fairy by Prefairy — J M Turner

1996 3(16),2(23),**U(-)**,1(23),**4(17)**

596 22/3 Horseheath (R) LAD 3m 4 F *made all, ran on gamely whn prssd last* 1 20
780 31/3 Fakenham (L) HC 3m 110yds 7 G *(fav) chsd ldr, left in ld 4 out, driven out, held on well.* 1 20
1284 29/4 Huntingdon (R) HC 3m 6 G *keen hold, cl up, chsd wnr 11th, rdn apr 2 out, 3rd and held when mstk two out, wknd.* 3 19
1529 18/5 Fakenham (L) HC 3m 110yds 9 G *made all, clr after 3 out, all out.* 1 23

Fair performer & well-placed in 97; best at easy 3m; should win Laides at 13; G-F 24

DROMIN MIST ch.g. 10 Over The River (FR) - Ten-Cents by Taste Of Honey — Dick Chapman

332 1/3 Eaton Hall (R) RES 3m 18 GS *mid to rear, nvr dang, p.u. 4 out* P 0

Looks to have no prospects now 0

DROMOD HERO (Irish) — **I** 3024, **I** 337F

DROMOD MAGIC (Irish) — **I** 20P, **I** 260P

DROMOD POINT (Irish) — **I** 361, **I** 932, **I** 1832, **I** 4082

DROUM ROSS(IRE) b.g. 6 Satco (FR) - Cloghersville by Sweet Revenge — Richard Mathias

644 22/3 Castle Of C' (R) MDO 3m 9 G *prom, ld 15th-3 out, 5th & wkng whn blnd nxt* 5 11

Placed in Irish Maiden 96; fair effort in weak race but vanished 11

DRUID BLUE gr.g. 15 Padro - Beauty's Pal by Charlie's Pal — Miss E J Kessler
1996 P(0),P(0)

1480	11/5 Ottery St M'	(L) MEM 3m	6	G	*disp to 6th, prom to 13th, wknd 3 out*	3	0
1579	26/5 Lifton	(R) CON 3m	9	G	*ld 6th-13th, no ext frm nxt*	5	0

No longer of any account 0

DRUID'S LODGE b.g. 10 Wolverlife - Taralote by Tarboosh (USA) — D J Lay
1996 5(15),1(16),7(17),2(15),2(20),2(20),U(-),5(16)

10	25/1 Cottenham	(R) INT 3m	7	GF	*rear, rdn apr 11th, lost tch 13th, p.u. nxt*	P	0
72	2/2 Higham	(L) INT 3m	4	GF	*chsd ldr, mstk 14th, ld nxt, jnd 2 out, hdd & no ext flat*	2	19
123	9/2 Cottenham	(R) INT 3m	13	GF	*chsd ldrs, 4th & outpcd frm 14th, kpt on to tk 3rd nr fin*	3	19
271	22/2 Ampton	(R) CON 3m	15	G	*chsd ldrs, mstk 7th, 5th & outpcd 14th, no dang aft*	5	12
321	1/3 Marks Tey	(L) INT 3m	10	G	*disp ld til f 9th*	F	-
497	15/3 Ampton	(R) CON 3m	9	GF	*alwys 1st 2, ld 15th, made rest, styd on strngly frm 2 out*	1	19
802	31/3 Marks Tey	(L) INT 3m	4	F	*(fav) chsd ldrs, prog ld 10th, rddn clr apr last, styd on wll flat*	1	19
1113	19/4 Higham	(L) MEM 3m	3	GF	*(fav) trckd ldr, just ld 11th, lft clr nxt, v easily*	1	19
1279	27/4 Fakenham P-'	(L) OPE 3m	7	G	*chsd ldr, ld 4th, made rest, rdn apr last, styd on well*	1	21
1430	10/5 Marks Tey	(L) CON 3m	7	G	*(fav) chsd ldrs, 4th at 9th, 2nd 14th, disp 4 out, sn outpcd,eased*	4	10

Enjoyed good season; stays, tough & consistent; injured last start but should win at 11; G/F-S 20

DRUMBANES PET ch.g. 8 Tina's Pet - Confetti Copse by Town And Country — Mrs C Lawrence
1996 4(10),3(0),3(0)

553	16/3 Ottery St M'	(L) MDN 3m	15	G	*alwys mid-div, lost tch 13th, outpcd aft*	4	0
1094	16/4 Hockworthy	(L) MDN 3m	11	GF	*slw jmp 4th, ld to 6 out, ld 3 out, hrd rdn & styd on*	1	13

Safe & found right opening; barely stays & Restricted looks unlikely 14

DRUMCAIRN(IRE) b.g. 9 Drumalis - Felin Geri by Silly Season — M D Noble
1996 **P(NH),11(NH)**

118	9/2 Wetherby Po'	(L) RES 3m	14	GF	*rear, lost tch 13th, t.o.*	10	0
230	22/2 Friars Haugh	(L) RES 3m	15	G	*alwys bhnd*	8	0
415	8/3 Dalston	(R) RES 3m	19	GS	*rear, prog & 8th hlfwy, effrt to chs ldrs 15th, no imp*	5	11
584	17/3 Newcastle	(L) HC 2 1/2m	11	GF	*blnd 1st, soon t.o..*	8	0
1406	5/5 Witton Cast'	(R) RES 3m	10	GS	*rear, strgglng 12th, t.o. 14th*	5	0
1509	17/5 Corbridge	(R) INT 3m	10	GS	*rear, dtchd frm 7th, t.o. & p.u. 10th*	P	0
1586	28/5 Cartmel	(L) HC 3 1/4m	10	GF	*(bl) n.j.w., in tch, prom 7th, driven along and wknd 12th, blnd next, p.u. before 14th.*	P	0

Ran passably 3rd start but miles behind other efforts; looks safely ignored 10

DRUMCEVA b or br.g. 11 Salluceva - Drumvision by Brave Invader (USA) — M S Wilesmith
1996 F(-),U(-),6(0),r(-),1(20),2(18),F(-)

3	19/1 Barbury Cas'	(L) XX 3m	14	GF	*alwys bhnd, blnd 7th, t.o. & u.r. 12th*	U	-
85	2/2 Wolverhampt'	(L) LAD 3m	11	GS	*bhnd, prog 9th, wknd 12th, t.o. & p.u. 3 out*	P	0
362	2/3 Garnons	(L) OPE 3m	11	GS	*chsd ldrs til lost tch 11th, t.o. & p.u. 3 out*	P	0
703	29/3 Upper Sapey	(R) OPE 3m	5	GF	*cls 3rd/4th til pce qcknd hlfwy, wnt clr 3rd 14th, outpcd*	3	14
1060	13/4 Maisemore P'	(L) MEM 3m	5	GF	*chsd ldr 3-11th, outpcd 13th, kpt on to tk 2nd apr last*	2	15
1236	26/4 Brampton Br'	(R) LAD 3m	4	G	*alwys 3rd, outpcd frm 7th, no ch frm 12th*	3	0

Members winner 96; below form 97 & well-beaten; hard to win at 12 16

DRUMFAIR VI (Irish) — **I** 329P

DRUMILLER HILL LAD (Irish) — **I** 113P, **I** 124P, **I** 252F, **I** 290P, **I** 3673

DRUMLONGFIELD (Irish) — **I** 284, **I** 664, **I** 945, **I** 118F

DRUMMER BOY(IRE) br.g. 9 Royal Fountain - More Expense by Energist — C G M Lloyd-Baker

6	19/1 Barbury Cas'	(L) LAD 3m	13	GF	*bhnd, 9th & t.o. hlfwy*	5	11
218	16/2 Heythrop	(R) INT 3m	21	G	*in tch, outpcd 3 out, styd on onepcd apr last*	3	18
293	1/3 Didmarton	(L) INT 3m	16	G	*alwys prom, still chsng ldrs whn p.u. aft 2 out, lame*	P	0

Dual winner 95; missed 96; problems again last start & best watched if returning in 98 17

DRUMREE (Irish) — **I** 178F, **I** 251P, **I** 2926, **I** 366F, **I** 4631

DRUMROCK LADY (Irish) — **I** 112F, **I** 250P, **I** 3292, **I** 4722, **I** 556F

DRUSILLA (Irish) — **I** 544F, **I** 591P

DRUSO(USA) b.g. 13 Raise A Cup (USA) - Pretty Pride (USA) by Kentucky Pride — Joint Ownership Terminated

472	9/3 Southwell P'	(L) MEM 3m	3	G	*w.w. clsd 11th, ld nxt, drew clr 3 out, easily*	1	10

Doddled home under novice rider & could repeat at 14 10

DUAL OR BUST(IRE) b.g. 6 Going Broke - Dual's Delight by Dual — J S Ruddy

1193	20/4 Garthorpe	(R) MDO 3m	9	GF	*in tch, ld 11th, 4l clr & going wll whn u.r. 2 out*	U	16
1380	5/5 Northaw	(L) MDO 3m	4	F	*(fav) made all, rdn clr aft last, comf*	1	15

Won a poor race but looks better than bare form & Restricted should be in sight in 98; G-F, so far 18

DUBLIN HILL(IRE) b.g. 7 Roselier (FR) - Deep Link by Deep Run — R H Knowles

1996 **3(NH),P(NH),P(NH)**

1101	19/4	Hornby Cast'	(L)	RES	3m	14	G	*reluctant to race & v slwly away, alwys t.o., p.u. last*	P	0
1250	26/4	Easingwold	(L)	RES	3m	15	GS	*bhnd early, prog 10th, fdd whn u.r. 4 out*	U	-
1348	3/5	Gisburn	(R)	RES	3m	10	GF	*hld up, ld 14th, styd on wll whn chal apr last*	1	16
1509	17/5	Corbridge	(R)	INT	3m	10	GS	*mid-div, prog 12th, ev ch 2 out, sn wknd, 3rd & u.r. last*	U	-

Irish Maiden winner 96; temperamental but scored only effort on fast ground; may win Confined 17

DUCHESS OF PADUA(IRE) b.f. 7 Duky - Anndanrose — R Mason

1996 **6(NH),5(NH),6(NH),9(NH),11(NH)**

187	15/2	Erw Lon	(L)	OPE	3m	16	G	*jmpd bdly, last whn p.u. 6th, lame*	P	0

Irish pointing winner 96; a brief & unfortunate English season 0

DUCHESS OF TUBBER(IRE) b.m. 9 Buckskin (FR) - Unforgetabubble by Menelek — R J S Linne

1996 P(0),4(14),1(20),2(22),**3(22)**

49	1/2	Wadebridge	(L)	LAD	3m	5	G	*wll bhnd frm 10th, p.u. 2 out*	P	0
99	8/2	Great Treth'	(R)	LAD	3m	10	GS	*rear, wknd & p.u. 11th*	P	0

Ladies winner 96; season lasted week in 97 & showed nothing; best watched; G-F 17

DUCKIN-N-DIVING b.m. 7 Hasty Word - Cosmic Occasion by Space King — J M Bowen

625	22/3	Kilworthy	(L)	MDN	3m	14	G	*bhnd til p.u. apr 4 out*	P	0
741	29/3	Higher Kilw'	(L)	MDN	3m	12	GF	*bhnd, hit 12th, t.o. & p.u. last*	P	0

No show either start & season lasted a week 0

DUKE OF IMPNEY b.g. 10 Roscoe Blake - Top Secret by Manacle — Peter Saville

1996 P(0),8(0),6(0),3(0),r(-),3(15),3(16),3(0),**F(-)**

200	15/2	Weston Park	(L)	CON	3m	16	G	*mid-div, wknd hlfwy, p.u. 3 out*	P	0

Beaten last 22 outings & may be finished now 10

DUKE OF LANCASTER(IRE) br.g. 8 Lancastrian - Chake-Chake by Goldhill — R C Irving

1996 **5(NH),F(NH),17(NH),3(NH),4(NH),3(NH),3(NH),3(NH),3(NH),P(NH)**

60	1/2	Kingston Bl'	(L)	MDN	3m	17	GF	*(fav) sn wll bhnd, prog frm 13th, poor 6th 15th, qcknd to ld flat*	1	13
222	16/2	Heythrop	(R)	RES	3m	17	G	*chsd ldrs, outpcd 14th, no dang aft*	5	0
372	2/3	Mollington	(R)	RES	3m	19	G	*rear grp, no ch frm 11th, t.o. 13th, ran on wll frm 2 out*	4	0
661	22/3	Badbury Rin'	(L)	RES	3m	6	F	*(bl) ld to 13th, styd on agn frm 2 out*	3	11
921	5/4	Larkhill	(R)	RES	3m	3	F	*(fav) (bl) last, slw jmp 3rd, wll bhnd whn blnd & u.r. 6th*	U	-
1058	13/4	Hackwood Pa'	(L)	RES	3m	6	GF	*rear, mstk 11th, no dang*	4	10
1275	27/4	Little Wind'	(R)	RES	3m	9	GF	*jmpd slwly in rear, kpt on frm 14th, nrst fin*	3	12
1449	10/5	Kingston Bl'	(L)	RES	3m	8	G	*ld to 4th, ld 6th, 2nd nxt, ld 10th-nxt, wknd 12th*	5	13
1567	25/5	Kingston Bl'	(L)	RES	3m	8	GF	*chsng grp, no prog 15th, wknd 3 out*	5	0

Slow & unenthusiastic; plods badly & blinkers no help; Restricted most unlikely 13

DUKE OF PLUMSTEAD gr.g. 12 Alanrod - Natalgo by Native Admiral (USA) — P J Williams

433	8/3	Upton-On-Se'	(R)	RES	3m	18	G	*rear frm 3rd, lost tch & p.u. 10th*	P	0

Rarely seen & worthless 0

DUKE OF TULLA (Irish) — **I** 103^{F}, **I** 158^{F}, **I** 196^{P}, **I** 275^{U}

DUKES SON ch.g. 10 The Parson - Dukes Darling by Duky — D P Smith

1996 3(16),P(0),3(14)

3	19/1	Barbury Cas'	(L)	XX	3m	14	GF	*in tch, 6th hlfwy, wknd frm 3 out*	7	10

Placed twice in 96 but fragile & vanished 1st day of 97 14

DUKESTOWN (Irish) — **I** 142^{P}, **I** 483^{5}, **I** 534^{1}

DULA MODEL b.m. 9 Latest Model - Mandula by Mandamus — J E Fear

1996 P(0),U(-),P(0),U(-),U(-),r(-),F(-)

1045	12/4	Cothelstone	(L)	MDO	3m	6	GF	*s.s. plld hrd, ld 5-9th, wknd rpdly, t.o. & p.u. 4 out*	P	0
1216	26/4	Woodford	(L)	MDN	3m	13	G	*ld 3rd, clr nxt, hdd 13th, wknd, t.o.*	6	0
1314	3/5	Holnicote	(L)	MDO	3m	8	G	*ld to 12th, wknd rpdly*	6	0
1492	14/5	Cothelstone	(L)	MEM	3m	4	GF	*ld 6th til hdd & blnd 12th, sn wknd, p.u. 2 out*	P	0

Last on only 2 completions from 16 starts 94-7 0

DUNAMANAGH EXPRESS (Irish) — **I** 221^{P}, **I** 526^{F}, **I** 586^{P}

DUNAMASE DANDY(IRE) ch.g. 8 Torus - Southern Dandy by Menelek — Mrs P Perriss

1996 **7(NH)**

22	25/1	Badbury Rin'	(L)	RES	3m	3	GF	*ld til p.u. apr 4th, saddle slppd*	P	0
59	1/2	Kingston Bl'	(L)	RES	3m	16	GF	*prom, ld aft 5th til mstk & hdd 10th, wknd, p.u. last*	P	0

Irish Maidenw inner 96; season lasted a week & showed nothing 10

DUNAREE (Irish) — **I** 219^{3}

DUNBOY CASTLE(IRE) b.g. 9 Carlingford Castle - Many Miracles by Le Moss — Miss Gi Chown
1996 1(22),U(-),1(23),1(21),U(-),U(-)

26	26/1	Marks Tey	(L)	LAD	3m	8 GF	*in tch, rdn 2 out, ev ch last, unable qckn flat*	2	23

Won 3 Ladies in 96; decent run only start 97 but vanished; may be best watched; F-G/S 22

DUNCAHA HERO b.g. 11 Golden Love - Arctic Jungle — R Barrow
1996 **8(NH)**

211	16/2	Southwell P'	(L)	MDO	3m	15 GS	*alwys bhnd, some late prog, nvr dang*	4	0
451	8/3	Newton Brom'	(R)	MDN	3m	8 G	*ld 2nd-10th, ld 12th-nxt, ld 14th, made rest, drvn clr*	1	13
927	6/4	Garthorpe	(R)	RES	3m	9 GF	*rear 4th, t.o. 8th, p.u. 10th*	P	0
1076	13/4	Guilsborough	(L)	MEM	3m	9 GF	*made most to 13th, effrt & ev ch 16th til wknd apr last*	3	14

Novice ridden; won a soft race; good stable; Restricted at 12 needs more 15

DUNCANS DREAM b.g. 12 Ayyabaan - Clifton Frolic by Ballynockan — Ms C Wilson
1996 1(0),5(0),P(0)

155	15/2	Lanark	(R)	MEM	3m	4 G	*lft in ld aft 4th, hdd 6th, outpcd frm 14th*	2	0

Members winner 96 & just a hunter now 0

DUNFORD BRIDGE(USA) b.g. 8 Sovereign Don (USA) - National Bay (USA) by Mo Bay (USA) — A T P Harrison

421	8/3	Charm Park	(L)	MEM	3m	6 GF	*mid-div til ld 3rd, hdd 6th & fdd 12th*	4	10
623	22/3	Hutton Rudby	(L)	MDO	3m	9 GF	*mid-div, outpcd 12th, prog 14th, wknd 2 out*	3	10

Not disgraced either start 97 but rarely seen & time passing 11

DUNHILL LADY (Irish) — **I** 270^{P}, **I** 401^{P}

DUNTURK VIEW (Irish) — **I** 120^{P}, **I** 122^{P}

DURBO b.g. 13 Bustino - Durun by Run The Gantlet (USA) — Mrs E J Champion
1996 1(19),3(14),4(11),3(18),3(15)

280	23/2	Charing	(L)	LAD	3m	12 G	*trckd ldrs going wll til not qckn frm 16th, onepcd*	4	17
968	6/4	Penshurst	(L)	LAD	3m	5 F	*ld to 3rd, cls aft, ld 13th, hdd 3 out, rlld flat, alwys hld*	2	16

Ladies winner 96; safe & consistent; goes well fresh; may still have chances at 14; F-G/S 16

DURHAM DELIGHT b.m. 8 Idiot's Delight - Dyna Drueni by Law Of The Wise — Eddy Luke
1996 **19(NH),11(NH)**

358	2/3	Great Stain'	(L)	MDO	3m	14 S	*ld, sn clr, u.r. 5th*	U	-

No ability under Rules & soon vanished from points 0

DURHAM GLINT b.g. 6 Glint Of Gold - Jem Jen by Great Nephew — Eddy Luke

32	26/1	Alnwick	(L)	RES	3m	11 G	*mstks, alwys last, t.o. & p.u. 13th*	P	0
131	9/2	Alnwick	(L)	RES	3m	13 G	*alwys bhnd, t.o. & p.u. 3 out*	P	0
1409	5/5	Witton Cast'	(R)	MDO	3m	15 GS	*rear & sn detached, t.o. 7th, p.u. 3 out*	P	0
1429	10/5	Aspatria	(L)	MDO	3m	15 G	*rear, effrt 11th, 5th & no ch whn f 13th*	F	-
1513	17/5	Corbridge	(R)	MDO	3m	13 GS	*mid-div,prog 6th,chsng ldr whn blnd 12th, mstk 2 out,sn btn*	3	12

First form last start but blunders his way round at present; should do better if jumping ironed out 13

DURZI b.g. 12 High Line - Sookera (USA) by Roberto (USA) — Mrs R E Walker
1996 P(0),P(0),4(10),P(0)

572	16/3	Garnons	(L)	INT	3m	13 G	*s.s. rdn into mid-div 7th, wknd & p.u. 10th*	P	0
650	22/3	Siddington	(L)	CON	3m	8 F	*ref & u.r. 1st*	R	-
1403	5/5	Ashorne	(R)	CON	3m	14 G	*ref 1st*	R	-

No longer of any account 0

DUSKANTO (Irish) — **I** 332^{P}

DUSKY RUN (Irish) — **I** 45^{F}, **I** 497^{P}, **I** 541^{P}, **I** 591^{F}

DUST OF LIFE b.m. 7 War Hero - Yellow Wagtail by Paddy's Stream — T E Pocock

527	15/3	Cothelstone	(L)	MDN	3m	14 GS	*twrds rear til p.u. 15th*	P	0
1040	12/4	Cothelstone	(L)	MEM	3m	3 GF	*alwys 3rd, handy to 13th, lost tch nxt, t.o. 3 out*	3	0

Yet to show any ability 0

DUSTY FURLONG b.g. 9 Button Bright (USA) - Poppy Furlong by Armagnac Monarch — Mrs Katie Squire
1996 6(0),2(10),F(-),4(0)

740	29/3	Higher Kilw'	(L)	MDN	3m	15 GF	*t.o. & p.u. 12th*	P	0
794	31/3	Bishopsleigh	(R)	MDO	3m	12 G	*prom early, lost tch 7th, t.o. & p.u. 16th*	P	0
1110	19/4	Flete Park	(R)	LAD	3m	9 GF	*sn rear, jmpd lft, t.o. & p.u. 14th*	P	0
1260	27/4	Black Fores'	(R)	MDO	3m	12 F	*nvr nr ldrs, fin 4th*	0	0
1399	5/5	High Bickin'	(R)	MDO	3m	12 G	*raced wd, 6th hlfwy, mstk 12th, wll bhnd frm nxt*	4	0
1485	11/5	Ottery St M'	(L)	MDO	3m	13 G	*alwys mid-div, nvr on trms, outpcd*	5	0

1584	26/5	Lifton	(R)	MDO	3m	13	G	*ld/disp 5th til drew clr 2 out, hdd last, sn wknd*	3	11
1610	7/6	Umberleigh	(L)	MEM	3m	3	F	*(fav) trckd ldr, ld apr 13th, sn clr, drvn & all out, lame*	1	0

Long-standing Maiden till found dreadful race last day of season - will not win again 10

DUSTY ROSE (Irish) — I 61[4], I 138[2], I 188[F], I 273[P], I 296[P], I 488[2], I 499[4]

DVVIT (Irish) — I 184[5], I 285[P]

DYNAMIC DESIGN (Irish) — I 40[1]

DYNAMITE DAN(IRE) b.g. 9 Ballinamona Boy - Aliceion by Tanfirion — B Kennedy

1996 U(-),1(18)

24	26/1	Marks Tey	(L)	MEM	3m	6	GF	*(fav) ld to 3rd, chsd wnr aft, 3l down 2 out, no ext*	2	13
123	9/2	Cottenham	(R)	INT	3m	13	GF	*hld up, prog & in tch 13th, sn btn, p.u. 16th*	P	0
193	15/2	Higham	(L)	CON	3m	14	G	*mid-div till f 5th*	F	-
319	1/3	Marks Tey	(L)	CON	3m	11	G	*chsd ldrs to 15th, sn wknd, t.o.*	5	0
441	8/3	Higham	(L)	INT	3m	7	G	*cls up,clsng whn ran wd apr 3 out,rallied to ld nr fin*	1	19
594	22/3	Horseheath	(R)	XX	3m	2	F	*(fav) nrrw ld to 5th, disp aft til qcknd clr last*	1	16

Members winner 96; best at easy 3m & slow to find form 97; can win Confined in right conditions; G-F 19

DYNASTIE D'AUGE(FR) br.m. 6 Cyborg (FR) - Pinzuta (FR) by Carvin — Miss Z A Green

613	22/3	Friars Haugh	(L)	MDN	3m	12	GF	*f 3rd*	F	-
815	31/3	Tranwell	(L)	MDO	2 1/2m	14	G	*mid-div, no imp on ldrs final m*	7	0
1429	10/5	Aspatria	(L)	MDO	3m	15	G	*mstk 5th, alwys bhnd, t.o. 12th, p.u. last*	P	0

Well-beaten on only completion & shows no great signs yet 0

DYSART ABBEY (Irish) — I 60[F], I 105[P], I 138[P], I 227[5], I 273[P]

DYSART O'DEA (Irish) — I 530[2], I 587[F]

EADIE (Irish) — I 61[F]

EAGLE BID(IRE) b.g. 9 Auction Ring (USA) - Gay Folly by Wolver Hollow — Mrs D H McCarthy

194	15/2	Higham	(L)	OPE	3m	12	G	*(fav) (vis) mid-div, jnd ldrs 10th, going wll whn p.u. aft 13th, dsmntd*	P	0
585	18/3	Fontwell	(R)	HC	2m 3f	7	GF	*(vis) held up in tch, hdwy 9th, wknd 2 out.*	4	16

H/Chase winner 95; missed 96; stable out of form 97; sold & best watched early 98 18

EAGLE VAIL (Irish) — I 347[P], I 438[F]

EARL BOON gr.g. 9 Baron Blakeney - Miss Boon by Road House II — J A Keighley

1996 2(22),1(26),5(12),P(0)

2	19/1	Barbury Cas'	(L)	XX	3m	14	GF	*mid-div, 6th & pshd alng hlfwy, no prog*	5	17
395	8/3	Barbury Cas'	(L)	XX	3m	9	G	*w.w. prog 9th, slght ld 2 out, hdd & wknd und pres flat*	4	17
862	31/3	Kingston St'	(R)	CON	3m	7	F	*held up, prog 16th, ld aft 3 out, clr til cght nr post*	2	18
929	6/4	Charlton Ho'	(L)	MEM	3m	5	G	*mstk 9th,trckd ldrs,ld 12-14th,ralld und pres last,jst fld*	2	24
1271	27/4	Little Wind'	(R)	OPE	3m	3	GF	*(fav) trckd ldr, ld 14th, qcknd clr 16th, easily*	1	22
1440	10/5	Holnicote	(L)	OPE	3m	3	G	*(fav) ld 2nd-aft nxt, ld aft 10th, forged clr frm 3 out*	1	22
1593	31/5	Bratton Down	(L)	XX	3m	5	F	*(fav) ld to 8th, trckd ldr, ld aft 16th, clr last, comf*	1	24
1611	7/6	Umberleigh	(L)	OPE	3m	8	F	*(fav) j.w. trckd ldr, ld 8th-aft 12th, ld 3 out, sn clr, easily*	1	0

Novice-ridden early season but returned to best after; top stable; can win more; G-F 26

EARL GRAY gr.g. 10 Baron Blakeney - Conveyor Belle by Gunner B — Mrs A Lockwood

1996 6(13),8(0),4(0),U(-),P(0),P(0),7(0),6(0),P(0),5(13),P(0),6(10)

118	9/2	Wetherby Po'	(L)	RES	3m	14	GF	*rear, lost tch 10th, t.o.*	8	0
167	15/2	Witton Cast'	(R)	RES	3m	7	F	*alwys prom, 2nd 7th, disp 10th, ld 4 out, sn drew clr*	1	16
264	22/2	Duncombe Pa'	(R)	MEM	3m	9	G	*hld up in tch, prog 9th, wnt 2nd 11th,ld apr last,ran on wll*	1	16
353	2/3	Great Stain'	(L)	CON	3m	9	S	*mid-div, outpcd 12th, prog 14th, ev ch 2 out, no imp*	2	14
476	9/3	Southwell P'	(L)	XX	3m	6	G	*mid-div, 4th & rdn 14th, no prog*	5	0
619	22/3	Hutton Rudby	(L)	INT	3m	8	GF	*alwys rear, lost tch 3 out*	6	13
694	29/3	Stainton	(R)	CON	3m	11	F	*mid-div, prog to chs ldrs 8th, outpcd frm 4 out*	5	17
897	5/4	Wetherby Po'	(L)	INT	3m	3	F	*(fav) trckd ldr, ld 5th, clr 7th, 20l up whn blnd & u.r. 2 out*	U	15
1071	13/4	Whitwell-On'	(R)	CON	3m	10	G	*mid-div, rdn 9th, lost tch 12th, wll bhnd whn p.u. 2 out*	P	0
1247	26/4	Easingwold	(L)	CON	3m	9	GS	*mid-div, hit 13th, onepcd, nvr dang*	5	15
1405	5/5	Witton Cast'	(R)	CON	3m	10	GS	*prom til lost plcd 5th, rear 8th, lost tch 15th, t.o.*	9	0
1419	10/5	Easingwold	(L)	CON	3m	8	GF	*(bl) ld to 14th, sn rdn, wknd nxt, t.o. & p.u. 2 out*	P	0
1589	31/5	Market Rasen	(R)	HC	2 3/4m 110yds	10	GF	*(bl) soon bhnd, nvr on terms.*	5	12

Broke losing sequence of 25 with early season double; struggling since & Members best hope in 98 ... 15

EARL OF MIRTH (Irish) — I 53[P]

EARLSWOOD b.g. 7 Kinglet - Flashgun by King's Troop — Mrs Karen Jones

741	29/3	Higher Kilw'	(L)	MDN	3m	12	GF	*prom whn blnd & u.r. 5th*	U	-
1035	12/4	Lifton	(R)	MDN	3m	11	F	*nvr a factor, wll bhnd whn p.u. aft 12th*	P	0
1112	19/4	Flete Park	(R)	MDN	3m	13	GF	*b.d. 1st*	B	-

Unfortunate to date 0

EARLYDUE b.g. 10 Bustineto - Princesspry by Pry — T W Moore

1996 **10(13),F(-)**

63	1/2	Horseheath	(R)	OPE	3m	5	GF	*ld to 2nd, in tch, hit 12th, 4th & no ch frm 14th*	4	16
322	1/3	Marks Tey	(L)	OPE	3 1/2m	9	G	*mstks, ld 5-10th, blndrd 12th, 3rd & outpcd frm 17th*	3	20

Dual Irish pointing winner 96; passable runs both starts but vanished; best watched at 11 18

EARLY MAN b.g. 10 Mandalus - Early Start by Wrekin Rambler — Mrs John Grist

1996 **P(NH),8(NH)**

279	23/2	Charing	(L)	CON	3m	10	G	*trckd ldng pair til eased & p.u. 16th*	P	0
302	1/3	Parham	(R)	CON	3m	14	G	*(fav) 6s-2s, handy, ld apr 3 out, hdd nxt, wknd*	2	18
1504	16/5	Folkestone	(R)	HC	3m 7f	5	G	*settld in 3rd, chsd ldr 13th till mstk next, mistake and wknd 15th, p.u. before 3 out.*	P	0

Failed when the money went down & does not stay; will need fortune to win, even in SE 16

EARTHMOVER(IRE) ch.g. 6 Mister Lord (USA) - Clare's Crystal by Tekoah — R M Penny

1996 1(14),1(18),2(16),2(22)

97	8/2	Great Treth'	(R)	INT	3m	13	GS	*trckd ldr 7th, ld 14th, clr apr 2 out, imprssv*	1	28
296	1/3	Didmarton	(L)	LAD	3m	13	G	*(fav) w.w. out of tch, clsd 13th, ld 2 out, shkn up & ran on well*	1	28
645	22/3	Castle Of C'	(R)	LAD	3m	6	G	*(fav) hld up, prog to ld 8th, made rest, qcknd clr 2 out, easily*	1	28
1090	16/4	Hockworthy	(L)	LAD	3m	8	GF	*(fav) w.w. prog 8th, trckd ldr 3 out, ld aft nxt, pshd clr*	1	26
1213	26/4	Woodford	(L)	LAD	3m	6	G	*(fav) chsd ldr, disp 13th, rdn 3 out, sn ld, styd on strngly*	1	28
1490	13/5	Chepstow	(L)	HC	3m	7	G	*(fav) held up, hdwy to track ldr apr 7th, ld after 13th, mstk 2 out, shaken up and qcknd clr run-in.*	1	30
1588	30/5	Stratford	(L)	HC	3 1/2m	9	G	*(fav) held up in mid-field, hit 13th, steady prog from 16th, ld after 3 out, soon clr, ran on well.*	1	33

Cracking performer; stays & quickens well; proved himself last start & hard to beat 98; G-S 36

EASBY ROC(IRE) b.g. 9 Bulldozer - Lady Mell by Milan — Mrs C M A Dook

1996 3(10)

836	31/3	Thorpe Lodge	(L)	OPE	3m	7	F	*alwys prom, ld 5th-7th & 5 out, chsd wnr nxt, outpcd 2 out*	3	14
1267	27/4	Southwell P'	(L)	MEM	3m	4	G	*ld til apr 5th, chsd wnr aft, wknd rpdly 3 out, p.u.last*	P	0

Very lightly raced; modest at best & problems again last start 14

EASTER BARD (Irish) — **I** 163[1], **I** 240[3], **I** 345[6], **I** 494[P], **I** 523[1]

EASTERN PLEASURE gr.g. 10 Absalom - First Pleasure by Dominion — Ian Emmerson

1996 **P(NH),6(NH)**

133	9/2	Alnwick	(L)	OPE	3m	6	G	*hld up in tch, prog 9th, outpcd apr 4 out, t.o.*	4	0
166	15/2	Witton Cast'	(R)	OPE	3m	8	F	*keen hld, prom, 2nd at 9th, u.r. nxt*	U	-
353	2/3	Great Stain'	(L)	CON	3m	9	S	*prom, ld 11th, drew clr 2 out, v easily*	1	17
562	16/3	Lanark	(R)	OPE	3m	8	GS	*alwys hndy, ch apr 3 out, wknd qckly*	4	10
732	29/3	Alnwick	(L)	CON	3m	6	F	*chsd ldr, lft in ld 3rd, jnd 2 out, hdd last, no ext flat*	3	18
1099	19/4	Stratford	(L)	HC	2m 5f 110yds	14	G	*prom till wknd 4 out.*	3	10
1405	5/5	Witton Cast'	(R)	CON	3m	10	GS	*prom, chsd ldr 14th, wknd apr 4 out*	6	12
1571	26/5	Wetherby	(L)	HC	2 1/2m 110yds	15	GF	*prom, rdn along 4 out, weakening when f 2 out.*	F	-

Winning hurdler 94; found easy chance when winning (only run on Soft); struggles to stay 17

EASTLANDS HI-LIGHT ch.g. 8 Saxon Farm - Light O' Love by Lighter — J G Staveley

1996 U(-),1(15),4(13),3(15),2(16),2(17),5(0),2(15),**2(18)**

157	15/2	Lanark	(R)	RES	3m	11	G	*mid-div, rpd prog to ld 3 out, 2l clr last, hdd & no ext flt*	2	17
230	22/2	Friars Haugh	(L)	RES	3m	15	G	*alwys in tch, no ext frm 3 out*	3	17
383	5/3	Catterick	(L)	HC	3m 1f 110yds	10	G	*chsd ldrs, rdn along 4 out, soon one pace, blnd 2 out.*	4	19

Maiden winner 96; genuine, safe & one paced; Restricted possible but finished early 97; G/S-F 17

EASTWOOD LAD b.g. 7 Impecunious - Another Dandie by Communication — D W Holdway

539	16/3	Erw Lon	(L)	RES	3m	8	GF	*lft, t.n.p.*	0	0
841	31/3	Lydstep	(L)	MDO	3m	8	F	*trckd ldrs, tiring whn f 3 out*	F	-
1183	20/4	Lydstep	(L)	MDO	3m	8	GF	*mid-div, no ch whn p.u. 2 out*	P	0

An inauspicious start 0

EASY FEELIN (Irish) — **I** 176[F]

EBBZEADO WILLFURR(IRE) b.g. 6 Tidaro (USA) - Lady Ffizz by Gleason (USA) — J N R Billinge

131	9/2	Alnwick	(L)	RES	3m	13	G	*cls up, 3rd whn mssd mrkr aft 9th, cont, fin 8th*	r	-
230	22/2	Friars Haugh	(L)	RES	3m	15	G	*alwys ldng grp, 2nd whn slppd apr 2 out, kpt on well*	4	17
415	8/3	Dalston	(R)	RES	3m	19	GS	*mstk 4th,wll bhnd,poor 13th hlfwy,ran on 14th,too mch to do*	3	15
607	22/3	Friars Haugh	(L)	RES	3m	8	GF	*not fluent, wnt 3rd 9th, strgglng frm 12th*	4	11
947	6/4	Friars Haugh	(L)	RES	3m	6	GF	*3rd mstly frm 8th, wnt 4l clr apr 4 out, no ext frm nxt*	2	13

Irish Maiden winner 96; good enough to win Restricted but badly ridden & ground agaisnt mostly; Soft 17

ECOLOGIC (Irish) — **I** 107[2], **I** 161[1]

EDDIE (Irish) — **I** 94[2], **I** 148[1]

EDEN'S CLOSE ch.g. 8 Green Dancer (USA) - Royal Agreement (USA) by Vaguely Noble — Mrs A Villar

124	9/2	Cottenham	(R)	OPE	3m	9	GF	*prssd wnr to 10th, sn wknd, t.o. & p.u. 15th*	P	0

Winning hurdler; no chance of staying 3m & soon vanished 13

EDERMINE SUNSET (Irish) — **I** 344[B], **I** 407[P]

EDINA(IRE) b.m. 7 The Parson - Dukes Darling by Duky — Dennis Yardy

1996 **F(NH)**,**U(NH)**,**P(NH)**,**F(NH)**,**4(NH)**

88	2/2	Wolverhampt'	(L)	MDO	3m	13	GS	*chsd ldr to 6th, wkng whn mstk 8th, t.o. & p.u. 12th, lame*	P	0

Not an ab-fab season 0

EDINBURGH REEL ALE b.m. 6 Scottish Reel - Report 'em (USA) by Staff Writer (USA) — Mrs Richard Pilkington

1996 3(0),3(0)

30	26/1	Marks Tey	(L)	MDN	3m	9	GF	*(fav) jmpd rght, prom, ld 11th, in cmmnd whn lft wll clr 3 out*	1	15
222	16/2	Heythrop	(R)	RES	3m	17	G	*prom til wknd 14th, p.u. 2 out*	P	0
1081	13/4	Guilsborough	(L)	RES	3m	13	GF	*wll in rear, effrt & rdn whn mstk 12th, btn nxt, p.u. 3 out*	P	0

Changed hands 97 & found poor chance 1st time out; well-beaten after & more needed 14

EDUCATE ME(IRE) b.g. 6 Hollow Hand - Widdy — S Burley

1996 **P(NH)**

252	22/2	Brocklesby '	(L)	MDO	3m	9	G	*alwys last, t.o. 10th, p.u. 5 out*	P	0
478	9/3	Southwell P'	(L)	MDO	3m	17	G	*mid-div, ch whn hmpd 15th, sn outpcd*	4	0
839	31/3	Thorpe Lodge	(L)	MDO	3m	15	F	*(Jt fav) alwys prom 3rd/4th, outpcd by 1st pair frm 6 out*	3	0
1003	12/4	Alpraham	(R)	MDO	2 1/2m	10	GF	*alwys mid-div, styd on onepcd 3 out, nvr dang*	3	0
1268	27/4	Southwell P'	(L)	MDO	3m	13	G	*mid-div, prog 6th, ev ch 4 out, outpcd*	3	0
1345	3/5	Gisburn	(R)	MDN	3m	13	GF	*cls up, ld 3 out til apr last, outpcd*	2	14

Safe but very one paced; best run in 7m+ race last start & may plod to victory 98 13

EILID ANOIR ch.g. 8 King Goldwyn - Hartfell by Lord Nelson (FR) — J Shearer

1996 3(0),P(0),**3(12)**,**4(0)**,1(12)

584	17/3	Newcastle	(L)	HC	2 1/2m	11	GF	*in tch till wknd before 4 out, t.o..*	7	0
944	6/4	Friars Haugh	(L)	INT	3m	5	GF	*ld til aft 3 out, no ext frm nxt*	2	11

Lucky winner of short Maiden in 96; does not stay 3m & Restricted prospects very slim 13

EL BAE b.g. 11 Lord Ha Ha - Shanaway by Moss Court — Mrs Barbara Brown

1996 P(0),P(0),11(0),5(17),P(0),6(10),P(0),6(0),**10(0)**,P(0)

271	22/2	Ampton	(R)	CON	3m	15	G	*rr div, mstk 6th, nvr nr ldrs*	8	0
319	1/3	Marks Tey	(L)	CON	3m	11	G	*prom, 4th & ch 16th, outpcd frm nxt*	3	10
497	15/3	Ampton	(R)	CON	3m	9	GF	*alwys rr div, nvr nr ldrs*	6	0
799	31/3	Marks Tey	(L)	OPE	3m	5	F	*midfld, cls up 10th, outpcd frm 14th*	3	12

Well beaten all 14 starts 96/7 & sure to extend the sequence 12

ELDER HAYS ch.g. 7 Alias Smith (USA) - Melton Grange by Song — G G Tawell

445	8/3	Newton Brom'	(R)	MEM	3m	3	G	*blnd 2nd & rdr lost irons, u.r. bef nxt*	U	-
450	8/3	Newton Brom'	(R)	MDN	3m	7	G	*2nd outing, sn bhnd, p.u. 6th*	P	0

Season lasted one day of calamity 0

ELDER PRINCE ch.g. 11 Final Straw - Particular Miss by Luthier — Brian Gee

1996 1(22),1(24),3(17),2(17),**5(14)**

76	2/2	Market Rase'	(L)	XX	3m	12	GF	*(fav) hld up, hit 5th, prog 14th, lft 3rd 2 out, nvr nr*	3	20
350	2/3	Market Rase'	(L)	CON	3m	11	GF	*trckd ldrs, ev ch 14th, rdn & wknd apr last*	3	19
673	23/3	Brocklesby '	(L)	CON	3m	8	GF	*w.w. mid-div, prog 12th, ev ch apr 3 out, 4th & btn, f last*	F	-
836	31/3	Thorpe Lodge	(L)	OPE	3m	7	F	*(fav) 4th/5th for 2 m, 3rd 4 out, ran on frm 2 out,not rch wnr*	2	16

Dual winner 96; below best 97; barely stays; likes Market Rasen; could win again 19

ELECTRIC AVENUE (Irish) — **I** 141[P], **I** 195[2], **I** 305[P]

ELECTRIC BRIDGE (Irish) — **I** 534[P], **I** 559[P]

ELECTRIC CAN (Irish) — **I** 19[P], **I** 46[P], **I** 90[P], **I** 263[F], **I** 338[U]

ELECTRIC COMMITTEE(IRE) ch.g. 7 Lancastrian - Mary Black by Ardoon — James R Kearsley

142	9/2	Tweseldown	(R)	MEM	3m	8	GF	*ld, sn clr, tk wrong course bend aft 7th*	r	-
177	15/2	Larkhill	(R)	MEM	3m	6	G	*ref to race, tk no part*	R	-
267	22/2	Duncombe Pa'	(R)	OPE	3m	8	G	*plld hrd, ld & sn clr, hdd 14th, wknd qckly, f 4 out*	F	-
389	8/3	Sandown	(R)	HC	2 1/2m 110yds	6	G	*ld, clr from 3rd, hdd apr 2 out, wknd approaching last.*	4	14

678 25/3 Sandown (R) HC 2 1/2m 110yds 6 GF *ld 3rd, slight mstks 6th and 14th, rdn and styd on well run-in.* 1 20

Selling hurdle winner; all over the place but found soft H/Chase; impossible to place now 18

ELECTRIC EDDIE (Irish) — **I** 353P
ELECTRIC FENCER (Irish) — **I** 148P
ELECTRIC JOHNJO (Irish) — **I** 287P, **I** 391F, **I** 413P
ELECTRIC SPARK (Irish) — **I** 317P

ELECTROFANE(IRE) b or br.g. 9 Teofane - Clanwilla by Pauper — Miss N Joynes
1996 P(0),2(11),3(0)
648 22/3 Castle Of C' (R) RES 3m 8 G *in tch, rdn & outpcd 11th, t.o. & p.u. 15th* P 0
687 29/3 Little Wind' (R) MEM 3m 5 GF *s.s. alwys t.o.* 4 0

Lightly-raced maiden & likely to stay that way 0

ELECTROLYTE b.g. 7 Electric - This Sensation by Balidar — G Austin
1996 P(0),U(-),P(0),7(11),U(-),9(0),P(0),3(0),5(0),U(-),F(-)
3 19/1 Barbury Cas' (L) XX 3m 14 GF *chsd ldrs, 6th & wkng whn u.r. 13th* U -
98 8/2 Great Treth' (R) OPE 3m 14 GS *last pair, t.o. 7th, p.u. 16th* P 0
256 22/2 Newtown (L) OPE 3m 17 G *rear main grp, effrt 12th, sn outpcd & no ch* 8 0
400 8/3 Llanfrynach (R) OPE 3m 10 G *alwys mid-div, nvr dang* 5 13
537 16/3 Erw Lon (L) OPE 3m 9 GF *(bl) alwys mid-div, no dang* 5 14

Well beaten when completing & no real prospects in even modest company 13

ELEGANT ISLE (Irish) — **I** 249P, **I** 288^4, **I** 327P

ELEGANT SUN ch.g. 15 Sunyboy - Arctic Elegance by Articulate — Mrs F Lockyer
1996 2(10),F(-)
657 22/3 Badbury Rin' (L) MEM 3m 4 F *ld/disp to 14th, clr nxt, hdd & no ext flat* 2 11
1022 12/4 Badbury Rin' (L) LAD 3m 3 F *(fav) ld, mstk 4th, hdd 11th, sn wknd, t.o. 3 out* 3 0

Astonishing favourite last start & looks finished now 0

EL GUAPO ch.g. 7 Stanford - Puff Pastry by Reform — A Chinnery
276 22/2 Ampton (R) MDO 3m 12 G *pllng, lft in ld 3rd, hdded 13th, wkng whn blnd nxt & p.u.* P 0
320 1/3 Marks Tey (L) MEM 3m 4 G *ld to 9th, lost plc, wnt 3rd 15th, btn 2 out* 3 0
439 8/3 Higham (L) MDO 3m 11 G *sn rear, outpcd 8th, t.o. & p.u. 16th* P 0

Well-beaten in poor race & shows nothing - novice-ridden 0

ELI PECKANPAH(IRE) b.g. 7 Supreme Leader - Grove Girl by Stetchworth (USA) — Mrs Jean McGregor
386 7/3 Ayr (L) HC 2m 5f 110yds 7 S *v unruly start and dismntd, deemed to have ref to race.* 0 0

Rarely seen & could not have done less! 0

ELLE FLAVADOR b.m. 7 El Conquistador - Flavirostris by Grisaille — Mrs A B Watts
1996 P(0),1(15),3(12),2(10)
23 25/1 Badbury Rin' (L) RES 3m 8 GF *(fav) mstk 5th, chsd ldr, mstk 3 out, wknd & lost 2nd nxt* 3 13
106 8/2 Milborne St' (L) RES 3m 12 GF *hld up, prog 11th, ld 15th-3 out, outpcd frm nxt* 4 12
557 16/3 Ottery St M' (L) RES 3m 9 G *handy, 2nd at 13th, disp 4 out til lft in ld last* 1 16
862 31/3 Kingston St' (R) CON 3m 7 F *(fav) hdwy to disp aft 16th, ev ch til wknd rpdly aft 3 out* 3 14
1156 20/4 Stafford Cr' (R) INT 3m 6 GF *alwys prom, cls 3rd til outpcd frm 2 out* 3 13
1438 10/5 Holnicote (L) LAD 3m 7 G *keen hld, prom, 2nd whn mstk 14th, wknd 3 out, mstk last* 5 17
1608 1/6 Dingley (R) INT 3m 11 GF *raced in 5th, mstk 8th, ran on 14th, chal 2 out, no ext last* 4 19

Maiden winner 96; possibly fortunate winner & struggles to stay; ran well last start & may win again ... 19

ELLEN'S PRIDE (Irish) — **I** 596F

ELLERTON HILL br.g. 14 Potent Councillor - Kenny by Royal Pennant — T W Thompson
1996 1(26),**6(18)**,F(-),2(22)
163 15/2 Witton Cast' (R) MEM 3m 5 F *(fav) ld til apr 4 out, rdn whn lft clr nxt* 1D 19

Very useful in his day but ideal swan-song win foiled by technicality 19

ELLERTON PARK b.g. 10 Politico (USA) - Sweet Clare by Suki Desu — J F Thompson
1996 4(17),U(-),4(14),P(0)
348 2/3 Market Rase' (L) RES 3m 13 GF *ld, mstk 10th, hdd 3 out, wknd nxt* 6 12
424 8/3 Charm Park (L) RES 3m 12 GF *prom, outpcd 9th, wknd 13th, p.u. 4 out (lame)* P 0

Maiden winner 94; missed 95 & problems again 97 13

ELLERTON TONY b.g. 5 Ardar - Ellerton Song by Cree Song — T W Thompson
269 22/2 Duncombe Pa' (R) MDO 3m 16 G *alwys in rear, wll bhnd 14th, p.u. 2 out* P 0
620 22/3 Hutton Rudby (L) MDO 3m 10 GF *alwys strgglng, t.o. 11th, p.u. nxt* P 0

Shows nothing yet **0**

ELLFIEDICK gr.m. 6 Alfie Dickins - Tabellion by Tabbas — Mrs F M Gray

1514 17/5 Corbridge (R) MDO 3m 17 GS *alwys rear, t.o. 7th, p.u. 10th* P 0

No encouragement from one run late season **0**

ELL GEE ch.m. 7 Ra Nova - Evening Song by True Song — Paul Townsley

1996 **13(NH),8(NH),13(NH)**

151 12/2 Lingfield (L) HC 3m 13 HY *third when f 7th.* F -
225 19/2 Folkestone (R) HC 2m 5f 10 S *chsd ldrs till hit 9th, soon bhnd, t.o..* 6 0

Very lightly-raced & season lasted a week of no consequence **0**

ELLIES PRIDE (Irish) — I 126P, I 2091, I 3263, I 466P

ELMERS MARSH gr.m. 6 Lighter - Yankee Silver by Yankee Gold — A J Lawes

303 1/3 Parham (R) RES 3m 10 G *(bl) alwys last, t.o. & p.u. 10th* P 0

Unpromising **0**

ELMORE ch.g. 10 Le Moss - Be Nice by Bowsprit — Mike Roberts

1996 1(13),P(0)

198 15/2 Higham (L) RES 3m 14 G *conf rdn, made virt all, pshd clr 4 out, easily* 1 23
380 4/3 Leicester (R) HC 3m 9 G *(Jt fav) ld to 4th, led four out, hdd next, outpcd from last.* 2 17
983 12/4 Ascot (R) HC 3m 110yds 14 GF *mid div, dropped rear 10th, mstk 12th, p.u. before 3 out.* P 0

Maiden winner 96; bombed home in Restricted but aimed too high after; Confined likely if fit 98 .... **21**

ELWILL GLORY (Irish) — I 163, I 5183, I 5602, I 5985

EMARRCEEVEESS (Irish) — I 24P, I 59P

EMBU-MERU b.g. 9 Scorpio (FR) - Rosie Tudor by Tudor Treasure — R G Owen

1996 7(0),2(13),1(14),U(-),P(0)

260 22/2 Newtown (L) RES 3m 16 G *alwys wll bhnd, t.o. 10th* 6 0
325 1/3 Eaton Hall (R) MEM 3m 3 GS *(fav) ld to 12th, hdd 13th, in tch 3 out, outpcd, ref last* R -

Maiden winner 96; season lasted week in 97 & looks to have problems **11**

EMERALD BREFFNI (Irish) — I 120F, I 180P, I 2546, I 316U, I 3663, I 4642, I 5021, I 584F

EMERALD CHARM(IRE) b.m. 9 Mister Lord (USA) - Ko Mear by Giolla Mear — M P Wiggin

1996 **F(NH),12(NH),11(NH)**

261 22/2 Newtown (L) MDN 3m 16 G *w.w. prog 9th, btn frm 15th, lft 2nd 2 out* 2 10
435 8/3 Upton-On-Se' (R) MDO 3m 14 G *rear frm 10th, some prog 14th, no ch frm 3 out* 5 0
754 29/3 Brampton Br' (R) MDN 3m 9 GF *(fav) clr ldr frm 6th, 30l up 15th, hdd 3 out, kpt on und pres* 3 12
1019 12/4 Bitterley (L) MDO 3m 12 GF *trckd ldrs, 2l 3rd 14th, rdn to chal last, ld flat* 1 16
1202 25/4 Ludlow (R) HC 2 1/2m 5 GF *chsd ldrs till wknd 10th, t.o. when p.u. before 4 out.* P 0
1392 5/5 Cursneh Hill (L) RES 3m 6 GF *(fav) held up, efft to chs wnnr 13th, mstk & no ext frm 2 out* 2 16

Beat subsequent winners when scoring; barely stays but may find Restricted in 98; G-F **17**

EMERALD KNIGHT(IRE) ch.g. 7 Sandalay - Fort Etna by Be Friendly — Ken Liscombe

1996 1(20),2(21),**6(NH)**

725 29/3 Sandon (L) OPE 3m 4 GF *(fav) ld at slow pace to 5th, outpcd by wnr 11th, nvr nr aft* 2 15
939 6/4 Tabley (R) LAD 3m 9 G *rear, prog to trckd ldrs 15th, onepcd apr 2 out* 3 19

Useful prospect 96; changed hands & disappointing now; season lasted 8 days; best watched **16**

EMERALD MOON b.g. 10 Auction Ring (USA) - Skyway by Skymaster — R S Eagleton

1996 **4(NH),9(NH),5(NH),4(NH),4(NH),8(NH)**

376 3/3 Windsor (R) HC 3m 11 GF *in tch till wknd 13th, t.o. when blnd and u.r. 3 out.* U -
576 16/3 Detling (L) MEM 3m 10 F *ld 2nd-5th, lft in ld 7th, hdd aft 2 out, no ext* 2 11
1447 10/5 Peper Harow (L) CON 3m 6 GF *ld 2nd, sn clr, blnd 7th, hdd apr 13th, wknd, p.u. 15th* P 0
1506 16/5 Folkestone (R) HC 2m 5f 8 G *in tch to 10th, soon outpcd and bhnd.* 5 13

Winning hurdler 94; does not stay 3m & winning prospects in points very bleak **10**

EMERALD RULER b.g. 10 Tender King - Blue Gulf by Gay Fandango (USA) — Roger Nicholls

1996 **11(NH),7(NH),3(NH),8(NH),10(NH),4(NH)**

432 8/3 Upton-On-Se' (R) MXO 3m 7 G *4l 3rd at 12th, 2l 3rd whn u.r. 3 out* U -
1099 19/4 Stratford (L) HC 2m 5f 110yds 14 G *alwys in rear, t.o. and p.u. before 6 out.* P 0
1488 12/5 Towcester (R) HC 2m 110yds 16 GS *in tch, rdn 4 out, soon wknd.* 7 14

Fair run on debut but disappointing & does not stay 3m; can only be watched **14**

EMMA'S GAMBLE (Irish) — I 467P

EMMAS GAMBLE (Irish) — I 113P, I 129P, I 330P

EMPOWERMENT (Irish) — I 18P

EMRYS ch.g. 14 Welsh Pageant - Sun Approach by Sun Prince — David Bond

781 31/3 Hereford (R) HC 2m 3f 9 GF *chsd ldrs, wknd 8th, t.o. when p.u. before 2 out.* P 0

Emerged from retirement to no effect ... 0

EMSEE-H b.g. 12 Paddy's Stream - Kincsem by Nelcius — J M Turner

1996 2(16),4(0),**5(0)**,1(20),**6(0)**

64 1/2 Horseheath (R) LAD 3m 7 GF *mid-div, prog 11th, cls 3rd 13th, onepcd frm 3 out* 3 18
154 14/2 Fakenham (L) HC 2m 5f 110yds 10 G *held up, t.o. after 12th.* 6 0
271 22/2 Ampton (R) CON 3m 15 G *w.w. prog 7th, chsd wnr 3 out, sn rdn & no ex* 2 20
444 8/3 Higham (L) CON 3m 8 G *mstly 3rd/4th,2nd aft 11th,20l down 15th,ld apr last,sn clr* 1 19

Repeated 96 Higham Confined win; hard ride & often disappoints; may land hat-trick in 98; G/S-G/F ... 19

EMU PARK gr.g. 9 Mansingh (USA) - Gun Tana (FR) by Tanerko — J D Thompson

1996 P(0),P(0),7(0),P(0),4(0),2(16),**8(0)**

609 22/3 Friars Haugh (L) LAD 3m 11 GF *s.s., nvr dang* 7 13
945 6/4 Friars Haugh (L) LAD 3m 6 GF *2nd mstly til wknd 4 out, poor 4th whn u.r. 2 out* U -
994 12/4 Tranwell (L) LAD 3m 5 F *lft in ld 4th til hdd 6th, ev ch til demoted to 3rd 3 out* 3 17
1220 26/4 Balcormo Ma' (R) OPE 3m 2 F *trckd ldr til ld 2 out, held on wll* 1 10
1297 3/5 Hexham (L) HC 3m 1f 8 F *in tch till wknd from 10th, t.o..* 5 0
1545 24/5 Cartmel (L) HC 3 1/4m 14 G *bhnd, hdwy 9th (water), in tch when hit 12th, wknd 4 out (water).* 7 0

Lost Maiden certificate in joke contest & that spells end of winning chances ... 13

EMYVALE BOY (Irish) — I 430P, I 548P, I 579P, I 594P

ENCHANTED MAN b.g. 13 Enchantment - Queen's Treasure by Queen's Hussar — Mrs J M Morris

1996 F(-),P(0),**3(12)**,P(0),2(16)

781 31/3 Hereford (R) HC 2m 3f 9 GF *bhnd 6th, t.o. when p.u. before 3 out.* P 0

Does not stay & too old now ... 0

END OF THE RUN b.g. 6 Pragmatic - Its Now Up To You by Deep Run — E F Birchall

1996 F(-)

263 22/2 Newtown (L) MDN 3m 11 G *pllng, in tch til ran out 6th* r -

Two runs in 2 seasons & nothing yet ... 0

ENGAGING b.g. 10 Black Minstrel - Ko Mear by Giolla Mear — A Jackson

1996 2(11),6(0),P(0),3(13),P(0),P(0)

265 22/2 Duncombe Pa' (R) CON 3m 15 G *prom til lost plc qckly & p.u. 7th* P 0

Placed twice in 96 but clearly problems in 97 ... 10

ENSIGN EWART(IRE) ch.g. 6 Buckskin (FR) - Clonea Fog by Laurence O — Major M W Sample

1996 3(0),5(10),1(16),1(17)

229 22/2 Friars Haugh (L) CON 3m 9 G *hld up, ldng grp frm 13th, chsd wnr 3 out, no imp* 2 20
611 22/3 Friars Haugh (L) CON 3m 11 GF *(Jt fav) mstly 2nd til ld 5 out,hdd brfly nxt,styd on wll frm 3 out* 1 21
972 7/4 Kelso (L) HC 3m 1f 12 GF *(fav) held up, steady hdwy 14th, chsd ldrs 3 out, effort and rdn next, styd on same pace.* 2 22
1201 24/4 Perth (R) HC 3m 14 G *towards rear, steady hdwy from 12th, styd on well to ld final 100 yards, all out.* 1 25

Very promising; improving, stays well & genuine; more H/Chases likely 98; G/S-G/F ... 27

EOINS LAD (Irish) — I 397², I 440, , I 468²

EOSTRE b.g. 8 Saxon Farm - Herald The Dawn by Dubassoff (USA) — Mrs J M Lancaster

1996 2(10),F(-),2(14),1(14)

157 15/2 Lanark (R) RES 3m 11 G *cls up frm hlfwy, qcknd wll to ld flat* 1 18
414 8/3 Dalston (R) XX 3m 9 GS *mstk 3rd, nvr going wll, lost tch 12th, t.o.* 5 0
778 31/3 Carlisle (R) HC 3 1/4m 14 G *ld to 3rd, lost pl 11th, p.u. before 4 out.* P 0

Maiden winner 96; improved to win Restricted but clearly problems after & best watched ... 16

EQUATIME b.m. 11 Turn Back The Time (USA) - Equa by Cheval — T K Williams

1996 P(0),P(0),U(-),P(0),4(0),3(0)

399 8/3 Llanfrynach (R) CON 3m 11 G *mid-div, styd on onepcd* 6 10
538 16/3 Erw Lon (L) RES 3m 5 GF *chsd wnr, nvr able to chal* 3 10
1008 12/4 St Hilary (R) RES 3m 11 GF *ld til f 12th* F -
1135 19/4 Bonvilston (R) RES 3m 14 G *ld to 12th, prom aft til wknd 3 out* 6 0
1227 26/4 Pyle (R) RES 3m 15 GS *wth ldrs to 10th, sn wknd, p.u. 15th* P 0
1467 11/5 Erw Lon (L) MEM 3m 3 GS *ld to 15th, jmpd rght, btn whn mstk 2 out* 2 0

Maiden winner 94; rarely completes now & well-beaten when she does ... 0

ERIK THE VIKING b.g. 6 Leading Star - Gay Viking by Wingspread — R J Armson

775	29/3	Dingley	(R)	MDO	2m 5f	10	G	*rear hlf til u.r. 4th*	U	-
941	6/4	Tabley	(R)	MDO	3m	11	G	*rear, mstk 6th, prog & in tch whn f 13th*	F	-
1209	26/4	Clifton On '	(L)	MDO	3m	16	GS	*alwys last trio, outpcd 6 out*	9	0

Showed a little 2nd start but not yet threatening to plunder 0

ERINSBOROUGH (Irish) — **I** 83^P^, **I** 189^P^

ERLEMO b.g. 8 Mummy's Game - Empress Catherine by Welsh Pageant — Miss Sarah George

1996 **6(NH),9(NH),8(NH),3(NH),5(NH),2(NH),11(NH)**

568	16/3	Garnons	(L)	CON	3m	12	G	*alwys rear, last at 9th, styd on onepcd frm 14th*	5	15
751	29/3	Brampton Br'	(R)	XX	3m	5	GF	*(bl) not fluent, rdn 15th, chal 3 out, sn btn*	2	18
1099	19/4	Stratford	(L)	HC	2m 5f 110yds	14	G	*(bl) started slowly, alwys well bhnd.*	7	0

Selling hurdle winner 95; beat only 3 others in 97 & not likely to win a point 14

ERME ROSE(IRE) br.m. 8 Callernish - Rose Money by Roselier (FR) — Mrs B C Willcocks

1996 2(17),1(18),3(16),2(19),1(18),3(21)

456	8/3	Great Treth'	(R)	INT	3m	11	S	*ld til 5th, lost plc 14th, p.u. apr 2 out*	P	0
631	22/3	Kilworthy	(L)	INT	3m	8	G	*lost plc & rmmndrs apr 12th, bhnd whn p.u. apr last*	P	0
1092	16/4	Hockworthy	(L)	XX	3m	5	GF	*ld to 8th, wknd 12th, t.o. & p.u. 2 out*	P	0

dual winner 96 but fell to pieces 97 & can only be watched if reappearing 12

ESERIE DE CORES(USA) b.g. 7 Gold Crest (USA) - April Blues by Cure The Blues (USA) — F R Bown

1996 P(0),U(-),4(12),4(0)

102	8/2	Great Treth'	(R)	MDO	3m	8	GS	*prom, cls 2nd whn f 14th*	F	-
238	22/2	Lemalla	(R)	LAD	3m	9	S	*rear whn f 12th*	F	-
460	8/3	Great Treth'	(R)	MDO	3m	13	S	*bhnd, wnt poor 3rd 15th, disp 3rd whn p.u. apr last*	P	0
625	22/3	Kilworthy	(L)	MDN	3m	14	G	*alwys prom, cls 4th 11th, ev ch last, not qckn*	2	14
740	29/3	Higher Kilw'	(L)	MDN	3m	15	GF	*cls 2nd til ld 9th, 4l clr 3 out, ct flat, no ext*	2	15
1112	19/4	Flete Park	(R)	MDN	3m	13	GF	*prog 12th, 5th at 16th, lft in ld 3 out, kpt on*	1	15
1339	3/5	Flete Park	(R)	RES	3m	6	G	*(fav) handy, ld 13th, styd on strngly*	1	18
1550	24/5	Mounsey Hil'	(R)	INT	3m	9	G	*in tch, chsd ldr 14th, ev ch 3 out, rdn nxt,unable qckn flat*	2	20

Swept aside all doubters 97 & improved each start; stays & tries now; can win Confined; G-F 20

ESPLEY NIPPER b.g. 6 North Briton - Muna by Thatch (USA) — Ian Carmichael

1996 **P(NH)**

612	22/3	Friars Haugh	(L)	MDN	3m	14	GF	*strgglng whn f 12th*	F	-
815	31/3	Tranwell	(L)	MDO	2 1/2m	14	G	*cls 4th hlfwy, wknd qckly & lost tch frm 2 out*	10	0

Season lasted 9 days & well-beaten when completing 0

ESPY b.g. 14 Pitpan - Minorette by Miralgo — C James

1996 F(-),3(12),1(16),P(0),F(-)

58	1/2	Kingston Bl'	(L)	MEM	3m	5	GF	*alwys prom, chsd ldr 9th, styd on onepcd*	2	17
397	8/3	Barbury Cas'	(L)	XX	3m	10	G	*mid-div, prog to 2nd 2 out, hrd rdn apr last, no ext*	2	16
868	31/3	Hackwood Pa'	(L)	MEM	3m	2	F	*(fav) mstk 1st, disp til lft alone 3 out*	1	0
1054	13/4	Hackwood Pa'	(L)	CON	3m	4	GF	*2nd frm 3rd, going wll & narrow ld whn lft clr 2 out*	1	19
1214	26/4	Woodford	(L)	OPE	3m	5	G	*cls up, ld aft 15th, hdd nxt, outpcd 2 out*	2	20
1462	11/5	Tweseldown	(R)	CON	3m	6	GF	*(fav) j.w. w.w. ld 13th, drvn out flat*	1	19
1564	25/5	Kingston Bl'	(L)	CON	3m	7	GF	*(fav) w.w. prog to 3rd frm 10th, rdn & not qckn aft 3 out*	3	19

Old character; well-ridden in 97 to land Sandhurst treble; can win similar at 15; Any 19

ESQUIMAU (Irish) — **I** 152^3^

ESTEVEZ (Irish) — **I** 447^F^, **I** 481^P^, **I** 545,

ETHELWOOD VI (Irish) — **I** 354^P^

EUPABA (Irish) — **I** 481^P^, **I** 594^P^

EURO FORUM ch.g. 5 Deploy - Unique Treasure by Young Generation — John Dunsdon

1211	26/4	Woodford	(L)	MEM	3m	8	G	*mid-div, prog to 3rd at 10th, blnd 12th, wknd 15th, p.u.2out*	P	0

Well-backed & not disgraced; placed in decent Flat races 95 & may do better in points if he stays 14

EUROGAL (Irish) — **I** 143^P^, **I** 519^P^

EUROLINKHELLRAISER(IRE) b or br.g. 6 Mandalus - Lady Lucifer by Lucifer (USA) — Richard Barber

1996 **6(NH),9(NH)**

101	8/2	Great Treth'	(R)	MDO	3m	9	GS	*w.w. jnd ldrs 13th, wknd & mstks frm 15th, poor 2nd & f 2out*	F	-
458	8/3	Great Treth'	(R)	MDO	3m	15	S	*prom til lost plc 10th, t.o. p.u. apr 15th*	P	0
643	22/3	Castle Of C'	(R)	MDO	3m	12	G	*w.w. mstk 2nd, prog whn blnd 13th, btn nxt, p.u. 2 out*	P	0

Rare dud for top stable & blundered his way around 10

EUROMILL STAR ch.m. 7 White Mill — Mrs C Howells

1996 F(-),P(0),R(-)

540	16/3	Erw Lon	(L)	MDN	3m	13	GF	*blnd 1st, ref 2nd*	R	-
845	31/3	Lydstep	(L)	RES	3m	5	F	*mid-div whn f 6th*	F	-
1185	20/4	Lydstep	(L)	RES	3m	5	GF	*(bl) 4th whn f 7th*	F	-

Never completes 0

EURO THYNE(IRE) ch.g. 7 Good Thyne (USA) - Cappagh Lady by Al Sirat (USA) T D Easterby

1996 **12(NH),P(NH),8(NH)**

269	22/2	Duncombe Pa'	(R)	MDO	3m	16	G	*(fav) mid-div whn mstk 13th, sn fdd, p.u. bfr last, dismntd*	P	0

Good stable but obvious problem only start in points 12

EVARIS VI (Irish) — **I** 557^{P}, **I** 586^{U}

EVEN CALL (Irish) — **I** 408^{F}

EVERLAUGHING (Irish) — **I** 264^{P}, **I** 319^{3}, **I** 378^{4}, **I** 479^{5}, **I** 564^{5}

EVERSO IRISH b.g. 8 Hatim (USA) - Ever So by Mummy's Pet Miss J Lewis

1996 P(0),5(10),4(13),**4(14)**

1008	12/4	St Hilary	(R)	RES	3m	11	GF	*cls up in 3rd, went 2nd 3 out, styd on onepcd*	2	14
1135	19/4	Bonvilston	(R)	RES	3m	14	G	*cls up early, wknd 15th, p.u. last*	P	0
1210	26/4	Woodford	(L)	RES	3m	14	G	*prom, blnd 5th, wth wnr 4 out, sn rdn, wknd 2 out*	4	14
1458	11/5	Maisemore P'	(L)	XX	3m	6	G	*cls up, outpcd 13th, effrt to chs wnr 15th, no imp 2 out*	2	19
1526	17/5	Bredwardine	(R)	RES	3m	13	G	*hld up, prog & in tch 12th, 4th & outpcd 14th, no prog aft*	4	12
1587	29/5	Uttoxeter	(L)	HC	2m 5f	11	GF	*alwys bhnd.*	5	0

Maiden winner 95; ran well twice in 97 but struggles to stay & may need fortune to win Restricted 15

EXARCH(USA) b.g. 8 His Majesty (USA) - Velvet (USA) by Sir Ivor Robert J Foster

319	1/3	Marks Tey	(L)	CON	3m	11	G	*hld up in tch, gng wll whn f 14th*	F	-
501	15/3	Ampton	(R)	OPE	3m	4	GF	*hld up, wnt 2nd 14th, ev ch 3 out, sn outpcd.*	2	18
799	31/3	Marks Tey	(L)	OPE	3m	5	F	*held up,prog disp ld 14th,hdd nxt,ev ch 3 out,btn mstk 2 out*	2	14

Appeared to run well but beat only 2 others in small races & stamina doubts 17

EXCLUSIVE EDITION(IRE) ch.m. 7 Bob Back (USA) - Nielsine by Czaravich (USA) Mrs Cheryl Foster

1996 4(15),4(20),2(16),3(19),2(17),1(16),P(0)

70	2/2	Higham	(L)	OPE	3m	5	GF	*(fav) hld up bhnd, clsd 11th, 3rd 13th, disp 4 out, outpcd 2 out*	2	18
193	15/2	Higham	(L)	CON	3m	14	G	*(fav) cls up, effrt 16th, kpt on last, not trbl wnr*	2	19
444	8/3	Higham	(L)	CON	3m	8	G	*mid-div,prog to ld 11th,clr 15th,wknd rpdly nxt,hdd apr last*	2	17
710	29/3	High Easter	(L)	OPE	3m	5	F	*trkd ldrs, cls 3rd 14th, outpcd frm nxt*	3	15

Members winner 96; consistent but non-stayer; finished early; could find small race 98 18

EXCUSE ME SIR (Irish) — **I** 165^{1}

EXECUTIVE BABE (Irish) — **I** 178^{R}

EXECUTIVE FLAME (Irish) — **I** 335^{P}, **I** 510^{2}, **I** 551^{4}, **I** 588^{F}

EXECUTIVE FONTAINE (Irish) — **I** 243^{P}, **I** 459^{P}, **I** 490^{P}, **I** 551^{P}

EXECUTIVE OPAL (Irish) — **I** 163^{F}, **I** 207^{P}, **I** 277^{3}, **I** 295,

EXHIBITION PRINCE(IRE) b.g. 6 Exhibitioner - Glenardina by Furry Glen R J Brown

917	5/4	Larkhill	(R)	MDO	2 1/2m	6	F	*chsd ldrs to 7th, lost tch nxt, p.u. 4 out*	P	0
1446	10/5	Peper Harow	(L)	MDO	3m	7	GF	*chsd ldr to 3rd,jmpd slwly nxt,4th & rdn 13th,t.o.& p.u.3out*	P	0

Pulled up in dire races & shows nothing 0

EXILE ON MAIN ST (Irish) — **I** 549^{P}

EXPLORE MONDIAL(IRE) b.g. 6 Alzao (USA) - Organdy by Blakeney Stephen Ramsay

1996 **8(NH),F(NH),U(NH),3(NH),2(NH),P(NH),P(NH),P(NH),P(NH)**

155	15/2	Lanark	(R)	MEM	3m	4	G	*u.r. 2nd*	U	-
233	22/2	Friars Haugh	(L)	MDO	3m	13	G	*hld up, prog to ld brfly 4 out, no ext apr last*	3	13

Placed under Rules; not beaten far 2nd start but season lasted a week 13

EXPRESSMENT br.g. 13 Battlement - Ruby Express by Pony Express Miss A S Ross

1996 6(0),2(20),**3(19)**,5(12),3(20),1(18),**2(20)**,**1(22)**

173	15/2	Ottery St M'	(L)	CON	3m	7	G	*hld up, prog 14th, chal apr last, sn ld & ran on well*	1	21
285	26/2	Taunton	(R)	HC	4 1/4m 110yds	16	GS	*hit 6th, bhnd from 12th, t.o..*	5	0
591	21/3	Newbury	(L)	HC	3m	7	GF	*alwys bhnd, t.o..*	5	0
1243	26/4	Bratton Down	(L)	OPE	3m	6	GS	*chsng grp til no ext frm 2 out*	3	12
1484	11/5	Ottery St M'	(L)	OPE	3m	7	G	*hld up, prog 14th, rdn 3 out, tk 2nd cls hm*	2	20
1544	21/5	Newton Abbot	(L)	HC	3 1/4m 110yds	11	G	*alwys bhnd, t.o..*	7	0

H/Chase winner 96; found right race to start 97 but outclassed after; ground against; hard at 14; sft ... 20

EXPRESSO DRUMMER b.g. 7 Sergeant Drummer (USA) - Free Expression by Kind Of Hush Capt T A Forster

527	15/3	Cothelstone	(L) MDN 3m	14 GS	*handy, cls 2nd 16th, ev ch 2 out, no ext, promising*	4	11
1015	12/4	Bitterley	(L) MDO 3m	12 GF	*(fav) blnd & u.r. 2nd*	U	-
1246	26/4	Bratton Down	(L) MDO 3m	16 GS	*(fav) mstks, nvr trbld ldrs, p.u. apr 2 out*	P	0
1521	17/5	Bratton Down	(L) MDO 3m	16 GS	*prog to 5th at 11th, 4th at 14th, fdd, p.u. flat*	P	0

Decent debut but mistakes after & failed to capitalise; may do better 13

EXTRASPECIAL BREW br.g. 10 Afzal - Totally Tiddly by French Vine Mrs T Ritson

1996 P(0),5(10),U(-)

663	23/3	Eaton Hall	(R) MEM 3m	2 GF	*2nd til f 6th*	F	-

No longer of any account 0

EYRE EILE (Irish) — **I** 574P

EYRE POINT(IRE) b.g. 8 Le Bavard (FR) - Betty Sue by Menelek John Honeyball

1996 **4(NH),P(NH),4(NH),P(NH),3(NH),R(NH)**

2	19/1	Barbury Cas'	(L) XX 3m	14 GF	*alwys wll bhnd, last & t.o. hlfwy*	9	0
111	8/2	Milborne St'	(L) MDN 3m	8 GF	*rear, prog 15th, styd on wll 2 out, nrst fin*	2	12
244	22/2	Lemalla	(R) MDO 3m	12 S	*(fav) hld up mid-div, prog to 2nd 3 out, ld apr last, ran on wll*	1	14
532	15/3	Wadebridge	(L) RES 3m	9 GF	*alwys prom, kpt on onepcd apr last*	3	15
688	29/3	Little Wind'	(R) RES 3m	5 GF	*in tch, effrt to chs wnr 4 out, no imp apr 2 out*	2	13
1108	19/4	Flete Park	(R) RES 3m	14 GF	*mid-div til blnd & u.r. 11th*	U	-

Modest but generally safe; consistent; novice-ridden; could find small Restricted; Soft 16

EYTON ROCK ch.g. 12 Menelaus - Hectic by Eastern Lyric J W Beddoes

81	2/2	Wolverhampt'	(L) MDN 3m	13 GS	*rear, t.o. whn f 11th*	F	-
260	22/2	Newtown	(L) RES 3m	16 G	*rear whn u.r. 8th*	U	-
332	1/3	Eaton Hall	(R) RES 3m	18 GS	*alwys rear, t.o. & p.u. aft 11th*	P	0
1381	5/5	Eyton-On-Se'	(L) MEM 3m	5 GF	*hndy to 4th, qckly lost tch 6th, p.u. nxt*	P	0

Of no account 0

FACE THE MUSIC ch.g. 10 True Song - Ginger Fury by Fury Royal Miss J Stevens

212	16/2	Southwell P'	(L) MDO 3m	14 GS	*bhnd frm 8th, t.o. & p.u. 14th*	P	0
347	2/3	Market Rase'	(L) MDO 3m	9 GF	*ld to 5th, ld 10th-15th, wknd*	5	0
1193	20/4	Garthorpe	(R) MDO 3m	9 GF	*bhnd, t.o. frm 14th, lft bad 3rd 2 out, ref last, cont*	3	0

Lightly raced & of no account 0

FAHA MOSS(IRE) b.g. 7 Le Moss - Varamond by Vulgan N W Padfield

498	15/3	Ampton	(R) MDO 3m	8 GF	*w.w.disp ld 13th,ld & jmpd lft 3 out,gng best whn lft clrnxt*	1	13
798	31/3	Marks Tey	(L) RES 3m	7 F	*(fav) mstks in rear,slght prog to 5th 9th,wknd 11th,p.u. aft 12th*	P	0
1355	4/5	Dingley	(R) RES 3m	12 G	*last whn mstk 6th, t.o. & p.u. 14th*	P	0

Ex-Irish; won bad Maiden & showed nothing after; will struggle to win again 12

FAHA POINT(IRE) b.m. 5 Electric - Killinure Point by Smooth Stepper Miss Julia Oakey

467	8/3	Eyton-On-Se'	(L) RES 3m	15 G	*t.o. 5th, p.u. 9th*	P	0
1016	12/4	Bitterley	(L) MDO 3m	14 GF	*prom til p.u. aft 4th, saddle slppd*	P	0
1240	26/4	Brampton Br'	(R) MDO 3m	12 G	*prom whn mstk 8th, f 10th*	F	-
1304	3/5	Weston Park	(L) MDO 3m	8 G	*alwys rear, t.o. 11th, p.u. 15th, school*	P	0

Ex-Irish; unpromising so far 0

FAHOORA (Irish) — **I** 167F

FAIR AND SQUARE b.m. 5 All Fair - Anditover by Spitsbergen Mrs Jane M Wickett

1035	12/4	Lifton	(R) MDN 3m	11 F	*t.o. whn p.u. aft 10th*	P	0
1394	5/5	High Bickin'	(R) MEM 3m	4 G	*jmpd novicey, disp 2nd whn f 8th*	F	-
1583	26/5	Lifton	(R) MDO 3m	11 G	*mostly rear, p.u. aft 12th*	P	0

Makes mistakes & yet to get involved 0

FAIR CAPRICE b.m. 6 Pablond - Capelena by Mon Fetiche G Evans

582	16/3	Detling	(L) MDN 3m	16 F	*trckng ldrs whn f 8th*	F	-

A brief start 0

FAIRCREST (Irish) — **I** 339P

FAIR CROSSING ch.g. 11 Over The River (FR) - Golden Chestnut by Green Shoon Michael Emmanuel

1996 1(24)

446	8/3	Newton Brom'	(R) CON 3m	8 G	*alwys chsg ldrs, 3rd apr 16th, tk 2nd 2 out, onepcd*	2	21
651	22/3	Siddington	(L) OPE 3m	7 F	*chsd wnr, not qckn aft 3 out, kpt on*	2	22
758	29/3	Kimble	(L) OPE 3m	6 GF	*alwys 1st pair, ld 4th, made rest, qcknd clr 15th*	1	24
1098	19/4	Bangor	(L) HC 3m 110yds	9 G	*in tch, prom 7th, losing ground when pkd 10th, t.o. when p.u. before 3 out.*	P	0

Won only start 96; useful but very lightly-raced; novice-ridden; goes well fresh; can win at 12 22

FAIR FONTAINE (Irish) — I 48^{5}, I 80^{1}

FAIR GRAND b.g. 7 Primitive Rising (USA) - Grand Queen by Grand Conde (FR) Mrs J M Reynard

1996 P(0),U(-),P(0),P(0)

209	16/2	Southwell P'	(L)	MDO	3m	7	GS	*hld up, prog & mstk 9th, rdn 14th, wknd*	3	0
358	2/3	Great Stain'	(L)	MDO	3m	14	S	*(bl) rear, lost tch 10th, t.o. 3 out, p.u. nxt*	P	0
510	15/3	Dalton Park	(R)	MDO	3m	14	GF	*(bl) mid-div whn u.r. 6th*	U	-
1074	13/4	Whitwell-On'	(R)	MDO	2 1/2m 88yds	16	G	*(bl) alwys rear, nvr dang*	6	0
1105	19/4	Hornby Cast'	(L)	MDO	3m	11	G	*rear, rddn 10th, wll bhnd 14th, p.u. 4 out*	P	0
1252	26/4	Easingwold	(L)	MDO	3m	9	GS	*mid-div, 5th 4 out, nvr dang*	5	0
1345	3/5	Gisburn	(R)	MDN	3m	13	GF	*(bl) rear, nvr bynd mid-div*	5	0

Always well-beaten & no prospects 0

FAIR NOTICE (Irish) — I 346^{P}, I 501^{4}

FAIR OPHELIA (Irish) — I 80^{P}, I 141^{P}, I 590,

FAIR REVIVAL (Irish) — I 5^{4}, I 41^{P}, I 257^{P}

FAIRTREE (Irish) — I 127^{P}, I 247^{6}, I 371^{3}

FAITHFUL PAL (Irish) — I 138^{P}, I 235^{3}, I 319^{4}, I 419^{P}

FAITHFUL STAR b.g. 12 Tilden - Star Relation by Star Gazer R S Hunnisett

1996 3(12),U(-),3(22),1(25),1(28),1(28),1(31),1(29),1(30),**U(-)**

9	25/1	Cottenham	(R)	OPE	3m	3	GF	*ld, mstk 7th, hdd 14th, no ch whn blnd 3 out, t.o.*	3	14
138	9/2	Thorpe Lodge	(L)	OPE	3m	5	GF	*ldng grp going wll til wknd rpdly 3 out*	5	0
547	16/3	Garthorpe	(R)	XX	3m	7	GF	*in tch til 6th & outpcd 12th, t.o. whn u.r. 3 out*	U	-
771	29/3	Dingley	(R)	OPE	3m	10	G	*cls up til wknd 10th, bhnd whn p.u. last*	P	0

Top pointer in 96; changed hands & a disaster in 97; can only be watched now 13

FALSE ECONOMY ch.g. 12 Torus - Vulvic by Vulgan Miss K Scorgie

1996 3(20),U(-),3(16),3(19),5(14),5(14),2(18),P(0),4(10),6(11)

174	15/2	Ottery St M'	(L)	LAD	3m	9	G	*rear, nvr on trms, outpcd frm 4 out*	5	18
311	1/3	Clyst St Ma'	(L)	LAD	3m	9	HY	*made most, ran on well frm 3 out*	1	20
627	22/3	Kilworthy	(L)	LAD	3m	7	G	*lost ground stdly frm 11th, no ch*	5	14
689	29/3	Little Wind'	(R)	LAD	3m	5	GF	*prssd ldr, ld 9-11th, not qckn frm 15th*	4	14
1036	12/4	Lifton	(R)	LAD	3m	4	F	*(fav) ld/disp to 11th, clr 12th, no ext whn chal*	2	13
1110	19/4	Flete Park	(R)	LAD	3m	9	GF	*disp to 5th, prom til wklnd 15th*	4	16
1490	13/5	Chepstow	(L)	HC	3m	7	G	*prom to 7th, t.o. when ref 4 out.*	R	-

Good schoolmaster & ground ideal when winning; lucky to repeat at 13; G-Hy 16

FALSE TAIL(IRE) b.g. 5 Roselier (FR) - Its Good Ere by Import J A Keighley

41	1/2	Larkhill	(R)	MDO	3m	13	GF	*hld up,prog 12th,3rd & no prog 15th,lft in ld & u.r. last*	U	15
297	1/3	Didmarton	(L)	MDN	3m	11	G	*(fav) trckd ldr til f 9th*	F	-
644	22/3	Castle Of C'	(R)	MDO	3m	9	G	*cls up, ld apr 13th-15th, ev ch & rdn 2 out, no ext*	4	12
933	6/4	Charlton Ho'	(L)	MDO	3m	12	G	*w.w prog 13th, mstk nxt, ld 15th, rdn & qcknd flat*	1	15
1157	20/4	Stafford Cr'	(R)	RES	3m	11	GF	*(fav) prom, 3rd at 11th, chsd wnr & slppd final bnd, no prog aft*	2	15

Top stable but hard ride & well-handled when winning; should improve but Restricted no certainty 17

FAMILIAR FRIEND gr.g. 11 John French - Bidula by Manacle M H G Lang

1996 P(0),4(13),**6(0),5(17),1(19),1(20),4(16),4(18)**

587	19/3	Ludlow	(R)	HC	2 1/2m	18	GF	*(bl) mid div, wknd 5 out, t.o..*	11	12
679	26/3	Ascot	(R)	HC	2m 3f 110yds	9	G	*(bl) trckd ldrs, wknd 10th, t.o. when mstk 3 out, p.u. before next.*	P	0
781	31/3	Hereford	(R)	HC	2m 3f	9	GF	*(bl) in tch, pressed wnr from 3 out, no ext from last.*	2	20
1293	30/4	Cheltenham	(L)	HC	2m 110yds	5	GF	*(bl) ld to 3rd, led 7th till 3 out, wknd apr last.*	4	17
1296	3/5	Hereford	(R)	HC	2m 3f	11	G	*(bl) held up, hdwy 9th, wknd apr 3 out, left poor 2nd last.*	2	21
1488	12/5	Towcester	(R)	HC	2m 110yds	16	GS	*(bl) prom till wknd quickly 3 out, p.u. before last.*	P	0

Dual H/Chase winner 96; outclassed mostly 97; best 2m; likes Hereford; hard ride 18

FAMILYVALUE (Irish) — I 169^{P}, I 488^{P}

FAMOUS STOUT (Irish) — I 59^{P}, I 92^{P}, I 115^{P}, I 173^{3}

FANCYTALKINTINKER(IRE) b.g. 7 Bold Owl - Our Ena by Tower Walk J N Dalton

1996 F(-),P(0)

327	1/3	Eaton Hall	(R)	MDN	3m	11	GS	*rear, nvr dang, p.u. 5 out*	P	0
470	8/3	Eyton-On-Se'	(L)	MDN	2 1/2m	12	G	*s.s. mostly rear, some late prog*	6	0
1016	12/4	Bitterley	(L)	MDO	3m	14	GF	*hld up, prog 12th, cls 2nd nxt, ev ch til wknd 3 out,p.u.nxt*	P	0

Well-beaten on only completion 96/7 & looks non-stayer 10

FANTASTIC FLEET(IRE) b.g. 5 Woodman (USA) - Gay Fantastic by Ela-Mana-Mou Mrs R Mackness & Mrs Vanessa Ramm

1996 **9(NH),6(NH),3(NH),5(NH),1(NH),P(NH),P(NH),2(NH),4(NH),5(NH),1(NH),4(NH),B(NH)**

6	19/1	Barbury Cas'	(L)	LAD	3m	13	GF	*prssd wnr til grad wknd apr 2 out*	4	22
85	2/2	Wolverhampt'	(L)	LAD	3m	11	GS	*trckd ldrs, blnd 9th, no imp ldrs frm 12th, lft 3rd 3 out*	3	17
145	9/2	Tweseldown	(R)	LAD	3m	10	GF	*ld to 5th, wknd frm 14th, p.u. 3 out*	P	0
490	10/3	Stratford	(L)	HC	3m	12	G	*held up, hdwy when blundd and u.r. 13th.*	U	-
817	31/3	Paxford	(L)	CON	3m	3	F	*(fav) hld up rear, prog to 2nd at 12th, ld 3 out, qcknd flat*	1	16
960	6/4	Pantyderi	(L)	OPE	3m	1	F	*walked over*	1	0
1293	30/4	Cheltenham	(L)	HC	2m 110yds	5	GF	*mstks, ld 3rd till 7th, mistake 4 out and lost pl, rallied und pres apr 2 out, soon not qckn.*	3	16
1456	11/5	Maisemore P'	(L)	LAD	3m	5	G	*hld up, trckd wnr 14th, ev ch apr last, not qckn*	2	19
1525	17/5	Bredwardine	(R)	LAD	3m	9	G	*hld up, not fluent, in tch 13th, outpcd frm 14th*	4	16

Winning hurdler; quite able but irresolute & does not stay; soft contests again needed in 98 18

FANTUS b.g. 10 Green Shoon - Brave Dorney by Brave Invader (USA) J A Keighley

180	15/2	Larkhill	(R)	MXO	3m	6	G	*(fav) chsd ldr to 3rd & frm 11th,ld 2 out,hdd last,no ext,lame*	2	30
295	1/3	Didmarton	(L)	OPE	3m	9	G	*(fav) prog 8th,prssd wnr & pshd alng 13th,4l down & btn whn f last*	F	29
494	13/3	Cheltenham	(L)	HC	3 1/4m 110yds	18	G	*in tch, pressing ldrs when hit 16th, ld after next, strly pressed last, kept on gamely.*	1	38

Cheltenham Foxhunters winner 95; missed 96; brilliantly trained to grab top prize again; best on Sft ... 39

FARADAY b.g. 7 Electric - Muffet's Gold by Cavo Doro G B Foot

1996 **20(NH),P(NH),P(NH),F(NH)**

314	1/3	Clyst St Ma'	(L)	MDN	3m	11	HY	*rear,prog 11th, 3rd 3 out, wknd nxt, p.u. last*	P	0
525	15/3	Cothelstone	(L)	MDN	3m	15	GS	*prom, ld 12th-16th, cls 3rd apr 2 out, wknd*	3	11
866	31/3	Kingston St'	(R)	MDO	3m	7	F	*(fav) hit 15th, wnt 2nd nxt, ld apr 3 out, drew clr*	1	16
1041	12/4	Cothelstone	(L)	RES	3m	4	GF	*(fav) disp til clr ldr 5th, jnd 2 out, ld last, ran on well*	1	17
1269	27/4	Little Wind'	(R)	MEM	3m	3	GF	*(fav) made all, mstk 5th, clr whn lft solo aft 14th*	1	15
1372	5/5	Cotley Farm	(L)	INT	3m	3	GF	*(Jt fav) ld/disp to 12th, chsd wnnr aft, lost tch frm 3 out*	2	10

Enjoyed good season but won only soft races & may struggle when upgraded in 98; G-F 18

FARDROSS b.g. 11 Fidel - Miss Maraise by Grange Melody G W Briscoe

938	6/4	Tabley	(R)	OPE	3m	9	G	*prom, ld 7th, rddn & drew clr apr last, comf*	1	20

Winning chaser; retained from long absence & won well; can win at 12 if fit; Good 22

FARDRUM (Irish) — I 25^{P}

FARINGO b.g. 12 Rustingo - Royal Marie by Alba Rock Aintree Challenge Partnership

1996 **P(0)**,1(17),**4(0)**,**U(-)**,**2(12)**,**10(0)**,1(21)

151	12/2	Lingfield	(L)	HC	3m	13	HY	*t.o. from 5th, p.u. before 4 out.*	P	0
281	23/2	Charing	(L)	OPE	3m	12	G	*alwys rear, lost tch 12th, t.o.*	8	0
376	3/3	Windsor	(R)	HC	3m	11	GF	*alwys bhnd, soon t.o..*	7	0
890	4/4	Aintree	(L)	HC	2 3/4m	14	G	*bhnd, not fluent, t.o. hfwy.*	9	0
1415	9/5	Stratford	(L)	HC	3m	6	G	*jmpd slowly 2nd, alwys bhnd, left poor 3rd at last.*	3	24
1503	16/5	Folkestone	(R)	HC	3 1/4m	7	G	*(bl) ld to 5th, soon pushed along, chsd ldr to 11th, wknd after next, left poor 2nd 2 out.*	2	17

Dual points winner 96; novice-ridden & fell to pieces 97; looks safely ignored now 12

FARLOUGH LADY (Irish) — I 31^{P}, I 366^{F}, I 586^{R}

FARMER TOM ch.g. 13 Tom Noddy - Gay Ghana by Accra Mrs J M Hinder

522	15/3	Cothelstone	(L)	CON	3m	14	GS	*prom, ld brfly aft 5th, p.u. aft nxt, dsmntd*	P	0

Won 3 in 92 & an unfortunate revival 0

FARM TRACK b.m. 8 Saxon Farm - Earlsgift by Dusky Boy H W Humble

565	16/3	Lanark	(R)	MDO	3m	10	GS	*sn bhnd, p.u. 11th*	P	0

Missed 96 & looks virtually impossible to keep on a track 0

FARRAN GARRETT (Irish) — I 10^{1}

FARRIANA ch.m. 9 Dutch Treat - By Midnight by By Rights W S Layton

754	29/3	Brampton Br'	(R)	MDN	3m	9	GF	*mid-div, lost tch 9th, p.u. nxt*	P	0
1018	12/4	Bitterley	(L)	MDO	3m	13	GF	*mid-div to 10th, lost tch 13th, p.u. 15th*	P	0
1238	26/4	Brampton Br'	(R)	MDO	3m	10	G	*cls 4th at 8th, ld 15th til hdd 2 out, wknd flat*	4	10

Missed 96; 1st ever form last start in modest race & more needed for a win 11

FARRIERS FANTASY ch.m. 5 Alias Smith (USA) - Little Hut by Royal Palace Mrs N Hope

1996 **4(NH)**

136	9/2	Alnwick	(L)	MDO	3m	16	G	*(Jt fav) mid-div whn blnd & u.r. 4th*	U	-
340	1/3	Corbridge	(R)	MDN	3m	10	G	*rear & outpcd 12th, t.o. & p.u. 3 out*	P	0

Good stable but soon disappeared & best watched 10

FARRIERS FAVOURITE gr.m. 8 Alias Smith (USA) - Farm Consultation by Farm Walk Mrs J Leckenby

1996 1(19),2(18),3(19)

130	9/2	Alnwick	(L)	INT	3m	7	G	*hld up, effrt apr 4 out, kpt on onepcd frm nxt*	3 0
335	1/3	Corbridge	(R)	CON	3m	7	G	*rear, prog 3 out, ev ch last, onepcd*	2 19
411	8/3	Dalston	(R)	CON	3m	16	GS	*w.w. prog 12th, lft 2nd aft 3 out, ld last, drvn out flat*	1 19

Restricted winner 96; lightly-raced & did well to win Confined; consistent; one paced; may win again .. 20

FAR TOO LOUD b.g. 10 Taufan (USA) - Octet by Octavo (USA) Miss A S Ross

1996 5(16),4(14),5(0),R(-),R(-),R(-),R(-)

738	29/3	Higher Kilw'	(L)	CON	3m	8	GF	*ld whn ref 2nd, cont, t.o. & p.u. 3 out*	P 0
1033	12/4	Lifton	(R)	CON	3m	6	F	*ref 1st*	R -
1481	11/5	Ottery St M'	(L)	CON	3m	12	G	*ref 1st*	R -

Refused last 7 races & that should be the end 0

FAR TOO RISKY b.g. 12 Prince Tenderfoot (USA) - Red For Go by Tanfirion Trevor Trigg

742	29/3	Barbury Cas'	(L)	MEM	3m	5	F	*bhnd frm 7th, t.o. & p.u. aft 10th*	P 0

Of no account 0

FASTER OR ELSE(NZ) gr.g. 9 Super Gray (USA) - Reese's Pride (NZ) by Trelay (NZ) Reg Jones

103	8/2	Great Treth'	(R)	MDO	3m	9	GS	*33s-12s, chsg grp, rdn & wknd 15th, t.o. & p.u. 2 out*	P 0
461	8/3	Great Treth'	(R)	MDO	3m	12	S	*7th hlfwy, bhnd p.u. apr 3 out*	P 0
1034	12/4	Lifton	(R)	MDN	3m	7	F	*towrds rear early, gd prog 12th, chal last, ld cls home*	1 14

Missed 96; found weak race when scrambling home & more needed for Restricted hopes 15

FAST FLOW(IRE) ch.m. 5 Over The River (FR) - Hi Cal by Callernish Mrs C Day

1473	11/5	Erw Lon	(L)	MDO	3m	13	GS	*f 4th*	F -

Brief start 0

FAST FUN b.g. 9 Germont - Fearful Fun by Harwell M J Walton

343	1/3	Corbridge	(R)	MDO	3m	14	G	*prom til fdd 8th, t.o. & p.u. 2 out*	P 0
411	8/3	Dalston	(R)	CON	3m	16	GS	*alwys bhnd, t.o. last whn p.u. 12th*	P 0
613	22/3	Friars Haugh	(L)	MDN	3m	12	GF	*ld brfly 4th, cls up til no ext frm 4 out*	4 0
734	29/3	Alnwick	(L)	MDN	3m	6	F	*chsd ldng pair, lft 2nd 10th, und pres 2 out, rallied flat*	2 13
996	12/4	Tranwell	(L)	MDO	3m	8	F	*(fav) mid-div 1st ctt,hdwy & lft in ld 13th til hdd 3 out, no ext*	2 13
1172	20/4	Hexham Poin'	(L)	MDO	3m	4	GF	*(fav) ld til jnd 12th-16th, sn hdd, outpcd frm 2 out*	2 0
1297	3/5	Hexham	(L)	HC	3m 1f	8	F	*chsd ldrs to 7th, soon lost pl and bhnd, t.o. when p.u. before 3 out.*	P 0
1429	10/5	Aspatria	(L)	MDO	3m	15	G	*alwys bhnd, t.o. & p.u. 12th*	P 0
1514	17/5	Corbridge	(R)	MDO	3m	17	GS	*mid-div, wknd 4 out, t.o.*	7 0

Missed 95/6; 2nd in 3 poor races on Firm & will need fortune to win 12

FAST STUDY b.g. 12 Crash Course - Mary May by Little Buskins S J Robinson

1996 3(16),2(17),2(16),4(17),P(0),P(0),5(15)

166	15/2	Witton Cast'	(R)	OPE	3m	8	F	*not fluent, prom, fdd frm 14th*	5 15
353	2/3	Great Stain'	(L)	CON	3m	9	S	*prom, lft in ld 4th, hdd 11th, wknd 2 out*	3 11
492	11/3	Sedgefield	(L)	HC	3m 3f	7	G	*jmpd badly, held up, imp 8th, struggling 13th, t.o..*	5 10
812	31/3	Tranwell	(L)	OPE	3m	7	G	*alwys rear, no imp final ctt, tk poor 6th run in*	6 0
1103	19/4	Hornby Cast'	(L)	OPE	3m	5	G	*rear, rddn 10th, wknd 14th, sn t.o.*	3 0
1248	26/4	Easingwold	(L)	OPE	3m	8	GS	*mid-div, onepcd, tk 4th run in*	4 0
1407	5/5	Witton Cast'	(R)	OPE	3m	4	GS	*settld in 3rd til chsd wnr 3rd,disp 7th,hdd & outpcd 4 out*	2 15
1512	17/5	Corbridge	(R)	OPE	3m	10	GS	*prom til u.r. 10th*	U -

Beaten all 15 races 96/7 & showed little in 97; likely to extend losing sequence 11

FATHER MALONE(IRE) b.g. 8 Ovac (ITY) - Belle Fillette by Beau Chapeau D Luxton

1996 P(0),P(0),P(0)

525	15/3	Cothelstone	(L)	MDN	3m	15	GS	*p.u. apr 4th*	P 0
1088	16/4	Hockworthy	(L)	MEM	3m	6	GF	*cls up til mstk & wknd 11th, blnd nxt & p.u.*	P 0
1437	10/5	Holnicote	(L)	MDO	3m	14	G	*in tch to 14th, wkng whn hit 17th, no ch aft*	5 0

Last on only completion & shows little 0

FATHER O'CALLAGHAN(IRE) br.g. 8 Touch Boy - Xiara by Callernish J W Hughes

38	26/1	Alnwick	(L)	MDO	3m	14	G	*rear, prog hlfwy, 6th & in tch whn mstk & u.r. 12th*	U -
135	9/2	Alnwick	(L)	MDO	3m	12	G	*rear of main grp, ran on 4 out, 4th whn f last*	F -
234	22/2	Friars Haugh	(L)	MDO	3m	15	G	*6th hlfwy, sn lost tch*	8 0
613	22/3	Friars Haugh	(L)	MDN	3m	12	GF	*nvr rchd ldrs*	6 0
1051	13/4	Lockerbie	(R)	MDN	3m	10	F	*cls up til 3 out, wknd rpdly, p.u. last*	P 0

Tailed off both completions; novice-ridden; looks non-stayer 0

FATHER O'REILLY (Irish) — I 1[3], I 20[5], I 52[F], I 135, , I 238[P]

FATHER PAT (Irish) — I 44[4]

FATHER-PAT (Irish) — I 259,

FATHERS FOOTPRINTS b.g. 9 Roc Imp - Mayo Melody by Highland Melody — Peter Diggle

1996 P(0),2(11),P(0),3(10),1(15),**5(0)**,**8(0)**,**2(16)**,P(0)

230	22/2	Friars Haugh	(L)	RES	3m	15	G	*sn bhnd, p.u. 3 out*	P 0

Maiden winner 96; changed hands & soon disappeared 97; best watched 11

FAUX PAVILLON ch.g. 13 Alias Smith (USA) - Beech Tree by Fighting Ship — Mrs J G Retter

554	16/3	Ottery St M'	(L)	CON	3m	7	G	*handy to 13th, wknd nxt & p.u.*	P 0

No longer of any account 0

FAVLIENT b.m. 7 Farajullah - Valiant Dancer by Northfields (USA) — Miss C Sparkes

1996 F(-),2(0),B(-)

297	1/3	Didmarton	(L)	MDN	3m	11	G	*in tch til b.d. 8th*	B -
390	8/3	Barbury Cas'	(L)	MDN	3m	15	G	*mstks, blnd 2nd, alwys rear, last whn p.u. 13th*	P 0

Beaten a distance on only completion from 5 starts 96/7 0

FAWSLEY MANOR ch.m. 7 St Columbus - True Manor by True Song — G B Tarry

1352	4/5	Dingley	(R)	MDO	2 1/2m	9	G	*prog 9th, ld 11th, pkd nxt, hdd 13th, ev ch whn f 3 out*	F -
1452	10/5	Kingston Bl'	(L)	MDO	3m	9	G	*rear whn ran throgh wing 4th*	r -
1609	1/6	Dingley	(R)	MDO	3m	14	GF	*mid-div,prog & mstk 11th,ran on & ld aft 2out,sn clr,rdn out*	1 13

Clear-cut win from large but bad field; stable's usually improve & Restricted possible 98 17

FAY LIN (Irish) — I 211[P], I 249[P], I 364[1], I 374, , I 433[6], I 465[2]

FEARLESS BERTIE b.g. 6 Fearless Action (USA) - Rambert by Mandamus — Miss J Johnston

1996 P(0)

775	29/3	Dingley	(R)	MDO	2m 5f	10	G	*prom til u.r. 4th*	U -
1081	13/4	Guilsborough	(L)	RES	3m	13	GF	*mid-div, 9th & just in tch whn f 14th*	F -
1352	4/5	Dingley	(R)	MDO	2 1/2m	9	G	*rear, pshd alng 9th, outpcd 11th, wnt 2nd 2 out, ld nr fin*	1 13

Unlucky not to be given outright verdict in weak race - 1st form; should improve - needs to 15

FEARSOME gr.g. 11 Formidable (USA) - Seriema by Petingo — G W Penfold

1996 4(16),3(16),3(19),1(14),1(20),3(18),2(20),1(21),3(19),2(19),6(15)

48	1/2	Wadebridge	(L)	OPE	3m	5	G	*trckd ldrs, ld last, styd on well flat*	1 19
171	15/2	Ottery St M'	(L)	OPE	3m	9	G	*hld up, went 2nd 15th, rdn aft, no imp wnr*	2 21
530	15/3	Wadebridge	(L)	OPE	3m	4	GF	*alwys 2nd, not pace to trbl wnr*	2 19
554	16/3	Ottery St M'	(L)	CON	3m	7	G	*(Jt fav) in tch, ld 4 out, sn clr*	1 20
793	31/3	Bishopsleigh	(R)	OPE	3m	7	G	*(fav) hld up, prog 17th, chal 2 out, hrd rdn last, ld cls hm*	1 21
1091	16/4	Hockworthy	(L)	OPE	3m	4	GF	*w.w. ld 11-14th, no ch wth wnr aft 2 out, kpt on*	2 19
1256	27/4	Black Fores'	(R)	OPE	3m	4	F	*trckd ldrs, no ext frm 3 out*	4 19
1396	5/5	High Bickin'	(R)	MXO	3m	7	G	*rmndrs 8th, 5th hlfwy, nvr dang, styd on clsng stgs*	4 15
1482	11/5	Ottery St M'	(L)	LAD	3m	5	G	*chsd ldng pair, rdn 3 out, not qckn nxt*	3 20
1517	17/5	Bratton Down	(L)	MXO	3m	8	GS	*handy, 2nd brfly aft 13th, sn wknd, t.o.*	7 0

Won 6, placed 13 of 21 races 96/7 & most consistent; should win again at 12; Any 21

FEILE NA HINSE b.g. 14 Cidrax (FR) - Hildamay by Cantab Or Sale Time — Miss Anna Bucknall

1996 P(0)

521	15/3	Cothelstone	(L)	OPE	3m	8	GS	*in tch, went 3rd 17th, no ext*	3 18
1493	14/5	Cothelstone	(L)	OPE	3m	2	GF	*wth ldr, ld 15th, jnd 2 out, lft clr aft last*	1 16

Revived in 97 & handed match on plate; unlikely to achieve much at 15 15

FELL MIST b.g. 14 Silly Prices - Minimist by Bilsborrow — Mrs W D Sykes

1996 2(22),2(18),1(21),**P(0)**,**4(13)**,**P(0)**

1302	3/5	Weston Park	(L)	LAD	3m	5	G	*ld to 4th, chsd wnr to 4 out, wknd & onepcd nxt*	3 10
1525	17/5	Bredwardine	(R)	LAD	3m	9	G	*cls up, wkng whn blnd 13th, p.u. nxt*	P 0

Consistent Ladies pointer in his time but late to appear 97 & looks finished now 10

FELLOW SIOUX ch.g. 10 Sunley Builds - Sue Lark by Sir Lark — T B Stevens

1996 5(13),1(18),1(19),F(-),5(12)

1311	3/5	Holnicote	(L)	MEM	3m	7	G	*bhnd, gd prog frm 13th, ld 3 out, shkn up flat*	1 18
1416	10/5	Newton Abbot	(L)	HC	2m 5f 110yds	14	G	*pulld hrd, prom till wknd 10th, t.o. when p.u. before 2 out.*	P 0
1550	24/5	Mounsey Hil'	(R)	INT	3m	9	G	*(fav) w.w. going wll, prog to ld 17th, hrd rdn & hld on wll flat*	1 20
1614	7/6	Umberleigh	(L)	CON	3m	3	F	*(fav) hld up, ld 8th, clr aft 13th, easily*	1 0

Restricted winner 96; improved 97; won 5 of last 7 points; never appears till late season; G-F 22

FELTHAM MISTRESS ch.m. 7 Sula Bula - Tycoons Belle by Tycoon II — Donald C Tucker

111	8/2	Milborne St'	(L)	MDN	3m	8	GF	*handy til 13th, lost tch nxt, t.o. & p.u. 4 out*	P	0
366	2/3	Garnons	(L)	MDO	2 1/2m	13	GS	*wth ldrs, cls 2nd at 12th, wknd 3 out*	6	0
585	18/3	Fontwell	(R)	HC	2m 3f	7	GF	*bhnd till hdwy 10th, wknd apr 3 out, p.u. before last.*	P	0
892	5/4	Hereford	(R)	HC	2m	11	GF	*in tch, 4th when f 7th.*	F	-
1139	19/4	Larkhill	(R)	MEM	3m	2	F	*jmpd rght, blnd 5th, jnd ldr 13th, ld 2 out, rdn out*	1	0
1275	27/4	Little Wind'	(R)	RES	3m	9	GF	*3rd whn u.r. 5th*	U	-
1488	12/5	Towcester	(R)	HC	2m 110yds	16	GS	*held up, hdwy 4 out, rdn apr 2 out, one pace.*	4	16
1613	7/6	Umberleigh	(L)	RES	3m	13	F	*chsng grp, 5th & no ch 14th, styd on to tk 3rd 2 out*	3	0

Won a joke race but ran passably last 2 starts; dodgy stayer & more needed for Restricted chance 15

FENNORHILL b or br.g. 13 Al Sirat (USA) - Choralgina by Choral Society — R Ward-Dutton

1996 P(0),P(0),8(0),P(0)

464	8/3	Eyton-On-Se'	(L)	INT	3m	12	G	*rear & t.o. 10th, p.u. 13th*	P	0
574	16/3	Garnons	(L)	RES	3m	14	G	*s.u. bend bef 2nd*	S	-
726	29/3	Sandon	(L)	CON	3m	8	GF	*ld to 3rd, fdd rpdly 8th, p.u. 4 out*	P	0

No longer of any account 0

FENTON BRIDGE b.g. 13 Gleason (USA) - Divine Drapes by Divine Gift — A G Tutton

925	6/4	Garthorpe	(R)	LAD	3m	7	GF	*cls up 8th, sn wknd, bhnd & p.u. 2 out*	P	0
1078	13/4	Guilsborough	(L)	LAD	3m	11	GF	*pllng, ld to 7th, wknd frm 14th, t.o. & p.u. last*	P	0
1161	20/4	Mollington	(R)	LAD	3m	3	GF	*jmpd lft, ld to 5th, last frm 13th, wknd rpdly, p.u. last*	P	0
1207	26/4	Clifton On '	(L)	LAD	3m	6	GS	*cls 2nd to 8th, wknd rpdly, t.o. last whn p.u. 5 out*	P	0

Schoolmaster in 97 0

FERGAL'S DELIGHT b.g. 14 Welsh Chanter - Telamonia by Ballymoss — Mrs Caroline Chadney

1996 **5(0)**,5(0),6(0),1(15),3(12),3(11),4(0)

1391	5/5	Cursneh Hill	(L)	LAD	3m	4	GF	*(bl) ld til hdd 9th, wknd & p.u. 14th*	P	0

Members winner 96 but looks finished now 0

FERNBOY (Irish) — I 261^{P}, I 317^{P}, I 378, , I 447^{P}

FERNISKY (Irish) — I 372^{P}, I 432^{P}, I 585^{P}

FERRITERS PUB (Irish) — I 60^{4}, I 138^{4}, I 339^{4}, I 388^{4}

FESTIVE TEAK (Irish) — I 261^{F}

FETHARD ORCHID (Irish) — I 13^{P}, I 75^{P}, I 130^{5}, I 208, , I 309^{P}, I 427^{4}, I 454^{6}, I 541^{5}

FEVER PITCH gr.g. 7 Kalaglow - Seragsbee by Sagaro — W G Gooden

146	9/2	Tweseldown	(R)	MDO	3m	10	GF	*plld, ld to 3rd & 6-11th, sn btn, p.u. 3 out*	P	0
243	22/2	Lemalla	(R)	MDO	3m	12	S	*5th hlfwy, lost tch 16th, poor 4th whn ref last*	R	-
643	22/3	Castle Of C'	(R)	MDO	3m	12	G	*cls up, 3rd & ev ch 14th, wknd apr 2 out, fin tired*	3	0
933	6/4	Charlton Ho'	(L)	MDO	3m	12	G	*mstk 3rd, in tch, wth wnr 15th-2 out, wknd rpdly*	6	0
1158	20/4	Stafford Cr'	(R)	MDO	3m	5	GF	*(fav) disp to 4 out, outpcd frm 2 out, tk 2nd nr fin*	2	11

Well-beaten in poor race last start & does not stay 10

FIBREGUIDE TECH b.g. 14 Uncle Pokey - Starcat by Avocat — Mrs T R Kinsey

849	31/3	Eyton-On-Se'	(L)	OPE	3m	7	GF	*ld 13th, ran on wll und pres frm 2 out*	1	20
1098	19/4	Bangor	(L)	HC	3m 110yds	9	G	*alwys in rear, t.o. when p.u. before 2 out.*	P	0
1383	5/5	Eyton-On-Se'	(L)	OPE	3m	3	GF	*held up bhnd 1st 2, lft 2nd 4 out, cls up 3 out,not qckn*	2	18
1508	17/5	Bangor	(L)	HC	3m 110yds	12	G	*midfield till f 10th.*	F	-

Well-revived 97 to land modest Open; could still win a point at 15 if ready 18

FIDDLERS BLADE b.m. 6 Broadsword (USA) - Fiddlers Bee by Idiot's Delight — Mike Roberts

197	15/2	Higham	(L)	MDO	3m	12	G	*(Jt fav) hld up, prog to ld 11th, ev ch 3 out, no ext last*	3	15

Good stable & promising debut; should win if ready in 98 14

FIDDLERS BRAE br.g. 7 Baron Blakeney - Mildenstone by Milan — Miss D M M Calder

1996 7(0),r(-)

235	22/2	Friars Haugh	(L)	MDO	3m	10	G	*ld 4th-7th, 15l down whn lft in ld 2 out*	1	13
1169	20/4	Hexham Poin'	(L)	RES	3m	9	GF	*nvr nr ldrs, styd on frm 4 out, tk poor 4th last*	4	0
1424	10/5	Aspatria	(L)	RES	3m	17	G	*sn wll bhnd,gd prog frm 12th,chsd ldng pair 3 out,ran on*	3	18

Fortunate winner 1st start; ran well last start (owner-ridden) & Restricted likely in 98; stays 17

FIDDLERS GOODWILL ch.g. 8 Scorpio (FR) - Course Weed by Crash Course — J A Wales

10	25/1	Cottenham	(R)	INT	3m	7	GF	*bhnd til f 11th*	F	-
126	9/2	Cottenham	(R)	RES	3m	14	GF	*alwys bhnd, t.o. & p.u. 2 out*	P	0
276	22/2	Ampton	(R)	MDO	3m	12	G	*wth ldrs, mstk 7th, lst pl 11th, wll bhnd whn p.u. 17th*	P	0

479 9/3 Southwell P' (L) MDO 3m 15 G *chsd ldrs, rdn & wknd 10th, t.o. & p.u. 12th* P 0

Promise 94; missed 95/6 & showed nothing in 97 0

FIDDLERS KNAP br.g. 7 Queen's Soldier (USA) - Sharp Reef by Milford C P Hobbs
1996 P(0),F(-),2(14),P(0)

147 9/2 Tweseldown (R) MDO 3m 12 GF *ld to 2nd, alwys prom, ran on to ld apr last, all out* 1 14

Placed in 96; found weak race only start 97; novice-ridden; more needed for Restricteds if fit 98 15

FIDDLERS PIKE b.g. 16 Turnpike - Fiddlers Bee by Idiot's Delight Mrs R G Henderson
1996 **3(NH),P(NH),P(NH)**

149 10/2 Hereford (R) HC 3m 1f 110yds 18 GS *prom to 9th, t.o. when p.u. before 3 out.* P 0
237 22/2 Lemalla (R) CON 3m 13 S *j.w. in tch, cls 3rd 16th, ld nxt, drew clr 2 out, styd on* 1 21
384 6/3 Towcester (R) HC 3m 1f 7 GS *pulld hrd, trckd wnr from hfwy, ev ch 2 out, one pace after.* 2 24
586 19/3 Exeter (R) HC 3 1/4m 12 GF *b.d. 1st.* B -
628 22/3 Kilworthy (L) CON 3m 12 G *ld 10th, lkd wnnr til hdd aft last, kpt on gamely* 2 24

Gallant veteran combination & fantastically revived; unlucky twice; can win at 17; best in Soft 22

FIDDLERS THREE ch.g. 14 Orchestra - Kirin by Tyrant (USA) R Gaden
1996 1(24),1(27),**6(13)**

362 2/3 Garnons (L) OPE 3m 11 GS *(fav) prom, cls 3rd whn f 11th* F -

Good pointer in 96 but vanished after fall; well into veteran stage now 21

FIDDLE THE BOOKS b.g. 9 Sergeant Drummer (USA) - Golden Home by Homing S D Harper

345 2/3 Market Rase' (L) MDO 3m 13 GF *bhnd frm 3rd, t.o. 9th, p.u. 11th* P 0

No sign of ability 0

FIFTH AMENDMENT b.g. 12 The Parson - Biowen by Master Owen Lease Terminated

151 12/2 Lingfield (L) HC 3m 13 HY *(bl) chsd ldrs, 5th when blnd 12th, no ch after.* 3 12
227 21/2 Kempton (R) HC 3m 6 G *(bl) pressed ldrs 3rd and raced wd, wknd 10th, jmpd poorly and tried to refuse in rear till blnd and u.r. 12th.* U -
489 10/3 Plumpton (L) HC 3m 1f 110yds 7 GS *(bl) ld 7th to 16th, wknd quickly, 5th and no ch when ref next.* R -
1201 24/4 Perth (R) HC 3m 14 G *(bl) hmpd 1st, mstk 5th, lost tch and p.u. before 13th.* P 0
1359 5/5 Southwell (L) HC 3m 110yds 7 GS *(bl) ld and soon well clr, rdn along 5 out, hdd after 3 out, soon wknd.* 3 12

Always unreliable & turned it in in 97; 1st time out only chance in 98; G-S 15

FIFTH FUSILIER ch.g. 10 Sunley Builds - Creggana by Malinowski (USA) Miss Camilla Courtenay
1996 **P(NH),5(NH),5(NH),5(NH),P(NH)**

954 6/4 Black Fores' (R) RES 3m 4 G *1st ride, prom to 13th, lost tch, t.o. 3 out* 3 0

No longer of any account 0

FIGHTING FOR GOOD(IRE) b.g. 7 Lancastrian - Breeze Dancer by Torus C N Nimmo
1996 P(0)

224 16/2 Heythrop (R) MDN 3m 16 G *14s-8s, prog 7th, ld 11-13th, wknd 15th, p.u. 2 out* P 0
451 8/3 Newton Brom' (R) MDN 3m 8 G *(fav) hld up, cls 4th & ev ch whn hmpd & u.r. 15th* U -
498 15/3 Ampton (R) MDO 3m 8 GF *(fav) (bl) trkd ldrs, ld 11th til 3 out, sn rdn & btn* 2 10
1353 4/5 Dingley (R) MDO 2 1/2m 9 G *chsd ldrs til 4th & wknng 12th, t.o. 2 out* 4 0
1380 5/5 Northaw (L) MDO 3m 4 F *(bl) chsd ldr to 8th & agn 14th, rdn 2 out, onepcd* 2 12
1577 26/5 Chaddesley ' (L) MDO 3m 11 F *(bl) chsd ldr to aft 11th, cls 3rd whn f 12th* F -
1615 7/6 Umberleigh (L) MDO 3m 11 F *(bl) prom, wth wnr 14th-nxt, wknd rpdly aft 3 out, p.u. last* P 0

Placed in poor races; not improving & does not stay; hard to win 11

FIGHTING MARINER b.g. 10 Julio Mariner - Dark Pearl by Harwell Mrs J H Westrope
1996 P(0)

926 6/4 Garthorpe (R) OPE 3m 10 GF *prom, cls 2nd at 6th, grad lost tch, p.u. 3 out* P 0
1162 20/4 Mollington (R) CON 3m 7 GF *(bl) prom to 3 out, wknd rpdly nxt* 6 0
1404 5/5 Ashorne (R) MEM 3m 7 G *(bl) prom,lft in ld apr 13th,lost plc rpdly nxt,s.u.bnd apr 2 out* S -
1576 26/5 Chaddesley ' (L) XX 3m 12 F *(bl) made most to 9th, wknd 12th, lft poor 3rd apr last* 3 0

No real form 96/7 & looks a lost cause now 0

FIGHT TO WIN(USA) b.g. 9 Fit To Fight (USA) - Spark Of Life (USA) by Key To The Mint (USA) Bernard Partridge

1292 30/4 Cheltenham (L) HC 2m 5f 12 GF *prom, ev ch and going easily 13th, fd after 4 out.* 5 19
1544 21/5 Newton Abbot (L) HC 3 1/4m 110yds 11 G *waited with, imp 13th, lost pl 15th, styd on to take poor 2nd 2 out, t.o..* 2 17

Does not stay 3m but ran well long way at Cheltenham & may surprise in short H/Chase 98 19

FILL THE BOOT(IRE) br.g. 7 Mandalus - Lady O' The Grange by Stanford Mrs Ian McKie

369	2/3	Mollington	(R)	MEM	3m	13	G	*alwys bhnd, t.o. & p.u. 3 out*	P	0
653	22/3	Siddington	(L)	RES	3m	10	F	*prom, chsd wnr 10th, mstk 12th, rdn & ev ch 15th, wknd nxt*	4	13
761	29/3	Kimble	(L)	MDO	3m	12	GF	*(fav) sttld mid-div, prog 15th, ld apr last, hrd rdn, jnd post*	1	15
1531	18/5	Mollington	(R)	MEM	3m	6	GS	*(fav) mstk 6th,hldup,prog to ld 2 out,hng lft,wknd & hdd flat*	2	13

Struggles to stay so far; novice-ridden; should have Restricted chances if getting trip better 98; GF 17

FINAL EXPRESS ch.m. 9 Pony Express - Sansem by New Member — J A G Meaden

1996 4(13),1(14),6(14),2(18),P(0),6(14),P(0),2(21)

106	8/2	Milborne St'	(L)	RES	3m	12	GF	*mid-div, lost tch 12th, plodded round*	7	0
179	15/2	Larkhill	(R)	CON	3m	12	G	*nvr bttr than mid-div, mod 5th 12th, nvr dang, t.o.*	5	0
285	26/2	Taunton	(R)	HC	4 1/4m 110yds	16	GS	*bhnd from 6th, t.o..*	6	0
661	22/3	Badbury Rin'	(L)	RES	3m	6	F	*in tch to 13th, outpcd nxt, no dang aft*	5	0
688	29/3	Little Wind'	(R)	RES	3m	5	GF	*sn pshd alng, bhnd frm 11th, t.o.*	3	0
1275	27/4	Little Wind'	(R)	RES	3m	9	GF	*(bl) lft 2nd aft 7th, pshd alng frm 12th, no imp, dmtd 3 out*	4	11
1483	11/5	Ottery St M'	(L)	RES	3m	15	G	*(bl) alwys mid-div, no ch whn p.u. 14th*	P	0

Maiden winner 96; fell to pieces 97 & blinkers no help 0

FINAL HOPE(IRE) ch.g. 9 Burslem - Mesnil Warren by Connaught — R Tate

1996 3(20),1(20),1(22),**F(-)**,**2(19)**,**2(17)**,3(19),2(18),**3(NH)**

117	9/2	Wetherby Po'	(L)	LAD	3m	10	GF	*hld up rear, prog und pres 13th, kpt on onepcd frm 3 out*	3	20
249	22/2	Brocklesby '	(L)	LAD	3m	4	G	*(fav) made all, 3l clr 3 out, ran on gmly*	1	20
355	2/3	Great Stain'	(L)	LAD	3m	9	S	*prom, prog 4 out, no imp frm 2 out*	4	18
583	17/3	Newcastle	(L)	HC	3m	8	GF	*chsd ldrs, ld 13th, styd on well und pres from last.*	1	23
1072	13/4	Whitwell-On'	(R)	MXO	4m	21	G	*mid-div, mstk 6th, prog 16th, chsd wnr 4 out, onepcd*	3	20
1346	3/5	Gisburn	(R)	LAD	3m	5	GF	*(fav) not fluent,cls 2nd 7th-2 out,wknd rpdly,p.u. last,lame*	P	0

Quite useful at best & consistent; badly lame last start; best watched if reappearing 98; Any 21

FINALLY FANTAZIA ch.m. 8 True Song - Catherine Bridge by Pitpan — Miss K Holmes

1996 5(10),8(0)

219	16/2	Heythrop	(R)	LAD	3m	16	G	*in tch in rear to 7th, t.o. 12th*	10	0
371	2/3	Mollington	(R)	LAD	3m	9	G	*mid-div, outpced 11th, effrt whn mstk 15th, no dang aft*	4	12
988	12/4	Kingston Bl'	(L)	LAD	3m	7	GF	*lft 3rd at 4th, rdn & no imp ldrs 12th, lft poor 2nd 14th*	2	13

Does not stay & outlcassed in Ladies company 13

FINAL OPTION(IRE) b.g. 9 Quayside - Death Or Glory by Hasdrubal — G A Fynn

1996 P(0),U(-),**P(0)**,2(0),4(0),4(0),9(0)

184	15/2	Erw Lon	(L)	MDN	3m	14	G	*sn wll bhnd, poor 8th at 13th, ran on aft, fin strngly*	2	10
408	8/3	Llanfrynach	(R)	MDN	3m	12	G	*alwys last, t.o. hlfwy*	7	0
718	29/3	Llanvapley	(L)	RES	3m	13	GF	*last pair til ran on wll frm 3 out*	4	0
1005	12/4	St Hilary	(R)	CON	3m	10	GF	*last til ran on frm 3 out past btn hrss*	5	0
1138	19/4	Bonvilston	(R)	MDO	3m	9	G	*ld brfly 7th, cls 2nd aft til onepcd frm 2 out*	3	11
1324	3/5	Bonvilston	(R)	MDO	3m	16	G	*prom, ld 13th til hdd & no ext flat*	2	12
1555	24/5	Bassaleg	(R)	MEM	3m	6	G	*lost tch frm 8th, tk bad 3rd 13th, no dang*	3	0
1602	31/5	Bassaleg	(R)	INT	3m	5	F	*alwys last, lost tch 11th, no ch 14th, p.u. 2 out, dsmntd*	P	0

Often flatters but placed 8 times 96/7 & likely to continue to frustrate 11

FINAL PRIDE b.m. 11 Push On - Final Answer by Honour Bound — Grahame Barrett

1996 **6(NH)**,**4(NH)**,**4(NH)**

296	1/3	Didmarton	(L)	LAD	3m	13	G	*prssd ldr to 13th, 3rd & btn aft nxt, wknd 2 out*	3	18
494	13/3	Cheltenham	(L)	HC	3 1/4m 110yds	18	G	*set str pace, blnd and hdd 9th, lost tch after 4 out, soon btn.*	6	22
716	29/3	Llanvapley	(L)	LAD	3m	5	GF	*(fav) made all, sn wll clr, easily*	1	24
1194	22/4	Chepstow	(L)	HC	3m	11	GF	*(fav) j.w, made all, soon clr, easily.*	1	32
1495	14/5	Cothelstone	(L)	LAD	3m	6	GF	*(fav) made all, drew clr & blnd 13th, dist up 3 out, imprssv*	1	29
1590	31/5	Stratford	(L)	HC	3m	9	G	*(fav) with ldr, ld 3rd till hdd after 6 out, pressed wnr after, kept on same pace from 2 out.*	2	24

Returned to best 97; speedy, front-runner; best easy 3m; well-ridden; likely to go summer jumping 29

FINAL STATEMENT (Irish) — **I** 385^{P}, **I** 405^{6}, **I** 484^{P}, **I** 595^{P}

FIND OUT MORE (Irish) — **I** 27^{4}, **I** 116^{U}, **I** 173^{5}

FINE AFFAIR (Irish) — **I** 13^{3}

FINESSE THE KING(IRE) b.g. 9 King's Ride - Candy Slam by Candy Cane — Ms Marcella Bayliss

435	8/3	Upton-On-Se'	(R)	MDO	3m	14	G	*hmpd 2nd, rcvrd, prom to 12th, wkng whn u.r. 15th*	P	0

Of no account & rarely seen 0

FINGAL b.g. 8 Fingora - Alpro by Count Albany — Mrs L J Skitt

241	22/2	Lemalla	(R)	RES	3m	11	S	*last whn ran out 4th*	r	-
1245	26/4	Bratton Down	(L)	INT	3m	9	GS	*bhnd til p.u. 10th*	P	0
1483	11/5	Ottery St M'	(L)	RES	3m	15	G	*alwys rear, t.o. & p.u. 14th*	P	0
1521	17/5	Bratton Down	(L)	MDO	3m	16	GS	*in tch, 4th at 12th, wknd nxt, bhnd & p.u. 3 out, lame*	P	0

1584 26/5 Lifton (R) MDO 3m 13 G *ld/disp 5th-2 out, lkd btn aft, rallied to ld und pres flat* 1 12
1613 7/6 Umberleigh (L) RES 3m 13 F *alwys rear, 9th at 7th, wknd & p.u. 11th* P 0

Won a poor race - 1st sign of any ability & improvement needed for Restricted chance 11

FINNIGAN FREE ch.g. 7 Los Cerrillos (ARG) - Philly-Free by Avocat G E Rich
1996 3(13)
589 20/3 Wincanton (R) HC 2m 5f 9 GF *rear when p.u. before 7th.* P 0

Promise on only start in 96 but soon disappeared in 97 13

FINNISK DREAM (Irish) — **I** 517[P], **I** 559[P]

FINNOW THYNE (Irish) — **I** 17[3]

FIRE AND REIGN(IRE) b.g. 9 Sandhurst Prince - Fine Form (USA) by Fachendon Neil King
286 27/2 Huntingdon (R) HC 3m 8 GS *n.j.w., feeling pace when f 4th.* F -

Of no account 0

FIREBLENDS (Irish) — **I** 19[F], **I** 46[F], **I** 98[F]

FIRE KING b.g. 11 Furry Glen - Foolish Lady (USA) by Signa Infesta E S Collins
1996 **11(NH)**,**7(NH)**,**10(NH)**
201 15/2 Weston Park (L) OPE 3m 16 G *prom to 10th, p.u. 13th* P 0
258 22/2 Newtown (L) RES 3m 14 G *wth ldr til f 6th* F -
467 8/3 Eyton-On-Se' (L) RES 3m 15 G *mid-div, cls order 10th, no imp frm 4 out* 4 13
753 29/3 Brampton Br' (R) RES 3m 9 GF *ld to 9th, lost pld 12th, kpt on onepcd frm 16th* 4 10
1135 19/4 Bonvilston (R) RES 3m 14 G *prom til wknd frm 14th, p.u. flat* P 0
1237 26/4 Brampton Br' (R) RES 3m 13 G *ld/disp 7th-15th, not qckn nxt, kpt on onepcd* 4 12
1526 17/5 Bredwardine (R) RES 3m 13 G *mid-div, lost tch 13th, no dang aft* 5 0

Generally well-beaten & looks unlikely to win at 12 14

FIRESTARTER ch.g. 8 Seymour Hicks (FR) - I'm Still Waiting by Remainder Man Mrs S L Goodman
435 8/3 Upton-On-Se' (R) MDO 3m 14 G *sn rear, lost tch & p.u. 13th* P 0
901 5/4 Howick (L) RES 3m 6 F *n.j.w. wll bhnd frm 9th, t.o.* 5 0
1065 13/4 Maisemore P' (L) MDO 3m 13 GF *ran out & u.r. 2nd* r -
1240 26/4 Brampton Br' (R) MDO 3m 12 G *cls up, chsd ldrs 12th til mstk & u.r. 15th* U -
1459 11/5 Maisemore P' (L) MDO 3m 12 G *rear, prog 10th, lost tch 14th, poor 4th whn f last* F -
1541 18/5 Wolverhampt' (L) MDO 3m 15 GS *mid to rear, no ch whn p.u. 5 out* P 0

Does not stay & jumps poorly 0

FIRST BASH(IRE) ch.g. 7 Ragabash - Colette's First by Buckskin (FR) A S Jones
390 8/3 Barbury Cas' (L) MDN 3m 15 G *f 1st* F -
513 15/3 Larkhill (R) MDO 3m 10 GF *hld up last, prog 12th, jnd wnr apr last, rdn & not qckn* 2 16

Ex-Irish; ran well 2nd start but season lasted week; good enough to win but not 100% genuine 15

FIRST COMMAND(NZ) b.g. 10 Captain Jason (NZ) - Lady Of The Dawn (NZ) by Princely Note Rob Newey
1996 5(0),8(0),3(0),3(10),1(15)
59 1/2 Kingston Bl' (L) RES 3m 16 GF *mostly mid-div, no ch whn p.u. 15th* P 0
213 16/2 Southwell P' (L) RES 3m 16 GS *mid-div, in tch, 6th & outpcd whn blnd 14th, kpt on* 4 15
727 29/3 Sandon (L) RES 3m 6 GF *(fav) prom, ld 14th, going wll whn f 2 out* F -
1208 26/4 Clifton On ' (L) RES 3m 4 GS *(fav) alwys last, rmndrs 9th-10th, t.o. 6 out* 4 0
1392 5/5 Cursneh Hill (L) RES 3m 6 GF *trckd ldrs til prog 12th, ld frm nxt, pshd out flat* 1 17
1507 16/5 Stratford (L) HC 3m 10 G *chsd ldrs till wknd 12th, t.o. when p.u. before 3 out.* P 0

Maiden winner 96; non-stayer but found soft Restricted; both wins Cursneh; Confined there hope 98 .. 16

FIRST DESIGN b.g. 10 Rustingo - Designer by Celtic Cone P D Jones
1996 2(12),F(-)
170 15/2 Ottery St M' (L) MEM 3m 6 G *in tch, chsd ldrs to 14th, outpcd aft* 3 13
454 8/3 Great Treth' (R) LAD 3m 7 S *3rd frm hlfwy, no ch frm 14th* 3 12
792 31/3 Bishopsleigh (R) RES 3m 13 G *alwys prom, disp 4 out til outpcd flat* 2 17
1109 19/4 Flete Park (R) OPE 4m 9 GF *handy, went 2nd 20th, ev ch til no ext aft 3 out* 2 19
1340 3/5 Flete Park (R) LAD 4m 5 G *trckd ldrs in 3rd, lost tch frm 19th* 3 11
1519 17/5 Bratton Down (L) RES 3m 15 GS *6th hlfwy, prog 15th, went 3rd 3 out, fin strngly* 2 18

Maiden winner 93; safe & placed 15 times since win but frustrating 17

FIRST HARVEST b.g. 10 Oats - Celtic Blade by Celtic Cone C J Bennett
1996 **4(18)**,6(0),1(20),**5(17)**,3(18)
201 15/2 Weston Park (L) OPE 3m 16 G *disp 10th-4 out, outpcd frm 2 out, kpt on* 3 17
431 8/3 Upton-On-Se' (R) CON 3m 9 G *ld frm 3rd, prssd 3 out, clr last, eased flat* 1 23
496 15/3 Hereford (R) HC 3m 1f 110yds 10 GF *hdwy 7th, chsd ldrs when blnd 14th, soon wknd.* 5 0
749 29/3 Brampton Br' (R) OPE 3m 4 GF *(fav) 1/3-4/7, cls up, ld 8th, drew wll clr frm 15th* 1 22

Fair performer at best & won 3 of last 5 points; likes Brampton; should win again; G/F-S 23

FIRST MOHIKIN (Irish) — I 17^6, I 82^P, I 87^P, I 307^P

FISCAL POLICY b.g. 9 Politico (USA) - Moschata by Star Moss — H P Trotter

1996 P(0),2(15),2(15),1(15),7(0),1(18),2(16),2(19),P(0)

34	26/1 Alnwick	(L) OPE	3m	9	G	*mstk & u.r. 1st*	U	-
130	9/2 Alnwick	(L) INT	3m	7	G	*ld til aft 3rd, chsd ldrs, went 2nd 3 out, styd on*	2	0
159	15/2 Lanark	(R) OPE	3m	3	G	*(fav) ld to 10th, cls up, ld agn 3 out, sn clr*	1	21
228	22/2 Friars Haugh	(L) MEM	3m	4	G	*(fav) ld frm 4th, 2l up whn lft clr last*	1	20
610	22/3 Friars Haugh	(L) OPE	3m	6	GF	*alwys just bhnd ldrs, kpt on onepce*	3	22
1412	7/5 Uttoxeter	(L) HC	3 1/4m	10	GS	*blnd and u.r. 1st.*	U	-
1426	10/5 Aspatria	(L) OPE	3m	9	G	*alwys prom, ld 14th, clr 2 out, kpt on wll*	1	22
1512	17/5 Corbridge	(R) OPE	3m	10	GS	*mid-div, prog 5th, disp 7th-10th, ld 4 out, lft clr last*	1	24

dual winner 96; improved 97; novice-ridden; stays well; can win more Opens; G-S 23

FISH QUAY ch.g. 14 Quayside - Winkle by Whistler — Mrs K M Lamb

1996 4(17),4(18),**3(19)**,6(12),4(16),**5(10)**,**R(-)**,3(13),**P(0)**,6(0),**11(0)**

35	26/1 Alnwick	(L) CON	3m	10	G	*rear, last & wll bhnd 9th, prog 13th, mstk 15th, wknd*	8	0
152	12/2 Musselburgh	(R) HC	3m	8	GS	*ld 2nd to 4th, mstk 10th, soon lost tch, t.o..*	4	0
387	7/3 Market Rasen	(R) HC	3m 1f	5	G	*imp to chase wnr after 4th, blnd and lost pl 10th, soon t.o., ref 2 out.*	R	-
611	22/3 Friars Haugh	(L) CON	3m	11	GF	*last by 8th, nvr dang*	6	0
891	4/4 Sedgefield	(L) HC	3m 3f	5	GF	*in tch, lost pl 13th, soon struggling, p.u. after 2 out.*	P	0
1287	29/4 Huntingdon	(R) HC	2 1/2m 110yds	14	G	*alwys bhnd, t.o. from 9th.*	10	0

No longer of any account 0

FIVE CIRCLES(IRE) g. 7 Legal Circles (USA) - Classy Chassis — Robert Puddick

1996 **F(NH)**

59	1/2 Kingston Bl'	(L) RES	3m	16	GF	*nvr rchd ldrs, wll bhnd whn p.u. last*	P	0
222	16/2 Heythrop	(R) RES	3m	17	G	*nvr nr ldrs, wll bhnd whn p.u. 3 out*	P	0
300	1/3 Didmarton	(L) RES	3m	23	G	*sn prom, outpcd 14th, kpt on onepcd frm 3 out*	3	16
574	16/3 Garnons	(L) RES	3m	14	G	*cls up in mid-div to 11th, 20l 4th 14th, p.u. 2 out*	P	0

Irish Maiden winner 96; ran well 3rd start but generally disappointing & finished early 15

FIVE MILE DANCER (Irish) — I 274^P, I 438^P

FIXED LIABILITY ch.g. 10 Slippered - Adamstown Girl by Lucifer (USA) — D G Alers-Hankey

1996 P(0),2(16),3(12),U(-),1(14),8(0)

97	8/2 Great Treth'	(R) INT	3m	13	GS	*mid-div,blnd 9th,sn outpcd,poor 4th whn hng rght aft 3 out*	4	12
294	1/3 Didmarton	(L) INT	3m	20	G	*s.s. alwys wll bhnd, no prog frm 11th*	7	0
522	15/3 Cothelstone	(L) CON	3m	14	GS	*(bl) bhnd til p.u. 13th, b.b.v.*	P	0

Restricted winner 96; changed hands but real problems now & looks safely ignored 12

FIX THE SPEC(IRE) ch.g. 7 Burslem - Foolish Lady (USA) — Darren Page

1996 **8(NH)**,**F(NH)**,**6(NH)**,**4(NH)**,**0(NH)**

44	1/2 Larkhill	(R) MDO	3m	9	GF	*chsd ldr 9th til wknd 13th, wll bhnd whn p.u. 15th*	P	0
127	9/2 Cottenham	(R) MDO	3m	11	GF	*alwys bhnd, t.o. & p.u. 13th*	P	0

Of no account in points 0

FLAME OF GOLD (Irish) — I 125^P, I 179^P, I 360^U, I 370^P, I 416^P, I 467^P, I 507^P

FLAME O'FRENSI b.m. 11 Tudor Flame - Regal Rage by Fury Royal — P J Clarke

1996 1(26),2(22),**1(25)**,2(23),2(24),1(23),4(20),**5(0)**,1(26),1(23),5(14)

1	19/1 Barbury Cas'	(L) XX	3m	11	GF	*ld to 9th, chsd ldr to 15th, lft 2nd nxt, fin tired*	2	16
94	7/2 Newbury	(L) HC	2 1/2m	12	G	*ld to 6th, wknd 10th.*	6	0
522	15/3 Cothelstone	(L) CON	3m	14	GS	*ld apr 11th til f 15th*	F	-
791	31/3 Bishopsleigh	(R) CON	3m	6	G	*j.w. made all, kpt on wll frm 3 out*	1	23

Game still but below best in 97; won 17 of 31 points 93-7; should find more chances 23

FLANAGHANS WAY (Irish) — I 114^3, I 176^U, I 328^2

FLAPPING FREDA(IRE) ch.m. 9 Carlingford Castle - Just Darina by Three Dons — B G Clark

15	25/1 Cottenham	(R) MDN	3m	7	GF	*prom til f 3rd*	F	-
69	2/2 Higham	(L) MDO	3m	8	GF	*hld up rear, last at 12th, clsd 14th, wknd nxt, t.o.*	3	0
196	15/2 Higham	(L) MDO	3m	12	G	*alwys wll in rear, t.o. & p.u. 2 out*	P	0
317	1/3 Marks Tey	(L) MDN	3m	13	G	*mid-div, prog 10th, 3rd 15th, wknd nxt, fin tired*	3	0
598	22/3 Horseheath	(R) MDO	3m	3	F	*alwys 3rd, not pace to chal, blnd 15th, sn btn*	3	0
1283	27/4 Fakenham P-'	(L) MDO	3m	9	G	*jmpd slwly, alwys bhnd, t.o. 12th, p.u. 3 out*	P	0
1379	5/5 Northaw	(L) RES	3m	6	F	*jmpd slwly, t.o 4th til p.u. appr 11th*	P	0
1431	10/5 Marks Tey	(L) MDO	3m	6	G	*(Jt fav) (bl) made virt all, jmpd rght, prssd 2 out, drew clr last, easily*	1	10

Basically of little account & found terrible race last start (blinkers); Restricted looks impossible 11

FLASHING ROCK (Irish) — I 87^P

FLASHING STEEL (Irish) — I 24[1], I 59[1]

FLASHLIGHT ch.g. 6 Lighter - Altun Ha by Morston (FR) A G Bonas

1996 P(0),U(-)

116 9/2 Wetherby Po' (L) MDO 3m 14 GF *disp to 10th, trckd ldr aft, not qckn frm 3 out* 3 13

First ever form only start 97 but 3 runs in 2 seasons so far; go close if ready 98 14

FLASHY BUCK b.g. 13 Buckskin (FR) - Flashy Money by Even Money Mrs S J Stearn

193 15/2 Higham (L) CON 3m 14 G *cls up, chal & ld 3 out, made rest, ran on well* 1 20

444 8/3 Higham (L) CON 3m 8 G *(fav) sn rear, nvr going wll, virt t.o. 11th, plodded on* 3 0

Confined winner 95; missed 96; decent winner on return but ground too firm after; can win at 14; G-S 19

FLASHY LEADER (Irish) — I 61[P]

FLAXRIDGE b.g. 12 Amoristic (USA) - Pitpans Star by Pitpan Miss E J Tamplin

1996 U(-),F(-),6(0),B(-),S(-),F(-),9(0),P(0)

189 15/2 Erw Lon (L) RES 3m 14 G *in tch in rear, mstk 14th, sn btn, walked in* 8 0

405 8/3 Llanfrynach (R) RES 3m 15 G *tongue-strap, ld til f 5th* F -

539 16/3 Erw Lon (L) RES 3m 8 GF *tongue-strap, ld to aft 13th, onepcd* 4 11

1135 19/4 Bonvilston (R) RES 3m 14 G *towrds rear, p.u. last* P 0

1227 26/4 Pyle (R) RES 3m 15 GS *pllng, made most 2nd-10th, wknd rpdly 12th, p.u. 15th* P 0

1555 24/5 Bassaleg (R) MEM 3m 6 G *chsd wnr 4th, ld 9-11th, no imp aft 3 out* 2 12

Maiden winner 95; no threat now & no chances at 13 0

FLEDERMAUS b.g. 6 Joligeneration - Flamber by Hot Brandy Mrs T Yandle

1315 3/5 Holnicote (L) MDO 3m 7 G *bhnd & rdn 12th, styd on onepcd frm 3 out* 3 0

1521 17/5 Bratton Down (L) MDO 3m 16 GS *6th hlfwy, no ch ldrs, just hld 3rd* 3 0

Late to appear but not disgraced both starts; should go close in 98 12

FLEECED b.g. 7 Gambler's Cup (USA) - Shepherd Valley by Arrigle Valley C D G Wilson

1996 P(0),4(0),7(0),P(0)

437 8/3 Upton-On-Se' (R) MDO 3m 15 G *prom to 4th, wknd rpdly, t.o. & p.u. 10th* P 0

933 6/4 Charlton Ho' (L) MDO 3m 12 G *last frm 9th, t.o. & p.u. 12th* P 0

Of no account 0

FLIGHTS LANE b.m. 7 Norwick (USA) - Farceuse by Comedy Star (USA) B J Vernoum

1996 P(0),4(0)

147 9/2 Tweseldown (R) MDO 3m 12 GF *alwys rear, p.u. 12th* P 0

Rarely seen & shows nothing 0

FLIGHTY LEADER (Irish) — I 602[P]

FLINTERS b.g. 10 Deep Run - En Clair by Tarqogan John Halewood

1996 U(-),2(14),2(12),2(14),1(15),P(0),**P(NH)**

204 15/2 Weston Park (L) RES 3m 13 G *(bl) prom, ld 4-5th, 2nd aft til ld 3 out, ran on well* 1 18

333 1/3 Eaton Hall (R) INT 3m 10 GS *(bl) cls up, 3rd 10th, chsd wnr 11th, onepcd frm 13th* 5 10

671 23/3 Eaton Hall (R) INT 3 3/4m 8 GF *(bl) cls up to 12th, btn 4 out, p.u. 2 out* P 0

766 29/3 Whittington (L) INT 3m 10 S *(bl) chsd ldr, cls 2nd whn f 14th* F -

998 12/4 Alpraham (R) MEM 3m 4 GF *(bl) cls up, jmpd slwly 5th & rmndrs, wknd rpdly 3 out* 3 0

1349 3/5 Gisburn (R) CON 3m 11 GF *(bl) alwys last trio, t.o. 8th, p.u. 14th* P 0

1538 18/5 Wolverhampt' (L) CON 3m 8 GS *(bl) prom early, mid-div 9th, wknd rpdly, p.u. 13th* P 0

Maiden winner 96; started 97 well but fell to pieces after fall; best watched 98; Soft 14

FLIP THE LID(IRE) b or br.m. 8 Orchestra - Punters Gold by Yankee Gold Peter Sawney

1996 2(19),1(19),3(16),1(23),1(22),1(23)

119 9/2 Wetherby Po' (L) OPE 3m 15 GF *plld hrd, disp til ld 3rd, hdd 4 out, wknd, p.u. flat, lame* P 0

267 22/2 Duncombe Pa' (R) OPE 3m 8 G *mid-div,prog 9th,wnt 2nd 4 out,lft in ld nxt,hld on wll flat* 1 25

Won 4 in 96; game winner 2nd start but vanished; can win more if fit 98; G/F-S 24

FLOCKMASTER(IRE) ch.g. 6 Accordion - Only A Laugh by Torus M G Jones

543 16/3 Erw Lon (L) MDN 3m 11 GF *u.r. 6th in mid-div* U -

1136 19/4 Bonvilston (R) MDO 3m 15 G *last til p.u. 3 out* P 0

1324 3/5 Bonvilston (R) MDO 3m 16 G *rear til p.u. 13th* P 0

1528 17/5 Bredwardine (R) MDO 3m 17 G *alwys bhnd, t.o. & p.u. 10th* P 0

Shows no ability yet 0

FLODART (Irish) — I 112[P], I 375[1], I 466[2], I 503[S]

FLORIDA LIGHT (Irish) — I 22[2], I 103[3]

FLORIDA MIST (Irish) — I 354[P]

FLORIDA OR BUST (Irish) — I 119[P], I 180[6], I 214[2], I 315[U]

FLORIDA WAY (Irish) — I 582[P]

FLORUCEVA (Irish) — I 113[U], I 125[F], I 251[2]

FLOWERHILL ch.g. 10 Decent Fellow - Tamerandy by Tamerlane — M F Harding

44	1/2 Larkhill	(R) MDO 3m	9	GF	*prom to 10th, wknd 12th, blnd 13th & p.u.*	P	0
487	9/3 Tweseldown	(R) MDO 3m	12	G	*7th & out of tch whn u.r. 7th*	U	-
706	29/3 Upper Sapey	(R) MDO 3m	15	GF	*cls 5th til 11th, unable to qckn wth ldrs frm 14th*	5	10
907	5/4 Howick	(L) MDN 3m	4	F	*(fav) prom,ld 14th-3 out,btn whn lft in ld apr last,wknd & hdd flt*	2	0
1200	23/4 Andoversford	(R) MDO 3m	8	F	*prom, ev ch 3 out, sn rdn, btn nxt, dsmntd aft fin*	5	10

Gave up the ghost in desperate race 4th start & problems last outing; non-stayer 10

FLOWER OF DUNBLANE ch.m. 6 Ardross - Anita's Choice by Shantung — Mrs Jean McGregor

1996 **8(NH),5(NH),8(NH),9(NH),8(NH)**

234	22/2 Friars Haugh	(L) MDO 3m	15	G	*sn bhnd, p.u. 2 out*	P	0
566	16/3 Lanark	(R) MDO 3m	10	GS	*u.r. 2nd*	U	-
1051	13/4 Lockerbie	(R) MDN 3m	10	F	*bhnd til prog 4 out, not rch ldng pair*	3	13
1222	26/4 Balcormo Ma'	(R) MDO 3m	6	F	*(fav) ld frm 11th, made rest comf*	1	12
1424	10/5 Aspatria	(L) RES 3m	17	G	*alwys rear, t.o & p.u. 3 out*	P	0

Poor under Rules; got her act together for weak Maiden win; further improvement needed for Restricted 14

FLOWERY FERN (Irish) — I 45[P], I 378[P]

FLOWING GOLD (Irish) — I 594[F]

FLOWING RIVER(USA) b.g. 11 Irish River (FR) - Honey's Flag (USA) by Hoist The Flag (USA) — Piers Butler

1996 **6(NH),4(NH),6(NH),4(NH),6(NH)**

94	7/2 Newbury	(L) HC 2 1/2m	12	G	*in tch, staying on in 4th when hmpd 12th, soon btn.*	4	10
679	26/3 Ascot	(R) HC 2m 3f 110yds	9	G	*held up, blnd 8th, bhnd from 10th, t.o..*	4	12
1292	30/4 Cheltenham	(L) HC 2m 5f	12	GF	*mid div, lost tch with ldrs 12th, no prog after.*	9	14
1416	10/5 Newton Abbot	(L) HC 2m 5f 110yds	14	G	*(bl) prom, ld 4th to 10th, weakend quickly, t.o. when p.u. before 2 out.*	P	0

Winning hurdler; non-stayer & disappointing in H/Chases; blinkers no help 12

FLY FOR US b.m. 11 Cut Above - Flying Spice by Charlottown — C G Taylor

1996 3(22),2(21),F(-)

355	2/3 Great Stain'	(L) LAD 3m	9	S	*mid-div, prog 8th, wknd 4 out, p.u. nxt*	P	0
1573	26/5 Chaddesley '	(L) LAD 3m	6	F	*w.w. prog 10th, prssd wnr aft nxt, rdn & no ext 2 out*	2	22
1606	1/6 Dingley	(R) LAD 3m	13	GF	*cls up, chal 3 out, wknd aft nxt, 5th & btn whn p.u. last*	P	0

Brief campaigns now; retains ability & ran well 2nd start; can win Ladies at 12 if fit 21

FLY FRED b.g. 12 Red Sunset - The Flying Sputnik — Miss H Lewis

187	15/2 Erw Lon	(L) OPE 3m	16	G	*alwys rear, t.o. & p.u. 13th*	P	0
713	29/3 Llanvapley	(L) MEM 3m	4	GF	*(fav) made all, clr hlfwy, easily*	1	12
1321	3/5 Bonvilston	(R) MXO 3m	10	G	*2nd til lft in ld 7th-12th, styd on onepcd*	2	18
1524	17/5 Bredwardine	(R) OPE 3m	8	G	*chsd ldrs, 3rd & wkng 13th, t.o. & p.u. last*	P	0

Confined winner 95; missed 96; doddle in Members & ran well 3rd start; Members possible at 13; G-F 15

FLYING FELLOW(IRE) gr.g. 6 Noalto - Decent Vulgan by Decent Fellow — Miss Catherine Tuke

775	29/3 Dingley	(R) MDO 2m 5f	10	G	*4th whn u.r. 3rd*	U	-
915	5/4 Cottenham	(R) MDO 3m	6	F	*3rd whn ran out 5th*	r	-

Novice-ridden & an unpromising start 0

FLYING IMP b.g. 6 Faustus (USA) - Quenlyn by Welsh Pageant — Mrs Jane Galpin

1996 **11(NH),4(NH),9(NH)**

110	8/2 Milborne St'	(L) MDN 3m	7	GF	*hld up, prog 11th, 3rd at 15th, ld apr last, ran on*	1	16
488	9/3 Tweseldown	(R) RES 3m	10	G	*w.w. rear, mstk 10th, wll bhnd 13th, ran on wll frm 2 out*	2	12

Well-beaten in hurdles 96; good start in modest race; stays extra well; stamina Restricted if fit 98 16

FLYING IN THE GALE (Irish) — I 453[1]

FLYING LINNET gr.m. 6 Neltino - Queen May by Rugantino — Mrs Gillian Duffield

478	9/3 Southwell P'	(L) MDO 3m	17	G	*rear, blnd 5th, t.o. & p.u. aft 11th*	P	0
776	29/3 Dingley	(R) MDO 2m 5f	10	G	*prom whn f 3rd*	F	-
928	6/4 Garthorpe	(R) MDO 3m	8	GF	*u.r. 1st*	U	-
1353	4/5 Dingley	(R) MDO 2 1/2m	9	G	*mstk 4th, jnd ldrs 7th, p.u. qckly 12th, (lame)*	P	0

Yet to complete & problems to boot 0

FLYING LION b.g. 12 Flying Tyke - Comedy Spring by Comedy Star (USA) — John Mackley

1996 2(12),3(17),2+(18),U(-),5(16),1(17),4(18)

164	15/2 Witton Cast'	(R) INT 3m	6	F	*trckd ldrs til onepcd frm 15th*	3	14
352	2/3 Great Stain'	(L) MEM 3m	5	S	*(fav) prom, outpcd 14th, styd on 2 out, clsng whn lft clr last*	1	14

619 22/3 Hutton Rudby (L) INT 3m 8 GF *mid-div til styd on wll frm 2 out* 4 14
694 29/3 Stainton (R) CON 3m 11 F *alwys chsng ldrs, ev ch 16th, onepcd frm 3 out* 3 19
1072 13/4 Whitwell-On' (R) MXO 4m 21 G *rear, styd on frm 4 out, nvr dang* 4 17
1100 19/4 Hornby Cast' (L) CON 3m 9 G *prom, jnd ldr 4 out, outpcd nxt* 3 15
1405 5/5 Witton Cast' (R) CON 3m 10 GS *mid-div,chsd ldrs 6th,mstk 11th,lost plc & strggling 13th,t.o* 7 0
1422 10/5 Easingwold (L) LAD 3m 7 GF *1st ride, mid-div, drppd rear 7th, t.o. 13th* 4 0

Ultra-safe & completed 34 of last 35 starts; Members at 13 only hope now 16

FLYING MARIA br.m. 6 Neltino - Flying Mistress by Lear Jet J S Papworth
1996 r(-),4(0),2(14)

105 8/2 Great Treth' (R) MDO 3m 15 GS *hld up last, just in tch 12th, no ch whn p.u. 16th* P 0
531 15/3 Wadebridge (L) MDO 3m 14 GF *prom early, bhnd in 6th whn f last* F -
625 22/3 Kilworthy (L) MDN 3m 14 G *hdwy 5th, cls 2nd 10th, ld 2 out, ran on wll* 1 15
954 6/4 Black Fores' (R) RES 3m 4 G *hld up in tch, prog 11th, ld 14th, kpt on, comf* 1 15

Confirmed 96 promise; good Maiden win but more needed when upgraded in 98; Good 18

FLYING QUEST b.g. 8 Salmon Leap (USA) - Aspatia by Henbit (USA) J W Lockwood

252 22/2 Brocklesby ' (L) MDO 3m 9 G *nvr dang, 5th outpcd 5 out, ran on* 4 11
344 2/3 Market Rase' (L) MEM 3m 3 GF *ld/disp til ld apr 14th, sn clr, hdd last, rallied,jst faild* 1 18
425 8/3 Charm Park (L) RES 3m 12 GF *hld up, mstk 3rd, prog 10th, styd on stdly frm 3 out, prmsng* 4 10
676 23/3 Brocklesby ' (L) RES 3m 14 GF *net-muzzle, hld up, prog to 3rd aft 15th, rdn 2 out, fin wll* 3 19
838 31/3 Thorpe Lodge (L) RES 3m 5 F *(fav) 3rd/4th hrd held til 2nd frm 12th,ld 3 out,sprntd flat,clvy* 1 16

Quite able but hard ride & well-ridden; can upgrade if all goes well in 98; G-F 20

FLYPIE b.g. 9 Current Magic - Southlandmargarete Vii Mrs C Strang Steel
1996 4(10),**3(0)**,4(13),r(-),**U(-)**,4(11),**9(0)**

162 15/2 Lanark (R) MDO 3m 16 G *bhnd til p.u. 14th* P 0
230 22/2 Friars Haugh (L) RES 3m 15 G *alwys bhnd* 9 0
415 8/3 Dalston (R) RES 3m 19 GS *alwys rear, 14th & t.o. hlfwy* 10 0
613 22/3 Friars Haugh (L) MDN 3m 12 GF *ld frm 8th, made rest, styd on strgly* 1 13
947 6/4 Friars Haugh (L) RES 3m 6 GF *cls 3rd whn u.r. 8th* U -
995 12/4 Tranwell (L) RES 3m 6 F *rear div 1st ctt, wnt 4th 2 out, no impssn on ldrs apr last* 4 0
1331 3/5 Mosshouses (L) MEM 3m 5 F *(fav) went 2nd at 10th, grad lost tch frm nxt* 2 0

Usually well-beaten & 50/1 winner (novice-ridden); hard to see a repeat 13

FLY THE HEIGHTS gr.g. 6 Malaspina - Flying by Head For Heights Mrs Fiona Denniff

478 9/3 Southwell P' (L) MDO 3m 17 G *alwys rear, t.o. & p.u. 14th* P 0
777 29/3 Dingley (R) MDO 2m 5f 8 G *mostly 5th til outpcd 6 out, p.u. last* P 0
1074 13/4 Whitwell-On' (R) MDO 2 1/2m 88yds 16 G *rear, rmndr 7th, sn t.o., p.u. 2 out* P 0

Not yet tuned up but may do better 0

FOHERISH MIST (Irish) — I 561^{P}, I 570^{P}, I 599, , I 603^{3}, I 610^{P}

FOLK DANCE b.g. 15 Alias Smith (USA) - Enchanting Dancer (FR) by Nijinsky (CAN) F R Jackson
1996 5(0),1(18),P(0),3(0),**7(0)**,**5(0)**

144 9/2 Tweseldown (R) OPE 3m 9 GF *hld up, prog 9th, 3rd & ev ch 3 out, wknd nxt, p.u. last* P 0
281 23/2 Charing (L) OPE 3m 12 G *mid-div to 8th, rear aft, t.o.* 7 0
484 9/3 Tweseldown (R) OPE 3m 10 G *alwys last, wll bhnd frm 13th, t.o.* 6 11
683 29/3 Charing (L) OPE 3m 5 F *alwys rear, in tch to 15th, lft poor 3rd 3 out* 3 0

Open winner 96; well-beaten all starts 97 & looks finished now 0

FONTANA LAD (Irish) — I 197^{P}, I 301^{1}

FOOLISH FANTASY b.g. 9 Idiot's Delight - In A Dream by Caruso Mrs G A Spencer
1996 P(0),7(0),5(0),P(0)

84 2/2 Wolverhampt' (L) MEM 3m 9 GS *ran in sntchs, in tch 11th, wknd nxt, virt p.u. flat* 6 0
203 15/2 Weston Park (L) RES 3m 11 G *mid-div, some prog frm 5 out, nrst fin* 4 0
348 2/3 Market Rase' (L) RES 3m 13 GF *chsd ldrs, outpcd apr 14th, 5th & no ch apr last* 5 12
670 23/3 Eaton Hall (R) RES 3m 15 GF *(vis) rear, nvr in race* 10 0
1177 20/4 Sandon (L) LAD 3m 4 GF *cls 3rd at 10th, fdd rpdly 4 out, ref last (twice)* R -

Maiden winner 95 (blinkers); struggling since & last race suggests given up the battle 0

FOOLISH SOPRANO b or br.m. 11 Idiot's Delight - Indian Diva by Indian Ruler Mrs G V Mackay
1996 3(0),3(11),P(0)

394 8/3 Barbury Cas' (L) LAD 3m 5 G *chsd ldng trio 3rd, mstk 6th, jmpd slwly nxt,wknd & p.u.11th* P 0

Placed 5 times 95/6 but disappointing & an elderly maiden now 0

FOOLSANDTHEIRMONEY (Irish) — I 40^{P}, I 104^{P}, I 371^{P}

FOOLS COURAGE (Irish) — I 91^{P}

FOOLS WITH HORSES (Irish) — I 105^{4}, I 157^{4}

FORABBY (Irish) — **I** 34^{F}, **I** 56^{P}, **I** 99^{P}, **I** 155^{3}

FORCE EIGHT b.g. 10 Strong Gale - Belle Kisco by Ballyciptic — Mrs E W Wilson

887	1/4	Flagg Moor	(L)	XX	3m	8	G	*(fav) ld 6th, clr apr 2 out, comf*	1	21
1078	13/4	Guilsborough	(L)	LAD	3m	11	GF	*(fav) trckd ldr, ld 7th, clr whn mstk 2 out, styd on*	1	23
1189	20/4	Garthorpe	(R)	LAD	3m	6	GF	*(fav) prom, mstk 2nd, 2nd whn f 6th*	F	-
1207	26/4	Clifton On '	(L)	LAD	3m	6	GS	*(fav) made most, drew clr frm 2 out, easily*	1	23
1476	11/5	Garthorpe	(R)	LAD	3m	5	GS	*(fav) chsd ldng pair, went 2nd 13th, ld apr 3 out, hdd last,onepcd*	2	20
1606	1/6	Dingley	(R)	LAD	3m	13	GF	*(fav) ld to 5th, ld aft 13th-2 out, wknd, lame*	4	17

Well-revived after missing 96 & useful Ladies horse at best; badly lame again last start 24

FORD CLASSIC (Irish) — **I** 321^{P}, **I** 418^{P}, **I** 478^{5}, **I** 539^{P}, **I** 566^{U}, **I** 606^{F}

FORDSTOWN(IRE) ch.g. 8 Le Bavard (FR) - Gortroe Queen by Simbir — Jamie Alexander

1996 7(0),1(21),2(17),3(13),4(18),1(23),4(16),1(16)

67	1/2	Wetherby	(L)	HC	3m 1f	10	G	*soon bhnd, kept on from 13th, n.d..*	4	19
156	15/2	Lanark	(R)	CON	3m	7	G	*(fav) ld, mstk 11th, outpcd frm 3 out*	2	19
289	28/2	Kelso	(L)	HC	3m 1f	8	GS	*ld to 6th, jmpd slowly and lost pl 9th, rallied to chal 14th, driven and no ext between last 2.*	5	17
492	11/3	Sedgefield	(L)	HC	3m 3f	7	G	*disp ld, ld 8th to 15th, outpcd 4 out, styd on from last.*	3	23
611	22/3	Friars Haugh	(L)	CON	3m	11	GF	*strgglng in 5th whn u.r. 12th*	U	-
890	4/4	Aintree	(L)	HC	2 3/4m	14	G	*chsd ldrs, struggling hfwy, soon t.o..*	8	0
1201	24/4	Perth	(R)	HC	3m	14	G	*ld till hdd 6th, chsd ldrs after, one paced from 15th.*	4	18
1569	26/5	Fontwell	(R)	HC	3 1/4m 110yds	10	GF	*ld to 3rd, mstk and outpcd 16th, styd on from 2 out.*	3	19
1586	28/5	Cartmel	(L)	HC	3 1/4m	10	GF	*prom, ld after 6th, hdd 4 out (water), one pace.*	2	21

Dual winner 96; outclassed in H/Chases; more options 98 & Confineds likely; G/F-S 22

FORESHORE MAN (Irish) — **I** 87^{F}, **I** 152^{2}, **I** 287^{1}

FOREST FLIGHT(IRE) ch.g. 5 Standaan (FR) - Camanime by Hello Gorgeous (USA) — A W S Contracts (G B)

542	16/3	Erw Lon	(L)	MDN	3m	15	GF	*mid-div, mstk 6th, p.u. nxt*	P	0
719	29/3	Llanvapley	(L)	MDN	3m	14	GF	*ld til ran out aft 8th*	r	-
1229	26/4	Pyle	(R)	MDO	3m	11	GS	*f 1st*	F	-

No promise yet 0

FOREST FOUNTAIN(IRE) b or br.g. 6 Royal Fountain - Forest Gale by Strong Gale — J D Callow

1996 P(0),1(16),1(19)

149	10/2	Hereford	(R)	HC	3m 1f 110yds	18	GS	*held up, effort 9th, soon bhnd, p.u. before 3 out.*	P	0
464	8/3	Eyton-On-Se'	(L)	INT	3m	12	G	*cls up, ev ch whn f 12th*	F	-
572	16/3	Garnons	(L)	INT	3m	13	G	*hld up til prog 8th, rdn to chal 15th, kpt on und pres*	2	22
724	29/3	Sandon	(L)	LAD	3m	4	GF	*(fav) hld up, prog 12th, ld 3 out, sn in cmmnd*	1	22

Dual winner 96; pitched in deep end 97; found right level last start & more wins likely 98 if fit 23

FOREST ORE (Irish) — **I** 485^{F}

FOREST RANGER b.g. 15 The Parson - Nora Grany by Menelek — Barrington M Robinson

1996 P(0)

432	8/3	Upton-On-Se'	(R)	MXO	3m	7	G	*lost tch 6th, t.o. & p.u. 11th*	P	0
637	22/3	Howick	(L)	OPE	3m	7	GF	*last til p.u. 13th*	P	0

No longer of any account 0

FOREST TRIBE (Irish) — **I** 233^{1}

FOREVER DREAMING(IRE) b.g. 6 Le Moss - On A Dream by Balinger — Mrs M Cooper

208	16/2	Southwell P'	(L)	MDO	3m	9	GS	*(fav) w.w. steady prog 11th,went 2nd apr 3 out,ran on,nt rch wnr*	2	15
767	29/3	Whittington	(L)	MDO	3m	9	S	*(fav) mstks,lft 3rd 13th,20l down 3 out,ran on strgly to ld last*	1	14

Good start but struggled to win 6 weeks later; looks thorough stayer; should upgrade; good stable 18

FOREVER FREDDY b.g. 9 Lepanto (GER) - My Belleburd by Twilight Alley — J M Valdes-Scott

1996 P(0),P(0),P(0),4(14),U(-),**P(0)**,F(-),R(-),P(0)

65	1/2	Horseheath	(R)	RES	3m	10	GF	*in tch to 6th, reluc & losing plc whn ref & u.r. nxt*	R	-

Some ability but mulish & quickly disappeared in 97 0

FOREVER GOLD (Irish) — **I** 325^{P}, **I** 375^{4}, **I** 431^{2}

FOREVER GREY (Irish) — **I** 111^{U}, **I** 179^{2}, **I** 251^{P}, **I** 329^{P}, **I** 462^{2}, **I** 506^{1}

FOREVER IN DEBT b.m. 7 Pragmatic - Deep In Debt by Deep Run — M R Clough

1996 R(-),P(0),P(0),r(-)

840	31/3	Lydstep	(L)	MEM	3m	6	F	*(vis) in rear whn ref 6th*	R	-

Yet to complete & unpromising 0

FORGET THE REST ro.g. 12 Palm Track - Precipienne by Precipice Wood R Wycherley

200	15/2 Weston Park	(L) CON 3m	16 G	*prom early, btn aft 9th, p.u. 11th*	P	0
330	1/3 Eaton Hall	(R) CON 3m	16 GS	*prom thruout, 2nd whn f 13th*	F	-
465	8/3 Eyton-On-Se'	(L) OPE 3m	13 G	*chsng grp, strggld whn pce increased 4 out*	5	12

Very lightly-raced & showed little in 3 points; best watched 10

FORGOODNESSJAKE VI (Irish) — **I** 65P, **I** 109P, **I** 2644, **I** 344P, **I** 388, , **I** 4533, **I** 5144, **I** 5752, **I** 6112

FORMAL b.g. 11 Cidrax (FR) - Late Challange by Tekoah R A Owen

1996 4(15),6(0)

200	15/2 Weston Park	(L) CON 3m	16 G	*chsd ldrs, btn whn pace incrsd 5 out*	6	0
325	1/3 Eaton Hall	(R) MEM 3m	3 GS	*cls 2nd til wnt on 13th 10l clr whn lft solo last*	1	12
766	29/3 Whittington	(L) INT 3m	10 S	*alwys cls up, ev ch 3 out, styd on onepcd*	3	17
1264	27/4 Southwell P'	(L) INT 3m	9 G	*rear, dtchd 7th, hmpd 9th, sn wll bhnd, p.u. 3 out*	P	0
1347	3/5 Gisburn	(R) OPE 3m	8 GF	*mid-div, nvr trbld ldrs*	4	15
1426	10/5 Aspatria	(L) OPE 3m	9 G	*chsd ldrs, 6th & strggling 11th, no ch aft*	5	10

Non-stayer & generallt outclassed but best season 97 & could repeat Members at 12 15

FOR MICHAEL b.g. 10 Orchestra - Pampered Sue by Pampered King Miss J Houldey

1996 P(0)

262	22/2 Newtown	(L) RES 3m	15 G	*rear, lost tch 11th, kpt on onepcd frm 14th, no dang*	5	0
331	1/3 Eaton Hall	(R) RES 3m	17 GS	*mid-div, some late prog 5 out, nrst fin*	2	17
575	16/3 Garnons	(L) RES 3m	12 G	*cls up whn blnd & u.r. 6th*	U	-
878	1/4 Upton-On-Se'	(R) XX 3m	11 GF	*rear, prog 7th, 3rd & outpcd frm 10th, wknd 15th, p.u. last*	P	0

Maiden winner 94; top stable 97 but novice-ridden to little effect & unlikely to win at 11 15

FORNIDO (Irish) — **I** 5716, **I** 595P

FOROLD (Irish) — **I** 182P, **I** 265P, **I** 301P

FOR PAUL (Irish) — **I** 77P, **I** 450P, **I** 595F

FORREST FUSE (Irish) — **I** 261U, **I** 335F

FORT ALICIA b.m. 10 Helluvafella - Fortalice by Saucy Kit W H O Hutchison

1996 3(12)

234	22/2 Friars Haugh	(L) MDO 3m	15 G	*4th hlfwy, cls up whn f 11th*	F	-
949	6/4 Friars Haugh	(L) MDN 3m	10 GF	*prssd ldr frm 4 out til p.u. lame apr 2 out*	P	0

Promise only start 96 but problems now & could be finished 10

FORT DIANA br.g. 11 Julio Mariner - Blue Delphinium by Quorum L R Vine

1996 U(-),P(0),F(-),3(0),P(0),P(0),2(0),F(-),1(12),F(-),P(0),P(0)

126	9/2 Cottenham	(R) RES 3m	14 GF	*chsng grp til wknd 13th, t.o. & p.u. 3 out*	P	0
278	23/2 Charing	(L) RES 3m	17 G	*mid-div, wknd 11th, t.o. & p.u. 14th*	P	0
462	8/3 Charing	(L) RES 3m	10 G	*prom, ld 5-7th, wknd nxt, bhnd whn p.u. 12th*	P	0
580	16/3 Detling	(L) RES 3m	11 F	*in tch to 15th, p.u. 3 out*	P	0
682	29/3 Charing	(L) RES 3m	5 F	*(vis) in tch, chsd ldng pair 15th, wknd 3 out*	3	0

Won a desperate Maiden in 96 & totally outclassed in Restricteds 0

FORT GALE(IRE) b.g. 6 Strong Gale - Only Gorgeous D J Clapham

1996 **P(NH),U(NH),4(NH),7(NH)**

1239	26/4 Brampton Br'	(R) MDO 3m	9 G	*(fav) sttld mid-div, prog 14th, ld 3 out, hdd & f nxt*	F	-
1367	5/5 Pantyderi	(L) MDO 3m	7 G	*(fav) mid-div, prog 12th, disp ld 2 out, hrd rdn & no ext last*	2	13
1460	11/5 Maisemore P'	(L) MDO 3m	16 G	*(fav) alwys cls up, prog to chal ldr aft 3 out, hrd rdn to ld post*	1	15
1605	1/6 Dingley	(R) RES 3m	13 GF	*(fav) conf rdn in rear, smooth prog to ld apr 2 out, pshd out flat*	1	17

Promising; improved each start & good win last outing; should upgrade; well-ridden; G-G/F 21

FORTINAS FLYER b.m. 11 Helluvafella - Fortalice by Saucy Kit Paul Reid

1996 U(-)

413	8/3 Dalston	(R) OPE 3m	9 GS	*(bl) t.o. & last til p.u. 14th*	P	0
729	29/3 Alnwick	(L) RES 3m	10 F	*(bl) alwys rear, t.o. 9th, p.u. nxt*	P	0
949	6/4 Friars Haugh	(L) MDN 3m	10 GF	*p.u. aft 1st*	P	0
1218	26/4 Balcormo Ma'	(R) RES 3m	5 F	*ld to 2nd, lost tch by 10th, p.u. aft 11th*	P	0
1429	10/5 Aspatria	(L) MDO 3m	15 G	*n.j.w. last & t.o. til p.u. 11th*	P	0
1514	17/5 Corbridge	(R) MDO 3m	17 GS	*(bl) rear, wll bhnd whn p.u. 7th*	P	0

No prospects now 0

FORTITUDE STAR b.m. 7 Morgans Choice - Fort Courage by Cash And Carry M G Smale

1996 **19(NH)**

105	8/2 Great Treth'	(R) MDO 3m	15 GS	*mid-div, 7th at 12th, wll btn whn f 16th*	F	-
243	22/2 Lemalla	(R) MDO 3m	12 S	*prom, 2nd 7th-11th, lost plc & rmndrs 13th, t.o. & p.u. 16th*	P	0
461	8/3 Great Treth'	(R) MDO 3m	12 S	*mid-div, sm hdwy 4th 12th, p.u. apr 3 out*	P	0
625	22/3 Kilworthy	(L) MDN 3m	14 G	*rear & rmmndrs 10th, t.o. p.u. apr 4 out*	P	0
1400	5/5 High Bickin'	(R) MDO 3m	14 G	*sn bhnd & rmndrs, not fluent, t.o. & p.u. 12th*	P	0

No ability & not keen 0

FORTUNES CAST (Irish) — I 60⁶, I 228⁶, I 287⁶

FORTUNES LEAP br.g. 5 Puissance - Lucky Starkist by Lucky Wednesday — Mrs D J Jones

1561 24/5 Bassaleg (R) MDO 3m 9 G *mstks, ld to 12th, wknd rpdly, p.u. 14th* P 0

Poor in hurdles & no chance of staying 3m 0

FORT VIEW (Irish) — I 24⁴, I 54⁵

FORWARD VIEW b.g. 11 Crash Course - Burl's Sister by Burlington II — C R Millington

477 9/3 Southwell P' (L) RES 3m 10 G *sn wll bhnd, t.o. & p.u. 13th* P 0
1081 13/4 Guilsborough (L) RES 3m 13 GF *mstks 4th & 8th, in tch to 14th, t.o. & p.u. 2 out* P 0
1191 20/4 Garthorpe (R) RES 3m 8 GF *rear, prog to mid-div 9th, outpcd 13th, kpt on 3 out* 4 0
1355 4/5 Dingley (R) RES 3m 12 G *prom til p.u. 8th (lame)* P 0
1474 11/5 Garthorpe (R) MEM 3m 6 GS *cls up, chsd wnr 5-7th, rdn 10th, wknd 13th, p.u. 2 out* P 0
1604 1/6 Dingley (R) MEM 3m 4 GF *mstks 6th & 14th, lft in ld 8th, disp aft til no ext 2 out* 2 0

Maiden winner 94; missed 95/6 & of no account now 0

FOSABUD b.g. 11 Dubassoff (USA) - Two Mm's by Manicou — G T Kittow

1996 F(-),P(0),R(-),5(0)

525 15/3 Cothelstone (L) MDN 3m 15 GS *f 1st* F -
1244 26/4 Bratton Down (L) CON 3m 14 GS *sn bhnd til p.u. aft 12th* P 0
1314 3/5 Holnicote (L) MDO 3m 8 G *prom, ld 12th-16th, grad wknd* 5 0
1497 14/5 Cothelstone (L) MDO 3m 10 GF *prom, lft 2nd 13th, jnd ldr 3 out til wknd apr last* 5 11
1553 24/5 Mounsey Hil' (R) MDO 3m 11 G *chsd ldrs, 5th & wkng whn p.u. 15th* P 0

Not beaten far 4th start but struggles to stay & form very weak; unlikely to win at 12 11

FOSBURY b.g. 12 Kambalda - Joyful Luck by Master Buck — H B Geddes

1996 4(17),3(18),4(0),2(25),F(-),**5(22)**,1(24),1(28),1(29),1(30)

19 25/1 Badbury Rin' (L) OPE 3m 8 GF *last & outpcd 3rd, nvr plcd to chal aft* 4 13
98 8/2 Great Treth' (R) OPE 3m 14 GS *prom, 2nd & rdn 13th, wknd frm 16th, walked in* 6 17
920 5/4 Larkhill (R) MXO 4m 4 F *(fav) trckd ldr, disp 5 out, ld nxt, sn clr, eased flat* 1 23
1148 19/4 Chaddesley ' (L) LAD 3m 5 GF *(Jt fav) nvr going wll, bhnd & pshd alng 12th, no prog, t.o., b.b.v.* 3 0
1316 3/5 Holnicote (L) MXO 3m 4 G *raced off pace, prog to ld 13th, disp aft til ld agn nr fin* 1 25
1517 17/5 Bratton Down (L) MXO 3m 8 GS *j.w. ld 2nd, slght ld til hdd 100yrds out, ld agn nr fin* 1 26
1596 31/5 Bratton Down (L) OPE 4m 5 F *(fav) j.w. ld 7th, abt 6l clr final cct, easily* 1 26

Very useful pointer late season; stays; jumps well; can win handicaps; G-F 28

FOSSY BEAR br.m. 5 Lir - Full Spirit by Bay Spirit — Miss K Young

1554 24/5 Mounsey Hil' (R) MDO 3m 14 G *schoold, alwys bhnd, p.u. 11th* P 0
1584 26/5 Lifton (R) MDO 3m 13 G *alwys bhnd, p.u. aft 9th* P 0

Two schools in two days 0

FOUNTAIN BID (Irish) — I 40ᴾ, I 444ᴾ, I 515ᴾ

FOUNTAIN MOSS (Irish) — I 46ᴾ, I 48ᴾ, I 166ᴾ

FOUR FROM THE EDGE b.g. 14 Pollerton - Honeytoi by Carlburg — Mrs T Pritchard

751 29/3 Brampton Br' (R) XX 3m 5 GF *cls 4th whn mstk 8th, not qckn 14th, kpt on onepcd frm 16th* 3 15

Returned from many years absence - ran passably but too old for real chances in 98 12

FOUR HEARTS(IRE) br.g. 8 Mandalus - Daisy Owen by Master Owen — T D B Barlow

1996 P(0),1(15),P(0),3(16),**P(0)**

83 2/2 Wolverhampt' (L) RES 3m 8 GS *prog 8th, cls up til outpcd 3 out, lft 2nd nxt* 2 15
468 8/3 Eyton-On-Se' (L) RES 3m 11 G *(fav) alwys 1st trio, ld 9-11th,cls up whn lft clr 12th,ran on wll* 1 18
667 23/3 Eaton Hall (R) CON 3m 10 GF *prom, 3rd at 6th, lost tch & p.u. 4 out* P 0

Maiden winner 96; maintained progress to win Restricted; finished early; could find Intermediate;G-F .. 19

FOUR LEAF CLOVER ch.m. 10 Sunyboy - National Clover by National Trust — Mrs K A Hanbury

1996 2(14),F(-),U(-),2(14),2(15),C(-),4(11)

1095 16/4 Hockworthy (L) MDN 3m 11 GF *(fav) made all, drew wll clr apr last, drvn out flat* 1 18
1275 27/4 Little Wind' (R) RES 3m 9 GF *(fav) ld to 3rd, lft in ld aft 7th, clr 15th, easily* 1 19
1398 5/5 High Bickin' (R) INT 3m 7 G *(fav) hld up, f 4th* F -
1441 10/5 Holnicote (L) CON 3m 7 G *(fav) sn prom, disp 9th til ld 12th, mstk 15th, drew clr 2 out* 1 21

Changed hands & much improved 97; good stable; can upgrade further at 11; H/Chase possible; G-F ... 25

FOUR NORTH (Irish) — I 210ᴾ

FOUR RIVERS b.g. 12 Relkino - Crystal Fountain by Great Nephew — Mrs A M Murray

1996 **P(0)**,**P(0)**,U(-),5(13)

655 22/3 Siddington (L) RES 3m 10 F *cls up, effrt to chs wnr 13th, ev ch 3 out, rdn & no ext aft* 4 14

Won 2 weak races 95; modest form 96/7 & becoming very lightly-raced now 14

FOUR ZEROS (Irish) — I 156F, I 185P, I 282,

FOWLING PIECE ch.g. 12 Kinghaven - Bonny Hollow by Wolver Hollow — Phillip E Legge

1996 7(13),U(-),4(14),8(0),P(0),3(17),2(14),F(-),P(0),4(15),5(14)

148	9/2 Tweseldown	(R) XX	3m	12 GF	*alwys prom, ld 13th til jnd last, styd on flat, just hld*	2	17
282	23/2 Charing	(L) INT	3m	7 G	*novice-rdn, immed bhnd, mstk 5th, t.o. nxt*	4	0
302	1/3 Parham	(R) CON	3m	14 G	*in tch to hlfwy, t.o. 3 out*	7	0
869	31/3 Hackwood Pa'	(L) XX	3m	6 F	*u.r. 1st*	U	-
1461	11/5 Tweseldown	(R) MEM	3m	3 GF	*jmpd delib in rear, t.o. 6th, lft remote 2nd 3 out*	2	0
1565	25/5 Kingston Bl'	(L) OPE	3m	4 GF	*cls up til lft bhnd aft 13th, no ch aft*	4	10

Changed hands (again) 97; remarkable 1st run but novice-ridden after & fell to pieces 0

FOXBOW(IRE) b.g. 7 Mandalus - Lady Bow by Deep Run — J M Turner

1996 **13(NH),3(NH),6(NH)**

193	15/2 Higham	(L) CON	3m	14 G	*chsd ldrs in tch, chal 4 out, kpt on well frm 2 out*	3	19
322	1/3 Marks Tey	(L) OPE	3 1/2m	9 G	*in tch, rdn apr 12th, sn bhnd, t.o.*	6	12
495	14/3 Fakenham	(L) HC	2m 5f 110yds	10 G	*f 3rd.*	F	-
595	22/3 Horseheath	(R) OPE	3m	5 F	*alwys 4th, outpcd 14th*	4	17
1117	19/4 Higham	(L) CON	3m	5 GF	*nvr going or jmpng wll, lost tch aft 11th, t.o.13th*	5	0
1433	10/5 Marks Tey	(L) OPE	3m	4 G	*(bl) chsd ldrs,disp 7th,clr nxt,drvn 3 out,wknd last, jst hld on*	1	18
1503	16/5 Folkestone	(R) HC	3 1/4m	7 G	*(bl) chsd ldr, ld 5th, rdn and joined when f 2 out.*	F	-

Winning hurdler 95; showed little till blinkers applied; could win again if in mood 98; Good 20

FOXES DANCE ch.m. 6 Vin St Benet - Jeanjim by Homeric — The Hon Mrs L A Henniker-Major

270	22/2 Ampton	(R) MEM	3m	8 G	*sn wll bhnd, t.o. & p.u. 12th*	P	0

Showed no promise 0

FOX POINTER b.g. 12 Healaugh Fox - Miss Warwick by Stupendous — Mrs L T J Evans

1996 **U(-),U(-),4(24),2(27),2(25)**

288	27/2 Ludlow	(R) HC	3m	8 G	*soon trckd ldr, ld apr 5 out, hdd 2 out, one pace.*	2	24
591	21/3 Newbury	(L) HC	3m	7 GF	*(fav) j.w, made all, shaken up apr last, qcknd clr.*	1	26
982	9/4 Ludlow	(R) HC	3m	6 F	*(fav) in tch, chsd wnr from 5th till dived 7th, wknd apr 3 out.*	3	23
1099	19/4 Stratford	(L) HC	2m 5f 110yds	14 G	*(fav) ld to 4th, wknd 5 out.*	4	10

Placed in 4 H/Chases prior to deserved win; below best after; could find another at 13; G/S-F 24

FOYLE BOREEN (Irish) — I 72F

FOYLE VALLEY LADY (Irish) — I 228, , I 350[4]

FRACTION ch.g. 6 Fearless Action (USA) - Amerian County by Amerian (USA) — Mrs F J Marriott

299	1/3 Didmarton	(L) MDN	3m	14 G	*last whn hmpd & u.r. 2nd*	U	-
761	29/3 Kimble	(L) MDO	3m	12 GF	*mid-div, 8th hlfwy, rear whn p.u. 16th*	P	0
980	8/4 Heythrop	(R) MDO	3m	2 F	*(Jt fav) disp ld til ld appr last, rddn & drw clr flat*	1	0
1164	20/4 Mollington	(R) RES	3m	10 GF	*sn bhnd, mstk 9th, clsd 13th, sn outpcd, kpt on frm 2 out*	5	10

Beat reluctant opponent in desperate match; some promise next start & should do better in 98 13

FRAGMENT(IRE) b.g. 7 Glint Of Gold - Mouletta by Moulton — Mrs V Simpson

1996 P(0),P(0),U(-)

915	5/4 Cottenham	(R) MDO	3m	6 F	*1st ride, chsd clr ldr to 9th, t.o. & p.u. 15th*	P	0
1118	19/4 Higham	(L) MDO	3m	9 GF	*last aft 1st, t.o. 3rd, 2 fncs bhnd whn p.u. 3 out*	P	0
1310	3/5 Cottenham	(R) MDO	3m	2 F	*set funereal pace to 4th, ld 6th-3 out, immed btn*	2	0
1431	10/5 Marks Tey	(L) MDO	3m	6 G	*(bl) trckd wnr, chal & ev ch whn mstk 2 out, hld aft*	2	0

Improved slightly with blinkers last start (could not have got worse) & just scrapes a rating 10

FRAGRANT LORD b.g. 8 Germont - Tiger Feet by Pongee — Mrs V Jackson

1996 P(0)

37	26/1 Alnwick	(L) MDO	3m	15 G	*alwys bhnd, no dang frm 14th*	5	0
235	22/2 Friars Haugh	(L) MDO	3m	10 G	*u.r. 7th*	U	-
566	16/3 Lanark	(R) MDO	3m	10 GS	*bhnd by 11th, p.u. bfr last*	P	0

Well-beaten on only completion & finished early 0

FRANCIS FARRELLY b.g. 12 Tudor Rhythm - Cave Lass by Orange Bay — R Bewley

606	22/3 Friars Haugh	(L) MEM	3m	9 GF	*alwys bhnd*	4	0

Rarely seen & of no account 0

FRANCOPHILE(IRE) ch.g. 6 Caribo - French Miss by Golden Love — J Walford

480	9/3 Southwell P'	(L) MDO	3m	17 G	*schoold rear; nvr nr ldrs, t.o. 15th*	8	0

Good stable & should do better in time 10

FRANK BE LUCKY b.g. 11 Mandalus - Bramble Leaf by Even Money — Ms Barbara Ashby-Jones

1996 **2(NH),4(NH)**

874	1/4	Uttoxeter	(L)	HC	2m 7f	9 GF	*chal 3rd till ld 5th, hdd apr 2 out, wknd rpdly and p.u. before last.*	P	0
1099	19/4	Stratford	(L)	HC	2m 5f 110yds	14 G	*prom, mstks, wknd 5 out, p.u. before 2 out.*	P	0
1292	30/4	Cheltenham	(L)	HC	2m 5f	12 GF	*pressed ldr to 9th, cl up after til rdn and wknd after 4 out.*	6	16

Winning chaser; bang there each race but stopped alarmingly; needs Soft but still best watched 18

FRANK RICH b.g. 10 King's Ride - Hill Invader by Brave Invader (USA) — D J Lay

1996 P(0),U(-),2(14),5(12)

444	8/3	Higham	(L)	CON	3m	8 G	*mid-div, dist 3rd aft 11th, not keen 14th, t.o. & p.u. 2 out*	P	0

Ungenuine & an undistinguished appearance in 97 0

FRANK THE SWANK b.g. 6 Dunbeath (USA) - Dark Amber by Formidable (USA) — T C Gittins

1996 F(-),P(0),P(0),P(0),P(0),P(0),5(0)

200	15/2	Weston Park	(L)	CON	3m	16 G	*jmpd slwly, sn t.o., p.u. 14th*	P	0
326	1/3	Eaton Hall	(R)	MDN	3m	14 GS	*ld to 5th, in tch 8th, wknd qckly, p.u. 11th*	P	0

No stamina & unpromising 0

FREDDIE FOX b.g. 11 Scallywag - Gouly Duff by Party Mink — Mrs A B Garton

1996 **3(15)**,1(18),2(19),**1(20),5(0)**

84	2/2	Wolverhampt'	(L)	MEM	3m	9 GS	*(fav) chsd ldr 9th, pshd alng frm 11th, kpt on to ld flat, gamely*	1	18
490	10/3	Stratford	(L)	HC	3m	12 G	*bhnd from 6th, p.u. before 12th.*	P	0
725	29/3	Sandon	(L)	OPE	3m	4 GF	*w.w. alwys 3rd, nvr able to chal*	3	14
936	6/4	Tabley	(R)	MEM	3m	9 G	*(fav) chsd ldr, ld apr 14-15th, 3rd & wll btn & p.u. 2 out*	P	0
1123	19/4	Whittington	(L)	OPE	3m	4 F	*chsd ldr, ld 7th-nxt, cls up til blnd 12th, wknd nxt*	3	17
1301	3/5	Weston Park	(L)	OPE	3m	4 G	*alwys 3rd & onepcd, lft 2nd at last*	2	10
1539	18/5	Wolverhampt'	(L)	OPE	3m	5 GS	*in tch, onepcd frm 3 out*	4	0

Stays, onepaced but ultra-safe; declined in 97 & Members again best hope at 12; G/F-S 15

FRED LAD ch.g. 9 Starch Reduced - Prim Catherine by Chestergate — E H Crow

999	12/4	Alpraham	(R)	MDO	3m	8 GF	*whppd round strt & u.r., t.n.p.*	0	0

Good stable - worst possible start 0

FREE AND EQUAL (Irish) — **I** 397^5

FREEMANSTOWN (Irish) — **I** 214^F

FREESTYLER (Irish) — **I** 57, , **I** 84^3, **I** 184^P, **I** 220^P, **I** 285^P, **I** 409, , **I** 496,

FREE TRANSFER(IRE) b.g. 8 Dara Monarch - Free Reserve (USA) by Tom Rolfe — D J Fairbairn

1996 2(22),U(-),1(21),3(14),**2(23)**

152	12/2	Musselburgh	(R)	HC	3m	8 GS	*in tch, blnd 12th, soon outpcd, rallied before 4 out, mstk 2 out, no ch after.*	3	15
375	3/3	Doncaster	(L)	HC	2m 3f 110yds	11 GF	*in tch, rdn along to chase ldrs when blnd and u.r. 11th.*	U	-
583	17/3	Newcastle	(L)	HC	3m	8 GF	*in tch, outpcd when hmpd 14th, some hdwy after 3 out, wknd after next, fin lame.*	5	14

Confined winner 96; struggled in H/Chases & problems as well; not 100% genuine; easy 3m; best watched 19

FRENCH GALE (Irish) — **I** 335^P

FRENCH INVASION b.m. 8 Nader - Lyme Bay II by Incredule — Mrs Marilyn Burrough

1996 P(0),U(-)

461	8/3	Great Treth'	(R)	MDO	3m	12 S	*mid-div whn f 9th*	F	-
644	22/3	Castle Of C'	(R)	MDO	3m	9 G	*rear, mstk 5th, outpcd 14th, no ch frm 3 out*	7	0
1157	20/4	Stafford Cr'	(R)	RES	3m	11 GF	*mid-div, u.r. 7th*	U	-
1269	27/4	Little Wind'	(R)	MEM	3m	3 GF	*chsd wnr 8th til blnd nxt, wknd 12th, crwld 14th & p.u.*	P	0
1498	14/5	Cothelstone	(L)	MDO	3m	9 GF	*mstks, chsd ldr to 13th, sn btn*	5	0

Of absolutely no account 0

FRENCH MYLE(IRE) ch.g. 9 Le Bavard (FR) - Myle Avenue by Push On — Mrs Rebecca Smith

207	16/2	Southwell P'	(L)	MEM	3m	3 GS	*not fluent, ld to 5th, chsd wnr aft, rdn 15th, onepcd*	2	12
507	15/3	Dalton Park	(R)	OPE	3m	8 GF	*prom til outpcd 14th, blnd 3 out, 4th & no ch whn u.r. nxt*	U	-

Lightly raced under Rules & no real achievements in points 12

FRENCH PLEASURE gr.m. 11 Dawn Johnny (USA) - Perfect Day by Roan Rocket — A J Mason

1996 1(17),3(10),3(16)

218	16/2	Heythrop	(R)	INT	3m	21 G	*trckd ldrs til outpcd 15th, kpt on*	4	15

396 8/3 Barbury Cas' (L) CON 3m 9 G *rear, 7th & pshd alng 10th, no prog, blnd 12th, p.u. aft* P 0
649 22/3 Siddington (L) MEM 3m 6 F *trckd ldrs, mstk 12th & rdn, btn whn nrly ref 15th & p.u.* P 0

Intermediate winner 96; below form 97; 1st time out 98 may be only chance now; Good 15

FRENCH STICK ch.g. 9 Sula Bula - French Highway by Duc D'Orleans Mrs J P Spencer
1996 P(0),2(17)

633 22/3 Howick (L) RES 3m 8 GF *(Jt fav) ld to 7th, 2nd til ld agn 12th, in cmmnd frm 2 out* 1 17
906 5/4 Howick (L) INT 3m 2 F *(fav) trckd wnr, no imp 3 out, btn whn blnd nxt* 2 11
1574 26/5 Chaddesley ' (L) CON 3m 8 F *ld to 14th, outpcd frm nxt* 3 12

Maiden winner 95; found modest Restricted but struggling after; lightly-raced; may win again 17

FRESH ICE(IRE) ch.g. 7 Aristocracy - Quefort by Quayside G Vergette
1996 P(0),F(-),1(14),2(17)

28 26/1 Marks Tey (L) RES 3m 9 GF *prom, ld 16th, lft clr 3 out, wknd rpdly apr last, hdd flat* 3 14
449 8/3 Newton Brom' (R) XX 3m 13 G *alwys cls up, effrt 2 out, not pace to chal* 2 17
548 16/3 Garthorpe (R) RES 3m 10 GF *(Jt fav) cls up, ld gng wll 3 out, hdd last, nt qckn flat* 2 18

D/H for Maiden 96; ran well each time but folded closing stages & may have a problem 17

FRESH PRINCE b.g. 9 Balinger - Lasses Nightshade by Deadly Nightshade Mrs Vanessa Ramm
1996 F(-),5(0),P(0),P(0),1(12),1(19),P(0)

5 19/1 Barbury Cas' (L) OPE 3m 11 GF *ld til ran out & u.r. bend apr 12th* r -
220 16/2 Heythrop (R) OPE 3m 20 G *chsd ldr, ld 11th, clr 14th, prssd 2 out, ran on well last* 1 26

Dual winner 96; vastly improved 2nd start 97 but vanished; win more opens if fit 98; Good 25

FRIARS ISLAND (Irish) — **I** 148^{F}, **I** 184^{P}, **I** 285^{P}, **I** 393^{2}, **I** 438^{3}, **I** 522^{3}, **I** 551^{1}, **I** 578^{P}

FRIAR STREET(IRE) b.g. 7 Carmelite House (USA) - Madam Slaney by Prince Tenderfoot (USA) A Witcomb
1996 **16(NH)**,**12(NH)**

75 2/2 Market Rase' (L) CON 3m 10 GF *hld up bhnd, prog to 3rd 10th, blndrd 13th, sn wknd, t.o.* 8 0

Tailed off last & disappeared; no prospects 0

FRIDAYS CHILD b.m. 5 Bold Fox - Fassbinder by El-Birillo Keith Kelso

842 31/3 Lydstep (L) MDO 3m 12 F *trckd ldr til f 10th* F -
964 6/4 Pantyderi (L) MDN 3m 4 F *ld til aft 15th, fdd rpdly* 3 0
1230 26/4 Pyle (R) MDO 3m 10 GS *prom til wknd rpdly 6th, p.u. 8th* P 0

Seems to stay about a mile & tailed off last on only completion 0

FRIENDLY LADY b.m. 13 New Member - Friendly Glow by Pal O Mine J Grant Cann
1996 F(-),8(10),6(11),5(0),3(20),U(-),2(18),1(20)

3 19/1 Barbury Cas' (L) XX 3m 14 GF *cls up til outpcd frm 12th, kpt on agn frm 2 out* 4 13
174 15/2 Ottery St M' (L) LAD 3m 9 G *sn bhnd, t.o. whn u.r. 4 out* U -
238 22/2 Lemalla (R) LAD 3m 9 S *sn rear, last at 13th, nrst fin* 5 14
1153 20/4 Stafford Cr' (R) CON 3m 10 GF *mid-div, nvr on trms wth ldrs* 3 12
1244 26/4 Bratton Down (L) CON 3m 14 GS *bhnd til some late prog, not near to chal* 5 10

Confined winner 96; formerly very useful but time seems to be catching up now 14

FRIENDLY VIKING ch.g. 7 Viking (USA) - Ale Water by Be Friendly Mrs J Holden-White
1996 P(0),R(-),F(-)

629 22/3 Kilworthy (L) OPE 3m 5 G *nvr dang, wll btn 3rd whn ref 15th* R -
1035 12/4 Lifton (R) MDN 3m 11 F *alwys abt same plc, kpt on onepcd frm 2 out* 4 11
1416 10/5 Newton Abbot (L) HC 2m 5f 110yds 14 G *alwys bhnd, t.o. when p.u. after 9th.* P 0
1521 17/5 Bratton Down (L) MDO 3m 16 GS *rear, 10th at 12th, p.u. apr nxt* P 0
1583 26/5 Lifton (R) MDO 3m 11 G *nvr nrr, fin own time* 4 0

Has completed 3 of 10 races; not disgraced 2nd start but unlikely to achieve anything 10

FRIGHTENING CHILD (Irish) — **I** 7^{P}, **I** 74^{P}, **I** 167^{3}

FROME BOY ch.g. 12 New Member - Groundsel by Reform Peter Johnson
1996 P(0),B(-),r(-),F(-)

423 8/3 Charm Park (L) OPE 3m 7 GF *rear, mstks 2nd & 3rd, sn bhnd, t.o. 10th, p.u. nxt* P 0
618 22/3 Hutton Rudby (L) OPE 3m 10 GF *rear & rmmndrs 6th, alwys strgglng, t.o.* 6 0
896 5/4 Wetherby Po' (L) OPE 3m 1 F *walked over* 1 0
1072 13/4 Whitwell-On' (R) MXO 4m 21 G *rear, lost tch 6th, t.o. & u.r. 17th* U -
1248 26/4 Easingwold (L) OPE 3m 8 GS *alwys rear, t.o. 13th, late efft* 6 0
1420 10/5 Easingwold (L) OPE 3m 5 GF *mid-div, rdn 4th, sn strgglng, t.o. 8th* 4 0

No longer of any account 0

FRONT COVER b.m. 7 Sunyboy - Roman Lilly by Romany Air Stewart Pike
1996 U(-),3(15),F(-),1(16),2(20),1(20)

18 25/1 Badbury Rin' (L) LAD 3m 9 GF *4th whn f 6th* F -

46	1/2	Larkhill	(R)	XX	3m	3	GF	*mstk 2nd, jmpd lft, outpcd 13th, went 2nd 2 out, no ch wnr*	2 19
218	16/2	Heythrop	(R)	INT	3m	21	G	*(fav) cls up, trckd ldrs 12th, chal & lft in ld 2 out, sn clr,comf*	1 23
647	22/3	Castle Of C'	(R)	INT	3m	7	G	*(fav) chsd ldr 3-8th & 12th,ev ch & rdn 3 out,btn whn lft clr last*	1 22
1148	19/4	Chaddesley '	(L)	LAD	3m	5	GF	*(Jt fav) prom til blnd & u.r. 8th*	U -
1272	27/4	Little Wind'	(R)	LAD	3m	2	GF	*(fav) trckd ldr, ld 3 out, blnd nxt, rdn out*	1 20
1412	7/5	Uttoxeter	(L)	HC	3 1/4m	10	GS	*(Jt fav) trckd ldrs, shaken up after 16th, ld next, soon clr, easily.*	1 24
1500	16/5	Aintree	(L)	HC	3m 1f	6	G	*(fav) nvr far away, reminder apr 5 out, soon ld, clr 3 out, unchal.*	1 29

Very useful now; won 7 of last 11; jumped better in H/Chases & win more in 98; G/S-G/F 29

FROSTBITTEN (Irish) — **I** 95², **I** 152ᶠ, **I** 219², **I** 343¹

FROSTY MORN (Irish) — **I** 48ᶠ, **I** 234ᴾ

FROSTY RECEPTION ch.g. 12 What A Guest - Stormy Queen by Typhoon — Miss C C Stucley1996 4(0),12(0),1(18)

791	31/3	Bishopsleigh	(R)	CON	3m	6	G	*(bl) chsd ldr to 17th, wknd nxt, fin tired*	3 10
1042	12/4	Cothelstone	(L)	MXO	3m	2	GF	*(bl) ld til blnd 13th, chsd wnr vainly aft, blnd last*	2 15
1090	16/4	Hockworthy	(L)	LAD	3m	8	GF	*ld to 4th, chsd ldrs til outpcd 12th, nvr on trms aft*	5 13
1311	3/5	Holnicote	(L)	MEM	3m	7	G	*mid-div, grad fdd frm 15th*	4 0
1441	10/5	Holnicote	(L)	CON	3m	7	G	*(bl) in tch til lost plc 8th, no ch frm 11th*	5 0
1496	14/5	Cothelstone	(L)	CON	3m	9	GF	*in tch to 10th, wll bhnd 13th, f 3 out*	F -

Shock winner of Confined 96; modest form 97 & suffered heavy fall last start 12

FROZEN PIPE b.m. 9 Majestic Maharaj - Celtic Ice by Celtic Cone — Alan P Brewer
1996 2(15),F(-),1(17),5(0),P(0)

360	2/3	Garnons	(L)	CON	3m	10	GS	*trckd ldrs, prog 15th, ld & lft clr 2 out*	1 21
568	16/3	Garnons	(L)	CON	3m	12	G	*trckd ldrs, chal 2 out, ld last, pshd out flat*	1 22
1064	13/4	Maisemore P'	(L)	CON	3m	13	GF	*w.w. prog 12th, went 3rd 3 out, no prog aft*	3 21
1212	26/4	Woodford	(L)	INT	3m	8	G	*in tch, blnd 12th, ev ch 2 out, unable qckn und pres*	3 20
1458	11/5	Maisemore P'	(L)	XX	3m	6	G	*chsd wnr to 15th, p.u. nxt, lame*	P 0

Restricted winner 96; improved & ran well 97; problems last start; can win again if fit 98; G/S 22

FROZEN STIFF(IRE) ro.g. 9 Carlingford Castle - Run Wardasha by Run The Gantlet (USA) — A J Brown
1996 1(15),1(19)

386	7/3	Ayr	(L)	HC	2m 5f 110yds	7	S	*chsd ldrs, mstks 5th and 14th, fd from 4 out.*	3 11
778	31/3	Carlisle	(R)	HC	3 1/4m	14	G	*chsd ldrs, struggling when hit 10th, soon btn, p.u. 5 out.*	P 0
1500	16/5	Aintree	(L)	HC	3m 1f	6	G	*(bl) almost u.r. 1st, held up, blnd and u.r. rider 4th.*	U -
1546	24/5	Hexham	(L)	HC	2 1/2m 110yds	10	GF	*soon t.o., p.u. before 9th.*	P 0

Dual winner early 96; all over the shop in H/Chases 97; can only be watched now 14

FRUIT FIELD gr.m. 6 Roselier (FR) - Fruit Farm by Twiberry — E H Crow

258	22/2	Newtown	(L)	RES	3m	14	G	*schoold & mstks,bhnd,some prog 13th,poor 4th whn p.u.2 out*	P 0

Reasonable performance & good stable but not seen after 13

FRUIT OF OAK(IRE) b.g. 7 Lancastrian - Fruit Farm by Twiberry — A McKay

325	1/3	Eaton Hall	(R)	MEM	3m	3	GS	*alwys 3rd in tch, 2l down whn f 12th*	F -
768	29/3	Whittington	(L)	MDO	3m	10	S	*n.j.w., alwys last pair, t.o. 14th, f 3 out*	F -
941	6/4	Tabley	(R)	MDO	3m	11	G	*rear, blndrd 6th, prog 11th, wnt 3rd 16th, outpcd 3 out*	3 0
1386	5/5	Eyton-On-Se'	(L)	MDO	2 1/2m	8	GF	*hit 2nd hrd & u.r.*	U -
1473	11/5	Erw Lon	(L)	MDO	3m	13	GS	*alwys prom, 2nd & btn whn f last*	F -

Possibly unlucky 2nd start but jumping needs to improve to be sure of winning 14

FRUMERTY b.g. 5 Nicholas Bill - Zulu Dancer by Sula Bula — Mrs A M Easterby

80	2/2	Market Rase'	(L)	MDO	2m 5f	9	GF	*hld up in rr til blndrd & u.r. 4th*	U -
116	9/2	Wetherby Po'	(L)	MDO	3m	14	GF	*(fav) chsd ldrs, fdd frm 4 out*	5 0

Good stable but season lasted a week & suffered mishap 2nd start 11

FUANNAE(IRE) b.g. 8 Aristocracy - Lottie's Charm by Charlottesville — F J Brennan

60	1/2	Kingston Bl'	(L)	MDN	3m	17	GF	*alwys prom, ld 8th til f 14th*	F -
374	2/3	Mollington	(R)	MDN	3m	14	G	*trckd ldrs, pshd alng 11th, sn outpcd, no imp frm 15th*	5 0
1568	25/5	Kingston Bl'	(L)	MDO	3m	11	GF	*prom til blnd 7th & 8th, sn rear, no ch 13th, t.o.*	5 0

Well-beaten both completions & makes mistakes; prospects modest 10

FULL ALIRT ch.m. 9 Lir - Full Tan by Dairialatan — B R J Young
1996 U(-),1(20),**F(-)**,4(19)

491	10/3	Taunton	(R)	HC	3m	8	G	*ld 5th, made rest, hrd pressed last, ran on well.*	1 23
586	19/3	Exeter	(R)	HC	3 1/4m	12	GF	*chsd ldrs to 6 out, soon wknd, bhnd when p.u. before 4 out.*	P 0
1242	26/4	Bratton Down	(L)	LAD	3m	6	GS	*alwys prom, efft to chal 15th, no ext frm nxt*	3 15
1416	10/5	Newton Abbot	(L)	HC	2m 5f 110yds	14	G	*held up in rear, hdwy 9th, one pace from 3 out.*	3 23

Members winner 96; quite able; best fresh; H/Chase success makes placing hard; G-Hy 23

FULL HOLIDAY (Irish) — **I** 61^U, **I** 202^U, **I** 355, , **I** 401^F

FULL MOON FEVER (Irish) – **I** 301^P, **I** 452,

FULL SCORE(IRE) b.g. 8 Orchestra - Country Character by Furry Glen — Ms K A Mansbridge

1996 P(0)

60	1/2	Kingston Bl'	(L)	MDN	3m	17	GF	*alwys prom, chsd ldrs frm 13th, styd on wll flat*	3	12

Rarely appears; ran reasonably only start 97 but time passing 12

FULL SONG b.m. 9 idiot's Delight - Into Song by True Song — G Coombe

1996 10(0),3(0),3(10),4(0),0(0),2(12),4(0),P(0)

372	2/3	Mollington	(R)	RES	3m	19	G	*prom to 11th, sn wknd, bhnd whn p.u. 3 out*	P	0
549	16/3	Garthorpe	(R)	MDO	3m	16	GF	*prom, lft in ld 3 out, rddn nxt, hdded & unable to qckn flat*	2	13
883	1/4	Flagg Moor	(L)	MDO	3m	12	G	*(fav) bhnd whn mstk 7th, lost tch 13th, t.o. & p.u. 3 out*	P	0
1193	20/4	Garthorpe	(R)	MDO	3m	9	GF	*chsd ldrs, ld 8-11th, rdn 13th, 4l down whn lft clr 2 out*	1	14
1355	4/5	Dingley	(R)	RES	3m	12	G	*(bl) ld, clr 2nd, rddn & reluc 10th, hdd 12th, wknd, p.u. 14th*	P	0
1475	11/5	Garthorpe	(R)	XX	3m	13	GS	*disp to 8th, 5th hlfwy, wknd 12th, t.o. & p.u. 2 out*	P	0
1605	1/6	Dingley	(R)	RES	3m	13	GF	*prom til wknd 14th, bhnd whn p.u. 2 out*	P	0

Won on 25th attempt (lucky) & soundly thrashed in Restricted after 12

FUNCTION DREAM (Irish) — **I** 140^3, **I** 519^1

FUNDY(IRE) b.g. 8 Arapahos (FR) - S T Blue by Bluerullah — A J Brazier

988	12/4	Kingston Bl'	(L)	LAD	3m	7	GF	*(fav) in tch til followed ldr out at 4th*	r	-
1148	19/4	Chaddesley '	(L)	LAD	3m	5	GF	*prom, cls 3rd whn f 12th*	F	-
1384	5/5	Eyton-On-Se'	(L)	LAD	3m	6	GF	*(fav) ld to 6th, 2nd to 12th, ld 13th, sn in commd, easily*	1	22
1450	10/5	Kingston Bl'	(L)	LAD	3m	7	G	*(fav) ld til aft 5th, ld 9th, made rest, drew clr frm 2 out,easily*	1	22

Dual Irish pointing winner 96; useful & won weak races easily; should win in better company 98 24

FUNNY FARM ch.g. 7 Funny Man - Ba Ba Belle by Petit Instant — Mrs Jane Walter

1996 P(0),r(-),2(13)

643	22/3	Castle Of C'	(R)	MDO	3m	12	G	*(Jt fav) in tch, cls 5th whn b.d. 8th*	B	-

Promise 96 but disappeared after mishap 97 13

FUNNY FEELINGS b.g. 7 Feelings (FR) - Miami Star by Miami Springs — Mrs J R Scott

1996 4(0),1(14),F(-),2(15),5(0),1D(17),U(-)

231	22/2	Friars Haugh	(L)	LAD	3m	13	G	*ld 4th-9th, rmnd handy, ev ch 2 out, no ext apr last*	2	20
415	8/3	Dalston	(R)	RES	3m	19	GS	*(fav) t.d.e. mstk 6th, prom til outpcd aft 3 out, sn btn*	6	11
609	22/3	Friars Haugh	(L)	LAD	3m	11	GF	*mstly 2nd til wknd frm 14th*	5	14
811	31/3	Tranwell	(L)	LAD	3m	3	G	*(fav) chsd ldr til hd 5th,ld agn 7th til mstk & hd last,not rcvrd*	2	15
1218	26/4	Balcormo Ma'	(R)	RES	3m	5	F	*(fav) in tch in 3rd plc til wknd qckly apr 2 out*	3	0
1334	3/5	Mosshouses	(L)	RES	3m	5	F	*(fav) alwys cls up, mstk 7th, ld 3 out, just hld on*	1	16
1509	17/5	Corbridge	(R)	INT	3m	10	GS	*prom til outpcd 11th, f nxt*	F	-

Disqualified from Restricted 96; finally gained reward in weak race; more needed now upgraded 16

FUNNY YE KNOW (Irish) — **I** 115^1, **I** 249^3, **I** 374^4, **I** 505^3

FURRY BEAR gr.g. 12 Rymer - Blueberry Pie — Mrs Sarah Hawker

109	8/2	Milborne St'	(L)	XX	3m	8	GF	*alwys last, t.o. & p.u. 4 out*	P	0
221	16/2	Heythrop	(R)	RES	3m	15	G	*alwys bhnd, t.o. hlfwy*	8	0

Of no account 0

FURRY ISLAND (Irish) — **I** 204^4, **I** 245^1, **I** 299^F, **I** 357^6, **I** 427^F

FURRY KNOWE b.g. 12 Furry Glen - I Know by Crespino — David Pritchard

1996 4(11),**4(0)**,5(12),5(13),**U(-)**,U(-),**P(0)**,P(0)

92	6/2	Wincanton	(R)	HC	3m 1f 110yds	6	GF	*mstks 3rd and 4th, hit 8th, hdwy and hit next, fourth and in tch when f 11th.*	F	-

Blundered around only start 97 & looks finished now 10

FURRY STAR (Irish) — **I** 185^2, **I** 284^B, **I** 346^3, **I** 439^1, **I** 577^P

GABRIELLE'S BOY (Irish) — **I** 24^P, **I** 30^P

GAELIC CHANCE (Irish) — **I** 529^P, **I** 580^2, **I** 594^B

GAELIC GLEN (Irish) — **I** 74^2, **I** 135^3, **I** 206^2, **I** 337, , **I** 536^1

GAELIC WARRIOR b.g. 10 Belfort (FR) - Practicality by Weavers' Hall — Mrs D Ibbotson

1996 P(0),2(19),U(-),2(15),2(20),**F(-)**

216	16/2	Southwell P'	(L)	OPE	3m	12	GS	*alwys rear, lost tch 10th, p.u. 12th*	P	0
354	2/3	Great Stain'	(L)	OPE	3m	7	S	*prom, ld 3-8th, lft in ld 12th, hdd 15th, onepcd aft*	2	18
618	22/3	Hutton Rudby	(L)	OPE	3m	10	GF	*disp ld to 6th, chsng ldrs whn hit 4 out, onepcd frm 2 out*	3	17
1072	13/4	Whitwell-On'	(R)	MXO	4m	21	G	*prom til wknd 16th, t.o. & p.u. 19th*	P	0

1253	26/4	Easingwold	(L)	MEM	3m	7 GS	*ld 5-14th, hdd, disp last, just btn flat*	2	19
1420	10/5	Easingwold	(L)	OPE	3m	5 GF	*prom, ld 3rd, drew clr 2 out, comf*	1	20
1571	26/5	Wetherby	(L)	HC	2 1/2m 110yds	15 GF	*mid-divisoon, hdwy to chase ldrs 10th, rdn after next and weakening when p.u. after 4 out.*	P	0

Open winner 95; broke losing sequence of 19 in soft race; similar needed to win again; G/F-Hy 18

GALACHLAW b.g. 7 Primitive Rising (USA) - Oaklands Lady by Smokey Rockett — A R Trotter

418	8/3	Dalston	(R)	MDO	2 1/2m	10 GS	*bhnd, mstk 6th, t.o. & p.u. 9th*	P	0
730	29/3	Alnwick	(L)	MDO	2 1/2m	9 F	*mid-div, wknd 10th, plggd on onepcd*	3	0

Beaten miles on only completion & much more needed for any hopes 0

GALACTIC GRAHAM b.g. 7 Sweet Monday - Vulrory's Lass by Saucy Kit — Mrs A Phipps

435	8/3	Upton-On-Se'	(R)	MDO	3m	14 G	*cls up til wknd 7th, t.o. & p.u. 14th*	P	0

Not yet of any account 0

GALANNICK (Irish) — **I** 176P, **I** 275P

GALE DANTE (Irish) — **I** 83P, **I** 264P, **I** 384P, **I** 419P

GALE GRIFFIN (Irish) — **I** 69¹, **I** 116P, **I** 211⁵, **I** 368F

GALES FOUNTAIN (Irish) — **I** 96P

GALE TAN (Irish) — **I** 73F

GALLANT EFFORT(IRE) b.g. 9 Thatching - Meeting Adjourned by General Assembly (USA) — Ian Snowden

2	19/1	Barbury Cas'	(L)	XX	3m	14 GF	*alwys bhnd, 11th & t.o. hlfwy*	8	11
39	1/2	Larkhill	(R)	CON	3m	6 GF	*prom, chsd ldr 10-12th, wknd frm 15th*	5	0
178	15/2	Larkhill	(R)	CON	3m	9 G	*(bl) chsd ldrs to 13th, sn outpcd*	5	0
309	1/3	Clyst St Ma'	(L)	CON	3m	7 HY	*in tch to 3 out, outpcd*	4	13
662	22/3	Badbury Rin'	(L)	CON	3m	8 F	*prom early, lost plc 12th, t.o. 15th*	5	10
920	5/4	Larkhill	(R)	MXO	4m	4 F	*ld to 5 out, blnd nxt, no ext frm 3 out*	2	17
1153	20/4	Stafford Cr'	(R)	CON	3m	10 GF	*chsd ldr, disp 2nd whn lft clr 2nd 14th, no imp*	2	20

Safe & best effort last start but generally modest & may need fortune to win Confined; Any 18

GALLANT GALE (Irish) — **I** 182P

GALLANTS DELIGHT b.m. 7 Idiot's Delight - Miss Gallant by Gallo Gallante — Mrs C Johnston

1996 **8(NH),5(NH)**

37	26/1	Alnwick	(L)	MDO	3m	15 G	*ld, clr hlfwy, 30l up whn f 3 out*	F	17
161	15/2	Lanark	(R)	MDO	2m 5f	14 G	*(fav) handy, chsd clr ldr 4 out, ld 2 out, sn clr*	1	20
413	8/3	Dalston	(R)	OPE	3m	9 GS	*(fav) mstks, hld up, prog to chs wnr 3 out, ran on wll, alwys hld*	2	20
563	16/3	Lanark	(R)	RES	3m	8 GS	*(fav) alwys in tch, ld 3 out, comf*	1	19
972	7/4	Kelso	(L)	HC	3m 1f	12 GF	*chsd ldrs, hit 12th, hdwy 14th, chased lder and blnd 3 out, ld last, styd on well.*	1	25
1507	16/5	Stratford	(L)	HC	3m	10 G	*(fav) held up, hdwy when mstk 10th, hit 12th, rallied 5 out, btn 3rd when blnd and u.r. last.*	U	23

Quite promising; improved each race; mistakes; good run last start & could win H/Chase again 98; GF/S 26

GALLOPING GIGGS (Irish) — **I** 100P

GALWAYS GRANITE (Irish) — **I** 206⁴, **I** 337,

GALZIG b.g. 9 Alzao (USA) - Idabella (FR) by Carwhite — Mrs D E H Turner

1996 P(0),2(16),P(0),1(17),**4(19)**

383	5/3	Catterick	(L)	HC	3m 1f 110yds	10 G	*ld to 12th, wknd before 4 out, bhnd when p.u. before 2 out.*	P	0
495	14/3	Fakenham	(L)	HC	2m 5f 110yds	10 G	*pressed ldr, ld 9th to 11th, ev ch 4 out, rdn and kept on one pace after 2 out.*	2	21
678	25/3	Sandown	(R)	HC	2 1/2m 110yds	6 GF	*rear, hdwy and hit 6th, mstk next, blnd and wknd 13th, 5th and no ch when p.u. apr 3 out.*	P	0
779	31/3	Fakenham	(L)	HC	2m 5f 110yds	9 G	*chsd ldrs, rdn and one pace from 3 out.*	3	19
1097	19/4	Bangor	(L)	HC	2 1/2m 110yds	11 G	*midfield, mstk 6th, effort to chase ldrs 10th, btn from 4 out.*	4	14

Awarded Confined 96; generally outclassed in H/Chases 97; needs modest Confined to win 98; G-F 18

GAMAY b.g. 7 Rymer - Darling Rose by Darling Boy — J J Boulter

1996 U(-),U(-),1(15)

303	1/3	Parham	(R)	RES	3m	10 G	*rear, jnd ldrs & blnd 8th & 9th, wknd 2 out, blnd last,tired*	4	0
523	15/3	Cothelstone	(L)	RES	3m	14 GS	*hld up, prog to 2nd 13th, ld 2 out til hdd flat*	2	19

Maiden winner 96; fair run 2nd start; won hurdle June 97 20

GAMBLERS REFRAIN b.g. 12 Blue Refrain - Blue Fire Lady by Pitcairn — R W Pincombe

1996 P(0),U(-),R(-),R(-),7(0),2(13)

104	8/2	Great Treth'	(R)	MDO	3m	9 GS	*ld to 5th, prom aft, wknd 3 out, wll btn whn p.u. last*	P	0

314 1/3 Clyst St Ma' (L) MDN 3m 11 HY *ld to 5th, lost tch 10th, ref 12th* R -
740 29/3 Higher Kilw' (L) MDN 3m 15 GF *prom, rdn 10th, wkng whn tried to ref 12th, p.u. nxt* P 0
795 31/3 Bishopsleigh (R) MDO 3m 12 G *mid-div til ref 13th* R -
1400 5/5 High Bickin' (R) MDO 3m 14 G *ld til s.u. bend apr 2nd* S -
1497 14/5 Cothelstone (L) MDO 3m 10 GF *ld to 6th, wknd 12th, nrly ref nxt, p.u. 14th* P 0

Finished 2 of last 19 starts & generally horrible 0

GAMBLING MAN b.g. 6 St David - Lady Corbel by Some Hand — Charles Smith

1584 26/5 Lifton (R) MDO 3m 13 G *alwys bhnd, p.u. aft 13th* P 0

Tailed off throughout on late season debut 0

GAMBLING ROYAL ch.g. 14 Royal Match - Chance Belle by Foggy Bell — Mrs T Pritchard

1996 **P(NH)**

151 12/2 Lingfield (L) HC 3m 13 HY *second when blnd 9th, 4th when blunded 12th, t.o. when p.u. before 3 out.* P 0
376 3/3 Windsor (R) HC 3m 11 GF *chsd ldr, left in ld 13th, hdd after 4 out, wknd next.* 3 16
679 26/3 Ascot (R) HC 2m 3f 110yds 9 G *trckd ldrs, mstk 11th, one pace apr 4 out.* 3 20
981 9/4 Chepstow (L) HC 3m 6 F *soon tracking ldr, chal 8th till ld 10th, hdd after 14th, wknd after 3 out.* 3 13

Winning chaser; tried hard in H/Chases but too old to win one now 16

GAME FAIR b.g. 10 Lighter - Stagbury by National Trust — William Cook

1996 P(0),4(0),P(0),2(14),P(0),2(17),3(15),P(0)

516 15/3 Larkhill (R) RES 3m 7 GF *cls up to 14th, wknd rpdly, crwld 3 out & p.u.* P 0
742 29/3 Barbury Cas' (L) MEM 3m 5 F *rear 6th, t.o. 10th, btn 2f* 3 0
1058 13/4 Hackwood Pa' (L) RES 3m 6 GF *alwys 2nd/3rd, chal 2 out, no imp* 2 14
1210 26/4 Woodford (L) RES 3m 14 G *chsd ldrs to 7th, last frm 12th, t.o.* 9 0
1494 14/5 Cothelstone (L) RES 3m 11 GF *prom to 6th, sn wknd, t.o. & p.u. 13th* P 0

Members winner 94; beaten all 19 starts 95-7; occasional fair run but sequence likely to extend 11

GANDON LADY (Irish) — I 224^{F}, I 344^{P}

GANDOUGES LASS (Irish) — I 472^{P}

GARACILLIN (Irish) — I 53^{P}, I 221^{5}, I 273^{3}, I 348^{6}

GARDENIA'S SONG ch.g. 6 True Song - Gardenia Lady by Mummy's Game — Mrs A Harker

699 29/3 Stainton (R) MDO 3m 7 F *rear, prog 8th, in tch whn saddle slppd 10th & p.u.* P 0
860 31/3 Charm Park (L) MDO 3m 12 F *alwys rear, nvr dang, p.u. 13th* P 0
1106 19/4 Hornby Cast' (L) MDO 3m 10 G *mid-div, prog 4 out, wknd 2 out, eased flat* 4 0
1409 5/5 Witton Cast' (R) MDO 3m 15 GS *mid-div til wknd 13th, t.o. whn p.u. 15th* P 0

Well-beaten only completion & lacks stamina 0

GARRAMOSS (Irish) — I 49^{F}, I 75, , I 134^{6}, I 194^{P}, I 382^{1}, I 446^{U}, I 480^{P}

GARRISON FRIENDLY (Irish) — I 332^{P}, I 489^{1}, I 517^{1}, I 587^{F}

GARRYLUCAS ch.g. 11 Bishop Of Orange - Susy Karne by Woodville II — J D Lomas

1996 2(21),1(26),2(22),2(24)

201 15/2 Weston Park (L) OPE 3m 16 G *ld to 2nd, prom hlfwy, outpcd 4 out* 5 12
256 22/2 Newtown (L) OPE 3m 17 G *mstk 3d, cls up to 13th, wknd* 9 10
380 4/3 Leicester (R) HC 3m 9 G *held up, hrd rdn 3 out, nvr able to chal.* 4 11
569 16/3 Garnons (L) OPE 3m 7 G *cls up til outpcd by 1st pair frm 13th, nrly sntchd 2nd* 3 16
748 29/3 Brampton Br' (R) MEM 3m 6 GF *1/1-5/2, made all, rdn 3 out, styd on strngly* 1 18
1014 12/4 Bitterley (L) OPE 3m 9 GF *rdn alng frm 10th, no prog 13th, p.u. 15th* P 0
1328 3/5 Chaddesley ' (L) OPE 3m 2 GF *disp til blnd 3rd, hit 12th, rdn apr 3 out, no real imp* 2 18
1524 17/5 Bredwardine (R) OPE 3m 8 G *in tch, rdn 12th, sn btn, jmpd slwly 14th, t.o. 3 out* 4 0
1575 26/5 Chaddesley ' (L) OPE 3m 10 F *chsd ldrs,mstk 9th,effrt 12th,2nd 14th-nxt,wknd,crwld last* 3 11

Open winner 96; deteriorated 97 & ground against; best watched at 13; G-S 16

GARRYROSS (Irish) — I 7^{P}, I 53^{P}, I 262^{4}, I 317^{3}, I 378^{5}

GARRYSPILLANE (Irish) — I 196^{4}, I 294^{U}, I 352^{2}

GASMARK(IRE) br.g. 6 Rontino - Heatherogan by Tarqogan — D Pugh

81 2/2 Wolverhampt' (L) MDN 3m 13 GS *mstk 1st, prom, ld 8-10th, 2nd whn f nxt* F -
205 15/2 Weston Park (L) MDN 3m 10 G *(fav) cls 2nd going wll whn lft clr 9th, solo aft* 1 15
940 6/4 Tabley (R) RES 3m 9 G *ld, sn clr, jmp lft 6th, hdd 16th, wknd 2 out* 3 13
1237 26/4 Brampton Br' (R) RES 3m 13 G *made most frm 6th til hdd 3 out, p.u. last* P 0
1574 26/5 Chaddesley ' (L) CON 3m 8 F *12s-13/2,trckd ldr 3rd,ld & qcknd 14th,rdn 3 out,ran on wll* 1 21

Barely stays & course & going ideal last start; has ability & can win more when conditions suit 22

GATHERING TIME ch.g. 11 Deep Run - Noble Gathering by Artaius (USA) — Miss Carol Richardson

1996 **8(NH),r(NH),3(NH),6(NH),6(NH),S(NH)**

583 17/3 Newcastle (L) HC 3m 8 GF *soon lost tch, t.o..* 7 0

No longer of any account 0

GAWNGADINN (Irish) — **I** 293^{P}

GAYE BARD (Irish) — **I** 13^{6}, **I** 41^{2}, **I** 75^{4}, **I** 145^{1}, **I** 516^{2}

GAYLEY GALE (Irish) — **I** 110^{S}

GAY MUSE b.m. 8 Scorpio (FR) - La Tricoteuse by Le Tricolore — J G Charlton
1996 P(0)

513 15/3 Larkhill (R) MDO 3m 10 GF *alwys rear, no ch frm 4 out, sn wll bhnd* 5 0
934 6/4 Charlton Ho' (L) MDO 3m 10 G *alwys rear, 7th & no ch whn blnd 11th, p.u. 3 out* P 0

Rarely runs & last on only completion 0

GAY RUFFIAN b.g. 11 Welsh Term - Alcinea (FR) by Sweet Revenge — Mrs D J Dyson
1996 2(17),4(16),**6(0)**

286 27/2 Huntingdon (R) HC 3m 8 GS *alwys chasing ldrs, went handy after one cct, struggling 6 out, soon lost tch, t.o..* 5 11
496 15/3 Hereford (R) HC 3m 1f 110yds 10 GF *hdwy 8th, wknd 13th.* 4 10
1213 26/4 Woodford (L) LAD 3m 6 G *in tch to 14th, sn strgglng, lft poor 3rd 4 out* 3 16
1525 17/5 Bredwardine (R) LAD 3m 9 G *prom to 13th, sn outpcd & btn* 5 14

Safe & completed all starts 96/7 but not threatening to win; novice-ridden 16

GAYSUN b.g. 5 Lir - Indomitable (FR) by Indian King (USA) — R G Gay

625 22/3 Kilworthy (L) MDN 3m 14 G *sn bhnd, t.o. til p.u. apr 3 out* P 0
808 31/3 Wadebridge (L) MDO 3m 8 F *alwys chsng ldrs, kpt on frm 3 out, promsng* 3 0
1035 12/4 Lifton (R) MDN 3m 11 F *ld 1st-4th, ld agn 7th, grdly wknd, p.u. 4 out* P 0
1343 3/5 Flete Park (R) MDO 3m 13 G *sn twrds rear, t.o. & p.u. 16th* P 0

Last when completing & yet to show the expected improvement 10

G DEREK br.g. 14 Derek H - Bonnie Lorraine by Sea Wolf — P M Halder
1996 3(0),P(0),2(10),P(0)

266 22/2 Duncombe Pa' (R) RES 3m 19 G *rear & lost tch 9th, t.o. whn p.u. 13th* P 0
424 8/3 Charm Park (L) RES 3m 12 GF *mid-div til lost tch 11th, t.o. & p.u. last* P 0

No longer of any account 0

GEE DOUBLE YOU ch.g. 11 Tap On Wood - Repicado Rose (USA) by Repicado (CHI) — J D Watkins
1996 P(0),6(0),4(0),1(14),1(20),**P(0)**,1(21),**U(-)**

220 16/2 Heythrop (R) OPE 3m 20 G *mid-div, prog 11th, chnce 2 out, onepcd aft* 2 22

Won 3 in 96; ran well only start 97 but vanished; best watched early 98; G-F 20

GEE THANKS (Irish) — **I** 64^{U}, **I** 219^{6}, **I** 347,

GENERAL ARI (Irish) — **I** 106^{P}, **I** 197^{2}, **I** 301^{3}, **I** 353^{4}

GENERAL BRANDY b.g. 11 Cruise Missile - Brandy's Honour by Hot Brandy — E W & M Tuer
1996 F(-)

119 9/2 Wetherby Po' (L) OPE 3m 15 GF *handy whn u.r. 7th* U -
166 15/2 Witton Cast' (R) OPE 3m 8 F *ld til disp 4 out, hdd 2 out, onepcd* 3 20
354 2/3 Great Stain' (L) OPE 3m 7 S *sttld 3rd, wknd 14th, t.o. & p.u. 2 out* P 0
618 22/3 Hutton Rudby (L) OPE 3m 10 GF *mid-div, prog 8th, wnt 2nd 11th, ld 16th, pshd out flat* 1 21
1071 13/4 Whitwell-On' (R) CON 3m 10 G *mid-div, prog 10th, disp 13th-nxt, sn outpcd* 4 16

Generally disappointing but comfortable winner 4th start (20/1); hard to assess prospects at 12; GF ... 19

GENERAL DELIGHT gr.g. 10 General Ironside - Mistress Anna by Arapaho — Mrs A R Wood
1996 1(16),6(0)

337 1/3 Corbridge (R) RES 3m 11 G *mid-div, prog 9th, not qckn 3 out* 3 14
584 17/3 Newcastle (L) HC 2 1/2m 11 GF *bhnd early, tk clr order hfwy, effort before 3 out, chsd wnr from next, no impn.* 2 18
778 31/3 Carlisle (R) HC 3 1/4m 14 G *mid div, rdn 11th, outpcd before 5 out.* 6 12

Members winner 96; runner-up in poor H/Chase & should stick to Restricteds 16

GENERAL JACK b.g. 9 Liberated - Ganges Trial by Kadir Cup — Miss Nicola Dixon
1996 P(0),U(-)

948 6/4 Friars Haugh (L) MDO 3m 7 GF *alwys rear* 4 0
1051 13/4 Lockerbie (R) MDN 3m 10 F *ld 8th-13th, sn wknd* 6 0
1427 10/5 Aspatria (L) INT 3m 7 G *bhnd frm 7th, t.o. 11th, p.u. 13th* P 0
1514 17/5 Corbridge (R) MDO 3m 17 GS *prom, ld 9th, disp 11th til ld 14th, hdd nxt, wknd rpdly* 8 0

Best season in 97 but still failed to beat another horse 0

GENERAL JACKIE(IRE) b.g. 7 Supreme Leader - Carry On Jackie by David Jack — R Mair

1996 **10(NH),13(NH),P(NH),7(NH),5(NH)**

284	23/2	Charing	(L)	MDO	3m	17	G	*u.r. 1st*	U	-
582	16/3	Detling	(L)	MDN	3m	16	F	*rear whn p.u. 6th*	P	0

A brief season of no promise 0

GENERAL PERK (Irish) — I 153P

GENERAL PICTON b.g. 11 Cut Above - Bodnant by Welsh Pageant — Mrs C S Knowles

1996 U(-),3(14),2(17),2(17),**F(-)**,2(16),1(16)

321	1/3	Marks Tey	(L)	INT	3m	10	G	*(vis) disp ld til lft clr 9th, jnd 3 out, hdd nxt, wknd apr last*	4	17

Restricted winner 96; fair run only start 97; ungenuine; best watched at 12 16

GENERAL TROY ro.g. 11 General Ironside - Silly Twit by Deep Run — N B Jones

187	15/2	Erw Lon	(L)	OPE	3m	16	G	*mid-div, wknd 12th, t.o. & p.u. 15th*	P	0
294	1/3	Didmarton	(L)	INT	3m	20	G	*in tch in rear whn blnd bdly 7th, sn bhnd, p.u. 15th*	P	0
535	16/3	Erw Lon	(L)	CON	3m	12	GF	*mstk 3rd, in rear aft, p.u. 10th*	P	0
714	29/3	Llanvapley	(L)	CON	3m	15	GF	*rear, bad mstk 12th, p.u. 3 out*	P	0

Restricted winner 94; missed 95/6 & looks finished now 0

GENERATOR BOY b or br.g. 9 My Treasure Chest - Barley Fire by Prince Barle — T King

1996 P(0),F(-),P(0)

222	16/2	Heythrop	(R)	RES	3m	17	G	*mstk 4th, alwys rear, t.o. & p.u. 15th*	P	0
260	22/2	Newtown	(L)	RES	3m	16	G	*ld 3-9th, wknd 13th, t.o. & p.u. 2 out*	P	0
633	22/3	Howick	(L)	RES	3m	8	GF	*mid-div, some prog frm 12th, not rch ldrs*	4	0
1061	13/4	Maisemore P'	(L)	RES	3m	12	GF	*mid-div, wknd apr 14th, no ch whn f 2 out*	F	-
1210	26/4	Woodford	(L)	RES	3m	14	G	*bhnd, 10th hlfwy, kpt on frm 4 out, nvr nrr*	3	15
1494	14/5	Cothelstone	(L)	RES	3m	11	GF	*hld up bhnd, steady prog 13th, went 2nd 2 out, no ch wth wnr*	2	14

Won dire Maiden 95; improved 97 but non-stayer & Restricted win still odds against 15

GENEVA STEELE (Irish) — I 2072

GEN-TECH b.g. 10 Star Appeal - Targa (GER) by Stani — Dick Chapman

1996 8(0),1(19),3(15),4(18),**5(13),4(0),7(0)**

333	1/3	Eaton Hall	(R)	INT	3m	10	GS	*rear, some prog frm hlfwy, onepcd frm 3 out*	4	12

Restricted winner 96; safe & slow & a brief appearance 97 15

GENTLE JESTER br.m. 8 Reesh - Mirthful by Will Somers — Chris J Buckerfield

1	19/1	Barbury Cas'	(L)	XX	3m	11	GF	*f 4th*	F	-
110	8/2	Milborne St'	(L)	MDN	3m	7	GF	*sn rear, t.o. 5th, p.u. 3 out*	P	0
315	1/3	Clyst St Ma'	(L)	MDN	3m	5	HY	*f 1st*	F	-

Rarely seen & does not last long when she does appear 0

GEORGE FINGLAS (Irish) — I 579P, I 593P, I 6116

GEORGE LANE b.g. 9 Librate - Queen Of The Kop by Queen's Hussar — Miss A L Barnett

1996 **6(NH),4(NH),3(NH),6(NH),1(NH),3(NH),8(NH),U(NH),U(NH),U(NH),7(NH)**

1257	27/4	Black Fores'	(R)	LAD	3m	5	F	*ld/disp to 6th, ld 9th, hdd & no ext aft last*	2	15

Selling hurdle winner 96; beaten in poor Ladies & unlikely to win a point 14

GEORGIE PORGIE b.g. 5 Emarati (USA) - Running Cool by Record Run — C G Newman

1996 **15(NH)**

110	8/2	Milborne St'	(L)	MDN	3m	7	GF	*prom, ld 5th til jnd 12th, f nxt*	F	-

Ran green on debut & may do better 0

GERAGH ROAD (Irish) — I 7P, I 74, , I 1334, I 2626, I 3175, I 558P, I 601P

GERRY DELIGHT (Irish) — I 3703

GERRYS DELIGHT (Irish) — I 32F, I 634, I 97P, I 126F, I 312B

GET CRACKING (Irish) — I 145P, I 259, , I 336,

GET ON LOTTIE b.m. 8 Doctor Wall - Pennulli by Sir Nulli — Miss Jane Goddard

833	31/3	Heathfield	(R)	MDO	3m	7	F	*last pr, mstks 2nd & 6th, lsng tch & j.s 8th, t.o & p.u 10th*	P	0
1446	10/5	Peper Harow	(L)	MDO	3m	7	GF	*mid-div to 8th, wll bhnd frm 10th, p.u. 13th*	P	0

Of no account 0

GET STEPPING ch.g. 11 Posse (USA) - Thanks Edith by Gratitude — W H Whitley

1996 U(-),P(0),3(10)

692	29/3	Little Wind'	(R)	MDO	3m	8	GF	*mstk 4th, cls up, ld 10th, lft clr 3 out, wknd & hdd flat*	2	12
956	6/4	Black Fores'	(R)	MDO	3m	4	G	*(fav) ld til aft 2 out, outpcd aft*	2	12
1112	19/4	Flete Park	(R)	MDN	3m	13	GF	*ld 7th, disp 10-11th, 10l 2nd & wkng whn f 17th*	F	-
1261	27/4	Black Fores'	(R)	MDO	3m	12	F	*(Jt fav) prom, outpcd 3 out, rallied last, just faild*	2	13

1486 11/5 Ottery St M' (L) MDO 3m 17 G *handy to 14th, lost tch nxt, p.u. 3 out* P 0
1521 17/5 Bratton Down (L) MDO 3m 16 GS *prom, cls 3rd at 12th, chsd ldr 16th, no imp* 2 10

Non-stayer but tries hard & twice came close in 97; luck needed to win at 12 12

GIBRALTAR QUEEN b.m. 5 Kinglet - Gibraltar Girl by True Song J T Bailey

224 16/2 Heythrop (R) MDN 3m 16 G *hld up, prog to jn ldrs 10th, wknd aft 14th, p.u. 2 out* P 0
549 16/3 Garthorpe (R) MDO 3m 16 GF *in tch til 12th, lft poor 5th 3 out, kpt on* 4 0

Well-bred & showed enough to suggest some hope in 98 12

GIDGEGANNUP b.g. 11 Magnolia Lad - Vulrory's Lass by Saucy Kit Mrs A Phipps

260 22/2 Newtown (L) RES 3m 16 G *in tch to 12th, 7th & no ch whn hmpd 14th & p.u.* P 0
550 16/3 Garthorpe (R) MDO 3m 11 GF *in tch to 12th, poor 4th 3 out, ran on wll, nt rch ldrs* 3 11
1192 20/4 Garthorpe (R) MDO 3m 6 GF *w.w. prog to 2nd 12th, chal 2 out, ran on to ld nr fin* 1 13
1475 11/5 Garthorpe (R) XX 3m 13 GS *mid-div, prog 9th, disp apr 3 out, wknd nxt* 3 14

Very lightly-raced; made reliability count; unlikely to win Restricted at 12 15

GIGI BEACH(IRE) ch.g. 6 Roselier (FR) - Cranagh Lady by Le Bavard (FR) Mrs Susan Humphreys

1996 U(-),6(12),4(0),1(16)

100 8/2 Great Treth' (R) RES 3m 14 GS *(fav) trckd ldrs, mstk 9th, ld 16th, drew clr last, comf* 1 19
293 1/3 Didmarton (L) INT 3m 16 G *hld up bhnd, lost tch 10th, t.o. & p.u. 14th* P 0
647 22/3 Castle Of C' (R) INT 3m 7 G *rmndr 8th, ld 10th, hrd rdn 3 out, in cmmnd whn u.r. last* U 25
930 6/4 Charlton Ho' (L) INT 3m 8 G *(fav) hld up, prog 9th, ld 13th, pshd out flat* 1 23

Useful prospect; top stable; stays; Opens in 98; G-S (too firm 2nd start) 25

G I JOE (Irish) — **I** 68³, **I** 118¹, **I** 174ᶠ, **I** 252ᴾ

GILLIE'S FOUNTAIN b.g. 6 Baron Blakeney - Florella by Royal Fountain J D Callow

1996 5(0),4(10)

115 9/2 Wetherby Po' (L) MDO 3m 8 GF *(Jt fav) mid-div, prog 11th, disp nxt, ld 14th, sn drew clr, eased* 1 16
467 8/3 Eyton-On-Se' (L) RES 3m 15 G *(fav) hld up mid-div, cls order 12th, und pres 5 out, p.u. 3 out* P 0
670 23/3 Eaton Hall (R) RES 3m 15 GF *w.w. prog & ev ch 4 out, ran on, just held* 2 18
1263 27/4 Southwell P' (L) RES 3m 9 G *(fav) hld up rear,prog 11th,went 2nd 3 out,ld nxt,hdd last,nt qckn* 2 17
1412 7/5 Uttoxeter (L) HC 3 1/4m 10 GS *settld rear, in tch till rdn and wknd 4 out, left poor 3rd 2 out.* 3 0
1526 17/5 Bredwardine (R) RES 3m 13 G *prom til rdn & btn 13th, wll bhnd whn p.u. 2 out* P 0

Confirmed 96 promise when winning; not progressed; may be suspect in finish; ought to win Restricted 17

GILSON'S COVE b.g. 10 Netherkelly - Realm Wood by Precipice Wood A Merriam

1996 1(14),5(0),3(15),4(18),U(-)

68 2/2 Higham (L) MEM 3m 4 GF *(fav) made all, drew clr 10th, easily* 1 13
195 15/2 Higham (L) LAD 3m 14 G *mid-div, not pace to trbl ldrs* 5 14

Repeated 96 Members win but outclassed in better company now & finished early; Firm 14

GINGER PINK b.g. 11 Strong Gale - Zitas Toi by Chinatown C Cottingham

1996 2(14),4(10),U(-),10(0),1(17),6(0)

75 2/2 Market Rase' (L) CON 3m 10 GF *chsd ldr to 6th, bhnd frm 10th, t.o. & p.u. 3 out* P 0
248 22/2 Brocklesby ' (L) CON 3m 10 G *cls up mstly 3rd til wknd 5 out* 9 0
547 16/3 Garthorpe (R) XX 3m 7 GF *last frm 8th t.o. & p.u 15th* P 0

Restricted winner 96; never reliable & gave up entirely in 97 0

GINGERS GIRL (Irish) — **I** 274ᶠ

GIORGIONE(FR) b.g. 8 Zino - Restless Nell W J Turcan

1996 **P(NH),P(NH)**

77 2/2 Market Rase' (L) RES 3m 9 GF *jmpt lft, prom til jmp slwly 11th, p.u. aft 12th* P 0

Irish Maiden winner 96; not much to enthuse about now 0

GIRLOUGH CASTLE (Irish) — **I** 135⁵, **I** 238ᴾ

GIRLS IN BUSINESS b.m. 7 Sula Bula - Grade Well by Derring-Do Mrs V Barber

1996 P(0),5(0),P(0)

1094 16/4 Hockworthy (L) MDN 3m 11 GF *chsng grp, mstk 8th, clsd 3 out, rdn & wknd nxt* 4 0
1270 27/4 Little Wind' (R) MDO 2 1/2m 10 GF *sn bhnd, t.o. & p.u. aft 11th, dsmntd* P 0

Top stable but looks no good & problems to boot 0

GIVE IT A BASH(IRE) b.m. 9 Gianchi - Marzia Fabbricotti by Ribero Miss S Wilson

1996 1(13),5(0),4(10),P(0)

28 26/1 Marks Tey (L) RES 3m 9 GF *alwys mid-div, 5th & no ch apr 15th* 6 0
198 15/2 Higham (L) RES 3m 14 G *mid-div, wknd 14th, t.o.* 6 0
711 29/3 High Easter (L) RES 3m 6 F *cls up til f 12th* F -
798 31/3 Marks Tey (L) RES 3m 7 F *mstk 1st,hdwy to go 2nd 11th,ld 3 out,jnd nxt,hd last,ran on* 2 14
1286 29/4 Huntingdon (R) HC 3m 10 G *chsd ldrs, jmpd slowly 11th, soon wknd, t.o. and p.u. before 2 out.* P 0
1430 10/5 Marks Tey (L) CON 3m 7 G *hld up, prog 7th, disp 3 out, ld nxt, ran on wll last* 1 17

Maiden winner 96; found modest Confined & usually well-beaten; mistakes; hard to win again; Good ... 17

GIVE IT A WHIRL ch.g. 8 Revolutionary (USA) - No Love by Bustiki — Ross Haddow
1996 1(13),F(-),U(-),P(0)

477	9/3 Southwell P'	(L)	RES	3m	10	G	*ld aft 1st, hdd 2 out, onepcd und pres*	2	17
676	23/3 Brocklesby '	(L)	RES	3m	14	GF	*disp til ld 5th, hdd 2 out, kpt on gamely und pres*	2	20

Maiden winner 96; improved both starts 97 & win Restricted that form in 98 if fit ... 18

GIVEMEYOURHAND (Irish) — **I** 21², **I** 108²

GIVOWER b.g. 9 Kinglet - River Valley by Apollonius — A J Smith
1996 6(0),3(0),1(12)

232	22/2 Friars Haugh	(L)	OPE	3m	6	G	*last til some prog 9th, lost tch 4 out*	5	11

Members winner 96; appearing infrequently now & Restricted chance slipping by; G-F ... 14

GIVUS A HAND ch.g. 7 Nearly A Hand - Chanelle by The Parson — Mrs J M Bailey
1996 P(0),P(0),B(-)

246	22/2 Lemalla	(R)	MDO	3m	4	S	*lost tch 13th, t.o. & p.u. 16th*	P	0
525	15/3 Cothelstone	(L)	MDN	3m	15	GS	*cls 4th hlfwy, lost plc 13th, ran on agn clsng stgs*	4	10
1270	27/4 Little Wind'	(R)	MDO	2 1/2m	10	GF	*ld to 3rd, prom, mstk 13th, rdn to ld apr 2 out, drvn out*	1	14

Steadily improved & found weak Maiden; may upgrade in 98 if staying ... 15

GLACIAL DANCER (Irish) — **I** 255⁴, **I** 424²

GLACIAL KING (Irish) — **I** 58ᴾ, **I** 84ᴾ, **I** 184ᴾ, **I** 285³, **I** 390¹

GLACIAL LADY (Irish) — **I** 460ᴾ, **I** 552ᶠ, **I** 574ᴾ, **I** 588⁴

GLAD SHE'S GONE gr.g. 6 Move Off - Absent Lady by Absalom — Mrs A Lockwood

479	9/3 Southwell P'	(L)	MDO	3m	15	G	*raced wd, chsd ldr to 4th, wkng whn f 6th*	F	-

No signs of ability ... 0

GLADSTONE (Irish) — **I** 182², **I** 273ᵁ, **I** 300¹

GLAMOROUS GUY ch.g. 10 Orchestra - Glamorous Night by Sir Herbert — Mrs D Du Feu
1996 5(0),2(0),8(0),P(0),P(0)

460	8/3 Great Treth'	(R)	MDO	3m	13	S	*t.o. p.u. apr 10th*	P	0
522	15/3 Cothelstone	(L)	CON	3m	14	GS	*u.r. 1st*	U	-
648	22/3 Castle Of C'	(R)	RES	3m	8	G	*chsd ldr to 4th, last whn blnd 12th, p.u. nxt*	P	0
1552	24/5 Mounsey Hil'	(R)	RES	3m	12	G	*alwys bhnd, last whn blnd & u.r. 9th*	U	-

Failed to finish last 6 races & no prospects ... 0

GLASTRYTURN (Irish) — **I** 440², **I** 507³

GLEEMING LACE (Irish) — **I** 83, , **I** 132³, **I** 189²

GLENALLA BELLA (Irish) — **I** 113ᴾ, **I** 125², **I** 178², **I** 250³, **I** 329⁵

GLENAVEY b.g. 16 Cantab - Dancing Flame by Dead Ahead — C J Hall
1996 10(0),3(11),1(13),P(0)

305	1/3 Parham	(R)	OPE	3m	9	G	*alwys last, t.o. hlfwy, p.u. 3 out*	P	0
503	15/3 Ampton	(R)	XX	3m	11	GF	*bhnd frm 5th, nvr nr ldrs*	6	0
828	31/3 Heathfield	(R)	MEM	3m	5	F	*cls up, ld 9-14th, ld agn 4 out, hd prssd whn lft clr last*	1	10

Schoolmaster now; won Members 95-7 & only chance of another win at 17 ... 11

GLENBOWER QUEEN (Irish) — **I** 130ᴾ, **I** 257ᴾ, **I** 320, , **I** 420ᴾ, **I** 446⁴, **I** 477³, **I** 518ᴾ, **I** 567ᴾ

GLENBRICKEN b.g. 11 Furry Glen - Kilbricken Money by Even Money — Kevin Williams
1996 5(0),P(0),6(12),**2(16)**,1(15),**P(0)**,3(16)

66	1/2 Horseheath	(R)	MEM	3m	7	GF	*1st ride,chsd ldrs,outpcd 12th,styd on 15th,ld last,sn clr*	1	15
597	22/3 Horseheath	(R)	RES	3m	8	F	*(fav) cls up, ld 11th, made rest, kpt on frm 2 out*	1	17

Changed hands 97; fairytale win for new owner; improved; one paced; stays; G-F ... 18

GLENCAOIN (Irish) — **I** 277ᴾ, **I** 296ᴾ

GLEN CHERRY b.g. 11 Furry Glen - Our Cherry by Tarqogan — P A D Scouller
1996 1(18)

142	9/2 Tweseldown	(R)	MEM	3m	8	GF	*chsd ldr, lost plc frm 10th, mstk 15th, sn btn*	3	12
577	16/3 Detling	(L)	CON	3m	18	F	*prom to 10th, wll in rear whn ref 3 out*	R	-
872	31/3 Hackwood Pa'	(L)	CON	3m	4	F	*ld early, 2nd to 11th, wknd, p.u. last*	P	0

Members winner only start 96; showed very little 97 & finished early ... 12

GLENCOE BOY b.g. 14 Pry - Rainella by Bahrain — P D Jones
1996 U(-)

48	1/2 Wadebridge	(L)	OPE	3m	5	G	*bhnd frm 2nd, wknd 12th, p.u. 14th, dead*	P	0

Dead 0

GLENCUSH PEAK (Irish) — I 300P, I 359P

GLENFINSH (Irish) — I 169P

GLENFORM b.g. 10 Glenstal (USA) - In Form by Formidable (USA) A Cole

1996 4(0),5(11),4(12),4(10),4(13),3(18)

48	1/2	Wadebridge	(L)	OPE	3m	5	G	*wll bhnd, lft 3rd 14th*	3	12
171	15/2	Ottery St M'	(L)	OPE	3m	9	G	*alwys mid-div, outpcd frm 15th*	5	0
455	8/3	Great Treth'	(R)	OPE	3m	8	S	*ld 2nd-13th, wknd, t.o.*	6	0
530	15/3	Wadebridge	(L)	OPE	3m	4	GF	*(bl) 3rd frm 2nd, cls up til lost tch 12th*	3	0
1579	26/5	Lifton	(R)	CON	3m	9	G	*(bl) nvr trbld ldrs, p.u. 13th*	P	0

Safe but does not threaten to win in points & declined in 97 12

GLENHUGH (Irish) — I 289P, I 331P

GLENMERE PRINCE b.g. 11 Prince Tenderfoot (USA) - Ashbourne Lass by Ashmore (FR) P J Ikin

1996 P(0),F(-)

1176	20/4	Sandon	(L)	OPE	3m	5	GF	*rear 2nd, blnd nxt, ref 4th*	R	-

No longer of any account 0

GLENMORE STAR (Irish) — I 487P, I 572P, I 608P

GLEN OAK b.g. 12 Glenstal (USA) - Neeran by Wollow R J Mansell

1996 6(16),3(19),7(0),3(19),4(11),4(18)

226	21/2	Haydock	(L)	HC	3m	11	G	*n.j.w., hdwy and in tch 4 out, fd 2 out.*	3	22
379	4/3	Leicester	(R)	HC	3m	7	G	*alwys prom, reminder 10th, cl up when hmpd 3 out, styd on same pace apr last.*	3	20
492	11/3	Sedgefield	(L)	HC	3m 3f	7	G	*nvr far away, hit 5 out, styd on before last to ld near fin.*	1	23
680	29/3	Towcester	(R)	HC	3m 1f	8	GF	*chsd ldrs, rdn apr 2 out, styd on same pace.*	5	19
1289	30/4	Cheltenham	(L)	HC	3m 1f 110yds	6	GF	*waited with, pushed along after 11th, prog to chase ldrs 13th, not qckn after 3 out, styd on to chase wnr run-in.*	2	24
1454	11/5	Maisemore P'	(L)	MEM	3m	5	G	*(fav) chsd ldr to 6th & frm 13th, ld 15th, blnd nxt, sn clr*	1	18
1504	16/5	Folkestone	(R)	HC	3m 7f	5	G	*(fav) waited with, prog to chase ldr after 14th, pushed along 3 out, ld after next, styd on well.*	1	24
1591	31/5	Stratford	(L)	HC	3 1/2m	11	G	*chsd ldrs, feeling pace and driven along final cct, no impn on lders from 4 out.*	4	26

Changed hands & revived 97; one paced; stays; won modest H/Chases; may find another; G/F-S 24

GLEN OF BARGY (Irish) — I 167P, I 221⁴, I 407¹, I 495⁴, I 587P

GLENPINE (Irish) — I 32P, I 113P, I 228³, I 286U, I 349F, I 392², I 472³, I 525², I 576, , I 591F

GLENROE GAL (Irish) — I 92F, I 185P, I 249, , I 346⁴

GLENROWAN(IRE) b.g. 9 Euphemism - Deity by Red God R Thomas

199	15/2	Weston Park	(L)	MEM	3m	7	G	*alwys mid-div, nvr trbld 1st pair*	3	17
666	23/3	Eaton Hall	(R)	MDO	3m	10	GF	*chsd ldr, strng run flat, ld fin*	1	14
884	1/4	Flagg Moor	(L)	CON	3m	6	G	*w.w. lft 3rd 14th, ld 3 out, rdn & forged clr apr last*	1	19
1300	3/5	Weston Park	(L)	CON	3m	8	G	*hld up, 20l bhnd 4 out, ran on wll und pres, just faild*	2	20
1508	17/5	Bangor	(L)	HC	3m 110yds	12	G	*alwys well bhnd, nvr a factor.*	7	0

Missed 96; stays well & much improved; can win another Confined; Good 21

GLENSELIER (Irish) — I 7², I 54P, I 74³, I 135, , I 262³

GLENSHANE PASS (Irish) — I 69³, I 115⁴, I 121, , I 211P, I 291F, I 374P, I 433P, I 505⁵, I 582F

GLENSTAL FOREST (Irish) — I 424⁵, I 489³

GLEN TAYLOR g. 11 Glenorum (CAN) - Tambi by Bivouac Mrs G A Spencer

1996 4(0),6(0),4(0),4(0),U(-),5(0),1(0),P(0)

204	15/2	Weston Park	(L)	RES	3m	13	G	*alwys rear, fin own time*	4	0
332	1/3	Eaton Hall	(R)	RES	3m	18	GS	*mid-div, ran on onepcd frm 5 out*	5	0
670	23/3	Eaton Hall	(R)	RES	3m	15	GF	*strgglng in rear aft 8th*	9	0
727	29/3	Sandon	(L)	RES	3m	6	GF	*hld up, onepcd frm 14th, no ch 1st pair*	3	0
1000	12/4	Alpraham	(R)	RES	3m	8	GF	*chsd ldrs to 10th, wknd, t.o. 15th, tk 6th flat*	6	0
1299	3/5	Weston Park	(L)	MEM	3m	4	G	*ld to 3rd, 3rd & outpcd frm 5th, no dang aft*	3	11

Left solo when winning Members in 96 & similar needed to win again 0

GLENTORALDA (Irish) — I 261³, I 558, , I 564³

GLENVIEW ROSE (Irish) — I 131², I 494², I 600⁴

GLENVILLE BREEZE(IRE) g. 8 Kambalda - Vina's Last G Greenhaf

1065	13/4	Maisemore P'	(L)	MDO	3m	13	GF	*trckd ldrs, wknd 11th, t.o. & p.u. 3 out*	P	0
1473	11/5	Erw Lon	(L)	MDO	3m	13	GS	*(Co fav) mid-div, prog 14th, chsd wnr 2 out, no imp*	2	0

Ex-Irish; placed in weak race but at least shows some ability; may have chances in 98 12

GLIDING AWAY (Irish) — I 227P, I 272², I 591³

GLIN CASTLE (Irish) — I 103P

GLISTENING WATERS (Irish) — I 6U, I 61F, I 139P, I 167P

GLITTERBIRD br.m. 10 Glint Of Gold - Dovetail by Brigadier Gerard — Mrs Caroline Chadney

1996 2(17),P(0)

262	22/2 Newtown	(L) RES	3m	15 G	*prom til wknd aft 13th, poor 5th whn p.u. 2 out*	P	0
363	2/3 Garnons	(L) XX	3m	6 GS	*prom, 4th & in tch whn blnd 11th, p.u. nxt*	P	0
877	1/4 Upton-On-Se'	(R) RES	3m	17 GF	*prom til 4th & outpcd frm 12th, no prog aft*	3	12
1149	19/4 Chaddesley '	(L) RES	3m	6 GF	*made all, styd on well frm 3 out*	1	19
1575	26/5 Chaddesley '	(L) OPE	3m	10 F	*not fluent,prom,lft 2nd aft 6th,ld 11th,pshd clr apr last*	1	21

Makes mistakes but came good in 97; Open win limits options in 98; G-F 21

GLITTER GIRL (Irish) — I 19P, I 45P, I 109, , I 138F, I 305P, I 338³, I 443², I 519⁴

GLITTER PADDY (Irish) — I 409⁵

GLITZY LADY(IRE) b.m. 8 Strong Gale - Shady Lady by Proverb — G Smith

1996 3(14),1(21),2(20),P(0),4(17),4(18)

2	19/1 Barbury Cas'	(L) XX	3m	14 GF	*mid-div, 7th & effrt hlfwy, nvr on trms*	6	17
214	16/2 Southwell P'	(L) CON	3m	10 GS	*b.d. 2nd*	B	-

Winner in 96 but form tailed off then & soon vanished in 97; best watched 17

GLUAIS LINN (Irish) — I 38, , I 48P, I 258P

GLYNN BRAE(IRE) b.g. 7 Spin Of A Coin - Bright Toro by Proverb — D Davies

1136	19/4 Bonvilston	(R) MDO	3m	15 G	*alwys mid-div*	7	0
1231	26/4 Pyle	(R) MDO	3m	7 GS	*ld til mstk 5th, ld 7th-aft 13th, rdn & reluc aft, sn btn*	4	0
1361	5/5 Pantyderi	(L) MEM	3m	4 G	*chsd wnr to 10th, wknd, p.u. 14th*	P	0
1562	24/5 Bassaleg	(R) MDO	3m	8 G	*mostly 2nd frm 5th, rdn & not qckn 3 out, not run on nxt*	3	0

A little ability but nasty & safely ignored 0

GO AGAIN(IRE) b.g. 8 Febrino - Miss Avoca — R Luders-Gibbs

84	2/2 Wolverhampt'	(L) MEM	3m	9 GS	*ld 2-3rd, t.o. & p.u. 8th*	P	0

Of no account 0

GOING AROUND b.g. 9 Baron Blakeney - Elect by New Member — J R Buchanan

1996 **P(NH),F(NH),15(NH),9(NH)**

216	16/2 Southwell P'	(L) OPE	3m	12 GS	*prom til wknd apr 12th, t.o. & p.u. 3 out*	P	0
370	2/3 Mollington	(R) OPE	3m	6 G	*trckd ldrs going wll, chal 15th, rdn & wknd aft nxt*	3	17
547	16/3 Garthorpe	(R) XX	3m	7 GF	*in tch til outpcd 12th, no ch frm nxt*	4	15
769	29/3 Dingley	(R) CON	3m	14 G	*abt 5th for 2m, wknd 6 out, 8th 5 out, fin own time*	5	0
1162	20/4 Mollington	(R) CON	3m	7 GF	*mstks, chsd ldrs, effrt apr 2 out, onepcd*	4	15
1403	5/5 Ashorne	(R) CON	3m	14 G	*trckd ldrs, effrt 15th, rdn to chal 2 out,mstk last,styd on*	2	19
1532	18/5 Mollington	(R) CON	3m	11 GS	*trckd ldrs, not qckn 15th, no prog aft*	4	15

Winning hurdler 94; safe & consistent but does not stay & will need fortune to win 17

GO JENNY (Irish) — I 126P

GOLD CHOICE b.g. 12 Crooner - Coffee Bob by Espresso — Victor Ogden

1996 P(0),P(0),4(0),U(-)

120	9/2 Wetherby Po'	(L) MDO	3m	18 GF	*plld hrd, made all, sn wll clr, unchal*	1	17

Change of rider reaped dividends & bolted home; win Restricted if back at 13 17

GOLD DAM(IRE) ch.g. 9 Le Bavard (FR) - Miss Feacle by Bargello — P T Hollins

664	23/3 Eaton Hall	(R) MDO	3m	12 GF	*(bl) ld to 13th, onepcd aft, sn btn*	8	0
883	1/4 Flagg Moor	(L) MDO	3m	12 G	*(bl) ld to apr 3 out, wknd rpdly, p.u. last, dsmntd*	P	0

Unlucky once in 95 but missed 96 & problems again now 10

GOLD DIVER ch.g. 10 Main Reef - Ice Baby by Grundy — Linden Rogers

1996 9(0),4(16),P(0),P(0),1(18),4(13)

6	19/1 Barbury Cas'	(L) LAD	3m	13 GF	*rear, 7th & no ch hlfwy, p.u. 14th*	P	0
401	8/3 Llanfrynach	(R) LAD	3m	14 G	*cls up, wknd 14th, p.u. 3 out*	P	0
537	16/3 Erw Lon	(L) OPE	3m	9 GF	*mid-div, btn whn p.u. 13th*	P	0
1006	12/4 St Hilary	(R) LAD	3m	7 GF	*mostly 2nd, ld 14th, hdd nxt, ran on onepcd*	2	15
1132	19/4 Bonvilston	(R) CON	3m	9 G	*cls up, lost post hlfwy, styd on late*	3	10
1226	26/4 Pyle	(R) OPE	3m	6 GS	*ld to 6th, rdn & wknd nxt, p.u. 11th*	P	0
1321	3/5 Bonvilston	(R) MXO	3m	10 G	*ld to 5th, wknd & p.u. 3 out*	P	0
1573	26/5 Chaddesley '	(L) LAD	3m	6 F	*prom, ld whn blnd & u.r. 4th*	U	-

Ladies winner 96; well below form 97; only one fair run; hard to win again now 13

GOLDEN BAR (Irish) — I 371², I 468F, I 508¹

GOLDEN FARE ch.g. 12 Scallywag - Katie Fare by Ritudyr — A L Wallace

1996 P(0),**P(0)**,6(0),5(11),3(10),6(0),2(11),P(0)

330	1/3	Eaton Hall	(R)	CON	3m	16	GS	*mid to rear, p.u. 5 out*	P	0
669	23/3	Eaton Hall	(R)	LAD	3m	5	GF	*rear by 4th, t.o. & p.u. 11th*	P	0
848	31/3	Eyton-On-Se'	(L)	MEM	3m	6	GF	*cls up 8th, lost tch 12th, wll bhnd whn p.u. bfr last*	P	0
1384	5/5	Eyton-On-Se'	(L)	LAD	3m	6	GF	*cls up in tch to 13th, fdd & p.u. 3 out*	P	0
1540	18/5	Wolverhampt'	(L)	LAD	3m	5	GS	*made most to 10th & 11-14th, fdd 4 out*	4	11
1606	1/6	Dingley	(R)	LAD	3m	13	GF	*prom til b.d. 6th*	B	-

No longer of any account 0

GOLDEN FELLOW(IRE) ch.g. 9 Buckskin (FR) - Miss Argument by No Argument — Keith Coe

1996 1(15),F(-)

24	26/1	Marks Tey	(L)	MEM	3m	6	GF	*pllng, ld 3rd, made rest, blnd 12th, rdn & styd on wll last*	1	15
65	1/2	Horseheath	(R)	RES	3m	10	GF	*(fav) mstks, prog to ld 11th, blnd nxt, hdd 15th, btn 2 out*	3	14

Maiden winner 96; very lightly-raced & looked in trouble 2nd start 97 15

GOLDEN MAC ch.g. 10 Court Macsherry - Prett Damsel by Prince Hansel — R L Fanshawe

1996 P(0),5(0),1(18),**3(15)**,6(10),P(0),4(12)

285	26/2	Taunton	(R)	HC	4 1/4m 110yds	16	GS	*prom, wknd 17th, t.o. and virtually p.u. run-in.*	7	0
388	7/3	Sandown	(R)	HC	3m 110yds	7	G	*chsd ldrs to 12th, soon bhnd, t.o. when blnd and u.r. 6 out.*	U	-

Restricted winner 96; out of his depth 97 & can only be watched now 13

GOLDEN MIST (Irish) — I 31[U], I 227[F], I 394[6]

GOLDEN MOSS ch.g. 12 Le Moss - Call Bird by Le Johnstan — C Cottingham

1996 F(-),1(19),2(22),2(15),**F(-)**,7(0)

74	2/2	Market Rase'	(L)	MEM	3m	4	GF	*chsd wnr til 11th, rmnd 13th, sn lost, tld off*	3	0
137	9/2	Thorpe Lodge	(L)	MEM	3m	9	GF	*rear early, nvr able to rch ldrs*	4	0
250	22/2	Brocklesby '	(L)	OPE	3m	6	G	*disp brfly, fdd, t.o. 10th, p.u. 3 out, re-stt, completed*	4	0
545	16/3	Garthorpe	(R)	CON	3m	12	GF	*alwys bhnd, no ch frm 11th*	8	0

Open winner 95/6; beat only 2 others in 97 & looks finished now 0

GOLDEN NEWS b.g. 6 Newski (USA) - Golden Rochas by Golden Shields — J F Symes

1996 **P(NH)**

458	8/3	Great Treth'	(R)	MDO	3m	15	S	*f 3rd*	F	-
512	15/3	Larkhill	(R)	MDO	3m	6	GF	*hld up last, u.r. 7th*	U	-
866	31/3	Kingston St'	(R)	MDO	3m	7	F	*rear, blndrd 7th, p.u. bfr nxt*	P	0
1246	26/4	Bratton Down	(L)	MDO	3m	16	GS	*prom early, grdly wknd & p.u. 11th*	P	0

Yet to compete & of no account 0

GOLDEN PELE b.g. 16 Golden Love - Feale-Side Nook by Laurence O — Mrs B Ansell

1996 P(0),F(-),P(0),P(0),P(0)

682	29/3	Charing	(L)	RES	3m	5	F	*alwys rear, t.o. 2 out*	4	0

Deserves retirement now 0

GOLDEN RECORD ch.g. 9 Nicholas Bill - Halmsgiving by Free State — Ms Hanna Walsgrove

372	2/3	Mollington	(R)	RES	3m	19	G	*ld to 10th, sn wknd, walked in*	9	0

Novice-ridden & tailed off last 0

GOLDEN STAR(IRE) ch.g. 6 Salse (USA) - Tight Spin by High Top — Rick Beauchamp

928	6/4	Garthorpe	(R)	MDO	3m	8	GF	*(fav) ld 4th-6th, steadied, lft clr 5 out, ran on well*	1	12
1355	4/5	Dingley	(R)	RES	3m	12	G	*chsd ldrs, ld 12th, rddn & styd on wll frm 2 out*	1	20

Poor hurdler 94/5; fair prospect in points; beat subsequent H/Chase winner & should upgrade in 98 ... 21

GOLDEN START (Irish) — I 113[P], I 126[1], I 174[P], I 252[3], I 314[F], I 368[2], I 376[3]

GOLD LEADER (Irish) — I 120[P], I 178[4], I 250[1], I 290[6], I 376[5], I 504[F]

GOLD'N SHROUD(IRE) b.g. 6 Shy Groom (USA) - Launch The Raft by Home Guard (USA) — J W Delahay

255	22/2	Newtown	(L)	CON	3m	14	G	*mid-div, wknd hlfwy, last & t.o. whn p.u. 14th*	P	0
431	8/3	Upton-On-Se'	(R)	CON	3m	9	G	*chsd ldrs, outpcd 13th, remote 5th whn p.u. 3 out*	P	0
568	16/3	Garnons	(L)	CON	3m	12	G	*15l 5th at 12th, lost tch 14th, remote 7th whn u.r. 2 out*	U	-
1233	26/4	Brampton Br'	(R)	CON	3m	8	G	*rear til ran on 16th, nrst fin*	4	17
1523	17/5	Bredwardine	(R)	CON	3m	7	G	*cls up, chsd wnr 14th-apr 2 out, kpt on und pres*	3	17

Winning hurdler 94; 2 fair runs but struggles to stay & win in points hard to find 18

GOLD OR BUST b.m. 7 Amazing Bust - Going After Gold by King's Ride — A Jackson

135	9/2	Alnwick	(L)	MDO	3m	12	G	*rear, mstk 4th, prog & ran wd apr 10th, wknd 12th,p.u.3out*	P	0

No real signs yet **0**

GOLD SIGNAL (Irish) — I 248P, I 372P

GOLD SWORD ch.g. 6 Broadsword (USA) - Dunton Lady by Extra — D H Roberts

774 29/3 Dingley (R) MDO 2m 5f 10 G *7th & in tch to 9th, 5th & outpcd 6 out, bhnd & f 3 out* F -
928 6/4 Garthorpe (R) MDO 3m 8 GF *mid-div hlfwy, 4tha t 12th, went 2nd 3 out, not rch wnr* 2 10

Not disgraced behind fair prospect 2nd start & may go close in 98 .... **14**

GOLD TALISMAN b.m. 8 Scorpio (FR) - Jyponica by Wabash — P T Hollins
1996 P(0),P(0),P(0)

120 9/2 Wetherby Po' (L) MDO 3m 18 GF *mid-div, wknd 12th, t.o. & p.u. 14th* P 0
767 29/3 Whittington (L) MDO 3m 9 S *ldng grp, lft 2nd 13th, onepcd aft* 3 10

First form last start but more needed to score in 98 if fit **12**

GOLD TIP ch.m. 11 Billion (USA) - Gamblers Ace — Miss R Williams
1996 P(0),P(0),P(0),2(0),3(10),P(0),2(12),4(0),P(0)

543 16/3 Erw Lon (L) MDN 3m 11 GF *trckd ldrs to 12th, wknd, p.u. 2 out* P 0

Safely ignored now **0**

GOLFING MAN (Irish) — I 128P, I 175U, I 248, , I 2934

GO LIKE THE DEVIL (Irish) — I 219P, I 3473

GOLLY MISS MOLLY (Irish) — I 251, I 2086, I 2405, I 299P, I 401F, I 494F, I 5463, I 569P

GO MAGIC b.g. 8 Rustingo - Ruths Magic by Current Magic — Mrs E A Squirrell
1996 P(0),P(0),P(0)

30 26/1 Marks Tey (L) MDN 3m 9 GF *blnd & u.r. 1st* U -
65 1/2 Horseheath (R) RES 3m 10 GF *hld up, prog 8th, blnd 11th, bhnd whn p.u. 3 out* P 0

Yet to complete & season lasted 6 days **0**

GONALSTON PERCY gr.g. 9 Dawn Johnny (USA) - Porto Louise by Porto Bello — F S Jackson
1996 P(0),P(0)

345 2/3 Market Rase' (L) MDO 3m 13 GF *alwys bhnd, t.o. 9th, p.u. 11th* P 0
480 9/3 Southwell P' (L) MDO 3m 17 G *hmpd 2nd, sn wll bhnd, t.o. 6th* 9 0
834 31/3 Thorpe Lodge (L) MEM 3m 3 F *(bl) mstly 5l 2nd, prssd ldr frm 6 out, outpcd last, eased* 2 0
1086 14/4 Southwell (L) HC 3m 110yds 11 G *(bl) started slowly, alwys in rear, t.o. and p.u. before 10th.* P 0

Of no account & 2nd in slowly run race **0**

GONE FOR LUNCH br.g. 6 Presidium - Border Mouse by Border Chief — John Whyte
1996 **9(NH),F(NH),11(NH),4(NH),1(NH),9(NH)**

192 15/2 Higham (L) MEM 3m 3 G *(fav) ld 3rd-10th, cls 2nd til no ext 3 out* 2 0
495 14/3 Fakenham (L) HC 2m 5f 110yds 10 G *whipped round start, v slowly away, t.o. when jmpd slowly 5th and p.u..* P 0

Hurdle winner 96; one to avoid now **0**

GOOD BOY CHARLIE ch.g. 6 Wonderful Surprise - Jenny's Joy by Le Bavard (FR) — N B Jones
1996 P(0),P(0),U(-)

185 15/2 Erw Lon (L) MDN 3m 14 G *sn prom, chsd wnr 13th, 2nd & btn whn f 3 out* F -
720 29/3 Llanvapley (L) MDN 3m 8 GF *(fav) towrds rear, some prog 13th, onepcd aft* 4 11
1009 12/4 St Hilary (R) MDN 3m 11 GF *mid-div, blnd & u.r. 10th* U -
1136 19/4 Bonvilston (R) MDO 3m 15 G *rear early, styd on onepcd frm 3 out* 6 0

Promise not yet developed; may still do better in 98 .... **11**

GOOD BOY FRED b.g. 5 Itsu (USA) - Karen Kelly by Pitskelly — Mrs J Williams

365 2/3 Garnons (L) MDO 2 1/2m 14 GS *nvr nr ldrs, styd on frm 11th, tk 2nd cls hm* 2 0
719 29/3 Llanvapley (L) MDN 3m 14 GF *(Jt fav) cls up, blndrd & u.r. 6th* U -
1136 19/4 Bonvilston (R) MDO 3m 15 G *(fav) trckd ldrs, 2nd 13th, strng chal apr last, alwys held* 2 14
1231 26/4 Pyle (R) MDO 3m 7 GS *(fav) trckd ldrs, ld 3 out, clr nxt, pshd out* 1 13

Steady improvement & comfortable winner of weak race; should have Restricted prospects **16**

GOOD COUNSEL (Irish) — I 4562

GOODHEAVENS MRTONY b.g. 10 Carwhite - Golden October by Young Generation — Mrs Carole Sykes

212 16/2 Southwell P' (L) MDO 3m 14 GS *prom to 8th, bhnd 12th, t.o. & p.u. 3 out* P 0
358 2/3 Great Stain' (L) MDO 3m 14 S *prom, lft in ld 5th, hdd 7th, sn fdd* 4 0
510 15/3 Dalton Park (R) MDO 3m 14 GF *mid-div, outpcd 9th, t.o. 12th* 4 0
698 29/3 Stainton (R) MDO 3m 6 F *settld in 3rd, mstk 7th, outpcd 15th* 3 0
1068 13/4 Whitwell-On' (R) RES 3m 12 G *mid-div, effrt 13th, no prog frm 4 out* 4 13
1105 19/4 Hornby Cast' (L) MDO 3m 11 G *prom,disp 6th,ld 9th & disp 13th,ld agn 3 out,styd on wllnxt* 1 14
1263 27/4 Southwell P' (L) RES 3m 9 G *prom, rdn 11th, strgglng frm 3 out, t.o.* 5 0

1406 5/5 Witton Cast' (R) RES 3m 10 GS *alwys hndy, chal 14th, outpcd frm 4 out, fin tired* 3 13
1421 10/5 Easingwold (L) RES 3m 8 GF *prom til outpcd & rmndrs 11th, mstk 13th, t.o. & p.u. last* P 0
1571 26/5 Wetherby (L) HC 2 1/2m 110yds 15 GF *reminders in rear hfwy, soon well bhnd.* 9 0

Safe & reliability won the day in weak Maiden; struggling since 13

GOOD KING HENRY b.g. 11 St Columbus - Cooks' Knife by Perhapsburg — I J Widdicombe
1996 3(0),P(0),3(12),4(12),**4(13)**,**2(20)**,**P(0)**
493 12/3 Newton Abbot (L) HC 2m 5f 110yds 11 HY *in tch till wknd 10th, t.o..* 3 0
889 3/4 Taunton (R) HC 3m 7 F *held up, jmpd slowly 5th, well bhnd from 14th, t.o. when p.u. before 2 out.* P 0

Placed in H/Chase in 96 but vanished after poor run on Firm in 97; best watched 13

GOOD LOOKING GUY ch.g. 8 Cruise Missile - Saxon Belle by Deep Run — Mrs Judy Young
1996 6(10),3(10),U(-),3(0),7(10),2(15),1(16),**U(-)**
7 19/1 Barbury Cas' (L) RES 3m 14 GF *rear, 9th hlfwy, no prog* 5 0
45 1/2 Larkhill (R) RES 3m 14 GF *w.w. in rear, prog 14th, strng chal last 100 yrds, just hld* 2 19
221 16/2 Heythrop (R) RES 3m 15 G *(fav) w.w. prog to prss wnr 3 out, ev ch aft, not qckn flat* 2 18

Maiden winner 96; one paced, stays & twice ran well 97; finished early but Restricted if fit 98 18

GOOD LORD FRANK (Irish) — **I** 39[1]

GOOD OMEN b.g. 7 No Evil - Palladian Nymph by Column (USA) — J Vaughan
541 16/3 Erw Lon (L) MDN 3m 10 GF *rear, ran green, p.u. 11th* P 0

Rarely runs & shows nothing 0

GOOD PROFIT ch.g. 8 Meadowbrook - Night Profit by Carnival Night — W G Young
1996 P(0),**F(-)**,F(-),P(0),5(0),U(-),3(0),**7(NH)**
565 16/3 Lanark (R) MDO 3m 10 GS *t.o. by 9th, p.u. bfr nxt* P 0

Of no account 0

GOOD TIME ABBEY (Irish) — **I** 332[5], **I** 517[4]

GOOD VIEW (Irish) — **I** 533[U]

GOODWILL HILL b.g. 9 State Diplomacy (USA) - Cessy by Burglar — Mrs S J Gospel
1996 7(0),6(10),1(13),P(0),12(0),6(11),4(0)
118 9/2 Wetherby Po' (L) RES 3m 14 GF *prom til wknd 13th, t.o. & p.u. 4 out* P 0
167 15/2 Witton Cast' (R) RES 3m 7 F *trckd ldr, mstk 11th, wknd 15th, t.o. & p.u. 3 out* P 0

Maiden winner 96; well beaten since & 97 season lasted 6 days 10

GOOLDS DIAMOND (Irish) — **I** 81[F], **I** 132[U]

GOOLDS GOLD ch.g. 11 Le Moss - Marie Goold by Arapaho — David Brace
1996 1(25),**6(27)**,1(27),**3(21)**,1(26),U(-),1(26),**4(18)**,S(-)
188 15/2 Erw Lon (L) LAD 3m 8 G *(fav) hld up, 6th whn p.u. 6th, lame* P 0

Won 4 points in 96 but broke down only start 97 & hard to come back at 12 22

GOOLDS OPAL (Irish) — **I** 48[P], **I** 79[3], **I** 305[P]

GORDONS BAY (Irish) — **I** 274[P]

GORDONSTOUN b.g. 9 Royal Vulcan - Mishabo by Royalty — Ronald A Heath
854 31/3 Eyton-On-Se' (L) MDO 3m 10 GF *cls up 5th, sn mid-div, schooling* 6 0

Just an educational run but time already passing 0

GORMLESS(IRE) b.g. 9 Torus - Fine Thing by Camden Town — Sir Richard Cooper
1996 P(0),5(13),P(0),1(13)
396 8/3 Barbury Cas' (L) CON 3m 9 G *chsd ldrs to 10th, 5th & outpcd 12th, hmpd nxt & p.u.* P 0
662 22/3 Badbury Rin' (L) CON 3m 8 F *in tch to 14th, wknd nxt, t.o. & p.u. 3 out* P 0
1242 26/4 Bratton Down (L) LAD 3m 6 GS *ld 6-12th, wknd qckly, p.u. 3 out* P 0

Intermediate winner 96; disappointing & runs as if something is amiss now 0

GORTROE GUY (Irish) — **I** 76[5], **I** 239[3], **I** 322[S], **I** 425[F]

GOWAN GOWAN (Irish) — **I** 297[2], **I** 425[4], **I** 527[U]

GO WILLIE GO b.g. 7 Domitor (USA) - Native Chant by Gone Native — Miss L J Smale
1035 12/4 Lifton (R) MDN 3m 11 F *bhnd til ref 7th* R -
1108 19/4 Flete Park (R) RES 3m 14 GF *s.s. last whn ref 2nd* R -
1246 26/4 Bratton Down (L) MDO 3m 16 GS *u.r. 1st* U -
1400 5/5 High Bickin' (R) MDO 3m 14 G *bhnd whn u.r. 3rd* U -
1437 10/5 Holnicote (L) MDO 3m 14 G *s.s. t.o. & ref 3rd* R -

1498	14/5 Cothelstone	(L) MDO 3m	9 GF	*t.o. & ref 2nd*	R	-
1554	24/5 Mounsey Hil'	(R) MDO 3m	14 G	*sn wll bhnd, t.o. & p.u. 7th*	P	0
1583	26/5 Lifton	(R) MDO 3m	11 G	*mid-div, f 9th*	F	-
1615	7/6 Umberleigh	(L) MDO 3m	11 F	*rear, 7th whn f 7th, dead*	F	-

Dead **0**

GOWLAUN b.g. 8 Electric - Tura W J Moore

474 9/3 Southwell P' (L) LAD 3m 12 G *chsd ldrs, mstk 12th, cls 3rd & blnd 14th, wknd* 6 0

Rarely seen & well beaten last only start 97 .... **0**

GRA-BRI (Irish) — I 547^P, I 590^F

GRADLE (Irish) — I 100^P, I 275^4, I 351^6, I 398^1

GRAFY HILL (Irish) — I 35^F, I 100^2, I 123^4

GRAHAM'S CHOICE b.m. 8 Jalmood (USA) - Constanza by Sun Prince Mrs A M Bell

211 16/2 Southwell P' (L) MDO 3m 15 GS *schoold, sn t.o., p.u. 12th* P 0

No promise on debut **0**

GRAIN MERCHANT b.g. 11 Blakeney - Epilogue by Right Royal V J W Walmsley

1996 F(-),1(14),7(0)

12	25/1 Cottenham	(R) RES 3m	3 GF	*ld to 4th, 8l 3rd apr 2 out, strng run flat to ld nr fin*	1	14
113	9/2 Wetherby Po'	(L) CON 3m	10 GF	*mid-div, gd prog to trck ldrs 4 out, lft in ld nxt, hdd flat*	1	20
265	22/2 Duncombe Pa'	(R) CON 3m	15 G	*(fav) alwys prom, not qckn frm 3 out*	4	18

Maiden winner 96; improved 97; finished early but could win Confined if fit at 12; Good **20**

GRAMPAS' GIRL(IRE) b.m. 7 Callernish - Miss Posy by Pitskelly J R Jones

1996 **21(NH),P(NH)**

185	15/2 Erw Lon	(L) MDN 3m	14 G	*prom, 5th & in tch whn ref & u.r. 12th*	R	-
368	2/3 Garnons	(L) MDO 2 1/2m	13 GS	*mid-div whn u.r. 5th*	U	-
542	16/3 Erw Lon	(L) MDN 3m	15 GF	*mid-div, no ch whn p.u. 15th*	P	0
841	31/3 Lydstep	(L) MDO 3m	8 F	*mid-div, no ch whn p.u. 15th*	P	0

Shows no ability **0**

GRAND CANYON (Irish) — I 589^3

GRAND ENTRY ch.g. 7 Le Coq D'Or - Balayer by Balidar Mrs Mary A Meek

1996 **P(NH),6(NH)**

1173 20/4 Hexham Poin' (L) MDO 2 1/2m 9 GF *ld, svrl mstks, mainly 4l up frm 3 out, hld on gamely flat* 1 14

Hard ride but held on to win weak race; may improve - needs to for Restricteds **15**

GRAND VALUE ch.g. 14 Kambalda - Candy Slam by Candy Cane Mrs S J Coupe

1996 4(0),3(0),U(-),F(-)

370	2/3 Mollington	(R) OPE 3m	6 G	*wth wnr til wknd rpdly 11th, t.o. & p.u. 14th*	P	0
978	8/4 Heythrop	(R) CON 3m	3 F	*ld til hdd aft 2 out, no ex*	2	12
986	12/4 Kingston Bl'	(L) CON 3m	10 GF	*ld 6-11th, lost tch frm 13th, t.o.*	4	0
1198	23/4 Andoversford	(R) OPE 3m	5 F	*ld 1st, sn hdd, 4th & outpcd aft, kpt on frm 2 out*	4	13
1403	5/5 Ashorne	(R) CON 3m	14 G	*lft in ld apr 3rd til 4th, wknd 8th, t.o. & p.u. 3 out*	P	0
1448	10/5 Kingston Bl'	(L) CON 3m	9 G	*ld to 2nd, wknd 6th, rear whn p.u. 12th*	P	0

Won 1 of last 36 starts & no prospects of another now **10**

GRANGE MISSILE b.m. 9 Cruise Missile - Peticienne by Mummy's Pet Ian Gilbert

1996 P(0),8(0)

550	16/3 Garthorpe	(R) MDO 3m	11 GF	*chsd ldrs 7th, ld 11th, clr 13th, hdded appr 3 out, wknd*	4	0
770	29/3 Dingley	(R) RES 3m	18 G	*mid-div, fdd 12th, remote 8th whn p.u. last*	P	0
1083	13/4 Guilsborough	(L) MDN 3m	15 GF	*in tch, blnd 13th, sn wknd, t.o. & p.u. last*	P	0
1350	4/5 Dingley	(R) MEM 3m	5 G	*hit 3rd,wnt 2nd 9th,lft in ld 12th,clr whn blnd & u.r. 15th*	U	-
1479	11/5 Garthorpe	(R) MDO 3m	12 GS	*chsd ldrs to 11th, sn wknd, p.u. 15th*	P	0

Does not stay & lost golden chance 4th start - unlikely to get another **0**

GRANGE PINE (Irish) — I 137^F, I 169^U, I 263^P, I 321^P, I 445^P, I 566^5

GRANGEWICK KELLY b.m. 7 Netherkelly - Better Spoken by Articulate J L Marks

276	22/2 Ampton	(R) MDO 3m	12 G	*bhnd 4th, prog 7th, lst pl 11th, t.o. & p.u. 14th*	P	0
450	8/3 Newton Brom'	(R) MDN 3m	7 G	*cls 3rd whn u.r. 6th*	U	-
498	15/3 Ampton	(R) MDO 3m	8 GF	*alwys last, wll bhnd & p.u. 10th*	P	0

No signs of ability yet **0**

GRANNY BID (Irish) — I 105^5, I 200^5

GRANNYS COTTAGE (Irish) — I 426^P, I 541^P

GRANTS CAROUSE ch.g. 10 Carlingford Castle - Clashawley by Deep Run A J Baillie

83	2/2	Wolverhampt'	(L)	RES	3m	8	GS	*jmpd slwly 8th, drppd last 10th, wknd 15th*	4	0
203	15/2	Weston Park	(L)	RES	3m	11	G	*rear early, no prog frm 12th, wll bhnd & p.u. 2 out*	P	0
473	9/3	Southwell P'	(L)	CON	3m	10	G	*jmpd lft,ld,jmpd slwly 5th,hdd 11th,ev ch & hit 14th,wknd*	5	13

Ex-Irish; no stamina & disappeared after only show of form 12

GRAN TURISMO (Irish) — I 489²

GRANVILLE GRILL b.g. 12 Furry Glen - Glamorous Night by Sir Herbert — E W Smith

1996 2(21),1(22),2(21),3(17),1(25),1(24)

5	19/1	Barbury Cas'	(L)	OPE	3m	11	GF	*prom, 5th hlfwy, btn whn p.u. 12th*	P	0
220	16/2	Heythrop	(R)	OPE	3m	20	G	*chsd ldrs til wknd frm 15th*	7	12
292	1/3	Didmarton	(L)	MEM	3m	9	G	*ld 3rd, clr whn blnd & u.r. 6th*	U	-
393	8/3	Barbury Cas'	(L)	OPE	3m	7	G	*t.d.e. jmpd lft,ld/disp to 10th,wknd & hit 14th,fin 3rd,disq*	4D	0
651	22/3	Siddington	(L)	OPE	3m	7	F	*made all, drew clr aft 3 out, mstk last, rdn out*	1	24
819	31/3	Paxford	(L)	OPE	3m	5	F	*t.d.e. ld to 3rd, chsd ldr til wknd 13th, onepcd aft*	3	15
976	8/4	Heythrop	(R)	OPE	4m	7	F	*t.d.e. jmpd lft, ld til hdd sn aft last, no ex*	2	23
1198	23/4	Andoversford	(R)	OPE	3m	5	F	*t.d.e. jmpd lft, ld 3rd, made rest, clr 2 out, styd on wll*	1	25
1474	11/5	Garthorpe	(R)	MEM	3m	6	GS	*(fav) t.d.e. jmpd lft, made all, hld on gamely flat*	1	20

Solid, consistent pointer; won 10 of last 20; front-runner; much prefers Firm; can mwin more at 13 24

GRANVILLE GUEST ch.g. 11 Deep Run - Miss Furlong by Fury Royal — Mrs Bridget Nicholls

1996 1(26),2(29),**4(16)**

109	8/2	Milborne St'	(L)	XX	3m	8	GF	*(fav) 1st ride, hld up, prog 10th, disp 11th til blnd & u.r. 14th*	U	-
286	27/2	Huntingdon	(R)	HC	3m	8	GS	*settld with chasing gp, gd hdwy to join lding pair after 3 out, effort and wandered run-in, no ext.*	2	26
491	10/3	Taunton	(R)	HC	3m	8	G	*(fav) alwys handy, chsd wnr from 12th, str chal when hit last, edged left and wknd run-in.*	2	23
1413	7/5	Uttoxeter	(L)	HC	4 1/4m	7	GS	*trckd ldrs going well till rdn and no response 18th, t.o. and p.u. before 4 out.*	P	0

Able but irresolute & flatters to deceive in H/Chases; points best hope at 12; G-S 22

GRAPHIC DESIGNER(IRE) b.g. 8 Sheer Grit - Kates Princess by Pitpan — J J Hazeltine

1996 **F(NH),P(NH),P(NH)**

605	22/3	Parham	(R)	MDO	3m	7	F	*hld up, jnd wnr 12th, chal 4 out, lvl 2 out, kpt on wll*	2	11
829	31/3	Heathfield	(R)	XX	3m	5	F	*trkd ldrs, ld brfly apr 4 out, wknd qkly apr 3 out*	3	0

Fair pointing debut but season lasted 9 days; novice-ridden; may find a chance if fit 98 12

GRASSINGTON(IRE) gr.g. 8 Roselier (FR) - Private Affair by Julio Mariner — Scott Quirk

1996 2(12),4(0),5(0),4(0),3(11),1(13)

274	22/2	Ampton	(R)	RES	3m	10	G	*in tch, prog 7th, 3rd & rdn 3 out, onepcd*	3	15
449	8/3	Newton Brom'	(R)	XX	3m	13	G	*prom, lost plc 7th, went 3rd agn 11th, styd on onepcd*	3	15
597	22/3	Horseheath	(R)	RES	3m	8	F	*prssd ldr, ld brfly 7-8th, outpcd 15th, ran on agn last*	2	15
913	5/4	Cottenham	(R)	RES	3m	4	F	*made most til ran wd 10th, last frm 13th,t.o. & p.u. 2 out*	P	0
1286	29/4	Huntingdon	(R)	HC	3m	10	G	*alwys rear, no ch from 11th.*	6	13
1503	16/5	Folkestone	(R)	HC	3 1/4m	7	G	*(vis) trckd ldrs, 4th when f 7th.*	F	-

Dead 14

GREATFULL FRED ch.g. 12 Reppin Castle - Kellet Lane by Sandford Lad — Howard J Pickersgill

1996 5(0),2(0),3(0)

622	22/3	Hutton Rudby	(L)	MDO	3m	10	GF	*mid-div, wknd 11th, t.o. & p.u. 13th*	P	0
1106	19/4	Hornby Cast'	(L)	MDO	3m	10	G	*mid-div, drppd to rear 8th, sn strggling*	6	0
1418	10/5	Easingwold	(L)	MEM	3m	6	GF	*chsd ldr, lft in ld 7th, hdd & lost plc 11th, u.r. 14th*	U	-

Placed in 96 but too old to win now 0

GREAT GUSTO b.g. 11 Windjammer (USA) - My Music by Sole Mio (USA) — R C H Racing

587	19/3	Ludlow	(R)	HC	2 1/2m	18	GF	*held up rear, hdwy 11th, one pace apr 4 out.*	5	20
950	6/4	Black Fores'	(R)	MEM	3m	7	G	*(fav) handy, ld 9th, went clr 12th, easily*	1	22
1202	25/4	Ludlow	(R)	HC	2 1/2m	5	GF	*(fav) chsd ldrs, ld apr 10th, clr 5 out, styd on well.*	1	25
1571	26/5	Wetherby	(L)	HC	2 1/2m 110yds	15	GF	*(fav) trckd ldrs, hdwy 8th, cl up when blnd 10th, rdn along apr 4 out, wknd before next.*	7	14
1612	7/6	Umberleigh	(L)	LAD	3m	5	F	*(fav) prom, ld 10th, sn clr, unchal*	1	0

Lightly-raced but useful at best; best under 3m on Firm; can win points & H/Chase at 12 26

GREAT POKEY b or br.g. 12 Uncle Pokey - Mekhala by Menelek — Miss Nell Courtenay

1996 5(19),4(11),2(17),1(21),2(18),2(22),**2(23)**

99	8/2	Great Treth'	(R)	LAD	3m	10	GS	*ld to 4th & 8-10th, wknd rpdly 13th, p.u. nxt*	P	0
174	15/2	Ottery St M'	(L)	LAD	3m	9	G	*ld/disp til blnd & u.r. 4 out*	U	-
491	10/3	Taunton	(R)	HC	3m	8	G	*ld 3rd to 5th, remained prom till wknd from 12th, t.o. when p.u. before 3 out.*	P	0
587	19/3	Ludlow	(R)	HC	2 1/2m	18	GF	*slowly away, t.o. 3rd.*	12	0
678	25/3	Sandown	(R)	HC	2 1/2m 110yds	6	GF	*ld to 3rd, outpcd 14th, rallied and ran on run-in.*	2	19
890	4/4	Aintree	(L)	HC	2 3/4m	14	G	*soon ld, hdd 5th, mstk 10th (Becher's), soon well bhnd, t.o..*	7	0

1090 16/4 Hockworthy (L) LAD 3m 8 GF *wth ldr frm 4th-15th, outpcd aft nxt* 3 16
1292 30/4 Cheltenham (L) HC 2m 5f 12 GF *alwys rear, t.o. from 13th.* 10 0

Ladies winner 96; struggled in H/Chases; novice-ridden; needs to revert to points but barely stays 17

GREAT REMINDER (Irish) — I 181^{F}, I 219^{P}

GREAT SIMPLICITY ch.g. 10 Simply Great (FR) - Affaire D'Amour by Tudor Music — Michael Appleby

6 19/1 Barbury Cas' (L) LAD 3m 13 GF *t.o. till p.u. 14th* P 0
55 1/2 Kingston Bl' (L) CON 3m 15 GF *(bl) chsd ldrs til f 8th* F -
219 16/2 Heythrop (R) LAD 3m 16 G *(bl) rear, t.o. & p.u. 12th* P 0
376 3/3 Windsor (R) HC 3m 11 GF *(bl) alwys in rear, p.u. before 9th.* P 0

No longer of any account 0

GREAT UNCLE b.g. 9 Uncle Pokey - Petrinella by Mummy's Pet — Miss E Oram

1996 **7(0),P(0)**,3(10),3(11),5(0),**5(NH),5(NH),5(NH)**

431 8/3 Upton-On-Se' (R) CON 3m 9 G *drppd last 9th, lost tch 12th, t.o. 15th* 5 0
645 22/3 Castle Of C' (R) LAD 3m 6 G *wth ldr to 7th, 4th & outpcd 13th, last whn p.u. aft 2 out* P 0
952 6/4 Black Fores' (R) LAD 3m 3 G *j.w. disp to 3rd, 2nd aft, chal 2 out, ld apr last,ran on wl* 1 12
1146 19/4 Chaddesley ' (L) CON 3m 6 GF *in tch in rear til outpcd 13th, sn t.o.* 4 0
1384 5/5 Eyton-On-Se' (L) LAD 3m 6 GF *chsd ldrs, nvr bttr thn 3rd, strgglng frm 3 out* 3 11
1540 18/5 Wolverhampt' (L) LAD 3m 5 GS *chsng grp, cls up 5 out, lost tch nxt* 5 11

Novice-ridden & found terrible race when winning; no other prospects now 11

GRECIAN LARK b.g. 9 Crested Lark - Grecian Lace by Spartan General — J White

1996 1(17),1(23),1(18),**F(-)**

55 1/2 Kingston Bl' (L) CON 3m 15 GF *hld up in tch, nvr able to rch ldrs* 3 20
201 15/2 Weston Park (L) OPE 3m 16 G *mid-div, prog 10th, strng chal to ld 3 out, ran on wll* 1 23
758 29/3 Kimble (L) OPE 3m 6 GF *(fav) hld up, mstk 6th, 2nd aft 2 out, no ch wnr* 2 16
1354 4/5 Dingley (R) MXO 3m 3 G *(fav) w.w., chsd ldr 14th, sn rddn alng, not pce to chal* 2 21
1451 10/5 Kingston Bl' (L) OPE 3m 5 G *(fav) hld up in mid-div, qcknd to ld 15th-nxt, ld 2 out, drvn out* 1 20

Solid pointer & won 5 of last 8; stays well; win more Opens 98; G-S 24

GRECIANLID gr.g. 9 Lidhame - Grecian Charter by Runnymede — L A E Hopkins

1996 P(0),P(0),U(-),7(0),5(0),5(0)

467 8/3 Eyton-On-Se' (L) RES 3m 15 G *chsng grp to 10th, no ch whn p.u. 5 out* P 0
727 29/3 Sandon (L) RES 3m 6 GF *prom hlfwy, onepcd aft* 4 0
1000 12/4 Alpraham (R) RES 3m 8 GF *cls up to 14th, fdd rpdly, walked in* 7 0

No longer of any account 0

GREEDY JOHNO (Irish) — I 34^{P}, I 155^{P}, I 222^{P}

GREENACRE GIRL b.m. 7 Lightning Dealer - Deep Love by Deep Run — J R Kearsley

1996 R(-)

205 15/2 Weston Park (L) MDN 3m 10 G *mid to rear, no ch whn p.u. 13th* P 0
326 1/3 Eaton Hall (R) MDN 3m 14 GS *t.o. aft ctt, p.u. bfr 12th* P 0

Not the best of starts 0

GREENACRES ROSE b.m. 7 Derring Rose - New Cherry by New Brig — R W Phizacklea

1996 **P(NH),P(NH),4(NH),P(NH)**

141 9/2 Thorpe Lodge (L) MDN 3m 12 GF *mid to rear, some late prog frm 3 out, nvr nrr* 3 10
775 29/3 Dingley (R) MDO 2m 5f 10 G *alwys 1st pair, chsd wnr frm 4 out, alwys hld* 2 10
1084 13/4 Guilsborough (L) MDN 3m 11 GF *ld 2nd-8th, ld 15th, clr 3 out, wknd & hdd last* 2 12

Modest & novice-ridden but safe & may find a chance in 98 14

GREENAN HILL (Irish) — I 123^{P}

GREEN ARCHER b.g. 14 Hardgreen (USA) - Mittens by Run The Gantlet (USA) — Mrs S D Walter

1996 1(21),F(-),2(20),4(19),**U(-)**,3(19)

57 1/2 Kingston Bl' (L) LAD 3m 13 GF *wll bhnd til mod prog frm 14th, nrst fin* 4 18
219 16/2 Heythrop (R) LAD 3m 16 G *jmpd slwly, rear by 6th, t.o. 12th, no ch aft* 8 11
272 22/2 Ampton (R) LAD 3m 7 G *bhnd & j.s 5th, prog to ld 9th, made rest, j.s.2 out,styd on* 1 22
379 4/3 Leicester (R) HC 3m 7 G *alwys in rear.* 5 16
546 16/3 Garthorpe (R) LAD 3m 11 GF *(fav) sn bhnd, j.s. 3rd, sn rddn, poor 8th 15th, styd on, nvr nrr* 5 11
988 12/4 Kingston Bl' (L) LAD 3m 7 GF *lft 2nd 4th, rdn 11th, jnd & lft wll clr 14th, unchal* 1 21

Old stager but retains much of ability; stays; inconsistent; best Soft; can win at 15 21

GREENFIELD MAID(IRE) ch.m. 8 Red Johnnie - Cuan Maid by Whistling Top — J V C Davenport

407 8/3 Llanfrynach (R) MDN 3m 11 G *mid-div, f 8th* F -
706 29/3 Upper Sapey (R) MDO 3m 15 GF *alwys rear, 8th 11th, p.u. 15th* P 0
1138 19/4 Bonvilston (R) MDO 3m 9 G *alwys rear* 5 0
1324 3/5 Bonvilston (R) MDO 3m 16 G *prom, lost tch hlfwy, lft 3rd by dfctns* 3 0
1527 17/5 Bredwardine (R) MDO 3m 13 G *prom til wknd rpdly 13th, p.u. 15th* P 0

Beat only one other in 2 completions & has no scope 0

GREENFIELD TIGER(IRE) ch.g. 9 Good Thyne (USA) - Bangleore by Condorcet (FR) Mrs N Sharpe

189	15/2	Erw Lon	(L)	RES	3m	14	G	*alwys last, mstk 7th, t.o. & p.u. 13th*	P	0
406	8/3	Llanfrynach	(R)	RES	3m	13	G	*mid-div, p.u. 12th*	P	0
575	16/3	Garnons	(L)	RES	3m	12	G	*prom til outpcd 7th, t.o. in 7th whn p.u. flat*	P	0
713	29/3	Llanvapley	(L)	MEM	3m	4	GF	*n.j.w., alwys 3rd, ran on onepce*	3	0
1008	12/4	St Hilary	(R)	RES	3m	11	GF	*rear, no ch whn p.u. 16th*	P	0
1134	19/4	Bonvilston	(R)	MXO	4m	10	G	*alwys towrds rear*	6	0

Ex-Irish; a real disappointment & showed nothing 0

GREENFLAG PRINCESS (Irish) — **I** 10³, **I** 46^F, **I** 90⁴, **I** 143¹, **I** 236¹, **I** 380¹

GREENHILL FLY AWAY b.g. 9 Cruise Missile - April Fortune by Maystreak Mrs S Dench

1996 U(-),U(-),P(0)

282	23/2	Charing	(L)	INT	3m	7	G	*ld to 13th, wknd 15th*	3	0
462	8/3	Charing	(L)	RES	3m	10	G	*prom, chsd wnr 8th, lost tch 13th, lost 2nd apr last*	3	0
1379	5/5	Northaw	(L)	RES	3m	6	F	*(fav) ld til appr 8th, sn p.u. (lame)*	P	0

Dual winner 95; lightly raced; little form 96/7 & problems now 11

GREEN HILLS GLORY (Irish) — **I** 47^P, **I** 76^P

GREENHILLS RUBY br.m. 6 Green Ruby (USA) - Tiki's Affair by Bustiki Mrs G Lancina

1996 F(-),P(0),7(0)

261	22/2	Newtown	(L)	MDN	3m	16	G	*rear, wknd 10th, t.o. & p.u. 12th*	P	0
570	16/3	Garnons	(L)	MDN	2 1/2m	14	G	*alwys mid-div, kpt on steadily frm 14th*	6	0
853	31/3	Eyton-On-Se'	(L)	MDO	3m	13	GF	*chsd ldrs, 3rd 10-14th, no ch whn p.u. 4 out*	P	0

A hint of ability last start & may do better 0

GREENHIL PATCHWORK ro.g. 7 Baron Blakeney - Greenhil Jazz Time by Music Boy Mrs Giles Lacey

1996 **10(NH),F(NH)**

141	9/2	Thorpe Lodge	(L)	MDN	3m	12	GF	*mid-div whn f 10th*	F	-
549	16/3	Garthorpe	(R)	MDO	3m	16	GF	*mstks, bhnd frm 5th, t.o. & p.u. 3 out*	P	0

No ability under Rules & nothing in points either 0

GREENMOUNT LAD(IRE) ch.g. 9 Fidel - Deep Chariot by Deep Run J Cornforth

1996 F(-),P(0),3(16),3(14),1(15),6(0),4(14)

32	26/1	Alnwick	(L)	RES	3m	11	G	*mid-div, prog 9th, sn wth ldrs, wknd aft 3 out*	4	14
78	2/2	Market Rase'	(L)	RES	3m	8	GF	*(fav) bhnd, hit 4th, prog 7th, u.r. 11th*	U	-
213	16/2	Southwell P'	(L)	RES	3m	16	GS	*hld up, prog 11th, jnd ldr 3 out, ld cls home*	1	19
267	22/2	Duncombe Pa'	(R)	OPE	3m	8	G	*rear & detachd 9th, wll bhnd whn p.u. 13th*	P	0
383	5/3	Catterick	(L)	HC	3m 1f 110yds	10	G	*alwys cl up, disp ld 13th, blnd 4 out, ld next, rdn 2 out, hdd and not qckn after last.*	2	23
509	15/3	Dalton Park	(R)	XX	3m	13	GF	*prom whn ran out 3rd*	r	-
619	22/3	Hutton Rudby	(L)	INT	3m	8	GF	*chsd ldrs, disp 10th til ld apr last, ran on strgly*	1	19
891	4/4	Sedgefield	(L)	HC	3m 3f	5	GF	*(fav) chsd clr ldr, ld 6 out, hrd pressed final 2, ran on well.*	1	20
1086	14/4	Southwell	(L)	HC	3m 110yds	11	G	*held up, hdwy 9th, styd on from 2 out, not reach wnr.*	2	24
1414	9/5	Sedgefield	(L)	HC	2m 5f	6	GF	*nvr far away, rdn after 13th, slight ld between last 2, hdd and hit last, soon ld again, styd on well.*	1	23
1588	30/5	Stratford	(L)	HC	3 1/2m	9	G	*held up, mstks 7th and next, soon bhnd, t.o..*	5	0

Members winner 96; much improved 97; stays; one paced; best in H/Chases but hard to place now; Good 24

GREEN SHEEN(IRE) ch.g. 9 Green Shoon - Hill Sixty by Slippered Ernie Fenwick

131	9/2	Alnwick	(L)	RES	3m	13	G	*u.r. 2nd*	U	-
157	15/2	Lanark	(R)	RES	3m	11	G	*alwys handy, no ext apr last*	3	16
778	31/3	Carlisle	(R)	HC	3 1/4m	14	G	*prom till outpcd 12th, p.u. 3 out.*	P	0

Highly promising in 94 but missed 95/6 & unable to recpature form now 14

GREEN'S VAN GOYEN(IRE) b.g. 9 Lyphard's Special (USA) - Maiden Concert by Condorcet (FR) Mrs D H McCarthy

1996 5(21),F(-),1(24),**U(-)**

91	6/2	Huntingdon	(R)	HC	3m	10	G	*ld to 3rd, chsd ldrs till wknd after 11th, bhnd when p.u. before 5 out.*	P	0
484	9/3	Tweseldown	(R)	OPE	3m	10	G	*6/4-3s, trckd ldrs, lost plc hlfwy, sn wll bhnd, p.u. last*	P	0
967	6/4	Penshurst	(L)	OPE	3m	4	F	*ld til p.u. lame 12th*	P	0

Useful pointer at best but stable out of form 97 & fell to pieces; can only be watched 15

GREEN TIMES ch.g. 12 Green Shoon - Time And A Half by No Time Major General C A Ramsay

1996 4(11),1(19),**U(NH),3(22)**,**7(16)**,3(19),**4(22)**,**4(22)**,**P(0)**

611	22/3	Friars Haugh	(L)	CON	3m	11	GF	*nvr rchd ldrs*	5	0
946	6/4	Friars Haugh	(L)	OPE	3m	5	GF	*hld up, wnt cls 3rd 4 out, wknd qckly frm nxt*	3	11

1096 18/4 Ayr (L) HC 3m 3f 110yds 7 G *prom till lost pl 12th and soon bhnd, t.o. 5 out.* 5 0
1294 30/4 Kelso (L) HC 3m 1f 6 GF *soon bhnd, n.d..* 4 13
1426 10/5 Aspatria (L) OPE 3m 9 G *rear, 7th & strggIng 11th, no ch aft* 6 0
1512 17/5 Corbridge (R) OPE 3m 10 GS *prom til rdn & wknd 10th, sn wll bhnd, p.u. last* P 0

Confined winner 96; declined greatly in 97 & well-beaten; hard to win again 12

GREENWINE(USA) br.h. 11 Green Dancer (USA) - Princesse Margo by Targowice (USA) D Underhill
1996 4(21),**P(0)**,3(18),3(20),2(19),1(16),3(14)

47 1/2 Wadebridge (L) MEM 3m 4 G *chsng pair, lft 2nd 10th, u.r. 12th* U -
520 15/3 Cothelstone (L) LAD 3m 12 GS *nov rdn, not fluent, rear til p.u. 15th* P 0
628 22/3 Kilworthy (L) CON 3m 12 G *nov rddn, in tch, outpcd 15th, kpt on clsng stgs* 3 22
1292 30/4 Cheltenham (L) HC 2m 5f 12 GF *cl up, chsd ldr 9th til jmpd slowly next, rdn and not qckn after 4 out.* 4 21

Won 2 soft races 95/6; usually finishes but ungenuine & prefers not to win 18

GREET THE GREEK (Irish) — **I** 120P, **I** 254, , **I** 289P, **I** 372³, **I** 508⁶

GREYBURY LANE(IRE) b.g. 9 Roselier (FR) - Troyside by Quayside Dr D B A Silk

225 19/2 Folkestone (R) HC 2m 5f 10 S *blnd and u.r. 2nd.* U -
305 1/3 Parham (R) OPE 3m 9 G *wll in tch to 10th, wll bhnd whn p.u. 3 out* P 0

Promising in 94; missed 95/6 & unable to recover; can only be watched 12

GREYBURY STAR(IRE) b.g. 9 Roselier (FR) - Diamond Angel by Diamonds Are Trump (USA) Mrs D B A Silk

284 23/2 Charing (L) MDO 3m 17 G *10s-6s, prom, lft in ld 14th, reluc frm 4 out, all out* 1 10
303 1/3 Parham (R) RES 3m 10 G *cls up, 2nd 3 out, outpcd by wnr* 3 12
1286 29/4 Huntingdon (R) HC 3m 10 G *chsd ldrs, struggling when mstk 12th, soon lost tch.* 5 14

Staggered home in bad Maiden (not stay & reluctant) & hard to win again 14

GREY GUESTINO gr.g. 11 Ivotino (USA) - Wedding Guest by Sanbal Mrs A Delve
1996 6(15),P(0),4(0),3(13),5(0),6(14),7(0)

737 29/3 Higher Kilw' (L) LAD 3m 5 GF *ld/disp til lost plc rpdly 7th, sn strgglng, t.o.* 4 0
950 6/4 Black Fores' (R) MEM 3m 7 G *ld to 9th, 2nd to 13th, wknd nxt* 4 0
1043 12/4 Cothelstone (L) INT 3m 7 GF *prom early, lost plc 12th, onepcd frm 4 out* 5 0
1395 5/5 High Bickin' (R) RES 3m 9 G *trckd ldr, wknd 14th, sn outpcd* 7 0
1494 14/5 Cothelstone (L) RES 3m 11 GF *chsd ldr to 11th, wknd 13th, sn wll bhnd* 5 0
1581 26/5 Lifton (R) LAD 3m 7 G *nvr trbld ldrs, onepcd* 4 16

1 win from 35 starts; safe but non-stayer & usually outclassed 11

GREY HORIZON (Irish) — **I** 50F, **I** 87F

GREY HUSSAR(NZ) gr.g. 11 War Hawk - Poi (NZ) by Native Turn (USA) Mrs S Gray
1996 P(0),8(13),1(10)

248 22/2 Brocklesby ' (L) CON 3m 10 G *alwys last pair, rmmndrs 8-9th, gave up 4 out* P 0
505 15/3 Dalton Park (R) MEM 3m 6 GF *mid-div, went 2nd 13th, rdn 16th, outpcd 2 out* 3 10

Members winner 96; well beaten in same 97 & no real prospects now 11

GREY JERRY gr.g. 6 Kinglet - Orphan Grey by Crash Course Sir Richard Cooper
1996 P(0),P(0),P(0)

525 15/3 Cothelstone (L) MDN 3m 15 GS *f 1st* F -
557 16/3 Ottery St M' (L) RES 3m 9 G *sn rear, t.o. & p.u. 14th* P 0
1246 26/4 Bratton Down (L) MDO 3m 16 GS *ld/disp til 12th, kpt on onepcd run in* 4 11

Last on 1st completion but may do better in 98 12

GREY REALM ch.m. 9 Grey Desire - Miss Realm by Realm R E Barr
1996 2(18),3(17),U(-),3(20),5(15),5(15),1(21),3(17)

619 22/3 Hutton Rudby (L) INT 3m 8 GF *disp 4th til lost plcd 6th,prog 5 out,gng wll whn f nxt* F -
694 29/3 Stainton (R) CON 3m 11 F *held up, prog 12th, wnt 2nd 3 out, chal nxt, not qckn flat* 2 21
1070 13/4 Whitwell-On' (R) XX 3m 9 G *prom, disp 6th til ld 9-11th, ld 13th, ran on strngly 2 out* 1 20
1103 19/4 Hornby Cast' (L) OPE 3m 5 G *(fav) j.w., ld til 12th, ld agn 14th, qcknd clr 3 out, easily* 1 22

Confined winner 96; improved again; stays better; can win more Opens 98; G-F 23

GREY ROCK(IRE) gr.m. 6 Roselier (FR) - Leallen by Le Bavard (FR) Mrs B E Miller

815 31/3 Tranwell (L) MDO 2 1/2m 14 G *n.j.w., rear div, styd on gmly frm 4 out* 8 0
949 6/4 Friars Haugh (L) MDN 3m 10 GF *u.r. 2nd* U -
1051 13/4 Lockerbie (R) MDN 3m 10 F *made most to 8th, ld agn 15th, cosily* 1 15
1424 10/5 Aspatria (L) RES 3m 17 G *(fav) alwys prom, trckd wnr 4 out, rdn & ev ch 2 out, just faild* 2 20
1510 17/5 Corbridge (R) RES 3m 13 GS *(fav) disp to 4th, chsd ldr til disp 10th-12th, onepcd* 3 17

Quite promising; touched off in fair Restricted 4th start & should soon go one better; G-F 20

GREYSTYLE b.g. 7 Grey Desire - Riverstyle by River Knight (FR) Denys Smith

168 15/2 Witton Cast' (R) MDO 3m 4 F *(fav) sttld in 3rd, swishd tail 13th, 2nd nxt, hrd rdn & not qckn* 2 0

Beaten in bad race & finished lame - may do better on softer ground 11

GREY TIDE (Irish) — **I** 359^{1}

GREY TUDOR gr.g. 10 Import - Grey Morley by Pongee Noel Warner

1996 P(0),P(0),F(-),P(0),4(10),**P(0)**,U(-)

650 22/3 Siddington (L) CON 3m 8 F *chsd ldr to 9th, outpcd 14th, 6l 3rd whn blnd & u.r. nxt* U -

1064 13/4 Maisemore P' (L) CON 3m 13 GF *last whn u.r. 5th* U -

Flat winner; of no account in points 10

GREY VENTURE (Irish) — **I** 265^{3}, **I** 430^{6}, **I** 490^{1}

GRIMLEY GALE(IRE) br.m. 8 Strong Gale - Zauditu by Menelek R M Phillips

1996 1(23),3(19),1(19)

148 9/2 Tweseldown (R) XX 3m 12 GF *(Jt fav) mid-div, mstk 9th, prog 4 out, disp last, ld nr fin, all out* 1 19

294 1/3 Didmarton (L) INT 3m 20 G *cls up whn u.r. 8th* U -

484 9/3 Tweseldown (R) OPE 3m 10 G *(fav) in tch, blnd 11th, ld 14th, sn clr, ran on well* 1 24

700 29/3 Upper Sapey (R) MEM 3m 8 GF *(fav) ld to 4th, imprvd to ld agn 15th, lft wll clr nxt, easily* 1 21

1013 12/4 Bitterley (L) CON 3m 14 GF *(fav) hld up, prog 8th, rdn to ld last, eased nr fin* 1 21

1236 26/4 Brampton Br' (R) LAD 3m 4 G *(fav) trckd ldr 4th, ld brfly 11th, ld 13th, rdn clr frm 3 out* 1 22

1391 5/5 Cursneh Hill (L) LAD 3m 4 GF *(fav) ld 1st & frm 9th, drew clr aft 14th, not extnd* 1 22

1463 11/5 Tweseldown (R) MXO 3m 5 GF *(fav) hld up, prog 10th, ld 14th, mstk last, easily* 1 23

1535 18/5 Mollington (R) LAD 3m 6 GS *(fav) ld to 4th, prssd ldr, rdn to ld 3 out, clr nxt, ran on wll* 1 25

1573 26/5 Chaddesley ' (L) LAD 3m 6 F *(fav) prom, ld 6th, made rest, ran on well frm 3 out* 1 24

Sustained improvement; won 11 of last 13; stays; tough; win plenty more in 98; G/S-F 28

GRINDLEY BROOK b.g. 12 Over The River (FR) - Cullagh's Girl by Tepukei Dick Chapman

330 1/3 Eaton Hall (R) CON 3m 16 GS *t.o., p.u. 11th* P 0

468 8/3 Eyton-On-Se' (L) RES 3m 11 G *wth ldrs whn ran out 6th* r -

667 23/3 Eaton Hall (R) CON 3m 10 GF *prom to 10th, wknd rpdly, p.u. 12th* P 0

936 6/4 Tabley (R) MEM 3m 9 G *(bl) wll bhnd, poor 6th whn u.r. 12th* U -

1000 12/4 Alpraham (R) RES 3m 8 GF *(bl) ld 3rd, 6l clr whn f nxt* F -

No longer of any account 0

GROMIT(NZ) gr.g. 9 Captain Jason (NZ) - Larksleve (NZ) by Grey Bird (NZ) Miss Sarah Eaton

1996 1(15),P(0),1(19),1(19)

572 16/3 Garnons (L) INT 3m 13 G *mid-div, effrt 14th, kpt on onepcd frm nxt* 4 13

704 29/3 Upper Sapey (R) INT 3m 4 GF *efft to disp ld frm 13th, wnt 2l clr apr last, ran on strgly* 1 20

1064 13/4 Maisemore P' (L) CON 3m 13 GF *hld up in rear, poor 7th & no ch 13th* 6 0

1536 18/5 Mollington (R) INT 3m 8 GS *sttld rear,rdn & prog 10th,effrt to chal & ev ch last,no ext* 3 17

1574 26/5 Chaddesley ' (L) CON 3m 8 F *(Jt fav) trckd ldrs,effrt 12th,chsd wnr 15th,rdn 3 out,ran on onepcd* 2 20

Won 3 out of 4 in 96; fair runs 97 but not improved; easy 3m essential; can win Confined; G/S-F 20

GROVE CROSS (Irish) — **I** 452^{P}

GT HAYES POMMARD b.g. 7 Trampler - Great Hayes Bene by Night Thought D Howells

1996 U(-),P(0),U(-),F(-),4(0),P(0)

3 19/1 Barbury Cas' (L) XX 3m 14 GF *rear whn u.r. 2nd* U -

23 25/1 Badbury Rin' (L) RES 3m 8 GF *s.s. t.o. til p.u. 12th* P 0

222 16/2 Heythrop (R) RES 3m 17 G *ld to 7th, 4th whn u.r. 10th* U -

299 1/3 Didmarton (L) MDN 3m 14 G *13th whn f 2nd* F -

391 8/3 Barbury Cas' (L) MEM 3m 6 G *raced wd, jmpd rght, ld to apr 12th, ld last, ran on well* 1 10

865 31/3 Kingston St' (R) RES 3m 3 F *ld til jmp slwly 6th, 3rd whn blndrd & u.r. 8th* U -

50/1 when winning (2nd completion from 15 races) & no hope of a repeat 10

GUARENA(USA) b.g. 12 Run The Gantlet (USA) - Trenton North (USA) by Herbager M Lewis

1996 P(0),P(0)

258 22/2 Newtown (L) RES 3m 14 G *wll bhnd, t.o. 10th, tk poor 3rd nr fin* 3 0

574 16/3 Garnons (L) RES 3m 14 G *rear frm 5th, lost tch 11th, t.o. & p.u. 2 out* P 0

634 22/3 Howick (L) RES 3m 7 GF *hld up, prog 11th, drvn alng 13th, disp 3 out, ld last,qcknd* 1 14

1063 13/4 Maisemore P' (L) XX 3m 13 GF *rear, rmndr 5th, mstk 12th, nvr dang* 7 0

1132 19/4 Bonvilston (R) CON 3m 9 G *alwys rear* 6 0

1319 3/5 Bonvilston (R) INT 3m 8 G *rear & rmndrs hlfwy, t.o. & p.u. 2 out* P 0

Looked finished 96 but found bad Restricted 3rd start 97; will not find another chance now 12

GUITING GRAY gr.g. 10 Carlingford Castle - Very Pleased (USA) by Al Hattab (USA) A M Mason

1996 1(20),4(18),1(24),2(19),1(27)

396 8/3 Barbury Cas' (L) CON 3m 9 G *made all, hit 2nd & 6th, drew clr apr 3 out, easily* 1 27

Very useful; won hot Confined only start 97; hard to beat if fit 98; G/S-F 28

GULER-A b.g. 9 King Of Spain - Wayleave by Blakeney P F Gibbon

1996 **8(NH)**,**4(NH)**,**7(NH)**

120 9/2 Wetherby Po' (L) MDO 3m 18 GF *alwys rear, t.o. & p.u. 14th* P 0
343 1/3 Corbridge (R) MDO 3m 14 G *prom til b.d. 10th* B -

Placed in novice chase 96; should be able to figure in Maidens but soon vanished 10

GUNNER BOON b.g. 7 Gunner B - Miss Boon — David Brace

1996 r(-),6D(14),2(12),2(15),F(-)

102 8/2 Great Treth' (R) MDO 3m 8 GS *(fav) made all, drew clr aft 2 out, comf* 1 16
262 22/2 Newtown (L) RES 3m 15 G *(fav) made virt all, drew clr apr last, comf* 1 21
363 2/3 Garnons (L) XX 3m 6 GS *ld til jnd 14th, wknd frm 3 out* 2 16
846 31/3 Lydstep (L) INT 3m 4 F *(fav) ld to 14th, no ch wnr aft* 2 19
1086 14/4 Southwell (L) HC 3m 110yds 11 G *prom till blnd badly and u.r. 6 out.* U -
1133 19/4 Bonvilston (R) INT 3m 8 G *(fav) cls up, lft 2nd 15th, ld 2 out, qcknd clr* 1 21
1228 26/4 Pyle (R) INT 3m 5 GS *ld 7-8th, ld aft 14th, rdn & jnd last, hdd post* 2 21
1319 3/5 Bonvilston (R) INT 3m 8 G *(fav) chsd ldr, ld 2 out, hdd last, outpcd flat* 2 23
1468 11/5 Erw Lon (L) INT 3m 7 GS *ld to 14th, lft in ld 16th, drew clr 2 out* 1 20

Made up for 96 ill-luck with a vengeance; consistent & genuine; Confineds, at least, in 98; G/F-G/S 23

GUNNERS DAWN b.m. 6 Rustingo - Gunner Go by Gunner B — Mrs S V Corbin

433 8/3 Upton-On-Se' (R) RES 3m 18 G *lost tch 7th, t.o. & p.u. 3 out* P 0

No show on only start 0

GUNNER STREAM ch.g. 13 Gunner B - Golfers Dream by Carnoustie — Mrs A G Sims

1996 U(-),**7(NH)**,**U(NH)**,P(0),4(0),4(0)

916 5/4 Larkhill (R) MEM 3m 3 F *(fav) alwys 2nd, dist bhnd whn blnd & u.r. last, rmntd* 3 0
1142 19/4 Larkhill (R) OPE 3m 3 F *cls up, mstk & rdr lost irons 2nd, p.u. nxt, rtrcd, p.u. 7th* P 0
1371 5/5 Cotley Farm (L) MXO 3m 2 GF *ld/disp to 3 out, outpcd aft* 2 0

Last on both completions & of no account now 0

GUS MCCRAE gr.g. 11 Parole - Golden Grove by Roan Rocket — Miss P Philipps

1996 2(14),1(17),4(0),P(0)

296 1/3 Didmarton (L) LAD 3m 13 G *alwys bhnd, 11th whn u.r. 10th* U -
536 16/3 Erw Lon (L) LAD 3m 9 GF *(Jt fav) cls up til fdd frm 11th* 6 0
846 31/3 Lydstep (L) INT 3m 4 F *alwys 3rd, no dang* 3 12

Restricted winner 96; brief season 97 & showed virtually nil; best watched at 12; G-F 13

GUSTY VENTURE (Irish) — **I** 356F

GYMCRAK DAWN b.g. 12 Rymer - Edwina's Dawn by Space King — A W Perkins

1996 4(0),P(0),2(16),1(17),6(14),2(13),P(0),P(0),P(0),2(18),P(0)

47 1/2 Wadebridge (L) MEM 3m 4 G *bhnd frm 2nd, 25l down whn lft in ld 12th* 1 14
805 31/3 Wadebridge (L) OPE 3m 5 F *alwys prom, prssd wnr frm 15th til no ext run in* 2 18

Confined winner 96; fortunate Members win & finished early; Members again only hope at 13 14

GYPSY BLUES b.m. 7 Sula Bula - Pine Gypsy by Workboy — Mrs J V Wilkinson

1996 **10(NH)**,**20(NH)**,**6(NH)**

182 15/2 Larkhill (R) MDO 3m 12 G *u.r. 1st* U -

No ability under Rules & the briefest of starts to pointing 0

GYPSY GERRY b.g. 7 Sunyboy - La Chunga by Queen's Hussar — C de P Berry

54 1/2 Wadebridge (L) MDO 3m 13 G *(Co fav) alwys wll plcd, ld 15th, made rest, styd on well* 1 15
176 15/2 Ottery St M' (L) RES 3m 17 G *hld up, prog 12th, went 2nd 14th, ev ch 4 out, outpcd aft* 2 19
532 15/3 Wadebridge (L) RES 3m 9 GF *(fav) alwys cls up, 3rd at 12th, ld 14th, made rest, comf* 1 19
791 31/3 Bishopsleigh (R) CON 3m 6 G *(fav) hld up, 3rd at 14th, effrt 3 out, not qckn frm 2 out, eased* 2 21

Good start & ran well each race; finished early but should upgrade if fit 98; Good 21

GYPSY KING(IRE) b.g. 9 Deep Run - Express Film by Ashmore (FR) — The Gypsy King Partnership

1996 3(20),**2(26)**,**4(20)**

225 19/2 Folkestone (R) HC 2m 5f 10 S *chsd ldrs till wknd 3 out.* 5 15
495 14/3 Fakenham (L) HC 2m 5f 110yds 10 G *alwys chasing ldrs, ev ch 4 out, jmpd slowly next, kept on one pace.* 3 20
801 31/3 Marks Tey (L) CON 3m 8 F *(fav) midfld,wnt 3rd 11th,chsd wnr 15th,ev ch 2 out,styd on wll* 2 18
1432 10/5 Marks Tey (L) MEM 3m 2 G *(fav) made all at sedate pace, drew clr 12th, canter* 1 12

Consistent 96/7 but hard to win with & only success in doddle; may find another chance; F-S 19

GYPSY LUCK b.m. 8 Sula Bula - Pine Gypsy by Workboy — J Grant Cann

1996 F(-),5(11)

1 19/1 Barbury Cas' (L) XX 3m 11 GF *rear, poor 6th hlfwy, kpt on, nrst fin* 3 11
50 1/2 Wadebridge (L) RES 3m 10 G *(fav) alwys cls up, ld 11-14th, just outpcd clsng stgs* 3 14
106 8/2 Milborne St' (L) RES 3m 12 GF *handy early, losng tch whn u.r. 15th* U -
175 15/2 Ottery St M' (L) RES 3m 15 G *handy, mostly 3rd, outpcd frm 3 out* 3 14

806 31/3 Wadebridge (L) RES 3m 6 F *(fav) bhnd til prog 15th, not pce to trbl wnnr* 2 13

Maiden winner 95; no real progress in 97 & finished early; may find Restricted if ready 98 15

GYPSY ROVER (Irish) — I 222P

HACKETT'S FARM ch.g. 12 Deep Run - Anitacat by No Argument Miss Barbara Wilce

1996 4(14),F(-),2(16),1(18),5(17),4(13),5(14),2(18),4(15),1(19)

56 1/2 Kingston Bl' (L) OPE 3m 13 GF *alwys prom, lft 2nd 15th, outpcd aft* 3 17
148 9/2 Tweseldown (R) XX 3m 12 GF *(Jt fav) mid-div, onepcd frm 15th* 7 0
294 1/3 Didmarton (L) INT 3m 20 G *in tch to 10th, wll btn whn p.u. 14th* P 0
430 8/3 Upton-On-Se' (R) MEM 3m 4 G *made most frm 5th til 3 out, rallied last, no ext flat* 2 17
880 1/4 Upton-On-Se' (R) CON 3m 6 GF *prom, cls up 12th, sn outpcd by 1st pair* 3 12
976 8/4 Heythrop (R) OPE 4m 7 F *last frm 4th, t.o frm 14th, p.u. 2 out* P 0
1146 19/4 Chaddesley ' (L) CON 3m 6 GF *(fav) ld/disp,qcknd 13th,drew clr 4 out,hrd rdn & lft wl clr 2 out* 1 18
1388 5/5 Cursneh Hill (L) CON 3m 4 GF *ld 1st & agn 7th, hdd aft 14th, no ext und pres* 2 17
1576 26/5 Chaddesley ' (L) XX 3m 12 F *trckd ldrs til 5th & lost tch 11th, p.u. nxt* P 0

Dual winner 96; declined 97 & usually well-beaten; goes best for Julian Pritchard; may struggle 98 17

HAGAR ch.g. 8 Viking (USA) - Blue Mistral (USA) by Monteverdi Ian Emmerson

1996 **2(NH)**

229 22/2 Friars Haugh (L) CON 3m 9 G *alwys handy, ld 3 out, sn clr, comf* 1 23
339 1/3 Corbridge (R) OPE 3m 5f 11 G *mid-div, gd prog 3 out, ld last, ran on strngly* 1 25
610 22/3 Friars Haugh (L) OPE 3m 6 GF *(fav) hld up, wnt 2nd 4 out, ld nxt, styd on strgly* 1 25

Modest hurdle winner 95; good pointer 97; stays very well; win more if ready 98; Good 26

HALCO (Irish) — I 285P

HALF A CHANCE b.g. 6 Contest (USA) - Solar Hope Vii by Damsire Unregistered Miss J Ashby

451 8/3 Newton Brom' (R) MDN 3m 8 G *cls 3rd til wknd aft 13th, hmpd 15th & p.u.* P 0
775 29/3 Dingley (R) MDO 2m 5f 10 G *cls 3rd frm 6th, p.u. sddnly 11th* P 0
1084 13/4 Guilsborough (L) MDN 3m 11 GF *sn rear, t.o. & p.u. 12th* P 0
1352 4/5 Dingley (R) MDO 2 1/2m 9 G *wth ldrs to 7th, wknng whn hit 9th, p.u. aft* P 0

Shows no stamina yet but could conceivably improve 0

HALF A SOV b.g. 13 Kinglet - Hudsons Hill by Eborneezer Mrs Anne Butler

1996 P(0),P(0),1(10),U(-),**P(0)**

320 1/3 Marks Tey (L) MEM 3m 4 G *chsd ldr, ld 9th-2 out, onepcd und pres* 2 10
798 31/3 Marks Tey (L) RES 3m 7 F *mid-div,und pres 12th,outpcd 14th,styd on agn 3 out,nrst fin* 4 14
1278 27/4 Fakenham P-' (L) RES 3m 11 G *(bl) ld 2nd-12th, wknd, p.u. 15th* P 0
1379 5/5 Northaw (L) RES 3m 6 F *chsd ldr, ld appr 8th,hdd appr 3 out, no ch whn f last, rmtd* 2 0

Members winner 96 & only effective in that class 11

HALF EACH b.m. 5 Weld - Golden Valley by Hotfoot Mrs G B Walford

345 2/3 Market Rase' (L) MDO 3m 13 GF *f 1st* F -
479 9/3 Southwell P' (L) MDO 3m 15 G *schoold, sn wll bhnd, t.o. 4th, p.u. 3 out* P 0
621 22/3 Hutton Rudby (L) MDO 3m 10 GF *prom whn ran out 13th* r -
1074 13/4 Whitwell-On' (R) MDO 2 1/2m 88yds 16 G *prom, wknd 9th, u.r. nxt* U -
1268 27/4 Southwell P' (L) MDO 3m 13 G *prom til grad fdd frm 14th* 4 0

Well beaten on only completion; good stable & may do better 10

HALF MOON SPINNEY br.g. 7 True Song - Dane Hole by Past Petition Miss C Holliday

284 23/2 Charing (L) MDO 3m 17 G *sn wll bhnd, t.o. 8th, p.u. 13th* P 0
581 16/3 Detling (L) MDO 3m 12 F *mid-div, jnd ldrs 10th, ld 3 out-last, onepcd* 2 14

Not beaten far in one of area's better Maidens & should certainly find a chance in 98 14

HALF SCOTCH (Irish) — I 72³, I 122¹, I 252P, I 288¹, I 376⁶, I 465,

HALF SHARP ch.m. 7 Broadsword (USA) - Semi-Colon by Colonist II R A Jeffery

209 16/2 Southwell P' (L) MDO 3m 7 GS *in tch, prog going wll 11th, 4th & btn whn f 13th* F -
1084 13/4 Guilsborough (L) MDN 3m 11 GF *mstks, sn rear, t.o. 13th, p.u. 3 out* P 0
1209 26/4 Clifton On ' (L) MDO 3m 16 GS *prom to 10th, fdd, outpcd 6 out* 8 0
1452 10/5 Kingston Bl' (L) MDO 3m 9 G *t.d.e. mid-div, f 5th* F -

Well-beaten in only completion & jumping needs improving 0

HALLS BURN b.g. 9 Beverley Boy - Wintersgame by Game Warden J D Telfer

1337 3/5 Mosshouses (L) MDO 3m 7 F *jmpd violently rght 1st, out of control, p.u. 5th* P 0

Rarely seen, never completes & mad 0

HALL'S MILL (Irish) — I 124², I 213⁴

HAL'S PRINCE b.g. 10 Le Moss - Hal's Pauper by Official T L Jones

184 15/2 Erw Lon (L) MDN 3m 14 G *(fav) made all, lft clr 3 out, ran on well, unchal* 1 15
258 22/2 Newtown (L) RES 3m 14 G *(fav) mstks 2nd & 11th, ld to 13th, 3rd & btn whn blnd & u.r. 3out* U -
406 8/3 Llanfrynach (R) RES 3m 13 G *ld 8th, hdd 2 out, onepcd* 2 12
1061 13/4 Maisemore P' (L) RES 3m 12 GF *disp clr ld til ld 4th-12th, 2nd whn blnd 15th, p.u. aft* P 0
1365 5/5 Pantyderi (L) RES 3m 10 G *(Jt fav) 2nd at 3rd & 11th, hrd rdn & ld last* 1 18
1555 24/5 Bassaleg (R) MEM 3m 6 G *(fav) ld to 9th, ld 11th, mstk 14th, clr 2 out, rdn out* 1 14

Improved 97; likes to dominate & barely stays; well-ridden; may find Intermediate; Good 19

HALSWAY LANE (Irish) — **I** 271^{2}
HANDBALL (Irish) — **I** 546^{F}, **I** 587^{P}
HANDFAST POINT b.g. 6 Golden Heights - Typhoo Warning by Broadsword (USA) C J Vale

252 22/2 Brocklesby ' (L) MDO 3m 9 G *mid-div, imprvng whn slppd lndg 12th* F -
480 9/3 Southwell P' (L) MDO 3m 17 G *mid-div in tch, styd on frm 15th, fin wll, not rch wnr* 2 14

Beat 7 other finishers 2nd start & looks ready-made for success if fit in 98 16

HAND OUT b.m. 13 Spare A Dime - Stolen Ember by Burglar Colin Raymond

1093 16/4 Hockworthy (L) RES 3m 16 GF *prom to 10th, wknd rpdly, t.o. & p.u. last* P 0

No longer of any account 0

HANDY SALLY (Irish) — **I** 162^{P}, **I** 228^{2}, **I** 278^{1}, **I** 357^{5}, **I** 546^{B}, **I** 587^{P}
HANG IN THERE (Irish) — **I** 245^{P}
HANIGANS BRIDGE (Irish) — **I** 11^{4}, **I** 50^{P}, **I** 86^{6}
HANLEYS CALL(IRE) b.g. 7 Amazing Bust - Cumin Call by Super Slip I R Gibson

36 26/1 Alnwick (L) MDO 3m 15 G *chsd ldrs, 4th whn f 7th* F -

Finished on the 2nd Sunday of the season 0

HANSEL'S STREAK br.g. 5 Majestic Streak - Hansel's Meadow Vii by Damsire Unregistered Mrs A J McMath

815 31/3 Tranwell (L) MDO 2 1/2m 14 G *u.r. 1st* U -

Could not have done less 0

HANUKKAH b.m. 8 Oats - Badsworth Girl by Arch Sculptor P Ansell

1996 U(-),P(0),6(0),5(0),3(10)
97 8/2 Great Treth' (R) INT 3m 13 GS *t.d.e. alwys wll in rear, t.o. whn mstk 13th, p.u. 15th* P 0
456 8/3 Great Treth' (R) INT 3m 11 S *s.s., bhnd til p.u. apr 15th* P 0
625 22/3 Kilworthy (L) MDN 3m 14 G *s.s., towrds rear til b.d. 8th* B -
805 31/3 Wadebridge (L) OPE 3m 5 F *nvr bttr plc, kpt on onepcd* 3 0

Poor performances in 98 & should stick to Maidens 10

HAPPY HENRY(IRE) ch.g. 7 Arapahos (FR) - Pike Run by Deep Run B Dennett

1996 P(0),F(-),F(-),F(-),U(-)
243 22/2 Lemalla (R) MDO 3m 12 S *(fav) ld, jnd & f 16th* F -

Ability but never finishes & vanished after usual fall only start 97 13

HAPPY HULA GIRL (Irish) — **I** 90^{P}, **I** 204^{P}, **I** 263^{F}, **I** 423^{U}, **I** 479^{P}, **I** 539^{5}
HAPPY PADDY ch.g. 14 Paddy's Stream - Inch Tape by Prince Hansel Mrs G M Summers

1996 P(0),4(0),P(0)
381 4/3 Leicester (R) HC 2m 1f 13 G *(bl) bhnd from 5 out.* 7 0
892 5/4 Hereford (R) HC 2m 11 GF *in tch, mstk and wknd 5th, t.o..* 8 0

No longer of any account 0

HAPPY VALLEY b.m. 9 Cruise Missile - Valley Mist by Perhapsburg Captain M B Baker

1996 6(0),8(0),P(0),3(10),2(14)
458 8/3 Great Treth' (R) MDO 3m 15 S *prom early, rear frm 7th, t.o.* 7 0
626 22/3 Kilworthy (L) MDN 3m 14 G *bhnd til p.u. apr 16th* P 0
956 6/4 Black Fores' (R) MDO 3m 4 G *chsd ldr to 10th, 3rd aft, outpcd & no imp 2 out* 3 10
1112 19/4 Flete Park (R) MDN 3m 13 GF *f 1st* F -
1343 3/5 Flete Park (R) MDO 3m 13 G *in tch, mstk 12th, 4th whn hit 3 out, onepcd* 3 10
1486 11/5 Ottery St M' (L) MDO 3m 17 G *sn rear, t.o. & p.u. 14th* P 0
1584 26/5 Lifton (R) MDO 3m 13 G *nvr nr ldrs to chal* 6 0
1615 7/6 Umberleigh (L) MDO 3m 11 F *bhnd, 10th whn hmpd & f 7th* F -

Placed in Maidens 96/7 but worse in 97; novice-ridden & not threatening to win now 11

HARBOUR LEADER (Irish) — **I** 8^{P}, **I** 76^{3}, **I** 85^{1}, **I** 168^{1}, **I** 259^{2}
HARBOUR LIGHT(IRE) ch.g. 6 Dry Dock - Lady Siobhan by Laurence O A Howland Jackson

61 1/2 Horseheath (R) MDO 3m 9 GF *mid-div, mstk 7th, 4th & outpcd 14th, not pshd* 4 0

Good debut but not seen after; should go close if ready in 98 12

HARDEN GLEN b.g. 6 Respect - Polly Peril by Politico (USA) — M H Walton

1996 2(10),3(11),U(-)

420	8/3	Dalston	(R)	MDO 2 1/2m	8	GS	*made all, clr 3 out, easily*	1	16
608	22/3	Friars Haugh	(L)	XX 3m	6	GF	*(fav) ld to 3 out, ev ch whn no ext flat*	2	18
813	31/3	Tranwell	(L)	RES 3m	7	G	*(fav) cls 2nd til disp ld 2nd-10th,hdd nxt,disp ld 2 out,hdd last*	2	18
1499	15/5	Perth	(R)	HC 2 1/2m 110yds	8	GS	*mstks, chsd lding bunch till blnd and lost tch 5 out.*	6	0

Bolted up seasonal debut; failed to last home after; mistakes; should win Restricted; G-S 18

HARDTOBEGOOD (Irish) — I 188^{P}, I 217^{P}, I 388^{B}, I 407^{2}, I 432^{3}, I 576, , I 611^{P}

HARD TO BREAK b.g. 6 High Season - Frogmore Sweet by Morston (FR) — M W A Coffey

1996 **P(NH),P(NH)**

116	9/2	Wetherby Po'	(L)	MDO 3m	14	GF	*s.s. rpd prog to go prom 3rd, fdd 10th, t.o. & p.u. 15th*	P	0
1105	19/4	Hornby Cast'	(L)	MDO 3m	11	G	*ld, disp 6th til hdd 9th, not qckn frm 3 out*	3	10

Placed in poor race 2nd start but may do better with experience 11

HARDY CRACKER (Irish) — I 493^{F}, I 539^{F}

HARDY WOLF ch.g. 6 Little Wolf - Sister Corruption by Bribe — W A P Layton

718	29/3	Llanvapley	(L)	RES 3m	13	GF	*last til p.u. 5th*	P	0
908	5/4	Howick	(L)	MDN 3m	7	F	*jmpd slwly 4th, alwys bhnd, stppd aft 11th*	P	0

Looks hopeless so far 0

HARINGTON HUNDREDS ch.g. 7 Tacheron - Spring Clear by Perspex — Mrs Jean R Bishop

1996 **P(NH)**

284	23/2	Charing	(L)	MDO 3m	17	G	*prom til wknd 11th, wll bhnd & p.u. 14th*	P	0

Very lightly raced & disappeared after showing no great promise 0

HARKEN PREMIER gr.g. 12 Hard Fought - Maraquiba (FR) by Kenmare (FR) — A Jeffries

1996 P(0),P(0),F(-),F(-),P(0),4(0)

1320	3/5	Bonvilston	(R)	CON 3m	8	G	*rear til p.u. 2 out*	P	0

Flat winner 89; no stamina for points 0

HARLEQUIN BAY b.g. 7 Remezzo - New Columbine by New Member — P N Baldwin

643	22/3	Castle Of C'	(R)	MDO 3m	12	G	*s.s. rshd to ld 3rd til apr 7th, 2nd whn f 8th, dead*	F	-

Dead 0

HARMONY RIVER(IRE) ch.m. 9 Orchestra - Serene River by Over The River (FR) — Miss C Holliday

278	23/2	Charing	(L)	RES 3m	17	G	*chsd ldrs, hmpd 8th, lost tch & p.u. 16th*	P	0
462	8/3	Charing	(L)	RES 3m	10	G	*nvr dang, styd on to tk dist 2nd apr last*	2	0
1129	19/4	Penshurst	(L)	RES 3m	6	GF	*trckd ldrs, chal 4 out, ld nxt, styd on strngly*	1	17

Missed 96; recovered form last start - fair performance & can win again; G/F-S, best Soft 19

HARMONY'S CHOICE ch.g. 6 Morgans Choice - Beera Harmony by Shannon Boy — M E Hawkins

1996 P(0),F(-),5(0)

105	8/2	Great Treth'	(R)	MDO 3m	15	GS	*rear, prog to 8th at 12th, lost tch ldrs 14th, p.u. last*	P	0
245	22/2	Lemalla	(R)	MDO 3m	11	S	*prog 9th, 2nd at 15th, disp 3 out, wknd nxt*	2	14
458	8/3	Great Treth'	(R)	MDO 3m	15	S	*b.d. 3rd*	B	-
1485	11/5	Ottery St M'	(L)	MDO 3m	13	G	*(Jt fav) handy, ld 14th, wknd & hdd nr fin*	2	14
1521	17/5	Bratton Down	(L)	MDO 3m	16	GS	*(fav) in tch til f 9th*	F	-

Just beaten in modest race 4th start & should be able to gain reward in 98 15

HARMONY WALK(IRE) b.g. 9 Flair Path - Peaceful Girl by Keep The Peace — H Morton

1996 P(0),4(0)

1077	13/4	Guilsborough	(L)	CON 3m	16	GF	*mid-div, rdn 9th, sn btn, t.o. & p.u. 2 out*	P	0
1351	4/5	Dingley	(R)	CON 3m	7	G	*rear, mod 3rd & rddn 10th, t.o. & p.u. 15th*	P	0
1475	11/5	Garthorpe	(R)	XX 3m	13	GS	*prom, chsd ldr 7th, ld 13th, clr 2 out, styd on wll*	1	19

Restricted winner 95; looked lost cause till finding right ground last start (33/1); can win again 98 20

HARRY FROM BARRY b.g. 9 Cree Song - Lyptosol Gold by Lepanto (GER) — Gwyn R Davies

1996 P(0),P(0),2(0),F(-),1(13)

633	22/3	Howick	(L)	RES 3m	8	GF	*7s-7/2, rear til p.u. 14th*	P	0
1004	12/4	St Hilary	(R)	MEM 3m	4	GF	*3rd til went 2nd 16th, hld whn ref last*	R	-
1227	26/4	Pyle	(R)	RES 3m	15	GS	*last trio til p.u. 6th*	P	0
1556	24/5	Bassaleg	(R)	RES 3m	13	G	*ld 3rd til jinked & u.r. apr 7th*	U	-

Won a bad Maiden in 96 & showed nothing in 97 - non-stayer 0

HARRY'S SECRET (Irish) — I 147^{P}, I 367^{4}

HARRYS SPECIAL(IRE) b.g. 7 Orchestra - Bramble Princess by Gleason (USA) E Tuer
1996 **F(NH),F(NH),F(NH),10(NH),P(NH)**
114 9/2 Wetherby Po' (L) MDO 3m 8 GF *plld hrd, alwys prom, 2nd 3 out, hrd rdn to ld nr fin* 1 15
266 22/2 Duncombe Pa' (R) RES 3m 19 G *(fav) prom, wnt 3rd 14th, ev ch whn u.r. 2 out* U -
1406 5/5 Witton Cast' (R) RES 3m 10 GS *towrds rear, lost tch 13th, p.u. 15th* P 0
Scrambled home in reasonable race 1st start but season interrupted; Restricted chances if fit 98 16

HARRY TARTAR b.g. 6 Cisto (FR) - Tartar Holly Vii by Damsire Unregistered J D Parker
1996 P(0),P(0),4(0),6(0)
61 1/2 Horseheath (R) MDO 3m 9 GF *chsd ldrs to 9th, last whn mstk 12th, p.u. 14th* P 0
275 22/2 Ampton (R) MDO 3m 10 G *u.r. 5th* U -
318 1/3 Marks Tey (L) MDN 3m 13 G *f 3rd* F -
499 15/3 Ampton (R) MDO 3m 9 GF *rr, mstks 5th & 7th, rpd prog to cls 3rd 3 out,onepcd aft* 4 12
1281 27/4 Fakenham P-' (L) MDO 3m 8 G *(fav) rear,jnd ldrs 8th,mstk 13th & outpcd,kpt on to poor 2nd flat* 2 0
1356 4/5 Dingley (R) MDO 3m 9 G *in tch til outpcd 9th, rddn 11th, no resp, p.u. 15th* P 0
Beaten only 2l 4th start (poor race) but usually struggling & is very slow 10

HARVEST HOME(IRE) b.g. 5 Dromod Hill - Carlys Bank by Saucy Kit W P Harper
1037 12/4 Lifton (R) OPE 3m 5 F *alwys bhnd til f 12th* F -
Never figured in only run 0

HARVEST SINGER b.m. 7 Barley Hill - Song Bird by True Song Mrs C T Forber
940 6/4 Tabley (R) RES 3m 9 G *bhnd, last & blndrd 7th, f nxt* F -
1003 12/4 Alpraham (R) MDO 2 1/2m 10 GF *rear whn u.r. 6th* U -
Season lasted 6 days & gave no encouragement 0

HARVEST TIME (Irish) — **I** 33^{4}, **I** 109^{2}
HARVEYSLAND (Irish) — **I** 59^{P}, **I** 92^{2}, **I** 149^{3}, **I** 216, , **I** 386^{3}, **I** 410^{1}, **I** 498^{3}, **I** 543^{U}
HARWALL QUEEN b.m. 14 Tobique - Knights Queen by Arctic Chevalier Miss D Harries
1996 9(0),P(0)
188 15/2 Erw Lon (L) LAD 3m 8 G *1st ride, t.o. frm 8th* 6 0
401 8/3 Llanfrynach (R) LAD 3m 14 G *rear whn f 7th* F -
536 16/3 Erw Lon (L) LAD 3m 9 GF *in rear whn f 15th* F -
844 31/3 Lydstep (L) LAD 3m 6 F *twrds rear, p.u. aft 11th, leather broke* P 0
No longer of any account 0

HARWELD ch.g. 5 Weld - Fruit Farm by Twiberry E H Crow
942 6/4 Tabley (R) MDO 3m 8 G *in tch, jmp slwly 7th, hit 14th, lost tch, p.u. apr 2 out* P 0
1386 5/5 Eyton-On-Se' (L) MDO 2 1/2m 8 GF *(fav) held up,prog frm 8th,strng late run frm 2 out,ld flat,allout* 1 15
Won a weak race but well-regarded by stable & should upgrade in 98 16

HASTY HOURS (Irish) — **I** 36^{F}, **I** 61, , **I** 222^{5}, **I** 344^{2}, **I** 401^{1}
HA-TO-SIEE(IRE) b.g. 9 Burslem - Ingrid Volley (ITY) by Romolo Augusto (USA) Mrs Charlotte Cooke
1996 P(0)
927 6/4 Garthorpe (R) RES 3m 9 GF *cls up 6th, wknd 9th, p.u. 12th* P 0
1278 27/4 Fakenham P-' (L) RES 3m 11 G *ld to 2nd, wknd 9th, t.o. & p.u. 15th* P 0
No longer of any account 0

HATTERILL RIDGE br.g. 7 Rustingo - Nun Owen by Owen Anthony A C James
1996 1(11),P(0),F(-),P(0),P(0),4(0)
190 15/2 Erw Lon (L) RES 3m 11 G *in tch, mstk 9th, sn wknd, t.o. & p.u. 13th* P 0
260 22/2 Newtown (L) RES 3m 16 G *(bl) ld to 3rd, wknd 9th, t.o. & p.u. aft 13th* P 0
Members winner 1st start 96; finished only 1 of next 7 races & 97 season lasted a week 0

HATTON CLOUD b.m. 7 Governor General - Piglet by Kemal (FR) Mrs G A Spencer
665 23/3 Eaton Hall (R) MDO 3m 11 GF *alwys rear, t.o. & p.u. 4 out, school* P 0
Rarely seen & shows nothing 0

HAVEAFEWMANNERS (Irish) — **I** 32^{F}, **I** 62^{P}, **I** 125^{1}, **I** 325^{3}, **I** 434^{F}
HAVE ANOTHER (Irish) — **I** 242^{P}
HAVEN ch.g. 7 North Street - Tandys Tonic by Full Of Beans B F W Rendell
1996 R(-)
795 31/3 Bishopsleigh (R) MDO 3m 12 G *mid-div til ran out 7th* r -
1485 11/5 Ottery St M' (L) MDO 3m 13 G *ran out 1st* r -
1520 17/5 Bratton Down (L) MDO 3m 17 GS *s.s. bhnd & jmpd poorly til ref 3rd* R -
Nasty 0

HAVEN LIGHT b.g. 10 Flower Robe - Points Review by Major Point — Mrs J P Spencer
1996 U(-),1(16)

700	29/3	Upper Sapey	(R)	MEM	3m	8	GF	*ld frm 4th, 3l clr 10th, disp ld whn f 3 out*	F	-
1014	12/4	Bitterley	(L)	OPE	3m	9	GF	*ld frm 4th, 10l up 12th, ct aft 14th, wknd & p.u. 2 out*	P	0
1235	26/4	Brampton Br'	(R)	INT	3m	10	G	*hld up, prog 9th, effrt 14th, no ch wth 1st pair frm 16th*	3	0
1390	5/5	Cursneh Hill	(L)	INT	3m	4	GF	*(Jt fav) cls 2nd/disp til efft to ld 14th, wknd qckly & p.u. aft nxt*	P	0
1523	17/5	Bredwardine	(R)	CON	3m	7	G	*hld up bhnd, prog 7th, chsd wnr apr 2 out, no ext flat*	2	18
1576	26/5	Chaddesley '	(L)	XX	3m	12	F	*hld up,prog 7th,ld 12-14th & 15th-nxt,ld apr last,drvn out*	1	23

Barely stays but change of tactics worked & won fair race; win again in right conditions 98; Firm 21

HAVEN'T AN OCEAN (Irish) — I 55[1], I 93[1]

HAWAIIAN PRINCE b.g. 13 Hawaiian Return (USA) - Wrong Decision by No Argument — Miss Tina Hammond
1996 2(0)

1167	20/4	Hexham Poin'	(L)	MEM	3m	5	GF	*ld to 3rd, 2l 3rd 15th, outpcd apr 3 out, lost tch*	3	0

Turns out for an annual constitutional 0

HAWAIIAN REEF b.g. 10 Henbit (USA) - Raffmarie by Raffingora — M W Wells
1996 P(0)

445	8/3	Newton Brom'	(R)	MEM	3m	3	G	*(fav) ld til ref 4th, cont, ref 6th twice & u.r.*	R	-

Rarely seen & favourite for a non-event 0

HAYDON HILL ch.m. 6 Hadeer - Coppice by Pardao — Mrs E Gosling
1996 P(0),1(15),P(0),3(17)

989	12/4	Kingston Bl'	(L)	INT	3m	7	GF	*s.s. sn prom, mstk 3rd, ld 6-15th, wknd 2 out*	4	14
1450	10/5	Kingston Bl'	(L)	LAD	3m	7	G	*s.v.s. last til aft 5th, some prog, wknd 8th, p.u. aft 15th*	P	0

Maiden winner 96; changed hands; ran well 1st start but tricky ride; still has Restricted chance 15

HAYESTOWN HOPE (Irish) — I 61[U], I 224[P]

HAYNE LASS b.m. 9 Nearly A Hand - Holcombe Lass by Baltus — William R H Barons

740	29/3	Higher Kilw'	(L)	MDN	3m	15	GF	*rear, mstk 2nd, t.o. & p.u. 5th*	P	0

Soon vanished 0

HAZY MIST (Irish) — I 8[P], I 79[P], I 234[P]

HAZY SEA (Irish) — I 260[P], I 564[2]

HEALING THOUGHT (Irish) — I 353[P], I 610[1]

HEARTS ARE WILD ch.g. 10 Scallywag - Henry's True Love by Random Shot — Miss Polly Gundry
1996 **8(NH),15(NH),4(NH)**

818	31/3	Paxford	(L)	LAD	3m	3	F	*chsd ldr, ld 8th-14th, ld nxt, drew clr 3 out, easily*	1	20

Winning chaser; bolted home in virtual non-event only start; could win proper race if fit 98 21

HEATHER BOY b.g. 8 Whistlefield - Calfstown Maid by Master Buck — Miss K Leake
1996 P(0),2(0),3(13),F(-),5(0),4(16),4(10)

409	8/3	Llanfrynach	(R)	MDN	3m	12	G	*(fav) ld 5th-13th, 2nd aft til wknd rpdly 3 out*	5	0
540	16/3	Erw Lon	(L)	MDN	3m	13	GF	*chsd wnr to 9th, wknd, rear & p.u. 2 out*	P	0
1186	20/4	Lydstep	(L)	MDO	3m	7	GF	*ld to 10th, wknd rpdly, p.u. 14th*	P	0

Changed hands 97 & looks a lost cause now 0

HEATHER QUEEN (Irish) — I 227[U], I 350[F]

HEATHERTON PARK b.m. 6 El Conquistador - Opt Out by Spartan General — H Wellstead
1996 U(-),P(0),3(14),F(-)

182	15/2	Larkhill	(R)	MDO	3m	12	G	*chsd ldrs, went 2nd 9th, ld apr 13th til ran out 3 out*	r	-

Promise in 96 but looks impossible to settle & suffered mishap only start 97 15

HEATHER WOOD br.m. 7 Lighter - Irish Rose by Soldier Rose — R Benbow
1996 P(0)

262	22/2	Newtown	(L)	RES	3m	15	G	*last & n.j.w., t.o. & p.u. 14th*	P	0
1015	12/4	Bitterley	(L)	MDO	3m	12	GF	*ld til ran out 5th*	r	-
1065	13/4	Maisemore P'	(L)	MDO	3m	13	GF	*mstks, prom, lost plc 8th, t.o. & u.r. 13th*	U	-
1238	26/4	Brampton Br'	(R)	MDO	3m	10	G	*ld frm 5th til hdd aft 12th, wknd & p.u. 15th*	P	0

Makes mistakes & no signs of ability 0

HEATHVIEW b.g. 10 Pitpan - Whosview by Fine Blade (USA) — Mrs Peter Corbett
1996 **3(NH),2(NH),3(NH),8(NH)**

396	8/3	Barbury Cas'	(L)	CON	3m	9	G	*mid-div, 6th & outpcd 11th, lft poor 4th 14th, p.u. nxt*	P	0
742	29/3	Barbury Cas'	(L)	MEM	3m	5	F	*made all, clr 12th, unchal*	1	15
872	31/3	Hackwood Pa'	(L)	CON	3m	4	F	*ld 4th, jmpd rght, qcknd & 6l up whn lft clr last*	1	19

1054 13/4 Hackwood Pa' (L) CON 3m 4 GF *(fav) jmpd rght, mstk 12th, ld til hdd & f 2 out* F 17
1569 26/5 Fontwell (R) HC 3 1/4m 110yds 10 GF *hdwy 9th, ld 12th to 15th, mstk next, led apr 3 out to last, soon outpcd.* 2 20

Winning chaser 95; found 2 weak contests; not entirely genuine; should win again; R/H?; Firm 20

HEAVENLY HOOFER b.g. 14 Dance In Time (CAN) - Heavenly Chord by Hittite Glory Miss E Johnston
1996 P(0),3(0)
1423 10/5 Aspatria (L) MEM 3m 3 G *last til prog to ld 15th-16th, rdn & wknd 2 out* 3 0

No longer of any account 0

HECTORS WAY ch.g. 6 Doctor Wall - Ty-Pren by Precipice Wood S J Smith
435 8/3 Upton-On-Se' (R) MDO 3m 14 G *in tch to 8th, lost plc & outpcd 10th, t.o. & p.u. 15th* P 0
876 1/4 Upton-On-Se' (R) MEM 3m 7 GF *prom,blnd 9th,ld 15th,blnd & nrly ran off course nxt,nt rcvr* 3 0
1016 12/4 Bitterley (L) MDO 3m 14 GF *cls 6th at 12th, wknd 14th, no ch whn p.u. 3 out, dsmntd* P 0

Looked unlucky 2nd start but problem after; may find a chance if fit 98 14

HEDDON VALLEY b.g. 6 Nearly A Hand - Arctic Mission by The Parson Mrs N G Smyth
175 15/2 Ottery St M' (L) RES 3m 15 G *rear whn p.u. 11th* P 0
313 1/3 Clyst St Ma' (L) RES 3m 10 HY *rear, f 6th* F -
526 15/3 Cothelstone (L) MDN 3m 15 GS *in tch whn f hvly 6th* F -
1095 16/4 Hockworthy (L) MDN 3m 11 GF *bhnd, poor 7th at 10th, sn t.o., fin well* 4 0

Jumps badly but glimpse of better to come last start 11

HE IS ch.g. 7 Gunner B - Barvadel by Le Bavard (FR) T Hamlin
1996 3(12),1(15)
240 22/2 Lemalla (R) RES 3m 11 S *alwys prom, disp 11th-14th, outpcd nxt, lft 2nd last* 2 17
524 15/3 Cothelstone (L) RES 3m 10 GS *prog 9th, lft 2nd 12th, ld nxt, sn clr, comf* 1 18

Maiden winner 96; romped home in Restricted 97; only 5 runs to date & should upgrade; G-S 21

HELD TO RANSOM ch.g. 5 Revlow - Chantage by Sweet Revenge Mrs M Brown
599 22/3 Horseheath (R) MDO 3m 4 F *n.j.w. lost tch 10th, p.u. nxt* P 0
1282 27/4 Fakenham P-' (L) MDO 3m 8 G *alwys bhnd, rdn 14th, sn no ch* 4 0

Beaten miles 2nd start & yet to learn to jump 0

HELLOFAHOOLY (Irish) — **I** 55^{P}, **I** 156^{1}, **I** 215^{P}
HELLUVAGALE (Irish) — **I** 265^{F}, **I** 496^{5}, **I** 574^{P}
HEMERO (Irish) — **I** 352^{P}, **I** 425^{5}, **I** 449^{2}, **I** 510^{4}
HENCEYEM(IRE) ch.g. 9 Fine Blade (USA) - What Vision by Golden Vision J M Walker
1996 P(0),4(0),P(0)
120 9/2 Wetherby Po' (L) MDO 3m 18 GF *rear, mstk 4th, nvr dang, t.o.* 5 0

Beaten miles only start 97 & looks a dud 0

HENLEYDOWN (Irish) — **I** 144^{2}, **I** 208^{2}, **I** 448^{3}
HENLEY KNAPP (Irish) — **I** 269^{P}
HENNERWOOD OAK b.m. 7 Lighter - Welsh Log by King Log Cyril Thomas
1996 P(0),3(0),F(-),1(15),P(0),5(12),**U(-)**
90 5/2 Ludlow (R) HC 2 1/2m 6 G *patiently rdn, smooth hdwy to chal from 4 out, ev ch till hit 2 out, kept on same pace run-in.* 2 20
254 22/2 Newtown (L) MEM 3m 6 G *chsd wnr 4th-12th, wknd, t.o.* 4 0
587 19/3 Ludlow (R) HC 2 1/2m 18 GF *mstk 4th, alwys bhnd, t.o. when p.u. before 2 out.* P 0

Maiden winner 96; does not stay & H/Chase 2nd worth little; hard to find a chance now 14

HENRIETTA BOO BOO br.m. 7 Jupiter Island - Kadra by High Top G J Green
1996 **6(NH)**
570 16/3 Garnons (L) MDN 2 1/2m 14 G *nvr nr ldrs, wll btn whn p.u. last* P 0
1240 26/4 Brampton Br' (R) MDO 3m 12 G *cls up to 13th, wknd 15th, p.u. 2 out* P 0
1386 5/5 Eyton-On-Se' (L) MDO 2 1/2m 8 GF *alwys cls up, ld 4 out til hdd run in, ran on wll.* 2 13
1541 18/5 Wolverhampt' (L) MDO 3m 15 GS *(fav) chsng grp, 3rd at 14th, sn btn, p.u. 3 out* P 0

Touched off in weak race & may not have handled ground after; should have chances in 98 14

HENRY DARLING b.g. 11 Tudorville - Custard by Darling Boy Mrs B F Abraham
1996 2(14),3(10),1(15),9(0),F(-)
213 16/2 Southwell P' (L) RES 3m 16 GS *mid-div, went prom 9th, outpcd frm 14th* 6 12
348 2/3 Market Rase' (L) RES 3m 13 GF *mid-div, 4th 2 out, styd on, not trbl wnr* 2 16
676 23/3 Brocklesby ' (L) RES 3m 14 GF *mid-div, 7th & just in tch whn f 12th* F -

Maiden winner 96; ground against 97 & lame last start; best watched at 12 15

HENRY GALE b.g. 10 Strong Gale - Bams Crown by Young Emperor — P D F Strawson

247	22/2 Brocklesby '	(L) MEM 3m	4	G	*disp, ld 6th/7th & frm 5 out, drew clr frm nxt*	1	0

Won a joke race 10

HENRY HIGGINS b.g. 7 Gambler's Cup (USA) - Poor Girl by Richboy — Mrs G Hunter

341	1/3 Corbridge	(R) MDN 3m	10	G	*rear whn u.r. 1st*	U	-
419	8/3 Dalston	(R) MDO 2 1/2m	10	GS	*s.v.s. school & bhnd, t.o. 10th, p.u. last*	P	0
730	29/3 Alnwick	(L) MDO 2 1/2m	9	F	*handy 4th til lost tch frm 6th, sn t.o.*	6	0

Last & beaten imles on only completion 0

HENRYMYSON b.g. 9 Sunyboy - Toumanova by High Line — F D Cornes

1996 **U(-),5(0)**

204	15/2 Weston Park	(L) RES 3m	13	G	*rear whn p.u. 14th*	P	0
258	22/2 Newtown	(L) RES 3m	14	G	*wll bhnd, t.o. 13th, lft poor 3rd 3 out, wknd*	4	0
332	1/3 Eaton Hall	(R) RES 3m	18	GS	*rear whn u.r. 11th*	U	-
664	23/3 Eaton Hall	(R) MDO 3m	12	GF	*mid to rear, last whn p.u. 3 out*	P	0
849	31/3 Eyton-On-Se'	(L) OPE 3m	7	GF	*ld 4-12th, fdd 5 out, no ch whn ref last*	R	-

Beaten miles on only completion & looks to have no prospects 0

HENRYS NO PUSHOVER b.g. 8 Push On - Shylyn by Hay Chas — F G Hollis

558	16/3 Ottery St M'	(L) INT 3m	6	G	*handy til wknd 9th, p.u. aft nxt*	P	0
631	22/3 Kilworthy	(L) INT 3m	8	G	*in tch, 3rd whn mstk 10th, blndrd & u.r. nxt*	U	-
1484	11/5 Ottery St M'	(L) OPE 3m	7	G	*n.j.w. chsd ldrs, 2nd at 12th, tired 2 out, dmtd flat*	4	18

Last but not disgraced final outing & may find a race in 98 18

HENRY THE LAD (Irish) — I 601[P]

HENSUE b.g. 8 Henricus (ATA) - Sue Ming Vii — Miss P J Boundy

1996 P(0),P(0),1(19),2(19),1(16),3(15),3(15),2(14)

171	15/2 Ottery St M'	(L) OPE 3m	9	G	*in tch to 12th, wknd nxt, p.u. 14th*	P	0
310	1/3 Clyst St Ma'	(L) INT 3m	9	HY	*in tch to 13th, outpcd frm 3 out*	3	14
863	31/3 Kingston St'	(R) OPE 3m	4	F	*(Jt fav) hndy, disp aft 4 out, ev ch til no ext 2 out*	2	16
1043	12/4 Cothelstone	(L) INT 3m	7	GF	*alwys mid-div, lft 2nd 14th, outpcd frm 3 out*	3	17
1244	26/4 Bratton Down	(L) CON 3m	14	GS	*alwys prom, ev ch 3 out, no ext cls home*	4	13
1440	10/5 Holnicote	(L) OPE 3m	3	G	*hld up, went 2nd apr 11th, ev ch til no ext frm 3 out*	2	16
1547	24/5 Mounsey Hil'	(R) MEM 3m	9	G	*(fav) chsd ldrs, ld 9th, made rest, blnd last, hld on und pres*	1	16
1594	31/5 Bratton Down	(L) INT 3m	10	F	*ld 6th-9th, lost plc 12th, strggling frm 15th*	6	14
1611	7/6 Umberleigh	(L) OPE 3m	8	F	*in tch in rear til s.u. btwn 4th & 5th*	S	-

Dual winner 96; safe but one paced & struggled mostly 97; Members best hope again; Any 17

HERB SUPERB (Irish) — I 34[F], I 99[F], I 275[1], I 395[2], I 437[1]

HERE COMES CHARTER b.g. 12 Le Moss - Windtown Fancy by Perspex — E Pennock

1996 5(0),3(12),2(13),6(0),1(13),P(0)

77	2/2 Market Rase'	(L) RES 3m	9	GF	*hld up, nvr on trms, t.o. frm 12th*	5	0
266	22/2 Duncombe Pa'	(R) RES 3m	19	G	*plld hrd,prom,ld 4th til hd bfr 10th,sn wknd,t.o.& p.u.14th*	P	0
422	8/3 Charm Park	(L) CON 3m	8	GF	*prom til fdd 13th, lft remt 3rd 3 out*	3	13
855	31/3 Charm Park	(L) MEM 3m	3	F	*trckd ldr, disp 4 out, ld nxt, hdd 2 out, outpcd flat*	2	14
1072	13/4 Whitwell-On'	(R) MXO 4m	21	G	*mid-div, strggling 14th, t.o. 19th, p.u. 2 out*	P	0
1250	26/4 Easingwold	(L) RES 3m	15	GS	*alwys rear, no ext, p.u. 14th*	P	0

Members winner 96; outlcassed 97 & Members again only real chance in 98 13

HERE NOW (Irish) — I 202[P], I 512[1], I 546[P]

HERES HOLLY (Irish) — I 270[P], I 349[F], I 458[P], I 531[3], I 547[P], I 590[5]

HERHORSE ch.m. 10 Royal Vulcan - Ditchling Beacon by High Line — Mrs K Garcia-Olmo

1996 4(11),P(0),P(0),P(0)

172	15/2 Ottery St M'	(L) MDN 3m	14	G	*alwys mid-div, nvr on trms*	5	0
243	22/2 Lemalla	(R) MDO 3m	12	S	*cls 5th at 10th, lft 3rd 16th, styd on, tk 2nd nr fin*	2	12
493	12/3 Newton Abbot	(L) HC 2m 5f 110yds	11	HY	*chsd ldrs, hit 6th, soon rcvred ld 2 out, left well clr last.*	1	24
1416	10/5 Newton Abbot	(L) HC 2m 5f 110yds	14	G	*held up, hdwy when hit 5 out, weakening when mstk 3 out.*	5	22

Went from maiden pointer to H/Chase winner in one leap; off 2 months after; hard to place 98; S-Hy ... 23

HERONIMUS BOSCH (Irish) — I 20[F]

HETTY BELL gr.m. 5 Say Primula - Queen Bell by King Sitric — K Waters

160	15/2 Lanark	(R) MDO 2m 5f	10	G	*sn wll bhnd, p.u. 2 out*	P	0
340	1/3 Corbridge	(R) MDN 3m	10	G	*sn wll bhnd, p.u. 12th*	P	0
564	16/3 Lanark	(R) MDO 2 1/2m	13	GS	*strgglng whn f 8th*	F	-
815	31/3 Tranwell	(L) MDO 2 1/2m	14	G	*alwys rear div*	9	0

Beaten long way only completion & no promise yet 0

HEY BINGO b.m. 8 Welsh Captain - Mindblowing by Pongee — Tom S L Joule

13 25/1 Cottenham (R) MDO 3m 10 GF *wll bhnd 10th, t.o. & p.u. 12th* P 0

No promise & gone by 2nd weekend 0

HEY CHIEF (Irish) — **I** 155⁴, **I** 366ᵁ, **I** 536ᴾ, **I** 550², **I** 594²

HICKELTON LAD ch.g. 13 Black Minstrel - Lupreno by Hugh Lupus — Miss B W Palmer

1996 **P(0),F(NH),4(18),1(20),R(NH),F(-)**

90 5/2 Ludlow (R) HC 2 1/2m 6 G *chsd ldrs, hrd at work to keep up 5 out, soon lost tch, t.o..* 4 0
389 8/3 Sandown (R) HC 2 1/2m 110yds 6 G *blnd 1st, hdwy 10th, wknd apr 3 out.* 5 14
588 19/3 Towcester (R) HC 2 3/4m 4 GF *ld after 1st to 5th, ev ch apr 2 out, kept on same pace run-in.* 2 16
782 31/3 Towcester (R) HC 2 3/4m 3 GF *alwys 3rd, lost tch 8th, mstk next, t.o..* 3 0
1488 12/5 Towcester (R) HC 2m 110yds 16 GS *alwys bhnd, t.o. when p.u. before 2 out.* P 0
1590 31/5 Stratford (L) HC 3m 9 G *struggling and well bhnd before hfwy, t.o. when p.u. before 2 out.* P 0

H/Chase winner 96; outclassed now & no real prospects at 14 14

HICKEYS TAVERN (Irish) — **I** 303⁴, **I** 424³, **I** 597³

HICKORY HOLLOW ch.g. 6 Lighter - Caubeen by Scottish Rifle — Mrs J K Peutherer

259 22/2 Newtown (L) MDN 3m 18 G *n.j.w. wll bhnd, t.o. & p.u. 9th* P 0

No promise 0

HICKY JIGGER b or br.m. 8 Riberetto - Middletown Girl by Steel City — R Teague

848 31/3 Eyton-On-Se' (L) MEM 3m 6 GF *cls up to 13th, outpcd 4 out, p.u. 3 out* P 0

Showed up for a long way but nothing concrete yet 0

HIDDEN DOLLAR ch.g. 13 Buckskin (FR) - Famous Lady by Prefairy — G Heal

1996 1(13)

239 22/2 Lemalla (R) OPE 3m 7 S *prom, 2nd hlfwy, outpcd 15th, 4th 3 out, no ext* 5 16
552 16/3 Ottery St M' (L) OPE 3m 6 G *trckd ldr to 14th, rdn 4 out, no respns* 3 17
628 22/3 Kilworthy (L) CON 3m 12 G *f 1st, (destroyed)* F -

Dead 15

HIDDEN HOLLOW (Irish) — **I** 94¹, **I** 215², **I** 367¹

HI DIXIE (Irish) — **I** 72¹

HIGH BEACON ch.g. 10 High Line - Flaming Peace by Queen's Hussar — N J Pewter

272 22/2 Ampton (R) LAD 3m 7 G *(bl) wth ldrs til wknd qkly 7th, p.u. appr nxt, lame* P 0

Of no account & problems to boot 0

HIGH CHARGES (Irish) — **I** 18ᴾ

HIGH CHURCH ANNIE (Irish) — **I** 312ᶠ, **I** 329ᶠ, **I** 370ᴾ

HIGHFURLONG(IRE) ch.g. 7 Doulab (USA) - Cheerful Heart by Petingo — Mrs A Kemp

1209 26/4 Clifton On ' (L) MDO 3m 16 GS *mid-div, 9th at 10th, wknd & p.u. 5 out* P 0
1353 4/5 Dingley (R) MDO 2 1/2m 9 G *chsd ldrs til 3rd & outpcd frm 12th* 3 0

Well-beaten in modest race 2nd start & improvement needed to figure in 98 0

HIGH GUARDIAN ch.g. 8 Amerian (USA) - Hypetra by One Little Boy — Mrs J Greenhaf

3 19/1 Barbury Cas' (L) XX 3m 14 GF *blnd 6th, alwys bhnd, t.o. 11th* 9 0
185 15/2 Erw Lon (L) MDN 3m 14 G *alwys rear, no ch 13th, kpt on* 4 0
409 8/3 Llanfrynach (R) MDN 3m 12 G *mid-div, gd prog 14th, onepcd frm nxt* 4 10

Missed 96; not disgraced last start but finished early; more needed for a win 11

HIGH HOPES ch.g. 6 Lyphento (USA) - Ma-Bellona by Sweet Revenge — Miss D M M Calder

417 8/3 Dalston (R) MDO 2 1/2m 11 GS *ld to 4th, ld 8th, mstk nxt, clr 2 out, pshd out* 1 16

Good start & clear-cut win; could prove aptly named in ready in 98 18

HIGH INTAKE b.g. 5 Primitive Rising (USA) - Cornetta by Cornuto — Mrs K Tutty

210 16/2 Southwell P' (L) MDO 3m 15 GS *alwys rear, lost tch 11th, p.u. nxt* P 0
620 22/3 Hutton Rudby (L) MDO 3m 10 GF *rear, prog 13th, wnt 2nd 16th, ev ch last, outpcd* 2 13

Showed enough 2nd start for winning hopes if ready in 98 14

HIGH ISLAND (Irish) — **I** 459ᴾ, **I** 482ᴾ, **I** 545,

HIGHLAND BUCK (Irish) — **I** 122ᴾ, **I** 173⁶, **I** 246³, **I** 331³, **I** 417², **I** 526³

HIGHLAND CALL (Irish) — **I** 19, , **I** 166⁵, **I** 235², **I** 384ᴾ

HIGHLAND CHASE ch.g. 8 Kaytu - Thetford Chase by Relkino M J Jackson
1996 5(0),P(0),P(0)
1387 5/5 Cursneh Hill (L) MEM 3m 3 GF *ld 2n-5th, 10l 3rd 13th, ld brfly apr 3 out, sn outpcd* 3 0
Of no account **0**

HIGHLANDER(IRE) b.g. 8 Shernazar - Bonny Brae by Cure The Blues (USA) Yoshiki Akazawa
1996 **3(NH),5(NH),5(NH),2(NH),1(NH),3(NH),4(NH)**
1187 20/4 Garthorpe (R) MEM 3m 9 GF *sn wll bhnd, t.o. & jmpd slwly 4th, p.u. 13th* P 0
.... **0**

HIGHLAND FRIEND ch.g. 9 Highlands - Friendly Wonder by Be Friendly Henry Bell
1996 4(11),1(13),4(12),1(22),**7(0)**,3(21),**P(0)**
119 9/2 Wetherby Po' (L) OPE 3m 15 GF *rear, strgglng 4th, lost tch 10th, t.o. & p.u. 3 out* P 0
159 15/2 Lanark (R) OPE 3m 3 G *(bl) 2nd to 8th, lost tch 4 out, poor 3rd whn f 2 out* F -
Dead **17**

HIGHLANDMAN b.g. 11 Florida Son - Larne by Giolla Mear Mrs Hugh Fraser
1996 **7(NH),P(NH),8(NH)**
67 1/2 Wetherby (L) HC 3m 1f 10 G *in tch till outpcd hfwy, no ch after.* 7 17
379 4/3 Leicester (R) HC 3m 7 G *alwys prom, ld 10th to 6 out, left in ld after 3 out, soon hdd, led run-in, driven out.* 1 21
583 17/3 Newcastle (L) HC 3m 8 GF *ld, hdd 13th, disp ld till outpcd apr last, styd on well und pres towards fin.* 2 23
890 4/4 Aintree (L) HC 2 3/4m 14 G *midfield, chsd ldrs 8th, outpcd after 12th (Canal Turn), styd on apr 2 out, unable to chal.* 2 22
Winning chaser; very one paced; fortunate winner but ran well after; may win at 12; stays **24**

HIGHLAND TALK ch.g. 11 Le Bavard (FR) - Kintrout by Little Buskins Miss J S S Garrett
877 1/4 Upton-On-Se' (R) RES 3m 17 GF *jmpd bdly, bhnd whn ref 6th* R -
1497 14/5 Cothelstone (L) MDO 3m 10 GF *jmpd slwly 6th, sn bhnd, t.o. 13th* 6 0
Rarely seen & runs badly each time **0**

HIGH PILGRIM (Irish) — **I** 429[5], **I** 512[4]
HIGH RIVER DEN (Irish) — **I** 416[P], **I** 467[P], **I** 508[P]
HIGH STAR (Irish) — **I** 177[1], **I** 465[1]
HIGH THYNE (Irish) — **I** 226[3], **I** 347[5], **I** 398[2]
HIGHWAY FIVE(IRE) ch.g. 9 Carlingford Castle - Final Triumph by Laurence O Lady Susan Brooke
257 22/2 Newtown (L) LAD 3m 12 G *mid-div, mstk 9th, outpcd frm 13th, no ch aft* 7 0
382 5/3 Bangor (L) HC 3m 110yds 6 GS *bhnd and niggld along 5th, cl up 9th, led 4 out to next, pressed ldr, styd on to ld close home.* 1 19
496 15/3 Hereford (R) HC 3m 1f 110yds 10 GF *soon bhnd, t.o. when p.u. before 15th.* P 0
890 4/4 Aintree (L) HC 2 3/4m 14 G *f 1st.* F -
1098 19/4 Bangor (L) HC 3m 110yds 9 G *alwys bhnd, t.o. when p.u. before 13th.* P 0
H/Chase winner 95; struggled home in another weak contest & no other form; hard to win again **17**

HIGHWAY JIM b.g. 12 Dubassoff (USA) - Hilda's Way by Royal Highway Miss M D Burrough
1996 3(14),U(-),3(16),1(10),4(14),3(17),**U(-)**
1153 20/4 Stafford Cr' (R) CON 3m 10 GF *1st ride, alwys last, t.o. whn ref 12th* R -
1274 27/4 Little Wind' (R) XX 3m 8 GF *chsd ldrs til wknd 14th, t.o. & p.u. 2 out* P 0
1369 5/5 Cotley Farm (L) MEM 3m 4 GF *in tch, chal 4 out, disp nxt, rddn & just held* 2 12
1495 14/5 Cothelstone (L) LAD 3m 6 GF *outpcd, t.o. 6th, bad 4th whn u.r. last* U -
1550 24/5 Mounsey Hil' (R) INT 3m 9 G *bhnd, last frm 11th, p.u. 16th* P 0
Schoolmaster & only form in Members now **10**

HIGHWAY LAD b.g. 8 Nearly A Hand - Hilda's Way by Royal Highway M White
1996 5(12),U(-)
43 1/2 Larkhill (R) MDO 3m 10 GF *mstk 6th, ld to 8th, prom aft, outpcd 2 out, fin strngly* 2 14
175 15/2 Ottery St M' (L) RES 3m 15 G *in tch, prog 15th, chal apr last, ld flat, ran on well* 1 17
310 1/3 Clyst St Ma' (L) INT 3m 9 HY *(fav) w.w. prog 11th, chal 13th, rdn 2 out, alwys hld* 2 17
647 22/3 Castle Of C' (R) INT 3m 7 G *chsd ldrs,mstk & lost plc 9th,rdn 14th,no ch & lft 2nd last* 2 12
1156 20/4 Stafford Cr' (R) INT 3m 6 GF *ld 3rd til hdd last, onepcd aft* 2 18
1369 5/5 Cotley Farm (L) MEM 3m 4 GF *(fav) ld til 4 out, hdd & wknd frm 3 out* 3 0
Improved & consistent form till last start; could win modest Intermediate at best; G-Hy **18**

HI HI YOUNG FELLA (Irish) — **I** 407[P], **I** 488[P], **I** 499[U]
HI JAMIE (Irish) — **I** 70[F], **I** 285[1]

HIL LADY b.m. 6 Arctic Lord - First Attempt by Proverb — Miss G Gibson

1996 P(0),U(-),3(0)

405	8/3	Llanfrynach	(R)	RES	3m	15	G	*alwys rear, p.u. 2 out*	P	0
541	16/3	Erw Lon	(L)	MDN	3m	10	GF	*prom, ld 8-10th, ld & f 14th*	U	-
842	31/3	Lydstep	(L)	MDO	3m	12	F	*(Jt fav) twrds rear, prog 14th, sn ev ch, no imp wnr aft*	3	10
1010	12/4	St Hilary	(R)	MDN	3m	10	GF	*(Co fav) cls up, lft 2nd 14th, ran on onepcd*	2	10

Improving slightly but placed in modest races & more needed for a win 13

HILL CRUISE ch.g. 8 Cruise Missile - Danah's Lacquer by Chinese Lacquer — Mrs May Collins

314	1/3	Clyst St Ma'	(L)	MDN	3m	11	HY	*alwys prom, lft in ld 3 out, clr whn f last*	F	13
460	8/3	Great Treth'	(R)	MDO	3m	13	S	*(fav) in tch, ld apr 14th, clr 3 out, easily*	1	15
630	22/3	Kilworthy	(L)	RES	3m	16	G	*(fav) mid-div & not fluent, p.u. apr 14th*	P	0
1275	27/4	Little Wind'	(R)	RES	3m	9	GF	*chsd ldrs, 4th whn f 11th*	F	-

Romped home when winning; ground against after; could win Restricted early 98; Soft 17

HILL DIAMOND (Irish) — **I** 481[P]

HILL FARM KATIE b.m. 6 Derrylin - Kate Brook by Nicholas Bill — D J Miller

1996 **17(NH)**

191	15/2	Erw Lon	(L)	CON	3m	13	G	*prom to 6th, sn wknd, t.o. & p.u. 10th*	P	0
536	16/3	Erw Lon	(L)	LAD	3m	9	GF	*ran out 2nd*	r	-
958	6/4	Pantyderi	(L)	CON	3m	3	F	*p.u. aft 4th*	P	0

Of no account & very hard to steer 0

HILL FORT(IRE) ch.g. 9 Carlingford Castle - Lismoyney Hill by Giolla Mear — F P Luff

1996 4(0),5(0),6(12),3(16),P(0)

4	19/1	Barbury Cas'	(L)	OPE	3m	9	GF	*t.o. 3rd, p.u. 8th*	P	0
183	15/2	Erw Lon	(L)	MEM	3m	3	G	*last til jnd ldrs 13th, sn hrd rdn, ld last, all out*	1	12
260	22/2	Newtown	(L)	RES	3m	16	G	*mid-div, outpcd 13th, 6th & no ch whn blnd & u.r. 14th*	U	-
404	8/3	Llanfrynach	(R)	INT	3m	17	G	*alwys mid-div, onepcd*	7	0
538	16/3	Erw Lon	(L)	RES	3m	5	GF	*chsd wnr, no imp frm 3 out*	2	12
1185	20/4	Lydstep	(L)	RES	3m	5	GF	*alwys chsng wnr, hrd rdn 2 out, alwys hld*	2	13
1227	26/4	Pyle	(R)	RES	3m	15	GS	*chsd ldrs, no prog frm 14th, sn btn*	5	0
1365	5/5	Pantyderi	(L)	RES	3m	10	G	*5th at 3rd, 7th at 11th, no dang aft*	4	14
1472	11/5	Erw Lon	(L)	XX	3m	9	GS	*3rd whn c.o. 5th*	C	-
1556	24/5	Bassaleg	(R)	RES	3m	13	G	*rear, f 3rd*	F	-
1559	24/5	Bassaleg	(R)	XX	3m	4	G	*2nd outing,n.j.w. bhnd frm 9th,t.o.12th,r.o. aft last,cont*	3	0

Changed hands 97; won a poor race & usually well-beaten now; Members only hope again 98 11

HILL ISLAND br.g. 10 Strong Gale - Affordalot by Fordham (USA) — Colin Gee

1996 P(0),6(0),U(-),1(23),1(21),1(23),1(22)

58	1/2	Kingston Bl'	(L)	MEM	3m	5	GF	*(fav) ld 5-9th, wknd rpdly, dist 3rd frm 12th*	3	0
256	22/2	Newtown	(L)	OPE	3m	17	G	*ld to 15th, sn outpcd, rallied 2 out, ran on flat*	2	23
370	2/3	Mollington	(R)	OPE	3m	6	G	*(fav) made virt all, drew clr aft 2 out, rdn out*	1	23
446	8/3	Newton Brom'	(R)	CON	3m	8	G	*(fav) hld up rear, 3rd at 9th, disp 11th, ld aft 16th, styd on*	1	24
1079	13/4	Guilsborough	(L)	OPE	3m	6	GF	*ld 3rd-3 out, ran on wll, no imp wnr*	2	23
1206	26/4	Clifton On '	(L)	OPE	3m	3	GS	*(fav) cls 2nd, jmpd rght, ld 2 out, drew clr*	1	24
1289	30/4	Cheltenham	(L)	HC	3m 1f 110yds	6	GF	*ld 6th to 12th, led again 15th, rdn and hdd 2 out, no ext last*	3	23
1415	9/5	Stratford	(L)	HC	3m	6	G	*(fav) chsd ldr most of way till ld 14th, rdn, still slight ld but held when f 2 out.*	F	21
1534	18/5	Mollington	(R)	OPE	3m	7	GS	*(fav) trckd ldrs, ld 13th-2 out, ev ch flat, no ext und pres*	2	21

Useful pointer; won 7 of last 11; needs a race; more Opens 98 & could win H/Chase; G/F-G/S 24

HILLMILLY b.m. 5 Wonderful Surprise - Snarry Hill by Vitiges (FR) — Roy Robinson

421	8/3	Charm Park	(L)	MEM	3m	6	GF	*rear, detached 2nd, lost tch 10th, t.o. & p.u. 13th*	P	0
623	22/3	Hutton Rudby	(L)	MDO	3m	9	GF	*mid-div, jmp slwly 4th, sn lost tch, p.u. 11th*	P	0
860	31/3	Charm Park	(L)	MDO	3m	12	F	*alwys prom, chsd wnr 13th, alwys hld*	2	12

Good effort last start & looks likely to go one better if ready in 98 15

HILL OF GRACE (Irish) — **I** 25[P], **I** 31[U]

HILL OF TULLA (Irish) — **I** 594[F]

HILLTOP DUKE (Irish) — **I** 57[P], **I** 85[F]

HILLTOWN HOUSE (Irish) — **I** 418[F]

HILL VIEW COTTAGE (Irish) — **I** 13[P], **I** 41, , **I** 49[B]

HILLVIEW LAD br.g. 11 Northern Tempest (USA) - Lady Grosvenor by Above Suspicion — Keith Thomas

1996 P(0),P(0),P(0),U(-),2(0)

118	9/2	Wetherby Po'	(L)	RES	3m	14	GF	*rear, sn dtchd, t.o. & p.u. 14th*	P	0

Placed Irish Maidens 94; no form in England 0

HILLVIEW LASS (Irish) — I 83⁴, I 189ᶠ, I 318⁴, I 383ᴾ

HILLVIEW LIZZIE (Irish) — I 251ᴾ, I 292ᴾ

HILLVIEW SUSIE (Irish) — I 250ᴾ, I 329ᴾ, I 377ᶠ, I 467ᴾ, I 504²

HILTON MILL (Irish) — I 113², I 325¹

HILTONSTOWN LASS (Irish) — I 67, , I 116ᴾ, I 213ᶠ, I 365ˢ, I 376⁴

HINTERTUX b.g. 7 Risk Me (FR) - Linn O' Dee by King Of Spain — Mrs V Thompson

234	22/2	Friars Haugh	(L) MDO 3m	15	G	*prom early, bhnd whn p.u. 13th*	P	0
612	22/3	Friars Haugh	(L) MDN 3m	14	GF	*mstly 2nd til wknd frm 10th*	5	0

May conceivably do better 0

HIRAM B BIRDBATH b.g. 11 Ragapan - At The King's Side (USA) by Kauai King — Steven Astaire

6	19/1	Barbury Cas'	(L) LAD 3m	13	GF	*prom whn blnd & u.r. 4th*	U	-
57	1/2	Kingston Bl'	(L) LAD 3m	13	GF	*(bl) cls up early, bhnd whn p.u. 15th*	P	0
280	23/2	Charing	(L) LAD 3m	12	G	*(bl) mid-div, 6th & wkng whn p.u. 14th*	P	0
850	31/3	Eyton-On-Se'	(L) LAD 3m	6	GF	*(bl) ld to 3rd, ld 5th, made rest, ran on gmly und pres*	1	17
988	12/4	Kingston Bl'	(L) LAD 3m	7	GF	*(bl) lft in ld 4th, jnd whn blnd & u.r. 14th*	U	-
1384	5/5	Eyton-On-Se'	(L) LAD 3m	6	GF	*(bl) prom 5th, ld 7-12th, hdd & wknd 13th, not run on frm 3 out*	4	0
1450	10/5	Kingston Bl'	(L) LAD 3m	7	G	*(bl) mid-div, clsd 7th, no ch frm 12th, rear whn p.u. last*	P	0
1566	25/5	Kingston Bl'	(L) LAD 3m	5	GF	*(bl) made most to 3 out, sn outpcd*	3	11

Missed 96; surprisingly co-operated when winning but usually throws it in now; hard to win again 14

HIS SONG (Irish) — I 333¹

HI-WAY'S GALE (Irish) — I 426⁵, I 454, , I 511⁶, I 569⁵

HOBNOBBER br.g. 10 True Song - Speakalone by Articulate — J H Docker

1996 P(0),2(17),r(-),3(21),**2(19),2(19)**

94	7/2	Newbury	(L) HC 2 1/2m	12	G	*some hdwy from 3 out, not trbl ldrs.*	3	11

Ungenuine & threw away 4 winning chances 96; can only be watched after brief 97 season 18

HODDERS FOLLY (Irish) — I 335ᶠ

HOD WOOD b.m. 6 Lighter - Pamaris by Pamroy — A D Gale

1996 P(0),P(0)

110	8/2	Milborne St'	(L) MDN 3m	7	GF	*rear, lost tch 11th, t.o. & p.u. 13th*	P	0
311	1/3	Clyst St Ma'	(L) LAD 3m	9	HY	*sn bhnd, t.o. & p.u. 2 out*	P	0
555	16/3	Ottery St M'	(L) LAD 3m	10	G	*sn last, jmpd lswly, p.u. 5th*	P	0

Yet to complete the course 0

HOISTTHESTANDARD ch.m. 10 Stanford - Precious Mite by Tambourine II — J R Wright

1996 7(10),F(-),2(13),P(0),4(0),S(-),6(0)

32	26/1	Alnwick	(L) RES 3m	11	G	*mstk 8th, alwys rear, t.o. 15th*	7	0
167	15/2	Witton Cast'	(R) RES 3m	7	F	*rear, prog to chs ldrs 11th, fdd 15th, t.o.*	4	0
429	8/3	Charm Park	(L) MDO 3m	14	GF	*mid-div, imprvd 9th, outpcd 12th & sn lost tch, t.o.*	6	0
616	22/3	Hutton Rudby	(L) RES 3m	14	GF	*s.i.s., rear, wll bhnd frm 3 out, t.o.*	10	0
1100	19/4	Hornby Cast'	(L) CON 3m	9	G	*prom, disp 6th, ld 9-12th, wknd qckly, t.o. whn p.u. 3 out*	P	0

Placed in 4 of 23 starts 93-7 & looks destined to remain a maiden 0

HOLCOMBE HANDFUL ch.g. 8 Nearly A Hand - Holcombe Jane by Baltus — J R Wescott

956	6/4	Black Fores'	(R) MDO 3m	4	G	*hld up, prog to 2nd 11th, chal 2 out, qcknd clr*	1	15

Won a bad race but did it in style & should upgrade in 98 17

HOLCOMBE IDEAL ch.m. 10 Sharp Deal - Holcombe Jane by Baltus — J R Wescott

955	6/4	Black Fores'	(R) MDO 3m	2	G	*(fav) made all, blnd 11th, dist clr nxt, unchal*	1	10
1093	16/4	Hockworthy	(L) RES 3m	16	GF	*mstks, alwys rear, no ch frm 9th, p.u. 5 out*	P	0
1519	17/5	Bratton Down	(L) RES 3m	15	GS	*3rd hlfwy, wknd 13th, t.o. & p.u. 16th*	P	0
1552	24/5	Mounsey Hil'	(R) RES 3m	12	G	*alwys mid-div, no ch frm 15th*	6	0

Won a terrible match & totally outclassed in Restricteds 0

HOLDING THE ACES b.g. 7 Uncle Pokey - Carr-Daile by New Brig — G Vergette

1996 5(12),2(0),F(-),F(-),U(-),U(-)

15	25/1	Cottenham	(R) MDN 3m	7	GF	*ld to 10th, ev ch 16th, wknd 3 out, lft 2nd nxt*	2	0
128	9/2	Cottenham	(R) MDO 3m	10	GF	*mstk 10th, made most to 11th, wknd rpdly, p.u. 14th*	P	0
478	9/3	Southwell P'	(L) MDO 3m	17	G	*mid-div to 4th, lost plc rpdly 7th, p.u. nxt*	P	0
1281	27/4	Fakenham P-'	(L) MDO 3m	8	G	*ld to 13th, ld apr 3 out, sn clr, rdn out*	1	13

Does not stay & has been a disappointment but found bad race last start; follow-up unlikely 13

HOLD THE QUEEN (Irish) — I 322ᴾ, I 384ᴾ

HOLIDAY TIME (Irish) — I 6ᴾ, I 19ᴾ, I 140ᴾ, I 207ᴾ, I 234³, I 302, , I 319ᴾ, I 538³

HOLLAND HOUSE b.g. 11 Sunyboy - Norma Can by Normandy — E Knight

1996 U(-),4(24),**1(32)**,**5(28)**,**1(35)**,**1(35)**

151	12/2	Lingfield	(L)	HC	3m	13	HY	*(fav) chsd ldrs, 3rd when stumbld and u.r. apr 3 out.*	U	-
290	28/2	Newbury	(L)	HC	3m	6	GS	*(fav) made all, hit 5 out and next, clr when mstk 3 out, unchal.*	1	33
494	13/3	Cheltenham	(L)	HC	3 1/4m 110yds	18	G	*held up, pushed along 10th, bhnd when p.u. 6 out.*	P	0
1413	7/5	Uttoxeter	(L)	HC	4 1/4m	7	GS	*(fav) mstks, ld 7th to 19th, weakening when blnd 3 out, 4th and well btn when f last.*	F	-

Very good H/Chaser at best; ground mostly against 97; poor run last start; vulnerable at 12; G-Hy 27

HOLLOW SOUND(IRE) ch.m. 8 Orchestra - Bells Hollow by Rarity — T D Sproat

1996 **11(NH)**,**6(NH)**,**5(NH)**,**F(NH)**,**F(NH)**,**13(NH)**,**P(NH)**,**8(NH)**

540	16/3	Erw Lon	(L)	MDN	3m	13	GF	*made all, unchal frm 14th*	1	16
1008	12/4	St Hilary	(R)	RES	3m	11	GF	*(fav) 2nd til lft in ld 12th, qcknd 3 out, sn clr*	1	18
1181	20/4	Lydstep	(L)	INT	3m	3	GF	*(fav) ld 8-10th, cls up til aft 3 out, fdd, p.u. nxt, dsmntd*	P	0

Ex-Irish; started well (modest races) but problem last start; should upgrade if fit 98 19

HOLLOW SUSPICION(IRE) br.g. 8 Teofane - Little Rastro by Above Suspicion — Miss D A Cruddas

810	31/3	Tranwell	(L)	CON	3m	5	G	*j.w., ld 3rd til hdd & wknd into 3rd 3 out, lost tch frm nxt*	3	0
1511	17/5	Corbridge	(R)	LAD	3m	10	GS	*mid-div, prog to ld 5th-9th, ev ch til wknd 3 out*	8	0

Irish pointing winner 96 (beat Rolier); stamina giving way so far & disappointing 10

HOLLY COURT ch.m. 6 Vital Season - Ambacourt by Leander — Miss Sarah George

753	29/3	Brampton Br'	(R)	RES	3m	9	GF	*taken steadily in rear til f 6th*	F	-

A brief beginning 0

HOLLY FARE b.g. 11 Holly Fern - Last Farewell by Palm Track — C J Wilton Jnr

1996 R(-),P(0),P(0),6(0)

95	8/2	Great Treth'	(R)	MEM	3m	4	GS	*ld 4th til ref & u.r. 7th*	R	-
100	8/2	Great Treth'	(R)	RES	3m	14	GS	*2nd outing, alwys rear, no ch 14th, lft 4th by dfctns, t.o.*	4	0
236	22/2	Lemalla	(R)	INT	3m	12	S	*mstks, rear frm 7th, t.o. & ref 16th*	R	-
1259	27/4	Black Fores'	(R)	RES	3m	7	F	*mid-div til prog 3 out, fin fast*	2	15
1483	11/5	Ottery St M'	(L)	RES	3m	15	G	*mid-div, prog 14th, ev ch 4 out, outpcd aft*	4	14
1579	26/5	Lifton	(R)	CON	3m	9	G	*nvr bttr than mid-div, styd on onepcd flat*	4	15

Maiden winner 93; looked lost cause till last 3 starts but Restricted still unlikely at 12 14

HOLLYMEAD (Irish) — I 31[P]

HOLMBY MILL b.g. 8 Neltino - Truella by True Song — C R Saunders

28	26/1	Marks Tey	(L)	RES	3m	9	GF	*(fav) ld,jmpd slwly 1st,ld agn 3rd,blnd & hdd 9th, wknd 15th,t.o.*	7	0
140	9/2	Thorpe Lodge	(L)	RES	3m	7	GF	*(fav) n.j.w. prom, disp 10th-3 out, onepcd*	3	12
449	8/3	Newton Brom'	(R)	XX	3m	13	G	*j.w. made all, drew clr 2 out, imprssv*	1	20
1077	13/4	Guilsborough	(L)	CON	3m	16	GF	*(fav) ld to 2nd, ld 9th-16th, wknd, 6th whn p.u. 2 out*	P	0

Maiden winner 95; missed 96; only one good run 97; mistakes; likely to atone if fit 98 20

HOMO DORNEY (Irish) — I 303[U], I 333[P]

HONOR MISSION (Irish) — I 332[U], I 399[U], I 460[F], I 539[F], I 588[2]

HOOK LINE'N'SINKER b.g. 11 Kabour - Valpolicella by Lorenzaccio — Ian McLaughlin

1996 **P(0)**,3(15),3(17),**P(0)**,2(18),5(0)

1064	13/4	Maisemore P'	(L)	CON	3m	13	GF	*ld to 2nd, chsd ldrs to 10th, bhnd whn p.u. 15th*	P	0
1146	19/4	Chaddesley '	(L)	CON	3m	6	GF	*cls up til outpcd 13th, sn t.o.*	3	0
1329	3/5	Chaddesley '	(L)	CON	3m	5	GF	*4th whn blnd & u.r. 3rd*	U	-
1403	5/5	Ashorne	(R)	CON	3m	14	G	*in tch, rmndr aft 11th, wknd 14th*	6	10
1574	26/5	Chaddesley '	(L)	CON	3m	8	F	*rear, mstk 10th & rdn, sn wnd, p.u. 13th*	P	0

Just goes through the motions now 0

HOOKY'S TREAT b.m. 6 Dutch Treat - Hookah Girl by Hubble Bubble — Mrs H O Graham

136	9/2	Alnwick	(L)	MDO	3m	16	G	*alwys rear, nvr dang*	9	0
235	22/2	Friars Haugh	(L)	MDO	3m	10	G	*4th hlfwy, sn wknd, p.u. 3 out*	P	0
341	1/3	Corbridge	(R)	MDN	3m	10	G	*rear, prog 10th, not qckn frm 4 out*	2	10
411	8/3	Dalston	(R)	CON	3m	16	GS	*chsd ldrs to 14th, wknd aft 3 out*	7	0
612	22/3	Friars Haugh	(L)	MDN	3m	14	GF	*nvr rchd ldrs, p.u. 4 out*	P	0
733	29/3	Alnwick	(L)	MDN	3m	5	F	*alwys handy, wknd to 8th 3rd at 14th, rallied 4 out, onepcd*	3	10
1171	20/4	Hexham Poin'	(L)	LAD	3m	3	GF	*cls up til mstk 16th, outpcd 3 out*	3	0
1429	10/5	Aspatria	(L)	MDO	3m	15	G	*u.r. 2nd*	U	-
1514	17/5	Corbridge	(R)	MDO	3m	17	GS	*alwys in mid-div, strggling 4 out*	5	0

Very modest, if safe, & looks unlikely to win 10

HOPEFULL DRUMMER b or br.g. 8 Sergeant Drummer (USA) - Hopeful Leigh by Flandre II — W Westacott

1996 F(-),P(0)

50	1/2	Wadebridge	(L)	RES	3m	10	G	*alwys prom, chal 2 out, unable qckn*	2 15
176	15/2	Ottery St M'	(L)	RES	3m	17	G	*mid-div, wknd 14th, p.u. 4 out*	P 0
532	15/3	Wadebridge	(L)	RES	3m	9	GF	*rear early, gd prog 15th, ev ch 2 out, no ext*	4 14
806	31/3	Wadebridge	(L)	RES	3m	6	F	*ld 7th, clr 13th, ran on wll*	1 16

Dual winner 95; revived somewhat 97 & found modest race; more needed when upgraded; G-F 16

HOPEFULLY TRUE (Irish) — I 244, , I 427^{3}, I 451^{P}, I 567^{F}, I 613^{5}

HOPE'S DELIGHT (Irish) — I 546^{1}, I 598^{4}

HORACE b.g. 12 True Song - Spartan Daisy by Spartan General — Mrs A Vaughan-Jones

1996 F(-)

10	25/1	Cottenham	(R)	INT	3m	7	GF	*pckd 1st,ld 3rd,hit 3 out,hdd nxt, wknd last, bttr for race*	4 16
62	1/2	Horseheath	(R)	CON	3m	5	GF	*ld to 5th, lft in ld apr 14th, rdn & hdd 2 out, outpcd*	2 17
123	9/2	Cottenham	(R)	INT	3m	13	GF	*mid-div, prog 11th, 3rd & outpcd 15th, no imp ldrs aft*	4 18
319	1/3	Marks Tey	(L)	CON	3m	11	G	*(fav) in tch,jnd ldrs 10th,chsd wnr frm 16th,onepcd und pres*	2 14
593	22/3	Horseheath	(R)	CON	3m	3	F	*made all, hld on gamely flat*	1 18
769	29/3	Dingley	(R)	CON	3m	14	G	*prom bhnd ldrs, 4th 6 out-4 out, outpcd nxt*	6 0
910	5/4	Cottenham	(R)	CON	3m	3	F	*(fav) ld til apr 10th, ld 13th, kpt on und pres flat*	1 17
1190	20/4	Garthorpe	(R)	INT	3m	8	GF	*chsd ldrs, 3rd & ev ch apr 3 out, onepcd und pres*	3 15

Consistent but slow & found 2 small races; genuine & reliability may see another chance 98 17

HORCUM b or br.g. 12 Sweet Monday - Charlie's Sunshine by Jimsun — Mrs Jayne Barton

1996 F(-),3(0),2(11),P(0),1(16),4(11)

760	29/3	Kimble	(L)	RES	3m	7	GF	*hld up rear, 4th hlfwy, 5th at 15th, btn & p.u. nxt*	P 0
975	8/4	Heythrop	(R)	INT	3m	3	F	*alwys last, lst tch 12th, t.o.*	3 0
989	12/4	Kingston Bl'	(L)	INT	3m	7	GF	*chsd ldrs, wknd aft 13th, sn bhnd*	6 0
1199	23/4	Andoversford	(R)	INT	3m	5	F	*chsd ldrs 5th-8th, last frm 10th, no ch 15th*	5 0
1531	18/5	Mollington	(R)	MEM	3m	6	GS	*in tch til last & jmpd slwly 13th, kpt on frm 2 out*	4 11

Maiden winner 96; ground against 97 & well-beaten; novice-ridden; no real prospects at 13 12

HORNBLOWER b.g. 10 Noalto - Hot Lips Moll by Firestreak — N J Barrowclough

1996 2(21),2(23),1(19),1(22),F(-)

412	8/3	Dalston	(R)	LAD	3m	8	GS	*alwys prom, prssd wnr 3 out, unable to qckn apr last*	3 19
669	23/3	Eaton Hall	(R)	LAD	3m	5	GF	*(fav) chsg grp til ld 2 out, sn in cmmnd, comf*	1 21
885	1/4	Flagg Moor	(L)	LAD	3m	5	G	*(fav) w.w. 2nd at 15th, ld 3 out, rdn apr last, kpt on*	1 20
939	6/4	Tabley	(R)	LAD	3m	9	G	*(fav) prom, ld 13-16th, rddn to ld apr last, styd on*	1 23
1122	19/4	Whittington	(L)	LAD	3m	3	F	*(fav) ld to 14th & frm 16th, ran on wll whn chal last*	1 22
1302	3/5	Weston Park	(L)	LAD	3m	5	G	*(fav) chsng grp, ld 4th, unchal*	1 23
1586	28/5	Cartmel	(L)	HC	3 1/4m	10	GF	*(fav) (vis) ld till after 6th, remained cl up, regained ld 4 out (water), drew clr from last, pushed out.*	1 25

Decent Ladies horse; won 8 of last 10; game; win plenty more in 98; G/S-F 24

HORSETRADER b.g. 5 Aragon - Grovette by Derring-Do — John W Meredith

87	2/2	Wolverhampt'	(L)	MDO	3m	11	GS	*alwys bhnd, mstk 10th, t.o. & p.u. 12th*	P 0

No promise on debut 0

HORTON ch.g. 7 Rafolon (FR) - Salmonway Song by Salmonway Spirit — Mrs Christine M Spurgeon

1485	11/5	Ottery St M'	(L)	MDO	3m	13	G	*sn rear, bhnd whn p.u. 8th*	P 0

Looked less than ready for the fray 0

HORTON COUNTRY br.m. 7 Town And Country - Horton Helen by Flatbush — R J Francome

1996 P(0),P(0),3(0),P(0)

181	15/2	Larkhill	(R)	MDO	3m	17	G	*f 1st*	F -
297	1/3	Didmarton	(L)	MDN	3m	11	G	*in tch, mstk 5th, hmpd 8th & 9th, sn bhnd, p.u. last*	P 0
513	15/3	Larkhill	(R)	MDO	3m	10	GF	*alwys rear, t.o. last whn p.u. 4 out*	P 0

Well beaten in bad race on only completion from 7 starts 96/7 0

HORWOOD DRUMMER b.m. 6 Sergeant Drummer (USA) - Bubbling Spirit by Hubble Bubble — A W Congdon

459	8/3	Great Treth'	(R)	MDO	3m	9	S	*rear, hmpd 11th, t.o. p.u. apr 14th*	P 0
630	22/3	Kilworthy	(L)	RES	3m	16	G	*11th hlfwy, t.o.*	11 0

Last & beaten miles 2nd start 0

HOSTETLER ch.g. 8 Fit To Fight (USA) - Diana's Bow by Great Nephew — Mrs Sally Norris

1996 P(0),P(0),3(0),5(0),9(0),F(-)

545	16/3	Garthorpe	(R)	CON	3m	12	GF	*in tch to 6th, sn bhnd, no ch frm 11th*	9 0
924	6/4	Garthorpe	(R)	CON	3m	6	GF	*mid-div, lft 3rd 10th, went 2nd flat, no ch wnr*	2 11
1076	13/4	Guilsborough	(L)	MEM	3m	9	GF	*alwys rear, strgglng frm 12th, no prog 16th*	6 11
1205	26/4	Clifton On '	(L)	CON	3m	13	GS	*alwys abt 8th, rdn frm 9th, outpcd 5 out*	8 0
1475	11/5	Garthorpe	(R)	XX	3m	13	GS	*prom to 4th, sn bhnd, last hlfwy, t.o.*	7 0
1604	1/6	Dingley	(R)	MEM	3m	4	GF	*disp frm 9th til plodded clr aft 2 out*	1 0

No aptitude & struggled home in desperate race last start - no further prospects 0

HOT MOVE ch.g. 6 Move Off - Hotwave by Hotfoot — Miss G T Lee

621 22/3 Hutton Rudby (L) MDO 3m 10 GF *rear, mstk 1st, efft 11th, outpcd 15th, t.o. whn p.u. 3 out* P 0

Green but showed just a hint of ability 0

HOT SUMMERS (Irish) — **I** 123F

HOUSELOPE BECK ch.g. 7 Meadowbrook - Hallo Cheeky by Flatbush — F V White

1996 P(0),P(0),4(0),F(-),3(15),1(17),2(20),U(-),**4(14)**

33 26/1 Alnwick (L) LAD 3m 12 G *ld to 7th, prom til fdd frm 15th* 5 17

Ladies winner 96; finished 2nd weekend 97 & best watched 17

HOUSELOPE BROOK ch.m. 6 Meadowbrook - Hallo Cheeky by Flatbush — F V White

1996 **8(NH)**

564 16/3 Lanark (R) MDO 2 1/2m 13 GS *not fluent, bhnd whn p.u. 2 out* P 0
728 29/3 Alnwick (L) MEM 3m 4 F *green, alwys last pair, t.o. final m* 3 0
949 6/4 Friars Haugh (L) MDN 3m 10 GF *sn wll bhnd* 4 0
997 12/4 Tranwell (L) MDO 2 1/2m 8 F *alwys prom, wnt 2nd 3 out, 2l down & lft in ld last, ran on* 1 14
1334 3/5 Mosshouses (L) RES 3m 5 F *mostly 2nd frm 11th, kpt on wll flat, just faild* 2 16
1510 17/5 Corbridge (R) RES 3m 13 GS *twrds rear, blnd 13th, f nxt* F -

Got to grips mid-season; form in modest races & fortunate winner; mistakes; may upgrade 15

HOWARYADOON b or br.g. 11 Good Thyne (USA) - Butler's Daughter by Rett Butler — Dr S G F Cave

179 15/2 Larkhill (R) CON 3m 12 G *mid-div til u.r. 6th* U -
304 1/3 Parham (R) LAD 3m 10 G *handy, ld 13th-2 out, ld last, ct line* 2 21
759 29/3 Kimble (L) LAD 3m 4 GF *prog 13th, ld 15th-3 out, no ext aft* 3 19
1396 5/5 High Bickin' (R) MXO 3m 7 G *mstk 7th, prog to chs wnr 16th, wknd nr fin* 3 19
1445 10/5 Peper Harow (L) LAD 3m 6 GF *(fav) in tch, disp 11th, ld 3 out, hit last, rdn out* 1 19
1525 17/5 Bredwardine (R) LAD 3m 9 G *prom til 3rd & outpcd frm 14th, no imp ldrs aft* 3 18
1569 26/5 Fontwell (R) HC 3 1/4m 110yds 10 GF *blnd 3rd, rear after, bhnd when p.u. before 3 out.* P 0

Ladies winner 95; missed 96; not as good now & won weak race; may struggle at 12 19

HOWARYA HARRY(IRE) b.g. 8 Abednego - Bruna Magli by Brave Invader (USA) — P S Burke

1996 **F(NH)**,**2(NH)**

84 2/2 Wolverhampt' (L) MEM 3m 9 GS *jmpd rght, ld 7th, clr 3 out, hng rght & hdd flat, not qckn* 2 16
333 1/3 Eaton Hall (R) INT 3m 10 GS *w.w. late prog, running on fin, nvr plcd to chal* 3 12

Ex-Irish pointer; threw away Members & looks one to avoid if reappearing 16

HOWARYASUN(IRE) b.g. 9 Derring Rose - Suny Salome by Sunyboy — M R Watkins

1996 1(21),**F(-)**,**1(27)**,**1(29)**,**4(18)**,**3(24)**,**1(28)**

153 13/2 Sandown (R) HC 2 1/2m 110yds 6 G *(vis) ld to 4th, cl up, led 3 out till soon after last, no ext.* 2 29

Won 3 H/Chases 96; useful but hard ride; disappeared after good run; can win again if fit 98; Any 27

HOWAYMAN b.g. 7 Faustus (USA) - Our Mable by Posse (USA) — Dennis Waggott

1996 1(19),1(19),1(0),**F(-)**

152 12/2 Musselburgh (R) HC 3m 8 GS *trckd ldrs, ld 4 out, styd on und pres.* 1 22
289 28/2 Kelso (L) HC 3m 1f 8 GS *held up, hdwy hfwy, 2nd when hit 2 out, hmpd last, no ext.* 3 22
562 16/3 Lanark (R) OPE 3m 8 GS *(fav) in tch, ld aft 4 out, sn clr, pshd out flat* 1 23
888 3/4 Aintree (L) HC 3m 1f 9 G *in tch, not fluent 4th, trckd ldrs hfwy till outpcd four out, no ch with wnr.* 2 22
1201 24/4 Perth (R) HC 3m 14 G *(fav) prom, ld 13th till hdd final 100 yards, kept on.* 2 26
1499 15/5 Perth (R) HC 2 1/2m 110yds 8 GS *cl up, disp ld from 8th, ld before 3 out, hdd towards fin.* 2 26
1546 24/5 Hexham (L) HC 2 1/2m 110yds 10 GF *(fav) held up, left 3rd 3 out, ld before last, soon clr.* 1 27

Useful; won 7 of last 8 points & upgraded well to H/Chases; best under 3m; should win more; G/F-S 26

HOWESSHECUTTING (Irish) — **I** 277F, **I** 356P, **I** 394P

HOW FRIENDLY ch.g. 7 Gabitat - Bucks Fizz Music by Be Friendly — R J Mansell

1996 F(-),2(17),P(0),3(15),5(14)

381 4/3 Leicester (R) HC 2m 1f 13 G *chsd ldrs till f 5 out.* F -
575 16/3 Garnons (L) RES 3m 12 G *cls up frm 11th, ev ch 15th, no ext nxt, lost 2nd cls hm* 3 15
701 29/3 Upper Sapey (R) RES 3m 6 GF *15l last by 6th, efft frm 14th, ran on to take 3rd frm 3 out* 3 10
962 6/4 Pantyderi (L) RES 3m 3 F *ld til u.r. 2nd* U -
1196 23/4 Andoversford (R) CON 3m 6 F *prom, ld 3-8th, chsd ldr 13th, styd on gamely to ld flat* 1 17
1319 3/5 Bonvilston (R) INT 3m 8 G *mid-div, prog to 4th at 12th, wknd & p.u. last* P 0
1559 24/5 Bassaleg (R) XX 3m 4 G *(fav) ld to 3rd, trckd ldr 5th, ld 15th, hld on flat* 1 14
1602 31/5 Bassaleg (R) INT 3m 5 F *(fav) w.w. chsd wnr 13th, rdn whn squeezed 3 out, alwys hld,dsmntd* 2 16

Maiden winner 95; modest till well-ridden to land 5th start; problem last run; may struggle in 98 17

HOWS SHE GOING (Irish) — I 60F

HOW SUIR(IRE) ch.g. 9 Carlingford Castle - Suir Lady by Push On — J W Radnor

259 22/2 Newtown (L) MDN 3m 18 G *chsd ldrs, 5th at 10th, wknd 12th, t.o. & p.u. 2 out* 0 0

No threat & soon vanished 0

HUCKLEBERRY FRIEND ch.m. 9 Karlinsky (USA) - Katie Too by Amber Light — Mrs M G Howie

1996 2(0),P(0),F(-),4(0)

284 23/2 Charing (L) MDO 3m 17 G *mid-div, 8th & out of tch whn u.r. 9th* U -
580 16/3 Detling (L) RES 3m 11 F *alwys rear, mstk 15th, p.u. nxt* P 0
829 31/3 Heathfield (R) XX 3m 5 F *alwys last, hit 6th, lsng tch & hit 10th, t.o. & p.u. 2 out* P 0
965 6/4 Penshurst (L) MEM 3m 3 F *set v sedated pce, hvly restrained, hdd 12th,chsd wnr aft* 2 0
1130 19/4 Penshurst (L) MDO 3m 5 GF *ld til p.u. aft 13th, dead* P 0

Dead 0

HUFFIN AND PUFFIN b or br.g. 5 Sulaafah (USA) - Ragsi by Amerian (USA) — Mrs P G Wilkins

630 22/3 Kilworthy (L) RES 3m 16 G *bhnd & schooling til p.u. apr 15th* P 0

Just an educational run to date 0

HUGLI ch.g. 10 Relkino - Hors Serie (USA) by Vaguely Noble — G Hearse

1996 2(18),P(0),3(14)

6 19/1 Barbury Cas' (L) LAD 3m 13 GF *bhnd, 8th & no ch hlfwy, t.o.* 7 0
296 1/3 Didmarton (L) LAD 3m 13 G *alwys bhnd, t.o. 11th, fin fast* 5 10
636 22/3 Howick (L) CON 3m 12 GF *rear, steady prog hlfwy, not rch ldrs* 4 16
1007 12/4 St Hilary (R) OPE 3m 10 GF *prom, went 2nd 16th, cls up & ev ch whn s.u. bnd apr 3 out* S -
1223 26/4 Pyle (R) MEM 3m 6 GS *in tch,slw jmp 8th,outpcd 13th,ran on agn 2 out,onepcd* 3 15
1320 3/5 Bonvilston (R) CON 3m 8 G *(Jt fav) cls up, ld 9th-11th, ld 3 out, qcknd clr* 1 21
1469 11/5 Erw Lon (L) OPE 3m 6 GS *chsd wnr, disp brfly 15th, ev ch 3 out, drvn & wknd nxt* 4 20

Disappointing till change of rider woke him up last 2 starts; may repeat in 98; G/S-F 20

HUGO HENRY (Irish) — I 3², I 82¹, I 256³

HULA b.g. 9 Broadsword (USA) - Blakes Lass by Blakeney — P J Scott Plummer

233 22/2 Friars Haugh (L) MDO 3m 13 G *ldng grp til wknd 4 out* 6 0
415 8/3 Dalston (R) RES 3m 19 GS *prom, ld 12th-aft 3 out, wknd rpdly, 9th whn f 2 out* F -
606 22/3 Friars Haugh (L) MEM 3m 9 GF *cls up whn u.r. flat apr 8th* U -
972 7/4 Kelso (L) HC 3m 1f 12 GF *in tch, hdwy 13th, rdn along and blnd 16th, 4th when b.d. 3 out.* B -

Ran reasonably last start (100/1) & Maiden chances clear on that form if staying in 98 13

HUM 'N' HAW (Irish) — I 65³, I 127¹

HUMPHREY ch.g. 6 Lighter - Woodbury Lane by Sir Nulli — Mrs S M Newell

1528 17/5 Bredwardine (R) MDO 3m 17 G *t.o. 10th, p.u. 12th* P 0

Soon dropped out on debut 0

HUNGRY JACK b.g. 9 Germont - Kale Brig by New Brig — J A T de Giles

1996 5(11),P(0),P(0),2(14),4(10),3(12),1(15),P(0)

45 1/2 Larkhill (R) RES 3m 14 GF *in tch in rear, effrt 14th, styd on onepcd frm nxt* 4 16

Maiden winner 96 (blinkered); changed hands 97; disappeared after passable run 15

HUNTERS CHORUS (Irish) — I 354¹

HURRICANE LINDA b.m. 10 Strong Gale - El Reine by Bargello — Lady Hewitt

1996 F(-),F(-)

1072 13/4 Whitwell-On' (R) MXO 4m 21 G *alwys rear, t.o. whn p.u. 4 out* P 0
1100 19/4 Hornby Cast' (L) CON 3m 9 G *held up, prog 9th, gng wll 4 out, ld apr nxt, ran on strgly* 1 20
1264 27/4 Southwell P' (L) INT 3m 9 G *hld up rear, prog 11th, ld 2 out, drvn & hld on wll nr fin* 1 21
1405 5/5 Witton Cast' (R) CON 3m 10 GS *(fav) held up in rear, prog 3 out, chal last, ld flat, drvn out* 1 22

Returned to form 97; won decent races; Opens possible at 11; game; stays; G/F-G/S 23

HURRICANE MURPHY (Irish) — I 491F, I 548⁴, I 595⁴

HURRICANE RYAN(IRE) b.g. 9 Lafontaine (USA) - Etesian by Tumble Wind (USA) — I McMath

1996 F(-)

36 26/1 Alnwick (L) MDO 3m 15 G *7s-7/2, set mad gallop til ran out apr 7th* r -
338 1/3 Corbridge (R) RES 3m 10 G *keen hld, rear, prog 4th, ld 6th, clr whn p.u. 11th* P 0

May have ability but finds ways of disguising it 0

HYDROPIC b.g. 10 Kabour - Hydrangea by Warpath — Mrs B E Miller

1996 4(0),6(0),7(0),6(0),8(0),5(10),7(0),4(11)

130 9/2 Alnwick (L) INT 3m 7 G *ld aft 3rd to 13th, wknd apr 4 out, p.u. 2 out* P 0
410 8/3 Dalston (R) MEM 3m 5 GS *cls up, ld 12th, sn clr, hdd & wknd aft 3 out* 4 14

611 22/3 Friars Haugh (L) CON 3m 11 GF *u.r. 3rd* U -

Won 1 of last 34 starts; gave it a go in Members but no real chances now 11

HYELORD (Irish) — **I** 3^{1}, **I** 89^{P}, **I** 215^{U}, **I** 495^{1}

HYPERBOLE ch.g. 12 Bali Dancer - Third Lady by Bonne Noel — Dick Chapman

723 29/3 Sandon (L) MDO 3m 6 GF *ld, set str pace, f 11th* F -
999 12/4 Alpraham (R) MDO 3m 8 GF *4th whn f 3rd* F -
1178 20/4 Sandon (L) XX 3m 6 GF *ld at strng pace to 10th, wknd rpdly, p.u. 4 out* P 0
1300 3/5 Weston Park (L) CON 3m 8 G *ld at strng pace to 10th, btn frm 12th, t.o. nxt, p.u. 14th* P 0

Useless - and that's no exaggeration 0

I BLAME THEPARENTS b.m. 10 Celtic Cone - Foxwell by Healaugh Fox — P J Corbett
1996 2(13),5(0),F(-),1(16),4(13)

190 15/2 Erw Lon (L) RES 3m 11 G *prom, ev ch whn p.u. 14th, lame* P 0

Quite promising Maiden winner 96; obvious problem only outing 97 16

ICANTSAY (Irish) — **I** 11^{P}, **I** 74^{P}, **I** 135^{6}, **I** 260^{P}, **I** 378^{3}, **I** 558^{4}, **I** 564^{6}

ICARUS(USA) b.g. 11 Wind And Wuthering (USA) - Cedar Waxwing (USA) by Tom Fool — D H Brown

154 14/2 Fakenham (L) HC 2m 5f 110yds 10 G *(bl) chsd clr ldr, left 2nd 10th, f next, dead.* F -

Dead 0

ICECAPADE(BEL) b.g. 9 Moulouki - Furryrush by Furry Glen — P Riddick
1996 6(0),P(0),1(10),3(0),1(16),F(-),P(0),3(0),F(-)

714 29/3 Llanvapley (L) CON 3m 15 GF *mid-div, f 3rd* F -
903 5/4 Howick (L) CON 3m 6 F *disp to 8th, lost plc nxt, effrt 12th, btn aft 15th* 3 0
1005 12/4 St Hilary (R) CON 3m 10 GF *rear til p.u. 16th* P 0
1133 19/4 Bonvilston (R) INT 3m 8 G *prom early, wknd frm 13th, p.u. 2 out* P 0
1318 3/5 Bonvilston (R) MEM 3m 9 G *prom early, lost plc hlfwy, p.u. 2 out* P 0
1557 24/5 Bassaleg (R) CON 3m 9 G *trckd ldng grp,3rd frm 11th,ran on 2 out,fin wll,just faild* 2 19
1602 31/5 Bassaleg (R) INT 3m 5 F *chsd ldr 4th,ld 12th,rdn 3 out,clr whn blnd last,rdn out* 1 17

Dual winner 96; looked totally out of sorts 97 till last 2 starts; non-stayer; may find race 98 17

ICED GINGER ch.g. 13 Ginger Boy - Snowdrift by Frigid Aire — D Evatt

146 9/2 Tweseldown (R) MDO 3m 10 GF *mid-div, lost ground hlfwy, p.u. aft 11th* P 0
600 22/3 Parham (R) MEM 3m 7 F *(vis) mstks, wll in rear whn p.u. 12th* P 0
833 31/3 Heathfield (R) MDO 3m 7 F *(vis) disp til lft in ld 4th, hdd & blnd 14th, lft poor 2nd last* 2 0

Poor old thing 0

ICKY'S FIVE b.g. 13 Dawn Review - Reengaroga by Brave Invader (USA) — Miss T Habgood
1996 P(0),4(0),7(0),4(10),4(0),8(0),5(0),4(15),**P(0)**,5(10)

217 16/2 Heythrop (R) MEM 3m 4 G *alwys last, bhnd frm hlfwy, no ch aft* 4 0
371 2/3 Mollington (R) LAD 3m 9 G *ld to 2nd, wknd frm 10th, t.o.* 7 0
652 22/3 Siddington (L) LAD 3m 5 F *in tch to 10th, t.o. 14th, went dist 3rd 2 out* 3 0
819 31/3 Paxford (L) OPE 3m 5 F *1st ride, alwys last, sn t.o.* 5 0
988 12/4 Kingston Bl' (L) LAD 3m 7 GF *alwys outpcd, t.o. 11th, lft remote 3rd 14th* 3 0
1531 18/5 Mollington (R) MEM 3m 6 GS *cls up til outpcd frm 15th, kpt on 2 out* 3 11
1566 25/5 Kingston Bl' (L) LAD 3m 5 GF *1st ride, mstk 8th, sn bhnd, t.o. 13th* 5 0

Safe as houses but of no real account now 0

IDEAL b.g. 12 Salluceva - Hurry Miss by Royal Buck — Richard Mathias
1996 **U(-)**,2(19),7(0),3(18),P(0)

647 22/3 Castle Of C' (R) INT 3m 7 G *jmpd rght, ld to 10th, last & no ch frm 14th* 4 11
793 31/3 Bishopsleigh (R) OPE 3m 7 G *ld to 10th, 2nd aft til wknd 17th* 4 14
938 6/4 Tabley (R) OPE 3m 9 G *prom, 4th & rddn apr 2 out, no ext* 3 17
1133 19/4 Bonvilston (R) INT 3m 8 G *ld til hdd apr 15th & f* F -
1228 26/4 Pyle (R) INT 3m 5 GS *ld to 7th, cls up aft, rdn 3 out, wknd nxt* 3 12
1319 3/5 Bonvilston (R) INT 3m 8 G *ld to 2 out, styd on onepcd* 3 20
1536 18/5 Mollington (R) INT 3m 8 GS *mstk 6th, chsd clr ldr to 11th, sn wknd, t.o. & p.u. 2 out* P 0
1560 24/5 Bassaleg (R) OPE 3m 7 G *ld to 12th, strgglng frm 14th* 4 11
1602 31/5 Bassaleg (R) INT 3m 5 F *2nd whn ran out 3rd* r -

Dual winner 95; very inconsistent now & just 2 good runs; best watched at 13; G-S 15

IDEAL PARTNER(IRE) ch.g. 8 Ovac (ITY) - Castle Demon by Tiepolo II — T And J A Curry

287 27/2 Huntingdon (R) HC 3m 13 GS *waited with, imp 9th, wknd 3 out, t.o..* 4 14
490 10/3 Stratford (L) HC 3m 12 G *(bl) prom, driven along 4 out, wknd apr 2 out.* 3 21

Professionally-trained & not disgraced but looks slow & season lasted 11 days; best watched 20

IDENTIFY IN CRISIS (Irish) — **I** 40^{F}, **I** 76^{P}

IDIOMATIC b.g. 8 Idiot's Delight - Young Mistress by Young Emperor Mrs S M Shone

204	15/2	Weston Park	(L)	RES	3m	13	G	*t.o. & p.u. 13th*	P 0
666	23/3	Eaton Hall	(R)	MDO	3m	10	GF	*disp to 4th, wknd 10th, p.u. 5 out*	P 0
874	1/4	Uttoxeter	(L)	HC	2m 7f	9	GF	*t.o. from 5th, p.u. before 10th.*	P 0
999	12/4	Alpraham	(R)	MDO	3m	8	GF	*chsd ldrs, wknd 11th, p.u. 2 out*	P 0

Of no account 0

IDIOTIC br.g. 9 Idiot's Delight - Norma Can by Normandy E Knight

1996 **1(26),B(-)**

94	7/2	Newbury	(L)	HC	2 1/2m	12	G	*(fav) f 2nd.*	F -
154	14/2	Fakenham	(L)	HC	2m 5f 110yds	10	G	*lost tch after 11th, soon bhnd.*	5 15
874	1/4	Uttoxeter	(L)	HC	2m 7f	9	GF	*hdwy to chase ldrs 10th, chal 3 out, blnd next, rallied last, rdn to ld near fin.*	1 27
1087	16/4	Cheltenham	(L)	HC	3 1/4m 110yds	8	GF	*hdwy 7th, mstk and lost pl 10th, rallied 12th, rdn when hit 3 out, fd run-in.*	4 20
1284	29/4	Huntingdon	(R)	HC	3m	6	G	*(Jt fav) not fluent, held up, prog 12th, rdn to chase wnr after 3 out, ev ch last, veered left und pres run-in, not qckn.*	2 27

H/Chase winner 96; useful but hard ride & mistakes; needs L/H; best under 3m; can win again; Good .. 28

IDIOT'S SURPRISE (Irish) — **I** 10⁴, **I** 139, , **I** 235ᴾ, **I** 295,

I HAVEN'T A BUCK (Irish) — **I** 105²

I HAVEN'T A BUCK(IRE) ch.g. 9 Buckskin (FR) - Lovely Colour Ian Anderson

1996 **6(NH)**

938	6/4	Tabley	(R)	OPE	3m	9	G	*trckd ldrs gng wll, wnt 2nd 3 out, sn rddn, onepcd*	2 17
1233	26/4	Brampton Br'	(R)	CON	3m	8	G	*trckd ldrs, cls 5th at 9th, wknd 15th, p.u. 3 out*	P 0

Irish pointing winner 96; fair 1st run but disappointing after; best watched 16

I HAVE YOU NOW (Irish) — **I** 499¹, **I** 546⁴

ILIKEHIM b.g. 10 Orange Reef - Coffee by Warpath Mrs Lorraine Lamb

211	16/2	Southwell P'	(L)	MDO	3m	15	GS	*prom to 6th, sn wknd, t.o. & p.u. 10th*	P 0
345	2/3	Market Rase'	(L)	MDO	3m	13	GF	*t.d.e. ld til apr 4th,lft clr 6th,hdd apr 11th,wknd,p.u.13th*	P 0
478	9/3	Southwell P'	(L)	MDO	3m	17	G	*ld aft 1st, jmpd slwly & hdd 6th, bhnd & p.u. 12th*	P 0
839	31/3	Thorpe Lodge	(L)	MDO	3m	15	F	*ld to 13th, 4th outpcd frm nxt*	4 0
1268	27/4	Southwell P'	(L)	MDO	3m	13	G	*ld to 6th, disp 9th-nxt, wknd rpdly 12th, p.u. 3 out*	P 0

Storms off but always stops long before the finish 0

I LIKE THE DEAL b.m. 6 Lighter - Skidmore by Paddy's Stream B Ayre

1996 P(0),3(10),P(0)

1246	26/4	Bratton Down	(L)	MDO	3m	16	GS	*alwys prom, wnt 2nd 2 out, styd on, promsng*	2 14
1486	11/5	Ottery St M'	(L)	MDO	3m	17	G	*hld up,prog 9th,lft in ld 4 out,jnd nxt,p.u. 2 out, dsmntd*	P 0
1597	31/5	Bratton Down	(L)	MDO	3m	12	F	*(fav) jmpd slwly 2nd, immed lost tch, t.o. last & p.u. aft 5th*	P 0

Twice ran well but beset by problems & worrying last start; good enough for a win at best 14

I'LL BE BOUND b.g. 6 Beveled (USA) - Treasurebound by Beldale Flutter (USA) Miss C A Roberts

244	22/2	Lemalla	(R)	MDO	3m	12	S	*disp til 7th, cls 2nd till f 15th*	F -
314	1/3	Clyst St Ma'	(L)	MDN	3m	11	HY	*(fav) handy, ev ch whn blnd & u.r. 13th*	U -
525	15/3	Cothelstone	(L)	MDN	3m	15	GS	*(bl) disp 10-11th, mstks nxt 2, lost tch rpdly & p.u. 15th*	P 0
1094	16/4	Hockworthy	(L)	MDN	3m	11	GF	*(vis) bhnd,mstk 3rd,gd prog frm 6 out,3rd & ch whn hit 2 out,wknd*	3 0
1439	10/5	Holnicote	(L)	RES	3m	9	G	*(vis) rear, 8th hlfwy, bhnd whn p.u. 14th*	P 0
1547	24/5	Mounsey Hil'	(R)	MEM	3m	9	G	*keen hld, in tch, prog 11th, 4th & btn frm 17th*	4 0

Some ability but does not stay & win looks unlikely 11

I'LL SAY NOTHING (Irish) — **I** 86¹, **I** 194¹

I'LL SKIN THEM(IRE) br.m. 9 Buckskin (FR) - Stormy Wave by Gulf Pearl M Lee

1996 P(0),4(11)

666	23/3	Eaton Hall	(R)	MDO	3m	10	GF	*mstks, mid to rear, t.o. & p.u. 3 out*	P 0
762	29/3	Whittington	(L)	MEM	3m	5	S	*j.s., 2nd 6th, ld/disp frm 9th, lft wll clr 15th*	1 12
1050	13/4	Lockerbie	(R)	RES	3m	5	F	*last at 10th, nvr nr wnr*	3 13
1424	10/5	Aspatria	(L)	RES	3m	17	G	*alwys wll in rear, no ch frm 13th, p.u. 15th*	P 0

Virtual solo when winning; not yet threatening to follow up 13

I LOVE TO FLY (Irish) — **I** 63ᴾ, **I** 92⁵, **I** 147³, **I** 283ᴾ

I'M A BUTE b.m. 7 Abutammam - Haselbech by Spartan General T R R Farr

1996 P(0),5(0),P(0),P(0),F(-),4(0),r(-),4(0),4(0)

184	15/2	Erw Lon	(L)	MDN	3m	14	G	*t.d.e. mstks, chsd ldrs til wknd 13th*	5 0
408	8/3	Llanfrynach	(R)	MDN	3m	12	G	*cls up, 5th at 14th, sn btn*	4 0
540	16/3	Erw Lon	(L)	MDN	3m	13	GF	*nvr nr ldrs*	4 0
640	22/3	Howick	(L)	MDN	3m	10	GF	*cls up til wknd 13th, styd on agn late*	2 0

907	5/4 Howick	(L) MDN	3m	4	F	*ld to 13th,3rd & outpcd aft,lft 2nd apr last,ld flat,all out*	1	10
1135	19/4 Bonvilston	(R) RES	3m	14	G	*t.o. frm hlfwy, p.u. 3 out*	P	0
1472	11/5 Erw Lon	(L) XX	3m	9	GS	*alwys twrds rear, onepcd*	4	0
1559	24/5 Bassaleg	(R) XX	3m	4	G	*ld 4th til ran out nxt*	r	-

Handed ghastly Maiden 5th start (should have been 3rd) - remarkable feat to win even that 10

IMAGE BOY(IRE) br.h. 9 Flash Of Steel - Gay Pariso by Sir Gaylord — Mrs R D Greenwood
1996 2(0),P(0),2(13),1(14)

223	16/2 Heythrop	(R) RES	3m	19	G	*alwys rear, t.o. & p.u. 14th*	P	0
488	9/3 Tweseldown	(R) RES	3m	10	G	*in tch, rdn 9th, outpcd 12th, wknd, t.o. & p.u. last*	P	0

Maiden winner 96; no show either run 97 & finished early 11

I'M FOXY b.m. 6 Joligeneration - Tinker's Quest by Romany Air — Mrs A Frank

1246	26/4 Bratton Down	(L) MDO	3m	16	GS	*prom early, mid-div whn ran out thru wing 14th*	r	-
1399	5/5 High Bickin'	(R) MDO	3m	12	G	*mid-div, 8th at 10th, p.u. 12th*	P	0
1520	17/5 Bratton Down	(L) MDO	3m	17	GS	*mid-div, 10th hlfwy, bhnd & p.u. 3 out, schooling*	P	0
1554	24/5 Mounsey Hil'	(R) MDO	3m	14	G	*(bl) t.d.e. ld 3rd,clr whn blnd 16th,hdd aft 3 out,wknd,p.u. nxt*	P	0
1597	31/5 Bratton Down	(L) MDO	3m	12	F	*(bl) hld up in chsng grp, prom 12th, wknd aft 14th, no ch aft*	5	0

Shows speed but headstrong & no stamina yet 10

I'M FREE(IRE) b.g. 6 Aristocracy - Glenbalda by Kambalda — M J Gingell

439	8/3 Higham	(L) MDO	3m	11	G	*mid-div, outpcd 7th, dtchd whn p.u. nxt*	P	0
776	29/3 Dingley	(R) MDO	2m 5f	10	G	*disp to 10th, 3rd frm 6 out, no ext frm 2 out*	3	11

Last to finish when 3rd but may do better in time 11

I'M HAPPY NOW (Irish) — **I** 336[P], **I** 448[P], **I** 562[P]

IMIKE ch.g. 7 Gunner B - Joe's Fancy by Apollo Eight — N Poacher
1996 P(0),P(0)

43	1/2 Larkhill	(R) MDO	3m	10	GF	*trckd ldrs, 4th & still in tch whn f 3 out, dead*	F	-

Dead 0

I'MINONIT b.g. 7 Rolfe (USA) - Lorrensino by Laurence O — P S Macrae
1996 F(-),1(15),P(0)

241	22/2 Lemalla	(R) RES	3m	11	S	*hld up in tch, prog to disp 16th, hdd nxt, ld last, styd on*	1	20

Maiden winner 96; good performance only start 97 & can upgrade if fit 98; stays; Soft 21

I'M JOKING ch.g. 7 True Song - Sancal by Whistlefield — A R Trotter
1996 P(0),P(0)

38	26/1 Alnwick	(L) MDO	3m	14	G	*bhnd, prog & just in tch 13th, sn wknd, p.u. 3 out*	P	0

Lightly raced & yet to complete 0

IMLISTENING (Irish) — **I** 98[P], **I** 151[P], **I** 218[1]

IMMEDIATE ACTION (Irish) — **I** 317[6]

IMPECCABLE BUCK (Irish) — **I** 93[F]

IMPERIAL DAWN (Irish) — **I** 132[5], **I** 171[P], **I** 275[3], **I** 482[P], **I** 527[1]

IMPETUOUS DREAMER b.m. 6 Impecunious - Flaming Matilda by Tudor Flame — Miss Elizabeth Harris

244	22/2 Lemalla	(R) MDO	3m	12	S	*rear, n.j.w. f 4th*	F	-
316	1/3 Clyst St Ma'	(L) MDN	3m	6	HY	*ld to 2nd, lost tch 5th, blnd 12th & p.u.*	P	0

Shows no sign of ability 0

I'M THE GAFFER ch.g. 6 Lighter - City's Sister by Maystreak — F J Brennan
1996 **10(NH)**

823	31/3 Lockinge	(L) MDO	3m	4	F	*cls up, ld 7th-16th, lft in ld final bnd, drvn out*	1	11
1041	12/4 Cothelstone	(L) RES	3m	4	GF	*mostly 3rd, nvr on trms wth ldrs, outpcd frm 4 out*	3	0

Won a bad race (fortunate) & well beaten next time; much more needed 11

I'M TOBY b.g. 10 Celtic Cone - Easter Tinkle by Hot Brandy — P Scaramanga
1996 **U(NH),P(NH),11(NH),4(NH),12(NH),5(NH),P(NH)**

3	19/1 Barbury Cas'	(L) XX	3m	14	GF	*wll in rear, poor 9th hlfwy, prog 13th, clsd 2 out, nrst fin*	3	18
55	1/2 Kingston Bl'	(L) CON	3m	15	GF	*ld 2nd-5th, outpcd frm 13th*	6	12
369	2/3 Mollington	(R) MEM	3m	13	G	*alwys rear, no ch frm 13th, kpt on*	6	14
650	22/3 Siddington	(L) CON	3m	8	F	*alwys last pair, t.o. 10th, ref 2 out*	R	-
1096	18/4 Ayr	(L) HC	3m 3f 110yds	7	G	*alwys bhnd, t.o. when f 15th.*	F	-

Fair run 1st time out but soon lost interest & best watched now 15

IMULARI b.g. 6 Say Primula - Ribera by Ribston — Mrs Gilbert Robinson

1996 **10(NH)**

418	8/3 Dalston	(R) MDO 2 1/2m	10 GS	*made most to 3 out, wknd & p.u. nxt*	P	0
614	22/3 Friars Haugh	(L) MDN 3m	13 GF	*alwys bhnd*	6	0
809	31/3 Tranwell	(L) MEM 3m	5 G	*in tch 1st ctt, cls 2nd & even ch 4 out, wknd into 3rd 2 out*	3	0

No stamina yet & last when 3rd 0

IMUSTAMIT b.g. 7 Sula Bula - You Can Be Sure by Major Point — Mrs F Kehoe

224	16/2 Heythrop	(R) MDN 3m	16 G	*mid-div, outpcd frm 12th, kpt on onepcd frm 3 out, no dang*	3	0
1084	13/4 Guilsborough	(L) MDN 3m	11 GF	*(Jt fav) prom, ld 8th, blnd 14th, hdd nxt, wknd, no ch & p.u. last*	P	0

Modest form when 3rd & mistakes next time; more needed for winning chance 13

INACTUALFACT (Irish) — **I** 35³, **I** 122, , **I** 232ᴾ, **I** 254², **I** 316³, **I** 330¹

INCH CHAMPION (Irish) — **I** 8ᴾ, **I** 84⁴, **I** 322³, **I** 378ᴾ, **I** 423ᴾ

INCH CROSS (Irish) — **I** 3ᴾ, **I** 29ᴾ, **I** 152ᶠ, **I** 220², **I** 311¹, **I** 374¹, **I** 469², **I** 498¹

INCH EMPRESS(IRE) b.m. 8 Cataldi - African Moon by Tobrouk (FR) — D J Miller

1996 P(0)

404	8/3 Llanfrynach	(R) INT 3m	17 G	*cls up, ld 14th, hrd rdn & hdd nr fin*	2	17
1322	3/5 Bonvilston	(R) RES 3m	9 G	*(fav) 2s-1/1, mid-div, blnd 8th, p.u. 11th*	P	0

Irish Maiden winner 94; very lightly-raced; ran well 97 debut but problem after 15

INCH FOUNTAIN(IRE) br.g. 6 Royal Fountain - The Priory by Oats — M J Parr

1996 1(18)

200	15/2 Weston Park	(L) CON 3m	16 G	*w.w. mid-div, prog 3 out, lvl last, no ext cls home*	2	24

Restricted winner only start 96; ran really well only outing 97; useful if fit 98 23

INCH HILL (Irish) — **I** 187ᶠ

INCH HOSTESS (Irish) — **I** 566ᶠ

INCH MAID b.m. 11 Le Moss - Annie Augusta by Master Owen — S A Brookshaw

1996 U(-),2(19),2(19),1(23),1(23),r(-),**2(24)**,3(20)

93	7/2 Bangor	(L) HC 2 1/2m 110yds	11 G	*held up, hdwy after 6th, ld 3 out, styd on well.*	1	26
288	27/2 Ludlow	(R) HC 3m	8 G	*(fav) prom till lost pl 5 out, styd on from 2 out.*	3	24
466	8/3 Eyton-On-Se'	(L) LAD 3m	7 G	*(fav) j.w., made all, ran on wll, not extnd*	1	24

Won twice in 96; novice-ridden; successful season; can win more Ladies at 12; G-F 24

INCH WAY (Irish) — **I** 390⁴, **I** 470ᶠ, **I** 496⁴, **I** 574²

INCONCLUSIVE b.g. 10 Roselier (FR) - Kilbride Madam by Mandalus — R T Dennis

1996 **F(NH),8(NH),4(NH),7(NH),4(NH)**

353	2/3 Great Stain'	(L) CON 3m	9 S	*rear, losing tch whn p.u. 11th*	P	0
618	22/3 Hutton Rudby	(L) OPE 3m	10 GF	*s.i.s.,hld up in rear,sn wll bhnd,rddn 13th,t.o. & p.u. 15th*	P	0
1349	3/5 Gisburn	(R) CON 3m	11 GF	*mid-div, rdn 12th, nvr dang*	6	0
1426	10/5 Aspatria	(L) OPE 3m	9 G	*10s-5s, chsd ldrs til 5th & wkng 11th, t.o. & p.u. 16th*	P	0
1512	17/5 Corbridge	(R) OPE 3m	10 GS	*mid-div til outpcd 9th, wll bhnd frm 4 out*	5	13

Fair pointer 95 but declined considerably now & unlikely to achieve much at 11 13

IN DEMAND b.g. 6 Nomination - Romantic Saga by Prince Tenderfoot (USA) — A J Balmer

1996 2(13),1(16),1(20),4(0)

335	1/3 Corbridge	(R) CON 3m	7 G	*(fav) hld up mid-div, f 12th*	F	-
411	8/3 Dalston	(R) CON 3m	16 GS	*(fav) jmpd slwly 4th, nvr going wll, lost tch & btn frm 15th*	6	0
608	22/3 Friars Haugh	(L) XX 3m	6 GF	*u.r. 1st*	U	-
611	22/3 Friars Haugh	(L) CON 3m	11 GF	*alwys hndy, ch 3 out, no ext frm nxt*	3	18

Promising dual winner 96; never got to grips 97; finished early; may revive 98; G-F 20

INDEPENDENCE DAY (Irish) — **I** 107,

INDEXIA (Irish) — **I** 174ᴾ, **I** 214, , **I** 253,

INDIAN CROW b.g. 10 Revolutionary (USA) - Hindu Queen by Indian Ruler — P J H Wills

1448	10/5 Kingston Bl'	(L) CON 3m	9 G	*in tch to hlfwy, grad wknd, bhnd whn p.u. last*	P	0

Maiden winner 95 (promising); missed 96 & one late appearance of no note in 97 14

INDIAN KNIGHT b.g. 12 Kinglet - Indian Whistle by Rugantino — C A Green

1996 2(18),3(18),U(-),4(15),**4(20)**,**7(15)**

39	1/2 Larkhill	(R) CON 3m	6 GF	*trckd ldrs, ld 15th, mstk & jnd last, hld on well*	1	20
179	15/2 Larkhill	(R) CON 3m	12 G	*(fav) mid-div til ran out & u.r. 7th*	r	-
514	15/3 Larkhill	(R) MXO 3m	6 GF	*cls up, ld 13-15th, wknd 3 out*	3	16
659	22/3 Badbury Rin'	(L) OPE 3m	2 F	*(fav) trckd ldr, chal 3 out, blnd nxt, no ext aft*	2	12
918	5/4 Larkhill	(R) CON 3m	1 F	*walked over*	1	0
1142	19/4 Larkhill	(R) OPE 3m	3 F	*(fav) trckd ldr, ld apr 15th, sn clr, canter*	1	18

1214 26/4 Woodford (L) OPE 3m 5 G *rear, in tch to 15th, no dang aft* 5 10
1358 5/5 Exeter (R) HC 2m 7f 110yds 8 G *trckd ldr to 9th, weakening when hit 5 out, t.o.* 6 0
1570 26/5 Hereford (R) HC 3m 1f 110yds 14 G *in rear when blnd and u.r. 6 out.* U -

Broke losing sequence of 18 but 3 wins very flattering; easily beaten now; G-F 17

INDIAN LANGUAGE b.g. 8 Creetown - Florence Mary by Mandamus — Mrs Anne Carter

553 16/3 Ottery St M' (L) MDN 3m 15 G *bhnd, outpcd & no ch frm 13th* 6 0
740 29/3 Higher Kilw' (L) MDN 3m 15 GF *4th hlfwy, lost ground 13th, blnd 3 out, p.u. nxt* P 0
1095 16/4 Hockworthy (L) MDN 3m 11 GF *chsd ldng pair to 9th, sn wknd, t.o. & p.u. last* P 0
1260 27/4 Black Fores' (R) MDO 3m 12 F *alwys bhnd, fin 8th* 0 0

Missed 96 & returned to no effect 0

INDIAN RABI gr.g. 7 Northern Game - Acoras Prediction by Scallywag — Mrs E M Roberts
1996 P(0),1(14)

240 22/2 Lemalla (R) RES 3m 11 S *keen hld, in tch, 5th at 9th, lost plc aft mstk 13th* 4 0
457 8/3 Great Treth' (R) RES 3m 8 S *6th hlfwy wnt 3rd apr 3 out, not rch ldrs* 3 13
556 16/3 Ottery St M' (L) RES 3m 12 G *mid-div, prog 15th, outpcd 3 out, not trbl wnr aft* 2 13
792 31/3 Bishopsleigh (R) RES 3m 13 G *alwys mid-div, effrt 17th, unable rch ldrs* 4 0
1395 5/5 High Bickin' (R) RES 3m 9 G *made virt all, ran on wll clsng stgs* 1 16
1516 17/5 Bratton Down (L) CON 3m 6 GS *ld to 7th, wkng whn mstks 12th & 13th, t.o. 15th* 3 0
1550 24/5 Mounsey Hil' (R) INT 3m 9 G *cls up, hit 6th, 5th & outpcd 13th, no dang aft, tk 3rd 2out* 3 14

Maiden winner 96; ran in competitive races; both wins High Bickington & Confined possible there 98 .. 18

INDIAN RIVER(IRE) b.g. 9 Indian King (USA) - Chaldea by Tamerlane — Robert Miller-Bakewell
1996 P(0),6(0)

36 26/1 Alnwick (L) MDO 3m 15 G *last pair & t.o. til p.u. 4th, dsmntd* P 0
136 9/2 Alnwick (L) MDO 3m 16 G *ld 3rd-12th, sn wknd, t.o. & p.u. 4 out* P 0
234 22/2 Friars Haugh (L) MDO 3m 15 G *nvr rchd ldrs* 5 0
343 1/3 Corbridge (R) MDO 3m 14 G *mid-div, wknd 11th, t.o.* 6 0
565 16/3 Lanark (R) MDO 3m 10 GS *bhnd early, stdy hdwy frm 11th, not rch ldng pair* 3 13
612 22/3 Friars Haugh (L) MDN 3m 14 GF *bhnd by 8th, nvr nr ldrs* 4 0
728 29/3 Alnwick (L) MEM 3m 4 F *(fav) j.w. chsd ldr til ld 4th, qcknd clr 11th, canter* 1 10

Fianlly found some ability & won dire race; much more needed for Restricted chance 12

INDIE ROCK b.g. 7 Hadeer - Song Test (USA) by The Minstrel (CAN) — R Tate
1996 r(-),3(18),1(21),P(0),r(-),1(20),2(20),F(-)

165 15/2 Witton Cast' (R) LAD 3m 6 F *hld up rear, some prog in 4th whn u.r. 14th* U -
426 8/3 Charm Park (L) LAD 3m 12 GF *hld up in rear, prog 4 out, ev ch 2 out, not qckn* 3 21
617 22/3 Hutton Rudby (L) LAD 3m 9 GF *hld up in rear, prog 3 out, ev ch nxt, wknd* 5 18
1102 19/4 Hornby Cast' (L) LAD 3m 7 G *held up in mid-div,chal2 out,ld last,ran on wll undpres flat* 1 21
1476 11/5 Garthorpe (R) LAD 3m 5 GS *patiently rdn, prog to 2nd 3 out, ld last, ran on well* 1 21
1571 26/5 Wetherby (L) HC 2 1/2m 110yds 15 GF *mid div, hdwy 4 out, soon rdn and no impn from next.* 6 13
1589 31/5 Market Rasen (R) HC 2 3/4m 110yds 10 GF *chsd ldrs, ld 4 out, hit last, soon hdd, kept on well.* 2 24

Useful Ladies horse on day; inconsistent; barely stays; win more, possible H/Chase sub 3m; G/S-G/F .. 24

INDIWAY ch.g. 9 Broadsword (USA) - Artalinda by Indiaro — Mrs S E Haydon
1996 P(0),U(-)

833 31/3 Heathfield (R) MDO 3m 7 F *in tch lft 3rd 12th, wknd 4 out, lft poor 3rd last* 3 0
1283 27/4 Fakenham P-' (L) MDO 3m 9 G *mid-div in tch, mstk 9th, wknd 12th, p.u. 15th, lame* P 0

No signs of ability & problems 0

INGLEBROOK br.g. 6 Meadowbrook - Inglebrig by New Brig — D Williams
1996 P(0),U(-)

81 2/2 Wolverhampt' (L) MDN 3m 13 GS *s.s. hld up & t.o., ran on 13th, nvr nrr, hopeless task* 3 10

Promise in 96; given odd ride only start 97 & vanished; sure to win if racing regularly 14

INGLEBY FLYER b.m. 9 Valiyar - Fardella (ITY) by Molvedo — Mrs S Frank
1996 P(0),6(11),3(0),B(-),F(-),3(0)

120 9/2 Wetherby Po' (L) MDO 3m 18 GF *mid-div, wknd 13th, t.o. & p.u. 4 out* P 0

Placed twice in 96 but has never threatened to win 10

INHURST b.m. 8 Remezzo - Passionate by Dragonara Palace (USA) — D G Dixon
1996 U(-)

212 16/2 Southwell P' (L) MDO 3m 14 GS *in tch, went prom 8th, wknd apr 12th, p.u. 3 out* P 0

Rarely seen & no stamina 0

INIS CARA (Irish) — I 297[1]

INJUNCTION(IRE) ch.g. 6 Glenstal (USA) - Laide Festa (ITY) by Teodoro Trivulzio — R Cowie
1996 **U(NH),2(NH),U(NH),4(NH),1(NH),14(NH)**

849	31/3	Eyton-On-Se'	(L)	OPE	3m	7 GF	*(bl) w.w.,cls order 10th,chal whn bad mstk 4 out,4th whn u.r.last*	U	-
1176	20/4	Sandon	(L)	OPE	3m	5 GF	*(bl) alwys prom, 2nd at 9th, chsd wnr, hrd rdn 2 out, alwys hld*	2	18
1301	3/5	Weston Park	(L)	OPE	3m	4 G	*(fav) (bl) cls 2nd til ld 13th-2 out, reluc whn lft clr last*	1	17

Hurdles winner 96; able but ungenuine & handed last race on plate; sure to frustrate in future 18

INKY b or br.m. 8 Impecunious - Latanett by Dairialatan — M J Hart
1996 4(0),F(-)

436	8/3	Upton-On-Se'	(R)	MDO	3m	17 G	*w.w. prog 10th, 6th & no ch 15th, p.u. nxt*	P	0
754	29/3	Brampton Br'	(R)	MDN	3m	9 GF	*30l 4th at 8th, 30l 2nd at 13th, ran on to ld 3 out, comf*	1	14

Very lightly-raced now but gained deserved win; barely stays; may have chance if fit 98 16

INNER SNU gr.m. 8 Vital Season - Grey Receipt by Rugantino — S L Mitchell
1996 F(-),3(0),U(-),4(0),P(0),2(15)

658	22/3	Badbury Rin'	(L)	MDN	3m	6 F	*(fav) hld up, prog 14th, chal 2 out, ld last, ran on und pres*	1	14

Improved 96 & beat subsequent winners only start 97; go close in Restricted if back in 98 16

INNISCEIN (Irish) — **I** 13², **I** 49⁵, **I** 236²

INNISHFEA (Irish) — **I** 519^F, **I** 559^P, **I** 565⁵

INSULATE ch.m. 7 Sula Bula - Penny Catcher by Barolo — Stephen March
1996 F(-),U(-),2(10)

128	9/2	Cottenham	(R)	MDO	3m	10 GF	*in tch in rear til outpcd 14th, no imp ldrs aft*	3	0
499	15/3	Ampton	(R)	MDO	3m	9 GF	*alwys mid div, 6th & rdn 16th, nt pace to rch ldrs*	5	12

Not beaten far in poor race last start but more needed for winning chance 11

INTEABADUN ch.g. 5 Hubbly Bubbly (USA) - Madam Taylor by Free State — T S Wallace
1996 **P(NH),8(NH),0(NH)**

1577	26/5	Chaddesley '	(L)	MDO	3m	11 F	*jmpd slwly, in tch til wknd 11th, t.o. & p.u. 13th*	P	0

Late to appear & may be aptly named 0

INTEGRITY BOY b.g. 10 Touching Wood (USA) - Powderhall by Murrayfield — Richard P Watts
1996 2(21),1(19),2(21)

268	22/2	Duncombe Pa'	(R)	LAD	3m	5 G	*disp ld to 3rd,in tch whn lft 2nd 4 out,chal last onepcd*	2	21
349	2/3	Market Rase'	(L)	LAD	3m	5 GF	*(fav) in tch, lft in ld 12th, drew clr apr 2 out, easily*	1	21
426	8/3	Charm Park	(L)	LAD	3m	12 GF	*mid-div, prog 5 out, ev ch 3 out, not qckn frm nxt*	4	20
697	29/3	Stainton	(R)	LAD	3m	5 F	*chsd ldrs, outpcd 10th, cls up brfly 16th, wknd 3 out*	3	16

Consistent Ladies pointer; won/placed all starts 96/7; best L/H; stays; win at 11; G/F-G/S 21

IN THE CHOIR b.m. 9 Chief Singer - In The Shade by Bustino — H Carrothers
1996 4(10)

20	25/1	Badbury Rin'	(L)	MDN	3m	9 GF	*jmpd rght 2nd, last pair til ran on frm 2 out, no dang*	3	0
177	15/2	Larkhill	(R)	MEM	3m	6 G	*bhnd, in tch til apr 13th, jmpd slwly 3 out, tk mod 3rd last*	3	0
517	15/3	Larkhill	(R)	RES	3m	10 GF	*jmpd v slwly, t.o. til p.u. 13th*	P	0

Novice-ridden & well-beaten when completing 0

IN THE STOCKING (Irish) — **I** 14⁶, **I** 40⁴, **I** 84⁶, **I** 444⁴, **I** 515^F, **I** 574³, **I** 602¹

IN THE WATER ch.g. 10 Carlingford Castle - Cardamine by Indigenous — Mrs B Brown
1996 7(0),6(0),U(-),U(-),P(0)

263	22/2	Newtown	(L)	MDN	3m	11 G	*prom, wth ldr 10-12th, wknd 15th*	3	0
409	8/3	Llanfrynach	(R)	MDN	3m	12 G	*trckd ldrs, ld 14th, jnd 2 out, all out flat*	1	13
634	22/3	Howick	(L)	RES	3m	7 GF	*(fav) mid-div, drvn 11th, ran on onepcd*	4	0
1014	12/4	Bitterley	(L)	OPE	3m	9 GF	*in chsng grp, wknd frm 13th, p.u. 15th*	P	0
1232	26/4	Brampton Br'	(R)	MEM	3m	4 G	*slw jmp & last frm 3rd, lost tch frm 12th*	3	0
1389	5/5	Cursneh Hill	(L)	OPE	3m	2 GF	*chsd wnnr, rddn 12th, lost tch frm nxt*	2	0

Improved with stronger handling 97 & scrambled home in poor race; Restricted most unlikely 12

INTO THE CLAN (Irish) — **I** 8^P, **I** 57⁵, **I** 335³, **I** 456¹

INVADER GENERAL (Irish) — **I** 153^P, **I** 219^P, **I** 403^P

INVER RED (Irish) — **I** 289¹, **I** 361¹, **I** 433², **I** 503¹

IONA FLYER (Irish) — **I** 110², **I** 159¹, **I** 240^F, **I** 357⁴

IRBEE b.g. 5 Gunner B - Cupids Bower by Owen Dudley — Mrs I Breese
1996 **5(NH)**

210	16/2	Southwell P'	(L)	MDO	3m	15 GS	*(fav) chsd ldrs, mstk 15th, ev ch nxt, no ext nr fin*	2	16
437	8/3	Upton-On-Se'	(R)	MDO	3m	15 G	*s.s. cls 7th at 10th, 2nd 13th, ld 2 out, clr last*	1	14

Decent start & clear-cut winner; every chance of upgrading if fit 98 17

IREBY VI (Irish) — **I** 68^{U}, **I** 118^{P}, **I** 127^{P}

IRENE'S CALL (Irish) — **I** 334^{2}, **I** 420^{1}

IRISH DISPLAY (Irish) — **I** 136^{F}, **I** 242^{P}, **I** 429^{P}

IRISH FROLIC (Irish) — **I** 8^{4}, **I** 40^{3}, **I** 77^{2}, **I** 335^{5}, **I** 425^{1}, **I** 530^{1}, **I** 598^{2}

IRISH GENT br.g. 11 Andretti - Seana Sheo by Seana Sgeal — Sir Sanderson Temple

1996 **1(NH),7(NH)**

939	6/4	Tabley	(R)	LAD	3m	9	G	*alwys last, u.r. 16th*	U	-
1123	19/4	Whittington	(L)	OPE	3m	4	F	*alwys rear, nvr dang*	4	0
1426	10/5	Aspatria	(L)	OPE	3m	9	G	*not fluent in last, no ch frm 11th, kpt on*	4	10
1512	17/5	Corbridge	(R)	OPE	3m	10	GS	*rear, strgglng 9th, t.o. 12th*	4	13
1575	26/5	Chaddesley '	(L)	OPE	3m	10	F	*alwys bhnd, t.o. 12th, nvr nrr*	5	0

Winning chaser 96; very poor pointing runs on unsuitable ground; best watched; Soft 13

IRISH PRIDE (Irish) — **I** 561^{P}, **I** 572^{P}, **I** 599^{6}, **I** 607^{4}

IRISH ROVER (Irish) — **I** 73^{4}, **I** 171^{5}, **I** 324^{P}

IRISH SPIRIT (Irish) — **I** 47^{P}, **I** 140^{P}

IRISH STOUT (Irish) — **I** 59^{P}, **I** 112^{F}

IRISH THINKER b.g. 6 Derring Rose - Irish Holiday by Simbir — W Tudor

1996 P(0),U(-),U(-),U(-)

186	15/2	Erw Lon	(L)	MDN	3m	13	G	*in tch, chsd wnr 12th, no imp 3 out, wknd & lost 2nd last*	3	0
540	16/3	Erw Lon	(L)	MDN	3m	13	GF	*tongue-strap, mid-div, prog aft 9th, ev ch 13th, wknd 15th*	3	0
1229	26/4	Pyle	(R)	MDO	3m	11	GS	*prssd wnr, ev ch whn mstk 15th, sn rdn, btn 2 out, eased*	2	10
1368	5/5	Pantyderi	(L)	MDO	3m	8	G	*(Jt fav) rear, prog 10th, chsd wnr 12th, hrd rdn 2 out, no imp*	2	13
1561	24/5	Bassaleg	(R)	MDO	3m	9	G	*(fav) cls up, ld 12th, clr 2 out, pshd out*	1	14

Gradually improved & reliability saw weak race landed; barely stays; more needed for Restricted 15

IRISH VENTURE(IRE) b.g. 6 Meneval (USA) - Mystery Gift by Guillaume Tell (USA) — W Ralph Thomas

258	22/2	Newtown	(L)	RES	3m	14	G	*hmdp & u.r. 1st*	U	-
404	8/3	Llanfrynach	(R)	INT	3m	17	G	*alwys rear, p.u. 3 out*	P	0

Season lasted 2 weeks & no promise 0

IRREGULAR PLANTING (Irish) — **I** 66^{P}, **I** 300^{3}, **I** 459^{2}, **I** 529^{F}

ISHEREAL(IRE) gr.g. 6 Carlingford Castle - Boreenace by Boreen (FR) — Mrs Jane Smith

470	8/3	Eyton-On-Se'	(L)	MDN	2 1/2m	12	G	*mid to rear, no ch whn p.u. 4 out*	P	0
722	29/3	Sandon	(L)	MDO	3m	10	GF	*mid-div, prog 9th, disp 2nd & going wll whn b.d. 2 out*	B	-
1073	13/4	Whitwell-On'	(R)	MDO	2 1/2m 88yds	17	G	*rear, prog 4 out, ev ch 2 out, not qckn*	3	13

Ran reasonably last start & should have chances in 98 14

ISHMA(IRE) b.g. 6 Kambalda - Scat-Cat by Furry Glen — Darren Page

1996 **P(NH),P(NH),P(NH),P(NH),P(NH),P(NH)**

43	1/2	Larkhill	(R)	MDO	3m	10	GF	*ref & u.r. 5th*	R	-
128	9/2	Cottenham	(R)	MDO	3m	10	GF	*bhnd frm 3rd, t.o. whn crawld 16th & p.u.*	P	0
284	23/2	Charing	(L)	MDO	3m	17	G	*sn wll bhnd, t.o. 8th, lft 4th aft 14th, kpt on*	3	0
582	16/3	Detling	(L)	MDN	3m	16	F	*towrds rear whn b.d. 8th*	B	-
605	22/3	Parham	(R)	MDO	3m	7	F	*cls up, prssd wnr 9th til c.o. loose horse 13th*	C	-
681	29/3	Charing	(L)	MEM	3m	5	F	*prsd wnr frm 8th,rdn & up sides whn jmp slwly 4 out,no dang*	2	0
1130	19/4	Penshurst	(L)	MDO	3m	5	GF	*(fav) rear, rmndrs & prog 13th, ld aft 3 out, kpt on*	1	0
1359	5/5	Southwell	(L)	HC	3m 110yds	7	GS	*in rear, blnd 2nd, bhnd when ref 9th.*	R	-
1505	16/5	Folkestone	(R)	HC	2m 5f	8	G	*prom to 3rd, soon wknd, t.o. and p.u. before 9th.*	P	0

Won a diabolical race & no other prospects outside Members 10

ISLAND ECHO (Irish) — **I** 81^{4}, **I** 87^{3}, **I** 206^{3}, **I** 337^{2}, **I** 443^{3}, **I** 551^{P}, **I** 596^{1}

ISLAND HARRIET (Irish) — **I** 120^{F}, **I** 250^{P}, **I** 329^{6}, **I** 467^{3}, **I** 508^{5}, **I** 554^{F}, **I** 586^{4}

ISOLA FARNESE b.m. 10 Hotfoot - Immaculate Girl by Habat — Mrs Julie Johnson

345	2/3	Market Rase'	(L)	MDO	3m	13	GF	*mid-div, mstk 4th, blnd & u.r. 6th*	U	-
549	16/3	Garthorpe	(R)	MDO	3m	16	GF	*jmpd poorly, ld 4th, clr whn u.r. 8th*	U	-
839	31/3	Thorpe Lodge	(L)	MDO	3m	15	F	*2nd til mstk 10th, wknd qckly, p.u. 13th*	P	0
1083	13/4	Guilsborough	(L)	MDN	3m	15	GF	*sn rear, wll bhnd 9th, t.o. & p.u. 13th*	P	0

Of no account 0

IS RED THERE b.g. 5 Lord David S (USA) - Another Pin by Pinza — Charlie Peckitt

428	8/3	Charm Park	(L)	MDO	3m	10	GF	*mid-div, disp remt 3rd 8th, wknd 10th, t.o. & p.u. 12th*	P	0
860	31/3	Charm Park	(L)	MDO	3m	12	F	*bhnd, nvr a fctr, p.u. 12th*	P	0
1073	13/4	Whitwell-On'	(R)	MDO	2 1/2m 88yds	17	G	*mid-div, rmndrs 5th, sn strgglng, wll bhnd whn p.u. 2 out*	P	0

Shows no stamina or promise yet **0**

IS SHE QUICK ch.m. 7 Norwick (USA) - Get Involved by Shiny Tenth G M Flynn

1996 5(11),F(-),3(0),P(0),F(-)

299	1/3	Didmarton	(L)	MDN	3m	14	G	*alwys bhnd, t.o. 10th, p.u. 14th*	P 0
570	16/3	Garnons	(L)	MDN	2 1/2m	14	G	*mid-div to 5th, drppd rear, t.o. & p.u. 12th*	P 0

Fair debut 96 but finished 1 of next 6 races & brief season 97 .... **0**

IS THIS THE ONE (Irish) — **I** 34[F], **I** 119[S], **I** 180[F], **I** 507[F], **I** 557[P]

IT AIN'T EASY (Irish) — **I** 67[2]

ITALIAN MAN(IRE) b.g. 9 Don Orazio - Via Del Tabacco by Ballymoss G W Penfold

1996 **5(NH),5(NH),P(NH),5(NH),4(NH)**

101	8/2	Great Treth'	(R)	MDO	3m	9	GS	*in tch til outpcd by wnr 15th, lft clr 2nd 2 out*	2 10
172	15/2	Ottery St M'	(L)	MDN	3m	14	G	*mid-div early, 4th at 13th, effrt 4 out, no ext frm nxt*	2 14
553	16/3	Ottery St M'	(L)	MDN	3m	15	G	*made all, kpt on wll frm 4 out*	1 17

No real ability under Rules; solid in points & beat subsequent winners; can upgrade **18**

ITA'S FELLOW(IRE) ch.g. 9 Decent Fellow - Castle Ita by Midland Gayle R Prince

1996 U(-),1(17),1(17)

330	1/3	Eaton Hall	(R)	CON	3m	16	GS	*mid-div, prog 5 out, up sides 2 out,slght ld last,ran on wll*	1 20
726	29/3	Sandon	(L)	CON	3m	8	GF	*(fav) ld 4th, sn in cmmnd, easily*	1 20
1002	12/4	Alpraham	(R)	CON	3m	4	GF	*(fav) ld 6th, clr 14th, easily*	1 20
1412	7/5	Uttoxeter	(L)	HC	3 1/4m	10	GS	*(Jt fav) keen hold, cl up, mstk 7th, b.d. 8th.*	B -
1508	17/5	Bangor	(L)	HC	3m 110yds	12	G	*midfield, effort to chase ldrs 13th, soon no impn.*	4 14

Promising & won 6 of last 7 points; beaten in hot H/Chase last start; Opens, at least, 98; G/F-G/S **23**

ITS A DODDLE ch.m. 7 Prince Of Peace - Bossy Cleo by Proud Challenge Mrs J Marsh

1996 P(0),P(0),P(0),F(-)

540	16/3	Erw Lon	(L)	MDN	3m	13	GF	*tongue-strap, rear, p.u. 10th*	P 0
719	29/3	Llanvapley	(L)	MDN	3m	14	GF	*rear, f 11th*	F -
1131	19/4	Bonvilston	(R)	MEM	3m	6	G	*alwys rear, no ch frm hlfwy*	4 0
1324	3/5	Bonvilston	(R)	MDO	3m	16	G	*rear, p.u. 2 out*	P 0

Hopeless & beaten miles on only completion **0**

ITSAJUNGLEOUTTHERE (Irish) — **I** 17[F], **I** 54[2]

ITSALLTHEONETODEV(IRE) b.g. 7 Phardante (FR) - Cappahard by Record Run A R Trotter

35	26/1	Alnwick	(L)	CON	3m	10	G	*mstks, ld til ran wd bnd aft 9th, wknd rpdly 15th,p.u.2out*	P 0
133	9/2	Alnwick	(L)	OPE	3m	6	G	*t.d.e. hld up, chsd ldr 13th-14th, 3rd & btn whn u.r. 3 out*	U -
156	15/2	Lanark	(R)	CON	3m	7	G	*raced in 4th, lost tch 14th, poor 3rd whn p.u. 3 out*	P 0

Unbeaten in 2 Irish points 96; out of control in England & no stamina; best watched **13**

IT'S A SCOOP ch.g. 7 Afzal - Secret Stolen (USA) by Sassafras (FR) B L Lay

373	2/3	Mollington	(R)	MDN	3m	14	G	*race wd, made most til ran out 9th*	r -
1166	20/4	Mollington	(R)	MDO	3m	9	GF	*ld til p.u. 8th, dsmntd*	P 0

No real promise & problem last start **0**

ITSGONEOFF br.g. 8 Neltino - The Beginning by Goldhill Mrs E Kennedy

286	27/2	Huntingdon	(R)	HC	3m	8	GS	*ld and soon clr, not fluent final cct, hdd after 3 out, 3rd when p.u. before next, broke down, destroyed.*	P 0

Dead **33**

ITS MURPHY MAN ch.g. 8 Itsu (USA) - Gaie Pretense (FR) by Pretendre David J Murphy

1996 3(14),P(0),4(10),P(0)

78	2/2	Market Rase'	(L)	RES	3m	8	GF	*prom to 11th, grad lost pl*	4 0
217	16/2	Heythrop	(R)	MEM	3m	4	G	*(fav) made all, lft clr 3 out, comf*	1 14
300	1/3	Didmarton	(L)	RES	3m	23	G	*s.s. prom to 13th, bhnd whn p.u. 2 out*	P 0
653	22/3	Siddington	(L)	RES	3m	10	F	*trckd ldrs, outpcd 14th, 5th whn p.u. nxt*	P 0
1164	20/4	Mollington	(R)	RES	3m	10	GF	*blnd 1st, in tch, onepcd frm 3 out*	4 13

Non-stayer & found bad race to break duck; Restricted prospects poor **14**

IT'S NOT MY FAULT(IRE) b.g. 9 Red Sunset - Glas Y Dorlan by Sexton Blake P D Jones

1996 **5(NH),3(NH),P(NH),P(NH),13(NH)**

99	8/2	Great Treth'	(R)	LAD	3m	10	GS	*rear, lost tch wth ldrs 13th, onepcd aft*	5 15
238	22/2	Lemalla	(R)	LAD	3m	9	S	*5th at 9th, outpcd 15th, 5th & wkng 2 out, walked in*	7 0
453	8/3	Great Treth'	(R)	CON	3m	13	S	*ld/disp 5-14th, ev ch til not qckn aft 3 out*	3 18
793	31/3	Bishopsleigh	(R)	OPE	3m	7	G	*handy, mostly 3rd, disp 4 out-last, no ext nr fin*	3 21
1111	19/4	Flete Park	(R)	CON	3m	5	GF	*(fav) hld up in tch, ev ch til wknd apr 2 out, eased flat*	2 14
1338	3/5	Flete Park	(R)	MEM	3m	1	G	*walked over*	1 0

1481 11/5 Ottery St M' (L) CON 3m 12 G *alwys prom, disp 4th-4 out, ev ch nxt, onepcd 2 out* 3 19
1580 26/5 Lifton (R) OPE 3m 8 G *chsng grp frm hlfwy, nvr able to chal wnr* 2 16

Selling hurdles winner 95; disappointing in points; ungenuine; won chase in June 19

IT'SNOTSIMPLE (Irish) — I 70[1]

ITSPANTOTIME b.m. 7 Itsu (USA) - Panto Girl by Lepanto (GER) John Jones

1367 5/5 Pantyderi (L) MDO 3m 7 G *nvr nrr than 5th, p.u. 16th* P 0

A wishy-washy start 0

IT'S POGO b.g. 6 Remezzo - County Clare by Vimadee L A R Lynch

574 16/3 Garnons (L) RES 3m 14 G *rear frm 11th, no ch whn p.u. 15th* P 0

No great bounce yet 0

ITSSTORMINGNORMA b.m. 7 Itsu (USA) - Norman Currency by Normandy John Jones
1996 P(0),3(0),4(11)

720 29/3 Llanvapley (L) MDN 3m 8 GF *mstly 3rd/4th, strng chal frm 3 out, just outpcd* 2 13
1009 12/4 St Hilary (R) MDN 3m 11 GF *(fav) cls up in 3rd/4th, onepcd frm 3 out* 4 0
1137 19/4 Bonvilston (R) MDO 3m 13 G *mid-div, prog to 4th 15th, onepce aft* 5 0
1368 5/5 Pantyderi (L) MDO 3m 8 G *mid-div, effrt 13th, fdd rpdly 15th* 5 0

Placed 4 times 96/7 but no improvement & stamina problems; win hard to find 11

ITSTHEJONESBOY ch.g. 7 Itsu (USA) - Maella (FR) by Traffic John Jones

1527 17/5 Bredwardine (R) MDO 3m 13 G *made most to 15th, sn wknd, fair debut* 4 0
1584 26/5 Lifton (R) MDO 3m 13 G *(Jt fav) ld 1st til almost ran out aft 5th, no dang aft, p.u. 4 out* P 0

Decent enough debut & 2nd run may have come too quickly; could do better 98 12

ITSUPTOME VI (Irish) — I 211[P], I 249, , I 313[P], I 327[3], I 414[4]

IVEAGH LADY (Irish) — I 72[P], I 119[P], I 123[P], I 432, , I 464[P]

IVE CALLED TIME b.g. 9 Sergeant Drummer (USA) - Alice Rairthorn by Romany Air C M Shadbolt
1996 P(0),2(15),1(16),3(19),1(19),2(16),**P(0)**,2(18),1(19)

236 22/2 Lemalla (R) INT 3m 12 S *prom whn blnd & u.r. 1st* U -
310 1/3 Clyst St Ma' (L) INT 3m 9 HY *in tch to 12th, lost plc nxt, t.o. & p.u. 2 out* P 0
522 15/3 Cothelstone (L) CON 3m 14 GS *mid-div, 6th at 14th, ran on steadily, nrst fin* 3 13
691 29/3 Little Wind' (R) INT 3m 5 GF *made most to 2 out, unable to qckn und pres last* 2 19
1089 16/4 Hockworthy (L) CON 3m 7 GF *chsd ldrs, outpcd frm 10th, no dang aft* 4 11

Won 3 in 96; mostly disappointing 97; ground against; could revive in wet year 20

I'VE COPPED IT(IRE) br.g. 7 Corvaro (USA) - Diamond Glow Richard Mathias
1996 P(0)

254 22/2 Newtown (L) MEM 3m 6 G *t.o. 4th, p.u. 2 out* P 0
1016 12/4 Bitterley (L) MDO 3m 14 GF *prom to 13th, not qckn nxt, rdn & no ext frm 15th* 5 0
1230 26/4 Pyle (R) MDO 3m 10 GS *chsd ldrs, lost tch hlfwy, t.o. 13th, tk poor 3rd nr fin* 3 0

Does not stay & no real chances 0

I'VEGOTYOUNOW (Irish) — I 337[5]

IVY MIST (Irish) — I 233[2]

JACK DORY (Irish) — I 3[4], I 76[F], I 192[2]

JACK HACKETT (Irish) — I 132[4]

JACK SOUND b.g. 11 Mister Lord (USA) - Dale Road by Le Tricolore E L Harries

42 1/2 Larkhill (R) MXO 3m 7 GF *made most to apr 13th, wknd rpdly, p.u. last* P 0
187 15/2 Erw Lon (L) OPE 3m 16 G *chsd ldrs, effrt 13th, rdn & btn nxt* 3 14
400 8/3 Llanfrynach (R) OPE 3m 10 G *ld/disp til ld 14th, alwys in cmmnd aft* 1 25
637 22/3 Howick (L) OPE 3m 7 GF *(fav) cls up, ld 11th, qcknd 3 out, in cmmnd aft* 1 23
843 31/3 Lydstep (L) OPE 3m 4 F *(fav) ld to 15th, ld agn last, hrd rdn flat, just hld on* 1 21
1007 12/4 St Hilary (R) OPE 3m 10 GF *(fav) 2nd til ld 13th, wknd rpdly apr last, hdd flat* 2 21
1363 5/5 Pantyderi (L) OPE 3m 4 G *(fav) in ld 3rd, disp 11th, 2nd & hrd rdn last, no ext* 2 24
1491 14/5 Hereford (R) HC 3m 1f 110yds 11 G *chsd ldr to 3 out, soon wknd.* 4 19

Missed 96; still useful pointer at best; won 14 of 23; likes Llanfrynach; win more in 98; F-S 23

JACK SUN br.g. 7 Sunyboy - Miss Craigie by New Brig Ian Snowden
1996 P(0),F(-)

44 1/2 Larkhill (R) MDO 3m 9 GF *ld 2nd, clr 9th, hdd 3 out, kpt on, no ch wth wnr* 2 13
182 15/2 Larkhill (R) MDO 3m 12 G *(fav) prom til pckd & u.r. 3rd* U -
315 1/3 Clyst St Ma' (L) MDN 3m 5 HY *(fav) ld to 3rd, handy, ld 13th, sn clr* 1 12
661 22/3 Badbury Rin' (L) RES 3m 6 F *(fav) lft 30l start, prog 11th, disp 13th-nxt, effrt 3 out,nt qckn* 2 14

Ran creditably but novice-ridden & needs stronger handling to win average Restricted; Any 16

JACK THE TD(IRE) b.g. 8 Rochebrun (FR) - Lily Of Dunmoon by Prince Regent (FR) J R Cornwall

1996 **U(NH),4(NH),6(NH),8(NH),3(NH),6(NH)**

88	2/2	Wolverhampt'	(L)	MDO	3m	13	GS	*mstk 10th, ld to aft 13th, sn btn, kpt on to tk 2nd post*	2	10
211	16/2	Southwell P'	(L)	MDO	3m	15	GS	*ld aft 1st, sn wll clr, hit 12th, hdd 2 out, btn & blnd last*	2	11
381	4/3	Leicester	(R)	HC	2m 1f	13	G	*ld, hdd when unsighted and u.r. 2 out.*	U	-
1268	27/4	Southwell P'	(L)	MDO	3m	13	G	*f 1st*	F	-

Blazes the trail but does not stay & a win hard to see 12

JADS LAD gr.g. 13 Warpath - Alexandra by Song R D Pullar

1996 7(0),4(0),5(0),6(0)

131	9/2	Alnwick	(L)	RES	3m	13	G	*wth ldr, ld 6th-8th, ev ch 4 out, kpt on onepcd*	3	0
415	8/3	Dalston	(R)	RES	3m	19	GS	*alwys bhnd, last & t.o. hlfwy, p.u. 14th*	P	0
729	29/3	Alnwick	(L)	RES	3m	10	F	*(bl) mid-div, lost tch 12th, p.u. 3 out*	P	0

No longer of any account 0

JAKE THE PEG (Irish) — I 140[P], I 239[P], I 302,

JAKI'S ROULETTE ch.m. 9 Rolfe (USA) - Stephouette by Stephen George D L Evans

1230	26/4	Pyle	(R)	MDO	3m	10	GS	*blnd 1st, t.o. whn ref 4th*	R	-

Rarely runs & 97's effort particularly useless 0

JANUARY DON b.h. 12 Hold Your Peace (USA) - Meg's Pride by Sparkler J S Warner

1996 5(0),2(19),3+(19),2(18),P(0),**P(0)**,3(11),1(11),3(11)

98	8/2	Great Treth'	(R)	OPE	3m	14	GS	*(bl) prom to 7th, sn wknd, t.o. & p.u. 3 out*	P	0
220	16/2	Heythrop	(R)	OPE	3m	20	G	*(bl) slw jmp 1st, sn rear, t.o. 12th*	10	0
484	9/3	Tweseldown	(R)	OPE	3m	10	G	*(bl) ld to 3rd, mstk 11th, outpcd 13th, no dang aft, kpt on*	4	15
705	29/3	Upper Sapey	(R)	CON	3m	4	GF	*(bl) 10l clr 5th, rmmndrs 11th, wknd frm 15th*	2	13
976	8/4	Heythrop	(R)	OPE	4m	7	F	*(bl) chsd ldrs, rmdrs 6th, 4th & drvn 15th, no ch frm 19th*	4	11
1055	13/4	Hackwood Pa'	(L)	OPE	3m	4	GF	*(bl) alwys cls up, chal frm 2 out, just hld*	2	17
1196	23/4	Andoversford	(R)	CON	3m	6	F	*(bl) ld, rmndrs 1st, hdd 3rd, rdn 10th, wknd 3 out*	4	0
1321	3/5	Bonvilston	(R)	MXO	3m	10	G	*(bl) rear & rdn alng, not trbl ldrs*	4	0

Becoming more reluctant each year; ultra-safe but unlikely to consent enough to win at 13 14

JAPODENE b.m. 9 Uncle Pokey - Another Denetop by Another River John Mackley

352	2/3	Great Stain'	(L)	MEM	3m	5	S	*ld til jnd 3 out, hdd nxt, 2nd & hld whn f last*	F	12
622	22/3	Hutton Rudby	(L)	MDO	3m	10	GF	*disp til ld 7th, disp 13th til hdd 3 out, unable to qckn*	2	13
1106	19/4	Hornby Cast'	(L)	MDO	3m	10	G	*(fav) ld til 5th, ld agn 8th, hdd 2 out, not qckn*	2	12
1571	26/5	Wetherby	(L)	HC	2 1/2m 110yds	15	GF	*alwys rear, well bhnd when p.u. before 4 out.*	P	0

Beat 9 others when placed & ought to be up to a win in 98 14

JAYANDOUBLEU(IRE) b.g. 8 Buckskin (FR) - Lucky House by Pollerton W A Crozier

1996 1(14),F(-)

337	1/3	Corbridge	(R)	RES	3m	11	G	*mid-div, mod prog 4 out, sn wknd*	6	10
415	8/3	Dalston	(R)	RES	3m	19	GS	*alwys prom, ld 11-12th, ev ch 3 out, sn onepcd*	4	13
1424	10/5	Aspatria	(L)	RES	3m	17	G	*made virt all, rdn & jnd 2 out, hld on gamely nr fin*	1	20
1509	17/5	Corbridge	(R)	INT	3m	10	GS	*(fav) prom, ld 4th, 3l clr & going wll whn f last, rmntd*	4	21
1545	24/5	Cartmel	(L)	HC	3 1/4m	14	G	*ld to 12th, cl up, outpcd last, kept on one pace straight, no impn on wnr.*	2	19

Maiden winner 96; improved 97 & unlucky in fair race 4th start; compensation awaits 98; G-S 22

J B LAD b.g. 11 Lighter - Cherry Fizz by Master Buck Mrs M J Tuck

1996 P(0)

45	1/2	Larkhill	(R)	RES	3m	14	GF	*in tch whn f 5th*	F	-
149	10/2	Hereford	(R)	HC	3m 1f 110yds	18	GS	*bhnd 9th, p.u. before 3 out.*	P	0
288	27/2	Ludlow	(R)	HC	3m	8	G	*prom to 6th, bhnd when mstk 9th, t.o..*	4	12
523	15/3	Cothelstone	(L)	RES	3m	14	GS	*prom til wknd 15th*	5	0
889	3/4	Taunton	(R)	HC	3m	7	F	*held up, hdwy 14th, hit next, staying on when carried left run-in.*	3	18
1211	26/4	Woodford	(L)	MEM	3m	8	G	*raced wd, ld 9th, wide & hdd 11th, outpcd frm 15th*	3	13
1289	30/4	Cheltenham	(L)	HC	3m 1f 110yds	6	GF	*mstks, ld 4th till 6th, weakening when blnd 14th, t.o. and p.u. before 17th.*	P	0
1491	14/5	Hereford	(R)	HC	3m 1f 110yds	11	G	*hdwy 12th, wknd 4 out.*	6	17
1544	21/5	Newton Abbot	(L)	HC	3 1/4m 110yds	11	G	*prom, jmpd slowly 4th, bhnd from 11th, t.o. when hit 16th, blnd and u.r. next.*	U	-

Completely out of his depth but at least reliability earned some cash in H/Chases 14

JEEPERS (Irish) — I 43[1]

JEMBATO (Irish) — I 217[P], I 406[P]

JENAWAY (Irish) — I 10[F], I 19[6], I 139[P], I 318[P], I 401[3], I 493[4], I 544[F], I 548,

JENNYS PEARL (Irish) — I 169P, I 384P, I 428U, I 445P

JENNY WOOD ch.m. 6 Derrylin - Dancing Jenny by Goldhill — Miss C E J Dawson

161 15/2 Lanark (R) MDO 2m 5f 14 G *f 1st* F -

Could not have done less 0

JENOBI (Irish) — I 547F

JEROME JEROME b.g. 5 Arctic Lord - Polaris Song by True Song — G K Hullett

459 8/3 Great Treth' (R) MDO 3m 9 S *hld up, 6th 14th, lft 3rd 2 out, imprvd* 3 0
1094 16/4 Hockworthy (L) MDN 3m 11 GF *ran out & u.r. 3rd* r -
1246 26/4 Bratton Down (L) MDO 3m 16 GS *among chsng grp whn b.d. 14th* B -

Last when finishing & yet to capitalise; should do better with experience 11

JERRIGO b.g. 12 Reformed Character - High Jean by Arrigle Valley — S F Knowles

1996 P(0),3(16),5(0),2(20),2(15),U(-)

769 29/3 Dingley (R) CON 3m 14 G *alwys rear div, p.u. 4 out* P 0
1076 13/4 Guilsborough (L) MEM 3m 9 GF *wth ldr, lost plc 11th, effrt to ld 15th-3 out, btn nxt* 4 13

Steady but modest pointer; good ride for novice; likes Ampton; struggle to win again 15

JESTASTAR b.g. 6 Jester - Mickley Spacetrail by Space King — Mrs J Bush

1996 U(-),P(0)

181 15/2 Larkhill (R) MDO 3m 17 G *prom to 13th, wknd nxt, t.o. & p.u. 2 out* P 0

Three runs in 2 seasons & nothing yet 0

JESTER'S MOON ch.m. 5 Jester - Ice Moon by Ballymoss — M F Jones

748 29/3 Brampton Br' (R) MEM 3m 6 GF *jmpd novicey, prog to 20l 4th whn f flat aft 11th, dead* F -

Dead 0

JET JOCKEY b.g. 8 Relkino - Fen Mist by Deep Run — E Wonnacott

456 8/3 Great Treth' (R) INT 3m 11 S *towrds rear whn f 9th* F -
557 16/3 Ottery St M' (L) RES 3m 9 G *n.j.w. plld hrd in rear, mstk 11th, p.u. nxt* P 0
740 29/3 Higher Kilw' (L) MDN 3m 15 GF *rear whn blnd & u.r. 3rd* U -
795 31/3 Bishopsleigh (R) MDO 3m 12 G *ld to 17th, wknd rpdly nxt, p.u. last* P 0
1093 16/4 Hockworthy (L) RES 3m 16 GF *chsd ldrs, ld 10th-4 out, wknd nxt* 6 0
1260 27/4 Black Fores' (R) MDO 3m 12 F *made all, sn clr, unchal* 0 16

Very unlucky last start (void race); non-stayer but should find win on easy track in 98; Firm 15

JIGTIME b.m. 8 Scottish Reel - Travel Again by Derrylin — J W Hughes

1996 1(18),**1(28)**

289 28/2 Kelso (L) HC 3m 1f 8 GS *(fav) cl up, ld 12th, strly pressed from 2 out, driven clr after last.* 1 30
590 21/3 Kelso (L) HC 3 1/2m 5 G *(fav) trckd ldng pair, hdwy 16th, ld 3 out, rdn last, ran on strly.* 1 29
1096 18/4 Ayr (L) HC 3m 3f 110yds 7 G *(fav) chsd ldr, ld 10th, clr 4 out, kept on.* 1 29

Good H/Chaser; unbeaten 96/7; jumps & stays well; should aim higher 98; G-S 31

JILLY WIG(IRE) b.m. 5 Strong Gale - Music Interpreter by Kampala — Count K Goess-Saurau

656 22/3 Siddington (L) MDN 3m 7 F *jmpd slwly early, prom, ld 12th-aft 3 out, wknd apr last* 3 12

Promising debut in weak race & must have winning prospects if ready in 98 15

JIM CROW b.g. 8 Bay Spirit - Sinsinawa VI by Menelek — J M Salter

1996 P(0),U(-)

460 8/3 Great Treth' (R) MDO 3m 13 S *prom, 3rd hlfwy, losng grnd in 5th whn p.u. apr 15th* P 0
644 22/3 Castle Of C' (R) MDO 3m 9 G *made most to apr 13th, rdn 2 out, ld last, hld on gamely* 1 14
935 6/4 Charlton Ho' (L) RES 3m 7 G *in tch to 10th, wknd & p.u. 13th* P 0
1152 20/4 Stafford Cr' (R) MEM 3m 4 GF *(fav) disp til lft clr 4th, lft solo last* 1 10

Improved & won poor races on only completions; may still progress but needs to for Restricteds 15

JIMMY CONE ch.g. 14 Celtic Cone - True Member by New Member — Miss J Russell

1996 U(-),F(-)

108 8/2 Milborne St' (L) MXO 3m 6 GF *rear, outpcd frm 13th* 4 16
311 1/3 Clyst St Ma' (L) LAD 3m 9 HY *rear, prog 12th, ev ch 3 out, outpcd aft* 3 18
555 16/3 Ottery St M' (L) LAD 3m 10 G *prom early, lost tch 12th, bhnd frm 4 out* 6 0
929 6/4 Charlton Ho' (L) MEM 3m 5 G *t.o. til p.u. 8th* P 0

Staged brief revival early 97 but looks finished now 14

JIMMY DAN (Irish) — I 142, , I 261⁴, I 379U, I 474¹

JIMMY MAC JIMMY b.g. 10 Carriage Way - Tuthill Bello by Porto Bello — D R Barnard

1996 P(0),5(13),1(0),1(20),P(0),3(16),2(19),**P(0)**

63 1/2 Horseheath (R) OPE 3m 5 GF *prom, chsd wnr 6th-14th, no dang aft* 3 17
194 15/2 Higham (L) OPE 3m 12 G *mid-div, chsd ldrs 11th, no ch 1st pair aft 4 out, kpt on* 3 12
271 22/2 Ampton (R) CON 3m 15 G *mstks, chsd ldrs to 6th, no ch & j.s 14th, t.o.* 9 0
322 1/3 Marks Tey (L) OPE 3 1/2m 9 G *mid-div, 4th & ch 17th, wknng whn blndrd nxt* 4 16
707 29/3 High Easter (L) MEM 3m 2 F *nt fluent, slt ld to 14th, ld agn 2 out, kpt on* 1 13

Dual winner 96; struggling in Opens& weak Confined only possible in 98; Any 18

JIMMY MORREL br.g. 6 Baron Blakeney - Tower Bay by Tower Walk A Hollingsworth

224 16/2 Heythrop (R) MDN 3m 16 G *schoold in last, wll bhnd til p.u. 13th* P 0
261 22/2 Newtown (L) MDN 3m 16 G *bhnd, 13th whn u.r. 8th* U -
881 1/4 Upton-On-Se' (R) MDN 3m 13 GF *schoold rear, bhnd frm 12th, p.u. 3 out* P 0

Educational outings to date 0

JIMMY THE TAILOR (Irish) — **I** 1^{2}
JIMYRIL (Irish) — **I** 210^{F}
JINGLE JACK (Irish) — **I** 129^{P}
JINXEY GLEN (Irish) — **I** 251^{P}, **I** 292^{F}, **I** 370^{P}
JJ'S HOPE b.g. 13 Corawice - Harry's Hope N Holland

727 29/3 Sandon (L) RES 3m 6 GF *ld to 14th, sn btn, p.u. last* P 0
936 6/4 Tabley (R) MEM 3m 9 G *ld, blndrd 9th, hdd apr 14th, wknd, lft poor 3rd 2 out* 3 0
1175 20/4 Sandon (L) CON 3m 8 GF *alwys prom, outpcd frm 3 out* 4 12
1349 3/5 Gisburn (R) CON 3m 11 GF *chsd ldrs, 7l 5th at 12th, rmndrs 14th, btn 6th & p.u. 16th* P 0

Ex-Irish pointer; very modest form & no threat 11

JOBINGO b or br.g. 9 Rustingo - Ruths Image by Grey Love Mrs C M Poland

1996 P(0),6(0),5(10),5(0)

146 9/2 Tweseldown (R) MDO 3m 10 GF *mstks 3rd & 11th, ld nxt til wknd rpdly aft 2 out* 5 0
283 23/2 Charing (L) MDO 3m 16 G *blnd 2nd, prom til wknd 15th, t.o. & p.u. last* P 0
871 31/3 Hackwood Pa' (L) MDO 3m 7 F *nvr bttr than mid-div, wknd & p.u. 14th* P 0
1465 11/5 Tweseldown (R) MDO 3m 2 GF *ld, ran wd bend aft 14th & hdd, btn 2 out* 2 0
1568 25/5 Kingston Bl' (L) MDO 3m 11 GF *jmpd rght,hld up,prog to ld 10th,lft clr 13th,unchal aft* 1 13

Bombed home in weak race last start but doubtful stayer & Restricted unlikely; summer jumping 15

JOCTOR DON(IRE) b or br.g. 5 Pitpan - Thats Irish by Furry Glen Mrs Derek Strauss

225 19/2 Folkestone (R) HC 2m 5f 10 S *f 1st.* F -

The briefest of debuts 0

JOE PENNY gr.g. 8 Impecunious - Roberts Girl by Mount Hagen (FR) P J Kerley

1996 F(-),P(0),P(0)

20 25/1 Badbury Rin' (L) MDN 3m 9 GF *prom, cls 4th whn f 14th* F -
40 1/2 Larkhill (R) MDO 3m 5 GF *f 1st* F -

Dead 0

JOE RATTLE (Irish) — **I** 268^{P}, **I** 343^{P}, **I** 379^{P}
JOES FAVOURITE (Irish) — **I** 456^{4}, **I** 470^{2}, **I** 574^{P}
JOESTONE b.g. 12 Healaugh Fox - Our Fluff by Petit Instant Miss E B Godfrey

769 29/3 Dingley (R) CON 3m 14 G *rear div, mstk 3rd, t.o. 8th, p.u. 11th* P 0
924 6/4 Garthorpe (R) CON 3m 6 GF *mid-div, prog to 2nd 3 out, no ext & dmtd flat* 3 11
1187 20/4 Garthorpe (R) MEM 3m 9 GF *in tch, outpcd 12th, no ch frm 15th* 5 0
1205 26/4 Clifton On ' (L) CON 3m 13 GS *alwys 6th/7th, outpcd 5 out* 6 11

Revived after 3 years absence but unable to recapture form now 10

JOHN IRELAND (Irish) — **I** 190^{1}
JOHNNY CLAW (Irish) — **I** 76^{P}, **I** 104^{P}, **I** 203^{P}
JOHNNY'S ECHO (Irish) — **I** 82^{3}, **I** 146^{P}, **I** 301^{F}, **I** 544^{P}
JOHNNY THE FOX(IRE) ch.g. 9 Hardboy - Miss Cheyne by Mansingh (USA) C C Bennett

1996 **2(NH),2(NH),2(NH),4(24)**

180 15/2 Larkhill (R) MXO 3m 6 G *t.d.e. lost tch 10th, t.o. 14th, p.u. 2 out* P 0
305 1/3 Parham (R) OPE 3m 9 G *rear til u.r. 9th* U -
888 3/4 Aintree (L) HC 3m 1f 9 G *u.r. 1st.* U -
1203 26/4 Worcester (L) HC 2m 7f 110yds 10 S *mstk 1st, bhnd from 6th, t.o. when p.u. before 10th.* P 0

Ex-useful Irish pointer-H/Chaser; all over the place in England & can only be watched 15

JOHN ROBIN b.g. 5 Green Adventure (USA) - Pamaris by Pamroy Mrs D A Smith

44 1/2 Larkhill (R) MDO 3m 9 GF *pllng, in tch til f 5th* F -
127 9/2 Cottenham (R) MDO 3m 11 GF *s.s. & green, prog to prss ldr 8th, wknd 16th* 4 0

Some promise but vanished after an 8 days season 12

JOHN ROGER b.g. 11 Impecunious - Romany Serenade by Romany Air — H J Manners

1996 F(-),P(0),1+(14)

No	Date	Course		Race	Dist	Rnrs	Going	Comment	Pl	Rtg
295	1/3	Didmarton	(L)	OPE	3m	9	G	*last pair & t.o. til u.r. 9th*	U	-
397	8/3	Barbury Cas'	(L)	XX	3m	10	G	*prom, blnd 7th, 5th & outpcd 14th, no dang aft, t.o.*	6	0
655	22/3	Siddington	(L)	RES	3m	10	F	*rear, p.u. 5th*	P	0
1144	19/4	Larkhill	(R)	RES	3m	3	F	*alwys 2nd, 5l down & rdn 3 out, kpt on flat, nt rch wnr*	2	11
1449	10/5	Kingston Bl'	(L)	RES	3m	8	G	*in tch, 2nd at 5th, wll bhnd frm 7th, styd on*	7	10
1563	25/5	Kingston Bl'	(L)	MEM	3m	5	GF	*trckd ldng trio, jmpd slwly 11th, wknd aft 13th*	4	0

Dead/heated in Maiden 96; novice-ridden & very disappointing; safely ignored now 10

JOHN'S RIGHT (Irish) — **I** 41, , **I** 75^{6}, **I** 256^{5}, **I** 320^{2}, **I** 382^{2}, **I** 420^{3}, **I** 448^{2}

JOHNSTHEMAN (Irish) — **I** 64^{4}, **I** 106^{2}, **I** 160^{1}, **I** 229^{1}, **I** 279^{2}, **I** 358^{3}

JOINT ACCOUNT ch.g. 7 Sayyaf - Dancing Clara by Billion (USA) — Mrs F E Needham

1996 P(0),U(-),F(-),U(-),P(0),F(-)

No	Date	Course		Race	Dist	Rnrs	Going	Comment	Pl	Rtg
253	22/2	Brocklesby '	(L)	MDO	3m	6	G	*made all, jmpng vntly rght, bttr spd on flat*	1	14
424	8/3	Charm Park	(L)	RES	3m	12	GF	*pulld hrd, alwys prom, ev ch 3 out, onepcd*	5	15
676	23/3	Brocklesby '	(L)	RES	3m	14	GF	*keen hld, chsd ldrs, 3rd whn u.r. 6th*	U	-
856	31/3	Charm Park	(L)	RES	3m	8	F	*cls up, 2nd 4 out, chsd wnr, mstk 2 out, alwys hld*	2	18
1101	19/4	Hornby Cast'	(L)	RES	3m	14	G	*prom, trckd ldr 6th, disp 8th, ld 4 out, hdd 2 out,rlld last*	2	18
1421	10/5	Easingwold	(L)	RES	3m	8	GF	*(fav) mid-div, prog 12th, chal going wll 2 out, rdn & ran on flat*	1	17

Failed to complete 96; more amenable & much improved 97; fair form; can upgrade 98; G-F 19

JOKERS PATCH ch.g. 10 Hotfoot - Rhythmical by Swing Easy (USA) — Mrs D L Gillies

1996 P(0),4(0),6(0),P(0),3(0),4(0),5(0),P(0)

No	Date	Course		Race	Dist	Rnrs	Going	Comment	Pl	Rtg
454	8/3	Great Treth'	(R)	LAD	3m	7	S	*last frm 7th, t.o. p.u. apr 14th*	P	0

Schoolmaster & no stamina - just potters around the back 0

JOLI HIGH NOTE b.m. 8 Senang Hati - Major Symphony by Trombone — Mrs C Barnett

1996 P(0),U(-),P(0),2(12),3(10),8(0)

No	Date	Course		Race	Dist	Rnrs	Going	Comment	Pl	Rtg
527	15/3	Cothelstone	(L)	MDN	3m	14	GS	*sn rear, bhnd & p.u. 13th*	P	0

Placed in weak Maidens 96 & soon disappeared in 97 10

JOLLY DECENT (Irish) — **I** 39^{4}, **I** 322^{1}

JOLLY FELLOW b.g. 13 Pimpernels Tune - Jolie Fille — Miss S M Ward

1996 8(0),2(16),6(12),**11(0)**,2(17)

No	Date	Course		Race	Dist	Rnrs	Going	Comment	Pl	Rtg
163	15/2	Witton Cast'	(R)	MEM	3m	5	F	*rear, lost tch 7th, kpt on flat*	2	0
352	2/3	Great Stain'	(L)	MEM	3m	5	S	*mid-div, 2nd 7th, disp 3 out, ld nxt, 2l up whn f last*	F	14
694	29/3	Stainton	(R)	CON	3m	11	F	*rear & sn strggling, t.o. 12th, u.r. 14th*	U	-
1169	20/4	Hexham Poin'	(L)	RES	3m	9	GF	*prog frm rear to 4th at 12th, chal 3 out, ld last, styd on*	1	16
1221	26/4	Balcormo Ma'	(R)	INT	3m	1	F	*walked over*	1	0
1332	3/5	Mosshouses	(L)	INT	3m	4	F	*hld up, went 2nd 13th, outpcd frm 2 out*	2	10
1427	10/5	Aspatria	(L)	INT	3m	7	G	*last & wll bhnd 7th, t.o. 11th, cont mls bhnd*	5	0
1509	17/5	Corbridge	(R)	INT	3m	10	GS	*(bl) rear, prog 10th, chsd ldr 11th til f nxt, dead*	F	-

Dead 13

JOLLY GHOST b.g. 8 Grey Ghost - Pamolie by Pamroy — Miss S Haykin

No	Date	Course		Race	Dist	Rnrs	Going	Comment	Pl	Rtg
266	22/2	Duncombe Pa'	(R)	RES	3m	19	G	*rear, lost tch 8th, t.o. 11th, p.u. 14th*	P	0
357	2/3	Great Stain'	(L)	MDO	3m	15	S	*alwys prom, ev ch 2 out, onepcd*	3	14
429	8/3	Charm Park	(L)	MDO	3m	14	GF	*prom, lft 2nd 10th, ld brfly 2 out til apr last, outpcd*	2	14
693	29/3	Stainton	(R)	MEM	3m	3	F	*(fav) trckd ldr,ld 4th til hdd 8th,ld 16th,drew clr frm 2 out,easy*	1	12

Missed 96; found dire race to break duck & needs to step up for Restricted hopes 15

JOLLY JAPE (Irish) — **I** 66^{P}, **I** 107^{P}, **I** 324^{3}, **I** 452^{2}, **I** 490^{2}

JOLLY LAD (Irish) — **I** 86^{P}, **I** 146^{F}, **I** 324^{P}, **I** 422^{1}

JOLLY MAN (Irish) — **I** 85^{P}, **I** 142^{1}

JOLLY PADDY (Irish) — **I** 85^{P}, **I** 192^{5}, **I** 261^{P}, **I** 317^{P}, **I** 378, , **I** 515^{P}

JOLLY SENSIBLE gr.m. 8 Pragmatic - Jolly Regal by Jolly Good — W H Whitley

1996 4(12),P(0)

No	Date	Course		Race	Dist	Rnrs	Going	Comment	Pl	Rtg
54	1/2	Wadebridge	(L)	MDO	3m	13	G	*(bl) nvr bttr than mid-div*	5	10
553	16/3	Ottery St M'	(L)	MDN	3m	15	G	*rear til f 7th*	F	-
1034	12/4	Lifton	(R)	MDN	3m	7	F	*(bl) alwys front rank, prssd ldr 14th, no ext frm nxt*	3	13

Not beaten far 3rd start but finished lame; may strike lucky if fit 98 13

JOLLY SHORT NECK (Irish) — **I** 303, , **I** 399^{2}, **I** 489^{P}, **I** 609^{5}

JOLLY SWAGMAN b.g. 6 Governor General - Armour Of Light by Hot Spark — B R Hughes

1996 P(0),P(0),P(0),P(0),F(-),P(0),4(10)

184	15/2 Erw Lon	(L) MDN 3m	14 G	*mstks, chsd wnr to 6th, cls up 12th, wknd rpdly 14th,p.u.nxt*	P	0
404	8/3 Llanfrynach	(R) INT 3m	17 G	*mid-div, 7th at 11th, wknd & p.u. 2 out*	P	0
639	22/3 Howick	(L) MDN 3m	15 GF	*ld, wll clr 8th, wknd rpdly 13th, f nxt*	F	-
841	31/3 Lydstep	(L) MDO 3m	8 F	*mid-div, prog 13th, ld 15th, unchal aft*	1	15
1008	12/4 St Hilary	(R) RES 3m	11 GF	*hld up rear, went 4th hlfwy, no frthr prog*	4	0
1227	26/4 Pyle	(R) RES 3m	15 GS	*rear,gd prog to chs ldrs 13th, wknd rpdly & p.u. nxt*	P	0
1322	3/5 Bonvilston	(R) RES 3m	9 G	*prom,3rd at 9th, ld apr 13th, hdd nxt,poor 4th & p.u.flat*	P	0
1468	11/5 Erw Lon	(L) INT 3m	7 GS	*nvr nrr than 3rd, onepcd*	3	0

Bombed home in bad race; finished 4 of 15 starts & non-stayer; Restricted prospects slim 14

JONES gr.g. 7 Alias Smith (USA) - Miss Prospect by Sweet Story — Mrs C Croxford-Adams

340	1/3 Corbridge	(R) MDN 3m	10 G	*rear, lost tch 7th, t.o. 10th, p.u. 12th*	P	0
417	8/3 Dalston	(R) MDO 2 1/2m	11 GS	*unruly pddck, s.s. jmpd bdly, t.o. 11th*	5	0
730	29/3 Alnwick	(L) MDO 2 1/2m	9 F	*alwys last pair, t.o. final cct, p.u. 3 out*	P	0

Shows no aptitude yet 0

JORODEC (Irish) — **I** 64U, **I** 261U

JOSALADY (Irish) — **I** 32U, **I** 61P, **I** 3446, **I** 3896

JOSH THE BOSS (Irish) — **I** 4002

JOSIE'S TURN (Irish) — **I** 218P, **I** 497P

JO-SU-KI b.g. 10 Strong Gale - Glenalass by Deep Diver — Peter Saville

1996 P(0),6(0),P(0),4(0),1(15),**P(0)**

464	8/3 Eyton-On-Se'	(L) INT 3m	12 G	*u.r. 2nd*	U	-
667	23/3 Eaton Hall	(R) CON 3m	10 GF	*mid-div early, t.o. 11th, p.u. nxt*	P	0
851	31/3 Eyton-On-Se'	(L) INT 3m	8 GF	*ld, 25l clr whn u.r. 4th*	U	-
937	6/4 Tabley	(R) CON 3m	10 G	*wiped round start, t.o. whn tried to ref & u.r. 7th*	U	-
1002	12/4 Alpraham	(R) CON 3m	4 GF	*rear, 10l 4th whn f 13th, dead*	F	-

Dead 13

JOURNEYS FRIEND(IRE) b.g. 9 Green Shoon - Carry On Polly by Pollerton — J N Dalton

1996 **U(NH),2(NH),U(NH),1(NH)**

330	1/3 Eaton Hall	(R) CON 3m	16 GS	*(fav) wth ldrs whn f 7th*	F	-

Novice chase winner 96; vanished after fall & best watched initially 98 17

JOURNO'S JOY b.m. 7 First Footman - Levotesse by Levmoss — Mrs M A Goldsworthy

185	15/2 Erw Lon	(L) MDN 3m	14 G	*mstk 2nd, sn rear, t.o. & p.u. 13th*	P	0
405	8/3 Llanfrynach	(R) RES 3m	15 G	*mid-div, prog 15th, nrst fin*	4	13

Ran well in decent Restricted last start & Maiden likely if fit 98 14

JOYCES HOPE (Irish) — **I** 388P, **I** 407P, **I** 501P, **I** 591U

JOYFUL HERO b.m. 7 War Hero - Joy Travel by Ete Indien (USA) — R Dench

1996 P(0),F(-),4(0),3(0),0(0)

61	1/2 Horseheath	(R) MDO 3m	9 GF	*(fav) keen hld, hld up, prog 9th, btn 14th, p.u. 3 out*	P	0
686	29/3 Charing	(L) MDO 2 1/2m	5 F	*not fluent, chsd ldrs final ctt, lft 2nd 4 out,rddn & no imp*	2	0
1380	5/5 Northaw	(L) MDO 3m	4 F	*alwys last, in tch til rdn & btn 3 out, p.u. last*	P	0

Placed 4 times but all dire races & nowhere near a win 0

JOYFUL JOAN(IRE) b.m. 6 Viteric (FR) - Nana's Gift by Side Track — Mrs Richard Pilkington

1996 F(-),P(0)

196	15/2 Higham	(L) MDO 3m	12 G	*mid-div, chsd ldrs 15th, wknd rpdly nxt*	3	0
438	8/3 Higham	(L) MDO 3m	8 G	*(fav) handy in 3rd/4th, not qckn 16th, wknd 3 out*	3	0

Beaten long way both starts & finished early; no real prospects yet 0

JOYNEY br.m. 10 Harlow (USA) - Whipper Snapper by Menelek — Miss Kathryn Guard

1996 S(-),P(0),P(0),3(14),3(12),2(13),3(10)

87	2/2 Wolverhampt'	(L) MDO 3m	11 GS	*rear, prog 9th, chsd wnr 2 out, no imp, fin tired*	2	10

261	22/2	Newtown	(L) MDN 3m	16	G	*chsd ldrs to 12th, wknd, p.u. 3 out*	P	0
437	8/3	Upton-On-Se'	(R) MDO 3m	15	G	*prog 12th, 10l 4th whn mstk 3 out, kpt on onepcd*	2	11
706	29/3	Upper Sapey	(R) MDO 3m	15	GF	*(fav) effrt frm 12th to go 4l 3rd 17th, unable to trbl wnnr*	2	14
1150	19/4	Chaddesley '	(L) MDO 3m	7	GF	*rear & not fluent,effrt to chs wnr 4 out,12l down & u.r.2out*	U	-
1402	5/5	Ashorne	(R) MDO 3m	11	G	*(fav) prog 10th,lft 2nd 15th,ld 2 out,hrd rdn & hdd nr fin*	2	14
1528	17/5	Bredwardine	(R) MDO 3m	17	G	*alwys handy, ld 13th-15th, styd on onepcd frm 2 out*	3	12

Placed in 9 of last 11 starts but most frustrating; non-stayer & finds little; may find a chance 13

JOY STREET b.m. 6 Derring Rose - Not Negotiable by Sir Deamon — G J T Olver

1246	26/4	Bratton Down	(L) MDO 3m	16	GS	*bhnd whn p.u. 13th*	P	0
1399	5/5	High Bickin'	(R) MDO 3m	12	G	*rear til p.u. 12th*	P	0
1554	24/5	Mounsey Hil'	(R) MDO 3m	14	G	*bhnd frm 8th, t.o. & p.u. aft 11th*	P	0

No sign of ability yet 0

JUDGEROGER b.g. 11 Decent Fellow - Carnation Cruise by Dual — Keith Lewis

1996 1(17),3(18)

377	4/3	Leicester	(R) HC 2 1/2m 110yds	15	G	*bhnd from 5th, p.u. before 3 out.*	P	0
1086	14/4	Southwell	(L) HC 3m 110yds	11	G	*bhnd from 10th, p.u. before 5 out.*	P	0

Useful in 94 but only 4 races since & soon tailed off both starts 97 13

JUDY LINE b.m. 8 Funny Man - Deirdre's Choice by Golden Love — K C Lewis

1996 4(10),1(16),2(10),U(-),5(13)

149	10/2	Hereford	(R) HC 3m 1f 110yds	18	GS	*bhnd hfwy, p.u. before 3 out.*	P	0
257	22/2	Newtown	(L) LAD 3m	12	G	*hld up in tch, lost plc 13th, sn bhnd, ran on agn 2 out*	6	14
399	8/3	Llanfrynach	(R) CON 3m	11	G	*mid-div, steady prog 13th, ld 3 out, sn clr*	1	20
572	16/3	Garnons	(L) INT 3m	13	G	*alwys chsng ldrs, not qckn 15th, styd on wll 2 out*	3	21
982	9/4	Ludlow	(R) HC 3m	6	F	*held up, well bhnd from 10th, t.o. when p.u. before 4 out.*	P	0

Restricted winner 96; improved & won fair Confined; more chances in 98 when ready; Good 21

JUDYS THIGH (Irish) — I 333P

JULIAS BOY (Irish) — I 169P

JULIES JOY (Irish) — I 263F, I 338P

JULY SCHOON b.g. 12 Green Shoon - Aghavine by Orchardist — T D B Underwood

1996 **P(NH),3(NH),6(NH),U(NH),5(NH)**

601	22/3	Parham	(R) RES 3m	4	F	*(fav) hld up, effrt 13th, outpcd 3 out, saddle slppd*	3	10
873	31/3	Hackwood Pa'	(L) RES 3m	6	F	*(fav) hld up going wll, clsd 2 out, ld apr last, easily*	1	19
989	12/4	Kingston Bl'	(L) INT 3m	7	GF	*hld up,prog 9th,not qckn 14th,ran on & ld aft 2 out,sn clr*	1	21
1160	20/4	Mollington	(R) INT 3m	9	GF	*w.w. prog 13th, effrt to chs wnr aft 2 out, no imp last*	2	20
1196	23/4	Andoversford	(R) CON 3m	6	F	*w.w. prog 11th, hit 16th, 3rd & rdn 2 out, kpt on*	3	17
1300	3/5	Weston Park	(L) CON 3m	8	G	*(fav) w.w. rear 4th, steady prog, 2nd 13th, ld aft 2 out,ran on*	1	20
1444	10/5	Peper Harow	(L) OPE 3m	5	GF	*hld up bhnd, prog 12th, chnc 3 out, 4th & hld whn blnd nxt*	4	18
1532	18/5	Mollington	(R) CON 3m	11	GS	*hld up,prog 5th,lost plc 11th,no imp 13th, bhnd & p.u.last*	P	0
1574	26/5	Chaddesley '	(L) CON 3m	8	F	*hld up, outpcd aft 11th, no ch aft*	4	0

Ex-Irish; remarkably improved at 12; stays & consistent; could win at 13; G-F 19

JUNCTION TWENTYTWO ch.g. 7 Local Suitor (USA) - Pollinella by Charlottown — C G Major

1996 **14(NH),15(NH),14(NH),15(NH)**

749	29/3	Brampton Br'	(R) OPE 3m	4	GF	*cls up, rdn to chs wnr 13th, mstk & wknd nxt, p.u. last*	P	0
1062	13/4	Maisemore P'	(L) MXO 3m	12	GF	*(bl) chsd ldrs, 4th & rdn 11th, wknd, t.o. & p.u. 2 out*	P	0
1454	11/5	Maisemore P'	(L) MEM 3m	5	G	*(bl) ld to 15th, hrd rdn & wknd, fin exhausted*	2	10

No prospects 0

JUNIPER LODGE br.g. 9 Impecunious - Miss Ticklemouse by Rhodomantade — Mrs W Jarrett

1996 F(-),F(-),3(0),3(10),3(12)

43	1/2	Larkhill	(R) MDO 3m	10	GF	*mstk 1st,prom,ld 8-13th,chal & lft in ld aft last,all out*	1	14
178	15/2	Larkhill	(R) CON 3m	9	G	*prom, mstk 2nd, chsd ldr 9th-13th, wknd apr 3 out*	4	10
516	15/3	Larkhill	(R) RES 3m	7	GF	*wth ldr, ld 8-13th, 2nd aft til mstk 2 out, wknd*	4	11
1157	20/4	Stafford Cr'	(R) RES 3m	11	GF	*prom til 9th, p.u. apr 11th*	P	0

Probably fortunate but deserved win; may be problems last start; Restricted unlikely 14

JUPITER MOON b.g. 8 Jupiter Island - Troy Moon by Troy — John D Higgs

1996 U(-),5(0),F(-),1(13),4(14)

92	6/2	Wincanton	(R) HC 3m 1f 110yds	6	GF	*soon bhnd, t.o. 9th, p.u. before 12th.*	P	0
376	3/3	Windsor	(R) HC 3m	11	GF	*nvr far away, hdwy to chase wnr from 2 out.*	2	21
489	10/3	Plumpton	(L) HC 3m 1f 110yds	7	GS	*chsd ldrs, ld 16th, hung left run-in, held on well.*	1	22

1087 16/4 Cheltenham (L) HC 3 1/4m 110yds 8 GF *held up, blnd and u.r. 5th.* U -
1098 19/4 Bangor (L) HC 3m 110yds 9 G *in tch, outpcd from 5 out, soon no dngr.* 3 19

Confined winner 96; well-ridden to land soft H/Chase; very hard to place in 98; G-S 21

JUST A BREEZE (Irish) — I 26[1], I 37[1], I 244[4], I 455[2], I 492[2], I 573[3], I 598,

JUST A KING b.g. 6 Rakaposhi King - Karmelanna by Silly Season Miss G Poad

899 5/4 Wetherby Po' (L) MDO 3m 3 F *sttld 3rd,trckd ldr 14th,rdn 3 out,2l down whn lft clr 2 out* 1 10

Meaningless win & much to prove yet 10

JUST A MADAM(IRE) gr.m. 7 Roselier (FR) - La Bise by Callernish M J Gingell

1996 2(14),2(13),3(16),1(17),5(10),**3(NH)**

10 25/1 Cottenham (R) INT 3m 7 GF *ld to 3rd, outpcd 14th, 4th whn blnd 2 out, kpt on flat* 3 18

Maiden winner 96; ran well only start 97 but vanished; novice-ridden to no effect 18

JUST A PLAYBOY (Irish) — I 40[P], I 77[P], I 261[P], I 321[3], I 534[3], I 568[P]

JUST A SINGLE(IRE) b.g. 6 Adbass (USA) - Sniggy by Belfort (FR) M J Brown

1996 **8(NH)**

264 22/2 Duncombe Pa' (R) MEM 3m 9 G *plld hrd in rear, outpcd 10th, t.o. 13th* 5 0
428 8/3 Charm Park (L) MDO 3m 10 GF *ld til hdd last, ran v wd final bnd, rlld fin* 2 13
623 22/3 Hutton Rudby (L) MDO 3m 9 GF *(fav) prom,ld frm 5th,hung bdly rght apr 7th & 13th whn ran out* r -

Shows ability but steering problems & finished early; L/H may be essential 14

JUST BE LUCKY (Irish) — I 48[P], I 80[F], I 140[P], I 264[1]

JUST BEN br.g. 9 Oats - Kayella by Fine Blade (USA) R L Persey

1996 P(0),1(20),P(0),4(13),1(20),5(15),2(20),1(19)

236 22/2 Lemalla (R) INT 3m 12 S *handy, 3rd at 11th, wll plcd til wknd 3 out, bttr for race* 4 19
456 8/3 Great Treth' (R) INT 3m 11 S *lft in ld 11th, hdd 14th, sn outpcd* 2 14
631 22/3 Kilworthy (L) INT 3m 8 G *ld 10th, blndrd & lost plc 14th, styd on wll clsng stgs* 2 21
1089 16/4 Hockworthy (L) CON 3m 7 GF *nvr going wll, lost plc 8th, wll bhnd whn p.u. 13th* P 0
1244 26/4 Bratton Down (L) CON 3m 14 GS *(fav) ld 5th, made rest, pshd out cls home* 1 19
1441 10/5 Holnicote (L) CON 3m 7 G *disp 9th-12th, cls up & ev ch til outpcd 2 out* 2 19
1544 21/5 Newton Abbot (L) HC 3 1/4m 110yds 11 G *chsd ldrs to 12th, soon wknd, t.o..* 6 0

Won 3 in 96; not progressed & burdened with penalties 97; best sharp tracks; do better 98; G-S 21

JUST BERT(IRE) b.g. 7 Kambalda - Cappagh Flier by Lock Diamond Mrs J Alford

1996 1(22),U(-),2(19),U(-)

51 1/2 Wadebridge (L) CON 3m 4 G *(fav) trckd ldrs, ld 3 out, grad asserted* 1 20
174 15/2 Ottery St M' (L) LAD 3m 9 G *alwys rear, no ch frm 4 out, nrst fin* 6 16
238 22/2 Lemalla (R) LAD 3m 9 S *alwys prom, 2nd frm 9th til ld aft 3 out, ev ch, no ext last* 2 23
529 15/3 Wadebridge (L) LAD 3m 2 GF *(fav) ld/disp til drew clr frm 2 out* 1 21
1340 3/5 Flete Park (R) LAD 4m 5 G *bhnd frm 12th, f 17th* F -

Useful prospect in 96; interrupted season 97; can win more in wet year; G-Hy 23

JUST CHARLIE b.g. 8 Bustino - Derring Miss by Derrylin Mrs Susan E Mason

1996 3(19),1(23),6(11),1(21),4(17),2(22),**2+(NH)**

75 2/2 Market Rase' (L) CON 3m 10 GF *sn wl bhnd, prog 11th, ld 2 out, hld on, und pres flat* 1 24
164 15/2 Witton Cast' (R) INT 3m 6 F *(fav) trckd ldr, disp 8th, mstk nxt, ld 14th, prssd 2 out, qcknd* 1 21
422 8/3 Charm Park (L) CON 3m 8 GF *(Jt fav) ld to 4th, lft in ld 7th, jnd 4 out, lft wll clr nxt, easily* 1 23
506 15/3 Dalton Park (R) CON 3m 16 GF *(fav) prom, ld 6th, made rest, comf* 1 23
696 29/3 Stainton (R) OPE 3m 5 F *(fav) trckd ldr,lost plc qckly 4th,t.o. 11th,ran on strgly 2 out* 3 18
1247 26/4 Easingwold (L) CON 3m 9 GS *in tch, disp 11-14th, ld nxt, made all aft, comf* 1 25
1407 5/5 Witton Cast' (R) OPE 3m 4 GS *(fav) ld, disp 7th, ld 4 out, drew clr 2 out, eased flat* 1 22
1420 10/5 Easingwold (L) OPE 3m 5 GF *(fav) sttld in 3rd, blnd 6th & lost plc, prog to 2nd 12th, f 14th* F -

Dual winner 96; good pointer now; consistent; hard to beat in Opens 98; G/S-F 26

JUST CHICA gr.g. 6 Siberian Express (USA) - Lightening Reef by Bon Sang (FR) Russell G Abrey

439 8/3 Higham (L) MDO 3m 11 G *mid-div, outpcd aft 11th, rear & p.u. 15th* P 0
1282 27/4 Fakenham P-' (L) MDO 3m 8 G *ld, jmpd rght 2nd, hdd nxt, disp 3 out-apr last, onepcd* 3 12

Not beaten far in weak race & should be able to find a chance in 98 14

JUST COMING b.g. 7 Primitive Rising (USA) - Fair Louise by Blakeney R G P Mason

429 8/3 Charm Park (L) MDO 3m 14 GF *mid-div, prog 12th, ld apr last, sn drew clr, comf* 1 17

Missed 96; clear-cut winner (decent time) only start; can certainly upgrade if fit 98 19

JUST DONALD b.g. 10 Politico (USA) - Brox Treasure by Broxted John Honeyball

1996 2(0),P(0),6(0),U(-),5(0),r(-),U(-)

23	25/1	Badbury Rin'	(L)	RES	3m	8	GF	*rear, lost tch 12th, t.o.*	5	0
106	8/2	Milborne St'	(L)	RES	3m	12	GF	*alwys rear, t.o. 4 out*	6	0
313	1/3	Clyst St Ma'	(L)	RES	3m	10	HY	*rear til f 11th*	F	-

No longer of any account 0

JUST FOR KICKS br.g. 11 Saher - Kix by King Emperor (USA) Mrs Nicki Craggs

1425	10/5	Aspatria	(L)	LAD	3m	6	G	*in tch, chsd ldng pair 14th, no imp, kpt on flat*	3	17
1511	17/5	Corbridge	(R)	LAD	3m	10	GS	*rear, dtchd 4th, rpd prog 4 out, ld last, hdd nr fin*	2	22
1606	1/6	Dingley	(R)	LAD	3m	13	GF	*rear, hmpd 6th, 9th & no ch hlfwy, ran on 3 out, nrst fin*	3	20

Missed 95/6; ran well on return in decent races; good enough to win fair race at 12; G-S 22

JUST FOR ME(IRE) b.g. 8 Callernish - Just Reward by Choral Society J A Moore

1996 **P(NH),P(NH),P(NH),P(NH)**

120	9/2	Wetherby Po'	(L)	MDO	3m	18	GF	*alwys rear, t.o. & p.u. 11th*	P	0
357	2/3	Great Stain'	(L)	MDO	3m	15	S	*prom, fdd 12th, t.o. & p.u. 3 out*	P	0
778	31/3	Carlisle	(R)	HC	3 1/4m	14	G	*chsd ldrs, hit 8th, outpcd last 5.*	7	0
1545	24/5	Cartmel	(L)	HC	3 1/4m	14	G	*midfield, hit 7th, rdn apr 4 out, kept on one pace, no impn on ldrs.*	5	17

Beaten 7l in weak H/Chase last start & Maiden a formality IF reproduced in 98 16

JUST HANG ON (Irish) — **I** 219^{P}

JUST HARVEY (Irish) — **I** 160^{B}, **I** 206^{P}

JUST HOLD ON (Irish) — **I** 58^{F}, **I** 589^{4}

JUST JACK br.g. 11 Ovac (ITY) - Precision Chopper by Menelek P Jonason

1996 7(0),**4(16)**,**U(-)**,**5(14)**,2(18),**P(0)**

70	2/2	Higham	(L)	OPE	3m	5	GF	*trckd ldng pair, chal 4 out, ld aft nxt, qcknd clr, eased*	1	19
154	14/2	Fakenham	(L)	HC	2m 5f 110yds	10	G	*chsd ldrs from 10th til wknd after 5 out.*	4	15
444	8/3	Higham	(L)	CON	3m	8	G	*cls up, hit 9th, blnd & u.r. 11th*	U	-
503	15/3	Ampton	(R)	XX	3m	11	GF	*(fav) in tch, prog to chs wnr 16th, wknd 3 out, fin tired*	4	0
780	31/3	Fakenham	(L)	HC	3m 110yds	7	G	*in tch, rdn and one pace from 3 out.*	5	12
1279	27/4	Fakenham P-'	(L)	OPE	3m	7	G	*in tch, prog 9th, went 2nd 13th, chal 2 out, no ext last*	2	20
1506	16/5	Folkestone	(R)	HC	2m 5f	8	G	*mstk 2nd, prom, chsd ldr after 8th till 10th, outpcd from next.*	4	13

H/Chase winner 95; found weak Open & usually outclassed now; hard to place at 12; Good 18

JUST JEEVES ch.g. 7 Homeboy - Nom de Plume by Aureole H Hill

837	31/3	Thorpe Lodge	(L)	LAD	3m	5	F	*last til u.r. 6th*	U	-

No promise 0

JUST JESSICA br.m. 8 State Diplomacy (USA) - Harpalyce by Don't Look Lady Susan Watson

1996 F(-),P(0),P(0)

120	9/2	Wetherby Po'	(L)	MDO	3m	18	GF	*mid-div, lost tch 6th, t.o. & p.u. 10th*	P	0
346	2/3	Market Rase'	(L)	MDO	3m	10	GF	*mid-div, lft 3rd 6th, lost tch apr 13th, t.o.*	4	0
1069	13/4	Whitwell-On'	(R)	RES	3m	12	G	*prom til fdd frm 12th*	8	0

Ran prominently 97 but has only beaten one other finisher to date 0

JUST JOE (Irish) — **I** 152^{F}, **I** 220^{P}

JUST JOHNIE ch.g. 7 Meadowbrook - Just Diamonds by Laurence O R G Watson

1996 P(0),P(0)

429	8/3	Charm Park	(L)	MDO	3m	14	GF	*prom, wnt 3rd 12th, ev ch 3 out, sn outpcd*	3	12
510	15/3	Dalton Park	(R)	MDO	3m	14	GF	*(fav) prom, ld & going wll whn f 15th*	F	-
1073	13/4	Whitwell-On'	(R)	MDO	2 1/2m 88yds	17	G	*(fav) alwys prom, ev ch 3 out, onepcd*	4	12
1105	19/4	Hornby Cast'	(L)	MDO	3m	11	G	*(fav) mid-div, prog 9th, wknd 3 out*	4	0

Proving expensive & failed in weak races last 2 starts; may win but you can afford to miss it 13

JUST LIKE MADGE b.m. 6 Cruise Missile - Madge Spartan S J Woolley

1996 P(0),P(0)

1537	18/5	Mollington	(R)	MDO	3m	14	GS	*t.d.e.,in tch,prssd ldr 13th,ld aft 3 out,lkd wnr & u.r. nxt*	U	14

Would have won poor race only start 97; not easy ride but should atone in 98 15

JUST MAI-BEE gr.g. 5 Chilibang - Just Maisy by Broadsword (USA) D L Claydon

275	22/2	Ampton	(R)	MDO	3m	10	G	*n.j.w. bhnd til p.u. 12th*	P	0
317	1/3	Marks Tey	(L)	MDN	3m	13	G	*bhnd 8th, t.o. & jmp slwly 11th, p.u. 13th*	P	0
499	15/3	Ampton	(R)	MDO	3m	9	GF	*mstks, disp ld to 7th, wknd 13th, t.o.*	8	0

Tailed off last on only completion 0

JUST MARMALADE ch.g. 8 Noalto - Kitty Come Home by Monsanto (FR) Mrs A D Williams

1996 1(15),4(16),3(14),1(18),3(15),3(16),P(0)

255 22/2 Newtown (L) CON 3m 14 G *chsd ldrs, pshd alng 10th, no imp frm 14th* 5 15
1013 12/4 Bitterley (L) CON 3m 14 GF *chsd ldr, ld 7th, rdn & no ext whn hdd 2 out* 2 19
1264 27/4 Southwell P' (L) INT 3m 9 G *alwys prom, ld 10th til hdd & wknd 3 out* 4 15
1412 7/5 Uttoxeter (L) HC 3 1/4m 10 GS *chsd lding pair till cannoned into by loose horse and b.d. 8th.* B -

Dual winner 96; changed hands; interrupted season & ground against; can win Confined; G-S 19

JUST MY BILL ch.g. 11 Nicholas Bill - Misnomer by Milesian Mrs K Heard

1996 2(17),0(0),2(20),**2(22)**,**4(18)**

237 22/2 Lemalla (R) CON 3m 13 S *s.s. prog 9th, went 3rd aft 16th, tk 2nd apr last, no ch wnr* 2 18
1033 12/4 Lifton (R) CON 3m 6 F *lft 2nd apr 4th til wknd aft last* 3 14
1256 27/4 Black Fores' (R) OPE 3m 4 F *mostly 2nd, slght ld 14th-nxt, outpcd aft* 3 20
1342 3/5 Flete Park (R) CON 3m 6 G *ld/disp 10th til slght ld 3 out, drew clr und pres nxt* 1 19
1484 11/5 Ottery St M' (L) OPE 3m 7 G *w.w. prog 13th, ran on und pres frm 3 out* 3 18
1579 26/5 Lifton (R) CON 3m 9 G *(Jt fav) s.s. mid-div hlfwy, prog 15th, chal 2 out, kpt on wll flat* 2 18

2 wins from last 25 starts; most consistent but very hard to win with; may find another Confined; GF ... 19

JUST MY HARRY (Irish) — **I** 354, , **I** 430[4], **I** 490[P], **I** 532[3], **I** 554[3], **I** 593[P]

JUST RALPH b.h. 12 Welsh Saint - Gully by Dike (USA) H C Coldicott

1064 13/4 Maisemore P' (L) CON 3m 13 GF *t.o. 8th, p.u. 10th* P 0
1212 26/4 Woodford (L) INT 3m 8 G *ld til apr 7th, wkng & rdn 10th, t.o. 12th, p.u. 3 out* P 0

No longer of any account 0

JUST RUFFLED b.g. 8 Rough Lad - Deep Harmony by White Hart Lane Mrs P A Hooper

840 31/3 Lydstep (L) MEM 3m 6 F *rear whn ref 5th* R -

A brief appearance 0

JUST SHIRLEY b.m. 7 Primitive Rising (USA) - Harpalyce by Don't Look Lady Susan Watson

79 2/2 Market Rase' (L) MDO 2m 5f 9 GF *alwys rr, t.o. & p.u. 11th* P 0
1074 13/4 Whitwell-On' (R) MDO 2 1/2m 88yds 16 G *rear, strgglng 8th, t.o. & p.u. 10th* P 0

No promise on either start 0

JUST SUPREME (Irish) — **I** 29[F]

JUST TAKETHE MICKY b.g. 7 Gay Meadow - Oujarater by Adropejo Lady Susan Watson

1996 P(0),U(-),P(0),F(-)

36 26/1 Alnwick (L) MDO 3m 15 G *jmp rght,chsd ldr,lft in ld apr 7th,hdd & wknd 13th,p.u.2out* P 0

Blazed away only start 97 & yet to complete the course 10

KABANCY b.g. 6 Kabour - Nikancy by Castlenik Miss P Zygmant

345 2/3 Market Rase' (L) MDO 3m 13 GF *keen hld, chsd ldr, blnd 3rd, ld apr nxt til f 6th* F -
479 9/3 Southwell P' (L) MDO 3m 15 G *raced wd, blnd 5th, t.o. 8th, p.u. 12th* P 0
549 16/3 Garthorpe (R) MDO 3m 16 GF *pulling, rr, prog to mid div whn hmpd & u.r. 8th* U -
771 29/3 Dingley (R) OPE 3m 10 G *abt 8th 1st m, t.o. 10th, p.u. 6 out* P 0
886 1/4 Flagg Moor (L) OPE 3m 3 G *schoold,immed t.o.,went 2nd 3 out,fin full of rnng,stewards* 2 0
928 6/4 Garthorpe (R) MDO 3m 8 GF *prom, ld 6th, going wll whn f 5 out* F -
1077 13/4 Guilsborough (L) CON 3m 16 GF *mstk 5th, last pair & t.o. til p.u. 13th* P 0
1310 3/5 Cottenham (R) MDO 3m 2 F *(fav) plld hrd, ld 4-6th, rstrnd til ld 3 out, sn wll clr* 1 0
1433 10/5 Marks Tey (L) OPE 3m 4 G *s.s. alwys last, mstk 3rd, wknd 10th, p.u. 12th* P 0
1575 26/5 Chaddesley ' (L) OPE 3m 10 F *alwys bhnd, t.o. & p.u. 12th, dsmntd* P 0

Very hard ride & found non-event when winning; badly campaigned & another win unlikely 11

KABWEE STAR (Irish) — **I** 57[P], **I** 148[2], **I** 297[4]

KACEY'S ANNIE (Irish) — **I** 195[F], **I** 321[F]

KALA DAWN b.m. 10 Kala Shikari - Morning Heather by Langton Heath Mrs B Everall

1996 3(15),2(14),3(12),5(0)

487 9/3 Tweseldown (R) MDO 3m 12 G *ld to 2nd, chsd wnr aft, no ch frm 15th, wknd flat* 4 0
658 22/3 Badbury Rin' (L) MDN 3m 6 F *in tch til blnd & u.r. 6th* U -
1021 12/4 Badbury Rin' (L) MEM 3m 2 F *jmp lft,made most til jnd 10th,mstk 16th,hd aft 2 out,onepcd* 2 0
1315 3/5 Holnicote (L) MDO 3m 7 G *ld, clr 12th, hdd 4 out, grad wknd* 5 0
1486 11/5 Ottery St M' (L) MDO 3m 17 G *alwys mid-div, nvr on trms* 4 0
1577 26/5 Chaddesley ' (L) MDO 3m 11 F *in tch til lost plc 9th, went poor 3rd aft 13th, plodded on* 3 10

Placed 7 times 96/7 but always well-beaten; novice-ridden; great fortune needed to win 11

KALAVO (Irish) — **I** 433[P]

KALOKAGATHOS b.g. 8 King Of Spain - Kip's Sister by Cawston's Clown Miss Nell Courtenay

1996 3(0),3(0),P(0),P(0)

736 29/3 Higher Kilw' (L) RES 3m 10 GF *bhnd til p.u. 14th* P 0

Placed twice in 96 but a brief appearance in 97 10

KALOORE ch.g. 8 Ore - Cool Straight by Straight Lad — Mrs J Alford

1996 2(22),1(25),1(23)

98	8/2	Great Treth'	(R)	OPE	3m	14 GS	*(fav) rear, prog 11th, hrd rdn to chs ldr 16th, ld last,jst hld on*	1	25
171	15/2	Ottery St M'	(L)	OPE	3m	9 G	*in tch, chsd alng frm 12th, outpcd frm 3 out*	3	19
493	12/3	Newton Abbot	(L)	HC	2m 5f 110yds	11 HY	*(Jt fav) in rear, rdn and hdwy 6 out, weakening when left 2nd last.*	2	20
628	22/3	Kilworthy	(L)	CON	3m	12 G	*(fav) (bl) mstk 13th,wnt 3rd 14th,cls 2nd nxt til hrd rdn to ld run in*	1	25
1341	3/5	Flete Park	(R)	OPE	3m	5 G	*(bl) sn rear, alwys bhnd, lft 2nd last*	2	18

Useful but disappointing season 97; ground against; thorough stayer; can do better 98; G-S 26

KAMADORA ch.g. 10 Kambalda - Icydora by Arctic Slave — Milson Robinson

1996 1(14),6(11),F(-),3(0),P(0),r(-)

140	9/2	Thorpe Lodge	(L)	RES	3m	7 GF	*rear, lsng tch whn ref 6th*	R	-

Won bad Maiden 96; signs unpromising now 0

KAMATRA EYRE (Irish) — I 90P

KAMBALDA BAY (Irish) — I 317F

KAMBALDA RAMBLER b or br.g. 13 Kambalda - Stroan Lass by Brave Invader (USA) — H Morton

1996 1(27),P(0),**2(23)**,**3(21)**,**U(-)**,1(23)

250	22/2	Brocklesby '	(L)	OPE	3m	6 G	*ld 5th, drew clr frm 4 out, wll clr whn f last, remntd*	3	25
378	4/3	Leicester	(R)	HC	2 1/2m 110yds	6 G	*raced keenly, soon chasing ldrs, ev ch 2 out, wknd last.*	4	22
1287	29/4	Huntingdon	(R)	HC	2 1/2m 110yds	14 G	*mid div, lost tch with ldrs 10th, kept on one pace from 3 out, no dngr.*	4	16
1359	5/5	Southwell	(L)	HC	3m 110yds	7 GS	*held up and bhnd, gd hdwy before 4 out, chal 2 out, ev ch last, kept on.*	2	22
1589	31/5	Market Rasen	(R)	HC	2 3/4m 110yds	10 GF	*nvr far away, ev ch 4 out, outpcd after next.*	3	23

Retains much ability but hard to place; best under 3m but H/Chase win unlikely at 14; G/F-G/S 22

KAN-ANN (Irish) — I 179F, I 212P

KANHA br.m. 5 Sousa - Alcassa (FR) by Satingo — Mrs B E Rounsevell

531	15/3	Wadebridge	(L)	MDO	3m	14 GF	*bhnd whn u.r. 12th*	U	-
808	31/3	Wadebridge	(L)	MDO	3m	8 F	*alwys towrds rear til p.u. bfr 4 out*	P	0
1034	12/4	Lifton	(R)	MDN	3m	7 F	*alwys rear til p.u. 14th*	P	0
1108	19/4	Flete Park	(R)	RES	3m	14 GF	*bhnd frm 10th*	7	0
1343	3/5	Flete Park	(R)	MDO	3m	13 G	*6th hlfwy, not rch ldrs*	5	0

beaten only 2 others when completing but showed marginal improvement last start 0

KANJO OLDA gr.m. 7 Scallywag - Devine Lady by The Parson — M A Lloyd

1996 P(0),P(0)

367	2/3	Garnons	(L)	MDO	2 1/2m	9 GS	*ld 4th til aft 12th, not qckn nxt, fin 3rd, disq*	0	11

Ran passably but rarely seen & more needed for a win 11

KARENS KING (Irish) — I 302[5], I 337, , I 430P, I 515P

KAREN'S LEADER (Irish) — I 115P, I 251P, I 360F, I 432[3]

KARICLEIGH BOY ch.g. 9 Nearly A Hand - Duvessa by Glen Quaich — Philip Rogers

1996 F(-),F(-),2(19)

236	22/2	Lemalla	(R)	INT	3m	12 S	*hdwy 12th, 4th at 15th, wknd nxt, bhnd & p.u. last*	P	0
456	8/3	Great Treth'	(R)	INT	3m	11 S	*prom, ld whn blnrd & u.r. 11th*	U	-
558	16/3	Ottery St M'	(L)	INT	3m	6 G	*sn bhnd, no ch frm 14th*	4	12
631	22/3	Kilworthy	(L)	INT	3m	8 G	*cls 2nd 10th til ld 14th,hdd last,wknd,disq lost wtcloth*	3D	20
1258	27/4	Black Fores'	(R)	INT	3m	5 F	*ld til ran out 3rd*	r	-
1342	3/5	Flete Park	(R)	CON	3m	6 G	*ld/disp til aft 3 out, wknd nxt, lost tack & p.u. last*	P	0
1582	26/5	Lifton	(R)	INT	3m	10 G	*ld 2nd-4th, ld 7th, made rest, just hld on*	1	16

Accident-prone but better than figures suggest & deserved win; Confined possible at best; G-S 19

KARLIMAY b.m. 7 Karlinsky (USA) - Mayspring by Silly Season — Mrs R Fell

1996 P(0),F(-),5(10),3(11),1(15),1(17),2(15),2(17)

96	8/2	Great Treth'	(R)	CON	3m	7 GS	*(fav) hld up, prog to remote 3rd at 15th, nvr nr ldrs, wknd 2 out*	4	12
454	8/3	Great Treth'	(R)	LAD	3m	7 S	*lost tch 12th, no ch frm 14th, t.o.*	4	0
555	16/3	Ottery St M'	(L)	LAD	3m	10 G	*rear, t.o. & p.u. 14th*	P	0

Dual winner 96; below form in 97 & finished early; best watched; G-S 17

KARLIN'S QUEST b.g. 6 Karlinsky (USA) - Lost Valley by Perdu — S C Horn

1996 **12(NH)**

236	22/2	Lemalla	(R)	INT	3m	12 S	*ld & mstk 1st, sn rear, bhnd & p.u. 10th*	P	0

624 22/3 Kilworthy (L) MEM 3m 7 G *mstk 1st, rear whn crashed thru wing 8th* r -
738 29/3 Higher Kilw' (L) CON 3m 8 GF *in tch in 3rd til outpcd frm 3 out* 3 15

Novice-ridden but showed 1st form last start; should try Maidens - chance if repeating form 14

KATE GALE (Irish) — I 396³

KATES CASTLE b.m. 10 Carlingford Castle - Nadezda by Menelek Ben Van Praagh

1996 P(0),4(17),3(14),1(19),1(19),P(0),**3(19)**

279 23/2 Charing (L) CON 3m 10 G *made most, blnd 3 out, mstk nxt, hdd & wknd last* 4 16
305 1/3 Parham (R) OPE 3m 9 G *ld to 12th, agn 4 out, ran on well frm 2 out* 1 20
600 22/3 Parham (R) MEM 3m 7 F *(fav) 6/4-4/6,ld to 7th & 10-13th,styd on strngly to ld 2 out,easy* 1 20
830 31/3 Heathfield (R) MXO 3m 6 F *(fav) ld/disp til ld 16th, 8l clr & hit 3 out, hit nxt, hdd flat* 3 18
1444 10/5 Peper Harow (L) OPE 3m 5 GF *ld, hit 10th, hdd 12th, sn rdn, wknd 3 out, p.u. last* P 0
1501 16/5 Folkestone (R) HC 3 1/4m 10 G *prom till 4th and weakening when blnd 3 out, no ch after.* 4 11

Won 4 of last 8 points; moderate but can win again; moderately ridden; Any 19

KATE'S MACHINE (Irish) — I 493ᴾ, I 531ᴾ

KATIE KITOFF ch.m. 5 Weld - Sea Rambler by Menelek C H Birch

941 6/4 Tabley (R) MDO 3m 11 G *prom, chsd ldr 7-13th, wknng whn ref & u.r. nxt* R -
1262 27/4 Southwell P' (L) MDO 3m 15 G *prom, disp 9th, mstk 13th & sn lost plc, t.o.* 7 0

Tailed off last when completing but may strip fitter in 98 0

KATIE PARSON ch.m. 10 The Parson - Little Welly by Little Buskins Mrs S E Vaughan

1996 4(11)

1013 12/4 Bitterley (L) CON 3m 14 GF *rear frm 8th, no ch whn p.u. aft 14th* P 0
1149 19/4 Chaddesley ' (L) RES 3m 6 GF *mstks, bhnd frm 9th, p.u. 12th* P 0

No longer of any account 0

KATIES ARGUMENT br.m. 12 St Columbus - Royaldyne by No Argument Miss J E Wilson

1996 4(15),3(11),6(13),7(0),2(19),B(-),U(-),P(0)

264 22/2 Duncombe Pa' (R) MEM 3m 9 G *ld to 3rd, rmnd prom, outpcd 12th, kpt on frm 3 out* 2 16
356 2/3 Great Stain' (L) INT 3m 9 S *rear & plenty to do 13th, prog 2 out, ran on well flat* 2 14
476 9/3 Southwell P' (L) XX 3m 6 G *rear, in tch to 12th, outpcd, went poor 3rd 3 out* 3 10
766 29/3 Whittington (L) INT 3m 10 S *alwys bhnd, tk 4th aft 2 out* 4 10
1072 13/4 Whitwell-On' (R) MXO 4m 21 G *rear, strgglng whn blnd 13th, sn t.o., p.u. 16th* P 0

Lost last 19 starts; needs a real stamina test; getting old now. 13

KATREE RUNNER b.g. 8 Scorpio (FR) - Last Run by Deep Run A J Scrimgeour

101 8/2 Great Treth' (R) MDO 3m 9 GS *in tch til wknd frm 14th, t.o.* 4 0
243 22/2 Lemalla (R) MDO 3m 12 S *nov rddn,chsd ldr 12th til lft in ld 16th, hdd 2 out,eased* 3 12

Decent performance 2nd start but vanished after; should win in 98 if ready 15

KAYAK POINT ch.g. 8 Remezzo - Snipe Shooter by Le Coq D'Or Mrs J E Goodall

204 15/2 Weston Park (L) RES 3m 13 G *rear, t.o. & p.u. aft 12th* P 0
347 2/3 Market Rase' (L) MDO 3m 9 GF *(bl) cls up, disp 6th-nxt, wknd 13th, p.u. nxt, lame* P 0

No encouragement & problems as well 0

KAZMAR (Irish) — I 405⁵

K C'S DANCER ch.g. 12 Buckskin (FR) - Lorna Lass by Laurence O D L Weaver

1996 **P(NH),6(NH),5(NH),7(NH),3(NH),5(NH)**

890 4/4 Aintree (L) HC 2 3/4m 14 G *held up, cld 6th, lost tch 13th (Valentine's), styd on same pace from 3 out.* 4 21
1290 30/4 Cheltenham (L) HC 4m 1f 10 GF *chsd wnr 12th till 20th, wknd 4 out, bhnd when p.u. before 2 out.* P 0

Winning hcaser; ran passably at Aintree but unlikely to achieve much at 13; stays 17

KEELSON (Irish) — I 41ᴾ, I 56²

KEEP A SECRET b.g. 6 Moor House - Potterway by Velvet Prince D G Atkinson

36 26/1 Alnwick (L) MDO 3m 15 G *last trio, t.o. & p.u. 12th* P 0
338 1/3 Corbridge (R) RES 3m 10 G *rear & bhnd, t.o. & p.u. last* P 0
622 22/3 Hutton Rudby (L) MDO 3m 10 GF *prom, mstk 12th, fdd nxt* 4 0

Tailed off in fair Maiden & could do better with experience 0

KEEPER'S CALL(IRE) b.g. 5 Mandalus - Thistletopper by Le Bavard (FR) R G Makin

1428 10/5 Aspatria (L) MDO 3m 11 G *schoold & mstks,prog 12th,2nd 14th,ld 2 out,ran on well* 1 14

Ideal start & runner-up won subsequently; could prove quite useful 18

KEEP FLOWING(IRE) ch.g. 6 Castle Keep - Flowing Tide by Main Reef David Brace

54 1/2 Wadebridge (L) MDO 3m 13 G *(Co fav) ld 5th & agn 12th-15th, styd on und pres* 3 12

368 2/3 Garnons (L) MDO 2 1/2m 13 GS *alwys prom, 3rd 12th, not qckn frm nxt* 3 14
542 16/3 Erw Lon (L) MDN 3m 15 GF *(fav) ld 2nd-5th, ld frm 13th, in cmmnd aft* 1 14
1135 19/4 Bonvilston (R) RES 3m 14 G *(fav) mid-div, p.u. 13th (stewards)* P 0
1227 26/4 Pyle (R) RES 3m 15 GS *(fav) mstk 9th,ld nxt-12th,mstk 15th,ran on to ld apr last,all out* 1 17

Ex-Irish; steady improvement & showed right attitude in modest races; should upgrade; well-ridden ... 19

KEEPTHEMGUESSING (Irish) — I 23P

KEEP THEM KEEN(IRE) ch.g. 9 Carlingford Castle - Some Gift by Avocat K O'Meara
1996 P(0)

768 29/3 Whittington (L) MDO 3m 10 S *bhnd, nvr dang, p.u. 2 out* P 0
941 6/4 Tabley (R) MDO 3m 11 G *mstks, mid-div, lost tch 12th, lft poor 4th 3 out* 4 0
999 12/4 Alpraham (R) MDO 3m 8 GF *rear, in tch til wknd 12th, p.u. 2 out* P 0
1428 10/5 Aspatria (L) MDO 3m 11 G *rear, lost tch 11th, t.o. last whn f 16th* F -

Last on only completion 97 & no prospects 0

KEERAGH (Irish) — I 218P, I 270P

KEIROSE b.m. 7 Derring Rose - Keira by Keren R Paisley
1996 R(-),P(0),P(0)

160 15/2 Lanark (R) MDO 2m 5f 10 G *alwys handy, cls 2nd whn u.r. 3 out* U -
341 1/3 Corbridge (R) MDN 3m 10 G *chsd ldrs, outpcd 4 out* 3 0
614 22/3 Friars Haugh (L) MDN 3m 13 GF *nvr nr ldrs, p.u. 4 out* P 0

Ran prominently 1st start but makes mistakes & stamina lacking 10

KELBURNE LAD(IRE) ch.g. 8 Cardinal Flower - Ross Lady by Master Buck Mrs D B A Silk
1996 3(0),F(-),F(-),1(12),U(-),3(14),**4(12)**

277 23/2 Charing (L) MEM 3m 6 G *hld up, effrt 11th, wkind 15th, poor 4th & p.u. 2 out* P 0
682 29/3 Charing (L) RES 3m 5 F *(fav) ld apr 3rd, mstk 10th, clr 15th, kpt on whn chal 3 out* 1 13
969 6/4 Penshurst (L) INT 3m 3 F *(fav) ld to 2nd agn 6th, 4l up 2 out, mstks last 2, hdd flat* 2 13

Maiden winner 96; non-stayer & effective only in poor races; hard to win again 14

KELLING b.g. 10 Blakeney - Domicile by Dominion Tony Millard

191 15/2 Erw Lon (L) CON 3m 13 G *alwys bhnd, t.o. & p.u. 13th* P 0
296 1/3 Didmarton (L) LAD 3m 13 G *chsd ldrs, 5th whn f 8th* F -

Rarely seen now & looks finished 0

KELLYS DIAMOND ch.g. 8 Netherkelly - Just Diamonds by Laurence O Mrs P A Russell
1996 4(17),1(19),2(14),3(0),3(15)

117 9/2 Wetherby Po' (L) LAD 3m 10 GF *mid-div, some prog 14th, wknd 3 out, t.o.* 5 13
215 16/2 Southwell P' (L) LAD 3m 12 GS *mid-div, prog 7th, 4th & onepcd frm 12th* 4 16
265 22/2 Duncombe Pa' (R) CON 3m 15 G *hld up,prog 9th,wnt 3rd 4 out,rddn & ran on strgly,ld nr fin* 1 20
474 9/3 Southwell P' (L) LAD 3m 12 G *mid-div, prog 12th, chal apr 3 out, ld nxt, hld on well* 1 20
617 22/3 Hutton Rudby (L) LAD 3m 9 GF *mid-div, prog 4 out, disp nxt, ld apr last, hdd nr line* 2 21
764 29/3 Whittington (L) LAD 3m 5 S *(fav) held up, 2nd 15th, ev ch 2 out, no ext* 2 20
1075 13/4 Whitwell-On' (R) MEM 3m 9 G *prom, ld 9th, disp 13th, ld 2 out, rdn & hdd post* 2 21
1249 26/4 Easingwold (L) LAD 3m 6 GS *(Jt fav) mid-div, prog, tk 2nd 4 out, fdd aft* 4 16
1408 5/5 Witton Cast' (R) LAD 3m 5 GS *chsd wnr to 10th,outpcd 13th,prog into 2nd 4 out,onepcd last* 3 21
1422 10/5 Easingwold (L) LAD 3m 7 GF *mid-div, prog 14th, ev ch 3 out, outpcd nxt* 3 18

Restricted winner 96; improved, consistent & good ride for novice; should win again; G/F-G/S 21

KELLY'S MANOR ch.g. 11 Netherkelly - Petite Cressida by Crown Again Steve Hulse

1276 27/4 Fakenham P-' (L) MEM 3m 7 G *bhnd & blnd 1st, t.o. 5th* 4 0

Rarely seen & no ability 0

KELLYS NAP ch.g. 8 Netherkelly - Nepal by Indian Ruler Major E W O'F Wilson
1996 3(16)

69 2/2 Higham (L) MDO 3m 8 GF *pllng in mid-div,mstk 5th,prog to ld 15th,hdd & no ext flat* 2 12
196 15/2 Higham (L) MDO 3m 12 G *(fav) prom, ld aft 15th, wknd rpdly & p.u. nxt* P 0
1276 27/4 Fakenham P-' (L) MEM 3m 7 G *blnd 8th, chsd wnr to 11th, wknd apr 3 out, dsmntd aft fin* 3 0

Only 9 runs in 4 seasons; could win Maiden at best but problems again last start 12

KELLY'S PERK (Irish) — I 40⁵, I 568P

KELLYTINO gr.m. 8 Neltino - Kelly's Maid by Netherkelly J C Sharp

480 9/3 Southwell P' (L) MDO 3m 17 G *hmpd & u.r. 2nd* U -
1417 10/5 Warwick (L) HC 3 1/4m 8 G *held up, hdwy and in tch when blnd and u.r. 12th.* U -

Some ability but rarely appears 14

KEMYS COMMANDER ch.g. 12 Monksfield - Rockwood Lady by Aeolian G J Smith

473 9/3 Southwell P' (L) CON 3m 10 G *in tch, losng plc whn blnd 11th, t.o. & p.u. nxt* P 0
673 23/3 Brocklesby ' (L) CON 3m 8 GF *ld to 5th, cls up whn u.r. 12th* U -

834	31/3	Thorpe Lodge	(L)	MEM	3m	3	F	*(fav) made all, ran on strngly flat*	1	10
924	6/4	Garthorpe	(R)	CON	3m	6	GF	*ld til f 10th*	F	-
1063	13/4	Maisemore P'	(L)	XX	3m	13	GF	*ld to 14th, sn outpcd by wnr, onepcd*	4	14
1205	26/4	Clifton On '	(L)	CON	3m	13	GS	*prom, 2nd/disp til 3rd frm 9th, 2nd agn 4 out, wknd nxt*	5	11
1351	4/5	Dingley	(R)	CON	3m	7	G	*ld 1st, last frm 5th til p.u. 8th*	P	0
1377	5/5	Northaw	(L)	OPE	3m	3	F	*ld, clr 9th, fence ahd whn lft solo 14th*	1	0

Of very little account now & found 2 non-events - similar needed in 98 to win again 13

KENDOR PASS(IRE) b.g. 9 Hard Fought - Proceeding by Monsanto (FR) — Dr M P Tate

13	25/1	Cottenham	(R)	MDO	3m	10	GF	*chsd ldng pair to 10th, no dang frm 13th*	3	10
211	16/2	Southwell P'	(L)	MDO	3m	15	GS	*prom in chsng grp, lost plc 11th, ran on 3 out, fin well*	3	11
252	22/2	Brocklesby '	(L)	MDO	3m	9	G	*ld to 4th & 8th-6 out, outpcd nxt, ran on agn 3 out*	2	14
478	9/3	Southwell P'	(L)	MDO	3m	17	G	*(fav) ld til aft 1st, grad lost plc, styd on 3 out, not trbl wnr*	2	11
620	22/3	Hutton Rudby	(L)	MDO	3m	10	GF	*chsd ldrs til ld apr 14th, qcknd clr whn chal last, easily*	1	15
1068	13/4	Whitwell-On'	(R)	F.ES	3m	12	G	*(Jt fav) trckd ldr, disp 4-8th, ld 13th-nxt, wknd 3 out*	3	16
1263	27/4	Southwell P'	(L)	RES	3m	9	G	*trckd ldr til lost plc 10th, onepcd frm 3 out*	3	12

Quite promising but owner-ridden to poor effect; Restricted only possible unless rider change 17

KENSTOWN(IRE) ch.g. 9 Le Bavard (FR) - Maureens Dote by David Jack — P J King

1996 4(0),P(0)

556	16/3	Ottery St M'	(L)	RES	3m	12	G	*ran out 1st*	r	-
738	29/3	Higher Kilw'	(L)	CON	3m	8	GF	*prom, jmpd rght 5th, lost plc 10th, t.o. & p.u. 12th*	P	0
956	6/4	Black Fores'	(R)	MDO	3m	4	G	*sttld 3rd, outpcd 14th, no ext 3 out, lame*	4	0

Last on only completion 97 & problems to boot; can only be watched 10

KENTISH PIPER br.g. 12 Black Minstrel - Toombeola by Raise You Ten — The Hon Mrs R E Wharton

1996 **12(NH),6(NH),5(NH),4(NH),P(NH),5(NH)**

174	15/2	Ottery St M'	(L)	LAD	3m	9	G	*alwys last, t.o. whn tried to run out & u.r. 4 out*	U	-
309	1/3	Clyst St Ma'	(L)	CON	3m	7	HY	*u.r. 2nd*	U	-

Winning chaser; of no account now 0

KERDIFF PARK (Irish) — **I** 532P

KERRIES JAKE (Irish) — **I** 166P, **I** 305P

KERRY HILL ch.g. 11 Scallywag - Katie Fare by Ritudyr — Mrs D J Jackson

1996 P(0),2(14),6(11),5(13),P(0),8(0)

878	1/4	Upton-On-Se'	(R)	XX	3m	11	GF	*alwys wll bhnd, t.o. 11th*	5	0
1237	26/4	Brampton Br'	(R)	RES	3m	13	G	*alwys rear, wknd 11th, t.o. & p.u. 3 out*	P	0

No longer of any account 0

KERRY MY HOME ch.g. 10 Le Moss - Sno-Sleigh by Bargello — M J Norman

1996 P(0),3(0),2(12),1(14),P(0),7(0),2(10),4(0),2(17)

548	16/3	Garthorpe	(R)	RES	3m	10	GF	*rr, last & rddn 10th, no resp, t.o. & p.u. aft 15th*	P	0
770	29/3	Dingley	(R)	RES	3m	18	G	*twrds rear whn f 3rd*	F	-
1191	20/4	Garthorpe	(R)	RES	3m	8	GF	*jmpd lft, alwys rear, rmndrs 12th, sn lost tch, t.o.*	7	0
1278	27/4	Fakenham P-'	(L)	RES	3m	11	G	*rear 5th, rmndrs 8th, no rspns, t.o. & p.u. 13th*	P	0
1309	3/5	Cottenham	(R)	RES	3m	4	F	*jmpd lft 1st cct, ld 10th-3 out, kpt on no ch wth wnr*	2	12
1474	11/5	Garthorpe	(R)	MEM	3m	6	GS	*chsd wnr to 5th & 8-9th, 3rd & outpcd frm 13th, lame*	3	0

Maiden winner 96; disappointing & unenthusiastic now & looks lost cause 10

KERRY SOLDIER BLUE gr.g. 8 Fine Blue - Kerry Maid by Maestoso — Mrs Margaret Price

1996 P(0)

185	15/2	Erw Lon	(L)	MDN	3m	14	G	*schoold & wll bhnd, ran on 13th, lft 2nd 3 out, no ext last*	2	14
398	8/3	Llanfrynach	(R)	MEM	3m	6	G	*2nd til ld 10th, jnd last, qcknd flat*	1	16

Brief but promising season; only 3 runs in career; Restricted possible if fit 98 17

KERSTIN'S CHOICE b.m. 6 Abutammam - Kick About by Rugantino — Mrs B W D Llewellyn

1996 P(0),P(0),3(0),P(0)

184	15/2	Erw Lon	(L)	MDN	3m	14	G	*1st ride, in tch to 13th, poor 6th whn f 2 out*	F	-
368	2/3	Garnons	(L)	MDO	2 1/2m	13	GS	*rear whn u.r. 10th*	U	-
542	16/3	Erw Lon	(L)	MDN	3m	15	GF	*mstks, alwys rear*	6	0
841	31/3	Lydstep	(L)	MDO	3m	8	F	*trckd ldr early, wknd 13th, onepcd*	4	0
963	6/4	Pantyderi	(L)	MDN	3m	6	F	*mid-div thruout, nvr near to chal, lft 2nd 2 out*	2	0
1180	20/4	Lydstep	(L)	MEM	3m	2	GF	*jmpd novicey, ld brfly 10th, chsd wnr aft, kpt on wll*	2	0
1230	26/4	Pyle	(R)	MDO	3m	10	GS	*chsd ldr til wknd aft 12th, t.o. & p.u. 14th*	P	0
1365	5/5	Pantyderi	(L)	RES	3m	10	G	*4th at 3rd, rear at 11th, p.u. 3 out*	P	0
1471	11/5	Erw Lon	(L)	RES	3m	9	GS	*alwys twrds rear, t.o.*	5	0
1562	24/5	Bassaleg	(R)	MDO	3m	8	G	*wth ldr whn blnd 4th, p.u. nxt, dead*	P	0

Dead 0

KETTLES b.m. 10 Broadsword (USA) - Penny's Affair by Chingnu — Mrs M R Daniell

1996 3(15),1(19),1(22),7(18),**4(23)**

149 10/2 Hereford (R) HC 3m 1f 110yds 18 GS *nvr better than mid div, rear when blnd and u.r. 3 out.* U -
285 26/2 Taunton (R) HC 4 1/4m 110yds 16 GS *alwys in tch, effort to cl on ldrs 16th, styd on same pace from 3 out.* 3 20
976 8/4 Heythrop (R) OPE 4m 7 F *(fav) hld up wll bhnd,prog 15th,blnd 20th,chal last,sn ld,styd on* 1 24
1290 30/4 Cheltenham (L) HC 4m 1f 10 GF *(Jt fav) not alwys fluent, waited with, effort after 15th, nvr reach ldrs, no ch from 22nd.* 7 0

Quite useful staying pointer; repeated Heythrop win & could complete treble; Any, best G-S 23

KEY IDEA (Irish) — **I** 50^{P}, **I** 496^{P}

KEY OF THE NILE (Irish) — **I** 62^{P}, **I** 98^{P}, **I** 339^{P}

KHANDYS SLAVE(IRE) ch.m. 9 Le Johnstan - Snow Sweet by Arctic Slave — K M Stanworth

1996 P(0),4(0),5(0),P(0)

300 1/3 Didmarton (L) RES 3m 23 G *rear, wknd rpdly & p.u. 12th* P 0
408 8/3 Llanfrynach (R) MDN 3m 12 G *hld up, gd prog 14th, ld 3 out, hdd & no ext last* 2 13
1137 19/4 Bonvilston (R) MDO 3m 13 G *(Jt fav) alwys cls up, ld 12th, made rest, comf* 1 15
1322 3/5 Bonvilston (R) RES 3m 9 G *ld to 8th, grad wknd, no ch frm 13th, fin 3rd, plcd 2nd* 2 11

Improved 97; beat subsequent winners but form weak; may find Restricted if maintaining progress 16

KHATTAF b.g. 13 Kris - Hanna Alta (FR) by Busted — Mrs H C Johnson

1996 1(23),2(24),1(24),1(24),1(25),2(21),1(22)

174 15/2 Ottery St M' (L) LAD 3m 9 G *(fav) cls up, disp 12th til lft clr 4 out, blnd last* 1 25
627 22/3 Kilworthy (L) LAD 3m 7 G *ld 2nd, disp 13-14th, cls 2nd & ev ch whn not qckn flat* 2 23
790 31/3 Bishopsleigh (R) LAD 3m 7 G *(fav) j.w. ld 5th, kpt on wll frm 4 out* 1 23
1110 19/4 Flete Park (R) LAD 3m 9 GF *(fav) j.w. made most, lft clr apr last, comf* 1 23
1396 5/5 High Bickin' (R) MXO 3m 7 G *jmpd rght, prog 10th, cls 2nd 12th-15th, 3rd aft, ran on fin* 2 20
1581 26/5 Lifton (R) LAD 3m 7 G *(fav) rear, prog 10th, wknd 13th, p.u. nxt, lame* P 0

Tremendous veteran; won 11 of last 16 but disaster last start may spell the end 23

KICKLES LASS b.m. 8 Broadsword (USA) - Ditchling Beacon by High Line — D R Walsh

374 2/3 Mollington (R) MDN 3m 14 G *prom to 11th, wknd rpdly & f 13th* F -
1209 26/4 Clifton On ' (L) MDO 3m 16 GS *rear hlf whn f 6th* F -
1357 4/5 Dingley (R) MDO 3m 5 G *mstks, in tch, wknng & blnd 14th, rn wd 2 out, walked in* 4 0

Tailed off in desperate race & has no prospects 0

KILARA (Irish) — **I** 51^{4}, **I** 168^{P}

KILBRICKEN SUNSET (Irish) — **I** 126^{P}, **I** 472^{P}, **I** 556^{1}, **I** 614,

KILCANNON SOPHIE (Irish) — **I** 46^{2}, **I** 83^{P}, **I** 166^{2}, **I** 286^{U}, **I** 318^{P}

KILCAW (Irish) — **I** 14^{F}, **I** 58^{F}

KILCOUNTY(IRE) ch.m. 7 Arapahos (FR) - Andy's Pet by Laurence O — D L Claydon

797 31/3 Marks Tey (L) MDO 3m 4 F *pllng, last to 12th, prog trckd ldrs 14th, chal 2 out,outpcd* 2 0

Placed in 2 poor races from only 3 starts 95-7; should do better if racing regularly 12

KILCOUNTY COLLEEN (Irish) — **I** 317^{P}

KILCULLY JAKE (Irish) — **I** 8^{P}, **I** 47^{P}, **I** 85^{4}, **I** 203^{4}, **I** 308^{5}

KILCULLYS-PRIDE (Irish) — **I** 205^{U}, **I** 236^{5}, **I** 320^{P}

KILDEA DUCHESS (Irish) — **I** 25^{4}, **I** 514, , **I** 547^{P}

KILFANE (Irish) — **I** 406^{1}

KILGOBBIN(IRE) ch.g. 6 Kambalda - Paldamask by Native Prince — O J Stephens

1067 13/4 Maisemore P' (L) MDO 3m 8 GF *(fav) keen hld, hld up, went 2nd 12th, ev ch 3 out, not qckn last* 2 10
1230 26/4 Pyle (R) MDO 3m 10 GS *(fav) trckd ldrs,3rd & in tch 13th, no imp nxt, wknd, sddl slppd* 4 0
1527 17/5 Bredwardine (R) MDO 3m 13 G *hld up rear, prog to chs ldng pair aft 15th, no imp 2 out* 3 0

Ex-Irish; best run in modest race last start gives some hope for winning chance 98 13

KILLALIGAN KIM (Irish) — **I** 97^{F}

KILLARNEY MAN br.g. 11 Pragmatic - Lilly Of Killarney by Sunny Way — Miss V H Smith

1996 7(0),F(-)

462 8/3 Charing (L) RES 3m 10 G *alwys bhnd, t.o. 14th* 4 0
576 16/3 Detling (L) MEM 3m 10 F *alwys last, t.o. whn ref last* R -
783 31/3 Aldington (L) RES 3m 4 HD *last frm 6th, lost tch 12th* 4 0

No longer of any account 0

KILLATTY PLAYER(IRE) b.m. 7 The Noble Player (USA) - Tiefland by Right Tack — Ian Anderson

199 15/2 Weston Park (L) MEM 3m 7 G *handy, ld 13th, in cmmnd 3 out, ran on well* 1 20
467 8/3 Eyton-On-Se' (L) RES 3m 15 G *hld up mid-div, prog 10th, cls up & ev ch 4 out, onepcd* 3 16
574 16/3 Garnons (L) RES 3m 14 G *alwys cls up, rdn to chs ldr 15th, styd on to ld flat* 1 19

671	23/3 Eaton Hall	(R)	INT	3 3/4m	8	GF	*hld up rear, prog 15th, cls up 4 out, no imp aft, p.u. last*	P	0
884	1/4 Flagg Moor	(L)	CON	3m	6	G	*(fav) lft in ld aft 5th, hdd 7th, 4l down whn blnd & u.r. 14th*	U	-
1002	12/4 Alpraham	(R)	CON	3m	4	GF	*svrl mstks,ld to 6th,lost plc,tk 2nd 3 out,not trbl wnr*	2	15
1175	20/4 Sandon	(L)	CON	3m	8	GF	*(fav) prom, 2nd whn u.r. 7th*	U	-
1300	3/5 Weston Park	(L)	CON	3m	8	G	*n.j.w. in tch 4 out, rdn & no rspns, 5th & p.u. last*	P	0

Irish Maiden winner 96; good start but jumping fell to pieces after; may revive on easier ground 98 19

KILLBALLY CASTLE (Irish) — I 201P

KILLEANEY CARR(IRE) b.g. 6 Yashgan - Barrack Lady by Ragapan — C Dawson

358	2/3 Great Stain'	(L)	MDO	3m	14	S	*mid-div, lost tch 9th, wll bhnd 11th, t.o. & p.u. 13th*	P	0
419	8/3 Dalston	(R)	MDO	2 1/2m	10	GS	*rear,t.o. 10th,kpt on 3 out,3rd & btn whn f last,rmntd*	3	11
623	22/3 Hutton Rudby	(L)	MDO	3m	9	GF	*prom,lft 2nd 14th,ch whn mstk last,rlld,just faild,plc 1st*	1	14
813	31/3 Tranwell	(L)	RES	3m	7	G	*cls up 1st ctt, 1l 2nd 14th & even ch, wknd into 3rd nxt*	3	16

Fortunate to be awarded verdict but ran passably in Restricted & may win on merit in 98 if staying 16

KILLELAN LAD br.g. 15 Kambalda - Dusky Glory by Dusky Boy — Miss K Di Marte

1996 3(10),1(12)

1358	5/5 Exeter	(R)	HC	2m 7f 110yds	8	G	*alwys in rear, hit 10th, t.o. when p.u. before 4 out.*	P	0
1491	14/5 Hereford	(R)	HC	3m 1f 110yds	11	G	*slowly away and jmpd poorly in rear, soon t.o., p.u. before 8th.*	P	0

No longer of any account 0

KILLENAGH MOSS (Irish) — I 92P, I 149F, I 185P, I 306F, I 387⁴, I 410², I 498P

KILLENA STAR (Irish) — I 590F, I 608P

KILLERY HARBOUR b.g. 10 Cardinal Flower - Clockonocra by Shall We Dance — W T Fagg

320	1/3 Marks Tey	(L)	MEM	3m	4	G	*(fav) alwys gng wll, wnt 2nd 10th, ld 2 out, rddn clr flat*	1	12
597	22/3 Horseheath	(R)	RES	3m	8	F	*narrw ld til 11th, 2nd to 14th, wknd nxt, no ch 3 out*	5	0

Promise in 94; missed 95/6; won bad race & well beaten other start 13

KILLIMOR CASTLE (Irish) — I 527P

KILLIMOR LAD b.g. 10 Tina's Pet - Jeldi by Tribal Chief — Mrs D C Samworth

215	16/2 Southwell P'	(L)	LAD	3m	12	GS	*chsd ldrs to 6th, sn wknd, t.o. & p.u. 11th*	P	0
474	9/3 Southwell P'	(L)	LAD	3m	12	G	*in tch to 14th, sn outpcd*	5	0
546	16/3 Garthorpe	(R)	LAD	3m	11	GF	*chsd ldrs til ran wde appr 12th, grad lot tch*	6	0
674	23/3 Brocklesby '	(L)	LAD	3m	5	GF	*ld 2nd, sn clr, hdd apr 3 out, onepcd*	3	15
837	31/3 Thorpe Lodge	(L)	LAD	3m	5	F	*tried to make all,brushed aside bfr 3 out,eased whn ch gone*	2	11
1287	29/4 Huntingdon	(R)	HC	2 1/2m 110yds	14	G	*alwys bhnd, t.o. from 9th.*	9	0
1488	12/5 Towcester	(R)	HC	2m 110yds	16	GS	*alwys bhnd. y*	8	11
1606	1/6 Dingley	(R)	LAD	3m	13	GF	*ld 5th-aft 13th, wknd aft 3 out*	6	13

Outclassed in Ladies & H/Chases & no winning prospects now 13

KILLINANE BEAUTY (Irish) — I 295P, I 514P

KILLINEY GRADUATE (Irish) — I 59P, I 92³, I 149F, I 284², I 346⁶, I 410P

KILLINEY'S IMAGE(IRE) b.f. 7 Amazing Bust - Just Killiney — S G Jones

1996 **10(NH),13(NH)**

1209	26/4 Clifton On '	(L)	MDO	3m	16	GS	*abt 9th til f 6th*	F	-

Brief appearance 0

KILLMURRAY BUCK (Irish) — I 212¹

KILLONE RIVER (Irish) — I 25P, I 277⁴, I 356F, I 487P, I 531¹

KILLYMAN(IRE) b.g. 9 Remainder Man - Saxon Princess by English Prince — Peter Mathias

718	29/3 Llanvapley	(L)	RES	3m	13	GF	*mid-div, 10l 4th wnn mstk 15th, no further prog*	5	0
1004	12/4 St Hilary	(R)	MEM	3m	4	GF	*ld to 6th, 2nd to 15th, wknd rpdly, p.u. 3 out*	P	0
1227	26/4 Pyle	(R)	RES	3m	15	GS	*alwys twrds rear, wll bhnd aft 13th, p.u. 3 out*	P	0
1472	11/5 Erw Lon	(L)	XX	3m	9	GS	*trckd ldrs, ev ch 15th, wknd rpdly 2 out*	3	0

Promising in 95; missed 96, changed hands & of no account now 0

KILMINFOYLE b.g. 10 Furry Glen - Loreto Lady by Brave Invader (USA) — Mrs S H Shirley-Beavan

1996 P(0),3(19),F(-),1(20),**5(20)**

152	12/2 Musselburgh	(R)	HC	3m	8	GS	*bhnd when mstk 4th, mistake and u.r. next.*	U	-
229	22/2 Friars Haugh	(L)	CON	3m	9	G	*hld up, prog frm 14th, no imp whn mstk last*	3	20
339	1/3 Corbridge	(R)	OPE	3m 5f	11	G	*rear, mstk 4th, t.o. 13th, p.u. 15th*	P	0

Ladies winner 96; novice-ridden in points 97 & finished early; best watched; G-S 17

KILMISTEN BREEZE (Irish) — I 55P, I 92P, I 216P, I 342², I 387P, I 411³

KILMURRAY BUCK (Irish) — I 97[4]

KILONE ABBESS (Irish) — I 31[2]

KILTROSE LAD b.g. 8 Soldier Rose - Kiltish by Pamroy — Mrs E A Gutteridge

1996 F(-),3(12),2(11),2(14),1(16),2(18)

670	23/3	Eaton Hall	(R)	RES	3m	15 GF	*alwys mid-div, nvr rchd ldrs*	6	10
749	29/3	Brampton Br'	(R)	OPE	3m	4 GF	*ld to 7th, rdn & not qckn 13th, went 2nd 15th, blnd last*	2	16
975	8/4	Heythrop	(R)	INT	3m	3 F	*(bl) ld, mstk 7th & 10th, hdd appr last, onepcd und press*	2	17

Maiden winner 96; safe & consistent but very one paced & placed in small fields 17

KILTROUM(FR) gr.g. 8 Courtroom (FR) - Kiltie by Habat — A E Tacy

769	29/3	Dingley	(R)	CON	3m	14 G	*t.o. 1st, f 8th*	F	-
926	6/4	Garthorpe	(R)	OPE	3m	10 GF	*hrd hld in rear, no rspns whn let go 4th, p.u. 10th*	P	0
1079	13/4	Guilsborough	(L)	OPE	3m	6 GF	*last whn f 2nd*	F	-

Of no account 0

KIMBROSS ch.g. 6 Ardross - Kate Kimberley by Sparkler — Mrs J Robshaw

1996 **11(NH),14(NH)**

526	15/3	Cothelstone	(L)	MDN	3m	15 GS	*plld hrd, ld 9th-13th, sn wknd, p.u. 15th*	P	0
795	31/3	Bishopsleigh	(R)	MDO	3m	12 G	*alwys mid-div, nvr any ch, bhnd & p.u. 4 out*	P	0
933	6/4	Charlton Ho'	(L)	MDO	3m	12 G	*bhnd,blnd 11th,effrt 13th,rdn 3 out,ran on strngly apr last,lkd 3rd*	2	14

First form last start in modest race & ought to have winning chances in 98 14

KINCORA (Irish) — I 160[2], I 243[2]

KIND OF CHIC ch.m. 6 Kind Of Hush - Arras Style by Nicholas Bill — Mrs Susan E Mason

80	2/2	Market Rase'	(L)	MDO	2m 5f	9 GF	*blnd 3rd, prssd ldr 4th, outpcd 11th, lft poor 2nd 2 out*	2	0
428	8/3	Charm Park	(L)	MDO	3m	10 GF	*(fav) kn hld,stld 3rd til lft 2nd 5th,ld last,lft clr flat,kpt on*	1	14

Good stable & won readily; should upgrade if ready in 98 17

KINESIOLOGY(IRE) b or br.g. 9 Boreen (FR) - Ardellis Lady by Pollerton — A J Sendell

1996 2(20)

298	1/3	Didmarton	(L)	RES	3m	15 G	*prom, ld 10-11th, wknd frm 15th*	4	10
648	22/3	Castle Of C'	(R)	RES	3m	8 G	*ld 5th til apr 15th, rdn 3 out, swtchd last, rallied flat*	2	18
1061	13/4	Maisemore P'	(L)	RES	3m	12 GF	*(fav) chsd ldr 6th, blnd 11th, rdn apr 2 out, unable qckn apr last*	2	18
1439	10/5	Holnicote	(L)	RES	3m	9 G	*(fav) ld to 14th, ld agn aft nxt, ev ch til not qckn apr last*	2	17

Second in 4 of 5 races 96/7 & deserves Restricted win; good enough to win most at best 17

KINGARRIFF GIRL (Irish) — I 506[P]

KINGARTH b.g. 5 Kinglet - Hinton Bairn by Balinger — Miss S Bannatyne

318	1/3	Marks Tey	(L)	MDN	3m	13 G	*rear & rmmndrs 3rd, alwys bhnd, t.o. & p.u. 11th*	P	0
498	15/3	Ampton	(R)	MDO	3m	8 GF	*mid div, in tch til 6th & outpcd 16th, t.o. & p.u. 3 out*	P	0
1281	27/4	Fakenham P-'	(L)	MDO	3m	8 G	*mstks, chsd ldr to 8th, sn bhnd, t.o. & p.u. 12th*	P	0

Shows no promise yet 0

KING CASH b.g. 11 Kambalda - Lisgarvan Highway by Dusky Boy — Roger Anderson

271	22/2	Ampton	(R)	CON	3m	15 G	*hld up, prog to mid-div 14th, nvr rchd ldrs*	7	11
319	1/3	Marks Tey	(L)	CON	3m	11 G	*hld up, prog 9th, rddn alng 13th, wknd apr 16th, p.u. 2 out*	P	0

Season lasted a week & of no real account now 11

KING EDWARD(IRE) b.g. 6 Royal Fountain - Duchess-A-Dee by Lord Ha Ha — Sir John Barlow Bt

469	8/3	Eyton-On-Se'	(L)	MDN	2 1/2m	9 G	*alwys rear, p.u. 8th*	P	0
763	29/3	Whittington	(L)	CON	3m	9 S	*alwys mid-div, 40l 5th whn p.u. 11th*	P	0
1003	12/4	Alpraham	(R)	MDO	2 1/2m	10 GF	*mstly 2nd to 8th, grad wknd frm 11th*	5	0
1345	3/5	Gisburn	(R)	MDN	3m	13 GF	*ldng grp, wknd 14th, p.u. 16th*	P	0

Probably just learning but well beaten only completion 0

KINGEOCHY b.g. 11 Forties Field (FR) - Mrs McQuaid by Mick McQuaid — A Rogers

927	6/4	Garthorpe	(R)	RES	3m	9 GF	*chsd ldrs to hlfwy, lost tch 12th, no dang aft*	4	0
1080	13/4	Guilsborough	(L)	RES	3m	11 GF	*prom, ld 9-13th, wknd & p.u. 16th, dsmntd*	P	0

Irish Maiden winner 96; season lasted a week & ended with problems 10

KINGFISHER BAY b.g. 12 Try My Best (USA) - Damiya (FR) by Direct Flight — D W Chilcott

1996 **P(0)**,9(0),P(0),4(13),P(0),2(0),**6(0)**,6(0),**9(0)**

288	27/2	Ludlow	(R)	HC	3m	8 G	*bhnd when blnd 11th, soon t.o..*	6	0
400	8/3	Llanfrynach	(R)	OPE	3m	10 G	*chsd ldrs to 11th, wknd*	6	0
496	15/3	Hereford	(R)	HC	3m 1f 110yds	10 GF	*bhnd from 11th, t.o. when p.u. before 13th.*	P	0
715	29/3	Llanvapley	(L)	OPE	3m	8 GF	*ld to 5th, grdly lost plc, p.u. 13th*	P	0

900	5/4	Howick	(L)	MEM	3m	4	F	*(vis) ld to 4th, effrt to ld 11-15th, rallied und pres flat*	2	11
1007	12/4	St Hilary	(R)	OPE	3m	10	GF	*ld to 12th, lost plc, ran on 15th, ld flat*	1	19
1194	22/4	Chepstow	(L)	HC	3m	11	GF	*alwys bhnd, t.o. from 11th.*	7	0
1455	11/5	Maisemore P'	(L)	CON	3m	8	G	*ld to 2nd, rdn & wknd aft 11th, t.o. & p.u. 15th*	P	0

Generally tailed off & useless but 50/1 shock winner from good horse; unlikely to repeat 13

KING FOWLER(IRE) gr.g. 7 King's Ride - Chicchick by Smartset — A J Williams

1459	11/5	Maisemore P'	(L)	MDO	3m	12	G	*w.w. prog 8th, jnd ldrs 13th, ev ch whn f nxt*	F	-

Little show under Rules; going well when falling only start & should have chances in 98 13

KING HIGH b.h. 10 Shirley Heights - Regal Twin (USA) by Majestic Prince — Mrs Nigel Wrighton

225	19/2	Folkestone	(R)	HC	2m 5f	10	S	*chsd ldrs, one pace from 3 out.*	3	17
1078	13/4	Guilsborough	(L)	LAD	3m	11	GF	*last pair, t.o. 8th, p.u. 15th*	P	0

Ran passably in H/Chase but showed no interest other start; best watched 12

KING KEITH ch.g. 8 Sunley Builds - The Flying Cleo by Native Admiral (USA) — Mrs C E Whiteway

1996 2(12),P(0),2(13),4(0),U(-)

480	9/3	Southwell P'	(L)	MDO	3m	17	G	*w.w. in tch, mstk 12th, no hdwy frm 15th*	5	0
665	23/3	Eaton Hall	(R)	MDO	3m	11	GF	*svrl slw jmps, chsng grp, ev ch 3 out, ran on flat, lkd 2nd*	3	14
723	29/3	Sandon	(L)	MDO	3m	6	GF	*(fav) (bl) hld up,lft 2nd 11th,ld 2 out,v slw last,hdd,ld agn post*	1	13
1000	12/4	Alpraham	(R)	RES	3m	8	GF	*chsd ldr 11th-3 out, no ext*	4	11
1191	20/4	Garthorpe	(R)	RES	3m	8	GF	*mstks, prog & in tch 11th, sn strgglng, no ch frm 15th*	6	0

Very suspect & just failed to throw away winning chance in bad race; Restricted most unlikely 13

KING LOUIS b.g. 9 Kinglet - Sunyone by Sunyboy — Mrs E Y N Barber

198	15/2	Higham	(L)	RES	3m	14	G	*mid-div to 11th, wknd nxt, p.u. 14th*	P	0

Dead 0

KING OF CAIRO ch.g. 9 Sunyboy - Queen Of The Nile by Hittite Glory — Charles Smith

453	8/3	Great Treth'	(R)	CON	3m	13	S	*1st ride, sn bhnd, t.o. & p.u. 3 out*	P	0
626	22/3	Kilworthy	(L)	MDN	3m	14	G	*nov rddn, alwys bhnd*	5	0
740	29/3	Higher Kilw'	(L)	MDN	3m	15	GF	*rear whn u.r. 7th*	U	-

Missed 96 & novice-ridden to no great effect in 97 0

KING OF CLARE (Irish) — **I** 103[P], **I** 297, , **I** 532[P], **I** 550[1]

KING OF GLEN (Irish) — **I** 347[F], **I** 496[2], **I** 540[1]

KINGOFNOBLES(IRE) ch.g. 8 King Persian - Eau D'Amour by Tall Noble (USA) — K B Rogers

1996 P(0),3(12),8(10),2(16),**P(0)**,2(13),P(0)

56	1/2	Kingston Bl'	(L)	OPE	3m	13	GF	*rear, prog hlfwy, lft 3rd 15th. tk 2nd nr fin*	2	19
254	22/2	Newtown	(L)	MEM	3m	6	G	*chsd wnr to 4th,lost tch 10th,ran on 14th,2nd 2 out,nvr nrr*	2	18
1061	13/4	Maisemore P'	(L)	RES	3m	12	GF	*bhnd frm 8th, t.o. & p.u. 12th*	P	0

Maiden winner 95; ran well 1st 2 starts 97 but ungenuine & unlikely to win Restricted 15

KING OF SHADOWS b or br.g. 10 Connaught - Rhiannon by Welsh Pageant — Ceri James

1996 P(0),**P(0)**,**P(0)**,**5(16)**,**1(21)**,**3(23)**

93	7/2	Bangor	(L)	HC	2 1/2m 110yds	11	G	*bhnd when b.d. 5th.*	B	-
288	27/2	Ludlow	(R)	HC	3m	8	G	*ld to 5th, mstk 11th, soon bhnd, t.o. when p.u. before 2 out.*	P	0
587	19/3	Ludlow	(R)	HC	2 1/2m	18	GF	*chsd ldrs till wknd 12th.*	8	16
874	1/4	Uttoxeter	(L)	HC	2m 7f	9	GF	*made most to 5th, wknd 10th, no ch when blnd 12th, t.o..*	4	0
1097	19/4	Bangor	(L)	HC	2 1/2m 110yds	11	G	*chsd ldrs, lost pl 6th, soon bhnd, t.o. when p.u. before 2 out.*	P	0
1488	12/5	Towcester	(R)	HC	2m 110yds	16	GS	*prom to 5th, t.o. when p.u. before 3 out.*	P	0

H/Chase winner 96; outclassed & well below form 97; best watched now 12

KING OF THE CLOUDS b.g. 12 Sonnen Gold - Misfired by Blast — J Hammond

1996 6(0),P(0),2(16),3(17),P(0),U(-),P(0)

221	16/2	Heythrop	(R)	RES	3m	15	G	*ld 4th til hdd & f 11th*	F	-
300	1/3	Didmarton	(L)	RES	3m	23	G	*ld 2nd-13th, sn outpcd by ldrs*	6	10
878	1/4	Upton-On-Se'	(R)	XX	3m	11	GF	*ld 4th, sn clr, hdd 15th, cls engh 2 out, sn btn*	2	14
1129	19/4	Penshurst	(L)	RES	3m	6	GF	*plld to ld 3rd,hdd & mstk 12th,3rd aft,kpt on,tk 2nd last*	2	14
1326	3/5	Chaddesley '	(L)	RES	3m	3	GF	*chsd wnr 3-5th & agn 7th, lft ev ch last, onepcd*	2	14

Novice-ridden now; still runs consistently but non-winner for 5 years 13

KING OF THE MICKS ch.g. 7 Revlow - Gypsey Lea by Gambling Debt — Mrs Peter Wakely

867	31/3	Kingston St'	(R)	MDO	3m	6	F	*plld hrd,trckd ldr,not fluent,efft & ran on to ld cls home*	1	16

No form in hurdles 94; ideal start in bad race & something to prove in Restricteds still 15

KING OF THE SUIR (Irish) — I 22^{P}, I 196^{2}, I 275^{6}

KINGOFTHESWINGERS br.g. 10 Swinging Rebel - Fair Sara by McIndoe — M Gallemore

1996 F(-),F(-)

882 1/4 Flagg Moor (L) MEM 3m 8 G — 4 0

Headstrong and clumsy 0

KING ON THE RUN (Irish) — I 303^{1}

KING PADDY(IRE) b.g. 5 King's Ride - Nebechal by Native Bazaar — Mrs S A Evans

571 16/3 Garnons (L) MDN 2 1/2m 13 G *rear frm 6th, t.o. & p.u. aft 10th* — P 0
1066 13/4 Maisemore P' (L) MDO 3m 9 GF *chsd ldrs,4th & rdn 7th,lft poor 4th 12th,nrly ref nxt,p.u.* — P 0

No signs of ability yet 0

KINGQUILLO(IRE) b.g. 8 Henbit (USA) - Friendly Polly by Be Friendly — Mrs B Shaw

1996 1(16),F(-)

1264 27/4 Southwell P' (L) INT 3m 9 G *disp to 4th, prom til wknd rpdly 7th, wll bhnd & p.u. 9th* — P 0

Maiden winner 96; only seen twice since & clearly problems now 12

KINGS ALIBI (Irish) — I 61^{6}, I 98^{F}, I 163^{2}, I 201^{2}, I 225^{F}, I 350^{1}

KINGS CHOIR ch.g. 5 Kinglet - Singing Story by True Song — Mrs R Prosser

775 29/3 Dingley (R) MDO 2m 5f 10 G *last til ref 5th* — R -
1082 13/4 Guilsborough (L) MDN 3m 14 GF *t.o. til p.u. 9th* — P 0

Unpromising 0

KING'S MAVERICK(IRE) b.g. 9 King's Ride - Lawless Secret by Meadsville — D L Ashby

1996 F(-),P(0),2(17),1(17)

282 23/2 Charing (L) INT 3m 7 G *hld up in tch, wknd rpdly 15th, p.u. nxt* — P 0

Won 2 bad races 95/96; clearly in trouble in 97 & best watched if reappearing 13

KING SOL (Irish) — I 117^{P}, I 128^{P}

KING SPRING br.g. 12 Royal Fountain - K-King by Fury Royal — Miss C E J Dawson

1996 4(0)

34 26/1 Alnwick (L) OPE 3m 9 G *rear, prog 12th, chsd wnr 15th-3 out, onepcd* — 4 19
159 15/2 Lanark (R) OPE 3m 3 G *2nd frm 8th, ld 10th-3 out, no ext* — 2 16
1217 26/4 Balcormo Ma' (R) MEM 3m 4 F *(fav) jmp slwly, wll bhnd thruout* — 3 0
1499 15/5 Perth (R) HC 2 1/2m 110yds 8 GS *alwys bhnd and detatched, t.o. when p.u. before 4 out.* — P 0
1545 24/5 Cartmel (L) HC 3 1/4m 14 G *alwys bhnd, t.o. when p.u. before 4 out (water).* — P 0

Declined rapidly in 97 & novice-ridden in Members which may have been last winning chance 12

KINGS RANK br.g. 12 Tender King - Jhansi Ki Rani (USA) by Far North (CAN) — Mrs L P Vaughan

1996 4(22),P(0),7(0),P(0),R(-)

359 2/3 Garnons (L) MEM 3m 3 GS *jmpd delib, chal 12th, ld nxt, drew clr frm 15th* — 1 14
702 29/3 Upper Sapey (R) LAD 3m 4 GF *(bl) hmp 1st, 10l 3rd whn ref 4th* — R -
1062 13/4 Maisemore P' (L) MXO 3m 12 GF *(bl) jmpd slwly, t.o. 9th, some late prog, nvr dang* — 5 13
1196 23/4 Andoversford (R) CON 3m 6 F *(bl) rear & jmpd slwly 4th, last whn ref nxt* — R -

Winning hurdler; soon loses interest & 1st time out only chance again in 98 14

KINGS RESPONSE (Irish) — I 510^{P}

KINGS RUN (Irish) — I 304^{P}

KINGS STRIDE (Irish) — I 285^{4}, I 311^{4}

KINGSTHORPE ch.g. 9 Brotherly (USA) - Miss Kewmill by Billion (USA) — Mervyn Jones

1996 P(0),B(-),4(11),1(15),F(-),P(0),7(0)

222 16/2 Heythrop (R) RES 3m 17 G *alwys rear, no ch frm 14th* — 6 0
258 22/2 Newtown (L) RES 3m 14 G *mid-div, prog 9th, chsd ldrs 13th, 4th & btn whn f 15th* — F -
433 8/3 Upton-On-Se' (R) RES 3m 18 G *trckd ldrs, effrt to 4th & ev ch 14th, wknd 3 out, p.u. last* — P 0
701 29/3 Upper Sapey (R) RES 3m 6 GF *prog 3rd to 3l 2nd 9th, ev ch whn outpcd frm 2 out* — 2 17
1061 13/4 Maisemore P' (L) RES 3m 12 GF *chsd ldrs, 2nd whn blnd 14th, kpt on onepcd frm 3 out* — 4 16
1237 26/4 Brampton Br' (R) RES 3m 13 G *mid-div, effrt to chs ldrs whn hit 13th, wknd 15th, p.u.3out* — P 0
1392 5/5 Cursneh Hill (L) RES 3m 6 GF *cls up til lost plc 7th, efft & ev ch 13th, wknd frm nxt* — 4 10

Maiden winner 96; barely stays; generally struggling & will need fortune to win Restricted 15

KINGS TOKEN b.g. 7 Rakaposhi King - Pro-Token by Proverb — Mrs F T Walton

1996 P(0),5(0),3(13),P(0),4(13),1(15)

230 22/2 Friars Haugh (L) RES 3m 15 G *steadied start, plld to ld & f 2nd* — F -
337 1/3 Corbridge (R) RES 3m 11 G *prom, mstk 2nd, wknd 10th, t.o. & p.u. 2 out* — P 0
1169 20/4 Hexham Poin' (L) RES 3m 9 GF *rear, prog 15th, tk poor 3rd apr last* — 3 0
1424 10/5 Aspatria (L) RES 3m 17 G *hld up, prog to trck ldrs 11th, lost plc & p.u. 15th* — P 0

1546 24/5 Hexham (L) HC 2 1/2m 110yds 10 GF *soon t.o., p.u. before 9th.* P 0

Steady improvement; won poor race and needs to improve; good stable. 14

KING'S TREASURE(USA) b.g. 8 King Of Clubs - Crown Treasure (USA) by Graustark — Mrs I A Balding
1996 U(-),**2(26)**,**2(22)**,**1(30)**,**1(30)**,**1(29)**

490 10/3 Stratford (L) HC 3m 12 G *(fav) chsd ldrs, ld 5th, hdd 3 out, outpcd apr last.* 2 24
589 20/3 Wincanton (R) HC 2m 5f 9 GF *(fav) prom, 3rd when f 6th.* F -

Very good H/Chaser 96; tubed; problems 97; young enough to recover; 2-3m 27

KINGTON DOWN b.g. 8 Town And Country - Wild Queen by Levanter — B B Akerman

218 16/2 Heythrop (R) INT 3m 21 G *blnd & u.r. 1st* U -

The briefest of seasons 0

KING TORUS(IRE) b.g. 7 Torus - Kam A Dusk — Nick Viney

7 19/1 Barbury Cas' (L) RES 3m 14 GF *prssd ldr clr of rest, ld 3 out, sn clr, ran on well* 1 21
97 8/2 Great Treth' (R) INT 3m 13 GS *wll in tch, chsd wnr 14th, no imp apr 2 out* 2 23
236 22/2 Lemalla (R) INT 3m 12 S *(fav) went 2nd 7th, ld/disp 10th, ev ch til wknd und pres last* 2 23
515 15/3 Larkhill (R) INT 3m 8 GF *made virt all, clr aft 2 out, hrd rdn & hng lft flat,all out* 1 24
1241 26/4 Bratton Down (L) MEM 3m 4 GS *(fav) made virt all, eased near fin* 1 20
1416 10/5 Newton Abbot (L) HC 2m 5f 110yds 14 G *(fav) alwys prom, ld 10th, rdn 2 out, all out.* 1 27
1518 17/5 Bratton Down (L) XX 3m 7 GS *(fav) ld to 9th, cls 2nd til ld agn 2 out, kpt on gamely und pres* 1 25
1587 29/5 Uttoxeter (L) HC 2m 5f 11 GF *(fav) chsd ldrs, ld apr 4 out, comf.* 1 28

Ex-Irish; very useful; best easy 3m & win more H/Chases 98; F-S, best GF 28

KINGUSSIE FLOWER br.m. 5 Scottish Reel - Kins Token by Relkino — Mrs Vanessa Ramm

1323 3/5 Bonvilston (R) MDO 3m 14 G *prom, ld 4 out, qcknd clr 2 out* 1 15

Ran green but ideal start in bad race; should have further prospects at 6 16

KINLEA b.g. 7 Meadowbrook - Faskin by Fez — Peter Diggle
1996 2(17),1(18)

35 26/1 Alnwick (L) CON 3m 10 G *alwys prom, ld 11-15th, chal 2 out, unable qckn flat* 3 18

Restricted winner 96; very lightly-raced; ran well only start & win Confined if fit 98 20

KINLET CREST ch.m. 6 Brotherly (USA) - Galway Lady Vii by Damsire Unregistered — J E Hector

437 8/3 Upton-On-Se' (R) MDO 3m 15 G *rear, t.o. 9th, p.u. 12th* P 0
723 29/3 Sandon (L) MDO 3m 6 GF *mid to rear, f 10th* F -

No promise yet 0

KINLET SPARK b.m. 8 Riberetto - Galway Lady Vii — J E Hector

1019 12/4 Bitterley (L) MDO 3m 12 GF *in tch til eased & p.u. 8th* P 0

Missed 96; only finished 1 of 8 starts to date 0

KINLOCHALINE b.m. 7 Silver Season - Teviot Lady by New Brig — Mrs C E Murray

338 1/3 Corbridge (R) RES 3m 10 G *swrvd & u.r. start* U -
418 8/3 Dalston (R) MDO 2 1/2m 10 GS *t.o. 5th, p.u. 11th* P 0
564 16/3 Lanark (R) MDO 2 1/2m 13 GS *prom til wknd frm 10th* 6 0
730 29/3 Alnwick (L) MDO 2 1/2m 9 F *rear, t.o. final cct, dead* 5 0

Dead 0

KINLOGH GALE(IRE) b.g. 9 Strong Gale - Kinlogh Maid by Random Shot — W J Evans
1996 2(13),6(0),3(11),4(0),3(12)

536 16/3 Erw Lon (L) LAD 3m 9 GF *(bl) ld aft 12th, kckd clr, hdd aft last, onepcd* 2 17
847 31/3 Lydstep (L) MDO 3m 5 F *(fav) (bl) sttld mid-div, prog 12th, ld 14th, sn in cmmnd* 1 12
962 6/4 Pantyderi (L) RES 3m 3 F *(fav) (bl) lft in ld 2nd, unchal aft* 1 13
1366 5/5 Pantyderi (L) INT 3m 6 G *(bl) chsd ldrs, effrt aft 15th, sn onepcd* 4 0

Safe & found 2 poor races; not 100% genuine; may struggle now upgraded; try Ladies again 15

KINNAHALLA (Irish) — **I** 91^P^, **I** 150^4^, **I** 186^1^, **I** 267^2^, **I** 494^4^, **I** 542^2^, **I** 587^1^
KINNEFAD KING (Irish) — **I** 65^P^, **I** 95^P^, **I** 459^P^, **I** 529^F^, **I** 577^P^, **I** 595,

KINO b.g. 10 Niniski (USA) - Relkina (FR) by Relkino — Andrew J Martin

93 7/2 Bangor (L) HC 2 1/2m 110yds 11 G *ld to 4th, wknd after 7th, lost tch and p.u. before 9th.* P 0
220 16/2 Heythrop (R) OPE 3m 20 G *rear, prog to chs ldrs 13th, no imp 15th, wknd & p.u. 2 out* P 0
369 2/3 Mollington (R) MEM 3m 13 G *chsd ldrs, outpcd 13th, ran on wll frm 3 out, nrst fin* 4 18
587 19/3 Ludlow (R) HC 2 1/2m 18 GF *alwys bhnd.* 9 15
926 6/4 Garthorpe (R) OPE 3m 10 GF *chsng grp, ld 13th, sn in cmmnd, ran on well* 1 22

1284 29/4 Huntingdon (R) HC 3m 6 G *waited with, hmpd 12th and lost tch, rpd prog and mstk next, gradually wknd from 15th.* 4 12
1415 9/5 Stratford (L) HC 3m 6 G *outpcd 6th, hdwy to chase ldr 11th, wknd 3 out, left poor 2nd after 2 out, left in ld last, lucky.* 1 18
1544 21/5 Newton Abbot (L) HC 3 1/4m 110yds 11 G *made most to 7th, weakening when hit 15th, t.o. when blnd badly and almost u.r. 3 out, p.u. before next.* P 0

Incredibly lucky H/Chase winner (looked 4th best) but 5th start suggests points possible in 98; G-F 21

KINTINO gr.m. 7 Neltino - King's Lavender by King's Troop J Tredwell
1996 **12(NH)**
1083 13/4 Guilsborough (L) MDN 3m 15 GF *f 2nd* F -

Brief appearance 0

KIRAMANDA br.m. 6 Kirchner - Annamanda by Tycoon II T Long
526 15/3 Cothelstone (L) MDN 3m 15 GS *lost tch 9th, t.o. & p.u. 11th* P 0
1095 16/4 Hockworthy (L) MDN 3m 11 GF *sn wll bhnd, t.o. 8th, p.u. 5 out* P 0
1261 27/4 Black Fores' (R) MDO 3m 12 F *alwys rear, p.u. 3 out* P 0
1437 10/5 Holnicote (L) MDO 3m 14 G *keen hld, prom til lost ground 14th, wkng whn f 16th* F -

Shows no promise yet 0

KIRI'S ROSE(IRE) b.m. 7 Roselier (FR) - Kiri's Return by Hawaiian Return (USA) Brian Gee
1996 **13(NH),3(NH),4(NH),3(NH),4(NH),8(NH)**
141 9/2 Thorpe Lodge (L) MDN 3m 12 GF *f 2nd* F -
345 2/3 Market Rase' (L) MDO 3m 13 GF *(fav) in tch, went 2nd 11th, ld apr last, qcknd clr, easily* 1 16
676 23/3 Brocklesby ' (L) RES 3m 14 GF *chsd ldrs, prog 12th, went 3rd brfly apr 3 out, sn wknd* 4 13
835 31/3 Thorpe Lodge (L) INT 3m 7 F *(fav) cls up, ld 7th & 10-11th, 2nd to 6 out, onepcd nxt* 5 13
1267 27/4 Southwell P' (L) MEM 3m 4 G *(fav) trckd ldrs, ld 10th, drew clr 13th, unchal* 1 14
1421 10/5 Easingwold (L) RES 3m 8 GF *prom, lft in ld 7th, jnd 2 out, styd on wll flat* 1 17
1608 1/6 Dingley (R) INT 3m 11 GF *mstks,chsd ldng trio frm 8th,no imp 15th,wknd 2 out,p.u.last* P 0

Placed in hurdles 96; good season but form modest & may struggle in better class now 18

KIRSTY'S PAL b.g. 8 Karlinsky (USA) - Last Farewell by Palm Track Mrs L Bloomfield
1996 **P(NH)**
243 22/2 Lemalla (R) MDO 3m 12 S *ran out bend aft 2nd* r -
460 8/3 Great Treth' (R) MDO 3m 13 S *bhnd whn p.u. apr 9th* P 0

Not the best of starts 0

KISSANES PRIDE (Irish) — **I** 103[P]

KITES HARDWICKE b.g. 10 Sunyboy - Kitty Stobling by Goldhill Mrs Camilla Behrens
1996 U(-),2(19),U(-),1+(17),**4(0)**,U(-),3(11)
215 16/2 Southwell P' (L) LAD 3m 12 GS *alwys rear, last frm 11th* 8 0
371 2/3 Mollington (R) LAD 3m 9 G *mid-div, outpcd 11th, clsd & in tch 13th, wknd rpdly 2 out* 5 12
448 8/3 Newton Brom' (R) LAD 3m 5 G *chsd ldrs, 3rd at 14th, styd on well* 3 16
773 29/3 Dingley (R) LAD 3m 11 G *w.w. 5th & rdn 10th, 3rd 6 out, chsd wnr nxt, outpcd 2 out* 2 18
986 12/4 Kingston Bl' (L) CON 3m 10 GF *w.w. prog 12th, clsd 3 out, chal last, not qckn flat* 2 18
1207 26/4 Clifton On ' (L) LAD 3m 6 GS *alwys last pair, outpcd 4 out* 5 12

Dead/Heated in Ladies 96; consistent but one paced & needs give; could surprise right conditions 98 .. 17

KITSBEL ro.g. 9 Belfort (FR) - Fair Kitty by Saucy Kit D F Donegan
462 8/3 Charing (L) RES 3m 10 G *t.d.e. immed dtchd, alwys last, p.u. 10th* P 0

Unpromising 0

KITS PRIDE b.m. 5 Abutammam - Bauneen Oge by Master Buck Caleb Davies
367 2/3 Garnons (L) MDO 2 1/2m 9 GS *declined 1st* R -
542 16/3 Erw Lon (L) MDN 3m 15 GF *(bl) ref 2nd* R -
842 31/3 Lydstep (L) MDO 3m 12 F *(bl) ref 2nd* R -
1561 24/5 Bassaleg (R) MDO 3m 9 G *jmpd slwly 8th,prog 11th,chsd wnr nxt,unable qckn aft 3 out* 2 12

Looked ghastly till last effort (weak race); could have chances if behaving herself 98 12

KITZBERG (Irish) — **I** 212,

KLAGUNFURT (Irish) — **I** 383[F]

KLONDYKE MAID ch.m. 6 Flying Tyke - Winchester Lass by Mandamus Stuart Wilson
427 8/3 Charm Park (L) MDO 3m 10 GF *prom early, outpcd 8th, wll bhnd 12th, p.u. 4 out* P 0

No signs of ability yet 0

KNIFEBOARD b.g. 11 Kris - Catalpa by Reform Paul O J Hosgood
586 19/3 Exeter (R) HC 3 1/4m 12 GF *trckd ldrs til wknd after 4 out, p.u. before 2 out.* P 0
1292 30/4 Cheltenham (L) HC 2m 5f 12 GF *waited with in rear, gd prog from 10th, mstk 4 out, chsd wnr and mistake last, ran on.* 2 26

1544 21/5 Newton Abbot (L) HC 3 1/4m 110yds 11 G *held up, hdwy 8th, outpcd apr 15th, t.o..* 4 12

Able but fragile & lightly raced; best under 3m; ran well Cheltenham & still chances at 12 if fit 24

KNIGHTLY ARGUS ch.g. 10 Le Moss - Cala San Vicente by Gala Performance (USA) M R Rollett

650 22/3 Siddington (L) CON 3m 8 F *keen hld, jmpd rght, chsd ldr 9th, disp 13th-3 out, kpt on* 2 16
880 1/4 Upton-On-Se' (R) CON 3m 6 GF *chsd ldrs, mstk 7th, sn pshd alng, bhnd frm 13th* 4 0

Flattered when 2nd & well beaten other start; season lasted 10 days; best watched 14

KNIGHT OF PASSION b.g. 5 Arctic Lord - Lovelek by Golden Love G J Harris

316 1/3 Clyst St Ma' (L) MDN 3m 6 HY *f 1st* F -
527 15/3 Cothelstone (L) MDN 3m 14 GS *sn rear, not fluent, bhnd & p.u. 13th* P 0
1094 16/4 Hockworthy (L) MDN 3m 11 GF *mstks 5th & 9th, rear, t.o. & p.u. 4 out* P 0

Mistakes to date & no signs of ability yet 0

KNIGHT'S SPUR(USA) b.g. 10 Diesis - Avoid (USA) by Buckpasser Mrs Mary Henderson
1996 4(14),2(20),2(20),**6(13)**

546 16/3 Garthorpe (R) LAD 3m 11 GF *mid div, prog 11th, outpcd 15th, 4th & no ch frm 3 out* 4 14

Placed in 8 of 11 races 95-7 but frustrating & soon vanished in 97 17

KNOCANS PRIDE (Irish) — **I** 67,
KNOCKADOOMA (Irish) — **I** 17⁵, **I** 64ᴾ, **I** 476³, **I** 563ᴾ, **I** 615,
KNOCKANARD (Irish) — **I** 484³
KNOCKANNIG BAY (Irish) — **I** 23ᴾ, **I** 161ᴾ
KNOCKANORAN (Irish) — **I** 35ᵁ, **I** 99³, **I** 135ᴾ, **I** 221², **I** 341², **I** 405¹
KNOCK IT BACK (Irish) — **I** 191³, **I** 308¹
KNOCKLAWN (Irish) — **I** 142ᴾ, **I** 195ᴾ
KNOCK LEADER (Irish) — **I** 83¹
KNOCKNACARRA LAD (Irish) — **I** 455¹, **I** 528², **I** 560¹, **I** 567⁵, **I** 605¹
KNOCKNAGORE (Irish) — **I** 533ᶠ, **I** 563ᴾ, **I** 608ᴾ
KNOCK ROAD (Irish) — **I** 329ᴾ, **I** 377ᴾ
KNOCKTORAN LADY (Irish) — **I** 299ᴾ, **I** 357ᴾ, **I** 454ᴾ, **I** 494ᶠ, **I** 562ᴾ

KNOWE HEAD b.g. 13 Beau Charmeur (FR) - Niagara Lass by Prince Hansel J Hodgson
1996 3(18),2(17),3(12),S(-),**1(26)**

696 29/3 Stainton (R) OPE 3m 5 F *ld til hdd & wknd 4 out* 4 13
1248 26/4 Easingwold (L) OPE 3m 8 GS *ld & made all to last, hdd outpcd run in* 2 20
1414 9/5 Sedgefield (L) HC 2m 5f 6 GF *(fav) ld till hdd between last 2, no ext.* 3 18
1546 24/5 Hexham (L) HC 2 1/2m 110yds 10 GF *cl up, mstk 7th, struggling final cct, t.o. when p.u. before last.* P 0

H/Chase winner 96; time looks to be catching up on him now; best under 3m & hard to place now; G-F 17

KNOW SOMETHING VI (Irish) — **I** 569¹

KOWLOON BAY(IRE) b.g. 7 Abednego - Kowloon by No Argument P Armitage

116 9/2 Wetherby Po' (L) MDO 3m 14 GF *rear, strgglng 7th, t.o. 9th, p.u. 12th* P 0
269 22/2 Duncombe Pa' (R) MDO 3m 16 G *alwys rear, t.o. whn p.u. 10th* P 0
358 2/3 Great Stain' (L) MDO 3m 14 S *sn dtchd, t.o. & p.u. 12th* P 0

No sign of ability & soon tailed off each time 0

KRISAN b.m. 7 Krisinsky (USA) - Mandana by Extra J L Burt

1082 13/4 Guilsborough (L) MDN 3m 14 GF *in tch to 11th, wll bhnd frm 13th, p.u. 15th* P 0
1209 26/4 Clifton On ' (L) MDO 3m 16 GS *prom to 10th, fdd, outpcd 6 out* 10 0
1353 4/5 Dingley (R) MDO 2 1/2m 9 G *in tch, blnd 10th, last aft, t.o. & p.u. 2 out* P 0

No promise to date 0

KRISTAL HAZE b.m. 5 Krisinsky (USA) - Brilliant Haze Vii by Damsire Unregistered Mrs K M Dando

367 2/3 Garnons (L) MDO 2 1/2m 9 GS *rear frm 4th, p.u. 9th* P 0
541 16/3 Erw Lon (L) MDN 3m 10 GF *ptntly rdn, prog 3 out, ld aft nxt, ran on* 1 13
717 29/3 Llanvapley (L) RES 3m 13 GF *held up in rear, prog 13th, fin wll, to much to do* 3 10
1131 19/4 Bonvilston (R) MEM 3m 6 G *held up in rear, prog & lft 2nd 14th, alwys held* 2 11
1322 3/5 Bonvilston (R) RES 3m 9 G *rear, p.u. 11th* P 0

Found weak race 2nd start; not given hard time & may improve in 98 14

KUMADA b.g. 10 Vision (USA) - Fan The Flame by Grundy Mrs J K Marriage
1996 3(16),1(18),F(-),2(20),1(21),2(20),9(0)

193 15/2 Higham (L) CON 3m 14 G *handy, pshd alng 11th, wkng whn p.u. 15th* P 0

444	8/3	Higham	(L)	CON	3m	8	G	*ld to 11th, hit nxt, qckly bhnd, t.o. 16th*	4	0
707	29/3	High Easter	(L)	MEM	3m	2	F	*(fav) wth wnr til ld 14th, hdd 2 out, nt qkn und press*	2	13
912	5/4	Cottenham	(R)	LAD	3m	3	F	*ld to 5th, ld 11th-14th, ev ch 3 out, ran on to ld nr fin*	1	17
1029	12/4	Horseheath	(R)	LAD	3m	3	HD	*(fav) ld to 4th, chsd wnr, 2l dwn & hit 15th, no ch wth wnr aft*	2	17
1280	27/4	Fakenham P-'	(L)	LAD	3m	6	G	*ld til jmpd slwly 3rd,ld 8-12th & 15th,blnd & hdd nxt,onepcd*	2	17
1378	5/5	Northaw	(L)	LAD	3m	5	F	*ld 4-8th,ld 10th til mstk & hdd 15th,sn rdn, no ex apr last*	4	16
1502	16/5	Folkestone	(R)	HC	2m 5f	10	G	*nvr going well, alwys bhnd, t.o. 8th, p.u. before 3 out.*	P	0

Dual winner 96; changed hands 97; best easy 3m on Firm; may find another small race 18

KUSHBALOO b.g. 12 Kambalda - Cushla by Zabeg — Mr & Mrs Raymond Anderson Green

1996 **4(NH),2(NH),1(NH),4(NH)**

67	1/2	Wetherby	(L)	HC	3m 1f	10	G	*chsd ldrs to hfwy, soon bhnd, t.o..*	9	0
492	11/3	Sedgefield	(L)	HC	3m 3f	7	G	*(fav) slight ld to 8th, ld again 15th, clr 3 out, shaken up and hdd near fin.*	2	25
973	7/4	Kelso	(L)	HC	3m 1f	5	GF	*ld, rdn along and blnd 2 out, hdd last 50 yards, no ext.*	3	23
1284	29/4	Huntingdon	(R)	HC	3m	6	G	*(Jt fav) trckd ldr 5th, ld after 8th, rdn apr last, styd on well run-in.*	1	26

Good winning chaser; unlucky twice & made amends; one paced & may struggle at 13 in H/Chases 23

K WALK ch.m. 7 K-Battery - Burri Walk by Tower Walk — Mrs M Armstrong

1996 P(0),8(0),P(0)

161	15/2	Lanark	(R)	MDO	2m 5f	14	G	*bhnd whn p.u. 11th*	P	0
815	31/3	Tranwell	(L)	MDO	2 1/2m	14	G	*mid-div til p.u. 7th*	P	0
1173	20/4	Hexham Poin'	(L)	MDO	2 1/2m	9	GF	*chsd ldrs, no imp final cct, t.o.*	5	0
1409	5/5	Witton Cast'	(R)	MDO	3m	15	GS	*chsd ldr til wknd qckly 4 out, t.o. whn p.u. last*	P	0

Tailed off last on only completion 97 & shows no stamina 0

KYLE LAMP (Irish) — **I** 218[P]

LABURNUM gr.g. 9 Glint Of Gold - Lorelene (FR) by Lorenzaccio — Robert Barr

1996 P(0),P(0),**P(0)**,1(18),3(15),**P(0)**,P(0)

71	2/2	Higham	(L)	LAD	3m	6	GF	*mid-div, prog 11th, wknd rpdly 13th, p.u. nxt*	P	0
194	15/2	Higham	(L)	OPE	3m	12	G	*alwys rear, wll bhnd 13th*	7	0
440	8/3	Higham	(L)	OPE	3m	5	G	*cls 2nd at 4th, rmndrs 10th, blnd & wknd 14th, t.o.,dsmntd*	4	0

Open winner 96; looks finished now 12

LAC DE GRAS(IRE) gr.g. 6 Henbit (USA) - I've No Idea by Nishapour (FR) — E Pennock

1996 **11(NH),5(NH),P(NH),5(NH),2(NH),P(NH),2(NH)**

345	2/3	Market Rase'	(L)	MDO	3m	13	GF	*jmpd bdly, sn wll bhnd, t.o. & p.u. 10th*	P	0
506	15/3	Dalton Park	(R)	CON	3m	16	GF	*mid-div, f 1st*	F	-
675	23/3	Brocklesby '	(L)	OPE	3m	6	GF	*jmpd rght, t.o. frm 2nd*	5	0
860	31/3	Charm Park	(L)	MDO	3m	12	F	*in tch, 5th at 8th, wknd, f 13th*	F	-
1251	26/4	Easingwold	(L)	MDO	3m	9	GS	*in tch, error 4th, wknd, p.u. 14th*	P	0

Placed in hurdles but cannot jump in points 0

LA CHARENTE (Irish) — **I** 12[P], **I** 136[F], **I** 171[1]

LACKEN BEAU (Irish) — **I** 116[P], **I** 211[3], **I** 249[6], **I** 362[1], **I** 374[6], **I** 433[4]

LACKEN CROSS (Irish) — **I** 51[3]

LACKEN STAR (Irish) — **I** 485[4]

LAD LANE b or br.g. 13 Proverb - Quarry Lane by Bargello — J Borradaile

1996 P(0),4(0),3(0),12(0),9(0)

978	8/4	Heythrop	(R)	CON	3m	3	F	*chsd ldr til j.s. 6th, last aft, t.o. frm 3 out*	3	0
1403	5/5	Ashorne	(R)	CON	3m	14	G	*t.o. 4th, p.u. 11th*	P	0
1532	18/5	Mollington	(R)	CON	3m	11	GS	*alwys last pair, t.o. 12th, p.u. 3 out*	P	0

No longer of any account 0

LADY ELISE (Irish) — **I** 5[2]

LADY FLECK (Irish) — **I** 228[5], **I** 277[F], **I** 298[P], **I** 557[3], **I** 576[P]

LADY KILTON b.m. 7 Welsh Captain - Kilton Jill by Adropejo — Mrs D Cowley

1401	5/5	Ashorne	(R)	MDO	3m	15	G	*s.s. jmpd bdly, t.o. til p.u. 9th*	P	0
1537	18/5	Mollington	(R)	MDO	3m	14	GS	*alwys rear, t.o. 12th, p.u. 2 out*	P	0

.... **0**

LADY LEIGH b.m. 8 Henricus (ATA) - Calverleigh by Tudor Flame — R J Chanin

737	29/3	Higher Kilw'	(L)	LAD	3m	5	GF	*ld/disp to 8th, wknd, p.u. 12th, school*	P	0
950	6/4	Black Fores'	(R)	MEM	3m	7	G	*plld hrd, t.o. & p.u. 10th*	P	0
1400	5/5	High Bickin'	(R)	MDO	3m	14	G	*rmndrs 5th, t.o. 9th, p.u. 12th*	P	0

No promise yet & time already passing 0

LADY LIR ch.m. 8 Lir - Kimberley Ann by St Columbus — M D Rusden

1996 P(0),6(0),6(0),P(0),1(15)

100	8/2	Great Treth'	(R)	RES	3m	14 GS	*in tch, prog to trck ldr 10th til wknd 14th,no ch whn f last*	F	-
457	8/3	Great Treth'	(R)	RES	3m	8 S	*hdwy 10th, losng grnd in 5th whn p.u. apr 15th*	P	0
628	22/3	Kilworthy	(L)	CON	3m	12 G	*prog to 5th 13th, ev ch 3 out, onepce*	4	22
1039	12/4	Lifton	(R)	RES	3m	8 F	*chsd ldrs til grdly wknd 5 out, p.u. 2 out*	P	0

Maiden winner 96; excellent 3rd run but problems last start; Restricted possible if fit 98 17

LADY LLANFAIR b.m. 11 Prince Tenderfoot (USA) - Picnic Time by Silly Season — N G Anderson

1996 3(20),P(0),4(19),P(0)

257	22/2	Newtown	(L)	LAD	3m	12 G	*in tch to 12th, sn wknd, p.u. aft 3 out*	P	0
296	1/3	Didmarton	(L)	LAD	3m	13 G	*rear main grp, no prog 11th, t.o. & p.u. last*	P	0
401	8/3	Llanfrynach	(R)	LAD	3m	14 G	*cls up, lost plc hlfwy, no ch aft*	6	16

Formerly decent but looks ready for retirement now 14

LADY MOUSE b or br.m. 7 Derring Rose - All Our Yesterdays by Jimsun — Mrs N Clothier

106	8/2	Milborne St'	(L)	RES	3m	12 GF	*sn rear, blnd 7th, t.o. & p.u. nxt*	P	0
642	22/3	Castle Of C'	(R)	MEM	3m	4 G	*hld up, mstk 6th, prog 11th, btn whn jmpd slwly 15th,p.u.nxt*	P	0
933	6/4	Charlton Ho'	(L)	MDO	3m	12 G	*jmpd slwly 6th, prom to 8th, rear whn blnd 11th & p.u.*	P	0

Yet to learn to jump & looks unpromising 0

LADY OF GORTMERRON (Irish) — I 246[P], I 312[P], I 377[P], I 416[P], I 461[3], I 506[P]

LADY OF IRON (Irish) — I 46[3], I 74[P], I 90[5], I 263[1], I 309[P], I 380[S]

LADY OF MEANS (Irish) — I 10[6], I 60, , I 137[4], I 166, , I 384[5], I 479[4]

LADY ORR(IRE) ch.m. 6 Ore - Better Again by Deep Run — Rhoss Davies

1996 P(0)

407	8/3	Llanfrynach	(R)	MDN	3m	11 G	*hld up mid-div, prog to disp 3 out, ran out bend apr nxt*	P	0
841	31/3	Lydstep	(L)	MDO	3m	8 F	*sttld rear, prog 14th, nvr nr engh to chal*	3	0
1323	3/5	Bonvilston	(R)	MDO	3m	14 G	*rear til p.u. 2 out*	P	0
1367	5/5	Pantyderi	(L)	MDO	3m	7 G	*ld/disp to 13th, wknd, p.u. 2 out*	P	0
1603	31/5	Bassaleg	(R)	MDO	3m	6 F	*hld up,prog 10th,2nd & going wll whn crawld 13th,p.u. lame*	P	0

Unlucky & lost golden chance in desperate race last start 10

LADY PENDRAGON b.m. 8 Oats - Impressive Reward (USA) by Impressive — D Mansell

1996 **9(NH),11(NH),6(NH)**

430	8/3	Upton-On-Se'	(R)	MEM	3m	4 G	*hld up in tch, 3rd 3 out, nvr able to chal*	3	13
664	23/3	Eaton Hall	(R)	MDO	3m	12 GF	*prom, 2nd at 7th, disp 10th, wknd 13th, p.u. 3 out*	P	0

Ran well enough on pointing debut but disappointing next start & vanished 10

LADY POKEY br.m. 7 Uncle Pokey - Lady Buttons by New Brig — S Edwards

1996 P(0),P(0)

81	2/2	Wolverhampt'	(L)	MDN	3m	13 GS	*mstks, prom til wknd 12th, t.o. & p.u. 15th*	P	0
327	1/3	Eaton Hall	(R)	MDN	3m	11 GS	*chsng grp, 3rd 9th, ev ch 5 out, not qckn*	5	10

Tailed off in only completion from 4 starts 96/7 0

LADY ROMANCE(IRE) b.m. 9 Brewery Boy (AUS) - Romantic Rhapsody by Ovac (ITY) — M G Jones

1996 2(11),3(10),F(-),2(12),3(12),P(0),3(10)

407	8/3	Llanfrynach	(R)	MDN	3m	11 G	*prom early, wknd & p.u. 3 out*	P	0
541	16/3	Erw Lon	(L)	MDN	3m	10 GF	*nvr nr ldrs, p.u. 3 out*	P	0
963	6/4	Pantyderi	(L)	MDN	3m	6 F	*4th/5th thruout, p.u. bfr last*	P	0
1137	19/4	Bonvilston	(R)	MDO	3m	13 G	*rear, p.u. 3 out*	P	0
1323	3/5	Bonvilston	(R)	MDO	3m	14 G	*cls up, lost plc hlfwy, lft 3rd by dfctns*	3	0
1527	17/5	Bredwardine	(R)	MDO	3m	13 G	*prom to 10th, rear frm 13th, sn t.o.*	5	0

Placed 7 times but no rateable form in 97 & win looks impossible 0

LADY SPARKY (Irish) — I 487[P], I 519[P]

LADY STEEL(IRE) gr.m. 8 Roselier (FR) - Roses In June by Timobriol — Miss S E Baxter

84	2/2	Wolverhampt'	(L)	MEM	3m	9 GS	*ld 3rd-7th, prom to 11th, sn outpcd*	4	10
213	16/2	Southwell P'	(L)	RES	3m	16 GS	*s.s. f 2nd*	F	-
724	29/3	Sandon	(L)	LAD	3m	4 GF	*ld to 6th, 2nd to 12th, 3rd aft, onepcd*	3	17
939	6/4	Tabley	(R)	LAD	3m	9 G	*severall postitions, disp ld 14th-nxt, wknd 3 out*	5	15
1177	20/4	Sandon	(L)	LAD	3m	4 GF	*cls 2nd whn slppd bnd aft 2nd*	S	-

Irish Maiden winner 96; modest form in Ladies & stamina suspect; unlikely to win 14

LADY SYLVIE (Irish) — I 31[F], I 96[3], I 151[2], I 286[2], I 349[1], I 415[1], I 465[P], I 528[U], I 542[4], I 605[P]

LADY ZAFFARAN (Irish) — I 111[P], I 227[F], I 292, , I 413[P], I 461[6], I 506, , I 586[5]

LAEMNI (Irish) — I 490[P], I 532[4], I 580[5]

LA FONTAINBLEAU(IRE) gr.g. 9 Lafontaine (USA) - Alsong by Al Sirat (USA) — D H Brown

1996 **2(NH),6(NH),5(NH)**

119 9/2 Wetherby Po' (L) OPE 3m 15 GF *prom til lost ground 5th, wll bhnd 10th, t.o.* 5 11
250 22/2 Brocklesby ' (L) OPE 3m 6 G *alwys last, rmmdrs 8-9th, t.o. 10th, p.u. 4 out* P 0
287 27/2 Huntingdon (R) HC 3m 13 GS *alwys in rear, t.o. when p.u. before 5 out.* P 0

Hurdles winner 95; of no account in points 0

LAGANSIDE (Irish) — **I** 303⁶, **I** 332⁶, **I** 485⁵

LAKEFIELD RAMBLER (Irish) — **I** 104³

LAKELAND EDITION gr.m. 6 Respect - Miss Lakeland by Pongee K Eve

33 26/1 Alnwick (L) LAD 3m 12 G *u.r. 2nd* U -
134 9/2 Alnwick (L) MDO 3m 11 G *sn wll bhnd, t.o. frm 3rd* 5 0
156 15/2 Lanark (R) CON 3m 7 G *wll bhnd by 7th, p.u. 12th* P 0

Shows nothing & finished early 0

LAKELAND VENTURE ch.m. 7 Respect - Miss Lakeland by Pongee P E Clark

1996 r(-),P(0),5(0),P(0)

168 15/2 Witton Cast' (R) MDO 3m 4 F *keen hld, trckd ldr, ld 7th-13th, sn wknd, t.o.* 3 0
269 22/2 Duncombe Pa' (R) MDO 3m 16 G *rear, p.u. 7th, lame* P 0

Last on both completions 96/7 & problems to add to the misery 0

LAKE MARINER b.m. 10 Julio Mariner - Lillytip by Tepukei Mrs Lyn Brafield

1996 2(10),1(13),P(0),P(0)

176 15/2 Ottery St M' (L) RES 3m 17 G *mid-div til blnd & u.r. 12th* U -
312 1/3 Clyst St Ma' (L) RES 3m 8 HY *prom, ld 8th til s.u. bend aft 12th* S -
523 15/3 Cothelstone (L) RES 3m 14 GS *prom til lost plc 15th, bhnd whn p.u. 2 out* P 0
648 22/3 Castle Of C' (R) RES 3m 8 G *in tch, chsd ldr brfly 13th, wknd 15th* 5 0
1043 12/4 Cothelstone (L) INT 3m 7 GF *hld up, prog 12th, 4th & ev ch whn hmpd & u.r. nxt* U -
1317 3/5 Holnicote (L) RES 3m 5 G *sn bhnd, t.o. 2nd, some prog whn u.r. 2 out* U -
1496 14/5 Cothelstone (L) CON 3m 9 GF *prog & prom 8th, outpcd frm 13th, no imp frm 16th* 5 11
1551 24/5 Mounsey Hil' (R) RES 3m 13 G *hld up mid-div, prog to 3rd at 17th, btn 2 out, dmtd flat* 4 11

Maiden winner 96; only finished 5 of 20 races 94-7; struggling now 11

LAKE MISSION b.g. 12 Blakeney - Missed Blessing by So Blessed C T Nash

1996 **4(NH),5(NH),2(NH),9(NH),8(NH),6(NH)**

57 1/2 Kingston Bl' (L) LAD 3m 13 GF *alwys prom, chsd wnr last cct, no imp, lost 2nd flat* 3 21
219 16/2 Heythrop (R) LAD 3m 16 G *ld 4th,prssd but going bttr frm 2 out, hdd & not qckn nr fin* 2 26
296 1/3 Didmarton (L) LAD 3m 13 G *set fast pace til hdd 2 out, ran on well flat* 2 26

Well-revived & ran 3 tremendous races in top Ladies contests (novice-ridden); could win if fit at 13 23

LAKENHEATHER(NZ) b.g. 11 Lakenheath (USA) - Monanne by Pharamond Mrs Pat Mullen

1996 U(-),2(13),2(0),U(-),1(13)

463 8/3 Eyton-On-Se' (L) MEM 3m 1 G *walked over* 1 0
465 8/3 Eyton-On-Se' (L) OPE 3m 13 G *rear 10th, t.o. 5 out, p.u. 3 out* P 0

Restricted winner 96; very modest at best & unlikely to win another race 12

LAKESIDE LAD b.g. 5 St Columbus - Beyond The Trimm by Trimmingham A Wright

1996 **8(NH),0(NH)**

365 2/3 Garnons (L) MDO 2 1/2m 14 GS *mid-div, kpt on steadily frm 11th* 4 0
570 16/3 Garnons (L) MDN 2 1/2m 14 G *prog 9th, rdn & chnc 3 out, no ext frm nxt* 2 10
1015 12/4 Bitterley (L) MDO 3m 12 GF *cls up to 9th, 10l 6th whn f 3 out* F -

Not disgraced each start & should go close in 98 13

LA KESTREL (Irish) — **I** 166, , **I** 235ᶠ, **I** 305ᶠ, **I** 478ᶠ, **I** 519ᴾ, **I** 561⁵, **I** 608⁴

LAKE TEEREEN ch.g. 12 Callernish - Gusserane Lark by Napoleon Bonaparte T D B Underwood

1996 **P(NH),P(NH),11(NH),5(NH),6(NH),P(NH)**

17 25/1 Badbury Rin' (L) CON 3m 9 GF *mstks, in tch in rear til u.r. 10th* U -
55 1/2 Kingston Bl' (L) CON 3m 15 GF *prom early, no ch frm 13th* 9 0
142 9/2 Tweseldown (R) MEM 3m 8 GF *outpcd in rear, some prog 12th, blnd & btn 3 out, p.u. nxt* P 0
577 16/3 Detling (L) CON 3m 18 F *p.u. 4th* P 0

Winning chaser; last start suggests the end may be nigh 12

LA LAC(IRE) b.m. 9 Kings Lake (USA) - La Cita by Le Levanstell Mrs E A Eagles

525 15/3 Cothelstone (L) MDN 3m 15 GS *rear, blnd 6th, t.o. til p.u. 4 out* P 0

No promise & already in middle-age 0

LA MAJA(IRE) b.m. 8 Lafontaine (USA) - Eiger Sanctions by St Alphage Mrs N C Wilson

117 9/2 Wetherby Po' (L) LAD 3m 10 GF *sn lost tch, completed own time* 6 0
474 9/3 Southwell P' (L) LAD 3m 12 G *pckd 3rd, prog to ld & f 9th* F -

609 22/3 Friars Haugh (L) LAD 3m 11 GF *s.s., alwys wll bhnd* 9 0
891 4/4 Sedgefield (L) HC 3m 3f 5 GF *jmpd right thrght, held up, imp after 13th, chal 2 out, hit last, kept on same pace.* 2 17
1075 13/4 Whitwell-On' (R) MEM 3m 9 G *rear, dtchd whn u.r. 10th* U -
1247 26/4 Easingwold (L) CON 3m 9 GS *rear, mstk 8th, wll bhnd whn ref last* R -
1406 5/5 Witton Cast' (R) RES 3m 10 GS *rear, prog 7th, disp 10th til hdd & wknd 14th, p.u. 3 out* P 0

Irish Maiden winner 96; form only in poor H/Chase & looks one to steer clear of 12

LAMANAUGH LADY VI (Irish) — **I** 234^{F}, **I** 302^{P}, **I** 356^{F}

LA MANCHA BOY (Irish) — **I** 36^{P}, **I** 72^{5}, **I** 214, , **I** 253^{3}, **I** 366^{4}

LANCASTRIAN JET(IRE) b.g. 6 Lancastrian - Kilmurray Jet by Le Bavard (FR) Capt T A Forster
1996 **11(NH)**
1016 12/4 Bitterley (L) MDO 3m 14 GF *(fav) alwys prom, mstk 13th, ld 3 out, qcknd clr* 1 14

Impressive winner on pointing debut; worth watching when next appearing 19

LAND FORLORN (Irish) — **I** 251^{P}, **I** 310^{F}, **I** 364^{3}, **I** 464^{P}, **I** 556^{P}, **I** 586^{2}

LANDSKER ALFRED ch.g. 11 Push On - April Fooldus by Haven Dr P P Brown
1996 1(19),2(23),1(22),1(21),1(22)
363 2/3 Garnons (L) XX 3m 6 GS *w.w. went cls 3rd 9th, ev ch 13th, wknd nxt, walked in* 3 0
568 16/3 Garnons (L) CON 3m 12 G *(fav) cls up, rdn 2 out, ev ch last, no ext und pres* 2 22
880 1/4 Upton-On-Se' (R) CON 3m 6 GF *mstly chsd wnr, jmpd lft 10th, rdn & no imp 3 out* 2 18
1064 13/4 Maisemore P' (L) CON 3m 13 GF *chsd ldrs, went 2nd 15th, 3l down apr 2 out, btn nxt* 2 21
1211 26/4 Woodford (L) MEM 3m 8 G *(fav) chsd ldrs, ld 11th, made rest, drew clr frm 3 out, easily* 1 22
1455 11/5 Maisemore P' (L) CON 3m 8 G *blnd 4th, effrt to chs wnr 12th-3 out, 3rd & btn aft* 3 16
1576 26/5 Chaddesley ' (L) XX 3m 12 F *(fav) prom,slw jmp 4th,ld 9-12th,ld 3 out-last,rallied flat* 2 22

Moderate but very consistent; top stable; easily beaten by fair horses; should win again; L/H; F-S 21

LANDSKER MISSILE b.m. 8 Cruise Missile - Gemmerly Jane by Bally Russe W J Evans
46 1/2 Larkhill (R) XX 3m 3 GF *ld to 13th, btn whn mstk 3 out, wknd, ref last* R -
191 15/2 Erw Lon (L) CON 3m 13 G *ld, mstk 13th, hdd 3 out, sn btn, lost 2nd last* 3 17
587 19/3 Ludlow (R) HC 2 1/2m 18 GF *chsd wnr thrght, held when blnd 2 out, not rcvr.* 2 25
781 31/3 Hereford (R) HC 2m 3f 9 GF *(fav) prom, ld 7th, hrd pressed from 3 out till driven clr from last.* 1 26
958 6/4 Pantyderi (L) CON 3m 3 F *(fav) made all, unchal* 1 22
1182 20/4 Lydstep (L) OPE 3m 3 GF *(fav) ld 2nd, unchal* 1 24
1226 26/4 Pyle (R) OPE 3m 6 GS *(fav) ld 7-14th, sn btn, mstk 3 out, wknd & eased* 2 17
1296 3/5 Hereford (R) HC 2m 3f 11 G *(fav) alwys prom, rdn 4 out, wknd next, left 3rd last.* 3 21

Winning chaser 95; quite useful; best under 3m; below form last 2 but should win again; G-F 24

LANGRETTA (Irish) — **I** 519^{P}, **I** 599^{5}

LANMIRE (Irish) — **I** 255^{1}

LANNGARA (Irish) — **I** 56^{S}, **I** 152^{P}

LAN-PAULA (Irish) — **I** 111^{P}, **I** 178^{P}, **I** 292^{3}, **I** 372^{S}

LANTERN PIKE ch.g. 11 Full Of Hope - Tiddles Twopence by Royal Bay A H L Michael
1996 2(16),1(19),3(14),1(20),**2(21)**,1(24),**4(13)**
194 15/2 Higham (L) OPE 3m 12 G *ld 3rd, brfly hdd 11th, hdd & wknd aft 4 out, bttr for race* 4 11

Won 3 in 96 but disappeared early 97; best at 12 19

LANTERN SPARK(IRE) b.m. 7 The Parson - La Dragoniere by Hot Spark R L Clifton-Brown
197 15/2 Higham (L) MDO 3m 12 G *rear, losng tch whn ref 14th* R -
318 1/3 Marks Tey (L) MDN 3m 13 G *f 4th* F -
439 8/3 Higham (L) MDO 3m 11 G *mid-div, bhnd frm 11th, t.o. & reluc 14th, p.u. nxt* P 0
599 22/3 Horseheath (R) MDO 3m 4 F *3rd til lft 2nd aft 9th, prssd wnr 11-16th,u.r. 2out, rmntd* 2 0
914 5/4 Cottenham (R) MDO 3m 4 F *(Jt fav) (bl) ld 5th, clr 8th, blnd 3 out, hdd nxt, ev ch last, no ext* 2 0
1282 27/4 Fakenham P-' (L) MDO 3m 8 G *(bl) chsd ldrs, mstk 1st, jmpd slwly 4th, 4th & btn whn u.r. 2out* U -
1380 5/5 Northaw (L) MDO 3m 4 F *(bl) keen hold, mstks, chsd ldr 8-14th, rdn 15th, onepcd* 3 11

Placed in bad races & ungenuine; blinkers no help & luck needed for a win 10

LANTON MOOR br.m. 8 Liberated - Daleside Heather by St Alphage W Spence
1429 10/5 Aspatria (L) MDO 3m 15 G *blnd 6th, t.o. nxt, p.u. 12th* P 0

Rarely runs & shows nothing 0

LARAS BOY (Irish) — **I** 66^{P}, **I** 101^{U}, **I** 152^{F}, **I** 198^{P}

LARK RIVER (Irish) — **I** 185^{P}, **I** 458^{4}, **I** 487^{1}

LARKROSS b.g. 6 Crested Lark - Banbury Cake by Seaepic (USA) Sir Michael Connell
1996 **14(NH),13(NH),5(NH),P(NH)**
224 16/2 Heythrop (R) MDN 3m 16 G *ld 2-5th, prom to 13th, bhnd whn p.u. 2 out* P 0
451 8/3 Newton Brom' (R) MDN 3m 8 G *alwys prom, ld 10th-12th & 13th-nxt, onepcd 3 out* 2 10
823 31/3 Lockinge (L) MDO 3m 4 F *(fav) keen hld & rstrnd, cls up, ev ch 14th, not qckn frm 16th* 3 0

Hard ride & looks less than keen; unlikely to find a race 11

LARKY MCILROY b.m. 11 Rymer - Forest Row by Royal Highway D Luxton
1996 2(18),3(16),2(15),1(17),U(-),2(18)
49 1/2 Wadebridge (L) LAD 3m 5 G *ld/disp til ld aft 9th, mstk 3 out, ran on well* 1 20
99 8/2 Great Treth' (R) LAD 3m 10 GS *mid-div, 5th whn mstk 13th, btn frm nxt* 7 10
Members winner 96; found weak Ladies but season lasted only a week 19

LARRIGAN (Irish) — I 275^{5}, I 300^{P}, I 532^{F}

LARRY THE LAMB ch.g. 12 St Columbus - Florence Eliza by Floriana Mrs F E Chown
1996 2(21),1+(24),1(23),1(25),2(23),F(-),2(19)
57 1/2 Kingston Bl' (L) LAD 3m 13 GF *wll bhnd, styd on frm 14th, tk 2nd nr fin* 2 23
272 22/2 Ampton (R) LAD 3m 7 G *f 2nd* F -
Won 3 in 96 & useful Ladies at best; can only be watched if returning at 13 20

LARS ON TOUR (Irish) — I 14^{P}, I 47^{P}, I 84^{P}, I 142^{P}

LARTINGTON LAD ch.g. 11 Dalsaan - Rarest Flower (USA) by Carlemont Miss J Goodyear
1996 4(0),6(0),6(0)
266 22/2 Duncombe Pa' (R) RES 3m 19 G *rear whn u.r. 4th* U -
429 8/3 Charm Park (L) MDO 3m 14 GF *mid-div, fdd 8th, t.o. 10th, p.u. 12th* P 0
Well beaten all 3 completions in 96 & worse in 97 0

LASTOFTHE LITTLES b.g. 5 Lighter - Little Nun by Crozier C J Hitchings
1528 17/5 Bredwardine (R) MDO 3m 17 G *u.r. 1st* U -
Appeared late - blinked & you missed him 0

LAST OPTION br.g. 5 Primitive Rising (USA) - Saint Motunde by Tyrant (USA) R Tate
509 15/3 Dalton Park (R) XX 3m 13 GF *rear & sn wll bhnd, t.o. & p.u. 12th* P 0
622 22/3 Hutton Rudby (L) MDO 3m 10 GF *rear & bhnd, mstk 8th, wknd 14th, t.o.* 6 0
1106 19/4 Hornby Cast' (L) MDO 3m 10 G *prom, blndrd 13th, chal 3 out, ld nxt, ran green, kpt on wll* 1 14
1348 3/5 Gisburn (R) RES 3m 10 GF *cls up, ld 6th-8th, cls 2nd & ev ch whn f 3 out* F -
1406 5/5 Witton Cast' (R) RES 3m 10 GS *mid-div,prog 12th,disp 15th,ld 3 out,prssd flat,ran on wll* 1 18
1477 11/5 Garthorpe (R) XX 3m 6 GS *(fav) trckd ldrs, mstks 6th & 14th, lft in ld apr 2 out, u.r. 2out* U 17
Promising; mistakes but improving; should certainly upgrade & could prove useful 22

LATHERON(IRE) b.g. 7 Reference Point - La Romance (USA) by Lyphard (USA) J Sisterson
1996 1(15),U(-),2(22),1(20),1(19),3(20),1(20)
76 2/2 Market Rase' (L) XX 3m 12 GF *w.w., rmdr 6th,prog nxt,ld 14th,lft wll clr 2 out,eased flat* 1 23
166 15/2 Witton Cast' (R) OPE 3m 8 F *(fav) hld up & bhnd, prog 14th, hrd rdn & styd on wll 2 out,nvr nr* 2 21
Won 4 in 96 & promising; disppeared after below-par run on Firm in 97; hopefully return; G-S 24

LAUDATION(IRE) ch.g. 5 Bold Arrangement - Hooray Lady by Ahonoora R Mason
400 8/3 Llanfrynach (R) OPE 3m 10 G *n.j.w. in last, p.u. 11th* P 0
543 16/3 Erw Lon (L) MDN 3m 11 GF *trckd ldr to 9th, fdd, p.u. 12th* P 0
964 6/4 Pantyderi (L) MDN 3m 4 F *(fav) wll in rear, jmp rght, rpd prog aft 15th,ev ch last,onepcd* 2 0
1137 19/4 Bonvilston (R) MDO 3m 13 G *rear & n.j.w., p.u. 15th* P 0
1473 11/5 Erw Lon (L) MDO 3m 13 GS *ld to 12th, wknd rpdly, p.u. nxt* P 0
Cannot jump yet & 2nd in a desperate contest 0

LAUDER SQUARE gr.g. 9 Pragmatic - Royal Ruby by Rubor Mrs T D C Dun
1996 **12(NH),P(NH),P(NH)**
233 22/2 Friars Haugh (L) MDO 3m 13 G *alwys wll bhnd* 7 0
343 1/3 Corbridge (R) MDO 3m 14 G *mid-div, kpt on frm 2 out, ran on well flat* 2 0
416 8/3 Dalston (R) RES 3m 12 GS *rear, lost tch 14th, ran on wll frm 3 out, nrst fin* 2 14
613 22/3 Friars Haugh (L) MDN 3m 12 GF *(fav) alwys bhnd* 8 0
Promising 2nd in weak Restricted but problems last start; should win if fit at 10; G-S 15

LAURA'S MELODY (Irish) — I 589^{P}

LAURELHILL LADY (Irish) — I 460^{3}, I 461^{2}

LAURELVALE (Irish) — I 36^{F}, I 72^{F}, I 232^{4}, I 287^{3}, I 397^{P}, I 526^{1}, I 592^{4}

LAURINTINIUM (Irish) — I 172^{P}, I 262^{B}, I 302^{6}

LAVALIGHT b.g. 10 Lighter - Laval by Cheval R Lane
1996 P(0),5(13),**3(12),7(12),P(0),U(NH),3(NH),F(NH),4(NH)**
1022 12/4 Badbury Rin' (L) LAD 3m 3 F *jmp rght, trckd ldr til ld apr 11th, hdd last, no ext* 2 12
1141 19/4 Larkhill (R) LAD 3m 4 F *disp to 9th, prssd wnr til apr 13th, grad wknd* 3 0
1495 14/5 Cothelstone (L) LAD 3m 6 GF *chsd ldng pair, dist bhnd whn ran out 6th* r -
1548 24/5 Mounsey Hil' (R) LAD 3m 10 G *chsd ldrs, jmpd slwly 5th, 3rd & wkng 16th, dmtd fin* 4 16

1612	7/6 Umberleigh	(L) LAD 3m	5 F	*(bl) prom til lost tch frm 9th, 3rd & no prog final cct*	3	0

Well beaten all 14 starts 96/7 & sure to extend sequence 12

LAWD OF BLISLAND ch.g. 8 Celtic Cone - Foxwell by Healaugh Fox — Paul C N Heywood

1996 5(14),P(0),2(11),4(0),3(0)

54	1/2 Wadebridge	(L) MDO 3m	13 G	*(Co fav) alwys chsng ldrs, hrd rdn 4 out, no ext*	7	0
245	22/2 Lemalla	(R) MDO 3m	11 S	*ld to 6th,blnd 10th, disp 11-12th, wknd, poor 4th whn f last*	F	-

Placed 3 times in 96 but finished early 97; form modest 12

LAWNSWOOD QUAY ch.g. 7 Bairn (USA) - Miss Quay by Quayside — G C Musgrave

621	22/3 Hutton Rudby	(L) MDO 3m	10 GF	*strng hold, ld til hdd 3 out, 3rd & btn whn f last*	F	-

Bombed off but injured when falling & best watched if returning 0

LAW PURSUIT (Irish) — I 220P

LAYSTON D'OR ch.g. 8 Le Coq D'Or - Water Crescent by No Mercy — J W Russell

1996 1(16),4(15)

260	22/2 Newtown	(L) RES 3m	16 G	*prom, f 5th*	F	-
567	16/3 Garnons	(L) MEM 3m	3 G	*(fav) w.w. tk clsr ordr 12th, ld 15th, clr 2 out, eased flat*	1	16
1491	14/5 Hereford	(R) HC 3m 1f 110yds	11 G	*alwys bhnd.*	7	16

Members winner 96; repeated trick but lightly-raced; hat-trick best hope in 97 16

LAYSTON PINZAL b.m. 6 Afzal - Clever Pin by Pinza — J W Russell

1996 S(-),2(14)

259	22/2 Newtown	(L) MDN 3m	18 G	*wll bhnd, effrt whn mstk 12th, nvr on trms aft*	4	0

Promising 2nd in 96 but no chance to progress yet; still time if fit 98 14

LAZY ACRES (Irish) — I 422⁵, I 447P

LAZZARETTO b.g. 9 Ballacashtal (CAN) - Florence Mary by Mandamus — Mrs J Brook-Saunders

1996 P(0),P(0),P(0),P(0),P(0)

44	1/2 Larkhill	(R) MDO 3m	9 GF	*ld to 2nd, bhnd frm 12th, t.o. 15th, tk poor 3rd nr fin*	3	0
186	15/2 Erw Lon	(L) MDN 3m	13 G	*rear, styd on frm 13th, tk poor 2nd last*	2	0
285	26/2 Taunton	(R) HC 4 1/4m 110yds	16 GS	*t.o. from 5th, p.u. before 23rd.*	P	0
639	22/3 Howick	(L) MDN 3m	15 GF	*hld up, ran on to 2nd at 15th, onepcd aft*	3	0

Placings are virtually worthless & a miracle needed for a win 10

LEAMLARA JET (Irish) — I 12P, I 73P

LEAMLARA ROSE (Irish) — I 48P, I 143P, I 166P, I 263², I 338⁶

LEANE (Irish) — I 251¹

LEANNES MAN(IRE) b.g. 8 Tale Quale - Spring Of Patricia by High Top — Mrs G Reed

337	1/3 Corbridge	(R) RES 3m	11 G	*made all, drew clr frm 2 out, easily*	1	19
732	29/3 Alnwick	(L) CON 3m	6 F	*(fav) ld til c.o. by loose horse 3rd*	C	-
972	7/4 Kelso	(L) HC 3m 1f	12 GF	*ld to 7th, chsd ldr, blnd 9th, driven along in 3rd when f 3 out.*	F	-

Irish Maiden winner 96; started well but unlucky, then mistakes in H/Chase; should win Confined 98 ... 20

LEAPING THREE (Irish) — I 19², I 91¹, I 208³

LEAP YEAR MAN (Irish) — I 77P, I 142P, I 302U

LEARNER DRIVER b.g. 10 Crash Course - Broken Mirror by Push On — B Dowling

69	2/2 Higham	(L) MDO 3m	8 GF	*alwys mid-div, wknd rpdly 8th, p.u. 10th*	P	0
126	9/2 Cottenham	(R) RES 3m	14 GF	*n.j.w. & reluc, alwys bhnd, t.o. & p.u. 3 out*	P	0
317	1/3 Marks Tey	(L) MDN 3m	13 G	*chsd ldrs to 9th, wknng whn blndrd 13th, t.o. & f 17th*	F	-
770	29/3 Dingley	(R) RES 3m	18 G	*alwys rear hlf, outpcd 6 out, p.u. 3 out*	P	0
1283	27/4 Fakenham P-'	(L) MDO 3m	9 G	*mid-div, mstks 6th & 11th, lost tch, p.u. 3 out*	P	0

Failed the test 0

LEDWYCHE GATE b.g. 10 Roscoe Blake - Ledwyche by Pamroy — L Evans

1996 4(16),4(0),1(18),2(18),**2(23),P(0)**

333	1/3 Eaton Hall	(R) INT 3m	10 GS	*chsng grp, ev ch 10th, fdd, p.u. 4 out*	P	0
464	8/3 Eyton-On-Se'	(L) INT 3m	12 G	*(bl) hld up,20l 3rd 3 out,ran on strgly frm 2 out,lft in ld last*	1	20
671	23/3 Eaton Hall	(R) INT 3 3/4m	8 GF	*(bl) ld to 3rd, cls up to 4 out, rdn & sn btn nxt*	3	13
851	31/3 Eyton-On-Se'	(L) INT 3m	8 GF	*mstly 2nd/3rd til outpcd 12th*	5	0
1012	12/4 Bitterley	(L) MEM 3m	6 GF	*(bl) ld to 13th, ev ch til no ext frm 3 out, eased flat*	2	15

Quite able but quirky; below best mostly 97 & ground too firm; could win at 11; likes Bitterley 19

LEE HIGHWAY (Irish) — I 289P, I 363P, I 461F, I 585²

LEEJAY LUKI ch.g. 7 Farajullah - Subook by Salmon Leap (USA) — Mrs S K Notley

1437	10/5 Holnicote	(L) MDO 3m	14 G	*twrds rear, bhnd whn b.d. 16th*	B	-
1521	17/5 Bratton Down	(L) MDO 3m	16 GS	*mid-div, 7th at 12th, bhnd & p.u. flat*	P	0
1584	26/5 Lifton	(R) MDO 3m	13 G	*nvr bttr than mid-div, no dang 3 out*	7	0

Tailed off on only completion 0

LEESWOOD b.g. 9 Little Wolf - Tina's Gold by Goldhill — M M Allen

1996 **6(NH)**

199	15/2 Weston Park	(L) MEM 3m	7 G	*(vis) prom to 12th, outpcd & no ext frm 4 out*	4	16
414	8/3 Dalston	(R) XX 3m	9 GS	*(vis) chsd ldr,mstks 14 & 15,3rd & btn whn hit mrkr & u.r.apr 2out*	U	-
781	31/3 Hereford	(R) HC 2m 3f	9 GF	*(vis) alwys bhnd, struggling from hfwy, nvr a factor.*	4	0

Does not stay & ran badly in short H/Chase - hard to see a win 15

LEGAL AFFAIR b.m. 6 El Conquistador - Legal Aid by Legal Eagle — P R Hill

1996 P(0),B(-),R(-)

172	15/2 Ottery St M'	(L) MDN 3m	14 G	*rear early, prog 14th, nrst fin*	3	11
553	16/3 Ottery St M'	(L) MDN 3m	15 G	*handy, 2nd at 13th, chsd alng 4 out, 2l down whn f nxt*	F	-
741	29/3 Higher Kilw'	(L) MDN 3m	12 GF	*(fav) hld up, prog 10th, cls 2nd 12th til ld 15th, lft clr last*	1	14
1093	16/4 Hockworthy	(L) RES 3m	16 GF	*in tch, prog & ev ch 4 out, wkng whn blnd 2 out & p.u.*	P	0

Confirmed ability in weak race; not disgraced last start; may prefer G-S 15

LEGAL PICNIC gr.g. 14 Roselier (FR) - Margo's Pal — Ms C Bryan

1996 3(12),5(14),3(18)

520	15/3 Cothelstone	(L) LAD 3m	12 GS	*sn rear, t.o. frm 15th*	6	12
645	22/3 Castle Of C'	(R) LAD 3m	6 G	*in tch, outpcd 12th, lft poor 3rd 14th, demoted 2 out*	4	11
689	29/3 Little Wind'	(R) LAD 3m	5 GF	*ld to 9th, 3rd frm 13th, onepcd frm 15th*	3	15
1022	12/4 Badbury Rin'	(L) LAD 3m	3 F	*hdl up last, prog frm 14th, ld apr last, pshd out*	1	14
1272	27/4 Little Wind'	(R) LAD 3m	2 GF	*ld to 3 out, ev ch aft nxt, btn whn mstk last*	2	17
1391	5/5 Cursneh Hill	(L) LAD 3m	4 GF	*mostly last, chal for 2nd frm 15th, onepcd*	3	15

Schoolmaster; very safe & found terrible Ladies - similar needed for win at 15 15

LEGAL WHISPER (Irish) — I 128P, I 1984, I 311U, I 3515

LE GARCON D'OR b.g. 14 Goldhills Pride - Nautique by Windjammer (USA) — Mrs C R Hurst

454	8/3 Great Treth'	(R) LAD 3m	7 S	*rear frm 10th, t.o. p.u. apr 16th*	P	0
790	31/3 Bishopsleigh	(R) LAD 3m	7 G	*sn rear, wll bhnd frm 14th*	5	0

Only 7 runs since 91 & looks finished now 0

LEGGANHALL (Irish) — I 96F, I 124P, I 2274, I 286, , I 3505

LE HEARTY STEP (Irish) — I 39P

LEIGH BOY(USA) b.g. 11 Bates Motel (USA) - Afasheen by Sheshoon — P H Thomas

1996 3(13),3(22),5(20)

431	8/3 Upton-On-Se'	(R) CON 3m	9 G	*mid-div, lost tch 12th, no ch frm nxt*	4	0
751	29/3 Brampton Br'	(R) XX 3m	5 GF	*cls up, effrt 11th, sn wknd, p.u. 15th*	P	0
1292	30/4 Cheltenham	(L) HC 2m 5f	12 GF	*reminder 6th, bhnd from 10th, t.o. and p.u. before 2 out.*	P	0

Declined considerably in 97 & looks finished now 10

LEINTHALL THISTLE(IRE) b.m. 8 Mandalus - Phantom Thistle by Deep Run — D P Carpenter

1996 **P(NH)**

1562	24/5 Bassaleg	(R) MDO 3m	8 G	*alwys bhnd, t.o. 12th*	6	0
1603	31/5 Bassaleg	(R) MDO 3m	6 F	*7s-3s, alwys wll bhnd, blnd 9th, lost tch 11th, p.u. 14th*	P	0

Ran in 2 poor Maidens & showed nothing 0

LEITRIM COTTAGE(IRE) b.g. 6 Yashgan - New Talent by The Parson — Mrs D B A Silk

1996 **15(NH)**

197	15/2 Higham	(L) MDO 3m	12 G	*cls up, chal aft 16th, ev ch til no ext last, improve*	2	15
306	1/3 Parham	(R) MDN 3m	12 G	*in tch, rmndrs 9th, strggIng aft, 4th & wll btn whn p.u.3out*	P	0
582	16/3 Detling	(L) MDN 3m	16 F	*mid-div, 5th & btn 3 out, p.u. aft nxt*	P	0

Decent debut but yet to develop; may do better in 98 11

LE JACOBIN br.g. 14 Rare One - Cooleen by Tarqogan — Major Charles Lambert

395	8/3 Barbury Cas'	(L) XX 3m	9 G	*ld 2nd-apr 4th, wknd 10th, t.o. & p.u. last*	P	0
824	31/3 Lockinge	(L) CON 3m	8 F	*mstk 2nd, chsd wnr to 5th, sn wknd, t.o. & p.u. 13th*	P	0
1199	23/4 Andoversford	(R) INT 3m	5 F	*chsd ldr 3-11th, 4th & wkng apr 2 out*	4	0

No longer of any account 0

LENNIE THE LION b.g. 6 Krisinsky (USA) - Leaning Tower by Menelek — T R R Farr

1996 P(0),F(-),F(-),F(-)

633	22/3 Howick	(L) RES 3m	8 GF	*last & n.j.w., p.u. 9th*	P	0

717 29/3 Llanvapley (L) RES 3m 13 GF *last til p.u. 4th* P 0
908 5/4 Howick (L) MDN 3m 7 F *disp mod 3rd frm 7th, no ch frm 12th* 3 0
1009 12/4 St Hilary (R) MDN 3m 11 GF *ld to 14th, ld agn 3 out, ran on well* 1 10
1322 3/5 Bonvilston (R) RES 3m 9 G *rear, no prog frm hlfwy* 5 0
1556 24/5 Bassaleg (R) RES 3m 13 G *rear whn u.r. 6th* U -
1598 31/5 Bassaleg (R) MEM 3m 2 F *mstks, ld to 2nd, blnd 15th, rdn & ev ch last, onepcd* 2 10

Looked useless till springing 33/1 shock win; unlikely to roar again 10

LEON GARCIA (Irish) — I 534F

LE PICCOLAGE b.g. 13 The Parson - Daithis Coleen by Carnival Night P H Morris
1996 3(14),2(17),1(20),**5(0)**,P(0)

199 15/2 Weston Park (L) MEM 3m 7 G *alwys rear, btn whn p.u. last, sore* P 0
667 23/3 Eaton Hall (R) CON 3m 10 GF *disp to 3rd, lft 2nd at 10th, no ext 3 out* 4 12
725 29/3 Sandon (L) OPE 3m 4 GF *cls up, ld 6th, kckd clr 11th, unchal* 1 19
938 6/4 Tabley (R) OPE 3m 9 G *rear, some prog to 5th 2 out, nvr trbld ldrs* 5 15

Confined winner 96; well-ridden to land poor race 2nd start; hard to see win at 14 17

LESLIESHILL (Irish) — I 254P, I 293P, I 330P, I 377P

LETHEM LAIRD b.g. 6 Germont - Lawsuitlaw by Cagirama Tim Butt
1996 P(0)

135 9/2 Alnwick (L) MDO 3m 12 G *ld to 9th, wknd 12th, p.u. 14th* P 0
161 15/2 Lanark (R) MDO 2m 5f 14 G *sn wll bhnd* 8 0
340 1/3 Corbridge (R) MDN 3m 10 G *mid-div, outpcd 12th, t.o. & p.u. 2 out* P 0
565 16/3 Lanark (R) MDO 3m 10 GS *nvr rch ldrs, p.u. 3 out* P 0
1051 13/4 Lockerbie (R) MDN 3m 10 F *disp ld early, wknd frm 13th, p.u. 2 out* P 0

Beaten miles on only completion from 6 starts 96/7 0

LETS TWIST AGAIN(IRE) ch.g. 7 Glenstal (USA) - Gorgeous Twist by Hello Gorgeous (USA) Mrs S Bird

435 8/3 Upton-On-Se' (R) MDO 3m 14 G *ld 11th, prssd 3 out, in cmmnd whn lft clr last* 1 15
655 22/3 Siddington (L) RES 3m 10 F *(fav) hld up, prog to ld 10th, drew clr apr 2 out, comf* 1 18
880 1/4 Upton-On-Se' (R) CON 3m 6 GF *(fav) made all, jmpd lft 9th, clr 2 out, pshd out* 1 21
1060 13/4 Maisemore P' (L) MEM 3m 5 GF *(fav) ld, blnd 11th, hdd 15th, sn rdn & swshd tail, sn btn* 3 12
1212 26/4 Woodford (L) INT 3m 8 G *hld up, prog 10th, ld apr 4 out-last, no ext* 2 21
1329 3/5 Chaddesley ' (L) CON 3m 5 GF *(fav) w.w. went 2nd 12th, pshd alng nxt,jnd ldr 4 out,f nxt,rmntd* 2 0
1523 17/5 Bredwardine (R) CON 3m 7 G *(fav) ld 4-6th, ld 12th, prssd frm 2 out, pshd out flat* 1 19

Ex-Irish; well-ridden & consistent; suspect under pressure; may find Open chances; G-F 23

LEVEL VIBES ch.g. 8 Scorpio (FR) - Embuscade by Random Shot Mrs M D Abrahams
1996 **7(NH)**

266 22/2 Duncombe Pa' (R) RES 3m 19 G *mid-div whn u.r. 6th* U -
342 1/3 Corbridge (R) MDO 3m 12 G *prom, ld 6th-4 out, wknd rpdly, p.u. 2 out* P 0
510 15/3 Dalton Park (R) MDO 3m 14 GF *ld to 14th, wknd* 3 0
1104 19/4 Hornby Cast' (L) MEM 3m 6 G *disp til 6th, chsd ldr aft til outpcd frm 12th* 3 11
1345 3/5 Gisburn (R) MDN 3m 13 GF *ld 5th-15th, no ext* 3 0

Well beaten in each placing & stamina lacking; vibes not too strong for a win 12

LE VIENNA(IRE) b.g. 8 Le Bavard (FR) - Northern Push by Push On S Currey
1996 P(0),P(0),P(0),5(0),2(0),3(11),2(0)

221 16/2 Heythrop (R) RES 3m 15 G *tongue-strap, alwys bhnd, t.o. & p.u. 15th* P 0
364 2/3 Garnons (L) XX 3m 7 GS *alwys rear, lost tch 11th, t.o. & p.u. 2 out* P 0
406 8/3 Llanfrynach (R) RES 3m 13 G *tongue-strap, alwys rear, fin own time* 6 0
639 22/3 Howick (L) MDN 3m 15 GF *alwys rear* 6 0
1138 19/4 Bonvilston (R) MDO 3m 9 G *rear til some late prog* 4 0
1216 26/4 Woodford (L) MDN 3m 13 G *alwys bhnd, 8th & no ch hlfwy, t.o.* 5 0
1323 3/5 Bonvilston (R) MDO 3m 14 G *last til p.u. 2 out* P 0
1562 24/5 Bassaleg (R) MDO 3m 8 G *alwys bhnd, svrl slw jmps, t.o. 12th* 5 0

Basically useless 0

LEWESDON PRINCESS b.m. 9 Kinglet - Lewesdon Lass by My Lord M P Haigh
1996 U(-),P(0),P(0),P(0),P(0),4(0),P(0)

1308 3/5 Cottenham (R) LAD 3m 5 F *chsd wnr 3-5th, last frm 7th, no ch 14th* 5 11
1445 10/5 Peper Harow (L) LAD 3m 6 GF *keen hld, chsd ldrs to 6th, last frm 9th, no ch frm 12th* 4 0
1567 25/5 Kingston Bl' (L) RES 3m 8 GF *chsng grp, wknd 3 out* 6 0

Ran better by her standards in 97 but future prospects still zero 0

LIBERTY JAMES ch.g. 10 Remezzo - Lady Cheval by Cheval Mrs J Brooks
1996 F(-),5(0),2(16),2(15),2(12),3(10),**P(NH)**,**P(NH)**,**P(NH)**

50 1/2 Wadebridge (L) RES 3m 10 G *s.s. alwys bhnd, p.u. aft 13th* P 0
1093 16/4 Hockworthy (L) RES 3m 16 GF *nvr dang, wll bhnd whn p.u. 5 out* P 0
1245 26/4 Bratton Down (L) INT 3m 9 GS *nvr bttr then mid-div* 5 0
1315 3/5 Holnicote (L) MDO 3m 7 G *(Jt fav) bhnd & mstks, stdy prog 3 out, no ch wnr, lft 2nd nxt* 2 10

1485 11/5 Ottery St M' (L) MDO 3m 13 G *rear, nvr on trms, bhnd & p.u. 3 out* P 0
1521 17/5 Bratton Down (L) MDO 3m 16 GS *f 8th, dead* F -

Dead **0**

LIFE OF A KING (Irish) — I 30², I 59²

LIFE PEERAGE(USA) b.g. 12 Roberto (USA) - Countess Tully by Hotfoot M J Hayes

522 15/3 Cothelstone (L) CON 3m 14 GS *alwys bhnd* 5 0
645 22/3 Castle Of C' (R) LAD 3m 6 G *rear, lost tch 12th, kpt on to tk poor 3rd 2 out* 3 14
1040 12/4 Cothelstone (L) MEM 3m 3 GF *ld to 6th,ld 12th,disp 4 out-2 out,hdd, ld apr last, ran on* 1 10
1244 26/4 Bratton Down (L) CON 3m 14 GS *midfld whn u.r. 5th* U -
1313 3/5 Holnicote (L) CON 3m 7 G *mid div whn u.r. 3rd* U -

Deserved win in poor race but no prospects in competitive company now **11**

LIFES TREASURE (Irish) — I 91^F

LIGHT ARGUMENT (Irish) — I 105³, I 244^P, I 276²

LIGHTENING NEWS b.m. 6 Newski (USA) - Microlighter by Lighter Mrs L Glanville

1152 20/4 Stafford Cr' (R) MEM 3m 4 GF *u.r. 1st* U -

Briefest of starts **0**

LIGHTEN THE LOAD b.g. 10 Lighter - Princess Charybdis by Ballymoss J S Payne

1996 F(-),F(-),1(21),1(21),**P(0)**,1(23),6(19)

56 1/2 Kingston Bl' (L) OPE 3m 13 GF *chsd ldrs, no imp frm 15th* 4 16
149 10/2 Hereford (R) HC 3m 1f 110yds 18 GS *alwys rear, p.u. before 3 out.* P 0
256 22/2 Newtown (L) OPE 3m 17 G *hld up, prog 9th, in tch 13th, onepcd frm nxt* 6 15
400 8/3 Llanfrynach (R) OPE 3m 10 G *rear, styd on frm 2 out, no dang* 4 15
1134 19/4 Bonvilston (R) MXO 4m 10 G *prom to 17th, grdly wknd & p.u. last* P 0
1318 3/5 Bonvilston (R) MEM 3m 9 G *(fav) rear & rmndrs hlfwy, 30l last 4 out, hrd rdn nxt, ld flat* 1 14
1560 24/5 Bassaleg (R) OPE 3m 7 G *w.w. clsd 12th, rdn nxt, onepcd frm 15th* 3 15

Won 3 in 96 but well below form in 97; all out to win poor race; best watched **15**

LIGHTER LORD b.g. 6 Lighter - Lady Vulmid by Sir Lark R C Pudd

841 31/3 Lydstep (L) MDO 3m 8 F *alwys 2nd/3rd, no imp wnr, improve* 2 0

Reasonable debut in modest race & should go closer in 98 .... **11**

LIGHTERS CONFUSION ch.m. 13 Lighter - Bluecon by Majority Blue Ms Michelle Millar

207 16/2 Southwell P' (L) MEM 3m 3 GS *s.s. jmpd lft, sn wll bhnd, t.o. & p.u. 10th* P 0

Of no account **0**

LILAC TIME b.m. 11 Town And Country - Harp Strings (FR) by Luthier Mrs J Baker

148 9/2 Tweseldown (R) XX 3m 12 GF *trckd ldrs, ch 15th, onepcd* 5 0

Rarely seen & looks to have no prospects now **10**

LILLIEPLANT(IRE) b.m. 5 Aristocracy - Canute Princess by Torenaga A Plant

185 15/2 Erw Lon (L) MDN 3m 14 G *prom til u.r. 9th* U -

No concrete evidence of ability yet **0**

LILLYBROOK gr.m. 8 Scallywag - Blue Gift by Hasty Word J Townson

83 2/2 Wolverhampt' (L) RES 3m 8 GS *cls up, chal 3 out, ld & going best whn f nxt* F 19
348 2/3 Market Rase' (L) RES 3m 13 GF *(Jt fav) mid-div, prog 10th, rdn 15th, went 2nd 2 out, no imp wnr* 4 14

Maiden winner 95; missed 96; unlucky 1st start 97 & would win Restricted if fit 98; Soft **18**

LILY LANE ch.g. 5 Town And Country - My Pride by Petit Instant Les Bennett

181 15/2 Larkhill (R) MDO 3m 17 G *rear, jmpd slwly 7th, lost tch 12th, p.u. 15th* P 0
297 1/3 Didmarton (L) MDN 3m 11 G *6s-4s, n.j.w. in tch to 10th, sn wknd, t.o.* 4 0

Well thought of but jumped badly when money was down; could do better **11**

LILY THE LARK b.m. 9 Crested Lark - Florence Eliza by Floriana Miss H M Irving

1996 F(-),1(16),5(10),3(14),5(12),1(20)

57 1/2 Kingston Bl' (L) LAD 3m 13 GF *chsd ldrs, wknd frm 14th* 6 11
219 16/2 Heythrop (R) LAD 3m 16 G *prom til outpcd frm 4 out, no prog aft* 4 18
371 2/3 Mollington (R) LAD 3m 9 G *(fav) cls up, trckd ldr 10th-15th, onepcd aft* 3 20

Ladies winner 96; inconsistent & one good run 97; finished early; may struggle now; G-F **19**

LIMERIDGE (Irish) — I 249, , I 362⁴

LIME TREE ROAD (Irish) — I 424^F, I 456^F

LINANTIC b.g. 9 Full Of Hope - Contessa (HUN) by Peleid — John Rees

1996 5(10),2(15),P(0),P(0)

404	8/3	Llanfrynach	(R)	INT	3m	17	G	*rear whn p.u. 11th*	P	0
717	29/3	Llanvapley	(L)	RES	3m	13	GF	*trckd ldr, onepcd frm 13th*	2	10

Members winner 95; mainly disappointing & disappeared after modest 2nd 97 14

LINDA BABE (Irish) — I 187[1]

LINDALIGHTER bl.m. 7 Lighter - Linda's Wish by Harvest Spirit — M F Howard

1996 F(-),F(-),5(13),P(0),**P(0)**

365	2/3	Garnons	(L)	MDO	2 1/2m	14	GS	*alwys cls up, rdn into 2nd & ev ch 12th, wknd 2 out*	3	0
571	16/3	Garnons	(L)	MDN	2 1/2m	13	G	*chsd ldrs, rdn 3 out, styd on flat, just hld*	2	15
644	22/3	Castle Of C'	(R)	MDO	3m	9	G	*(fav) w.w. in tch, cls 3rd & ev ch 2 out, unable qckn flat*	3	13
1016	12/4	Bitterley	(L)	MDO	3m	14	GF	*prog to 5th at 12th, ev ch 15th, not qckn frm nxt*	2	11
1240	26/4	Brampton Br'	(R)	MDO	3m	12	G	*(fav) hld up frm 4th, effrt wth wnr 13th, no ext frm 2 out*	2	11

Safe now & consistent but struggles to stay & short Maidens not available in 98; may strike lucky 14

LINDA'S PRINCE(IRE) b.g. 8 Prince Bee - Linda Martin by Furry Glen — Mrs V Barber

1996 **8(NH)**

242	22/2	Lemalla	(R)	MDO	3m	10	S	*prog to ld 9th, clr whn f 16th*	F	-
692	29/3	Little Wind'	(R)	MDO	3m	8	GF	*(fav) mstks, hld up, prog to 2nd 16th, clsng whn blnd & u.r. nxt*	U	-

Unfortunate both starts & clear round should see success 16

LINDON RUN b.g. 8 Cruise Missile - Trial Run by Deep Run — T D Donaldson

1996 P(0),F(-),F(-),5(0),2(15),1(14)

157	15/2	Lanark	(R)	RES	3m	11	G	*ld til 4 out, kpt on onepcd*	4	14
338	1/3	Corbridge	(R)	RES	3m	10	G	*ld to 6th, prom til lft in ld 11th, hdd nxt, fdd 3 out*	3	11
584	17/3	Newcastle	(L)	HC	2 1/2m	11	GF	*in tch when blnd and u.r. 9th.*	U	-
813	31/3	Tranwell	(L)	RES	3m	7	G	*made virt all, 1l up last & ran on strngly*	1	19
972	7/4	Kelso	(L)	HC	3m 1f	12	GF	*chsd ldrs, hit 12th, rdn along and blnd 15th, soon wknd and hmpd 3 out, bhnd when f last.*	F	-
1405	5/5	Witton Cast'	(R)	CON	3m	10	GS	*ld til 5th, chsd ldr aft, wknd 14th, t.o.*	8	0
1427	10/5	Aspatria	(L)	INT	3m	7	G	*chsd wnr to 10th, sn rdn, 4th & wkng whn p.u. 14th*	P	0

Maiden winner 96; inconsistent in 97; both wins Tranwell; may have Confined chance, at best 18

LINEKER (Irish) — I 281[2]

LINFORD(IRE) b.g. 7 Supreme Leader - Miss Furlong — E E Williams

1996 **6(NH)**,**12(NH)**,**5(NH)**

38	26/1	Alnwick	(L)	MDO	3m	14	G	*(Jt fav) mstks, alwys prom, btn 3 out, disp 3rd whn f last*	F	-

Some ability under Rules but blundered round only point & disappeared 14

LINGCOOL b.m. 7 Uncle Pokey - Cooling by Tycoon II — R Morley

1996 P(0),U(-),F(-),P(0),2(12),P(0),P(0),P(0)

116	9/2	Wetherby Po'	(L)	MDO	3m	14	GF	*rear, lost tch 10th, p.u. nxt*	P	0
269	22/2	Duncombe Pa'	(R)	MDO	3m	16	G	*ld to 3rd, prom til fdd 14th, hmpd 3 out, t.o.*	3	0
357	2/3	Great Stain'	(L)	MDO	3m	15	S	*(fav) made all, drew clr apr last, ran on und pres*	1	15
421	8/3	Charm Park	(L)	MEM	3m	6	GF	*prom, ld 6th til rddr lost irons & wd 11th, hdd onepcd 4 out*	3	12

Made stamina pay in modest race; novice-ridden last start; Restricted possible on long course 98 16

LINGER BALINDA ch.m. 11 Balinger - Artalinda by Indiaro — Mrs S Haydon

1996 P(0)

828	31/3	Heathfield	(R)	MEM	3m	5	F	*chsd ldrs, mstks 10th & 14th, rdn apr 3 out, wl btn nxt*	4	0
1130	19/4	Penshurst	(L)	MDO	3m	5	GF	*alwys cls up, many rmndrs, ld 13th-3 out, hld aft*	2	0
1446	10/5	Peper Harow	(L)	MDO	3m	7	GF	*chsd ldr 4th, ld & blnd 12th, hdd 15th, sn hrd rdn, outpcd*	2	0
1501	16/5	Folkestone	(R)	HC	3 1/4m	10	G	*(bl) prom to 10th, weakening in 5th when blnd 13th, t.o. and p.u. before 3 out.*	P	0

Placed in dire races & no real prospect of a win 0

LINGER HILL br.g. 10 Netherkelly - Ballyvelour by Ballyciptic — Miss S Bannatyne

66	1/2	Horseheath	(R)	MEM	3m	7	GF	*in tch, mstk & rmndr 8th, outpcd 12th, kpt on frm 3 out*	3	13
324	1/3	Marks Tey	(L)	RES	3m	16	G	*in tch til 11th, lost tch 14th, t.o.*	8	0

Maiden winner 95; missed 96 & showed very little in 97 11

LINGERING HOPE(IRE) b.g. 9 Strong Gale - My Only Hope by Brave Invader (USA) — R J Rowsell

1996 **P(NH)**

402	8/3	Llanfrynach	(R)	INT	3m	7	G	*f 1st*	F	-

Did not linger long in 97 0

LINGERING ON (Irish) — I 172[P], I 262[P], I 337, , I 378, , I 447[P]

LINGER JET (Irish) — I 551[P], I 610[P]

LINK COPPER ch.g. 8 Whistlefield - Letitica by Deep Run — Mrs E J Taplin

1996 P(0),2(18),P(0),F(-),P(0),P(0),3(15),3(16)

523	15/3	Cothelstone	(L)	RES	3m	14	GS	*prom til lost ground 11th, p.u. 13th*	P	0
792	31/3	Bishopsleigh	(R)	RES	3m	13	G	*hld up, prog 17th, 3rd 2 out, chal & ld aft last*	1	17
1043	12/4	Cothelstone	(L)	INT	3m	7	GF	*hld up, prog 4 out, tk 2nd 2 out, nrst fin*	2	18
1258	27/4	Black Fores'	(R)	INT	3m	5	F	*ld 6th til blnd 11th,ld 15th,jnd 2 out,styd on wll flat*	1	18
1485	6/5	Wincanton	(R)	HC	2m 5f	4	F	*alwys chasing wnr, chal 9th and 4 out, rallied again last, one pace.*	2	0
1570	26/5	Hereford	(R)	HC	3m 1f 110yds	14	G	*hit 1st, bhnd from 5th, p.u. before 6 out.*	P	0
1594	31/5	Bratton Down	(L)	INT	3m	10	F	*ld 5th til mstk nxt,3rd & outpcd 15th,styd on flat,jst faild*	2	20

Maiden winner 94; improved 97; hard ride tactically but should win Confined if in the mood 98; Any 21

LINLAKE LIGHTNING b.m. 10 St Columbus - Bright Exploit by Exploitation — Miss H M Irving

1996 P(0),4(14),4(10),5(13),P(0),P(0)

59	1/2	Kingston Bl'	(L)	RES	3m	16	GF	*(bl) cls up early, fdd & p.u. last*	P	0
278	23/2	Charing	(L)	RES	3m	17	G	*(bl) alwys rear, t.o.*	6	0
449	8/3	Newton Brom'	(R)	XX	3m	13	G	*(bl) tongue-strap, sn prom, wknd 10th, sn bhnd*	7	0
676	23/3	Brocklesby '	(L)	RES	3m	14	GF	*(bl) sn wll bhnd, t.o. & p.u. 11th*	P	0
826	31/3	Lockinge	(L)	RES	3m	4	F	*(bl) ld to 8th & 11-12th, 3rd & btn aft 14th*	3	11
989	12/4	Kingston Bl'	(L)	INT	3m	7	GF	*(bl) ld 4-6th, bhnd frm 10th, t.o.*	7	0
1207	26/4	Clifton On '	(L)	LAD	3m	6	GS	*mostly 3rd, disp 2nd 4 out, outpcd nxt*	4	16
1450	10/5	Kingston Bl'	(L)	LAD	3m	7	G	*tongue-strap, 2nd til aft 7th, chsd ldrs, not qckn frm 15th*	3	12
1535	18/5	Mollington	(R)	LAD	3m	6	GS	*in tch, pshd alng 10th, lft bhnd frm 12th, t.o.*	4	0
1606	1/6	Dingley	(R)	LAD	3m	13	GF	*ldng grp til grad fdd frm 15th*	5	16

Maiden winner 94; ultra-safe now but never threatens to win again 14

LINLITHGOW PALACE ch.g. 15 Royal Palace - Moonbreaker by Twilight Alley — Mrs J Morrison

275	22/2	Ampton	(R)	MDO	3m	10	G	*mid-div, outpcd 11th, no ch whn u.r. last*	U	-
450	8/3	Newton Brom'	(R)	MDN	3m	7	G	*s.s. cls up til wknd aft 10th, rear & p.u. 15th*	P	0

No longer of any account 0

LINRED b.g. 12 Politico (USA) - Denwick Bambi by Hamood — Mrs R H Bott

1996 5(18),3(19),2(19)

302	1/3	Parham	(R)	CON	3m	14	G	*mid-div to hlfwy, lost tch & p.u. 14th*	P	0
503	15/3	Ampton	(R)	XX	3m	11	GF	*in tch,chsd wnr 13-16th,agn 3 out, hd rdn 2 out, kpt on*	2	14
829	31/3	Heathfield	(R)	XX	3m	5	F	*(fav) disp til j.s.4th, ld 9th til hdd last, onepcd und press flat*	2	12

Quite useful to 96 but changed hands & declined rapidly; unlikely to figure again 12

LINTON b.m. 7 St David - Follifoot's Folly by Comedy Star (USA) — Miss Jill F Diggory

95	8/2	Great Treth'	(R)	MEM	3m	4	GS	*8s-4s, mstk 4th, bhnd whn hmpd 7th, t.o. & p.u. 14th*	P	0
453	8/3	Great Treth'	(R)	CON	3m	13	S	*sb bhnd, t.o. whn p.u. apr 15th*	P	0
531	15/3	Wadebridge	(L)	MDO	3m	14	GF	*alwys rear, p.u. 4 out*	P	0

No real signs of ability yet 0

LION OF VIENNA b.g. 10 Bulldozer - Lucky Favour by Ballyciptic — A Dawson

1996 F(-),7(0)

35	26/1	Alnwick	(L)	CON	3m	10	G	*(fav) 6s-3s, rear, strgglng whn mstk 11th, effrt 15th, nvr on trms*	6	11
133	9/2	Alnwick	(L)	OPE	3m	6	G	*chsd ldrs, disp 10th-12th, strgglng & mstk nxt, no dang aft*	3	0
229	22/2	Friars Haugh	(L)	CON	3m	9	G	*prom to hlfwy, sn lost tch*	7	0
411	8/3	Dalston	(R)	CON	3m	16	GS	*20s-12s, alwys rear, t.o. 15th*	9	0
943	6/4	Friars Haugh	(L)	MEM	3m	5	GF	*sn bhnd, tk remote 3rd btw last 2*	3	0
1048	13/4	Lockerbie	(R)	LAD	3m	6	F	*(bl) alwys last, t.o. & p.u. 4 out*	P	0

Winning hurdler; often well-backed in points but shows no interest at all 0

LIPSTICK LADY (Irish) — I 45^{P}, I 62^{P}, I 97^{P}, I 217^{P}, I 344, , I 388^{P}

LISDOYLELADY (Irish) — I 255^{2}, I 333^{3}, I 424^{F}

LISDUFF PRIDE (Irish) — I 36^{P}, I 162^{3}, I 201^{4}, I 277^{1}, I 336^{1}, I 427^{P}, I 528^{3}, I 573^{6}, I 587^{P}

LISGARVAN LAD(IRE) b.g. 5 Kambalda - Lisgarvan Highway by Dusky Boy — Mrs P Grainger

367	2/3	Garnons	(L)	MDO	2 1/2m	9	GS	*rear frm 3rd, rdn 8th, lost tch & p.u. 3 out*	P	0
436	8/3	Upton-On-Se'	(R)	MDO	3m	17	G	*u.r. start, rear & rdn 8th, t.o. & p.u. 15th*	P	0

Schooling so far & makes mistakes; season lasted 6 days 0

LISLARY LAD (Irish) — I 30, , I 59^{5}

LISSELAN LASS (Irish) — I 20^{6}, I 48^{P}, I 143^{P}, I 207^{P}, I 238^{P}, I 338, , I 419^{P}

LISSNASHE (Irish) — I 277^{P}

LISTRAKELT (Irish) — I 72^{2}, I 120^{4}, I 173^{2}, I 246^{1}

LITTLE BUCKIE (Irish) — I 39^{6}

LITTLE BY LITTLE b.g. 7 Derring Rose - April Fortune by Maystreak — D Pugh
1996 3(10),r(-),3(11),1(13),6(0),6(0),**3(NH)**,**2(NH)**,**3(NH)**

332	1/3	Eaton Hall	(R)	RES	3m	18 GS	*mid to rear, no ch whn p.u. 5 out*	P	0
467	8/3	Eyton-On-Se'	(L)	RES	3m	15 G	*mid-div, p.u. 3rd*	P	0
852	31/3	Eyton-On-Se'	(L)	RES	3m	11 GF	*mid-div, styng on onepce frm 5 out*	4	0
1000	12/4	Alpraham	(R)	RES	3m	8 GF	*s.s. 30l bhnd by 1st, prog to 10l 5th 14th, no frthr hdwy*	5	0
1303	3/5	Weston Park	(L)	RES	3m	6 G	*prog 12th, chsd wnr 4 out, ran on onepcd*	2	14
1385	5/5	Eyton-On-Se'	(L)	RES	3m	4 GF	*alwys cls 3rd, ld 4 out, hrd rddn frm 2 out, just held on*	1	16

Maiden winner 96; scrambled home in small race & much more required 98; doubtful stamina 16

LITTLE DUKE (Irish) — **I** 335[2]

LITTLE EASE(IRE) b.m. 5 Little Bighorn - River Tay by Crash Course — D Davies

436	8/3	Upton-On-Se'	(R)	MDO	3m	17 G	*t.o. 4th, btn 3 fncs*	5	0
643	22/3	Castle Of C'	(R)	MDO	3m	12 G	*prom to 4th, grad lost plc, mstk 7th, last whn u.r. 11th*	U	-
907	5/4	Howick	(L)	MDN	3m	4 F	*bhnd & mstks frm 8th, btn 2 fncs*	3	0
1067	13/4	Maisemore P'	(L)	MDO	3m	8 GF	*s.s. in tch 7th, last & wkng 13th, p.u. nxt*	P	0

Ghastly 0

LITTLE GENERAL ch.g. 14 General Ironside - Coolentallagh by Perhapsburg — Mrs D McCormack
1996 **P(0)**,P(0)

35	26/1	Alnwick	(L)	CON	3m	10 G	*prom til onepcd apr 3 out*	5	16
289	28/2	Kelso	(L)	HC	3m 1f	8 GS	*in tch, dropped rear 13th, struggling apr 2 out, soon no dngr.*	6	12
561	16/3	Lanark	(R)	LAD	3m	7 GS	*4th 10th, nvr rchd ldrs*	5	0
732	29/3	Alnwick	(L)	CON	3m	6 F	*(vis) alwys prom, 3rd at 12th, ld last, ran on strngly*	1	18

Staged mini revival 97 & visor helped to win; hard to repeat at 15 16

LITTLE GLEN b.g. 9 Germont - Glendyke by Elvis — A B Crozier
1996 5(0),4(15),2(14),2(16),U(-),**9(0)**,2(19),4(14)

1047	13/4	Lockerbie	(R)	INT	3m	4 F	*ld 5th-15th, jnd wnr last, no ext cls hm*	2	18

Consistent Confined horse; touched off only start 97; may win if fit 98; G-F 18

LITTLE HAWK 7 — John Carr
1996 P(0),P(0),P(0)

815	31/3	Tranwell	(L)	MDO	2 1/2m	14 G	*6th hlfwy, wknd 10th & lost tch wth ldrs*	11	0
997	12/4	Tranwell	(L)	MDO	2 1/2m	8 F	*rear div, wnt 5th 10th, no imprssn on ldrs frm nxt,p.u. last*	P	0
1173	20/4	Hexham Poin'	(L)	MDO	2 1/2m	9 GF	*disp handy 3rd whn ran out 4th*	r	-
1409	5/5	Witton Cast'	(R)	MDO	3m	15 GS	*ld til hdd 11th, wknd qckly, t.o. whn p.u. 4 out*	P	0

Last on only completion from 7 starts 96/7 0

LITTLE IDIOT b.m. 6 Idiot's Delight - Miss Rubbish by Rubor — T Brockbank

767	29/3	Whittington	(L)	MDO	3m	9 S	*alwys rear, t.o. 9th, p.u. 11th*	P	0
1052	13/4	Lockerbie	(R)	MDN	3m	10 F	*alwys wll bhnd, p.u. 3 out*	P	0

Just schooling & may do better 0

LITTLE LEN (Irish) — **I** 155[U], **I** 221[P], **I** 391, , **I** 405[F], **I** 500,

LITTLE MINUTE (Irish) — **I** 66[1], **I** 147[F], **I** 215[F]

LITTLE MONKSIDE(IRE) b.m. 6 Castle Keep - Dunmain Stream by Paddy's Stream — R H Walton

997	12/4	Tranwell	(L)	MDO	2 1/2m	8 F	*hndy 5th 6th, nvr nrr ldrs final ctt*	5	0

Last to finish in poor race - may improve 0

LITTLE PADDLE (Irish) — **I** 572[P]

LITTLE RED b.g. 6 Dreams To Reality (USA) - Qualitairess by Kampala — Mrs B Orkney
1996 **24(NH)**,**P(NH)**

79	2/2	Market Rase'	(L)	MDO	2m 5f	9 GF	*stdyd rr til blndrd & u.r. 3rd*	U	-
428	8/3	Charm Park	(L)	MDO	3m	10 GF	*mid-div, prog 10th, wnt remt 3rd 3 out, nvr nrr*	3	10
620	22/3	Hutton Rudby	(L)	MDO	3m	10 GF	*prog 7th,chsd ldrs 14th,wknd qckly 16th,t.o & p.u. 3 out*	P	0
1073	13/4	Whitwell-On'	(R)	MDO	2 1/2m 88yds	17 G	*prom, ld 7th-11th, sn wknd, t.o. & p.u. 2 out*	P	0
1105	19/4	Hornby Cast'	(L)	MDO	3m	11 G	*s.s., rear whn u.r. 2nd*	U	-

Not disgraced when modest 3rd but no real signs of stamina yet 10

LITTLE ROO (Irish) — **I** 79[P], **I** 204[2], **I** 380[P]

LITTLE SANTA (Irish) — **I** 80[B], **I** 383[P], **I** 419[4], **I** 479[P]

LITTLE SIMBA (Irish) — **I** 140[P], **I** 167[P], **I** 235[F], **I** 305[U], **I** 355[P]

LITTLE WENLOCK b.g. 13 Tycoon II - Oujarater by Adropejo — Mrs D S C Gibson
1996 3(15),U(-),2(18),1(17),**1(24)**,**1(21)**,**4(20)**,**F(-)**,**P(0)**

152	12/2	Musselburgh	(R)	HC	3m	8 GS	*bhnd hfwy, t.o. when p.u. before 2 out.*	P	0

289 28/2 Kelso (L) HC 3m 1f 8 GS *held up in tch, pushed along to chase lding gp 3 out, one pace between last 2.* 4 22
583 17/3 Newcastle (L) HC 3m 8 GF *bhnd, hdwy before 3 out, chal last, no ext und pres clsg stgs.* 2 23
973 7/4 Kelso (L) HC 3m 1f 5 GF *chsd ldrs till p.u. lame after 9th, dead.* P 0

Dead 23

LIVE CONNECTION(IRE) b.g. 6 Electric - Strong Wings by Strong Gale M G Sheppard

1281 27/4 Fakenham P-' (L) MDO 3m 8 G *jmpd bdly, sn bhnd, t.o. whn blnd 9th, p.u. aft* P 0

Very green on debut 0

LIVE WIRE(IRE) b.g. 6 Electric - Green Gale by Strong Gale C C Trietline

1996 P(0),1(15),3(14)

7 19/1 Barbury Cas' (L) RES 3m 14 GF *alwys bhnd, last & t.o. hlfwy, p.u. 2 out* P 0
59 1/2 Kingston Bl' (L) RES 3m 16 GF *nvr bttr than mid-div, styd on onepcd* 6 0
468 8/3 Eyton-On-Se' (L) RES 3m 11 G *chsd wnr to 5th, lft 2nd 13th, onepcd frm 4 out* 5 10
524 15/3 Cothelstone (L) RES 3m 10 GS *rmndrs 11th, 3rd at 14th, went 2nd 2 out, fin tired* 2 0

Maiden winner 96; well beaten when 2nd & not progressed; finished early 12

LIVIN JOY (Irish) — **I** 22P, **I** 102,

LIXWM b.m. 8 Scorpio (FR) - Connaughts' Trump by Connaught Miss J Winch

21 25/1 Badbury Rin' (L) MDN 3m 7 GF *(Jt fav) sn wll clr,fnc ahd 15th,tired rpdly 2 out,f last, winded* F -
284 23/2 Charing (L) MDO 3m 17 G *(fav) trckd ldrs til f 10th* F -
390 8/3 Barbury Cas' (L) MDN 3m 15 G *hld up, prog to chs ldrs 8th, 2nd 10th til wknd 2 out* 3 14

Can go a real gallop but stamina suspect; ran well last start & could win if fit 98 14

LIZAPET(IRE) b.m. 5 Petorius - Sybaris by Crowned Prince (USA) S R Green

1996 **P(NH),14(NH)**

821 31/3 Paxford (L) MDO 3m 6 F *hld up rear, f 9th* F -
1082 13/4 Guilsborough (L) MDN 3m 14 GF *rear, lost tch 11th, t.o. & p.u. 3 out* P 0
1209 26/4 Clifton On ' (L) MDO 3m 16 GS *last frm 10th, p.u. 5 out* P 0
1401 5/5 Ashorne (R) MDO 3m 15 G *mid-div, effrt 12th, wknd nxt, t.o.* 4 0
1609 1/6 Dingley (R) MDO 3m 14 GF *ld to 2nd, wknd aft 11th, sn t.o.* 6 0

Shows no ability at all 0

LIZZIE BOON b.m. 5 Le Moss - Miss Boon by Road House II David Brace

1183 20/4 Lydstep (L) MDO 3m 8 GF *nvr nrr than 7th, p.u. 8th* P 0
1231 26/4 Pyle (R) MDO 3m 7 GS *schoold, cls up frm 6th, ev ch whn f 13th* F -
1324 3/5 Bonvilston (R) MDO 3m 16 G *rear, f 6th* F -

Showed enough 2nd start to suggest better to come when jumping improves 10

LIZZIES CORNER (Irish) — **I** 251F, **I** 292F, **I** 363F, **I** 461F

LIZZY GECKO b.m. 9 Majestic Maharaj - Daring Liz by Dairialatan Christopher Cox

624 22/3 Kilworthy (L) MEM 3m 7 G *mstk 10th, p.u. apr 14th, cont & ran out immed* P 0
1034 12/4 Lifton (R) MDN 3m 7 F *prom til wknd 12th, p.u. 2 out* P 0

No promise & already past her prime 0

LLES LE BUCFLOW ch.g. 9 Little Wolf - Elsell by Grey Mirage Jeffrey A Smith

1996 P(0),P(0),6(0)

405 8/3 Llanfrynach (R) RES 3m 15 G *prom til outpcd 3 out, p.u. last* P 0
635 22/3 Howick (L) RES 3m 7 GF *whppd round start, tk no part* 0 0
753 29/3 Brampton Br' (R) RES 3m 9 GF *prog to chal 11th, rdn 16th, ld 2 out, all out* 1 16
1013 12/4 Bitterley (L) CON 3m 14 GF *mid-div whn b.d. 7th* B -
1235 26/4 Brampton Br' (R) INT 3m 10 G *s.s. nvr rchd ldrs, no ch whn p.u. 15th* P 0
1390 5/5 Cursneh Hill (L) INT 3m 4 GF *chsd ldrs, rddn 12th, styd on to ld last* 1 21
1522 17/5 Bredwardine (R) MEM 3m 2 G *(fav) not fluent, cls 2nd, jnd ldr & lft alone 14th, reluc nxt* 1 10

Maidenw inner 95; has ability & good season but reluctant & should struggle when upgraded 17

LOACH CROGA (Irish) — **I** 136³, **I** 169³, **I** 337⁴, **I** 447P, **I** 520P

LOCAL CUSTOMER b.g. 12 Le Bavard (FR) - Penny Bar by Bargello Mrs J Barber

362 2/3 Garnons (L) OPE 3m 11 GS *ld/disp to 11th, wknd 13th, p.u. 15th* P 0
536 16/3 Erw Lon (L) LAD 3m 9 GF *mid-div, prog 11th, rdn 3 out, onepcd* 3 16
1225 26/4 Pyle (R) LAD 3m 6 GS *hld up, outpcd apr 14th, mstk 15th, t.o. & p.u. 2 out* P 0
1363 5/5 Pantyderi (L) OPE 3m 4 G *alwys rear* 4 11
1470 11/5 Erw Lon (L) LAD 3m 9 GS *ld 5-11th, ev ch to 15th, onepcd aft* 5 0
1525 17/5 Bredwardine (R) LAD 3m 9 G *mstk 9th, in tch to 12th, sn wknd, t.o. 15th* 6 0
1558 24/5 Bassaleg (R) LAD 3m 5 G *clr ldr til wknd & hdd apr 14th, t.o.* 4 10

Formerly useful but well past it now & win win at 13 looks impossible 12

LOCAL MANOR ch.g. 10 Le Bavard (FR) - Blackrath Girl by Bargello J L Dunlop

1996 4(10),1(15),3(14),r(-),1(15),3(13),**U(-)**

148	9/2	Tweseldown	(R)	XX	3m	12	GF	*mid-div, prog 12th, ev ch 2 out, no ext*	3	14
302	1/3	Parham	(R)	CON	3m	14	G	*mid-div, prog to chal apr 3 out, ld nxt, ran on well*	1	20
600	22/3	Parham	(R)	MEM	3m	7	F	*s.i.s. sn trckd ldrs, 3rd & pshd alng 3 out, wknd nxt,eased*	3	0

Dual winner 96; decent win 2nd start but vanished after poor run; novice-ridden; best watched 18

LOCAL RACE(IRE) b.g. 8 Welsh Term - Regretable J M Brook

1996 **10(NH),9(NH),7(NH)**

1077	13/4	Guilsborough	(L)	CON	3m	16	GF	*prom to 9th, sn lost plc, p.u. 13th*	P	0
1205	26/4	Clifton On '	(L)	CON	3m	13	GS	*disp/ld to 6 out, onepcd frm 4 out*	4	14
1404	5/5	Ashorne	(R)	MEM	3m	7	G	*t.d.e. ld to 12th, s.u. bend apr nxt*	S	-

Ex-Irish; very modest form & unlikely to find a race 12

LOCAL WHISPER (Irish) — I 439^{3}

LOCATION b.g. 10 Blakeney - Green Teable (FR) by Green Dancer (USA) J Down

1996 3(11)

1520	17/5	Bratton Down	(L)	MDO	3m	17	GS	*prom til 7th, rear whn p.u. 13th*	P	0
1553	24/5	Mounsey Hil'	(R)	MDO	3m	11	G	*bhnd frm 5th, lost tch 10th, p.u. 15th*	P	0

Very lightly-raced; some promise at start of 96 but late to appear 97 & nothing 0

LOCH BRAN LAD (Irish) — I 397^{P}, I 526, , I 557^{P}, I 579^{P}, I 594,

LOCH GARANNE br.m. 9 Lochnager - Raperon by Rapid River P G Watkins

1996 P(0),12(0),0(0),0(0),5(0),0(0),0(0),0(0),R(-)

1213	26/4	Woodford	(L)	LAD	3m	6	G	*s.v.s. trotted to 1st, 2f bhnd whn ref 2nd*	R	-

Maintained her record & hopefully we've seen the last of her 0

LOCH GARMAN ARMS (Irish) — I 385^{1}, I 408^{P}, I 486^{P}, I 495^{P}

LOCHINVAR LORD b.g. 10 Callernish - Side Wink by Quayside D J Renney

1996 P(0),3(0),1(13),3(0),7(0)

372	2/3	Mollington	(R)	RES	3m	19	G	*(bl) ldng grp til wknd 11th, no ch whn u.r. 15th, stirrup broke*	U	-
517	15/3	Larkhill	(R)	RES	3m	10	GF	*cls up to 14th, sn wknd, t.o. in 4th whn p.u. last, lame*	P	0

Maiden winner 96; unlucky in 97 & problems too; novice-ridden 12

LOCH IRISH(IRE) b.m. 8 Lancastrian - Pure Spec by Fine Blade (USA) N W Padfield

1996 F(-),P(0),6(0),3(10),3(0)

318	1/3	Marks Tey	(L)	MDN	3m	13	G	*chsd ldrs to 10th, wknd 13th, t.o. & p.u. 17th*	P	0
452	8/3	Newton Brom'	(R)	MDN	3m	9	G	*ld to 4th, ld 7th-aft 15th, btn whn mstk last, demoted*	3	11
712	29/3	High Easter	(L)	MDO	3m	4	F	*(fav) chsd ldr til ld 10th, hdd 2 out, onepcd und press*	2	12
990	12/4	Kingston Bl'	(L)	MDN	3m	11	GF	*(fav) cls up, chsd wnr aft 13th, rdn & btn aft 15th*	4	0
1118	19/4	Higham	(L)	MDO	3m	9	GF	*ld to 7th, sn lost plc, wknd 12th, p.u. 3 out*	P	0

Placed 5 times but form very weak & a daft favourite twice 10

LOCH LOMOND (Irish) — I 159^{6}, I 245^{3}, I 383^{P}, I 538^{P}

LOCHNAVER b.m. 8 Lochnager - Annamanda by Tycoon II Mrs A Trollope-Bellew

1996 P(0),F(-),P(0),P(0),4(0)

102	8/2	Great Treth'	(R)	MDO	3m	8	GS	*prom til f 4th*	F	-
519	15/3	Cothelstone	(L)	MEM	3m	5	GS	*bhnd hlfwy, t.o.*	3	0

Of no account 0

LOCH SALAND (Irish) — I 72^{U}, I 125^{P}, I 360^{6}, I 432^{F}, I 467^{S}, I 585^{5}

LOFTY DEED(USA) b.g. 7 Shadeed (USA) - Soar Aloft (USA) by Avatar (USA) G M Thomson

1996 **3(NH),10(NH),6(NH),2(NH),11(NH),5(NH),3(NH),8(NH),7(NH),2(NH),5(NH)**

987	12/4	Kingston Bl'	(L)	OPE	3m	4	GF	*jmpd v slwly, lost tch 13th, t.o.*	3	0
1403	5/5	Ashorne	(R)	CON	3m	14	G	*crwld 3rd, mstk nxt, alwys bhnd, t.o. & p.u. 2 out*	P	0
1451	10/5	Kingston Bl'	(L)	OPE	3m	5	G	*2nd til aft 9th, cls up, ld aft 13th,sn hdd, kpt on flat*	3	15
1565	25/5	Kingston Bl'	(L)	OPE	3m	4	GF	*w.w. chsd wnr 13th, rdn aft 3 out, unable to chal*	2	18
1607	1/6	Dingley	(R)	OPE	3m	9	GF	*ref & u.r. 1st*	R	-
1611	7/6	Umberleigh	(L)	OPE	3m	8	F	*ref 1st (twice)*	R	-

Winning hurdler; ran passably twice but showed true colours after & best avoided 0

LOGICAL FUN b.g. 9 Nishapour (FR) - Thimblerigger by Sharpen Up Mrs R Crank

1996 P(0),2(19),4(10)

202	15/2	Weston Park	(L)	LAD	3m	13	G	*mid-div early, sn btn, no ch whn p.u. 2 out*	P	0
329	1/3	Eaton Hall	(R)	LAD	3m	10	GS	*chsng grp, 2nd 11th, ld 12th, hdd 4 out, ran on onepce*	3	16
724	29/3	Sandon	(L)	LAD	3m	4	GF	*(bl) cls 2nd, ld 11th, hdd 3 out, not qckn*	2	19
939	6/4	Tabley	(R)	LAD	3m	9	G	*(bl) ld to 6th & agn 10-13th, wknd, p.u. last*	P	0
1234	26/4	Brampton Br'	(R)	OPE	3m	4	G	*(bl) alwys last, clsd to 6l 4th at 10th, outpcd 12th, p.u. 2 out*	P	0

Winning hurdler; placed in small races & unlikely to win a Ladies 15

LOMOND HILL (Irish) — I 479^{P}

LONDON HILL b.g. 9 Little Wolf - Bambag by Goldhill — Mrs A Kemp

1996 **P(NH),F(NH),10(NH)**

249	22/2	Brocklesby '	(L)	LAD	3m	4	G	*2nd frm 5th, chsd wnnr last m, just held off*	2	19
448	8/3	Newton Brom'	(R)	LAD	3m	5	G	*3rd whn mstk & u.r. 2nd*	U	-
674	23/3	Brocklesby '	(L)	LAD	3m	5	GF	*mstks, chsd ldrs, went 2nd 7th, ld 3 out, kpt on und pres*	1	19

Ran well twice & unlucky not to be given outright win last start; finished early; G-F 21

LONELY CASTLE (Irish) — I 220^{P}

LONESOME STEP b.m. 10 Pas de Seul - Phalaborwa by Oats — A Gardner

1996 P(0),7(0),P(0),3(0)

294	1/3	Didmarton	(L)	INT	3m	20	G	*alwys rear, t.o. 11th, p.u. 13th*	P	0
903	5/4	Howick	(L)	CON	3m	6	F	*rear, prog to jn ldr 10th, wknd 15th, poor 4th whn p.u. last*	P	0
1228	26/4	Pyle	(R)	INT	3m	5	GS	*bhnd frm 4th, t.o. & p.u. 14th*	P	0

No longer of any account 0

LONESOME TRAVELLER(NZ) b.g. 8 Danzatore (CAN) - Honey Doll by Rheingold — Reg Hand

1996 4(13),2(19),5(11),5(11),1(17),**9(0)**,4(19),3(14),3(15)

237	22/2	Lemalla	(R)	CON	3m	13	S	*lost ground steadily frm 9th, rmndrs 12th, wll btn aft*	5	12
456	8/3	Great Treth'	(R)	INT	3m	11	S	*mid-div, just in tch frm 14th, no ch frm 16th*	4	0
628	22/3	Kilworthy	(L)	CON	3m	12	G	*mid-div, 6th & rddn 14th, no ch ldrs*	5	19
952	6/4	Black Fores'	(R)	LAD	3m	3	G	*(fav) disp to 3rd, disp 2nd aft, prog 14th, ran on, lkd 2nd*	3	10
1398	5/5	High Bickin'	(R)	INT	3m	7	G	*chsd ldr, slppd bend apr 14th, ev ch 3 out, styd on onepcd*	2	15
1481	11/5	Ottery St M'	(L)	CON	3m	12	G	*ld/disp to 3 out, rallied apr last, ran on to ld nr fin*	1	20
1490	13/5	Chepstow	(L)	HC	3m	7	G	*in tch till wknd 13th, t.o..*	4	0

Restricted winner 96; always finishes but needs stamina test; could do better if 98 wet; G-Hy 20

LONE SURVIVOR (Irish) — I 354^{F}, I 544^{F}

LONGMORE BOY (Irish) — I 72^{U}, I 119^{4}, I 180^{5}, I 289, , I 366^{2}, I 436^{1}

LOOKING b.g. 10 Kinglet - Chance A Look by Don't Look — P C Caudwell

1996 5(0),3+(0),F(-),P(0)

147	9/2	Tweseldown	(R)	MDO	3m	12	GF	*sweating, prom, ld 8-11th, ev ch 3 out, sn wknd*	3	10
223	16/2	Heythrop	(R)	RES	3m	19	G	*chsd ldrs, wknd frm 14th*	4	0
485	9/3	Tweseldown	(R)	MDO	3m	11	G	*prom,mstk 10th & lost plc,outpcd 15th,ran on 2 out,nvr nrr*	2	13
1402	5/5	Ashorne	(R)	MDO	3m	11	G	*mstks, ld/disp to 14th, onepcd frm 3 out*	4	11
1452	10/5	Kingston Bl'	(L)	MDO	3m	9	G	*ld 1st, ld 5-8th, ran out bend apr nxt*	r	-

Placed 5 times 96/7 but ungenuine & most unlikely to win 11

LOOKING AHEAD (Irish) — I 78, , I 131^{P}, I 259^{U}, I 320^{4}, I 427^{F}, I 454^{3}, I 477^{2}, I 535^{1}, I 567^{3}

LOOK SHARPE b.g. 6 Looking Glass - Washburn Flyer by Owen Dudley — T S Sharpe

1996 **2(NH),7(NH)**

115	9/2	Wetherby Po'	(L)	MDO	3m	8	GF	*s.s. hld up, plld hrd, prog 9th, ev ch whn f 4 out*	F	-
269	22/2	Duncombe Pa'	(R)	MDO	3m	16	G	*mid-div, prog 12th, 3rd & ev ch whn f 4 out*	F	-
427	8/3	Charm Park	(L)	MDO	3m	10	GF	*(fav) virt ref to race, stt wll bhnd, alwys t.o. & p.u. 13th*	P	0
1069	13/4	Whitwell-On'	(R)	RES	3m	12	G	*reluc to race, t.o. til jnd main grp 10th, kpt on frm 4 out*	5	10
1106	19/4	Hornby Cast'	(L)	MDO	3m	10	G	*keen hold, alwys prom, ev ch 3 out, onepcd*	3	11
1513	17/5	Corbridge	(R)	MDO	3m	13	GS	*alwys twrds rear, onepcd frm 3 out, nvr dang*	5	10

Some ability but temperamental; good enough to win but not to be trusted; ran in NH Flat after 13

LOOKS LIKE TROUBLE (Irish) — I 73^{2}

LOOSE WHEELS b.g. 11 Strong Gale - Kylogue Daisy by Little Buskins — Miss K Makinson

1996 4(0),5(0),1(15),4(11),7(0),4(0),3(14)

448	8/3	Newton Brom'	(R)	LAD	3m	5	G	*made most til 3 out, no ext*	2	17
773	29/3	Dingley	(R)	LAD	3m	11	G	*cls up to 11th, 5th & outpcd 6 out*	5	0
1189	20/4	Garthorpe	(R)	LAD	3m	6	GF	*prom to 3rd, sn bhnd, last & t.o. 8th*	4	0

Won dire match in 96 & outclassed in 97 14

LORD-A-DEE (Irish) — I 333^{4}

LORD AMETHYST (Irish) — I 154^{4}, I 221^{P}, I 341^{P}

LORD BASIL (Irish) — I 114^{F}, I 175^{1}

LORD COOLROE (Irish) — I 593^{P}

LORD EGROSS (Irish) — I 172^{P}, I 260^{P}, I 423^{P}, I 559,

LORD ESKER (Irish) — I 22^{P}

LORD GEORGE ch.g. 5 Lord Bud - Mini Gazette by London Gazette — D G Atkinson

269	22/2	Duncombe Pa'	(R)	MDO	3m	16	G	*alwys strgglng, t.o. whn p.u. 13th*	P	0
358	2/3	Great Stain'	(L)	MDO	3m	14	S	*mid-div, fdd 7th, p.u. 9th*	P	0
621	22/3	Hutton Rudby	(L)	MDO	3m	10	GF	*alwys in rear, lost tch 13th, t.o.*	4	0

1104 19/4 Hornby Cast' (L) MEM 3m 6 G *plld hrd in rear, blndrd 11th, t.o. 13th, p.u. 4 out* P 0

Well beaten on only completion - may do better 0

LORD HARRY (Irish) — I 421³, I 448¹, I 516¹, I 598³

LORDINTHESKY (Irish) — I 89ᴾ, I 134³, I 170³, I 309ᴾ

LORD KILTON ch.g. 9 Crested Lark - Kilton Jill by Adropejo Mrs D Cowley

1996 r(-),P(0),P(0)

1298 3/5 Warwick (L) HC 2 1/2m 110yds 2 GF *keen hold early, chsd ldr, not fluent 3rd, lost tch 10th, rallied between final 2, ld run-in, ran on.* 1 10

Of no account but handed season's most astonishing win - no further prospects 10

LORD KNOX(IRE) ch.g. 7 Tale Quale - Lady Knox by Dalsaan B G Clark

61 1/2 Horseheath (R) MDO 3m 9 GF *ld to 6th, ld agn 15th, made rest, styd on strngly* 1 13
274 22/2 Ampton (R) RES 3m 10 G *prom, ld 8-12th, 5th & wkng 16th, t.o. & p.u. 2 out* P 0

Ex-Irish; won a poor Maiden & finished early; best watched 13

LORD LANKIE(IRE) b.g. 6 Lancastrian - Blue Misty Eyes by Welsh Chanter W K Hooper

374 2/3 Mollington (R) MDN 3m 14 G *in tch to 11th, bhnd whn p.u. 15th* P 0
761 29/3 Kimble (L) MDO 3m 12 GF *chsd ldrs, 5th at 12th, wknd & p.u. 3 out* P 0

Just a couple of educational runs & may do better 0

LORD OF ALL (Irish) — I 38¹

LORD RELIC(NZ) b.g. 11 Zamazaan (FR) - Morning Order (NZ) by Bismark Mrs H J Clarke

1996 **P(NH),P(NH),6(NH)**

93 7/2 Bangor (L) HC 2 1/2m 110yds 11 G *trckd ldrs, ld 8th till hdd 3 out, chsd wnr after, no impn.* 2 25
226 21/2 Haydock (L) HC 3m 11 G *(fav) cl up, ld 2 out, pushed clr after last.* 1 32
291 1/3 Warwick (L) HC 3 1/4m 6 G *(fav) chsd clr ldr, imp to ld apr 7 out, jmpd slowly next, hdd 4 out, rallied from last, fin lame.* 2 29
494 13/3 Cheltenham (L) HC 3 1/4m 110yds 18 G *held up, struggling 14th, bhnd when p.u. 6 out.* P 0

Revived well to win decent H/Chase; always fragile & soon disappeared; can win if fit 98; G-S 27

LORD SAMMY (Irish) — I 436ᴾ, I 507⁶, I 583⁴

LORD SPIDER b.g. 5 Town And Country - Lolly Spider by Rugantino J Grant Cann

1520 17/5 Bratton Down (L) MDO 3m 17 GS *bhnd, last at 10th, gd prog 13th, chsd wnr 3 out, promising* 2 14

Went into every notebook & looks sure to win in 98 16

LORD VINCE (Irish) — I 381ᴾ, I 484ᴾ, I 608ᴾ

LORGLANE LADY (Irish) — I 167ᶠ, I 264ᴾ, I 383ᶠ, I 561ᴾ

LOSLOMOS (Irish) — I 103⁵, I 142³, I 196³, I 294¹

LOST COIN (Irish) — I 98ᴾ, I 221⁶, I 339², I 388¹, I 411¹, I 480⁴, I 498⁴

LOST FORTUNE ch.g. 14 Nearly A Hand - Opt Out by Spartan General H W Wheeler

1996 1(22),1(23)

308 1/3 Clyst St Ma' (L) OPE 3m 7 HY *(fav) hld up, prog 15th, 2nd nxt, ld 3 out, kpt on* 1 21
432 8/3 Upton-On-Se' (R) MXO 3m 7 G *cls 2nd at 8th, 8l 4th 13th, effrt nxt, no ext aft 3 out* 2 21

Lightly-raced now but has won 14 of last 19; goes well fresh & may win 1st time out at 15; G-S 23

LOSTYNDYKE (Irish) — I 54ᴾ, I 341ᶠ, I 449³, I 548ᴾ

LOTHIAN COMMODORE ro.g. 7 Alias Smith (USA) - Lothian Lightning by Lighter D A Whitaker

1996 **7(NH),P(NH)**

972 7/4 Kelso (L) HC 3m 1f 12 GF *in tch, rdn along 15th, soon wknd.* 5 12

Professionally-trained but rarely appears & shows little yet 14

LOTHIAN MAGIC (Irish) — I 163³, I 245², I 295³, I 509ᴾ, I 576⁴, I 615ᴾ

LOTHIAN PILOT ro.g. 10 Alias Smith (USA) - Lothian Lightning by Lighter Mrs B Warres

158 15/2 Lanark (R) LAD 3m 8 G *ld til u.r. 5th* U -
335 1/3 Corbridge (R) CON 3m 7 G *ld to 5th, wth wnr 13th til wknd rpdly 2 out* 4 12
413 8/3 Dalston (R) OPE 3m 9 GS *prom, chsd wnr 11th-3 out, wknd nxt, blnd last* 5 12
943 6/4 Friars Haugh (L) MEM 3m 5 GF *2nd frm 10th, ld 3 out, grdly forged clr* 1 17

Doddled home in Members but struggled in better class; Members again best hope 98 16

LOTTIE THE LOTUS ch.m. 8 Crested Lark - Florence Eliza by Floriana G B Tarry

1402 5/5 Ashorne (R) MDO 3m 11 G *schoold,prog 10th,chsd ldrs aft,nvr askd to chal,fin strngly* 3 13

Highly promising debut under novice rider & sure to win in 98 16

LOTTOLEIGH (Irish) — **I** 24[3]

LOTTOVER (Irish) — **I** 201[1]

LOUDY ROWDY (Irish) — **I** 269[P], **I** 391[P], **I** 459[1]

LOUGHLANDER (Irish) — **I** 452[1]

LOUGH LEIN SPIRIT (Irish) — **I** 15[1], **I** 236[F]

LOUGHLINSTOWN BOY b.g. 12 Ela-Mana-Mou - Tante Yvonne by Crowned Prince (USA) — J A Riddell

1996 5(0),6(0),**P(0)**,**P(0)**,**P(0)**,1(20),1(21),3(13),1(19),1(19),**7(20)**

232	22/2	Friars Haugh	(L)	OPE	3m	6	G	*2nd til 13th, sn lost tch*	6 13
339	1/3	Corbridge	(R)	OPE	3m 5f	11	G	*mid-div, drppd rear 10th, t.o. & p.u. 13th*	P 0
610	22/3	Friars Haugh	(L)	OPE	3m	6	GF	*ld to 8th, sn lost tch, p.u. 4 out*	P 0

Won 4 in 96; best late season & well below form in 97; best watched now 14

LOUGH MORNE b.g. 9 Welsh Captain - Souris Francais by Decoy Boy — N Lock

516	15/3	Larkhill	(R)	RES	3m	7	GF	*dtchd last whn mstk & u.r. 2nd*	U -
706	29/3	Upper Sapey	(R)	MDO	3m	15	GF	*t.o. by 6th, last by 12th, p.u. 15th*	P 0
1195	23/4	Andoversford	(R)	MEM	3m	4	F	*jmpd lft, lost tch 4th, t.o. 8th*	3 0
1609	1/6	Dingley	(R)	MDO	3m	14	GF	*cls up, mstk 15th, wknd aft, p.u. 2 out*	P 0

Does not stay & shows nothing under novice rider 0

LOUIS DE PALMER (Irish) — **I** 55, , **I** 100[P], **I** 156[4], **I** 223[F], **I** 273[2], **I** 341[3], **I** 391[F], **I** 500[4], **I** 545[4], **I** 580,

LOVABLE OUTLAW (Irish) — **I** 93[3], **I** 147[P], **I** 387[1]

LOVEABLE LADY (Irish) — **I** 46[F], **I** 339, , **I** 388[P]

LOVE ACTINIUM(IRE) b.m. 6 Actinium (FR) - Flashing Gaze — D McComb

35	26/1	Alnwick	(L)	CON	3m	10	G	*in tch, prog 11th, wth wnr 15th, not qckn nxt, styd on*	2 18
131	9/2	Alnwick	(L)	RES	3m	13	G	*chsd ldrs to 4 out, no hdwy aft*	6 0

Irish Maiden winner 96; fair start but vanished; novice-ridden; best watched 17

LOVELY HURLING (Irish) — **I** 238, , **I** 308,

LOYAL GAIT(NZ) ch.g. 9 Gaiter (NZ) - Lotsydamus (NZ) by Auk (USA) — P Atkins

1996 1(16),**F(-)**

592	22/3	Lingfield	(L)	HC	3m	5	GF	*prom, ld after 4th to 7th, wknd from 11th, t.o. when p.u. before 3 out.*	P 0
983	12/4	Ascot	(R)	HC	3m 110yds	14	GF	*mid div when blnd badly 4th (water), bhnd from hfwy, t.o. when p.u. before 15th.*	P 0
1285	29/4	Huntingdon	(R)	HC	3m	10	G	*mstk 8th, alwys rear, t.o. and p.u. before 16th.*	P 0
1567	25/5	Kingston Bl'	(L)	RES	3m	8	GF	*mostly chsd wnr til aft 3 out, 3rd & wll btn whn f nxt.*	F -

Maiden winner 96; silly campaign 97 & Restricted less than likely 98; Firm 13

LOYAL NOTE ch.g. 9 Royal Vulcan - Maynote by Maystreak — R Andrews

1996 7(14),**1(22)**,**5(14)**,F(-)

150	10/2	Plumpton	(L)	HC	3m 1f 110yds	5	GS	*disp ld, not fluent 15th, hit next, ld apr last, ran on well.*	1 25
286	27/2	Huntingdon	(R)	HC	3m	8	GS	*not fluent, in tch, went handy after one cct, struggling 6 out, no impn after.*	4 22
489	10/3	Plumpton	(L)	HC	3m 1f 110yds	7	GS	*hdwy 8th, str chal from 2 out, kept on well.*	2 24
1290	30/4	Cheltenham	(L)	HC	4m 1f	10	GF	*chsd ldrs, pushed along 18th, blnd 22nd, rdn and no impn next.*	4 18

H/Chase winner 96; stays well; both H/Chase wins Plumpton; may find another; G-Hy 25

LUCIMAN(IRE) b.g. 7 Mandalus - Lucylet by Kinglet — William Corrigan

1996 **4(NH)**

540	16/3	Erw Lon	(L)	MDN	3m	13	GF	*(fav) mid-div to 6th, prog & cls up 14th, onepcd*	2 10

Placed in novice hurdle 96 (Mary Reveley); not disgraced but may prove disappointing 13

LUCKIESHIEL b.m. 9 Broadsword (USA) - Mildenstone by Milan — Miss D M M Calder

228	22/2	Friars Haugh	(L)	MEM	3m	4	G	*s.s. alwys t.o.*	2 0
414	8/3	Dalston	(R)	XX	3m	9	GS	*pllng,ld to 2nd,4th & outpcd frm 13th,lft poor 3rd apr 2 out*	3 10
608	22/3	Friars Haugh	(L)	XX	3m	6	GF	*alwys wll bhnd, t.o.*	4 0
1047	13/4	Lockerbie	(R)	INT	3m	4	F	*cls up til wknd frm 14th*	3 10

Dual winner 95; missed 96; not recover form in 97; G-Hy 11

LUCKY CHRISTOPHER b.g. 12 St Columbus - Lucky Story by Lucky Sovereign — G B Tarry

1996 P(0),2(25),**3(20)**,1(24),2(20),1(24),1(22),**1(25)**,1(28),1(30)

56	1/2	Kingston Bl'	(L)	OPE	3m	13	GF	*chsd ldr,ld 4-6th,sn ld agn,hdd 13th,jnd wnr & ran out 15th*	r -
138	9/2	Thorpe Lodge	(L)	OPE	3m	5	GF	*(fav) hld up, jnd ldr 3 out, clr nxt, ran on well*	1 24
273	22/2	Ampton	(R)	OPE	3m	7	G	*(fav) prom, no room on inner whn trd to ref & u.r. 12th*	U -
447	8/3	Newton Brom'	(R)	OPE	3m	6	G	*(Jt fav) hld up rear, 3rd at 9th, ld 2 out, qcknd clr, easily*	1 24

1079 13/4 Guilsborough (L) OPE 3m 6 GF *(fav) w.w. trckd ldr 16th, ld 3 out, shkn up & sn in cmmnd* 1 25
1163 20/4 Mollington (R) OPE 3m 4 GF *(fav) made most, qcknd clr 15th, canter* 1 20
1489 12/5 Towcester (R) HC 3m 1f 6 GS *(fav) alwys in tch, trckd ldr, short of room and switched left on bend apr 2 out, rdn and kept on one pace.* 2 27
1591 31/5 Stratford (L) HC 3 1/2m 11 G *struggling to go pace when nearly u.r. 7th, hit next, t.o. till p.u. between last 2.* P 0

Very useful; won 9 of last 12 points; consistent, stays and can quicken; sure to win more; G/F-S 27

LUCKY FIFTEEN (Irish) — I 109F, I 162P, I 200P, I 278F, I 338, , I 608P

LUCKY HERO (Irish) — I 545[1]

LUCKY JEFF (Irish) — I 317P, I 381P, I 484P, I 536P

LUCKY LANDING(IRE) b.g. 8 Lancastrian - Twice Lucky by Condorcet (FR) Nigel Taylor

1996 **P(NH),P(NH),P(NH)**

927 6/4 Garthorpe (R) RES 3m 9 GF *ld 3rd-12th, wknd rpdly, no ch whn p.u. 3 out* P 0
1160 20/4 Mollington (R) INT 3m 9 GF *keen hld, prom to 11th, wknd 13th, t.o. & p.u. 15th* P 0
1287 29/4 Huntingdon (R) HC 2 1/2m 110yds 14 G *mid div, lost tch 9th, t.o. and p.u. before 12th.* P 0
1355 4/5 Dingley (R) RES 3m 12 G *chsd ldrs to 11th, t.o. & p.u. 2 out* P 0
1488 12/5 Towcester (R) HC 2m 110yds 16 GS *alwys towards rear, t.o. when p.u. before last.* P 0

Of no account 0

LUCKY OLE SON b.g. 10 Old Lucky - Drake's Beauty by Captain Drake David Brace

1996 2(20),4(13),8(0),1(18),4(0),2(18),1(19),1+(18),P(0),4(0),U(-),3(16),3(0),P(0)

49 1/2 Wadebridge (L) LAD 3m 5 G *(fav) disp 2nd-9th, grad lost tch 12th, ran on agn flat* 3 15
191 15/2 Erw Lon (L) CON 3m 13 G *jmpd slwly, bhnd frm 6th, t.o. & p.u. aft 12th* P 0
536 16/3 Erw Lon (L) LAD 3m 9 GF *(Jt fav) sttld mid-div, prog to ld aft last, rdn out* 1 18
638 22/3 Howick (L) LAD 3m 10 GF *rear, rdn & no prog frm 13th* 6 0
844 31/3 Lydstep (L) LAD 3m 6 F *alwys strgglng, p.u. last, lame* P 0
905 5/4 Howick (L) LAD 3m 4 F *chsd wnr to 12th & frm 15th, rdn & no imp* 2 15
1184 20/4 Lydstep (L) LAD 3m 4 GF *(fav) dist 2nd til clsd 3 out, ld apr last where left clr* 1 18
1364 5/5 Pantyderi (L) LAD 3m 5 G *4th at 3rd, 3rd at 11th, p.u. 2 out* P 0
1472 11/5 Erw Lon (L) XX 3m 9 GS *twrds rear, rpd prog 2 out, fin fast, lft 2nd last* 2 10
1559 24/5 Bassaleg (R) XX 3m 4 G *ld 3-4th, lft in ld nxt-15th, ev ch & blnd 2 out,ran on flat* 2 14
1606 1/6 Dingley (R) LAD 3m 13 GF *prom, 4th whn f 6th* F -

Won 5 of 25 races 96/7; only goes for Pip Jones but broke her leg last start; summer jumping 17

LUCKY STATEMENT (Irish) — I 56P, I 99P, I 155P

LUCKY TOWN (Irish) — I 49[2], I 75[3], I 256[2], I 357[1], I 427[1], I 492[1], I 592[1]

LUCKY VIENNA b.m. 7 Lucky Wednesday - Lady Sangara by Sagaro J H Henderson

1027 12/4 Horseheath (R) MDO 3m 2 HD *(Jt fav) j.s 1st, ld & j.s 3rd, 30l clr 9th, lft solo 11th* 1 0
1263 27/4 Southwell P' (L) RES 3m 9 G *rear, jmpd slwly 5th, sn wll bhnd, p.u. 12th* P 0
1305 3/5 Cottenham (R) MEM 3m 4 F *last & jmpd slwly, t.o. 11th, tk dist 3rd 3 out* 3 0

Won one of season's many dire matches & has no further prospects 0

LUDDEN CHIEF (Irish) — I 190[3], I 274F, I 332[3]

LUDOVICIANA b.m. 8 Oats - Crafty Look by Don't Look G W Paul

1996 2(16)

29 26/1 Marks Tey (L) MDN 3m 10 GF *t.d.e. ld to 4th, ld 15th-3 out, onepcd und pres aft* 3 15
69 2/2 Higham (L) MDO 3m 8 GF *(fav) ld til blnd 2nd, ld nxt til f 11th* F -
317 1/3 Marks Tey (L) MDN 3m 13 G *(fav) ld 4th, made rest, drew wll clr frm 15th, easy* 1 15
443 8/3 Higham (L) RES 3m 7 G *f 1st* F -
502 15/3 Ampton (R) RES 3m 5 GF *prom, ld 8th til appr 2 out, no ex* 2 17

Confirmed promise in weak race; should win Restricted; probably best on easy 3m; G-F 18

LUKS AKURA b.g. 9 Dominion - Pacificus (USA) by Northern Dancer W James Morgan

1996 **8(NH),7(NH),P(NH),P(NH)**

202 15/2 Weston Park (L) LAD 3m 13 G *alwys mid-div* 7 0

Tailed off last & no prospects 0

LUNEY RIVER b.m. 8 Idiot's Delight - Perfect Saint by St Paddy R Tonks

103 8/2 Great Treth' (R) MDO 3m 9 GS *clr ldr, blnd 11th, wknd & hdd aft 13th, p.u. 15th* P 0
245 22/2 Lemalla (R) MDO 3m 11 S *keen hold, prom, ld 6th, hdd & wknd 12th, blnd nxt, p.u.* P 0
460 8/3 Great Treth' (R) MDO 3m 13 S *chsd ldr, hit 7th, sn lost plc, t.o. p.u. apr 13th* P 0
531 15/3 Wadebridge (L) MDO 3m 14 GF *made most to 15th, fdd* 4 12
808 31/3 Wadebridge (L) MDO 3m 8 F *plld hrd, race into clr ld til u.r. 12th (ditch)* U -
1034 12/4 Lifton (R) MDN 3m 7 F *raced wd, alwys towrds rear* 5 0
1242 26/4 Bratton Down (L) LAD 3m 6 GS *ld to 6th, ran wd, grdly lost tch, p.u. 12th* P 0
1343 3/5 Flete Park (R) MDO 3m 13 G *keen hld, ld til p.u. aft 6th* P 0

Missed 96 & has only finished 2 of 10 races 10

L'UOMO PIU b.g. 13 Paddy's Stream - Easter Vigil by Arctic Slave — Lease Terminated

1996 **8(NH),5(NH),5(NH),P(NH),6(NH),5(NH),5(NH),4(NH),5(NH),3(NH),P(NH),4(NH),P(NH)**

311	1/3	Clyst St Ma'	(L)	LAD	3m	9	HY	*hld up, prog whn mssd mrkr & p.u. 13th*	P	0
520	15/3	Cothelstone	(L)	LAD	3m	12	GS	*nov rdn, rear grp, t.o. 16th*	7	0
862	31/3	Kingston St'	(R)	CON	3m	7	F	*ld til ran out 7th*	r	-
889	3/4	Taunton	(R)	HC	3m	7	F	*made all, hit 12th, driven out.*	1	19
1087	16/4	Cheltenham	(L)	HC	3 1/4m 110yds	8	GF	*prom, chsd ldr from 6th to 10th, bhnd from 12th, t.o. when p.u. before 4 out.*	P	0
1441	10/5	Holnicote	(L)	CON	3m	7	G	*ld 2-8th, sn wknd, bhnd frm 11th, p.u. 2 out*	P	0

Brilliantly ridden to win poor H/Chase but no real prospects at 14 15

LUPY MINSTREL br.g. 12 Black Minstrel - Lupreno by Hugh Lupus — Miss D Hall

1996 **P(NH),3(NH),5(NH),1(NH),F(NH),7(NH)**

33	26/1	Alnwick	(L)	LAD	3m	12	G	*(fav) trckd ldrs going wll, not quckn 13th, ran on onepcd frm 3out*	3	21
132	9/2	Alnwick	(L)	LAD	3m	9	G	*mid-div, outpcd & rmndr 12th, kpt on onepcd frm 3 out*	3	0
339	1/3	Corbridge	(R)	OPE	3m 5f	11	G	*alwys prom, ld 3 out, hdd last, kpt on*	2	24
731	29/3	Alnwick	(L)	MXO	4m	7	F	*alwys ldng trio, outpcd 21st, rallied wll flat, not rch wnr*	2	23
1048	13/4	Lockerbie	(R)	LAD	3m	6	F	*(fav) cls up til outpcd frm 14th*	2	19
1122	19/4	Whittington	(L)	LAD	3m	3	F	*j.w. ld 14th-nxt, ev ch last, not qckn nr fin*	2	22
1489	12/5	Towcester	(R)	HC	3m 1f	6	GS	*ld to 4th, led 8th till hdd apr 2 out, rdn and kept on one pace.*	3	25
1586	28/5	Cartmel	(L)	HC	3 1/4m	10	GF	*held up, mstk 10th, effort 13th, nvr troubld ldrs.*	5	13

Winning chaser 96; able & consistent but finds little & likely to frustrate again at 13 21

LURRIGA GLITTER(IRE) gr.g. 9 General Ironside - Glitter On by Even Money — M P Wareing

91	6/2	Huntingdon	(R)	HC	3m	10	G	*held up, hdwy 11th, ld 13th to 6 out, rdn and rallied 2 out, not qckn.*	2	20
287	27/2	Huntingdon	(R)	HC	3m	13	GS	*waited with, imp 11th, wknd apr 4 out, t.o..*	6	13
384	6/3	Towcester	(R)	HC	3m 1f	7	GS	*prom, chsd ldrs, wknd 4 out, t.o..*	3	13
888	3/4	Aintree	(L)	HC	3m 1f	9	G	*bhnd, mstk 9th, t.o. 11th.*	5	17
983	12/4	Ascot	(R)	HC	3m 110yds	14	GF	*(bl) chsd ldrs, blnd 12th, lost pl next, hdwy 4 out, styd on well from 2 out, mstk last, no impn.*	2	24
1290	30/4	Cheltenham	(L)	HC	4m 1f	10	GF	*(bl) prog to chase ldrs 8th, no impn from 17th, one pace from 22nd.*	6	11
1570	26/5	Hereford	(R)	HC	3m 1f 110yds	14	G	*(bl) soon well bhnd, p.u. before 4 out.*	P	0

Ex-Irish; ran 2 good races but badly apart & blinkers soon wore off; one to be wary of 19

LUVLY BUBBLY b.g. 9 Carlingford Castle - Mill Shine by Milan — C Hall

1996 F(-),P(0),2(10)

233	22/2	Friars Haugh	(L)	MDO	3m	13	G	*prom early, bhnd by 10th, p.u. 3 out*	P	0
342	1/3	Corbridge	(R)	MDO	3m	12	G	*rear, prog 7th, ld 4 out, hdd nxt, ev ch last, kpt on*	2	13
614	22/3	Friars Haugh	(L)	MDN	3m	13	GF	*(fav) alwys bhnd*	7	0

Touched off 2nd start but tailed off after; best watched 11

LYDEBROOK b.g. 8 Scallywag - Bahama by Bali Dancer — John R Wilson

1996 U(-),U(-),4(0)

81	2/2	Wolverhampt'	(L)	MDN	3m	13	GS	*in tch in rear til u.r. 7th*	U	-
204	15/2	Weston Park	(L)	RES	3m	13	G	*ld 6th-4 out, no ext frm 2 out*	3	13

Has only beaten 2 other finishers & very lightly-raced 10

LYME GOLD(IRE) ch.g. 8 Phardante (FR) - Mad For Her Beer by Proverb — J M Turner

1996 **5(NH),2(NH),1(NH),3(NH),4(NH)**

323	1/3	Marks Tey	(L)	LAD	3m	7	G	*ld to 5th, cls up, ev ch 17th, onepcd frm nxt*	4	10
780	31/3	Fakenham	(L)	HC	3m 110yds	7	G	*not fluent early, mstk 9th, wknd 14th, p.u. before last.*	P	0
1279	27/4	Fakenham P-'	(L)	OPE	3m	7	G	*chsd ldrs, lost plc & rdn 7th, mstk 10th, last & p.u. 14th*	P	0
1433	10/5	Marks Tey	(L)	OPE	3m	4	G	*(bl) prom, ld & mstk 4th, jnd 7th, hdd nxt, blnd 10th, wknd 15th*	3	12
1529	18/5	Fakenham	(L)	HC	3m 110yds	9	G	*(bl) alwys in rear.*	7	0

Winning chaser 96; showed no interest in 97 12

LYNINGO ch.g. 10 Rustingo - Lyns Legend by Marengo — Mrs M J Ward

1996 F(-),2(15),1(15),6(10),5(12),5(13)

425	8/3	Charm Park	(L)	RES	3m	12	GF	*sn in rear, strggng & lost tch 12th*	5	0
615	22/3	Hutton Rudby	(L)	MEM	3m	8	GF	*mid-div, prog 11th, mstk 14th, outpcd 3 out, kpt on flat*	2	14
856	31/3	Charm Park	(L)	RES	3m	8	F	*alwys mid-div, nvr a fctr*	5	15
1068	13/4	Whitwell-On'	(R)	RES	3m	12	G	*rear, outpcd 10th, sn wll bhnd, p.u. 4 out*	P	0
1250	26/4	Easingwold	(L)	RES	3m	15	GS	*mid-div, fdd 10th, p.u. 14th*	P	0
1348	3/5	Gisburn	(R)	RES	3m	10	GF	*chsng ldrs, ev ch 12th, no dang to 1st pair aft*	3	12
1510	17/5	Corbridge	(R)	RES	3m	13	GS	*(bl) mid-div, mstk 2nd, rmndrs 11th, sn wknd, t.o.*	5	10

Maiden winner 96; safe but struggling in Restricteds & unlikely to win one 12

LYNNES DANIELLA(IRE) b.m. 6 Carlingford Castle - Lily Gale (IRE) by Strong Gale Mrs P Rees

543 16/3 Erw Lon (L) MDN 3m 11 GF *alwys rear, p.u. 6th* P 0
964 6/4 Pantyderi (L) MDN 3m 4 F *ref 3rd* R -
1010 12/4 St Hilary (R) MDN 3m 10 GF *rear til p.u. 13th* P 0
1183 20/4 Lydstep (L) MDO 3m 8 GF *(bl) nvr nrr than 5th, p.u. 4 out* P 0
1323 3/5 Bonvilston (R) MDO 3m 14 G *(bl) mid-div, p.u. 7th* P 0
1367 5/5 Pantyderi (L) MDO 3m 7 G *trckd ldrs, f 8th* F -
1471 11/5 Erw Lon (L) RES 3m 9 GS *rear, p.u. 9th* P 0
1562 24/5 Bassaleg (R) MDO 3m 8 G *mstks, chsd ldrs, wknd 13th, t.o. & p.u. 2 out* P 0

Devoid of ability 0

LYNPHORD GIRL ch.m. 6 Lyphento (USA) - Woodlands Angel by Levanter A Cayford
1996 **15(NH),7(NH)**

524 15/3 Cothelstone (L) RES 3m 10 GS *prom, lft in ld 12th, hdd nxt, btn 3rd whn p.u. 2 out* P 0
933 6/4 Charlton Ho' (L) MDO 3m 12 G *20s-4s, wth ldr to 13th, lost plc, ran on agn 2 out, fin wll, lkd 2nd* 3 14

Ran well in modest race & should have winning chances if fit 98 15

LYRICAL SEAL b.m. 7 Dubassoff (USA) - Sea-Rosemary by Seaepic (USA) Mrs J Dening
1996 **P(NH),P(NH),4(NH),3(NH)**

20 25/1 Badbury Rin' (L) MDN 3m 9 GF *w.w. 6th & in tch whn hmpd & u.r. 14th* U -
181 15/2 Larkhill (R) MDO 3m 17 G *in tch to 14th, outpcd frm nxt* 5 0

Modest form under Rules; should be capable of figuring in Maidens but finished early 10

MABOY LADY 10 D J Hooper
1996 P(0),F(-),U(-),5(10),6(13)

789 31/3 Bishopsleigh (R) MEM 3m 5 G *lft in ld 3rd, disp 5 out til hdd & no ext last* 2 0
1108 19/4 Flete Park (R) RES 3m 14 GF *ld to 7th, chsd ldr til wknd 3 out* 5 11
1259 27/4 Black Fores' (R) RES 3m 7 F *ld/disp to 6th, grad wknd, p.u. 2 out* P 0

Irish Maiden winne 95; beaten by a remounter in members; winning chances slim. 12

MACCARRONS RUN (Irish) — **I** 125P, **I** 179P, **I** 250P, **I** 360P

MACFARLY (Irish) — **I** 303P, **I** 6093

MACKABEE(IRE) b or br.g. 8 Supreme Leader - Donegal Queen by Quayside P B Williams
1996 4(0),1(15),F(-),2(16),4(14),S(-)

189 15/2 Erw Lon (L) RES 3m 14 G *in tch in rear to 13th, t.o. & p.u. 2 out* P 0
262 22/2 Newtown (L) RES 3m 15 G *mid-div, prog 11th, mstk 13th, cls up nxt, sn onepcd* 3 13
398 8/3 Llanfrynach (R) MEM 3m 6 G *(fav) hld up, prog 10th, jnd wnr last, no ext flat* 2 15
575 16/3 Garnons (L) RES 3m 12 G *chsd ldrs til outpcd frm 14th* 4 10
633 22/3 Howick (L) RES 3m 8 GF *(Jt fav) hld up mid-div, prog to 2nd 12th, mstk 3 out, hld aft* 2 15
753 29/3 Brampton Br' (R) RES 3m 9 GF *prog to cls 5th at 15th, wknd aft nxt* 5 0

Members winner 96; consistent in modest races; weak Restricted possible;G/S-G/F. 15

MACK A DAY (Irish) — **I** 785, **I** 1492, **I** 1934, **I** 3203, **I** 5182, **I** 5674

MACKEN MONEY (Irish) — **I** 32F, **I** 98F, **I** 1113, **I** 2864, **I** 312F, **I** 4623

MACKLETTE (Irish) — **I** 10, , **I** 454, **I** 903, **I** 1372, **I** 3041, **I** 3805, **I** 4756, **I** 5623

MAC'S BLADE(USA) ch.g. 5 Imp Society (USA) - Safety Razor (USA) by Blade (USA) T R Brown

616 22/3 Hutton Rudby (L) RES 3m 14 GF *n.j.w., rear & sn t.o., ref 7th* R -
897 5/4 Wetherby Po' (L) INT 3m 3 F *sttld 3rd,strggIng 13th,lft 2nd 2 out,rallied flat,just hld* 2 10
1105 19/4 Hornby Cast' (L) MDO 3m 11 G *mstks,mid-div,prog 5th,lost plcd 8th,blndrd 11th,f 14th* F -
1247 26/4 Easingwold (L) CON 3m 9 GS *alwys wll in rear, errors, t.o., p.u. 10th* P 0
1409 5/5 Witton Cast' (R) MDO 3m 15 GS *prom, disp 4 out til hdd & 2l down whn f last* F 15

Last when completing but shows promise; needs to jump better 14

MAC'S BOY b.g. 8 Macmillion - Tender Manx by Owen Dudley Julian P Allen
1996 P(0),1(15),3(17),5(0),P(0),U(-),**F(-)**

7 19/1 Barbury Cas' (L) RES 3m 14 GF *prom, 3rd hlfwy, grad wknd, 5th & no ch whn p.u. last* P 0
100 8/2 Great Treth' (R) RES 3m 14 GS *5s-2s, ld to 5th, lost plc & blnd 12th, bhnd whn p.u. 16th* P 0

Maiden winner 96; finished early 97; win Restricted if fit in 98; stays; mistakes; G/F-S. 18

MAC'S GAMBLE br.g. 8 Macmillion - Galitino by Rontino R J Davis

1062 13/4 Maisemore P' (L) MXO 3m 12 GF *jmpd rght, alwys last, t.o. & p.u. 12th* P 0

No show on debut 0

MAC'S LEGEND (Irish) — **I** 2431

MADAM ASIDE (Irish) — **I** 14, **I** 91P, **I** 321P

MADAME BECK b.m. 8 Meadowbrook - My Mimosa by Cagirama R Michael Smith
1996 F(-),P(0),**4(0)**,4(13),2(13),U(-),**U(-)**

566 16/3 Lanark (R) MDO 3m 10 GS *kpt on stdly frm 14th, nvr rchd ldrs* 4 0
778 31/3 Carlisle (R) HC 3 1/4m 14 G *held up, imp to chase ldrs 12th, struggling 5 out, p.u. last.* P 0
1050 13/4 Lockerbie (R) RES 3m 5 F *in tch til wknd 13th, p.u. 3 out* P 0
1337 3/5 Mosshouses (L) MDO 3m 7 F *alwys handy, made most frm 13th til hdd apr last* 2 14
1513 17/5 Corbridge (R) MDO 3m 13 GS *prom, rmndrs 10th, ev ch apr last, not qckn* 2 13

Placed 6 of last 10 starts; stays but onepaced; has run tubed; deserves a win 14

MADAME DEFARGE b or br.m. 6 Vital Season - La Tricoteuse by Le Tricolore — Mrs C M Leech

623 22/3 Hutton Rudby (L) MDO 3m 9 GF *rear, lost tch 11th, t.o. nxt, p.u. 14th* P 0
898 5/4 Wetherby Po' (L) MDO 3m 7 F *trckd ldr, lost plc 5th, outpcd 10th, ran on wll frm 2 out* 2 0
1051 13/4 Lockerbie (R) MDN 3m 10 F *bhnd til some late prog, nvr rchd ldrs* 4 11

Beaten 12 lengths minimum (last start); both places on long tracks; go close in 98. 12

MADAM SIOUX (Irish) — I 332^{4}

MADE OF TALENT br.m. 8 Supreme Leader - Cedor's Daughter by Pallard Court — E H Crow

1996 2(16),F(-),2(16)

204 15/2 Weston Park (L) RES 3m 13 G *chsng grp, rdn & no prog 5 out, p.u. 3 out* P 0
332 1/3 Eaton Hall (R) RES 3m 18 GS *alwys rear, t.o. & p.u. 12th* P 0

Maiden winner 95; disappointing 96 & surely problems in97; best watched. 13

MADIYAN(USA) ch.g. 8 Sharastani (USA) - Meadow Glen Lady (USA) by Believe It (USA) — J H Forbes

1996 3(12),3(12),4(12),6(12)

45 1/2 Larkhill (R) RES 3m 14 GF *in tch in rear til wknd apr 15th* 6 0

Won poor Maiden 94; very moderate & finished early in 97; unlikely to win again. 12

MADRAJ(IRE) b or br.g. 9 Double Schwartz - Poka Poka (FR) by King Of Macedon — Bruce Sarson

1996 **7(NH)**

11 25/1 Cottenham (R) LAD 3m 2 GF *disp til lft solo 8th* 1 0
195 15/2 Higham (L) LAD 3m 14 G *mid-div til u.r. 6th* U -
296 1/3 Didmarton (L) LAD 3m 13 G *alwys bhnd, t.o. & p.u. 13th* P 0
825 31/3 Lockinge (L) MXO 3m 3 F *prssd wnr, ld 13-16th, sn wknd, lame* 2 10
1062 13/4 Maisemore P' (L) MXO 3m 12 GF *(bl) cls up to 6th, wknd 13th, t.o. & p.u. 2 out* P 0
1197 23/4 Andoversford (R) LAD 3m 5 F *(bl) in tch, ld 12th-13th, 3rd & wkng apr 2 out, fin tired* 3 10

Winning hurdler; won joke race; does not stay and need same to score again. 12

MAESGWYN BACH b.m. 9 Leading Man - Fairlina by Quality Fair — R T Tudor

1996 P(0),P(0),P(0)

723 29/3 Sandon (L) MDO 3m 6 GF *rear, t.o. 12th, p.u. 5 out* P 0
942 6/4 Tabley (R) MDO 3m 8 G *chsd ldrs to 9th, last & blndrd 14th, p.u. 16th* P 0
1304 3/5 Weston Park (L) MDO 3m 8 G *mid-div to hlfwy, 3rd 5 out, lost tch nxt, p.u. 3 out* P 0

No signs of ability 0

MAES GWYN DREAMER b.g. 7 Dreams To Reality (USA) - Fairlina by Quality Fair — Ms M Teague

1996 P(0),P(0),F(-),P(0)

82 2/2 Wolverhampt' (L) MDN 3m 11 GS *chsd ldrs, 4th whn f 8th* F -

Yet to complete and a brief 97; no real signs yet. 0

MAEVE'S MAGIC (Irish) — I 440^{P}

MAGGIES FELLOW(IRE) ch.g. 8 Decent Fellow - Gentle Maggie by Tarqogan — John Eaton

1996 1(16)

521 15/3 Cothelstone (L) OPE 3m 8 GS *cls up to 13th, bhnd whn p.u. 16th* P 0

Maiden winner 96; very lightly raced (3 runs 94-97); more needed for Restricted. 16

MAGGIE TEE b.m. 9 Lepanto (GER) - Grey Receipt by Rugantino — R L Scorgie

1996 **P(NH)**

630 22/3 Kilworthy (L) RES 3m 16 G *ld & ran out 3rd, saddle slpd* r -
1483 11/5 Ottery St M' (L) RES 3m 15 G *mid-div til p.u. 14th* P 0
1597 31/5 Bratton Down (L) MDO 3m 12 F *sn rear of chsng grp, lost tch 12th, t.o. & p.u. aft 14th* P 0

Shown no ability under rules or in points as yet. 0

MAGICAL APPROACH (Irish) — I 50^{1}, I 108^{1}

MAGICAL MANOR ch.m. 8 St Columbus - True Manor by True Song — G B Tarry

374 2/3 Mollington (R) MDN 3m 14 G *last pair til u.r. 4th* U -
1082 13/4 Guilsborough (L) MDN 3m 14 GF *in tch to 12th, sn wknd, t.o. & p.u. 3 out* P 0
1165 20/4 Mollington (R) MDO 3m 9 GF *in tch in rear, effrt 11th, not rch ldrs, wknd apr 3 out* 5 0
1401 5/5 Ashorne (R) MDO 3m 15 G *chsd ldrs, outpcd 13th, 5th & btn whn f 15th* F -

Beaten 30 lengths plus when completing; good stable and should do better 12

MAGIC MOLE b.m. 5 Sulaafah (USA) - Kite's Nest by Nicholas Bill — Richard J Hill

657	22/3	Badbury Rin'	(L)	MEM	3m	4	F	*(Jt fav) prom, blnd 3 out, strng run nxt, ld flat*	1	11

Won weak Members on debut; much more needed for Restricted; firm so far. 12

MAGIC SONG b.m. 9 Cree Song - Magic Chat by Le Bavard (FR) — R W Swiers

1996 r(-),3(0),P(0)

357	2/3	Great Stain'	(L)	MDO	3m	15	S	*prom til wknd 14th, t.o. & p.u. 3 out*	P	0
510	15/3	Dalton Park	(R)	MDO	3m	14	GF	*rear, lost tch 11th, t.o. & p.u. 13th*	P	0

Well beaten when placed in 96; brief 97 and not worth a rating yet 0

MAGIKOOPA (Irish) — **I** 148[P], **I** 184[P], **I** 285[P]

MAGILLEN (Irish) — **I** 94[P], **I** 226[1]

MAGNOLIA MAN b.g. 11 Red Man - Roman Candy by Roman Candle — Mrs D B Lunt

1996 F(-),1(20),1(23),2(17),2(17),F(-),3(18),2(17),P(0),P(0)

98	8/2	Great Treth'	(R)	OPE	3m	14	GS	*prog 9th, ld apr 14th, hdd last, rallied wll, just faild*	2	25
239	22/2	Lemalla	(R)	OPE	3m	7	S	*hld up in tch, cls 3rd 17th, qcknd to ld apr last, sn clr*	1	23
455	8/3	Great Treth'	(R)	OPE	3m	8	S	*(fav) hld up, prog 12th, strng run frm 2 out, just faild*	2	23
953	6/4	Black Fores'	(R)	OPE	3m	2	G	*(fav) made all, v easily*	1	20
1088	16/4	Hockworthy	(L)	MEM	3m	6	GF	*(fav) hld up, prog 8th, ld 14th, clr aft 2 out, easily*	1	23
1256	27/4	Black Fores'	(R)	OPE	3m	4	F	*(fav) hld up, rpd prog 5 out, ld aft last, rdn out*	1	24
1489	12/5	Towcester	(R)	HC	3m 1f	6	GS	*held up, steady hdwy from 11th, ld apr 2 out, styd on strly.*	1	28
1591	31/5	Stratford	(L)	HC	3 1/2m	11	G	*soon struggling, t.o. when p.u. before 4 out.*	P	0

Improved & useful now; consistent; can win another H/chase; best with cut in the ground. 28

MAGNUM EXPRESS (Irish) — **I** 75[P], **I** 387[2]

MAGONEY (Irish) — **I** 436[P]

MAGSOOD ch.g. 12 Mill Reef (USA) - Shark Song by Song — Hugh Ellison

1996 **8(NH),2(NH),13(NH)**

304	1/3	Parham	(R)	LAD	3m	10	G	*alwys rear, wll bhnd whn p.u. 3 out*	P	0

Winning chaser; brief season in 97; best watched. 14

MAIDEN'S QUEST b.m. 5 Green Adventure (USA) - Melly May by Melodic Air — Mrs M R Daniell

368	2/3	Garnons	(L)	MDO	2 1/2m	13	GS	*prog to 2nd whn bad mstk 6th, p.u. aft 10th*	P	0
570	16/3	Garnons	(L)	MDN	2 1/2m	14	G	*alwys rear, lost tch & p.u. aft 10th*	P	0
1460	11/5	Maisemore P'	(L)	MDO	3m	16	G	*alwys rear, p.u. 11th*	P	0

Only learning so far. 0

MAID FOR DANCING (Irish) — **I** 30[F], **I** 63[1]

MAID O'TULLY (Irish) — **I** 126[3], **I** 179[3], **I** 360[2], **I** 370[F], **I** 432[P]

MAINSHEAR (Irish) — **I** 416[P]

MAISON ROUGE b.g. 6 K-Battery - Bowery Babe by Tantivy — J R Knight

473	9/3	Southwell P'	(L)	CON	3m	10	G	*in tch til f 9th*	F	-
774	29/3	Dingley	(R)	MDO	2m 5f	10	G	*nvr dang, 6th & rmndrs 8th, no respns, p.u. 4 out*	P	0

.. 0

MAJESTIC RIDE b.g. 13 Palm Track - Lakeland Lady by Leander — Rob Woods

1996 0(0),P(0),2(14),6(10),1(14),9(0),3(15)

673	23/3	Brocklesby '	(L)	CON	3m	8	GF	*hld up, prog 12th, cls up whn blnd & u.r. 15th*	U	-
835	31/3	Thorpe Lodge	(L)	INT	3m	7	F	*cls up 3rd/4th, chal 4 out, outpcd 2 out, hit last, wknd*	4	14
1190	20/4	Garthorpe	(R)	INT	3m	8	GF	*rear, prog & in tch 11th, 4th & outpcd 15th, kpt on*	4	13
1206	26/4	Clifton On '	(L)	OPE	3m	3	GS	*outpcd frm 4th*	3	13
1306	3/5	Cottenham	(R)	INT	3m	4	F	*mod 3rd til chsd ldr 14th,blnd 3 out,ld last,all out*	1	18
1474	11/5	Garthorpe	(R)	MEM	3m	6	GS	*hld up, jmpd slwly 7th, blnd 12th, mod 4th nxt, nvr on trms*	4	0
1570	26/5	Hereford	(R)	HC	3m 1f 110yds	14	G	*prom to 9th, bhnd when p.u. before 3 out.*	P	0
1608	1/6	Dingley	(R)	INT	3m	11	GF	*bhnd, 7th whn hit 8th, t.o. & mstk 11th, p.u. nxt*	P	0
1611	7/6	Umberleigh	(L)	OPE	3m	8	F	*alwys rear, lost tch 12th, t.o. & ref 2 out, cont*	6	0

Won weak Confined; quirky & stamina problems; not one to trust & need luck to score again. 13

MAJESTIC SPIRIT gr.g. 11 Majestic Maharaj - Runquest by Runnymede — Alan Raymond

1996 P(0),3(14),P(0),6(14),1(22),2(18),3(21)

454	8/3	Great Treth'	(R)	LAD	3m	7	S	*made most, blndrd bdly 12th, clr 14th, styd on strgly*	1	22
790	31/3	Bishopsleigh	(R)	LAD	3m	7	G	*ld to 5th, 2nd to 14th, wknd, p.u. 17th*	P	0

Able but inconsistent; needs easy courses; finished early 97 (ground?); can win again; needs cut. 23

MAJIC BELLE b.m. 9 Majestic Maharaj - Ankerdine Belle by Paddy Boy — D J B Denny

1996 P(0),P(0),3(13),5(0),P(0)

435	8/3	Upton-On-Se'	(R)	MDO	3m	14	G	*(bl) prom til wknd 11th, t.o. & p.u. 3 out*	P	0
587	19/3	Ludlow	(R)	HC	2 1/2m	18	GF	*(bl) f 2nd.*	F	-
664	23/3	Eaton Hall	(R)	MDO	3m	12	GF	*(bl) chsd ldrs to 12th, grad wknd*	6	0
1400	5/5	High Bickin'	(R)	MDO	3m	14	G	*b.d. bend apr 2nd*	B	-
1553	24/5	Mounsey Hil'	(R)	MDO	3m	11	G	*prom, ld 12th-15th, 2nd & btn whn swrvd & u.r. 17th*	U	-

Placed in bad race 96; ran passably last start but not worth a rating so far. 0

MAJOR ABOVE ALL (Irish) — I 43P, I 87P

MAJOR BERT(IRE) b.g. 9 Kemal (FR) - African Nelly by Pitpan — Richard Field

1996 3(0),2(0),**P(0)**,P(0)

262	22/2	Newtown	(L)	RES	3m	15	G	*mid-div, lost tch 12th, t.o. & p.u. nxt*	P	0
313	1/3	Clyst St Ma'	(L)	RES	3m	10	HY	*handy, 2nd to 4 out, wknd nxt*	4	0
1061	13/4	Maisemore P'	(L)	RES	3m	12	GF	*chsd ldrs 10th, 5th & chnce 3 out, onepcd*	5	15

Dual winner 95; very disappointing since & not threatening to win now. 13

MAJOR BILL (Irish) — I 42P, I 83, , I 189F, I 243P, I 324P

MAJOR BUGLER(IRE) b.g. 8 Thatching - Bugle Sound by Bustino — Michael Kerr-Dineen

1996 **15(NH),10(NH),6(NH),2(NH),7(NH)**

220	16/2	Heythrop	(R)	OPE	3m	20	G	*alwys last pair, t.o. & p.u. 12th*	P	0
292	1/3	Didmarton	(L)	MEM	3m	9	G	*in tch til outpcd 11th, tk poor 2nd apr 2 out*	2	11

Former useful hurdler; lost interest under rules and well beaten in Members; best watched. 12

MAJOR INQUIRY(USA) b.g. 11 The Minstrel (CAN) - Hire A Brain (USA) by Seattle Slew (USA) — N J Pewter

1996 9(0),2(13),7(0),5(0),P(0),7(0),**P(0)**

25	26/1	Marks Tey	(L)	CON	3m	5	GF	*alwys rear, lost tch 14th, t.o. & p.u. 3 out*	P	0
124	9/2	Cottenham	(R)	OPE	3m	9	GF	*sn rear, 7th & no ch whn u.r. 14th*	U	-
270	22/2	Ampton	(R)	MEM	3m	8	G	*trkd ldrs, 4th & btn whn p.u. 17th*	P	0
497	15/3	Ampton	(R)	CON	3m	9	GF	*chsd ldrs to 10th, wll bhnd frm 16th*	7	0
710	29/3	High Easter	(L)	OPE	3m	5	F	*last frm 4th, lsng tch whn p.u. 11th*	P	0
801	31/3	Marks Tey	(L)	CON	3m	8	F	*rear main grp, wknd frm 16th, t.o.*	5	0
1029	12/4	Horseheath	(R)	LAD	3m	3	HD	*last frm 4th, outpcd 13th, r.o. 3 out, retraced*	3	0
1280	27/4	Fakenham P-'	(L)	LAD	3m	6	G	*(bl) prom, ld 3-8th, wknd apr 15th*	3	11
1378	5/5	Northaw	(L)	LAD	3m	5	F	*(bl) in tch, last & outpcd 12th,clsd apr 3 out, wnt 3rd nr fin*	3	16
1434	10/5	Marks Tey	(L)	LAD	3m	3	G	*(bl) chsd wnr,ld 4th-11th,ld 14th,clr 4 out,hdd last,ran on flat*	2	14

Perked up late season; lost last 27 starts; ungenuine but capable of a surprise; blinkers. 15

MAJOR MAC b.g. 10 Mandalus - Ullard Lady by Official — D L Williams

151	12/2	Lingfield	(L)	HC	3m	13	HY	*t.o. when p.u. before 4 out.*	P	0
285	26/2	Taunton	(R)	HC	4 1/4m 110yds	16	GS	*chsd ldrs to 11th, lost tch 15th, t.o. when p.u. before 3 out.*	P	0
384	6/3	Towcester	(R)	HC	3m 1f	7	GS	*bhnd, effort 11th, wknd next, t.o..*	5	0
931	6/4	Charlton Ho'	(L)	OPE	3m	6	G	*in tch til wknd rpdly 13th, t.o. & p.u. 3 out*	P	0

Promise 95; missed 96; ambitiously campaigned & showed nothing in 97; best watched now. 13

MAJOR MAN(IRE) ch.g. 7 Le Moss - Carradyne Touch by Gleason (USA) — Miss C Wates

148	9/2	Tweseldown	(R)	XX	3m	12	GF	*ld, hit 2nd, u.r. 7th*	9	0
302	1/3	Parham	(R)	CON	3m	14	G	*trckd ldrs, mstk 5th, cls 3rd 4 out, wknd aft*	5	11
1129	19/4	Penshurst	(L)	RES	3m	6	GF	*(fav) rear, mstks, 4th final cct, nvr dang, p.u. last*	P	0

Irish Maiden winner 96; not disgraced in Confined; mistakes; should stick to Restricteds. 14

MAJOR NEAVE b.g. 10 Royal Vulcan - Park Springs by Brigadier Gerard — J D Jamieson

1996 3(15),1(17),P(0),**P(0)**

123	9/2	Cottenham	(R)	INT	3m	13	GF	*mstk 3rd, p.u. nxt, dsmntd*	P	0

Restricted winner 96; not completed since & vanished quickly in 97; can only be watched. 17

MAJOR SHARPE(IRE) b.g. 5 Phardante (FR) - Winsome Doe by Buckskin (FR) — Mrs Bridget Nicholls

527	15/3	Cothelstone	(L)	MDN	3m	14	GS	*hld up, steady prog 14th, slght ld last, ran on well*	1	15
1210	26/4	Woodford	(L)	RES	3m	14	G	*(fav) hld up rear, in tch whn f 8th*	F	-

Beat subsequent winner on debut; top stable and looks sure to progress. G-G/S so far. 18

MAJOR SPONSOR (Irish) — I 114[1]

MAKE A LINE b.g. 9 High Line - Another Packet by Main Reef — C H A Denny

266	22/2	Duncombe Pa'	(R)	RES	3m	19	G	*mid-div thruout, onepcd frm 3 out*	6	10
425	8/3	Charm Park	(L)	RES	3m	12	GF	*prom til outpcd frm 4 out*	6	0
616	22/3	Hutton Rudby	(L)	RES	3m	14	GF	*mid-div, outpcd 14th*	5	13
695	29/3	Stainton	(R)	RES	3m	11	F	*alwys rear, wll bhnd 16th, t.o. & p.u. 3 out*	P	0
1069	13/4	Whitwell-On'	(R)	RES	3m	12	G	*alwys prom, ld 11th til hdd & wknd 4 out*	7	0
1101	19/4	Hornby Cast'	(L)	RES	3m	14	G	*mid-div til slppd up bnd apr 8th*	S	-
1253	26/4	Easingwold	(L)	MEM	3m	7	GS	*alwys rear, 5th frm 14th, onepcd*	5	0

Ex Irish; looks woefully onepaced and well short of a win. 10

MAKE A MOVE (Irish) — I 31[F], I 98[2], I 188[2]

MAKE UP YOUR MIND (Irish) — I 184[P], I 268[P]

MAKIN' DOO(IRE) ch.g. 7 Black Minstrel - Ariannrun by Deep Run — R G Makin

1996 P(0),3(0)

14	25/1	Cottenham	(R)	MDO	3m	7	GF	*chsd ldng pair, jnd ldr 14th, ld apr last, styd on und pres*	1	15
131	9/2	Alnwick	(L)	RES	3m	13	G	*(fav) 7/2-2s, w.w. prog to ld 4 out, hdd last, rallied to ld fin*	1	0
414	8/3	Dalston	(R)	XX	3m	9	GS	*(fav) alwys going wll, trckd ldrs, ld apr 2 out, rdn out flat*	1	22
766	29/3	Whittington	(L)	INT	3m	10	S	*(fav) held up, 4l 5th & gng wll whn b.d. 14th*	B	-
1426	10/5	Aspatria	(L)	OPE	3m	9	G	*(fav) in tch, prog 12th, ev ch 14th-3 out, no ext und pres*	2	21

Useful & progressive youngster; stays and safe; go close in Nov H/chase 98; G/F-S. 24

MAKING THE CUT (Irish) — I 48[P]

MAKING TIME gr.m. 10 Furry Glen - Arctic Border by Arctic Slave — R Shepherd

1996 P(0),4(0),P(0),1(18),2(18),**3(19),5(0),P(0)**

371	2/3	Mollington	(R)	LAD	3m	9	G	*cls up, trckd ldr 15th, ld last, rdn out*	1	22
977	8/4	Heythrop	(R)	LAD	3m 5f	1	F	*walked over*	1	0
983	12/4	Ascot	(R)	HC	3m 110yds	14	GF	*held up, hdwy 10th, mstk 12th, soon wknd, p.u. before 3 out.*	P	0
1161	20/4	Mollington	(R)	LAD	3m	3	GF	*w.w. chsd wnr 13th, no imp aft 2 out*	2	19
1287	29/4	Huntingdon	(R)	HC	2 1/2m 110yds	14	G	*mstks, alwys bhnd, t.o. and p.u. before 13th.*	P	0
1535	18/5	Mollington	(R)	LAD	3m	6	GS	*trckd ldng pair, mstk 6th, outpcd & mstk 12th, sn t.o.*	3	12

Consistent in points; outclassed & mistakes in H/chases; likes fast ground; should find another win. ... 20

MAKS DREAM (Irish) — I 215, , I 345[4], I 541[P]

MALACHITE GREEN b.g. 7 Lochnager - Rhiannon by Welsh Pageant — B Kennedy

1996 2(17),2(18)

25	26/1	Marks Tey	(L)	CON	3m	5	GF	*trckd ldrs, blnd 11th, lost tch 15th, t.o.*	4	0
801	31/3	Marks Tey	(L)	CON	3m	8	F	*alwys prom, cls 2nd 4 out, outpcd nxt, styd on apr last*	3	18

Winning selling hurdler; lightly raced; beaten under 2 lengths last start; can find a small win. 17

MALENSKI(IRE) b.g. 7 Strong Statement (USA) - Hi Cal by Callernish — P J Millington

478	9/3	Southwell P'	(L)	MDO	3m	17	G	*chsd ldrs, hit 10th, went 2nd 13th, wknd 15th, p.u. 2 out*	P	0
777	29/3	Dingley	(R)	MDO	2m 5f	8	G	*cls up, 3rd frm 6 out, just outpcd apr last*	3	10
899	5/4	Wetherby Po'	(L)	MDO	3m	3	F	*(fav) ld/disp, ld 8th, 2l up whn ran out & u.r. 2 out, rmntd*	3	11
1083	13/4	Guilsborough	(L)	MDN	3m	15	GF	*rear, prog 13th, ev ch 15th, wknd aft 3 out*	5	10
1187	20/4	Garthorpe	(R)	MEM	3m	9	GF	*in tch, chsd ldr 12th-nxt, 4th & wkng 15th*	4	0
1357	4/5	Dingley	(R)	MDO	3m	5	G	*(fav) hld up, in tch, cls 3rd & gng wll whn f 3 out*	F	-
1479	11/5	Garthorpe	(R)	MDO	3m	12	GS	*w.w. prog to 3rd at 15th, no imp aft*	3	0
1541	18/5	Wolverhampt'	(L)	MDO	3m	15	GS	*hld up, prog 5 out, ran on, nrst fin*	2	11
1609	1/6	Dingley	(R)	MDO	3m	14	GF	*prom, chsd ldr 15th, ev ch aft 2 out, sn no ext, fin tired*	2	0

Unlucky in two awful races but overall form is weak; stamina doubts & more needed. 12

MALINGERER gr.m. 6 Petong - Crystal Gael by Sparkler — R Thomson

1996 r(-),F(-),P(0)

128	9/2	Cottenham	(R)	MDO	3m	10	GF	*pllng, prom to 11th, sn wknd, p.u. 14th*	P	0
605	22/3	Parham	(R)	MDO	3m	7	F	*alwys prom, pshd alng in 3rd frm 14th, btn 2 out*	3	0

Ungenuine on the Flat; last when completing(an achievement in itself); makes no appeal. 0

MALLOW INNOCENCE b.g. 7 Abutammam - Phyllis Jane by Lepanto (GER) — Mrs Lorraine Lamb

114	9/2	Wetherby Po'	(L)	MDO	3m	8	GF	*s.s. dtchd by 3rd, t.o. 10th, p.u. 14th*	P	0
210	16/2	Southwell P'	(L)	MDO	3m	15	GS	*cls up til apr 12th, grad lost plc, kpt on agn 2 out*	4	0
480	9/3	Southwell P'	(L)	MDO	3m	17	G	*in tch, wknd 12th, t.o. & p.u. 3 out*	P	0
777	29/3	Dingley	(R)	MDO	2m 5f	8	G	*2nd to 9th, 4th & outpcd 6 out, ran on strngly 3 out,ld last*	1	12
1068	13/4	Whitwell-On'	(R)	RES	3m	12	G	*mid-div, outpcd 10th, sn wll bhnd, p.u. 14th*	P	0
1263	27/4	Southwell P'	(L)	RES	3m	9	G	*mid-div, mstk 14th, strgglng 3 out*	4	12

Won slowly run short Maiden; does not stay 3 miles; so another win looks tough. 13

MAL'S CASTLE(IRE) ch.m. 8 Heraldiste (USA) - Listooder Girl by Wolverlife — S Clark

1996 P(0),F(-)

37	26/1	Alnwick	(L)	MDO	3m	15	G	*n.j.w. prom to 8th, wknd 10th, t.o. & p.u. 15th*	P	0
353	2/3	Great Stain'	(L)	CON	3m	9	S	*mid-div, mstk 3rd, bhnd 6th, t.o. & p.u. 11th*	P	0
429	8/3	Charm Park	(L)	MDO	3m	14	GF	*plld hrd, not fluent, alwys rear, lost tch 8th, p.u. 12th*	P	0

No signs of ability. 0

MALTBY SON b.g. 5 Infantry - Top Soprano by High Top — Mrs R Smith

839	31/3	Thorpe Lodge	(L)	MDO	3m	15	F	*cls up 3rd,chsd wnr 6 out,level 3 out-last,just outpcd,prom*	2	16

1209 26/4 Clifton On ' (L) MDO 3m 16 GS *(fav) 3rd frm 6th, mstk 4 out, ran on to chal 2 out, all out* 1 15

Beat large but moderate bunch; still young & can improve; needs to; F-G/S. 17

MALTESE CROSS (Irish) — I 54P, I 135P, I 447P, I 482⁴, I 520P

MALTHOUSE LAD b.g. 9 Ayyabaan - Flaming Sun by Tudor Flame A L Roberts

362 2/3 Garnons (L) OPE 3m 11 GS *in tch to 10th, wknd & p.u. aft 13th* P 0
406 8/3 Llanfrynach (R) RES 3m 13 G *mid-div, outpcd frm 14th* 5 0
639 22/3 Howick (L) MDN 3m 15 GF *10s-6s, mid-div, prog 14th, 2nd 3 out, not rch wnr* 2 0
717 29/3 Llanvapley (L) RES 3m 13 GF *cls up, ran out 5th* r -
1065 13/4 Maisemore P' (L) MDO 3m 13 GF *chsd ldrs, 3rd whn blnd 11th, sn rdn & wknd, p.u. last* P 0
1138 19/4 Bonvilston (R) MDO 3m 9 G *cls up, ld 14th til hdd flat* 2 12
1216 26/4 Woodford (L) MDN 3m 13 G *chsd ldrs, wknd 15th, t.o. & p.u. 3 out* P 0

Beaten 2 lengths on penultimate start (very short course); stamina gives out elsewhere; need luck.sm 12

MALT MAN (Irish) — I 28³

MALVERN CANTINA b.g. 9 Royal Vulcan - My Martina by My Swallow M J Hill

1996 P(0),P(0),F(-),F(-),1(14)

32 26/1 Alnwick (L) RES 3m 11 G *hld up, mid-div hlfwy, no prog whn blnd & u.r. 14th* U -
77 2/2 Market Rase' (L) RES 3m 9 GF *w.w., prog 7th, chsd wnr 3 out, hrd rdn nxt, no imp* 2 15
118 9/2 Wetherby Po' (L) RES 3m 14 GF *mid-div whn f 14th* F -
348 2/3 Market Rase' (L) RES 3m 13 GF *hld up wll bhnd, prog 11th, mstk 4 out, styd on, nvr nrr* 3 15
616 22/3 Hutton Rudby (L) RES 3m 14 GF *rear, strgglng 14th, t.o. whn p.u. last* P 0
695 29/3 Stainton (R) RES 3m 11 F *rear, blndrd 12th, wll bhnd whn p.u. 3 out, dismntd* P 0

Maiden winner 96; struggling now upgraded; mistakes & hard ride; weak Restricted only possible. 15

MAMNOON(USA) b.g. 6 Nijinsky (CAN) - Continual (USA) by Damascus (USA) Rob Woods

1996 **9(NH),5(NH),13(NH),P(NH)**

141 9/2 Thorpe Lodge (L) MDN 3m 12 GF *f 3rd* F -
347 2/3 Market Rase' (L) MDO 3m 9 GF *mid-div, prog 12th, rdn to ld 15th, styd on well 2 out* 1 14
548 16/3 Garthorpe (R) RES 3m 10 GF *hld up, nvr nr ldrs, no ch frm 13th* 7 0
1149 19/4 Chaddesley ' (L) RES 3m 6 GF *chsd ldrs, rdn 13th, strgglng frm 15th* 4 0
1477 11/5 Garthorpe (R) XX 3m 6 GS *in tch, ld 11-13th, wknd apr 15th, lft poor 3rd 2 out, tired* 3 0
1507 16/5 Stratford (L) HC 3m 10 G *bhnd, rdn after 10th, p.u. after next.* P 0
1605 1/6 Dingley (R) RES 3m 13 GF *cls up til wknd 14th, sn bhnd* 6 0
1613 7/6 Umberleigh (L) RES 3m 13 F *last & sn mls bhnd, jmpd slwly 5th, t.o. aft* 5 0

Ex selling hurdler; beat subsequent winner in short Maiden; does not stay and prospects are nil. 11

MANACURED (Irish) — I 274³, I 390², I 460¹

MANARD b.m. 6 Ardross - Sweet Mandy by Normandy Mrs J Woodward

1996 **10(NH)**

259 22/2 Newtown (L) MDN 3m 18 G *nvr nr ldrs, t.o. & p.u. 13th* P 0
365 2/3 Garnons (L) MDO 2 1/2m 14 GS *made most, drew clr 3 out, styd on well* 1 14
404 8/3 Llanfrynach (R) INT 3m 17 G *prom, 3rd at 15th, wknd rpdly & p.u. 2 out* P 0
1145 19/4 Chaddesley ' (L) MEM 3m 6 GF *chsd ldng pair, went 2nd 14th, no imp, wknd & lost 2nd flat* 3 14
1237 26/4 Brampton Br' (R) RES 3m 13 G *slppd bdly 1st, nvr rchd ldrs, p.u. 3 out* P 0

Won short Maiden (slow time); stamina suspect & much more needed. 13

MANCHA BOY (Irish) — I 99F

MANDINGO (Irish) — I 112P, I 180, , I 254⁴, I 331², I 468P

MANDOORA (Irish) — I 10P, I 83⁶, I 139F, I 189F, I 383P, I 538P

MANDRIL (Irish) — I 429³

MANDYS LAD ch.g. 8 Sula Bula - Sweet Mandy by Normandy S J Robinson

1996 P(0),1(15),F(-),5(0),P(0)

118 9/2 Wetherby Po' (L) RES 3m 14 GF *j.w. ld & sn wll clr, hdd & wknd rpdly 2 out* 4 13
356 2/3 Great Stain' (L) INT 3m 9 S *plld hrd, ld & sn clr, slw jmp 14th, sn hdd & wknd* 7 0
416 8/3 Dalston (R) RES 3m 12 GS *pllng, ld 5th til mstk 14th, blnd nxt, nt rcvr & p.u.* P 0

Maiden winner96; changed hands; headstrong front runner & another win looks tough. 13

MANDYS SPECIAL ch.m. 11 Roman Warrior - Petite Mandy by Mandamus R M Thorne

1996 P(0),P(0),F(-),2(0),U(-)

157 15/2 Lanark (R) RES 3m 11 G *bhnd by 8th, p.u. 13th* P 0
337 1/3 Corbridge (R) RES 3m 11 G *bhnd frm 6th, t.o. 12th* 8 0
415 8/3 Dalston (R) RES 3m 19 GS *chsd ldrs, 7th hlfwy, sn wknd, t.o.* 12 0
813 31/3 Tranwell (L) RES 3m 7 G *in tch 1st ctt, cls 5th 9th til outpcd & lost tch 12th* 5 0

Maiden winner 93; looks past it now. 0

MANDY STILL (Irish) — I 286, , I 344B

MANDY'S TREASURE (Irish) — I 41P

MANHATTAN JEWEL (Irish) — I 249P

MANHATTAN PRINCE (Irish) — **I** 27^{P}, **I** 113^{1}, **I** 129^{2}, **I** 252^{4}, **I** 555^{P}, **I** 605^{P}, **I** 613^{3}

MANKIND b.g. 6 Rakaposhi King - Mandarling by Mandalus — J A T de Giles

1996 **15(NH)**

299	1/3	Didmarton	(L)	MDN	3m	14	G	*prom, blnd 11th & wknd, p.u. 14th*	P 0
1099	19/4	Stratford	(L)	HC	2m 5f 110yds	14	G	*chsd ldrs, ld 4th to 9th, led 2 out, rdn out.*	1 22
1296	3/5	Hereford	(R)	HC	2m 3f	11	G	*in tch to 8th, soon bhnd, t.o. when p.u. before 3 out.*	P 0

66/1 shocker in weak H/chase; still plenty to prove and hard to place next season.Summer jumping. ... 24

MANLEY GIRL (Irish) — **I** 110,

MANLEY GIRL(IRE) b.f. 6 Mandalus - Arctic Express — J W Evans

1996 **18(NH)**

1240	26/4	Brampton Br'	(R)	MDO	3m	12	G	*rear frm 3rd, wknd 13th, p.u. 15th*	P 0

No signs yet but can do better. 0

MANNIX (Irish) — **I** 122^{F}, **I** 253^{P}, **I** 289^{P}, **I** 366^{P}, **I** 467^{F}

MAN OF HOPE (Irish) — **I** 171^{6}, **I** 242^{P}, **I** 512^{P}, **I** 563^{P}, **I** 571, , **I** 601,

MAN OF IRON (Irish) — **I** 366^{1}, **I** 439^{2}

MAN OF MOREEF b.g. 10 Miramar Reef - Coliemore by Coliseum — Mrs A R Wood

1996 3(13)

162	15/2	Lanark	(R)	MDO	3m	16	G	*alwys handy, ld 2 out, hdd & no ext flat*	2 15

Plenty of promise but only appears annually; win no problem if fit in 98. 15

MAN OF MYSTERY b.g. 11 Torus - Queen's Folly by King's Bench — D G Field

1996 **3(NH),3(NH)**

85	2/2	Wolverhampt'	(L)	LAD	3m	11	GS	*bhnd frm 8th, last & t.o. 11th, p.u. 3 out*	P 0
215	16/2	Southwell P'	(L)	LAD	3m	12	GS	*chsd clr ldr to 7th, grad wknd, p.u. 12th*	P 0
268	22/2	Duncombe Pa'	(R)	LAD	3m	5	G	*disp til ld 3rd,just ahd whn lft clr 4 out,hd last,onepcd*	3 21
426	8/3	Charm Park	(L)	LAD	3m	12	GF	*prom, ev ch 4 out, sn fdd*	6 17
546	16/3	Garthorpe	(R)	LAD	3m	11	GF	*ld to 2 out, onepcd aft*	3 17
773	29/3	Dingley	(R)	LAD	3m	11	G	*first pair, mstly ld to 11th, wknd rpdly 5 out, p.u. 2 out*	P 0
837	31/3	Thorpe Lodge	(L)	LAD	3m	5	F	*(fav) trckd ldr, qcknd 4 out, clr nxt, v easily*	1 19
925	6/4	Garthorpe	(R)	LAD	3m	7	GF	*ld to 11th, chsd wnr aft, unable to cls frm 15th*	2 18
1189	20/4	Garthorpe	(R)	LAD	3m	6	GF	*prom, ld 4th-15th, wknd nxt*	3 14
1266	27/4	Southwell P'	(L)	LAD	3m	5	G	*sttld in 3rd, chsd wnr 10th, wknd 4 out, p.u. nxt*	P 0
1476	11/5	Garthorpe	(R)	LAD	3m	5	GS	*chsd ldr til ld 3-13th, wknd rpdly, p.u. 3 out*	P 0

Winning chaser; modest Ladies pointer; best easy 3 miles; may find another weak event.G/F-G/S. 16

MAN OF STEELE (Irish) — **I** 332^{1}

MAN OF WISLEY(IRE) b.g. 7 Mandalus - Sabura by Busted — Mrs J R Buckley

208	16/2	Southwell P'	(L)	MDO	3m	9	GS	*rcd freely,ld aft 1st, sn clr, mstks 7 & 10th, hdd 12th,wknd*	3 0
346	2/3	Market Rase'	(L)	MDO	3m	10	GF	*blnd 1st, hvly rstrnd in rear, p.u. 4th*	P 0

Very headstrong & no prospects as a pointer 0

MANOR'S MAID ch.m. 5 St Columbus - Blazing Manor by True Song — M R Keith

451	8/3	Newton Brom'	(R)	MDN	3m	8	G	*last til b.d. 6th*	B -
1165	20/4	Mollington	(R)	MDO	3m	9	GF	*alwys bhnd, t.o. 13th, p.u. 15th*	P 0

Only learning so far. 0

MANVER (Irish) — **I** 58^{U}, **I** 84^{5}, **I** 184^{1}

MAN WITH A PLAN VI (Irish) — **I** 164^{2}, **I** 224^{2}, **I** 357^{P}

MAPALAK ch.m. 7 Buckley - Sound Run by Deep Run — A Dawson

1996 r(-),P(0),F(-),P(0),3(10),6(0),F(-),F(-),P(0),2(13)

36	26/1	Alnwick	(L)	MDO	3m	15	G	*chsd ldrs til grad wknd frm 14th*	4 0

Disappointing & finished early in 97; not easy to find a win. 12

MARA ASKARI b.g. 9 Night Shift (USA) - Madam Cody by Hot Spark — Mrs J Knapp

1996 P(0),U(-),P(0)

70	2/2	Higham	(L)	OPE	3m	5	GF	*(vis) ld 2nd-7th, wknd rpdly 12th, blnd 15th & p.u.*	P 0
195	15/2	Higham	(L)	LAD	3m	14	G	*(vis) rear, not pace ldrs, wll bhnd whn p.u. 15th*	P 0
577	16/3	Detling	(L)	CON	3m	18	F	*(vis) alwys rear, losng tch whn p.u. 14th*	P 0

Winning hurdler; shows no aptitude for pointing. 0

MARBLE CITY (Irish) — **I** 190^{2}, **I** 274^{2}

MARCH GATE b.g. 7 Lancastrian - March Fly by Sousa — Mrs M D W Wilson

88	2/2	Wolverhampt'	(L)	MDO	3m	13	GS	*rear, prog 9th, ld aft 13th, clr 2 out, ran on well*	1 15

877 1/4 Upton-On-Se' (R) RES 3m 17 GF *(fav) alwys rear, no ch frm 9th, wll bhnd whn p.u. 13th* P 0

Romped home in poor race; flopped next time; best watched. 15

MARDON (Irish) — I 48[1]

MARGINAL MARGIE b.m. 10 Majestic Maharaj - Vulrory's Lass by Saucy Kit — Mrs A Phipps

41 1/2 Larkhill (R) MDO 3m 13 GF *bhnd, kpt on frm 13th, no ch whn lft 2nd last, styd on* 2 11
261 22/2 Newtown (L) MDN 3m 16 G *bmpd & f 2nd* F -
653 22/3 Siddington (L) RES 3m 10 F *jmpd slwly 1st, schoold in rear, nvr dang* 5 0
1479 11/5 Garthorpe (R) MDO 3m 12 GS *rear, prog to chs ldr 12th,ev ch & outjmpd 3 out, onepcd aft* 2 12

Beaten by very good horse last start; possibly flattered but loooks good to score in 98. 15

MARIANS OWN (Irish) — I 263[3], I 383[B], I 558[U]

MARIES CALL (Irish) — I 33[3], I 120[F], I 227[2], I 310[4], I 458[1]

MARINERS MAID b.m. 10 Julio Mariner - Copamour by Bold As Brass — J Hart

1996 4(0)

485 9/3 Tweseldown (R) MDO 3m 11 G *prssd ldr 4-10th, wknd rpdly 13th, p.u. 15th* P 0

Very lightly raced; would have chance in her Members if fit in 98.bers if fit 97 0

MARINERS QUEST (Irish) — I 56[U], I 98[P], I 187[P], I 339,

MARINO ROSE (Irish) — I 125[U], I 312[F]

MARION'S OWN(IRE) ch.g. 7 Duky - Estrella by Virginia Boy — Mrs M B Keighley

103 8/2 Great Treth' (R) MDO 3m 9 GS *(fav) chsng grp, disp 16th til lft clr 2 out, all out* 1 15
300 1/3 Didmarton (L) RES 3m 23 G *(fav) prog to jn ldrs 13th,not qckn 15th,lft 2nd & hmpd last,no ex* 2 17
648 22/3 Castle Of C' (R) RES 3m 8 G *jnd ldrs 9th, ld 15th, hrd rdn apr last, hng lft, all out* 1 18
930 6/4 Charlton Ho' (L) INT 3m 8 G *hld up, prog 10th, rdn 15th, chsd wnr 2 out, not qckn last* 2 21
1156 20/4 Stafford Cr' (R) INT 3m 6 GF *(fav) (bl) hld up, prog 10th, went 2nd 4 out, chal last, ran on,ld flat* 1 20
1518 17/5 Bratton Down (L) XX 3m 7 GS *(vis) hld up, prog to 4th at 14th, p.u. nxt, lame* P 0

Proving expensive but top stable & should make amends early in 96 20

MARKED CARD b.g. 9 Busted - Winter Queen by Welsh Pageant — Mrs M A Kendall

1996 **12(NH),4(NH),8(NH),6(NH),P(NH)**

136 9/2 Alnwick (L) MDO 3m 16 G *tubed, bhnd frm 6th, no dang aft* 7 0
342 1/3 Corbridge (R) MDO 3m 12 G *rear, plenty to do 4 out, rdp prog 2 out, ld flat, hld on wl* 1 13
410 8/3 Dalston (R) MEM 3m 5 GS *ld 6-9th, chsd ldr, ld aft 3 out, ran on well flat* 1 17
563 16/3 Lanark (R) RES 3m 8 GS *last 11th, nvr near ldrs* 4 11
766 29/3 Whittington (L) INT 3m 10 S *6l 3rd whn u.r. 7th* U -
947 6/4 Friars Haugh (L) RES 3m 6 GF *strgglng in rear frm 12th* 5 0
1424 10/5 Aspatria (L) RES 3m 17 G *chsd ldrs, outpcd frm 13th, no imp frm 16th* 4 12

Ex N/H; has problems & inconsistent; both wins R/H; weak Restrictsd possible. 16

MARKED WELL (Irish) — I 222[P]

MARKHAM LAD b.g. 7 Revolutionary (USA) - Markham Lady by Athens Wood — David Pritchard

429 8/3 Charm Park (L) MDO 3m 14 GF *virt ref to race, stt 2 fences bhnd, alwys t.o. & p.u. 8th* P 0
506 15/3 Dalton Park (R) CON 3m 16 GF *rear whn u.r. 3rd* U -
677 23/3 Brocklesby ' (L) MDN 3m 8 GF *rear of main grp, clsd 8th, wknd & mstk 12th, u.r. nxt* U -
859 31/3 Charm Park (L) MDO 3m 4 F *in tch to 10th, outpcd 12th, t.o. aft* 3 0
1252 26/4 Easingwold (L) MDO 3m 9 GS *ref 2nd* R -
1348 3/5 Gisburn (R) RES 3m 10 GF *alwys rear, t.o. 5th, p.u. 9th* P 0

Last & beaten miles when completing; signs not good. 0

MARMALADE ch.g. 8 Oats - Le Tequila by Lear Jet — M H D Barlow

1209 26/4 Clifton On ' (L) MDO 3m 16 GS *alwys last trio, p.u. 5 out* P 0
1452 10/5 Kingston Bl' (L) MDO 3m 9 G *alwys prom, 5l 2nd at 9th, lost plc nxt, onepcd frm 15th* 2 0
1568 25/5 Kingston Bl' (L) MDO 3m 11 GF *in tch, lft 2nd 13th, no imp on wnr, dmtd & onepcd frm 15th* 3 0

Beat 5 others on last start; reasonable start but needs a little more. 13

MARTHA'S BOY(IRE) b.g. 6 Supreme Leader - Madame Martha by Carlingford Castle — D C Robinson

284 23/2 Charing (L) MDO 3m 17 G *prom, ld 11th, drawing clr whn f 14th* F -
582 16/3 Detling (L) MDN 3m 16 F *(fav) prom whn blndrd & u.r. 7th* U -

Ex Irish; looked unlucky 1st outing; should have no problem scoring when jumping is sorted out. 15

MARTIN DE PORRES (Irish) — I 36[P], I 59[P], I 101[4], I 122[P]

MARTIN'S FRIEND br.g. 14 Noble Imp - Indian Madness by Indian Ruler — Mrs L Bloomfield

1996 **F(NH)**

528 15/3 Wadebridge (L) CON 3m 5 GF *prom til mstk 12th (ditch), wknd rpdly, p.u. nxt* P 0

Looks finished now. 0

MARTIYA b.m. 9 Martinmas - Tia Song by Acrania — R Williams

1996 P(0),3(0)

1318	3/5	Bonvilston	(R)	MEM	3m	9	G	*rear til p.u. 12th*	P 0

Of no account. 0

MARY HAND (Irish) — I 385^{5}, I 493^{F}, I 501^{2}, I 576^{5}, I 606^{P}

MARY MARRY ME (Irish) — I 79^{P}, I 322^{P}

MARYS DELIGHT (Irish) — I 90^{P}, I 188^{P}

MARYS FRIEND (Irish) — I 6^{F}, I 73, , I 167^{P}, I 234^{5}, I 304^{F}, I 384^{6}, I 519^{6}, I 561^{P}

MARYS TWIN (Irish) — I 317^{P}, I 538^{5}

MASK RIVER (Irish) — I 202^{4}, I 231^{3}, I 280^{2}, I 296^{5}, I 397^{3}

MASTER BRACKEN ch.g. 8 Grey Desire - Maha by Northfields (USA) — P Newth

880	1/4	Upton-On-Se'	(R)	CON	3m	6	GF	*hld up, lost tch 11th, wknd, walked in*	5 0

Won bumper 94 (1m5f); no show on point debut; unpromising. 12

MASTER BUCKLEY b.g. 7 Buckley - Ivy Hill by Cantab — Mrs V M Robinson

1996 P(0),P(0)

526	15/3	Cothelstone	(L)	MDN	3m	15	GS	*mid-div, no ch frm 13th*	5 0
1095	16/4	Hockworthy	(L)	MDN	3m	11	GF	*chsd ldrs, 5th at 8th, lost plc & p.u. nxt*	P 0
1260	27/4	Black Fores'	(R)	MDO	3m	12	F	*nvr dang, fin 5th*	0 0
1486	11/5	Ottery St M'	(L)	MDO	3m	17	G	*(bl) f 1st*	F -
1554	24/5	Mounsey Hil'	(R)	MDO	3m	14	G	*chsd clr ldrs, 2nd & hrd rdn 2 out, ev ch last, no ext flat*	2 13

Just beaten in weak race; looking suspect now & needs more to win. 12

MASTER CORNET ch.g. 12 Celtic Cone - Yogurt by Saint Denys — W A Bethell

265	22/2	Duncombe Pa'	(R)	CON	3m	15	G	*ld til disp 10th, hdd 4 out, steadd fdd*	6 16
505	15/3	Dalton Park	(R)	MEM	3m	6	GF	*(fav) trckd ldr, ld 9th, blnd nxt, hdd last, kpt on*	2 11
1072	13/4	Whitwell-On'	(R)	MXO	4m	21	G	*prom til fdd 14th, t.o. & p.u. 19th*	P 0

Winning chaser 92; placed in weak Members; that looks his only hope now. 13

MASTER CROZINA br.g. 9 Uncle Pokey - Miss Crozina by Crozier — J Cornforth

1996 F(-),1(14),5(14),P(0),**P(0)**

381	4/3	Leicester	(R)	HC	2m 1f	13	G	*mstk 3rd, alwys in rear, bhnd when p.u. before 2 out.*	P 0
584	17/3	Newcastle	(L)	HC	2 1/2m	11	GF	*in tch till wknd before 4 out, t.o..*	5 0
694	29/3	Stainton	(R)	CON	3m	11	F	*prom til ld 6th, hdd 15th, fdd frm 3 out*	4 18
995	12/4	Tranwell	(L)	RES	3m	6	F	*j.w., ld/disp 5-8th, 1l up 9-14th, drew clr frm 2 out*	1 17
1247	26/4	Easingwold	(L)	CON	3m	9	GS	*disp, ld 9th-nxt, disp 11-14th, hdd no ext*	3 17

Improved; consistent in points; needs easy 3 miles; should find a Confined; F-G/S.18 17

MASTER CRUSADER b.g. 11 Mandalus - Abi's Dream by Paddy's Stream — The Laugh A Minute Racing Club

1293	30/4	Cheltenham	(L)	HC	2m 110yds	5	GF	*held up last, gd prog to press wnr 3 out, ev ch next, rallied and edged left run-in, styd on.*	2 19

Placed in weak H/chase; won Novice chase since & future is there. 21

MASTER DANCER b.g. 10 Mashhor Dancer (USA) - Silent Dancer by Quiet Fling (USA) — Mrs D J Dyson

1996 P(0),P(0),P(0),P(0)

432	8/3	Upton-On-Se'	(R)	MXO	3m	7	G	*chsd ldr, cls 2nd 10th, not qckn frm 14th, kpt on*	3 18
1017	12/4	Bitterley	(L)	LAD	3m	4	GF	*ld to 3rd, cls up til outpcd 14th, walked in*	3 0
1403	5/5	Ashorne	(R)	CON	3m	14	G	*chsd ldrs, 5th & in tch 15th, onepcd aft*	4 17
1523	17/5	Bredwardine	(R)	CON	3m	7	G	*ld to 4th & 6th-12th, wknd 15th*	4 11

Confined winner 95; revived in 97 but another win looks hard; stays. 16

MASTER DECOY b.g. 6 Green Ruby (USA) - Decoyanne by Decoy Boy — M K J Reed

554	16/3	Ottery St M'	(L)	CON	3m	7	G	*mid-div whn f 4th*	F -
861	31/3	Kingston St'	(R)	MEM	3m	2	F	*trckd wnr, eft 3 out, ev ch last not qckn*	2 10
1088	16/4	Hockworthy	(L)	MEM	3m	6	GF	*cls up til f 7th*	F -
1246	26/4	Bratton Down	(L)	MDO	3m	16	GS	*ld/disp til 12th, ev ch whn f 2 out*	F -
1486	11/5	Ottery St M'	(L)	MDO	3m	17	G	*(Co fav) alwys mid-div, nvr on trms, p.u. 3 out*	P 0
1553	24/5	Mounsey Hil'	(R)	MDO	3m	11	G	*trckd ldrs,disp 13th,ld 15th,fence clr whn f last,rmtd in ld*	1 15

Remarkable win; one clear round in six attempts; has scope & can upgrade when jumping better. 16

MASTER DEMPSEY (Irish) — I 397^{P}, I 579^{P}

MASTER DONNINGTON br.g. 9 Julio Mariner - Lor Darnie by Dumbarnie — M S Wilesmith

1996 7(10),4(0),5(15),2(14)

255	22/2	Newtown	(L)	CON	3m	14	G	*prom to 11th, wknd 13th, p.u. 3 out*	P 0
293	1/3	Didmarton	(L)	INT	3m	16	G	*made most to 9th, prom til wknd 3 out, fin tired*	4 0
589	20/3	Wincanton	(R)	HC	2m 5f	9	GF	*in tch till wknd 13th.*	5 15

1064 13/4 Maisemore P' (L) CON 3m 13 GF *chsd ldrs, 5th whn hit 14th, no dang aft* 5 12

Dual winner 95; disappointing 96/97 & not threatening to win now; best watched. 16

MASTER ERYL b.g. 14 Anax - Blackberry Hill by Sovereign Path Mrs Roger Guilding

1996 **F(NH)**

187 15/2 Erw Lon (L) OPE 3m 16 G *chsd ldrs, outpcd 13th, went poor 3rd 2 out, wknd* 4 12
256 22/2 Newtown (L) OPE 3m 17 G *rear, mstks 7 & 8th, t.o. & p.u. 11th* P 0
431 8/3 Upton-On-Se' (R) CON 3m 9 G *ld to 2nd, cls 4th at 11th, outpcd 13th, dist 4th & u.r.2out* U -
879 1/4 Upton-On-Se' (R) MXO 3m 4 GF *ld to 8th, effrt to cs wnr & mstk 3 out, wknd, walked in* 4 0

H/Chase winner 93; looks finished now. 12

MASTER FINBAR (Irish) — I 23[P], I 28, , I 64, , I 182[P], I 265[6], I 343[F], I 459[P]
MASTER JAKE (Irish) — I 11[P], I 74[5], I 87[5], I 601[F]
MASTER JULIAN (Irish) — I 56[3], I 281[1]
MASTER KEMAL (Irish) — I 44[5], I 88[6]

MASTER KIT(IRE) b.g. 8 Lancastrian - Katie Proverb by Proverb J N R Billinge

1996 U(-),1(20),1(21),S(-),F(-),1(24),1(25),**1(28)**

152 12/2 Musselburgh (R) HC 3m 8 GS *(fav) keen, ld 7th till after 14th, chsd 1st 2 after, mstk 3 out, rdn after next, no impn when f last.* F 21
226 21/2 Haydock (L) HC 3m 11 G *str hold, chsd ldrs from 5th, 6th and struggling when u.r. 4 out.* U -
1201 24/4 Perth (R) HC 3m 14 G *held up early, gd hdwy to ld 6th, mstk 11th (water), hdd 13th, wknd quickly, t.o., virtually p.u. run-in.* 8 0
1499 15/5 Perth (R) HC 2 1/2m 110yds 8 GS *cl up on outside till wknd before 2 out.* 3 20
1546 24/5 Hexham (L) HC 2 1/2m 110yds 10 GF *nvr far away, left 2nd 3 out, ld next, hdd before last, soon outpcd.* 3 19

Bubble burst in 97; ran better last start(jockey change); needs confidence restoring; win points 98. 21

MASTER LAUGHTER b.g. 6 Sulaafah (USA) - Miss Comedy by Comedy Star (USA) J Scott

557 16/3 Ottery St M' (L) RES 3m 9 G *schoold mid-div til p.u. 12th* P 0
1261 27/4 Black Fores' (R) MDO 3m 12 F *bhnd frm 3rd, p.u. aft 10th* P 0
1486 11/5 Ottery St M' (L) MDO 3m 17 G *alwys mid-div, bhnd whn p.u. 3 out* P 0
1553 24/5 Mounsey Hil' (R) MDO 3m 11 G *bhnd frm 6th, lost tch 11th, p.u. 14th* P 0

Hasn't raised a laugh yet. 0

MASTER MATHEW ch.g. 10 Claude Monet (USA) - Kettisha by Wolver Hollow Mrs S Walby

729 29/3 Alnwick (L) RES 3m 10 F *ld/disp til 3rd frm 13th, kpt on wll frm 3 out* 3 17
1424 10/5 Aspatria (L) RES 3m 17 G *mstk 7th, prssd wnr to 12th, wknd 14th* 9 0

Dual winner 92; novice chasing since; has ability but a frustrating sort; may surprise. 16

MASTER MUFFLER b.g. 5 Seymour Hicks (FR) - Miss Mufsi by One Day Soon David A Smith

853 31/3 Eyton-On-Se' (L) MDO 3m 13 GF *mid-div hlfwy, t.o. whn p.u. 4 out* P 0

Only learning on debut. 0

MATCHLESSLY b.g. 14 Royal Match - Mayfield Girl by Le Prince Mrs R E Walker

1996 6(0),5(0),5(0),P(0),7(0),5(0),3(10)

221 16/2 Heythrop (R) RES 3m 15 G *ld to 4th, cls up aft til fdd frm 15th* 4 12
436 8/3 Upton-On-Se' (R) MDO 3m 17 G *prom, cls 4th at 12th, outpcd frm 14th* 4 0
821 31/3 Paxford (L) MDO 3m 6 F *ld to 2nd, chsd ldrs, onepcd frm 15th* 3 0

A non-staying veteran maiden & will remain so. 10

MATCHMAKER SEAMUS (Irish) — I 23[P], I 87[2]

MATRACE ch.m. 12 Mummy's Game - Sospirae by Sandford Lad K Little

1996 4(10)

561 16/3 Lanark (R) LAD 3m 7 GS *3rd 10th, sn wknd, p.u. 13th* P 0
1046 13/4 Lockerbie (R) MEM 3m 4 F *cls 2nd frm 14th, no ext flat* 2 12

Maiden winner; lightly raced & Members only hope. 10

MATT REID ch.g. 13 Abednego - Abbey Lodge by Master Owen W G N Morgan

1996 **9(NH),8(NH),3(NH)**

67 1/2 Wetherby (L) HC 3m 1f 10 G *in tch, trckd ldr from 10th, ev ch 4 out, fd.* 3 24
387 7/3 Market Rasen (R) HC 3m 1f 5 G *bhnd, effort after 12th, outpcd before 4 out, no dngr after.* 3 21
890 4/4 Aintree (L) HC 2 3/4m 14 G *(bl) f 1st.* F -

Winning chaser; out & out stayer; well beaten in H/chases & unlikely to win again. 20

MATURE APRIL b.m. 6 Daring March - Mature by Welsh Pageant Stuart Wilson

357 2/3 Great Stain' (L) MDO 3m 15 S *alwys rear, t.o. & p.u. 4 out* P 0
620 22/3 Hutton Rudby (L) MDO 3m 10 GF *rear, rddn 7th, outpcd 11th, t.o.* 3 0

Well beaten when completing; young but much more needed. 0

MAURAS GIRL (Irish) — **I** 97F

MAXINE'S FOUNTAIN (Irish) — **I** 141³, **I** 203³, **I** 302², **I** 379¹, **I** 537²

MAX LAD (Irish) — **I** 43F, **I** 81⁵, **I** 94³, **I** 153²

MAYDAY MIRACLE b.m. 11 Superlative - Mayday Melody by Highland Melody — R Lush

194	15/2 Higham	(L) OPE 3m	12 G	*in rear til p.u. aft 11th*	P	0
319	1/3 Marks Tey	(L) CON 3m	11 G	*pllng, ld 3rd-7th, wknng & blndrd 10th, p.u. 13th*	P	0

Flat winner 88; no prospects in points. 0

MAYFAIR MAIDEN b.m. 10 Fairy King (USA) - De Narde by Auction Ring (USA) — F V Higgins

278	23/2 Charing	(L) RES 3m	17 G	*s.s. schoold in last & t.o. til p.u. 13th*	P	0
581	16/3 Detling	(L) MDO 3m	12 F	*prom, ld 11-15th, wknng whn f nxt*	F	-

Some promise but more stamina needed. 10

MAYPOLE FOUNTAIN (Irish) — **I** 13P, **I** 49⁴, **I** 134P

MAY RUN b.f. 11 Cruise Missile - Trial Run by Deep Run — W R Middleton

1996 4(13),1(13),P(0)

411	8/3 Dalston	(R) CON 3m	16 GS	*made most to 11th, wknd 14th, t.o. & p.u. aft 3 out*	P	0
809	31/3 Tranwell	(L) MEM 3m	5 G	*(fav) alwys prom,mainly 3l 2nd 9-14th,qcknd to ld 2 out,6l up last*	1	14

Completed Members double 95/96; outclassed in competitive races. 13

MAYTOWN ch.g. 11 Town And Country - Mayotte by Little Buskins — A J Thomas

1996 P(0),U(-),3(0),3(0),U(-)

639	22/3 Howick	(L) MDN 3m	15 GF	*alwys rear, p.u. 13th*	P	0
718	29/3 Llanvapley	(L) RES 3m	13 GF	*mid-div, f 9th*	F	-
907	5/4 Howick	(L) MDN 3m	4 F	*cls up,ld 13th-nxt,ld 3 out,clr whn u.r. apr last,sddl slppd*	U	11

A long standing maiden & robbed of his moment of glory in dire race; need same again to win. 11

MAZIES CHOICE b.m. 6 Morgans Choice - Amazement by Chinese Lacquer — D E Tucker

245	22/2 Lemalla	(R) MDO 3m	11 S	*unruly start, rear, blnd 10th, t.o. & p.u. 13th*	P	0
314	1/3 Clyst St Ma'	(L) MDN 3m	11 HY	*mid-div, blnd & u.r. 7th*	U	-
458	8/3 Great Treth'	(R) MDO 3m	15 S	*not fluent, rear frm 10th, t.o. p.u. apr 15th*	P	0
789	31/3 Bishopsleigh	(R) MEM 3m	5 G	*in tch to 14th, outpcd aft, no ch 4 out*	3	0
1261	27/4 Black Fores'	(R) MDO 3m	12 F	*alwys rear, nvr dang*	7	0

Beaten a long way in her Members; no where near a rating yet. 0

MAZZARD(IRE) b or br.g. 6 Gildoran - Cherry Morello by Bargello — Mrs L Treloggen

297	1/3 Didmarton	(L) MDN 3m	11 G	*prom, lft 2nd 9th, no imp whn mstk 3 out, lft 2nd agn flat*	2	10
526	15/3 Cothelstone	(L) MDN 3m	15 GS	*ld 6th-9th, ld 13th-17th, sn outpcd*	2	13
1314	3/5 Holnicote	(L) MDO 3m	8 G	*(fav) rear, prog 12th, rdn last, ld nr fin*	1	14

Won weak race but a satisfactory debut season; can improve; needs to for Restricteds. 15

MCAULEY JO (Irish) — **I** 70P

MCCARTNEY b.g. 11 Tug Of War - Red Cross by Pitpan — Miss S Goodhand

1996 P(0),5(0),5(10),F(-),**6(0)**,2(16),**3(20)**

76	2/2 Market Rase'	(L) XX 3m	12 GF	*chsd ldrs to 11th, sn stugg*	7	11
214	16/2 Southwell P'	(L) CON 3m	10 GS	*alwys rear, last frm 10th, p.u. 13th*	P	0
1530	18/5 Fakenham	(L) HC 2m 5f 110yds	11 G	*mid-divison, hdwy and hit 11th, wknd apr 4 out.*	7	0

Restricted winner 95; interrupted 97 & below par; Confined chances if fit in 98. 17

MCCLATCHEY (Irish) — **I** 67⁵, **I** 124P

MCFEPEND (Irish) — **I** 41⁶, **I** 320¹, **I** 420², **I** 477¹, **I** 535P

MCILHATTON (Irish) — **I** 57²

MCMAHON'S RIVER ch.m. 10 Over The River (FR) - Kanndaya (FR) by Venture Vii — J V C Davenport

1996 P(0),**P(0)**,3(13),3(16),1(19),P(0)

360	2/3 Garnons	(L) CON 3m	10 GS	*prom til wknd 11th, t.o. 15th, p.u. nxt*	P	0
705	29/3 Upper Sapey	(R) CON 3m	4 GF	*8l 3rd 14th, efft apr 3 out, lft clr last*	1	17

Won poor Open 96 (4 miles); lightly raced 97; ground wrong; best soft; hard to place in 98. 18

MCNAY b.g. 10 Montreal Boy - Zo-Zo by Hamood — Christopher Graham

1996 4(0)

31	26/1 Alnwick	(L) MEM 3m	4 G	*alwys last, lost tch 10th, abt 12l 3rd whn f 15th*	F	-
613	22/3 Friars Haugh	(L) MDN 3m	12 GF	*cls up til wknd 12th*	7	0
948	6/4 Friars Haugh	(L) MDO 3m	7 GF	*ld, mstk 11th, hdd nxt, rmnd cls up, outpcd frm 2 out*	2	13

Busier than normal in 97; last start shows that a small win is possible. **14**

MEADOW COTTAGE ch.g. 11 Callernish - Miss Madam by Black Tarquin — N F Williams

1996 F(-),1(14),2(14),2(18),S(-)

126	9/2	Cottenham	(R)	RES	3m	14	GF	*chsng grp, mstk 6th, no prog 13th, onepcd*	4	0
260	22/2	Newtown	(L)	RES	3m	16	G	*prom, ld 9-13th, onepcd frm 3 out*	3	17
433	8/3	Upton-On-Se'	(R)	RES	3m	18	G	*cls up 10th, ev ch whn hit 13th, wknd 15th, p.u. last*	P	0
1526	17/5	Bredwardine	(R)	RES	3m	13	G	*mid-div, u.r. 4th*	U	-
1605	1/6	Dingley	(R)	RES	3m	13	GF	*w.w. prog to ld & pckd 14th, hdd apr 2 out, onepcd*	3	12
1613	7/6	Umberleigh	(L)	RES	3m	13	F	*ld to 2nd, prom in chsng grp, chsd wnr 13th, nvr any imp*	2	0

Maiden winner 96; stays but onepaced; hard to win with but should find weak Restricted; F-G/S. **17**

MEANDYOU (Irish) — **I** 517[P], **I** 559[P]

MECADO b.g. 10 Ballacashtal (CAN) - Parma Nova by Dominion — Mrs D Yardley

493	12/3	Newton Abbot	(L)	HC	2m 5f 110yds	11	HY	*(vis) held up, hdwy 8th, wknd 6 out, t.o. when ref 2 out.*	R	-
1064	13/4	Maisemore P'	(L)	CON	3m	13	GF	*(vis) rear & jmpd slwly 7th, wll bhnd & p.u. 14th*	P	0
1266	27/4	Southwell P'	(L)	LAD	3m	5	G	*(vis) rear, mstk 3rd, rdn 10th, wknd 14th, t.o.*	4	12

Selling hurdle winner; unpromising pointer; has returned to hurdling. **13**

MEDIANE(USA) b.g. 12 Dust Commander (USA) - Mlle Quille (USA) by On-And-On — Miss Annabel Wilson

91	6/2	Huntingdon	(R)	HC	3m	10	G	*prom when mstk 8th, soon wknd, t.o. after 12th, p.u. after 5 out.*	P	0
227	21/2	Kempton	(R)	HC	3m	6	G	*reluctant to line up, chsd ldrs 6th, chal 10th to 14th, outpcd after 4 out, styd on again to take 2nd run-in.*	2	22
290	28/2	Newbury	(L)	HC	3m	6	GS	*(vis) unruly start, ref to race.*	0	0
385	6/3	Wincanton	(R)	HC	3m 1f 110yds	6	G	*(vis) ref to race.*	0	0
393	8/3	Barbury Cas'	(L)	OPE	3m	7	G	*s.s. sn rcvrd, ld 4th, clr whn f nxt*	F	-
514	15/3	Larkhill	(R)	MXO	3m	6	GF	*trckd ldrs, prssd wnr 2 out, ev ch til not qckn flat*	2	21

Winning hurdler; obvious ability but very temperamental; could win but best avoided. **20**

MEDIAS MAID b.m. 7 Mas Media - Silleys Maid by Continuation — R T Grant

1996 F(-),2(10),F(-),6(0),P(0),1(13)

532	15/3	Wadebridge	(L)	RES	3m	9	GF	*in 4th at 14th, grad fdd*	7	0
806	31/3	Wadebridge	(L)	RES	3m	6	F	*2nd 7-13th, grdly fdd*	4	0
1089	16/4	Hockworthy	(L)	CON	3m	7	GF	*alwys last, t.o. & p.u. 13th*	P	0
1245	26/4	Bratton Down	(L)	INT	3m	9	GS	*ld/disp til wknd 12th, p.u. bfr 3 out*	P	0
1339	3/5	Flete Park	(R)	RES	3m	6	G	*(bl) not fluent, lost tch 12th, p.u. apr 3 out*	P	0
1519	17/5	Bratton Down	(L)	RES	3m	15	GS	*prog to 3rd at 12th, 2nd whn mstk 14th, wknd rpdly*	6	11
1581	26/5	Lifton	(R)	LAD	3m	7	G	*prssd ldr til wknd 12th, p.u. 2 out*	P	0
1612	7/6	Umberleigh	(L)	LAD	3m	5	F	*hld up, chsd wnr 11th, no imp, mstk 2 out, fin tired*	2	0

Won poor Maiden 96; does not stay & outclassed now upgraded; prospects are very slim. **11**

MEDIEVAL QUEEN ch.m. 12 Jester - Cookstown Lady — Mrs J Mathias

1996 6(16),4(15),2(16),2(11)

535	16/3	Erw Lon	(L)	CON	3m	12	GF	*in tch til blnd 7th, fdd, p.u. 3 out*	P	0
840	31/3	Lydstep	(L)	MEM	3m	6	F	*alwys twrds rear, nvr dang*	3	0

Last won in 95 & most unlikely to do so again. **13**

MEGANS MYSTERY(IRE) b.g. 7 Corvaro (USA) - Megans Choice by Furry Glen — J S Haldane

1996 P(0),3(11),4(0),6(0)

235	22/2	Friars Haugh	(L)	MDO	3m	10	G	*ld 7th, sn clr, mstk 4 out, 15l up whn u.r. 2 out*	U	15
420	8/3	Dalston	(R)	MDO	2 1/2m	8	GS	*(fav) chsd wnr 6th, mstk 8th, wknd aft 3 out*	4	0
1429	10/5	Aspatria	(L)	MDO	3m	15	G	*prom til wknd rpdly 10th, t.o. & p.u. 13th*	P	0
1514	17/5	Corbridge	(R)	MDO	3m	17	GS	*mid-div, prog 12th, f nxt*	F	-

Unlucky 1st start; jumping & stamina problems after; can win when these are ironed out. **14**

MEIGS BATTLE (Irish) — **I** 349[P], **I** 501[P], **I** 539[U]

MELDANTE VI (Irish) — **I** 160[P], **I** 243[P], **I** 509[1], **I** 546[5], **I** 587[3], **I** 614,

MELDON b.g. 10 Paddy's Stream - Enchanted Evening by Warpath — M R Lilley

878	1/4	Upton-On-Se'	(R)	XX	3m	11	GF	*rear, effrt to poor 4th at 12th, kpt on, nvr dang*	3	10

Hurdles winner 93; retains some ability but hardly ever runs & not threatening to win now. **12**

MELLEFONT (Irish) — **I** 488[P], **I** 572, , **I** 599,

MELLICOMETTI ch.g. 9 Giacometti - Mellifluous by Midsummer Night II — Mrs Anne Carter

795	31/3	Bishopsleigh	(R)	MDO	3m	12	G	*sn bhnd, no ch & p.u. 17th*	P	0
1094	16/4	Hockworthy	(L)	MDN	3m	11	GF	*pllng, hld up, nvr on trms, t.o. 4 out*	6	0
1261	27/4	Black Fores'	(R)	MDO	3m	12	F	*twrds rear of ldrs, onepcd frm 3 out*	5	0
1311	3/5	Holnicote	(L)	MEM	3m	7	G	*prom early, 3rd & losing tch whn u.r. 15th*	U	-

1520 17/5 Bratton Down (L) MDO 3m 17 GS *prom, ld 11th-13th, wknd rpdly 16th, p.u. nxt* P 0
1597 31/5 Bratton Down (L) MDO 3m 12 F *rear of chsng grp, lost tch 12th, t.o. & p.u. 15th* P 0

Shows speed but no stamina; no real prospects. 0

MELLING b.g. 6 Thowra (FR) - Miss Melmore by Nishapour (FR) Miss R Dobson
1996 2(0),P(0),F(-),4D(14),C(-),3(13)
110 8/2 Milborne St' (L) MDN 3m 7 GF *(fav) ld to 4th, handy til outpcd frm 4 out* 3 13
245 22/2 Lemalla (R) MDO 3m 11 S *(fav) mid-div, rdn 12th, no prog, bhnd & p.u. 16th* P 0
392 8/3 Barbury Cas' (L) MDN 3m 9 G *w.w. prog to 3rd 11th, mstk 14th, rdn 2 out, ld nr fin* 1 14
877 1/4 Upton-On-Se' (R) RES 3m 17 GF *alwys rear, no ch frm 10th, t.o. & p.u. 15th* P 0
935 6/4 Charlton Ho' (L) RES 3m 7 G *(bl) mid-div, prog to ld 12th-14th, wknd rpdly apr 2 out* 4 10

Won weak Maiden; stamina doubts & signs not encouraging now; need poor race to win again. 14

MELODIC LADY (Irish) — **I** 37^{P}, **I** 96^{5}
MELSONBY br.g. 15 Politico (USA) - Melmin by Comandeer R Hankey
1996 4(10),P(0),P(0)
936 6/4 Tabley (R) MEM 3m 9 G *1st ride, alwys mid-div, outpcd frm 10th, t.o.* 4 0

Safely got a debutante round but of no account now. 0

MEMBERS CRUISE ch.g. 7 Cruise Missile - Members Joy by New Member E W Smith
1996 F(-),F(-)
7 19/1 Barbury Cas' (L) RES 3m 14 GF *prom, 4th hlfwy, onepcd final cct* 4 14
299 1/3 Didmarton (L) MDN 3m 14 G *prom, disp 10th, 3rd & outpcd aft 14th* 3 12
654 22/3 Siddington (L) MDN 3m 10 F *(Jt fav) jmpd rght, chsd ldr 6th, ld 15th, blnd nxt, kpt on und pres* 1 15

Won modest race but going the right way; successful stable and should upgrade; G-F so far. 16

MEMBERS RIGHTS ch.m. 12 New Member - Mistress Rights by Master Spiritus M Keel
1996 8(0),P(0),3(14),4(0)
362 2/3 Garnons (L) OPE 3m 11 GS *chsd ldrs to 10th, lost tch nxt, t.o. & p.u. 3 out* P 0
433 8/3 Upton-On-Se' (R) RES 3m 18 G *cls 3rd at 7th, outpcd 12th, no ch whn p.u. 2 out* P 0
877 1/4 Upton-On-Se' (R) RES 3m 17 GF *chsd ldr to 5th, outpcd frm 10th, no ch aft* 4 11
1145 19/4 Chaddesley ' (L) MEM 3m 6 GF *ld 2nd til aft 13th, strgglng whn mstk nxt, wknd* 4 10
1326 3/5 Chaddesley ' (L) RES 3m 3 GF *chsd wnr til blnd 3rd & agn 5-7th,mstk 10th,sn bhnd,u.r.14th* U -
1455 11/5 Maisemore P' (L) CON 3m 8 G *bhnd frm 8th, t.o. aft 13th, kpt on frm 3 out* 4 0

Maiden winner 93; lost all 18 starta 94-97 and will extend the sequence; mistakes. 11

MEMBER THAT (Irish) — **I** 460, , **I** 531^{U}, **I** 591^{2}, **I** 606^{4}
MENALMA (Irish) — **I** 166^{4}, **I** 258^{2}, **I** 317^{4}, **I** 487^{2}, **I** 519^{3}, **I** 561^{1}
MENATURE(IRE) ch.g. 8 Meneval (USA) - Speedy Venture by Bargello J D V Seth-Smith
1996 P(0),8(0),F(-),6(0),1(17),**3(NH),3(NH)**
218 16/2 Heythrop (R) INT 3m 21 G *in tch to 11th, wll bhnd whn p.u. 3 out* P 0
446 8/3 Newton Brom' (R) CON 3m 8 G *chsd ldrs, cls 2nd at 6th, 3rd 11th, wknd rpdly, p.u. 2 out* P 0
545 16/3 Garthorpe (R) CON 3m 12 GF *bhnd, brf eff 11th, t.o. & p.u. 2 out* P 0
1077 13/4 Guilsborough (L) CON 3m 16 GF *s.v.s. grad prog frm 6th, tk 4th 2 out, no hdwy aft* 5 18
1160 20/4 Mollington (R) INT 3m 9 GF *s.s. alwys last, t.o. 10th, p.u. 13th* P 0
1350 4/5 Dingley (R) MEM 3m 5 G *cls up til blnd & u.r. 6th* U -
1474 11/5 Garthorpe (R) MEM 3m 6 GS *in tch til 5th & outpcd apr 13th, t.o.* 5 0
1530 18/5 Fakenham (L) HC 2m 5f 110yds 11 G *held up, hdwy 12th wknd next.* 5 0

Members winner 96; placed summer jumping; awful & looked troubled in 97; best watched. 14

MENDIP SON b.g. 7 Hallgate - Silver Surprise by Son Of Silver Mrs H E Rees
1996 P(0),P(0),P(0),r(-),**7(NH)**
176 15/2 Ottery St M' (L) RES 3m 17 G *rear til p.u. 3 out* P 0
312 1/3 Clyst St Ma' (L) RES 3m 8 HY *in tch, effrt 3 out, outpcd nxt* 2 14
557 16/3 Ottery St M' (L) RES 3m 9 G *hd up in tch, effrt 3 out, onpcd frm nxt, lft 2nd last* 2 15
794 31/3 Bishopsleigh (R) MDO 3m 12 G *(fav) hld up, lft in ld 12th, kpt on und pres whn chal* 1 14

Much more amenable now; beat subsequent winner & should go close in Restricted; G-Hy. 17

MENEDUKE (Irish) — **I** 240^{6}
MENESTREAM (Irish) — **I** 453^{P}, **I** 493^{P}
MERGER MANIA b.g. 5 Precocious - Scrummage by Workboy W I Owens
1996 **P(NH),14(NH)**
403 8/3 Llanfrynach (R) INT 3m 8 G *ran out 3rd* r -
572 16/3 Garnons (L) INT 3m 13 G *prom, ld 9th-13th, mstk & wknd nxt, p.u. 3 out* P 0
853 31/3 Eyton-On-Se' (L) MDO 3m 13 GF *cls up, ld 3rd-5th, outpcd, p.u. 5 out* P 0
1016 12/4 Bitterley (L) MDO 3m 14 GF *hld up rear, gd prog 14th, wknd frm 3 out* 7 0
1239 26/4 Brampton Br' (R) MDO 3m 9 G *pllng, cls up til lost tch 15th, no ch nxt, fin fast* 3 0
1393 5/5 Cursneh Hill (L) MDO 3m 9 GF *held up, cls 5th 11th, 8l 5th 13th, no ch frm 15th* 5 0
1528 17/5 Bredwardine (R) MDO 3m 17 G *rear of main grp, ran on 15th, ld apr 2 out, sn clr, eased* 1 15

Scooted home from 8 others; needs holding up; hard to assess but still young & can progress. 17

MERITMOORE b.g. 14 Moorestyle - More Treasure by Ballymore J Pearce
1996 P(0),P(0),8(0),1(16)
474 9/3 Southwell P' (L) LAD 3m 12 G *alwys wll bhnd, t.o. & p.u. 12th, dsmntd* P 0

Ladies winner 96 (25/1); problems 97 & looks finished now. 0

MERLIN THE MONKEY b.g. 7 Royben - Targa (GER) by Stani Mrs J Perry
1260 27/4 Black Fores' (R) MDO 3m 12 F *alwys bhnd, f 12th* 0 0
1399 5/5 High Bickin' (R) MDO 3m 12 G *bhnd til p.u. 8th, school* P 0

Only learning so far. 0

MERLYNS CHOICE b.g. 13 Ovac (ITY) - Liffey's Choice by Little Buskins A Woodward
1996 P(0),P(0),5(0),5(0),11(0)
86 2/2 Wolverhampt' (L) OPE 3m 9 GS *bhnd, poor 7th at 11th, styd on well frm nxt, nrst fin* 3 18
216 16/2 Southwell P' (L) OPE 3m 12 GS *prom in chsng grp, outpcd apr 12th, no dang aft* 5 16
364 2/3 Garnons (L) XX 3m 7 GS *cls up, went 5l 3rd 14th, chsd wnr nxt, kpt on onepcd* 2 18
473 9/3 Southwell P' (L) CON 3m 10 G *mid-div, prog to cls 3rd 12th, kpt on onepcd frm 15th* 3 16
771 29/3 Dingley (R) OPE 3m 10 G *last to 8th, remote 7th at 11th, steady prog to d/h 2nd post* 2 18
887 1/4 Flagg Moor (L) XX 3m 8 G *last & dtchd 5th, styd on 14th, chnc 3 out, no imp aft* 2 17
1351 4/5 Dingley (R) CON 3m 7 G *bhnd, wnt mod 3rd 12th, styd on to ld apr last, sn drew clr* 1 19
1539 18/5 Wolverhampt' (L) OPE 3m 5 GS *(fav) sn rear, nvr going wll, wll t.o. 6 out, ran on to 3rd flat* 3 10
1607 1/6 Dingley (R) OPE 3m 9 GF *sn pshd alng, outpcd frm 5th, wll bhnd 8th, kpt on frm 3 out* 3 13

Revived in 97; novice ridden; safe, stays but onepaced; hard to find a win at 14. 19

MERRY CASTLE (Irish) — **I** 45^P^

MERRY MORN b.m. 6 Nearly A Hand - Dale Road by Le Tricolore E L Harries
405 8/3 Llanfrynach (R) RES 3m 15 G *f 2nd* F -
842 31/3 Lydstep (L) MDO 3m 12 F *f 1st* F -
1009 12/4 St Hilary (R) MDN 3m 11 GF *twrds rear til p.u. 15th* P 0
1230 26/4 Pyle (R) MDO 3m 10 GS *in tch, prssd ldr 14th, rdn apr last, styd on to ld flat* 1 14
1365 5/5 Pantyderi (L) RES 3m 10 G *rear, f 7th* F -

Won weak Maiden; the problem is obvious & needs more practice before upgrading. 14

MERRY NOELLE b.m. 7 Scorpio (FR) - Merry Jane by Rymer M P Wiggin
1996 **3(NH),4(NH),13(NH)**
259 22/2 Newtown (L) MDN 3m 18 G *(fav) trckd ldrs, 3rd at 10th, no imp 1st pair frm 3 out* 3 11
436 8/3 Upton-On-Se' (R) MDO 3m 17 G *(fav) ld/disp to 6th, ev ch 14th, wknd aft 3 out, lft 2nd* 2 0
1015 12/4 Bitterley (L) MDO 3m 12 GF *cls up til ld 12th, hdd & wknd aft 2 out* 4 0
1238 26/4 Brampton Br' (R) MDO 3m 10 G *cls up 11th, chal 3 out, ran on und pres to ld last* 1 12

Placed nov hurdles; finally came good in slow race; stamina doubts & needs more to upgrade. 15

MERRY RIVER (Irish) — **I** 166^B^, **I** 235^4^, **I** 319^2^, **I** 479^3^

MERRY SCORPION ch.g. 8 Scorpio (FR) - Merry Jane by Rymer T D Marlow
1996 U(-),C(-),3(11),1(13),1(16)
465 8/3 Eyton-On-Se' (L) OPE 3m 13 G *f 1st* F -

Dead 17

MERSEY RACING (Irish) — **I** 417^F^

METRO FASHION (Irish) — **I** 82^U^, **I** 132^2^, **I** 181^U^, **I** 220^P^, **I** 307^2^

METROSTYLE gr.g. 14 Roselier (FR) - Changing Gears by Master Owen C H Warner
1996 2(17),P(0),2(16),2(18),3(14),**P(0)**
3 19/1 Barbury Cas' (L) XX 3m 14 GF *alwys bhnd, 10th & no ch hlfwy, sn t.o.* 10 0

Solid form in 96; vanished after day one in 97 & looks finished now. 13

MET STATION b.g. 14 Royal Fountain - Lido Light by Good Light J J Boulter
109 8/2 Milborne St' (L) XX 3m 8 GF *(bl) alwys rear, u.r. 9th* U -
395 8/3 Barbury Cas' (L) XX 3m 9 G *(bl) prom, ld apr 4th til aft 11th, wkng whn blnd nxt, p.u. 15th* P 0

H/chase winner 95; missed 96 & looks finished now. 12

MHEMEANLES br.g. 7 Jalmood (USA) - Folle Idee (USA) by Foolish Pleasure (USA) Frank Nicholls
1996 **4(NH),F(NH),U(NH),1(NH),13(NH)**
226 21/2 Haydock (L) HC 3m 11 G *jmpd poorly, alwys well bhnd, t.o. when p.u. 5 out.* P 0
587 19/3 Ludlow (R) HC 2 1/2m 18 GF *chsd ldrs to 9th, weakening when blnd and u.r. 11th.* U -
938 6/4 Tabley (R) OPE 3m 9 G *(bl) s.s., t.o. 2nd til f 6th* F -

Winning selling hurdler; stamina suspect & makes no appeal. 13

MIAMI BEAR b.g. 11 Miami Springs - Belinda Bear by Ragstone Mrs L M Fahey

1996 1(17),**7(NH)**

264	22/2	Duncombe Pa'	(R)	MEM	3m	9	G	*chsd ldr til ld 3rd,sn wll clr,tired 4 out,hd apr last,wknd*	4	11
423	8/3	Charm Park	(L)	OPE	3m	7	GF	*hld up in rear,prog 4 out,ev ch 2 out,wknng whn lft 2nd last*	2	20
506	15/3	Dalton Park	(R)	CON	3m	16	GF	*rear, prog 9th, trckd ldrs going wll whn f 15th*	F	-

Members winner 96; capable pointer & Members/Confined still likely at 12; mistakes. 18

MICHAEL'S SOCIETY (Irish) — **I** 571,

MICHELLES CRYSTAL b.m. 6 Ovac (ITY) - Lochlairey by Lochnager — Paul Wise

1996 P(0),P(0)

381	4/3	Leicester	(R)	HC	2m 1f	13	G	*blnd and u.r. 2nd.*	U	-
892	5/4	Hereford	(R)	HC	2m	11	GF	*slowly away, f 3rd.*	F	-

Appalling in points & H/chases; gone nov hurdling now. 0

MICKEYS DREAM (Irish) — **I** 81[P]

MICKLIMAR (Irish) — **I** 369[F], **I** 461[1], **I** 584[4]

MICKTHECUTAWAY (Irish) — **I** 191[U], **I** 285[F], **I** 351[1], **I** 555[P], **I** 578[P]

MICROTELLE ROSE (Irish) — **I** 212[F], **I** 292[P], **I** 329[P], **I** 464[5], **I** 508[2]

MICRO VILLA (Irish) — **I** 25[P], **I** 271[3], **I** 296[1], **I** 402[2], **I** 494[P], **I** 541[1]

MIDDLEHAM PEARL b.m. 7 Loch Pearl - Twice Nice by Double Jump — L Turnbull

1996 **12(NH),P(NH)**

210	16/2	Southwell P'	(L)	MDO	3m	15	GS	*mstk 3rd, bhnd 9th, no dang aft*	7	0

No signs of ability under rules or in points. 0

MIDFIELDER ch.g. 11 Formidable (USA) - Pampas Flower by Pampered King — B A Savage

3	19/1	Barbury Cas'	(L)	XX	3m	14	GF	*mid-div, prog & 5th hlfwy, no imp 3 out, sn btn*	8	0
49	1/2	Wadebridge	(L)	LAD	3m	5	G	*chsng grp, prog 11th, no ext frm nxt*	2	17
145	9/2	Tweseldown	(R)	LAD	3m	10	GF	*chsd ldrs, lost tch 12th, p.u. 3 out*	P	0
637	22/3	Howick	(L)	OPE	3m	7	GF	*ld to 11th, cls up 3 out, onepcd*	4	15

Winning hurdler/chaser; stamina suspect & easy 3 miles essential; hard to find a win. 15

MIDGE b.m. 10 Reformed Character - Alpro by Count Albany — Mrs P P Wright

1996 P(0),P(0),P(0),P(0),5(14),U(-),C(-),F(-)

251	22/2	Brocklesby '	(L)	RES	3m	16	G	*alwys rear hlf, outpcd 6 out, p.u. 3 out*	P	0
349	2/3	Market Rase'	(L)	LAD	3m	5	GF	*rear, losing tch whn u.r. 13th*	U	-
508	15/3	Dalton Park	(R)	LAD	3m	4	GF	*rear, lost tch 7th, wll bhnd 11th*	3	12
674	23/3	Brocklesby '	(L)	LAD	3m	5	GF	*ld to 2nd, mstk 6th, chsd ldrs til wknd apr 3 out*	4	14
695	29/3	Stainton	(R)	RES	3m	11	F	*rear, prog into mid-div 8th, mstk 13th, outpcd frm 4 out*	5	13
1075	13/4	Whitwell-On'	(R)	MEM	3m	9	G	*mid-div, prog to ld 7th, hdd 9th, grad fdd, lost tch 4 out*	4	0
1250	26/4	Easingwold	(L)	RES	3m	15	GS	*rear early, mstks, p.u. 11th*	P	0
1348	3/5	Gisburn	(R)	RES	3m	10	GF	*cls up to 13th, wknd aft*	4	10
1419	10/5	Easingwold	(L)	CON	3m	8	GF	*prom early, rear & strgglng 8th, t.o. 10th, p.u. 14th*	P	0

Very moderate; 1 win last 34 starts; need fortune to score again. 11

MIDNIGHT BOB b.g. 6 Derring Rose - Anner Amanda by Mandamus — J F Weldhen

1996 **6(NH),15(NH)**

101	8/2	Great Treth'	(R)	MDO	3m	9	GS	*4th whn u.r. 7th*	U	-
244	22/2	Lemalla	(R)	MDO	3m	12	S	*ld aft 7th, clr 3 out, hdd apr last, kpt on*	2	14
458	8/3	Great Treth'	(R)	MDO	3m	15	S	*hndy, 3rd 3 out, wnt 2nd 2 out, no ext cls home, imprvd*	3	10
626	22/3	Kilworthy	(L)	MDN	3m	14	G	*(Jt fav) hdwy whn hit 11th, disp 15th til jmp lft, swrvd & u.r. 2 out*	U	14
737	29/3	Higher Kilw'	(L)	LAD	3m	5	GF	*cls up in 3rd, ev ch til onepcd frm 3 out*	3	19
1035	12/4	Lifton	(R)	MDN	3m	11	F	*(fav) bhnd til tk cls order 5 out, efft 2 out, no ext aft*	2	14
1110	19/4	Flete Park	(R)	LAD	3m	9	GF	*cls 2nd frm 7th-3 out, ev ch til outpcd nxt*	3	18
1257	27/4	Black Fores'	(R)	LAD	3m	5	F	*hld up, steady prog 13th, ev ch last, just outpcd*	3	14

Best form in Ladies but not produce that in Maidens; finds little at the finish looks suspect. 15

MIDNIGHT MAGIC (Irish) — **I** 337[F], **I** 381[F]

MIDNIGHT MIRACLE ch.m. 7 Sunley Builds - Midnight Diamond by Legal Tender — R Garvin

223	16/2	Heythrop	(R)	RES	3m	19	G	*mstks 1st & 2nd, p.u. nxt*	P	0

Blundering around in the dark so far. 0

MIDNIGHT SERVICE(IRE) b.g. 8 The Parson - Stringfellows — Mrs D E H Turner

78	2/2	Market Rase'	(L)	RES	3m	8	GF	*in tch, bln 7th, last frm nxt, p.u. 14th*	P	0
477	9/3	Southwell P'	(L)	RES	3m	10	G	*alwys bhnd, lost tch 7th, nvr on trms*	7	0
1191	20/4	Garthorpe	(R)	RES	3m	8	GF	*chsd ldrs to 4th, 4th & outpcd 13th, no ch aft*	5	0
1263	27/4	Southwell P'	(L)	RES	3m	9	G	*(bl) prom, trckd ldr 10th, ld apr 12th-2 out, rallied to ld last*	1	18
1474	11/5	Garthorpe	(R)	MEM	3m	6	GS	*(bl) chsd ldrs, went 2nd 9th, pckd 3 out, ev ch last, no ext*	2	18
1576	26/5	Chaddesley '	(L)	XX	3m	12	F	*(bl) mstk 5th, alwys rear, t.o. & p.u. 12th*	P	0

Irish Maiden winner; blinkers worked the oracle; needs cut; can win again. 19

MIDNIGHT SOCIETY (Irish) — **I** 294^{4}, **I** 338^{2}, **I** 428^{P}, **I** 570^{P}

MIGHTY EXPRESS b.g. 8 Bay Express - Astral Suite by On Your Mark — Mrs C Park

230	22/2	Friars Haugh	(L)	RES	3m	15	G	*nvr nr ldrs, p.u. 3 out*	P	0
343	1/3	Corbridge	(R)	MDO	3m	14	G	*mid-div, f 3rd*	F	-
411	8/3	Dalston	(R)	CON	3m	16	GS	*alwys bhnd, t.o. last whn p.u. 3 out*	P	0
566	16/3	Lanark	(R)	MDO	3m	10	GS	*bhnd by 11th, kpt on without threatng ldrs*	5	0
698	29/3	Stainton	(R)	MDO	3m	6	F	*(fav) (3s-4/5)rear & nvr gng wll, outpcd 13th, t.o. whn p.u. 4 out*	P	0
1172	20/4	Hexham Poin'	(L)	MDO	3m	4	GF	*cls up, disp 15th til ld aft nxt, qcknd clr 2 out*	1	10
1424	10/5	Aspatria	(L)	RES	3m	17	G	*alwys rear, t.o. & p.u. 15th*	P	0
1510	17/5	Corbridge	(R)	RES	3m	13	GS	*rear, lost tch 14th, t.o. & p.u. nxt*	P	0

Repaid supporters in 7 mins plus race; no other form; more needed. 14

MIGHTY FALCON b.g. 12 Comedy Star (USA) - Lettuce by So Blessed — Miss Emma Tory

1996 2(14),2(20),4(12),4(0),2(17)

39	1/2	Larkhill	(R)	CON	3m	6	GF	*made most to 15th, sn btn*	4	11
107	8/2	Milborne St'	(L)	MEM	3m	8	GF	*(fav) hld up, prog 12th, ld nxt, ran on well frm 3 out*	1	15
397	8/3	Barbury Cas'	(L)	XX	3m	10	G	*(Jt fav) bhnd 4th, prog 11th, went poor 4th 14th, styd on, nvr nrr*	4	15
511	15/3	Larkhill	(R)	CON	3m	3	GF	*disp til ld 13th, clr nxt, easily*	1	19
869	31/3	Hackwood Pa'	(L)	XX	3m	6	F	*(fav) mostly 2nd til ld 12th, disp aft til hdd last, ran on*	2	15
1090	16/4	Hockworthy	(L)	LAD	3m	8	GF	*chsd ldrs, outpcd 14th, kpt on frm 2 out*	4	16
1274	27/4	Little Wind'	(R)	XX	3m	8	GF	*cls up, ld aft 14th, clr nxt, styd on strngly*	1	20
1358	5/5	Exeter	(R)	HC	2m 7f 110yds	8	G	*soon in tch, ld 9th to 11th, rallied to go 2nd 3 out, chal next, kept on und pres.*	2	24
1495	14/5	Cothelstone	(L)	LAD	3m	6	GF	*outpcd, t.o. 6th, kpt on frm 16th, nvr nrr*	3	17
1569	26/5	Fontwell	(R)	HC	3 1/4m 110yds	10	GF	*ld 3rd till mstk and hdd 10th, lost pl 13th, rear 15th, plenty to do 4 out, gd hdwy to ld last, soon clr.*	1	22

Enjoyed fine season; safe & stays; harder to place now; below Ladies class; F-G. 22

MIGHTY GALE(IRE) b.g. 6 Strong Gale - Swanee Mistress by My Swanee — E Dauncey

1996 **14(NH)**

1498	14/5	Cothelstone	(L)	MDO	3m	9	GF	*(fav) n.j.w. in tch, chsd ldr 13th, ld 2 out, pshd out*	1	12
1552	24/5	Mounsey Hil'	(R)	RES	3m	12	G	*chsd ldrs, wknd apr 14th, last whn p.u. 3 out*	P	0

Won desperate Maiden on debut despite mistakes,needs more experience; huge improvement needed. 13

MIGHTY HAGGIS b.g. 10 Glen Quaich - Willie Pat by Pitpan — Sir Sanderson Temple

1996 P(0)

231	22/2	Friars Haugh	(L)	LAD	3m	13	G	*s.v.s. f 6th*	F	-
331	1/3	Eaton Hall	(R)	RES	3m	17	GS	*ld to 2nd, prom to 12th, onepcd frm 5 out*	5	14
563	16/3	Lanark	(R)	RES	3m	8	GS	*losng tch whn f 13th*	F	-
762	29/3	Whittington	(L)	MEM	3m	5	S	*s.s., ld aft 1st, clr 5th, missd mrkr bef nxt*	P	0
937	6/4	Tabley	(R)	CON	3m	10	G	*whppd round start, rear whn f 4th*	F	-

Irish Maiden winner 92; tricky ride & Members looks his only hope. 12

MIGHTY MARBLE (Irish) — **I** 531^{U}, **I** 576^{2}, **I** 590^{4}

MIGHTY MERC ch.g. 9 Shaab - Cornish Saffron by Spitsbergen — Mrs Beryl K Broad

119	9/2	Wetherby Po'	(L)	OPE	3m	15	GF	*wth ldrs til fdd 13th, t.o. & p.u. 3 out*	P	0
348	2/3	Market Rase'	(L)	RES	3m	13	GF	*chsd ldr to 9th, t.o. & p.u. 15th*	P	0
1406	5/5	Witton Cast'	(R)	RES	3m	10	GS	*prom, disp 4th, ld nxt, disp 10th, hdd & fdd 14th*	4	13
1419	10/5	Easingwold	(L)	CON	3m	8	GF	*rear, prog to 2nd at 4th, steadily wknd frm 14th*	4	14

Maiden winner 94; placed nov chase 95; stamina suspect & not threatening to win a Restricted. 13

MIGHTY STATEMENT (Irish) — **I** 498^{R}, **I** 594^{P}

MILE MILL (Irish) — **I** 153^{P}

MILES MORE FUN b.m. 8 Idiot's Delight - Mary Mile by Athenius — Edward Retter

1996 P(0),U(-),U(-)

96	8/2	Great Treth'	(R)	CON	3m	7	GS	*16s-6s, w.w. prog to ld 15th, clr 3 out, easily*	1	24
170	15/2	Ottery St M'	(L)	MEM	3m	6	G	*(fav) plld hrd, ld 5th, sn clr, easily*	1	23
586	19/3	Exeter	(R)	HC	3 1/4m	12	GF	*held up, pushed along after 7 out, soon wknd, bhnd when p.u. before 4 out.*	P	0
1037	12/4	Lifton	(R)	OPE	3m	5	F	*(fav) slght ld to 15th, hdd & lkd btn whn f last, rmt*	3	0

Shrewd stable landed touch impressively; ran well after; can land Open 98. 22

MILEY PIKE b.g. 10 Amboise - Cornetta by Cornuto — Mrs K Tutty

1996 4(17),2(15),6(0)

213	16/2	Southwell P'	(L)	RES	3m	16	GS	*in tch to 10th, bhnd whn p.u. 14th*	P	0
266	22/2	Duncombe Pa'	(R)	RES	3m	19	G	*mid-div til outpcd 10th, t.o. whn p.u. 14th*	P	0
616	22/3	Hutton Rudby	(L)	RES	3m	14	GF	*prom til wknd qckly 3 out*	6	11
1069	13/4	Whitwell-On'	(R)	RES	3m	12	G	*mid-div, rdn 9th, sn strgglng, t.o. 13th*	9	0

Maiden winner 92; needs stamina test; showed nothing in 97; may surprise when conditions suit. 14

MILITARY MAN ch.g. 7 Broadsword (USA) - Pearl Bride by Spartan General — A W Argent

365	2/3	Garnons	(L)	MDO	2 1/2m	14	GS	*(fav) cls up, chsd wnr 11th-3 out, wknd nxt*	5	0
643	22/3	Castle Of C'	(R)	MDO	3m	12	G	*mid-div, chsd ldr 13th, rdn & blnd 2 out, kpt on und pres*	2	15
755	29/3	Brampton Br'	(R)	MDN	3m	5	GF	*(fav) ld 5th til hdd aft 16th, kpt on onepcd und pres*	2	10
1016	12/4	Bitterley	(L)	MDO	3m	14	GF	*prom whn f 10th*	F	-
1239	26/4	Brampton Br'	(R)	MDO	3m	9	G	*cls up til wknd 15th, p.u. 3 out*	P	0
1401	5/5	Ashorne	(R)	MDO	3m	15	G	*hmpd & u.r. 1st*	U	-
1528	17/5	Bredwardine	(R)	MDO	3m	17	G	*prom, ld 15th til apr 2 out, no ext aft*	2	12

Missed 96; placed 4 0f 10 starts; finds little under pressure; may win on easy course. 13

MILLAS DELIGHT (Irish) — **I** 347[P], **I** 430[5]

MILLBROOK ROAD (Irish) — **I** 462[P]

MILLBROOK WARRIOR (Irish) — **I** 450, , **I** 489, , **I** 559[4], **I** 597[4], **I** 609[4]

MILLED OATS ch.g. 9 Oats - Mid-Day Milli by Midsummer Night II — Mrs A C Martin

100	8/2	Great Treth'	(R)	RES	3m	14	GS	*unruly pddck, alwys prom, ev ch 2 out, no ch wnr last*	2	17
241	22/2	Lemalla	(R)	RES	3m	11	S	*unruly pddck, mid-div, 6th & rmndrs 13th, 3rd & no ch 2 out*	3	19
457	8/3	Great Treth'	(R)	RES	3m	8	S	*hdwy 9th, strng run to ld 2 out, styd on wll*	1	19
522	15/3	Cothelstone	(L)	CON	3m	14	GS	*cls 5th hlfwy, disp 3 out, 2l 2nd nxt, fin well*	2	23
631	22/3	Kilworthy	(L)	INT	3m	8	G	*(fav) hld up, efft 3 out, ld last, ran on strgly*	1	22
1089	16/4	Hockworthy	(L)	CON	3m	7	GF	*sn pshd alng,rdn to chs wnr 13th,no imp,lost poor 2nd flat*	3	13
1516	17/5	Bratton Down	(L)	CON	3m	6	GS	*handy, went 2nd apr 12th, chsd wnr, fin 2nd, disq*	2D	23
1593	31/5	Bratton Down	(L)	XX	3m	5	F	*not fluent, ld 8th-aft 16th, outpcd aft 2 out, lft 2nd last*	2	19

Missed 96; changed hands; consistent; needs soft; beaten by good horses; can win again. 22

MILLER KING (Irish) — **I** 27[2], **I** 67[F], **I** 93[F], **I** 147[2], **I** 314[4], **I** 345[3]

MILLERMAN (Irish) — **I** 129[P], **I** 176[F]

MILLER'S CHAP br.g. 10 Teofane - Millar's Gayle — Mrs A G Rogers

545	16/3	Garthorpe	(R)	CON	3m	12	GF	*chsd ldrs 7th, wnt 2nd 12th,ld 2 out til hdd & no ex cls hme*	2	19
769	29/3	Dingley	(R)	CON	3m	14	G	*prom 1st cct, 3rd at 11th, wknd 6 out, p.u. last*	P	0
1077	13/4	Guilsborough	(L)	CON	3m	16	GF	*mstk 6th, mid-div, btn frm 12th, p.u. 15th*	P	0
1189	20/4	Garthorpe	(R)	LAD	3m	6	GF	*ld 2nd-4th, 3rd whn f 6th*	F	-
1205	26/4	Clifton On '	(L)	CON	3m	13	GS	*abt 6th whn f 5th*	F	-
1351	4/5	Dingley	(R)	CON	3m	7	G	*ld 2nd-4th, disp 2nd whn f 8th*	F	-

Winning Irish chaser; just caught on debut; fall apart after & can only be watched now. 14

MILLSOFBALLYSODARE (Irish) — **I** 28[P]

MILLSTOCK b.m. 7 Interrex (CAN) - Millingdale by Tumble Wind (USA) — N J Stallard

259	22/2	Newtown	(L)	MDN	3m	18	G	*alwys rear, t.o. 13th, p.u. 2 out*	P	0
366	2/3	Garnons	(L)	MDO	2 1/2m	13	GS	*ld 6-8th, cls 2nd 11th, wknd aft nxt, p.u. last*	P	0
568	16/3	Garnons	(L)	CON	3m	12	G	*lft 15l, prog to mid-div 8th, lost tch 13th, p.u. 2 out*	P	0
706	29/3	Upper Sapey	(R)	MDO	3m	15	GF	*s.s., efft to go 6th 11th, grdly lost tch*	7	0
1063	13/4	Maisemore P'	(L)	XX	3m	13	GF	*t.d.e. s.s. alwys rear*	8	0
1454	11/5	Maisemore P'	(L)	MEM	3m	5	G	*chsd ldr 6-9th,outpcd12th,ran on 2 out,disp 2nd & f last*	F	10

Ex nov hurdler; novice-ridden; does not stay & well below winning standard. 10

MILLWOOD b.g. 5 Macmillion - Nightwood by Sparkler — J Alford

54	1/2	Wadebridge	(L)	MDO	3m	13	G	*alwys rear, p.u. 4 out*	P	0
625	22/3	Kilworthy	(L)	MDN	3m	14	G	*(fav) hld up, prog 16th, disp 3rd whn f last*	F	13

Showed plenty of promise; should progress & win in 98. 15

MILLYHENRY b.g. 6 White Prince (USA) - Milly's Chance by Mljet — L G Tizzard

40	1/2	Larkhill	(R)	MDO	3m	5	GF	*(fav) blnd 3rd,bhnd,prog to chs wnr 11th,clsng whn blnd & u.r.3out*	U	-
643	22/3	Castle Of C'	(R)	MDO	3m	12	G	*(Jt fav) hld up rear, prog & hmpd 8th, wknd apr 15th, p.u. 2 out*	P	0
1151	19/4	Chaddesley '	(L)	MDO	3m	5	GF	*hld up, f 3rd*	F	-
1315	3/5	Holnicote	(L)	MDO	3m	7	G	*alwys rear, some prog 13th, onepcd frm nxt*	4	0
1437	10/5	Holnicote	(L)	MDO	3m	14	G	*ld/disp frm 4th, ld 16th-3 out, ld agn nxt, sn clr*	1	14
1519	17/5	Bratton Down	(L)	RES	3m	15	GS	*prog 9th, ld 13th-16th, disp nxt til pshd clr apr last*	1	20

Progressive youngster; romped home when winning; successful stable & looks worth following. looks wog 20

MILO BOY b.g. 6 Jester - Miss Cervinia by Memling — A J M Norris

1996 **P(NH),P(NH),3(NH),U(NH),P(NH),P(NH)**

677	23/3	Brocklesby '	(L)	MDN	3m	8	GF	*w.w. prog 9th, 3rd & chnc 15th, btn whn f nxt*	F	-
839	31/3	Thorpe Lodge	(L)	MDN	3m	15	F	*(Jt fav) mid-div, remmndrs 12-13th, outpcd 5th frm 6 out*	5	0
1073	13/4	Whitwell-On'	(R)	MDO	2 1/2m 88yds	17	G	*mid-div, mstk 7th, outpcd frm 4 out*	5	0
1268	27/4	Southwell P'	(L)	MDO	3m	13	G	*trckd ldr, ld 6th til disp 9th, ld 10-12th, wknd 4 out*	5	0
1356	4/5	Dingley	(R)	MDO	3m	9	G	*chsd ldrs, lft poor 4th 14th, kpt on frm 2 out, not rch ldrs*	3	0
1479	11/5	Garthorpe	(R)	MDO	3m	12	GS	*rear, prog to mid-div whn blnd 11th, no ch aft*	5	0

Poor nov hurdler; safe enough but very onepaced; reliability may see him home one day. 11

MINEHILL b.g. 10 Tug Of War - Red Cross by Pitpan — Mrs Jill McVay

66 1/2 Horseheath (R) MEM 3m 7 GF *(fav) ld to 12th, blnd nxt, rdn 3 out, ev ch whn f nxt* F -

Irish Maiden winner 96; would not have won his Members; go close in Restricted if fit in 98. 16

MINELLA EXPRESS(IRE) b.g. 8 The Parson - Dream Toi by Carlburg — Mrs Liz Brazier

1996 **5(NH),1(NH),1(NH)**

215	16/2 Southwell P'	(L) LAD	3m	12 GS	*jmpd lft, ld, hdd 3 out, sn outpcd*	3	22
257	22/2 Newtown	(L) LAD	3m	12 G	*ld 2-5th & frm 9th, mstk 11th, made rest, pshd out*	1	28
378	4/3 Leicester	(R) HC	2 1/2m 110yds	6 G	*(fav) ld, jmpd left, hdd 6 out, ev ch 2 out, styd on same pace run-in.*	2	25
587	19/3 Ludlow	(R) HC	2 1/2m	18 GF	*(fav) alwys prom, one pace apr 4 out.*	3	25
1147	19/4 Chaddesley '	(L) OPE	3m	7 GF	*ld to 11th & 13th-15th, ev ch & mstk 4 out, sn wknd*	5	15
1327	3/5 Chaddesley '	(L) LAD	3m	3 GF	*alwys 3rd, hit 4th & 15th, effrt apr 3 out, no prog nxt*	3	15

Useful ex chaser; won hot Ladies; disappointing after; may revive when fresh; best L/H. 23

MINELLA LASS (Irish) — I 481[1]
MINERAL AL (Irish) — I 42[P], I 87[F], I 182[F], I 215[P], I 343[P]
MINERAL RIVER (Irish) — I 181[P], I 484[P], I 543[4], I 592[F]
MINERS BAY (Irish) — I 127[P], I 175[F], I 328, , I 371[P]
MINERS FORTUNE(IRE) b.g. 9 Miner's Lamp - Banish Misfortune by Master Owen — M A Lloyd

1996 1(22),S(-),P(0)

200 15/2 Weston Park (L) CON 3m 16 G *cls up & going wll til fdd 12th, p.u. 14th* P 0

Confined winner 96; lightly raced & vanished quickly in 97; best watched initially in 98. 20

MINERS MEDIC(IRE) b.g. 6 Miner's Lamp - Suny Furlong by Sunyboy — Dr D B A Silk

1996 P(0)

306 1/3 Parham (R) MDN 3m 12 G *mid-div, p.u. 10th* P 0

Yet to show anything but only learning & may do better. 0

MINERS MELODY (Irish) — I 134[P], I 193[3], I 276[1]
MINER'S SON (Irish) — I 96[F]
MINERS SUNSET (Irish) — I 31[P]
MINE'S A GIN(IRE) gr.g. 6 Roselier (FR) - Cathedral Street by Boreen Beag — Mrs H C Johnson

1996 P(0),P(0),P(0),6(0),1(15)

100	8/2 Great Treth'	(R) RES	3m	14 GS	*prom, ld 6th-16th, wknd nxt, no ch whn p.u. last*	P	0
300	1/3 Didmarton	(L) RES	3m	23 G	*in tch, cls 5th whn mstk 12th, sn btn, p.u. last*	P	0
523	15/3 Cothelstone	(L) RES	3m	14 GS	*8th hlfwy, rear whn blnd 13th, p.u. nxt*	P	0
630	22/3 Kilworthy	(L) RES	3m	16 G	*hdwy 12th, ld 14th, disp 15th, qcknd clr run in*	1	17
1092	16/4 Hockworthy	(L) XX	3m	5 GF	*jmpd rght, wth ldr, ld 8-11th, disp 2nd aft, sn outpcd*	2	16
1398	5/5 High Bickin'	(R) INT	3m	7 G	*prog to 3rd at 12th, wknd 15th, no ch clsng stgs*	4	10
1481	11/5 Ottery St M'	(L) CON	3m	12 G	*mid-div, prog 12th, ev ch 3 out, not qckn nxt*	4	18
1582	26/5 Lifton	(R) INT	3m	10 G	*prom til lost ground 9th, rallied 4 out, unable to chal*	3	15

slow to reach peak; needs good ground still young & can progress further; good stable. 18

MINIBRIG b.m. 11 Le Coq D'Or - Millymeeta by New Brig — Mrs Jane Clark

1996 1(21),2(12),**F(-)**,3(11),3(15),3(13)

231	22/2 Friars Haugh	(L) LAD	3m	13 G	*nvr quite rchd ldrs*	5	18
336	1/3 Corbridge	(R) LAD	3m 5f	9 G	*mid-div, prog 10th, ev ch 16th, onepcd whn u.r. 2 out*	U	-
609	22/3 Friars Haugh	(L) LAD	3m	11 GF	*alwys abt same plc, nvr dang*	4	15
1219	26/4 Balcormo Ma'	(R) LAD	3m	3 F	*trckd wnnr frm 9th, chal 2 out, no ext flat*	2	19

Below best in 97; inconsistent; goes best fresh & could surprise 1st time out in 98; Good. 19

MINI CRUISE ch.g. 7 Cruise Missile - Mini Pie by Dike (USA) — Miss J Fisher

1996 **18(NH)**

1334	3/5 Mosshouses	(L) RES	3m	5 F	*ld til wknd 3 out*	3	0
1513	17/5 Corbridge	(R) MDO	3m	13 GS	*ld til jnd 4 out, hdd nxt, wknd rpdly, p.u. last*	P	0

Shows speed but well short of stamina as yet. 10

MINIKINO b.g. 8 Relkino - Minimint by Menelek — C J Vale

253	22/2 Brocklesby '	(L) MDO	3m	6 G	*(fav) alwys 2nd, chsd wnnr last m, alwys held*	2	13
1083	13/4 Guilsborough	(L) MDN	3m	15 GF	*prom, wkng whn hmpd 14th, p.u. nxt*	P	0

Showed promise in 95; missed 96; placed in weak race; can land smalll win if appearing more often. ... 13

MINILEADER (Irish) — I 324[P], I 422[P], I 478[3], I 571[3], I 615[P]
MINOR SETBACK (Irish) — I 599[P]
MINSTRALS BOYO ch.g. 10 Black Minstrel - Sweater Girl by Blue Cashmere — A Cole

1996 F(-)

735 29/3 Higher Kilw' (L) MEM 3m 5 GF *prom til wknd rpdly 13th, t.o. & p.u. 3 out* P 0

Some hope in 96 but signs not encouraging now. 0

MINSTRELS QUAY (Irish) — I 7[P], I 43[F], I 74[U], I 86[U], I 262, , I 324[4], I 378[2], I 482[P], I 558[P], I 564[1], I 604[4]
MINTULYAR br.g. 6 Broadsword (USA) - Minimint by Menelek — The Ridings Partnership

326 1/3 Eaton Hall (R) MDN 3m 14 GS *mid-div, some late prog, nrst at fin* 2 10
1015 12/4 Bitterley (L) MDO 3m 12 GF *ld 6th til ran out 12th* r -

Well beaten on debut but shows plenty of promise; should go very close in 98. 14

MIRAMAC b.g. 16 Relkino - Magical by Aggressor R N Bateman

170 15/2 Ottery St M' (L) MEM 3m 6 G *cls up to 5th, lost tch 11th, t.o. 13th* 6 0

Of no account now. 0

MIRROMARK (Irish) — **I** 106[P]

MIRROR IMAGE br.m. 8 Mansingh (USA) - Havenwood Lady by Fair Season Mrs V Francis

321 1/3 Marks Tey (L) INT 3m 10 G *alwys rear div, t.o. & p.u. 13th* P 0
438 8/3 Higham (L) MDO 3m 8 G *alwys rear, outpcd 13th, wll bhnd 16th* 6 0
498 15/3 Ampton (R) MDO 3m 8 GF *chsd ldrs, rdn & btn appr 17th, lft poor 3rd 2 out* 3 0
971 6/4 Penshurst (L) MDO 3m 5 F *(fav) ld to 9th, prssd wnnr aft til no ext 2 out* 2 0

Placed in dire Maidens; more needed before winning. 10

MIRROR MELODY b.m. 8 Mirror Boy - Celia by Grange Melody Robert Robinson

342 1/3 Corbridge (R) MDO 3m 12 G *ld to 6th, prom, ev ch 2 out, sn wknd* 3 11

Promise in94/95; missed 96; ran well & vanished again; needs more. 12

MISCHIEVOUS ANDY (Irish) — **I** 30[6], **I** 59[P], **I** 282[6]

MISCHIEVOUS IMP br.g. 6 Impecunious - Mutual Aunt by Mutual Interest D J Line

7 19/1 Barbury Cas' (L) RES 3m 14 GF *alwys bhnd, 12th & t.o. hlfwy, p.u. 2 out* P 0

No signs & not seen after day one. 0

MIS-E-FISHANT b.m. 9 Sunyboy - Alpine Orchid by Mon Capitaine H Turberfield

1996 P(0),F(-),5(0),P(0),5(0)

263 22/2 Newtown (L) MDN 3m 11 G *cls up to 12th, wknd, t.o. & p.u. 2 out* P 0
436 8/3 Upton-On-Se' (R) MDO 3m 17 G *alwys chsng ldrs, 4th 14th, lft 2nd 2 out, lft in ld last* 1 11
671 23/3 Eaton Hall (R) INT 3 3/4m 8 GF *rear, t.o. 11th, no ch whn p.u. 5 out* P 0
877 1/4 Upton-On-Se' (R) RES 3m 17 GF *last & t.o. til p.u. 11th* P 0

Beat two subsequent winners (very lucky); no other form & most unlikely to win again. 11

MISMETALLIC ch.m. 6 True Song - Misprite by Master Stephen Mrs T Cowper

655 22/3 Siddington (L) RES 3m 10 F *schoold in rear, outpcd 10th, t.o.* 7 0

Only learning on debut. 0

MISS ACCOUNTS(IRE) gr.m. 6 Roselier (FR) - Tara Weed by Tarqogan Richard P Watts

427 8/3 Charm Park (L) MDO 3m 10 GF *rear, mstk 2nd, prog 8th, wknd 13th, t.o. frm 3 out* 5 0
1074 13/4 Whitwell-On' (R) MDO 2 1/2m 88yds 16 G *prom whn u.r. 5th* U -
1173 20/4 Hexham Poin' (L) MDO 2 1/2m 9 GF *handy in 4th til no imp final cct, lft poor 3rd 2 out* 3 0
1345 3/5 Gisburn (R) MDN 3m 13 GF *hld up, prog 10th, ld aft 2 out, styd on well* 1 15

Steady progress; won 7 mins plus Maiden; more needed but looks capable of better. 16

MISS ANNAGAUL (Irish) — **I** 31[F], **I** 281[4], **I** 350[F]

MISS BARNAMIRE (Irish) — **I** 97[P], **I** 283[P], **I** 310[F], **I** 339, , **I** 389[4], **I** 406[4]

MISS BETSY (Irish) — **I** 138[P], **I** 166[P]

MISS CATHERINE (Irish) — **I** 207[P], **I** 479[P]

MISS CLARE b.m. 9 Cruise Missile - Claredel by Saucy Kit I D S Jones

1996 P(0),P(0),F(-),P(0),F(-)

408 8/3 Llanfrynach (R) MDN 3m 12 G *alwys rear, p.u. 3 out* P 0
754 29/3 Brampton Br' (R) MDN 3m 9 GF *rear frm 4th, ran on steadily frm 15th, nrst fin* 4 11
1238 26/4 Brampton Br' (R) MDO 3m 10 G *alwys mid-div, effrt 16th, no ext frm nxt* 5 0
1393 5/5 Cursneh Hill (L) MDO 3m 9 GF *chsd ldrs, cls 6th whn mstk & u.r. 11th* U -
1528 17/5 Bredwardine (R) MDO 3m 17 G *chsd ldng pair to 12th, outpcd 15th, no imp ldrs aft* 6 0

At least shes getting round now but moderate & more needed. 10

MISS CONSTRUE b.m. 10 Rymer - Miss Behave by Don't Look Mrs Kit Martin

1996 1(17),4(15),**10(0)**,3(13)

441 8/3 Higham (L) INT 3m 7 G *alwys rear, outpcd aft 12th* 5 14

Restricted winner 96; lightly raced & finished early 97; not easy to win again. 16

MISS CRESTA b.m. 8 Master Willie - Sweet Snow (USA) by Lyphard (USA) R Wale

1996 3(12),1(15),6(11),4(12),6(12)

140 9/2 Thorpe Lodge (L) RES 3m 7 GF *ld 2nd, 20l clr 8th, 10l clr whn f 10th* F -

Lucky Maiden winner96; stamina problems; not seen after falling; Restricted looks tough. 15

MISS CULLANE(IRE) b.m. 9 Duky - Cheeky Dame by Golden Love Robert Neill

1996 8(0),1(15),F(-),P(0),3(12),P(0)

131 9/2 Alnwick (L) RES 3m 13 G *ld to 2nd, bhnd frm 9th, t.o. & p.u. 3 out* P 0

228 22/2 Friars Haugh (L) MEM 3m 4 G *u.r. 3rd* U -

Won decent Maiden 96; disappointed after & brief 97; best watched. 14

MISS DAY (Irish) — I 223^{P}, I 287, , I 458^{P}, I 500^{5}, I 575^{P}

MISS DIOR b.m. 7 Chaparly (FR) - Sirette by Great Nephew M F Harding

222 16/2 Heythrop (R) RES 3m 17 G *alwys bhnd, t.o. & p.u. 14th* P 0
570 16/3 Garnons (L) MDN 2 1/2m 14 G *ld 4th-5th, chsd clr ldr til wknd grad 14th* 5 0
821 31/3 Paxford (L) MDO 3m 6 F *chsd wnr til f 9th* F -
908 5/4 Howick (L) MDN 3m 7 F *ld 3-4th, chsd wnr aft, no ch frm 13th, fin tired* 2 0
1216 26/4 Woodford (L) MDN 3m 13 G *chsd ldr 9th, ld 13th, wll clr apr 4 out, hdd 2 out,fin tird* 2 0
1460 11/5 Maisemore P' (L) MDO 3m 16 G *prom til mstk & u.r. 11th* U -
1554 24/5 Mounsey Hil' (R) MDO 3m 14 G *(fav) t.d.e. rear of main grp, 6th whn blnd 17th, kpt on, nvr nrr* 4 10
1615 7/6 Umberleigh (L) MDO 3m 11 F *ld aft 5th-14th,lost plc,ran on to chs wnr 2 out,clsng flat* 2 0

Form is modest but is going the right way; easy course looks essential; can win small race. 14

MISS FASHION (Irish) — I 204^{P}, I 606,

MISS FLORIDA (Irish) — I 514^{F}, I 566^{1}

MISS GRUNTLED b.m. 6 Arctic Lord - Sweet Move by Corvaro (USA) Mrs G M S Slater

1996 **P(NH),8(NH)**

524 15/3 Cothelstone (L) RES 3m 10 GS *5th whn hit 13th, bhnd & p.u. 3 out* P 0
867 31/3 Kingston St' (R) MDO 3m 6 F *bhnd til p.u. apr 2 out* P 0
1270 27/4 Little Wind' (R) MDO 2 1/2m 10 GF *jmpd v slwly, sn bhnd, t.o. & p.u. 9th* P 0
1373 5/5 Cotley Farm (L) MDO 3m 6 GF *ld/disp to 13th, lost tch nxt, outpcd frm 3 out* 4 0
1553 24/5 Mounsey Hil' (R) MDO 3m 11 G *blnd 4th, bhnd aft, 10th whn ref 11th* R -

Last when completing & looks unpromising. 0

MISS HUNTCLIFFE ch.m. 10 Deep Run - Woodcliffe by Harwell Mrs G R Dun

613 22/3 Friars Haugh (L) MDN 3m 12 GF *loose bfr start, strgglng whn f 10th* F -

No signs yet. 0

MISSILE MAN b.g. 8 Cruise Missile - Into Song by True Song Mrs J A I'anson

1996 8(15),3(19),5(14),5(14),3(15)

251 22/2 Brocklesby ' (L) RES 3m 16 G *rear div, outpcd 6 out, p.u. 2 out* P 0
616 22/3 Hutton Rudby (L) RES 3m 14 GF *rear, lost tch 8th, t.o. whn p.u. 14th* P 0
1072 13/4 Whitwell-On' (R) MXO 4m 21 G *rear, lost tch 13th, t.o. & p.u. 16th* P 0

Maiden winner 95(finished alone); no form 96; needs soft; may surprise when conditions suit. 14

MISSING LADY (Irish) — I 37^{3}, I 115^{P}, I 173^{1}, I 230^{1}, I 313^{3}, I 346^{2}

MISSING MAMA (Irish) — I 258^{P}, I 317^{P}

MISSISSIPPISTEAMER(IRE) b or br.g. 8 Henbit (USA) - Kekova by Kythnos M E David

1011 12/4 St Hilary (R) MDN 3m 10 GF *whppd round strt, tk no part* 0 0
1137 19/4 Bonvilston (R) MDO 3m 13 G *rear til p.u. 12th* P 0
1323 3/5 Bonvilston (R) MDO 3m 14 G *mid-div early, lost tch whn p.u. 2 out* P 0
1473 11/5 Erw Lon (L) MDO 3m 13 GS *f 4th* F -
1615 7/6 Umberleigh (L) MDO 3m 11 F *chsd ldrs, nvr able to chal, wknd & blnd 3 out, t.o.* 5 0

Tailed off when completing; of no real account. 0

MISS JAKE (Irish) — I 201^{6}, I 226^{4}, I 278^{P}, I 394^{P}

MISS JCB(IRE) b.f. 7 Bulldozer - Busted Angel A Oliver

1996 P(0),0(0),U(-)

259 22/2 Newtown (L) MDN 3m 18 G *n.j.w. bhnd, rdn frm 9th, wll t.o. whn p.u. 3 out* P 0

Temperamental; of no account. 0

MISS JEDD gr.m. 10 Scallywag - Leckywil by Menelek W G Young

413 8/3 Dalston (R) OPE 3m 9 GS *prssd wnr til blnd & nrly u.r. 9th, nt rcvr, p.u. 3 out* P 0
562 16/3 Lanark (R) OPE 3m 8 GS *bhnd by 11th, t.o. whn p.u. 2 out* P 0
946 6/4 Friars Haugh (L) OPE 3m 5 GF *10l 4th whn f 8th* F -

Hurdles winner 95; missed 96; showed nothing in points; unpromising. 12

MISS JOSEPHINE (Irish) — I 19^{4}, I 38^{5}, I 487^{P}, I 538^{P}, I 599,

MISS LURGAN (Irish) — I 55, , I 97^{1}, I 498^{P}, I 573^{1}

MISS LYNCH (Irish) — I 163^{P}, I 200^{P}, I 278^{P}

MISS MADELON gr.m. 5 Absalom - Larive by Blakeney Mrs J C Cooper

347 2/3 Market Rase' (L) MDO 3m 9 GF *hld up bhnd, mstks 4 & 12th, t.o. & p.u. nxt* P 0
699 29/3 Stainton (R) MDO 3m 7 F *made all, qcknd apr last, comf* 1 13
1250 26/4 Easingwold (L) RES 3m 15 GS *(fav) ld & made all to 2 out, hdd & no ext* 3 14

No ability under rules; front runs; easy course looks essential; still young & should progress. 16

MISS MAGIC b.m. 12 Cruise Missile - Magic Mountain by Menelek — F J Brennan

1	19/1	Barbury Cas'	(L)	XX	3m	11	GF	*chsd ldrs, poor 4th hlfwy, no prog*	4	0
59	1/2	Kingston Bl'	(L)	RES	3m	16	GF	*s.s. alwys rear, wll bhnd & p.u. aft 13th*	P	0
221	16/2	Heythrop	(R)	RES	3m	15	G	*cls up, prssd wnr 12th-15th, wknd rpdly*	7	0
585	18/3	Fontwell	(R)	HC	2m 3f	7	GF	*trckd ldr, hit 6th, mstk 10th, soon btn.*	6	0
649	22/3	Siddington	(L)	MEM	3m	6	F	*prom, chsd wnr 9-14th, rdn & btn 3 out, wknd*	3	10
824	31/3	Lockinge	(L)	CON	3m	8	F	*chsd wnr 6th, ld 10-13th, wknd & v tired frm 16th*	2	13
921	5/4	Larkhill	(R)	RES	3m	3	F	*disp to 2nd, ld 4th, sn clr, easily*	1	15
1142	19/4	Larkhill	(R)	OPE	3m	3	F	*disp til ld 3rd, hdd aft 14th, blnd nxt, sn btn*	2	0

Missed 96; found a bad race; barely stays & need same to win again. 14

MISS MALACHITE ch.m. 5 Gildoran - Shining by Golden Dipper — Mrs S Nash

297	1/3	Didmarton	(L)	MDN	3m	11	G	*in tch til blnd & u.r. 8th*	U	-
761	29/3	Kimble	(L)	MDO	3m	12	GF	*in tch early, last at 8th, t.o. & p.u. aft 11th*	P	0

Only learning so far. 0

MISS METAL (Irish) — I 83, , I 166[F], I 487[4], I 514[3], I 561[P]

MISS MILLBROOK b.m. 9 Meadowbrook - Broadwater by Cawston's Clown — D T Goldsworthy

1996 P(0),1(18),3(15),1(18),2(19),**1(28),F(-)**

149	10/2	Hereford	(R)	HC	3m 1f 110yds	18	GS	*held up, hdwy 7th, ld 12th, clr 3 out, blnd last.*	1	31
290	28/2	Newbury	(L)	HC	3m	6	GS	*held up, mstk 3rd, blnd and lost pl 11th, left third 3 out, styd on to go 2nd run-in.*	2	28
494	13/3	Cheltenham	(L)	HC	3 1/4m 110yds	18	G	*in tch, pushed along when hit 15th and next, soon btn, bhnd when p.u. 2 out.*	P	0
715	29/3	Llanvapley	(L)	OPE	3m	8	GF	*(fav) trckd ldr, hrd rdn to disp last, got up cls home*	1	26
1194	22/4	Chepstow	(L)	HC	3m	11	GF	*hdwy 10th, went 2nd and hit 2 out, nvr near wnr.*	2	26
1289	30/4	Cheltenham	(L)	HC	3m 1f 110yds	6	GF	*(fav) trckd ldr 7th, ld 12th till mstk 15th, rdn and mistake 4 out, rallied to ld 2 out, driven out.*	1	26
1491	14/5	Hereford	(R)	HC	3m 1f 110yds	11	G	*(fav) hdwy 10th, ld 14th, driven out run-in.*	1	29

Improved; useful; tough; best with give; just below top horses; win more in 98. 29

MISS MILLIE b.m. 10 Homeboy - Lynebury by Ilbury — W W Stroud

650	22/3	Siddington	(L)	CON	3m	8	F	*schoold, last til p.u. 10th*	P	0

A late starter; showed nothing. 0

MISS MONTGOMERY(IRE) b.m. 6 Montekin - Cherry Avenue by King's Ride — Mrs S M Farr

1996 F(-),4(0),3(0),4(0),3(0),F(-),P(0),2(10)

185	15/2	Erw Lon	(L)	MDN	3m	14	G	*mid-div, 6th & out of tch whn u.r. 11th*	U	-
720	29/3	Llanvapley	(L)	MDN	3m	8	GF	*trckd ldr, ld 12th, made rest, qcknd whn chal apr last*	1	14
1008	12/4	St Hilary	(R)	RES	3m	11	GF	*mid-div, wknd frm 15th*	6	0
1135	19/4	Bonvilston	(R)	RES	3m	14	G	*mid-div, wknd hlfwy, t.o.*	8	0
1184	20/4	Lydstep	(L)	LAD	3m	4	GF	*s.u. bef 6th in rear*	S	-
1225	26/4	Pyle	(R)	LAD	3m	6	GS	*prssd ldr,ld apr 3 out-2 out,rdn whn hmpd last,no ext flat*	2	16
1364	5/5	Pantyderi	(L)	LAD	3m	5	G	*2nd at 3rd, 6l 2nd at 11th, ld & clr last*	1	16
1558	24/5	Bassaleg	(R)	LAD	3m	5	G	*n.j.w. cls up to 11th, wknd rpdly, p.u. 15th*	P	0

Improved; probably fortunate in Ladies; needs easy track; harder to place now. 17

MISS OUTLAW (Irish) — I 163[P], I 202[U], I 231[F], I 280[P]

MISS PANDY b or br.m. 9 Pitpan - Polly Major by Politico (USA) — A O Ashford

306	1/3	Parham	(R)	MDN	3m	12	G	*ld to 8th, grad wknd, bhnd whn p.u. 4 out*	P	0
582	16/3	Detling	(L)	MDN	3m	16	F	*mid-div whn u.r. 11th*	U	-
833	31/3	Heathfield	(R)	MDO	3m	7	F	*disp ld til f 4th*	F	-
1130	19/4	Penshurst	(L)	MDO	3m	5	GF	*nvr dang, tk 3rd last*	3	0

Beaten 6 lengths in one of the seasons worst races; at least she managed a clear round. 0

MISS PANOO ch.m. 6 Presidium - Miss Skindles by Taufan (USA) — O T Lloyd

1240	26/4	Brampton Br'	(R)	MDO	3m	12	G	*rear frm 4th, in tch til mstk 13th, eased & p.u. nxt*	P	0
1324	3/5	Bonvilston	(R)	MDO	3m	16	G	*rear, p.u. 9th*	P	0
1527	17/5	Bredwardine	(R)	MDO	3m	13	G	*mstks, cls up to 12th, wknd, t.o. & p.u. 2 out*	P	0

A glimmer of hope & looks capable of better. 10

MISS PRECOCIOUS b.m. 9 Precocious - Hissy Missy by Bold Lad (IRE) — R C Harper

1996 P(0),P(0)

761	29/3	Kimble	(L)	MDO	3m	12	GF	*cls 3rd frm 6th til wknd 15th, p.u. 2 out*	P	0
1083	13/4	Guilsborough	(L)	MDN	3m	15	GF	*alwys rear, t.o. 14th, p.u. 3 out*	P	0
1166	20/4	Mollington	(R)	MDO	3m	9	GF	*prom, disp whn blnd 11th, effrt agn 14th, sn btn*	3	0

1401 5/5 Ashorne (R) MDO 3m 15 G *cls up, ev ch 15th, wknd nxt, poor 3rd whn u.r. last* U -

Only 2 completions in 12 starts; well beaten in 97 & win looks unlikely. 12

MISS RICUS b.m. 6 Henricus (ATA) - Sue Ming Vii by Damsire Unregistered — Miss P J Boundy

1996 P(0),P(0),3(10),1(14)

175 15/2 Ottery St M' (L) RES 3m 15 G *u.r. 2nd* U -
312 1/3 Clyst St Ma' (L) RES 3m 8 HY *(Jt fav) handy, prog 11th, lft in ld 13th, styd on well* 1 17
522 15/3 Cothelstone (L) CON 3m 14 GS *bhnd til p.u. 12th* P 0
862 31/3 Kingston St' (R) CON 3m 7 F *lft in ld 7th, slght ld til f 16th* F -
1245 26/4 Bratton Down (L) INT 3m 9 GS *mid-div til moved up 3 out, efft short lived* 4 0

Improved; stays but mistakes; not disgraced last 2 starts; needs more for Inter/Confined. 18

MISS SARAJEVO (Irish) — I 384^P

MISS SHAW b.m. 11 Cruise Missile - Fernshaw by Country Retreat — Mrs R Crank

1996 2(15),3(15),2(10),3(11),3(12),**F(-)**,3(12)

83 2/2 Wolverhampt' (L) RES 3m 8 GS *ld to 14th, chal agn 3 out, ev ch whn b.d. nxt* B 18
203 15/2 Weston Park (L) RES 3m 11 G *ld to 11th, onepcd frm nxt, outpcd by 1st pair* 3 10
332 1/3 Eaton Hall (R) RES 3m 18 GS *20s-8s, chsng grp, 2nd at last, ran on und pres to ld flat* 1 19
667 23/3 Eaton Hall (R) CON 3m 10 GF *1st ride, mid-div til prog 14th, ran on onepcd* 3 13
936 6/4 Tabley (R) MEM 3m 9 G *chsd ldrs, mstk 12th, ld 15th, clr 3 out, comf* 1 16
1300 3/5 Weston Park (L) CON 3m 8 G *mid-div 12th, prog nxt, ev ch & rdn 2 out, ran on* 3 19

Showed improvement 97; won 3 placed 13 of last 19 starts; capable of winning again. 19

MISS SIMITAR b.m. 6 Broadsword (USA) - Miss Barle by Prince Barle — Dudley C Moore

24 26/1 Marks Tey (L) MEM 3m 6 GF *bhnd frm 3rd, t.o. & p.u. 17th* P 0
128 9/2 Cottenham (R) MDO 3m 10 GF *in tch til wknd 13th, t.o. & p.u. 16th* P 0

Only learning so far. 0

MISS SOLITAIRE ch.m. 9 St Columbus - Tlucky Diamond by Eborneezer — Mrs M Goodwin

1996 P(0),F(-),2(15),3(11),4(11)

140 9/2 Thorpe Lodge (L) RES 3m 7 GF *mstks, mid-div, nrst fin* 2 13
274 22/2 Ampton (R) RES 3m 10 G *n.j.w. sn wll bhnd, t.o. & p.u. 9th* P 0
449 8/3 Newton Brom' (R) XX 3m 13 G *alwys rear, wll bhnd whn p.u. 3 out* P 0
1076 13/4 Guilsborough (L) MEM 3m 9 GF *cls up, wth ldr 13th, mstk nxt, chal 3 out, alwys hld* 2 18
1164 20/4 Mollington (R) RES 3m 10 GF *ld to 5th, prom, chsd ldr 3 out, no ext nxt* 3 14

Maiden winner 95; poor jumper & needs strong handling; can win modest Restricted on best form. 18

MISS THIMBLE (Irish) — I 167^P

MISTAKEN IDENTITY b.g. 6 Rough Lad - Mickley Vulmoss by Sea Moss — Mrs J E Harries

542 16/3 Erw Lon (L) MDN 3m 15 GF *mstk 3rd, rear, p.u. 12th* P 0
1473 11/5 Erw Lon (L) MDO 3m 13 GS *alwys twrds rear, p.u. 12th* P 0

Schooled round for 2 miles on both outings so far. 0

MISTER BLACK(IRE) ch.g. 9 Mister Lord (USA) - Minstrel Top by Black Minstrel — Mrs N J Hollows

1996 **5(NH),4(NH),3(NH),5(NH),10(NH)**

123 9/2 Cottenham (R) INT 3m 13 GF *chsd ldr 5th, ld aft 10th til 3 out, ev ch last, wknd* 2 21
333 1/3 Eaton Hall (R) INT 3m 10 GS *j.w. w.w. bhnd runaway ldr, lft clr 10th, unchal* 1 20
464 8/3 Eyton-On-Se' (L) INT 3m 12 G *(fav) ld/disp thruout,hdd 3 out,ran on und pres last,f heavily* F 20

Winning Irish pointer & placed hurdles; interesting recruit; stays; win again if fit in 98. 22

MISTER BUZIOS ch.g. 9 Import - Leonora by Leander — Miss D L Wightman

343 1/3 Corbridge (R) MDO 3m 14 G *ld til u.r. 10th* U -
612 22/3 Friars Haugh (L) MDN 3m 14 GF *ld til 4 out, no ext frm nxt* 3 0

Well beaten when placed; front runs and a little more stamina needed. 12

MISTER CHIPPENDALE b.g. 10 Floriferous - Midi Skirt by Kabale — Mrs D S R Watson

1996 P(0),P(0),1(12),4(10),F(-)

74 2/2 Market Rase' (L) MEM 3m 4 GF *last whn hit 7th, t.o. & p.u. 4 out* P 0
472 9/3 Southwell P' (L) MEM 3m 3 G *(fav) chsd ldr, blnd 5th & rmndr, ld brfly apr 12th, wll btn 2 out* 2 0
887 1/4 Flagg Moor (L) XX 3m 8 G *mid-div, 5th & rdn 11th, wknd whn blnd 12th & p.u.* P 0

Finished alone in Members96; shows minimal interest now & looks finished. 10

MISTER GEBO b.g. 12 Strong Gale - Miss Goldiane by Baragoi — Mrs D J Dyson

1996 3(18),3(0),6(14),2(21)

878 1/4 Upton-On-Se' (R) XX 3m 11 GF *(fav) in tch, trckd ldr 8th, ld 15th, drew clr apr last* 1 17
1148 19/4 Chaddesley ' (L) LAD 3m 5 GF *ld to 3rd & 5th-15th, ld nxt, hdd & blnd 2 out, no ch aft* 2 17
1327 3/5 Chaddesley ' (L) LAD 3m 3 GF *ld to 3rd, prssd wnr til 15th, onepcd aft* 2 18
1490 13/5 Chepstow (L) HC 3m 7 G *alwys bhnd, t.o. when p.u. before 2 out.* P 0

1590	31/5	Stratford	(L)	HC	3m	9	G	*struggling and driven along after one cct, relentless prog to chase ldng pair final circuit, kept on one pace from 3 out.*	4	21

3 wins, 13 places, 94-7; found right opening 97; needs things his own way & getting on now. 19

MISTER HORATIO b.g. 7 Derring Rose - Miss Horatio by Spartan General — W D Lewis

1996 1(20),2(22),1(20),1(23),2(15),**6(0)**

187	15/2	Erw Lon	(L)	OPE	3m	16	G	*prssd ldr, ld 11th, drew clr 15th, rdn out flat*	1	26
295	1/3	Didmarton	(L)	OPE	3m	9	G	*mstk 5th, chsd ldrs, 4th & btn frm 12th til f 2 out*	F	-
715	29/3	Llanvapley	(L)	OPE	3m	8	GF	*j.w., ld 6th, jnd last, just outpcd final 50yds*	2	26
1086	14/4	Southwell	(L)	HC	3m 110yds	11	G	*(Jt fav) chsd ldrs, ld apr 3 out, clr next.*	1	26
1295	2/5	Bangor	(L)	HC	3m 110yds	4	G	*prom, jmpd slowly 3rd, outpcd when hit 14th, rdn to chase clr wnr apr 3 out, no ch when mstk last.*	2	20
1416	10/5	Newton Abbot	(L)	HC	2m 5f 110yds	14	G	*held up, hdwy 9th, wknd apr 2 out.*	4	24
1588	30/5	Stratford	(L)	HC	3 1/2m	9	G	*prom, chsd ldr from 16th, challenging when blnd and u.r. 4 out.*	U	-

Improved; novice ridden; mistakes; running well last start; could prove useful in the right hands. 27

MISTER JAY DAY b.g. 7 Domitor (USA) - Habille by On Your Mark — William John Day

1996 P(0),P(0),3(10),P(0)

367	2/3	Garnons	(L)	MDO	2 1/2m	9	GS	*ld to 3rd, wknd rpdly 11th, p.u. 3 out*	P	0
409	8/3	Llanfrynach	(R)	MDN	3m	12	G	*cls up, gd prog 15th, 3rd & ev ch whn f 2 out*	F	-
719	29/3	Llanvapley	(L)	MDN	3m	14	GF	*2nd/3rd til clr 2nd frm 11th, onepcd frm 3 out*	3	10
1136	19/4	Bonvilston	(R)	MDO	3m	15	G	*3rd/4th til ld 13th, made rest, qcknd whn chal flat*	1	15

Maintained steady progress; easily won modest race; more needed but should keep progressing. 15

MISTER KINGSTON ch.g. 6 Kinglet - Flaxen Tina by Beau Tudor — Mrs S Gee

208	16/2	Southwell P'	(L)	MDO	3m	9	GS	*chsng grp, prog to 3rd apr 12th, f 14th*	F	-
372	2/3	Mollington	(R)	RES	3m	19	G	*trckd ldrs, outpcd 12th, no prog, poor 5th whn p.u. 2 out*	P	0
550	16/3	Garthorpe	(R)	MDO	3m	11	GF	*ld/disp to 11th,ld appr 3 out, rddn & styd on wll frm 2 out*	1	15
1081	13/4	Guilsborough	(L)	RES	3m	13	GF	*(Jt fav) trckd ldng pair, outpcd aft 16th, no ch aft, onepcd*	4	10

Subsequent winner behind when winning; scopey; top stable & looks sure to progress. 18

MISTER MAIN MAN(IRE) ch.g. 9 Remainder Man - Mainstown Belle by Peacock (FR) — Sir Chippendale Keswick

1996 5(23),2(21),3(20)

271	22/2	Ampton	(R)	CON	3m	15	G	*(fav) cls up, ld 3rd, made rest, shkn up & drw clr appr 2 out,easy*	1	23
389	8/3	Sandown	(R)	HC	2 1/2m 110yds	6	G	*(fav) blnd 4th, hdwy 12th, ev ch when hit last, kept on same pace run-in.*	2	22
926	6/4	Garthorpe	(R)	OPE	3m	10	GF	*prom, 3rd 6th-12th, went 2nd apr 2 out, ran on onepcd*	2	21
1079	13/4	Guilsborough	(L)	OPE	3m	6	GF	*w.w. cls engh 15th, outpcd 3 out, no dang aft*	3	20
1354	4/5	Dingley	(R)	MXO	3m	3	G	*made all, 5l clr 2 out, rddn out*	1	23
1501	16/5	Folkestone	(R)	HC	3 1/4m	10	G	*(fav) ld to 3 out, led again next, rdn last, held on und pres run- in.*	1	21

Consistent solid; stays, jumps, best r/h; win Opens & another modest H/chase possible in 98. 23

MISTER MALONE (Irish) — **I** 585,

MISTER MCGASKILL ch.g. 8 Itsu (USA) - Deep Depression by Weathercock — P L Thomas

1996 P(0),P(0),6(0),1(14)

45	1/2	Larkhill	(R)	RES	3m	14	GF	*prom, disp whn f 5th*	F	-
190	15/2	Erw Lon	(L)	RES	3m	11	G	*made most to 9th, sn wknd, t.o. & p.u. 13th*	P	0
539	16/3	Erw Lon	(L)	RES	3m	8	GF	*rear, prog frm 14th, nvr able to chal*	2	14
845	31/3	Lydstep	(L)	RES	3m	5	F	*(fav) sttld rear, prog 4 out, nvr thrtnd wnr*	2	11

Maiden winner 96; placed in weak Restricteds; needs longer tracks; should find a race. 15

MISTER ONE b or br.g. 6 Buckley - Miss Redlands by Dubassoff (USA) — Paul K Barber

44	1/2	Larkhill	(R)	MDO	3m	9	GF	*(fav) hld up, prog 13th, ld 3 out, easily*	1	16
298	1/3	Didmarton	(L)	RES	3m	15	G	*(fav) trckd ldrs,ld 11th,hdd apr last,lft in ld last,hdd nr fin*	2	20

Half brother to See More Business; top stable; just pipped by H/chase winner; one to watch. 23

MISTER RAINMAN br.g. 8 Morston's Heir - Artwogan by Tarqogan — G H Barber

1996 F(-),P(0),2(12),F(-)

30	26/1	Marks Tey	(L)	MDN	3m	9	GF	*w.w. prog 9th, chsd wnr 17th, 5l down whn f 3 out*	F	-
317	1/3	Marks Tey	(L)	MDN	3m	13	G	*hld up, prog 8th, outpcd apr 15th, t.o. & p.u. 17th*	P	0
796	31/3	Marks Tey	(L)	MDO	3m	6	F	*chsd ldrs,wknd last 9th,prog und pres 11th,p.u. dismntd 13th*	P	0

2nd in bad race 96; no other completions & problems last start; more needed. 12

MISTER SPECTATOR(IRE) br.g. 8 Mandalus - Focal Point by Hawaiian Sound (USA) — Paddy Hughes

1996 F(-),r(-),F(-)

13	25/1	Cottenham	(R)	MDO	3m	10	GF	*made all, clr 5th, hit last, unchal*	1	21
126	9/2	Cottenham	(R)	RES	3m	14	GF	*(fav) made all, drew clr aft 2 out, ran on well*	1	21
911	5/4	Cottenham	(R)	OPE	3m	3	F	*made all, shkn up & drew clr 3 out, hrd hld*	1	23

1286 29/4 Huntingdon (R) HC 3m 10 G *ld 2nd to 8th, pressed wnr after, mstk 12th, ev ch 3 out, wknd next, well btn when blnd last.* 2 20
1502 16/5 Folkestone (R) HC 2m 5f 10 G *(fav) n.j.w. and nvr going well, lost pl 5th, well bhnd when p.u. before 7th, lame.* P 0

Much improved for new riders; useful pointer; excuses last start & H/chase likely if fit in 97. 22

MISTIC HIGHWAY (Irish) — **I** 278^{P}

MISTI HUNTER(IRE) gr.g. 8 Roselier (FR) - Lovely Stranger by Le Bavard (FR) Mrs D Ibbotson
1996 **1(NH)**

166 15/2 Witton Cast' (R) OPE 3m 8 F *rear, some prog 15th, no hdwy aft* 6 14
267 22/2 Duncombe Pa' (R) OPE 3m 8 G *reluctant to race & v slwly away,alwys wll bhd,p.u. 13th* P 0
423 8/3 Charm Park (L) OPE 3m 7 GF *prom til stdly fdd frm 3 out, lft 3rd last* 3 19
696 29/3 Stainton (R) OPE 3m 5 F *mid-div,2nd 4th,outpcd 16th,ran on strgly apr last,ld flat* 1 19
1071 13/4 Whitwell-On' (R) CON 3m 10 G *hld up, prog 11th, ev ch last, rallied nr fin* 2 22

Winning chaser; quirky & needs strong handling; stays & quite capable of another win. 21

MISTRESS DASHER b.m. 7 Relkino - Bengal Lady by Celtic Cone Colin Gee

776 29/3 Dingley (R) MDO 2m 5f 10 G *disp, ld 10th-4 out, ev ch whn f nxt* F -

Showed speed on debut & should go close if fit in 98. 11

MISTRESS GALE (Irish) — **I** 428^{6}, **I** 453^{4}, **I** 514^{5}, **I** 572^{5}, **I** 599, , **I** 608^{5}

MISTRESS LINNET b.m. 7 Crested Lark - Master Suite by Master Owen A S Templeton

318 1/3 Marks Tey (L) MDN 3m 13 G *bhnd, lost tch 8th, t.o. & p.u. apr 11th* P 0
499 15/3 Ampton (R) MDO 3m 9 GF *trkd ldrs, cls 3rd & gng wll 15th, btn appr 2 out* 6 11

Lightly raced; 1st signs on last start; beaten under 4 lengths under tender ride. 12

MISTY(NZ) b.g. 10 Ivory Hunter (USA) - Our Loaming (NZ) by Sovereign Edition Mrs J E Milne
1996 1(14),**4(15)**,5(0),4(14),4(0),5(0),**2(0)**,**P(0)**

59 1/2 Kingston Bl' (L) RES 3m 16 GF *nvr nr ldrs* 7 0
285 26/2 Taunton (R) HC 4 1/4m 110yds 16 GS *chsd ldrs to 11th, t.o. when p.u. before 3 out.* P 0

Won poor race in the mud 96; hard ride & future prospects virtually nil. 14

MISTY NIGHT gr.m. 9 Grey Desire - Maha by Northfields (USA) Mrs M A Bowie

132 9/2 Alnwick (L) LAD 3m 9 G *chsd ldrs, lft in ld 11th, made rest, lft clr 3 out, styd on* 1 0
336 1/3 Corbridge (R) LAD 3m 5f 9 G *(fav) mid-div, prog 12th, ld 14th-16th, ld last, ran on strngly* 1 22
606 22/3 Friars Haugh (L) MEM 3m 9 GF *(fav) not fluent, 3rd 9th, ld apr 4 out, pshd out flat* 1 20
731 29/3 Alnwick (L) MXO 4m 7 F *(fav) nvr going wll, losing tch whn p.u. 17th, lame* P 0

Missed 96; returned in great form but problems last start; win more Ladies if fit in 98. 22

MISWISKERS br.m. 7 Reesh - That Space by Space King Tom Dawson

408 8/3 Llanfrynach (R) MDN 3m 12 G *tongue-strap, rear, p.u. 8th* P 0
575 16/3 Garnons (L) RES 3m 12 G *ld to 6th, wknd 8th, p.u. 12th* P 0

Showed early speed but no stamina & unpromising. 0

MITCHELLS BEST br.g. 11 True Song - Emmalina by Doubtless II A Hollingsworth
1996 P(0),4(11),4(17),4(10),4(14),1(19),3(19),3(19)

218 16/2 Heythrop (R) INT 3m 21 G *bhnd, lost tch 12th, styd on frm 3 out, nrst fin* 6 14
256 22/2 Newtown (L) OPE 3m 17 G *rear, prog 10th, outpcd 15th, ran on 2 out, fin well* 3 22
380 4/3 Leicester (R) HC 3m 9 G *prom, rdn apr 3 out, styd on same pace.* 3 13
879 1/4 Upton-On-Se' (R) MXO 3m 4 GF *cls up til outpcd 12th, kpt on to tk 2nd aft last* 2 16
1214 26/4 Woodford (L) OPE 3m 5 G *ld to 12th, last & rdn apr 4 out, kpt on onepcd* 3 17

One win from last 26 starts (Members); consistent but very onepaced & easily beaten by Open horses. 20

MITCHELSTOWN RIVER (Irish) — **I** 147^{P}, **I** 230^{4}, **I** 439^{P}

MITIDEBE (Irish) — **I** 52^{F}, **I** 102^{5}

MITTENWALD(IRE) b.g. 8 Denel (FR) - Garden Of Roses by London Bells (CAN) Mrs J E Tamplin
1996 **6(NH)**,**5(NH)**,**11(NH)**,**3(NH)**

408 8/3 Llanfrynach (R) MDN 3m 12 G *cls up, 4th at 14th, rpd prog 2 out, ld last* 1 14
718 29/3 Llanvapley (L) RES 3m 13 GF *(fav) mid-div, p.u. 10th & dismntd* P 0

Placed nov hurdles; beat 6 others but hit trouble next time; needs more. 15

MOBILE MESSENGER(NZ) b.g. 9 Ring The Bell (NZ) - Sleepy Slipper (NZ) by Avaray (FR) Mrs D C Samworth
1996 **F(NH)**,**4(NH)**,**P(NH)**,**3(NH)**,**3(NH)**,**2(NH)**,**2(NH)**,**2(NH)**,**P(NH)**

226 21/2 Haydock (L) HC 3m 11 G *ld to 4th, 5th and in tch when f 9th.* F -
383 5/3 Catterick (L) HC 3m 1f 110yds 10 G *prom till outpcd and bhnd from hfwy.* 6 13
1290 30/4 Cheltenham (L) HC 4m 1f 10 GF *alwys bhnd, t.o. from 17th, p.u. run-in, lame.* P 0

Long standing Maiden under rules; novice ridden & outclassed in H/chases; problems now. 14

MOCKLERSHILL LADY (Irish) — **I** 91[P], **I** 159[P], **I** 186[U], **I** 271[P], **I** 296[P]

MOHERA KING (Irish) — **I** 141[P]

MOLE STAR (Irish) — **I** 506[F], **I** 552[P]

MOLLS CHOICE (Irish) — **I** 15[3], **I** 63[2], **I** 108[P], **I** 131[4]

MOLLY GREY(IRE) gr.m. 6 Boreen (FR) - Golden Robe by Yankee Gold — P Monteith

386 7/3 Ayr (L) HC 2m 5f 110yds 7 S *blnd 3rd, bhnd, mstks, t.o. when p.u. before 4 out.* P 0
564 16/3 Lanark (R) MDO 2 1/2m 13 GS *sn bhnd, p.u. 2 out* P 0

Too many jumping errors so far. 0

MONARROW(IRE) b.g. 9 Carlingford Castle - Christy's Arrow by Mon Capitaine — Miss S Buckley
1996 P(0),2(14),1(14),3(13)

77 2/2 Market Rase' (L) RES 3m 9 GF *1st ride, last frm 11th, t.o.* 6 0
213 16/2 Southwell P' (L) RES 3m 16 GS *bhnd, prog 9th, chsd ldrs 13th, no hdwy frm nxt* 5 14

Dead 15

MONDAY'S NEWS (Irish) — **I** 601[4], **I** 602[P]

MONEY DON'T MATTER br.m. 5 Arctic Lord - Raheny by Sir Herbert — S W Rudge

1239 26/4 Brampton Br' (R) MDO 3m 9 G *nrly f 2nd, in tch til wknd & ran off course aft 11th* r -
1460 11/5 Maisemore P' (L) MDO 3m 16 G *rear, in tch whn mstk 12th, 5th & wll btn whn u.r. 15th* U -
1528 17/5 Bredwardine (R) MDO 3m 17 G *mstk 8th, alwys bhnd, t.o. 12th* 8 0
1609 1/6 Dingley (R) MDO 3m 14 GF *jmpd badly, t.o. til p.u. 10th* P 0

Jumped awfully so far and looks unpromising. 0

MONEY MATTERS (Irish) — **I** 171[P], **I** 515[2]

MONKSFORT b.g. 11 Monksfield - Karamble by Karabas — Miss C Holliday
1996 P(0),1(15),P(0),1(24)

125 9/2 Cottenham (R) LAD 3m 11 GF *wll in tch, prog to jn ldrs whn u.r. 13th* U -
279 23/2 Charing (L) CON 3m 10 G *(fav) t.d.e. prssd ldr, chal & lvl last, not qckn flat* 2 18
577 16/3 Detling (L) CON 3m 18 F *ld 6-13th, chsd wnr aft, stdly outpcd, wknd 2 out* 4 14
604 22/3 Parham (R) CON 3m 3 F *(fav) made all, styd on wll frm 3 out* 1 20

Won 3 of 8 starts pointing; likes to dictate & struggles in Ladies; should win again; Good. 20

MONOROSE b.m. 8 Nomination - Phoenix Rose by Frankincense — Mrs Sandra C Morton

700 29/3 Upper Sapey (R) MEM 3m 8 GF *last by 2nd, imprvd 6th hlfwy, t.o. & p.u. 15th* P 0
1018 12/4 Bitterley (L) MDO 3m 13 GF *alwys rear, t.o. 8th* 7 0

Last when completing; needs huge improvement 0

MONTEBA (Irish) — **I** 40[2], **I** 85[2], **I** 169[1]

MONTYKOSKY b.g. 10 Montekin - Reliable Rosie by Relko — A L Wallace
1996 3(0),P(0)

466 8/3 Eyton-On-Se' (L) LAD 3m 7 G *trckd ldrs to 10th, lost tch 12th, p.u. 4 out* P 0
1538 18/5 Wolverhampt' (L) CON 3m 8 GS *mid-div, t.o. 9th, p.u. nxt* P 0

Restricted winner 94; only 4 runs 95-7 & shows nothing now. 10

MONTYS DELIGHT (Irish) — **I** 28[F], **I** 57[1]

MONYNUT ch.m. 8 Celtic Cone - Mount St Mary's by Lochnager — Miss Sally Harding
1996 P(0),P(0),7(0),**P(0)**,P(0)

36 26/1 Alnwick (L) MDO 3m 15 G *rear grp, no prog whn hmpd & u.r. 13th* U -
134 9/2 Alnwick (L) MDO 3m 11 G *mid-div, blnd 9th, p.u. nxt* P 0

No sign of ability yet 0

MOONBAY LADY b.m. 7 State Diplomacy (USA) - Burntwood Lady by Royal Buck — Gary Andrew
1996 P(0),P(0),U(-),3(0),P(0),P(0),P(0)

242 22/2 Lemalla (R) MDO 3m 10 S *rear, lft remote 3rd by dfctrs 15th, completed own time* 3 0
808 31/3 Wadebridge (L) MDO 3m 8 F *alwys towrds rear til p.u. aft 9th* P 0

Beaten miles when finishing & looks a forlorn hope. 0

MOONLIGHT CRUISE b.m. 9 Cruise Missile - Saucy Moon by Saucy Kit — Miss T Hughes
1996 4(0),P(0),2(10),3(10),3(13),1(13)

189 15/2 Erw Lon (L) RES 3m 14 G *cls up, effrt 14th, sn outpcd, kpt on to tk 2nd flat* 2 15
298 1/3 Didmarton (L) RES 3m 15 G *in tch whn f 7th* F -
405 8/3 Llanfrynach (R) RES 3m 15 G *mostly 4th/5th, styd on onepcd frm 3 out* 3 13
1227 26/4 Pyle (R) RES 3m 15 GS *lost plc 4th, sn wll in rear, t.o. last whn p.u. 12th* P 0

1365 5/5 Pantyderi (L) RES 3m 10 G *rear at 3rd, 9th at 11th, ran on aft last, not rch wnr* 2 17
1471 11/5 Erw Lon (L) RES 3m 9 GS *mid-div whn f 12th* F -

Won 1 placed 9 last 16 starts; tries hard & should find a weak Restricted; G-S. 16

MOONLIGHT STORY b.g. 6 Rolfe (USA) - Fixby Story by Sweet Story Miss E C S Daniels

1082 13/4 Guilsborough (L) MDN 3m 14 GF *t.o. til ref 7th* R -

Stopped after a mile on debut. 0

MOON MONKEY(IRE) b.g. 9 Derring Rose - Paiukiri by Ballyciptic Mrs D Butler

14 25/1 Cottenham (R) MDO 3m 7 GF *bhnd whn mstks 6th & 7th, t.o. frm 11th* 6 0
223 16/2 Heythrop (R) RES 3m 19 G *wll bhnd, kpt on frm 15th, no dang* 6 0
380 4/3 Leicester (R) HC 3m 9 G *chsd ldrs, rdn 9th, wknd 11th, bhnd when mstk and u.r. 2 out.* U -

Poor novice hurdler/chaser; needs to concentrate on Maidens but needs more before winning. 11

MOONVOOR (Irish) — I 42F, I 50F, I 172P, I 324P, I 484[1], I 541[4], I 604[1]

MOOR HILL LASS(IRE) b.f. 7 King Persian - Sevens Wild P J Roberts

1996 **10(NH),P(NH)**

406 8/3 Llanfrynach (R) RES 3m 13 G *f 4th* F -
540 16/3 Erw Lon (L) MDN 3m 13 GF *prom to 9th, wknd aft* 5 0
720 29/3 Llanvapley (L) MDN 3m 8 GF *1st ride, 2nd til f 7th* F -
908 5/4 Howick (L) MDN 3m 7 F *ld 4th, mstk 10th, wll clr 13th, unchal* 1 15
1131 19/4 Bonvilston (R) MEM 3m 6 G *(Jt fav) ld til f 14th* F -
1227 26/4 Pyle (R) RES 3m 15 GS *wth ldrs, disp whn ran out & u.r. 6th* r -

No ability under rules; romped home in poor race; headstrong & mistakes; needs more to upgrade. 14

MOORLAND MAGIC(IRE) b.m. 5 Common Grounds - Red Magic by Red God Mrs Diana Bibby

459 8/3 Great Treth' (R) MDO 3m 9 S *ld 8-10th, lost grnd 13th, p.u. apr 16th, imprvd* P 0
643 22/3 Castle Of C' (R) MDO 3m 12 G *mid-div, cls 5th at 12th, wknd nxt, p.u. 14th* P 0
795 31/3 Bishopsleigh (R) MDO 3m 12 G *prom, 2nd to 14th, wknd & p.u. 17th* P 0

Shows some promise but needs more stamina; can improve. 10

MOORLOUGH BAY(IRE) ch.g. 7 Abednego - Monica's Pet by Sovereign Gleam A Leigh

1138 19/4 Bonvilston (R) MDO 3m 9 G *(fav) prom early, ld 10th, hdd nxt, wknd qckly & p.u. last* P 0
1216 26/4 Woodford (L) MDN 3m 13 G *bhnd, poor 7th hlfwy, grad clsd, ld 2 out, sn clr* 1 14
1439 10/5 Holnicote (L) RES 3m 9 G *chsd ldr to 13th, lost ground aft 15th, p.u. last* P 0

ex Irish N/H; outstayed rivals when winning; needs stamina test; Resticted possible; G-S. 16

MOPHEAD KELLY ch.g. 8 Netherkelly - Trois Filles by French Marny P R Whiston

1996 P(0),P(0),2(13)

81 2/2 Wolverhampt' (L) MDN 3m 13 GS *chsd ldrs til wknd 12th, t.o. & p.u. 14th* P 0
468 8/3 Eyton-On-Se' (L) RES 3m 11 G *j.s., rear early, cls order 10th, wknd, p.u. 2 out* P 0
664 23/3 Eaton Hall (R) MDO 3m 12 GF *mid-div, prog to disp 3 out, not qckn aft* 4 10
1304 3/5 Weston Park (L) MDO 3m 8 G *ld 10-12th, wknd, p.u. 15th* P 0

Placed in 2 weak Maidens 96/97; stamina suspect & needs more. 10

MORAN BRIG ch.g. 7 Bustino - Aunt Judy by Great Nephew Guy Luck

1996 P(0),P(0),6(0),U(-),4(0)

306 1/3 Parham (R) MDN 3m 12 G *mid-div til u.r. 8th* U -

Only beaten one horse so far & vanished quickly in 97; barely rateable but in a very weak area. 10

MORANS FORGE (Irish) — I 113P, I 209U, I 330P, I 377P

MORCHARD GEM ch.m. 5 Out Of Hand - Border Gem by Border Chief R T Grant

1481 11/5 Ottery St M' (L) CON 3m 12 G *rear whn ran out 6th* r -
1520 17/5 Bratton Down (L) MDO 3m 17 GS *twrds rear whn f 10th* F -
1583 26/5 Lifton (R) MDO 3m 11 G *nvr going wll, bhnd whn p.u. 12th* P 0
1597 31/5 Bratton Down (L) MDO 3m 12 F *last when f heavily 8th* F -

An awful debut season. 0

MORCHARD MILL b.g. 5 Out Of Hand - Dorothy Jane by He Loves Me R T Grant

1485 11/5 Ottery St M' (L) MDO 3m 13 G *bhnd whn f 7th* F -
1521 17/5 Bratton Down (L) MDO 3m 16 GS *u.r. 2nd* U -

Yet to get beyond a mile. 0

MORCHARD MILLY br.m. 10 Remezzo - Border Gem by Border Chief R T Grant

1996 6(0),2(10),U(-),5(11),3(13),1(16),3(19)

533 15/3 Wadebridge (L) INT 3m 5 GF *trckd ldrs til u.r. 12th* U -
804 31/3 Wadebridge (L) INT 3m 6 F *ld 14th til no ext cls home* 2 16
1039 12/4 Lifton (R) RES 3m 8 F *ld 7th til hdd 3 out, kpt on und press* 2 15

1093	16/4	Hockworthy	(L)	RES	3m	16	GF	*chsd ldrs, lost plc & rdn hlfwy, sn no ch, kpt on 2 out*	3	11
1241	26/4	Bratton Down	(L)	MEM	3m	4	GS	*cls up til lost ground 4 out*	3	0
1483	11/5	Ottery St M'	(L)	RES	3m	15	G	*mid-div early, 4th at 13th, lost tch 15th, blnd 2 out & p.u.*	P	0
1547	24/5	Mounsey Hil'	(R)	MEM	3m	9	G	*ld to 7th, chsd wnr aft 9th, ev ch 3 out, btn last*	3	15
1582	26/5	Lifton	(R)	INT	3m	10	G	*cls up til wknd 4 out, kpt on onepcd frm 2 out*	6	10
1613	7/6	Umberleigh	(L)	RES	3m	13	F	*alwys wll bhnd, 11th & t.o. whn u.r. 12th*	U	

1 win 17 places from 35 points; moderate & need fortune to find Restricted; Members best hope. 14

MORE BANTER b.g. 7 Politico (USA) - Little Ginger by Cawston's Clown — R Barr

1996 **9(NH),4(NH),6(NH),2(NH),6(NH)**

1331	3/5	Mosshouses	(L)	MEM	3m	5	F	*2nd til 10th, sn strgglng, t.o. & p.u. aft 12th*	P	0

Placed Irish hurdles/chases; no encouragement on points debut over here. 0

MORE BOOZE (Irish) — **I** 615^{P}

MORE MANNERS b.h. 12 Buzzards Bay - Dewberry by Bay Express — Miss M Bragg

586	19/3	Exeter	(R)	HC	3 1/4m	12	GF	*chsd ldrs, mstk 7 out, soon wknd, bhnd when p.u. after 5 out.*	P	0

Resricted winner 93; hardly runs now; looks finished. 14

MORE OF IT b.g. 12 Furry Glen - Homewrecker by Wrekin Rambler — Christopher Hall

1996 **11(NH),18(NH),P(NH)**

282	23/2	Charing	(L)	INT	3m	7	G	*trckd ldr, ld 13-14th, wknd nxt, p.u. 16th*	P	0
579	16/3	Detling	(L)	OPE	4m	9	F	*mstly mid-div til wknd 19th, no ch whn p.u. 22nd*	P	0
830	31/3	Heathfield	(R)	MXO	3m	6	F	*chsd ldrs, 3rd & rdn 15th, blnd nxt, kpt on frm 2 out*	4	17

Winning hurdler; beaten under 5 lengths in weak Open; hard to find a win; Members worth a try. 14

MORE PEOPLE (Irish) — **I** 484^{P}, **I** 568^{3}

MORE RAIN(IRE) br.g. 6 Tidaro (USA) - Hasty Years by Hul A Hul — P F Craggs

1173	20/4	Hexham Poin'	(L)	MDO	2 1/2m	9	GF	*6th whn p.u. 6th*	P	0
1428	10/5	Aspatria	(L)	MDO	3m	11	G	*chsd ldrs, 4th & outpcd 13th, no prog aft, t.o.*	3	0
1513	17/5	Corbridge	(R)	MDO	3m	13	GS	*prom til wknd 3 out, f nxt*	F	-

Well beaten when completing; can do better & go close 98. 11

MORGANTWO b.g. 11 Montekin - Heure de Pointe (FR) by Le Fabuleux — J T Evans

568	16/3	Garnons	(L)	CON	3m	12	G	*ld 1st, cls up til outpcd 9th, t.o. & p.u. last*	P	0

Irish Chase winner 92; rarely runs & of no real account now. 0

MORRAJAY (Irish) — **I** 390^{P}, **I** 483^{P}, **I** 595^{5}

MORSTONS MAGIC b.g. 9 Morston's Heir - Sdenka Royal by Queen's Hussar — G H Barber

24	26/1	Marks Tey	(L)	MEM	3m	6	GF	*1st ride, bhnd til u.r. 9th*	U	-
797	31/3	Marks Tey	(L)	MDO	3m	4	F	*ld til jnd 14th, hdd 16th, wknd qckly nxt, t.o. & f 2 out*	F	-

Ran prominently in bad race but much more needed. 0

MORSTONS STAR b.g. 6 Morston's Heir - Honourable Girl by Sunyboy — G H Barber

796	31/3	Marks Tey	(L)	MDO	3m	6	F	*s.s., last whn ran thru wing 3rd*	r	-

No star turn on debut. 0

MO'S CHORISTER b.g. 11 Lir - Revelstoke by North Stoke — Mrs J Marsh

1996 3(13),2(15),P(0),4(10)

491	10/3	Taunton	(R)	HC	3m	8	G	*ld till f 1st.*	F	-
536	16/3	Erw Lon	(L)	LAD	3m	9	GF	*ld 1st, trckd ldrs aft, onepcd frm 9th*	4	15
716	29/3	Llanvapley	(L)	LAD	3m	5	GF	*alwys last, fin own time*	3	0
1133	19/4	Bonvilston	(R)	INT	3m	8	G	*rear, no ch frm hlfwy*	5	0
1225	26/4	Pyle	(R)	LAD	3m	6	GS	*mstk 7th, sn last, no ch frm 14th*	4	0

Dual winner 93; lightly raced now; losing sequence of 11 will be extended. 11

MOSCOW SQUEAKER (Irish) — **I** 255^{P}

MOSES MAN (Irish) — **I** 117^{P}, **I** 127^{4}, **I** 247, , **I** 293^{5}, **I** 463^{3}, **I** 508^{P}, **I** 554^{F}, **I** 583^{U}

MO'S KELIRO b.m. 5 Lir - Bossy Cleo by Proud Challenge — Mrs J Marsh

719	29/3	Llanvapley	(L)	MDN	3m	14	GF	*rear, p.u. 3 out*	P	0
1136	19/4	Bonvilston	(R)	MDO	3m	15	G	*rear til f 10th*	F	-
1229	26/4	Pyle	(R)	MDO	3m	11	GS	*mstks, last & wkng whn ran out & u.r. 12th*	r	-
1323	3/5	Bonvilston	(R)	MDO	3m	14	G	*rear, styd on onepcd frm 3 out*	5	0

Beaten 65 lengths when completing; at least she got round but far more needed. 0

MOSS BEE br.g. 10 Zambrano - Brown Bee III by Marcus Superbus — W G Reed

34 26/1 Alnwick (L) OPE 3m 9 G *prom to 7th, sn wknd, t.o. & p.u. 12th* P 0

Winning chaser; last won in 94; rarely seen now & can only be watched. 0

MOSSIDE ch.g. 8 Le Moss - Eight Of Diamonds by Silent Spring — B W Gillbard

1996 3(13),2(13),1(15),4(11),U(-),P(0),P(0)

313 1/3 Clyst St Ma' (L) RES 3m 10 HY *(fav) in tch, 2nd 3 out, no imp on wnr* 2 13
556 16/3 Ottery St M' (L) RES 3m 12 G *alwys mid-div, p.u. 13th* P 0
1108 19/4 Flete Park (R) RES 3m 14 GF *8th at 10th, prog 15th, kpt on und pres clsng stgs* 4 16
1339 3/5 Flete Park (R) RES 3m 6 G *mstk & lost plc 12th, t.o. & p.u. 15th* P 0

No form under Rules; won poor Maiden; looks suspect; struggling in Restricteds since 14

MOSSIMAN(IRE) b.g. 9 Le Moss - Suparoli by Super Sam — Nicholas Alexander

1996 7(0)

416 8/3 Dalston (R) RES 3m 12 GS *alwys rear, t.o. whn f 3 out* F -

Very lightly raced; shows nothing. 0

MOSS PAC (Irish) — **I** 74F

MOSS TREE (Irish) — **I** 497F

MOST INTERESTING b.m. 12 Music Boy - Quick Glance by Oats — Mrs R Jones

1996 **5(NH),4(NH),9(NH)**

1525 17/5 Bredwardine (R) LAD 3m 9 G *in tch to 12th, t.o. 15th, p.u. last* P 0

Winning hurdler; last won in 90/91 & no prospects as a pointer. 0

MOST VITAL b.g. 6 Vital Season - Flavirostris by Grisaille — Major R P Thorman

22 25/1 Badbury Rin' (L) RES 3m 3 GF *lft disp apr 4th til 3 out, ran on agn flat, just faild* 2 13
111 8/2 Milborne St' (L) MDN 3m 8 GF *(fav) in tch, cls 3rd whn f 15th* F -
390 8/3 Barbury Cas' (L) MDN 3m 15 G *n.j.w. blnd 2nd, alwys rear, t.o. & p.u. 2 out* P 0
512 15/3 Larkhill (R) MDO 3m 6 GF *keen hld, trckd ldr til blnd & u.r. 9th* U -
917 5/4 Larkhill (R) MDO 2 1/2m 6 F *(fav) unruly start, lft 30l, ran out 2nd* r -
1024 12/4 Badbury Rin' (L) MDO 3m 3 F *not fluent in rear, rddn 13th, hld in 2nd whn ran out 16th* r -

Beaten in a crawl on debut; jumped poorly & went downhill after; best watched initially. 11

MOSTYN ch.g. 6 Astral Master - Temple Rock by Melody Rock — R J Weaver

1996 4(0),7(0),3(0)

40 1/2 Larkhill (R) MDO 3m 5 GF *jmpd lft, made all & sn clr, tiring whn lft wll clr 3 out* 1 15
298 1/3 Didmarton (L) RES 3m 15 G *n.j.w. ld 2-7th, blnd 9th, wknd, t.o. & p.u. 2 out* P 0
901 5/4 Howick (L) RES 3m 6 F *cls up,ld 13th-3 out, qcknd to ld agn flat* 1 16
1390 5/5 Cursneh Hill (L) INT 3m 4 GF *(Jt fav) made most til hdd 15th, ld agn 2 out, no ext apr last* 2 15

Improved; won weak races(lucky once); safe; game but onepaced; needs more for Confined;F-G. 15

MOUNTAIN HALL (Irish) — **I** 11[1], **I** 75[1]

MOUNTAIN-LINNET b.g. 10 Vital Season - Flavirostris by Grisaille — Major R P Thorman

1996 F(-),P(0),4(0),5(0),3(11)

658 22/3 Badbury Rin' (L) MDN 3m 6 F *handy to 14th, lost tch nxt, outpcd* 4 0
692 29/3 Little Wind' (R) MDO 3m 8 GF *prom til wknd frm 15th* 5 0
934 6/4 Charlton Ho' (L) MDO 3m 10 G *mid-div, effrt to chs ldrs 11th, no imp 13th, t.o.* 4 0
1139 19/4 Larkhill (R) MEM 3m 2 F *(fav) ld, jnd 13th, hdd & mstk 2 out, onepcd* 2 0
1314 3/5 Holnicote (L) MDO 3m 8 G *mid-div, prog 12th, ev ch last, just outpcd nr fin* 2 14
1465 11/5 Tweseldown (R) MDO 3m 2 GF *(fav) trckd ldr, mstk 13th, ld 15th, easily* 1 12
1551 24/5 Mounsey Hil' (R) RES 3m 13 G *chsd ldrs til f 14th* F -
1613 7/6 Umberleigh (L) RES 3m 13 F *prom in chsng grp, chsd wnr 7th-13th, wknd, p.u. 2 out* P 0

Beat subsequent winner in a match; very moderate & does not stay; need fortune for another win.G-F. 14

MOUNTAIN MASTER b.g. 11 Furry Glen - Leney Girl by Seminole II — Mrs Sue Rowe

1996 5(0),2(16),**U(-)**,P(0),2(19),3(11),3(0),1(15),2(16)

50 1/2 Wadebridge (L) RES 3m 10 G *alwys cls up, ld brfly 10th, ld 14th, made rest, ran on well* 1 17
173 15/2 Ottery St M' (L) CON 3m 7 G *handy, 4th at 13th, wknd 15th, btn 5th whn u.r. last* U -
533 15/3 Wadebridge (L) INT 3m 5 GF *(fav) ld/disp til ld 11th-14th, onepcd aft* 3 12
804 31/3 Wadebridge (L) INT 3m 6 F *(Jt fav) alwys cls up til onepcd aft last* 3 16
1241 26/4 Bratton Down (L) MEM 3m 4 GS *prssd wnnr frm 12th, styd on onepce frm nxt* 2 16
1481 11/5 Ottery St M' (L) CON 3m 12 G *prom early, lost tch 10th, t.o. & p.u. 2 out* P 0

Members winner 96; onepaced & options limited now; Members best hope again; L/H; Any. 15

MOUNTAINOUS VALLEY(IRE) ch.g. 9 Crash Course - Victor's Valley by Deep Run — N W Padfield

278 23/2 Charing (L) RES 3m 17 G *chsd clr ldr, ld 16th, mstk nxt, drvn out* 1 19
577 16/3 Detling (L) CON 3m 18 F *nvr nr ldrs, efft 16th, 4th frm 4 out, tk 3rd flat* 3 15
986 12/4 Kingston Bl' (L) CON 3m 10 GF *(fav) prom, ld 13th, jnd nxt, hdd 3 out, no ext nxt* 3 17
1375 5/5 Northaw (L) MEM 3m 5 F *(fav) disp ld til f 9th* F -

Irish Maiden winner 96; solid season; should win a Confined; L/H only in 97; G-F. 19

MOUNTAIN SLAVE b.m. 8 First Footman - Levotesse by Levmoss — Mrs June Howells
1996 P(0),P(0)

540	16/3 Erw Lon	(L) MDN 3m	13 GF	*mid-div, prog whn f 14th*	F	-
1136	19/4 Bonvilston	(R) MDO 3m	15 G	*rear til p.u. 3 out*	P	0
1229	26/4 Pyle	(R) MDO 3m	11 GS	*chsd ldrs, no ch frm 12th, poor 4th whn u.r. 2 out*	U	-
1368	5/5 Pantyderi	(L) MDO 3m	8 G	*alwys rear, p.u. 14th*	P	0

No real signs yet. 0

MOUNT FABER b.g. 7 Headin' Up - Wise Lady by Law Of The Wise — R G Watson
1996 P(0),3(11),2(11),4(0),1(16),P(0),P(0)

251	22/2 Brocklesby '	(L) RES 3m	16 G	*alwys last trio, outpcd 6 out, p.u. 3 out*	P	0
425	8/3 Charm Park	(L) RES 3m	12 GF	*mid-div, lost tch 5 out, t.o.*	9	0
616	22/3 Hutton Rudby	(L) RES 3m	14 GF	*chsd ldrs til outpcd 14th, prog & ev ch 3 out, onepcd*	3	17
1101	19/4 Hornby Cast'	(L) RES 3m	14 G	*(bl) prom, ld 3rd, disp 8th til hdd & wknd 4 out*	5	13
1250	26/4 Easingwold	(L) RES 3m	15 GS	*(bl) mid-div, 4th 3 out, nvr dang*	4	0
1421	10/5 Easingwold	(L) RES 3m	8 GF	*(bl) rear, prog 8th, chsd ldr 11th, outpcd frm 2 out*	3	14

Maiden winner 96; inconsistent; blinkers & best L/H; capable of surprising in weak Restricted. 15

MOUNT FALCON br.g. 15 Paico - Lady Mell by Milan — Miss Carolyn Morgan
1996 8(0),6(0),8(14),U(-),6(0),3(10),8(0),4(10),4(0)

844	31/3 Lydstep	(L) LAD 3m	6 F	*alwys rear, no dang*	3	0
957	6/4 Pantyderi	(L) MEM 3m	3 F	*1st ride, ld to 8th, sn wknd*	3	0

Members winner 94-95; mega safe but surely too old to win again. 0

MOUNTHENRY STAR (Irish) — I 199[4], I 244[P], I 306[2]

MOUNT KINABALU b.g. 10 Head For Heights - Kaisersage (FR) by Exbury — H Turberfield

201	15/2 Weston Park	(L) OPE 3m	16 G	*alwys rear, t.o. & p.u. 14th*	P	0
437	8/3 Upton-On-Se'	(R) MDO 3m	15 G	*ld to 5th, wknd 11th, t.o. & p.u. 3 out*	P	0

Shows speed but no stamina; unpromising. 0

MOUNT NUGENT JACK (Irish) — I 3[B], I 23[3]

MOUNT PATRICK b.g. 13 Paddy's Stream - Hills Of Fashion by Tarqogan — C J Lawson
1996 8(0),P(0),P(0),10(0),P(0),U(-),4(0),4(0),3(0),1(10)

10	25/1 Cottenham	(R) INT 3m	7 GF	*wll bhnd frm 6th, t.o. & p.u. 9th*	P	0
143	9/2 Tweseldown	(R) XX 3m	3 GF	*j.w. made most til jnd 3 out, hdd & btn nxt*	3	0
278	23/2 Charing	(L) RES 3m	17 G	*alwys bhnd, t.o.*	8	0

1 win last 36 starts; most unlikely to repeat the trick & finished early in 97.eeded to win again 10

MOUNTSHANNON b.g. 11 Pry - Tara Ogan by Tarqogan — Mrs T J Hill
1996 2(23),4(22)

125	9/2 Cottenham	(R) LAD 3m	11 GF	*trckd ldrs, disp 13th til ld aft 3 out, hdd flat, rallied*	2	23
448	8/3 Newton Brom'	(R) LAD 3m	5 G	*(fav) hld up, cls up til ld 3 o ut, ran on strngly*	1	22
652	22/3 Siddington	(L) LAD 3m	5 F	*ld to 5th, ld 9th-3 out, not qckn aft*	2	19

Winning hurdler; lightly raced; not 100% genuine; stays; can win another weak Ladies. 22

MOURNE MINER (Irish) — I 122[P], I 178[P], I 250[5], I 372[2], I 432[2], I 507[1], I 584[5]

MOVE IN STYLE ch.g. 6 Move Off - Sheer Panache by Fury Royal — Mrs R Gibbon

428	8/3 Charm Park	(L) MDO 3m	10 GF	*trckd ldr whn f 5th*	F	-

Crashed on debut; still young. 0

MOVING FORCE b.g. 10 Muscatite - Saint Simbir by Simbir — Miss C E Williams
1996 5(13),U(-),3(22),4(18),U(-),5(14),2(15),1(22),U(-)

1184	20/4 Lydstep	(L) LAD 3m	4 GF	*ld til s.u. flat apr 6th*	S	-
1364	5/5 Pantyderi	(L) LAD 3m	5 G	*3rd at 3rd, p.u. aft mssd 8th*	P	0
1472	11/5 Erw Lon	(L) XX 3m	9 GS	*ld, ran wd bend & mssd 5th*	r	-
1524	17/5 Bredwardine	(R) OPE 3m	8 G	*pllng, ld to apr 10th, wknd rpdly, p.u. 12th*	P	0

Open winner 96; needs short course & firm ground; below par 97; may win again when conditions suit. 14

MOYA'S TIP TOP b.m. 11 Prince Titian - Moya's Star by Top Star — Kenneth R Owen
1996 P(0),P(0),P(0),U(-)

202	15/2 Weston Park	(L) LAD 3m	13 G	*chsng grp, cls 3rd whn u.r. 12th*	U	-
329	1/3 Eaton Hall	(R) LAD 3m	10 GS	*mid-div, 4th 4 out, wknd qckly, p.u. last*	P	0
466	8/3 Eyton-On-Se'	(L) LAD 3m	7 G	*mid-div in tch 10th, rear & strglng 12th, rlld,ran on 2 out*	5	12
669	23/3 Eaton Hall	(R) LAD 3m	5 GF	*chsng grp til lost tch 4 out*	4	0
850	31/3 Eyton-On-Se'	(L) LAD 3m	6 GF	*cls up & ev ch 5 out, sn wknd*	4	0

Non-staying Maiden; totally outclassed in Ladies. 11

MOYAVO LAD (Irish) — I 331[P], I 375[P]

MOYBEG (Irish) — I 365^{P}, I 557^{P}

MOYGREHAN GIRL (Irish) — I 412^{F}, I 437^{P}, I 525^{F}, I 575^{P}

MOYLE ROVER (Irish) — I 539^{B}, I 590^{P}

MOYNALVY FUTURE VI (Irish) — I 35^{P}, I 100^{P}

MOYNE CROSS br.g. 10 Furry Glen - Swan Of The Bride by Orchardist — Miss D M M Calder

1428	10/5 Aspatria	(L) MDO 3m		11	G	*alwys rear, last & t.o. whn p.u. 15th*	P	0

Lightly raced & shown nothing since 94. 0

MOZE TIDY b.g. 12 Rushmere - Church Belle by Spartan General — Denis Williams

1996 5(16),1(17),2(13),**7(0)**,3(12),P(0),1(19)

170	15/2 Ottery St M'	(L) MEM 3m		6	G	*hld up, chsd wnr 10th, outpcd 4 out, blnd 2 out, no imp*	2	16
237	22/2 Lemalla	(R) CON 3m		13	S	*sn prom, cls 3rd hlfwy, ld 14th-17th, wknd 2 out*	4	15
551	16/3 Ottery St M'	(L) MEM 3m		4	G	*(fav) trckd ldr, chal 4 out, wknd nxt, outpcd*	3	12

Dual winner 96; inconsistent; brief 97; members best hope at 13; Good. 16

MR BALDA (Irish) — I 56^{P}, I 99^{P}, I 385^{3}, I 405^{P}, I 593^{P}

MR BARNEY (Irish) — I 359^{2}

MR BOBBIT(IRE) b.g. 7 Over The River (FR) - Orient Breeze by Deep Run — S J P Furniss

1996 F(-),1(16),2(14),2(16),U(-)

204	15/2 Weston Park	(L) RES	3m	13	G	*(fav) chsng grp in tch, wknd rpdly 4 out, p.u. nxt*	P	0
467	8/3 Eyton-On-Se'	(L) RES	3m	15	G	*chsng grp, hld up, 2nd 12th, ld 5 out, ran on wll und pres*	1	20
851	31/3 Eyton-On-Se'	(L) INT	3m	8	GF	*chsng grp, rdn 3 out, not qckn und pres frm 2 out*	3	17
1014	12/4 Bitterley	(L) OPE	3m	9	GF	*chsd ldrs, 12l 4th at 13th, kpt on onepcd frm 15th*	3	18
1235	26/4 Brampton Br'	(R) INT	3m	10	G	*mid-div, cls 5th whn ran out 14th*	r	-
1382	5/5 Eyton-On-Se'	(L) INT	3m	7	GF	*cls up, lft in ld 6th, jnd 3 out, ran on wll frm 2 out*	1	20
1507	16/5 Stratford	(L) HC	3m	10	G	*prom early, hit 6th, t.o.when p.u. after 3 out.*	P	0

Improving; likes Eyton; stays; best L/H; needs a little more for Confineed.G-G/F. 18

MR BOCO ch.g. 7 Boco (USA) - Fiesta Day by Weathercock — Mrs J J Andrews

797	31/3 Marks Tey	(L) MDO 3m		4	F	*chsd ldr, brfly disp 14th, ev ch 4 out, wknd nxt*	3	0

Last in bad race on debut; looks capable of better. 10

MR BOSTON b.g. 12 Halyudh (USA) - Edith Rose by Cheval — M K Oldham

1996 **4(NH),F(NH)**

153	13/2 Sandown	(R) HC	2 1/2m 110yds	6	G	*(Jt fav) held up in cl tch, shaken up apr 2 out, ld soon after last, pushed out, ran on well.*	1	30
286	27/2 Huntingdon	(R) HC	3m	8	GS	*(fav) patiently rdn, steady hdwy to chase ldr final cct, ld before 2 out, styd on strly run-in.*	1	30
387	7/3 Market Rasen	(R) HC	3m 1f	5	G	*(fav) nvr far away, imp and ev ch final cct, edged right and ld before 3 out, drew clr.*	1	30
890	4/4 Aintree	(L) HC	2 3/4m	14	G	*(fav) jmpd right, ld 5th, slight ld and going well when f 2 out.*	F	30
1591	31/5 Stratford	(L) HC	3 1/2m	11	G	*waited with, tk clr order hfwy, driven along when pace qcknd final cct, no impn from 4 out.*	3	30

Former useful chaser; professionally trained; stays very well; unlucky at Aintree; win more. 31

MR BRANIGAN(IRE) b.g. 7 Cataldi - Silver Doll by Sovereign Gleam — G T H Bailey

1996 U(-),1(14),1(24),2(23)

214	16/2 Southwell P'	(L) CON	3m	10	GS	*(Jt fav) in tch, hit 5th, ev ch 15th, onepcd und pres frm 2 out*	2	23
321	1/3 Marks Tey	(L) INT	3m	10	G	*(fav) alwys gng wll, lft 2nd 9th, ld 2 out, drew clr flat*	1	22
769	29/3 Dingley	(R) CON	3m	14	G	*(fav) alwys 1st pair, ld 10th, drew away 2 out, comf*	1	22

Progressing steadily; good stable; reach Opens/nov H/chases in 98; G-G/S. 24

MR BUSKER(IRE) b.g. 8 Orchestra - Kavali by Blakeney — C J B Barlow

1996 3(10),2(0),F(-),1(15),U(-),5(14)

332	1/3 Eaton Hall	(R) RES	3m	18	GS	*prom, ev ch 4 out, no ext 2 out*	3	17
467	8/3 Eyton-On-Se'	(L) RES	3m	15	G	*prom,2nd to 5th,ran on wll frm 4 out,tk 2nd last,just outpcd*	2	19
663	23/3 Eaton Hall	(R) MEM	3m	2	GF	*(fav) ld, lft solo 6th*	1	12
940	6/4 Tabley	(R) RES	3m	9	G	*(fav) prom, wnt 2nd 9th, ld 16th til apr 2 out, onepcd*	2	20
1098	19/4 Bangor	(L) HC	3m 110yds	9	G	*held up, hdwy to chase wnr before 3 out, no impn.*	2	23

Improved; stays; safe but onepaced; beaten by good horses last 2 starts; Restricted a formality; G-S. .. 22

MR BUSTER (Irish) — I 268^{P}

MR CAMPUS (Irish) — I 106^{F}, I 294^{P}, I 353^{P}, I 452^{6}

MR CHATAWAY (Irish) — I 29^{3}, I 283^{2}, I 351^{U}

MR CONNIE VEE (Irish) — I 301^{P}, I 337^{P}, I 595^{F}, I 608^{1}

MR COSMO(IRE) b.g. 7 Abednego - Miss Alex by No Argument — J N R Billinge

1996 **10(NH),5(NH),2(NH),6(NH)**

161 15/2 Lanark (R) MDO 2m 5f 14 G *in chsng grp, no prog frm 4 out* 5 0
338 1/3 Corbridge (R) RES 3m 10 G *prom, prssng ldr whn ran out 5th* r -
419 8/3 Dalston (R) MDO 2 1/2m 10 GS *chsd ldr 6-10th, lft 2nd 3 out, hld whn u.r. last* U 12
566 16/3 Lanark (R) MDO 3m 10 GS *ld til apr 2 out, no ext* 3 11
730 29/3 Alnwick (L) MDO 2 1/2m 9 F *(fav) alwys prom, ld 9th, clr 3 out, styd on strngly* 1 15
944 6/4 Friars Haugh (L) INT 3m 5 GF *2nd til 9th, btn 3rd whn ran out 4 out* r -

Placed Irish bumpers; novice ridden; headstrong & stamina doubtful; more needed for Restricted. 15

MR DENNEHY(IRE) ch.g. 8 Callernish - Down By The River by Over The River (FR) M A Butcher

255 22/2 Newtown (L) CON 3m 14 G *1st ride, last til some prog 9th, no ch whn u.r. 15th* U -
431 8/3 Upton-On-Se' (R) CON 3m 9 G *prom, chsd ldr 5-11th, wknd 13th, p.u. 3 out* P 0
1145 19/4 Chaddesley ' (L) MEM 3m 6 GF *wll bhnd, poor 4th hlfwy, ran on 4 out, tk 2nd flat* 2 14
1330 3/5 Chaddesley ' (L) MDN 3m 6 GF *in tch whn s.u. aft 6th* S -
1402 5/5 Ashorne (R) MDO 3m 11 G *8th whn f 7th* F -
1452 10/5 Kingston Bl' (L) MDO 3m 9 G *(fav) sn prom, chsd ldr til blnd & u.r. 7th* U -

Ex Irish; beat subsequent winner when placed in Members; novice ridden; mistakes; needs more. 12

MR DICK gr.g. 7 Absalom - Red Spider by Red God Mrs J Cooper

1996 2(12),4(12),1(16),F(-),1(18)

350 2/3 Market Rase' (L) CON 3m 11 GF *(fav) in tch, disp ld 14th-nxt, chal & ld last, ran on* 1 22
422 8/3 Charm Park (L) CON 3m 8 GF *(Jt fav) hld up in rear, prog 14th, outpcd 4 out, lft poor 2nd 3 out* 2 18
619 22/3 Hutton Rudby (L) INT 3m 8 GF *(fav) prom, disp 5th til rddn & hdd apr last, rlld flat* 2 19
694 29/3 Stainton (R) CON 3m 11 F *(fav) alwys prom, ld 15th, prssd 2 out, rddn ran on wll flat* 1 22
1075 13/4 Whitwell-On' (R) MEM 3m 9 G *(fav) prom, disp 13th til hdd 2 out, hrd drvn to ld post* 1 21
1247 26/4 Easingwold (L) CON 3m 9 GS *(fav) mid-div, tk 4th 14th, styd on same pce* 4 19
1405 5/5 Witton Cast' (R) CON 3m 10 GS *towrds rear, ran wd apr 13th, wknd 3 out* 5 15
1419 10/5 Easingwold (L) CON 3m 8 GF *alwys prom, ev ch 2 out, styd on wll flat* 2 21

Improved; solid; consistent; below Open standard but win more Confineds; G-G/F. 21

MR DRAKE(IRE) b.g. 7 Salluceva - Salambos by Doon M J Tuckey

1996 P(0),P(0),3(12)

1059 13/4 Hackwood Pa' (L) MDO 3m 6 GF *(fav) 3rd til lft 2nd 11th, vain pursuit aft* 2 0

Well beaten by subsequent H/chase winner; vanished after; weak Maiden still possible if fit 98. 13

MR DUNCAN (Irish) — I 293P, I 366F, I 417P, I 436P, I 464F

M-REG b.g. 8 Politico (USA) - Heckley Surprise by Foggy Bell G Cazenove

1996 1(15),1(20),1(22),P(0)

522 15/3 Cothelstone (L) CON 3m 14 GS *nov rdn, bhnd til p.u. 2 out* P 0
1594 31/5 Bratton Down (L) INT 3m 10 F *sn last, t.o. 9th, f 14th* F -

3 wins 96; problems last start 96 & changed hands after; can only be watched now. 12

MR FFITCH b.g. 11 Hays - Lady Topknot by High Top M Howells

1996 U(-),3(0),F(-),3(12)

963 6/4 Pantyderi (L) MDN 3m 6 F *trckd ldr to 14th, sn wknd, fin tired* 3 0
1137 19/4 Bonvilston (R) MDO 3m 13 G *prom early, lost plc hlfwy, ran on frm 3 out, onepcd* 2 12
1324 3/5 Bonvilston (R) MDO 3m 16 G *5s-3s, chsd ldrs, ran on frm 2 out, ld flat* 1 13
1526 17/5 Bredwardine (R) RES 3m 13 G *in tch, wknd 8th, t.o. & p.u. 11th* P 0
1613 7/6 Umberleigh (L) RES 3m 13 F *rear & sn pshd alng, t.o. 12th, p.u. 3 out* P 0

Deserved a win(desperate race); struggling now upgraded & need luck to win again. 13

MR FIVE WOOD (Irish) — I 116², I 211²

MR FLOWERS (Irish) — I 574P

MR FREEBIE(DEN) b.g. 7 Viking (USA) - Sirenivo (USA) by Sir Ivor Mrs M C Banks

141 9/2 Thorpe Lodge (L) MDN 3m 12 GF *mid to rear, btn whn p.u. 10th* P 0
210 16/2 Southwell P' (L) MDO 3m 15 GS *rear, prog 9th, outpcd apr 12th, t.o. & p.u. 2 out* P 0
478 9/3 Southwell P' (L) MDO 3m 17 G *hld up, blnd 3rd, prog & in tch 12th, no hdwy 15th* 6 0
775 29/3 Dingley (R) MDO 2m 5f 10 G *4th of 5 survivors at 7th, 3rd nxt, ld 4 out, ran on well* 1 13
1080 13/4 Guilsborough (L) RES 3m 11 GF *wll in tch to 15th, grad wknd* 5 0

Won weak short Maiden; not disgraced after; scopey & can improve; G-G/S. 15

MR FREEMAN (Irish) — I 82², I 107⁶, I 140², I 206F, I 302¹

MR GEE b.g. 12 Crooner - Miss Desla by Light Thrust M W Conway

1996 r(-),2(15),1(15),F(-),5(0),5(11)

213 16/2 Southwell P' (L) RES 3m 16 GS *in tch til apr 12th, no dang aft* 8 0
477 9/3 Southwell P' (L) RES 3m 10 G *rear of main grp til outpcd frm 14th* 5 0
548 16/3 Garthorpe (R) RES 3m 10 GF *in tch, 5th, & rddn 12th, outpcd frm 15th* 4 11
770 29/3 Dingley (R) RES 3m 18 G *alwys rear hlf, last pair at 10th, wll bhnd whn p.u. last* P 0
1077 13/4 Guilsborough (L) CON 3m 16 GF *alwys rear, no ch 13th, t.o.* 6 10
1187 20/4 Garthorpe (R) MEM 3m 9 GF *in tch, mstk 3rd, prog 11th, went 2nd 3 out,rdn to ld nr fin* 1 15

1208	26/4	Clifton On '	(L)	RES	3m	4 GS	*cls up til disp 7 out, ld 4 out, ran on gamely*	1	15
1403	5/5	Ashorne	(R)	CON	3m	14 G	*w.w. prog 13th, gd run to ld aft last, ran on well*	1	20
1536	18/5	Mollington	(R)	INT	3m	8 GS	*w.w. rear, grad prog frm 13th, chal & ev ch last,onepcd flat*	2	18
1608	1/6	Dingley	(R)	INT	3m	11 GF	*bhnd,poor 7th at 10th,ran on 13th,styd on wl flat,nt rch wnr*	2	20

Hot streak late season; moody & needs things his own way; hard to place now; G/S-G/F. 20

MR GOLDFINGER b.g. 10 Beau Charmeur (FR) - Miss Dollar by Lucifer (USA) Miss P Fitton

333	1/3	Eaton Hall	(R)	INT	3m	10 GS	*mid to rear, no ch whn p.u. 5 out*	P	0
414	8/3	Dalston	(R)	XX	3m	9 GS	*rear, effrt 11th, sn btn, t.o. whn crwld 3 out & p.u.*	P	0

Lightly raced; of no account. 0

MR GOLIGHTLY gr.g. 10 Lighter - Go Gently by New Member Mrs B I Cobden
1996 **P(0),U(-),1(30),1(32),2(33),P(0)**

494	13/3	Cheltenham	(L)	HC	3 1/4m 110yds	18 G	*jmpd poorly in rear, t.o. when p.u. 10th.*	P	0

Very useful H/Chaser; problems & finished early 97; below top class but win more if fit 98; G/F-Hy. 30

MR GOODBYE (Irish) — **I** 50P, **I** 85P, **I** 133³, **I** 192⁴, **I** 321¹

MR HATCHET(IRE) ch.g. 6 Executive Perk - Aubretia (USA) by Hatchet Man (USA) A Hollingsworth
1996 **4(NH),4(NH)**

259	22/2	Newtown	(L)	MDN	3m	18 G	*pllng, hld up, ran out & u.r. 7th*	r	-
367	2/3	Garnons	(L)	MDO	2 1/2m	9 GS	*alwys prom, cls 2nd 10th, disp 3 out-nxt, no ext*	2	13

Placed in N/H flat; beaten by good horse; stamina doubtful but short Maiden looks a formality. 15

MR HOOK b.g. 5 Primitive Rising (USA) - Miss Puck by Tepukei W Brown

358	2/3	Great Stain'	(L)	MDO	3m	14 S	*mid-div, lost tch 8th, p.u. nxt*	P	0
427	8/3	Charm Park	(L)	MDO	3m	10 GF	*mid-div, mstk 5th, lost tch 8th, p.u. nxt*	P	0
622	22/3	Hutton Rudby	(L)	MDO	3m	10 GF	*mid-div til fdd 12th, t.o. & p.u. 14th*	P	0
860	31/3	Charm Park	(L)	MDO	3m	12 F	*alwys wll in rear, not fluent, p.u. 10th*	P	0
1106	19/4	Hornby Cast'	(L)	MDO	3m	10 G	*alwys in rear, nvr dang*	5	0
1251	26/4	Easingwold	(L)	MDO	3m	9 GS	*mid-div, prog 14th, lft dist 3rd 3 out*	3	0
1514	17/5	Corbridge	(R)	MDO	3m	17 GS	*rear, prog 3 out, ev ch nxt, outpcd by wnr*	2	11

Steady progress; 6 horses behind last start; should find a race. 14

MR KEVERNAIR b.g. 7 High Season - Mena Gold by Golden Passenger P A Tylor

531	15/3	Wadebridge	(L)	MDO	3m	14 GF	*nvr trbld ldrs, bhnd whn p.u. 2 out*	P	0
1486	11/5	Ottery St M'	(L)	MDO	3m	17 G	*mid-div, nvr on trms, p.u. 15th*	P	0

Only learning; can do better. 0

MR K'S WINTERBLUES (Irish) — **I** 44²

MR MAD b.g. 9 Good Times (ITY) - Mistress Bowen by Owen Anthony Gwynne Phillips
1996 1(16),2(18)

298	1/3	Didmarton	(L)	RES	3m	15 G	*rear, lost tch 11th, t.o. & p.u. 2 out*	P	0
404	8/3	Llanfrynach	(R)	INT	3m	17 G	*hld up rear, prog 14th, went 2nd 2 out, onepcd aft*	5	12
534	16/3	Erw Lon	(L)	MEM	3m	3 GF	*(fav) cls up whn f 12th*	F	-
1008	12/4	St Hilary	(R)	RES	3m	11 GF	*rear til p.u. 14th*	P	0
1135	19/4	Bonvilston	(R)	RES	3m	14 G	*rear early, prog 15th, no ext apr last*	5	11
1365	5/5	Pantyderi	(L)	RES	3m	10 G	*(Jt fav) 6th at 3rd, 3rd at 11th, onepcd aft last*	3	16
1471	11/5	Erw Lon	(L)	RES	3m	9 GS	*ld to 4th, wn lost plc, p.u. 15th*	P	0

Members winner 96; lost his way & disappointing 97; may revive; stays; G/F-S. 17

MR ORIENTAL b.g. 7 Skyliner - Sybilly by Nicholas Bill Giuseppe G Gigantesco
1996 **P(NH),16(NH),4(NH),P(NH)**

1127	19/4	Penshurst	(L)	OPE	3m	7 GF	*in tch, wkng whn p.u. aft 9th*	P	0
1379	5/5	Northaw	(L)	RES	3m	6 F	*nt fluent, lft poor 3rd appr 8th, p.u. 10th*	P	0
1502	16/5	Folkestone	(R)	HC	2m 5f	10 G	*mstks, rear from 6th, t.o. when f 9th.*	F	-
1569	26/5	Fontwell	(R)	HC	3 1/4m 110yds	10 GF	*mid div, jmpd slowly 2nd, rear when bridle slpd and u.r. after next.*	U	-

Hopeless under rules; needs to concentrate on Maidens but signs not good; novice ridden. 0

MR PEOPLES (Irish) — **I** 363P, **I** 435²

MR PINBALL b.g. 10 Balinger - Pin Hole by Parthia Mrs D Cowley

761	29/3	Kimble	(L)	MDO	3m	12 GF	*(bl) prom til blnd 12th, lost plc, not rcvr*	5	0
1285	29/4	Huntingdon	(R)	HC	3m	10 G	*(bl) n.j.w., soon t.o., p.u. before 16th.*	P	0
1452	10/5	Kingston Bl'	(L)	MDO	3m	9 G	*(bl) ld 2nd-5th, ld 9th-13th, ld aft 14th, styd on*	1	11

Missed 96; won poor 2 finisher race (25/1); blinkers; well below Restricted class. 12

MR PIPE MAN(IRE) ch.g. 8 Orchestra - Bernish Lass D Rogers
1996 **P(NH)**

851 31/3 Eyton-On-Se' (L) INT 3m 8 GF *hndy, disp 4-2 out, no ext apr last* 2 20
938 6/4 Tabley (R) OPE 3m 9 G *(fav) mstks, cls up, blndrd 8th, hrd rddn & btn 2 out* 4 15
1381 5/5 Eyton-On-Se' (L) MEM 3m 5 GF *(fav) w.w.,2nd 10th,chal & ev ch 4 out,3rd & btn whn ref last* R -
1538 18/5 Wolverhampt' (L) CON 3m 8 GS *mid-div, prog 13th, ran on frm 3 out, not rch wnr* 2 14

Winning Irish pointer 96; good debut but disappointing after; win confined if reviving 98; G/F-G/S. 19

MR PRIMETIME(IRE) b.g. 7 Phardante (FR) - Bavette by Le Bavard (FR) N W A Bannister

1996 **F(NH),2(NH),3(NH),1(NH),6(NH),F(NH),P(NH),F(NH)**

675 23/3 Brocklesby ' (L) OPE 3m 6 GF *chsd ldrs, went 2nd 14th-3 out, onepcd aft* 4 21
937 6/4 Tabley (R) CON 3m 10 G *chsd ldng pair thruout, rddn apr 2 out, kpt on, nvr nr wnnr* 2 16
1070 13/4 Whitwell-On' (R) XX 3m 9 G *mid-div, prog 4th, ld 11th-13th, rdn & outpcd 3 out* 3 17
1344 3/5 Gisburn (R) MEM 3m 3 GF *(fav) ld 7th, clr 14th, dist up whn ref & u.r. 16th* R -

Winning novice/chaser; has ability but ungenuine; blew a gift last start; will continue to frustrate 17

MRS DANIELS (Irish) — I 390, , I 485[3], I 539[F]

MR SETASIDE br.g. 12 Royal Fountain - Cregg Park by Orchardist D J Coates

1996 **P(NH),P(NH)**

354 2/3 Great Stain' (L) OPE 3m 7 S *mid-div, went 2nd 12th, outpcd frm 4 out* 3 17

Won in remarkable fashion on pointing debut (lucky); young enough to improve 16

MRS GREEN ch.m. 7 Fearless Action (USA) - Pritchards by Idiot's Delight Mrs Julie Rawle

1246 26/4 Bratton Down (L) MDO 3m 16 GS *f 3rd* F -
1399 5/5 High Bickin' (R) MDO 3m 12 G *schoold rear til p.u. 9th* P 0

Only learning so far. 0

MRS MAGINN (Irish) — I 481[P]

MRS MCCLUSKY(IRE) b.m. 5 Mandalus - Clodagh's Treasure by Tarqogan Mrs Nerys Dutfield

1996 **10(NH)**

461 8/3 Great Treth' (R) MDO 3m 12 S *schoold rear til p.u. aft 13th* P 0
736 29/3 Higher Kilw' (L) RES 3m 10 GF *in tch to 13th, wknd 15th, p.u. 3 out, improve* P 0

No show in N/H flat; showed promise & looks sure to do better. 0

MRS MOPPIT b.m. 8 Pitpan - Motif by St Elmo R Cope

60 1/2 Kingston Bl' (L) MDN 3m 17 GF *bhnd, prog hlfwy, lft in ld aft 3 out, hdd nr fin* 2 13
756 29/3 Kimble (L) MEM 3m 3 GF *(fav) ld/disp, qcknd clr 16th, idld, hdd apr last, u.r. last* U -

Lightly raced; missed 96; placed in large field; form is weak but every chance of a small win. 14

MRS SOMEBODY b.m. 8 Right Regent - Moorland Gal by Baragoi Mrs M A Simpson

172 15/2 Ottery St M' (L) MDN 3m 14 G *rear whn f 7th* F -
553 16/3 Ottery St M' (L) MDN 3m 15 G *sn last, t.o. & ref 7th* R -

Missed 96; shows nothing. 0

MR SUNNYSIDE b.g. 11 Sunyboy - Firella by Firestreak S J Claisse

1996 F(-),6(0),3(11),5(0),U(-),P(0)

23 25/1 Badbury Rin' (L) RES 3m 8 GF *chsd ldrs to 12th, wknd, t.o.* 6 0
45 1/2 Larkhill (R) RES 3m 14 GF *cls up, hmpd & f 5th* F -

Maiden winner 92; placed in poor races 96; slow & not thretening to win now. 11

MR SUSPICIOUS(IRE) b.g. 9 Le Moss - Caffra Mills by Pitpan M P Jones

259 22/2 Newtown (L) MDN 3m 18 G *rear, hmpd 9th, no dang aft* 5 0
640 22/3 Howick (L) MDN 3m 10 GF *mid-div, cls 4th whn f 14th* F -

Missed 96; glimmer of hope in poor race; more needed. 10

MRS WUMPKINS(IRE) b.m. 6 Phardante (FR) - Mr Jersey by Crash Course G Piper

1996 P(0),1(14),P(0),P(0),P(0),P(0),P(0),U(-)

50 1/2 Wadebridge (L) RES 3m 10 G *disp to 2nd, ld 9th-10th, no ext clsng stgs* 4 13
190 15/2 Erw Lon (L) RES 3m 11 G *wth ldr, ld 9-13th, chsd wnr 3 out, chal flat, just hld* 2 19
405 8/3 Llanfrynach (R) RES 3m 15 G *(fav) cls up in 3rd, went 2nd 3 out, outpcd* 2 14

Won weak Maiden 96; improved & gets round now; young & can find a Restricted; Good. 16

MR TITTLE TATTLE b.g. 11 Le Bavard (FR) - Mille Fleurs (USA) by Floribunda H A Shone

1996 P(0),2(23),3(12),1(25),1(19),2(19)

465 8/3 Eyton-On-Se' (L) OPE 3m 13 G *(bl) ld til hdd 11th, ran on onepce, lost tch & p.u. bfr last* P 0
765 29/3 Whittington (L) OPE 3m 6 S *(bl) ld mstly to 8th, cls up til wknd aft 3 out* 4 0
938 6/4 Tabley (R) OPE 3m 9 G *(bl) prom to 12th, 5th & wknng 14th, t.o.* 6 0
1123 19/4 Whittington (L) OPE 3m 4 F *(fav) (bl) ld to 7th & frm nxt, clr 3 out, easily* 1 23
1347 3/5 Gisburn (R) OPE 3m 8 GF *(bl) made all, hld on wll whn chal flat* 1 23

Front runner; moody & needs to dominate; blinkers essential; needs a run; win more 98; G-S. 22

MR WHALEBONE (Irish) — I 456^F, I 484^P

MR WHO (Irish) — I 38, , I 258^P

MR WILBUR br.g. 11 Sit In The Corner (USA) - Hargan by Harwell — J D Callow

88	2/2 Wolverhampt'	(L) MDO 3m	13 GS	*chsd ldr 6-10th, wkng whn mstk 12th & p.u.*	P	0
212	16/2 Southwell P'	(L) MDO 3m	14 GS	*prom, chsd ldr 5th til 3 out, wknd*	3	0
345	2/3 Market Rase'	(L) MDO 3m	13 GF	*chsd ldrs, lft 2nd 6th, ld 10th-apr last, no ext*	2	13
575	16/3 Garnons	(L) RES 3m	12 G	*ld 7th-15th, wknd rpdly, p.u. 2 out*	P	0
1018	12/4 Bitterley	(L) MDO 3m	13 GF	*w.w. prog to ld 14th, kpt on, rdn out flat*	1	15
1175	20/4 Sandon	(L) CON 3m	8 GF	*hld up mid-div, 3rd 5 out, ld 3 out, in cmmnd apr last, comf*	1	19
1329	3/5 Chaddesley '	(L) CON 3m	5 GF	*hld up, prog whn f 11th*	F	-
1574	26/5 Chaddesley '	(L) CON 3m	8 F	*(Jt fav) not fluent,hld up,outpcd aft 11th,no ch aft,mstk 2 out &p.u.*	P	0

Missed 96; improved; won modest races; barely stays & hard to place now; G/F-G. 17

MR WOODCOCK b.g. 12 Sit In The Corner (USA) - Grey Bird by Eastern Venture — P A Tylor

1996 **2(NH)**

442	8/3 Higham	(L) LAD 3m	8 G	*conf rdn, ld 6th, made rest, qcknd clr flat*	1	25
759	29/3 Kimble	(L) LAD 3m	4 GF	*(fav) ld 4-11th, & nxt-15th, ld 3 out-nxt, disp last, styd on wll*	1	21
1213	26/4 Woodford	(L) LAD 3m	6 G	*ld to 13th, sn wknd, disp poor 3rd whn u.r. 4 out*	U	-

Former useful chaser; well travelled; problems last start; stays; win again if fit 98; G-G/F best. 24

MSADI MHULU (Irish) — I 166, , I 301^P, I 349^5

MS TAAFFE b.m. 9 Country Retreat - Queen's Colonsay Vii — Mrs M Bellamy

211	16/2 Southwell P'	(L) MDO 3m	15 GS	*nvr bttr than mid-div, 5th & no ch whn u.r. last*	U	-
549	16/3 Garthorpe	(R) MDO 3m	16 GF	*nvr nr ldrs, no ch frm 12th*	6	0
772	29/3 Dingley	(R) MEM 3m	4 G	*mostly 4l 3rd, rdn 6 out, f nxt*	F	-

Missed 96; only beaten one horse so far; unpromising. 0

M T POCKETS (Irish) — I 55^P, I 282^5, I 348, , I 468^F

MUCKY MAN (Irish) — I 303^P, I 379^P, I 424^P, I 540^P

MUDDLE HEAD(IRE) br.g. 8 Royal Fountain - Cairita by Pitcairn — B Kennedy

1996 F(-),P(0),P(0),P(0)

69	2/2 Higham	(L) MDO 3m	8 GF	*hld up, prog to 4th at 11th, wknd 15th, t.o. & p.u. 2 out*	P	0

Placed in 95; shown nothing since; hard puller; prospects look bleak. 0

MUFFLED MIST b.m. 6 Ayyabaan - Keep Fighting by Baltus — Mrs R Harry

1047	13/4 Lockerbie	(R) INT 3m	4 F	*alwys last, lost tch 13th, p.u. 4 out*	P	0

No show on debut. 0

MULLAGHEA LASS (Irish) — I 33^F, I 60^P

MULLINELLO (Irish) — I 459^P, I 491^4, I 557^2

MULTI LINE ch.m. 7 High Line - Waterford Cream by Proverb — Mrs S Brazier

1996 5(0),3(11)

287	27/2 Huntingdon	(R) HC 3m	13 GS	*sluggish start, rcvred to race in tch to 13th, lost pl, t.o..*	8	0

Lightly raced; a little promise in 96; outclassed & finished early 97; weak Maiden possible if fit 98 14

MULTIPOWER b.g. 8 Lightning Dealer - Tintern Abbey by Star Appeal — Mrs S Brazier

761	29/3 Kimble	(L) MDO 3m	12 GF	*chsd ldrs to hlfwy, in tch whn mstk & u.r. 13th*	U	-

Some signs of hope on debut. 0

MUNTA (Irish) — I 91^P, I 488^P, I 565^P

MURDER MOSS(IRE) ch.g. 7 Doulab (USA) - Northern Wind by Northfields (USA) — S Coltherd

1996 P(0),P(0),7(0),2(12),P(0),P(0),1(15),1(18)

35	26/1 Alnwick	(L) CON 3m	10 G	*rear, lost tch 11th, effrt 15th, sn wknd*	7	0
130	9/2 Alnwick	(L) INT 3m	7 G	*chsd ldr 6th, ld 13th, sn clr, blnd 2 out, rdn out*	1	0
152	12/2 Musselburgh	(R) HC 3m	8 GS	*held up, cld hfwy, ld after 14th to 4 out, chsd wnr after, no impn.*	2	19

Improving sort; novice ridden; stays; ran well H/chase; not seen again; can win again; G-Hy. 22

MURIELS PRIDE (Irish) — I 304^P

MURPHYS CROSS (Irish) — I 187^U, I 217^P, I 265^P, I 344^F

MURTON HEIGHTS ch.g. 7 Primitive Rising (USA) - Cornetta by Cornuto — Mrs K Tutty

167	15/2 Witton Cast'	(R) RES 3m	7 F	*(fav) alwys prom, 2nd 3 out, no imp whn p.u. flat, lame*	P	0

Maiden winner 96 (heavy); missed 96 & more problems in 97; can only be watched. 14

MUSCOATES b.g. 6 Domynsky - Mescalin by Politico (USA) W Brown
1996 P(0),U(-),P(0),r(-),P(0),6(0),P(0)

115 9/2 Wetherby Po' (L) MDO 3m 8 GF *trckd ldrs til wknd frm 13th, virt p.u. flat* 3 0

Yet to beat another horse & finished early 97; unpromising. 0

MUSICAL BREEZE (Irish) — **I** 435P

MUSICAL MAIL b.g. 10 Rymer - Blue Mail by Pony Express J R Sutcliffe
1996 F(-),U(-),P(0),P(0),S(-),4(10),4(0)

88 2/2 Wolverhampt' (L) MDO 3m 13 GS *alwys bhnd, t.o. & p.u. 12th* P 0
211 16/2 Southwell P' (L) MDO 3m 15 GS *ld til aft 1st, chsd ldrs, wkng whn blnd 12th, t.o.* 6 0
436 8/3 Upton-On-Se' (R) MDO 3m 17 G *ld/disp to 6th, wknd 12th, p.u. 3 out* P 0
723 29/3 Sandon (L) MDO 3m 6 GF *in tch,lft in ld 11th,hdd 2 out,lft in ld aft last, hdd post* 2 13
1209 26/4 Clifton On ' (L) MDO 3m 16 GS *prom in abt 4th til no ext frm 10th, outpcd 6 out* 6 0
1393 5/5 Cursneh Hill (L) MDO 3m 9 GF *cls up til just outpcd 13th, styd on to 3rd aft 2 out* 3 13
1460 11/5 Maisemore P' (L) MDO 3m 16 G *alwys prom, ld 9th-14th, wknd aft 3 out* 3 10
1572 26/5 Chaddesley ' (L) MEM 3m 3 F *(fav) trckd ldr, ld 13th, clr 15th, pshd out* 1 10

Very moderate; does not stay; won awful Members; need same to win again. 12

MUSICAL SLING (Irish) — **I** 485P

MUSICAL VOCATION(IRE) ch.m. 6 Orchestra - Kentucky Calling by Pry G L Edwards
1996 **7(NH),8(NH),8(NH),P(NH),12(NH),F(NH),P(NH)**

88 2/2 Wolverhampt' (L) MDO 3m 13 GS *mstk 6th, rear til effrt 11th, 5th & no ch whn p.u. 3 out* P 0
206 15/2 Weston Park (L) MDN 3m 9 G *ld 4-6th, ev ch til wknd 4 out, p.u. in 4th flat* P 0
470 8/3 Eyton-On-Se' (L) MDN 2 1/2m 12 G *alwys chsng grp, ev ch 4 out, onepcd* 3 10
853 31/3 Eyton-On-Se' (L) MDO 3m 13 GF *(fav) prom, ld 6th, 30l clr 12th, ran on wll, eased run in, imp* 1 16

Poor & suspect under rules; sluiced in but loks tricky & plenty to prove yet. 17

MUSICAL WAVES (Irish) — **I** 27F, **I** 111F, **I** 226F, **I** 286P, **I** 350F, **I** 392[4]

MUSIC BOX ch.g. 11 Orchestra - Pearl Locket by Gulf Pearl Mrs J D Railton

993 12/4 Tranwell (L) OPE 3m 5 F *alwys prom, 2l 2nd 4 out, disp ld last, no ext last 100yds* 2 18

Winning chaser; just pipped in poor Open; hardly runs now & hard to find a win. 14

MUSIC IN THE NIGHT ch.g. 9 True Song - Look Back by Country Retreat Mrs N Price
1996 2(18)

251 22/2 Brocklesby ' (L) RES 3m 16 G *(fav) alwys rear hlf, outpcd 10th, p.u. 2 out* P 0
372 2/3 Mollington (R) RES 3m 19 G *alwys prom, ld 3 out, clr last, rdn out nr fin* 1 19
476 9/3 Southwell P' (L) XX 3m 6 G *(fav) 2nd frm 4th,chal & stmbld 3 out,rdn & hit nxt,ld last,ran on* 1 19
1160 20/4 Mollington (R) INT 3m 9 GF *(Jt fav) trckd ldrs, cls 3rd 13th, wknd & p.u. 15th, lame* P 0

Dead. 20

MUSIC OF MOURNE(IRE) ch.m. 8 Orchestra - Deladeuce by Le Bavard (FR) W W Dennis

626 22/3 Kilworthy (L) MDN 3m 14 G *chsd ldr til 14th,lft in slght ld 2 out,no ext apr last,prom* 2 13

Very promising debut (modest race); not seen again but should go one better. 15

MUSKERRY MISS(IRE) b.m. 9 Bishop Of Orange - Muskerry Mary by Mon Capitaine Charles Cox

1449 10/5 Kingston Bl' (L) RES 3m 8 G *alwys bhnd, t.o. & p.u. aft 13th* P 0
1567 25/5 Kingston Bl' (L) RES 3m 8 GF *prom in chsng grp, 2nd brfly 14th, sn no prog & dmtd* 3 0

Irish Maiden winner 93; lightly raced; well beaten when placed & short of Restricted class. 13

MUSKERRY MOYA(IRE) ch.m. 8 Rising - Muskerry Mary by Mon Capitaine N W Rimington
1996 F(-),P(0),U(-)

110 8/2 Milborne St' (L) MDN 3m 7 GF *cls up, disp 12th til ld 14th, hdd apr last, rallied flat* 2 16
283 23/2 Charing (L) MDO 3m 16 G *hld up bhnd, lost tch 13th, t.o.* 5 0
485 9/3 Tweseldown (R) MDO 3m 11 G *trckd ldrs, 4th & outpcd 15th, no imp ldrs aft* 5 10
871 31/3 Hackwood Pa' (L) MDO 3m 7 F *alwys 1st trio, wknd apr 2 out, lft poor 2nd last* 2 0
1059 13/4 Hackwood Pa' (L) MDO 3m 6 GF *jmpd rght, made all, qcknd clr aft 3 out* 1 16
1317 3/5 Holnicote (L) RES 3m 5 G *ld, clr 13th, unchal aft* 1 18
1505 16/5 Folkestone (R) HC 2m 5f 8 G *made all, joined 2 out, shaken up and ran on well apr last.* 1 19
1587 29/5 Uttoxeter (L) HC 2m 5f 11 GF *ld to apr 4 out, wknd next, fin lame.* 3 15

Much improved; found weak races; front runs; problems last start & hard to place now. 19

MUSKORA(IRE) b.g. 8 Muscatite - Singing Wren by Julio Mariner Mrs F Percy-Davis
1996 **16(NH),5(NH),2(NH),1(NH),5(NH),3(NH),U(NH),P(NH)**

609 22/3 Friars Haugh (L) LAD 3m 11 GF *(fav) (bl) j.w. in ld, styd on wll* 1 23
945 6/4 Friars Haugh (L) LAD 3m 6 GF *(fav) (bl) sh wll clr, 15l up 3 out, only 3l up whn lft clr 2 out* 1 23
1408 5/5 Witton Cast' (R) LAD 3m 5 GS *(fav) (vis) made all, drew clr 14th, hrd drvn & styd on wll flat* 1 23

Winning hurdler/chaser; front runs; best easy 3 miles; headgear essential; worth a try in H/chase. 24

MUST BE MURPHY(IRE) br.g. 6 Gallic Heir - Tricias Pet by Mandalus Mrs J K Peutherer

1996 P(0),P(0)

210	16/2	Southwell P'	(L)	MDO	3m	15	GS	*prom to 11th, sn rdn & wknd, p.u. 14th*	P	0
722	29/3	Sandon	(L)	MDO	3m	10	GF	*in tch, outpcd 4 out, lft 3rd 2 out*	3	0
1304	3/5	Weston Park	(L)	MDO	3m	8	G	*alwys rear, t.o. 5th, p.u. 10th*	P	0
1459	11/5	Maisemore P'	(L)	MDO	3m	12	G	*in tch whn mstk 11th, wknd & p.u. 13th*	P	0

Well beaten when placed; still young but much more needed. 0

MUTUAL DECISION (Irish) — **I** 125^{3}

MUTUAL MEMORIES b.g. 9 Relkino - Mindblowing by Pongee — D Morgan

1996 **F(NH),P(NH),9(NH),P(NH)**

196	15/2	Higham	(L)	MDO	3m	12	G	*set slow pace, ld 5-15th, wknd rpdly, p.u. aft nxt*	P	0
439	8/3	Higham	(L)	MDO	3m	11	G	*mid-div, hit 7th, chsd ldrs 11th, cls up 14th, onepcd 3 out*	3	0
1118	19/4	Higham	(L)	MDO	3m	9	GF	*trckd ldrs, 2nd at 15th, ld apr 2 out, sn clr*	1	15
1278	27/4	Fakenham P-'	(L)	RES	3m	11	G	*hld up, prog to 2nd & going wll 13th, wknd apr 2 out*	4	0
1505	16/5	Folkestone	(R)	HC	2m 5f	8	G	*keen hold, chsd ldrs, mstk 9th, soon struggling, tk poor 3rd und pres near fin.*	3	0

Lightly raced; beat a debutante in 2 finisher race; stamina problems; hard to find a Restricted.G/F 15

MYALUP (Irish) — **I** 334^{P}, **I** 382^{4}, **I** 446^{2}, **I** 480^{2}, **I** 535^{3}, **I** 560^{3}, **I** 612^{3}

MY BELIEF (Irish) — **I** 496^{P}, **I** 551^{P}, **I** 589^{P}

MY BEST MAN br.g. 10 True Song - Eventime by Hot Brandy — Alan Hill

1996 1(15),**7(0)**,1(24),1(19)

220	16/2	Heythrop	(R)	OPE	3m	20	G	*hld up, no prog whn p.u. 11th*	P	0
370	2/3	Mollington	(R)	OPE	3m	6	G	*trckd ldrs, rdn frm 10th, chal und pres 15th, btn 2 out*	2	20
547	16/3	Garthorpe	(R)	XX	3m	7	GF	*prom, hit 7th, sn drvn alng, lost tch wth ldrs 12th, t.o.*	3	13
1450	10/5	Kingston Bl'	(L)	LAD	3m	7	G	*cls up, 3rd at 5th, wknd nxt, t.o. & p.u. aft 15th*	P	0

Won 3 in 96; disappointing in 97; poor jumper; needs strong handling; another win not easy to find. 18

MY FIRST MAN ch.g. 9 Starch Reduced - Clover Honey Bee by Winden — Mrs J M Worthington

940	6/4	Tabley	(R)	RES	3m	9	G	*chsd ldrs to 5th, wknd 7th, t.o. & p.u. apr 11th*	P	0
1179	20/4	Sandon	(L)	MDN	3m	6	GF	*alwys 3rd, nvr able to chal*	3	0
1304	3/5	Weston Park	(L)	MDO	3m	8	G	*ld to 3rd, wknd rpdly 8th, p.u. 10th*	P	0
1541	18/5	Wolverhampt'	(L)	MDO	3m	15	GS	*rear, t.o. 12th, p.u. nxt*	P	0

Last when completing; unpromising. 0

MYHAMET b.g. 10 Gorytus (USA) - Honey Bridge by Crepello — Paul C N Heywood

1996 1(20),F(-),**2(24)**,**10(0)**,4(22)

47	1/2	Wadebridge	(L)	MEM	3m	4	G	*(fav) ld til u.r. 12th*	U	-
174	15/2	Ottery St M'	(L)	LAD	3m	9	G	*chsd ldrs, lft 2nd 4 out, no imp frm nxt*	2	22
311	1/3	Clyst St Ma'	(L)	LAD	3m	9	HY	*(fav) in tch, effrt 3 out, no prog nxt*	4	16
528	15/3	Wadebridge	(L)	CON	3m	5	GF	*(fav) ld 6th, steadily drew clr, easily*	1	22
738	29/3	Higher Kilw'	(L)	CON	3m	8	GF	*(fav) handy, disp 13th til ld 16th, sn clr, easily*	1	20
1033	12/4	Lifton	(R)	CON	3m	6	F	*(fav) lft in ld apr 4th, clr nxt, unchal*	1	22
1342	3/5	Flete Park	(R)	CON	3m	6	G	*(fav) hld up in tch, prog 16th, ev ch til no ext 2 out*	2	20
1416	10/5	Newton Abbot	(L)	HC	2m 5f 110yds	14	G	*held up, hdwy 5 out, nvr near to chal.*	6	21
1579	26/5	Lifton	(R)	CON	3m	9	G	*(Jt fav) ld 13th-2 out, outpcd aft*	3	19

Winning hurdler; solid Confined horse; penalties make life harder now; can win more; G-F best. 21

MYITSU ch.g. 8 Itsu (USA) - Maella (FR) by Traffic — John Jones

1996 F(-)

1583	26/5	Lifton	(R)	MDO	3m	11	G	*ld 2nd to 4 out, 2nd & lkd btn whn u.r. nxt*	U	-

Very lightly raced; 1st signs in 97 go close if appearing more regularly. 12

MY KEY SILCA ch.g. 12 Deep Run - La Flamenca by Brave Invader (USA) — G Heal

627	22/3	Kilworthy	(L)	LAD	3m	7	G	*nov rddn, s.s., blndrd & u.r. 2nd*	U	-
793	31/3	Bishopsleigh	(R)	OPE	3m	7	G	*u.r. 3rd*	U	-
953	6/4	Black Fores'	(R)	OPE	3m	2	G	*n.j.w. blnd 6th, 6l down whn p.u. 2 out, dead*	P	0

Dead. 0

MY MAN (Irish) — **I** 174^{P}, **I** 247^{3}

MY MAN ON DUNDRUM(IRE) ch.g. 8 Orchestra - Pargio by Parthia — Richard Barber

104	8/2	Great Treth'	(R)	MDO	3m	9	GS	*prom, ld & blnd 11th, clr 2 out, blnd last, styd on well*	1	15
240	22/2	Lemalla	(R)	RES	3m	11	S	*handy, disp 15th, ev ch but hrd rdn whn ran out last*	r	20
557	16/3	Ottery St M'	(L)	RES	3m	9	G	*(fav) alwys prom, disp 4 out til hit last & u.r.*	U	-
1093	16/4	Hockworthy	(L)	RES	3m	16	GF	*(fav) trckd ldrs, prog to ld 4 out, clr 2 out, drvn out flat*	1	19

Improving; top stable; won good Restricted; needs strong handling; sure to win more; G/F-S. 21

MY MEADOWSWEET ch.g. 7 Meadowbrook - My Mimosa by Cagirama — Roland W Telford

1996 2(10),6(0),3(0)

36	26/1 Alnwick	(L) MDO 3m	15	G	*trckd ldrs, ld 13th-3 out, 2nd & hld whn f nxt*	F	-
234	22/2 Friars Haugh	(L) MDO 3m	15	G	*(fav) 3rd hlfwy, clsd on wnr frm 3 out, just faild*	2	15

Improving steadily; just pipped in modest race; not seen after; can go one better. 15

MY MOONA b.m. 6 Ballacashtal (CAN) - Salala by Connaught — David Walker

582	16/3 Detling	(L) MDN 3m	16	F	*ld til ref & u.r. 6th*	R	-
917	5/4 Larkhill	(R) MDO 2 1/2m	6	F	*plld hrd, ld 3rd til blnd & u.r. 4 out*	U	-

Headstrong & needs to settle before progressing. 0

MY NEW MERC (Irish) — I 109⁴, I 200¹, I 240P, I 454⁴

MY NOMINEE b.g. 9 Nomination - Salala by Connaught — D E Nicholls

1996 P(0),**9(0)**,5(19),2(22),**F(-)**,1(24),2(24),**1(28)**,**1(33)**,**1(31)**,**3(20)**,**3(20)**

93	7/2 Bangor	(L) HC 2 1/2m 110yds	11	G	*(Jt fav) (bl) prom, ld 7th to 8th, wknd after 12th, t.o..*	3	14
226	21/2 Haydock	(L) HC 3m	11	G	*(bl) ld 4th, pushed along and hdd 2 out, soon wandered, fd apr last.*	4	22
328	1/3 Eaton Hall	(R) OPE 3m	6	GS	*(fav) alwys 2nd/3rd, nvr on trms wth wnr, ran on onepce frm 4 out*	2	24
494	13/3 Cheltenham	(L) HC 3 1/4m 110yds	18	G	*(bl) cl up, rdn and outpcd 6 out, bhnd when p.u. 2 out.*	P	0
668	23/3 Eaton Hall	(R) OPE 3m	3	GF	*(fav) (bl) made all, lft 25l clr 5 out, eased nr fin*	1	24
874	1/4 Uttoxeter	(L) HC 2m 7f	9	GF	*(fav) (bl) in tch, rdn to chal 3 out, ld next, ridden and ct run- in.*	2	27
982	9/4 Ludlow	(R) HC 3m	6	F	*(bl) ld to 2nd, regained ld next, made rest, hrd pressed from 4 out, all out.*	1	27
1097	19/4 Bangor	(L) HC 2 1/2m 110yds	11	G	*(fav) (bl) made all, well clr 4 out, eased down run-in.*	1	28
1292	30/4 Cheltenham	(L) HC 2m 5f	12	GF	*(fav) (bl) jmpd right, made most till after 3 out, rdn and unable to qckn.*	3	27
1491	14/5 Hereford	(R) HC 3m 1f 110yds	11	G	*(bl) hdwy 11th, wknd 14th.*	8	10
1571	26/5 Wetherby	(L) HC 2 1/2m 110yds	15	GF	*(bl) prom, ld after 7th, hit 3 out, rdn next and styd on gamely.*	1	23

Useful; slow to reach peak; quirky; blinkers; sure to win more; G/F-S. 26

MY PILOT b.g. 13 Al Sirat (USA) - Dandyville by Vulgan — J Turnbull

1996 11(0),3(18)

402	8/3 Llanfrynach	(R) INT 3m	7	G	*alwys 4th, no ch frm hlfwy*	4	0

Completed Lydstep hat-trick 95; lightly raced now & unlikely ti win again. 16

MY PRIDES WAY b.m. 8 Prince Of Peace - My Always by Kalimnos — M G Gloyn

1996 F(-),6(0),F(-)

243	22/2 Lemalla	(R) MDO 3m	12	S	*mid-div, prog whn blnd 9th, immed p.u.*	P	0
460	8/3 Great Treth'	(R) MDO 3m	13	S	*8th hlfwy, poor 5th 15th, lft 3rd apr last*	3	0
625	22/3 Kilworthy	(L) MDN 3m	14	G	*towrds rear til f 8th*	F	-
740	29/3 Higher Kilw'	(L) MDN 3m	15	GF	*rear & strgglng til p.u. 12th*	P	0

Yet to beat another horse & barely worth a rating. 10

MYRTLEFIELD ANN (Irish) — I 129P, I 288P, I 370P

MY SHOUT b.g. 5 Nicholas Bill - Ruth's River by Young Man (FR) — G T H Bailey

276	22/2 Ampton	(R) MDO 3m	12	G	*hld up, in tch, 6th & ch 16th, outpcd 3 out, p.u. last*	P	0
549	16/3 Garthorpe	(R) MDO 3m	16	GF	*(fav) w.w prog 13th, lft 4th 3 out, ev ch nxt, ld flat, clvly*	1	14

Won weak Maiden (cosily); good stable; has scope & looks sure to upgrade. 18

MYSTERIOUS BEAU (Irish) — I 112P, I 124P, I 252P, I 365P

MYSTERIOUS RUN(IRE) ch.g. 9 Deep Run - Misty Venture — Mrs D C Samworth

1996 U(-),P(0),4(0),1(13),P(0)

137	9/2 Thorpe Lodge	(L) MEM 3m	9	GF	*disp whn ran out 3rd*	r	-
213	16/2 Southwell P'	(L) RES 3m	16	GS	*prom, nrly u.r. 5th, wknd 11th, t.o. & p.u. 2 out*	P	0
473	9/3 Southwell P'	(L) CON 3m	10	G	*mid-div, cls 4th at 12th, outpcd 14th, kpt on*	4	15
544	16/3 Garthorpe	(R) MEM 3m	6	GF	*ld 3rd til u.r. 9th*	U	-

Maiden wiiner 96; novice ridden; mistakes; weak Restricted possible with stronger handling. 15

MYSTERIOUS WOMAN (Irish) — I 390P, I 470P

MYSTERYS PRIDE (Irish) — I 287P

MYSTICAL LORD (Irish) — I 228P, I 312P, I 394P

MYSTIC MAJOR b.g. 5 Wace (USA) - Mystic Mintet by King Log — Miss I Dady

326	1/3 Eaton Hall	(R) MDN 3m	14	GS	*prom, 2nd 8-14th, sn btn, p.u. 3 out*	P	0

A satisfactory debut; looks sure to do better. 0

MYSTIC MOMENT (Irish) — I 125^{P}, I 227^{1}, I 290^{3}, I 368^{1}

MYSTIC ROSE (Irish) — I 112^{F}

MY TRUE CLOWN ch.g. 11 True Song - Tudor Clown by Ritudyr — Mrs Peter Seels

1996 1(0),P(0)

121	9/2	Wetherby Po'	(L)	MEM	3m	2	GF	*(fav) disp at slow pace, just outpced apr last*	2	0
248	22/2	Brocklesby '	(L)	CON	3m	10	G	*last til gained 2 plcs on flat*	7	0
506	15/3	Dalton Park	(R)	CON	3m	16	GF	*lost tch 7th, t.o.*	7	0
835	31/3	Thorpe Lodge	(L)	INT	3m	7	F	*last frm 5th, t.o. 7th, p.u. 12th*	P	0
894	5/4	Wetherby Po'	(L)	RES	3m	6	F	*mid-div, lost plc 8th, rdn 10th, wll bhnd frm 13th*	5	0

Won joke Members 96; could not follow up & outclassed in proper races. 0

MY UNCLE BATT (Irish) — I 22^{P}, I 77^{F}, I 85^{F}, I 241^{3}, I 297^{5}, I 425^{S}, I 450^{3}

MYVERYGOODFRIEND b.g. 10 Swing Easy (USA) - Darymoss by Ballymoss — S Cobden

1996 5(14),U(-),P(0)

483	9/3	Tweseldown	(R)	CON	3m	8	G	*prom, ld 10-15th, prssd wnr aft, onepcd apr last*	2	16
659	22/3	Badbury Rin'	(L)	OPE	3m	2	F	*j.w. ld to 4 out, disp nxt til ld 2 out, ran on well*	1	13
1055	13/4	Hackwood Pa'	(L)	OPE	3m	4	GF	*(fav) ld 6th, jmpd slwly 14th, ld agn 16th, all out*	1	17
1463	11/5	Tweseldown	(R)	MXO	3m	5	GF	*chsd ldrs, outpcd frm 12th, sn btn*	4	16

Winning hurdler/chaser; won 2 bad Opens; hard to place now but local area very weak; G-F. 17

MY WEE MAN(IRE) b.g. 6 Carlingford Castle - Pollerun Slave by Pollerton — G Barfoot-Saunt

570	16/3	Garnons	(L)	MDN	2 1/2m	14	G	*mid-div, prog to 2nd 14th, ld last, sn clr*	1	14
1093	16/4	Hockworthy	(L)	RES	3m	16	GF	*n.j.w. alwys rear, t.o.*	7	0
1215	26/4	Woodford	(L)	CON	3m	3	G	*jmpd rght, w.w. went 2nd 14th, sn outpcd by wnr*	2	13
1494	14/5	Cothelstone	(L)	RES	3m	11	GF	*prog 9th, chsd ldr 15th, lft clr apr nxt, comf*	1	19

Impressively won modest races; mistakes; can improve; needs to for Confineds. 19

MY YOUNG MAN b.g. 12 Young Man (FR) - Hampsruth by Sea Hawk II — Mrs S Towler

93	7/2	Bangor	(L)	HC	2 1/2m 110yds	11	G	*(Jt fav) ld 4th to 6th, lost tch before 10th, t.o. when p.u. before 3 out.*	P	0
291	1/3	Warwick	(L)	HC	3 1/4m	6	G	*ld and soon well clr, slowed and hdd apr 7 out, wknd rpdly 5 out, t.o. when p.u. before 2 out.*	P	0
1287	29/4	Huntingdon	(R)	HC	2 1/2m 110yds	14	G	*ld and set gd pace, mstk 9th, hdd and wknd apr 2 out.*	3	19
1296	3/5	Hereford	(R)	HC	2m 3f	11	G	*ld 2nd rdn and hdd 3 out, ev ch till hit and u.r. last.*	U	-
1488	12/5	Towcester	(R)	HC	2m 110yds	16	GS	*hdwy 3rd, ld 5th to 7th, hit 3 out, no hdway after.*	2	21

Former decent chaser; professionally trained; does not stay 3 miles; hard to find a race now. 22

NABURN LOCH b.m. 7 Lochnager - Balgownie by Prince Tenderfoot (USA) — J D Hankinson

258	22/2	Newtown	(L)	RES	3m	14	G	*alwys wl bhnd, t.o. & p.u. 13th*	P	0
313	1/3	Clyst St Ma'	(L)	RES	3m	10	HY	*prom, lost tch 10th, p.u. 12th*	P	0
644	22/3	Castle Of C'	(R)	MDO	3m	9	G	*chsd ldr, ld brfly 6th, wknd 12th, t.o. & p.u. 15th*	P	0
823	31/3	Lockinge	(L)	MDO	3m	4	F	*blnd 1st, made most to 7th, wknd 14th, p.u. 4 out*	P	0
1065	13/4	Maisemore P'	(L)	MDO	3m	13	GF	*nvr bttr than mid-div, p.u. 15th*	P	0
1216	26/4	Woodford	(L)	MDN	3m	13	G	*ld 2nd-3rd, chsd ldr to 9th, sn wknd, t.o. & p.u. 3 out*	P	0

No stamina; running on the flat now. 0

NADANNY(IRE) ch.g. 8 The Noble Player (USA) - Bradden by King Emperor (USA) — M E David

1996 P(0)

1186	20/4	Lydstep	(L)	MDO	3m	7	GF	*sttld mid-div, prog 12th, ev ch 3 out, onepcd aft, fin sore*	2	10
1324	3/5	Bonvilston	(R)	MDO	3m	16	G	*(fav) cls up, ld 12th, hdd nxt, lsng tch & p.u. 2 out*	P	0

Placed in a bad race (no winners behind); plenty to prove yet. 10

NADIAD b.g. 11 Darshaan - Naveen by Sir Gaylord — D McCain

1097	19/4	Bangor	(L)	HC	2 1/2m 110yds	11	G	*bhnd, hdwy to chase ldrs 6th, reminders apr 10th, wknd next, no ch when blnd last, t.o..*	5	0
1295	2/5	Bangor	(L)	HC	3m 110yds	4	G	*cl up, outpcd and bhnd 14th, no ch when pkd 2 out.*	3	17

Placed in a novice chase; professionally trained; outclassed in H/chases. 13

NA MOILLTEAR (Irish) — I 66^{P}, I 185^{P}

NANCY HANKS (Irish) — I 539^{1}

NANCY HILL (Irish) — I 125^{P}, I 179^{P}, I 212^{P}

NANCY'S LAST b.m. 7 Peter Wrekin - Nancy Scot by Fleche Bleu — Mrs L Heysham

331	1/3	Eaton Hall	(R)	RES	3m	17	GS	*mid to rear, no ch whn p.u. 4 out*	P	0
469	8/3	Eyton-On-Se'	(L)	MDN	2 1/2m	9	G	*chsng grp, cls up 9th, fdd 4 out, p.u. 2 out*	P	0

A little hope but more stamina needed. 0

NANDA DEVI b.g. 6 Scorpio (FR) - Muskcat Rambler by Pollerton — John Knowles

324	1/3	Marks Tey	(L)	RES	3m	16	G	*alwys rear, last whn f 11th*	F	-
549	16/3	Garthorpe	(R)	MDO	3m	16	GF	*chsd ldrs til wknd 11th, t.o. & p.u. 3 out*	P	0
928	6/4	Garthorpe	(R)	MDO	3m	8	GF	*mid-div, lost tch 10th, ran on onepcd*	3	0

Well beaten when placed; big rangy sort; can improve. **10**

NANDA MOON b.g. 10 Henbit (USA) - Red Nanda by Status Seeker — C F C Jackson

1996 P(0),P(0)

430	8/3	Upton-On-Se'	(R)	MEM	3m	4	G	*ld/disp til grad wknd frm 14th*	4	0
750	29/3	Brampton Br'	(R)	LAD	3m	5	GF	*mostly 2nd, rdn 16th, prog nxt, qcknd to ld flat*	1	17
1141	19/4	Larkhill	(R)	LAD	3m	4	F	*jmpd slwly early,lost tch 6th,clsd 15th,2nd apr last,nvr nrr*	2	10
1391	5/5	Cursneh Hill	(L)	LAD	3m	4	GF	*cls up, chsd ldr 13th, lost tch nxt, held on for 2nd*	2	15
1558	24/5	Bassaleg	(R)	LAD	3m	5	G	*held up last, effrt 11th, outpcd nxt, t.o.*	3	11

Winning hurdler; revived & won poor Ladies; does not really stay; hard to win again. **14**

NAN'S PET (Irish) — **I** 7^{1}, **I** 41^{4}

NASH NA HABHAINN (Irish) — **I** 545^{F}, **I** 575, , **I** 591^{5}, **I** 608^{P}

NATIVE BLOOD VI (Irish) — **I** 93^{P}, **I** 123^{P}, **I** 282^{F}

NATIVE CANNON (Irish) — **I** 489^{F}, **I** 597^{2}

NATIVE CHIEF (Irish) — **I** 527^{3}, **I** 589^{P}

NATIVE COVE (Irish) — **I** 127^{3}, **I** 248^{2}, **I** 311, , **I** 373^{3}

NATIVE ISLE(IRE) ch.g. 5 Be My Native (USA) - Shuil Ard by Quayside — D J Caro

571	16/3	Garnons	(L)	MDN	2 1/2m	13	G	*alwys rear, no ch 11th, kpt on frm 3 out*	4	10

Beaten 18 lengths on debut; looks sure to go close in 98. .... **11**

NATIVE MONY(IRE) b.g. 8 Bulldozer - Native Wings by Al-'alawi — B Kennedy

1996 **6(NH),F(NH),2(NH),4(NH)**

13	25/1	Cottenham	(R)	MDO	3m	10	GF	*mid-div, 4th whn mstk 13th, wll btn whn p.u. 3 out*	P	0
197	15/2	Higham	(L)	MDO	3m	12	G	*cls up til disp 4th to 3 out, wknd nxt*	4	12

Placed in novice hurdles/chases; brief season & lookeed suspect; may need blinkers. **10**

NATIVE OASIS (Irish) — **I** 394^{3}, **I** 458^{P}

NATIVE PRINCE (Irish) — **I** 293^{F}

NATIVE RAMBLER(IRE) ch.g. 7 Le Bavard (FR) - Native Shot by Random Shot — Mrs A Price

1996 **P(NH),4(NH),F(NH),4(NH)**

93	7/2	Bangor	(L)	HC	2 1/2m 110yds	11	G	*towards rear when f 5th.*	F	-
399	8/3	Llanfrynach	(R)	CON	3m	11	G	*2nd to 12th, grad lost tch*	7	0

.... **0**

NATLASH (Irish) — **I** 337^{P}

NATTICO (Irish) — **I** 262^{U}, **I** 307^{P}, **I** 381^{P}, **I** 484^{P}, **I** 570^{6}, **I** 608^{3}

NATURE PERFECTED (Irish) — **I** 254^{P}, **I** 316^{F}, **I** 464^{P}, **I** 502^{P}

NATURES GENTLEMAN (Irish) — **I** 403^{4}, **I** 447^{2}

NATURES STORM (Irish) — **I** 460^{F}

NAUGHTY NELLIE b.m. 6 Neltino - Hayburnwyke by Pretty Form — C D Dawson

1996 1(13),F(-),P(0)

139	9/2	Thorpe Lodge	(L)	LAD	3m	4	GF	*2nd/3rd til disp 4 out, kpt on onepcd frm 3 out*	2	15
249	22/2	Brocklesby '	(L)	LAD	3m	4	G	*alwys last, not fluent, outpcd 6 out, p.u. 3 out*	P	0
349	2/3	Market Rase'	(L)	LAD	3m	5	GF	*chsd ldr 3rd-11th, lft 2nd nxt, btn 2 out, blnd last*	2	12
1422	10/5	Easingwold	(L)	LAD	3m	7	GF	*rear,prog to ld 6th, sn wll clr, ran out apr 9th,rjnd,f 13th*	F	-

Won short Maiden 96; headstrong & not progressing; good stable; best watched till settling better. **16**

NEARCTIC BAY(USA) b.g. 11 Explodent (USA) - Golferette (USA) by Mr Randy — G B Barlow

1996 P(0),6(0)

763	29/3	Whittington	(L)	CON	3m	9	S	*alwys rear, t.o. 6th, p.u. 11th*	P	0
936	6/4	Tabley	(R)	MEM	3m	9	G	*tubed, alwys bhnd, t.o. frm 7th*	5	0

Of no account. **0**

NEARLY A MERMAID b.m. 8 Nearly A Hand - Mermaids Daughter by Crozier — R E Nuttall

1996 U(-),P(0),4(11),4(10)

106	8/2	Milborne St'	(L)	RES	3m	12	GF	*cls up early, lost tch 13th, t.o. & p.u. 2 out*	P	0
517	15/3	Larkhill	(R)	RES	3m	10	GF	*ld to 3rd, rear whn f 10th*	F	-

Maiden winner 94 (lucky); lightly raced & not progrss since; can only be watched now. **13**

NEARLY AN EYE ch.g. 6 Nearly A Hand - Kitty Come Home by Monsanto (FR) — Paul K Barber

1996 **6(NH)**

181	15/2	Larkhill	(R)	MDO	3m	17 G	*crashd thro wng & u.r. 3rd*	r	-
299	1/3	Didmarton	(L)	MDN	3m	14 G	*(fav) w.w. prog to ld 14th, clr whn nrly f last, nt rcvr, unlcky*	2	17
525	15/3	Cothelstone	(L)	MDN	3m	15 GS	*(fav) ptntly rdn, prog 13th, cls 2nd 3 out, ld apr nxt, sn clr*	1	16
935	6/4	Charlton Ho'	(L)	RES	3m	7 G	*(fav) hld up,trckd ldr 7th,ld 14th,mstk nxt,shkn up 2 out,rdn out*	1	20
1212	26/4	Woodford	(L)	INT	3m	8 G	*(fav) w.w. went 2nd 12th, rdn to ld & jmpd lft last, styd on*	1	21

Progressive youngster; will run under rules now. 24

NEARLY AT SEA ch.m. 8 Nearly A Hand - Culm Port by Port Corsair — C J Down

1996 F(-),1(14)

1093	16/4	Hockworthy	(L)	RES	3m	16 GF	*hld up, gd prog frm 6 out, chsd wnr 2 out, ev ch, just hld*	2	19
1259	27/4	Black Fores'	(R)	RES	3m	7 F	*hld up, prog 5 out, ld last, ran on wll und pres*	1	17
1507	16/5	Stratford	(L)	HC	3m	10 G	*mstks in rear, t.o. when p.u. after 11th.*	P	0

Maiden winner 96; lightly raced; can improve; mistakes in H/chase; win more points; G-F. 20

NEARLY FAIR ch.m. 6 Nearly A Hand - Fair Cone by Celtic Cone — Mrs S M Trump

105	8/2	Great Treth'	(R)	MDO	3m	15 GS	*alwys bhnd, t.o. 13th, p.u. nxt*	P	0
461	8/3	Great Treth'	(R)	MDO	3m	12 S	*rear til p.u. apr 3 out*	P	0
794	31/3	Bishopsleigh	(R)	MDO	3m	12 G	*mid-div, effrt 17th, 3rd nxt, dmtd apr last*	4	0

Not disgraced on last start; going the right way & can go closer in 98. 12

NEARLY SPLENDID br.g. 12 Nearly A Hand - Splentynna by John Splendid — S R Stevens

1996 4(26),P(0),1(20),1(28),**4(25)**,3(21)

42	1/2	Larkhill	(R)	MXO	3m	7 GF	*blnd 2nd, p.u. nxt*	P	0
98	8/2	Great Treth'	(R)	OPE	3m	14 GS	*ld 4th til apr 14th, sn outpcd, kpt on*	4	18
285	26/2	Taunton	(R)	HC	4 1/4m 110yds	16 GS	*hit 6th, blnd 8th, hdwy 17th, t.o. when p.u. before 2 out.*	P	0
629	22/3	Kilworthy	(L)	OPE	3m	5 G	*tried to make all, jnd & jmp lft last, no ext flat*	2	23
793	31/3	Bishopsleigh	(R)	OPE	3m	7 G	*nvr going wll, bhnd whn p.u. 10th*	P	0
1109	19/4	Flete Park	(R)	OPE	4m	9 GF	*(Jt fav) made all, j.w. clsng stgs, styd on strngly*	1	24
1340	3/5	Flete Park	(R)	LAD	4m	5 G	*(fav) chsd wnr, ev ch til no ext 2 out, fin tired*	2	20

Grand servant but deteriorating now; stays well; can still win at 13; Any. 22

NEAT AND TIDY b.g. 12 Dubassoff (USA) - Spic And Span by Crisp And Even — Miss L A Davis

1996 **P(NH),P(NH),4(NH),P(NH),5(NH)**

647	22/3	Castle Of C'	(R)	INT	3m	7 G	*in tch, ran out & u.r. 5th*	r	-
867	31/3	Kingston St'	(R)	MDO	3m	6 F	*3rd whn ran out 6th*	r	-

Poor under rules; too much of a handful for novice rider; unpromising. 0

NECTANEBO(IRE) b or br.c. 9 Persian Bold - Dancing Sally by Sallust — Mrs R E Parker

892	5/4	Hereford	(R)	HC	2m	11 GF	*held up and alwys going well, hdwy 6th, chal 3 out till ld after next, soon clr.*	1	21
1293	30/4	Cheltenham	(L)	HC	2m 110yds	5 GF	*keen hold, held up, in tch when u.r. 7th.*	U	-
1488	12/5	Towcester	(R)	HC	2m 110yds	16 GS	*mstks, held up in rear, hdwy from 4 out, one pace from 2 out.*	3	18

Missed96; found his niche in short H/chases; won a bad one & opportunities limited. 22

NEED A LADDER b.g. 10 Highlands - Munster Glen by Furry Glen — Mrs R Birtwistle

1996 P(0),P(0),P(0),B(-),P(0)

996	12/4	Tranwell	(L)	MDO	3m	8 F	*last 3rd, t.o. 9th & p.u. nxt*	P	0

Of no account. 0

NEEDSMORETIME (Irish) — **I** 311[P], **I** 438[P], **I** 470[P]

NEEDWOOD JOKER b.g. 6 Picea - Mey Madam by Song — Miss S Goodhand

1996 **13(NH),7(NH),8(NH)**

677	23/3	Brocklesby '	(L)	MDN	3m	8 GF	*disp til ld 6th, 2l up whn u.r. 14th*	U	-
1479	11/5	Garthorpe	(R)	MDO	3m	12 GS	*hld up in tch, lost tch 12th, t.o. & p.u. 2 out*	P	0
1589	31/5	Market Rasen	(R)	HC	2 3/4m 110yds	10 GF	*alwys well bhnd.*	7	0

Placed in novice hurdle; promise on debut but interrupted season; chances if fit in 98. 12

NEEDWOOD NEPTUNE b.g. 7 Rolfe (USA) - Needwood Nymph by Bold Owl — P A Bennett

1996 2(15),1(15),3(14)

372	2/3	Mollington	(R)	RES	3m	19 G	*(Jt fav) w.w. prog 10th, effrt 13th, 3rd & no imp 3 out, fin tired*	3	10
548	16/3	Garthorpe	(R)	RES	3m	10 GF	*mid div, 6th whn mstk 11th, no ch frm nxt*	6	0
1204	26/4	Clifton On '	(L)	MEM	3m	6 GS	*last pair for 2m,chsd ldng pair frm 11th, unable to cls*	3	15

Maiden winner 96; lightly raced; not progress & suspect; more needed for Restricted. 16

NEELISAGIN(IRE) b.g. 6 Wylfa - Mystrique by Streak W J Turcan

210 16/2 Southwell P' (L) MDO 3m 15 GS *mid-div, prog 11th, chsd ldrs 14th, outpcd apr 3 out* 3 10

480 9/3 Southwell P' (L) MDO 3m 17 G *alwys prom, chal apr 3 out, wknd nxt* 3 10

774 29/3 Dingley (R) MDO 2m 5f 10 G *(fav) alwys prom, 3rd 3 out, chsd wnr nxt, no imp* 2 13

923 6/4 Garthorpe (R) MEM 3m 4 GF *handy, ld 13th, jnd 2 out, just hdd und pres flat* 2 15

1166 20/4 Mollington (R) MDO 3m 9 GF *(fav) mid-div, lost tch 13th, t.o. & p.u. 3 out* P 0

Steady progress; changed hands after 4th start; can win if fit in 98; needs easy course at present. 14

NEELY (Irish) — **I** 115^{P}, **I** 289^{5}, **I** 331^{4}, **I** 366, , **I** 417^{B}, **I** 464^{3}, **I** 507^{U}, **I** 583^{U}

NEETO (Irish) — **I** 406^{P}, **I** 501,

NEILY JOE (Irish) — **I** 39^{F}, **I** 47^{P}, **I** 142^{5}, **I** 443^{5}, **I** 478^{2}, **I** 596^{5}

NELLIE GALE (Irish) — **I** 263^{P}, **I** 305^{4}, **I** 487^{P}, **I** 519^{5}

NELLS DELIGHT b.m. 6 Idiot's Delight - Coolek by Menelek S Clark

427 8/3 Charm Park (L) MDO 3m 10 GF *rear & sn strgglng, wll bhnd 9th, f 11th* F -

No signs on debut. 0

NELPHA (Irish) — **I** 4^{P}, **I** 34^{P}, **I** 100^{P}, **I** 405,

NEMURO(USA) b or br.g. 9 Northrop (USA) - Determined One by Determined King (USA) P A D Scouller

1996 **F(NH),8(NH),5(NH),5(NH),1(NH),F(NH),1(NH),U(NH),4(NH)**

144 9/2 Tweseldown (R) OPE 3m 9 GF *plld, rear, t.o. 9th, ref & u.r. 11th* R -

281 23/2 Charing (L) OPE 3m 12 G *trckd ldrs, pshd alng frm 12th, nvr able to chal* 5 16

870 31/3 Hackwood Pa' (L) MXO 3m 4 F *disp to 8th,steadied,ld & mstk 15th,hdd nxt,mstk last,ran on* 2 21

Useful hurdler & winning novice chaser; able but quirky; can win Open if reproducing last run. 20

NEPE'S MELODY (Irish) — **I** 507^{U}, **I** 525^{P}

NERVOUS KATE (Irish) — **I** 98^{F}, **I** 150^{2}, **I** 217^{P}

NETHERBY CHEESE b.g. 10 Say Primula - Netherby Maid by Derek H Mrs K Smith

1996 P(0),3(0),4(0),2(11),P(0)

576 16/3 Detling (L) MEM 3m 10 F *chsd ldrs, wknd 4 out, p.u. 2 out* P 0

Placed in poor Maidens 96; finished early 97; will need fortune to win. 10

NETHER GOBIONS br.g. 11 Netherkelly - Madame de Luce by Don't Look P Clutterbuck

1996 5(11),P(0),3(20),1(23),F(-),1(23),1(25)

220 16/2 Heythrop (R) OPE 3m 20 G *ld to 11th, chsd wnr aft, chnce 2 out, no ext* 3 22

819 31/3 Paxford (L) OPE 3m 5 F *(fav) hld up, ld 6th-12th, ld 3 out, clr nxt, fin tired* 1 21

1198 23/4 Andoversford (R) OPE 3m 5 F *ld & hit 2nd, hdd nxt, prssd wnr, blnd 12th,rdn & btn 2 out* 2 22

1389 5/5 Cursneh Hill (L) OPE 3m 2 GF *(fav) made all, 4l up 10th, fence ahd frm 2 out* 1 20

1524 17/5 Bredwardine (R) OPE 3m 8 G *(fav) chsd ldr, ld apr 10th, made rest, styd on wll frm 2 out* 1 24

1575 26/5 Chaddesley ' (L) OPE 3m 10 F *(fav) prom,ld & slppd up bend aft 6th,rmntd,cont til p.u. 15th* P 0

Solid; consistent; won 8 of last 17; front runs; mistakes; top training & riding; win more.F-S. 23

NEVER HEARD (Irish) — **I** 43^{U}, **I** 106^{P}, **I** 140^{P}, **I** 206^{1}, **I** 309^{P}, **I** 336^{6}

NEVILLE br.g. 11 Full Of Hope - Viduli by Firestreak J F Heslop

1996 U(-),P(0),4(12),4(16)

516 15/3 Larkhill (R) RES 3m 7 GF *ld to 8th, wth ldr to 12th, outpcd 14th, kpt on last* 3 15

935 6/4 Charlton Ho' (L) RES 3m 7 G *in tch,outpcd 14th,ran on to chs wnr 2 out,chnc last,no ext* 2 18

1058 13/4 Hackwood Pa' (L) RES 3m 6 GF *s.s. f 2nd* F -

Maiden winner 94; lightly raced; changed hands; can run well & weak race possible; G/F-S. 17

NEWBOG LAD (Irish) — **I** 152^{4}, **I** 219^{P}, **I** 343^{5}, **I** 391^{3}

NEWBRANO gr.m. 10 Zambrano - Fanny Adams by Sweet Ration Ian Carmichael

1996 3(0),3(12),P(0)

342 1/3 Corbridge (R) MDO 3m 12 G *mid-div, wknd 12th, t.o. & p.u. 2 out* P 0

415 8/3 Dalston (R) RES 3m 19 GS *(bl) mid-div, 11th hlfwy, sn btn, t.o. & p.u. 3 out* P 0

614 22/3 Friars Haugh (L) MDN 3m 13 GF *made most frm 3rd til 5 out, wll hld frm nxt, lft 2nd last* 2 0

809 31/3 Tranwell (L) MEM 3m 5 G *ld til hdd 5th, ld agn 12th til hdd 2 out, outpcd last* 2 11

996 12/4 Tranwell (L) MDO 3m 8 F *ld 3rd-5th, lft 2nd 13th, qcknd to ld 3 out, hld on gamely* 1 14

Improved; jumping better now; won weak race & needs more for Confined. 14

NEWCHURCH LAD gr.g. 6 Motivate - Miss Rem's Girl Vii by Damsire Unregistered L J Remnant

720 29/3 Llanvapley (L) MDN 3m 8 GF *last til f 4th* F -

1136 19/4 Bonvilston (R) MDO 3m 15 G *rear til p.u. 3 out* P 0

No signs of ability yet. 0

NEW CRUISER b.m. 7 Cruise Missile - New Dawning by Deep Run G L Edwards

1996 6(0),4(0)

326 1/3 Eaton Hall (R) MDN 3m 14 GS *chsd ldrs frm 5 out, no imp clsng stgs* 3 0

Lightly raced; well beaten but at least gets round safely; successful stable; can go closer. 13

NEW FLAME b.m. 7 Lighter - Water Eaton Gal by Legal Eagle K W Walker

1 19/1 Barbury Cas' (L) XX 3m 11 GF *alwys bhnd, t.o. & p.u. last* P 0
224 16/2 Heythrop (R) MDN 3m 16 G *alwys rear, t.o. & p.u. 15th* P 0
299 1/3 Didmarton (L) MDN 3m 14 G *mid-div, no prog 12th, bhnd whn p.u. 14th* P 0

No real signs yet. 0

NEW GHOST ch.g. 12 New Member - St Mary Axe by Metropolis G W Giddings

486 9/3 Tweseldown (R) XX 3m 3 G *mstks, ld to 15th, prssd wnr aft, unable qckn flat* 2 13
1462 11/5 Tweseldown (R) CON 3m 6 GF *(vis) made most to mstk 13th, wknd rpdly, p.u. 4 out, lame* P 0

Hardly runs now; last when finishing & problems last start. 11

NEWMAN'S CONQUEST ch.m. 5 El Conquistador - Newman's Girl by New Member Mrs A M Reed

657 22/3 Badbury Rin' (L) MEM 3m 4 F *alwys last, blnd 14th, tk 3rd nr fin* 3 0

Placed in dire Members; young but needs huge improvement for proper races. 10

NEWMARKET CHEDDAR (Irish) — **I** 76^P, **I** 132^F, **I** 308^P, **I** 444^U, **I** 515^F

NEW PROBLEM b.m. 10 New Member - Light Of Zion by Pieces Of Eight R Michael Smith

1996 S(-),U(-)

559 16/3 Lanark (R) MEM 3m 3 GS *ld brfly 7th, lost tch 11th, p.u. aft nxt* P 0
949 6/4 Friars Haugh (L) MDN 3m 10 GF *ld til 4 out, sn btn* 3 0
1052 13/4 Lockerbie (R) MDN 3m 10 F *sn clr 2nd, wknd frm 14th, p.u. 3 out* P 0
1335 3/5 Mosshouses (L) OPE 3m 4 F *ld 4th-7th, wknd rpdly 11th, p.u. aft nxt* P 0

Speed but no stamina; looks hopeless. 0

NEWSKI EXPRESS bl.m. 12 Newski (USA) - Mint Express by Pony Express John Lister

1996 U(-),1(15),2(17)

1339 3/5 Flete Park (R) RES 3m 6 G *blnd 2nd, prog 13th, cls up til wknd 3 out, p.u. nxt* P 0
1416 10/5 Newton Abbot (L) HC 2m 5f 110yds 14 G *f 2nd.* F -

Maiden winner 96; lightly raced; has ability but time running out now. 17

NEWSTARSKY b.g. 11 New Member - Star Beauty by Jock Scot R G Westacott

1996 P(0),P(0),**F(-)**

176 15/2 Ottery St M' (L) RES 3m 17 G *mid-div, lost tch 14th, t.o. nxt* 4 0
298 1/3 Didmarton (L) RES 3m 15 G *alwys rear, t.o. & p.u. 2 out* P 0
1261 27/4 Black Fores' (R) MDO 3m 12 F *10s-4s, alwys prom, ld 14th, made rest, hld on gamely* 1 13
1483 11/5 Ottery St M' (L) RES 3m 15 G *t.d.e. s.s. alwys mid-div, nvr on trms, p.u. 15th* P 0
1494 14/5 Cothelstone (L) RES 3m 11 GF *rear whn blnd & u.r. 3rd* U -
1552 24/5 Mounsey Hil' (R) RES 3m 12 G *bhnd frm 11th, blnd 13th, p.u. 15th* P 0
1612 7/6 Umberleigh (L) LAD 3m 5 F *20s-6s, rear whn mstk 7th, sn wll bhnd, t.o.* 4 0

Placed 7 times before winning bad race; barely stays & unlikely to win again; crazy punt last start. 14

NEWTON WOLD ch.m. 5 Scorpio (FR) - Pretty Lass by Workboy R H Mason

1251 26/4 Easingwold (L) MDO 3m 9 GS *slow jmp 1st, rear, ref 6th* R -
1268 27/4 Southwell P' (L) MDO 3m 13 G *rear, wll bhnd 12th, p.u. 14th* P 0

Only learning so far. 0

NEWTOWN HENRY (Irish) — **I** 311^P, **I** 413^F

NEWTOWN RAMBLER(IRE) br.g. 7 Step Together (USA) - Knocknahour Windy Vii by Damsire Unregistered W K Hooper

60 1/2 Kingston Bl' (L) MDN 3m 17 GF *rear, steady prog to 2nd at 14th, wknd* 5 0

Ex Irish; vanished after one run; plenty to prove. 12

NEWTOWN ROAD (Irish) — **I** 117^3

NEW YORK BOY b.g. 9 Sergeant Drummer (USA) - Auction Ring by Track Spare R O Bishop

28 26/1 Marks Tey (L) RES 3m 9 GF *sn wll bhnd, t.o. & p.u. 14th* P 0
126 9/2 Cottenham (R) RES 3m 14 GF *sn bhnd, t.o. 12th, ran on frm 3 out, fin wll* 6 0
198 15/2 Higham (L) RES 3m 14 G *mid-div til blnd & u.r. 12th* U -
443 8/3 Higham (L) RES 3m 7 G *mid-div, mstk 16th, ran on 3 out, chal last, ran on,just hld* 2 18
711 29/3 High Easter (L) RES 3m 6 F *in tch,lft 3rd 12th,outpcd 3 out,2nd & wll hld whn mstk nxt* 2 12
1114 19/4 Higham (L) RES 3m 5 GF *(fav) trckd wnr, no imp frm 16th, wknd last* 2 12
1278 27/4 Fakenham P-' (L) RES 3m 11 G *mstk 5th, bhnd frm 10th, t.o. & p.u. 2 out* P 0
1445 10/5 Peper Harow (L) LAD 3m 6 GF *bhnd frm 4th, pshd alng 10th, nvr nr ldrs* 5 0

Maiden winner 95; missed 96; one good run; mistakes & overall form poor; likes Higham; need luck to win 14

NGALA (Irish) — **I** 71^{3}, **I** 112, , **I** 126^{2}, **I** 250^{P}, **I** 312^{3}, **I** 360^{4}, **I** 416^{3}, **I** 432^{P}

NIAMHS DREAM (Irish) — **I** 394^{P}, **I** 437^{P}

NIAMHS GLORY (Irish) — **I** 225^{F}, **I** 438^{P}

NIBBLE b.g. 9 Nicholas Bill - Sigh by Highland Melody — G I Cooper

1996 1(15),4(10),1(17)

64	1/2	Horseheath	(R)	LAD	3m	7	GF	*hmpd & nrly u.r. 1st, prog 7th, cls up whn f 9th*	F	-
271	22/2	Ampton	(R)	CON	3m	15	G	*chsd ldrs, 4th & rdn appr 3 out, onepcd aft*	4	18
497	15/3	Ampton	(R)	CON	3m	9	GF	*trkcd ldrs, gng wll, ev ch & blnd 17th, rdn & btn appr 2 out*	3	17
800	31/3	Marks Tey	(L)	LAD	3m	3	F	*mstks in rear, last 10th, outpcd 16th, styd on frm 3 out*	3	16

Lightly raced; stays; consistent but mistakes; can win modest Confined; likes Marks Tey; Good. 18

NICE APPROACH (Irish) — **I** 274^{P}, **I** 333^{2}

NICE TO NO ch.g. 9 Cisto (FR) - Noneed by Duneed — G M Leeves

1996 P(0),P(0),4(0),5(0),5(0)

175	15/2	Ottery St M'	(L)	RES	3m	15	G	*alwys mid-div, t.o. & p.u. 15th*	P	0
312	1/3	Clyst St Ma'	(L)	RES	3m	8	HY	*cls up to 8th, lost tch & p.u. 12th*	P	0
527	15/3	Cothelstone	(L)	MDN	3m	14	GS	*wll in tch to 14th, wknd, p.u. 2 out*	P	0

Well beaten when completing 96; not progress in 97; much more needed. 10

NICHOLLS CROSS (Irish) — **I** 57^{6}, **I** 220^{1}

NICKAMY FOUNTAIN(IRE) b.g. 7 Royal Fountain - Devon Ann by Black Minstrel — K O'Meara

853	31/3	Eyton-On-Se'	(L)	MDO	3m	13	GF	*ran out 3rd*	r	-
1429	10/5	Aspatria	(L)	MDO	3m	15	G	*(bl) t.o. 7th, p.u. 12th*	P	0
1541	18/5	Wolverhampt'	(L)	MDO	3m	15	GS	*(bl) mid to rear, p.u. 4 out*	P	0

Signs are not encouraging. 0

NICKNAVAR ch.g. 12 Raga Navarro (ITY) - Bay Girl by Persian Bold — Mrs P A Tetley

1996 F(-)

70	2/2	Higham	(L)	OPE	3m	5	GF	*prom whn stirrup broke aft 1st & p.u.*	P	0
194	15/2	Higham	(L)	OPE	3m	12	G	*sn rear, nvr going wll, wll bhnd & p.u. 15th*	P	0

Very lightly raced & of no real account now. 0

NICK THE BISCUIT b.g. 6 Nicholas Bill - Maryland Cookie (USA) by Bold Hour — S W Rudge

1996 **3(NH),2(NH),P(NH),12(NH)**

365	2/3	Garnons	(L)	MDO	2 1/2m	14	GS	*chsd ldrs to 9th, wknd 12th, walked in*	6	0
706	29/3	Upper Sapey	(R)	MDO	3m	15	GF	*cls 3rd/4th til mstk 15th, no ext frm 2 out*	6	0
1016	12/4	Bitterley	(L)	MDO	3m	14	GF	*alwys mid-div, effrt 13th, no prog frm 15th*	6	0
1460	11/5	Maisemore P'	(L)	MDO	3m	16	G	*in tch,prog 11th,ld 15th,jnd apr 2 out,kpt on wll, hdd post*	2	15
1527	17/5	Bredwardine	(R)	MDO	3m	13	G	*w.w.prog to ld 15th-nxt, chsd wnr aft, not qckn last*	2	12
1578	26/5	Chaddesley '	(L)	MDO	3m	7	F	*(fav) ld to 2nd, chsd ldr, ld 13th, wll clr 3 out, comf*	1	13
1605	1/6	Dingley	(R)	RES	3m	13	GF	*w.w. prog to ld 13th-14th, outpcd aft nxt, kpt on*	4	12

Ex selling hurdler; sluiced home & not disgraced after; lacks scope & needs more for Restricted.G-F. .. 16

NICOLE'S HOPE (Irish) — **I** 467^{P}, **I** 507^{P}

NICOLINSKY b.m. 7 Krisinsky (USA) - Game Spinney by Precipice Wood — Mrs S J Biggin

1996 P(0),P(0)

392	8/3	Barbury Cas'	(L)	MDN	3m	9	G	*last whn blnd & u.r. 2nd*	U	-
513	15/3	Larkhill	(R)	MDO	3m	10	GF	*ld to 3rd, wknd 7th, sn bhnd, p.u. 3 out*	P	0
917	5/4	Larkhill	(R)	MDO	2 1/2m	6	F	*last til clsd 3 out, ran on to ld nr fin*	1	11

Won one of the seasons worst races; mega improvement needed now. 11

NIGHTS IMAGE(IRE) br.g. 7 Corvaro (USA) - Lysanders Lady by Saulingo — T Blane

1996 7(0),U(-),2(12)

81	2/2	Wolverhampt'	(L)	MDN	3m	13	GS	*(fav) 7s-7/4, prom, cls 3rd whn f 11th*	F	-
206	15/2	Weston Park	(L)	MDN	3m	9	G	*(fav) cls up, ld 7th til 4 out, outpcd frm 2 out*	2	15
327	1/3	Eaton Hall	(R)	MDN	3m	11	GS	*(fav) n.j.w., cls 2nd 6th, in tch til wknd cls home*	3	13
470	8/3	Eyton-On-Se'	(L)	MDN	2 1/2m	12	G	*chsd ldrs., wll in tch whn u.r. 6 out*	U	-
665	23/3	Eaton Hall	(R)	MDO	3m	11	GF	*(fav) f 3rd*	F	-
768	29/3	Whittington	(L)	MDO	3m	10	S	*held up, styd prog to ld apr 3 out, hdd nxt, no ext*	3	12
942	6/4	Tabley	(R)	MDO	3m	8	G	*w.w., prog 3rd 9th, rddn & btn apr 2 out, blndrd last*	3	0

Dead 13

NIGHT WIND b.g. 10 Strong Gale - Kylogue Lady by London Gazette — Mrs P Tollit

1996 2(20),6(12),2(18),F(-)

520	15/3	Cothelstone	(L)	LAD	3m	12	GS	*ld 1st, prom, 3rd but no prog frm hlfwy*	3	21
818	31/3	Paxford	(L)	LAD	3m	3	F	*(fav) hld up last, went 2nd 13th, hit 15th, wknd, t.o.*	3	0
1013	12/4	Bitterley	(L)	CON	3m	14	GF	*prom, cls 3rd whn f 13th*	F	-
1266	27/4	Southwell P'	(L)	LAD	3m	5	G	*rear, effrt to go 2nd 4 out, onepcd nxt*	2	19
1302	3/5	Weston Park	(L)	LAD	3m	5	G	*3rd, prog 4 out, ran on, not rch wnr*	2	20

Chase winner 94; consistent but easily beaten by good horses; may find weak Ladies; not firm. 21

NIJAPAJO (Irish) — I 247^P, I 328^P

NIKAROO b or br.m. 11 Chukaroo - Nikali by Siliconn — Mrs Carrie Janaway

1996 **7(NH),6(NH),4(NH),2(NH),4(NH)**

41	1/2	Larkhill	(R) MDO 3m	13	GF	*ld 2nd-10th, outpcd 14th, no ch whn blnd 2 out*	4	0
390	8/3	Barbury Cas'	(L) MDN 3m	15	G	*chsd ldrs til wknd 11th, t.o. & p.u. 2 out*	P	0
871	31/3	Hackwood Pa'	(L) MDO 3m	7	F	*alwys rear, poor 4th last, p.u. flat, dead*	P	0

Dead. 0

NIKITASECONDCHANCE ch.m. 10 Push On - Chiquita Beatle by Beat Group — S Bamford

186	15/2	Erw Lon	(L) MDN 3m	13	G	*schoold, t.o. til p.u. 10th*	P	0
260	22/2	Newtown	(L) RES 3m	16	G	*u.r. 1st*	U	-
437	8/3	Upton-On-Se'	(R) MDO 3m	15	G	*cls 8th at 10th, outpcd 13th, dist 6th whn p.u. last*	P	0
543	16/3	Erw Lon	(L) MDN 3m	11	GF	*alwys rear, p.u. 12th*	P	0
877	1/4	Upton-On-Se'	(R) RES 3m	17	GF	*rear, 9th & wll bhnd at 11th, p.u. 15th, dsmntd*	P	0
1186	20/4	Lydstep	(L) MDO 3m	7	GF	*alwys mid-div, ran on aft last to tk 3rd flat*	3	0

Beaten 30 lengths plus when completing; a step in the right direction but much more needed. 0

NIKOLAYEVICH b.g. 10 Niniski (USA) - Rexana by Relko — A M Turner

312	1/3	Clyst St Ma'	(L) RES 3m	8	HY	*sn bhnd, t.o. & p.u. 11th*	P	0
526	15/3	Cothelstone	(L) MDN 3m	15	GS	*bhnd til u.r. 16th*	U	-
795	31/3	Bishopsleigh	(R) MDO 3m	12	G	*alwys rear, t.o. & p.u. 12th*	P	0
1436	10/5	Holnicote	(L) MEM 3m	5	G	*ld/disp til outpcd aft 3 out, ran on & lft in ld last,hdd fn*	2	13

Missed 96; just pipped in slow Members; chances in weak Maiden if reproducing it. 13

NINETEENOFIVE (Irish) — I 103^P, I 261^P, I 343^P, I 390^P

NIORD b.g. 7 Nishapour (FR) - Pro Scania by Niniski (USA) — B Davies

1996 P(0),P(0),F(-),6(0),F(-),3(0)

82	2/2	Wolverhampt'	(L) MDN 3m	11	GS	*alwys bhnd, t.o. & p.u. 11th*	P	0
469	8/3	Eyton-On-Se'	(L) MDN 2 1/2m	9	G	*cls up til f 9th*	F	-
1003	12/4	Alpraham	(R) MDO 2 1/2m	10	GF	*made all, rdn out whn chal flat*	1	13
1303	3/5	Weston Park	(L) RES 3m	6	G	*chsd wnr, mstks & tiring 4 out, p.u. 2 out*	P	0

Won poor short Maiden; does not stay 3 miles & future prospects are nil. 12

NIRALDA (Irish) — I 496,

NISHKINA b.g. 9 Nishapour (FR) - Varishkina by Derring-Do — C J Cundall

1996 4(13),F(-),6(15),3(12),7(0),5(16)

265	22/2	Duncombe Pa'	(R) CON 3m	15	G	*prom, til wknd 11th, blndrd 14th, t.o. & p.u. 3 out*	P	0
421	8/3	Charm Park	(L) MEM 3m	6	GF	*disp til hdd 3rd, ld 11th & disp nxt, ld 15th, kpt on flat*	1	14
857	31/3	Charm Park	(L) MXO 3m	3	F	*20l 3rd at 5th, trckd ldr 11th, ld 4 out-2 out, outpcd*	2	15

Confined winner 95; safe but usually easily beaten; Members best hope again; Any. 16

NISSAN STAR (Irish) — I 79^P, I 234^6

NOBBUTJUST(IRE) ch.m. 7 Sandalay - Kam Hill by Kambalda — Countess Goess-Saurau

1996 4(10),P(0),1D(10),1(13)

45	1/2	Larkhill	(R) RES 3m	14	GF	*alwys prom, outpcd 3 out, strng chal last 100 yrds, just hld*	3	19
222	16/2	Heythrop	(R) RES 3m	17	G	*prog 9th, cls up 14th, wknd 3 out, p.u. nxt*	P	0
516	15/3	Larkhill	(R) RES 3m	7	GF	*cls up til mstk & u.r. 11th*	U	-
653	22/3	Siddington	(L) RES 3m	10	F	*(Jt fav) hld up, mstk 3rd, effrt 12th, nvr rchd ldrs, btn & p.u.3 out*	P	0
1080	13/4	Guilsborough	(L) RES 3m	11	GF	*w.w. prog 14th, styd on to chs wnr apr last, nrst fin*	2	16
1210	26/4	Woodford	(L) RES 3m	14	G	*mid-div, 7th hlfwy, styd on frm 4 out, not trbl wnr*	2	16
1466	11/5	Tweseldown	(R) RES 3m	5	GF	*(fav) trckd ldrs, rmndrs hlfwy, 2nd 4 out, ev ch last, no ext*	2	16
1552	24/5	Mounsey Hil'	(R) RES 3m	12	G	*nvr bttr than mid-div, 8th at 13th, no prog*	5	0

Won weak Maiden 96; stays; good enogh to win but frustrating now; slog in mud may suit. 16

NOBLE ANGEL(IRE) b.g. 9 Aristocracy - Be An Angel by Be Friendly — P R Whiston

1996 P(0),P(0),**F(-)**,U(-),**P(0)**

82	2/2	Wolverhampt'	(L) MDN 3m	11	GS	*ld to 16th, sn outpcd & no ch wth wnr aft*	2	11
211	16/2	Southwell P'	(L) MDO 3m	15	GS	*chsd clr ldr to 15th, wknd rpdly, p.u. nxt*	P	0
377	4/3	Leicester	(R) HC 2 1/2m 110yds	15	G	*pulld hrd, led 4th to apr 6th, weakening when f 9th.*	F	-
665	23/3	Eaton Hall	(R) MDO 3m	11	GF	*whppd round strt, lost 50l, grad made ground, tk 4th flat*	4	0
854	31/3	Eyton-On-Se'	(L) MDO 3m	10	GF	*mid-div, disp 3rd-4th-13th, ran on wll frm 3 out*	2	12
1381	5/5	Eyton-On-Se'	(L) MEM 3m	5	GF	*cls up,ld 3rd,made rest,ran on und pres frm 3 out.*	1	18
1508	17/5	Bangor	(L) HC 3m 110yds	12	G	*prom, ld apr 3rd till hdd 5th, mstk and lost pl 9th, soon lost tch, t.o. when p.u. before 12th.*	P	0

Improving now settling bettr; likes Eyton; Restricted likely if maintaining progress.G/F. 17

NOBLE COMIC b.g. 6 Silly Prices - Barony by Ribston — R E Dimond

1996 P(0),3(14),P(0)

392 8/3 Barbury Cas' (L) MDN 3m 9 G *(fav) plIng, prom 5th, chsd ldr 12th, wknd rpdly 2 out, p.u. last* P 0
526 15/3 Cothelstone (L) MDN 3m 15 GS *f 1st* F -
933 6/4 Charlton Ho' (L) MDO 3m 12 G *w.w. trckd ldrs going wll 14th, wknd rpdly & p.u. 2 out* P 0
1270 27/4 Little Wind' (R) MDO 2 1/2m 10 GF *trckd ldrs, ev ch 13th, 4th & btn whn blnd & u.r. nxt* U -
1485 11/5 Ottery St M' (L) MDO 3m 13 G *hld up, prog 14th, 2nd 3 out, chal last, ran on to ld nr fin* 1 14
1552 24/5 Mounsey Hil' (R) RES 3m 12 G *hld up bhnd, prog 12th, chsd ldng pair 17th, btn nxt, tired* 3 13

Hard puller & win owes much to the rider; does not stay; follow up hard to find; G-G/F. 15

NOBLE JAKEY b.g. 7 Baron Blakeney - Joscilla by Joshua Edward Retter

1034 12/4 Lifton (R) MDN 3m 7 F *alwys cls up til rddn frm 3 out, promsng* 4 0

Asatisfactory start; good stable & should go very close in 98. 12

NOBLE KNIGHT(IRE) ch.g. 9 Boyne Valley - Nano's View by Carnival Night C Jarvis

63 1/2 Horseheath (R) OPE 3m 5 GF *ld 2nd-5th, last frm 9th, t.o. & p.u. 13th* P 0
123 9/2 Cottenham (R) INT 3m 13 GF *last & sn wll bhnd, t.o. 10th* 6 0
270 22/2 Ampton (R) MEM 3m 8 G *ld 3-5th, blnd 15th, ev ch 17th, wknd appr 2 out* 4 0
438 8/3 Higham (L) MDO 3m 8 G *disp 3rd, ld 4-7th, ld 16th, drew clr 2 out, v easily* 1 15
503 15/3 Ampton (R) XX 3m 11 GF *chsd ldr, ld 10th, made rest, clr 3 out, hld on gamely flat* 1 15

Ex Irish; novice ridden; won modest races; front runs; every chance of weak local Restricted. 16

NOBLE LEADER (Irish) — **I** 154^{P}, **I** 181^{F}
NOBLE MELODY (Irish) — **I** 185^{5}, **I** 339^{P}, **I** 499^{U}, **I** 572^{P}
NOBLE PROPOSAL (Irish) — **I** 576^{P}
NOBLE PROTECTOR(IRE) ch.g. 7 Aristocracy - Inveigle G F Wheeler

1996 **16(NH)**

181 15/2 Larkhill (R) MDO 3m 17 G *bdly hmpd & u.r. 1st* U -
316 1/3 Clyst St Ma' (L) MDN 3m 6 HY *ld 3-11th,wknd nxt,lft bttr by dfctns, kpt on to ld flat* 1 0
517 15/3 Larkhill (R) RES 3m 10 GF *ld 3rd, jnd whn f 12th* F -
688 29/3 Little Wind' (R) RES 3m 5 GF *25s-5s,keen hld,mstks,ld to aft 14th,sn wknd,t.o. & p.u.last* P 0
1275 27/4 Little Wind' (R) RES 3m 9 GF *jmpd bdly, in tch to 12th, last whn f 3 out, dead* F -

Dead. 11

NOBLE STAR b.g. 5 Jester - Mickley Spacetrail by Space King Mrs J Bush

297 1/3 Didmarton (L) MDN 3m 11 G *blnd 6th, wknd 10th, t.o. & p.u. 13th* P 0

Only learning on debut. 0

NOBODYWANTSME (Irish) — **I** 413^{3}, **I** 471^{3}
NODDIS DILEMMA (Irish) — **I** 11^{P}, **I** 54^{4}, **I** 135^{1}
NODFORMS DILEMMA(USA) ch.g. 14 State Dinner (USA) - Princess Jo Jo Mrs C A Hollinshead

1996 4(17),3(18),3(18),4(18)

202 15/2 Weston Park (L) LAD 3m 13 G *mid-div, p.u. aft 5th* P 0
466 8/3 Eyton-On-Se' (L) LAD 3m 7 G *hld up, cls order to 2nd 9th, wknd qckly, p.u. 13th* P 0
850 31/3 Eyton-On-Se' (L) LAD 3m 6 GF *rear to 12th, cls order 4 out, lkd held in 3rd 2 out* 2 11
1299 3/5 Weston Park (L) MEM 3m 4 G *ld 4th-13th, chsd wnr at onepcd aft, lame* 2 15

Won 9 points 92-4; schoolmaster now; unlikely to win again & problems last start. 13

NODFORMS INFERNO b.g. 8 Idiot's Delight - River Linnet by Forlorn River R G Turvey

1996 **11(NH),8(NH)**

175 15/2 Ottery St M' (L) RES 3m 15 G *plld hrd, ld 5th til f 11th* F -
526 15/3 Cothelstone (L) MDN 3m 15 GS *twrds rear til p.u. 14th* P 0
866 31/3 Kingston St' (R) MDO 3m 7 F *plIng, ld til hdd apr 3 out, wknd, walked in* 2 0

No ability under rules; too headstrong so far. 0

NODFORM WONDER b.g. 10 Cut Above - Wonder by Tekoah D A Malam

1996 **2(NH),2(NH),4(NH),6(NH),7(NH),r(NH)**

200 15/2 Weston Park (L) CON 3m 16 G *ld to 9th, cls up to 4 out, outpcd 2 out* 4 16
330 1/3 Eaton Hall (R) CON 3m 16 GS *made all, chal strngly by wnr 2 out, jmp lft last, not rcvr* 2 19
667 23/3 Eaton Hall (R) CON 3m 10 GF *(fav) made most, clr 4th, unchal, easily* 1 21
937 6/4 Tabley (R) CON 3m 10 G *(fav) disp til ld 4th, made rest, drew clr frm 3 out, easily* 1 25
1098 19/4 Bangor (L) HC 3m 110yds 9 G *(fav) ld to 4th, led 7th to 8th, led again 10th, mstk 3 out, clr when pkd last, comf.* 1 27
1508 17/5 Bangor (L) HC 3m 110yds 12 G *(fav) ld till apr 3rd, regained ld 5th, pkd badly 10th, clr from 12th, unchal.* 1 32

Ex hurdler; very useful; strong galloper; front runs; sure to win more; G/F-G/S. 32

NO DOZING(IRE) b.g. 8 Bulldozer - Miss Pet Tina by Choral Society Joseph Byrne

221 16/2 Heythrop (R) RES 3m 15 G *wll bhnd, t.o. 12th, ran on frm 2 out, fin strngly* 5 11

391 8/3 Barbury Cas' (L) MEM 3m 6 G *alwys rear, jmpd slwly 2nd lost tch 10th, no ch frm 12th* 5 0

Poor novice hurdler; subsequent winner behind 1st start but needs more. 13

NO HANKY PANKY ch.g. 6 Lighter - Karafair by Karabas — Mrs Susan E Busby

59 1/2 Kingston Bl' (L) RES 3m 16 GF *sn wll bhnd, t.o. whn ref & u.r. 10th* R -
221 16/2 Heythrop (R) RES 3m 15 G *prom to 6th, sn lost plc, p.u. 11th* P 0
827 31/3 Lockinge (L) MDO 3m 3 F *jmpd slwly & rght, lost tch 11th, p.u. nxt, dsmntd* P 0

No signs yet; may do better. 0

NO INHIBITIONS ch.h. 10 Exhibitioner - Australite by Realm — L J Bowman

302 1/3 Parham (R) CON 3m 14 G *ld to 5th, wknd 9th, rear & p.u. 13th* P 0
1506 16/5 Folkestone (R) HC 2m 5f 8 G *prom, chsd ldr briefly 10th, outpcd when mstk next, no dngr after.* 3 17
1569 26/5 Fontwell (R) HC 3 1/4m 110yds 10 GF *chsd ldrs till wknd quickly 4 out, bhnd when p.u. before last.* P 0

Won awful H/chase 95; missed 96; outclassed in 97; should concentrate on points. 16

NOISY WELCOME b.g. 11 The Parson - Lady Pitpan by Pitpan — M P Jones

1996 6(0),F(-),6(0),6(0),5(0),F(-)

285 26/2 Taunton (R) HC 4 1/4m 110yds 16 GS *f 4th.* F -
567 16/3 Garnons (L) MEM 3m 3 G *ld til mstk & hdd 15th, kpt on onepcd aft* 2 11
636 22/3 Howick (L) CON 3m 12 GF *last early, some late prog, ran on onepcd* 5 13
749 29/3 Brampton Br' (R) OPE 3m 4 GF *alwys 4th, 10l down & rdn 12th, went remote 3rd 3 out* 3 14
903 5/4 Howick (L) CON 3m 6 F *(fav) made most, rdn 2 out, hdd last, rallied flat, just faild* 2 13
1134 19/4 Bonvilston (R) MXO 4m 10 G *towrds rear til p.u. 3 out* P 0

Restricted winner 95 beaten in bad races 97 & need fortune to win now. 14

NO JOKER(IRE) b.g. 9 Jester - Canta Lair by The Parson — Brigadier R W S Hall

1996 **U(-),3(21),F(-),U(-),2(21),2(20),U(-)**

91 6/2 Huntingdon (R) HC 3m 10 G *mstk 1st, ld 3rd to next, weakening when u.r. 11th.* U -
388 7/3 Sandown (R) HC 3m 110yds 7 G *ld to 4th, wknd after 12th, soon t.o., no ch when blnd four out.* 5 13
1203 26/4 Worcester (L) HC 2m 7f 110yds 10 S *trckd ldrs, hit 10th, soon bhnd, t.o. when p.u. before 3 out.* P 0
1501 16/5 Folkestone (R) HC 3 1/4m 10 G *trckd wnr till after 12th, effort to ld 3 out, hdd next, mstk last, rallied well und pres.* 2 21
1570 26/5 Hereford (R) HC 3m 1f 110yds 14 G *(fav) bhnd, hdwy 4 out, ld last, styd on well.* 1 22

Won 4 points 94/5; stronger handling brought reward; mistakes; stays; hard to place in 98; F-S. 21

NO JUSTICE b.g. 8 Alleging (USA) - Bright Stream by Cure The Blues (USA) — Mrs Karen McLintock

38 26/1 Alnwick (L) MDO 3m 14 G *last & mstk 1st,effrt 10th,7th & btn whn mstk 15th,p.u. nxt* P 0
614 22/3 Friars Haugh (L) MDN 3m 13 GF *hndy, cls 2nd whn f 12th* F -
948 6/4 Friars Haugh (L) MDO 3m 7 GF *(33's-8's), 3rd whn f 6th* F -
1051 13/4 Lockerbie (R) MDN 3m 10 F *cls up, ld 13th-15th, sn wknd, p.u. last* P 0

Shows some hope; can do better. 11

NOMEROSE (Irish) — I 423P, I 534P

NO MORE THE FOOL ch.g. 11 Jester - Prima Bella by High Hat — Lee Brennan

1996 **P(NH),6(NH),P(NH),11(0),4(0)**

200 15/2 Weston Park (L) CON 3m 16 G *alwys rear, p.u. 14th* P 0
330 1/3 Eaton Hall (R) CON 3m 16 GS *mid to rear, p.u. 5 out* P 0
726 29/3 Sandon (L) CON 3m 8 GF *mid-div, nvr dang* 4 13
938 6/4 Tabley (R) OPE 3m 9 G *in tch, rmmndr 12th, sn outpcd, t.o.* 7 0
1175 20/4 Sandon (L) CON 3m 8 GF *s.s. mid-div 5th, ld 11th-4 out, ran on onepcd* 2 17
1300 3/5 Weston Park (L) CON 3m 8 G *mid-div, prog 11th, mstk & wknd 5 out, p.u. 2 out* P 0
1508 17/5 Bangor (L) HC 3m 110yds 12 G *slowly into stride, alwys bhnd, t.o. 12th, p.u. before 5 out.* P 0

Very moderate; placed in poor Confined; most unlikely to win. 13

NO MORE TRIX b.g. 11 Kemal (FR) - Blue Trix by Blue Chariot — W M Burnell

154 14/2 Fakenham (L) HC 2m 5f 110yds 10 G *in tch when blnd and u.r. 4th.* U -
351 2/3 Market Rase' (L) OPE 3m 10 GF *prom, disp 4th & btn whn f 14th* F -
1248 26/4 Easingwold (L) OPE 3m 8 GS *mstk 3rd, rear aft, p.u. 4 out* P 0
1349 3/5 Gisburn (R) CON 3m 11 GF *mid-div, prog 14th, strng chal aft 2 out, outpcd aft* 2 18
1420 10/5 Easingwold (L) OPE 3m 5 GF *ld to 3rd, chsd wnr aft, lost plc 12th, sn strggling* 3 10

Winning chaser 94/95; missed 95/96; ran well once; outclassed in Opens; may find modest Confined. .. 17

NONEOFYOURBUSINESS(IRE) b.m. 6 Salluceva - Roriston Queen by Furry Glen — R W Jewitt

730 29/3 Alnwick (L) MDO 2 1/2m 9 F *prom, 2l 2nd 6th, outpcd & remote 3rd whn p.u. 3 out* P 0

997 12/4 Tranwell (L) MDO 2 1/2m 8 F *cls 6th 6th, grdly lost tch final ctt, t.o. & p.u. 4 out* P 0
1167 20/4 Hexham Poin' (L) MEM 3m 5 GF *(fav) 15l 3rd at 6th, prog 10th, ld 2 out, ran on well* 1 10

Won a dreadful race (probably lucky); way below Restricted standard. 11

NONNY'S BOY b.g. 7 Rakaposhi King - Geminera by Rymer — B Wilberforce

205 15/2 Weston Park (L) MDN 3m 10 G *s.s. nvr in race, p.u. 10th* P 0

No show on debut. 0

NO ONE KNOWS (Irish) — **I** 62^{5}, **I** 281^{3}

NO OTHER HILL (Irish) — **I** 95^{F}, **I** 226^{2}, **I** 285^{P}, **I** 393^{4}, **I** 522^{4}, **I** 552^{2}

NO PANIC b.g. 13 Pitpan - Scirea by Cantab — C R Johnson
1996 P(0),U(-),P(0),P(0)

191 15/2 Erw Lon (L) CON 3m 13 G *alwys bhnd, t.o. 13th* 6 0
363 2/3 Garnons (L) XX 3m 6 GS *10l 5th at 8th, lost tch 11th, p.u. 15th* P 0
399 8/3 Llanfrynach (R) CON 3m 11 G *nvr bynd mid-div, p.u. 2 out* P 0
535 16/3 Erw Lon (L) CON 3m 12 GF *ld to 2nd, cls up to 11th, fdd* 5 11
843 31/3 Lydstep (L) OPE 3m 4 F *cls up to 12th, no ch aft* 4 0
958 6/4 Pantyderi (L) CON 3m 3 F *2nd thruout, nvr near to chal* 2 14
1182 20/4 Lydstep (L) OPE 3m 3 GF *popped around in rear* 3 0
1224 26/4 Pyle (R) CON 3m 7 GS *prom, mstk 5th, chsd ldr 9-12th, sn wknd, t.o.* 4 0
1362 5/5 Pantyderi (L) CON 3m 4 G *in rear, mstk 3rd, dist 3rd at fin* 3 0
1467 11/5 Erw Lon (L) MEM 3m 3 GS *chsd ldr, mstk 14th, ld nxt, easily* 1 10
1491 14/5 Hereford (R) HC 3m 1f 110yds 11 G *hdwy 11th, soon wknd, t.o. when blnd and u.r. 4 out.* U -
1590 31/5 Stratford (L) HC 3m 9 G *t.o. before hfwy, virtually p.u. after last.* 7 0

Very moderate; fortunate to win Members; no prospects in proper races. 11

NO PROBLEM (Irish) — **I** 1^{1}, **I** 236^{3}

NORAS GALE (Irish) — **I** 83^{P}

NORDIC FLASH b.g. 10 Nordico (USA) - Rosemore by Ashmore (FR) — Miss H Bevan
1996 **P(NH),2(NH)**

220 16/2 Heythrop (R) OPE 3m 20 G *alwys bhnd, t.o. & p.u. 12th* P 0
293 1/3 Didmarton (L) INT 3m 16 G *(bl) prom, blnd & wknd 13th, wll bhnd whn ref last* R -

Winning selling hurdler; no prospects as a pointer. 11

NORDROSS b.m. 9 Ardross - Noreena by Nonoalco (USA) — M A Lloyd
1996 P(0),2(13),4(10)

1018 12/4 Bitterley (L) MDO 3m 13 GF *trckd ldrs, effrt 12th, ld nxt, not qckn frm 14th* 4 10

Lightly raced; shows ability but vanished quickly in 97; may need a long track. 12

NOREASONATALL b.m. 5 Lord David S (USA) - Grand Queen by Grand Conde (FR) — A G Knowles

768 29/3 Whittington (L) MDO 3m 10 S *mstks, rear, p.u. 11th* P 0
1073 13/4 Whitwell-On' (R) MDO 2 1/2m 88yds 17 G *alwys rear, t.o. & p.u. 2 out* P 0
1262 27/4 Southwell P' (L) MDO 3m 15 G *prom til lost plc 11th, sn strggling* 6 0

A glimmer of hope; much more needed. 0

NO REFUND (Irish) — **I** 143^{P}, **I** 166, , **I** 305^{P}, **I** 338^{F}, **I** 538^{P}, **I** 561^{3}

NO REPLY b.g. 11 Tumble Gold - Santa Luna by Saint Crespin — A Simpson
1996 P(0),4(0),5(0),5(0),3(10),4(0),P(0),3(0)

921 5/4 Larkhill (R) RES 3m 3 F *ld 2nd-4th, cls up to 10th, outpcd aft* 2 0
1059 13/4 Hackwood Pa' (L) MDO 3m 6 GF *sweating, 2nd til p.u. 11th* P 0

Placed 11 times 94-7; brief season 97 & most unlikely to win at 12. 10

NORMAN ROAD (Irish) — **I** 201^{P}, **I** 245^{P}, **I** 295^{P}

NORMANS PROFIT ch.g. 7 Meadowbrook - Night Profit by Carnival Night — W G Young
1996 5(0),P(0)

160 15/2 Lanark (R) MDO 2m 5f 10 G *ldng grp til wknd 4 out* 4 0
564 16/3 Lanark (R) MDO 2 1/2m 13 GS *nvr nr ldrs, p.u. 3 out* P 0

Well beaten when completing; way below standard as yet. 0

NORMEAD LASS b.m. 9 Norwick (USA) - Meads Lass by Saritamer (USA) — Ms Felicity Ashfield
1996 **P(NH),4(NH),6(NH),9(NH)**

1 19/1 Barbury Cas' (L) XX 3m 11 GF *alwys bhnd, t.o. & p.u. 14th* P 0
14 25/1 Cottenham (R) MDO 3m 7 GF *mid-div, lost tch 10th, t.o.* 5 0
146 9/2 Tweseldown (R) MDO 3m 10 GF *trckd ldrs,prog to 2nd 15th,ld aft 2 out,mstk last,drvn out* 1 13
278 23/2 Charing (L) RES 3m 17 G *mid-div, lost tch & p.u. 16th* P 0
483 9/3 Tweseldown (R) CON 3m 8 G *chsd ldrs, rdn 8th, wknd 14th, t.o.* 5 0

Ex novice hurdler; 25/1 when scoring; does not stay & follow up looks impossible. 12

NORMOUS (Irish) — I 36², I 123ᴾ, I 232², I 348,
NORTHCHA LADY (Irish) — I 90ᶠ, I 186ᶠ
NORTH CITY (Irish) — I 118ᴾ, I 311⁶, I 413⁵

NORTHERN BLUFF b.g. 7 Precocious - Mainmast by Bustino — W D Francis
1996 2(12),U(-),1(16),1(20),1(16),1(19),**1(25)**

400	8/3	Llanfrynach	(R)	OPE	3m	10	G	*(fav) ld/disp til clr 2nd frm 14th, 4l down & hld whn f last*	F -
537	16/3	Erw Lon	(L)	OPE	3m	9	GF	*(fav) alwys prom, chsd wnr last, ev ch flat, onepcd*	2 21

H/chase winner 96; not disgraced in brief 96; good stable; can win Opens 98;L/H best. 23

NORTHERN BRIDE ch.m. 9 Northern Game - Brampton Bride by Bribe — Miss L Clisby Brown
1996 P(0),P(0),P(0),P(0)

807	31/3	Wadebridge	(L)	LAD	3m	4	F	*ld 7-8th, efft short livd, grdly lost tch*	3 0
1090	16/4	Hockworthy	(L)	LAD	3m	8	GF	*n.j.w. s.s., t.o. til p.u. 15th*	P 0

Of no account. 0

NORTHERN CODE br.g. 10 Funny Man - Dialling Code by Don't Look — G J Smith

28	26/1	Marks Tey	(L)	RES	3m	9	GF	*chsd ldr, lft in ld 9th, mstk 11th, hdd 16th, btn whn f 3out*	F -
147	9/2	Tweseldown	(R)	MDO	3m	12	GF	*(fav) ld 3rd til blnd bdly 7th, wknd rpdly, p.u. 12th*	P 0
345	2/3	Market Rase'	(L)	MDO	3m	13	GF	*chsd ldrs to 6th, mid-div whn p.u. 9th*	P 0

Very lightly raced; shows some speed but stamina suspect; unlikely to win. 10

NORTHERN QUAY b.f. 13 Quayside - Northern Quest — Miss L R McFarlane

748	29/3	Brampton Br'	(R)	MEM	3m	6	GF	*strgglng frm 6th, t.o. 13th*	4 0

Members winner 94; too old now. 0

NORTHERN SENSATION b.m. 8 Northern Game - Dark Sensation by Thriller — J Down
1996 P(0),3(12),P(0),3(10)

1039	12/4	Lifton	(R)	RES	3m	8	F	*nvr trbld ldrs, p.u. aft 13th*	P 0
1259	27/4	Black Fores'	(R)	RES	3m	7	F	*ld/disp, clr 7th, hdd last, no ext*	3 15
1519	17/5	Bratton Down	(L)	RES	3m	15	GS	*mid-div, 8th at 10th, bhnd & p.u. 2 out*	P 0
1551	24/5	Mounsey Hil'	(R)	RES	3m	13	G	*bhnd frm 11th, t.o. & p.u. 15th*	P 0

Maiden winner 95; the odd good run but does not stay & struggling; should try Members. 13

NORTHERN TALENT (Irish) — I 423ᴾ, I 517ᴾ, I 609ᴾ

NORTHERN VILLAGE ch.g. 10 Norwick (USA) - Merokette by Blast — L P Dace
1996 **8(NH),3(NH),4(NH)**

302	1/3	Parham	(R)	CON	3m	14	G	*mid-div whn f 2nd*	F -
489	10/3	Plumpton	(L)	HC	3m 1f 110yds	7	GS	*chsd ldrs, mstk 14th, wknd next.*	4 0
589	20/3	Wincanton	(R)	HC	2m 5f	9	GF	*rear, hrd rdn 8th, styd on from 4 out, nvr near ldrs.*	3 18
680	29/3	Towcester	(R)	HC	3m 1f	8	GF	*held up, mstk 2nd, hdwy 11th, chsd ldr 2 out, styd on to ld near fin.*	1 22
983	12/4	Ascot	(R)	HC	3m 110yds	14	GF	*with ldrs early, soon held up in mid div, mstk 11th, blnd 15th, soon wknd.*	6 16
1444	10/5	Peper Harow	(L)	OPE	3m	5	GF	*(fav) chsd ldrs, jmpd slwly 3rd & 4th, blnd 14th, unable qckn 2out*	3 20

Winning hurdler; inconsistent; mistakes; needs stamina test; hard to place now. 21

NORTH KILKENNY (Irish) — I 153ᶠ, I 265²
NORTON'S BRIDGE (Irish) — I 123¹
NO SPEED LIMIT (Irish) — I 151ᴾ, I 186ᴾ, I 388ᵁ
NO SUCH PARSON (Irish) — I 136ᴾ, I 242², I 301², I 353ᴾ, I 476², I 533²
NO SWAP (Irish) — I 15², I 63ᴾ, I 130ᵁ, I 237ᴾ

NOTANOTHERONE(IRE) b.g. 9 Mazaad - Maltese Pet by Dragonara Palace (USA) — Mrs J L Livermore
1996 5(0),4(13),**P(0)**,**P(0)**,1(19),4(21)

1062	13/4	Maisemore P'	(L)	MXO	3m	12	GF	*chsd ldrs, hit 10th, went mod 4th 14th, not trbl ldrs*	4 17

Restricted winner 96; vanished quickly in 97; win Confined if fit 98; G-F. 20

NOT A PROBLEM ch.g. 14 Main Reef - Tobeylina by Red Alert — D Knights

1060	13/4	Maisemore P'	(L)	MEM	3m	5	GF	*s.s. sn rcvrd, blnd 4th, t.o. 6th, p.u. 14th*	P 0

Of no account. 0

NOT A RAZU (Irish) — I 21⁶, I 513¹, I 555¹

NOTARIUS(FR) b.g. 9 Deep Roots - Lady Ring by Tachypous — Mrs A E Juliet Barnett

343 1/3 Corbridge (R) MDO 3m 14 G *sn rear, lost tch 9th, t.o.* 5 0
621 22/3 Hutton Rudby (L) MDO 3m 10 GF *mid div, prog 12th, ld 3 out, sn clr* 1 14
894 5/4 Wetherby Po' (L) RES 3m 6 F *hld up, mstk 2nd, prog 10th, ld 3 out, drvn out flat* 1 17
1100 19/4 Hornby Cast' (L) CON 3m 9 G *(Jt fav) held up in rear, efft 14th, wknd nxt* 4 12

Missed 96; lightly raced; improved; won weak races & much more needed for Confineds. 16

NOTARY-NOWELL b.g. 11 Deep Run - Hamers Flame by Green Shoon Mrs Richard Pilkington

1996 P(0),3(18),4(14),**7(12)**,2(14),**4(0)**,3(12)

66 1/2 Horseheath (R) MEM 3m 7 GF *1st ride, chsd ldrs to 11th, sn bhnd, t.o. & p.u. 3 out* P 0
125 9/2 Cottenham (R) LAD 3m 11 GF *mid-div, lost tch 11th, t.o. 14th* 6 0
272 22/2 Ampton (R) LAD 3m 7 G *(bl) wth ldrs, rn wde aft 1st, bhnd & rdn 14th, no resp, t.o.* 5 0
442 8/3 Higham (L) LAD 3m 8 G *mid-div til u.r. 5th* U -
578 16/3 Detling (L) LAD 3m 11 F *alwys towrds rear, u.r. 14th* U -
837 31/3 Thorpe Lodge (L) LAD 3m 5 F *in t.o. pair mstly 4th til ran out 13th (ditch)* r -
1117 19/4 Higham (L) CON 3m 5 GF *(bl) cls up, ev ch til rdn aft 13th, sn outpcd* 3 11
1285 29/4 Huntingdon (R) HC 3m 10 G *(bl) mid div, effort to chase lding pair 13th, no impn.* 4 0
1375 5/5 Northaw (L) MEM 3m 5 F *(bl) trckd ldrs til blnd & u.r. 5th* U -

Ungenuine; lost last 28 starts and will extend the sequence. 12

NOT CONVINCED (Irish) — **I** 300², **I** 430², **I** 512ᴾ

NOT FOR PARROT (Irish) — **I** 14³, **I** 47ᶠ, **I** 297ᴾ

NOT FOR PROFIT (Irish) — **I** 483ᴾ, **I** 552ᴾ

NOT FOUND YET (Irish) — **I** 117ᴾ, **I** 175⁴, **I** 585,

NOTHINGTOTELLME(IRE) gr.g. 6 Roselier (FR) - Tower Road by Polaroid R A Bartlett

1996 2+(14),3(13)

135 9/2 Alnwick (L) MDO 3m 12 G *(fav) conf rdn, prog 14th, ld 2 out, lft in cmmnd last, ran on* 1 0
337 1/3 Corbridge (R) RES 3m 11 G *(fav) rear, mod prog 11th, blnd 14th, sn wknd, p.u. 2 out* P 0

Lightly raced; winners behind when scoring; has scpoe & can progress to Restricted if fit in 98. 16

NOTHING VENTURED b.g. 8 Sonnen Gold - Dream Venture by Giolla Mear Countess Goess-Saurau

1996 P(0),4(0),2(14),1(14),1(16)

203 15/2 Weston Park (L) RES 3m 11 G *(fav) alwys handy, ld/disp frm 12th, 3l clr 2 out, ran on* 1 20
293 1/3 Didmarton (L) INT 3m 16 G *trckd ldrs, effrt 3 out, sn outpcd, lft 2nd last* 2 18
515 15/3 Larkhill (R) INT 3m 8 GF *cls up, wth wnr 13th til aft 3 out, styd on wll flat* 2 24
1160 20/4 Mollington (R) INT 3m 9 GF *(Jt fav) wth ldr, ld 10th, drew clr aft 2 out, comf* 1 24
1383 5/5 Eyton-On-Se' (L) OPE 3m 3 GF *prom, cls 2nd whn lft in ld 4 out, ran on wll, comf* 1 23
1508 17/5 Bangor (L) HC 3m 110yds 12 G *in tch, hdwy to chase wnr 9th, no ch with clr winner from 12th.* 2 21

Still improving; beaten by good horse last start; worth perservering in H/chases; staysG/S-G/F. 25

NOT MY LINE(IRE) gr.g. 8 Entre Nous - Uno Navarro by Raga Navarro (ITY) P C Caudwell

1996 F(-)

91 6/2 Huntingdon (R) HC 3m 10 G *hdwy 7th, ld 9th to 11th, soon wknd, bhnd when p.u. before 13th.* P 0
149 10/2 Hereford (R) HC 3m 1f 110yds 18 GS *prom, ld after 6th to 12th, wknd 4 out.* 4 14
490 10/3 Stratford (L) HC 3m 12 G *mid div, rdn apr 5 out, soon lost tch.* 6 0
779 31/3 Fakenham (L) HC 2m 5f 110yds 9 G *held up, joined ldr 13th, ld after 2 out, all out.* 1 21
1086 14/4 Southwell (L) HC 3m 110yds 11 G *prom, joined ldr 12th, ld 4 out, soon hdd, one pace from next.* 4 20
1287 29/4 Huntingdon (R) HC 2 1/2m 110yds 14 G *chsd ldrs, no prog from 12th.* 5 12
1488 12/5 Towcester (R) HC 2m 110yds 16 GS *ld to 5th, led 7th, styd on well.* 1 25
1571 26/5 Wetherby (L) HC 2 1/2m 110yds 15 GF *ld to 3rd, cl up, effort and ev ch 4 out, driven next, held when blnd last.* 4 19

Ex Irish; suited by short H/chases; owes much to rider; harder to place now;G/F-G/S. 23

NOT SO PRIM b.m. 5 Primitive Rising (USA) - Sobriquet by Roan Rocket Mrs D Ibbotson

1996 **6(NH)**

210 16/2 Southwell P' (L) MDO 3m 15 GS *bhnd, prog & in tch whn blnd & u.r. 9th* U -
357 2/3 Great Stain' (L) MDO 3m 15 S *prom, fdd 7th, t.o. & p.u. nxt* P 0
1074 13/4 Whitwell-On' (R) MDO 2 1/2m 88yds 16 G *prom, disp 8th-10th, wknd rpdly, p.u. 2 out* P 0
1252 26/4 Easingwold (L) MDO 3m 9 GS *prom, ld 10-14th, hdd, no ext aft* 4 0

Shows some hope but more stamina needed. 10

NOTTAREX b.g. 8 Right Regent - Baresca by Bargello B J C Wright

1996 U(-),U(-),5(0),5(0),U(-),U(-),P(0)

556 16/3 Ottery St M' (L) RES 3m 12 G *prom early, lost tch 10th, t.o. & p.u. 3 out* P 0
792 31/3 Bishopsleigh (R) RES 3m 13 G *mid-div, blnd 8th, rdr lost irons, p.u. nxt* P 0
934 6/4 Charlton Ho' (L) MDO 3m 10 G *alwys bhnd, t.o. 10th* 6 0

1095 16/4 Hockworthy (L) MDN 3m 11 GF *mid-div, poor 8th hlfwy, sn t.o.* 5 0
1261 27/4 Black Fores' (R) MDO 3m 12 F *alwys mid-div, no dang* 4 0
1400 5/5 High Bickin' (R) MDO 3m 14 G *b.d. bend apr 2nd* B -
1521 17/5 Bratton Down (L) MDO 3m 16 GS *rear, poor 8th at 14th, t.o.* 6 0
1554 24/5 Mounsey Hil' (R) MDO 3m 14 G *chsd ldrs to 6th, grad lost plc, kpt on frm 3 out* 5 10
1597 31/5 Bratton Down (L) MDO 3m 12 F *mstk 7th, chsng grp til wknd 12th, t.o. 14th* 6 0

Novice ridden; safe but need a miracle to win. 0

NOT THE NADGER b.g. 6 Aragon - Broken Accent by Busted — R T Dennis

1996 P(0),F(-),P(0)

169 15/2 Witton Cast' (R) MDO 3m 5 F *plld hrd, rear, prog to ld 6th, hdd 10th, wknd, p.u. 13th* P 0
480 9/3 Southwell P' (L) MDO 3m 17 G *chsd ldr til ld 5th, hdd apr 12th, p.u. qckly nxt, lame* P 0
615 22/3 Hutton Rudby (L) MEM 3m 8 GF *made all, sn clr, steady 7th, qcknd 3 out, drvn clr flat* 1 15
1250 26/4 Easingwold (L) RES 3m 15 GS *cls up, outpcd hlfwy, p.u. 4 out* P 0
1348 3/5 Gisburn (R) RES 3m 10 GF *ld to 6th, wknd 12th, p.u. 15th, lame* P 0

Dictated slowly run Members; stamina problems & way below Restricted class at present. 13

NOVA NITA b.m. 7 Ra Nova - Jovenita by High Top — Robert Black

1996 1(13),2(16)

230 22/2 Friars Haugh (L) RES 3m 15 G *alwys handy, ld 4 out, sn clr, easily* 1 22
560 16/3 Lanark (R) CON 3m 8 GS *(fav) 3rd hlfwy,wnt 2nd 14th,mstk 3 out,kpt on und 10der handling* 2 20
944 6/4 Friars Haugh (L) INT 3m 5 GF *(fav) hld up, wnt 2nd 9th, ld aft 3 out, comf* 1 17
1427 10/5 Aspatria (L) INT 3m 7 G *(fav) w.w. prog to chs wnr 13th, no imp, dmtd 2 out* 3 13
1509 17/5 Corbridge (R) INT 3m 10 GS *mid-div, prog 10th, chsd ldr 13th, hld whn lft clr last* 1 20

Improved; stays; should progress; needs more for Opens; G/F-S. 21

NOVA STAR gr.m. 6 Ra Nova - Tullymore Dew Vii by Damsire Unregistered — B P Sillis

1996 U(-),P(0)

147 9/2 Tweseldown (R) MDO 3m 12 GF *mstk 1st, t.o. 7th, p.u. 3 out* P 0

Some promise 96; very brief 97 & much more needed. 10

NOVASUN ch.g. 7 Sunley Builds - Owenova by Owen Anthony — J W Elliott

582 16/3 Detling (L) MDN 3m 16 F *alwys rear, lost tch 16th, p.u. 3 out* P 0

No signs on debut. 0

NOVATARA ch.g. 5 Ra Nova - Asphaltara by Scallywag — Mrs T H Regis

450 8/3 Newton Brom' (R) MDN 3m 7 G *rear, prog 12th, wknd 14th, p.u. nxt* P 0
775 29/3 Dingley (R) MDO 2m 5f 10 G *(fav) mid-div, ran out 4th* r -

Good stable; can do better. 0

NOWHISKI b.g. 9 Petoski - Be Faithful by Val de Loir — Tim Tarratt

1996 P(0),5(0),4(0),**U(-)**,P(0),1(18),1(20),1(23)

139 9/2 Thorpe Lodge (L) LAD 3m 4 GF *(fav) ld to 11th, in tch whn blnd 4 out, not rcvr* 3 14
381 4/3 Leicester (R) HC 2m 1f 13 G *chsd ldrs, rdn apr 2 out, no ext run-in.* 2 19

Won 3 Ladies 96; vanished after godd H/chase run; win Ladies if fit 98; front runs; game; G-F. 22

NO WORD b or br.g. 10 Oats - Rapenna by Straightdad — S P Hudson

1996 **10(NH)**,**8(NH)**,**11(NH)**,**P(NH)**

67 1/2 Wetherby (L) HC 3m 1f 10 G *pulld hrd, led 5th to 10th, wknd quickly, t.o. when blnd 4 out, p.u. before next.* P 0
216 16/2 Southwell P' (L) OPE 3m 12 GS *wth ldr to 4th, 2nd whn p.u. 7th* P 0
375 3/3 Doncaster (L) HC 2m 3f 110yds 11 GF *cl up, ld 3rd and soon clr, hdd 9th, wknd after next.* 6 0
507 15/3 Dalton Park (R) OPE 3m 8 GF *prom til lost plc 8th, bdly hmpd & p.u. 11th* P 0
857 31/3 Charm Park (L) MXO 3m 3 F *ld to 10th, fdd, t.o. 13th* 3 0
1488 12/5 Towcester (R) HC 2m 110yds 16 GS *alwys bhnd, t.o..* 10 0
1571 26/5 Wetherby (L) HC 2 1/2m 110yds 15 GF *cl up, ld 3rd to after 7th, wknd 10th, bhnd when p.u. lame before 2 out.* P 0

Winning chase; no stamina & hopeless in points/H/chases. 0

NOW YOUNG MAN(IRE) br.g. 8 Callernish - Claddagh Pride by Bargello — Grant C Mitchell

973 7/4 Kelso (L) HC 3m 1f 5 GF *in tch till outpcd and rdn along 15th, styd on apr last, ridden run-in to ld near fin.* 1 23
1096 18/4 Ayr (L) HC 3m 3f 110yds 7 G *held up, pushed along and hdwy when hit 15th, soon rdn and btn 4 out.* 4 21

Winning hurdler; good start; likes Kelso; professionally trained; options limited; stays. 23

NUCKLEWOOD (Irish) — I 349^3, I 547^3

NUTCASE b.m. 8 Idiot's Delight - Real Beauty by Kinglet — N Shutts

1996 2(15),1(15),2(10)

190	15/2 Erw Lon	(L)	RES	3m	11	G	*(fav) trckd ldrs,ld 14th,in cmmnd 2 out,prssd flat, rdn & hld on*	1	19
360	2/3 Garnons	(L)	CON	3m	10	GS	*ld 1st & 4-6th, chsd ldr 15th, lft in btn 2nd whn f 2 out*	F	-
434	8/3 Upton-On-Se'	(R)	INT	3m	4	G	*hld up, mstk 10th, prog 12th, chal 3 out, no ext nxt*	3	18
645	22/3 Castle Of C'	(R)	LAD	3m	6	G	*trckd ldrs, chsd wnr 9th, rdn & ev ch 3 out, wknd nxt*	2	19
1017	12/4 Bitterley	(L)	LAD	3m	4	GF	*hld up, effrt 12th, ev ch til just outpcd frm 15th*	2	19
1472	11/5 Erw Lon	(L)	XX	3m	9	GS	*ld 9th, in cmmnd whn lft clr last, fin tired*	1	19
1538	18/5 Wolverhampt'	(L)	CON	3m	8	GS	*(fav) chsd wnr, lvl 4 out, outpcd & btn nxt*	3	12

Improved; consistent; staya but onepaced; harder to place now; needs more for Confined; G/F-S. 18

OAKLANDS WORD br.g. 8 Hasty Word - Salvo's Grace (FR) by Salvo — F P Luff

1996 2(14),1(22),**1(28)**,**1(28)**

256	22/2 Newtown	(L)	OPE	3m	17	G	*(fav) prom, trckd ldr 11th, ld 15th, sn clr, drvn out flat*	1	26

Dual H/chase winner 96; useful; brief 97; sure to win more if fit 98; G-S. 30

OATFLAKE (Irish) — I 183³, I 215, , I 267ᴾ, I 345ᴾ

OATS FOR NOTES b.m. 7 Oats - Run In Tune by Deep Run — Mrs R F Knipe

1996 B(-),4(13),**6(NH)**,**8(NH)**,**4(NH)**

88	2/2 Wolverhampt'	(L)	MDO	3m	13	GS	*(fav) in tch, chsd ldr 10th, ev ch aft 13th, wknd 2 out, dmtd post*	3	10
359	2/3 Garnons	(L)	MEM	3m	3	GS	*trckd ldrs, effrt 15th, wknd aft 2 out*	3	0
570	16/3 Garnons	(L)	MDN	2 1/2m	14	G	*mid-div, effrt 11th, gd prog nxt, wknd & p.u. 2 out*	P	0
751	29/3 Brampton Br'	(R)	XX	3m	5	GF	*chsd wnr 3rd, chal 15th, wknd aft nxt, p.u. last*	P	0
892	5/4 Hereford	(R)	HC	2m	11	GF	*alwys bhnd, no ch when mstk 3 out.*	7	0

Placed N/H flat summer 96; lacking in stamina & needs more. 11

OBIE'S TRAIN ch.g. 11 Buckskin (FR) - Whisper Moon by Chinatown — Mrs A E Lee

1996 5(13)

503	15/3 Ampton	(R)	XX	3m	11	GF	*alwys bhnd, t.o. & p.u. 17th*	P	0
769	29/3 Dingley	(R)	CON	3m	14	G	*disp brfly on outside, sn outpcd, bhnd whn u.r. 5th*	U	-
887	1/4 Flagg Moor	(L)	XX	3m	8	G	*chsd ldrs, 3rd whn u.r. 3rd*	U	-
1159	20/4 Mollington	(R)	MEM	3m	4	GF	*ld brfly 2nd, bhnd frm 4th, lft dist 2nd 11th, ref 3 out*	R	-
1448	10/5 Kingston Bl'	(L)	CON	3m	9	G	*alwys wll bhnd, t.o. 8th, p.u. aft 11th*	P	0
1564	25/5 Kingston Bl'	(L)	CON	3m	7	GF	*(bl) ld 3rd til ran off course apr nxt*	r	-

Of no account. 0

OCEAN ROSE gr.m. 10 Baron Blakeney - Deep Ocean by Deep Run — W M Burnell

1996 6(15),1(14),4(15),2(16)

76	2/2 Market Rase'	(L)	XX	3m	12	GF	*prom, cls 3rd 11th, outpcd frm 13th*	6	14
163	15/2 Witton Cast'	(R)	MEM	3m	5	F	*keen hold, chsd ldr til outpcd 14th, lft 2nd 3 out*	1	13

Restricted winner 96; very onepaced & struggling now; Members best hope. 16

OCEAN SOVEREIGN b.g. 11 Smackover - Pacific Crown Vii — Mrs Fiona Denniff

1996 6(0),P(0),P(0),2(12),9(0)

251	22/2 Brocklesby '	(L)	RES	3m	16	G	*u.r. 1st*	U	-
476	9/3 Southwell P'	(L)	XX	3m	6	G	*ld aft 1st, clr 4th, hdd apr 12th, no ch whn blnd last*	4	0
884	1/4 Flagg Moor	(L)	CON	3m	6	G	*ld til ran wd & hdd aft 5th, last aft, t.o. & p.u. 15th*	P	0
1267	27/4 Southwell P'	(L)	MEM	3m	4	G	*sttld 3rd, ld apr 5th-10th, onepcd frm 13th*	3	0

Won weak Maiden 95; not threatening now upgraded. 10

O CURRY KING (Irish) — I 275ᴾ, I 425ᴾ

O'DONNELL ABU (Irish) — I 81², I 87ᴾ, I 161³, I 300, , I 353ᶠ, I 452⁴, I 529⁵

OFFENSIVE WEAPON ch.g. 10 Homing - Chuchilla by Comedy Star (USA) — Mrs J P Bissill

1996 5(0)

852	31/3 Eyton-On-Se'	(L)	RES	3m	11	GF	*mid-div to 5th, rear 8th, t.o. 12th, p.u. 4 out*	P	0
1526	17/5 Bredwardine	(R)	RES	3m	13	G	*rear & rdn 11th, sn t.o., p.u. 3 out*	P	0

Maiden winner 95; lightly raced; showed nothing 97 & can only be watched now. 12

OFFLEY LASS b.m. 8 Remezzo - Barby's Girl by Barbaro — M S Wilesmith

706	29/3 Upper Sapey	(R)	MDO	3m	15	GF	*j.w. in mid-div til p.u. 12th*	P	0

Only learning on debut; can do better. 0

O GHLUIN GO GHLUIN (Irish) — I 216⁵

OH DONNA (Irish) — I 151ᶠ, I 217ᴾ, I 389¹

OH LORD(IRE) b.g. 8 Mister Lord (USA) - Arctic Survivor by Hard Run — Mrs S Barber

1996 P(0),5(10)

259	22/2 Newtown	(L)	MDN	3m	18	G	*chsd ldrs, 4th whn blnd 11th, sn btn, p.u. 14th*	P	0

Showed some hope in 96; very lightly raced & time passing him by. 11

OH SO GRUMPY (Irish) — I 59^{3}, I 284^{1}

OH SO QUIET ch.g. 5 Kind Of Hush - Clear As Crystal by Whitstead — Mrs P A Tory

795 31/3 Bishopsleigh (R) MDO 3m 12 G *schoold til p.u. 14th* P 0
1094 16/4 Hockworthy (L) MDN 3m 11 GF *chsng grp, effrt hlfwy, sn no prog, no ch 3 out* 5 0

No real signs; young enough & may do better. 0

OH SO VITAL ch.g. 8 Vital Season - Rosie Oh by Laurence O — P Venner

324 1/3 Marks Tey (L) RES 3m 16 G *mid-div, prog to 3rd 15th, btn 17th, no ch whn blndrd 2 out* 6 10

Maiden winner 95; 1 run last 2 seasons & can only be watched now. 14

OH SO WINDY b.m. 10 Oats - Tempest Girl by Caliban — Rupert Cottrell

1996 3(14),1(15),1(20),5(13)

521 15/3 Cothelstone (L) OPE 3m 8 GS *chsd wnr til mstk & strggling frm 16th* 4 10
879 1/4 Upton-On-Se' (R) MXO 3m 4 GF *cls up, wth wnr 10-13th, outpcd whn mstk 15th, lost 2nd flat* 3 16
1092 16/4 Hockworthy (L) XX 3m 5 GF *cls up to 11th, sn wknd, no ch & p.u. aft 3 out, lame* P 0

Dual winner 96; not disgraced but big problems last start; best watched if returning. 17

OISIN DUBH(IRE) b.g. 8 Supreme Leader - Gaoth Na Bride — J M B Cookson

1996 **9(NH)**

809 31/3 Tranwell (L) MEM 3m 5 G *chsd ldr til ld 5th, mstk & hdd 11th, disp 2nd whn f 13th* F -

Placed in Irish Maiden 95; capsized in Members; plenty to prove yet. 0

OJONNYO(IRE) br.g. 7 Spin Of A Coin - Follow Lightly by Light Thrust — S P Tindall

1996 **3(NH),4(NH),4(NH),R(NH),7(NH)**

306 1/3 Parham (R) MDN 3m 12 G *(fav) cls up, ld 8th-3 out, chal last, rdn clr* 1 14
580 16/3 Detling (L) RES 3m 11 F *(fav) ld to 12th, jmp slwly 14th, wknng whn p.u. 16th* P 0

Disappointing under rules; won weak race; suspect & vanished after next start. 13

OK CORRAL(USA) gr.g. 10 Malinowski (USA) - Tiger Trap (USA) by Al Hattab (USA) — D R Greig

1996 **13(NH),5(NH)**

124 9/2 Cottenham (R) OPE 3m 9 GF *in tch til outpcd 14th, no imp on ldrs frm 3 out* 4 17
279 23/2 Charing (L) CON 3m 10 G *in tch til rdn & wknd 14th, t.o. & p.u. 16th* P 0
577 16/3 Detling (L) CON 3m 18 F *trckd ldrs,chsd clr ld in 3rd 4 out,kpt on to take 2nd 2 out* 2 19
911 5/4 Cottenham (R) OPE 3m 3 F *in tch, rdn 13th, no ch frm 3 out* 3 15

Winning chaser; capable of running well but ungenuine & unlikely to consent to win again. 18

OKDO (Irish) — I 78, , I 134^{5}, I 168^{4}, I 306^{4}, I 320^{P}

OKEETEE b.g. 14 Raise You Ten - Peppardstown by Javelot — B T Crawford

1996 P(0),2(18),5(11),2(17),3(15),2(18)

248 22/2 Brocklesby ' (L) CON 3m 10 G *mstly 2nd to 5 out, chsd 1st pair gmly, just outpcd* 3 19
545 16/3 Garthorpe (R) CON 3m 12 GF *alwys prom, 4th & ch appr 2 out, onepcd aft* 3 18
925 6/4 Garthorpe (R) LAD 3m 7 GF *chsd ldr, ld 12th, 4l clr 14th, ran on strngly 3 out* 1 20

Consistent; honest veteran; won modest Ladies; could still win(Members especially) at 15;G/F-S. 19

O K FLO JO gr.m. 6 K-Battery - Minster Scally by Scallywag — Mrs Ruth Crank

999 12/4 Alpraham (R) MDO 3m 8 GF *hld up, 3rd 12th, ld aft 3 out, clr nxt* 1 16

Romped home on debut(subsequent winner behind); ample stamina; interesting prospect. 15

OLD BRIG br.g. 11 Roscoe Blake - Hunter's Treasure by Tudor Treasure — Mrs H M Bridges

484 9/3 Tweseldown (R) OPE 3m 10 G *prom, wth ldr 12th, outpcd by wnr 15th, kpt on* 3 19

Novice chase winner 93; ran well but promptly vanished again; can only be watched if reappearing. 18

OLD DECENCY (Irish) — I 3^{F}, I 64^{1}

OLD DUNDALK b.g. 13 Derrylin - Georgiana by Never Say Die — R Oliver Smith

1996 5(14),12(0),1(15),4(16),2(20)

8 25/1 Cottenham (R) CON 3m 5 GF *bhnd frm 3rd, t.o. & p.u. 14th* P 0
270 22/2 Ampton (R) MEM 3m 8 G *(bl) rr, lsng tch & blnd 7th,rdn 12th, no resp, t.o. & p.u. 16th* P 0
322 1/3 Marks Tey (L) OPE 3 1/2m 9 G *(bl) rear, lost tch 13th, t.o.* 7 10
495 14/3 Fakenham (L) HC 2m 5f 110yds 10 G *(bl) mstk 7th, soon well bhnd, t.o. when p.u. before last.* P 0
968 6/4 Penshurst (L) LAD 3m 5 F *1st ride, ld 3rd-8th agn 10-13th, fdd aft* 4 0
1078 13/4 Guilsborough (L) LAD 3m 11 GF *in tch to 10th, sn strgglng, t.o.* 5 0

Members winner 96; moody & looks ready for retirement now. 12

OLDE CRESCENT br.g. 11 Kambalda - Bush Mistress by Will Somers — T D B Underwood

1996 2(14),3(17),P(0),U(-),P(0),1(19),1(17),P(0),P(0)

715 29/3 Llanvapley (L) OPE 3m 8 GF *alwys 3rd/4th, ran on onepce* 4 0

1007 12/4 St Hilary (R) OPE 3m 10 GF *twrds rear, styd on onepcd* 5 0
1226 26/4 Pyle (R) OPE 3m 6 GS *bhnd frm 7th, t.o. 12th, p.u. 3 out* P 0
1321 3/5 Bonvilston (R) MXO 3m 10 G *ld 6th til ran out nxt, rjnd, p.u. 9th* P 0
1601 31/5 Bassaleg (R) MXO 3m 2 F *ld, clr 4th, hdd 12th, sn btn, blnd 14th, t.o.* 2 0

Won 2 poor races 96; changed hands; showed nothing in 97. 0

OLD FATHER TIME b.g. 10 The Parson - Scotch News by London Gazette Mrs Sarah Richmond-Watson

373 2/3 Mollington (R) MDN 3m 14 G *wth ldrs to 12th, wknd rpdly, t.o. & p.u. last* P 0
550 16/3 Garthorpe (R) MDO 3m 11 GF *disp ld to 4th, 4th & outpcd 15th, kpt on frm 2 out* 5 0
1083 13/4 Guilsborough (L) MDN 3m 15 GF *chsd ldrs, pshd alng in cls 5th whn f 14th* F -
1200 23/4 Andoversford (R) MDO 3m 8 F *prom, ld 9th, hdd apr last, onepcd und pres* 2 11

Disappointing ex hurdler/chaser; has ability but finds little; need luck to win; sold Ascot June. 11

OLD HARRY'S WIFE b.m. 7 Idiot's Delight - Blakesware Gift by Dominion Mrs J E Purdie
1996 4(0),P(0),5(0)

43 1/2 Larkhill (R) MDO 3m 10 GF *cls up, mstk 11th, outpcd 2 out, ran on agn flat* 4 13
181 15/2 Larkhill (R) MDO 3m 17 G *ld/disp til ld 5th, made rest, 2l up whn f last* F 16
512 15/3 Larkhill (R) MDO 3m 6 GF *(fav) set slw pace, hmpd by loose hrs apr 10th, hdd 2 out, no ext* 2 10
1497 14/5 Cothelstone (L) MDO 3m 10 GF *hld up, lost tch 10th, no prog 15th, p.u. 2 out* P 0

Has ability; unlucky 2nd outing; lacks speed but should find compensation. 14

OLDHILL WOOD(IRE) ch.g. 7 Salluceva - Davinsky Rose by Stradavinsky E Tuer
1996 **8(NH),12(NH),4(NH),5(NH),4(NH),4(NH),5(NH)**

113 9/2 Wetherby Po' (L) CON 3m 10 GF *plld hrd, rear, prog 11th, wknd 14th, t.o.* 6 0

Winning hurdler (2 miles); stamina looks a major problem. 13

OLD MILL STREAM br.g. 11 Rapid River - Daleena by Dalesa Richard Barber

18 25/1 Badbury Rin' (L) LAD 3m 9 GF *pllng, ld 2nd til blnd & u.r. 5th* U -
864 31/3 Kingston St' (R) LAD 3m 6 F *(fav) keen hold, ld 6th til p.u. lame aft 16th* P 0
1155 20/4 Stafford Cr' (R) LAD 3m 6 GF *plld hrd, ld 4th-3 out, disp nxt, rdn & ran on well* 1 26
1438 10/5 Holnicote (L) LAD 3m 7 G *(fav) j.w. ld frm 5th, drew clr apr 2 out, comf* 1 25
1590 31/5 Stratford (L) HC 3m 9 G *driven along with chasing gp, effort hfwy, struggling final cct, nvr a threat.* 5 14

Missed 96; changed hands; good Ladies horse; needs easy 3 miles; can win more;G-F. 26

OLD MONEY b.g. 11 Furry Glen - Many Views by Bargello A W Pickering
1996 **12(NH),7(NH),3(NH),12(NH),5(NH),5(NH),5(NH),3(NH),1(NH),6(NH)**

351 2/3 Market Rase' (L) OPE 3m 10 GF *disp to 5th, wknd 10th, t.o. & p.u. 12th* P 0
836 31/3 Thorpe Lodge (L) OPE 3m 7 F *ld 3rd-4th & 12th til hit 5 out, wknd qckly, walked in* 4 0
926 6/4 Garthorpe (R) OPE 3m 10 GF *nvr bttr than mid-div, no dang* 5 10
1188 20/4 Garthorpe (R) OPE 3m 9 GF *in tch, 4th & blnd 14th, sn lost tch* 4 0
1265 27/4 Southwell P' (L) OPE 3m 8 G *prom, disp 5-8th, rdn 11th, wknd rpdly 14th, p.u. 3 out* P 0

Winning chaser(2m5f); does not stay & no real prospects. 11

OLD ROAD(USA) b.g. 11 Regal And Royal (USA) - Raise Me (USA) by Mr Prospector (USA) Mrs S Keating-Coyne
1996 P(0),9(0),7(0),2(0),5(0),5(10),2(10),2(13)

483 9/3 Tweseldown (R) CON 3m 8 G *prssd wnr, ld 9-10th, wknd rpdly 15th* 4 0
824 31/3 Lockinge (L) CON 3m 8 F *chsd ldrs, 3rd & outpcd 11th, no imp aft, wknd 16th* 4 0
1464 11/5 Tweseldown (R) XX 3m 7 GF *cls up, onepcd 15th, sn btn* 3 0
1565 25/5 Kingston Bl' (L) OPE 3m 4 GF *ld to 10th, last aft nxt, lft bhnd frm 13th* 3 11

Winning chaser; non stayer; need miracle to win. 0

OLD TRAFFORD (Irish) — **I** 42[1], **I** 108[4]

OLIVE BASKET b.m. 6 Neltino - Casket by Pannier P L Southcombe
1996 P(0),F(-),5(0),5(11),U(-),P(0)

523 15/3 Cothelstone (L) RES 3m 14 GS *bhnd til p.u. 14th* P 0
687 29/3 Little Wind' (R) MEM 3m 5 GF *mstk 5th, chsd ldr to 10th, sn wknd, t.o. 14th, p.u. 2 out* P 0
933 6/4 Charlton Ho' (L) MDO 3m 12 G *prom, ld 13th-15th, wknd apr 2 out* 7 0
1158 20/4 Stafford Cr' (R) MDO 3m 5 GF *prom til outpcd 15th, lost tch nxt, ran on agn clsng stgs* 4 10

Only beaten one horse so far; needs to concentrate on Maidens; can do better. 11

OLIVE BRANCH br.m. 9 Le Moss - Olive Press by Ragapan A H Mactaggart
1996 3(10),3(14),4(11)

37 26/1 Alnwick (L) MDO 3m 15 G *chsd ldrs, no prog 14th, lft 2nd 3 out, styd on* 2 12

Well-bred; lightly raced & time slipping by now; may eventually win but is becoming frustrating. 14

OLIVER HIMSELF b.g. 6 Strong Gale - Sparticone by Celtic Cone Mrs Judy Wilson
1996 P(0),4(0),6(0),F(-)

80 2/2 Market Rase' (L) MDO 2m 5f 9 GF *(fav) ld to 4th, hit 8th, ev ch 11th, rdn 3 out, lft clr nxt* 1 13
449 8/3 Newton Brom' (R) XX 3m 13 G *(fav) rear, prog hlfwy, 3rd 13th, no ext 2 out* 4 0

1076 13/4 Guilsborough (L) MEM 3m 9 GF *hld up last, lost tch 11th, ran on frm 3 out, fin well* 5 13

Won weak short Maiden; good stable; stays; can improve & every chance of weak Restricted. 16

OLIVER'S MATE(IRE) b.g. 7 Over The River (FR) - African Swan by African Sky P J Dennis

1996 **17(NH)**

116 9/2 Wetherby Po' (L) MDO 3m 14 GF *prom til wknd 4 out* 6 0
169 15/2 Witton Cast' (R) MDO 3m 5 F *disp to 6th, cls up, disp 13th, ld 3 out, styd on strngly* 1 10
425 8/3 Charm Park (L) RES 3m 12 GF *mid-div, rddn 11th, rear whn f 12th* F -
615 22/3 Hutton Rudby (L) MEM 3m 8 GF *(fav) nvr gng wll, rear, strgglng 4 out, sn lost tch, p.u. 2 out* P 0

Won bad Maiden (very slow time); struggling now &much more needed for Restricted. 13

OLLARDALE(IRE) b.g. 9 Abednego - Kauai-Ka-Zum by Kauai King Wilfred S Littleworth

1996 2(17),3(14),3(17)

380 4/3 Leicester (R) HC 3m 9 G *prom, hit 2nd, soon lost pl, pushed along 8th, lost tch 10th, t.o. when p.u. before 5 out.* P 0
1237 26/4 Brampton Br' (R) RES 3m 13 G *rear frm 8th, lost tch 13th, p.u. 3 out* P 0
1526 17/5 Bredwardine (R) RES 3m 13 G *(bl) mstks, prom, ld 9th, kicked clr 14th, unchal, eased flat* 1 19

Dual winner 95; blinkers worked & zoomed home in modest race; win again if in same mood; G/F-S. ... 19

OLLAR HOUSE (Irish) — I 176P, I 210P, I 247F, I 371F
OLLAR LADY (Irish) — I 179P, I 251P, I 360P
OLLIES BOY (Irish) — I 28[5], I 64[3], I 226P, I 436F, I 463[2], I 507P
OLYMPIC CLASS b.g. 7 Strong Gale - Olympic Course Simon J Robinson

1996 F(-),8(0),3(13),F(-),F(-),5(0)

116 9/2 Wetherby Po' (L) MDO 3m 14 GF *disp til ld 10th, hdd & nt qckn nr fin* 2 15
169 15/2 Witton Cast' (R) MDO 3m 5 F *(fav) disp to 6th, ld 10th til disp 13th, hdd & wknd 2 out, lame* 3 0

Placed 3 of last 6 starts; stays; finished early 97; deserves a small win but not easy to find. 12

OLYMPIC LADY (Irish) — I 187R
OMIDJOY(IRE) ch.m. 7 Nishapour (FR) - Fancy Finish by Final Straw Mrs Nigel Wrighton

1996 **4(NH),5(NH),3(NH),4(NH)**

64 1/2 Horseheath (R) LAD 3m 7 GF *mid-div, prog 9th, disp 2nd 10th-12th, sn outpcd* 4 0
125 9/2 Cottenham (R) LAD 3m 11 GF *last pair & alwys wll bhnd, t.o. 10th* 5 0
323 1/3 Marks Tey (L) LAD 3m 7 G *(bl) prom, disp ld 15th, ld 17th, 3l clr last, hdd cls home* 2 14
709 29/3 High Easter (L) LAD 3m 2 F *(bl) chsd wnr, ev ch 15th, onepcd aft* 2 15
1078 13/4 Guilsborough (L) LAD 3m 11 GF *(bl) in tch to 10th, sn wknd, t.o.* 6 0
1280 27/4 Fakenham P-' (L) LAD 3m 6 G *(bl) bdly hmpd & u.r. 1st* U -
1378 5/5 Northaw (L) LAD 3m 5 F *(bl) chsd ldrs, rmdrs 9th, 3rd & outpcd 12th, last & btn 3 out* 5 12

Winning hurdler; ungenuine & placed umpteen times; safe; hard to find a win; best in blinkers. 12

ON DEADLY GROUND (Irish) — I 29[1]
ONE CLEAN SWEEP (Irish) — I 517P
ONEEDIN GLORY (Irish) — I 118[3]
ONE ELEVEN (Irish) — I 210P, I 311U, I 328F, I 371P, I 467P, I 585P
ONE FOR THE CHIEF b.g. 9 Chief Singer - Action Belle by Auction Ring (USA) M A Kemp

1996 P(12),5(10),6(16),r(-),1(18),4(14),**4(NH)**

26 26/1 Marks Tey (L) LAD 3m 8 GF *chsd ldr 9th, ld 14th, rdn apr last, hld on wll flat* 1 23
64 1/2 Horseheath (R) LAD 3m 7 GF *cls up, ld 6th, made rest, clr frm 15th, comf* 1 23

Restricted winner 96; changed hands; improved; finished early; hard to beat in local Ladies 98.G-G/F .. 24

ONE FOR THE CROSS(IRE) ch.g. 9 The Parson - Dora-Elliven by Sweet Revenge L W Wickett

1996 P(0),P(0)

175 15/2 Ottery St M' (L) RES 3m 15 G *sn bhnd, t.o. & p.u. 14th* P 0
244 22/2 Lemalla (R) MDO 3m 12 S *rear, rmndrs 8th, bhnd & p.u. 12th* P 0

Placed 5 times 94/5; non finisher 96/97; does not stay & prospects virtually nil. 10

ONEMANS CHOICE (Irish) — I 253P, I 289P, I 331P, I 436P
ONEMOREANWEGO b.m. 9 Celtic Cone - Foxwell by Healaugh Fox P J Corbett

1996 P(0),1(16)

258 22/2 Newtown (L) RES 3m 14 G *sn trckd ldrs, mstk 11th, jnd wnr 15th, swtchd 2 out, no ext* 2 17
404 8/3 Llanfrynach (R) INT 3m 17 G *(fav) alwys 3rd/4th, outpcd frm 3 out* 3 17
670 23/3 Eaton Hall (R) RES 3m 15 GF *u.r. 3rd* U -
753 29/3 Brampton Br' (R) RES 3m 9 GF *w.w. prog 8th, 4l 3rd 13th, 10l 3rd whn p.u. aft 16th, lame* P 0

Maiden winner 96; ran passably; problems last start; can win modest Restricted if fit 98. 17

ONEOFOUROWN (Irish) — I 102[1], I 256[4], I 336F, I 426[3]
ONEOFTHECLAN (Irish) — I 222P

ONEOVERTHEIGHT br.g. 12 Sousa - Western Melody by West Partisan — Miss K Cook

1996 2(17),8(0),P(0),5(10),P(0),2(15),7(0),4(15),1(11),P(0),3(10)

51	1/2	Wadebridge	(L)	CON	3m	4	G	*ld 2nd-14th, grad fdd*	3 16
310	1/3	Clyst St Ma'	(L)	INT	3m	9	HY	*in tch to 13th, outpcd aft*	4 0
528	15/3	Wadebridge	(L)	CON	3m	5	GF	*ld 2nd-6th, styd prom, rdn 12th, no imp aft*	2 15
804	31/3	Wadebridge	(L)	INT	3m	6	F	*ld til mssd marker aft 14th*	r -
1033	12/4	Lifton	(R)	CON	3m	6	F	*lft remote 3rd apr 4th, ran on to take 2nd cls home*	2 15
1243	26/4	Bratton Down	(L)	OPE	3m	6	GS	*alwys chsng grp, tk 2nd 3 out, not trbl wnnr*	2 13
1484	11/5	Ottery St M'	(L)	OPE	3m	7	G	*alwys last, t.o. & p.u. 14th*	P 0
1550	24/5	Mounsey Hil'	(R)	INT	3m	9	G	*ld to 17th, 3rd & btn nxt, blnd & dmtd 2 out*	4 14
1580	26/5	Lifton	(R)	OPE	3m	8	G	*rear, some late prog, nrst fin*	3 15
1614	7/6	Umberleigh	(L)	CON	3m	3	F	*lft in ld aft 6th-8th,blnd 13th,no ch aft, rdn & reluc 2 out*	2 0

1 one win last 32 starts (very fortunate); mega safe but need luck to win again. 13

ONE WOMAN (Irish) — **I** 46[1], **I** 131[F], **I** 170[2], **I** 408[1]

ONGOING DILEMMA (Irish) — **I** 275[F], **I** 297[P], **I** 425[P]

ON HIS OWN br.g. 14 Paico - Luvvy Duvvy by Levmoss — P L Southcombe

1996 P(0),2(20),4(17),3(17),2(16),2(20),3(16),4(16),1(21)

145	9/2	Tweseldown	(R)	LAD	3m	10	GF	*outpcd in rear, t.o. 12th*	5 11
238	22/2	Lemalla	(R)	LAD	3m	9	S	*prom, pckd 10th, lost ground 12th, wll btn frm 17th*	4 16
482	9/3	Tweseldown	(R)	LAD	3m	5	G	*chsd ldrs, no ch frm 13th, mstk 3 out*	3 11
864	31/3	Kingston St'	(R)	LAD	3m	6	F	*prog 16th, lft in ld apr nxt, clr til virt cght nr post*	1 17
1155	20/4	Stafford Cr'	(R)	LAD	3m	6	GF	*rear til prog 14th, lft 3rd last, nvr dang*	3 13

Deteriorating now; won weak Ladies; best R/H; hard to find a win a 15. 16

ONLY FOR IF (Irish) — **I** 485[1]

ONLY FOUR (Irish) — **I** 441[2]

ONLY HARRY ch.g. 6 Derrylin - Running For Gold by Rymer — J Alford

103	8/2	Great Treth'	(R)	MDO	3m	9	GS	*schoold, wll bhnd frm 7th, t.o. & p.u. 11th*	P 0
172	15/2	Ottery St M'	(L)	MDN	3m	14	G	*alwys mid-div, nvr on trms wth ldrs*	6 0

Well beaten but only learning so far & can do better. 10

ONLY IN IRELAND b.g. 11 Bulldozer - Welsh Wise by Welsh Saint — Capt R J Inglesant

360	2/3	Garnons	(L)	CON	3m	10	GS	*ld 2nd-nxt, wknd 10th, p.u. 12th*	P 0
665	23/3	Eaton Hall	(R)	MDO	3m	11	GF	*ld 3rd til f 12th*	F -
1013	12/4	Bitterley	(L)	CON	3m	14	GF	*ld to 6th, wknd 8th, p.u. 12th*	P 0
1150	19/4	Chaddesley '	(L)	MDO	3m	7	GF	*ld, clr to 14th, tired whn hdd & f 16th*	F -
1239	26/4	Brampton Br'	(R)	MDO	3m	9	G	*ld til 14th, ld nxt, wknd rpdly & p.u. aft 16th*	P 0
1541	18/5	Wolverhampt'	(L)	MDO	3m	15	GS	*handy, ld 6th-4 out, sn wknd*	5 0
1575	26/5	Chaddesley '	(L)	OPE	3m	10	F	*made most to 11th, wknd 14th, poor 4th whn f 2 out*	F -

Blazes the trail but no prospects of staying 3 miles. 10

ONLY ONE (Irish) — **I** 21[3], **I** 30[3], **I** 69, , **I** 112[5], **I** 183[4], **I** 471[2]

ONMEOWN (Irish) — **I** 90[P], **I** 140[P]

ON THE FLY b.g. 6 Bustino - My Greatest Star by Great Nephew — M J Brown

1996 **10(NH)**

114	9/2	Wetherby Po'	(L)	MDO	3m	8	GF	*prom, ld apr 4th, ran wd 7th, hdd 11th, wknd, p.u. 13th*	P 0
266	22/2	Duncombe Pa'	(R)	RES	3m	19	G	*lost many l stt,rear whn crashd thru wing & u.r. 7th*	U -
356	2/3	Great Stain'	(L)	INT	3m	9	S	*prom, wknd 8th, blnd & p.u. aft nxt*	P 0
424	8/3	Charm Park	(L)	RES	3m	12	GF	*prom, ld 4th til hdd 2 out, kpt on wll*	3 16
620	22/3	Hutton Rudby	(L)	MDO	3m	10	GF	*(fav) u.r. on way to post,trckd ldrs,disp 5th,hd apr 14th sn wknd*	4 0
860	31/3	Charm Park	(L)	MDO	3m	12	F	*cls up, ld 11th, made rest, styd on*	1 13
1068	13/4	Whitwell-On'	(R)	RES	3m	12	G	*prom, cls 3rd whn f 8th*	F -
1101	19/4	Hornby Cast'	(L)	RES	3m	14	G	*prom whn ran out 5th rejnd, alwys t.o., p.u. 4 out*	P 0

Plenty of ability but wayward; good enough for Restricted if going the right way. 16

ONTHELIST (Irish) — **I** 438[U], **I** 470[1]

ON THE QUIET gr.g. 5 Alias Smith (USA) - Cindy's Princess by Electric — Jeremy Mason

452	8/3	Newton Brom'	(R)	MDN	3m	9	G	*mid-div, wknd 11th, p.u. 14th*	P 0

Not yet of any account 0

ON YOUR WAY b.g. 15 Ragapan - Fourteen Carat by Sterling Bay (SWE) — A A Gilby

1996 P(0),3(0),3(0),4(0)

763	29/3	Whittington	(L)	CON	3m	9	S	*s.s., alwys t.o., 2 fences bhnd 6th*	4 0
1119	19/4	Whittington	(L)	MEM	3m	5	F	*cls up til wknd 9th, t.o. 11th*	4 0

No longer of any account 0

OPALS SON b.g. 6 Rabdan - Opal Fancy by Kibenka — Mrs A Price

361 2/3 Garnons (L) LAD 3m 7 GS *alwys rear, t.o. 9th, p.u. 11th* P 0
573 16/3 Garnons (L) LAD 3m 8 G *cls 3rd at 5th, wknd & p.u. 10th* P 0
750 29/3 Brampton Br' (R) LAD 3m 5 GF *last frm 4th, t.o. 12th, p.u. nxt* P 0
1236 26/4 Brampton Br' (R) LAD 3m 4 G *disp to 2nd, ran wd aft 4th, t.o. & p.u. 12th* P 0

No stamina as yet.No stamina as yet. 0

OPENING QUOTE (Irish) — I 68^{U}, I 128^{P}, I 311^{P}

OPULENT TRAPPINGS ch.m. 6 Foolish Ways - Piglet by Kemal (FR) C H Birch

666 23/3 Eaton Hall (R) MDO 3m 10 GF *chsng grp, 2nd at 9th, mstk nxt, sn btn, p.u. 3 out* P 0
1541 18/5 Wolverhampt' (L) MDO 3m 15 GS *ref 1st* R -

Not yet of any account 0

ORAFENO (Irish) — I 90^{P}

ORAGAS b.g. 11 Sagaro - Maranatha by Le Prince G J L Orchard

1996 1(19),2(12),F(-),4(0),2(14),5(0)

255 22/2 Newtown (L) CON 3m 14 G *chsd ldrs til lost tch 11th, no prog aft* 8 0
360 2/3 Garnons (L) CON 3m 10 GS *chsd ldrs til outpcd 11th, lft dist 3rd, tk 2nd flat* 2 12
740 29/3 Brampton Br' (R) MEM 3m 6 GF *alwys 3rd, 20l down 15th, sntchd 2nd flat* 2 11

50/1 Restricted winner 96; hard ride & shown little since; can only be watched. 15

ORANGE RAGUSA ch.g. 11 Orange Reef - Poncho by Ragusa S H Shirley-Beavan

156 15/2 Lanark (R) CON 3m 7 G *trckd ldng pair, ld apr 3 out, sn clr* 1 25
412 8/3 Dalston (R) LAD 3m 8 GS *(fav) j.w. keen hld, ld 4th, made rest, pshd out & ran on well* 1 22
590 21/3 Kelso (L) HC 3 1/2m 5 G *ld, rdn along 4 out, hdd next, driven and one pace last.* 3 23
1098 19/4 Bangor (L) HC 3m 110yds 9 G *prom, ld 4th to 7th, led 8th to 10th, wknd from 13th.* 5 16

Missed 96; fair pointer; retains ability; win more points; game; G/F-S. 23

ORA PRONOBIS b.g. 11 Kambalda - Let's Compromise R Hancox

1996 3(11)

1018 12/4 Bitterley (L) MDO 3m 13 GF *ld to 8th, styd prom, rdn 2 out, no ext* 2 14

Rarely seen; has ability & beat 5 others in 97; deserves a win but time getting on. 13

ORCHESTRAL SUITE(IRE) br.g. 9 Orchestra - Sweetly Stung by Master Rocky Exors Of The Late Mr G Pidgeon

1996 1(21)

91 6/2 Huntingdon (R) HC 3m 10 G *(fav) alwys handy, ld 5 out, styd on well from 2 out.* 1 24
490 10/3 Stratford (L) HC 3m 12 G *chsd ldrs, ld 3 out, styd on strly.* 1 29
888 3/4 Aintree (L) HC 3m 1f 9 G *(fav) chsd ldrs, f 3rd.* F -

Improved & now useful; lightly raced; 6 wins last 8 starts; win more; good stable; G-S. 28

ORDAIN (Irish) — I 35^{4}, I 100^{P}, I 119^{3}, I 123^{6}, I 180^{4}, I 214^{P}, I 315^{5}, I 331^{P}, I 362^{5}

ORE GALORE (Irish) — I 304^{P}, I 487^{F}, I 519^{2}

ORIEL DANCER (Irish) — I 470^{F}

ORIENTAL BEAUTY (Irish) — I 45^{2}, I 98^{1}

ORIGAMI ch.g. 12 Horage - Demeter by Silly Season E Rhodes

1996 2(13),3(13),5(13),P(0),1(18),P(0),3(10)

2 19/1 Barbury Cas' (L) XX 3m 14 GF *rear til u.r. 5th* U -
187 15/2 Erw Lon (L) OPE 3m 16 G *alwys rear, no ch whn ran out 14th* r -
257 22/2 Newtown (L) LAD 3m 12 G *in tch, 6th & outpcd 13th, no ch aft, ref last* R -
535 16/3 Erw Lon (L) CON 3m 12 GF *(bl) alwys rear, p.u. 15th* P 0
843 31/3 Lydstep (L) OPE 3m 4 F *trckd ldrs, ev ch 3 out, onepcd aft, lame* 3 10

Won 2 of last 29 starts; moody & declining now; Members looks only hope now; Any. 13

ORINOCO VENTURE(IRE) br.g. 6 Doyoun - Push A Button by Bold Lad (IRE) D A Malam

1996 **P(NH)**,**8(NH)**

347 2/3 Market Rase' (L) MDO 3m 9 GF *hld up, prog 10th, lost tch 13th, bhnd & p.u. 3 out* P 0

Placed novice hurdles; no real signs on debut; vanished after; successful stable & may do better. 12

ORLAS CHOICE (Irish) — I 458^{F}

ORLAS FANCY (Irish) — I 401^{4}

OROGALE (Irish) — I 501^{P}

ORPHAN OLLY b.g. 7 Relkino - Austrian Maid by Faberge II R H York

1996 3(0),F(-),F(-),P(0),F(-),U(-)

20 25/1 Badbury Rin' (L) MDN 3m 9 GF *made all, styd on well frm 2 out, comf* 1 13
59 1/2 Kingston Bl' (L) RES 3m 16 GF *ld to 3rd, chsd wnr to 11th, rallied flat* 3 18
580 16/3 Detling (L) RES 3m 11 F *alwys prom, ld 14th,made rest,ran on wll whn prssd frm 3 out* 1 18

872 31/3 Hackwood Pa' (L) CON 3m 4 F *(fav) alwys last, hrd rdn & mstk 13th, t.o. & lft poor 2nd last* 2 0

Much improved; gamely won competitive Restricted; L/H looks essential; can win again;G/F-F so far. .. 17

ORPHAN SPA (Irish) — I 153P, I 181U, I 2203

ORTON HOUSE b.g. 10 Silly Prices - Who's Free by Sit In The Corner (USA) Mrs A P Kelly

1996 3(10),**P(0)**,F(-),**P(0)**,3(15),1(15),**6(0)**,**U(-)**

83 2/2 Wolverhampt' (L) RES 3m 8 GS *chsd ldr, ld 14th, hdd & lft clr 2 out, drvn out* 1 18
200 15/2 Weston Park (L) CON 3m 16 G *mid-div, nvr pace to rch ldrs* 5 12
382 5/3 Bangor (L) HC 3m 110yds 6 GS *prom, ld 9th to 4 out, pushed along and wknd apr 2 out.* 4 13
496 15/3 Hereford (R) HC 3m 1f 110yds 10 GF *bhnd from 9th, t.o. when p.u. before 15th.* P 0
1098 19/4 Bangor (L) HC 3m 110yds 9 G *cl up to 4th, outpcd final cct.* 4 17
1288 30/4 Cheltenham (L) HC 2m 5f 10 GF *prom to 8th, weakening when mstk 11th, t.o. when hmpd 14th.* 5 0
1539 18/5 Wolverhampt' (L) OPE 3m 5 GS *handy, prog to ld 4 out, ran on strngly nxt, comf* 1 17
1545 24/5 Cartmel (L) HC 3 1/4m 14 G *alwys bhnd, struggling from 13th, nvr a factor.* 8 0

Maiden winner 96; outclassed in H/chases; weak Open win makes life very tough now. 19

ORUJO(IRE) b.g. 9 Try My Best (USA) - Oyace (ITY) by Hogarth (ITY) Miss C Gordon

1996 2(17),**9(0)**,6(10),4(10)

4 19/1 Barbury Cas' (L) OPE 3m 9 GF *chsd ldrs, outpcd 12th, onepcd aft, fin 4th, disq* 4D 20
94 7/2 Newbury (L) HC 2 1/2m 12 G *prom, ld 6th to 10th, weakening when hmpd 12th.* 7 0
514 15/3 Larkhill (R) MXO 3m 6 GF *cls up, jnd wnr 15th, wknd 2 out* 4 16
822 31/3 Lockinge (L) MEM 3m 4 F *chsd clr ldr, clsd frm 3 out, chnc whn outjmpd last,nt qckn* 2 16
1292 30/4 Cheltenham (L) HC 2m 5f 12 GF *mstks, bhnd, effort 10th, soon btn, t.o. and p.u. before 2 out.* P 0

Non-stayer; beaten in bad Members & hard to see him finding a race. 15

ORWELL ROSS(IRE) b.g. 9 Roselier (FR) - Orwell Brief by Lucky Brief D F Crockford

1996 **P(NH)**

262 22/2 Newtown (L) RES 3m 15 G *rear, wll bhnd frm 10th, t.o. & p.u. 14th* P 0
433 8/3 Upton-On-Se' (R) RES 3m 18 G *alwys rear, t.o. 8th, p.u. 11th* P 0
567 16/3 Garnons (L) MEM 3m 3 G *chsd ldr til outpcd 9th, t.o.* 3 0
1439 10/5 Holnicote (L) RES 3m 9 G *bhnd frm 5th, p.u. 14th* P 0

.. 0

OSCARS LINK (Irish) — I 3, , I 874

OSGATHORPE ch.g. 10 Dunbeath (USA) - Darlingka by Darling Boy R Tate

1996 P(0),F(-),3(17),2(17),P(0),**4(16)**,**5(NH)**

508 15/3 Dalton Park (R) LAD 3m 4 GF *s.s. trckd ldr, ld 12-14th, ld agn 3 out, sn clr, hld on fin* 1 19
857 31/3 Charm Park (L) MXO 3m 3 F *(fav) 20l 2nd at 5th, prog aft, ld 11-15th, ld 2 out, sn clr, easy* 1 19
1103 19/4 Hornby Cast' (L) OPE 3m 5 G *hvly rstrnd in 3rd, chsd ldr 14th, outpcd 3 out, fin tired* 2 16
1249 26/4 Easingwold (L) LAD 3m 6 GS *in tch, ld 3 out, styd on wll* 1 22
1408 5/5 Witton Cast' (R) LAD 3m 5 GS *settld 3rd, chsd wnr 10th til wknd qckly 4 out* 4 12
1422 10/5 Easingwold (L) LAD 3m 7 GF *chsd ldrs, disp 11th-14th, ld agn last, styd on wll* 1 20

Revived in 96; solid; consistent; needs easy 3 miles; likes Easingwold; win more; G/S-F. 21

OSMOSIS b.g. 11 Green Shoon - Milparinka by King's Equity K A Nelmes

1996 **15(NH)**

17 25/1 Badbury Rin' (L) CON 3m 9 GF *s.s. pllng, ld 6th til nrly u.r. 10th, wknd 13th, p.u. 15th* P 0
308 1/3 Clyst St Ma' (L) OPE 3m 7 HY *evented round, t.o. 2nd* 4 0
931 6/4 Charlton Ho' (L) OPE 3m 6 G *s.s. alwys t.o.* 4 0
1153 20/4 Stafford Cr' (R) CON 3m 10 GF *mid-div, lost tch 12th, t.o. 4 out* 6 0
1274 27/4 Little Wind' (R) XX 3m 8 GF *mstk 9th,w.w.,steady prog to chs ldrs 15th,wknd nxt,walkd in* 4 0

Winning hurdler; does not stay & no prospects in points. 0

O SO BOSSY ch.g. 7 Sousa - Bubbling Spirit by Hubble Bubble A W Congdon

556 16/3 Ottery St M' (L) RES 3m 12 G *hld up, prog 12th, chnce 14th, wknd aft 4 out, gd effrt* 4 0

Last but showed potential: go close in 98. 12

OSSIE MURPHY (Irish) — I 27P, I 119P

OTTER RIVER ch.g. 8 Celtic Cone - Ottery News by Pony Express O J Carter

290 28/2 Newbury (L) HC 3m 6 GS *alwys bhnd, lost tch after hit 7th, blnd 12th, t.o. when p.u. before last.* P 0

Well-bred; thrown in the deep end & shown nothing so far. 0

OUL LARRY ANDY (Irish) — I 351, I 229F

OUNAVARRA CREEK (Irish) — I 304, I 266U, I 334P, I 374, , I 4803, I 5352, I 5923

OUR BREW (Irish) — I 409P, I 497F, I 545P

OURMANJAC b.g. 7 Relkino - Sirenia by Biskrah — Mrs Nicola Turner

776 29/3 Dingley (R) MDO 2m 5f 10 G *(fav) nvr dang, 5th 6 out-3 out, wknd, p.u. last* P 0
1080 13/4 Guilsborough (L) RES 3m 11 GF *rear, mstk 6th, lsng tch whn mstk 13th & p.u.* P 0

Lightly raced; showed nothing in 97. 0

OUR NENO(NZ) ch.g. 5 Roman Empire - Polly's Sister (NZ) by Hasty Cloud — D H Barons

172 15/2 Ottery St M' (L) MDN 3m 14 G *hld up rear, prog 12th, 6th at nxt, outpcd 3 out* 4 11

Subsequent H/chase winner behind on debut; good stable; can score if fit 98. 14

OUR SURVIVOR b.g. 13 Trimmingham - Lougharue by Deep Run — Harry White

1996 C(-),1(18),3(17),P(0),4(12),**P(0)**

280 23/2 Charing (L) LAD 3m 12 G *trckd ldrs, rdn 16th, styd on wll flat, just faild* 2 21

Won modest Ladies 96; just pipped in same 97; lightly raced & hard to find another win at 14; Good. ... 18

OUR TEDDIS b.g. 7 Henricus (ATA) - Ted's Choice by Royal Smoke — E Sussex

1996 F(-),3(11),1(14),3(14)

630 22/3 Kilworthy (L) RES 3m 16 G *ld til aft 2nd, c.o. apr nxt* C -
736 29/3 Higher Kilw' (L) RES 3m 10 GF *ld to 8th, wknd, rear & p.u. 13th* P 0
792 31/3 Bishopsleigh (R) RES 3m 13 G *ld til ran out 7th* r -

Won weak Maiden 96; going wrong way now & best watched for signs of revival. 15

OUR WYN-STON ch.g. 5 Hard Fought - Wyn-Bank by Green God — Mrs P A Russell

1996 **6(NH),11(NH)**

80 2/2 Market Rase' (L) MDO 2m 5f 9 GF *chsd ldrs til ran out 4th* r -
116 9/2 Wetherby Po' (L) MDO 3m 14 GF *prom, ev ch 4 out, onepcd* 4 13
478 9/3 Southwell P' (L) MDO 3m 17 G *mid-div in tch, hmpd 15th, no ch aft* 5 0
768 29/3 Whittington (L) MDO 3m 10 S *nvr bynd mid-div, p.u. 2 out* P 0
1074 13/4 Whitwell-On' (R) MDO 2 1/2m 88yds 16 G *alwys prom, chal last, ran on wll flat, just faild* 2 16
1251 26/4 Easingwold (L) MDO 3m 9 GS *(fav) cls up, hit 13th, disp 2 out, ld last, drew clr, comf* 1 14
1421 10/5 Easingwold (L) RES 3m 8 GF *twrds rear, prog 10th,blnd 13th,wknd apr 3 out,p.u. nxt,lame* P 0

Dead 15

OUTCROP br.m. 9 Oats - Night Out III by Metropolis — Capt P S R Kennedy

361 2/3 Garnons (L) LAD 3m 7 GS *prom, 10l 2nd whn f 8th* F -
433 8/3 Upton-On-Se' (R) RES 3m 18 G *disp cls 3rd whn f 5th* F -
573 16/3 Garnons (L) LAD 3m 8 G *ld 1st, cls 2nd whn f 3rd* F -
701 29/3 Upper Sapey (R) RES 3m 6 GF *5l 2nd til hlfwy, wknd, distant last whn f 3 out* F -
1012 12/4 Bitterley (L) MEM 3m 6 GF *cls up, mstks 5 & 7th, wknd 12th, t.o. whn nrly u.r. last* 4 0

Won a poor Maiden 95; missed 96; calamitious now & can only be watched. 0

OUT FOR FUN ch.g. 11 Relkino - Cherry Picking by Queen's Hussar — Miss G A March

1996 **F(-),F(-)**

89 4/2 Warwick (L) HC 3 1/4m 4 GF *ld, given breather 6 out, qckknd next, blnd last, hdd and one pace run-in.* 2 26

Impressive debut winner 94; very lightly raced; H/chase still possible but time going by; G/F-S. 28

OUT OF ACTONS (Irish) — **I** 95^F

OUT OF LINE b.m. 6 Sunyboy - Hold The Line by New Brig — Mrs A Holman

193 15/2 Higham (L) CON 3m 14 G *twrds rear whn f 5th* F -
1028 12/4 Horseheath (R) CON 3m 3 HD *alwys last, lsng tch & hit 11th, t.o. & p.u. 3 out* P 0
1277 27/4 Fakenham P-' (L) CON 3m 10 G *rear, jmpd slwly 3rd, t.o. 8th, p.u. 13th* P 0

Not yet of any account 0

OUT OF THE CLOUDS (Irish) — **I** 552^P, **I** 585^P

OUT ON THE TOWN ch.m. 7 Town And Country - Bank House Lodge by Funny Man — Keith James

543 16/3 Erw Lon (L) MDN 3m 11 GF *rear, p.u. 12th* P 0
842 31/3 Lydstep (L) MDO 3m 12 F *alwys rear, p.u. 2 out* P 0
1010 12/4 St Hilary (R) MDN 3m 10 GF *mid-div, dist 3rd whn ref 3 out* R -
1323 3/5 Bonvilston (R) MDO 3m 14 G *mid-div, wknd & p.u. 2 out* P 0
1473 11/5 Erw Lon (L) MDO 3m 13 GS *prom til ld 13th, clr 2 out, styd on wll* 1 13

Stunning improvement to land modest race; hard to assess; can improve needs to for Restricteds. 15

OUT THE DOOR(IRE) br.g. 8 Lepanto (GER) - Pejays Princess by Pumps (USA) — M Mann

1996 U(-),2(22),1(22),1(24),3(20),1(24),2(22),1(18),1(22),1(22)

85 2/2 Wolverhampt' (L) LAD 3m 11 GS *prom, chsd ldr 9th, chal & lft clr 3 out, comf* 1 24

Useful Ladies pointer; well handled; finished early 97; win more if fit 98; L/H; G/S-G/F. 25

OUT THE NAV (Irish) — I 383^{F}, I 500^{F}, I 607^{S}

OUT THE WAY (Irish) — I 570^{4}

OVAHANDY MAN ch.g. 6 Ovac (ITY) - Langton Lass by Nearly A Hand — J L Gledson

135	9/2 Alnwick	(L) MDO 3m	12 G	*in tch, prog 12th, ev ch nxt, wknd 3 out*	5	0
564	16/3 Lanark	(R) MDO 2 1/2m	13 GS	*(fav) not fluent, 4th frm hlfwy, nvr threaten 1st 2*	4	0

Promising debut season; sure to improve & should score in 98. 14

OVER EAGER (Irish) — I 22^{P}, I 47^{3}, I 103^{F}, I 133^{1}, I 170^{1}

OVERSTEP ch.g. 11 Over The River (FR) - Madam Exbury by Homeric — R Douglas

1996 1(14),P(0)

1510	17/5 Corbridge	(R) RES 3m	13 GS	*jmpd lft, rear, t.o. 7th, p.u. 13th*	P	0

Won weak Maiden 96; very lightly raced; vanished early & can only be watched now. 13

OVER THE BARROW (Irish) — I 156^{2}, I 221^{P}, I 341^{P}

OVER THE COUNTRY (Irish) — I 490^{3}, I 559^{1}

OVER THE DOOR gr.m. 5 Over The River (FR) - Barnist by Dumbarnie — M Mann

1543	18/5 Wolverhampt'	(L) MEM 3m	2 GS	*(fav) hld up, ld apr 3 out, 3l up whn lft alone 3 out*	1	0

Finished solo in awful race; young; successful stable; huge improvement needed. 10

OVER THE EDGE ch.g. 11 Over The River (FR) - Banish Misfortune by Master Owen — Christopher Sporborg

1996 2(24),1(23),**1(23)**,**11(11)**,1(24),6(13),1(23),**1(22)**

27	26/1 Marks Tey	(L) OPE 3m	6 GF	*prom, 3rd & rdn 17th, styd on wll flat, not rch wnr*	2	24
151	12/2 Lingfield	(L) HC 3m	13 HY	*bhnd from 9th, t.o. when p.u. before 3 out.*	P	0
273	22/2 Ampton	(R) OPE 3m	7 G	*made all, pushed clr 3 out, nt extnd*	1	23
388	7/3 Sandown	(R) HC 3m 110yds	7 G	*chsd ldrs, lost pl after 12th, styd on one pace after 4 out.*	3	19
501	15/3 Ampton	(R) OPE 3m	4 GF	*(fav) made all, drw clr appr 2 out, easily*	1	23
595	22/3 Horseheath	(R) OPE 3m	5 F	*(fav) made all in nrrw ld, qcknd clr last*	1	23
710	29/3 High Easter	(L) OPE 3m	5 F	*(fav) j.w. made all, drw clr appr last, easily*	1	24
911	5/4 Cottenham	(R) OPE 3m	3 F	*(fav) chsd wnr, outpcd 3 out, kpt on flat*	2	18
1030	12/4 Horseheath	(R) OPE 3m	2 HD	*(fav) disp ld til ld 13th, clr frm nxt, rdn flat, just hld on*	1	20
1279	27/4 Fakenham P-'	(L) OPE 3m	7 G	*(fav) ld to 4th, 3rd whn mstk & rmndr 13th, no imp 3 out*	3	16
1433	10/5 Marks Tey	(L) OPE 3m	4 G	*(fav) ld to 4th,went 2nd 12th,outpcd 3 out,styd on nxt,just faild*	2	18

Fair pointer; jumps; stays; likes to dictate; win more local Opens; dislikes Fakenham;G-Hd. 21

OVER THE GLEN (Irish) — I 90^{P}, I 150^{F}, I 218^{5}, I 388^{2}, I 406^{2}

OVER THE HILL (Irish) — I 522^{P}, I 574^{P}, I 595^{P}

OVER THE LAKE(IRE) ch.m. 8 Over The River (FR) - Castle Lake by Orchardist — A Tredwell

1996 2(0)

60	1/2 Kingston Bl'	(L) MDN 3m	17 GF	*alwys wll bhnd, t.o. & p.u. 3 out*	P	0
275	22/2 Ampton	(R) MDO 3m	10 G	*rr, rmdrs & hdwy 9th, outpcd 14th, no ch & p.u. 3 out, lame*	P	0

Of no account 0

OVER THE PLOUGH (Irish) — I 226^{F}

OVER THE TAVERN (Irish) — I 97^{P}, I 217^{P}, I 286^{P}

OWEN GOWLA (Irish) — I 498^{P}

OXBOW b.g. 10 Trojan Fen - Shannon Princess by Connaught — D D Davies

281	23/2 Charing	(L) OPE 3m	12 G	*(bl) hld up, rdn & no prog 13th, t.o. & p.u. last*	P	0
966	6/4 Penshurst	(L) CON 3m	7 F	*ld to 9th, p.u. aft nxt lame*	P	0

Winning hurdler; stable out of form 97; no stamina & problems last start. 0

OXFORD PLACE br.g. 13 Derrylin - Garden Party by Reform — Miss P S Richardson

426	8/3 Charm Park	(L) LAD 3m	12 GF	*(bl) rear & lost tch 9th, t.o. 12th, p.u. 3 out*	P	0
505	15/3 Dalton Park	(R) MEM 3m	6 GF	*(bl) prom, mstk 3rd, wknd 13th, sn bhnd, t.o.*	4	0
1071	13/4 Whitwell-On'	(R) CON 3m	10 G	*(bl) prom til lost plc 9th, wll bhnd whn u.r. 11th*	U	-

No longer of any account 0

OZIER HILL (Irish) — I 27^{3}, I 78^{1}, I 149^{1}, I 216^{1}, I 386^{1}

OZZIE JONES b.g. 6 Formidable (USA) - Distant Relation by Great Nephew — Keith R Pearce

1996 **12(NH)**,**8(NH)**,**3(NH)**,**4(NH)**,**5(NH)**,**3(NH)**

534	16/3 Erw Lon	(L) MEM 3m	3 GF	*ld to 6th, ld 9th, unchal frm 12th*	1	14
638	22/3 Howick	(L) LAD 3m	10 GF	*cls up, ld 13th, qcknd clr, ran on well*	1	20
844	31/3 Lydstep	(L) LAD 3m	6 F	*(fav) ld/disp til ld 11th, sn in cmmnd*	1	21
961	6/4 Pantyderi	(L) LAD 3m	2 F	*(fav) ld til ran out 14th*	r	-

Winning hurdler; had busy career; sluiced home & looks sure to be hard to beat in local Ladies. 21

PABELO (Irish) — I 554P, I 593P

PABLOWMORE b.g. 7 Pablond - Carrowmore by Crozier — R W Green

1996 2(11),2(12),3(14)

134	9/2	Alnwick	(L)	MDO	3m	11	G	*(fav) pllng, prom & hit 2nd, lost plc 7th, t.o. 10th, ran on flat*	4	0
160	15/2	Lanark	(R)	MDO	2m 5f	10	G	*(fav) not alwys fluent, bhnd til prog 4 out, chal & lft clr 2 out*	1	15
230	22/2	Friars Haugh	(L)	RES	3m	15	G	*nvr rchd ldrs*	7	0
338	1/3	Corbridge	(R)	RES	3m	10	G	*prom, 2nd 13th, ld nxt, clr whn mstk last, styd on well*	1	17
411	8/3	Dalston	(R)	CON	3m	16	GS	*jmpd slwly & bhnd, prog frm 14th, styd on wll 2 out,nrst fin*	3	17
810	31/3	Tranwell	(L)	CON	3m	5	G	*ld til hdd 3rd, trckd ldrs til disp ld 3 out,qcknd 5l up nxt*	1	20

Progressive; mistakes & tricky; best easy 3 miles; more needed for Opens; Good. 20

PABREY gr.g. 11 Pablond - Grey Receipt by Rugantino — S L Mitchell

1996 3(14),7(0)

107	8/2	Milborne St'	(L)	MEM	3m	8	GF	*rear early, prog 12th, prssd wnr 4 out, onepcd frm 2 out*	2	14
310	1/3	Clyst St Ma'	(L)	INT	3m	9	HY	*sn bhnd, nvr rchd ldrs*	5	0
662	22/3	Badbury Rin'	(L)	CON	3m	8	F	*10s-4s, hld up, prog 12th, ld 13th-nxt, cls 3rd whn f 3 out*	F	-
920	5/4	Larkhill	(R)	MXO	4m	4	F	*5s-2s, last, jmpd slwly 10th, p.u. nxt, b.b.v*	P	0
1372	5/5	Cotley Farm	(L)	INT	3m	3	GF	*alwys 3rd, wll bhnd whn ref 2 out*	R	-

Won 3 in 95; lost form in 97 & signs not looking good now; best watched. 13

PACIFICBLUE (Irish) — I 241P, I 297P

PACIFIC RAMBLER(IRE) b.g. 7 Riberetto - Cooleen by Tarqogan — Richard Barry

1996 **P(NH),7(NH)**

114	9/2	Wetherby Po'	(L)	MDO	3m	8	GF	*prom, ld 14th til hdd & nt qckn nr fin*	3	15

No ability under rules; winner behind when just caught; vanished after; win if fit in 98. 14

PACO'S BOY b.g. 12 Good Thyne (USA) - Jeremique by Sunny Way — R H York

1996 3(0),3(0),**4(11)**,**3(19)**,3(18),**6(15)**,**6(10)**,2(10),**5(11)**

3	19/1	Barbury Cas'	(L)	XX	3m	14	GF	*alwys prom, chsd ldr 12th, ld flat, lkd hdd nr fin*	1	19
56	1/2	Kingston Bl'	(L)	OPE	3m	13	GF	*in tch early, wll bhnd frm hlfwy*	5	0
302	1/3	Parham	(R)	CON	3m	14	G	*(bl) prom, ld 11th-4 out, 3rd aft, steadily wknd, lost 3rd fin*	4	15
481	9/3	Tweseldown	(R)	MEM	3m	6	G	*(fav) (bl) j.w. chsd ldr, ld apr last, easily*	1	15
870	31/3	Hackwood Pa'	(L)	MXO	3m	4	F	*(bl) disp to 8th, hmpd 10th-12th, wknd*	3	10
1054	13/4	Hackwood Pa'	(L)	CON	3m	4	GF	*chsd ldrs, wknd rpdly bef 2 out, lft poor 2nd*	2	10
1127	19/4	Penshurst	(L)	OPE	3m	7	GF	*trckd ldrs, 3rd & ev ch 4 out, wknd 2 out*	3	14
1462	11/5	Tweseldown	(R)	CON	3m	6	GF	*sn outpcd in rear, rdn 10th, no ch frm 14th*	4	0

Won 5 placed 12 last 23 starts; finds some soft races; need same to score again. 15

PADDY A GO GO br.m. 5 Queen's Soldier (USA) - Master Suite by Master Owen — Bruce Andrews

796	31/3	Marks Tey	(L)	MDO	3m	6	F	*bhnd,mstk 2nd,prog to 3rd 11th,wknd frm 14th,t.o. & p.u.16th*	P	0
1118	19/4	Higham	(L)	MDO	3m	9	GF	*alwys rear, jmpd poorly, t.o. 12th, p.u. 15th*	P	0
1432	10/5	Marks Tey	(L)	MEM	3m	2	G	*chsd wnr, jmpd delib, lost tch 12th*	2	0

Jumped badly & unpromising so far. 0

PADDY CASEY (Irish) — I 184P

PADDY RED (Irish) — I 36F, I 119F, I 180P, I 231[4], I 554P, I 579[2], I 583,

PADDY'S POCKET br.g. 11 Ovac (ITY) - High Arctic by Rum (USA) — P Hudson

345	2/3	Market Rase'	(L)	MDO	3m	13	GF	*chsd ldrs 7th, 4th & outpcd apr 14th, t.o.*	4	0
550	16/3	Garthorpe	(R)	MDO	3m	11	GF	*mid div, hit 5th, 4th & hit 14th, wknd, p.u. 2 out*	P	0
770	29/3	Dingley	(R)	RES	3m	18	G	*disp brfly to 3rd, sn fdd, last pair 10th, p.u. nxt*	P	0
1187	20/4	Garthorpe	(R)	MEM	3m	9	GF	*ld, 10l clr 15th, rdn apr last, ct nr fin*	2	14
1577	26/5	Chaddesley '	(L)	MDO	3m	11	F	*ld to 12th, chsd wnr aft, wknd 3 out, fin tired*	2	10
1609	1/6	Dingley	(R)	MDO	3m	14	GF	*ld 2nd til aft 2 out, wknd & slw jmp last, fin tired*	3	0

Missed 96; tries hard but does not stay; ldeserves a win but looks very hard now. 12

PADDYS RING (Irish) — I 307P

PALACE KING(IRE) ch.g. 8 Great Eastern - Fancy Girl by Mon Capitaine — Mrs P Strawbridge

1996 P(0),0(0),P(0),5(0),P(0),2(18),6(0),8(0)

457	8/3	Great Treth'	(R)	RES	3m	8	S	*prom til lost plc 12th, btn 6th whn p.u. apr 15th*	P	0
661	22/3	Badbury Rin'	(L)	RES	3m	6	F	*alwys prom, ld 14th, clr whn blnd 3 out, hdd nxt, onepcd*	4	10
1108	19/4	Flete Park	(R)	RES	3m	14	GF	*5th hlfwy, no ch frm 15th*	6	0
1369	5/5	Cotley Farm	(L)	MEM	3m	4	GF	*held up, prog 4 out, disp nxt, ld last, all out*	1	12
1494	14/5	Cothelstone	(L)	RES	3m	11	GF	*alwys bhnd, t.o. & p.u. 13th*	P	0
1551	24/5	Mounsey Hil'	(R)	RES	3m	13	G	*trckd ldrs, outpcd 15th, btn whn blnd 17th, t.o.*	5	0

Members winner 95 & 97; outclassed in other races & only hope again. 11

PALACE WOLF(NZ) b.g. 13 Star Wolf - Castle Star (NZ) by Indian Order — Mrs N M Coombe

481	9/3	Tweseldown	(R)	MEM	3m	6	G	*ran out 2nd*	r	-

Winning Irish chaser; past it now. 0

PALAMAN b.g. 10 Mandalus - Pallas Breeze by Shackleton — Charles Aikenhead

1996 P(0),5(0),U(-),P(0),P(0),1(0)

873	31/3	Hackwood Pa'	(L)	RES	3m	6	F	*ld 7-12th, mstks 3 out & nxt, fdd*	3	10
1053	13/4	Hackwood Pa'	(L)	MEM	3m	2	GF	*ld 7th, qcknd 6l clr 4 out, rdn apr last, wknd & hdd flat*	2	13

Won awful Members 95/96; only effective in the poorest races; need luck to win again. 10

PALLADANTE(IRE) b or br.m. 6 Phardante (FR) - Pallastown Run by Deep Run — P B Williamson

1996 **18(NH)**

327	1/3	Eaton Hall	(R)	MDN	3m	11	GS	*ldng grp, cls 3rd 10th, fdd, p.u. 4 out*	P	0
666	23/3	Eaton Hall	(R)	MDO	3m	10	GF	*mid to rear, no ch whnp.u. 3 out*	P	0
850	31/3	Eyton-On-Se'	(L)	LAD	3m	6	GF	*cls up, ld 4th, 2nd whn f 6th*	F	-

Shows some speed but much more needed. 0

PALLINGHAM LAD(IRE) b.g. 7 Torenaga - Star Mill by Milan — Mrs Lynne Jones

1996 **10(NH)**

316	1/3	Clyst St Ma'	(L)	MDN	3m	6	HY	*prom, ld 13th til apr last, blnd & u.r. last*	U	-
519	15/3	Cothelstone	(L)	MEM	3m	5	GS	*prom, cls 2nd whn f 13th*	F	-

No form under rules; ran passably on debut but race was dreadful & much more needed. 0

PALMED OFF b.m. 6 Palm Track - Alpro by Count Albany — R T Dennis

506	15/3	Dalton Park	(R)	CON	3m	16	GF	*mid-div, lost tch 5th, ran out nxt*	r	-
949	6/4	Friars Haugh	(L)	MDN	3m	10	GF	*6th but just in tch whn f 9th*	F	-

An unfortunate start. 0

PALMERSTON'S FOLLY b.m. 6 Brianston Zipper - Fortis by Bribe — Mrs M O'Sullivan

306	1/3	Parham	(R)	MDN	3m	12	G	*n.j.w. alwys last, t.o. & p.u. 10th*	P	0
661	22/3	Badbury Rin'	(L)	RES	3m	6	F	*handy til f 8th*	F	-
1158	20/4	Stafford Cr'	(R)	MDO	3m	5	GF	*sn rear, lost tch 12th, p.u. aft 15th*	P	0
1373	5/5	Cotley Farm	(L)	MDO	3m	6	GF	*sn rear, t.o. whn p.u. 4 out*	P	0

Not yet of any account 0

PALM READER b.g. 13 Palm Track - Carbia by Escart III — Lord Mostyn

1996 5(0),2(15)

93	7/2	Bangor	(L)	HC	2 1/2m 110yds	11	G	*soon well bhnd, t.o. when p.u. before 10th.*	P	0

lightly raced now & looks past it now. 12

PALMROCK QUEEN (Irish) — I 25^{F}, I 32^{P}

PALMURA (Irish) — I 230, , I 266^{P}, I 395^{P}, I 414^{3}, I 439^{P}, I 524^{P}, I 578^{P}

PAMELA'S LAD ch.g. 11 Dalsaan - La Margarite by Bonne Noel — P R Burling

1996 3(19),4(16),**2(21)**,**F(-)**,2(16),**3(18)**,3(16)

377	4/3	Leicester	(R)	HC	2 1/2m 110yds	15	G	*alwys in rear.*	9	0
849	31/3	Eyton-On-Se'	(L)	OPE	3m	7	GF	*held up in rear, 3rd 3 out, p.u. 2 out*	P	0
937	6/4	Tabley	(R)	CON	3m	10	G	*prog to chs ldr 10th, rddn & btn 3 out, lost 2nd run in*	4	15
1301	3/5	Weston Park	(L)	OPE	3m	4	G	*hld up rear, prog to 2nd at 14th, ld 2 out, f last,rmntd*	3	19
1508	17/5	Bangor	(L)	HC	3m 110yds	12	G	*bhnd, hdwy to chase ldrs 13th, no impn und pres.*	3	17

Has ability but lost last 22 & blew a gift penultimate start; barely stays; best avoided. 19

PAMELLAS STAR (Irish) — I 570^{P}, I 590^{P}

PANCHO'S TANGO (Irish) — I 18^{1}, I 49^{P}, I 193^{1}

PANCRATIC b.g. 14 Pitpan - Paddys Flyer by Paddy's Stream — C R Millington

771	29/3	Dingley	(R)	OPE	3m	10	G	*3rd brfly to 3rd, sn fdd, t.o. 10th, p.u. 2 out*	P	0
926	6/4	Garthorpe	(R)	OPE	3m	10	GF	*alwys rear, no imp, p..u 8th*	P	0
1077	13/4	Guilsborough	(L)	CON	3m	16	GF	*alwys last pair, t.o.*	7	0
1350	4/5	Dingley	(R)	MEM	3m	5	G	*disp til ld 4th, 4l clr whn f 12th*	F	-
1604	1/6	Dingley	(R)	MEM	3m	4	GF	*made most til 8l clr & s.u. bend apr 9th*	S	-

Missed 96; front runs; probably unlucky in 2 bad Members 97; same only hope in 98. 12

PANDA NOVA (Irish) — I 118^{P}, I 176^{2}, I 248^{6}, I 289^{4}, I 375^{5}

PANDA SHANDY b.m. 9 Nearly A Hand - Panda Pops by Cornuto — Mrs R H Woodhouse

1996 1(21),P(0),1(21)

385	6/3	Wincanton	(R)	HC	3m 1f 110yds	6	G	*hmpd 9th and lost position, hdwy 13th, chsd wnr 15th, chal 4 out till f next.*	F	-
660	22/3	Badbury Rin'	(L)	LAD	3m	2	F	*(fav) trckd ldr, chal 2 out, onepcd apr last*	2	25
870	31/3	Hackwood Pa'	(L)	MXO	3m	4	F	*(fav) j.w. rear til ld brfly 14th, ld 3 out, ran on well*	1	22

Won 6 of last 11 95/97; still improving; unlucky in H/chase; can win modest one;F-G. 25

PANTO LADY br.m. 11 Lepanto (GER) - Dusky Damsel by Sahib — Mrs K M Lamb
1996 P(0),U(-),**9(0)**,**5(0)**,P(0),**5(NH)**,**P(NH)**,**7(NH)**,**7(0)**

131	9/2	Alnwick	(L)	RES	3m	13	G	*sn wll bhnd, t.o. frm 7th, p.u. 3 out*	P 0
944	6/4	Friars Haugh	(L)	INT	3m	5	GF	*sn bhnd, t.o. whn p.u. aft 9th*	P 0
995	12/4	Tranwell	(L)	RES	3m	6	F	*n.j.w., 20l last 9th, lost tch 11th, t.o. & p.u. 3 out*	P 0
1169	20/4	Hexham Poin'	(L)	RES	3m	9	GF	*mid-div to 12th, wknd 15th, p.u. last*	P 0
1332	3/5	Mosshouses	(L)	INT	3m	4	F	*3rd to 6th, t.o. 12th, p.u. 2 out*	P 0

Won poor Maiden 95; of no account now. 0

PAPER FAIR b.m. 12 Paper Cap - Trefair by Graig Hill Master — W C D James
1996 P(0),3(0),P(0)

713	29/3	Llanvapley	(L)	MEM	3m	4	GF	*alwys chsng wnnr, no imp frm hlfwy*	2 0

Members winner 92; shown nothing since. 0

PAPERWORK BOY ch.g. 12 Buckskin (FR) - Orinda Way by Deep Run — Miss N Berry

280	23/2	Charing	(L)	LAD	3m	12	G	*alwys last pair, t.o. & p.u. 16th*	P 0

Winning hurdler; of no account now. 0

PAPS LAST HOPE (Irish) — I 101^{3}, I 186^{3}, I 286^{3}, I 344^{3}, I 438^{U}, I 472^{1}, I 546^{P}, I 605^{5}, I 614^{5}

PAPUITE (Irish) — I 50^{U}, I 90^{P}, I 264^{P}

PARAPLUIE ch.m. 8 Sunyboy - Mandycap by Mandamus — Mrs J Brazington

433	8/3	Upton-On-Se'	(R)	RES	3m	18	G	*losing tch 7th, t.o. 11th, p.u. 2 out*	P 0
934	6/4	Charlton Ho'	(L)	MDO	3m	10	G	*mstk 3rd, alwys bhnd, t.o. 10th*	5 0
1066	13/4	Maisemore P'	(L)	MDO	3m	9	GF	*alwys mid-div, blnd 9th, lft poor 4th 14th, t.o.*	4 0
1460	11/5	Maisemore P'	(L)	MDO	3m	16	G	*f 1st*	F -
1577	26/5	Chaddesley '	(L)	MDO	3m	11	F	*last & sn dtchd, t.o. 12th*	4 0

Beaten miles when completing; massive improvement needed. 0

PARDITINO b.g. 9 Pardigras - Happy Tino by Rugantino — Mrs K R J Nicholas
1996 U(-),3(12)

241	22/2	Lemalla	(R)	RES	3m	11	S	*rear, mstks, bhnd whn crawld 16th, p.u. nxt*	P 0
313	1/3	Clyst St Ma'	(L)	RES	3m	10	HY	*j.w. made all, unchal*	1 18
554	16/3	Ottery St M'	(L)	CON	3m	7	G	*mstks, prom til lost plc 14th, rallied 3 out, no imp aft*	2 14
862	31/3	Kingston St'	(R)	CON	3m	7	F	*prom, ld 16th til aft 3 out, lkd btn til rlld to ld nr post*	1 18
1088	16/4	Hockworthy	(L)	MEM	3m	6	GF	*ld 5th-14th, rdn & onepcd frm 2 out*	2 17
1245	26/4	Bratton Down	(L)	INT	3m	9	GS	*alwys prom, efft 2 out, no imprssn*	2 10
1313	3/5	Holnicote	(L)	CON	3m	7	G	*ld 5th-9th, ld nxt, clr whn blnd last, not rcvr, hdd flat*	2 21
1481	11/5	Ottery St M'	(L)	CON	3m	12	G	*(fav) alwys rear & outpcd, no ch whn p.u. 2 out*	P 0
1496	14/5	Cothelstone	(L)	CON	3m	9	GF	*cls up, ld 8th, jnd 13th-aft 3 out, clr nxt, comf*	1 21
1548	24/5	Mounsey Hil'	(R)	LAD	3m	10	G	*blnd & u.r. 2nd*	U -
1581	26/5	Lifton	(R)	LAD	3m	7	G	*mid-div, prog 3 out, chal nxt, ld last, ran on und pres*	1 22

Much improved; novice ridden; game; mistakes; harder to place but can win again; Any. 21

PARDON ME MUM ch.g. 12 The Parson - Please Mum by Kabale — Dr D B A Silk
1996 U(-),1(20),1(21),3(20),4(20)

195	15/2	Higham	(L)	LAD	3m	14	G	*cls up in ldng 4, prssd ldr 12-14th, ev ch til outpcd 16th*	4 19
578	16/3	Detling	(L)	LAD	3m	11	F	*(fav) alwys prom, 3rd 2 out, hrd rddn to ld last*	1 19

Consistent Ladies pointer; needs easy 3 miles & best L/H; can win again if fit 98;G-F. 20

PARISH RANGER (Irish) — I 41^{P}, I 75^{P}, I 88^{3}, I 193^{P}, I 320^{5}

PARK DRIFT ch.g. 11 Say Primula - Kerera by Keren — G Thornton
1996 5(17),2(21),1(25),3(22),1(23),1(24),1(24),**P(0)**

250	22/2	Brocklesby '	(L)	OPE	3m	6	G	*w.w., prog 8th, 2nd frm 12th til p.u. qckly bfr last*	P 0
507	15/3	Dalton Park	(R)	OPE	3m	8	GF	*hld up rear, effrt 15th, not qckn 3 out*	3 17
618	22/3	Hutton Rudby	(L)	OPE	3m	10	GF	*(fav) chsd ldrs, wnt 2nd 3 out, wknd nxt*	4 16
696	29/3	Stainton	(R)	OPE	3m	5	F	*rear, prog 4th, ld 4 out, hdd & onepcd flat*	2 18
1085	14/4	Hexham	(L)	HC	3m 1f	5	F	*trckd ldrs, effort 4 out, rdn next and soon wknd.*	4 13
1248	26/4	Easingwold	(L)	OPE	3m	8	GS	*cls up, tk 3rd 2 out, no ch ldng pair*	3 12

Won 6 95/96; below par 97; needs easy 3 miles; may need Confined to win at 12.F- G/S. 17

PARKERS HILLS(IRE) b.g. 8 Mister Lord (USA) - Annies Pet by Normandy — Christopher Sporborg
1996 6(10),P(0),6(0),1(17),4(16),P(0),7(0)

321	1/3	Marks Tey	(L)	INT	3m	10	G	*(tuped), mid-div, lost tch 14th, t.o. & p.u. 17th*	P 0

Lucky winner 96; tubed & finished early 97; can only be watched if reappearing. 13

PARK WEST (Irish) — I 161^{P}, I 202^{P}, I 231^{P}, I 280^{P}

PARLIAMENT HALL gr.g. 11 Piling (USA) - Miss Carribean by Sea Hawk II — S H Shirley-Beavan
1996 1(24),2(21),**P(0)**,P(0)

158	15/2	Lanark	(R)	LAD	3m	8	G	*(fav) mstks & lost plc hlfwy, prog & chnce 3 out, wknd apr nxt*	5 0

764 29/3 Whittington (L) LAD 3m 5 S *ld to 9th & frm 14th, styd on wll whn chal apr 2 out* 1 23
1425 10/5 Aspatria (L) LAD 3m 6 G *(fav) not fluent, ld, wll clr frm 5th til wknd & hdd aft 3 out* 4 15

Former useful chaser; able but inconsistent; best early season; likes soft; may win again. 21

PARMAN (Irish) — I 175[P], I 248, , I 293[3], I 328[4], I 508[F], I 554[2], I 583[3]

PAROS LEADER (Irish) — I 48[P], I 139[P], I 235[P], I 263[P], I 338[P], I 561[P], I 571[P]

PARSON FLYNN b.g. 10 Mandalus - Flynn's Field by The Parson Mrs M J Trickey
1996 2(14),2(15),P(0),F(-),1(16)

433 8/3 Upton-On-Se' (R) RES 3m 18 G *mid-div, effrt 12th, not chal ldrs* 4 0
630 22/3 Kilworthy (L) RES 3m 16 G *lft in ld 3rd-5th, cls up til wknd und pres frm 16th* 7 10
1244 26/4 Bratton Down (L) CON 3m 14 GS *ldng grp til grdly wknd 12th,stop to walk run in, (dead)* 6 0

Dead. 15

PARSONS BRIG b.g. 11 The Parson - Tumlin Brig by New Brig J S Haldane

33 26/1 Alnwick (L) LAD 3m 12 G *trckd ldrs til blnd & u.r. 8th* U -
132 9/2 Alnwick (L) LAD 3m 9 G *(fav) in tch, 3rd & hit 13th, ev ch 4 out, btn whn lft 2nd nxt* 2 0
231 22/2 Friars Haugh (L) LAD 3m 13 G *(Jt fav) ld/disp frm 10th, slght ld 2 out, styd on wll* 1 21
945 6/4 Friars Haugh (L) LAD 3m 6 GF *strgglng 10th, wnt 3rd 3 out, lft 2nd 2 out, no ch wth wnnr* 2 20

Useful ex Irish chaser; consistent; ran under rules after(Scottish national); can win again. 21

PARSON'S CORNER b.g. 10 The Parson - Arctic Rhapsody by Bargello Miss C E Williams
1996 P(0),5(0),2(0),3(0)

665 23/3 Eaton Hall (R) MDO 3m 11 GF *mid to rear, p.u. 4 out* P 0
854 31/3 Eyton-On-Se' (L) MDO 3m 10 GF *cls up, outpcd frm 4 out* 4 0
1019 12/4 Bitterley (L) MDO 3m 12 GF *nvr going pace, t.o. & p.u. 5th* P 0
1479 11/5 Garthorpe (R) MDO 3m 12 GS *ld to 5th, chsd ldrs to 11th, wkng & blnd 13th, t.o.* 6 0

Placed in 3 of last 8 starts but not progressing; win looks unlikely now. 0

PARSONS FORT (Irish) — I 397[4], I 452[P], I 512[2], I 548[1], I 587[6]

PARSONS GREEN BOY (Irish) — I 76[P], I 104[P], I 297[P], I 400[1], I 448[P]

PARSON'S WAY b.g. 10 The Parson - Daithis Coleen by Carnival Night Mrs K A Heywood
1996 6(0),P(0),1(20),1(23)

554 16/3 Ottery St M' (L) CON 3m 7 G *(Jt fav) (bl) ld to 4 out, onepcd frm nxt* 3 12
739 29/3 Higher Kilw' (L) OPE 3m 3 GF *(bl) chsd wnr, no ch frm 4 out* 2 0
1037 12/4 Lifton (R) OPE 3m 5 F *(bl) trckd ldr til ld 15th, made rest readly* 1 20
1256 27/4 Black Fores' (R) OPE 3m 4 F *ld 2nd, hdd 14th, slght ld agn nxt-last, no ext flat* 2 23
1396 5/5 High Bickin' (R) MXO 3m 7 G *(bl) ld to 9th, prom til wknd 14th, no ch 16th* 5 10
1581 26/5 Lifton (R) LAD 3m 7 G *made most til hdd last, no ext flat* 2 22

won 3 Opens 96/97; quirky; best in blinkers; has good jockeys; can win again; F-S. 20

PARTYONJASON (Irish) — I 254[P], I 316[B], I 436, , I 468[P], I 579[P]

PASSIM b.m. 5 Kind Of Hush - Sigwells Miss by Tender King C Hendrie

136 9/2 Alnwick (L) MDO 3m 16 G *alwys wll bhnd, t.o. 7th, p.u. 3 out* P 0
233 22/2 Friars Haugh (L) MDO 3m 13 G *nvr nr ldrs, p.u. 3 out* P 0
417 8/3 Dalston (R) MDO 2 1/2m 11 GS *alwys rear, no ch 11th, t.o.* 8 0

last when completing; much more needed. 0

PASSING FAIR b.m. 6 Pablond - Joyful's Girl by White Prince (USA) Mrs C Wilson
1996 3(14),F(-),2(12),2(15)

105 8/2 Great Treth' (R) MDO 3m 15 GS *(fav) pllng, ld 3rd-15th & 3 out, lkd wnr nxt, kpt on, hdd nr fin* 2 17
368 2/3 Garnons (L) MDO 2 1/2m 13 GS *(fav) ld til jnd 2 out, switchd rght & no ext flat* 2 15
526 15/3 Cothelstone (L) MDN 3m 15 GS *(fav) keen hld, hld up in tch, ld 3 out, drew clr* 1 16
736 29/3 Higher Kilw' (L) RES 3m 10 GF *(fav) 3s-6/4, cls up, ld 15th, drew clr 2 out, ran on strngly* 1 20
1044 12/4 Cothelstone (L) XX 3m 2 GF *(fav) made all, lft solo 14th* 1 0
1235 26/4 Brampton Br' (R) INT 3m 10 G *(fav) prog to cls 3rd 13th,chsd ldr 15th, ld 3 out,kpt on und pres* 1 19

Much improved; well placed & yet to meet good horses; good stable; can progress further;G/F-G/S. 21

PASTORAL PRIDE(USA) b.g. 13 Exceller (USA) - Pastoral Miss by Northfields (USA) M R Scott
1996 **5(17),F(-),3(21),7(15)**

90 5/2 Ludlow (R) HC 2 1/2m 6 G *ld, clr 4th, p.u. after 8th, broke blood vessel.* P 0
781 31/3 Hereford (R) HC 2m 3f 9 GF *ld to 7th, lost pl quickly 9th, bhnd when p.u. before next.* P 0

Formerly decent but very fragile; probably finished now. 16

PAT ALASKA b.g. 14 Ovac (ITY) - Indicate by Mustang Miss C Wates
1996 2(11),U(-),P(0),**4(16),P(0)**

301 1/3 Parham (R) MEM 3m 3 G *(fav) ld to 3 out, onepcd* 2 0

Members winner 95; beaten in bad renewal 97; surely too old now. 11

PAT CULLEN b.g. 12 The Parson - Duhallow Hazel — D C White

1996 3(12),3(15),**5(12)**

362	2/3	Garnons	(L)	OPE	3m	11	GS	*in tch til outpcd 11th, styd on to tk 3rd flat*	3	14

Confined winner 95; lightly raced & declining now; likes Ilanvapley but hard to find another win. 15

PATEY COURT gr.m. 6 Grey Desire - Mrs Meyrick by Owen Dudley — D Gill

1996 P(0),P(0),P(0),P(0)

357	2/3	Great Stain'	(L)	MDO	3m	15	S	*rear, prog 10th, wknd 4 out, t.o. & p.u. 2 out*	P	0
427	8/3	Charm Park	(L)	MDO	3m	10	GF	*prom, ev ch 4 out, fddng whn mstks last 2*	3	0
621	22/3	Hutton Rudby	(L)	MDO	3m	10	GF	*(fav) mid-div, lost tch 4 out, p.u. nxt*	P	0
860	31/3	Charm Park	(L)	MDO	3m	12	F	*(bl) ld to 10th, 2nd whn f 12th*	F	-
1073	13/4	Whitwell-On'	(R)	MDO	2 1/2m 88yds	17	G	*(bl) mid-div, rdn 6th, prog 8th, ld 11th, kpt on wll flat*	1	15
1101	19/4	Hornby Cast'	(L)	RES	3m	14	G	*(bl) mid-div, rddn 6th, lost tch 11th, t.o. whn p.u. 4 out*	P	0
1406	5/5	Witton Cast'	(R)	RES	3m	10	GS	*j.s.1st,mid-div,rear 6th,sn strgglng,wll bhnd whn p.u. 13th*	P	0

Won poor short Maiden; blinkers look essential; stamina very doubtful; needs much more. 14

PATS BOREEN (Irish) — I 118^{F}

PATS CROSS(IRE) b.g. 8 Abednego - No Hunting by No Time — James Byrne

1996 **2(NH)**,**7(NH)**

78	2/2	Market Rase'	(L)	RES	3m	8	GF	*lft in ld 3rd, made rest, lft clr 3 out, styd on*	1	17
267	22/2	Duncombe Pa'	(R)	OPE	3m	8	G	*chsd clr ldr til ld 14th, 3l ld whn u.r. 3 out*	U	-
354	2/3	Great Stain'	(L)	OPE	3m	7	S	*ld to 3rd, ld agn 8th til crshd thro wing & u.r. 12th*	U	-
423	8/3	Charm Park	(L)	OPE	3m	7	GF	*keen hold, ld just ahd & gng best whn u.r. last*	U	23
855	31/3	Charm Park	(L)	MEM	3m	3	F	*(fav) ld to 15th, disp nxt, hdd, ld 2 out, hld on*	1	16
1072	13/4	Whitwell-On'	(R)	MXO	4m	21	G	*ldng grp til wknd frm 18th, t.o.*	11	0

Irish Maiden winner 96; novice ridden; should have won 4; could prove decent in right hands; Any. 21

PATS FAREWELL (Irish) — I 36^{F}, I 59^{P}, I 122^{F}, I 253^{1}

PATTER MERCHANT ch.g. 8 Import - El Chaperall by Scottish Rifle — P B Hall

1996 **6(NH)**,**r(NH)**

411	8/3	Dalston	(R)	CON	3m	16	GS	*reluc to race, wll bhnd til p.u. 14th*	P	0
559	16/3	Lanark	(R)	MEM	3m	3	GS	*not fluent, made most to 11th, lost tch & p.u. aft 14th*	P	0

Not yet of any account 0

PAULS POINT (Irish) — I 119^{2}, I 253^{P}, I 330^{2}, I 464^{1}, I 581^{S}

PAY THE PIPER (Irish) — I 514^{P}

PAY-U-CASH b.g. 11 Winden - Abbots Delight by Welsh Abbot — W T D Perkins

1996 7(13)

187	15/2	Erw Lon	(L)	OPE	3m	16	G	*alwys bhnd, t.o. whn ran out 11th*	r	-
294	1/3	Didmarton	(L)	INT	3m	20	G	*alwys rear, t.o.*	9	0
535	16/3	Erw Lon	(L)	CON	3m	12	GF	*in rear, mstk 10th, no dang aft*	7	0
636	22/3	Howick	(L)	CON	3m	12	GF	*alwys rear, fin own time*	7	0
846	31/3	Lydstep	(L)	INT	3m	4	F	*(bl) prom to 7th, sn strgglng*	4	0
1005	12/4	St Hilary	(R)	CON	3m	10	GF	*alwys last pair*	7	0
1134	19/4	Bonvilston	(R)	MXO	4m	10	G	*cls up, wknd 16th, ran on onepce*	5	0
1366	5/5	Pantyderi	(L)	INT	3m	6	G	*ld til aft 2nd, sn lost plc, no dang*	3	0
1582	26/5	Lifton	(R)	INT	3m	10	G	*lost tch 6 out, t.o. & p.u. 2 out*	P	0

Dual winner 95; very moderate & only beat 2 horses in 97; need a miracle to win again. 10

PEAFIELD (Irish) — I 323^{P}, I 382^{6}, I 475^{4}, I 562^{5}, I 614^{2}

PEAJADE b.g. 13 Buckskin (FR) - Kaminaki by Deep Run — Mrs Pauline Vernon

1996 1(21),**2(25)**,1(23),2(22),**2(24)**,1(24),**3(24)**

67	1/2	Wetherby	(L)	HC	3m 1f	10	G	*soon bhnd.*	6	18
379	4/3	Leicester	(R)	HC	3m	7	G	*ld to 10th, led apr 2 out, hdd run-in, styd on und pres.*	2	21
680	29/3	Towcester	(R)	HC	3m 1f	8	GF	*chsd ldrs, ld 7th to 9th, led 11th to apr 2 out, styd on same pace.*	3	20
1078	13/4	Guilsborough	(L)	LAD	3m	11	GF	*cls up, chsd wnr 10-12th, 2nd agn 3 out, styd on wll,nvr nrr*	2	22
1249	26/4	Easingwold	(L)	LAD	3m	6	GS	*(Jt fav) cls up, ld 4 out, hdd, no ext run in*	3	19
1413	7/5	Uttoxeter	(L)	HC	4 1/4m	7	GS	*mstks 7th and 8th, struggling after, t.o. and p.u. before 19th.*	P	0

Good Ladies horse; stays very well; declining now; stamina test offers best hope; soft best. 21

PEANUTS PET b.g. 12 Tina's Pet - Sinzinbra by Royal Palace — J W Walmsley

1996 2(25),2(22),10(12),2(23),2(20),1(25),2(25)

9	25/1	Cottenham	(R)	OPE	3m	3	GF	*chsd ldr, mstk 5th, ld 14th til apr last, onepcd*	2	24
119	9/2	Wetherby Po'	(L)	OPE	3m	15	GF	*wth ldng grp, 2nd 11th, ld apr last, ran on strngly*	1	28
267	22/2	Duncombe Pa'	(R)	OPE	3m	8	G	*(fav) hld up,gd prog 4 out,lft in 2nd 3 out,chal flat,not qckn*	2	26
423	8/3	Charm Park	(L)	OPE	3m	7	GF	*prom, wnt 2nd 10th, prssng ldr & rddn whn lft clr last*	1	23
507	15/3	Dalton Park	(R)	OPE	3m	8	GF	*(fav) hld up mid-div, prssd ldr 11th, ld 16th, qcknd clr, easily*	1	25
1071	13/4	Whitwell-On'	(R)	CON	3m	10	G	*(fav) prom, disp 13th, ld nxt, prssd last, hld on wll nr fin*	1	22
1147	19/4	Chaddesley '	(L)	OPE	3m	7	GF	*w.w. effrt 14th, chsd ldrs, 4 out, kpt on onepcd*	3	20

1248 26/4 Easingwold (L) OPE 3m 8 GS *(fav) trcks ldr, error 13th, drvn out flat, styd on wll* 1 22
1347 3/5 Gisburn (R) OPE 3m 8 GF *(fav) alwys cls up, 2nd 12th, ev ch & rdn apr last, not qckn* 2 23

Decent pointer; won 6 placed 9 last 15; stays; win more at 13; G/F-S. 23

PEARL DANTE (Irish) — **I** 75[5], **I** 168[P], **I** 257[B], **I** 323[1], **I** 480[6], **I** 535[4], **I** 567[2]

PEAT POTHEEN b.g. 7 Derring Rose - Sally Potheen P J Sheppard
1996 U(-),4(0),P(0)

184 15/2 Erw Lon (L) MDN 3m 14 G *u.r. 1st* U -
366 2/3 Garnons (L) MDO 2 1/2m 13 GS *prog 9th, wknd aft 11th, no ch whn s.u. apr 3 out* S -
409 8/3 Llanfrynach (R) MDN 3m 12 G *mid-div, prog 15th, disp 2 out, ev ch, just faild* 2 13

Improving; winners behind when just pipped; finished early; go one better if fit in 98. 14

PEDE GALE (Irish) — **I** 97[P]

PEELINICK b.g. 7 Meadowbrook - Jed Again by Cagirama Mrs R L Elliot
1996 S(-),5(0)

135 9/2 Alnwick (L) MDO 3m 12 G *mstks, ld 11th-2 out, ev ch whn blnd last, no ext* 3 0
233 22/2 Friars Haugh (L) MDO 3m 13 G *(fav) alwys handy, no ext frm 3 out* 4 12
341 1/3 Corbridge (R) MDN 3m 10 G *disp til u.r. 4th* U -
416 8/3 Dalston (R) RES 3m 12 GS *chsd ldrs, 5th whn u.r. 12th* U -
614 22/3 Friars Haugh (L) MDN 3m 13 GF *hld up,hdwy 9th,ld 5 out,in cmmnd whn lft virt solo last* 1 16
729 29/3 Alnwick (L) RES 3m 10 F *(Jt fav) alwys prom, went 2nd 13th,ld 4 out,jnd 2 out,hdd last,no ext* 2 18

Improving with better jumping; beat subsequent winner; has scope & capable of upgrading. 17

PEGGYS LEG (Irish) — **I** 19[P], **I** 263[F], **I** 338,

PEJAWI br.m. 10 Strong Gale - Beau St by Will Somers Miss J Winch
1996 4(18),r(-),P(0),2(10),U(-),2(14),7(0),5(14)

18 25/1 Badbury Rin' (L) LAD 3m 9 GF *jmpd lft & sn bhnd,efft 10th,sn btn,poor 4th whn u.r.2 out* U -
219 16/2 Heythrop (R) LAD 3m 16 G *alwys rear, wll bhnd & no ch frm 12th* 6 12
394 8/3 Barbury Cas' (L) LAD 3m 5 G *last frm 3rd, t.o. 9th, u.r. 13th* U -
869 31/3 Hackwood Pa' (L) XX 3m 6 F *hld up, smooth prog to jn ldrs 2 out, styd on wll frm last* 1 17
1056 13/4 Hackwood Pa' (L) LAD 3m 3 GF *went 2nd at 11th, no ch wth wnr* 2 19
1274 27/4 Little Wind' (R) XX 3m 8 GF *plld into ld 8-9th, steadied, effrt to chs wnr 3 out, no imp* 2 15
1464 11/5 Tweseldown (R) XX 3m 7 GF *j.w. ld 9th, mstk 12th, rdn out flat* 1 17
1563 25/5 Kingston Bl' (L) MEM 3m 5 GF *j.w. made all, ran on wll frm 2 out* 1 19

Schoolmaster; conistent; only modest & finds soft races; well ridden 97; may find another opening. 18

PEJAYS DUCA (Irish) — **I** 47[P], **I** 158[F], **I** 297[P]

PENBOLA(IRE) b.g. 5 Pennine Walk - Sciambola by Great Nephew Horace Nicholls
1996 **6(NH)**,**12(NH)**,**7(NH)**

81 2/2 Wolverhampt' (L) MDN 3m 13 GS *prom, ld 10th-16th, wknd, no ch whn mstk 2 out* 4 0
666 23/3 Eaton Hall (R) MDO 3m 10 GF *mid to rear, losng tch whn p.u. 3 out* P 0

Poor novice hurdler; showed some hope on debut; but stamina doubts & more needed. 11

PENDIL'S DELIGHT b.m. 8 Scorpio (FR) - Pendella by Pendragon N F Williams
1996 3(12),1(14),1(19),1(20),**P(NH)**

255 22/2 Newtown (L) CON 3m 14 G *rear, 9th & no ch at 13th, ran on 15th, nrst fin* 4 18

Won 3 96; changed hands; ran well enough but vanished after; Confined chances if fit 98; G-S. 21

PENGUIN br.m. 6 Arctic Lord - Seal Marine by Harwell H Messer-Bennetts
1996 **12(NH)**,**9(NH)**

105 8/2 Great Treth' (R) MDO 3m 15 GS *in tch, mstk 9th, 6th at 12th, btn 14th, p.u. 3 out* P 0
458 8/3 Great Treth' (R) MDO 3m 15 S *hmp 3rd, ld 12th, clr aft 3 out, unchal, imp* 1 17
736 29/3 Higher Kilw' (L) RES 3m 10 GF *prom, hng rght thrght, hit 11th, ran out 13th* r -
1108 19/4 Flete Park (R) RES 3m 14 GF *(fav) ld 7th til ran wd & lost plc bnd aft 3 out,rallied flat* 2 18
1395 5/5 High Bickin' (R) RES 3m 9 G *(fav) hld up, prog 11th, mstks 13th & nxt, 5th whn u.r. 2 out* U -

WON fair Maiden(good time); tricky & R/H looks essential; good enough for Restricted; G/F-S. 17

PENLEA LADY b.m. 10 Leading Man - Pen Quill by Pendragon Mrs S G Addinsell

496 15/3 Hereford (R) HC 3m 1f 110yds 10 GF *in tch, mstk 10th, bumped and nearly u.r. 12th, styd on to chase ldr 15th, shaken up and qcknd to ld cl home.* 1 22

Won 2 novice chases 94; absent until winning modest H/chase; not seen again; hard to place now. 24

PENLET b.g. 9 Kinglet - Pensun by Jimsun R G Weaving
1996 1(25),2(16),1(23),3(21),2(23),2(22)

216 16/2 Southwell P' (L) OPE 3m 12 GS *prom to 2nd, rdn 11th, prog 13th, chsd ldrs 3 out, no imp* 4 17
380 4/3 Leicester (R) HC 3m 9 G *(Jt fav) held up, mstk 6th, hdwy 10th, rdn and btn when pkd 3 out.* 5 10
447 8/3 Newton Brom' (R) OPE 3m 6 G *hld up last, prog to cls 4th at 14th, ld nxt-2 out, no ext* 2 22
771 29/3 Dingley (R) OPE 3m 10 G *(fav) mostly 6th, rdn frm 10th, ran on 6 out, not rch 1st trio* 4 16

987	12/4 Kingston Bl'	(L) OPE 3m	4 GF	*(fav) chsd wnr 11th,ev ch 15th,rdn whn slppd bnd aft 3out,sn btn*	2	17
1478	11/5 Garthorpe	(R) OPE 3m	2 GS	*ld to 11th, ev ch 3 out, unable qckn aft*	2	18
1534	18/5 Mollington	(R) OPE 3m	7 GS	*last, lost tch 10th, t.o. 13th, p.u. 2 out*	P	0

Won 5 in 95/96; out of sorts & disappointing 97; stays; best watched initially in 98;G/F-S. 18

PENLLYNE'S PRIDE ch.g. 16 Tachypous - Fodens Eve by Dike (USA) J S Chilton

1996 P(0),P(0),U(-),U(-),3(14),U(-),6(0)

1062	13/4 Maisemore P'	(L) MXO 3m	12 GF	*chsd ldrs to 6th, sn lost plc, p.u. 10th*	P	0
1178	20/4 Sandon	(L) XX 3m	6 GF	*chsd ldr clr of rest to 10th, sn strgglng*	3	0
1233	26/4 Brampton Br'	(R) CON 3m	8 G	*in tch til wknd 11th, crwld nxt & p.u.*	P	0
1325	3/5 Chaddesley '	(L) MEM 3m	1 GF	*walked over*	1	0
1381	5/5 Eyton-On-Se'	(L) MEM 3m	5 GF	*(bl) ld to 2nd, cls up in tch 10th,sn outpcd,t.o. 12th,btn fence*	3	0
1538	18/5 Wolverhampt'	(L) CON 3m	8 GS	*ref to race*	0	0
1576	26/5 Chaddesley '	(L) XX 3m	12 F	*(vis) s.s. sn prom, wknd 10th, t.o. 12th*	5	0
1607	1/6 Dingley	(R) OPE 3m	9 GF	*(vis) ld 2nd-3rd, wknd 9th, cont mls t.o.*	5	0

Well past it now. 0

PENLY b.g. 7 Netherkelly - Pensun by Jimsun R G Weaving

1996 1(10),7(0),P(0),P(0)

877	1/4 Upton-On-Se'	(R) RES 3m	17 GF	*prom, blnd 8th, sn strgglng, wll bhnd & p.u. 15th*	P	0
986	12/4 Kingston Bl'	(L) CON 3m	10 GF	*mstks, trckd ldrs til 4th & outpcd aft 13th, t.o.*	5	0
1164	20/4 Mollington	(R) RES 3m	10 GF	*bhnd frm 8th, brf efft 13th, sn wknd, p.u. last*	P	0
1404	5/5 Ashorne	(R) MEM 3m	7 G	*chsd ldrs, lft 2nd 13th,ev ch 15th,wknd,rdr lost irons*	2	0
1533	18/5 Mollington	(R) XX 3m	8 GS	*prom to 11th, sn wknd, 6th & t.o. whn u.r. 2 out*	U	-

Won bad Maiden (lucky) 96; does not stay & struggling now upgraded; prospects are virtually nil. 0

PENNINE VIEW ch.g. 10 Slim Jim - Salvia by Salvo J J Dixon

1996 7(0),4(14),1(15),3(14),1(17),2(19),**P(0)**

410	8/3 Dalston	(R) MEM 3m	5 GS	*(fav) w.w. prog 15th,jnd wnr 2 out,ev ch & veerd lft flat,nt qckn*	2	16
584	17/3 Newcastle	(L) HC 2 1/2m	11 GF	*cl up, disp ld 4 out, ch 2 out, kept on same pace.*	3	18
763	29/3 Whittington	(L) CON 3m	9 S	*(fav) chsd ldr, ld 7th, lft wll clr 15th, eased flat*	1	18
972	7/4 Kelso	(L) HC 3m 1f	12 GF	*chsd ldr, ld 7th, rdn 2 out, hdd and hit last. wknd run-in.*	3	20

Dual winner 96; stays; suspect in a finish; has good jockeys; can win again; Any. 20

PENNY BRIDE (Irish) — **I** 131^{F}

PENNY BUG (Irish) — **I** 60^{P}, **I** 339, , **I** 499^{P}, **I** 561^{P}

PEN-SHILMON b.h. 5 Shaab - Cornish Mona Lisa by Damsire Unregistered P Mann

239	22/2 Lemalla	(R) OPE 3m	7 S	*blnd 1st, jmpd novicey til p.u. 8th*	P	0
455	8/3 Great Treth'	(R) OPE 3m	8 S	*lost grnd frm 12th, last whn p.u. apr 15th*	P	0
531	15/3 Wadebridge	(L) MDO 3m	14 GF	*prom early, grad lost tch, bhnd & p.u. last*	P	0
626	22/3 Kilworthy	(L) MDN 3m	14 G	*lost tch frm 13th, t.o.*	6	0

Yet to beat another horse & much more needed. 0

PENSTAL LADY (Irish) — **I** 166^{1}, **I** 215, , **I** 299^{P}, **I** 495^{2}

PENYLAN GOLD ch.m. 7 Broadsword (USA) - Barlady by Bargello Mrs D J Hughes

406	8/3 Llanfrynach	(R) RES 3m	13 G	*unruly pddck, rear, p.u. 2nd*	P	0
1004	12/4 St Hilary	(R) MEM 3m	4 GF	*(bl) 4th til f 10th*	F	-
1137	19/4 Bonvilston	(R) MDO 3m	13 G	*rear, p.u. 14th*	P	0
1323	3/5 Bonvilston	(R) MDO 3m	14 G	*(bl) prom to 7th, wknd rpdly, p.u. 11th*	P	0

Placed N/H flat 95; signs not good & most unpromising. 0

PEPSA MORFEE (Irish) — **I** 96^{P}, **I** 178^{1}, **I** 252^{6}

PERAMBULATE(NZ) br.g. 5 Oregon (USA) - French Flavour (NZ) by Zamazaan (FR) D H Barons

243	22/2 Lemalla	(R) MDO 3m	12 S	*not alwys fluent, prog 11th, lft 2nd 16th, ld 2 out, sn clr*	1	15
453	8/3 Great Treth'	(R) CON 3m	13 S	*(6s-3s), ld 14th til blndrd bdly 2 out, ld agn last, gamely*	1	20

Very promising youngster; stays & battles; could jump better; good stable; one to watch; Soft so far 22

PERCUSIONIST (Irish) — **I** 56^{P}, **I** 99^{F}, **I** 154^{P}, **I** 231^{P}, **I** 281, , **I** 351^{3}, **I** 548^{P}

PERCY PIT b.g. 8 Pitpan - Technical Merit by Gala Performance (USA) Mrs D McCormack

1996 **5(NH),8(NH),F(NH),5(NH),6(NH),F(NH),R(NH),P(NH),12(NH)**

479	9/3 Southwell P'	(L) MDO 3m	15 G	*ld, hit 1st, sn wll clr, wknd & hdd apr 12th, p.u. 3 out*	P	0
1514	17/5 Corbridge	(R) MDO 3m	17 GS	*plld hrd, ld & sn clr, wknd rpdly & hdd 9th, p.u. nxt*	P	0
1546	24/5 Hexham	(L) HC 2 1/2m 110yds	10 GF	*ld to 8th, p.u. before 10th.*	P	0

A tearaway; changed hands after 1st run; no prospects. 0

PERCY SPECIAL(IRE) b.g. 7 Royal Fountain - Vickies Rambler by Wrekin Rambler Craig Wanless

418	8/3 Dalston	(R) MDO 2 1/2m	10 GS	*last & t.o. til ran out 4th*	r	-
623	22/3 Hutton Rudby	(L) MDO 3m	9 GF	*alwys prom, wknd 3 out, t.o.*	4	0

730 29/3 Alnwick (L) MDO 2 1/2m 9 F *nvr nr ldrs, remote 4th frm 10th til p.u. 3 out* P 0

Well beaten when completing; looks capable of better. 0

PERFECT LIGHT b.g. 8 Salmon Leap (USA) - Sheer Gold by Yankee Gold R Lee

1996 **4(NH)**

77 2/2 Market Rase' (L) RES 3m 9 GF *(fav) jmpd rght, made all, sn clr, hit last, unchal* 1 19
254 22/2 Newtown (L) MEM 3m 6 G *(fav) pllng, jmpd rght, made all & sn clr, unchal* 1 20
333 1/3 Eaton Hall (R) INT 3m 10 GS *(fav) ld, fast pace, 8l up whn f 10th* F -

Placed in good novice chase; lightly raced; novice ridden; headstrong; can win again if fit 98. 20

PERFECT STRANGER b.g. 13 Wolver Hollow - Mrs Walmsley by Lorenzaccio T A J McCoy

1996 4(0),2(20),5(0),5(14)

551 16/3 Ottery St M' (L) MEM 3m 4 G *chsd wnr, chal 4 out-nxt, no imp aft* 2 15
627 22/3 Kilworthy (L) LAD 3m 7 G *wll in tch, disp 13-14th, onepcd frm 3 out* 3 22
1482 11/5 Ottery St M' (L) LAD 3m 5 G *hld up, prog 12th, nvr on trms frm 4 out* 4 15

Winning hurdler/chaser; retains ability but hard to find a win at 14; worth another try in Members. 17

PERHAPS(USA) b or br.m. 6 Lord Avie (USA) - Allegedly Flashing (USA) by Alleged (USA) Mrs P Tollit

1996 **3(NH),1(NH),2(NH),5(NH),4(NH)**

201 15/2 Weston Park (L) OPE 3m 16 G *mid-div, some late prog, nrst fin* 4 14
1265 27/4 Southwell P' (L) OPE 3m 8 G *mid-div, prog to 2nd at 9th, lft in ld 2 out, styd on* 1 22

Winning hurdler/chaser; interrupted season; fortunate in weak Open; young but hard to place now. 22

PERKY LAD (Irish) — **I** 76[1]

PERKYS PLONKER (Irish) — **I** 218,

PERMIT b.m. 9 Leander - Perversity by French Beige D H Bennett

653 22/3 Siddington (L) RES 3m 10 F *crawld fences, t.o. til p.u. 6th* P 0
1067 13/4 Maisemore P' (L) MDO 3m 8 GF *jmpd slwly, ld to 4th, lost plc 10th, last whn f nxt* F -
1216 26/4 Woodford (L) MDN 3m 13 G *prom to 3rd, sn lost plc, t.o. last at 11th, p.u. nxt* P 0
1437 10/5 Holnicote (L) MDO 3m 14 G *6th hlfwy, bhnd 13th til p.u. 16th* P 0

No signs of ability. 0

PERRIPAGE ch.g. 6 Nearly A Hand - Perrimay by Levanter R N Miller

643 22/3 Castle Of C' (R) MDO 3m 12 G *rear & jmpd slwly 4th, last whn blnd 7th, p.u. nxt* P 0
692 29/3 Little Wind' (R) MDO 3m 8 GF *prom, mstk 10th, sn wknd, p.u. aft 14th* P 0
1437 10/5 Holnicote (L) MDO 3m 14 G *prom til lost plc 11th, bhnd whn p.u. 16th* P 0

Only learning so far; can do better. 0

PERRYLINE b.m. 8 Capricorn Line - Perryville by New Brig R Fellows

1996 P(0),1(15),F(-),U(-)

260 22/2 Newtown (L) RES 3m 16 G *hld up, prog 9th, ld 2 out, all out* 1 19
360 2/3 Garnons (L) CON 3m 10 GS *prom, ev ch til wknd 15th, p.u. 3 out* P 0
704 29/3 Upper Sapey (R) INT 3m 4 GF *efft frm 15th, strng run to hold ev ch 2 out, wknd run in* 3 18
1062 13/4 Maisemore P' (L) MXO 3m 12 GF *hld up, some prog to poor 7th at 9th, nvr on trms, p.u.2 out* P 0
1390 5/5 Cursneh Hill (L) INT 3m 4 GF *prog frm rear 11th, ld 15th, slw jmp nxt, sn bttn* 3 15

Maiden winner 96; won competitive race; ran poorly after(ground?); stamina doubts; below Confineds. 16

PERSEVERANCE b.g. 11 Pardigras - Perplexity by Pony Express D H Bennett

1996 4(11),3(12),1(17),P(0),4(17)

1212 26/4 Woodford (L) INT 3m 8 G *chsd ldr 4th, ld apr 7th-apr 4 out, sn wknd* 5 0
1438 10/5 Holnicote (L) LAD 3m 7 G *4th whn stirrup iron broke & u.r. 12th* U -

Restricted winner; 96; brief 97; slow & hard to find another win. 15

PERSIAN (Irish) — **I** 73[P]

PERSIAN LIFE (Irish) — **I** 417[F], **I** 468[1], **I** 521[1], **I** 577[2]

PERSIAN LION br.g. 8 Reesh - Parijoun by Manado A Jackson

1996 **8(NH)**

120 9/2 Wetherby Po' (L) MDO 3m 18 GF *rear, sn dtchd, wll bhnd whn p.u. 14th* P 0
429 8/3 Charm Park (L) MDO 3m 14 GF *ld til f 10th* F -
620 22/3 Hutton Rudby (L) MDO 3m 10 GF *ld, disp 5th til hdd 13th, 3rd & fddng whn f 15th* F -
693 29/3 Stainton (R) MEM 3m 3 F *keen, ld til hdd 4th, ld 8th-16th, sn outpcd* 2 0
898 5/4 Wetherby Po' (L) MDO 3m 7 F *(fav) made all, drew clr 3 out, unchal* 1 14
1069 13/4 Whitwell-On' (R) RES 3m 12 G *trckd ldr, wknd rpdly 14th, t.o. & p.u. 3 out* P 0
1250 26/4 Easingwold (L) RES 3m 15 GS *prom early, fdd 12th, onepcd aft* 6 0
1406 5/5 Witton Cast' (R) RES 3m 10 GS *ld, disp 4th to nxt, chsd ldr til fdd 11th,t.o. & p.u. 4 out* P 0
1421 10/5 Easingwold (L) RES 3m 8 GF *disp to 3rd, chsd ldr aft, wknd 13th, t.o. 3 out* 4 0
1510 17/5 Corbridge (R) RES 3m 13 GS *prom til fdd 14th, t.o.* 6 0

Plodded home in slow Maiden; stamina suspect & struggling now upgraded; Members best hope. 13

PERSIAN MOSS (Irish) — **I** 295, , **I** 428^{2}, **I** 514^{2}

PERSIAN PACKER (Irish) — **I** 260^{2}, **I** 378^{1}, **I** 486^{4}

PETER POINTER br.g. 9 Relkino - Housemistress by New Member — A J Williams

1996 **P(NH),9(NH)**

361	2/3	Garnons	(L)	LAD	3m	7	GS	*ld 2nd, sn clr, just ld 15th, sn hdd & wknd, p.u. flat*	P	0
573	16/3	Garnons	(L)	LAD	3m	8	G	*ld 2nd, set fast pace til ct 10th, wknd & p.u. 3 out*	P	0
1460	11/5	Maisemore P'	(L)	MDO	3m	16	G	*ld to 9th, ld 14th-nxt, wknd 3 out*	5	0

Shows plenty of speed but 3 miles too far; surely worth a try in a short Maiden. 11

PETE'S SAKE b.g. 12 Scorpio (FR) - Pete's Money (USA) by Caucasus (USA) — Mrs Michael Ennever

1996 6(11),2(13),1(20),1(20)

484	9/3	Tweseldown	(R)	OPE	3m	10	G	*prom, ld 10-14th, sn outpcd, kpt on*	2	20
1203	26/4	Worcester	(L)	HC	2m 7f 110yds	10	S	*hit 6th, alwys bhnd, t.o. when p.u. before 13th.*	P	0
1564	25/5	Kingston Bl'	(L)	CON	3m	7	GF	*hld up, prog to chs wnr 10th, ev ch 3 out, rdn & no ext nxt*	2	19

Won 4 of last 9 95/97; lightly raced; well placed; can find another local race; G-F. 19

PETIT PRIMITIVE b.m. 6 Primitive Rising (USA) - Highmoor Scallyann by Scallywag — Mrs K Ratcliffe

346	2/3	Market Rase'	(L)	MDO	3m	10	GF	*rear, lft 5th at 6th, prog to 3rd 14th, nvr dang*	3	0
427	8/3	Charm Park	(L)	MDO	3m	10	GF	*mid-div, prog 9th, ld 4 out, sn wll clr*	1	13
766	29/3	Whittington	(L)	INT	3m	10	S	*mstk 1st, mid-div whn f 6th*	F	-
887	1/4	Flagg Moor	(L)	XX	3m	8	G	*hld up, 6th whn f 6th*	F	-

Romped home in a weak race (slow time); neds to improve for Restricted. 14

PHAEDAIR b.g. 7 Strong Gale - Festive Season by Silly Season — Mrs O Hubbard

1996 **5(NH),U(NH),P(NH),3(NH)**

284	23/2	Charing	(L)	MDO	3m	17	G	*prom til f 10th*	F	-
582	16/3	Detling	(L)	MDN	3m	16	F	*trckd ldrs, ld & mstk 4 out, drew clr apr last*	1	15
1443	10/5	Peper Harow	(L)	RES	3m	3	GF	*(Jt fav) u.r. going to strt, ld til stmbld & u.r. 14th*	U	-

Poor novice chaser; front runner; can win a modest Restricted; do better with stronger handling; G-F .. 15

PHARAOH BLUE ch.g. 13 Blue Cashmere - Phaedima by Darius — M Shears

455	8/3	Great Treth'	(R)	OPE	3m	8	S	*lost tch 9th, bhnd whn p.u. apr 15th*	P	0
554	16/3	Ottery St M'	(L)	CON	3m	7	G	*(bl) in tch to 7th, t.o. 13th*	4	0
791	31/3	Bishopsleigh	(R)	CON	3m	6	G	*alwys bhnd, t.o. & p.u. 15th*	P	0
951	6/4	Black Fores'	(R)	CON	3m	3	G	*in tch, disp 7th, 2nd aft, dmtd apr last*	3	10
1109	19/4	Flete Park	(R)	OPE	4m	9	GF	*5th whn mstk 13th, t.o. 17th til u.r. 2 out*	U	-
1254	27/4	Black Fores'	(R)	MEM	3m	2	F	*(fav) (bl) made all, alwys in cmmnd*	1	10

Won 2 joke races 95 7 97; missed 96; ungenuine & no hope in proper races. 11

PHARAVO (Irish) — **I** 32^{3}, **I** 163^{P}, **I** 197^{1}, **I** 240^{2}, **I** 299^{2}

PHARBROOK LAD (Irish) — **I** 117^{P}, **I** 210^{1}, **I** 361^{4}

PHARCEBOS (Irish) — **I** 453^{P}, **I** 547^{P}

PHAR DESERT (Irish) — **I** 43^{4}, **I** 73, , **I** 262^{5}, **I** 324^{P}

PHARDING (Irish) — **I** 318^{P}, **I** 419^{3}

PHARDITU (Irish) — **I** 134^{4}, **I** 237^{2}, **I** 299^{3}, **I** 334^{3}

PHARLINDO(IRE) b.g. 6 Phardante (FR) - Linda Martin — Mrs J W Furness

1996 **10(NH),r(NH),5(NH),8(NH),10(NH),P(NH),8(NH),10(NH)**

114	9/2	Wetherby Po'	(L)	MDO	3m	8	GF	*trckd ldrs, disp 3rd, blnd & u.r. nxt*	U	-
269	22/2	Duncombe Pa'	(R)	MDO	3m	16	G	*keen, prom, ld 6th, qcknd clr last, comf*	1	15
509	15/3	Dalton Park	(R)	XX	3m	13	GF	*plld hrd, ld, ran wd apr 3rd, disp 10th-14th, f nxt*	F	-
695	29/3	Stainton	(R)	RES	3m	11	F	*held up early, prog 4th, ld 7th, clr 16th, pshd out flat*	1	19

Ex Irish; found his niche in points; headstrong & tricky ride; can progress; G-F. 19

PHARMACY TRIO (Irish) — **I** 110^{6}, **I** 547^{2}, **I** 590^{B}

PHARNISKEY (Irish) — **I** 247^{P}

PHARN N WIDE (Irish) — **I** 317^{P}, **I** 514^{F}, **I** 561,

PHARRAGO(IRE) ch.g. 8 Phardante (FR) - Garry Move On by Le Bavard (FR) — Miss E Saunders

1996 r(-),P(0),P(0),P(0),**8(0)**,2(0),U(-),P(0),1(13),P(0),P(0),2(0),**5(NH),2(NH),2(NH),2(NH),P(NH)**

7	19/1	Barbury Cas'	(L)	RES	3m	14	GF	*alwys bhnd, 11th hlfwy, t.o. & p.u. 14th*	P	0
149	10/2	Hereford	(R)	HC	3m 1f 110yds	18	GS	*bhnd when p.u. before 8th.*	P	0
240	22/2	Lemalla	(R)	RES	3m	11	S	*mstk 4th, rear, 8th hlfwy, bhnd & p.u. 15th*	P	0
406	8/3	Llanfrynach	(R)	RES	3m	13	G	*mid-div, p.u. 12th*	P	0
633	22/3	Howick	(L)	RES	3m	8	GF	*last pair til ran out 7th*	r	-

Won bad Maiden 96; placed H'cap chases summer 96(professionally trained); shows nothing now. 0

PHARTOOMANNY (Irish) — I 162^{P}, I 167^{1}, I 237^{F}, I 257^{F}, I 380^{6}

PHAR TOO TOUCHY ch.m. 10 Mister Lord (USA) - Bridgitte Browne by Mon Fetiche — Miss R A Francis

1996 U(-),1(18),1(23),1(23),1(26),1(22),2(21),1(24),1(25),1(27),1(28),1(20)

1	19/1	Barbury Cas'	(L)	XX	3m	11	GF	*(fav) prssd ldr, ld 9th, wll clr whn blnd & u.r. 3 out*	U	-
1203	26/4	Worcester	(L)	HC	2m 7f 110yds	10	S	*(fav) chsd ldr, ld 6th, made rest, clr from 10th, hit 12th and 2 out, unchal.*	1	29
1411	7/5	Chepstow	(L)	HC	3m	4	G	*(fav) made all, shaken up run-in, ran on well.*	1	28
1544	21/5	Newton Abbot	(L)	HC	3 1/4m 110yds	11	G	*(fav) hdwy to go prom 5th, ld 7th, hit next, mstk and hdd 16th, soon wknd, t.o., fin distressed.*	5	11
1588	30/5	Stratford	(L)	HC	3 1/2m	9	G	*prom, mstk 2nd, hit 13th, soon bhnd, p.u. before 16th.*	P	0

Won 10 points 96; useful; interrupted season; excuses last 2 starts; sure to win more; any. 30

PHARWAYS (Irish) — I 323^{P}, I 382^{3}, I 475^{3}

PHELIOFF ch.g. 13 Dubassoff (USA) - Darymoss by Ballymoss — Miss Sarah A Dawson

1996 1+(17),4(0),6(0),3(16),U(-),5(11),P(0)

219	16/2	Heythrop	(R)	LAD	3m	16	G	*cls up to 8th, wll bhnd frm 12th*	7	12
482	9/3	Tweseldown	(R)	LAD	3m	5	G	*chsd wnr, no ch frm 14th*	2	14
1197	23/4	Andoversford	(R)	LAD	3m	5	F	*chsd ldr, ld 5th-12th, sn lost plc, t.o. 16th*	4	0
1308	3/5	Cottenham	(R)	LAD	3m	5	F	*chsd wnr to 3rd, mstk 11th, sn lost tch*	4	11
1463	11/5	Tweseldown	(R)	MXO	3m	5	GF	*mostly cls 2nd to 11th, outpcd & sn btn, t.o. 4 out*	5	0
1606	1/6	Dingley	(R)	LAD	3m	13	GF	*rear whn hmpd & u.r. 6th*	U	-

Safe but declined; hard to find a win at 14; G-F. 12

PHILDANTE (Irish) — I 445^{1}, I 569,

PHILELWYN(IRE) br.m. 6 Strong Gale - Miss Kamsy by Kambalda — P E Griffiths

1996 P(0),P(0)

261	22/2	Newtown	(L)	MDN	3m	16	G	*mid-div til wknd & p.u. 10th*	P	0
365	2/3	Garnons	(L)	MDO	2 1/2m	14	GS	*alwys rear, lost tch 7th, t.o. & p.u. 3 out*	P	0
570	16/3	Garnons	(L)	MDN	2 1/2m	14	G	*nvr rchd ldrs, runnng on in 6th whn u.r. 12th*	U	-
1016	12/4	Bitterley	(L)	MDO	3m	14	GF	*ld 6th til hdd 3 out, kpt on onepcd*	3	10
1393	5/5	Cursneh Hill	(L)	MDO	3m	9	GF	*(Jt fav) ld frm 4th til wknd & jmp lft last, sn bttn*	2	14
1528	17/5	Bredwardine	(R)	MDO	3m	17	G	*(fav) w.w. prog to trck ldrs 13th, no imp 3 out, wknd & p.u. last*	P	0

Improved; stamina limited & easy 3 miles essential; should find a race. 13

PHOZA MOYA(IRE) b.g. 6 Lancastrian - Annes Grove by Raise You Ten — J N Llewellen Palmer

1996 P(0),R(-),P(0),6(0)

1513	17/5	Corbridge	(R)	MDO	3m	13	GS	*prom til wknd rpdly 12th, ref 14th*	R	-

Late to appear; showed speed but plenty to prove yet. 0

PHROSE b.g. 7 Pharly (FR) - Rose Chanelle by Welsh Pageant — A W Pickering

1996 4(0),3(15)

137	9/2	Thorpe Lodge	(L)	MEM	3m	9	GF	*prom, ev ch 5 out, not qckn aft*	5	0

Hurdles winner 95; lightly raced now; last on only start 7 not threatening to win; Soft. 16

PICK-N-CRUISE b.m. 5 Cruise Missile - Pickled Tink by Tickled Pink — Mrs C W Middleton

570	16/3	Garnons	(L)	MDN	2 1/2m	14	G	*alwys rear, no ch frm 10th, p.u. 3 out*	P	0

Learning on debut. 0

PICK'N HILL(IRE) b.g. 9 Kind Of Hush - Shagra by Sallust — A R Price

1996 4(0),5(10),U(-)

189	15/2	Erw Lon	(L)	RES	3m	14	G	*in tch in rear, mstk 11th, outpcd frm 14th*	7	0

Maiden winner 95; lightly raced & struggling since; Restricted unlikely. 12

PICTON (Irish) — I 114^{F}, I 176^{P}

PIERPOINTS CHOICE (Irish) — I 97^{P}, I 186^{4}, I 286, , I 312^{F}

PIGEON HILL BUCK (Irish) — I 412^{3}, I 440^{F}, I 579^{P}, I 593^{P}

PIGEONSTOWN (Irish) — I 280^{F}, I 352^{3}, I 490^{P}, I 527^{2}, I 589^{P}

PILGRIM'S MISSION(IRE) b.g. 7 Carlingford Castle - Hill Invader by Brave Invader (USA) — A G Masters

1996 **12(NH),8(NH),13(NH)**

242	22/2	Lemalla	(R)	MDO	3m	10	S	*5th hlfwy, lft 15l 2nd 16th, v tired whn blnd last*	2	0
453	8/3	Great Treth'	(R)	CON	3m	13	S	*alwys mid-div*	6	0
553	16/3	Ottery St M'	(L)	MDN	3m	15	G	*mid-div, prog 10th, in tch til wknd 3 out*	3	11
1112	19/4	Flete Park	(R)	MDN	3m	13	GF	*prog to disp 12th, ld apr 15th, clr whn f 3 out*	F	-
1486	11/5	Ottery St M'	(L)	MDO	3m	17	G	*mid-div, styd on frm 15th, not rch ldrs*	3	14
1520	17/5	Bratton Down	(L)	MDO	3m	17	GS	*(fav) handy, ld 14th, clr 3 out, hld on wll, all out*	1	15
1582	26/5	Lifton	(R)	INT	3m	10	G	*mstks 1st 4 fncs, mid-div aft,effrt 4 out,no ext frm 2 out*	5	13

Steady progress; beat large but weak field; stays; onepaced; needs more for Restricted; G/F-S. 15

PIMA (Irish) — **I** 167[2]

PIMPERNELS SPREAD (Irish) — **I** 529[P], **I** 594[P]

PINBALL ROCK (Irish) — **I** 570[P], **I** 601[P]

PINES EXPRESS(IRE) b.g. 7 Mister Lord (USA) - Autumn Spirit by Deep Run — Mrs Audrey Kley

1996 B(-),P(0),6(0),P(0),P(0),P(0)

7	19/1	Barbury Cas'	(L)	RES	3m	14	GF	*mid-div, 6th hlfwy, ran on strngly aft last, tk 2nd nr fin*	2	15
45	1/2	Larkhill	(R)	RES	3m	14	GF	*(fav) ld 3rd, made most aft, jnd 100 yrds out, hld on well*	1	19
236	22/2	Lemalla	(R)	INT	3m	12	S	*mid-div, strgglng 12th, rear whn p.u. 15th*	P	0

Maiden winner 95; changed yards; revived & won fair race; finished early; needs more for Confined. ... 18

PINEWOOD LAD b.g. 10 Caribo - Rose Of The West by Royal Buck — David Ford

1996 4(15),2(18),4(17),**7(0)**,4(14),6(13),P(0)

422	8/3	Charm Park	(L)	CON	3m	8	GF	*prom, ld 4th til ran v wd & p.u. 7th*	P	0
763	29/3	Whittington	(L)	CON	3m	9	S	*mid-div whn u.r. 3rd*	U	-
1071	13/4	Whitwell-On'	(R)	CON	3m	10	G	*rear, lost tch 9th, t.o. nxt*	6	0
1104	19/4	Hornby Cast'	(L)	MEM	3m	6	G	*disp, ld 6th til wknd qckly frm 4 out, t.o.*	4	0
1405	5/5	Witton Cast'	(R)	CON	3m	10	GS	*rear, detached whn u.r. 7th*	U	-

Irish chase winner 94; changed hands; novice ridden & showed nothing in 97. 12

PINGO SLOO (Irish) — **I** 32[U], **I** 66[P]

PINTAIL BAY b.g. 11 Buzzards Bay - Pin Hole by Parthia — J C Sweetland

1996 3(19),3(10),1(15)

171	15/2	Ottery St M'	(L)	OPE	3m	9	G	*(bl) in tch, 6th at 13th, wknd 15th, outpcd aft*	6	0
239	22/2	Lemalla	(R)	OPE	3m	7	S	*(vis) 6th but in tch 9th, outpcd 15th, nrst fin*	4	17
308	1/3	Clyst St Ma'	(L)	OPE	3m	7	HY	*(vis) w.w. 3rd at 13th, slw jmp 16th, kpt on und pres 3 out*	2	17
552	16/3	Ottery St M'	(L)	OPE	3m	6	G	*(vis) chsd ldrs, outpcd frm 4 out*	4	16
931	6/4	Charlton Ho'	(L)	OPE	3m	6	G	*(vis) w.w. in rear, prog 13th, disp 2nd 3 out, wknd aft nxt*	3	16
1153	20/4	Stafford Cr'	(R)	CON	3m	10	GF	*mid-div, went 3rd 12th, rdn 2 out, lost 3rd flat*	4	10

Won 1 placed 12 last 17 starts; easily beaten by good horses; frustrating & hard to find another win 17

PINTEX (Irish) — **I** 89[P], **I** 131[P], **I** 170[4], **I** 309[4]

PIN UP BOY b.g. 8 Afzal - Clever Pin by Pinza — Mrs P Tollit

1996 P(0),1(18),F(-),P(0)

200	15/2	Weston Park	(L)	CON	3m	16	G	*alwys chsng grp, no ch wth 1st pair frm 3 out*	3	18
572	16/3	Garnons	(L)	INT	3m	13	G	*cls 3rd whn u.r. 2nd*	U	-
763	29/3	Whittington	(L)	CON	3m	9	S	*ld to 7th, 10l 3rd & lkd btn whn f 14th*	F	-
1264	27/4	Southwell P'	(L)	INT	3m	9	G	*disp til ld 4th, disp 6-10th, fdd rpdly, p.u. 2 out*	P	0

Restricted winner 96; stays well; mistakes; need stamina test to win Inter/Confined; G-S. 18

PIO'R (Irish) — **I** 322[P]

PIPER O'DRUMMOND ch.g. 10 Ardross - Skelbrooke by Mummy's Pet — Mrs L Walby

1996 F(-),4(11),1(22),4(15)

336	1/3	Corbridge	(R)	LAD	3m 5f	9	G	*hld up rear, mstk 8th, prog 12th, chal last, not qckn*	2	21
583	17/3	Newcastle	(L)	HC	3m	8	GF	*in tch, effort before 3 out, kept on same pace from next.*	4	21

Ladies winner 96; lightly raced; unreliable; capable of winning again; Good. 20

PIXIE IN PURPLE(IRE) ch.g. 6 Executive Perk - Glint Of Baron by Glint Of Gold — D Stephens

1996 r(-),8(0),1(17)

241	22/2	Lemalla	(R)	RES	3m	11	S	*in tch, 5th whn f 14th*	F	-
1483	11/5	Ottery St M'	(L)	RES	3m	15	G	*hld up, cls 3rd at 10th, p.u. 12th, dsmntd*	P	0

Maiden winner 96; has ability but problems & not progress in 97; still young enough to revive. 16

PLAIN SAILING(FR) b.g. 7 Slip Anchor - Lassalia by Sallust — J Sluggett

1996 3(0),P(0)

98	8/2	Great Treth'	(R)	OPE	3m	14	GS	*went prom 10th, cls up til wknd 15th, walked in*	7	15

Selling hurdle winner 94; ran well in hot race but hardly ever runs; can only be watched. 15

PLAN-A(IRE) br.g. 7 Creative Plan (USA) - Faravaun Rose by Good Thyne (USA) — R W Edwards

1996 P(0),F(-),F(-),2(19),2(16),3(13)

45	1/2	Larkhill	(R)	RES	3m	14	GF	*in tch whn hmpd & u.r. 5th*	U	-
106	8/2	Milborne St'	(L)	RES	3m	12	GF	*(fav) mid-div, prog 10th, 3rd at 15th, ld 2 out, ran on well*	1	19
293	1/3	Didmarton	(L)	INT	3m	16	G	*prog 6th,ld 9th,hdd aft 2 out,rallied & ev ch whn r.o. last*	r	23
515	15/3	Larkhill	(R)	INT	3m	8	GF	*trckd ldrs,mstk 8th,strgglng 13th,no ch whn ref & u.r. 3 out*	R	-
691	29/3	Little Wind'	(R)	INT	3m	5	GF	*(bl) cls up,ld & ran off course aft 14th,cont,ran out & u.r.3 out*	r	-

Maiden winner 95; able but a nightmare ride; won novice chase after pointing. 20

PLANNING GAIN b.g. 6 Blakeney - Romantiki (USA) by Giboulee (CAN) — James Baxter

1996 **7(NH)**,**13(NH)**,**9(NH)**

386	7/3 Ayr	(L) HC	2m 5f 110yds	7	S	*started slowly, soon in tch, raced wd, n.j.w., lost touch after 14th, 4th and staying on when f 3 out.*	F	-
609	22/3 Friars Haugh	(L) LAD	3m	11	GF	*bhnd by 7th, nvr dang*	6	14

N/H flat winner; not disgraced both starts; needs more practice before winning. 15

PLAS-HENDY ch.g. 11 Celtic Cone - Little Cindy II by Nine One — P M Rich

1996 P(0),P(0),P(0),7(0),F(-)

300	1/3 Didmarton	(L) RES 3m	23	G	*alwys rear, t.o. & p.u. 14th*	P	0
640	22/3 Howick	(L) MDN 3m	10	GF	*12s-6s, cls up, ld & clr 13th, blnd 15th, hdd & btn aft*	3	0
717	29/3 Llanvapley	(L) RES 3m	13	GF	*(fav) ld til qcknd clr 13th, easily*	1	17
1194	22/4 Chepstow	(L) HC 3m	11	GF	*chsd wnr till wknd 12th.*	8	0

Stunning improvement on 18th start; needs more for Confineds. 16

PLATEMAN ch.g. 10 True Song - Spartan Clover by Spartan General — K Hutsby

1996 U(-),4(10),P(0),1(11),P(0)

59	1/2 Kingston Bl'	(L) RES 3m	16	GF	*s.s. prog to 2nd at 6th, cls 4th whn f 13th*	F	-
222	16/2 Heythrop	(R) RES 3m	17	G	*prom, ld 7th, jnd 2 out, hld on gamely flat*	1	19

Won bad Maiden 96; improved & found weak Restricted; honest but barely stays; more needed. 19

PLAYBOY 10

1996 U(-)

1075	13/4 Whitwell-On'	(R) MEM 3m	9	G	*carried 13st 6lbs, rear, bhnd 11th, t.o. & f 4 out*	F	-

Of no account 0

PLAYING THE FOOL b.m. 7 Idiot's Delight - Celtic Blade by Celtic Cone — C J Bennett

1996 P(0),F(-),P(0),4(0)

570	16/3 Garnons	(L) MDN 2 1/2m	14	G	*ld 6th, clr frm 10th, wknd & hdd 2 out, fin tired*	4	0
1066	13/4 Maisemore P'	(L) MDO 3m	9	GF	*keen hld, chsd wnr 8th, ev ch apr 2 out, unable qckn*	2	16
1240	26/4 Brampton Br'	(R) MDO 3m	12	G	*hld up, prog 9th, ld 15th, qcknd clr apr last*	1	15

Won weak Maiden; improved; staying better now; needs more for Restricted. 17

PLAYMORE (Irish) — I 86P, I 169P, I 324P, I 381⁵, I 447,

PLAYPEN b.g. 13 Sit In The Corner (USA) - Blue Nursery by Bluerullah — Miss S E Crook

1996 2(14),3(18),4(15),2(16),3(16),2(17),2(18)

99	8/2 Great Treth'	(R) LAD 3m	10	GS	*rear, rpd prog to chal 14th, ev ch 2 out, wknd*	3	19
551	16/3 Ottery St M'	(L) MEM 3m	4	G	*in tch til stmbld & u.r. bend aft 14th*	U	-

Ladies winner 95; novice ridden; finished early 97; unlikely to win at 14. 16

PLAY POKER(IRE) ch.g. 9 Buckskin (FR) - Trulos by Three Dons — S W Dusting

1996 F(-),2(17),2(16),F(-)

100	8/2 Great Treth'	(R) RES 3m	14	GS	*rear, mstk 11th, prog to chs ldrs 14th,4th & btn whn f 2out*	F	-
1594	31/5 Bratton Down	(L) INT 3m	10	F	*trckd ldrs, not qckn 14th, mod 6th 2 out, fin well*	4	16

Maiden winner 94; lightly raced; lost last 10 & finds little; will continue to frustrate; Good. 18

PLAY RISKY(IRE) b.g. 8 Risk Me (FR) - Palucca (GER) by Orsini — P H Guard

1996 4(0),8(0),U(-),2(0)

789	31/3 Bishopsleigh	(R) MEM 3m	5	G	*cls up to 12th, lost tch 14th, p.u. aft nxt*	P	0

Of no account 0

PLEASEDASPUNCH(IRE) br.g. 5 Convinced - Ferdee Free by Netherkelly — C Storey

340	1/3 Corbridge	(R) MDN 3m	10	G	*mid-div, wknd 8th, t.o. & p.u. 11th*	P	0
420	8/3 Dalston	(R) MDO 2 1/2m	8	GS	*schoold & wll in rear, nvr nrr, improve*	5	0
815	31/3 Tranwell	(L) MDO 2 1/2m	14	G	*rear til hdwy into 5th 8th,wnt 2nd 2 out,fin strgly run in*	1	15

Progressive; beat 10 finishers when winning; good stable; stamina untested but looks sure to progress 17

PLUCKY PUNTER b.g. 9 Idiot's Delight - Birds Of A Feather by Warpath — J R Jones

1996 P(0)

183	15/2 Erw Lon	(L) MEM 3m	3	G	*(fav) ld to 13th, wknd rpdly, t.o.*	3	0
543	16/3 Erw Lon	(L) MDN 3m	11	GF	*ld til aft 2 out, onepcd*	3	12
1011	12/4 St Hilary	(R) MDN 3m	10	GF	*made all, ran on strngly whn chal 2 out*	1	15
1185	20/4 Lydstep	(L) RES 3m	5	GF	*(fav) made all, in no dang frm 3 out, easily*	1	17

Changed hands 7 much improved 97; front runner; likes easy 3 miles; can win again; G/F. 17

PLUNDERING STAR(IRE) b or br.g. 9 The Parson - Laud by Dual — D A Malam

1996 P(0),3(12)

332	1/3 Eaton Hall	(R) RES 3m	18	GS	*mid to rear, p.u. 5 out*	P	0
671	23/3 Eaton Hall	(R) INT 3 3/4m	8	GF	*mid-div, rdn & no imp 14th, wknd & p.u. 16th*	P	0
940	6/4 Tabley	(R) RES 3m	9	G	*(bl) f 3rd*	F	-

Maiden winner 95; very lightly raced now & shows nothing. **13**

POLUVIUS (Irish) — **I** 14F, **I** 39P, **I** 423²

POACHERS LAMP (Irish) — **I** 20S, **I** 42⁴, **I** 81⁶, **I** 418⁴

PO CAP EEL b.m. 7 Uncle Pokey - Hejera by Cantab — Mrs T R Kinsey

1996 P(0),P(0)

326	1/3	Eaton Hall	(R) MDN	3m	14	GS	*mid to rear, nvr dang*	4	0
664	23/3	Eaton Hall	(R) MDO	3m	12	GF	*mid-div, prog 12th, ran on und pres 2 out, lkd 2nd*	3	13
942	6/4	Tabley	(R) MDO	3m	8	G	*prom, disp ld 7th til ld 10th, hdd 15th, wknd*	4	0

Improved but last twice & needs to speed up; more needed. **13**

POINCIANA b.g. 8 Big Spruce (USA) - Andrushka (USA) by Giboulee (CAN) — Miss J S Lewis

360	2/3	Garnons	(L) CON	3m	10	GS	*ld frm 7th, 3l up 15th, hdd & f 2 out*	F	19
636	22/3	Howick	(L) CON	3m	12	GF	*cls up til ld 13th, jnd 3 out, hdd nxt, just outpcd*	2	19
1062	13/4	Maisemore P'	(L) MXO	3m	12	GF	*cls up, 3rd & mstk 12th, sn rdn, outpcd by ldng pair aft*	3	20

Flat winner; very lightly raced; retains ability & good enough for Confined;G/S-G/F. **18**

POKEY GRANGE b.g. 9 Uncle Pokey - Sudden Surrender by The Brianstan — S N Burt

1996 5(0),2(11),1(10)

251	22/2	Brocklesby '	(L) RES	3m	16	G	*ld to 10th, 2nd to 5 out, outpcd nxt*	5	13
377	4/3	Leicester	(R) HC	2 1/2m 110yds	15	G	*bhnd from 9th.*	10	0
676	23/3	Brocklesby '	(L) RES	3m	14	GF	*disp to 5th, chsd ldr to 14th, wknd*	5	0

Won bad Maiden 96; safe but very slow & need luck to win again; any. **13**

POLAR ANA(IRE) b.m. 8 Pollerton - O Ana by Laurence O — Mrs P A McIntyre

1996 F(-),7(0),U(-),P(0),3(10),1(12),2(16),2(14)

324	1/3	Marks Tey	(L) RES	3m	16	G	*rear, prog 13th, mod 6th 15th, wnt 2nd last, nvr nrr*	2	15
580	16/3	Detling	(L) RES	3m	11	F	*mid-div, hdwy 4 out, 3rd & ev ch nxt, onepce*	4	15
831	31/3	Heathfield	(R) RES	3m	2	F	*(fav) j.w. made all, rdn apr last, kpt on*	1	13
968	6/4	Penshurst	(L) LAD	3m	5	F	*(fav) hndy, chal 14th, ld 3 out, pshd out flat*	1	18
1128	19/4	Penshurst	(L) LAD	3m	8	GF	*(Jt fav) conf rdn,rear,smooth prog 13th,ld 3 out, sn clr, eased flat*	1	19
1501	16/5	Folkestone	(R) HC	3 1/4m	10	G	*jmpd left, in tch, prog to chase wnr after 12th till 15th, ev ch after 3 out, soon wknd.*	3	16

Improved further; won weak races; not disgraced in weak H/chase; win more; best L/H;G-F. **20**

POLAR REGION br.g. 11 Alzao (USA) - Bonny Hollow by Wolver Hollow — C Marner

1996 **P(NH),P(NH),P(NH),4(NH),6(NH),2(NH),4(NH),P(NH),5(NH)**

1563	25/5	Kingston Bl'	(L) MEM	3m	5	GF	*7s-5/2, jmpd slwly, chsd wnr to 6th, outpcd frm 14th*	3	12

Winning chaser; well beaten when punted in Members; unlikely to win at 12. .... **14**

POLISH RIDER(USA) ch.g. 9 Danzig Connection (USA) - Missy T (USA) by Lt Stevens — T G Morgan

188	15/2	Erw Lon	(L) LAD	3m	8	G	*ld 2-8th, wknd 10th, sn t.o.*	5	0
844	31/3	Lydstep	(L) LAD	3m	6	F	*3rd til chsd wnr 15th, no imp*	2	12
1006	12/4	St Hilary	(R) LAD	3m	7	GF	*hld up mid-div, rpd prog to ld 15th, hdd 3 out, wknd rpdly*	3	13
1364	5/5	Pantyderi	(L) LAD	3m	5	G	*rear at 3rd & 11th, no dang to wnr last*	2	15
1470	11/5	Erw Lon	(L) LAD	3m	9	GS	*rear, f 10th*	F	-

Winning hurdler 94; lightly raced since; does not stay & need fortune to win Ladies. **13**

POLITICAL BELLE ch.m. 7 Politico (USA) - Trial Run by Deep Run — R W Middleton

341	1/3	Corbridge	(R) MDN	3m	10	G	*mid-div, prog 10th, wknd 3 out, t.o.*	4	0
565	16/3	Lanark	(R) MDO	3m	10	GS	*prom to 10th, strgglng whn p.u. 12th*	P	0
613	22/3	Friars Haugh	(L) MDN	3m	12	GF	*mstk & p.u. aft 2nd*	P	0
734	29/3	Alnwick	(L) MDN	3m	6	F	*alwys strgglng, t.o. & p.u. 9th*	P	0

Last on debut; not progress after; plenty more needed. **0**

POLITICAL DIAMOND b.m. 6 Politico (USA) - Hejera by Cantab — J W Robson

235	22/2	Friars Haugh	(L) MDO	3m	10	G	*sn t.o., p.u. 14th*	P	0
340	1/3	Corbridge	(R) MDN	3m	10	G	*rear & sn outpcd, t.o. & p.u. 12th*	P	0
614	22/3	Friars Haugh	(L) MDN	3m	13	GF	*nvr nr ldrs, p.u. 4 out*	P	0
728	29/3	Alnwick	(L) MEM	3m	4	F	*alwys last piar, t.o. & mstk 2 out, p.u. last*	P	0

Not yet of any account **0**

POLITICAL FIELD b.m. 7 Politico (USA) - Miss Broadfields by Bivouac — R G Watson

1996 5(0),2(11),1(15)

348	2/3	Market Rase'	(L) RES	3m	13	GF	*alwys rear, blnd 6th, rdn & no rspns 13th, p.u. nxt*	P	0
509	15/3	Dalton Park	(R) XX	3m	13	GF	*rear, lost tch 14th, t.o. & p.u. 2 out*	P	0
1068	13/4	Whitwell-On'	(R) RES	3m	12	G	*rear, strgglng & rmndrs 10th, t.o. 12th, p.u. 14th*	P	0

Won modest Maiden 96; showed nothing in 97 & can only be watched now. **13**

POLITICAL ISSUE b.g. 13 Politico (USA) - Red Stockings by Red Pins — T L A Robson
1996 3(21),P(0),**2(19)**,**P(0)**

35	26/1 Alnwick	(L) CON	3m	10	G	*cls up til outpcd 13th, ran on agn 3 out, not qckn nxt*	4	18
152	12/2 Musselburgh	(R) HC	3m	8	GS	*ld to 2nd, led 4th to 7th, lost tch 11th, t.o. when p.u. before four out.*	P	0

H.chase winner 92; very lightly raced & unable to fulfil; ran well 1st start; try Members;G-S. 16

POLITICAL SAM ch.g. 8 Politico (USA) - Samonia by Rolfe (USA) — J W Barker
1996 1(16),U(-),2(19),6(0),3(0)

118	9/2 Wetherby Po'	(L) RES	3m	14	GF	*chsng grp, prog 13th, ld 2 out, styd on wll, jnd line*	1	19
383	5/3 Catterick	(L) HC	3m 1f 110yds	10	G	*cl up, hit 9th, ld 12th till rdn and hdd apr 3 out, gradually wknd.*	5	14

Maiden winner 96; improving; likes Wetherby; can find Confined; stays;G/F-S. 20

POLITICAL TROUT ch.m. 7 Politico (USA) - Elf Trout by Elf-Arrow — R W Stephenson
1996 P(0)

1075	13/4 Whitwell-On'	(R) MEM	3m	9	G	*rear, strggnlg 7th, t.o. 11th, p.u. 14th*	P	0

Not yet of any account 0

POLITICO POT br.g. 10 Politico (USA) - Another Pin by Pinza — Charlie Peckitt
1996 **P(0)**,1(19),1(18),**4(18)**,4(15),**P(0)**,P(0)

34	26/1 Alnwick	(L) OPE	3m	9	G	*mstks, prom til wknd & mstk 14th, t.o. & p.u. last*	P	0
119	9/2 Wetherby Po'	(L) OPE	3m	15	GF	*mid-div, wknd 10th, t.o. & p.u. 12th*	U	-

Dual Open winner 96(weak races); likes soft & finished early 97; hard to place now; G-S. 16

POLLS GALE (Irish) — I 281[P], I 344[5], I 407[5], I 544[2]

POLLY CINDERS gr.m. 6 Alias Smith (USA) - Political Prospect by Politico (USA) — J D Goodfellow
1996 **7(NH)**

234	22/2 Friars Haugh	(L) MDO	3m	15	G	*5th hlfwy, sn lost tch*	7	0
417	8/3 Dalston	(R) MDO	2 1/2m	11	GS	*rear, no ch 11th, t.o. & p.u. 3 out*	P	0

Not yet of any account 0

POLLY PRINGLE ch.m. 12 Scallywag - Pollywella by Welham — Mrs C E Goldsworthy
1996 2(16),5(13),1(20),2(19),1(18),2(19),1(15)

191	15/2 Erw Lon	(L) CON	3m	13	G	*(fav) rear, no ch frm 12th, styd on 3 out, nvr plcd to chal*	4	12
399	8/3 Llanfrynach	(R) CON	3m	11	G	*hld up, prog 13th, 3rd 3 out, not rch 1st pair*	3	17
715	29/3 Llanvapley	(L) OPE	3m	8	GF	*alwys last pair, no ch hlfwy, p.u. 2 out*	P	0
1133	19/4 Bonvilston	(R) INT	3m	8	G	*held up towrds rear, ran on wll frm 3 out, nrst fin*	3	17
1224	26/4 Pyle	(R) CON	3m	7	GS	*7s-4s, mstks, ld to 4th, chsd wnr 14th,hrd rdn & no imp last*	2	19
1319	3/5 Bonvilston	(R) INT	3m	8	G	*nvr bynd mid-div, no dang*	4	18

Won 3 in 96; consistent confined horse; best easy 3 miles; can win again; G-S. 19

POLLY'S LADY ch.m. 7 Mirror Boy - Terrona Lady by Damsire Unregistered — J John Paterson

1337	3/5 Mosshouses	(L) MDO	3m	7	F	*bhnd frm 4th, t.o.*	5	0

Not yet of any account 0

POLLYTICKLE gr.m. 9 Politico (USA) - No Don't by Don't Look — G J Smith

212	16/2 Southwell P'	(L) MDO	3m	14	GS	*ld to 4th, in tch, prog to 4th at 13th, no hdwy aft*	5	0
347	2/3 Market Rase'	(L) MDO	3m	9	GF	*prom to 5th, in tch, lft 3rd 14th, onepcd frm 3 out*	3	10
478	9/3 Southwell P'	(L) MDO	3m	17	G	*prom, chsd ldr 8-13th, cls up whn u.r. 15th*	U	-

Ex novice hurdler; lightly raced; has some ability; chances of weak Midlands Maiden if fit in 98. 13

POLYDEUCES b.g. 11 Swan's Rock - Mary Morison by Ragusa — Capt R J Inglesant

1014	12/4 Bitterley	(L) OPE	3m	9	GF	*cls up, 8l 3rd at 10th, wknd rpdly, p.u. aft 12th*	P	0
1149	19/4 Chaddesley '	(L) RES	3m	6	GF	*cls up to 11th, sn wknd, t.o. & p.u. 2 out*	P	0
1417	10/5 Warwick	(L) HC	3 1/4m	8	G	*held up in tch, jmpd right 4th and 5th, chsd wnr next, wknd 12th, p.u. before 14th.*	P	0

Does not stay; of no account. 0

POLYNTH b.g. 8 Politico (USA) - Miss Trixie by Le Tricolore — Mrs V Cunningham
1996 2(18),1(18),7(14),P(0),2(18),P(0)

119	9/2 Wetherby Po'	(L) OPE	3m	15	GF	*mid-div whn u.r. 4th*	U	-
267	22/2 Duncombe Pa'	(R) OPE	3m	8	G	*rear, jmp slwly 7th, wll bhnd 10th, p.u. 12th*	P	0
356	2/3 Great Stain'	(L) INT	3m	9	S	*mid-div, rdn 11th, outpcd nxt*	5	10
492	11/3 Sedgefield	(L) HC	3m 3f	7	G	*jmpd badly in tch, mstk and lost pl 6th, t.o. final cct, p.u. before last.*	P	0

Restricted winner 96; disappointing since; stays well; may surprise in mud. 16

PONDERNOT (Irish) — **I** 220[F], **I** 497[4], **I** 545[2], **I** 594[3]

PONT DE PAIX b.g. 11 Cheval - Mattie B by Sea Moss — Exors Of The Late Col A Clerke-Brown

1996 P(0),2(24),**5(17)**,P(0)

57	1/2	Kingston Bl'	(L)	LAD	3m	13	GF	*ld to 13th, grad wknd*	5	15
202	15/2	Weston Park	(L)	LAD	3m	13	G	*mstks, mid-div, ran on frm 4 out, nrst fin*	3	17
442	8/3	Higham	(L)	LAD	3m	8	G	*trckd ldrs, outpcd 16th*	3	21
744	29/3	Barbury Cas'	(L)	LAD	3m	2	F	*(fav) made all, mstks 5th & 13th, easily*	1	19
824	31/3	Lockinge	(L)	CON	3m	8	F	*(fav) mstks, ld to 10th, ld agn 13th, clr 16th, comf*	1	21

Formerly decent; revived somewhat; well placed; mistakes; good stable; find more openings.G/S-F. 20

POOR SKIN (Irish) — **I** 547[P], **I** 575[3]

POORS WOOD b.g. 10 Martinmas - Lyaaric by Privy Seal — F R Jackson

1996 **6(NH)**

153	13/2	Sandown	(R)	HC	2 1/2m 110yds	6	G	*ld 4th to 3 out, hrd rdn apr last, wknd.*	4	21
227	21/2	Kempton	(R)	HC	3m	6	G	*held up, hdwy and hit 12th, chsd wnr from 4 out till wknd run-in.*	3	18
679	26/3	Ascot	(R)	HC	2m 3f 110yds	9	G	*held up bhnd, hdwy 10th, ld 4 out, clr 2 out, ran on.*	1	23
983	12/4	Ascot	(R)	HC	3m 110yds	14	GF	*pulld hrd, held up, p.u. before 10th, dismntd.*	P	0

Winning hurdler; lightly raced; won weak H/chase; best under 3 miles; problems last start. 23

POPON b.m. 9 Push On - Chiquita Beatle by Beat Group — Mrs L T J Evans

184	15/2	Erw Lon	(L)	MDN	3m	14	G	*mid-div, mstk 8th, sn strgglng, wll bhnd & p.u. 14th*	P	0

Missed 96; hardly runs now & shows nothing. 0

POPS ACADEMY (Irish) — **I** 381[1]

POP SONG b.g. 13 High Season - Top Of The Pops II by Hanover — G Roe

1996 **3(NH)**,**P(NH)**,**P(NH)**

96	8/2	Great Treth'	(R)	CON	3m	7	GS	*ld to 12th & 14th-nxt,btn whn blnd 3 out,wknd,lost 2nd last*	3	16
173	15/2	Ottery St M'	(L)	CON	3m	7	G	*ld til apr last, outpcd by wnr*	2	17
237	22/2	Lemalla	(R)	CON	3m	13	S	*(fav) ld to 5th, disp 9th-13th, cls 2nd 16th, wknd rpdly, p.u.last*	P	0
738	29/3	Higher Kilw'	(L)	CON	3m	8	GF	*lft in ld 2nd, ld til disp 13th, hdd 15th, wknd, p.u. 2 out*	P	0

Winning chaser; ran well but hard to find a win now; try Members. 15

PORCHA (Irish) — **I** 462[R]

PORTER TASTES NICE (Irish) — **I** 37[P], **I** 96[P], **I** 218[3], **I** 388[3], **I** 406,

PORTLAND ROW (Irish) — **I** 274[1], **I** 376[P]

POSSTICK MILL b.m. 5 Meadowbrook - Hope Of Oak by Leander — Mrs N Hope

37	26/1	Alnwick	(L)	MDO	3m	15	G	*hld up bhnd,prog & mstk 10th,chsd ldr 14th,lft clr 3 out*	1	14

Fortunate to win on debut (slow time); not seen again; good stable; plenty to prove yet. 16

POTATO FOUNTAIN(IRE) b.m. 7 Royal Fountain - Ski Cap by Beau Chapeau — M J Roberts

1996 P(0),U(-),2(10)

201	15/2	Weston Park	(L)	OPE	3m	16	G	*chsng grp whn u.r. 8th*	U	-
255	22/2	Newtown	(L)	CON	3m	14	G	*alwys bhnd, t.o. whn ref 3 out*	R	-
700	29/3	Upper Sapey	(R)	MEM	3m	8	GF	*dist 4th 10th, stdy prog frm 3 out gained 3rd run in*	3	0

Well beaten in 2 placing 96/97; should concentrate on Midens; barely worth a rating as yet. 11

POTIPHAR br.g. 11 Warpath - Zulaika Hopwood by Royalty — Mrs J M Worthington

1996 P(0)

204	15/2	Weston Park	(L)	RES	3m	13	G	*cls up to 12th, wknd rpdly, p.u. nxt*	P	0

Pulled up all starts 95/97; looks finished now. 0

POULGILLIE (Irish) — **I** 36[F], **I** 56[P], **I** 223[P], **I** 281[6]

POWERSURGE b.g. 10 Electric - Ladysave by Stanford — R B J Harrison

125	9/2	Cottenham	(R)	LAD	3m	11	GF	*rear whn u.r. 1st*	U	-
195	15/2	Higham	(L)	LAD	3m	14	G	*rear, prog to jnd ldrs 11th,chsd ldrs 14th,kpt on to 2nd fin*	2	22
304	1/3	Parham	(R)	LAD	3m	10	G	*trckd ldrs, wknd rpdly 12th, t.o. & p.u. 3 out*	P	0
578	16/3	Detling	(L)	LAD	3m	11	F	*cls up, blndrd 11th, grdly wknd frm 14th*	8	0

Missed 95/96; beaten a length in good Ladies but still a maiden; stamina doubts; unlikely to win. 17

POYNDER PARK(IRE) b.g. 6 Mandalus - So Deep by Deep Run — Mrs V A Stevenson

1046	13/4	Lockerbie	(R)	MEM	3m	4	F	*alwys last, lost tch by 13th, p.u. 2 out*	P	0

Only learning on debut; can do better. 0

PRANKSTER ch.g. 11 Don - Social Partner by Sparkler — T Atkinson

17	25/1	Badbury Rin'	(L)	CON	3m	9	GF	*prom, wth ldr 14th, wknd aft nxt, t.o.*	4	0
107	8/2	Milborne St'	(L)	MEM	3m	8	GF	*cls up, handy 4th whn f 13th*	F	-
178	15/2	Larkhill	(R)	CON	3m	9	G	*rear, in tch, strgglng whn hit 14th, t.o. & p.u. last*	P	0
397	8/3	Barbury Cas'	(L)	XX	3m	10	G	*bhnd frm 4th, no ch whn u.r. 15th*	U	-
662	22/3	Badbury Rin'	(L)	CON	3m	8	F	*prom, ev ch 15th, onepcd frm 2 out*	4	17
863	31/3	Kingston St'	(R)	OPE	3m	4	F	*hit 7th, lost tch 13th, blndrd & u.r. 15th*	U	-

Irish bumper winner; does not stay & most unlikely to find a race. 14

PRAYON PARSON (Irish) — **I** 49, , **I** 89^{P}, **I** 306^{6}, **I** 402^{3}, **I** 451^{3}

PRECARIUM(IRE) b.g. 9 The Parson - Bonne Bouche by Bonne Noel — Miss S Leach

33	26/1	Alnwick	(L)	LAD	3m	12	G	*prssd ldr, ld 7-9th, prom til wknd apr 3 out*	7	12
117	9/2	Wetherby Po'	(L)	LAD	3m	10	GF	*prom whn u.r. 2nd*	U	-
158	15/2	Lanark	(R)	LAD	3m	8	G	*made most frm 5th, hrd prssd frm 2 out, hld on wll*	1	21
268	22/2	Duncombe Pa'	(R)	LAD	3m	5	G	*settld in 3rd, whn 2nd 6th, prssng ldr whn f 4 out*	F	-

Winning Irish chaser 94/95; lightly raced; novice ridden & mistakes; may find another modest Ladies. .. 20

PREMIUM BRAND (Irish) — **I** 160^{P}, **I** 202^{2}, **I** 232^{1}, **I** 298^{2}, **I** 395^{6}, **I** 491^{2}, **I** 578^{2}

PRESELI VIEW b.m. 6 Still Time Left - Jacqueline by Harvest Sun — W D Lewis

1996 6(0),5(0),2(0),5(0)

184	15/2	Erw Lon	(L)	MDN	3m	14	G	*in tch, prog 12th, chsd wnr 14th, chnce whn f 3 out*	F	-
540	16/3	Erw Lon	(L)	MDN	3m	13	GF	*5th whn mstk 6th, lost reins, p.u. nxt*	P	0
842	31/3	Lydstep	(L)	MDO	3m	12	F	*(Jt fav) sttld rear, prog 13th, ld 16th, in cmmnd aft, eased flat*	1	14
1227	26/4	Pyle	(R)	RES	3m	15	GS	*mid-div,prog 13th,rdn 3 out,drvn to chal & mstk last,no ext*	2	16

Improving; ran well in competitive Restricted; can win one in 98; stays; F-G/S. 18

PRESS FOR ACTION b.g. 12 Croghan Hill - Ballynavin Money by Even Money — Mrs S H Shirley-Beavan

414	8/3	Dalston	(R)	XX	3m	9	GS	*ld 2nd, set gd pace, hdd apr 2 out, kpt on well*	2	19
561	16/3	Lanark	(R)	LAD	3m	7	GS	*made most til wknd qckly apr 3 out*	3	11
943	6/4	Friars Haugh	(L)	MEM	3m	5	GF	*(fav) ld til 3 out, no ext*	2	14
1097	19/4	Bangor	(L)	HC	2 1/2m 110yds	11	G	*prom, jmpd right 7th, wknd 9th, t.o. when p.u. before 4 out.*	P	0
1414	9/5	Sedgefield	(L)	HC	2m 5f	6	GF	*chsd ldr to 11th, wknd quickly after next.*	5	0

Won weak H/Chase 94; missed 96; front runner; declining now; another win looks tough. 15

PRESS TO STING b.g. 8 Scorpio (FR) - Olive Press by Ragapan — A H Mactaggart

38	26/1	Alnwick	(L)	MDO	3m	14	G	*ld 6th til apr 3 out, wknd rpdly*	4	0
767	29/3	Whittington	(L)	MDO	3m	9	S	*ld to 9th, cls 2nd whn f 12th*	F	-
1429	10/5	Aspatria	(L)	MDO	3m	15	G	*9s-5s,prom,3rd frm 10th til chsd wnr & 6l 2nd 16th,btn nxt*	2	10
1514	17/5	Corbridge	(R)	MDO	3m	17	GS	*(fav) prom, disp 11th-14th, ld nxt, qcknd clr last, easily*	1	16

Progressive; beat large field impressively; looks sure to upgrade; stays; G-S. 17

PRESTIGE LORD (Irish) — **I** 14, , **I** 77^{F}, **I** 203^{1}

PRETORIA DANCER b.g. 5 Dancing Brave (USA) - Pretoria by Habitat — R J Mansell

1996 **13(NH),6(NH),3(NH),3(NH),4(NH)**

1321	3/5	Bonvilston	(R)	MXO	3m	10	G	*mid-div, rmndrs hlfwy, wknd & p.u. 2 out*	P	0
1455	11/5	Maisemore P'	(L)	CON	3m	8	G	*chsd wnr 10-12th & agn 3 out, chnc nxt, btn & slw jmp last*	2	18
1524	17/5	Bredwardine	(R)	OPE	3m	8	G	*hld up last, sn wll bhnd, t.o. 8th, p.u. 12th*	P	0
1607	1/6	Dingley	(R)	OPE	3m	9	GF	*ld 3-5th, chsd wnr to 12th,, wknd & mstk nxt, fin tired*	4	0

Flat winner 95; ran well in good Confined; ungenuine & not reproduce; one to avoid. 15

PRETTYMAID (Irish) — **I** 90^{P}, **I** 151^{P}, **I** 218,

PRICELESS BUCK (Irish) — **I** 55^{3}, **I** 267^{P}

PRICE WAR b.g. 8 Silly Prices - Verona Queen by Majestic Streak — J G Bell

1996 4(11)

38	26/1	Alnwick	(L)	MDO	3m	14	G	*(Jt fav) 5th whn blnd & u.r. 6th*	U	-
162	15/2	Lanark	(R)	MDO	3m	16	G	*ld/disp early, sn lost tch, p.u. 2 out*	P	0
612	22/3	Friars Haugh	(L)	MDN	3m	14	GF	*bhnd by 7th, p.u. 4 out*	P	0

Showed promise in 96 but no progress in97; needs to regain the plot. 10

PRICKLY TROUT ch.m. 8 Politico (USA) - Elf Trout by Elf-Arrow — R W Stephenson

1996 P(0),P(0),P(0)

429	8/3	Charm Park	(L)	MDO	3m	14	GF	*rear & sn outpcd, wll bhnd 9th, t.o. 12th*	5	0
859	31/3	Charm Park	(L)	MDO	3m	4	F	*u.r. 2nd*	U	-
1071	13/4	Whitwell-On'	(R)	CON	3m	10	G	*rear, lost tch 4th, t.o. 8th, p.u. 10th*	P	0

Not yet of any account 0

PRIDEAUX PRINCE b.g. 11 Prince Regent (FR) - Fairy by Prefairy — Mrs C L Goodinson

300 1/3 Didmarton (L) RES 3m 23 G *prom,outpcd 14th,ran on 3 out,btn whn lft in ld last,ran on* 1 19
515 15/3 Larkhill (R) INT 3m 8 GF *wth wnr to 12th, wknd nxt, poor 4th & p.u. last* P 0
1013 12/4 Bitterley (L) CON 3m 14 GF *alwys rear, rmndrs aft 10th, rdn & no prog 13th* 6 0

Maiden winner 92; hardly runs now; fortunate to land Restricted; Confined looks to tough. 17

PRIDE OF POZNAN (Irish) — I 460P
PRIDEWOOD GOLDING ch.g. 10 Soldier Rose - Quick Reply by Tarqogan E A Thomas

1018 12/4 Bitterley (L) MDO 3m 13 GF *ld frm 9th, blnd nxt, hit marker & u.r. apr 13th* U -
1239 26/4 Brampton Br' (R) MDO 3m 9 G *w.w. prog 8th, ld 14th, ev ch til wknd 2 out* 4 0
1393 5/5 Cursneh Hill (L) MDO 3m 9 GF *alwys cls up, cls 3rd & ev ch 15th, wknd frm nxt* 4 11
1528 17/5 Bredwardine (R) MDO 3m 17 G *ld to 13th, steadily wknd* 7 0
1577 26/5 Chaddesley ' (L) MDO 3m 11 F *hld up, rpd prog to ld 12th, clr aft 15th, mstk 2 out, tired* 1 14

Ex novice hurdler; does not stay & beat a bunch of non stayers; way below Restricted class. 14

PRIDEWOOD TARGET ch.g. 9 Oats - Quick Reply by Tarqogan Mrs B Morris
1996 6(0),P(0)

1186 20/4 Lydstep (L) MDO 3m 7 GF *sttld rear, prog 12th, nvr nr to chal, lost 3rd flat, dsmntd* 4 0

Shows some ability; very lightly raced & time passing by. 10

PRIESTHILL(IRE) ch.g. 8 Ovac (ITY) - Shady Grove by Deep Run Mrs E Kulbicki
1996 **9(NH),P(NH),F(NH),P(NH)**

575 16/3 Garnons (L) RES 3m 12 G *rear whn u.r. 5th* U -
639 22/3 Howick (L) MDN 3m 15 GF *alwys rear, p.u. 14th* P 0
717 29/3 Llanvapley (L) RES 3m 13 GF *prom til lost plc 12th, p.u. 15th* P 0
900 5/4 Howick (L) MEM 3m 4 F *ld 4-8th, last whn u.r. aft 11th* U -
1011 12/4 St Hilary (R) MDN 3m 10 GF *mid-div, onepcd frm 15th* 4 0
1229 26/4 Pyle (R) MDO 3m 11 GS *chsd ldrs, mstk 8th, wknd rpdly aft 12th, p.u. aft nxt* P 0
1324 3/5 Bonvilston (R) MDO 3m 16 G *hld up mid-div, prog to 2nd at 11th, sn lost tch* 4 0
1460 11/5 Maisemore P' (L) MDO 3m 16 G *in tch to 10th, sn wknd, t.o. & p.u. 14th* P 0
1603 31/5 Bassaleg (R) MDO 3m 6 F *in tch, 4th whn u.r. 4th* U -

Does not stay & looks hopeless. 0

PRIMA-COSA (Irish) — I 223P, I 447P
PRIME COURSE(IRE) b.g. 8 Crash Course - Prime Mistress by Skymaster E J Farrant
1996 F(-),1(14),3(0)

278 23/2 Charing (L) RES 3m 17 G *prom to 11th, wknd & p.u. 14th* P 0
1355 4/5 Dingley (R) RES 3m 12 G *mid-div, 6th & wknng 12th, p.u. apr 2 out* P 0
1443 10/5 Peper Harow (L) RES 3m 3 GF *chsd ldr, lft in ld 14th, slppd apr 2 out, hdd last, no ext* 2 11
1570 26/5 Hereford (R) HC 3m 1f 110yds 14 G *mstk 3rd, bhnd from 9th, p.u. before 6 out.* P 0

Dead-heated in weak Maiden 96; shown nothing since & beaten in bad race 97; best watched. 14

PRIME STYLE ch.g. 8 Say Primula - Sheer Panache by Fury Royal Norman Manners

157 15/2 Lanark (R) RES 3m 11 G *(fav) ldng grp, mstk 11th, cls up whn f 4 out* F -
425 8/3 Charm Park (L) RES 3m 12 GF *ld, mstk 1st, blndrd & hdd 11th, wknd qckly 13th, t.o.* 10 0

Dual winner 95; missed 96; finished early in 97; can only be watched now. 16

PRIMITIVE GIRL ch.m. 6 Primitive Rising (USA) - Bitofagirl by Habitual Lady Arabella Casey

299 1/3 Didmarton (L) MDN 3m 14 G *rear, prog whn blnd 12th, 4th & no imp frm 14th* 4 0

Last on debut(well beaten); not without hope & should do better. 12

PRIMITIVE KING b.g. 5 Primitive Rising (USA) - Middlestone Queen by Tumble Wind (USA) M D Reed

306 1/3 Parham (R) MDN 3m 12 G *mid-div, clsng whn blnd 14th & p.u.* P 0
581 16/3 Detling (L) MDO 3m 12 F *(fav) rear,prog to trck ldrs 15th,rdn to chal apr last,ld flat* 1 14

Won poor race; young & should improve; needs to for Restricted. 14

PRIMITIVE STAR b.m. 6 Primitive Rising (USA) - Bill's Daughter by Nicholas Bill J Cornforth
1996 P(0),P(0),5(0)

37 26/1 Alnwick (L) MDO 3m 15 G *not fluent, chsd clr ldr, disp 2nd & wkng whn f 14th* F -
76 2/2 Market Rase' (L) XX 3m 12 GF *ld to 10th, wkng whn u.r. 12th* U -
168 15/2 Witton Cast' (R) MDO 3m 4 F *ld to 7th, ld 13th, rdn clr frm 2 out, styd on well* 1 10
266 22/2 Duncombe Pa' (R) RES 3m 19 G *prom,disp 11th,outpcd 13th,rlld 3 out,ev ch whn f 2 out* F -
695 29/3 Stainton (R) RES 3m 11 F *prom, disp ld 3rd-7th, grdly fdd* 7 0

Improved; won weak race; mistakes & needs easy 3 miles; needs a little more for Restricteds.G-F. 15

PRIMITIVE STREAK b.g. 6 Primitive Rising (USA) - Purple Streak by Majestic Streak J L Gledson

419 8/3 Dalston (R) MDO 2 1/2m 10 GS *trckd ldrs going wll, ld 12th, 4l up whn u.r. aft nxt* U -
566 16/3 Lanark (R) MDO 3m 10 GS *(fav) alwys hndy, chal 2 out, no ext flat* 2 14

Subsequent winner behind when placed; looks sure to go one better. 15

PRIMITIVE WAY b.g. 5 Primitive Rising (USA) - Potterway by Velvet Prince — D G Atkinson

357	2/3	Great Stain'	(L)	MDO	3m	15	S	*rear, wll bhnd 14th, p.u. 2 out*	P	0
1074	13/4	Whitwell-On'	(R)	MDO	2 1/2m 88yds	16	G	*prom til wknd apr 3 out*	4	12
1348	3/5	Gisburn	(R)	RES	3m	10	GF	*alwys bhnd, nvr trbld ldrs*	5	0
1514	17/5	Corbridge	(R)	MDO	3m	17	GS	*alwys prom, ev ch 3 out, sn wknd*	3	10

Beaten 12 lengths minimum; reasonable start; little more stamina needed; can improve. 12

PRINCE BUCK(IRE) b.g. 7 Buckskin (FR) - Rechime by Prince Regent (FR) — Mike Roberts

1996 r(-),2(12)

276	22/2	Ampton	(R)	MDO	3m	12	G	*(fav) mstks, chsd ldrs, wnt 2nd 13th, ld 2 out, styd on und press*	1	15
303	1/3	Parham	(R)	RES	3m	10	G	*(fav) made all, styd on well 2 out, drew clr*	1	20
592	22/3	Lingfield	(L)	HC	3m	5	GF	*(fav) ld till after 4th, led 7th to next, one l 2nd and rdn when f 2 out.*	F	26
1417	10/5	Warwick	(L)	HC	3 1/4m	8	G	*(fav) made all, mstk 2nd, styd on strly.*	1	31
1588	30/5	Stratford	(L)	HC	3 1/2m	9	G	*in tch, chsd ldr from 8th to 16th, wknd from 3 out, tiring when mstk next.*	4	25

Much improved novice; stays; not disgraced last start; good stable; sure to win more; Good. 29

PRINCE ITSU b.g. 9 Itsu (USA) - Beige Princess by French Beige — John Jones

1996 P(0)

641	22/3	Howick	(L)	MDN	3m	9	GF	*rear til ran out 7th*	r	-
1067	13/4	Maisemore P'	(L)	MDO	3m	8	GF	*t.d.e. keen hld, ld 4th, made rest, styd on strngly flat*	1	11
1318	3/5	Bonvilston	(R)	MEM	3m	9	G	*trckd ldrs, ld 3 out, blnd nxt, not rcvr*	4	0

Easily won weak & slow race; possibly unlucky after; hard ride but learning & can progress. 15

PRINCE NEPAL b.g. 13 Kinglet - Nepal by Indian Ruler — Terry Hopkins

1996 U(-),5(18),P(0),5(11),P(0),3(12),3(11),2(16),R(-),S(-)

5	19/1	Barbury Cas'	(L)	OPE	3m	11	GF	*prom, 4th hlfwy, sn wknd, t.o.*	6	0
171	15/2	Ottery St M'	(L)	OPE	3m	9	G	*chsd wnr to 14th, blnd nxt, p.u. 16th*	P	0
308	1/3	Clyst St Ma'	(L)	OPE	3m	7	HY	*ld/disp to 13th, wknd rpdly, nxt, t.o. & ref 2 out*	R	-
491	10/3	Taunton	(R)	HC	3m	8	G	*left in ld 1st, hit next, hdd 3rd, mstks 6th and next, wknd 13th.*	5	0
646	22/3	Castle Of C'	(R)	OPE	3m	5	G	*chsd ldr, ld 9th, clr 13th, hdd nxt, wll btn whn blnd 3 out*	4	11
715	29/3	Llanvapley	(L)	OPE	3m	8	GF	*rear early, prog to 3rd 11th, no ch wth 1st 2*	3	14
904	5/4	Howick	(L)	OPE	3m	3	F	*ld, reluc & ran out apr 10th, cont & ref 10th*	R	-
1007	12/4	St Hilary	(R)	OPE	3m	10	GF	*mid-div, f 4th*	F	-
1134	19/4	Bonvilston	(R)	MXO	4m	10	G	*mid-div, imprvd to 2nd hlfwy, no further prog*	4	11
1211	26/4	Woodford	(L)	MEM	3m	8	G	*ld to 3rd, lft in ld 5th-9th, sn wknd, t.o. & p.u. 3 out*	P	0
1321	3/5	Bonvilston	(R)	MXO	3m	10	G	*cls up, ld 13th til hdd 2 out, wknd rpdly*	3	10
1484	11/5	Ottery St M'	(L)	OPE	3m	7	G	*cls up to 13th, lost tch 15th, t.o. & p.u. 2 out*	P	0

Can run well but never threatens to win now. 12

PRINCE OF VERONA b or br.g. 10 Zambrano - Verona Queen by Majestic Streak — Mrs T Stopford-Sackville

180	15/2	Larkhill	(R)	MXO	3m	6	G	*prom, chsd wnr 7-11th, 3rd & outpcd 13th, no dang aft*	3	15
496	15/3	Hereford	(R)	HC	3m 1f 110yds	10	GF	*(fav) soon outpcd and bhnd, effort 10th, soon wknd, t.o. when p.u. before 15th.*	P	0

Decent prospect 94; absent since & unable to recover form 97; can only be watched. 19

PRINCE OWEN (Irish) — **I** 18[P], **I** 54[P], **I** 136[6]

PRINCE ROSSINI(IRE) br.g. 9 Roselier (FR) - Auragne (FR) by Crowned Prince (USA) — R Thorburn

1996 F(-),F(-),P(0),6(0),8(0)

134	9/2	Alnwick	(L)	MDO	3m	11	G	*nvr bttr than mid-div, t.o. whn f 4 out*	F	-
162	15/2	Lanark	(R)	MDO	3m	16	G	*prom to hlfwy*	10	0
234	22/2	Friars Haugh	(L)	MDO	3m	15	G	*nvr rchd ldrs*	4	0
342	1/3	Corbridge	(R)	MDO	3m	12	G	*(bl) prom, rmndrs 10th, sn wknd, t.o. 12th, p.u. 2 out*	P	0

Only once better than last 96/97; barely worth a rating. 10

PRINCE RUA ch.g. 11 Wrens Hill - Oldtown Princess VI by Chou Chin Chou — R Williams

1996 P(0),P(0),3(0),U(-),4(0)

1613	7/6	Umberleigh	(L)	RES	3m	13	F	*alwys last pair, t.o. & p.u. aft 12th*	P	0

Won a dreadful Members 95; changed hands; of no account now. 0

PRINCE'S COURT b.g. 14 Kinglet - Court Scene by Royal Levee (USA) — S Kimber

1996 U(-),5(12),7(11),U(-),U(-)

869	31/3	Hackwood Pa'	(L)	XX	3m	6	F	*cls up to 8th, wknd, rear last cct*	4	0
1063	13/4	Maisemore P'	(L)	XX	3m	13	GF	*bhnd, some prog 14th, went mod 5th 2 out, nvr nrr*	5	10
1205	26/4	Clifton On '	(L)	CON	3m	13	GS	*alwys rear, t.o. frm 9th*	7	0

Winning hurdler; not threatening to win now. 10

PRINCE'S GIFT b.g. 8 Scorpio (FR) - Burton Princess by Prince Barle — Dave Dixon

1996 U(-),P(0),P(0),P(0)

106	8/2	Milborne St'	(L)	RES	3m	12	GF	*in tch, 4th at 15th, chal 2 out, hld flat*	2	18
278	23/2	Charing	(L)	RES	3m	17	G	*(fav) w.w. prog 12th, 5th & in tch 16th, kpt on onepcd*	3	17
517	15/3	Larkhill	(R)	RES	3m	10	GF	*(Jt fav) mstk 7th, nvr going wll, lost tch 13th, p.u. 15th*	P	0

Maiden winner 95; disappointing since & not progress; may find a Restricted one day. 16

PRINCE SOLOMAN br.g. 11 Lir - Cornish Princess by True Code — Miss Tracy Turner

1996 3(0),4(16),1(17),3(18),P(0),**P(0)**,3(11),4(16)

51	1/2	Wadebridge	(L)	CON	3m	4	G	*alwys last pair, drvn 3 out, kpt on onepcd*	4	14
96	8/2	Great Treth'	(R)	CON	3m	7	GS	*bhnd frm 6th, t.o. 14th, p.u. 2 out*	P	0

Confined winner 96; struggling since & season only lasted a week; can only be watched now. 14

PRINCESS AMANDA (Irish) — I 286^{P}, I 350^{2}, I 438^{2}, I 472^{P}, I 575^{P}

PRINCESS BAVARD (Irish) — I 88^{P}, I 134^{P}

PRINCESS CATALDI (Irish) — I 178^{P}, I 251^{P}, I 310^{P}

PRINCESS DIGA (Irish) — I 7^{P}, I 73^{P}, I 167^{P}, I 538^{P}, I 558^{P}, I 599^{P}

PRINCESS LETITIA br.m. 7 Kinglet - Lady Scamp by Scallywag — J W Stephenson

1996 R(-),R(-)

777	29/3	Dingley	(R)	MDO	2m 5f	8	G	*alwys last, t.o. 8th, p.u. 5 out*	P	0
1083	13/4	Guilsborough	(L)	MDN	3m	15	GF	*t.o. til p.u. 6th*	P	0

Awful. 0

PRINCESS LU(IRE) b.g. 7 Nordance (USA) - Beau Lieu by Red God — M G Jones

1996 **F(NH)**,**11(NH)**,**P(NH)**,**9(NH)**

537	16/3	Erw Lon	(L)	OPE	3m	9	GF	*nvr nr ldrs, p.u. 13th*	P	0
714	29/3	Llanvapley	(L)	CON	3m	15	GF	*cls up, styd on onepce frm 3 out*	4	12
1132	19/4	Bonvilston	(R)	CON	3m	9	G	*mid-div, prog to cls 2nd 15th, wknd qckly nxt*	4	0
1318	3/5	Bonvilston	(R)	MEM	3m	9	G	*lft in ld 7th, hdd 3 out, wknd rpdly, p.u. last*	P	0

Won Irish novice chase 95(2 miles); looks well short of stamina. 12

PRINCESS POLLY b.m. 9 Prince Of Peace - Mingold by Klondyke Bill — P D Rogers

172	15/2	Ottery St M'	(L)	MDN	3m	14	G	*alwys mid-div, nvr on trms, btn 6th whn u.r. last*	U	-
741	29/3	Higher Kilw'	(L)	MDN	3m	12	GF	*mid-div, 8th hlfwy, nvr nr to chal*	4	0
1343	3/5	Flete Park	(R)	MDO	3m	13	G	*mid-div, bhnd whn p.u. apr 2 out*	P	0

Some promise in 94; absent since & showed little 97; slog in mud looks her best chance. 12

PRINCESS THYNE (Irish) — I 90^{P}, I 189^{F}, I 264^{P}, I 538^{P}, I 566^{4}, I 606^{6}

PRINCESS WENLLYAN b.m. 12 White Prince (USA) - Prince's Daughter by Black Prince — R L Black

54	1/2	Wadebridge	(L)	MDO	3m	13	G	*alwys rear*	8	0
285	26/2	Taunton	(R)	HC	4 1/4m 110yds	16	GS	*hdwy 14th, wknd 18th, t.o. when p.u. before 3 out.*	P	0
525	15/3	Cothelstone	(L)	MDN	3m	15	GS	*ld, mstk 2nd, hdd 10th, wknd 15th, p.u. 3 out*	P	0
1314	3/5	Holnicote	(L)	MDO	3m	8	G	*sn bhnd, p.u. 10th*	P	0
1554	24/5	Mounsey Hil'	(R)	MDO	3m	14	G	*ld to 3rd, clr 2nd aft, blnd 15th, wknd 17th, p.u. 2 out*	P	0

Very lightly raced; no stamina & too old to win now. 0

PRINCE THEO b.g. 10 Teofane - Clyda Princess by Pry — Miss E F Goldsworthy

1996 P(0),P(0),P(0),C(-)

541	16/3	Erw Lon	(L)	MDN	3m	10	GF	*ld 8th, ld 11-13th, fdd aft*	3	10
840	31/3	Lydstep	(L)	MEM	3m	6	F	*ld to 11th, sn wknd, p.u. 14th, lame*	P	0

Last when completing; does not stay; problems last start. 10

PRINCE WARRIOR b.g. 6 Prince Of Peace - What An Experiance by Chance Meeting — A Cole

735	29/3	Higher Kilw'	(L)	MEM	3m	5	GF	*n.j.w. went 2nd 13th, wknd 15th, btn whn f 2 out, winded*	F	-

Blundered his way round on debut 0

PRINCE YAZA (Irish) — I 249^{P}, I 362^{2}, I 505^{6}

PRINCE ZEUS br.g. 18 Prince de Galles - Zeus Girl by Zeus Boy — D G Knowles

1996 1(10),2(16),**B(-)**

788	31/3	Aldington	(L)	MEM	3m	1	HD	*walked over*	1	0
1128	19/4	Penshurst	(L)	LAD	3m	8	GF	*alwys rear, wll bhnd frm 3 out*	6	0

Grand old servant; Members is always dire but surely too old now; Firm. 10

PRINCIPAL PEACE (Irish) — I 111^{F}

PRINCIPLE MUSIC(USA) ch.g. 9 Palace Music (USA) - Principle (USA) by Viceregal (CAN) — Nick Shutts

1996 3(16)

94 7/2 Newbury (L) HC 2 1/2m 12 G *hdwy 8th, ld 10th, clr apr 12th, hdd 3 out, styd on one pace run-in.* 2 19
290 28/2 Newbury (L) HC 3m 6 GS *held up, hdwy when hit 9th, chsd wnr next to 5 out, btn 3rd when blnd and u.r. 3 out.* U -
431 8/3 Upton-On-Se' (R) CON 3m 9 G *(Jt fav) w.w. prog 12th, chal 3 out, rdn & no ext apr nxt* 2 20

Irish hurdle winner 93; ran well; Confined on easy course possible. 21

PRI NEUKIN br.g. 10 Mufrij - Cessy by Burglar — Mrs S J Gospel
1996 P(0),P(0),P(0)

120 9/2 Wetherby Po' (L) MDO 3m 18 GF *alwys rear, t.o. & p.u. 11th* P 0

Of no account 0

PRINZAL b or br.g. 10 Afzal - Delvin Princess by Aglojo — Mrs Pam Froud
1996 **1(30),3(24),4(NH)**

154 14/2 Fakenham (L) HC 2m 5f 110yds 10 G *mstks, ld, clr after 4th, blnd and u.r. 8th.* U -
376 3/3 Windsor (R) HC 3m 11 GF *slowly away, blnd and u.r. 1st.* U -
1099 19/4 Stratford (L) HC 2m 5f 110yds 14 G *held up, hdwy 5 out, wknd next, p.u. before 3 out.* P 0

H/chase winner 96; lightly raced; novice ridden & not show form in 97; best below 3 miles; Good. 17

PRIOR'S CORNER b.m. 6 Idiot's Delight - Miss Paveh by Paveh Star — R Hawker
1996 **P(NH),15(NH)**

299 1/3 Didmarton (L) MDN 3m 14 G *mstk 4th, cls up whn blnd & u.r. 6th* U -
437 8/3 Upton-On-Se' (R) MDO 3m 15 G *mid-div to 10th, not qckn frm 12th, no ch whn f 3 out* F -

No ability under rules or in points so far. 0

PRIORY PIPER b.g. 8 Maris Piper - Priory Girl by Rugantino — Mrs L Ward
1996 **U(NH),F(NH),P(NH)**

574 16/3 Garnons (L) RES 3m 14 G *prom to 10th, wknd nxt, p.u. 15th* P 0
721 29/3 Sandon (L) MEM 3m 6 GF *(Jt fav) t.o. 9th, 5th & clsng 14th, ran on 2 out, ld last, conf rdn* 1 11
1000 12/4 Alpraham (R) RES 3m 8 GF *hld up rear,4th at 15th,styd on to chal & mstk last,jst fld* 2 18
1237 26/4 Brampton Br' (R) RES 3m 13 G *hld up, prog 12th, ld 3 out, hit nxt & hdd, kpt on flat* 3 15
1382 5/5 Eyton-On-Se' (L) INT 3m 7 GF *(fav) n.j.w., w.w. in rear, found nil frm 4 out* 5 14
1586 28/5 Cartmel (L) HC 3 1/4m 10 GF *steadied start, bhnd, mstk 3rd, nvr on terms.* 6 11

Ex hurdler/chaser; won bad race; tricky but every chance of Restricted; G-G/F. 17

PRIORY STREET (Irish) — **I** 388, , **I** 458[P]

PRIVATE JET(IRE) b.g. 8 Dara Monarch - Torriglia (USA) by Nijinsky (CAN) — P H Sanders
1996 5(0),2(12),5(0),F(-),3(14),**2(19),3(16)**

264 22/2 Duncombe Pa' (R) MEM 3m 9 G *(fav) prom, in chsng grp whn u.r. 6th* U -

Placed in 2 weak H/chases 96; vanished quickly 97; good enough to win but has had plenty of chances. 16

PRIVATE POWER (Irish) — **I** 175[3], **I** 248[4]

PROAN HILL (Irish) — **I** 369[P], **I** 462[F]

PROBATION b.g. 8 Nomination - Ballagarrow Girl by North Stoke — S W May

244 22/2 Lemalla (R) MDO 3m 12 S *in tch, 7th hlfwy, wknd, p.u. last* P 0
459 8/3 Great Treth' (R) MDO 3m 9 S *hld up in tch, cls 3rd 16th, ld apr 2 out, ran on wll* 1 13
630 22/3 Kilworthy (L) RES 3m 16 G *pllng & blndrd 2nd, 10th hlfwy, t.o.* 10 0
1108 19/4 Flete Park (R) RES 3m 14 GF *gd hdwy 3 out, cls 2nd & ev ch last, not qckn* 3 17
1339 3/5 Flete Park (R) RES 3m 6 G *slght ld to 13th, lost tch steadily frm 15th* 3 10

Missed 95/96ogged home; placed in weak Restricted; stays; needs more. 15

PRO BONO(IRE) ch.g. 7 Tale Quale - Quality Suite by Prince Hansel — P C Caudwell
1996 P(0),**2(23),1(22)**

94 7/2 Newbury (L) HC 2 1/2m 12 G *with ldrs 6th, chal 10th to 11th, 3rd and rdn when f next.* F -
154 14/2 Fakenham (L) HC 2m 5f 110yds 10 G *left in ld 8th, hdd 4 out, styd on one pace.* 3 21
378 4/3 Leicester (R) HC 2 1/2m 110yds 6 G *chsd ldrs, mstk 8th, wknd 6 out, p.u. before 2 out.* P 0
592 22/3 Lingfield (L) HC 3m 5 GF *held up bhnd ldrs, 4th when blnd and u.r. 8th.* U -
874 1/4 Uttoxeter (L) HC 2m 7f 9 GF *soon chasing ldrs, chal from 10th, hit 11th, ev ch 3 out, wknd next.* 3 20
1099 19/4 Stratford (L) HC 2m 5f 110yds 14 G *alwys prom, ld 9th, hdd and mstk 2 out, styd on same pace.* 2 21
1293 30/4 Cheltenham (L) HC 2m 110yds 5 GF *(fav) held up in cl tch, mstk 5th, ld 3 out, pushed clr last, hrd rdn and kept on near fin.* 1 21

Won 2 weak H/chases 96/97; best below 3 miles; need same to win again. 22

PROFESSOR LONGHAIR br.g. 10 Strong Gale - Orient Conquest by Dual — A J Papworth
1996 **5(16),3(16),13(0),7(10),P(0),1(21),5(15)**

71 2/2 Higham (L) LAD 3m 6 GF *chsd ldrs, outpcd 12th, styd on wll 4 out, tk 2nd cls hm* 2 19
195 15/2 Higham (L) LAD 3m 14 G *immed rear, t.o. 11th, u.r. 15th* U -
323 1/3 Marks Tey (L) LAD 3m 7 G *(fav) hld up, chsd ldrs 11th, 4th 2 out, strng run to ld cls home* 1 15
442 8/3 Higham (L) LAD 3m 8 G *disp to 2nd, 4th aft, in tch whn hit 13th, no ch aft* 4 15
596 22/3 Horseheath (R) LAD 3m 4 F *mostly 3rd, blnd 12th, no ch aft* 3 17
800 31/3 Marks Tey (L) LAD 3m 3 F *last to 7th, prog disp 10th, ev ch 3 out, outpcd nxt* 2 17
1276 27/4 Fakenham P-' (L) MEM 3m 7 G *blnd 1st, chsd wnr 11th, ev ch 3 out, no ext apr last* 2 14
1378 5/5 Northaw (L) LAD 3m 5 F *ld to 2nd, last & outpcd 10th,hdwy 13th, chall last, ld flat* 1 19
1434 10/5 Marks Tey (L) LAD 3m 3 G *(fav) ld to 4th,mstk 9th,ld 11th-14th,outpcd,ran on to ld last* 1 15
1606 1/6 Dingley (R) LAD 3m 13 GF *bhnd whn hmpd 6th, t.o. aft, no prog* 7 13

H/Chase winner 96; changed hands; excellent schoolmaster; stays; best L/H; win more;G-F. 19

PROFLIGATE ch.h. 12 Shack (USA) - Reshuffle by Sassafras (FR) R Dench
1996 2(14),6(10),P(0),2(12)
26 26/1 Marks Tey (L) LAD 3m 8 GF *hld up, lost tch 14th, t.o.* 6 0
125 9/2 Cottenham (R) LAD 3m 11 GF *rear, lost tch hlfwy, kpt on onepcd frm 15th* 4 12
280 23/2 Charing (L) LAD 3m 12 G *alwys last pair, t.o. 12th* 7 0
578 16/3 Detling (L) LAD 3m 11 F *trckd ldrs, rddn & ev ch whn bad mstk 3 out,btn whn p.u. nxt* P 0
681 29/3 Charing (L) MEM 3m 5 F *(fav) hld up, lft in ld apr 8th, kpt on strgly frm 2 out* 1 12

Moderate; won bad Members; outclassed in competitive races; Firm. 13

PROJECT'S MATE br.g. 10 Rustingo - Lyricist by Averof P H Richards
1996 **17(NH),9(NH),P(NH)**
399 8/3 Llanfrynach (R) CON 3m 11 G *last pair til p.u. 11th* P 0
569 16/3 Garnons (L) OPE 3m 7 G *cls up to 6th, wknd 9th, t.o. & p.u. 3 out* P 0
713 29/3 Llanvapley (L) MEM 3m 4 GF *(bl) in 2nd whn blndrd & u.r. 3rd* U -
1006 12/4 St Hilary (R) LAD 3m 7 GF *rear til p.u. 2out* P 0
1134 19/4 Bonvilston (R) MXO 4m 10 G *nvr bynd mid-div, p.u. 2 out* P 0
1321 3/5 Bonvilston (R) MXO 3m 10 G *(bl) nvr bynd mid-div, no dang* 5 0
1523 17/5 Bredwardine (R) CON 3m 7 G *(bl) mstk 6th, sn drppd out, t.o. & p.u. 11th* P 0

Winning hurdler 93; of no account now. 0

PROPER CORNISH ch.g. 6 Morgans Choice - Helen's Way by Scorpio (FR) Mrs S J Gummow
1996 **13(NH),P(NH),P(NH)**
460 8/3 Great Treth' (R) MDO 3m 13 S *dwelt, ran out 3rd* r -

Not a good start. 0

PROPHET'S CHOICE gr.g. 11 Warpath - Queen's Melody by Highland Melody M Haigh
1996 F(-),F(-),5(0),r(-),P(0),4(11),2(0),3(13)
429 8/3 Charm Park (L) MDO 3m 14 GF *prom, lft in ld 10th, hdd 2 out, wknd qckly* 4 10
510 15/3 Dalton Park (R) MDO 3m 14 GF *prom,mstk 8th, prog to disp 14th, lft in ld nxt, hld on flat* 1 14
856 31/3 Charm Park (L) RES 3m 8 F *ld 5-10th, wknd, hit 12th, sn rear* 8 0
1069 13/4 Whitwell-On' (R) RES 3m 12 G *mid-div most of way, not qckn frm 4 out* 6 0
1250 26/4 Easingwold (L) RES 3m 15 GS *prom early, mstks, fdd frm hlfwy* 8 0
1419 10/5 Easingwold (L) CON 3m 8 GF *not fluent, rear, wll bhnd 8th, t.o. 10th, p.u. nxt* P 0

Found weak race(probably fortunate); barely stays & will struggle to follow up. 13

PROPHETS THUMB (Irish) — I 4[3], I 18[4], I 53[5], I 136[4], I 238[F]

PROPLUS ch.g. 15 Proverb - Castle Treasure by Perspex Mrs A E Lee
1996 4(0)
1063 13/4 Maisemore P' (L) XX 3m 13 GF *prom to 5th, bhnd 12th, p.u. 15th* P 0
1205 26/4 Clifton On ' (L) CON 3m 13 GS *rear div frm 4th, t.o. frm 9th* 9 0
1464 11/5 Tweseldown (R) XX 3m 7 GF *prom, lft in ld 7-9th, wknd 13th* 4 0
1576 26/5 Chaddesley ' (L) XX 3m 12 F *prom til wknd 8th, t.o. frm 12th* 4 0

No longer of any account 0

PROSCENIUM (Irish) — I 257[P], I 421[F], I 475[P]

PROSPECT STAR (Irish) — I 42[5], I 161[P], I 593[4], I 610[5]

PROUD CARLINGFORD (Irish) — I 261[P], I 302, , I 443[P]

PROUD PRINCESS (Irish) — I 33[P], I 60[2], I 96[4], I 228[4], I 310[1]

PROVINCIAL RETREAT ch.g. 5 Town And Country - Dingley Dell by Saucy Kit C G Squance
605 22/3 Parham (R) MDO 3m 7 F *in tch til wknd & p.u. aft 2 out* P 0
1446 10/5 Peper Harow (L) MDO 3m 7 GF *(fav) 5/2-5/4,chsd ldrs,went 2nd & hit 13th, ld 15th, rdn clr flat* 1 10

Won poor race; looks the part & will improve; needs to for Restricted. 13

PRUDENCE SARN (Irish) — I 75[F], I 256[F]

PSAMEAD ch.g. 5 Master Trader - Servalan by Souvran R H York
283 23/2 Charing (L) MDO 3m 16 G *s.s. schoold & t.o. til p.u. 12th* P 0
581 16/3 Detling (L) MDO 3m 12 F *alwys rear, last & pshd alng final ctt, bhnd whn p.u. 17th* P 0

686	29/3	Charing	(L)	MDO 2 1/2m	5	F	*trckd ldrs, 3rd & btn whn ran out 2 out*	r	-
990	12/4	Kingston Bl'	(L)	MDN 3m	11	GF	*(bl) cls up to 9th, wll bhnd whn nrly ref 14th, p.u. nxt*	P	0

A most unpromising beginning. 0

PUBLIC INTEREST (Irish) — I 423^{P}

PUDDING br.m. 5 Infantry - Spring Tide by Take A Reef — Paul Rackham

441	8/3	Higham	(L)	INT 3m	7	G	*immed last, t.o. 4th, p.u. aft 11th*	P	0

Only learning on debut. 0

PUKKA SAHIB b.g. 10 Jalmood (USA) - So True by So Blessed — Mrs S K Edmunds

1996 **12(NH),12(NH)**

60	1/2	Kingston Bl'	(L)	MDN 3m	17	GF	*sn prom, chsd ldrs til wknd 14th*	7	0
252	22/2	Brocklesby '	(L)	MDO 3m	9	G	*plld hrd, ld 5-7th, 4th outpcd 5 out*	5	0
485	9/3	Tweseldown	(R)	MDO 3m	11	G	*last pair, prog whn mstk 13th, sn lost tch, no dang aft*	6	0
990	12/4	Kingston Bl'	(L)	MDN 3m	11	GF	*prssd ldr, ld brfly 13th, wknd nxt*	6	0
1193	20/4	Garthorpe	(R)	MDO 3m	9	GF	*keen hld, cls 4th & rdn 13th, wknd, t.o. & p.u. 3 out*	P	0

Safe enough but no stamina. 0

PULL THE LEVER (Irish) — I 175^{2}, I 210^{P}, I 364^{2}, I 373^{2}, I 463^{P}

PULLTHEPLUG b.g. 6 Reesh - Stop Gap by Hasty Word — Mrs J A Burton

1996 F(-),P(0),F(-)

206	15/2	Weston Park	(L)	MDN 3m	9	G	*ld to 3rd, cls up til wknd rpdly 5 out, p.u. 3 out*	P	0
327	1/3	Eaton Hall	(R)	MDN 3m	11	GS	*prom to hlfwy, wknd qckly, p.u. 5 out*	P	0
470	8/3	Eyton-On-Se'	(L)	MDN 2 1/2m	12	G	*mstks, mid-div, onepcd frm 4 out*	5	0
665	23/3	Eaton Hall	(R)	MDO 3m	11	GF	*prom, in tch to 5 out, wknd & onepcd aft*	5	0

Only beaten one horse so far but gradually getting the message and can do better. 11

PUNNETT'S TOWN br.m. 7 Sulaafah (USA) - Queen's Bronze by King's Troop — Mrs L P Baker

196	15/2	Higham	(L)	MDO 3m	12	G	*disp to 3rd, cls 2nd til lost plc 8th, ran out nxt*	r	-
324	1/3	Marks Tey	(L)	RES 3m	16	G	*s.s., bhnd, jmp rght 4th, t.o. & p.u. 12th*	P	0
582	16/3	Detling	(L)	MDN 3m	16	F	*ran out 1st*	r	-

Wayward so far. 0

PUNTERS FORTUNE (Irish) — I 28^{P}

PURBECK POLLY ch.m. 7 Pollerton - Warwick Air by True Song — Mrs Angela Davis

110	8/2	Milborne St'	(L)	MDN 3m	7	GF	*in tch til blnd & u.r. 5th*	U	-
182	15/2	Larkhill	(R)	MDO 3m	12	G	*last pair,wll bhnd,prog 10th,lft 3rd & chnc whn f 3 out,rmnt*	3	0
312	1/3	Clyst St Ma'	(L)	RES 3m	8	HY	*hld up, prog 11th, 2nd 13th, ev ch 2 out, wknd apr last*	3	12
692	29/3	Little Wind'	(R)	MDO 3m	8	GF	*in tch,mstk 7th,outpcd 15th,styd on wll apr last,ld nr fin*	1	12
1157	20/4	Stafford Cr'	(R)	RES 3m	11	GF	*rear whn f 6th*	F	-

Gamely won a poor Maiden; can improve but needs much more for Restricted. 14

PURCELL (Irish) — I 441^{P}, I 471^{P}, I 521^{P}

PURE AIR (Irish) — I 76^{R}, I 85^{P}, I 142^{2}, I 298^{5}

PURE ENERGY (Irish) — I 4^{P}, I 38^{6}, I 258^{P}, I 317^{P}

PURE MADNESS(USA) b.g. 7 Northern Prospect (USA) - Icy Oddsmaker (USA) by Icecapade (USA) — D R Greig

1996 P(0),R(-),3(0),3(0),3(14),2(14),1(15),1(19),**P(0)**

483	9/3	Tweseldown	(R)	CON 3m	8	G	*hld up last, jmpd left, t.o. 9th, ran out 11th*	r	-
603	22/3	Parham	(R)	OPE 3m	2	F	*wth rvl to 3rd, not keen aft & drvn alng, t.o. 13th*	2	0

Dual winner 96; highly suspect previously; changed hands & unlikely ti achieve much now. 0

PURPLE MELODY(IRE) ch.g. 7 Orchestra - Violate by Continuation — A J Brazier

1996 2(13),1(14)

260	22/2	Newtown	(L)	RES 3m	16	G	*(fav) prom 5th, ld 15th-2 out, ran on flat, just faild*	2	19
574	16/3	Garnons	(L)	RES 3m	14	G	*(fav) 7/4-evens, nvr rchd ldrs, effrt 14th, no prog, p.u. 3 out*	P	0

Won hot race 96; changed hands; finished early 97; still young; win Restricted if fit 98;G-S. 17

PUSH ALONG ch.g. 10 Push On - Pollywella by Welham — G T Goldsworthy

1996 4(0),5(0),1(20),3(14),2(22),F(-)

256	22/2	Newtown	(L)	OPE 3m	17	G	*in tch in rear to 10th, sn strgglng, t.o.*	11	0
402	8/3	Llanfrynach	(R)	INT 3m	7	G	*2nd til ld 15th, hdd 2 out, alwys hld*	2	17
714	29/3	Llanvapley	(L)	CON 3m	15	GF	*mid-div, no prog frm 13th*	7	0

Restricted winner 96; brief 97; likes Llanfrynach; chance there if fit 98; Soft best. 17

PUSH GENTLY (Irish) — I 6^{4}, I 32^{P}, I 61^{2}, I 97^{2}, I 139^{1}, I 215^{4}, I 314^{1}, I 411^{2}, I 495^{5}, I 543, , I 573^{5}, I 604^{2}, I 612^{P}

PUTTINGONTHESTYLE ch.g. 10 Enchantment - Straightaway Style by Anax — John Nicholas

1996 P(0),P(0),R(-),r(-),3(0)

185	15/2	Erw Lon	(L)	MDN	3m	14	G	*lost plc 3rd, wknd rpdly & p.u. 9th*	P	0

Of no account 0

PYRO PENNANT b.g. 12 Official - Courtney Pennant by Angus — Mrs J Brook-Saunders

1996 U(-),P(0),8(0),P(0),4(0),4(0),**P(0)**,6(0),4(0),4(0),3(0)

2	19/1	Barbury Cas'	(L)	XX	3m	14	GF	*alwys rear, 9th hlfwy, t.o. & p.u. 14th*	P	0
87	2/2	Wolverhampt'	(L)	MDO	3m	11	GS	*cls up, 2nd brfly aft 11th, sn outpcd, fin tired*	4	10
244	22/2	Lemalla	(R)	MDO	3m	12	S	*ld/disp to 7th, cls up til onepcd frm 3 out*	4	12
408	8/3	Llanfrynach	(R)	MDN	3m	12	G	*mid-div, no prog frm 14th*	5	0
847	31/3	Lydstep	(L)	MDO	3m	5	F	*ld/disp to 13th, ev ch 4 out, wknd rpdly*	4	0
1231	26/4	Pyle	(R)	MDO	3m	7	GS	*2nd whn mstk 8th, sn bhnd, kpt on onepcd frm 15th*	3	0

Lost all 26 starts 95/97; ran best ever 3rd start but need a miracle to win. 0

QANNAAS br.g. 13 Kris - Red Berry by Great Nephew — Mrs Ann Leat

1996 1(22),1(25),1(25),**1(26)**

482	9/3	Tweseldown	(R)	LAD	3m	5	G	*(fav) (bl) j.w. made all, easily*	1	24

Useful; won last 8; front runs; blinkers; finished early 97; win more if fit 98; G-F. 25

QUAH (Irish) — I 460[F], I 501[5], I 539[P], I 591[P]

QUAKER PEP ch.g. 7 Scallywag - Jo Matanza by Adropejo — T H Gibbon

1996 P(0),P(0)

540	16/3	Erw Lon	(L)	MDN	3m	13	GF	*alwys rear, p.u. 13th*	P	0
639	22/3	Howick	(L)	MDN	3m	15	GF	*(vis) mid-div, f 8th, dead*	F	-

Dead. 0

QUALITAIR MEMORY(IRE) ch.g. 8 Don't Forget Me - Whist Awhile by Caerleon (USA) — C L Tizzard

1996 5(0),2(22),1(20),1(21),3(24),F(-),1(23),1(22)

5	19/1	Barbury Cas'	(L)	OPE	3m	11	GF	*prom, 2nd hlfwy, lft in ld apr 12th, hdd 2 out, just hld*	2	25
42	1/2	Larkhill	(R)	MXO	3m	7	GF	*prssd ldr to 12th,outpcd 14th,ran on 2 out,disp 2nd & f last*	F	27
220	16/2	Heythrop	(R)	OPE	3m	20	G	*(fav) chsd ldrs, strgglng frm 15th, no ch aft*	8	10
239	22/2	Lemalla	(R)	OPE	3m	7	S	*ld til jnd 17th, disp 2 out, wknd apr last*	3	22
522	15/3	Cothelstone	(L)	CON	3m	14	GS	*(fav) handy, disp 3 out, ld nxt, pshd out*	1	24
646	22/3	Castle Of C'	(R)	OPE	3m	5	G	*ld to 9th, mstk 11th, ld 14th, rdn 3 out, hdd & no ext flat*	2	24
929	6/4	Charlton Ho'	(L)	MEM	3m	5	G	*(fav) mstk 7th,ld to 12th,ld agn 14th,hrd rdn flat,just hld on*	1	24
1042	12/4	Cothelstone	(L)	MXO	3m	2	GF	*(fav) trckd ldr, ld 14th, easily*	1	23
1154	20/4	Stafford Cr'	(R)	OPE	3m	2	GF	*(fav) made all, ran on wll whn chal frm last*	1	22
1316	3/5	Holnicote	(L)	MXO	3m	4	G	*(fav) ld/disp til hdd & just outpcd flat*	2	25

Solid; consistent; now useful; beaten by good horses; sure to win more;G/F-S. 25

QUARTER MARKER(IRE) br.g. 9 Celio Rufo - Palatine Lady by Pauper — Richard Lee

1996 P(0),P(0),P(0),F(-),P(0),F(-),U(-),P(0),3(0),**P(0)**

257	22/2	Newtown	(L)	LAD	3m	12	G	*alwys rear, t.o. last whn p.u. 14th*	P	0
381	4/3	Leicester	(R)	HC	2m 1f	13	G	*in tch till wknd 3 out.*	6	0

Of no account 0

QUAYSIDE BUOY (Irish) — I 78[P], I 144[P], I 306, , I 420[P], I 477[P], I 535[P]

QUEEN BIDDY (Irish) — I 539[U], I 566[3]

QUEENOFCLUBS (Irish) — I 7[F], I 45[1], I 75[P], I 170[F], I 240[P], I 380[4]

QUEEN OF SILVER (Irish) — I 274[P]

QUEEN OFTHE KNOWES b.m. 5 Rakaposhi King - Fast Lady by Push On — Mrs D Walton

1424	10/5	Aspatria	(L)	RES	3m	17	G	*schoold in last til u.r. 5th*	U	-
1513	17/5	Corbridge	(R)	MDO	3m	13	GS	*rear, t.o. 9th, p.u. nxt*	P	0

Only learning so far. 0

QUEEN'S CHAPLAIN b.g. 13 The Parson - Reginasway by Flair Path — Miss Rebecca Heal

1996 4(12),4(0),P(0),**F(-)**,**R(-)**

237	22/2	Lemalla	(R)	CON	3m	13	S	*mstk 5th, prog to 6th at 9th, lost plc 12th, ref 16th*	R	-
528	15/3	Wadebridge	(L)	CON	3m	5	GF	*(bl) lost tch 5th, p.u. 10th*	P	0

No longer of any account 0

QUEEN'S EQUA b or br.m. 7 Queen's Soldier (USA) - Equa by Cheval — Mrs B J Harkins

1996 P(0),P(0),F(-),P(0),P(0),P(0)

186	15/2	Erw Lon	(L)	MDN	3m	13	G	*in tch to 11th, wknd, blnd 14th & p.u.*	P	0
403	8/3	Llanfrynach	(R)	INT	3m	8	G	*rear, p.u. 9th*	P	0
542	16/3	Erw Lon	(L)	MDN	3m	15	GF	*mid-div, nvr a fctr*	5	0
720	29/3	Llanvapley	(L)	MDN	3m	8	GF	*mid-div, prog 3 out, no ext aft*	3	11
1009	12/4	St Hilary	(R)	MDN	3m	11	GF	*mid-div, wknd 12th, p.u. 15th*	P	0

1136	19/4 Bonvilston	(R) MDO 3m	15 G	*ld til ran out apr 13th*	r	-
1323	3/5 Bonvilston	(R) MDO 3m	14 G	*10s-6s, rear, prog hlfwy, nrst fin*	4	0
1562	24/5 Bassaleg	(R) MDO 3m	8 G	*chsd ldrs til lost tch 12th, jmpd slwly aft, t.o.*	4	0

Beaten 8 lengths on 4th start; barely worth a rating & much more needed. 0

QUEENS SERMON (Irish) — **I** 552⁴, **I** 574ᴾ

QUERRIN LODGE b.g. 11 Furry Glen - Opel Kadett by Steel Heart — P J Gratton

1996 P(0),P(0),3(10),P(0),P(0),3(0),4(0)

237	22/2 Lemalla	(R) CON 3m	13 S	*last frm 6th, wll bhnd whn p.u. last*	P	0
309	1/3 Clyst St Ma'	(L) CON 3m	7 HY	*sn bhnd, t.o. & p.u. 12th*	P	0
628	22/3 Kilworthy	(L) CON 3m	12 G	*8th hlfwy, nvr dang*	7	10
951	6/4 Black Fores'	(R) CON 3m	3 G	*in tch, disp 7th, 3rd aft, tk 2nd apr last*	2	10
1258	27/4 Black Fores'	(R) INT 3m	5 F	*cls up to 11th, sn bhnd*	3	0
1480	11/5 Ottery St M'	(L) MEM 3m	6 G	*in tch to 10th, losng ground whn p.u. 13th*	P	0

Restricted winner 95; disappointing since & best avoided now. 11

QUICKER JACK b.g. 6 Crawter - Royal Promise by King Morgan — Mrs A Delve

524	15/3 Cothelstone	(L) RES 3m	10 GS	*s.s. alwys t.o.*	4	0
740	29/3 Higher Kilw'	(L) MDN 3m	15 GF	*sn wll bhnd, t.o. & p.u. 15th*	P	0

Much quicker jack. 0

QUICK QUICK SLOE b.m. 8 Scallywag - Cherry Morello by Bargello — Dr S G F Cave

1996 U(-),2(15),U(-),P(0)

303	1/3 Parham	(R) RES 3m	10 G	*mid-div, 6th & losing tch whn p.u. 14th*	P	0
524	15/3 Cothelstone	(L) RES 3m	10 GS	*not alwys fluent, lost tch 9th, p.u. 12th*	P	0

Maiden winner 95; lightly raced & unable to progress since; can only be watched now. 14

QUICK SILVER BOY gr.g. 7 Kalaglow - Safidar by Roan Rocket — P Riddick

1996 **P(NH),3(NH)**

399	8/3 Llanfrynach	(R) CON 3m	11 G	*cls up early, grad wknd*	8	0

Winning hurdler; last to finish & plenty to prove. 0

QUIET CONFIDENCE(IRE) b.m. 7 Pennine Walk - Northern Wisdom by Northfields (USA) — Mrs S Kerley

1996 3(17),U(-),1(15),1(19)

179	15/2 Larkhill	(R) CON 3m	12 G	*made all, clr 2nd, drew rght away frm 12th, unchal, imprssv*	1	29
376	3/3 Windsor	(R) HC 3m	11 GF	*(fav) ld, clr 10th, hit 13th, u.r..*	U	-
679	26/3 Ascot	(R) HC 2m 3f 110yds	9 G	*(fav) ld 3rd till hdd 4 out, one pace.*	2	22
932	6/4 Charlton Ho'	(L) LAD 3m	6 G	*chsd ldr, ld 9th, clr 13th, hdd 2 out, unable qckn*	2	26

Much improved; front runs; speedy; novice ridden; useful; can win H/chase; G-F. 26

QUINCE CROSS b.m. 6 Pitpan - Minnie The Moocher by Prince Hansel — Mrs Sarah Faulks

316	1/3 Clyst St Ma'	(L) MDN 3m	6 HY	*prom, ld 12-13th, outpcd, lft clr last, wknd & hdd flat*	2	0
526	15/3 Cothelstone	(L) MDN 3m	15 GS	*plld hrd, f 1st*	F	-
644	22/3 Castle Of C'	(R) MDO 3m	9 G	*mid-div, prog to jn ldrs & blnd 10th, wknd 15th, p.u. 2 out*	P	0

Last in a joke race; much more needed. 0

QUITE A MISS b.m. 7 True Song - Nitty's Girl by Spartan General — C W Loggin

1996 P(0)

758	29/3 Kimble	(L) OPE 3m	6 GF	*alwys bhnd, t.o. & p.u. 13th*	P	0
1160	20/4 Mollington	(R) INT 3m	9 GF	*chsd ldrs, wknd 12th, t.o. & p.u. 3 out*	P	0
1386	5/5 Eyton-On-Se'	(L) MDO 2 1/2m	8 GF	*mid-div early,rear 8th,some late prog,rnng on*	3	12
1537	18/5 Mollington	(R) MDO 3m	14 GS	*prom,ld 8th-aft 3 out,lft 2nd nxt,styd on to ld flat*	1	13

Improved; fortunate to win bad Maiden; much more needed. 13

QUOTE ch.m. 10 Oats - Queen Hill by Crozier — Mrs Terence Sims

1996 **F(NH),P(NH)**

692	29/3 Little Wind'	(R) MDO 3m	8 GF	*lft 2 fences, cont t.o. til f 11th*	F	-
916	5/4 Larkhill	(R) MEM 3m	3 F	*alwys 3rd, dist bhnd whn lft 2nd last*	2	0
1024	12/4 Badbury Rin'	(L) MDO 3m	3 F	*plld, ld til apr 14th, sn wknd, lft remote 2nd 16th*	2	0

Flattered by her form figures; only beat a remounter; hopeless. 0

RABA RIBA gr.g. 12 Oats - Erica Alba by Yukon Eric (CAN) — J Spearing

125	9/2 Cottenham	(R) LAD 3m	11 GF	*prom, cls 3rd whn mstk & u.r. 10th*	U	-

Winning chaser; returned & won H/chase after brief sojourn pointing. 22

RABBLE ROUSER b.g. 10 Politico (USA) - Penny Pink by Spartan General — M J Brown

1996 2(13),U(-),r(-),2(12),1(16),P(0)

118 9/2 Wetherby Po' (L) RES 3m 14 GF *rear, prog 6th, blnd 10th, sn strggl ng, t.o.* 9 0
164 15/2 Witton Cast' (R) INT 3m 6 F *hld up rear, effrt 14th, sn outpcd, blnd 4 out & p.u.* P 0
353 2/3 Great Stain' (L) CON 3m 9 S *mid-div, went 2nd 5th, disp nxt-11th, sn wknd* 4 0

Maiden winner 96(well ridden); mistakes & struggling now upgraded; hard to find another win. 14

RACE AGAINST TIME b.m. 11 Latest Model - Gemini Miss by My Swanee — Mrs D D Scott
1996 P(0),F(-),F(-)
556 16/3 Ottery St M' (L) RES 3m 12 G *n.j.w. mid-div, lost plc 10th, p.u. nxt* P 0
1395 5/5 High Bickin' (R) RES 3m 9 G *prom til wknd rpdly 7th, last whn jmpd slwly 14th, p.u. nxt* P 0

Gave it a go last start but yet to show any tangible ability 0

RACE TO THE RHYTHM gr.m. 10 Deep Run - Mother Cluck by Energist — Andrew Davis
211 16/2 Southwell P' (L) MDO 3m 15 GS *hld up, lost tch 10th, p.u. 12th* P 0
712 29/3 High Easter (L) MDO 3m 4 F *trckd ldrs, 4th & strugg whn hit 16th, no ch aft* 4 0

placed novice hurdles; lightly raced now & nothing rateable in 97. 0

RACHELS PLAN (Irish) — I 63^{S}, I 96^{P}, I 187^{P}, I 218^{6}, I 270^{F}, I 339^{6}, I 388^{P}
RADICAL DUAL (Irish) — I 282, , I 351^{2}, I 437^{3}, I 526, , I 580^{3}, I 594^{P}
RADICAL RIVER (Irish) — I 259^{6}, I 382^{P}, I 475^{2}, I 516^{P}
RADICAL-TIMES (Irish) — I 4^{P}, I 52^{1}, I 145^{3}, I 236^{4}, I 569^{2}, I 603^{2}
RADICAL VIEWS b.g. 12 Radical - Regency View by Royal Highway — M A Walter
1996 **8(0)**,5(10),2(15),1(16),2(18),B(-)
759 29/3 Kimble (L) LAD 3m 4 GF *2nd hlfwy, lost plc, qcknd to ld 2 out, jnd last, hdd nr fin* 2 21
1078 13/4 Guilsborough (L) LAD 3m 11 GF *not fluent, nvr going wll, rear til p.u. 13th* P 0
1451 10/5 Kingston Bl' (L) OPE 3m 5 G *blnd 2nd, hld up, qcknd to ld 14th, hdd nxt, wknd rpdly* 4 10
1534 18/5 Mollington (R) OPE 3m 7 GS *w.w. cls up 14th, pshd alng nxt, ev ch apr 2 out,wknd last* 3 18

Reains ability; finds little & hard to win with but can find another opening;G/F-S. 20

RADIO DAYS(IRE) ch.g. 6 Boreen (FR) - Sensible Sue by Orchestra — T D Sproat
185 15/2 Erw Lon (L) MDN 3m 14 G *(fav) ld to 2nd & frm 5th, clr 2 out, shkn up & ran on wll flat* 1 16
538 16/3 Erw Lon (L) RES 3m 5 GF *(fav) made all, easily* 1 18
1005 12/4 St Hilary (R) CON 3m 10 GF *(fav) hld up in 3rd, prog to ld 3 out, just hld on und pres flat* 1 20
1180 20/4 Lydstep (L) MEM 3m 2 GF *(fav) ld to 10th, sn ld agn, in cmmnd aft, pshd out* 1 15

Ex Irish; unbeaten in modest races; good stable; can progress to Opens in 98. 21

RAGLAN ROAD b.g. 13 Furry Glen - Princess Concorde by Great Heron (USA) — Mark Johnson
1996 **5(NH)**,**6(NH)**,**7(NH)**,**6(NH)**,**2(NH)**
142 9/2 Tweseldown (R) MEM 3m 8 GF *not fluent, outpcd in rear, some prog 12th,sn wknd,p.u.3 out* P 0

Won 3 L adies 94; no show in Members; won 2 H/chases after. 18

RAGTIME BOY b.g. 9 Sunyboy - Ragtime Dance by Ragstone — Mrs Jo Clarke
1996 **F(-)**,2(20),1D(20),**F(-)**
242 22/2 Lemalla (R) MDO 3m 10 S *(fav) w.w. prog 9th, 2nd 13th, lft clr 16th, mstk last, unchal* 1 16
491 10/3 Taunton (R) HC 3m 8 G *held up, hdwy 13th, wknd from 4 out.* 3 15
736 29/3 Higher Kilw' (L) RES 3m 10 GF *handy, chsd wnr 15th, no ext und pres frm 3 out* 2 18
1088 16/4 Hockworthy (L) MEM 3m 6 GF *w.w. cls engh 14th, not qckn apr 2 out, kpt on* 3 17
1519 17/5 Bratton Down (L) RES 3m 15 GS *(bl) mid-div, mstk 8th, rmndrs 11th, bhnd & p.u. 14th* P 0
1613 7/6 Umberleigh (L) RES 3m 13 F *out of tch til jnd chsng grp 7th, 6th & no ch 14th, styd on* 4 0

Won weak Maiden; should have won long before; hard ride & needs strong handling; could win again. .. 17

RAGTIMER b.g. 7 Nearly A Hand - Ragtime Dance by Ragstone — W Bush
1996 P(0),U(-)
292 1/3 Didmarton (L) MEM 3m 9 G *3rd whn blnd & u.r. 3rd* U -

Lightly raced & yet to show anything. 10

RAGTIME SONG b.g. 8 Dunbeath (USA) - Kelowna (USA) by Master Derby (USA) — J S Ruddy
1996 **F(NH)**,**14(NH)**,**3(NH)**,**8(NH)**,**9(NH)**
194 15/2 Higham (L) OPE 3m 12 G *chsd ldrs to 12th, wknd, wll bhnd & p.u. 16th* P 0
271 22/2 Ampton (R) CON 3m 15 G *prom to 7th, grad lst pl, t.o.* 12 0
442 8/3 Higham (L) LAD 3m 8 G *disp/ld to 5th, last by 8th, hit 13th, t.o.* 5 0
799 31/3 Marks Tey (L) OPE 3m 5 F *(bl) mstk 1st,slw jmp 7th,hdd nxt,wknd qckly 9th,t.o. & p.u. 11th* P 0

Flat winner 93; poor novice hurdler; no prospects. 0

RAHEEN CROSS (Irish) — I 63^{P}, I 97^{F}, I 370^{F}
RAIKE IT IN b.m. 7 Silly Prices - Caravan Centre by Nelcius — J Hugill
1996 P(0),4(12),2(12)
429 8/3 Charm Park (L) MDO 3m 14 GF *(fav) rear & sn bhnd, t.o. 9th, p.u. nxt* P 0

1073 13/4 Whitwell-On' (R) MDO 2 1/2m 88yds 17 G *ld to 7th, wknd rpdly, p.u. 11th* P 0

Some promise in 96; looked troubled 97 & best watched initially in 98. .... **11**

RAINBOW FANTASIA(IRE) b.g. 8 Orchestra - Rovral Flo by Whistling Deer J H Wingfield Digby
1996 R(-),F(-),2(10),P(0),3(0),4(0),6(0),4(0)
111 8/2 Milborne St' (L) MDN 3m 8 GF *j.w. handy, 2nd frm 11th til ld aft 2 out, styd on well,lame* 1 13

Change dhands & found bad race; problems now & well below Restricted standard. **13**

RAINBOW TRIX (Irish) — I 186F, I 271F

RAINCHECK b.h. 6 Mtoto - Lashing (USA) by Storm Bird (CAN) Mrs Georgina Worsley
1996 **P(NH),0(NH),P(NH),P(NH),2(NH),F(NH),U(NH),U(NH)**
14 25/1 Cottenham (R) MDO 3m 7 GF *hld up, prog to ld 14-16th, ld, blnd & hdd 2 out, onepcd flt* 3 14

Disappointing under rules; looked unlucky in only point; unreliable but good enough to win if fit 98 ..... **14**

RAINPROOF (Irish) — I 162P, I 201³, I 295⁵

RAISE A LOAN br.g. 7 Impecunious - Lizzie The Twig by Precipice Wood Mrs C Bailey
1996 1(15),F(-),1(19)
62 1/2 Horseheath (R) CON 3m 5 GF *j.w. ld 6th til p.u. apr 14th, lame* P 0

Dead **22**

RAISE AN ARGUMENT b.g. 18 No Argument - Ten Again by Raise You Ten Mrs J H Docker
1996 3(0),1(18),3(19),1(20),1(20),3(15),r(-)
138 9/2 Thorpe Lodge (L) OPE 3m 5 GF *1st ride, j.w. ld til jnd 3 out, ran on onepcd aft* 2 20
250 22/2 Brocklesby ' (L) OPE 3m 6 G *ld 4th, 4th outpcd frm 6 out, lft 2nd 2 last* 2 18
771 29/3 Dingley (R) OPE 3m 10 G *j.w.chsd ldrs, effrt to 2nd 2 out, ran on gamely* 2 19
1204 26/4 Clifton On ' (L) MEM 3m 6 GS *(fav) j.w. tried to make all, hdd aft 2 out, onepcd* 2 17
1475 11/5 Garthorpe (R) XX 3m 13 GS *rear frm 4th, 9th hlfwy, t.o.* 8 0

Retired. **15**

RAKEIRA b.m. 5 Rakaposhi King - Keira by Keren R Paisley
161 15/2 Lanark (R) MDO 2m 5f 14 G *sn bhnd, p.u. 10th* P 0
418 8/3 Dalston (R) MDO 2 1/2m 10 GS *alwys rear, t.o. & p.u. 10th* P 0
564 16/3 Lanark (R) MDO 2 1/2m 13 GS *nvr nr ldrs* 5 0

Beaten out of sight when completing; can do better. **0**

RAKI CRAZY ch.g. 6 Lyphento (USA) - Tom's Nap Hand by Some Hand O J Carter
1485 11/5 Ottery St M' (L) MDO 3m 13 G *10s-4s, mid-div, nvr on trms, p.u. 2 out* P 0
1530 18/5 Fakenham (L) HC 2m 5f 110yds 11 G *bhnd when blnd 3rd, hdwy 10th, wknd 4 out.* 6 0

Stables usual eccentric campaign; ran passsably in H/chase; can win a point. **13**

RAKISH QUEEN b.m. 10 Joshua - Cognac Queen by Armagnac Monarch R W Phizacklea
1996 U(-),P(0)
770 29/3 Dingley (R) RES 3m 18 G *alwys rear hlf, outpcd 6 out, p.u. nxt* P 0
1081 13/4 Guilsborough (L) RES 3m 13 GF *rear frm 10th, t.o. 14th, p.u. 2 out* P 0
1355 4/5 Dingley (R) RES 3m 12 G *rcd wd, prog 10th, chsd ldng pr 3 out, no prog aft* 3 16
1475 11/5 Garthorpe (R) XX 3m 13 GS *raced wd, in tch to 8th, t.o. & p.u. last* P 0
1542 18/5 Wolverhampt' (L) RES 3m 6 GS *rear, prog 14th, chsd wnr nxt, no imp frm 2 out* 2 13
1605 1/6 Dingley (R) RES 3m 13 GF *pllng, raced wd, cls up til not qckn aft 15th* 5 11

Maiden winner 94; novice ridden; inconsistent; need a poor race to win again. **14**

RALEAGH MUGGINS (Irish) — I 112³, I 252⁵, I 326², I 503⁴, I 555³

RALEAGH NATIVE (Irish) — I 369P, I 462¹

RALLYE STRIPE gr.g. 13 Buckskin (FR) - Petit Bleu by Abernant Col S R Allen
1996 P(0),5(0),6(0),P(0),F(-),F(-),P(0),6(0)
1274 27/4 Little Wind' (R) XX 3m 8 GF *ld to 6th, sn wknd, t.o. 10th, p.u. 3 out* P 0
1498 14/5 Cothelstone (L) MDO 3m 9 GF *prom, mstk 12th, 3rd & chnc 16th, wknd 2 out* 4 0
1597 31/5 Bratton Down (L) MDO 3m 12 F *s.s. sn prom in chsng grp, wknd 11th, t.o. 14th* 7 0

Does not stay **0**

RALLYING CRY(IRE) b.g. 9 Last Tycoon - Clarina by Klairon Mrs J Seymour
1996 P(0),**4(0)**,P(0),6(0)
1222 26/4 Balcormo Ma' (R) MDO 3m 6 F *(bl) held up, wnt 2nd brfly 3 out, wknd apr nxt* 3 0
1336 3/5 Mosshouses (L) MDO 3m 7 F *(fav) not alwys fluent, some prog frm 3 out, not rch ldng pair* 3 11
1513 17/5 Corbridge (R) MDO 3m 13 GS *(bl) mid-div, jmpd slwly 6th, wknd 11th, p.u. 14th* P 0
1586 28/5 Cartmel (L) HC 3 1/4m 10 GF *(bl) bhnd, mstk 2nd and 4th, lost tch 6th, p.u. after 8th, dismntd.* P 0

Dead **10**

RAMBLING-GIRL b or br.m. 6 Rambling River - Kerera by Keren — John E Wright

269 22/2 Duncombe Pa' (R) MDO 3m 16 G *prom, jmp slwly 1st, fdd 10th, lost tch 12th, p.u. 4 out* P 0

Not yet of any account 0

RAMBLING LORD(IRE) b.g. 9 Mister Lord (USA) - Vickies Gold by Golden Love — G J Smith

1996 U(-),1(16),1(20)

216 16/2 Southwell P' (L) OPE 3m 12 GS *rear, prog 10th, lost tch apr 12th, p.u. 15th* P 0
351 2/3 Market Rase' (L) OPE 3m 10 GF *chsd ldr 11th,blnd nxt,outpcd 14th,3rd & no ch whn blnd last* 3 16
490 10/3 Stratford (L) HC 3m 12 G *held up, n.d..* 7 0
887 1/4 Flagg Moor (L) XX 3m 8 G *chsd ldrs, 2nd 4 out-2 out, wll btn whn blnd last* 3 13
1187 20/4 Garthorpe (R) MEM 3m 9 GF *(fav) in tch, chsd ldr 13th-3 out, btn whn blnd nxt* 3 13

Dual winner 96; changed hands; well beaten & disappointing in97; best watched now; Good. 14

RAMBLING OATS gr.g. 8 Oats - Ramelton by Precipice Wood — R J Owen

1996 **P(NH),U(NH)**

120 9/2 Wetherby Po' (L) MDO 3m 18 GF *chsng grp, wknd 12th, t.o. & p.u. 2 out* P 0
768 29/3 Whittington (L) MDO 3m 10 S *alwys prom, ld 2 out, wknd qckly nxt* 4 0

N o form under rules; 1st signs on last start; may do better; easier course would help. 12

RAMBLING SAM (Irish) — **I** 248[1]

RAMONA STYLE (Irish) — **I** 165[2], **I** 255[P]

RAMSTAR ch.g. 9 Import - Meggies Dene by Apollo Eight — A Loze

1996 **7(NH),3(NH),5(NH),2(NH),5(NH),7(NH),3(NH),5(NH),1(NH),1(NH),3(NH),6(NH),3(NH)**

94 7/2 Newbury (L) HC 2 1/2m 12 G *hdwy 10th, wknd after 12th, t.o. when p.u. before last.* P 0
587 19/3 Ludlow (R) HC 2 1/2m 18 GF *chsd ldrs, mstk 5th, wknd 11th.* 7 18

Winning chaser; does not stay 3 miles; opportunities limited & hard to find H/chase. 18

RAPID RASCAL b.h. 12 Rapid Pass - Sue Ming Vii — Miss P J Boundy

1996 7(0),5(12),U(-),4(0),3(17),B(-),F(-),4(12),5(14),5(14),P(0),4(0)

109 8/2 Milborne St' (L) XX 3m 8 GF *prom, disp 5-10th, lost tch & outpcd aft* 4 12
520 15/3 Cothelstone (L) LAD 3m 12 GS *ld 2nd-6th, sn wknd, p.u. 14th* P 0
864 31/3 Kingston St' (R) LAD 3m 6 F *ld to 6th,lost pl,ran on agn apr last,strng run flat,unlucky* 2 17
1141 19/4 Larkhill (R) LAD 3m 4 F *(fav) disp clr ld til ld 9th, drew clr apr 13th, unchal* 1 16
1257 27/4 Black Fores' (R) LAD 3m 5 F *(fav) trckd ldrs, ld 7th-9th, drppd bck, rallied to ld agn flat* 1 16
1438 10/5 Holnicote (L) LAD 3m 7 G *slght ld 2-6th, wll in tch til outpcd 15th, kpt on* 3 18
1492 14/5 Cothelstone (L) MEM 3m 4 GF *(fav) ld to 6th, ld 12th, rdn & hdd last, not qckn* 2 15
1548 24/5 Mounsey Hil' (R) LAD 3m 10 G *chsd ldr to 13th, sn drpppd out, t.o.* 6 12
1595 31/5 Bratton Down (L) LAD 3m 5 F *mstk 9th, prssd ldr to 11th, outpcd frm 15th* 4 0

Won 3 of 21 starts 96/97; novice ridden; onepaced; may find another weak race; any. 16

RAPID REGENT b.g. 10 Rapid Pass - Kamella II — Mrs P Visick

120 9/2 Wetherby Po' (L) MDO 3m 18 GF *alwys rear, t.o. & p.u. 11th* P 0
345 2/3 Market Rase' (L) MDO 3m 13 GF *mid-div to 8th, sn wll bhnd, t.o. & p.u. 12th* P 0
544 16/3 Garthorpe (R) MEM 3m 6 GF *ld to 3rd, prom til u.r. 9th* U -
839 31/3 Thorpe Lodge (L) MDO 3m 15 F *ldng pair whn f 2nd* F -
1191 20/4 Garthorpe (R) RES 3m 8 GF *prom to 9th, last & wkng 12th, p.u. nxt* P 0

Of no account 0

RAP UP FAST(USA) b.g. 8 Eskimo (USA) - Naomi's Flash (USA) by Ray Jeter (USA) — R T Baimbridge

1996 5(12),F(-),4(10)

1066 13/4 Maisemore P' (L) MDO 3m 9 GF *(fav) ld aft 2nd, clr nxt, kpt on und pres frm 2 out* 1 16

Beat subsequent winner; barely stays; shrewd stable may find another opening;G-F. 15

RARE FIRE b.g. 13 Rarity - El Diana by Tarboosh (USA) — Mrs R Davison

1996 P(0),P(0)

231 22/2 Friars Haugh (L) LAD 3m 13 G *ld to 4th, sn wknd, p.u. 13th* P 0
411 8/3 Dalston (R) CON 3m 16 GS *t.o. 8th, p.u. 10th* P 0
608 22/3 Friars Haugh (L) XX 3m 6 GF *2nd til 7th, lost tch by 9th, t.o.* 5 0
809 31/3 Tranwell (L) MEM 3m 5 G *alwys last, t.o. & p.u. 6th* P 0

No longer of any account 0

RARE FLUTTER b.m. 10 Sunyboy - Wings Ground by Murrayfield — D J Renney

1996 P(0),4(0),U(-),P(0),1(19),4(16),U(-)

294 1/3 Didmarton (L) INT 3m 20 G *mid-div, outpcd 11th, 7th & keeping on onepcd whn u.r. 3 out* U -
395 8/3 Barbury Cas' (L) XX 3m 9 G *alwys rear, mstk 7th, no ch frm 12th, t.o. & p.u. 2 out* P 0
1264 27/4 Southwell P' (L) INT 3m 9 G *mid-div, rdn 10th, wll bhnd 12th, p.u. 2 out* P 0

Won 3 points 95/96 for top stable; changed hands; novice ridden & hard to win again. 14

RARE HARVEST (Irish) — **I** 333[P]

RARE HOUSE (Irish) — **I** 94P, **I** 128P

RARELY AT ODDS b.g. 13 Tyrnavos - Carol Service by Daring Display (USA) Mrs S A Sansom

1996 8(0),7(0),4(0),5(0),4(0),4(0),7(0),8(0)

123 9/2 Cottenham (R) INT 3m 13 GF *in tch to 11th, sn wknd, t.o. & p.u. 16th* P 0
577 16/3 Detling (L) CON 3m 18 F *alwys rear, t.o. by hlfwy, p.u. 4 out* P 0
685 29/3 Charing (L) XX 3m 3 F *alwys chsng ldr, kpt on same pce frm 3 out* 3 14
829 31/3 Heathfield (R) XX 3m 5 F *prom, 3rd & rdn apr 4 out, ld last, ran on strngly* 1 13
969 6/4 Penshurst (L) INT 3m 3 F *ld 2nd-6th, wth ldr whn sltly hmp & u.r. 7th* U -
1128 19/4 Penshurst (L) LAD 3m 8 GF *alwys prom, pshd alng in 5th frm 12th, kpt on onepcd* 4 12
1447 10/5 Peper Harow (L) CON 3m 6 GF *tongue-strap, chsd ldrs, 4th & in tch whn u.r. 12th* U -

Changed hands; novice ridden; won desperate race; need same to win at 14; G/S-F. 12

RARE SALLY (Irish) — **I** 472P, **I** 525⁴, **I** 575P

RASCALLY gr.m. 7 Scallywag - Blue Gift by Hasty Word J Townson

1996 **7(NH),6(NH),7(NH),3(NH),1(NH),1(NH),2(NH),2(NH)**

475 9/3 Southwell P' (L) OPE 3m 7 G *mid-div, 5th & jmpd slwly 12th, sn rdn, no prog, p.u. 14th* P 0

Winning hurdler; returned to that sphere & won again after brief pointing career. 15

RASHKIN (Irish) — **I** 347¹

RASTA MAN b.g. 9 Ore - Bellino by Andrea Mantegna J Heard

173 15/2 Ottery St M' (L) CON 3m 7 G *(fav) in tch, chal 4 out, no ext frm 2 out* 3 17
453 8/3 Great Treth' (R) CON 3m 13 S *prom, disp 12-14th, no prog frm 3 out* 4 17
628 22/3 Kilworthy (L) CON 3m 12 G *ld 4-10th, cls up til wknd 15th* 6 17
789 31/3 Bishopsleigh (R) MEM 3m 5 G *(fav) ld til nrly ref & u.r. 3rd, rmntd, disp 5 out,ld last,ran on* 1 0
1398 5/5 High Bickin' (R) INT 3m 7 G *handy, 2nd at 14th, mstk nxt, ld 16th, sn clr, pshd out* 1 19
1481 11/5 Ottery St M' (L) CON 3m 12 G *hld up, prog 13th, ld 3 out, wknd flat, hdd nr fin* 2 20

Missed 96; won 4 of last 11; headstrong & hard ride; good enough for Confined; G-S. 20

RATHER SHARP b.g. 11 Green Shoon - Rather Special by Varano S D Watson

1996 **9(NH),P(NH),3(NH),4(NH),6(NH),2(NH),3(NH),F(NH),P(NH)**

924 6/4 Garthorpe (R) CON 3m 6 GF *prom, 2nd at 11th, fdd, p.u. 3 out* P 0
1097 19/4 Bangor (L) HC 2 1/2m 110yds 11 G *alwys bhnd, lost tch 9th, t.o. when p.u. before next.* P 0

Winning chaser; does not stay & no real prospects. 0

RATHMICHAEL b.g. 11 Petorius - Always Smiling by Prominer M S Rose

1996 4(0),1(19),2(18),4(17)

17 25/1 Badbury Rin' (L) CON 3m 9 GF *ld to 3rd, in tch til outpcd aft 13th, tk poor 3rd flat* 3 10
108 8/2 Milborne St' (L) MXO 3m 6 GF *disp early, wknd 10th, t.o. & p.u. 4 out* P 0

Intermediate winner 96; not 100% genuine

anged hands & hard to find another win; G-Hy. 16

RATICOSA b.m. 5 Hallgate - Rose Meadow by Mummy's Game Ms J Dunn

1262 27/4 Southwell P' (L) MDO 3m 15 G *rear, mstk 10th, t.o. 14th, p.u. 4 out* P 0
1409 5/5 Witton Cast' (R) MDO 3m 15 GS *rear, wll bhnd whn jmp v slwly 14th & p.u.* P 0

No signs yet 0

RATOATH GALE (Irish) — **I** 488P, **I** 565⁴, **I** 606¹

RAT RACE (Irish) — **I** 345⁵, **I** 412P

RAVENSDALE LAD ch.g. 9 Balinger - Minimint by Menelek W G Jordan

1996 4(10),2(14),1(14),2(14),2(18)

59 1/2 Kingston Bl' (L) RES 3m 16 GF *mid-div, 4th hlfwy, chsd wnr 11th, ran on onepcd* 2 18
262 22/2 Newtown (L) RES 3m 15 G *cls up, ch 14th, sn wknd* 4 0
433 8/3 Upton-On-Se' (R) RES 3m 18 G *chsd ldrs, effrt 12th, no prog 15th, p.u. 2 out* P 0

Maiden winner 96; ran well 1st outing; flopped after; Restricted chances if returning to form. 16

RAYMAN(IRE) ch.g. 9 Callernish - Clare's Hansel by Prince Hansel Alan Hill

1996 P(0),2(0),F(-),5(12),**4(19),3(17),6(14)**

126 9/2 Cottenham (R) RES 3m 14 GF *pllng, chsd ldng pair til wknd & blnd 14th, t.o.* 7 0
300 1/3 Didmarton (L) RES 3m 23 G *prom to 12th, bhnd whn p.u. last* P 0
495 14/3 Fakenham (L) HC 2m 5f 110yds 10 G *bhnd 8th, brief effort after 10th, soon behind.* 7 0
873 31/3 Hackwood Pa' (L) RES 3m 6 F *rear til prog to ld 13th, hdd 2 out, no ch wth wnr* 2 15
1058 13/4 Hackwood Pa' (L) RES 3m 6 GF *rear, clsd 13th, mstk nxt, wknd* 3 12
1450 10/5 Kingston Bl' (L) LAD 3m 7 G *rear, prog to ld aft 5th-9th, cls 2nd til outpcd 2 out* 2 15
1533 18/5 Mollington (R) XX 3m 8 GS *prog 5th, ld aft 8th-15th, ld nxt-apr 2 out, no ext* 2 16
1566 25/5 Kingston Bl' (L) LAD 3m 5 GF *(fav) hld up in tch, qcknd on innr to ld 3 out, sn clr, comf* 1 19

Romped home in bad Ladies; does not stay; best L/H; need same to win again; summer jumping; G/S-F 18

RAYMAR DANCER (Irish) — **I** 363^{P}

READ THE NEWS ch.m. 5 Mirror Boy - Craigies Girl by Germont — Mrs J P Copeland

1052	13/4	Lockerbie	(R)	MDN	3m	10	F	*sn last, t.o. & p.u. 3 out*	P	0
1429	10/5	Aspatria	(L)	MDO	3m	15	G	*alwys bhnd, t.o. & p.u. 14th*	P	0

No sign of making headlines 0

READY STEADY ch.g. 15 Bivouac - Very Merry by Lord Of Verona — Lady Temple

1996 6(12),F(-),4(0),1(20),U(-),1(22),1(21),2(21),F(-)

33	26/1	Alnwick	(L)	LAD	3m	12	G	*alwys bhnd, nvr a fctr*	8	0
132	9/2	Alnwick	(L)	LAD	3m	9	G	*chsd ldr to 4 out, wknd apr nxt*	5	0
158	15/2	Lanark	(R)	LAD	3m	8	G	*bhnd by 4th, jnd ldrs 11th, outpcd frm 3 out*	4	13
336	1/3	Corbridge	(R)	LAD	3m 5f	9	G	*hld up rear, prog 14th, no imp whn u.r. 2 out*	U	-
412	8/3	Dalston	(R)	LAD	3m	8	GS	*ld to 4th, prom til mstk 13th, sn btn, t.o. & p.u. last*	P	0

Won 6 95/96; anno domini looks to be winning now 14

REAL CLASS b.g. 14 Deep Run - Our Cherry by Tarqogan — T E Osborne

1996 2(18),2(19),6(0),2(17),2(19),1(18)

2	19/1	Barbury Cas'	(L)	XX	3m	14	GF	*sn wll bhnd, 10th hlfwy, nvr a fctr*	7	11

Won 4 95/96; changed hands & looks finished now 14

REAL GENT br.g. 7 Mandalus - Gentle Madam by Camden Town — Jonathan A Lee

1996 F(-)

199	15/2	Weston Park	(L)	MEM	3m	7	G	*mid-div, no ch wth ldng pair frm 4 out*	5	14
326	1/3	Eaton Hall	(R)	MDN	3m	14	GS	*mid-div, f 14th*	F	-
467	8/3	Eyton-On-Se'	(L)	RES	3m	15	G	*f 3rd*	F	-
574	16/3	Garnons	(L)	RES	3m	14	G	*prom, chsd ldr 13th, kpt on onepcd frm 3 out*	3	15
883	1/4	Flagg Moor	(L)	MDO	3m	12	G	*chsd ldr to 6th & frm 11th, styd on und pres to ld flat*	1	15

Improving; beat subsequent winner; game; stays well; can upgrade; Good. 17

REALLY NEAT gr.m. 11 Alias Smith (USA) - Tiddley by Filiberto (USA) — G M Beilby

1996 **10(NH),P(NH)**

314	1/3	Clyst St Ma'	(L)	MDN	3m	11	HY	*prom, ld 6th til blnd & u.r. 11th*	U	-
526	15/3	Cothelstone	(L)	MDN	3m	15	GS	*mid-div, hmpd & u.r. 6th*	U	-
862	31/3	Kingston St'	(R)	CON	3m	7	F	*rear til f 15th*	F	-

An elderly & clumsy maiden 0

REAL TO REAL (Irish) — **I** 297^{P}, **I** 425^{P}, **I** 551^{P}, **I** 568^{S}, **I** 595^{P}

REAL VALUE (Irish) — **I** 482^{P}, **I** 515^{P}

REAPER b.g. 9 Lightning Dealer - Deep Love — G Vergette

1996 P(0)

1268	27/4	Southwell P'	(L)	MDO	3m	13	G	*twrds rear whn b.d. 1st*	B	-
1409	5/5	Witton Cast'	(R)	MDO	3m	15	GS	*f 1st (dead)*	F	-

Dead. 0

REAPERS REWARD b.m. 9 Oats - Red Ragusa by Homeric — H J Barton

406	8/3	Llanfrynach	(R)	RES	3m	13	G	*ld to 7th, prom aft til outpcd 15th*	3	0
582	16/3	Detling	(L)	MDN	3m	16	F	*alwys prom, ld 10th-4 out, wknd*	3	0

Missed 96; placed 5 of last 14 starts; form weak & more needed 12

REBEL YELL(IRE) b.m. 6 Noalto - Domestic Goddess by Roselier (FR) — N Jones

640	22/3	Howick	(L)	MDN	3m	10	GF	*rear, p.u. 12th*	P	0
1010	12/4	St Hilary	(R)	MDN	3m	10	GF	*rear til p.u. 13th*	P	0
1136	19/4	Bonvilston	(R)	MDO	3m	15	G	*rear, sm prog 14th, ran on onepcd*	4	0
1323	3/5	Bonvilston	(R)	MDO	3m	14	G	*rear til p.u. 3 out*	P	0

Well beaten when finishing; only learning & can do better 0

RECKLESS LORD(IRE) ch.g. 7 Mister Lord (USA) - Strelorus by Black Minstrel — E H Crow

1996 U(-),P(0)

331	1/3	Eaton Hall	(R)	RES	3m	17	GS	*hld up bhnd ldrs, ld 10th, prssd whn f 2 out*	F	-

Maiden winner 95; lightly raced & not fulfil; still young enough but best watched. 17

RECLUSE b.g. 6 Last Tycoon - Nomadic Pleasure by Habitat — G McGuinness

1996 **12(NH),P(NH)**

156	15/2	Lanark	(R)	CON	3m	7	G	*bhnd by 4th, p.u. aft 10th*	P	0
611	22/3	Friars Haugh	(L)	CON	3m	11	GF	*(bl) in tch to hlfwy, bhnd whn p.u. 4 out*	P	0
943	6/4	Friars Haugh	(L)	MEM	3m	5	GF	*(bl) 2nd frm 3rd til lost tch frm 10th*	4	0

Flat winner; well beaten in points; running on the flat after. 0

RED CHANNEL(IRE) b.g. 7 Import - Winscarlet North by Garland Knight R A Crawley
1996 **9(NH),6(NH),4(NH)**
69 2/2 Higham (L) MDO 3m 8 GF *s.i.s. disp 5th, lft in ld 11th, hdd 15th, btn whn f 3 out* F -
283 23/2 Charing (L) MDO 3m 16 G *s.s. plld hrd, hld up, some prog 11th, no ch whn p.u. 14th* P 0
686 29/3 Charing (L) MDO 2 1/2m 5 F *(fav) ld frm 2nd, alwys gng wll, lft clr 4 out, in command aft* 1 12
1114 19/4 Higham (L) RES 3m 5 GF *plld to ld 3rd, made rest, 8l clr 15th, kpt on 3 out, comf* 1 16
1505 16/5 Folkestone (R) HC 2m 5f 8 G *started slowly, pulld hrd and held up, prog to chase ldrs 7th, mstk 11th, wknd 3 out.* 4 0
poor under rules; hard puller; does not stay & found bad races; hard to place now. G/F-F. 15

REDCLYFFE(USA) b.g. 9 Secreto (USA) - Regal Heiress by English Prince B J Vernoum
176 15/2 Ottery St M' (L) RES 3m 17 G *mid-div, lost tch 12th, p.u. 14th* P 0
313 1/3 Clyst St Ma' (L) RES 3m 10 HY *sn rear, t.o. & p.u. 12th* P 0
556 16/3 Ottery St M' (L) RES 3m 12 G *cls up to 13th, wknd nxt, p.u. 4 out* P 0
Maiden winner 94; missed 96 & showing nothing now. 10

REDELVA b.m. 10 Fidel - Whisky Afric by African Sky Mrs D Rowell
1996 4(18),3(12),4(0),2(17),U(-),4(10)
304 1/3 Parham (R) LAD 3m 10 G *last & dtchd whn u.r. 8th* U -
577 16/3 Detling (L) CON 3m 18 F *alwys rear, in tch to 15th* 7 0
600 22/3 Parham (R) MEM 3m 7 F *prom, ld aft 7th-10th, wknd 4 out, bhnd & p.u. 2 out* P 0
Restricted winner 95; moderate; no form in 97; need luck to win again. 11

REDHAVEN LIGHT ch.m. 6 Lighter - Lady Redhaven by Red Man Jerry Baker
182 15/2 Larkhill (R) MDO 3m 12 G *mid-div til f 10th* F -
487 9/3 Tweseldown (R) MDO 3m 12 G *sn bhnd, t.o. last whn f 10th* F -
Not yet of any account 0

RED HOT BOOGIE(IRE) b.g. 8 Abednego - Boogie Woogie by No Argument Mrs J M Hollands
1996 8(0),P(0),5(0)
136 9/2 Alnwick (L) MDO 3m 16 G *chsd ldrs, hmpd 9th, rdn 4 out, kpt on onepcd aft* 4 0
235 22/2 Friars Haugh (L) MDO 3m 10 G *5th hlfwy, lft 2nd 2 out, no imp wnr* 2 12
613 22/3 Friars Haugh (L) MDN 3m 12 GF *made most to 8th, remaind cls up, no ext frm 3 out* 3 10
733 29/3 Alnwick (L) MDN 3m 5 F *(fav) chsd ldr, ld/disp 10-13th, outpcd nxt, not rch wnr aft* 2 11
Improved; consistent but stamina problems; should find a Maiden 12

RED HUGH (Irish) — **I** 441^{P}

RED IS THE ROSE br.m. 10 Bustinetto - Red Rose by Saint Denys C Gillbard
1996 **U(NH),5(NH),P(NH)**
1261 27/4 Black Fores' (R) MDO 3m 12 F *prom to 7th, lost plc, nvr nr ldrs aft* 6 0
1373 5/5 Cotley Farm (L) MDO 3m 6 GF *in tch, 3rd 10th, ev ch 3 out, wknd & outpcd frm nxt* 3 10
1497 14/5 Cothelstone (L) MDO 3m 10 GF *mid-div til u.r. 7th* U -
1520 17/5 Bratton Down (L) MDO 3m 17 GS *slght ld to 9th, wknd, bhnd & p.u. 14th* P 0
1592 31/5 Bratton Down (L) MEM 3m 4 F *chsd wnr to 14th, sn wknd, t.o. & ref last* R -
Non stayer; poor jumper; no prospects 0

RED MOLLIE (Irish) — **I** 139^{P}, **I** 188^{P}, **I** 458^{2}, **I** 556^{P}, **I** 576^{3}, **I** 590^{6}

RED NECK ch.g. 6 Nishapour (FR) - Roda Haxan by Huntercombe Mrs C E Goldsworthy
1324 3/5 Bonvilston (R) MDO 3m 16 G *rear til p.u. 2 out* P 0
1561 24/5 Bassaleg (R) MDO 3m 9 G *t.d.e. last & schoold, t.o. & p.u. 12th* P 0
Learning so far 0

REDORAN b.m. 6 Gildoran - Red Spirit by Starch Reduced T G Morgan
1996 P(0),F(-),U(-),P(0)
840 31/3 Lydstep (L) MEM 3m 6 F *chsd ldrs, nvr able to chal* 2 11
1009 12/4 St Hilary (R) MDN 3m 11 GF *prom, went 2nd 16th, ran on onepcd* 2 0
1183 20/4 Lydstep (L) MDO 3m 8 GF *in tch, onepcd frm 4 out* 3 0
Getting round now but form is very weak; needs more. 11

RED REBEL gr.g. 5 Scallywag - Little Red Flower by Blakeney Mrs M E Moody
210 16/2 Southwell P' (L) MDO 3m 15 GS *plng, raced wd, hld up, prog to cls 3rd whn f 13th* F -
347 2/3 Market Rase' (L) MDO 3m 9 GF *(fav) keen hld, prog to ld 9th-10th, cls 3rd whn ran out 14th* r -
478 9/3 Southwell P' (L) MDO 3m 17 G *hld up, stdy prog 9th, ld 3 out, sn clr, canter* 1 17
766 29/3 Whittington (L) INT 3m 10 S *held up, 15l 6th apr 14th, strggld aft* 5 0
Beat 3 subsequent winners; headstrong & plenty to learn yet; looks sure to upgrade; stays;G-S. 17

RED RHAPSODY b.m. 8 Sizzling Melody - The Firebird by Busted R J Rowsell
404 8/3 Llanfrynach (R) INT 3m 17 G *rear, f 5th* F -

538 16/3 Erw Lon (L) RES 3m 5 GF *nvr nr ldrs, p.u. 12th* P 0
717 29/3 Llanvapley (L) RES 3m 13 GF *mid-div, wknd & p.u. 3 out* P 0
902 5/4 Howick (L) RES 3m 2 F *disp to 3rd,ld 9th til blnd 13th,rdr lost irons & p.u.,cont* 2 0
1138 19/4 Bonvilston (R) MDO 3m 9 G *ld early, wknng whn bad mstk 11th & p.u.* P 0
1323 3/5 Bonvilston (R) MDO 3m 14 G *nvr bynd mid-div, no dang* 6 0
1561 24/5 Bassaleg (R) MDO 3m 9 G *in tch to 11th, 5th & wkng whn f 13th* F -

Missed 96; does not stay & of no account 0

REDS PARADISE (Irish) — **I** 176[P], **I** 248[P], **I** 369[5], **I** 435[U], **I** 462[P]

RED SPRUCE b.g. 6 Symbolic - Giant Redwood by Vaigly Great — K A Clemmit

855 31/3 Charm Park (L) MEM 3m 3 F *in tch to hlfwy, fdd, bhnd 12th, p.u. 14th* P 0

No signs on debut 0

REDWOOD BOY ch.g. 7 Highlands - October Woods by Precipice Wood — C B Taylor

1996 P(0),P(0)

621 22/3 Hutton Rudby (L) MDO 3m 10 GF *rear, lost tch 13th, t.o.* 5 0
859 31/3 Charm Park (L) MDO 3m 4 F *chsd wnr, 20l down 10th, no imp, mstk 2 out* 2 0
1173 20/4 Hexham Poin' (L) MDO 2 1/2m 9 GF *alwys rear, styd on to remote 4th 2 out* 4 0
1513 17/5 Corbridge (R) MDO 3m 13 GS *mid-div, drppd rear 8th, wll bhnd frm 4 out* 6 0

Safe but only beaten 2 horses so far; needs to speed up. 0

REED b.h. 12 Dara Monarch - Angelica (SWE) by Hornbeam — Mrs Lyal Provan

1996 3(11),5(13),5(13),6(0),5(0)

1499 15/5 Perth (R) HC 2 1/2m 110yds 8 GS *cl up, ld 8th till hdd before 3 out, btn when blnd badly 2 out.* 5 11
1546 24/5 Hexham (L) HC 2 1/2m 110yds 10 GF *bhnd, rdn hfwy, nvr on terms.* 4 12

Dual winner 93; totally outclassed in H/chases; unlikely to win again 14

REEF LARK b.g. 12 Mill Reef (USA) - Calandra (USA) by Sir Ivor — Mrs Jane Galpin

1996 5(12)

394 8/3 Barbury Cas' (L) LAD 3m 5 G *chsd ldrs, mstk 9th, ev ch whn blnd 3 out, kpt on nr fin* 2 22
555 16/3 Ottery St M' (L) LAD 3m 10 G *alwys rear, nvr any ch* 5 10
932 6/4 Charlton Ho' (L) LAD 3m 6 G *outpcd, last & pshd alng hlfwy, t.o. 3 out* 4 0
1155 20/4 Stafford Cr' (R) LAD 3m 6 GF *alwys rear, no ch frm 12th* 4 0
1340 3/5 Flete Park (R) LAD 4m 5 G *mostly 4th, lost tch 19th* 4 0
1595 31/5 Bratton Down (L) LAD 3m 5 F *s.s. not fluent, outpcd 10th, effrt 14th, onepcd frm 3 out* 3 10

Ran well fresh but quickly lost interest; prospects slim; weak Ladies when fresh best hope. 14

REEL RASCAL gr.m. 7 Scallywag - My Music by Sole Mio (USA) — Mrs A Villar

1996 F(-),3(10),3(0),P(0)

275 22/2 Ampton (R) MDO 3m 10 G *mid-div, stdy prog to ld appr 3 out, clr nxt, rdn out* 1 13

Beat a poor bunch; not seen again; much more needed; P. Keane first winner. 13

REGAL ABSENCE (Irish) — **I** 14[2], **I** 39[3]

REGAL BAY b.g. 7 Scorpio (FR) - Pendle Princess by Broxted — David Wales

1996 P(0),3(0),5(0)

29 26/1 Marks Tey (L) MDN 3m 10 GF *bhnd frm 10th, t.o. & p.u. 15th* P 0
127 9/2 Cottenham (R) MDO 3m 11 GF *cls up, trckd ldr 16th, chal 2 out, drvn to ld flat* 1 15
324 1/3 Marks Tey (L) RES 3m 16 G *w.w., prog & pckd 9th, chsd wnr 16th, onepcd und pres* 3 15
449 8/3 Newton Brom' (R) XX 3m 13 G *mid-div, effrt to 5th at 13th, no prog aft* 6 0
1191 20/4 Garthorpe (R) RES 3m 8 GF *chsd ldrs 7th, chal 3 out, ld last, hld on gamely flat* 1 16
1477 11/5 Garthorpe (R) XX 3m 6 GS *w.w. in tch, rdn & wknd apr 13th, p.u. 3 out* P 0

Improved; gutsy; has scope & needs to improve for Confineds; G/F-G/S. 17

REGAL FELLOW (Irish) — **I** 154[P], **I** 283[3], **I** 348[4]

REGAL GOSSIP (Irish) — **I** 83[P], **I** 143[3], **I** 235[P], **I** 304[5], **I** 419[P], **I** 561[2]

REGAL MIST (Irish) — **I** 607[B]

REGAL OPTIMIST (Irish) — **I** 398[F], **I** 580[P]

REGAL SHADOW gr.g. 8 Scorpio (FR) - Pendle Princess by Broxted — David Wales

1996 P(0),P(0)

479 9/3 Southwell P' (L) MDO 3m 15 G *hld up, prog 10th, wknd rpdly & p.u. 12th* P 0
915 5/4 Cottenham (R) MDO 3m 6 F *jmpd rght, ld, sn clr, hdd 2 out, wknd* 3 0
1193 20/4 Garthorpe (R) MDO 3m 9 GF *ld to 8th, wknd 10th, t.o. & p.u. 13th* P 0

Rarely runs & looks devoid of stamina 0

REGAR (Irish) — **I** 247[P]

REGENCY COTTAGE b.g. 7 Relkino - Sunny Cottage by Sunyboy — David Wales

30 26/1 Marks Tey (L) MDN 3m 9 GF *rear, prog 9th, 4th & outpcd 14th, lft poor 2nd 3 out* 2 0
128 9/2 Cottenham (R) MDO 3m 10 GF *wth ldrs, 3rd frm 13th til lft 2nd 2 out, no imp wnr* 2 11
777 29/3 Dingley (R) MDO 2m 5f 8 G *ld to 5 out, disp to 2 out, onepcd apr last* 4 10
1282 27/4 Fakenham P-' (L) MDO 3m 8 G *ld 3rd, made rest, jnd 3 out, ld & gd jmp last, styd on* 1 13

Gradual progress; won poor race; can improve further; needs to for Restricted 14

REGENT CROSS b.g. 12 Prince Regent (FR) - Holy Cross by Arcticeelagh — Miss Jill Wormall

474 9/3 Southwell P' (L) LAD 3m 12 G *ld/disp to 5th, cls up til wknd 13th, t.o. & p.u. 3 out* P 0

Won 3 in 93; lightly raced now & looks finished 11

REGENT SON b.g. 11 Right Regent - Moorland Gal by Baragoi — Mrs M A Simpson

1996 P(0),P(0),P(0)

172 15/2 Ottery St M' (L) MDN 3m 14 G *rear whn ref 7th* R -

Of no account 0

REGULAR BEAT (Irish) — **I** 99^{P}, **I** 202^{F}, **I** 225^{P}, **I** 353^{P}, **I** 557^{F}, **I** 580^{P}

REGULAR ROSE (Irish) — **I** 344^{P}, **I** 389^{P}, **I** 501^{6}

REIGN DANCE ch.g. 6 Kinglet - Gay Criselle by Decoy Boy — Mrs D H McCarthy

1996 P(0),P(0),P(0)

196 15/2 Higham (L) MDO 3m 12 G *n.j.w. in last til p.u. 8th* P 0
284 23/2 Charing (L) MDO 3m 17 G *8s-4s, made most to 6th, wknd & p.u. 14th, lame* P 0

Has ability; stable out of form & problems in 97; best watched initially if returning in 98 10

REINSKEA (Irish) — **I** 200^{4}, **I** 278^{3}, **I** 296^{P}

REJECTS REPLY b.g. 7 Balliol - Fair Dino by Thatch (USA) — M A Lloyd

1996 2(0),P(0),4(0)

205 15/2 Weston Park (L) MDN 3m 10 G *in tch whn f hvly 4th* F -
327 1/3 Eaton Hall (R) MDN 3m 11 GS *hld up in rear, jmp delib, ran on onepce, not keen* 4 10
575 16/3 Garnons (L) RES 3m 12 G *hld up, prog to cls 4th at 15th, wknd frm nxt* 5 0
1151 19/4 Chaddesley ' (L) MDO 3m 5 GF *hmpd 3rd, lft 2nd 11th, ev ch 4 out, btn nxt* 2 10
1238 26/4 Brampton Br' (R) MDO 3m 10 G *rear til gd prog 14th, ev ch frm 3 out, no ext cls hm* 2 12
1459 11/5 Maisemore P' (L) MDO 3m 12 G *hld up,prog frm 10th, chsd wnr 15th, rdn & chnc 2 out,no ext* 2 14
1527 17/5 Bredwardine (R) MDO 3m 13 G *hld up last, nvr put in race, ref 8th* R -
1578 26/5 Chaddesley ' (L) MDO 3m 7 F *pllng,in tch,3rd & mstk 14th,sn outpcd,went 2nd 2 out,no imp* 2 10

Ungenuine; 2nd in 5 of 11 starts; will continue to frustrate 12

REJMAS (Irish) — **I** 62^{P}

REMALONE ch.m. 8 Remezzo - Marilone by Maris Piper — Mrs T A Halliwell

1996 U(-),P(0),4(0),P(0),r(-),P(0),P(0)

139 9/2 Thorpe Lodge (L) LAD 3m 4 GF *alwys rear, lsng tch whn p.u. 14th* P 0
474 9/3 Southwell P' (L) LAD 3m 12 G *bhnd & rdn 4th, mstk 6th, t.o. 9th, p.u. 12th* P 0
925 6/4 Garthorpe (R) LAD 3m 7 GF *mid-div to 5th, sn rear, t.o. 11th, p.u. 3 out* P 0
1078 13/4 Guilsborough (L) LAD 3m 11 GF *mstks, sn wll bhnd, t.o. last whn u.r. 13th* U -

Of no account 0

REMEMBER MAC b.g. 9 My Dad Tom (USA) - Sur Les Roches by Sea Break — Mrs J Hayes

1996 P(0),P(0),P(0),P(0),5(0),3(10),3(0),6(0),P(0)

792 31/3 Bishopsleigh (R) RES 3m 13 G *(bl) prom early, mid-div 10th, outpcd aft* 6 0
1093 16/4 Hockworthy (L) RES 3m 16 GF *(bl) prom to 7th, sn bhnd, t.o. & p.u. 10th* P 0
1241 26/4 Bratton Down (L) MEM 3m 4 GS *(bl) 20l bhnd frm 6th, nvr nrr* 4 0
1317 3/5 Holnicote (L) RES 3m 5 G *(bl) bhnd, rpd prog 12th, styd prom til no ext frm 16th* 2 11
1439 10/5 Holnicote (L) RES 3m 9 G *(bl) sn twrds rear, bhnd frm 12th* 5 0
1547 24/5 Mounsey Hil' (R) MEM 3m 9 G *(bl) blnd 2nd & 5th, bhnd aft, 5th & no ch frm 15th* 5 0

Maiden winner 94; mega safe but lost last 20 & will will extend the sequence 0

REMILAN(IRE) b.g. 6 Remainder Man - Alice Milan by Milan — M G Sheppard

1996 3(0),P(0)

29 26/1 Marks Tey (L) MDN 3m 10 GF *w.w. prog 11th, btn apr 3 out, eased* 5 0
318 1/3 Marks Tey (L) MDN 3m 13 G *alwys mid-div, lost tch 15th, t.o. & p.u. 3 out* P 0

Lightly raced & well beaten when completing; can do better 12

REMMY CRUZ (Irish) — **I** 42^{P}, **I** 82^{5}, **I** 86^{P}, **I** 146^{P}

REMO GROVE(IRE) b.g. 9 Remainder Man - Garbally Girl by Mugatpura — Miss D J Ross

8 25/1 Cottenham (R) CON 3m 5 GF *made all, drew clr apr 14th, unchal, fin lame* 1D 20

Winning chaser; won weak race (later disqualified); not seen again; can only be watched if returning ... 20

RENARD QUAY b or br.g. 14 Quayside - Donegal Lady by Indigenous — B Wilberforce

1996 5(13),5(13),3(15),3(12),3(11),5(15)

199 15/2 Weston Park (L) MEM 3m 7 G *cls up to 12th, rdn & wknd 4 out* 6 0

Ladies winner 95; probably finished now 11

RENSHAW INGS ch.g. 8 Kirchner - Spot On Pink by Perhapsburg — R Barrow

1996 F(-),F(-),P(0)

314 1/3 Clyst St Ma' (L) MDN 3m 11 HY *rear, t.o. & p.u. 11th* P 0
643 22/3 Castle Of C' (R) MDO 3m 12 G *prom, ld apr 7th-9th, wknd 11th, p.u. 13th* P 0

Not yet of any account 0

RENTY (Irish) — **I** 356F, **I** 428P, **I** 449⁴, **I** 514P, **I** 550³

REPTILE PRINCESS b.m. 11 Majestic Maharaj - Daring Liz by Dairialatan — Miss Wizzy Hartnoll

1996 4(0),5(0),9(0),4(0)

172 15/2 Ottery St M' (L) MDN 3m 14 G *mid-div, bhnd whn p.u. 3 out* P 0
531 15/3 Wadebridge (L) MDO 3m 14 GF *bhnd frm 6th, p.u. 12th* P 0
626 22/3 Kilworthy (L) MDN 3m 14 G *tongue strap, prom early, sn wknd, bhnd frm 12th* 4 0
741 29/3 Higher Kilw' (L) MDN 3m 12 GF *(bl) tongue-strap, prom, ld 7th-12th, wknd 14th, sn lost tch* 5 0
1109 19/4 Flete Park (R) OPE 4m 9 GF *(bl) tongue-strap, sn bhnd, n.j.w. t.o. & p.u. 3 out* P 0

beaten miles when completing; hopeless 0

REPUBLICAN LADY b.m. 5 Battle Hymn - Sweet Helen by No Mercy — C Drew

318 1/3 Marks Tey (L) MDN 3m 13 G *mstks, t.o. frm 7th til p.u. 10th* P 0

Jumped poorly on debut. 0

RESKUE LINE ro.g. 7 Respect - Kiku by Faberge II — Allan Shaw

1996 8(0)

341 1/3 Corbridge (R) MDN 3m 10 G *mid-div, fdd 12th, f nxt* F -

Rarely runs; shows nothing 0

RESPECTABLE LAURA b.m. 6 Respect - Laura Lyshill Wood by Master Spiritus — J S Haldane

233 22/2 Friars Haugh (L) MDO 3m 13 G *sn bhnd, p.u. 3 out* P 0

Only learning on debut 0

RESTLESS STAR ch.m. 10 Star Appeal - Restive by Relic — Eddy Luke

510 15/3 Dalton Park (R) MDO 3m 14 GF *rear, strgglng whn ran out 15th* r -

Very wayward; of no account 0

RESTRAINT b.m. 7 Bustino - Queens Message by Town Crier — J Barnes

36 26/1 Alnwick (L) MDO 3m 15 G *alwys rear, t.o. 15th, f last* F -
161 15/2 Lanark (R) MDO 2m 5f 14 G *alwys bhnd* 6 0
417 8/3 Dalston (R) MDO 2 1/2m 11 GS *ld 4-8th, outpcd frm 12th, no imp ldrs aft* 4 10
730 29/3 Alnwick (L) MDO 2 1/2m 9 F *ld 2nd-9th, outpcd & 4l 2nd 4 out, no ext* 2 12
1423 10/5 Aspatria (L) MEM 3m 3 G *ld, mstk 14th, hdd nxt, ld 16th, pshd out* 1 11

Steady progress; form poor & members win makes things hard now; huge improvement needed 13

RETRIEVING MISSION(IRE) ch.g. 6 Executive Perk - Our Siveen by Deep Run — Mrs Sarah Faulks

1045 12/4 Cothelstone (L) MDO 3m 6 GF *ref & u.r. 1st* R -
1246 26/4 Bratton Down (L) MDO 3m 16 GS *in chsng grp whn f 14th* F -
1437 10/5 Holnicote (L) MDO 3m 14 G *(fav) cls 3rd at 10th, cls 2nd whn hit 16th, p.u. nxt, dead* P 0

Dead. 0

REVEREND BROWN(IRE) b.g. 7 The Parson - Let The Hare Sit by Politico (USA) — J M Turner

1996 **4(NH),15(NH),8(NH),3(NH)**

127 9/2 Cottenham (R) MDO 3m 11 GF *(fav) made most, some slw jmps, jnd last, hdd & no ext flat* 2 14
318 1/3 Marks Tey (L) MDN 3m 13 G *(fav) chsng grp,wnt 2nd 14th,rdn 3 out,jst ld & lft clr nxt,rdnout* 1 16
779 31/3 Fakenham (L) HC 2m 5f 110yds 9 G *(fav) not fluent early, kept on one pace from 3 out.* 4 16
1278 27/4 Fakenham P-' (L) RES 3m 11 G *(fav) prom, ld apr 13th, rdn apr last, styd on* 1 18
1505 16/5 Folkestone (R) HC 2m 5f 8 G *(fav) chsd wnr, mstk 9th, rdn 3 out, joined winner next, wknd rpdly and jmpd last slowly, lame.* 2 15

Disappointing under rules; quirky & well ridden; stays; problems last start; win again if fit 98 19

RHINE RIVER(USA) br.g. 7 Riverman (USA) - Fruhlingstag (FR) by Orsini — Brian Eardley

1996 P(0),1(10),P(0),1(10),P(0)

887 1/4 Flagg Moor (L) XX 3m 8 G *(bl) ld to 6th, prssd wnr til wknd 15th, p.u. 3 out* P 0
1539 18/5 Wolverhampt' (L) OPE 3m 5 GS *(bl) ld to 5 out, not qckn, btn frm nxt* 2 13

Won 3 bad races 95/96; brief 97; inconsistent & has acquired blinkers; need luck to win again. 14

RHU NA HAVEN b or br.g. 13 Le Bavard (FR) - Shuil Dubh by Black Tarquin — James Buckle

1113 19/4 Higham (L) MEM 3m 3 GF *3rd & not fluent, lft 2nd aft 11th, nvr pace to chal, t.o.* 2 0
1277 27/4 Fakenham P-' (L) CON 3m 10 G *rear, t.o. frm 8th* 7 0

Member swinner 94/95; missed 96 & looks past it now 10

RHYME AND CHIME b.g. 6 Rymer - Belle Deirdrie by Mandamus — Mrs R Kennen
1996 P(0),U(-),U(-)

102 8/2 Great Treth' (R) MDO 3m 8 GS *mstks,bhnd,effrt 7th,wknd 10th,sn t.o.,blnd last* 4 0
243 22/2 Lemalla (R) MDO 3m 12 S *c.o. bend aft 2nd, cont t.o. til p.u. 7th* P 0
626 22/3 Kilworthy (L) MDN 3m 14 G *(bl) in tch, efft to disp 3 out, f nxt* F 14

1st signs last start (blinkers); has ability but poor jump; can win if learning 15

RHYMING MOPPET b.m. 8 Rymer - Deep Moppet by Deep Run — E R Hanbury
1996 7(0)

480 9/3 Southwell P' (L) MDO 3m 17 G *f 2nd* F -
548 16/3 Garthorpe (R) RES 3m 10 GF *sn bhnd, t.o. & p.u. 9th* P 0
722 29/3 Sandon (L) MDO 3m 10 GF *w.w. clsd 4 out, ld nxt, sn clr* 1 15

Lightly raced; stunning improvement & romped home in poor race; hard to assess but more needed. ... 15

RIAS RASCAL (Irish) — I 116P

RIBINGTON b.g. 8 Riberetto - By Midnight by By Rights — W S Layton

259 22/2 Newtown (L) MDN 3m 18 G *prom til f 9th* F -
409 8/3 Llanfrynach (R) MDN 3m 12 G *prom, outpcd frm 3 out* 3 11
666 23/3 Eaton Hall (R) MDO 3m 10 GF *chsd ldrs, ev ch 4 out, not qckn* 4 11
1019 12/4 Bitterley (L) MDO 3m 12 GF *cls up to 10th, wknd & p.u. 12th* P 0
1150 19/4 Chaddesley ' (L) MDO 3m 7 GF *chsd ldrs to 14th, wknd 16th, lft poor 2nd 2 out* 2 0
1238 26/4 Brampton Br' (R) MDO 3m 10 G *ld to 4th, prom til wknd 15th, p.u. aft nxt* P 0
1387 5/5 Cursneh Hill (L) MEM 3m 3 GF *made most at v slow pcd frm 6th, qcknd apr last, just hld on* 1 0
1556 24/5 Bassaleg (R) RES 3m 13 G *chsd ldng pair 8th, rdn & btn 12th, t.o. & p.u. 2 out* P 0

Non-stayer; won a crawl (well ridden); Restricted looks impossible 10

RICHARD HUNT b.g. 13 Celtic Cone - Member's Mistress by New Member — Mrs P Rowe
1996 1(26),1(24),1(22),U(-),**2(23)**,1+(24),1(25),2(23)

125 9/2 Cottenham (R) LAD 3m 11 GF *(fav) rear, prog 10th, chal 2 out, ld flat, just hld on* 1 23
286 27/2 Huntingdon (R) HC 3m 8 GS *struggling to keep up after one cct, t.o. when p.u. apr 3 out.* P 0

Won 24 points & 1 H/chase; has been retired. 24

RICHVILLE b.g. 11 Kemal (FR) - Golden Ingot by Prince Hansel — Victor Dartnall
1996 **6(NH),8(NH),8(NH),4(NH),P(NH),4(NH)**

2 19/1 Barbury Cas' (L) XX 3m 14 GF *prom, ld 10th-2 out, sn wknd* 4 17
174 15/2 Ottery St M' (L) LAD 3m 9 G *not fluent, chsd ldrs, 5th at 13th, no ext frm 3 out* 3 20
397 8/3 Barbury Cas' (L) XX 3m 10 G *(Jt fav) hld up going wll, prog to 2nd 15th, ld apr 2 out, rdn out* 1 19
555 16/3 Ottery St M' (L) LAD 3m 10 G *1st ride, alwys mid-div, no ch frm 13th* 4 11

Winning chaser; safe but barely stays; found right race; good stable & can find another opening 21

RIDEMORE BALLADEER gr.g. 6 Malaspina - Balitree by Balidar — D Barron
1996 3(11),2(15),1(15)

7 19/1 Barbury Cas' (L) RES 3m 14 GF *(fav) hld up, prog & 5th hlfwy, lost plc & p.u. 13th* P 0
517 15/3 Larkhill (R) RES 3m 10 GF *(Jt fav) wth ldr 5th til lft in ld 12th, jnd nxt, hdd & f last, lame* F -

Maiden winner 96; top stable ; problems & not progress 97; young enough to revive; Good 18

RIDING HILLS GIRL gr.m. 8 Meadowbrook - Briahill by The Brianstan — Mrs D McCormack

343 1/3 Corbridge (R) MDO 3m 14 G *rear whn f 11th* F -
565 16/3 Lanark (R) MDO 3m 10 GS *3rd hlfwy, disp 2 out, slght ld last, just hld on* 1 13
729 29/3 Alnwick (L) RES 3m 10 F *mid-div, wknd 12th, lost tch & p.u. 2 out* P 0

Landed weak race by minimum margin(slow time); needs more exprience before upgrading 14

RIDWAN b.g. 10 Rousillon (USA) - Ring Rose by Relko — K V Bonser
1996 2(21),2(21),4(10),3(12)

137 9/2 Thorpe Lodge (L) MEM 3m 9 GF *(fav) n.j.w. outpcd to hlfwy, prog und pres nr fin* 3 15
1207 26/4 Clifton On ' (L) LAD 3m 6 GS *mid-div, disp 2nd 4 out, outpcd 2 out* 3 18

Winning hurdler; stays well but onepaced; slog in mud offers best hope 18

RIGGLEDOWN REGENT b.g. 11 Right Regent - Blinding Light by Fury Royal — R W Pincombe
1996 r(-),P(0)

54 1/2 Wadebridge (L) MDO 3m 13 G *nvr trbld ldrs, mstk 10th, p.u. nxt* P 0
794 31/3 Bishopsleigh (R) MDO 3m 12 G *sn rear, p.u. 10th* P 0

Never completed; hopeless 0

RIGHT AND REASON (Irish) — I 389^{P}

RIGHTEYE (Irish) — I 114^{P}, I 127^{P}, I 248^{3}

RIGHT THEN ROSIE (Irish) — I 45^{3}, I 90^{P}, I 189^{4}, I 305^{P}

RIGHT WELL(IRE) br.g. 5 Royal Fountain - Right Hand by Oats — W J Turcan

776 29/3 Dingley (R) MDO 2m 5f 10 G *alwys rear, t.o. 7th at 9th, p.u. 2 out* P 0
1082 13/4 Guilsborough (L) MDN 3m 14 GF *in tch to 11th, wll bhnd whn p.u. 16th* P 0
1352 4/5 Dingley (R) MDO 2 1/2m 9 G *alwys rear, t.o. & p.u. apr 11th* P 0

Looks the part but shown nothing yet; can do better 0

RI NA GAOITHE (Irish) — I 322^{F}

RINGAHEEN (Irish) — I 95^{3}, I 153^{3}, I 219^{4}, I 268^{2}

RING BANK b.g. 6 Humdoleila - Butchers Barn by Space King — S Edwards

1996 P(0),R(-),5(0),P(0),P(0),U(-),F(-)

82 2/2 Wolverhampt' (L) MDN 3m 11 GS *chsd ldrs til wknd 11th, t.o. & p.u. 15th* P 0
205 15/2 Weston Park (L) MDN 3m 10 G *ld, clr going wll whn u.r. 9th* U -
549 16/3 Garthorpe (R) MDO 3m 16 GF *ld to 4th,lft in ld 8th til aft 15th,ld agn brfly nxt,sn wkd* 5 0
722 29/3 Sandon (L) MDO 3m 10 GF *ld to 4 out, disp 2nd & lkd hld whn b.d. 2 out* B -

Shows speed but stamina highly suspect; much more needed 11

RING MAM (Irish) — I 63^{P}, I 163^{F}, I 245^{4}, I 271^{5}, I 296^{6}

RINKY DINKY DOO b.g. 11 Oats - County Clare by Vimadee — Miss Denise Foode

1996 4(0),P(0),**3(0)**,4(0),F(-),P(0),6(0),**P(0)**

467 8/3 Eyton-On-Se' (L) RES 3m 15 G *ld to 5th, btn 12th, p.u. 5 out* P 0
726 29/3 Sandon (L) CON 3m 8 GF *mid to rear, nvr dang* 5 0
1176 20/4 Sandon (L) OPE 3m 5 GF *cls up to 9th, fdd 14th* 3 0
1303 3/5 Weston Park (L) RES 3m 6 G *3rd to 13th, rear whn p.u. 5 out* P 0

Maiden winner 95; well beaten in 97 & no real prospects now 0

RIO CISTO ch.m. 8 Cisto (FR) - Rio Princess by Prince Hansel — Mrs B J Harkins

1996 P(0),P(0),P(0)

293 1/3 Didmarton (L) INT 3m 16 G *alwys rear, t.o. & p.u. 15th* P 0
406 8/3 Llanfrynach (R) RES 3m 13 G *rear whn f 4 out* F -

No signs of ability; yet to complete 0

RIO'S KING (Irish) — I 474^{2}, I 515,

RIOS KING (Irish) — I 142^{4}

RIO STAR (Irish) — I 73^{3}, I 234^{2}, I 318^{2}, I 383^{3}, I 558^{6}

RIOT LADY(IRE) b.m. 6 Riot Helmet - Golden Eily by Golden Love — H A Shone

854 31/3 Eyton-On-Se' (L) MDO 3m 10 GF *prom to 9th, lost tch, p.u. 3 out* P 0
942 6/4 Tabley (R) MDO 3m 8 G *prom to 11th, rmmdrs 13th, sn bhnd, no ch, p.u. last* P 0
1386 5/5 Eyton-On-Se' (L) MDO 2 1/2m 8 GF *wll in tch wth ldr to 10th, no ext clsng stgs* 4 10
1541 18/5 Wolverhampt' (L) MDO 3m 15 GS *alwys ldng quartet, no ext frm 4 out* 4 0

Placed in Irish Maidens 96; disappointing & stamina looks the problem; much more needed 10

RIP THE CALICO(IRE) b.m. 9 Crash Course - Rocky's Dream by Aristocracy — Mrs Jo Duckett

1996 P(0),6(10),4(12),5(0)

219 16/2 Heythrop (R) LAD 3m 16 G *mid-div, effrt to chs ldng 5 at 14th, no imp, wknd 3 out* 9 0
296 1/3 Didmarton (L) LAD 3m 13 G *alwys bhnd, t.o. 12th* 6 0
1197 23/4 Andoversford (R) LAD 3m 5 F *w.w. prog to 2nd at 16th, sn outpcd, dsmntd aft fin* 2 15

Selling hurdle winner; does not stay & not threatening to win a Ladies 14

RIP VAN WINKLE br.g. 10 Le Bavard (FR) - Flying Silver by Master Buck — Dr P P Brown

1996 F(-),1(21),1(22),1(24),2(25),1(25)

393 8/3 Barbury Cas' (L) OPE 3m 7 G *(fav) chsd ldrs, lft disp 5th, ld 10th, made rest, clr 2 out, easy* 1 25
703 29/3 Upper Sapey (R) OPE 3m 5 GF *(fav) made all, drew clr frm 15th* 1 25
1197 23/4 Andoversford (R) LAD 3m 5 F *(fav) alwys going wll, ld 13th, drew clr frm 3 out, v easily* 1 24
1525 17/5 Bredwardine (R) LAD 3m 9 G *(fav) ld aft 5th, made rest, shkn up last, ran on well* 1 25
1548 24/5 Mounsey Hil' (R) LAD 3m 10 G *(fav) chsd ldng pair, prog to ld 14th, sn clr, unextndd* 1 25

Very useful Ladies horse; top stable; sure to keep winning; F-S 26

RI RA b.m. 7 Derring Rose - Cat Meadow by Town And Country — Miss Sandra E Bowerman

1996 **11(NH),10(NH)**

549 16/3 Garthorpe (R) MDO 3m 16 GF *alwys rr, t.o. & p.u 3 out* P 0
853 31/3 Eyton-On-Se' (L) MDO 3m 13 GF *mid-div, losng tch whn p.u. 5 out* P 0
1352 4/5 Dingley (R) MDO 2 1/2m 9 G *chsd ldrs, blnd 4th, strgglng whn blnd & u.r. 12th* U -
1609 1/6 Dingley (R) MDO 3m 14 GF *prom, 4th whn u.r. 6th* U -

No ability under rules & same story in points so far 0

RISE ABOVE IT(IRE) ch.g. 7 Aristocracy - Castle Tyne by Good Thyne (USA) — Mrs P M Jibson
1996 P(0),P(0),F(-),2(0),2(15)

859	31/3	Charm Park	(L)	MDO	3m	4	F	*(fav) made all, easily*	1	10
1068	13/4	Whitwell-On'	(R)	RES	3m	12	G	*ld/disp to 11th, sn wknd, fin tired*	5	0

Won dreadful Maiden; headstrong; stamina doubts; plenty to find for restricted; best L/H. 14

RISE TO IT (Irish) — **I** 393^{3}

RISING PADDY (Irish) — **I** 268^{P}

RISING SAP ch.g. 7 Brotherly (USA) - Miss Kewmill by Billion (USA) — J D Downes
1996 2(13),1(15)

91	6/2	Huntingdon	(R)	HC	3m	10	G	*held up, hdwy 9th, ld 11th till after 12th, mstk 4 out, weakening when p.u. before next.*	P	0
285	26/2	Taunton	(R)	HC	4 1/4m 110yds	16	GS	*hit 6th, hdwy 13th, wknd 18th, t.o. when p.u. before 3 out.*	P	0
490	10/3	Stratford	(L)	HC	3m	12	G	*held up, hdwy 10th, wknd 4 out.*	8	0
874	1/4	Uttoxeter	(L)	HC	2m 7f	9	GF	*bhnd when blnd badly 8th, hdwy 11th, hit 4 out, wknd quickley, t.o. when p.u. before last.*	P	0

Won modest Maiden 96; outclassed in H/chases; should concentrate on Restricteds; chances; Good ... 16

RISK-A-DINGE (Irish) — **I** 71^{P}, **I** 126^{F}, **I** 212^{F}

RISK OF THUNDER (Irish) — **I** 105^{1}, **I** 199^{1}, **I** 358^{1}, **I** 395^{1}

RISKY BID b.m. 7 Risk Me (FR) - Crammond Brig by New Brig — J R Thomas
1996 P(0),5(0),2(12),P(0)

175	15/2	Ottery St M'	(L)	RES	3m	15	G	*n.j.w. rear til p.u. 15th*	P	0
532	15/3	Wadebridge	(L)	RES	3m	9	GF	*ld 7-14th, wknd rpdly, p.u. nxt*	P	0

Placed in weak Maiden 96; no other form; mistakes; finished early 97; needs more 10

RITH DUBH (Irish) — **I** 191^{U}

RIVA(NZ) ch.g. 10 Beechcraft (NZ) - Bronze Penny (NZ) by Patron Saint — Paul Thorman

296	1/3	Didmarton	(L)	LAD	3m	13	G	*chsd ldng pair, wkng whn f 11th*	F	-
521	15/3	Cothelstone	(L)	OPE	3m	8	GS	*w.w. went 2nd 16th, tried to chal, alwys hld*	2	20
1440	10/5	Holnicote	(L)	OPE	3m	3	G	*raced keenly, ld & clr by 6th, wknd rpdly, blnd 10th,p.u.nxt*	P	0

Winning hurdler; lightly raced now; flattered when placed & sugns not good last start; hard to win 16

RIVER BARGY (Irish) — **I** 222^{6}, **I** 405, , **I** 482^{3}, **I** 545, , **I** 594^{4}

RIVERDANCE ROSIE (Irish) — **I** 370^{2}, **I** 472^{P}, **I** 575^{F}, **I** 586^{1}

RIVER DON ch.g. 5 Over The River (FR) - Jane's Daughter by Pitpan — Mrs A M Easterby

79	2/2	Market Rase'	(L)	MDO	2m 5f	9	GF	*hld up, mstk 7th, smth prog to ld 2 out, readily*	1	16

Hacked up (19 seconds faster than div II); right connections; one to watch; could be useful. 20

RIVERFORT (Irish) — **I** 389^{P}, **I** 407^{4}

RIVER MAGNET (Irish) — **I** 113^{F}

RIVER MELODY ch.m. 10 Over The River (FR) - Deep Solare by Deep Run — T W Moore
1996 1(27),2(23),2(19),1(23),1(18),2(21)

62	1/2	Horseheath	(R)	CON	3m	5	GF	*(fav) hld up, lft 2nd apr 14th, ld 2 out, cruised clr*	1	25
124	9/2	Cottenham	(R)	OPE	3m	9	GF	*(fav) cls up,trckd wnr aft 3 out,chal last,nt mch room,found nil*	2	24
273	22/2	Ampton	(R)	OPE	3m	7	G	*cls up til badly hmpd & u.r. 12th*	U	-
440	8/3	Higham	(L)	OPE	3m	5	G	*(fav) pllng,ld 1st,sttld 3rd,clr wth wnr 16th, blnd 2 out,nt rcvr*	2	22
595	22/3	Horseheath	(R)	OPE	3m	5	F	*rstrnd in 3rd, clr wth wnr frm 14th, onepcd last*	2	21
708	29/3	High Easter	(L)	CON	3m	3	F	*(fav) jmpd rt, ld to 6th, ld agn 15th rdn & hdd last, sn btn*	2	18
1307	3/5	Cottenham	(R)	OPE	3m	2	F	*(fav) prssd ldr, ld 7th, clr frm 12th, easily*	1	22

8 wins 12 places last 21 starts; goes well fresh; found little & easily beaten 97; can win again; F-S 21

RIVER OF DREAMS (Irish) — **I** 157^{3}, **I** 298^{1}

RIVER RAMBLE b.m. 7 Rambling River - Oregano by Track Spare — Mrs G Sunter
1996 F(-),4(0),P(0),2(12),3(11)

38	26/1	Alnwick	(L)	MDO	3m	14	G	*prom, ld 4-6th, blnd 8th, ld apr 3 out where blnd, styd on*	1	15
131	9/2	Alnwick	(L)	RES	3m	13	G	*ld 2nd-6th, prom to 14th, outpcd frm nxt*	7	0
266	22/2	Duncombe Pa'	(R)	RES	3m	19	G	*rear, prog 10th, chsd ldrs & ev ch whn u.r. 3 out*	U	-
337	1/3	Corbridge	(R)	RES	3m	11	G	*rear whn f 4th*	F	-
425	8/3	Charm Park	(L)	RES	3m	12	GF	*mid-div, wknd 11th, t.o. & p.u. 4 out*	P	0

Won modest Maiden; mistakes; struggling now & below Restricted class at present 15

RIVERRUNSTHROUGHIT (Irish) — **I** 339^{F}, **I** 388^{6}, **I** 406^{6}

RIVERS END(IRE) ch.g. 8 Over The River (FR) - Ballymore Status by Status Seeker — I R Mann
1996 **F(NH),3(NH),P(NH),6(NH),P(NH),6(NH)**

373 2/3 Mollington (R) MDN 3m 14 G *prom, ld 9-12th, chsd wnr aft, wknd rpdly aft 2 out* 4 0
550 16/3 Garthorpe (R) MDO 3m 11 GF *in tch, prog 9th, ev ch 3 out, no ex und press frm nxt* 2 12
915 5/4 Cottenham (R) MDO 3m 6 F *(fav) hld up, went 2nd 11th, ld 2 out, hdd last, onepcd* 2 10

Ex Nov/chaser; tries but stamina problems; good stable; should find a race. 13

RIVERSIDE BOY ch.g. 14 Funny Man - Tamorina by Quayside Miss M E Sherrington
1996 **8(NH),P(NH),5(NH),12(NH)**

328 1/3 Eaton Hall (R) OPE 3m 6 GS *(bl) jmp wll, cls 2nd to 8th, ld 9th, ran on wll frm 4 out, comf* 1 25
569 16/3 Garnons (L) OPE 3m 7 G *(fav) ld til 15th, styd on, forged clr flat* 1 23
886 1/4 Flagg Moor (L) OPE 3m 3 G *(fav) (bl) ld, sn clr, drew rght away 3 out, heavily eased flat* 1 20
1383 5/5 Eyton-On-Se' (L) OPE 3m 3 GF *(fav) alwys ld & 2l clr whn hit 4 out & f* F -

Former useful stayer; moody but revived in points; can win again at 15; G/F-S 24

RIVER STREAM b.m. 10 Paddy's Stream - River Belle by Divine Gift Mrs Sarah Faulks
1996 P(0),P(0),4(0),7(0),P(0),P(0)

1547 24/5 Mounsey Hil' (R) MEM 3m 9 G *t.d.e. prom til wknd 12th, p.u. 16th* P 0
1615 7/6 Umberleigh (L) MDO 3m 11 F *alwys bhnd, t.o. final cct, tk poor 4th 2 out* 4 0

Tailed off when completing; does not stay; summer jumping now 0

RIVER SUNSET(IRE) ch.g. 9 Over The River (FR) - Sunset Princess by Prince Hansel J Foster

82 2/2 Wolverhampt' (L) MDN 3m 11 GS *alwys bhnd, t.o. 10th, p.u. 15th* P 0
204 15/2 Weston Park (L) RES 3m 13 G *mid to rear, no ch whn p.u. 3 out* P 0
332 1/3 Eaton Hall (R) RES 3m 18 GS *prom to hlfwy, fdd, p.u. 4 out* P 0
550 16/3 Garthorpe (R) MDO 3m 11 GF *disp ld 4-11th, wknd appr 13th* 7 0
854 31/3 Eyton-On-Se' (L) MDO 3m 10 GF *alwys ldng quintet, onepcd frm 3 out* 5 0
999 12/4 Alpraham (R) MDO 3m 8 GF *alwys mid-div, styd on onepcd, not rch ldrs* 3 0
1299 3/5 Weston Park (L) MEM 3m 4 G *alwys rear, no ch whn p.u. 4 out* P 0

Missed 96; very poor; only beat one horse in 97; finds little & win looks impossible. 10

RIVER THRUST(IRE) br.g. 7 Over The River (FR) - Ballygoman Maid by Light Thrust C I C Munro
1996 **15(NH)**

147 9/2 Tweseldown (R) MDO 3m 12 GF *rear, sn outpcd, t.o. 12th* 5 0
297 1/3 Didmarton (L) MDN 3m 11 G *rear, wll bhnd frm 11th, tk poor 3rd flat* 3 0
747 29/3 Barbury Cas' (L) MDO 3m 3 F *(fav) prom, wknd 11th, p.u. 13th* P 0

Tailed off when completing; much more needed;(favourite last start?) 0

RIVER WILD (Irish) — **I** 24[P], **I** 53[P], **I** 107[U], **I** 202[F], **I** 242[5], **I** 353[P]

R N COMMANDER b.g. 11 Full Of Hope - Dectette by Quartette J R Cornwall
1996 **U(-),5(0),5(0),P(0),P(0)**,P(0),5(13)

137 9/2 Thorpe Lodge (L) MEM 3m 9 GF *ld/disp to 5th, cls up, ld 5 out-nxt, no ext frm 2 out* 2 15
387 7/3 Market Rasen (R) HC 3m 1f 5 G *ld to 3rd, cl up till lost pl 11th, struggling last 5.* 4 0
875 1/4 Wetherby (L) HC 3m 1f 5 GF *lost tch from hfwy, well t.o..* 5 0

Won 1 of 25 starts 93/97; safe but woefully onepaced; need fortune to win again 13

ROAMING SHADOW gr.g. 10 Rymer - Silver Shadow by Birdbrook J D Hankinson
1996 6(15),3(13),4(14),1(15),P(0),P(0),3(17),U(-),6(12),5(10)

39 1/2 Larkhill (R) CON 3m 6 GF *hld up, prog to prss ldr 13th, outpcd frm 2 out* 3 14
179 15/2 Larkhill (R) CON 3m 12 G *hld up, lost tch 7th, some prog frm 14th, nvr on trms, t.o.* 4 0
391 8/3 Barbury Cas' (L) MEM 3m 6 G *(fav) in tch, chsd ldr 6th, ld apr 12th, blnd & hdd last, wknd* 2 0
1025 12/4 Badbury Rin' (L) INT 3m 2 F *j.w., disp til narrow adv 12th, outpcd & hdd cls home* 2 11
1199 23/4 Andoversford (R) INT 3m 5 F *w.w. in tch, prog 3 out, went 2nd last, no imp flat* 2 14
1360 5/5 Towcester (R) HC 2 3/4m 7 GF *ld after 4th till after 7th and wknd rpdly, t.o. when p.u. before 2 out.* P 0
1550 24/5 Mounsey Hil' (R) INT 3m 9 G *rear, in tch to 15th, wll bhnd whn p.u. 2 out* P 0
1594 31/5 Bratton Down (L) INT 3m 10 F *wll in tch til outpcd aft 14th, wknd 2 out, dsmntd* 7 0

Won 3 weak races 95/96; moderate; barely stays & finds soft races; Members best hope again.F-G/S. .. 13

ROARK'S CHUKKA 10 D P Smith
1996 P(0),P(0),P(0),P(0),P(0)

60 1/2 Kingston Bl' (L) MDN 3m 17 GF *cls up, ld 4th til f 7th* F -
223 16/2 Heythrop (R) RES 3m 19 G *alwys bhnd, t.o. & p.u. 12th* P 0
373 2/3 Mollington (R) MDN 3m 14 G *in tch, cls up 10th, sn btn, walked in* 6 0
656 22/3 Siddington (L) MDN 3m 7 F *ld to 12th, ld agn aft 3 out, ran on wll nxt* 1 15

Looked devoid of stamina till surprising on short course; follow looks highly unlikely 14

ROBBIE'S BOY b.g. 10 Sunley Builds - Lucys Willing by Will Hays (USA) J L Brown
1996 2(10),**8(13)**,2(18),1(18),F(-),4(13)

535 16/3 Erw Lon (L) CON 3m 12 GF *alwys mid-div, bttr for race* 6 10

Rsetricted winnner 96; finished early 97; still Confined chances if fit 98; G-S. 19

ROBEHEN b.m. 7 All Fair - Flame Song by True Song — Mrs S A Murch

792	31/3	Bishopsleigh	(R) RES 3m	13	G	*mid-div, no show, p.u. 16th*	P	0
1035	12/4	Lifton	(R) MDN 3m	11	F	*alwys bhnd, t.o. frm 7th*	5	0

Well beaten so far & much more needed 0

ROBERO b.g. 6 Robellino (USA) - Copt Hall Princess by Crowned Prince (USA) — Tom Hayes

1996 **6(NH),5(NH),10(NH),3(NH),F(NH),10(NH)**

222	16/2	Heythrop	(R) RES 3m	17	G	*wll bhnd, t.o. 12th, nvr nrr, school*	4	0
1527	17/5	Bredwardine	(R) MDO 3m	13	G	*(fav) w.w. prog 13th, ld 3 out, rdn out flat*	1	13

Poor & disappointing under rules; interrupted season; modest win; lacks scope; needs more 15

ROBERTS ROYAL ch.g. 6 Royal Vulcan - Michele My Belle by Lochnager — A R West

209	16/2	Southwell P'	(L) MDO 3m	7	GS	*prom, ld apr 5-8th, wknd rpdly & p.u. 12th*	P	0
480	9/3	Southwell P'	(L) MDO 3m	17	G	*prom til wknd 13th, bhnd & p.u. 3 out*	P	0

Shows speed but no stamins so far; can do better 0

ROBIN OF LOXLEY (Irish) — **I** 83^{3}, **I** 563^{P}, **I** 570^{1}, **I** 600^{5}

ROBINSTOWN (Irish) — **I** 184^{F}, **I** 268^{P}

ROBUSTI ch.g. 15 Bustino - Juliette Marny by Blakeney — S Turner

1996 8(0),4(15)

5	19/1	Barbury Cas'	(L) OPE 3m	11	GF	*bhnd, 8th hlfwy, nvr dang*	5	13
359	2/3	Garnons	(L) MEM 3m	3	GS	*(fav) ld to 12th, outpcd frm 15th, styd on und pres flat*	2	14
401	8/3	Llanfrynach	(R) LAD 3m	14	G	*tubed, alwys rear*	8	13
714	29/3	Llanvapley	(L) CON 3m	15	GF	*(vis) (tubed), prom early, 3rd 11th, grdly wknd*	5	0

Ladies winner 95; lightly raced; has problems & surely to old to win now. 12

ROCCO b.g. 10 King's Ride - Ladycastle by Pitpan — K Tork

1996 **U(NH),U(NH),7(NH),2(NH)**

305	1/3	Parham	(R) OPE 3m	9	G	*n.j.w. prom to 5th, bhnd whn p.u. 14th*	P	0
486	9/3	Tweseldown	(R) XX 3m	3	G	*alwys last, lost tch whn ref 2 out*	R	-
1125	19/4	Penshurst	(L) MEM 3m	3	GF	*cls up whn u.r. 6th*	U	-
1377	5/5	Northaw	(L) OPE 3m	3	F	*reluc to race, lft 200 yds, ref 2nd*	R	-

Winning Hurdler/Chaser; awful in 97 & best avoided 0

ROC DE PRINCE(FR) br.g. 14 Djarvis (FR) - Haute Volta II (FR) by Beau Fixe — P A D Scouller

17	25/1	Badbury Rin'	(L) CON 3m	9	GF	*bhnd frm 5th, t.o. & p.u. 11th*	P	0

Dead 19

ROCKET MAN (Irish) — **I** 369^{4}

ROCKET RADAR b.g. 6 Vouchsafe - Courtney Pennant by Angus — R Bunn

1996 6(0),3(14)

263	22/2	Newtown	(L) MDN 3m	11	G	*(fav) trckd ldrs, ld 13th, clr 3 out, easily*	1	13
433	8/3	Upton-On-Se'	(R) RES 3m	18	G	*cls up 8th, prog 13th, ld 3 out, drew clr nxt*	1	18
851	31/3	Eyton-On-Se'	(L) INT 3m	8	GF	*(fav) rear, in tch 7th, 3rd 3th, ld 5 out, ran on wll und pres*	1	22

Progressive youngster; fastest time of the day last start; can reach Opens 98; could prove useful 22

ROCKHOLM LAD (Irish) — **I** 22^{P}, **I** 158^{2}

ROCK ON BUD (Irish) — **I** 28^{2}, **I** 68^{2}, **I** 117^{2}, **I** 176^{3}, **I** 328^{3}, **I** 375^{B}

ROCK ON LORD (Irish) — **I** 14^{F}, **I** 48^{P}, **I** 79^{2}, **I** 519^{P}, **I** 565^{6}

ROCK ON ROSIES (Irish) — **I** 6^{5}, **I** 60^{P}

ROGER(IRE) ch.g. 5 Magical Strike (USA) - Saint Simbir by Simbir — Miss E Saunders

88	2/2	Wolverhampt'	(L) MDO 3m	13	GS	*alwys bhnd, mstk 11th, t.o. & p.u. nxt*	P	0
245	22/2	Lemalla	(R) MDO 3m	11	S	*in tch, 6th hlfwy, wknd 12th, bhnd & p.u. 16th*	P	0
407	8/3	Llanfrynach	(R) MDN 3m	11	G	*f 2nd*	F	-
641	22/3	Howick	(L) MDN 3m	9	GF	*ld 6th-13th, wknd rpdly, f 3 out*	U	-
842	31/3	Lydstep	(L) MDO 3m	12	F	*u.r. 2nd*	U	-
1229	26/4	Pyle	(R) MDO 3m	11	GS	*chsd ldrs til wknd 8th, t.o. & p.u. 14th*	P	0

No stamina so far; unpromising 0

ROGERSON ch.g. 9 Green-Fingered - Town Belle by Town Crier — S H Sweetland

1996 P(0),P(0),P(0),U(-),2(12)

315	1/3	Clyst St Ma'	(L) MDN 3m	5	HY	*cls up, lft in ld 8-12th, wknd 2 out, tired & ref last*	R	-
527	15/3	Cothelstone	(L) MDN 3m	14	GS	*rpd prog to ld 6th, slght ld whn ref 15th*	R	-

Placed in weak race 96; signs not good now & best watched 12

ROLIER(IRE) gr.g. 7 Roselier (FR) - Countess Tudor — T A B Scott

1996 **12(NH)**

206	15/2	Weston Park	(L)	MDN	3m	9	G	*mid-div, prog 8th, ld 4 out, sn clr, easily*	1	18
348	2/3	Market Rase'	(L)	RES	3m	13	GF	*(Jt fav) cls up til slppd & u.r. 5th*	U	-
753	29/3	Brampton Br'	(R)	RES	3m	9	GF	*(fav) mid-div whn ran thro' wing 5th*	r	-
940	6/4	Tabley	(R)	RES	3m	9	G	*mid-div, ld apr 2 out, ran on strngly*	1	23
1178	20/4	Sandon	(L)	XX	3m	6	GF	*(fav) hld up rear, clsd 3 out, disp nxt, ld last & lft clr*	1	21
1264	27/4	Southwell P'	(L)	INT	3m	9	G	*(fav) hld up rear, prog 8th, ld 3 out-nxt, rallied wll flat*	2	19
1299	3/5	Weston Park	(L)	MEM	3m	4	G	*(fav) alwys handy, 2nd 10th, ld 5 out, sn in cmmnd, easily*	1	23

Ex Irish; improving; decent prospect; stays ; can win Opens 98; worth watching;G-G/F 23

ROLL WITH IT (Irish) — **I** 527^{4}, **I** 589^{U}

ROLY PRIOR b.g. 8 Celtic Cone - Moonduster by Sparkler — Ian Hamilton

1996 3(14),2(15),F(-),4(0),2(15),1(16),6(13),P(0)

33	26/1	Alnwick	(L)	LAD	3m	12	G	*cls up til lost tch wth ldrs 14th, styd on wll frm 2 out*	4	18
158	15/2	Lanark	(R)	LAD	3m	8	G	*bhnd by 4th, gd prog frm 4 out, chal 2 out, just hld*	2	21
336	1/3	Corbridge	(R)	LAD	3m 5f	9	G	*alwys prom, ev ch whn f 16th*	F	-
412	8/3	Dalston	(R)	LAD	3m	8	GS	*prom, chsd wnr 11th-3 out, rallied apr last, ran on*	2	20
561	16/3	Lanark	(R)	LAD	3m	7	GS	*(fav) not fluent, wnt 2nd 9th, disp frm 12th, drew clr 3 out*	1	22
778	31/3	Carlisle	(R)	HC	3 1/4m	14	G	*bhnd and rdn along, imp 6 out, no impn final 4.*	4	18
1048	13/4	Lockerbie	(R)	LAD	3m	6	F	*ld 3rd-11th, ld 14th, sn clr*	1	22
1219	26/4	Balcormo Ma'	(R)	LAD	3m	3	F	*(fav) 10l 2nd whn lft in ld 9th, made rest, pshd out flat*	1	21

Improved & now decent Ladies pointer; stays well; well ridden; sure to win more;G/S-F 23

ROMAN GALE (Irish) — **I** 75^{P}, **I** 421^{1}, **I** 518^{F}

ROMAN ROMANY ch.g. 8 Sir Patrick - Roman Lass by Roi Soleil — D R E Bevan

654	22/3	Siddington	(L)	MDN	3m	10	F	*f 3rd*	F	-
1151	19/4	Chaddesley '	(L)	MDO	3m	5	GF	*ld til ref & u.r. 6th*	R	
1165	20/4	Mollington	(R)	MDO	3m	9	GF	*made virt all, clr 14th, pshd out flat*	1	15
1326	3/5	Chaddesley '	(L)	RES	3m	3	GF	*(fav) made all,hit 1st,slw jmp 4th,in cmmnd whn blnd last,drvn out*	1	14
1536	18/5	Mollington	(R)	INT	3m	8	GS	*ld, clr to 11th, hdd & wknd 2 out, p.u. last*	P	0

Won weak races; front runs; mistakes & well ridden; can improve; needs to for Confineds 17

ROMANY ANNE b.m. 9 Button Bright (USA) - Romany Charm by Romany Air — L Bond

1996 P(0),P(0),6(0),3(11),P(0),2(10)

105	8/2	Great Treth'	(R)	MDO	3m	15	GS	*ld to 3rd, prom til outpcd 14th, no ch whn p.u. last*	P	0
242	22/2	Lemalla	(R)	MDO	3m	10	S	*wll bhnd til p.u. 13th*	P	0
625	22/3	Kilworthy	(L)	MDN	3m	14	G	*ld aft 3rd til 17th, disp 3rd & wkng whn f last*	F	12
740	29/3	Higher Kilw'	(L)	MDN	3m	15	GF	*wll out of tch, fin strngly, too mch to do*	4	0
1036	12/4	Lifton	(R)	LAD	3m	4	F	*hld up, gd prog 15th, ld aft last, comf*	1	15
1394	5/5	High Bickin'	(R)	MEM	3m	4	G	*ld 5th, mssd mrkr aft 7th, cont in ld, eased, disq*	0D	0
1438	10/5	Holnicote	(L)	LAD	3m	7	G	*5th hlfwy, lost ground 11th, ran on cls home*	4	18
1548	24/5	Mounsey Hil'	(R)	LAD	3m	10	G	*alwys mid-div, some prog to 4th at 14th, nvr nr ldrs*	5	13
1596	31/5	Bratton Down	(L)	OPE	4m	5	F	*last til prog 13th, chsd wnr 4 out-2 out, wknd, dsmntd*	3	17

Won bad Ladies; consistent but moderate & hard to find another win; Members best hope 15

ROMANY ARK b.g. 11 Arkan - Romany Charm by Romany Air — Mrs A Bell

214	16/2	Southwell P'	(L)	CON	3m	10	GS	*alwys bhnd, t.o. whn blnd 3 out*	5	0
350	2/3	Market Rase'	(L)	CON	3m	11	GF	*chsd ldrs, outpcd apr 14th, lft 4th nxt, kpt on*	4	16
545	16/3	Garthorpe	(R)	CON	3m	12	GF	*hld up,stdy prog 11th, chall last, ran on to ld cls hme*	1	20
780	31/3	Fakenham	(L)	HC	3m 110yds	7	G	*dropped rear 4th, hdwy when mstk 13th, no ext from 3 out.*	4	16

Won 3 in 94; missed 95/96; retains ability; every chance of Confined at 12; G/F-S 19

ROMILEY MILL b.g. 6 Derring Rose - Night Beat by Meldrum — Miss C Billington

418	8/3	Dalston	(R)	MDO	2 1/2m	10	GS	*prssd ldr, ld 3 out, rdn & wknd flat, hdd nr fin*	3	15
763	29/3	Whittington	(L)	CON	3m	9	S	*mid-div, lft dist 2nd 15th, styd on wll, not trble wnnr*	2	10
1345	3/5	Gisburn	(R)	MDN	3m	13	GF	*(fav) ld to 5th, cls 2nd whn u.r. nxt*	U	-

Beaten 25 lengths in Confined; poor horses behind; should find a Maiden 15

RONALDSWAY b.g. 6 Slip Anchor - Western Star by Alcide — James Buckle

193	15/2	Higham	(L)	CON	3m	14	G	*trckd ldr til blnd & u.r. 8th*	U	-
439	8/3	Higham	(L)	MDO	3m	11	G	*trckd ldrs, prog 11th, ld 16th, sn clr, comf*	1	15
711	29/3	High Easter	(L)	RES	3m	6	F	*(fav) ld to 12th, chsd wnr aft til wknd 3 out, lost 2nd 2 out*	3	11
913	5/4	Cottenham	(R)	RES	3m	4	F	*chsd ldr, ld 10th-13th, 3rd & btn whn u.r. 3 out*	U	-

Won weak Maiden; struggling after; stamina suspect; can improve; needs to for Restricted 14

RONKINO (Irish) — **I** 48^{P}, **I** 91^{4}, **I** 143^{P}, **I** 169^{F}, **I** 599^{F}

RONNIES WEDDING(IRE) ch.g. 5 King Luthier - Balacco by Balidar — Miss C Billington

420	8/3	Dalston	(R)	MDO	2 1/2m	8	GS	*alwys last, t.o. whn tried ref 4th, school aft*	6	0

Learning on debut 0

ROOK'S ROCK (Irish) — I 53^{P}

ROOM TO MANOUVER(IRE) ch.g. 8 Le Bavard (FR) - She's A Model by Caribo — R Lush

1996 P(0),4(0),P(0),U(-),4(0)

498	15/3	Ampton	(R)	MDO 3m	8	GF	*rcd wde, cls up to 8th, bhnd frm 11th, t.o. whn ref 2 out*	R	-

Novice-ridden; shows nothing & finished early 97 0

ROO'S LEAP(IRE) b.m. 9 Leap High (USA) - Island More by Mugatpura — Tom Hayes

1018	12/4	Bitterley	(L)	MDO 3m	13	GF	*rear frm 11th, lost tch & p.u. 15th*	P	0
1296	3/5	Hereford	(R)	HC 2m 3f	11	G	*bhnd from 7th, t.o. when p.u. before 9th.*	P	0

Not yet of any account 0

ROOTSMAN(IRE) b.g. 7 Glenstal (USA) - Modena by Sassafras (FR) — Mrs J Morgan

436	8/3	Upton-On-Se'	(R)	MDO 3m	17	G	*rear of ldng grp 9th, in tch til no prog 12th, p.u. 3 out*	P	0
1015	12/4	Bitterley	(L)	MDO 3m	12	GF	*hld up rear, prog 3 out, qcknd to ld last, sn clr*	1	14
1237	26/4	Brampton Br'	(R)	RES 3m	13	G	*(fav) hld up, prog 15th, qcknd to ld last, sn clr*	1	17

Ex novice hurdler; won modest races; imprving; quickens; can win Confineds; G-G/F so far 19

ROSA'S REVENGE b or br.m. 9 Pony Express - Royal Brief by Eborneezer — G W Johnson

1996 P(0),6(0),1(14),6(11)

176	15/2	Ottery St M'	(L)	RES 3m	17	G	*alwys prom, outpcd 14th, kpt on onepcd frm 4 out*	3	17
630	22/3	Kilworthy	(L)	RES 3m	16	G	*(bl) 7th hlfwy, no ch last m*	9	0
1107	19/4	Flete Park	(R)	MEM 3m	2	GF	*(bl) ld til 15th, ld 17th til mstk 2 out, no ext*	2	18
1339	3/5	Flete Park	(R)	RES 3m	6	G	*(bl) raced wd, cls 2nd mstly, fdd frm 2 out*	2	15

Maiden winner 96; finds little & blinkers essential; struggling in Restricteds; Members best hope 15

ROSCOE'S GEMMA b.m. 13 Roscoe Blake - Ash Copse by Golden Love — N K Thick

1996 P(0),6(0),2(12),5(0)

263	22/2	Newtown	(L)	MDN 3m	11	G	*ld to 4th, p.u. nxt*	P	0

Problems & vanished quickly in 97; too old to win now 10

ROSCOLVIN(IRE) g. 5 Prince Rupert (FR) - Chepstow House (USA) by Northern Baby (CAN) — Mrs Julie Read

1996 **4(NH),6(NH),16(NH)**

15	25/1	Cottenham	(R)	MDN 3m	7	GF	*(fav) trckd ldng pair, smooth prog to cls 2nd whn f 2 out,rmntd*	4	0
439	8/3	Higham	(L)	MDO 3m	11	G	*(fav) trckd ldr, wknd aft 11th, lost plc nxt, no ch & p.u. 2 out*	P	0
915	5/4	Cottenham	(R)	MDO 3m	6	F	*keen hld, hld up, prog 3 out, ld last, qcknd clr flat*	1	11
1309	3/5	Cottenham	(R)	RES 3m	4	F	*(fav) hld up in tch, trckd ldr 14th, ld 3 out, hrd hld*	1	15
1502	16/5	Folkestone	(R)	HC 2m 5f	10	G	*mstks, held up, bhnd from 7th, t.o. and p.u. before 2 out.*	P	0

Ex Irish Flat/NH; plenty of ability but tricky & needs things his way; won soft races; can win again 16

ROSCOMMON LAD(IRE) b.g. 5 Groom Dancer (USA) - Preoccupy by Habitat — F L Matthews

1996 **P(NH),P(NH),11(NH),P(NH),P(NH)**

470	8/3	Eyton-On-Se'	(L)	MDN 2 1/2m	12	G	*alwys rear, p.u. 9th*	P	0

No ability under rules; no show on debut & not seen again 0

ROSCRILY WILLIAM (Irish) — I 248^{5}, I 328^{6}, I 431^{3}, I 508^{3}, I 583^{P}

ROSEA PLENA ch.m. 13 Leander - Indian Cash by Indian Ruler — Miss L Clisby Brown

1244	26/4	Bratton Down	(L)	CON 3m	14	GS	*midfld whn u.r. 5th*	U	-
1517	17/5	Bratton Down	(L)	MXO 3m	8	GS	*lost tch 11th, jmpd rght 13th, t.o. & p.u. 16th*	P	0

Of no account 0

ROSEBERRY STAR b.m. 9 Alfie Dickins - Sweet Roseberry by Derek H — P Cowey

1996 F(-),2(0),3(0),P(0),4(0),6(0)

510	15/3	Dalton Park	(R)	MDO 3m	14	GF	*rear, sn wll bhnd, t.o. 6th, p.u. 12th*	P	0
622	22/3	Hutton Rudby	(L)	MDO 3m	10	GF	*prom til wknd 14th, t.o.*	5	0
693	29/3	Stainton	(R)	MEM 3m	3	F	*settld in last plc, outpcd 8th, sn lost tch, t.o. 15th*	3	0

Does not stay & well beaten when completing; prospects very slim 0

ROSE GREY (Irish) — I 506^{F}

ROSELAND (Irish) — I 55^{5}, I 98^{F}, I 218^{2}, I 296^{3}, I 389^{5}, I 497^{6}, I 591^{1}

ROSELYNHILL (Irish) — I 112^{P}, I 126^{P}, I 212,

ROSE MALT (Irish) — I 565^{P}

ROSEMARY ANN (Irish) — I 250^{P}, I 312^{P}, I 556^{P}, I 586^{P}

ROSE OF MACMILLION b.m. 8 Macmillion - Tic-On-Rose by Celtic Cone — K R Howse

178	15/2	Larkhill	(R)	CON 3m	9	G	*wth ldr, blnd 3rd, lost plc 8th, last whn f 10th*	F	-
293	1/3	Didmarton	(L)	INT 3m	16	G	*alwys rear, t.o. last whn p.u. 11th*	P	0
512	15/3	Larkhill	(R)	MDO 3m	6	GF	*in tch, chsd ldr brfly apr 13th, 3rd whn f 14th*	F	-

649 22/3 Siddington (L) MEM 3m 6 F *ld 3-9th, wknd rpdly, t.o. & p.u. 13th* P 0
1065 13/4 Maisemore P' (L) MDO 3m 13 GF *hld up rear, lft 3rd 14th, lft 2nd 3 out, ld last, all out* 1 14
1322 3/5 Bonvilston (R) RES 3m 9 G *last early, some prog 7th, p.u. 12th* P 0
1594 31/5 Bratton Down (L) INT 3m 10 F *n.j.w. in tch in rear to 11th, wkng whn p.u. 13th* P 0

Ex novice hurdler; won bad 2 finisher race(well ridden); mistakes; does not stay; very hard now 13

ROSEOREE (Irish) — **I** 329^{P}, **I** 370^{P}, **I** 472^{P}, **I** 556^{F}

ROSES IN MAY b.m. 11 Mummy's Game - Ma Famille by Welsh Saint R J S Linne
1996 3(0),1(13),P(0)
804 31/3 Wadebridge (L) INT 3m 6 F *trcks ldrs til grdly wknd frm 3 out* 5 10

Won Restricted 96 (match); finished early 97 & most unlikely to win again 11

ROSE'S LADY DAY b.m. 6 Old Jocus - Rose's Final by Crawter Mrs J Goudge
1996 U(-),P(0),P(0),P(0)
53 1/2 Wadebridge (L) MDO 3m 3 G *ran around own pace* 2 0
105 8/2 Great Treth' (R) MDO 3m 15 GS *alwys bhnd, t.o. & p.u. 13th* P 0
244 22/2 Lemalla (R) MDO 3m 12 S *f 1st* F
808 31/3 Wadebridge (L) MDO 3m 8 F *nvr a factor, p.u. 4 out* P 0
1584 26/5 Lifton (R) MDO 3m 13 G *nvr nr ldrs, p.u. 10th* P 0

Hopeless 0

ROSES LUCK (Irish) — **I** 323^{F}, **I** 448^{P}, **I** 486^{P}

ROSETOWN GIRL (Irish) — **I** 33^{2}, **I** 109^{3}, **I** 162^{1}, **I** 208^{5}, **I** 299^{1}, **I** 511^{2}

ROSEVALLEY(IRE) b.g. 7 Boyne Valley - Rosebrook by Brother Birdbrook A J Whiting
297 1/3 Didmarton (L) MDN 3m 11 G *ld, in cmmnd & clr whn u.r. 100 yrds frm fin* U 14
821 31/3 Paxford (L) MDO 3m 6 F *(fav) ld 2nd, made rest, unchal* 1 16
1061 13/4 Maisemore P' (L) RES 3m 12 GF *mstks, disp til blnd 4th, ld 12th-2 out, no ext* 3 16
1211 26/4 Woodford (L) MEM 3m 8 G *w.w. in tch whn blnd 10th, 5th & wkng 13th, p.u. 15th* P 0

Ex Irish; winner behind in weak race; ran well after but too many errors; weak Restricted possible 16

ROSIE BLUE b.m. 7 Ardar - Hotwave by Hotfoot Miss G T Lee
510 15/3 Dalton Park (R) MDO 3m 14 GF *rear & sn lost tch, t.o. 6th, p.u. 9th* P 0
623 22/3 Hutton Rudby (L) MDO 3m 9 GF *rear & sn strgglng, t.o. 12th, p.u. 3 out* P 0
699 29/3 Stainton (R) MDO 3m 7 F *prom,chsd ldr 6th,fdd 12th,wknd,t.o. broke leg & p.u. 4 out* P 0

Dead. 0

ROSIEPLANT b.m. 7 Queen's Soldier (USA) - Sweet Saskia by Spitsbergen A Plant
1996 P(0),4(0),1(14)
189 15/2 Erw Lon (L) RES 3m 14 G *prom, ld 10th-3 out, no ch wnr aft, lost 2nd flat* 4 14
404 8/3 Llanfrynach (R) INT 3m 17 G *prom early, grad wknd, p.u. 2 out* P 0
718 29/3 Llanvapley (L) RES 3m 13 GF *rear,imprvd to trck ldrs frm 12th,2l down 2 out,alwys held* 2 15
1135 19/4 Bonvilston (R) RES 3m 14 G *rear early, prog 3 out, nvr nrr* 4 14
1224 26/4 Pyle (R) CON 3m 7 GS *w.w. prog to jn ldrs 13th, wknd rpdly nxt, p.u. 3 out* P 0

Maiden winner 96; good stable; inconsistent & not progress 97; may eventually find a Restricted 15

ROSMERE (Irish) — **I** 272^{6}, **I** 389, , **I** 458^{6}, **I** 548^{6}

ROSSI BEG (Irish) — **I** 384^{3}

ROSSODISERA ch.g. 9 Scottish Reel - Iceni Star by Firestreak Giuseppe G Gigantesco
488 9/3 Tweseldown (R) RES 3m 10 G *lft start, crwld 1st & 2nd, ref 3rd, cont, stppd 5th* R -

Not a good start 0

ROSS QUAY (Irish) — **I** 156^{F}, **I** 221^{1}, **I** 257^{1}

ROSS VENTURE b.g. 12 Monksfield - Fitz's Buck by Master Buck Lee Brennan
1996 P(0),**2(20)**,3(11)
149 10/2 Hereford (R) HC 3m 1f 110yds 18 GS *chsd ldrs, rdn and wknd 6 out.* P 0

Winning chaser; lightly raced; finished early 97 & most unlikely to win again 15

ROSSY ORCHESTRA (Irish) — **I** 159^{P}, **I** 453^{F}, **I** 510^{P}, **I** 547^{6}, **I** 576^{6}

ROUGH AURA b.g. 7 Just A Monarch - Lucy Aura by Free State C G Martin
1996 P(0)
279 23/2 Charing (L) CON 3m 10 G *last & t.o. til p.u. 10th* P 0
306 1/3 Parham (R) MDN 3m 12 G *alwys rear, t.o. & p.u. 10th* P 0
581 16/3 Detling (L) MDO 3m 12 F *ld to 6th, wll bhnd 15th, p.u. 3 out* P 0
605 22/3 Parham (R) MDO 3m 7 F *ld to 3rd, last frm 6th, lost tch whn u.r. 4 out* U -

Of no account 0

ROUGH EDGE b.g. 9 Broadsword (USA) - Mini Gazette by London Gazette — David Wales

770 29/3 Dingley (R) RES 3m 18 G *alwys rear hlf, outpcd 6 out, remote 7th whn p.u. last* P 0
1080 13/4 Guilsborough (L) RES 3m 11 GF *mstks, in tch, effrt to chs ldrs 15th, sn outpcd, kpt on wll* 3 13
1276 27/4 Fakenham P-' (L) MEM 3m 7 G *(fav) made all, rdn apr last, styd on well* 1 13
1355 4/5 Dingley (R) RES 3m 12 G *w.w., mstk 6th, prog 8th, ev ch 2 out, unable to qckn last* 2 19
1435 10/5 Marks Tey (L) INT 3m 8 G *hld up rear,prog 10th,chsd ldr 4 out,chal 2 out,ld last,r.o.* 1 18
1530 18/5 Fakenham (L) HC 2m 5f 110yds 11 G *(fav) held up, hdwy 10th, hit next, chsd ldr 3 out, ld last, styd on well.* 1 22

Maiden winner 94; missed 96; improved; H/chase makes liofe tough now; needs more for Opens; G/F-G 20

ROUGH HOUSE b.g. 6 Homeboy - Course Weed by Crash Course — Robert Robinson

1996 4(0),3(0),P(0)

417 8/3 Dalston (R) MDO 2 1/2m 11 GS *prom, mstk 11th, sn wknd, t.o. & p.u. 2 out* P 0
612 22/3 Friars Haugh (L) MDN 3m 14 GF *nvr nr ldrs* 6 0
1046 13/4 Lockerbie (R) MEM 3m 4 F *ld to 6th, cls 2nd til 14th, lost tch 3 out* 3 0

Well beaten when completing; still young but much more needed 0

ROUGHSHOD (Irish) — I 14^{4}, I 85^{U}

ROUGH TOR ch.g. 10 Riot Helmet - Lisnafulla Lady by Golden Love — Mrs M D Hartley

173 15/2 Ottery St M' (L) CON 3m 7 G *chsd ldr, ev ch 4 out, wknd rpdly aft nxt* 5 0

Potentially useful 95; only one run since & can only be watched now 21

ROUND OF DRINKS b.g. 7 Pollerton - Dusky Nancy by Red Sunset — P Sanders

531 15/3 Wadebridge (L) MDO 3m 14 GF *ref to race, t.n.p.* 0 0
741 29/3 Higher Kilw' (L) MDN 3m 12 GF *ran green, pllng, ld 2nd-7th, cls up whn f 11th* F -
1585 26/5 Lifton (R) MEM 3m 2 G *20l bhnd whn u.r. 3rd* U -

No cause for celebration yet 0

ROUND POUND (Irish) — I 18^{P}

ROUND TOWER LADY (Irish) — I 13^{P}, I 41^{P}, I 75^{P}, I 194^{P}, I 421^{5}

ROUSILLON TO BE b.g. 10 Rousillon (USA) - Triple Bar by Jimmy Reppin — David Iveson

11 25/1 Cottenham (R) LAD 3m 2 GF *(fav) disp til u.r. 8th* U -
272 22/2 Ampton (R) LAD 3m 7 G *ld/disp til ld 7-9th, lst tch wth 1st 2 frm nxt, t.o.* 3 10
448 8/3 Newton Brom' (R) LAD 3m 5 G *rear, last at 14th, sn bhnd* 4 0
546 16/3 Garthorpe (R) LAD 3m 11 GF *(bl) chsd ldrs til wknd qkly appr 3 out, t.o. & p.u. last* P 0
1077 13/4 Guilsborough (L) CON 3m 16 GF *(bl) ld 2nd-9th, sn btn, p.u. 15th* P 0

Members winner 95; missed 96; blew a gift 1st start; outclassed otherwise; need luck to win again 11

ROVAC b.g. 10 Ovac (ITY) - Open You Eyes by Beau Charmeur (FR) — Mrs G Fryer

212 16/2 Southwell P' (L) MDO 3m 14 GS *hld up, prog 10th, 4th & outpcd 13th, kpt on* 4 0
480 9/3 Southwell P' (L) MDO 3m 17 G *mid-div, prog 10th, 4th & rdn 14th, wll btn apr 3 out* 6 0

Ex Irish; missed 95/96; well beaten & needs more to win; time passing him by 11

ROVET (Irish) — I 72^{P}, I 119^{P}, I 232^{5}, I 315^{U}, I 417^{P}, I 437^{5}, I 471^{4}, I 526^{2}, I 554^{P}

ROVING GYPSY b or br.m. 5 Newski (USA) - Proven Gypsy by Ampney Prince — Mrs A P Wakeham

1343 3/5 Flete Park (R) MDO 3m 13 G *sn rear, bhnd whn p.u. 12th* P 0
1481 11/5 Ottery St M' (L) CON 3m 12 G *rear whn u.r. 3rd* U -
1520 17/5 Bratton Down (L) MDO 3m 17 GS *rear til p.u. 14th, schooling* P 0

Learning so far 0

ROVING REBEL b.g. 10 Prince Of Peace - Proven Gypsy by Ampney Prince — Mrs A P Wakeham

1996 P(0),P(0)

237 22/2 Lemalla (R) CON 3m 13 S *prom, ld 5th, disp 9-11th, lost plc nxt, p.u. aft 16th* P 0
557 16/3 Ottery St M' (L) RES 3m 9 G *mid-div til p.u. 12th* P 0

Maiden winner 94; lightly raced & of no account now 0

ROVING REPORT gr.g. 10 Celio Rufo - Black Rapper by Le Tricolore — Mrs A Rucker

1996 P(0),2(21),2(14),2(22),2(20),2(19),1(19),0(0),2(21)

18 25/1 Badbury Rin' (L) LAD 3m 9 GF *outpcd in mid-div, effrt 11th, sn btn, t.o. 15th* 4 10
143 9/2 Tweseldown (R) XX 3m 3 GF *(fav) hld up last, prog to ld on bit 2 out, easily* 1 16
255 22/2 Newtown (L) CON 3m 14 G *bhnd frm 6th, no dang aft* 7 11
482 9/3 Tweseldown (R) LAD 3m 5 G *t.n.p.* 0 0
638 22/3 Howick (L) LAD 3m 10 GF *mid-div, went 3rd 12th, chal 3 out, alwys hld* 2 18
702 29/3 Upper Sapey (R) LAD 3m 4 GF *f 1st* F -

3 wins 11 places last 19 starts; declined in 97; quirky; may revive with strong handling;F-S 18

ROVING VAGABOND b.g. 13 Newski (USA) - Proven Gypsy by Ampney Prince — Mrs A P Wakeham

1996 P(0),F(-),P(0),P(0),3(0),F(-)

1036	12/4	Lifton	(R) LAD	3m	4	F	*slght ld 1st, sn lost tch, bhnd whn ref 14th*	R	-

Maiden winner 95(finished solo); outclassed since; no prospects 0

ROWDLEDY (Irish) — I 296^{P}, I 428^{3}

ROYAL ARCTIC (Irish) — I 52^{2}, I 100^{1}, I 147^{1}, I 216^{F}, I 266^{2}

ROYAL ARISTOCRAT (Irish) — I 290, , I 434^{1}, I 584^{3}

ROYAL BALINGER ch.m. 7 Balinger - Ginger Fury by Fury Royal — I P Crane

479	9/3	Southwell P'	(L) MDO	3m	15	G	*nvr bttr than mid-div, 4th & no ch frm 14th*	4	10
776	29/3	Dingley	(R) MDO	2m 5f	10	G	*disp, lft in ld 3 out, hdd & outpcd apr last*	2	12
1082	13/4	Guilsborough	(L) MDN	3m	14	GF	*prom, disp 13th-16th, sn btn, 4th & no ch whn p.u. last*	P	0
1193	20/4	Garthorpe	(R) MDO	3m	9	GF	*chsd ldrs, p.u. 5th, lame*	P	0

Missed 96; only beat one horse but promise when placed; problems last start 12

ROYAL BARGE (Irish) — I 4^{1}, I 89^{F}, I 147^{F}, I 194^{3}

ROYAL BATTLE b.m. 9 Broadsword (USA) - Non Such Valley by Colonist II — M R Flinton

438	8/3	Higham	(L) MDO	3m	8	G	*jmpd rght, rear, nvr going wll*	5	0

Ex-novice hurdler; hardly ever runs; does not stay & no real prospects 0

ROYAL BULA b.g. 9 Sula Bula - Clan Royal by Royal Smoke — G I Isaac

1996 P(0),P(0),P(0),U(-),3(0),P(0)

223	16/2	Heythrop	(R) RES	3m	19	G	*alwys bhnd, t.o. & p.u. 12th*	P	0
574	16/3	Garnons	(L) RES	3m	14	G	*last frm 9th, t.o. & p.u. 15th*	P	0

Last on only completion; looks hopeless 0

ROYAL CHAPEAU (Irish) — I 143^{2}, I 245^{P}, I 305^{P}, I 383^{2}

ROYAL CHARGER(IRE) b.g. 5 Euphemism - Royal Brigade by Light Brigade — Harry Atkinson

620	22/3	Hutton Rudby	(L) MDO	3m	10	GF	*mid-div, in tch whn b.d. 15th*	B	-
1073	13/4	Whitwell-On'	(R) MDO	2 1/2m 88yds	17	G	*prom til wknd 4 out, t.o. & p.u. 2 out*	P	0

A glimmer of hope; young & should do better 0

ROYAL CURRAGH (Irish) — I 517^{2}

ROYAL DADDA br.g. 7 Denel (FR) - Royal Typhoon by Royal Fountain — M P Avery

1996 **9(NH)**,**P(NH)**

60	1/2	Kingston Bl'	(L) MDN	3m	17	GF	*s.s. alwys wll bhnd, p.u. 3 out*	P	0
224	16/2	Heythrop	(R) MDN	3m	16	G	*blnd 5th, in tch, rdn to disp & mstk 9th, sn btn, p.u. 2 out*	P	0
374	2/3	Mollington	(R) MDN	3m	14	G	*in tch, rdn aft 10th, effrt 14th, nvr rchd ldrs*	4	10
549	16/3	Garthorpe	(R) MDO	3m	16	GF	*chsd ldrs, 3rd & rddn 11th, wknd nxt, hit 14th, p.u. 3 out*	P	0
756	29/3	Kimble	(L) MEM	3m	3	GF	*ld/disp, out jmpd, rdn 17th, ld apr last, lft solo*	1	10
986	12/4	Kingston Bl'	(L) CON	3m	10	GF	*svrl slw jmps, sn pshd alng, rdn & no prog 10th, p.u. 15th*	P	0
1453	10/5	Kingston Bl'	(L) MEM	3m	3	G	*ld to 3rd, ld nxt, ld/disp til outpcd aft 3 out*	2	0

Ex novice hurdler; finished alone in Members; does not stay; mistakes; hard to find another win 11

ROYAL DALE (Irish) — I 137^{P}, I 169^{5}, I 379^{5}

ROYAL DARKNESS(IRE) br.g. 6 King Luthier - Dusky Servilla by Callernish — D G Field

479	9/3	Southwell P'	(L) MDO	3m	15	G	*nvr bttr than mid-div, 6th & no ch whn blnd 13th, f nxt*	F	-
928	6/4	Garthorpe	(R) MDO	3m	8	GF	*mid-div, u.r. 8th*	U	-

Not yet of any account 0

ROYAL DILEMMA (Irish) — I 96^{F}

ROYAL EXHIBITION ch.g. 13 Le Bavard (FR) - The Brown Link by Rugged Man — Ms Jayne Barton

1996 1(13)

371	2/3	Mollington	(R) LAD	3m	9	G	*last pair & alwys t.o.*	8	0
449	8/3	Newton Brom'	(R) XX	3m	13	G	*alwys bhnd, t.o.*	8	0
820	31/3	Paxford	(L) RES	3m	4	F	*mostly 2nd, effrt 3 out, ld nxt, styd on well*	1	12
985	12/4	Kingston Bl'	(L) MEM	3m	4	GF	*last & out of tch til u.r. bnd aft 8th*	U	-

Won 2 bad races 96/97; well below Confineds; very hard to find another race at 14 12

ROYAL FIFE br.m. 11 Royal Fountain - Aunt Bertha by Blandford Lad — Mrs C G Braithwaite

1996 F(-),4(0),U(-),U(-),2(13),1(15),4(11),7(10)

157	15/2	Lanark	(R) RES	3m	11	G	*nvr rchd ldrs*	5	0
415	8/3	Dalston	(R) RES	3m	19	GS	*last pair & nvr in race, t.o. & p.u. 15th*	P	0
945	6/4	Friars Haugh	(L) LAD	3m	6	GF	*bhnd by 7th, p.u. aft 9th*	P	0
1218	26/4	Balcormo Ma'	(R) RES	3m	5	F	*in tch til 13th, strggling whn p.u. apr 15th*	P	0

Won Maiden 96(73/4 mins); struggling badly since & unlikely to follow up; Soft 11

ROYAL FIREWORKS ch.g. 10 Royal Vulcan - Bengal Lady by Celtic Cone — Mrs N R Nutting

1996 P(0),**F(-)**,**P(NH)**

301	1/3	Parham	(R)	MEM	3m	3	G	*trckd ldr til blnd & u.r. 11th*	U	-
601	22/3	Parham	(R)	RES	3m	4	F	*ld, blnd 2nd, hdd 6th, ld 14th-apr last, wknd*	2	10

Maiden winner 94; rarely runs; beat subsequent winner when placed but still makes little appeal 0

ROYAL ICING b.m. 5 White Prince (USA) - Princess Straight by True Song — C J Bennett

87	2/2	Wolverhampt'	(L)	MDO	3m	11	GS	*schoold & bhnd, effrt 6th, just in tch whn f nxt*	F	-
366	2/3	Garnons	(L)	MDO	2 1/2m	13	GS	*prom to 8th, wknd 11th, p.u. 4 out*	P	0

No real signs yet 0

ROYAL IRISH ch.g. 13 Le Bavard (FR) - Leuze by Vimy — A C Ayres

1996 **2(19)**,**2(19)**,**2(18)**,**4(0)**,**P(0)**,**7(0)**,**P(NH)**

153	13/2	Sandown	(R)	HC	2 1/2m 110yds	6	G	*mstk 2nd, lost tch 7th, p.u. before 10th.*	P	0
304	1/3	Parham	(R)	LAD	3m	10	G	*nvr trbld ldrs, 4th final cct, lft 3rd last*	3	14
489	10/3	Plumpton	(L)	HC	3m 1f 110yds	7	GS	*in tch till rdn and outpcd 13th, soon bhnd, p.u. before 4 out.*	P	0
1054	13/4	Hackwood Pa'	(L)	CON	3m	4	GF	*chsd ldrs, wknd apr 2 out, ran out & u.r. last*	U	-
1442	10/5	Peper Harow	(L)	MEM	3m	4	GF	*jmpd slwly 3rd,ld to 12th,ev ch & rdn 3 out,blnd nxt,onepcd*	2	11

Irish bumper winner; ungenuine; never won over jumps & most unlikely to consent to 13

ROYAL JESTER b.g. 13 Royal Fountain - Tormina by Tormento — Mrs A D Wauchope

1996 2(24),**2(25)**,**1(23)**,**1(28)**,**1(27)**,**2(27)**

133	9/2	Alnwick	(L)	OPE	3m	6	G	*(fav) ld to 2 out, unable to qckn und pres*	2	0
289	28/2	Kelso	(L)	HC	3m 1f	8	GS	*alwys handy, chal 10th, pushed along from 3 out, styd on same pace.*	2	26
590	21/3	Kelso	(L)	HC	3 1/2m	5	G	*cl up, rdn along and outpcd apr 4 out, styd on from last, not reach wnr.*	2	26
973	7/4	Kelso	(L)	HC	3m 1f	5	GF	*(fav) chsd ldr, rdn along apr 3 out, styd on approaching last, ridden and ev ch run-in, no ext near fin.*	2	23
1096	18/4	Ayr	(L)	HC	3m 3f 110yds	7	G	*trckd ldrs, hdwy to chase wnr 15th, rdn 3 out, kept on.*	2	27
1413	7/5	Uttoxeter	(L)	HC	4 1/4m	7	GS	*rear, struggling from 16th, t.o. from 5 out.*	4	0

Decent H/chaser; (6 wins at Kelso); consistent; needs to return to points to win at 14; G/F-S 24

ROYAL LEADER (Irish) — **I** 243^{3}, **I** 300^{P}, **I** 509^{2}, **I** 579^{P}

ROYAL OASIS (Irish) — **I** 65^{1}

ROYAL OATS b.m. 12 Oats - Knights Queen by Arctic Chevalier — E Tudor Harries

1996 3(11),1(17),4(14),5(0),2(18),4(11),P(0)

191	15/2	Erw Lon	(L)	CON	3m	13	G	*prom til 4th & strgglng frm 12th, no prog aft*	5	11
403	8/3	Llanfrynach	(R)	INT	3m	8	G	*chsd wnr to 14th, wknd rpdly*	4	11
840	31/3	Lydstep	(L)	MEM	3m	6	F	*(fav) chsd ldr, ld 11th, easily*	1	16
1194	22/4	Chepstow	(L)	HC	3m	11	GF	*f 6th.*	F	-

Won good Restricted 96; inconsistent; lightly raced 97; likes Soft; Members best hope again 98 15

ROYAL ORCHARD ch.g. 7 Regal Steel - Windfall VI by Master Owen — Mrs F J Marriott

224	16/2	Heythrop	(R)	MDN	3m	16	G	*last pair & alwys bhnd, t.o. & p.u. 13th*	P	0

Only learning on debut 0

ROYAL QUARRY b.g. 11 Royal Fountain - True Friend by Bilsborrow — A Eaton

1996 P(0),U(-),5(0),4(0),3(11)

122	9/2	Cottenham	(R)	MEM	3m	6	GF	*1st ride, raced wd, sn wll bhnd, t.o. last hlfwy*	5	0
276	22/2	Ampton	(R)	MDO	3m	12	G	*mstks, wll bhnd frm 10th, t.o. & p.u. 16th*	P	0
478	9/3	Southwell P'	(L)	MDO	3m	17	G	*chsd ldrs to 7th, rdn & wknd 11th, t.o.*	7	0
839	31/3	Thorpe Lodge	(L)	MDO	3m	15	F	*rear hlf, t.o. 6th 12th, p.u. nxt*	P	0

Placed in poor race 96; no other rateable form & most unlikely to win 10

ROYAL SEGOS b.g. 10 High Line - Segos by Runnymede — A J Baillie

1996 **4(NH)**,**2(NH)**,**P(NH)**

212	16/2	Southwell P'	(L)	MDO	3m	14	GS	*(fav) ld 4th, made rest, drew clr frm 3 out, easily*	1	17
331	1/3	Eaton Hall	(R)	RES	3m	17	GS	*trckd ldrs, chal & lft clr 2 out, ran on und pres*	1	17
490	10/3	Stratford	(L)	HC	3m	12	G	*ld till 5th, rdn and wknd 4 out.*	4	15
937	6/4	Tabley	(R)	CON	3m	10	G	*alwys mid-div, blndrd 8th, nvr rchd ldrs*	5	13
1264	27/4	Southwell P'	(L)	INT	3m	9	G	*prom, disp 6th-10th, chsd ldr aft, fdd 14th, t.o.*	5	10
1412	7/5	Uttoxeter	(L)	HC	3 1/4m	10	GS	*ld to 4 out, rdn and one pace from next.*	2	19

Ex N/H; won modest races; not disgraced H/chases; win Confineds; ignore if owner ridden; stays well 19

ROYAL STAR (Irish) — **I** 37^{P}, **I** 62^{P}, **I** 93^{F}, **I** 437^{P}

ROYAL STOCK (Irish) — **I** 265^{U}

ROYAL SWEEP b.g. 8 Swing Easy (USA) - Lillylee Lady (USA) by Shecky Greene (USA) — E Lord

1150	19/4	Chaddesley '	(L)	MDO 3m	7	GF	*ref 1st, cont til ref 6th*	R	-
1211	26/4	Woodford	(L)	MEM 3m	8	G	*raced freely, ld & blnd 3rd, ran out & u.r. 5th*	r	-
1216	26/4	Woodford	(L)	MDN 3m	13	G	*2nd outing, chsd ldrs til u.r. 6th*	U	-
1330	3/5	Chaddesley '	(L)	MDN 3m	6	GF	*hld up, 5th whn blnd & u.r. 3rd*	U	-
1455	11/5	Maisemore P'	(L)	CON 3m	8	G	*jmpd slwly, t.o. til ref 4th*	R	-

A wild ride **0**

ROYAL SWINGER ch.m. 9 Royal Match - Easy Swinger by Swing Easy (USA) — E Lord

1996 P(0),U(-),P(0),B(-),4(10),P(0),P(0)

296	1/3	Didmarton	(L)	LAD 3m	13	G	*pcdk 7th, rear, wknd & p.u. 12th*	P	0
1216	26/4	Woodford	(L)	MDN 3m	13	G	*u.r. 2nd*	U	-
1330	3/5	Chaddesley '	(L)	MDN 3m	6	GF	*raced freely,prom,blnd 6th,sn bhnd, went poor 3rd 12th,t.o.*	2	0
1459	11/5	Maisemore P'	(L)	MDO 3m	12	G	*mstk 5th, lost tch 9th, 10th whn u.r. 11th*	U	-

Does not stay & no prospects **0**

ROYAL TOMMY (Irish) — I 191[P], I 482[1]

ROYAL TURN b.g. 10 Turn Back The Time (USA) - Royal Blast by Royal Palm — John Honeyball

1996 5(0),7(0),4(12),3(14)

41	1/2	Larkhill	(R)	MDO 3m	13	GF	*hmpd & u.r. 1st*	U	-
147	9/2	Tweseldown	(R)	MDO 3m	12	GF	*rear, mstks 5 & 7th, styd on onepcd frm 14th*	4	0
246	22/2	Lemalla	(R)	MDO 3m	4	S	*w.w. disp 12th, drew clr apr last, pshd out*	1	12
457	8/3	Great Treth'	(R)	RES 3m	8	S	*wnt 3rd 10th, rddn & wknd aft 16th*	4	0
630	22/3	Kilworthy	(L)	RES 3m	16	G	*hld up, gd hdwy 13th, wnt 3rd 15th, styd on wll*	3	16
861	31/3	Kingston St'	(R)	MEM 3m	2	F	*(fav) made virt all at mod pce, pshd out*	1	10
1041	12/4	Cothelstone	(L)	RES 3m	4	GF	*w.w. prog 12th, 2nd nxt, chal 2 out, outpcd flat*	2	16
1157	20/4	Stafford Cr'	(R)	RES 3m	11	GF	*rear, prog 12th, outpcd frm 3 out*	3	13
1374	5/5	Cotley Farm	(L)	RES 3m	7	GF	*w.w., prog 14th, disp 4 out, ev ch 2 out, rddn & held aft*	2	19
1439	10/5	Holnicote	(L)	RES 3m	9	G	*hld up in tch, effrt 15th, ld apr last, styd on strngly*	1	19
1496	14/5	Cothelstone	(L)	CON 3m	9	GF	*trckd ldrs, jnd wnr 13th til aft 3 out, wknd apr last*	3	17
1582	26/5	Lifton	(R)	INT 3m	10	G	*(fav) rear, prog 4 out, chal 2 out, sn btn*	4	15

Improved; consistent & solid now; onepaced & needs a little more for Confineds but can win again;F-S **20**

ROYAL VICTOR (Irish) — I 409[F]

ROYLE BURCHLIN b.g. 11 Roscoe Blake - Miss Evelin by Twilight Alley — R A Royle

1996 P(0),P(0),U(-),3(0),2(13)

204	15/2	Weston Park	(L)	RES 3m	13	G	*rear & strgglng, p.u. 3 out*	P	0
332	1/3	Eaton Hall	(R)	RES 3m	18	GS	*ld, 3l clr last, veered lft flat, hdd nr fin*	2	19
766	29/3	Whittington	(L)	INT 3m	10	S	*(bl) ld to 15th & apr 2 out, hdd last, outpcd flat*	2	19
998	12/4	Alpraham	(R)	MEM 3m	4	GF	*(fav) (bl) made all, clr 3 out, easily*	1	17
1120	19/4	Whittington	(L)	INT 3m	2	F	*(fav) (bl) jmpd rght, made all, alwys in cmmnd*	1	16
1349	3/5	Gisburn	(R)	CON 3m	11	GF	*(bl) ld to 5th & 12th-14th, ld 16th, hdd & wknd nxt*	3	17
1538	18/5	Wolverhampt'	(L)	CON 3m	8	GS	*made all, prssd 4 out, ran on wll frm nxt*	1	18

Maiden winner 92; greatly revived; needs strong handling & likes to dictate; may win again;F-S. **18**

ROYLE SPEEDMASTER ch.g. 13 Green Shoon - Cahermone Ivy by Perspex — Miss S J Cutcliffe

1996 F(-),1(22),2(23),3(15),4(19)

393	8/3	Barbury Cas'	(L)	OPE 3m	7	G	*sn wll bhnd, nvr nr ldrs, lft poor 2nd last*	2	13
745	29/3	Barbury Cas'	(L)	OPE 3m	3	F	*alwys prom, pshd up 4 out, unable qckn*	2	16
976	8/4	Heythrop	(R)	OPE 4m	7	F	*alwys bhnd, poor 6th whn p.u & dismntd 16th*	P	0

Open winner 96; thorough stayer but problems last start & looks finished now **16**

RUALMIT(IRE) b.m. 8 Mister Lord (USA) - Demanoluma by Golden Love — Mrs R White

1996 **7(NH),5(NH),2(NH),2(NH),11(NH),1(NH),4(NH),3(NH)**

117	9/2	Wetherby Po'	(L)	LAD 3m	10	GF	*(fav) 7/2-6/4, prom whn u.r. 2nd*	U	-
214	16/2	Southwell P'	(L)	CON 3m	10	GS	*prom, ld 11th-15th, ld agn 2 out, styd on strngly*	1	25

Novice chase winner; won hot race; vanished after; win Opens; maybe H/chase if fit 98; G/S-G/F **26**

RUBBLEE BUBBLEE b.g. 8 Doctor Wall - May Snow by Hornet — R Mason

541	16/3	Erw Lon	(L)	MDN 3m	10	GF	*in tch to 10th, fdd, p.u. 12th*	P	0
718	29/3	Llanvapley	(L)	RES 3m	13	GF	*mid-div p.u. 3 out*	P	0

No signs of luvlee jubblee for rubblee bubblee **0**

RUBEN JAMES (Irish) — I 483[P]

RUBIKA(FR) b.g. 14 Saumon (FR) - Eureka III (FR) by Vieux Chateau — Mrs Sarah Shoemark

1996 6(0),2(10),P(0),6(0)

55	1/2	Kingston Bl'	(L)	CON 3m	15	GF	*ld to 2nd, grad wknd*	7	0
219	16/2	Heythrop	(R)	LAD 3m	16	G	*sn rear, t.o. & p.u. 12th*	P	0
396	8/3	Barbury Cas'	(L)	CON 3m	9	G	*prom to 2nd, sn bhnd, lft poor 4th 15th, t.o.*	4	0
822	31/3	Lockinge	(L)	MEM 3m	4	F	*made all, sn clr, tired 2 out, gd jmp last, hld on*	1	17

Won pooor Members; novice-ridden; outclassed in other races **14**

RUBY'S GIRL b.m. 7 Sula Bula - Rugamour by Rugantino — B Higham

1996 **P(NH),F(NH),6(NH),3(NH)**

485 9/3 Tweseldown (R) MDO 3m 11 G *mstk 1st, made most to 11th, wknd rpdly, t.o. & p.u. 2 out* P 0
656 22/3 Siddington (L) MDN 3m 7 F *rear, lost tch 11th, bhnd aft, p.u. 2 out* P 0

No ability under rules; stamina looks the problem **0**

RUCK 'N MAUL (Irish) — **I** 352^{P}, **I** 450,

RUECASTLE b.g. 9 Politico (USA) - Topazolite by Hessonite — Miss Simone Park

1996 P(0),1(15),P(0),9(0)

411 8/3 Dalston (R) CON 3m 16 GS *prom to 8th, wknd 11th, t.o.* 8 0
607 22/3 Friars Haugh (L) RES 3m 8 GF *ld/disp to 8th, wknng whn u.r. 4 out* U -
947 6/4 Friars Haugh (L) RES 3m 6 GF *in tch til no ext frm 4 out* 4 0
995 12/4 Tranwell (L) RES 3m 6 F *disp ld 2nd-3rd, hdd nxt, 3l 3rd 9-14th, outpcd frm nxt* 5 0

Won poor Maiden 96; struggling now & not threatening to win Reatricted; Firm best **14**

RUE DE FORT gr.g. 9 Belfort (FR) - Royal Huntress by Royal Avenue — Ms M Teague

203 15/2 Weston Park (L) RES 3m 11 G *chsng grp 5th, wknd aft 12th, p.u. 14th* P 0
331 1/3 Eaton Hall (R) RES 3m 17 GS *lft in ld 5th, hdd 9th, sn btn, p.u. 14th* P 0
467 8/3 Eyton-On-Se' (L) RES 3m 15 G *cls up, ld 6th-4 out, lost tch & p.u. 2 out* P 0
670 23/3 Eaton Hall (R) RES 3m 15 GF *ld 5th-4 out, unable qckn nxt, no ext last* 3 17
848 31/3 Eyton-On-Se' (L) MEM 3m 6 GF *(fav) made all til cght apr last, no ext run in* 2 15

Maiden winner 94; lightly raced ; revived last two; barely stays; Members best hope if fit 98 .... **15**

RUFF ACCOUNT b.g. 10 Ruffo (USA) - Dutch Account Vii — R G Brader

1996 1(16),1(17),7(11),3(15)

118 9/2 Wetherby Po' (L) RES 3m 14 GF *chsd clr ldr, mstk 11th, onepcd frm 3 out* 3 15
251 22/2 Brocklesby ' (L) RES 3m 16 G *3rd to 4th, fdd 7th 5 out, outpcd nxt, p.u. 2 out* P 0
425 8/3 Charm Park (L) RES 3m 12 GF *prom til outpcd frm 4 out* 7 0
1069 13/4 Whitwell-On' (R) RES 3m 12 G *(fav) ld to 11th, steadily wknd 4 out* 4 11

Dual winner 96; not progress 97 (ground wrong); may revive with give; stays; G-S **16**

RUFFINSWICK gr.g. 11 Baron Blakeney - Indiscreet by Stupendous — O A Little

1320 3/5 Bonvilston (R) CON 3m 8 G *last til p.u. 10th* P 0
1459 11/5 Maisemore P' (L) MDO 3m 12 G *alwys rear, lost tch 9th, t.o. & p.u. 15th* P 0
1561 24/5 Bassaleg (R) MDO 3m 9 G *in tch to 11th, wknd rpdly nxt, t.o. aft til p.u. 2 out* P 0
1603 31/5 Bassaleg (R) MDO 3m 6 F *prom, ld 6th-10th, wknd apr 12th, lft poor 2nd aft nxt* 2 0

No stamina; hopeless **0**

RUFO'S COUP br.g. 10 Celio Rufo - Wadowice by Targowice (USA) — T M Rayner

1996 11(0)

332 1/3 Eaton Hall (R) RES 3m 18 GS *mid to rear, nvr in race, p.u. 13th* P 0

Hardly ever runs; shows nothing **0**

RUFO'S RAPPER (Irish) — **I** 215^{P}, **I** 340^{P}

RUGRAT b.m. 7 Another Realm - Gay Hostess (FR) by Direct Flight — G L Edwards

1996 **5(NH)**

326 1/3 Eaton Hall (R) MDN 3m 14 GS *u.r. 5th* U -
883 1/4 Flagg Moor (L) MDO 3m 12 G *chsd ldrs, 6th & wkng 4 out, t.o. & p.u. last* P 0
999 12/4 Alpraham (R) MDO 3m 8 GF *bhnd, 2nd at 8th, ld 14th-3 out, no ext* 2 12
1541 18/5 Wolverhampt' (L) MDO 3m 15 GS *alwys prom, smooth prog to ld apr 3 out, ran on wll* 1 15

Romped home in poor race; stays well; can improve; needs to for Restricted; G/F-G/S **15**

RUM CUSTOMER b.g. 6 Morgans Choice - Man Maid by Mandamus — Mrs L Roberts

1996 **U(NH),3(NH),2(NH)**

41 1/2 Larkhill (R) MDO 3m 13 GF *(fav) mid-div, outpcd frm 14th, no ch whn lft 3rd last* 3 0
104 8/2 Great Treth' (R) MDO 3m 9 GS *(fav) in tch wil wknd frm 16th, walked in* 3 0

Placed N/H Flat; season only lasted a week; needs more stamina **11**

RUM REBEL br.g. 6 Silly Prices - Rebrona by Rebel Prince — Mrs F T Walton

1996 **9(NH),10(NH),11(NH),P(NH)**

1513 17/5 Corbridge (R) MDO 3m 13 GS *alwys rear, t.o. 3 out, p.u. last* P 0

No ability under rules or points yet; successful stable & may do better **0**

RUNABOUT (Irish) — **I** 108^{5}, **I** 164^{P}, **I** 357^{2}, **I** 426^{4}

RUNACO (Irish) — **I** 121^{P}, **I** 178^{P}, **I** 212^{6}, **I** 312^{P}, **I** 329^{P}, **I** 432^{6}, **I** 506^{4}, **I** 585^{6}

RUN FOR BROWNIE(IRE) b.g. 7 Tale Quale - Parson's Dream by The Parson A R Parrish

283 23/2 Charing (L) MDO 3m 16 G *prom to 5th, wknd rpdly, p.u. 8th* P 0

Ran out of puff after a mile on debut 0

RUN FOR FREE b.g. 13 Deep Run - Credit Card by Current Coin Alan Hill

55 1/2 Kingston Bl' (L) CON 3m 15 GF *prom to hlfwy, wkng whn p.u. 3 out* P 0
475 9/3 Southwell P' (L) OPE 3m 7 G *chsd wnr apr 5th, 2l down 15th, hng lft frm nxt, kpt on* 2 23
592 22/3 Lingfield (L) HC 3m 5 GF *held up, jmpd slowly 10th, soon bhnd, t.o. from 13th, left poor 2nd 2 out.* 2 15
1077 13/4 Guilsborough (L) CON 3m 16 GF *alwys prom,jnd ldr 12th,ld 16th,sn clr,hung lft frm 3 out* 1 24
1206 26/4 Clifton On ' (L) OPE 3m 3 GS *slght ld on innr hanging lft, hdd & outpcd frm 2 out* 2 20
1448 10/5 Kingston Bl' (L) CON 3m 9 G *(fav) hld up, prog 6th, ld 11th-aft 2 out, drvn to ld last,lft clr* 1 23
1532 18/5 Mollington (R) CON 3m 11 GS *(fav) cls up,pshd alng 14th,ld apr 2 out,hng lft aft, hdd flat* 2 23
1606 1/6 Dingley (R) LAD 3m 13 GF *hmpd 6th, nvr going wll aft, poor 8th hlfwy, p.u. 13th* P 0

Former very useful chaser; able but hard ride; L/H best; stays well; win again with strong handling 22

RUN FOR FUN (Irish) — I 21^{5}, I 37^{F}, I 56^{5}, I 130^{F}
RUN FOR NIALL (Irish) — I 51^{P}, I 134^{P}, I 266^{3}, I 404^{1}, I 492^{P}
RUNNING FRAU ch.m. 10 Deep Run - Suzi Hegi by Mon Capitaine T R M Oakey

1996 P(0),U(-),4(0),5(14),6(0)

329 1/3 Eaton Hall (R) LAD 3m 10 GS *rear, not go early pce* 4 12
412 8/3 Dalston (R) LAD 3m 8 GS *last pair, losng tch whn blnd & u.r. 14th* U -
561 16/3 Lanark (R) LAD 3m 7 GS *sn bhnd, kpt on frm 4 out, not rch ldrs* 4 11
764 29/3 Whittington (L) LAD 3m 5 S *rear til ran on strgly frm 3 out, fin fast* 3 17
984 12/4 Kingston Bl' (L) MEM 3m 4 GF *(fav) trckd ldrs, outpcd 14th, ran on 3 out, ld apr last, sn clr* 1 12
1122 19/4 Whittington (L) LAD 3m 3 F *chsd ldrs, 6l 3rd whn blnd & u.r. 13th* U -
1347 3/5 Gisburn (R) OPE 3m 8 GF *bhnd, some prog 12th, wknd 15th* 7 10
1511 17/5 Corbridge (R) LAD 3m 10 GS *rear, dtchd 4th, t.o. 11th* 7 0
1574 26/5 Chaddesley ' (L) CON 3m 8 F *raced wd, in tch to 10th, wknd aft nxt, t.o. 15th* 5 0

Won Pegasus Members; outpaced in other races; novice-ridden; Members only real hope 98 13

RUNNING ON THYNE (Irish) — I 150^{F}, I 187^{U}, I 217^{P}, I 339^{F}, I 407^{P}, I 501^{F}
RUNNING SOLO (Irish) — I 83^{P}, I 189^{P}, I 260^{P}
RUNNING WOLF (Irish) — I 20^{P}, I 85^{P}, I 423^{4}
RUN TO FORM br.g. 12 Deep Run - Let The Hare Sit by Politico (USA) M S Wilesmith

1996 P(0),5(0),5(12),3(20),1(21),1(23)

6 19/1 Barbury Cas' (L) LAD 3m 13 GF *chsd ldrs, 5th & effrt hlfwy, wknd & p.u. 15th* P 0
57 1/2 Kingston Bl' (L) LAD 3m 13 GF *rear, no ch frm 11th* 7 10
257 22/2 Newtown (L) LAD 3m 12 G *prom, cls 4th whn mstk 14th, sn outpcd* 5 18
361 2/3 Garnons (L) LAD 3m 7 GS *prom to 5th, 25l 2nd 9th, kpt on onepcd 15th* 3 16
397 8/3 Barbury Cas' (L) XX 3m 10 G *chsd ldrs 8th, ld 11th-apr 2 out, onepcd* 3 15

Dual winner 96; declined in 97; easily beaten by good horses; hard to find another win at 13; G/S-G. ... 17

RUPERTS CHOICE(IRE) ch.g. 5 Phardante (FR) - Miss Nancy by Giolla Mear Christopher Sporborg

29 26/1 Marks Tey (L) MDN 3m 10 GF *mstks, rear, prog 12th, ev ch & blnd 2 out, ran on wll flat* 2 16

Fine debut; 5 subsequent winners left behind; may have won if jumping better; win if fit 98 16

RURAL RUN (Irish) — I 493^{1}
RUSHHOME gr.m. 10 Rushmere - Doon Silver by Doon Mrs G Drury

1996 2(13),P(0),**P(NH)**,**F(NH)**,**R(NH)**

462 8/3 Charing (L) RES 3m 10 G *in tch to 9th, p.u. 11th* P 0
581 16/3 Detling (L) MDO 3m 12 F *mid-div til wknd & p.u. 14th* P 0

Possibly unlucky 96; changed hands; suspect & time passing by 0

RUSHING BURN b.m. 11 Royal Fountain - Money Penny by Even Money F D A Snowden

1996 P(0),1(17),5(12),1(16)

158 15/2 Lanark (R) LAD 3m 8 G *ld brfly 11th, sn lost plc, bhnd whn p.u. 4 out* P 0
231 22/2 Friars Haugh (L) LAD 3m 13 G *nvr nr ldrs, p.u. 3 out* P 0
778 31/3 Carlisle (R) HC 3 1/4m 14 G *blnd 1st, imp to chase ldrs 8th, fd 5 out, t.o..* 8 0
1425 10/5 Aspatria (L) LAD 3m 6 G *chsng grp til wknd 11th, t.o. 15th* 5 0
1545 24/5 Cartmel (L) HC 3 1/4m 14 G *soon bhnd, t.o..* 9 0

Dual winner 96(both Friars Haugh); outclassed 97; needs Soft; worth a try in her Members 98; G-S 14

RUSHING WATERS (Irish) — I 35^{2}, I 53^{1}, I 93^{F}, I 157^{1}
RUSHMORE (Irish) — I 483^{P}
RUSSELL LODGE (Irish) — I 127^{P}, I 175^{P}, I 247^{P}, I 328, , I 377^{P}, I 435^{4}, I 461^{4}
RUSTIC CRAFT(IRE) ch.g. 7 Thatching - Western Goddess by Red God Andrew Brown

1996 **P(NH),U(NH),U(NH),P(NH),P(NH)**

886	1/4	Flagg Moor	(L)	OPE	3m	3	G	*chsd wnr, wknd rpdly 3 out, exhstd whn stppd nxt*	R	-
1188	20/4	Garthorpe	(R)	OPE	3m	9	GF	*sn wll bhnd, t.o. 7th, p.u. 15th*	P	0
1205	26/4	Clifton On '	(L)	CON	3m	13	GS	*alwys last, t.o. frm 7th*	10	0

Debut winner at Ascot as 2yo; hopeless over fences 0

RUSTIC LORD br.g. 5 Town And Country - Trecauldah by Treboro (USA) — Richard Barber

182	15/2	Larkhill	(R)	MDO	3m	12	G	*schoold, alwys rear, last & p.u. 14th*	P	0
644	22/3	Castle Of C'	(R)	MDO	3m	9	G	*trckd ldrs going wll, ld 2 out, ran wd & hdd last, kpt on*	2	14
933	6/4	Charlton Ho'	(L)	MDO	3m	12	G	*(fav) w.w. prog 13th, ev ch apr 2 out, not qckn last*	4	13

Top stable; should have won 2nd start; novice-ridden; may need stronger handling; should find a race 13

RUSTIC RAMBLE br.g. 11 Rusticaro (FR) - Swizzle Stick by Tumble Wind (USA) — Peter Tipples

1996 1(14),1(15),**P(0)**,P(0)

577	16/3	Detling	(L)	CON	3m	18	F	*hld up, prog 15th, poor 5th frm 3 out*	5	12
685	29/3	Charing	(L)	XX	3m	3	F	*(fav) held up, rddn 4 out, bttr jmp last, ld & drew clr flat*	1	17
1127	19/4	Penshurst	(L)	OPE	3m	7	GF	*(fav) trckd ldrs, chal 3 out, ld apr nxt, rdn out*	1	18
1501	16/5	Folkestone	(R)	HC	3 1/4m	10	G	*started slowly, nvr going well, t.o. and p.u. before 13th.*	P	0

Won 5 of last 10 95/97; likes Firm & finds soft races; outclassed in H/chases; can win again 16

RUSTIC SUNSET b.g. 11 Furry Glen - Nicky's Bird by Will Hays (USA) — Mrs I N McCallum

179	15/2	Larkhill	(R)	CON	3m	12	G	*chsd ldrs, 3rd frm 6th, wkng whn jmpd slwly 13th, t.o.*	3	11
295	1/3	Didmarton	(L)	OPE	3m	9	G	*chsd wnr to 8th, 5th & wkng whn u.r. 10th*	U	-

Won Maiden Chase 94/95; lightly raced & shows nothing now 13

RUSTINO ch.g. 11 Bustino - Miss Britain by Tudor Melody — S B Clark

1996 **12(NH),11(NH),P(NH),P(NH)**

33	26/1	Alnwick	(L)	LAD	3m	12	G	*cls up, mstk 12th, effrt to 3rd whn pckd 15th, wknd 2 out*	6	15
165	15/2	Witton Cast'	(R)	LAD	3m	6	F	*mid-div, prog 10th, kpt on to go remote 2nd 2 out*	2	14
268	22/2	Duncombe Pa'	(R)	LAD	3m	5	G	*alwys rear, strgglng 11th, t.o. whn p.u. 14th*	4	13
617	22/3	Hutton Rudby	(L)	LAD	3m	9	GF	*(bl) rear & bhnd, brf efft 14th, wknd 16th, t.o.*	8	10
895	5/4	Wetherby Po'	(L)	LAD	3m	2	F	*made most, clr 5th, prssd 4 out, hdd nxt, outpcd*	2	13
1072	13/4	Whitwell-On'	(R)	MXO	4m	21	G	*prom, went 2nd 13th, ld 16th-18th, no ext*	6	17

Winning hurdler/chaser; safe but ungenuine & not threatening to win now; running under rules again .. 16

RUSTY BLADE b.g. 8 Broadsword (USA) - Sea Sand by Sousa — Mrs M I Nisbet

1201	24/4	Perth	(R)	HC	3m	14	G	*soon bhnd, t.o. when p.u. before 3 out.*	P	0
1294	30/4	Kelso	(L)	HC	3m 1f	6	GF	*chsd ldr, blnd 9th, rdn after 13th, ch last, kept on same pace.*	3	20

Won 3 nov/chases 94/95; placed in weak H/chase & went back under rules again; stays; hard to win ... 18

RUSTY BRIDGE b.g. 10 Rustingo - Bridge Ash by Normandy — I K Johnson

1996 **3(15),B(-),5(0),5(0),5(22),6(NH),2(23),2(26),3(23),3(NH),8(11),5(NH),4(NH),7(NH),U(NH)**

4	19/1	Barbury Cas'	(L)	OPE	3m	9	GF	*strgglng frm 8th, sn wll bhnd*	5	16
86	2/2	Wolverhampt'	(L)	OPE	3m	9	GS	*ld 3rd-5th, sn pshd alng, outpcd 11th, kpt on frm 13th*	4	19
149	10/2	Hereford	(R)	HC	3m 1f 110yds	18	GS	*ld, hit 6th and hdd, wknd six out.*	3	17
285	26/2	Taunton	(R)	HC	4 1/4m 110yds	16	GS	*made all, clr from 9th, hit 3 out, styd on well.*	1	28
586	19/3	Exeter	(R)	HC	3 1/4m	12	GF	*ld to 12th, lost pl, rdn and rallied after 6 out, kept on one pace*	4	19
889	3/4	Taunton	(R)	HC	3m	7	F	*(fav) chsd wnr, mstk 4th, rdn when hit 2 out, edged left and kept on run-in.*	2	18
981	9/4	Chepstow	(L)	HC	3m	6	F	*(fav) ld to 10th, soon pushed along, outpcd apr 14th, rallied and hit 4 out, chsd wnr 2 out, one pace run-in.*	2	21
1087	16/4	Cheltenham	(L)	HC	3 1/4m 110yds	8	GF	*ld to 3rd, rdn and lost pl 11th, kept on one pace from 2 out.*	3	21
1290	30/4	Cheltenham	(L)	HC	4m 1f	10	GF	*(Jt fav) ld to 20th, pressed ldr after, rdn 4 out, led again last, driven and held on gamely.*	1	27
1413	7/5	Uttoxeter	(L)	HC	4 1/4m	7	GS	*ld to 7th, lost pl 11th, rdn and lost tch 18th, kept on und pres from 4 out.*	3	22
1491	14/5	Hereford	(R)	HC	3m 1f 110yds	11	G	*ld till after 1st, rdn from 10th, styd on again from 2 out, tk 3rd run-in.*	3	21
1591	31/5	Stratford	(L)	HC	3 1/2m	11	G	*ld till hdd 10th, lost pl quickly final cct, t.o..*	7	14

Tough as teak; hard ride; out & out stayer; has good jockeys; every chance of another marathon; F-G ... 24

RUSTY FELLOW b.g. 7 Rustingo - Sallisses by Pamroy — Mrs G M Shail

1996 U(-),B(-),R(-),R(-),7(0),U(-),U(-),2(13)

261	22/2	Newtown	(L)	MDN	3m	16	G	*rear, lost tch frm 13th, styd on 2 out, nrst fin*	3	0
435	8/3	Upton-On-Se'	(R)	MDO	3m	14	G	*prom, chsd ldr 14th, lkd hld in 3l 2nd whn f last*	F	13
653	22/3	Siddington	(L)	RES	3m	10	F	*rear,effrt 12th,prog to chal 2 out,outjmpd & not qckn aft*	2	19
881	1/4	Upton-On-Se'	(R)	MDN	3m	13	GF	*chsd ldrs, effrt 3 out, disp 2 out til qcknd clr aft last*	1	16
1061	13/4	Maisemore P'	(L)	RES	3m	12	GF	*nvr going wll, t.o. 4th, stewards*	7	0

Has ability & penny finally dropping; only goes for D Mansell; could win in 97 if in the mood 16

RUSTY HALL ch.m. 5 Risk Me (FR) - Happy Snap by Jalmood (USA) Miss C Lynch

1996 **4(NH),6(NH)**

1	19/1	Barbury Cas'	(L)	XX	3m	11	GF	*blnd 2nd, bhnd til f 6th*	F -
186	15/2	Erw Lon	(L)	MDN	3m	13	G	*ran out 2nd*	r -
409	8/3	Llanfrynach	(R)	MDN	3m	12	G	*rear, p.u. 10th*	P 0

Placed N/H flat; not a good start in points 0

RUSTY MUSIC b.g. 11 Rustingo - Lyricist by Averof P Richards

191	15/2	Erw Lon	(L)	CON	3m	13	G	*jmpd bdly, alwys bhnd, t.o. 12th, p.u. last*	P 0
256	22/2	Newtown	(L)	OPE	3m	17	G	*in tch to 9th, t.o. whn p.u. 3 out*	P 0
364	2/3	Garnons	(L)	XX	3m	7	GS	*prom, 4l 3rd at 9th, lost tch 13th*	5 0
399	8/3	Llanfrynach	(R)	CON	3m	11	G	*alwys rear, some late prog frm 15th*	5 11
632	22/3	Howick	(L)	MEM	3m	2	GF	*ld, jnd last, hdd & no ext nr fin*	2 12
714	29/3	Llanvapley	(L)	CON	3m	15	GF	*rear, fin in own time*	6 0
903	5/4	Howick	(L)	CON	3m	6	F	*in tch,pshd alng 11th,2nd 15th,rdn to ld last,jst hld on*	1 13
1134	19/4	Bonvilston	(R)	MXO	4m	10	G	*mid-div, rddn alng hlfwy, tk 3rd 3 out, no ch wth wnnr*	3 14
1472	11/5	Erw Lon	(L)	XX	3m	9	GS	*f 4th*	F -
1557	24/5	Bassaleg	(R)	CON	3m	9	G	*sn dtchd, wll bhnd in 7th whn u.r. 10th*	U -
1600	31/5	Bassaleg	(R)	CON	3m	3	F	*ld to 8th, last nxt, regained 2nd 13th, no ch wth wnr*	2 13

Missed 96; very moderate & won bad race; likes Howick but need luck to score again 13

RUTH'S BOY(IRE) br.g. 8 Lord Ha Ha - Club Belle by Al Sirat (USA) Capt T A Forster

1996 2(16),F(-),2(13),1(17),F(-),2(17)

433	8/3	Upton-On-Se'	(R)	RES	3m	18	G	*(fav) ld til hdd & not qckn 3 out, btn frm nxt*	2 14
523	15/3	Cothelstone	(L)	RES	3m	14	GS	*(fav) ld til mstk 15th, sn wknd, p.u. 2 out*	P 0
935	6/4	Charlton Ho'	(L)	RES	3m	7	G	*chsd ldr to 7th, rdn & effrt 13th, no imp 2 out, eased*	3 14
1093	16/4	Hockworthy	(L)	RES	3m	16	GF	*ld to 10th, prom aft til wknd 3 out*	4 10
1374	5/5	Cotley Farm	(L)	RES	3m	7	GF	*ld to 14th, hdd & outpcd aft*	5 15
1613	7/6	Umberleigh	(L)	RES	3m	13	F	*(fav) (bl) 3s-2s, ld aft 4th, sn clr, 25l up 13th, blnd 3 out, imprssv*	1 0

Maiden winner96; galvanised by blinkers; front runs; sold to run under rules 21

RYDERS WELLS gr.g. 10 Warpath - The Lathkill by Clear River E F Astley-Arlington

1996 5(14),2(16),3(12),U(-),2(14),**2(22)**,**P(0)**,**P(0)**

78	2/2	Market Rase'	(L)	RES	3m	8	GF	*in tch, rdn 13th, hit nxt, lft 2nd 3 out, no prog*	3 12
140	9/2	Thorpe Lodge	(L)	RES	3m	7	GF	*ld to 2nd, lft in ld 10th, disp aft, 2nd & hld whn u.r.2 out*	U -
348	2/3	Market Rase'	(L)	RES	3m	13	GF	*prom, chsd ldr 9th, ld 3 out, rdn clr, easily*	1 22
476	9/3	Southwell P'	(L)	XX	3m	6	G	*ld til aft 1st,ld apr 12th,und pres 2 out,hdd last,not qckn*	2 19
673	23/3	Brocklesby '	(L)	CON	3m	8	GF	*(fav) chsd ldrs, blnd bdly 6th, went 2nd 8th-15th, rdn & btn nxt*	4 15
835	31/3	Thorpe Lodge	(L)	INT	3m	7	F	*ld 1st-7th & frm 12th, drew clr frm 2 out, comf*	1 19
1086	14/4	Southwell	(L)	HC	3m 110yds	11	G	*soon in rear, hit 6th, bhnd when p.u. before 12th.*	P 0
1412	7/5	Uttoxeter	(L)	HC	3 1/4m	10	GS	*jinked and u.r. 2nd.*	U -

Capable but inconsistent; mistakes & hard ride; good enough for another Confined; G-F 18

RYME AND RUN b.m. 11 Rymer - Altaghaderry Run by Deep Run Mrs C J Enser

1996 P(0)

532	15/3	Wadebridge	(L)	RES	3m	9	GF	*ld 4th-7th, grad lost tch*	5 11
806	31/3	Wadebridge	(L)	RES	3m	6	F	*ld to 6th, drppd bck, ran on agn clsng stgs*	3 12
1039	12/4	Lifton	(R)	RES	3m	8	F	*alwys mid-div, kpt on onepce*	3 11
1259	27/4	Black Fores'	(R)	RES	3m	7	F	*nvr nrr*	4 12
1483	11/5	Ottery St M'	(L)	RES	3m	15	G	*sn bhnd, t.o. & p.u. 14th*	P 0
1552	24/5	Mounsey Hil'	(R)	RES	3m	12	G	*chsd ldrs, went 2nd 15th, ld nxt, clr 2 out, styd on*	1 18
1595	31/5	Bratton Down	(L)	LAD	3m	5	F	*(fav) trckd ldr 11th, ld 14th, clr 3 out, easily*	1 19

Maiden winner 94; changed hands; won poor Ladies; harder to place next year; G-F 18

RYMEROLE 7 C D Dawson

1996 2(0)

247	22/2	Brocklesby '	(L)	MEM	3m	4	G	*(fav) disp, hrd hld til p.u. qckly 7th*	P 0

Good stable; lightly raced & problems 97; still young enough to revive 12

RYMING CUPLET b.g. 12 Rymer - Leisure Bay by Jock Scot Gerald Tanner

1996 4(15),2(27),1(25),**1(33)**,**P(0)**

19	25/1	Badbury Rin'	(L)	OPE	3m	8	GF	*mid-div, pshd alng hlfwy, sn outpcd, no dang aft*	5 12
98	8/2	Great Treth'	(R)	OPE	3m	14	GS	*rear whn blnd 4th, rdr lost irons & p.u. nxt*	P 0
385	6/3	Wincanton	(R)	HC	3m 1f 110yds	6	G	*disp ld, ld and mstk 6th, hdd 9th, led next, hrd pressed and rdn when left clr 3 out, driven and held on well run-in.*	1 20
591	21/3	Newbury	(L)	HC	3m	7	GF	*alwys bhnd, unable to chal final cct.*	3 15
1291	30/4	Cheltenham	(L)	HC	3 1/4m 110yds	4	GF	*chsd ldrs, blnd 5th, lost tch lding pair from 14th, soon bhnd.*	3 21

1413 7/5 Uttoxeter (L) HC 4 1/4m 7 GS *reminder 4th, prog 10th, chsd ldr 12th to 19th, chased wnr after next, styd on und pres.* 2 27

Useful H/chaser; inconsistent & declined in 97; need to return to points for chances; stays well; 25

RYTON GUARD br.g. 12 Strong Gale - Gardez Le Reste by Even Money G B Barlow
1996 P(0),P(0),5(11),3(15),P(0),**P(NH)**

885 1/4 Flagg Moor (L) LAD 3m 5 G *3rd wh blnd 5th, last frm nxt, t.o. whn blnd & u.r. 12th* U -

Dead 12

SAAHI(USA) b.g. 8 Lyphard (USA) - Dumtadumtadum (USA) by Grey Dawn II Mrs Jan Wood
1996 6(0)

117 9/2 Wetherby Po' (L) LAD 3m 10 GF *prom, ld 3rd til disp 8th, hdd 11th, sn wknd, p.u. 13th* P 0
329 1/3 Eaton Hall (R) LAD 3m 10 GS *mid-div, lft 3rd 12th, 2nd 2 out, not qckn cls home* 2 18
764 29/3 Whittington (L) LAD 3m 5 S *alwys 3rd/4th, 9l down whn f 14th* F -
939 6/4 Tabley (R) LAD 3m 9 G *chsd ldrs til wknd frm 15th* 6 11
1097 19/4 Bangor (L) HC 2 1/2m 110yds 11 G *well bhnd, styd on from 3 out, nvr a factor.* 3 17
1384 5/5 Eyton-On-Se' (L) LAD 3m 6 GF *hld up in rear,prog 13th,2nd 4 out,ran on onepcd,alwys held* 2 18

Winning A/W hurdler; runs passably; placed in weak Ladies & may eventually find one 18

SABBAQ(USA) ch.g. 7 Theatrical - Cancan Madame (USA) by Mr Prospector (USA) A J Dowrick
1996 **16(NH),P(NH),12(NH),9(NH)**

103 8/2 Great Treth' (R) MDO 3m 9 GS *prom in chsng grp, disp 16th, ev ch whn f 2 out* F 15
366 2/3 Garnons (L) MDO 2 1/2m 13 GS *(fav) w.w. 6th at 11th, gd prog nxt, ev ch til nt qckn aft 3 out* 2 12
461 8/3 Great Treth' (R) MDO 3m 12 S *(fav) trckd ldr, efft & ld aft 2 out, styd on strgly* 1 16
648 22/3 Castle Of C' (R) RES 3m 8 G *trckd ldrs, mstk 9th, prog & ev ch 15th, onepcd frm 2 out* 4 15
1374 5/5 Cotley Farm (L) RES 3m 7 GF *(fav) w.w., prog 12th, wnt 2nd nxt, ld 4 out, ran on wll, easily* 1 21
1516 17/5 Bratton Down (L) CON 3m 6 GS *hld up, prog 14th, disp 3rd whn blnd & u.r. 3 out* U -

No ability under rules; improving; stays; can upgrade; G/F-S 20

SABRE KING ch.g. 9 Broadsword (USA) - King's Lavender by King's Troop J Tredwell
1996 2(12),1(14),1(18),P(0)

369 2/3 Mollington (R) MEM 3m 13 G *(bl) prom, chsd ldr 10th, ld aft last, hdd post* 2 20
1077 13/4 Guilsborough (L) CON 3m 16 GF *(bl) trckd ldrs, blnd 11th, outpcd 13th, no ch & p.u. 2 out* P 0
1160 20/4 Mollington (R) INT 3m 9 GF *(bl) ld to 10th, chsd wnr aft, chnc whn mstk 2 out, wknd rpdly* 3 15

Dual winner 96; blinkers essential & hard ride; best in Soft; modest Confined still possible; stays 19

SADDLER'S CHOICE b.g. 12 Buckskin (FR) - Lady Perry by David Jack J Colston

362 2/3 Garnons (L) OPE 3m 11 GS *alwys rear, lost tch 11th, styd on onepcd* 5 13
878 1/4 Upton-On-Se' (R) XX 3m 11 GF *mid-div, no ch frm 9th, wknd 15th, cllpsd aft race* 6 0

Winning chaser; lightly raced & probably finished now 10

SAFFRON FLAME(IRE) b.g. 7 Sandalay - Tip The Gold by Harwell M G Sheppard
1996 6(0),1(15),1(17),3(20),1(20),4(13)

25 26/1 Marks Tey (L) CON 3m 5 GF *w.w. mstk 9th, 3rd & ch 3 out, btn nxt, eased flat* 3 19

Progressive & won 3 96; ran well 97 but disappeared after; win Confined if fit 98; F-G/S 22

SAFFRON MOSS ch.g. 7 Le Moss - Saffron's Daughter by Prince Hansel T R R Farr
1996 8(0),P(0),6(0),6(10),F(-),P(0),3(14),4(0),2(13)

189 15/2 Erw Lon (L) RES 3m 14 G *in tch til wknd & blnd 11th, wll bhnd whn u.r. 3 out* U -
406 8/3 Llanfrynach (R) RES 3m 13 G *chsd ldrs, lost tch 15th* 4 0
539 16/3 Erw Lon (L) RES 3m 8 GF *trckd ldr til fdd 13th, rdn into 3rd flat* 3 11
635 22/3 Howick (L) RES 3m 7 GF *cls 2nd, disp 3 out, mstk nxt, no ext* 2 14
1006 12/4 St Hilary (R) LAD 3m 7 GF *mid-div, prog to 3rd at 14th, f 16th* F -
1185 20/4 Lydstep (L) RES 3m 5 GF *alwys 3rd, no imp wnr* 3 11
1319 3/5 Bonvilston (R) INT 3m 8 G *twrds rear, rmndrs 12th, no prog aft* 5 10

Maiden winner 95; very moderate & struggling badly since; need bad race to win again 12

SAFFRON SPIRIT ch.m. 9 Town And Country - Port'n Lemon by Hot Brandy E W Lewis

877 1/4 Upton-On-Se' (R) RES 3m 17 GF *mid-div, lost tch 9th, poor 8th at 11th, p.u. 13th, dsmntd* P 0

Maiden winner 95; only one run 96/97 & can only be watched now 12

SAGARO BELLE ch.m. 11 Sagaro - La Chunga by Queen's Hussar Miss J Fisher
1996 **10(NH),10(NH),4(NH)**

136 9/2 Alnwick (L) MDO 3m 16 G *in tch to 10th, bhnd frm 13th* 10 0
162 15/2 Lanark (R) MDO 3m 16 G *prom til wknd frm 12th* 9 0
234 22/2 Friars Haugh (L) MDO 3m 15 G *nvr rchd ldrs* 6 0
1337 3/5 Mosshouses (L) MDO 3m 7 F *ld 9th-13th, wknd apr 2 out* 4 10
1514 17/5 Corbridge (R) MDO 3m 17 GS *prom, lost plc 12th, sn strgglng* 6 0

Poor form under rules; safe but not threatening to win 0

SAGAVILLE(IRE) b.g. 7 Mister Lord (USA) - Beautiful Glen by Furry Glen — R H Pedrick
1996 **P(NH),12(NH),U(NH)**
105 8/2 Great Treth' (R) MDO 3m 15 GS *alwys prom, blnd 11th, outpcd 14th, tk poor 3rd nr fin* 3 0
242 22/2 Lemalla (R) MDO 3m 10 S *ld 2nd-6th, disp to 9th, 3rd whn stmbld aft 14th & p.u.* P 0
no ability under rules; well beaten in good race; not seen again; go closer if fit 98 13

SAIGON LADY(IRE) b.m. 9 Scorpio (FR) - Fair Detail by Fine Blade (USA) — J C Clark
1996 3+(0),0(0),P(0),F(-)
342 1/3 Corbridge (R) MDO 3m 12 G *mid-div, outpcd 13th, t.o. & p.u. 2 out* P 0
612 22/3 Friars Haugh (L) MDN 3m 14 GF *strgglng whn f 10th* F -
814 31/3 Tranwell (L) MDO 3m 9 G *prom 1st ctt,2l 2nd 9th,wknd into 6th 14th,t.o. & p.u. last* P 0
1331 3/5 Mosshouses (L) MEM 3m 5 F *cls 3rd whn f 11th* F -
Well beaten when completing; clumsy & stamina doubts; much more needed 10

SAIL ON SAM (Irish) — **I** 100[F]

SAINT BENE'T(IRE) b.g. 9 Glenstal (USA) - Basilea (FR) by Frere Basile (FR) — George Prodromou
1996 4(19),**7(0)**,4(19),2(18),4(19),1(22),3(19),**4(16)**,**8(10)**,**3(NH)**,**5(NH)**,**4(NH)**,**8(NH)**
322 1/3 Marks Tey (L) OPE 3 1/2m 9 G *(bl) wth ldrs, lost plc qckly 5th, t.o. nxt, p.u. apr 12th* P 0
504 15/3 Ampton (R) MEM 3m 2 GF *(fav) (bl) chsd ldr, disp ld 12-14th, rmdr 16th, ld appr 3 out, sn clr* 1 13
780 31/3 Fakenham (L) HC 3m 110yds 7 G *(bl) dropped rear 5th, lost tch 14th, styd on well from 2 out.* 3 16
1290 30/4 Cheltenham (L) HC 4m 1f 10 GF *(vis) rdn 8th, alwys bhnd, t.o. 17th, p.u. before 3 out.* P 0
Won 2 of last 20; won joke Members; moody & hard ride; unlikely to win proper races 14

SAINT JOSEPH ch.g. 7 Lir - Kimberley Ann by St Columbus — B R J Young
1996 P(0),P(0),F(-),P(0),P(0),P(0)
97 8/2 Great Treth' (R) INT 3m 13 GS *alwys bhnd, t.o. & p.u. 11th* P 0
245 22/2 Lemalla (R) MDO 3m 11 S *prom, ld 15th, disp 3 out til drew clr apr last* 1 16
630 22/3 Kilworthy (L) RES 3m 16 G *prog to disp 7-11th, lost ground stdly* 6 11
1245 26/4 Bratton Down (L) INT 3m 9 GS *alwys gng wll, ld 14th, drew clr, imprssv* 1 19
1397 5/5 High Bickin' (R) CON 3m 3 G *(fav) went 2nd 10th, cls up whn lft clr 3 out, comf* 1 20
1517 17/5 Bratton Down (L) MXO 3m 8 GS *in tch, 5th & outpcd aft 16th, styd on wll clsng stgs* 3 21
Much improved; beaten in hot race last start; stays; worth a try in H/chase 98; G-S 23

SALACHY RUN(IRE) b.g. 8 Fine Blade (USA) - Just Had It by No Argument — Mrs Patrick Cooper
1996 P(0),P(0),1(10),2(17),2(13),3(15),P(0)
444 8/3 Higham (L) CON 3m 8 G *rear, ran out bnd bfr 9th* r -
502 15/3 Ampton (R) RES 3m 5 GF *alwys last, t.o & p.u. 13th* P 0
1113 19/4 Higham (L) MEM 3m 3 GF *ld to 11th, ran out bend apr nxt* r -
1305 3/5 Cottenham (R) MEM 3m 4 F *ran wd on bnds, ld to 7th, wknd 13th, t.o. & p.u. aft 3 out* P 0
1430 10/5 Marks Tey (L) CON 3m 7 G *ld 1st, 6l clr 6th, tried to run out & hdd aft 10th, sn btn* 5 0
Maiden winner 96; changed hands; headstrong; novice-ridden & can only be watched now 0

SALCANTAY ch.m. 6 High Line - Sunylyn by Sunyboy — M J Tuckey
823 31/3 Lockinge (L) MDO 3m 4 F *jmpd slwly 1st, cls up, ld 16th til ran wd final bnd,nt rcvr* 2 10
Unlucky in awful race on debut; much more needed for competitive races 12

SALEMHADY(IRE) ch.g. 8 Lancastrian - Lucille Lady — Dr D B A Silk
278 23/2 Charing (L) RES 3m 17 G *mstks, in tch, prog 13th, cls up 3 out, no ext* 4 15
Irish Maiden winner 96; ran passably; not seen after(Ground?); must have chances in local Restricted 16

SALLY MEADOWS (Irish) — **I** 195[F]

SALLY'S CALL (Irish) — **I** 574[P], **I** 587[P]

SALLY'S IMAGE (Irish) — **I** 351[P], **I** 394[P], **I** 472[P]

SALLY SMITH b.m. 8 Alias Smith (USA) - Salira by Double Jump — Miss M J Benson
1996 4(0),P(0),F(-),**P(NH)**
814 31/3 Tranwell (L) MDO 3m 9 G *cls up 1st ctt, lost wth ldrs tch frm 4 out* 5 10
Lightly raced; well beaten when completing & well short of a win yet 0

SALLY WILLOWS (Irish) — **I** 32[2], **I** 188[B]

SALMON MEAD(IRE) b.g. 8 Lancastrian - New Brook by Paddy's Stream — Christopher Sporborg
1996 F(-),1(14),P(0),4(0),P(0),3(14),2(17),3(16)
10 25/1 Cottenham (R) INT 3m 7 GF *mid-div, prog 10th, rdn & outpcd 14th, styd on flat* 2 19
73 2/2 Higham (L) RES 3m 3 GF *(fav) trckd ldr, ld 9th-11th, ld 4 out, sn clr, easily* 1 18
123 9/2 Cottenham (R) INT 3m 13 GF *rear, nvr on trms wth ldrs, wll bhnd whn p.u. 14th* P 0
319 1/3 Marks Tey (L) CON 3m 11 G *cls up, disp ld 11th, ld 15th, clr 2 out, styd on wll* 1 19
497 15/3 Ampton (R) CON 3m 9 GF *(fav) in tch, jnd ldrs 7th, mstk 9th, rdn & btn 16th, p.u. 3 out* P 0
801 31/3 Marks Tey (L) CON 3m 8 F *mid-div, imprvd disp ld 10th, hdd nxt, wknd frm 4 out* 4 13

910 5/4 Cottenham (R) CON 3m 3 F *chsd ldr, ld apr 10th-13th, rdn nxt, btn apr last* 3 12
1026 12/4 Horseheath (R) MEM 3m 1 HD *walked over* 1 0
1031 12/4 Horseheath (R) INT 3m 3 HD *w.w. lft 2nd 11th, ld 3 out, 8l clr nxt, hit last, all out* 1 16
1115 19/4 Higham (L) OPE 3m 4 GF *disp to 4th, ld aft til hdd 15th, sn outpcd, no ch 4 out* 2 14
1376 5/5 Northaw (L) CON 3m 3 F *ld 5-7th, ld agn 14th, clr 3 out, blnd last,hld on und press* 1 18

Won 8 points 94/97; well placed; below Open standard; may find more chances; G/F-Hd; Sold 17

SALMON POUTCHER ch.m. 8 Brando - Heythrop Vii J N Cochrane-Barnett
1996 P(0),P(0),2(13)

654 22/3 Siddington (L) MDN 3m 10 F *trckd ldrs, outpcd 11th, no ch 14th, poor 4th & p.u. last* P 0
979 8/4 Heythrop (R) MDO 3m 2 F *(fav) ld to 3rd & 11-14th, ld appr 2 out, clr last, easily* 1 10
1210 26/4 Woodford (L) RES 3m 14 G *ld to 1st, prom, chsd ldr 14th-apr 4 out, grad wknd* 7 10
1449 10/5 Kingston Bl' (L) RES 3m 8 G *ld 4th, sn hdd, lost plc, 6th 2 out, ran on wll flat* 4 14
1570 26/5 Hereford (R) HC 3m 1f 110yds 14 G *bhnd from 7th, p.u. after 10th.* P 0

Won poor 2 runner Maiden; needs much more for Restricted 14

SALTY BAY (Irish) — I 338[5], I 419[2], I 479[F], I 538[F]

SALTY SNACKS(IRE) b.g. 8 Callernish - Salty Sea by Sir Herbert J S Ruddy

123 9/2 Cottenham (R) INT 3m 13 GF *ld 3rd til aft 10th, wknd frm 14th* 5 11
193 15/2 Higham (L) CON 3m 14 G *ld til 3 out, wknd rpdly* 4 15
441 8/3 Higham (L) INT 3m 7 G *hld up mid-div, nvr on trms ldrs, outpcd 16th* 4 17
1190 20/4 Garthorpe (R) INT 3m 8 GF *ld/disp to 12th, wknd, last frm 15th, p.u. last* P 0
1375 5/5 Northaw (L) MEM 3m 5 F *disp ld til lft solo 9th* 1 0

Winning Irish pointer; looks a non-stayer; finished solo in Members; best hope again 12

SALUTING WALTER(USA) b.g. 9 Verbatim (USA) - Stage Hour (USA) by Stage Director (USA) Mrs D H McCarthy

279 23/2 Charing (L) CON 3m 10 G *plld hrd, prom til wknd 8th, stppd 11th* P 0
577 16/3 Detling (L) CON 3m 18 F *alwys rear, t.o. whn p.u. 3 out* P 0

No ability under rules; does not stay; no prospects 0

SALVO ch.g. 6 K-Battery - Saleander by Leander W H Whitley
1996 **5(NH)**,**2(NH)**

589 20/3 Wincanton (R) HC 2m 5f 9 GF *keen hold, ld 3rd to 13th, cl up when left in ld, mstk and u.r. 4 out.* U -
1482 11/5 Ottery St M' (L) LAD 3m 5 G *chsd ldr, disp 10th-14th, onepcd aft* 2 20

Winning hurdler; interrupted season; stamina doubts; probably need to concentrate on short H/chases 21

SAME DIFFERENCE(IRE) b.g. 9 Seymour Hicks (FR) - Santa Fe (GER) by Orsini Christopher Shankland
1996 **5(NH)**,**8(NH)**,**2(NH)**,**10(NH)**,**P(NH)**,**5(NH)**

18 25/1 Badbury Rin' (L) LAD 3m 9 GF *last whn nrly u.r. 3rd, t.o. aft til u.r. 12th* U -

Winning hurdler; vanished after one run; makes little appeal 0

SAMETOYOU (Irish) — I 112[P], I 252[P]

SAMINSKI (Irish) — I 534[P], I 559[P]

SAMMY SUNSHINE (Irish) — I 161[P], I 242[3], I 301[6], I 353[P], I 509[3], I 548,

SAM QUALE (Irish) — I 22[P], I 141[P], I 294, , I 379[3], I 425[3], I 568[2]

SAMS HERITAGE b.g. 13 National Trust - Taberella by Aberdeen C G Smedley
1996 P(0),**3(0)**,2(13),8(16)

6 19/1 Barbury Cas' (L) LAD 3m 13 GF *w.w. prog & 6th hlfwy, styd on frm 14th, nrst fin* 3 24
18 25/1 Badbury Rin' (L) LAD 3m 9 GF *(fav) w.w. prog 10th, chsd wnr 15th, styd on, no imp aft last* 2 24
202 15/2 Weston Park (L) LAD 3m 13 G *(fav) hld up in tch, ld 5 out, sn in cmmnd, comf* 1 24
364 2/3 Garnons (L) XX 3m 7 GS *(fav) cls up, ld 7th, alwys in cmmnd, pshd out flat* 1 22
652 22/3 Siddington (L) LAD 3m 5 F *(fav) cls up, trckd ldr 10th, ld 3 out, comf* 1 21
879 1/4 Upton-On-Se' (R) MXO 3m 4 GF *(fav) trckd ldr, ld 8th, qcknd frm 13th, easily* 1 21
1213 26/4 Woodford (L) LAD 3m 6 G *trckd ldrs,disp 14th-3 out,blnd nxt,tired whn jmpd lft last* 2 23
1490 13/5 Chepstow (L) HC 3m 7 G *held up, hdwy 9th, went 2nd after 13th, ev ch last, outpcd run-in.* 2 27
1590 31/5 Stratford (L) HC 3m 9 G *chsd clr lding pair till p.u. lame before 12th.* P 0

Baimbridge magic again; well revived; beaten by good horses; problems last start; win if fit 98 26

SAM'S SUCCESSOR b.g. 6 Old Jocus - Melanie Lass Vii by Damsire Unregistered Mrs J R Hellier
1996 P(0),P(0),P(0),P(0)

1246 26/4 Bratton Down (L) MDO 3m 16 GS *mid-div til gd hdwy 15th, styd on up hill fin* 3 11
1437 10/5 Holnicote (L) MDO 3m 14 G *mid-div, 7th at 12th, nvr dang* 4 0
1547 24/5 Mounsey Hil' (R) MEM 3m 9 G *bhnd frm 10th, lost tch 12th, t.o. & p.u. 16th* P 0
1597 31/5 Bratton Down (L) MDO 3m 12 F *prom in chsng grp, 2nd brfly 10th, lost plc 13th, p.u. 15th* P 0

Beaten 14 lengths on debut; not reproduce after(ground?); young & can go closer; G/S 12

SAMSWORD ch.g. 8 Broadsword (USA) - True Divine by True Song Brian Gurney

1996 1(15)

273 22/2 Ampton (R) OPE 3m 7 G *blnd badly 2nd, lft 2nd 12th, rdn 3 out, kpt on onepcd* 2 18
377 4/3 Leicester (R) HC 2 1/2m 110yds 15 G *alwys in rear, p.u. before 2 out.* P 0
757 29/3 Kimble (L) INT 3m 3 GF *ld frm 3rd,qcknd clr aft 15th,12l ld whn slpd & u.r.apr last* U 16
1077 13/4 Guilsborough (L) CON 3m 16 GF *mid-div, wknd 13th, bhnd whn p.u. 2 out* P 0
1403 5/5 Ashorne (R) CON 3m 14 G *ref to race* 0 0
1475 11/5 Garthorpe (R) XX 3m 13 GS *disp til ld 8-13th, wknd, t.o. & p.u. last* P 0

Restricted winner 96; unreliable; blew a gift a Kimble; best fresh but hard to find another win 13

SAMULE gr.g. 7 Another Realm - Dancing Kathleen by Green God Mrs M Harding
1996 3(14)

571 16/3 Garnons (L) MDN 2 1/2m 13 G *(fav) chsd ldrs, prog 11th, ld 3 out, kpt on und pres* 1 15
1210 26/4 Woodford (L) RES 3m 14 G *u.r. 3rd* U -
1439 10/5 Holnicote (L) RES 3m 9 G *tongue-strap, 4th whn hit 10th, 5th at 13th, kpt on* 3 15
1551 24/5 Mounsey Hil' (R) RES 3m 13 G *5s-11/4, in tch, chsd ldr 15th, ld 2 out, hdd last, ld post* 1 19

Improving; battles & won modest Restricted; can improve; needs to for Confined; Good 19

SANAMAR ch.g. 13 Hello Gorgeous (USA) - Miss Markey by Gay Fandango (USA) Mrs T A Halliwell
1996 F(-),6(0),P(0),3(0),6(0),P(0)

837 31/3 Thorpe Lodge (L) LAD 3m 5 F *t.o. mstly 3rd frm 3rd, lft remote 3rd 13th* 3 0

Of no account 0

SANCREED b.g. 12 Shaab - St Barbe by Galeopsis Miss L Long
1996 4(15),3(0),6(15),5(0),5(14),P(0),5(17),5(0)

453 8/3 Great Treth' (R) CON 3m 13 S *rear frm 8th til p.u. & dismntd apr 13th* P 0

Members winner 94; lost last 22 races; problems 97 & looks finished now 13

SANDAIG b.g. 11 Kemal (FR) - Pride Of Croghan by Raise You Ten Miss Sarah Wills

393 8/3 Barbury Cas' (L) OPE 3m 7 G *ld to 4th, wknd 9th, last whn p.u. 11th* P 0

Winning chaser; lightly raced & shows nothing now 0

SAND DE VINCE (Irish) — **I** 176^P, **I** 325^F, **I** 436^4, **I** 508^F, **I** 581^2

SAND DIRECT(IRE) ch.g. 6 Le Bavard (FR) - Karazend by Karabas T Pickering

1409 5/5 Witton Cast' (R) MDO 3m 15 GS *in rear whn f 4th* F -
1428 10/5 Aspatria (L) MDO 3m 11 G *chsd ldr 8th-15th, wknd rpdly & mstks aft, p.u. 2 out* P 0

Ran well enough last start; should do better 10

SANDFAIR (Irish) — **I** 147^P, **I** 215^3

SANDFORD ORCAS b.g. 11 Shrivenham - Miss Rosewyn by Wynkell P G Bevins
1996 2(14)

112 8/2 Milborne St' (L) INT 3m 4 GF *hld up in 3rd, outpcd frm 3 out* 4 14
391 8/3 Barbury Cas' (L) MEM 3m 6 G *chsd ldrs til 4th & outpcd 15th, no dang aft* 4 0

Dual winner 95; only 3 runs 96/97 & not recover form; stays; can only be watched now 13

SANDI DEVIL ch.g. 6 Devil To Play - Kandilove by Kabale Mrs S J Smith

839 31/3 Thorpe Lodge (L) MDO 3m 15 F *rear hlf, t.o. 7th 12th, p.u. nxt* P 0
1179 20/4 Sandon (L) MDN 3m 6 GF *nvr nr ldrs, kpt on frm 2 out, lft 2nd last* 2 0

Beaten a long way when placed; much more needed 0

SANDS OF GOLD(IRE) ch.g. 9 Le Moss - Twice Lucky by Condorcet (FR) Brett Badham

225 19/2 Folkestone (R) HC 2m 5f 10 S *ld till rdn and hdd 2 out, kept on one pace.* 2 21
287 27/2 Huntingdon (R) HC 3m 13 GS *ld to 13th, wknd apr 3 out, t.o..* 5 14
888 3/4 Aintree (L) HC 3m 1f 9 G *held up, niggld along hfwy, mstk 12th, bhnd when jmpd slowly next, t.o..* 4 18
1545 24/5 Cartmel (L) HC 3 1/4m 14 G *alwys prom, hit 3 out, hrd driven to ld entering straight, kept on.* 1 20

Maiden winner 95; missed 96; improved; stays well; game; hard to place now; G-S 21

SANDY BEAU ch.g. 11 Beau Charmeur (FR) - Straight Sprite by Three Wishes Mrs Vanessa Ramm
1996 3(15),2(20),3(0),3(17),1(22),6(14),3(22)

364 2/3 Garnons (L) XX 3m 7 GS *made most to 6th, chsd wnr til wknd 14th* 3 10
569 16/3 Garnons (L) OPE 3m 7 G *bhnd til prog 8th, 30l 4th at 12th, t.o. & p.u. 3 out* P 0
1063 13/4 Maisemore P' (L) XX 3m 13 GF *s.s. alwys rear, nvr dang* 9 0
1320 3/5 Bonvilston (R) CON 3m 8 G *rear til p.u. 11th* P 0
1458 11/5 Maisemore P' (L) XX 3m 6 G *bhnd frm 8th, t.o. & p.u. 15th* P 0
1555 24/5 Bassaleg (R) MEM 3m 6 G *lost tch 8th, mstks & t.o. final cct* 4 0

Won weak Open 96; showed nothing in 97 & best watched now 0

SANDYBRAES ch.g. 12 Kambalda - Kinsella's Choice by Middle Temple — H Hutsby

1403	5/5	Ashorne	(R)	CON	3m	14	G	*prom,trckd ldr 10th,ld 15th til wknd & hdd aft last*	3	18
1529	18/5	Fakenham	(L)	HC	3m 110yds	9	G	*chsd wnr thrght, hit 13th, blnd 3 out, rdn apr last, no impn.*	2	19
1571	26/5	Wetherby	(L)	HC	2 1/2m 110yds	15	GF	*bhnd and rdn along 6th, p.u. before next.*	P	0

Dual H/chase winner 95; missed 96; ran passably but more problems now; hard to win again 22

SANDY ETNA(IRE) gr.m. 8 Sandalay - Fort Etna by Be Friendly — M H Dare

1996 4(0),P(0),2(14)

527	15/3	Cothelstone	(L)	MDN	3m	14	GS	*ld 2nd-5th, lost plc 13th, eased, t.o.*	6	0
643	22/3	Castle Of C'	(R)	MDO	3m	12	G	*cls up til b.d. 8th*	B	-

Just beaten in poor race 96; finished early 97; needs more to win 13

SANDY KING(IRE) ch.g. 8 Sandalay - Comeallye by Kambalda — A J Baillie

1996 F(-),5(0)

211	16/2	Southwell P'	(L)	MDO	3m	15	GS	*rear, t.o. 7th, p.u. 9th*	P	0
346	2/3	Market Rase'	(L)	MDO	3m	10	GF	*(bl) prom til apr 7th, sn bhnd, last & p.u. 12th*	P	0
665	23/3	Eaton Hall	(R)	MDO	3m	11	GF	*mid-div, lost tch 12th, p.u. 4 out*	P	0
1174	20/4	Sandon	(L)	MEM	3m	4	GF	*rear, disp 3rd/4th, 3rd frm 2 out, no dang*	3	0
1268	27/4	Southwell P'	(L)	MDO	3m	13	G	*prom til wknd 9th, t.o. nxt, p.u. 12th*	P	0

Not yet of any account 0

SANDY PEARL TWO (Irish) — **I** 41^{P}, **I** 130, , **I** 215, , **I** 340^{1}, **I** 410^{3}, **I** 542^{3}, **I** 573^{4}

SANDYS GIRL (Irish) — **I** 207^{P}

SANFORD HEIGHTS (Irish) — **I** 27^{P}

SAN-FRANCE (Irish) — **I** 278^{2}, **I** 394^{1}

SAN REMO b.g. 10 Sexton Blake - Rockwood Lady by Aeolian — Mrs D C Samworth

1996 10(0),**P(0)**,P(0),F(-),7(0),1(14)

1077	13/4	Guilsborough	(L)	CON	3m	16	GF	*alwys rear, t.o. & p.u. 15th*	P	0
1189	20/4	Garthorpe	(R)	LAD	3m	6	GF	*prom,went 2nd 3 out,ld last,lkd wnr til hdd flat,rallied fin*	2	18
1266	27/4	Southwell P'	(L)	LAD	3m	5	G	*ld til apr 5th,chsd wnr,lost plc 10th, rallied 4 out,sn wknd*	3	14
1476	11/5	Garthorpe	(R)	LAD	3m	5	GS	*ld to 3rd, hit 11th, ld 13th-apr 3 out, wknd, p.u. nxt*	P	0
1500	16/5	Aintree	(L)	HC	3m 1f	6	G	*(bl) cl up till outpcd 11th, soon well bhnd, t.o..*	4	0

Won bad Confined 96; has ability but unreliable; unlucky 2nd start; could surprise again 16

SANSNIP b.g. 7 Impecunious - Sansem by New Member — G W Giddings

1315	3/5	Holnicote	(L)	MDO	3m	7	G	*alwys rear, u.r. 16th*	U	-
1498	14/5	Cothelstone	(L)	MDO	3m	9	GF	*rear, mstk 13th, nvr rchd ldrs, styd on to tk 3rd last*	3	0

Beaten 16 lengths in bad race; reasonable start but more needed 10

SANTA JET (Irish) — **I** 43^{2}, **I** 482^{F}, **I** 554^{1}, **I** 587^{2}

SAOL SONA (Irish) — **I** 53^{6}

SAPLING b.m. 6 Infantry - Lady Bedale by Comedy Star (USA) — J Jiggens

1281	27/4	Fakenham P-'	(L)	MDO	3m	8	G	*rear, prog 11th, hit nxt, last & strggIng whn f 15th*	F	-
1431	10/5	Marks Tey	(L)	MDO	3m	6	G	*alwys rear, some prog to 3rd at 11th, outpcd 14th, p.u. 3out*	P	0

Not yet of any account 0

SAPPHIRE 'N' SILVER (Irish) — **I** 215^{P}

SARATOGA SAL (Irish) — **I** 139^{F}, **I** 272^{P}

SARAVILLE ch.m. 10 Kemal (FR) - Golden Ingot by Prince Hansel — David Wales

1996 **6(NH)**,**4(NH)**

447	8/3	Newton Brom'	(R)	OPE	3m	6	G	*chsd ldrs, ld 4th-6th, ev ch 14th, wknd nxt*	4	15

Winning chaser; lightly raced now; last on only start & can only be watched now 16

SARAZAR(USA) ch.g. 8 Shahrastani (USA) - Sarshara by Habitat — N J Pewter

1996 4(0),U(-),4(16),3(12),P(0),3(11),3(0)

26	26/1	Marks Tey	(L)	LAD	3m	8	GF	*alwys last, t.o. & p.u. 11th*	P	0
64	1/2	Horseheath	(R)	LAD	3m	7	GF	*jmpd rght 1st, rear, prog 10th, sn lost tch, t.o.*	5	0
271	22/2	Ampton	(R)	CON	3m	15	G	*bhnd, last & p.u. 10th*	P	0
1028	12/4	Horseheath	(R)	CON	3m	3	HD	*nt fluent, disp ld til 15th, sn outpcd*	2	0
1277	27/4	Fakenham P-'	(L)	CON	3m	10	G	*(vis) blnd 1st, chsd ldrs, lost plc 9th, p.u. apr 15th*	P	0
1376	5/5	Northaw	(L)	CON	3m	3	F	*(vis) alwys last, lsng tch whn blnd & lst irons 12th, p.u. aft*	P	0

Of no account 0

SARCOID (Irish) — **I** 52^{3}, **I** 107^{3}, **I** 140^{1}, **I** 336^{3}

SARGEANTS CHOICE b.g. 8 Le Solaret (FR) - Rose Dante by Tiran (HUN) — John Sargeant

1996 P(0),6(0),C(-),r(-),2(12),U(-),1(15),8(0)

83	2/2	Wolverhampt'	(L)	RES	3m	8	GS	*in tch til wknd rpdly 14th, nrly ref nxt & p.u.*	P	0
203	15/2	Weston Park	(L)	RES	3m	11	G	*cls 2nd to 10th, btn frm 4 out*	5	0
348	2/3	Market Rase'	(L)	RES	3m	13	GF	*chsd ldrs to 14th, no ch whn s.u. apr last*	S	-
548	16/3	Garthorpe	(R)	RES	3m	10	GF	*chsd ldrs, cls 4th 12th, outpcd frm 14th*	5	0
727	29/3	Sandon	(L)	RES	3m	6	GF	*cls up, lft in ld 2 out, hdd apr last, wknd*	2	12

Won weak Maiden 96; inconsistent; does not stay & need luck to win again; G-F 13

SARONA SMITH ch.m. 10 Alias Smith (USA) - Sarona by Lord Of Verona — Mrs F T Walton

1996 P(0),4(11),**P(0)**,5(0),2(11),3(0)

338	1/3	Corbridge	(R)	RES	3m	10	G	*mid-div, lost plc 5th, wll bhnd whn u.r. 10th*	U	-
1334	3/5	Mosshouses	(L)	RES	3m	5	F	*sn rear, t.o. 9th, p.u. aft 12th*	P	0
1424	10/5	Aspatria	(L)	RES	3m	17	G	*prom to 5th, sn wknd, t.o. & p.u. 12th*	P	0
1515	17/5	Corbridge	(R)	MEM	3m	5	GS	*ld & sn clr,steadied 5th,hdd 4 out,rallied to ld last,hld on*	1	10

Maiden winner 94; safe but slow & Members only hope again 12

SARONICA-R 7 — L J Remnant

1996 U(-)

639	22/3	Howick	(L)	MDN	3m	15	GF	*rear, p.u. 12th*	P	0
719	29/3	Llanvapley	(L)	MDN	3m	14	GF	*1st ride, alwys last, fin own time*	5	0

Not yet of any account 0

SATALDA (Irish) — **I** 55[6], **I** 349[2]

SATCO PRINCE (Irish) — **I** 435[F]

SATQUAID (Irish) — **I** 148[P], **I** 219[P], **I** 390[6], **I** 409[P], **I** 496[P], **I** 540[P]

SAUCY MINT ch.m. 7 Respect - Cool Kit by Saucy Kit — Mrs D Walton

340	1/3	Corbridge	(R)	MDN	3m	10	G	*trckd ldrs, fdd 13th*	4	0
728	29/3	Alnwick	(L)	MEM	3m	4	F	*ld to 4th, outpcd & wll bhnd frm 11th*	2	0
996	12/4	Tranwell	(L)	MDO	3m	8	F	*prom, ld 5th til hdd nxt, cls 3rd 9th, gng wll whn f 13th*	F	-
1336	3/5	Mosshouses	(L)	MDO	3m	7	F	*made most til 13th, no ext frm 3 out*	4	11

Short of stamina & only beaten 2 horses so far; more needed 10

SAUN(CZE) b.g. 11 Silver - Szunda (HUN) by Suc (FR) — J Shaw

1996 3(0),U(-),1(12)

304	1/3	Parham	(R)	LAD	3m	10	G	*b.d. 2nd*	B	-
580	16/3	Detling	(L)	RES	3m	11	F	*alwys rear, mstk 15th, p.u. nxt*	P	0

Won poor Maiden 96; brief 97 & will struggle to follow up 11

SAVAGE OAK b.g. 8 Cruise Missile - Savage Sally by Owen Anthony — D Gwyn Williams

298	1/3	Didmarton	(L)	RES	3m	15	G	*rear frm 10th, t.o. & p.u. 14th*	P	0
718	29/3	Llanvapley	(L)	RES	3m	13	GF	*alwys 3rd/4th, wnt 2nd 12th-3 out, onepcd*	3	12
902	5/4	Howick	(L)	RES	3m	2	F	*(fav) disp til ld 3-9th, lft solo 13th, ambld home*	1	10
1132	19/4	Bonvilston	(R)	CON	3m	9	G	*prom, wnt 2nd 3 out, chal last, no ext flat*	2	19
1228	26/4	Pyle	(R)	INT	3m	5	GS	*ld 8th-aft 14th, rdn & mstk nxt, wknd, p.u. last, lame*	P	0

Finished solo in both wins 95 & 97; needs easy 3 miles; problems last start; weak Confined possible ... 17

SAVOY ch.g. 10 Callernish - Dream Daisy by Choral Society — Robert Ogden

1996 **2(NH)**,**3(NH)**,**3(NH)**,**2(NH)**

289	28/2	Kelso	(L)	HC	3m 1f	8	GS	*held up, hit 6th, cld hfwy, pressing wnr when f last.*	F	-
1411	7/5	Chepstow	(L)	HC	3m	4	G	*held up, hdwy to chase wnr from 9th, reminders apr 2 out, no impn.*	2	25
1499	15/5	Perth	(R)	HC	2 1/2m 110yds	8	GS	*(fav) nvr far away, effort before 2 out, styd on well to ld near fin.*	1	25

Able but not 100% genuine; ran on to win after rider dropped whip; harder in 98; G/F-S 26

SAXON LASS b.m. 9 Martinmas - Khatti Hawk by Hittite Glory — M N J Sparkes

1996 P(0),P(0),P(0),2(15),1(15),2(21)

221	16/2	Heythrop	(R)	RES	3m	15	G	*prom, ld 11th, jnd 3 out, ran on gamely und pres flat*	1	19
293	1/3	Didmarton	(L)	INT	3m	16	G	*f 1st*	F	-
396	8/3	Barbury Cas'	(L)	CON	3m	9	G	*blnd 1st, chsd ldr to 11th, 4th & wkng whn f 13th*	F	-

Deservedly won modest Restricted; barely stays; finished after falls; more needed for Confineds; good 18

SAXON SMILE b.g. 9 Saxon Farm - Columboola by Rapid River — A J Godfrey

1996 F(-),P(0),U(-),4(0)

754	29/3	Brampton Br'	(R)	MDN	3m	9	GF	*wth chsg grp, 3rd frm 11-16th, wknd & p.u. flat*	P	0
1019	12/4	Bitterley	(L)	MDO	3m	12	GF	*prom to 8th, lost tch 10th, p.u. aft nxt*	P	0
1238	26/4	Brampton Br'	(R)	MDO	3m	10	G	*cls up to 8th, lost plc & p.u. 11th*	P	0
1393	5/5	Cursneh Hill	(L)	MDO	3m	9	GF	*ld 2nd til p.u. & dismntd bfr 4th*	P	0

No signs of ability & problems last start 0

SAY DAPHNE gr.m. 7 Say Primula - Ellaron by Abwah C Dawson

352 2/3 Great Stain' (L) MEM 3m 5 S *rear,blnd 3 out,sn t.o.,lft remote 2nd & guided round last* 2 0
418 8/3 Dalston (R) MDO 2 1/2m 10 GS *wll in tch til wknd aft 3 out* 4 0
621 22/3 Hutton Rudby (L) MDO 3m 10 GF *chsd ldr thruout, ev ch 3 out, onepcd nxt* 2 10
815 31/3 Tranwell (L) MDO 2 1/2m 14 G *held up til hdwy into cls 3rd 8th, no imp on ldrs frm 3 out* 4 0

Beaten 12 lengths minimum in modest races; safe & reliability should see her home one day 12

SAYIN NOWT b.m. 9 Nicholas Bill - Greyburn by Saintly Song Dennis Waggott
1996 1(17),1(19)

232 22/2 Friars Haugh (L) OPE 3m 6 G *(fav) hld up, prog 4 out, just ld 2 out, just hld on* 1 23
383 5/3 Catterick (L) HC 3m 1f 110yds 10 G *(fav) not fluent, held up and bhnd, steady hdwy 14th, blnd 3 out, chal next, rdn to ld after last, styd on strly.* 1 24
610 22/3 Friars Haugh (L) OPE 3m 6 GF *hld up, mstk 5th & 3 out, no dang aft* 4 20

Improving; stays; game; won 5 of last 6; won modest H/chase; can win more Opens; all wins on Good .. 23

SAY NOWT (Irish) — **I** 269P

SAYYURE(USA) b.g. 11 Lydian (FR) - Periquito (USA) by Olden Times A G Harris
1996 1(20),1(0),1(25),3(14)

432 8/3 Upton-On-Se' (R) MXO 3m 7 G *mostly 4th/5th, outpcd 13th, p.u. 3 out* P 0
932 6/4 Charlton Ho' (L) LAD 3m 6 G *chsd ldrs, went 2nd 12th-aft 15th, wknd apr 2 out* 3 14

Useful in 96; brief 97 & not produce best; needs strong handling; best watched now; Any 20

SCALE DOWN(IRE) b.g. 8 Lancastrian - Willie Pat by Pitpan P A Bennett

380 4/3 Leicester (R) HC 3m 9 G *ld 4th till f 12th.* F -

Irish Maiden winner 94; retains some ability but impossible to assess 17

SCALLYBUCK (Irish) — **I** 102P, **I** 352[1]

SCALLY HILL gr.m. 6 Scallywag - Madge Hill by Spartan General Mrs B Johnson
1996 P(0),2(0)

327 1/3 Eaton Hall (R) MDN 3m 11 GS *prom early, t.o. 11th, p.u. 14th* P 0
469 8/3 Eyton-On-Se' (L) MDN 2 1/2m 9 G *unruly start, lft a fence, p.u. 5th* P 0
722 29/3 Sandon (L) MDO 3m 10 GF *restrnd mid-div, lft 4th 2 out, no prog* 4 0
941 6/4 Tabley (R) MDO 3m 11 G *chsd ldr 7th til wknd 13th, t.o. whn f 3 out* F -

Beaten out of sight when completing; looks reluctant; best avoided 0

SCALLYKENNING gr.g. 9 Scallywag - Delegation by Articulate J F Weldhen
1996 P(0),P(0),4(14),U(-),P(0),r(-),U(-),6(0),2(12)

53 1/2 Wadebridge (L) MDO 3m 3 G *made all, ran out 7th & 14th, rjnd in ld both times, easily* 1 0
176 15/2 Ottery St M' (L) RES 3m 17 G *(bl) handy early, lost tch 12th, p.u. 14th* P 0
240 22/2 Lemalla (R) RES 3m 11 S *(bl) mid-div, 7th whn hit 10th, blnd 13th, p.u. nxt* P 0
532 15/3 Wadebridge (L) RES 3m 9 GF *(bl) prom early, grad wknd, bhnd frm 15th* 8 0
806 31/3 Wadebridge (L) RES 3m 6 F *(bl) alwys prom, trckd ldrs til fdd frm 4 out* 5 0

Won awful race; despite doing his best to lose; not one to trust; best avoided 11

SCALLY LASS gr.m. 8 Scallywag - Wexford Lass Vii by Damsire Unregistered R F Rimmer
1996 P(0)

331 1/3 Eaton Hall (R) RES 3m 17 GS *mid to rear, p.u. 4 out* P 0
666 23/3 Eaton Hall (R) MDO 3m 10 GF *cls up to 8th, lost tch 10th, t.o. & p.u. 14th* P 0
767 29/3 Whittington (L) MDO 3m 9 S *rear, t.o. 11th, last whn u.r. 13th* U -
941 6/4 Tabley (R) MDO 3m 11 G *mstks, lost tch 11th, p.u. aft 13th* P 0

Not yet of any account 0

SCALLY MUIRE ro.m. 13 Scallywag - Coroin Muire by Perspex G L Edwards
1996 2(20),1(22),1(21),2(23),1(27),1(24),1(24),**1(28),3(23)**

86 2/2 Wolverhampt' (L) OPE 3m 9 GS *(fav) pckd 2nd, bhnd, prog 11th, chsd wnr nxt, ch 3 out,sn btn* 2 21
201 15/2 Weston Park (L) OPE 3m 16 G *(fav) mid-div in tch, p.u. 7th, lame, retired* P 0

Retired 26

SCALP HUNTER (Irish) — **I** 510F

SCARED STIFF b.m. 9 Electric - Petrify by Air Trooper Barton L Williams

401 8/3 Llanfrynach (R) LAD 3m 14 G *ref to race* 0 0
636 22/3 Howick (L) CON 3m 12 GF *alwys rear, p.u. 13th* P 0
714 29/3 Llanvapley (L) CON 3m 15 GF *mid-div, p.u. 10th* P 0
1132 19/4 Bonvilston (R) CON 3m 9 G *alwys rear* 5 0
1224 26/4 Pyle (R) CON 3m 7 GS *rear, mstk 7th, t.o. & p.u. 13th* P 0
1321 3/5 Bonvilston (R) MXO 3m 10 G *rear whn s.u. flat aft 6th* S -
1456 11/5 Maisemore P' (L) LAD 3m 5 G *jmpd slwly, rear til ran out & u.r. 7th* r -
1557 24/5 Bassaleg (R) CON 3m 9 G *sn dtchd, t.o. 11th, p.u. 15th* P 0

Flat winner 91; awful in points; 0

SCARE MCCLARE ch.m. 6 Town And Country - The Donething by Nearly A Hand — Harry Hobson

127	9/2	Cottenham	(R)	MDO	3m	11 GF	*10s-5s, in tch in rear, wkng whn mstk 15th, t.o. & p.u. 3out*	P	0

Learning on debut; can do better 0

SCARLET BERRY br.m. 9 Zambrano - Scarlet Letch by New Brig — P J Sanderson

1996 6(0),1(15),4(10),2(16),4(15)

258	22/2	Newtown	(L)	RES	3m	14 G	*nt alwys fluent, prom, ld 13th, hrd rdn 2 out, drew clr last*	1	19
403	8/3	Llanfrynach	(R)	INT	3m	8 G	*made all, in cmmnd frm 3 out*	1	19
671	23/3	Eaton Hall	(R)	INT	3 3/4m	8 GF	*(fav) ld 3rd, strngly chal 3 out, ran on wll und pres*	1	19
976	8/4	Heythrop	(R)	OPE	4m	7 F	*prom, chsd ldr 7th, ev ch frm 3 out, kpt on onepcd und press*	3	23
1236	26/4	Brampton Br'	(R)	LAD	3m	4 G	*disp til ld 3rd, hdd 11th, ld nxt-13th, not qckn frm 15th*	2	17

Improved; thorough stayer & needs stamina test; mistakes; can win again; F-S 23

SCARLETT O'HARA b.m. 5 Ardross - Deirdre's Choice by Golden Love — Christopher Sporborg

15	25/1	Cottenham	(R)	MDN	3m	7 GF	*hmpd 2nd, jmpd slwly 4th, 4th & btn whn ref 3 out*	R	-

Showed some hope on debut; not seen again; can do better 0

SCARNING GIZMO br.m. 12 Mandrake Major - Sew And Sew by Hard Tack — Miss D Greengrow

1996 U(-),5(0),6(0),4(0),2(11)

681	29/3	Charing	(L)	MEM	3m	5 F	*rear f 2nd*	F	-

Placed in awful races 96; briefest of seasons 97 & well short of a win 0

SCARRA DARRAGH(IRE) b.m. 7 Phardante (FR) - The Black Rattler by Black Minstrel — Mrs Angela Smith

917	5/4	Larkhill	(R)	MDO	2 1/2m	6 F	*ld to 3rd, 2nd aft, ld 3 out, crwld 2 out & last, hdd nr fin*	2	11
1200	23/4	Andoversford	(R)	MDO	3m	8 F	*keen hld, chsd ldrs, blnd 6th, wknd apr 2 out*	6	0
1460	11/5	Maisemore P'	(L)	MDO	3m	16 G	*w.w. rear, mstk 12th, sn btn, wll bhnd & p.u. 14th*	P	0
1505	16/5	Folkestone	(R)	HC	2m 5f	8 G	*several slow jumps, alwys bhnd, t.o. from 11th.*	6	0

Just caught in one of the seasons worst races; mistakes; no stamina; summer jumping now? 0

SCARTEEN LOWER (Irish) — **I** 144^{P}, **I** 237^{P}, **I** 256^{6}, **I** 309^{3}, **I** 336^{4}, **I** 421^{4}

SCHEAMIN N DREAMIN (Irish) — **I** 242^{P}, **I** 354^{P}, **I** 452^{P}, **I** 548^{P}, **I** 593^{P}

SCHNAPPS (Irish) — **I** 468^{F}, **I** 521^{P}, **I** 580^{P}

SCHWEPPES TONIC br.g. 11 Persian Bold - Gay Shadow by Northfields (USA) — J P Seymour

33	26/1	Alnwick	(L)	LAD	3m	12 G	*mstk 2nd, u.r. 4th*	U	-
132	9/2	Alnwick	(L)	LAD	3m	9 G	*chsd ldrs to 9th, sn wknd, t.o. & p.u. 3 out*	P	0
231	22/2	Friars Haugh	(L)	LAD	3m	13 G	*ld brfly 9th, sn wknd, t.o.*	7	0
336	1/3	Corbridge	(R)	LAD	3m 5f	9 G	*mid-div, ld 4th-8th, prom til fdd 14th, t.o. & p.u. last*	P	0
412	8/3	Dalston	(R)	LAD	3m	8 GS	*in tch to 14th, sn wknd, t.o.*	5	0
609	22/3	Friars Haugh	(L)	LAD	3m	11 GF	*hndy, wnt 2nd 14th, wknd qckly frm nxt*	8	0
945	6/4	Friars Haugh	(L)	LAD	3m	6 GF	*in chsng trio til wknd qckly 4 out*	3	12
994	12/4	Tranwell	(L)	LAD	3m	5 F	*cls up til ld 6th, hdd 8th, ev ch 14th til wknd 4th 3 out*	4	17
1171	20/4	Hexham Poin'	(L)	LAD	3m	3 GF	*cls up til went 2nd 16th, not rch wnr flat*	2	16
1333	3/5	Mosshouses	(L)	LAD	3m	2 F	*trckd wnr, ld brfly aft 3 out, mstk last, no ext*	2	13

Winning hurdler; safe but flattered by placing (only beat 2 horses); need luck to win; G-F 14

SCKLEPP (Irish) — **I** 25^{3}, **I** 31^{P}, **I** 110^{4}, **I** 159^{5}, **I** 186^{U}, **I** 356^{P}, **I** 460^{P}, **I** 493^{P}

SCOIL HILL (Irish) — **I** 251^{3}, **I** 470^{3}

SCOLE b.g. 12 Deep Run - Verbana by Boreen (FR) — Miss A Hinch

1996 **4(NH),8(NH),2(NH),U(NH),2(NH),5(NH)**

75	2/2	Market Rase'	(L)	CON	3m	10 GF	*ld to 3rd, grad lost pl, t.o. frm 14th*	6	0
473	9/3	Southwell P'	(L)	CON	3m	10 G	*last frm 5th, t.o. 9th, p.u. 3 out*	P	0
546	16/3	Garthorpe	(R)	LAD	3m	11 GF	*chsd ldrs to 4th, grad lst pl, no ch frm 12th*	8	0
923	6/4	Garthorpe	(R)	MEM	3m	4 GF	*2nd til 5th, chsd ldrs, ev ch 5 out, not qckn*	3	10

Winning chaser; safe but not threatening to win now 11

SCORPOTINA b.m. 8 Scorpio (FR) - Ablula by Abwah — Mrs T R Kinsey

1996 2(12)

854	31/3	Eyton-On-Se'	(L)	MDO	3m	10 GF	*chsng grp, in tch til pce increased 4 out*	3	0

Very lightly raced; has some ability but needs to run more before winning 12

SCOTCH LAW br.g. 9 Little Wolf - Scotch Dawn by Jock Scot — B J Champion

1996 U(-),F(-)

581	16/3	Detling	(L)	MDO	3m	12 F	*prom to 11th, bhnd whn p.u. 14th*	P	0

Of no account 0

SCOTTISH MATCH (Irish) — **I** 271^{P}, **I** 401^{6}, **I** 531^{F}, **I** 556^{P}

SCOTTS CROSS (Irish) — **I** 72^{P}, **I** 120^{P}, **I** 214^{6}, **I** 253^{P}, **I** 310^{F}, **I** 366^{P}, **I** 436, , **I** 507, , **I** 586^{3}

SCRAHAN CROSS (Irish) — I 568[6]

SCRAPTASTIC ch.g. 6 Scallywag - Rusty To Reign by General Ironside — Mrs A Bell

769	29/3	Dingley	(R)	CON	3m	14	G	*prom 1st m, fdd, p.u. 11th*	P	0
779	31/3	Fakenham	(L)	HC	2m 5f 110yds	9	G	*ld 3rd to 7th, rear when f 10th.*	F	-
1190	20/4	Garthorpe	(R)	INT	3m	8	GF	*in tch, 5th & outpcd apr 3 out, kpt on onepcd*	6	12
1351	4/5	Dingley	(R)	CON	3m	7	G	*rcd wd, chsd ldrs til f 4th*	F	-
1477	11/5	Garthorpe	(R)	XX	3m	6	GS	*hit 1st, ld to 11th, wknd 13th, p.u. 3 out*	P	0

Shows promise but strange choice of races; must have Maiden chances 13

SCRIVEN BOY b.g. 10 Lafontaine (USA) - Miss Bula by Master Buck — R M Billing

1996 P(0),U(-),2(12),2(18),F(-)

294	1/3	Didmarton	(L)	INT	3m	20	G	*alwys bhnd, t.o. & p.u. 13th*	P	0
572	16/3	Garnons	(L)	INT	3m	13	G	*lost tch 8th, t.o. & p.u. 11th*	P	0
642	22/3	Castle Of C'	(R)	MEM	3m	4	G	*chsd wnr, rdn 3 out, onepcd*	2	11
1043	12/4	Cothelstone	(L)	INT	3m	7	GF	*cls up, 2nd frm 11th til blnd & u.r. 13th*	U	-
1133	19/4	Bonvilston	(R)	INT	3m	8	G	*alwys last*	6	0
1212	26/4	Woodford	(L)	INT	3m	8	G	*chsd ldrs to 11th, 6th & wkng 14th, t.o. & p.u. last*	P	0

Dual winner 95; disappointing since & best watched now 11

SCROUTHEA (Irish) — I 12[3], I 54[P], I 483[2]

SEA BRETA (Irish) — I 10[P], I 83[5], I 189[3], I 234[F], I 487[P], I 611[P]

SEA DREAMS(IRE) b.g. 6 Midyan (USA) - Davill by Record Token — J D Hankinson

19	25/1	Badbury Rin'	(L)	OPE	3m	8	GF	*mstks, prom, 3rd whn f 10th*	F	-
256	22/2	Newtown	(L)	OPE	3m	17	G	*f 2nd*	F	-
308	1/3	Clyst St Ma'	(L)	OPE	3m	7	HY	*bhnd, t.o. & p.u. 13th*	P	0
521	15/3	Cothelstone	(L)	OPE	3m	8	GS	*rear til p.u. 11th*	P	0

Italian flat winner 93; no apptitude for points 0

SEAN CONNORS (Irish) — I 485[P]

SEA PATROL b.g. 10 Shirley Heights - Boathouse by Habitat — Miss B M Barton

1996 **P(NH),P(NH),4(NH),12(NH),3(NH),3(NH),3(NH),P(NH)**

188	15/2	Erw Lon	(L)	LAD	3m	8	G	*prom til wknd aft 12th, t.o. nxt*	4	0
401	8/3	Llanfrynach	(R)	LAD	3m	14	G	*nvr bynd mid-div*	9	10
576	16/3	Detling	(L)	MEM	3m	10	F	*(fav) (bl) cls up, ld 5th til ran out 7th*	r	-
784	31/3	Aldington	(L)	CON	3m	2	HD	*chsd rival til ran out & u.r. 9th*	r	-
957	6/4	Pantyderi	(L)	MEM	3m	3	F	*(bl) sttld rear, impvd 10th, ld 2 out, ran on*	1	12

Won poor Members; needs strong handling; won Ascot novice chase after & future lies there 11

SEARCY b.g. 9 Good Times (ITY) - Fee by Mandamus — Mrs E J Richards

1996 3(22),r(-),**5(10)**,**5(13)**,1(20),P(0)

99	8/2	Great Treth'	(R)	LAD	3m	10	GS	*rear, no prog frm 14th, onepcd*	6	14
174	15/2	Ottery St M'	(L)	LAD	3m	9	G	*alwys handy, 3rd at 13th, outpcd frm 4 out*	4	20
311	1/3	Clyst St Ma'	(L)	LAD	3m	9	HY	*(bl) in tch, chal 2 out-last, not run on*	2	19
555	16/3	Ottery St M'	(L)	LAD	3m	10	G	*chsd ldrs, no ch frm 4 out*	3	15
1155	20/4	Stafford Cr'	(R)	LAD	3m	6	GF	*chsd ldrs, 3rd frm 9th, wll btn in 3rd whn f last*	F	-
1441	10/5	Holnicote	(L)	CON	3m	7	G	*6s-7/2, twrds rear, 5th hlfwy, poor 4th frm 11th, some prog*	4	0
1495	14/5	Cothelstone	(L)	LAD	3m	6	GF	*(bl) prssd wnr to 12th, no ch frm 14th, wknd 3 out, fin tired*	2	19
1548	24/5	Mounsey Hil'	(R)	LAD	3m	10	G	*(bl) ld, clr 5th, hdd 14th, no ch wth wnr aft, blnd last, tired*	2	18

Dual winner 95; disappointing now & ungenuine; unlikely to win again; F-S 18

SEA SEARCH ch.g. 10 Deep Run - Gift Seeker by Status Seeker — C R Johnson

1996 P(0),P(0),4(0),5(0),2(15),F(-),1(13),**3(18)**,2(16),2(18),**3(18)**,**7(20)**,**8(NH)**

189	15/2	Erw Lon	(L)	RES	3m	14	G	*wth ldr to 10th, sn lost plc, t.o. & p.u. 2 out*	P	0
300	1/3	Didmarton	(L)	RES	3m	23	G	*nvr nr ldrs, wll bhnd whn p.u. last, dsmntd*	P	0

Maiden winner 96; problems & finished early 97; not 100% reliable; best watched initially in 98 14

SEASIDE LADY (Irish) — I 488[P], I 501[P], I 539[P]

SEA SKY gr.m. 10 Oats - Seajan by Mandamus — G Coombe

449	8/3	Newton Brom'	(R)	XX	3m	13	G	*chsd ldr til wknd 13th, bhnd whn p.u. 15th*	P	0
1187	20/4	Garthorpe	(R)	MEM	3m	9	GF	*chsd ldr to 11th, wknd nxt, p.u. 14th*	P	0

Maiden winner 93; lightly raced since & can only be watched now 0

SEA SPIRIT gr.m. 5 Nearly A Hand - Uncornered (USA) by Silver Series (USA) — Mrs E M Elliot

740	29/3	Higher Kilw'	(L)	MDN	3m	15	GF	*mid-div, 6th whn blkd & u.r. 12th*	U	-
1112	19/4	Flete Park	(R)	MDN	3m	13	GF	*sn rear, 8th at 12th, bhnd whn p.u. 17th*	P	0

Only learning so far 0

SEATON MILL b.g. 9 Scorpio (FR) - Maygo — N P Morgan

1996 F(-),U(-),F(-)

772 29/3 Dingley (R) MEM 3m 4 G *alwys 1st pair,ld 6th-12th,outpcd 2 out,p.u.last,stewards* P 0
1192 20/4 Garthorpe (R) MDO 3m 6 GF *keen hld, in tch, chsd ldr 9-12th, wknd apr 3 out* 3 0
1356 4/5 Dingley (R) MDO 3m 9 G *chsd ldrs, 3rd whn f 6th* F -
1479 11/5 Garthorpe (R) MDO 3m 12 GS *prom, ld 5-11th, sn wknd, p.u. 15th* P 0
1537 18/5 Mollington (R) MDO 3m 14 GS *in tch til wknd & p.u. 11th* P 0
1609 1/6 Dingley (R) MDO 3m 14 GF *rear, lost tch 10th, p.u. nxt* P 0

Well beaten when completing; mistakes; headstrong & no stamina so far 0

SEBASTOPOL b.g. 8 Royal Match - Saucy Sprite by Balliol — Derrick Page

1996 **7(NH),2(NH),9(NH),P(NH),9(NH),P(NH)**

293 1/3 Didmarton (L) INT 3m 16 G *in tch to 11th, sn wknd, t.o. & p.u. 15th* P 0
402 8/3 Llanfrynach (R) INT 3m 7 G *u.r. 2nd* U -
568 16/3 Garnons (L) CON 3m 12 G *rear til some prog 12th, no ch frm 15th, t.o.* 7 0
637 22/3 Howick (L) OPE 3m 7 GF *alwys mid-div* 5 11
900 5/4 Howick (L) MEM 3m 4 F *(fav) prom, ld 15th, hrd rdn 2 out, just hld on* 1 11
1132 19/4 Bonvilston (R) CON 3m 9 G *rear til p.u. 13th* P 0

Placed over hurdles; won a desperate race; need same to score again 10

SEBRIMAR (Irish) — **I** 371^{P}, **I** 436, , **I** 463^{P}, **I** 507^{P}, **I** 585,

SECRET BAY b.g. 8 Zambrano - Secret Storm by Secret Ace — Stuart Dent

120 9/2 Wetherby Po' (L) MDO 3m 18 GF *alwys in chsng grp, went 2nd 8th, kpt on steadily frm 2 out* 2 15
343 1/3 Corbridge (R) MDO 3m 14 G *(fav) chsd ldrs, lft in ld 10th, drew clr 4 out, v easily* 1 16
425 8/3 Charm Park (L) RES 3m 12 GF *(fav) sttld mid-div,smth prog 15th,ld 2 out,sn qcknd clr,eased flt* 1 17
858 31/3 Charm Park (L) INT 3m 1 F *walked over* 1 0
1085 14/4 Hexham (L) HC 3m 1f 5 F *(fav) ld to 4 out, led again 2 out, rdn clr apr last.* 1 28
1285 29/4 Huntingdon (R) HC 3m 10 G *(fav) ld to 4th, steadied, trckd ldr 8th, led 15th, soon clr, v easily.* 1 31

Top class recruit; stays; quickens; well ridden; could challenge the best in 98; F-G so far 32

SECRET CASTLE b.g. 9 Castle Keep - Excavator Lady by Most Secret — Mrs L A Love

1996 **P(NH)**

464 8/3 Eyton-On-Se' (L) INT 3m 12 G *rear, p.u. 13th* P 0
851 31/3 Eyton-On-Se' (L) INT 3m 8 GF *cls up, ld 5-11th, sn btn, p.u. 13th* P 0
1099 19/4 Stratford (L) HC 2m 5f 110yds 14 G *started slowly, alwys bhnd, p.u. before 9th.* P 0

Ex selling hurdler; no apptitude for points 0

SECRET DOOR (Irish) — **I** 112^{F}, **I** 126^{P}, **I** 251^{P}, **I** 292^{1}, **I** 368^{3}, **I** 466^{P}

SECRET FOUR b.g. 11 My Top - Secret Top by African Sky — P Masterson

1996 **P(NH),P(NH),2(NH),5(NH)**

99 8/2 Great Treth' (R) LAD 3m 10 GS *prom, ld aft 13th, drew clr last, ran on well* 1 23
238 22/2 Lemalla (R) LAD 3m 9 S *hld up in tch, prog 13th, chal & ld aft 2 out, pshd clr* 1 25
627 22/3 Kilworthy (L) LAD 3m 7 G *(fav) hndy, ld 14th, ran on wll clsng stgs* 1 25
1090 16/4 Hockworthy (L) LAD 3m 8 GF *svrl slw jmps, made most frm 4th til aft 2 out,no ch wnr aft* 2 21
1242 26/4 Bratton Down (L) LAD 3m 6 GS *(fav) alwys cls up, ld 12th, made rest, kpt on wll run in* 1 24

Winning hurdler; useful Ladies horse; beaten by top class horse; sure to win more; G-S 25

SECRET MUSIC b.g. 6 Southern Music - Secret Rebel by Rebel Prince — J D Parker

1996 F(-),2(0),P(0)

127 9/2 Cottenham (R) MDO 3m 11 GF *prom, blnd 10th, 3rd whn f nxt* F -
197 15/2 Higham (L) MDO 3m 12 G *mid-div, wknd rpdly 15th, t.o. & p.u. 3 out* P 0
599 22/3 Horseheath (R) MDO 3m 4 F *ld 1st, cls 2nd aft til u.r. aft 9th* U -
915 5/4 Cottenham (R) MDO 3m 6 F *keen hld, lft 3rd at 5th, wknd 16th, t.o.* 4 0
1118 19/4 Higham (L) MDO 3m 9 GF *rear, jmpd poorly, nvr dang, t.o. 13th, p.u. 16th* P 0
1278 27/4 Fakenham P-' (L) RES 3m 11 G *chsd ldrs to 9th, bhnd frm 13th, nrly ref 15th & p.u.* P 0
1353 4/5 Dingley (R) MDO 2 1/2m 9 G *(bl) mstk 2nd, prom til f 11th* F -

Yet to beat another horse; bad jumper & well short of a win 0

SECRET TRUTH ch.m. 8 Nestor - Another Nitty by Country Retreat — Andrew J Martin

1996 P(0),P(0),U(-),P(0)

1163 20/4 Mollington (R) OPE 3m 4 GF *pllng, chsd wnr, no dang, wknd apr last* 3 0
1357 4/5 Dingley (R) MDO 3m 5 G *pllng, ld 3rd til apr 2 out, no ext und pres* 2 0
1489 12/5 Towcester (R) HC 3m 1f 6 GS *mstk 1st, ld 4th to 8th, wakened quickly, t.o. when p.u. before 11th.* P 0
1589 31/5 Market Rasen (R) HC 2 3/4m 110yds 10 GF *chsd wnr, weakening when hit 10th, t.o. when p.u. before 3 out.* P 0

Strange campaign; headstrong; does not stay & beaten in desperate Maiden; need miracle to win 0

SEEK AND DESTROY ch.g. 7 Destroyer - Over Dinsdale by Rubor — Mrs P Claxton

129 9/2 Alnwick (L) MEM 3m 2 G *(Jt fav) trckd wnr, ev ch 3 out, unable qckn flat* 2 0

Beaten by fair horse in a slowly run match; more needed but has scope **10**

SEE MORE ACTION ch.g. 5 Seymour Hicks (FR) - Singing Kettle by True Song — S G Adams

357 2/3 Great Stain' (L) MDO 3m 15 S *mid-div, drppd rear 10th, t.o. & p.u. 12th* P 0
721 29/3 Sandon (L) MEM 3m 6 GF *u.r. apr 1st* U -
1541 18/5 Wolverhampt' (L) MDO 3m 15 GS *ld til ran out 5th* r -

Not a good start **0**

SEE MORE CASTLES b.m. 6 Seymour Hicks (FR) - Golden Valley by Hotfoot — S Clark

898 5/4 Wetherby Po' (L) MDO 3m 7 F *plld hrd, alwys rear, outpcd 10th, blnd 12th, p.u. nxt* P 0

Not yet of any account **0**

SEGUNDO (Irish) — I 270[5]
SELKOLINE (Irish) — I 185[4], I 216, , I 266[P]
SEMINOLE PRINCESS b.m. 9 Ahonoora - Ballys Princess by Salvo — Miss Meregan Turner

1996 **8(NH),3(NH),P(NH),10(NH),P(NH)**

223 16/2 Heythrop (R) RES 3m 19 G *mid-div, wknd 12th, p.u. 15th* P 0
392 8/3 Barbury Cas' (L) MDN 3m 9 G *ld to 4th, last frm 6th, jmpd slwly 8th, t.o. & p.u. 13th* P 0

Poor under rules; unpromising **0**

SEND IT IN (Irish) — I 52[F], I 354[2], I 529[1]
SENEGALAIS(FR) b.g. 13 Quart de Vin (FR) - Divonne (FR) by Vieux Chateau — M S Venner

1996 4(0),3(19),2(17),F(-),F(-),6(15),1(21)

96 8/2 Great Treth' (R) CON 3m 7 GS *mid-div, outpcd 12th, kpt on frm 3 out, tk 2nd last* 2 18
237 22/2 Lemalla (R) CON 3m 13 S *rear whn mstk & u.r. 10th* U -
453 8/3 Great Treth' (R) CON 3m 13 S *in tch to 13th, wknd* 7 0

Won 1 of last 16 starts; very onepaced & needs mud; hard to find another win **17**

SENOR TOMAS b.g. 14 Sparkler - Pearlemor by Gulf Pearl — Mrs M J Trickey

1996 3(0)

1548 24/5 Mounsey Hil' (R) LAD 3m 10 G *alwys bhnd, t.o. & p.u. 13th* P 0

Flat winner; too old now **0**

SENSO(IRE) b.g. 6 Persian Heights - Flosshilde by Rheingold — R Green

1996 **4(NH),6(NH),5(NH)**

116 9/2 Wetherby Po' (L) MDO 3m 14 GF *rear, lost tch 10th, t.o.* 7 0
247 22/2 Brocklesby ' (L) MEM 3m 4 G *w.w., last cls up til u.r. 5 out (ditch)* U -
677 23/3 Brocklesby ' (L) MDN 3m 8 GF *alwys last, lost tch 10th, t.o.* 4 0

Ex selling hurdler; last when completing & much more needed **0**

SENTIMENTAL CRUSH (Irish) — I 26[P], I 138[P], I 200[F]
SENTIMENTALSCALLY b.m. 5 Scallywag - Sentimental Me by Precipice Wood — L A E Hopkins

1003 12/4 Alpraham (R) MDO 2 1/2m 10 GF *bhnd whn s.u. flat aft 3rd* S -
1541 18/5 Wolverhampt' (L) MDO 3m 15 GS *cls up to 6th, lost tch 13th, btn whn u.r. 5 out* U -

Not yet of any account **0**

SERDARLI b.m. 15 Miami Springs - Run Swift by Run The Gantlet (USA) — Michael Culleton

88 2/2 Wolverhampt' (L) MDO 3m 13 GS *ref 1st* R -

Of no account **0**

SERENADE STAR (Irish) — I 529[P], I 594[P]
SERENAS SERENADE (Irish) — I 109[P], I 207[P], I 294,
SERGEANT PEPPER ch.g. 7 Mandrake Major - Party Cloak by New Member — Mrs D N B Pearson

1996 3(0),P(0),1(11)

424 8/3 Charm Park (L) RES 3m 12 GF *hld up & bhnd, prog 10th, mstk 14th, outpcd frm 2 out* 6 12
695 29/3 Stainton (R) RES 3m 11 F *plld hrd, held up in rear, prog 8th, mid-div whn p.u. 14th* P 0
1250 26/4 Easingwold (L) RES 3m 15 GS *mid-div, hit 11th, nvr a factor, 5th 13th* 5 0
1421 10/5 Easingwold (L) RES 3m 8 GF *s.s. rear til p.u. 5th, lame* P 0

Won poor Maiden winner 96; struggling badly now & well below Restricted class **12**

SERIOUS MONEY(USA) ch.g. 12 Plugged Nickle (USA) - Broadway Hit by Hittite Glory — Mrs Angus Campbell

283 23/2 Charing (L) MDO 3m 16 G *1st ride, s.s. t.o. til p.u. 15th* P 0
581 16/3 Detling (L) MDO 3m 12 F *(bl) ref 1st* R -
681 29/3 Charing (L) MEM 3m 5 F *ld, jmp slwly 1st, hdd aft 7th, hmp & u.r. bnd bfr 8th* C -
785 31/3 Aldington (L) LAD 3m 1 HD *walked over* 1 0
968 6/4 Penshurst (L) LAD 3m 5 F *sn rear, many slow jmps, t.o. & p.u. aft 13th* P 0

1127 19/4 Penshurst (L) OPE 3m 7 GF *(bl) prom til jmpd slwly 4th, n.j.w. aft, wll bhnd whn p.u. 8th* P 0
1501 16/5 Folkestone (R) HC 3 1/4m 10 G *jmpd v slowly, alwys t.o., ref 13th.* R -

Of no account **0**

SERIOUS NOTE (Irish) — **I** 113P, **I** 1293, **I** 2882, **I** 3761, **I** 4422

SERLA SISTER (Irish) — **I** 1475

SET A WAY (Irish) — **I** 156F, **I** 223P, **I** 500F, **I** 5952, **I** 610U

SEVEN CRUISE ch.g. 8 Cruise Missile - Seven Ways by Seven Bells — Mrs C A Biddle

1996 P(0),P(0),2(0),P(0),4(0)

1232 26/4 Brampton Br' (R) MEM 3m 4 G *ld 3rd-nxt, cls 3rd whn blnd & u.r. 11th* U -
1388 5/5 Cursneh Hill (L) CON 3m 4 GF *ld 2nd-6th, wknd 11th, mstk nxt, t.o. & p.u. 15th* P 0
1528 17/5 Bredwardine (R) MDO 3m 17 G *sn wll in rear, bhnd whn u.r. bend apr 10th* U -
1577 26/5 Chaddesley ' (L) MDO 3m 11 F *chsd ldrs til wknd aft 11th, t.o. & p.u. 3 out* P 0

Of no account **0**

SEVENTH LOCK b.g. 11 Oats - Barge Mistress by Bargello — K L Dare

1996 3(16),2(13),2(18),4(15)

309 1/3 Clyst St Ma' (L) CON 3m 7 HY *ld/disp to 11th, chsd wnr aft til wknd 3 out* 3 15
493 12/3 Newton Abbot (L) HC 2m 5f 110yds 11 HY *trckd ldr, blnd 6th, wknd next, t.o. when p.u. before 4 out.* P 0
738 29/3 Higher Kilw' (L) CON 3m 8 GF *in tch to 12th, sn wknd* 4 0
950 6/4 Black Fores' (R) MEM 3m 7 G *handy to 10th, went 2nd 14th, outpcd frm 2 out* 3 14
1111 19/4 Flete Park (R) CON 3m 5 GF *ld 7th til wd bnd aft 3 out, 2l 2nd whn f 2 out* F -
1396 5/5 High Bickin' (R) MXO 3m 7 G *rmndrs hlfwy, rear, p.u. apr 16th* P 0
1481 11/5 Ottery St M' (L) CON 3m 12 G *alwys mid-div, nvr on trms, p.u. 2 out* P 0

Winning hurdler; weak finisher; lost last 15 & most unlikely to break the sequence **13**

SEVERE STORM ch.g. 7 Fort Nayef - Able Abbe by Absalom — D J Fairbairn

1996 **8(NH),8(NH)**

134 9/2 Alnwick (L) MDO 3m 11 G *hld up, prog 9th, nvr rchd ldrs, lft poor 2nd 4 out, tired* 2 0

Finished exhausted in weak race; not seen again; much more needed **10**

SEVERN INVADER b.g. 12 Al Sirat (USA) - Wunder Madchen by Brave Invader (USA) — Mrs Miles Gosling

1996 5(16),3(22),3+(19),3(22),1(21),1(22)

218 16/2 Heythrop (R) INT 3m 21 G *prom, outpcd aft 14th, btn whn hmpd & u.r. 2 out* U -
446 8/3 Newton Brom' (R) CON 3m 8 G *sttld rear, last frm 9th, effrt 14th, fin well* 4 18
596 22/3 Horseheath (R) LAD 3m 4 F *(fav) cls 2nd, outpcd frm 14th, ran on agn last, just faild* 2 20
978 8/4 Heythrop (R) CON 3m 3 F *(fav) trkd ldr frm 6th, ld aft 2 out, sn clr, unextnd* 1 19
1162 20/4 Mollington (R) CON 3m 7 GF *sttld dtchd last til rpd prog 2 out, ran on wll to ld nr fin* 1 20
1360 5/5 Towcester (R) HC 2 3/4m 7 GF *(fav) plenty to do 4 out, steady hdwy from next, styd on to ld after 2 out, readily.* 1 23

Solid; consistent pointer; easily won weak H/chase; harder to place now but can win again; Firm best .. **23**

SEYMOUR FIDDLES b.m. 6 King's Holt - Kidcello by Bybicello — J P Seymour

1996 4(0),U(-)

37 26/1 Alnwick (L) MDO 3m 15 G *mid-div, lost tch 13th, kpt on 3 out, nrst fin* 3 0
612 22/3 Friars Haugh (L) MDN 3m 14 GF *3rd whn u.r. 5th* U -
972 7/4 Kelso (L) HC 3m 1f 12 GF *mstks, in rear till f 11th.* F -
1052 13/4 Lockerbie (R) MDN 3m 10 F *bhnd til prog frm 12th, ch 3 out, wknd apr nxt* 3 10

Some improvement; form weak & more needed to win **12**

SEYMOURS SECRET b.m. 5 Seymour Hicks (FR) - Stanton Queen by Most Secret — Mrs B A Edwards

469 8/3 Eyton-On-Se' (L) MDN 2 1/2m 9 G *t.o. & no ch whn u.r. 6th* U -
665 23/3 Eaton Hall (R) MDO 3m 11 GF *mid to rear, no ch whn p.u. 4 out* P 0

Not yet of any account **0**

SHADOW WALKER b.g. 13 Bigivor - Panatate by Panco — A Hollingsworth

1996 P(0),3(18),4(0),4(15),3(14),P(0),9(0),5(19),5(12)

56 1/2 Kingston Bl' (L) OPE 3m 13 GF *in tch early, sn fdd* 8 0
220 16/2 Heythrop (R) OPE 3m 20 G *alwys rear, t.o. 12th* 9 0
364 2/3 Garnons (L) XX 3m 7 GS *alwys rear, effrt 13th, no prog 15th* 4 0
568 16/3 Garnons (L) CON 3m 12 G *mid-div til lost tch 13th, no ch whn p.u. last* P 0
878 1/4 Upton-On-Se' (R) XX 3m 11 GF *1st ride, alwys bhnd, t.o. 11th, kpt on* 4 0
1145 19/4 Chaddesley ' (L) MEM 3m 6 GF *sn wll bhnd, no ch frm hlfwy* 5 0

1 win last 24 starts; declining now & most unlikely to win again **13**

SHADRACH b.g. 6 Neltino - Fay Valantine by Foggy Bell — T J Sunderland

774 29/3 Dingley (R) MDO 2m 5f 10 G *cls up, ld 6 out, clr 2 out, promising* 1 16

Perfect start; good time but no winners behind; must have Restricted hopes at least 98 .... **17**

SHADY PRINCE (Irish) — I 74[P]

SHAKE FIVE(IRE) br.g. 6 Tremblant - Five Swallows by Crash Course Mrs C H Sporborg

1996 1(17),5(0),2(18),1(16)

198 15/2 Higham (L) RES 3m 14 G *(fav) chsd ldrs 11th, lft disp 3rd nxt, nvr able to chal* 3 0
443 8/3 Higham (L) RES 3m 7 G *(fav) cls up, disp 3 out, jnd last, ran on wll flat, all out* 1 18
593 22/3 Horseheath (R) CON 3m 3 F *(fav) hld up in 3rd, went 2nd 14th, not qckn 2 out, ran on flat* 2 17
1117 19/4 Higham (L) CON 3m 5 GF *(Jt fav) cls up, disp 8-11th, chsd wnr aft, onepcd 2 out* 2 17
1305 3/5 Cottenham (R) MEM 3m 4 F *(fav) w.w. trckd ldr 12th,chal last,rdn & found little flat,ld fin* 1 15
1435 10/5 Marks Tey (L) INT 3m 8 G *hld up, prog 11th, 3rd & ev ch 3 out, sn outpcd* 3 13

Won 4 of 10 starts; won weak races & slightly disappointing 97; may prefer give; can win more 18

SHAKINALLOVER(IRE) b.g. 5 Tremblant - Corston Velvet by Bruni Mrs P Grainger

1262 27/4 Southwell P' (L) MDO 3m 15 G *alwys rear, t.o. & p.u. 2 out* P 0
1527 17/5 Bredwardine (R) MDO 3m 13 G *hld up rear,lost tch 13th, 6th & no ch whn p.u. 3 out,school* P 0

Learning so far; looks the part 10

SHAMELESS LADY b.m. 7 Bold Owl - Spartan's Girl by Spartan General Richard C Darke

1996 **6(NH),U(NH)**

170 15/2 Ottery St M' (L) MEM 3m 6 G *ld to 4th, lost tch 14th, outpcd aft* 4 0
461 8/3 Great Treth' (R) MDO 3m 12 S *hndy, 3rd & ev ch 14th, sn outpcd* 3 0
741 29/3 Higher Kilw' (L) MDN 3m 12 GF *cls up til ld 12th-15th, onepcd und pres, lft 2nd last* 2 11
1343 3/5 Flete Park (R) MDO 3m 13 G *(fav) hld up in tch, ld 11th, styd on wll clsng stgs* 1 15

Improving; stays; beat a poor lot & needs more for Restricted 15

SHAMRON (Irish) — I 167[F], I 319[1], I 380,

SHANACOOLE PRIDE (Irish) — I 220[F], I 515[P]

SHANAGORE HILL(IRE) ch.g. 7 Torus - Port La Joie by Charlottown M C Wells

284 23/2 Charing (L) MDO 3m 17 G *ld 6-11th, lft 2nd 14th, plodded on* 2 0
485 9/3 Tweseldown (R) MDO 3m 11 G *dtchd last whn u.r. 1st* U -

Dead 0

SHANDONAGH BRIDGE (Irish) — I 30[P]

SHANECRACKEN (Irish) — I 177[P], I 249[5], I 313[5], I 374[4], I 433[1]

SHANES BAY (Irish) — I 98[R], I 126[P], I 212[P], I 310[3]

SHANNON GLEN b.g. 11 Furry Glen - Shannon Ville by Deep Run R H Dalgety

1996 **3(NH),8(NH),11(NH),2(NH),7(NH),4(NH),3(NH),5(NH)**

2 19/1 Barbury Cas' (L) XX 3m 14 GF *(bl) alwys prom, 3rd hlfwy, 5th whn blnd 3 out, styd on wll* 3 22
220 16/2 Heythrop (R) OPE 3m 20 G *(bl) prom til wknd frm 15th* 6 13

Dual Open winner 95; moody & quickly loses interest; changed hands; novice-ridden & unlikely to win 16

SHANNON KING(IRE) ch.g. 9 Boyne Valley - Miss Royal by King's Company B J Nicholson

1996 P(0),P(0),5(0)

213 16/2 Southwell P' (L) RES 3m 16 GS *chsd ldrs, ld 11th-13th, wknd, p.u. 2 out* P 0
433 8/3 Upton-On-Se' (R) RES 3m 18 G *prog 6th, cls 3rd 9th, wknd 12th, p.u. 14th* P 0

Maiden winner 94; missed 95 & not able to recover form for new connections; best watched 10

SHANTALLOW (Irish) — I 212[P], I 250[P], I 292, , I 432[P], I 504[P]

SHARED FORTUNE(IRE) b or br.g. 9 Strong Gale - Reaper's Run by Deep Run R Gould

1996 P(0),P(0),F(-),F(-),F(-),P(0)

16 25/1 Badbury Rin' (L) MEM 3m 2 GF *wth wnr to 9th, sn wknd, fence bhnd whn s.u. bnd apr last* S -
581 16/3 Detling (L) MDO 3m 12 F *ld 6th, blndrd bdly 17th, hdd 3 out, wknd* 5 10
743 29/3 Barbury Cas' (L) RES 3m 1 F *walked over* 1 0
930 6/4 Charlton Ho' (L) INT 3m 8 G *ld to 13th, sn rdn & btn, wknd 2 out* 6 0
1156 20/4 Stafford Cr' (R) INT 3m 6 GF *ld to 3rd, prom to 9th, lost tch frm 14th* 5 0
1564 25/5 Kingston Bl' (L) CON 3m 7 GF *pllng, in tch to 13th, sn wknd, poor 5th whn p.u. last* P 0

Jumped much better but a walk over was about the only way he was going to win; no real hopes now .. 10

SHAREEF STAR b.g. 9 Shareef Dancer (USA) - Ultra Vires by High Line Paul Wise

1996 **P(0),F(-)**,P(0),**F(-)**,9(0),**10(0)**,P(0)

569 16/3 Garnons OPE 3m 7 G *last frm 7th, completed own time* 4 0
781 31/3 Hereford (R) HC 2m 3f 9 GF *(bl) n.j.w., alwys well bhnd, t.o. when p.u. before 4 out.* P 0
1014 12/4 Bitterley (L) OPE 3m 9 GF *alwys last, t.o. 7th, p.u. 14th* P 0
1360 5/5 Towcester (R) HC 2 3/4m 7 GF *(vis) jmpd badly till tried to refuse and f 4th.* F -

Selling hurdle winner 92; of no account now 0

SHAREZA RIVER (Irish) — I 108[3], I 157[2], I 244[3], I 357[3]

SHARGAN (Irish) — I 588[P]

SHARIMAGE (Irish) — I 112^{1}, I 174^{1}

SHARINSKI ch.g. 10 Niniski (USA) - Upanishad by Amber Rama (USA) — Mrs Jo Yeomans

1996 5(15),1(21),1(25),P(0)

220	16/2	Heythrop	(R)	OPE	3m	20	G	*chsd ldrs til wknd 13th, bhnd whn p.u. 2 out*	P	0
430	8/3	Upton-On-Se'	(R)	MEM	3m	4	G	*(fav) trckd ldrs, chal 14th, ld 3 out, jnd last, drvn out flat*	1	18
703	29/3	Upper Sapey	(R)	OPE	3m	5	GF	*disp 7-11th, wknd & eased frm 15th*	4	10
1147	19/4	Chaddesley '	(L)	OPE	3m	7	GF	*cls up til wknd apr 14th, bhnd & p.u. 16th*	P	0
1234	26/4	Brampton Br'	(R)	OPE	3m	4	G	*cls up in 3rd, 4l down 9th, lost tch 12th, t.o. & p.u. 3 out*	P	0
1575	26/5	Chaddesley '	(L)	OPE	3m	10	F	*mstk 3rd, alwys bhnd, rdn & no rspns 10th, t.o. & p.u. 12th*	P	0
1607	1/6	Dingley	(R)	OPE	3m	9	GF	*(bl) prom til rdn & reluc frm 9th, t.o. & p.u. 12th*	P	0

Dudley cup winner 96; completly jacked it in 97; can only be watched now;G-S 0

SHARLENE (Irish) — I 217^{F}, I 350^{F}

SHARONS CHOICE (Irish) — I 222^{F}

SHAROUJACK (Irish) — I 5^{3}, I 26^{4}, I 49, , I 88^{P}, I 306, , I 382^{P}, I 446^{3}, I 477^{4}

SHARP ALICE b.m. 6 Lighter - Scamper by Abwah — A Hollingsworth

224	16/2	Heythrop	(R)	MDN	3m	16	G	*rear, wknd 12th, t.o. & p.u. nxt*	P	0
1212	26/4	Woodford	(L)	INT	3m	8	G	*sn bhnd, t.o. & p.u. 12th*	P	0
1401	5/5	Ashorne	(R)	MDO	3m	15	G	*alwys rear, t.o. 11th, p.u. 14th*	P	0

Not yet of any account 0

SHARP CHALLENGE b.g. 10 Roselier (FR) - Young Canute by Jupiter Pluvius — Miss J M Stephenson

335	1/3	Corbridge	(R)	CON	3m	7	G	*prom, ld 5th, disp ld whn f 12th*	F	-
732	29/3	Alnwick	(L)	CON	3m	6	F	*mstk & u.r. 1st*	U	-
897	5/4	Wetherby Po'	(L)	INT	3m	3	F	*jmpd rght, ld to 5th, outpcd 7th, poor 2nd whn lft clr 2 out*	1	10

Luckily won poor 2 finisher race; no real prospects of upgrading 12

SHARPLAW b.m. 6 Mandalus - Mossfield by Le Moss — J P Elliot

235	22/2	Friars Haugh	(L)	MDO	3m	10	G	*sn bhnd, some prog frm hlfwy, bhnd agn whn p.u. 2 out*	P	0
949	6/4	Friars Haugh	(L)	MDN	3m	10	GF	*15l 3rd 3 out, strng run apr nxt, ld last, sn clr*	1	16

Stormed home; beating subsequent winner; decent prospect & looks sure to progress 16

SHARP OPINION b.g. 14 Le Bavard (FR) - Arctic Tack by Arctic Slave — Mrs L Walby

1996 P(0),2(19),4(10),4(10),P(0),3(13)

334	1/3	Corbridge	(R)	MEM	3m	7	G	*sttld 3rd, lft 2nd 10th, ld last, ran on well*	1	17
411	8/3	Dalston	(R)	CON	3m	16	GS	*rear & nvr going wll, lost tch 11th, p.u. 15th*	P	0

Gallant veteran; retains ability but only hope if reappearing at 15; G-Hy 15

SHARP PERFORMER(IRE) br.g. 8 Sharpo - Husnah (USA) by Caro — Miss Michelle Taylor

1996 **5(NH),P(NH),4(NH)**

109	8/2	Milborne St'	(L)	XX	3m	8	GF	*plld hrd, ld til ran out bend apr 5th*	r	-
514	15/3	Larkhill	(R)	MXO	3m	6	GF	*ld to 13th, wknd rpdly 15th, p.u. 2 out*	P	0

Novice chase winner 95 (2m 5f); headstrong & stamina is the problem 12

SHARPRIDGE ch.g. 13 Nearly A Hand - Maria's Piece by Rose Knight — M B Mawhinney

1996 5(12),P(0),P(0),U(-),P(0),P(0),2(0),F(-),4(0)

164	15/2	Witton Cast'	(R)	INT	3m	6	F	*trckd ldr, outpcd 14th, lost tch nxt*	4	10
265	22/2	Duncombe Pa'	(R)	CON	3m	15	G	*rear & lost tch 8th, t.o. 10th, p.u. 12th*	P	0
562	16/3	Lanark	(R)	OPE	3m	8	GS	*bhnd whn p.u. aft 8th*	P	0
619	22/3	Hutton Rudby	(L)	INT	3m	8	GF	*rear, f 7th*	F	-
694	29/3	Stainton	(R)	CON	3m	11	F	*prom til lost plc 8th, sn strgglng, t.o. & p.u. 15th*	P	0
1070	13/4	Whitwell-On'	(R)	XX	3m	9	G	*mid-div, lost tch 5th, t.o. 9th, p.u. 11th*	P	0
1100	19/4	Hornby Cast'	(L)	CON	3m	9	G	*rear, outpcd 8th, sn strgglng, t.o. 12th, p.u. 3 out*	P	0
1248	26/4	Easingwold	(L)	OPE	3m	8	GS	*alwys wll bhnd, p.u. 8th*	P	0
1418	10/5	Easingwold	(L)	MEM	3m	6	GF	*rear, lost tch 7th, t.o. 9th*	4	0

Dual winner 95; of no account now 0

SHARP THYNE(IRE) b.g. 7 Good Thyne (USA) - Cornamcula — Mrs R L Matson

457	8/3	Great Treth'	(R)	RES	3m	8	S	*in tch til 10th, rear whn p.u. apr 14th*	P	0

Ex Irish N/H flat; very brief 97 & showed nothing 0

SHARP TO OBLIGE ch.g. 10 Dublin Taxi - Please Oblige by Le Levanstell — Miss Sara Jane Rodgers

1996 F(-),5(0),P(0),1(15),P(0),F(-),4(10)

251	22/2	Brocklesby '	(L)	RES	3m	16	G	*alwys rear hlf, outpcd 6 out, ran on onepce*	6	11
424	8/3	Charm Park	(L)	RES	3m	12	GF	*ld to 4th, prom whn f 11th*	F	-
616	22/3	Hutton Rudby	(L)	RES	3m	14	GF	*(bl) rear, efft 13th, outpcd & lost tch 16th, t.o.*	9	0
1068	13/4	Whitwell-On'	(R)	RES	3m	12	G	*rear whn u.r. 2nd*	U	-

Won bad Maiden; does not really stay & struggling badly now 13

SHARSMAN(IRE) b.g. 7 Callernish - Another Dutchess by Master Buck — E H Crow
1996 F(-),2(10)

327	1/3 Eaton Hall	(R) MDN 3m	11 GS	*made all, ran on strngly frm 3 out*	1	16
1000	12/4 Alpraham	(R) RES 3m	8 GF	*(fav) ld to 3rd & 4-11th, rdn 3 out, no ext*	3	14

Lightly raced; won modest race; well beaten after & needs more for Restricted; stays well; G/S 16

SHAWS CROSS (Irish) — I 13^{P}, I 41^{3}

SHEDOES ch.m. 8 True Song - Shewill by Evening Trial — Mrs E C Cockburn

1082	13/4 Guilsborough	(L) MDN 3m	14 GF	*in tch, wkng whn blnd 12th & p.u.*	P	0
1165	20/4 Mollington	(R) MDO 3m	9 GF	*chsd ldrs til wknd 14th, t.o.*	6	0
1402	5/5 Ashorne	(R) MDO 3m	11 G	*chsd ldrs to 12th, wknd & p.u. 14th*	P	0

No signs of ability 0

SHEEGHEE (Irish) — I 609^{1}

SHEER HOPE ro.g. 9 Hope Anchor - Sheer Romance by Precipice Wood — D Hays
1996 P(0),5(0)

24	26/1 Marks Tey	(L) MEM 3m	6 GF	*pllng, n.j.w. prom early, bhnd 9th, t.o. & p.u. 13th*	P	0
196	15/2 Higham	(L) MDO 3m	12 G	*cls up til wknd rpdly 16th, p.u. 2 out*	P	0
317	1/3 Marks Tey	(L) MDN 3m	13 G	*(bl) f 1st*	F	-
498	15/3 Ampton	(R) MDO 3m	8 GF	*keen hold, prom, blnd 6th,wth wnnr but und press whn f 2 out*	F	-

1st real signs last start (bad race); mistakes & needs strong handling; need fortune to win 10

SHEER JEST b.g. 12 Mummy's Game - Tabasheer (USA) by Indian Chief II — Mrs Judy Wilson
1996 1(32),**1(36)**,**F(-)**,**2(32)**,**2(33)**,**1(30)**,**3(33)**

9	25/1 Cottenham	(R) OPE 3m	3 GF	*(fav) hld up, went 2nd 15th, ld apr last, rdn & kpt on flat*	1	27
375	3/3 Doncaster	(L) HC 2m 3f 110yds	11 GF	*(fav) held up, smooth hdwy 5 out, cl 3rd when p.u. lame after 3 out.*	P	0

Dead. 32

SHEER MISCHIEF (Irish) — I 172^{P}, I 260^{P}, I 381^{2}, I 572^{2}

SHEER POWER(IRE) b.g. 8 Exhibitioner - Quality Blake by Blakeney — Mrs J L Games
1996 P(0),P(0),6(0),P(0)

261	22/2 Newtown	(L) MDN 3m	16 G	*alwys bhnd, t.o. 12th, p.u. last*	P	0
755	29/3 Brampton Br'	(R) MDN 3m	5 GF	*last til went 8l 4th at 12th, 30l last 16th, walked in*	3	0
1186	20/4 Lydstep	(L) MDO 3m	7 GF	*trckd ldrs to 11th, fdd, fin tired*	5	0

Of no account 0

SHEGOES (Irish) — I 614,

SHE GOES ch.m. 10 Royal Boxer - Village Beauty by Gregalach's Nephew — William John Day
1996 P(0)

543	16/3 Erw Lon	(L) MDN 3m	11 GF	*prom, ld aft 2 out, ran on gamely*	1	13
1318	3/5 Bonvilston	(R) MEM 3m	9 G	*hld up mid-div, prog 14th, ev ch 2 out, onepcd*	3	0
1471	11/5 Erw Lon	(L) RES 3m	9 GS	*trckd ldr, ev ch 16th, easily hld aft*	2	13

Lightly raced; won weak Maiden; game but barely stays; need poor Restricted to win again 14

SHELLEY'S DREAM b.m. 7 Impecunious - Badinage by Brigadier Gerard — D J Dando
1996 F(-)

222	16/2 Heythrop	(R) RES 3m	17 G	*mstk 1st, sn prom, 2nd whn f 10th*	F	-
297	1/3 Didmarton	(L) MDN 3m	11 G	*in tch whn u.r. aft 6th*	U	-
390	8/3 Barbury Cas'	(L) MDN 3m	15 G	*rear, blnd & u.r. 10th*	U	-
1065	13/4 Maisemore P'	(L) MDO 3m	13 GF	*mstks, hld up, prog to 2nd 12th, 3rd & btn whn f 14th*	F	-

Shows some ability but confidence must be shattered 0

SHELMALIER (Irish) — I 389^{3}, I 407^{3}, I 458^{F}

SHENANIGANS (Irish) — I 3^{3}, I 42^{U}, I 50^{2}, I 86^{3}, I 133^{F}, I 172^{3}, I 484^{2}, I 515^{1}

SHEPPIE'S REALITY b.g. 7 Dreams To Reality (USA) - Manshecango by Saucy Kit — Mrs Jane Smith
1996 P(0),P(0),P(0),6(0)

326	1/3 Eaton Hall	(R) MDN 3m	14 GS	*mid to rear, nvr dang, p.u. 12th*	P	0
464	8/3 Eyton-On-Se'	(L) INT 3m	12 G	*prom to 8th, sn lost tch, p.u. 4 out*	P	0
670	23/3 Eaton Hall	(R) RES 3m	15 GF	*ld to 4th, lost tch 14th, p.u. 3 out*	P	0
883	1/4 Flagg Moor	(L) MDO 3m	12 G	*(bl) hld up rear, in tch whn f 9th*	F	-

Non-stayer; no prospects 0

SHERBROOKS b.g. 11 Millfontaine - Candolcis by Candy Cane — M Hoskins
1996 6(13),P(0),5(0),4(14),3(0),3(16),5(0)

50	1/2 Wadebridge	(L) RES 3m	10 G	*nvr bttr than mid-div*	8	0
241	22/2 Lemalla	(R) RES 3m	11 S	*rear whn mstk 10th, bhnd & p.u. 15th*	P	0
308	1/3 Clyst St Ma'	(L) OPE 3m	7 HY	*prom, disp 6th til ld 14th, hdd 3 out, outpcd*	3	15

Maiden winner 95; beaten in last 15 races; woefully onepaced & Restricted looks too tough now; G-S .. 14

SHERIFF'S BAND ch.g. 10 Posse (USA) - Willis (FR) by Lyphard (USA) — P J King

207	16/2 Southwell P'	(L) MEM 3m	3 GS	*(fav) trckd ldr til ld 5th, made rest, rdn out*	1	13
350	2/3 Market Rase'	(L) CON 3m	11 GF	*ld to 14th, 4th & btn whn f nxt, dead*	F	-

Dead. 17

SHERWIN (Irish) — **I** 210^{4}, **I** 293^{2}, **I** 369^{1}

SHESADINGER (Irish) — **I** 13^{5}, **I** 41, , **I** 49^{6}, **I** 88^{5}, **I** 130^{1}, **I** 306^{P}

SHE'S A FLYER (Irish) — **I** 390^{P}, **I** 501^{P}, **I** 590^{P}

SHESAGUD GIRL b.m. 9 Andy Rew - Khotso by Alcide — E J Pearse

259	22/2 Newtown	(L) MDN 3m	18 G	*jmpd bdly, t.o. whn ran out 5th*	r	-
575	16/3 Garnons	(L) RES 3m	12 G	*alwys rear, t.o. 12th*	6	0
718	29/3 Llanvapley	(L) RES 3m	13 GF	*lft start, tk no part*	0	0

Oh no shes not 0

SHES BIZARRE (Irish) — **I** 66^{F}, **I** 228, , **I** 286^{U}, **I** 349^{P}

SHESHIA (Irish) — **I** 280^{F}, **I** 355^{F}, **I** 453^{F}, **I** 531^{F}, **I** 557^{P}

SHILGROVE PLACE ch.g. 15 Le Bavard (FR) - Petmon by Eudaemon — Col S R Allen

1996 F(-)

107	8/2 Milborne St'	(L) MEM 3m	8 GF	*ld to 11th, wknd & outpcd aft, t.o.*	6	0
178	15/2 Larkhill	(R) CON 3m	9 G	*sn wll bhnd, p.u. 5th*	P	0
309	1/3 Clyst St Ma'	(L) CON 3m	7 HY	*sn bhnd, t.o. & p.u. 14th*	P	0
662	22/3 Badbury Rin'	(L) CON 3m	8 F	*sn rear, p.u. 6th*	P	0

No longer of any account 0

SHILLELAGH OAK (Irish) — **I** 55, , **I** 100^{3}, **I** 154^{1}

SHIMANO (Irish) — **I** 52, , **I** 100^{P}, **I** 154^{5}, **I** 222^{4}, **I** 341^{P}

SHINE A LIGHT ch.g. 7 K-Battery - Lady Jay by Double Jump — Neil Bennett

1996 P(0),4(0)

564	16/3 Lanark	(R) MDO 2 1/2m	13 GS	*ld frm 5th, mstk 4 out, hdd nxt, no ext*	2	10
815	31/3 Tranwell	(L) MDO 2 1/2m	14 G	*(fav) made virt all til hdd run in*	2	14
1294	30/4 Kelso	(L) HC 3m 1f	6 GF	*trckd ldrs, blnd 8th, wknd quickly after 13th, t.o. when p.u. before last.*	P	0
1429	10/5 Aspatria	(L) MDO 3m	15 G	*prom, ld/disp 8th-13th, blnd nxt, wknd 4 out*	3	0

Improving; beat 9 others at Tranwell; stamina unproven; must have chances in short Maiden 14

SHINING LEADER (Irish) — **I** 82^{4}

SHINING PENNY b.g. 10 Sunyboy - Quickapenny by Espresso — S D Watson

212	16/2 Southwell P'	(L) MDO 3m	14 GS	*in tch til f 7th*	F	-
345	2/3 Market Rase'	(L) MDO 3m	13 GF	*(bl) w.w. steady prog 9th, ev ch 13th, btn apr 2 out*	3	10
478	9/3 Southwell P'	(L) MDO 3m	17 G	*(bl) hld up rear, rdn & effrt 11th, sn btn, p.u. 15th*	P	0
549	16/3 Garthorpe	(R) MDO 3m	16 GF	*(bl) swrd start, prog to mid div whn blnd & u.r. 7th*	U	-
1262	27/4 Southwell P'	(L) MDO 3m	15 G	*alwys mid-div, onepcd frm 3 out*	4	0
1359	5/5 Southwell	(L) HC 3m 110yds	7 GS	*bhnd and mstk 5th, blnd 12th and p.u. after.*	P	0

Poor & disappointing under rules; not disgraced when placed but suspect & mistakes; more needed ... 12

SHIP OF SHAME (Irish) — **I** 3^{F}, **I** 47^{4}, **I** 241^{2}, **I** 294^{2}, **I** 551^{1}

SHIP THE BUILDER ch.g. 8 Politico (USA) - Early Run by Deep Run — The Shipmates

1996 F(-),5(0),S(-),2(13)

622	22/3 Hutton Rudby	(L) MDO 3m	10 GF	*(Jt fav) hld up in mid-div, prog to go 3rd 13th, ev ch 3 out, onepcd*	3	12
1268	27/4 Southwell P'	(L) MDO 3m	13 G	*(Jt fav) hld up, prog 11th, chsd wnr 3 out, not qckn*	2	12
1359	5/5 Southwell	(L) HC 3m 110yds	7 GS	*prom, chsd ldr 4th till f 11th.*	F	-
1500	16/5 Aintree	(L) HC 3m 1f	6 G	*bhnd, some hdwy and mod 3rd when blnd and u.r. 13th.*	U	-
1589	31/5 Market Rasen	(R) HC 2 3/4m 110yds	10 GF	*jmpd badly in rear, soon struggling, t.o. when p.u. before 2 out.*	P	0

Knocking on the door in Maidens; onepaced; strange late season races; can win a race 14

SHIRGALE (Irish) — **I** 78, , **I** 130^{6}, **I** 193^{2}, **I** 306,

SHOON WIND b.g. 14 Green Shoon - Gone by Whistling Wind — J N Dalton

1996 3(16),2(22),3(14),1(23),1(23),2(24),1(22),1(25),F(-)

200	15/2 Weston Park	(L) CON 3m	16 G	*(fav) hld up, ld 10th, ran on strgnly whn jnd 3 out, ld nr fin*	1	25
351	2/3 Market Rase'	(L) OPE 3m	10 GF	*(fav) chsd ldrs, 3rd & rdn apr 14th, went 2nd nxt, unable chal*	2	17
751	29/3 Brampton Br'	(R) XX 3m	5 GF	*(fav) made all, qcknd clr 2 out, readily*	1	24
1014	12/4 Bitterley	(L) OPE 3m	9 GF	*ld to 3rd, prog to chal 2 out, disp last, rdn out flat*	1	22

1234 26/4 Brampton Br' (R) OPE 3m 4 G *(fav) ld to 12th, chsd wnr aft, rallied 2 out, eased flat* 2 21
1607 1/6 Dingley (R) OPE 3m 9 GF *(fav) j.w. ld to 2nd & frm 5th, clr 3 out, pshd out* 1 24

Won 8 placed 7 of last 16; honest; solid performer; stable in good form 97; win again at 15; G-F 23

SHORT CIRCUIT (Irish) — I 17^{2}, I 81^{3}, I 238^{6}, I 418^{3}

SHOULDOFDONE gr.g. 8 Alias Smith (USA) - Snare by Poaching — Miss H Vickers
1996 3(11)

546 16/3 Garthorpe (R) LAD 3m 11 GF *prog to chs ldr 7th til appr 12th, sn wknd* 7 0
773 29/3 Dingley (R) LAD 3m 11 G *abt 9th til f 6th* F -
1078 13/4 Guilsborough (L) LAD 3m 11 GF *raced wd, prom to 9th, sn wknd, t.o. & p.u. 16th* P 0

Lightly raced; no real prospects in Ladies 12

SHOVE OVER (Irish) — I 350^{F}, I 438^{4}

SHREWD THOUGHT(USA) ch.g. 6 Lyphard's Wish (FR) - Tamed Shrew (USA) by Sir Ivor — George Ball
1996 **6(NH),12(NH)**

172 15/2 Ottery St M' (L) MDN 3m 14 G *(fav) j.w. made all, ran on well frm 2 out* 1 17
624 22/3 Kilworthy (L) MEM 3m 7 G *(fav) prom, ld 9th, slght ld whn f 14th* F -
1483 11/5 Ottery St M' (L) RES 3m 15 G *(fav) ld til blnd & jnd 3 out, ran on agn frm nxt* 1 19

Improving; front runner; good stable & can progress to Confineds; Good 19

SHUIL FLOSSY (Irish) — I 25^{U}, I 45^{F}, I 110^{P}, I 163^{F}, I 245^{P}, I 295^{6}, I 338,

SHUIL MOR (Irish) — I 29^{F}, I 118^{P}, I 247^{P}, I 365^{P}, I 377^{P}

SHUIL NA MHUIRE (Irish) — I 10^{5}, I 38^{4}, I 207^{4}, I 258^{1}, I 323^{2}

SHUIL SAOR b.g. 10 Fairbairn - Shuil Comeragh by Laurence O — Miss P Fitton
1996 **9(NH),P(NH),3(NH),5(NH)**

1121 19/4 Whittington (L) CON 3m 4 F *alwys 3rd, ev ch 3 out, no ext* 3 10
1349 3/5 Gisburn (R) CON 3m 11 GF *alwys rear, nvr trbld ldrs, p.u. 3 out* P 0
1488 12/5 Towcester (R) HC 2m 110yds 16 GS *alwys bhnd, t.o..* 9 0
1512 17/5 Corbridge (R) OPE 3m 10 GS *rear, t.o. 11th, p.u. 13th* P 0
1571 26/5 Wetherby (L) HC 2 1/2m 110yds 15 GF *held up, steady hdwy 11th, prom next, rdn 2 out, kept on.* 2 19
1589 31/5 Market Rasen (R) HC 2 3/4m 110yds 10 GF *held up, steady hdwy 9th, rdn 4 out, blnd next, soon btn.* 4 18

Winning hurdler; quite able & ran blinder last start but totally unreliable & not to be trusted 15

SHUIL'S STAR(IRE) b.g. 6 Henbit (USA) - Shuil Run by Deep Run — R Mason
1996 2(0),1(13),1(18)

294 1/3 Didmarton (L) INT 3m 20 G *s.s. wll in rear, no ch 13th, rpd prog aft, nvr nrr* 4 20
403 8/3 Llanfrynach (R) INT 3m 8 G *(fav) hld up rear, prog 15th, too mch to do* 2 17
1319 3/5 Bonvilston (R) INT 3m 8 G *mostly 3rd/4th, prog 3 out, ld last, qcknd flat* 1 23
1469 11/5 Erw Lon (L) OPE 3m 6 GS *made all, clr 3 out, ran on well* 1 23
1588 30/5 Stratford (L) HC 3 1/2m 9 G *held up and bhnd, hit 6th, gd hdwy 16th, cl 3rd when hmpd 4 out, one pace from next.* 3 29

Much improved; ran well in top novice H/chase; win one in 98; stays; Good 28

SIAMSA BRAE (Irish) — I 101^{2}, I 156^{3}, I 232^{P}, I 283^{6}, I 341^{4}, I 499^{2}

SIDE BRACE(NZ) gr.g. 13 Mayo Mellay (NZ) - Grey Mist (NZ) by Karayar — J S Swindells
1996 P(0),4(15),**4(13)**,2(18),2(16),**5(12)**

84 2/2 Wolverhampt' (L) MEM 3m 9 GS *alwys bhnd, t.o. & p.u. 12th* P 0
492 11/3 Sedgefield (L) HC 3m 3f 7 G *n.j.w., bhnd, t.o. final cct.* 6 0
667 23/3 Eaton Hall (R) CON 3m 10 GF *mid to rear, poor 6th 4 out, p.u. nxt* P 0
884 1/4 Flagg Moor (L) CON 3m 6 G *(vis) chsd ldr 3rd, ld 7th-3 out, wknd, fin 3rd, disq* 3D 10
1001 12/4 Alpraham (R) MXO 3m 3 GF *chsd ldr to 13th, strgglng aft* 2 0

Lost last 25; safe but ungenuine & sure to extend the sequence 12

SIDELINER ch.g. 9 Green Shoon - Emmalina by Doubtless II — A Hollingsworth
1996 5(0),6(0),5(15),3(15),8(0),4(12)

222 16/2 Heythrop (R) RES 3m 17 G *prog 8th, prssd wnr 15th, ev ch last, no ext nr fin* 2 18
300 1/3 Didmarton (L) RES 3m 23 G *mid-div, effrt & prog whn f 11th* F -
433 8/3 Upton-On-Se' (R) RES 3m 18 G *rear of main grp 9th, blkd & p.u. bef nxt* P 0
701 29/3 Upper Sapey (R) RES 3m 6 GF *5th 1st ctt, strggld frm 9th, p.u. 12th* P 0
877 1/4 Upton-On-Se' (R) RES 3m 17 GF *mid-div, effrt 9th, went 5th at 11th, no prog, lft 2nd last* 2 13

Maiden winner 95; non-stayer & struggling since; ran well debut & may surprise on easy course 16

SIDEWAYS SALLY (Irish) — I 209^{3}, I 365^{2}, I 442^{1}, I 469^{3}

SIGN gr.g. 8 Sharrood (USA) - Polly Packer by Reform — Philip Newton

10 25/1 Cottenham (R) INT 3m 7 GF *(fav) prom, prssd ldr 14th, rdn apr 3 out, ld nxt, styd on* 1 21
123 9/2 Cottenham (R) INT 3m 13 GF *(fav) trckd ldrs, chal 15th, mstk nxt, ld 3 out, ran on well* 1 24

Won 5 of 8 starts 95/97; missed 96; mistakes; stays & battles; finished early 97; win if fit 98; 24

SILENT POND (Irish) — I 430P, I 443P, I 5293, I 5964

SILENT SNEEZE (Irish) — I 262, I 786

SILK OATS ch.m. 7 Oats - Celtic Silk by Celtic Cone — M S Wilesmith

1996 P(0),5(0)

365	2/3 Garnons	(L) MDO 2 1/2m	14 GS	*prom to 4th, lost tch 10th, p.u. nxt*	P	0
1065	13/4 Maisemore P'	(L) MDO 3m	13 GF	*(fav) prog 8th, chsd ldrs 10th, wknd 12th, p.u. 15th*	P	0

Last on only completion & no real signs yet; (crazy favourite) 11

SILK RASCAL b.m. 6 Scallywag - Bid-Up by Royal Smoke — T E Vaughan

186	15/2 Erw Lon	(L) MDN 3m	13 G	*ref 2nd*	R	-
298	1/3 Didmarton	(L) RES 3m	15 G	*sn t.o. in last, p.u. 13th*	P	0

Not yet of any account 0

SILKS DOMINO ch.g. 12 Dominion - Bourgeonette by Mummy's Pet — M Hyslop

1996 8(0),P(0),P(0),P(0),U(-)

350	2/3 Market Rase'	(L) CON 3m	11 GF	*rear, t.o. whn blnd 6th, p.u. 13th*	P	0

No longer of any account 0

SILLY PET b.g. 7 Silly Prices - Tierna's Pet by Laurence O — C T Pogson

210	16/2 Southwell P'	(L) MDO 3m	15 GS	*nrly ref 1st, last whn succeeded nxt*	R	-
914	5/4 Cottenham	(R) MDO 3m	4 F	*ld til hmpd 2nd, jmpd slwly 4th, lost tch 13th, no ch aft*	3	0
1262	27/4 Southwell P'	(L) MDO 3m	15 G	*mid-div, prog to disp 4th, hdd 9th, fdd, t.o. & p.u. 3 out*	P	0

Well beaten in awful race; plenty to learn yet 0

SILLY SOVEREIGN b.m. 10 Just A Monarch - Minalto by Thriller — Mrs Angus Campbell

1996 P(0),P(0),P(0)

284	23/2 Charing	(L) MDO 3m	17 G	*sn wll bhnd, t.o. 8th, lft poor 3rd aft 14th, no prog*	4	0

No signs of any ability 0

SILLY TINKER b.g. 7 Silly Prices - Gypsy For Sure by Ascertain (USA) — R W Swiers

116	9/2 Wetherby Po'	(L) MDO 3m	14 GF	*alwys handy, ev ch whn blnd & u.r. 3 out*	U	-
1074	13/4 Whitwell-On'	(R) MDO 2 1/2m 88yds	16 G	*mid-div, prog 10th, ev ch 3 out, wknd rpdly*	5	10
1105	19/4 Hornby Cast'	(L) MDO 3m	11 G	*prom, chsd ldr 3 out, mstk nxt, onepcd*	2	13
1251	26/4 Easingwold	(L) MDO 3m	9 GS	*prom, 3rd whn f 3 out, lkd btn*	F	-

Beaten in weak races but a reasonable start; needs a little more but can improve 13

SILVER AGE(USA) b.g. 11 Silver Hawk (USA) - Our Paige (USA) by Grand Revival (USA) — Mrs C Day

1996 **4(NH),P(NH),P(NH),P(NH)**

256	22/2 Newtown	(L) OPE 3m	17 G	*blnd & u.r. 2nd*	U	-
586	19/3 Exeter	(R) HC 3 1/4m	12 GF	*blnd and u.r. 1st.*	U	-

Placed in novice/chases but hardly inspires confidence now 0

SILVER BUCKLE (Irish) — I 55, , I 89P, I 147P

SILVER CONCORD gr.g. 9 Absalom - Boarding House by Shack (USA) — Mrs C J Enser

1996 P(0),1(10),1(16),2(19)

735	29/3 Higher Kilw'	(L) MEM 3m	5 GF	*(fav) rear, p.u. aft 6th, lame*	P	0

Won 2 weak races 96; changed hands; problems now & can only be watched if returning 15

SILVER FIG ch.m. 10 True Song - Spartan Clown by Spartan General — J Mahon

1996 P(0),1(16),3(17),2(18)

468	8/3 Eyton-On-Se'	(L) RES 3m	11 G	*clr ldr to 8th,hd 9th,just ld & gng wll whn u.r.12th*	U	-

Maiden winner 96; brief 97; tricky & finds little; Restricted not easy to find; G-S 17

SILVER GALE (Irish) — I 5336

SILVERSPINA gr.m. 6 Malaspina - Silver Cirrus by General Ironside — Major R G Wilson

1276	27/4 Fakenham P-'	(L) MEM 3m	7 G	*chsd ldrs, jmpd slwly 3rd, wkng whn slw jmp 10th, p.u. 15th*	P	0
1431	10/5 Marks Tey	(L) MDO 3m	6 G	*(Jt fav) last whn ref 1st*	R	-
1435	10/5 Marks Tey	(L) INT 3m	8 G	*2nd outing,mid-div,slw jmps 1st & 2nd,wknd 10th,p.u.13th*	P	0

Jumped poorly & shown nothing yet; (favourite once?) 0

SIMON JOSEPH b or br.g. 10 Tower Walk - Lady Bess by Straight Lad — Mrs Yda Morgan

1996 **11(NH),P(NH)**

411	8/3 Dalston	(R) CON 3m	16 GS	*trckd ldr, ld 11-14th, lft in ld aft 3 out, hdd last,kpt on*	2	18

560	16/3 Lanark	(R) CON	3m	8	GS	*2nd hlfwy, 3rd & lkd held 3 out, kpt on to ld flat*	1	20
1049	13/4 Lockerbie	(R) OPE	3m	3	F	*(fav) ld & alwys abt 3l up, comf*	1	19

Novice/chase winner 95; lightly raced; won modest Open; stays; can win again; G/S best 21

SIMPLY A STAR(IRE) ch.g. 7 Simply Great (FR) - Burren Star by Hardgreen (USA) M W Easterby

1996 U(-),4(17),1(21),3(19),**8(NH)**

113	9/2 Wetherby Po'	(L) CON	3m	10	GF	*mid-div, outpcd 10th, t.o. 14th, p.u. 2 out*	P	0
265	22/2 Duncombe Pa'	(R) CON	3m	15	G	*mid-div, mstk 5th, rider lost reins & p.u. nxt*	P	0
351	2/3 Market Rase'	(L) OPE	3m	10	GF	*alwys rear, brf effrt 11th, sn strgglng, t.o. & p.u. last*	P	0
1075	13/4 Whitwell-On'	(R) MEM	3m	9	G	*(bl) prom til outpcd frm 3 out*	3	18
1103	19/4 Hornby Cast'	(L) OPE	3m	5	G	*(bl) trckd ldr, ld 12-14th, in tch whn f nxt*	F	-
1265	27/4 Southwell P'	(L) OPE	3m	8	G	*(bl) prom til wklnd 13th, wll bhnd 4 out, t.o.*	3	0

Confined winner 96; disappointin g & signs not good 97; needs test of stamina; may revive; G/S-Hy 16

SIMPLY JOYFUL b.m. 10 Idiot's Delight - Royal Pam by Pamroy Mrs G Greenwood

1996 2(12),6(0),U(-),P(0),3(0)

244	22/2 Lemalla	(R) MDO	3m	12	S	*in tch til lost plc 15th*	5	11
485	9/3 Tweseldown	(R) MDO	3m	11	G	*last pair, lost tch 14th, 7th & no ch 3 out, fin strngly*	4	11
1314	3/5 Holnicote	(L) MDO	3m	8	G	*mid-div, prog 10th, no ext apr last*	4	11
1437	10/5 Holnicote	(L) MDO	3m	14	G	*ld/disp to 13th, lost plc 16th, onepcd clsng stgs*	3	0

Placed 8 times 94-97; form is weak & still needs more improvement 12

SIMPLY PERFECT b.g. 11 Wassl - Haneena by Habitat J S Swindells

1996 **2(22)**,2(21),**6(0)**,2(18),**4(12),2(20),3(17),2(20)**

466	8/3 Eyton-On-Se'	(L) LAD	3m	7	G	*mid-div early, 3rd 7th, 2nd 10th, ev ch, not qckn frm 3 out*	3	16
587	19/3 Ludlow	(R) HC	2 1/2m	18	GF	*bhnd, nvr on terms.*	6	17
1097	19/4 Bangor	(L) HC	2 1/2m 110yds	11	G	*blnd and u.r. 1st.*	U	-
1292	30/4 Cheltenham	(L) HC	2m 5f	12	GF	*mstk 6th, lost pl 8th, nvr on terms after.*	8	14
1508	17/5 Bangor	(L) HC	3m 110yds	12	G	*midfield, effort 13th, nvr reached challenging position.*	5	11
1571	26/5 Wetherby	(L) HC	2 1/2m 110yds	15	GF	*alwys chasing ldrs, effort and ev ch 4 out, rdn next, one pace and hit last.*	3	18

Ladies winner 95; lost last 16 & will not win H/chase; should try Ladies; G/F-S 18

SIMPSONS KID (Irish) — I 227[F], I 312[F], I 460[P]

SINGH SONG b.m. 7 True Song - Regal Ranee by Indian Ruler Richard Chandler

1996 P(0)

79	2/2 Market Rase'	(L) MDO	2m 5f	9	GF	*in tch til blndrd & u.r. 3rd*	U	-

Not yet of any account 0

SINGING PROFIT b.m. 5 Gold Song - Gold Profit by Rubor W G Young

1996 **18(NH),9(NH),10(NH)**

949	6/4 Friars Haugh	(L) MDN	3m	10	GF	*losng tch whn u.r. 10th*	U	-
1222	26/4 Balcormo Ma'	(R) MDO	3m	6	F	*in tch til 4 out, bhnd whn p.u. bfr 2 out*	P	0
1336	3/5 Mosshouses	(L) MDO	3m	7	F	*sn bhnd, 15l 4th at 9th, nvr rchd ldrs, p.u. 2 out*	P	0
1428	10/5 Aspatria	(L) MDO	3m	11	G	*n.j.w. alwys bhnd, last whn p.u. 12th*	P	0

No ability under rules; mistakes & no real signs yet 0

SINGING SAM b.g. 12 Tudor Rhythm - Saxon Slave by Be Friendly Mrs Vicky Cunningham

1418	10/5 Easingwold	(L) MEM	3m	6	GF	*sttld 3rd, lft 2nd 7th, disp 11th-nxt, sn wknd*	3	11

Winning chaser; hardly runs now; a jolly round in his Members but will not be winning now 0

SIOBHANS PRINCESS (Irish) — I 460[P], I 525[6], I 556[3], I 591[6]

SIP OF BRANDY (Irish) — I 534[P], I 597[F]

SIRAIDAN (Irish) — I 185[P], I 285[P], I 409, , I 496,

SIR FREDERICK (Irish) — I 53[P]

SIR GANDOUGE (Irish) — I 397, , I 468[P], I 554[F], I 583[6]

SIR HARRY RINUS ch.g. 11 Golden Love - Teresa Jane by My Swanee Mrs Andrea Fisher

1996 2(10),4(0)

383	5/3 Catterick	(L) HC	3m 1f 110yds	10	G	*chsd ldrs, blnd 10th and soon lost pl, bhnd when blunded 12th and p.u. after.*	P	0
778	31/3 Carlisle	(R) HC	3 1/4m	14	G	*jmpd badly in rear, t.o. when p.u. before 2 out.*	P	0

Still a Maiden & outclassed in H/chases; a little ability but time passsing by 10

SIRISAT ch.g. 13 Cisto (FR) - Gay Ruin by Master Spiritus Miss T O Blazey

1996 5(18),6(0),1(17),3(14),2(19),2(19),2(15)

3	19/1 Barbury Cas'	(L) XX	3m	14	GF	*ld to 4th, chsd ldr to 12th, grad wknd frm 3 out*	5	12

89 4/2 Warwick (L) HC 3 1/4m 4 GF *chsd ldng pair, feeling pace when hit 8 out, one pace last 4, no impn.* 3 21
219 16/2 Heythrop (R) LAD 3m 16 G *alwys prom, outpcd by ldng pair 3 out, kpt on wll, gd effrt* 3 23
285 26/2 Taunton (R) HC 4 1/4m 110yds 16 GS *chsd ldrs, blnd 11th, styd on again from 14th, one pace from 3 out.* 4 21
586 19/3 Exeter (R) HC 3 1/4m 12 GF *held up, hdwy 10th, chsd ldrs from 6 out, kept on one pace.* 2 23
1504 16/5 Folkestone (R) HC 3m 7f 5 G *ld till after 2 out, not qckn, wknd run-in.* 2 19
1591 31/5 Stratford (L) HC 3 1/2m 11 G *well pld for a cct, lost tch quickly apr 6 out, t.o..* 8 12

WON 1 placed 9 last 16 starts; novice-ridden; safe but very onepaced; may find a point at 14; Any 22

SIR KRISPIN b.g. 7 Kris - Lady Tippins (USA) by Star de Naskra (USA) J M Wildman

1166 20/4 Mollington (R) MDO 3m 9 GF *last til prog to jn ldrs 9th, wknd 12th, p.u. 15th* P 0
1401 5/5 Ashorne (R) MDO 3m 15 G *12s-4s, rear, prog to chs ldrs 12th, wknd nxt, p.u. 2 out* P 0

A little hope so far; well supported 2nd start & can improve 10

SIR LARRY (Irish) — **I** 66P, **I** 94P

SIR L MUNNY (Irish) — **I** 605P

SIRRAH ARIS(IRE) b.g. 6 Buckskin (FR) - Sirrah Madam by Tug Of War M J Parr

84 2/2 Wolverhampt' (L) MEM 3m 9 GS *rear, mstk 11th & rdn, no respnse, t.o. & p.u. nxt* P 0
667 23/3 Eaton Hall (R) CON 3m 10 GF *disp to 3rd, 10l 2nd whn f 10th* F -
937 6/4 Tabley (R) CON 3m 10 G *alwys mid-div, brf efft to 4th 13th, nvr dang* 6 12

Won 2 Irish points 96 (fast ground); showed nothing in 97; worth another chance; G-F 16

SISTER EMU b.m. 10 Buckskin (FR) - Hill Master by Master Owen M D Gichero

1996 1(19),U(-),3(13),5(0)

572 16/3 Garnons (L) INT 3m 13 G *prom to 8th, wknd frm 12th, p.u. 2 out* P 0
1382 5/5 Eyton-On-Se' (L) INT 3m 7 GF *made running til f 6th* F -
1538 18/5 Wolverhampt' (L) CON 3m 8 GS *rear, t.o. whn f 4 out* F -

Slogged through mud to win 96; disappointing since & can only be watched now; Soft 12

SISTER GALE br.m. 5 Strong Gale - Saffron's Daughter by Prince Hansel Ben Van Praagh

1996 **7(NH),4(NH)**

306 1/3 Parham (R) MDN 3m 12 G *prog to prss ldr 13th, ld 3 out-last, no ext* 2 13

Placed Novice hurdle 96; promising start in 3 finisher race; high hopes of local Maiden if fit 98 14

SISTER LARK ch.m. 8 True Song - Seeker's Sister by Ashmore (FR) N B Jones

1996 5(0),4(10),P(0),P(0),2(14),4(0),4(0),3(10),2(12),**7(0)**,1(13),P(0)

189 15/2 Erw Lon (L) RES 3m 14 G *prom, ev ch 14th, sn outpcd, styd on agn flat* 3 14
300 1/3 Didmarton (L) RES 3m 23 G *alwys rear, t.o. & p.u. 14th* P 0
404 8/3 Llanfrynach (R) INT 3m 17 G *trckd ldr, ld 11-13th, onepcd aft* 4 16
539 16/3 Erw Lon (L) RES 3m 8 GF *prom to 12th, wknd, p.u. nxt* P 0

Won weak Maiden 96; non-stayer & things tough now; need luck to win Restricted 14

SISTERLY b.m. 11 Brotherly (USA) - Wee Jennie by Vimadee Peter Nash

1996 F(-),2(20),3(19),1(19)

255 22/2 Newtown (L) CON 3m 14 G *prom, cls 3rd at 14th, wknd rpdly frm nxt* 9 0
434 8/3 Upton-On-Se' (R) INT 3m 4 G *(fav) ld til jnd 3 out, 2l up last, not qckn & hdd flat* 2 20
703 29/3 Upper Sapey (R) OPE 3m 5 GF *efft to take 2nd 11th, ev ch whn outpcd frm 3 out* 2 21
1063 13/4 Maisemore P' (L) XX 3m 13 GF *chsd ldr 7th, ld 14th, kckd clr, hit last, unchal* 1 19
1233 26/4 Brampton Br' (R) CON 3m 8 G *(fav) cls up, ld 13th til hdd aft 3 out, rallied und pres flat* 3 19
1388 5/5 Cursneh Hill (L) CON 3m 4 GF *(fav) trckd ldr cls up til ld 15th, pshd clr 2 out, comf* 1 20
1472 11/5 Erw Lon (L) XX 3m 9 GS *(fav) ld 5-9th, chsd wnr aft, hld whn f last* F 17
1576 26/5 Chaddesley ' (L) XX 3m 12 F *prom, ld 14th-nxt, wknd 3 out, 3rd & no ch whn p.u. last* P 0

Won 4 94-97; solid; consistent; needs easy 3 miles; can win Confined at 12; G/S-F 20

SISTER NORA (Irish) — **I** 32[1], **I** 112F, **I** 124P, **I** 376[2], **I** 466[1]

SISTER SEVEN(IRE) b.m. 6 Henbit (USA) - Bonne Royale by Bonne Noel M H Walton

129 9/2 Alnwick (L) MEM 3m 2 G *(Jt fav) made all at steady pace, rdn & qcknd clr flat* 1 0
335 1/3 Corbridge (R) CON 3m 7 G *handy, disp 10th til lft in ld 12th, styd on wll* 1 20
810 31/3 Tranwell (L) CON 3m 5 G *(fav) alwys prom,hdwy to disp ld 3 out,outpcd & 5l 2nd nxt,no ext* 2 17
992 12/4 Tranwell (L) INT 3m 1 F *walked over* 1 0
994 12/4 Tranwell (L) LAD 3m 5 F *(fav) hld up 1st ctt,smth hdwy frm 14th to ld 3 out,ran on wll* 1 19

Ilrish Maiden winner 96; well placed & won modest races; young but more needed for good Ladies; G-F 20

SIT TIGHT b.g. 8 Buckley - Chaise Longue by Full Of Hope Miss S Pilkington

1996 5(0),2(14),U(-),U(-),P(0),P(0),2(11)

21 25/1 Badbury Rin' (L) MDN 3m 7 GF *(Jt fav) hld up, prog to chs clr ldr 13th, clsd & lft in clr ld last* 1 13
148 9/2 Tweseldown (R) XX 3m 12 GF *rear whn u.r. 11th* U -
198 15/2 Higham (L) RES 3m 14 G *prom to 11th, lft disp 3rd aft nxt, wknd 16th, p.u. 2 out* P 0
877 1/4 Upton-On-Se' (R) RES 3m 17 GF *alwys rear, t.o. & p.u. 11th* P 0

1210 26/4 Woodford (L) RES 3m 14 G *prom til wknd apr 4 out* 8 0
1355 4/5 Dingley (R) RES 3m 12 G *w.w.,prog to 4th 10th,wknng whn blnd 3 out,t.o. & p.u. last* P 0

Placed 4 times prior to winning poor race; poor jumper & very hard to find Restricted 12

SIXTH IN LINE(IRE) ch.g. 9 Deep Run - Yellow Lotus by Majority Blue R G Chapman
1996 P(0),P(0),P(0),4(0),4(0),4(13),6(0),F(-)
625 22/3 Kilworthy (L) MDN 3m 14 G *mstk 2nd, 8th 11th, t.o.* 6 0
736 29/3 Higher Kilw' (L) RES 3m 10 GF *bhnd til p.u. 12th* P 0
1035 12/4 Lifton (R) MDN 3m 11 F *front rank til wknd 12th, p.u. aft 14th* P 0
1260 27/4 Black Fores' (R) MDO 3m 12 F *f 9th* 0 0
1400 5/5 High Bickin' (R) MDO 3m 14 G *c.o. bend apr 2nd* C -
1521 17/5 Bratton Down (L) MDO 3m 16 GS *rear, 10th at 12th, nrst fin* 4 0
1584 26/5 Lifton (R) MDO 3m 13 G *rear, steady prog frm 13th, onepcd frm 3 out* 5 0

Rarely completes & went backwards in 97; unlikely to win 10

SKERRY MEADOW b.g. 13 Anfield - Mi Tia by Great Nephew O J Carter
1996 **P(0)**,U(-),3(0),**5(15)**,**P(0)**
1482 11/5 Ottery St M' (L) LAD 3m 5 G *alwys last, t.o. 15th* 5 0
1529 18/5 Fakenham (L) HC 3m 110yds 9 G *hit 1st, soon well bhnd, blnd 6th, p.u. after 10th.* 9 0

Formerly useful; shows nothing now 12

SKIDROW RIVER (Irish) — I 65^{U}, I 82^{F}, I 153^{P}, I 219^{P}

SKI LADY b.m. 9 Myjinski (USA) - Lady Jay by Double Jump Mrs J Horner
1996 **15(NH)**,**7(NH)**,**7(NH)**,**P(NH)**
120 9/2 Wetherby Po' (L) MDO 3m 18 GF *mid-div, mstk 8th, t.o. & p.u. nxt* P 0
355 2/3 Great Stain' (L) LAD 3m 9 S *rear & lost tch 10th, t.o. & p.u. 12th* P 0
426 8/3 Charm Park (L) LAD 3m 12 GF *mid-div, lost tch 10th, t.o. 13th* 9 0
615 22/3 Hutton Rudby (L) MEM 3m 8 GF *rear, mstk 5th, outpcd 7th, nvr dang* 4 0
698 29/3 Stainton (R) MDO 3m 6 F *ld til hdd 12th, ld 15th-3 out, wknd* 2 10
1106 19/4 Hornby Cast' (L) MDO 3m 10 G *saddle slppd & u.r. bfr 1st* U -
1252 26/4 Easingwold (L) MDO 3m 9 GS *rear, mstks, completed own time* 6 0
1345 3/5 Gisburn (R) MDN 3m 13 GF *mid-div, nvr trbld ldrs* 4 0

Poor under rules; safe enough but not threatening to win; big improvement needed 10

SKIMABIT (Irish) — I 43^{3}, I 133^{F}, I 169^{2}, I 262^{2}

SKINNHILL b.g. 13 Final Straw - Twenty Two (FR) by Busted Mrs T Binnington
1996 7(0),4(11),7(11),5(15),3(15),U(-),1(16),2(19),3(16),4(13)
2 19/1 Barbury Cas' (L) XX 3m 14 GF *(bl) prom, 4th hlfwy, 5th & btn whn u.r. last* U -
16 25/1 Badbury Rin' (L) MEM 3m 2 GF *(fav) made most, drew clr frm 10th, mstk 3 out, easily* 1 16
109 8/2 Milborne St' (L) XX 3m 8 GF *(bl) mid-div, some prog 15th, nvr on trms* 3 17
302 1/3 Parham (R) CON 3m 14 G *(bl) alwys rear, lost tch 14th* 6 11
662 22/3 Badbury Rin' (L) CON 3m 8 F *ld to 13th, agn 14th-3 out, outpcd aft* 3 18
745 29/3 Barbury Cas' (L) OPE 3m 3 F *ld to 11th, ran on agn 3 out, lkd to fin 2nd* 3 16
869 31/3 Hackwood Pa' (L) XX 3m 6 F *(bl) rear & sn rdn, clsd 7th, disp 12th, outpcd 2 out* 3 12
1055 13/4 Hackwood Pa' (L) OPE 3m 4 GF *(bl) rdn alng, ld to 6th, ld brfly 15th, ran on* 3 15
1274 27/4 Little Wind' (R) XX 3m 8 GF *(bl) ld 6-8th, ld 10th til aft 14th, rdn & onepcd aft* 3 15
1464 11/5 Tweseldown (R) XX 3m 7 GF *(bl) chsd ldrs, pshd alng 13th, styd on onepcd frm 3 out, retired* 2 14

Has been retired 16

SKINNY MINNIE (Irish) — I 120^{P}, I 251^{P}, I 292^{P}

SKI NUT b.g. 10 Sharpo - Saint Cynthia by Welsh Saint K D Wright
1996 U(-),P(0),P(0),2(18),7(10),3(0),2(11)
145 9/2 Tweseldown (R) LAD 3m 10 GF *outpcd in rear, t.o. 15th* 6 10
645 22/3 Castle Of C' (R) LAD 3m 6 G *ld to 8th, 3rd & outpcd whn blnd & u.r. 14th* U -
824 31/3 Lockinge (L) CON 3m 8 F *sn wll bhnd, no ch hlfwy, t.o. & p.u. last* P 0

Not disgraced but outclased in competitive races; surely worth a try in his Members 12

SKIPCARL (Irish) — I 488^{P}, I 561^{4}, I 565^{F}

SKIPPING CHICK (Irish) — I 167^{P}, I 378^{F}, I 445^{4}, I 538^{1}, I 614^{1}

SKIPPING GALE b.g. 12 Strong Gale - Skiporetta by Even Money G W Barker
1996 P(0),P(0),5(11),2(19),3(13),3(15)
113 9/2 Wetherby Po' (L) CON 3m 10 GF *prom til wknd rpdly 10th, sn t.o., p.u. 4 out* P 0
164 15/2 Witton Cast' (R) INT 3m 6 F *ld til disp 8th, hdd 14th, rallied 2 out, sn outpcd* 2 19
265 22/2 Duncombe Pa' (R) CON 3m 15 G *prom, disp ld 10th, wknd 14th, t.o.* 8 0
356 2/3 Great Stain' (L) INT 3m 9 S *prom to 9th, sn lost tch* 6 0
506 15/3 Dalton Park (R) CON 3m 16 GF *ld/disp to 6th, outpcd 11th, styd on agn 3 out* 3 15
619 22/3 Hutton Rudby (L) INT 3m 8 GF *ld, disp 4-10th, rmnd prom til fdd frm 3 out* 3 15
694 29/3 Stainton (R) CON 3m 11 F *ld til hdd 6th, rmnd prom til grdly fdd frm 4 out* 7 15
1100 19/4 Hornby Cast' (L) CON 3m 9 G *rear, rmmndrs 11th, sn outpcd, t.o. 3 out, p.u. last* P 0
1247 26/4 Easingwold (L) CON 3m 9 GS *disp to 8th, fdd, p.u. 2 out* P 0

Losing sequence of 18 since last win in 94; most unlikely to win again **14**

SKIPTHECUDDLES (Irish) — **I** 195³, **I** 304⁶, **I** 401²

SKOLERN b.g. 13 Lochnager - Piethorne by Fine Blade (USA) T H Pounder

165 15/2 Witton Cast' (R) LAD 3m 6 F *s.s. rear, blnd 5th, lost tch 8th, t.o.* 5 0
426 8/3 Charm Park (L) LAD 3m 12 GF *(bl) lost many l stt, alwys wll bhnd, p.u. 3 out* P 0
617 22/3 Hutton Rudby (L) LAD 3m 9 GF *(vis) disp ld til wknd qckly 3 out, t.o.* 9 0
1102 19/4 Hornby Cast' (L) LAD 3m 7 G *prom, jmp slwly 7th, lost plcd 12th, wknd 4 out, t.o.* 5 12

Winning selling hurdler; reluctant & no prospects now **0**

SKYE WEDDING(IRE) b or br.m. 8 Fine Blade (USA) - Nimble Ninepence by London Gazette Nicholas Alexander

162 15/2 Lanark (R) MDO 3m 16 G *sn t.o., p.u. 11th* P 0
949 6/4 Friars Haugh (L) MDN 3m 10 GF *sn bhnd, t.o. whn p.u. 10th* P 0

Not yet of any account **0**

SKYLARK SONG b.m. 6 True Song - Copperclown by Spartan General A Godrich

1996 **14(NH)**,**7(NH)**

544 16/3 Garthorpe (R) MEM 3m 6 GF *s.s. last whn u.r. 2nd* 0 0
770 29/3 Dingley (R) RES 3m 18 G *plld hrd, cls up til u.r. 8th* U -

No ability under rules & not a good start **0**

SKY MISSILE b.m. 8 Cruise Missile - Over Dinsdale by Rubor Gavin Douglas

1996 5(0),6(0),9(0)

134 9/2 Alnwick (L) MDO 3m 11 G *ld to 4th, chsd ldrs, 3rd & btn whn lft wll clr 4 out* 1 0

Reliability saw him home(fortunate); vanished after; more needed for Restricted **13**

SKY RAINBOW (Irish) — **I** 98ᶠ, **I** 222ᴾ, **I** 339ᴾ

SKY RUNNER ch.g. 6 Scallywag - Space Drama by Space King R G E Owen

1996 P(0),P(0),P(0)

81 2/2 Wolverhampt' (L) MDN 3m 13 GS *in tch, mstk 14th, prog to ld apr 2 out, clr last, pshd out* 1 15
331 1/3 Eaton Hall (R) RES 3m 17 GS *alwys rear, t.o. & p.u. 13th* P 0
1542 18/5 Wolverhampt' (L) RES 3m 6 GS *ld til blnd 9th, sn wknd, p.u. 4 out* P 0

Won weak race; pulled up all other starts; can only be watched **12**

SKYVAL ch.m. 7 Domynsky - Derry Island by Varano T Peace

1996 6(0),5(0),1(13),P(0)

77 2/2 Market Rase' (L) RES 3m 9 GF *hld up bhnd, nvr on trms, t.o. frm 13th* 4 0
264 22/2 Duncombe Pa' (R) MEM 3m 9 G *rear, lost tch 9th, wll bhnd 12th, t.o. whn p.u. 3 out* P 0
1070 13/4 Whitwell-On' (R) XX 3m 9 G *rear, mstk 4th, outpcd 7th, wll bhnd 10th, p.u. 4 out* P 0
1101 19/4 Hornby Cast' (L) RES 3m 14 G *alwys in rear, jnd rght 2nd, wll bhnd 11th,t.o. & p.u. 4 out* P 0
1250 26/4 Easingwold (L) RES 3m 15 GS *mid-div, 10th 10th, same plc thruout* 7 0
1406 5/5 Witton Cast' (R) RES 3m 10 GS *alwys in rear, strgglng 12th, t.o. & p.u. 4 out* P 0

Won bad Maiden 96; outclassed now upgraded & little hope of another success **12**

SKY VENTURE ch.g. 13 Paddy's Stream - Mijette by Pauper Barry Briggs

1996 3(18),5(0),1(21),4(15),4(13),2(17)

142 9/2 Tweseldown (R) MEM 3m 8 GF *hld up, prog to ld 11th, hdd 4 out, styd on onepcd* 2 16
279 23/2 Charing (L) CON 3m 10 G *trckd ldrs, rdn 14th, sn wknd, p.u. last* P 0
484 9/3 Tweseldown (R) OPE 3m 10 G *trckd ldrs going wll, 4th & outpcd whn blnd 15th, wknd* 5 10
604 22/3 Parham (R) CON 3m 3 F *trckd wnr, jmpd slwly 6th, pshd alng 13th, outpcd* 2 15
966 6/4 Penshurst (L) CON 3m 7 F *trckd ldrs, efft 4 out, kpt on onepce* 3 15
1127 19/4 Penshurst (L) OPE 3m 7 GF *ld 7-12th, agn 4 out-nxt, onepcd* 4 12

Won 3 in 95; consistent & Solid & deserved win; struggle to find another at 13; G-F **14**

SLADE VALLEY HIGH (Irish) — **I** 472ᴾ

SLADE VALLEY LADY (Irish) — **I** 525ᴾ, **I** 575ᴾ, **I** 591ᴾ

SLANEY BACON (Irish) — **I** 284ᵁ, **I** 386ᴾ

SLANEY CUISINE (Irish) — **I** 486ᴾ

SLANEY DELIGHT (Irish) — **I** 287ᴾ, **I** 429ᴾ

SLANEY ENCORE (Irish) — **I** 78ᴾ

SLANEY FAYRE (Irish) — **I** 202ᴾ, **I** 337¹

SLANEY FOOD br.g. 10 Strong Gale - Martones Chance by Golden Love Capt T A Forster

99 8/2 Great Treth' (R) LAD 3m 10 GS *(fav) prom, chsd wnr 14th, ev ch 2 out, sn btn, eased* 2 21
520 15/3 Cothelstone (L) LAD 3m 12 GS *trckd ldr 7th til lft in ld 14th, just ld last, ran on wll* 1 26
1017 12/4 Bitterley (L) LAD 3m 4 GF *(fav) trckd wnr 4th,chal 15th,cls 2nd & hld whn f last,dead* F -

Dead. 26

SLANEY FRANCE(IRE) b or br.g. 9 Over The River (FR) - Kitty Quin by Saucy Kit Mrs Jane Lovelace
1996 **P(NH),P(NH),4(NH),P(NH)**

107	8/2 Milborne St'	(L) MEM	3m	8	GF	*in tch to 12th, outpcd 15th, kpt on frm 2 out*	3	0
179	15/2 Larkhill	(R) CON	3m	12	G	*nvr nr ldrs, t.o. frm 12th*	7	0
397	8/3 Barbury Cas'	(L) XX	3m	10	G	*bhnd frm 6th, t.o. 12th, p.u. last*	P	0
1370	5/5 Cotley Farm	(L) XX	3m	4	GF	*cls 4th til 12th, wnt 2nd 14th, no further prog frm 2 out*	2	13
1458	11/5 Maisemore P'	(L) XX	3m	6	G	*pckd 2nd, t.o. 7th, p.u. 11th*	P	0
1518	17/5 Bratton Down	(L) XX	3m	7	GS	*svrl pstns, in tch to 13th, wll btn frm 16th*	4	0
1593	31/5 Bratton Down	(L) XX	3m	5	F	*cls up to 9th, wknd 12th, t.o. 15th, tk poor 3rd agn fin*	3	0

Decent Irish pointer; novice ridden overhere & beaten in poor races & not threatening to win 12

SLANEY GOODNESS (Irish) — **I** 27[5], **I** 78[P], **I** 185[1], **I** 224[3], **I** 404[2], **I** 549[2], **I** 577[3], **I** 605[3], **I** 613[4]

SLANEY PROJECT(IRE) b.g. 5 Project Manager - Sundrive by Status Seeker Miss A L Wright

683	29/3 Charing	(L) OPE	3m	5	F	*ld 5th til blndrd & u.r. 11th*	U	-

Irish flat winner; thrown in at the deep end; plenty to prove yet 0

SLANEY SAUCE (Irish) — **I** 408[4], **I** 457[U], **I** 491[3], **I** 542[5], **I** 614[3]
SLANEY SAUCY (Irish) — **I** 340[F]
SLANEY STREAM (Irish) — **I** 18[P], **I** 35[6]
SLANEY SUPREME (Irish) — **I** 284[3], **I** 340[P]
SLANEY WIND (Irish) — **I** 134[1], **I** 216[2], **I** 386[P], **I** 613[2]

SLAUGHT BOY(IRE) ch.g. 9 Pauper - Fantastic Madame by Fantastic Light B W Gupwell

881	1/4 Upton-On-Se'	(R) MDN	3m	13	GF	*cls up til f 5th*	F	-

Abrief debut 10

SLAVICA (Irish) — **I** 13[4], **I** 41[1], **I** 62[1]
SLEEPY ROCK (Irish) — **I** 256,
SLEMISH MIST (Irish) — **I** 37[F]
SLIABH LUCHRA BOY (Irish) — **I** 132[P], **I** 260[P], **I** 352[P]

SLIEVENAMON MIST ch.g. 11 Thatching - La Generale by Brigadier Gerard Nick Viney
1996 P(0),1(24),**1(33)**

94	7/2 Newbury	(L) HC	2 1/2m	12	G	*hdwy and hit 9th, trckd ldr 12th, chal 4 out, slight ld from next, driven out run-in.*	1	25
375	3/3 Doncaster	(L) HC	2m 3f 110yds	11	GF	*in tch, hdwy to chase ldr 6th, ld 9th, clr 2 out, styd on well.*	1	28
1287	29/4 Huntingdon	(R) HC	2 1/2m 110yds	14	G	*(fav) held up, prog to chase lding pair 11th, ld apr 2 out where mstk, driven clr.*	1	28
1506	16/5 Folkestone	(R) HC	2m 5f	8	G	*(fav) held up bhnd, prog to chase ldr after 10th, ld apr 2 out, soon clr, eased run-in.*	1	31

Very useful H/chaser; lightly raced; best below 3 miles; good stable & sure to win more; Good 32

SLIGHT PANIC b.m. 9 Lighter - Midnight Panic by Panco Miss J H Wickens
1996 F(-),3(12),6(10),**6(NH)**

442	8/3 Higham	(L) LAD	3m	8	G	*in tch in rear whn u.r. 10th*	U	-
578	16/3 Detling	(L) LAD	3m	11	F	*wll in rear til rpdly jnd pack 6th,in tch final ctt,onepcd*	6	12
684	29/3 Charing	(L) LAD	3m	2	F	*ld aft 7th,u.r. 8th,evntlly rejnd,ld 4 out to nxt,ev ch*	2	0
968	6/4 Penshurst	(L) LAD	3m	5	F	*last, rpd prog to ld 8-10th, prom aft, wknd 3 out*	3	10
1128	19/4 Penshurst	(L) LAD	3m	8	GF	*cls up, mstk 11th, chsd wnr 3 out, wknd last*	3	14
1308	3/5 Cottenham	(R) LAD	3m	5	F	*chsd wnr 5th til blnd 10th,2nd agn 3 out,no imp,dmtd nr fin*	3	17

Maiden winner 95; changed hands; stamina suspect; placed in modest Ladies; hard to find a race 14

SLIGO CHAMPION (Irish) — **I** 507[5]

SLIM CHANCE b.m. 6 Al Amead - Maria Slim by Owen Dudley J Latham

263	22/2 Newtown	(L) MDN	3m	11	G	*mstk 3rd, t.o. last til p.u. 12th*	P	0
570	16/3 Garnons	(L) MDN	2 1/2m	14	G	*t.o. 5th, p.u. 10th*	P	0

Well named on the evidence so far 0

SLIM KING b.g. 9 Slim Jim - Bromley Rose by Rubor Mrs S E Woodward
1996 P(0),4(0)

415	8/3 Dalston	(R) RES	3m	19	GS	*chsd ldrs, 6th hlfwy, sn wknd, t.o. & f 2 out*	F	-
698	29/3 Stainton	(R) MDO	3m	6	F	*sweating, chsd ldr til wknd 11th, sn wll bhnd*	4	0

Well beaten when completing & not worth a rating 0

SLOW BEET (Irish) — **I** 101[P], **I** 155[P], **I** 223[4], **I** 550[P]

SLUMBERHILL(IRE) b.g. 6 Roselier (FR) - Shuil Ronan by Deep Run P J Millington

208 16/2 Southwell P' (L) MDO 3m 9 GS *chsd ldng pair 7th-apr 12th, wkng whn blnd 13th, p.u. 3 out* P 0

Vanished after reasonable debut 0

SMART AS (Irish) — I 312^{P}, I 394^{P}

SMART BEAT ch.g. 8 True Song - Clear Thinking by Articulate R H Woodward

449 8/3 Newton Brom' (R) XX 3m 13 G *cls up, wknd hlfwy, rear & p.u. 15th* P 0

Maiden winner 95; missed 96 & very brief 97; can only be watched now 14

SMART MOVER ch.g. 8 Vaigly Great - Presentable by Sharpen Up Mrs J M Reynard

212 16/2 Southwell P' (L) MDO 3m 14 GS *hld up in tch, strgglng whn f 12th* F -
429 8/3 Charm Park (L) MDO 3m 14 GF *prom til wknd 9th, lost tch 12th, t.o. & p.u. last* P 0
623 22/3 Hutton Rudby (L) MDO 3m 9 GF *ld-5th,2nd & lft in ld 14th,made rest,hld on wll fin,plc 2nd* 2 14
948 6/4 Friars Haugh (L) MDO 3m 7 GF *2nd mstly til 12th, wknd frm 4 out, poor 4th whn u.r. last* U -
1104 19/4 Hornby Cast' (L) MEM 3m 6 G *rear, mstk 3rd, rmmndrs 13th, strgglng nxt,t.o. & p.u. 2 out* P 0
1251 26/4 Easingwold (L) MDO 3m 9 GS *ld to 3 out, disp nxt, hdd, outpcd flat* 2 12
1409 5/5 Witton Cast' (R) MDO 3m 15 GS *(fav) prom til fdd frm 4 out* 3 0

Robbed on 3rd start; all form on easy tracks; should find compensation; G-F 13

SMART PAL b.g. 12 Balinger - Smart Bird by Stephen George B Knox

1996 P(0),4(11),4(13)

62 1/2 Horseheath (R) CON 3m 5 GF *chsd ldr to 5th, last & losing tch whn f 12th* F -
193 15/2 Higham (L) CON 3m 14 G *in rear, sn strgglng & nt fluent, p.u. 12th* P 0
271 22/2 Ampton (R) CON 3m 15 G *mid-div, prog 7th, j.s. 9th, 6th & outpcd 14th, no dang aft* 6 11
319 1/3 Marks Tey (L) CON 3m 11 G *chsd ldrs to 8th, lost plc 10th, rlld 15th, no hdwy frm nxt* 4 0
497 15/3 Ampton (R) CON 3m 9 GF *disp ld to 3rd, prom to 12th, wkng & j.s. 14th, no dang aft* 5 10
593 22/3 Horseheath (R) CON 3m 3 F *cls 2nd til outpcd 14th, no ch frm nxt* 3 13
802 31/3 Marks Tey (L) INT 3m 4 F *ld 1st, hdd 6th, ld agn nxt, hdd 10th, ev ch 2 out, no ext* 3 16
1190 20/4 Garthorpe (R) INT 3m 8 GF *bhnd 7th, jmpd slwly 11th, no ch frm 15th* 7 0
1285 29/4 Huntingdon (R) HC 3m 10 G *chsd ldrs till wknd 12th, soon t.o..* 5 0
1435 10/5 Marks Tey (L) INT 3m 8 G *alwys prom, ld brfly 16th, sn outpcd, onepcd 2 out* 5 12

Dual winner 94; losing sequence of 16 since & unlikely to win again 13

SMART RHYTHM ch.m. 9 True Song - Clear Thinking by Articulate R H Woodward

1996 1(15),P(0),P(0),4(0)

546 16/3 Garthorpe (R) LAD 3m 11 GF *alwys rr div, t.o frm 10th* 10 0
773 29/3 Dingley (R) LAD 3m 11 G *alwys last, t.o. 10th, p.u. last* P 0
1204 26/4 Clifton On ' (L) MEM 3m 6 GS *prom, 2nd 1st m, fdd, last frm 9th, t.o. 11th* 4 0
1355 4/5 Dingley (R) RES 3m 12 G *chsd ldrs to 7th, last frm 11th, t.o. & ref last* R -

Fortunate Maiden winner 96; not better than last since & best avoided 0

SMART SONG b.g. 6 True Song - New World by St Columbus Mrs S Cartridge

1996 P(0),P(0)

210 16/2 Southwell P' (L) MDO 3m 15 GS *ld/disp til apr 12th, grad lost plc* 6 0
435 8/3 Upton-On-Se' (R) MDO 3m 14 G *prom til not qckn 12th, lost tch & p.u. 3 out* P 0

Only learning so far; may do better 0

SMART TEACHER(USA) b or br.h. 7 Smarten (USA) - Finality (USA) by In Reality Mrs N R Matthews

1996 P(0)

369 2/3 Mollington (R) MEM 3m 13 G *pllng, prom to 8th, wknd rpdly & p.u. 12th* P 0

Not yet of any account 0

SMASHING VIEW ch.g. 8 Saxon Farm - Edwina's Law by Ercolano (USA) R M Hartley

676 23/3 Brocklesby ' (L) RES 3m 14 GF *chsd ldrs to 10th, 8th & wkng whn hmpd 12th, t.o.* 6 0
1069 13/4 Whitwell-On' (R) RES 3m 12 G *rear, prog 8th, ev ch 14th, unable qckn nxt* 2 14
1345 3/5 Gisburn (R) MDN 3m 13 GF *nvr bynd mid-div, wll btn 4th whn ran out wing last* r -

Lightly raced; beat 7 others when placed(poor lot); obviously good enough for Maiden if reproducing ... 14

SMILING MINSTREL (Irish) — I 29^{P}, I 94^{4}, I 219^{P}

SMITH'S MELODY b.g. 9 Alias Smith (USA) - Queen's Melody by Highland Melody M Haigh

120 9/2 Wetherby Po' (L) MDO 3m 18 GF *mid-div, wknd 10th, t.o. & p.u. nxt* P 0
264 22/2 Duncombe Pa' (R) MEM 3m 9 G *prom, wnt 2nd 9th, rddn & outpcd 11th, sn wll bhnd, t.o.* 6 0
357 2/3 Great Stain' (L) MDO 3m 15 S *mid-div, f 4th* F -
424 8/3 Charm Park (L) RES 3m 12 GF *prom til wknd 11th, sn lost tch, t.o.* 7 0

Of no account 0

SMITTEN NOT BITTEN (Irish) — I 497^{P}

SMOKEY THUNDER(IRE) br.g. 7 Miner's Lamp - Moorstown Lady Mrs Fiona Gordon

1996 **P(NH),F(NH)**

107	8/2 Milborne St'	(L) MEM 3m	8	GF	*prom to 12th, outpcd nxt, blnd 15th, t.o. 2 out*	5	0
488	9/3 Tweseldown	(R) RES 3m	10	G	*5th whn blnd 7th, lost tch 11th, t.o. & p.u. 16th*	P	0

No real signs of ability yet 0

SNAPPER b.g. 6 Gunner B - Fortalice by Saucy Kit — R H Black

1996 2(14),1(15)

32	26/1 Alnwick	(L) RES 3m	11 G	*pllng, chsd wnr 3rd-3 out, 3rd & btn whn f 2 out*	F	-
157	15/2 Lanark	(R) RES 3m	11 G	*cls up whn f 8th*	F	-
416	8/3 Dalston	(R) RES 3m	12 GS	*(fav) hld up, prog 8th, chsd ldrs & outpcd 3 out, sn btn*	3	0
1050	13/4 Lockerbie	(R) RES 3m	5 F	*cls up to 13th, sn lost tch, virt p.u. flat*	4	0

Won 73/4 mins Maiden 96; nothing 97 but still young; stamina test best hope; G/S-S 13

SNIPPETOFF b.g. 9 Dubassoff (USA) - Snippet by Ragstone — P Senter

1996 7(0),3(0),F(-)

877	1/4 Upton-On-Se'	(R) RES 3m	17 GF	*mstks, sn in rear, wll bhnd whn p.u. 15th*	P	0
1066	13/4 Maisemore P'	(L) MDO 3m	9 GF	*mstks, prog 9th, lft 3rd 12th, sn lost tch, t.o.*	3	0

Lightly raced; well beaten when completing; mistakes; will struggle to win 10

SNITTON STREAM b.g. 7 Domitor (USA) - Cala Di Volpe by Hardiran — W H Whitley

1996 **F(NH),18(NH),P(NH)**

456	8/3 Great Treth'	(R) INT 3m	11 S	*ld 5th til f 10th*	F	-
556	16/3 Ottery St M'	(L) RES 3m	12 G	*ld to 14th, wknd rpdly nxt, p.u. 3 out*	P	0
1553	24/5 Mounsey Hil'	(R) MDO 3m	11 G	*raced freely, clr wth ldr, ld 8-12th, wknd, p.u. 14th*	P	0
1597	31/5 Bratton Down	(L) MDO 3m	12 F	*j.w. made all, 30l clr hlfwy, unchal*	1	18

Stunning performance last start; weak race but good time; firm & easy course needed; can upgrade ... 17

SNOBS CASINO (Irish) — **I** 31^{P}, **I** 179^{P}

SNOWBERRY RIVER (Irish) — **I** 99^{P}, **I** 123^{5}

SNOWTOWN ACTRESS (Irish) — **I** 33^{P}, **I** 310^{2}, **I** 472^{P}

SNUGVILLE SALLY (Irish) — **I** 25^{P}, **I** 110^{1}, **I** 157^{5}

SOCIAL VISION(IRE) b.g. 7 Parliament - Elegant Miss by Prince Tenderfoot (USA) — R Fellows

1996 P(0)

201	15/2 Weston Park	(L) OPE 3m	16 G	*t.o. til kpt on frm 4 out*	8	0
435	8/3 Upton-On-Se'	(R) MDO 3m	14 G	*in tch in rear, prog 11th, kpt on, lft 2nd last*	2	11
881	1/4 Upton-On-Se'	(R) MDN 3m	13 GF	*hld up, lost tch ldrs 11th, nvr on trms aft*	5	0

Lightly raced; subsequent winner behind when placed; needs a little more but can improve 13

SOCIETY LAD (Irish) — **I** 220^{P}, **I** 269^{P}, **I** 403, , **I** 409^{4}, **I** 481^{2}, **I** 497^{P}

SOCIETY MEMBER ch.g. 12 New Member - Key Biscayne by Deep Run — Mrs S M Jones

456	8/3 Great Treth'	(R) INT 3m	11 S	*5th hlfwy, p.u. aft 13th*	P	0

Won 4 points 92/93; very lightly raced & probably finished now 14

SOCIETYS STREAM(IRE) b.f. 7 Deep Society - Pampered Sally by Paddy's Stream — Mrs Ruth Crank

206	15/2 Weston Park	(L) MDN 3m	9 G	*blnd & u.r. 2nd*	U	-
326	1/3 Eaton Hall	(R) MDN 3m	14 GS	*f 5th*	F	-

Floundering so far 0

SOCK HOP (Irish) — **I** 275^{P}, **I** 354^{P}

SODA POPINSKI(USA) b.g. 9 Sir Ivor - Four Runs (USA) by Reviewer (USA) — C J Vale

214	16/2 Southwell P'	(L) CON 3m	10 GS	*ld 4th, sn clr, hit 8th, hdd 11th, wknd rpdly, p.u. nxt*	P	0
350	2/3 Market Rase'	(L) CON 3m	11 GF	*mid-div, mstk 6th, 6th & btn whn f 14th*	F	-
836	31/3 Thorpe Lodge	(L) OPE 3m	7 F	*cls up 2nd/disp til fdd 8th, t.o. 5th 10th, p.u. 6 out*	P	0

Winning A/W hurdler; does not stay & no hopes in points 0

SO ISLE ch.m. 13 Nicholas Bill - Radar Girl by Bleep-Bleep — M H Gingell

8	25/1 Cottenham	(R) CON 3m	5 GF	*chsd ldr to 6th, 3rd & outpcd 14th, no dang aft, subs promoted*	2	12
125	9/2 Cottenham	(R) LAD 3m	11 GF	*ld to 13th, wknd rpdly & p.u. bef nxt*	P	0

Won 5 points 92; hardly runs now & looks finished 13

SOLAR CASTLE(IRE) b.f. 7 Carlingford Castle - Cornahinch — L A E Hopkins

1996 **8(NH),10(NH),10(NH),6(NH)**

82	2/2 Wolverhampt'	(L) MDN 3m	11 GS	*slw jmp 2nd, nrly u.r. nxt, t.o. 6th*	4	0
206	15/2 Weston Park	(L) MDN 3m	9 G	*mid to rear, no ch whn u.r. 14th*	U	-
469	8/3 Eyton-On-Se'	(L) MDN 2 1/2m	9 G	*w.w. smooth prog to ld 2 out, ran on well*	1	15
852	31/3 Eyton-On-Se'	(L) RES 3m	11 GF	*mstk 2nd, f 4th*	F	-

940	6/4	Tabley	(R)	RES	3m	9	G	*w.w., prog 11th, 4th & bttn 3 out, blndrd last, p.u. flat*	P	0
1178	20/4	Sandon	(L)	XX	3m	6	GF	*nvr dang, p.u. 4 out*	P	0
1381	5/5	Eyton-On-Se'	(L)	MEM	3m	5	GF	*prom, outpcd hlfwy, ran on frm 5 out*	2	17
1542	18/5	Wolverhampt'	(L)	RES	3m	6	GS	*hld up in tch, clsd on ldrs 4 out, onepcd frm nxt*	3	13

Ex Irish; won weak race; needs easy 3 miles & likes Eyton; Members best hope 98; G/F best 14

SOLAR GEM b.g. 10 Easter Topic - River Gem by Arctic Judge — W J Palmer

56	1/2	Kingston Bl'	(L)	OPE	3m	13	GF	*mostly last, t.o. hlfwy*	10	0
223	16/2	Heythrop	(R)	RES	3m	19	G	*wll bhnd, effrt 12th, nvr on trms, wknd 2 out*	7	0
273	22/2	Ampton	(R)	OPE	3m	7	G	*j.s. 1st, in tch, lft 4th 12th, rdn 17th, kpt on*	3	16
384	6/3	Towcester	(R)	HC	3m 1f	7	GS	*jmpd poorly in rear, blnd 10th, t.o. when hit 3 out, u.r..*	U	-
548	16/3	Garthorpe	(R)	RES	3m	10	GF	*(bl) ld til ran wde & hdded appr 4th, cls up til f 9th*	F	-
680	29/3	Towcester	(R)	HC	3m 1f	8	GF	*(bl) mstk 1st, in rear when hit 8th, t.o. and p.u. before 6 out.*	P	0
1164	20/4	Mollington	(R)	RES	3m	10	GF	*alwys last, t.o. 6th, p.u. 3 out*	P	0

Maiden winner 94; novice-ridden in points; moody & very unlikely to consent to win again 11

SOLID(IRE) b.g. 9 Glenstal (USA) - Reine de Chypre (FR) by Habitat — H Hill

122	9/2	Cottenham	(R)	MEM	3m	6	GF	*ld 5th-2 out, kpt on onepcd flat*	2	12
271	22/2	Ampton	(R)	CON	3m	15	G	*ld to 3rd, wknd 12th, t.o. & p.u. 3 out*	P	0
475	9/3	Southwell P'	(L)	OPE	3m	7	G	*bhnd frm 5th, t.o. 12th, p.u. 2 out*	P	0
771	29/3	Dingley	(R)	OPE	3m	10	G	*alwys last pair, t.o. last at 10th, p.u. last*	P	0

Winning A/W hurdler; placed in weak Members; does not stay & no prospects in competitive races 11

SOLO MINSTREL (Irish) — **I** 401[P]

SOLVANG (Irish) — **I** 219[1]

SOLWAYSANDS b.g. 7 Germont - Castle Point by Majestic Streak — K Little

1996 3(10),5(0),1(14),1(12),P(0)

157	15/2	Lanark	(R)	RES	3m	11	G	*ldng grp, ld brfly 4 out, wknd frm nxt*	7	0
337	1/3	Corbridge	(R)	RES	3m	11	G	*prom, chsd ldr 12th, ev ch 2 out, not qckn*	2	15
413	8/3	Dalston	(R)	OPE	3m	9	GS	*prom til outpcd frm 3 out, sn no ch*	3	14
778	31/3	Carlisle	(R)	HC	3 1/4m	14	G	*chsd ldrs, struggling final cct, p.u. 4 out.*	P	0
1046	13/4	Lockerbie	(R)	MEM	3m	4	F	*(fav) ld 6th, made rest, kpt on well*	1	13
1169	20/4	Hexham Poin'	(L)	RES	3m	9	GF	*(fav) ld/disp til hdd last, no ext flat*	2	14
1424	10/5	Aspatria	(L)	RES	3m	17	G	*prom to 13th, wknd rpdly, walked in*	11	0

Won 3 poor racse 96/7 (2 Members); stays; likes fast ground; may find another chance 14

SOME DAY (Irish) — **I** 476[P], **I** 519[P], **I** 572[P]

SOME MAN (Irish) — **I** 66[6], **I** 118[2], **I** 210[6]

SOME OTHER KNIGHT (Irish) — **I** 132[P]

SOME SHOCK (Irish) — **I** 263[P], **I** 384[P], **I** 538[P], **I** 566[2]

SOME SWOP (Irish) — **I** 107[P], **I** 301[5], **I** 403[5], **I** 449[1], **I** 513[3]

SOMETIMES QUICKLY (Irish) — **I** 305[P]

SOME TOURIST(IRE) b.g. 9 Torus - Noellespir by Bargello — Nigel Benstead

59	1/2	Kingston Bl'	(L)	RES	3m	16	GF	*wll bhnd, steady prog 13th, wll btn whn lft 4th last*	4	16
277	23/2	Charing	(L)	MEM	3m	6	G	*1st ride, wth ldr to 7th, 3rd & outpcd frm 15th*	3	11
303	1/3	Parham	(R)	RES	3m	10	G	*alwys wll bhnd, p.u. 2 out*	P	0
1286	29/4	Huntingdon	(R)	HC	3m	10	G	*slowly into stride, alwys bhnd, t.o. and p.u. before 3 out.*	P	0

Winninh Irish pointer; safe but well beaten in points; won a timber race in 97 11

SOME-TOY ch.g. 11 Arkan - Cedar Of Galaxy by Bauble — John Squire

1996 1(23),3(17),1(25),**U(-)**,3(20),**1(25)**

149	10/2	Hereford	(R)	HC	3m 1f 110yds	18	GS	*nvr trbl ldrs.*	6	0
238	22/2	Lemalla	(R)	LAD	3m	9	S	*(fav) 6th hlfwy, prog 13th, outpcd 15th, blnd nxt, wknd rpdly*	6	13
589	20/3	Wincanton	(R)	HC	2m 5f	9	GF	*in tch when mstk 11th, soon rdn and lost pl.*	4	17
737	29/3	Higher Kilw'	(L)	LAD	3m	5	GF	*not fluent, prog to chs wnr 9th, ev ch 3 out, sn outpcd*	2	21
981	9/4	Chepstow	(L)	HC	3m	6	F	*steady hdwy from 13th, ld after next, shaken up and ran on well run-in.*	1	22
1087	16/4	Cheltenham	(L)	HC	3 1/4m 110yds	8	GF	*held up, hdwy to chase wnr 10th, rdn when hit 3 out, one pace.*	2	25
1291	30/4	Cheltenham	(L)	HC	3 1/4m 110yds	4	GF	*chsd ldrs, mstk 9th, struggling from 12th, soon t.o..*	4	20
1544	21/5	Newton Abbot	(L)	HC	3 1/4m 110yds	11	G	*alwys bhnd, t.o. 8th, p.u. before 4 out.*	P	0

Useful 96; won modest H/chase but below par in 97; mistakes; hard to place now; F-S 25

SOME VIEW (Irish) — **I** 67[1], **I** 290[2], **I** 441[P]

SONNAURA b.m. 7 Sonnen Gold - Centaura by Centaurus — P Morgan

1996 **4D(NH),8(NH),U(NH),4(NH),P(NH)**

54 1/2 Wadebridge (L) MDO 3m 13 G *nvr bttr than mid-div, p.u. aft 14th* P 0

No ability under rules & unpromising so far 0

SONNEN GIFT b.m. 7 Sonnen Gold - Hopeful Gift by Bounteous G L Edwards

1996 **19(NH),8(NH)**

1003 12/4 Alpraham (R) MDO 2 1/2m 10 GF *rear whn ref 2nd* R -

None finisher in 4 outings 95 & 97; signs bad now 0

SONNY'S SONG b.g. 11 True Song - Zaratune by Badedas Alan Clarke

1996 P(0),8(0),6(0),5(0),6(0),P(0),P(0)

568 16/3 Garnons (L) CON 3m 12 G *alwys rear, lost tch 12th, p.u. 15th* P 0
881 1/4 Upton-On-Se' (R) MDN 3m 13 GF *keen hld, mstk 7th,prom to 10th, wknd, p.u. 15th* P 0
1402 5/5 Ashorne (R) MDO 3m 11 G *(vis) wll bhnd frm 8th, cont t.o.* 6 0
1528 17/5 Bredwardine (R) MDO 3m 17 G *(bl) alwys rear, t.o. 12th, p.u. 14th* P 0
1577 26/5 Chaddesley ' (L) MDO 3m 11 F *alwys rear, t.o. frm 12th* 5 0

Hopeless 0

SONOFAGIPSY b.g. 13 Sunyboy - Zingarella by Romany Air Mrs B Whettam

1996 **3(24),2(21),6(21),2(23),4(19),5(12)**

92 6/2 Wincanton (R) HC 3m 1f 110yds 6 GF *in 3rd most of way, rdn from 14th, soon no ch.* 3 19
376 3/3 Windsor (R) HC 3m 11 GF *in tch till wknd apr 4 out.* 5 12
981 9/4 Chepstow (L) HC 3m 6 F *(bl) prom till wknd 7th, n.d. after.* 6 0

H/Chase winner 95; declined & reluctant now; looks ready for retirement; Firm 16

SOON BE BACK b.g. 7 St Columbus - Up With The Lark by Be Friendly Miss N L Sell

13 25/1 Cottenham (R) MDO 3m 10 GF *mstks, wll bhnd, some prog frm 14th, nvr dang* 4 10
128 9/2 Cottenham (R) MDO 3m 10 GF *(fav) prom, ld 11th, 5l clr whn f 2 out* F 14
283 23/2 Charing (L) MDO 3m 16 G *f 2nd* F -
439 8/3 Higham (L) MDO 3m 11 G *t.o. last at 2nd, schoold rear til ran on 2 out, stewards* 4 0

Unlucky in bad race; confidence booster last start; chances in weak race if learning 13

SOONER STILL b.g. 13 Tachypous - Sooner Or Later by Sheshoon R F Rimmer

1996 3(13),F(-),5(10),3(11),3(14),4(17)

329 1/3 Eaton Hall (R) LAD 3m 10 GS *(bl) chsd ldrs, 2nd 13th, ld 4 out, ran on und pres frm 2 out* 1 19
669 23/3 Eaton Hall (R) LAD 3m 5 GF *chsng grp, disp 2nd 3 out, outpcd apr last* 3 16
939 6/4 Tabley (R) LAD 3m 9 G *(bl) prom, ld 6-10th, lost plcd & rddn 12th, no dang aft* 7 0

Winning chaser; won Ladies (favourites departed); stays; blinkers best; hard to win at 14 18

SOUL SURVIVOR(IRE) b.g. 8 Andretti - La Mont R Dunsford

54 1/2 Wadebridge (L) MDO 3m 13 G *ld to 5th, grad wknd* 6 0

Ran well on only start; beaten 15 lengths; chances if fit in 98 12

SOUND BARRIER (Irish) — **I** 429^{4}, **I** 585^{F}

SOUND FORECAST b.g. 9 Hill's Forecast - Miss Soundly by Maelsheachlainn Mrs S A Evans

1996 **14(NH),9(NH),7(NH),7(NH),6(NH),3(NH),8(NH),3(NH),6(NH),4(NH),4(NH)**

85 2/2 Wolverhampt' (L) LAD 3m 11 GS *bnhd, poor 7th at 11th, kpt on frm nxt, no dang* 4 14
257 22/2 Newtown (L) LAD 3m 12 G *last til prog 12th, no ch aft nxt, styd on wll frm 3 out* 4 18

Short Maiden winner 94; under rules since; has ability but disappointing & unlikely to win 18

SOUNDS CONFIDENT (Irish) — **I** 179^{F}, **I** 277^{U}, **I** 296^{2}, **I** 363^{1}

SOUND VISION (Irish) — **I** 277^{P}, **I** 355^{P}

SOUTHERLY BUSTER b.g. 14 Strong Gale - Southern Slave by Arctic Slave Simon White

1996 U(-)

98 8/2 Great Treth' (R) OPE 3m 14 GS *alwys rear, t.o. 14th, p.u. 3 out* P 0
239 22/2 Lemalla (R) OPE 3m 7 S *cls 4th 11th, lost tch wth ldrs 16th* 6 13
395 8/3 Barbury Cas' (L) XX 3m 9 G *prom, ld apr 12th, mstk & hdd 14th, 5th & btn whn u.r. 2 out* U -
646 22/3 Castle Of C' (R) OPE 3m 5 G *last & jmpd slwly 5th,lost tch 14th,kpt on to poor 3rd flat* 3 12
1244 26/4 Bratton Down (L) CON 3m 14 GS *alwys prom, chal 2 out, kpt on wd cls home* 2 17
1436 10/5 Holnicote (L) MEM 3m 5 G *in tch til outpcd 17th, ran on clsng stgs* 3 12
1516 17/5 Bratton Down (L) CON 3m 6 GS *raced wd, in tch til outpcd 15th, lft 3rd 3 out, kpt on* 2 16
1580 26/5 Lifton (R) OPE 3m 8 G *nvr nr ldrs, rdn 13th, no prog* 5 11

Dual winner 95; changed hands; schoolmaster now; still tries but win looks too tough now 14

SOUTHERNCROSSPATCH ch.g. 6 Ra Nova - Southern Bird by Shiny Tenth Keith R Pearce

1996 **13(NH),4(NH),13(NH)**

963 6/4 Pantyderi (L) MDN 3m 6 F *(fav) trckd ldrs, ld 3 out, f 2 out, unlucky* F -
1137 19/4 Bonvilston (R) MDO 3m 13 G *n.j.w., in mid-div, wknd frm 14th* 6 0

1367 5/5 Pantyderi (L) MDO 3m 7 G *ld/disp, ran on best aft last* 1 14

Poor under rules; beat subsequent dual winner; all runs easy tracks; local Restricted likely; G-F 15

SOUTHERN FLIGHT b.g. 8 Southern Music - Fly Blackie by Dear Gazelle Mrs K J Cumings
1996 U(-),1(20),1(20)

97 8/2 Great Treth' (R) INT 3m 13 GS *chsd ldrs til poor 4th & no imp frm 13th* 5 12
293 1/3 Didmarton (L) INT 3m 16 G *ldng grp, effrt 15th, outpcd 3 out, kpt on* 3 18
558 16/3 Ottery St M' (L) INT 3m 6 G *prom, disp 4 out-nxt, ev ch 2 out, outpcd* 2 22

Lightly raced; beaten by good horses & still improving; stays; likes Soft; can win in 98 23

SOUTHERN MINSTREL ch.g. 14 Black Minstrel - Jadida (FR) by Yelapa (FR) N Chamberlain
1996 **4(24)**,1(22),**1(26)**,**8(16)**,**3(23)**,**3(22)**,**9(15)**,**5(0)**

33 26/1 Alnwick (L) LAD 3m 12 G *in tch,trckd ldr 13th, outpcd 3 out, ran on last, got up fin* 1 23
67 1/2 Wetherby (L) HC 3m 1f 10 G *in tch till gradually wknd from 12th.* 5 18
355 2/3 Great Stain' (L) LAD 3m 9 S *rear, prog 8th, outpcd 3 out, kpt on apr last* 3 19
590 21/3 Kelso (L) HC 3 1/2m 5 G *in tch, effort and rdn along 5 out, soon outpcd.* 4 21
1096 18/4 Ayr (L) HC 3m 3f 110yds 7 G *held up, hdwy 14th, rdn 5 out, one pace.* 3 23
1359 5/5 Southwell (L) HC 3m 110yds 7 GS *in tch, rdn along 13th, bhnd from 4 out.* 4 0
1586 28/5 Cartmel (L) HC 3 1/4m 10 GF *bhnd, some hdwy final cct, n.d..* 4 16

H/chase winner 96; declining now; best L/H; Ladies looks too tough now; G-S 20

SOUTH STACK b.g. 11 Daring March - Lady Henham by Breakspear II T Laxton
1996 P(0),P(0),2(0),3(0)

412 8/3 Dalston (R) LAD 3m 8 GS *last pair, lsng tch whn hmpd & u.r. 14th* U -
764 29/3 Whittington (L) LAD 3m 5 S *cls 2nd til ld 9th, hdd 14th, wknd qckly* 4 10

Beaten miles when placed & of no account now 10

SOVEREIGN COTTAGE (Irish) — **I** 559[6]

SOVEREIGNS MATCH b.g. 9 Royal Match - Sovereign's Folly by Sovereign Bill J McKinnon
1996 P(14)

162 15/2 Lanark (R) MDO 3m 16 G *made most to 7th, wknd 4 out, eased flat* 8 0
411 8/3 Dalston (R) CON 3m 16 GS *prom, ld 14th, 4l clr whn p.u. aft 3 out* P 0
875 1/4 Wetherby (L) HC 3m 1f 5 GF *ld, jmpd slowly 4 out, joined next and rdn, hdd run-in, rallied towards fin.* 2 19
1294 30/4 Kelso (L) HC 3m 1f 6 GF *ld, clr 2 out, wknd quickly and hdd last, soon btn.* 5 12

Lightly raced; headstrong; unlucky & deserves a win; a certainty for a Maiden. 19

SOVEREIGN SPRAY(IRE) b.g. 7 Celio Rufo - Countess Spray by Even Say S P Tindall
1996 P(0),1(12),1(19)

282 23/2 Charing (L) INT 3m 7 G *(fav) trckd ldrs, ld 14th, hrd rdn aft 3 out, all out* 1 18
832 31/3 Heathfield (R) INT 3m 2 F *(fav) w.w. effort to chall 4 out, rdn nxt, wll btn apr last* 2 14

Won 3 of 5 starts; improving but yet to beat anything decent; should progress to Confineds; G-F 19

SPACE MAN ch.g. 14 True Song - Perfect Day by Roan Rocket Miss Scarlett J Crew
1996 2(19),2(19),3(14),**8(0)**,6(11),2(23)

187 15/2 Erw Lon (L) OPE 3m 16 G *chsd ldrs, outpcd frm 12th, no dang aft* 6 0
483 9/3 Tweseldown (R) CON 3m 8 G *nvr going wll, alwys rear, btn 10th, t.o. & p.u. last* P 0

Formerly fair stayer; hard to win with & looks finished now 14

SPACE MOLLY b.m. 8 Capitano - Space Speaker by Space King T Frost
1996 F(-),P(0),P(0),U(-),P(0),P(0)

373 2/3 Mollington (R) MDN 3m 14 G *wth ldr til wknd rpdly 9th, t.o. & p.u. 15th* P 0
653 22/3 Siddington (L) RES 3m 10 F *(bl) made most to 4th, wth wnr to 9th, sn wknd, t.o.* 7 0
892 5/4 Hereford (R) HC 2m 11 GF *t.o. from 4th, p.u. before 3 out.* P 0
1083 13/4 Guilsborough (L) MDN 3m 15 GF *(bl) sn ld, kpt on wll frm 3 out, hdd apr last, no ext flat* 2 15
1285 29/4 Huntingdon (R) HC 3m 10 G *(bl) ld 4th to 6th, wknd 8th, well bhnd when f 12th.* F -

2 completions from 15 starts; good enogh to win but totally unreliable; blinkers 14

SPACIAL(USA) b.g. 13 Star Appeal - Abeer (USA) by Dewan (USA) Richard J Hill
1996 3(20),1(24),1(25),1(26)

18 25/1 Badbury Rin' (L) LAD 3m 9 GF *chsd ldr 5th-15th, grad fdd* 3 22
145 9/2 Tweseldown (R) LAD 3m 10 GF *j.w. prom, ld 2 out, imprssv* 1 27
394 8/3 Barbury Cas' (L) LAD 3m 5 G *prssd wnr, ev ch apr 2 out, rdn & btn apr last* 3 22
660 22/3 Badbury Rin' (L) LAD 3m 2 F *ld to 3 out, disp nxt, ran on best und pres* 1 27

Useful Ladies horse on fast ground; front runs; needs easy 3 miles; still win at 14; G-F 25

SPALEASE br.m. 7 Strong Gale - Batease by Quiet Fling (USA) Mrs Judy Wilson
1996 1(15),6(0)

251 22/2 Brocklesby ' (L) RES 3m 16 G *mid-div, 6th 5 out, outpcd nxt, p.u. 2 out* P 0
770 29/3 Dingley (R) RES 3m 18 G *prom bhnd ldrs til outpcd frm 6 out, fin own time* 5 0

Maiden winner 96; lightly raced & nothing since; good stable but can only be watched 16

SPANISH JEST b.g. 6 Jester - Donnacelli by Don Carlos Mrs Marilyn Burrough

1246 26/4 Bratton Down (L) MDO 3m 16 GS *bhnd whn p.u. 10th* P 0
1486 11/5 Ottery St M' (L) MDO 3m 17 G *sn rear, t.o. & p.u. 11th* P 0

Not yet of any account 0

SPANISH MONEY gr.g. 10 Scallywag - Morgan's Money by David Jack Russel H Lee

1996 **P(0),F(NH),P(NH),P(NH)**

1101 19/4 Hornby Cast' (L) RES 3m 14 G *rear, lost tch 6th, t.o. 10th, p.u. nxt* P 0

Won dire Maiden 95; shows nothing now; prospects nil 0

SPANISH PAL(IRE) b.g. 7 Spanish Place (USA) - Pallatess by Pall Mall J S S Hollins

284 23/2 Charing (L) MDO 3m 17 G *s.s. t.o. til p.u. 11th* 0 0
582 16/3 Detling (L) MDN 3m 16 F *towrds rear whn c.o. by loose horse 8th* C -
605 22/3 Parham (R) MDO 3m 7 F *3rd whn u.r. 2nd* U -
686 29/3 Charing (L) MDO 2 1/2m 5 F *alwys last, lost tch 7th, p.u. 4 out* P 0
971 6/4 Penshurst (L) MDO 3m 5 F *trckng ldrs whn hmp & f 5th* F -
1130 19/4 Penshurst (L) MDO 3m 5 GF *rear, 3rd 14th, not pace to chal* 4 0
1446 10/5 Peper Harow (L) MDO 3m 7 GF *hld up, prog to 4th & in tch whn blnd & u.r. 10th* U -
1568 25/5 Kingston Bl' (L) MDO 3m 11 GF *alwys last trio, t.o. 13th* 8 0

Not better than last; local area serves up some poor races but much more needed 0

SPANISH RIVER g. 11 Mrs Sarah-Jane Baxter

1996 **17(NH)**

392 8/3 Barbury Cas' (L) MDN 3m 9 G *rear, in tch to 8th, p.u. 11th* P 0

Of no account 0

SPANISH ROUGE ch.g. 13 - Sparwood by Spartan General A R Ford

1996 3(0),P(0),7(0),r(-)

633 22/3 Howick (L) RES 3m 8 GF *2nd til ld 8th-12th, onepcd aft* 3 10

Maiden winner 93; placed 6 times since but Restricted chance has gone; barely stays 13

SPAR COPSE ch.g. 14 Pablond - Ringarose by Rose Knight P E Froud

1996 P(0),5(0),2(12),**3(13)**,2(10),2(10)

929 6/4 Charlton Ho' (L) MEM 3m 5 G *lost tch 7th, t.o. 12th, p.u. 3 out* P 0
1024 12/4 Badbury Rin' (L) MDO 3m 3 F *(fav) trckd ldr,cls up frm 11th,ld 14th,lft clr 16th,pshd out* 1 10
1144 19/4 Larkhill (R) RES 3m 3 F *(fav) made all, 4l clr whn jmpd slwly 2 out, kpt on* 1 12
1436 10/5 Holnicote (L) MEM 3m 5 G *1st ride, lost tch 6th, t.o.* 5 0

Broke his duck in 2 awful races; does not really stay & need same to win again; G-F 12

SPARKES CROSS (Irish) — **I** 223ᴾ, **I** 344ᴾ, **I** 389ᶠ, **I** 406ᴾ, **I** 500ᴾ

SPARKLING CLOWN ch.m. 8 True Song - Copperclown by Spartan General Miss C Arthers

1996 6(0)

212 16/2 Southwell P' (L) MDO 3m 14 GS *mstk 1st, bhnd til u.r. 9th* U -

Has some ability but lightly raced & unable to fulfill. 10

SPARKLING ROSIE (Irish) — **I** 349[6], **I** 394[5], **I** 416[F], **I** 472[F], **I** 525[1], **I** 573[2], **I** 604[3], **I** 614,

SPARKLING SPIRIT b.m. 9 Sparkling Boy - Spartan Spirit by Spartan General I Marsh

1996 **F(NH),3(NH),6(NH),6(NH)**

65 1/2 Horseheath (R) RES 3m 10 GF *chsd ldrs to 13th, sn strggling, no ch whn u.r. last* U -
197 15/2 Higham (L) MDO 3m 12 G *(Jt fav) cls up going wll, effrt 2 out, sn ld, ran on well* 1 16

Placed Novice/chases; won weak Maiden; novice-ridden; vanished after; needs more to upgrade 15

SPARKY BROWN(IRE) b.g. 6 Double Schwartz - Pride And Joy (FR) by Miami Springs Mrs P Edwards-Harrison

266 22/2 Duncombe Pa' (R) RES 3m 19 G *rear & lost tch 5th, t.o. whn p.u. 8th* P 0
358 2/3 Great Stain' (L) MDO 3m 14 S *prom, ran out 3rd* r -
428 8/3 Charm Park (L) MDO 3m 10 GF *mid-div, fdd 7th, sn lost tch, t.o. & p.u. 9th* P 0

Very unpromising 0

SPARKY JOE (Irish) — **I** 12[P], **I** 42[P]

SPARNOVA ch.m. 7 Ra Nova - Spartaca by Spartan General V T Bradshaw

1996 P(0),1(14),3(16),3(10),3(15)

221 16/2 Heythrop (R) RES 3m 15 G *mid-div, effrt to chs ldrs 12th, btn 14th, p.u. nxt* P 0
449 8/3 Newton Brom' (R) XX 3m 13 G *3rd early, sn lost plc, bhnd & p.u. 3 out* P 0

826	31/3 Lockinge	(L) RES	3m	4	F	*(bl) alwys last, effrt 10th, outpcd & mstks frm 13th*	4	0
985	12/4 Kingston Bl'	(L) MEM	3m	4	GF	*(bl) mstks, chsd wnr to 5th & frm 10th, sn rdn, no imp*	2	13
1164	20/4 Mollington	(R) RES	3m	10	GF	*(bl) mstks, cls up to 14th, lost tch und pres, p.u. last*	P	0
1450	10/5 Kingston Bl'	(L) LAD	3m	7	G	*sn bhnd, last frm 5th, t.o. & p.u. aft 15th*	P	0

Maiden winner 96; mistakes; moody & going the wrong way now; best watched now 12

SPARTAN JULIET b.m. 9 Julio Mariner - Miss Spartan by Spartan General — H S Fletcher

1996 5(0),P(0),P(0),7(0),3(15),2+(17)

118	9/2 Wetherby Po'	(L) RES	3m	14	GF	*prom til wknd 14th, t.o.*	7	0
266	22/2 Duncombe Pa'	(R) RES	3m	19	G	*rear, mstk 11th, kpt on frm 3 out*	4	12
425	8/3 Charm Park	(L) RES	3m	12	GF	*rear most of the way, strggng 4 out,wll btn whn blndrd 2 out*	8	0
695	29/3 Stainton	(R) RES	3m	11	F	*disp ld to 2nd, settld mid-div, mstk 13th, sn strgglng*	6	10
1072	13/4 Whitwell-On'	(R) MXO	4m	21	G	*alwys rear, nvr a fctr*	9	11

Members winner 94; safe but never involved at the business end now; need luck to win; Good 14

SPARTAN PARK (Irish) — **I** 365[P], **I** 431[P]

SPARTAN PETE ch.g. 9 Peter Wrekin - Spartan Madam by Spartan General — Mrs J A Burton

1996 P(0),P(0),4(14)

218	16/2 Heythrop	(R) INT	3m	21	G	*in tch til grad wknd frm 14th*	7	12
331	1/3 Eaton Hall	(R) RES	3m	17	GS	*mid to rear, p.u. 4 out*	P	0
465	8/3 Eyton-On-Se'	(L) OPE	3m	13	G	*rear 10th, some late prog, not trbl ldrs*	4	13
664	23/3 Eaton Hall	(R) MDO	3m	12	GF	*mid-div, rmndrs, p.u. 8th*	P	0

Has ability but strange choice of races; must have chances in Maiden 13

SPARTANS CONQUEST b.g. 7 Baron Blakeney - Spartella by Spartan General — O Vaughan-Jones

1996 P(0),P(0),P(0),1(13)

65	1/2 Horseheath	(R) RES	3m	10	GF	*ld to 5th, cls up, ld & blnd 2 out, clr last*	1	19

Improving; won modest races; stays; needs more for Confineds; can improve further 20

SPARTANS DINA b.m. 6 Newski (USA) - Spartan Mariner by Spartan General — P D Rogers

1996 F(-),C(-),P(0),F(-),P(0),4(0)

105	8/2 Great Treth'	(R) MDO	3m	15	GS	*blnd 7th, in tch in rear til blnd 12th & p.u.*	P	0
315	1/3 Clyst St Ma'	(L) MDN	3m	5	HY	*ld 4th til f 8th*	F	-
460	8/3 Great Treth'	(R) MDO	3m	13	S	*not fluent, 9th hlfwy, t.o. p.u. apr 14th*	P	0
531	15/3 Wadebridge	(L) MDO	3m	14	GF	*rear til prog 13th, kpt on onepcd frm nxt*	5	0
808	31/3 Wadebridge	(L) MDO	3m	8	F	*chsd ldr til lft in ld 12th-last, no ext whn chal*	2	10
1035	12/4 Lifton	(R) MDN	3m	11	F	*ld 4-6th agn 8-11th, poor jmp 14th, wknd qckly*	3	12
1261	27/4 Black Fores'	(R) MDO	3m	12	F	*(Jt fav) t.d.e. pllng, ran out 3rd*	r	-

Placed in poor races; mistakes & stamina suspect; needs more to win 13

SPARTAN SILVER ch.g. 11 Warpath - Spartan Spirit by Spartan General — Lord Somerleyton

1996 **P(NH)**

154	14/2 Fakenham	(L) HC	2m 5f 110yds	10	G	*prom to 5th, t.o. 8th, p.u. before 10th.*	P	0
319	1/3 Marks Tey	(L) CON	3m	11	G	*ld til apr 11th, wknd qckly, blndrd 12th, p.u. nxt*	P	0

Novice/chase winner; hardly runs now & looks finished 0

SPARTAN'S SAINT b.g. 12 St Columbus - Spartan Lace by Spartan General — G B Tarry

1996 P(0),4(11),2(11)

372	2/3 Mollington	(R) RES	3m	19	G	*alwys bhnd, t.o. & p.u. 12th*	P	0

Maiden winner 93; only 8 runs since & can only be watched now 10

SPECIALARRANGEMENT(IRE) br.g. 8 Strong Gale - Batease by Quiet Fling (USA) — Mrs Judy Wilson

248	22/2 Brocklesby '	(L) CON	3m	10	G	*(fav) mid-div, prog 10th, 2nd 5 out, ld 3 out, comf*	1	24
515	15/3 Larkhill	(R) INT	3m	8	GF	*(fav) w.w. prog to 3rd whn mstk 13th, sn btn, p.u. 3 out*	P	0
851	31/3 Eyton-On-Se'	(L) INT	3m	8	GF	*w.w., cls order to ld 12th, hdd 5 out, p.u. qckly 4 out*	P	0
1351	4/5 Dingley	(R) CON	3m	7	G	*(fav) chsd ldrs,ld aft 11th,slppd & hdd nxt,wknd 3 out,p.u.last*	P	0

Dead 22

SPECIAL COMPANY(IRE) b.m. 6 Phardante (FR) - Sweet Proverb by Proverb — C W Booth

123	9/2 Cottenham	(R) INT	3m	13	GF	*mid-div, 7th & in tch whn blnd & u.r. 10th*	U	-
294	1/3 Didmarton	(L) INT	3m	20	G	*chsd ldrs, 6th & outpcd whn blnd 11th, nt rcvr*	8	0

Dead 18

SPECKLED GLEN (Irish) — **I** 55[4]

SPECTACULAR STAR(IRE) ch.g. 8 Good Thyne (USA) - Cailin Alainn by Sweet Revenge — D Branton

104	8/2 Great Treth'	(R) MDO	3m	9	GS	*6s-3s, in tch til wknd 16th, wll btn whn p.u. last*	P	0
740	29/3 Higher Kilw'	(L) MDN	3m	15	GF	*(Jt fav) cls 5th whn blnd & u.r. 6th*	U	-

Placed Novice hurdles; some ability but stamina doubts & not certain to repay supporters; 12

SPEEDY O'DEE (Irish) — I 95P, I 148P, I 219P

SPEIGHTSTOWN BOY (Irish) — I 137P, I 169[4], I 242[4], I 308[3], I 520[4], I 563P, I 611P

SPERRIN VIEW ch.m. 11 Fidel - Baroness Vimy by Barrons Court — Mrs Helen Mobley

1996 1(21),1(20),1(22),2(26),2(22),1(26),2(19)

57	1/2	Kingston Bl'	(L)	LAD	3m	13	GF	*(fav) prom whn u.r. 2nd*	U -
280	23/2	Charing	(L)	LAD	3m	12	G	*(fav) not fluent, trckd ldrs, ld apr 16th til apr last, sn btn*	3 19
779	31/3	Fakenham	(L)	HC	2m 5f 110yds	9	G	*rear most of way.*	5 14
1606	1/6	Dingley	(R)	LAD	3m	13	GF	*raced wd,alwys prom,ld going well 2 out,sn clr, easily*	1 27

Useful Ladies horse; back to best last start; well ridden; sure to win more Ladies; G/F-S 26

SPIKES THE MAN (Irish) — I 23F, I 29P, I 64P, I 95[1], I 282[2]

SPINANS HILL (Irish) — I 405P, I 529[4], I 579[3]

SPINAYAB b.m. 8 King Of Spain - Pallomere by Blue Cashmere — J H Mead

41	1/2	Larkhill	(R)	MDO	3m	13	GF	*alwys bhnd, t.o. 12th, p.u. 3 out*	P 0
177	15/2	Larkhill	(R)	MEM	3m	6	G	*in tch, hit 7th, chsd ldr 11th-nxt, 3rd & outpcd apr 15th*	4 0

Lightly raced; of no real account 0

SPIN CITY (Irish) — I 568F, I 588F

SPIRIT PRINCE b.g. 5 White Prince (USA) - Anascend by Ascendant — Miss C Voyce

87	2/2	Wolverhampt'	(L)	MDO	3m	11	GS	*tried to ref & u.r. 1st*	U -
190	15/2	Erw Lon	(L)	RES	3m	11	G	*unruly pddck, jmpd bdly, t.o. til p.u. 13th*	P 0
263	22/2	Newtown	(L)	MDN	3m	11	G	*pllng, just in tch to 12th, t.o. & p.u. 15th*	P 0
571	16/3	Garnons	(L)	MDN	2 1/2m	13	G	*cls up frm 8th, ev ch 11th, wknd frm nxt*	6 0

Unpleasent so far 0

SPITFIRE JUBILEE b.g. 11 Chief Singer - Altana by Grundy — Mrs Z S Clark

1996 1(23),3(12),2(23),1(22),1(18)

108	8/2	Milborne St'	(L)	MXO	3m	6	GF	*ld/disp to 13th, rdn 15th, disp 3 out, ran on wll frm nxt*	1 21
585	18/3	Fontwell	(R)	HC	2m 3f	7	GF	*(fav) ld to 4th, lost pl 9th, styd on from 2 out.*	3 16
1023	12/4	Badbury Rin'	(L)	OPE	3m	2	F	*(fav) j.w., made all, sn clr, v easy*	1 20
1198	23/4	Andoversford	(R)	OPE	3m	5	F	*chsd ldng pair, rdn 13th, nvr able to chal*	3 17
1358	5/5	Exeter	(R)	HC	2m 7f 110yds	8	G	*ld to 9th, rdn and wknd 3 out.*	5 15

Fair pointer; needs easy 3 miles; finds soft races; front runs; can win again; G-F 20

SPLASHMAN(USA) ch.h. 11 Riverman (USA) - L'extravagante (USA) by Le Fabuleux — John Livock

1187	20/4	Garthorpe	(R)	MEM	3m	9	GF	*last whn ref 1st (twice)*	R -

.. 0

SPLINT b.g. 7 Relkino - Chancer's Last by Foggy Bell — Count K Goess-Saurau

1996 **15(NH),9(NH)**

1386	5/5	Eyton-On-Se'	(L)	MDO	2 1/2m	8	GF	*chsng grp, wll in tch 10th, sn btn, p.u. 2 out*	P 0

Not yet of any account 0

SPLIT SECOND b.g. 8 Damister (USA) - Moment In Time by Without Fear (FR) — Mrs P J Willis

1996 1(21),1(22),1(27)

257	22/2	Newtown	(L)	LAD	3m	12	G	*(fav) trckd ldrs, chsd wnr 3 out, no imp apr last*	2 26
520	15/3	Cothelstone	(L)	LAD	3m	12	GS	*hld up, 5th hlfwy, nvr on trms*	4 18
1017	12/4	Bitterley	(L)	LAD	3m	4	GF	*ld 4th, in cmmnd whn lft clr last*	1 23
1456	11/5	Maisemore P'	(L)	LAD	3m	5	G	*(fav) trckd ldrs, ld 13th, rdn aft 2 out, ran on well*	1 20

Won 7 of last 9; useful Ladies horse; top stable; sure to win more; G/S-G/F 25

SPORADIC VERSE (Irish) — I 241F, I 297[6], I 425[2]

SPORTING SPIRIT br.g. 7 Dunbeath (USA) - Silent Plea by Star Appeal — M P Kneafsey

76	2/2	Market Rase'	(L)	XX	3m	12	GF	*rr & hit 9th, last frm 13th, t.o.*	9 0
350	2/3	Market Rase'	(L)	CON	3m	11	GF	*prom, chsd ldr 4th til f 12th*	F -

Flat winner 94; no real signs in points yet 0

SPRING BEAU (Irish) — I 56P

SPRING CALL(IRE) br.g. 7 Mandalus - Miss Cuckoo by Never Slip — C T Pogson

1996 **P(NH),4(NH),5(NH),1(NH),9(NH),4(NH)**

351	2/3	Market Rase'	(L)	OPE	3m	10	GF	*disp 5th til apr 14th, wknd, t.o. & p.u. last*	P 0
673	23/3	Brocklesby '	(L)	CON	3m	8	GF	*chsd ldr, ld 5th, mstk & rmndr 10th, hdd 2 out, no ext*	3 18

Winning hurdler; ran well in modest race; not seen again; local Confined possible if fit 98 18

SPRINGCOMBE ch.m. 9 Vital Season - Triscombe Stone by Pharaoh Hophra — Mrs E Eames

1996 P(0),4(0),P(0),P(0),4(0),10(0),P(0),U(-),1(13),P(0),U(-),4(14)

100	8/2	Great Treth'	(R)	RES	3m	14	GS	*rear,prog 12th,in tch 14th,wknd 16th,6th & no ch, u.r. 2 out*	U	-
240	22/2	Lemalla	(R)	RES	3m	11	S	*ld, clr early, wknd & hdd 11th, 5th whn mstk 16th, kpt on*	3	0

Won poor race 96; novice-ridden; up against it now; Members best hope 14

SPRINGFIELD LAD ch.g. 11 Golden Love - Barnaderg Lass by Bargello — Miss L Robbins

1996 2(17),1(20),**P(0)**,8(0),4(10)

218	16/2	Heythrop	(R)	INT	3m	21	G	*ldng grp, outpcd 15th, kpt on to tk 2nd flat*	2	20
1147	19/4	Chaddesley '	(L)	OPE	3m	7	GF	*rear, lost tch & rdn 12th, t.o. & p.u. 16th*	P	0
1532	18/5	Mollington	(R)	CON	3m	11	GS	*in tch in rear to 15th, kpt on agn frm 2 out*	5	15
1576	26/5	Chaddesley '	(L)	XX	3m	12	F	*alwys bhnd, t.o. & p.u. 12th*	P	0

Confined winner 96; goes well fresh & quickly loses intererest; hard to find a win now 15

SPRINGFIELD PET b.m. 8 Oedipus Complex - Scarlet Coon by Tycoon II — Mrs C W Pinney

1996 P(0),3(0)

13	25/1	Cottenham	(R)	MDO	3m	10	GF	*n.j.w. alwys bhnd, t.o. & p.u. 3 out*	P	0
137	9/2	Thorpe Lodge	(L)	MEM	3m	9	GF	*alwys rear, t.o. hlfwy, p.u. 11th*	P	0
672	23/3	Brocklesby '	(L)	MEM	3m	1	GF	*walked over*	1	0

Yet to beat another horse; no chance of a Restricted 0

SPRINGFIELD REX ch.g. 6 Oedipus Complex - Scarlet Coon by Tycoon II — Mrs C W Pinney

14	25/1	Cottenham	(R)	MDO	3m	7	GF	*bhnd, t.o. 10th, p.u. 13th*	P	0
141	9/2	Thorpe Lodge	(L)	MDN	3m	12	GF	*mid to rear, kpt on frm 4 out, nrst fin*	4	10
346	2/3	Market Rase'	(L)	MDO	3m	10	GF	*mid-div til b.d. 6th*	B	-
677	23/3	Brocklesby '	(L)	MDN	3m	8	GF	*chsd ldrs, 4th & outpcd 12th, lft poor 3rd 3 out*	3	0
1262	27/4	Southwell P'	(L)	MDO	3m	15	G	*prom, disp 9th til ld 3 out, going wll whn f 2 out*	F	15
1352	4/5	Dingley	(R)	MDO	2 1/2m	9	G	*(fav) chsd ldrs, blnd 11th,lft 2nd & blnd 3 out,btn nxt,p.u. last*	P	0

Steady progress; jumped poorly & disappointed last start; must have chances 98 15

SPRINGFORD (Irish) — I 40^{6}, I 85^{P}, I 260^{3}

SPRING FUN b.g. 14 Over The River (FR) - Russian Fun by Zabeg — David Young

1996 4(13),**P(0)**,4(0),1(16),3(15),2(17),**4(0)**

109	8/2	Milborne St'	(L)	XX	3m	8	GF	*alwys prom, disp 5th til ld 2 out, ct post*	1	18

H/Chase winner 94; novice-ridden; won 2 weak races 96/7; gaqmeMembers only hope if returning in 98 15

SPRING MARATHON(USA) b.g. 7 Topsider (USA) - April Run by Run The Gantlet (USA) — Mrs Nerys Dutfield

455	8/3	Great Treth'	(R)	OPE	3m	8	S	*j.w.,in tch, cls 3rd 14th, slght ld 2 out, hld on wll*	1	24
629	22/3	Kilworthy	(L)	OPE	3m	5	G	*(fav) w.w., trckng ldr, efft til disp last, pshd clr*	1	25
1243	26/4	Bratton Down	(L)	OPE	3m	6	GS	*(fav) bhnd, mstk (ditch), p.u. & dismntd 12th*	P	0

Former useful hurdler; won good races & very useful; stays; problems last start; G-S 26

SPRING SABRE ch.g. 7 Broadsword (USA) - Karafair by Karabas — Mrs K Lawther

1996 P(0),r(-),5(0),r(-),r(-)

60	1/2	Kingston Bl'	(L)	MDN	3m	17	GF	*(bl) mid-div, prog 6th, lft in ld 14th til ran out bnd apr 2 out*	r	-
224	16/2	Heythrop	(R)	MDN	3m	16	G	*(bl) pllng, chsd ldrs to 14th, wknd, 4th & no ch whn p.u. 2 out*	P	0
917	5/4	Larkhill	(R)	MDO	2 1/2m	6	F	*hld up, prog 10th, lft 2nd 4 out, ld apr nxt & ran out*	r	-
1401	5/5	Ashorne	(R)	MDO	3m	15	G	*(bl) lft strt, cont t.o. til p.u. 5th*	P	0
1453	10/5	Kingston Bl'	(L)	MEM	3m	3	G	*reluc to start, cls 3rd til ref 9th*	R	-

Has some ability but a nightmare ride; can only be watched 0

SPRINGTIME MIST (Irish) — I 25^{F}, I 33^{P}, I 109^{P}, I 159^{4}, I 187^{3}, I 271^{P}, I 355^{P}

SPRING TRIX (Irish) — I 125^{P}, I 179^{P}, I 310^{F}

SPRINGVILLA(IRE) b.g. 9 Invited (USA) - Rooske Loraine by Vulgan — C A Green

1996 F(-)

871	31/3	Hackwood Pa'	(L)	MDO	3m	7	F	*(Jt fav) ld 5th, narrow ld whn pckd & u.r. last, unlucky*	F	13
1210	26/4	Woodford	(L)	RES	3m	14	G	*hld up, last hlfwy, prog 15th, kpt on, nvr nrr*	5	12
1486	11/5	Ottery St M'	(L)	MDO	3m	17	G	*(Co fav) hld up, prog 4 out, chal 2 out, no ext aft*	2	15
1568	25/5	Kingston Bl'	(L)	MDO	3m	11	GF	*(fav) not fluent, prom, 3l 2nd whn blnd & u.r. 13th*	U	-

2 completions from 12 starts; good enough but hardly inspires confidence; barely stays 15

SPRITLY LADY (Irish) — I 97^{F}, I 188^{4}, I 217^{2}, I 344^{U}, I 385^{2}, I 407^{P}, I 545^{5}, I 591^{4}

SPRUCEFIELD ch.g. 14 Pamroy - Vacuna by Bargello — M H D Barlow

1996 P(0),8(0),5(0),4(0),5(10),2(19)

55	1/2	Kingston Bl'	(L)	CON	3m	15	GF	*cls up early, wknd aft hlfwy*	8	0
218	16/2	Heythrop	(R)	INT	3m	21	G	*alwys rear, wll bhnd whn p.u. last*	P	0
369	2/3	Mollington	(R)	MEM	3m	13	G	*rear, no ch frm 13th, kpt on frm 3 out*	5	15
446	8/3	Newton Brom'	(R)	CON	3m	8	G	*ld 2nd-3rd, chsd ldrs, ld 7th, hdd 16th, lost 2nd 2 out*	3	18
757	29/3	Kimble	(L)	INT	3m	3	GF	*ld aft 1st-3rd, outpcd 13th, no ch whn lft clr bend apr last*	1	12
1162	20/4	Mollington	(R)	CON	3m	7	GF	*j.w. ld to 13th, styd on to ld apr last, hdd nr fin*	3	17

1448 10/5 Kingston Bl' (L) CON 3m 9 G *chsd ldrs to 11th, wknd rpdly, p.u. 15th* P 0
1531 18/5 Mollington (R) MEM 3m 6 GS *ld to aft 2nd, wth ldr, ld 10th-2 out, styd on to ld flat* 1 14

Revived 97; won weak races (lucky once); novice-ridden; hard to fin d awin at 15;G/F-S 17

SPY'S DELIGHT b.g. 11 Idiot's Delight - Ida Spider by Ben Novus Mrs A R Hewitt
1996 **18(NH)**
93 7/2 Bangor (L) HC 2 1/2m 110yds 11 G *blnd and u.r. 2nd.* U -
330 1/3 Eaton Hall (R) CON 3m 16 GS *f 1st* F -
546 16/3 Garthorpe (R) LAD 3m 11 GF *w.w prog 10th, ld 2 out til hdded & no ex cls hme* 2 18
937 6/4 Tabley (R) CON 3m 10 G *bhnd, kpt on frm 3 out, wnt 3rd flat, nvr nrr* 3 15
1001 12/4 Alpraham (R) MXO 3m 3 GF *(fav) hld up rear, clsd 13th, lft wll clr apr 2 out* 1 18
1347 3/5 Gisburn (R) OPE 3m 8 GF *alwys mid-div, nvr dang* 5 14
1508 17/5 Bangor (L) HC 3m 110yds 12 G *in tch, mstk 5th, hmpd by faller 10th, lost touch from 5 out, t.o..* 8 0

Won 3 awful races 95/7; changed hands after 3rd start; hard to find another win ; G-F 16

SQUERREY ch.g. 6 Royal Vulcan - Dark Rosheen by Rushmere Mrs T C Betts
1996 **P(NH)**
582 16/3 Detling (L) MDN 3m 16 F *rear whn ref 8th* R -
971 6/4 Penshurst (L) MDO 3m 5 F *in tch in rear,3rd & rddn 14th,no ch whn p.u. lame aft 3 out* P 0

No signs yet & problems last start 0

SQUIRES TALE(IRE) b.g. 9 Kemal (FR) - Darren's Heather by Menelek J G Howse
1996 **4(NH),P(NH)**
113 9/2 Wetherby Po' (L) CON 3m 10 GF *chsd ldrs, mstk 4th, fdd frm 4 out, t.o.* 5 0
265 22/2 Duncombe Pa' (R) CON 3m 15 G *mid-div,prog 9th,chsd ldrs 4 out,ld last,hdd & no ext nr fin* 2 20
336 1/3 Corbridge (R) LAD 3m 5f 9 G *prom, drppd rear 13th, kpt on onepcd frm 3 out* 4 18
509 15/3 Dalton Park (R) XX 3m 13 GF *prom, prog to 2nd 16th, qcknd to ld apr last, lft wll clr* 1 20
694 29/3 Stainton (R) CON 3m 11 F *mid-div til outpcd 9th, sn strgglng, wll bhnd whh p.u. 16th* P 0

NH Flat winner 93; tricky; likes things his own way; capable of another win; G-G/F 20

SQUIRRELLSDAUGHTER gr.m. 10 Black Minstrel - Grey Squirell by Golden Gorden J W Beddoes
1996 **U(-),1(20),P(0),2(19),F(-),4(NH),P(NH),5(NH),5(NH)**
849 31/3 Eyton-On-Se' (L) OPE 3m 7 GF *(fav) held up, cls order 7th, 2nd 10th, ev ch 5 out, onepcd* 2 19
1177 20/4 Sandon (L) LAD 3m 4 GF *(fav) hld up, ld 7th til hdd & f last, rmntd* 2 14

Won poor H/chase 96; moderate; mistakes & hard to place now; barely stays; Any 19

SRIVIJAYA b.g. 10 Kris - Princess Pati by Top Ville K Holder
618 22/3 Hutton Rudby (L) OPE 3m 10 GF *plld hrd,disp 6th & ld nxt,hdd & wknd 16th,t.o. & p.u. last* P 0

Winning hurdler; headstrong & little prospects in points 0

STACKIE BOY (Irish) — **I** 180^{P}, **I** 254^{P}, **I** 316^{U}, **I** 365^{P}

STAG FIGHT b.g. 7 Primitive Rising (USA) - Gamewood by Ascertain (USA) Mrs J A Scott
1996 5(16),2(17),2(17),3(0),1(19),4(13),F(-)
255 22/2 Newtown (L) CON 3m 14 G *ld to 5th & frm 12th, clr 3 out, ran on strngly* 1 23
1145 19/4 Chaddesley ' (L) MEM 3m 6 GF *(fav) ld to 2nd, ld aft 13th, sn clr, eased flat* 1 20
1328 3/5 Chaddesley ' (L) OPE 3m 2 GF *(fav) disp til ld 3rd, 4l clr 4 out, rdn nxt,drvn out,dsmntd aft* 1 19

Changed hands; stays well; onepaced; well placed 97 & penalties make life tough next year; G/F-S 25

STAGS ROCK (Irish) — **I** 146^{P}, **I** 238^{4}, **I** 337^{6}, **I** 418^{2}, **I** 536^{2}, **I** 572^{3}, **I** 603^{P}

STAIGUE FORT(IRE) b.g. 9 Torus - Lady Beecham by Laurence O T R P S Norton
1996 **5(NH),3(NH),P(NH),2(NH),2(NH),2(NH)**
232 22/2 Friars Haugh (L) OPE 3m 6 G *ld to 4 out, wknd frm nxt* 3 18
610 22/3 Friars Haugh (L) OPE 3m 6 GF *cls up til lost tch 4 out* 5 12
812 31/3 Tranwell (L) OPE 3m 7 G *ld 3rd-7th, mnly 8l 2nd 8th-2 out, wknd into 3rd last* 3 18
946 6/4 Friars Haugh (L) OPE 3m 5 GF *ld, mstk 6th, hdd 12th, outpcd frm 3 out* 2 19
1335 3/5 Mosshouses (L) OPE 3m 4 F *ld to 4th, made most frm 7th, kpt on wll flat* 1 22

Novice chase winner 95; consistent; stays well; novice-ridden; another modest Open possible;G-F 19

STAINLESS STEEL ch.g. 10 Crawter - Culmleigh Princess by Solar Duke S H Sweetland
1996 2(10),P(0),2(16)
176 15/2 Ottery St M' (L) RES 3m 17 G *rear til p.u. 14th* P 0
307 1/3 Clyst St Ma' (L) MEM 3m 3 HY *ld to 3 out, outpcd aft, fin tired* 2 10
792 31/3 Bishopsleigh (R) RES 3m 13 G *prom early, lost tch 17th, outpcd* 5 0
1152 20/4 Stafford Cr' (R) MEM 3m 4 GF *chsd wnr, effrt 2 out, ev ch whn p.u. last, lame* P 0

Members winner 95; outclassed in competitive races & problem last start 11

STALBRIDGE BILL b.g. 7 El Conquistador - Abridged by Nearly A Hand Mrs J Frankland

1996 1(16),6(10)

7 19/1 Barbury Cas' (L) RES 3m 14 GF *mid-div, prog frm 11th, clsng on ldrs whn blnd & u.r. 3 out* U -
148 9/2 Tweseldown (R) XX 3m 12 GF *mid-div, u.r. 3rd* U -
278 23/2 Charing (L) RES 3m 17 G *hld up, prog 12th, ev ch whn mstk 3 out, ran on* 2 18
488 9/3 Tweseldown (R) RES 3m 10 G *(fav) wth ldr, ld & qcknd clr 12th, unchal aft* 1 20
1463 11/5 Tweseldown (R) MXO 3m 5 GF *chsd ldrs, outpcd frm 12th, no ch frm 15th* 3 16

Improved; not disgraced last start after 2 month break; be placed to win in 98; G/S-G/F 21

STALBRIDGE GOLD ch.m. 8 Vital Season - Abridged by Nearly A Hand C J Barnes
1996 P(0),2(14),1(14),P(0),P(0),3(13)

23 25/1 Badbury Rin' (L) RES 3m 8 GF *hld up,prog 11th, chsd clr ldr 2 out, styd on wll to ld flat* 1 19
112 8/2 Milborne St' (L) INT 3m 4 GF *hld up in 2nd, chal to ld aft 2 out, hdd flat, ran on* 2 18
282 23/2 Charing (L) INT 3m 7 G *w.w. trckd wnr 14th, chal & mstk 16th, not qckn 2 out* 2 17
515 15/3 Larkhill (R) INT 3m 8 GF *in tch in rear to 13th, wll bhnd whn p.u. 3 out* P 0
691 29/3 Little Wind' (R) INT 3m 5 GF *cls up, jmpd slwly 8th & 9th, ev ch 15th, wknd 3 out* 3 12
919 5/4 Larkhill (R) INT 3m 1 F *walked over* 1 0
1025 12/4 Badbury Rin' (L) INT 3m 2 F *(fav) disp to 12th, qcknd to ld cls home, all out* 1 12
1316 3/5 Holnicote (L) MXO 3m 4 G *rear, prog 14th, not qckn frm 3 out* 3 21
1438 10/5 Holnicote (L) LAD 3m 7 G *6th hlfwy, prog 11th, went 2nd 15th, rdn & no ext 2 out* 2 20
1581 26/5 Lifton (R) LAD 3m 7 G *rear, rdn 11th, no prog, p.u. last* P 0

Improved; won 4 placed 7 last 16 starts; rab blinders at Holnicote; connections will find more races ... 20

STALMONTA (Irish) — **I** 271[4], **I** 428[4]

ST AMOUR b.g. 6 Broadsword (USA) - Mini Gazette by London Gazette J J And L M Boulter
1996 U(-),**16(NH)**,**9(NH)**

111 8/2 Milborne St' (L) MDN 3m 8 GF *n.j.w. last til p.u. 4th* P 0

No signs yet; successful stable & may do better 0

STAND ALONE (Irish) — **I** 242[R], **I** 294,

STANFORD BOY b.g. 12 Stanford - Gothic Lady by Godswalk (USA) G N Andrew
1996 5(0),4(15),B(-),4(16),2(18),**5(0)**

56 1/2 Kingston Bl' (L) OPE 3m 13 GF *alwys last pair, t.o. hlfwy* 9 0
255 22/2 Newtown (L) CON 3m 14 G *wll bhnd 5th, t.o. 13th, kpt on aft, nrst fin* 6 11
1063 13/4 Maisemore P' (L) XX 3m 13 GF *chsd ldrs, 6th & wkng whn f 15th* F -
1523 17/5 Bredwardine (R) CON 3m 7 G *rear, last but in tch whn u.r. 11th* U -
1575 26/5 Chaddesley ' (L) OPE 3m 10 F *alwys bhnd, t.o. 12th, p.u. 14th* P 0

Dual winner 94; declined in97 & unlikely to win again 12

STANLEY STEAMER (Irish) — **I** 112[4], **I** 174[2], **I** 267[1]

STANWICK BUCKFAST ch.g. 8 Crested Lark - Stanwick Twister by Netherkelly Mrs S Dean

550 16/3 Garthorpe (R) MDO 3m 11 GF *rr, lsing tch whn p.u. appr 12th* P 0
839 31/3 Thorpe Lodge (L) MDO 3m 15 F *cls up 5th til f 11th* F -
1082 13/4 Guilsborough (L) MDN 3m 14 GF *prog 9th, ld/disp 10-16th, sn outpcd, ran on strngly 2 out* 2 12
1193 20/4 Garthorpe (R) MDO 3m 9 GF *(fav) w.w. prog 10th, 3rd & rdn 15th, wll btn whn lft 2nd 2 out* 2 10

Beaten 11/2 lengths 3rd start; next race too quick? can improve & should find a race 14

STANWICK FARLAP ch.m. 11 St Columbus - Stanwick Twister by Netherkelly T F G Marks
1996 P(0),8(17),3(17),1(18),3(15),1(15),2(16),3(18),2(16)

8 25/1 Cottenham (R) CON 3m 5 GF *(fav) in tch, pshd alng 11th, no dang frm 13th, fin 4th, subs promoted* 3 10
70 2/2 Higham (L) OPE 3m 5 GF *ld to 2nd, ld 7th, jnd 4 out, ev ch nxt, onepcd aft* 3 17
193 15/2 Higham (L) CON 3m 14 G *mid-div, nvr on trms* 6 11
351 2/3 Market Rase' (L) OPE 3m 10 GF *rear, in tch to 12th, bhnd frm 14th* 6 12
835 31/3 Thorpe Lodge (L) INT 3m 7 F *mstly 3rd, ld 8-9th, outpcd by ldng pair 3 out, tk 2nd flat* 2 15
909 5/4 Cottenham (R) MEM 3m 2 F *(fav) ld 5th, rdn & hld on flat* 1 11
1190 20/4 Garthorpe (R) INT 3m 8 GF *ld/disp til ld 12th, hdd apr 3 out, onepcd und pres* 2 15
1279 27/4 Fakenham P-' (L) OPE 3m 7 G *chsd ldrs, 4th & pshd alng 12th, no dang frm 15th* 4 13
1305 3/5 Cottenham (R) MEM 3m 4 F *trckd ldr, ld 7th, rdn 2 out, kpt on onepcd, hdd nr fin* 2 15
1475 11/5 Garthorpe (R) XX 3m 13 GS *chsd ldrs, 4th & rdn apr 3 out, onepcd* 4 11

3 wins 17 places last 26 races; woefully onepaced; Members best hope again 98; Any 15

STANWICK FORT b.m. 8 Belfort (FR) - Allez Stanwick by Goldhill Mrs Helen Dickson
1996 F(-),**P(NH)**

814 31/3 Tranwell (L) MDO 3m 9 G *ld 3rd til ran out nxt* r -
996 12/4 Tranwell (L) MDO 3m 8 F *cls up,ld 6th til ran wd aft 11th & dmtd to last,f 13th* F -
1167 20/4 Hexham Poin' (L) MEM 3m 5 GF *n.j.w. ld 3rd til ran wd & hdd 2 out, not rcvr* 2 0
1514 17/5 Corbridge (R) MDO 3m 17 GS *prom whn u.r. 2nd* U -

Lightly raced; mistakes; unlucky in poor Members; below normal winning standard 11

STARCHY'S QUEST b.g. 5 Starch Reduced - Karousa Girl by Rouser Robert Barr

1996 **19(NH),P(NH)**

68	2/2	Higham	(L)	MEM	3m	4	GF	*pllng, ran out 2nd, cont, mstk & u.r. 4th*	U	-

No ability under rules; an entertaining debut 0

STAR FLYER (Irish) — **I** 178^{F}, **I** 250^{4}, **I** 292^{4}, **I** 366^{P}, **I** 432^{5}, **I** 504^{U}

STAR HAND (Irish) — **I** 385^{P}, **I** 459^{P}, **I** 474^{4}, **I** 515^{P}

STAR LEA ch.g. 7 Scorpio (FR) - Rose Bridges by Calpurnius — B Stonehouse

36	26/1	Alnwick	(L)	MDO	3m	15	G	*chsd ldr 7th til mstk 11th, lft 2nd agn 2 out, styd on flat*	2	15
136	9/2	Alnwick	(L)	MDO	3m	16	G	*(Jt fav) prom, ld 3 out, steadied last, hld on*	1	0
338	1/3	Corbridge	(R)	RES	3m	10	G	*chsd ldrs, outpcd 13th*	4	0
416	8/3	Dalston	(R)	RES	3m	12	GS	*trckd ldrs, prog 14th, ld & f 2 out*	F	17
729	29/3	Alnwick	(L)	RES	3m	10	F	*alwys prom, handy 4th frm 13th, no imp ldrs aft*	4	16

Missed 96; Improved; consistent; likes Alnwick; Restricted should come; G/S-F 17

STARLIGHT FOUNTAIN (Irish) — **I** 21^{F}, **I** 108^{F}, **I** 205^{P}, **I** 358^{2}, **I** 427^{P}, **I** 511^{P}

STAR OATS ch.g. 11 Oats - Starproof by Comedy Star (USA) — Hayden Phillips

1996 **U(NH),P(NH),P(NH),U(NH)**

6	19/1	Barbury Cas'	(L)	LAD	3m	13	GF	*ld till blnd & u.r. 2nd*	U	-
57	1/2	Kingston Bl'	(L)	LAD	3m	13	GF	*cls up til u.r. 10th*	U	-
144	9/2	Tweseldown	(R)	OPE	3m	9	GF	*pllng, trckd ldrs, ld 11th, hdd apr last, no ext*	2	21
288	27/2	Ludlow	(R)	HC	3m	8	G	*hit 3rd, ld 5th, soon clr, hit 9th, hdd apr 5 out, wknd quickly, p.u. before next, lame.*	P	0
588	19/3	Towcester	(R)	HC	2 3/4m	4	GF	*held up, hdwy to ld 2 out, rdn out and styd on well.*	1	17
679	26/3	Ascot	(R)	HC	2m 3f 110yds	9	G	*started slowly, held up in last pl, n.j.w., taild of when p.u. before 2 out.*	P	0
1099	19/4	Stratford	(L)	HC	2m 5f 110yds	14	G	*prom, hit 10th, blnd next, soon wknd, p.u. before 4 out.*	P	0

Won 2 poor H/chases 96-7; bad jumper; best below 3 miles; tough to find another win now; G-F 19

STAR OF ANNAGH (Irish) — **I** 335^{P}, **I** 533^{P}

STAR TRAVELLER b.g. 6 Norwick (USA) - Star Of Parnassus by Star Appeal — Mrs Richard Strachan

549	16/3	Garthorpe	(R)	MDO	3m	16	GF	*t.o. frm 5th til p.u. 3 out*	P	0
775	29/3	Dingley	(R)	MDO	2m 5f	10	G	*2nd/disp til f 5 out*	F	-
1083	13/4	Guilsborough	(L)	MDN	3m	15	GF	*rear, lost tch 13th, sn t.o., styd on frm 2 out*	6	0
1205	26/4	Clifton On '	(L)	CON	3m	13	GS	*w.w. 8th at 9th, ran on 6 out, 5th 3 out, ld last, hld on*	1	19
1350	4/5	Dingley	(R)	MEM	3m	5	G	*(fav) rcd wd, disp to 4th, lft 2nd 12th, lft wll clr 15th*	1	10

Won modest races; novice-ridden; sold & won Novice/chase after 17

STATE MEDLAR ro.g. 6 Pragmatic - Lizzie The Twig by Precipice Wood — Mrs R J Horton

792	31/3	Bishopsleigh	(R)	RES	3m	13	G	*alwys mid-div, btn 6th whn ran out last*	r	-

Only learning on debut; looks sure to improve 10

STATFOLD SOLVA gr.m. 8 Oats - Statfold Pride by Precipice Wood — Mrs Pat Hewitt

927	6/4	Garthorpe	(R)	RES	3m	9	GF	*prom to 6th, sn bhnd, t.o. & p.u. 10th*	P	0
1187	20/4	Garthorpe	(R)	MEM	3m	9	GF	*chsd ldrs til rdn & wknd aft 11th, p.u. nxt*	P	0

No signs of ability 0

STATION EXPRESS(IRE) b.g. 9 Rusticaro (FR) - Vallee D'O (FR) by Polyfoto — Miss Laura J Horsey

1996 **P(NH),8(NH),7(NH),13(NH),9(NH)**

454	8/3	Great Treth'	(R)	LAD	3m	7	S	*towrds rear, btn 5th whn p.u. apr 15th*	P	0
555	16/3	Ottery St M'	(L)	LAD	3m	10	G	*prom to 12th, lsng tch whn f 15th*	F	-
864	31/3	Kingston St'	(R)	LAD	3m	6	F	*alwys rear, rnng on in 4th whn f last*	F	-

Winning selling hurdler; not disgraced in poor Ladies last start but not threatening to win 12

STATION MAN (Irish) — **I** 30^{P}, **I** 156^{P}, **I** 272^{P}, **I** 455^{3}, **I** 549^{4}, **I** 580^{P}, **I** 592^{5}

STAYS FRESH b.g. 7 Gambler's Cup (USA) - Cassandra Moor Vii by Damsire Unregistered — D Westwood

1996 P(0),U(-),7(0),5(10),5(0),3(0)

252	22/2	Brocklesby '	(L)	MDO	3m	9	G	*alwys last trio, t.o. 6 out, p.u. 4 out*	P	0

Well beaten when placed 96; vanished quickly in 97 & plenty to prove yet 10

STAY WEST (Irish) — **I** 165^{F}

STEADY MAN gr.g. 6 Belfort (FR) - Fair Kitty by Saucy Kit — Mrs J D Bulman

161	15/2	Lanark	(R)	MDO	2m 5f	14	G	*u.r. 4th*	U	-
230	22/2	Friars Haugh	(L)	RES	3m	15	G	*rear til p.u. 11th*	P	0
417	8/3	Dalston	(R)	MDO	2 1/2m	11	GS	*s.s. rear til crshd thro wing 4th*	r	-
564	16/3	Lanark	(R)	MDO	2 1/2m	13	GS	*ld til 5th, sn wknd, p.u. 3 out*	P	0

Very unsteady so far 0

STEADY WOMAN (Irish) — **I** 80P, **I** 195P

STEDE QUARTER b.g. 10 Cruise Missile - Dragon Lass by Cheval — Mrs S Dench

1996 U(-),3(20),1(18),2(14),4(0),F(-),1(17),P(0),4(14),2(15),**1(18)**,**P(0)**

27	26/1	Marks Tey	(L)	OPE	3m	6	GF	*trckd ldrs, ev ch 3 out, ld brfly nxt, onepcd aft*	3	23
91	6/2	Huntingdon	(R)	HC	3m	10	G	*chsd ldrs, ld after 12th to next, wknd quickly after 5 out. t.o..*	4	10
281	23/2	Charing	(L)	OPE	3m	12	G	*prom, ld 12th, made rest, rdn clr apr last*	1	22
579	16/3	Detling	(L)	OPE	4m	9	F	*prssd ldr,ld 22nd,hdd 25th,2nd aft,tired & whn blndrd last*	2	20
683	29/3	Charing	(L)	OPE	3m	5	F	*(fav) alwys cls, lft in ld 11th, ran on wll whn chal 3 out*	1	21
967	6/4	Penshurst	(L)	OPE	3m	4	F	*(fav) trcks ldr, lft disp 12th til blndrd 14th & p.u. (dead)*	P	0

Dead **22**

STEELE JUSTICE ch.g. 13 Avocat - Strandhill by Bargello — W Manners

1996 2(20),1(21),5(15)

994	12/4	Tranwell	(L)	LAD	3m	5	F	*ld 8th til jnd 10th, hdd 3 out, outpcd & 3l down nxt*	2	17
1171	20/4	Hexham Poin'	(L)	LAD	3m	3	GF	*(fav) made all, mostly 2l up frm 16th, kpt on wll flat*	1	17

Formerly useful; lightly raced now; well ridden & still beats 2nd raters; should find a win at 14 19

STEEL ICE ch.g. 9 Broadsword (USA) - Iced Tea by Pappatea — Mrs A J McVay

1996 P(0)

196	15/2	Higham	(L)	MDO	3m	12	G	*cls up, blnd 7th, wth ldrs 15th, ev ch & rdn 2 out, no ext*	2	14

Just beaten in poor race; hardly ever runs & time passing him by 13

STEEL STREET(IRE) b.g. 7 The Parson - Lady Siobhan by Laurence O — E J Parrott

1996 5(0)

876	1/4	Upton-On-Se'	(R)	MEM	3m	7	GF	*t.o. 4th, btn 3 fncs*	4	0

Rarely runs & yet to beat another horse 0

STEEL VALLEY(IRE) ch.m. 9 Orchestra - Caddy Girl by Avocat — T White

1996 3(0),F(-),P(0),2(10),P(0),S(-),3(12)

1131	19/4	Bonvilston	(R)	MEM	3m	6	G	*t.o. frm 5th til p.u. 12th*	P	0
1231	26/4	Pyle	(R)	MDO	3m	7	GS	*ld 5-7th, wknd 13th, t.o.*	5	0

Placed in poor races 96; stamina doubts; finished early 97 & more needed 10

STEFFI LIZ (Irish) — **I** 355³, **I** 493P, **I** 575¹

STELINJO (Irish) — **I** 23P, **I** 29P, **I** 65⁶, **I** 181P, **I** 268⁴, **I** 343², **I** 459³, **I** 529²

STELZER b.g. 11 Carlingford Castle - Gabis Lady by Reformed Character — A G Bonas

265	22/2	Duncombe Pa'	(R)	CON	3m	15	G	*mid-div, wknd 10th, t.o. & p.u. aft 12th*	P	0
1247	26/4	Easingwold	(L)	CON	3m	9	GS	*mid-div, wknd 12th, p.u. 3 out*	P	0

Restricted winner 94; lightly raced now & shows nothing now 13

STEPHENS PET ch.g. 14 Piaffer (USA) - Mrs Stephens by Master Stephen — Dr P P Brown

1996 1(23),1(24),1(24),1(23)

329	1/3	Eaton Hall	(R)	LAD	3m	10	GS	*(fav) 4th gng easily whn rddr k/o in mid air 10th*	U	-
702	29/3	Upper Sapey	(R)	LAD	3m	4	GF	*(fav) made all, drew clr frm 3 out, eased flat*	1	20
1161	20/4	Mollington	(R)	LAD	3m	3	GF	*(fav) ld 5th, drew clr aft 2 out, easily*	1	23
1535	18/5	Mollington	(R)	LAD	3m	6	GS	*ld 5th-3 out, eased whn btn apr last, collapsed & died aft*	2	20

Dead. **25**

STEP IN LINE (Irish) — **I** 321⁴, **I** 423¹

STERLING BUCK(USA) b.g. 10 Buckfinder (USA) - Aged (USA) by Olden Times — D J Clapham

1996 2(14),4(10),2(15),1(16),1(20)

218	16/2	Heythrop	(R)	INT	3m	21	G	*in tch to 11th, wll in rear whn p.u. 2 out*	P	0
255	22/2	Newtown	(L)	CON	3m	14	G	*(fav) cls up, prssd wnr 12th-14th, onepcd aft*	3	19
434	8/3	Upton-On-Se'	(R)	INT	3m	4	G	*2nd/3rd til rdn 11th, ev ch whn ptchd lndg 14th, wknd rpdly*	4	0
572	16/3	Garnons	(L)	INT	3m	13	G	*mid-div, effrt apr 14th, no prog frm nxt*	5	0
704	29/3	Upper Sapey	(R)	INT	3m	4	GF	*4l last but ch 17th, ran on strgly to take 2nd flat*	2	18
959	6/4	Pantyderi	(L)	INT	3m	2	F	*(fav) disp to 3 out, in comm aft, easy*	1	16
1064	13/4	Maisemore P'	(L)	CON	3m	13	GF	*prog 9th, 4th & rdn 11th, sn wknd, p.u. 2 out*	P	0
1181	20/4	Lydstep	(L)	INT	3m	3	GF	*ld 5-7th, ld 11th, clr 2 out, easily*	1	16
1363	5/5	Pantyderi	(L)	OPE	3m	4	G	*chsd ldr, disp 11th, 3rd & btn last*	3	13
1560	24/5	Bassaleg	(R)	OPE	3m	7	G	*(fav) prom, wth wnr 12th-nxt, sn outpcd, no imp frm 15th*	2	16
1601	31/5	Bassaleg	(R)	MXO	3m	2	F	*(fav) chsd rival, rmndr 11th, ld nxt, sn drew clr*	1	17
1611	7/6	Umberleigh	(L)	OPE	3m	8	F	*ld to 8th & aft 12th-3 out, sn btn*	3	0

Likes things his own way; finds soft late season races; should win again; well ridden; G-F 20

ST GREGORY b.g. 9 Ardross - Crymlyn by Welsh Pageant — A Howland Jackson

1996 6(14),2(20),5(17),1(22),1(20),3(14),1(24),1(20),2(24),U(-),1(20)

26	26/1	Marks Tey	(L)	LAD	3m	8	GF	*(fav) (bl) ld to 2nd, prom, rdn & blnd 2 out, onepcd aft*	3	22
64	1/2	Horseheath	(R)	LAD	3m	7	GF	*(fav) (bl) mstks, ld 2nd-6th, chsd wnr 13th-3 out, kpt on*	2	20

195 15/2 Higham (L) LAD 3m 14 G *mstks, cls up, clr wth ldr 16th, ld nxt, drvn clr, wll rdn* 1 23
272 22/2 Ampton (R) LAD 3m 7 G *(fav) (bl) chsd wnr frm 7th, 4l down 16th, hd rdn nxt, styd on run in* 2 21
442 8/3 Higham (L) LAD 3m 8 G *(bl) disp to 3rd, 2nd agn 11th, chsd wnr, chal last, not qckn* 2 23
500 15/3 Ampton (R) LAD 3m 4 GF *(fav) (bl) ld to 2nd, chsd wnr, ld 13th til blnd & u.r. nxt* U -
709 29/3 High Easter (L) LAD 3m 2 F *(fav) (bl) made all, blnd & rmdr 13th, j.s. nxt, clr 2 out,eased nr fin* 1 20
800 31/3 Marks Tey (L) LAD 3m 3 F *(fav) made all, sight mstk 12th, rddn clr apr last, easily* 1 21
1116 19/4 Higham (L) LAD 3m 2 GF *(fav) (bl) made all, eased clr frm 12th, eased flat* 1 20
1280 27/4 Fakenham P-' (L) LAD 3m 6 G *(fav) (bl) prom, mstk 6th, ld 12-15th, ld 3 out, drew clr frm nxt* 1 20
1308 3/5 Cottenham (R) LAD 3m 5 F *(fav) (bl) made all, clr apr last, pshd out flat* 1 20
1378 5/5 Northaw (L) LAD 3m 5 F *(fav) (bl) w.r.s. lst 30l, ld 8-10th, agn 15th, rdn 3 out, hdd flat* 2 20

Won 11 of last 23 races; tough; hard ride; mistakes; best L/H; blinkers; sure to win more; Any 22

STICKWITHTHEHAND b.g. 6 Nearly A Hand - Royal Rushes by Royal Palace Mrs J Sidebottom
1996 **7(NH)**
403 8/3 Llanfrynach (R) INT 3m 8 G *rear, p.u. 11th* P 0

Not yet of any account 0

STIFF DRINK ch.g. 6 Starch Reduced - Karousa Girl by Rouser K A Williams
409 8/3 Llanfrynach (R) MDN 3m 12 G *clr ldr til ran out 5th* r -
719 29/3 Llanvapley (L) MDN 3m 14 GF *pllng in rear, rpd prog frm 6th, lft in ld aft 8th,f 10th* F -
1010 12/4 St Hilary (R) MDN 3m 10 GF *2nd til ld 11th, f 14th* F -
1229 26/4 Pyle (R) MDO 3m 11 GS *disp whn blnd & u.r. 1st* U -
1318 3/5 Bonvilston (R) MEM 3m 9 G *ld til ran out apr 7th* r -

Thats what his jockeys need at present 0

STILL IN BUSINESS b.g. 9 Don Enrico (USA) - Mill Miss by Typhoon R G Williams
1996 2(30),**2(25)**,**3(19)**,**5(15)**,1(26),F(-),1(25),**3(21)**,1(24),1(28)
5 19/1 Barbury Cas' (L) OPE 3m 11 GF *(fav) prog & 3rd hlfwy, ld 2 out, drvn out flat* 1 25
42 1/2 Larkhill (R) MXO 3m 7 GF *(fav) mstk 1st, hld up, prog 7th, ld 15th, clr 2 out, eased flat* 1 29
494 13/3 Cheltenham (L) HC 3 1/4m 110yds 18 G *u.r. 1st.* U -
690 29/3 Little Wind' (R) OPE 3m 4 GF *(fav) hld up, ld 10th, drew clr apr 3 out, eased flat* 1 28
1147 19/4 Chaddesley ' (L) OPE 3m 7 GF *(fav) hld up,prog 10th,ev ch 4 out,wknd rpdly nxt,crawld last* 4 16

Useful pointer; top stable; fences problem in H/chases; not stay last start; win more 98; G/S-F 28

STILLMORE BUSINESS ch.g. 6 Don Enrico (USA) - Mill Miss by Typhoon R G Williams
1996 P(0),U(-),U(-),P(0),3(15)
513 15/3 Larkhill (R) MDO 3m 10 GF *(fav) trckd ldr 7th, ld aft 4 out, jnd apr last, rdn & styd on wll* 1 17

Improving; winners behind when scoring; not seen again; should upgrade if fit 98; top stable; G/S-G/F 17

STILLTODO gr.m. 10 Grey Ghost - River Sirene by Another River W R Wilson
1996 P(0),4(0),1+(13),**r(-)**,**4(19)**,**3(10)**,**3(18)**
1410 5/5 Witton Cast' (R) MEM 3m 3 GS *(fav) made all, qcknd clr 2 out, pshd out* 1 15
1415 9/5 Stratford (L) HC 3m 6 G *ld to 14th, soon wknd, tailed of.* 5 0

Dead-heated in poor race 96; front runs; safe; managed an annual win 95-7; can maintain if fit 98 18

ST JULIEN(IRE) b.g. 7 Le Bavard (FR) - Johns County by Crash Course J J And L M Boulter
1996 P(0),9(0),4(0),4(0)
1583 26/5 Lifton (R) MDO 3m 11 G *nvr trbld ldrs, t.o. 6th, p.u. 12th* P 0

Promise in 96; very late appearing 97 & unable to progress; successful stable & can do better 12

ST LARRY (Irish) — I 3^{P}

ST LAYCAR b.g. 12 St Columbus - Lady Carinya by Heswall Honey D R Greig
1996 6(15)
579 16/3 Detling (L) OPE 4m 9 F *alwys rear, rddn & btn 19th, p.u. 22nd & dismntd* P 0
1115 19/4 Higham (L) OPE 3m 4 GF *4th & off pace, went 3rd at 10th, rdn 12th, no imp ldrs* 3 0
1442 10/5 Peper Harow (L) MEM 3m 4 GF *trckd ldrs, 3rd & rdn 13th, btn 3 out, p.u. last, lame* P 0

Formerly useful; lightly raced now & problems last start; most unlikely to win again 12

STONEYACRE (Irish) — I 99^{P}

STONEYISLAND(IRE) b.g. 8 Ovac (ITY) - Solinika M J Bloom
69 2/2 Higham (L) MDO 3m 8 GF *prom, lft in ld 2nd, hdd nxt, prom whn mstk & u.r. 13th* U -
196 15/2 Higham (L) MDO 3m 12 G *mid-div, lost plc 11th, rear & p.u. 3 out* P 0
504 15/3 Ampton (R) MEM 3m 2 GF *ld til appr 3 out, sn wknd* 2 0
712 29/3 High Easter (L) MDO 3m 4 F *ld to 10th, 3rd & wkng 3 out* 3 0
1283 27/4 Fakenham P-' (L) MDO 3m 9 G *ld to 14th, sn wknd, p.u. 3 out* P 0

Ex Irish; only beat one horse in 97; does not stay & no real prospects 0

STONEY PIPER (Irish) — I 56^{P}, I 223^{P}, I 385^{4}, I 405^{P}, I 452^{P}, I 478^{1}, I 495^{P}

STONY MISSILE br.m. 8 Cruise Missile - Stonybridge by Perhapsburg — S C Horn

1996 **P(NH),11(NH)**

105	8/2	Great Treth'	(R) MDO 3m	15	GS	*mstks, alwys wll bhnd, t.o. 11th, p.u. 16th*	P	0
243	22/2	Lemalla	(R) MDO 3m	12	S	*sn bhnd, jmpd slwly, t.o. whn p.u. last*	P	0
458	8/3	Great Treth'	(R) MDO 3m	15	S	*ld til 10th, lost plc 12th, bhnd, p.u. 2 out*	P	0
624	22/3	Kilworthy	(L) MEM 3m	7	G	*blndrd & u.r. 7th*	U	-
740	29/3	Higher Kilw'	(L) MDN 3m	15	GF	*ld 1st, lost plc 8th, t.o. frm 10th*	5	0
1110	19/4	Flete Park	(R) LAD 3m	9	GF	*n.j.w. in rear, t.o. & p.u. 12th*	P	0
1343	3/5	Flete Park	(R) MDO 3m	13	G	*5th hlfwy, wknd 15th, t.o.*	7	0

Jumps poorly; no stamina; unpromising 0

STORM ALIVE(IRE) b.g. 6 Electric - Gaileen by Boreen (FR) — Mrs Richard Arthur

1996 P(0),P(0)

37	26/1	Alnwick	(L) MDO 3m	15	G	*alwys wll bhnd, t.o. & p.u. 15th*	P	0
135	9/2	Alnwick	(L) MDO 3m	12	G	*bhnd, prog 9th, lost tch 11th, no dang aft*	6	0
334	1/3	Corbridge	(R) MEM 3m	7	G	*chsd ldr, disp 9th til lft clr nxt, wknd & hdd last*	2	15
418	8/3	Dalston	(R) MDO 2 1/2m	10	GS	*(Jt fav) trckd ldrs, hrd rdn & effrt aft 3 out, styd on to ld nr fin*	1	15
972	7/4	Kelso	(L) HC 3m 1f	12	GF	*chsd ldrs, hit 9th and soon bhnd, blnd 11th, soon t.o..*	6	0
1169	20/4	Hexham Poin'	(L) RES 3m	9	GF	*disp 3rd-9th, cls up til wknd apr 3 out, p.u. last*	P	0

Improved; won modest short Maiden; stamina doubts & much more needed for Restricted 14

STORM DAI FENCE(IRE) b.m. 5 Glacial Storm (USA) - Firing by Tarboosh (USA) — D Rees

963	6/4	Pantyderi	(L) MDN 3m	6	F	*alwys in rear & t.o. whn p.u. 10th*	P	0
1009	12/4	St Hilary	(R) MDN 3m	11	GF	*twrs rear til p.u. 3 out*	P	0
1229	26/4	Pyle	(R) MDO 3m	11	GS	*rear, pshd alng 10th, went poor 3rd 13th, no dang*	3	0
1368	5/5	Pantyderi	(L) MDO 3m	8	G	*mid-div, rpd prog frm 15th, styd on wll flat*	3	12
1473	11/5	Erw Lon	(L) MDO 3m	13	GS	*(Co fav) rear, jmpd novicey, p.u. 12th*	P	0

Novice-ridden; only beaten 4 lengths penultimate race; chances if jumping better 98 12

STORMEY TUNE (Irish) — I 332^{2}, I 517^{3}

STORMHEAD ch.g. 9 Move Off - Young Lamb by Sea Hawk II — A C R Stubbs

1996 U(-)

328	1/3	Eaton Hall	(R) OPE 3m	6	GS	*f 1st*	F	-
763	29/3	Whittington	(L) CON 3m	9	S	*alwys cls up, 1l 2nd whn f 16th*	F	-

Winning hurdler; running well last start but has'nt managed a clear round yet; best watched 14

STORMHILL RECRUIT b.g. 7 Welsh Captain - Miss Oxstall's by The Brianstan — Mrs A Price

1996 F(-),U(-),5(0),3(10)

366	2/3	Garnons	(L) MDO 2 1/2m	13	GS	*ld to 3rd, cls up & ev ch 12th, kpt on onepcd frm nxt*	3	11
407	8/3	Llanfrynach	(R) MDN 3m	11	G	*(fav) trckd ldrs, disp 3 out, lft in ld apr nxt, all out*	1	14
568	16/3	Garnons	(L) CON 3m	12	G	*chsd ldrs, rdn & outpcd frm 14th*	6	13
753	29/3	Brampton Br'	(R) RES 3m	9	GF	*cls 7th at 11th, lost tch 15th, p.u. aft nxt*	P	0
1013	12/4	Bitterley	(L) CON 3m	14	GF	*rear frm 11th, no ch frm 14th*	7	0
1237	26/4	Brampton Br'	(R) RES 3m	13	G	*in tch til outpcd 13th, t.o. & p.u. last*	P	0
1392	5/5	Cursneh Hill	(L) RES 3m	6	GF	*drppd last 8th, strgglng 11th, p.u. 13th*	P	0

Fortunate to win poor Maiden; struggling badly now & well short of Restricted class 12

STORMING LADY b.m. 7 Strong Gale - Drom Lady by Royalty — Mike Roberts

1282	27/4	Fakenham P-'	(L) MDO 3m	8	G	*(fav) cls up whn bmpd & u.r. 2nd*	U	-
1479	11/5	Garthorpe	(R) MDO 3m	12	GS	*(fav) trckd ldrs 8th, ld 11th, clr 3 out, styd on, comf*	1	15
1502	16/5	Folkestone	(R) HC 2m 5f	10	G	*alwys going well, trckd ldr 10th, ld after next, drew well clr after 3 out, impressive.*	1	31

Hugely impressive; beat nothing but fast time; exciting prospect; sure to win more 30

STORMING ROY b.g. 7 Strong Gale - Book Token by Proverb — J G Nicholson

1996 **F(NH),6(NH)**

276	22/2	Ampton	(R) MDO 3m	12	G	*prom, ld 13th-2 out, kpt on wll*	2	14
452	8/3	Newton Brom'	(R) MDN 3m	9	G	*(fav) ld 4th-7th, ld aft 15th, drew clr 2 out*	1	16
548	16/3	Garthorpe	(R) RES 3m	10	GF	*(Jt fav) ld 4th, made most aft, blnd & hdded 3 out, ld last, styd on*	1	18
769	29/3	Dingley	(R) CON 3m	14	G	*mid-div, prog 9th, 3rd 5 out-2 out, no ext*	4	17
1077	13/4	Guilsborough	(L) CON 3m	16	GF	*trckd ldrs, outpcd & mstk 13th, no prog til kpt on frm 2 out*	4	18

Decent recruit; stays; game; not disgraced in Confineds; can win one 98; G-G/F so far 20

STORMIN TO GLORY (Irish) — I 485^{P}

STORM MAN (Irish) — I 197^{P}, I 568^{P}

STORM OF PROTEST (Irish) — I 295^{4}

STORM REEF (Irish) — I 135^{P}

STORMY FASHION b.g. 10 Strong Gale - Belle Chanel by Moyrath Jet — G F Wheeler

1996 P(0),U(-),P(0),F(-),**P(0)**

487	9/3	Tweseldown	(R)	MDO	3m	12	G	*sn wll bhnd, t.o. whn blnd 11th & p.u.*	P	0
934	6/4	Charlton Ho'	(L)	MDO	3m	10	G	*chsd ldr to 9th, sn outpcd, t.o. 3 out*	3	0
1373	5/5	Cotley Farm	(L)	MDO	3m	6	GF	*7s-4s, ld/disp til wnt clr 14th, ran on wll frm 3 out*	1	15
1494	14/5	Cothelstone	(L)	RES	3m	11	GF	*jmpd rght, ld to 14th, onepcd aft*	3	14
1552	24/5	Mounsey Hil'	(R)	RES	3m	12	G	*tubed, ld to 5th, ld 11-16th, wknd rpdly, p.u. 3 out*	P	0
1613	7/6	Umberleigh	(L)	RES	3m	13	F	*hld up, sn wll bhnd, no prog hlfwy, poor 5th & p.u. last*	P	0

Won weak race; headstrong & has problems; much more needed for Restricted 14

STRAIGHT ANGLE (Irish) — **I** 239P

STRAIGHT BAT b.g. 14 Dragonara Palace (USA) - Camdamus by Mandamus — Miss S Sadler

1996 3(0),3(0),P(0)

816	31/3	Paxford	(L)	MEM	3m	3	F	*carried 14st, ld til f 15th*	U	-

No longer of any account 0

STRAIGHT TOUCH b.m. 5 Touch Of Grey - Straight Gin by Ginger Boy — A J Taylor

283	23/2	Charing	(L)	MDO	3m	16	G	*alwys rear, t.o. & p.u. 12th*	P	0

No signs on debut 0

STRANGE SECRET (Irish) — **I** 10P, **I** 45P, **I** 483, **I** 1891

STRATA RIDGE (Irish) — **I** 59P, **I** 101P

STRATHFIELD LASS (Irish) — **I** 150P, **I** 186P, **I** 411P

STRATTON PARK (Irish) — **I** 520P, **I** 563P, **I** 570F, **I** 601P

STRAWBERRY LAMP (Irish) — **I** 411P, **I** 497F, **I** 590P

STRETCHIT b.g. 7 Full Extent (USA) - Snippet by Ragstone — G W Penfold

1996 **F(NH),P(NH),9(NH),6(NH)**

54	1/2	Wadebridge	(L)	MDO	3m	13	G	*rear til gd prog frm 5 out, nvr nrr*	4	11
103	8/2	Great Treth'	(R)	MDO	3m	9	GS	*n.j.w. in chsng grp, no prog frm 16th*	4	0
458	8/3	Great Treth'	(R)	MDO	3m	15	S	*alwys mid-div*	5	0
794	31/3	Bishopsleigh	(R)	MDO	3m	12	G	*in tch, 4th at 10th, chal 3 out, no ext aft last*	2	14
1095	16/4	Hockworthy	(L)	MDN	3m	11	GF	*hld up, went mod 3rd at 9th, no imp 1st pair aft*	3	0
1246	26/4	Bratton Down	(L)	MDO	3m	16	GS	*alwys cls up, disp ld 12th til lft in ld 2 out, ran on wll*	1	15
1395	5/5	High Bickin'	(R)	RES	3m	9	G	*handy, rmndr 15th, hdwy nxt, chal und pres 3 out, styd on*	2	15
1481	11/5	Ottery St M'	(L)	CON	3m	12	G	*mid-div, prog 14th, ev ch 3 out, outpcd frm nxt*	5	17
1551	24/5	Mounsey Hil'	(R)	RES	3m	13	G	*mid-div, prog to ld apr 15th, hdd 2 out, ld last, hdd post*	2	19

Ex Novice/chaser; safe; consistent but onepaced; knocking on the door & should find Restricted 17

STRIDE TO GLORY(IRE) b.g. 6 Superpower - Damira (FR) by Pharly (FR) — R Coward

1996 P(0),3(0),1(14),U(-),10(0),8(0)

251	22/2	Brocklesby '	(L)	RES	3m	16	G	*alwys rear div, outpcd 6 out*	8	0
348	2/3	Market Rase'	(L)	RES	3m	13	GF	*chsd ldrs, blnd & u.r. 8th*	U	-
424	8/3	Charm Park	(L)	RES	3m	12	GF	*prom, ld 2 out-last, not qckn*	4	15
616	22/3	Hutton Rudby	(L)	RES	3m	14	GF	*rear, lost tch 3 out*	7	10
856	31/3	Charm Park	(L)	RES	3m	8	F	*ld to 4th, ld 10-13th, onepcd, lkd 3rd*	4	17
1068	13/4	Whitwell-On'	(R)	RES	3m	12	G	*(bl) mid-div, outpcd 11th, sn lost tch, t.o. & f hvly last*	F	-

Maiden winner 96; inconsistent & suspect; likes Charm Park; more needed for Restricted;G-F 15

STRONG ACCOUNT(IRE) ch.g. 8 Strong Statement (USA) - Clare's Hansel by Prince Hansel — Andrew Mobley

1996 U(-),P(0),U(-)

374	2/3	Mollington	(R)	MDN	3m	14	G	*ld til ran out thro wing 6th*	r	-
927	6/4	Garthorpe	(R)	RES	3m	9	GF	*ld to 2nd, cls up, ev ch 4 out, outpcd apr nxt*	3	11
1084	13/4	Guilsborough	(L)	MDN	3m	11	GF	*(Jt fav) ld to 2nd, prom, chsd ldr 15th, wknd 2 out*	3	0
1209	26/4	Clifton On '	(L)	MDO	3m	16	GS	*made most, jnd 2 out, just outpcd flat*	2	15
1401	5/5	Ashorne	(R)	MDO	3m	15	G	*(fav) ld 6-9th & frm 14th, hrd rdn last, hdd nr fin*	2	15

Much improved; tries hard but onepaced; reliability should see him home one day 15

STRONG AMBITION (Irish) — **I** 7P, **I** 48P, **I** 378P, **I** 4452, **I** 5583, **I** 564,

STRONG CHAIRMAN(IRE) br.g. 6 Strong Gale - The Furnituremaker by Mandalus — J A Keighley

1996 F(-),1(18),3(21)

178	15/2	Larkhill	(R)	CON	3m	9	G	*(fav) hld up, jnd ldrs 13th, ld 2 out, drvn & qcknd clr flat*	1	24
293	1/3	Didmarton	(L)	INT	3m	16	G	*(fav) w.w. prog 12th, rdn 15th, ld apr last where lft clr*	1	24
646	22/3	Castle Of C'	(R)	OPE	3m	5	G	*(fav) jmpd lft,trckd ldrs, chal 15th,swtch apr last,ld flat,clvrly*	1	24
931	6/4	Charlton Ho'	(L)	OPE	3m	6	G	*(fav) sttld 3rd, effrt to chs ldr 3 out, ld last, pshd out*	1	22
1214	26/4	Woodford	(L)	OPE	3m	5	G	*(fav) alwys going wll, ld 4 out, rdn clr 2 out, easily*	1	24

Tpo stable; quickens; best L/H; going to run under rules 98 28

STRONG DREAM (Irish) — **I** 601, **I** 891, **I** 131P, **I** 340U, **I** 3875

STRONG MEASURE(IRE) b.g. 9 Strong Gale - Inch Tape by Prince Hansel — Mrs M Armstrong

1996 **P(NH),6(NH),17(NH)**

133	9/2	Alnwick	(L)	OPE	3m	6	G	*keen hld, wth ldr to 10th, wknd 13th, t.o. & p.u. 3 out*	P	0
334	1/3	Corbridge	(R)	MEM	3m	7	G	*keen hld, ld to 9th, disp whn f nxt*	F	-
562	16/3	Lanark	(R)	OPE	3m	8	GS	*made most til 9th, bhnd by 11th, p.u. 2 out*	P	0
611	22/3	Friars Haugh	(L)	CON	3m	11	GF	*alwys bhnd*	7	0
810	31/3	Tranwell	(L)	CON	3m	5	G	*in tch 1st ctt, wknd to 4th 12th, outpcd & lost tch frm nxt*	4	0
993	12/4	Tranwell	(L)	OPE	3m	5	F	*disp ld 3rd-10th,hdd nxt,mstk & wknd into 4th 14th,last 3out*	5	0

Winning hurdler; does not stay; no prospects 0

STRONG RED PINE (Irish) — I 47^{P}

STRONG TIME (Irish) — I 117^{F}, I 127^{P}

STRONG TRACE(IRE) b.g. 8 Strong Gale - Royal Inheritance by Will Somers — David Ian Tuckley

1996 P(0)

262	22/2	Newtown	(L)	RES	3m	15	G	*unruly pddck, in tch to 11th, t.o. & p.u. 14th*	P	0
468	8/3	Eyton-On-Se'	(L)	RES	3m	11	G	*mid-div, some late prog, nrst fin*	4	10
852	31/3	Eyton-On-Se'	(L)	RES	3m	11	GF	*rear, poor last 11th, t.o. 13th, p.u. 5 out*	P	0

Won short Maiden 95; lightly raced since & not progress; best watched now 13

STRONG VIEWS b.g. 10 Remainder Man - Gokatiego by Huntercombe — E Haddock

1996 5(10),P(0)

724	29/3	Sandon	(L)	LAD	3m	4	GF	*alwys 3rd/4th, t.o. 4 out, no ch whn p.u. aft 2 out*	P	0

Winning chaser93; lightly raced & of little account now 11

STRONG WISHES (Irish) — I 110^{5}

STRONG WORDS b.g. 6 Say Primula - Potent Polly by Potent Councillor — S A Pinder

1996 **22(NH),20(NH)**

422	8/3	Charm Park	(L)	CON	3m	8	GF	*mid-div whn u.r. 3rd*	U	-
509	15/3	Dalton Park	(R)	XX	3m	13	GF	*s.s. alwys rear, wll bhnd 13th, p.u. 15th*	P	0
1074	13/4	Whitwell-On'	(R)	MDO	2 1/2m 88yds	16	G	*disp to 6th, steadily fdd, t.o. & p.u. 2 out*	P	0
1253	26/4	Easingwold	(L)	MEM	3m	7	GS	*ld to 4th, fdd, hit 11th, p.u. 13th*	P	0

No signs of stamina or ability 0

STRUGGLES GLORY(IRE) b.g. 6 Kamehameha (USA) - Another Struggle by Cheval — D C Robinson

277	23/2	Charing	(L)	MEM	3m	6	G	*(fav) prom, ld 8th til mstk 11th, ld 14th, sn clr, ran on strngly*	1	20
462	8/3	Charing	(L)	RES	3m	10	G	*(fav) cls up, ld 8th, clr 12th, unchal*	1	0
577	16/3	Detling	(L)	CON	3m	18	F	*(fav) cls up, ld frm 13th, stdly drew clr frm 17th, unchal*	1	29
983	12/4	Ascot	(R)	HC	3m 110yds	14	GF	*(fav) cl up, ld 10th, made rest, styd on well.*	1	29
1286	29/4	Huntingdon	(R)	HC	3m	10	G	*(fav) ld to 2nd, led 8th, drew clr 2 out, ran on strly.*	1	30
1588	30/5	Stratford	(L)	HC	3 1/2m	9	G	*ld till after 3 out, styd on run-in.*	2	32

Top class novice; veteran ridden; stays; jumps; go far in right hands; G-F 34

STUARTS POINT (Irish) — I 445^{P}, I 599^{P}

STUDENT BENEFIT b.g. 7 Electric - Balmenoch by Queen's Hussar — The Blowingstone Partnership

1195	23/4	Andoversford	(R)	MEM	3m	4	F	*in tch whn nrly ref 3rd, jmpd slwly nxt, last whn ref 5th*	R	-

A stuttering start 0

STUD STILE GIRL b.m. 6 Wonderful Surprise - Little Smeaton by Velvet Prince — Ms W Hanley

168	15/2	Witton Cast'	(R)	MDO	3m	4	F	*jmpd bdly in rear, lost tch 8th, t.o. & p.u. 12th, dsmntd*	P	0
358	2/3	Great Stain'	(L)	MDO	3m	14	S	*f 1st*	F	-

Jumped badly & unpromising so far 0

STUNNING STUFF b.g. 12 Boreen (FR) - Mayfield Grove by Khalkis — C St V Fox

1996 **P(NH),P(NH),4(NH),P(NH)**

309	1/3	Clyst St Ma'	(L)	CON	3m	7	HY	*ld/disp til clr 12th, wll clr 3 out, tired & crwld last*	1	16
522	15/3	Cothelstone	(L)	CON	3m	14	GS	*in tch, 5th at 14th, 3rd 3 out, eased nr fin*	4	12
690	29/3	Little Wind'	(R)	OPE	3m	4	GF	*ld to 7th, prssd wnr 12th til rdn & outpcd apr 3 out*	2	22
1091	16/4	Hockworthy	(L)	OPE	3m	4	GF	*wth ldr, ld 8-11th, rdn 3 out, kpt on onepcd*	3	19
1271	27/4	Little Wind'	(R)	OPE	3m	3	GF	*ld to 14th, rdn & not qckn 16th, no ch wnr aft*	2	18

Winning chaser; stays well but not 100% genuine; well ridden; not easy to win again; Any 19

STYLISH GENT br.g. 10 Vitiges (FR) - Squire's Daughter by Bay Express — R D Griffiths

1996 **16(NH),P(NH)**

201	15/2	Weston Park	(L)	OPE	3m	16	G	*mid to rear, u.r. 12th*	U	-
587	19/3	Ludlow	(R)	HC	2 1/2m	18	GF	*blnd and u.r. 4th.*	U	-
1012	12/4	Bitterley	(L)	MEM	3m	6	GF	*alwys cls up, prog to chal 15th, wknd frm 2 out*	3	13
1146	19/4	Chaddesley '	(L)	CON	3m	6	GF	*cls up,3rd & outpcd 13th,ran on 4 out,6l down & clsng,f 2out*	F	16
1202	25/4	Ludlow	(R)	HC	2 1/2m	5	GF	*held up, raced keenly, outpcd 10th, soon well bhnd.*	3	0
1523	17/5	Bredwardine	(R)	CON	3m	7	G	*jmps slwly 7th, in tch to 12th, wknd, t.o. & p.u.3 out, lame*	P	0

Winning hurdler; mistakes; does not stay; problems now & little hope of a win 15

STYLISH STEPPER (Irish) — I 92[4], I 284[P]

SUAVE (Irish) — I 104[P], I 133[P], I 241[P], I 352[P], I 490[P]

SUBA LIN b.m. 8 Sula Bula - Tula Lin by Tula Rocket — Mrs Carolyn Atyeo

1996 P(0),P(0),U(-),P(0)

522	15/3 Cothelstone	(L)	CON	3m	14	GS	*bhnd til p.u. 12th*	P	0
795	31/3 Bishopsleigh	(R)	MDO	3m	12	G	*mid-div, chsd ldrs 17th, nvr on trms*	4	0
1045	12/4 Cothelstone	(L)	MDO	3m	6	GF	*sttld rear, no ch frm 4 out, nrst fin*	4	10
1400	5/5 High Bickin'	(R)	MDO	3m	14	G	*mid-div, 5th hlfwy, poor 3rd frm 16th*	3	0
1497	14/5 Cothelstone	(L)	MDO	3m	10	GF	*hld up last,wll bhnd 12th,rpd prog 3 out,chnc apr last,no ex*	4	11
1554	24/5 Mounsey Hil'	(R)	MDO	3m	14	G	*chsd ldng pair til p.u. 14th, lame*	P	0

Getting round now but form is very weak; problems last start & more needed 13

SUBSONIC(IRE) b.g. 9 Be My Guest (USA) - Broken Wide by Busted — Tim Tarratt

1996 P(0),7(0)

474	9/3 Southwell P'	(L)	LAD	3m	12	G	*chsd ldrs, 4th & outpcd apr 3 out, onepcd aft*	4	14
500	15/3 Ampton	(R)	LAD	3m	4	GF	*hld up, lft 2nd 14th-nxt, outpcd aft 3 out, kpt on flat*	2	14

Flat winner; runs passably but not threatening to win a Ladies 15

SUDANOR(IRE) b.g. 8 Khartoum (USA) - Alencon by Northfields (USA) — Mrs Jo Yeomans

1996 P(0),1(21)

218	16/2 Heythrop	(R)	INT	3m	21	G	*ld 5th to 2 out, 2nd & btn whn blnd last, wknd*	5	15
431	8/3 Upton-On-Se'	(R)	CON	3m	9	G	*(Jt fav) last til some prog 8th, no ch 13th, p.u. 15th*	P	0
704	29/3 Upper Sapey	(R)	INT	3m	4	GF	*(fav) ld til mstk 16th, recvrd wll but outpcd apr last*	4	17
1146	19/4 Chaddesley '	(L)	CON	3m	6	GF	*ld/disp, qcknd 13th, hdd 16th, wknd rpdly, lft 2nd 2 out*	2	0
1235	26/4 Brampton Br'	(R)	INT	3m	10	G	*ld til hdd & rdn 15th, wknd frm nxt*	4	0
1296	3/5 Hereford	(R)	HC	2m 3f	11	G	*in tch when blnd 8th, soon bhnd, t.o. when p.u. before 4 out.*	P	0

Restricted winner 96; front runs but barely stays; mistakes; not progress 97 & best watche now 16

SUDDEN SALLY(IRE) b.m. 6 Bustomi - Donnabimba by Don (ITY) — J W Hughes

231	22/2 Friars Haugh	(L)	LAD	3m	13	G	*s.v.s. t.o. til p.u. 3 out*	P	0
1048	13/4 Lockerbie	(R)	LAD	3m	6	F	*in tch til wknd frm 14th, p.u. apr last*	P	0

Thrown in at the deep end; showed some hope; should try Maidens 0

SUE'S QUEST b.m. 7 El Conquistador - Parisian Piaffer by Piaffer (USA) — Mrs S E Wall

1996 P(0),4(0),3(0)

106	8/2 Milborne St'	(L)	RES	3m	12	GF	*in tch early, outpcd frm 12th, t.o. & p.u. 4 out*	P	0
527	15/3 Cothelstone	(L)	MDN	3m	14	GS	*jmpd rght, rear hlfwy til p.u. 2 out*	P	0
1045	12/4 Cothelstone	(L)	MDO	3m	6	GF	*last til prog 13th, hrd rdn 2 out, tk 2nd flat*	2	10
1158	20/4 Stafford Cr'	(R)	MDO	3m	5	GF	*disp to 3 out, hdd, rnwd effrt nxt, ld apr last, ran on wll*	1	14
1494	14/5 Cothelstone	(L)	RES	3m	11	GF	*(fav) chsd ldrs, 5th & rdn 12th, sn btn & bhnd*	6	0

Won poor race; last next time & much more needed for Restricted 13

SUGI g. 8 Oats - Ledee — Ian Wynne

1996 F(-),F(-),r(-),3(10)

435	8/3 Upton-On-Se'	(R)	MDO	3m	14	G	*cls up 8th, chsd ldrs til not qckn 13th, lft 3rd*	3	10
768	29/3 Whittington	(L)	MDO	3m	10	S	*alwys cls up, 2l 2nd last, qcknd wll flat*	1	14
1424	10/5 Aspatria	(L)	RES	3m	17	G	*rear, outpcd frm 12th, no ch aft, kpt on frm 3 out*	6	12

Improved & beat subsquent winner; lightly raced & can improve; needs to for upgrade; stays; G-S 15

SUITE COTTAGE LADY (Irish) — I 318[P]

SULASON b.g. 7 Sulaafah (USA) - Perrimay by Levanter — R N Miller

1996 P(0),P(0),F(-),3(11)

20	25/1 Badbury Rin'	(L)	MDN	3m	9	GF	*cls up,lost plc 11th,ralld und pres 15th,wknd 3out,p.u.last*	P	0
181	15/2 Larkhill	(R)	MDO	3m	17	G	*prom to 14th, wknd, t.o. & p.u. 2 out*	P	0
1270	27/4 Little Wind'	(R)	MDO	2 1/2m	10	GF	*prom to 11th, wknd rpdly 13th, last whn ref 3 out*	R	-

Does not stay & never best than last yet 0

SULTAN OF SWING b.g. 8 Idiot's Delight - Tropical Swing by Swing Easy (USA) — Mrs Carrie Zetter-Wells

43	1/2 Larkhill	(R)	MDO	3m	10	GF	*hdstr, hld up, ld 13th til blnd nxt, nt rcvr, p.u.3 out*	P	0
390	8/3 Barbury Cas'	(L)	MDN	3m	15	G	*(fav) mid-div, prog 8th, 3rd 3 out, strng run apr last, ld nr fin*	1	17
688	29/3 Little Wind'	(R)	RES	3m	5	GF	*(fav) hng & jmpd lft, hld up, prog to ld 15th, clr 2 out*	1	17
1092	16/4 Hockworthy	(L)	XX	3m	5	GF	*w.w. effrt to chs wnr 14th, no imp 2 out, demoted aft*	3	14
1273	27/4 Little Wind'	(R)	INT	3m	2	GF	*jmpd lft, trckd wnr, pshd alng 16th, rdn & no imp apr 2 out*	2	16

Won good races; hard ride; hangs; sold very cheaply Ascot June; can only be watched 18

SULTAN'S SON b.g. 11 Kings Lake (USA) - Get Ahead by Silly Season — J J V Phillips

1062	13/4 Maisemore P'	(L)	MXO	3m	12	GF	*50s-12s, 2nd til jnd ldr 13th, ld apr last, ran on well*	1	24

1203	26/4	Worcester	(L)	HC	2m 7f 110yds	10	S	*held up, lost tch from 8th, went poor 3rd 3 out, blnd and u.r. last.*	U	-
1411	7/5	Chepstow	(L)	HC	3m	4	G	*in cl tch till outpcd after 8th, t.o..*	4	12
1469	11/5	Erw Lon	(L)	OPE	3m	6	GS	*cls up, ev ch 4 out, hrd rdn, onepcd 2 out*	3	21

Winning hurdler; beat good horse to land punt; ground wrong after; can win more Opens; G/F best 21

SUMAKANO (Irish) — I 78, , I 257^{P}, I 336^{P}, I 537^{1}, I 567^{1}

SUMMERHILL EXPRESS (Irish) — I 13^{1}, I 130^{3}

SUMMERHILL FLIER (Irish) — I 226^{F}

SUMMERTHETIME ch.g. 8 Vital Season - Triscombe Stone by Pharaoh Hophra — Mrs E Eames

104	8/2	Great Treth'	(R)	MDO	3m	9	GS	*n.j.w. t.o. 7th, p.u. 10th*	P	0
866	31/3	Kingston St'	(R)	MDO	3m	7	F	*last whn f 6th*	F	-
1369	5/5	Cotley Farm	(L)	MEM	3m	4	GF	*last til lost cth 10th, wknd & p.u. apr 12th*	P	0
1498	14/5	Cothelstone	(L)	MDO	3m	9	GF	*alwys rear, t.o. & u.r. 10th*	U	-
1520	17/5	Bratton Down	(L)	MDO	3m	17	GS	*prog 5th, ld 9-10th, wd bnd apr nxt, mstk 12th, p.u. 14th*	P	0

Yet to complete; unpromising 0

SUMPT'N SMART b.g. 10 Starlan - Laragh by Fray Bentos — Mrs Yda Morgan

131	9/2	Alnwick	(L)	RES	3m	13	G	*in tch, prog to chs ldrs 13th, btn apr 4 out, p.u. nxt*	P	0
230	22/2	Friars Haugh	(L)	RES	3m	15	G	*handy til f 10th*	F	-
563	16/3	Lanark	(R)	RES	3m	8	GS	*ld brfly 5th, t.o. whn p.u. 2 out*	P	0
995	12/4	Tranwell	(L)	RES	3m	6	F	*disp ld 5-8th, mnly 1l 2nd 9-14th, outpcd frm 2 out*	2	14
1218	26/4	Balcormo Ma'	(R)	RES	3m	5	F	*ld frm 2nd til apr 2 out, no ext*	2	16
1424	10/5	Aspatria	(L)	RES	3m	17	G	*mid-div, no prog 13th, kpt on onepcd*	5	12
1510	17/5	Corbridge	(R)	RES	3m	13	GS	*prom til outpcd frm 4 out*	4	15

Irish Maiden winner; missed 96; consistent but weak finisher; may find Restricted one day 15

SUNCZECH (Irish) — I 356^{3}, I 453^{P}, I 590^{2}

SUNDAY POINTER b.g. 8 Pragmatic - Solo Waltz by Quiet Fling (USA) — John Threadgall

733	29/3	Alnwick	(L)	MDN	3m	5	F	*ld 2nd-10th, wkng in 4th 13th, p.u. 3 out*	P	0

showed speed but much more needed 0

SUNGIA(IRE) b.g. 8 Orchestra - Lysanders Lady by Saulingo — Graeme Roe

1996 **F(NH),P(NH)**

655	22/3	Siddington	(L)	RES	3m	10	F	*prom til wknd rpdly 14th, t.o.*	6	0

Of no account 0

SUNKALA SHINE ch.g. 9 Kalaglow - Allander Girl by Miralgo — S B Clark

1996 **P(NH)**

14	25/1	Cottenham	(R)	MDO	3m	7	GF	*ld 4-14th & 16th til aft 3 out,lft in ld nxt,hdd last,no ext*	2	14
120	9/2	Wetherby Po'	(L)	MDO	3m	18	GF	*(fav) mid-div,prog 10th,remote 3rd 13th,blnd nxt,sn wknd,p.u.4 out*	P	0
1105	19/4	Hornby Cast'	(L)	MDO	3m	11	G	*mid-div,prog into 2nd 12th,disp nxt,blndrd 4 out,sn wknd*	5	0

Ex novice/hurdler; lightly raced; stamina suspect but must have chances on easy course 13

SUNLEY STREET b.m. 9 Sunley Builds - Kerry Street by Dairialatan — J Scammell

1996 2(20),2(22)

294	1/3	Didmarton	(L)	INT	3m	20	G	*(bl) nvr nr ldr4s, t.o. frm 14th*	6	10
434	8/3	Upton-On-Se'	(R)	INT	3m	4	G	*(bl) 2nd/3rd,outpcd 12th, 15l 3rd 3 out,ran on strngly to ld flat*	1	20
929	6/4	Charlton Ho'	(L)	MEM	3m	5	G	*(bl) mstk 10th,prssd ldr to 12th,ev ch 3 out,wknd nxt,eased*	3	18
1153	20/4	Stafford Cr'	(R)	CON	3m	10	GF	*(fav) (bl) 7/2-9/4, chsd ldr, disp 2nd til blnd 12th, p.u. aft*	P	0
1582	26/5	Lifton	(R)	INT	3m	10	G	*blnd 1st, alwys bhnd aft, p.u. 2 out*	P	0

Won 4 of last 11; mistakes; tricky; blinkers; good enough for Confined; Good 21

SUNNY MOUNT b.g. 11 Furry Glen - Up The Hill by Light Thrust — J E Greenall

27	26/1	Marks Tey	(L)	OPE	3m	6	GF	*(fav) prom, mstks 1st & 11th, ld 3 out, rdn & ran on strngly last*	1	25
150	10/2	Plumpton	(L)	HC	3m 1f 110yds	5	GS	*(fav) held up, prog 13th, ev ch 2 out, one pace.*	3	22

Very useful 94; only three runs since; retains ability; could still win Open if fit 98 26

SUN OF CHANCE b.g. 13 Sunyboy - Chance A Look by Don't Look — Miss M Ree

1996 4(18),1(19),P(0),P(0)

400	8/3	Llanfrynach	(R)	OPE	3m	10	G	*mid-div, onepcd 3rd frm 14th, lft 2nd last*	2	17
714	29/3	Llanvapley	(L)	CON	3m	15	GF	*cls up, ld 6-11th, cls 2nd aft, ld 2 out,blndrd whn clr last*	1	20
1007	12/4	St Hilary	(R)	OPE	3m	10	GF	*hld up mid-div, some prog 3 out, ran on wll, nrst fin*	3	16
1224	26/4	Pyle	(R)	CON	3m	7	GS	*mstk 6th, ld 5th-14th, 3rd & btn aft, wknd*	3	11

Confined winner 96; consistent; below Open class; may find another Confined; G-S 18

SUNSET RUN b.g. 11 Deep Run - Sunset Queen by Arctic Slave — Miss Catherine Tuke

1996 3(17),r(-)

65	1/2	Horseheath	(R)	RES	3m	10 GF	*keen hld, chsd ldrs, mstk 9th, 4th & btn whn ran out 3 out*	r	-
779	31/3	Fakenham	(L)	HC	2m 5f 110yds	9 G	*(bl) bhnd till p.u. before 7th.*	P	0

Dead 12

SUN SETTING ch.g. 6 Sunyboy - Nosey's Daughter by Song — C J R Sweeting

1996 F(-)

774	29/3	Dingley	(R)	MDO	2m 5f	10 G	*in tch til outpcd 6 out, f 3 out*	F	-
1015	12/4	Bitterley	(L)	MDO	3m	12 GF	*alwys prom, ev ch 3 out, kpt on to tk 2nd flat*	2	11
1537	18/5	Mollington	(R)	MDO	3m	14 GS	*(fav) trckd ldrs til f 5th*	F	-

Subsequent winner behind on only completion; capable of scoring when jumping better 14

SUNSHINE MANOR ch.g. 13 Le Soleil - Manor Lady by Eastern Venture — G B Tarry

1996 P(0),3(21),3(21),F(-),2(21)

1532	18/5	Mollington	(R)	CON	3m	11 GS	*pllng, ld to apr 2 out, wknd rpdly, walked in*	7	0
1564	25/5	Kingston Bl'	(L)	CON	3m	7 GF	*mstk 2nd,ld to 3rd,lft in ld nxt,qcknd aft 2 out,pshd out*	1	21
1608	1/6	Dingley	(R)	INT	3m	11 GF	*(fav) ld to aft 10th, mstks final cct, rallied 2 out, no ext last*	3	19

Lightly raced now; front runner; retains ability, and solid Confined horse; can win at 14; G/F-G 21

SUNWIND b.g. 11 Windjammer (USA) - Mrewa by Runnymede — David Heath

1996 3(10),5(14),4(12),7(0),B(-)

50	1/2	Wadebridge	(L)	RES	3m	10 G	*nvr trbld ldrs*	6	11
532	15/3	Wadebridge	(L)	RES	3m	9 GF	*alwys prom, onepcd frm 3 out*	2	15
803	31/3	Wadebridge	(L)	MEM	3m	3 F	*ld 3rd-5th, chsd wnr aft, no imp*	2	14
1039	12/4	Lifton	(R)	RES	3m	8 F	*bhnd til prog 15th, smooth run to ld 3 out,ran on strngly*	1	17
1156	20/4	Stafford Cr'	(R)	INT	3m	6 GF	*hld up, cls 4th & going wll whn u.r. 14th*	U	-
1398	5/5	High Bickin'	(R)	INT	3m	7 G	*hld up, went 4th at 16th, lft 3rd 3 out, tired & mstk nxt*	3	11

Members winner 95; well ridden to win Restricted; barely stays; below Confined standard 16

SUNYLAD b.g. 9 Sunyboy - Rowane by Ginger Boy — John Studd

487	9/3	Tweseldown	(R)	MDO	3m	12 G	*mstk 2nd, chsd ldng pair, wknd 13th, tired & p.u. aft 3 out*	P	0

Showed a glimmer of hope; can do better 10

SUNY ROSE b.m. 6 Sunyboy - Rostra by Legal Eagle — Miss E M Hewitt

839	31/3	Thorpe Lodge	(L)	MDO	3m	15 F	*f 2nd*	F	-
898	5/4	Wetherby Po'	(L)	MDO	3m	7 F	*rear, rdn & strggling 10th, wll bhnd & p.u. 13th*	P	0
1262	27/4	Southwell P'	(L)	MDO	3m	15 G	*alwys rear, mstk 8th, t.o. 3 out, p.u. last*	P	0

Not yet of any account 0

SUP A BRANDY (Irish) — **I** 79^{P}, **I** 141^{P}

SUPERFORCE b.g. 10 Superlative - Loup de Mer by Wolver Hollow — A B Coogan

1996 P(0),P(0),P(0),U(-),R(-)

30	26/1	Marks Tey	(L)	MDN	3m	9 GF	*(bl) mstks, rmndrs 3rd, t.o. & p.u. 6th, b.b.v.*	P	0

Of no account 0

SUPERIOR CALL (Irish) — **I** 3^{P}

SUPREMCAN (Irish) — **I** 478^{P}

SUPREME CAUTION (Irish) — **I** 305^{U}

SUPREME CITIZEN (Irish) — **I** 77^{3}, **I** 515^{F}, **I** 533^{P}

SUPREME DEALER ch.g. 12 The Parson - Vul's Money by Even Money — L J Bowman

1996 P(0)

577	16/3	Detling	(L)	CON	3m	18 F	*ld to 6th, cls aft, mstk 13th, 3rd whn f 15th*	F	-
1126	19/4	Penshurst	(L)	CON	3m	6 GF	*(Jt fav) ld to 2nd, lft in ld 7-9th, no dang 4 out, onepcd*	4	12
1447	10/5	Peper Harow	(L)	CON	3m	6 GF	*ld to 2nd, ld apr 13th, kpt on gamely frm 2 out*	1	14
1502	16/5	Folkestone	(R)	HC	2m 5f	10 G	*chsd ldr till after 6th, weakening when mstk 9th, soon well bhnd.*	4	0

Dual winner 93; lightly raced now; found a bad Confined and needs same to score again 15

SUPREME DREAM(IRE) b.m. 8 Supreme Leader - Rock Solid by Hardboy — Mrs Pauline Adams

1996 4(0),U(-),U(-),5(10),1(15),3(16),F(-),F(-)

449	8/3	Newton Brom'	(R)	XX	3m	13 G	*ran in sntchs, last at 7th, effrt 3 out, fin well*	5	0
546	16/3	Garthorpe	(R)	LAD	3m	11 GF	*in tch, chsd ldr 12th to 3 out, rallied appr last,ld cls hme*	1	19
773	29/3	Dingley	(R)	LAD	3m	11 G	*nvr dang, 5th/6th for 2m, 4th & onepcd frm 4 out*	4	14
1076	13/4	Guilsborough	(L)	MEM	3m	9 GF	*(Jt fav) trckd ldrs, lost plc 12th, prog 16th, ld 3 out, ran on well*	1	19
1207	26/4	Clifton On '	(L)	LAD	3m	6 GS	*cls up,ld brfly 7-8th, outpcd 5 out, ran on 3 out,nt rch wnr*	2	19
1476	11/5	Garthorpe	(R)	LAD	3m	5 GS	*last frm 3rd, pckd 8th, went mod 3rd apr 2 out, nvr dang*	3	15
1573	26/5	Chaddesley '	(L)	LAD	3m	6 F	*in tch til 4th & outpcd 12th, no imp ldrs aft*	4	16
1604	1/6	Dingley	(R)	MEM	3m	4 GF	*(fav) cls up til u.r. 5th*	U	-

Consistent performer; safer in 97; stays well; should win again; G/F-G/S 19

SUPREME FLIGHT (Irish) — I 329^{U}, I 467^{P}
SUPREME FORWARD (Irish) — I 7^{3}, I 86^{P}
SUPREME FOUNTAIN (Irish) — I 304^{3}, I 558^{P}
SUPREME GOLD (Irish) — I 98^{P}, I 151^{S}, I 217^{1}
SUPREME LANCER (Irish) — I 377^{P}, I 413^{F}, I 507^{2}, I 583^{1}
SUPREME ODDS (Irish) — I 7^{P}, I 73^{1}, I 130^{4}, I 194^{P}, I 569^{P}
SUPREME SHAMROCK (Irish) — I 77^{P}

SUPREME WARRIOR b.g. 11 Simply Great (FR) - Sindo by Derring-Do — Miss L Blackford
1996 4(10)

1399	5/5	High Bickin'	(R)	MDO	3m	12	G	*mid-div, mstk 9th, p.u. 12th*	P	0

Very lightly raced; a little ability, but time passing by 11

SURE PRIDE(USA) b.g. 9 Bates Motel (USA) - Coquelicot (CAN) by L'enjoleur (CAN) — A G Russell
1996 P(0),4(0),**U(-),7(11),P(0)**

828	31/3	Heathfield	(R)	MEM	3m	5	F	*lft in ld aft 4th-9th & 14th-4 out, onepcd und press*	3	0
1506	16/5	Folkestone	(R)	HC	2m 5f	8	G	*alwys bhnd, t.o. from 9th.*	5	13

Winning hurdler; ran passably in poor Members but not threatening to win 10

SURPRISE VIEW b.m. 5 Picture Post - Tilloujo by Ovac (ITY) — Mrs S Gibson

80	2/2	Market Rase'	(L)	MDO	2m 5f	9	GF	*bhnd & mstk 7th, ran out nxt*	r	-
357	2/3	Great Stain'	(L)	MDO	3m	15	S	*mid-div, lost tch 12th, p.u. 3 out*	P	0
428	8/3	Charm Park	(L)	MDO	3m	10	GF	*alwys in rear, lost tch aft 8th, t.o. & p.u. 10th*	P	0
860	31/3	Charm Park	(L)	MDO	3m	12	F	*sn bhnd, p.u. 10th*	P	0
1073	13/4	Whitwell-On'	(R)	MDO	2 1/2m 88yds	17	G	*mid-div, outpcd 6th, f nxt*	F	-

No signs yet 0

SUSIES DELIGHT (Irish) — I 281^{P}, I 350^{P}, I 416^{P}

SUSIES PRINCE br.g. 7 Prince Of Peace - What An Experiance by Chance Meeting — P R Whiston

853	31/3	Eyton-On-Se'	(L)	MDO	3m	13	GF	*alwys rear, schooling, p.u. 5 out*	P	0

Only learning on debut 0

SUTTON LASS ch.m. 14 Politico (USA) - Selborne Lass by Deep Run — H C Harper
1996 P(0),4(0),6(0),5(0),5(0),6(0)

372	2/3	Mollington	(R)	RES	3m	19	G	*alwys bhnd, t.o. & p.u. 11th*	P	0
676	23/3	Brocklesby '	(L)	RES	3m	14	GF	*bhnd, t.o. & p.u. 9th*	P	0
820	31/3	Paxford	(L)	RES	3m	4	F	*chsd ldrs, mstks 4 & 7th, blnd 9th, lost irons, ran out 10th*	r	-
986	12/4	Kingston Bl'	(L)	CON	3m	10	GF	*jmpd slwly, sn bhnd, t.o. 13th, p.u. 2 out*	P	0
1532	18/5	Mollington	(R)	CON	3m	11	GS	*sn last, t.o. 9th, mls bhnd whn ref last*	R	-

Veteran novice ridden 97; of no account 0

SWANEES TUNE (Irish) — I 353^{P}, I 428^{P}
SWAN POINT (Irish) — I 58^{P}, I 114^{F}, I 175^{F}, I 247^{1}

SWANSEA GOLD(IRE) ch.m. 6 Torus - Show M How by Ashmore (FR) — Mrs H E North
1996 1(15)

298	1/3	Didmarton	(L)	RES	3m	15	G	*mstk 1st, ld 7-10th, sn outpcd, kpt on frm 3 out*	3	13
523	15/3	Cothelstone	(L)	RES	3m	14	GS	*keen hld, ld 15th, hdd 2 out, ran on to ld flat, gamely*	1	20
1507	16/5	Stratford	(L)	HC	3m	10	G	*ld to 4th, led 8th, clr four out, wknd and hdd 2 out, rallied gamely run-in.*	2	25

Improving; both wins Cotherstone; front runs and battles when headed; will win H/chase 26

SWEENEY LEE (Irish) — I 106^{P}, I 202^{5}, I 353^{5}, I 429^{P}
SWEET CASTLEHYDE (Irish) — I 66^{5}, I 110^{F}

SWEET KILDARE ch.m. 10 Parole - Lady Royal by Sharpen Up — V J Thomas
1996 1(16),1(17),2(19),1(14)

1005	12/4	St Hilary	(R)	CON	3m	10	GF	*hld up in mid-div, prog to 4th 3 out, styd on onepcd*	4	0
1133	19/4	Bonvilston	(R)	INT	3m	8	G	*mid-div, nvr plcd to chal*	4	11
1366	5/5	Pantyderi	(L)	INT	3m	6	G	*ld 5th-7th, chsd wnr aft, no ch frm 15th*	2	11
1557	24/5	Bassaleg	(R)	CON	3m	9	G	*ld to 7th, wknd 11th, sn t.o.*	5	0
1598	31/5	Bassaleg	(R)	MEM	3m	2	F	*(fav) jmpd lft, ld 2nd, clr 4th, pshd out whn chal last, comf*	1	13
1611	7/6	Umberleigh	(L)	OPE	3m	8	F	*wll in rear til prog 13th, styd on to go 2nd aft 2 out,no ch*	2	0

Won 4 of last 10; slow to reach form 97; ran well last start; should find another opening; F-G/S 19

SWEET MARINER ch.g. 11 Julio Mariner - Sweet Bush by The Brianstan — Michael H Ings

408	8/3	Llanfrynach	(R)	MDN 3m	12	G	*ld to 14th, wknd rpdly, p.u. 2 out*	P	0
639	22/3	Howick	(L)	MDN 3m	15	GF	*4th/5th til outpcd frm 14th*	5	0

Well beaten when finishing; surely too old to win now 0

SWEET MERENDA(IRE) b.m. 6 Lancastrian - Merendas Sister by Pauper — B Kennedy

28	26/1	Marks Tey	(L)	RES 3m	9	GF	*mid-div,poor 6th 14th,lft 3rd 3 out,strng run last,ld nr fin*	1	15
282	23/2	Charing	(L)	INT 3m	7	G	*prom til f 10th*	F	-
321	1/3	Marks Tey	(L)	INT 3m	10	G	*w.w., lft 4th 9th, ev ch 17th, onepcd und pres*	3	18

Irish Maiden winner 96; won modest Restricted; stays well but needs more for Inter/Confined; Good ... 17

SWEETMOUNT LAD (Irish) — **I** 64[P]

SWEET PERK (Irish) — **I** 65[F], **I** 96[P], **I** 218[F], **I** 295[P], **I** 344[P]

SWEET SANDRA (Irish) — **I** 389[P]

SWEPT ASIDE (Irish) — **I** 165[F]

SWIFT REWARD b.m. 8 Kinglet - Swift Wood by Precipice Wood — David Wales

1996 P(0)

65	1/2	Horseheath	(R)	RES 3m	10	GF	*mid-div, rdn & lost plc 9th, t.o. & p.u. 3 out*	P	0
126	9/2	Cottenham	(R)	RES 3m	14	GF	*(bl) chsg grp, lost tch 12th, kpt on frm 3 out, tk 3rd flat*	3	0
278	23/2	Charing	(L)	RES 3m	17	G	*mid-div, lost tch 15th, t.o.*	5	0
477	9/3	Southwell P'	(L)	RES 3m	10	G	*chsd ldr to 5th, rdn & wknd apr 12th*	6	0
597	22/3	Horseheath	(R)	RES 3m	8	F	*hld up, prog to 2nd at 13th, chsd wnr, no ch 2 out, lost 2nd*	3	15

Maiden winner 95 (blinkers); ungenerous and well short of Restricted standard 14

SWINGING SONG b.g. 10 True Song - Grissy by Grisaille — Mrs E Gilman

1996 P(0),P(0),2(0),3(0),1(15)

140	9/2	Thorpe Lodge	(L)	RES 3m	7	GF	*mid to rear, t.o. & p.u. 15th*	P	0
838	31/3	Thorpe Lodge	(L)	RES 3m	5	F	*tried to make all, hdd & onepcd 3 out*	3	11

Won poor Maiden 96; headstrong and tricky; need weak Restricted to win again 14

SWING TO THE LEFT(IRE) gr.m. 7 Corvaro (USA) - Ballinoe Lass by Captain James — J Pryce

1996 P(0),1(14),3(13),3(11)

7	19/1	Barbury Cas'	(L)	RES 3m	14	GF	*bhnd, 10th hlfwy, p.u. 14th*	P	0
100	8/2	Great Treth'	(R)	RES 3m	14	GS	*mid-div, prog 14th, jnd wnr 3 out til wknd apr last*	3	16
241	22/2	Lemalla	(R)	RES 3m	11	S	*prom, disp 9-14th, lost plc 16th, 5th whn p.u. 2 out*	P	0
556	16/3	Ottery St M'	(L)	RES 3m	12	G	*in tch, ld 14th, disp 4 out til f 3 out*	F	-
792	31/3	Bishopsleigh	(R)	RES 3m	13	G	*(fav) prom, ld 7th til hdd aft last, no ext*	3	15
1519	17/5	Bratton Down	(L)	RES 3m	15	GS	*tubed, rear, blnd 11th, t.o. & p.u. 14th*	P	0

Maiden winner 96; inconsistent and signs not good last start; best watched now; stays; G-HY 15

SWISS THYNE (Irish) — **I** 278[F], **I** 356[1]

SWORDBENDER (Irish) — **I** 524[2]

SYBILLABEE br.m. 9 Sula Bula - Upham Jubilee by Murrayfield — Mrs D Buckett

1996 4(10),F(-),3(10),F(-),1(16)

106	8/2	Milborne St'	(L)	RES 3m	12	GF	*prom early, outpcd 12th, no ext frm 4 out*	5	0
488	9/3	Tweseldown	(R)	RES 3m	10	G	*in tch, chsd wnr 12th, sn no imp, wknd & lost 2nd flat*	4	12
516	15/3	Larkhill	(R)	RES 3m	7	GF	*w.w. prog to ld 13th, clr 3 out, easily*	1	18
989	12/4	Kingston Bl'	(L)	INT 3m	7	GF	*(fav) prom, prssd ldr 7-13th, outpcd nxt, ran on onepcd 2 out*	2	17
1372	5/5	Cotley Farm	(L)	INT 3m	3	GF	*(Jt fav) ld/disp til wnt clr 12th, ran on wll frm 3 out, easily*	1	20

Maiden winner 96; improved & well placed; needs more for Confindes; best easy 3 miles; G/F 19

SYCAMORE COVE (Irish) — **I** 597,

SYD GREEN(IRE) b.g. 9 Green Shoon - Gone by Whistling Wind — P M Hodges

1996 P(0),U(-),1(18),**1(24)**,**2(25)**

1265	27/4	Southwell P'	(L)	OPE 3m	8	G	*(fav) hld up, prog 11th, ld going easily 3 out, f nxt*	F	24

Improved & won H/chase 96; late to appear & no luck 97; sure to win if fit 98; G-F 24

SYLVAN SIROCCO b.g. 10 Known Fact (USA) - Juddmonte by Habitat — A G L Taylor

1996 U(-),5(12),**10(0)**,**P(0)**

437	8/3	Upton-On-Se'	(R)	MDO 3m	15	G	*prom to 2nd, rstrnd, ld 13th-3 out, wknd nxt*	3	0
881	1/4	Upton-On-Se'	(R)	MDN 3m	13	GF	*chsd ldrs to 15th, grad wknd frm 3 out*	4	0
1065	13/4	Maisemore P'	(L)	MDO 3m	13	GF	*ld, clr 6th, blnd 14th, hdd apr last, no ext*	2	13
1216	26/4	Woodford	(L)	MDN 3m	13	G	*(fav) ld to 1st, chsd ldr 14th-3 out, no imp aft*	3	0

Beat 7 others when 5th & should try Maidens - would have a squeak 12

SYMBOL OF SUCCESS(IRE) b.g. 6 Red Sunset - Simbella by Simbir — D L Williams

91	6/2	Huntingdon	(R)	HC	3m	10	G	*(vis) held up, went 3rd after 4 out, rdn after next, styd on between last 2.*	3	20

Winning hurdler; not seen after good H/chase run; has the ability to win one 23

SYRUS P TURNTABLE b.g. 11 King Of Spain - Lizabeth Chudleigh by Imperial Fling (USA) Miss P Fitton

1996 2(18),5(13),**5(11)**

328	1/3	Eaton Hall	(R)	OPE	3m	6	GS	*nvr bttr thn 4th, losng tch whn p.u. 13th*	P	0
413	8/3	Dalston	(R)	OPE	3m	9	GS	*alwys bhnd, t.o. 15th*	6	0
507	15/3	Dalton Park	(R)	OPE	3m	8	GF	*rear, prog 12th, fdd 16th, t.o.*	5	12
618	22/3	Hutton Rudby	(L)	OPE	3m	10	GF	*rear & sn detached, t.o.*	7	0
765	29/3	Whittington	(L)	OPE	3m	6	S	*alwys 3rd/4th, nvr trbld ldrs*	3	10
875	1/4	Wetherby	(L)	HC	3m 1f	5	GF	*chsd ldrs till wknd after 14th, t.o..*	3	0
1072	13/4	Whitwell-On'	(R)	MXO	4m	21	G	*rear, wll bhnd 18th, p.u. 4 out*	P	0
1344	3/5	Gisburn	(R)	MEM	3m	3	GF	*ld to 7th, cls up til wknd 14th, lft clr 16th, fin tired*	1	0
1489	12/5	Towcester	(R)	HC	3m 1f	6	GS	*prom, reminders after 9th, soon wknd, t.o. when p.u. before last.*	P	0
1571	26/5	Wetherby	(L)	HC	2 1/2m 110yds	15	GF	*bhnd from hfwy.*	10	0

Won a joke race (lucky); safe as houses but needs same to score again 12

TABLE ROCK (Irish) — **I** 51⁵

TACK ROOM LADY (Irish) — **I** 13ᴾ, **I** 62³, **I** 89ᶠ, **I** 131ᴾ, **I** 237¹

TACONAS GIFT (Irish) — **I** 125ᶠ, **I** 292ᴾ, **I** 360ᴾ

TAFADALI (Irish) — **I** 536ᴾ

TAILS U WIN b.g. 11 Spin Of A Coin - Soldier Girl by Queen's Hussar Paul Morris

331	1/3	Eaton Hall	(R)	RES	3m	17	GS	*mid to rear, p.u. 5 out*	P	0
575	16/3	Garnons	(L)	RES	3m	12	G	*rear til mstk & u.r. 9th*	U	-
727	29/3	Sandon	(L)	RES	3m	6	GF	*w.w. prog frm rear & lft 2nd 2 out, ld apr last, ran on well*	1	16

Very lightly raced; 16/1 when winning desperate race (lucky); really up against it now 14

TAKAHASHI(IRE) ch.g. 7 Henbit (USA) - North North West Mrs M G Wallace

398	8/3	Llanfrynach	(R)	MEM	3m	6	G	*p.u. aft 2nd, dsmntd*	P	0
640	22/3	Howick	(L)	MDN	3m	10	GF	*hld up, prog 13th, lft 2nd 15th, disp & f 2 out*	F	13
1010	12/4	St Hilary	(R)	MDN	3m	10	GF	*(Co fav) prom, lft in ld 14th, qcknd clr 3 out*	1	12
1227	26/4	Pyle	(R)	RES	3m	15	GS	*prom, ld 12th-2 out, wknd rpdly, walked in*	6	0
1365	5/5	Pantyderi	(L)	RES	3m	10	G	*8th at 3rd, 5th at 11th, fin 2nd, disq*	0D	0

Won modest 2 finisher race; easy 3 miles looks essential; hopes in weak Restricted; G/F-G 15

TAKE ACHANCE ON ME b.g. 5 Arctic Lord - Rockin Berry by Daybrook Lad Bill Davies

1578	26/5	Chaddesley '	(L)	MDO	3m	7	F	*slw jmps 1st & 2nd, in tch til wnd 12th, t.o.*	4	0

Only learning on debut 0

TAKE A LITTLE (Irish) — **I** 574ᴾ

TAKE A RIGHT b.g. 5 Skyliner - Miss Colenca by Petong Mrs J Cornes

1996 **15(NH),14(NH),P(NH)**

853	31/3	Eyton-On-Se'	(L)	MDO	3m	13	GF	*ld to 2nd, chsng grp to 10th, sn wknd, p.u. 4 out*	P	0

No ability under Rules; showed speed but no stamina on debut 0

TAKE BY STORM(IRE) b.g. 8 Bluebird (USA) - Laurel Express by Bay Express M R Williams

1996 **P(NH),6(NH)**

521	15/3	Cothelstone	(L)	OPE	3m	8	GS	*hdwy 12th, 4th at 16th, no ch whn p.u. aft 2 out*	P	0
931	6/4	Charlton Ho'	(L)	OPE	3m	6	G	*chsd ldr til blnd 3 out, not rcvr & p.u. nxt, lame*	P	0

Placed in Novice/chases; problems now & can only be watched now 15

TAKEITHANDY (Irish) — **I** 75ᴾ, **I** 298⁴

TAKE MY SIDE (Irish) — **I** 22ᴾ, **I** 393¹

TAKE THE TOWN b.g. 12 Pollerton - Rose Of Spring by Golden Vision M Jones

1996 P(0),F(-),6(0),5(15),U(-)

194	15/2	Higham	(L)	OPE	3m	12	G	*mid-div, not pace to trbl ldrs, kpt on frm 3 out*	5	0
281	23/2	Charing	(L)	OPE	3m	12	G	*prom, ld 7th-12th, mstk 14th, outpcd frm nxt*	4	16

Winning Irish chaser; struggling over here; not threatening to win 14

TALE OF ENDURANCE(IRE) b.g. 9 Ovac (ITY) - Black Tulip by Pals Passage D G Field

1996 **4(NH),P(NH),U(NH)**

86	2/2	Wolverhampt'	(L)	OPE	3m	9	GS	*alwys bhnd, t.o. & p.u. 12th*	P	0
475	9/3	Southwell P'	(L)	OPE	3m	7	G	*(bl) chsd wnr to 5th, 4th & outpcd 13th, no ch frm nxt*	5	0
545	16/3	Garthorpe	(R)	CON	3m	12	GF	*chsd ldrs, wnt 2nd aft 15th til nxt, 5th & btn whn f last*	F	17

Winning Irish chaser; stamins suspect; finished early & prospects look slim 12

TALL ORDER(IRE) br.g. 8 Prince Bee - Rosie Probert by Captain's Gig (USA) J F Weldhen
1996 **5(NH)**,**2(NH)**
105 8/2 Great Treth' (R) MDO 3m 15 GS *mstk 2nd, wth ldrs, 3rd at 12th, wknd 15th, lost 3rd nr fin* 4 0
Placed Irish Novice/chase; last & well beaten in hot race on debut; chances if fit 98 13

TAMAIMO(IRE) b.g. 6 Electric - Tino's Love by Rugantino Mrs Susan Humphreys
1996 P(0),P(0)
105 8/2 Great Treth' (R) MDO 3m 15 GS *prom, ld 15th-3 out, lkd btn nxt, rallied to ld nr fin* 1 17
648 22/3 Castle Of C' (R) RES 3m 8 G *(fav) w.w. in tch, prog to 3rd 15th, unable qckn apr last* 3 17
Improving; top stable; lightly raced; game; winner behind in Restricted; sure to win one in 98 20

TAMBORITO(IRE) b.g. 8 Thatching - Vera Musica (USA) by Stop The Music (USA) Mrs M Rigg
1996 P(0),U(-),P(0)
306 1/3 Parham (R) MDN 3m 12 G *alwys rear, lost tch whn p.u. aft 14th* P 0
1128 19/4 Penshurst (L) LAD 3m 8 GF *prom to 5th, n.j.w., t.o. 13th* 7 0
Looks hopeless 0

TAMER'S RUN (Irish) — I 281[P]

TAMMY'S FRIEND b.g. 10 Deep Run - Cinderwood by Laurence O Mrs L M Kemble
1996 4(22)
780 31/3 Fakenham (L) HC 3m 110yds 7 G *(bl) ld, mstk 6th, blnd and u.r. 4 out.* U -
1277 27/4 Fakenham P-' (L) CON 3m 10 G *(bl) rear, jmpd slwly 4th, blnd nxt, prog 10th, nvr nr ldrs* 5 11
1284 29/4 Huntingdon (R) HC 3m 6 G *(bl) not fluent, ld till after 8th, mstk next, cl up when u.r. 12th.* U -
1529 18/5 Fakenham (L) HC 3m 110yds 9 G *(bl) prom, outpcd 3 out, styd on apr last.* 4 17
1569 26/5 Fontwell (R) HC 3 1/4m 110yds 10 GF *(bl) keen hold, prom, ld 10th to 12th, wknd apr last.* 5 15
Winning chaser; likes things his own way; blinkers; could still win Confined if in the mood 17

TANGLE BARON gr.g. 9 Baron Blakeney - Spartangle by Spartan General P J Clarke
1996 5(20),P(0),**3(22)**,3(14),4(17),**6(0)**,1(20),2(22),1D(23),2(18)
6 19/1 Barbury Cas' (L) LAD 3m 13 GF *prom till 4th & strgglng hlfwy, sn no ch* 6 0
52 1/2 Wadebridge (L) INT 3m 4 G *(fav) prssd wnr til outpcd 4 out, styd on wll agn frm last* 2 19
294 1/3 Didmarton (L) INT 3m 20 G *alwys prom, ev ch 15th, kpt on onepcd* 3 22
490 10/3 Stratford (L) HC 3m 12 G *prom, mstk 11th, wknd 5 out.* 5 15
888 3/4 Aintree (L) HC 3m 1f 9 G *soon chasing ldr, lost pl 6 out, wknd quickly after next, t.o..* 6 15
1033 12/4 Lifton (R) CON 3m 6 F *3rd 1st-2nd, cls 2nd whn slppd up bnd apr 4th* S -
1038 12/4 Lifton (R) INT 3m 4 F *(fav) 2nd run, made all, lft wll clr 13th, canter* 1 21
1245 26/4 Bratton Down (L) INT 3m 9 GS *(fav) ld/disp to 14th, outpcd frm nxt* 3 11
1311 3/5 Holnicote (L) MEM 3m 7 G *(fav) made most to 3 out, outpcd aft, kpt on und pres* 2 18
1496 14/5 Cothelstone (L) CON 3m 9 GF *rear & nvr going wll, wll bhnd frm 13th, t.o.* 6 0
1594 31/5 Bratton Down (L) INT 3m 10 F *prom, ld 9th, styd on wll frm 2 out, just hld on* 1 22
1614 7/6 Umberleigh (L) CON 3m 3 F *ld til ran out aft 6th* r -
Fair firm ground performer; not 100% reliable; below Open class but should win again late season 20

TANGLE KELLY b.g. 8 Netherkelly - Spartangle by Spartan General Michael Lanz
1996 P(0),F(-),3(12),1(15),P(0),2(0),P(0)
524 15/3 Cothelstone (L) RES 3m 10 GS *alwys prom, cls 2nd whn blnd & u.r. 12th* U -
865 31/3 Kingston St' (R) RES 3m 3 F *disp 6th, cls up til ld aft 16th,clr whn lft alone apr 3 out* 1 17
1038 12/4 Lifton (R) INT 3m 4 F *alwys bhnd, lft 2nd 13th, kpt on onepcd* 2 10
1156 20/4 Stafford Cr' (R) INT 3m 6 GF *prom to 13th, lost tch 15th, no ch aft* 4 0
1312 3/5 Holnicote (L) INT 3m 3 G *made most til outjmpd 2 out, no ch wnr aft* 2 15
1398 5/5 High Bickin' (R) INT 3m 7 G *prom, cls 3rd at 11th, hit 13th, lost tch 14th, p.u.aft 16th* P 0
1441 10/5 Holnicote (L) CON 3m 7 G *ld 1st, prom til ld 8-9th, grad fdd frm 12th* 3 11
1550 24/5 Mounsey Hil' (R) INT 3m 9 G *prom, chsd ldr 9-14th, sn strgglng, p.u. 2 out* P 0
Finished solo when winning Restricted; disappointing overall and will struggle to win again 14

TANGO TOM ch.g. 12 New Member - Dance Partner by Manicou John J Smith
1996 4(13),F(-),P(0),3(10),5(12)
395 8/3 Barbury Cas' (L) XX 3m 9 G *rear, last whn blnd 8th, soon lost tch, p.u. 11th* P 0
Dual winner 93; shows nothing now & looks finished 13

TANHONEY (Irish) — I 6[1]

TANNER b.g. 7 Impecunious - Tantaliser II by Tenterhooks Mrs S E Vaughan
1996 P(0),2(0),P(0),1(10),P(0)
258 22/2 Newtown (L) RES 3m 14 G *f 1st* F -
405 8/3 Llanfrynach (R) RES 3m 15 G *trckd ldrs, outpcd frm hlfwy* 7 0
574 16/3 Garnons (L) RES 3m 14 G *chsd ldrs, outpcd 14th, plodded on frm 3 out* 4 0
1232 26/4 Brampton Br' (R) MEM 3m 4 G *(fav) ld to 2nd, ld 5th-13th, rdn & no ext 15th* 2 0

Won joke Members 96; totally outclassed in proper races 10

TANNOCK BROOK b.g. 9 Meadowbrook - Miss Sunny by Sunyboy W G Macmillan

1996 P(0),U(-),P(0)

158	15/2	Lanark	(R)	LAD	3m	8	G	*bhnd by 4th, t.o. & p.u. 4 out*	P	0
230	22/2	Friars Haugh	(L)	RES	3m	15	G	*made most til 4 out, sn wknd*	5	12
337	1/3	Corbridge	(R)	RES	3m	11	G	*prom til outpcd 9th, kpt on frm 2 out*	5	10

Maiden winner 95; lightly raced & disappointing since; best watched now 14

TANTALUM b.m. 7 Rakaposhi King - Tantrum by Leading Man W Spence

1052	13/4	Lockerbie	(R)	MDN	3m	10	F	*alwys bhnd, p.u. 3 out*	P	0
1222	26/4	Balcormo Ma'	(R)	MDO	3m	6	F	*disp ld frm 6-9th, cls 2nd whn f nxt*	F	-
1336	3/5	Mosshouses	(L)	MDO	3m	7	F	*alwys 1st trio, ld 13th til apr last, no ext*	2	13

Satisfactory 1st season; beaten 4 lengths last start & can score; Firm only so far 13

TANTUM BONUM (Irish) — I 21, , I 49[P], I 199[2], I 276[3], I 358[4], I 451[4]

TAP DANCING ch.g. 11 Sallust - Amorak by Wolver Hollow Neil Allen

1996 P(0),P(0),3(15),**P(0)**

202	15/2	Weston Park	(L)	LAD	3m	13	G	*mid-div, no ch wth ldng trio frm 3 out*	6	0
296	1/3	Didmarton	(L)	LAD	3m	13	G	*rear main grp, t.o. 12th, p.u. 14th*	P	0

Confined winner 95; outclassed in Ladies; stays but hard to win again; G-F 14

TAP PRACTICE (Irish) — I 29[P], I 57,

TARA BOY b.g. 12 Rusticaro (FR) - Flosshilde by Rheingold Mrs Richard Cambray

1996 5(12),F(-),4(18),4(15),6(12),6(0),5(0),4(14),2(0)

200	15/2	Weston Park	(L)	CON	3m	16	G	*alwys rear, p.u. 4 out*	P	0
330	1/3	Eaton Hall	(R)	CON	3m	16	GS	*chsng grp, no imp frm 4 out, onepcd*	5	0
465	8/3	Eyton-On-Se'	(L)	OPE	3m	13	G	*mid-div, ran on frm 5 out, nrst at fin*	3	16
668	23/3	Eaton Hall	(R)	OPE	3m	3	GF	*10l 3rd at 10th, lft 2nd 5 out, no imp wnr*	2	15
848	31/3	Eyton-On-Se'	(L)	MEM	3m	6	GF	*(bl) prom early, steadd 4th, prog 4 out, ran on wll to ld last*	1	17
1175	20/4	Sandon	(L)	CON	3m	8	GF	*(bl) mid-div, t.o. 12th, p.u. 4 out*	P	0
1292	30/4	Cheltenham	(L)	HC	2m 5f	12	GF	*rear, jmpd slowly 5th, rdn 8th, soon well bhnd, kept on und pres from 3 out.*	7	15
1415	9/5	Stratford	(L)	HC	3m	6	G	*rear and mstk 5th, nvr reached ldrs, left poor 2nd when hmpd 2 out, soon one pace.*	2	16
1508	17/5	Bangor	(L)	HC	3m 110yds	12	G	*alwys in rear, struggling 5 out, nvr a factor.*	6	10

Broke losing sequence of 17 & won poor Members; onepaced & easily beaten in competitive races 17

TARA'S UNYOKE (Irish) — I 482[P], I 497[P]

TARGET PRACTICE (Irish) — I 606[5]

TARGET TIME b.m. 7 Faustus (USA) - Alicia Markova by Habat B Neaves

1996 F(-),P(0),U(-),F(-),F(-),F(-)

581	16/3	Detling	(L)	MDO	3m	12	F	*hdwy to 4th 14th, outpcd 4 out, ran on strgly flat*	3	12
787	31/3	Aldington	(L)	MDO	3m	1	HD	*walked over*	1	0
970	6/4	Penshurst	(L)	RES	3m	4	F	*alwys last, jmp slwly 14th, t.o. aft, ran on frm 2 out*	4	0

Improved with better jumping; form very weak & needs another drought year for Restricted hopes 11

TARKA TRAIL b.g. 6 Old Jocus - My Kizzy by The Ditton John Squire

175	15/2	Ottery St M'	(L)	RES	3m	15	G	*rear til hmpd & p.u. 11th*	P	0
460	8/3	Great Treth'	(R)	MDO	3m	13	S	*mid-div, wnt 2nd 14th, sn rddn & no imp frm 3 out*	2	0
625	22/3	Kilworthy	(L)	MDN	3m	14	G	*prom til 15th, 6th & no ch 16th, fin wll*	5	0
794	31/3	Bishopsleigh	(R)	MDO	3m	12	G	*mid-div, slght chnc 4 out, outpcd aft*	3	10

Beaten 12 lengths minimum; improving steadily & go much closer in 98 12

TARRY AWHILE ch.g. 11 Crested Lark - Lucky Sandy by St Columbus Sir Michael Connell

1996 F(-),5(0),2(18),4(14),2(17),**2(20)**,**3(12)**,8(0),3(18)

58	1/2	Kingston Bl'	(L)	MEM	3m	5	GF	*prom to 10th, t.o. & p.u. 2 out*	4	0
148	9/2	Tweseldown	(R)	XX	3m	12	GF	*prom, lft in ld 7th, hdd 12th, no ext frm 3 out*	4	10
655	22/3	Siddington	(L)	RES	3m	10	F	*prom, ld 7-10th, cls up aft, styd on onepcd frm 2 out*	2	15
826	31/3	Lockinge	(L)	RES	3m	4	F	*trckd ldr, ld 8-11th, chsd wnr 14th, not qckn & no imp*	2	12
1081	13/4	Guilsborough	(L)	RES	3m	13	GF	*mstks, in tch whn blnd 6th, rear aft, t.o. 14th*	7	0
1164	20/4	Mollington	(R)	RES	3m	10	GF	*(bl) chsd ldrs til wknd 14th, walked in*	7	0
1286	29/4	Huntingdon	(R)	HC	3m	10	G	*soon pushed along in mid div, lost tch from 11th, no ch after.*	7	0
1466	11/5	Tweseldown	(R)	RES	3m	5	GF	*mostly cls 2nd, ld 4 out, all out flat*	1	17
1608	1/6	Dingley	(R)	INT	3m	11	GF	*ldng trio til wknd apr 2 out, p.u. last*	P	0

Won one well of last 28; novice ridden; safe but very one paced; struggle to win again; F-S 15

TARTAN BUCK(IRE) b.m. 6 Buckskin (FR) - Lovely Tartan by Push On C Dawson

997 12/4 Tranwell (L) MDO 2 1/2m 8 F *prom, hndy 4th 10th-2 out, outpcd & lft poor 3rd last* 3 0

Beaten 25 lengths on debut; can improve & go closer 11

TARTAN GLORY b.m. 7 Roman Glory - Spartan Flame by Owen Anthony R R Ledger

1996 P(0),P(0)

283 23/2 Charing (L) MDO 3m 16 G *alwys bhnd, t.o. & p.u. 15th* P 0

Shown nothing yet 0

TARTAN TORNADO b.g. 11 Strong Gale - Frankford Run by Deep Run W J Laws

1996 P(0),4(18),2(12),**8(0)**,4(15),3(18),2(13),P(0),**8(0)**

232 22/2 Friars Haugh (L) OPE 3m 6 G *alwys twrds rear* 4 16
339 1/3 Corbridge (R) OPE 3m 5f 11 G *mid-div, drppd rear 16th, sn t.o.* 5 16
492 11/3 Sedgefield (L) HC 3m 3f 7 G *prom, outpcd 4 out, no impn final 2.* 4 21
590 21/3 Kelso (L) HC 3 1/2m 5 G *mstks, alwys rear, bhnd 16th.* 5 0
812 31/3 Tranwell (L) OPE 3m 7 G *alwys rear, outpcd final ctt, wnt poor 5th 3 out* 5 12
993 12/4 Tranwell (L) OPE 3m 5 F *towrds rear,wnt 3l 4th 9th,ld 11th,jnd last,ld last 100yds* 1 19
1220 26/4 Balcormo Ma' (R) OPE 3m 2 F *(fav) set mod pce, hdd 2 out, kpt on onepce* 2 10
1335 3/5 Mosshouses (L) OPE 3m 4 F *sn bhnd, went 2nd 14th, chal 3 out, outpcd apr last* 2 21
1512 17/5 Corbridge (R) OPE 3m 10 GS *rear, wll bhnd 6th, t.o. & p.u. 4 out* P 0

H/chase winner in 95; safe but moderate; won awful Open & will struggle to win again 15

TASHALIN (Irish) — **I** 368P, **I** 432P, **I** 5253, **I** 575P, **I** 586,

TASMANITE br.g. 8 Lighter - Minirocket by Space King Miss S Garratt

1996 P(0),P(0),P(0),P(0),F(-)

126 9/2 Cottenham (R) RES 3m 14 GF *alwys bhnd, last & t.o. whn p.u. 12th* P 0
283 23/2 Charing (L) MDO 3m 16 G *chsd ldrs, rdn & wknd 12th, 7th whn p.u. 14th* P 0

Of no account 0

TASSAGH BOY (Irish) — **I** 120B, **I** 2465

TATTLEJACK(IRE) ch.g. 9 Le Bavard (FR) - Bonne Fille by Bonne Noel M Silcock

1996 5(0),**F(-)**,7(0),2(16),3(12),6(0),5(11)

356 2/3 Great Stain' (L) INT 3m 9 S *hld up, prog 13th, went 2nd 4 out, ld apr last, ran on well* 1 17
671 23/3 Eaton Hall (R) INT 3 3/4m 8 GF *mid-div, nvr dang* 4 0
1047 13/4 Lockerbie (R) INT 3m 4 F *(fav) (bl) disp to 5th, ld 15th, jnd last, found ext cls hm* 1 18
1121 19/4 Whittington (L) CON 3m 4 F *(fav) (vis) made most frm 3rd, clr 3 out, easily* 1 19

Changed hands & revived 97; well ridden & placed; stays well; Any; sold Ascot June 18

TAU ch.g. 12 Kambalda - Mystry Tour by Master Buck Miss Felicity McLachlan

1996 P(0),P(0),4(12),3(14),1(15),**4(0)**

576 16/3 Detling (L) MEM 3m 10 F *blnrd & u.r. 2nd* U -
969 6/4 Penshurst (L) INT 3m 3 F *chsd ldr 7th, drvn up to chal last, ld flat* 1 14
1127 19/4 Penshurst (L) OPE 3m 7 GF *ld to 7th, wth ldr to 12th, rdn & outpcd 4 out, p.u. last* P 0
1285 29/4 Huntingdon (R) HC 3m 10 G *rear, lost tch 11th, kept on und pres from 3 out.* 3 17
1504 16/5 Folkestone (R) HC 3m 7f 5 G *chsd ldr to 13th, soon wknd, no ch from 15th, tk poor 3rd near fin.* 3 11

Moderate; won 2 bad races 96/97; stays; onepaced; needs same to score again 16

TAURA'S RASCAL b.g. 8 Scallywag - Centaura by Centaurus K P Brennan

1996 1(15)

287 27/2 Huntingdon (R) HC 3m 13 GS *chasing ldrs when f 7th.* F -
760 29/3 Kimble (L) RES 3m 7 GF *rear, prog to ld 11th-2 out, drvn to ld flat* 1 16
1043 12/4 Cothelstone (L) INT 3m 7 GF *n.j.w. made all, clr whn blnd 3 out, kpt on wll und pres* 1 19
1286 29/4 Huntingdon (R) HC 3m 10 G *trckd ldrs, blnd 12th, rdn and in tch 15th, wknd 2 out, fin tired.* 3 19
1360 5/5 Towcester (R) HC 2 3/4m 7 GF *chsd ldrs, hit 7th and 11th, hit 3 out and soon wknd, no ch when jmpd badly right last.* 4 0
1588 30/5 Stratford (L) HC 3 1/2m 9 G *mid div, hit 10th, blnd badly 15th, bhnd when p.u. before 17th.* P 0

Improved; speedy but many blunders; good enough for Confinds; stays & battles; G-G/F 21

TAUREAN TYCOON b.g. 13 Octogenarian - Eastling by Tycoon II D L Williams

1996 **P(NH)**,**P(NH)**,**P(NH)**

361 2/3 Garnons (L) LAD 3m 7 GS *30l 4th at 7th, effrt to 12l 3rd 14th, won race for 2nd* 2 16
389 8/3 Sandown (R) HC 2 1/2m 110yds 6 G *not fluent, bhnd from 7th.* 6 11
520 15/3 Cothelstone (L) LAD 3m 12 GS *alwys mid-div* 5 17
824 31/3 Lockinge (L) CON 3m 8 F *chsd wnr 5-6th, 4th & outpcd 11th, no imp ldrs aft* 3 10
1056 13/4 Hackwood Pa' (L) LAD 3m 3 GF *chsd wnr to 11th, wknd rpdly 3 out* 3 10

Dead 12

TAURIAN PRINCESS b.m. 8 Electric - Facetious by Malicious G D Hanmer

1996 P(0),3(16)

939 6/4 Tabley (R) LAD 3m 9 G *w.w. in tch, 5th & outpcd 3 out, kpt on* 4 16

Hurdles winner 92; lightly raced; ran well when placed 96/97 but unlikely to win a Ladies 16

TBILISI b.g. 10 Roscoe Blake - Big Maggie by Master Owen — G D Hanmer

381	4/3	Leicester	(R)	HC	2m 1f	13 G	*reluctant to race, alwys well bhnd, p.u. before 4 out.*	P	0
1179	20/4	Sandon	(L)	MDN	3m	6 GF	*ld, just ld whn f last*	F	11
1304	3/5	Weston Park	(L)	MDO	3m	8 G	*hrd hld, ld 4th til ref to race apr 8th*	R	-
1382	5/5	Eyton-On-Se'	(L)	INT	3m	7 GF	*ref to race*	R	-
1541	18/5	Wolverhampt'	(L)	MDO	3m	15 GS	*ref to race*	0	0

Has ability but overwhelmed by his temperament; best avoided 0

TEA BOX (Irish) — I 181[2], I 268[3]

TEA CEE KAY ch.g. 7 True Song - Fort Ditton by The Ditton — C O King

1996 3(15),4(18),4(14),2(15),3(12),1(15),**6(12)**,**3(16)**

7	19/1	Barbury Cas'	(L)	RES	3m	14 GF	*ld to 3 out, wknd apr last*	3	15
23	25/1	Badbury Rin'	(L)	RES	3m	8 GF	*cls up,ld 9th,clr 16th,stmbld bnd apr last,hdd & no ext flat*	2	18
94	7/2	Newbury	(L)	HC	2 1/2m	12 G	*bhnd 6th.*	5	10
222	16/2	Heythrop	(R)	RES	3m	17 G	*chsd ldrs, outpcd frm 15th, ran on apr last, nrst fin*	3	18
585	18/3	Fontwell	(R)	HC	2m 3f	7 GF	*alwys prom, ld 4th to 13th, kept on one pace from 2 out.*	2	19
779	31/3	Fakenham	(L)	HC	2m 5f 110yds	9 G	*well pld till rear 8th, soon lost tch.*	6	0
1080	13/4	Guilsborough	(L)	RES	3m	11 GF	*(fav) ld to 9th, ld 13th, kckd clr 2 out, styd on*	1	17
1203	26/4	Worcester	(L)	HC	2m 7f 110yds	10 S	*ld to 6th, chsd wnr after till outpcd 8th, went poor 2nd 3 out, t.o..*	2	17
1360	5/5	Towcester	(R)	HC	2 3/4m	7 GF	*ld till after 4th, styd with ldr till led again after 7th, rdn and hdd after 2 out, stayed on same pace.*	2	19

Won 2 placed 11 last 17 starts; can win Confined but H/chase unlikely; well ridden; G-F 21

TEADS BOREEN (Irish) — I 83[2], I 136[1], I 257[2], I 323[4], I 486[P], I 598[F]

TEAPLANTER b.g. 14 National Trust - Miss India by Indian Ruler — R G Russell

1996 1(31),**1(34)**,**2(34)**,**1(35)**,**2(32)**,**1(34)**,**1(34)**,**4(20)**

67	1/2	Wetherby	(L)	HC	3m 1f	10 G	*ld to 5th, mstk 8th, led 10th, mistake 4 out, hdd final 100 yards, no ext.*	2	32
227	21/2	Kempton	(R)	HC	3m	6 G	*(fav) ld to 3rd, in trbl and rdn 10th, hit 12th and wknd.*	4	15
384	6/3	Towcester	(R)	HC	3m 1f	7 GS	*(fav) made most, kept on gamely from 2 out.*	1	27
782	31/3	Towcester	(R)	HC	2 3/4m	3 GF	*(fav) ld to 7th, styd tracking ldr, chal 4 out, led, blnd and hdd next, led again apr last, stayed on gamely.*	1	25

Wonderful campaigner; has been retired 30

TEARAWAY KING (Irish) — I 5[1], I 30[1], I 164[1]

TEARFULL (Irish) — I 419[1], I 475[P], I 562[P], I 603[1]

TEATRADER b.g. 11 Baron Blakeney - Miss India by Indian Ruler — Miss T O Blazey

1996 **3(NH)**,**2(NH)**,**5(NH)**,**P(NH)**,**4(NH)**,**U(NH)**,**3(NH)**,**3(NH)**,**P(NH)**

42	1/2	Larkhill	(R)	MXO	3m	7 GF	*prom til outpcd 12th, wll bhnd frm 14th*	3	20
178	15/2	Larkhill	(R)	CON	3m	9 G	*made most, jnd 3 out, hdd nxt, ev ch last, onepcd*	2	21
382	5/3	Bangor	(L)	HC	3m 110yds	6 GS	*ld to 9th, remained prom, led again 3 out, hrd pressed, slightly hmpd run-in by loose horse, hdd cl home.*	2	18
496	15/3	Hereford	(R)	HC	3m 1f 110yds	10 GF	*hit 6th and bhnd, t.o. when p.u. before 4 out.*	P	0
591	21/3	Newbury	(L)	HC	3m	7 GF	*in tch, bhnd final cct.*	4	13
680	29/3	Towcester	(R)	HC	3m 1f	8 GF	*prom to 11th, soon lost pl, t.o..*	7	11
1289	30/4	Cheltenham	(L)	HC	3m 1f 110yds	6 GF	*ld to 4th, wknd 12th, t.o. and p.u. before 3 out.*	P	0
1448	10/5	Kingston Bl'	(L)	CON	3m	9 G	*cls up, ld 6th, sn hdd, chsd ldrs, 4th 2 out, ran on*	2	16
1503	16/5	Folkestone	(R)	HC	3 1/4m	7 G	*bhnd, hmpd 7th, no prog from 13th, soon t.o., left poor 3rd 2 out.*	3	15
1570	26/5	Hereford	(R)	HC	3m 1f 110yds	14 G	*ld to 3rd, wknd 4 out.*	5	0

Won 5 in 95; novice ridden; safe but onepaced & hard to win with; may find another race 16

TED'S KNIGHT(IRE) ch.g. 6 Mister Lord (USA) - Annie Panny by Take A Reef — Dave Dixon

1996 F(-),P(0),2(14),**P(0)**,**P(0)**

20	25/1	Badbury Rin'	(L)	MDN	3m	9 GF	*(fav) alwys prom, mstk 10th, lft 2nd 2 out, no imp wnr flat*	2	11
146	9/2	Tweseldown	(R)	MDO	3m	10 GF	*(fav) blnd badly 1st, rear, styd on thro' btn hrss 4 out, nvr nrr*	3	10

Placed in modest Maidens 96/97; finsiehed early 97; still young & could yet repay supporters 13

TEDSTONE FOX b.g. 5 Bold Fox - Royal Wren by Blast — Mrs E Weaver

365	2/3	Garnons	(L)	MDO	2 1/2m	14 GS	*mid-div, blnd & u.r. 4th*	U	-
571	16/3	Garnons	(L)	MDN	2 1/2m	13 G	*rear whn blnd & u.r. 5th*	U	-

No signs yet 0

TEDUET b.g. 7 Teofane - Lovers Duet by Jimmy The Singer — T F G Marks

777 29/3 Dingley (R) MDO 2m 5f 8 G *alwys rear, outpcd 6 out, p.u. last* P 0
928 6/4 Garthorpe (R) MDO 3m 8 GF *mid-div, t.o. & p.u. 4 out* P 0
1281 27/4 Fakenham P-' (L) MDO 3m 8 G *chsd ldr 8th, ld 13th til apr 3 out, no ext* 3 0

Beaten 15 lengths in poor race; rangy & can do better; needs to 10

TEE AITCH KAY (Irish) — **I** 369[P]

TEETON HEAVENS b.m. 6 Sunley Builds - Angels Are Near by Floriferous Mrs Joan Tice

450 8/3 Newton Brom' (R) MDN 3m 7 G *rear, 15l 4th at 7th, effrt 12th, onepcd frm 16th* 2 12
1082 13/4 Guilsborough (L) MDN 3m 14 GF *(fav) mstks, w.w. in tch whn blnd 15th, 5th & no ch whn p.u. last* P 0
1356 4/5 Dingley (R) MDO 3m 9 G *(Jt fav) mstks,2nd whn blnd 12th,lft in ld 14th-2 out,ld last,ran on* 1 12

Fortunate in weak maiden; hampered by jumping; can improve; needs to for Restricted 14

TEETON MILL gr.g. 8 Neltino - Celtic Well by Celtic Cone C R Saunders

1996 F(-),1(20)

216 16/2 Southwell P' (L) OPE 3m 12 GS *w.w. lft 2nd 7th, ld 4 out, styd on well* 1 28
377 4/3 Leicester (R) HC 2 1/2m 110yds 15 G *(fav) held up, hdwy 6th, ld 9th, driven out.* 1 26

Improving; good stable; stays; sure to improve further; one to watch; S-G 29

TEIGR PREN b.g. 6 Tigerwood - Official Lady by Official Mrs B W D Llewellyn

365 2/3 Garnons (L) MDO 2 1/2m 14 GS *t.o. 5th, nrly f nxt & p.u.* P 0
539 16/3 Erw Lon (L) RES 3m 8 GF *mstk 1st, ran green & alwys bhnd* 5 0
842 31/3 Lydstep (L) MDO 3m 12 F *alwys rear, f 15th* F -
1367 5/5 Pantyderi (L) MDO 3m 7 G *mstks, alwys mid-div, wll btn & p.u. 3 out* P 0
1473 11/5 Erw Lon (L) MDO 3m 13 GS *n.j.w. alwys rear, p.u. 12th* P 0
1556 24/5 Bassaleg (R) RES 3m 13 G *n.j.w. sn wll bhnd, t.o. & p.u. 11th* P 0

Jumped poorly & reveals no ability 0

TEKLA(FR) b.g. 12 Toujours Pret (USA) - Hekla Des Sacart (FR) by Laniste E H Lodge

1996 F(-),4(17),3(0),4(0),1(15),**5(0)**,**P(0)**,**8(0)**,**P(0)**

1535 18/5 Mollington (R) LAD 3m 6 GS *immed dtchd, t.o. 7th, p.u. 11th* P 0

Won Members 96, vanished quickly 97; does not really stay & most unlikely to win again 11

TEKROC (Irish) — **I** 20[P], **I** 132[F], **I** 171[3], **I** 307[4], **I** 536[P]

TELECOM AFFAIR (Irish) — **I** 104[P], **I** 158[1], **I** 298[F]

TELEPHONE b.g. 8 Sonnen Gold - Bellekino by Relkino R J Hamer

1996 5(0),P(0),P(0),1(14),P(0),3(15)

300 1/3 Didmarton (L) RES 3m 23 G *alwys last grp, t.o. & p.u. 3 out, dsmntd* P 0
539 16/3 Erw Lon (L) RES 3m 8 GF *mid-div, prog frm 11th, gd jmp 14th, ld 2 out, easily* 1 17
714 29/3 Llanvapley (L) CON 3m 15 GF *ld early, grdly wknd, p.u. & dismntd 13th* P 0

Maiden winner 96; won modest Restricted; inconsistent; may be has a problem; more needed now 16

TELLAPORKY b.g. 8 Bold Fort - Ab Dabh by Spanish Gold T Hind

1996 **P(NH)**,**P(NH)**

490 10/3 Stratford (L) HC 3m 12 G *held up, mstk 3rd, hdwy 7th, blundd and u.r. 11th.* U -
495 14/3 Fakenham (L) HC 2m 5f 110yds 10 G *ld to 9th, pressed ldr, led 11th to 2 out, soon wknd.* 4 17
679 26/3 Ascot (R) HC 2m 3f 110yds 9 G *held up, mstks 6th and next, hrd rdn after 9th, bhnd next, t.o..* 6 0
1099 19/4 Stratford (L) HC 2m 5f 110yds 14 G *slowly into stride, alwys bhnd.* 6 0
1296 3/5 Hereford (R) HC 2m 3f 11 G *(bl) slowly away, n.j.w., t.o. from 6th.* 4 0
1530 18/5 Fakenham (L) HC 2m 5f 110yds 11 G *held up, hdwy 4 out, not reach ldrs.* 3 17
1587 29/5 Uttoxeter (L) HC 2m 5f 11 GF *well bhnd til styd on from 2 out, nvr nrr.* 4 11

Shows some ability; novice ridden & needs to lower his sights; stamina unproven 16

TELL TALE(IRE) b.g. 5 Tale Quale - Loobagh Bridge by River Beauty G H Barber

1435 10/5 Marks Tey (L) INT 3m 8 G *rear whn hmpd 2nd, mstk nxt, last 10th, p.u. nxt* P 0
1568 25/5 Kingston Bl' (L) MDO 3m 11 GF *mid-div, prog 13th, chsd wnr 15th, no imp til ran on flat* 2 0

Late to appear; beat 6 others in weak Maiden; should be capable of going one better 13

TELL THE BOYS(IRE) b.g. 9 Montelimar (USA) - Disco Beat by No Mercy A J Mobley

374 2/3 Mollington (R) MDN 3m 14 G *(fav) cls up going wll, chsd wnr 15th, chal last, no ext nr fin* 2 15

Ex novice Hurdler; just pipped in fair Maiden; obviously good enough but not seen after 15

TEMPESTUOUS LADY (Irish) — **I** 31[1], **I** 313[1], **I** 346[1]

TEMPLAND b.g. 6 Respect - Miss Sunny by Sunyboy W G Macmillan

1052	13/4	Lockerbie	(R)	MDN	3m	10	F	*chsng grp whn p.u. 10th*	P 0

Only learning so far 0

TEMPLEMARTIN (Irish) — I 58^{U}

TEMPLE MARY ch.g. 10 Roman Warrior - Cavendish by Kalamoun — Andrew Eveleigh

108	8/2	Milborne St'	(L)	MXO	3m	6	GF	*handy to 13th, lost tch nxt, outpcd*	5 12
690	29/3	Little Wind'	(R)	OPE	3m	4	GF	*ld 7-10th, lost tch aft 14th, wll bhnd whn blnd 2 out*	3 13
1021	12/4	Badbury Rin'	(L)	MEM	3m	2	F	*(fav) restrained, disp 10th, blndrd 3 out, wnt aft nxt, rddn out*	1 10

Ex-Irish chase winner 92; lightly raced; does not really stay; won a match & outclassed otherwise 15

TEMPLEPATRICK (Irish) — I 363^{P}, I 435^{6}

TEMPLERAINEY(IRE) b.g. 9 Welsh Term - Saharan by Tarboosh (USA) — Richard J Smith

179	15/2	Larkhill	(R)	CON	3m	12	G	*s.s. went prom 5th, 4th & wkng 12th, p.u. nxt*	P 0
292	1/3	Didmarton	(L)	MEM	3m	9	G	*in tch, cls 2nd at 11th, sn btn, lost poor 2nd apr 2 out*	3 0
746	29/3	Barbury Cas'	(L)	CON	3m	2	F	*trckd ldr, ld 13th, qcknd clr, easily*	1 15

Winning hurdler; won a desperate match; does not stay & most unlikely to follow up 12

TEMPLEVALLEY (Irish) — I 483^{4}, I 568,

TEN BOB DOWN (Irish) — I 42^{F}

TEN BOB NOTE b.g. 8 True Song - Castelira by Castle — Richard J Smith

43	1/2	Larkhill	(R)	MDO	3m	10	GF	*jmpd slwly 1st & 2nd, ref & u.r. nxt*	R -
392	8/3	Barbury Cas'	(L)	MDN	3m	9	G	*(bl) j.w. ld 4th, 10l clr 12th, wknd 2 out, hdd nr fin*	2 14

Has ability & just caught in weak race; chances if reproducing but one to treat with caution 13

TEN CASTLES (Irish) — I 533^{4}, I 596^{3}

TENDERMAN(IRE) b.g. 6 Tender King - Mayrhofen by Don — J M Turner

1996 P(0),P(0),2(16)

324	1/3	Marks Tey	(L)	RES	3m	16	G	*t.d.e., in tch to 10th, t.o. & p.u. 15th*	P 0
597	22/3	Horseheath	(R)	RES	3m	8	F	*alwys rear, bhnd whn p.u. aft 15th, dsmntd*	P 0

Irish maiden winner; problems & finished early 97; young but best watched if reappearing 11

TENELORD ch.g. 10 True Song - Tenella by Wrekin Rambler — C R Saunders

1996 4(16),P(0),2(15),1(15),3(16),1(18),P(0)

473	9/3	Southwell P'	(L)	CON	3m	10	G	*chsd ldr to 3rd, 6th & wkng 12th, t.o. & p.u. 2 out, dsmntd*	P 0
769	29/3	Dingley	(R)	CON	3m	14	G	*ld/disp til wknd frm 12th, 5th & outpcd 5 out, p.u. last*	P 0
1076	13/4	Guilsborough	(L)	MEM	3m	9	GF	*not fluent, w.w. prog & cls up 14th, wknd nxt, p.u. 2 out*	P 0

Dual winner 96; barely stays; showed nothing in 97 & can only be watched now 13

TEN PAST ELEVEN (Irish) — I 407^{F}

TEN PENCE PRINCESS (Irish) — I 548^{5}

TERRORISA ch.m. 6 Alias Smith (USA) - Tyne Bridge by Red Bridge — Mrs J D Percy

612	22/3	Friars Haugh	(L)	MDN	3m	14	GF	*sn t.o., p.u. 4 out*	P 0
1513	17/5	Corbridge	(R)	MDO	3m	13	GS	*rear, prog into mid-div 10th, outpcd frm 4 out*	4 10

Satisfactory start beaten 15 lengths in modest race; looks sure to go closer 98 12

TERRY MCCANN (Irish) — I 107^{P}, I 161^{P}, I 301^{P}, I 353^{F}

TEST THE JOCKEY (Irish) — I 232^{F}, I 280^{B}, I 295, , I 398^{P}

THADYS REMEDY (Irish) — I 109^{1}, I 130^{P}, I 240^{4}, I 299^{4}

THAMESDOWN TOOTSIE b.m. 12 Comedy Star (USA) - Lizzie Lightfoot by Hotfoot — Miss V S Lyon

1996 5(0),2(21),2(24)

280	23/2	Charing	(L)	LAD	3m	12	G	*made most to 8th, outpcd frm 16th*	5 15
304	1/3	Parham	(R)	LAD	3m	10	G	*(Jt fav) ld to 13th, 3rd & btn whn stmbld & u.r. last*	U 18
573	16/3	Garnons	(L)	LAD	3m	8	G	*cls up frm 10th, chal 13th, not qckn frm 3 out*	4 18
885	1/4	Flagg Moor	(L)	LAD	3m	5	G	*chsd ldr 2-15th, onepcd aft*	3 18
1078	13/4	Guilsborough	(L)	LAD	3m	11	GF	*cls up, chsd wnr 12th-3 out, onepcd aft*	3 18

Former uesful Ladies horse; declining now; novice ridden; needs Soft & unlikely to win again 18

THANK U JIM b.g. 9 Bootsman Bains (GER) - Oregano by Track Spare — Mrs G Sunter

1072	13/4	Whitwell-On'	(R)	MXO	4m	21	G	*ld to 15th, grad fdd*	5 17
1201	24/4	Perth	(R)	HC	3m	14	G	*blnd and u.r. 1st.*	U -
1346	3/5	Gisburn	(R)	LAD	3m	5	GF	*made all, clr aft 2 out, easily*	1 20
1422	10/5	Easingwold	(L)	LAD	3m	7	GF	*(fav) ld to 6th, trckng ldr whn s.u. bef nxt*	S -
1511	17/5	Corbridge	(R)	LAD	3m	10	GS	*disp to 5th,chsd ldr aft, ld 9th-4 out, rallied last, ld fin*	1 22
1546	24/5	Hexham	(L)	HC	2 1/2m 110yds	10	GF	*with ldr, ld 8th, f 3 out.*	F -

1590	31/5 Stratford	(L) HC	3m	9	G	*ld to 3rd, styd upsides till regained ld after 6 out, set str pace after, stayed on well from 2 out.*	1	25

Missed 96; speedy; misiakes; beat good horse in H/chase; harder to place now; win Ladies 98; G-F 24

THATS DEDICATION (Irish) — **I** 285²

THEAIRYMAN (Irish) — **I** 302ᴾ, **I** 337ᴾ, **I** 429ᴾ, **I** 443ᶠ, **I** 533¹, **I** 569ᴾ

THE ALLEYCAT(IRE) b.g. 6 Tidaro (USA) - Allitess by Mugatpura — Mrs S H Shirley-Beavan

161	15/2 Lanark	(R) MDO	2m 5f	14	G	*sn wll bhnd, p.u. 10th*	P	0
341	1/3 Corbridge	(R) MDN	3m	10	G	*rear, t.o. 4th, p.u. 12th*	P	0
417	8/3 Dalston	(R) MDO	2 1/2m	11	GS	*prom, prssd wnr frm 8th, no imp aft 3 out*	2	12
767	29/3 Whittington	(L) MDO	3m	9	S	*lft in clr ld 13th,15l up whn mstk 3 out,wknd & hdd apr last*	2	12
1051	13/4 Lockerbie	(R) MDN	3m	10	F	*(fav) last at 9th, prog to chal 2 out, alwys just hld*	2	15

Half brother to Fiftysevenchannels; improving & knocking on the door; should score in 98 14

THE ANNOUNCER ch.g. 11 Le Bavard (FR) - Maeves Choice — Mrs V Anderson

836	31/3 Thorpe Lodge	(L) OPE	3m	7	F	*alwys last, rdn frm 5th, t.o. 10th, p.u. 13th*	P	0

Of no account 0

THE APPRENTICE ch.g. 11 Torus - Bog View by African Sky — Robert Williams

1996 1(15),P(0),2(16),P(0),1(16),P(0)

97	8/2 Great Treth'	(R) INT	3m	13	GS	*ld to 7th, wknd rpdly, p.u. 11th*	P	0

Dual winner 96; barely stays; very brief 97 & best watched if returning 15

THE ARCHORIAN b.g. 8 Sula Bula - My Name Is Nobody by Push On — J Young

1996 **7(NH),P(NH)**

78	2/2 Market Rase'	(L) RES	3m	8	GF	*ld, clr whn f 3rd, dead*	F	-

Dead 0

THE ARTFUL RASCAL b.g. 13 Scallywag - Quick Exit by David Jack — M A Kemp

1996 1(26)

63	1/2 Horseheath	(R) OPE	3m	5	GF	*(fav) ld 5th, made rest, drew wll clr 14th, easily*	1	27
322	1/3 Marks Tey	(L) OPE	3 1/2m	9	G	*(fav) cls up, ld frm 11th, drew wll clr frm 17th, easy*	1	26
579	16/3 Detling	(L) OPE	4m	9	F	*(fav) patiently rdn, prog frm rear 18th, ld 25th, clr 2 out*	1	28

Useful Pointer; very lightly raced; well handled; stays well; sure to win more; F-S 28

THE AUCTIONEER gr.g. 7 Neltino - Floral Palm by Floribunda — Mrs P Rowe

209	16/2 Southwell P'	(L) MDO	3m	7	GS	*ld to 4th & 8th til apr 3 out, rallied nxt, no ext nr fin*	2	17
450	8/3 Newton Brom'	(R) MDN	3m	7	G	*(fav) made virt all, styd on well frm 2 out*	1	13
770	29/3 Dingley	(R) RES	3m	18	G	*(fav) ld to 3rd, 2nd til blnd & u.r. 10th*	U	-

Missed 96; improving; good stable; stays; no problem in finding Restricted; G-G/S 17

THE BANDON CAR (Irish) — **I** 233ᶠ

THE BELL TREE (Irish) — **I** 133ᶠ, **I** 184⁴, **I** 322ᴾ, **I** 400ᴾ

THE BIG BAY MARE (Irish) — **I** 538ᴾ, **I** 599ˢ

THE BIG FELLA (Irish) — **I** 12ᴾ, **I** 82ᴾ, **I** 86⁵, **I** 146ᴾ, **I** 269²

THE BIRDIE SONG b.m. 7 Little Wolf - Katebird by Birdbrook — Mrs G M Summers

1996 F(-)

1165	20/4 Mollington	(R) MDO	3m	9	GF	*alwys rear, lost tch 13th, t.o. & p.u. last*	P	0
1357	4/5 Dingley	(R) MDO	3m	5	G	*n.j.w., disp ld to 2nd, outpcd 14th, no dang aft*	3	0
1537	18/5 Mollington	(R) MDO	3m	14	GS	*mstks in rear, lost tch 13th, t.o.*	5	0

Placed in dire race; needs to jump better to have any chances 0

THE BISHOPS SISTER (Irish) — **I** 393ᴾ, **I** 438ᵁ, **I** 470ᴾ, **I** 552ᵁ

THE BLEARY FLYER (Irish) — **I** 71ᵁ, **I** 112ᵁ, **I** 126ᴾ, **I** 178, , **I** 375ᶠ, **I** 467ᴾ

THE BLIND JUDGE b.g. 8 Baron Blakeney - Fernessa by Roman Warrior — J S Warner

1996 U(-),5(0),F(-),P(0)

261	22/2 Newtown	(L) MDN	3m	16	G	*alwys bhnd, t.o. 12th, p.u. aft nxt*	P	0
485	9/3 Tweseldown	(R) MDO	3m	11	G	*prom til mstk 9th, wknd 11th, last whn f 14th*	F	-
1059	13/4 Hackwood Pa'	(L) MDO	3m	6	GF	*in rear til u.r. 4 out*	U	-
1200	23/4 Andoversford	(R) MDO	3m	8	F	*alwys bhnd, jmpd slwly 4th, p.u. 12th*	P	0
1324	3/5 Bonvilston	(R) MDO	3m	16	G	*alwys rear, p.u. 12th*	P	0
1454	11/5 Maisemore P'	(L) MEM	3m	5	G	*jmpd slwly 3rd & sn t.o., 2 fncs bhnd whn f last*	F	-

Of no account 0

THE BODHRAN(IRE) b.g. 7 Bowling Pin - Punch Bowl by Tarboosh (USA) — T J C Seegar

1996 **4(NH)**

176 15/2 Ottery St M' (L) RES 3m 17 G *cls up, 3rd whn f 12th* F -
316 1/3 Clyst St Ma' (L) MDN 3m 6 HY *(fav) hld up, prog 11th, ld apr last, f last, unlucky* F 12
527 15/3 Cothelstone (L) MDN 3m 14 GS *w.w. in tch, ev ch 2 out, not qckn* 3 14
591 21/3 Newbury (L) HC 3m 7 GF *f 4th.* F -
794 31/3 Bishopsleigh (R) MDO 3m 12 G *mid-div, outpcd 16th, lost tch nxt, p.u. 3 out* P 0

Unlucky in poor race & ran much better next time; good enough to win; best runs with give 14

THE BOILER WHITE(IRE) ch.g. 9 Deep Run - Cill Dara by Lord Gayle (USA) Miss J Froggatt
1996 **7(NH),10(NH),6(NH),P(NH),2(NH)**

85 2/2 Wolverhampt' (L) LAD 3m 11 GS *bhnd, last whn u.r. 8th* U -
139 9/2 Thorpe Lodge (L) LAD 3m 4 GF *j.w. 2nd/3rd til ld 6 out, ran on strngly whn chal 2 out* 1 17
202 15/2 Weston Park (L) LAD 3m 13 G *chsng grp, nvr rchd ldrs, kpt on* 5 0
329 1/3 Eaton Hall (R) LAD 3m 10 GS *mid to rear, outpcd, styng on frm 3 out* 5 12
546 16/3 Garthorpe (R) LAD 3m 11 GF *alwys wll bhnd, t.o. frm 10th* 9 0

Winning chaser; novice ridden; won poor Ladies; moody & inconsistent; needs same to win again 14

THE BOLD ABBOT b.g. 7 Derring Rose - Canford Abbas by Hasty Word R A Lissack
1996 P(0),5(0),F(-),B(-),2(12),6(0),4(11),8(0)

41 1/2 Larkhill (R) MDO 3m 13 GF *4th whn mstk & u.r. 5th* U -
181 15/2 Larkhill (R) MDO 3m 17 G *alwys prom, ev ch 3 out, lft 2nd last, unable qckn* 2 14
299 1/3 Didmarton (L) MDN 3m 14 G *nvr nr ldrs, wll bhnd whn u.r. 14th* U -
556 16/3 Ottery St M' (L) RES 3m 12 G *mid-div, lft 3rd 3 out, nvr bttr* 3 12
643 22/3 Castle Of C' (R) MDO 3m 12 G *ld to 3rd, ld 9th, made rest, clr apr last, styd on* 1 16

Changed hands; improved; novice ridden; stays but onepaced; needs more for Restricted 15

THE BOOLYA (Irish) — I 115^{2}, I 121^{3}, I 211^{4}, I 249^{2}, I 327^{U}, I 374^{U}, I 433^{3}, I 465^{4}

THE BOUNDER b.g. 7 Uncle Pokey - Young Romance by King's Troop L G Tizzard
1996 **3(NH),8(NH),1(NH),2(NH),7(NH),3(NH),2(NH),3(NH)**

4 19/1 Barbury Cas' (L) OPE 3m 9 GF *prssd ldr, brthr aft 12th, rnwd effrt to ld 2 out, ran on wl* 1 30
171 15/2 Ottery St M' (L) OPE 3m 9 G *(fav) j.w. made all, not extndd* 1 32
295 1/3 Didmarton (L) OPE 3m 9 G *j.w. made all, qcknd clr aft 2 out, lft wll clr last* 1 30
521 15/3 Cothelstone (L) OPE 3m 8 GS *(fav) made all, modest pace, alwys in cmmnd, clvrly* 1 26

Winning hurdler; a revelation & top class Pointer; well handled; H/chases surely in 98; G/S-G/F 35

THE BREAK (Irish) — I 310^{P}

THE BUACHAILL(IRE) ch.g. 8 Le Bavard (FR) - Many Views by Bargello Mrs Alix Stevenson
1996 1(14),3(15),4(10)

131 9/2 Alnwick (L) RES 3m 13 G *prom, ld 8th-4 out, onepcd und pres aft* 4 0
338 1/3 Corbridge (R) RES 3m 10 G *(fav) rear, prog 7th, ld 12th-14th, onepcd frm 2 out* 2 15
415 8/3 Dalston (R) RES 3m 19 GS *trckd ldrs, mstk 13th, ld aft 3 out, hld on und pres* 1 17
1425 10/5 Aspatria (L) LAD 3m 6 G *t.d.e. chsd ldr, mstk 11th, clsd 16th, ld aft 3 out, sn clr* 1 21
1511 17/5 Corbridge (R) LAD 3m 10 GS *(fav) prom til outpcd 9th,prog 12th,ld 4 out til wknd & hdd last* 5 18

Improving; interrupted season & can be excused last run; win more Ladies 98; stays; G-S 23

THE BUCK PONY (Irish) — I 25^{2}, I 150^{F}, I 187^{P}, I 263^{P}, I 406^{5}

THE BUG HILL (Irish) — I 55, , I 100^{P}, I 154^{P}, I 341^{P}, I 391^{P}, I 405^{2}, I 459^{4}, I 500^{2}, I 548^{3}, I 593^{U}

THE BUTLER ch.g. 11 Roman Warrior - Just Nicola by Eborneezer J Sluggett
1996 P(0),F(-),6(0),P(0)

50 1/2 Wadebridge (L) RES 3m 10 G *disp to 2nd, prom, ev ch 3 out, wknd last* 5 13
97 8/2 Great Treth' (R) INT 3m 13 GS *mid-div til rear & no ch 13th, p.u. nxt* P 0
532 15/3 Wadebridge (L) RES 3m 9 GF *ld to 4th, sn bhnd* 6 0
736 29/3 Higher Kilw' (L) RES 3m 10 GF *ld 8-14th, hld in 3rd whn blnd & u.r. 3 out* U -
1039 12/4 Lifton (R) RES 3m 8 F *prom til wknd 14th, p.u. 2 out* P 0
1157 20/4 Stafford Cr' (R) RES 3m 11 GF *prom early, lost tch 14th, onepcd aft* 4 0
1313 3/5 Holnicote (L) CON 3m 7 G *nvr nr ldrs, t.o. 10th* 5 0
1483 11/5 Ottery St M' (L) RES 3m 15 G *chsd ldr to 13th, wknd 4 out, p.u. 2 out* P 0
1494 14/5 Cothelstone (L) RES 3m 11 GF *chsd ldrs, 6th & rdn 12th, poor 4th & no ch frm 16th* 4 10

Maiden winner 95; non-stayer & lost last 18; will extend the sequence 11

THE CAFFLER(IRE) b.g. 7 Mandalus - Creagh by Sky Boy Major General C A Ramsay

228 22/2 Friars Haugh (L) MEM 3m 4 G *ld to 4th, chsd wnr aft, 2l down whn u.r. last* U 17
607 22/3 Friars Haugh (L) RES 3m 8 GF *ld 8th til apr 3 out, hld & 3rd whn b.d. last* B 14
995 12/4 Tranwell (L) RES 3m 6 F *(fav) trckd ldrs 1st ctt, disp 3l 3rd 14th, mstk & outpcd 2 out* 3 13
1218 26/4 Balcormo Ma' (R) RES 3m 5 F *cls 2nd frm 11th, ld apr 2 out, comf* 1 18

Irish maiden winner 96; consistent but needs more for Confinds; can improve; Any 17

THE CAMAIR FLYER(IRE) b.g. 7 Wylfa - Merrybash by Pinzari Colin W German
1996 F(-),F(-),F(-)

115 9/2 Wetherby Po' (L) MDO 3m 8 GF *disp ld whn u.r. 2nd* U -
233 22/2 Friars Haugh (L) MDO 3m 13 G *ld to 5th, wknd frm 10th* 8 0

815 31/3 Tranwell (L) MDO 2 1/2m 14 G *alwys prom, 2l 2nd & ev ch 11th, wknd into 3rd 2 out* 3 10
997 12/4 Tranwell (L) MDO 2 1/2m 8 F *(Jt fav) disp ld to 8th,ld nxt,2l up whn ran out thruwing last* r -
1173 20/4 Hexham Poin' (L) MDO 2 1/2m 9 GF *(fav) prom, went 2nd 6th, 4l down frm 3 out til rallied flat* 2 14
1409 5/5 Witton Cast' (R) MDO 3m 15 GS *prom, ld 11th-4 out, lft 2nd last, kpt on* 2 14

Speedy & unlucky in weak race; stamina limited but should find a race 13

THE CASS MAN (Irish) — **I** 4^{P}, **I** 36^{4}, **I** 56^{P}, **I** 155^{P}, **I** 265^{4}, **I** 341, , **I** 459^{P}

THE CHAIRMAN(IRE) b.g. 6 Last Tycoon - Bhama (FR) by Habitat V C Webster

980 8/4 Heythrop (R) MDO 3m 2 F *(Jt fav) disp ld til appr last, hung lft last, nt run on* 2 0
1166 20/4 Mollington (R) MDO 3m 9 GF *pllng, trckd ldrs, prssd wnr 13th, ev ch last, not run on* 2 12
1401 5/5 Ashorne (R) MDO 3m 15 G *cls up, trckd ldr 15th, chal last, pshd out to ld nr fin* 1 15
1536 18/5 Mollington (R) INT 3m 8 GS *hld up, last & lost tch 8th, p.u. aft 10th* P 0

Ex-hurdler; ungenuine & well ridden to win; sure to frustrate & Restricted looks too tough 15

THE CHAP br.g. 14 Tanfirion - Bay Tree (FR) by Relko R S Lochman

1996 7(0),P(0),P(0),5(11),P(0),P(0)

251 22/2 Brocklesby ' (L) RES 3m 16 G *alwys rear div, outpcd 6 out, completed own time* 7 0
422 8/3 Charm Park (L) CON 3m 8 GF *prom,jnd slwly 8th & 9th,wknd qckly 14th,t.o. whn ref 4 out* R -
676 23/3 Brocklesby ' (L) RES 3m 14 GF *sn wll bhnd, t.o. 6th, p.u. 3 out* P 0
856 31/3 Charm Park (L) RES 3m 8 F *mid-div to hlfwy, rear & onepcd aft* 7 0
1072 13/4 Whitwell-On' (R) MXO 4m 21 G *mid-div, strgglng 13th, t.o. & p.u. 16th* P 0
1101 19/4 Hornby Cast' (L) RES 3m 14 G *alwys rear, t.o. 11th, p.u. last* P 0
1253 26/4 Easingwold (L) MEM 3m 7 GS *bhnd early, 4th frm 14th, nvr a factor* 4 0
1347 3/5 Gisburn (R) OPE 3m 8 GF *alwys rear, wknd 12th, p.u. 15th* P 0

Of no account 0

THE COCKERTOO b.g. 6 Rakaposhi King - More Rheola by Morston (FR) Mrs J M Bailey

1996 **9(NH),3(NH)**

182 15/2 Larkhill (R) MDO 3m 12 G *jmpd lft, ld to 4th, cls 2nd whn ref & u.r. 7th* R -
299 1/3 Didmarton (L) MDN 3m 14 G *chsd ldr, ld 11-14th, btn whn lft in ld aft last, hld on* 1 16
1210 26/4 Woodford (L) RES 3m 14 G *keen hld, made most frm 4th, drew clr 3 out, not extndd* 1 19

Placed N/H Flat; improving; tricky & needs strong handling; stays; has the ability to progress 21

THE COMMITTEE (Irish) — **I** 30, , **I** 115^{F}

THE COMMUNICATOR b.g. 11 Black Minstrel - Patricias Pet by Battle Burn M A Hill

375 3/3 Doncaster (L) HC 2m 3f 110yds 11 GF *(bl) ld to 3rd, lost pl 8th, t.o. when p.u. before 3 out.* P 0
587 19/3 Ludlow (R) HC 2 1/2m 18 GF *(bl) rear when p.u. after 9th.* P 0
892 5/4 Hereford (R) HC 2m 11 GF *chsd ldrs, hit 4 out, soon wknd.* 6 0

Won short Maiden 93; missed 96; does not stay 3 miles & will not win a H/Chase now 10

THE CONAWAREY (Irish) — **I** 173^{P}, **I** 254^{P}

THE CONVINCER (Irish) — **I** 113^{P}, **I** 124^{P}, **I** 213^{F}, **I** 466^{P}

THE COPPEEN LORD (Irish) — **I** 255^{P}, **I** 517^{5}

THE COPPER KEY b.g. 12 Park Row - Menhaden by Menelek Mrs S M Trump

1996 6(0),U(-),4(0),3(10),P(0),4(0),10(0),1(18),2(19),7(0)

97 8/2 Great Treth' (R) INT 3m 13 GS *alwys bhnd, t.o. & p.u. 14th* P 0
307 1/3 Clyst St Ma' (L) MEM 3m 3 HY *2nd whn f 7th* F -
456 8/3 Great Treth' (R) INT 3m 11 S *hndy, hld in 3rd but styd on stdly clsng stgs* 3 10
631 22/3 Kilworthy (L) INT 3m 8 G *ld til 3rd, lost plc 11th, bhnd whn hit 2 out* 5 10
738 29/3 Higher Kilw' (L) CON 3m 8 GF *rear, 5th 3 out, styd on to tk 2nd apr last* 2 15
950 6/4 Black Fores' (R) MEM 3m 7 G *alwys prom, lost plc 10th, rnwd effrt 13th, tk 2nd apr last* 2 14
1111 19/4 Flete Park (R) CON 3m 5 GF *5th & in tch whn p.u. 11th, lame* P 0

Restricted winner 96; inconsistent; stays well & best in soft; problems now & unlikely to win at 13 15

THE COUNTRY TRADER br.g. 11 Furry Glen - Lady Girand by Raise You Ten J Borradaile

1996 **F(-),4(NH)**

3 19/1 Barbury Cas' (L) XX 3m 14 GF *alwys bhnd, t.o. last hlfwy, p.u. & u.r. apr 2 out* P 0
56 1/2 Kingston Bl' (L) OPE 3m 13 GF *alwys rear* 7 0
220 16/2 Heythrop (R) OPE 3m 20 G *last pair & sn t.o.* 12 0
295 1/3 Didmarton (L) OPE 3m 9 G *(bl) in tch to 8th, t.o. 12th, lft poor 3rd last* 3 0
397 8/3 Barbury Cas' (L) XX 3m 10 G *ld 2nd-8th, 6th & outpcd 12th, no dang aft, t.o.* 5 0
651 22/3 Siddington (L) OPE 3m 7 F *chsd ldrs to 8th, wknd 10th, t.o. whn u.r. apr 15th* U -
819 31/3 Paxford (L) OPE 3m 5 F *nvr nrr, onepcd* 4 13
974 8/4 Heythrop (R) MEM 3m 5 F *mstk 5th, chsd ldr 8th, ld last, ran on wll, dism aft fin* 1 14
1196 23/4 Andoversford (R) CON 3m 6 F *in tch to 12th, sn strgglng, no ch frm 14th* 5 0
1475 11/5 Garthorpe (R) XX 3m 13 GS *nvr bttr than mid-div, mod 6th at 13th, kpt on, nt rch ldrs* 5 10
1534 18/5 Mollington (R) OPE 3m 7 GS *(bl) ld 2nd, sn clr, hdd 13th, sn wknd* 6 0

Winning chaser; novice ridden; safe & won weak Members; needs easy 3 miles; struggle to win again .. 13

THE COVENTRY FLYER b.m. 8 Seymour Hicks (FR) - Easterly Gael by Tudor Music Mrs Jackie Masters

1996 **10(NH)**

1216 26/4 Woodford (L) MDN 3m 13 G *jmpd bdly, t.o. last whn ref & u.r. 5th* R -
1577 26/5 Chaddesley ' (L) MDO 3m 11 F *jmpd badly, alwys rear, t.o. whn f 13th* F -

Absolutely awful so far 0

THE CRAZY CHICK (Irish) — **I** 65^{P}, **I** 162^{P}, **I** 514^{P}

THE CRIOSRA(IRE) gr.g. 8 Carlingford Castle - Whisky Path by Warpath A J Bateman

310 1/3 Clyst St Ma' (L) INT 3m 9 HY *1st ride, blnd & u.r. 2nd* U -
519 15/3 Cothelstone (L) MEM 3m 5 GS *nov rdn, rear, lft poor 2nd 13th, no imp* 2 0
862 31/3 Kingston St' (R) CON 3m 7 F *rear, lost tch 15th, t.o.* 4 0
1153 20/4 Stafford Cr' (R) CON 3m 10 GF *alwys bhnd, t.o. 15th* 5 0
1258 27/4 Black Fores' (R) INT 3m 5 F *nvr trbld ldrs, t.o. 9th* 4 0
1441 10/5 Holnicote (L) CON 3m 7 G *sn trailing, t.o. 3rd, p.u. 2 out* P 0

Novice ridden & beaten miles when completing; well short of winning standard 0

THE CRUCIBLE (Irish) — **I** 390^{P}

THE DANCE (Irish) — **I** 281^{P}

THE DANCING PARSON b.m. 10 The Parson - Quayville by Quayside T B Brown

1996 5(16),4(14),8(0)

256 22/2 Newtown (L) OPE 3m 17 G *in tch, mstk 6th, sn bhnd, t.o. & p.u. last* P 0

Winning Irish Pointer; lightly raced over here & most unlikely to win now 12

THE DEFENDER (Irish) — **I** 357^{P}, **I** 426^{P}, **I** 555^{P}

THE DIFFERENCE b.g. 10 Cruise Missile - Brandy's Honour by Hot Brandy M G Chatterton

1996 P(0),F(-),1(17),8(0),B(-),U(-),1(17)

138 9/2 Thorpe Lodge (L) OPE 3m 5 GF *mostly 5th & strgglng, ran on frm 3 out, nvr dang* 4 15
214 16/2 Southwell P' (L) CON 3m 10 GS *prom to 4th, mid-div aft, nvr trbld ldrs* 4 15
380 4/3 Leicester (R) HC 3m 9 G *alwys in rear.* 6 0
923 6/4 Garthorpe (R) MEM 3m 4 GF *(fav) hld up, ld 7-12th, lvl 2 out, ran on best flat* 1 15
1072 13/4 Whitwell-On' (R) MXO 4m 21 G *mid-div, prog 4 out, styd on wll 2 out* 2 20
1265 27/4 Southwell P' (L) OPE 3m 8 G *alwys rear, t.o. 4 out* 4 0

Won 3 modest races 96/97; ran best-ever over 4 miles; Confined possible now penalties annulled;G/S-F 18

THE ELK b.g. 9 Relkino - Growing Wild by Free State Richard J Smith

390 8/3 Barbury Cas' (L) MDN 3m 15 G *in tch, mstk 7th, cls 4th at 12th, onepcd frm 3 out* 4 14

Last but only beaten 11 lengths in good race; late starter but has the ability to win 13

THE EXECUTRIX (Irish) — **I** 63^{P}, **I** 96^{B}, **I** 187^{F}, **I** 349^{4}

THEFIRSTONE (Irish) — **I** 67^{P}, **I** 112, , **I** 213^{P}

THE FLUTER ch.g. 6 Cruise Missile - Queenlet Ella by Kinglet W E O Gladwin

644 22/3 Castle Of C' (R) MDO 3m 9 G *last pair, steady prog frm 3 out, nvr plcd to chal* 6 10

Beaten under 10 lengths on gentle debut (weak race & slow time); will surely go close in 98 13

THE FORTIES ch.g. 12 Bybicello - Fanny Adams by Sweet Ration N C Earnshaw

1996 9(0),6(0),11(0),4(0)

144 9/2 Tweseldown (R) OPE 3m 9 GF *made most to 9th, wknd rpdly, t.o. 4 out* 6 11
305 1/3 Parham (R) OPE 3m 9 G *prom early, lost tch 12th, blnd & t.o. 3 out* 5 0
577 16/3 Detling (L) CON 3m 18 F *alwys rear, last & lost tch 11th* 9 0
829 31/3 Heathfield (R) XX 3m 5 F *tubed, disp til ld 4th-9th, 4th & wkng whn blnd & u.r. 14th* U -
1442 10/5 Peper Harow (L) MEM 3m 4 GF *tubed, prssd ldr to 9th, wknd 11th, lft poor 3rd last* 3 0

Winning staying chaser; of no account now 0

THE FROSTY FOX(IRE) gr.g. 6 King Luthier - No Breeze by Strong Gale Mrs L A Syckelmoore

512 15/3 Larkhill (R) MDO 3m 6 GF *jmpd slwly 1st, in tch to 13th, wknd rpdly, p.u. 3 out* P 0

A steady debut; can do better 0

THE GENERAL'S DRUM b.g. 10 Sergeant Drummer (USA) - Scottswood by Spartan General Mrs R Fell

1996 1(21),1(22),2(21),**1(26)**,2(28),1(24),2(25),1(28),1(24),3(20),2(22),**5(23)**

98 8/2 Great Treth' (R) OPE 3m 14 GS *bhnd, prog 10th, chsd ldng pair 16th, no imp nxt* 3 22
239 22/2 Lemalla (R) OPE 3m 7 S *(fav) wll in tch, 2nd 10th, effrt to disp 3 out, no ext und pres* 2 23
552 16/3 Ottery St M' (L) OPE 3m 6 G *(fav) hld up, prog 10th, disp 14th-nxt, ld 16th, styd on well* 1 25
629 22/3 Kilworthy (L) OPE 3m 5 G *p.u. & dismntd aft 2nd* P 0
1107 19/4 Flete Park (R) MEM 3m 2 GF *(fav) trckd ldr, ld 15th-17th & aft 2 out, unimprssv* 1 20
1489 12/5 Towcester (R) HC 3m 1f 6 GS *held up in rear, mstk 6th, wknd 4 out, t.o..* 4 13
1517 17/5 Bratton Down (L) MXO 3m 8 GS *prog to 3rd at 15th, outpcd 3 out, sn wknd & eased* 4 19
1580 26/5 Lifton (R) OPE 3m 8 G *alwys bhnd, past btn horses nr fin* 4 12

Decent stayer; below par late season; can revive when conditions suit & still win Opens; G-Hy 23

THE GOLAM (Irish) — **I** 122P, **I** 2141, **I** 3145, **I** 4413

THE GOLFING CURATE ch.g. 12 Avocat - Donnarabella by Bluerullah — T Wheeler

1996 **P(NH),5(NH),9(NH),6(NH),5(NH)**

519	15/3 Cothelstone	(L) MEM 3m	5 GS	*(fav) ld til f 13th*	F	-
863	31/3 Kingston St'	(R) OPE 3m	4 F	*cls 3rd whn f 6th*	F	-
1089	16/4 Hockworthy	(L) CON 3m	7 GF	*w.w. rear, 6th & out of tch hlfwy, kpt on to tk 2nd nr fin*	2	13
1341	3/5 Flete Park	(R) OPE 3m	5 G	*steady prog 14th, chsd ldr 16th, lft in ld last*	1	22
1517	17/5 Bratton Down	(L) MXO 3m	8 GS	*prog 14th, in tch 16th, onepcd frm nxt*	5	18

Winning hurdler; probably fortuante to win; ran well in hot race after; should find another win 20

THE GOLLY OLLYBIRD ch.g. 8 Ballacashtal (CAN) - Persian Air by Persian Bold — J C Swinburn

1996 P(0),P(0)

120	9/2 Wetherby Po'	(L) MDO 3m	18 GF	*rear, n.j.w. t.o. & p.u. 11th*	P	0
163	15/2 Witton Cast'	(R) MEM 3m	5 F	*rear, not fluent, lost tch 7th, t.o. & p.u. 4 out*	P	0

No signs of ability. 0

THEGOOSE b.g. 12 Windjammer (USA) - Space Dancer by Roan Rocket — A Palmer

1996 4(15),1(19),2(22),2(22),1(19)

515	15/3 Larkhill	(R) INT 3m	8 GF	*hld up rear, prog to chs ldng pair 14th,no imp aft,wknd last*	3	18
930	6/4 Charlton Ho'	(L) INT 3m	8 G	*hld up, prog 6th, wth wnr 13th-15th, onepcd frm 2 out*	3	19
1109	19/4 Flete Park	(R) OPE 4m	9 GF	*(Jt fav) hld up bhnd, prog 17th, went 3rd last, fin well*	3	18
1312	3/5 Holnicote	(L) INT 3m	3 G	*(fav) j.w. hld up in 3rd, jmpd into ld 2 out, sn clr*	1	19
1518	17/5 Bratton Down	(L) XX 3m	7 GS	*cls 3rd frm 8th til outpcd 3 out, eased flat*	3	16

Solid; consistent; beaten by good horses; can win at 13; worth another try in Flete 4 miler; G-F 21

THE GOTHIC (Irish) — **I** 601P

THE GREY MAJOR (Irish) — **I** 221U, **I** 287F, **I** 3481

THE HAIRY LORD (Irish) — **I** 110P, **I** 245P, **I** 296P

THE HOLLOW(IRE) b.m. 7 Phardante (FR) - Fairy Hollow by Furry Glen — G C Evans

1996 F(-),P(0)

368	2/3 Garnons	(L) MDO 2 1/2m	13 GS	*trckd ldrs in tch, blnd 12th, no ch aft*	5	0
1460	11/5 Maisemore P'	(L) MDO 3m	16 G	*wll in tch to 12th, sn wknd, wll bhnd & p.u. 3 out*	P	0
1528	17/5 Bredwardine	(R) MDO 3m	17 G	*mstk 6th, chsd ldrs to 12th, wknd & p.u. 15th*	P	0

Well beaten on only completion & much more needed 0

THE HOLY GOLFER br.g. 10 Avocat - Taitu by Menelek — C Smyth

1996 P(0),6(0),4(0),6(11),1(11),7(0),5(10),P(0),1(17)

822	31/3 Lockinge	(L) MEM 3m	4 F	*alwys last, t.o. 13th, p.u. 2 out*	P	0

Won 3 weak Points 95/96; barely seen in 97 & can only be watched now 13

THE HON COMPANY b.g. 11 Silly Prices - Derigold by Hunter's Song — Mrs R E Walker

1996 P(0),P(0)

223	16/2 Heythrop	(R) RES 3m	19 G	*prom, ld 10th til aft 2 out, no ch wth wnr aft*	2	14
300	1/3 Didmarton	(L) RES 3m	23 G	*mstk 6th, in tch to 11th, wll bhnd whn p.u. 15th*	P	0
433	8/3 Upton-On-Se'	(R) RES 3m	18 G	*cls 5th at 8th, outpcd 14th, no ch frm 3 out*	5	0
1210	26/4 Woodford	(L) RES 3m	14 G	*chsd ldrs, wknd 15th, t.o. & p.u. 3 out*	P	0
1449	10/5 Kingston Bl'	(L) RES 3m	8 G	*bhnd, last at 7th, prog 11th, 5th at 15th, nrst fin*	3	14

Maiden winner 94; revived & ran well well placed but not easy to win at 12; Members best hope 15

THE HONEST POACHER(IRE) b or br.g. 7 Saronicos - Shanaway by Moss Court — F M Green

332	1/3 Eaton Hall	(R) RES 3m	18 GS	*chsd ldrs, going wll whn f 4 out*	F	-

Maiden winner 95; capsized when going well in good Restricted; vanished after; can upgrade if fit 98 .. 17

THE HON ROSE ro.m. 8 Baron Blakeney - Roseitess by Royal And Regal (USA) — Ms Monica Yates

1461	11/5 Tweseldown	(R) MEM 3m	3 GF	*chsd wnr, ev ch whn f 3 out*	F	-

Unlucky in Members; promising & sure to gain quick compensation in 98 15

THE H'PENNY MARVEL (Irish) — **I** 59P, **I** 275F, **I** 348, , **I** 5321

THE HUMBLE TILLER b.g. 14 Rarity - Bardicate by Bargello — P G Bevins

1996 1(19),2(19),P(0),1(18),U(-)

107	8/2 Milborne St'	(L) MEM 3m	8 GF	*mid-div til blnd & u.r. 8th*	U	-
178	15/2 Larkhill	(R) CON 3m	9 G	*prom til ran out 4th*	r	-
869	31/3 Hackwood Pa'	(L) XX 3m	6 F	*ld til hdd & f 12th*	F	-
1153	20/4 Stafford Cr'	(R) CON 3m	10 GF	*sn rear, t.o. & u.r. 15th*	U	-
1518	17/5 Bratton Down	(L) XX 3m	7 GS	*not fluent, sn strgglng, t.o.*	6	0

Members winner 96; moody & looks past it now 0

THE JOGGER b.g. 12 Deep Run - Pollychant by Politico (USA) — Mrs P Tizzard

1996 3(12),3(17),2(17),2(20),1(18),1(22),2(12),**1(23)**,**1(20)**

19	25/1	Badbury Rin'	(L)	OPE	3m	8	GF	*(fav) ld to 11th, ld 15th, drew clr 2 out, easily*	1 27
227	21/2	Kempton	(R)	HC	3m	6	G	*with ldr till ld 3rd, came clr from 4 out, readily.*	1 30
494	13/3	Cheltenham	(L)	HC	3 1/4m 110yds	18	G	*chsd ldrs, chal hfwy, driven along 5 out, soon btn.*	7 15

Useful H/Chaser; consistent 96/97; outclassed in top race; well ridden & can win again; Any 28

THE KIMBLER ch.g. 9 Lir - Kimberley Ann by St Columbus — B R J Young

1996 P(0),5(17),1(17),P(0),4(0),P(0),P(0)

95	8/2	Great Treth'	(R)	MEM	3m	4	GS	*(fav) ld to 4th, lft in ld 7th, made rest, rdn out*	1 13
790	31/3	Bishopsleigh	(R)	LAD	3m	7	G	*handy, 2nd at 15th, chsd wnr vainly aft*	2 22
1579	26/5	Lifton	(R)	CON	3m	9	G	*alwys prom, ld 2 out, ran on well*	1 19

Confined winner 96; stays; improved; sure to win Ladies 98; G-S 23

THE LAST MISTRESS b.m. 10 Mandalus - Slinky Persin by Jupiter Pluvius — A J Cook

1996 P(0),P(0),P(0),5(0),**4(NH)**,**7(NH)**

399	8/3	Llanfrynach	(R)	CON	3m	11	G	*last pair til p.u. 3 out*	P 0
906	5/4	Howick	(L)	INT	3m	2	F	*made all, clr 3 out, comf*	1 16
1005	12/4	St Hilary	(R)	CON	3m	10	GF	*ld to 11th, disp to 15th, wknd frm nxt*	3 14
1194	22/4	Chepstow	(L)	HC	3m	11	GF	*nvr better than middle division.*	5 20

Dual winner 94; disappointing since; needs firm & another easy race possible 16

THE LAUGHING LORD b.g. 11 Lord Ha Ha - Celtic Serenity by Proverb — Miss Rachel Shiell

1996 **3(NH)**,**4(NH)**,**5(NH)**,**P(NH)**

33	26/1	Alnwick	(L)	LAD	3m	12	G	*alwys last, t.o. & p.u. 12th*	P 0
132	9/2	Alnwick	(L)	LAD	3m	9	G	*ld til f 11th*	F -
231	22/2	Friars Haugh	(L)	LAD	3m	13	G	*nvr nr ldrs, p.u. 3 out*	P 0
609	22/3	Friars Haugh	(L)	LAD	3m	11	GF	*nvr a threat, p.u. 4 out*	P 0
943	6/4	Friars Haugh	(L)	MEM	3m	5	GF	*cls 2nd whn u.r. 3rd*	U -

Winning hurdler/chaser; novice ridden & showed nothing in 97; can only be watched 10

THE LORRYMAN(IRE) ch.g. 9 Avocat - Perception by Star Moss — J J Boulter

1996 **P(NH)**,**12(NH)**,**P(NH)**,**P(NH)**

55	1/2	Kingston Bl'	(L)	CON	3m	15	GF	*alwys prom, not qckn clsng stgs*	4 18
179	15/2	Larkhill	(R)	CON	3m	12	G	*alwys chsng wnr, clsd 9th, outpcd apr 13th, no dang aft*	2 17
552	16/3	Ottery St M'	(L)	OPE	3m	6	G	*ld 3rd-13th, disp aft til hdd 4 out, onepcd aft*	2 21
931	6/4	Charlton Ho'	(L)	OPE	3m	6	G	*ld, 5l clr 3 out, hdd last, ran on*	2 21
1064	13/4	Maisemore P'	(L)	CON	3m	13	GF	*prssd wnr, blnd 12th, 4th & wkng 3 out*	4 15
1287	29/4	Huntingdon	(R)	HC	2 1/2m 110yds	14	G	*mstks, mid div, lost tch 9th, t.o..*	8 0

Winning chaser; able but ungenuine; tail swisher; will continue to frustrate 19

THE MAJOR GENERAL b.g. 10 Pollerton - Cornamucla by Lucky Guy — Robert Ogden

1996 **4(12)**,**1(22)**,**1(28)**

226	21/2	Haydock	(L)	HC	3m	11	G	*held up, hdwy and in tch 9th, blnd 13th and next, well bhnd when p.u. 3 out.*	P 0
1415	9/5	Stratford	(L)	HC	3m	6	G	*held up in tch, lost position 11th, hdwy to chase ldr 4 out, going well upsides when left clr 2 out, u.r. last, rmt.*	4 23

Lightly raced; professionally trained; stays; unlucky 97; can win again if fit 98; G-S 26

THE MAJORS HOLLOW (Irish) — I 122F

THE MALAKARMA b.g. 11 St Columbus - Impinge (USA) by Impressive — Charles Dixey

1996 **8(NH)**,**10(NH)**,**4(NH)**

89	4/2	Warwick	(L)	HC	3 1/4m	4	GF	*(fav) chsd ldr, nigglд along after one cct, joined lder 6 out, outpcd and rdn 4 out, styd on gamely to lead run-in.*	1 29
291	1/3	Warwick	(L)	HC	3 1/4m	6	G	*patiently rdn, steady hdwy final cct, jmpd ahd 4 out, styd on strly from between last 2.*	1 31
586	19/3	Exeter	(R)	HC	3 1/4m	12	GF	*trckd ldr, ld 12th to 6 out, led again 5 out to next, soon rdn and unable to qckn.*	3 24
1087	16/4	Cheltenham	(L)	HC	3 1/4m 110yds	8	GF	*held up, wknd 11th, t.o..*	6 11
1290	30/4	Cheltenham	(L)	HC	4m 1f	10	GF	*chsd wnr to 12th, rdn to go 2nd again 18th, ld 20th, soon hrd ridden, hdd last, styd on gamely.*	2 27
1413	7/5	Uttoxeter	(L)	HC	4 1/4m	7	GS	*(bl) alwys prom and going well, ld 19th, clr 3 out, rdn out run- in.*	1 30

Useful staying H/Chaser; 4 miles ideal; good stable; well ridden; can win again; G/F-S 29

THE MAN FROM CLARE(IRE) b.g. 9 Roselier (FR) - Restless Saint by Saint Denys — Mrs R C Matheson

1996 P(0),F(-),6(0),1(14)

213	16/2	Southwell P'	(L)	RES	3m	16	GS	*chsd ldrs to 11th, sn strgglng, no ch nxt*	7 0
300	1/3	Didmarton	(L)	RES	3m	23	G	*mid-div, no ch frm 14th, wll bhnd whn p.u. last*	P 0
517	15/3	Larkhill	(R)	RES	3m	10	GF	*chsd ldrs, 3rd & rdn 2 out, ran on to ld last, drvn out*	1 16

822 31/3 Lockinge (L) MEM 3m 4 F *(fav) mstks, chsd clr ldr, rdn frm 14th, 3rd & btn 3 out* 3 13

Maiden winner 96; lightly raced; 20/1 when winning modest Restricted; much more needed for Confinds 15

THE MAN FROM LYRE(IRE) b.g. 7 King's Ride - Lathanona W J Tolhurst

195 15/2 Higham (L) LAD 3m 14 G *mid-div till f 13th* F -

323 1/3 Marks Tey (L) LAD 3m 7 G *u.r. 1st* U -

443 8/3 Higham (L) RES 3m 7 G *hld up rear,rpd prog to ld 16th,hit nxt,ev ch last,fin lame* 4 17

Winning Irish Pointer; looked unlucky last start; good enough for Restricted if fit 98; pulls 16

THE MERRY NUN(IRE) ch.m. 8 Lancastrian - Katebeaujolais by Politico (USA) M F Loggin

1996 **P(NH)**

451 8/3 Newton Brom' (R) MDN 3m 8 G *lost plc 6th, ran on hlfwy, cls 3rd whn f 15th* F -

1537 18/5 Mollington (R) MDO 3m 14 GS *rear til hmpd & u.r. 5th* U -

No ability under Rules; showed some hope but needs to jump better before winning 13

THE MILL HEIGHT(IRE) ch.g. 7 Callernish - Cherry Gamble by Meadsville K Tork

1996 3(11),2(10),1(14)

462 8/3 Charing (L) RES 3m 10 G *mid-div whn blnd & u.r. 2nd* U -

678 25/3 Sandown (R) HC 2 1/2m 110yds 6 GF *in tch to 6th, t.o. 8th, p.u. before 12th.* P 0

Maiden winner 96; changed hands & can only be watched now 0

THE MODERATOR (Irish) — I 99^{P}, I 155^{P}

THEMOREYOUKNOW b.g. 8 Boco (USA) - Odic by Hopeful Venture M H Weston

479 9/3 Southwell P' (L) MDO 3m 15 G *disp 2nd bhnd clr ldr, ld apr 12th, hdd apr 2 out, wknd* 3 12

1356 4/5 Dingley (R) MDO 3m 9 G *(Jt fav) ld, hit 12th, 10l clr & gng wll whn f 14th* F -

1459 11/5 Maisemore P' (L) MDO 3m 12 G *(fav) ld to 2nd, trckd ldrs, ld 13th, ran on well frm 2 out* 1 15

Poor under Rules; interrupted season; won modest race; must have Restricted chances 98; Good 17

THE ODIN LINE(IRE) b or br.g. 8 Odin (FR) - Knockboy Glor by I'm A Star W Kerr

1996 **9(NH),2(NH),3(NH),3(NH),2(NH),3(NH)**

1331 3/5 Mosshouses (L) MEM 3m 5 F *made all, drew clr frm 11th, v easily* 1 16

1510 17/5 Corbridge (R) RES 3m 13 GS *disp til ld 4th, disp 10th til ld 10th, hdd & onepcd 2 out* 2 18

Placed Irish chases 96; romped home in two-finisher race; must have every chance of Restricted 98 ... 18

THE OXFORD DON gr.g. 9 Baron Blakeney - Oxford Lane by Clever Fella R S Hunnisett

358 2/3 Great Stain' (L) MDO 3m 14 S *(fav) alwys prom, went 2nd 11th, disp 3 out, ld apr last, ran on* 1 16

509 15/3 Dalton Park (R) XX 3m 13 GF *(Jt fav) trckd ldr, disp 10th, ld 14th, lft clr nxt,hdd apr last & f* F 18

856 31/3 Charm Park (L) RES 3m 8 F *(fav) rear, prog 10th, ld 14th, made rest, comf* 1 21

1608 1/6 Dingley (R) INT 3m 11 GF *2nd whn f 2nd* F -

Improving novice; changed hands after third startw novice ridden & at the crossroadsst watched 16

THE PARISH PUMP(IRE) br.g. 9 Bustinetto - Ladies Gazette by London Gazette R Burgess

1996 **F(NH),P(NH)**

329 1/3 Eaton Hall (R) LAD 3m 10 GS *ld/disp to 6th, 2nd whn u.r. 10th* U -

413 8/3 Dalston (R) OPE 3m 9 GS *made all, clr 2 out, pshd out flat* 1 22

765 29/3 Whittington (L) OPE 3m 6 S *(fav) ld 8th, wnt clr aft 3 out, eased flat* 1 23

Winning Irish Pointer; stays well; well ridden; sure to win more; H/chase worth a try; G/S-Hy 24

THE PHARSIDE(IRE) b.g. 6 Phardante (FR) - Cloughoola Lady by Black Minstrel Mrs Alix Stevenson

161 15/2 Lanark (R) MDO 2m 5f 14 G *sn wll bhnd* 7 0

419 8/3 Dalston (R) MDO 2 1/2m 10 GS *(fav) mstks, 4th whn f 6th* F -

No real signs yet; good stable & can do better 0

THE POACHER b.g. 10 Balinger - Queen Francesca by Frankincense Mrs B Dukes

21 25/1 Badbury Rin' (L) MDN 3m 7 GF *mstks, prom in chsng grp til ran out & u.r. 13th* r -

41 1/2 Larkhill (R) MDO 3m 13 GF *blnd 1st, last whn u.r. 6th* U -

580 16/3 Detling (L) RES 3m 11 F *n.j.w., t.o. whn p.u. 15th* P 0

Jumps poorly & unpromising 0

THE PODGER (Irish) — I 152^{F}, I 260^{P}, I 391, , I 497^{3}, I 545^{6}

THE POINT IS ch.g. 10 Major Point - Babble by Forlorn River P S Hewitt

1996 1(24),U(-),U(-),F(-),1(23)

216 16/2 Southwell P' (L) OPE 3m 12 GS *ld, sn clr, hdd 4 out, wknd rpdly, p.u. nxt* P 0

475 9/3 Southwell P' (L) OPE 3m 7 G *t.d.e. ld, sn clr, kpt on gamely frm 3 out* 1 24

675 23/3 Brocklesby ' (L) OPE 3m 6 GF *made all, kpt on gamely frm 2 out* 1 24

1086 14/4 Southwell (L) HC 3m 110yds 11 G *(Jt fav) ld, hdd 4 out, soon wknd, p.u. before 2 out.* P 0

Fair Pointer; headstrong & well handled; front runs; best left-handed; can win again; G/F-S 23

THE PORTSOY LOON b.g. 10 Miami Springs - Glittering Gem by Silly Season D R Greig
1996 2(25),3(24),3(19),2(17),4(13),2(0),**P(0)**

281 23/2 Charing (L) OPE 3m 12 G *wth ldrs til rdn & lost plc 12th, wll bhnd whn p.u. last* P 0
604 22/3 Parham (R) CON 3m 3 F *trckd ldr, rdn 12th, btn 3 out* 3 11

Winning novice chaser; finished quickly 97; ungenuine & best avoided 13

THE PRIOR b.g. 11 Monksfield - Merry Rambler by Wrekin Rambler P J Rowe
1996 U(-),P(0),P(0),2(0)

30 26/1 Marks Tey (L) MDN 3m 9 GF *rear, prog & in tch 10th, outpcd 13th, t.o. & p.u. 3 out* P 0
276 22/2 Ampton (R) MDO 3m 12 G *bhnd, prog 11th, ev ch 17th, no ex appr 2 out* 3 10
318 1/3 Marks Tey (L) MDN 3m 13 G *w.w., stdd prog 11th, 4th 16th, lft 2nd 2 out, no imp on wnr* 2 13
499 15/3 Ampton (R) MDO 3m 9 GF *(fav) ld/disp to 17th, unable to qkn appr last* 2 13

Placed 5 times 95/97; knocking on the door; better with give; novice ridden; deserves a win 14

THE PULPIT (Irish) — I 13P, I 75P, I 89P, I 1302, I 2373, I 3206, I 516P, I 5622, I 6122
THE REAL BAVARD (Irish) — I 27, , I 122P
THE REBEL PARISH(IRE) b.g. 7 Strong Gale - Belle Kisco by Ballyciptic Mrs E W Wilson

774 29/3 Dingley (R) MDO 2m 5f 10 G *n.j.w. alwys last pair, t.o. & p.u. aft 2 out* P 0
1081 13/4 Guilsborough (L) RES 3m 13 GF *prom, lost plc 13th, eased & p.u. 3 out, improve* P 0
1353 4/5 Dingley (R) MDO 2 1/2m 9 G *(fav) ld til blnd & hdd 12th, ld agn 3 out, styd on strngly* 1 15

Good stable; benefited from quiet introduction; loads of scope & looks sure to progress 18

THE RED DEVIL(IRE) b.g. 6 Mandalus - Judy Go Easy by Avocat Paul Rackham

676 23/3 Brocklesby ' (L) RES 3m 14 GF *mid-div to 7th,bhnd & rdn 11th,no ch nxt, p.u.3 out,dsmntd* P 0

Irish Maiden winner 96; problems only start 97; still young enough to revive; plenty to prove yet 14

THE REPROBATE(IRE) ch.g. 8 Orchestra - Heather-Can by Cantab Mrs R E Walker

569 16/3 Garnons (L) OPE 3m 7 G *wth ldrs to 7th, wknd & p.u. aft 11th* P 0

N/H Flat winner 94; very lightly raced & shows nothing now 0

THEREWEGO(IRE) br.g. 9 Mandalus - Knockscovane by Carlburg Mrs R Corn
1996 P(0),7(0)

333 1/3 Eaton Hall (R) INT 3m 10 GS *hld up in tch, chsd wnr 13th, unable to chal* 2 17
651 22/3 Siddington (L) OPE 3m 7 F *mstk 3rd, alwys last, t.o. & p.u. 15th* P 0
878 1/4 Upton-On-Se' (R) XX 3m 11 GF *rear, jmpd lft 9th, ran out & u.r. nxt* r -
1160 20/4 Mollington (R) INT 3m 9 GF *cls up, rdn 11th, mstk 13th, outpcd frm nxt* 4 0

Won 2 Irish points 94; ran well debut; needs give; hard to find a win 14

THEREYOUGO b.g. 6 Touch Of Grey - Young Lady by Young Generation Mrs P King
1996 P(0),P(0)

317 1/3 Marks Tey (L) MDN 3m 13 G *w.w., some prog 11th, just in tch whn f 14th* F -

Shown nothing yet 0

THE RIGHT ATTITUDE (Irish) — I 113, I 52P
THE RISING BUCK VI (Irish) — I 239P, I 534P, I 559P
THE RUM MARINER gr.g. 10 Julio Mariner - Decorum by Quorum T A Rogers
1996 P(0),1(20),P(0),3(15),1(20),P(0),1(21),2(16),2(20)

149 10/2 Hereford (R) HC 3m 1f 110yds 18 GS *prom till wknd 6 out, p.u. before 3 out.* P 0
399 8/3 Llanfrynach (R) CON 3m 11 G *(Jt fav) 3rd to 10th, disp nxt, ld 14th, hdd 3 out, no ext* 2 19
496 15/3 Hereford (R) HC 3m 1f 110yds 10 GF *ld, rdn 3 out, hdd and no ext cl home.* 2 21
668 23/3 Eaton Hall (R) OPE 3m 3 GF *6l 2nd & lkd hld whn u.r. 5 out* U -
1233 26/4 Brampton Br' (R) CON 3m 8 G *ld to 12th, rdn 15th, not qckn nxt, kpt on frm 2 out* 5 17
1500 16/5 Aintree (L) HC 3m 1f 6 G *ld, jmpd right thrght, mstk 13th, hdd 5 out, wknd apr 3 out, soon no dngr.* 2 17
1570 26/5 Hereford (R) HC 3m 1f 110yds 14 G *ld 3rd to 9th, led 11th to 6 out, wknd 4 out.* 4 12

Solid; consistent; best when front-running; placed in weak H/Chases; can win Confinds still; Any 20

THE RURAL DEAN (Irish) — I 3711
THE SCRUB (Irish) — I 234
THE SHADE MATCHER br.g. 11 Black Minstrel - Dursey Sound by Royal Highway Mrs Alix Stevenson

1996 4(14),1(20),2(18)

156 15/2 Lanark (R) CON 3m 7 G *trckd ldr, upsides whn p.u. aft 14th, lame* P 0

Winning hurdler; won modest race 96ghtly raced & more problems nowak Confined possible if fit 19

THE SLIPPERY BEAR (Irish) — **I** 106[P], **I** 160[F], **I** 202[F]

THE SMILING GIRL b.m. 7 Broadsword (USA) - Slipalong by Slippered — P J Jones

1996 **10(NH),B(NH)**

181 15/2 Larkhill (R) MDO 3m 17 G *u.r. 3rd* U -
299 1/3 Didmarton (L) MDN 3m 14 G *alwys bhnd, t.o. whn ref 13th* R -
867 31/3 Kingston St' (R) MDO 3m 6 F *(bl) 5th whn blndrd & u.r. 11th* U -

Nothing to smile about yet 0

THE SNUFFMAN (Irish) — **I** 18[P], **I** 42[P]

THE STAG (Irish) — **I** 146[F], **I** 238[2], **I** 337[P], **I** 476[1]

THE SUTTY FOX (Irish) — **I** 440[3], **I** 507[P]

THE TERRITORIAN (Irish) — **I** 50[3], **I** 100[F], **I** 242[1], **I** 323[3], **I** 486[1], **I** 567[P]

THE TIDE RACE b.m. 9 Politico (USA) - Brox Treasure by Broxted — G H Dook

839 31/3 Thorpe Lodge (L) MDO 3m 15 F *alwys rear hlf, wll bhnd whn p.u. aft 12th* P 0
1069 13/4 Whitwell-On' (R) RES 3m 12 G *rear, strgglng 9th, t.o. 13th, p.u. nxt* P 0
1268 27/4 Southwell P' (L) MDO 3m 13 G *mid-div, wknd 8th, t.o. 10th, p.u. 12th* P 0

Not yet of any account 0

THE TOOR TRAIL (Irish) — **I** 29[P]

THE UGLY DUCKLING br.g. 7 Lir - Dule Darkie by Bay Spirit — D W Heard

1996 r(-),P(0),2(0),P(0),U(-),P(0),3(0),5(0)

103 8/2 Great Treth' (R) MDO 3m 9 GS *prom in chsng grp, ld aft 13th-3 out, no ext* 3 12
246 22/2 Lemalla (R) MDO 3m 4 S *(fav) ld/disp, ev ch til no ext apr last* 2 11
459 8/3 Great Treth' (R) MDO 3m 9 S *made most til 15th, ev ch til not qckn apr 2 out* 2 12
624 22/3 Kilworthy (L) MEM 3m 7 G *cls up, in tch whn b.d. 14th, remntd* 3 0
795 31/3 Bishopsleigh (R) MDO 3m 12 G *alwys prom, 3rd at 15th, nvr on trms frm 4 out* 3 10
1112 19/4 Flete Park (R) MDN 3m 13 GF *handy, 5th hlfwy, lft 10l 3rd 3 out, onepcd* 3 0
1261 27/4 Black Fores' (R) MDO 3m 12 F *ld/disp frm 7th, clr 10th, hdd 14th, fdd frm 2 out* 3 11
1485 11/5 Ottery St M' (L) MDO 3m 13 G *ld to 14th, cls up aft, not qckn 2 out, fin 3rd, disq* 3D 13
1584 26/5 Lifton (R) MDO 3m 13 G *alwys prom, found nil frm 2 out* 4 10

Improved; placed 11 times & will not or cannot find anything under pressure; best avoided 13

THE ULTIMATE BUCK b.g. 15 Buckskin (FR) - Royal Gertrude by Royal Buck — Mrs P Visick

118 9/2 Wetherby Po' (L) RES 3m 14 GF *mid-div, wknd rpdly & p.u. 11th* P 0
350 2/3 Market Rase' (L) CON 3m 11 GF *rear, lost tch 11th, t.o.* 6 0
835 31/3 Thorpe Lodge (L) INT 3m 7 F *alwys last trio, t.o. 6 out, comp own time* 6 0

Of no account 10

THE VILLAGE WAY (Irish) — **I** 12[2], **I** 146[1]

THE WAYWARD GUNNER ch.g. 6 Gunner B - Lady Letitia by Le Bavard (FR) — David Chown

452 8/3 Newton Brom' (R) MDN 3m 9 G *chsd ldrs, in tch whn f 15th* F -
761 29/3 Kimble (L) MDO 3m 12 GF *hld up, prog to prss ldrs 16th, onepcd aft* 3 10

Ex-N/H Flat; reasonable start; beaten 15 lengths (winner behind); should go closer in 98 13

THE WHIP ch.g. 10 Fine Blade (USA) - Phayre Vulgan by Vulgan — The Hon Mrs C Yeates

1996 **3(NH),5(NH),5(NH)**

304 1/3 Parham (R) LAD 3m 10 G *handy, chsd ldr 14th, ld brfly 2 out, rallied flat, ld line* 1 21
602 22/3 Parham (R) LAD 3m 1 F *walked over* 1 0
830 31/3 Heathfield (R) MXO 3m 6 F *ld/disp til 15th, 2nd & btn whn f 3 out* F -

Winning chaser (2m 5f max); won modest Ladies; stamina limited, every chance of another local Ladies 20

THE WHOLE LOT b.g. 7 Hotfoot - Selborne Lass by Deep Run — James Buckle

1996 **19(NH),P(NH)**

914 5/4 Cottenham (R) MDO 3m 4 F *u.r. 1st* U -
1027 12/4 Horseheath (R) MDO 3m 2 HD *(Jt fav) n.j.w. ld ti j.s & hdd 3rd, lst tch 6th, t.o. whn ref 11th* R -
1118 19/4 Higham (L) MDO 3m 9 GF *rear, hmnpd & u.r. 6th* U -
1282 27/4 Fakenham P-' (L) MDO 3m 8 G *cls up, jmpd slwly 3rd, 5th whn blnd 13th, wknd, p.u. 15th* P 0

No signs of ability 0

THE WORKS (Irish) — **I** 107[P]

THEY ALL FORGOT ME b.g. 10 Tender King - African Doll by African Sky — Mrs D J Dyson

1996 P(0),2(12),4(16),2(12),4(15),4(14),**10(NH),7(NH),4(NH),7(NH),3(NH),7(NH),3(NH),F(NH)**

702 29/3 Upper Sapey (R) LAD 3m 4 GF *chsd ldr in 2nd plc frm start,8l down mstk 3 out,ran on flat* 2 15

Winning chaser; safe & consistent; does not really stay & unlikely to find a win; finished early 97 16

THIEF'S ROAD b.g. 10 Royal Fountain - Mildenstone by Milan — Miss D M M Calder

1996 2(0),4(0)

38	26/1	Alnwick	(L)	MDO	3m	14	G	*in tch in rear to 14th, bhnd whn p.u. 3 out*	P 0
234	22/2	Friars Haugh	(L)	MDO	3m	15	G	*ld 5th, clr 3 out, just hld on*	1 15
337	1/3	Corbridge	(R)	RES	3m	11	G	*prom til fdd 10th, t.o. 12th*	7 0

Lightly raced; won at ninth attempt; needs much more for Restricteds 13

THIEVING SANDS (Irish) — I 217^{F}, I 389^{U}, I 407^{P}, I 525^{P}

THINKABOUTTHAT(IRE) br.g. 8 Roselier (FR) - Rossian by Silent Spring — J F W Muir

235	22/2	Friars Haugh	(L)	MDO	3m	10	G	*ld to 4th, poor 5th whn u.r. 13th*	U -
415	8/3	Dalston	(R)	RES	3m	19	GS	*ld 2-11th, prom til wknd 3 out*	7 11
566	16/3	Lanark	(R)	MDO	3m	10	GS	*alwys ldng trio, ld apr 2 out, drew clr flat*	1 16
606	22/3	Friars Haugh	(L)	MEM	3m	9	GF	*ld jmpng wll, blndrd 10th, hdd 4 out, kpt on wll*	2 17
729	29/3	Alnwick	(L)	RES	3m	10	F	*(Jt fav) ld/disp to 4 out,prog agn to disp& mstk 2 out,ld last,ran on*	1 19
944	6/4	Friars Haugh	(L)	INT	3m	5	GF	*nvr gng wll, poor 4th 9th, lft 3rd 4 out*	3 0
1332	3/5	Mosshouses	(L)	INT	3m	4	F	*2nd til 13th, sn btn*	3 0
1427	10/5	Aspatria	(L)	INT	3m	7	G	*bhnd frm 7th, t.o. 11th, kpt on frm 3 out*	4 10
1509	17/5	Corbridge	(R)	INT	3m	10	GS	*prom, chsd ldr 4th til fdd 10th, wll btn*	3 13

Ex-Irish; won 2 competitive races; stays; likes to dictate; struggling now; Members best hope 98 18

THIRD MELODY b.m. 11 Leander - Baynton Melody by Romany Air — Brian S Heath

1996 **P(NH)**,**P(NH)**,**P(NH)**

313	1/3	Clyst St Ma'	(L)	RES	3m	10	HY	*alwys rear, nvr on trms*	5 0
523	15/3	Cothelstone	(L)	RES	3m	14	GS	*alwys bhnd*	4 0
935	6/4	Charlton Ho'	(L)	RES	3m	7	G	*n.j.w. alwys bhnd, t.o. & p.u. 3 out*	P 0
1061	13/4	Maisemore P'	(L)	RES	3m	12	GF	*alwys bhnd, no ch frm 14th*	6 0

Maiden winner 94; nor form under Rules after; does not stay & no prospects 0

THIS I'LL DO US(IRE) ch.g. 9 Boyne Valley - Sweater Girl by Blue Cashmere — A J Morley

1996 3(17),U(-),6(11)

467	8/3	Eyton-On-Se'	(L)	RES	3m	15	G	*t.o. 5th, p.u. 9th*	P 0
523	15/3	Cothelstone	(L)	RES	3m	14	GS	*rear, 8th at 15th, ran on steadily, nrst fin*	3 11

Irish Maiden winner 93; lightly raced; well beaten 97; weak Restricted possible but time passing 16

THISTLE MONARCH b.g. 12 Rontino - Lavender Blue by Silly Season — S B Clark

1996 1(21),1(24),1(19),2(22),P(0)

215	16/2	Southwell P'	(L)	LAD	3m	12	GS	*hld up, prog to mod 6th at 12th, no hdwy aft, p.u. 3 out*	P 0
355	2/3	Great Stain'	(L)	LAD	3m	9	S	*chsd ldr, ld 2 out, sn clr, wknd & hdd flat*	2 20
508	15/3	Dalton Park	(R)	LAD	3m	4	GF	*(fav) sttld 3rd,mstk 10th,ld 15th-4 out,outpcd nxt,ran on wll flat*	2 19

Lightly raced; won 3 Points 96; stays; best with cut; Confined possible at 13 19

THORNHILL b.m. 7 Pollerton - Crowebrass by Crowned Prince (USA) — F L Matthews

1996 **U(-)**,**F(-)**,**F(-)**,F(-)

256	22/2	Newtown	(L)	OPE	3m	17	G	*alwys bhnd, t.o. & p.u. 13th*	P 0
368	2/3	Garnons	(L)	MDO	2 1/2m	13	GS	*nvr rchd ldrs, t.o. 11th*	6 0
854	31/3	Eyton-On-Se'	(L)	MDO	3m	10	GF	*rear, t.o. 12th, p.u. 5 out*	P 0
1097	19/4	Bangor	(L)	HC	2 1/2m 110yds	11	G	*bhnd, reminders 9th and lost tch, t.o. when p.u. before 3 out.*	P 0
1296	3/5	Hereford	(R)	HC	2m 3f	11	G	*slowly away, in rear when f 5th.*	F -
1543	18/5	Wolverhampt'	(L)	MEM	3m	2	GS	*ld til apr 3 out, btn whn u.r. 3 out*	U -
1587	29/5	Uttoxeter	(L)	HC	2m 5f	11	GF	*t.o. from 5th, p.u. before 6 out.*	P 0

One completion from 11 starts; looks hopeless 0

THORNPARK LEADER (Irish) — I 308^{6}

THOUGHTFUL CHOICE ch.m. 7 Baron Blakeney - Choice Secret by The Dane — Mrs W A Orchard

1015	12/4	Bitterley	(L)	MDO	3m	12	GF	*rear til prog 12th, 15l 5th whn f 2 out*	F -

A reasonable enough debut; can do better 13

THOUGHT READER(IRE) b.g. 7 Prince Rupert (FR) - Kolomelskoy Palace by Royal Palace — R T Sturgis

177	15/2	Larkhill	(R)	MEM	3m	6	G	*prom til ran out 9th*	r -
262	22/2	Newtown	(L)	RES	3m	15	G	*cls up to 8th, wknd 12th, t.o. & p.u. 14th*	P 0
292	1/3	Didmarton	(L)	MEM	3m	9	G	*in tch to 10th, sn strggling*	4 0

... 0

THREEANDABIT (Irish) — I 55^{U}, I 286^{6}

THREE AND A HALF b.g. 8 Nearly A Hand - Miss Comedy by Comedy Star (USA) — J Scott

1996 4(10),0(16),6(0),8(0)

101	8/2	Great Treth'	(R)	MDO	3m	9	GS	*prom, ld 11th, drew rght away frm 15th, unchal*	1	19
240	22/2	Lemalla	(R)	RES	3m	11	S	*(fav) prom, disp 15th, ld und pres aft 2 out, lft clr last*	1	20
456	8/3	Great Treth'	(R)	INT	3m	11	S	*(fav) hld up, prog 10th, ld 14th, sn clr, easily*	1	20
1258	27/4	Black Fores'	(R)	INT	3m	5	F	*(fav) bhnd til prog 7th, ld 11th-15th,jnd wnr 2 out,wknd flat,lame*	2	18
1313	3/5	Holnicote	(L)	CON	3m	7	G	*(fav) ld to 5th, cls up aft, no ext frm 3 out*	3	17
1518	17/5	Bratton Down	(L)	XX	3m	7	GS	*prom til ld 9th, hdd 2 out, styd on wll und pres flat*	2	23
1594	31/5	Bratton Down	(L)	INT	3m	10	F	*(fav) trckd ldrs,rdn to prss wnr 14th,ev ch til no ext last,dsmntd*	3	20

Much improved; stays; cut looks essential; worth a try in Nov H/Chase 98; G/S-S 26

THREE B'S b.m. 7 Baron Blakeney - Bealsmead by Rugantino — Mrs G Drury

971	6/4	Penshurst	(L)	MDO	3m	5	F	*in tch in rear til outpcd 14th, lft poor 3rd aft 3 out*	3	0

Beaten over a fence in a bad race; huge improvement needed 0

THREE TOWN ROCK (Irish) — I 113^{P}, I 251, , I 329^{1}

THURLES PICKPOCKET(IRE) b.g. 6 Hollow Hand - Sugar Lady by Dalsaan — G I Cooper

1996 P(0)

61	1/2	Horseheath	(R)	MDO	3m	9	GF	*f 2nd*	F	-
276	22/2	Ampton	(R)	MDO	3m	12	G	*chsd ldrs, ev ch 17th, wknd 3 out*	4	0
499	15/3	Ampton	(R)	MDO	3m	9	GF	*in tch, disp ld 13th, slt ld frm 17th, hld on gamely flat*	1	13

Steady improvement; stays; won weak race; can improve enough for Restricted hopes 15

TICKET TO THE MOON b.m. 7 Pollerton - Spring Rocket by Harwell — Mrs Janita Scott

1996 P(0),1(17),3(18)

236	22/2	Lemalla	(R)	INT	3m	12	S	*hld up in tch, prog to 3rd 3 out, styng on whn hmpd apr last*	3	22
453	8/3	Great Treth'	(R)	CON	3m	13	S	*(fav) cls 5th hlfwy, ld aft 2 out til outjmpd last, no ext*	2	19
558	16/3	Ottery St M'	(L)	INT	3m	6	G	*(fav) hld up, chal & ld 3 out, styd on well*	1	22
1416	10/5	Newton Abbot	(L)	HC	2m 5f 110yds	14	G	*held up in tch, hdwy to press wnr from 4 out, no ext apr last.*	2	26

Maintained progress; interrupted season; ran in good races; stays; should win H/Chase; G-Hy 26

TICKLEBAY b.m. 6 Rolfe (USA) - Profusion Of Pink by Tickled Pink — Keith Coe

1996 P(0)

15	25/1	Cottenham	(R)	MDN	3m	7	GF	*alwys bhnd, last & jmpd slwly 13th, lft poor 3rd 2 out*	3	0
275	22/2	Ampton	(R)	MDO	3m	10	G	*chsd ldrs, disp ld 13th til appr 3 out, wknd 2 out*	3	10

Beaten 10l in poor race last start; may progress but needs to for a win & finished early 11

TIDAL REEF(IRE) br.g. 5 Tidaro (USA) - Windsor Reef by Take A Reef — R Fielder

1379	5/5	Northaw	(L)	RES	3m	6	F	*last whn nrly ref 2nd, succeeded nxt*	R	-
1446	10/5	Peper Harow	(L)	MDO	3m	7	GF	*alwys bhnd, jmpd slwly 3rd, t.o. & p.u. 13th*	P	0
1568	25/5	Kingston Bl'	(L)	MDO	3m	11	GF	*prog & prom 9th, wknd 13th, t.o. & p.u. 15th*	P	0

Ran better last start (could not have done worse) & local races offer even bad horses a chance 0

TIDARO FAIRY (Irish) — I 43^{P}, I 311^{P}, I 398^{F}, I 468^{4}, I 507^{4}, I 580^{4}, I 595^{P}

TIDERUNNER(IRE) b.g. 9 Deep Run - Boherdeel by Boreen (FR) — Mrs M Morris

253	22/2	Brocklesby '	(L)	MDO	3m	6	G	*mstly 4th, outpcd 5 out, p.u. 2 out*	P	0
479	9/3	Southwell P'	(L)	MDO	3m	15	G	*mid-div, prog to 4th at 11th, went 2nd & rdn 2 out, onepcd*	2	14
677	23/3	Brocklesby '	(L)	MDN	3m	8	GF	*trckd ldrs, lft in ld 14th, sn hdd, ld agn 2 out, ran on wll*	1	14
770	29/3	Dingley	(R)	RES	3m	18	G	*mid-div, 5th/6th to 12th, outpcd nxt, p.u. 3 out*	P	0
927	6/4	Garthorpe	(R)	RES	3m	9	GF	*(fav) alwys mid-div, nvr dang*	5	0
1263	27/4	Southwell P'	(L)	RES	3m	9	G	*rear, strgglng 13th, sn lost tch, p.u. 4 out*	P	0

Lightly raced; comfortable winner but struggling after; weak Restricted only possible; Good 15

TIERFERGUS (Irish) — I 178^{P}, I 250^{P}, I 360, , I 467^{4}

TIERNYS ISLAND (Irish) — I 245^{F}, I 304^{P}, I 428^{P}, I 453^{5}

TIGER BRIGHT b.h. 8 Seymour Hicks (FR) - Commander Alice by Spartan General — Miss G L D Hardy

1179	20/4	Sandon	(L)	MDN	3m	6	GF	*mid-div, t.o. 8th, p.u. 11th*	P	0

No sign of ability yet 0

TIGER DOLLY (Irish) — I 123^{P}, I 179^{P}, I 254^{P}, I 360^{5}, I 436^{3}

TIGER LORD bl.g. 6 Tigerwood - Roushane by Rustingo — William John Day

1996 P(0),P(0),P(0),P(0)

365	2/3	Garnons	(L)	MDO	2 1/2m	14	GS	*rear frm 4th, t.o. & p.u. 3 out*	P	0
408	8/3	Llanfrynach	(R)	MDN	3m	12	G	*alwys mid-div, no ch frm 14th*	6	0
542	16/3	Erw Lon	(L)	MDN	3m	15	GF	*alwys mid-div, onepcd*	4	10
720	29/3	Llanvapley	(L)	MDN	3m	8	GF	*rear till p.u. 3 out*	P	0
1137	19/4	Bonvilston	(R)	MDO	3m	13	G	*rear, p.u. 3 out*	P	0
1473	11/5	Erw Lon	(L)	MDO	3m	13	GS	*alwys rear, p.u. 12th*	P	0

4th in a poor race & only completed 2 of 10 races to date 0

TIGER SALLY b.m. 6 Tigerwood - Sally Haven by Haven — E H Williams

542 16/3 Erw Lon (L) MDN 3m 15 GF *rear, u.r. 6th* U -
1009 12/4 St Hilary (R) MDN 3m 11 GF *rear, f 2nd* F -

Not the best of starts **0**

TIMBER TOPPER ch.g. 7 Crowning Honors (CAN) - Clairwood by Final Straw — P Wilkin
1996 P(0),U(-),7(0),P(0)

429 8/3 Charm Park (L) MDO 3m 14 GF *rear & sn strggling, t.o. 9th, p.u. 2 out* P 0
510 15/3 Dalton Park (R) MDO 3m 14 GF *prom, 4th & in tch whn b.d. 15th* B -
1073 13/4 Whitwell-On' (R) MDO 2 1/2m 88yds 17 G *prom til wknd 4 out, t.o. & p.u. 2 out* P 0
1409 5/5 Witton Cast' (R) MDO 3m 15 GS *prom, disp 4 out til ld & lft clr last, styd on wll* 1 16
1418 10/5 Easingwold (L) MEM 3m 6 GF *chsd ldrs, disp 11th, ld nxt-4out,prssd wnr 2 out,kpt on wll* 2 17
1510 17/5 Corbridge (R) RES 3m 13 GS *hld up,prog 9th,ld 2 out, clr & jmpd slwly last,ran on wll* 1 20

Much improved; won good Restricted; should be able to upgrade in 98; G/S-G/F **21**

TIM BOBBIN b.h. 15 Swing Easy (USA) - Rosalia by Tower Walk — J G Scott
1996 6(0)

606 22/3 Friars Haugh (L) MEM 3m 9 GF *alwys bhnd* 5 0

Of no account. **0**

TIMES LEADER b.g. 8 Politico (USA) - Our Hard Times by Damsire Unregistered — Mrs D M Hall
1996 **4(NH)**,**10(NH)**,**P(NH)**

122 9/2 Cottenham (R) MEM 3m 6 GF *in tch wth ldng pair to 10th, steadily wknd* 4 0
276 22/2 Ampton (R) MDO 3m 12 G *in tch, 5th & btn whn u.r. 3 out* U -
439 8/3 Higham (L) MDO 3m 11 G *ld 1st, hit 8th, hdd apr 16th, onepcd apr last* 2 11
1283 27/4 Fakenham P-' (L) MDO 3m 9 G *mid-div, 7th whn blnd 13th, sn lost tch, p.u. 3 out* P 0

Ex novice chaser; ran fair race when 2nd but looks slow & may struggle to find a win **12**

TIME TO BE (Irish) — **I** 287[4], **I** 351[P]

TIME TO SMILE (Irish) — **I** 188[P], **I** 282,

TIMMOSS(IRE) b.g. 6 Le Moss - Tangaroa by Lord Gayle (USA) — S B Bell
1996 **13(NH)**

357 2/3 Great Stain' (L) MDO 3m 15 S *prom, ev ch 3 out, onepcd nxt* 2 14

Ran well in modest race & vanished; should be up to winning if fit in 98 .... **14**

TIMMYJOHN (Irish) — **I** 515[P]

TIMMY TUFF (Irish) — **I** 82[P], **I** 238[P], **I** 474[3], **I** 533[5], **I** 615[3]

TIMS KICK(IRE) b.m. 6 Borovoe - La Paure by Pauper — R H P Williams
1996 P(0),P(0),1(14),P(0)

845 31/3 Lydstep (L) RES 3m 5 F *ld to 2nd, chsd wnr aft, wknd 2 out* 3 10
1008 12/4 St Hilary (R) RES 3m 11 GF *mid-div, wknd & p.u. 15th* P 0
1227 26/4 Pyle (R) RES 3m 15 GS *mid-div, wknd 13th, t.o. & p.u. 15th* P 0
1471 11/5 Erw Lon (L) RES 3m 9 GS *trckd ldr til mstk 14th, no ext aft* 4 12
1556 24/5 Bassaleg (R) RES 3m 13 G *lost tch 6th, ran wd bend aft 8th, p.u. nxt* P 0

Maiden winner 96; struggling badly since & looks to have little chance of Restricted win **12**

TINERANA BOY (Irish) — **I** 492[P], **I** 511[4]

TINKER HILL gr.g. 7 Scallywag - Sandra Bella by Crooner — W D S Murdoch

209 16/2 Southwell P' (L) MDO 3m 7 GS *prom to 7th, sn lost plc, t.o. & p.u. 11th* P 0
346 2/3 Market Rase' (L) MDO 3m 10 GF *cls up, 2nd whn f 6th* F -

Placed 95; missed 96; nothing in 97 .... **0**

TINKER TAILOR b.g. 5 Sergeant Drummer (USA) - Tinker's Quest by Romany Air — Mrs T White

526 15/3 Cothelstone (L) MDN 3m 15 GS *keen hld, in tch, cls 4th at 15th, no ext, eased, improve* 4 10
1094 16/4 Hockworthy (L) MDN 3m 11 GF *(fav) chsng grp, effrt to 4th 4 out, sn btn, t.o. & p.u. last* P 0

Promise on debut but looked & ran poorly next time; should improve at 6 .... **13**

TINOSMILL (Irish) — **I** 353[P], **I** 594[P]

TINOTOPS br.g. 7 Neltino - Topte by Copte (FR) — R H H Targett
1996 F(-),4(16),1(18),2(22),1(25),1(25)

6 19/1 Barbury Cas' (L) LAD 3m 13 GF *(fav) bhnd, gd prog to 15l 3rd hlfwy, chsd wnr 2 out, nrst fin* 2 25
97 8/2 Great Treth' (R) INT 3m 13 GS *(fav) prom, ld 7-14th, outpcd & mstk 16th, no prog aft* 3 20
363 2/3 Garnons (L) XX 3m 6 GS *(fav) trckd ldr 8th, ld 15th, 5l up nxt, drew clr* 1 25
586 19/3 Exeter (R) HC 3 1/4m 12 GF *(fav) trckd ldrs, went 2nd 12th, ld 6 out to next, led again 4 out, mstk 2 out, soon clr, driven out.* 1 28
1292 30/4 Cheltenham (L) HC 2m 5f 12 GF *cl up, trckd ldr 11th, ld after 3 out, driven out run-in.* 1 27
1517 17/5 Bratton Down (L) MXO 3m 8 GS *(fav) trckd ldr, rdn 2 out, ran on to ld 100 yrds out, hdd post* 2 26

Very useful tough & consistent; beaten only in hot races; win plenty more; stays well; G/F-S 30

TINRYLAND b.g. 13 Prince Regent (FR) - Tonduff Star by Royal Highway — Miss C Elderton

773 29/3 Dingley (R) LAD 3m 11 G *last pair til ref 8th* R -

No longer of any account 0

TINSUN b.g. 6 Neltino - Pensun by Jimsun — R G Weaving

1996 6(0)

774 29/3 Dingley (R) MDO 2m 5f 10 G *2nd to 9th, 4th & outpcd 4 out, ran on onepcd* 3 10
1082 13/4 Guilsborough (L) MDN 3m 14 GF *ld 3-10th, disp 13-16th, chsd wnr aft, onepcd 2 out* 3 11
1402 5/5 Ashorne (R) MDO 3m 11 G *chsd ldrs, rdn 11th, wknd & p.u. 13th, dead* P 0

Dead 13

T'INT(IRE) b.m. 9 Camden Town - Rue Del Peru by Linacre — S Burley

1996 4(17),3(13)

332 1/3 Eaton Hall (R) RES 3m 18 GS *mid-div, styd on frm 3 out, nrst fin* 4 0
887 1/4 Flagg Moor (L) XX 3m 8 G *chsd ldrs, mstk 12th, 2nd brfly apr 15th, wknd 3 out* 4 0

Maiden winner 95; lightly raced; safe but slow & hard to win again now 12

TIPP DOWN ch.g. 14 Crash Course - Caramore Lady by Deep Run — Mrs A E Astall

1996 P(0),P(0),4(0),U(-),**9(0),U(-)**

202 15/2 Weston Park (L) LAD 3m 13 G *alwys rear, p.u. 3 out* P 0
375 3/3 Doncaster (L) HC 2m 3f 110yds 11 GF *chsd ldrs till f 8th, dead.* F -

Dead 0

TIPPING AWAY (Irish) — **I** 510[1], **I** 600[P]

TIPS LAD b.g. 14 Seafields - Bonnie Lola by Gulf Pearl — D T Greenwood

762 29/3 Whittington (L) MEM 3m 5 S *lft 20l 3rd 6th, alwys bhnd aft, btn 1 fence* 2 0

No longer of any account 0

TIP THE SKIP (Irish) — **I** 122[4], **I** 202[F], **I** 315[4], **I** 348[5], **I** 417[3], **I** 468[F], **I** 580[1]

TIRLEY GALE b.g. 5 Strong Gale - Mascara Vii by Damsire Unregistered — Mrs W Smith

259 22/2 Newtown (L) MDN 3m 18 G *in tch in rear, u.r. aft 9th* U -

Just a quiet debut 0

TITATIUM (Irish) — **I** 103[6]

TITCHWELL MILLY b.m. 8 Baron Blakeney - Zaratella by Le Levanstell — A J Owen

1996 P(0),U(-),U(-),3(10),P(0)

211 16/2 Southwell P' (L) MDO 3m 15 GS *in tch to 11th, t.o. & p.u. 15th* P 0
487 9/3 Tweseldown (R) MDO 3m 12 G *sn wll bhnd,no ch hlfwy, kpt on frm 16th, went dist 3rd flat* 3 0
1165 20/4 Mollington (R) MDO 3m 9 GF *(fav) chsd wnr, no imp 3 out, 3rd & btn whn mstk nxt* 4 10

Placed in 3 of last 5 starts but form very weak & much more needed for winning chances 11

TOARLITE (Irish) — **I** 468[P], **I** 551[P], **I** 580[P], **I** 595[6]

TOASTER CRUMPET b.g. 8 Seymour Hicks (FR) - Lady Letitia by Le Bavard (FR) — Miss Pauline Robson

1996 6(0),2(17),5(0),1(18),3(18),3(16),3(14)

35 26/1 Alnwick (L) CON 3m 10 G *alwys prom, ld 15th, clr last, pshd out, comf* 1 20
130 9/2 Alnwick (L) INT 3m 7 G *(fav) alwys same plc, brf efft apr 4 out, wll btn nxt* 4 0
335 1/3 Corbridge (R) CON 3m 7 G *mid-div, prog 3 out, ev ch nxt, outpcd* 3 18
560 16/3 Lanark (R) CON 3m 8 GS *4th hlfwy, nvr rchd ldrs* 4 15
608 22/3 Friars Haugh (L) XX 3m 6 GF *hld up, wnt 2nd 4 out, slght ld frm nxt drvn out flat* 1 18
732 29/3 Alnwick (L) CON 3m 6 F *alwys prom, chsd ldr 12th-3 out, disp nxt, hdd & no ext last* 2 18
1427 10/5 Aspatria (L) INT 3m 7 G *chsd wnr 10-13th, no imp, kpt on to go 2nd agn 2 out* 2 16
1509 17/5 Corbridge (R) INT 3m 10 GS *rear whn f 3rd* F -

Consistent, ultra-safe & dour stayer; one paced but should find more chances in 98; F-G/S 20

TOBIN BRONZE b.g. 10 Sexton Blake - Pampered Julie by Le Bavard (FR) — G Thornton

1996 P(0),P(0),1(18),3(20)

119 9/2 Wetherby Po' (L) OPE 3m 15 GF *mid-div, prog 11th, kpt on frm 3 out* 3 21
166 15/2 Witton Cast' (R) OPE 3m 8 F *hld up rear, gd prog 14th, disp 4 out, ld 2 out, ran on wll* 1 22
339 1/3 Corbridge (R) OPE 3m 5f 11 G *hld up rear, prog 13th, went 2nd 4 out, wknd 2 out* 4 19
475 9/3 Southwell P' (L) OPE 3m 7 G *(fav) hld up, prog 10th, 8l 3rd apr 3 out, wll btn nxt* 3 13
673 23/3 Brocklesby ' (L) CON 3m 8 GF *w.w. prog 10th, 2nd apr 3 out, rdn nxt, onepced* 2 19
1253 26/4 Easingwold (L) MEM 3m 7 GS *(fav) trckd ldr, ld 4-2 out, disp last, styd on wll* 1 18

Consistent & fair pointer; won 3 of last 8; best on easy tracks; should find more chances 98; F-S 22

TO DARN HOT (Irish) — **I** 602[P]

TODCRAG b.g. 8 Feelings (FR) - Redetwig by Carlton Grange — Mrs D Scott

1996 1(15),2(16),1(19),1(20),1(23),1(23),1(22)

562	16/3	Lanark	(R)	OPE	3m	8	GS	*ld 9th-12th, cls up whn mstk 4 out, kpt on & no ch aft*	2	21
610	22/3	Friars Haugh	(L)	OPE	3m	6	GF	*ld 8th-3 out, kpt on wll*	2	24
812	31/3	Tranwell	(L)	OPE	3m	7	G	*(fav) j.w.,cls 2nd til ld 7th,mnly 8l up 8th-2 out,styd on strngly*	1	24
946	6/4	Friars Haugh	(L)	OPE	3m	5	GF	*(fav) 2nd til ld 12th, drew clr frm 3 out*	1	22
1170	20/4	Hexham Poin'	(L)	OPE	3m	2	GF	*(fav) ld til hdd & outpcd 2 out, 4l down last, no imp flat*	2	20

Won 6 in 96 & maintained progress; beaten by good horses 97; stays; consistent; worth H/Chase try ... 25

TODDLING INN b.m. 10 Pragmatic - Arconist by Welsh Pageant — R J R Symonds

1996 **F(NH),8(NH),6(NH),P(NH),U(NH),6(NH)**

45	1/2	Larkhill	(R)	RES	3m	14	GF	*rear whn hmpd 5th, sn t.o.*	7	0
177	15/2	Larkhill	(R)	MEM	3m	6	G	*jmpd lft, ld til apr 13th, chsd wnr vainly aft*	2	12

Irish Maiden winner 94; toddled round slowly 2nd start 11

TODDS HALL(IRE) gr.g. 9 Orchestra - Golden Robe by Yankee Gold — Andrew Munro

1996 6(0),6(0),R(-)

294	1/3	Didmarton	(L)	INT	3m	20	G	*prom til u.r. 8th*	U	-
488	9/3	Tweseldown	(R)	RES	3m	10	G	*ld to 12th, sn outpcd, wknd 16th, wll btn whn u.r. last*	U	-
742	29/3	Barbury Cas'	(L)	MEM	3m	5	F	*in tch til wknd rpdly 11th, t.o.*	2	0
1058	13/4	Hackwood Pa'	(L)	RES	3m	6	GF	*(bl) ld 3-10th, wknd rpdly, t.o. & p.u. aft 3 out*	P	0

Awarded Irish Maiden 95; does not stay & no hopes of a win 10

TOD LAW b.m. 9 Le Moss - Owenburn by Menelek — J P Elliot

1996 4(16),P(0)

231	22/2	Friars Haugh	(L)	LAD	3m	13	G	*f 2nd*	F	-
608	22/3	Friars Haugh	(L)	XX	3m	6	GF	*alwys hndy, no ext frm 3 out*	3	14
811	31/3	Tranwell	(L)	LAD	3m	3	G	*mnly 3rd 1st ctt, cls 2nd 11-14th, wknd to 3rd 2 out*	3	15
1297	3/5	Hexham	(L)	HC	3m 1f	8	F	*alwys bhnd, t.o. from hfwy.*	6	0
1425	10/5	Aspatria	(L)	LAD	3m	6	G	*chsng grp til mstk & wknd 11th, t.o. 15th*	6	0
1515	17/5	Corbridge	(R)	MEM	3m	5	GS	*(fav) sttld 3rd, prog to ld 4 out, faltered & hdd last, rallied*	2	10

Restricted winner 95; one paced & struggling since; hard to see where win comes from now 14

TOIAPAN(IRE) ch.g. 9 Ragapan - Deep Toi by Deep Run — Miss R F Gander

773	29/3	Dingley	(R)	LAD	3m	11	G	*plld hrd, ld 5th, ran out nxt*	r	-
1076	13/4	Guilsborough	(L)	MEM	3m	9	GF	*wth ldr, ld 13th, mstk nxt, hdd 15th, wknd & p.u. 3 out*	P	0
1609	1/6	Dingley	(R)	MDO	3m	14	GF	*rear whn hmpd & u.r. 2nd*	U	-

Missed 96 & unlikely to achieve much now 0

TOLMIN ch.g. 9 Topsider (USA) - Ivor's Honey by Sir Ivor — Andrew Dickman

1996 6(0),4(0),**9(0)**,3(10),3(13)

38	26/1	Alnwick	(L)	MDO	3m	14	G	*alwys bhnd, t.o. 10th, p.u. 3 out*	P	0
136	9/2	Alnwick	(L)	MDO	3m	16	G	*bhnd, prog & in tch 10th, outpcd apr 13th*	8	0
162	15/2	Lanark	(R)	MDO	3m	16	G	*nvr rchd ldrs*	6	0
343	1/3	Corbridge	(R)	MDO	3m	14	G	*mid-div, mod 3rd 11th, onepcd 2 out*	3	0
565	16/3	Lanark	(R)	MDO	3m	10	GS	*alwys hndy, ld 12th, jnd 2 out, hdd last, rlld nr line*	2	13
991	12/4	Tranwell	(L)	MEM	3m	3	F	*n.j.w., 6l last & u.r. 3rd*	U	-
1172	20/4	Hexham Poin'	(L)	MDO	3m	4	GF	*(bl) cls 2nd to 11th, disp 12th-14th, 3rd nxt, outpcd 3 out*	3	0
1337	3/5	Mosshouses	(L)	MDO	3m	7	F	*(bl) made most to 9th, hrd rdn to sty in tch, no ext frm 2 out*	3	11
1429	10/5	Aspatria	(L)	MDO	3m	15	G	*mid-div & out of tch, wknd & p.u. 12th*	P	0
1514	17/5	Corbridge	(R)	MDO	3m	17	GS	*rear whn p.u. 8th*	P	0

Placed 7 times 96/7; very modest; will need luck to win 10

TOMASINS CHOICE (Irish) — **I** 106P, **I** 133P, **I** 206P, **I** 300P

TOMBOLA gr.g. 6 Neltino - Asphaltara by Scallywag — Mrs T H Regis

452	8/3	Newton Brom'	(R)	MDN	3m	9	G	*rear, prog to 3rd 11th, ran on 2 out, tk 2nd nr fin*	2	11

Satisfactory debut in weak race; should improve; good stable 13

TOMCAPPAGH(IRE) br.g. 6 Riberetto - Shuil Suas by Menelek — Miss S French

1996 P(0)

57	1/2	Kingston Bl'	(L)	LAD	3m	13	GF	*alwys bhnd, p.u. 13th*	P	0
196	15/2	Higham	(L)	MDO	3m	12	G	*w.w. cls 2nd frm 8th, ld 16th, ran on wll whn chal flat*	1	14
324	1/3	Marks Tey	(L)	RES	3m	16	G	*cls up, blndrd 10th, 4th & outpcd 15th, no dang aft*	4	10

Improved & won on 1st completion (poor race); not disgraced next time & may have chances 98 14

TOM DEELY (Irish) — **I** 43P, **I** 1024, **I** 161P, **I** 2434, **I** 3005, **I** 3532

TOMEKO (Irish) — **I** 1474

TOM FURZE b.g. 10 Sula Bula - Bittleys Wood by Straight Lad — Mrs D Buckett

1996 **P(0),1(20)**

679	26/3	Ascot	(R)	HC	2m 3f 110yds	9	G	*ld to 3rd, with ldr to 11th, soon wknd, t.o. when blnd last.*	5	0
987	12/4	Kingston Bl'	(L)	OPE	3m	4	GF	*keen hld, ld 6th, jnd brfly 15th, clr 2 out, comf*	1	20
1298	3/5	Warwick	(L)	HC	2 1/2m 110yds	2	GF	*ld clr from 10th, in command when eased from 2 out, hdd run-in, rdn and ran on well, just failed.*	2	11

Very lightly raced; quite useful; H/Chase winner 96 & best under 3m; should win in 98; G/F-F 22

TOM HAGGARD (Irish) — **I** 34^{P}, **I** 120^{P}, **I** 254, , **I** 330^{P}, **I** 377^{P}, **I** 436^{6}, **I** 467^{F}, **I** 585^{P}

TOM LOG ch.g. 10 Politico (USA) - Shepherd Valley by Arrigle Valley — Mrs C M Wardroper

1996 4(20),3(18),2(19),7(0),6(0)

67	1/2	Wetherby	(L)	HC	3m 1f	10	G	*mstk 6th, soon bhnd, t.o..*	8	0
113	9/2	Wetherby Po'	(L)	CON	3m	10	GF	*(vis) alwys prom, 2nd at 11th, outpcd frm 3 out*	3	14
339	1/3	Corbridge	(R)	OPE	3m 5f	11	G	*(vis) keen hld, ld to 3 out, wknd rpdly*	6	12
509	15/3	Dalton Park	(R)	XX	3m	13	GF	*mid-div,lost plc 14th, effrt 16th, onepcd 3 out,lft 2nd last*	2	15
875	1/4	Wetherby	(L)	HC	3m 1f	5	GF	*mstk 6th, blnd next, soon lost tch, t.o..*	4	0
1072	13/4	Whitwell-On'	(R)	MXO	4m	21	G	*(bl) mid-div, mstk 15th, wknd 18th*	10	10
1253	26/4	Easingwold	(L)	MEM	3m	7	GS	*(bl) mid-div, outpcd by ldrs, dist 3rd 3 out*	3	0

Ultra-safe but slow & ground against 97; only chance in stamina test in 98; G-Hy 16

TOMMY-GUN b.g. 10 Cruise Missile - Joyeuse by Biskrah — Mrs J A C Lundgren

147	9/2	Tweseldown	(R)	MDO	3m	12	GF	*prom, wknd 9th, p.u. 12th*	P	0
600	22/3	Parham	(R)	MEM	3m	7	F	*prom early, rear whn p.u. 9th*	P	0

Some speed but no stamina so far 0

TOMMYKNOCKER(IRE) ch.g. 5 Woodman (USA) - Repercutionist (USA) by Beaudelaire (USA) — Ms L Sercombe

1996 **7(NH),8(NH)**

43	1/2	Larkhill	(R)	MDO	3m	10	GF	*alwys rear, t.o. 12th, p.u. 15th*	P	0
184	15/2	Erw Lon	(L)	MDN	3m	14	G	*last pair & t.o. til p.u. 14th*	P	0
408	8/3	Llanfrynach	(R)	MDN	3m	12	G	*rear, p.u. 14th*	P	0
639	22/3	Howick	(L)	MDN	3m	15	GF	*mid-div, ran on frm 14th, nrst fin*	4	0
719	29/3	Llanvapley	(L)	MDN	3m	14	GF	*towrds rear, ran on onepce*	4	0
908	5/4	Howick	(L)	MDN	3m	7	F	*disp mod 3rd frm 7th, no ch 12th, nvr plc to chal*	4	0

Yet to become seriously involved & given a strange ride last start; much more needed 10

TOMMY O'DWYER(IRE) b.g. 8 Black Minstrel - Collective by Pragmatic — A K Pritchard

1996 F(-),1(13),P(0),P(0),3(15)

300	1/3	Didmarton	(L)	RES	3m	23	G	*prog 10th, jnd ldr 14th, wknd aft nxt*	4	14
517	15/3	Larkhill	(R)	RES	3m	10	GF	*in tch to 13th, sn wknd, p.u. 15th*	P	0
760	29/3	Kimble	(L)	RES	3m	7	GF	*prssd ldrs, ld 2 out, jnd last, not qckn & hdd flat*	2	15
1081	13/4	Guilsborough	(L)	RES	3m	13	GF	*hld up,mstk 10th,prog nxt,chsd wnr 15th,btn 2 out,fin tired*	2	16

Maiden winner 96; ran in good races mainly 97 & outclassed; non-stayer but may find a chance 98 17

TOMMY PINK (Irish) — **I** 283^{P}

TOMMYS PRIDE (Irish) — **I** 192^{P}, **I** 261^{2}, **I** 352^{5}, **I** 444^{3}, **I** 533^{3}, **I** 559^{3}, **I** 602^{4}

TOMMYS WEBB(IRE) b.g. 9 Asir - Coleman Lass by Pry — A Hartgrove

375	3/3	Doncaster	(L)	HC	2m 3f 110yds	11	GF	*held up, hdwy to chase ldrs 5 out, soon rdn and no impn.*	4	16

Ran a more than passable race in decent H/Chase but failed to appear; could have chances 98 16

TOMMY THE DUKE (Irish) — **I** 16^{2}, **I** 51^{2}, **I** 144^{1}, **I** 168^{2}, **I** 244^{2}

TOMMY WYNN (Irish) — **I** 268^{1}

TOMPET b.g. 11 Le Bavard (FR) - Swanny Jane by Bargello — Sir Michael Connell

1996 4(12),6(10),3(0),5(14),r(-),3(18),S(-)

142	9/2	Tweseldown	(R)	MEM	3m	8	GF	*hld up, in tch whn blnd & u.r. 11th*	U	-
370	2/3	Mollington	(R)	OPE	3m	6	G	*hld up last, not keen & bhnd frm 12th, no imp aft*	4	12
446	8/3	Newton Brom'	(R)	CON	3m	8	G	*ld1st, disp 3rd-apr 7th, lost plc 11th, wknd*	6	12
650	22/3	Siddington	(L)	CON	3m	8	F	*not keen, ld to 13th, sn btn, lft 3rd 15th*	3	0
984	12/4	Kingston Bl'	(L)	MEM	3m	4	GF	*ld aft 5th til reluc & hdd 14th, sn outpcd, kpt on agn flat*	2	10
1162	20/4	Mollington	(R)	CON	3m	7	GF	*chsd ldrs, effrt & hit 2 out, kpt on wll flat*	2	17
1403	5/5	Ashorne	(R)	CON	3m	14	G	*chsd ldr 7-10th, not qckn aft frm 15th, kpt on*	5	15
1532	18/5	Mollington	(R)	CON	3m	11	GS	*jmpd lft, prssd ldr to 10th, wknd 15th*	6	10
1607	1/6	Dingley	(R)	OPE	3m	9	GF	*chsd ldrs,styd on frm 10th,3rd at 14th,chsd wnr last,nvr nrr*	2	21

Losing sequence now 20; occasionally makes an effort but generally very sullen & win most unlikely ... 17

TOM SAID (Irish) — **I** 204^{P}

TOM'S APACHE br.g. 8 Sula Bula - Tom's Nap Hand by Some Hand — O J Carter

1996 P(0)

493	12/3	Newton Abbot	(L)	HC	2m 5f 110yds	11	HY	*mstk 1st, t.o. when p.u. before 10th.*	P	0

892 5/4 Hereford (R) HC 2m 11 GF *ld, soon clr, hdd after 2 out, soon outpcd.* 2 19

Still a maiden but ran well in short H/Chase; very lightly raced & hard to find a win 14

TOM'S ARCTIC DREAM b.m. 9 Oats - Tom's Nap Hand by Some Hand Mrs J McCullough

176 15/2 Ottery St M' (L) RES 3m 17 G *f 1st* F -
242 22/2 Lemalla (R) MDO 3m 10 S *ld 1st, cls up til disp 6-9th, lost ground 11th, p.u. 13th* P 0
459 8/3 Great Treth' (R) MDO 3m 9 S *jmp rght, ld til 3rd, lost plc, hmp 11th, f 12th* F -
648 22/3 Castle Of C' (R) RES 3m 8 G *ld to 5th, prom til wknd 11th, t.o. & p.u. last* P 0
1152 20/4 Stafford Cr' (R) MEM 3m 4 GF *disp til p.u. bef 4th, reins broke* P 0
1486 11/5 Ottery St M' (L) MDO 3m 17 G *plld hrd, ld to 13th, disp nxt, ld 15th, going wll, f 4 out* F -
1553 24/5 Mounsey Hil' (R) MDO 3m 11 G *rcd freely,ld to 8th,chsd ldrs,3rd & btn whn u.r.3out,rmntd* 3 0

Has ability but runs himself into the ground; could win if learning to settle 14

TOMS CHOICE(IRE) gr.g. 8 Mandalus - Prior Engagement by Push On M F Harding

1996 3(14),2(15)

88 2/2 Wolverhampt' (L) MDO 3m 13 GS *prom to 4th, bhnd frm 11th, t.o. & p.u. nxt* P 0
654 22/3 Siddington (L) MDN 3m 10 F *(Jt fav) ld to 15th, sn rdn, ev ch 2 out, no ext* 2 14

Lightly raced; placed in 3 of last 4 but stamina doubts; may find a chance 14

TOM'S GEMINI STAR ch.g. 9 Celtic Cone - Je Dit by I Say O J Carter

1996 P(0),**6(NH)**,**P(NH)**

385 6/3 Wincanton (R) HC 3m 1f 110yds 6 G *pressing ldrs when f 9th.* F 22
493 12/3 Newton Abbot (L) HC 2m 5f 110yds 11 HY *bhnd when blnd and u.r. 6th.* U -
589 20/3 Wincanton (R) HC 2m 5f 9 GF *hdwy 12th, in tch when left cl 2nd and hmpd 4 out, ld next, pushed clr from 2 out.* 1 23
888 3/4 Aintree (L) HC 3m 1f 9 G *held up, f 3rd.* F -
983 12/4 Ascot (R) HC 3m 110yds 14 GF *held up in tch, hdwy to chase ldrs from 10th, rdn along 15th, driven and held in 4th when blnd and u.r. 2 out.* U -
1416 10/5 Newton Abbot (L) HC 2m 5f 110yds 14 G *held up, hdwy when blnd 4 out, p.u. before next.* P 0
1544 21/5 Newton Abbot (L) HC 3 1/4m 110yds 11 G *held up, hit 13th, soon lost tch, mod prog from 3 out, t.o..* 3 14
1588 30/5 Stratford (L) HC 3 1/2m 9 G *blnd 2nd, alwys bhnd, t.o. when f 4 out.* F -

33/1 when winning (lucky but subsequent winners behind); all over the place after; the future? 21

TOMSSON b.g. 7 My Dad Tom (USA) - Sophie's Star by Noalcoholic (FR) T B Chapman

261 22/2 Newtown (L) MDN 3m 16 G *bhnd, last whn u.r. 8th* U -

No encouragement yet 0

TOM'S TUNE (Irish) — **I** 133B, **I** 1982, **I** 275P, **I** 3544

TOM THE BOY VI (Irish) — **I** 238P

TOM THE TANK b.g. 7 Skyliner - Mistral Magic by Crofter (USA) D Gill

1996 4(0),1(15),2(19),1(19),P(0),2(18)

356 2/3 Great Stain' (L) INT 3m 9 S *(fav) mid-div,prog 11th,ld 15th, sn clr, hdd apr last, eased,lame* 3 15

Dual winner 96; obvious problem only start 97; could step up if fit 98 19

TONMARIE CHANCE (Irish) — **I** 195, **I** 79P, **I** 3554, **I** 6062

TONTO MACTAVISH br.g. 5 Tuam - Baynards Black Cat Vii by Damsire Unregistered G O Harper

1352 4/5 Dingley (R) MDO 2 1/2m 9 G *j.v.s., sn t.o., ref 4th thrice* R -

A daft name & performance to match 0

TONY'S FEELINGS b.g. 9 Feelings (FR) - Meg's Mantle by New Brig Mrs Linda Dyer

1996 **17(NH)**,**10(NH)**,**12(NH)**,**3(NH)**,**4(NH)**,**F(NH)**,**6(NH)**,**P(NH)**

156 15/2 Lanark (R) CON 3m 7 G *u.r. 1st* U -
229 22/2 Friars Haugh (L) CON 3m 9 G *nvr nr ldrs, t.o. & p.u. 2 out* P 0
560 16/3 Lanark (R) CON 3m 8 GS *sn bhnd, p.u. aft 11th* P 0
1219 26/4 Balcormo Ma' (R) LAD 3m 3 F *sn clr, 10l ahd whn ran out 9th* r -

Hurdle winner 95; no aptitude for pointing 0

TOO COVERS (Irish) — **I** 168P

TOO PHAR GONE ch.g. 5 Phardante (FR) - Timeless Flight by Prince Hansel K Cumings

792 31/3 Bishopsleigh (R) RES 3m 13 G *schoold in rear, p.u. 17th* P 0

A quiet introduction; good stable 0

TOOTH PICK (Irish) — **I** 1354, **I** 4292, **I** 4475, **I** 5203, **I** 5482

TOOTING TIMES ch.g. 11 Leading Man - Saucy by Saucy Kit R Dalton

1996 P(0)

265 22/2 Duncombe Pa' (R) CON 3m 15 G *mid-div, lost tch 8th, t.o. whn p.u. 12th* P 0
506 15/3 Dalton Park (R) CON 3m 16 GF *plld hrd, mid-div, prog 6th, rdn 12th, sn fdd, p.u. 2 out* P 0
695 29/3 Stainton (R) RES 3m 11 F *(bl) rear, rddn 7th, lost tch 11th, t.o. & p.u. 15th* P 0

Members winner 94; looks finished now 0

TOOZAN TAK b.g. 11 Sadler's Wells (USA) - Calandra (USA) by Sir Ivor — Major V Lloyd-Davies

606 22/3 Friars Haugh (L) MEM 3m 9 GF *(bl) alwys last* 7 0

No longer of any account 0

TOP BEAUTY b.m. 9 High Top - American Beauty by Mill Reef (USA) — C D Dawson

883 1/4 Flagg Moor (L) MDO 3m 12 G *mid-div, mstk 2nd, blnd & u.r. nxt* U -
1080 13/4 Guilsborough (L) RES 3m 11 GF *virt ref 1st & p.u. aft* P 0

Good stable but could scarcely have made a worse start 0

TOP FLIGHT TRAVEL (Irish) — I 62P, I 109[6]

TOP MISS b.m. 8 Celestial Storm (USA) - Crimson Ring by Persian Bold — A S Neaves

1996 **U(NH),P(NH),5(NH),9(NH),8(NH),5(NH),5(NH),R(NH),P(NH)**

323 1/3 Marks Tey (L) LAD 3m 7 G *pllng, ld 8-17th, no ext und pres apr last* 3 12
578 16/3 Detling (L) LAD 3m 11 F *mid-div til pshd alng & wknd 15th, p.u. aft 4 out* P 0

Very moderate under Rules; suspect stamina & unlikely to win a competitive point 11

TOP ODDER(IRE) b.g. 5 Doubletour (USA) - Miss Firion by Tanfirion — P J Millington

476 9/3 Southwell P' (L) XX 3m 6 G *sn wll bhnd, blnd 4th, t.o. & p.u. 11th* P 0
883 1/4 Flagg Moor (L) MDO 3m 12 G *blnd 1st, last frm nxt, t.o. 11th, p.u. 15th* P 0
898 5/4 Wetherby Po' (L) MDO 3m 7 F *mid-div, mstk 4th, prog 5 out, ev ch nxt, wknd* 3 0
1084 13/4 Guilsborough (L) MDN 3m 11 GF *rear, last whn f hvly 12th* F -
1281 27/4 Fakenham P-' (L) MDO 3m 8 G *jmpd slwly 3rd, chsd ldrs 8th, blnd 9th & 14th, btn 3 out* 4 0
1353 4/5 Dingley (R) MDO 2 1/2m 9 G *hld up, mstk 8th, outpcd 11th, last whn f 3 out* F -
1568 25/5 Kingston Bl' (L) MDO 3m 11 GF *mstk 2nd,rear,some prog to poor 4th & slw jmp 15th,fin tired* 4 0

Well beaten when completing & blunders his way round; prospects not appealing 10

TOP OF THE RANGE(IRE) ch.g. 7 Quayside - Dersina by Deep Run — P C Cornwell

1996 1(13),P(0),5(16)

324 1/3 Marks Tey (L) RES 3m 16 G *prom to 9th, bhnd whn p.u. 12th* P 0
502 15/3 Ampton (R) RES 3m 5 GF *ld to 8th, prom til 3 out, no ch whn blnd badly 2 out & p.u.* P 0
798 31/3 Marks Tey (L) RES 3m 7 F *cls up,ld 5th,hdd 7th,disp ld 2 out,just outpcd flat* 3 14

Maiden winner 96; beaten in poor Restricted last start & finished early; Restricted win unlikely 14

TOPPING-THE-BILL b.g. 12 Nicholas Bill - Top-N-Tale by Sweet Story — Mrs Emma Coveney

1996 1(21),2(22),4(14),1(18),2(19)

304 1/3 Parham (R) LAD 3m 10 G *prom early, bhnd whn p.u. 13th* P 0
1125 19/4 Penshurst (L) MEM 3m 3 GF *(fav) pllng & mstks, wth ldr, ld 3 out til apr last, wknd* 2 10

Fair Ladies horse to 96 but ran badly 97 & can only be watched early 98 14

TOP THE BID b.g. 10 Auction Ring (USA) - Funicular by Arctic Slave — M E Arthers

1996 P(0),P(0),4(0),5(0)

141 9/2 Thorpe Lodge (L) MDN 3m 12 GF *nvr bttr than mid-div* 7 0

Lightly raced & has only beaten one other finisher 0

TOP TOR b.m. 7 — R H P Williams

1996 P(0),2(12)

541 16/3 Erw Lon (L) MDN 3m 10 GF *mid-div, no ch whn p.u. 15th* P 0
640 22/3 Howick (L) MDN 3m 10 GF *(fav) hld up, lft in ld 15th, disp & lft clr 2 out* 1 15
962 6/4 Pantyderi (L) RES 3m 3 F *chsd wnr frm 2nd, clsng whn mstk 2 out, no ch aft* 2 11
1223 26/4 Pyle (R) MEM 3m 6 GS *blnd 1st, nvr going aft, bhnd frm 5th, p.u. 11th* P 0
1472 11/5 Erw Lon (L) XX 3m 9 GS *chsd ldrs to 11th, fdd, p.u. 15th* P 0
1599 31/5 Bassaleg (R) RES 3m 2 F *alwys 2nd, mstk 2nd, rdn apr 11th, sn t.o.* 2 0

Looked to be going the right way when winning but ran badly after; may revive but best watched 13

TORDUFF BAY (Irish) — I 150F, I 218P, I 377F, I 385P, I 501[3], I 539P

TORDUFF EXPRESS (Irish) — I 17[1], I 56P, I 147P, I 340F, I 387[3], I 457[1], I 480[1], I 543[1]

TORDUFF STAR (Irish) — I 150F, I 186[2], I 286[5]

TORR HEAD (Irish) — I 507,

TOSAWI'S GIRL(IRE) b.m. 6 Commanche Run - Madeira Lady by On Your Mark — Mrs A P Kelly

81 2/2 Wolverhampt' (L) MDN 3m 13 GS *in tch til wknd 7th, f nxt* F -
205 15/2 Weston Park (L) MDN 3m 10 G *alwys rear, t.o. & p.u. 14th* P 0

469 8/3 Eyton-On-Se' (L) MDN 2 1/2m 9 G *cls up, 2nd at 8th, mstk nxt, no dang aft* 4 0

Tailed off last on only completion to date 0

TOTALLY OPTIMISTIC b.g. 7 True Song - Wildly Optimistic by Hard Fact — Miss P Zygmant

1996 P(0),P(0),5(0)

990 12/4 Kingston Bl' (L) MDN 3m 11 GF *blnd 5th, last whn blnd 6th & p.u.* P 0

Not very good in 96 & a disastrous run 97 0

TO THE HILT (Irish) — **I** 155^{P}, **I** 185^{P}, **I** 341^{P}, **I** 405^{4}, **I** 499^{3}, **I** 570^{2}

TOT OF RUM ch.m. 7 Little Wolf - Decorum by Quorum — Mrs C M Rogers

1996 P(0)

408 8/3 Llanfrynach (R) MDN 3m 12 G *f 2nd* F -

570 16/3 Garnons (L) MDN 2 1/2m 14 G *last frm 5th, p.u. 7th* P 0

Yet to complete from 3 starts 96/7 0

TOUCHER(IRE) ch.g. 9 Fidel - Lealies Pride by Knotty Pine — David Morris

1996 U(-),P(0),P(0),P(0),U(-),3(0),P(0),4(0)

406 8/3 Llanfrynach (R) RES 3m 13 G *alwys rear, p.u. 8th* P 0

641 22/3 Howick (L) MDN 3m 9 GF *mid-div, b.d. 6th* B -

717 29/3 Llanvapley (L) RES 3m 13 GF *alwys rear, p.u. 3 out* P 0

1011 12/4 St Hilary (R) MDN 3m 10 GF *rear til p.u. 13th* P 0

1324 3/5 Bonvilston (R) MDO 3m 16 G *rear, p.u. 10th* P 0

Of no account 0

TOUCHING DOWN (Irish) — **I** 409^{P}, **I** 496^{1}

TOUCHING STAR b.g. 12 Touching Wood (USA) - Beaufort Star by Great Nephew — R Grant Sturges

1088 16/4 Hockworthy (L) MEM 3m 6 GF *(bl) bckwrd, made most to 5th, wknd 9th, t.o. & p.u. 13th* P 0

Winning chaser 94; looks finished now 0

TOUCH 'N' PASS ch.g. 9 Dominion - Hanglands by Bustino — R H P Williams

1996 U(-),2(12),5(14),1(23),**P(0)**,2(23),1(20),U(-),1(21),F(-)

98 8/2 Great Treth' (R) OPE 3m 14 GS *ld to 4th, wkng whn f 11th* F -

188 15/2 Erw Lon (L) LAD 3m 8 G *in tch, trckd ldr 14th, outjmpd last, ran on to ld nr fin* 1 24

401 8/3 Llanfrynach (R) LAD 3m 14 G *(fav) rear, no prog 13th* 5 18

537 16/3 Erw Lon (L) OPE 3m 9 GF *mid-div, prog 10th, ld aft 2 out, blnd last, styd on well* 1 23

637 22/3 Howick (L) OPE 3m 7 GF *rear, hrd rdn hlfwy, not rch ldrs, p.u. last* P 0

961 6/4 Pantyderi (L) LAD 3m 2 F *trckd dlr til lft alone 14th* 1 0

1006 12/4 St Hilary (R) LAD 3m 7 GF *(fav) hld up rear, rpd prog 16th, ld 3 out, sn clr* 1 20

1225 26/4 Pyle (R) LAD 3m 6 GS *(fav) hld up, prog 14th, ld 2 out, jmpd lft last, pshd out* 1 20

1364 5/5 Pantyderi (L) LAD 3m 5 G *(fav) in ld 3rd & 11th, f 3 out, rmntd* 3 0

1470 11/5 Erw Lon (L) LAD 3m 9 GS *(fav) sttld mid-div, prog 13th, ld 2 out, easily* 1 22

1540 18/5 Wolverhampt' (L) LAD 3m 5 GS *(fav) cls up, ld 10-11th, ld agn 5 out, ran on wll und pres* 1 21

1558 24/5 Bassaleg (R) LAD 3m 5 G *(fav) w.w. chsd ldr 14th, chal apr 2 out,ran wd bef last, no ext* 2 22

Consistent, tough; very game; suited by Ladies weights; sure to win more 98; G/F-G/S 24

TOUCH OF AUTUMN (Irish) — **I** 251^{P}, **I** 292, , **I** 329^{4}, **I** 370^{1}, **I** 504^{1}

TOUCH OF WINTER b or br.g. 11 Strong Gale - Ballyhoura Lady by Green Shoon — M W Kwiatkowski

1996 5(16),1(20),4(12),1(20),2(22),**U(-)**,7(0)

511 15/3 Larkhill (R) CON 3m 3 GF *(fav) disp til mstk 13th, found nil aft* 2 13

742 29/3 Barbury Cas' (L) MEM 3m 5 F *(fav) trckd wnr, saddl slppd & p.u. apr 9th* P 0

872 31/3 Hackwood Pa' (L) CON 3m 4 F *3rd to 11th, chsd wnr aft, p.u. flat* P 0

1271 27/4 Little Wind' (R) OPE 3m 3 GF *cls up in last til not qckn 15th, wknd nxt* 3 14

Dual winner 96 but took no interest 97 & looks safely ignored at 12 12

TOUGH MINDED ch.g. 8 Starch Reduced - Oujarater by Adropejo — Mrs P King

1996 3(20),2(14)

443 8/3 Higham (L) RES 3m 7 G *j.w. trckd ldrs, ld 11-15th, disp 3 out til p.u. nxt, lame* P 0

Maiden winner 94; problems now; Restricted standard if fit 98 16

TOUR BALLYEE (Irish) — **I** 554^{P}

TOURIG BIT (Irish) — **I** 132^{P}, **I** 191^{P}

TOWNGATE b.g. 7 Town And Country - Miss Buckstar by Master Buck — G Vergette

208 16/2 Southwell P' (L) MDO 3m 9 GS *jmpd big 1st, last & rdn 10th, t.o. & p.u. 12th* P 0

452 8/3 Newton Brom' (R) MDN 3m 9 G *rear, wknd 12th, p.u. 15th* P 0

550 16/3 Garthorpe (R) MDO 3m 11 GF *rr, lost tch 12th, t.o. & p.u. 14th* P 0

No signs of ability yet 0

TOYTOWN KING (Irish) — **I** 136^{P}, **I** 308^{4}, **I** 381^{4}, **I** 447^{P}, **I** 558^{2}, **I** 564^{F}, **I** 615^{2}

TRACEYTOWN (Irish) — I 151^{3}, I 187^{2}

TRACKMAN(IRE) b.g. 9 Remainder Man - Vitamin Maud — R E Evans
1996 **F(NH)**

186	15/2	Erw Lon	(L)	MDN	3m	13 G	*ld to 3rd, ld 7th, rdn clr 3 out, styd on well*	1	16
362	2/3	Garnons	(L)	OPE	3m	11 GS	*cls up, chal 12th, no ext frm 15th, wknd 3 out*	4	13
539	16/3	Erw Lon	(L)	RES	3m	8 GF	*(fav) prom, ld 14th-2 out, p.u. last, lame*	P	0

Ex-Irish; made ideal start but problem last start; Restricted chances if fit 98 16

TRACK O'PROFIT (Irish) — I 114^{P}, I 176^{P}, I 246^{2}, I 363^{2}, I 552^{F}

TRACTORIAS(IRE) br.g. 9 Aristocracy - My Serena — Mrs A Connal
1996 P(0),4(10),3(0)

21	25/1	Badbury Rin'	(L)	MDN	3m	7 GF	*rear, wknd 11th, t.o. & p.u. 15th*	P	0

No longer of any account 0

TRACYS TROT (Irish) — I 438^{U}

TRAKSWAYBOY (Irish) — I 520^{P}, I 558^{P}

TRAMPS HEARTBREAK (Irish) — I 405^{P}, I 500^{1}

TRANQUIL LORD(IRE) b.g. 8 Le Moss - Sedate by Green Shoon — D P Smith
1996 U(-),2(13),3(10),2(15),U(-),1(16)

372	2/3	Mollington	(R)	RES	3m	19 G	*(Jt fav) rear grp, no ch frm 11th, t.o. & p.u. 2 out*	P	0
974	8/4	Heythrop	(R)	MEM	3m	5 F	*(fav) mstks, w.w. prog 14th, ld aft 2 out, hdd last, no ex, lame*	2	13

Maiden winner 96; novice ridden; problems 97 & best watched if returning 98 14

TRANQUIL WATERS(USA) ch.g. 11 Diesis - Ebbing Tide (USA) by His Majesty (USA) — Mrs C Lawrence

791	31/3	Bishopsleigh	(R)	CON	3m	6 G	*alwys rear, t.o. 17th*	4	0
1397	5/5	High Bickin'	(R)	CON	3m	3 G	*2nd to 10th, in tch til rdn 15th, fdd*	3	0
1518	17/5	Bratton Down	(L)	XX	3m	7 GS	*in tch til rdn & wknd 14th*	5	0
1579	26/5	Lifton	(R)	CON	3m	9 G	*bhnd frm 7th, nvr dang*	6	0

Only beat 2 other finishers 97 & just going through the motions now 10

TRANSCENDENTAL(IRE) b.g. 7 Torenaga - Whistling Gold by Whistling Wind — Chester Bosomworth
1996 **6(NH),10(NH)**

79	2/2	Market Rase'	(L)	MDO	2m 5f	9 GF	*20s-5s, mid-div, prog to 3rd 10th, lost pl & p.u. nxt, lame*	P	0
116	9/2	Wetherby Po'	(L)	MDO	3m	14 GF	*mid-div, prog 14th, chal last, ran on to ld nr fin*	1	15
421	8/3	Charm Park	(L)	MEM	3m	6 GF	*(fav) hld up in mid-div, disp 12th,outpcd by wnr 15th,styd on flat*	2	14
616	22/3	Hutton Rudby	(L)	RES	3m	14 GF	*(Jt fav) rear & bhnd, out of tch whn p.u. 14th, saddld slpd*	P	0
1101	19/4	Hornby Cast'	(L)	RES	3m	14 G	*prom til lost plcd 11th, towrds rear whn u.r. 14th*	U	-

No form under Rules; won modest Maiden (7m+); may have chances in stamina Restricted 98 15

TRAVEL BOUND b.g. 12 Belfalas - Sugar Shaker by Quisling — Michael Mullineaux
1996 **6(NH),4(NH),P(NH)**

87	2/2	Wolverhampt'	(L)	MDO	3m	11 GS	*in tch to 11th, sn wll bhnd, ran on apr last, fin well*	3	10
226	21/2	Haydock	(L)	HC	3m	11 G	*(bl) chsd ldrs, lost pl hfwy, well bhnd 5 out.*	5	0
331	1/3	Eaton Hall	(R)	RES	3m	17 GS	*mid-div, nvr rchd ldrs*	6	0
464	8/3	Eyton-On-Se'	(L)	INT	3m	12 G	*settld mid-div, nvr plcd to chal*	3	10
665	23/3	Eaton Hall	(R)	MDO	3m	11 GF	*ld to 2nd, cls up, lft in ld 12th, hdd apr 3 out, kpt on*	2	14
941	6/4	Tabley	(R)	MDO	3m	11 G	*ld til blndrd & u.r. 1st*	U	-
999	12/4	Alpraham	(R)	MDO	3m	8 GF	*(fav) ld to 14th, wknd rpdly, p.u. 2 out*	P	0

An elderly maiden & likely to stay that way 12

TREASURE GALE (Irish) — I 593^{P}

TREATY BRIDGE ch.g. 10 Over The River (FR) - Diplomat's Tam by Tamariscifolia — A C Ayres
1996 P(0),U(-)

148	9/2	Tweseldown	(R)	XX	3m	12 GF	*prom, hit 3rd, hmpd & p.u. 5th, lame*	P	0

No longer of any account 0

TRECOMETTI b.m. 9 Giacometti - Balitree by Balidar — J A T de Giles
1996 5(0)

41	1/2	Larkhill	(R)	MDO	3m	13 GF	*pllng,in tch,chsd ldr 12th,chal 15th,1l down whn f last,dead*	F	16

Dead 0

TREMBLES CHOICE (Irish) — I 60^{P}

TREMBLING LADY (Irish) — I 280^{F}, I 296^{P}

TREMEIRCHION b.h. 11 Teenoso (USA) - Lady Waverton by Huntercombe — Mat Barnard

838	31/3	Thorpe Lodge	(L)	RES	3m	5 F	*back of bunch whn u.r. 2nd*	U	-
1032	12/4	Horseheath	(R)	RES	3m	2 HD	*mstks, wth wnr til wknd appr last*	2	0
1309	3/5	Cottenham	(R)	RES	3m	4 F	*ld to 10th, 3rd & in tch whn blnd 16th, wknd rpdly*	4	0

1435 10/5 Marks Tey (L) INT 3m 8 G *alwys rear, lost tch 10th, t.o. 13th, mstk & p.u. aft nxt* P 0

Maiden winner 95; missed 96; last on both completions 97 10

TRESPASSER(IRE) b.g. 8 Kambalda - Tip The Gold by Harwell Mrs M Armstrong
1996 **P(NH),P(NH),4(NH),U(NH),8(NH),4(NH),6(NH)**

130 9/2 Alnwick (L) INT 3m 7 G *bhnd & jmpd slwly 8th, reluc aft nxt, ran out 10th* r -
416 8/3 Dalston (R) RES 3m 12 GS *(bl) alwys rear, 10th & t.o. whn ref 13th* P 0
813 31/3 Tranwell (L) RES 3m 7 G *(bl) cls 3rd 4th, wknd into 6th 9th, outpcd & u.r. 12th* U -

Disappointing under Rules & worse in points 0

TREVVEETHAN(IRE) ch.g. 8 On Your Mark - Carrick Slaney by Red God Giles Smyly
1996 **6(NH),3(NH),8(NH),F(NH),3(NH)**

262 22/2 Newtown (L) RES 3m 15 G *chsd wnr 9th, chal 14th, rdn & no ext 2 out* 2 18
487 9/3 Tweseldown (R) MDO 3m 12 G *(fav) chsd ldng pair, disp 3rd whn f 10th* F -
1150 19/4 Chaddesley ' (L) MDO 3m 7 GF *(fav) w.w. prog to chs ldr 14th, ld & lft clr 16th, comf* 1 17
1288 30/4 Cheltenham (L) HC 2m 5f 10 GF *mstk 1st, held up, prog 8th, 5th and in tch when hmpd and u.r. 13th.* B -
1449 10/5 Kingston Bl' (L) RES 3m 8 G *(fav) mid-div, prog 10th, ld 12th-aft last, not qckn* 2 18
1533 18/5 Mollington (R) XX 3m 8 GS *(fav) hld up, prog to jn ldrs 13th, ld apr 2 out, clr last, comf* 1 19

Disappointing under Rules but came good in points; mistakes but progressive; can win Confined 98 ... 21

TRIAIL DO LAIMH (Irish) — I 461P, I 5403

TRICKSOME ch.g. 10 Nicholas Bill - Pranky by Bold Lad (IRE) J L Dunlop
1996 **B(NH),1(NH)**

142 9/2 Tweseldown (R) MEM 3m 8 GF *chsd ldr, lft in ld 8th, hdd 11th, btn whn f 3 out, dead* F -

Dead 23

TRIFAST LAD ch.g. 12 Scallywag - Cilla by Highland Melody Mike Roberts
1996 2(19),2(22)

150 10/2 Plumpton (L) HC 3m 1f 110yds 5 GS *made most, hit 16th, hdd apr last, one pace.* 2 22
225 19/2 Folkestone (R) HC 2m 5f 10 S *(fav) trckd ldr, chal 4 out, ld 2 out, styd on.* 1 22
378 4/3 Leicester (R) HC 2 1/2m 110yds 6 G *chsd ldrs, lost pl 3rd, tk clr order 9th, ld 2 out, mstk last, styd on well.* 1 26
890 4/4 Aintree (L) HC 2 3/4m 14 G *not fluent in rear, pkd 10th (Becher's), soon lost tch.* 6 14
1359 5/5 Southwell (L) HC 3m 110yds 7 GS *(fav) chsd clr ldr, hdwy 5 out, rdn to ld after 3 out, held on well from last.* 1 23
1491 14/5 Hereford (R) HC 3m 1f 110yds 11 G *hdwy 10th, chsd wnr from 3 out, styd on apr last but no impn on winner.* 2 28
1569 26/5 Fontwell (R) HC 3 1/4m 110yds 10 GF *(fav) settld towards rear, shaken up and hdwy 14th, effort and chal apr last, wknd run-in.* 4 20

Busiest season 97; very consistent & quite useful; effective from 21/2-3m+; can win at 13; Good 26

TRIMBUSH ch.g. 12 Flatbush - Miss Flymo by Guide K J Sims
1996 P(0),3(0),3(0)

390 8/3 Barbury Cas' (L) MDN 3m 15 G *ld to 6th, cls up til wknd 12th, last whn p.u. last* P 0

Looks destined to remain a maiden now 0

TRIMFOLD (Irish) — I 35P, I 72P, I 3771

TRIMMER LADY (Irish) — I 6P, I 605, I 139, , I 222, , I 3395, I 407U, I 4583, I 5006

TRIMMER PRINCESS (Irish) — I 27P, I 75P, I 147F, I 256, , I 387P, I 408, , I 494P, I 5466, I 587P, I 6146

TRIMMER WONDER (Irish) — I 37F, I 78, , I 1494, I 2166, I 306, , I 3865

TRINA'S COTTAGE(IRE) br.g. 8 Ovac (ITY) - Solar Cottage Miss Sarah A Dawson
1996 **9(NH),11(NH)**

13 25/1 Cottenham (R) MDO 3m 10 GF *alwys bhnd, t.o. & p.u. 3 out* P 0
60 1/2 Kingston Bl' (L) MDN 3m 17 GF *alwys bhnd, p.u. last* P 0
222 16/2 Heythrop (R) RES 3m 17 G *alwys bhnd, t.o. 12th* 7 0
487 9/3 Tweseldown (R) MDO 3m 12 G *sn bhnd, t.o. 11th, fin own time* 5 0
987 12/4 Kingston Bl' (L) OPE 3m 4 GF *ld to 6th, wknd 13th, t.o.* 4 0
1568 25/5 Kingston Bl' (L) MDO 3m 11 GF *made msot frm aft 2nd-10th, sn wknd, t.o.* 6 0

Safe enough but woefully lacking in ability 0

TRIPLE ACTION (Irish) — I 301S

TROJAN CALL b or br.g. 10 Trojan Fen - Breezy Answer by On Your Mark A Simpson
1996 **10(NH),6(NH),P(NH),2(NH),P(NH)**

302 1/3 Parham (R) CON 3m 14 G *mid-div, 5th & losing tch 15th, wll bhnd whn p.u. 2 out* P 0
481 9/3 Tweseldown (R) MEM 3m 6 G *ld, sn clr, hdd apr last, no ext* 2 10

Ran passably in Members but will not figure in proper races 10

TROJAN PLEASURE br.m. 10 Trojan Fen - Sweet Pleasure by Sweet Revenge — Mrs P Morris

333	1/3	Eaton Hall	(R)	INT	3m	10	GS	*t.o. & p.u. 9th*	P	0
670	23/3	Eaton Hall	(R)	RES	3m	15	GF	*mid to rear, no ch whn p.u. 3 out*	P	0
726	29/3	Sandon	(L)	CON	3m	8	GF	*chsg grp to hlfwy, sn btn*	7	0
940	6/4	Tabley	(R)	RES	3m	9	G	*b.d. 3rd*	B	-
1176	20/4	Sandon	(L)	OPE	3m	5	GF	*chsng grp to 9th, wknd, rear frm 12th*	4	0

No longer of any account 0

TROLLY gr.g. 6 Joli Wasfi (USA) - True Princess by Eastwood Prince — D J Norman

1996 P(0),P(0),F(-)

105	8/2	Great Treth'	(R)	MDO	3m	15	GS	*in tch, 5th at 12th, wknd & p.u. 15th*	P	0
244	22/2	Lemalla	(R)	MDO	3m	12	S	*in tch, cls 4th whn blnd 16th, wknd, no ch whn mstk last*	3	12
553	16/3	Ottery St M'	(L)	MDN	3m	15	G	*alwys rear, wll bhnd frm 14th*	5	0
794	31/3	Bishopsleigh	(R)	MDO	3m	12	G	*prom to 17th, wknd*	5	0

Has some ability but not really progressing & win unlikely at present 12

TROPICAL GABRIEL(IRE) ch.c. 9 Invited (USA) - Shimering Star by Mon Capitaine — Ken Liscombe

1996 3(0)

203	15/2	Weston Park	(L)	RES	3m	11	G	*mid to rear, btn aft hlfwy, no ch whn p.u. flat*	P	0

Rarely seen now & shows nothing 0

TROPICAL REEF(IRE) b.g. 7 Stalker - Superior Maid by Gay Fandango (USA) — H M Barnfather

160	15/2	Lanark	(R)	MDO	2m 5f	10	G	*hld up, lft poor 2nd 2 out, no imp, dmtd flat*	3	0

Beaten long way on debut & vanished; much more needed if fit 98 10

TROPNEVAD ch.g. 9 Alias Smith (USA) - Confident Girl by Quorum — P Spottiswood

1996 **14(NH)**,**12(NH)**,**5(NH)**,**6(NH)**

37	26/1	Alnwick	(L)	MDO	3m	15	G	*alwys bhnd, t.o. 10th*	6	0
814	31/3	Tranwell	(L)	MDO	3m	9	G	*(bl) alwys prom,cls 3rd 9th,styd on strngly last in to 2nd run in*	2	14

Ran well 2nd start but had plenty of chances under Rules & likely to disappoint 13

TROUBLED MAN (Irish) — **I** 372^{4}

TROUTLET b.m. 5 Supreme Leader - Lucky Trout by Beau Charmeur (FR) — Mrs P Grainger

210	16/2	Southwell P'	(L)	MDO	3m	15	GS	*w.w. prog & in tch 11th, 4th & outpcd apr 3 out*	5	0

A reasonable start & ought to be able to do better in 98 11

TRUE CENSATION ch.m. 6 True Song - Barton's Blush by Fury Royal — K M T Wilson

420	8/3	Dalston	(R)	MDO	2 1/2m	8	GS	*s.s. last whn tried to ref & u.r. 2nd*	U	-
622	22/3	Hutton Rudby	(L)	MDO	3m	10	GF	*alwys wll bhnd, t.o. & p.u. 13th*	P	0
898	5/4	Wetherby Po'	(L)	MDO	3m	7	F	*2nd frm 5th, blnd bdly 14th, not rcvr, p.u. nxt*	P	0
1345	3/5	Gisburn	(R)	MDN	3m	13	GF	*rear whn f 6th*	F	-
1513	17/5	Corbridge	(R)	MDO	3m	13	GS	*prom til lost plc 4th, wll bhnd 6th, p.u. 8th*	P	0

Un-censational so far 0

TRUE CHIMES ch.g. 6 True Song - Ballytina by Rugantino — Mrs E V Cardew

1996 **21(NH)**,**19(NH)**,**10(NH)**

127	9/2	Cottenham	(R)	MDO	3m	11	GF	*mstk 3rd, in tch, 4th 3 out, kpt on onepcd*	3	0

No ability under Rules; not seen after passable debut; may do better if ready in 98 11

TRUE FORTUNE b.g. 7 True Song - Cost A Fortune by Silver Cloud — D J Miller

1996 1(14)

189	15/2	Erw Lon	(L)	RES	3m	14	G	*(fav) mstks, w.w. prog 13th, ld 3 out, drew clr nxt, ran on well*	1	19
382	5/3	Bangor	(L)	HC	3m 110yds	6	GS	*handy till f 9th.*	F	-
1228	26/4	Pyle	(R)	INT	3m	5	GS	*(fav) w.w. trckd ldr 15th, hrd rdn to chal last,ld und pres post*	1	20
1417	10/5	Warwick	(L)	HC	3 1/4m	8	G	*alwys prom, chsd wnr 13th, rdn 3 out, soon btn.*	2	23
1545	24/5	Cartmel	(L)	HC	3 1/4m	14	G	*(fav) in tch, hdwy to go cl up 7th, f 11th.*	F	-
1587	29/5	Uttoxeter	(L)	HC	2m 5f	11	GF	*alwys prom, chsd wnr 4 out, styd on.*	2	24

Maiden winner only start 96; improving & quite useful; mistakes still but could win H/Chase in 98 24

TRUE FRED ch.g. 8 True Song - Silver Spartan by Spartan General — Mrs A Price

1996 P(0),U(-),P(0)

706	29/3	Upper Sapey	(R)	MDO	3m	15	GF	*cls 7th whn f 11th*	F	-
1018	12/4	Bitterley	(L)	MDO	3m	13	GF	*prom til lost plc 7th, blnd nxt, p.u. 10th*	P	0
1232	26/4	Brampton Br'	(R)	MEM	3m	4	G	*cls up, ld 13th, drew clr frm 16th*	1	10
1388	5/5	Cursneh Hill	(L)	CON	3m	4	GF	*wnt 2l 2nd 11th, ev ch til outpcd frm 14th*	3	14

Won a bad race; not disgraced next time but more needed for Restricted hopes 14

TRUE STEEL b.g. 11 Deep Run - Aran Tour by Arapaho — Jon Trice-Rolph

1996 P(0),2(18),**2(21)**,**2(NH)**

287	27/2	Huntingdon	(R)	HC	3m	13 GS	*alwys bhnd, t.o. when p.u. before 5 out.*	P	0
388	7/3	Sandown	(R)	HC	3m 110yds	7 G	*held up, hdwy when mstk 9th, ld 12th, mistake next, hdd 16th, wknd after 2 out, lost 2nd pl run-in, fin tired.*	4	15
678	25/3	Sandown	(R)	HC	2 1/2m 110yds	6 GF	*(fav) hdwy 7th, mstk next, jmpd slowly and lost pl 9th, btn 13th.*	4	10

Able but tricky ride; blew out in golden opportunity last start & should be treated with caution now 19

TRULY OPTIMISTIC b.m. 8 True Song - Wildly Optimistic by Hard Fact — Mrs R C Hayward

1996 P(0),P(0),F(-)

374	2/3	Mollington	(R)	MDN	3m	14 G	*prom, lft in ld 6th, hdd 12th, wknd rpdly, p.u. 3 out*	P	0
452	8/3	Newton Brom'	(R)	MDN	3m	9 G	*last til mod prog 10th, 4th & no imp 16th*	4	0

Well beaten on only completion from 5 starts 96/7 & no cause for optimism 0

TRUMPET HILL b.g. 8 Feelings (FR) - Faughill by Bronze Hill — H M Barnfather

1996 4(0),3(0),10(0),5(0)

36	26/1	Alnwick	(L)	MDO	3m	15 G	*out of tch in mid-div, no ch frm 15th, styd on 3 out,nvr nrr*	3	10
162	15/2	Lanark	(R)	MDO	3m	16 G	*mid-div, prog 4 out, styd on to ld flat*	1	15
410	8/3	Dalston	(R)	MEM	3m	5 GS	*alwys last, lost tch 15th, t.o. & p.u. nxt, dsmntd*	P	0

Safe & won fair Maiden; problems after; may revive if fit 98 15

TRUSTY FRIEND b.g. 15 True Song - Princess Camilla by Prince Barle — Andrew Brown

1996 7(13),4(0),6(14),U(-),3(0),3(0),5(14),5(0)

3	19/1	Barbury Cas'	(L)	XX	3m	14 GF	*mid-div, 8th hlfwy, no imp ldrs final cct*	6	11
138	9/2	Thorpe Lodge	(L)	OPE	3m	5 GF	*in tch, no ext frm 3 out*	3	16

Continues his steady descent into retirement now 10

TRY A BLUFF (Irish) — **I** 470[P], **I** 522[1]

TRYDAN ch.g. 9 Push On - Island Joy by Easter Island — Malcolm W Davies

1996 r(-),U(-),P(0)

409	8/3	Llanfrynach	(R)	MDN	3m	12 G	*rear, p.u. 11th*	P	0
640	22/3	Howick	(L)	MDN	3m	10 GF	*rear, p.u. 12th*	P	0
1011	12/4	St Hilary	(R)	MDN	3m	10 GF	*rear til p.u. 13th*	P	0

Completed 2 of 22 races (last both times); no prospects 0

TRY GOD gr.g. 10 Godswalk (USA) - Are You Sure by Lepanto (GER) — F Allan

249	22/2	Brocklesby '	(L)	LAD	3m	4 G	*2nd hrd hld to 4th, cls 3rd til wknd qckly bfr 3 out*	3	0
495	14/3	Fakenham	(L)	HC	2m 5f 110yds	10 G	*trckd ldrs, ev ch 5 out, rdn and wknd after next.*	6	10

Showed up well but non-stayer & finished early; prospects slim 13

TRY IT ALONE b.g. 15 Harvest Sun - Philemore by Philemon — M Biddick

1996 1(25),**9(0)**,F(-),3(18),4(18)

807	31/3	Wadebridge	(L)	LAD	3m	4 F	*ld 4-7th agn 9th, made rest comf*	1	19
1110	19/4	Flete Park	(R)	LAD	3m	9 GF	*w.w. gd prog 3 out, outpcd aft 2 out*	2	19
1358	5/5	Exeter	(R)	HC	2m 7f 110yds	8 G	*alwys bhnd, rdn apr 9th, t.o. when p.u. before 4 out.*	P	0
1580	26/5	Lifton	(R)	OPE	3m	8 G	*nvr on terms, p.u. aft 15th, lame*	P	0

Retains some ability & popped up with another modest success; last race could spell the end 17

TUDOR FABLE(IRE) b.g. 9 Lafontaine (USA) - Welsh Pride by Welsh Saint — C R R Sweeting

1996 **P(NH)**,**1(NH)**,**F(NH)**,**P(NH)**,**P(NH)**

771	29/3	Dingley	(R)	OPE	3m	10 G	*alwys prom, 3rd til 2nd 6 out-2 out, wknd rpdly, p.u. last*	P	0
1099	19/4	Stratford	(L)	HC	2m 5f 110yds	14 G	*alwys bhnd.*	5	0
1287	29/4	Huntingdon	(R)	HC	2 1/2m 110yds	14 G	*mid div, lost tch when mstk 9th, no dngr after.*	7	10

Winning chaser (quite decent); does not stay 3m & a disappointment now 13

TUDOR FLIGHT b.m. 6 Forzando - Tudor Pilgrim by Welsh Pageant — I A Brown

1996 **16(NH)**,**8(NH)**,**2(NH)**,**3(NH)**,**8(NH)**

80	2/2	Market Rase'	(L)	MDO	2m 5f	9 GF	*keen hold, ld 4th, 1/2l ld whn f 2 out*	F	13
358	2/3	Great Stain'	(L)	MDO	3m	14 S	*rear, prog 8th, ev ch whn f 12th*	F	-
620	22/3	Hutton Rudby	(L)	MDO	3m	10 GF	*prom whn ran out 4th*	r	-
699	29/3	Stainton	(R)	MDO	3m	7 F	*(Jt fav) prom, mstk 7th, chsd wnnr frm 12th, outpcd apr last*	2	11
1073	13/4	Whitwell-On'	(R)	MDO	2 1/2m 88yds	17 G	*rear til ran on wll 3 out, nrst fin*	2	14
1252	26/4	Easingwold	(L)	MDO	3m	9 GS	*(fav) in tch, 4th 6th, u.r. nxt*	U	-

Ex-selling hurdler; disappointing under Rules & may maintain the trend in points; sloppy jumper 13

TUDOR HENRY b.g. 12 Tudor Rhythm - Grebe by Hot Brandy — J W Mitchell

1996 P(0),3(15),3(18),3(19),2(18),4(0)

145	9/2	Tweseldown	(R)	LAD	3m	10	GF	*outpcd in rear, prog frm 9th, styd on onepcd frm 4 out*	3	20
280	23/2	Charing	(L)	LAD	3m	12	G	*nrly u.r. 2nd, ld 8th-apr 16th, ld apr last, just hld on*	1	21
1213	26/4	Woodford	(L)	LAD	3m	6	G	*w.w. in tch whn u.r. 9th*	U	-

Consistent & deserved win in Ladies; season interrupted & will find it hard to repeat success at 13 19

TUDOR OAKS b.m. 10 Ayyabaan - Sarah's Joy by Full Of Hope — S Gallagher

1996 7(0),P(0),P(0),1(13),3(0),5(0),5(0)

223	16/2	Heythrop	(R)	RES	3m	19	G	*ld 4th-10th, wknd 12th, t.o.*	8	0
634	22/3	Howick	(L)	RES	3m	7	GF	*ld til f 4th*	F	-
718	29/3	Llanvapley	(L)	RES	3m	13	GF	*ld til slppd up bnd aft 11th*	S	-
1199	23/4	Andoversford	(R)	INT	3m	5	F	*ld, sn clr, jmpd slwly 5th, mstk 15th, hdd apr last, no ext*	3	14
1392	5/5	Cursneh Hill	(L)	RES	3m	6	GF	*ld to 12th, wknd 14th, t.o. & p.u. 2 out*	P	0

Won 2 dire races 95/96; given the best of rides 97 but still failed 97 11

TUDOR ROYAL (Irish) — **I** 335^{P}

TUFFNUT GEORGE ch.g. 10 True Song - Arenig by New Member — Mrs S Cartridge

1996 2(16),P(0),**2(20)**,1(23),**3(20)**,**1(23)**,**1(NH)**

587	19/3	Ludlow	(R)	HC	2 1/2m	18	GF	*in tch, hdwy 8th, mstk 11th, no ch from 5 out.*	4	21
782	31/3	Towcester	(R)	HC	2 3/4m	3	GF	*trckd wnr, chal 6th, ld next, hdd 3 out but soon left in front again, hded 2 out, soon btn.*	2	18
1099	19/4	Stratford	(L)	HC	2m 5f 110yds	14	G	*prom till wknd 6 out, p.u. before 3 out.*	P	0
1296	3/5	Hereford	(R)	HC	2m 3f	11	G	*ld to 2nd, prom till wknd 9th, t.o. when p.u. before 2 out.*	P	0

H/Chase & handicap winner 96; alarming slump 97 & can only be watched now 17

TUFFNUT TOM ch.g. 8 Sergeant Drummer (USA) - Arenig by New Member — Mrs R Lamacraft

1311	3/5	Holnicote	(L)	MEM	3m	7	G	*prssd ldr to 9th, bhnd frm 15th, effrt 3 out, sn wknd*	3	13
1436	10/5	Holnicote	(L)	MEM	3m	5	G	*(fav) ld/disp til ld 2 out, blnd & hdd last, rallied to ld nr fin*	1	13
1550	24/5	Mounsey Hil'	(R)	INT	3m	9	G	*mid-div, 6th & in tch whn f 12th*	F	-
1593	31/5	Bratton Down	(L)	XX	3m	5	F	*trckd ldrs,effrt & pckd 2 out,went 5l 2nd & f last,rmntd*	5	19

Late starter; won slow-run Members but ran well last outing & can win again 19

TULIRA HILL (Irish) — **I** 198^{P}, **I** 243^{P}, **I** 294^{P}, **I** 403^{F}

TULLAGHFIN (Irish) — **I** 300^{6}

TULLAMORE (Irish) — **I** 114^{P}, **I** 175^{P}, **I** 210^{P}, **I** 328^{U}, **I** 435^{5}

TULLIBARDNICENEASY (Irish) — **I** 64^{5}, **I** 90^{1}, **I** 224^{F}

TULLYALLENSTAR (Irish) — **I** 71^{P}, **I** 125^{P}, **I** 250^{P}

TULLY BOY (Irish) — **I** 313, , **I** 392^{1}

TULLYHONIVER (Irish) — **I** 232^{P}, **I** 283^{P}, **I** 348^{F}

TULLYKYNE BELLS gr.g. 8 Le Solaret (FR) - Cowbells by Mountain Call — M A Kerley

1996 P(0),U(-),3(0),2(12),4(0)

21	25/1	Badbury Rin'	(L)	MDN	3m	7	GF	*mid-div, drppd rear 11th, no prog, lft 3rd last*	3	0
311	1/3	Clyst St Ma'	(L)	LAD	3m	9	HY	*sn bhnd, t.o. & p.u. 14th*	P	0
518	15/3	Larkhill	(R)	MEM	3m	1	GF	*walked over*	1	0
661	22/3	Badbury Rin'	(L)	RES	3m	6	F	*alwys prom, ld 13th-nxt, rnwd effrt to ld 2 out, kpt on wll*	1	13
691	29/3	Little Wind'	(R)	INT	3m	5	GF	*hld up, prog 8th, wknd 11th, t.o. 14th, p.u. 3 out*	P	0

Gamely won weak Restricted but no other chances of a win outside Members now 13

TULLYS BALL (Irish) — **I** 18^{3}, **I** 54^{P}, **I** 169^{F}, **I** 260^{1}

TULLY VIEW (Irish) — **I** 483^{P}, **I** 551^{F}

TUMLIN OOT(IRE) b.g. 8 Amazing Bust - Tumlin Brig by New Brig — Mrs Hugh Fraser

1996 **14(NH)**,**F(NH)**,**P(NH)**,**P(NH)**

381	4/3	Leicester	(R)	HC	2m 1f	13	G	*held up, hdwy 5 out, weakening when hmpd 2 out.*	5	13
584	17/3	Newcastle	(L)	HC	2 1/2m	11	GF	*bhnd, hdwy when blnd 10th, wknd before 4 out, t.o..*	6	0
972	7/4	Kelso	(L)	HC	3m 1f	12	GF	*held up, hit 4th, hdwy to chase ldrs and blnd 8th, blunded 13th and soon bhnd, t.o. when p.u. 3 out.*	P	0

Outclassed in H/Chases & no prospects of a win 11

TUNEFUL TOM b.g. 6 Sizzling Melody - Gay Shadow by Northfields (USA) — Miss V Burn

609	22/3	Friars Haugh	(L)	LAD	3m	11	GF	*s.s., t.o. whn p.u. 4 out*	P	0
730	29/3	Alnwick	(L)	MDO	2 1/2m	9	F	*last pair til prog 7th, sn btn, t.o.*	4	0
1167	20/4	Hexham Poin'	(L)	MEM	3m	5	GF	*alwys rear, no imp final cct*	4	0

Beaten miles when finishing 0

TU PIECE b.g. 8 Kaytu - Bikini Top by Formidable (USA) — P H Howse

1996 P(0),4(0)

5	19/1	Barbury Cas'	(L)	OPE	3m	11	GF	*bhnd, 10th hlfwy, p.u. 12th*	P	0
40	1/2	Larkhill	(R)	MDO	3m	5	GF	*chsd wnr 7-11th, sn wknd, lft poor 2nd 3 out*	2	0
146	9/2	Tweseldown	(R)	MDO	3m	10	GF	*rear, styd on onepcd frm 4 out*	4	10
392	8/3	Barbury Cas'	(L)	MDN	3m	9	G	*chsd ldrs,mstk 9th,5th & outpcd 14th,styd on agn 2 out*	3	13
654	22/3	Siddington	(L)	MDN	3m	10	F	*chsd ldrs, 6th whn f 8th*	F	-
1200	23/4	Andoversford	(R)	MDO	3m	8	F	*in tch, rmndr 12th, outpcd 16th, rallied 2 out, no imp last*	3	10

Placed in 5 of last 8 starts but form very weak & will need fortune to win 11

TURBULENT GALE(IRE) br.g. 8 Strong Gale - Turbo Run — E E Williams

1996 3(0),1(18),C(-)

32	26/1	Alnwick	(L)	RES	3m	11	G	*(fav) mstk 8th, ld to 3 out, rallied to ld last, just hld on*	1	19
199	15/2	Weston Park	(L)	MEM	3m	7	G	*(fav) ld to 12th, cls 2nd to 3 out, no ext frm nxt, lame*	2	18

Fair performer & won decent Restricted; should upgrade if overcoming problems in 98 19

TURN OF FOOT(IRE) b.g. 8 Sheer Grit - Animalean by Beau Chapeau — J N Llewellen Palmer

564	16/3	Lanark	(R)	MDO	2 1/2m	13	GS	*alwys t.o.*	7	0
729	29/3	Alnwick	(L)	RES	3m	10	F	*alwys rear, t.o. last hlfwy, p.u. 2 out*	P	0
1051	13/4	Lockerbie	(R)	MDN	3m	10	F	*alwys twrds rear*	5	0
1217	26/4	Balcormo Ma'	(R)	MEM	3m	4	F	*f 2nd*	F	-
1510	17/5	Corbridge	(R)	RES	3m	13	GS	*rear, dtchd 9th, t.o. & p.u. 13th*	P	0

Looks devoid of ability so far 0

TUSKAR FLOP (Irish) — **I** 27^{F}, **I** 100^{P}, **I** 231^{5}, **I** 282^{1}, **I** 314^{P}, **I** 412^{1}, **I** 441^{4}, **I** 469^{1}, **I** 524^{1}

TUTS LAD b.g. 6 Buzzards Bay - Floreat Regina by Rolfe (USA) — N Thomas

1452	10/5	Kingston Bl'	(L)	MDO	3m	9	G	*alwys bhnd, last at 5th, t.o. & p.u. aft 10th*	P	0

No promise on debut 0

TWELTH MAN b.g. 10 Remainder Man - Merry Cherry by Deep Run — W G Dutton

1996 P(0),P(0)

203	15/2	Weston Park	(L)	RES	3m	11	G	*prom to hlfwy, sn btn, p.u. 3 out*	P	0
331	1/3	Eaton Hall	(R)	RES	3m	17	GS	*mid-div, ran on onepcd 4 out*	4	15
433	8/3	Upton-On-Se'	(R)	RES	3m	18	G	*rear frm 6th, t.o. 11th, p.u. 3 out*	P	0

Ran surprisingly well 2nd start but usually shows nothing & unlikely to win Restricted 11

TWICE KNIGHTLY b.g. 6 Double Bed (FR) - Charter Belle by Runnymede — W H Whitley

1996 F(-)

954	6/4	Black Fores'	(R)	RES	3m	4	G	*blnd 1st, rdr lost irons & injured, p.u. nxt*	P	0
1093	16/4	Hockworthy	(L)	RES	3m	16	GF	*prom to 8th, sn wknd, bhnd whn p.u. 5 out*	P	0
1483	11/5	Ottery St M'	(L)	RES	3m	15	G	*alwys rear, t.o. & p.u. 2 out*	P	0

Of no account 0

TWILIGHT HOUR (Irish) — **I** 106^{P}, **I** 146^{P}, **I** 570^{P}

TWILIGHT INVADER (Irish) — **I** 123^{P}, **I** 436^{P}, **I** 464^{P}, **I** 508^{U}, **I** 583^{P}

TWILIGHT TOM ro.g. 8 Pragmatic - Starlight Beauty by Scallywag — L J Williams

1996 B(-),2(0),1(15)

190	15/2	Erw Lon	(L)	RES	3m	11	G	*in tch til lost plc & p.u. 5th*	P	0
718	29/3	Llanvapley	(L)	RES	3m	13	GF	*trckd ldr til lft in ld aft 11th, made rest, held on wll*	1	16

Maiden winner 96; very lightly raced & won modest Restricted; should have chances if back in 98 18

TWIN TRACK (Irish) — **I** 34^{P}, **I** 154^{F}, **I** 223^{3}, **I** 391^{6}, **I** 417^{1}, **I** 542^{F}

TWIST 'N' SCU ch.g. 9 Prince Sabo - Oranella by Orange Bay — Miss Lucy Smith

144	9/2	Tweseldown	(R)	OPE	3m	9	GF	*j.w. prom til wknd frm 4 out*	4	15
393	8/3	Barbury Cas'	(L)	OPE	3m	7	G	*in tch,prog 8th,chsd ldr 12th,2l down 3 out,sn btn,ref last*	R	17
1296	3/5	Hereford	(R)	HC	2m 3f	11	G	*jmpd slowly 5th, t.o. when p.u. before 10th.*	P	0
1462	11/5	Tweseldown	(R)	CON	3m	6	GF	*mostly cls 2nd, wknd 8th, p.u. 12th, lame*	P	0

Winning hurdler; does not stay & no real form in points; problems now 12

TWO COVERS (Irish) — **I** 549^{3}, **I** 577^{4}

TWO GENTS ch.g. 9 Netherkelly - Sorraia by El Ruedo — P H Morris

1179	20/4	Sandon	(L)	MDN	3m	6	GF	*rear, last & in tch whn f 3rd*	F	-
1345	3/5	Gisburn	(R)	MDN	3m	13	GF	*alwys last trio, p.u. 15th*	P	0

No signs of any ability 0

TWO IN TUNE (Irish) — **I** 205^{1}, **I** 598^{1}

TYO MO CHARA (Irish) — **I** 52^{P}, **I** 172^{F}, **I** 294^{6}, **I** 405^{P}

TYPICAL WOMAN(IRE) b or br.m. 6 Executive Perk - Beau Jo by Joshua — A H Bulled

1095	16/4	Hockworthy	(L)	MDN	3m	11	GF	*n.j.w. & wll bhnd, effrt to poor 6th hlfwy, t.o. & p.u.4 out*	P	0
1496	14/5	Cothelstone	(L)	CON	3m	9	GF	*pckd 6th, last whn mstk & u.r. 9th*	U	-

Not yet involved & needs to learn to jump 0

TYRELLA CLEAR VIEW (Irish) — **I** 72^{4}

TYTHERINGTON b or br.g. 13 New Member - Vespers II by The Monk — Miss S H Talbot

1996 **F(-)**,P(0),3(0),4(14),3(14)

466	8/3	Eyton-On-Se'	(L)	LAD	3m	7	G	*cls up gng wll 12th, outpcd frm 4 out*	4	13
652	22/3	Siddington	(L)	LAD	3m	5	F	*lft 25l, rcvrd to ld 5th-9th, wknd 11th, t.o.*	4	0
750	29/3	Brampton Br'	(R)	LAD	3m	5	GF	*s.s. cls up 4th, outpcd frm 12th, t.o. 15th*	4	0
1146	19/4	Chaddesley '	(L)	CON	3m	6	GF	*ld 3rd-4th, outpcd 13th, sn t.o.*	5	0
1329	3/5	Chaddesley '	(L)	CON	3m	5	GF	*prssd ldr to 10th,last 12th,lft poor 2nd 3 out,lft solo nxt*	1	0
1572	26/5	Chaddesley '	(L)	MEM	3m	3	F	*ld to 13th, not qckn aft nxt, kpt on*	2	0

Schoolmater now; safe but incredibly lucky winner & no other prospects now 10

ULLINGTON LORD b.g. 8 Afzal - Horsehay Annabelle Vii by Damsire Unregistered — Graham Treglown

1150	19/4	Chaddesley '	(L)	MDO	3m	7	GF	*alwys rear, rdn & wknd 11th, p.u. 13th*	P	0
1209	26/4	Clifton On '	(L)	MDO	3m	16	GS	*mid-div, 7th at 10th, fdd, p.u. 5 out*	P	0
1401	5/5	Ashorne	(R)	MDO	3m	15	G	*alwys rear, t.o. 11th, p.u. 13th*	P	0
1459	11/5	Maisemore P'	(L)	MDO	3m	12	G	*(bl) prom to 10th, wknd 12th, t.o. & p.u. 15th*	P	0

No sings of ability or stamina 0

ULTRASON IV(FR) b.g. 11 Quart de Vin (FR) - Jivati (FR) by Laniste — David A Smith

1996 6(0),1(16),P(0),U(-)

848	31/3	Eyton-On-Se'	(L)	MEM	3m	6	GF	*mid-div, cls order 10th, ev ch 3 out, not qckn*	3	0
1002	12/4	Alpraham	(R)	CON	3m	4	GF	*hld up, chsd wnr 14th-16th, no ext*	3	13
1233	26/4	Brampton Br'	(R)	CON	3m	8	G	*prog 8th, 15l 6th at 13th, no ch frm 16th, p.u. 2 out*	P	0
1382	5/5	Eyton-On-Se'	(L)	INT	3m	7	GF	*mstly 3rd, outpcd frm 3 out*	4	16
1508	17/5	Bangor	(L)	HC	3m 110yds	12	G	*handy till 9th, lost tch from 12th, t.o. when p.u. before last.*	P	0

Won weak Intermediate 96; stays but modest & win at 12 looks tough; G/F-S 15

UNA JUNA (Irish) — **I** 159^{P}

UNASSUMING ch.g. 9 Vaigly Great - Petard by Mummy's Pet — Mrs T A Halliwell

137	9/2	Thorpe Lodge	(L)	MEM	3m	9	GF	*cls up, ld 6-9th, wknd, p.u. 5 out*	P	0
1205	26/4	Clifton On '	(L)	CON	3m	13	GS	*last til p.u. 4th, lame*	P	0

Of no account 0

UNCLE ARCHIE (Irish) — **I** 192^{F}, **I** 258^{P}, **I** 321^{F}, **I** 602^{P}

UNCLE ART (Irish) — **I** 112^{2}, **I** 129^{P}, **I** 252^{P}, **I** 326^{P}, **I** 434^{2}, **I** 466^{P}, **I** 503^{5}, **I** 581^{1}

UNCLE BRUCE b.g. 7 Sula Bula - Saxon Belle by Deep Run — Mrs Judy Young

1996 F(-),R(-)

20	25/1	Badbury Rin'	(L)	MDN	3m	9	GF	*alwys prssng wnr, cls 2nd & ev ch whn f 2 out*	F	-
182	15/2	Larkhill	(R)	MDO	3m	12	G	*prom, 3rd whn f 5th*	F	-
298	1/3	Didmarton	(L)	RES	3m	15	G	*in tch to 9th, t.o. whn p.u. 2 out*	P	0
654	22/3	Siddington	(L)	MDN	3m	10	F	*mid-div, 3rd & outpcd frm 12th, kpt on steadily frm 15th*	3	10

Placed in modest event on 1st completion; more needed for a win in 98 12

UNCLE JAMES(IRE) br.g. 6 Young Man (FR) - Hampsruth by Sea Hawk II — Charles White

630	22/3	Kilworthy	(L)	RES	3m	16	G	*rear, ran on stdly frm 15th, fair debut*	8	0
1093	16/4	Hockworthy	(L)	RES	3m	16	GF	*hld up, last whn blnd & u.r. 3rd*	U	-
1343	3/5	Flete Park	(R)	MDO	3m	13	G	*gd prog 15th, went 2nd 3 out, ev ch nxt, not qckn, prmsng*	2	14
1497	14/5	Cothelstone	(L)	MDO	3m	10	GF	*prom, lft in ld 13th, jnd 3 out, hrd rdn & hdd nr fin*	2	13

Knocking on the door & just beaten in weak race last start; should win in 98 15

UNCLE TOM b.g. 6 Scallywag - Reebok by Scottish Rifle — Mrs M P Marfell

881	1/4	Upton-On-Se'	(R)	MDN	3m	13	GF	*schoold, rear, chsd ldng grp 13th, no prog & p.u. 3 out*	P	0

Showed enough to suggest much more to come in 98 12

UNDERWAY(FR) b.g. 11 Djarvis (FR) - Jamaica (FR) by Tryptic — G M Vergette

1479	11/5	Garthorpe	(R)	MDO	3m	12	GS	*mstks, alwys last, blnd 10th, p.u. aft*	P	0

Of no account 0

UNDERWYCHWOOD(IRE) b.g. 9 Try My Best (USA) - Sooner Or Later by Sheshoon — D Davies

1137	19/4	Bonvilston	(R)	MDO	3m	13	G	*towrds rear, steadd prog 15th, nrst fin*	3	10
1229	26/4	Pyle	(R)	MDO	3m	11	GS	*(fav) made virt all, rdn clr 2 out, eased flat*	1	14

1361	5/5 Pantyderi	(L)	MEM	3m	4	G	*(fav) rear til prog 11th, chsng wnr last, no imp*	2	12

Placed in novice chase 93; very lightly-raced; easy winner & Restricted chance 98 15

UNEVANO (Irish) — I 398^{F}, I 468^{P}, I 526^{F}, I 580^{P}

UNIQUE TRIBUTE b.g. 8 Celestial Storm (USA) - Fearless Felon (USA) by Bailjumper (USA) J D Parker

1996 1(20)

271	22/2 Ampton	(R)	CON	3m	15	G	*alwys rr, t.o. & p.u. 3 out*	P	0
1277	27/4 Fakenham P-'	(L)	CON	3m	10	G	*mid-div, lost tch 11th, p.u. 13th*	P	0

Restricted winner 96; stays & needs soft; lightly-raced; showed nothing in 97 13

UNLUCKY FOR SOME(IRE) b.g. 8 Dromod Hill - Red Gimmy Vii C J Harper

1996 3(12),4(11),F(-),P(0),P(0)

218	16/2 Heythrop	(R)	INT	3m	21	G	*alwys bhnd t.o. & p.u. 10th*	P	0
372	2/3 Mollington	(R)	RES	3m	19	G	*rear grp, no ch frm 11th, kpt on frm 15th, nrst fin*	5	0
820	31/3 Paxford	(L)	RES	3m	4	F	*nrly alwys last, no ch frm 15th, walked in*	3	0

Maiden winner 95; well-beaten since & disappointing; no real prospects now 12

UNSCRUPULOUS GENT ch.g. 15 Over The River (FR) - Even Lass by Even Money Mrs E Huttinger

1996 5(0),3(0),P(0),4(0)

1316	3/5 Holnicote	(L)	MXO	3m	4	G	*ld/disp to 13th, sn lost tch, t.o.*	4	0
1563	25/5 Kingston Bl'	(L)	MEM	3m	5	GF	*t.o. frm 6th, btn 3 fences*	5	0

No longer of any account 0

UNYOKE LADY (Irish) — I 539^{F}

UP AND RUNNING ch.g. 6 Ovac (ITY) - Water Eaton Gal by Legal Eagle J P Seymour

135	9/2 Alnwick	(L)	MDO	3m	12	G	*bhnd frm 6th, t.o. & p.u. 4 out*	P	0
335	1/3 Corbridge	(R)	CON	3m	7	G	*rear, jmpd slwly 1st, sn bhnd, rdn 10th, t.o. & p.u. 12th*	P	0
614	22/3 Friars Haugh	(L)	MDN	3m	13	GF	*losng tch whn f 12th*	F	-
948	6/4 Friars Haugh	(L)	MDO	3m	7	GF	*lost tch by 9th, u.r. 12th*	U	-
997	12/4 Tranwell	(L)	MDO	2 1/2m	8	F	*rear div, last 6th, styd on wll frm 4 out, not trbl ldrs*	4	0

Beaten 30l on 1st completion but at least a step in the right direction 0

UP AND UNDER (Irish) — I 34^{1}

UP FOR RANSOME(IRE) b.g. 8 Boyne Valley - Fauvette (USA) by Youth (USA) W M Wanless

1996 **9(NH),5(NH),4(NH)**

377	4/3 Leicester	(R)	HC	2 1/2m 110yds	15	G	*prom, rdn apr 2 out, ran on one pace.*	3	24
584	17/3 Newcastle	(L)	HC	2 1/2m	11	GF	*(fav) f 1st.*	F	-
779	31/3 Fakenham	(L)	HC	2m 5f 110yds	9	G	*in tch, hit 3rd, ld 12th till after 2 out, rallied run-in.*	2	21
1085	14/4 Hexham	(L)	HC	3m 1f	5	F	*cl up, ld 4 out, rdn next, hdd 2 out and one pace und pres apr last.*	2	21

Winning Irish pointer; consistent, one paced & may lack enough heart to win H/Chase 20

UPHAM CLOSE ch.m. 11 Oats - Real View by Royal Highway Reg Hand

1996 4(12)

92	6/2 Wincanton	(R)	HC	3m 1f 110yds	6	GF	*well bhnd 12th, hdwy 16th, chsd wnr 3 out to next, 3rd and weakening when f last.*	F	-
1110	19/4 Flete Park	(R)	LAD	3m	9	GF	*cls 3rd at 15th, chal & ev ch whn p.u. aft 2 out, lame*	P	0

Won 4 in 93; lost last 13 now & more problems last start could spell real trouble 17

UPSHEPOPS (Irish) — I 9^{P}, I 62^{2}, I 88^{2}, I 427^{P}, I 454^{1}, I 511^{3}

UP THE BANNER VI (Irish) — I 194^{P}, I 267^{P}, I 298^{U}, I 359^{3}

UP THE ROAD (Irish) — I 328^{P}, I 369, , I 375^{P}

UP THE ROCK (Irish) — I 341^{6}

UP THE SLANEY (Irish) — I 187^{P}, I 286^{1}

UPTON GALE(IRE) br.g. 7 Strong Gale - Newtown Colleen by Golden Love Mrs Jill Dennis

1996 P(0)

105	8/2 Great Treth'	(R)	MDO	3m	15	GS	*mid-div, wll in tch whn f 11th*	F	-

Two runs in 2 seasons; no real signs yet but stable not known for their duds 10

UPTON LASS(IRE) b.m. 8 Crash Course - Gorrue Lady by Furry Glen Mrs M Kimber

1996 **P(NH)**

374	2/3 Mollington	(R)	MDN	3m	14	G	*prom til wknd 15th, walked in*	7	0
549	16/3 Garthorpe	(R)	MDO	3m	16	GF	*prom, lft 2nd 8th, ev ch appr 3 out, wknd appr 2 out*	3	0
990	12/4 Kingston Bl'	(L)	MDN	3m	11	GF	*prom, ld aft 13th, rdn clr aft 2 out, kpt on*	1	13
1208	26/4 Clifton On '	(L)	RES	3m	4	GS	*cls up 2nd to 9th, chsd wnr frm 4 out, alwys hld*	2	13

1449 10/5 Kingston Bl' (L) RES 3m 8 G *mostly mid-div, prog to 2nd at 11th, 3rd at 15th, wknd* 6 11

Won weak Maiden in slow time & does not really stay; more needed for Restricted chance 14

UPWARD SURGE(IRE) ch.g. 7 Kris - Sizes Vary by Be My Guest (USA) R R Ledger

1996 **4(NH),2(NH),P(NH),3(NH),8(NH),10(NH),3(NH),7(NH)**

26 26/1 Marks Tey (L) LAD 3m 8 GF *bhnd frm 9th, t.o. & p.u. 16th* P 0
71 2/2 Higham (L) LAD 3m 6 GF *alwys prom, ld 11th, qcknd nxt, hdd & outpcd 16th, dmtd flat* 3 19
195 15/2 Higham (L) LAD 3m 14 G *ld to 3rd & 5-6th, cls 2nd til wknd rpdly 16th* 6 11
578 16/3 Detling (L) LAD 3m 11 F *cls up, ld 15th, wknd & hdd last* 2 18
1287 29/4 Huntingdon (R) HC 2 1/2m 110yds 14 G *chsd ldrs to 10th, soon wknd, t.o. and p.u. before 2 out.* P 0

Winning chaser (2m); speedy but stamina suspect; no show under Rules later in season 13

UPWELL b.g. 13 Tanfirion - Debnic by Counsel Robert Johnson

1996 9(0),2(11),7(0),**3(NH),5(NH),3(NH),2(NH),4(NH),6(NH)**

891 4/4 Sedgefield (L) HC 3m 3f 5 GF *ld till hdd 6 out, outpcd before 2 out.* 3 14

Very modest & no real chances at 14 11

VAIN MINSTREL (Irish) — **I** 335^F, **I** 534^P

VALANDER ch.m. 6 Master Trader - Servalan by Souvran R H York

147 9/2 Tweseldown (R) MDO 3m 12 GF *f 2nd* F -
682 29/3 Charing (L) RES 3m 5 F *mstks, in tch to 15th, t.o. 3 out* 5 0

Beaten over two fences 2nd start & shows nothing 0

VALATCH ch.g. 9 Valiyar - Love Match (USA) by Affiliate (USA) J H Henderson

1996 P(0),3(0),3(0),4(12)

122 9/2 Cottenham (R) MEM 3m 6 GF *4th & outpcd by 5th, no prog aft, tk poor 3rd last* 3 0
271 22/2 Ampton (R) CON 3m 15 G *bhnd frm 7th, t.o.* 10 0
473 9/3 Southwell P' (L) CON 3m 10 G *mid-div to 8th, bhnd frm 10th, t.o.* 6 0
545 16/3 Garthorpe (R) CON 3m 12 GF *(bl) nt fluent, alwys bhnd, no ch frm 11th* 7 0
923 6/4 Garthorpe (R) MEM 3m 4 GF *(bl) ld to 7th, mstk 11th, lost tch 13th, sn t.o.* 4 0

Safe but never threatens to win 0

VALE OF OAK b.m. 6 Meadowbrook - Farm Consultation by Farm Walk Miss Scarlett J Crew

1996 **9(NH)**

190 15/2 Erw Lon (L) RES 3m 11 G *alwys bhnd, t.o. hlfwy* 4 0
297 1/3 Didmarton (L) MDN 3m 11 G *rear, hmpd 9th & lost tch, ran on 12th, btn whn lft clr flat* 1 12

Fortunate winner; subsequent scorer behind but more needed if back in 98 12

VALE OF YORK gr.g. 9 Kabour - Amber Vale by Warpath S B Clark

1996 P(0),P(0),2(11),4(10)

266 22/2 Duncombe Pa' (R) RES 3m 19 G *rear, prog 7th,ld brfly 10th,sn fdd, wll bhnd whn p.u. 4 out* P 0
510 15/3 Dalton Park (R) MDO 3m 14 GF *s.s. mid-div, prog to remote 3rd 15th, no hdwy, p.u. last* P 0
698 29/3 Stainton (R) MDO 3m 6 F *mid-div, prog to ld 12th, hdd 15th, ld agn 3 out, sn wll clr* 1 13

Lightly raced; won modest race & needs easy 3m; more needed for Restricteds 14

VALIANT FRIEND b.g. 10 Hell's Gate - Fleur-De-Chriose by Dragonara Palace (USA) Mrs M E Barton

1996 3(0),P(0)

403 8/3 Llanfrynach (R) INT 3m 8 G *rear til p.u. 12th* P 0
580 16/3 Detling (L) RES 3m 11 F *(bl) alwys prom, ld 12-14th, 4th whn ref 17th* R -
783 31/3 Aldington (L) RES 3m 4 HD *(bl) ld,jmpd slwly 2nd, hdd 6th, ld 10-12th, 3rd frm 15th,onepcd* 3 10
959 6/4 Pantyderi (L) INT 3m 2 F *(bl) disp to 3 out, onepcd aft* 2 11
1008 12/4 St Hilary (R) RES 3m 11 GF *(bl) alwys rear* 7 0
1134 19/4 Bonvilston (R) MXO 4m 10 G *(bl) last til f 17th* F -
1468 11/5 Erw Lon (L) INT 3m 7 GS *(bl) cls up early, t.o. & p.u. 8th* P 0

Losing sequence now 22 & sure to be extended 0

VALIBUS(FR) b.g. 12 Labus (FR) - Valgrinette (FR) by Valdingran (FR) P A D Scouller

1996 P(0),2(10),1(20),1(15)

58 1/2 Kingston Bl' (L) MEM 3m 5 GF *ld to 5th, sn drppd out, t.o. & p.u. aft 13th* P 0
279 23/2 Charing (L) CON 3m 10 G *last pair & wll bhnd til p.u. 10th* P 0
579 16/3 Detling (L) OPE 4m 9 F *mid-div,jmp slwly 12th,jn ldr 19th,mstk nxt,btn whn p.u.22nd* P 0
986 12/4 Kingston Bl' (L) CON 3m 10 GF *ld to 6th, prom, jnd ldr 14th, ld 3 out, hld on well* 1 21
1444 10/5 Peper Harow (L) OPE 3m 5 GF *chsd ldr, ld 12th, made rest, styd on wll frm 2 out* 1 21

Either wins of pulls up; useful when "right" & can win at 13; G-F 21

VALLEY'S CHOICE ch.m. 8 Morgans Choice - Culm Valley by Port Corsair S R Stevens

1996 **P(NH),9(NH),13(NH),F(NH),7(NH)**

104 8/2 Great Treth' (R) MDO 3m 9 GS *in tch, chsd wnr 15th, chal aft 3 out, sn no imp* 2 11
307 1/3 Clyst St Ma' (L) MEM 3m 3 HY *(fav) hld up, prog 15th, ld 3 out, sn clr* 1 14

630 22/3 Kilworthy (L) RES 3m 16 G *in tch, rddn 13th, 5th & onepcd frm 15th* 5 11
1108 19/4 Flete Park (R) RES 3m 14 GF *alwys prom, cls 4tha t 15th, ld apr 2 out, hdl on well* 1 18

Poor under Rules but steady progress in points; handles all going & should upgrade in 98 20

VALLEY TINGO (Irish) — **I** 11P, **I** 423, **I** 642, **I** 87F

VALLY'S SPIRIT ch.g. 6 Sergeant Drummer (USA) - Evening Bar by Pardigras Mrs Sarah Shoemark

60 1/2 Kingston Bl' (L) MDN 3m 17 GF *s.s. sn t.o., p.u.* P 0
222 16/2 Heythrop (R) RES 3m 17 G *wll bhnd til p.u. 9th* P 0

No signs of ability & finished early 0

VALOVER (Irish) — **I** 460P, **I** 493P, **I** 501,

VALPARAISO (Irish) — **I** 383P, **I** 488P, **I** 519P

VANCOUVER ISLAND (Irish) — **I** 133F, **I** 206P

VANITY QUEST (Irish) — **I** 350F

VARYKINOV(IRE) b or br.g. 8 Roselier (FR) - Royal Handful by Some Hand Mark G Rimell

1996 **P(NH)**

260 22/2 Newtown (L) RES 3m 16 G *prom, disp whn blnd & u.r. 10th* U -
436 8/3 Upton-On-Se' (R) MDO 3m 17 G *7s-3s, prog to 2nd 10th, ld 13th, clr whn crmpld lndg last* F 15

Poor under Rules; unlucky not to land punt & should recoup if fit in 98 16

VELKA b or br.m. 8 Uncle Pokey - Miss Prague by Mon Capitaine R V Mair

1996 2(0),2(12),1(13),**5(0)**

126 9/2 Cottenham (R) RES 3m 14 GF *chsng grp, chsd ldng pair 14th, no imp, wknd flat* 5 0
280 23/2 Charing (L) LAD 3m 12 G *mid-div, 7th & losng tch whn f 12th* F -
580 16/3 Detling (L) RES 3m 11 F *trckd ldrs, imprvd to prssd wnr 3 out, no ext flat* 2 17
783 31/3 Aldington (L) RES 3m 4 HD *(fav) hld up, ld 15th, in cmmnd aft* 1 15
1447 10/5 Peper Harow (L) CON 3m 6 GF *chsd ldrs,mstk 10th,went 2nd 13th,ev ch & blnd 2 out,no ext* 2 13

Consistent, modest pointer; won 2 weak races 96/7; barely stays; more needed for another win 15

VENERDI SANTO (Irish) — **I** 3482

VENN BOY ch.g. 8 White Prince (USA) - Ace Chance by Blandford Lad L G Tizzard

1996 1(16),4(12),P(0),P(0)

175 15/2 Ottery St M' (L) RES 3m 15 G *(fav) ld to 4th & 11th til apr last, onepced flat* 2 16
241 22/2 Lemalla (R) RES 3m 11 S *(fav) ld to 9th, fdd rpdly aft 12th, rear & p.u. 15th* P 0
524 15/3 Cothelstone (L) RES 3m 10 GS *in tch til rdn 14th, wkng whn hit 3 out* 3 0
930 6/4 Charlton Ho' (L) INT 3m 8 G *hld up, outpcd 13th, nvr on trms aft* 5 14
1093 16/4 Hockworthy (L) RES 3m 16 GF *alwys rear, nvr a fctr* 5 10
1374 5/5 Cotley Farm (L) RES 3m 7 GF *in tch, chal 4 out, ev ch nxt, outpcd frm 2 out* 3 18
1494 14/5 Cothelstone (L) RES 3m 11 GF *prom, trckd ldr 11th, ld 14th, 1l up whn s.u. bnd apr 16th* S -
1551 24/5 Mounsey Hil' (R) RES 3m 13 G *(fav) mstks, chsd ldrs, 3rd & blnd 10th, 5th & no ch whn p.u.last* P 0

Maiden winner on debut in 96; disappointing since; makes mistakes; likely to frustrate in future 16

VERMONT RIVER (Irish) — **I** 324, **I** 119F, **I** 1881

VERNHAM WOOD b.g. 8 Electric - Bois Le Duc by Kalydon Mrs P H K McNaught

111 8/2 Milborne St' (L) MDN 3m 8 GF *ld til 2 out, wknd apr last* 3 11

Rarely seen but at least showed a smidgeon of ability only start 98 12

VERY BEST (Irish) — **I** 521P

VERY DARING b.g. 7 Derring Rose - La Verite by Vitiges (FR) Miss Rosalind Booth

1996 **P(0)**

721 29/3 Sandon (L) MEM 3m 6 GF *(Jt fav) ld to 3rd, in tch, ld 11th-last, no ext* 2 10
1177 20/4 Sandon (L) LAD 3m 4 GF *ld to 6th, 2nd aft, ld & lft clr last* 1 14
1288 30/4 Cheltenham (L) HC 2m 5f 10 GF *bhnd from 8th, t.o. when hmpd 14th.* 6 0
1412 7/5 Uttoxeter (L) HC 3 1/4m 10 GS *in tch till b.d. 8th.* B -
1417 10/5 Warwick (L) HC 3 1/4m 8 G *chsd ldrs, rdn after 13th, soon wknd, fin 3rd, pld 4th.* 4 11
1500 16/5 Aintree (L) HC 3m 1f 6 G *held up, struggling from hfwy, soon t.o..* 3 0
1587 29/5 Uttoxeter (L) HC 2m 5f 11 GF *alwys bhnd.* 6 0

Totally outclassed in H/Chases & won by virtue of a clear round; no real chances in 98 13

VERY EVIDENT(IRE) b.g. 8 Glenstal (USA) - Royal Daughter by High Top C Bird

1996 **6(NH),2(NH),5(NH),1(NH)**

158 15/2 Lanark (R) LAD 3m 8 G *alwys handy, no ext frm 3 out* 3 16
231 22/2 Friars Haugh (L) LAD 3m 13 G *nvr rchd ldrs* 6 17
412 8/3 Dalston (R) LAD 3m 8 GS *prog & prom 9th, outpcd 3 out, kpt on agn frm nxt* 4 17
561 16/3 Lanark (R) LAD 3m 7 GS *bhnd til wnt 3rd 11th, mstk 14th, kpt on, no ch wth wnnr* 2 14
609 22/3 Friars Haugh (L) LAD 3m 11 GF *alwys hndy, 2nd 4 out, no ext frm 2 out* 3 19
945 6/4 Friars Haugh (L) LAD 3m 6 GF *wnt 2nd 4 out, cls wll frm 3 out, 3l down whn u.r. 2 out* U 22
1048 13/4 Lockerbie (R) LAD 3m 6 F *ld til ran out 3rd* r -

Irish chase winner 96; novice-ridden; consistent; beaten by good horses; deserves a win 21

VERY RARE(IRE) ch.m. 8 Rare One - Mintra Lady by Quayside Miss C Holliday

283 23/2 Charing (L) MDO 3m 16 G *hmpd & u.r. 2nd* U -
306 1/3 Parham (R) MDN 3m 12 G *in tch whn f 14th* F -

Unlucky in weak race 95; missed 96; not much to rave about in 97 & soon vanished 10

VIA DEL QUATRO (Irish) — I 38³, I 79¹, I 131ᴾ

VICE CAPTAIN (Irish) — I 11ᴾ, I 66³, I 153ᴾ

VICEROY OF INDIA(CAN) b.g. 10 Vice Regent (CAN) - Damascene Lady (USA) by Damascus (USA) Mrs Caroline Dix

1996 **4(NH)**

718 29/3 Llanvapley (L) RES 3m 13 GF *rear til p.u. & dismntd 15th* P 0

Maiden winner 93; only 4 runs since & more problems in 97 0

VICKYBERTO b.m. 8 Laxton - Silberto by Dadda Bert E J Govan

1996 **P(NH),P(NH)**

266 22/2 Duncombe Pa' (R) RES 3m 19 G *sn detachd, jmp slwly 1st, ref nxt* R -
898 5/4 Wetherby Po' (L) MDO 3m 7 F *keen hld, prom, ev ch 4 out, rdn & wknd nxt, t.o.* 4 0
1106 19/4 Hornby Cast' (L) MDO 3m 10 G *mid-div, lost plcd 6th, mstk 8th, t.o. 13th, p.u. 2 out* P 0
1409 5/5 Witton Cast' (R) MDO 3m 15 GS *mid-div til lost plcd 7th, rddn nxt, t.o. whn p.u. 13th* P 0

No stamina & no prospects 0

VICOMPT DE VALMONT b.g. 12 Beau Charmeur (FR) - Wish Again by Three Wishes Mrs Bridget Nicholls

1996 **6(NH),2(NH),3(NH),6(NH),10(NH)**

151 12/2 Lingfield (L) HC 3m 13 HY *hdwy 8th, ld last, ran on well.* 1 30
285 26/2 Taunton (R) HC 4 1/4m 110yds 16 GS *(fav) soon well bhnd, rdn along from 7th, hit 22nd, styd on to go 2nd after 2 out, not reach wnr.* 2 25
489 10/3 Plumpton (L) HC 3m 1f 110yds 7 GS *(fav) (bl) bhnd, rdn 7th, promising hdwy 14th, chsd ldrs next, one pace from 4 out.* 3 20

Old staying chaser; moody & hard ride; 1st time up 98 may be only chance now; S-Hy 24

VICTIM OF SLANDER (Irish) — I 139⁵, I 207³, I 319ᴾ, I 380ᴾ, I 419ᴾ, I 458ᴾ

VICTOR CHARLIE ch.g. 7 Hard Fought - The Bean-Goose by King Sitric Mrs S A Sutton

37 26/1 Alnwick (L) MDO 3m 15 G *prom til grad wknd frm 13th, 7th & no ch whn u.r. 15th* U -
419 8/3 Dalston (R) MDO 2 1/2m 10 GS *chsd ldr to 6th, wknd & blnd 10th, t.o. 3 out, lft 2nd last* 2 0
815 31/3 Tranwell (L) MDO 2 1/2m 14 G *alwys prom, cls 2nd whn u.r. 7th* U -
1428 10/5 Aspatria (L) MDO 3m 11 G *pllng, mid-div, 5th & btn 13th, sn t.o.* 4 0

Tailed off on both completions & yet to show any real ability 0

VICTORIA'S BOY (Irish) — I 369²

VICTORY SONG (Irish) — I 220⁶, I 403¹

VIEW POINT(IRE) br.g. 7 Point North - Dangan View by Bargello Peter Smith

1996 P(0),U(-),5(0),B(-),3(10)

15 25/1 Cottenham (R) MDN 3m 7 GF *cls up whn f 2nd* F -
61 1/2 Horseheath (R) MDO 3m 9 GF *hld up, blnd 4th, prog to 3rd at 14th, no imp frm nxt* 3 0
122 9/2 Cottenham (R) MEM 3m 6 GF *jmpd slwly & reluc,bhnd,effrt 12th,sn wknd,t.o. & p.u.16th* P 0
438 8/3 Higham (L) MDO 3m 8 G *mid-div, prog to ld 8th til outpcd 16th, wknd rpdly 3 out* 4 0
774 29/3 Dingley (R) MDO 2m 5f 10 G *ld to 10th, 2nd to 3 out, 3rd & outpcd nxt* 4 0
1192 20/4 Garthorpe (R) MDO 3m 6 GF *hld up, chsd ldrs 6th, cls 4th whn f 15th* F -
1537 18/5 Mollington (R) MDO 3m 14 GS *in tch, jnd ldrs & jmpd slwly 13th, sn wknd, t.o. & p.u.2out* P 0

Placed in bad races; makes mistakes & looks most unlikely to win 0

VIKING BUOY (Irish) — I 47¹, I 157, , I 168ᶠ, I 193ᴾ, I 215⁵

VIKING FLAME ch.m. 8 Viking (USA) - Olympic Loser by Sassafras (FR) R C H Hall

221 16/2 Heythrop (R) RES 3m 15 G *alwys bhnd, t.o. & p.u. 14th* P 0
300 1/3 Didmarton (L) RES 3m 23 G *alwys rear, no dang frm 14th* 7 0
649 22/3 Siddington (L) MEM 3m 6 F *mstk 2nd, in tch til wknd 10th, mstk 11th & p.u.* P 0

Missed 96 & showed nothing on return; looks to be in trouble again 0

VIKING ROD (Irish) — I 141ᴾ, I 191, , I 241ᶠ, I 568ᴾ

VILLA ALBA (Irish) — I 102ᴾ, I 138ᶠ, I 200,

VILLAGE COPPER b.g. 5 Town And Country - Culm Valley by Port Corsair A Howland Jackson

127 9/2 Cottenham (R) MDO 3m 11 GF *16s-8s, in tch, 5th & ch 16th, wknd nxt* 5 0
318 1/3 Marks Tey (L) MDN 3m 13 G *chsd ldr to 5th, wknd 14th, t.o. & p.u. 3 out* P 0
1282 27/4 Fakenham P-' (L) MDO 3m 8 G *in tch, trckd ldrs 12th, outpcd 3 out, kpt on agn frm nxt* 2 12

Not beaten far in weak race last start & every chance of going one better in 98 14

VILLAGE REMEDY b.m. 7 Doctor Pangloss - Avill by Crozier — A G Tutton

224	16/2	Heythrop	(R)	MDN 3m	16	G	*ld 5th-11th, wknd frm 14th, t.o.*	4	0
373	2/3	Mollington	(R)	MDN 3m	14	G	*f 1st*	F	-
499	15/3	Ampton	(R)	MDO 3m	9	GF	*prom, disp ld 7-12th, wkng & hit 13th, no ch aft*	7	0
654	22/3	Siddington	(L)	MDN 3m	10	F	*alwys rear, t.o. 12th*	4	0
928	6/4	Garthorpe	(R)	MDO 3m	8	GF	*ld to 3rd, chsd ldrs aft, 5l 3rd whn f 2 out, rmntd*	4	0
990	12/4	Kingston Bl'	(L)	MDN 3m	11	GF	*ld to 13th, wknd nxt*	5	0
1352	4/5	Dingley	(R)	MDO 2 1/2m	9	G	*prom, disp ld 8-10th, wknd 12th, lft poor 3rd last*	3	0
1537	18/5	Mollington	(R)	MDO 3m	14	GS	*ld to 8th, wknd 10th, t.o. & p.u. last*	P	0

Flattered by her placings; does not stay & no real winning prospects 0

VILLAINS BRIEF(IRE) b.g. 8 Torus - Larrys Glen by Laurence O — Nick Quesnel

1996 **6(NH)**,**F(NH)**,**10(NH)**

294	1/3	Didmarton	(L)	INT 3m	20	G	*alwys bhnd, t.o. & p.u. 13th*	P	0
513	15/3	Larkhill	(R)	MDO 3m	10	GF	*(bl) chsd ldrs, 3rd & outpcd apr 14th, no ch aft*	3	0
827	31/3	Lockinge	(L)	MDO 3m	3	F	*(fav) (bl) disp at slow pace til drew clr aft 14th*	1	10
1164	20/4	Mollington	(R)	RES 3m	10	GF	*(bl) trckd ldrs, ld 14th, clr 3 out, hdd apr last, rallied flat*	2	17
1449	10/5	Kingston Bl'	(L)	RES 3m	8	G	*(bl) hld up, prog aft 5th, ld 7-10th, qcknd to ld flat*	1	18
1536	18/5	Mollington	(R)	INT 3m	8	GS	*(fav) (bl) chsng grp, prog & chsd ldr 13th, ld 2 out, ran on wll flat*	1	20
1563	25/5	Kingston Bl'	(L)	MEM 3m	5	GF	*(fav) 1st ride, trckd wnr 6th, mstk 15th, not qckn frm 2 out*	2	17

Improving; tricky & needs strong handling; blinkers essential; can upgrade; G/F-G/S 22

VIMCHASE ch.g. 11 Slim Jim - Vimys Pet by Lord Nelson (FR) — B Duke

137	9/2	Thorpe Lodge	(L)	MEM 3m	9	GF	*prom, ld 10th-6 out, in tch whn u.r. nxt*	U	-
251	22/2	Brocklesby '	(L)	RES 3m	16	G	*alwys rear hlf, outpcd 6 out, p.u. 3 out*	P	0
344	2/3	Market Rase'	(L)	MEM 3m	3	GF	*ld/disp til apr 14th, sn wll bhnd, t.o.*	3	0
770	29/3	Dingley	(R)	RES 3m	18	G	*mid-div whn u.r. 6th*	U	-

No longer of any account 0

VINTAGE CHOICE (Irish) — **I** 247², **I** 311³, **I** 506²

VINTAGE CLASSIC (Irish) — **I** 33¹

VIOLETS LORD (Irish) — **I** 200ᶠ

VIRIDIAN b.g. 12 Green Shoon - Cahermone Ivy by Perspex — Denis Hine

431	8/3	Upton-On-Se'	(R)	CON 3m	9	G	*mid-div, prog to cls 3rd 10th, not qckn frm 14th*	3	15
819	31/3	Paxford	(L)	OPE 3m	5	F	*ld 3-5th, ld 12th-3 out, chal 2 out, no ext flat*	2	21
1060	13/4	Maisemore P'	(L)	MEM 3m	5	GF	*in tch, mstk 9th, disp 12th, hit nxt, ld 15th, sn wll clr*	1	20
1234	26/4	Brampton Br'	(R)	OPE 3m	4	G	*trckd ldr, ld 13th, 2l up 16th, rdn & maintained adv*	1	23
1457	11/5	Maisemore P'	(L)	OPE 3m	2	G	*(fav) ld to 8th, ld 13th, canter*	1	20
1503	16/5	Folkestone	(R)	HC 3 1/4m	7	G	*(fav) chsd ldr 11th, chal from 5 out, level and going better when left well clr 2 out, eased run-in.*	1	23

Winning chaser; revived well in 97; modest H/Chase win makes placing harder in 98; stays 23

VISAGA b.g. 11 King's Ride - Subiacco by Yellow River — L Hellstenius

1996 **2(NH)**,**5(NH)**,**7(NH)**,**2(NH)**

92	6/2	Wincanton	(R)	HC 3m 1f 110yds	6	GF	*ld to 2nd, chal 8th, hit 12th, chald next, chsd wnr till apr 3 out, went second at last, one pace.*	2	20

Winning chaser 94; not disgraced on only start 97 but will find it hard to win at 12 19

VISIBLE DIFFERENCE (Irish) — **I** 216³

VISION OF LIGHT gr.m. 7 Lighter - Heron's Mirage by Grey Mirage — Mrs J Z Munday

1996 **6(NH)**,**14(NH)**,**10(NH)**

201	15/2	Weston Park	(L)	OPE 3m	16	G	*in rear, no ch whn p.u. 13th*	P	0
366	2/3	Garnons	(L)	MDO 2 1/2m	13	GS	*ld 4th-nxt, ev ch aft 11th, no ext nxt*	4	10
571	16/3	Garnons	(L)	MDN 2 1/2m	13	G	*trckd ldrs til outpcd frm 12th*	5	0
700	29/3	Upper Sapey	(R)	MEM 3m	8	GF	*20l 3rd 6th, lost tch wth 1st 2 frm 10th, lft 2nd 2 out*	2	10

Poor under Rules; looks short on stamina & ineligible for short Maidens in 98 12

VITAL ISSUE (Irish) — **I** 22¹

VITAL LEGACY b.g. 8 Vital Season - Unto Rose by Cornuto — J Bugg

1996 F(-),7(11),1(14),6(12),R(-)

106	8/2	Milborne St'	(L)	RES 3m	12	GF	*alwys rear, t.o. & p.u. 12th*	P	0
240	22/2	Lemalla	(R)	RES 3m	11	S	*t.o. whn ref 10th*	R	-

Maiden winner 96; not completed since & signs look ominous now 0

VITAL SHOT b.m. 8 Vital Season - Skilla by Mexico III — M C Hillier

1996 4(0),5(0),P(0),1(13),P(0)

873	31/3	Hackwood Pa'	(L)	RES 3m	6	F	*ld to 6th, cls up to 10th, p.u. nxt*	P	0
1020	12/4	Badbury Rin'	(L)	RES 3m	1	F	*walked over*	1	0
1141	19/4	Larkhill	(R)	LAD 3m	4	F	*jmpd slwly, alwys last, t.o. 7th*	4	0

Won poor Maiden in 96 & followed up the only way she was likely to 0

VITAL SONG b.g. 11 Vital Season - Tia Song by Acrania G Matthews
1996 3(17),2(23),1(22),1(24),2(24),2(26),2(24)

589	20/3 Wincanton	(R) HC	2m 5f	9 GF	*prom, slightly outpcd 13th, left in ld 4 out, btn when mstk last.*	2	21
1288	30/4 Cheltenham	(L) HC	2m 5f	10 GF	*made all, left clr 13th, mstk next, ran on well from 2 out.*	1	27
1491	14/5 Hereford	(R) HC	3m 1f 110yds	11 G	*ld after 1st till mstk and hdd 14th, wknd 4 out.*	5	19

Useful; needs to dominate; novice-ridden; harder to place now but can win Opens; G/S-F 26

VITAL TO ME b.g. 5 Vital Season - Pablena by Pablond D J Lay

1118	19/4 Higham	(L) MDO	3m	9 GF	*rear whn u.r. 1st*	U	-

The briefest of starts 0

VITAL WITNESS(CAN) b.g. 10 Val de L'orne (FR) - Friendly Witness (USA) by Northern Dancer D E Ingle
1996 3(18)

215	16/2 Southwell P'	(L) LAD	3m	12 GS	*mid-div, prog to 3rd 12th, ev ch 15th, outpcd 3 out, kpt on*	2	21
474	9/3 Southwell P'	(L) LAD	3m	12 G	*(fav) hld up, prog to mid-div whn b.d. 9th*	B	-

Hurdle winner 91; ran well 1st start but injured next time; win in 98 if fit 21

VOLCANIC ROC b.g. 7 Rustingo - La Chica by El Cid Mrs N A Warner

261	22/2 Newtown	(L) MDN	3m	16 G	*schoold & bhnd, effrt to 8th at 13th, nvr nr ldrs*	5	0
367	2/3 Garnons	(L) MDO	2 1/2m	9 GS	*cls up, 10l 5th at 11th, 4th & no prog whn f 3 out*	F	-
719	29/3 Llanvapley	(L) MDN	3m	14 GF	*cls up, lft in ld 10th, hdd 3 out, hrd rdn last, just held*	2	12
1137	19/4 Bonvilston	(R) MDO	3m	13 G	*cls up, wknd 14th, p.u. 2 out*	P	0
1368	5/5 Pantyderi	(L) MDO	3m	8 G	*steady prog to ld 11th, clr 15th, unchal*	1	15
1542	18/5 Wolverhampt'	(L) RES	3m	6 GS	*(fav) chsd ldr til ld 9th, made rest, comf*	1	17

Steadily improving; won modest races but loks likely to upgrade in 98; Good 18

VOLDI (Irish) — **I** 30⁵, **I** 121⁴, **I** 173⁴, **I** 230³, **I** 313⁶, **I** 395⁴, **I** 412², **I** 465⁵, **I** 524³, **I** 553⁴, **I** 577¹, **I** 582²

V'SOSKE GALE (Irish) — **I** 44³

VULGAN PRINCE b.g. 9 Scorpio (FR) - Burton Princess by Prince Barle D R Greig
1996 2(14),3(10),4(15),2(0),3(0),U(-)

605	22/3 Parham	(R) MDO	3m	7 F	*(fav) ld 3rd, made rest, styd on well whn prssd frm 4 out*	1	11

Placed 6 times prior to winning bad race; vanished after; more needed if back in 98 12

VULTHYNE (Irish) — **I** 46ᴾ, **I** 56ᴾ, **I** 139⁶, **I** 217³, **I** 270²

VULTORO b.g. 14 Torus - Vulace by Vulgan T D B Underwood
1996 P(0),3(10),P(0),U(-),4(13),2D(17)

870	31/3 Hackwood Pa'	(L) MXO	3m	4 F	*s.s. jmpd lft, ld 10th-12th, wknd, p.u. last*	P	0
966	6/4 Penshurst	(L) CON	3m	7 F	*immtly detached, p.u. 3rd*	P	0
1057	13/4 Hackwood Pa'	(L) XX	3m	4 GF	*ld 6th-2 out, outpcd flat*	3	15
1126	19/4 Penshurst	(L) CON	3m	6 GF	*immed dtchd, clsd 7th, ld 9th-apr 2 out, wknd und pres*	2	15
1447	10/5 Peper Harow	(L) CON	3m	6 GF	*(fav) tubed, hld up, wll bhnd, prog 12th, rdn 3 out, wll btn nxt*	3	0

Won 4 in 95 but non-winner 96/7 & will find even Sandhurst success hard to find at 15 13

WADDLE'S ROCK(IRE) b.f. 6 Lucky Mickmoosh - Burren Lass D Douglas
1996 **4(NH),13(NH)**

942	6/4 Tabley	(R) MDO	3m	8 G	*jmp slwly 2nd & 3rd, in tch til p.u. 12th*	P	0

Ex-Irish; just a school on pointing debut 0

WAITNOW (Irish) — **I** 28ᵁ, **I** 58¹, **I** 93ᶠ

WAKE UP LUV ch.g. 12 Some Hand - Arctic Ander by Leander R Williams
1996 **F(NH),3(NH),P(NH)**

638	22/3 Howick	(L) LAD	3m	10 GF	*2nd til ld 9th, hdd 13th, onepcd aft*	4	12
716	29/3 Llanvapley	(L) LAD	3m	5 GF	*2nd til wknd 13th, t.o. whn lft 2nd last*	2	14
905	5/4 Howick	(L) LAD	3m	4 F	*(fav) made all, clr 12th, unchal*	1	18
1194	22/4 Chepstow	(L) HC	3m	11 GF	*alwys prom, one pace from 4 out.*	4	21
1320	3/5 Bonvilston	(R) CON	3m	8 G	*ld 6th-8th, chsd ldrs aft, no prog 3 out*	4	0
1590	31/5 Stratford	(L) HC	3m	9 G	*struggling to go pace and well bhnd hfwy, str run from 3 out, fin well.*	3	21
1612	7/6 Umberleigh	(L) LAD	3m	5 F	*ld to 10th, sn strgglng, disp mod 3rd whn s.u. bnd apr 13th*	S	-

Winning Irish chaser 93; won weak Ladies; ran well in 2 H/Chases but outclassed in them 18

WALKERS POINT b.g. 11 Le Moss - Saltee Star by Arapaho Steven Astaire
1996 1(20),4(19),1(16),F(-),2(18),2(14),1(20)

55	1/2 Kingston Bl'	(L) CON	3m	15 GF	*nvr a fctr, p.u. aft 11th*	P	0
369	2/3 Mollington	(R) MEM	3m	13 G	*sn t.o.*	8	0

397 8/3 Barbury Cas' (L) XX 3m 10 G *ld to 2nd, ld 8-11th, sn outpcd, t.o. 15th* 7 0
925 6/4 Garthorpe (R) LAD 3m 7 GF *rear 8th, t.o. 11th, p.u. 2 out* P 0
1163 20/4 Mollington (R) OPE 3m 4 GF *sn hrd hld in last, ran on to 2nd last, no ch, rider retired* 2 12
1464 11/5 Tweseldown (R) XX 3m 7 GF *bhnd whn u.r. 7th* U -
1531 18/5 Mollington (R) MEM 3m 6 GS *made most aft 2nd-10th, wknd 15th, t.o.* 6 0

Won 3 in 96; changed hands 97; safely ignored now 10

WALKONTHEMOON ch.m. 8 Coquelin (USA) - Lunar Eclipse by Hot Spark M F Loggin
1996 P(0),5(0),6(0)

371 2/3 Mollington (R) LAD 3m 9 G *1st ride, t.o. in last pair til p.u. 3 out* P 0
573 16/3 Garnons (L) LAD 3m 8 G *prom in chsng grp, wknd 10th, t.o. & p.u. 14th* P 0
1535 18/5 Mollington (R) LAD 3m 6 GS *in tch, pshd alng 10th, sn wknd, t.o. & p.u. 13th* P 0
1566 25/5 Kingston Bl' (L) LAD 3m 5 GF *in tch to 13th, no imp nxt, wknd rpdly apr last* 4 0

Of no account 0

WALTER'S LAD b.g. 6 Derring Rose - Sweetwater Lass by Whitstead Mrs M J Wall
1996 **P(NH),P(NH),8(NH),15(NH),13(NH)**

85 2/2 Wolverhampt' (L) LAD 3m 11 GS *plld hrd, ld 3rd, mstk nxt, ran out & u.r. 5th* r -
215 16/2 Southwell P' (L) LAD 3m 12 GS *s.v.s. fence bhnd whn u.r. 5th* U -
329 1/3 Eaton Hall (R) LAD 3m 10 GS *rear thruout, no ch whn p.u. 12th* P 0
1384 5/5 Eyton-On-Se' (L) LAD 3m 6 GF *rear 6th, t.o. whn p.u. 13th* P 0

No ability under Rules; headstrong & no prospects in points 0

WALTERSTOWN BOY (Irish) — **I** 311U, **I** 347U, **I** 413F, **I** 470P, **I** 522[6], **I** 574P

WALTON THORNS b.g. 9 Leading Man - Jacqueline Jane by David Jack Brian A Robinson

40 1/2 Larkhill (R) MDO 3m 5 GF *chsd wnr to 7th, wknd 9th, t.o. & p.u. 13th* P 0
480 9/3 Southwell P' (L) MDO 3m 17 G *prog to trck ldrs 11th, 3rd & outpcd apr 3 out* 4 0
1065 13/4 Maisemore P' (L) MDO 3m 13 GF *prom, chsd ldr 10th, rdn 15th, p.u. rpdly nxt, lame* P 0

Very lightly-raced & more problems now could spell the end 10

WALYUNGA (Irish) — **I** 604P

WANG HOW b.g. 9 Nishapour (FR) - Killifreth by Jimmy Reppin J C Clark
1996 3(0),5(0),U(-)

233 22/2 Friars Haugh (L) MDO 3m 13 G *hld up, drvn to nrrw ld 3 out, kpt on well* 1 15
560 16/3 Lanark (R) CON 3m 8 GS *5th hlfwy, bhnd whn p.u. 2 out* P 0
729 29/3 Alnwick (L) RES 3m 10 F *mid-div, prog to 5th at 12th, outpcd frm nxt* 5 15
1334 3/5 Mosshouses (L) RES 3m 5 F *hld up in tch, chal 2 out, disp 2nd & hld whn f last* F -
1545 24/5 Cartmel (L) HC 3 1/4m 14 G *in tch early, bhnd and no ch when mstk 3 out.* 6 10

Beat subsequent winners when scoring but struggling in Restricteds since 13

WAR BARON ch.g. 8 Baron Blakeney - Red Lady by Warpath Mrs C E G Bonner
1996 P(0),P(0)

866 31/3 Kingston St' (R) MDO 3m 7 F *towrds rear, 30l 4th whn p.u. apr 13th* P 0
1095 16/4 Hockworthy (L) MDN 3m 11 GF *alwys bhnd, poor 9th hlfwy, mls bhnd final cct* 6 0

Looks devoid of ability 0

WARDY HILL b.m. 6 Lighter - Royal Seal by Privy Seal D J E Scott

195 15/2 Higham (L) LAD 3m 14 G *sn strgglng rear, p.u. 11th* P 0
323 1/3 Marks Tey (L) LAD 3m 7 G *prom, ld 5-8th, blndrd 11th, 5th in tch whn f 15th* F -
442 8/3 Higham (L) LAD 3m 8 G *rear & wd aft 1st, f 5th* F -

Too many mistakes & no real signs 0

WAR HEAD b.g. 14 Warpath - Foil by Bleep-Bleep T Collins
1996 P(0),P(0),P(0)

77 2/2 Market Rase' (L) RES 3m 9 GF *f 1st* F -
213 16/2 Southwell P' (L) RES 3m 16 GS *alwys bhnd, t.o. & p.u. aft 11th* P 0

Of no account 0

WAR HORSE b.g. 6 War Hero - Yellow Wagtail by Paddy's Stream A W Wood

509 15/3 Dalton Park (R) XX 3m 13 GF *rear, t.o. & p.u. 15th* P 0
1345 3/5 Gisburn (R) MDN 3m 13 GF *alwys rear, p.u. 13th* P 0

Yet to charge into battle 0

WARKSWOODMAN gr.g. 9 Zambrano - Amberama by Sweet Ration Mrs Helen Dickson
1996 5(0),3(13),3(14)

416 8/3 Dalston (R) RES 3m 12 GS *alwys last, t.o. 11th* 6 0
731 29/3 Alnwick (L) MXO 4m 7 F *mainly last pair, wknd final cct, p.u. 20th* P 0

Safe but slow & ran in wrong races 97 - unlikely to win a Maiden now 11

WARM RELATION(IRE) b.g. 6 Nepotism - Summerello by Bargello — N G King

1996 P(0),P(0),P(0),3(10)

366	2/3	Garnons	(L)	MDO	2 1/2m	13	GS	*mid-div, prog 10th, cls up 12th, wknd nxt*	5	0
571	16/3	Garnons	(L)	MDN	2 1/2m	13	G	*prog 11th, ev ch 3 out, wkng whn f nxt*	F	-
853	31/3	Eyton-On-Se'	(L)	MDO	3m	13	GF	*rear, p.u. 12th*	P	0

Looked to have possibilities last start 96 but nothing much 97 & does not stay 10

WARNER FOR SPORT b.g. 8 Mandalus - Joy Travel by Ete Indien (USA) — Mrs I J Bishop

1996 P(0),U(-)

125	9/2	Cottenham	(R)	LAD	3m	11	GF	*last pair & wll bhnd, mstk 5th, t.o. & p.u. 16th*	P	0
197	15/2	Higham	(L)	MDO	3m	12	G	*prom on outside til wknd rpdly 15th, t.o.*	6	0
439	8/3	Higham	(L)	MDO	3m	11	G	*s.s. rear, blnd 12th & p.u.*	P	0

Of no account 0

WARNING CALL (Irish) — **I** 9^{4}, **I** 88^{4}, **I** 145^{2}, **I** 259^{4}

WARREN BOY b.g. 7 Hotfoot - Artaius Rose (FR) by Artaius (USA) — F J Ayres

1996 1(16),1(19),P(0),1(16)

218	16/2	Heythrop	(R)	INT	3m	21	G	*ld 2-5th, wknd 11th, p.u. nxt*	P	0
257	22/2	Newtown	(L)	LAD	3m	12	G	*ld to 2nd & 5-9th, prom til wknd 14th, p.u. last*	P	0
399	8/3	Llanfrynach	(R)	CON	3m	11	G	*(Jt fav) ld til jnd 11th, ran on onepcd*	4	16
1320	3/5	Bonvilston	(R)	CON	3m	8	G	*(Jt fav) ld to 5th, grad lost tch, p.u. 2 out*	P	0

Won 3 in 96 & looked good prospect; looked troubled in 97; could revive but best watched start 98 16

WARRIOR BARD(IRE) ch.g. 7 Black Minstrel - Enco's War by Tug Of War — Mrs Robert Puddick

1996 1(19)

58	1/2	Kingston Bl'	(L)	MEM	3m	5	GF	*rear, trckd ldrs 6th, ld 9th, made rest, drvn out*	1	18
218	16/2	Heythrop	(R)	INT	3m	21	G	*alwys prom, chal aft 14th, just ld & f 2 out*	F	-
292	1/3	Didmarton	(L)	MEM	3m	9	G	*lft in ld 6th, clr 12th, easily*	1	21
572	16/3	Garnons	(L)	INT	3m	13	G	*(fav) prog 8th, cls up til ld 3 out, drew clr flat*	1	25

Has won each completed start in points & impressed last start; could prove very useful if fit 98 26

WARWICK ROAD b.g. 10 Soldier Rose - Wind Hill by Moulton — J W Haydon

526	15/3	Cothelstone	(L)	MDN	3m	15	GS	*in tch to 12th, rear whn p.u. 15th*	P	0
934	6/4	Charlton Ho'	(L)	MDO	3m	10	G	*chsd ldrs, mstk 5th, lost tch 13th, 6th whn p.u. nxt*	P	0
1094	16/4	Hockworthy	(L)	MDN	3m	11	GF	*ld chsng grp, blnd 9th, wknd 5 out, t.o. & p.u. 3 out*	P	0
1260	27/4	Black Fores'	(R)	MDO	3m	12	F	*(bl) alwys bhnd, t.o. & p.u. last*	P	0

Dead 0

WASHAKIE gr.g. 12 Warpath - Super Satin by Lord Of Verona — Mrs F T Walton

1996 1(21),1(25),**2(24)**,**4(19)**,1(22),**6(0)**,1(22)

31	26/1	Alnwick	(L)	MEM	3m	4	G	*(fav) chsd ldr to 5th & agn 13th, ld nxt, sn clr, eased flat*	1	18
133	9/2	Alnwick	(L)	OPE	3m	6	G	*conf rdn, prog 14th, ld 2 out, gd jmp last, ran on strngly*	1	0
339	1/3	Corbridge	(R)	OPE	3m 5f	11	G	*(fav) hld up mid-div, prog 3 out, ev ch nxt, onepcd*	3	20
583	17/3	Newcastle	(L)	HC	3m	8	GF	*(fav) lost tch from 8th, t.o..*	6	0
812	31/3	Tranwell	(L)	OPE	3m	7	G	*outpcd 1st ctt,gd hdwy frm 13th into 8l 2nd last,not rch wnr*	2	21
1170	20/4	Hexham Poin'	(L)	OPE	3m	2	GF	*alwys cls up, qcknd to ld 2 out, 4l up last, styd on strngly*	1	22
1294	30/4	Kelso	(L)	HC	3m 1f	6	GF	*(fav) soon bhnd, some hdwy to chase ldrs after 13th, styd on well from 2 out, ld last, all out.*	1	22
1512	17/5	Corbridge	(R)	OPE	3m	10	GS	*(fav) mid-div, prog 10th, chsd wnr 2 out, ev ch whn ran out last*	r	23

Decent pointer; consistent; won 7 of 10 in 96/7; likes Alnwick; found weak H/Chase; win at 13 24

WATCHIT LAD b.g. 7 El-Birillo - Watch Lady by Home Guard (USA) — Mrs A Price

1996 **F(-)**,**F(-)**,**U(-)**,6(0),F(-)

405	8/3	Llanfrynach	(R)	RES	3m	15	G	*mid-div, no prog hlfwy*	6	0
1528	17/5	Bredwardine	(R)	MDO	3m	17	G	*prssd ldr to 12th, lost plc 15th, kpt on agn 2 out*	4	10
1570	26/5	Hereford	(R)	HC	3m 1f 110yds	14	G	*in rear when hit 8th, t.o. and p.u. before 2 out.*	P	0

Some ability & fair run 2nd start but needs to concentrate on Maidens; may have chances 98 12

WATERCOMBE CRACKER b.m. 6 Naskracker (USA) - La Marquesa by Lepanto (GER) — P H Guard

1498	14/5	Cothelstone	(L)	MDO	3m	9	GF	*alwys rear, t.o. & p.u. 11th*	P	0

No cracker yet 0

WATERCOURSE (Irish) — **I** 149^{P}, **I** 185^{3}, **I** 410^{P}

WATER DANCER (Irish) — **I** 449,

WATERLOO ANDY b.g. 11 Le Moss - Bartlemy Hostess by Bargello — Miss J E Cook

1996 **6(NH)**,**6(NH)**,**3(NH)**

66	1/2	Horseheath	(R)	MEM	3m	7	GF	*1st ride, hld up, 5th & outpcd 13th, kpt on frm 3 out,nvr nr*	4	13
272	22/2	Ampton	(R)	LAD	3m	7	G	*sn wll bhnd, sme late prog, nrly snatched 3rd*	4	0

1116 19/4 Higham (L) LAD 3m 2 GF *in tch til not qckn 12th, wknd 14th, no ch aft* 2 11

Winning chaser; novice-ridden in points & not threatening to win one 13

WATERLOO KING (Irish) — I 51P, I 88P, I 144P

WAYDANTE (Irish) — I 332, , I 4852, I 5651

WAYFORWARD (Irish) — I 2835, I 3483, I 3971, I 521P, I 578F

WAY HOME (Irish) — I 24P

WAYS AND MEANS b.m. 10 Oedipus Complex - Snow Mountain by Mountain Call — Mrs S Mollett

1996 3(14),1(15),3(20),2(21),1(20)

74 2/2 Market Rase' (L) MEM 3m 4 GF *(fav) held up, chsd wnr 11th, ev ch 3 out, unable to qckn frm nxt* 2 18
248 22/2 Brocklesby ' (L) CON 3m 10 G *nvr dang, ran on pssd wknng rivals frm 7th-4 out* 4 13
344 2/3 Market Rase' (L) MEM 3m 3 GF *(fav) hld up last, went 2nd 14th, clsd 3 out, ld last, eased nr fn* 2 18
673 23/3 Brocklesby ' (L) CON 3m 8 GF *ptntly rdn, prog 14th, ld 2 out, clr last, rdn out* 1 19

Very consistent 2nd class pointer; unfortunate 3rd start; likes Market Rasen & can win in 98; G-G/F 20

WAYSIDE BOY b.g. 12 Deep Run - Ciotog by Varano — D J Caro

1996 **P(0)**,4(13)

1060 13/4 Maisemore P' (L) MEM 3m 5 GF *in tch, rmndr 5th, mstk 8th, rdn & lost tch 11th, p.u. 14th* P 0

Restricted winner 95; rarely seen now & looks past it 0

WAYSIDE SPIN (Irish) — I 124P, I 174P, I 290P, I 3675, I 466P

WAYWARD EDWARD ch.g. 11 Takachiho - Portate by Articulate — J Turnbull

1996 2(15),P(0)

185 15/2 Erw Lon (L) MDN 3m 14 G *prom, rdn 10th, outpcd 13th, no dang aft, lft 3rd 3 out* 3 0
407 8/3 Llanfrynach (R) MDN 3m 11 G *trckd ldrs, 3rd 3 out, rallied nxt, onepcd flat* 2 14
847 31/3 Lydstep (L) MDO 3m 5 F *ld/disp to 13th, onepcd aft* 3 0
1137 19/4 Bonvilston (R) MDO 3m 13 G *ld to 11th, hdd nxt, alwys chsng wnnr, wknd 2 out* 4 10

Long standing maiden; placed in 5 of 6 races 96/7 but unlikely to take the plunge 11

WAYWARD KING (Irish) — I 83, I 472, I 1371, I 2561, I 4271, I 5181

WEAK MOMENT (Irish) — I 1362, I 3071

WE ALL NEED DREAMS (Irish) — I 554F

WEAVERS WINDOW VI (Irish) — I 221P, I 3444, I 388F, I 406, , I 595P

WEDNESDAYS AUCTION(IRE) b.g. 9 Mazaad - Happy Always by Lucky Wednesday — Mrs M Rigg

284 23/2 Charing (L) MDO 3m 17 G *s.s. t.o. til p.u. 13th* P 0
828 31/3 Heathfield (R) MEM 3m 5 F *hld up, prog apr 3 out, 1l dwn & clsng whn blnd last,nt rcvr* 2 0
967 6/4 Penshurst (L) OPE 3m 4 F *alwys last, lost tch 10th, lft poor 2nd 14th, u.r. 3 out* U -
1502 16/5 Folkestone (R) HC 2m 5f 10 G *last when pkd 1st, soon well bhnd, t.o. 7th, kept on from 11th, tk poor 2nd after last.* 2 17

Blunders around but showed ability last start (flattered) & Maiden win ought to follow in 98 15

WEEKEND WARRIOR (Irish) — I 398P, I 526P

WEEKEND WORKER b.g. 6 Rustingo - Crystal Run Vii — V Y Gethin

1996 **7(NH),10(NH)**

146 9/2 Tweseldown (R) MDO 3m 10 GF *mid-div, in tch whn p.u. 13th, lame* P 0

Lightly raced to date & problems on pointing debut 0

WEE MACGREGOR ch.g. 9 Gypsy Castle - Secret Storm by Secret Ace — Mrs L P Vaughan

1066 13/4 Maisemore P' (L) MDO 3m 9 GF *bhnd frm 5th, no ch 10th, p.u. 14th* P 0

No ability under Rules & none on pointing debut 0

WEJEM (Irish) — I 13P, I 41P, I 752, I 1444

WELL BANK b.g. 10 Tudor Diver - Technical Merit by Gala Performance (USA) — Mrs C Hicks

1996 **P(NH),8(NH),5(NH),P(NH),F(NH),P(NH)**

258 22/2 Newtown (L) RES 3m 14 G *prom to 11th, wknd rpdly 13th, p.u. 15th* P 0
656 22/3 Siddington (L) MDN 3m 7 F *alwys prom, rdn & ev ch 15th, wknd aft 3 out* 4 0
1019 12/4 Bitterley (L) MDO 3m 12 GF *prom, ev ch 14th, wknd nxt, p.u. 2 out* P 0
1195 23/4 Andoversford (R) MEM 3m 4 F *keen hld, chsd wnr, mstk 14th, rdn & btn apr 2 out* 2 0
1288 30/4 Cheltenham (L) HC 2m 5f 10 GF *mstks, in tch till rdn and wknd 11th, no ch when f 14th.* F -
1402 5/5 Ashorne (R) MDO 3m 11 G *ld/disp to 14th, cls 2nd & ev ch whn f nxt* F -
1615 7/6 Umberleigh (L) MDO 3m 11 F *ld 2nd-aft 5th, wknd 12th, 5th & btn whn blnd & u.r. nxt* U -

Does not stay & clumsy; has completed 2 of 13 starts in points 92-7 10

WELL DOCTOR (Irish) — I 243P, I 300P, I 429P

WELLINGTON BROWN b.g. 13 Faraway Times (USA) - Chevulgan by Cheval — J W Mitchell

511 15/3 Larkhill (R) CON 3m 3 GF *cls up to 12th, btn & jmpd slwly frm nxt, lame* 3 0

Formerly top-class; looks finished now 0

WELL TED (Irish) — I 311[F], I 347[2], I 438[1]

WELSH CLOVER b.m. 9 Cruise Missile - National Clover by National Trust Michael H Ings

1996 P(0),R(-),P(0),P(0),P(0),P(0),P(0),2(0),P(0)

300 1/3 Didmarton (L) RES 3m 23 G *ld to 2nd, wll bhnd whn p.u. 3 out* P 0

Won poor Maiden 95; gone to pieces since 10

WELSH FAIR b.m. 7 Tigerwood - Trefair by Graig Hill Master Mrs E Egerton

365 2/3 Garnons (L) MDO 2 1/2m 14 GS *rear frm 6th, no ch 11th, t.o. & p.u. 3 out* P 0

Only an educational debut 0

WELSH LAD (Irish) — I 196[5], I 241[F]

WELSH LANE (Irish) — I 50[4], I 220[P], I 324[P], I 391, , I 497[F]

WELSH LIGHTNING b or br.g. 9 Lighter - Welsh Log by King Log A Gunther

1996 9(0),P(0)

87 2/2 Wolverhampt' (L) MDO 3m 11 GS *u.r. 1st* U -
223 16/2 Heythrop (R) RES 3m 19 G *chsd ldrs, btn frm 14th, disp poor 4th & u.r. last* U -
288 27/2 Ludlow (R) HC 3m 8 G *mstks in rear, t.o. from 12th.* 5 0
664 23/3 Eaton Hall (R) MDO 3m 12 GF *rear 12th, some late prog, nvr nrr* 5 0
1019 12/4 Bitterley (L) MDO 3m 12 GF *mid-div whn mstk & u.r. 4th* U -
1240 26/4 Brampton Br' (R) MDO 3m 12 G *cls up frm 7th, wknd 15th, no ch whn p.u. last* P 0
1393 5/5 Cursneh Hill (L) MDO 3m 9 GF *last frm 8th, lost tch & p.u. 11th* P 0

WEll beaten when completing; does not stay & no hopes 0

WELSHMANS CANYON (Irish) — I 72,

WELSH MARCH (Irish) — I 47[P], I 132[1], I 194[2], I 279[3]

WELSH RUPERT(IRE) b.g. 8 Orchestra - Welsh Tan by Welsh Saint Jon Trice-Rolph

373 2/3 Mollington (R) MDN 3m 14 G *trckd ldrs going easily, 3rd & chnce whn blnd 3 out, wknd* 5 0

Promise in Bumper in 94; could win if able to stand regular racing 13

WELSH SINGER ch.g. 11 Celtic Cone - Madam Butterfly by Deep Run K B Rogers

1996 3(18),4(19),2(18),2(18),1(19),3(17)

256 22/2 Newtown (L) OPE 3m 17 G *cls up to 11th, wknd 13th, no ch aft* 7 12
447 8/3 Newton Brom' (R) OPE 3m 6 G *lft in ld 2nd, hdd 4th, made most 6th 6th-14th, onepcd* 3 19
758 29/3 Kimble (L) OPE 3m 6 GF *hld up rear, f 4th* F -
1214 26/4 Woodford (L) OPE 3m 5 G *keen hld, chsd ldrs, ld 12th-15th, cls 3rd & blnd nxt, wknd* 4 16
1451 10/5 Kingston Bl' (L) OPE 3m 5 G *in tch, cls 2nd at 14th, ld 3 out-nxt, just outpcd* 2 20

Fair pointer at best but 1 win, 8 placings 96/7 & may find it tough to win at 12; G-S 19

WELSH SITARA (Irish) — I 179[1]

WELSH TREASURE(IRE) b.m. 5 Treasure Kay - Villars by Home Guard (USA) D J Miller

186 15/2 Erw Lon (L) MDN 3m 13 G *(fav) prom to 10th, no ch whn p.u. 14th* P 0
543 16/3 Erw Lon (L) MDN 3m 11 GF *(fav) cls up, mstk 10th, p.u. 12th* P 0
1229 26/4 Pyle (R) MDO 3m 11 GS *blnd 2nd, effrt to go 3rd whn mstk 11th, wknd & p.u. 13th* P 0
1368 5/5 Pantyderi (L) MDO 3m 8 G *n.j.w. rear til p.u. 7th* P 0

Good stable & highly thought-of but showed nothing & can only be watched at present 0

WESSHAUN b.m. 7 Shaunicken - Wessex Flyer by Pony Express Mrs A G Sims

1996 B(-),F(-),P(0),P(0)

390 8/3 Barbury Cas' (L) MDN 3m 15 G *cls up to 9th, sn wknd, t.o. & jmpd slwly 14th, p.u. 2 out* P 0
513 15/3 Larkhill (R) MDO 3m 10 GF *ld 3rd til aft 4 out, wkng whn blnd nxt, t.o.* 6 0
916 5/4 Larkhill (R) MEM 3m 3 F *made all, dist clr 13th, unchal* 1 10
1143 19/4 Larkhill (R) XX 3m 2 F *(fav) ld, 4l clr & in cmmnd whn f last* F 11
1370 5/5 Cotley Farm (L) XX 3m 4 GF *ld til 11th, hdd nxt, lost tch frm 4 out* 3 0

Improved but non-stayer & won silly race; placed in poor novice chase season's end 11

WEST COAST COOLER (Irish) — I 133[P], I 191[5], I 307[3], I 444[P], I 602[P]

WESTCOUNTRY LAD b.g. 7 General Surprise - Charmezzo by Remezzo Mrs P Bond

1996 P(0)

103 8/2 Great Treth' (R) MDO 3m 9 GS *chsng grp, effrt 3 out, lft 2nd nxt, kpt on well* 2 14
458 8/3 Great Treth' (R) MDO 3m 15 S *5th 12th, hit 14th, sn lost plc* 6 0
625 22/3 Kilworthy (L) MDN 3m 14 G *bad mstk 3rd, hdwy und pres 16th, onepce clsng stgs* 3 13
1399 5/5 High Bickin' (R) MDO 3m 12 G *handy, cls 4th at 14th, went 2nd und pres last, ran on* 2 16

Improving; 2nd in decent race last start & sure to win on that form in 98 16

WESTCOURT (Irish) — I 39P, I 58P, I 302,

WESTER LAD b.g. 8 Germont - Lawsuitlaw by Cagirama — Tim Butt

162 15/2 Lanark (R) MDO 3m 16 G *disp 7th, cls 3rd but hld whn f last* F -

Some promise 95; missed 96; vanished after fall; chances if fit 98 13

WESTERN FORT(IRE) ch.g. 7 Saher - Moon Away — R G Westacott

1996 **13(NH)**

104 8/2 Great Treth' (R) MDO 3m 9 GS *prom, ld 5th-11th, wknd 13th, p.u. 15th* P 0
175 15/2 Ottery St M' (L) RES 3m 15 G *mid-div early, t.o. 14th, p.u. 2 out* P 0

Showed up on debut but season lasted a week 10

WESTERN HARMONY ch.g. 9 Extra - Harmonica by St Paddy — R T Baimbridge

1996 1(15)

574 16/3 Garnons (L) RES 3m 14 G *ld, 3l up 14th, hdd & no ext flat* 2 18
701 29/3 Upper Sapey (R) RES 3m 6 GF *(fav) ld frm start, ran on strgly whn chal frm 3 out,drew clr flat* 1 19

Maiden winner 96 Baimbridge magic worked again; should be placed to win in 98 19

WESTERN PEARL(IRE) gr.g. 9 Sarab - Legs And Things by Three Legs — Mrs P J Price

1996 P(0)

88 2/2 Wolverhampt' (L) MDO 3m 13 GS *prom to 4th, wll bhnd whn p.u. 11th* P 0
263 22/2 Newtown (L) MDN 3m 11 G *ld 4-9th, lost plc, effrt to chs wnr aft 13th, btn 15th* 2 0
437 8/3 Upton-On-Se' (R) MDO 3m 15 G *prom, ld 6-12th, not qckn 14th, btn 5th whn f last* F -

Lightly raced; beaten 15l when placed & still short of winning standard; finished after fall 12

WEST KING br.g. 12 Kinglet - Indiscreet by Stupendous — O A Little

401 8/3 Llanfrynach (R) LAD 3m 14 G *last til p.u. 11th* P 0
638 22/3 Howick (L) LAD 3m 10 GF *last til p.u. 11th* P 0
717 29/3 Llanvapley (L) RES 3m 13 GF *last pair, p.u. 3 out* P 0
1135 19/4 Bonvilston (R) RES 3m 14 G *alwys rear, p.u. 13th* P 0
1319 3/5 Bonvilston (R) INT 3m 8 G *mid-div, f 5th* F -
1456 11/5 Maisemore P' (L) LAD 3m 5 G *cls up til wknd 14th, t.o.* 3 0
1557 24/5 Bassaleg (R) CON 3m 9 G *sn dtchd, t.o. 11th, stppd aft nxt* P 0

No longer of any account 0

WEST LUTTON b.g. 5 Scorpio (FR) - Crammond Brig by New Brig — Mrs A M Easterby

116 9/2 Wetherby Po' (L) MDO 3m 14 GF *prom til wknd 11th, t.o. & p.u. 3 out* P 0
269 22/2 Duncombe Pa' (R) MDO 3m 16 G *rear, mstk 3rd, u.r. nxt* U -
357 2/3 Great Stain' (L) MDO 3m 15 S *mid-div, f 3rd* F -
428 8/3 Charm Park (L) MDO 3m 10 GF *rear, prog to chsng grp 10th, mstk nxt, fdd 3 out* 4 0
621 22/3 Hutton Rudby (L) MDO 3m 10 GF *rear, efft 12th, outpcd 4 out, btn whn f 2 out* F -

WEll beaten only completion & clumsy to date; should do better 10

WEST OF THE MOON (Irish) — I 23F

WESTON MOON(IRE) b.m. 8 Le Moss - Lady Bluebird by Arapaho — N R J Bell

1996 1(13)

770 29/3 Dingley (R) RES 3m 18 G *ld 4th-12th, fdd nxt, 6th whn p.u. last* P 0
1081 13/4 Guilsborough (L) RES 3m 13 GF *mstk 9th, clr ldr til hdd 15th, wknd* 6 0
1208 26/4 Clifton On ' (L) RES 3m 4 GS *ld for 2m, hdd & wknd rpdly frm 4 out* 3 0

Maiden winner only start 96; very lightly raced; non-stayer & prospects look remote 12

WESTONS WAY (Irish) — I 40P

WEST ORIENT b.g. 12 Strong Gale - Bean Giolla by Giolla Mear — D Hiatt

1996 **F(NH),P(NH),13(NH)**

219 16/2 Heythrop (R) LAD 3m 16 G *ld to 4th, prom til wknd frm 15th* 5 13
371 2/3 Mollington (R) LAD 3m 9 G *jmpd lft, ld 2-10th, btn frm nxt* 6 0
818 31/3 Paxford (L) LAD 3m 3 F *ld to 8th, ld agn 14th-nxt, onepcd aft* 2 13
988 12/4 Kingston Bl' (L) LAD 3m 7 GF *clr ldr til ran out 4th* r -

Winning chaser (2m); does not stay & too old as well 10

WEST QUAY b.g. 11 Dubassoff (USA) - Elysium Dream Vii — C T Moate

1996 1(24),**2(24)**,**3(23)**,**F(-)**

589 20/3 Wincanton (R) HC 2m 5f 9 GF *ld to 3rd, led 13th till p.u. lame apr 4 out.* P 0

Useful but always lightly raced & disaster struck again only start 97 (would have won); best watched ... 24

WEST TRIX VI (Irish) — I 86, , I 153P

WEYCROFT VALLEY b.m. 6 North Street - Folly's Copes by Persian Plan (AUS) — G Herrod

1437 10/5 Holnicote (L) MDO 3m 14 G *sn bhnd, t.o. & p.u. 12th* P 0

1521 17/5 Bratton Down (L) MDO 3m 16 GS *t.o. & p.u. 11th* P 0

Not yet of any account 0

WHARFINGAR (Irish) — I 24^P, I 449^P

WHAT-A-BRAVE RUN b.g. 6 Mr Big John - Brave Colleen by Brave Invader (USA) Keith Tollick

487 9/3 Tweseldown (R) MDO 3m 12 G *out of tch in mid-div, poor 5th whn f 10th* F -
582 16/3 Detling (L) MDN 3m 16 F *alwys rear, f 14th* F -
833 31/3 Heathfield (R) MDO 3m 7 F *mstks, in tch til blnd & u.r. 12th* U -
979 8/4 Heythrop (R) MDO 3m 2 F *keen hold, ld 3-11th & 14-2 out, sn rddn & btn* 2 0

Beaten in a match & makes mistakes - no chances yet 0

WHAT A CHOICE (Irish) — I 26^6, I 295^2, I 355^1, I 454^5

WHATAFELLOW(IRE) ch.g. 7 Arapahos (FR) - Dara's March by March Parade Gareth Samuel

1996 1(18),U(-),3(19),1(20),1(20),4(16)

330 1/3 Eaton Hall (R) CON 3m 16 GS *w.w. rear, 10l 3rd 4 out, 2l 3rd & chal 2 out, no ext run in* 3 18
465 8/3 Eyton-On-Se' (L) OPE 3m 13 G *f 1st* F -

Won 3 in 96; ran well 1st outing but season lasted a week; can win again if fit 98 22

WHAT A HAND (Irish) — 494^3, I 9^1

WHATALOOK (Irish) — I 295^P

WHAT A MISS ch.m. 10 Move Off - Vinovia by Ribston Mrs A E Astall

1996 P(0),P(0),P(0),P(0),P(0)

201 15/2 Weston Park (L) OPE 3m 16 G *no ch whn p.u. 11th* P 0
330 1/3 Eaton Hall (R) CON 3m 16 GS *rear, t.o.& p.u. 11th* P 0
465 8/3 Eyton-On-Se' (L) OPE 3m 13 G *mid-div in tch, sn btn, p.u. 4 out* P 0
882 1/4 Flagg Moor (L) MEM 3m 8 G 3 0

Won 2 bad races in 95 but pulled up all stsarts 96/7 & could not even win the stone wall special 0

WHAT A STORM (Irish) — I 57^P, I 522^5

WHAT A TO DO b.g. 13 Le Bavard (FR) - Alfie's Wish by Three Wishes C J R Sweeting

1996 U(-),P(0),1(19),4(17),**1(23)**

219 16/2 Heythrop (R) LAD 3m 16 G *in tch to 9th, sn wknd, t.o. & p.u. last* P 0
384 6/3 Towcester (R) HC 3m 1f 7 GS *prom to 10th, btn 4th when blnd and u.r. last.* U -
773 29/3 Dingley (R) LAD 3m 11 G *abt 6th til outpcd & t.o. 10th, p.u. 2 out* P 0
825 31/3 Lockinge (L) MXO 3m 3 F *(fav) not fluent, made most to 13th, ld agn 16th, sn clr* 1 15
981 9/4 Chepstow (L) HC 3m 6 F *in tch till wknd 7th, lost touch from 10th.* 4 10

H/Chase winner 96; won poor race 97 & looks near to retirement now 15

WHATCANIDO (Irish) — I 247^P, I 293^1

WHAT CHANCE(IRE) ch.m. 9 Buckskin (FR) - Grainne Geal by General Ironside C W Booth

1996 1(15),2(18),2(23)

219 16/2 Heythrop (R) LAD 3m 16 G *pckd 1st, in tch til b.d. 10th* B -
371 2/3 Mollington (R) LAD 3m 9 G *prom, ld 10th-last, unable qckn flat* 2 21
495 14/3 Fakenham (L) HC 2m 5f 110yds 10 G *held up, hdwy to track ldrs after 9th, cld up after 3 out, ld next, styd on well.* 1 22
1414 9/5 Sedgefield (L) HC 2m 5f 6 GF *nvr far away, ld last, soon hdd, no ext.* 2 23
1590 31/5 Stratford (L) HC 3m 9 G *struggling and driven along before hfwy, t.o. final cct.* 6 0

Maiden winner 96; maintained improvement; weak H/Chase success suggests Ladies best option 98 .. 24

WHAT SAND (Irish) — I 532^2, I 601^B

WHATS ANOTHER ch.m. 10 Lord Ha Ha - Purranna by Mugatpura Mrs G M Bridge

1996 U(-),P(0),P(0),P(0),4(13),2(13)

26 26/1 Marks Tey (L) LAD 3m 8 GF *prom, ld 6-14th, grad wknd* 5 10
198 15/2 Higham (L) RES 3m 14 G *mid-div, not pace to rch ldrs, no ch 14th* 4 0
274 22/2 Ampton (R) RES 3m 10 G *chsd ldrs, chsd wnr & ev ch 3 out, onepcd frm nxt* 2 16
443 8/3 Higham (L) RES 3m 7 G *disp til ld 3-7th, cls up, chal 3 out, no ext last* 3 17
503 15/3 Ampton (R) XX 3m 11 GF *mstks, prom til 5th & outpcd 13th, wll bhnd whn p.u. last* P 0
711 29/3 High Easter (L) RES 3m 6 F *chsd ldrs, ld 12th, made rest, drw clr frm 3 out* 1 17
1031 12/4 Horseheath (R) INT 3m 3 HD *(fav) chsd ldr 6th, ld aft 10th, f nxt* U -

Placed 5 times 96/7 before landing poor Restricted (novice-ridden); safe & may find another chance ... 17

WHATS MONEY gr.m. 6 Scallywag - What A Coup by Malicious E H Crow

1996 P(0)

366 2/3 Garnons (L) MDO 2 1/2m 13 GS *prom, ld 9th-nxt, ev ch whn u.r. 11th* U -

Two runs in 2 seasons so far; showed ability only start 97 & may do better if fit 98 13

WHATS THE MARK (Irish) — I 24^P

WHATS YOUR GAME b.g. 14 Kambalda - Sugar Shaker by Quisling K Sheppard

1996 P(0),P(0)

194 15/2 Higham (L) OPE 3m 12 G *(bl) alwys rear* 8 0
370 2/3 Mollington (R) OPE 3m 6 G *(bl) pshd alng, prom to 10th, nrly u.r. 11th, t.o. & u.r. 15th* U -
1163 20/4 Mollington (R) OPE 3m 4 GF *(bl) mstly 3rd & not fluent, wknd 3 out* 4 0
1279 27/4 Fakenham P-' (L) OPE 3m 7 G *(bl) jmpd slwly, sn bhnd, t.o. & p.u. 6th* P 0
1464 11/5 Tweseldown (R) XX 3m 7 GF *(bl) n.j.w. t.o. whn ref 9th* R -

No longer of any account 0

WHATWILLBEWILLBE(IRE) b or br.g. 8 Long Pond - Cheap Fuel by Bluerullah P S Burke
1996 1(17),F(-)

83 2/2 Wolverhampt' (L) RES 3m 8 GS *(fav) w.w. prog 14th, jnd ldrs 3 out, wknd apr nxt* 3 10

Maiden winner 96; vanished after one run 97; still time to revive; Soft 17

WHERE'S SAM (Irish) — **I** 59^{P}, **I** 119^{F}, **I** 180^{P}, **I** 253^{2}, **I** 331^{P}, **I** 365^{F}, **I** 366^{P}, **I** 464^{P}, **I** 583^{2}, **I** 610^{3}

WHINSTONE MILL b.g. 9 Pablond - Carrowmore by Crozier Mrs Sally Thornton
1996 3(11),**P(0)**,P(0),5(0),P(0),1(17),2(20),**2(17)**,1(20),4(12)

119 9/2 Wetherby Po' (L) OPE 3m 15 GF *rear, prog 10th, wknd 4 out, p.u. nxt* P 0

Dual winner 96; hard ride & soon vanished 97; best watched if back in 98 16

WHINVEAGH (Irish) — **I** 363^{F}, **I** 370^{P}, **I** 506^{P}

WHISKEY DITCH ch.m. 6 Kinglet - Trailing Rose by Undulate (USA) S J Gospel
1996 **P(NH)**

115 9/2 Wetherby Po' (L) MDO 3m 8 GF *mstk 1st, rear, blnd 6th, lost tch 11th, p.u. nxt* P 0
427 8/3 Charm Park (L) MDO 3m 10 GF *prom til stdly fdd frm 14th, t.o. & p.u. last* P 0

A glimmer of hope on 2nd start 0

WHISPERS HILL ch.m. 6 Kind Of Hush - Snarry Hill by Vitiges (FR) Roy Robinson
1996 F(-),6(0),F(-),1(15)

118 9/2 Wetherby Po' (L) RES 3m 14 GF *prom til fdd 14th, t.o.* 6 10
167 15/2 Witton Cast' (R) RES 3m 7 F *rear, rdn 9th, prog 11th, outpcd 3 out, lft 2nd flat* 2 12

Maiden winner 96; season lasted only 6 days in 97; prospects if fit in 98 15

WHISTLING GIPSY ch.g. 12 Whistling Top - Denzil's Delight by Little Buskins N P Williams
1996 **7(NH),3(NH),3(NH),4(NH)**

76 2/2 Market Rase' (L) XX 3m 12 GF *mid-div, prog 10th, 4th & outpcd app 14th, t.o. & p.u. last* P 0
836 31/3 Thorpe Lodge (L) OPE 3m 7 F *midfld whn f 2nd* F -
1188 20/4 Garthorpe (R) OPE 3m 9 GF *ld, sn wll clr, blnd 8th, wkng whn blnd & u.r. 11th* U -
1280 27/4 Fakenham P-' (L) LAD 3m 6 G *plld hrd, hld up, blnd 13th, ev ch 2 out, btn whn u.r. last* U 15

Winning hurdler; headstrong & tricky; unlikely to achieve much at 13 14

WHITE BULLET(USA) ch.g. 10 Shadeed (USA) - Eye Drop (USA) by Irish River (FR) Miss Ruth Matthews

213 16/2 Southwell P' (L) RES 3m 16 GS *ld 2nd-7th, wknd rpdly 10th, p.u. 12th* P 0
251 22/2 Brocklesby ' (L) RES 3m 16 G *cls up, ld 11th-3 out, hdd & no ext 2 out* 3 18
477 9/3 Southwell P' (L) RES 3m 10 G *(fav) w.w. prog 7th, mstk 11th, cls 4th nxt, sn strgglng, p.u.14th* P 0
544 16/3 Garthorpe (R) MEM 3m 6 GF *hld up bhnd, lft poor 3rd 9th, nvr plcd to chall* 3 0
676 23/3 Brocklesby ' (L) RES 3m 14 GF *prom, lft 3rd 6th, chsd ldr 14th, ld 2 out, hld on und pres* 1 20
924 6/4 Garthorpe (R) CON 3m 6 GF *chsg grp, lft in ld 10th, 8l clr 13th, comf* 1 19

Missed 95/6 but revived well 97; won well twice & can find more chances in 98 if fit 21

WHITESTOWN BOY (Irish) — **I** 95^{P}

WHITMORE b.g. 9 Sula Bula - Damside by Shackleton E B S Farmer

647 22/3 Castle Of C' (R) INT 3m 7 G *blnd & u.r. 2nd* U -
934 6/4 Charlton Ho' (L) MDO 3m 10 G *prom,chsd ldr 9th,15l down 3 out,ran on to ld last,drvn out* 1 16
1149 19/4 Chaddesley ' (L) RES 3m 6 GF *(fav) hld up bhnd, prog to chs wnr 14th, chnc 4 out, no imp nxt* 2 17

Dead 17

WHITWORTH GREY gr.g. 9 Marching On - Grey Morley by Pongee Miss T Spilman

372 2/3 Mollington (R) RES 3m 19 G *alwys rear, t.o. & u.r. 15th* U -
452 8/3 Newton Brom' (R) MDN 3m 9 G *in tch to hlfwy, last whn p.u. 15th* P 0

No signs yet & season lasted 6 days 0

WHOCANTELLYA (Irish) — **I** 62^{P}, **I** 339^{F}, **I** 389^{P}

WHO DOCTORED WHO(IRE) b.g. 7 Tanfirion - Glenshesk by Furry Glen Mrs A P Kelly

883 1/4 Flagg Moor (L) MDO 3m 12 G *s.s. rear of main grp whn f 5th* F -
1124 19/4 Whittington (L) MDO 3m 2 F *lft 30l,n.j.w.,prog & cls 15th,outpcd,ran on& lft solo last* 1 0
1385 5/5 Eyton-On-Se' (L) RES 3m 4 GF *alwys rear, detached & p.u. 12th* P 0
1542 18/5 Wolverhampt' (L) RES 3m 6 GS *prom, 2nd at 10th, btn frm 14th, p.u. nxt* P 0

Handed a match on plate & really up against it now 0

WHOSGOTSILLYSSENSE gr.m. 8 Pragmatic - Achiever by Tarqogan — Mrs S Martin

416	8/3	Dalston	(R)	RES	3m	12	GS	*alwys rear, no ch 14th, t.o.*	4 0
607	22/3	Friars Haugh	(L)	RES	3m	8	GF	*hld up, some hdwy frm 4 out, not trbl wnnr*	2 14
814	31/3	Tranwell	(L)	MDO	3m	9	G	*(fav) alwys prom,cls 2nd 12-14th,1l down 2 out-last,no ext run in*	3 14

Missed 96; improved & subsequent winner behind last start; can win if fit 98 14

WHOSTHAT b.g. 11 Politico (USA) - Muffler by Haris II — D A Lamb

1996 **U(-),U(-),3(0)**

31	26/1	Alnwick	(L)	MEM	3m	4	G	*ld to 14th, mstk & btn nxt, kpt on*	2 12
136	9/2	Alnwick	(L)	MDO	3m	16	G	*ld, blnd 2nd, hdd nxt, prom whn f 9th*	F -
357	2/3	Great Stain'	(L)	MDO	3m	15	S	*prom til fdd 8th, lost tch 12th, sn bhnd*	4 0

Flattered when 2nd & struggling in Maidens 10

WHO'S YOUR MAN(IRE) br.g. 7 Strong Statement (USA) - Pennies River by Over The River (FR) — H Morris

368	2/3	Garnons	(L)	MDO	2 1/2m	13	GS	*prog 9th, ev ch 11th, wknd nxt*	4 0
408	8/3	Llanfrynach	(R)	MDN	3m	12	G	*(fav) mostly 2nd til outpcd frm 14th*	3 0
719	29/3	Llanvapley	(L)	MDN	3m	14	GF	*(Jt fav) j.w. in mid-div, prog 15th to ld nxt, just held on flat*	1 12
1008	12/4	St Hilary	(R)	RES	3m	11	GF	*prom, lft 2nd 12th, onepcd frm 3 out*	3 10
1203	26/4	Worcester	(L)	HC	2m 7f 110yds	10	S	*bhnd when blnd 7th, t.o. when p.u. before 9th.*	P 0
1522	17/5	Bredwardine	(R)	MEM	3m	2	G	*made most til jnd & f 14th, rmntd*	2 0

Placed Irish Maidens 96; beat 2 subsequent winners when scoring; weak Restricted needed in 98 15

WHY EMERALD (Irish) — I 61[P], I 139[3]

WICKED IMP ch.g. 5 Scallywag - Naughty Niece by Bribe — Peter Scott

512	15/3	Larkhill	(R)	MDO	3m	6	GF	*mstk 3rd, in tch, prssd ldr 13th, ld 2 out, rdn out flat*	1 11

Ideal start in weak & slow Maiden; form poor but good stable & should have prospects in 98 15

WICKED PIXIE(IRE) b.m. 5 Executive Perk - Quincy Bay by Buckskin (FR) — D Stephens

102	8/2	Great Treth'	(R)	MDO	3m	8	GS	*schoold, alwys bhnd, t.o. 4th, tk poor 3rd last*	3 0

Beaten miles on debut & vanished 0

WIGTOWN BAY br.g. 14 Young Nelson - Bonnie Bladnoch by Lord Of Verona — Mrs P C Stirling

1996 6(0),1+(13),F(-),2(16),P(0)

811	31/3	Tranwell	(L)	LAD	3m	3	G	*ld til hdd 5th, cls up til 2l 2nd 2 out, ld last, ran on wll*	1 16
1333	3/5	Mosshouses	(L)	LAD	3m	2	F	*(fav) slght ld virt thro'out, styd on gamely*	1 14

Beautifully placed to win two desperate contests & duly retired on a high 16

WILBAR (Irish) — I 34[P], I 115[3], I 180[2], I 254[1], I 326[1], I 374[2], I 437[2], I 471[1], I 521[2], I 553[1]

WILD ADVENTURE b or br.g. 8 Kabour - Magic Mover by Julio Mariner — J R Wright

36	26/1	Alnwick	(L)	MDO	3m	15	G	*mstks, prom, 5th whn f 13th*	F -
164	15/2	Witton Cast'	(R)	INT	3m	6	F	*plld hrd in rear, mstks 2 & 11th, wknd 14th*	5 0
352	2/3	Great Stain'	(L)	MEM	3m	5	S	*rear, lost tch 15th, f 4 out, dead*	F -

Dead 0

WILD BAVARD (Irish) — I 192[3], I 534[U], I 601[2]

WILD BUCK (Irish) — I 65[4], I 282[3]

WILD EDRIC b.g. 5 Weld - Paper Lady by Document — Mrs R M McFarlane

748	29/3	Brampton Br'	(R)	MEM	3m	6	GF	*4th til mstk & drppd last 6th, p.u. 12th*	P 0

No sign on debut but time on his side 0

WILD ILLUSION ch.g. 13 True Song - Fused Light by Fury Royal — Exors Of The Late Col A Clerke-Brown

1996 2(22),1(28),**1(30),3(20)**,**1(28),1(28),2(25)**

56	1/2	Kingston Bl'	(L)	OPE	3m	13	GF	*(fav) hld up in tch, ld aft 13th, jnd & lft clr 15th*	1 28
153	13/2	Sandown	(R)	HC	2 1/2m 110yds	6	G	*(Jt fav) cl up, rdn after 3 out, styd on apr last, one pace.*	3 28
385	6/3	Wincanton	(R)	HC	3m 1f 110yds	6	G	*(fav) disp ld to 6th, jmpd slowly 8th, ld 9th to next, jumped slowly 12th, rallied and ev ch last, styd on.*	2 19
675	23/3	Brocklesby '	(L)	OPE	3m	6	GF	*(fav) in tch, rdn alng 10th, chsd wnr 3 out-nxt, no imp apr last*	3 22
745	29/3	Barbury Cas'	(L)	OPE	3m	3	F	*(fav) w.w. ld 12th, skipped clr 15th, cosily*	1 22
982	9/4	Ludlow	(R)	HC	3m	6	F	*bhnd, hdwy apr 12th, wknd 14th, t.o. when p.u. before 4 out.*	P 0

Great campaigner; declined 97; may need points in 98 but still good enough to win at 14; G-F 23

WILDNITE b.g. 13 Whealden - Melinite by Milesian — Miss L Robbins

1996 P(0),1(14),6(0)

816	31/3	Paxford	(L)	MEM	3m	3	F	*trckd ldr, lft in ld 15th, ran on gamely*	1	10
1524	17/5	Bredwardine	(R)	OPE	3m	8	G	*in tch in rear, rdn & wknd 12th, p.u. 15th*	P	0
1574	26/5	Chaddesley '	(L)	CON	3m	8	F	*prom til wknd 12th, 4th & wll btn whn p.u. last, dsmntd*	P	0

Completed Members double but of no real account now & problems last start 10

WILD NOBLE (Irish) — **I** 91[P]

WILD RUDOLPH(IRE) ch.g. 6 Wood Chanter - More Energy by Little Sandy — D Sundin

38	26/1	Alnwick	(L)	MDO	3m	14	G	*alwys bhnd, t.o. & p.u. 10th*	P	0
233	22/2	Friars Haugh	(L)	MDO	3m	13	G	*alwys bhnd, p.u. 13th*	P	0

No signs of ability yet 0

WILD WEATHER ch.g. 7 Nearly A Hand - Miss Blakeney by Baron Blakeney — Mrs Stanley Perry

1996 **14(NH),P(NH)**

182	15/2	Larkhill	(R)	MDO	3m	12	G	*mid-div whn u.r. 5th*	U	-
299	1/3	Didmarton	(L)	MDN	3m	14	G	*ld to 11th, wknd rpdly, p.u. 14th*	P	0
525	15/3	Cothelstone	(L)	MDN	3m	15	GS	*s.s. alwys trailing*	6	0
933	6/4	Charlton Ho'	(L)	MDO	3m	12	G	*mstk 8th, alwys rear, last & lost tch whn p.u. 15th*	P	0

No stamina & looks unpromising 0

WILLBROOK (Irish) — **I** 106[P]

WILLIE B BRAVE (Irish) — **I** 29[F], **I** 117[F], **I** 128[1], **I** 174[P], **I** 345[2], **I** 473[1]

WILL IT LAST b.m. 11 Roi Guillaume (FR) - Golden Annie by Le Tricolore — F L Matthews

226	21/2	Haydock	(L)	HC	3m	11	G	*soon well bhnd, t.o. when p.u. 11th.*	P	0
291	1/3	Warwick	(L)	HC	3 1/4m	6	G	*(vis) jmpd slowly, soon t.o. and 2 fences bhnd, jumped slowly and u.r. 6 out.*	U	-
849	31/3	Eyton-On-Se'	(L)	OPE	3m	7	GF	*ld to 4th, sn btn, t.o. 9th, p.u. 5 out*	P	0

Hurdle winner 94; a waste of time now 0

WILLOW BELLE(IRE) b.m. 9 Bustinetto - Light Belle by Light Brigade — Mrs C Day

1996 P(0),P(0),2(0),P(0),4(0)

640	22/3	Howick	(L)	MDN	3m	10	GF	*ld to 12th, grad wknd*	4	0
900	5/4	Howick	(L)	MEM	3m	4	F	*ld 8-11th, cls 3rd whn s.u. bnd aft 15th*	S	-
1011	12/4	St Hilary	(R)	MDN	3m	10	GF	*2nd til lost plc 12th, p.u. 3 out*	P	0

Placed in dire races 95-7 & no prospects of a win 0

WILLOW BROOK(IRE) b.g. 6 Carlingford Castle - Loose Key by Distinctly (USA) — J R Holt

210	16/2	Southwell P'	(L)	MDO	3m	15	GS	*alwys rear, mstk 7th, t.o. & p.u. 12th*	P	0
372	2/3	Mollington	(R)	RES	3m	19	G	*rear grp, no ch frm 11th, t.o. & p.u. 3 out*	P	0

No cause for optimism yet 0

WILLSAN ch.g. 7 Nearly A Hand - Sanber by New Member — R Winslade

1996 P(0)

1373	5/5	Cotley Farm	(L)	MDO	3m	6	GF	*(fav) hld up,prog 11th,wnt 2nd4 out,ev ch 2out,wknd aft,eased flat*	2	12

Lightly raced;; well-bred; runner-up in poor race but should do better - needs to 13

WILL TRAVEL(IRE) b.g. 8 Mandalus - Kenga by Roman Warrior — D V Tate

167	15/2	Witton Cast'	(R)	RES	3m	7	F	*ld, disp 10th, hdd & fdd 4 out, wll btn whn p.u. last*	P	0
230	22/2	Friars Haugh	(L)	RES	3m	15	G	*nvr bttr tahn mid-div, bhnd whn p.u. 3 out*	P	0
356	2/3	Great Stain'	(L)	INT	3m	9	S	*mid-div, went 2nd 10th, rdn nxt, wknd 14th, p.u. 3 out*	P	0
563	16/3	Lanark	(R)	RES	3m	8	GS	*alwys hndy, kpt on wll frm 3 out*	3	17
607	22/3	Friars Haugh	(L)	RES	3m	8	GF	*hld up in tch, ld apr 3 out, styd on wll*	1	17
812	31/3	Tranwell	(L)	OPE	3m	7	G	*outpcd in 3rd 1st ctt, wknd into 4th 2 out*	4	17
991	12/4	Tranwell	(L)	MEM	3m	3	F	*(fav) ld til 5th,disp ld 8-9th,ld nxt,1/2l up 4out-2 out,kpt on*	1	16
1168	20/4	Hexham Poin'	(L)	CON	3m	3	GF	*cls up, disp 16th, 3l 2nd nxt, no imp wnr 2 out*	2	16
1297	3/5	Hexham	(L)	HC	3m 1f	8	F	*(fav) chsd wnr, rdn 4 out, wknd after next.*	3	19
1499	15/5	Perth	(R)	HC	2 1/2m 110yds	8	GS	*ld to 8th, struggling 5 out, t.o..*	4	12
1586	28/5	Cartmel	(L)	HC	3 1/4m	10	GF	*cl up till gradually wknd from 14th.*	7	11

Irish Maiden winner 96; won weak races & out of depth in H/Chases; may find another chance; Any 19

WILLY WEE (Irish) — **I** 71[1], **I** 113[3], **I** 213[3], **I** 361[2]

WILTON PARK b.m. 9 Majestic Streak - Cregg Park by Orchardist — G Young

634	22/3	Howick	(L)	RES	3m	7	GF	*last frm 12th til p.u. 14th*	P	0
1018	12/4	Bitterley	(L)	MDO	3m	13	GF	*rear of main grp, nvr able to chal*	5	0
1136	19/4	Bonvilston	(R)	MDO	3m	15	G	*held up, steadd prog 12th, 3rd 15th, styd on onepce*	3	0
1367	5/5	Pantyderi	(L)	MDO	3m	7	G	*3rd til mstk 11th, lost plc, styd on onepcd 3 out*	3	0
1527	17/5	Bredwardine	(R)	MDO	3m	13	G	*nrly ran out 2nd, in tch in rear whn ran out 8th*	r	-

Missed 95/6 & well beaten when completing in 97 0

WIND FORCE br.g. 12 Strong Gale - Richest by Richboy — Milson Robinson
1996 **6(NH),U(NH),8(NH),3(NH),F(NH),5(NH)**

76	2/2	Market Rase'	(L)	XX	3m	12 GF	*wth ldr to 10th, grad lost pl, no ch frm 14th*	5	16
675	23/3	Brocklesby '	(L)	OPE	3m	6 GF	*chsd ldr to 14th, rallied & 2nd agn 2 out, no imp flat*	2	23

Winning chaser; brief season; barely stays but ran well 2nd start; could win at 13 if fit 20

WINDGATES ZONE (Irish) — I 407^{6}, I 497^{F}, I 576^{1}
WINDMILL STAR (Irish) — I 71^{B}, I 112^{6}, I 126^{F}, I 179^{P}, I 292^{2}, I 329, , I 463^{4}
WIND OF GLORY (Irish) — I 119^{P}, I 129^{P}, I 253^{F}, I 330^{P}, I 467^{2}, I 583^{U}
WINDSOR FOUNTAIN (Irish) — I 461^{F}, I 586^{6}
WINDWHISTLE LAD b.g. 8 Sharp Deal - Maius Dancer by Full Of Beans — Mrs H J Churchill

523	15/3	Cothelstone	(L)	RES	3m	14 GS	*in tch, 5th at 13th, prog to 3rd whn f 3 out*	F	-
865	31/3	Kingston St'	(R)	RES	3m	3 F	*(fav) disp 6th, ld 11-16th, wknng & p.u. lame apr 3 out*	P	0

Dead 16

WINNIE LORRAINE b.m. 12 St Columbus - Win Green Hill by National Trust — R W Jewitt
1996 **4(NH),5(NH),5(NH),2(NH),P(NH),P(NH),U(NH)**

561	16/3	Lanark	(R)	LAD	3m	7 GS	*bhnd by 11th, t.o.*	6	0
993	12/4	Tranwell	(L)	OPE	3m	5 F	*(fav) disp ld 3rd-10th,hdd nxt,no imprssn frm 3 out,wknd run in*	4	0
1168	20/4	Hexham Poin'	(L)	CON	3m	3 GF	*cls up bhnd ldr, ld aft 16th, styd on well*	1	18
1335	3/5	Mosshouses	(L)	OPE	3m	4 F	*(fav) went 2nd 9th, ld brfly 11th, wknd 3 out*	3	12
1426	10/5	Aspatria	(L)	OPE	3m	9 G	*ld to 14th, sn wknd, no ch whn s.u. bnd apr 3 out*	S	-

Retired 15

WINNING RHYTHM (Irish) — I 150^{3}, I 344^{1}, I 442^{3}
WINTER BREEZE b.g. 10 Strong Gale - Ballyreidy Star by Mon Capitaine — R M Phillips

706	29/3	Upper Sapey	(R)	MDO	3m	15 GF	*prog frm 7th to go 2nd 15th, ev ch til onepcd frm 2 out*	4	12
1019	12/4	Bitterley	(L)	MDO	3m	12 GF	*prog to cls 2nd 12th, chsd ldr til wknd 2 out*	3	10
1239	26/4	Brampton Br'	(R)	MDO	3m	9 G	*alwys cls up, not qckn apr 3 out, lft 2nd nxt*	2	10
1393	5/5	Cursneh Hill	(L)	MDO	3m	9 GF	*(Jt fav) cls up, efft & rddn 14th, chal last, ld flat, all out*	1	15
1533	18/5	Mollington	(R)	XX	3m	8 GS	*alwys prom, ld 15th-nxt, onepcd apr 2 out*	3	15
1605	1/6	Dingley	(R)	RES	3m	13 GF	*wll in tch til p.u. 11th, dsmntd*	P	0
1613	7/6	Umberleigh	(L)	RES	3m	13 F	*6s-3s, chsng grp, effrt to 3rd at 14th, sn wknd, p.u. 2 out*	P	0

Late starter; subsequent winners behind when scoring but non-stayer & hard to find Restricted 15

WINTER RAMBLE (Irish) — I 364^{F}, I 375^{P}, I 583^{5}
WINTER'S LANE ch.g. 13 Leander - Roman Lilly by Romany Air — Granville Taylor
1996 P(0),5(0),**6(10)**,U(-),6(14),5(11),4(15),U(-),F(-)

587	19/3	Ludlow	(R)	HC	2 1/2m	18 GF	*bhnd, hit 10th, t.o. when p.u. before 12th*	P	0
1396	5/5	High Bickin'	(R)	MXO	3m	7 G	*prom til slppd bnd apr 7th,mstks 12 & nxt, lost tch,p.u.15th*	P	0

Formerly decent; looks finished now 12

WINTERS MELODY b.m. 7 Southern Music - Wintersgame by Game Warden — E Pennock
1996 F(-),P(0),U(-),r(-)

79	2/2	Market Rase'	(L)	MDO	2m 5f	9 GF	*chsd ldrs to 8th, sn wknd, t.o. frm 11th*	4	0
114	9/2	Wetherby Po'	(L)	MDO	3m	8 GF	*ld to 3rd, prom, ld 11th-14th, wknd rpdly*	4	0
346	2/3	Market Rase'	(L)	MDO	3m	10 GF	*prom, lft in ld 6th, drew wll clr apr 14th, unchal*	1	15
425	8/3	Charm Park	(L)	RES	3m	12 GF	*mid-div, prog 9th, ld 11th-15th, wknd, blndrd last*	3	11
894	5/4	Wetherby Po'	(L)	RES	3m	6 F	*prom, ld 3rd, disp 11th til hdd & wknd 14th, bhnd & p.u.2out*	P	0

Beat 2 subsequent winners when scoring; headstrong & mistakes; settle better to win Restricted 15

WINTRY WILLOW (Irish) — I 261^{P}, I 483^{1}
WIRED FOR SOUND b.g. 7 Sharpo - Swift Return by Double Form — Mrs Hazel Richardson
1996 P(0),P(0),U(-),6(0),3(11)

182	15/2	Larkhill	(R)	MDO	3m	12 G	*j.w. ld 4th til aft 12th, lft 2nd 3 out, sn ld, drew clr*	1	16
292	1/3	Didmarton	(L)	MEM	3m	9 G	*ld to 3rd, 2nd whn p.u. 5th, dsmntd*	P	0

All out to win 2 finisher race & problems other start; best watched 14

WISE FLORIZEL b.g. 8 Right Regent - Sage Mountain by Spitsbergen — M B Ogle
1996 **P(NH),P(NH)**

629	22/3	Kilworthy	(L)	OPE	3m	5 G	*last til p.u. apr 14th*	P	0
739	29/3	Higher Kilw'	(L)	OPE	3m	3 GF	*sn lost tch, t.o. & p.u. 13th*	P	0

No ability under Rules or in points so far 0

WISE POINT(IRE) b.g. 6 Abednego - Corely Point by Cantab — R Lush

61	1/2	Horseheath	(R)	MDO	3m	9 GF	*mstks, sn wll bhnd, t.o. & p.u. 10th*	P	0
276	22/2	Ampton	(R)	MDO	3m	12 G	*sn wll bhnd, t.o. whn r.o. 8th*	r	-

Novice ridden; no signs of ability 0

WISE WIZARD b.g. 8 Neltino - Learned Lady by Crozier — Mrs F E Gilman

251 22/2 Brocklesby ' (L) RES 3m 16 G *cls up, 3rd 4 out, chal nxt, ld 2 out, ran on wll* 1 19
544 16/3 Garthorpe (R) MEM 3m 6 GF *(fav) prom, lft in ld 9th, hdd 3 out, ld appr last, ran on wll* 1 18
924 6/4 Garthorpe (R) CON 3m 6 GF *(fav) hld up, wll in tch whn u.r. 10th* U -
1189 20/4 Garthorpe (R) LAD 3m 6 GF *chsd ldr 8th, ld 15th, hdd last, rallied to ld nr fin* 1 18

Maiden winner 95; missed 96; improving; won modest Ladies; game & may step up in 98 21

WISHING WILLIAM (Irish) — I 8P, I 771

WISSYWIS(IRE) b.m. 5 Waajib - Miss Sandman by Manacle — J E Price

1996 **P(NH)**,**P(NH)**,**6(NH)**,**3(NH)**

435 8/3 Upton-On-Se' (R) MDO 3m 14 G *b.d. 2nd* B -
635 22/3 Howick (L) RES 3m 7 GF *alwys rear, dist 5th at 10th, p.u. 3 out* P 0
705 29/3 Upper Sapey (R) CON 3m 4 GF *lost 20l start, last til p.u. 11th* P 0
901 5/4 Howick (L) RES 3m 6 F *disp mod 3rd til slppd & u.r. bnd aft 9th* U -
1136 19/4 Bonvilston (R) MDO 3m 15 G *cls up to 7th, wknd qckly, p.u. 15th* P 0
1200 23/4 Andoversford (R) MDO 3m 8 F *alwys last, t.o. 7th, u.r. 13th* U -
1572 26/5 Chaddesley ' (L) MEM 3m 3 F *alwys last, lost tch 12th, t.o.* 3 0
1605 1/6 Dingley (R) RES 3m 13 GF *bhnd, dtchd last whn f 8th* F -

Horse & rider make a sorry looking combination 0

WISTINO b.g. 12 Neltino - Pensive Princess by Kinglet — A W K Merriam

1996 6(11),3(16),**U(-)**,1(21),**3(0)**,3(20)

26 26/1 Marks Tey (L) LAD 3m 8 GF *pllng, ld 2-6th, chsd ldrs aft, wknd apr 3 out* 4 14
125 9/2 Cottenham (R) LAD 3m 11 GF *chsd ldr 6th, disp 13th til aft 3 out, wknd apr last* 3 19
474 9/3 Southwell P' (L) LAD 3m 12 G *ld/disp til apr 3 out, onepcd* 3 17

Ladies winner 96; consistent but moderate & will struggle to find a chance at 13 18

WITCH DOCTOR b or br.g. 9 Senang Hati - Cognac Queen by Armagnac Monarch — R W Phizacklea

1996 P(0),P(0),P(0),3(0),F(-)

1193 20/4 Garthorpe (R) MDO 3m 9 GF *raced wd, t.o. 8th, blnd 11th, p.u. nxt* P 0
1204 26/4 Clifton On ' (L) MEM 3m 6 GS *cls up 2nd, rdn & wknd 9th, t.o. 12th* 5 0
1357 4/5 Dingley (R) MDO 3m 5 G *disp ld to 3rd, chsd ldr til ld apr 2 out, ran on gamely* 1 0
1542 18/5 Wolverhampt' (L) RES 3m 6 GS *cls up early, 3rd at 10th, 2nd at 13th, mstk nxt, sn t.o.* 4 0

Won a dire contest; tailed off every other completion; no chances now 0

WITH INTENT b.g. 5 Governor General - Don't Loiter by Town And Country — A J Cottrell

1270 27/4 Little Wind' (R) MDO 2 1/2m 10 GF *(fav) pllng, ld 3rd til blnd & u.r. 8th* U -

Too headstrong on debut & also pulled in hurdle after; may do better when settling 12

WITHOUT A PENNY (Irish) — I 548P

WITH RESPECT ch.g. 6 Respect - Satinanda by Leander — Mrs F T Walton

1173 20/4 Hexham Poin' (L) MDO 2 1/2m 9 GF *last, clmbd 2nd & p.u.* P 0
1514 17/5 Corbridge (R) MDO 3m 17 GS *rear, t.o. 7th, p.u. 12th* P 0

No signs yet 0

WODEHOUSE b.g. 12 Sunyboy - Flammula by Wrekin Rambler — M H L Stevens

827 31/3 Lockinge (L) MDO 3m 3 F *disp at slow pace til wknd aft 14th* 2 0

An old maiden 0

WOLFHILL LAD(IRE) b.g. 8 Phardante (FR) - Lady Dikler by Even Money — Michael A Johnson

275 22/2 Ampton (R) MDO 3m 10 G *(fav) ld 2-4th & 6th mstk & rmdr 15th, hdded & wknd appr 3 out* 4 0
317 1/3 Marks Tey (L) MDN 3m 13 G *prom,lft 2nd 9th,chsd wnnr aft,btn whn jmp lft last 3,tired* 2 0

Placed Irish Maidens 95; missed 96; beat subsequent winners 2nd start & chances should follow in 98 13

WOLFIE SMITH b.g. 7 Little Wolf - Gillie's Daughter by Hardiran — Mrs Jim Houldey

1996 P(0),3(14),P(0),4(10)

259 22/2 Newtown (L) MDN 3m 18 G *ld to 5th, wknd 10th, t.o. & p.u. 14th* P 0
570 16/3 Garnons (L) MDN 2 1/2m 14 G *(fav) prom in chsng grp, not qckn 3 out, kpt on flat* 3 10
1066 13/4 Maisemore P' (L) MDO 3m 9 GF *ld to 2nd, wll bhnd 7th, t.o. & p.u. 11th* P 0

Placed in 3 of 7 starts; does not stay little chance of a win 10

WOLFIES WONDER ch.m. 9 Little Wolf - Sparwood by Spartan General — A R Ford

635 22/3 Howick (L) RES 3m 7 GF *last til blnd & u.r. 9th* U -

Of no account 0

WOLF TONE b.g. 8 Little Wolf - Tina's Gold by Goldhill — M M Allen

1996 **13(NH),5(NH),5(NH),P(NH)**

346	2/3	Market Rase'	(L)	MDO	3m	10 GF	*(fav) hld up, last whn bdly hmpd & u.r. 6th*	U	-

Ex-novice hurdler; has some ability but vanished after brief debut; best watched initially 98 12

WOLVER'S PET(IRE) ch.g. 9 Tina's Pet - Wolviston by Wolverlife — R W J Willcox

1996 3(10),F(-),P(0)

190	15/2	Erw Lon	(L)	RES	3m	11 G	*prom, chsd wnr 14th-3 out, rdn & effrt agn last, no ext*	3	18
406	8/3	Llanfrynach	(R)	RES	3m	13 G	*(fav) trckd ldr, qcknd to ld 2 o ut, drew clr*	1	18
535	16/3	Erw Lon	(L)	CON	3m	12 GF	*sttld rear, prog 11th, chsd ldrs & hrd rdn 14th, no imp*	3	17
846	31/3	Lydstep	(L)	INT	3m	4 F	*trckd ldrs, ld 14th, unchal, easily*	1	21
1086	14/4	Southwell	(L)	HC	3m 110yds	11 G	*held up, hit 8th, hdwy next, chsd wnr 3 out, styd on same pace.*	3	21

Revived & improved 97; ran well all starts; should win Confined, at least, if same form 98; F-S 23

WONDER DAWN (Irish) — I 354P

WONDERFUL NEWS (Irish) — I 459P, I 545B

WOODBINESANDROSES (Irish) — I 33P, I 973, I 1511, I 215, , I 387, , I 4086

WOODEN MINSTREL ch.m. 11 Black Minstrel - In The Wood by Proverb — Mrs J A Morley

575	16/3	Garnons	(L)	RES	3m	12 G	*cls up, ev ch til not qckn apr 3 out*	2	15
753	29/3	Brampton Br'	(R)	RES	3m	9 GF	*cls 4th at 11th, ev ch 15th, not qckn, kpt on*	3	14
1483	11/5	Ottery St M'	(L)	RES	3m	15 G	*handy, prog 13th, 2nd nxt, jnd wnr 3 out, outpcd aft*	2	17
1519	17/5	Bratton Down	(L)	RES	3m	15 GS	*ld 2nd, disp 3rd-9th, mstk 11th, wknd, t.o. & p.u. 2 out*	P	0

Members winner 94; very lightly raced since; tries but hard to win at 12 15

WOODFIELD BOSS (Irish) — I 7P, I 526, I 74F, I 3172, I 3786, I 6104

WOODHAY HILL br.g. 12 Oats - Firs Park by Crozier — John Knowles

1996 7(14),U(-),**2(23)**

271	22/2	Ampton	(R)	CON	3m	15 G	*cls up to 4th, lst pl nxt, t.o. frm 12th*	11	0

Has never fulfilled initial promise & looks finished now 0

WOODLANDS BEAU(IRE) b.g. 5 Beau Sher - Never Intended by Sayyaf — David Briers

181	15/2	Larkhill	(R)	MDO	3m	17 G	*ref 3rd*	R	-
513	15/3	Larkhill	(R)	MDO	3m	10 GF	*trckd ldrs til lost plc aft 12th, no dang aft, kpt on*	4	0
871	31/3	Hackwood Pa'	(L)	MDO	3m	7 F	*cls up 1st cct, in tch whn f 14th*	F	-
1270	27/4	Little Wind'	(R)	MDO	2 1/2m	10 GF	*prom, ld 11th til apr 2 out, ev ch last, no ext flat*	2	13
1497	14/5	Cothelstone	(L)	MDO	3m	10 GF	*mstks,rear,prog 14th,clsd 3 out,chal nxt,ran on,just hld fin*	3	13

Improving gradually & just beaten in weak races; should have winning chances in 98 14

WOODLANDS LADY b.m. 11 Oats - Sand Lady by Sandford Lad — John Pointon

772	29/3	Dingley	(R)	MEM	3m	4 G	*t.o. last thrght*	2	0

No longer of any account 0

WOODLANDS POWER b.g. 9 Celtic Cone - Surely Right by Giolla Mear — Miss M J Preece

1996 **P(NH),7(NH),3(NH),6(NH),P(NH),9(NH),F(NH),4(NH),P(NH)**

60	1/2	Kingston Bl'	(L)	MDN	3m	17 GF	*prom to hlfwy, fdd*	6	0
212	16/2	Southwell P'	(L)	MDO	3m	14 GS	*cls up, rdn & outpcd 11th, t.o. & p.u. last*	P	0
881	1/4	Upton-On-Se'	(R)	MDN	3m	13 GF	*ld/disp til ld 13th, hdd 2 out, hrd rdn & onepcd*	3	12
1083	13/4	Guilsborough	(L)	MDN	3m	15 GF	*(fav) chsd ldrs, rdn 11th, kpt on aft, nvr able to chal*	4	10
1401	5/5	Ashorne	(R)	MDO	3m	15 G	*(bl) keen hld,prom,ld 12-14th,wkng whn blnd nxt,lft poor 3rd last*	3	0

A maiden after 28 races & shows no sign of ending the drought 12

WOODLAWN EXPRESS (Irish) — I 398P

WOODVIEW LADY (Irish) — I 2945, I 3555

WOODVILLE NATIVE (Irish) — I 195U, I 263F, I 384P, I 479F, I 5393, I 576P

WOODVILLE PRINCESS (Irish) — I 91P, I 318P

WOODY DARE b.g. 7 Phardante (FR) - Woodland Pit by Pitpan — P Needham

1996 P(0),3(14)

386	7/3	Ayr	(L)	HC	2m 5f 110yds	7 S	*ld, blnd and hdd 12th, chasing wnr when blunded badly 4 out, no ch after.*	2	14
584	17/3	Newcastle	(L)	HC	2 1/2m	11 GF	*trckd ldrs, ld 4 out, styd on well from 2 out.*	1	19

Went from maiden pointer to H/Chase winner in one bound; poor race & hard to place in 98 if fit 19

WOODY WILL b.g. 11 Mandalus - Woodville Grove by Harwell — Mrs Emma Coveney

302	1/3	Parham	(R)	CON	3m	14 G	*rear, in tch to hlfwy, p.u. aft 15th*	P	0
577	16/3	Detling	(L)	CON	3m	18 F	*towrds rear, some hdwy 14th, 5th 4 out, wknd nxt*	6	10
966	6/4	Penshurst	(L)	CON	3m	7 F	*alwys cls up, chal 3 out, ld last, ran on wll*	1	16

1128	19/4	Penshurst	(L)	LAD	3m	8	GF	*(Jt fav) wll in tch, 4th frm 12th, rdn & styd on 2 out, tk 2nd flat*	2	16
1284	29/4	Huntingdon	(R)	HC	3m	6	G	*in tch to 12th, soon wknd, t.o. 3 out.*	5	0
1445	10/5	Peper Harow	(L)	LAD	3m	6	GF	*prssd ldr, ld 6th-3 out, kpt on wll, cllpsd & died aft race*	2	18

Dead 15

WOOLY TOWN b.m. 10 Town And Country - Something Slinky by Chingnu — John Binding

1996 P(0),P(0)

641	22/3	Howick	(L)	MDN	3m	9	GF	*ld to 6th, wknd & p.u. 12th*	P	0
717	29/3	Llanvapley	(L)	RES	3m	13	GF	*alwys rear, p.u. 3 out*	P	0
1136	19/4	Bonvilston	(R)	MDO	3m	15	G	*(bl) rear til p.u. 12th*	P	0
1561	24/5	Bassaleg	(R)	MDO	3m	9	G	*t.o. 6th, p.u. nxt*	P	0

Of no account 0

WORLD O GOOD (Irish) — I 431F

WORLESTON FARRIER b.g. 9 Looking Glass - Madame Serenity by What A Man — D Williams

1996 2(0),3(17),4(10),1(18),1(20)

938	6/4	Tabley	(R)	OPE	3m	9	G	*tubed,t.d.e.,ld to 6th,lost plcd nxt,no ch 3 out, p.u. last*	P	0
1175	20/4	Sandon	(L)	CON	3m	8	GF	*ld to 10th, ev ch til outpcd frm 2 out*	3	15
1300	3/5	Weston Park	(L)	CON	3m	8	G	*chsd ldr, ld 11th til aft 2 out, wknd apr last*	4	10
1545	24/5	Cartmel	(L)	HC	3 1/4m	14	G	*went to post early, cl up, hit 8th, ld 12th, clr after last till tired and hdd entering straight, no ext.*	3	19

Dual winner 96; below form 97 till fair run in weak H/Chase; stays; may win Confined 98; G/F-S 19

WORTAGAMBLE (Irish) — I 158F, I 171P, I 551P

WORTHY SPARK b.g. 12 Lighter - Sardan by Lauso — A J Balmer

1996 F(-),1(22),1(19),**2(20)**,3(16)

1168	20/4	Hexham Poin'	(L)	CON	3m	3	GF	*(fav) j.w. ld til jnd 16th, wknd nxt, rallied 2 out, no ext last*	3	16
1405	5/5	Witton Cast'	(R)	CON	3m	10	GS	*prom, ld 5th til disp 4 out, hdd & not qckn apr last*	3	20

Dual winner 96; goes well fresh; late to appear 97; can win if fit 98; G/F-S again; G/F-S. 19

WORTHY WAY b.g. 8 Fort Nayef - Worthy Heiress by Richboy — R J Kyle

342	1/3	Corbridge	(R)	MDO	3m	12	G	*rear, prog 9th going wll, ld 3 out, hdd & wknd last*	4	11
612	22/3	Friars Haugh	(L)	MDN	3m	14	GF	*(fav) alwys bhnd*	7	0

Promise on debut but only beaten one other finisher to date; may do better 98 12

WOTAMONA b.m. 9 Another Realm - Meadow Wood by Meadow Court — Mrs Clare Alderton

223	16/2	Heythrop	(R)	RES	3m	19	G	*in tch to 12th, wknd & p.u. 15th*	P	0
374	2/3	Mollington	(R)	MDN	3m	14	G	*prom, ld 12th, rdn & prssd 2 out, hld on gamely flat*	1	15
760	29/3	Kimble	(L)	RES	3m	7	GF	*chsd ldrs, 4th & not rch ldrs fin cct*	3	14
1081	13/4	Guilsborough	(L)	RES	3m	13	GF	*mid-div, outpcd 16th, styd on wll agn frm 2 out*	3	13

Missed 96; improved to win weak Maiden; stays & may find weak Restricted 98 16

WOT NO CASH gr.g. 5 Ballacashtal (CAN) - Madame Non by My Swanee — R C Harper

218	16/2	Heythrop	(R)	INT	3m	21	G	*alwys rear, t.o. & p.u. 10th*	P	0
369	2/3	Mollington	(R)	MEM	3m	13	G	*alwys bhnd, t.o. & p.u. 11th*	P	0
761	29/3	Kimble	(L)	MDO	3m	12	GF	*sn rear, 9th hlfwy, bhnd & p.u. 16th*	P	0
1082	13/4	Guilsborough	(L)	MDN	3m	14	GF	*ld to 3rd, in tch to 15th, wknd & p.u. 3 out*	P	0

No real signs yet but time on his side 0

WREKIN HILL b.g. 15 Duky - Cummin Hill by Wrekin Rambler — Mrs J V Wilkinson

1996 5(0),3(19),1(14),2(17),R(-),3(17),**4(15),3(15)**

17	25/1	Badbury Rin'	(L)	CON	3m	9	GF	*bhnd frm 4th, t.o. 11th*	5	0
39	1/2	Larkhill	(R)	CON	3m	6	GF	*mstks, chsd ldr to 10th, wknd 12th, t.o.*	6	0
396	8/3	Barbury Cas'	(L)	CON	3m	9	G	*sn wll bhnd, t.o. frm 9th*	5	0
744	29/3	Barbury Cas'	(L)	LAD	3m	2	F	*trckd wnr, effrt 14th, wknd nxt*	2	10
920	5/4	Larkhill	(R)	MXO	4m	4	F	*alwys 3rd, t.o. whn ref 3 out*	R	-

Looks ready for retirement now 0

WRENBURY FARMER ch.g. 7 Say Primula - Willow Path by Farm Walk — B Evans

1996 R(-),5(0),P(0)

700	29/3	Upper Sapey	(R)	MEM	3m	8	GF	*4th/5th til hlfwy, efft frm 12th,lft 3rd 3 out,outpcd run in*	4D	0
1065	13/4	Maisemore P'	(L)	MDO	3m	13	GF	*mid-div, mstk 6th, t.o. 12th, p.u. nxt*	P	0

Well-beaten when completing & much more needed 0

WRITE THE MUSIC b.g. 16 Riboboy (USA) - Zither by Vienna — I P Crane

1996 P(0),2(18),U(-),3D(18),3(11),1(13)

1188	20/4	Garthorpe	(R)	OPE	3m	9	GF	*(bl) sn bhnd, t.o. 4th, blnd & u.r. 9th*	U	-

Members winner 96 but must be finished now 0

WUNWABBITWUN (Irish) — **I** 96[P], **I** 150[P], **I** 218, , **I** 339[P], **I** 406[P]

WYNDAMS LAD(IRE) ch.g. 6 Phardante (FR) - Some Gale by Strong Gale — R J Cotton

641	22/3	Howick	(L)	MDN	3m	9	GF	*mid-div, b.d. 6th*	B	-
719	29/3	Llanvapley	(L)	MDN	3m	14	GF	*towrds rear, p.u. 3 out*	P	0
1527	17/5	Bredwardine	(R)	MDO	3m	13	G	*in tch whn ran out 8th*	r	-

Not yet of any account 0

YARRON KING b.g. 11 Push On - Baming by Barbin — G A Fynn

1996 P(0),3(0),5(0)

407	8/3	Llanfrynach	(R)	MDN	3m	11	G	*last pair early, late prog, nrst fin*	3	0
641	22/3	Howick	(L)	MDN	3m	9	GF	*(fav) hld up mid-div, prog to ld 15th, styd on*	1	11
901	5/4	Howick	(L)	RES	3m	6	F	*hld up last, wll bhnd 6th, sn t.o., tk remote 3rd post*	3	0
1135	19/4	Bonvilston	(R)	RES	3m	14	G	*alwys rear*	7	0
1322	3/5	Bonvilston	(R)	RES	3m	9	G	*rear, some late prog, no dang, fin 4th, plcd 3rd*	3	0
1556	24/5	Bassaleg	(R)	RES	3m	13	G	*p.u. aft 3rd, dsmntd*	P	0

Found a terrible race; ungenuine & no chance of a Restricted win 10

YASGOURRA(IRE) ch.f. 6 Yashgan - Kangourra — Paul Morris

1996 **13(NH)**

327	1/3	Eaton Hall	(R)	MDN	3m	11	GS	*alwys towrds rear, p.u. 13th*	P	0
470	8/3	Eyton-On-Se'	(L)	MDN	2 1/2m	12	G	*prom early, losng tch whn p.u. 4 out*	P	0
723	29/3	Sandon	(L)	MDO	3m	6	GF	*mostly last pair, f 4 out, rmntd*	3	0

No signs of ability yet 0

YENOORA(IRE) b.g. 8 Ahonoora - Beijing (USA) by Northjet — Mrs Sue Bell

1996 P(0),P(0),F(-),U(-),P(0),P(0),F(-)

560	16/3	Lanark	(R)	CON	3m	8	GS	*(bl) lost tch by 9th, p.u. aft nxt*	P	0
611	22/3	Friars Haugh	(L)	CON	3m	11	GF	*alwys bhnd*	8	0
732	29/3	Alnwick	(L)	CON	3m	6	F	*alwys last, 15l down 9th, t.o. final m*	4	0
946	6/4	Friars Haugh	(L)	OPE	3m	5	GF	*alwys last, t.o.*	4	0
993	12/4	Tranwell	(L)	OPE	3m	5	F	*rear div 1st ctt, 4th 3 out, styd on poor 3rd run in*	3	10
1103	19/4	Hornby Cast'	(L)	OPE	3m	5	G	*rear, mstk 11th, lost tch nxt, t.o. & p.u. last*	P	0

Flat winner 92; failed to finish 96 but at least getting round now 0

YEOMAN FARMER br.g. 13 Trombone - Ballykeel Owen by Master Owen — Miss P Wood

1996 P(0),3(12),3(16),3(18),6(14),5(14),3(16)

281	23/2	Charing	(L)	OPE	3m	12	G	*hld up, nvr rchd ldrs*	6	12
577	16/3	Detling	(L)	CON	3m	18	F	*rear thruout, in tch to 14th*	8	0
683	29/3	Charing	(L)	OPE	3m	5	F	*just ld 2nd-5th, chal 3 out, wknd last*	2	17
966	6/4	Penshurst	(L)	CON	3m	7	F	*(fav) hld up, drvn up to chal apr last, hld flat*	2	15
1126	19/4	Penshurst	(L)	CON	3m	6	GF	*hld up, prog to 3rd at 13th, rdn & no imp frm 4 out*	3	12
1447	10/5	Peper Harow	(L)	CON	3m	6	GF	*alwys rear, jmpd slwly 3rd, t.o. last at 9th, p.u. 12th*	P	0

Moderate pointer; declining now; lost last 15 & unlikely to break sequence 14

YES BOSS (Irish) — **I** 37[P], **I** 61[1], **I** 116[1]

YODELLER BILL ch.g. 6 Nicholas Bill - Over The Mountain by Over The River (FR) — M J Brown

115	9/2	Wetherby Po'	(L)	MDO	3m	8	GF	*twrds rear whn ran out 4th*	r	-
169	15/2	Witton Cast'	(R)	MDO	3m	5	F	*hld up in tch, prog to chal 2 out, unable qckn*	2	0
269	22/2	Duncombe Pa'	(R)	MDO	3m	16	G	*prom, wnt 2nd 10th, ev ch apr last, not qckn*	2	13
1073	13/4	Whitwell-On'	(R)	MDO	2 1/2m 88yds	17	G	*mid-div, prog 7th, wknd 3 out, wll bhnd whn p.u. last*	P	0

Beaten by decent prospect when 2nd & should have prospects if fit in 98 14

YOGI'S MISTRESS b.m. 6 Silly Prices - Colishine by Coliseum — Mrs S Frank

116	9/2	Wetherby Po'	(L)	MDO	3m	14	GF	*mid-div, jmpd slwly 4th, wknd 10th, t.o. & p.u. nxt*	P	0
169	15/2	Witton Cast'	(R)	MDO	3m	5	F	*chsd ldrs, slw jmp & lost ground 14th, wknd, t.o. & p.u.last*	P	0
428	8/3	Charm Park	(L)	MDO	3m	10	GF	*rear, prog to chsng grp 9th, wknd 3 out*	5	0
615	22/3	Hutton Rudby	(L)	MEM	3m	8	GF	*rear,efft 11th,losng tch & rdr lost iron,p.u. aft 15th*	P	0
1105	19/4	Hornby Cast'	(L)	MDO	3m	11	G	*prom til wknd qckly 11th, ref 13th*	R	-

Short of stamina at present 0

YOHANNA (Irish) — **I** 393[P]

YORKSHIRE POP br.m. 9 Politico (USA) - Record Mark by Record Run — Miss N J Rudge

878	1/4	Upton-On-Se'	(R)	XX	3m	11	GF	*last whn u.r. 1st*	U	-
1403	5/5	Ashorne	(R)	CON	3m	14	G	*ld til s.u. bnd apr 3rd*	S	-
1526	17/5	Bredwardine	(R)	RES	3m	13	G	*pllng, ld aft 2nd-9th, wknd rpdly, p.u. 12th*	P	0

No longer of any account 0

YOU BE KING b.g. 6 Kinglet - Right You Be by Sunyboy — Miss Jill Wormall

479	9/3	Southwell P'	(L)	MDO 3m	15	G	*u.r. 1st*	U	-
1083	13/4	Guilsborough	(L)	MDN 3m	15	GF	*rear whn mstk 9th, prog 11th, ev ch 16th, outpcd nxt, kpt on*	3	14
1262	27/4	Southwell P'	(L)	MDO 3m	15	G	*(fav) ld til disp 4th,hdd 3 out,lft disp nxt,hdd & no ex apr last*	2	12

Good enough debut season; stays; should find a race in 98 15

YOUCAT(IRE) b.g. 8 Yashgan - Vera Van Fleet by Cracksman — I Marsh

1996 **F(NH)**

62	1/2	Horseheath	(R)	CON 3m	5	GF	*in tch, chsd ldr brfly 11th, sn strgglng, btn whn mstk 3 out*	3	13
441	8/3	Higham	(L)	INT 3m	7	G	*ld 3rd, made rest til hdd nr fin*	2	19
769	29/3	Dingley	(R)	CON 3m	14	G	*prog 6 out, 5th 4 out, ran on well, nrst fin*	3	18
926	6/4	Garthorpe	(R)	OPE 3m	10	GF	*ld at gd pace to 12th, wknd nxt, kpt on frm 2 out*	4	14
1117	19/4	Higham	(L)	CON 3m	5	GF	*(Jt fav) cls up, disp 8th til ld 11th, qcknd clr 2 out, ran on wll*	1	20
1306	3/5	Cottenham	(R)	INT 3m	4	F	*(fav) jmpd slwly & nvr going, last frm 4th, t.o. & p.u. 13th*	P	0

Dual Irish pointing winner 96; consistent; novice-ridden; prefers give & may do better if wet in 98 21

YOU'LLBESUPRISED (Irish) — **I** 310[P]

YOUNG BEBE (Irish) — **I** 61[P], **I** 97[U], **I** 188[3], **I** 283[P], **I** 351[F]

YOUNG BLOSSOM (Irish) — **I** 223[P], **I** 287[P]

YOUNG BRAVE b.g. 11 Warpath - Mekhala by Menelek — David Young

1996 1(29),1(28),**1(24)**,**1(30)**

180	15/2	Larkhill	(R)	MXO 3m	6	G	*hld up last, losng tch & rmndr 11th, nvr nr ldrs*	3	15
385	6/3	Wincanton	(R)	HC 3m 1f 110yds	6	G	*in tch, hdwy 13th, chsd ldrs and mstk 17th, weakening when blnd 2 out.*	3	18
1087	16/4	Cheltenham	(L)	HC 3 1/4m 110yds	8	GF	*hd up, prog 17th, weakening when hit 3 out.*	5	19
1290	30/4	Cheltenham	(L)	HC 4m 1f	10	GF	*waited with, prog going easily 18th, trckd lding pair 22nd, ch 4 out, rdn and one pace after.*	3	22

Useful H/Chaser 96; well below form 97; stays 4m; best watched at 12 initially; G/S-F 22

YOUNG HERBERT(IRE) b.g. 8 Phardante (FR) - Revenue Reserve by Proverb — R W Pincombe

315	1/3	Clyst St Ma'	(L)	MDN 3m	5	HY	*fat, sn bhnd, t.o. & p.u. 13th*	P	0
789	31/3	Bishopsleigh	(R)	MEM 3m	5	G	*sttld rear, lost tch 14th, blnd 4 out, no ch aft*	4	0
1260	27/4	Black Fores'	(R)	MDO 3m	12	F	*alwys bhnd, fin 7th*	0	0

Last when completing (behind a remounter) & shows nothing 0

YOUNG INDIA br.m. 10 Indian King (USA) - Marfisa by Green God — Mrs G Howfield

714	29/3	Llanvapley	(L)	CON 3m	15	GF	*last til p.u. 13th*	P	0
903	5/4	Howick	(L)	CON 3m	6	F	*mstks, alwys rear, t.o. & p.u. 14th*	P	0
1007	12/4	St Hilary	(R)	OPE 3m	10	GF	*s.s. last til p.u. 15th*	P	0
1318	3/5	Bonvilston	(R)	MEM 3m	9	G	*rear til p.u. 13th*	P	0

Flat winner 89; no prospects in points 0

YOUNG MOSS b.g. 11 Le Moss - Young Ash Linn by Deep Run — Mrs C Lawson-Croome

1996 P(0),5(13),6(0),4(11)

35	26/1	Alnwick	(L)	CON 3m	10	G	*rear whn blnd 8th, t.o. 13th*	9	0
130	9/2	Alnwick	(L)	INT 3m	7	G	*jmpd rght, cls up to 2nd, sn bhnd, t.o. & p.u. 9th*	P	0

Maiden winner 95; struggling since & finished early 97; can only be watched 0

YOUNG NIMROD b.g. 10 Boreen (FR) - Noelbonne Femme by Bonne Noel — G J D Wragg

194	15/2	Higham	(L)	OPE 3m	12	G	*hld up, plld up to ldrs 10th, ld 16th-nxt, sn btn*	2	20
378	4/3	Leicester	(R)	HC 2 1/2m 110yds	6	G	*held up, effort apr 3 out, soon wknd.*	5	16
603	22/3	Parham	(R)	OPE 3m	2	F	*(fav) ld, clr 5th, unchal*	1	20
890	4/4	Aintree	(L)	HC 2 3/4m	14	G	*in tch, chsd ldr from hfwy, drew level 3 out, ld briefly next, driven and wknd run-in.*	5	20
1506	16/5	Folkestone	(R)	HC 2m 5f	8	G	*waited with, 6th when u.r. 5th.*	U	-

Ex-Irish winning pointer-H/Chaser; useful but needs better handling; best below 3m 23

YOUNG PARSON b.g. 11 The Parson - Dadooronron by Deep Run — T D Marlow

1996 5(0)

204	15/2	Weston Park	(L)	RES 3m	13	G	*mid-div whn u.r. 8th*	U	-
346	2/3	Market Rase'	(L)	MDO 3m	10	GF	*prom, lft 2nd 6th, outpcd by wnr apr 14th*	2	0
670	23/3	Eaton Hall	(R)	RES 3m	15	GF	*mid-div, prog 10th, trckd ldr til ld 3 out, ran on wll flat*	1	18
937	6/4	Tabley	(R)	CON 3m	10	G	*bhnd, rddn 12th, 5th & no ch whn u.r. 15th*	U	-
1235	26/4	Brampton Br'	(R)	INT 3m	10	G	*12l 6th at 8th, wkng whn blkd & f 14th*	F	-

Won competitive Restricted to break duck at 11; novice ridden; hard to predict in 98 17

YOUNG SPRING gr.m. 5 Buckley - Another Spring by Town Crier — C C Trietline

754	29/3	Brampton Br'	(R)	MDN 3m	9	GF	*schoold in rear, p.u. 11th*	P	0
1527	17/5	Bredwardine	(R)	MDO 3m	13	G	*ran wd bend apr 3rd & p.u., dsmntd*	P	0

1578 26/5 Chaddesley ' (L) MDO 3m 7 F *jmpd slwy 2nd, nrly ref 3rd & u.r. aft* U -

Unpromising start **0**

YOUR OPINION gr.g. 11 Cut Above - Dance Mistress by Javelot Mrs S M Walters

1996 P(0)

1061 13/4 Maisemore P' (L) RES 3m 12 GF *mid-div, lost tch 13th, p.u. 15th, dsmntd* P 0
1210 26/4 Woodford (L) RES 3m 14 G *prom, 3rd & rdn apr 3 out, wknd* 6 10
1502 16/5 Folkestone (R) HC 2m 5f 10 G *prom, cl 4th when blnd and u.r. 10th.* U -

Lightly raced now & unlikely to achieve anything at 12 .... **11**

YOU SAID IT (Irish) — I 120P, I 180P, I 254[5], I 331[1], I 466P

YQUEM(IRE) ch.g. 7 Henbit (USA) - Silent Run by Deep Run J J Boulter

1996 1(16),2(17)

1296 3/5 Hereford (R) HC 2m 3f 11 G *held up, hdwy 6th, ld 3 out, rdn when left clr last.* 1 24
1488 12/5 Towcester (R) HC 2m 110yds 16 GS *(fav) in tch till wknd quickly apr 2 out.* 5 16

Maiden winner 96; lightly raced; won modest H/Chase; best under 3m; summer jumping **23**

YUKON GALE(IRE) br.g. 9 Strong Gale - Lou by Arctic Chevalier J Aled Griffiths

1996 F(-),P(0)

83 2/2 Wolverhampt' (L) RES 3m 8 GS *hld up, mstk 4th, prog nxt, hrd rdn & wknd 16th, p.u. 3 out* P 0
203 15/2 Weston Park (L) RES 3m 11 G *w.w. prog 11th, disp 12th-3 out, rdn & not qckn nxt* 2 19
670 23/3 Eaton Hall (R) RES 3m 15 GF *(fav) w.w. prog 5 out, not qckn nxt, nvr able to chal* 4 16
852 31/3 Eyton-On-Se' (L) RES 3m 11 GF *(fav) ld to 2nd, cls up, ld 3 out, not qckn frm 2 out* 2 12
1178 20/4 Sandon (L) XX 3m 6 GF *alwys prom, ld 11th til hdd last, no ext* 2 15
1303 3/5 Weston Park (L) RES 3m 6 G *f heavily 1st* F -

Finds little & frustrating now; beaten by good horses & may find a chance in 98 .... **16**

ZAFFARAN RUN (Irish) — I 91[2], I 159[2], I 204[1]

ZAFFIELD (Irish) — I 28P, I 114[2]

ZAM BEE br.g. 11 Zambrano - Brown Bee III by Marcus Superbus Mrs A Bell

1996 1(21),0D(22),1(25),2(24),2(24),**2(21),2(26),5(23)**

75 2/2 Market Rase' (L) CON 3m 10 GF *(fav) ld 3rd, clr 6th, hdd 2 out, rld last, kept on flat* 2 24
216 16/2 Southwell P' (L) OPE 3m 12 GS *(fav) prom in chsng grp, ev ch 4 out, onepcd* 3 22

Decent pointer 96 but season over in a fortnight 97; stays; jumps; one paced; win if fit at 12 .... **22**

ZAMBRANO(USA) ch.g. 5 Strawberry Road (AUS) - Cloudy Day Sunny D L Williams

182 15/2 Larkhill (R) MDO 3m 12 G *in tch, chsd ldr 6th, disp 15th, lft in ld 2 out,sn hdd,wknd* 2 13
367 2/3 Garnons (L) MDO 2 1/2m 9 GS *(fav) trckd ldrs, prog 11th, ld apr last, pshd out* 1 16
524 15/3 Cothelstone (L) RES 3m 10 GS *(fav) crashd thro' wing 1st* r -
635 22/3 Howick (L) RES 3m 7 GF *(fav) hld up mid-div, steady prog 13th, ld 2 out, rdn clr* 1 16
930 6/4 Charlton Ho' (L) INT 3m 8 G *4s-2s, hld up, mstk 9th, outpcd frm 13th, effrt 3 out,no imp* 4 15
1147 19/4 Chaddesley ' (L) OPE 3m 7 GF *(vis) mstk 3rd,trckd ldrs, went 2nd 16th,ev ch 2 out,ran on onepcd* 2 24

Placed Irish Flat; much improved last start with visor; win fair races 98 if reproducing **24**

ZANAGALE (Irish) — I 181, , I 265[5], I 348, , I 608[6]

ZARANTE (Irish) — I 76P, I 84, , I 192F, I 262P

ZAUDANTE(IRE) ch.m. 6 Phardante (FR) - Zauditu by Menelek R M Phillips

436 8/3 Upton-On-Se' (R) MDO 3m 17 G *in tch to 10th, eased & p.u. 12th* P 0
706 29/3 Upper Sapey (R) MDO 3m 15 GF *lost tch wth ldrs by 12th, p.u. 15th* P 0
1016 12/4 Bitterley (L) MDO 3m 14 GF *alwys rear, lsng tch whn f 12th* F -

Schooling so far **0**

ZEROSE br.m. 5 Zero Watt (USA) - Bill's Daughter by Nicholas Bill J Cornforth

80 2/2 Market Rase' (L) MDO 2m 5f 9 GF *rr, t.o. 9th, p.u. last, cont'd* 3 0
210 16/2 Southwell P' (L) MDO 3m 15 GS *alwys bhnd, last frm 9th til p.u. 12th* P 0
428 8/3 Charm Park (L) MDO 3m 10 GF *prom in chsng grp, disp remt 3rd 8th, fddng whn u.r. 11th* U -

No signs of ability yet **0**

ZIEG (Irish) — I 372P

ZILFI(USA) b.g. 7 Lyphard (USA) - Over Your Shoulder (USA) by Graustark Mrs L Worley

1996 P(0),P(0),r(-),r(-)

302 1/3 Parham (R) CON 3m 14 G *alwys wll in rear, t.o. & p.u. 13th* P 0
681 29/3 Charing (L) MEM 3m 5 F *prom, just ld whn ran out bnd bfr 8th* r -

Flat winner; no go in points **0**

ZINZAN BANK (Irish) — I 315P, I 417P

ZOBEJO b.g. 5 Hallgate - Hydrangea by Warpath — Tony Fawcett

1996 **8(NH),7(NH),11(NH)**

427	8/3	Charm Park	(L)	MDO 3m	10	GF	*mid-div, prog 4th 4 out, styd on frm 2 out*	2	0
860	31/3	Charm Park	(L)	MDO 3m	12	F	*(fav) rear, prog 12th, 3rd nxt, fdng whn ref 15th*	R	-

No ability under Rules; promise on debut but flopped after; young enough to do better 12

ZODIAC PRINCE b.g. 5 Scorpio (FR) - Pendle Princess by Broxted — R H Philips

478	9/3	Southwell P'	(L)	MDO 3m	17	G	*mid-div, blnd 2nd & 3rd, in tch whn f 15th*	F	-
853	31/3	Eyton-On-Se'	(L)	MDO 3m	13	GF	*rear early, ran on frm 13th, nrst fin*	2	10
1151	19/4	Chaddesley '	(L)	MDO 3m	5	GF	*(fav) trckd ldr, lft in ld 6th, clr 2 out, blnd last*	1	13

Won weak race but looks the part & should have more chances in 98 16

ZOES PET ch.m. 6 Cisto (FR) - Pat's Pet by Autre Prince — N J Pewter

30	26/1	Marks Tey	(L)	MDN 3m	9	GF	*mstk 2nd, in tch til u.r. 8th*	U	-
128	9/2	Cottenham	(R)	MDO 3m	10	GF	*rcd wd,pllng,chsd ldr 11th,hld whn lft in ld 2 out,ran on*	1	12
274	22/2	Ampton	(R)	RES 3m	10	G	*cls up, disp ld 3-6th, 4th & mstk 17th, wll btn nxt*	4	11
500	15/3	Ampton	(R)	LAD 3m	4	GF	*prom, chsd wnr 15th, outpcd aft 3 out, lst 2nd flat*	3	14
1114	19/4	Higham	(L)	RES 3m	5	GF	*4th & in tch til outpcd aft 11th, last 13th, t.o. 3 out*	5	0

Fortunate winner; safe enough but well beaten after & unlikely to win Restricted 13

ZOFLO b.m. 9 Zambrano - Aunt Bertha by Blandford Lad — Mrs F J Drysdale

1996 P(0),7(0),P(0),4(0),P(0)

234	22/2	Friars Haugh	(L)	MDO 3m	15	G	*ld to 5th, cls up whn p.u. 8th*	P	0

Of no account 0

ZOOM b.m. 6 Zambrano - Triscombe Stone by Pharaoh Hophra — Mrs E Eames

1270	27/4	Little Wind'	(R)	MDO 2 1/2m	10	GF	*schoold in last, t.o. 5th, p.u. 9th*	P	0

A quiet introduction 0

STATISTICAL LEADERS 1997

LEADING HUNTER CHASE WINNERS

Slievenamon Mist	4
Trifast Lad	3
Miss Millbrook	3
My Nominee	3
The Malakarma	3
Bitofamixup (IRE)	3
Mr Boston	3
Jigtime	3
Howayman	2
Rusty Bridge	2
Greenmount Lad (IRE)	2
Glen Oak	2
Cab On Target	2
Teaplanter	2
Double Silk	2
Struggles Glory (IRE)	2
Cumberland Blues (IRE)	2
Dromin Leader	2
Orchestral Suite (IRE)	2
Denim Blue	2
Blue Cheek	2
Secret Bay	2
Tinotops	2
Phar Too Touchy	2
Not My Line (IRE)	2
Front Cover	2
Nodform Wonder	2
King Torus (IRE)	2
Earthmover (IRE)	2
Celtic Abbey	2

LEADING HUNTER CHASE RIDERS

P Hacking	8
S Swiers	7
B Pollock	6
J Jukes	6
R Burton	5
A Sansome	4
E Williams	4
M Bradburne	4
D S Jones	3
A Parker	3
J M Pritchard	3
R Thornton	3
C Vigors	3
W Wales	3
N Harris	3
R Ford	2
J Tizzard	2
Chris Wilson	2
P Cornforth	2
L Jefford	2
D C Robinson	2
D Alers-Hankey	2
F Hutsby	2
T Mitchell	2
N Bradley	2
R Bevis	2
L Baker	2

P-T-P LEADING GENTLEMEN RIDERS

Julian Pritchard	37
T Mitchell	33
J Jukes	28
E Williams	25
N Harris	22
A Dalton	20
S Sporborg	20
J Tizzard	19
L Jefford	14
A Farrant	14
D S Jones	13
A Crow	13
S Walker	13
S Swiers	12
N Wilson	12
M Rimell	12
R Morgan	10

P-T-P LEADING LADY RIDERS

Miss S Vickery	30
Miss P Jones	26
Miss A Dare	21
Miss P Curling	18
Mrs F Needham	13
Miss A Goschen	12
Mrs C Ford	12
Miss J Cumings	11
Miss L Blackford	10
Miss P Robson	9
Miss S Young	9
Miss P Gundry	8
Mrs J Dawson	7
Miss T Cave	7
Miss A Deniel	6
Mrs L Gibbon	6
Miss D Laidlaw	5
Mrs S Grant	5
Mrs V Jackson	5
Miss S Gladders	5
Miss L Rowe	5

LEADING P-T-P HORSES

Butler John (IRE)	10
Grimley Gale (IRE)	9
Touch 'N' Pass	7
St Gregory	6
Just Charlie	6
Peanuts Pet	5
Over The Edge	5
Salmon Mead (IRE)	5
Arctic Chill (IRE)	5
Hornblower	5
Doubting Donna	5
Earthmover (IRE)	5
Strong Chairman (IRE)	5
Rip Van Winkle	5
Gunner Boon	4
Parditino	4
Qualitair Memory (IRE)	4
Sams Heritage	4
Lets Twist Again (IRE)	4
Passing Fair	4
Magnolia Man	4
King Torus (IRE)	4
Shoon Wind	4
Earl Boon	4
Druid's Lodge	4
Avril Showers	4
Butofanatter	4
Carrick Lanes	4
Fiscal Policy	4
Sister Seven (IRE)	4
Secret Four	4

Desert Waltz (IRE)	4
Rolier (IRE)	4
Osgathorpe	4
Fosbury	4
The Bounder	4
Cardinal Richelieu	4
Radio Days (IRE)	4
Lucky Christopher	4

LEADING P-T-P AND HUNTER CHASE SIRES

Strong Gale (IRE)	65
Roselier (FR)	26
The Parson	26
Idiot's Delight	23
Le Bavard (FR)	23
Cruise Missile	21
Le Moss (IRE)	20
Mister Lord	20
Baron Blakeney	19
Scallywag	18
Carlingford Castle (IRE)	17
Lancastrian (IRE)	17
Mandalus	17
Sunyboy	17
Oats (IRE)	16
Over The River (FR)	16
Nearly A Hand	15
Torus	15
Buckskin (FR)	14
Callernish	14
Celtic Cone	14
Deep Run	14
Neltino	14
Orchestra	14
Glenstal (USA)	13
True Song	13
Uncle Pokey	13
Furry Glen	12
Green Shoon	12
Henbit (USA)	12
Meadowbrook	12
St. Columbus	12

AMATEUR RIDERS

The table below gives the weights of amateur riders, their number of winners of Hunter chases and Point-to-Points.
The criterion for inclusion is at least one winner in a Hunter chase or Point-to-Point.
All riders with weights had licences to ride under Rules.

	Weight	Hunter Chases	P-t-P
Mrs P Adams		0	2
D Alers-Hankey	10 12	3	2
E Andrewes		0	1
S R Andrews	11 7	1	9
Miss A Armitage	8 4	0	2
R Armson	10 7	0	3
R Atkinson		0	4
E Babington	9 7	0	1
E Bailey		0	1
A Baillie		0	1
Miss K Baily		0	2
J Baimbridge		0	2
G Baines	9 7	1	0
L Baker	9 0	2	0
Mrs R Baldwin		0	1
G Barfoot-Saunt	10 9	0	4
A Barlow		0	2
C Barlow	10 12	0	4
D Barlow	11 5	0	6
M Barnard		0	1
Miss H Barnard		0	1
J Barnes		0	2
Miss F Barnes	9 10	0	1
R Barrett	9 4	0	2
Mrs S Barrow		0	1
Miss R Barrow		0	1
T Barry	10 5	0	1
Miss B Barton		0	1
M Batters	11 7	0	2
Miss S Baxter		0	1
A Bealby		0	2
A Beedles	10 5	0	5
N Bell		0	1
C Bennett		0	2
I Bennett		0	2
R Bevis	10 0	2	5
J Billinge		0	1
Mrs S Bingham		0	1
S Blackwell	10 5	0	2
Miss L Blackford	10 9	2	10
N Bloom	11 2	0	7
A Bonson		0	2
J Borradaile		0	1
Miss A Bowie	9 7	0	4
M Bradburne	10 7	4	4
N Bradley	9 7	2	0

	Weight	Hunter Chases	P-t-P
F Brennan	10 2	0	4
Miss K Bridge		0	1
Miss H Brookshaw		1	1
Miss C Bryan		0	1
P Bull	10 6	0	5
W Burnell	10 0	0	3
R Burton	10 2	5	8
S Bush	11 0	0	1
J Byrne		0	2
R Cambray		0	1
J Carmichael		0	1
Miss T Cave	9 7	0	7
G Chanter		0	1
A Charles-Jones	10 1	1	3
S Charlton		0	2
M Chatterton		0	1
J Chilton		0	1
Miss G Chown		0	1
Miss R Clark	9 7	0	1
D Coates		0	1
S Cobden		0	1
A Coe	10 7	0	6
T Cole		0	1
S Coltherd		0	1
J Connell		0	2
Miss P Cooper		0	1
J Cornes	11 2	0	1
P Cornforth		2	4
K Cousins		0	1
Mrs E Coveney		0	2
S Cowell	11 0	0	4
M Cowley	10 9	1	1
P Cowley		0	1
T Cox		0	1
P Craggs	10 4	0	7
Miss K Crank		0	1
J Creighton	10 7	0	3
A Crow	10 11	0	13
Miss J Cumings	10 0	0	11
C Cundall		0	1
Miss P Curling	10 7	0	18
A Dalton	11 0	0	20
Miss A Dare	10 0	0	21
Miss I Dartnall		0	1
Mrs A Davis	9 0	0	1
Mrs J Dawson		0	7

	Weight	Hunter Chases	P-t-P
Miss H Delahooke		0	1
Miss A Deniel	9 0	2	6
Daniel Dennis		0	5
David Dennis		0	2
J Deutsch		0	3
J Dillon		0	1
B Dixon	10 12	0	2
J Docker	10 0	0	2
L Donnelly		0	1
I Dowrick	10.7	0	3
D Duggan		0	4
H Dunlop	10 10	0	1
S Durack	9 7	0	2
Miss K Durie		0	1
Miss C Dyson	9 7	0	1
D Easterby		0	5
S Edwards		0	1
R Edwards		0	1
Miss C Ellison		0	1
Miss J Elson		0	1
Miss A Embiricos	10 2	0	4
M Emmanuel	10 7	0	1
R Emmett		0	1
D Esden		0	1
J Evans		0	1
Miss C J Ewart		0	1
A Farrant	11 0	0	14
D Featherstone		0	1
M Fitzgerald	9 13	0	4
Mrs C Ford	9 0	1	12
R Ford	11 2	2	7
Miss S Forster	9 12	0	1
Miss L Foxton		0	2
Miss S French	10 0	0	1
M Frith	9 10	1	2
Miss J Froggatt		0	1
T Garton	11 7	0	1
P Gee	10 0	0	5
Mrs L Gibbon		0	6
B Gibson	9 7	0	1
K Giles		0	1
R Gill		0	1
Miss K Gilman		0	2
M Gingell	11 0	0	4
Miss S Gladders	9 7	0	5
T Glass		0	1
C Gordon		0	3
M Gorman		0	3
Miss A Goschen		1	12
Miss H Gosling		1	2
Mrs S Grant		0	5
Miss J Grant		0	2
T Greed	10 10	0	1
K Green	10 0	0	3
R Green		0	3
A Greig		0	1
Miss C Grissell		0	1
Miss S Gritton	9 7	0	1

	Weight	Hunter Chases	P-t-P
Miss P Gundry	9 12	2	8
Miss T Habgood		0	3
P Hacking	11 7	8	9
E Haddock		0	1
M Haigh	9 7	0	1
C Hall		0	1
P Hamer		0	4
M Hammond		0	2
Mrs M Hand	10 7	0	2
S Hanks		0	1
P Hanly	10 4	0	3
G Hanmer	11 4	0	5
Mrs K Hargreave		0	2
N Harris	10 0	3	22
M Harris	11 0	0	7
A Harvey		0	2
Miss F Hatfield		0	1
Miss D Hawkes		0	1
K Heard		0	6
C Heard		0	5
Mrs R Henderson	10 0	0	1
M Hewitt		0	2
A Hickman		0	5
A Hill	11 11	0	9
Miss M Hill	9 7	0	3
Mrs T Hill	10 7	0	4
T Hills	11 5	0	1
J Hobbs		0	1
A Holdsworth	9 5	0	2
Miss C Holliday		0	2
A Honeyball		0	4
Miss T Honeyball		0	1
Miss L Horner		0	1
D Howells		0	1
P Howse	11 4	0	3
R Hubbard		0	1
A Hunnisett		1	1
Miss J Hutchinson		0	1
F Hutsby		2	6
D Ingle		0	1
Miss H Irving	9 12	0	4
Mrs V Jackson	10 0	0	5
Miss T Jackson		1	4
Miss S Jackson	10 0	0	1
E James	10 0	1	2
A James		0	2
Miss E James	9 7	1	3
C Jarvis		0	2
L Jefford	9 12	2	14
I Johnson		0	2
P Johnson (Yorks)		0	1
P Johnson (Northern)	11 0	0	1
P Jonason		0	1
D S Jones	10 10	3	13
Miss E Jones	9 0	0	1
Miss P Jones	9 0	1	26
M Jones		0	3
M P Jones		0	3

	Weight	Hunter Chases	P-t-P
A Jordan		0	1
J Jukes	9 7	6	28
P Keane		0	2
J P Keen		0	2
Mrs M Kendall	9 7	0	2
N Kent	10 0	0	3
G Kerr		0	1
W Kerr		0	1
S Kidston		0	5
A Kinane	9 7	1	0
N King	10 12	0	1
P King		0	4
G Knowles		0	1
Miss D Laidlaw		0	5
T Lane		0	4
R Lawther	10 7	0	5
L Lay	11 0	1	4
Miss S Leach		0	1
R Lee		0	2
G Lewis		0	4
M Lewis	10 7	1	3
S Lloyd	11 2	1	3
Sgt C Lloyd		0	1
Miss S Lock		0	1
S Love		0	1
T Macfarlane		0	1
Miss M Maher		0	1
G Maloney		0	3
L Manners		0	1
D Mansell		0	3
S March		0	1
T Marks		1	3
I Marsh		0	2
A Martin		1	5
C Mason		0	1
G Matthews		1	0
G Maundrell		0	2
P McAllister	9 0	0	2
T McCarthy	10 0	1	2
Mrs C McCarthy		0	1
Miss T McCurrick		0	1
D McLeod		0	1
O McPhail	9 7	1	0
Miss A Meakins	10 0	0	1
Miss C Metcalfe	9 7	0	1
A Michael	9 8	0	1
M Miller	11 7	0	8
C Millington		0	1
N Mitchell	11 3	0	6
T Mitchell	11 12	2	33
Mrs C Mitchell		0	1
T Moore		0	5
R Morgan		0	10
C Morlock		0	1
S Morris		0	6
T Morrison	10 2	0	2
J Muir		0	2
C Mulhall	10 3	0	6
M Munrowd	10 7	0	3
H Naughton	9 7	0	1
Mrs F Needham	9 7	1	13
K Needham		0	8
Mrs H Needham		0	1
N Nicholson		0	3
Miss V Nicholas		0	4
R Nuttall	10 5	0	5
B O'Doherty		0	1
P O'Keeffe	10 4	0	3
T O'Leary		0	2
T Oates		0	2
A Ogden	10 7	1	4
J Owen		0	1
R Owen		0	2
D Page		0	1
Miss C Papworth		0	3
A Parker	10 4	3	9
Capt D Parker		0	1
D Parravani		0	1
R Payne	10 0	0	2
Miss L Pearce		0	4
G Penfold		0	8
M Pennell		0	1
A Pennock		0	1
Miss J Peercy		0	1
G Perkins		0	1
Miss H Pewter		0	1
A Phillips	10 2	1	6
Miss S Phizacklea		0	1
P Picton-Warlow		0	1
Miss A Plunkett	9 7	0	3
B Pollock	10 5	6	6
M Portman		0	6
J Van Praagh		0	4
A Price	11 7	0	5
J Price	11 9	0	5
M Prince		0	1
S Prior		0	1
Julian Pritchard	11 0	3	37
Miss R Ramsay		0	1
Miss C Ramsey		0	1
N Rayner		0	1
Miss N Richards		0	2
M Rimell	10 2	1	12
D Robinson		2	3
A Robson	10 10	1	4
Miss P Robson	9 3	2	9
Miss S Rodman		0	1
R Rogers		0	1
Miss L Rowe	10 0	0	5
Mrs A Rucker		0	3
M Ruddy		0	1
Miss V Russell	9 10	0	2
A Sansome	10 12	4	9
Miss A Sansom		0	1
Miss C Savell		0	1
J Saville		0	1

	Weight	Hunter Chases	P-t-P
Miss K Scorgie		0	1
T Scott	11 7	0	9
P Scott	9 10	1	0
P Scouller		0	3
J Sharp		0	3
Miss S Sharratt	10 4	0	3
P Shaw		0	2
M Shears		0	1
D Sherlock		0	1
R Shiels	11 4	0	3
S Shinton	11 0	0	1
Mrs S Shoemark		0	1
M Skinner		0	2
S Slade		0	2
D Smith		0	1
G Smith		0	2
N Smith	11 0	0	6
R Smith		0	1
J Snowden		0	1
Miss W Southcombe	8 0	0	1
Miss C Spearing	9 7	0	2
Miss T Spearing	9 0	0	2
S Sporborg	11 0	1	20
N Squires		0	1
Miss D Stafford		0	3
J Stephenson		0	1
T Stephenson		0	7
D Stephens		0	2
P Strang Steel		0	1
Miss N Stirling		0	2
C Stockton	11 7	0	9
B Stonehouse		0	1
C Storey	10 4	1	7
P Strawson		0	1
Miss C Stucley		0	1
Mrs K Sunderland	8 7	0	1
N Sutton		0	1
R Sweeting		0	4
Miss L Sweeting		0	1
S Swiers	10 5	7	12
Miss S Talbot		0	1
G Tarry		0	6
M Tate		0	1
J Tate		0	2
R Tate		0	2
W Tellwright		0	2
Miss C Thomas	9 7	0	1
H Thomas		0	1
R Thomas		0	1
J Thompson		0	1
R Thornton	9 7	3	0
Miss K Thory		0	1
J Tizzard	10 0	2	19
Miss E Tory		1	3
R Treloggen	10 10	1	3
J Trice-Rolph	11 0	1	4
H Trotter		0	2
R Trotter		0	2
J Tudor		0	3
G Tuer		0	5
N Tutty	11 0	0	2
T Underwood		0	6
T Vaughan		0	2
Miss S Vickery	9 0	4	30
C Vigors	10 2	3	2
C Wadland		0	3
R Wakley	9 9	1	1
W Wales	11 2	3	8
E Walker		0	1
Miss E Walker		0	1
S Walker	9 7	0	13
R Walmsley	11 0	0	7
M Walters	10 0	0	1
J Walton		1	5
Mrs S Walwin		0	1
C Ward	11 0	0	1
Mrs L Ward		0	2
Miss S Ward		0	2
C Ward Thomas	10 7	0	6
A Warr	11 0	0	2
Maj M Watson	11 0	0	4
Miss S West		0	3
Maj G Wheeler	10 10	0	2
H Wheeler		0	4
L Whiston		0	1
Miss L Whitaker		0	3
S Whitaker		0	1
K Whiting		0	1
I Widdicombe		0	2
M Wilesmith		0	2
E Williams	10 9	4	25
K Williams		0	1
P Williams		0	5
C Wilson	10 10	2	3
N Wilson	10 7	0	12
Miss F Wilson		0	1
J Wingfield-Digby		0	1
A Wintle	10 3	1	5
A Wood	10 10	1	0
D Wood		0	2
A Woodward		0	1
T Woolridge		0	2
M Worthington		0	1
I Wynne		0	1
P York		0	5
Miss S Young	10 7	1	9
J Young	10 0	0	3
Miss Y Young		0	1

LEADING POINT-TO-POINT RIDERS OF THE POST-WAR YEARS

	Wins
Turner, David	343
Llewellyn, John	270
Cunard, Sir Guy	268
Dare, Miss Alison	252
Felton, Mike	225
Ryall, Frank	218
Cann, Grant	217
Alner, Robert	211
Curling, Miss Polly	197
Miller, Richard	178
Scholfield, Philip	178
Daniell, John	175
Sheppard, Mrs. Josie (fly. Bothway née Turner)	173
Tollit, Mrs. Pat	171
Hacking, Robert (W.R.)	170
Sharp, John	167
Tarry, James	163
Greenall, Peter	160
Treloggen, Ron	154
Brookshaw, Steven	148
Bloom, Michael	145
Horton, Mrs. Sue (née Aston)	145
Rooney, Tim	144
Andrews, Simon	138
Pritchard, Julian	138
Crow, Alastair	137
Hill, Bertie (A.E.)	136
Guilding, Roger	135
Tatlow, David	133
Hamer, Paul	132
Jones, Tim	130
Hacking, Paul	129
Pidgeon, Miss Jenny	126
Bloom, Nigel	125
Farthing, Justin	124
Williams, Michael (Wales)	124
Dawson, Mrs. Jill	123
Mitchell, Tim	121
Craggs, Peter	119
French, Mrs. Sheilagh	119
Jones, Miss Pip	118
Down, Chris	116
Bryan, John	115
Gibbon, Mrs. Lucy	113
Jones, Bill	113
McKie, Ian	112
Greenway, Robin	111
Wales, David	110
Jukes, Jamie	109
Wilkin, Tommy	109
Scouller, Philip	108
Newton, Joey	107
Spencer, Col. C. R.	107
Hand, Mrs Mandy (née Turner)	106
Williams, Michael (Devon)	103

	Wins
Cooper, George	101
Macmillan, Charlie	101
Edwards, Ron (R.J.)	100
Tate, Robin	99
Woolley, Bob	99
Barber, Mick (G.M.)	97
Crank, Simon	97
Davies, Bob	97
Tutty, Nigel	97
Moore, Tim	96
Jeanes, Stuart (T.S.)	95
Hill, Alan	94
Gibson, David	91
Mathias, Fred	91
Vickery, Miss Shirley	91
Anderson, Kevin	90
Blackford, Miss Linda	90
Bush, Nicky	90
Holland-Martin, Tim	89
Stephens, David	89
Wheeler, Harry	89
Jones, Dai	88
Chugg, Robert	84
Duggan, Damien	84
Elliott, Harry (W.H.)	82
Shepherd, Richard	82
Fisher, Miss Pip	82
Ulyet, Alistair	82
Williams, Evan	82
Cumings, Miss Jo	81
Trice-Rolph, Jon	81
Dickinson, A	80+
Charlton, Alistair	80
Chown, Mrs. "Fizz" (D.)	80
Sowersby, Michael	80
Dufosee, John	79
Hickman, John	79
Arthers, Malcolm	78
Berry, Andrew	78
Bloomfield, R.A.	78
Cowell, Henry	77
Frost, Jimmy	76
McCarthy, Tim	76
Docker, John	75
Bryan, Willie	74
Cowell, Bob	74
Crouch, Mrs. Mary	74
Kinsella, David	74
Philby, Tommy	74
Turner, George	74
Mathias, Philip	72
Morgan, Miss Shan	72
Warren, Bruce	71
Foulkes, Billy (C.W.)	70
Rowe, Hunter	70

WINNERS OF MAJOR POINT-TO-POINT RACES

Four-Mile Men's Open for Lord Ashton of Hyde's Cup at the Heythrop

	Owner	*Horse*	*Rider*
1953	L. A. Coville	Dark Stranger	I. Kerwood
1954	S. C. Turner	Nylon	G. Morgan
1955	H. Phillips	Chandie IV	J. Jackson
1956	H. M. Ballard	Cash Account	W. Foulkes
1957	S. L. Maundrell	Star Bar	Owner
1958	S. L. Maundrell	Kolpham	P. Dibble
1959	R. J. Horton	Andy Pandy	D. Horton
1960	R. I. Johnson	Mascot III	R. Woolley
1961	Major H. P. Rushton	Holystone Oak	A. Biddlecombe
1962	W. H. Firkins	Everything's Rosy	D. Tatlow
1963	C. D. Collins	Wild Legend	Owner
1964	W. J. A. Shepherd	Straight Lady	R. J. Shepherd
1965	Mrs J. Brutton	Snowdra Queen	H. Oliver
1966	Miss V. Diment	Bob Sawyer	G. Dartnall
1967	J. Jordan	Barley Bree	D. Tatlow
1968	Major P. Ormrod	Winter Willow	D. W. Williams-Wynn
1969	Miss L. Jones	Bartlemy Boy	J. Daniell
1970	Mrs. J. Brutton	Lord Fortune	G. Hyatt
1971	J. S. Townsend	Creme Brule	R. Knipe
1972	M. H. Ings	Dunsbrook Lass	Owner
1973	Major M. R. Dangerfield	All A Myth	R. N. Miller
1974	A. E. Cowan	False Note	Owner
1975	(Div. 1) J. W. Brown	Take Cover	Owner
	(Div. 2) M. R. Churches	Rich Rose	R. N. Miller
1976	Mrs. J. Brutton	Lord Fortune	D. Edmunds
1977	Mrs. J. Brutton	Lord Fortune	D. Edmunds
1978	Mrs. P. Morris	Sparkford	J. Bryan
1979	E. J. Bufton	Headmaster	A. James
1980	H. Wellon	Spartan Scot	T. Houlbrooke
1981	J. B. Sumner	Nostradamus	I. McKie
1982	H. Wellon	Spartan Scot	T. Houlbrooke
1983	J. B. Sumner	Nostradamus	I. McKie
1984	Mrs. E. Dowling	Lay-The-Trump	B. Dowling
1985	J. B. Sumner	Nostradamus	I. McKie
1986	A. Perry and J. Deutsch	Paddy's Peril	J. Deutsch
1987	P. Hemelek and P. Barnes	Political Whip	D. Naylor-Leyland
1988	A. Perry and J. Deutsch	Paddy's Peril	J. Deutsch
1989	C. Main	Lolly's Patch	Owner
1990	J. Cullen	Polar Glen	M. Felton
1991	J Deutsch	Dromin Joker	J Deutsch
1992	Mrs. M.E. Terry	Speedy Boy	T. McCarthy
1993	Mrs. P. White	Uncle Raggy	R. Lawther
1994	E. Knight	Holland House	C. Vigors
1995	G. Nock	Sevens Out	E. James
1996	Mrs. J. Daniell	Kettles	A. Phillips
1997	Mrs. J. Daniell	Kettles	A. Phillips

From 1953 to 1982 the race was run at Fox Farm, Stow-on-the-Wold, and since then it has been run at Heythrop just outside Chipping Norton. For the last eleven years it has been sponsored by *The Sporting Life.*

The Lady Dudley Cup (Men's Open) at the Worcestershire (First competed for in 1897)

	Owner	Horse	Rider
1946	E. Holland-Martin	Hefty	T. Holland-Martin
1947	A. W. Garfield	Arod	Dr. D. J. K. McCarthy
1948	P. Kerby	Vinty	P. J. Kerby
1949	G. Hutsby	Sir Isumbras	Owner
1950	P. T. Cartridge	Maybe II	Owner
1951	A. H. Thomlinson	Paul Pry	W. A. Stephenson
1952	G. R. Maundrell	Right Again	D. Maundrell
1953	(Div. 1) G. R. Maundrell	Cottage Lace	D. Maundrell
	(Div. 2) H. Sumner	Flint Jack	J. Fowler
1954	(Div. 1) C. S. Ireland	Blenalad	C. Harty
	(Div. 2) H. Sumner	Flint Jack	J. Fowler
1955	(Div. 1) H. M. Ballard	Cash Account	M. Tate
	(Div. 2) C. Nixon	Creeola II	C. Harty
1956	(Div. 1) H. M. Ballard	Cash Account	W. Foulkes
	(Div. 2) G. A. Miles	Galloping Gold	C. Nesfield
1957	(Div. 1) H. M. Ballard	Cash Account	W. H. Wynn
	(Div. 2) J. R. Hindley	Prospero	P. Brookshaw
1958	(Div. 1) C. Davies	Master Copper	Owner
	(Div. 2) J. R. French	Domabelle	Owner
	(Div. 3) T. D. Rootes	Some Baby	M. J. Thorne
1959	(Div. 1) G. C. Llewellin	Clover Bud	D. Llewellin
	(Div. 2) Miss L. Jones	Flippant Lad	J. Daniell
1960	(Div. 1) K. Small	Precious Gem	G. Small
	(Div. 2) Miss L. Jones	Culleenpark	J. Daniell
1961	(Div. 1) Miss L. Jones	Corn Star	J. Daniell
1962	(Div. 1) T. D. Holland-Martin	Midnight Coup	Owner
	(Div. 2) Major J. L. Davenport	Pomme De Guerre	P. Davenport
1963	(Div. 1) R. P. Cooper	Foroughona	Owner
	(Div. 2) W. Shand Kydd	No Reward	Owner
1964	W. J. A. Shepherd	Straight Lady	R. Willis
1965	Mrs. J. Brutton	Snowdra Queen	H. Oliver
1966	T. G. Cambridge	Handsel	Owner
1967	Mrs. D. L. Freer	Tailorman	P. Hobbs
1968	G. A. C. Cure	Bright Willow	R. Chugg
1969	Abandoned. Course waterlogged		
1970	Mrs. E. C. Gaze	Frozen Dawn	H. Oliver
1971	D. T. Surnam	Real Rascal	G. Hyatt
1972	G. A. C. Cure	Mighty Red	J. Chugg
1973	G. A. C. Cure	Mighty Red	R. Woolley
1974	P. A. Rackham	Lake District	M. Bloom
1975	P. T. Brookshaw	Mickley Seabright	P. Brookshaw, Jnr.
1976	Mrs. P. Morris	Jim Lad	J. R. Bryan
1977	R. Wynn	Little Fleur	J. R. Bryan
1978	Miss J. Hey	Sporting Luck	T. Smith
1979	Mrs. P. Morris	Sparkford	J. R. Bryan
1980	W. R. J. Everall	Major Star	S. Brookshaw
1981	W. Price	Petite Mandy	N. Oliver
1982	D. L. Reed	Norman Case	P. Mathias
1983	Mrs. P. M. Jones	Clear Pride	D. Trow
1984	M. F. Howard	Darlingate	T. Jackson
1985	R. A. Phillips	Ridgeman	I. K. Johnson
1986	P. Greenall	Highland Blaze	Owner
1987	J. Harris, B. Leighton, K. Brooke, E. Rees and S. Merrick	Pride Of Tullow	T. Bowen
1988	J. Palmer	North Key	A. Ulyet
1989	P. Deal	Border Sun	S. Sweeting
1990	Mrs. S. A. Potter	Turn Mill	M. Hammond

	Owner	Horse	Rider
1991	P R Haley	The Red One	S Swiers
1992	R. J. Mansell	Brunico	R. Treloggen
1993	T. W. Raymond	Brunico	R. Treloggen
1994	R. Jones	Yahoo	M. Rimell
1995	P. Barber	Bond Jnr	T. Mitchell
1996	Mrs. J. Yeomans	Sharinski	M. Jackson
1997	R. Wilkins	Double Thriller	J. Tizzard

From 1946 to 1950, the race was run over a 3-mile course at Chaddesley Corbett, in 1951 and 1952 over a 3½-mile course at Upton-on-Severn, from 1953 to 1968 over a 3¼-mile course at Upton-on-Severn, in 1970 over a 3-mile 500 yds. course at Chaddesley Corbett, from 1971 to 1973 over a 3-mile 600 yds. course at Chaddesley Corbett, and from 1974 onwards over a 3-mile 520 yds. course at Chaddesley Corbett. For the last eleven years it has been sponsored by *The Sporting Life*.

The Lord Grimthorpe Gold Cup (Men's Open) at the Middleton

	Owner	Horse	Rider
1946	H. W. Metcalfe	San Michele	G. B. Metcalfe
1947	H. W. Metcalfe	San Michele	C. Metcalfe
1948	Mrs. H. M. Gilpin	Rolling River	Capt. C. MacAndrew
1949	(Div. 1) C. Chapman	Finolly	Major G. Cunard
	(Div. 2) A. Simpson	The Joker VII	W. R. Simpson
1950	W. A. Stephenson	General Ripple	Owner
1951	A. H. Thomlinson	Paul Pry	W. A. Stephenson
1952	G. F. Fawcett	Trusty	H. Elliott
1953	Miss V. Porter-Hargreaves	Turkish Prince	A. Dickinson
1954	Mrs. J. Makin	Kitty Brook	C. Smith
1955	W. A. Stephenson	Mr. Gay	Owner
1956	S. Webster	More Honour	Owner
1957	H. M. Ballard	Cash Account	W. Wynn
1958	R. W. Ratcliffe	Brown Sugar	P. Fox
1959	S. Webster	More Honour	Owner
1960	J. H. Thompson	Gay William	M. Thompson
1961	J. Peckitt	Glann	T. Wilkin
1962	R. Heaton	Brass Tacks	P. Brookshaw
1963	F. T. Gibbon	Harrow Hall	R. Moody
1964	Major G. Cunard	Ferncliffe	Owner
1965	R. A. H. Perkins	Faruno	Owner
1966	Mrs. R. G. Hutchison-Bradburne	Banjoe	J. Hutchinson-Bradburne
1967	Major G. Cunard	Puddle Jumper	Owner
1968	Mrs. A. E. Dickinson	Shandover	M. Dickinson
1969	C. B. Harper	My Night	J. Leadbetter
1970	D. E. Wilson	Young Highlander	D. Gibson
1971	Capt. R. M. Micklethwait	Kangaroo Jim	A. Berry
1972	J. W. Walton	Old Man Trouble	Owner
1973	F. D. Nicholson	Moyleen	A. Nicholson
1974	P. A. Rackham	Watch Night	M. Bloom
1975	Mrs. J. Gilmour	Falling Leaves	J. Gilmour
1976	L. H. Barker	Villa Court	L. Barker
1977	J. B. Walker	Escamist	J. Barton
1978	J. Scott-Aiton	Sea Petrel	I. Scott-Aiton
1979	T. M. Wilson	Rakamar	T. Smith
1980	A. W. Johnson	Scalby Cresta	G. Halder
1981	J. A. Cooper	Mountain Lad	J. Peckitt
1982	J. M. Evetts	Border Mark	Owner
1983	A. Sanderson	Lady Buttons	N. Tutty
1984	Race abandoned. Too firm ground		

	Owner	*Horse*	*Rider*
1985	J. D. Jemmeson	Salkeld	D. Kinsella
1986	Mrs. M. F. Strawson	Freddie Teal	P. Strawson
1987	Race abandoned. Waterlogging		
1988	Mrs. S. Frank	Ingleby Star	N. Tutty
1989	T. P. Bell	Old Nick	S. Whitaker
1990	R. G. Watson	Certain Rhythm	M. Sowersby
1991	Meeting abandoned.		
1992	B. Heywood	Ocean Day	Mrs. A. Farrell
1993	B. Heywood	Ocean Day	H. Brown
1994	Mrs. D. R. Brotherton	Across The Lake	Miss S. Brotherton
1995	P. Sawney	Duright	N. Tutty
1996	H. Bell	Highland Friend	P. Atkinson
1997	J. Burns	Ask Antony	N. Wilson

In 1952 the distance of this race was extended from 3½ miles to 4 miles; and in 1954, when it became known as the point-to-point Grand National, to 4½ miles. In 1982 the distance was reduced to 4¼ miles, in 1986 to 4 miles 1 furlong, and in 1989 to 3 miles 1 furlong. In 1990 the race was run over 3 miles 50 yards. In 1992 the race reverted to 4 miles and became a mixed open. The venue is Whitwell-on-the-Hill, mid-way between Malton and York.

LEADING HORSE AWARDS

	Owner	*Horse*	*Number of races won*
Grand Marnier Trophy			
1970	A. Gordon-Watson	Barty	10
1971	C. Hancock	Golden Batman	8
1972	Mrs. H. P. Rushton	Pensham	11
1973	J. M. Turner	Master Vesuvius	11
1974	J. M. Turner	Boy Bumble	12
1975	J. M. Turner	Even Harmony	11
1976	J. M. Turner	Hardcastle	9
1977	J. M. Turner	Hardcastle	11
1978	R. Wynn	Little Fleur	12
1979	P. Tylor	Hargan	10
1980	T. Hunnable	Florida King	8
1981	J. Sumner	Nostradamus	9
1982	R. Bulgin	Mac Kelly	8
1983	Mrs. B. Perry	Seine Bay	8
1984	D. Llewellin	National Clover	9
1985	Mrs. C. Foote-Forster	Brigadier Mouse	9
1986	C. Dawson, M.F.H.	Sweet Diana	9
1987	Mrs. C. Nicholas	Mantinolas	8
1988	T. F. G. Marks	Stanwick Lad	10
1989	J. F. Weldhen	For A Lark	10
The Daily Telegraph Trophy			
1990	W. J. Evans	Timber Tool	11
1991	Mrs L Wadham	Fort Hall	10
1992	R. J. Mansell	Brunico	12
1993	A. J. Papworth	Melton Park	12
Grand Marnier Trophy			
1994	A. J. Papworth	Melton Park	7
1995	E. Harries	Handsome Harvey	10
1996	Miss R. A. Francis	Phar Too Touchy	10
1997	N. Viney	Butler John	10

NATIONAL WINNERS 1997

Land Rover	Mrs. D. Lunt	Magnolia Man
Greig Middleton	R. M. Penny	Earthmover
Interlink Express	G. Keirle	Aller Moor

PPORA AWARDS 1997

Horse and Hound/PPORA Young Horse Award	M. Thorne & D. Hobbs	Arctic Chill
PPORA Mares	Mrs. & Mrs. R. Phillips	Grimley Gale
Leading Novice Riders	Anthony Honeyball	

DAILY TELEGRAPH CUP: LEADING GENTLEMAN POINT-TO-POINT RIDER
Winners and Runners-up

	Wins
1967	
David Tatlow	24
Roger Guilding	19
1968	
David Tatlow	18
David Gibson	14
1969	
Michael Bloom	19
Bill Shand Kydd	18
1970	
David Turner	19
Grant Cann	16
1971	
Bob Davies	29
Mike Villiers	18
1972	
Richard Miller	21
{John Docker	14
{David Turner	14
1973	
Richard Miller	23
David Turner	20
1974	
David Turner	26
Richard Miller	14
1975	
David Turner	24
{Grant Cann	14
{Robin Greenway	14
1976	
David Turner	22
John Bryan	16
1977	
David Turner	29
John Bryan	26
1978	
John Bryan	32
David Turner	19

	Wins
1979	
David Turner	17
John Bryan	15
1980	
{**Ian McKie**	20
{**David Turner**	20
1981	
Ian McKie	18
{Peter Greenall	16
{Tim Rooney	16
1982	
Peter Greenall	24
Jimmy Frost	18
1983	
John Llewellyn	19
Peter Greenall	17
1984	
David Turner	20
Peter Greenall	19
1985	
Peter Greenall	23
David Turner	15
1986	
Peter Greenall	28
Mike Felton	24
1987	
Mike Felton	26
Philip Scholfield	18
1988	
Philip Scholfield	37
Mike Felton	28
1989	
Mike Felton	26
John Llewellyn	18
1990	
Mike Felton	27
Philip Scholfield	20
1991	
Justin Farthing	26
Philip Scholfield	23

LEADING GENTLEMAN POINT-TO-POINT RIDER

	Wins
1992	
Robert Alner	31
Julian Pritchard	19
1993	
Alastair Crow	22
{Nigel Bloom	20
{Julian Pritchard	20
1994	
Nigel Bloom	22
Damien Duggan	21
1995	
Alastair Crow	30
Jimmy Tarry	25
1996	
Jamie Jukes	34
Alastair Crow	27
1997	
Julian Pritchard	37
Tim Mitchell	33

THE SPORTING LIFE CUP: LEADING LADY POINT-TO-POINT RIDER
Winners and Runners-up

	Wins
1967	
Mrs Pat Hinch	11
Mrs Pat Tollit	10
Mrs Avril Williams	10
1968	
Miss Sue Aston	15
Miss Rosemary Cadell	8
Miss Josie Turner	8
1969	
Miss Josie Turner	14
Miss Sue Aston	13
1970	
Miss Sue Aston	14
Mrs Pat Tollit	9
Miss Anne Greenwood	9
1971	
Miss Sue Aston	14
Mrs Pat Tollit	11
1972	
Miss Sue Aston	15
Mrs Pat Tollit	15
1973	
Mrs Mabel Forrest	17
Mrs Josie Bothway (née Turner)	12
1974	
Mrs Josie Bothway	20
Miss Diana Bishop	16
1975	
Mrs Josie Bothway	17
Mrs Mary Crouch	9
Mrs Anne Sturdy	9
1976	
Mrs Josie Bothway	17
Mrs Mary Crouch	15
1977	
Mrs Josie Sheppard (fly. Bothway)	17
Mrs Mary Crouch	14
1978	
Mrs Rosemary White	11
Miss Amanda Jemmeson	9
1979	
Miss Pip Fisher	10
Miss Katie Halswell	9
Mrs Josie Sheppard	9
1980	
Miss Lucy King (now Mrs David Gibbon)	14
Miss Pip Fisher	11
1981	
Miss Lucy King	14
Miss Jenny Pidgeon	10
1982	
Miss Jenny Pidgeon	18
Mrs Jenny Hembrow	15
1983	
Miss Jenny Pidgeon	18
Mrs Lucy Gibbon (née King)	8
Miss Mandy Lingard	8
1984	
Miss Jenny Pidgeon	13
Miss Mandy Lingard	13
1985	
Miss Jenny Pidgeon	18
Miss Lucy Crow	13
Miss Alison Dare	13
1986	
Miss Alison Dare	17
Miss Amanda Harwood	14
1987	
Miss Alison Dare	17
Miss Jenny Pidgeon	10
Mrs Lucy Gibbon	10
1988	
Mrs Jenny Litston	16
Miss Amanda Harwood	15
1989	
Miss Lucy Crow	15
Miss Mandy Turner	14
1990	
Miss Alison Dare	20
Miss Polly Curling	14
Mrs Jill Dawson	14

LEADING LADY POINT-TO-POINT RIDER

	Wins
1991	
Miss Alison Dare	26
Mrs P Nash	22
1992	
Miss Alison Dare	21
Miss Linda Blackford	16
1993	
Miss Polly Curling	25
Miss Mandy Turner	20
1994	
Miss Polly Curling	35
Miss Alison Dare	17
1995	
Miss Polly Curling	40
{ Miss Shirley Vickery	22
{ Miss Pip Jones	22
1996	
Miss Alison Dare	31
Miss Polly Curling	23
1997	
Miss Shirley Vickery	30
Miss Pip Jones	26

POINT-TO-POINT COURSES

ALDINGTON Kent
6m SE of Ashford, S of A20.
L/H; 19J; 7m 05s.
Undulating, galloping, test of stamina.
Good viewing.

ALNWICK Northumberland
3m E of Alnwick, near B1399.
L/H; 18J; 6m 35s.
Slightly undulating, galloping.
Excellent viewing.

ALPRAHAM Cheshire
3m SE of Tarporley, off A51.
R/H; 18J; 7m 20s.
Mostly flat, suits stayers.
Reasonable viewing.

AMPTON Suffolk
4m N of Bury St Edmunds, near A134.
R/H; 20J; 6m 55s.
Undulating, sharp but suits stayers.
Poor viewing.

ANDOVERSFORD Glos.
6m SE of Cheltenham, signposted from A40.
R/H; 19J; 6m 30s.
Undulating, uphill finish.
Reasonable viewing.

ASHORNE Warwicks
4m S of Warwick, off A41.
R/H; 18J; 6m 20s.
Slightly undulating, uphill finish.
Very good viewing.

ASPATRIA Cumbria
2m NE of town, on A596, Carlisle to Maryport Road.
L/H; 18J 6m 20s.
Undulating, galloping.
Good viewing.

BADBURY RINGS Dorset
5m SE of Blandford, Adj B3082.
L/H; 19J; 6m 30s.
Undulating, rectangular.
Good viewing

BALCORMO MAINS Fife
3m NE of Leven, off A915.
R/H; 18J; 7m 00s.
Gently undulating, galloping, suits stayers.
Good viewing.

BARBURY CASTLE Wilts
4m S of Swindon, Near Wroughton.
L/H; 18J; 6m 25s.
Galloping.
Excellent viewing.

BASSALEG Gwent
2m NW Junction 28 M4, near A468.
R/H; 18J; 6m 45s.
Undulating, galloping.
Excellent viewing.

BEXHILL E Sussex
½m N of town, off A269.
R/H; 19J; 7m 00s.
Undulating, stamina test, uphill finish.
Very good viewing.

BISHOPSLEIGH Devon
9m NE of Crediton, E of A377.
R/H; 19J; 6m 25s.
Undulating, not as testing as previously.
Course Revised: Viewing improved

BITTERLEY Shropshire
4m NE of Ludlow, N of A4117.
L/H; 18J; 6m 30s.
Almost flat, sharp, slight uphill finish.
Good viewing.

BLACKFOREST LODGE Devon
5m S Exeter.
R/H; 19J; 6m 05s.
Galloping.
Excellent viewing.

BONVILSTON S Glamorgan
4m S Cardiff, near A48.
R/H; 18J; 6m 00s.
Gently undulating, sharp.
Very good viewing.

BRAMPTON BRYAN Hereford & Worcs.
10m W of Ludlow, near A4113.
R/H; 18J; 6m 25s.
Flat, galloping.
Fair viewing.

BRATTON DOWN Devon
10m N of South Molton, Adj B3226.
L/H; 18J; 6m 15s.
Undulating, long uphill finish.
Mostly good viewing.

BREDWARDINE Hereford & Worcs.
7m E of Hay-on-Wye, E of B4352.
R/H; 18J; 6m 45s.
Flat, galloping.
Good viewing.

BROCKLESBY PARK Lincs.
10m W of Grimsby, Adj B1210.
L/H; 18J; 6m 25s.
Flat, slight uphill finish.
Good viewing.

CASTLE OF COMFORT Somerset
Off B3134, between Priddy & East Harptree.
R/H; 18J; 6m 35s.
Undulating, sharp.
Good viewing.

CHADDESLEY CORBETT Hereford & Worcs.
6m W of Bromsgrove, Adj A448.
L/H; 18J; 6m 15s; 20J, 6m 40s.
Gently undulating, galloping.
Very good viewing.

CHARING Kent
6m NW of Ashford, Adj A20.
L/H; 19J; 6m 35s.
Undulating, suits stayers.
Good viewing.

CHARLTON HORETHORNE Somerset
Off B3145, 6m SW of Wincanton.
R/H; 18J; 6m 50s.
Slightly undulating.
Good viewing.

CHARM PARK Yorkshire
At Wykeham, Adj A170, 5m SW of Scarborough.
L/H; 19J; 6m 40s.
Flat, galloping.
Very good viewing.

CLIFTON-ON-DUNSMORE Warwicks
3m NW of Junc 18 of M1; Adj A5.
L/H; 19J; 6m 10s.
Slightly undulating, galloping, old Rugby racecourse.
Very good viewing.

CLYST ST MARY Devon
5m E of Exeter, Nr A3052.
L/H; 22J; 7m 00s.
Mostly flat, sharp.
Very good viewing.
Course reported closed.

CORBRIDGE Northumberland
3m N of Town, near A68.
R/H; 18J; 6m 25s; (3m 5f, 22J, 8m 00s).
Undulating, galloping, uphill finish.
Good viewing.

COTHELSTONE Somerset
3m N of Taunton.
L/H; 18J; 6m 20s.
Undulating, sharp.
Good viewing.

COTLEY FARM Somerset
2m S of Chard, 1½m off A30.
L/H; 18J; 6m 45s.
Undulating, galloping, suits stayers.
Very good viewing.

COTTENHAM Cambs.
5m N of Cambridge, E of B1049.
R/H; 19J; 6m 10s.
Flat, galloping.
Very good viewing (including grandstand).

CURSNEH HILL Hereford & Worcs.
1m W of Leominster, off A44.
L/H; 18J; 6m 15s.
Very sharp, undulating.
Good viewing.

DALSTON Cumbria
5m S of Carlisle, Adj B5299.
R/H; 18J; 6m 40s.
Flat, galloping.
Good viewing.

DALTON PARK Yorkshire
5m NW of Beverley, W of B1248.
R/H; 19J; 7m 05s.
Almost flat, stamina test.
Fairly good viewing.

DETLING Kent
3m NE of Maidstone, N of A249.
L/H; 18J; 6m 30s; (4m, 24J, 8m 45s).
Almost flat, galloping, slight uphill finish.
Good viewing.

DIDMARTON Glos.
6m SW of Tetbury, Adj A433.
L/H; 18J; 6m 15s.
Undulating, downhill finish.
Very good viewing.

DINGLEY Northants.
2m E of Market Harborough, Adj A427.
R/H; 18J; 6m 35s.
Almost flat, sharp bend before last.
Excellent viewing.

DUNCOMBE PARK Yorkshire
1m SW of Helmsley, W of A170.
R/H; 18J; 6m 15s.
Undulating, long uphill finish.
Good viewing.

EASINGWOLD Yorkshire
13m NW of York, off A419.
L/H; 18J; 6m 00s.
Almost flat, sharp, suits non-stayers.
Fair viewing.

EATON HALL Cheshire
4m S of Chester, off A483.
R/H; 18J; 6m 45s.
Flat, galloping, stamina needed.
Reasonable viewing.

ERW LON Dyfed
10m N of Carmarthen, near B4459.
L/H; 18J; 6m 25s.
Flat, galloping.
Poor viewing.

EYTON-ON-SEVERN Shropshire
6m SE of Shrewsbury, near B4380.
L/H; 18J; 6m 25s.
Big, flat, galloping.
Very good viewing.

FAKENHAM Norfolk
2n SW of town.
L/H; 18J; 6m 15s.
Undulating, sharp, inside/outside NH course.
Excellent viewing.

FLAGG MOOR Derbyshire
6m SE of Buxton, E of A515.
L/H; 20J; 7m 40s.
Undulating, very testing, uphill finish.
Good viewing.

FLETE PARK Devon
2m N of Modbury, N of A379.
R/H; 19J; 6m 55s.
Undulating, stayers' course.
Reasonable viewing.

FRIARS HAUGH Borders
1m W of Kelso, off A699.
L/H; 19J; 6m 50s.
Flat, one sharp rise/fall, galloping, finish up centre shute.
Good viewing.

GARNONS Hereford & Worcs.
7m W of Hereford, N of A438.
L/H; 18J; 6m 40s.
Undulating, sharp.
Good viewing.

GARTHORPE Leics.
5m E of Melton Mowbray, Adj B676.
R/H; 18J; 6m 30s.
Undulating, last 3f flat.
Very good viewing.

GISBURN Lancs.
1m SW of town, off A59.
R/H; 18J; 7m 15s.
Sharp undulating, suits stayers.
Poor viewing.

GREAT STAINTON, Co. Durham
5m SW of Sedgefield, Handy A1(M).
R/H; 18J; 6m 10s.
Galloping
Good viewing.

GREAT TRETHEW Cornwall
3m SE of Liskeard.
R/H; 22J; 6m 30s.
Very undulating, quite testing, uphill finish.
Good viewing.

GUILSBOROUGH Northants.
10m N of Northampton, Adj A50.
L/H; 19J; 6m 30s.
Flat, sharp bends.
Fair viewing.

HACKWOOD PARK Hampshire
2m SE of Basingstoke; E of A339.
L/H; 18J; 6m 25s.
Flat, sharp.
Unsatisfactory viewing.

HEATHFIELD Sussex
1m E of town, Adj A265.
R/H; 20J; 7m 10s.
Undulating, twisty, suits stayers.
Very good viewing.

HEXHAM Northumberland
Inside NH course.
L/H; 18J; 7m 20s.
Undulating, stayers course.
Very good viewing.

HEYTHROP Oxfordshire
2m E of Chipping Norton, off A34.
R/H; 20J; 7m 00s. (4m, 25J, 8m 20s).
Slightly undulating; long course but suits front-runners.
Good viewing.

HIGH BICKINGTON Devon
9m S of Barnstaple, off B3217.
R/H; 18J; 6m 35s.
Sharp, twisty.
Good viewing.

HIGHAM Essex
7m NE of Colchester, W of A12.
L/H; 19J; 6m 15s.
Flat, galloping, suits front-runners.
Fair viewing.

HIGH EASTER Essex
Off A1060, between Bishops Stortford & Chelmsford.
L/H; 18J; 6m 20s.
Undulating, galloping, suits non-stayers.
Good viewing.

HIGHER KILWORTHY Devon
2m NE of Tavistock, N of A286.
L/H; 18J; 6m 35s.
Undulating, uphill finish.
Very good viewing.

HOCKWORTHY Devon
6m W of Wellington, between M5 & A361.
L/H; 18J; 6m 35s.
Undulating, uphill finish.
Good viewing.

HOLNICOTE Somerset
Adj. A39, 3m W of Minehead.
L/H; 20J; 6m 25s.
Undulating, sharp.
Very good viewing.

HORNBY CASTLE Yorkshire
3m S of Catterick, W of A1.
L/H; 18J; 6m 40s.
Slightly undulating, suits stayers.
Unsatisfactory viewing.

HORSEHEATH Cambs.
3m E of Linton, Adj. A604.
R/H; 18J; 6m 30s.
Undulating, galloping, suits stayers.
Quite good viewing.

HOWICK Gwent
2m W of Chepstow, near B4235.
L/H; 18J; 6m 45s.
Undulating, sharp bends.
Good viewing.

HUTTON RUDBY Yorkshire
4m SW Stokesley, near A19.
L/H; 20J; 6m 15s.
Undulating, sharp.
Good viewing.

KILWORTHY Devon
2m NE of Tavistock, N of A386.
L/H; 18J; 6m 40s.
Undulating, galloping, suits stayers.
Good viewing.

KIMBLE Bucks.
4m S of Aylesbury, near B4009.
L/H; 19J; 6m 35s.
Almost flat, galloping.
Reasonable viewing.

KINGSTON BLOUNT Oxfordshire
4m NE of Watlington; off B4009.
L/H; 18J; 6m 20s.
Undulating, steep rise/fall far end.
Good viewing.

KINGSTON ST MARY Somerset
3m N of Taunton, E of A358.
R/H; 18J; 6m 30s.
Undulating, twisting.
Reasonable viewing.

LANARK Strathclyde
1m E of town off A73 (old Lanark racecourse).
R/H; 18J; 6m 45s.
Galloping, suits stayers.
Good viewing.

LARKHILL Wiltshire
3m NW of Amesbury, W of A345.
R/H; 18J; 6m 10s.
Undulating, galloping, suits non-stayer.
Good but distant viewing.

LEMALLA Cornwall
6m SW of Launceston, S of A30.
R/H; 20J; 7m 00s.
Sharp, undulating.
Poor viewing.

LIFTON Devon
3m N of Launceston, 2m off A30.
R/H; 19J; 6m 30s.
Undulating, sharp.
Very good viewing.

LITTLE WINDSOR Dorset
4m S of Crewkerne, 2m W of A3066.
R/H; 19J; 6m 45s.
Undulating, galloping, uphill finish.
Good viewing.

LLANFRYNACH Powys
3m SE of Brecon, off B4558.
R/H; 18J; 6m 40s.
Flat, twisty.
Reasonable viewing.

LLANVAPLEY Gwent
4m E of Abergavenny, off B4223.
L/H; 18J; 6m 25s.
Flat, twisty.
Excellent viewing.

LOCKERBIE Dumfries & Galloway
2m SW of town, S of A709.
R/H; 19J; 7m 30s.
Flat, sharp, long trip.
Good viewing.

LOCKINGE Oxfordshire
2m S of Wantage, Adj B4494.
L/H; 19J; 6m 25s.
Undulating, galloping, very short run-in.
Excellent viewing.

LYDSTEP Dyfed
3m SW of Tenby, off A4139.
L/H; 19J; 6m 35s.
Gently undulating, sharp.
Excellent viewing.

MAISEMORE PARK Glos.
2m NW of Gloucester, Adj A417.
L/H; 18J; 6m 45s.
Flat, fairly sharp.
Very good viewing.

MARKET RASEN Lincs
Inside N.H. Course.
L/H; 18J; 6m 35s.
Sharp, undulating.
Excellent viewing.

MARKS TEY Essex
5m W of Colchester, Adj A12.
L/H; 19J; 6m 40s (3¼m, 20J, 7m 00s).
Galloping, uphill finish, suits stayers.
Good viewing.

MILBORNE ST ANDREW Dorset
4m E of Puddletown, S of A354.
L/H; 19J; 6m 30s.
Galloping, fairly flat.
Fair viewing.

MOLLINGTON Oxfordshire
5m N of Banbury, Adj A423.
R/H; 18J; 6m 30s.
Undulating, galloping, uphill finish.
Excellent viewing.

MOSSHOUSES Borders
4m N of Melrose, W of A68.
L/H; 18J; 6m 50s.
Undulating, galloping, suits stayers.
Very good viewing.

MOUNSEY HILL GATE Somerset
4m N of Dulverton, Adj B3223.
R/H; 20J; 6m 33s.
Flat, sharp.
Very poor viewing.

NEWTON BROMSWOLD Northants.
3m SE of Rushden, E of A6.
R/H; 19J; 6m 50s.
Slightly undulating, galloping, suits stayers.
Good viewing.

NEWTOWN Hereford & Worcs.
7m NE of Hereford, Adj A417/A4103.
L/H; 18J; 6m 30s.
Undulating, suits stayers.
Good viewing.

NORTHAW Herts.
2m NE of Potters Bar, Adj B156.
L/H; 18J; 6m 25s.
Slightly undulating.
Good viewing.

OTTERY ST. MARY Devon
1m SW of town, off B3174.
L/H; 19J; 6m 25s.
Flat, sharp.
Excellent viewing.

PANTYDERI Dyfed
7m NE of Newcastle Enlyn, Adj B4332.
L/H; 18J; 6m 40s.
Mostly flat.
Good viewing.

PARHAM Sussex
3m SE of Pulbrough, Adj A283.
R/H; 18J; 6m 35s.
Flat, galloping.
Good viewing.

PAXFORD Glos.
3m SE Chipping Camden, near B4479.
L/H; 18J; 6m 15s.
Galloping.
Very good viewing.

PENSHURST Kent
4m SW of Tonbridge, W of B2188.
L/H; 18J; 6m 45s.
Undulating, uphill finish.
Unsatisfactory viewing.

PEPER HAROW Surrey
2m W of Godalming, W of A3.
L/H; 18J; 6m 50s.
Flat, very sharp, finish up centre chute.
Very poor viewing.

PYLE W Glamorgan
At Margam Park, off M40, junction 38.
R/H; 18J; 6m 20s.
Undulating, sharp.
Good viewing.

SANDON Staffs.
4m SE of Stone, off A51.
L/H; 19J; 6m 50s.
Slightly undulating.
Excellent viewing.

SIDDINGTON Glos.
2m S of Cirencester, W of A419.
L/H; 18J; 6m 20s.
Flat, galloping.
Good viewing, but not of finish.

SOUTHWELL Notts.
1m SW of town.
L/H; 18J; 6m 30s.
Flat, sharp, inside of NH Course.
Excellent viewing.

STAFFORD CROSS Devon
3m W of Seaton, Adj A3052.
R/H; 18J; 6m 10s.
Flat, sharp, easy 3m.
Unsatisfactory viewing.

STAINTON Cleveland
1m S of Middlesbrough, off A19.
R/H; 18J; 6m 30s.
Sharp.
Fair viewing.

ST HILARY S Glamorgan
2m E of Cowbridge, S of A48.
R/H; 19J; 6m 20s.
Flat, sharp.
Good viewing.

TABLEY Cheshire
1m W Knutsford, near M6.
R/H; 19J; 6m 30s.
Sharp.
Good viewing.

THORPE LODGE Notts.
3m SW of Newark, S of A46.
L/H; 18J; 6m 40s.
Flat, fair.
Excellent viewing.

TRANWELL Northumberland
3m SW of Morpeth, S of B6524.
L/H; 18J; 6m 20s.
Flat, uphill finish in shute.
Reasonable viewing.

TWESELDOWN Hampshire
3m W of Aldershot, W of A325.
R/H; 19J; 6m 20s.
Undulating, triangular.
Excellent view of finish, but not much else.

UMBERLEIGH Devon
5m SE of Barnstaple, Adj A377.
L/H; 18J; 6m 25s.
Sharp, up & down side of hill.
Reasonable viewing, but mobility essential.

UPPER SAPEY Hereford & Worcs.
6m N of Bromyard, Adj B4203.
R/H; 18J; 6m 05s.
Very undulating.
Reasonable viewing.

UPTON-ON-SEVERN Hereford & Worcs.
5m N of Tewkesbury, W of A38.
R/H; 18J; 6m 35s.
Flat, galloping, suits stayers.
Excellent viewing.

WADEBRIDGE Cornwall
1m W of town, Adj A39 (Royal Showground).
L/H; 21J; 6m 30s.
Slightly undulating, twisty.
Reasonable viewing.

WESTON PARK Shropshire
6m E of Telford, S of A5.
L/H; 20J; 6m 35s.
Flat, sharp.
Reasonable viewing.

WETHERBY Yorkshire
8m SE of Harrogate, Adj A1.
L/H; 18J; 7m 00s.
Flat, suits stayers, inside NH course.
Excellent from grandstand.

WHITTINGTON Lancashire
2m S of Kirkby Lonsdale, off B6254.
L/H; 18J; 7m 10s.
Flat, galloping, stamina test.
Excellent viewing.

WHITWELL-ON-THE-HILL Yorkshire
6m SW of Malton, Adj A64.
R/H; 18J; 6m 45s.
Mainly flat, galloping, suits stayers.
Excellent viewing.

WITTON CASTLE Durham
3m W of Bishop Auckland, E of A68.
R/H; 21J; 6m 30s.
Flat, galloping.
Excellent viewing.

WOLVERHAMPTON Staffs.
Inside A/W Course.
L/H; 18J; 6m 40s.
Flat, sharp.
Excellent viewing.

WOODFORD Glos.
15m NE of Bristol, Adj A38.
L/H; 19J; 6m 25s.
Flat, galloping.
Fair viewing.

POINT-TO-POINT SECRETARIES' ASSOCIATION

CHAIRMAN: Andrew Merriam, Oaklawn House, Eye, Suffolk. IP23 7NN. Tel. (01379) 870362
VICE CHAIRMAN:
ADMINISTRATOR/SECRETARY: The Jockey Club, 42 Portman Square, London. W1H 0EN. Tel. 0171 486 4921

ADDRESSES FOR AREA SCHEDULES

Each Schedule lists name, address and telephone number of every Point-to-Point Secretary in its Area, and gives full details of every meeting and race planned for 1998 in that Area. They may be obtained by sending a SAE (at least 7 × 5 ins) to the following.

DEVON & CORNWALL: M. E. Hawkins Esq, Hunters Lodge, Newton St Cyres, Exeter, Devon. EX5 5BS. Tel. (01392) 851275.

EAST ANGLIA: W. Barber Esq, Barn Cottage, Sedgeford, Hunstanton, Norfolk. PE36 5LL. Tel. (01485) 518424.

MIDLANDS (Lincolnshire, Northants & Notts): Mrs. E. Gilman, Coppice Farmhouse, Church Lane, Glaston, Oakham, Rutland. LE15 9BN. Tel. (01572) 823476.

NORTHERN (Northumberland, Scotland): A. J. Hogarth Esq, Mosshouses, Galashields, Selkirkshire. TD1 2PG. Tel. (01896) 860242. Fax. (01896) 860295.

NORTH WEST (Shropshire, Cheshire): J. R. Wilson Esq. Huntington House, Little Wenlock, Telford, Salop. TF6 5BW. Tel. (01952) 502354.

SANDHURST (Surrey, Hampshire & Isle of Wight): Mrs. H. Murray, Kingston House, Kingston Blount, Oxon. OX9 4SH. Tel. (01844) 351216.

SOUTH EAST (Kent, Sussex & Surrey): Mrs. Nicky Featherstone, 28 Exeter Close, Tonbridge, Kent. TN10 4NT. Tel. (01732) 353518.

SOUTH MIDLANDS (Warwickshire, Oxon, Berks, Bucks): Mrs. H. Murray (as Sandhurst).

SOUTH & WEST WALES: I. Prichard Esq. Karlyn, St Hilary, Cowbridge, S. Glamorgan. Tel. (01446) 772335 (home) (01446) 774603 (office).

WELSH BORDER COUNTIES: J. R. Pike Esq, The Priory, Kilpeck, Hereford. HR2 9DN. Tel. (01981) 570366.

WESSEX (Somerset, Dorset, Wilts): F. G. Mathews Esq, Peak Ashes, Penselwood, Wincanton, Somerset. BA9 8LY. Tel. (01747) 840412.

WEST MIDLANDS (Gloucestershire, Worcestershire & Warwickshire): Mrs. K. Smith-Maxwell, Phepson Manor, Himbleton, nr. Droitwich, Worcs. WR9 7JE. Tel. (01905) 391206.

WEST WALES: I. Prichard (as South & West Wales).

YORKSHIRE: Mrs. C. M. Wardroper, High Osgoodby Grange, Thirsk, N. Yorks. YO7 2AW. Tel. (01845) 597226.

If any changes are made for 1998 after the publication of this annual, those listed above will pass on correspondence to any successor.

THE POINT-TO-POINT OWNERS' & RIDERS' ASSOCIATION

CHAIRMAN: M. J. R. Bannister, MFH, Coniston Hall, Coniston Cold, Skipton, N. Yorkshire. (Tel: Skipton [01756] 749551 Home; Skipton [01756] 748136 Office).

PRESIDENT and CHAIRMAN OF POINT-TO-POINT COMMITTEE: J. Mahon Esq, Bishopton Hill House, Bishopton, Stratford-on-Avon, Warwicks. (Tel: Stratford-on-Avon [01789] 299029).

SECRETARY: Mrs Jeanette Dawson, Horton Court, Westbere Lane, Westbere, Canterbury, Kent. CT2 0HJ. (Tel/Fax: [01227] 713080).

AREA REPRESENTATIVES

DEVON & CORNWALL: K. Cumings Esq, Eastwood, Bishops Nympton, South Molton, N. Devon. EX36 4PB. (Tel: [01769] 550528 Home; [01823] 432356 Office).

EAST ANGLIA: M. Bloom Esq, Kimberley Home Farm, Wymondham, Norfolk. NR18 0RW. (Tel: Wymondham [01953] 603137).

MIDLANDS: J. H. Docker Esq, Rookery Farm, Northbrook Road, Coundon, nr. Coventry, Warwicks. CV6 2AJ. (Tel: [01203] 332036).

NORTHERN: R. F. Minto Esq, Gilson, Spylaw Park, Kelso, Borders. TD5 8DS (Tel: [01573] 223162).

NORTH WEST: T. P. Brookshaw Esq, Mickley House Farm, Habberley, Pontesbury, Shrewsbury. SY5 0SQ. (Tel: [01743] 790083).

SANDHURST: J. Maxse Esq, Homestead Farm, Selborne, Alton, Hants. GU34 3LN. (Tel: [01420] 511216).

SOUTH EAST: W. A. Alcock Esq, The Willows, Brook, Ashford, Kent. TN25 5PD. (Tel: Wye [01233] 812613 Home; Wye [01233] 812761 Office).

SOUTH MIDLANDS: N. Price Esq, Manor Farmhouse, Maidford, nr. Towcester. NN12 8HB. (Tel: [01327] 860297).

SOUTH WALES: Mrs J. Tamplin, Cefn Llwyd Farm, Abertridwr, Caerphilly, Mid Glamorgan. (Tel: Caerphilly [01222] 830278).

WELSH BORDERS: G. Saveker Esq, 26 Cotswold Drive, Kings Acre, Hereford. HR4 0TG. (Tel: [01432] 343655).

WESSEX: J. J. Barber Esq, Peckmore Farm, Henley, Crewkerne, Somerset. TA18 8PQ. (Tel: [01460] 74943) *and* L. Vickery Esq, Knowle End, South Barrow, Yeovil, Somerset. BA22 7LN. (Tel: [01963] 440043).

WEST MIDLANDS: W. Bush Esq, Old Manor House, West Littleton, Chippenham, Wilts. SN14 8JE. (Tel: Bath [01225] 891683).

WEST WALES: Mrs C. Higgon, Newton Hall, Crundale, Haverfordwest, Dyfed. SA62 4EB. (Tel: Clarbeston [01437] 731239).

YORKSHIRE: Mrs A. Morshead, The Cottage, Foulrice Farm, Brandsby, York. YO6 4SB. (Tel: [01347] 888273).

NORTHERN JOCKEYS REPRESENTATIVE: S. Whitaker Esq, Hellwood Farm, Hellwood Lane, Scarcroft, Leeds. LS14 3BP. (Tel: Leeds [0113] 2892265).

SOUTHERN JOCKEYS REPRESENTATIVE: J. G. Cann Esq, Newland, Cullompton, Devon. EX15 1QQ. (Tel: Cullompton [01884] 32284).

The Point-to-Point Owners' & Riders' Association are dedicated to the advancement and promotion of point-to-pointing. Annual Subscription £10.00. Life Membership £100. For further information contact the secretary (above).

NOTES

NOTES

NOTES

NOTES

NOTES

NOTES

NOTES

NOTES

NOTES

NOTES

NOTES

NOTES

NOTES

NOTES

NOTES

NOTES

NOTES

NOTES

NOTES

NOTES

NOTES

NOTES

NOTES

NOTES

NOTES